The Literary
STUDY BIBLE

ESV
ENGLISH STANDARD VERSION

The Literary STUDY BIBLE

ESV

ENGLISH STANDARD VERSION

Containing the Old and New Testaments

General Editors

LELAND RYKEN & PHILIP GRAHAM RYKEN

CROSSWAY BIBLES
WHEATON, ILLINOIS

RRD		14		13		12		11		10		09		08		07
13	12	11	10	9	8	7	6	5	4	3	2					

CONTENTS
THE BOOKS OF THE BIBLE IN CANONICAL ORDER

THE OLD TESTAMENT

THE NEW TESTAMENT

THE BOOKS OF THE BIBLE IN ALPHABETICAL ORDER

EDITORS' PREFACE

This book is a literary guide to the entire Bible. We have defined the concept of literature very broadly as anything having to do with *how* biblical writers have expressed their content. The foundational premise of all verbal communication is that meaning is conveyed *through form*, starting with language itself but moving beyond that to a whole range of literary forms and genres. There is no meaning without the form in which a piece of writing is expressed.

This means that when we read the Bible, literary considerations are not optional features to which we might attend only if we have an interest in literary matters. We need to pay attention to the *how* of a Bible passage as preliminary to understanding *what* is said.

This literary Bible explains how biblical authors have embodied their messages in their chosen literary forms. The most important features of this book (the only one of its type in existence) are as follows:

- It is a study Bible in the sense of containing the text of the entire Bible, accompanied by commentary.

- It is unlike other study Bibles in that the commentary focuses on the literary features of the Bible, as distinct from historical, cultural, or linguistic features.

- It is also unlike conventional study Bibles in being a reader's guide to the Bible—a book that guides readers through the actual text of the Bible—rather than primarily a reference book about the Bible.

- It is a reader's Bible by virtue of dividing the Bible into units of a size that lends itself to daily reading or weekly group Bible study.

- The commentary and tips for reading appear at the head of passages instead of in footnotes.

- These lead-ins, moreover, move readers into the text that follows, instead of being a distraction from the text.

- The introductions to the books of the Bible provide a roadmap that points out what a reader most benefits from knowing about the book that follows.

- Literary commentary of the type provided in this book is particularly adept at showing the unity of Bible passages and the way in which they fit into the flow of a biblical book and the Bible as a whole.

- The commentary in this book is designed to draw readers into interaction with the biblical text instead of merely providing information about the Bible.

- A glossary at the back of the book provides definitions of literary terms and pointers about how to understand and interpret various literary genres.

As the foregoing list suggests, a literary Bible is distinctly different from other study Bibles. It is ideal as a first approach to the Bible because the content of the Bible can be mastered only if we pay attention to the forms in which that content is embodied. Further, the commentary that we provide is a guide *into* the Bible, not a reference source of information *about* the Bible. This literary commentary is thus a means to the end of equipping readers to renew their commitment to the Bible and to the living God who has revealed himself in the literary forms of the Bible.

INTRODUCTION

This book is both a reader's Bible and a literary Bible. It is a reader's Bible by virtue of its format, which is designed to facilitate sitting down and reading through the Bible. An important part of that format is that the biblical text has been divided into units of a length that invites devotional reading day by day, each preceded by helpful tips for reading the passage that follows.

This book is a study Bible as well as a reader's Bible. The commentary that appears before each passage contains tips for analysis as well as tips for reading. Furthermore, the format and commentary make this literary Bible ideal for use in group Bible studies. Study leaders can use the commentary to help organize their thoughts about a passage and formulate a series of discussion questions.

One of the greatest gifts of the literary approach to the Bible is that it enables readers to grasp a passage as a literary *whole*. Although this book preserves the traditional chapter and verse numbers for ease of reference, it omits the distraction of footnotes (except for the standard ESV notes dealing with translation issues). The reason for this omission is simple: a reader cannot read a passage as a flowing, unified composition while at the same time reading footnotes. Traditional study Bibles are reference books; this literary Bible is a reader's Bible. The single-column format enhances this purpose.

This book is also, as the title promises, a literary Bible. It is a guide to individual books and passages of the Bible that highlights the Bible's literary features. To explain this in more detail, we need to explore the concept that the Bible is literary and the question of what it means to approach the Bible in keeping with its literary nature.

Before we do that, however, we need to clarify a very important point: the content of any piece of writing is communicated *through form*. The concept of form needs to be construed very broadly here. It means anything having to do with *how* a writer has embodied his or her content, starting with the very words. Without literary form, no content can exist. We cannot extract the moral or theological meaning of a story without first assimilating the plot, setting, and characters of the story, or the meaning of a poem without first pondering the poem's images and figures of speech.

This means that a certain priority needs to be given to literary form—not a priority of importance but a priority in the sense of what comes first. To approach the Bible as literature as this literary Bible does is not like dessert—something pleasurable to add to more important aspects of the Bible. The literary approach is the first item on the agenda—the starting point for other approaches to the Bible. This has been a point of neglect among Bible readers and Bible scholars that this literary Bible aims to correct.

WHAT IT MEANS THAT THE BIBLE IS LITERATURE

▌Literary genres. The most customary way to define literature is by the external genres (types or kinds of writing) in which its content is expressed. The two main genres in the Bible are narrative and poetry. Numerous categories cluster under each of these. Narrative subtypes, for example, include hero story, Gospel, epic, tragedy, comedy (a U-shaped plot with a happy ending), and parable. Specific poetic genres keep multiplying as well: lyric, lament psalm, praise psalm, love poem, nature poem, epithalamion (wedding poem), and many others.

Still, these literary forms are only the tip of the iceberg. In addition to narrative and poetry, we find prophecy, visionary writing, apocalypse, pastoral, encomium, oratory, drama (the book of Job), satire, and epistle. Then if we start adding more specific forms like travel story, dramatic monologue, doom song, and Christ hymn, the number of literary genres in the Bible readily exceeds one hundred. Many of these genres are defined in the glossary at the back of this Bible. For entries in the glossary, the editors have placed an asterisk in front of each term the first time it appears in the commentary on a given book of the Bible.

The importance of genre to biblical interpretation is that genres have their own methods of procedure and rules of interpretation. An awareness of genre should program our encounter with a text, alerting us to what we can expect to find. For example, the most prevalent of all literary forms is narrative or story. To make adequate sense of a story, we need to know that it consists of plot or action, setting, and characters. These, in turn, constitute the basic grid through which we assimilate the story and talk about it.

In view of how many literary genres are present in the Bible, it is obvious that the overall literary form of the Bible is the anthology, as even the word *Bible* (Greek *biblia*, meaning "little books") hints. As an anthology, the Bible possesses the same kinds of unity that other anthologies exhibit: multiple authorship (approximately three dozen authors); diverse genres; a rationale for the assembling of this particular collection of materials (a unifying religious viewpoint and story of salvation history, as well as the fact that all the books except Luke and Acts were written by Jews); comprehensiveness; and an identifiable strategy of organization (a combination of historical chronology and groupings by genre). With belief in the inspiration of the Bible as a foundational premise, we can say that the Holy Spirit is the ultimate editor of the anthology that we know as the Bible.

■ **Literary subject matter.** Literature is also identifiable by its subject matter. It is differentiated from expository (informational) writing by the way in which it presents concrete human experience. Instead of stating abstract propositions, logical arguments, or bare facts, literature embodies what literary authors often call "the stuff of real life." We can profitably think of biblical writing as existing on a continuum, with abstract propositional discourse on one end and concrete presentation of human experience on the other. The more thoroughly a piece of writing falls on the experiential end of the spectrum, the more literary it is.

To illustrate, the command "you shall not murder" is an example of expository discourse. The story of Cain and Abel embodies the same truth in the form of characters in concrete settings performing physical and mental actions. Expository writing gives us the precept; literature gives us the example. "God's provision extends to all of our life" is a thematic summary of Psalm 23; the psalm, however, eschews such abstraction and incarnates the truth about providence in a pastoral poem that images the daily routine of a shepherd and his sheep.

The subject of literature is human experience rendered as concretely as possible. The result is that it possesses a universal quality. Whereas history and the daily news tell us what *happened*, literature tells us what *happens*—what is true for all people in all places and times. A text can be both, but the literary dimension of a text resides in its embodiment of recognizable human experience. While we rightly think of the Bible as revelatory (God's supernatural revelation of truth), the literary parts of the Bible are at the same time the human race's testimony to its own experience.

The goal of literature is to prompt a reader to share or relive an experience. The truth that literature imparts is not simply ideas that are true but *truthfulness to human experience*. The implication for interpretation is that Bible readers, teachers, and expositors need to be active in re-creating experiences in their imagination, identifying the recognizable human experiences in a text (thereby building bridges to life in the modern world), and resisting the impulse immediately to reduce a biblical passage to a set of theological ideas.

▌**Archetypes and motifs.** An archetype is a plot motif (such as initiation or quest), character type (such as the villain or trickster), or image (such as light or water) that recurs throughout literature and life. The presence of archetypes in a text signals a literary quality. When we read literature, we are continuously aware of such archetypes as the temptation motif, the dangerous valley, or the hero, whereas with other types of writing we are rarely aware of archetypes.

Archetypes are the building blocks of literature. Writers could not avoid them even if they tried. The Bible is the most complete repository of archetypes in the Western world, and this makes the Bible a universal and primeval book (reaching down to bedrock human experience). Awareness of archetypes helps us see the unity of the Bible (since we keep relating one instance of an archetype to other instances), the connections between the Bible and other literature, and the connections between the Bible and life.

▌**Stylistics and rhetoric.** Literature also uses distinctive resources of language that set it apart from ordinary expository discourse. The most obvious example is poetry. Poets speak a language all their own, consisting of images and figures of speech. The most important of the special resources of language that push a text into the category of literature include the following: imagery, metaphor, simile, symbol, allusion, irony, wordplay, hyperbole, apostrophe (direct address to someone or something absent as though present), personification, paradox, and pun.

The most concentrated repository of such language in the Bible is the books that are poetic in their basic format—the prophetic books, Job, Psalms, Proverbs, Ecclesiastes (a book of prose poems), Song of Solomon, Revelation. But literary resources of language are not limited to the obviously poetic books of the Bible. They appear on virtually every page of the Bible beyond the poetic books—most obviously in the discourses of Jesus and in the Epistles, but also, though less pervasively, in the narratives of the Bible.

A related literary phenomenon is rhetoric—arrangement of content in patterned ways and employment of conventional literary techniques or formulas. Parallelism of sentence elements, for example, is an instance of stylized rhetoric. Patterns of repetition—of words, phrases, or content units—is a distinguishing feature of the Bible. So are the aphoristic conciseness and memorability that continuously raise the Bible to a literary realm of eloquence far above everyday discourse. A specimen page from a New Testament epistle might include the presence of rhetorical questions, question-and-answer constructions, direct addresses to real or imaginary respondents, and repeated words or phrases within a passage, and we can depend on it that famous aphorisms will appear in abundance.

▌**Artistry.** Literature is an art form in which beauty of expression, craftsmanship, and verbal virtuosity are valued as rewarding and as an enhancement of effective communication. The one writer of the Bible to state his philosophy of composition portrays himself as, among other things, a self-conscious stylist and wordsmith who arranged his material "with great care" and who "sought to find words of delight" (Eccles. 12:9–10). Surely our impression is that the other writers of the Bible did the same.

The standard elements of artistic form include unity, theme-and-variation, pattern, design, progression, contrast, balance, recurrence, coherence, and symmetry. Authors cultivate artistry like this because it is important to their effect and intention. The Bible is an aesthetic as well as a utilitarian book, and we need to experience it as such, both for our understanding and for our enjoyment.

▌**Summary: Reading and interpreting the Bible as literature.** Any piece of writing needs to be assimilated and interpreted in terms of the kind of writing that it is. The Bible is a literary book in which theology and history are usually embodied in literary forms. Those forms include genres, the expression of human experience in concrete form, stylistic and rhetorical techniques, and artistry.

These literary features are not extraneous aspects of the text—not optional matters to consider if we have time or interest to do so after we have assimilated the message or content of a passage. Instead, they are the forms *through which* the content is mediated. If the writing of the Bible is the product of divine inspiration—if it represents what the Holy Spirit prompted the authors to write as they were carried along (2 Peter 1:21)—then the literary forms of the Bible have been inspired by God and need to be granted an importance in keeping with that inspiration.

APPROACHING THE BIBLE AS LITERATURE

We might think that acknowledging the literary nature of the Bible would automatically produce a literary approach to the material, but this has not been the case. Even scholars and commentators who subscribe to the literary nature of the Bible as outlined in the preceding section overwhelmingly ignore the Bible's literary features in their commentary. The concept of the Bible as literature has tended to be head knowledge only, without application to the text.

The goal of this literary Bible is to provide literary commentary and tips for reading the Bible in keeping with its literary features. Accordingly, the commentary provided in this book takes seriously the traits that make the Bible literary. Specifically, the critical apparatus that the editors have provided will do the following things:

- provide prompts to the human experiences that we find in the text
- identify the genre(s) of a passage
- name archetypes and motifs that permeate a passage
- comment on the style and rhetorical patterns of a passage
- make occasional observations regarding the artistry of a passage, with particular attention to the unity of passages
- show the flow of passages within themselves and also as they relate to the books of the Bible in which they appear and ultimately to the Bible as a whole

In all of these areas, the editors' commentary provides a starting point. It is up to readers to apply and extend what the commentary has begun.

FALLACIES ABOUT A LITERARY APPROACH TO THE BIBLE

Before we can embrace a literary approach to the Bible with enthusiasm, we of course need to be relieved of anxieties about viewing the Bible as literature. Resistance to viewing the Bible as literature has rested on misconceptions about what literature is, both in itself and as it relates to the Bible. Below are five false characterizations that have prevailed in some Christian and non-Christian circles, accompanied by an explanation of why the allegations are untrue.

▌Fallacy #1: Viewing the Bible as literature betrays a liberal theological bias.

It is untrue that viewing the Bible as literature means automatically adopting a liberal theological attitude toward the Bible. A survey of commentators who conduct literary analysis of the Bible shows the same range of viewpoint, from conservative to liberal, that other approaches to the Bible manifest. There is nothing inherent in a literary approach that requires a liberal perspective. In fact, it is entirely possible to begin a literary analysis of the Bible exactly where all study of the Bible should begin—by accepting as true all that biblical writers say about the Bible (its inspiration by God, its reliability, its complete truthfulness, etc.).

We need to remind ourselves that it is possible to approach the Bible theologically and miss the mark of truth, too. Theologizing by itself is no guarantee of truth. There has been as much false theology as there has been true theology, so a literary approach to the Bible is neither more nor less suspect than a theological approach.

▌Fallacy #2: The idea of the Bible as literature is a modern idea that is foreign to the Bible itself.

The idea of the Bible as literature began with the Bible itself. The writers of the Bible refer with technical precision to a whole range of literary genres in which they write—proverb, saying, chronicle, complaint (lament psalm), oracle, apocalypse, parable, song, epistle, and many another.

Furthermore, some of the forms that we find in the Bible correspond to the literary forms that were current in the authors' surrounding cultures. For example, the Ten Commandments are cast into the form of suzerainty treaties that ancient Near Eastern kings imposed on their subjects, and the New Testament epistles, despite unique features, show many affinities to Greek and Roman letters of the same era.

Mainly, though, we can look to the Bible itself to see the extent to which it is a literary book. Virtually every page of the Bible is replete with literary technique, and to possess the individual texts of the Bible fully, we need to read the Bible as literature, just as we need to read it theologically and (in the narrative parts) historically.

▌Fallacy #3: To speak of the Bible as literature is to claim that the Bible is fictional.

While fictionality is common in literature, it is not an essential ingredient of literature. The properties that make a text literary are unaffected by the historicity or fictionality of the material. A text is literary based on a writer's selectivity and molding of the material and the style of presentation, regardless of whether the details really happened or are made up.

Nor does the presence of convention and artifice in the Bible necessarily imply fictionality. The modern television genre of docudrama is filled with conventions (interviews of people, film clips of events, material from archives) that do not detract from the factuality of the account.

▌Fallacy #4: To approach the Bible as literature means approaching it only as literature.

Some people resist embracing the concept of the Bible as literature out of the fear that to speak of the Bible as literature necessarily means paying attention *only* to the Bible's literary features and ignoring its more important aspects. But the same argument might be used to preclude a study of the history or language of the Bible, since with these approaches, too, a person might remain fixed on those aspects only.

To analyze the Bible as literature need not entail abandoning the special authority that Christians ascribe to the Bible or the expectation that God will speak to us through it. Nor does it necessarily mean that the reader will not pay equal attention to other aspects of the Bible—its history, its language, its theology, its sociology, its psychology. The Bible requires multiple approaches, and the literary approach is one of them. A theological approach to the Bible by itself is incomplete. A literary approach seeks to complement other approaches, not to replace them. It is appropriate to say again, however, that the literary forms of the Bible are the means *through which* the content is expressed, and this means that literary analysis has a particular priority as the only adequate starting point for other kinds of analysis.

▌Fallacy #5: To say that the Bible is literature denies its divine inspiration. If we believe in the inspiration of the Bible by the Holy Spirit, we believe that whatever we find in the Bible is what God wanted us to know and possess. We do not believe in the inspiration of the Bible because of the content that we find there. It is actually the other way around: we begin with the premise of inspiration, so that whatever is in the Bible is what God the Holy Spirit inspired the human authors to compose.

If God moved the writers of the Bible to write as they did, the only plausible inference is that God inspired the forms of the Bible. We should not say he inspired "the forms of the Bible as well as its content," because the content is embodied *in* the forms. The three modes of writing that we find in the Bible—theological, historical, literary—are all equal in regard to inspiration. God inspired the writing of all three, and the writers of all three were equally dependent on inspiration by the Holy Spirit to write the truth.

Second Peter 1:21 tells us that the writers of Scripture wrote as they were "carried along by the Holy Spirit." Thus when the Bible gives us literary subject matter—the concrete embodiment of human experience—that subject matter is present through the agency of divine inspiration. So are the genres and forms of the Bible. If God inspired some writers to tell stories, others to write poems, others to write satire or letters or visions, then those forms deserve attention in keeping with their inspired nature.

TWELVE LITERARY FEATURES OF THE BIBLE

The Bible is not a totally unique book. In general, its literary forms function in the same way that these forms function beyond the Bible. A story is a story, whether in the Bible or beyond it. A metaphor is a metaphor. Nonetheless, it is possible to make generalizations about characteristic literary features of the Bible, with no implication that these features do not exist elsewhere. Below are twelve literary qualities or preferred literary techniques that we often find in the Bible.

1. A unifying story line. Although the overall genre of the Bible is the anthology of individual books and passages, the Bible possesses a unity far beyond that of other literary anthologies. The technical term for a unifying superstructure such as we find in the Bible is *metanarrative* (big or overarching story). In the Bible, the metanarrative is the story of salvation history—the events by which God worked out his plan to redeem humanity and the creation after they fell from original innocence. This story of salvation history is Christocentric in the sense that it focuses ultimately on the substitutionary sacrifice and atonement of Christ on the cross and his resurrection from death. The unifying story line of the Bible is a U-shaped story that moves from the creation of a perfect world, through the fall of that world into sin, then through fallen human history as it slowly and painfully makes its way toward consummation and arrives at the final destruction of evil and the eternal triumph of good.

2. The presence of a central character. All stories have a central character or protagonist, and in the overarching story of the Bible God is the protagonist. He is the unifying presence from the beginning of the Bible to the end. All creatures interact with this central and ultimate being. All events are related to him. The story of human history unfolds within the broader story of what God does. The result is a sense of ultimacy that comes through as we read the pages of the Bible.

3. Religious orientation. The subject of literature is human experience, and this is true of the Bible, too, but a distinctive feature of the Bible is that it overwhelmingly presents human experience in a religious and moral light. Events that other writers might treat in a purely human and natural light—a sunrise, a battle, a birth, a journey—are presented by the authors of the Bible within a moral or spiritual frame-work. Part of this moral and spiritual framework is the assumption of the biblical authors that a great conflict between good and evil is going on in our world and, further, that people are continually confronted with the need to choose between good and evil, between working for God's kingdom and going against God.

4. Variety of genres and styles. Every literary anthology of the Bible's magnitude displays a range of literary forms, but the Bible's range may well top them all. We need to be alert to this, because the religious uses to which we put the Bible can easily lull us into assuming that the Bible is all one type of writing. The list of individual forms, if we include such specific motifs as the homecoming story or trickster or love poem, keeps expanding. (A complete guide to these literary forms as we find them in the Bible is Leland Ryken, James C. Wilhoit, and Tremper Longman III, eds., *Dictionary of Biblical Imagery* [Downers Grove, Ill.: InterVarsity Press, 1998].) The variety that we find in the Bible stems partly from the large categories that converge—history, theology, and literature, for example, or prose and poetry, realism and fantasy, past and future, God and people.

5. Preference of the concrete over the abstract. While the New Testament contains a great deal of theological writing, the general preference of biblical authors is for concrete vocabulary. This is especially true of the Hebrew language of the Old Testament. In the Bible, God is portrayed as light and rock and thunder. Slander is a sharp knife. Living the godly life is like putting on a garment or suit of armor. Heaven is a landscape of jewels. To read the Bible well, we need to read with the "right side" of the brain—the part that is activated by sensory data.

6. Realism. The prophetic and apocalyptic parts of the Bible give us a steady diet of fantasy (flying scrolls, for example, and red horses), but the general tendency of the Bible is toward everyday realism. The Bible displays the flaws of even its best characters (Oliver Cromwell famously said that the biblical writers paint their characters "warts and all"). Although the Bible does not delineate the sordid experiences of life in the extreme detail that modern literary realism does, it nonetheless covers the same real experi-ences, such as violence, murder, sexuality, death, suffering, and famine. Of course the Bible differs from modern realism by showing us that there is a realism of grace as well as a realism of carnality. In other words, the Bible is not content to portray the degrada-tion of a world that has fallen into sin without also portraying the redemptive possibilities of a world that has been visited by the grace of God and is destined for glory.

7. Simplicity. Although the Bible is certainly not devoid of examples of the high style, especially in the poetic parts, its overall orientation is toward the simple. The prevailing narrative style is plain, unembellished, matter-of-fact prose. Shakespeare's vocabulary is approximately twenty thousand words, Milton's thirteen thousand, and English translations of the Bible six thousand. Biblical writers often work with such simplified dichotomies as good and evil, light and darkness, heroes and villains. Of course there is a simplicity that diminishes and a simplicity that enlarges. The simplicity of the Bible paradoxically produces an effect of majesty and authority.

8. Preference for the brief unit. Linked with this simplicity is a marked preference for the brief literary unit. Biblical poets tend to write brief lyrics, for example, not long narrative poems. Most long narratives in the Bible such as the story of Abraham or the Gospels are actually cycles of stories in which the individual episodes are briefer and more self-contained than what we find in a novel. The prophetic books are actually anthologies of self-contained oracles and snatches of narrative. Other familiar biblical genres reinforce this tendency toward simplicity—proverb or saying, parable, lists of individual commands or rules, summaries of what various kings did, occasional letters (epistles) in which the author responds to a list of questions that have been asked or a crisis that has arisen in a local church.

9. Elemental quality. The Bible is a book of universal human experience. It is filled with experiences and images that are the common human lot in all places and times. The Bible embraces the commonplace and repeatedly shows ordinary people engaged in the customary activities of life—planting, building, baking, fighting, worrying, celebrating, praying. The world that biblical characters inhabit is likewise stripped and elemental, consisting of such natural settings as day and night, field and desert, sky and earth. Even occupations have an elemental quality—king, priest, shepherd, homemaker, missionary.

10. Oral style. Even though the Bible that we read is a written book, in its original form much of it existed orally. This is true because ancient cultures were predominantly oral cultures in which information circulated chiefly by word of mouth. The literary forms of the Bible show this rootedness in an oral culture. The prevalence of dialogue (directly quoted speeches) in the Bible is without parallel in literature generally until we come to the novel. Everywhere we turn in the Bible, we hear voices speaking and replying. The spare, unembellished narrative style of the Bible arises from the situation of oral circulation of the stories. Additionally, many of the nonnarrative parts of the Bible show signs of oral speech—the prophetic discourses and oracles, the psalms (which were sung in temple worship), the epistles (which were read aloud in churches), and the Gospels (where the words of Jesus are a leading ingredient).

11. Aphoristic quality. An aphorism is a concise, memorable statement of truth—in the words of English poet Alexander Pope, "What oft was thought, but ne'er so well expressed." The Bible is the most aphoristic book of the Western world. It is filled with sayings that are part of the common storehouse of proverbs and idioms: "pride goes before destruction" (Prov. 16:18); seeing "eye to eye" (Isa. 52:8); a "house divided against itself" (Matt. 12:25). This quality is present not only in the wisdom literature of the Bible but in all parts of the Bible and most notably in the sayings of Jesus.

12. The literature of confrontation. When we read Shakespeare or Dickens, we find ourselves moved to agreement or disagreement, but we do not ordinarily feel that we have been confronted by someone or something that requires us to make a choice. By contrast, when we assimilate the Bible we feel as though we have been personally confronted with something that requires a response. While this choice is ultimately for or against God, the ideas of the Bible, too, require us to believe or disbelieve them. The Bible displays a vivid consciousness of values—of the difference between good and evil—with the result that it is virtually impossible to remain neutral about the ideas that confront us as we read the Bible.

▌**Summary.** Perhaps none of the twelve features noted above is unique in itself. But if we put them together, they produce a book that is unique. Reading the Bible is not just like reading another book. It has an affective power and aura of authority that cannot be duplicated. It possesses a quality of encounter that other books do not display, so that as we read we are confronted with the voice and presence of God and are virtually compelled to believe or disbelieve what we are reading. The Westminster Confession of Faith provides an apt summary of the things that make the Bible unique: "the heavenliness of the matter, the efficacy of the doctrine, the majesty of the style, the consent of all the parts, the scope of the whole [which is to give all glory to God], the full discovery it makes of the only way of man's salvation, the many other incomparable excellencies, and the entire perfection thereof, are arguments whereby it doth abundantly evidence itself to be the Word of God."

HOW TO USE THIS LITERARY BIBLE

This literary Bible is governed by a twofold goal: (1) to make the Bible reader friendly and (2) to show how application of literary tools of analysis helps in reading and understanding the Bible. We can apply these goals to two common uses that we make of the Bible.

First, we read the Bible devotionally. While this reading usually is not highly analytic in nature, we can nonetheless develop habits of reading that make our devotional reading more substantial than it often is. The literary prompts that appear in the introductions and headnotes of this literary Bible can become a "second sense" that we naturally put into practice as we read. Furthermore, even in devotional reading, we benefit from seeing the flow of a passage, and the lead-ins to individual passages in this literary Bible will help readers to perform that function.

Second, we study the Bible as well as read it devotionally. The commentary in this literary Bible provides analysis of individual passages and books of the Bible. Equally important, the critical apparatus of this Bible is filled with tools of literary analysis that can be applied to many passages. Much commentary on the Bible, including that found in conventional study Bibles, is more of a substitute for reading the Bible than a guide to studying it. This literary Bible is a guide to the Bible that pushes the reader into the text instead of providing mere summaries of the content that readily become substitutes for reading the Bible.

This literary Bible is an introduction to literary analysis. As noted above, we cannot assimilate the religious content of a Bible passage without first interacting with the form in which it has been embodied. Given that the Bible is a literary book, it cannot be studied and taught adequately if we do not start with analysis of the literary form of the passage we wish to explore. Thus the skills of literary analysis are themselves central to an informed experience of the Bible.

PREFACE

▮ **The Bible.** "This Book [is] the most valuable thing that this world affords. Here is Wisdom; this is the royal Law; these are the lively Oracles of God." With these words the Moderator of the Church of Scotland hands a Bible to the new monarch in Britain's coronation service. These words echo the King James Bible translators, who wrote in 1611: "God's sacred Word . . . is that inestimable treasure that excelleth all the riches of the earth." This assessment of the Bible is the motivating force behind the publication of the English Standard Version.

▮ **Translation Legacy.** The English Standard Version (ESV) stands in the classic mainstream of English Bible translations over the past half-millennium. The fountainhead of that stream was William Tyndale's New Testament of 1526; marking its course were the King James Version of 1611 (KJV), the English Revised Version of 1885 (RV), the American Standard Version of 1901 (ASV), and the Revised Standard Version of 1952 and 1971 (RSV). In that stream, faithfulness to the text and vigorous pursuit of accuracy were combined with simplicity, beauty, and dignity of expression. Our goal has been to carry forward this legacy for a new century.

To this end each word and phrase in the ESV has been carefully weighed against the original Hebrew, Aramaic, and Greek, to ensure the fullest accuracy and clarity and to avoid under-translating or overlooking any nuance of the original text. The words and phrases themselves grow out of the Tyndale–King James legacy, and most recently out of the RSV, with the 1971 RSV text providing the starting point for our work. Archaic language has been brought to current usage and significant corrections have been made in the translation of key texts. But throughout, our goal has been to retain the depth of meaning and enduring language that have made their indelible mark on the English-speaking world and have defined the life and doctrine of the church over the last four centuries.

▮ **Translation Philosophy.** The ESV is an "essentially literal" translation that seeks as far as possible to capture the precise wording of the original text and the personal style of each Bible writer. As such, its emphasis is on "word-for-word" correspondence, at the same time taking into account differences of grammar, syntax, and idiom between current literary English and the original languages. Thus it seeks to be transparent to the original text, letting the reader see as directly as possible the structure and meaning of the original.

In contrast to the ESV, some Bible versions have followed a "thought-for-thought" rather than "word-for-word" translation philosophy, emphasizing "dynamic equivalence" rather than the "essentially literal" meaning of the original. A "thought-for-thought" translation is of necessity more inclined to reflect the interpretive opinions of the translator and the influences of contemporary culture.

Every translation is at many points a trade-off between literal precision and readability, between "formal equivalence" in expression and "functional equivalence" in communication, and the ESV is no exception. Within this framework we have sought to be "as literal as possible" while maintaining clarity of expression and literary excellence. Therefore, to the extent that plain English permits and the meaning in each case allows, we have sought to use the same English word for important recurring words in the original; and, as far as grammar and syntax allow, we have rendered Old Testament passages cited in the New in ways that show their correspondence. Thus in each of these areas, as well as throughout the Bible as a whole, we have sought to capture the echoes and overtones of meaning that are so abundantly present in the original texts.

As an essentially literal translation, then, the ESV seeks to carry over every possible nuance of meaning in the original words of Scripture into our own language. As such, it is ideally suited for in-depth study of the Bible. Indeed, with its emphasis on literary excellence, the ESV is equally suited for public reading and preaching, for private reading and reflection, for both academic and devotional study, and for Scripture memorization.

▌**Translation Style.** The ESV also carries forward classic translation principles in its literary style. Accordingly it retains theological terminology—words such as grace, faith, justification, sanctification, redemption, regeneration, reconciliation, propitiation—because of their central importance for Christian doctrine and also because the underlying Greek words were already becoming key words and technical terms in New Testament times.

The ESV lets the stylistic variety of the biblical writers fully express itself—from the exalted prose that opens Genesis, to the flowing narratives of the historical books, to the rich metaphors and dramatic imagery of the poetic books, to the ringing rhetorical indictments in the prophetic books, to the smooth elegance of Luke, to the profound simplicities of John, and the closely reasoned logic of Paul.

In punctuating, paragraphing, dividing long sentences, and rendering connectives, the ESV follows the path that seems to make the ongoing flow of thought clearest in English. The biblical languages regularly connect sentences by frequent repetition of words such as "and," "but," and "for," in a way that goes beyond the conventions of literary English. Effective translation, however, requires that these links in the original be reproduced so that the flow of the argument will be transparent to the reader. We have therefore normally translated these connectives, though occasionally we have varied the rendering by using alternatives (such as "also," "however," "now," "so," "then," or "thus") when they better capture the sense in specific instances.

In the area of gender language, the goal of the ESV is to render literally what is in the original. For example, "anyone" replaces "any man" where there is no word corresponding to "man" in the original languages, and "people" rather than "men" is regularly used where the original languages refer to both men and women. But the words "man" and "men" are retained where a male meaning component is part of the original Greek or Hebrew. Likewise, the word "man" has been retained where the original text intends to convey a clear contrast between "God" on the one hand and "man" on the other hand, with "man" being used in the collective sense of the whole human race (see Luke 2:52). Similarly, the English word "brothers" (translating the Greek word *adelphoi*) is retained as an important familial form of address between fellow-Jews and fellow-Christians in the first century. A recurring note is included to indicate that the term "brothers" (*adelphoi*) was often used in Greek to refer to both men and women, and to indicate the specific instances in the text where this is the case. In addition, the English word "sons" (translating the Greek word *huioi*) is retained in specific instances because the underlying Greek term usually includes a male meaning component and it was used as a legal term in the adoption and inheritance laws of first-century Rome. As used by the apostle Paul, this term refers to the status of all Christians, both men and women, who, having been adopted into God's family, now enjoy all the privileges, obligations, and inheritance rights of God's children.

The inclusive use of the generic "he" has also regularly been retained, because this is consistent with similar usage in the original languages and because an essentially literal translation would be impossible without it. Similarly, where God and man are compared or contrasted in the original, the ESV retains the generic use of "man" as the clearest way to express the contrast within the framework of essentially literal translation.

In each case the objective has been transparency to the original text, allowing the reader to understand the original on its own terms rather than on the terms of our present-day culture.

▌ **The Translation of Specialized Terms.** In the translation of biblical terms referring to God, the ESV takes great care to convey the specific nuances of meaning of the original Hebrew and Greek terms. First, concerning terms that refer to God in the Old Testament: God, the Maker of heaven and earth, introduced himself to the people of Israel with the special, personal name, whose consonants are YHWH (see Exodus 3:14–15). Scholars call this the "Tetragrammaton," a Greek term referring to the four Hebrew letters YHWH. The exact pronunciation of YHWH is uncertain, because the Jewish people considered the personal name of God to be so holy that it should never be spoken aloud. Instead of reading the word YHWH, they would normally read the Hebrew word *adonai* ("Lord"), and the ancient translations into Greek, Syriac, and Aramaic also followed suit. When the vowels of the word *adonai* are placed with the consonants of YHWH, this results in the familiar word *Jehovah* that was used in some earlier English Bible translations. As is common among English translations today, the ESV usually renders the personal name of God (YHWH) with the word Lord (printed in small capitals). An exception to this is when the Hebrew word adonai appears together with YHWH, in which case the two words are rendered together as "the Lord [in lower case] God [in small capitals]." In contrast to the personal name for God (YHWH), the more general name for God in Old Testament Hebrew is *'elohim* and its related forms of *'el* or *'eloah*, all of which are normally translated "God" (in lower case letters). The use of these different ways to translate the Hebrew words for God is especially beneficial to the English reader, enabling the reader to see and understand the different ways that the *personal* name and the *general* name for God are both used to refer to the *One True God* of the Old Testament.

Second, in the New Testament, the Greek word *Christos* has been translated consistently as "Christ." Although the term originally meant "anointed," among Jews in New Testament times the term came to designate the Messiah, the great Savior that God had promised to raise up. In other New Testament contexts, however, especially among Gentiles, *Christos* ("Christ") was on its way to becoming a proper name. It is important, therefore, to keep the context in mind in understanding the various ways that *Christos* ("Christ") is used in the New Testament. At the same time, in accord with its "essentially literal" translation philosophy, the ESV has retained consistency and concordance in the translation of *Christos* ("Christ") throughout the New Testament.

A third specialized term, the word "behold," usually has been retained as the most common translation for the Hebrew word *hinneh* and the Greek word *idou*. Both of these words mean something like "Pay careful attention to what follows! This is important!" Other than the word "behold," there is no single word in English that fits well in most contexts. Although "Look!" and "See!" and "Listen!" would be workable in some contexts, in many others these words lack sufficient weight and dignity. Given the principles of "essentially literal" translation, it is important not to leave *hinneh* and *idou*

completely untranslated, and so to lose the intended emphasis in the original languages. The older and more formal word "behold" has usually been retained, therefore,
as the best available option for conveying the original sense of meaning.

▌**Textual Basis.** The ESV is based on the Masoretic text of the Hebrew Bible as found
in *Biblia Hebraica Stuttgartensia* (2nd ed., 1983), and on the Greek text in the 1993
editions of the *Greek New Testament* (4th corrected ed.), published by the United
Bible Societies (UBS), and *Novum Testamentum Graece* (27th ed.), edited by Nestle
and Aland. The currently renewed respect among Old Testament scholars for the
Masoretic text is reflected in the ESV's attempt, wherever possible, to translate difficult
Hebrew passages as they stand in the Masoretic text rather than resorting to emenda-
tions or to finding an alternative reading in the ancient versions. In exceptional, difficult
cases, the Dead Sea Scrolls, the Septuagint, the Samaritan Pentateuch, the Syriac
Peshitta, the Latin Vulgate, and other sources were consulted to shed possible light on
the text, or, if necessary, to support a divergence from the Masoretic text. Similarly, in
a few difficult cases in the New Testament, the ESV has followed a Greek text different
from the text given preference in the UBS/Nestle-Aland 27th edition. In this regard the
footnotes that accompany the ESV text are an integral part of the ESV translation,
informing the reader of textual variations and difficulties and showing how these have
been resolved by the ESV translation team. In addition to this, the footnotes indicate
significant alternative readings and occasionally provide an explanation for technical
terms or for a difficult reading in the text. Throughout, the translation team has
benefited greatly from the massive textual resources that have become readily available
recently, from new insights into biblical laws and culture, and from current advances in
Hebrew and Greek lexicography and grammatical understanding.

▌**Publishing Team.** The ESV publishing team includes more than a hundred people.
The fourteen-member Translation Oversight Committee has benefited from the work of
fifty biblical experts serving as Translation Review Scholars and from the comments of
the more than fifty members of the Advisory Council, all of which has been carried out
under the auspices of the Good News Publishers Board of Directors. This hundred-
member team, which shares a common commitment to the truth of God's Word and to
historic Christian orthodoxy, is international in scope and includes leaders in many
denominations.

▌**To God's Honor and Praise.** We know that no Bible translation is perfect or final; but
we also know that God uses imperfect and inadequate things to his honor and praise.
So to our triune God and to his people we offer what we have done, with our prayers
that it may prove useful, with gratitude for much help given, and with ongoing wonder
that our God should ever have entrusted to us so momentous a task.

Soli Deo Gloria!—To God alone be the glory!

*The Translation Oversight Committee**

*A complete list of the Translation Oversight Committee, the Translation Review
Scholars, and the Advisory Council, is available upon request from Crossway
Bibles, a publishing ministry of Good News Publishers.

FEATURES

The Literary Study Bible includes two valuable features, in addition to those listed in the Editors' Preface, to encourage the reading and study of the Bible: textual footnotes and cross-reference footnotes. A brief description is provided below explaining the purpose and use of these notes.

TEXTUAL FOOTNOTES

Several kinds of footnotes related to the ESV text are provided throughout *The Literary Study Bible* to assist the reader. These footnotes appear at the bottom of the page and are indicated in the ESV text by a superscript *number* that *follows* the word or phrase to which the footnote applies (e.g., "Isaac[2]").

The footnotes included in the ESV Bible are an integral part of the text and provide important information concerning the understanding and translation of the text. The footnotes fall mainly into four categories, as illustrated in the examples below.

(1) *Alternative Translations.* Footnotes of this kind provide alternative translations for specific words or phrases when there is a strong possibility that such words or phrases could be translated in another way, such as: "Or *keep awake*" (see Matt. 26:38); and "Or *down payment*" (see Eph. 1:14). In such cases, the translation deemed to have the stronger support is in the text while other possible renderings are given in the note.

(2) *Explanation of Greek and Hebrew Terms.* Notes of this kind relate primarily to the meaning of specific Greek or Hebrew terms, as illustrated by the following examples:

(a) Notes about the meaning of names in the original languages, such as: "*Isaac* means *he laughs*" (see Gen. 17:19); and "*Simeon* sounds like the Hebrew for *heard*" (see Gen. 29:33).

(b) Notes that give the literal translation of a Greek or Hebrew word or phrase deemed too awkward to be used in the English text, such as: "Greek *girding up the loins of your mind*" (see 1 Pet. 1:13).

(c) Notes indicating that absolute certainty of the meaning of a word or phrase is not possible given our best understanding of the original language (e.g., Hebrew words occurring so infrequently in the Old Testament that their meaning cannot be determined with certainty). Such words are identified with a note stating that "The meaning of the Hebrew is uncertain" (see, e.g., Josh. 17:11).

(d) Notes that indicate the specialized use of a Greek word, such as: "brothers," translating the Greek word *adelphoi* (see, e.g., the extended note on Rom. 1:13, corresponding to the first occurrence of *adelphoi* in any New Testament book, and the abbreviated note, e.g., on Rom. 7:1, corresponding to subsequent occurrences of *adelphoi* in any New Testament book); and "sons," translating the Greek word *huioi* (see, e.g., Rom. 8:14). See also the discussion of *adelphoi* and *huioi* in the preface.

(3) *Other Explanatory Notes.* Footnotes of this kind provide clarifying information as illustrated by the following examples:

(a) Notes clarifying additional meanings that may not otherwise be apparent in the text, such as: "*Leprosy* was a term for several skin diseases; see Leviticus 13."

(b) Notes clarifying important grammatical points that would not otherwise be apparent in English, such as: "In Hebrew *you* is plural in verses 1–5" (see Gen. 3:1).

(c) Notes clarifying when the referent for a pronoun has been supplied in the English text, such as: "Greek *he*" (see, e.g., Mark 1:43).

(d) Notes giving English equivalents for weights, measures, and monetary values.

(4) *Technical Translation Notes.* Footnotes of this kind indicate how decisions have been made in the translation of difficult Hebrew and Greek passages. Such notes occasionally include technical terms. For an explanation of these terms the reader is referred to standard Bible study reference works. See further the section in the preface on "Textual Basis" for an explanation of the original-language texts used in the translation of the ESV Bible and how the translation of difficult passages has been resolved.

CROSS-REFERENCE FOOTNOTES

In addition to the *numeric* (textual) footnotes, the New Testament portion of *The Literary Study Bible* includes two kinds of cross-reference notes. These are identified *alphabetically* and follow the numeric notes at the bottom of each page. These include (1) *direct quotations from the Old Testament* (indirect quotations and allusions are not included), and (2) *parallel passages in the four Gospels.* These cross-references are included to help the reader understand the relationship of the New Testament to the Old Testament, and the harmony of the Gospels in the New Testament.

The
OLD TESTAMENT

GENESIS

The book at a glance. 50 chapters, 1,533 verses. As its title signals, the book of Genesis is the Bible's book of beginnings. It is a foundational book that informs us about the first principles of the biblical faith—such first principles as how the world came into being, how sin entered the world, how God began to unfold his plan of salvation, and what people and human institutions (especially the family) are like. Although Genesis is a history book, its history is packaged in highly literary forms, the most dominant of which is *hero story. Because the history that is recounted in the book of Genesis reaches back to the primitive origins of the human race, it is particularly rich in universal, elemental human experience. Despite the seeming remoteness of the world of Genesis, the experiences are actually very close to our everyday lives.

▌**Genres.** The book of Genesis is very complex, with numerous *genres converging in it. We are on safest ground if we begin with the premise that Genesis is an anthology or collection of diverse works. This anthology is more highly unified than most anthologies, however, inasmuch as all the material falls into the overall genre of historical *narrative. But the history is not packaged like history books with which we are familiar. Instead, the book of Genesis is primarily a collection of *hero stories, with interspersed *genealogies. In keeping with the nature of heroic narrative, the heroes of Genesis, for all their uniqueness in the drama of salvation history, are also representatives of the human condition generally. As a result, we can see our own experiences in their stories, and their heroism is in many cases a model for us to emulate. The first three chapters belong to a genre known as the *story of origins. Also, because the story is one of universal history (chapters 1–11) and the origins of the nation of Israel (chapters 12–50), the book of Genesis has affinities with *epic. (For more information on items accompanied by an asterisk, see the glossary at the back of this Bible.)

▌**The literary concept of a hero.** A literary approach to the book of Genesis requires that we think correctly about the concept of a literary hero. Here are five crucial principles regarding a literary hero: (1) real life provides the materials for a hero, but the image of the hero is always a selection and distillation drawn from a larger body of information about a person; (2) cultures celebrate heroes as a way of codifying their ideals, values, and virtues; (3) literary heroes are representative of the culture producing them and of people universally; (4) to rank as a hero, a person must be generally admirable—an ideal character to whom we look up; (5) this does not mean, however, that heroes are wholly idealized, and in the Bible they rarely are wholly idealized. Much of what a storyteller aims to say about life is embodied in the character

Passage	Content	Contribution to the Story of Redemptive History	Type of History	Cast of Characters	Most Memorable Events or Characters
1:1–2:25	God's perfect creation	God blesses his creation			
3:1–24	Humanity's fall into sin				Four main events: creation, fall, flood, Tower of Babel
4:1–5:32	Cain, Abel, genealogies	The human race forfeits God's blessing	Primeval history	The whole human race	
6:1–9:29	Noah and the flood				
10:1–11:32	Dispersion of the nations				
12:1–25:18	Story of Abraham				
25:19–26:35	Story of Isaac				Four main characters: Abraham, Isaac, Jacob, Joseph
27:1–35:29	Story of Jacob	God unfolds a plan to bless his covenant people	Patriarchal history	A single family line	
36:1–43	Generations of Esau				
37:1–50:26	Story of Joseph and his brothers				

and experiences of the hero. As we read a hero story, we become the observant traveling companion of the hero, sharing his or her experiences and learning the lessons that the hero learned.

▌**The story lines.** Even though Genesis is an anthology of diverse (mainly narrative) units, there are underlying story lines that unify the book. The first eleven chapters tell the history of the entire human race and are called primeval history. The rest of the book gives us patriarchal history and tells the story of a single family line beginning with Abraham. Despite all the diversity, therefore, two main stories are told. Another unifying plot line is covenant history—the story of the binding agreements by which God relates to his people. Some of these are stated explicitly and others are inferred by the reader: the covenant of works with Adam and Eve (Genesis 2), in which their complete perfection depended on their continued obedience to God; the covenant with Noah (Gen. 9:1–17), in which God promised never to destroy the earth with a flood again; the covenant with Abraham, in which God promised to bless all nations. Within the context of the foregoing story lines, an additional one emerges: the story of individuals' choosing either to trust and obey God or to follow a path of expediency in which they behave according to their own inclinations (which are usually depraved).

▌**The cast of characters.** God is the only character who is present from start to finish, and in the overall story of Genesis God is the protagonist or central character. All the human characters in the story interact with this great protagonist and his designs. Even though the human scene in Genesis becomes crowded as the stories unfold, there are eight great heroes of Genesis: Adam, Abel, Enoch, Noah, Abraham, Isaac, Jacob, and Joseph. There are also five major heroines: Eve, Sarah, Rebekah, Leah, and Rachel. In a book where the arena of action is usually the family, five couples occupy much of our interest: Adam and Eve, Abraham and Sarah, Isaac and Rebekah, Jacob and Leah, Jacob and Rachel.

▍**Unifying motifs.** (1) The characterization of God and the story of his dealings with people. (2) The sinfulness of the human race and individuals. (3) The story of God's unfolding plan to redeem a people for himself despite human waywardness (to use John Milton's formula, "supernal grace contending with sinfulness of men"). (4) Hero story as the nearly constant genre. (5) An abundance of universal, recognizable human experience. (6) Characters, characters, characters: in both the narrative parts of Genesis and in the genealogies, we are continuously drawn into an encounter with unforgettable characters and their stories.

▍**Inferred literary intentions.** The book is designed to achieve the following literary purposes:

- acquaint us with first things—the events that happened first in human history and the foundational principles of human existence

- satisfy our taste for story by giving us stories that are the very touchstone of great narrative

- give us a full-fledged portrait of the character of God

- get us to share essential human experiences with the memorable characters of the book

- clue us in to the beginnings of God's covenant of redemption that culminated in the atoning sacrifice of Jesus

- show us how to live our daily lives in accordance with God's will for people

▍**Theological themes.** (1) Creation: early Genesis is the most important repository of biblical teaching on the physical world of nature. (2) The nature of God: the acts and attributes of God are so extensively portrayed that we can compile a theology just from this book. (3) The nature of people: Genesis is also the basic biblical text on what theologians call anthropology, or the nature of people. (4) Sin: Genesis is an anatomy of human sinfulness—an ever-expanding picture of how people do what is evil. (5) Covenant: Genesis traces the early phases of God's plan to redeem sinful humanity. (6) Providence: God guides the history of the world and of individuals (especially Joseph) to accomplish his purposes. (7) Faith: the heroic characters (especially Abraham) are examples of faith in God.

▍**Genesis as a chapter in the master story of the Bible.** The master story of the Bible begins in Genesis. Genesis is our introduction to the character of God and his plan for dealing with the human race. It is also the beginning of human history, starting with the state of innocence and then plummeting to the fallen state. The great struggle between good and evil begins in Genesis. A major strand in the master story of the Bible is the unfolding of God's covenant with the human race, and this covenant history starts with the book of Genesis. From the beginning, God's purpose for Abraham and his offspring is to bless all the nations. Genesis 3:15 is the first announcement of the master story of the Bible that finds its fulfillment in Christ.

The creation of the world [chapter 1]. Genesis 1 is a story of origins that narrates how the universe in which we live came into being. God is the only character in the story, which is structured as a catalog of his creative acts. The account is highly artistic in its patterning, with a general set of ingredients appearing in all six days of creation: (1) the announcement "and God said"; (2) a divine command using the formula "let there be" or some other form of "let"; (3) the report "and it was so"; (4) evaluation by means of the formula "God saw that it was good"; (5) placement in time, using the formula "there was evening and there was morning, the _____ day." Further patterning exists in the orderly arrangement of God's filling in the canvas as divine artist: first he creates three places or settings (light; sky and sea; dry land and vegetation), and then he fills each setting with the appropriate creatures (light bearers; birds and sea creatures; land animals and people).

1 In the beginning, God created the heavens and the earth. [2]The earth was without form and void, and darkness was over the face of the deep. And the Spirit of God was hovering over the face of the waters.

[3]And God said, "Let there be light," and there was light. [4]And God saw that the light was good. And God separated the light from the darkness. [5]God called the light Day, and the darkness he called Night. And there was evening and there was morning, the first day.

[6]And God said, "Let there be an expanse[1] in the midst of the waters, and let it separate the waters from the waters." [7]And God made[2] the expanse and separated the waters that were under the expanse from the waters that were above the expanse. And it was so. [8]And God called the expanse Heaven.[3] And there was evening and there was morning, the second day.

[9]And God said, "Let the waters under the heavens be gathered together into one place, and let the dry land appear." And it was so. [10]God called the dry land Earth,[4] and the waters that were gathered together he called Seas. And God saw that it was good.

[11]And God said, "Let the earth sprout vegetation, plants[5] yielding seed, and fruit trees bearing fruit in which is their seed, each according to its kind, on the earth." And it was so. [12]The earth brought forth vegetation, plants yielding seed according to their own kinds, and trees bearing fruit in which is their seed, each according to its kind. And God saw that it was good. [13]And there was evening and there was morning, the third day.

[14]And God said, "Let there be lights in the expanse of the heavens to separate the day from the night. And let them be for signs and for seasons,[6] and for days and years, [15]and let them be lights in the expanse of the heavens to give light upon the earth." And it was so. [16]And God made the two great lights—the greater light to rule

[1] Or a canopy; also verses 7, 8, 14, 15, 17, 20 [2] Or fashioned; also verse 16 [3] Or Sky; also verses 9, 14, 15, 17, 20, 26, 28, 30; 2:1 [4] Or Land; also verses 11, 12, 22, 24, 25, 26, 28, 30; 2:1 [5] Or small plants; also verses 12, 29 [6] Or appointed times

the day and the lesser light to rule the night—and the stars. ¹⁷And God set them in the expanse of the heavens to give light on the earth, ¹⁸to rule over the day and over the night, and to separate the light from the darkness. And God saw that it was good. ¹⁹And there was evening and there was morning, the fourth day.

²⁰And God said, "Let the waters swarm with swarms of living creatures, and let birds¹ fly above the earth across the expanse of the heavens." ²¹So God created the great sea creatures and every living creature that moves, with which the waters swarm, according to their kinds, and every winged bird according to its kind. And God saw that it was good. ²²And God blessed them, saying, "Be fruitful and multiply and fill the waters in the seas, and let birds multiply on the earth." ²³And there was evening and there was morning, the fifth day.

²⁴And God said, "Let the earth bring forth living creatures according to their kinds—livestock and creeping things and beasts of the earth according to their kinds." And it was so. ²⁵And God made the beasts of the earth according to their kinds and the livestock according to their kinds, and everything that creeps on the ground according to its kind. And God saw that it was good.

²⁶Then God said, "Let us make man² in our image, after our likeness. And let them have dominion over the fish of the sea and over the birds of the heavens and over the livestock and over all the earth and over every creeping thing that creeps on the earth."

²⁷   So God created man in his own image,
        in the image of God he created him;
        male and female he created them.

²⁸And God blessed them. And God said to them, "Be fruitful and multiply and fill the earth and subdue it and have dominion over the fish of the sea and over the birds of the heavens and over every living thing that moves on the earth." ²⁹And God said, "Behold, I have given you every plant yielding seed that is on the face of all the earth, and every tree with seed in its fruit. You shall have them for food. ³⁰And to every beast of the earth and to every bird of the heavens and to everything that creeps on the earth, everything that has the breath of life, I have given every green plant for food." And it was so. ³¹And God saw everything that he had made, and behold, it was very good. And there was evening and there was morning, the sixth day.

Life in Paradise [chapter 2]. Chapter 2 is not a duplicate creation story—still less a creation story that contradicts the one told in chapter 1. Rather, it takes the creation of the cosmos (chapter 1) for granted and narrates how within that cosmos God created the perfect environment for his human creatures. A new name for God appears: *Yahweh Elohim* (the Lord God), the personal and covenant name of God, to complement the name *Elohim* (the Mighty One) used in Genesis 1. The cast of characters expands from the single divine protagonist in chapter 1 to the inclusion of Adam and Eve. Dialogue now balances the list of divine acts, as God enters into relationship with his creatures. The cosmic setting of chapter 1 is replaced by the enclosed garden. The terms used for plants (v. 5) and animals (vv. 19–20) imply domesticated plants and animals (and there is no mention of sea creatures). We can organize the story around the motif of the things that God provided for his human creatures—physical life (v. 7); a perfect environment

¹ Or *flying things*; see Leviticus 11:19-20 ² The Hebrew word for *man* (*adam*) is the generic term for mankind and becomes the proper name *Adam*

that is both beautiful and functional (v. 9); food (v. 9); work (v. 15); moral choice (vv. 16–17); human companionship and marriage (vv. 20–24); overarching everything, communion with God.

2 Thus the heavens and the earth were finished, and all the host of them. ²And on the seventh day God finished his work that he had done, and he rested on the seventh day from all his work that he had done. ³So God blessed the seventh day and made it holy, because on it God rested from all his work that he had done in creation.

⁴   These are the generations
   of the heavens and the earth when they were created,
   in the day that the Lord God made the earth and the heavens.

⁵When no bush of the field[1] was yet in the land[2] and no small plant of the field had yet sprung up—for the Lord God had not caused it to rain on the land, and there was no man to work the ground, ⁶and a mist[3] was going up from the land and was watering the whole face of the ground— ⁷then the Lord God formed the man of dust from the ground and breathed into his nostrils the breath of life, and the man became a living creature. ⁸And the Lord God planted a garden in Eden, in the east, and there he put the man whom he had formed. ⁹And out of the ground the Lord God made to spring up every tree that is pleasant to the sight and good for food. The tree of life was in the midst of the garden, and the tree of the knowledge of good and evil.

¹⁰A river flowed out of Eden to water the garden, and there it divided and became four rivers. ¹¹The name of the first is the Pishon. It is the one that flowed around the whole land of Havilah, where there is gold. ¹²And the gold of that land is good; bdellium and onyx stone are there. ¹³The name of the second river is the Gihon. It is the one that flowed around the whole land of Cush. ¹⁴And the name of the third river is the Tigris, which flows east of Assyria. And the fourth river is the Euphrates.

¹⁵The Lord God took the man and put him in the garden of Eden to work it and keep it. ¹⁶And the Lord God commanded the man, saying, "You may surely eat of every tree of the garden, ¹⁷but of the tree of the knowledge of good and evil you shall not eat, for in the day that you eat[4] of it you shall surely die."

¹⁸Then the Lord God said, "It is not good that the man should be alone; I will make him a helper fit for[5] him." ¹⁹Now out of the ground the Lord God had formed[6] every beast of the field and every bird of the heavens and brought them to the man to see what he would call them. And whatever the man called every living creature, that was its name. ²⁰The man gave names to all livestock and to the birds of the heavens and to every beast of the field. But for Adam[7] there was not found a helper fit for him. ²¹So the Lord God caused a deep sleep to fall upon the man, and while he slept took one of his ribs and closed up its place with flesh. ²²And the rib that the Lord God had taken from the man he made[8] into a woman and brought her to the man. ²³Then the man said,

   "This at last is bone of my bones
       and flesh of my flesh;

---

[1] Or open country [2] Or earth; also verse 6 [3] Or spring [4] Or when you eat [5] Or corresponding to; also verse 20 [6] Or And out of the ground the Lord God formed [7] Or the man [8] Hebrew built

she shall be called Woman,
    because she was taken out of Man."[1]

[24]Therefore a man shall leave his father and his mother and hold fast to his wife, and they shall become one flesh. [25]And the man and his wife were both naked and were not ashamed.

The Fall [chapter 3]. Genesis 3 completes the Bible's three-part story of origins. Its contribution is to record how sin and suffering entered the world. The story encompasses multiple archetypal plot motifs, including temptation, the fall from innocence, crime and punishment, and initiation. Additionally, Genesis 3 is the prototypical literary tragedy in the Bible. Satan (in the form of a serpent) is the archetypal tempter; Adam and Eve are the archetypal guilty children; God is the judge who, as a divine parent, ferrets out the truth from reluctant children. Even though this is one of the saddest stories in the Bible, nonetheless loss is balanced by restoration and judgment by mercy. The mainspring of the plot is disobedience. The story is an anatomy of how sin works in people's lives and of the effects of sin. The theological center of the story is Adam and Eve's spiritual alienation from God through sin, but at the human level the story is also a psychological portrayal of the dynamics of guilt. This historical narrative tells us both what *happened* on that fateful day and how sin *happens* in our own lives.

3 Now the serpent was more crafty than any other beast of the field that the LORD God had made.
He said to the woman, "Did God actually say, 'You[2] shall not eat of any tree in the garden'?" [2]And the woman said to the serpent, "We may eat of the fruit of the trees in the garden, [3]but God said, 'You shall not eat of the fruit of the tree that is in the midst of the garden, neither shall you touch it, lest you die.'" [4]But the serpent said to the woman, "You will not surely die. [5]For God knows that when you eat of it your eyes will be opened, and you will be like God, knowing good and evil." [6]So when the woman saw that the tree was good for food, and that it was a delight to the eyes, and that the tree was to be desired to make one wise,[3] she took of its fruit and ate, and she also gave some to her husband who was with her, and he ate. [7]Then the eyes of both were opened, and they knew that they were naked. And they sewed fig leaves together and made themselves loincloths.

[8]And they heard the sound of the LORD God walking in the garden in the cool[4] of the day, and the man and his wife hid themselves from the presence of the LORD God among the trees of the garden. [9]But the LORD God called to the man and said to him, "Where are you?"[5] [10]And he said, "I heard the sound of you in the garden, and I was afraid, because I was naked, and I hid myself." [11]He said, "Who told you that you were naked? Have you eaten of the tree of which I commanded you not to eat?" [12]The man said, "The woman whom you gave to be with me, she gave me fruit of the tree, and I ate." [13]Then the LORD God said to the woman, "What is this that you have done?" The woman said, "The serpent deceived me, and I ate."

[14]The LORD God said to the serpent,

"Because you have done this,
    cursed are you above all livestock

---

[1] The Hebrew words for *woman* (*ishshah*) and *man* (*ish*) sound alike [2] In Hebrew *you* is plural in verses 1-5 [3] Or *to give insight* [4] Hebrew *wind* [5] In Hebrew *you* is singular in verses 9 and 11

and above all beasts of the field;
  on your belly you shall go,
    and dust you shall eat
    all the days of your life.
15   I will put enmity between you and the woman,
    and between your offspring¹ and her offspring;
  he shall bruise your head,
    and you shall bruise his heel."

¹⁶To the woman he said,

"I will surely multiply your pain in childbearing;
    in pain you shall bring forth children.
  Your desire shall be for² your husband,
    and he shall rule over you."

¹⁷And to Adam he said,

"Because you have listened to the voice of your wife
    and have eaten of the tree
  of which I commanded you,
    'You shall not eat of it,'
  cursed is the ground because of you;
    in pain you shall eat of it all the days of your life;
18   thorns and thistles it shall bring forth for you;
    and you shall eat the plants of the field.
19   By the sweat of your face
      you shall eat bread,
    till you return to the ground,
      for out of it you were taken;
  for you are dust,
    and to dust you shall return."

²⁰The man called his wife's name Eve, because she was the mother of all living.³ ²¹And the LORD God made for Adam and for his wife garments of skins and clothed them.

²²Then the LORD God said, "Behold, the man has become like one of us in knowing good and evil. Now, lest he reach out his hand and take also of the tree of life and eat, and live forever—" ²³therefore the LORD God sent him out from the garden of Eden to work the ground from which he was taken. ²⁴He drove out the man, and at the east of the garden of Eden he placed the cherubim and a flaming sword that turned every way to guard the way to the tree of life.

The story of Cain and Abel [chapter 4]. We can organize our experience of this story as an exploration of Cain's evil heart. In fact, the story is structured as an unfolding series of bad actions and attitudes on Cain's part. He is the archetypal criminal, and his story is a story of crime and punishment. It is the story of a person who did not master sin in his life (v. 7) and of the consequences of that failure. To read the story as literature, we

¹ Hebrew *seed;* so throughout Genesis ² Or *against* ³ *Eve* sounds like the Hebrew for *life-giver* and resembles the word for *living*

need to be receptive to the abundance of recognizable human experiences embodied in just a single chapter: domestic violence, sibling rivalry, murder, a guilty child, lying to a parent (God), lack of self-control, harboring a grudge, giving in to an evil impulse, anger at having gotten caught, an attempted cover-up, trial and sentencing. The action unfolds in these phases: the criminal's family, occupational, and religious background (vv. 1–4); the motive for the crime (vv. 4–5); the criminal's counseling history (vv. 6–7); the circumstances of the crime (v. 8); arrest, trial, and sentencing (vv. 9–12); appeal and modification of the sentence (vv. 13–15); serving the sentence (v. 16).

4 Now Adam knew Eve his wife, and she conceived and bore Cain, saying, "I have gotten[1] a man with the help of the Lord." [2]And again, she bore his brother Abel. Now Abel was a keeper of sheep, and Cain a worker of the ground. [3]In the course of time Cain brought to the Lord an offering of the fruit of the ground, [4]and Abel also brought of the firstborn of his flock and of their fat portions. And the Lord had regard for Abel and his offering, [5]but for Cain and his offering he had no regard. So Cain was very angry, and his face fell. [6]The Lord said to Cain, "Why are you angry, and why has your face fallen? [7]If you do well, will you not be accepted?[2] And if you do not do well, sin is crouching at the door. Its desire is for[3] you, but you must rule over it."

[8]Cain spoke to Abel his brother.[4] And when they were in the field, Cain rose up against his brother Abel and killed him. [9]Then the Lord said to Cain, "Where is Abel your brother?" He said, "I do not know; am I my brother's keeper?" [10]And the Lord said, "What have you done? The voice of your brother's blood is crying to me from the ground. [11]And now you are cursed from the ground, which has opened its mouth to receive your brother's blood from your hand. [12]When you work the ground, it shall no longer yield to you its strength. You shall be a fugitive and a wanderer on the earth." [13]Cain said to the Lord, "My punishment is greater than I can bear.[5] [14]Behold, you have driven me today away from the ground, and from your face I shall be hidden. I shall be a fugitive and a wanderer on the earth, and whoever finds me will kill me." [15]Then the Lord said to him, "Not so! If anyone kills Cain, vengeance shall be taken on him sevenfold." And the Lord put a mark on Cain, lest any who found him should attack him. [16]Then Cain went away from the presence of the Lord and settled in the land of Nod,[6] east of Eden.

[17]Cain knew his wife, and she conceived and bore Enoch. When he built a city, he called the name of the city after the name of his son, Enoch. [18]To Enoch was born Irad, and Irad fathered Mehujael, and Mehujael fathered Methushael, and Methushael fathered Lamech. [19]And Lamech took two wives. The name of the one was Adah, and the name of the other Zillah. [20]Adah bore Jabal; he was the father of those who dwell in tents and have livestock. [21]His brother's name was Jubal; he was the father of all those who play the lyre and pipe. [22]Zillah also bore Tubal-cain; he was the forger of all instruments of bronze and iron. The sister of Tubal-cain was Naamah.

[23]Lamech said to his wives:

"Adah and Zillah, hear my voice;
    you wives of Lamech, listen to what I say:

---

[1] *Cain* sounds like the Hebrew for *gotten* [2] Hebrew *will there not be a lifting up* [of your face]? [3] Or *against* [4] Hebrew; Samaritan, Septuagint, Syriac, Vulgate add *Let us go out to the field* [5] Or *My guilt is too great to bear* [6] *Nod* means *wandering*

I have killed a man for wounding me,
        a young man for striking me.
²⁴   If Cain's revenge is sevenfold,
        then Lamech's is seventy-sevenfold."

²⁵And Adam knew his wife again, and she bore a son and called his name Seth, for she said, "God has appointed[1] for me another offspring instead of Abel, for Cain killed him." ²⁶To Seth also a son was born, and he called his name Enosh. At that time people began to call upon the name of the LORD.

> **The genealogy of Adam** [chapter 5]. As we work our way through Genesis, we swing back and forth between overview and close-up. Chapter 5 is an overview that lists the generations of Adam. There are several ways to approach the *genealogies of the Bible: (1) we need to recognize that ancient cultures (and some modern ones) were very interested in family origins; (2) the genealogies fit into the biblical theme of the continuity of generations; (3) the genealogies show the importance that God places on every individual; (4) the genealogies demonstrate that the Bible is a historical rather than a fictional book; (5) the genealogies sometimes have hidden theological meanings (for example, embodying either true faith or sinfulness, thereby serving as an encouragement or warning to us).

5 This is the book of the generations of Adam. When God created man, he made him in the likeness of God. ²Male and female he created them, and he blessed them and named them Man[2] when they were created. ³When Adam had lived 130 years, he fathered a son in his own likeness, after his image, and named him Seth. ⁴The days of Adam after he fathered Seth were 800 years; and he had other sons and daughters. ⁵Thus all the days that Adam lived were 930 years, and he died.

⁶When Seth had lived 105 years, he fathered Enosh. ⁷Seth lived after he fathered Enosh 807 years and had other sons and daughters. ⁸Thus all the days of Seth were 912 years, and he died.

⁹When Enosh had lived 90 years, he fathered Kenan. ¹⁰Enosh lived after he fathered Kenan 815 years and had other sons and daughters. ¹¹Thus all the days of Enosh were 905 years, and he died.

¹²When Kenan had lived 70 years, he fathered Mahalalel. ¹³Kenan lived after he fathered Mahalalel 840 years and had other sons and daughters. ¹⁴Thus all the days of Kenan were 910 years, and he died.

¹⁵When Mahalalel had lived 65 years, he fathered Jared. ¹⁶Mahalalel lived after he fathered Jared 830 years and had other sons and daughters. ¹⁷Thus all the days of Mahalalel were 895 years, and he died.

¹⁸When Jared had lived 162 years he fathered Enoch. ¹⁹Jared lived after he fathered Enoch 800 years and had other sons and daughters. ²⁰Thus all the days of Jared were 962 years, and he died.

²¹When Enoch had lived 65 years, he fathered Methuselah. ²²Enoch walked with God[3] after he fathered Methuselah 300 years and had other sons and daughters. ²³Thus all the days of Enoch were 365 years. ²⁴Enoch walked with God, and he was not,[4] for God took him.

²⁵When Methuselah had lived 187 years, he fathered Lamech. ²⁶Methuselah lived

---

[1] Seth sounds like the Hebrew for *he appointed* [2] Hebrew *adam* [3] Septuagint *pleased God* [4] Septuagint *was not found*

after he fathered Lamech 782 years and had other sons and daughters. [27]Thus all the days of Methuselah were 969 years, and he died.

[28]When Lamech had lived 182 years, he fathered a son [29]and called his name Noah, saying, "Out of the ground that the LORD has cursed this one shall bring us relief[1] from our work and from the painful toil of our hands." [30]Lamech lived after he fathered Noah 595 years and had other sons and daughters. [31]Thus all the days of Lamech were 777 years, and he died.

[32]After Noah was 500 years old, Noah fathered Shem, Ham, and Japheth.

Events leading to the Flood [chapter 6]. The story of Noah and the flood occupies four chapters, which together constitute a complete action. Nonetheless, it is possible to divide the story into four successive phases. Chapter 6 is the prelude to the main action. In this prelude, we learn about why God sent the flood (vv. 1–7, 11–12); about the heroism of Noah that led God to choose him as an agent of rescue (vv. 8–10); about God's instructions for the ark as Noah becomes God's confidant (vv. 13–21); about Noah's obedience (v. 22). In effect, God gives Noah a survival kit and survival plan for the entire creation.

---

6 When man began to multiply on the face of the land and daughters were born to them, [2]the sons of God saw that the daughters of man were attractive. And they took as their wives any they chose. [3]Then the LORD said, "My Spirit shall not abide in[2] man forever, for he is flesh: his days shall be 120 years." [4]The Nephilim[3] were on the earth in those days, and also afterward, when the sons of God came in to the daughters of man and they bore children to them. These were the mighty men who were of old, the men of renown.

[5]The LORD saw that the wickedness of man was great in the earth, and that every intention of the thoughts of his heart was only evil continually. [6]And the LORD was sorry that he had made man on the earth, and it grieved him to his heart. [7]So the LORD said, "I will blot out man whom I have created from the face of the land, man and animals and creeping things and birds of the heavens, for I am sorry that I have made them." [8]But Noah found favor in the eyes of the LORD.

[9]These are the generations of Noah. Noah was a righteous man, blameless in his generation. Noah walked with God. [10]And Noah had three sons, Shem, Ham, and Japheth.

[11]Now the earth was corrupt in God's sight, and the earth was filled with violence. [12]And God saw the earth, and behold, it was corrupt, for all flesh had corrupted their way on the earth. [13]And God said to Noah, "I have determined to make an end of all flesh,[4] for the earth is filled with violence through them. Behold, I will destroy them with the earth. [14]Make yourself an ark of gopher wood.[5] Make rooms in the ark, and cover it inside and out with pitch. [15]This is how you are to make it: the length of the ark 300 cubits,[6] its breadth 50 cubits, and its height 30 cubits. [16]Make a roof[7] for the ark, and finish it to a cubit above, and set the door of the ark in its side. Make it with lower, second, and third decks. [17]For behold, I will bring a flood of waters upon the earth to destroy all flesh in which is the breath of life under heaven. Everything that is on the earth shall die. [18]But I will establish my covenant with you, and you shall come into the ark, you, your sons, your wife, and your sons' wives with you. [19]And of

---

[1] Noah sounds like the Hebrew for *rest* [2] Or *My Spirit shall not contend with* [3] Or *giants* [4] Hebrew *The end of all flesh has come before me* [5] An unknown kind of tree; transliterated from Hebrew [6] A *cubit* was about 18 inches or 45 centimeters [7] Or *skylight*

every living thing of all flesh, you shall bring two of every sort into the ark to keep them alive with you. They shall be male and female. ²⁰Of the birds according to their kinds, and of the animals according to their kinds, of every creeping thing of the ground, according to its kind, two of every sort shall come in to you to keep them alive. ²¹Also take with you every sort of food that is eaten, and store it up. It shall serve as food for you and for them." ²²Noah did this; he did all that God commanded him.

The flood [chapter 7]. This is one of the most famous stories in the Bible, and one that stretches our imagination. We have all known localized floods, but this one magnifies that a hundredfold. We need to experience the terror of the event, and the story itself can be regarded as a cosmic horror story, invested with spiritual experience because the terror that God sent on the earth was his judgment against human sinfulness. It is also a grand death-rebirth story, and in regard to the rebirth we need to thrill at the care that God took to ensure the perpetuation of animal and human life on the earth. The concluding verse is like the moment of calm after a long storm, as people survey the aftermath of the cataclysm.

7 Then the Lord said to Noah, "Go into the ark, you and all your household, for I have seen that you are righteous before me in this generation. ²Take with you seven pairs of all clean animals,¹ the male and his mate, and a pair of the animals that are not clean, the male and his mate, ³and seven pairs² of the birds of the heavens also, male and female, to keep their offspring alive on the face of all the earth. ⁴For in seven days I will send rain on the earth forty days and forty nights, and every living thing³ that I have made I will blot out from the face of the ground." ⁵And Noah did all that the Lord had commanded him.

⁶Noah was six hundred years old when the flood of waters came upon the earth. ⁷And Noah and his sons and his wife and his sons' wives with him went into the ark to escape the waters of the flood. ⁸Of clean animals, and of animals that are not clean, and of birds, and of everything that creeps on the ground, ⁹two and two, male and female, went into the ark with Noah, as God had commanded Noah. ¹⁰And after seven days the waters of the flood came upon the earth.

¹¹In the six hundredth year of Noah's life, in the second month, on the seventeenth day of the month, on that day all the fountains of the great deep burst forth, and the windows of the heavens were opened. ¹²And rain fell upon the earth forty days and forty nights. ¹³On the very same day Noah and his sons, Shem and Ham and Japheth, and Noah's wife and the three wives of his sons with them entered the ark, ¹⁴they and every beast, according to its kind, and all the livestock according to their kinds, and every creeping thing that creeps on the earth, according to its kind, and every bird, according to its kind, every winged creature. ¹⁵They went into the ark with Noah, two and two of all flesh in which there was the breath of life. ¹⁶And those that entered, male and female of all flesh, went in as God had commanded him. And the Lord shut him in.

¹⁷The flood continued forty days on the earth. The waters increased and bore up the ark, and it rose high above the earth. ¹⁸The waters prevailed and increased greatly on the earth, and the ark floated on the face of the waters. ¹⁹And the waters prevailed so mightily on the earth that all the high mountains under the whole heaven were

¹ Or *seven of each kind of clean animal* ² Or *seven of each kind* ³ Hebrew *all existence*; also verse 23

covered. ²⁰The waters prevailed above the mountains, covering them fifteen cubits¹ deep. ²¹And all flesh died that moved on the earth, birds, livestock, beasts, all swarming creatures that swarm on the earth, and all mankind. ²²Everything on the dry land in whose nostrils was the breath of life died. ²³He blotted out every living thing that was on the face of the ground, man and animals and creeping things and birds of the heavens. They were blotted out from the earth. Only Noah was left, and those who were with him in the ark. ²⁴And the waters prevailed on the earth 150 days.

The rescue [8:1–19]. The story of the flood is a U-shaped death-rebirth story in which the action descends into calamity, reaches the bottom, and then gradually winds its way upward toward a restored earth. In terms of physical action, the story of the flood is a pyramid in which the waters rise to cover the earth and then subside so the earth can reappear. Chapter 7 was a survival story, as Noah's family was protected from drowning. Chapter 8 is a rescue story in which the family that survived the flood is rescued from their confinement on the boat. As every child knows, this is a suspense story: every time we read it we wonder anew what will happen to the dove, and we thrill to the climactic detail that the dove did not return to the ark. Equally perpetual is the sense of renewal that we feel as we read about Noah's family leaving the boat into a springtime setting.

8 But God remembered Noah and all the beasts and all the livestock that were with him in the ark. And God made a wind blow over the earth, and the waters subsided. ²The fountains of the deep and the windows of the heavens were closed, the rain from the heavens was restrained, ³and the waters receded from the earth continually. At the end of 150 days the waters had abated, ⁴and in the seventh month, on the seventeenth day of the month, the ark came to rest on the mountains of Ararat. ⁵And the waters continued to abate until the tenth month; in the tenth month, on the first day of the month, the tops of the mountains were seen.

⁶At the end of forty days Noah opened the window of the ark that he had made ⁷and sent forth a raven. It went to and fro until the waters were dried up from the earth. ⁸Then he sent forth a dove from him, to see if the waters had subsided from the face of the ground. ⁹But the dove found no place to set her foot, and she returned to him to the ark, for the waters were still on the face of the whole earth. So he put out his hand and took her and brought her into the ark with him. ¹⁰He waited another seven days, and again he sent forth the dove out of the ark. ¹¹And the dove came back to him in the evening, and behold, in her mouth was a freshly plucked olive leaf. So Noah knew that the waters had subsided from the earth. ¹²Then he waited another seven days and sent forth the dove, and she did not return to him anymore.

¹³In the six hundred and first year, in the first month, the first day of the month, the waters were dried from off the earth. And Noah removed the covering of the ark and looked, and behold, the face of the ground was dry. ¹⁴In the second month, on the twenty-seventh day of the month, the earth had dried out. ¹⁵Then God said to Noah, ¹⁶"Go out from the ark, you and your wife, and your sons and your sons' wives with you. ¹⁷Bring out with you every living thing that is with you of all flesh—birds and animals and every creeping thing that creeps on the earth—that they may swarm on the earth, and be fruitful and multiply on the earth." ¹⁸So Noah went out, and his sons and his wife and his sons' wives with him. ¹⁹Every beast, every creeping thing, and every bird, everything that moves on the earth, went out by families from the ark.

---

¹ A *cubit* was about 18 inches or 45 centimeters

God's covenant with Noah [8:20–9:19]. The narrative excitement of the flood story now gives way to a passage that is heavy with theological vocabulary and significance. It is as though we have returned to the atmosphere that surrounds the first two chapters of Genesis, as God begins a new cycle of creation and a new covenant. The sequence is as follows: God responds to Noah's offering by promising never again to destroy the earth or interfere with its natural cycles (8:20–22); God blesses Noah and outlines certain foundational principles for human life in this world (9:1–7); God repeats his covenant promises and adds the rainbow as a sign of his covenant with Noah and the human race (9:8–17); brief genealogical note regarding the family of the heroic Noah (9:18–19).

²⁰Then Noah built an altar to the LORD and took some of every clean animal and some of every clean bird and offered burnt offerings on the altar. ²¹And when the LORD smelled the pleasing aroma, the LORD said in his heart, "I will never again curse¹ the ground because of man, for the intention of man's heart is evil from his youth. Neither will I ever again strike down every living creature as I have done. ²²While the earth remains, seedtime and harvest, cold and heat, summer and winter, day and night, shall not cease."

9 And God blessed Noah and his sons and said to them, "Be fruitful and multiply and fill the earth. ²The fear of you and the dread of you shall be upon every beast of the earth and upon every bird of the heavens, upon everything that creeps on the ground and all the fish of the sea. Into your hand they are delivered. ³Every moving thing that lives shall be food for you. And as I gave you the green plants, I give you everything. ⁴But you shall not eat flesh with its life, that is, its blood. ⁵And for your lifeblood I will require a reckoning: from every beast I will require it and from man. From his fellow man I will require a reckoning for the life of man.

⁶   "Whoever sheds the blood of man,
        by man shall his blood be shed,
    for God made man in his own image.

⁷And you,² be fruitful and multiply, teem on the earth and multiply in it."

⁸Then God said to Noah and to his sons with him, ⁹"Behold, I establish my covenant with you and your offspring after you, ¹⁰and with every living creature that is with you, the birds, the livestock, and every beast of the earth with you, as many as came out of the ark; it is for every beast of the earth. ¹¹I establish my covenant with you, that never again shall all flesh be cut off by the waters of the flood, and never again shall there be a flood to destroy the earth." ¹²And God said, "This is the sign of the covenant that I make between me and you and every living creature that is with you, for all future generations: ¹³I have set my bow in the cloud, and it shall be a sign of the covenant between me and the earth. ¹⁴When I bring clouds over the earth and the bow is seen in the clouds, ¹⁵I will remember my covenant that is between me and you and every living creature of all flesh. And the waters shall never again become a flood to destroy all flesh. ¹⁶When the bow is in the clouds, I will see it and remember the everlasting covenant between God and every living creature of all flesh that is on the earth." ¹⁷God said to Noah, "This is the sign of the covenant that I have established between me and all flesh that is on the earth."

---

¹ Or *dishonor* ² In Hebrew *you* is plural

¹⁸The sons of Noah who went forth from the ark were Shem, Ham, and Japheth. (Ham was the father of Canaan.) ¹⁹These three were the sons of Noah, and from these the people of the whole earth were dispersed.¹

> **The family tree of Noah** [9:20–10:32]. The story of Noah has been a hero story up to this point—the story of an exemplary character whom God chose for extraordinary service. At this point the historical impulse takes over. We begin with an event that deheroizes Noah (his drunkenness as narrated in 9:20). As famous as that sordid chapter in Noah's life is, it gets only one verse in the biblical account, where the primary focus is not on Noah's sin but on the differentiation of Noah's sons into the categories of good and bad (9:21–27). The life of the heroic Noah reaches closure with a brief obituary notice (9:28–29). The moral judgment that Noah pronounces on his three sons on the occasion of his waking up from his drunkenness reaches its outworking in the genealogies of chapter 10. Together the names in the genealogy constitute a Table of Nations, and their number, seventy (multiple of seven and ten, important numbers in Genesis), symbolizes totality (all the nations of the earth). The list implies the unity and interrelatedness of all people (who have a common ancestry and responsibility to their Creator) but also their diversity (they are divided by geography, language, ethnicity, and culture). We can also see evidence of God's preservation of the messianic line through both primeval and patriarchal history (a leading motif in Genesis).

²⁰Noah began to be a man of the soil, and he planted a vineyard.² ²¹He drank of the wine and became drunk and lay uncovered in his tent. ²²And Ham, the father of Canaan, saw the nakedness of his father and told his two brothers outside. ²³Then Shem and Japheth took a garment, laid it on both their shoulders, and walked backward and covered the nakedness of their father. Their faces were turned backward, and they did not see their father's nakedness. ²⁴When Noah awoke from his wine and knew what his youngest son had done to him, ²⁵he said,

"Cursed be Canaan;
a servant of servants shall he be to his brothers."

²⁶He also said,

"Blessed be the LORD, the God of Shem;
and let Canaan be his servant.
²⁷   May God enlarge Japheth,³
and let him dwell in the tents of Shem,
and let Canaan be his servant."

²⁸After the flood Noah lived 350 years. ²⁹All the days of Noah were 950 years, and he died.

10 These are the generations of the sons of Noah, Shem, Ham, and Japheth. Sons were born to them after the flood.
²The sons of Japheth: Gomer, Magog, Madai, Javan, Tubal, Meshech, and Tiras. ³The sons of Gomer: Ashkenaz, Riphath, and Togarmah. ⁴The sons of Javan: Elishah, Tarshish, Kittim, and Dodanim. ⁵From these the coastland peoples spread in their lands, each with his own language, by their clans, in their nations.

---

¹ Or from these the whole earth was populated ² Or Noah, a man of the soil, was the first to plant a vineyard ³ Japheth sounds like the Hebrew for enlarge

⁶The sons of Ham: Cush, Egypt, Put, and Canaan. ⁷The sons of Cush: Seba, Havilah, Sabtah, Raamah, and Sabteca. The sons of Raamah: Sheba and Dedan. ⁸Cush fathered Nimrod; he was the first on earth to be a mighty man.¹ ⁹He was a mighty hunter before the LORD. Therefore it is said, "Like Nimrod a mighty hunter before the LORD." ¹⁰The beginning of his kingdom was Babel, Erech, Accad, and Calneh, in the land of Shinar. ¹¹From that land he went into Assyria and built Nineveh, Rehoboth-Ir, Calah, and ¹²Resen between Nineveh and Calah; that is the great city. ¹³Egypt fathered Ludim, Anamim, Lehabim, Naphtuhim, ¹⁴Pathrusim, Casluhim (from whom² the Philistines came), and Caphtorim.

¹⁵Canaan fathered Sidon his firstborn and Heth, ¹⁶and the Jebusites, the Amorites, the Girgashites, ¹⁷the Hivites, the Arkites, the Sinites, ¹⁸the Arvadites, the Zemarites, and the Hamathites. Afterward the clans of the Canaanites dispersed. ¹⁹And the territory of the Canaanites extended from Sidon in the direction of Gerar as far as Gaza, and in the direction of Sodom, Gomorrah, Admah, and Zeboiim, as far as Lasha. ²⁰These are the sons of Ham, by their clans, their languages, their lands, and their nations.

²¹To Shem also, the father of all the children of Eber, the elder brother of Japheth, children were born. ²²The sons of Shem: Elam, Asshur, Arpachshad, Lud, and Aram. ²³The sons of Aram: Uz, Hul, Gether, and Mash. ²⁴Arpachshad fathered Shelah; and Shelah fathered Eber. ²⁵To Eber were born two sons: the name of the one was Peleg,³ for in his days the earth was divided, and his brother's name was Joktan. ²⁶Joktan fathered Almodad, Sheleph, Hazarmaveth, Jerah, ²⁷Hadoram, Uzal, Diklah, ²⁸Obal, Abimael, Sheba, ²⁹Ophir, Havilah, and Jobab; all these were the sons of Joktan. ³⁰The territory in which they lived extended from Mesha in the direction of Sephar to the hill country of the east. ³¹These are the sons of Shem, by their clans, their languages, their lands, and their nations.

³²These are the clans of the sons of Noah, according to their genealogies, in their nations, and from these the nations spread abroad on the earth after the flood.

The Tower of Babel [11:1–9]. The importance and literary richness of this story is disproportionate to its shortness. The genre is known as *etiology—a story about the origin of something (in this case the diversity of human languages and dispersion of the human race over the earth). But the story is much more than that. The story is timeless and a picture of our own culture—a picture of the following things: the human urge for fame and permanence; human self-reliance and aspiration; excitement about technology as the thing that will make the good life possible (kiln-fired bricks as opposed to quarried stone); human confidence that the city is the ultimate environment for society; the desire to control human destiny through a unified civilization; the skyscraper as a proud symbol of the triumph of technology. The Tower of Babel is a picture of utopian planning. The author's point of view, though, is *satiric, as he mocks the enterprise that the human race pursued with such energy. For example, we learn that the bricks are held together with bitumen or asphalt instead of mortar. The detail that God "came down" to have a look (v. 5) is also a put-down, suddenly making the skyscraper seem much less imposing than the human view that it could reach to heaven (v. 4). The whole story turns on the contrast between God's perspective on the human experiment in greatness and humanity's perspective. Because of God's intervention, the story turns on the plot device

---

¹ Or he began to be a mighty man on the earth ² Or from where ³ Peleg means division

of reversal, as the misguided vision of a unified human race ends in confusion and dispersion. In yet another narrative surprise, God frustrates the human attempt at autonomy not because it will not succeed but for the opposite reason—because its success is assured (v. 6). The interpretive key is therefore to ascertain why God thinks the great experiment outlined in verses 1–4 would be bad rather than good for the human race.

11 Now the whole earth had one language and the same words. [2]And as people migrated from the east, they found a plain in the land of Shinar and settled there. [3]And they said to one another, "Come, let us make bricks, and burn them thoroughly." And they had brick for stone, and bitumen for mortar. [4]Then they said, "Come, let us build ourselves a city and a tower with its top in the heavens, and let us make a name for ourselves, lest we be dispersed over the face of the whole earth." [5]And the LORD came down to see the city and the tower, which the children of man had built. [6]And the LORD said, "Behold, they are one people, and they have all one language, and this is only the beginning of what they will do. And nothing that they propose to do will now be impossible for them. [7]Come, let us go down and there confuse their language, so that they may not understand one another's speech." [8]So the LORD dispersed them from there over the face of all the earth, and they left off building the city. [9]Therefore its name was called Babel, because there the LORD confused[1] the language of all the earth. And from there the LORD dispersed them over the face of all the earth.

The family line of Abram [11:10–32]. The lead-in tells us that the genealogy that is about to unfold represents "the generations of Shem," the son of Noah (v. 10), but the interpretive clue to the importance of this particular family line comes at the end when the genealogy concludes with Abram and gives additional information about him and his immediate family (vv. 27–32). We need to read between the lines to pick up the story that is told at the end of the chapter about Abram's father Terah. Under circumstances that remain unrevealed, Terah "went forth . . . to go into the land of Canaan" (v. 31) but did not follow through on his quest, instead settling in Ur of the Chaldeans. Joshua 24:2 fills in the picture somewhat when it tells us that Abraham's ancestors, including Terah, "served other gods" (Josh. 24:2).

[10]These are the generations of Shem. When Shem was 100 years old, he fathered Arpachshad two years after the flood. [11]And Shem lived after he fathered Arpachshad 500 years and had other sons and daughters.

[12]When Arpachshad had lived 35 years, he fathered Shelah. [13]And Arpachshad lived after he fathered Shelah 403 years and had other sons and daughters.

[14]When Shelah had lived 30 years, he fathered Eber. [15]And Shelah lived after he fathered Eber 403 years and had other sons and daughters.

[16]When Eber had lived 34 years, he fathered Peleg. [17]And Eber lived after he fathered Peleg 430 years and had other sons and daughters.

[18]When Peleg had lived 30 years, he fathered Reu. [19]And Peleg lived after he fathered Reu 209 years and had other sons and daughters.

[20]When Reu had lived 32 years, he fathered Serug. [21]And Reu lived after he fathered Serug 207 years and had other sons and daughters.

---

[1] *Babel* sounds like the Hebrew for *confused*

²²When Serug had lived 30 years, he fathered Nahor. ²³And Serug lived after he fathered Nahor 200 years and had other sons and daughters.

²⁴When Nahor had lived 29 years, he fathered Terah. ²⁵And Nahor lived after he fathered Terah 119 years and had other sons and daughters.

²⁶When Terah had lived 70 years, he fathered Abram, Nahor, and Haran.

²⁷Now these are the generations of Terah. Terah fathered Abram, Nahor, and Haran; and Haran fathered Lot. ²⁸Haran died in the presence of his father Terah in the land of his kindred, in Ur of the Chaldeans. ²⁹And Abram and Nahor took wives. The name of Abram's wife was Sarai, and the name of Nahor's wife, Milcah, the daughter of Haran the father of Milcah and Iscah. ³⁰Now Sarai was barren; she had no child.

³¹Terah took Abram his son and Lot the son of Haran, his grandson, and Sarai his daughter-in-law, his son Abram's wife, and they went forth together from Ur of the Chaldeans to go into the land of Canaan, but when they came to Haran, they settled there. ³²The days of Terah were 205 years, and Terah died in Haran.

> **The call and obedience of Abram** [12:1–9]. The story of Abram (Abraham) begins here and runs through Genesis 25:18. It is a *hero story in which much of what the storyteller wants to say about life is embodied in the character and experiences of Abram. In addition to the emerging portrait of the hero, three other plot lines converge in the story of Abram: God's progressive revelation of his covenant; Abram's quest to secure a son, descendants, and a land; the conflict between faith and expediency within Abram himself. The central core of the story is the hero's quest to find fulfillment of God's covenant promises and the struggles, defeats, victories, and discoveries that he experienced in his pursuit of this quest. Genesis 12:1–9 is our introduction to all of these motifs. God announces the covenant for the first time (vv. 1–3). The quest motif begins when God tells Abraham to "go" (v. 1) and Abram "went" (v. 4). We are introduced to Abram as a hero of faith, a domestic hero (in ancient thinking, home meant possessions as well as family [v. 5]), a worshiper (vv. 7–8), and the archetypal traveler and wanderer on a quest.

12 Now the LORD said¹ to Abram, "Go from your country and your kindred and your father's house to the land that I will show you. ²And I will make of you a great nation, and I will bless you and make your name great, so that you will be a blessing. ³I will bless those who bless you, and him who dishonors you I will curse, and in you all the families of the earth shall be blessed."²

⁴So Abram went, as the LORD had told him, and Lot went with him. Abram was seventy-five years old when he departed from Haran. ⁵And Abram took Sarai his wife, and Lot his brother's son, and all their possessions that they had gathered, and the people that they had acquired in Haran, and they set out to go to the land of Canaan. When they came to the land of Canaan, ⁶Abram passed through the land to the place at Shechem, to the oak³ of Moreh. At that time the Canaanites were in the land. ⁷Then the LORD appeared to Abram and said, "To your offspring I will give this land." So he built there an altar to the LORD, who had appeared to him. ⁸From there he moved to the hill country on the east of Bethel and pitched his tent, with Bethel on the west and Ai on the east. And there he built an altar to the LORD and called upon the name of the LORD. ⁹And Abram journeyed on, still going toward the Negeb.

---

¹ Or had said ² Or by you all the families of the earth shall bless themselves ³ Or terebinth

The sojourn in Egypt [12:10–13:1]. The individual episodes in the stories of the Bible's hero stories have a more self-contained quality than is true of chapters in a novel. The story of Abraham's sojourn in Egypt is formally marked by the lead-in statement "Abram went down to Egypt" (12:10) and the concluding statement "Abram went up from Egypt" (13:1). For all the brevity of this story, it packs a huge voltage. Identifying the phases of action is the first thing we need to do to discern the pattern in the individual episodes in the life of Abram, and in this case it yields the following sequence: arrival (12:10)—danger or threat (implied)—fear (implied)—expediency (12:11–13)—disaster (12:14–16)—rescue by divine intervention (12:17–19)—departure (12:20–13:1). The story has many of the ingredients that readers like best in a story—danger, conflict, intrigue, suspense, dramatic irony, rescue. At the level of subject matter, the sexual dynamic of the event is also important. The key to the story's interpretation lies in the fact that God intervened to rescue Abram, in view of which Abram was guilty of a lapse of faith. In the conflict between faith and expediency, the latter scores an ignominious victory in this episode.

¹⁰Now there was a famine in the land. So Abram went down to Egypt to sojourn there, for the famine was severe in the land. ¹¹When he was about to enter Egypt, he said to Sarai his wife, "I know that you are a woman beautiful in appearance, ¹²and when the Egyptians see you, they will say, 'This is his wife.' Then they will kill me, but they will let you live. ¹³Say you are my sister, that it may go well with me because of you, and that my life may be spared for your sake." ¹⁴When Abram entered Egypt, the Egyptians saw that the woman was very beautiful. ¹⁵And when the princes of Pharaoh saw her, they praised her to Pharaoh. And the woman was taken into Pharaoh's house. ¹⁶And for her sake he dealt well with Abram; and he had sheep, oxen, male donkeys, male servants, female servants, female donkeys, and camels.

¹⁷But the LORD afflicted Pharaoh and his house with great plagues because of Sarai, Abram's wife. ¹⁸So Pharaoh called Abram and said, "What is this you have done to me? Why did you not tell me that she was your wife? ¹⁹Why did you say, 'She is my sister,' so that I took her for my wife? Now then, here is your wife; take her, and go." ²⁰And Pharaoh gave men orders concerning him, and they sent him away with his wife and all that he had.

13 So Abram went up from Egypt, he and his wife and all that he had, and Lot with him, into the Negeb.

The separation of Abram and Lot [13:2–18]. The story of separation is a standard narrative genre. Although the story begins with a conflict (vv. 5–7), it is not a conflict story but a story of choice. The brief narratives that make up much of the Bible regularly fall into three main phases—exposition or background information, central event, aftermath of the central event. The main point of such a story will rarely if ever be found in the opening phase of exposition, but rather in the central event and its outcome. In this story, Abram and Lot make life-determining choices. The central technique is the *foil—the contrast that heightens or sets off one character or event from another. At the level of character, Abram and Lot are opposites. Abram is godly (vv. 4, 18), generous (vv. 8–9), and self-effacing. Lot is selfish (vv. 10–11) and spiritually careless (vv. 12–13). Their choices are likewise foils to each other: Lot chooses material prosperity with a terrible moral price tag attached, while Abram is content with the promises of God (vv. 14–17). The narrative device of *poetic justice (virtue rewarded, vice punished) is a standard way by which we know whether a course of action is offered to us for approval and disapproval. The foreshadowing of the eventual destruction of Sodom and Gomorrah (v. 10) lets us know that we have observed the anatomy of a bad choice in the story of Lot, while the fact that God rewards Abram with a renewal of the covenant lets us know that Abram has made the right choice. This is a story about priorities and ultimate allegiance.

[2]Now Abram was very rich in livestock, in silver, and in gold. [3]And he journeyed on from the Negeb as far as Bethel to the place where his tent had been at the beginning, between Bethel and Ai, [4]to the place where he had made an altar at the first. And there Abram called upon the name of the Lord. [5]And Lot, who went with Abram, also had flocks and herds and tents, [6]so that the land could not support both of them dwelling together; for their possessions were so great that they could not dwell together, [7]and there was strife between the herdsmen of Abram's livestock and the herdsmen of Lot's livestock. At that time the Canaanites and the Perizzites were dwelling in the land.

[8]Then Abram said to Lot, "Let there be no strife between you and me, and between your herdsmen and my herdsmen, for we are kinsmen.[1] [9]Is not the whole land before you? Separate yourself from me. If you take the left hand, then I will go to the right, or if you take the right hand, then I will go to the left." [10]And Lot lifted up his eyes and saw that the Jordan Valley was well watered everywhere like the garden of the Lord, like the land of Egypt, in the direction of Zoar. (This was before the Lord destroyed Sodom and Gomorrah.) [11]So Lot chose for himself all the Jordan Valley, and Lot journeyed east. Thus they separated from each other. [12]Abram settled in the land of Canaan, while Lot settled among the cities of the valley and moved his tent as far as Sodom. [13]Now the men of Sodom were wicked, great sinners against the Lord.

[14]The Lord said to Abram, after Lot had separated from him, "Lift up your eyes and look from the place where you are, northward and southward and eastward and westward, [15]for all the land that you see I will give to you and to your offspring forever. [16]I will make your offspring as the dust of the earth, so that if one can count the dust of the earth, your offspring also can be counted. [17]Arise, walk through the length and the breadth of the land, for I will give it to you." [18]So Abram moved his tent and came and settled by the oaks[2] of Mamre, which are at Hebron, and there he built an altar to the Lord.

The hero as warrior [chapter 14]. In most heroic narrative from ancient times, the hero is a warrior, and the main action is battlefield combat. Chapter 14 is the only appearance of this motif in Genesis. The opening catalog of enemy kings (vv. 1–9) and story of battle (vv. 10–12) are exactly what we would expect in ancient hero stories. Abram's determination to rescue Lot (vv. 13–14) is an extension of his domestic identity, though we are perhaps surprised that he is the leader of a small army (v. 14), since this is the only time we see that side of the hero. Surprise enters the story when the battle itself gets only passing reference (vv. 15–16). What interests the storyteller more than the battle are two memorable encounters that Abram experiences as spin-offs from his

---

[1] Hebrew *we are men, brothers* [2] Or *terebinths*

military victory. We observe the hero as spiritual celebrity when the mysterious and awe-inspiring Melchizedek fetes Abram with bread and wine and blesses him (vv. 18–20). We see the hero as diplomat when he sidesteps sharing booty with the king of Sodom (vv. 17, 21–24).

14 In the days of Amraphel king of Shinar, Arioch king of Ellasar, Chedorlaomer king of Elam, and Tidal king of Goiim, ²these kings made war with Bera king of Sodom, Birsha king of Gomorrah, Shinab king of Admah, Shemeber king of Zeboiim, and the king of Bela (that is, Zoar). ³And all these joined forces in the Valley of Siddim (that is, the Salt Sea). ⁴Twelve years they had served Chedorlaomer, but in the thirteenth year they rebelled. ⁵In the fourteenth year Chedorlaomer and the kings who were with him came and defeated the Rephaim in Ashteroth-karnaim, the Zuzim in Ham, the Emim in Shaveh-kiriathaim, ⁶and the Horites in their hill country of Seir as far as El-paran on the border of the wilderness. ⁷Then they turned back and came to En-mishpat (that is, Kadesh) and defeated all the country of the Amalekites, and also the Amorites who were dwelling in Hazazon-tamar.

⁸Then the king of Sodom, the king of Gomorrah, the king of Admah, the king of Zeboiim, and the king of Bela (that is, Zoar) went out, and they joined battle in the Valley of Siddim ⁹with Chedorlaomer king of Elam, Tidal king of Goiim, Amraphel king of Shinar, and Arioch king of Ellasar, four kings against five. ¹⁰Now the Valley of Siddim was full of bitumen pits, and as the kings of Sodom and Gomorrah fled, some fell into them, and the rest fled to the hill country. ¹¹So the enemy took all the possessions of Sodom and Gomorrah, and all their provisions, and went their way. ¹²They also took Lot, the son of Abram's brother, who was dwelling in Sodom, and his possessions, and went their way.

¹³Then one who had escaped came and told Abram the Hebrew, who was living by the oaks¹ of Mamre the Amorite, brother of Eshcol and of Aner. These were allies of Abram. ¹⁴When Abram heard that his kinsman had been taken captive, he led forth his trained men, born in his house, 318 of them, and went in pursuit as far as Dan. ¹⁵And he divided his forces against them by night, he and his servants, and defeated them and pursued them to Hobah, north of Damascus. ¹⁶Then he brought back all the possessions, and also brought back his kinsman Lot with his possessions, and the women and the people.

¹⁷After his return from the defeat of Chedorlaomer and the kings who were with him, the king of Sodom went out to meet him at the Valley of Shaveh (that is, the King's Valley). ¹⁸And Melchizedek king of Salem brought out bread and wine. (He was priest of God Most High.) ¹⁹And he blessed him and said,

"Blessed be Abram by God Most High,
    Possessor² of heaven and earth;
²⁰ and blessed be God Most High,
    who has delivered your enemies into your hand!"

And Abram gave him a tenth of everything. ²¹And the king of Sodom said to Abram, "Give me the persons, but take the goods for yourself." ²²But Abram said to the king of Sodom, "I have lifted my hand³ to the LORD, God Most High, Possessor of heaven and earth, ²³that I would not take a thread or a sandal strap or anything that is yours,

¹ Or terebinths ² Or Creator; also verse 22 ³ Or I have taken a solemn oath

lest you should say, 'I have made Abram rich.' ²⁴I will take nothing but what the young men have eaten, and the share of the men who went with me. Let Aner, Eshcol, and Mamre take their share."

> **Further revelation of the covenant** [chapter 15]. One of the story lines in the story of Abram is the progressive revelation of the covenant. Not only does God's renewal of the covenant to Abram regularly punctuate the action, but God keeps giving more and more information about the covenant. The sequence of chapter 15 is as follows: Abram's doubt and anxiety occasioned by the slow fulfillment of God's promise to give him a son (vv. 1–3); God's informing Abram that the son of promise will be his own son, not the son of a slave, thereby eliminating a false possibility (vv. 4–5); Abram's faith in what God has disclosed (v. 6); the cutting of the covenant, an ancient ritual that was in effect a signing of a contract by the two parties (vv. 7–12); further revelation from God regarding the fulfillment of the covenant (vv. 13–20). The meaning of Abram's sleeping instead of walking with God through the path between the divided carcasses is that God takes responsibility for both sides of the bargain—he is the one who will keep the covenant to death.

15 After these things the word of the LORD came to Abram in a vision: "Fear not, Abram, I am your shield; your reward shall be very great." ²But Abram said, "O Lord GOD, what will you give me, for I continue¹ childless, and the heir of my house is Eliezer of Damascus?" ³And Abram said, "Behold, you have given me no offspring, and a member of my household will be my heir." ⁴And behold, the word of the LORD came to him: "This man shall not be your heir; your very own son² shall be your heir." ⁵And he brought him outside and said, "Look toward heaven, and number the stars, if you are able to number them." Then he said to him, "So shall your offspring be." ⁶And he believed the LORD, and he counted it to him as righteousness.

⁷And he said to him, "I am the LORD who brought you out from Ur of the Chaldeans to give you this land to possess." ⁸But he said, "O Lord GOD, how am I to know that I shall possess it?" ⁹He said to him, "Bring me a heifer three years old, a female goat three years old, a ram three years old, a turtledove, and a young pigeon." ¹⁰And he brought him all these, cut them in half, and laid each half over against the other. But he did not cut the birds in half. ¹¹And when birds of prey came down on the carcasses, Abram drove them away.

¹²As the sun was going down, a deep sleep fell on Abram. And behold, dreadful and great darkness fell upon him. ¹³Then the LORD said to Abram, "Know for certain that your offspring will be sojourners in a land that is not theirs and will be servants there, and they will be afflicted for four hundred years. ¹⁴But I will bring judgment on the nation that they serve, and afterward they shall come out with great possessions. ¹⁵As for yourself, you shall go to your fathers in peace; you shall be buried in a good old age. ¹⁶And they shall come back here in the fourth generation, for the iniquity of the Amorites is not yet complete."

¹⁷When the sun had gone down and it was dark, behold, a smoking fire pot and a flaming torch passed between these pieces. ¹⁸On that day the LORD made a covenant with Abram, saying, "To your offspring I give³ this land, from the river of Egypt to the great river, the river Euphrates, ¹⁹the land of the Kenites, the Kenizzites, the Kad-

¹ Or *I shall die* ² Hebrew *what will come out of your own loins* ³ Or *have given*

monites, ²⁰the Hittites, the Perizzites, the Rephaim, ²¹the Amorites, the Canaanites, the Girgashites and the Jebusites."

Another venture in expediency [chapter 16]. The episode of the birth of Ishmael delineates an anatomy of a bad decision. The quest to produce a son has by now become obsessive in the lives of Abram and Sarai. The unfolding sequence in this episode is as follows: a vexing problem (v. 1); an expedient solution (vv. 1–4); family conflict (vv. 4–5); expulsion (v. 6); rescue (vv. 7–14); return (vv. 15–16). The action reenacts the archetypal withdrawal and return pattern, and it is a cycle of futility as the characters return to domestic unrest at the end. We know how to interpret a decision that characters in a story make by its outcome; the decision to have a child by Hagar produces false pride (v. 4), false blame (v. 5), and false neutrality (v. 6). Everyone ends up a loser in this experiment in expediency, a variation on the biblical theme of works versus faith (in this case, Abram and Sarai rely on their own plan instead of waiting for God to work his plan).

16 Now Sarai, Abram's wife, had borne him no children. She had a female Egyptian servant whose name was Hagar. ²And Sarai said to Abram, "Behold now, the LORD has prevented me from bearing children. Go in to my servant; it may be that I shall obtain children¹ by her." And Abram listened to the voice of Sarai. ³So, after Abram had lived ten years in the land of Canaan, Sarai, Abram's wife, took Hagar the Egyptian, her servant, and gave her to Abram her husband as a wife. ⁴And he went in to Hagar, and she conceived. And when she saw that she had conceived, she looked with contempt on her mistress.² ⁵And Sarai said to Abram, "May the wrong done to me be on you! I gave my servant to your embrace, and when she saw that she had conceived, she looked on me with contempt. May the LORD judge between you and me!" ⁶But Abram said to Sarai, "Behold, your servant is in your power; do to her as you please." Then Sarai dealt harshly with her, and she fled from her.

⁷The angel of the LORD found her by a spring of water in the wilderness, the spring on the way to Shur. ⁸And he said, "Hagar, servant of Sarai, where have you come from and where are you going?" She said, "I am fleeing from my mistress Sarai." ⁹The angel of the LORD said to her, "Return to your mistress and submit to her." ¹⁰The angel of the LORD also said to her, "I will surely multiply your offspring so that they cannot be numbered for multitude." ¹¹And the angel of the LORD said to her,

> "Behold, you are pregnant
>   and shall bear a son.
> You shall call his name Ishmael,³
>   because the LORD has listened to your affliction.
> ¹² He shall be a wild donkey of a man,
>   his hand against everyone
>   and everyone's hand against him,
> and he shall dwell over against all his kinsmen."

¹³So she called the name of the LORD who spoke to her, "You are a God of seeing,"⁴ for she said, "Truly here I have seen him who looks after me."⁵ ¹⁴Therefore the well was called Beer-lahai-roi;⁶ it lies between Kadesh and Bered.

¹ Hebrew *be built up*, which sounds like the Hebrew for *children* ² Hebrew *her mistress was dishonorable in her eyes*; similarly in verse 5 ³ *Ishmael* means *God hears* ⁴ Or *You are a God who sees me* ⁵ Hebrew *Have I really seen him here who sees me?* or *Would I have looked here for the one who sees me?* ⁶ *Beer-lahai-roi* means *the well of the Living One who sees me*

[15]And Hagar bore Abram a son, and Abram called the name of his son, whom Hagar bore, Ishmael. [16]Abram was eighty-six years old when Hagar bore Ishmael to Abram.

Progressive revelation of the covenant [chapter 17]. This long chapter is devoted to God's renewal of the covenant, and a wealth of new information about it emerges for both Abram—with his new name, Abraham—and us as readers. The first half of the chapter is an elaborate statement from God regarding the covenant. Specific topics include the promise of a huge number of descendants, an everlasting covenant, and Canaan as a promised land (vv. 1–8); circumcision as the sign of the covenant (vv. 9–14); and bringing Sarai (now called Sarah) into the covenant in a direct way (vv. 15–16). This is followed by Abraham's famous laugh (v. 17), which in view of what immediately follows (vv. 18–19) is probably a gesture of pent-up incredulity, doubt, scorn, and even bitterness on Abraham's part. After rebuking Abraham, God proceeds to give further promises regarding the covenant, even including the specific information that Isaac will be born a year later (vv. 19–21). Abraham this time responds with faith, as signaled by his performing the covenant sign (vv. 22–27). Much of the meaning of this episode is encapsulated in the new names that four of the characters receive: God, who calls himself by a new name in Genesis (*El Shaddai* [God Almighty]); Abraham (father of a multitude); Sarah (which means the same as her former name, Sarai—"princess"); and Isaac (he laughs).

17 When Abram was ninety-nine years old the Lord appeared to Abram and said to him, "I am God Almighty;[1] walk before me, and be blameless, [2]that I may make my covenant between me and you, and may multiply you greatly." [3]Then Abram fell on his face. And God said to him, [4]"Behold, my covenant is with you, and you shall be the father of a multitude of nations. [5]No longer shall your name be called Abram,[2] but your name shall be Abraham,[3] for I have made you the father of a multitude of nations. [6]I will make you exceedingly fruitful, and I will make you into nations, and kings shall come from you. [7]And I will establish my covenant between me and you and your offspring after you throughout their generations for an everlasting covenant, to be God to you and to your offspring after you. [8]And I will give to you and to your offspring after you the land of your sojournings, all the land of Canaan, for an everlasting possession, and I will be their God."

[9]And God said to Abraham, "As for you, you shall keep my covenant, you and your offspring after you throughout their generations. [10]This is my covenant, which you shall keep, between me and you and your offspring after you: Every male among you shall be circumcised. [11]You shall be circumcised in the flesh of your foreskins, and it shall be a sign of the covenant between me and you. [12]He who is eight days old among you shall be circumcised. Every male throughout your generations, whether born in your house or bought with your money from any foreigner who is not of your offspring, [13]both he who is born in your house and he who is bought with your money, shall surely be circumcised. So shall my covenant be in your flesh an everlasting covenant. [14]Any uncircumcised male who is not circumcised in the flesh of his foreskin shall be cut off from his people; he has broken my covenant."

[15]And God said to Abraham, "As for Sarai your wife, you shall not call her name Sarai, but Sarah[4] shall be her name. [16]I will bless her, and moreover, I will give[5] you a

---

[1] Hebrew *El Shaddai* [2] *Abram* means *exalted father* [3] *Abraham* means *father of a multitude* [4] *Sarai* and *Sarah* mean *princess* [5] Hebrew *have given*

son by her. I will bless her, and she shall become nations; kings of peoples shall come from her." ¹⁷Then Abraham fell on his face and laughed and said to himself, "Shall a child be born to a man who is a hundred years old? Shall Sarah, who is ninety years old, bear a child?" ¹⁸And Abraham said to God, "Oh that Ishmael might live before you!" ¹⁹God said, "No, but Sarah your wife shall bear you a son, and you shall call his name Isaac.¹ I will establish my covenant with him as an everlasting covenant for his offspring after him. ²⁰As for Ishmael, I have heard you; behold, I have blessed him and will make him fruitful and multiply him greatly. He shall father twelve princes, and I will make him into a great nation. ²¹But I will establish my covenant with Isaac, whom Sarah shall bear to you at this time next year."

²²When he had finished talking with him, God went up from Abraham. ²³Then Abraham took Ishmael his son and all those born in his house or bought with his money, every male among the men of Abraham's house, and he circumcised the flesh of their foreskins that very day, as God had said to him. ²⁴Abraham was ninety-nine years old when he was circumcised in the flesh of his foreskin. ²⁵And Ishmael his son was thirteen years old when he was circumcised in the flesh of his foreskin. ²⁶That very day Abraham and his son Ishmael were circumcised. ²⁷And all the men of his house, those born in the house and those bought with money from a foreigner, were circumcised with him.

> **Entertaining angels unawares** [18:1–15]. This episode falls into the genre known as the *idyll—a pleasant domestic event occurring in a pastoral or rural setting. The exemplary action of the hero and heroine is their hospitality, a virtue that ancient cultures held in extremely high regard. The interlude is an image of the good life, including abundance and a sense of community. We know, as Abraham and Sarah did not, that the three visitors are God and two angels. The story may implicitly adhere to a pattern from ancient literature in which a childless couple is visited by supernatural beings as a test of their hospitality, followed by reward in the form of a prediction of child to the barren couple after they have been ideally hospitable. Sarah's laugh (v. 12) embodies some of the same tensions and doubts as Abraham's laugh had represented, but it is cast in an even more unfavorable light (Sarah is caught eavesdropping; she lies; she is rebuked by God).

18 And the LORD appeared to him by the oaks² of Mamre, as he sat at the door of his tent in the heat of the day. ²He lifted up his eyes and looked, and behold, three men were standing in front of him. When he saw them, he ran from the tent door to meet them and bowed himself to the earth ³and said, "O Lord,³ if I have found favor in your sight, do not pass by your servant. ⁴Let a little water be brought, and wash your feet, and rest yourselves under the tree, ⁵while I bring a morsel of bread, that you may refresh yourselves, and after that you may pass on—since you have come to your servant." So they said, "Do as you have said." ⁶And Abraham went quickly into the tent to Sarah and said, "Quick! Three seahs⁴ of fine flour! Knead it, and make cakes." ⁷And Abraham ran to the herd and took a calf, tender and good, and gave it to a young man, who prepared it quickly. ⁸Then he took curds and milk and the calf that he had prepared, and set it before them. And he stood by them under the tree while they ate.

⁹They said to him, "Where is Sarah your wife?" And he said, "She is in the tent."

---

¹ *Isaac means he laughs* ² Or *terebinths* ³ Or *My lord* ⁴ A *seah* was about 7 quarts or 7.3 liters

¹⁰The Lᴏʀᴅ said, "I will surely return to you about this time next year, and Sarah your wife shall have a son." And Sarah was listening at the tent door behind him. ¹¹Now Abraham and Sarah were old, advanced in years. The way of women had ceased to be with Sarah. ¹²So Sarah laughed to herself, saying, "After I am worn out, and my lord is old, shall I have pleasure?" ¹³The Lᴏʀᴅ said to Abraham, "Why did Sarah laugh and say, 'Shall I indeed bear a child, now that I am old?' ¹⁴Is anything too hard¹ for the Lᴏʀᴅ? At the appointed time I will return to you, about this time next year, and Sarah shall have a son." ¹⁵But Sarah denied it,² saying, "I did not laugh," for she was afraid. He said, "No, but you did laugh."

The hero as confidant of God [18:16–33]. The portrait of Abraham as hero is a dynamic one. With each successive episode, something new is added to the portrait. Often we see Abraham in a new role that advances the portrait over what has preceded. In this episode, God takes Abraham into his confidence in a way that we had not seen before (vv. 17–19), clueing Abraham in to an impending major act by God. Additionally, Abraham enters a role as intercessor for Sodom, in a small way fulfilling God's covenant prediction that through Abraham the nations of the earth would be blessed. The dialogue between God and Abraham becomes a bargaining session, and a story of suspense as well, as we wonder at what point Abraham will stop pressing his request that God spare the wicked city of Sodom.

¹⁶Then the men set out from there, and they looked down toward Sodom. And Abraham went with them to set them on their way. ¹⁷The Lᴏʀᴅ said, "Shall I hide from Abraham what I am about to do, ¹⁸seeing that Abraham shall surely become a great and mighty nation, and all the nations of the earth shall be blessed in him? ¹⁹For I have chosen³ him, that he may command his children and his household after him to keep the way of the Lᴏʀᴅ by doing righteousness and justice, so that the Lᴏʀᴅ may bring to Abraham what he has promised him." ²⁰Then the Lᴏʀᴅ said, "Because the outcry against Sodom and Gomorrah is great and their sin is very grave, ²¹I will go down to see whether they have done altogether⁴ according to the outcry that has come to me. And if not, I will know."

²²So the men turned from there and went toward Sodom, but Abraham still stood before the Lᴏʀᴅ. ²³Then Abraham drew near and said, "Will you indeed sweep away the righteous with the wicked? ²⁴Suppose there are fifty righteous within the city. Will you then sweep away the place and not spare it for the fifty righteous who are in it? ²⁵Far be it from you to do such a thing, to put the righteous to death with the wicked, so that the righteous fare as the wicked! Far be that from you! Shall not the Judge of all the earth do what is just?" ²⁶And the Lᴏʀᴅ said, "If I find at Sodom fifty righteous in the city, I will spare the whole place for their sake."

²⁷Abraham answered and said, "Behold, I have undertaken to speak to the Lord, I who am but dust and ashes. ²⁸Suppose five of the fifty righteous are lacking. Will you destroy the whole city for lack of five?" And he said, "I will not destroy it if I find forty-five there." ²⁹Again he spoke to him and said, "Suppose forty are found there." He answered, "For the sake of forty I will not do it." ³⁰Then he said, "Oh let not the Lord be angry, and I will speak. Suppose thirty are found there." He answered, "I will not do it, if I find thirty there." ³¹He said, "Behold, I have undertaken to speak to the Lord. Suppose twenty are found there." He answered, "For the sake of twenty I will

¹ Or wonderful ² Or acted falsely ³ Hebrew known ⁴ Or they deserve destruction; Hebrew they have made a complete end

not destroy it." ³²Then he said, "Oh let not the Lord be angry, and I will speak again but this once. Suppose ten are found there." He answered, "For the sake of ten I will not destroy it." ³³And the LORD went his way, when he had finished speaking to Abraham, and Abraham returned to his place.

> **The destruction of Sodom and Gomorrah** [chapter 19]. Even though this story focuses on Lot rather than Abraham, the storyteller does tie the action into the story of Abraham in verse 29, which tells us that God saved Lot because he "remembered Abraham." The overall pattern is the *rescue motif. Before and during the rescue, other motifs are prominent: conflict, danger, violence, degradation. Although the narrator nowhere says anything negative about Lot's behavior, he shows us what kind of person Lot has become indirectly—by hints as to how closely Lot has become aligned with the wicked city of Sodom and how reluctant he is to leave the city. The man who had reached for the stars in terms of success, prosperity, and affluence ends up as a caveman (v. 30). The only way to reconcile this very negative picture with the NT commentary on Lot as a righteous man (2 Peter 2:6–8) is to see Lot as having lived a compromised life with a very bad conscience. The literary mode of the chapter is *realism—the plain portrayal of human depravity. Archetypes are also important: the corrupt city; the rescue; cataclysmic destruction; the city street; home as the protected place; the cave; the person on the run. We also learn in Lot's later life that it is easier to get the family out of Sodom than it is to get Sodom out of the family.

19 The two angels came to Sodom in the evening, and Lot was sitting in the gate of Sodom. When Lot saw them, he rose to meet them and bowed himself with his face to the earth ²and said, "My lords, please turn aside to your servant's house and spend the night and wash your feet. Then you may rise up early and go on your way." They said, "No; we will spend the night in the town square." ³But he pressed them strongly; so they turned aside to him and entered his house. And he made them a feast and baked unleavened bread, and they ate.

⁴But before they lay down, the men of the city, the men of Sodom, both young and old, all the people to the last man, surrounded the house. ⁵And they called to Lot, "Where are the men who came to you tonight? Bring them out to us, that we may know them." ⁶Lot went out to the men at the entrance, shut the door after him, ⁷and said, "I beg you, my brothers, do not act so wickedly. ⁸Behold, I have two daughters who have not known any man. Let me bring them out to you, and do to them as you please. Only do nothing to these men, for they have come under the shelter of my roof." ⁹But they said, "Stand back!" And they said, "This fellow came to sojourn, and he has become the judge! Now we will deal worse with you than with them." Then they pressed hard against the man Lot, and drew near to break the door down. ¹⁰But the men reached out their hands and brought Lot into the house with them and shut the door. ¹¹And they struck with blindness the men who were at the entrance of the house, both small and great, so that they wore themselves out groping for the door.

¹²Then the men said to Lot, "Have you anyone else here? Sons-in-law, sons, daughters, or anyone you have in the city, bring them out of the place. ¹³For we are about to destroy this place, because the outcry against its people has become great before the LORD, and the LORD has sent us to destroy it." ¹⁴So Lot went out and said to his sons-

in-law, who were to marry his daughters, "Up! Get out of this place, for the LORD is about to destroy the city." But he seemed to his sons-in-law to be jesting.

[15]As morning dawned, the angels urged Lot, saying, "Up! Take your wife and your two daughters who are here, lest you be swept away in the punishment of the city." [16]But he lingered. So the men seized him and his wife and his two daughters by the hand, the LORD being merciful to him, and they brought him out and set him outside the city. [17]And as they brought them out, one said, "Escape for your life. Do not look back or stop anywhere in the valley. Escape to the hills, lest you be swept away." [18]And Lot said to them, "Oh, no, my lords. [19]Behold, your servant has found favor in your sight, and you have shown me great kindness in saving my life. But I cannot escape to the hills, lest the disaster overtake me and I die. [20]Behold, this city is near enough to flee to, and it is a little one. Let me escape there—is it not a little one?—and my life will be saved!" [21]He said to him, "Behold, I grant you this favor also, that I will not overthrow the city of which you have spoken. [22]Escape there quickly, for I can do nothing till you arrive there." Therefore the name of the city was called Zoar.[1]

[23]The sun had risen on the earth when Lot came to Zoar. [24]Then the LORD rained on Sodom and Gomorrah sulfur and fire from the LORD out of heaven. [25]And he over-threw those cities, and all the valley, and all the inhabitants of the cities, and what grew on the ground. [26]But Lot's wife, behind him, looked back, and she became a pil-lar of salt.

[27]And Abraham went early in the morning to the place where he had stood before the LORD. [28]And he looked down toward Sodom and Gomorrah and toward all the land of the valley, and he looked and, behold, the smoke of the land went up like the smoke of a furnace.

[29]So it was that, when God destroyed the cities of the valley, God remembered Abraham and sent Lot out of the midst of the overthrow when he overthrew the cities in which Lot had lived.

[30]Now Lot went up out of Zoar and lived in the hills with his two daughters, for he was afraid to live in Zoar. So he lived in a cave with his two daughters. [31]And the first-born said to the younger, "Our father is old, and there is not a man on earth to come in to us after the manner of all the earth. [32]Come, let us make our father drink wine, and we will lie with him, that we may preserve offspring from our father." [33]So they made their father drink wine that night. And the firstborn went in and lay with her father. He did not know when she lay down or when she arose.

[34]The next day, the firstborn said to the younger, "Behold, I lay last night with my father. Let us make him drink wine tonight also. Then you go in and lie with him, that we may preserve offspring from our father." [35]So they made their father drink wine that night also. And the younger arose and lay with him, and he did not know when she lay down or when she arose. [36]Thus both the daughters of Lot became pregnant by their father. [37]The firstborn bore a son and called his name Moab.[2] He is the father of the Moabites to this day. [38]The younger also bore a son and called his name Ben-ammi.[3] He is the father of the Ammonites to this day.

Déjà vu [chapter 20]. After one of the most sensational and intense stories in the entire book of Genesis, we now switch to an episode pitched at a lower emotional plane. Abraham undertakes another experiment in expediency as he tries to deceive another

---

[1] Zoar means little [2] Moab sounds like the Hebrew for from father [3] Ben-ammi means son of my people

foreign king with the same disguise trick that had failed with the king of Egypt. The scenario follows a parallel track to the earlier episode, except that it unfolds in a more leisurely manner and fuller detail. Our assessment of the hero is the same as earlier: he should have known better. As elsewhere in our experience, sinners often make the same mistake more than once.

20 From there Abraham journeyed toward the territory of the Negeb and lived between Kadesh and Shur; and he sojourned in Gerar. ²And Abraham said of Sarah his wife, "She is my sister." And Abimelech king of Gerar sent and took Sarah. ³But God came to Abimelech in a dream by night and said to him, "Behold, you are a dead man because of the woman whom you have taken, for she is a man's wife." ⁴Now Abimelech had not approached her. So he said, "Lord, will you kill an innocent people? ⁵Did he not himself say to me, 'She is my sister'? And she herself said, 'He is my brother.' In the integrity of my heart and the innocence of my hands I have done this." ⁶Then God said to him in the dream, "Yes, I know that you have done this in the integrity of your heart, and it was I who kept you from sinning against me. Therefore I did not let you touch her. ⁷Now then, return the man's wife, for he is a prophet, so that he will pray for you, and you shall live. But if you do not return her, know that you shall surely die, you and all who are yours."

⁸So Abimelech rose early in the morning and called all his servants and told them all these things. And the men were very much afraid. ⁹Then Abimelech called Abraham and said to him, "What have you done to us? And how have I sinned against you, that you have brought on me and my kingdom a great sin? You have done to me things that ought not to be done." ¹⁰And Abimelech said to Abraham, "What did you see, that you did this thing?" ¹¹Abraham said, "I did it because I thought, There is no fear of God at all in this place, and they will kill me because of my wife. ¹²Besides, she is indeed my sister, the daughter of my father though not the daughter of my mother, and she became my wife. ¹³And when God caused me to wander from my father's house, I said to her, 'This is the kindness you must do me: at every place to which we come, say of me, He is my brother.' "

¹⁴Then Abimelech took sheep and oxen, and male servants and female servants, and gave them to Abraham, and returned Sarah his wife to him. ¹⁵And Abimelech said, "Behold, my land is before you; dwell where it pleases you." ¹⁶To Sarah he said, "Behold, I have given your brother a thousand pieces of silver. It is a sign of your innocence in the eyes of all[1] who are with you, and before everyone you are vindicated." ¹⁷Then Abraham prayed to God, and God healed Abimelech, and also healed his wife and female slaves so that they bore children. ¹⁸For the LORD had closed all the wombs of the house of Abimelech because of Sarah, Abraham's wife.

The birth of Isaac and expulsion of Ishmael [21:1–21]. Most storytellers would have made the birth of the promised son the climax of the quest story. The writer of Genesis treats it almost as an anticlimax, alerting us that the story of Abraham is mainly a severe waiting in which the hero's testing and growth in faith during the twenty-five years leading up to the birth of Isaac are what matter most. In this brief episode, Abraham is the staid father figure, going about the rituals of fatherhood in formal manner,

---

[1] Hebrew *It is a covering of eyes for all*

while the portrait of Sarah is more human. The expulsion of Hagar and Ishmael echoes the earlier episode of Hagar's flight when she became pregnant with Ishmael. Here, too, we find the motifs of conflict between wives occasioned by Hagar's offspring; Abraham caught between two raw-boned women; a decision based on expediency. We need to read between the lines to catch the probable human motivations at various points: Ishmael may have been taunting Isaac as the initial provocation (vv. 8–9); Sarah acts as the guardian of Isaac's interests as the rightful heir (v. 10); Abraham is displeased at the prospect of expelling Hagar and Ishmael because of the natural feelings of a father for a wife and son (v. 11); God approves of the expulsion because Isaac rather than Ishmael is the child of covenant promise and because Ishmael will also be blessed by virtue of having been fathered by Abraham (vv. 12–13). The episode ends with touching moments—a scene of parting (v. 14); a scene of despair (vv. 15–16); a scene of divine comfort (vv. 17–19).

21

The Lord visited Sarah as he had said, and the Lord did to Sarah as he had promised. ²And Sarah conceived and bore Abraham a son in his old age at the time of which God had spoken to him. ³Abraham called the name of his son who was born to him, whom Sarah bore him, Isaac.¹ ⁴And Abraham circumcised his son Isaac when he was eight days old, as God had commanded him. ⁵Abraham was a hundred years old when his son Isaac was born to him. ⁶And Sarah said, "God has made laughter for me; everyone who hears will laugh over me." ⁷And she said, "Who would have said to Abraham that Sarah would nurse children? Yet I have borne him a son in his old age."

⁸And the child grew and was weaned. And Abraham made a great feast on the day that Isaac was weaned. ⁹But Sarah saw the son of Hagar the Egyptian, whom she had borne to Abraham, laughing.² ¹⁰So she said to Abraham, "Cast out this slave woman with her son, for the son of this slave woman shall not be heir with my son Isaac." ¹¹And the thing was very displeasing to Abraham on account of his son. ¹²But God said to Abraham, "Be not displeased because of the boy and because of your slave woman. Whatever Sarah says to you, do as she tells you, for through Isaac shall your offspring be named. ¹³And I will make a nation of the son of the slave woman also, because he is your offspring." ¹⁴So Abraham rose early in the morning and took bread and a skin of water and gave it to Hagar, putting it on her shoulder, along with the child, and sent her away. And she departed and wandered in the wilderness of Beersheba.

¹⁵When the water in the skin was gone, she put the child under one of the bushes. ¹⁶Then she went and sat down opposite him a good way off, about the distance of a bowshot, for she said, "Let me not look on the death of the child." And as she sat opposite him, she lifted up her voice and wept. ¹⁷And God heard the voice of the boy, and the angel of God called to Hagar from heaven and said to her, "What troubles you, Hagar? Fear not, for God has heard the voice of the boy where he is. ¹⁸Up! Lift up the boy, and hold him fast with your hand, for I will make him into a great nation." ¹⁹Then God opened her eyes, and she saw a well of water. And she went and filled the skin with water and gave the boy a drink. ²⁰And God was with the boy, and he grew up. He lived in the wilderness and became an expert with the bow. ²¹He lived in the wilderness of Paran, and his mother took a wife for him from the land of Egypt.

¹ *Isaac* means *he laughs* ² Possibly *laughing in mockery*

Dispute over a well [21:22–34]. Stories move back and forth according to a rhythm of increasing tension followed by decreasing tension. After the intensity of the birth and expulsion scenes, we subside into comparative calm with the episode involving a well. The story is a conflict story in which Abraham needs to negotiate with a clan leader about property rights. We can assimilate the episode as giving us a glimpse into the hero's life as a wanderer and a domestic hero whose daily life was taken up with looking after his animals and property. Abraham is a spiritual hero, but he did not live in an ethereal "other" world. He was distracted by the same types of daily details that occupy us.

²²At that time Abimelech and Phicol the commander of his army said to Abraham, "God is with you in all that you do. ²³Now therefore swear to me here by God that you will not deal falsely with me or with my descendants or with my posterity, but as I have dealt kindly with you, so you will deal with me and with the land where you have sojourned." ²⁴And Abraham said, "I will swear."

²⁵When Abraham reproved Abimelech about a well of water that Abimelech's servants had seized, ²⁶Abimelech said, "I do not know who has done this thing; you did not tell me, and I have not heard of it until today." ²⁷So Abraham took sheep and oxen and gave them to Abimelech, and the two men made a covenant. ²⁸Abraham set seven ewe lambs of the flock apart. ²⁹And Abimelech said to Abraham, "What is the meaning of these seven ewe lambs that you have set apart?" ³⁰He said, "These seven ewe lambs you will take from my hand, that this¹ may be a witness for me that I dug this well." ³¹Therefore that place was called Beersheba,² because there both of them swore an oath. ³²So they made a covenant at Beersheba. Then Abimelech and Phicol the commander of his army rose up and returned to the land of the Philistines. ³³Abraham planted a tamarisk tree in Beersheba and called there on the name of the LORD, the Everlasting God. ³⁴And Abraham sojourned many days in the land of the Philistines.

The offering of Isaac [chapter 22]. Abraham's willingness to offer Isaac to God is the climax of his story. All of the plot motifs converge here: we see the spiritual heroism of Abraham as a man of faith in its finest hour; the quest for a son and descendants is threatened and then secured; the inner conflict between faith and expediency that had dogged Abraham is decisively resolved in the direction of faith; as a reward, God renews his covenant with Abraham for the last time in the story. The genre is the story of testing, as the opening formula editorializes: "After these things God tested Abraham" (v. 1). We can organize the sequence around the test motif: the test announced (vv. 1–2); preparing for the test (vv. 3–8); taking the test (vv. 9–10); interruption of the test (vv. 11–12); interpreting the results of the test (vv. 12–18); returning home after the test (v. 19). Archetypes include the physical journey whose significance is spiritual (we can speak of the spiritual geography through which Abraham travels); the quest; meeting with God on a mountain; the sacrifice and substitute; suspense; the death-rebirth motif (see Heb. 11:19); the willingness to offer an only son.

22 After these things God tested Abraham and said to him, "Abraham!" And he said, "Here am I." ²He said, "Take your son, your only son Isaac, whom you love, and go to the land of Moriah, and offer him there as a burnt offering on one of

---

¹ Or you ² *Beersheba* means *well of seven* or *well of the oath*

the mountains of which I shall tell you." ³So Abraham rose early in the morning, saddled his donkey, and took two of his young men with him, and his son Isaac. And he cut the wood for the burnt offering and arose and went to the place of which God had told him. ⁴On the third day Abraham lifted up his eyes and saw the place from afar. ⁵Then Abraham said to his young men, "Stay here with the donkey; I and the boy¹ will go over there and worship and come again to you." ⁶And Abraham took the wood of the burnt offering and laid it on Isaac his son. And he took in his hand the fire and the knife. So they went both of them together. ⁷And Isaac said to his father Abraham, "My father!" And he said, "Here am I, my son." He said, "Behold, the fire and the wood, but where is the lamb for a burnt offering?" ⁸Abraham said, "God will provide for himself the lamb for a burnt offering, my son." So they went both of them together.

⁹When they came to the place of which God had told him, Abraham built the altar there and laid the wood in order and bound Isaac his son and laid him on the altar, on top of the wood. ¹⁰Then Abraham reached out his hand and took the knife to slaughter his son. ¹¹But the angel of the LORD called to him from heaven and said, "Abraham, Abraham!" And he said, "Here am I." ¹²He said, "Do not lay your hand on the boy or do anything to him, for now I know that you fear God, seeing you have not withheld your son, your only son, from me." ¹³And Abraham lifted up his eyes and looked, and behold, behind him was a ram, caught in a thicket by his horns. And Abraham went and took the ram and offered it up as a burnt offering instead of his son. ¹⁴So Abraham called the name of that place, "The LORD will provide";² as it is said to this day, "On the mount of the LORD it shall be provided."³

¹⁵And the angel of the LORD called to Abraham a second time from heaven ¹⁶and said, "By myself I have sworn, declares the LORD, because you have done this and have not withheld your son, your only son, ¹⁷I will surely bless you, and I will surely multiply your offspring as the stars of heaven and as the sand that is on the seashore. And your offspring shall possess the gate of his⁴ enemies, ¹⁸and in your offspring shall all the nations of the earth be blessed, because you have obeyed my voice." ¹⁹So Abraham returned to his young men, and they arose and went together to Beersheba. And Abraham lived at Beersheba.

²⁰Now after these things it was told to Abraham, "Behold, Milcah also has borne children to your brother Nahor: ²¹Uz his firstborn, Buz his brother, Kemuel the father of Aram, ²²Chesed, Hazo, Pildash, Jidlaph, and Bethuel." ²³(Bethuel fathered Rebekah.) These eight Milcah bore to Nahor, Abraham's brother. ²⁴Moreover, his concubine, whose name was Reumah, bore Tebah, Gaham, Tahash, and Maacah.

Burying a wife [chapter 23]. After the high voltage of the sacrifice scene, we swing back to something poignant but less suspenseful with the death and burial of Sarah. Abraham and Sarah are one of the "classic couples" of biblical history, and their marriage comes to an end with this episode, which is a dimension of the hero's domestic identity. The genre is the burial story, which in this case is also a story of faith in the covenant promise of the land of Canaan. The story begins with grief (vv. 1–2), but cutting the other way is the latent humor of the bargaining process by which Abraham pays an exorbitant price for a burial cave. Underlying the negotiation are bargaining rituals of the ancient Near East. Abraham and the Hittites play a straight-faced game of pretense

¹ Or *young man*; also verse 12 ² Or *will see* ³ Or *he will be seen* ⁴ Or *their*

in which everyone knows from the start that Abraham will pay an outlandish price for the cave. The irony is that Abraham already owns the entire land of Canaan by promise from God.

23 Sarah lived 127 years; these were the years of the life of Sarah. [2]And Sarah died at Kiriath-arba (that is, Hebron) in the land of Canaan, and Abraham went in to mourn for Sarah and to weep for her. [3]And Abraham rose up from before his dead and said to the Hittites,[1] [4]"I am a sojourner and foreigner among you; give me property among you for a burying place, that I may bury my dead out of my sight." [5]The Hittites answered Abraham, [6]"Hear us, my lord; you are a prince of God[2] among us. Bury your dead in the choicest of our tombs. None of us will withhold from you his tomb to hinder you from burying your dead." [7]Abraham rose and bowed to the Hittites, the people of the land. [8]And he said to them, "If you are willing that I should bury my dead out of my sight, hear me and entreat for me Ephron the son of Zohar, [9]that he may give me the cave of Machpelah, which he owns; it is at the end of his field. For the full price let him give it to me in your presence as property for a burying place."

[10]Now Ephron was sitting among the Hittites, and Ephron the Hittite answered Abraham in the hearing of the Hittites, of all who went in at the gate of his city, [11]"No, my lord, hear me: I give you the field, and I give you the cave that is in it. In the sight of the sons of my people I give it to you. Bury your dead." [12]Then Abraham bowed down before the people of the land. [13]And he said to Ephron in the hearing of the people of the land, "But if you will, hear me: I give the price of the field. Accept it from me, that I may bury my dead there." [14]Ephron answered Abraham, [15]"My lord, listen to me: a piece of land worth four hundred shekels[3] of silver, what is that between you and me? Bury your dead." [16]Abraham listened to Ephron, and Abraham weighed out for Ephron the silver that he had named in the hearing of the Hittites, four hundred shekels of silver, according to the weights current among the merchants.

[17]So the field of Ephron in Machpelah, which was to the east of Mamre, the field with the cave that was in it and all the trees that were in the field, throughout its whole area, was made over [18]to Abraham as a possession in the presence of the Hittites, before all who went in at the gate of his city. [19]After this, Abraham buried Sarah his wife in the cave of the field of Machpelah east of Mamre (that is, Hebron) in the land of Canaan. [20]The field and the cave that is in it were made over to Abraham as property for a burying place by the Hittites.

A story of courtship and marriage [chapter 24]. Chapter 24 is a love story, and we can note at the outset that the storyteller satisfies the human interest in love stories by devoting a whopping sixty-seven verses to the episode in which Isaac conducts the courtship of his wife by proxy. Even though the story may seem to belong to Isaac rather than Abraham, it is actually an extension of Abraham's domestic role, since it was his responsibility to find a suitable wife for his son. The spirit in which Abraham undertakes the quest for Isaac's wife surrounds it with religious significance (vv. 5–8). We are to understand that Abraham was concerned to protect the covenant line, which stipulated

[1] Hebrew *sons of Heth*; also verses 5, 7, 10, 16, 18, 20 [2] Or *a mighty prince* [3] A *shekel* was about 2/5 ounce or 11 grams

that the covenant would be perpetuated through his family. The two lead characters in this romance drama are the servant who undertakes the journey and Rebekah, the bride of choice. One way to bring the servant into focus is to ponder the litany of things that make him one of the most attractive minor characters in the Bible. We can get a grip on Rebekah's characterization by scrutinizing the story for details that would commend her as a future wife. The story has a nice abundance of suspense, and it is a drama in miniature with speeches and dialogue fully reported. The first meeting of Isaac and Rebekah (vv. 62–67) is a masterpiece of atmosphere, tenderness, and understated emotion.

24 Now Abraham was old, well advanced in years. And the LORD had blessed Abraham in all things. ²And Abraham said to his servant, the oldest of his household, who had charge of all that he had, "Put your hand under my thigh, ³that I may make you swear by the LORD, the God of heaven and God of the earth, that you will not take a wife for my son from the daughters of the Canaanites, among whom I dwell, ⁴but will go to my country and to my kindred, and take a wife for my son Isaac." ⁵The servant said to him, "Perhaps the woman may not be willing to follow me to this land. Must I then take your son back to the land from which you came?" ⁶Abraham said to him, "See to it that you do not take my son back there. ⁷The LORD, the God of heaven, who took me from my father's house and from the land of my kindred, and who spoke to me and swore to me, 'To your offspring I will give this land,' he will send his angel before you, and you shall take a wife for my son from there. ⁸But if the woman is not willing to follow you, then you will be free from this oath of mine; only you must not take my son back there." ⁹So the servant put his hand under the thigh of Abraham his master and swore to him concerning this matter.

¹⁰Then the servant took ten of his master's camels and departed, taking all sorts of choice gifts from his master; and he arose and went to Mesopotamia¹ to the city of Nahor. ¹¹And he made the camels kneel down outside the city by the well of water at the time of evening, the time when women go out to draw water. ¹²And he said, "O LORD, God of my master Abraham, please grant me success today and show steadfast love to my master Abraham. ¹³Behold, I am standing by the spring of water, and the daughters of the men of the city are coming out to draw water. ¹⁴Let the young woman to whom I shall say, 'Please let down your jar that I may drink,' and who shall say, 'Drink, and I will water your camels'—let her be the one whom you have appointed for your servant Isaac. By this² I shall know that you have shown steadfast love to my master."

¹⁵Before he had finished speaking, behold, Rebekah, who was born to Bethuel the son of Milcah, the wife of Nahor, Abraham's brother, came out with her water jar on her shoulder. ¹⁶The young woman was very attractive in appearance, a maiden³ whom no man had known. She went down to the spring and filled her jar and came up. ¹⁷Then the servant ran to meet her and said, "Please give me a little water to drink from your jar." ¹⁸She said, "Drink, my lord." And she quickly let down her jar upon her hand and gave him a drink. ¹⁹When she had finished giving him a drink, she said, "I will draw water for your camels also, until they have finished drinking." ²⁰So she quickly emptied her jar into the trough and ran again to the well to draw water, and she drew for all his camels. ²¹The man gazed at her in silence to learn whether the LORD had prospered his journey or not.

¹ Hebrew *Aram-naharaim* ² Or *By her* ³ Or *a woman of marriageable age*

²²When the camels had finished drinking, the man took a gold ring weighing a half shekel,[1] and two bracelets for her arms weighing ten gold shekels, ²³and said, "Please tell me whose daughter you are. Is there room in your father's house for us to spend the night?" ²⁴She said to him, "I am the daughter of Bethuel the son of Milcah, whom she bore to Nahor." ²⁵She added, "We have plenty of both straw and fodder, and room to spend the night." ²⁶The man bowed his head and worshiped the LORD ²⁷and said, "Blessed be the LORD, the God of my master Abraham, who has not forsaken his steadfast love and his faithfulness toward my master. As for me, the LORD has led me in the way to the house of my master's kinsmen." ²⁸Then the young woman ran and told her mother's household about these things.

²⁹Rebekah had a brother whose name was Laban. Laban ran out toward the man, to the spring. ³⁰As soon as he saw the ring and the bracelets on his sister's arms, and heard the words of Rebekah his sister, "Thus the man spoke to me," he went to the man. And behold, he was standing by the camels at the spring. ³¹He said, "Come in, O blessed of the LORD. Why do you stand outside? For I have prepared the house and a place for the camels." ³²So the man came to the house and unharnessed the camels, and gave straw and fodder to the camels, and there was water to wash his feet and the feet of the men who were with him. ³³Then food was set before him to eat. But he said, "I will not eat until I have said what I have to say." He said, "Speak on."

³⁴So he said, "I am Abraham's servant. ³⁵The LORD has greatly blessed my master, and he has become great. He has given him flocks and herds, silver and gold, male servants and female servants, camels and donkeys. ³⁶And Sarah my master's wife bore a son to my master when she was old, and to him he has given all that he has. ³⁷My master made me swear, saying, 'You shall not take a wife for my son from the daughters of the Canaanites, in whose land I dwell, ³⁸but you shall go to my father's house and to my clan and take a wife for my son.' ³⁹I said to my master, 'Perhaps the woman will not follow me.' ⁴⁰But he said to me, 'The LORD, before whom I have walked, will send his angel with you and prosper your way. You shall take a wife for my son from my clan and from my father's house. ⁴¹Then you will be free from my oath, when you come to my clan. And if they will not give her to you, you will be free from my oath.'

⁴²"I came today to the spring and said, 'O LORD, the God of my master Abraham, if now you are prospering the way that I go, ⁴³behold, I am standing by the spring of water. Let the virgin who comes out to draw water, to whom I shall say, "Please give me a little water from your jar to drink," ⁴⁴and who will say to me, "Drink, and I will draw for your camels also," let her be the woman whom the LORD has appointed for my master's son.'

⁴⁵"Before I had finished speaking in my heart, behold, Rebekah came out with her water jar on her shoulder, and she went down to the spring and drew water. I said to her, 'Please let me drink.' ⁴⁶She quickly let down her jar from her shoulder and said, 'Drink, and I will give your camels drink also.' So I drank, and she gave the camels drink also. ⁴⁷Then I asked her, 'Whose daughter are you?' She said, 'The daughter of Bethuel, Nahor's son, whom Milcah bore to him.' So I put the ring on her nose and the bracelets on her arms. ⁴⁸Then I bowed my head and worshiped the LORD and blessed the LORD, the God of my master Abraham, who had led me by the right way[2] to take the daughter of my master's kinsman for his son. ⁴⁹Now then, if you are going

---

[1] A *shekel* was about 2/5 ounce or 11 grams [2] Or *faithfully*

to show steadfast love and faithfulness to my master, tell me; and if not, tell me, that I may turn to the right hand or to the left."

⁵⁰Then Laban and Bethuel answered and said, "The thing has come from the LORD; we cannot speak to you bad or good. ⁵¹Behold, Rebekah is before you; take her and go, and let her be the wife of your master's son, as the LORD has spoken."

⁵²When Abraham's servant heard their words, he bowed himself to the earth before the LORD. ⁵³And the servant brought out jewelry of silver and of gold, and garments, and gave them to Rebekah. He also gave to her brother and to her mother costly ornaments. ⁵⁴And he and the men who were with him ate and drank, and they spent the night there. When they arose in the morning, he said, "Send me away to my master." ⁵⁵Her brother and her mother said, "Let the young woman remain with us a while, at least ten days; after that she may go." ⁵⁶But he said to them, "Do not delay me, since the LORD has prospered my way. Send me away that I may go to my master." ⁵⁷They said, "Let us call the young woman and ask her." ⁵⁸And they called Rebekah and said to her, "Will you go with this man?" She said, "I will go." ⁵⁹So they sent away Rebekah their sister and her nurse, and Abraham's servant and his men. ⁶⁰And they blessed Rebekah and said to her,

> "Our sister, may you become
>   thousands of ten thousands,
> and may your offspring possess
>   the gate of those who hate him!"¹

⁶¹Then Rebekah and her young women arose and rode on the camels and followed the man. Thus the servant took Rebekah and went his way.

⁶²Now Isaac had returned from Beer-lahai-roi and was dwelling in the Negeb. ⁶³And Isaac went out to meditate in the field toward evening. And he lifted up his eyes and saw, and behold, there were camels coming. ⁶⁴And Rebekah lifted up her eyes, and when she saw Isaac, she dismounted from the camel ⁶⁵and said to the servant, "Who is that man, walking in the field to meet us?" The servant said, "It is my master." So she took her veil and covered herself. ⁶⁶And the servant told Isaac all the things that he had done. ⁶⁷Then Isaac brought her into the tent of Sarah his mother and took Rebekah, and she became his wife, and he loved her. So Isaac was comforted after his mother's death.

The death of a domestic hero [25:1–18]. After the titanic experiences of Abraham's life, we end his story with quietude. The closing chapter of his life is domestic rather than explicitly spiritual. The account reads something like an obituary at a funeral: a list of children and where they lived (vv. 1–6); the age of the deceased (vv. 7–8); place of burial (vv. 9–10); a note regarding the primary son (v. 11); further list of descendants, this time through the line of Ishmael (vv. 12–18). There are overtones of fulfillment of the covenant promise in this obituary, with the mention of the promised son Isaac and the place of Abraham's burial in the Promised Land.

25 Abraham took another wife, whose name was Keturah. ²She bore him Zimran, Jokshan, Medan, Midian, Ishbak, and Shuah. ³Jokshan fathered Sheba and Dedan. The sons of Dedan were Asshurim, Letushim, and Leummim. ⁴The

¹ Or hate them

sons of Midian were Ephah, Epher, Hanoch, Abida, and Eldaah. All these were the children of Keturah. ⁵Abraham gave all he had to Isaac. ⁶But to the sons of his concubines Abraham gave gifts, and while he was still living he sent them away from his son Isaac, eastward to the east country.

⁷These are the days of the years of Abraham's life, 175 years. ⁸Abraham breathed his last and died in a good old age, an old man and full of years, and was gathered to his people. ⁹Isaac and Ishmael his sons buried him in the cave of Machpelah, in the field of Ephron the son of Zohar the Hittite, east of Mamre, ¹⁰the field that Abraham purchased from the Hittites. There Abraham was buried, with Sarah his wife. ¹¹After the death of Abraham, God blessed Isaac his son. And Isaac settled at Beer-lahai-roi.

¹²These are the generations of Ishmael, Abraham's son, whom Hagar the Egyptian, Sarah's servant, bore to Abraham. ¹³These are the names of the sons of Ishmael, named in the order of their birth: Nebaioth, the firstborn of Ishmael; and Kedar, Adbeel, Mibsam, ¹⁴Mishma, Dumah, Massa, ¹⁵Hadad, Tema, Jetur, Naphish, and Kedemah. ¹⁶These are the sons of Ishmael and these are their names, by their villages and by their encampments, twelve princes according to their tribes. ¹⁷(These are the years of the life of Ishmael: 137 years. He breathed his last and died, and was gathered to his people.) ¹⁸They settled from Havilah to Shur, which is opposite Egypt in the direction of Assyria. He settled¹ over against all his kinsmen.

Jacob and Esau: birth and early relationship [25:19–34]. Although the line of patriarchs runs from Abraham to Isaac to Jacob to Joseph, the stories of the latter three overlap. Even though the story of Jacob and Esau will be interrupted by a return to the story of Isaac, this unit is best considered as the beginning of the story of Jacob. Verses 19–26 belong to the genre known as a *birth story, and this particular birth story partly stresses the humorous aspect of the births (vv. 25–26). More important, certain details regarding Jacob constitute a strong note of foreshadowing. The oracle predicts that the younger sibling will supplant the older sibling (v. 23); this is so common in OT narrative that it becomes an *archetype, suggestive of how the ways of God often differ from human expectations. Second, Jacob receives his name (meaning "he takes by the heel" or "he cheats") from the circumstances of his birth, and one of the unifying traits of the hero in the story of Jacob is that he keeps living up to his name and essential identity as the one who contends and overcomes. The other defining moment in the early relationship between Jacob and Esau is the exchanged birthright (vv. 27–34). Jacob does not literally steal the birthright as he later does the blessing, but he is guilty of selfish and unbrotherly behavior, just as Esau is a profane, unholy, or irreligious person (Heb. 12:16) who despises or misprizes his birthright (Gen. 25:34)—a person with no ability to regard spiritual values as being more important than physical appetite. Important archetypes cluster in this story: conflict story, the trickster, the dupe, reversal of plot (the entire lives of the two brothers are reversed in just a few seconds). In the overall story of Jacob, the portrait of the protagonist is largely a satiric portrait, as the hero's character flaws are repeatedly exposed to view.

¹⁹These are the generations of Isaac, Abraham's son: Abraham fathered Isaac, ²⁰and Isaac was forty years old when he took Rebekah, the daughter of Bethuel the Aramean of Paddan-aram, the sister of Laban the Aramean, to be his wife. ²¹And Isaac prayed to the LORD for his wife, because she was barren. And the LORD granted

---

¹ Hebrew *fell*

his prayer, and Rebekah his wife conceived. ²²The children struggled together within her, and she said, "If it is thus, why is this happening to me?"¹ So she went to inquire of the LORD. ²³And the LORD said to her,

"Two nations are in your womb,
    and two peoples from within you² shall be divided;
the one shall be stronger than the other,
    the older shall serve the younger."

²⁴When her days to give birth were completed, behold, there were twins in her womb. ²⁵The first came out red, all his body like a hairy cloak, so they called his name Esau. ²⁶Afterward his brother came out with his hand holding Esau's heel, so his name was called Jacob.³ Isaac was sixty years old when she bore them.

²⁷When the boys grew up, Esau was a skillful hunter, a man of the field, while Jacob was a quiet man, dwelling in tents. ²⁸Isaac loved Esau because he ate of his game, but Rebekah loved Jacob.

²⁹Once when Jacob was cooking stew, Esau came in from the field, and he was exhausted. ³⁰And Esau said to Jacob, "Let me eat some of that red stew, for I am exhausted!" (Therefore his name was called Edom.⁴) ³¹Jacob said, "Sell me your birthright now." ³²Esau said, "I am about to die; of what use is a birthright to me?" ³³Jacob said, "Swear to me now." So he swore to him and sold his birthright to Jacob. ³⁴Then Jacob gave Esau bread and lentil stew, and he ate and drank and rose and went his way. Thus Esau despised his birthright.

> **The life of Isaac: like father, like son** [chapter 26]. In terms of space allotted to him, Isaac in his adult life is the forgotten patriarch of Genesis. Chapter 26 is the lone chapter devoted just to Isaac in his role as leader of his family or clan. Compared to the titanic spiritual experiences of the other patriarchs, the story of Isaac might seem anticlimactic, though it reinforces the important biblical theme that God is very interested in our commonplace lives. The sequence of events that the storyteller chose to present in this chapter echo events in the life of Isaac's father Abraham: coping with famine (vv. 1–2); receiving God's covenant promise (vv. 3–5); lying to Abimelech about the identity of his wife (vv. 6–11); the affluence of the hero and the difficulties it brings with the outside world (vv. 12–16); the life of a wanderer and the importance of wells in the nomadic life (vv. 17–22); God's reestablishment of the covenant amid a life of altar, tent, and well (vv. 25); the making of a treaty with a king and yet another landmark well (vv. 26–33); domestic unhappiness over a problem son (v. 34). We can also read this chapter as giving us a glimpse into the family background of Jacob: it was a covenant family that knew God personally, a home in which the father was capable of resorting to expediency when faced with a crisis, a home in which the father was industrious and had excellent business sense.

26 Now there was a famine in the land, besides the former famine that was in the days of Abraham. And Isaac went to Gerar to Abimelech king of the Philistines. ²And the LORD appeared to him and said, "Do not go down to Egypt; dwell in the land of which I shall tell you. ³Sojourn in this land, and I will be with you and will bless you, for to you and to your offspring I will give all these lands, and I will establish the oath that I swore to Abraham your father. ⁴I will multiply your offspring

¹ Or why do I live? ² Or from birth ³ Jacob means He takes by the heel, or He cheats ⁴ Edom sounds like the Hebrew for red

as the stars of heaven and will give to your offspring all these lands. And in your off-spring all the nations of the earth shall be blessed, ⁵because Abraham obeyed my voice and kept my charge, my commandments, my statutes, and my laws."

⁶So Isaac settled in Gerar. ⁷When the men of the place asked him about his wife, he said, "She is my sister," for he feared to say, "My wife," thinking, "lest the men of the place should kill me because of Rebekah," because she was attractive in appear-ance. ⁸When he had been there a long time, Abimelech king of the Philistines looked out of a window and saw Isaac laughing with¹ Rebekah his wife. ⁹So Abimelech called Isaac and said, "Behold, she is your wife. How then could you say, 'She is my sister'?" Isaac said to him, "Because I thought, 'Lest I die because of her.'" ¹⁰Abimelech said, "What is this you have done to us? One of the people might easily have lain with your wife, and you would have brought guilt upon us." ¹¹So Abimelech warned all the people, saying, "Whoever touches this man or his wife shall surely be put to death."

¹²And Isaac sowed in that land and reaped in the same year a hundredfold. The LORD blessed him, ¹³and the man became rich, and gained more and more until he became very wealthy. ¹⁴He had possessions of flocks and herds and many servants, so that the Philistines envied him. ¹⁵(Now the Philistines had stopped and filled with earth all the wells that his father's servants had dug in the days of Abraham his father.) ¹⁶And Abimelech said to Isaac, "Go away from us, for you are much mightier than we."

¹⁷So Isaac departed from there and encamped in the Valley of Gerar and settled there. ¹⁸And Isaac dug again the wells of water that had been dug in the days of Abraham his father, which the Philistines had stopped after the death of Abraham. And he gave them the names that his father had given them. ¹⁹But when Isaac's ser-vants dug in the valley and found there a well of spring water, ²⁰the herdsmen of Gerar quarreled with Isaac's herdsmen, saying, "The water is ours." So he called the name of the well Esek,² because they contended with him. ²¹Then they dug another well, and they quarreled over that also, so he called its name Sitnah.³ ²²And he moved from there and dug another well, and they did not quarrel over it. So he called its name Rehoboth,⁴ saying, "For now the LORD has made room for us, and we shall be fruitful in the land."

²³From there he went up to Beersheba. ²⁴And the LORD appeared to him the same night and said, "I am the God of Abraham your father. Fear not, for I am with you and will bless you and multiply your offspring for my servant Abraham's sake." ²⁵So he built an altar there and called upon the name of the LORD and pitched his tent there. And there Isaac's servants dug a well.

²⁶When Abimelech went to him from Gerar with Ahuzzath his adviser and Phicol the commander of his army, ²⁷Isaac said to them, "Why have you come to me, seeing that you hate me and have sent me away from you?" ²⁸They said, "We see plainly that the LORD has been with you. So we said, let there be a sworn pact between us, between you and us, and let us make a covenant with you, ²⁹that you will do us no harm, just as we have not touched you and have done to you nothing but good and have sent you away in peace. You are now the blessed of the LORD." ³⁰So he made them a feast, and they ate and drank. ³¹In the morning they rose early and exchanged oaths. And Isaac sent them on their way, and they departed from him in peace. ³²That same day Isaac's servants came and told him about the well that they had dug and

---

¹ Hebrew may suggest an intimate relationship ² *Esek* means *contention* ³ *Sitnah* means *enmity* ⁴ *Rehoboth* means *broad places,* or *room*

said to him, "We have found water." [33]He called it Shibah;[i] therefore the name of the city is Beersheba to this day.

[34]When Esau was forty years old, he took Judith the daughter of Beeri the Hittite to be his wife, and Basemath the daughter of Elon the Hittite, [35]and they made life bitter[2] for Isaac and Rebekah.

The stolen blessing [27:1–40]. This episode unfolds in full, leisurely detail, and it is one of the most famous stories in the Bible. The event is a drama in miniature, with an abundance of dialogue, stationing of characters in the setting, and implied gestures and inflections. The story has most of the ingredients that we love in a story—conflict, suspense, intrigue, dramatic irony (based on mistaken identity), a scene of discovery. There is an equal abundance of recognizable human experience—marital discord, sibling rivalry, parental favoritism, the trickster plying his trade, the anger that accompanies having been cheated. All five senses enter the action, enhancing still further our ability to relive the event in our imagination. It is possible to compile a brief character sketch of all four actors in this family drama, and the overall pattern is a balanced lack of sympathy among all four characters. Poetic justice marks the moral point of the story, as everyone ends up a loser in this sordid chapter of family history.

27

When Isaac was old and his eyes were dim so that he could not see, he called Esau his older son and said to him, "My son"; and he answered, "Here I am." [2]He said, "Behold, I am old; I do not know the day of my death. [3]Now then, take your weapons, your quiver and your bow, and go out to the field and hunt game for me, [4]and prepare for me delicious food, such as I love, and bring it to me so that I may eat, that my soul may bless you before I die."

[5]Now Rebekah was listening when Isaac spoke to his son Esau. So when Esau went to the field to hunt for game and bring it, [6]Rebekah said to her son Jacob, "I heard your father speak to your brother Esau, [7]'Bring me game and prepare for me delicious food, that I may eat it and bless you before the LORD before I die.' [8]Now therefore, my son, obey my voice as I command you. [9]Go to the flock and bring me two good young goats, so that I may prepare from them delicious food for your father, such as he loves. [10]And you shall bring it to your father to eat, so that he may bless you before he dies." [11]But Jacob said to Rebekah his mother, "Behold, my brother Esau is a hairy man, and I am a smooth man. [12]Perhaps my father will feel me, and I shall seem to be mocking him and bring a curse upon myself and not a blessing." [13]His mother said to him, "Let your curse be on me, my son; only obey my voice, and go, bring them to me."

[14]So he went and took them and brought them to his mother, and his mother prepared delicious food, such as his father loved. [15]Then Rebekah took the best garments of Esau her older son, which were with her in the house, and put them on Jacob her younger son. [16]And the skins of the young goats she put on his hands and on the smooth part of his neck. [17]And she put the delicious food and the bread, which she had prepared, into the hand of her son Jacob.

[18]So he went in to his father and said, "My father." And he said, "Here I am. Who are you, my son?" [19]Jacob said to his father, "I am Esau your firstborn. I have done as you told me; now sit up and eat of my game, that your soul may bless me." [20]But Isaac said to his son, "How is it that you have found it so quickly, my son?" He answered,

---

[1] Shibah sounds like the Hebrew for *oath* [2] Hebrew *they were bitterness of spirit*

"Because the LORD your God granted me success." ²¹Then Isaac said to Jacob, "Please come near, that I may feel you, my son, to know whether you are really my son Esau or not." ²²So Jacob went near to Isaac his father, who felt him and said, "The voice is Jacob's voice, but the hands are the hands of Esau." ²³And he did not recognize him, because his hands were hairy like his brother Esau's hands. So he blessed him. ²⁴He said, "Are you really my son Esau?" He answered, "I am." ²⁵Then he said, "Bring it near to me, that I may eat of my son's game and bless you." So he brought it near to him, and he ate; and he brought him wine, and he drank.

²⁶Then his father Isaac said to him, "Come near and kiss me, my son." ²⁷So he came near and kissed him. And Isaac smelled the smell of his garments and blessed him and said,

"See, the smell of my son
    is as the smell of a field that the LORD has blessed!
28   May God give you of the dew of heaven
        and of the fatness of the earth
        and plenty of grain and wine.
29   Let peoples serve you,
        and nations bow down to you.
    Be lord over your brothers,
        and may your mother's sons bow down to you.
    Cursed be everyone who curses you,
        and blessed be everyone who blesses you!"

³⁰As soon as Isaac had finished blessing Jacob, when Jacob had scarcely gone out from the presence of Isaac his father, Esau his brother came in from his hunting. ³¹He also prepared delicious food and brought it to his father. And he said to his father, "Let my father arise and eat of his son's game, that you may bless me." ³²His father Isaac said to him, "Who are you?" He answered, "I am your son, your firstborn, Esau." ³³Then Isaac trembled very violently and said, "Who was it then that hunted game and brought it to me, and I ate it all before you came, and I have blessed him? Yes, and he shall be blessed." ³⁴As soon as Esau heard the words of his father, he cried out with an exceedingly great and bitter cry and said to his father, "Bless me, even me also, O my father!" ³⁵But he said, "Your brother came deceitfully, and he has taken away your blessing." ³⁶Esau said, "Is he not rightly named Jacob?[1] For he has cheated me these two times. He took away my birthright, and behold, now he has taken away my blessing." Then he said, "Have you not reserved a blessing for me?" ³⁷Isaac answered and said to Esau, "Behold, I have made him lord over you, and all his brothers I have given to him for servants, and with grain and wine I have sustained him. What then can I do for you, my son?" ³⁸Esau said to his father, "Have you but one blessing, my father? Bless me, even me also, O my father." And Esau lifted up his *voice and wept.*

³⁹Then Isaac his father answered and said to him:

"Behold, away from[2] the fatness of the earth shall your dwelling be,
    and away from[3] the dew of heaven on high.
40   By your sword you shall live,
        and you shall serve your brother;

---

[1] *Jacob* means *He takes by the heel,* or *He cheats* [2] Or *Behold, of* [3] Or *and of*

but when you grow restless
>   you shall break his yoke from your neck."

Breakup of a family [27:41–28:9]. The grand experiment in expediency now reaps its bitter harvest. We look in on more negative but familiar human experiences—hatred, fear, family discord, leave-taking, and a son's bad marriages.

[41] Now Esau hated Jacob because of the blessing with which his father had blessed him, and Esau said to himself, "The days of mourning for my father are approaching; then I will kill my brother Jacob." [42] But the words of Esau her older son were told to Rebekah. So she sent and called Jacob her younger son and said to him, "Behold, your brother Esau comforts himself about you by planning to kill you. [43] Now therefore, my son, obey my voice. Arise, flee to Laban my brother in Haran [44] and stay with him a while, until your brother's fury turns away— [45] until your brother's anger turns away from you, and he forgets what you have done to him. Then I will send and bring you from there. Why should I be bereft of you both in one day?"

[46] Then Rebekah said to Isaac, "I loathe my life because of the Hittite women.[1] If Jacob marries one of the Hittite women like these, one of the women of the land, what good will my life be to me?"

28 Then Isaac called Jacob and blessed him and directed him, "You must not take a wife from the Canaanite women. [2] Arise, go to Paddan-aram to the house of Bethuel your mother's father, and take as your wife from there one of the daughters of Laban your mother's brother. [3] God Almighty[2] bless you and make you fruitful and multiply you, that you may become a company of peoples. [4] May he give the blessing of Abraham to you and to your offspring with you, that you may take possession of the land of your sojournings that God gave to Abraham!" [5] Thus Isaac sent Jacob away. And he went to Paddan-aram, to Laban, the son of Bethuel the Aramean, the brother of Rebekah, Jacob's and Esau's mother.

[6] Now Esau saw that Isaac had blessed Jacob and sent him away to Paddan-aram to take a wife from there, and that as he blessed him he directed him, "You must not take a wife from the Canaanite women," [7] and that Jacob had obeyed his father and his mother and gone to Paddan-aram. [8] So when Esau saw that the Canaanite women did not please Isaac his father, [9] Esau went to Ishmael and took as his wife, besides the wives he had, Mahalath the daughter of Ishmael, Abraham's son, the sister of Nebaioth.

Jacob's dream [28:10–22]. The archetype is that of the young hero undertaking a perilous journey of initiation. Jacob is a young man undergoing an identity crisis, and the story is a coming-of-age story. Archetypes include exile, the guilt-haunted wanderer, the fugitive fleeing for his life. The main motif is the divine-human encounter, with the dream serving as the means by which God encounters Jacob. God here confers the covenant blessing on Jacob (later conferring a covenant name). Nearly every detail assumes a symbolic and spiritual meaning—the ladder with two-way angelic traffic between heaven and earth (v. 12); God's speaking from the top of the ladder (vv. 13–15); the content of God's promise, namely, the covenant (vv. 13–15); Jacob's immediate identifi-

---

[1] Hebrew *daughters of Heth* [2] Hebrew *El Shaddai*

cation of the place upon awakening (vv. 16–17); and Jacob's ritual acts the next morning (vv. 18–22). Overall, God signals, and Jacob recognizes, that God is with Jacob in his wanderings.

[10]Jacob left Beersheba and went toward Haran. [11]And he came to a certain place and stayed there that night, because the sun had set. Taking one of the stones of the place, he put it under his head and lay down in that place to sleep. [12]And he dreamed, and behold, there was a ladder[1] set up on the earth, and the top of it reached to heaven. And behold, the angels of God were ascending and descending on it! [13]And behold, the LORD stood above it[2] and said, "I am the LORD, the God of Abraham your father and the God of Isaac. The land on which you lie I will give to you and to your offspring. [14]Your offspring shall be like the dust of the earth, and you shall spread abroad to the west and to the east and to the north and to the south, and in you and your offspring shall all the families of the earth be blessed. [15]Behold, I am with you and will keep you wherever you go, and will bring you back to this land. For I will not leave you until I have done what I have promised you." [16]Then Jacob awoke from his sleep and said, "Surely the LORD is in this place, and I did not know it." [17]And he was afraid and said, "How awesome is this place! This is none other than the house of God, and this is the gate of heaven."

[18]So early in the morning Jacob took the stone that he had put under his head and set it up for a pillar and poured oil on the top of it. [19]He called the name of that place Bethel,[3] but the name of the city was Luz at the first. [20]Then Jacob made a vow, saying, "If God will be with me and will keep me in this way that I go, and will give me bread to eat and clothing to wear, [21]so that I come again to my father's house in peace, then the LORD shall be my God, [22]and this stone, which I have set up for a pillar, shall be God's house. And of all that you give me I will give a full tenth to you."

Jacob's assimilation into Laban's family [29:1–30]. The writer of Genesis selected and molded the events of Jacob's life to form a circular, three-part movement in which an opening appearance by God foreshadows each phase. The phase of Jacob in his parental home began with an oracle pronounced to Rebekah predicting that Jacob would supplant Esau, and that is exactly what happened. In the dream at Bethel, God has conferred his covenant blessing on Jacob even though Jacob has done nothing that would merit such favor. The second phase consists of Jacob's life with Laban in Haran. The cycle of stories of Jacob's relations with Laban is an extended conflict story. Both Laban and Jacob are tricksters who richly deserve each other and who undertake a battle of wits to gain the advantage over one another. As we observe Jacob's arrival in Haran at the start of chapter 29, the hero reenacts a familiar role—the newly arrived stranger feeling his way. His meeting of Rachel at the well is a landmark event in his life and in the stories of Genesis. In fact, the meeting with one's future betrothed at a well is an OT archetype. Jacob is the greatest lover among the patriarchs, and his "courtship" of Leah and Rachel, odd by modern standards, is a classic love story in its own way. Jacob proves to be a resilient comic hero in all of the obstacles that appear, including the famous incident of the substitute bride.

---

[1] Or *a flight of steps* [2] Or *beside him* [3] *Bethel* means *the house of God*

29 Then Jacob went on his journey and came to the land of the people of the east. ²As he looked, he saw a well in the field, and behold, three flocks of sheep lying beside it, for out of that well the flocks were watered. The stone on the well's mouth was large, ³and when all the flocks were gathered there, the shepherds would roll the stone from the mouth of the well and water the sheep, and put the stone back in its place over the mouth of the well.

⁴Jacob said to them, "My brothers, where do you come from?" They said, "We are from Haran." ⁵He said to them, "Do you know Laban the son of Nahor?" They said, "We know him." ⁶He said to them, "Is it well with him?" They said, "It is well; and see, Rachel his daughter is coming with the sheep!" ⁷He said, "Behold, it is still high day; it is not time for the livestock to be gathered together. Water the sheep and go, pasture them." ⁸But they said, "We cannot until all the flocks are gathered together and the stone is rolled from the mouth of the well; then we water the sheep."

⁹While he was still speaking with them, Rachel came with her father's sheep, for she was a shepherdess. ¹⁰Now as soon as Jacob saw Rachel the daughter of Laban his mother's brother, and the sheep of Laban his mother's brother, Jacob came near and rolled the stone from the well's mouth and watered the flock of Laban his mother's brother. ¹¹Then Jacob kissed Rachel and wept aloud. ¹²And Jacob told Rachel that he was her father's kinsman, and that he was Rebekah's son, and she ran and told her father.

¹³As soon as Laban heard the news about Jacob, his sister's son, he ran to meet him and embraced him and kissed him and brought him to his house. Jacob told Laban all these things, ¹⁴and Laban said to him, "Surely you are my bone and my flesh!" And he stayed with him a month.

¹⁵Then Laban said to Jacob, "Because you are my kinsman, should you therefore serve me for nothing? Tell me, what shall your wages be?" ¹⁶Now Laban had two daughters. The name of the older was Leah, and the name of the younger was Rachel. ¹⁷Leah's eyes were weak,[1] but Rachel was beautiful in form and appearance. ¹⁸Jacob loved Rachel. And he said, "I will serve you seven years for your younger daughter Rachel." ¹⁹Laban said, "It is better that I give her to you than that I should give her to any other man; stay with me." ²⁰So Jacob served seven years for Rachel, and they seemed to him but a few days because of the love he had for her.

²¹Then Jacob said to Laban, "Give me my wife that I may go in to her, for my time is completed." ²²So Laban gathered together all the people of the place and made a feast. ²³But in the evening he took his daughter Leah and brought her to Jacob, and he went in to her. ²⁴(Laban gave[2] his female servant Zilpah to his daughter Leah to be her servant.) ²⁵And in the morning, behold, it was Leah! And Jacob said to Laban, "What is this you have done to me? Did I not serve with you for Rachel? Why then have you deceived me?" ²⁶Laban said, "It is not so done in our country, to give the younger before the firstborn. ²⁷Complete the week of this one, and we will give you the other also in return for serving me another seven years." ²⁸Jacob did so, and completed her week. Then Laban gave him his daughter Rachel to be his wife. ²⁹(Laban gave his female servant Bilhah to his daughter Rachel to be her servant.) ³⁰So Jacob went in to Rachel also, and he loved Rachel more than Leah, and served Laban for another seven years.

[1] Or soft [2] Or had given; also verse 29

Jacob's stressful life in Haran [29:31–30:43]. The literary mode known as *realism dominates the story of Jacob, especially in this segment. Just as Jacob's life in his parental home was dominated by sibling rivalry, his marriage is dominated by the same syndrome as Leah and Rachel vie for his favor, with childbearing as the chief weapon. If we remember that the birth stories that make up 29:31–30:24 recount the births of the progenitors of the twelve tribes of Israel, we can see a basis for verdicts from commentators to the effect that the story of Jacob once again shows God's choosing difficult and unpromising material to accomplish his purposes, that there is more shadow than light in the stories of Genesis, and that it was from an unedifying thicket of human passions that the twelve tribes arose.

³¹When the LORD saw that Leah was hated, he opened her womb, but Rachel was barren. ³²And Leah conceived and bore a son, and she called his name Reuben,¹ for she said, "Because the LORD has looked upon my affliction; for now my husband will love me." ³³She conceived again and bore a son, and said, "Because the LORD has heard that I am hated, he has given me this son also." And she called his name Simeon.² ³⁴Again she conceived and bore a son, and said, "Now this time my husband will be attached to me, because I have borne him three sons." Therefore his name was called Levi.³ ³⁵And she conceived again and bore a son, and said, "This time I will praise the LORD." Therefore she called his name Judah.⁴ Then she ceased bearing.

30 When Rachel saw that she bore Jacob no children, she envied her sister. She said to Jacob, "Give me children, or I shall die!" ²Jacob's anger was kindled against Rachel, and he said, "Am I in the place of God, who has withheld from you the fruit of the womb?" ³Then she said, "Here is my servant Bilhah; go in to her, so that she may give birth on my behalf,⁵ that even I may have children⁶ through her." ⁴So she gave him her servant Bilhah as a wife, and Jacob went in to her. ⁵And Bilhah conceived and bore Jacob a son. ⁶Then Rachel said, "God has judged me, and has also heard my voice and given me a son." Therefore she called his name Dan.⁷ ⁷Rachel's servant Bilhah conceived again and bore Jacob a second son. ⁸Then Rachel said, "With mighty wrestlings⁸ I have wrestled with my sister and have prevailed." So she called his name Naphtali.⁹

⁹When Leah saw that she had ceased bearing children, she took her servant Zilpah and gave her to Jacob as a wife. ¹⁰Then Leah's servant Zilpah bore Jacob a son. ¹¹And Leah said, "Good fortune has come!" so she called his name Gad.¹⁰ ¹²Leah's servant Zilpah bore Jacob a second son. ¹³And Leah said, "Happy am I! For women have called me happy." So she called his name Asher.¹¹

¹⁴In the days of wheat harvest Reuben went and found mandrakes in the field and brought them to his mother Leah. Then Rachel said to Leah, "Please give me some of your son's mandrakes." ¹⁵But she said to her, "Is it a small matter that you have taken away my husband? Would you take away my son's mandrakes also?" Rachel said, "Then he may lie with you tonight in exchange for your son's mandrakes." ¹⁶When Jacob came from the field in the evening, Leah went out to meet him and said, "You must come in to me, for I have hired you with my son's mandrakes." So he lay with her that night. ¹⁷And God listened to Leah, and she conceived and bore Jacob a fifth

---

¹ *Reuben* means *See, a son* ² *Simeon* sounds like the Hebrew for *heard* ³ *Levi* sounds like the Hebrew for *attached* ⁴ *Judah* sounds like the Hebrew for *praise* ⁵ Hebrew *on my knees* ⁶ Hebrew *be built up*, which sounds like the Hebrew for *children* ⁷ *Dan* sounds like the Hebrew for *judged* ⁸ Hebrew *With wrestlings of God* ⁹ *Naphtali* sounds like the Hebrew for *wrestling* ¹⁰ *Gad* sounds like the Hebrew for *good fortune* ¹¹ *Asher* sounds like the Hebrew for *happy*

son. [18]Leah said, "God has given me my wages because I gave my servant to my husband." So she called his name Issachar.[1]

[19]And Leah conceived again, and she bore Jacob a sixth son. [20]Then Leah said, "God has endowed me with a good endowment; now my husband will honor me, because I have borne him six sons." So she called his name Zebulun.[2] [21]Afterward she bore a daughter and called her name Dinah.

[22]Then God remembered Rachel, and God listened to her and opened her womb. [23]She conceived and bore a son and said, "God has taken away my reproach." [24]And she called his name Joseph,[3] saying, "May the LORD add to me another son!"

[25]As soon as Rachel had borne Joseph, Jacob said to Laban, "Send me away, that I may go to my own home and country. [26]Give me my wives and my children for whom I have served you, that I may go, for you know the service that I have given you." [27]But Laban said to him, "If I have found favor in your sight, I have learned by divination that[4] the LORD has blessed me because of you. [28]Name your wages, and I will give it." [29]Jacob said to him, "You yourself know how I have served you, and how your livestock has fared with me. [30]For you had little before I came, and it has increased abundantly, and the LORD has blessed you wherever I turned. But now when shall I provide for my own household also?" [31]He said, "What shall I give you?" Jacob said, "You shall not give me anything. If you will do this for me, I will again pasture your flock and keep it: [32]let me pass through all your flock today, removing from it every speckled and spotted sheep and every black lamb, and the spotted and speckled among the goats, and they shall be my wages. [33]So my honesty will answer for me later, when you come to look into my wages with you. Every one that is not speckled and spotted among the goats and black among the lambs, if found with me, shall be counted stolen." [34]Laban said, "Good! Let it be as you have said." [35]But that day Laban removed the male goats that were striped and spotted, and all the female goats that were speckled and spotted, every one that had white on it, and every lamb that was black, and put them in the charge of his sons. [36]And he set a distance of three days' journey between himself and Jacob, and Jacob pastured the rest of Laban's flock.

[37]Then Jacob took fresh sticks of poplar and almond and plane trees, and peeled white streaks in them, exposing the white of the sticks. [38]He set the sticks that he had peeled in front of the flocks in the troughs, that is, the watering places, where the flocks came to drink. And since they bred when they came to drink, [39]the flocks bred in front of the sticks and so the flocks brought forth striped, speckled, and spotted. [40]And Jacob separated the lambs and set the faces of the flocks toward the striped and all the black in the flock of Laban. He put his own droves apart and did not put them with Laban's flock. [41]Whenever the stronger of the flock were breeding, Jacob would lay the sticks in the troughs before the eyes of the flock, that they might breed among the sticks, [42]but for the feebler of the flock he would not lay them there. So the feebler would be Laban's, and the stronger Jacob's. [43]Thus the man increased greatly and had large flocks, female servants and male servants, and camels and donkeys.

Flight and pursuit [chapter 31]. Jacob's departure from Laban falls into the archetypal pattern of flight and chase. The story recounted in chapter 31 is another transition for Jacob, and it is reminiscent of the transition between the first and second phases of his

---

[1] *Issachar* sounds like the Hebrew for *wages*, or *hire* [2] *Zebulun* sounds like the Hebrew for *honor* [3] *Joseph* means *May he add*, and sounds like the Hebrew for *taken away* [4] Or *have become rich and*

life as the hero is again depicted as running away from a family member whom he has alienated. Other motifs also make it seem like a rerun of earlier action, as though Jacob has learned little from his twenty years in Haran: God's appearing in a dream that both informs and rebukes Jacob (vv. 2–13); conflict and trickery between Jacob and Laban; unsavory behavior on the part of Rachel (vv. 30–42); a truce rather than genuine reconciliation between warring family members (vv. 43–54); parting between family members (v. 55).

31

Now Jacob heard that the sons of Laban were saying, "Jacob has taken all that was our father's, and from what was our father's he has gained all this wealth." ²And Jacob saw that Laban did not regard him with favor as before. ³Then the Lord said to Jacob, "Return to the land of your fathers and to your kindred, and I will be with you."

⁴So Jacob sent and called Rachel and Leah into the field where his flock was ⁵and said to them, "I see that your father does not regard me with favor as he did before. But the God of my father has been with me. ⁶You know that I have served your father with all my strength, ⁷yet your father has cheated me and changed my wages ten times. But God did not permit him to harm me. ⁸If he said, 'The spotted shall be your wages,' then all the flock bore spotted; and if he said, 'The striped shall be your wages,' then all the flock bore striped. ⁹Thus God has taken away the livestock of your father and given them to me. ¹⁰In the breeding season of the flock I lifted up my eyes and saw in a dream that the goats that mated with the flock were striped, spotted, and mottled. ¹¹Then the angel of God said to me in the dream, 'Jacob,' and I said, 'Here I am!' ¹²And he said, 'Lift up your eyes and see, all the goats that mate with the flock are striped, spotted, and mottled, for I have seen all that Laban is doing to you. ¹³I am the God of Bethel, where you anointed a pillar and made a vow to me. Now arise, go out from this land and return to the land of your kindred.'" ¹⁴Then Rachel and Leah answered and said to him, "Is there any portion or inheritance left to us in our father's house? ¹⁵Are we not regarded by him as foreigners? For he has sold us, and he has indeed devoured our money. ¹⁶All the wealth that God has taken away from our father belongs to us and to our children. Now then, whatever God has said to you, do."

¹⁷So Jacob arose and set his sons and his wives on camels. ¹⁸He drove away all his livestock, all his property that he had gained, the livestock in his possession that he had acquired in Paddan-aram, to go to the land of Canaan to his father Isaac. ¹⁹Laban had gone to shear his sheep, and Rachel stole her father's household gods. ²⁰And Jacob tricked[1] Laban the Aramean, by not telling him that he intended to flee. ²¹He fled with all that he had and arose and crossed the Euphrates, and set his face toward the hill country of Gilead.

²²When it was told Laban on the third day that Jacob had fled, ²³he took his kinsmen with him and pursued him for seven days and followed close after him into the hill country of Gilead. ²⁴But God came to Laban the Aramean in a dream by night and said to him, "Be careful not to say anything to Jacob, either good or bad."

²⁵And Laban overtook Jacob. Now Jacob had pitched his tent in the hill country, and Laban with his kinsmen pitched tents in the hill country of Gilead. ²⁶And Laban said to Jacob, "What have you done, that you have tricked me and driven away my

---

[1] Hebrew *stole the heart of*; also verses 26, 27

daughters like captives of the sword? ²⁷Why did you flee secretly and trick me, and did not tell me, so that I might have sent you away with mirth and songs, with tambourine and lyre? ²⁸And why did you not permit me to kiss my sons and my daughters farewell? Now you have done foolishly. ²⁹It is in my power to do you harm. But the God of your¹ father spoke to me last night, saying, 'Be careful not to say anything to Jacob, either good or bad.' ³⁰And now you have gone away because you longed greatly for your father's house, but why did you steal my gods?" ³¹Jacob answered and said to Laban, "Because I was afraid, for I thought that you would take your daughters from me by force. ³²Anyone with whom you find your gods shall not live. In the presence of our kinsmen point out what I have that is yours, and take it." Now Jacob did not know that Rachel had stolen them.

³³So Laban went into Jacob's tent and into Leah's tent and into the tent of the two female servants, but he did not find them. And he went out of Leah's tent and entered Rachel's. ³⁴Now Rachel had taken the household gods and put them in the camel's saddle and sat on them. Laban felt all about the tent, but did not find them. ³⁵And she said to her father, "Let not my lord be angry that I cannot rise before you, for the way of women is upon me." So he searched but did not find the household gods.

³⁶Then Jacob became angry and berated Laban. Jacob said to Laban, "What is my offense? What is my sin, that you have hotly pursued me? ³⁷For you have felt through all my goods; what have you found of all your household goods? Set it here before my kinsmen and your kinsmen, that they may decide between us two. ³⁸These twenty years I have been with you. Your ewes and your female goats have not miscarried, and I have not eaten the rams of your flocks. ³⁹What was torn by wild beasts I did not bring to you. I bore the loss of it myself. From my hand you required it, whether stolen by day or stolen by night. ⁴⁰There I was: by day the heat consumed me, and the cold by night, and my sleep fled from my eyes. ⁴¹These twenty years I have been in your house. I served you fourteen years for your two daughters, and six years for your flock, and you have changed my wages ten times. ⁴²If the God of my father, the God of Abraham and the Fear of Isaac, had not been on my side, surely now you would have sent me away empty-handed. God saw my affliction and the labor of my hands and rebuked you last night."

⁴³Then Laban answered and said to Jacob, "The daughters are my daughters, the children are my children, the flocks are my flocks, and all that you see is mine. But what can I do this day for these my daughters or for their children whom they have borne? ⁴⁴Come now, let us make a covenant, you and I. And let it be a witness between you and me." ⁴⁵So Jacob took a stone and set it up as a pillar. ⁴⁶And Jacob said to his kinsmen, "Gather stones." And they took stones and made a heap, and they ate there by the heap. ⁴⁷Laban called it Jegar-sahadutha,² but Jacob called it Galeed.³ ⁴⁸Laban said, "This heap is a witness between you and me today." Therefore he named it Galeed, ⁴⁹and Mizpah,⁴ for he said, "The LORD watch between you and me, when we are out of one another's sight. ⁵⁰If you oppress my daughters, or if you take wives besides my daughters, although no one is with us, see, God is witness between you and me."

⁵¹Then Laban said to Jacob, "See this heap and the pillar, which I have set between you and me. ⁵²This heap is a witness, and the pillar is a witness, that I will not pass over this heap to you, and you will not pass over this heap and this pillar to me, to do harm. ⁵³The God of Abraham and the God of Nahor, the God of their father, judge

---

¹ The Hebrew for *your* is plural here ² Aramaic *the heap of witness* ³ Hebrew *the heap of witness* ⁴ *Mizpah* means *watchpost*

between us." So Jacob swore by the Fear of his father Isaac, ⁵⁴and Jacob offered a sacrifice in the hill country and called his kinsmen to eat bread. They ate bread and spent the night in the hill country.

^{55 1} Early in the morning Laban arose and kissed his grandchildren and his daughters and blessed them. Then Laban departed and returned home.

> **Jacob prepares to meet Esau** [chapter 32]. This is another high point in the story of Jacob. The sequence of action is a back-and-forth movement between good and bad behavior on Jacob's part, and the action is permeated by irony: ironic hope (vv. 1–5—ironic because meeting Esau will not happen as easily as Jacob here thinks); ironic fear (vv. 6–7—ironic because Jacob assumes that Esau is coming to destroy him, whereas it turns out that Esau will be lavishly forgiving); ironic self-reliance (vv. 7–8—ironic because it is not Jacob's scheming that will win the day for him); self-abnegation and self-transcendence, as Jacob for the first time takes the initiative in casting himself on God's covenant mercy (vv. 9–12); more ironic self-reliance and calculating (vv. 13–21—ironic because Jacob should not have resorted to such behavior after his prayer to God); Jacob's conversion (vv. 22–31). In the wrestling with the angel of God, Jacob finally comes to the end of himself. God's giving Jacob his covenant name Israel is the oracle that stands at the beginning of the last phase of Jacob's three-part life as narrated in Genesis, which is at the same time a founding event for Israel as a nation. The story of God's encounter with Jacob at the brook Jabbok is a paradigm of how God meets and transforms an individual. The unifying motif in Jacob's life as a whole is the hero's struggle to become a godly man; this event is pivotal in the story, even though Jacob's record continues to be less than we might hope for a patriarch of the covenant who has seen God face to face.

32 Jacob went on his way, and the angels of God met him. ²And when Jacob saw them he said, "This is God's camp!" So he called the name of that place Mahanaim.²

³And Jacob sent³ messengers before him to Esau his brother in the land of Seir, the country of Edom, ⁴instructing them, "Thus you shall say to my lord Esau: Thus says your servant Jacob, 'I have sojourned with Laban and stayed until now. ⁵I have oxen, donkeys, flocks, male servants, and female servants. I have sent to tell my lord, in order that I may find favor in your sight.'"

⁶And the messengers returned to Jacob, saying, "We came to your brother Esau, and he is coming to meet you, and there are four hundred men with him." ⁷Then Jacob was greatly afraid and distressed. He divided the people who were with him, and the flocks and herds and camels, into two camps, ⁸thinking, "If Esau comes to the one camp and attacks it, then the camp that is left will escape."

⁹And Jacob said, "O God of my father Abraham and God of my father Isaac, O LORD who said to me, 'Return to your country and to your kindred, that I may do you good,' ¹⁰I am not worthy of the least of all the deeds of steadfast love and all the faithfulness that you have shown to your servant, for with only my staff I crossed this Jordan, and now I have become two camps. ¹¹Please deliver me from the hand of my brother, from the hand of Esau, for I fear him, that he may come and attack me, the mothers with the children. ¹²But you said, 'I will surely do you good, and make your offspring as the sand of the sea, which cannot be numbered for multitude.'"

---

¹ Ch 32:1 in Hebrew ²*Mahanaim* means *two camps* ³ Or *had sent*

[13]So he stayed there that night, and from what he had with him he took a present for his brother Esau, [14]two hundred female goats and twenty male goats, two hundred ewes and twenty rams, [15]thirty milking camels and their calves, forty cows and ten bulls, twenty female donkeys and ten male donkeys. [16]These he handed over to his servants, every drove by itself, and said to his servants, "Pass on ahead of me and put a space between drove and drove." [17]He instructed the first, "When Esau my brother meets you and asks you, 'To whom do you belong? Where are you going? And whose are these ahead of you?' [18]then you shall say, 'They belong to your servant Jacob. They are a present sent to my lord Esau. And moreover, he is behind us.'" [19]He likewise instructed the second and the third and all who followed the droves, "You shall say the same thing to Esau when you find him, [20]and you shall say, 'Moreover, your servant Jacob is behind us.'" For he thought, "I may appease him[1] with the present that goes ahead of me, and afterward I shall see his face. Perhaps he will accept me."[2] [21]So the present passed on ahead of him, and he himself stayed that night in the camp.

[22]The same night he arose and took his two wives, his two female servants, and his eleven children,[3] and crossed the ford of the Jabbok. [23]He took them and sent them across the stream, and everything else that he had. [24]And Jacob was left alone. And a man wrestled with him until the breaking of the day. [25]When the man saw that he did not prevail against Jacob, he touched his hip socket, and Jacob's hip was put out of joint as he wrestled with him. [26]Then he said, "Let me go, for the day has broken." But Jacob said, "I will not let you go unless you bless me." [27]And he said to him, "What is your name?" And he said, "Jacob." [28]Then he said, "Your name shall no longer be called Jacob, but Israel,[4] for you have striven with God and with men, and have prevailed." [29]Then Jacob asked him, "Please tell me your name?" But he said, "Why is it that you ask my name?" And there he blessed him. [30]So Jacob called the name of the place Peniel,[5] saying, "For I have seen God face to face, and yet my life has been delivered." [31]The sun rose upon him as he passed Penuel, limping because of his hip. [32]Therefore to this day the people of Israel do not eat the sinew of the thigh that is on the hip socket, because he touched the socket of Jacob's hip on the sinew of the thigh.

Family reunion [chapter 33]. The meeting with Esau turns out to be anticlimactic after the extensive preparation for it, and therein lies an important part of the meaning of the event. Jacob had thought that his meeting with his brother was the crisis at hand, but the really crucial event was his relationship to God. Jacob and Esau are foils to each other yet again: Jacob is comically overorganized—the humble suppliant with a guilty conscience—while Esau is the impulsive and emotional brother who forgives his brother on the spot. We can contemplate the rival conceptions that the brothers give to the identical sentiment that they both affirm when they say, "I have enough" (vv. 9 and 11). The truce between the brothers is somewhat tenuous, inasmuch as Jacob claims that he will join up with Esau in Seir (vv. 12–14) but actually stops short of that (vv. 15–20). There is an added importance to Jacob's stopping at Shechem (vv. 18–19): God had directed Jacob to return to the land of his family origins (31:3, 13), which was also the Promised Land, but Jacob stopped outside the border of that land.

---

[1] Hebrew *appease his face* [2] Hebrew *he will lift my face* [3] Or *sons* [4] *Israel* means *He strives with God,* or *God strives* [5] *Peniel* means *the face of God*

33

And Jacob lifted up his eyes and looked, and behold, Esau was coming, and four hundred men with him. So he divided the children among Leah and Rachel and the two female servants. ²And he put the servants with their children in front, then Leah with her children, and Rachel and Joseph last of all. ³He himself went on before them, bowing himself to the ground seven times, until he came near to his brother.

⁴But Esau ran to meet him and embraced him and fell on his neck and kissed him, and they wept. ⁵And when Esau lifted up his eyes and saw the women and children, he said, "Who are these with you?" Jacob said, "The children whom God has graciously given your servant." ⁶Then the servants drew near, they and their children, and bowed down. ⁷Leah likewise and her children drew near and bowed down. And last Joseph and Rachel drew near, and they bowed down. ⁸Esau said, "What do you mean by all this company¹ that I met?" Jacob answered, "To find favor in the sight of my lord." ⁹But Esau said, "I have enough, my brother; keep what you have for yourself." ¹⁰Jacob said, "No, please, if I have found favor in your sight, then accept my present from my hand. For I have seen your face, which is like seeing the face of God, and you have accepted me. ¹¹Please accept my blessing that is brought to you, because God has dealt graciously with me, and because I have enough." Thus he urged him, and he took it.

¹²Then Esau said, "Let us journey on our way, and I will go ahead of² you." ¹³But Jacob said to him, "My lord knows that the children are frail, and that the nursing flocks and herds are a care to me. If they are driven hard for one day, all the flocks will die. ¹⁴Let my lord pass on ahead of his servant, and I will lead on slowly, at the pace of the livestock that are ahead of me and at the pace of the children, until I come to my lord in Seir."

¹⁵So Esau said, "Let me leave with you some of the people who are with me." But he said, "What need is there? Let me find favor in the sight of my lord." ¹⁶So Esau returned that day on his way to Seir. ¹⁷But Jacob journeyed to Succoth, and built himself a house and made booths for his livestock. Therefore the name of the place is called Succoth.³

¹⁸And Jacob came safely⁴ to the city of Shechem, which is in the land of Canaan, on his way from Paddan-aram, and he camped before the city. ¹⁹And from the sons of Hamor, Shechem's father, he bought for a hundred pieces of money⁵ the piece of land on which he had pitched his tent. ²⁰There he erected an altar and called it El-Elohe-Israel.⁶

The sordid incident of Dinah [chapter 34]. Realism makes another shocking appearance in an event that was important in the family history but that is only tangentially related to the story of Jacob as a hero. The sordidness comes into focus when we call the events by their modern names: violent rape, duplicity, genocidal massacre, and looting. The story material is R-rated, though the medium of narrative guarantees a degree of distance and reticence when compared to a movie version of the same material. To the degree to which we regard this as part of the story of Jacob, it portrays Jacob in a negative light; he is a weak father, passive when he should be active, offering a flimsy excuse (v. 30) for being angry about the massacre carried out by his sons. Further, if

---

¹ Hebrew camp ² Or along with ³ Succoth means booths ⁴ Or peacefully ⁵ Hebrew a hundred qesitah; a unit of money of unknown value ⁶ El-Elohe-Israel means God, the God of Israel

Jacob had moved to the land of his kindred as commanded by God, the rape of Dinah would never have happened.

34 Now Dinah the daughter of Leah, whom she had borne to Jacob, went out to see the women of the land. ²And when Shechem the son of Hamor the Hivite, the prince of the land, saw her, he seized her and lay with her and humiliated her. ³And his soul was drawn to Dinah the daughter of Jacob. He loved the young woman and spoke tenderly to her. ⁴So Shechem spoke to his father Hamor, saying, "Get me this girl for my wife."

⁵Now Jacob heard that he had defiled his daughter Dinah. But his sons were with his livestock in the field, so Jacob held his peace until they came. ⁶And Hamor the father of Shechem went out to Jacob to speak with him. ⁷The sons of Jacob had come in from the field as soon as they heard of it, and the men were indignant and very angry, because he had done an outrageous thing in Israel by lying with Jacob's daughter, for such a thing must not be done.

⁸But Hamor spoke with them, saying, "The soul of my son Shechem longs for your[1] daughter. Please give her to him to be his wife. ⁹Make marriages with us. Give your daughters to us, and take our daughters for yourselves. ¹⁰You shall dwell with us, and the land shall be open to you. Dwell and trade in it, and get property in it." ¹¹Shechem also said to her father and to her brothers, "Let me find favor in your eyes, and whatever you say to me I will give. ¹²Ask me for as great a bride price[2] and gift as you will, and I will give whatever you say to me. Only give me the young woman to be my wife."

¹³The sons of Jacob answered Shechem and his father Hamor deceitfully, because he had defiled their sister Dinah. ¹⁴They said to them, "We cannot do this thing, to give our sister to one who is uncircumcised, for that would be a disgrace to us. ¹⁵Only on this condition will we agree with you—that you will become as we are by every male among you being circumcised. ¹⁶Then we will give our daughters to you, and we will take your daughters to ourselves, and we will dwell with you and become one people. ¹⁷But if you will not listen to us and be circumcised, then we will take our daughter, and we will be gone."

¹⁸Their words pleased Hamor and Hamor's son Shechem. ¹⁹And the young man did not delay to do the thing, because he delighted in Jacob's daughter. Now he was the most honored of all his father's house. ²⁰So Hamor and his son Shechem came to the gate of their city and spoke to the men of their city, saying, ²¹"These men are at peace with us; let them dwell in the land and trade in it, for behold, the land is large enough for them. Let us take their daughters as wives, and let us give them our daughters. ²²Only on this condition will the men agree to dwell with us to become one people— when every male among us is circumcised as they are circumcised. ²³Will not their livestock, their property and all their beasts be ours? Only let us agree with them, and they will dwell with us." ²⁴And all who went out of the gate of his city listened to Hamor and his son Shechem, and every male was circumcised, all who went out of the gate of his city.

²⁵On the third day, when they were sore, two of the sons of Jacob, Simeon and Levi, Dinah's brothers, took their swords and came against the city while it felt secure and killed all the males. ²⁶They killed Hamor and his son Shechem with the sword and

---

[1] The Hebrew for *your* is plural here [2] Or *engagement present*

took Dinah out of Shechem's house and went away. [27] The sons of Jacob came upon the slain and plundered the city, because they had defiled their sister. [28] They took their flocks and their herds, their donkeys, and whatever was in the city and in the field. [29] All their wealth, all their little ones and their wives, all that was in the houses, they captured and plundered.

[30] Then Jacob said to Simeon and Levi, "You have brought trouble on me by making me stink to the inhabitants of the land, the Canaanites and the Perizzites. My numbers are few, and if they gather themselves against me and attack me, I shall be destroyed, both I and my household." [31] But they said, "Should he treat our sister like a prostitute?"

Further events in the life of a wanderer [chapter 35]. The archetype of the wanderer continues to be important at this relatively late phase of Jacob's life. The hero appears in a positive light as he finally moves to the Promised Land and renews his worship of God at Bethel. The action occurs on an idealized plane, with conspicuous emphasis on the building of altars, the putting away of idols, the worship of God, other ritual religious acts, and the birth of the final patriarch (Benjamin). The final verses abandon literary narrative in favor of diarylike entries in a family history (vv. 22–29).

35 God said to Jacob, "Arise, go up to Bethel and dwell there. Make an altar there to the God who appeared to you when you fled from your brother Esau." [2] So Jacob said to his household and to all who were with him, "Put away the foreign gods that are among you and purify yourselves and change your garments. [3] Then let us arise and go up to Bethel, so that I may make there an altar to the God who answers me in the day of my distress and has been with me wherever I have gone." [4] So they gave to Jacob all the foreign gods that they had, and the rings that were in their ears. Jacob hid them under the terebinth tree that was near Shechem.

[5] And as they journeyed, a terror from God fell upon the cities that were around them, so that they did not pursue the sons of Jacob. [6] And Jacob came to Luz (that is, Bethel), which is in the land of Canaan, he and all the people who were with him, [7] and there he built an altar and called the place El-bethel,[1] because there God had revealed himself to him when he fled from his brother. [8] And Deborah, Rebekah's nurse, died, and she was buried under an oak below Bethel. So he called its name Allon-bacuth.[2]

[9] God appeared[3] to Jacob again, when he came from Paddan-aram, and blessed him. [10] And God said to him, "Your name is Jacob; no longer shall your name be called Jacob, but Israel shall be your name." So he called his name Israel. [11] And God said to him, "I am God Almighty:[4] be fruitful and multiply. A nation and a company of nations shall come from you, and kings shall come from your own body.[5] [12] The land that I gave to Abraham and Isaac I will give to you, and I will give the land to your offspring after you." [13] Then God went up from him in the place where he had spoken with him. [14] And Jacob set up a pillar in the place where he had spoken with him, a pillar of stone. He poured out a drink offering on it and poured oil on it. [15] So Jacob called the name of the place where God had spoken with him Bethel.

[16] Then they journeyed from Bethel. When they were still some distance[6] from Ephrath, Rachel went into labor, and she had hard labor. [17] And when her labor was

---

[1] *El-bethel* means *God of Bethel* [2] *Allon-bacuth* means *oak of weeping* [3] Or *had appeared* [4] Hebrew *El Shaddai* [5] Hebrew *from your loins* [6] Or *about two hours' distance*

at its hardest, the midwife said to her, "Do not fear, for you have another son." [18]And
as her soul was departing (for she was dying), she called his name Ben-oni;[1] but his
father called him Benjamin.[2] [19]So Rachel died, and she was buried on the way to
Ephrath (that is, Bethlehem), [20]and Jacob set up a pillar over her tomb. It is the pillar
of Rachel's tomb, which is there to this day. [21]Israel journeyed on and pitched his tent
beyond the tower of Eder.

[22]While Israel lived in that land, Reuben went and lay with Bilhah his father's concubine. And Israel heard of it.

Now the sons of Jacob were twelve. [23]The sons of Leah: Reuben (Jacob's firstborn),
Simeon, Levi, Judah, Issachar, and Zebulun. [24]The sons of Rachel: Joseph and
Benjamin. [25]The sons of Bilhah, Rachel's servant: Dan and Naphtali. [26]The sons of
Zilpah, Leah's servant: Gad and Asher. These were the sons of Jacob who were born
to him in Paddan-aram.

[27]And Jacob came to his father Isaac at Mamre, or Kiriath-arba (that is, Hebron),
where Abraham and Isaac had sojourned. [28]Now the days of Isaac were 180 years.
[29]And Isaac breathed his last, and he died and was gathered to his people, old and
full of days. And his sons Esau and Jacob buried him.

The generations of Esau [chapter 36]. The narrative of Genesis is again interrupted
by a long genealogy. As modern readers, we no longer share the historical and family
interest in this lineage that the original audience of the book of Genesis would have
had. We need to read between the lines to pick up the spiritual tenor of the genealogy:
when judged by external signs, Esau was a virile and successful man of the world, but
he completely missed out on the spiritual blessings of the covenant because from his
teenage years he had no appreciation for spiritual things. Further, the history of the line
of Esau is the history of the Edomites, and if we trace that line through the Bible, we can
see that it was a race who hated the people of God.

36 These are the generations of Esau (that is, Edom). [2]Esau took his wives from
the Canaanites: Adah the daughter of Elon the Hittite, Oholibamah the
daughter of Anah the daughter[3] of Zibeon the Hivite, [3]and Basemath, Ishmael's
daughter, the sister of Nebaioth. [4]And Adah bore to Esau, Eliphaz; Basemath bore
Reuel; [5]and Oholibamah bore Jeush, Jalam, and Korah. These are the sons of Esau
who were born to him in the land of Canaan.

[6]Then Esau took his wives, his sons, his daughters, and all the members of his
household, his livestock, all his beasts, and all his property that he had acquired in
the land of Canaan. He went into a land away from his brother Jacob. [7]For their possessions were too great for them to dwell together. The land of their sojournings
could not support them because of their livestock. [8]So Esau settled in the hill country
of Seir. (Esau is Edom.)

[9]These are the generations of Esau the father of the Edomites in the hill country of
Seir. [10]These are the names of Esau's sons: Eliphaz the son of Adah the wife of Esau,
Reuel the son of Basemath the wife of Esau. [11]The sons of Eliphaz were Teman,
Omar, Zepho, Gatam, and Kenaz. [12](Timna was a concubine of Eliphaz, Esau's son;
she bore Amalek to Eliphaz.) These are the sons of Adah, Esau's wife. [13]These are the
sons of Reuel: Nahath, Zerah, Shammah, and Mizzah. These are the sons of

---

[1] Ben-oni could mean son of my sorrow, or son of my strength [2] Benjamin means son of the right hand [3] Hebrew; Samaritan, Septuagint, Syriac son; also
verse 14

Basemath, Esau's wife. [14]These are the sons of Oholibamah the daughter of Anah the daughter of Zibeon, Esau's wife: she bore to Esau Jeush, Jalam, and Korah.

[15]These are the chiefs of the sons of Esau. The sons of Eliphaz the firstborn of Esau: the chiefs Teman, Omar, Zepho, Kenaz, [16]Korah, Gatam, and Amalek; these are the chiefs of Eliphaz in the land of Edom; these are the sons of Adah. [17]These are the sons of Reuel, Esau's son: the chiefs Nahath, Zerah, Shammah, and Mizzah; these are the chiefs of Reuel in the land of Edom; these are the sons of Basemath, Esau's wife. [18]These are the sons of Oholibamah, Esau's wife: the chiefs Jeush, Jalam, and Korah; these are the chiefs born of Oholibamah the daughter of Anah, Esau's wife. [19]These are the sons of Esau (that is, Edom), and these are their chiefs.

[20]These are the sons of Seir the Horite, the inhabitants of the land: Lotan, Shobal, Zibeon, Anah, [21]Dishon, Ezer, and Dishan; these are the chiefs of the Horites, the sons of Seir in the land of Edom. [22]The sons of Lotan were Hori and Hemam; and Lotan's sister was Timna. [23]These are the sons of Shobal: Alvan, Manahath, Ebal, Shepho, and Onam. [24]These are the sons of Zibeon: Aiah and Anah; he is the Anah who found the hot springs in the wilderness, as he pastured the donkeys of Zibeon his father. [25]These are the children of Anah: Dishon and Oholibamah the daughter of Anah. [26]These are the sons of Dishon: Hemdan, Eshban, Ithran, and Cheran. [27]These are the sons of Ezer: Bilhan, Zaavan, and Akan. [28]These are the sons of Dishan: Uz and Aran. [29]These are the chiefs of the Horites: the chiefs Lotan, Shobal, Zibeon, Anah, [30]Dishon, Ezer, and Dishan; these are the chiefs of the Horites, chief by chief in the land of Seir.

[31]These are the kings who reigned in the land of Edom, before any king reigned over the Israelites. [32]Bela the son of Beor reigned in Edom, the name of his city being Dinhabah. [33]Bela died, and Jobab the son of Zerah of Bozrah reigned in his place. [34]Jobab died, and Husham of the land of the Temanites reigned in his place. [35]Husham died, and Hadad the son of Bedad, who defeated Midian in the country of Moab, reigned in his place, the name of his city being Avith. [36]Hadad died, and Samlah of Masrekah reigned in his place. [37]Samlah died, and Shaul of Rehoboth on the Euphrates[1] reigned in his place. [38]Shaul died, and Baal-hanan the son of Achbor reigned in his place. [39]Baal-hanan the son of Achbor died, and Hadar reigned in his place, the name of his city being Pau; his wife's name was Mehetabel, the daughter of Matred, daughter of Mezahab.

[40]These are the names of the chiefs of Esau, according to their clans and their dwelling places, by their names: the chiefs Timna, Alvah, Jetheth, [41]Oholibamah, Elah, Pinon, [42]Kenaz, Teman, Mibzar, [43]Magdiel, and Iram; these are the chiefs of Edom (that is, Esau, the father of Edom), according to their dwelling places in the land of their possession.

Joseph's exile from his parental home [chapter 37]. With chapter 37 the patriarchal baton is passed from Jacob to Joseph. At last we have a hero story that reads like a hero story. While some readers see a bit of negative characterization at the beginning of chapter 37, it is more likely that the storyteller selected details from Joseph's life that paint a picture of a wholly idealized hero. The overall pattern of Joseph's heroic life is that of a suffering servant—a person who undergoes undeserved suffering that is redemptive in the lives of others. The story is also a suspense story: the opening dreams of Joseph predict that his family will bow down to him, but we have no inkling at the

---

[1] Hebrew the River

outset of the story how this despised family member can ever attain such prominence. Literary realism dominates chapter 37, which is structured as a downward spiral into greater and greater depths of evil: hatred (vv. 4, 8); jealousy (v. 11); conspiracy to commit murder (vv. 18–20); moral callousness (vv. 23–24); moral indifference (v. 25); greed combined with callousness (vv. 26–28); duplicity and lying (vv. 31–32); hypocrisy (v. 35). The entire book of Genesis specializes in sibling rivalry and dysfunctional families as subject matter, but this chapter seems to sink even lower than the others. Within his own family, Joseph is the archetypal outcast. When he is sold into slavery, he embarks on a journey of initiation.

37 Jacob lived in the land of his father's sojournings, in the land of Canaan. [2]These are the generations of Jacob.

Joseph, being seventeen years old, was pasturing the flock with his brothers. He was a boy with the sons of Bilhah and Zilpah, his father's wives. And Joseph brought a bad report of them to their father. [3]Now Israel loved Joseph more than any other of his sons, because he was the son of his old age. And he made him a robe of many colors.[1] [4]But when his brothers saw that their father loved him more than all his brothers, they hated him and could not speak peacefully to him.

[5]Now Joseph had a dream, and when he told it to his brothers they hated him even more. [6]He said to them, "Hear this dream that I have dreamed: [7]Behold, we were binding sheaves in the field, and behold, my sheaf arose and stood upright. And behold, your sheaves gathered around it and bowed down to my sheaf." [8]His brothers said to him, "Are you indeed to reign over us? Or are you indeed to rule over us?" So they hated him even more for his dreams and for his words.

[9]Then he dreamed another dream and told it to his brothers and said, "Behold, I have dreamed another dream. Behold, the sun, the moon, and eleven stars were bowing down to me." [10]But when he told it to his father and to his brothers, his father rebuked him and said to him, "What is this dream that you have dreamed? Shall I and your mother and your brothers indeed come to bow ourselves to the ground before you?" [11]And his brothers were jealous of him, but his father kept the saying in mind.

[12]Now his brothers went to pasture their father's flock near Shechem. [13]And Israel said to Joseph, "Are not your brothers pasturing the flock at Shechem? Come, I will send you to them." And he said to him, "Here I am." [14]So he said to him, "Go now, see if it is well with your brothers and with the flock, and bring me word." So he sent him from the Valley of Hebron, and he came to Shechem. [15]And a man found him wandering in the fields. And the man asked him, "What are you seeking?" [16]"I am seeking my brothers," he said. "Tell me, please, where they are pasturing the flock." [17]And the man said, "They have gone away, for I heard them say, 'Let us go to Dothan.'" So Joseph went after his brothers and found them at Dothan.

[18]They saw him from afar, and before he came near to them they conspired against him to kill him. [19]They said to one another, "Here comes this dreamer. [20]Come now, let us kill him and throw him into one of the pits.[2] Then we will say that a fierce animal has devoured him, and we will see what will become of his dreams." [21]But when Reuben heard it, he rescued him out of their hands, saying, "Let us not take his life." [22]And Reuben said to them, "Shed no blood; throw him into this pit here in the wil-

---

[1] See Septuagint, Vulgate; or (with Syriac) *a robe with long sleeves.* The meaning of the Hebrew is uncertain; also verses 23, 32 [2] Or *cisterns;* also verses 22, 24

derness, but do not lay a hand on him"—that he might rescue him out of their hand to restore him to his father. ²³So when Joseph came to his brothers, they stripped him of his robe, the robe of many colors that he wore. ²⁴And they took him and threw him into a pit. The pit was empty; there was no water in it.

²⁵Then they sat down to eat. And looking up they saw a caravan of Ishmaelites coming from Gilead, with their camels bearing gum, balm, and myrrh, on their way to carry it down to Egypt. ²⁶Then Judah said to his brothers, "What profit is it if we kill our brother and conceal his blood? ²⁷Come, let us sell him to the Ishmaelites, and let not our hand be upon him, for he is our brother, our own flesh." And his brothers listened to him. ²⁸Then Midianite traders passed by. And they drew Joseph up and lifted him out of the pit, and sold him to the Ishmaelites for twenty shekels¹ of silver. They took Joseph to Egypt.

²⁹When Reuben returned to the pit and saw that Joseph was not in the pit, he tore his clothes ³⁰and returned to his brothers and said, "The boy is gone, and I, where shall I go?" ³¹Then they took Joseph's robe and slaughtered a goat and dipped the robe in the blood. ³²And they sent the robe of many colors and brought it to their father and said, "This we have found; please identify whether it is your son's robe or not." ³³And he identified it and said, "It is my son's robe. A fierce animal has devoured him. Joseph is without doubt torn to pieces." ³⁴Then Jacob tore his garments and put sackcloth on his loins and mourned for his son many days. ³⁵All his sons and all his daughters rose up to comfort him, but he refused to be comforted and said, "No, I shall go down to Sheol to my son, mourning." Thus his father wept for him. ³⁶Meanwhile the Midianites had sold him in Egypt to Potiphar, an officer of Pharaoh, the captain of the guard.

More violence and realism [chapter 38]. There is no reason to sanitize the realism of the Bible. It tells us something the writers of the Bible obviously think we need to know, so we should heed the lesson. The specific kind of realism that we encounter in chapter 38 is what today we call sex and violence. The mainspring of the plot is the machinations that Tamar was forced to employ in an effort to produce offspring after her husband's death left her a childless widow. But there are numerous other sexual angles to the story. Despite Judah's depravity in this episode, he is transformed into a hero when he offers to give himself as a substitute for Benjamin when the brothers stand accused before Joseph (44:14–34), and furthermore God chose the tribe of Judah as the one from which the Messiah would come (49:10).

38 It happened at that time that Judah went down from his brothers and turned aside to a certain Adullamite, whose name was Hirah. ²There Judah saw the daughter of a certain Canaanite whose name was Shua. He took her and went in to her, ³and she conceived and bore a son, and he called his name Er. ⁴She conceived again and bore a son, and she called his name Onan. ⁵Yet again she bore a son, and she called his name Shelah. Judah² was in Chezib when she bore him.

⁶And Judah took a wife for Er his firstborn, and her name was Tamar. ⁷But Er, Judah's firstborn, was wicked in the sight of the LORD, and the LORD put him to death. ⁸Then Judah said to Onan, "Go in to your brother's wife and perform the duty of a brother-in-law to her, and raise up offspring for your brother." ⁹But Onan knew that the offspring would not be his. So whenever he went in to his brother's wife he would

¹ A *shekel* was about 2/5 ounce or 11 grams ² Hebrew *He*

waste the semen on the ground, so as not to give offspring to his brother. ¹⁰And what
he did was wicked in the sight of the LORD, and he put him to death also. ¹¹Then
Judah said to Tamar his daughter-in-law, "Remain a widow in your father's house,
till Shelah my son grows up"—for he feared that he would die, like his brothers. So
Tamar went and remained in her father's house.

¹²In the course of time the wife of Judah, Shua's daughter, died. When Judah was
comforted, he went up to Timnah to his sheepshearers, he and his friend Hirah the
Adullamite. ¹³And when Tamar was told, "Your father-in-law is going up to Timnah
to shear his sheep," ¹⁴she took off her widow's garments and covered herself with a
veil, wrapping herself up, and sat at the entrance to Enaim, which is on the road to
Timnah. For she saw that Shelah was grown up, and she had not been given to him
in marriage. ¹⁵When Judah saw her, he thought she was a prostitute, for she had covered her face. ¹⁶He turned to her at the roadside and said, "Come, let me come in to
you," for he did not know that she was his daughter-in-law. She said, "What will you
give me, that you may come in to me?" ¹⁷He answered, "I will send you a young goat
from the flock." And she said, "If you give me a pledge, until you send it—" ¹⁸He said,
"What pledge shall I give you?" She replied, "Your signet and your cord and your
staff that is in your hand." So he gave them to her and went in to her, and she conceived by him. ¹⁹Then she arose and went away, and taking off her veil she put on the
garments of her widowhood.

²⁰When Judah sent the young goat by his friend the Adullamite to take back the
pledge from the woman's hand, he did not find her. ²¹And he asked the men of the
place, "Where is the cult prostitute¹ who was at Enaim at the roadside?" And they
said, "No cult prostitute has been here." ²²So he returned to Judah and said, "I have
not found her. Also, the men of the place said, 'No cult prostitute has been here.'"
²³And Judah replied, "Let her keep the things as her own, or we shall be laughed at.
You see, I sent this young goat, and you did not find her."

²⁴About three months later Judah was told, "Tamar your daughter-in-law has been
immoral.² Moreover, she is pregnant by immorality."³ And Judah said, "Bring her out,
and let her be burned." ²⁵As she was being brought out, she sent word to her father-
in-law, "By the man to whom these belong, I am pregnant." And she said, "Please
identify whose these are, the signet and the cord and the staff." ²⁶Then Judah identified them and said, "She is more righteous than I, since I did not give her to my son
Shelah." And he did not know her again.

²⁷When the time of her labor came, there were twins in her womb. ²⁸And when she
was in labor, one put out a hand, and the midwife took and tied a scarlet thread on
his hand, saying, "This one came out first." ²⁹But as he drew back his hand, behold,
his brother came out. And she said, "What a breach you have made for yourself!"
Therefore his name was called Perez.⁴ ³⁰Afterward his brother came out with the
scarlet thread on his hand, and his name was called Zerah.

Joseph's misfortunes in Potiphar's house [chapter 39]. Like Daniel, Joseph is a young
hero living in an alien country and in the political center of that country. The archetype
that he reenacts is familiar in English and American literature—the young man from the
country who is initiated into the sophistication and dangers of civilization (whether a city

¹ Hebrew *sacred woman;* a woman who served a pagan deity by prostitution; also verse 22 ² Or *has committed prostitution* ³ Or *by prostitution* ⁴ *Perez* means *a breach*

or a court). The experiences of Joseph in Potiphar's house follow a pyramid structure, as he begins as a mere servant, rises to the position of being supervisor of operations, and ends up in prison on a trumped-up charge of sexual harassment. Joseph fills several archetypal roles in the episode: idealized hero, honest servant, innocent victim. The plot revolves around the archetypal temptation motif. Potiphar's wife is the seductress, and Potiphar himself is the gullible dupe. Throughout his story, Joseph is such a talented person, and is so favored by God (vv. 2, 3, 5, 21), that he rises to a position of dominance in every successive episode—even when he is in prison (vv. 21–23). The God-centered perspective of the story is evident not only in the author's ascribing Joseph's success to God but also when Joseph resists sexual temptation because it would be "sin against God" (v. 9).

39 Now Joseph had been brought down to Egypt, and Potiphar, an officer of Pharaoh, the captain of the guard, an Egyptian, had bought him from the Ishmaelites who had brought him down there. [2]The LORD was with Joseph, and he became a successful man, and he was in the house of his Egyptian master. [3]His master saw that the LORD was with him and that the LORD caused all that he did to succeed in his hands. [4]So Joseph found favor in his sight and attended him, and he made him overseer of his house and put him in charge of all that he had. [5]From the time that he made him overseer in his house and over all that he had the LORD blessed the Egyptian's house for Joseph's sake; the blessing of the LORD was on all that he had, in house and field. [6]So he left all that he had in Joseph's charge, and because of him he had no concern about anything but the food he ate.

Now Joseph was handsome in form and appearance. [7]And after a time his master's wife cast her eyes on Joseph and said, "Lie with me." [8]But he refused and said to his master's wife, "Behold, because of me my master has no concern about anything in the house, and he has put everything that he has in my charge. [9]He is not greater in this house than I am, nor has he kept back anything from me except yourself, because you are his wife. How then can I do this great wickedness and sin against God?" [10]And as she spoke to Joseph day after day, he would not listen to her, to lie beside her or to be with her.

[11]But one day, when he went into the house to do his work and none of the men of the house was there in the house, [12]she caught him by his garment, saying, "Lie with me." But he left his garment in her hand and fled and got out of the house. [13]And as soon as she saw that he had left his garment in her hand and had fled out of the house, [14]she called to the men of her household and said to them, "See, he has brought among us a Hebrew to laugh at us. He came in to me to lie with me, and I cried out with a loud voice. [15]And as soon as he heard that I lifted up my voice and cried out, he left his garment beside me and fled and got out of the house." [16]Then she laid up his garment by her until his master came home, [17]and she told him the same story, saying, "The Hebrew servant, whom you have brought among us, came in to me to laugh at me. [18]But as soon as I lifted up my voice and cried, he left his garment beside me and fled out of the house."

[19]As soon as his master heard the words that his wife spoke to him, "This is the way your servant treated me," his anger was kindled. [20]And Joseph's master took him and put him into the prison, the place where the king's prisoners were confined, and

he was there in prison. ²¹But the LORD was with Joseph and showed him steadfast love and gave him favor in the sight of the keeper of the prison. ²²And the keeper of the prison put Joseph in charge of all the prisoners who were in the prison. Whatever was done there, he was the one who did it. ²³The keeper of the prison paid no attention to anything that was in Joseph's charge, because the LORD was with him. And whatever he did, the LORD made it succeed.

> **Interpreter of dreams** [chapter 40]. Hero stories typically place the protagonist into situations of testing that allow the hero to display his or her superior abilities. Tests of physical prowess have probably dominated the stories of the world, with battle action being a particularly crowded field. But stories in which the hero's moral integrity is tested are also prominent, as are stories in which the mental ability of the hero is tested. In the latter category, the ancient equivalent of the modern detective story is the hero who is skilled to interpret dreams. This constitutes the story material of chapter 40, which is a warm-up to the interpretation of the king's dreams that is coming up. Joseph's lack of reward for interpreting the cupbearer's dream fits into his career as a suffering servant, undergoing unmerited misery as part of a process that will eventually put him in the right position to save a civilization and the covenant people of God.

40 Some time after this, the cupbearer of the king of Egypt and his baker committed an offense against their lord the king of Egypt. ²And Pharaoh was angry with his two officers, the chief cupbearer and the chief baker, ³and he put them in custody in the house of the captain of the guard, in the prison where Joseph was confined. ⁴The captain of the guard appointed Joseph to be with them, and he attended them. They continued for some time in custody.

⁵And one night they both dreamed—the cupbearer and the baker of the king of Egypt, who were confined in the prison—each his own dream, and each dream with its own interpretation. ⁶When Joseph came to them in the morning, he saw that they were troubled. ⁷So he asked Pharaoh's officers who were with him in custody in his master's house, "Why are your faces downcast today?" ⁸They said to him, "We have had dreams, and there is no one to interpret them." And Joseph said to them, "Do not interpretations belong to God? Please tell them to me."

⁹So the chief cupbearer told his dream to Joseph and said to him, "In my dream there was a vine before me, ¹⁰and on the vine there were three branches. As soon as it budded, its blossoms shot forth, and the clusters ripened into grapes. ¹¹Pharaoh's cup was in my hand, and I took the grapes and pressed them into Pharaoh's cup and placed the cup in Pharaoh's hand." ¹²Then Joseph said to him, "This is its interpretation: the three branches are three days. ¹³In three days Pharaoh will lift up your head and restore you to your office, and you shall place Pharaoh's cup in his hand as formerly, when you were his cupbearer. ¹⁴Only remember me, when it is well with you, and please do me the kindness to mention me to Pharaoh, and so get me out of this house. ¹⁵For I was indeed stolen out of the land of the Hebrews, and here also I have done nothing that they should put me into the pit."

¹⁶When the chief baker saw that the interpretation was favorable, he said to Joseph, "I also had a dream: there were three cake baskets on my head, ¹⁷and in the uppermost basket there were all sorts of baked food for Pharaoh, but the birds were eating it out of the basket on my head." ¹⁸And Joseph answered and said, "This is its

interpretation: the three baskets are three days. ¹⁹In three days Pharaoh will lift up your head—from you!—and hang you on a tree. And the birds will eat the flesh from you."

²⁰On the third day, which was Pharaoh's birthday, he made a feast for all his servants and lifted up the head of the chief cupbearer and the head of the chief baker among his servants. ²¹He restored the chief cupbearer to his position, and he placed the cup in Pharaoh's hand. ²²But he hanged the chief baker, as Joseph had interpreted to them. ²³Yet the chief cupbearer did not remember Joseph, but forgot him.

Joseph's big chance [41:1–36]. Joseph's faithfulness in service, even while in prison, finally pays off when Pharaoh has two troubling dreams. The obtuse cupbearer finally remembers what Joseph had done for him by way of interpreting dreams, and Joseph finds himself standing before the king (after shaving and changing his clothes—note the realistic detail in v. 14). Joseph's role as witness to his faith takes the form of his repeated ascription of his ability to interpret dreams to God (vv. 16, 25, 32). Joseph is a hero's hero.

41 After two whole years, Pharaoh dreamed that he was standing by the Nile, ²and behold, there came up out of the Nile seven cows attractive and plump, and they fed in the reed grass. ³And behold, seven other cows, ugly and thin, came up out of the Nile after them, and stood by the other cows on the bank of the Nile. ⁴And the ugly, thin cows ate up the seven attractive, plump cows. And Pharaoh awoke. ⁵And he fell asleep and dreamed a second time. And behold, seven ears of grain, plump and good, were growing on one stalk. ⁶And behold, after them sprouted seven ears, thin and blighted by the east wind. ⁷And the thin ears swallowed up the seven plump, full ears. And Pharaoh awoke, and behold, it was a dream. ⁸So in the morning his spirit was troubled, and he sent and called for all the magicians of Egypt and all its wise men. Pharaoh told them his dreams, but there was none who could interpret them to Pharaoh.

⁹Then the chief cupbearer said to Pharaoh, "I remember my offenses today. ¹⁰When Pharaoh was angry with his servants and put me and the chief baker in custody in the house of the captain of the guard, ¹¹we dreamed on the same night, he and I, each having a dream with its own interpretation. ¹²A young Hebrew was there with us, a servant of the captain of the guard. When we told him, he interpreted our dreams to us, giving an interpretation to each man according to his dream. ¹³And as he interpreted to us, so it came about. I was restored to my office, and the baker was hanged."

¹⁴Then Pharaoh sent and called Joseph, and they quickly brought him out of the pit. And when he had shaved himself and changed his clothes, he came in before Pharaoh. ¹⁵And Pharaoh said to Joseph, "I have had a dream, and there is no one who can interpret it. I have heard it said of you that when you hear a dream you can interpret it." ¹⁶Joseph answered Pharaoh, "It is not in me; God will give Pharaoh a favorable answer."[1] ¹⁷Then Pharaoh said to Joseph, "Behold, in my dream I was standing on the banks of the Nile. ¹⁸Seven cows, plump and attractive, came up out of the Nile and fed in the reed grass. ¹⁹Seven other cows came up after them, poor and very ugly and thin, such as I had never seen in all the land of Egypt. ²⁰And the thin, ugly cows

---

[1] Or (compare Samaritan, Septuagint) *Without God it is not possible to give Pharaoh an answer about his welfare*

ate up the first seven plump cows, ²¹but when they had eaten them no one would have known that they had eaten them, for they were still as ugly as at the beginning. Then I awoke. ²²I also saw in my dream seven ears growing on one stalk, full and good. ²³Seven ears, withered, thin, and blighted by the east wind, sprouted after them, ²⁴and the thin ears swallowed up the seven good ears. And I told it to the magicians, but there was no one who could explain it to me."

²⁵Then Joseph said to Pharaoh, "The dreams of Pharaoh are one; God has revealed to Pharaoh what he is about to do. ²⁶The seven good cows are seven years, and the seven good ears are seven years; the dreams are one. ²⁷The seven lean and ugly cows that came up after them are seven years, and the seven empty ears blighted by the east wind are also seven years of famine. ²⁸It is as I told Pharaoh; God has shown to Pharaoh what he is about to do. ²⁹There will come seven years of great plenty throughout all the land of Egypt, ³⁰but after them there will arise seven years of famine, and all the plenty will be forgotten in the land of Egypt. The famine will consume the land, ³¹and the plenty will be unknown in the land by reason of the famine that will follow, for it will be very severe. ³²And the doubling of Pharaoh's dream means that the thing is fixed by God, and God will shortly bring it about. ³³Now therefore let Pharaoh select a discerning and wise man, and set him over the land of Egypt. ³⁴Let Pharaoh proceed to appoint overseers over the land and take one-fifth of the produce of the land¹ of Egypt during the seven plentiful years. ³⁵And let them gather all the food of these good years that are coming and store up grain under the authority of Pharaoh for food in the cities, and let them keep it. ³⁶That food shall be a reserve for the land against the seven years of famine that are to occur in the land of Egypt, so that the land may not perish through the famine."

Joseph's political prominence [41:37–57]. The problem posed at the very start of the story (how can the despised family outcast attain a position of dominance over this family?) is moving toward a solution. The pattern that unfolds in this segment is the rags-to-riches archetype. Yet again Joseph rises to a position of dominance in the situation in which he finds himself. The planning policies of Joseph are the means for a gigantic rescue story. It is a success story of the highest order.

³⁷This proposal pleased Pharaoh and all his servants. ³⁸And Pharaoh said to his servants, "Can we find a man like this, in whom is the Spirit of God?"² ³⁹Then Pharaoh said to Joseph, "Since God has shown you all this, there is none so discerning and wise as you are. ⁴⁰You shall be over my house, and all my people shall order themselves as you command.³ Only as regards the throne will I be greater than you." ⁴¹And Pharaoh said to Joseph, "See, I have set you over all the land of Egypt." ⁴²Then Pharaoh took his signet ring from his hand and put it on Joseph's hand, and clothed him in garments of fine linen and put a gold chain about his neck. ⁴³And he made him ride in his second chariot. And they called out before him, "Bow the knee!"⁴ Thus he set him over all the land of Egypt. ⁴⁴Moreover, Pharaoh said to Joseph, "I am Pharaoh, and without your consent no one shall lift up hand or foot in all the land of Egypt." ⁴⁵And Pharaoh called Joseph's name Zaphenath-paneah. And he gave him in marriage Asenath, the daughter of Potiphera priest of On. So Joseph went out over the land of Egypt.

---

¹ Or over the land and organize the land ² Or of the gods ³ Hebrew and according to your command all my people shall kiss the ground ⁴ Abrek, probably an Egyptian word, similar in sound to the Hebrew word meaning to kneel

⁴⁶Joseph was thirty years old when he entered the service of Pharaoh king of Egypt. And Joseph went out from the presence of Pharaoh and went through all the land of Egypt. ⁴⁷During the seven plentiful years the earth produced abundantly, ⁴⁸and he gathered up all the food of these seven years, which occurred in the land of Egypt, and put the food in the cities. He put in every city the food from the fields around it. ⁴⁹And Joseph stored up grain in great abundance, like the sand of the sea, until he ceased to measure it, for it could not be measured.

⁵⁰Before the year of famine came, two sons were born to Joseph. Asenath, the daughter of Potiphera priest of On, bore them to him. ⁵¹Joseph called the name of the firstborn Manasseh. "For," he said, "God has made me forget all my hardship and all my father's house."[1] ⁵²The name of the second he called Ephraim, "For God has made me fruitful in the land of my affliction."[2]

⁵³The seven years of plenty that occurred in the land of Egypt came to an end, ⁵⁴and the seven years of famine began to come, as Joseph had said. There was famine in all lands, but in all the land of Egypt there was bread. ⁵⁵When all the land of Egypt was famished, the people cried to Pharaoh for bread. Pharaoh said to all the Egyptians, "Go to Joseph. What he says to you, do."

⁵⁶So when the famine had spread over all the land, Joseph opened all the store-houses[3] and sold to the Egyptians, for the famine was severe in the land of Egypt. ⁵⁷Moreover, all the earth came to Egypt to Joseph to buy grain, because the famine was severe over all the earth.

Joseph's brothers make an appearance [chapter 42]. If we have been tracking with the element of suspense established by the youthful dreams of Joseph narrated at the beginning of the story, chapter 42 is an emotionally charged climax. The action in this chapter and the next two gets complicated, but the patterns at work make the action understandable. Dramatic irony pervades the story at this point, as we as readers know who Joseph is, while his brothers do not. Poetic justice takes the form of the evil brothers' getting their comeuppance. The test motif is prominent. Joseph is tested on several fronts—in his ability to feign emotional distance from those he loves, in his ability to keep his identity a secret, and in his willingness to forgive his brothers. The brothers are also tested: ostensibly it is their honesty that is tested, but what is really tested is their moral progress from the days when they had sold a brother into slavery. The first responsibility in mastering this story is to read slowly and reconstruct the order of events and the details of the action. The governing motif is that Joseph wishes to ensure that his brothers will return, this time with his younger brother Benjamin (see 43:3–7). Further, Joseph spares his brothers' lives when he could have killed them; he gives them food, he weeps over their presence, and he replaces their money as a gesture of love.

42 When Jacob learned that there was grain for sale in Egypt, he said to his sons, "Why do you look at one another?" ²And he said, "Behold, I have heard that there is grain for sale in Egypt. Go down and buy grain for us there, that we may live and not die." ³So ten of Joseph's brothers went down to buy grain in Egypt. ⁴But Jacob did not send Benjamin, Joseph's brother, with his brothers, for he feared that harm might happen to him. ⁵Thus the sons of Israel came to buy among the others who came, for the famine was in the land of Canaan.

⁶Now Joseph was governor over the land. He was the one who sold to all the people

of the land. And Joseph's brothers came and bowed themselves before him with their faces to the ground. ⁷Joseph saw his brothers and recognized them, but he treated them like strangers and spoke roughly to them. "Where do you come from?" he said. They said, "From the land of Canaan, to buy food." ⁸And Joseph recognized his brothers, but they did not recognize him. ⁹And Joseph remembered the dreams that he had dreamed of them. And he said to them, "You are spies; you have come to see the nakedness of the land." ¹⁰They said to him, "No, my lord, your servants have come to buy food. ¹¹We are all sons of one man. We are honest men. Your servants have never been spies."

¹²He said to them, "No, it is the nakedness of the land that you have come to see." ¹³And they said, "We, your servants, are twelve brothers, the sons of one man in the land of Canaan, and behold, the youngest is this day with our father, and one is no more." ¹⁴But Joseph said to them, "It is as I said to you. You are spies. ¹⁵By this you shall be tested: by the life of Pharaoh, you shall not go from this place unless your youngest brother comes here. ¹⁶Send one of you, and let him bring your brother, while you remain confined, that your words may be tested, whether there is truth in you. Or else, by the life of Pharaoh, surely you are spies." ¹⁷And he put them all together in custody for three days.

¹⁸On the third day Joseph said to them, "Do this and you will live, for I fear God: ¹⁹if you are honest men, let one of your brothers remain confined where you are in custody, and let the rest go and carry grain for the famine of your households, ²⁰and bring your youngest brother to me. So your words will be verified, and you shall not die." And they did so. ²¹Then they said to one another, "In truth we are guilty concerning our brother, in that we saw the distress of his soul, when he begged us and we did not listen. That is why this distress has come upon us." ²²And Reuben answered them, "Did I not tell you not to sin against the boy? But you did not listen. So now there comes a reckoning for his blood." ²³They did not know that Joseph understood them, for there was an interpreter between them. ²⁴Then he turned away from them and wept. And he returned to them and spoke to them. And he took Simeon from them and bound him before their eyes. ²⁵And Joseph gave orders to fill their bags with grain, and to replace every man's money in his sack, and to give them provisions for the journey. This was done for them.

²⁶Then they loaded their donkeys with their grain and departed. ²⁷And as one of them opened his sack to give his donkey fodder at the lodging place, he saw his money in the mouth of his sack. ²⁸He said to his brothers, "My money has been put back; here it is in the mouth of my sack!" At this their hearts failed them, and they turned trembling to one another, saying, "What is this that God has done to us?"

²⁹When they came to Jacob their father in the land of Canaan, they told him all that had happened to them, saying, ³⁰"The man, the lord of the land, spoke roughly to us and took us to be spies of the land. ³¹But we said to him, 'We are honest men; we have never been spies. ³²We are twelve brothers, sons of our father. One is no more, and the youngest is this day with our father in the land of Canaan.' ³³Then the man, the lord of the land, said to us, 'By this I shall know that you are honest men: leave one of your brothers with me, and take grain for the famine of your households, and go your way. ³⁴Bring your youngest brother to me. Then I shall know that you are not spies but honest men, and I will deliver your brother to you, and you shall trade in the land.'"

³⁵As they emptied their sacks, behold, every man's bundle of money was in his sack. And when they and their father saw their bundles of money, they were afraid. ³⁶And Jacob their father said to them, "You have bereaved me of my children: Joseph is no more, and Simeon is no more, and now you would take Benjamin. All this has come against me." ³⁷Then Reuben said to his father, "Kill my two sons if I do not bring him back to you. Put him in my hands, and I will bring him back to you." ³⁸But he said, "My son shall not go down with you, for his brother is dead, and he is the only one left. If harm should happen to him on the journey that you are to make, you would bring down my gray hairs with sorrow to Sheol."

The brothers' second trip to Egypt [chapter 43]. The story that occupies chapter 43 spills over into the next chapter as well. In this chapter, the action moves in a quieter mood, serving in this regard as a foil to the tense next chapter. The sequence is as follows: Jacob reluctantly allows his sons to travel to Egypt (vv. 1–15); the fearful brothers make a return appearance before Joseph, bearing a gift from home in hope of ingratiating themselves to Joseph (vv. 16–25); Joseph inquires about the welfare of his family and breaks down weeping in private (vv. 26–30); Joseph hosts his brothers at a meal (vv. 31–34).

43 Now the famine was severe in the land. ²And when they had eaten the grain that they had brought from Egypt, their father said to them, "Go again, buy us a little food." ³But Judah said to him, "The man solemnly warned us, saying, 'You shall not see my face unless your brother is with you.' ⁴If you will send our brother with us, we will go down and buy you food. ⁵But if you will not send him, we will not go down, for the man said to us, 'You shall not see my face, unless your brother is with you.'" ⁶Israel said, "Why did you treat me so badly as to tell the man that you had another brother?" ⁷They replied, "The man questioned us carefully about ourselves and our kindred, saying, 'Is your father still alive? Do you have another brother?' What we told him was in answer to these questions. Could we in any way know that he would say, 'Bring your brother down'?" ⁸And Judah said to Israel his father, "Send the boy with me, and we will arise and go, that we may live and not die, both we and you and also our little ones. ⁹I will be a pledge of his safety. From my hand you shall require him. If I do not bring him back to you and set him before you, then let me bear the blame forever. ¹⁰If we had not delayed, we would now have returned twice."

¹¹Then their father Israel said to them, "If it must be so, then do this: take some of the choice fruits of the land in your bags, and carry a present down to the man, a little balm and a little honey, gum, myrrh, pistachio nuts, and almonds. ¹²Take double the money with you. Carry back with you the money that was returned in the mouth of your sacks. Perhaps it was an oversight. ¹³Take also your brother, and arise, go again to the man. ¹⁴May God Almighty¹ grant you mercy before the man, and may he send back your other brother and Benjamin. And as for me, if I am bereaved of my children, I am bereaved."

¹⁵So the men took this present, and they took double the money with them, and Benjamin. They arose and went down to Egypt and stood before Joseph.

¹⁶When Joseph saw Benjamin with them, he said to the steward of his house,

¹ Hebrew *El Shaddai*

"Bring the men into the house, and slaughter an animal and make ready, for the men are to dine with me at noon." [17] The man did as Joseph told him and brought the men to Joseph's house. [18] And the men were afraid because they were brought to Joseph's house, and they said, "It is because of the money, which was replaced in our sacks the first time, that we are brought in, so that he may assault us and fall upon us to make us servants and seize our donkeys." [19] So they went up to the steward of Joseph's house and spoke with him at the door of the house, [20] and said, "Oh, my lord, we came down the first time to buy food. [21] And when we came to the lodging place we opened our sacks, and there was each man's money in the mouth of his sack, our money in full weight. So we have brought it again with us, [22] and we have brought other money down with us to buy food. We do not know who put our money in our sacks." [23] He replied, "Peace to you, do not be afraid. Your God and the God of your father has put treasure in your sacks for you. I received your money." Then he brought Simeon out to them. [24] And when the man had brought the men into Joseph's house and given them water, and they had washed their feet, and when he had given their donkeys fodder, [25] they prepared the present for Joseph's coming at noon, for they heard that they should eat bread there.

[26] When Joseph came home, they brought into the house to him the present that they had with them and bowed down to him to the ground. [27] And he inquired about their welfare and said, "Is your father well, the old man of whom you spoke? Is he still alive?" [28] They said, "Your servant our father is well; he is still alive." And they bowed their heads and prostrated themselves. [29] And he lifted up his eyes and saw his brother Benjamin, his mother's son, and said, "Is this your youngest brother, of whom you spoke to me? God be gracious to you, my son!" [30] Then Joseph hurried out, for his compassion grew warm for his brother, and he sought a place to weep. And he entered his chamber and wept there. [31] Then he washed his face and came out. And controlling himself he said, "Serve the food." [32] They served him by himself, and them by themselves, and the Egyptians who ate with him by themselves, because the Egyptians could not eat with the Hebrews, for that is an abomination to the Egyptians. [33] And they sat before him, the firstborn according to his birthright and the youngest according to his youth. And the men looked at one another in amazement. [34] Portions were taken to them from Joseph's table, but Benjamin's portion was five times as much as any of theirs. And they drank and were merry[1] with him.

Further testing of the brothers [chapter 44]. The episode begins with high tension as Benjamin is seized and brought back to Joseph's court in the incident of the "planted" cup (vv. 1–13). Ostensibly this is vindictive behavior on Joseph's part, but we need to follow the logic of his actions. The brother's moral progress is being tested, and Joseph even allows them to regain some of the self-esteem that they had lost in their shame over what they did to Joseph when they sold him into slavery. On that earlier occasion, Judah was the one who had proposed selling Joseph into slavery (37:26–27), and it is now Judah who offers himself as a substitute for Benjamin in a long and formal speech to Joseph (vv. 14–34). The storyteller's strategy of impeding the movement of the plot by quoting the entire speech in leisurely detail has the effect of heightening our suspense as we read.

[1] Hebrew *and became intoxicated*

44 Then he commanded the steward of his house, "Fill the men's sacks with food, as much as they can carry, and put each man's money in the mouth of his sack, ²and put my cup, the silver cup, in the mouth of the sack of the youngest, with his money for the grain." And he did as Joseph told him.

³As soon as the morning was light, the men were sent away with their donkeys. ⁴They had gone only a short distance from the city. Now Joseph said to his steward, "Up, follow after the men, and when you overtake them, say to them, 'Why have you repaid evil for good?[1] ⁵Is it not from this that my lord drinks, and by this that he practices divination? You have done evil in doing this.'"

⁶When he overtook them, he spoke to them these words. ⁷They said to him, "Why does my lord speak such words as these? Far be it from your servants to do such a thing! ⁸Behold, the money that we found in the mouths of our sacks we brought back to you from the land of Canaan. How then could we steal silver or gold from your lord's house? ⁹Whichever of your servants is found with it shall die, and we also will be my lord's servants." ¹⁰He said, "Let it be as you say: he who is found with it shall be my servant, and the rest of you shall be innocent." ¹¹Then each man quickly lowered his sack to the ground, and each man opened his sack. ¹²And he searched, beginning with the eldest and ending with the youngest. And the cup was found in Benjamin's sack. ¹³Then they tore their clothes, and every man loaded his donkey, and they returned to the city.

¹⁴When Judah and his brothers came to Joseph's house, he was still there. They fell before him to the ground. ¹⁵Joseph said to them, "What deed is this that you have done? Do you not know that a man like me can indeed practice divination?" ¹⁶And Judah said, "What shall we say to my lord? What shall we speak? Or how can we clear ourselves? God has found out the guilt of your servants; behold, we are my lord's servants, both we and he also in whose hand the cup has been found." ¹⁷But he said, "Far be it from me that I should do so! Only the man in whose hand the cup was found shall be my servant. But as for you, go up in peace to your father."

¹⁸Then Judah went up to him and said, "Oh, my lord, please let your servant speak a word in my lord's ears, and let not your anger burn against your servant, for you are like Pharaoh himself. ¹⁹My lord asked his servants, saying, 'Have you a father, or a brother?' ²⁰And we said to my lord, 'We have a father, an old man, and a young brother, the child of his old age. His brother is dead, and he alone is left of his mother's children, and his father loves him.' ²¹Then you said to your servants, 'Bring him down to me, that I may set my eyes on him.' ²²We said to my lord, 'The boy cannot leave his father, for if he should leave his father, his father would die.' ²³Then you said to your servants, 'Unless your youngest brother comes down with you, you shall not see my face again.'

²⁴"When we went back to your servant my father, we told him the words of my lord. ²⁵And when our father said, 'Go again, buy us a little food,' ²⁶we said, 'We cannot go down. If our youngest brother goes with us, then we will go down. For we cannot see the man's face unless our youngest brother is with us.' ²⁷Then your servant my father said to us, 'You know that my wife bore me two sons. ²⁸One left me, and I said, Surely he has been torn to pieces, and I have never seen him since. ²⁹If you take this one also from me, and harm happens to him, you will bring down my gray hairs in evil to Sheol.'

³⁰"Now therefore, as soon as I come to your servant my father, and the boy is not

---

[1] Septuagint (compare Vulgate) adds *Why have you stolen my silver cup?*

with us, then, as his life is bound up in the boy's life, ³¹as soon as he sees that the boy is not with us, he will die, and your servants will bring down the gray hairs of your servant our father with sorrow to Sheol. ³²For your servant became a pledge of safety for the boy to my father, saying, 'If I do not bring him back to you, then I shall bear the blame before my father all my life.' ³³Now therefore, please let your servant remain instead of the boy as a servant to my lord, and let the boy go back with his brothers. ³⁴For how can I go back to my father if the boy is not with me? I fear to see the evil that would find my father."

Family reunion [chapter 45]. In emotional intensity, this chapter belongs with such high points of Western narrative as the hero's homecoming in Homer's *Odyssey* and the convict's showing up in Pip's apartment in Charles Dickens's *Great Expectations* and Rev. Dimmesdale's belated confession on the scaffold in Nathaniel Hawthorne's *The Scarlet Letter*. The disclosure of a secret is the mainspring of the plot, and it comes with heightened impact because it has been delayed through the long process narrated in chapters 42–44. The stunning revelations are punctuated by Joseph's profusion of weeping (vv. 1–2), the brothers' stunned disbelief and fear (v. 3), and a family embrace (vv. 14–15). To heighten the crescendo of happy-ending celebration, the storyteller includes full details about the success story that Joseph charges his brothers to tell their father about his favorite son (vv. 9–13) and the details of the provisions that were made for moving Joseph's family to Egypt (vv. 16–25). Joseph's parting shot to his brothers that they should "not quarrel on the way" (v. 24) is a nice bit of psychological realism, alerting us that there might have been finger-pointing among the brothers in regard to their earlier misbehavior. The emotional voltage remains unabated as we read about Jacob's response to the news of Joseph (vv. 26–28). The theological meaning of the entire preceding action is editorialized by Joseph when he interprets all the misfortune that he endured as part of God's providential and redemptive design (vv. 5–8).

45 Then Joseph could not control himself before all those who stood by him. He cried, "Make everyone go out from me." So no one stayed with him when Joseph made himself known to his brothers. ²And he wept aloud, so that the Egyptians heard it, and the household of Pharaoh heard it. ³And Joseph said to his brothers, "I am Joseph! Is my father still alive?" But his brothers could not answer him, for they were dismayed at his presence.

⁴So Joseph said to his brothers, "Come near to me, please." And they came near. And he said, "I am your brother, Joseph, whom you sold into Egypt. ⁵And now do not be distressed or angry with yourselves because you sold me here, for God sent me before you to preserve life. ⁶For the famine has been in the land these two years, and there are yet five years in which there will be neither plowing nor harvest. ⁷And God sent me before you to preserve for you a remnant on earth, and to keep alive for you many survivors. ⁸So it was not you who sent me here, but God. He has made me a father to Pharaoh, and lord of all his house and ruler over all the land of Egypt. ⁹Hurry and go up to my father and say to him, 'Thus says your son Joseph, God has made me lord of all Egypt. Come down to me; do not tarry. ¹⁰You shall dwell in the land of Goshen, and you shall be near me, you and your children and your children's children, and your flocks, your herds, and all that you have. ¹¹There I will provide for you, for there are yet five years of famine to come, so that you and your household,

and all that you have, do not come to poverty.' [12]And now your eyes see, and the eyes of my brother Benjamin see, that it is my mouth that speaks to you. [13]You must tell my father of all my honor in Egypt, and of all that you have seen. Hurry and bring my father down here." [14]Then he fell upon his brother Benjamin's neck and wept, and Benjamin wept upon his neck. [15]And he kissed all his brothers and wept upon them. After that his brothers talked with him.

[16]When the report was heard in Pharaoh's house, "Joseph's brothers have come," it pleased Pharaoh and his servants. [17]And Pharaoh said to Joseph, "Say to your brothers, 'Do this: load your beasts and go back to the land of Canaan, [18]and take your father and your households, and come to me, and I will give you the best of the land of Egypt, and you shall eat the fat of the land.' [19]And you, Joseph, are commanded to say, 'Do this: take wagons from the land of Egypt for your little ones and for your wives, and bring your father, and come. [20]Have no concern for[1] your goods, for the best of all the land of Egypt is yours.'"

[21]The sons of Israel did so: and Joseph gave them wagons, according to the command of Pharaoh, and gave them provisions for the journey. [22]To each and all of them he gave a change of clothes, but to Benjamin he gave three hundred shekels[2] of silver and five changes of clothes. [23]To his father he sent as follows: ten donkeys loaded with the good things of Egypt, and ten female donkeys loaded with grain, bread, and provision for his father on the journey. [24]Then he sent his brothers away, and as they departed, he said to them, "Do not quarrel on the way."

[25]So they went up out of Egypt and came to the land of Canaan to their father Jacob. [26]And they told him, "Joseph is still alive, and he is ruler over all the land of Egypt." And his heart became numb, for he did not believe them. [27]But when they told him all the words of Joseph, which he had said to them, and when he saw the wagons that Joseph had sent to carry him, the spirit of their father Jacob revived. [28]And Israel said, "It is enough; Joseph my son is still alive. I will go and see him before I die."

Moving to Egypt [46:1–47:12]. Jacob has been a case study in resilience, and even in his old age he musters the courage to make a long-distance international move. The specific details here and elsewhere in Genesis give the book the authentic ring of a factual family history as well as literary narrative. Just as God promised his providential care over Jacob in a vision as he slept at Bethel, now he again appears to Jacob "in visions of the night" (46:2) and renews the covenant blessing (46:3–4). Right in the middle of the narrative we find another *genealogy (46:8–27), showing again how the historical and literary impulses converge in the book of Genesis and in fact throughout the Bible. The arrival of Jacob in Egypt is narrated in leisurely detail, partly because the unlikelihood by human standards that the patriarch would actually stand as a celebrity before the king of Egypt renders the event momentous in the family's history. As we read the summary statement in 47:12, we are led to consider how extensive the story of Jacob has been as narrated in the book of Genesis. The character of Jacob is so problematical that we might wonder how God could have chosen him as a patriarch, but it is indisputable that he is a "bigger-than-life" figure.

46 So Israel took his journey with all that he had and came to Beersheba, and offered sacrifices to the God of his father Isaac. [2]And God spoke to Israel in visions of the night and said, "Jacob, Jacob." And he said, "Here am I." [3]Then he said,

---

[1] Hebrew *Let your eye not pity* [2] A *shekel* was about 2/5 ounce or 11 grams

"I am God, the God of your father. Do not be afraid to go down to Egypt, for there I will make you into a great nation. ⁴I myself will go down with you to Egypt, and I will also bring you up again, and Joseph's hand shall close your eyes."

⁵Then Jacob set out from Beersheba. The sons of Israel carried Jacob their father, their little ones, and their wives, in the wagons that Pharaoh had sent to carry him. ⁶They also took their livestock and their goods, which they had gained in the land of Canaan, and came into Egypt, Jacob and all his offspring with him, ⁷his sons, and his sons' sons with him, his daughters, and his sons' daughters. All his offspring he brought with him into Egypt.

⁸Now these are the names of the descendants of Israel, who came into Egypt, Jacob and his sons. Reuben, Jacob's firstborn, ⁹and the sons of Reuben: Hanoch, Pallu, Hezron, and Carmi. ¹⁰The sons of Simeon: Jemuel, Jamin, Ohad, Jachin, Zohar, and Shaul, the son of a Canaanite woman. ¹¹The sons of Levi: Gershon, Kohath, and Merari. ¹²The sons of Judah: Er, Onan, Shelah, Perez, and Zerah (but Er and Onan died in the land of Canaan); and the sons of Perez were Hezron and Hamul. ¹³The sons of Issachar: Tola, Puvah, Yob, and Shimron. ¹⁴The sons of Zebulun: Sered, Elon, and Jahleel. ¹⁵These are the sons of Leah, whom she bore to Jacob in Paddan-aram, together with his daughter Dinah; altogether his sons and his daughters numbered thirty-three.

¹⁶The sons of Gad: Ziphion, Haggi, Shuni, Ezbon, Eri, Arodi, and Areli. ¹⁷The sons of Asher: Imnah, Ishvah, Ishvi, Beriah, with Serah their sister. And the sons of Beriah: Heber and Malchiel. ¹⁸These are the sons of Zilpah, whom Laban gave to Leah his daughter; and these she bore to Jacob—sixteen persons.

¹⁹The sons of Rachel, Jacob's wife: Joseph and Benjamin. ²⁰And to Joseph in the land of Egypt were born Manasseh and Ephraim, whom Asenath, the daughter of Potiphera the priest of On, bore to him. ²¹And the sons of Benjamin: Bela, Becher, Ashbel, Gera, Naaman, Ehi, Rosh, Muppim, Huppim, and Ard. ²²These are the sons of Rachel, who were born to Jacob—fourteen persons in all.

²³The sons of Dan: Hushim. ²⁴The sons of Naphtali: Jahzeel, Guni, Jezer, and Shillem. ²⁵These are the sons of Bilhah, whom Laban gave to Rachel his daughter, and these she bore to Jacob—seven persons in all.

²⁶All the persons belonging to Jacob who came into Egypt, who were his own descendants, not including Jacob's sons' wives, were sixty-six persons in all. ²⁷And the sons of Joseph, who were born to him in Egypt, were two. All the persons of the house of Jacob who came into Egypt were seventy.

²⁸He had sent Judah ahead of him to Joseph to show the way before him in Goshen, and they came into the land of Goshen. ²⁹Then Joseph prepared his chariot and went up to meet Israel his father in Goshen. He presented himself to him and fell on his neck and wept on his neck a good while. ³⁰Israel said to Joseph, "Now let me die, since I have seen your face and know that you are still alive." ³¹Joseph said to his brothers and to his father's household, "I will go up and tell Pharaoh and will say to him, 'My brothers and my father's household, who were in the land of Canaan, have come to me. ³²And the men are shepherds, for they have been keepers of livestock, and they have brought their flocks and their herds and all that they have.' ³³When Pharaoh calls you and says, 'What is your occupation?' ³⁴you shall say, 'Your servants have been keepers of livestock from our youth even until now, both we and our fathers,' in

order that you may dwell in the land of Goshen, for every shepherd is an abomination to the Egyptians."

47 So Joseph went in and told Pharaoh, "My father and my brothers, with their flocks and herds and all that they possess, have come from the land of Canaan. They are now in the land of Goshen." ²And from among his brothers he took five men and presented them to Pharaoh. ³Pharaoh said to his brothers, "What is your occupation?" And they said to Pharaoh, "Your servants are shepherds, as our fathers were." ⁴They said to Pharaoh, "We have come to sojourn in the land, for there is no pasture for your servants' flocks, for the famine is severe in the land of Canaan. And now, please let your servants dwell in the land of Goshen." ⁵Then Pharaoh said to Joseph, "Your father and your brothers have come to you. ⁶The land of Egypt is before you. Settle your father and your brothers in the best of the land. Let them settle in the land of Goshen, and if you know any able men among them, put them in charge of my livestock."

⁷Then Joseph brought in Jacob his father and stood him before Pharaoh, and Jacob blessed Pharaoh. ⁸And Pharaoh said to Jacob, "How many are the days of the years of your life?" ⁹And Jacob said to Pharaoh, "The days of the years of my sojourning are 130 years. Few and evil have been the days of the years of my life, and they have not attained to the days of the years of the life of my fathers in the days of their sojourning." ¹⁰And Jacob blessed Pharaoh and went out from the presence of Pharaoh. ¹¹Then Joseph settled his father and his brothers and gave them a possession in the land of Egypt, in the best of the land, in the land of Rameses, as Pharaoh had commanded. ¹²And Joseph provided his father, his brothers, and all his father's household with food, according to the number of their dependents.

Joseph's success as an administrator [47:13–26]. The life of Joseph is no less extraordinary than Jacob's. His assimilation into the inner circle of Pharaoh's court is astounding when we consider his racial and social status as an outsider. The king obviously viewed Joseph as a valued colleague, as Joseph was apparently not subjected to the religious discrimination that at so many moments in history would have dogged a person in his position. The land policies that are outlined in this unit, mysterious by modern standards, are implicitly offered as a final proof of the hero's political acumen.

¹³Now there was no food in all the land, for the famine was very severe, so that the land of Egypt and the land of Canaan languished by reason of the famine. ¹⁴And Joseph gathered up all the money that was found in the land of Egypt and in the land of Canaan, in exchange for the grain that they bought. And Joseph brought the money into Pharaoh's house. ¹⁵And when the money was all spent in the land of Egypt and in the land of Canaan, all the Egyptians came to Joseph and said, "Give us food. Why should we die before your eyes? For our money is gone." ¹⁶And Joseph answered, "Give your livestock, and I will give you food in exchange for your livestock, if your money is gone." ¹⁷So they brought their livestock to Joseph, and Joseph gave them food in exchange for the horses, the flocks, the herds, and the donkeys. He supplied them with food in exchange for all their livestock that year. ¹⁸And when that year was ended, they came to him the following year and said to him, "We will not hide from my lord that our money is all spent. The herds of livestock are my lord's.

There is nothing left in the sight of my lord but our bodies and our land. [19]Why should we die before your eyes, both we and our land? Buy us and our land for food, and we with our land will be servants to Pharaoh. And give us seed that we may live and not die, and that the land may not be desolate." [20]So Joseph bought all the land of Egypt for Pharaoh, for all the Egyptians sold their fields, because the famine was severe on them. The land became Pharaoh's. [21]As for the people, he made servants of them[1] from one end of Egypt to the other. [22]Only the land of the priests he did not buy, for the priests had a fixed allowance from Pharaoh and lived on the allowance that Pharaoh gave them; therefore they did not sell their land.

[23]Then Joseph said to the people, "Behold, I have this day bought you and your land for Pharaoh. Now here is seed for you, and you shall sow the land. [24]And at the harvests you shall give a fifth to Pharaoh, and four fifths shall be your own, as seed for the field and as food for yourselves and your households, and as food for your little ones." [25]And they said, "You have saved our lives; may it please my lord, we will be servants to Pharaoh." [26]So Joseph made it a statute concerning the land of Egypt, and it stands to this day, that Pharaoh should have the fifth; the land of the priests alone did not become Pharaoh's.

Jacob's last days [47:27–48:22]. The stories of Jacob and Joseph overlap, and the focus now shifts to Jacob, specifically to his preparations for death. The final actions of Jacob's life as narrated in Genesis are ritual actions—formal requests, bowing, swearing of oaths, placing of hands in blessing, and pronouncements of blessing. The two main actions are Jacob's request (expressing his faith in the covenant promise) to Joseph that he not be buried in Egypt (47:29–31) and his blessing of Joseph's sons (chapter 48). The speeches of Jacob are expressed in stately and formal language. Jacob's pronouncing the chief blessing on the younger of Joseph's sons rather than the older, interpreted by Joseph as a mistake but actually a deliberate action on Jacob's part, perpetuates an archetype of the OT in which the younger is given precedence over the older (an echo of Jacob's own experience in relation to Esau).

[27]Thus Israel settled in the land of Egypt, in the land of Goshen. And they gained possessions in it, and were fruitful and multiplied greatly. [28]And Jacob lived in the land of Egypt seventeen years. So the days of Jacob, the years of his life, were 147 years.

[29]And when the time drew near that Israel must die, he called his son Joseph and said to him, "If now I have found favor in your sight, put your hand under my thigh and promise to deal kindly and truly with me. Do not bury me in Egypt, [30]but let me lie with my fathers. Carry me out of Egypt and bury me in their burying place." He answered, "I will do as you have said." [31]And he said, "Swear to me"; and he swore to him. Then Israel bowed himself upon the head of his bed.[2]

48 After this, Joseph was told, "Behold, your father is ill." So he took with him his two sons, Manasseh and Ephraim. [2]And it was told to Jacob, "Your son Joseph has come to you." Then Israel summoned his strength and sat up in bed. [3]And Jacob said to Joseph, "God Almighty[3] appeared to me at Luz in the land of Canaan and blessed me, [4]and said to me, 'Behold, I will make you fruitful and multiply you,

---

[1] Samaritan, Septuagint, Vulgate; Hebrew *he removed them to the cities* [2] Hebrew; Septuagint *staff* [3] Hebrew *El Shaddai*

and I will make of you a company of peoples and will give this land to your offspring after you for an everlasting possession.' ⁵And now your two sons, who were born to you in the land of Egypt before I came to you in Egypt, are mine; Ephraim and Manasseh shall be mine, as Reuben and Simeon are. ⁶And the children that you fathered after them shall be yours. They shall be called by the name of their brothers in their inheritance. ⁷As for me, when I came from Paddan, to my sorrow Rachel died in the land of Canaan on the way, when there was still some distance¹ to go to Ephrath, and I buried her there on the way to Ephrath (that is, Bethlehem)."

⁸When Israel saw Joseph's sons, he said, "Who are these?" ⁹Joseph said to his father, "They are my sons, whom God has given me here." And he said, "Bring them to me, please, that I may bless them." ¹⁰Now the eyes of Israel were dim with age, so that he could not see. So Joseph brought them near him, and he kissed them and embraced them. ¹¹And Israel said to Joseph, "I never expected to see your face; and behold, God has let me see your offspring also." ¹²Then Joseph removed them from his knees, and he bowed himself with his face to the earth. ¹³And Joseph took them both, Ephraim in his right hand toward Israel's left hand, and Manasseh in his left hand toward Israel's right hand, and brought them near him. ¹⁴And Israel stretched out his right hand and laid it on the head of Ephraim, who was the younger, and his left hand on the head of Manasseh, crossing his hands (for Manasseh was the first-born). ¹⁵And he blessed Joseph and said,

> "The God before whom my fathers Abraham and Isaac walked,
>   the God who has been my shepherd all my life long to this day,
> ¹⁶ the angel who has redeemed me from all evil, bless the boys;
>   and in them let my name be carried on, and the name of my fathers Abraham and
>   Isaac;
>   and let them grow into a multitude² in the midst of the earth."

¹⁷When Joseph saw that his father laid his right hand on the head of Ephraim, it displeased him, and he took his father's hand to move it from Ephraim's head to Manasseh's head. ¹⁸And Joseph said to his father, "Not this way, my father; since this one is the firstborn, put your right hand on his head." ¹⁹But his father refused and said, "I know, my son, I know. He also shall become a people, and he also shall be great. Nevertheless, his younger brother shall be greater than he, and his offspring shall become a multitude³ of nations." ²⁰So he blessed them that day, saying,

> "By you Israel will pronounce blessings, saying,
>   'God make you as Ephraim and as Manasseh.'"

Thus he put Ephraim before Manasseh. ²¹Then Israel said to Joseph, "Behold, I am about to die, but God will be with you and will bring you again to the land of your fathers. ²²Moreover, I have given to you rather than to your brothers one mountain slope⁴ that I took from the hand of the Amorites with my sword and with my bow."

Jacob's blessing on his sons [chapter 49]. A father's pronouncement of a blessing on his sons on his deathbed was an ancient ritual. In the OT, such blessings were not wishes or prayers but an actual prediction and conferring of what was pronounced. In

---

¹ Or *about two hours' distance* ² Or *let them be like fish for multitude* ³ Hebrew *fullness* ⁴ Or *one portion of the land;* Hebrew *shekem,* which sounds like the town and district called *Shechem*

keeping with the formality of the event, poetry replaces prose as the literary form. While some of the blessings are purely earthly and temporal, others have a spiritual feel. Some are curses rather than blessings (vv. 5–7). The most significant item in the list is the messianic prophecy related to Judah (vv. 10–11). Following the formal pronouncement of the blessings, the narrative mode resumes with an account of Jacob's death (vv. 28–33).

49 Then Jacob called his sons and said, "Gather yourselves together, that I may tell you what shall happen to you in days to come.

² "Assemble and listen, O sons of Jacob,
    listen to Israel your father.

³ "Reuben, you are my firstborn,
    my might, and the firstfruits of my strength,
    preeminent in dignity and preeminent in power.
⁴ Unstable as water, you shall not have preeminence,
    because you went up to your father's bed;
    then you defiled it—he went up to my couch!

⁵ "Simeon and Levi are brothers;
    weapons of violence are their swords.
⁶ Let my soul come not into their council;
    O my glory, be not joined to their company.
For in their anger they killed men,
    and in their willfulness they hamstrung oxen.
⁷ Cursed be their anger, for it is fierce,
    and their wrath, for it is cruel!
I will divide them in Jacob
    and scatter them in Israel.

⁸ "Judah, your brothers shall praise you;
    your hand shall be on the neck of your enemies;
    your father's sons shall bow down before you.
⁹ Judah is a lion's cub;
    from the prey, my son, you have gone up.
He stooped down; he crouched as a lion
    and as a lioness; who dares rouse him?
¹⁰ The scepter shall not depart from Judah,
    nor the ruler's staff from between his feet,
until tribute comes to him;¹
    and to him shall be the obedience of the peoples.
¹¹ Binding his foal to the vine
    and his donkey's colt to the choice vine,
he has washed his garments in wine
    and his vesture in the blood of grapes.
¹² His eyes are darker than wine,
    and his teeth whiter than milk.

---

¹ By a slight revocalization; a slight emendation yields (compare Septuagint, Syriac, Targum) *until he comes to whom it belongs*; Hebrew *until Shiloh comes*, or *until he comes to Shiloh*

¹³ "Zebulun shall dwell at the shore of the sea;
　　he shall become a haven for ships,
　　and his border shall be at Sidon.

¹⁴ "Issachar is a strong donkey,
　　crouching between the sheepfolds.[1]
¹⁵ He saw that a resting place was good,
　　and that the land was pleasant,
　so he bowed his shoulder to bear,
　　and became a servant at forced labor.

¹⁶ "Dan shall judge his people
　　as one of the tribes of Israel.
¹⁷ Dan shall be a serpent in the way,
　　a viper by the path,
　that bites the horse's heels
　　so that his rider falls backward.
¹⁸ I wait for your salvation, O LORD.

¹⁹ "Raiders shall raid Gad,[2]
　　but he shall raid at their heels.

²⁰ "Asher's food shall be rich,
　　and he shall yield royal delicacies.

²¹ "Naphtali is a doe let loose
　　that bears beautiful fawns.[3]

²² "Joseph is a fruitful bough,
　　a fruitful bough by a spring;
　　his branches run over the wall.[4]
²³ The archers bitterly attacked him,
　　shot at him, and harassed him severely,
²⁴ yet his bow remained unmoved;
　　his arms[5] were made agile
　by the hands of the Mighty One of Jacob
　(from there is the Shepherd,[6] the Stone of Israel),
²⁵ by the God of your father who will help you,
　　by the Almighty[7] who will bless you
　　with blessings of heaven above,
　blessings of the deep that crouches beneath,
　　blessings of the breasts and of the womb.
²⁶ The blessings of your father
　　are mighty beyond the blessings of my parents,
　　up to the bounties of the everlasting hills.[8]
　May they be on the head of Joseph,
　　and on the brow of him who was set apart from his brothers.

---

[1] Or between its saddlebags [2] Gad sounds like the Hebrew for raiders and raid [3] Or he gives beautiful words, or that bears fawns of the fold [4] Or Joseph is a wild donkey, a wild donkey beside a spring, his wild colts beside the wall [5] Hebrew the arms of his hands [6] Or by the name of the Shepherd [7] Hebrew Shaddai [8] A slight emendation yields (compare Septuagint) the blessings of the eternal mountains, the bounties of the everlasting hills

[27] "Benjamin is a ravenous wolf,
     in the morning devouring the prey
     and at evening dividing the spoil."

[28]All these are the twelve tribes of Israel. This is what their father said to them as he blessed them, blessing each with the blessing suitable to him. [29]Then he commanded them and said to them, "I am to be gathered to my people; bury me with my fathers in the cave that is in the field of Ephron the Hittite, [30]in the cave that is in the field at Machpelah, to the east of Mamre, in the land of Canaan, which Abraham bought with the field from Ephron the Hittite to possess as a burying place. [31]There they buried Abraham and Sarah his wife. There they buried Isaac and Rebekah his wife, and there I buried Leah— [32]the field and the cave that is in it were bought from the Hittites." [33]When Jacob finished commanding his sons, he drew up his feet into the bed and breathed his last and was gathered to his people.

> **The death and funeral rites of Jacob** [50:1–14]. The heroic life of Jacob is rounded off with an account of his burial. Epic literature is replete with accounts of the funeral and mourning that follow the death of a hero. This unit fits that pattern in an accustomed way. In this instance, the funeral rites take on a spiritual symbolism, with Jacob being buried in the Promised Land instead of Egypt.

50 Then Joseph fell on his father's face and wept over him and kissed him. [2]And Joseph commanded his servants the physicians to embalm his father. So the physicians embalmed Israel. [3]Forty days were required for it, for that is how many are required for embalming. And the Egyptians wept for him seventy days.

[4]And when the days of weeping for him were past, Joseph spoke to the household of Pharaoh, saying, "If now I have found favor in your eyes, please speak in the ears of Pharaoh, saying, [5]My father made me swear, saying, 'I am about to die: in my tomb that I hewed out for myself in the land of Canaan, there shall you bury me.' Now therefore, let me please go up and bury my father. Then I will return." [6]And Pharaoh answered, "Go up, and bury your father, as he made you swear." [7]So Joseph went up to bury his father. With him went up all the servants of Pharaoh, the elders of his household, and all the elders of the land of Egypt, [8]as well as all the household of Joseph, his brothers, and his father's household. Only their children, their flocks, and their herds were left in the land of Goshen. [9]And there went up with him both chariots and horsemen. It was a very great company. [10]When they came to the threshing floor of Atad, which is beyond the Jordan, they lamented there with a very great and grievous lamentation, and he made a mourning for his father seven days. [11]When the inhabitants of the land, the Canaanites, saw the mourning on the threshing floor of Atad, they said, "This is a grievous mourning by the Egyptians." Therefore the place was named Abel-mizraim;[1] it is beyond the Jordan. [12]Thus his sons did for him as he had commanded them, [13]for his sons carried him to the land of Canaan and buried him in the cave of the field at Machpelah, to the east of Mamre, which Abraham bought with the field from Ephron the Hittite to possess as a burying place. [14]After he had buried his father, Joseph returned to Egypt with his brothers and all who had gone up with him to bury his father.

---

[1] *Abel-mizraim* means *mourning* (or *meadow*) *of Egypt*

Final days and death of Joseph [50:15–26]. A further note of closure is now sounded as the book of Genesis gives the last word on the life of Joseph. Joseph's interactions with his fearful brothers state once more the providential interpretation that this suffering servant gives to his life of undeserved suffering (vv. 15–21). Joseph here emerges as an idealized character one last time. And in keeping with the nature of Genesis as a historical chronicle, the writer ends with the historical facts surrounding the death and burial of Joseph (vv. 22–26). The same spiritual symbolism emerges that was present in the burial of Jacob, as now Joseph extracts a promise that even though he will be embalmed and put in a coffin in Egypt, his bones will eventually be buried in the Promised Land. The story of the patriarchs ends with an exercise of faith in the covenant promises of God.

[15]When Joseph's brothers saw that their father was dead, they said, "It may be that Joseph will hate us and pay us back for all the evil that we did to him." [16]So they sent a message to Joseph, saying, "Your father gave this command before he died, [17]'Say to Joseph, Please forgive the transgression of your brothers and their sin, because they did evil to you.' And now, please forgive the transgression of the servants of the God of your father." Joseph wept when they spoke to him. [18]His brothers also came and fell down before him and said, "Behold, we are your servants." [19]But Joseph said to them, "Do not fear, for am I in the place of God? [20]As for you, you meant evil against me, but God meant it for good, to bring it about that many people[1] should be kept alive, as they are today. [21]So do not fear; I will provide for you and your little ones." Thus he comforted them and spoke kindly to them.

[22]So Joseph remained in Egypt, he and his father's house. Joseph lived 110 years. [23]And Joseph saw Ephraim's children of the third generation. The children also of Machir the son of Manasseh were counted as Joseph's own.[2] [24]And Joseph said to his brothers, "I am about to die, but God will visit you and bring you up out of this land to the land that he swore to Abraham, to Isaac, and to Jacob." [25]Then Joseph made the sons of Israel swear, saying, "God will surely visit you, and you shall carry up my bones from here." [26]So Joseph died, being 110 years old. They embalmed him, and he was put in a coffin in Egypt.

---

[1] Or *a numerous people* [2] Hebrew *were born on Joseph's knees*

EXODUS

The book at a glance. 40 chapters, 1,213 verses. Exodus is the greatest adventure story ever told. After long centuries of slavery under Pharaoh, God remembered his covenant with Israel and delivered his people out of the land of Egypt, out of the house of bondage. The story of Israel's salvation has everything that anyone could ever want in an adventure story: a cruel villain (Pharaoh), an unlikely hero (Moses), fantastic disasters (the plagues), a spectacular deliverance (crossing the Red Sea), a long journey (through the wilderness), a mountaintop experience (where Moses receives the Ten Commandments), and a grand finale (when God comes down to fill the tabernacle with his glory). Along the way—as we might expect in an epic adventure—there are unexpected setbacks and unpredictable delays, magic tricks and miracles, feasts and festivals, music and dancing, and many close encounters with the living God. God's purpose in all of this was to show his glory by fulfilling the promises he made to his people in the covenant. The exodus is the archetypal deliverance of the Old Testament—the definitive salvation event that established the identity of Israel as the people of God and demonstrated the character of their Deliverer as the God who saves.

▌**Genres.** The book of Exodus is presented in the form of an *epic. Like most epics, it begins in the middle of things, with the Israelites languishing in slavery and their would-be deliverer born under the threat of death by drowning. The story proceeds along epic lines, with a cosmic confrontation between good and evil that is happily resolved through a mighty act of rescue and a long journey to freedom. Moses is the heroic (albeit imperfect) national leader who serves as the human instrument of a divine deliverance. Like many epics, Exodus is also the story of the founding of a nation. This helps to explain how the second half of the book connects to the first: once they are delivered from bondage, the people of God meet to receive a national constitution (the Ten Commandments) and to establish a place for their national assembly (the tabernacle). Within its epic framework, Exodus also contains a wealth of subgenres: *rescue story, *calling story, human-divine *encounter, diplomatic negotiation, plague story, *genealogy, institution of a festival, *song of victory, *travelogue, *miracle story, legal code, case law, covenant renewal ceremony, architectural blueprint, garment design, building narrative. (For more information on items accompanied by an asterisk, see the glossary at the back of this Bible.)

▌**Unifying elements.** The person of Moses provides Exodus with a strong sense of narrative unity. It is Moses who meets with God at the burning bush, demands that

Passage	Content	Theme	Location
1:1–22	God's people suffer in slavery	God not glorified because Pharaoh will not let God's people go	Israel in Egypt
2:1–25	Birth and exodus of Moses		
3:1–4:17	The call of Moses		
4:18–6:30	First audience with Pharaoh		
7–10	The first nine plagues	God glorified in judging Egypt	
11–13	Passover and the final plague	God glorified in redeeming his people	From Egypt to God's mountain
14:1–31	Crossing the Red Sea		
15:1–21	The song of salvation		
15:22–18:27	Journey through the wilderness	God glorified in providing for his people	
19–20	The Ten Commandments	God glorified in giving his people the Law	
21–23	The Book of the Covenant		
24:1–18	God makes a covenant with Israel		
25–31	Plans for the tabernacle and its priests	God glorified in worship	Israel at Mount Sinai
32:1–35	The golden calf		
33–34	God renews his covenant with Israel		
35–39	The tabernacle built according to plan		
40:1–38	God's glory fills the tabernacle		

Pharaoh let God's people go, leads Israel across the sea on dry land, sings the song of their salvation, comes down a mountain (twice) with the Law of God, leads Israel in worship, and finally sets up the tabernacle. Since Moses is a national leader, Exodus is also unified by its focus on Israel as the people of God. But the real hero of the story is God himself, and Exodus finds its most essential unity in his actions and attributes as the God who hears his people pray, delivers them from slavery, provides for them in the wilderness, instructs them how to live, invites them to worship him, and meets with them in all the power of his holy divine presence. To be even more specific, the main theme of Exodus is the *glory* of God. The initial plot conflict is that Pharaoh will not let God's people go out to glorify their God (see 9:1). When God plagues the Egyptians and drowns Pharaoh's armies at the bottom of the sea, he does it to gain glory for himself (see 14:4, 17–18)—a glory that Moses celebrates in his victory song (see 15:11). This divine glory is revealed in visible form many times throughout the book: at the burning bush, in the pillar of cloud (16:10), at the top of Mount Sinai (see 24:15–17), in the face of Moses (34:29–35), and most climactically in the completed tabernacle (40:34–35). The central message of Exodus is that God's people are saved for God's glory.

▌**Inferred literary intentions.** The book is designed to achieve the following literary purposes:

  ▌glorify God by telling the full story of how he delivered his people

  ▌establish Israel's identity by rehearsing its founding experiences as a nation

  ▌personify evil in the cruelty and tyranny of Pharaoh

  ▌present Moses as an ideal mediator for the people of God

  ▌present memorable images of divine judgment

  ▌provide a travel guide for a life of spiritual pilgrimage

  ▌record memorable instances of personal and national encounters with God

  ▌reveal God's will for his people, as summarized in the Ten Commandments

  ▌show how God's law relates to daily life, as exemplified in the Book of the Covenant (chapters 21–23)

  ▌formalize the true pattern of worship in the institution of Passover, the renewal of the covenant, the construction of the tabernacle, and the consecration of its priests

  ▌revel in the luxurious beauty of the tabernacle and its furnishings

  ▌warn against the spiritual dangers of grumbling against God or deciding to worship him our way rather than his way

  ▌convey a sense of reverence and awe for the holiness and majesty of God

  ▌captivate us with the story itself

▌**Theological themes.** (1) The sovereignty of God: God rules all nations, working in history to reveal his glory. (2) Revelation: God reveals his will and character in what he says and what he does, so that his people can know him as their God. (3) Salvation: God releases his people from captivity, redeems them from slavery, and adopts them as children. (4) Covenant: Israel is rescued because God remembers his covenant and restored because God renews his covenant—his everlasting love commitment to his people, sealed in blood. (5) Law: God's law is both a gracious gift for the people he has redeemed and a perfect standard for human behavior. (6) Holiness: God has set his people apart for holy service, and everything associated with his worship is to be kept perfectly sacred. (7) Judgment: God justly executes his wrath against his enemies. (8) Atonement: through the various offerings made at Passover, on Mount Sinai, and in the tabernacle, Exodus shows that God forgives sin only through a righteous sacrifice of blood offered in the place of sinners. (9) Worship: the goal of life is to glorify God, who has the right to tell us exactly how he wants to be served and worshiped.

The book of Exodus as a chapter in the master story of the Bible. The story of Israel's exodus from Egypt is the paradigm for salvation in the OT. It also sets the pattern for the full and final salvation that God has provided in Israel's Messiah. Jesus Christ became the new Moses of a greater exodus by going down into Egypt, passing through the waters of baptism, enduring temptation in the wilderness, and going up on the mountain to give people God's law (see Matthew 2–7). Like Moses, Jesus is the mediator of a new covenant (see Heb. 9:15). Like the Passover lamb or the offering sprinkled on the ark of the covenant, the blood of his sacrifice is the atonement for our sin. Like the tabernacle, he is the dwelling place of God with us (see John 1:14, where the word for "dwell" is the Greek word for tabernacle). Like Aaron the high priest, he brings us into the Most Holy Place, where we can meet with God. If we know Christ, therefore, we can trace the story of the exodus somewhere in the spiritual geography of our own souls. Through the waters of baptism, we have been delivered from our bondage to sin. Now God is guiding us on our pilgrimage through the wilderness, feeding us our daily bread, teaching us his law, receiving our worship, and leading us to his glory in the Promised Land.

Israel in Egypt [1:1–21]. Exodus picks up where Genesis left off. The sons of Jacob—the twelve tribes of Israel—are still in Egypt, where Joseph rescued them from famine and where they have grown from seventy people to become a great nation, thus fulfilling God's covenant promise to make a people from himself (vv. 1–7). But the sons of Israel have not yet returned to the Promised Land, and the need for their eventual homecoming is the book's opening plot conflict. A more serious threat emerges with the rise of a tyrannical new pharaoh who neither knows Joseph nor honors God. First Pharaoh presses the Israelites into slavery—the archetypal house of bondage. Then he begins a reign of terror by trying to kill their baby boys—a genocidal campaign that threatens the very existence of the people of God, not simply their return to their homeland. The closing vignette, in which the antagonist is outwitted by a pair of Hebrew midwives, has the *satiric and mocking tone of slave literature: far from decreasing, the Israelites continue to multiply.

1 These are the names of the sons of Israel who came to Egypt with Jacob, each with his household: ²Reuben, Simeon, Levi, and Judah, ³Issachar, Zebulun, and Benjamin, ⁴Dan and Naphtali, Gad and Asher. ⁵All the descendants of Jacob were seventy persons; Joseph was already in Egypt. ⁶Then Joseph died, and all his brothers and all that generation. ⁷But the people of Israel were fruitful and increased greatly; they multiplied and grew exceedingly strong, so that the land was filled with them.

⁸Now there arose a new king over Egypt, who did not know Joseph. ⁹And he said to his people, "Behold, the people of Israel are too many and too mighty for us. ¹⁰Come, let us deal shrewdly with them, lest they multiply, and, if war breaks out, they join our enemies and fight against us and escape from the land." ¹¹Therefore they set taskmasters over them to afflict them with heavy burdens. They built for Pharaoh store cities, Pithom and Raamses. ¹²But the more they were oppressed, the more they multiplied and the more they spread abroad. And the Egyptians were in dread of the people of Israel. ¹³So they ruthlessly made the people of Israel work as slaves ¹⁴and made

their lives bitter with hard service, in mortar and brick, and in all kinds of work in the field. In all their work they ruthlessly made them work as slaves. ¹⁵Then the king of Egypt said to the Hebrew midwives, one of whom was named Shiphrah and the other Puah, ¹⁶"When you serve as midwife to the Hebrew women and see them on the birthstool, if it is a son, you shall kill him, but if it is a daughter, she shall live." ¹⁷But the midwives feared God and did not do as the king of Egypt commanded them, but let the male children live. ¹⁸So the king of Egypt called the midwives and said to them, "Why have you done this, and let the male children live?" ¹⁹The midwives said to Pharaoh, "Because the Hebrew women are not like the Egyptian women, for they are vigorous and give birth before the midwife comes to them." ²⁰So God dealt well with the midwives. And the people multiplied and grew very strong. ²¹And because the midwives feared God, he gave them families.

The savior's deliverance and failure to deliver [1:22–2:22]. Pharaoh continues his reign of terror by ordering the Israelites to drown their baby boys in the Nile. The deliverance of Moses from this horrible fate foreshadows the main act of deliverance to follow: just as baby Moses is saved from the dark waters, so Israel will be saved from the watery depths of the Red Sea. Ironically, Moses will be raised in the very courts of the ruler that he will later defy. The protagonist's first attempt to deliver Israel (one Egyptian at a time) ends in failure and disgrace, as Moses commits murder and becomes a fugitive from justice, fleeing for his life from the wrath of Pharaoh (2:11–15). After rising to greatness, the hero born in obscurity has made a tragic choice that costs him everything except life itself. Yet in addition to giving him a new family, God provides water for Moses in the wilderness (2:16–22)—another foreshadowing of Israel's subsequent salvation.

²²Then Pharaoh commanded all his people, "Every son that is born to the Hebrews¹ you shall cast into the Nile, but you shall let every daughter live."

2 Now a man from the house of Levi went and took as his wife a Levite woman. ²The woman conceived and bore a son, and when she saw that he was a fine child, she hid him three months. ³When she could hide him no longer, she took for him a basket made of bulrushes² and daubed it with bitumen and pitch. She put the child in it and placed it among the reeds by the river bank. ⁴And his sister stood at a distance to know what would be done to him. ⁵Now the daughter of Pharaoh came down to bathe at the river, while her young women walked beside the river. She saw the basket among the reeds and sent her servant woman, and she took it. ⁶When she opened it, she saw the child, and behold, the baby was crying. She took pity on him and said, "This is one of the Hebrews' children." ⁷Then his sister said to Pharaoh's daughter, "Shall I go and call you a nurse from the Hebrew women to nurse the child for you?" ⁸And Pharaoh's daughter said to her, "Go." So the girl went and called the child's mother. ⁹And Pharaoh's daughter said to her, "Take this child away and nurse him for me, and I will give you your wages." So the woman took the child and nursed him. ¹⁰When the child grew up, she brought him to Pharaoh's daughter, and he became her son. She named him Moses, "Because," she said, "I drew him out of the water."³

¹¹One day, when Moses had grown up, he went out to his people and looked on

¹ Samaritan, Septuagint, Targum; Hebrew lacks to the Hebrews ² Hebrew papyrus reeds ³ Moses sounds like the Hebrew for draw out

their burdens, and he saw an Egyptian beating a Hebrew, one of his people.[1] [12]He looked this way and that, and seeing no one, he struck down the Egyptian and hid him in the sand. [13]When he went out the next day, behold, two Hebrews were struggling together. And he said to the man in the wrong, "Why do you strike your companion?" [14]He answered, "Who made you a prince and a judge over us? Do you mean to kill me as you killed the Egyptian?" Then Moses was afraid, and thought, "Surely the thing is known." [15]When Pharaoh heard of it, he sought to kill Moses. But Moses fled from Pharaoh and stayed in the land of Midian. And he sat down by a well.

[16]Now the priest of Midian had seven daughters, and they came and drew water and filled the troughs to water their father's flock. [17]The shepherds came and drove them away, but Moses stood up and saved them, and watered their flock. [18]When they came home to their father Reuel, he said, "How is it that you have come home so soon today?" [19]They said, "An Egyptian delivered us out of the hand of the shepherds and even drew water for us and watered the flock." [20]He said to his daughters, "Then where is he? Why have you left the man? Call him, that he may eat bread." [21]And Moses was content to dwell with the man, and he gave Moses his daughter Zipporah. [22]She gave birth to a son, and he called his name Gershom, for he said, "I have been a sojourner[2] in a foreign land."

Moses meets the Great I AM [2:23–3:22]. The key to all the ensuing action comes in the opening verses of this section: God hears the cries of his people, knows their need, and remembers the promises of his covenant (2:23–25). Israel's deliverance begins with the call of Moses, whose encounter with God at the burning bush is one of the signature scenes of the Old Testament. Already in this first encounter with God, we are standing on holy ground, where we sense the majesty of God's presence and the inapproachable glory of his divine being. God's call for Moses to deliver Israel out of Egypt comes with many assurances, but the prophet has two immediate objections, which he phrases in the form of two questions: "Who am I?" and "Who are you?" (see 3:11, 13). "I will be with you," God answers, and as for his identity, "I AM WHO I AM" (3:12, 14). The bush itself—because it keeps burning without being consumed—is a sign of this sacred divine name, in which God reveals his eternal self-sufficiency. God also reminds Moses of his promises in the covenant and announces his explicit intention to strike Egypt with many plagues before delivering his people at Pharaoh's expense.

[23]During those many days the king of Egypt died, and the people of Israel groaned because of their slavery and cried out for help. Their cry for rescue from slavery came up to God. [24]And God heard their groaning, and God remembered his covenant with Abraham, with Isaac, and with Jacob. [25]God saw the people of Israel—and God knew.

3 Now Moses was keeping the flock of his father-in-law, Jethro, the priest of Midian, and he led his flock to the west side of the wilderness and came to Horeb, the mountain of God. [2]And the angel of the LORD appeared to him in a flame of fire out of the midst of a bush. He looked, and behold, the bush was burning, yet it was not consumed. [3]And Moses said, "I will turn aside to see this great sight, why the bush is not burned." [4]When the LORD saw that he turned aside to see, God called to him out of the bush, "Moses, Moses!" And he said, "Here I am." [5]Then he said, "Do

---

[1] Hebrew *brothers* [2] *Gershom* sounds like the Hebrew for *sojourner*

not come near; take your sandals off your feet, for the place on which you are stand-ing is holy ground." ⁶And he said, "I am the God of your father, the God of Abraham, the God of Isaac, and the God of Jacob." And Moses hid his face, for he was afraid to look at God.

⁷Then the LORD said, "I have surely seen the affliction of my people who are in Egypt and have heard their cry because of their taskmasters. I know their sufferings, ⁸and I have come down to deliver them out of the hand of the Egyptians and to bring them up out of that land to a good and broad land, a land flowing with milk and honey, to the place of the Canaanites, the Hittites, the Amorites, the Perizzites, the Hivites, and the Jebusites. ⁹And now, behold, the cry of the people of Israel has come to me, and I have also seen the oppression with which the Egyptians oppress them. ¹⁰Come, I will send you to Pharaoh that you may bring my people, the children of Israel, out of Egypt." ¹¹But Moses said to God, "Who am I that I should go to Pharaoh and bring the children of Israel out of Egypt?" ¹²He said, "But I will be with you, and this shall be the sign for you, that I have sent you: when you have brought the people out of Egypt, you shall serve God on this mountain."

¹³Then Moses said to God, "If I come to the people of Israel and say to them, 'The God of your fathers has sent me to you,' and they ask me, 'What is his name?' what shall I say to them?" ¹⁴God said to Moses, "I AM WHO I AM."¹ And he said, "Say this to the people of Israel, 'I AM has sent me to you.'" ¹⁵God also said to Moses, "Say this to the people of Israel, 'The LORD,² the God of your fathers, the God of Abraham, the God of Isaac, and the God of Jacob, has sent me to you.' This is my name forever, and thus I am to be remembered throughout all generations. ¹⁶Go and gather the elders of Israel together and say to them, 'The LORD, the God of your fathers, the God of Abraham, of Isaac, and of Jacob, has appeared to me, saying, "I have observed you and what has been done to you in Egypt, ¹⁷and I promise that I will bring you up out of the affliction of Egypt to the land of the Canaanites, the Hittites, the Amorites, the Perizzites, the Hivites, and the Jebusites, a land flowing with milk and honey."' ¹⁸And they will listen to your voice, and you and the elders of Israel shall go to the king of Egypt and say to him, 'The LORD, the God of the Hebrews, has met with us; and now, please let us go a three days' journey into the wilderness, that we may sacrifice to the LORD our God.' ¹⁹But I know that the king of Egypt will not let you go unless com-pelled by a mighty hand.³ ²⁰So I will stretch out my hand and strike Egypt with all the wonders that I will do in it; after that he will let you go. ²¹And I will give this people favor in the sight of the Egyptians; and when you go, you shall not go empty, ²²but each woman shall ask of her neighbor, and any woman who lives in her house, for silver and gold jewelry, and for clothing. You shall put them on your sons and on your daughters. So you shall plunder the Egyptians."

Signs and wonders [chapter 4]. By this point in the conversation it is clear that Moses is trying to bargain with God. His third objection to serving as Israel's deliverer is that people will not believe him when he says that he is God's prophet (v. 1). God responds by giving Moses three miraculous signs to attest to his prophetic calling (vv. 2–9). However, the real issue is that Moses is unwilling to serve, as becomes clear when he refuses outright, on the grounds that he is not a very good public speaker (vv. 10–13). In

---

¹ Or I AM WHAT I AM, or I WILL BE WHAT I WILL BE ² The word LORD, when spelled with capital letters, stands for the divine name, YHWH, which is here connected with the verb hayah, "to be" in verse 14 ³ Septuagint, Vulgate; Hebrew go, not by a mighty hand

the end the prophet answers God's call and goes back to Egypt, where his brother Aaron becomes his spokesman and where the people of God see the first signs of their deliverance, to the glory of God. This commissioning scene fits a familiar narrative convention, namely, preparation for the central action—setting the stage for what is to follow. It also introduces the familiar biblical motif of the reluctant prophet.

4 Then Moses answered, "But behold, they will not believe me or listen to my voice, for they will say, 'The LORD did not appear to you.'" ²The LORD said to him, "What is that in your hand?" He said, "A staff." ³And he said, "Throw it on the ground." So he threw it on the ground, and it became a serpent, and Moses ran from it. ⁴But the LORD said to Moses, "Put out your hand and catch it by the tail"—so he put out his hand and caught it, and it became a staff in his hand— ⁵"that they may believe that the LORD, the God of their fathers, the God of Abraham, the God of Isaac, and the God of Jacob, has appeared to you." ⁶Again, the LORD said to him, "Put your hand inside your cloak."¹ And he put his hand inside his cloak, and when he took it out, behold, his hand was leprous² like snow. ⁷Then God said, "Put your hand back inside your cloak." So he put his hand back inside his cloak, and when he took it out, behold, it was restored like the rest of his flesh. ⁸"If they will not believe you," God said, "or listen to the first sign, they may believe the latter sign. ⁹If they will not believe even these two signs or listen to your voice, you shall take some water from the Nile and pour it on the dry ground, and the water that you shall take from the Nile will become blood on the dry ground."

¹⁰But Moses said to the LORD, "Oh, my Lord, I am not eloquent, either in the past or since you have spoken to your servant, but I am slow of speech and of tongue." ¹¹Then the LORD said to him, "Who has made man's mouth? Who makes him mute, or deaf, or seeing, or blind? Is it not I, the LORD? ¹²Now therefore go, and I will be with your mouth and teach you what you shall speak." ¹³But he said, "Oh, my Lord, please send someone else." ¹⁴Then the anger of the LORD was kindled against Moses and he said, "Is there not Aaron, your brother, the Levite? I know that he can speak well. Behold, he is coming out to meet you, and when he sees you, he will be glad in his heart. ¹⁵You shall speak to him and put the words in his mouth, and I will be with your mouth and with his mouth and will teach you both what to do. ¹⁶He shall speak for you to the people, and he shall be your mouth, and you shall be as God to him. ¹⁷And take in your hand this staff, with which you shall do the signs."

¹⁸Moses went back to Jethro his father-in-law and said to him, "Please let me go back to my brothers in Egypt to see whether they are still alive." And Jethro said to Moses, "Go in peace." ¹⁹And the LORD said to Moses in Midian, "Go back to Egypt, for all the men who were seeking your life are dead." ²⁰So Moses took his wife and his sons and had them ride on a donkey, and went back to the land of Egypt. And Moses took the staff of God in his hand.

²¹And the LORD said to Moses, "When you go back to Egypt, see that you do before Pharaoh all the miracles that I have put in your power. But I will harden his heart, so that he will not let the people go. ²²Then you shall say to Pharaoh, 'Thus says the LORD, Israel is my firstborn son, ²³and I say to you, "Let my son go that he may serve me." If you refuse to let him go, behold, I will kill your firstborn son.'"

²⁴At a lodging place on the way the LORD met him and sought to put him to death.

¹ Hebrew *into your bosom*; also verse 7 ² *Leprosy* was a term for several skin diseases; see Leviticus 13

²⁵Then Zipporah took a flint and cut off her son's foreskin and touched Moses'¹ feet with it and said, "Surely you are a bridegroom of blood to me!" ²⁶So he let him alone. It was then that she said, "A bridegroom of blood," because of the circumcision.

²⁷The LORD said to Aaron, "Go into the wilderness to meet Moses." So he went and met him at the mountain of God and kissed him. ²⁸And Moses told Aaron all the words of the LORD with which he had sent him to speak, and all the signs that he had commanded him to do. ²⁹Then Moses and Aaron went and gathered together all the elders of the people of Israel. ³⁰Aaron spoke all the words that the LORD had spoken to Moses and did the signs in the sight of the people. ³¹And the people believed; and when they heard that the LORD had visited the people of Israel and that he had seen their affliction, they bowed their heads and worshiped.

Bricks without straw [5:1–6:9]. Moses and Aaron go directly to Pharaoh with God's famous demand: "Let my people go" (5:1). But instead of letting the Israelites go, Pharaoh takes away the straw they use to make his bricks, without any reduction in their daily quotas. Thus the plot conflict is intensified: Pharaoh refuses to let God's people worship their God and demands that they work for him instead. Predictably, the Israelites blame Moses and Aaron for their added hardships (5:20–21), while Moses in turn blames the Lord, accusing him of failing to deliver his people as promised (5:22–23). This dialogue gives God the opportunity to rehearse the promises of the covenant and to reiterate his commitment to restore his people to their land (6:1–8). The literary effect of this episode is to heighten the dramatic tension of the narrative. Will God indeed deliver Israel? Will Pharaoh ever let God's people go?

5 Afterward Moses and Aaron went and said to Pharaoh, "Thus says the LORD, the God of Israel, 'Let my people go, that they may hold a feast to me in the wilderness.'" ²But Pharaoh said, "Who is the LORD, that I should obey his voice and let Israel go? I do not know the LORD, and moreover, I will not let Israel go." ³Then they said, "The God of the Hebrews has met with us. Please let us go a three days' journey into the wilderness that we may sacrifice to the LORD our God, lest he fall upon us with pestilence or with the sword." ⁴But the king of Egypt said to them, "Moses and Aaron, why do you take the people away from their work? Get back to your burdens." ⁵And Pharaoh said, "Behold, the people of the land are now many,² and you make them rest from their burdens!" ⁶The same day Pharaoh commanded the taskmasters of the people and their foremen, ⁷"You shall no longer give the people straw to make bricks, as in the past; let them go and gather straw for themselves. ⁸But the number of bricks that they made in the past you shall impose on them, you shall by no means reduce it, for they are idle. Therefore they cry, 'Let us go and offer sacrifice to our God.' ⁹Let heavier work be laid on the men that they may labor at it and pay no regard to lying words."

¹⁰So the taskmasters and the foremen of the people went out and said to the people, "Thus says Pharaoh, 'I will not give you straw. ¹¹Go and get your straw yourselves wherever you can find it, but your work will not be reduced in the least.'" ¹²So the people were scattered throughout all the land of Egypt to gather stubble for straw. ¹³The taskmasters were urgent, saying, "Complete your work, your daily task each day, as when there was straw." ¹⁴And the foremen of the people of Israel, whom

¹ Hebrew *his* ² Samaritan *they are now more numerous than the people of the land*

Pharaoh's taskmasters had set over them, were beaten and were asked, "Why have you not done all your task of making bricks today and yesterday, as in the past?" ¹⁵Then the foremen of the people of Israel came and cried to Pharaoh, "Why do you treat your servants like this? ¹⁶No straw is given to your servants, yet they say to us, 'Make bricks!' And behold, your servants are beaten; but the fault is in your own people." ¹⁷But he said, "You are idle, you are idle; that is why you say, 'Let us go and sacrifice to the Lᴏʀᴅ.' ¹⁸Go now and work. No straw will be given you, but you must still deliver the same number of bricks." ¹⁹The foremen of the people of Israel saw that they were in trouble when they said, "You shall by no means reduce your number of bricks, your daily task each day." ²⁰They met Moses and Aaron, who were waiting for them, as they came out from Pharaoh; ²¹and they said to them, "The Lᴏʀᴅ look on you and judge, because you have made us stink in the sight of Pharaoh and his servants, and have put a sword in their hand to kill us."

²²Then Moses turned to the Lᴏʀᴅ and said, "O Lord, why have you done evil to this people? Why did you ever send me? ²³For since I came to Pharaoh to speak in your name, he has done evil to this people, and you have not delivered your people at all."

6 But the Lᴏʀᴅ said to Moses, "Now you shall see what I will do to Pharaoh; for with a strong hand he will send them out, and with a strong hand he will drive them out of his land."

²God spoke to Moses and said to him, "I am the Lᴏʀᴅ. ³I appeared to Abraham, to Isaac, and to Jacob, as God Almighty,¹ but by my name the Lᴏʀᴅ I did not make myself known to them. ⁴I also established my covenant with them to give them the land of Canaan, the land in which they lived as sojourners. ⁵Moreover, I have heard the groaning of the people of Israel whom the Egyptians hold as slaves, and I have remembered my covenant. ⁶Say therefore to the people of Israel, 'I am the Lᴏʀᴅ, and I will bring you out from under the burdens of the Egyptians, and I will deliver you from slavery to them, and I will redeem you with an outstretched arm and with great acts of judgment. ⁷I will take you to be my people, and I will be your God, and you shall know that I am the Lᴏʀᴅ your God, who has brought you out from under the burdens of the Egyptians. ⁸I will bring you into the land that I swore to give to Abraham, to Isaac, and to Jacob. I will give it to you for a possession. I am the Lᴏʀᴅ.'" ⁹Moses spoke thus to the people of Israel, but they did not listen to Moses, because of their broken spirit and harsh slavery.

The staff that swallowed the serpents [6:10–7:13]. God's mind has not changed, so he sends his representatives back to Pharaoh with the same ultimatum. On this occasion Moses and Aaron are dignified with a formal genealogy (an epic catalog) that firmly establishes their identity as leaders for Israel (6:14–25). Moses is still the reluctant prophet, refusing to speak, so Aaron will serve as his spokesman (6:28–7:2). Once again, God tells his prophet what will happen to Egypt: Pharaoh's refusals will lead to divine reprisals, until finally God delivers his people and everyone acknowledges that he is God (7:3–5). The audience Moses has with Pharaoh is a miracle story that takes the form of a challenge: Aaron defies the magicians of Egypt by swallowing their serpents with his staff (7:8–12). The closing line in this section introduces an important motif in the book of Exodus: the hardening of Pharaoh's heart. This phase of the story turns upon

---

¹ Hebrew *El Shaddai*

the narrative motif of suspense, as we are led to wonder what it will take to get Pharaoh to ever approve of the Israelites' departure.

[10]So the LORD said to Moses, [11]"Go in, tell Pharaoh king of Egypt to let the people of Israel go out of his land." [12]But Moses said to the LORD, "Behold, the people of Israel have not listened to me. How then shall Pharaoh listen to me, for I am of uncircumcised lips?" [13]But the LORD spoke to Moses and Aaron and gave them a charge about the people of Israel and about Pharaoh king of Egypt: to bring the people of Israel out of the land of Egypt.

[14]These are the heads of their fathers' houses: the sons of Reuben, the firstborn of Israel: Hanoch, Pallu, Hezron, and Carmi; these are the clans of Reuben. [15]The sons of Simeon: Jemuel, Jamin, Ohad, Jachin, Zohar, and Shaul, the son of a Canaanite woman; these are the clans of Simeon. [16]These are the names of the sons of Levi according to their generations: Gershon, Kohath, and Merari, the years of the life of Levi being 137 years. [17]The sons of Gershon: Libni and Shimei, by their clans. [18]The sons of Kohath: Amram, Izhar, Hebron, and Uzziel, the years of the life of Kohath being 133 years. [19]The sons of Merari: Mahli and Mushi. These are the clans of the Levites according to their generations. [20]Amram took as his wife Jochebed his father's sister, and she bore him Aaron and Moses, the years of the life of Amram being 137 years. [21]The sons of Izhar: Korah, Nepheg, and Zichri. [22]The sons of Uzziel: Mishael, Elzaphan, and Sithri. [23]Aaron took as his wife Elisheba, the daughter of Amminadab and the sister of Nahshon, and she bore him Nadab, Abihu, Eleazar, and Ithamar. [24]The sons of Korah: Assir, Elkanah, and Abiasaph; these are the clans of the Korahites. [25]Eleazar, Aaron's son, took as his wife one of the daughters of Putiel, and she bore him Phinehas. These are the heads of the fathers' houses of the Levites by their clans.

[26]These are the Aaron and Moses to whom the LORD said: "Bring out the people of Israel from the land of Egypt by their hosts." [27]It was they who spoke to Pharaoh king of Egypt about bringing out the people of Israel from Egypt, this Moses and this Aaron.

[28]On the day when the LORD spoke to Moses in the land of Egypt, [29]the LORD said to Moses, "I am the LORD; tell Pharaoh king of Egypt all that I say to you." [30]But Moses said to the LORD, "Behold, I am of uncircumcised lips. How will Pharaoh listen to me?"

7 And the LORD said to Moses, "See, I have made you like God to Pharaoh, and your brother Aaron shall be your prophet. [2]You shall speak all that I command you, and your brother Aaron shall tell Pharaoh to let the people of Israel go out of his land. [3]But I will harden Pharaoh's heart, and though I multiply my signs and wonders in the land of Egypt, [4]Pharaoh will not listen to you. Then I will lay my hand on Egypt and bring my hosts, my people the children of Israel, out of the land of Egypt by great acts of judgment. [5]The Egyptians shall know that I am the LORD, when I stretch out my hand against Egypt and bring out the people of Israel from among them." [6]Moses and Aaron did so; they did just as the LORD commanded them. [7]Now Moses was eighty years old, and Aaron eighty-three years old, when they spoke to Pharaoh.

[8]Then the LORD said to Moses and Aaron, [9]"When Pharaoh says to you, 'Prove yourselves by working a miracle,' then you shall say to Aaron, 'Take your staff and

cast it down before Pharaoh, that it may become a serpent.'" ¹⁰So Moses and Aaron
went to Pharaoh and did just as the LORD commanded. Aaron cast down his staff
before Pharaoh and his servants, and it became a serpent. ¹¹Then Pharaoh summoned the wise men and the sorcerers, and they, the magicians of Egypt, also did the
same by their secret arts. ¹²For each man cast down his staff, and they became serpents. But Aaron's staff swallowed up their staffs. ¹³Still Pharaoh's heart was hardened, and he would not listen to them, as the LORD had said.

The plagues begin: blood, frogs, gnats [7:14–8:19]. By the time Pharaoh finally let
God's people go, the land of Egypt was struck with ten mighty blows (which is what the
word for plague means in Latin). The story of these plagues has affinities with the narrative genre of the horror story. The first nine plagues come in groups of three, in which
the first plague begins when Moses meets Pharaoh early in the morning (plagues 1, 4,
and 7), the second plague begins when Moses meets Pharaoh at his palace (plagues 2,
5, and 8), and the third plague begins without any warning at all (plagues 3, 6, and 9).
The literary effect of this pattern is to highlight the tenth and deadliest plague. Each
plague serves as a judgment against one or more of Egypt's gods (see 12:12). For example, by turning the Nile into blood, God defeats Hapi, Khnum, and the other river gods
that the Egyptians depended on for their financial prosperity. Similarly, the plague of
frogs demonstrates God's power over Heqet, the goddess of fertility and rebirth, who was
typically portrayed as a frog. Already in the first three plagues (blood, frogs, gnats) we
begin to see some progress in the response of the Egyptians. Somehow Pharaoh's magicians are able to replicate the miracles of the blood and the frogs (7:22; 8:7), but they
are confounded by the gnats, which they freely acknowledge as an act of God (8:18–19).
Pharaoh is still not willing to let God's people go, but when the frogs begin to hop up
on his royal person (see 8:4), he does at least ask Moses and Aaron for their prayers
(8:8–12). Is his hard heart starting to soften?

¹⁴Then the LORD said to Moses, "Pharaoh's heart is hardened; he refuses to let the
people go. ¹⁵Go to Pharaoh in the morning, as he is going out to the water. Stand on
the bank of the Nile to meet him, and take in your hand the staff that turned into a
serpent. ¹⁶And you shall say to him, 'The LORD, the God of the Hebrews, sent me to
you, saying, "Let my people go, that they may serve me in the wilderness. But so far,
you have not obeyed." ¹⁷Thus says the LORD, "By this you shall know that I am the
LORD: behold, with the staff that is in my hand I will strike the water that is in the
Nile, and it shall turn into blood. ¹⁸The fish in the Nile shall die, and the Nile will
stink, and the Egyptians will grow weary of drinking water from the Nile.'"' ¹⁹And the
LORD said to Moses, "Say to Aaron, 'Take your staff and stretch out your hand over the
waters of Egypt, over their rivers, their canals, and their ponds, and all their pools of
water, so that they may become blood, and there shall be blood throughout all the
land of Egypt, even in vessels of wood and in vessels of stone.'"

²⁰Moses and Aaron did as the LORD commanded. In the sight of Pharaoh and in
the sight of his servants he lifted up the staff and struck the water in the Nile, and all
the water in the Nile turned into blood. ²¹And the fish in the Nile died, and the Nile
stank, so that the Egyptians could not drink water from the Nile. There was blood
throughout all the land of Egypt. ²²But the magicians of Egypt did the same by their
secret arts. So Pharaoh's heart remained hardened, and he would not listen to them,

as the LORD had said. ²³Pharaoh turned and went into his house, and he did not take even this to heart. ²⁴And all the Egyptians dug along the Nile for water to drink, for they could not drink the water of the Nile.

²⁵Seven full days passed after the LORD had struck the Nile.

8 ¹ Then the LORD said to Moses, "Go in to Pharaoh and say to him, 'Thus says the LORD, "Let my people go, that they may serve me. ²But if you refuse to let them go, behold, I will plague all your country with frogs. ³The Nile shall swarm with frogs that shall come up into your house and into your bedroom and on your bed and into the houses of your servants and your people,² and into your ovens and your kneading bowls. ⁴The frogs shall come up on you and on your people and on all your servants."'" ⁵³ And the LORD said to Moses, "Say to Aaron, 'Stretch out your hand with your staff over the rivers, over the canals and over the pools, and make frogs come up on the land of Egypt!'" ⁶So Aaron stretched out his hand over the waters of Egypt, and the frogs came up and covered the land of Egypt. ⁷But the magicians did the same by their secret arts and made frogs come up on the land of Egypt.

⁸Then Pharaoh called Moses and Aaron and said, "Plead with the LORD to take away the frogs from me and from my people, and I will let the people go to sacrifice to the LORD." ⁹Moses said to Pharaoh, "Be pleased to command me when I am to plead for you and for your servants and for your people, that the frogs be cut off from you and your houses and be left only in the Nile." ¹⁰And he said, "Tomorrow." Moses said, "Be it as you say, so that you may know that there is no one like the LORD our God. ¹¹The frogs shall go away from you and your houses and your servants and your people. They shall be left only in the Nile." ¹²So Moses and Aaron went out from Pharaoh, and Moses cried to the LORD about the frogs, as he had agreed with Pharaoh.⁴ ¹³And the LORD did according to the word of Moses. The frogs died out in the houses, the courtyards, and the fields. ¹⁴And they gathered them together in heaps, and the land stank. ¹⁵But when Pharaoh saw that there was a respite, he hardened his heart and would not listen to them, as the LORD had said.

¹⁶Then the LORD said to Moses, "Say to Aaron, 'Stretch out your staff and strike the dust of the earth, so that it may become gnats in all the land of Egypt.'" ¹⁷And they did so. Aaron stretched out his hand with his staff and struck the dust of the earth, and there were gnats on man and beast. All the dust of the earth became gnats in all the land of Egypt. ¹⁸The magicians tried by their secret arts to produce gnats, but they could not. So there were gnats on man and beast. ¹⁹Then the magicians said to Pharaoh, "This is the finger of God." But Pharaoh's heart was hardened, and he would not listen to them, as the LORD had said.

Flies, disease, boils [8:20–9:12]. The second cycle of three plagues begins with another early morning encounter. By now these disaster narratives are following a predictable literary pattern: Moses demands freedom for God's people, Pharaoh refuses, God strikes Egypt with a plague, Pharaoh makes a false concession, Moses intercedes for the Egyptians, God relents, Pharaoh hardens his heart and refuses to let God's people go. However, the circumstances of each plague are unique, and the basic pattern serves to highlight the differences. The accounts of the fourth and fifth plagues make it clear that God's own people were miraculously spared from suffering flies (see 8:22–23)

---

¹ Ch 7:26 in Hebrew ² Or *among your people* ³ Ch 8:1 in Hebrew ⁴ Or *which he had brought upon Pharaoh*

or a disease on their livestock (see 9:4–6). The fourth plague account is distinguished by Pharaoh's attempt to negotiate with Moses; Israel's antagonist is looking for some bargaining room, but he is not yet ready to give in to God's demand. At the end of each plague Pharaoh's heart is as hard as ever, both by his own choice (see 8:32) and by God's sovereign will (see 9:12). Suspense continues to be an important quality of the narrative, as the reader wonders when God's people will ever escape from Egypt.

²⁰Then the LORD said to Moses, "Rise up early in the morning and present yourself to Pharaoh, as he goes out to the water, and say to him, 'Thus says the LORD, "Let my people go, that they may serve me. ²¹Or else, if you will not let my people go, behold, I will send swarms of flies on you and your servants and your people, and into your houses. And the houses of the Egyptians shall be filled with swarms of flies, and also the ground on which they stand. ²²But on that day I will set apart the land of Goshen, where my people dwell, so that no swarms of flies shall be there, that you may know that I am the LORD in the midst of the earth.¹ ²³Thus I will put a division² between my people and your people. Tomorrow this sign shall happen."'" ²⁴And the LORD did so. There came great swarms of flies into the house of Pharaoh and into his servants' houses. Throughout all the land of Egypt the land was ruined by the swarms of flies.

²⁵Then Pharaoh called Moses and Aaron and said, "Go, sacrifice to your God within the land." ²⁶But Moses said, "It would not be right to do so, for the offerings we shall sacrifice to the LORD our God are an abomination to the Egyptians. If we sacrifice offerings abominable to the Egyptians before their eyes, will they not stone us? ²⁷We must go three days' journey into the wilderness and sacrifice to the LORD our God as he tells us." ²⁸So Pharaoh said, "I will let you go to sacrifice to the LORD your God in the wilderness; only you must not go very far away. Plead for me." ²⁹Then Moses said, "Behold, I am going out from you and I will plead with the LORD that the swarms of flies may depart from Pharaoh, from his servants, and from his people, tomorrow. Only let not Pharaoh cheat again by not letting the people go to sacrifice to the LORD." ³⁰So Moses went out from Pharaoh and prayed to the LORD. ³¹And the LORD did as Moses asked, and removed the swarms of flies from Pharaoh, from his servants, and from his people; not one remained. ³²But Pharaoh hardened his heart this time also, and did not let the people go.

9 Then the LORD said to Moses, "Go in to Pharaoh and say to him, 'Thus says the LORD, the God of the Hebrews, "Let my people go, that they may serve me. ²For if you refuse to let them go and still hold them, ³behold, the hand of the LORD will fall with a very severe plague upon your livestock that are in the field, the horses, the donkeys, the camels, the herds, and the flocks. ⁴But the LORD will make a distinction between the livestock of Israel and the livestock of Egypt, so that nothing of all that belongs to the people of Israel shall die."'" ⁵And the LORD set a time, saying, "Tomorrow the LORD will do this thing in the land." ⁶And the next day the LORD did this thing. All the livestock of the Egyptians died, but not one of the livestock of the people of Israel died. ⁷And Pharaoh sent, and behold, not one of the livestock of Israel was dead. But the heart of Pharaoh was hardened, and he did not let the people go.

⁸And the LORD said to Moses and Aaron, "Take handfuls of soot from the kiln, and let Moses throw them in the air in the sight of Pharaoh. ⁹It shall become fine dust

---

¹ Or that I the LORD am in the land ² Septuagint, Vulgate; Hebrew *set redemption*

over all the land of Egypt, and become boils breaking out in sores on man and beast throughout all the land of Egypt." ¹⁰So they took soot from the kiln and stood before Pharaoh. And Moses threw it in the air, and it became boils breaking out in sores on man and beast. ¹¹And the magicians could not stand before Moses because of the boils, for the boils came upon the magicians and upon all the Egyptians. ¹²But the LORD hardened the heart of Pharaoh, and he did not listen to them, as the LORD had spoken to Moses.

Hail, locusts, darkness [9:13–10:29]. Although most of the plagues come in the form of naturally occurring phenomena, their intensity and timing (typically both the onset of the plague and its removal are prophesied in advance) clearly indicate that they are miraculous disasters. Before the plague of hail strikes, some of Pharaoh's servants get their livestock to safety; God is starting to make believers out of them. Pharaoh himself is not a believer, but this time he goes so far as to confess that he has sinned against God (9:27). Yet this confession, too, turns out to be false. The eighth plague (locusts) begins with God's reminding Moses why he is afflicting Egypt with all these plagues: for generations to come, his people will know that he is God (10:1–2). Here there are signs that Pharaoh is weakening. When his servants plead with him to let God's people go, he at least considers the possibility, if only until he discovers that the Israelites intend to take their women and children with them (10:7–11). Also, this time his words of repentance (however insincere) are more emphatic (10:16–20). The ninth plague (three days of absolute darkness) held special horror for the Egyptians, whose supreme deities were the gods and goddesses of the sun (Aten, Re, Atum). This time the sticking point in the negotiations for Israel's release is the livestock, which Pharaoh demands that the Israelites leave behind (10:24–29). If it's not one excuse for the despot of Egypt, it's another.

¹³Then the LORD said to Moses, "Rise up early in the morning and present yourself before Pharaoh and say to him, 'Thus says the LORD, the God of the Hebrews, "Let my people go, that they may serve me. ¹⁴For this time I will send all my plagues on you yourself,[1] and on your servants and your people, so that you may know that there is none like me in all the earth. ¹⁵For by now I could have put out my hand and struck you and your people with pestilence, and you would have been cut off from the earth. ¹⁶But for this purpose I have raised you up, to show you my power, so that my name may be proclaimed in all the earth. ¹⁷You are still exalting yourself against my people and will not let them go. ¹⁸Behold, about this time tomorrow I will cause very heavy hail to fall, such as never has been in Egypt from the day it was founded until now. ¹⁹Now therefore send, get your livestock and all that you have in the field into safe shelter, for every man and beast that is in the field and is not brought home will die when the hail falls on them."'" ²⁰Then whoever feared the word of the LORD among the servants of Pharaoh hurried his slaves and his livestock into the houses, ²¹but whoever did not pay attention to the word of the LORD left his slaves and his livestock in the field.

²²Then the LORD said to Moses, "Stretch out your hand toward heaven, so that there may be hail in all the land of Egypt, on man and beast and every plant of the field, in the land of Egypt." ²³Then Moses stretched out his staff toward heaven, and the LORD sent thunder and hail, and fire ran down to the earth. And the LORD rained hail upon

---

[1] Hebrew *on your heart*

the land of Egypt. ²⁴There was hail and fire flashing continually in the midst of the hail, very heavy hail, such as had never been in all the land of Egypt since it became a nation. ²⁵The hail struck down everything that was in the field in all the land of Egypt, both man and beast. And the hail struck down every plant of the field and broke every tree of the field. ²⁶Only in the land of Goshen, where the people of Israel were, was there no hail.

²⁷Then Pharaoh sent and called Moses and Aaron and said to them, "This time I have sinned; the Lord is in the right, and I and my people are in the wrong. ²⁸Plead with the Lord, for there has been enough of God's thunder and hail. I will let you go, and you shall stay no longer." ²⁹Moses said to him, "As soon as I have gone out of the city, I will stretch out my hands to the Lord. The thunder will cease, and there will be no more hail, so that you may know that the earth is the Lord's. ³⁰But as for you and your servants, I know that you do not yet fear the Lord God." ³¹(The flax and the barley were struck down, for the barley was in the ear and the flax was in bud. ³²But the wheat and the emmer¹ were not struck down, for they are late in coming up.) ³³So Moses went out of the city from Pharaoh and stretched out his hands to the Lord, and the thunder and the hail ceased, and the rain no longer poured upon the earth. ³⁴But when Pharaoh saw that the rain and the hail and the thunder had ceased, he sinned yet again and hardened his heart, he and his servants. ³⁵So the heart of Pharaoh was hardened, and he did not let the people of Israel go, just as the Lord had spoken through Moses.

10 Then the Lord said to Moses, "Go in to Pharaoh, for I have hardened his heart and the heart of his servants, that I may show these signs of mine among them, ²and that you may tell in the hearing of your son and of your grandson how I have dealt harshly with the Egyptians and what signs I have done among them, that you may know that I am the Lord."

³So Moses and Aaron went in to Pharaoh and said to him, "Thus says the Lord, the God of the Hebrews, 'How long will you refuse to humble yourself before me? Let my people go, that they may serve me. ⁴For if you refuse to let my people go, behold, tomorrow I will bring locusts into your country, ⁵and they shall cover the face of the land, so that no one can see the land. And they shall eat what is left to you after the hail, and they shall eat every tree of yours that grows in the field, ⁶and they shall fill your houses and the houses of all your servants and of all the Egyptians, as neither your fathers nor your grandfathers have seen, from the day they came on earth to this day.'" Then he turned and went out from Pharaoh.

⁷Then Pharaoh's servants said to him, "How long shall this man be a snare to us? Let the men go, that they may serve the Lord their God. Do you not yet understand that Egypt is ruined?" ⁸So Moses and Aaron were brought back to Pharaoh. And he said to them, "Go, serve the Lord your God. But which ones are to go?" ⁹Moses said, "We will go with our young and our old. We will go with our sons and daughters and with our flocks and herds, for we must hold a feast to the Lord." ¹⁰But he said to them, "The Lord be with you, if ever I let you and your little ones go! Look, you have some evil purpose in mind.² ¹¹No! Go, the men among you, and serve the Lord, for that is what you are asking." And they were driven out from Pharaoh's presence.

¹²Then the Lord said to Moses, "Stretch out your hand over the land of Egypt for the locusts, so that they may come upon the land of Egypt and eat every plant in the

¹ A type of wheat ² Hebrew *before your face*

land, all that the hail has left." ¹³So Moses stretched out his staff over the land of Egypt, and the LORD brought an east wind upon the land all that day and all that night. When it was morning, the east wind had brought the locusts. ¹⁴The locusts came up over all the land of Egypt and settled on the whole country of Egypt, such a dense swarm of locusts as had never been before, nor ever will be again. ¹⁵They covered the face of the whole land, so that the land was darkened, and they ate all the plants in the land and all the fruit of the trees that the hail had left. Not a green thing remained, neither tree nor plant of the field, through all the land of Egypt. ¹⁶Then Pharaoh hastily called Moses and Aaron and said, "I have sinned against the LORD your God, and against you. ¹⁷Now therefore, forgive my sin, please, only this once, and plead with the LORD your God only to remove this death from me." ¹⁸So he went out from Pharaoh and pleaded with the LORD. ¹⁹And the LORD turned the wind into a very strong west wind, which lifted the locusts and drove them into the Red Sea. Not a single locust was left in all the country of Egypt. ²⁰But the LORD hardened Pharaoh's heart, and he did not let the people of Israel go.

²¹Then the LORD said to Moses, "Stretch out your hand toward heaven, that there may be darkness over the land of Egypt, a darkness to be felt." ²²So Moses stretched out his hand toward heaven, and there was pitch darkness in all the land of Egypt three days. ²³They did not see one another, nor did anyone rise from his place for three days, but all the people of Israel had light where they lived. ²⁴Then Pharaoh called Moses and said, "Go, serve the LORD; your little ones also may go with you; only let your flocks and your herds remain behind." ²⁵But Moses said, "You must also let us have sacrifices and burnt offerings, that we may sacrifice to the LORD our God. ²⁶Our livestock also must go with us; not a hoof shall be left behind, for we must take of them to serve the LORD our God, and we do not know with what we must serve the LORD until we arrive there." ²⁷But the LORD hardened Pharaoh's heart, and he would not let them go. ²⁸Then Pharaoh said to him, "Get away from me; take care never to see my face again, for on the day you see my face you shall die." ²⁹Moses said, "As you say! I will not see your face again."

The deadliest plague [11:1–12:30]. The last plague is the deadliest, and also the one that finally proves effective for Israel's deliverance: the death of every firstborn son in Egypt. The angel of death will also visit the people of God, but for them there will be a way of escape through the spotless blood of a sacrificial lamb. When God sees the saving blood smeared on their doorposts as a sign of atonement, he will pass over them in safety. The lengthy description of the first Passover (12:1–28) is a story of origins, in which God institutes a sacramental festival (Passover and the Feast of Unleavened Bread) and explains its ongoing significance for Israel (see 12:14–27). The death of the firstborn (12:29–30) is reported with a minimum of detail, allowing the horror of the deadly plague to speak for itself.

11 The LORD said to Moses, "Yet one plague more I will bring upon Pharaoh and upon Egypt. Afterward he will let you go from here. When he lets you go, he will drive you away completely. ²Speak now in the hearing of the people, that they ask, every man of his neighbor and every woman of her neighbor, for silver and gold jewelry." ³And the LORD gave the people favor in the sight of the Egyptians. Moreover, the man Moses was very great in the land of Egypt, in the sight of Pharaoh's servants and in the sight of the people.

⁴So Moses said, "Thus says the LORD: About midnight I will go out in the midst of Egypt, ⁵and every firstborn in the land of Egypt shall die, from the firstborn of Pharaoh who sits on his throne, even to the firstborn of the slave girl who is behind the handmill, and all the firstborn of the cattle. ⁶There shall be a great cry throughout all the land of Egypt, such as there has never been, nor ever will be again. ⁷But not a dog shall growl against any of the people of Israel, either man or beast, that you may know that the LORD makes a distinction between Egypt and Israel. ⁸And all these your servants shall come down to me and bow down to me, saying, 'Get out, you and all the people who follow you.' And after that I will go out." And he went out from Pharaoh in hot anger. ⁹Then the LORD said to Moses, "Pharaoh will not listen to you, that my wonders may be multiplied in the land of Egypt."

¹⁰Moses and Aaron did all these wonders before Pharaoh, and the LORD hardened Pharaoh's heart, and he did not let the people of Israel go out of his land.

12 The LORD said to Moses and Aaron in the land of Egypt, ²"This month shall be for you the beginning of months. It shall be the first month of the year for you. ³Tell all the congregation of Israel that on the tenth day of this month every man shall take a lamb according to their fathers' houses, a lamb for a household. ⁴And if the household is too small for a lamb, then he and his nearest neighbor shall take according to the number of persons; according to what each can eat you shall make your count for the lamb. ⁵Your lamb shall be without blemish, a male a year old. You may take it from the sheep or from the goats, ⁶and you shall keep it until the fourteenth day of this month, when the whole assembly of the congregation of Israel shall kill their lambs at twilight.¹

⁷"Then they shall take some of the blood and put it on the two doorposts and the lintel of the houses in which they eat it. ⁸They shall eat the flesh that night, roasted on the fire; with unleavened bread and bitter herbs they shall eat it. ⁹Do not eat any of it raw or boiled in water, but roasted, its head with its legs and its inner parts. ¹⁰And you shall let none of it remain until the morning; anything that remains until the morning you shall burn. ¹¹In this manner you shall eat it: with your belt fastened, your sandals on your feet, and your staff in your hand. And you shall eat it in haste. It is the LORD's Passover. ¹²For I will pass through the land of Egypt that night, and I will strike all the firstborn in the land of Egypt, both man and beast; and on all the gods of Egypt I will execute judgments: I am the LORD. ¹³The blood shall be a sign for you, on the houses where you are. And when I see the blood, I will pass over you, and no plague will befall you to destroy you, when I strike the land of Egypt.

¹⁴"This day shall be for you a memorial day, and you shall keep it as a feast to the LORD; throughout your generations, as a statute forever, you shall keep it as a feast. ¹⁵Seven days you shall eat unleavened bread. On the first day you shall remove leaven out of your houses, for if anyone eats what is leavened, from the first day until the seventh day, that person shall be cut off from Israel. ¹⁶On the first day you shall hold a holy assembly, and on the seventh day a holy assembly. No work shall be done on those days. But what everyone needs to eat, that alone may be prepared by you. ¹⁷And you shall observe the Feast of Unleavened Bread, for on this very day I brought your hosts out of the land of Egypt. Therefore you shall observe this day, throughout

---

¹ Hebrew *between the two evenings*

your generations, as a statute forever. [18]In the first month, from the fourteenth day of the month at evening, you shall eat unleavened bread until the twenty-first day of the month at evening. [19]For seven days no leaven is to be found in your houses. If anyone eats what is leavened, that person will be cut off from the congregation of Israel, whether he is a sojourner or a native of the land. [20]You shall eat nothing leavened; in all your dwelling places you shall eat unleavened bread."

[21]Then Moses called all the elders of Israel and said to them, "Go and select lambs for yourselves according to your clans, and kill the Passover lamb. [22]Take a bunch of hyssop and dip it in the blood that is in the basin, and touch the lintel and the two doorposts with the blood that is in the basin. None of you shall go out of the door of his house until the morning. [23]For the LORD will pass through to strike the Egyptians, and when he sees the blood on the lintel and on the two doorposts, the LORD will pass over the door and will not allow the destroyer to enter your houses to strike you. [24]You shall observe this rite as a statute for you and for your sons forever. [25]And when you come to the land that the LORD will give you, as he has promised, you shall keep this service. [26]And when your children say to you, 'What do you mean by this service?' [27]you shall say, 'It is the sacrifice of the LORD's Passover, for he passed over the houses of the people of Israel in Egypt, when he struck the Egyptians but spared our houses.'" And the people bowed their heads and worshiped.

[28]Then the people of Israel went and did so; as the LORD had commanded Moses and Aaron, so they did.

[29]At midnight the LORD struck down all the firstborn in the land of Egypt, from the firstborn of Pharaoh who sat on his throne to the firstborn of the captive who was in the dungeon, and all the firstborn of the livestock. [30]And Pharaoh rose up in the night, he and all his servants and all the Egyptians. And there was a great cry in Egypt, for there was not a house where someone was not dead.

Out of Egypt [12:31–13:22]. The long-awaited exodus begins with Pharaoh's sharp dismissal, Israel's hasty departure, and the plundering of silver and gold from the Egyptians—an act of *poetic justice. This escape narrative has the didactic purpose of explaining important traditions in Israel, such as eating unleavened bread at Passover (see 12:39, 43–49; 13:3–10) and consecrating every firstborn son (13:1–2, 11–16). Although these explanations disrupt the dramatic flow of the narrative to some extent, they have the positive purpose of showing the ongoing significance of the exodus for Israel's spiritual life as a nation. The narrator is careful to mention that on the night God led Israel out of Egypt with pillars of cloud and fire, Moses carried the bones of Joseph with him (13:19). This important detail connects Exodus back to Genesis and confirms that God is keeping the covenant promises he made to the patriarchs. The speech of Moses (13:3–16) is a formal oration by the nation's leader, and it serves the purpose of providing an interpretive framework for the surrounding narrative.

[31]Then he summoned Moses and Aaron by night and said, "Up, go out from among my people, both you and the people of Israel; and go, serve the LORD, as you have said. [32]Take your flocks and your herds, as you have said, and be gone, and bless me also!"

[33]The Egyptians were urgent with the people to send them out of the land in haste. For they said, "We shall all be dead." [34]So the people took their dough before it was

leavened, their kneading bowls being bound up in their cloaks on their shoulders.
[35]The people of Israel had also done as Moses told them, for they had asked the
Egyptians for silver and gold jewelry and for clothing. [36]And the LORD had given the
people favor in the sight of the Egyptians, so that they let them have what they asked.
Thus they plundered the Egyptians.

[37]And the people of Israel journeyed from Rameses to Succoth, about six hundred
thousand men on foot, besides women and children. [38]A mixed multitude also went
up with them, and very much livestock, both flocks and herds. [39]And they baked
unleavened cakes of the dough that they had brought out of Egypt, for it was not leavened, because they were thrust out of Egypt and could not wait, nor had they prepared any provisions for themselves.

[40]The time that the people of Israel lived in Egypt was 430 years. [41]At the end of
430 years, on that very day, all the hosts of the LORD went out from the land of Egypt.
[42]It was a night of watching by the LORD, to bring them out of the land of Egypt; so
this same night is a night of watching kept to the LORD by all the people of Israel
throughout their generations.

[43]And the LORD said to Moses and Aaron, "This is the statute of the Passover: no
foreigner shall eat of it, [44]but every slave that is bought for money may eat of it after
you have circumcised him. [45]No foreigner or hired servant may eat of it. [46]It shall be
eaten in one house; you shall not take any of the flesh outside the house, and you
shall not break any of its bones. [47]All the congregation of Israel shall keep it. [48]If a
stranger shall sojourn with you and would keep the Passover to the LORD, let all his
males be circumcised. Then he may come near and keep it; he shall be as a native of
the land. But no uncircumcised person shall eat of it. [49]There shall be one law for the
native and for the stranger who sojourns among you."

[50]All the people of Israel did just as the LORD commanded Moses and Aaron. [51]And
on that very day the LORD brought the people of Israel out of the land of Egypt by
their hosts.

13 The LORD said to Moses, [2]"Consecrate to me all the firstborn. Whatever is the
first to open the womb among the people of Israel, both of man and of beast,
is mine."

[3]Then Moses said to the people, "Remember this day in which you came out from
Egypt, out of the house of slavery, for by a strong hand the LORD brought you out from
this place. No leavened bread shall be eaten. [4]Today, in the month of Abib, you are
going out. [5]And when the LORD brings you into the land of the Canaanites, the
Hittites, the Amorites, the Hivites, and the Jebusites, which he swore to your fathers to
give you, a land flowing with milk and honey, you shall keep this service in this
month. [6]Seven days you shall eat unleavened bread, and on the seventh day there
shall be a feast to the LORD. [7]Unleavened bread shall be eaten for seven days; no leavened bread shall be seen with you, and no leaven shall be seen with you in all your
territory. [8]You shall tell your son on that day, 'It is because of what the LORD did for
me when I came out of Egypt.' [9]And it shall be to you as a sign on your hand and as a
memorial between your eyes, that the law of the LORD may be in your mouth. For with
a strong hand the LORD has brought you out of Egypt. [10]You shall therefore keep this
statute at its appointed time from year to year.

[11]"When the LORD brings you into the land of the Canaanites, as he swore to you

and your fathers, and shall give it to you, ¹²you shall set apart to the LORD all that first opens the womb. All the firstborn of your animals that are males shall be the LORD's. ¹³Every firstborn of a donkey you shall redeem with a lamb, or if you will not redeem it you shall break its neck. Every firstborn of man among your sons you shall redeem. ¹⁴And when in time to come your son asks you, 'What does this mean?' you shall say to him, 'By a strong hand the LORD brought us out of Egypt, from the house of slavery. ¹⁵For when Pharaoh stubbornly refused to let us go, the LORD killed all the firstborn in the land of Egypt, both the firstborn of man and the firstborn of animals. Therefore I sacrifice to the LORD all the males that first open the womb, but all the firstborn of my sons I redeem.' ¹⁶It shall be as a mark on your hand or frontlets between your eyes, for by a strong hand the LORD brought us out of Egypt."

¹⁷When Pharaoh let the people go, God did not lead them by way of the land of the Philistines, although that was near. For God said, "Lest the people change their minds when they see war and return to Egypt." ¹⁸But God led the people around by the way of the wilderness toward the Red Sea. And the people of Israel went up out of the land of Egypt equipped for battle. ¹⁹Moses took the bones of Joseph with him, for Joseph¹ had made the sons of Israel solemnly swear, saying, "God will surely visit you, and you shall carry up my bones with you from here." ²⁰And they moved on from Succoth and encamped at Etham, on the edge of the wilderness. ²¹And the LORD went before them by day in a pillar of cloud to lead them along the way, and by night in a pillar of fire to give them light, that they might travel by day and by night. ²²The pillar of cloud by day and the pillar of fire by night did not depart from before the people.

The great escape [chapter 14]. The main narrative resumes its dramatic pace with Israel's crossing of the Red Sea—a miracle story, battle story, and rescue story all rolled into one. The main players in the drama act according to character. When Pharaoh realizes that he has lost the services of the Israelites, he changes his mind once again, hardens his heart, and pursues them with his armies (vv. 5–9). When the Israelites realize that they are trapped between Pharaoh and the deep blue sea, they turn against Moses for leading them out of Egypt (vv. 10–12). For his part, Moses trusts the Lord to bring the victory and raises his staff to divide the waters (vv. 13–22). The famous miracle of the parting of the Red Sea is at the same time both a mighty act of deliverance for Israel and a mighty act of judgment against Egypt (vv. 23–30). These events are all orchestrated by God to achieve his primary purpose of gaining glory for himself, showing both Egypt and Israel that he is truly Lord (see vv. 4, 18, 31). Based on Israel's response in verse 31, the crossing of the Red Sea is partly a *recognition story in which the people acknowledge the Lord to be their God and Moses to be his prophet.

14 Then the LORD said to Moses, ²"Tell the people of Israel to turn back and encamp in front of Pi-hahiroth, between Migdol and the sea, in front of Baal-zephon; you shall encamp facing it, by the sea. ³For Pharaoh will say of the people of Israel, 'They are wandering in the land; the wilderness has shut them in.' ⁴And I will harden Pharaoh's heart, and he will pursue them, and I will get glory over Pharaoh and all his host, and the Egyptians shall know that I am the LORD." And they did so.

⁵When the king of Egypt was told that the people had fled, the mind of Pharaoh and his servants was changed toward the people, and they said, "What is this we have done, that we have let Israel go from serving us?" ⁶So he made ready his chariot and

¹ Samaritan, Septuagint; Hebrew *he*

took his army with him, [7]and took six hundred chosen chariots and all the other chariots of Egypt with officers over all of them. [8]And the LORD hardened the heart of Pharaoh king of Egypt, and he pursued the people of Israel while the people of Israel were going out defiantly. [9]The Egyptians pursued them, all Pharaoh's horses and chariots and his horsemen and his army, and overtook them encamped at the sea, by Pi-hahiroth, in front of Baal-zephon.

[10]When Pharaoh drew near, the people of Israel lifted up their eyes, and behold, the Egyptians were marching after them, and they feared greatly. And the people of Israel cried out to the LORD. [11]They said to Moses, "Is it because there are no graves in Egypt that you have taken us away to die in the wilderness? What have you done to us in bringing us out of Egypt? [12]Is not this what we said to you in Egypt: 'Leave us alone that we may serve the Egyptians'? For it would have been better for us to serve the Egyptians than to die in the wilderness." [13]And Moses said to the people, "Fear not, stand firm, and see the salvation of the LORD, which he will work for you today. For the Egyptians whom you see today, you shall never see again. [14]The LORD will fight for you, and you have only to be silent."

[15]The LORD said to Moses, "Why do you cry to me? Tell the people of Israel to go forward. [16]Lift up your staff, and stretch out your hand over the sea and divide it, that the people of Israel may go through the sea on dry ground. [17]And I will harden the hearts of the Egyptians so that they shall go in after them, and I will get glory over Pharaoh and all his host, his chariots, and his horsemen. [18]And the Egyptians shall know that I am the LORD, when I have gotten glory over Pharaoh, his chariots, and his horsemen."

[19]Then the angel of God who was going before the host of Israel moved and went behind them, and the pillar of cloud moved from before them and stood behind them, [20]coming between the host of Egypt and the host of Israel. And there was the cloud and the darkness. And it lit up the night[1] without one coming near the other all night.

[21]Then Moses stretched out his hand over the sea, and the LORD drove the sea back by a strong east wind all night and made the sea dry land, and the waters were divided. [22]And the people of Israel went into the midst of the sea on dry ground, the waters being a wall to them on their right hand and on their left. [23]The Egyptians pursued and went in after them into the midst of the sea, all Pharaoh's horses, his chariots, and his horsemen. [24]And in the morning watch the LORD in the pillar of fire and of cloud looked down on the Egyptian forces and threw the Egyptian forces into a panic, [25]clogging[2] their chariot wheels so that they drove heavily. And the Egyptians said, "Let us flee from before Israel, for the LORD fights for them against the Egyptians."

[26]Then the LORD said to Moses, "Stretch out your hand over the sea, that the water may come back upon the Egyptians, upon their chariots, and upon their horsemen." [27]So Moses stretched out his hand over the sea, and the sea returned to its normal course when the morning appeared. And as the Egyptians fled into it, the LORD threw[3] the Egyptians into the midst of the sea. [28]The waters returned and covered the chariots and the horsemen; of all the host of Pharaoh that had followed them into the sea, not one of them remained. [29]But the people of Israel walked on dry ground through the sea, the waters being a wall to them on their right hand and on their left.

[30]Thus the LORD saved Israel that day from the hand of the Egyptians, and Israel saw the Egyptians dead on the seashore. [31]Israel saw the great power that the LORD

---

[1] Septuagint *and the night passed* [2] Or *binding* (compare Samaritan, Septuagint, Syriac); Hebrew *removing* [3] Hebrew *shook off*

used against the Egyptians, so the people feared the LORD, and they believed in the LORD and in his servant Moses.

> **The song of Moses and of Miriam** [15:1–21]. The story of Israel's salvation becomes a musical as first Moses and then Miriam lead the people in a song of triumph. After opening statements of praise (vv. 1–3), Moses uses vivid imagery to describe how Pharaoh's horses and riders met their doom at the bottom of the sea (vv. 4–12). As the divine warrior, God is praised both for delivering his people the Israelites and for destroying his enemies the Egyptians. The last section of the poem looks ahead to Israel's return to the Promised Land and eventual resettlement on God's mountain (vv. 13–18). Miriam's exuberant refrain is accompanied with tambourines and dancing. The song of Moses and of Miriam is neither an interlude nor an interruption. Rather, it is the very reason God saved his people: so that he would receive the glory of their praise. If we compare this poetic account of the Red Sea deliverance with the factual, prose narrative version of the same events, we see how *metaphoric, *hyperbolic, and nonliteral biblical poetry can be. Whereas chapter 14 presents a continuous flow of action, highlighted by the connectives *then* and *and*, the poetic version gives us a kaleidoscope of impressionistic snapshots.

15 Then Moses and the people of Israel sang this song to the LORD, saying,

"I will sing to the LORD, for he has triumphed gloriously;
  the horse and his rider[1] he has thrown into the sea.
2   The LORD is my strength and my song,
  and he has become my salvation;
 this is my God, and I will praise him,
  my father's God, and I will exalt him.
3   The LORD is a man of war;
  the LORD is his name.

4   "Pharaoh's chariots and his host he cast into the sea,
  and his chosen officers were sunk in the Red Sea.
5   The floods covered them;
  they went down into the depths like a stone.
6   Your right hand, O LORD, glorious in power,
  your right hand, O LORD, shatters the enemy.
7   In the greatness of your majesty you overthrow your adversaries;
  you send out your fury; it consumes them like stubble.
8   At the blast of your nostrils the waters piled up;
  the floods stood up in a heap;
  the deeps congealed in the heart of the sea.
9   The enemy said, 'I will pursue, I will overtake,
  I will divide the spoil, my desire shall have its fill of them.
  I will draw my sword; my hand shall destroy them.'
10   You blew with your wind; the sea covered them;
  they sank like lead in the mighty waters.

---

[1] Or *its chariot*; also verse 21

11 "Who is like you, O LORD, among the gods?
    Who is like you, majestic in holiness,
    awesome in glorious deeds, doing wonders?
12 You stretched out your right hand;
    the earth swallowed them.

13 "You have led in your steadfast love the people whom you have redeemed;
    you have guided them by your strength to your holy abode.
14 The peoples have heard; they tremble;
    pangs have seized the inhabitants of Philistia.
15 Now are the chiefs of Edom dismayed;
    trembling seizes the leaders of Moab;
    all the inhabitants of Canaan have melted away.
16 Terror and dread fall upon them;
    because of the greatness of your arm, they are still as a stone,
till your people, O LORD, pass by,
    till the people pass by whom you have purchased.
17 You will bring them in and plant them on your own mountain,
    the place, O LORD, which you have made for your abode,
    the sanctuary, O Lord, which your hands have established.
18 The LORD will reign forever and ever."

19 For when the horses of Pharaoh with his chariots and his horsemen went into the sea, the LORD brought back the waters of the sea upon them, but the people of Israel walked on dry ground in the midst of the sea. 20 Then Miriam the prophetess, the sister of Aaron, took a tambourine in her hand, and all the women went out after her with tambourines and dancing. 21 And Miriam sang to them:

"Sing to the LORD, for he has triumphed gloriously;
    the horse and his rider he has thrown into the sea."

Pilgrims through this barren land [15:22–16:36]. Israel's journey from the house of bondage to the mountain of God goes through the wilderness—a place of testing (see 16:4). Although the people's basic needs on this pilgrimage are physical (food and water), their temptations are spiritual. Will they trust God to meet their needs? Will they rest content with what he provides? God does indeed provide sweet water and daily bread, showing his glory (see 16:7, 10), but not before the people grumble about his meal plan, longing for the meats and spices of Egypt. The manna God sends from heaven is delivered according to a weekly schedule that includes a Sabbath. The people's failure to follow this routine (see 16:20, 27–29) shows their lack of contentment and faith and introduces the basic pattern for Israel's wanderings in the wilderness over the next forty years: although God faithfully provides, his people constantly complain. At every point we are aware that we are reading an epic—the story of a journeying nation that in the progress of its pilgrimage is being formed as a national entity.

22 Then Moses made Israel set out from the Red Sea, and they went into the wilderness of Shur. They went three days in the wilderness and found no water. 23 When they came to Marah, they could not drink the water of Marah because it was bitter;

therefore it was named Marah.[1] [24]And the people grumbled against Moses, saying, "What shall we drink?" [25]And he cried to the LORD, and the LORD showed him a log,[2] and he threw it into the water, and the water became sweet.

There the LORD[3] made for them a statute and a rule, and there he tested them, [26]saying, "If you will diligently listen to the voice of the LORD your God, and do that which is right in his eyes, and give ear to his commandments and keep all his statutes, I will put none of the diseases on you that I put on the Egyptians, for I am the LORD, your healer."

[27]Then they came to Elim, where there were twelve springs of water and seventy palm trees, and they encamped there by the water.

16

They set out from Elim, and all the congregation of the people of Israel came to the wilderness of Sin, which is between Elim and Sinai, on the fifteenth day of the second month after they had departed from the land of Egypt. [2]And the whole congregation of the people of Israel grumbled against Moses and Aaron in the wilderness, [3]and the people of Israel said to them, "Would that we had died by the hand of the LORD in the land of Egypt, when we sat by the meat pots and ate bread to the full, for you have brought us out into this wilderness to kill this whole assembly with hunger."

[4]Then the LORD said to Moses, "Behold, I am about to rain bread from heaven for you, and the people shall go out and gather a day's portion every day, that I may test them, whether they will walk in my law or not. [5]On the sixth day, when they prepare what they bring in, it will be twice as much as they gather daily." [6]So Moses and Aaron said to all the people of Israel, "At evening you shall know that it was the LORD who brought you out of the land of Egypt, [7]and in the morning you shall see the glory of the LORD, because he has heard your grumbling against the LORD. For what are we, that you grumble against us?" [8]And Moses said, "When the LORD gives you in the evening meat to eat and in the morning bread to the full, because the LORD has heard your grumbling that you grumble against him—what are we? Your grumbling is not against us but against the LORD."

[9]Then Moses said to Aaron, "Say to the whole congregation of the people of Israel, 'Come near before the LORD, for he has heard your grumbling.'" [10]And as soon as Aaron spoke to the whole congregation of the people of Israel, they looked toward the wilderness, and behold, the glory of the LORD appeared in the cloud. [11]And the LORD said to Moses, [12]"I have heard the grumbling of the people of Israel. Say to them, 'At twilight you shall eat meat, and in the morning you shall be filled with bread. Then you shall know that I am the LORD your God.'"

[13]In the evening quail came up and covered the camp, and in the morning dew lay around the camp. [14]And when the dew had gone up, there was on the face of the wilderness a fine, flake-like thing, fine as frost on the ground. [15]When the people of Israel saw it, they said to one another, "What is it?"[4] For they did not know what it was. And Moses said to them, "It is the bread that the LORD has given you to eat. [16]This is what the LORD has commanded: 'Gather of it, each one of you, as much as he can eat. You shall each take an omer,[5] according to the number of the persons that each of you has in his tent.'" [17]And the people of Israel did so. They gathered, some more, some less. [18]But when they measured it with an omer, whoever gathered much had nothing left over, and whoever gathered little had no lack. Each of them gathered as much as he

---

[1] *Marah* means *bitterness* [2] Or *tree* [3] Hebrew *he* [4] Or *"It is manna."* Hebrew *man hu* [5] An *omer* was about 2 quarts or 2 liters

could eat. ¹⁹And Moses said to them, "Let no one leave any of it over till the morning."
²⁰But they did not listen to Moses. Some left part of it till the morning, and it bred
worms and stank. And Moses was angry with them. ²¹Morning by morning they gathered it, each as much as he could eat; but when the sun grew hot, it melted.

²²On the sixth day they gathered twice as much bread, two omers each. And when
all the leaders of the congregation came and told Moses, ²³he said to them, "This is
what the LORD has commanded: 'Tomorrow is a day of solemn rest, a holy Sabbath to
the LORD; bake what you will bake and boil what you will boil, and all that is left over
lay aside to be kept till the morning.'" ²⁴So they laid it aside till the morning, as Moses
commanded them, and it did not stink, and there were no worms in it. ²⁵Moses said,
"Eat it today, for today is a Sabbath to the LORD; today you will not find it in the field.
²⁶Six days you shall gather it, but on the seventh day, which is a Sabbath, there will be
none."

²⁷On the seventh day some of the people went out to gather, but they found none.
²⁸And the LORD said to Moses, "How long will you refuse to keep my commandments
and my laws? ²⁹See! The LORD has given you the Sabbath; therefore on the sixth day
he gives you bread for two days. Remain each of you in his place; let no one go out of
his place on the seventh day." ³⁰So the people rested on the seventh day.

³¹Now the house of Israel called its name manna. It was like coriander seed, white,
and the taste of it was like wafers made with honey. ³²Moses said, "This is what the
LORD has commanded: 'Let an omer of it be kept throughout your generations, so that
they may see the bread with which I fed you in the wilderness, when I brought you
out of the land of Egypt.'" ³³And Moses said to Aaron, "Take a jar, and put an omer of
manna in it, and place it before the LORD to be kept throughout your generations."
³⁴As the LORD commanded Moses, so Aaron placed it before the testimony to be kept.
³⁵The people of Israel ate the manna forty years, till they came to a habitable land.
They ate the manna till they came to the border of the land of Canaan. ³⁶(An omer is
the tenth part of an ephah.)¹

Fightings within and fears without [chapter 17]. The grumbling continues at
Rephidim, where the Israelites insist that Moses give them water. Not only do they sin
against God by demanding his provision (v. 2), denying his protection (v. 3), and doubting his presence (v. 7), but they also threaten to kill his prophet (v. 4). In effect, they are
putting Moses (and God) on trial (the word *test* in verses 2 and 7 is the term for a covenant lawsuit). God proves himself by providing water from the rock and also by defeating their enemies in battle, in answer to the prayers of his prophet (vv. 8–16). Israel's
God is as faithful in giving protection as he is in making provision. Variety of adventure
is a particular virtue of the epic of Exodus, as locales shift and the nature of the ordeals
varies. Additionally, the motifs of testing and rescue dominate the story.

17 All the congregation of the people of Israel moved on from the wilderness of
Sin by stages, according to the commandment of the LORD, and camped at
Rephidim, but there was no water for the people to drink. ²Therefore the people
quarreled with Moses and said, "Give us water to drink." And Moses said to them,
"Why do you quarrel with me? Why do you test the LORD?" ³But the people thirsted
there for water, and the people grumbled against Moses and said, "Why did you
bring us up out of Egypt, to kill us and our children and our livestock with thirst?"

¹ An *ephah* was about 3/5 bushel or 22 liters

⁴So Moses cried to the LORD, "What shall I do with this people? They are almost ready to stone me." ⁵And the LORD said to Moses, "Pass on before the people, taking with you some of the elders of Israel, and take in your hand the staff with which you struck the Nile, and go. ⁶Behold, I will stand before you there on the rock at Horeb, and you shall strike the rock, and water shall come out of it, and the people will drink." And Moses did so, in the sight of the elders of Israel. ⁷And he called the name of the place Massah¹ and Meribah,² because of the quarreling of the people of Israel, and because they tested the LORD by saying, "Is the LORD among us or not?"

⁸Then Amalek came and fought with Israel at Rephidim. ⁹So Moses said to Joshua, "Choose for us men, and go out and fight with Amalek. Tomorrow I will stand on the top of the hill with the staff of God in my hand." ¹⁰So Joshua did as Moses told him, and fought with Amalek, while Moses, Aaron, and Hur went up to the top of the hill. ¹¹Whenever Moses held up his hand, Israel prevailed, and whenever he lowered his hand, Amalek prevailed. ¹²But Moses' hands grew weary, so they took a stone and put it under him, and he sat on it, while Aaron and Hur held up his hands, one on one side, and the other on the other side. So his hands were steady until the going down of the sun. ¹³And Joshua overwhelmed Amalek and his people with the sword.

¹⁴Then the LORD said to Moses, "Write this as a memorial in a book and recite it in the ears of Joshua, that I will utterly blot out the memory of Amalek from under heaven." ¹⁵And Moses built an altar and called the name of it, The LORD Is My Banner, ¹⁶saying, "A hand upon the throne³ of the LORD! The LORD will have war with Amalek from generation to generation."

Israel gets reorganized [chapter 18]. This chapter is partly the story of a family reunion between Moses, his wife, and his in-laws. This becomes a conversion story as Moses tells the story of the exodus and his father-in-law Jethro comes to faith in the God of Israel (vv. 8–12). This chapter is also a story of origins, as Moses follows Jethro's advice in establishing seventy elders to help him rule as a judge over Israel—an effective solution to a practical problem in organizational leadership at the national level (vv. 13–27). Epics typically focus on epoch-making events in the formation of a nation, and that is what we find in this chapter as the rudiments of social structure evolve in response to national circumstances.

18 Jethro, the priest of Midian, Moses' father-in-law, heard of all that God had done for Moses and for Israel his people, how the LORD had brought Israel out of Egypt. ²Now Jethro, Moses' father-in-law, had taken Zipporah, Moses' wife, after he had sent her home, ³along with her two sons. The name of the one was Gershom (for he said, "I have been a sojourner⁴ in a foreign land"), ⁴and the name of the other, Eliezer⁵ (for he said, "The God of my father was my help, and delivered me from the sword of Pharaoh"). ⁵Jethro, Moses' father-in-law, came with his sons and his wife to Moses in the wilderness where he was encamped at the mountain of God. ⁶And when he sent word to Moses, "I,⁶ your father-in-law Jethro, am coming to you with your wife and her two sons with her," ⁷Moses went out to meet his father-in-law and bowed down and kissed him. And they asked each other of their welfare and went into the tent. ⁸Then Moses told his father-in-law all that the LORD had done to Pharaoh and to the Egyptians for Israel's sake, all the hardship that had come upon

---

¹ *Massah* means *testing* ² *Meribah* means *quarreling* ³ A slight change would yield *upon the banner* ⁴ *Gershom* sounds like the Hebrew word for *sojourner* ⁵ *Eliezer* means *My God is help* ⁶ Hebrew; Samaritan, Septuagint, Syriac *behold*

them in the way, and how the Lord had delivered them. ⁹And Jethro rejoiced for all the good that the Lord had done to Israel, in that he had delivered them out of the hand of the Egyptians. ¹⁰Jethro said, "Blessed be the Lord, who has delivered you out of the hand of the Egyptians and out of the hand of Pharaoh and has delivered the people from under the hand of the Egyptians. ¹¹Now I know that the Lord is greater than all gods, because in this affair they dealt arrogantly with the people."[1] ¹²And Jethro, Moses' father-in-law, brought a burnt offering and sacrifices to God; and Aaron came with all the elders of Israel to eat bread with Moses' father-in-law before God.

¹³The next day Moses sat to judge the people, and the people stood around Moses from morning till evening. ¹⁴When Moses' father-in-law saw all that he was doing for the people, he said, "What is this that you are doing for the people? Why do you sit alone, and all the people stand around you from morning till evening?" ¹⁵And Moses said to his father-in-law, "Because the people come to me to inquire of God; ¹⁶when they have a dispute, they come to me and I decide between one person and another, and I make them know the statutes of God and his laws." ¹⁷Moses' father-in-law said to him, "What you are doing is not good. ¹⁸You and the people with you will certainly wear yourselves out, for the thing is too heavy for you. You are not able to do it alone. ¹⁹Now obey my voice; I will give you advice, and God be with you! You shall represent the people before God and bring their cases to God, ²⁰and you shall warn them about the statutes and the laws, and make them know the way in which they must walk and what they must do. ²¹Moreover, look for able men from all the people, men who fear God, who are trustworthy and hate a bribe, and place such men over the people as chiefs of thousands, of hundreds, of fifties, and of tens. ²²And let them judge the people at all times. Every great matter they shall bring to you, but any small matter they shall decide themselves. So it will be easier for you, and they will bear the burden with you. ²³If you do this, God will direct you, you will be able to endure, and all this people also will go to their place in peace."

²⁴So Moses listened to the voice of his father-in-law and did all that he had said. ²⁵Moses chose able men out of all Israel and made them heads over the people, chiefs of thousands, of hundreds, of fifties, and of tens. ²⁶And they judged the people at all times. Any hard case they brought to Moses, but any small matter they decided themselves. ²⁷Then Moses let his father-in-law depart, and he went away to his own country.

Israel at God's mountain [chapter 19]. The people of Israel reach the goal of their pilgrimage and camp at the foot of Mount Sinai (vv. 1–2). Moses alone goes up the mountain to meet with God, who invites his people to belong to him in the covenant and to be his treasured possession among the nations (vv. 3–6). The people accept this invitation and go through elaborate preparations to consecrate themselves for the holy worship of God. The tension in this chapter comes from the dangerous presence of God, who is so awesome that people may not even touch his holy mountain (vv. 12–13, 21) but can only tremble at the divine glory they see in fire and smoke and hear in the thundering voice of God (vv. 16–18). This dramatic portrayal of divine majesty serves to emphasize the crucial role of Moses as the mediator who goes between the people and God. The dominant

[1] Hebrew *with them*

literary motif is the *theophany—the appearance of the deity amid spectacular natural displays.

19 On the third new moon after the people of Israel had gone out of the land of Egypt, on that day they came into the wilderness of Sinai. ²They set out from Rephidim and came into the wilderness of Sinai, and they encamped in the wilderness. There Israel encamped before the mountain, ³while Moses went up to God. The LORD called to him out of the mountain, saying, "Thus you shall say to the house of Jacob, and tell the people of Israel: ⁴You yourselves have seen what I did to the Egyptians, and how I bore you on eagles' wings and brought you to myself. ⁵Now therefore, if you will indeed obey my voice and keep my covenant, you shall be my treasured possession among all peoples, for all the earth is mine; ⁶and you shall be to me a kingdom of priests and a holy nation. These are the words that you shall speak to the people of Israel."

⁷So Moses came and called the elders of the people and set before them all these words that the LORD had commanded him. ⁸All the people answered together and said, "All that the LORD has spoken we will do." And Moses reported the words of the people to the LORD. ⁹And the LORD said to Moses, "Behold, I am coming to you in a thick cloud, that the people may hear when I speak with you, and may also believe you forever."

When Moses told the words of the people to the LORD, ¹⁰the LORD said to Moses, "Go to the people and consecrate them today and tomorrow, and let them wash their garments ¹¹and be ready for the third day. For on the third day the LORD will come down on Mount Sinai in the sight of all the people. ¹²And you shall set limits for the people all around, saying, 'Take care not to go up into the mountain or touch the edge of it. Whoever touches the mountain shall be put to death. ¹³No hand shall touch him, but he shall be stoned or shot;[1] whether beast or man, he shall not live.' When the trumpet sounds a long blast, they shall come up to the mountain." ¹⁴So Moses went down from the mountain to the people and consecrated the people; and they washed their garments. ¹⁵And he said to the people, "Be ready for the third day; do not go near a woman."

¹⁶On the morning of the third day there were thunders and lightnings and a thick cloud on the mountain and a very loud trumpet blast, so that all the people in the camp trembled. ¹⁷Then Moses brought the people out of the camp to meet God, and they took their stand at the foot of the mountain. ¹⁸Now Mount Sinai was wrapped in smoke because the LORD had descended on it in fire. The smoke of it went up like the smoke of a kiln, and the whole mountain trembled greatly. ¹⁹And as the sound of the trumpet grew louder and louder, Moses spoke, and God answered him in thunder. ²⁰The LORD came down on Mount Sinai, to the top of the mountain. And the LORD called Moses to the top of the mountain, and Moses went up.

²¹And the LORD said to Moses, "Go down and warn the people, lest they break through to the LORD to look and many of them perish. ²²Also let the priests who come near to the LORD consecrate themselves, lest the LORD break out against them." ²³And Moses said to the LORD, "The people cannot come up to Mount Sinai, for you yourself warned us, saying, 'Set limits around the mountain and consecrate it.'" ²⁴And the LORD said to him, "Go down, and come up bringing Aaron with you. But do not let the

---

[1] That is, shot with an arrow

priests and the people break through to come up to the LORD, lest he break out against them." ²⁵So Moses went down to the people and told them.

> **The Ten Commandments** [20:1–17]. With the beginning of chapter 20, the book of Exodus shifts from narration to legislation. The whole moral law of God is summarized in ten "words" (v. 1) or commandments—also known as the Decalogue—that reveal his will for our relationship with him (commandments one through four, verses 3 to 11) and our relationships with one another (commandments five through ten, verses 12 to 17). Because they are based on the holy character of God, the Ten Commandments remain the permanent standard of righteousness for all people everywhere. It should be noted from the preamble, however, that they are not presented as a way to get right with God, or to earn his favor, but as a gift of guidance for people who have been saved by grace (see v. 2). The Decalogue is embodied in an ancient literary form known as a suzerainty treaty—the treaty extended by an ancient ruler to his people. The motifs of a suzerainty treaty include the following: a prologue in which the "great king" (the meaning of the word *suzerain*) identifies himself in exalted language; the historical context in which the king reminds his vassals of the benefits he has bestowed; a list of covenant obligations, including a demand for the vassals' exclusive loyalty to their king; statements of blessings and curses accompanying the commands.

20
And God spoke all these words, saying,
²"I am the LORD your God, who brought you out of the land of Egypt, out of the house of slavery.

³"You shall have no other gods before¹ me.

⁴"You shall not make for yourself a carved image, or any likeness of anything that is in heaven above, or that is in the earth beneath, or that is in the water under the earth. ⁵You shall not bow down to them or serve them, for I the LORD your God am a jealous God, visiting the iniquity of the fathers on the children to the third and the fourth generation of those who hate me, ⁶but showing steadfast love to thousands² of those who love me and keep my commandments.

⁷"You shall not take the name of the LORD your God in vain, for the LORD will not hold him guiltless who takes his name in vain.

⁸"Remember the Sabbath day, to keep it holy. ⁹Six days you shall labor, and do all your work, ¹⁰but the seventh day is a Sabbath to the LORD your God. On it you shall not do any work, you, or your son, or your daughter, your male servant, or your female servant, or your livestock, or the sojourner who is within your gates. ¹¹For in six days the LORD made heaven and earth, the sea, and all that is in them, and rested on the seventh day. Therefore the LORD blessed the Sabbath day and made it holy.

¹²"Honor your father and your mother, that your days may be long in the land that the LORD your God is giving you.

¹³"You shall not murder.³

¹⁴"You shall not commit adultery.

¹⁵"You shall not steal.

¹⁶"You shall not bear false witness against your neighbor.

¹⁷"You shall not covet your neighbor's house; you shall not covet your neighbor's wife, or his male servant, or his female servant, or his ox, or his donkey, or anything that is your neighbor's."

---

¹ Or *besides* ² Or *to the thousandth generation* ³ The Hebrew word also covers causing human death through carelessness or negligence

The Book of the Covenant [20:18–21:11]. The Ten Commandments are followed by more than a hundred specific rules and regulations that apply the law of God to daily life. Like the Ten Commandments, these case laws (or legal statutes for particular life situations) were given to Moses on the holy mountain, so that he could give them to the people of God (20:18–22). This section of Exodus is usually called "the Book of the Covenant" (see 24:7), with the term *covenant* referring to a formally established, binding commitment between God and his people. The Book of the Covenant is more like a guide to cases than a strict legal code. The regulations it contains and the punishments it mandates were never intended to cover every conceivable case but rather to establish legal precedents that wise leaders could use to adjudicate other situations as they arose. Although these laws were given to Israel as a nation under God and thus are no longer binding in all their detail, they are based on moral principles that teach us the character of God and can still help to guide society today. The first two sets of laws regulate altars for the proper worship of God (20:22–26) and the relationship between masters and slaves (21:1–11). Here it is important to know that because servitude was usually voluntary and intended to be temporary (people often worked as slaves to pay off their debts or to make restitution), the institution of slavery in Israel was different in some important ways from the degrading and dehumanizing practice of permanent, involuntary slavery that was later practiced in Africa and the West (note that 21:16 mandates the death penalty for anyone who kidnaps a slave, or owns a slave who has been kidnapped). The laws in this section are intended to protect the rights of slaves and their families.

[18]Now when all the people saw the thunder and the flashes of lightning and the sound of the trumpet and the mountain smoking, the people were afraid[1] and trembled, and they stood far off [19]and said to Moses, "You speak to us, and we will listen; but do not let God speak to us, lest we die." [20]Moses said to the people, "Do not fear, for God has come to test you, that the fear of him may be before you, that you may not sin." [21]The people stood far off, while Moses drew near to the thick darkness where God was.

[22]And the LORD said to Moses, "Thus you shall say to the people of Israel: 'You have seen for yourselves that I have talked with you from heaven. [23]You shall not make gods of silver to be with me, nor shall you make for yourselves gods of gold. [24]An altar of earth you shall make for me and sacrifice on it your burnt offerings and your peace offerings, your sheep and your oxen. In every place where I cause my name to be remembered I will come to you and bless you. [25]If you make me an altar of stone, you shall not build it of hewn stones, for if you wield your tool on it you profane it. [26]And you shall not go up by steps to my altar, that your nakedness be not exposed on it.'

21 "Now these are the rules that you shall set before them. [2]When you buy a Hebrew slave, he shall serve six years, and in the seventh he shall go out free, for nothing. [3]If he comes in single, he shall go out single; if he comes in married, then his wife shall go out with him. [4]If his master gives him a wife and she bears him sons or daughters, the wife and her children shall be her master's, and he shall go out alone. [5]But if the slave plainly says, 'I love my master, my wife, and my children; I will not go out free,' [6]then his master shall bring him to God, and he shall bring him to the

---

[1] Samaritan, Septuagint, Syriac, Vulgate; Masoretic Text *the people saw*

door or the doorpost. And his master shall bore his ear through with an awl, and he shall be his slave forever.

[7] "When a man sells his daughter as a slave, she shall not go out as the male slaves do. [8] If she does not please her master, who has designated her[1] for himself, then he shall let her be redeemed. He shall have no right to sell her to a foreign people, since he has broken faith with her. [9] If he designates her for his son, he shall deal with her as with a daughter. [10] If he takes another wife to himself, he shall not diminish her food, her clothing, or her marital rights. [11] And if he does not do these three things for her, she shall go out for nothing, without payment of money.

> **An eye for an eye** [21:12–22:15]. The case laws in this section relate to capital crimes (21:12–17), personal injury (21:18–27), criminal negligence (21:28–32), and personal property (21:33–22:15). The general progression is from greater to lesser crimes. The standards for retribution and restitution are based on the principle of proportionality: the greater the crime, the greater the punishment or payment. There is a strong emphasis on personal responsibility, going beyond the misdeeds people perpetrate with willful intent to address the wrongs they allow through negligence.

[12] "Whoever strikes a man so that he dies shall be put to death. [13] But if he did not lie in wait for him, but God let him fall into his hand, then I will appoint for you a place to which he may flee. [14] But if a man willfully attacks another to kill him by cunning, you shall take him from my altar, that he may die.

[15] "Whoever strikes his father or his mother shall be put to death.

[16] "Whoever steals a man and sells him, and anyone found in possession of him, shall be put to death.

[17] "Whoever curses[2] his father or his mother shall be put to death.

[18] "When men quarrel and one strikes the other with a stone or with his fist and the man does not die but takes to his bed, [19] then if the man rises again and walks outdoors with his staff, he who struck him shall be clear; only he shall pay for the loss of his time, and shall have him thoroughly healed.

[20] "When a man strikes his slave, male or female, with a rod and the slave dies under his hand, he shall be avenged. [21] But if the slave survives a day or two, he is not to be avenged, for the slave is his money.

[22] "When men strive together and hit a pregnant woman, so that her children come out, but there is no harm, the one who hit her shall surely be fined, as the woman's husband shall impose on him, and he shall pay as the judges determine. [23] But if there is harm,[3] then you shall pay life for life, [24] eye for eye, tooth for tooth, hand for hand, foot for foot, [25] burn for burn, wound for wound, stripe for stripe.

[26] "When a man strikes the eye of his slave, male or female, and destroys it, he shall let the slave go free because of his eye. [27] If he knocks out the tooth of his slave, male or female, he shall let the slave go free because of his tooth.

[28] "When an ox gores a man or a woman to death, the ox shall be stoned, and its flesh shall not be eaten, but the owner of the ox shall not be liable. [29] But if the ox has been accustomed to gore in the past, and its owner has been warned but has not kept it in, and it kills a man or a woman, the ox shall be stoned, and its owner also shall be put to death. [30] If a ransom is imposed on him, then he shall give for the redemption

---

[1] Or so that he has not designated her [2] Or dishonors; Septuagint reviles [3] Or so that her children come out and it is clear who was to blame, he shall be fined as the woman's husband shall impose on him, and he alone shall pay. If it is unclear who was to blame . . .

of his life whatever is imposed on him. ³¹If it gores a man's son or daughter, he shall be dealt with according to this same rule. ³²If the ox gores a slave, male or female, the owner shall give to their master thirty shekels¹ of silver, and the ox shall be stoned.

³³"When a man opens a pit, or when a man digs a pit and does not cover it, and an ox or a donkey falls into it, ³⁴the owner of the pit shall make restoration. He shall give money to its owner, and the dead beast shall be his.

³⁵"When one man's ox butts another's, so that it dies, then they shall sell the live ox and share its price, and the dead beast also they shall share. ³⁶Or if it is known that the ox has been accustomed to gore in the past, and its owner has not kept it in, he shall repay ox for ox, and the dead beast shall be his.

22 ² "If a man steals an ox or a sheep, and kills it or sells it, he shall repay five oxen for an ox, and four sheep for a sheep. ²³ If a thief is found breaking in and is struck so that he dies, there shall be no bloodguilt for him, ³but if the sun has risen on him, there shall be bloodguilt for him. He shall surely pay. If he has nothing, then he shall be sold for his theft. ⁴If the stolen beast is found alive in his possession, whether it is an ox or a donkey or a sheep, he shall pay double.

⁵"If a man causes a field or vineyard to be grazed over, or lets his beast loose and it feeds in another man's field, he shall make restitution from the best in his own field and in his own vineyard.

⁶"If fire breaks out and catches in thorns so that the stacked grain or the standing grain or the field is consumed, he who started the fire shall make full restitution.

⁷"If a man gives to his neighbor money or goods to keep safe, and it is stolen from the man's house, then, if the thief is found, he shall pay double. ⁸If the thief is not found, the owner of the house shall come near to God to show whether or not he has put his hand to his neighbor's property. ⁹For every breach of trust, whether it is for an ox, for a donkey, for a sheep, for a cloak, or for any kind of lost thing, of which one says, 'This is it,' the case of both parties shall come before God. The one whom God condemns shall pay double to his neighbor.

¹⁰"If a man gives to his neighbor a donkey or an ox or a sheep or any beast to keep safe, and it dies or is injured or is driven away, without anyone seeing it, ¹¹an oath by the LORD shall be between them both to see whether or not he has put his hand to his neighbor's property. The owner shall accept the oath, and he shall not make restitution. ¹²But if it is stolen from him, he shall make restitution to its owner. ¹³If it is torn by beasts, let him bring it as evidence. He shall not make restitution for what has been torn.

¹⁴"If a man borrows anything of his neighbor, and it is injured or dies, the owner not being with it, he shall make full restitution. ¹⁵If the owner was with it, he shall not make restitution; if it was hired, it came for its hiring fee.⁴

More case laws [22:16–23:9]. The laws at the end of chapter 22 are miscellaneous, ranging from sexual ethics, to perverse forms of false worship, to protection of the weakest members of society, to the honor that we owe to God. In one way or another, each regulation is an application of one of the Ten Commandments and teaches us something about the character of God, giving tangible expression to divine attributes like purity or

¹ A *shekel* was about 2/5 ounce or 11 grams ² Ch 21:37 in Hebrew ³ Ch 22:1 in Hebrew ⁴ Or *it is reckoned in* (Hebrew *comes into*) *its hiring fee*

compassion. The laws at the beginning of chapter 23 relate to the due process of law and are designed to preserve justice in legal matters.

¹⁶"If a man seduces a virgin¹ who is not betrothed and lies with her, he shall give the bride-price² for her and make her his wife. ¹⁷If her father utterly refuses to give her to him, he shall pay money equal to the bride-price for virgins.

¹⁸"You shall not permit a sorceress to live.

¹⁹"Whoever lies with an animal shall be put to death.

²⁰"Whoever sacrifices to any god, other than the LORD alone, shall be devoted to destruction.³

²¹"You shall not wrong a sojourner or oppress him, for you were sojourners in the land of Egypt. ²²You shall not mistreat any widow or fatherless child. ²³If you do mistreat them, and they cry out to me, I will surely hear their cry, ²⁴and my wrath will burn, and I will kill you with the sword, and your wives shall become widows and your children fatherless.

²⁵"If you lend money to any of my people with you who is poor, you shall not be like a moneylender to him, and you shall not exact interest from him. ²⁶If ever you take your neighbor's cloak in pledge, you shall return it to him before the sun goes down, ²⁷for that is his only covering, and it is his cloak for his body; in what else shall he sleep? And if he cries to me, I will hear, for I am compassionate.

²⁸"You shall not revile God, nor curse a ruler of your people.

²⁹"You shall not delay to offer from the fullness of your harvest and from the outflow of your presses. The firstborn of your sons you shall give to me. ³⁰You shall do the same with your oxen and with your sheep: seven days it shall be with its mother; on the eighth day you shall give it to me.

³¹"You shall be consecrated to me. Therefore you shall not eat any flesh that is torn by beasts in the field; you shall throw it to the dogs.

23 "You shall not spread a false report. You shall not join hands with a wicked man to be a malicious witness. ²You shall not fall in with the many to do evil, nor shall you bear witness in a lawsuit, siding with the many, so as to pervert justice, ³nor shall you be partial to a poor man in his lawsuit.

⁴"If you meet your enemy's ox or his donkey going astray, you shall bring it back to him. ⁵If you see the donkey of one who hates you lying down under its burden, you shall refrain from leaving him with it; you shall rescue it with him.

⁶"You shall not pervert the justice due to your poor in his lawsuit. ⁷Keep far from a false charge, and do not kill the innocent and righteous, for I will not acquit the wicked. ⁸And you shall take no bribe, for a bribe blinds the clear-sighted and subverts the cause of those who are in the right.

⁹"You shall not oppress a sojourner. You know the heart of a sojourner, for you were sojourners in the land of Egypt.

Holy worship in the Promised Land [23:10–33]. The laws at the end of chapter 23 relate to the worship of God. Some of these laws regulate the Sabbath and promote mercy on God's holy day of rest (vv. 10–12). Others regulate the pilgrim feasts of unleav-

---

¹ Or *a girl of marriageable age*; also verse 17 ² Or *engagement present*; also verse 17 ³ That is, set apart (devoted) as an offering to the Lord (for destruction)

ened bread, harvest, and ingathering (vv. 14–19). Still others pertain to idolatry—specifically, to God's absolute prohibition against worshiping any of the pagan gods (vv. 24–33). The last set of laws also comes with a promise that God will complete the conquest of the Promised Land through the guardian power of his conquering angel (vv. 20–23). This whole legislative section of the book of Exodus has affinities to the literary genre of *utopian literature, inasmuch as the rules give us glimpses of a good society to be established in a promised land, along with the institutional key to that society, namely, obedience to God's rules for living.

[10]"For six years you shall sow your land and gather in its yield, [11]but the seventh year you shall let it rest and lie fallow, that the poor of your people may eat; and what they leave the beasts of the field may eat. You shall do likewise with your vineyard, and with your olive orchard.

[12]"Six days you shall do your work, but on the seventh day you shall rest; that your ox and your donkey may have rest, and the son of your servant woman, and the alien, may be refreshed.

[13]"Pay attention to all that I have said to you, and make no mention of the names of other gods, nor let it be heard on your lips.

[14]"Three times in the year you shall keep a feast to me. [15]You shall keep the Feast of Unleavened Bread. As I commanded you, you shall eat unleavened bread for seven days at the appointed time in the month of Abib, for in it you came out of Egypt. None shall appear before me empty-handed. [16]You shall keep the Feast of Harvest, of the firstfruits of your labor, of what you sow in the field. You shall keep the Feast of Ingathering at the end of the year, when you gather in from the field the fruit of your labor. [17]Three times in the year shall all your males appear before the Lord GOD.

[18]"You shall not offer the blood of my sacrifice with anything leavened, or let the fat of my feast remain until the morning.

[19]"The best of the firstfruits of your ground you shall bring into the house of the LORD your God.

"You shall not boil a young goat in its mother's milk.

[20]"Behold, I send an angel before you to guard you on the way and to bring you to the place that I have prepared. [21]Pay careful attention to him and obey his voice; do not rebel against him, for he will not pardon your transgression, for my name is in him.

[22]"But if you carefully obey his voice and do all that I say, then I will be an enemy to your enemies and an adversary to your adversaries.

[23]"When my angel goes before you and brings you to the Amorites and the Hittites and the Perizzites and the Canaanites, the Hivites and the Jebusites, and I blot them out, [24]you shall not bow down to their gods nor serve them, nor do as they do, but you shall utterly overthrow them and break their pillars in pieces. [25]You shall serve the LORD your God, and he[j] will bless your bread and your water, and I will take sickness away from among you. [26]None shall miscarry or be barren in your land; I will fulfill the number of your days. [27]I will send my terror before you and will throw into confusion all the people against whom you shall come, and I will make all your enemies turn their backs to you. [28]And I will send hornets before you, which shall drive out the Hivites, the Canaanites, and the Hittites from before you. [29]I will not drive them out from before you in one year, lest the land become desolate and the wild beasts

[j] Septuagint, Vulgate *I*

multiply against you. [30]Little by little I will drive them out from before you, until you have increased and possess the land. [31]And I will set your border from the Red Sea to the Sea of the Philistines, and from the wilderness to the Euphrates, for I will give the inhabitants of the land into your hand, and you shall drive them out before you. [32]You shall make no covenant with them and their gods. [33]They shall not dwell in your land, lest they make you sin against me; for if you serve their gods, it will surely be a snare to you."

> **The covenant confirmed** [chapter 24]. The covenant proposed in chapter 19 and stipulated in chapters 20–23 is ratified in chapter 24—a worship service of covenant renewal. The biblical covenants are binding promises between God and his people; typically they are sworn by oath and sealed in blood. Here the covenant is articulated in essentially the same form as an ancient treaty between a great lord and one of his vassals, with a preamble that identifies the parties to the agreement, a prologue that explains the history of their relationship, and a list of stipulations that explain their reciprocal responsibilities. God is the great King who sets the legal terms for Israel as the nation he has rescued and now calls into his royal service. This covenant is ratified in public worship that includes the reading of God's Word (vv. 3, 7); a confession of faith (v. 3); the sprinkling of sacrificial blood, both on the altar of God and on the people who are bound to him in the covenant (vv. 4–8); and the celebration of a sacramental meal that Moses, Aaron, and the seventy elders eat in the presence of God (!), halfway up the mountain (vv. 1–2, 9–11). Once the covenant is confirmed, Moses the mediator goes to the summit alone to receive God's law—the Ten Commandments, written in stone (v. 12)—and also to behold the glory of God (vv. 15–18). In addition to setting the basic biblical pattern for worship, the events in this chapter give us a picture of salvation, in which God bridges the distance between us and him by providing a blood sacrifice and finally drawing us up into his glory.

24 Then he said to Moses, "Come up to the LORD, you and Aaron, Nadab, and Abihu, and seventy of the elders of Israel, and worship from afar. [2]Moses alone shall come near to the LORD, but the others shall not come near, and the people shall not come up with him."

[3]Moses came and told the people all the words of the LORD and all the rules.[1] And all the people answered with one voice and said, "All the words that the LORD has spoken we will do." [4]And Moses wrote down all the words of the LORD. He rose early in the morning and built an altar at the foot of the mountain, and twelve pillars, according to the twelve tribes of Israel. [5]And he sent young men of the people of Israel, who offered burnt offerings and sacrificed peace offerings of oxen to the LORD. [6]And Moses took half of the blood and put it in basins, and half of the blood he threw against the altar. [7]Then he took the Book of the Covenant and read it in the hearing of the people. And they said, "All that the LORD has spoken we will do, and we will be obedient." [8]And Moses took the blood and threw it on the people and said, "Behold the blood of the covenant that the LORD has made with you in accordance with all these words."

[9]Then Moses and Aaron, Nadab, and Abihu, and seventy of the elders of Israel went up, [10]and they saw the God of Israel. There was under his feet as it were a pave-

---

[1] Or *all the just decrees*

ment of sapphire stone, like the very heaven for clearness. ¹¹And he did not lay his hand on the chief men of the people of Israel; they beheld God, and ate and drank.

¹²The LORD said to Moses, "Come up to me on the mountain and wait there, that I may give you the tablets of stone, with the law and the commandment, which I have written for their instruction." ¹³So Moses rose with his assistant Joshua, and Moses went up into the mountain of God. ¹⁴And he said to the elders, "Wait here for us until we return to you. And behold, Aaron and Hur are with you. Whoever has a dispute, let him go to them."

¹⁵Then Moses went up on the mountain, and the cloud covered the mountain. ¹⁶The glory of the LORD dwelt on Mount Sinai, and the cloud covered it six days. And on the seventh day he called to Moses out of the midst of the cloud. ¹⁷Now the appearance of the glory of the LORD was like a devouring fire on the top of the mountain in the sight of the people of Israel. ¹⁸Moses entered the cloud and went up on the mountain. And Moses was on the mountain forty days and forty nights.

Furnishing God's sanctuary [chapter 25]. This chapter marks the beginning of the detailed instructions that Moses received to build a house for the worship of God. After the high drama of Israel's exodus from Egypt, these chapters may seem anticlimactic. However, since the tabernacle is a place where people meet with God (vv. 8, 22), it has a drama all its own. The tabernacle is to be constructed with materials the Israelites present as a freewill offering to God (vv. 1–7), following the pattern that God gave to Moses on the mountain (vv. 9, 40). Its internal furnishings are all to be made of royal gold. These include the holy ark of the covenant, symbolizing the throne of God, on which the blood of atonement was sprinkled at the mercy seat (vv. 10–22); the table for the bread of the Presence, symbolizing God's fellowship with his people and provision for their needs; and the golden lampstand, symbolizing the light and the life of God (vv. 31–39). The material in this chapter is presented in the form of an inventory. The main motif is the sacred—an accumulation of spectacular sensory objects that together set a designated space apart from ordinary uses and consecrate it for the worship of God. The wealth of sensory details conveys a sense of spiritual richness and affirms the aesthetic value of visual beauty.

25 The LORD said to Moses, ²"Speak to the people of Israel, that they take for me a contribution. From every man whose heart moves him you shall receive the contribution for me. ³And this is the contribution that you shall receive from them: gold, silver, and bronze, ⁴blue and purple and scarlet yarns and fine twined linen, goats' hair, ⁵tanned rams' skins, goatskins,¹ acacia wood, ⁶oil for the lamps, spices for the anointing oil and for the fragrant incense, ⁷onyx stones, and stones for setting, for the ephod and for the breastpiece. ⁸And let them make me a sanctuary, that I may dwell in their midst. ⁹Exactly as I show you concerning the pattern of the tabernacle, and of all its furniture, so you shall make it.

¹⁰"They shall make an ark of acacia wood. Two cubits² and a half shall be its length, a cubit and a half its breadth, and a cubit and a half its height. ¹¹You shall overlay it with pure gold, inside and outside shall you overlay it, and you shall make on it a molding of gold around it. ¹²You shall cast four rings of gold for it and put them on its four feet, two rings on the one side of it, and two rings on the other side of it. ¹³You shall make poles of acacia wood and overlay them with gold. ¹⁴And you shall put the poles into the rings on the sides of the ark to carry the ark by them.

¹ Uncertain; possibly *dolphin skins*, or *dugong skins*; compare 26:14 ² A *cubit* was about 18 inches or 45 centimeters

¹⁵The poles shall remain in the rings of the ark; they shall not be taken from it. ¹⁶And you shall put into the ark the testimony that I shall give you.

¹⁷"You shall make a mercy seat¹ of pure gold. Two cubits and a half shall be its length, and a cubit and a half its breadth. ¹⁸And you shall make two cherubim of gold; of hammered work shall you make them, on the two ends of the mercy seat. ¹⁹Make one cherub on the one end, and one cherub on the other end. Of one piece with the mercy seat shall you make the cherubim on its two ends. ²⁰The cherubim shall spread out their wings above, overshadowing the mercy seat with their wings, their faces one to another; toward the mercy seat shall the faces of the cherubim be. ²¹And you shall put the mercy seat on the top of the ark, and in the ark you shall put the testimony that I shall give you. ²²There I will meet with you, and from above the mercy seat, from between the two cherubim that are on the ark of the testimony, I will speak with you about all that I will give you in commandment for the people of Israel.

²³"You shall make a table of acacia wood. Two cubits shall be its length, a cubit its breadth, and a cubit and a half its height. ²⁴You shall overlay it with pure gold and make a molding of gold around it. ²⁵And you shall make a rim around it a handbreadth² wide, and a molding of gold around the rim. ²⁶And you shall make for it four rings of gold, and fasten the rings to the four corners at its four legs. ²⁷Close to the frame the rings shall lie, as holders for the poles to carry the table. ²⁸You shall make the poles of acacia wood, and overlay them with gold, and the table shall be carried with these. ²⁹And you shall make its plates and dishes for incense, and its flagons and bowls with which to pour drink offerings; you shall make them of pure gold. ³⁰And you shall set the bread of the Presence on the table before me regularly.

³¹"You shall make a lampstand of pure gold. The lampstand shall be made of hammered work: its base, its stem, its cups, its calyxes, and its flowers shall be of one piece with it. ³²And there shall be six branches going out of its sides, three branches of the lampstand out of one side of it and three branches of the lampstand out of the other side of it; ³³three cups made like almond blossoms, each with calyx and flower, on one branch, and three cups made like almond blossoms, each with calyx and flower, on the other branch—so for the six branches going out of the lampstand. ³⁴And on the lampstand itself there shall be four cups made like almond blossoms, with their calyxes and flowers, ³⁵and a calyx of one piece with it under each pair of the six branches going out from the lampstand. ³⁶Their calyxes and their branches shall be of one piece with it, the whole of it a single piece of hammered work of pure gold. ³⁷You shall make seven lamps for it. And the lamps shall be set up so as to give light on the space in front of it. ³⁸Its tongs and their trays shall be of pure gold. ³⁹It shall be made, with all these utensils, out of a talent³ of pure gold. ⁴⁰And see that you make them after the pattern for them, which is being shown you on the mountain.

The blueprint for the tabernacle [chapter 26]. After telling Moses what goes inside the tabernacle, God proceeds to tell him how to make the tent of meeting itself. The many instructions about curtains and coverings—including the sacred veil that separates the Holy Place from the Most Holy Place (vv. 31–35)—show that access to the tabernacle was limited. Although this was the place for people to meet with God, it was shrouded in numinous mystery, giving the Israelites a constant reminder of God's holy majesty.

---

¹ Or cover ² A *handbreadth* was about 3 inches or 7.5 centimeters ³ A *talent* was about 75 pounds or 34 kilograms

26 "Moreover, you shall make the tabernacle with ten curtains of fine twined linen and blue and purple and scarlet yarns; you shall make them with cherubim skillfully worked into them. ²The length of each curtain shall be twenty-eight cubits,¹ and the breadth of each curtain four cubits; all the curtains shall be the same size. ³Five curtains shall be coupled to one another, and the other five curtains shall be coupled to one another. ⁴And you shall make loops of blue on the edge of the outermost curtain in the first set. Likewise you shall make loops on the edge of the outermost curtain in the second set. ⁵Fifty loops you shall make on the one curtain, and fifty loops you shall make on the edge of the curtain that is in the second set; the loops shall be opposite one another. ⁶And you shall make fifty clasps of gold, and couple the curtains one to the other with the clasps, so that the tabernacle may be a single whole.

⁷"You shall also make curtains of goats' hair for a tent over the tabernacle; eleven curtains shall you make. ⁸The length of each curtain shall be thirty cubits, and the breadth of each curtain four cubits. The eleven curtains shall be the same size. ⁹You shall couple five curtains by themselves, and six curtains by themselves, and the sixth curtain you shall double over at the front of the tent. ¹⁰You shall make fifty loops on the edge of the curtain that is outermost in one set, and fifty loops on the edge of the curtain that is outermost in the second set.

¹¹"You shall make fifty clasps of bronze, and put the clasps into the loops, and couple the tent together that it may be a single whole. ¹²And the part that remains of the curtains of the tent, the half curtain that remains, shall hang over the back of the tabernacle. ¹³And the extra that remains in the length of the curtains, the cubit on the one side, and the cubit on the other side, shall hang over the sides of the tabernacle, on this side and that side, to cover it. ¹⁴And you shall make for the tent a covering of tanned rams' skins and a covering of goatskins on top.

¹⁵"You shall make upright frames for the tabernacle of acacia wood. ¹⁶Ten cubits shall be the length of a frame, and a cubit and a half the breadth of each frame. ¹⁷There shall be two tenons in each frame, for fitting together. So shall you do for all the frames of the tabernacle. ¹⁸You shall make the frames for the tabernacle: twenty frames for the south side; ¹⁹and forty bases of silver you shall make under the twenty frames, two bases under one frame for its two tenons, and two bases under the next frame for its two tenons; ²⁰and for the second side of the tabernacle, on the north side twenty frames, ²¹and their forty bases of silver, two bases under one frame, and two bases under the next frame. ²²And for the rear of the tabernacle westward you shall make six frames. ²³And you shall make two frames for corners of the tabernacle in the rear; ²⁴they shall be separate beneath, but joined at the top, at the first ring. Thus shall it be with both of them; they shall form the two corners. ²⁵And there shall be eight frames, with their bases of silver, sixteen bases; two bases under one frame, and two bases under another frame.

²⁶"You shall make bars of acacia wood, five for the frames of the one side of the tabernacle, ²⁷and five bars for the frames of the other side of the tabernacle, and five bars for the frames of the side of the tabernacle at the rear westward. ²⁸The middle bar, halfway up the frames, shall run from end to end. ²⁹You shall overlay the frames with gold and shall make their rings of gold for holders for the bars, and you shall overlay the bars with gold. ³⁰Then you shall erect the tabernacle according to the plan for it that you were shown on the mountain.

---

¹ A *cubit* was about 18 inches or 45 centimeters

³¹"And you shall make a veil of blue and purple and scarlet yarns and fine twined linen. It shall be made with cherubim skillfully worked into it. ³²And you shall hang it on four pillars of acacia overlaid with gold, with hooks of gold, on four bases of silver. ³³And you shall hang the veil from the clasps, and bring the ark of the testimony in there within the veil. And the veil shall separate for you the Holy Place from the Most Holy. ³⁴You shall put the mercy seat on the ark of the testimony in the Most Holy Place. ³⁵And you shall set the table outside the veil, and the lampstand on the south side of the tabernacle opposite the table, and you shall put the table on the north side.

³⁶"You shall make a screen for the entrance of the tent, of blue and purple and scarlet yarns and fine twined linen, embroidered with needlework. ³⁷And you shall make for the screen five pillars of acacia, and overlay them with gold. Their hooks shall be of gold, and you shall cast five bases of bronze for them.

> **The courtyard to God** [27:1–19]. The tabernacle was surrounded by a perimeter fence (vv. 9–19), which formed the courtyard where ordinary Israelites could meet with God. Thus there were three levels of access: everyone could enter the courtyard to the tabernacle, but only the priests could go inside the Holy Place, and only the high priest ever entered the Most Holy Place of all. The central object in the courtyard was the large bronze altar (vv. 1–8) where the people made their sacrifices to God.

27 "You shall make the altar of acacia wood, five cubits¹ long and five cubits broad. The altar shall be square, and its height shall be three cubits. ²And you shall make horns for it on its four corners; its horns shall be of one piece with it, and you shall overlay it with bronze. ³You shall make pots for it to receive its ashes, and shovels and basins and forks and fire pans. You shall make all its utensils of bronze. ⁴You shall also make for it a grating, a network of bronze, and on the net you shall make four bronze rings at its four corners. ⁵And you shall set it under the ledge of the altar so that the net extends halfway down the altar. ⁶And you shall make poles for the altar, poles of acacia wood, and overlay them with bronze. ⁷And the poles shall be put through the rings, so that the poles are on the two sides of the altar when it is carried. ⁸You shall make it hollow, with boards. As it has been shown you on the mountain, so shall it be made.

⁹"You shall make the court of the tabernacle. On the south side the court shall have hangings of fine twined linen a hundred cubits long for one side. ¹⁰Its twenty pillars and their twenty bases shall be of bronze, but the hooks of the pillars and their fillets shall be of silver. ¹¹And likewise for its length on the north side there shall be hangings a hundred cubits long, its pillars twenty and their bases twenty, of bronze, but the hooks of the pillars and their fillets shall be of silver. ¹²And for the breadth of the court on the west side there shall be hangings for fifty cubits, with ten pillars and ten bases. ¹³The breadth of the court on the front to the east shall be fifty cubits. ¹⁴The hangings for the one side of the gate shall be fifteen cubits, with their three pillars and three bases. ¹⁵On the other side the hangings shall be fifteen cubits, with their three pillars and three bases. ¹⁶For the gate of the court there shall be a screen twenty cubits long, of blue and purple and scarlet yarns and fine twined linen, embroidered with needlework. It shall have four pillars and with them four bases.

¹ A *cubit* was about 18 inches or 45 centimeters

¹⁷All the pillars around the court shall be filleted with silver. Their hooks shall be of silver, and their bases of bronze. ¹⁸The length of the court shall be a hundred cubits, the breadth fifty, and the height five cubits, with hangings of fine twined linen and bases of bronze. ¹⁹All the utensils of the tabernacle for every use, and all its pegs and all the pegs of the court, shall be of bronze.

Fit for a priest [27:20–28:43]. One of the regular duties of the priests (Aaron and his sons) was to tend the eternal flame on the lampstand of God (27:20–21)—a symbol of the worship in heaven that never ends. As they went about their priestly duties, these men wore sacred garments that testified to the beauty, the holiness, and the glory of God (28:1–5; 40–41). The ephod (28:6–14) was something like an apron—a pair of holy linen overalls—with stone shoulderpieces engraved with the names of the twelve tribes of Israel. This showed that as the high priest went about his duties, he represented the people before God (28:12). Similarly, the breastpiece (28:15–30) attached to the ephod was sewn with twelve precious or semiprecious gems, symbolizing the twelve tribes that the high priest carried close to his heart (see 28:29). This part of the outfit was also called "the breastpiece of judgment" because it held the Urim and Thummim, which the high priest used to cast lots that would indicate God's will for his people (28:30). The high priest's seamless blue robe (28:31–35) was decorated with golden bells; these would indicate whether the high priest was still alive when he went into the (dangerously) holy presence of God. The entire outfit was topped off with a turban engraved with the words "Holy to the Lord" (28:36–38). This is what the high priest's whole wardrobe was intended to indicate, right down to his undergarments (28:42–43): here was a man set apart for the holy service of God.

²⁰"You shall command the people of Israel that they bring to you pure beaten olive oil for the light, that a lamp may regularly be set up to burn. ²¹In the tent of meeting, outside the veil that is before the testimony, Aaron and his sons shall tend it from evening to morning before the Lord. It shall be a statute forever to be observed throughout their generations by the people of Israel.

28 "Then bring near to you Aaron your brother, and his sons with him, from among the people of Israel, to serve me as priests—Aaron and Aaron's sons, Nadab and Abihu, Eleazar and Ithamar. ²And you shall make holy garments for Aaron your brother, for glory and for beauty. ³You shall speak to all the skillful, whom I have filled with a spirit of skill, that they make Aaron's garments to consecrate him for my priesthood. ⁴These are the garments that they shall make: a breastpiece, an ephod, a robe, a coat of checker work, a turban, and a sash. They shall make holy garments for Aaron your brother and his sons to serve me as priests. ⁵They shall receive gold, blue and purple and scarlet yarns, and fine twined linen.

⁶"And they shall make the ephod of gold, of blue and purple and scarlet yarns, and of fine twined linen, skillfully worked. ⁷It shall have two shoulder pieces attached to its two edges, so that it may be joined together. ⁸And the skillfully woven band on it shall be made like it and be of one piece with it, of gold, blue and purple and scarlet yarns, and fine twined linen. ⁹You shall take two onyx stones, and engrave on them the names of the sons of Israel, ¹⁰six of their names on the one stone, and the names of the remaining six on the other stone, in the order of their birth. ¹¹As a jeweler

engraves signets, so shall you engrave the two stones with the names of the sons of Israel. You shall enclose them in settings of gold filigree. ¹²And you shall set the two stones on the shoulder pieces of the ephod, as stones of remembrance for the sons of Israel. And Aaron shall bear their names before the Lord on his two shoulders for remembrance. ¹³You shall make settings of gold filigree, ¹⁴and two chains of pure gold, twisted like cords; and you shall attach the corded chains to the settings.

¹⁵"You shall make a breastpiece of judgment, in skilled work. In the style of the ephod you shall make it—of gold, blue and purple and scarlet yarns, and fine twined linen shall you make it. ¹⁶It shall be square and doubled, a span¹ its length and a span its breadth. ¹⁷You shall set in it four rows of stones. A row of sardius,² topaz, and carbuncle shall be the first row; ¹⁸and the second row an emerald, a sapphire, and a diamond; ¹⁹and the third row a jacinth, an agate, and an amethyst; ²⁰and the fourth row a beryl, an onyx, and a jasper. They shall be set in gold filigree. ²¹There shall be twelve stones with their names according to the names of the sons of Israel. They shall be like signets, each engraved with its name, for the twelve tribes. ²²You shall make for the breastpiece twisted chains like cords, of pure gold. ²³And you shall make for the breastpiece two rings of gold, and put the two rings on the two edges of the breastpiece. ²⁴And you shall put the two cords of gold in the two rings at the edges of the breastpiece. ²⁵The two ends of the two cords you shall attach to the two settings of filigree, and so attach it in front to the shoulder pieces of the ephod. ²⁶You shall make two rings of gold, and put them at the two ends of the breastpiece, on its inside edge next to the ephod. ²⁷And you shall make two rings of gold, and attach them in front to the lower part of the two shoulder pieces of the ephod, at its seam above the skillfully woven band of the ephod. ²⁸And they shall bind the breastpiece by its rings to the rings of the ephod with a lace of blue, so that it may lie on the skillfully woven band of the ephod, so that the breastpiece shall not come loose from the ephod. ²⁹So Aaron shall bear the names of the sons of Israel in the breastpiece of judgment on his heart, when he goes into the Holy Place, to bring them to regular remembrance before the Lord. ³⁰And in the breastpiece of judgment you shall put the Urim and the Thummim, and they shall be on Aaron's heart, when he goes in before the Lord. Thus Aaron shall bear the judgment of the people of Israel on his heart before the Lord regularly.

³¹"You shall make the robe of the ephod all of blue. ³²It shall have an opening for the head in the middle of it, with a woven binding around the opening, like the opening in a garment,³ so that it may not tear. ³³On its hem you shall make pomegranates of blue and purple and scarlet yarns, around its hem, with bells of gold between them, ³⁴a golden bell and a pomegranate, a golden bell and a pomegranate, around the hem of the robe. ³⁵And it shall be on Aaron when he ministers, and its sound shall be heard when he goes into the Holy Place before the Lord, and when he comes out, so that he does not die.

³⁶"You shall make a plate of pure gold and engrave on it, like the engraving of a signet, 'Holy to the Lord.' ³⁷And you shall fasten it on the turban by a cord of blue. It shall be on the front of the turban. ³⁸It shall be on Aaron's forehead, and Aaron shall bear any guilt from the holy things that the people of Israel consecrate as their holy gifts. It shall regularly be on his forehead, that they may be accepted before the Lord.

---

¹ A *span* was about 9 inches or 22 centimeters ²The identity of some of these stones is uncertain ³The meaning of the Hebrew word is uncertain; possibly *coat of mail*

[39]"You shall weave the coat in checker work of fine linen, and you shall make a turban of fine linen, and you shall make a sash embroidered with needlework.

[40]"For Aaron's sons you shall make coats and sashes and caps. You shall make them for glory and beauty. [41]And you shall put them on Aaron your brother, and on his sons with him, and shall anoint them and ordain them and consecrate them, that they may serve me as priests. [42]You shall make for them linen undergarments to cover their naked flesh. They shall reach from the hips to the thighs; [43]and they shall be on Aaron and on his sons when they go into the tent of meeting or when they come near the altar to minister in the Holy Place, lest they bear guilt and die. This shall be a statute forever for him and for his offspring after him.

The ordination of the priests [chapter 29]. The priests were set apart for their sacred duties through the following rituals of consecration: the preparation of holy sacrifices (vv. 1–3); the cleansing of the priests with water (v. 4); the investiture of the priests in their sacred garments, with the holy anointing of oil (vv. 5–9); and the offering of bulls and rams during seven days of sacrifices (vv. 10–37). The careful attention to the details of these rituals—to be followed in perpetuity (vv. 29–30)—conveys the sacredness of the priestly calling; the large number of sacrifices shows that these men had as much need for atonement as the people they served. The chapter ends with instructions for the sacrifices the priests were to offer at the tabernacle every day (vv. 38–42) and a reminder of God's purpose for their ministry: the priests were consecrated to serve God in the sanctuary he sanctified by his glory, so that God could dwell with the people he saved in love (vv. 43–46).

29 "Now this is what you shall do to them to consecrate them, that they may serve me as priests. Take one bull of the herd and two rams without blemish, [2]and unleavened bread, unleavened cakes mixed with oil, and unleavened wafers smeared with oil. You shall make them of fine wheat flour. [3]You shall put them in one basket and bring them in the basket, and bring the bull and the two rams. [4]You shall bring Aaron and his sons to the entrance of the tent of meeting and wash them with water. [5]Then you shall take the garments, and put on Aaron the coat and the robe of the ephod, and the ephod, and the breastpiece, and gird him with the skillfully woven band of the ephod. [6]And you shall set the turban on his head and put the holy crown on the turban. [7]You shall take the anointing oil and pour it on his head and anoint him. [8]Then you shall bring his sons and put coats on them, [9]and you shall gird Aaron and his sons with sashes and bind caps on them. And the priesthood shall be theirs by a statute forever. Thus you shall ordain Aaron and his sons.

[10]"Then you shall bring the bull before the tent of meeting. Aaron and his sons shall lay their hands on the head of the bull. [11]Then you shall kill the bull before the LORD at the entrance of the tent of meeting, [12]and shall take part of the blood of the bull and put it on the horns of the altar with your finger, and the rest of[1] the blood you shall pour out at the base of the altar. [13]And you shall take all the fat that covers the entrails, and the long lobe of the liver, and the two kidneys with the fat that is on them, and burn them on the altar. [14]But the flesh of the bull and its skin and its dung you shall burn with fire outside the camp; it is a sin offering.

[15]"Then you shall take one of the rams, and Aaron and his sons shall lay their hands on the head of the ram, [16]and you shall kill the ram and shall take its blood

---

[1] Hebrew all

and throw it against the sides of the altar. [17]Then you shall cut the ram into pieces, and wash its entrails and its legs, and put them with its pieces and its head, [18]and burn the whole ram on the altar. It is a burnt offering to the LORD. It is a pleasing aroma, a food offering[1] to the LORD.

[19]"You shall take the other ram, and Aaron and his sons shall lay their hands on the head of the ram, [20]and you shall kill the ram and take part of its blood and put it on the tip of the right ear of Aaron and on the tips of the right ears of his sons, and on the thumbs of their right hands and on the great toes of their right feet, and throw the rest of the blood against the sides of the altar. [21]Then you shall take part of the blood that is on the altar, and of the anointing oil, and sprinkle it on Aaron and his garments, and on his sons and his sons' garments with him. He and his garments shall be holy, and his sons and his sons' garments with him.

[22]"You shall also take the fat from the ram and the fat tail and the fat that covers the entrails, and the long lobe of the liver and the two kidneys with the fat that is on them, and the right thigh (for it is a ram of ordination), [23]and one loaf of bread and one cake of bread made with oil, and one wafer out of the basket of unleavened bread that is before the LORD. [24]You shall put all these on the palms of Aaron and on the palms of his sons, and wave them for a wave offering before the LORD. [25]Then you shall take them from their hands and burn them on the altar on top of the burnt offering, as a pleasing aroma before the LORD. It is a food offering to the LORD.

[26]"You shall take the breast of the ram of Aaron's ordination and wave it for a wave offering before the LORD, and it shall be your portion. [27]And you shall consecrate the breast of the wave offering that is waved and the thigh of the priests' portion that is contributed from the ram of ordination, from what was Aaron's and his sons'. [28]It shall be for Aaron and his sons as a perpetual due from the people of Israel, for it is a contribution. It shall be a contribution from the people of Israel from their peace offerings, their contribution to the LORD.

[29]"The holy garments of Aaron shall be for his sons after him; they shall be anointed in them and ordained in them. [30]The son who succeeds him as priest, who comes into the tent of meeting to minister in the Holy Place, shall wear them seven days.

[31]"You shall take the ram of ordination and boil its flesh in a holy place. [32]And Aaron and his sons shall eat the flesh of the ram and the bread that is in the basket in the entrance of the tent of meeting. [33]They shall eat those things with which atonement was made at their ordination and consecration, but an outsider shall not eat of them, because they are holy. [34]And if any of the flesh for the ordination or of the bread remain until the morning, then you shall burn the remainder with fire. It shall not be eaten, because it is holy.

[35]"Thus you shall do to Aaron and to his sons, according to all that I have commanded you. Through seven days shall you ordain them, [36]and every day you shall offer a bull as a sin offering for atonement. Also you shall purify the altar, when you make atonement for it, and shall anoint it to consecrate it. [37]Seven days you shall make atonement for the altar and consecrate it, and the altar shall be most holy. Whatever touches the altar shall become holy.

[38]"Now this is what you shall offer on the altar: two lambs a year old day by day regularly. [39]One lamb you shall offer in the morning, and the other lamb you shall offer at twilight. [40]And with the first lamb a tenth seah[2] of fine flour mingled with a

---

[1] Or an offering by fire; also verses 25, 41 [2] A seah was about 7 quarts or 7.3 liters

fourth of a hin¹ of beaten oil, and a fourth of a hin of wine for a drink offering. ⁴¹The other lamb you shall offer at twilight, and shall offer with it a grain offering and its drink offering, as in the morning, for a pleasing aroma, a food offering to the LORD. ⁴²It shall be a regular burnt offering throughout your generations at the entrance of the tent of meeting before the LORD, where I will meet with you, to speak to you there. ⁴³There I will meet with the people of Israel, and it shall be sanctified by my glory. ⁴⁴I will consecrate the tent of meeting and the altar. Aaron also and his sons I will consecrate to serve me as priests. ⁴⁵I will dwell among the people of Israel and will be their God. ⁴⁶And they shall know that I am the LORD their God, who brought them out of the land of Egypt that I might dwell among them. I am the LORD their God.

> **Final instructions for tabernacle worship** [chapters 30–31]. Most of the information in this section relates to the worship of God in his holy sanctuary, as carried out by Aaron and the other ordained priests. There are instructions for: an altar of incense the priests would use in offering daily prayers in the Holy Place (30:1–10); a sanctuary tax that symbolized the redemption of Israel and went for the ongoing maintenance of the tabernacle (30:11–16); a bronze basin in the courtyard to use for ritual cleansing (30:17–21); the preparation of anointing oil and sacred incense (30:22–38); the calling of Bezalel and Oholiab as master craftsmen to lead in the work of building the tabernacle (31:1–11); and the ongoing observance of a weekly Sabbath (31:12–17). The literary genre of this section of Exodus is an instructional manual for priests.

30 "You shall make an altar on which to burn incense; you shall make it of acacia wood. ²A cubit² shall be its length, and a cubit its breadth. It shall be square, and two cubits shall be its height. Its horns shall be of one piece with it. ³You shall overlay it with pure gold, its top and around its sides and its horns. And you shall make a molding of gold around it. ⁴And you shall make two golden rings for it. Under its molding on two opposite sides of it you shall make them, and they shall be holders for poles with which to carry it. ⁵You shall make the poles of acacia wood and overlay them with gold. ⁶And you shall put it in front of the veil that is above the ark of the testimony, in front of the mercy seat that is above the testimony, where I will meet with you. ⁷And Aaron shall burn fragrant incense on it. Every morning when he dresses the lamps he shall burn it, ⁸and when Aaron sets up the lamps at twilight, he shall burn it, a regular incense offering before the LORD throughout your generations. ⁹You shall not offer unauthorized incense on it, or a burnt offering, or a grain offering, and you shall not pour a drink offering on it. ¹⁰Aaron shall make atonement on its horns once a year. With the blood of the sin offering of atonement he shall make atonement for it once in the year throughout your generations. It is most holy to the LORD."

¹¹The LORD said to Moses, ¹²"When you take the census of the people of Israel, then each shall give a ransom for his life to the LORD when you number them, that there be no plague among them when you number them. ¹³Each one who is numbered in the census shall give this: half a shekel³ according to the shekel of the sanctuary (the shekel is twenty gerahs),⁴ half a shekel as an offering to the LORD. ¹⁴Everyone who is numbered in the census, from twenty years old and upward, shall give the LORD's offering. ¹⁵The rich shall not give more, and the poor shall not give less, than the half

---

¹ A *hin* was about 4 quarts or 3.5 liters ² A *cubit* was about 18 inches or 45 centimeters ³ A *shekel* was about 2/5 ounce or 11 grams ⁴ A *gerah* was about 1/50 ounce or 0.6 gram

shekel, when you give the LORD's offering to make atonement for your lives. [16]You shall take the atonement money from the people of Israel and shall give it for the service of the tent of meeting, that it may bring the people of Israel to remembrance before the LORD, so as to make atonement for your lives."

[17]The LORD said to Moses, [18]"You shall also make a basin of bronze, with its stand of bronze, for washing. You shall put it between the tent of meeting and the altar, and you shall put water in it, [19]with which Aaron and his sons shall wash their hands and their feet. [20]When they go into the tent of meeting, or when they come near the altar to minister, to burn a food offering[1] to the LORD, they shall wash with water, so that they may not die. [21]They shall wash their hands and their feet, so that they may not die. It shall be a statute forever to them, even to him and to his offspring throughout their generations."

[22]The LORD said to Moses, [23]"Take the finest spices: of liquid myrrh 500 shekels, and of sweet-smelling cinnamon half as much, that is, 250, and 250 of aromatic cane, [24]and 500 of cassia, according to the shekel of the sanctuary, and a hin[2] of olive oil. [25]And you shall make of these a sacred anointing oil blended as by the perfumer; it shall be a holy anointing oil. [26]With it you shall anoint the tent of meeting and the ark of the testimony, [27]and the table and all its utensils, and the lampstand and its utensils, and the altar of incense, [28]and the altar of burnt offering with all its utensils and the basin and its stand. [29]You shall consecrate them, that they may be most holy. Whatever touches them will become holy. [30]You shall anoint Aaron and his sons, and consecrate them, that they may serve me as priests. [31]And you shall say to the people of Israel, 'This shall be my holy anointing oil throughout your generations. [32]It shall not be poured on the body of an ordinary person, and you shall make no other like it in composition. It is holy, and it shall be holy to you. [33]Whoever compounds any like it or whoever puts any of it on an outsider shall be cut off from his people.'"

[34]The LORD said to Moses, "Take sweet spices, stacte, and onycha, and galbanum, sweet spices with pure frankincense (of each shall there be an equal part), [35]and make an incense blended as by the perfumer, seasoned with salt, pure and holy. [36]You shall beat some of it very small, and put part of it before the testimony in the tent of meeting where I shall meet with you. It shall be most holy for you. [37]And the incense that you shall make according to its composition, you shall not make for yourselves. It shall be for you holy to the LORD. [38]Whoever makes any like it to use as perfume shall be cut off from his people."

31

The LORD said to Moses, [2]"See, I have called by name Bezalel the son of Uri, son of Hur, of the tribe of Judah, [3]and I have filled him with the Spirit of God, with ability and intelligence, with knowledge and all craftsmanship, [4]to devise artistic designs, to work in gold, silver, and bronze, [5]in cutting stones for setting, and in carving wood, to work in every craft. [6]And behold, I have appointed with him Oholiab, the son of Ahisamach, of the tribe of Dan. And I have given to all able men ability, that they may make all that I have commanded you: [7]the tent of meeting, and the ark of the testimony, and the mercy seat that is on it, and all the furnishings of the tent, [8]the table and its utensils, and the pure lampstand with all its utensils, and the altar of incense, [9]and the altar of burnt offering with all its utensils, and the basin and its stand, [10]and the finely worked garments,[3] the holy garments for Aaron the priest and the garments of his sons, for their service as priests, [11]and the anointing oil and the

---

[1] Or an offering by fire [2] A hin was about 4 quarts or 3.5 liters [3] Or garments for worship

fragrant incense for the Holy Place. According to all that I have commanded you, they shall do."

¹²And the LORD said to Moses, ¹³"You are to speak to the people of Israel and say, 'Above all you shall keep my Sabbaths, for this is a sign between me and you throughout your generations, that you may know that I, the LORD, sanctify you. ¹⁴You shall keep the Sabbath, because it is holy for you. Everyone who profanes it shall be put to death. Whoever does any work on it, that soul shall be cut off from among his people. ¹⁵Six days shall work be done, but the seventh day is a Sabbath of solemn rest, holy to the LORD. Whoever does any work on the Sabbath day shall be put to death. ¹⁶Therefore the people of Israel shall keep the Sabbath, observing the Sabbath throughout their generations, as a covenant forever. ¹⁷It is a sign forever between me and the people of Israel that in six days the LORD made heaven and earth, and on the seventh day he rested and was refreshed.'"

¹⁸And he gave to Moses, when he had finished speaking with him on Mount Sinai, the two tablets of the testimony, tablets of stone, written with the finger of God.

Aaron's sacred cow [chapter 32]. Moses was up on God's mountain. Meanwhile, back at the camp, Aaron was setting up an alternative worship service, featuring pagan revels and the infamous idol of a golden calf. The overarching contrast is between God-centered worship (the carefully regulated rituals Moses has been receiving from God himself) and human-centered worship (what Aaron and the people of Israel come up with on their own initiative). The mood of this unhappy episode in Israel's pilgrimage is heavily ironic and highly pejorative. The people give Moses up for dead at the very time he is making his way down the mountain (v. 1). The first commandments in the law prohibit worshiping other gods or making graven images, but these are the very first things the Israelites want to do (vv. 1–6). Having been delivered from the gods of Egypt, they make for themselves the same kind of graven image that the Egyptians worshiped. And so on. The puzzlement of Joshua ("It is not the sound of shouting for victory, or the sound of the cry of defeat, but the sound of singing that I hear," v. 18) and the poor excuse of Aaron ("I threw it into the fire, and out came this calf," v. 24) are sure signs that something has gone badly wrong. The actions of Moses are decisive in turning away the wrath of God and restoring true worship to Israel. As the mediator, he patiently intercedes for Israel on the basis of the covenant (vv. 7–14), even to the point of offering his own life for their sin (vv. 30–35); angrily makes the people taste the bitter consequences of their sin (vv. 15–20); sternly calls his brother to account (vv. 21–24); and courageously mobilizes the Levites to execute God's vengeance (vv. 25–29).

32 When the people saw that Moses delayed to come down from the mountain, the people gathered themselves together to Aaron and said to him, "Up, make us gods who shall go before us. As for this Moses, the man who brought us up out of the land of Egypt, we do not know what has become of him." ²So Aaron said to them, "Take off the rings of gold that are in the ears of your wives, your sons, and your daughters, and bring them to me." ³So all the people took off the rings of gold that were in their ears and brought them to Aaron. ⁴And he received the gold from their hand and fashioned it with a graving tool and made a golden¹ calf. And they said, "These are your gods, O Israel, who brought you up out of the land of Egypt!" ⁵When Aaron saw this, he built an altar before it. And Aaron made proclamation and said,

¹ Hebrew *cast metal*; also verse 8

"Tomorrow shall be a feast to the LORD." ⁶And they rose up early the next day and offered burnt offerings and brought peace offerings. And the people sat down to eat and drink and rose up to play.

⁷And the LORD said to Moses, "Go down, for your people, whom you brought up out of the land of Egypt, have corrupted themselves. ⁸They have turned aside quickly out of the way that I commanded them. They have made for themselves a golden calf and have worshiped it and sacrificed to it and said, 'These are your gods, O Israel, who brought you up out of the land of Egypt!'" ⁹And the LORD said to Moses, "I have seen this people, and behold, it is a stiff-necked people. ¹⁰Now therefore let me alone, that my wrath may burn hot against them and I may consume them, in order that I may make a great nation of you."

¹¹But Moses implored the LORD his God and said, "O LORD, why does your wrath burn hot against your people, whom you have brought out of the land of Egypt with great power and with a mighty hand? ¹²Why should the Egyptians say, 'With evil intent did he bring them out, to kill them in the mountains and to consume them from the face of the earth'? Turn from your burning anger and relent from this disaster against your people. ¹³Remember Abraham, Isaac, and Israel, your servants, to whom you swore by your own self, and said to them, 'I will multiply your offspring as the stars of heaven, and all this land that I have promised I will give to your offspring, and they shall inherit it forever.'" ¹⁴And the LORD relented from the disaster that he had spoken of bringing on his people.

¹⁵Then Moses turned and went down from the mountain with the two tablets of the testimony in his hand, tablets that were written on both sides; on the front and on the back they were written. ¹⁶The tablets were the work of God, and the writing was the writing of God, engraved on the tablets. ¹⁷When Joshua heard the noise of the people as they shouted, he said to Moses, "There is a noise of war in the camp." ¹⁸But he said, "It is not the sound of shouting for victory, or the sound of the cry of defeat, but the sound of singing that I hear." ¹⁹And as soon as he came near the camp and saw the calf and the dancing, Moses' anger burned hot, and he threw the tablets out of his hands and broke them at the foot of the mountain. ²⁰He took the calf that they had made and burned it with fire and ground it to powder and scattered it on the water and made the people of Israel drink it.

²¹And Moses said to Aaron, "What did this people do to you that you have brought such a great sin upon them?" ²²And Aaron said, "Let not the anger of my lord burn hot. You know the people, that they are set on evil. ²³For they said to me, 'Make us gods who shall go before us. As for this Moses, the man who brought us up out of the land of Egypt, we do not know what has become of him.' ²⁴So I said to them, 'Let any who have gold take it off.' So they gave it to me, and I threw it into the fire, and out came this calf."

²⁵And when Moses saw that the people had broken loose (for Aaron had let them break loose, to the derision of their enemies), ²⁶then Moses stood in the gate of the camp and said, "Who is on the LORD's side? Come to me." And all the sons of Levi gathered around him. ²⁷And he said to them, "Thus says the LORD God of Israel, 'Put your sword on your side each of you, and go to and fro from gate to gate throughout the camp, and each of you kill his brother and his companion and his neighbor.'" ²⁸And the sons of Levi did according to the word of Moses. And that day about three thousand men of the people fell. ²⁹And Moses said, "Today you have been ordained

for the service of the LORD, each one at the cost of his son and of his brother, so that he might bestow a blessing upon you this day."

³⁰The next day Moses said to the people, "You have sinned a great sin. And now I will go up to the LORD; perhaps I can make atonement for your sin." ³¹So Moses returned to the LORD and said, "Alas, this people has sinned a great sin. They have made for themselves gods of gold. ³²But now, if you will forgive their sin—but if not, please blot me out of your book that you have written." ³³But the LORD said to Moses, "Whoever has sinned against me, I will blot out of my book. ³⁴But now go, lead the people to the place about which I have spoken to you; behold, my angel shall go before you. Nevertheless, in the day when I visit, I will visit their sin upon them."

³⁵Then the LORD sent a plague on the people, because they made the calf, the one that Aaron made.

Stay or go? [chapter 33]. This section of Exodus is unified by its concern for God's presence with his people. When God threatens not to go with his people to the Promised Land, lest they should be consumed by his wrath (vv. 1–3), the people go into mourning (vv. 4–6). The goal of their exodus is now threatened by the problem of their sin. But Moses goes into the tent of meeting (vv. 7–11), where he meets with God face to face and successfully argues that unless God goes with them, there is little point in their going at all (vv. 12–15). Indeed, the presence of God is the thing that sets Israel apart from all other nations (see v. 16). Emboldened by God's acceptance (v. 17), Moses audaciously asks to see the glory of God (v. 18). But since this is a sight that no sinful mortal can survive, God agrees to show Moses only his goodness, which is the backside of his glory (vv. 19–23). The narrative motif is again the divine-human *encounter.

33 The LORD said to Moses, "Depart; go up from here, you and the people whom you have brought up out of the land of Egypt, to the land of which I swore to Abraham, Isaac, and Jacob, saying, 'To your offspring I will give it.' ²I will send an angel before you, and I will drive out the Canaanites, the Amorites, the Hittites, the Perizzites, the Hivites, and the Jebusites. ³Go up to a land flowing with milk and honey; but I will not go up among you, lest I consume you on the way, for you are a stiff-necked people."

⁴When the people heard this disastrous word, they mourned, and no one put on his ornaments. ⁵For the LORD had said to Moses, "Say to the people of Israel, 'You are a stiff-necked people; if for a single moment I should go up among you, I would consume you. So now take off your ornaments, that I may know what to do with you.'" ⁶Therefore the people of Israel stripped themselves of their ornaments, from Mount Horeb onward.

⁷Now Moses used to take the tent and pitch it outside the camp, far off from the camp, and he called it the tent of meeting. And everyone who sought the LORD would go out to the tent of meeting, which was outside the camp. ⁸Whenever Moses went out to the tent, all the people would rise up, and each would stand at his tent door, and watch Moses until he had gone into the tent. ⁹When Moses entered the tent, the pillar of cloud would descend and stand at the entrance of the tent, and the LORD¹ would speak with Moses. ¹⁰And when all the people saw the pillar of cloud standing at the entrance of the tent, all the people would rise up and worship, each at his tent door. ¹¹Thus the LORD used to speak to Moses face to face, as a man speaks to his

¹ Hebrew *he*

friend. When Moses turned again into the camp, his assistant Joshua the son of Nun, a young man, would not depart from the tent.

¹²Moses said to the Lord, "See, you say to me, 'Bring up this people,' but you have not let me know whom you will send with me. Yet you have said, 'I know you by name, and you have also found favor in my sight.' ¹³Now therefore, if I have found favor in your sight, please show me now your ways, that I may know you in order to find favor in your sight. Consider too that this nation is your people." ¹⁴And he said, "My presence will go with you, and I will give you rest." ¹⁵And he said to him, "If your presence will not go with me, do not bring us up from here. ¹⁶For how shall it be known that I have found favor in your sight, I and your people? Is it not in your going with us, so that we are distinct, I and your people, from every other people on the face of the earth?"

¹⁷And the Lord said to Moses, "This very thing that you have spoken I will do, for you have found favor in my sight, and I know you by name." ¹⁸Moses said, "Please show me your glory." ¹⁹And he said, "I will make all my goodness pass before you and will proclaim before you my name 'The Lord.' And I will be gracious to whom I will be gracious, and will show mercy on whom I will show mercy. ²⁰But," he said, "you cannot see my face, for man shall not see me and live." ²¹And the Lord said, "Behold, there is a place by me where you shall stand on the rock, ²²and while my glory passes by I will put you in a cleft of the rock, and I will cover you with my hand until I have passed by. ²³Then I will take away my hand, and you shall see my back, but my face shall not be seen."

The glory and the covenant [chapter 34]. The two stone tablets of the Ten Commandments—the tablets that Moses angrily broke when he saw the Israelites dancing around their golden calf—still need to be replaced. So Moses goes back up the mountain alone for another forty days and forty nights (vv. 1–4, 28). There the mediator has another encounter with God. He stands in God's presence to hear God proclaim the full meaning of his gracious name (vv. 5–9) and to receive a fresh transcription of the Ten Commandments, with the Book of the Covenant (vv. 10–28). Upon making his descent, Moses discovers that his face is still shining with the reflection of God's glory (vv. 29–35). This visible display of divine radiance distinguishes Moses as the mediator and marks a further development in the glory of God as the main theme of Exodus. Human beings are made to bear the glory of God, even if at present such glory is too dazzling for mortal eyes to see. The veil as an image of the numinous or transcendent is a literary archetype.

34 The Lord said to Moses, "Cut for yourself two tablets of stone like the first, and I will write on the tablets the words that were on the first tablets, which you broke. ²Be ready by the morning, and come up in the morning to Mount Sinai, and present yourself there to me on the top of the mountain. ³No one shall come up with you, and let no one be seen throughout all the mountain. Let no flocks or herds graze opposite that mountain." ⁴So Moses cut two tablets of stone like the first. And he rose early in the morning and went up on Mount Sinai, as the Lord had commanded him, and took in his hand two tablets of stone. ⁵The Lord descended in the cloud and stood with him there, and proclaimed the name of the Lord. ⁶The Lord passed before him and proclaimed, "The Lord, the Lord, a God merciful and gracious, slow to anger, and abounding in steadfast love and faithfulness, [7]keeping steadfast love for thousands,[1] forgiving iniquity and transgression and sin, but who will by no means clear the guilty, visiting the iniquity of the fathers on the children and the children's children, to the third and the fourth generation." [8]And Moses quickly bowed his head toward the earth and worshiped. [9]And he said, "If now I have found favor in your sight, O Lord, please let the Lord go in the midst of us, for it is a stiff-necked people, and pardon our iniquity and our sin, and take us for your inheritance."

[10]And he said, "Behold, I am making a covenant. Before all your people I will do marvels, such as have not been created in all the earth or in any nation. And all the people among whom you are shall see the work of the LORD, for it is an awesome thing that I will do with you.

[11]"Observe what I command you this day. Behold, I will drive out before you the Amorites, the Canaanites, the Hittites, the Perizzites, the Hivites, and the Jebusites. [12]Take care, lest you make a covenant with the inhabitants of the land to which you go, lest it become a snare in your midst. [13]You shall tear down their altars and break their pillars and cut down their Asherim [14](for you shall worship no other god, for the LORD, whose name is Jealous, is a jealous God), [15]lest you make a covenant with the inhabitants of the land, and when they whore after their gods and sacrifice to their gods and you are invited, you eat of his sacrifice, [16]and you take of their daughters for your sons, and their daughters whore after their gods and make your sons whore after their gods.

[17]"You shall not make for yourself any gods of cast metal.

[18]"You shall keep the Feast of Unleavened Bread. Seven days you shall eat unleavened bread, as I commanded you, at the time appointed in the month Abib, for in the month Abib you came out from Egypt. [19]All that open the womb are mine, all your male[2] livestock, the firstborn of cow and sheep. [20]The firstborn of a donkey you shall redeem with a lamb, or if you will not redeem it you shall break its neck. All the firstborn of your sons you shall redeem. And none shall appear before me empty-handed.

[21]"Six days you shall work, but on the seventh day you shall rest. In plowing time and in harvest you shall rest. [22]You shall observe the Feast of Weeks, the firstfruits of wheat harvest, and the Feast of Ingathering at the year's end. [23]Three times in the year shall all your males appear before the LORD God, the God of Israel. [24]For I will cast out nations before you and enlarge your borders; no one shall covet your land, when you go up to appear before the LORD your God three times in the year.

[25]"You shall not offer the blood of my sacrifice with anything leavened, or let the sacrifice of the Feast of the Passover remain until the morning. [26]The best of the firstfruits of your ground you shall bring to the house of the LORD your God. You shall not boil a young goat in its mother's milk."

[27]And the LORD said to Moses, "Write these words, for in accordance with these words I have made a covenant with you and with Israel." [28]So he was there with the LORD forty days and forty nights. He neither ate bread nor drank water. And he wrote on the tablets the words of the covenant, the Ten Commandments.[3]

[29]When Moses came down from Mount Sinai, with the two tablets of the testimony in his hand as he came down from the mountain, Moses did not know that the skin of his face shone because he had been talking with God.[4] [30]Aaron and all the people

---

[1] Or to the thousandth generation [2] Septuagint, Theodotion, Vulgate, Targum; the meaning of the Hebrew is uncertain [3] Hebrew the ten words
[4] Hebrew him

of Israel saw Moses, and behold, the skin of his face shone, and they were afraid to come near him. ³¹But Moses called to them, and Aaron and all the leaders of the congregation returned to him, and Moses talked with them. ³²Afterward all the people of Israel came near, and he commanded them all that the LORD had spoken with him in Mount Sinai. ³³And when Moses had finished speaking with them, he put a veil over his face.

³⁴Whenever Moses went in before the LORD to speak with him, he would remove the veil, until he came out. And when he came out and told the people of Israel what he was commanded, ³⁵the people of Israel would see the face of Moses, that the skin of Moses' face was shining. And Moses would put the veil over his face again, until he went in to speak with him.

> **Freewill offering** [35:1–29]. Finally the Israelites are ready to fabricate and erect the tabernacle for which God gave Moses the blueprints on Mount Sinai. The material in chapters 35–39 repeats much of the material in chapters 25–31, in some cases verbatim. This repetition is instructive, however, because it shows how carefully the Israelites followed God's instructions (in obvious contrast to the disastrous incident with the golden calf, when they decided to do their own thing). The project begins with a freewill offering, in which the Israelites contribute all of the gold, silver, bronze, blue, purple, scarlet, wood, gems, oil, spices, and animal skins that are needed to make the tabernacle (vv. 4–9, 20–28). According to their God-given ability, some of the Israelites also offer their skill with arts and crafts (vv. 10–19, 26). Although most of this passage is simply a catalog of materials, a strong emphasis falls on the people's willing service in offering their gifts and their possessions to God (vv. 5, 21, 22, 29).

35 Moses assembled all the congregation of the people of Israel and said to them, "These are the things that the LORD has commanded you to do. ²Six days work shall be done, but on the seventh day you shall have a Sabbath of solemn rest, holy to the LORD. Whoever does any work on it shall be put to death. ³You shall kindle no fire in all your dwelling places on the Sabbath day."

⁴Moses said to all the congregation of the people of Israel, "This is the thing that the LORD has commanded. ⁵Take from among you a contribution to the LORD. Whoever is of a generous heart, let him bring the LORD's contribution: gold, silver, and bronze; ⁶blue and purple and scarlet yarns and fine twined linen; goats' hair, ⁷tanned rams' skins, and goatskins;¹ acacia wood, ⁸oil for the light, spices for the anointing oil and for the fragrant incense, ⁹and onyx stones and stones for setting, for the ephod and for the breastpiece.

¹⁰"Let every skillful craftsman among you come and make all that the LORD has commanded: ¹¹the tabernacle, its tent and its covering, its hooks and its frames, its bars, its pillars, and its bases; ¹²the ark with its poles, the mercy seat, and the veil of the screen; ¹³the table with its poles and all its utensils, and the bread of the Presence; ¹⁴the lampstand also for the light, with its utensils and its lamps, and the oil for the light; ¹⁵and the altar of incense, with its poles, and the anointing oil and the fragrant incense, and the screen for the door, at the door of the tabernacle; ¹⁶the altar of burnt offering, with its grating of bronze, its poles, and all its utensils, the basin and its stand; ¹⁷the hangings of the court, its pillars and its bases, and the screen for the gate of the court; ¹⁸the pegs of the tabernacle and the pegs of the court, and their cords;

¹ The meaning of the Hebrew word is uncertain; also verse 23; compare 25:5

[19] the finely worked garments for ministering[1] in the Holy Place, the holy garments for Aaron the priest, and the garments of his sons, for their service as priests."

[20] Then all the congregation of the people of Israel departed from the presence of Moses. [21] And they came, everyone whose heart stirred him, and everyone whose spirit moved him, and brought the LORD's contribution to be used for the tent of meeting, and for all its service, and for the holy garments. [22] So they came, both men and women. All who were of a willing heart brought brooches and earrings and signet rings and armlets, all sorts of gold objects, every man dedicating an offering of gold to the LORD. [23] And every one who possessed blue or purple or scarlet yarns or fine linen or goats' hair or tanned rams' skins or goatskins brought them. [24] Everyone who could make a contribution of silver or bronze brought it as the LORD's contribution. And every one who possessed acacia wood of any use in the work brought it. [25] And every skillful woman spun with her hands, and they all brought what they had spun in blue and purple and scarlet yarns and fine twined linen. [26] All the women whose hearts stirred them to use their skill spun the goats' hair. [27] And the leaders brought onyx stones and stones to be set, for the ephod and for the breastpiece, [28] and spices and oil for the light, and for the anointing oil, and for the fragrant incense. [29] All the men and women, the people of Israel, whose heart moved them to bring anything for the work that the LORD had commanded by Moses to be done brought it as a freewill offering to the LORD.

A beautiful house for God [35:30–36:38]. Bezalel and Oholiab were first introduced back in chapter 31, where they were filled with the Holy Spirit and called by God to use the full range of their artistic gifts in constructing the tabernacle. They are the first people in Scripture explicitly said to be "filled . . . with the Spirit of God" (35:31; cf. 31:3)—a fact that serves to emphasize both the importance of the tabernacle as a sanctuary for God and the value that God places on truth, beauty, and excellence in art. Here Bezalel and Oholiab are publicly set apart for service (35:30–36:1) and begin to exercise their gifts, leading the whole artistic community in making the curtains (36:8–19), frame (36:20–34), and veils (36:35–38) for God's beautiful house (36:8–38). Happily, the people have brought so many material contributions for the tabernacle that Moses must tell them not to make any more offerings (36:2–7). A good way to assimilate the chapter is to imagine oneself present at the event. The mood of the passage is joyous and industrious.

[30] Then Moses said to the people of Israel, "See, the LORD has called by name Bezalel the son of Uri, son of Hur, of the tribe of Judah; [31] and he has filled him with the Spirit of God, with skill, with intelligence, with knowledge, and with all craftsmanship, [32] to devise artistic designs, to work in gold and silver and bronze, [33] in cutting stones for setting, and in carving wood, for work in every skilled craft. [34] And he has inspired him to teach, both him and Oholiab the son of Ahisamach of the tribe of Dan. [35] He has filled them with skill to do every sort of work done by an engraver or by a designer or by an embroiderer in blue and purple and scarlet yarns and fine twined linen, or by a weaver—by any sort of workman or skilled designer.

---

[1] Or *garments for worship*; see 31:10

36 "Bezalel and Oholiab and every craftsman in whom the LORD has put skill and intelligence to know how to do any work in the construction of the sanctuary shall work in accordance with all that the LORD has commanded."

²And Moses called Bezalel and Oholiab and every craftsman in whose mind the LORD had put skill, everyone whose heart stirred him up to come to do the work. ³And they received from Moses all the contribution that the people of Israel had brought for doing the work on the sanctuary. They still kept bringing him freewill offerings every morning, ⁴so that all the craftsmen who were doing every sort of task on the sanctuary came, each from the task that he was doing, ⁵and said to Moses, "The people bring much more than enough for doing the work that the LORD has commanded us to do." ⁶So Moses gave command, and word was proclaimed throughout the camp, "Let no man or woman do anything more for the contribution for the sanctuary." So the people were restrained from bringing, ⁷for the material they had was sufficient to do all the work, and more.

⁸And all the craftsmen among the workmen made the tabernacle with ten curtains. They were made of fine twined linen and blue and purple and scarlet yarns, with cherubim skillfully worked. ⁹The length of each curtain was twenty-eight cubits,¹ and the breadth of each curtain four cubits. All the curtains were the same size. ¹⁰He coupled five curtains to one another, and the other five curtains he coupled to one another. ¹¹He made loops of blue on the edge of the outermost curtain of the first set. Likewise he made them on the edge of the outermost curtain of the second set. ¹²He made fifty loops on the one curtain, and he made fifty loops on the edge of the curtain that was in the second set. The loops were opposite one another. ¹³And he made fifty clasps of gold, and coupled the curtains one to the other with clasps. So the tabernacle was a single whole.

¹⁴He also made curtains of goats' hair for a tent over the tabernacle. He made eleven curtains. ¹⁵The length of each curtain was thirty cubits, and the breadth of each curtain four cubits. The eleven curtains were the same size. ¹⁶He coupled five curtains by themselves, and six curtains by themselves. ¹⁷And he made fifty loops on the edge of the outermost curtain of the one set, and fifty loops on the edge of the other connecting curtain. ¹⁸And he made fifty clasps of bronze to couple the tent together that it might be a single whole. ¹⁹And he made for the tent a covering of tanned rams' skins and goatskins.

²⁰Then he made the upright frames for the tabernacle of acacia wood. ²¹Ten cubits was the length of a frame, and a cubit and a half the breadth of each frame. ²²Each frame had two tenons for fitting together. He did this for all the frames of the tabernacle. ²³The frames for the tabernacle he made thus: twenty frames for the south side. ²⁴And he made forty bases of silver under the twenty frames, two bases under one frame for its two tenons, and two bases under the next frame for its two tenons. ²⁵For the second side of the tabernacle, on the north side, he made twenty frames ²⁶and their forty bases of silver, two bases under one frame and two bases under the next frame. ²⁷For the rear of the tabernacle westward he made six frames. ²⁸He made two frames for corners of the tabernacle in the rear. ²⁹And they were separate beneath but joined at the top, at the first ring. He made two of them this way for the two corners. ³⁰There were eight frames with their bases of silver: sixteen bases, under every frame two bases.

³¹He made bars of acacia wood, five for the frames of the one side of the taberna-

---

¹ A *cubit* was about 18 inches or 45 centimeters

cle, ³²and five bars for the frames of the other side of the tabernacle, and five bars for the frames of the tabernacle at the rear westward. ³³And he made the middle bar to run from end to end halfway up the frames. ³⁴And he overlaid the frames with gold, and made their rings of gold for holders for the bars, and overlaid the bars with gold.

³⁵He made the veil of blue and purple and scarlet yarns and fine twined linen; with cherubim skillfully worked into it he made it. ³⁶And for it he made four pillars of acacia and overlaid them with gold. Their hooks were of gold, and he cast for them four bases of silver. ³⁷He also made a screen for the entrance of the tent, of blue and purple and scarlet yarns and fine twined linen, embroidered with needlework, ³⁸and its five pillars with their hooks. He overlaid their capitals, and their fillets were of gold, but their five bases were of bronze.

In God's house [chapter 37]. The building project continues with Bezalel's making everything inside the tabernacle according to God's plan: the ark of the covenant, with cherubim representing the throne room of God and a mercy seat for making atonement (vv. 1–9); the table for the bread of the Presence, representing fellowship with God (vv. 10–16); the golden lampstand, representing the light and the life that come from God (vv. 17–24); and the altar of incense, where prayer was to be offered for God's people (vv. 25–29). These items of furniture signify the blessings that come from knowing God, such as forgiveness for sin, provision for daily needs, and access to God through prayer. They are all made of gold, because the inside of the earthly tabernacle was the royal dwelling place of God. After the earlier gathering of materials, the actual building of the tabernacle assumes the qualities of a narrative climax.

37 Bezalel made the ark of acacia wood. Two cubits¹ and a half was its length, a cubit and a half its breadth, and a cubit and a half its height. ²And he overlaid it with pure gold inside and outside, and made a molding of gold around it. ³And he cast for it four rings of gold for its four feet, two rings on its one side and two rings on its other side. ⁴And he made poles of acacia wood and overlaid them with gold ⁵and put the poles into the rings on the sides of the ark to carry the ark. ⁶And he made a mercy seat of pure gold. Two cubits and a half was its length, and a cubit and a half its breadth. ⁷And he made two cherubim of gold. He made them of hammered work on the two ends of the mercy seat, ⁸one cherub on the one end, and one cherub on the other end. Of one piece with the mercy seat he made the cherubim on its two ends. ⁹The cherubim spread out their wings above, overshadowing the mercy seat with their wings, with their faces one to another; toward the mercy seat were the faces of the cherubim.

¹⁰He also made the table of acacia wood. Two cubits was its length, a cubit its breadth, and a cubit and a half its height. ¹¹And he overlaid it with pure gold, and made a molding of gold around it. ¹²And he made a rim around it a handbreadth² wide, and made a molding of gold around the rim. ¹³He cast for it four rings of gold and fastened the rings to the four corners at its four legs. ¹⁴Close to the frame were the rings, as holders for the poles to carry the table. ¹⁵He made the poles of acacia wood to carry the table, and overlaid them with gold. ¹⁶And he made the vessels of pure gold that were to be on the table, its plates and dishes for incense, and its bowls and flagons with which to pour drink offerings.

¹⁷He also made the lampstand of pure gold. He made the lampstand of hammered

---

¹ A *cubit* was about 18 inches or 45 centimeters ² A *handbreadth* was about 3 inches or 7.5 centimeters

work. Its base, its stem, its cups, its calyxes, and its flowers were of one piece with it. ¹⁸And there were six branches going out of its sides, three branches of the lampstand out of one side of it and three branches of the lampstand out of the other side of it; ¹⁹three cups made like almond blossoms, each with calyx and flower, on one branch, and three cups made like almond blossoms, each with calyx and flower, on the other branch—so for the six branches going out of the lampstand. ²⁰And on the lampstand itself were four cups made like almond blossoms, with their calyxes and flowers, ²¹and a calyx of one piece with it under each pair of the six branches going out of it. ²²Their calyxes and their branches were of one piece with it. The whole of it was a single piece of hammered work of pure gold. ²³And he made its seven lamps and its tongs and its trays of pure gold. ²⁴He made it and all its utensils out of a talent¹ of pure gold.

²⁵He made the altar of incense of acacia wood. Its length was a cubit, and its breadth was a cubit. It was square, and two cubits was its height. Its horns were of one piece with it. ²⁶He overlaid it with pure gold, its top and around its sides and its horns. And he made a molding of gold around it, ²⁷and made two rings of gold on it under its molding, on two opposite sides of it, as holders for the poles with which to carry it. ²⁸And he made the poles of acacia wood and overlaid them with gold.

²⁹He made the holy anointing oil also, and the pure fragrant incense, blended as by the perfumer.

Outside the tabernacle [chapter 38]. Everything outside the tabernacle was also made according to God's plan: the bronze altar for burnt offerings (vv. 1–7), the bronze basin for cleansing (v. 8), and the fences for the courtyard where people went to meet with God (vv. 9–20). The furnishings in the courtyard were made of bronze, rather than gold, because this was only the entranceway to God and not his actual dwelling place. They showed that in order to gain access to God, people need atonement and cleansing for sin. Exodus ends its building record for the tabernacle with another inventory, which carefully accounts for all the valuable materials that went into its construction (vv. 21–31).

38 He made the altar of burnt offering of acacia wood. Five cubits² was its length, and five cubits its breadth. It was square, and three cubits was its height. ²He made horns for it on its four corners. Its horns were of one piece with it, and he overlaid it with bronze. ³And he made all the utensils of the altar, the pots, the shovels, the basins, the forks, and the fire pans. He made all its utensils of bronze. ⁴And he made for the altar a grating, a network of bronze, under its ledge, extending halfway down. ⁵He cast four rings on the four corners of the bronze grating as holders for the poles. ⁶He made the poles of acacia wood and overlaid them with bronze. ⁷And he put the poles through the rings on the sides of the altar to carry it with them. He made it hollow, with boards.

⁸He made the basin of bronze and its stand of bronze, from the mirrors of the ministering women who ministered in the entrance of the tent of meeting.

⁹And he made the court. For the south side the hangings of the court were of fine twined linen, a hundred cubits; ¹⁰their twenty pillars and their twenty bases were of bronze, but the hooks of the pillars and their fillets were of silver. ¹¹And for the north

---

¹ A *talent* was about 75 pounds or 34 kilograms ² A *cubit* was about 18 inches or 45 centimeters

side there were hangings of a hundred cubits, their twenty pillars, their twenty bases were of bronze, but the hooks of the pillars and their fillets were of silver. [12]And for the west side were hangings of fifty cubits, their ten pillars, and their ten bases; the hooks of the pillars and their fillets were of silver. [13]And for the front to the east, fifty cubits. [14]The hangings for one side of the gate were fifteen cubits, with their three pillars and three bases. [15]And so for the other side. On both sides of the gate of the court were hangings of fifteen cubits, with their three pillars and their three bases. [16]All the hangings around the court were of fine twined linen. [17]And the bases for the pillars were of bronze, but the hooks of the pillars and their fillets were of silver. The overlaying of their capitals was also of silver, and all the pillars of the court were filleted with silver. [18]And the screen for the gate of the court was embroidered with needlework in blue and purple and scarlet yarns and fine twined linen. It was twenty cubits long and five cubits high in its breadth, corresponding to the hangings of the court. [19]And their pillars were four in number. Their four bases were of bronze, their hooks of silver, and the overlaying of their capitals and their fillets of silver. [20]And all the pegs for the tabernacle and for the court all around were of bronze.

[21]These are the records of the tabernacle, the tabernacle of the testimony, as they were recorded at the commandment of Moses, the responsibility of the Levites under the direction of Ithamar the son of Aaron the priest. [22]Bezalel the son of Uri, son of Hur, of the tribe of Judah, made all that the LORD commanded Moses; [23]and with him was Oholiab the son of Ahisamach, of the tribe of Dan, an engraver and designer and embroiderer in blue and purple and scarlet yarns and fine twined linen.

[24]All the gold that was used for the work, in all the construction of the sanctuary, the gold from the offering, was twenty-nine talents and 730 shekels,[1] by the shekel of the sanctuary. [25]The silver from those of the congregation who were recorded was a hundred talents and 1,775 shekels, by the shekel of the sanctuary: [26]a beka[2] a head (that is, half a shekel, by the shekel of the sanctuary), for everyone who was listed in the records, from twenty years old and upward, for 603,550 men. [27]The hundred talents of silver were for casting the bases of the sanctuary and the bases of the veil; a hundred bases for the hundred talents, a talent a base. [28]And of the 1,775 shekels he made hooks for the pillars and overlaid their capitals and made fillets for them. [29]The bronze that was offered was seventy talents and 2,400 shekels; [30]with it he made the bases for the entrance of the tent of meeting, the bronze altar and the bronze grating for it and all the utensils of the altar, [31]the bases around the court, and the bases of the gate of the court, all the pegs of the tabernacle, and all the pegs around the court.

> **Just as God said** [chapter 39]. Care was also taken to make the priestly garments according to the pattern that God showed Moses on the mountain (v. 1), including the ephod (vv. 2–7), the breastpiece (vv. 8–21), the robe (vv. 22–26), and the turban (vv. 27–31). The high priest was holy from head to toe. The chapter ends by saying—three times, no less—what should be evident already, that the people of Israel made the tabernacle exactly the way that God told them to make it (vv. 32, 42–43). This is a notable example—all too rare—of full obedience to the revealed will of God.

---

[1] A *talent* was about 75 pounds or 34 kilograms; a *shekel* was about 2/5 ounce or 11 grams [2] A *beka* was about 1/5 ounce or 5.5 grams

39 From the blue and purple and scarlet yarns they made finely woven garments,[1] for ministering in the Holy Place. They made the holy garments for Aaron, as the LORD had commanded Moses.

[2]He made the ephod of gold, blue and purple and scarlet yarns, and fine twined linen. [3]And they hammered out gold leaf, and he cut it into threads to work into the blue and purple and the scarlet yarns, and into the fine twined linen, in skilled design. [4]They made for the ephod attaching shoulder pieces, joined to it at its two edges. [5]And the skillfully woven band on it was of one piece with it and made like it, of gold, blue and purple and scarlet yarns, and fine twined linen, as the LORD had commanded Moses.

[6]They made the onyx stones, enclosed in settings of gold filigree, and engraved like the engravings of a signet, according to the names of the sons of Israel. [7]And he set them on the shoulder pieces of the ephod to be stones of remembrance for the sons of Israel, as the LORD had commanded Moses.

[8]He made the breastpiece, in skilled work, in the style of the ephod, of gold, blue and purple and scarlet yarns, and fine twined linen. [9]It was square. They made the breastpiece doubled, a span[2] its length and a span its breadth when doubled. [10]And they set in it four rows of stones. A row of sardius, topaz, and carbuncle was the first row; [11]and the second row, an emerald, a sapphire, and a diamond; [12]and the third row, a jacinth, an agate, and an amethyst; [13]and the fourth row, a beryl, an onyx, and a jasper. They were enclosed in settings of gold filigree. [14]There were twelve stones with their names according to the names of the sons of Israel. They were like signets, each engraved with its name, for the twelve tribes. [15]And they made on the breastpiece twisted chains like cords, of pure gold. [16]And they made two settings of gold filigree and two gold rings, and put the two rings on the two edges of the breastpiece. [17]And they put the two cords of gold in the two rings at the edges of the breastpiece. [18]They attached the two ends of the two cords to the two settings of filigree. Thus they attached it in front to the shoulder pieces of the ephod. [19]Then they made two rings of gold, and put them at the two ends of the breastpiece, on its inside edge next to the ephod. [20]And they made two rings of gold, and attached them in front to the lower part of the two shoulder pieces of the ephod, at its seam above the skillfully woven band of the ephod. [21]And they bound the breastpiece by its rings to the rings of the ephod with a lace of blue, so that it should lie on the skillfully woven band of the ephod, and that the breastpiece should not come loose from the ephod, as the LORD had commanded Moses.

[22]He also made the robe of the ephod woven all of blue, [23]and the opening of the robe in it was like the opening in a garment, with a binding around the opening, so that it might not tear. [24]On the hem of the robe they made pomegranates of blue and purple and scarlet yarns and fine twined linen. [25]They also made bells of pure gold, and put the bells between the pomegranates all around the hem of the robe, between the pomegranates— [26]a bell and a pomegranate, a bell and a pomegranate around the hem of the robe for ministering, as the LORD had commanded Moses.

[27]They also made the coats, woven of fine linen, for Aaron and his sons, [28]and the turban of fine linen, and the caps of fine linen, and the linen undergarments of fine twined linen, [29]and the sash of fine twined linen and of blue and purple and scarlet yarns, embroidered with needlework, as the LORD had commanded Moses.

[30]They made the plate of the holy crown of pure gold, and wrote on it an inscrip-

---

[1] Or *garments for worship* [2] A *span* was about 9 inches or 22 centimeters

tion, like the engraving of a signet, "Holy to the LORD." ³¹And they tied to it a cord of blue to fasten it on the turban above, as the LORD had commanded Moses.

³²Thus all the work of the tabernacle of the tent of meeting was finished, and the people of Israel did according to all that the LORD had commanded Moses; so they did. ³³Then they brought the tabernacle to Moses, the tent and all its utensils, its hooks, its frames, its bars, its pillars, and its bases; ³⁴the covering of tanned rams' skins and goatskins, and the veil of the screen; ³⁵the ark of the testimony with its poles and the mercy seat; ³⁶the table with all its utensils, and the bread of the Presence; ³⁷the lampstand of pure gold and its lamps with the lamps set and all its utensils, and the oil for the light; ³⁸the golden altar, the anointing oil and the fragrant incense, and the screen for the entrance of the tent; ³⁹the bronze altar, and its grating of bronze, its poles, and all its utensils; the basin and its stand; ⁴⁰the hangings of the court, its pillars, and its bases, and the screen for the gate of the court, its cords, and its pegs; and all the utensils for the service of the tabernacle, for the tent of meeting; ⁴¹the finely worked garments for ministering in the Holy Place, the holy garments for Aaron the priest, and the garments of his sons for their service as priests. ⁴²According to all that the LORD had commanded Moses, so the people of Israel had done all the work. ⁴³And Moses saw all the work, and behold, they had done it; as the LORD had commanded, so had they done it. Then Moses blessed them.

When glory came down [chapter 40]. The last chapter of Exodus, in which Moses sets up the tabernacle step by step, may at first seem rather mundane. The prophet very methodically follows God's directions for assembly (vv. 1–8), starting with the tent of meeting and its furnishings (vv. 16–28) and then working his way all the way out to the courtyard fence (vv. 29–33). With holy oil he anoints every part of the tabernacle (vv. 9–11) and every priest who serves in the tabernacle (vv. 12–15) for the sacred worship of God. The suspense builds as each item is set in place: will God really dwell with his people? That question is decisively answered when Moses finishes his work and God fills the tabernacle with his glory (vv. 34–38). Ironically, the mediator cannot even enter the tent where he is supposed to meet with God because it is too full of glory! This is the final climax of the book of Exodus. God is with his people; he has come down in all his glory, to go with them wherever they go. Epics usually end with the motif of empire, as the hero and his nation win a final battle and establish or regain a kingdom. The epic of Exodus ends with the glory of God overwhelming a nation in the form of the cloud and fire of divine presence.

---

40 The LORD spoke to Moses, saying, ²"On the first day of the first month you shall erect the tabernacle of the tent of meeting. ³And you shall put in it the ark of the testimony, and you shall screen the ark with the veil. ⁴And you shall bring in the table and arrange it, and you shall bring in the lampstand and set up its lamps. ⁵And you shall put the golden altar for incense before the ark of the testimony, and set up the screen for the door of the tabernacle. ⁶You shall set the altar of burnt offering before the door of the tabernacle of the tent of meeting, ⁷and place the basin between the tent of meeting and the altar, and put water in it. ⁸And you shall set up the court all around, and hang up the screen for the gate of the court.

⁹"Then you shall take the anointing oil and anoint the tabernacle and all that is in it, and consecrate it and all its furniture, so that it may become holy. ¹⁰You shall also

anoint the altar of burnt offering and all its utensils, and consecrate the altar, so that
the altar may become most holy. ¹¹You shall also anoint the basin and its stand, and
consecrate it. ¹²Then you shall bring Aaron and his sons to the entrance of the tent of
meeting and shall wash them with water ¹³and put on Aaron the holy garments. And
you shall anoint him and consecrate him, that he may serve me as priest. ¹⁴You shall
bring his sons also and put coats on them, ¹⁵and anoint them, as you anointed their
father, that they may serve me as priests. And their anointing shall admit them to a
perpetual priesthood throughout their generations."

¹⁶This Moses did; according to all that the LORD commanded him, so he did. ¹⁷In
the first month in the second year, on the first day of the month, the tabernacle was
erected. ¹⁸Moses erected the tabernacle. He laid its bases, and set up its frames, and
put in its poles, and raised up its pillars. ¹⁹And he spread the tent over the tabernacle
and put the covering of the tent over it, as the LORD had commanded Moses. ²⁰He took
the testimony and put it into the ark, and put the poles on the ark and set the mercy
seat above on the ark. ²¹And he brought the ark into the tabernacle and set up the veil
of the screen, and screened the ark of the testimony, as the LORD had commanded
Moses. ²²He put the table in the tent of meeting, on the north side of the tabernacle,
outside the veil, ²³and arranged the bread on it before the LORD, as the LORD had commanded Moses. ²⁴He put the lampstand in the tent of meeting, opposite the table on
the south side of the tabernacle, ²⁵and set up the lamps before the LORD, as the LORD
had commanded Moses. ²⁶He put the golden altar in the tent of meeting before the
veil, ²⁷and burned fragrant incense on it, as the LORD had commanded Moses. ²⁸He
put in place the screen for the door of the tabernacle. ²⁹And he set the altar of burnt
offering at the entrance of the tabernacle of the tent of meeting, and offered on it the
burnt offering and the grain offering, as the LORD had commanded Moses. ³⁰He set
the basin between the tent of meeting and the altar, and put water in it for washing,
³¹with which Moses and Aaron and his sons washed their hands and their feet.
³²When they went into the tent of meeting, and when they approached the altar, they
washed, as the LORD commanded Moses. ³³And he erected the court around the tabernacle and the altar, and set up the screen of the gate of the court. So Moses finished
the work.

³⁴Then the cloud covered the tent of meeting, and the glory of the LORD filled the
tabernacle. ³⁵And Moses was not able to enter the tent of meeting because the cloud
settled on it, and the glory of the LORD filled the tabernacle. ³⁶Throughout all their
journeys, whenever the cloud was taken up from over the tabernacle, the people of
Israel would set out. ³⁷But if the cloud was not taken up, then they did not set out till
the day that it was taken up. ³⁸For the cloud of the LORD was on the tabernacle by day,
and fire was in it by night, in the sight of all the house of Israel throughout all their
journeys.

LEVITICUS

> **The book at a glance.** 27 chapters, 859 verses. Leviticus tells the story of how God wanted the OT covenant nation of Israel to order its religious life and practices, especially in regard to worship and the sacrifices that were the basis of God's relationship to his people. But even though the book tells the story of how God wanted Israel to live the life of faith, the format of the book is not that of *narrative. Instead, Leviticus consists largely of rules and regulations. Although the book's title (which means "that which pertains to the Levites") might seem to indicate that the book is a set of guidelines for the priests of Israel, only part of the book is addressed to the Levites. Most of the regulations are addressed to the nation. A good reading strategy is to look for the implied stories and human experiences of people living within the system—experiences like the terror of discovering some type of contamination in one's house and having to report it to the priests, possibly for disinfection of the house or even full-scale dismantlement (14:33–47).

▌Genres. The opening verse implies that the origin of the book was the convocation of the fledgling nation of Israel at Mount Sinai. Within that context, Leviticus gives a blueprint for a whole society, and the literary genre that we should have in mind is *utopian literature. The genre known as utopia gets its title from a Greek phrase meaning "good place," which in turn denotes "good society." Utopias not only portray a good society but offer an explanation of the institutions and practices that produce such a society. That is what the book of Leviticus does: it both portrays how people act in God's ideal commonwealth and lets us know what practices (the rules and regulations that God commands) and institutional scaffolding (the Levitical priesthood) will produce the good society. While utopias usually contain detailed regulations, implying that people will not innately do what is right, the book of Leviticus nonetheless tugs away from the utopian genre by its more extreme awareness of human sinfulness, for which the whole system of laws is intended to serve as a remedy before God. Additional genres include the following: a manual for worship; a law code; an outline of community health regulations; a liturgical calendar; *narrative. (For more information on items accompanied by an asterisk, see the glossary at the back of this Bible.)

▌Format and rhetoric. Leviticus is filled with direct commands that come from the authoritative voice of God. Accordingly, the dominant rhetorical pattern is the oracular directive from a divine lawgiver. The commands are addressed by God to Moses; in fact, the formula "and the LORD spoke to Moses" is repeated so often that the Hebrew title for the book simply repeats the opening words of the book ("the LORD called").

Passage	Main Content	Specific Topics	Theme
1:1–6:7	Offerings brought by the laity	Burnt offerings (1), grain offerings (2), peace offerings, (3) sin and guilt offerings (4:1–6:7)	Approaching a holy God: offerings and sacrifices
6:8–7:38	Instructions to the priests	How the priests processed the people's offerings	
8–10	Institution of the priesthood	Ordination of priests (8), inauguration of priestly ministry (9), judgment on priests for misbehavior (10)	
11–15	Uncleanness and its treatment	Unclean animals (11), uncleanness after childbirth (12), diseases and discharges (13–15)	
16	Atonement	Day of Atonement instituted	
17–27	Holiness Code	Sacrifice and food (17), sexual behavior (18), moral rules (19), serious offenses (20), rules for priests (21:1–22:16), offerings, festivals, sabbatical, jubilee (22:17–25:55); blessings and curses (26); vows (27)	Pleasing a holy God: a multitude of wide-ranging rules

Tips for reading. We need to abandon all expectation that we will be reading a story when we read Leviticus. We mainly read compilations of rules and regulations. It is a literary principle that literature portrays the universal by means of the particular. We therefore need to note the literal details that are presented, at the same time extrapolating general moral and spiritual principles from the concrete particulars. There is no way to avoid being struck and sometimes shocked by the huge gap between our own way of living and the practices of ancient cultures; this gap is evident when we observe the Bible's total lack of reserve in descriptions of the slaughter of animals, human diseases, bodily functions, and sexual behavior. The literary term for such material is *realism.

What you need to know about the kinds of Old Testament laws. The laws of the Mosaic covenant fall into three categories: (1) ceremonial laws that were fulfilled and terminated with the redemptive life and atoning death of Christ (see the NT book of Hebrews on this subject); (2) civil laws that were mainly limited to the OT nation of Israel and apply today only insofar as they embody general principles of justice; (3) moral laws that are timeless because they are founded on the character of God and his purpose for people. It is important to identify the category into which a given command falls and to apply it accordingly, in an awareness that even when a ceremonial or civil law is no longer literally practiced, it embodies a universal spiritual or moral principle that can still be applied to our lives.

Inferred literary intentions. The book is designed to achieve the following literary purposes:

- appeal to our imagination with its sheer quantity of particularized details

- put us in touch with a wide range of human experience, both good and bad

- portray a utopian "good place" and offer an explanation of how such a society will function

- paint an indirect picture of God based on the commands that he gives

- awaken our sense of the holy or numinous (four categories of the sacred emerge from the book—sacred persons like the priests; sacred rituals; sacred places and objects; sacred seasons and times)

▌Theological themes. (1) Holiness: the rules and practices prescribed in Leviticus are a picture of the holiness of God and the guidelines by which his covenant people could be holy, separate from surrounding nations. (2) Atonement: much of the Levitical code prescribes a system of blood sacrifice by which God provides sinful humanity access to himself. (3) Covenant: Leviticus is a handbook specifically for the covenant nation of Israel. (4) Ethics: many of the rules govern how people were intended to deal with their fellow humans and with their community.

▌The book of Leviticus as a chapter in the master story of the Bible. In the Old Covenant, God's salvation focused on a covenant nation that God called to be obedient to him as Shepherd and King. Leviticus pictures the system of practices and sacrifices by which God provided a path to holiness and atonement for his wayward people. Further, underlying Leviticus is a biblical principle known as *typology*. This means that OT characters, events, practices, and sacrifices often symbolize something for which Christ was God's chosen fulfillment from the very beginning of his plan of salvation. In particular, the system of offerings and sacrifices and the Day of Atonement point to the life that Jesus offered in obedience to God and the death that he died as the atonement for his people's sin.

Rules governing burnt offerings [chapter 1]. The first five chapters of Leviticus constitute a unit describing the offerings that God prescribed for the laity to bring to the priests for processing; chapters 6–7 then outline how the priests were supposed to process the people's offerings. So there is a sense in which the first seven chapters are a manual for offerings in OT worship. The way to move beyond the abstract lists of instructions is to imagine ourselves going through the procedures as we read them. Chapter 1 delineates how people were required to bring animals for slaughter and burning on an altar. If we read closely, we can differentiate which aspects of the handling of the animals and their slaughter were done by the person making the offering and which actions were performed by the priests. Nowhere in the chapter do we read what function the burnt offering served, but if we draw upon the whole system of blood sacrifice in the OT sacrificial system, we can infer that the function was expiation for sin as the basis of God's forgiveness.

1 The Lord called Moses and spoke to him from the tent of meeting, saying, [2]"Speak to the people of Israel and say to them, When any one of you brings an offering to the Lord, you shall bring your offering of livestock from the herd or from the flock.

[3]"If his offering is a burnt offering from the herd, he shall offer a male without blemish. He shall bring it to the entrance of the tent of meeting, that he may be accepted before the Lord. [4]He shall lay his hand on the head of the burnt offering, and it shall be accepted for him to make atonement for him. [5]Then he shall kill the bull before the Lord, and Aaron's sons the priests shall bring the blood and throw the blood against the sides of the altar that is at the entrance of the tent of meeting. [6]Then he shall flay the burnt offering and cut it into pieces, [7]and the sons of Aaron the priest shall put fire on the altar and arrange wood on the fire. [8]And Aaron's sons the priests shall arrange the pieces, the head, and the fat, on the wood that is on the fire on the altar; [9]but its entrails and its legs he shall wash with water. And the priest shall burn all of it on the altar, as a burnt offering, a food offering[1] with a pleasing aroma to the Lord.

[10]"If his gift for a burnt offering is from the flock, from the sheep or goats, he shall bring a male without blemish, [11]and he shall kill it on the north side of the altar before the Lord, and Aaron's sons the priests shall throw its blood against the sides of the altar. [12]And he shall cut it into pieces, with its head and its fat, and the priest shall arrange them on the wood that is on the fire on the altar, [13]but the entrails and the legs he shall wash with water. And the priest shall offer all of it and burn it on the altar; it is a burnt offering, a food offering with a pleasing aroma to the Lord.

[14]"If his offering to the Lord is a burnt offering of birds, then he shall bring his offering of turtledoves or pigeons. [15]And the priest shall bring it to the altar and wring off its head and burn it on the altar. Its blood shall be drained out on the side of the altar. [16]He shall remove its crop with its contents[2] and cast it beside the altar on the east side, in the place for ashes. [17]He shall tear it open by its wings, but shall not sever it completely. And the priest shall burn it on the altar, on the wood that is on the fire. It is a burnt offering, a food offering with a pleasing aroma to the Lord.

Grain offerings [chapter 2]. The rhetorical form of this chapter remains the same as that in chapter 1—a list of instructions divided between what the layperson did with the grain or cereal that was offered and what the priests did with it. As the offerings continue to unfold in the opening chapters of Leviticus, we need to note that consistently the offerings were to be the best of a flock or crop, never something inferior. The principle that emerges is that the offerings were expected to be a genuine sacrifice, with the further implication that the person making the sacrifice benefited spiritually from the act of giving something up. Although the text does not explicitly state what function the grain offerings served, they may have been considered a gift offered to God out of gratitude for his provision, though the formula that the offering was presented "to the Lord" (v. 1) also appears in instructions for the other categories of offerings (e.g., 1:14).

2 "When anyone brings a grain offering as an offering to the Lord, his offering shall be of fine flour. He shall pour oil on it and put frankincense on it [2]and bring it to Aaron's sons the priests. And he shall take from it a handful of the fine flour and oil, with all of its frankincense, and the priest shall burn this as its memorial portion on the altar, a food offering with a pleasing aroma to the LORD. ³But the rest of the grain offering shall be for Aaron and his sons; it is a most holy part of the LORD's food offerings.

⁴"When you bring a grain offering baked in the oven as an offering, it shall be unleavened loaves of fine flour mixed with oil or unleavened wafers smeared with oil. ⁵And if your offering is a grain offering baked on a griddle, it shall be of fine flour unleavened, mixed with oil. ⁶You shall break it in pieces and pour oil on it; it is a grain offering. ⁷And if your offering is a grain offering cooked in a pan, it shall be made of fine flour with oil. ⁸And you shall bring the grain offering that is made of these things to the LORD, and when it is presented to the priest, he shall bring it to the altar. ⁹And the priest shall take from the grain offering its memorial portion and burn this on the altar, a food offering with a pleasing aroma to the LORD. ¹⁰But the rest of the grain offering shall be for Aaron and his sons; it is a most holy part of the LORD's food offerings.

¹¹"No grain offering that you bring to the LORD shall be made with leaven, for you shall burn no leaven nor any honey as a food offering to the LORD. ¹²As an offering of firstfruits you may bring them to the LORD, but they shall not be offered on the altar for a pleasing aroma. ¹³You shall season all your grain offerings with salt. You shall not let the salt of the covenant with your God be missing from your grain offering; with all your offerings you shall offer salt.

¹⁴"If you offer a grain offering of firstfruits to the LORD, you shall offer for the grain offering of your firstfruits fresh ears, roasted with fire, crushed new grain. ¹⁵And you shall put oil on it and lay frankincense on it; it is a grain offering. ¹⁶And the priest shall burn as its memorial portion some of the crushed grain and some of the oil with all of its frankincense; it is a food offering to the LORD.

Peace offerings [chapter 3]. We continue to read about the rituals by which OT worshipers presented their offerings, and in this chapter we return to animal sacrifices. Again the bringer of the sacrifice and the priests divide the activities between them. We are not told what function was served by the peace offerings, but the very title implies a fellowship meal signifying reconciliation between the worshiper and God. The implied function is that the offering was an occasion for a festive meal of meat.

3 "If his offering is a sacrifice of peace offering, if he offers an animal from the herd, male or female, he shall offer it without blemish before the LORD. ²And he shall lay his hand on the head of his offering and kill it at the entrance of the tent of meeting, and Aaron's sons the priests shall throw the blood against the sides of the altar. ³And from the sacrifice of the peace offering, as a food offering to the LORD, he shall offer the fat covering the entrails and all the fat that is on the entrails, ⁴and the two kidneys with the fat that is on them at the loins, and the long lobe of the liver that he shall remove with the kidneys. ⁵Then Aaron's sons shall burn it on the altar on top of the burnt offering, which is on the wood on the fire; it is a food offering with a pleasing aroma to the LORD.

⁶"If his offering for a sacrifice of peace offering to the LORD is an animal from the flock, male or female, he shall offer it without blemish. ⁷If he offers a lamb for his offering, then he shall offer it before the LORD, ⁸lay his hand on the head of his offer-

ing, and kill it in front of the tent of meeting; and Aaron's sons shall throw its blood against the sides of the altar. [9]Then from the sacrifice of the peace offering he shall offer as a food offering to the LORD its fat; he shall remove the whole fat tail, cut off close to the backbone, and the fat that covers the entrails and all the fat that is on the entrails [10]and the two kidneys with the fat that is on them at the loins and the long lobe of the liver that he shall remove with the kidneys. [11]And the priest shall burn it on the altar as a food offering to the LORD.

[12]"If his offering is a goat, then he shall offer it before the LORD [13]and lay his hand on its head and kill it in front of the tent of meeting, and the sons of Aaron shall throw its blood against the sides of the altar. [14]Then he shall offer from it, as his offering for a food offering to the LORD, the fat covering the entrails and all the fat that is on the entrails [15]and the two kidneys with the fat that is on them at the loins and the long lobe of the liver that he shall remove with the kidneys. [16]And the priest shall burn them on the altar as a food offering with a pleasing aroma. All fat is the LORD's. [17]It shall be a statute forever throughout your generations, in all your dwelling places, that you eat neither fat nor blood."

Sin offerings [4:1–5:13]. The opening formula "if anyone sins unintentionally . . ." (4:2) signals that the sin offerings were designed to expiate or make amends for specific categories of sins. A new complexity enters our reading of this chapter as we ponder specific occasions for sin offerings. In addition to the prescribed ingredients for the sacrifices and the actions that the layperson and the priests performed, we need to pay attention to the function of expiation of sin that is intermingled with the descriptive aspect of the sacrifices. Repeatedly we read that the sin offerings were for sins committed unintentionally (4:2, 13, 22, 27). Further complexity emerges from such things as the following: specific groups that are named in the passage (for example, 4:3, 13, 22, 27); specific types of sins (5:1–6); gradations based on the economic status of the person bringing the offering (5:7–13).

4 And the LORD spoke to Moses, saying, [2]"Speak to the people of Israel, saying, If anyone sins unintentionally[1] in any of the LORD's commandments about things not to be done, and does any one of them, [3]if it is the anointed priest who sins, thus bringing guilt on the people, then he shall offer for the sin that he has committed a bull from the herd without blemish to the LORD for a sin offering. [4]He shall bring the bull to the entrance of the tent of meeting before the LORD and lay his hand on the head of the bull and kill the bull before the LORD. [5]And the anointed priest shall take some of the blood of the bull and bring it into the tent of meeting, [6]and the priest shall dip his finger in the blood and sprinkle part of the blood seven times before the LORD in front of the veil of the sanctuary. [7]And the priest shall put some of the blood on the horns of the altar of fragrant incense before the LORD that is in the tent of meeting, and all the rest of the blood of the bull he shall pour out at the base of the altar of burnt offering that is at the entrance of the tent of meeting. [8]And all the fat of the bull of the sin offering he shall remove from it, the fat that covers the entrails and all the fat that is on the entrails [9]and the two kidneys with the fat that is on them at the loins and the long lobe of the liver that he shall remove with the kidneys [10](just as these are taken from the ox of the sacrifice of the peace offerings); and the priest shall burn them on the altar of burnt offering. [11]But the skin of the bull and all its

[1] Or by mistake; so throughout Leviticus

flesh, with its head, its legs, its entrails, and its dung— ¹²all the rest of the bull—he shall carry outside the camp to a clean place, to the ash heap, and shall burn it up on a fire of wood. On the ash heap it shall be burned up.

¹³"If the whole congregation of Israel sins unintentionally¹ and the thing is hidden from the eyes of the assembly, and they do any one of the things that by the LORD's commandments ought not to be done, and they realize their guilt,² ¹⁴when the sin which they have committed becomes known, the assembly shall offer a bull from the herd for a sin offering and bring it in front of the tent of meeting. ¹⁵And the elders of the congregation shall lay their hands on the head of the bull before the LORD, and the bull shall be killed before the LORD. ¹⁶Then the anointed priest shall bring some of the blood of the bull into the tent of meeting, ¹⁷and the priest shall dip his finger in the blood and sprinkle it seven times before the LORD in front of the veil. ¹⁸And he shall put some of the blood on the horns of the altar that is in the tent of meeting before the LORD, and the rest of the blood he shall pour out at the base of the altar of burnt offering that is at the entrance of the tent of meeting. ¹⁹And all its fat he shall take from it and burn on the altar. ²⁰Thus shall he do with the bull. As he did with the bull of the sin offering, so shall he do with this. And the priest shall make atonement for them, and they shall be forgiven. ²¹And he shall carry the bull outside the camp and burn it up as he burned the first bull; it is the sin offering for the assembly.

²²"When a leader sins, doing unintentionally any one of all the things that by the commandments of the LORD his God ought not to be done, and realizes his guilt, ²³or the sin which he has committed is made known to him, he shall bring as his offering a goat, a male without blemish, ²⁴and shall lay his hand on the head of the goat and kill it in the place where they kill the burnt offering before the LORD; it is a sin offering. ²⁵Then the priest shall take some of the blood of the sin offering with his finger and put it on the horns of the altar of burnt offering and pour out the rest of its blood at the base of the altar of burnt offering. ²⁶And all its fat he shall burn on the altar, like the fat of the sacrifice of peace offerings. So the priest shall make atonement for him for his sin, and he shall be forgiven.

²⁷"If anyone of the common people sins unintentionally in doing any one of the things that by the LORD's commandments ought not to be done, and realizes his guilt, ²⁸or the sin which he has committed is made known to him, he shall bring for his offering a goat, a female without blemish, for his sin which he has committed. ²⁹And he shall lay his hand on the head of the sin offering and kill the sin offering in the place of burnt offering. ³⁰And the priest shall take some of its blood with his finger and put it on the horns of the altar of burnt offering and pour out all the rest of its blood at the base of the altar. ³¹And all its fat he shall remove, as the fat is removed from the peace offerings, and the priest shall burn it on the altar for a pleasing aroma to the LORD. And the priest shall make atonement for him, and he shall be forgiven.

³²"If he brings a lamb as his offering for a sin offering, he shall bring a female without blemish ³³and lay his hand on the head of the sin offering and kill it for a sin offering in the place where they kill the burnt offering. ³⁴Then the priest shall take some of the blood of the sin offering with his finger and put it on the horns of the altar of burnt offering and pour out all the rest of its blood at the base of the altar. ³⁵And all its fat he shall remove as the fat of the lamb is removed from the sacrifice of peace offerings, and the priest shall burn it on the altar, on top of the LORD's food

¹ Or makes a mistake ² Or suffer for their guilt, or are guilty; also verses 22, 27, and chapter 5

offerings. And the priest shall make atonement for him for the sin which he has committed, and he shall be forgiven.

5 "If anyone sins in that he hears a public adjuration to testify, and though he is a witness, whether he has seen or come to know the matter, yet does not speak, he shall bear his iniquity; ²or if anyone touches an unclean thing, whether a carcass of an unclean wild animal or a carcass of unclean livestock or a carcass of unclean swarming things, and it is hidden from him and he has become unclean, and he realizes his guilt; ³or if he touches human uncleanness, of whatever sort the uncleanness may be with which one becomes unclean, and it is hidden from him, when he comes to know it, and realizes his guilt; ⁴or if anyone utters with his lips a rash oath to do evil or to do good, any sort of rash oath that people swear, and it is hidden from him, when he comes to know it, and he realizes his guilt in any of these; ⁵when he realizes his guilt in any of these and confesses the sin he has committed, ⁶he shall bring to the LORD as his compensation¹ for the sin that he has committed, a female from the flock, a lamb or a goat, for a sin offering. And the priest shall make atonement for him for his sin.

⁷"But if he cannot afford a lamb, then he shall bring to the LORD as his compensation for the sin that he has committed two turtledoves or two pigeons,² one for a sin offering and the other for a burnt offering. ⁸He shall bring them to the priest, who shall offer first the one for the sin offering. He shall wring its head from its neck but shall not sever it completely, ⁹and he shall sprinkle some of the blood of the sin offering on the side of the altar, while the rest of the blood shall be drained out at the base of the altar; it is a sin offering. ¹⁰Then he shall offer the second for a burnt offering according to the rule. And the priest shall make atonement for him for the sin that he has committed, and he shall be forgiven.

¹¹"But if he cannot afford two turtledoves or two pigeons, then he shall bring as his offering for the sin that he has committed a tenth of an ephah³ of fine flour for a sin offering. He shall put no oil on it and shall put no frankincense on it, for it is a sin offering. ¹²And he shall bring it to the priest, and the priest shall take a handful of it as its memorial portion and burn this on the altar, on the LORD's food offerings; it is a sin offering. ¹³Thus the priest shall make atonement for him for the sin which he has committed in any one of these things, and he shall be forgiven. And the remainder⁴ shall be for the priest, as in the grain offering."

Guilt offerings [5:14–6:7]. Thus far in Leviticus four types of offerings have been covered—burnt offerings, grain offerings, peace offerings, and sin offerings. This final unit dealing with the offerings brought by the laity adds a fifth category—guilt offerings. These are like the other blood offerings in serving the purpose of atonement for sins. The ground rules for assimilating the chapter are identical to what we have had thus far: we need to pay attention to the elements of the offerings, the conditions under which the offerings are required, the combined actions of the laity and the priests, and statements about atonement as the purpose of the offerings.

¹⁴The LORD spoke to Moses, saying, ¹⁵"If anyone commits a breach of faith and sins unintentionally in any of the holy things of the LORD, he shall bring to the LORD as his

¹ Hebrew *his guilt penalty;* so throughout Leviticus ² Septuagint *two young pigeons;* also verse 11 ³ An *ephah* was about 3/5 bushel or 22 liters
⁴ Septuagint; Hebrew *it*

compensation, a ram without blemish out of the flock, valued[1] in silver shekels,[2] according to the shekel of the sanctuary, for a guilt offering. [16]He shall also make restitution for what he has done amiss in the holy thing and shall add a fifth to it and give it to the priest. And the priest shall make atonement for him with the ram of the guilt offering, and he shall be forgiven.

[17]"If anyone sins, doing any of the things that by the Lord's commandments ought not to be done, though he did not know it, then realizes his guilt, he shall bear his iniquity. [18]He shall bring to the priest a ram without blemish out of the flock, or its equivalent for a guilt offering, and the priest shall make atonement for him for the mistake that he made unintentionally, and he shall be forgiven. [19]It is a guilt offering; he has indeed incurred guilt before[3] the Lord."

6 [1]The Lord spoke to Moses, saying, [2]"If anyone sins and commits a breach of faith against the Lord by deceiving his neighbor in a matter of deposit or security, or through robbery, or if he has oppressed his neighbor [3]or has found something lost and lied about it, swearing falsely—in any of all the things that people do and sin thereby— [4]if he has sinned and has realized his guilt and will restore what he took by robbery or what he got by oppression or the deposit that was committed to him or the lost thing that he found [5]or anything about which he has sworn falsely, he shall restore it in full and shall add a fifth to it, and give it to him to whom it belongs on the day he realizes his guilt. [6]And he shall bring to the priest as his compensation to the Lord a ram without blemish out of the flock, or its equivalent for a guilt offering. [7]And the priest shall make atonement for him before the Lord, and he shall be forgiven for any of the things that one may do and thereby become guilty."

Instructions to the priests on how to perform the offerings [6:8–7:38]. Up to this point, the book of Leviticus has outlined the offerings that the ordinary people of Israel were required to bring to God. In this new unit, God instructs Moses regarding what the priests need to do with the various offerings that have been brought. A good way to assimilate the material is simply to imagine yourself as a priest performing the various commands and rituals. The last two verses of this unit (7:37–38) summarize the types of offerings and sacrifices that have been covered.

[8][5] The Lord spoke to Moses, saying, [9]"Command Aaron and his sons, saying, This is the law of the burnt offering. The burnt offering shall be on the hearth on the altar all night until the morning, and the fire of the altar shall be kept burning on it. [10]And the priest shall put on his linen garment and put his linen undergarment on his body, and he shall take up the ashes to which the fire has reduced the burnt offering on the altar and put them beside the altar. [11]Then he shall take off his garments and put on other garments and carry the ashes outside the camp to a clean place. [12]The fire on the altar shall be kept burning on it; it shall not go out. The priest shall burn wood on it every morning, and he shall arrange the burnt offering on it and shall burn on it the fat of the peace offerings. [13]Fire shall be kept burning on the altar continually; it shall not go out.

[14]"And this is the law of the grain offering. The sons of Aaron shall offer it before the Lord in front of the altar. [15]And one shall take from it a handful of the fine flour of the grain offering and its oil and all the frankincense that is on the grain offering

---

[1] Or flock, or its equivalent [2] A shekel was about 2/5 ounce or 11 grams [3] Or he has paid full compensation to [4] Ch 5:20 in Hebrew [5] Ch 6:1 in Hebrew

and burn this as its memorial portion on the altar, a pleasing aroma to the LORD. [16]And the rest of it Aaron and his sons shall eat. It shall be eaten unleavened in a holy place. In the court of the tent of meeting they shall eat it. [17]It shall not be baked with leaven. I have given it as their portion of my food offerings. It is a thing most holy, like the sin offering and the guilt offering. [18]Every male among the children of Aaron may eat of it, as decreed forever throughout your generations, from the LORD's food offerings. Whatever touches them shall become holy."

[19]The LORD spoke to Moses, saying, [20]"This is the offering that Aaron and his sons shall offer to the LORD on the day when he is anointed: a tenth of an ephah[1] of fine flour as a regular grain offering, half of it in the morning and half in the evening. [21]It shall be made with oil on a griddle. You shall bring it well mixed, in baked[2] pieces like a grain offering, and offer it for a pleasing aroma to the LORD. [22]The priest from among Aaron's sons, who is anointed to succeed him, shall offer it to the LORD as decreed forever. The whole of it shall be burned. [23]Every grain offering of a priest shall be wholly burned. It shall not be eaten."

[24]The LORD spoke to Moses, saying, [25]"Speak to Aaron and his sons, saying, This is the law of the sin offering. In the place where the burnt offering is killed shall the sin offering be killed before the LORD; it is most holy. [26]The priest who offers it for sin shall eat it. In a holy place it shall be eaten, in the court of the tent of meeting. [27]Whatever touches its flesh shall be holy, and when any of its blood is splashed on a garment, you shall wash that on which it was splashed in a holy place. [28]And the earthenware vessel in which it is boiled shall be broken. But if it is boiled in a bronze vessel, that shall be scoured and rinsed in water. [29]Every male among the priests may eat of it; it is most holy. [30]But no sin offering shall be eaten from which any blood is brought into the tent of meeting to make atonement in the Holy Place; it shall be burned up with fire.

7 "This is the law of the guilt offering. It is most holy. [2]In the place where they kill the burnt offering they shall kill the guilt offering, and its blood shall be thrown against the sides of the altar. [3]And all its fat shall be offered, the fat tail, the fat that covers the entrails, [4]the two kidneys with the fat that is on them at the loins, and the long lobe of the liver that he shall remove with the kidneys. [5]The priest shall burn them on the altar as a food offering to the LORD; it is a guilt offering. [6]Every male among the priests may eat of it. It shall be eaten in a holy place. It is most holy. [7]The guilt offering is just like the sin offering; there is one law for them. The priest who makes atonement with it shall have it. [8]And the priest who offers any man's burnt offering shall have for himself the skin of the burnt offering that he has offered. [9]And every grain offering baked in the oven and all that is prepared on a pan or a griddle shall belong to the priest who offers it. [10]And every grain offering, mixed with oil or dry, shall be shared equally among all the sons of Aaron.

[11]"And this is the law of the sacrifice of peace offerings that one may offer to the LORD. [12]If he offers it for a thanksgiving, then he shall offer with the thanksgiving sacrifice unleavened loaves mixed with oil, unleavened wafers smeared with oil, and loaves of fine flour well mixed with oil. [13]With the sacrifice of his peace offerings for thanksgiving he shall bring his offering with loaves of leavened bread. [14]And from it he shall offer one loaf from each offering, as a gift to the LORD. It shall belong to the priest who throws the blood of the peace offerings. [15]And the flesh of the sacrifice of

[1] An *ephah* was about 3/5 bushel or 22 liters [2] The meaning of the Hebrew is uncertain

his peace offerings for thanksgiving shall be eaten on the day of his offering. He shall not leave any of it until the morning. ¹⁶But if the sacrifice of his offering is a vow offering or a freewill offering, it shall be eaten on the day that he offers his sacrifice, and on the next day what remains of it shall be eaten. ¹⁷But what remains of the flesh of the sacrifice on the third day shall be burned up with fire. ¹⁸If any of the flesh of the sacrifice of his peace offering is eaten on the third day, he who offers it shall not be accepted, neither shall it be credited to him. It is tainted, and he who eats of it shall bear his iniquity.

¹⁹"Flesh that touches any unclean thing shall not be eaten. It shall be burned up with fire. All who are clean may eat flesh, ²⁰but the person who eats of the flesh of the sacrifice of the LORD's peace offerings while an uncleanness is on him, that person shall be cut off from his people. ²¹And if anyone touches an unclean thing, whether human uncleanness or an unclean beast or any unclean detestable creature, and then eats some flesh from the sacrifice of the LORD's peace offerings, that person shall be cut off from his people."

²²The LORD spoke to Moses, saying, ²³"Speak to the people of Israel, saying, You shall eat no fat, of ox or sheep or goat. ²⁴The fat of an animal that dies of itself and the fat of one that is torn by beasts may be put to any other use, but on no account shall you eat it. ²⁵For every person who eats of the fat of an animal of which a food offering may be made to the LORD shall be cut off from his people. ²⁶Moreover, you shall eat no blood whatever, whether of fowl or of animal, in any of your dwelling places. ²⁷Whoever eats any blood, that person shall be cut off from his people."

²⁸The LORD spoke to Moses, saying, ²⁹"Speak to the people of Israel, saying, Whoever offers the sacrifice of his peace offerings to the LORD shall bring his offering to the LORD from the sacrifice of his peace offerings. ³⁰His own hands shall bring the LORD's food offerings. He shall bring the fat with the breast, that the breast may be waved as a wave offering before the LORD. ³¹The priest shall burn the fat on the altar, but the breast shall be for Aaron and his sons. ³²And the right thigh you shall give to the priest as a contribution from the sacrifice of your peace offerings. ³³Whoever among the sons of Aaron offers the blood of the peace offerings and the fat shall have the right thigh for a portion. ³⁴For the breast that is waved and the thigh that is contributed I have taken from the people of Israel, out of the sacrifices of their peace offerings, and have given them to Aaron the priest and to his sons, as a perpetual due from the people of Israel. ³⁵This is the portion of Aaron and of his sons from the LORD's food offerings, from the day they were presented to serve as priests of the LORD. ³⁶The LORD commanded this to be given them by the people of Israel, from the day that he anointed them. It is a perpetual due throughout their generations."

³⁷This is the law of the burnt offering, of the grain offering, of the sin offering, of the guilt offering, of the ordination offering, and of the peace offering, ³⁸which the LORD commanded Moses on Mount Sinai, on the day that he commanded the people of Israel to bring their offerings to the LORD, in the wilderness of Sinai.

Ordaining of the priests [chapter 8]. Chapters 8–10 constitute a unit that tells the story of how Aaron and his sons began their priestly calling and practices. This is the part of the book where the title ("that which pertains to the Levites") is most obviously relevant. The consecration of the priests was an occasion of high solemnity and elaborate ritual, commensurate with their holy calling to the service of God. Chapter 8 records the ordination ceremonies that preceded the priests' beginning of their duties. The narrative is straightforward, and although the rituals were elaborate, we can relive the event simply by reading slowly and piecing the actions together. We should also ponder what the rituals teach us about the character of God and the requirements of his holy service.

8 The LORD spoke to Moses, saying, [2]"Take Aaron and his sons with him, and the garments and the anointing oil and the bull of the sin offering and the two rams and the basket of unleavened bread. [3]And assemble all the congregation at the entrance of the tent of meeting." [4]And Moses did as the LORD commanded him, and the congregation was assembled at the entrance of the tent of meeting.

[5]And Moses said to the congregation, "This is the thing that the LORD has commanded to be done." [6]And Moses brought Aaron and his sons and washed them with water. [7]And he put the coat on him and tied the sash around his waist and clothed him with the robe and put the ephod on him and tied the skillfully woven band of the ephod around him, binding it to him with the band.[1] [8]And he placed the breastpiece on him, and in the breastpiece he put the Urim and the Thummim. [9]And he set the turban on his head, and on the turban, in front, he set the golden plate, the holy crown, as the LORD commanded Moses.

[10]Then Moses took the anointing oil and anointed the tabernacle and all that was in it, and consecrated them. [11]And he sprinkled some of it on the altar seven times, and anointed the altar and all its utensils and the basin and its stand, to consecrate them. [12]And he poured some of the anointing oil on Aaron's head and anointed him to consecrate him. [13]And Moses brought Aaron's sons and clothed them with coats and tied sashes around their waists and bound caps on them, as the LORD commanded Moses.

[14]Then he brought the bull of the sin offering, and Aaron and his sons laid their hands on the head of the bull of the sin offering. [15]And he[2] killed it, and Moses took the blood, and with his finger put it on the horns of the altar around it and purified the altar and poured out the blood at the base of the altar and consecrated it to make atonement for it. [16]And he took all the fat that was on the entrails and the long lobe of the liver and the two kidneys with their fat, and Moses burned them on the altar. [17]But the bull and its skin and its flesh and its dung he burned up with fire outside the camp, as the LORD commanded Moses.

[18]Then he presented the ram of the burnt offering, and Aaron and his sons laid their hands on the head of the ram. [19]And he killed it, and Moses threw the blood against the sides of the altar. [20]He cut the ram into pieces, and Moses burned the head and the pieces and the fat. [21]He washed the entrails and the legs with water, and Moses burned the whole ram on the altar. It was a burnt offering with a pleasing aroma, a food offering for the LORD, as the LORD commanded Moses.

[22]Then he presented the other ram, the ram of ordination, and Aaron and his sons laid their hands on the head of the ram. [23]And he killed it, and Moses took some of its blood and put it on the lobe of Aaron's right ear and on the thumb of his right hand and on the big toe of his right foot. [24]Then he presented Aaron's sons, and Moses put some of the blood on the lobes of their right ears and on the thumbs of their right

---

[1] Hebrew *with it* [2] Probably Aaron or his representative; possibly Moses; also verses 16-23

hands and on the big toes of their right feet. And Moses threw the blood against the sides of the altar. ²⁵Then he took the fat and the fat tail and all the fat that was on the entrails and the long lobe of the liver and the two kidneys with their fat and the right thigh, ²⁶and out of the basket of unleavened bread that was before the LORD he took one unleavened loaf and one loaf of bread with oil and one wafer and placed them on the pieces of fat and on the right thigh. ²⁷And he put all these in the hands of Aaron and in the hands of his sons and waved them as a wave offering before the LORD. ²⁸Then Moses took them from their hands and burned them on the altar with the burnt offering. This was an ordination offering with a pleasing aroma, a food offering to the LORD. ²⁹And Moses took the breast and waved it for a wave offering before the LORD. It was Moses' portion of the ram of ordination, as the LORD commanded Moses.

³⁰Then Moses took some of the anointing oil and of the blood that was on the altar and sprinkled it on Aaron and his garments, and also on his sons and his sons' garments. So he consecrated Aaron and his garments, and his sons and his sons' garments with him.

³¹And Moses said to Aaron and his sons, "Boil the flesh at the entrance of the tent of meeting, and there eat it and the bread that is in the basket of ordination offerings, as I commanded, saying, 'Aaron and his sons shall eat it.' ³²And what remains of the flesh and the bread you shall burn up with fire. ³³And you shall not go outside the entrance of the tent of meeting for seven days, until the days of your ordination are completed, for it will take seven days to ordain you. ³⁴As has been done today, the LORD has commanded to be done to make atonement for you. ³⁵At the entrance of the tent of meeting you shall remain day and night for seven days, performing what the LORD has charged, so that you do not die, for so I have been commanded." ³⁶And Aaron and his sons did all the things that the LORD commanded by Moses.

The priests begin their ministry [chapter 9]. With the seven-day consecration ceremonies completed, Aaron and his sons began their ministry on the eighth day (v. 1). As with the events narrated in chapter 8, there is a once-only quality to the inauguration of the priestly ministry. We are familiar with inaugurations in our own culture, and the same flavor of ceremony and formality is present in chapter 9. We get the impression of leaders' observing formal protocol and of God's taking seriously anything having to do with the leadership of public worship. The emphasis in the inauguration of the priestly ministry is on sacrifices and atonement for sin. The chapter should be read as a gradual lead-up to the climactic appearance of divine glory at the end (v. 23), where we see that worship and the priesthood exist for the glory of God.

9 On the eighth day Moses called Aaron and his sons and the elders of Israel, ²and he said to Aaron, "Take for yourself a bull calf for a sin offering and a ram for a burnt offering, both without blemish, and offer them before the LORD. ³And say to the people of Israel, 'Take a male goat for a sin offering, and a calf and a lamb, both a year old without blemish, for a burnt offering, ⁴and an ox and a ram for peace offerings, to sacrifice before the LORD, and a grain offering mixed with oil, for today the LORD will appear to you.'" ⁵And they brought what Moses commanded in front of the tent of meeting, and all the congregation drew near and stood before the LORD. ⁶And Moses said, "This is the thing that the LORD commanded you to do, that the

glory of the LORD may appear to you." ⁷Then Moses said to Aaron, "Draw near to the altar and offer your sin offering and your burnt offering and make atonement for yourself and for the people, and bring the offering of the people and make atonement for them, as the LORD has commanded."

⁸So Aaron drew near to the altar and killed the calf of the sin offering, which was for himself. ⁹And the sons of Aaron presented the blood to him, and he dipped his finger in the blood and put it on the horns of the altar and poured out the blood at the base of the altar. ¹⁰But the fat and the kidneys and the long lobe of the liver from the sin offering he burned on the altar, as the LORD commanded Moses. ¹¹The flesh and the skin he burned up with fire outside the camp.

¹²Then he killed the burnt offering, and Aaron's sons handed him the blood, and he threw it against the sides of the altar. ¹³And they handed the burnt offering to him, piece by piece, and the head, and he burned them on the altar. ¹⁴And he washed the entrails and the legs and burned them with the burnt offering on the altar.

¹⁵Then he presented the people's offering and took the goat of the sin offering that was for the people and killed it and offered it as a sin offering, like the first one. ¹⁶And he presented the burnt offering and offered it according to the rule. ¹⁷And he presented the grain offering, took a handful of it, and burned it on the altar, besides the burnt offering of the morning.

¹⁸Then he killed the ox and the ram, the sacrifice of peace offerings for the people. And Aaron's sons handed him the blood, and he threw it against the sides of the altar. ¹⁹But the fat pieces of the ox and of the ram, the fat tail and that which covers the entrails and the kidneys and the long lobe of the liver— ²⁰they put the fat pieces on the breasts, and he burned the fat pieces on the altar, ²¹but the breasts and the right thigh Aaron waved for a wave offering before the LORD, as Moses commanded.

²²Then Aaron lifted up his hands toward the people and blessed them, and he came down from offering the sin offering and the burnt offering and the peace offerings. ²³And Moses and Aaron went into the tent of meeting, and when they came out they blessed the people, and the glory of the LORD appeared to all the people. ²⁴And fire came out from before the LORD and consumed the burnt offering and the pieces of fat on the altar, and when all the people saw it, they shouted and fell on their faces.

Shaky beginnings for the priesthood [chapter 10]. After two awe-inspiring chapters devoted to the ordination and inauguration of the priests, the concluding chapter in the three-part narrative is a distinct letdown, as we observe priestly disobedience and negligence. The disappointing sequence unfolds as follows: Nadab and Abihu (sons of Aaron) use unauthorized coals of fire for a sacrifice and are destroyed by God (vv. 1–2); Moses orders the removal of the two bodies from camp (vv. 3–7); God commands the priests to abstain from wine before serving and to "distinguish between the holy and the common," which can be taken as a leading theme of the book of Leviticus, with the implication that this distinction had been violated by Nadab and Abihu (vv. 8–10); Moses orders Eleazar and Ithamar to perform sacrifices and to eat the elements with their families in a holy place (vv. 11–15); Moses is angry when he discovers that the sacrificial elements have been burned instead of eaten (vv. 16–18); Aaron offers an explanation that placates Moses (vv. 19–20). We get a very human picture of people feeling their way in a new venture, and of some carelessly disregarding the clear commands of God, to the destruction of themselves.

10 Now Nadab and Abihu, the sons of Aaron, each took his censer and put fire in it and laid incense on it and offered unauthorized[1] fire before the LORD, which he had not commanded them. ²And fire came out from before the LORD and consumed them, and they died before the LORD. ³Then Moses said to Aaron, "This is what the LORD has said, 'Among those who are near me I will be sanctified, and before all the people I will be glorified.'" And Aaron held his peace.

⁴And Moses called Mishael and Elzaphan, the sons of Uzziel the uncle of Aaron, and said to them, "Come near; carry your brothers away from the front of the sanctuary and out of the camp." ⁵So they came near and carried them in their coats out of the camp, as Moses had said. ⁶And Moses said to Aaron and to Eleazar and Ithamar his sons, "Do not let the hair of your heads hang loose, and do not tear your clothes, lest you die, and wrath come upon all the congregation; but let your brothers, the whole house of Israel, bewail the burning that the LORD has kindled. ⁷And do not go outside the entrance of the tent of meeting, lest you die, for the anointing oil of the LORD is upon you." And they did according to the word of Moses.

⁸And the LORD spoke to Aaron, saying, ⁹"Drink no wine or strong drink, you or your sons with you, when you go into the tent of meeting, lest you die. It shall be a statute forever throughout your generations. ¹⁰You are to distinguish between the holy and the common, and between the unclean and the clean, ¹¹and you are to teach the people of Israel all the statutes that the LORD has spoken to them by Moses."

¹²Moses spoke to Aaron and to Eleazar and Ithamar, his surviving sons: "Take the grain offering that is left of the LORD's food offerings, and eat it unleavened beside the altar, for it is most holy. ¹³You shall eat it in a holy place, because it is your due and your sons' due, from the LORD's food offerings, for so I am commanded. ¹⁴But the breast that is waved and the thigh that is contributed you shall eat in a clean place, you and your sons and your daughters with you, for they are given as your due and your sons' due from the sacrifices of the peace offerings of the people of Israel. ¹⁵The thigh that is contributed and the breast that is waved they shall bring with the food offerings of the fat pieces to wave for a wave offering before the LORD, and it shall be yours and your sons' with you as a due forever, as the LORD has commanded."

¹⁶Now Moses diligently inquired about the goat of the sin offering, and behold, it was burned up! And he was angry with Eleazar and Ithamar, the surviving sons of Aaron, saying, ¹⁷"Why have you not eaten the sin offering in the place of the sanctuary, since it is a thing most holy and has been given to you that you may bear the iniquity of the congregation, to make atonement for them before the LORD? ¹⁸Behold, its blood was not brought into the inner part of the sanctuary. You certainly ought to have eaten it in the sanctuary, as I commanded." ¹⁹And Aaron said to Moses, "Behold, today they have offered their sin offering and their burnt offering before the LORD, and yet such things as these have happened to me! If I had eaten the sin offering today, would the LORD have approved?" ²⁰And when Moses heard that, he approved.

[1] Or strange

Clean and unclean animals for eating [chapter 11]. This chapter begins a five-chapter block dealing with uncleanness and its treatment. The long eleventh chapter deals with the specific subcategory of distinguishing between animals that could be eaten and those that could not. The first thing that should impress us as we read through the list is the intimate knowledge of animals that underlies the catalog. Further, we are confronted with the basic rule of literary writing that literature embodies the conceptual (ceremonial cleanness as opposed to ceremonial uncleanness, in this case) in concrete form. The abstractions "clean" and "unclean" receive a "local habitation and a name" (as Shakespeare called the imagination's way of presenting reality). The main spiritual principle underlying the division of animals into clean and unclean is the need for God's people to be holy (v. 45). Secondarily, the rules governing animals may have served a health purpose.

11 And the LORD spoke to Moses and Aaron, saying to them, ²"Speak to the people of Israel, saying, These are the living things that you may eat among all the animals that are on the earth. ³Whatever parts the hoof and is cloven-footed and chews the cud, among the animals, you may eat. ⁴Nevertheless, among those that chew the cud or part the hoof, you shall not eat these: The camel, because it chews the cud but does not part the hoof, is unclean to you. ⁵And the rock badger, because it chews the cud but does not part the hoof, is unclean to you. ⁶And the hare, because it chews the cud but does not part the hoof, is unclean to you. ⁷And the pig, because it parts the hoof and is cloven-footed but does not chew the cud, is unclean to you. ⁸You shall not eat any of their flesh, and you shall not touch their carcasses; they are unclean to you.

⁹"These you may eat, of all that are in the waters. Everything in the waters that has fins and scales, whether in the seas or in the rivers, you may eat. ¹⁰But anything in the seas or the rivers that has not fins and scales, of the swarming creatures in the waters and of the living creatures that are in the waters, is detestable to you. ¹¹You shall regard them as detestable; you shall not eat any of their flesh, and you shall detest their carcasses. ¹²Everything in the waters that has not fins and scales is detestable to you.

¹³"And these you shall detest among the birds;¹ they shall not be eaten; they are detestable: the eagle,² the bearded vulture, the black vulture, ¹⁴the kite, the falcon of any kind, ¹⁵every raven of any kind, ¹⁶the ostrich, the nighthawk, the sea gull, the hawk of any kind, ¹⁷the little owl, the cormorant, the short-eared owl, ¹⁸the barn owl, the tawny owl, the carrion vulture, ¹⁹the stork, the heron of any kind, the hoopoe, and the bat.

²⁰"All winged insects that go on all fours are detestable to you. ²¹Yet among the winged insects that go on all fours you may eat those that have jointed legs above their feet, with which to hop on the ground. ²²Of them you may eat: the locust of any kind, the bald locust of any kind, the cricket of any kind, and the grasshopper of any kind. ²³But all other winged insects that have four feet are detestable to you.

²⁴"And by these you shall become unclean. Whoever touches their carcass shall be unclean until the evening, ²⁵and whoever carries any part of their carcass shall wash his clothes and be unclean until the evening. ²⁶Every animal that parts the hoof but is not cloven-footed or does not chew the cud is unclean to you. Everyone who touches them shall be unclean. ²⁷And all that walk on their paws, among the animals that go

¹ Or *things that fly*; compare Genesis 1:20 ² The identity of many of these birds is uncertain

on all fours, are unclean to you. Whoever touches their carcass shall be unclean until the evening, ²⁸and he who carries their carcass shall wash his clothes and be unclean until the evening; they are unclean to you.

²⁹"And these are unclean to you among the swarming things that swarm on the ground: the mole rat, the mouse, the great lizard of any kind, ³⁰the gecko, the monitor lizard, the lizard, the sand lizard, and the chameleon. ³¹These are unclean to you among all that swarm. Whoever touches them when they are dead shall be unclean until the evening. ³²And anything on which any of them falls when they are dead shall be unclean, whether it is an article of wood or a garment or a skin or a sack, any article that is used for any purpose. It must be put into water, and it shall be unclean until the evening; then it shall be clean. ³³And if any of them falls into any earthenware vessel, all that is in it shall be unclean, and you shall break it. ³⁴Any food in it that could be eaten, on which water comes, shall be unclean. And all drink that could be drunk from every such vessel shall be unclean. ³⁵And everything on which any part of their carcass falls shall be unclean. Whether oven or stove, it shall be broken in pieces. They are unclean and shall remain unclean for you. ³⁶Nevertheless, a spring or a cistern holding water shall be clean, but whoever touches a carcass in them shall be unclean. ³⁷And if any part of their carcass falls upon any seed grain that is to be sown, it is clean, ³⁸but if water is put on the seed and any part of their carcass falls on it, it is unclean to you.

³⁹"And if any animal which you may eat dies, whoever touches its carcass shall be unclean until the evening, ⁴⁰and whoever eats of its carcass shall wash his clothes and be unclean until the evening. And whoever carries the carcass shall wash his clothes and be unclean until the evening.

⁴¹"Every swarming thing that swarms on the ground is detestable; it shall not be eaten. ⁴²Whatever goes on its belly, and whatever goes on all fours, or whatever has many feet, any swarming thing that swarms on the ground, you shall not eat, for they are detestable. ⁴³You shall not make yourselves detestable with any swarming thing that swarms, and you shall not defile yourselves with them, and become unclean through them. ⁴⁴For I am the Lᴏʀᴅ your God. Consecrate yourselves therefore, and be holy, for I am holy. You shall not defile yourselves with any swarming thing that crawls on the ground. ⁴⁵For I am the Lᴏʀᴅ who brought you up out of the land of Egypt to be your God. You shall therefore be holy, for I am holy."

⁴⁶This is the law about beast and bird and every living creature that moves through the waters and every creature that swarms on the ground, ⁴⁷to make a distinction between the unclean and the clean and between the living creature that may be eaten and the living creature that may not be eaten.

Purification of women after childbirth [chapter 12]. The combination of concern for spiritual purity and concern for physical health is also evident in the ceremonies governing the practices of mothers in the weeks immediately after having given birth to a baby.

12 The Lᴏʀᴅ spoke to Moses, saying, ²"Speak to the people of Israel, saying, 'If a woman conceives and bears a male child, then she shall be unclean seven days. As at the time of her menstruation, she shall be unclean. ³And on the eighth day the flesh of his foreskin shall be circumcised. ⁴Then she shall continue for thirty-three days in the blood of her purifying. She shall not touch anything holy, nor come into the sanctuary, until the days of her purifying are completed. ⁵But if she bears a female child, then she shall be unclean two weeks, as in her menstruation. And she shall continue in the blood of her purifying for sixty-six days.

⁶"'And when the days of her purifying are completed, whether for a son or for a daughter, she shall bring to the priest at the entrance of the tent of meeting a lamb a year old for a burnt offering, and a pigeon or a turtledove for a sin offering, ⁷and he shall offer it before the LORD and make atonement for her. Then she shall be clean from the flow of her blood. This is the law for her who bears a child, either male or female. ⁸And if she cannot afford a lamb, then she shall take two turtledoves or two pigeons,ⁱ one for a burnt offering and the other for a sin offering. And the priest shall make atonement for her, and she shall be clean.'"

Regulations for skin diseases [chapter 13]. Beginning here and continuing for two additional chapters, we need to abandon all squeamishness about bodily functions. These chapters give us variations on the theme of "the thousand natural shocks that flesh is heir to" (to borrow Hamlet's famous phrase). They are an ever-expanding picture of the ways in which the fall affected the human body, and we need to remember additionally that ancient cultures did not have the medical advantages that aid healing in the modern world. Chapter 13 deals with what the ancient world called leprosy, which included a range of skin ailments—rashes, scaliness, open sores, and suchlike. The chapter is a guide to the diagnosis and treatment of skin diseases—a health code, as we term it. We should note that the priests were both the religious leaders and health exam officers of the covenant community; if we add the pictures of slaughtering and cutting sacrificial animals earlier in Leviticus, we sense what a demanding role the priesthood was.

13 The LORD spoke to Moses and Aaron, saying, ²"When a person has on the skin of his body a swelling or an eruption or a spot, and it turns into a case of leprous² disease on the skin of his body, then he shall be brought to Aaron the priest or to one of his sons the priests, ³and the priest shall examine the diseased area on the skin of his body. And if the hair in the diseased area has turned white and the disease appears to be deeper than the skin of his body, it is a case of leprous disease. When the priest has examined him, he shall pronounce him unclean. ⁴But if the spot is white in the skin of his body and appears no deeper than the skin, and the hair in it has not turned white, the priest shall shut up the diseased person for seven days. ⁵And the priest shall examine him on the seventh day, and if in his eyes the disease is checked and the disease has not spread in the skin, then the priest shall shut him up for another seven days. ⁶And the priest shall examine him again on the seventh day, and if the diseased area has faded and the disease has not spread in the skin, then the priest shall pronounce him clean; it is only an eruption. And he shall wash his clothes and be clean. ⁷But if the eruption spreads in the skin, after he has shown himself to the priest for his cleansing, he shall appear again before the priest. ⁸And the priest shall look, and if the eruption has spread in the skin, then the priest shall pronounce him unclean; it is a leprous disease.

⁹"When a man is afflicted with a leprous disease, he shall be brought to the priest,

¹ Septuagint *two young pigeons* ² *Leprosy* was a term for several skin diseases

¹⁰and the priest shall look. And if there is a white swelling in the skin that has turned the hair white, and there is raw flesh in the swelling, ¹¹it is a chronic leprous disease in the skin of his body, and the priest shall pronounce him unclean. He shall not shut him up, for he is unclean. ¹²And if the leprous disease breaks out in the skin, so that the leprous disease covers all the skin of the diseased person from head to foot, so far as the priest can see, ¹³then the priest shall look, and if the leprous disease has covered all his body, he shall pronounce him clean of the disease; it has all turned white, and he is clean. ¹⁴But when raw flesh appears on him, he shall be unclean. ¹⁵And the priest shall examine the raw flesh and pronounce him unclean. Raw flesh is unclean, for it is a leprous disease. ¹⁶But if the raw flesh recovers and turns white again, then he shall come to the priest, ¹⁷and the priest shall examine him, and if the disease has turned white, then the priest shall pronounce the diseased person clean; he is clean.

¹⁸"If there is in the skin of one's body a boil and it heals, ¹⁹and in the place of the boil there comes a white swelling or a reddish-white spot, then it shall be shown to the priest. ²⁰And the priest shall look, and if it appears deeper than the skin and its hair has turned white, then the priest shall pronounce him unclean. It is a case of leprous disease that has broken out in the boil. ²¹But if the priest examines it and there is no white hair in it and it is not deeper than the skin, but has faded, then the priest shall shut him up seven days. ²²And if it spreads in the skin, then the priest shall pronounce him unclean; it is a disease. ²³But if the spot remains in one place and does not spread, it is the scar of the boil, and the priest shall pronounce him clean.

²⁴"Or, when the body has a burn on its skin and the raw flesh of the burn becomes a spot, reddish-white or white, ²⁵the priest shall examine it, and if the hair in the spot has turned white and it appears deeper than the skin, then it is a leprous disease. It has broken out in the burn, and the priest shall pronounce him unclean; it is a case of leprous disease. ²⁶But if the priest examines it and there is no white hair in the spot and it is no deeper than the skin, but has faded, the priest shall shut him up seven days, ²⁷and the priest shall examine him the seventh day. If it is spreading in the skin, then the priest shall pronounce him unclean; it is a case of leprous disease. ²⁸But if the spot remains in one place and does not spread in the skin, but has faded, it is a swelling from the burn, and the priest shall pronounce him clean, for it is the scar of the burn.

²⁹"When a man or woman has a disease on the head or the beard, ³⁰the priest shall examine the disease. And if it appears deeper than the skin, and the hair in it is yellow and thin, then the priest shall pronounce him unclean. It is an itch, a leprous disease of the head or the beard. ³¹And if the priest examines the itching disease and it appears no deeper than the skin and there is no black hair in it, then the priest shall shut up the person with the itching disease for seven days, ³²and on the seventh day the priest shall examine the disease. If the itch has not spread, and there is in it no yellow hair, and the itch appears to be no deeper than the skin, ³³then he shall shave himself, but the itch he shall not shave; and the priest shall shut up the person with the itching disease for another seven days. ³⁴And on the seventh day the priest shall examine the itch, and if the itch has not spread in the skin and it appears to be no deeper than the skin, then the priest shall pronounce him clean. And he shall wash his clothes and be clean. ³⁵But if the itch spreads in the skin after his cleansing, ³⁶then the priest shall examine him, and if the itch has spread in the skin, the priest need not seek for the yellow hair; he is unclean. ³⁷But if in his eyes the itch is unchanged

and black hair has grown in it, the itch is healed and he is clean, and the priest shall pronounce him clean.

³⁸"When a man or a woman has spots on the skin of the body, white spots, ³⁹the priest shall look, and if the spots on the skin of the body are of a dull white, it is leukoderma that has broken out in the skin; he is clean.

⁴⁰"If a man's hair falls out from his head, he is bald; he is clean. ⁴¹And if a man's hair falls out from his forehead, he has baldness of the forehead; he is clean. ⁴²But if there is on the bald head or the bald forehead a reddish-white diseased area, it is a leprous disease breaking out on his bald head or his bald forehead. ⁴³Then the priest shall examine him, and if the diseased swelling is reddish-white on his bald head or on his bald forehead, like the appearance of leprous disease in the skin of the body, ⁴⁴he is a leprous man, he is unclean. The priest must pronounce him unclean; his disease is on his head.

⁴⁵"The leprous person who has the disease shall wear torn clothes and let the hair of his head hang loose, and he shall cover his upper lip¹ and cry out, 'Unclean, unclean.' ⁴⁶He shall remain unclean as long as he has the disease. He is unclean. He shall live alone. His dwelling shall be outside the camp.

⁴⁷"When there is a case of leprous disease in a garment, whether a woolen or a linen garment, ⁴⁸in warp or woof of linen or wool, or in a skin or in anything made of skin, ⁴⁹if the disease is greenish or reddish in the garment, or in the skin or in the warp or the woof or in any article made of skin, it is a case of leprous disease, and it shall be shown to the priest. ⁵⁰And the priest shall examine the disease and shut up that which has the disease for seven days. ⁵¹Then he shall examine the disease on the seventh day. If the disease has spread in the garment, in the warp or the woof, or in the skin, whatever be the use of the skin, the disease is a persistent leprous disease; it is unclean. ⁵²And he shall burn the garment, or the warp or the woof, the wool or the linen, or any article made of skin that is diseased, for it is a persistent leprous disease. It shall be burned in the fire.

⁵³"And if the priest examines, and if the disease has not spread in the garment, in the warp or the woof or in any article made of skin, ⁵⁴then the priest shall command that they wash the thing in which is the disease, and he shall shut it up for another seven days. ⁵⁵And the priest shall examine the diseased thing after it has been washed. And if the appearance of the diseased area has not changed, though the disease has not spread, it is unclean. You shall burn it in the fire, whether the rot is on the back or on the front.

⁵⁶"But if the priest examines, and if the diseased area has faded after it has been washed, he shall tear it out of the garment or the skin or the warp or the woof. ⁵⁷Then if it appears again in the garment, in the warp or the woof, or in any article made of skin, it is spreading. You shall burn with fire whatever has the disease. ⁵⁸But the garment, or the warp or the woof, or any article made of skin from which the disease departs when you have washed it, shall then be washed a second time, and be clean."

⁵⁹This is the law for a case of leprous disease in a garment of wool or linen, either in the warp or the woof, or in any article made of skin, to determine whether it is clean or unclean.

---

¹ Or mustache

Purification rites for those with skin diseases [14:1–32]. Chapter 13 deals mainly with the diagnosis of skin ailments, the quarantining of diseased people, and the destruction of contaminated clothing. The first half of chapter 14 balances that with the procedures for restoring people to the community after they have recovered. The emphasis is not at all on the medical aspect of healing but wholly on religious rituals. The intention of the rites was thus spiritual and symbolic, ensuring that the covenant community saw the hand of God in recovery from illness. Additionally, the rituals were occasions for the ongoing sacrificial system by which the Israelites acknowledged their sinfulness and received forgiveness from God.

14 The LORD spoke to Moses, saying, [2]"This shall be the law of the leprous person for the day of his cleansing. He shall be brought to the priest, [3]and the priest shall go out of the camp, and the priest shall look. Then, if the case of leprous disease is healed in the leprous person, [4]the priest shall command them to take for him who is to be cleansed two live[1] clean birds and cedarwood and scarlet yarn and hyssop. [5]And the priest shall command them to kill one of the birds in an earthenware vessel over fresh[2] water. [6]He shall take the live bird with the cedarwood and the scarlet yarn and the hyssop, and dip them and the live bird in the blood of the bird that was killed over the fresh water. [7]And he shall sprinkle it seven times on him who is to be cleansed of the leprous disease. Then he shall pronounce him clean and shall let the living bird go into the open field. [8]And he who is to be cleansed shall wash his clothes and shave off all his hair and bathe himself in water, and he shall be clean. And after that he may come into the camp, but live outside his tent seven days. [9]And on the seventh day he shall shave off all his hair from his head, his beard, and his eyebrows. He shall shave off all his hair, and then he shall wash his clothes and bathe his body in water, and he shall be clean.

[10]"And on the eighth day he shall take two male lambs without blemish, and one ewe lamb a year old without blemish, and a grain offering of three tenths of an ephah[3] of fine flour mixed with oil, and one log[4] of oil. [11]And the priest who cleanses him shall set the man who is to be cleansed and these things before the LORD, at the entrance of the tent of meeting. [12]And the priest shall take one of the male lambs and offer it for a guilt offering, along with the log of oil, and wave them for a wave offering before the LORD. [13]And he shall kill the lamb in the place where they kill the sin offering and the burnt offering, in the place of the sanctuary. For the guilt offering, like the sin offering, belongs to the priest; it is most holy. [14]The priest shall take some of the blood of the guilt offering, and the priest shall put it on the lobe of the right ear of him who is to be cleansed and on the thumb of his right hand and on the big toe of his right foot. [15]Then the priest shall take some of the log of oil and pour it into the palm of his own left hand [16]and dip his right finger in the oil that is in his left hand and sprinkle some oil with his finger seven times before the LORD. [17]And some of the oil that remains in his hand the priest shall put on the lobe of the right ear of him who is to be cleansed and on the thumb of his right hand and on the big toe of his right foot, on top of the blood of the guilt offering. [18]And the rest of the oil that is in the priest's hand he shall put on the head of him who is to be cleansed. Then the priest shall make atonement for him before the LORD. [19]The priest shall offer the sin offering, to make atonement for him who is to be cleansed from his uncleanness.

---

[1] Or *wild* [2] Or *running*; Hebrew *living*; also verses 6, 50, 51, 52 [3] An *ephah* was about 3/5 bushel or 22 liters [4] A *log* was about 1/3 quart or 0.3 liter

And afterward he shall kill the burnt offering. ²⁰And the priest shall offer the burnt offering and the grain offering on the altar. Thus the priest shall make atonement for him, and he shall be clean.

²¹"But if he is poor and cannot afford so much, then he shall take one male lamb for a guilt offering to be waved, to make atonement for him, and a tenth of an ephah of fine flour mixed with oil for a grain offering, and a log of oil; ²²also two turtledoves or two pigeons, whichever he can afford. The one shall be a sin offering and the other a burnt offering. ²³And on the eighth day he shall bring them for his cleansing to the priest, to the entrance of the tent of meeting, before the Lord. ²⁴And the priest shall take the lamb of the guilt offering and the log of oil, and the priest shall wave them for a wave offering before the Lord. ²⁵And he shall kill the lamb of the guilt offering. And the priest shall take some of the blood of the guilt offering and put it on the lobe of the right ear of him who is to be cleansed, and on the thumb of his right hand and on the big toe of his right foot. ²⁶And the priest shall pour some of the oil into the palm of his own left hand, ²⁷and shall sprinkle with his right finger some of the oil that is in his left hand seven times before the Lord. ²⁸And the priest shall put some of the oil that is in his hand on the lobe of the right ear of him who is to be cleansed and on the thumb of his right hand and on the big toe of his right foot, in the place where the blood of the guilt offering was put. ²⁹And the rest of the oil that is in the priest's hand he shall put on the head of him who is to be cleansed, to make atonement for him before the Lord. ³⁰And he shall offer, of the turtledoves or pigeons, whichever he can afford, ³¹one¹ for a sin offering and the other for a burnt offering, along with a grain offering. And the priest shall make atonement before the Lord for him who is being cleansed. ³²This is the law for him in whom is a case of leprous disease, who cannot afford the offerings for his cleansing."

Regulations governing contamination in houses [14:33–57]. From the terrors of the body we turn to the terrors of homeowning. This unit expressly looks forward to the time when the nation would "come into the land of Canaan" (v. 34). The generic phrase "leprous disease in a house" (v. 34) might have covered anything from lingering fungus or germs to mold and mildew. Again spiritual and hygienic aspects merge. The last four verses (vv. 54–57) serve as a helpful summary of chapters 13–14.

³³The Lord spoke to Moses and Aaron, saying, ³⁴"When you come into the land of Canaan, which I give you for a possession, and I put a case of leprous disease in a house in the land of your possession, ³⁵then he who owns the house shall come and tell the priest, 'There seems to me to be some case of disease in my house.' ³⁶Then the priest shall command that they empty the house before the priest goes to examine the disease, lest all that is in the house be declared unclean. And afterward the priest shall go in to see the house. ³⁷And he shall examine the disease. And if the disease is in the walls of the house with greenish or reddish spots, and if it appears to be deeper than the surface, ³⁸then the priest shall go out of the house to the door of the house and shut up the house seven days. ³⁹And the priest shall come again on the seventh day, and look. If the disease has spread in the walls of the house, ⁴⁰then the priest shall command that they take out the stones in which is the disease and throw them into an unclean place outside the city. ⁴¹And he shall have the inside of the house

---

¹ Septuagint, Syriac; Hebrew *afford, ³¹such as he can afford,* one

scraped all around, and the plaster that they scrape off they shall pour out in an unclean place outside the city. ⁴²Then they shall take other stones and put them in the place of those stones, and he shall take other plaster and plaster the house.

⁴³"If the disease breaks out again in the house, after he has taken out the stones and scraped the house and plastered it, ⁴⁴then the priest shall go and look. And if the disease has spread in the house, it is a persistent leprous disease in the house; it is unclean. ⁴⁵And he shall break down the house, its stones and timber and all the plaster of the house, and he shall carry them out of the city to an unclean place. ⁴⁶Moreover, whoever enters the house while it is shut up shall be unclean until the evening, ⁴⁷and whoever sleeps in the house shall wash his clothes, and whoever eats in the house shall wash his clothes.

⁴⁸"But if the priest comes and looks, and if the disease has not spread in the house after the house was plastered, then the priest shall pronounce the house clean, for the disease is healed. ⁴⁹And for the cleansing of the house he shall take two small birds, with cedarwood and scarlet yarn and hyssop, ⁵⁰and shall kill one of the birds in an earthenware vessel over fresh water ⁵¹and shall take the cedarwood and the hyssop and the scarlet yarn, along with the live bird, and dip them in the blood of the bird that was killed and in the fresh water and sprinkle the house seven times. ⁵²Thus he shall cleanse the house with the blood of the bird and with the fresh water and with the live bird and with the cedarwood and hyssop and scarlet yarn. ⁵³And he shall let the live bird go out of the city into the open country. So he shall make atonement for the house, and it shall be clean."

⁵⁴This is the law for any case of leprous disease: for an itch, ⁵⁵for leprous disease in a garment or in a house, ⁵⁶and for a swelling or an eruption or a spot, ⁵⁷to show when it is unclean and when it is clean. This is the law for leprous disease.

Bodily discharges [chapter 15]. Again we need to abandon all squeamishness about the physical body and its discharges. A byproduct of these regulations is that we are given to understand that God created people as biological creatures and that we need to come to terms with our physical bodies. The immediately preceding chapters dealt with illness and were a health code designed for a community that lived in close proximity, but this chapter deals mainly with the normally functioning body, so that the theme is personal cleanliness more than health precautions. Overriding these physical considerations, though, is the pervasive spiritual symbolism of the need to purify oneself before God.

15 The LORD spoke to Moses and Aaron, saying, ²"Speak to the people of Israel and say to them, When any man has a discharge from his body,¹ his discharge is unclean. ³And this is the law of his uncleanness for a discharge: whether his body runs with his discharge, or his body is blocked up by his discharge, it is his uncleanness. ⁴Every bed on which the one with the discharge lies shall be unclean, and everything on which he sits shall be unclean. ⁵And anyone who touches his bed shall wash his clothes and bathe himself in water and be unclean until the evening. ⁶And whoever sits on anything on which the one with the discharge has sat shall wash his clothes and bathe himself in water and be unclean until the evening. ⁷And whoever touches the body of the one with the discharge shall wash his clothes and

¹ Hebrew *flesh*; also verse 3

bathe himself in water and be unclean until the evening. ⁸And if the one with the discharge spits on someone who is clean, then he shall wash his clothes and bathe himself in water and be unclean until the evening. ⁹And any saddle on which the one with the discharge rides shall be unclean. ¹⁰And whoever touches anything that was under him shall be unclean until the evening. And whoever carries such things shall wash his clothes and bathe himself in water and be unclean until the evening. ¹¹Anyone whom the one with the discharge touches without having rinsed his hands in water shall wash his clothes and bathe himself in water and be unclean until the evening. ¹²And an earthenware vessel that the one with the discharge touches shall be broken, and every vessel of wood shall be rinsed in water.

¹³"And when the one with a discharge is cleansed of his discharge, then he shall count for himself seven days for his cleansing, and wash his clothes. And he shall bathe his body in fresh water and shall be clean. ¹⁴And on the eighth day he shall take two turtledoves or two pigeons and come before the Lᴏʀᴅ to the entrance of the tent of meeting and give them to the priest. ¹⁵And the priest shall use them, one for a sin offering and the other for a burnt offering. And the priest shall make atonement for him before the Lᴏʀᴅ for his discharge.

¹⁶"If a man has an emission of semen, he shall bathe his whole body in water and be unclean until the evening. ¹⁷And every garment and every skin on which the semen comes shall be washed with water and be unclean until the evening. ¹⁸If a man lies with a woman and has an emission of semen, both of them shall bathe themselves in water and be unclean until the evening.

¹⁹"When a woman has a discharge, and the discharge in her body is blood, she shall be in her menstrual impurity for seven days, and whoever touches her shall be unclean until the evening. ²⁰And everything on which she lies during her menstrual impurity shall be unclean. Everything also on which she sits shall be unclean. ²¹And whoever touches her bed shall wash his clothes and bathe himself in water and be unclean until the evening. ²²And whoever touches anything on which she sits shall wash his clothes and bathe himself in water and be unclean until the evening. ²³Whether it is the bed or anything on which she sits, when he touches it he shall be unclean until the evening. ²⁴And if any man lies with her and her menstrual impurity comes upon him, he shall be unclean seven days, and every bed on which he lies shall be unclean.

²⁵"If a woman has a discharge of blood for many days, not at the time of her menstrual impurity, or if she has a discharge beyond the time of her impurity, all the days of the discharge she shall continue in uncleanness. As in the days of her impurity, she shall be unclean. ²⁶Every bed on which she lies, all the days of her discharge, shall be to her as the bed of her impurity. And everything on which she sits shall be unclean, as in the uncleanness of her menstrual impurity. ²⁷And whoever touches these things shall be unclean, and shall wash his clothes and bathe himself in water and be unclean until the evening. ²⁸But if she is cleansed of her discharge, she shall count for herself seven days, and after that she shall be clean. ²⁹And on the eighth day she shall take two turtledoves or two pigeons and bring them to the priest, to the entrance of the tent of meeting. ³⁰And the priest shall use one for a sin offering and the other for a burnt offering. And the priest shall make atonement for her before the Lᴏʀᴅ for her unclean discharge.

³¹"Thus you shall keep the people of Israel separate from their uncleanness, lest they die in their uncleanness by defiling my tabernacle that is in their midst."

³²This is the law for him who has a discharge and for him who has an emission of semen, becoming unclean thereby; ³³also for her who is unwell with her menstrual impurity, that is, for anyone, male or female, who has a discharge, and for the man who lies with a woman who is unclean.

The Day of Atonement instituted [chapter 16]. Whereas the first fifteen chapters have been most obviously moral and social in their surface details, with a theological substructure implied, with chapter 16 theology becomes explicit and dominant. The Day of Atonement shows what God requires for dealing with the problem of human sin. The day is preeminent in the Jewish covenant calendar, and here we actually observe (and can imaginatively relive) the establishment of this great event. The format is once again God's instruction to Moses regarding how the Day of Atonement is to be practiced. The chapter is the midpoint in Leviticus, symbolic of its climactic importance. We can appropriate the theological meaning of the material by analyzing the underlying principles (such as blood sacrifice and the idea of a substitutionary atonement) and then reflecting on how Christ fulfilled them. The Day of Atonement was the most important day of the year because it dealt with people's most important problem: sin.

16 The Lord spoke to Moses after the death of the two sons of Aaron, when they drew near before the Lord and died, ²and the Lord said to Moses, "Tell Aaron your brother not to come at any time into the Holy Place inside the veil, before the mercy seat that is on the ark, so that he may not die. For I will appear in the cloud over the mercy seat. ³But in this way Aaron shall come into the Holy Place: with a bull from the herd for a sin offering and a ram for a burnt offering. ⁴He shall put on the holy linen coat and shall have the linen undergarment on his body, and he shall tie the linen sash around his waist, and wear the linen turban; these are the holy garments. He shall bathe his body in water and then put them on. ⁵And he shall take from the congregation of the people of Israel two male goats for a sin offering, and one ram for a burnt offering.

⁶"Aaron shall offer the bull as a sin offering for himself and shall make atonement for himself and for his house. ⁷Then he shall take the two goats and set them before the Lord at the entrance of the tent of meeting. ⁸And Aaron shall cast lots over the two goats, one lot for the Lord and the other lot for Azazel.[1] ⁹And Aaron shall present the goat on which the lot fell for the Lord and use it as a sin offering, ¹⁰but the goat on which the lot fell for Azazel shall be presented alive before the Lord to make atonement over it, that it may be sent away into the wilderness to Azazel.

¹¹"Aaron shall present the bull as a sin offering for himself, and shall make atonement for himself and for his house. He shall kill the bull as a sin offering for himself. ¹²And he shall take a censer full of coals of fire from the altar before the Lord, and two handfuls of sweet incense beaten small, and he shall bring it inside the veil ¹³and put the incense on the fire before the Lord, that the cloud of the incense may cover the mercy seat that is over the testimony, so that he does not die. ¹⁴And he shall take some of the blood of the bull and sprinkle it with his finger on the front of the mercy seat on the east side, and in front of the mercy seat he shall sprinkle some of the blood with his finger seven times.

---

[1] The meaning of *Azazel* is uncertain; possibly the name of a place or a demon, traditionally a scapegoat; also verses 10, 26

[15]"Then he shall kill the goat of the sin offering that is for the people and bring its blood inside the veil and do with its blood as he did with the blood of the bull, sprinkling it over the mercy seat and in front of the mercy seat. [16]Thus he shall make atonement for the Holy Place, because of the uncleannesses of the people of Israel and because of their transgressions, all their sins. And so he shall do for the tent of meeting, which dwells with them in the midst of their uncleannesses. [17]No one may be in the tent of meeting from the time he enters to make atonement in the Holy Place until he comes out and has made atonement for himself and for his house and for all the assembly of Israel. [18]Then he shall go out to the altar that is before the LORD and make atonement for it, and shall take some of the blood of the bull and some of the blood of the goat, and put it on the horns of the altar all around. [19]And he shall sprinkle some of the blood on it with his finger seven times, and cleanse it and consecrate it from the uncleannesses of the people of Israel.

[20]"And when he has made an end of atoning for the Holy Place and the tent of meeting and the altar, he shall present the live goat. [21]And Aaron shall lay both his hands on the head of the live goat, and confess over it all the iniquities of the people of Israel, and all their transgressions, all their sins. And he shall put them on the head of the goat and send it away into the wilderness by the hand of a man who is in readiness. [22]The goat shall bear all their iniquities on itself to a remote area, and he shall let the goat go free in the wilderness.

[23]"Then Aaron shall come into the tent of meeting and shall take off the linen garments that he put on when he went into the Holy Place and shall leave them there. [24]And he shall bathe his body in water in a holy place and put on his garments and come out and offer his burnt offering and the burnt offering of the people and make atonement for himself and for the people. [25]And the fat of the sin offering he shall burn on the altar. [26]And he who lets the goat go to Azazel shall wash his clothes and bathe his body in water, and afterward he may come into the camp. [27]And the bull for the sin offering and the goat for the sin offering, whose blood was brought in to make atonement in the Holy Place, shall be carried outside the camp. Their skin and their flesh and their dung shall be burned up with fire. [28]And he who burns them shall wash his clothes and bathe his body in water, and afterward he may come into the camp.

[29]"And it shall be a statute to you forever that in the seventh month, on the tenth day of the month, you shall afflict yourselves[1] and shall do no work, either the native or the stranger who sojourns among you. [30]For on this day shall atonement be made for you to cleanse you. You shall be clean before the LORD from all your sins. [31]It is a Sabbath of solemn rest to you, and you shall afflict yourselves; it is a statute forever. [32]And the priest who is anointed and consecrated as priest in his father's place shall make atonement, wearing the holy linen garments. [33]He shall make atonement for the holy sanctuary, and he shall make atonement for the tent of meeting and for the altar, and he shall make atonement for the priests and for all the people of the assembly. [34]And this shall be a statute forever for you, that atonement may be made for the people of Israel once in the year because of all their sins." And Moses did as the LORD commanded him.

[1] Or shall fast; also verse 31

Rules for the slaughter and eating of animals [chapter 17]. It is customary to call the entire remainder of the book of Leviticus "the Holiness Code." This code covers an immense range of diverse rules and regulations. Chapter 17 takes animal slaughter as its subject, and even here the range of material requires our close attention. God's commands to Moses (vv. 1–2) concerning the slaughter and eating of animals cover three specific topics: a strict rule that all sacrificial animals must be slaughtered by the priests at the tabernacle and not at shrines of people's own choosing (vv. 3–9); an equally strict prohibition against ingesting the blood of animals (vv. 10–14); required purification rituals for people who eat animals that have not had the blood drained from them (vv. 15–16).

17 And the Lord spoke to Moses, saying, ²"Speak to Aaron and his sons and to all the people of Israel and say to them, This is the thing that the Lord has commanded. ³If any one of the house of Israel kills an ox or a lamb or a goat in the camp, or kills it outside the camp, ⁴and does not bring it to the entrance of the tent of meeting to offer it as a gift to the Lord in front of the tabernacle of the Lord, blood-guilt shall be imputed to that man. He has shed blood, and that man shall be cut off from among his people. ⁵This is to the end that the people of Israel may bring their sacrifices that they sacrifice in the open field, that they may bring them to the Lord, to the priest at the entrance of the tent of meeting, and sacrifice them as sacrifices of peace offerings to the Lord. ⁶And the priest shall throw the blood on the altar of the Lord at the entrance of the tent of meeting and burn the fat for a pleasing aroma to the Lord. ⁷So they shall no more sacrifice their sacrifices to goat demons, after whom they whore. This shall be a statute forever for them throughout their generations.

⁸"And you shall say to them, Any one of the house of Israel, or of the strangers who sojourn among them, who offers a burnt offering or sacrifice ⁹and does not bring it to the entrance of the tent of meeting to offer it to the Lord, that man shall be cut off from his people.

¹⁰"If any one of the house of Israel or of the strangers who sojourn among them eats any blood, I will set my face against that person who eats blood and will cut him off from among his people. ¹¹For the life of the flesh is in the blood, and I have given it for you on the altar to make atonement for your souls, for it is the blood that makes atonement by the life. ¹²Therefore I have said to the people of Israel, No person among you shall eat blood, neither shall any stranger who sojourns among you eat blood.

¹³"Any one also of the people of Israel, or of the strangers who sojourn among them, who takes in hunting any beast or bird that may be eaten shall pour out its blood and cover it with earth. ¹⁴For the life of every creature[1] is its blood: its blood is its life.[2] Therefore I have said to the people of Israel, You shall not eat the blood of any creature, for the life of every creature is its blood. Whoever eats it shall be cut off. ¹⁵And every person who eats what dies of itself or what is torn by beasts, whether he is a native or a sojourner, shall wash his clothes and bathe himself in water and be unclean until the evening; then he shall be clean. ¹⁶But if he does not wash them or bathe his flesh, he shall bear his iniquity."

---

[1] Hebrew *all flesh* [2] Hebrew *it is in its life*

Prohibited sexual activities [chapter 18]. Every culture protects what it values most with rules. The list of prohibited sexual practices in this chapter is designed to protect the legitimate sexual practices of chastity and married sexuality. The moral code of forbidden practices (vv. 6–23) has as its bookends (vv. 1–5 and 24–30) similar statements about the need to avoid behaving as the unbelieving nations behaved and to obey God out of devotion to him.

18 And the LORD spoke to Moses, saying, ²"Speak to the people of Israel and say to them, I am the LORD your God. ³You shall not do as they do in the land of Egypt, where you lived, and you shall not do as they do in the land of Canaan, to which I am bringing you. You shall not walk in their statutes. ⁴You shall follow my rules¹ and keep my statutes and walk in them. I am the LORD your God. ⁵You shall therefore keep my statutes and my rules; if a person does them, he shall live by them: I am the LORD.

⁶"None of you shall approach any one of his close relatives to uncover nakedness. I am the LORD. ⁷You shall not uncover the nakedness of your father, which is the nakedness of your mother; she is your mother, you shall not uncover her nakedness. ⁸You shall not uncover the nakedness of your father's wife; it is your father's nakedness. ⁹You shall not uncover the nakedness of your sister, your father's daughter or your mother's daughter, whether brought up in the family or in another home. ¹⁰You shall not uncover the nakedness of your son's daughter or of your daughter's daughter, for their nakedness is your own nakedness. ¹¹You shall not uncover the nakedness of your father's wife's daughter, brought up in your father's family, since she is your sister. ¹²You shall not uncover the nakedness of your father's sister; she is your father's relative. ¹³You shall not uncover the nakedness of your mother's sister, for she is your mother's relative. ¹⁴You shall not uncover the nakedness of your father's brother, that is, you shall not approach his wife; she is your aunt. ¹⁵You shall not uncover the nakedness of your daughter-in-law; she is your son's wife, you shall not uncover her nakedness. ¹⁶You shall not uncover the nakedness of your brother's wife; it is your brother's nakedness. ¹⁷You shall not uncover the nakedness of a woman and of her daughter, and you shall not take her son's daughter or her daughter's daughter to uncover her nakedness; they are relatives; it is depravity. ¹⁸And you shall not take a woman as a rival wife to her sister, uncovering her nakedness while her sister is still alive.

¹⁹"You shall not approach a woman to uncover her nakedness while she is in her menstrual uncleanness. ²⁰And you shall not lie sexually with your neighbor's wife and so make yourself unclean with her. ²¹You shall not give any of your children to offer them² to Molech, and so profane the name of your God: I am the LORD. ²²You shall not lie with a male as with a woman; it is an abomination. ²³And you shall not lie with any animal and so make yourself unclean with it, neither shall any woman give herself to an animal to lie with it: it is perversion.

²⁴"Do not make yourselves unclean by any of these things, for by all these the nations I am driving out before you have become unclean, ²⁵and the land became unclean, so that I punished its iniquity, and the land vomited out its inhabitants. ²⁶But you shall keep my statutes and my rules and do none of these abominations, either the native or the stranger who sojourns among you ²⁷(for the people of the land, who

¹ Or *my just decrees*; also verse 5 ² Hebrew *to make them pass through* [the fire]

were before you, did all of these abominations, so that the land became unclean), ²⁸lest the land vomit you out when you make it unclean, as it vomited out the nation that was before you. ²⁹For everyone who does any of these abominations, the persons who do them shall be cut off from among their people. ³⁰So keep my charge never to practice any of these abominable customs that were practiced before you, and never to make yourselves unclean by them: I am the LORD your God."

> **Rules for covenant living** [chapter 19]. The moral emphasis continues with a list of wide-ranging rules. First, we can appreciate the importance that God attaches to the conduct of life in very specific and down-to-earth matters. As part of that, we get a distinct picture from this chapter that holiness extends to all of life. Additionally, this law code expresses the values of the divine lawgiver, so we can read the material with a view toward understanding what God approves and disapproves. Along with that, we can ponder why God approves and disapproves of these things. Finally, we need to remember the affinities of the book of Leviticus with utopian literature: this is a blueprint for a good society, accompanied by a delineation of the external forms that will ensure its goodness.

19 And the LORD spoke to Moses, saying, ²"Speak to all the congregation of the people of Israel and say to them, You shall be holy, for I the LORD your God am holy. ³Every one of you shall revere his mother and his father, and you shall keep my Sabbaths: I am the LORD your God. ⁴Do not turn to idols or make for yourselves any gods of cast metal: I am the LORD your God.

⁵"When you offer a sacrifice of peace offerings to the LORD, you shall offer it so that you may be accepted. ⁶It shall be eaten the same day you offer it or on the day after, and anything left over until the third day shall be burned up with fire. ⁷If it is eaten at all on the third day, it is tainted; it will not be accepted, ⁸and everyone who eats it shall bear his iniquity, because he has profaned what is holy to the LORD, and that person shall be cut off from his people.

⁹"When you reap the harvest of your land, you shall not reap your field right up to its edge, neither shall you gather the gleanings after your harvest. ¹⁰And you shall not strip your vineyard bare, neither shall you gather the fallen grapes of your vineyard. You shall leave them for the poor and for the sojourner: I am the LORD your God.

¹¹"You shall not steal; you shall not deal falsely; you shall not lie to one another. ¹²You shall not swear by my name falsely, and so profane the name of your God: I am the LORD.

¹³"You shall not oppress your neighbor or rob him. The wages of a hired servant shall not remain with you all night until the morning. ¹⁴You shall not curse the deaf or put a stumbling block before the blind, but you shall fear your God: I am the LORD.

¹⁵"You shall do no injustice in court. You shall not be partial to the poor or defer to the great, but in righteousness shall you judge your neighbor. ¹⁶You shall not go around as a slanderer among your people, and you shall not stand up against the life¹ of your neighbor: I am the LORD.

¹⁷"You shall not hate your brother in your heart, but you shall reason frankly with your neighbor, lest you incur sin because of him. ¹⁸You shall not take vengeance or bear a grudge against the sons of your own people, but you shall love your neighbor as yourself: I am the LORD.

¹ Hebrew blood

[19]"You shall keep my statutes. You shall not let your cattle breed with a different kind. You shall not sow your field with two kinds of seed, nor shall you wear a garment of cloth made of two kinds of material.

[20]"If a man lies sexually with a woman who is a slave, assigned to another man and not yet ransomed or given her freedom, a distinction shall be made. They shall not be put to death, because she was not free; [21]but he shall bring his compensation to the LORD, to the entrance of the tent of meeting, a ram for a guilt offering. [22]And the priest shall make atonement for him with the ram of the guilt offering before the LORD for his sin that he has committed, and he shall be forgiven for the sin that he has committed.

[23]"When you come into the land and plant any kind of tree for food, then you shall regard its fruit as forbidden.[1] Three years it shall be forbidden to you; it must not be eaten. [24]And in the fourth year all its fruit shall be holy, an offering of praise to the LORD. [25]But in the fifth year you may eat of its fruit, to increase its yield for you: I am the LORD your God.

[26]"You shall not eat any flesh with the blood in it. You shall not interpret omens or tell fortunes. [27]You shall not round off the hair on your temples or mar the edges of your beard. [28]You shall not make any cuts on your body for the dead or tattoo yourselves: I am the LORD.

[29]"Do not profane your daughter by making her a prostitute, lest the land fall into prostitution and the land become full of depravity. [30]You shall keep my Sabbaths and reverence my sanctuary: I am the LORD.

[31]"Do not turn to mediums or necromancers; do not seek them out, and so make yourselves unclean by them: I am the LORD your God.

[32]"You shall stand up before the gray head and honor the face of an old man, and you shall fear your God: I am the LORD.

[33]"When a stranger sojourns with you in your land, you shall not do him wrong. [34]You shall treat the stranger who sojourns with you as the native among you, and you shall love him as yourself, for you were strangers in the land of Egypt: I am the LORD your God.

[35]"You shall do no wrong in judgment, in measures of length or weight or quantity. [36]You shall have just balances, just weights, a just ephah, and a just hin:[2] I am the LORD your God, who brought you out of the land of Egypt. [37]And you shall observe all my statutes and all my rules, and do them: I am the LORD."

Rules governing serious offenses [chapter 20]. The topics continue to be wide ranging, but the general tenor is that the offenses that are prohibited in this chapter are particularly serious ones. The prohibited offenses are as follows: sacrificing children to idols (vv. 1–5); consulting mediums and necromancers (vv. 6, 27); cursing one's father and mother (v. 9); adultery, sexual perversions, and sexual misconduct (vv. 10–21). Additionally, we find positive commands to obey God and avoid the behavior of pagan societies (vv. 7–8, 22–26). The chief command underlying all the specifics is the need to be holy to God (v. 26).

---

[1] Hebrew *as its uncircumcision* [2] An *ephah* was about 3/5 bushel or 22 liters; a *hin* was about 4 quarts or 3.5 liters

20 The LORD spoke to Moses, saying, ²"Say to the people of Israel, Any one of the people of Israel or of the strangers who sojourn in Israel who gives any of his children to Molech shall surely be put to death. The people of the land shall stone him with stones. ³I myself will set my face against that man and will cut him off from among his people, because he has given one of his children to Molech, to make my sanctuary unclean and to profane my holy name. ⁴And if the people of the land do at all close their eyes to that man when he gives one of his children to Molech, and do not put him to death, ⁵then I will set my face against that man and against his clan and will cut them off from among their people, him and all who follow him in whoring after Molech.

⁶"If a person turns to mediums and necromancers, whoring after them, I will set my face against that person and will cut him off from among his people. ⁷Consecrate yourselves, therefore, and be holy, for I am the LORD your God. ⁸Keep my statutes and do them; I am the LORD who sanctifies you. ⁹For anyone who curses his father or his mother shall surely be put to death; he has cursed his father or his mother; his blood is upon him.

¹⁰"If a man commits adultery with the wife of¹ his neighbor, both the adulterer and the adulteress shall surely be put to death. ¹¹If a man lies with his father's wife, he has uncovered his father's nakedness; both of them shall surely be put to death; their blood is upon them. ¹²If a man lies with his daughter-in-law, both of them shall surely be put to death; they have committed perversion; their blood is upon them. ¹³If a man lies with a male as with a woman, both of them have committed an abomination; they shall surely be put to death; their blood is upon them. ¹⁴If a man takes a woman and her mother also, it is depravity; he and they shall be burned with fire, that there may be no depravity among you. ¹⁵If a man lies with an animal, he shall surely be put to death, and you shall kill the animal. ¹⁶If a woman approaches any animal and lies with it, you shall kill the woman and the animal; they shall surely be put to death; their blood is upon them.

¹⁷"If a man takes his sister, a daughter of his father or a daughter of his mother, and sees her nakedness, and she sees his nakedness, it is a disgrace, and they shall be cut off in the sight of the children of their people. He has uncovered his sister's nakedness, and he shall bear his iniquity. ¹⁸If a man lies with a woman during her menstrual period and uncovers her nakedness, he has made naked her fountain, and she has uncovered the fountain of her blood. Both of them shall be cut off from among their people. ¹⁹You shall not uncover the nakedness of your mother's sister or of your father's sister, for that is to make naked one's relative; they shall bear their iniquity. ²⁰If a man lies with his uncle's wife, he has uncovered his uncle's nakedness; they shall bear their sin; they shall die childless. ²¹If a man takes his brother's wife, it is impurity.² He has uncovered his brother's nakedness; they shall be childless.

²²"You shall therefore keep all my statutes and all my rules and do them, that the land where I am bringing you to live may not vomit you out. ²³And you shall not walk in the customs of the nation that I am driving out before you, for they did all these things, and therefore I detested them. ²⁴But I have said to you, 'You shall inherit their land, and I will give it to you to possess, a land flowing with milk and honey.' I am the LORD your God, who has separated you from the peoples. ²⁵You shall therefore separate the clean beast from the unclean, and the unclean bird from the clean. You shall not make yourselves detestable by beast or by bird or by anything with which the

¹ Hebrew repeats *if a man commits adultery with the wife of* ² Literally *menstrual impurity*

ground crawls, which I have set apart for you to hold unclean. ²⁶You shall be holy to me, for I the LORD am holy and have separated you from the peoples, that you should be mine.

²⁷"A man or a woman who is a medium or a necromancer shall surely be put to death. They shall be stoned with stones; their blood shall be upon them."

A brief manual for priests [21:1–22:16]. As a follow-up to the instructions for how individuals were required to behave morally, we find a similar list of instructions addressed specifically to priests and their families. We might ponder how the requirements for the priests are more specific and more demanding than those for others, and also how the stipulations add up to a picture of holiness.

21 And the LORD said to Moses, "Speak to the priests, the sons of Aaron, and say to them: No one shall make himself unclean for the dead among his people, ²except for his closest relatives, his mother, his father, his son, his daughter, his brother, ³or his virgin sister (who is near to him because she has had no husband; for her he may make himself unclean). ⁴He shall not make himself unclean as a husband among his people and so profane himself. ⁵They shall not make bald patches on their heads, nor shave off the edges of their beards, nor make any cuts on their body. ⁶They shall be holy to their God and not profane the name of their God. For they offer the LORD's food offerings, the bread of their God; therefore they shall be holy. ⁷They shall not marry a prostitute or a woman who has been defiled, neither shall they marry a woman divorced from her husband, for the priest is holy to his God. ⁸You shall sanctify him, for he offers the bread of your God. He shall be holy to you, for I, the LORD, who sanctify you, am holy. ⁹And the daughter of any priest, if she profanes herself by whoring, profanes her father; she shall be burned with fire.

¹⁰"The priest who is chief among his brothers, on whose head the anointing oil is poured and who has been consecrated to wear the garments, shall not let the hair of his head hang loose nor tear his clothes. ¹¹He shall not go in to any dead bodies nor make himself unclean, even for his father or for his mother. ¹²He shall not go out of the sanctuary, lest he profane the sanctuary of his God, for the consecration of the anointing oil of his God is on him: I am the LORD. ¹³And he shall take a wife in her virginity.¹ ¹⁴A widow, or a divorced woman, or a woman who has been defiled, or a prostitute, these he shall not marry. But he shall take as his wife a virgin² of his own people, ¹⁵that he may not profane his offspring among his people, for I am the LORD who sanctifies him."

¹⁶And the LORD spoke to Moses, saying, ¹⁷"Speak to Aaron, saying, None of your offspring throughout their generations who has a blemish may approach to offer the bread of his God. ¹⁸For no one who has a blemish shall draw near, a man blind or lame, or one who has a mutilated face or a limb too long, ¹⁹or a man who has an injured foot or an injured hand, ²⁰or a hunchback or a dwarf or a man with a defect in his sight or an itching disease or scabs or crushed testicles. ²¹No man of the offspring of Aaron the priest who has a blemish shall come near to offer the LORD's food offerings; since he has a blemish, he shall not come near to offer the bread of his God. ²²He may eat the bread of his God, both of the most holy and of the holy things, ²³but he shall not go through the veil or approach the altar, because he has a blemish,

¹ Or a young wife ² Hebrew young woman

that he may not profane my sanctuaries, for I am the LORD who sanctifies them." ²⁴So Moses spoke to Aaron and to his sons and to all the people of Israel.

22 And the LORD spoke to Moses, saying, ²"Speak to Aaron and his sons so that they abstain from the holy things of the people of Israel, which they dedicate to me, so that they do not profane my holy name: I am the LORD. ³Say to them, 'If any one of all your offspring throughout your generations approaches the holy things that the people of Israel dedicate to the LORD, while he has an uncleanness, that person shall be cut off from my presence: I am the LORD. ⁴None of the offspring of Aaron who has a leprous disease or a discharge may eat of the holy things until he is clean. Whoever touches anything that is unclean through contact with the dead or a man who has had an emission of semen, ⁵and whoever touches a swarming thing by which he may be made unclean or a person from whom he may take uncleanness, whatever his uncleanness may be— ⁶the person who touches such a thing shall be unclean until the evening and shall not eat of the holy things unless he has bathed his body in water. ⁷When the sun goes down he shall be clean, and afterward he may eat of the holy things, because they are his food. ⁸He shall not eat what dies of itself or is torn by beasts, and so make himself unclean by it: I am the LORD.' ⁹They shall therefore keep my charge, lest they bear sin for it and die thereby when they profane it: I am the LORD who sanctifies them.

¹⁰"A lay person shall not eat of a holy thing; no foreign guest of the priest or hired servant shall eat of a holy thing. ¹¹but if a priest buys a slave as his property for money, the slave¹ may eat of it, and anyone born in his house may eat of his food. ¹²If a priest's daughter marries a layman, she shall not eat of the contribution of the holy things. ¹³But if a priest's daughter is widowed or divorced and has no child and returns to her father's house, as in her youth, she may eat of her father's food; yet no lay person shall eat of it. ¹⁴And if anyone eats of a holy thing unintentionally, he shall add the fifth of its value to it and give the holy thing to the priest. ¹⁵They shall not profane the holy things of the people of Israel, which they contribute to the LORD, ¹⁶and so cause them to bear iniquity and guilt, by eating their holy things: for I am the LORD who sanctifies them."

Acceptable and unacceptable sacrifices [22:17–33]. Following the section of instructions to the priests, this brief outline of acceptable and unacceptable sacrifices is addressed to both the priests and "all the people of Israel" (v. 18). We need to look beyond the details to the spiritual principles, which include the following: God is the one who prescribes how he is to be worshiped; God deserves the best that people can offer; conversely, people should not shortchange God; sacrifices are a way of honoring God (vv. 31–33).

¹⁷And the LORD spoke to Moses, saying, ¹⁸"Speak to Aaron and his sons and all the people of Israel and say to them, When any one of the house of Israel or of the sojourners in Israel presents a burnt offering as his offering, for any of their vows or freewill offerings that they offer to the LORD, ¹⁹if it is to be accepted for you it shall be a male without blemish, of the bulls or the sheep or the goats. ²⁰You shall not offer anything that has a blemish, for it will not be acceptable for you. ²¹And when anyone offers a sacrifice of peace offerings to the LORD to fulfill a vow or as a freewill offer-

---

¹ Hebrew *he*

ing from the herd or from the flock, to be accepted it must be perfect; there shall be no blemish in it. ²²Animals blind or disabled or mutilated or having a discharge or an itch or scabs you shall not offer to the LORD or give them to the LORD as a food offering on the altar. ²³You may present a bull or a lamb that has a part too long or too short for a freewill offering, but for a vow offering it cannot be accepted. ²⁴Any animal that has its testicles bruised or crushed or torn or cut you shall not offer to the LORD; you shall not do it within your land, ²⁵neither shall you offer as the bread of your God any such animals gotten from a foreigner. Since there is a blemish in them, because of their mutilation, they will not be accepted for you."

²⁶And the LORD spoke to Moses, saying, ²⁷"When an ox or sheep or goat is born, it shall remain seven days with its mother, and from the eighth day on it shall be acceptable as a food offering to the LORD. ²⁸But you shall not kill an ox or a sheep and her young in one day. ²⁹And when you sacrifice a sacrifice of thanksgiving to the LORD, you shall sacrifice it so that you may be accepted. ³⁰It shall be eaten on the same day; you shall leave none of it until morning: I am the LORD.

³¹"So you shall keep my commandments and do them: I am the LORD. ³²And you shall not profane my holy name, that I may be sanctified among the people of Israel. I am the LORD who sanctifies you, ³³who brought you out of the land of Egypt to be your God: I am the LORD."

> **The main holy days and festivals of OT religion** [chapter 23]. This chapter is a summary of the days and weeks that were the highlights of the weekly and annual liturgical life of OT Israel. The holy points in the Jewish calendar were as follows: the weekly Sabbath (vv. 1–3); the Passover (vv. 4–8); the Feast of Firstfruits (vv. 9–14); the Feast of Weeks (vv. 15–22); the Feast of Trumpets (vv. 23–25); the Day of Atonement (vv. 26–32); the Feast of Booths (vv. 33–43). Verse 44 rounds out the narrative. As we reflect on each of these, we can discern separate functions for each one: rest from work combined with the worship of God (Sabbath and Feast of Trumpets); acknowledging God's redemption of his people through the agency of blood (Passover and the Day of Atonement); the need to give God our first and our best (Firstfruits); celebrating God's bounty in harvest (Weeks); recalling God's providence during the journey through the wilderness (Booths).

23

The LORD spoke to Moses, saying, ²"Speak to the people of Israel and say to them, These are the appointed feasts of the LORD that you shall proclaim as holy convocations; they are my appointed feasts.

³"Six days shall work be done, but on the seventh day is a Sabbath of solemn rest, a holy convocation. You shall do no work. It is a Sabbath to the LORD in all your dwelling places.

⁴"These are the appointed feasts of the LORD, the holy convocations, which you shall proclaim at the time appointed for them. ⁵In the first month, on the fourteenth day of the month at twilight,¹ is the LORD's Passover. ⁶And on the fifteenth day of the same month is the Feast of Unleavened Bread to the LORD; for seven days you shall eat unleavened bread. ⁷On the first day you shall have a holy convocation; you shall not do any ordinary work. ⁸But you shall present a food offering to the LORD for seven days. On the seventh day is a holy convocation; you shall not do any ordinary work."

⁹And the LORD spoke to Moses, saying, ¹⁰"Speak to the people of Israel and say to

---

¹ Hebrew *between the two evenings*

them, When you come into the land that I give you and reap its harvest, you shall bring the sheaf of the firstfruits of your harvest to the priest, ¹¹and he shall wave the sheaf before the Lord, so that you may be accepted. On the day after the Sabbath the priest shall wave it. ¹²And on the day when you wave the sheaf, you shall offer a male lamb a year old without blemish as a burnt offering to the Lord. ¹³And the grain offering with it shall be two tenths of an ephah¹ of fine flour mixed with oil, a food offering to the Lord with a pleasing aroma, and the drink offering with it shall be of wine, a fourth of a hin.² ¹⁴And you shall eat neither bread nor grain parched or fresh until this same day, until you have brought the offering of your God: it is a statute forever throughout your generations in all your dwellings.

¹⁵"You shall count seven full weeks from the day after the Sabbath, from the day that you brought the sheaf of the wave offering. ¹⁶You shall count fifty days to the day after the seventh Sabbath. Then you shall present a grain offering of new grain to the Lord. ¹⁷You shall bring from your dwelling places two loaves of bread to be waved, made of two tenths of an ephah. They shall be of fine flour, and they shall be baked with leaven, as firstfruits to the Lord. ¹⁸And you shall present with the bread seven lambs a year old without blemish, and one bull from the herd and two rams. They shall be a burnt offering to the Lord, with their grain offering and their drink offerings, a food offering with a pleasing aroma to the Lord. ¹⁹And you shall offer one male goat for a sin offering, and two male lambs a year old as a sacrifice of peace offerings. ²⁰And the priest shall wave them with the bread of the firstfruits as a wave offering before the Lord, with the two lambs. They shall be holy to the Lord for the priest. ²¹And you shall make proclamation on the same day. You shall hold a holy convocation. You shall not do any ordinary work. It is a statute forever in all your dwelling places throughout your generations.

²²"And when you reap the harvest of your land, you shall not reap your field right up to its edge, nor shall you gather the gleanings after your harvest. You shall leave them for the poor and for the sojourner: I am the Lord your God."

²³And the Lord spoke to Moses, saying, ²⁴"Speak to the people of Israel, saying, In the seventh month, on the first day of the month, you shall observe a day of solemn rest, a memorial proclaimed with blast of trumpets, a holy convocation. ²⁵You shall not do any ordinary work, and you shall present a food offering to the Lord."

²⁶And the Lord spoke to Moses, saying, ²⁷"Now on the tenth day of this seventh month is the Day of Atonement. It shall be for you a time of holy convocation, and you shall afflict yourselves and present a food offering to the Lord. ²⁸And you shall not do any work on that very day, for it is a Day of Atonement, to make atonement for you before the Lord your God. ²⁹For whoever is not afflicted on that very day shall be cut off from his people. ³⁰And whoever does any work on that very day, that person I will destroy from among his people. ³¹You shall not do any work. It is a statute forever throughout your generations in all your dwelling places. ³²It shall be to you a Sabbath of solemn rest, and you shall afflict yourselves. On the ninth day of the month beginning at evening, from evening to evening shall you keep your Sabbath."

³³And the Lord spoke to Moses, saying, ³⁴"Speak to the people of Israel, saying, On the fifteenth day of this seventh month and for seven days is the Feast of Booths³ to the Lord. ³⁵On the first day shall be a holy convocation; you shall not do any ordinary work. ³⁶For seven days you shall present food offerings to the Lord. On the eighth day

---

¹ An *ephah* was about 3/5 bushel or 22 liters ² A *hin* was about 4 quarts or 3.5 liters ³ Or *tabernacles*

you shall hold a holy convocation and present a food offering to the Lord. It is a solemn assembly; you shall not do any ordinary work.

[37]"These are the appointed feasts of the Lord, which you shall proclaim as times of holy convocation, for presenting to the Lord food offerings, burnt offerings and grain offerings, sacrifices and drink offerings, each on its proper day, [38]besides the Lord's Sabbaths and besides your gifts and besides all your vow offerings and besides all your freewill offerings, which you give to the Lord.

[39]"On the fifteenth day of the seventh month, when you have gathered in the produce of the land, you shall celebrate the feast of the Lord seven days. On the first day shall be a solemn rest, and on the eighth day shall be a solemn rest. [40]And you shall take on the first day the fruit of splendid trees, branches of palm trees and boughs of leafy trees and willows of the brook, and you shall rejoice before the Lord your God seven days. [41]You shall celebrate it as a feast to the Lord for seven days in the year. It is a statute forever throughout your generations; you shall celebrate it in the seventh month. [42]You shall dwell in booths for seven days. All native Israelites shall dwell in booths, [43]that your generations may know that I made the people of Israel dwell in booths when I brought them out of the land of Egypt: I am the Lord your God."

[44]Thus Moses declared to the people of Israel the appointed feasts of the Lord.

Two tabernacle rituals and two moral laws [chapter 24]. This chapter is an interlude between units dealing with landmarks in the national calendar. We should allow our imagination to be inspired by pictures of a perpetual fire in the tabernacle (vv. 1–4) and a dozen specially baked loaves of bread put on display in the tabernacle every Sabbath (vv. 5–9). These pictures of spiritual holiness are then balanced by two pictures of moral holiness in the form of the prescription of death for the sin of blasphemy (vv. 10–16, 23) and the rule of fair retribution known as "an eye for an eye" (vv. 17–22).

24 The Lord spoke to Moses, saying, [2]"Command the people of Israel to bring you pure oil from beaten olives for the lamp, that a light may be kept burning regularly. [3]Outside the veil of the testimony, in the tent of meeting, Aaron shall arrange it from evening to morning before the Lord regularly. It shall be a statute forever throughout your generations. [4]He shall arrange the lamps on the lampstand of pure gold[1] before the Lord regularly.

[5]"You shall take fine flour and bake twelve loaves from it; two tenths of an ephah[2] shall be in each loaf. [6]And you shall set them in two piles, six in a pile, on the table of pure gold[3] before the Lord. [7]And you shall put pure frankincense on each pile, that it may go with the bread as a memorial portion as a food offering to the Lord. [8]Every Sabbath day Aaron shall arrange it before the Lord regularly; it is from the people of Israel as a covenant forever. [9]And it shall be for Aaron and his sons, and they shall eat it in a holy place, since it is for him a most holy portion out of the Lord's food offerings, a perpetual due."

[10]Now an Israelite woman's son, whose father was an Egyptian, went out among the people of Israel. And the Israelite woman's son and a man of Israel fought in the camp, [11]and the Israelite woman's son blasphemed the Name, and cursed. Then they brought him to Moses. His mother's name was Shelomith, the daughter of Dibri, of

[1] Hebrew *the pure lampstand* [2] An *ephah* was about 3/5 bushel or 22 liters [3] Hebrew *the pure table*

the tribe of Dan. ¹²And they put him in custody, till the will of the Lord should be clear to them.

¹³Then the Lord spoke to Moses, saying, ¹⁴"Bring out of the camp the one who cursed, and let all who heard him lay their hands on his head, and let all the congregation stone him. ¹⁵And speak to the people of Israel, saying, Whoever curses his God shall bear his sin. ¹⁶Whoever blasphemes the name of the Lord shall surely be put to death. All the congregation shall stone him. The sojourner as well as the native, when he blasphemes the Name, shall be put to death.

¹⁷"Whoever takes a human life shall surely be put to death. ¹⁸Whoever takes an animal's life shall make it good, life for life. ¹⁹If anyone injures his neighbor, as he has done it shall be done to him, ²⁰fracture for fracture, eye for eye, tooth for tooth; whatever injury he has given a person shall be given to him. ²¹Whoever kills an animal shall make it good, and whoever kills a person shall be put to death. ²²You shall have the same rule for the sojourner and for the native, for I am the Lord your God." ²³So Moses spoke to the people of Israel, and they brought out of the camp the one who had cursed and stoned him with stones. Thus the people of Israel did as the Lord commanded Moses.

Sabbatical and Jubilee years [chapter 25]. This chapter is a combination of additional sacred seasons and moral rules to protect the marginalized members of society. The two are related because the moral rules in this chapter coincide with certain cycles of time. First we read about two special seasons—the Sabbath Year every seven years (vv. 1–7) and the Year of Jubilee every fifty years (vv. 8–24). The regulations for the Year of Jubilee telescope outward into further rules governing the redemption of property (vv. 23–34), the lending of money to a fellow Israelite (vv. 35–38), and the hiring and releasing of servants (vv. 39–55).

25 The Lord spoke to Moses on Mount Sinai, saying, ²"Speak to the people of Israel and say to them, When you come into the land that I give you, the land shall keep a Sabbath to the Lord. ³For six years you shall sow your field, and for six years you shall prune your vineyard and gather in its fruits, ⁴but in the seventh year there shall be a Sabbath of solemn rest for the land, a Sabbath to the Lord. You shall not sow your field or prune your vineyard. ⁵You shall not reap what grows of itself in your harvest, or gather the grapes of your undressed vine. It shall be a year of solemn rest for the land. ⁶The Sabbath of the land shall provide food for you, for yourself and for your male and female slaves and for your hired servant and the sojourner who lives with you, ⁷and for your cattle and for the wild animals that are in your land: all its yield shall be for food.

⁸"You shall count seven weeks¹ of years, seven times seven years, so that the time of the seven weeks of years shall give you forty-nine years. ⁹Then you shall sound the loud trumpet on the tenth day of the seventh month. On the Day of Atonement you shall sound the trumpet throughout all your land. ¹⁰And you shall consecrate the fiftieth year, and proclaim liberty throughout the land to all its inhabitants. It shall be a jubilee for you, when each of you shall return to his property and each of you shall return to his clan. ¹¹That fiftieth year shall be a jubilee for you; in it you shall neither

¹ Or Sabbaths

sow nor reap what grows of itself nor gather the grapes from the undressed vines. [12]For it is a jubilee. It shall be holy to you. You may eat the produce of the field.[1]

[13]"In this year of jubilee each of you shall return to his property. [14]And if you make a sale to your neighbor or buy from your neighbor, you shall not wrong one another. [15]You shall pay your neighbor according to the number of years after the jubilee, and he shall sell to you according to the number of years for crops. [16]If the years are many, you shall increase the price, and if the years are few, you shall reduce the price, for it is the number of the crops that he is selling to you. [17]You shall not wrong one another, but you shall fear your God, for I am the LORD your God.

[18]"Therefore you shall do my statutes and keep my rules and perform them, and then you will dwell in the land securely. [19]The land will yield its fruit, and you will eat your fill and dwell in it securely. [20]And if you say, 'What shall we eat in the seventh year, if we may not sow or gather in our crop?' [21]I will command my blessing on you in the sixth year, so that it will produce a crop sufficient for three years. [22]When you sow in the eighth year, you will be eating some of the old crop; you shall eat the old until the ninth year, when its crop arrives.

[23]"The land shall not be sold in perpetuity, for the land is mine. For you are strangers and sojourners with me. [24]And in all the country you possess, you shall allow a redemption of the land.

[25]"If your brother becomes poor and sells part of his property, then his nearest redeemer shall come and redeem what his brother has sold. [26]If a man has no one to redeem it and then himself becomes prosperous and finds sufficient means to redeem it, [27]let him calculate the years since he sold it and pay back the balance to the man to whom he sold it, and then return to his property. [28]But if he has not sufficient means to recover it, then what he sold shall remain in the hand of the buyer until the year of jubilee. In the jubilee it shall be released, and he shall return to his property.

[29]"If a man sells a dwelling house in a walled city, he may redeem it within a year of its sale. For a full year he shall have the right of redemption. [30]If it is not redeemed within a full year, then the house in the walled city shall belong in perpetuity to the buyer, throughout his generations; it shall not be released in the jubilee. [31]But the houses of the villages that have no wall around them shall be classified with the fields of the land. They may be redeemed, and they shall be released in the jubilee. [32]As for the cities of the Levites, the Levites may redeem at any time the houses in the cities they possess. [33]And if one of the Levites exercises his right of redemption, then the house that was sold in a city they possess shall be released in the jubilee. For the houses in the cities of the Levites are their possession among the people of Israel. [34]But the fields of pastureland belonging to their cities may not be sold, for that is their possession forever.

[35]"If your brother becomes poor and cannot maintain himself with you, you shall support him as though he were a stranger and a sojourner, and he shall live with you. [36]Take no interest from him or profit, but fear your God, that your brother may live beside you. [37]You shall not lend him your money at interest, nor give him your food for profit. [38]I am the LORD your God, who brought you out of the land of Egypt to give you the land of Canaan, and to be your God.

[39]"If your brother becomes poor beside you and sells himself to you, you shall not make him serve as a slave: [40]he shall be with you as a hired servant and as a sojourner. He shall serve with you until the year of the jubilee. [41]Then he shall go out

[1] Or countryside

from you, he and his children with him, and go back to his own clan and return to the possession of his fathers. ⁴²For they are my servants,¹ whom I brought out of the land of Egypt; they shall not be sold as slaves. ⁴³You shall not rule over him ruthlessly but shall fear your God. ⁴⁴As for your male and female slaves whom you may have: you may buy male and female slaves from among the nations that are around you. ⁴⁵You may also buy from among the strangers who sojourn with you and their clans that are with you, who have been born in your land, and they may be your property. ⁴⁶You may bequeath them to your sons after you to inherit as a possession forever. You may make slaves of them, but over your brothers the people of Israel you shall not rule, one over another ruthlessly.

⁴⁷"If a stranger or sojourner with you becomes rich, and your brother beside him becomes poor and sells himself to the stranger or sojourner with you or to a member of the stranger's clan, ⁴⁸then after he is sold he may be redeemed. One of his brothers may redeem him, ⁴⁹or his uncle or his cousin may redeem him, or a close relative from his clan may redeem him. Or if he grows rich he may redeem himself. ⁵⁰He shall calculate with his buyer from the year when he sold himself to him until the year of jubilee, and the price of his sale shall vary with the number of years. The time he was with his owner shall be rated as the time of a hired servant. ⁵¹If there are still many years left, he shall pay proportionately for his redemption some of his sale price. ⁵²If there remain but a few years until the year of jubilee, he shall calculate and pay for his redemption in proportion to his years of service. ⁵³He shall treat him as a servant hired year by year. He shall not rule ruthlessly over him in your sight. ⁵⁴And if he is not redeemed by these means, then he and his children with him shall be released in the year of jubilee. ⁵⁵For it is to me that the people of Israel are servants.² They are my servants whom I brought out of the land of Egypt: I am the LORD your God.

Blessings and curses [chapter 26]. In the ongoing flow of Leviticus, this is the chapter toward which the story of God's covenant expectations has been moving all along. With the long lists of commands ringing in our ears, the main point of the specific details falls into place as with a camera click. Obedience to God's commands brings blessing, while disobedience brings a curse into personal and national life. The repeated rhetorical pattern that gives the chapter its eloquence is the formula "if . . . then . . . ," showing that actions have consequences. The concluding verse summarizes the entire plot of the implied story told in Leviticus: "These are the statutes and rules and laws that the LORD made between him and the people of Israel through Moses on Mount Sinai."

26 "You shall not make idols for yourselves or erect an image or pillar, and you shall not set up a figured stone in your land to bow down to it, for I am the LORD your God. ²You shall keep my Sabbaths and reverence my sanctuary: I am the LORD.

³"If you walk in my statutes and observe my commandments and do them, ⁴then I will give you your rains in their season, and the land shall yield its increase, and the trees of the field shall yield their fruit. ⁵Your threshing shall last to the time of the grape harvest, and the grape harvest shall last to the time for sowing. And you shall eat your bread to the full and dwell in your land securely. ⁶I will give peace in the land, and you shall lie down, and none shall make you afraid. And I will remove

¹ Hebrew *slaves* ² Or *slaves*

harmful beasts from the land, and the sword shall not go through your land. ⁷You shall chase your enemies, and they shall fall before you by the sword. ⁸Five of you shall chase a hundred, and a hundred of you shall chase ten thousand, and your enemies shall fall before you by the sword. ⁹I will turn to you and make you fruitful and multiply you and will confirm my covenant with you. ¹⁰You shall eat old store long kept, and you shall clear out the old to make way for the new. ¹¹I will make my dwelling¹ among you, and my soul shall not abhor you. ¹²And I will walk among you and will be your God, and you shall be my people. ¹³I am the LORD your God, who brought you out of the land of Egypt, that you should not be their slaves. And I have broken the bars of your yoke and made you walk erect.

¹⁴"But if you will not listen to me and will not do all these commandments, ¹⁵if you spurn my statutes, and if your soul abhors my rules, so that you will not do all my commandments, but break my covenant, ¹⁶then I will do this to you: I will visit you with panic, with wasting disease and fever that consume the eyes and make the heart ache. And you shall sow your seed in vain, for your enemies shall eat it. ¹⁷I will set my face against you, and you shall be struck down before your enemies. Those who hate you shall rule over you, and you shall flee when none pursues you. ¹⁸And if in spite of this you will not listen to me, then I will discipline you again sevenfold for your sins, ¹⁹and I will break the pride of your power, and I will make your heavens like iron and your earth like bronze. ²⁰And your strength shall be spent in vain, for your land shall not yield its increase, and the trees of the land shall not yield their fruit.

²¹"Then if you walk contrary to me and will not listen to me, I will continue striking you, sevenfold for your sins. ²²And I will let loose the wild beasts against you, which shall bereave you of your children and destroy your livestock and make you few in number, so that your roads shall be deserted.

²³"And if by this discipline you are not turned to me but walk contrary to me, ²⁴then I also will walk contrary to you, and I myself will strike you sevenfold for your sins. ²⁵And I will bring a sword upon you, that shall execute vengeance for the covenant. And if you gather within your cities, I will send pestilence among you, and you shall be delivered into the hand of the enemy. ²⁶When I break your supply² of bread, ten women shall bake your bread in a single oven and shall dole out your bread again by weight, and you shall eat and not be satisfied.

²⁷"But if in spite of this you will not listen to me, but walk contrary to me, ²⁸then I will walk contrary to you in fury, and I myself will discipline you sevenfold for your sins. ²⁹You shall eat the flesh of your sons, and you shall eat the flesh of your daughters. ³⁰And I will destroy your high places and cut down your incense altars and cast your dead bodies upon the dead bodies of your idols, and my soul will abhor you. ³¹And I will lay your cities waste and will make your sanctuaries desolate, and I will not smell your pleasing aromas. ³²And I myself will devastate the land, so that your enemies who settle in it shall be appalled at it. ³³And I will scatter you among the nations, and I will unsheathe the sword after you, and your land shall be a desolation, and your cities shall be a waste.

³⁴"Then the land shall enjoy³ its Sabbaths as long as it lies desolate, while you are in your enemies' land; then the land shall rest, and enjoy its Sabbaths. ³⁵As long as it lies desolate it shall have rest, the rest that it did not have on your Sabbaths when you were dwelling in it. ³⁶And as for those of you who are left, I will send faintness into their hearts in the lands of their enemies. The sound of a driven leaf shall put

---

¹ Hebrew *tabernacle* ² Hebrew *staff* ³ Or *pay for*; twice in this verse; also verse 43

them to flight, and they shall flee as one flees from the sword, and they shall fall when none pursues. [37] They shall stumble over one another, as if to escape a sword, though none pursues. And you shall have no power to stand before your enemies. [38] And you shall perish among the nations, and the land of your enemies shall eat you up. [39] And those of you who are left shall rot away in your enemies' lands because of their iniquity, and also because of the iniquities of their fathers they shall rot away like them.

[40] "But if they confess their iniquity and the iniquity of their fathers in their treachery that they committed against me, and also in walking contrary to me, [41] so that I walked contrary to them and brought them into the land of their enemies—if then their uncircumcised heart is humbled and they make amends for their iniquity, [42] then I will remember my covenant with Jacob, and I will remember my covenant with Isaac and my covenant with Abraham, and I will remember the land. [43] But the land shall be abandoned by them and enjoy its Sabbaths while it lies desolate without them, and they shall make amends for their iniquity, because they spurned my rules and their soul abhorred my statutes. [44] Yet for all that, when they are in the land of their enemies, I will not spurn them, neither will I abhor them so as to destroy them utterly and break my covenant with them, for I am the LORD their God. [45] But I will for their sake remember the covenant with their forefathers, whom I brought out of the land of Egypt in the sight of the nations, that I might be their God: I am the LORD."

[46] These are the statutes and rules and laws that the LORD made between himself and the people of Israel through Moses on Mount Sinai.

> **Laws about vows** [chapter 27]. Chapter 27 backs off from the grandeur of the pronouncement of blessings and curses with an unexpected addendum dealing with vows made to God. Since it is the author's last word, we can profitably explore it as embodying spiritual principles that sum up the main themes of the book as a whole. Here are some starting thoughts: God's prerogative to give the laws by which he expects people to live; the detailed instructions that God has given for people to order their individual and corporate lives; the specificity of God's laws revealed in Leviticus; the ordering of life and its regulations according to a range of categories (e.g., animals, land, people); God's requirement of holiness; the importance of religious rituals in OT worship; God's concern for the moral principles by which people relate to each other (and not simply to him).

27 The LORD spoke to Moses, saying, [2] "Speak to the people of Israel and say to them, If anyone makes a special vow to the LORD involving the valuation of persons, [3] then the valuation of a male from twenty years old up to sixty years old shall be fifty shekels[1] of silver, according to the shekel of the sanctuary. [4] If the person is a female, the valuation shall be thirty shekels. [5] If the person is from five years old up to twenty years old, the valuation shall be for a male twenty shekels, and for a female ten shekels. [6] If the person is from a month old up to five years old, the valuation shall be for a male five shekels of silver, and for a female the valuation shall be three shekels of silver. [7] And if the person is sixty years old or over, then the valuation for a male shall be fifteen shekels, and for a female ten shekels. [8] And if someone is too poor to pay the valuation, then he shall be made to stand before the priest, and the priest shall value him; the priest shall value him according to what the vower can afford.

---

[1] A *shekel* was about 2/5 ounce or 11 grams

⁹"If the vow¹ is an animal that may be offered as an offering to the LORD, all of it that he gives to the LORD is holy. ¹⁰He shall not exchange it or make a substitute for it, good for bad, or bad for good; and if he does in fact substitute one animal for another, then both it and the substitute shall be holy. ¹¹And if it is any unclean animal that may not be offered as an offering to the LORD, then he shall stand the animal before the priest, ¹²and the priest shall value it as either good or bad; as the priest values it, so it shall be. ¹³But if he wishes to redeem it, he shall add a fifth to the valuation.

¹⁴"When a man dedicates his house as a holy gift to the LORD, the priest shall value it as either good or bad; as the priest values it, so it shall stand. ¹⁵And if the donor wishes to redeem his house, he shall add a fifth to the valuation price, and it shall be his.

¹⁶"If a man dedicates to the LORD part of the land that is his possession, then the valuation shall be in proportion to its seed. A homer² of barley seed shall be valued at fifty shekels of silver. ¹⁷If he dedicates his field from the year of jubilee, the valuation shall stand, ¹⁸but if he dedicates his field after the jubilee, then the priest shall calculate the price according to the years that remain until the year of jubilee, and a deduction shall be made from the valuation. ¹⁹And if he who dedicates the field wishes to redeem it, then he shall add a fifth to its valuation price, and it shall remain his. ²⁰But if he does not wish to redeem the field, or if he has sold the field to another man, it shall not be redeemed anymore. ²¹But the field, when it is released in the jubilee, shall be a holy gift to the LORD, like a field that has been devoted. The priest shall be in possession of it. ²²If he dedicates to the LORD a field that he has bought, which is not a part of his possession, ²³then the priest shall calculate the amount of the valuation for it up to the year of jubilee, and the man shall give the valuation on that day as a holy gift to the LORD. ²⁴In the year of jubilee the field shall return to him from whom it was bought, to whom the land belongs as a possession. ²⁵Every valuation shall be according to the shekel of the sanctuary: twenty gerahs³ shall make a shekel.

²⁶"But a firstborn of animals, which as a firstborn belongs to the LORD, no man may dedicate; whether ox or sheep, it is the LORD's. ²⁷And if it is an unclean animal, then he shall buy it back at the valuation, and add a fifth to it; or, if it is not redeemed, it shall be sold at the valuation.

²⁸"But no devoted thing that a man devotes to the LORD, of anything that he has, whether man or beast, or of his inherited field, shall be sold or redeemed; every devoted thing is most holy to the LORD. ²⁹No one devoted, who is to be devoted for destruction⁴ from mankind, shall be ransomed; he shall surely be put to death.

³⁰"Every tithe of the land, whether of the seed of the land or of the fruit of the trees, is the LORD's; it is holy to the LORD. ³¹If a man wishes to redeem some of his tithe, he shall add a fifth to it. ³²And every tithe of herds and flocks, every tenth animal of all that pass under the herdsman's staff, shall be holy to the LORD. ³³One shall not differentiate between good or bad, neither shall he make a substitute for it; and if he does substitute for it, then both it and the substitute shall be holy; it shall not be redeemed."

³⁴These are the commandments that the LORD commanded Moses for the people of Israel on Mount Sinai.

---

¹ Hebrew *it* ² A *homer* was about 6 bushels or 220 liters ³ A *gerah* was about 1/50 ounce or 0.6 gram ⁴ That is, set apart (devoted) as an offering to the Lord (for destruction)

NUMBERS

The book at a glance. 36 chapters, 1,288 verses. While the title of the book might lead us to expect numbered lists of things and people, this accounts for a relatively small proportion of the book (two census summaries, supplemented by the numbers of items contained in the offerings to the tabernacle in chapter 7). Like the rest of the Pentateuch, the book of Numbers is partly a *narrative or story and partly a manual of laws and instructions. The author was a faithful recorder of God's instructions to Moses and a master storyteller of Israel's wilderness wanderings. As we encounter the abundance of religious rituals and sacrifices that are described in this book, we should view them as expressing religious truths in visual form.

▌**Genre.** The overall *genre of the book of Numbers is the historical chronicle—a record book of historical data. Consistent with historical writing, the bulk of the book is devoted to narrative, and these parts require the usual types of narrative analysis, with primary attention to *plot, *character, and *setting. But we cannot regard the book of Numbers simply as an anthology of stories, for the narrative sections alternate regularly with lists and collections of laws. We can legitimately call the latter material a religious instruction manual. (For more information on items accompanied by an asterisk, see the glossary at the back of this Bible.)

▌**Structure and format.** Although the book of Numbers might seem to be a maze of divergent material, it actually follows a simple plan. It is based on a predictable rhythm back and forth between sections of lists, instructions, and regulations on the one hand and narrative material on the other. The nonnarrative units should not be read as interruptions of the narrative. They should be viewed as complementary material in a historical chronicle. The law-giving sections are often phrased in quasi-narrative terms as what God told Moses, following the formula "the LORD spoke to Moses." Additionally, the sections of regulations can be viewed as telling the "story" (though not in narrative form) of a nation's religious practices.

▌**The story.** The narrative sections add up to a grand *travel story. The things to look for in a travel story include the following: variety of adventure and locale; encounters with places, people, and nations; conflict (including conflicts within the traveling community as well as conflicts with external forces such as environment and hostile natives); the *motifs of danger, suspense, risk, and testing. The travel story recounted in Numbers begins as a *quest story but becomes a story of wandering. Because this particular story is the story of a traveling nation caught at a formative moment in its

Passage	Content	Type of Material	Contribution to the Travel Story
1–4	Census of warriors (1); positioning of tribes in camp (2); census and duties of Levites (3–4)	Records and instructions	Preparations for the journey
5–6	General rules (5); laws for Nazirites and the Aaronic benediction (6)	Regulations	
7:1–9:14	Dedication of tabernacle (7); instructions for conduct of the Levites (8); the Passover (9:1–14)	Worship practices	
9:15–10:10	Cloud of guidance (9:15–23); silver trumpets (10:1–10)	Final travel preparations	
10:11–14:45	Marching, complaining, rebelling, judgment, rescue	Travel narrative	The journey in the wilderness
15	Law-giving interlude: offerings and Regulations	Rules	
16–17	Challenge to Aaron's priesthood	Narrative	
18–19	Law-giving interlude: duties of the Levites (19); purification rituals (19)	Rules	
20–25	Marching, complaining, rescue, the failure of Moses, Balaam's prophecy	Travel narrative	
26–30	Second census (26); issues of inheritance and succession (27); offerings and laws (28–30)	Rules	
31	Conquest of the Midianites	Battle story	At the edge of the Promised Land
32	Settling of tribes east of the Jordan	Settlement narrative	
33:1–49	Summary of campsites on the journey	Retrospective	
33:50–36:13	Instructions for settling in Canaan	Prospective	

national history, it is also an *epic. Because Moses is the central character in the epic, the narratives of Numbers have characteristics of a *hero story as well, with Moses as the heroic and representative protagonist. The main antagonists in the story of the nation are (1) the physical locales in which the traveling group finds itself, (2) other nations with whom the Israelites come into contact, and (3) the nation itself (often in conflict with its leader Moses). In regard to the internal conflicts that often make the Israelites their own worst enemies, we might say that the story of God's dealings with Israel illustrates John Milton's formula in *Paradise Lost*—"supernal grace contending with sinfulness of men."

▌ **1 Corinthians 10:1–13 as an interpretive framework.** First Corinthians 10:1–13 makes the following assertions about the story of the journey of the Israelites, and we can use these statements as an interpretive grid: (1) drastic events happened to the Israelites "as an example" to them (v. 11); (2) these events are also "examples for us" (v. 6); (3) God caused the events to be "written down for our instruction" (v. 11); (4) the lesson that we need to learn is "not [to] desire evil as they did" (v. 6).

▌ **Inferred literary intentions.** The book is designed to achieve the following literary purposes:

- tell the story of Israel's journey from Mount Sinai to Canaan in a manner that both instructs us and satisfies our literary taste for exciting narrative

- balance the narrative sections with sections of record keeping and law giving, the general effect of which is to foreshadow how a good society was to be constructed in the Promised Land

- record history in such a way that we can often see universal human experiences embodied in the stories of real-life individuals

- recount the journey by means of the familiar conventions of a travel story

- introduce God so aggressively into the action that we will never be in doubt that the worldview of the book is God-centered

- enable us to see timeless spiritual principles embodied in both the stories and the laws that make up the book

- show how, in spite of their many failures, God's people were divinely prepared to enter and possess the Promised Land

▌ **Theological themes.** (1) Theology: the book gives us many pictures of what God is like and of what he loves and hates. (2) Covenant: both narrative and law-giving sections picture God's expectations of his covenant people. (3) Human depravity: epics usually paint a flattering picture of the author's nation, but this one is a mainly negative portrayal of the Israelites, and it elevates God rather than a person to the status of ultimate hero. (4) Providence: God is ultimately the one who guides the nation on its journey and provides for its physical and spiritual needs. (5) Ethics: many of the laws are elements of a moral code that stipulates how people should relate to their fellow humans. (6) Sanctification: other laws outline how God's people can relate properly to a holy God.

▌ **The book of Numbers as a chapter in the master story of the Bible.** The master story of the Bible is partly the history of a covenant nation as the OT manifestation of the kingdom of God on earth. Another part of that story is the system of religious practices by which God's people can receive his blessing and by faith participate in his salvation. Both the narrative and the law-giving sections of Numbers tell these stories. Within this story of redemption, the incident of the bronze serpent (21:4–9) is a symbolic, foreshadowing picture of redemption through Christ (John 3:14–15).

Preparations for the journey [chapter 1]. The chapter unfolds according to the following sequence: instructions from God to Moses about the need to take a census of the nation, along with the names of the census takers (vv. 1–16); the numbering of Israel (summary of the census, vv. 17–46); the exemption of the Levites from the census, along with a brief summary of their duties (vv. 47–54). We need to remember the context of this somewhat strange event: the new nation of Israel is in the wilderness near Sinai, early in its quest for the Promised Land, and is being instructed by God about how to conduct its national affairs. In another context, the list of numbers of the tribes might seem like governmental record keeping of the type conducted in the United States every ten years. But in the context of the nation of Israel at Sinai, the opening chapter of Numbers can be read as a preparation for the journey to follow. A good way to assimilate the material is to enter into the world of the story, imagining yourself a participant and sensing the excitement of the venture. A side lesson is that God intends human society to conduct its national and religious life in an orderly fashion.

1 The LORD spoke to Moses in the wilderness of Sinai, in the tent of meeting, on the first day of the second month, in the second year after they had come out of the land of Egypt, saying, ²"Take a census of all the congregation of the people of Israel, by clans, by fathers' houses, according to the number of names, every male, head by head. ³From twenty years old and upward, all in Israel who are able to go to war, you and Aaron shall list them, company by company. ⁴And there shall be with you a man from each tribe, each man being the head of the house of his fathers. ⁵And these are the names of the men who shall assist you. From Reuben, Elizur the son of Shedeur; ⁶from Simeon, Shelumiel the son of Zurishaddai; ⁷from Judah, Nahshon the son of Amminadab; ⁸from Issachar, Nethanel the son of Zuar; ⁹from Zebulun, Eliab the son of Helon; ¹⁰from the sons of Joseph, from Ephraim, Elishama the son of Ammihud, and from Manasseh, Gamaliel the son of Pedahzur; ¹¹from Benjamin, Abidan the son of Gideoni; ¹²from Dan, Ahiezer the son of Ammishaddai; ¹³from Asher, Pagiel the son of Ochran; ¹⁴from Gad, Eliasaph the son of Deuel; ¹⁵from Naphtali, Ahira the son of Enan." ¹⁶These were the ones chosen from the congregation, the chiefs of their ancestral tribes, the heads of the clans of Israel.

¹⁷Moses and Aaron took these men who had been named, ¹⁸and on the first day of the second month, they assembled the whole congregation together, who registered themselves by clans, by fathers' houses, according to the number of names from twenty years old and upward, head by head, ¹⁹as the LORD commanded Moses. So he listed them in the wilderness of Sinai.

²⁰The people of Reuben, Israel's firstborn, their generations, by their clans, by their fathers' houses, according to the number of names, head by head, every male from twenty years old and upward, all who were able to go to war: ²¹those listed of the tribe of Reuben were 46,500.

²²Of the people of Simeon, their generations, by their clans, by their fathers' houses, those of them who were listed, according to the number of names, head by head, every male from twenty years old and upward, all who were able to go to war: ²³those listed of the tribe of Simeon were 59,300.

²⁴Of the people of Gad, their generations, by their clans, by their fathers' houses,

according to the number of the names, from twenty years old and upward, all who were able to go to war: [25]those listed of the tribe of Gad were 45,650.

[26]Of the people of Judah, their generations, by their clans, by their fathers' houses, according to the number of names, from twenty years old and upward, every man able to go to war: [27]those listed of the tribe of Judah were 74,600.

[28]Of the people of Issachar, their generations, by their clans, by their fathers' houses, according to the number of names, from twenty years old and upward, every man able to go to war: [29]those listed of the tribe of Issachar were 54,400.

[30]Of the people of Zebulun, their generations, by their clans, by their fathers' houses, according to the number of names, from twenty years old and upward, every man able to go to war: [31]those listed of the tribe of Zebulun were 57,400.

[32]Of the people of Joseph, namely, of the people of Ephraim, their generations, by their clans, by their fathers' houses, according to the number of names, from twenty years old and upward, every man able to go to war: [33]those listed of the tribe of Ephraim were 40,500.

[34]Of the people of Manasseh, their generations, by their clans, by their fathers' houses, according to the number of names, from twenty years old and upward, every man able to go to war: [35]those listed of the tribe of Manasseh were 32,200.

[36]Of the people of Benjamin, their generations, by their clans, by their fathers' houses, according to the number of names, from twenty years old and upward, every man able to go to war: [37]those listed of the tribe of Benjamin were 35,400.

[38]Of the people of Dan, their generations, by their clans, by their fathers' houses, according to the number of names, from twenty years old and upward, every man able to go to war: [39]those listed of the tribe of Dan were 62,700.

[40]Of the people of Asher, their generations, by their clans, by their fathers' houses, according to the number of names, from twenty years old and upward, every man able to go to war: [41]those listed of the tribe of Asher were 41,500.

[42]Of the people of Naphtali, their generations, by their clans, by their fathers' houses, according to the number of names, from twenty years old and upward, every man able to go to war: [43]those listed of the tribe of Naphtali were 53,400.

[44]These are those who were listed, whom Moses and Aaron listed with the help of the chiefs of Israel, twelve men, each representing his fathers' house. [45]So all those listed of the people of Israel, by their fathers' houses, from twenty years old and upward, every man able to go to war in Israel— [46]all those listed were 603,550.

[47]But the Levites were not listed along with them by their ancestral tribe. [48]For the LORD spoke to Moses, saying, [49]"Only the tribe of Levi you shall not list, and you shall not take a census of them among the people of Israel. [50]But appoint the Levites over the tabernacle of the testimony, and over all its furnishings, and over all that belongs to it. They are to carry the tabernacle and all its furnishings, and they shall take care of it and shall camp around the tabernacle. [51]When the tabernacle is to set out, the Levites shall take it down, and when the tabernacle is to be pitched, the Levites shall set it up. And if any outsider comes near, he shall be put to death. [52]The people of Israel shall pitch their tents by their companies, each man in his own camp and each man by his own standard. [53]But the Levites shall camp around the tabernacle of the testimony, so that there may be no wrath on the congregation of the people of Israel. And the Levites shall keep guard over the tabernacle of the testimony." [54]Thus did the people of Israel; they did according to all that the LORD commanded Moses.

Positioning of tribes in the camp [chapter 2]. This chapter, too, can be regarded as a preparation for the ensuing journey. The chapter is a reminder that the history of Israel was national and patriotic literature as well as religious writing. If God moved the writer to include the facts of the story of the journey, we should throw ourselves with zest into reliving the events that are recorded. The religious meaning resides partly in the fact that the tents on all four sides of the campsite faced the sacred Tent of Meeting in the center. Additionally, the nation portrayed here is God's covenant people, the fulfillment of God's promises to Jacob.

2 The LORD spoke to Moses and Aaron, saying, ²"The people of Israel shall camp each by his own standard, with the banners of their fathers' houses. They shall camp facing the tent of meeting on every side. ³Those to camp on the east side toward the sunrise shall be of the standard of the camp of Judah by their companies, the chief of the people of Judah being Nahshon the son of Amminadab, ⁴his company as listed being 74,600. ⁵Those to camp next to him shall be the tribe of Issachar, the chief of the people of Issachar being Nethanel the son of Zuar, ⁶his company as listed being 54,400. ⁷Then the tribe of Zebulun, the chief of the people of Zebulun being Eliab the son of Helon, ⁸his company as listed being 57,400. ⁹All those listed of the camp of Judah, by their companies, were 186,400. They shall set out first on the march.

¹⁰"On the south side shall be the standard of the camp of Reuben by their companies, the chief of the people of Reuben being Elizur the son of Shedeur, ¹¹his company as listed being 46,500. ¹²And those to camp next to him shall be the tribe of Simeon, the chief of the people of Simeon being Shelumiel the son of Zurishaddai, ¹³his company as listed being 59,300. ¹⁴Then the tribe of Gad, the chief of the people of Gad being Eliasaph the son of Reuel, ¹⁵his company as listed being 45,650. ¹⁶All those listed of the camp of Reuben, by their companies, were 151,450. They shall set out second.

¹⁷"Then the tent of meeting shall set out, with the camp of the Levites in the midst of the camps; as they camp, so shall they set out, each in position, standard by standard.

¹⁸"On the west side shall be the standard of the camp of Ephraim by their companies, the chief of the people of Ephraim being Elishama the son of Ammihud, ¹⁹his company as listed being 40,500. ²⁰And next to him shall be the tribe of Manasseh, the chief of the people of Manasseh being Gamaliel the son of Pedahzur, ²¹his company as listed being 32,200. ²²Then the tribe of Benjamin, the chief of the people of Benjamin being Abidan the son of Gideoni, ²³his company as listed being 35,400. ²⁴All those listed of the camp of Ephraim, by their companies, were 108,100. They shall set out third on the march.

²⁵"On the north side shall be the standard of the camp of Dan by their companies, the chief of the people of Dan being Ahiezer the son of Ammishaddai, ²⁶his company as listed being 62,700. ²⁷And those to camp next to him shall be the tribe of Asher, the chief of the people of Asher being Pagiel the son of Ochran, ²⁸his company as listed being 41,500. ²⁹Then the tribe of Naphtali, the chief of the people of Naphtali being Ahira the son of Enan, ³⁰his company as listed being 53,400. ³¹All those listed of the camp of Dan were 157,600. They shall set out last, standard by standard."

³²These are the people of Israel as listed by their fathers' houses. All those listed in

the camps by their companies were 603,550. ³³But the Levites were not listed among the people of Israel, as the LORD commanded Moses.

³⁴Thus did the people of Israel. According to all that the LORD commanded Moses, so they camped by their standards, and so they set out, each one in his clan, according to his fathers' house.

> **Census and duties of the Levites** [chapters 3–4]. The nation of Israel was a theocracy in which religious concerns were the top priority. The large amount of space given to the Levites, the professional clerics of ancient Israel, is an index to what mattered most in this holy commonwealth: the worship and service of God. The main theme of these two long chapters is the special status and duties of this priestly caste. We can regard the specific details as variations on that theme. The importance of religious ritual in OT worship and lavish attention to the aesthetic beauty of the tabernacle (4:4–16) are important subthemes. The attention to the minute details of the tabernacle and its service is breathtaking. Intermittent references to carrying the tabernacle remind us that the overall narrative is a travel story.

3 These are the generations of Aaron and Moses at the time when the LORD spoke with Moses on Mount Sinai. ²These are the names of the sons of Aaron: Nadab the firstborn, and Abihu, Eleazar, and Ithamar. ³These are the names of the sons of Aaron, the anointed priests, whom he ordained to serve as priests. ⁴But Nadab and Abihu died before the LORD when they offered unauthorized fire before the LORD in the wilderness of Sinai, and they had no children. So Eleazar and Ithamar served as priests in the lifetime of Aaron their father.

⁵And the LORD spoke to Moses, saying, ⁶"Bring the tribe of Levi near, and set them before Aaron the priest, that they may minister to him. ⁷They shall keep guard over him and over the whole congregation before the tent of meeting, as they minister at the tabernacle. ⁸They shall guard all the furnishings of the tent of meeting, and keep guard over the people of Israel as they minister at the tabernacle. ⁹And you shall give the Levites to Aaron and his sons; they are wholly given to him from among the people of Israel. ¹⁰And you shall appoint Aaron and his sons, and they shall guard their priesthood. But if any outsider comes near, he shall be put to death."

¹¹And the LORD spoke to Moses, saying, ¹²"Behold, I have taken the Levites from among the people of Israel instead of every firstborn who opens the womb among the people of Israel. The Levites shall be mine, ¹³for all the firstborn are mine. On the day that I struck down all the firstborn in the land of Egypt, I consecrated for my own all the firstborn in Israel, both of man and of beast. They shall be mine: I am the LORD."

¹⁴And the LORD spoke to Moses in the wilderness of Sinai, saying, ¹⁵"List the sons of Levi, by fathers' houses and by clans; every male from a month old and upward you shall list." ¹⁶So Moses listed them according to the word of the LORD, as he was commanded. ¹⁷And these were the sons of Levi by their names: Gershon and Kohath and Merari. ¹⁸And these are the names of the sons of Gershon by their clans: Libni and Shimei. ¹⁹And the sons of Kohath by their clans: Amram, Izhar, Hebron, and Uzziel. ²⁰And the sons of Merari by their clans: Mahli and Mushi. These are the clans of the Levites, by their fathers' houses.

²¹To Gershon belonged the clan of the Libnites and the clan of the Shimeites; these were the clans of the Gershonites. ²²Their listing according to the number of all the

males from a month old and upward was[1] 7,500. [23]The clans of the Gershonites were to camp behind the tabernacle on the west, [24]with Eliasaph, the son of Lael as chief of the fathers' house of the Gershonites. [25]And the guard duty of the sons of Gershon in the tent of meeting involved the tabernacle, the tent with its covering, the screen for the entrance of the tent of meeting, [26]the hangings of the court, the screen for the door of the court that is around the tabernacle and the altar, and its cords—all the service connected with these.

[27]To Kohath belonged the clan of the Amramites and the clan of the Izharites and the clan of the Hebronites and the clan of the Uzzielites; these are the clans of the Kohathites. [28]According to the number of all the males, from a month old and upward, there were 8,600, keeping guard over the sanctuary. [29]The clans of the sons of Kohath were to camp on the south side of the tabernacle, [30]with Elizaphan the son of Uzziel as chief of the fathers' house of the clans of the Kohathites. [31]And their guard duty involved the ark, the table, the lampstand, the altars, the vessels of the sanctuary with which the priests minister, and the screen; all the service connected with these. [32]And Eleazar the son of Aaron the priest was to be chief over the chiefs of the Levites, and to have oversight of those who kept guard over the sanctuary.

[33]To Merari belonged the clan of the Mahlites and the clan of the Mushites: these are the clans of Merari. [34]Their listing according to the number of all the males from a month old and upward was 6,200. [35]And the chief of the fathers' house of the clans of Merari was Zuriel the son of Abihail. They were to camp on the north side of the tabernacle. [36]And the appointed guard duty of the sons of Merari involved the frames of the tabernacle, the bars, the pillars, the bases, and all their accessories; all the service connected with these; [37]also the pillars around the court, with their bases and pegs and cords.

[38]Those who were to camp before the tabernacle on the east, before the tent of meeting toward the sunrise, were Moses and Aaron and his sons, guarding the sanctuary itself, to protect[2] the people of Israel. And any outsider who came near was to be put to death. [39]All those listed among the Levites, whom Moses and Aaron listed at the commandment of the LORD, by clans, all the males from a month old and upward, were 22,000.

[40]And the LORD said to Moses, "List all the firstborn males of the people of Israel, from a month old and upward, taking the number of their names. [41]And you shall take the Levites for me—I am the LORD—instead of all the firstborn among the people of Israel, and the cattle of the Levites instead of all the firstborn among the cattle of the people of Israel." [42]So Moses listed all the firstborn among the people of Israel, as the LORD commanded him. [43]And all the firstborn males, according to the number of names, from a month old and upward as listed were 22,273.

[44]And the LORD spoke to Moses, saying, [45]"Take the Levites instead of all the firstborn among the people of Israel, and the cattle of the Levites instead of their cattle. The Levites shall be mine: I am the LORD. [46]And as the redemption price for the 273 of the firstborn of the people of Israel, over and above the number of the male Levites, [47]you shall take five shekels[3] per head; you shall take them according to the shekel of the sanctuary (the shekel of twenty gerahs[4]), [48]and give the money to Aaron and his sons as the redemption price for those who are over." [49]So Moses took the redemption money from those who were over and above those redeemed by the Levites. [50]From the firstborn of the people of Israel he took the money, 1,365 shekels, by the shekel of

---

[1] Hebrew *their listing was* [2] Hebrew *guard* [3] A *shekel* was about 2/5 ounce or 11 grams [4] A *gerah* was about 1/50 ounce or 0.6 gram

the sanctuary. ⁵¹And Moses gave the redemption money to Aaron and his sons, according to the word of the LORD, as the LORD commanded Moses.

4 The LORD spoke to Moses and Aaron, saying, ²"Take a census of the sons of Kohath from among the sons of Levi, by their clans and their fathers' houses, ³from thirty years old up to fifty years old, all who can come on duty, to do the work in the tent of meeting. ⁴This is the service of the sons of Kohath in the tent of meeting: the most holy things. ⁵When the camp is to set out, Aaron and his sons shall go in and take down the veil of the screen and cover the ark of the testimony with it. ⁶Then they shall put on it a covering of goatskin¹ and spread on top of that a cloth all of blue, and shall put in its poles. ⁷And over the table of the bread of the Presence they shall spread a cloth of blue and put on it the plates, the dishes for incense, the bowls, and the flagons for the drink offering; the regular showbread also shall be on it. ⁸Then they shall spread over them a cloth of scarlet and cover the same with a covering of goatskin, and shall put in its poles. ⁹And they shall take a cloth of blue and cover the lampstand for the light, with its lamps, its tongs, its trays, and all the vessels for oil with which it is supplied. ¹⁰And they shall put it with all its utensils in a covering of goatskin and put it on the carrying frame. ¹¹And over the golden altar they shall spread a cloth of blue and cover it with a covering of goatskin, and shall put in its poles. ¹²And they shall take all the vessels of the service that are used in the sanctuary and put them in a cloth of blue and cover them with a covering of goatskin and put them on the carrying frame. ¹³And they shall take away the ashes from the altar and spread a purple cloth over it. ¹⁴And they shall put on it all the utensils of the altar, which are used for the service there, the fire pans, the forks, the shovels, and the basins, all the utensils of the altar; and they shall spread on it a covering of goatskin, and shall put in its poles. ¹⁵And when Aaron and his sons have finished covering the sanctuary and all the furnishings of the sanctuary, as the camp sets out, after that the sons of Kohath shall come to carry these, but they must not touch the holy things, lest they die. These are the things of the tent of meeting that the sons of Kohath are to carry.

¹⁶"And Eleazar the son of Aaron the priest shall have charge of the oil for the light, the fragrant incense, the regular grain offering, and the anointing oil, with the oversight of the whole tabernacle and all that is in it, of the sanctuary and its vessels."

¹⁷The LORD spoke to Moses and Aaron, saying, ¹⁸"Let not the tribe of the clans of the Kohathites be destroyed from among the Levites, ¹⁹but deal thus with them, that they may live and not die when they come near to the most holy things: Aaron and his sons shall go in and appoint them each to his task and to his burden, ²⁰but they shall not go in to look on the holy things even for a moment, lest they die."

²¹The LORD spoke to Moses, saying, ²²"Take a census of the sons of Gershon also, by their fathers' houses and by their clans. ²³From thirty years old up to fifty years old, you shall list them, all who can come to do duty, to do service in the tent of meeting. ²⁴This is the service of the clans of the Gershonites, in serving and bearing burdens: ²⁵they shall carry the curtains of the tabernacle and the tent of meeting with its covering and the covering of goatskin that is on top of it and the screen for the entrance of the tent of meeting ²⁶and the hangings of the court and the screen for the entrance of the gate of the court that is around the tabernacle and the altar, and their cords and all the equipment for their service. And they shall do all that needs to be done

---

¹ The meaning of the Hebrew word is uncertain; compare Exodus 25:5

with regard to them. ²⁷All the service of the sons of the Gershonites shall be at the command of Aaron and his sons, in all that they are to carry and in all that they have to do. And you shall assign to their charge all that they are to carry. ²⁸This is the service of the clans of the sons of the Gershonites in the tent of meeting, and their guard duty is to be under the direction of Ithamar the son of Aaron the priest.

²⁹"As for the sons of Merari, you shall list them by their clans and their fathers' houses. ³⁰From thirty years old up to fifty years old, you shall list them, everyone who can come on duty, to do the service of the tent of meeting. ³¹And this is what they are charged to carry, as the whole of their service in the tent of meeting: the frames of the tabernacle, with its bars, pillars, and bases, ³²and the pillars around the court with their bases, pegs, and cords, with all their equipment and all their accessories. And you shall list by name the objects that they are required to carry. ³³This is the service of the clans of the sons of Merari, the whole of their service in the tent of meeting, under the direction of Ithamar the son of Aaron the priest."

³⁴And Moses and Aaron and the chiefs of the congregation listed the sons of the Kohathites, by their clans and their fathers' houses, ³⁵from thirty years old up to fifty years old, everyone who could come on duty, for service in the tent of meeting; ³⁶and those listed by clans were 2,750. ³⁷This was the list of the clans of the Kohathites, all who served in the tent of meeting, whom Moses and Aaron listed according to the commandment of the LORD by Moses.

³⁸Those listed of the sons of Gershon, by their clans and their fathers' houses, ³⁹from thirty years old up to fifty years old, everyone who could come on duty for service in the tent of meeting— ⁴⁰those listed by their clans and their fathers' houses were 2,630. ⁴¹This was the list of the clans of the sons of Gershon, all who served in the tent of meeting, whom Moses and Aaron listed according to the commandment of the LORD.

⁴²Those listed of the clans of the sons of Merari, by their clans and their fathers' houses, ⁴³from thirty years old up to fifty years old, everyone who could come on duty, for service in the tent of meeting— ⁴⁴those listed by clans were 3,200. ⁴⁵This was the list of the clans of the sons of Merari, whom Moses and Aaron listed according to the commandment of the LORD by Moses.

⁴⁶All those who were listed of the Levites, whom Moses and Aaron and the chiefs of Israel listed, by their clans and their fathers' houses, ⁴⁷from thirty years old up to fifty years old, everyone who could come to do the service of ministry and the service of bearing burdens in the tent of meeting, ⁴⁸those listed were 8,580. ⁴⁹According to the commandment of the LORD through Moses they were listed, each one with his task of serving or carrying. Thus they were listed by him, as the LORD commanded Moses.

General laws and regulations [chapter 5]. Some parts of Numbers read like a sequel to Leviticus, with its instructions from God to Moses regarding the rules and regulations of the nation. Chapters 5–6 constitute one of those units. Chapter 5 addresses three areas of communal life: rules covering the ceremonially and hygienically unclean (vv. 1–4); rules regarding restitution for wrongs committed (vv. 5–10); the law concerning how to deal with a husband who suspects his wife of infidelity (vv. 11–31). An epic always embodies the values of a culture. One approach to this triad of regulations is to ponder the underlying values that are protected by the rules, including purity, justice, and marital fidelity.

5 The LORD spoke to Moses, saying, [2]"Command the people of Israel that they put out of the camp everyone who is leprous[1] or has a discharge and everyone who is unclean through contact with the dead. [3]You shall put out both male and female, putting them outside the camp, that they may not defile their camp, in the midst of which I dwell." [4]And the people of Israel did so, and put them outside the camp; as the LORD said to Moses, so the people of Israel did.

[5]And the LORD spoke to Moses, saying, [6]"Speak to the people of Israel, When a man or woman commits any of the sins that people commit by breaking faith with the LORD, and that person realizes his guilt, [7]he shall confess his sin that he has committed.[2] And he shall make full restitution for his wrong, adding a fifth to it and giving it to him to whom he did the wrong. [8]But if the man has no next of kin to whom restitution may be made for the wrong, the restitution for wrong shall go to the LORD for the priest, in addition to the ram of atonement with which atonement is made for him. [9]And every contribution, all the holy donations of the people of Israel, which they bring to the priest, shall be his. [10]Each one shall keep his holy donations: whatever anyone gives to the priest shall be his."

[11]And the LORD spoke to Moses, saying, [12]"Speak to the people of Israel, If any man's wife goes astray and breaks faith with him, [13]if a man lies with her sexually, and it is hidden from the eyes of her husband, and she is undetected though she has defiled herself, and there is no witness against her, since she was not taken in the act, [14]and if the spirit of jealousy comes over him and he is jealous of his wife who has defiled herself, or if the spirit of jealousy comes over him and he is jealous of his wife, though she has not defiled herself, [15]then the man shall bring his wife to the priest and bring the offering required of her, a tenth of an ephah[3] of barley flour. He shall pour no oil on it and put no frankincense on it, for it is a grain offering of jealousy, a grain offering of remembrance, bringing iniquity to remembrance.

[16]"And the priest shall bring her near and set her before the LORD. [17]And the priest shall take holy water in an earthenware vessel and take some of the dust that is on the floor of the tabernacle and put it into the water. [18]And the priest shall set the woman before the LORD and unbind the hair of the woman's head and place in her hands the grain offering of remembrance, which is the grain offering of jealousy. And in his hand the priest shall have the water of bitterness that brings the curse. [19]Then the priest shall make her take an oath, saying, 'If no man has lain with you, and if you have not turned aside to uncleanness while you were under your husband's authority, be free from this water of bitterness that brings the curse. [20]But if you have gone astray, though you are under your husband's authority, and if you have defiled yourself, and some man other than your husband has lain with you, [21]then' (let the priest make the woman take the oath of the curse, and say to the woman) 'the LORD make you a curse and an oath among your people, when the LORD makes your thigh fall away and your body swell. [22]May this water that brings the curse pass into your bowels and make your womb swell and your thigh fall away.' And the woman shall say, 'Amen, Amen.'

---

[1] *Leprosy* was a term for several skin diseases; see Leviticus 13 [2] Hebrew *they shall confess their sin that they have committed* [3] An ephah was about 3/5 bushel or 22 liters

²³"Then the priest shall write these curses in a book and wash them off into the water of bitterness. ²⁴And he shall make the woman drink the water of bitterness that brings the curse, and the water that brings the curse shall enter into her and cause bitter pain. ²⁵And the priest shall take the grain offering of jealousy out of the woman's hand and shall wave the grain offering before the Lord and bring it to the altar. ²⁶And the priest shall take a handful of the grain offering, as its memorial portion, and burn it on the altar, and afterward shall make the woman drink the water. ²⁷And when he has made her drink the water, then, if she has defiled herself and has broken faith with her husband, the water that brings the curse shall enter into her and cause bitter pain, and her womb shall swell, and her thigh shall fall away, and the woman shall become a curse among her people. ²⁸But if the woman has not defiled herself and is clean, then she shall be free and shall conceive children.

²⁹"This is the law in cases of jealousy, when a wife, though under her husband's authority, goes astray and defiles herself, ³⁰or when the spirit of jealousy comes over a man and he is jealous of his wife. Then he shall set the woman before the Lord, and the priest shall carry out for her all this law. ³¹The man shall be free from iniquity, but the woman shall bear her iniquity."

Rules for Nazirites and the institution of the Aaronic benediction [chapter 6]. Chapter 5 covered ordinary members of the community; chapter 6 balances that with the religious elite of the community. Nazirites were people who undertook strict ascetic vows for a limited time and a specific occasion. There is no need to go to a Bible dictionary to get additional information regarding Nazirite vows; the information is right here in the primary text. After the complicated instructions governing Nazirite vows, the Aaronic benediction and instructions for its pronouncement (vv. 22–27) are simplicity personified. The benediction is based on the literary pattern of threefold repetition, enshrined in *parallel construction. Three pairs of items unfold in rhythmic cadence. Each sentence begins with the subject of the clause named ("the Lord"), followed by a compound verb construction naming what God will do for the person on whom the blessing is pronounced.

6 And the Lord spoke to Moses, saying, ²"Speak to the people of Israel and say to them, When either a man or a woman makes a special vow, the vow of a Nazirite,¹ to separate himself to the Lord, ³he shall separate himself from wine and strong drink. He shall drink no vinegar made from wine or strong drink and shall not drink any juice of grapes or eat grapes, fresh or dried. ⁴All the days of his separation² he shall eat nothing that is produced by the grapevine, not even the seeds or the skins.

⁵"All the days of his vow of separation, no razor shall touch his head. Until the time is completed for which he separates himself to the Lord, he shall be holy. He shall let the locks of hair of his head grow long.

⁶"All the days that he separates himself to the Lord he shall not go near a dead body. ⁷Not even for his father or for his mother, for brother or sister, if they die, shall he make himself unclean, because his separation to God is on his head. ⁸All the days of his separation he is holy to the Lord.

⁹"And if any man dies very suddenly beside him and he defiles his consecrated head, then he shall shave his head on the day of his cleansing; on the seventh day he

---

¹ Nazirite means one separated, or one consecrated ² Or Naziriteship

shall shave it. ¹⁰On the eighth day he shall bring two turtledoves or two pigeons to the priest to the entrance of the tent of meeting, ¹¹and the priest shall offer one for a sin offering and the other for a burnt offering, and make atonement for him, because he sinned by reason of the dead body. And he shall consecrate his head that same day ¹²and separate himself to the LORD for the days of his separation and bring a male lamb a year old for a guilt offering. But the previous period shall be void, because his separation was defiled.

¹³"And this is the law for the Nazirite, when the time of his separation has been completed: he shall be brought to the entrance of the tent of meeting, ¹⁴and he shall bring his gift to the LORD, one male lamb a year old without blemish for a burnt offering, and one ewe lamb a year old without blemish as a sin offering, and one ram without blemish as a peace offering, ¹⁵and a basket of unleavened bread, loaves of fine flour mixed with oil, and unleavened wafers smeared with oil, and their grain offering and their drink offerings. ¹⁶And the priest shall bring them before the LORD and offer his sin offering and his burnt offering, ¹⁷and he shall offer the ram as a sacrifice of peace offering to the LORD, with the basket of unleavened bread. The priest shall offer also its grain offering and its drink offering. ¹⁸And the Nazirite shall shave his consecrated head at the entrance of the tent of meeting and shall take the hair from his consecrated head and put it on the fire that is under the sacrifice of the peace offering. ¹⁹And the priest shall take the shoulder of the ram, when it is boiled, and one unleavened loaf out of the basket and one unleavened wafer, and shall put them on the hands of the Nazirite, after he has shaved the hair of his consecration, ²⁰and the priest shall wave them for a wave offering before the LORD. They are a holy portion for the priest, together with the breast that is waved and the thigh that is contributed. And after that the Nazirite may drink wine.

²¹"This is the law of the Nazirite. But if he vows an offering to the LORD above his Nazirite vow, as he can afford, in exact accordance with the vow that he takes, then he shall do in addition to the law of the Nazirite."

²²The LORD spoke to Moses, saying, ²³"Speak to Aaron and his sons, saying, Thus you shall bless the people of Israel: you shall say to them,

²⁴   The LORD bless you and keep you;
²⁵   the LORD make his face to shine upon you and be gracious to you;
²⁶   the LORD lift up his countenance¹ upon you and give you peace.

²⁷"So shall they put my name upon the people of Israel, and I will bless them."

The dedication of the tabernacle [chapter 7]. Narrative reenters the book with the account of the dedication of the tabernacle. The lead-in (vv. 1–11) sets up the main action, which is a blow-by-blow account of the gifts that the leaders of the respective tribes presented on twelve successive days (vv. 12–83), followed by a summary of the gifts (vv. 84–88) and the climactic voice of God over the mercy seat (v. 89). The first item on our agenda is to picture ourselves present at the event, allowing ourselves to be dazzled by the lavishness of the gifts that were brought. Then we can identify underlying principles, such as the importance of giving to God, God's worthiness to be exalted, the importance of places of worship (including their aesthetics), and the need for the believing community to set apart some of its resources for public worship.

¹ Or face

7 On the day when Moses had finished setting up the tabernacle and had anointed and consecrated it with all its furnishings and had anointed and consecrated the altar with all its utensils, ²the chiefs of Israel, heads of their fathers' houses, who were the chiefs of the tribes, who were over those who were listed, approached ³and brought their offerings before the Lᴏʀᴅ, six wagons and twelve oxen, a wagon for every two of the chiefs, and for each one an ox. They brought them before the tabernacle. ⁴Then the Lᴏʀᴅ said to Moses, ⁵"Accept these from them, that they may be used in the service of the tent of meeting, and give them to the Levites, to each man according to his service." ⁶So Moses took the wagons and the oxen and gave them to the Levites. ⁷Two wagons and four oxen he gave to the sons of Gershon, according to their service. ⁸And four wagons and eight oxen he gave to the sons of Merari, according to their service, under the direction of Ithamar the son of Aaron the priest. ⁹But to the sons of Kohath he gave none, because they were charged with the service of the holy things that had to be carried on the shoulder. ¹⁰And the chiefs offered offerings for the dedication of the altar on the day it was anointed; and the chiefs offered their offering before the altar. ¹¹And the Lᴏʀᴅ said to Moses, "They shall offer their offerings, one chief each day, for the dedication of the altar."

¹²He who offered his offering the first day was Nahshon the son of Amminadab, of the tribe of Judah. ¹³And his offering was one silver plate whose weight was 130 shekels,¹ one silver basin of 70 shekels, according to the shekel of the sanctuary, both of them full of fine flour mixed with oil for a grain offering; ¹⁴one golden dish of 10 shekels, full of incense; ¹⁵one bull from the herd, one ram, one male lamb a year old, for a burnt offering; ¹⁶one male goat for a sin offering; ¹⁷and for the sacrifice of peace offerings, two oxen, five rams, five male goats, and five male lambs a year old. This was the offering of Nahshon the son of Amminadab.

¹⁸On the second day Nethanel the son of Zuar, the chief of Issachar, made an offering. ¹⁹He offered for his offering one silver plate whose weight was 130 shekels, one silver basin of 70 shekels, according to the shekel of the sanctuary, both of them full of fine flour mixed with oil for a grain offering; ²⁰one golden dish of 10 shekels, full of incense; ²¹one bull from the herd, one ram, one male lamb a year old, for a burnt offering; ²²one male goat for a sin offering; ²³and for the sacrifice of peace offerings, two oxen, five rams, five male goats, and five male lambs a year old. This was the offering of Nethanel the son of Zuar.

²⁴On the third day Eliab the son of Helon, the chief of the people of Zebulun: ²⁵his offering was one silver plate whose weight was 130 shekels, one silver basin of 70 shekels, according to the shekel of the sanctuary, both of them full of fine flour mixed with oil for a grain offering; ²⁶one golden dish of 10 shekels, full of incense; ²⁷one bull from the herd, one ram, one male lamb a year old, for a burnt offering; ²⁸one male goat for a sin offering; ²⁹and for the sacrifice of peace offerings, two oxen, five rams, five male goats, and five male lambs a year old. This was the offering of Eliab the son of Helon.

³⁰On the fourth day Elizur the son of Shedeur, the chief of the people of Reuben: ³¹his offering was one silver plate whose weight was 130 shekels, one silver basin of 70 shekels, according to the shekel of the sanctuary, both of them full of fine flour mixed with oil for a grain offering; ³²one golden dish of 10 shekels, full of incense; ³³one bull from the herd, one ram, one male lamb a year old, for a burnt offering; ³⁴one male goat for a sin offering; ³⁵and for the sacrifice of peace offerings, two oxen,

---

¹ A *shekel* was about 2/5 ounce or 11 grams

five rams, five male goats, and five male lambs a year old. This was the offering of Elizur the son of Shedeur.

³⁶On the fifth day Shelumiel the son of Zurishaddai, the chief of the people of Simeon: ³⁷his offering was one silver plate whose weight was 130 shekels, one silver basin of 70 shekels, according to the shekel of the sanctuary, both of them full of fine flour mixed with oil for a grain offering; ³⁸one golden dish of 10 shekels, full of incense; ³⁹one bull from the herd, one ram, one male lamb a year old, for a burnt offering; ⁴⁰one male goat for a sin offering; ⁴¹and for the sacrifice of peace offerings, two oxen, five rams, five male goats, and five male lambs a year old. This was the offering of Shelumiel the son of Zurishaddai.

⁴²On the sixth day Eliasaph the son of Deuel, the chief of the people of Gad: ⁴³his offering was one silver plate whose weight was 130 shekels, one silver basin of 70 shekels, according to the shekel of the sanctuary, both of them full of fine flour mixed with oil for a grain offering; ⁴⁴one golden dish of 10 shekels, full of incense; ⁴⁵one bull from the herd, one ram, one male lamb a year old, for a burnt offering; ⁴⁶one male goat for a sin offering; ⁴⁷and for the sacrifice of peace offerings, two oxen, five rams, five male goats, and five male lambs a year old. This was the offering of Eliasaph the son of Deuel.

⁴⁸On the seventh day Elishama the son of Ammihud, the chief of the people of Ephraim: ⁴⁹his offering was one silver plate whose weight was 130 shekels, one silver basin of 70 shekels, according to the shekel of the sanctuary, both of them full of fine flour mixed with oil for a grain offering; ⁵⁰one golden dish of 10 shekels, full of incense; ⁵¹one bull from the herd, one ram, one male lamb a year old, for a burnt offering; ⁵²one male goat for a sin offering; ⁵³and for the sacrifice of peace offerings, two oxen, five rams, five male goats, and five male lambs a year old. This was the offering of Elishama the son of Ammihud.

⁵⁴On the eighth day Gamaliel the son of Pedahzur, the chief of the people of Manasseh: ⁵⁵his offering was one silver plate whose weight was 130 shekels, one silver basin of 70 shekels, according to the shekel of the sanctuary, both of them full of fine flour mixed with oil for a grain offering; ⁵⁶one golden dish of 10 shekels, full of incense; ⁵⁷one bull from the herd, one ram, one male lamb a year old, for a burnt offering; ⁵⁸one male goat for a sin offering; ⁵⁹and for the sacrifice of peace offerings, two oxen, five rams, five male goats, and five male lambs a year old. This was the offering of Gamaliel the son of Pedahzur.

⁶⁰On the ninth day Abidan the son of Gideoni, the chief of the people of Benjamin: ⁶¹his offering was one silver plate whose weight was 130 shekels, one silver basin of 70 shekels, according to the shekel of the sanctuary, both of them full of fine flour mixed with oil for a grain offering; ⁶²one golden dish of 10 shekels, full of incense; ⁶³one bull from the herd, one ram, one male lamb a year old, for a burnt offering; ⁶⁴one male goat for a sin offering; ⁶⁵and for the sacrifice of peace offerings, two oxen, five rams, five male goats, and five male lambs a year old. This was the offering of Abidan the son of Gideoni.

⁶⁶On the tenth day Ahiezer the son of Ammishaddai, the chief of the people of Dan: ⁶⁷his offering was one silver plate whose weight was 130 shekels, one silver basin of 70 shekels, according to the shekel of the sanctuary, both of them full of fine flour mixed with oil for a grain offering; ⁶⁸one golden dish of 10 shekels, full of incense; ⁶⁹one bull from the herd, one ram, one male lamb a year old, for a burnt

offering; ⁷⁰one male goat for a sin offering; ⁷¹and for the sacrifice of peace offerings, two oxen, five rams, five male goats, and five male lambs a year old. This was the offering of Ahiezer the son of Ammishaddai.

⁷²On the eleventh day Pagiel the son of Ochran, the chief of the people of Asher: ⁷³his offering was one silver plate whose weight was 130 shekels, one silver basin of 70 shekels, according to the shekel of the sanctuary, both of them full of fine flour mixed with oil for a grain offering; ⁷⁴one golden dish of 10 shekels, full of incense; ⁷⁵one bull from the herd, one ram, one male lamb a year old, for a burnt offering; ⁷⁶one male goat for a sin offering; ⁷⁷and for the sacrifice of peace offerings, two oxen, five rams, five male goats, and five male lambs a year old. This was the offering of Pagiel the son of Ochran.

⁷⁸On the twelfth day Ahira the son of Enan, the chief of the people of Naphtali: ⁷⁹his offering was one silver plate whose weight was 130 shekels, one silver basin of 70 shekels, according to the shekel of the sanctuary, both of them full of fine flour mixed with oil for a grain offering; ⁸⁰one golden dish of 10 shekels, full of incense; ⁸¹one bull from the herd, one ram, one male lamb a year old, for a burnt offering; ⁸²one male goat for a sin offering; ⁸³and for the sacrifice of peace offerings, two oxen, five rams, five male goats, and five male lambs a year old. This was the offering of Ahira the son of Enan.

⁸⁴This was the dedication offering for the altar on the day when it was anointed, from the chiefs of Israel: twelve silver plates, twelve silver basins, twelve golden dishes, ⁸⁵each silver plate weighing 130 shekels and each basin 70, all the silver of the vessels 2,400 shekels according to the shekel of the sanctuary, ⁸⁶the twelve golden dishes, full of incense, weighing 10 shekels apiece according to the shekel of the sanctuary, all the gold of the dishes being 120 shekels; ⁸⁷all the cattle for the burnt offering twelve bulls, twelve rams, twelve male lambs a year old, with their grain offering; and twelve male goats for a sin offering; ⁸⁸and all the cattle for the sacrifice of peace offerings twenty-four bulls, the rams sixty, the male goats sixty, the male lambs a year old sixty. This was the dedication offering for the altar after it was anointed.

⁸⁹And when Moses went into the tent of meeting to speak with the Lᴏʀᴅ, he heard the voice speaking to him from above the mercy seat that was on the ark of the testimony, from between the two cherubim; and it spoke to him.

Instructions for Aaron and the Levites [chapter 8]. The format now turns from narrative to a religious instruction manual. The rhetorical formula that begins the section is the same as it was in the book of Leviticus, "the Lᴏʀᴅ spoke to Moses," with sections of instruction followed by narrative assurances that the instructions were implemented (vv. 3, 20–22). Again the emphasis is on sacred rituals and differentiating the sacred from the common. The regulations cover three things: the lamps of the tabernacle (vv. 1–4), purification of the Levites (vv. 5–22), and the ages of service for the Levites (vv. 23–26).

8 Now the Lᴏʀᴅ spoke to Moses, saying, ²"Speak to Aaron and say to him, When you set up the lamps, the seven lamps shall give light in front of the lampstand." ³And Aaron did so: he set up its lamps in front of the lampstand, as the Lᴏʀᴅ commanded Moses. ⁴And this was the workmanship of the lampstand, hammered work

of gold. From its base to its flowers, it was hammered work; according to the pattern that the LORD had shown Moses, so he made the lampstand.

⁵And the LORD spoke to Moses, saying, ⁶"Take the Levites from among the people of Israel and cleanse them. ⁷Thus you shall do to them to cleanse them: sprinkle the water of purification upon them, and let them go with a razor over all their body, and wash their clothes and cleanse themselves. ⁸Then let them take a bull from the herd and its grain offering of fine flour mixed with oil, and you shall take another bull from the herd for a sin offering. ⁹And you shall bring the Levites before the tent of meeting and assemble the whole congregation of the people of Israel. ¹⁰When you bring the Levites before the LORD, the people of Israel shall lay their hands on the Levites, ¹¹and Aaron shall offer the Levites before the LORD as a wave offering from the people of Israel, that they may do the service of the LORD. ¹²Then the Levites shall lay their hands on the heads of the bulls, and you shall offer the one for a sin offering and the other for a burnt offering to the LORD to make atonement for the Levites. ¹³And you shall set the Levites before Aaron and his sons, and shall offer them as a wave offering to the LORD.

¹⁴"Thus you shall separate the Levites from among the people of Israel, and the Levites shall be mine. ¹⁵And after that the Levites shall go in to serve at the tent of meeting, when you have cleansed them and offered them as a wave offering. ¹⁶For they are wholly given to me from among the people of Israel. Instead of all who open the womb, the firstborn of all the people of Israel, I have taken them for myself. ¹⁷For all the firstborn among the people of Israel are mine, both of man and of beast. On the day that I struck down all the firstborn in the land of Egypt I consecrated them for myself, ¹⁸and I have taken the Levites instead of all the firstborn among the people of Israel. ¹⁹And I have given the Levites as a gift to Aaron and his sons from among the people of Israel, to do the service for the people of Israel at the tent of meeting and to make atonement for the people of Israel, that there may be no plague among the people of Israel when the people of Israel come near the sanctuary."

²⁰Thus did Moses and Aaron and all the congregation of the people of Israel to the Levites. According to all that the LORD commanded Moses concerning the Levites, the people of Israel did to them. ²¹And the Levites purified themselves from sin and washed their clothes, and Aaron offered them as a wave offering before the LORD, and Aaron made atonement for them to cleanse them. ²²And after that the Levites went in to do their service in the tent of meeting before Aaron and his sons; as the LORD had commanded Moses concerning the Levites, so they did to them.

²³And the LORD spoke to Moses, saying, ²⁴"This applies to the Levites: from twenty-five years old and upward they¹ shall come to do duty in the service of the tent of meeting. ²⁵And from the age of fifty years they shall withdraw from the duty of the service and serve no more. ²⁶They minister² to their brothers in the tent of meeting by keeping guard, but they shall do no service. Thus shall you do to the Levites in assigning their duties."

God's instructions to Moses regarding the Passover [9:1–14]. The Passover is the central religious ceremony of the OT covenant. Rules governing it appear in multiple OT books, and this is the account of it in Numbers. After we have relived the literal objects and practices that made up the Passover, we can reflect on the symbolism of various

---

¹ Hebrew *he*; also verses 25, 26 ² Hebrew *He ministers*

aspects of it, with a view toward understanding what the Passover teaches us about God's way of salvation.

9 And the LORD spoke to Moses in the wilderness of Sinai, in the first month of the second year after they had come out of the land of Egypt, saying, ²"Let the people of Israel keep the Passover at its appointed time. ³On the fourteenth day of this month, at twilight, you shall keep it at its appointed time; according to all its statutes and all its rules you shall keep it." ⁴So Moses told the people of Israel that they should keep the Passover. ⁵And they kept the Passover in the first month, on the fourteenth day of the month, at twilight, in the wilderness of Sinai; according to all that the LORD commanded Moses, so the people of Israel did. ⁶And there were certain men who were unclean through touching a dead body, so that they could not keep the Passover on that day, and they came before Moses and Aaron on that day. ⁷And those men said to him, "We are unclean through touching a dead body. Why are we kept from bringing the LORD's offering at its appointed time among the people of Israel?" ⁸And Moses said to them, "Wait, that I may hear what the LORD will command concerning you."

⁹The LORD spoke to Moses, saying, ¹⁰"Speak to the people of Israel, saying, If any one of you or of your descendants is unclean through touching a dead body, or is on a long journey, he shall still keep the Passover to the LORD. ¹¹In the second month on the fourteenth day at twilight they shall keep it. They shall eat it with unleavened bread and bitter herbs. ¹²They shall leave none of it until the morning, nor break any of its bones; according to all the statute for the Passover they shall keep it. ¹³But if anyone who is clean and is not on a journey fails to keep the Passover, that person shall be cut off from his people because he did not bring the LORD's offering at its appointed time; that man shall bear his sin. ¹⁴And if a stranger sojourns among you and would keep the Passover to the LORD, according to the statute of the Passover and according to its rule, so shall he do. You shall have one statute, both for the sojourner and for the native."

Final preparations for the journey [9:15–10:10]. As we now reach the final preparations for the march through the wilderness, we can see that the mixture of narrative and instruction that has preceded has served the narrative function of setting up the preparations for the journey. It is true that many of the ceremonies were carried forward after the nation settled in the Promised Land, but they were first instituted when the nation was on a journey to that destination. Two dramatic events constitute the lead-up to the march. One is the appearance of a numinous fire by night and cloud by day (9:15–23), which appear on the day that the tabernacle is set up and demonstrate the presence of God with his people on their journey. Making the cloud even more stupendous is the fact that God uses it to guide the nation on its march. When the cloud remains over the tabernacle, the camp stays in the place. When the cloud moves, the people follow it. Only slightly less dramatic are the two silver trumpets that God commands Moses to forge (10:1–10). Their purpose is multiple, as the unit outlines.

¹⁵On the day that the tabernacle was set up, the cloud covered the tabernacle, the tent of the testimony. And at evening it was over the tabernacle like the appearance

of fire until morning. [16]So it was always: the cloud covered it by day[1] and the appearance of fire by night. [17]And whenever the cloud lifted from over the tent, after that the people of Israel set out, and in the place where the cloud settled down, there the people of Israel camped. [18]At the command of the LORD the people of Israel set out, and at the command of the LORD they camped. As long as the cloud rested over the tabernacle, they remained in camp. [19]Even when the cloud continued over the tabernacle many days, the people of Israel kept the charge of the LORD and did not set out. [20]Sometimes the cloud was a few days over the tabernacle, and according to the command of the LORD they remained in camp; then according to the command of the LORD they set out. [21]And sometimes the cloud remained from evening until morning. And when the cloud lifted in the morning, they set out, or if it continued for a day and a night, when the cloud lifted they set out. [22]Whether it was two days, or a month, or a longer time, that the cloud continued over the tabernacle, abiding there, the people of Israel remained in camp and did not set out, but when it lifted they set out. [23]At the command of the LORD they camped, and at the command of the LORD they set out. They kept the charge of the LORD, at the command of the LORD by Moses.

10 The LORD spoke to Moses, saying, [2]"Make two silver trumpets. Of hammered work you shall make them, and you shall use them for summoning the congregation and for breaking camp. [3]And when both are blown, all the congregation shall gather themselves to you at the entrance of the tent of meeting. [4]But if they blow only one, then the chiefs, the heads of the tribes of Israel, shall gather themselves to you. [5]When you blow an alarm, the camps that are on the east side shall set out. [6]And when you blow an alarm the second time, the camps that are on the south side shall set out. An alarm is to be blown whenever they are to set out. [7]But when the assembly is to be gathered together, you shall blow a long blast, but you shall not sound an alarm. [8]And the sons of Aaron, the priests, shall blow the trumpets. The trumpets shall be to you for a perpetual statute throughout your generations. [9]And when you go to war in your land against the adversary who oppresses you, then you shall sound an alarm with the trumpets, that you may be remembered before the LORD your God, and you shall be saved from your enemies. [10]On the day of your gladness also, and at your appointed feasts and at the beginnings of your months, you shall blow the trumpets over your burnt offerings and over the sacrifices of your peace offerings. They shall be a reminder of you before your God: I am the LORD your God."

The journey begins [10:11–36]. The function of this episode is to re-create the excitement of breaking camp at Mount Sinai and beginning the journey through the wilderness, with Canaan as the goal. The episode is told in relatively complete detail, so that we are invited to relive the event as we read. The account is orderliness personified. A warmly human note enters when Moses appeals to his Midianite brother-in-law to travel with the group to "serve as eyes" for them in the wilderness (vv. 29–32). The specifically religious nature of the journey becomes clear with the references to God's guidance at the end of the chapter (vv. 33–36). It is an event that one might well wish to have experienced.

[11]In the second year, in the second month, on the twentieth day of the month, the cloud lifted from over the tabernacle of the testimony, [12]and the people of Israel set out by stages from the wilderness of Sinai. And the cloud settled down in the wilder-

---
[1] Septuagint, Syriac, Vulgate; Hebrew lacks by day

ness of Paran. ¹³They set out for the first time at the command of the LORD by Moses. ¹⁴The standard of the camp of the people of Judah set out first by their companies, and over their company was Nahshon the son of Amminadab. ¹⁵And over the company of the tribe of the people of Issachar was Nethanel the son of Zuar. ¹⁶And over the company of the tribe of the people of Zebulun was Eliab the son of Helon.

¹⁷And when the tabernacle was taken down, the sons of Gershon and the sons of Merari, who carried the tabernacle, set out. ¹⁸And the standard of the camp of Reuben set out by their companies, and over their company was Elizur the son of Shedeur. ¹⁹And over the company of the tribe of the people of Simeon was Shelumiel the son of Zurishaddai. ²⁰And over the company of the tribe of the people of Gad was Eliasaph the son of Deuel.

²¹Then the Kohathites set out, carrying the holy things, and the tabernacle was set up before their arrival. ²²And the standard of the camp of the people of Ephraim set out by their companies, and over their company was Elishama the son of Ammihud. ²³And over the company of the tribe of the people of Manasseh was Gamaliel the son of Pedahzur. ²⁴And over the company of the tribe of the people of Benjamin was Abidan the son of Gideoni.

²⁵Then the standard of the camp of the people of Dan, acting as the rear guard of all the camps, set out by their companies, and over their company was Ahiezer the son of Ammishaddai. ²⁶And over the company of the tribe of the people of Asher was Pagiel the son of Ochran. ²⁷And over the company of the tribe of the people of Naphtali was Ahira the son of Enan. ²⁸This was the order of march of the people of Israel by their companies, when they set out.

²⁹And Moses said to Hobab the son of Reuel the Midianite, Moses' father-in-law, "We are setting out for the place of which the LORD said, 'I will give it to you.' Come with us, and we will do good to you, for the LORD has promised good to Israel." ³⁰But he said to him, "I will not go. I will depart to my own land and to my kindred." ³¹And he said, "Please do not leave us, for you know where we should camp in the wilderness, and you will serve as eyes for us. ³²And if you do go with us, whatever good the LORD will do to us, the same will we do to you."

³³So they set out from the mount of the LORD three days' journey. And the ark of the covenant of the LORD went before them three days' journey, to seek out a resting place for them. ³⁴And the cloud of the LORD was over them by day, whenever they set out from the camp.

³⁵And whenever the ark set out, Moses said, "Arise, O LORD, and let your enemies be scattered, and let those who hate you flee before you." ³⁶And when it rested, he said, "Return, O LORD, to the ten thousand thousands of Israel."

A complaining community [chapter 11]. The positive note of the story of breaking camp quickly gives way to negative experiences. In a story where complaining or "murmuring" (King James Version) will become the most salient characteristic of the Israelites, we are given an early glimpse of that national trait in this episode. The sequence is this: the people complain about misfortune, and the fire of God burns in response (vv. 1–3); the people complain about the manna that God has sent to sustain them (vv. 4–9); Moses responds to the complaint of the people by complaining to God (vv. 10–15); God instructs Moses to appoint seventy elders and also announces that he will send meat until the Israelites are weary of it (vv. 16–25); there is objection when the elders on whom God has sent his Spirit prophesy (vv. 26–30); God sends quail and a plague to punish the people for their lack of restraint (vv. 31–35). This is a picture of disharmony, and it introduces the anti-epic note into the story. The story that Numbers tells is, to be sure, an epic story of the quest of a traveling nation. But epics ordinarily celebrate the superior virtues of the writer's nation. The epic of exodus that spans the last four books of the Pentateuch consistently portrays the author's nation in an unfavorable light, with the characterization of God serving as a foil. We can also evoke the genre of *satire as a good explanation for what we find in Numbers, as the behavior of the Israelites is held up to satiric exposure and rebuke.

11 And the people complained in the hearing of the LORD about their misfortunes, and when the LORD heard it, his anger was kindled, and the fire of the LORD burned among them and consumed some outlying parts of the camp. [2]Then the people cried out to Moses, and Moses prayed to the LORD, and the fire died down. [3]So the name of that place was called Taberah,[1] because the fire of the LORD burned among them.

[4]Now the rabble that was among them had a strong craving. And the people of Israel also wept again and said, "Oh that we had meat to eat! [5]We remember the fish we ate in Egypt that cost nothing, the cucumbers, the melons, the leeks, the onions, and the garlic. [6]But now our strength is dried up, and there is nothing at all but this manna to look at."

[7]Now the manna was like coriander seed, and its appearance like that of bdellium. [8]The people went about and gathered it and ground it in handmills or beat it in mortars and boiled it in pots and made cakes of it. And the taste of it was like the taste of cakes baked with oil. [9]When the dew fell upon the camp in the night, the manna fell with it.

[10]Moses heard the people weeping throughout their clans, everyone at the door of his tent. And the anger of the LORD blazed hotly, and Moses was displeased. [11]Moses said to the LORD, "Why have you dealt ill with your servant? And why have I not found favor in your sight, that you lay the burden of all this people on me? [12]Did I conceive all this people? Did I give them birth, that you should say to me, 'Carry them in your bosom, as a nurse carries a nursing child,' to the land that you swore to give their fathers? [13]Where am I to get meat to give to all this people? For they weep before me and say, 'Give us meat, that we may eat.' [14]I am not able to carry all this people alone; the burden is too heavy for me. [15]If you will treat me like this, kill me at once, if I find favor in your sight, that I may not see my wretchedness."

[16]Then the LORD said to Moses, "Gather for me seventy men of the elders of Israel, whom you know to be the elders of the people and officers over them, and bring them to the tent of meeting, and let them take their stand there with you. [17]And I will come down and talk with you there. And I will take some of the Spirit that is on you and put it on them, and they shall bear the burden of the people with you, so that you may not bear it yourself alone. [18]And say to the people, 'Consecrate yourselves for tomorrow, and you shall eat meat, for you have wept in the hearing of the LORD, saying, "Who will give us meat to eat? For it was better for us in Egypt." Therefore the LORD will give you meat, and you shall eat. [19]You shall not eat just one day, or two

---

[1] *Taberah* means *burning*

days, or five days, or ten days, or twenty days, ²⁰but a whole month, until it comes out
at your nostrils and becomes loathsome to you, because you have rejected the LORD
who is among you and have wept before him, saying, "Why did we come out of
Egypt?"'" ²¹But Moses said, "The people among whom I am number six hundred
thousand on foot, and you have said, 'I will give them meat, that they may eat a whole
month!' ²²Shall flocks and herds be slaughtered for them, and be enough for them?
Or shall all the fish of the sea be gathered together for them, and be enough for
them?" ²³And the LORD said to Moses, "Is the LORD's hand shortened? Now you shall
see whether my word will come true for you or not."

²⁴So Moses went out and told the people the words of the LORD. And he gathered
seventy men of the elders of the people and placed them around the tent. ²⁵Then the
LORD came down in the cloud and spoke to him, and took some of the Spirit that was
on him and put it on the seventy elders. And as soon as the Spirit rested on them, they
prophesied. But they did not continue doing it.

²⁶Now two men remained in the camp, one named Eldad, and the other named
Medad, and the Spirit rested on them. They were among those registered, but they
had not gone out to the tent, and so they prophesied in the camp. ²⁷And a young man
ran and told Moses, "Eldad and Medad are prophesying in the camp." ²⁸And Joshua
the son of Nun, the assistant of Moses from his youth, said, "My lord Moses, stop
them." ²⁹But Moses said to him, "Are you jealous for my sake? Would that all the
LORD's people were prophets, that the LORD would put his Spirit on them!" ³⁰And
Moses and the elders of Israel returned to the camp.

³¹Then a wind from the LORD sprang up, and it brought quail from the sea and let
them fall beside the camp, about a day's journey on this side and a day's journey on
the other side, around the camp, and about two cubits¹ above the ground. ³²And the
people rose all that day and all night and all the next day, and gathered the quail.
Those who gathered least gathered ten homers.² And they spread them out for themselves all around the camp. ³³While the meat was yet between their teeth, before it
was consumed, the anger of the LORD was kindled against the people, and the LORD
struck down the people with a very great plague. ³⁴Therefore the name of that place
was called Kibroth-hattaavah,³ because there they buried the people who had the
craving. ³⁵From Kibroth-hattaavah the people journeyed to Hazeroth, and they
remained at Hazeroth.

The vindication of the epic hero [chapter 12]. Internal conflicts are often as prevalent in travel stories as external conflicts are. The story of Miriam and Aaron's challenge
to Moses' authority is a story of rebellion, crime and punishment, expulsion and reas-
similation, and testing and confirmation of the hero. The narrative is as brief as the
experience was unpleasant.

12 Miriam and Aaron spoke against Moses because of the Cushite woman
whom he had married, for he had married a Cushite woman. ²And they said,
"Has the LORD indeed spoken only through Moses? Has he not spoken through us
also?" And the LORD heard it. ³Now the man Moses was very meek, more than all people who were on the face of the earth. ⁴And suddenly the LORD said to Moses and to
Aaron and Miriam, "Come out, you three, to the tent of meeting." And the three of

¹ A *cubit* was about 18 inches or 45 centimeters ² A *homer* was about 6 bushels or 220 liters ³ *Kibroth-hattaavah* means *graves of craving*

them came out. [5]And the LORD came down in a pillar of cloud and stood at the entrance of the tent and called Aaron and Miriam, and they both came forward. [6]And he said, "Hear my words: If there is a prophet among you, I the LORD make myself known to him in a vision; I speak with him in a dream. [7]Not so with my servant Moses. He is faithful in all my house. [8]With him I speak mouth to mouth, clearly, and not in riddles, and he beholds the form of the LORD. Why then were you not afraid to speak against my servant Moses?" [9]And the anger of the LORD was kindled against them, and he departed.

[10]When the cloud removed from over the tent, behold, Miriam was leprous,[1] like snow. And Aaron turned toward Miriam, and behold, she was leprous. [11]And Aaron said to Moses, "Oh, my lord, do not punish us[2] because we have done foolishly and have sinned. [12]Let her not be as one dead, whose flesh is half eaten away when he comes out of his mother's womb." [13]And Moses cried to the LORD, "O God, please heal her—please." [14]But the LORD said to Moses, "If her father had but spit in her face, should she not be shamed seven days? Let her be shut outside the camp seven days, and after that she may be brought in again." [15]So Miriam was shut outside the camp seven days, and the people did not set out on the march till Miriam was brought in again. [16]After that the people set out from Hazeroth, and camped in the wilderness of Paran.

> **Spy saga** [chapters 13–14]. This is another of the famous episodes from Numbers that deeply impresses the childhood imagination. Analyzing childhood responses remains a valuable channel toward getting a grip on the stories of the Bible. Almost every aspect of the story yields vivid pictures—the dangerous mission of the spies, the gigantic cluster of grapes that requires two men to carry, the stock description "a land that flows with milk and honey," the giants in the land who make the weak-faithed spies feel like grasshoppers, the courage of Joshua and Caleb, the negative report of the ten ignominious spies, Moses and Aaron's futile attempt to instill faith in the people, God's anger and Moses' intercession, God's declaration that the generation of the faithless will die in the wilderness during a forty-year delay in entering the Promised Land, and a concluding military defeat that rounds out a sordid chapter in the national anti-epic of Numbers.

13 The LORD spoke to Moses, saying, [2]"Send men to spy out the land of Canaan, which I am giving to the people of Israel. From each tribe of their fathers you shall send a man, every one a chief among them." [3]So Moses sent them from the wilderness of Paran, according to the command of the LORD, all of them men who were heads of the people of Israel. [4]And these were their names: From the tribe of Reuben, Shammua the son of Zaccur; [5]from the tribe of Simeon, Shaphat the son of Hori; [6]from the tribe of Judah, Caleb the son of Jephunneh; [7]from the tribe of Issachar, Igal the son of Joseph; [8]from the tribe of Ephraim, Hoshea the son of Nun; [9]from the tribe of Benjamin, Palti the son of Raphu; [10]from the tribe of Zebulun, Gaddiel the son of Sodi; [11]from the tribe of Joseph (that is, from the tribe of Manasseh), Gaddi the son of Susi; [12]from the tribe of Dan, Ammiel the son of Gemalli; [13]from the tribe of Asher, Sethur the son of Michael; [14]from the tribe of Naphtali, Nahbi the son of Vophsi; [15]from the tribe of Gad, Geuel the son of Machi. [16]These were the names of the men whom Moses sent to spy out the land. And Moses called Hoshea the son of Nun Joshua.

---

[1] *Leprosy* was a term for several skin diseases; see Leviticus 13 [2] Hebrew *do not lay sin upon us*

[17]Moses sent them to spy out the land of Canaan and said to them, "Go up into the Negeb and go up into the hill country, [18]and see what the land is, and whether the people who dwell in it are strong or weak, whether they are few or many, [19]and whether the land that they dwell in is good or bad, and whether the cities that they dwell in are camps or strongholds, [20]and whether the land is rich or poor, and whether there are trees in it or not. Be of good courage and bring some of the fruit of the land." Now the time was the season of the first ripe grapes.

[21]So they went up and spied out the land from the wilderness of Zin to Rehob, near Lebo-hamath. [22]They went up into the Negeb and came to Hebron. Ahiman, Sheshai, and Talmai, the descendants of Anak, were there. (Hebron was built seven years before Zoan in Egypt.) [23]And they came to the Valley of Eshcol and cut down from there a branch with a single cluster of grapes, and they carried it on a pole between two of them; they also brought some pomegranates and figs. [24]That place was called the Valley of Eshcol,[1] because of the cluster that the people of Israel cut down from there.

[25]At the end of forty days they returned from spying out the land. [26]And they came to Moses and Aaron and to all the congregation of the people of Israel in the wilderness of Paran, at Kadesh. They brought back word to them and to all the congregation, and showed them the fruit of the land. [27]And they told him, "We came to the land to which you sent us. It flows with milk and honey, and this is its fruit. [28]However, the people who dwell in the land are strong, and the cities are fortified and very large. And besides, we saw the descendants of Anak there. [29]The Amalekites dwell in the land of the Negeb. The Hittites, the Jebusites, and the Amorites dwell in the hill country. And the Canaanites dwell by the sea, and along the Jordan."

[30]But Caleb quieted the people before Moses and said, "Let us go up at once and occupy it, for we are well able to overcome it." [31]Then the men who had gone up with him said, "We are not able to go up against the people, for they are stronger than we are." [32]So they brought to the people of Israel a bad report of the land that they had spied out, saying, "The land, through which we have gone to spy it out, is a land that devours its inhabitants, and all the people that we saw in it are of great height. [33]And there we saw the Nephilim (the sons of Anak, who come from the Nephilim), and we seemed to ourselves like grasshoppers, and so we seemed to them."

14 Then all the congregation raised a loud cry, and the people wept that night. [2]And all the people of Israel grumbled against Moses and Aaron. The whole congregation said to them, "Would that we had died in the land of Egypt! Or would that we had died in this wilderness! [3]Why is the LORD bringing us into this land, to fall by the sword? Our wives and our little ones will become a prey. Would it not be better for us to go back to Egypt?" [4]And they said to one another, "Let us choose a leader and go back to Egypt."

[5]Then Moses and Aaron fell on their faces before all the assembly of the congregation of the people of Israel. [6]And Joshua the son of Nun and Caleb the son of Jephunneh, who were among those who had spied out the land, tore their clothes [7]and said to all the congregation of the people of Israel, "The land, which we passed through to spy it out, is an exceedingly good land. [8]If the LORD delights in us, he will bring us into this land and give it to us, a land that flows with milk and honey. [9]Only do not rebel against the LORD. And do not fear the people of the land, for they are

---

[1] Eshcol means cluster

bread for us. Their protection is removed from them, and the LORD is with us; do not fear them." ¹⁰Then all the congregation said to stone them with stones. But the glory of the LORD appeared at the tent of meeting to all the people of Israel.

¹¹And the LORD said to Moses, "How long will this people despise me? And how long will they not believe in me, in spite of all the signs that I have done among them? ¹²I will strike them with the pestilence and disinherit them, and I will make of you a nation greater and mightier than they."

¹³But Moses said to the LORD, "Then the Egyptians will hear of it, for you brought up this people in your might from among them, ¹⁴and they will tell the inhabitants of this land. They have heard that you, O LORD, are in the midst of this people. For you, O LORD, are seen face to face, and your cloud stands over them and you go before them, in a pillar of cloud by day and in a pillar of fire by night. ¹⁵Now if you kill this people as one man, then the nations who have heard your fame will say, ¹⁶'It is because the LORD was not able to bring this people into the land that he swore to give to them that he has killed them in the wilderness.' ¹⁷And now, please let the power of the Lord be great as you have promised, saying, ¹⁸'The LORD is slow to anger and abounding in steadfast love, forgiving iniquity and transgression, but he will by no means clear the guilty, visiting the iniquity of the fathers on the children, to the third and the fourth generation.' ¹⁹Please pardon the iniquity of this people, according to the greatness of your steadfast love, just as you have forgiven this people, from Egypt until now."

²⁰Then the LORD said, "I have pardoned, according to your word. ²¹But truly, as I live, and as all the earth shall be filled with the glory of the LORD, ²²none of the men who have seen my glory and my signs that I did in Egypt and in the wilderness, and yet have put me to the test these ten times and have not obeyed my voice, ²³shall see the land that I swore to give to their fathers. And none of those who despised me shall see it. ²⁴But my servant Caleb, because he has a different spirit and has followed me fully, I will bring into the land into which he went, and his descendants shall possess it. ²⁵Now, since the Amalekites and the Canaanites dwell in the valleys, turn tomorrow and set out for the wilderness by the way to the Red Sea."

²⁶And the LORD spoke to Moses and to Aaron, saying, ²⁷"How long shall this wicked congregation grumble against me? I have heard the grumblings of the people of Israel, which they grumble against me. ²⁸Say to them, 'As I live, declares the LORD, what you have said in my hearing I will do to you: ²⁹your dead bodies shall fall in this wilderness, and of all your number, listed in the census from twenty years old and upward, who have grumbled against me, ³⁰not one shall come into the land where I swore that I would make you dwell, except Caleb the son of Jephunneh and Joshua the son of Nun. ³¹But your little ones, who you said would become a prey, I will bring in, and they shall know the land that you have rejected. ³²But as for you, your dead bodies shall fall in this wilderness. ³³And your children shall be shepherds in the wilderness forty years and shall suffer for your faithlessness, until the last of your dead bodies lies in the wilderness. ³⁴According to the number of the days in which you spied out the land, forty days, a year for each day, you shall bear your iniquity forty years, and you shall know my displeasure.' ³⁵I, the LORD, have spoken. Surely this will I do to all this wicked congregation who are gathered together against me: in this wilderness they shall come to a full end, and there they shall die."

³⁶And the men whom Moses sent to spy out the land, who returned and made all

the congregation grumble against him by bringing up a bad report about the land— ³⁷the men who brought up a bad report of the land—died by plague before the Lord. ³⁸Of those men who went to spy out the land, only Joshua the son of Nun and Caleb the son of Jephunneh remained alive.

³⁹When Moses told these words to all the people of Israel, the people mourned greatly. ⁴⁰And they rose early in the morning and went up to the heights of the hill country, saying, "Here we are. We will go up to the place that the Lord has promised, for we have sinned." ⁴¹But Moses said, "Why now are you transgressing the command of the Lord, when that will not succeed? ⁴²Do not go up, for the Lord is not among you, lest you be struck down before your enemies. ⁴³For there the Amalekites and the Canaanites are facing you, and you shall fall by the sword. Because you have turned back from following the Lord, the Lord will not be with you." ⁴⁴But they presumed to go up to the heights of the hill country, although neither the ark of the covenant of the Lord nor Moses departed out of the camp. ⁴⁵Then the Amalekites and the Canaanites who lived in that hill country came down and defeated them and pursued them, even to Hormah.

Instruction interlude on offerings and regulations [chapter 15]. Here narrative takes a break in the back-and-forth rhythm that makes up the book of Numbers. A law-giving section lays out supplemental rules and rituals. The brief instruction manual covers multiple subjects: instructions concerning diverse offerings (vv. 1–21); rules governing unintentional sins (vv. 22–31); the law regarding Sabbath breakers (vv. 32–36); stipulations regarding tassels on garments (vv. 37–41). Two good avenues to understanding this law-giving interlude are these: (1) look for connections between the ethos or worldview embodied in the laws of Israel and that of the narrative sections, and (2) operate on the premise that the ceremonial laws of Numbers are visual embodiments of spiritual realities.

15 The Lord spoke to Moses, saying, ²"Speak to the people of Israel and say to them, When you come into the land you are to inhabit, which I am giving you, ³and you offer to the Lord from the herd or from the flock a food offering¹ or a burnt offering or a sacrifice, to fulfill a vow or as a freewill offering or at your appointed feasts, to make a pleasing aroma to the Lord, ⁴then he who brings his offering shall offer to the Lord a grain offering of a tenth of an ephah² of fine flour, mixed with a quarter of a hin³ of oil; ⁵and you shall offer with the burnt offering, or for the sacrifice, a quarter of a hin of wine for the drink offering for each lamb. ⁶Or for a ram, you shall offer for a grain offering two tenths of an ephah of fine flour mixed with a third of a hin of oil. ⁷And for the drink offering you shall offer a third of a hin of wine, a pleasing aroma to the Lord. ⁸And when you offer a bull as a burnt offering or sacrifice, to fulfill a vow or for peace offerings to the Lord, ⁹then one shall offer with the bull a grain offering of three tenths of an ephah of fine flour, mixed with half a hin of oil. ¹⁰And you shall offer for the drink offering half a hin of wine, as a food offering, a pleasing aroma to the Lord.

¹¹"Thus it shall be done for each bull or ram, or for each lamb or young goat. ¹²As many as you offer, so shall you do with each one, as many as there are. ¹³Every native Israelite shall do these things in this way, in offering a food offering, with a pleasing aroma to the Lord. ¹⁴And if a stranger is sojourning with you, or anyone is living per-

¹ Or *an offering by fire*; so throughout Numbers ² An *ephah* was about 3/5 bushel or 22 liters ³ A *hin* was about 4 quarts or 3.5 liters

manently among you, and he wishes to offer a food offering, with a pleasing aroma to the Lord, he shall do as you do. ¹⁵For the assembly, there shall be one statute for you and for the stranger who sojourns with you, a statute forever throughout your generations. You and the sojourner shall be alike before the Lord. ¹⁶One law and one rule shall be for you and for the stranger who sojourns with you."

¹⁷The Lord spoke to Moses, saying, ¹⁸"Speak to the people of Israel and say to them, When you come into the land to which I bring you ¹⁹and when you eat of the bread of the land, you shall present a contribution to the Lord. ²⁰Of the first of your dough you shall present a loaf as a contribution; like a contribution from the threshing floor, so shall you present it. ²¹Some of the first of your dough you shall give to the Lord as a contribution throughout your generations.

²²"But if you sin unintentionally,¹ and do not observe all these commandments that the Lord has spoken to Moses, ²³all that the Lord has commanded you by Moses, from the day that the Lord gave commandment, and onward throughout your generations, ²⁴then if it was done unintentionally without the knowledge of the congregation, all the congregation shall offer one bull from the herd for a burnt offering, a pleasing aroma to the Lord, with its grain offering and its drink offering, according to the rule, and one male goat for a sin offering. ²⁵And the priest shall make atonement for all the congregation of the people of Israel, and they shall be forgiven, because it was a mistake, and they have brought their offering, a food offering to the Lord, and their sin offering before the Lord for their mistake. ²⁶And all the congregation of the people of Israel shall be forgiven, and the stranger who sojourns among them, because the whole population was involved in the mistake.

²⁷"If one person sins unintentionally, he shall offer a female goat a year old for a sin offering. ²⁸And the priest shall make atonement before the Lord for the person who makes a mistake, when he sins unintentionally, to make atonement for him, and he shall be forgiven. ²⁹You shall have one law for him who does anything unintentionally, for him who is native among the people of Israel and for the stranger who sojourns among them. ³⁰But the person who does anything with a high hand, whether he is native or a sojourner, reviles the Lord, and that person shall be cut off from among his people. ³¹Because he has despised the word of the Lord and has broken his commandment, that person shall be utterly cut off; his iniquity shall be on him."

³²While the people of Israel were in the wilderness, they found a man gathering sticks on the Sabbath day. ³³And those who found him gathering sticks brought him to Moses and Aaron and to all the congregation. ³⁴They put him in custody, because it had not been made clear what should be done to him. ³⁵And the Lord said to Moses, "The man shall be put to death; all the congregation shall stone him with stones outside the camp." ³⁶And all the congregation brought him outside the camp and stoned him to death with stones, as the Lord commanded Moses.

³⁷The Lord said to Moses, ³⁸"Speak to the people of Israel, and tell them to make tassels on the corners of their garments throughout their generations, and to put a cord of blue on the tassel of each corner. ³⁹And it shall be a tassel for you to look at and remember all the commandments of the Lord, to do them, not to follow² after your own heart and your own eyes, which you are inclined to whore after. ⁴⁰So you shall remember and do all my commandments, and be holy to your God. ⁴¹I am the Lord your God, who brought you out of the land of Egypt to be your God: I am the Lord your God."

---

¹ Or by mistake; also verses 24, 27, 28, 29 ² Hebrew to spy out

Aaron's priesthood challenged and vindicated [chapters 16–17]. This episode is told in epic fullness, signaling its importance in the storyteller's scheme of things (the rule of proportionate space is that writers often show the relative importance of an event by the amount of space they give to it). The first thing to do is identify the plot conflicts and the cast of leading characters. Then we can analyze the principles involved in this conflict story—issues of leadership, jealousy, disrespect for legitimate authority, presumption, and divine judgment. Expansive epics organize themselves in our imaginations partly around vivid images and events. Examples in this story include these: the ground splits apart to swallow up the rebels and all that belonged to them; God's fire consumes 250 men who have offered unauthorized incense; Aaron and Moses run with incense into the congregation to stop the spread of the plague; Aaron's rod blossoms. These were God's means of teaching spiritual lessons in visual form, and according to 1 Corinthians 10:11, God sent them as a warning to the Israelites and as instruction to us.

16 Now Korah the son of Izhar, son of Kohath, son of Levi, and Dathan and Abiram the sons of Eliab, and On the son of Peleth, sons of Reuben, took men. ²And they rose up before Moses, with a number of the people of Israel, 250 chiefs of the congregation, chosen from the assembly, well-known men. ³They assembled themselves together against Moses and against Aaron and said to them, "You have gone too far! For all in the congregation are holy, every one of them, and the LORD is among them. Why then do you exalt yourselves above the assembly of the LORD?" ⁴When Moses heard it, he fell on his face, ⁵and he said to Korah and all his company, "In the morning the LORD will show who is his,¹ and who is holy, and will bring him near to him. The one whom he chooses he will bring near to him. ⁶Do this: take censers, Korah and all his company; ⁷put fire in them and put incense on them before the LORD tomorrow, and the man whom the LORD chooses shall be the holy one. You have gone too far, sons of Levi!" ⁸And Moses said to Korah, "Hear now, you sons of Levi: ⁹is it too small a thing for you that the God of Israel has separated you from the congregation of Israel, to bring you near to himself, to do service in the tabernacle of the LORD and to stand before the congregation to minister to them, ¹⁰and that he has brought you near him, and all your brothers the sons of Levi with you? And would you seek the priesthood also? ¹¹Therefore it is against the LORD that you and all your company have gathered together. What is Aaron that you grumble against him?"

¹²And Moses sent to call Dathan and Abiram the sons of Eliab, and they said, "We will not come up. ¹³Is it a small thing that you have brought us up out of a land flowing with milk and honey, to kill us in the wilderness, that you must also make yourself a prince over us? ¹⁴Moreover, you have not brought us into a land flowing with milk and honey, nor given us inheritance of fields and vineyards. Will you put out the eyes of these men? We will not come up." ¹⁵And Moses was very angry and said to the LORD, "Do not respect their offering. I have not taken one donkey from them, and I have not harmed one of them."

¹⁶And Moses said to Korah, "Be present, you and all your company, before the LORD, you and they, and Aaron, tomorrow. ¹⁷And let every one of you take his censer and put incense on it, and every one of you bring before the LORD his censer, 250 censers; you also, and Aaron, each his censer." ¹⁸So every man took his censer and

¹ Septuagint *The LORD knows those who are his*

put fire in them and laid incense on them and stood at the entrance of the tent of meeting with Moses and Aaron. ¹⁹Then Korah assembled all the congregation against them at the entrance of the tent of meeting. And the glory of the Lord appeared to all the congregation.

²⁰And the Lord spoke to Moses and to Aaron, saying, ²¹"Separate yourselves from among this congregation, that I may consume them in a moment." ²²And they fell on their faces and said, "O God, the God of the spirits of all flesh, shall one man sin, and will you be angry with all the congregation?" ²³And the Lord spoke to Moses, saying, ²⁴"Say to the congregation, Get away from the dwelling of Korah, Dathan, and Abiram."

²⁵Then Moses rose and went to Dathan and Abiram, and the elders of Israel followed him. ²⁶And he spoke to the congregation, saying, "Depart, please, from the tents of these wicked men, and touch nothing of theirs, lest you be swept away with all their sins." ²⁷So they got away from the dwelling of Korah, Dathan, and Abiram. And Dathan and Abiram came out and stood at the door of their tents, together with their wives, their sons, and their little ones. ²⁸And Moses said, "Hereby you shall know that the Lord has sent me to do all these works, and that it has not been of my own accord. ²⁹If these men die as all men die, or if they are visited by the fate of all mankind, then the Lord has not sent me. ³⁰But if the Lord creates something new, and the ground opens its mouth and swallows them up with all that belongs to them, and they go down alive into Sheol, then you shall know that these men have despised the Lord."

³¹And as soon as he had finished speaking all these words, the ground under them split apart. ³²And the earth opened its mouth and swallowed them up, with their households and all the people who belonged to Korah and all their goods. ³³So they and all that belonged to them went down alive into Sheol, and the earth closed over them, and they perished from the midst of the assembly. ³⁴And all Israel who were around them fled at their cry, for they said, "Lest the earth swallow us up!" ³⁵And fire came out from the Lord and consumed the 250 men offering the incense.

³⁶¹ Then the Lord spoke to Moses, saying, ³⁷"Tell Eleazar the son of Aaron the priest to take up the censers out of the blaze. Then scatter the fire far and wide, for they have become holy. ³⁸As for the censers of these men who have sinned at the cost of their lives, let them be made into hammered plates as a covering for the altar, for they offered them before the Lord, and they became holy. Thus they shall be a sign to the people of Israel." ³⁹So Eleazar the priest took the bronze censers, which those who were burned had offered, and they were hammered out as a covering for the altar, ⁴⁰to be a reminder to the people of Israel, so that no outsider, who is not of the descendants of Aaron, should draw near to burn incense before the Lord, lest he become like Korah and his company—as the Lord said to him through Moses.

⁴¹But on the next day all the congregation of the people of Israel grumbled against Moses and against Aaron, saying, "You have killed the people of the Lord." ⁴²And when the congregation had assembled against Moses and against Aaron, they turned toward the tent of meeting. And behold, the cloud covered it, and the glory of the Lord appeared. ⁴³And Moses and Aaron came to the front of the tent of meeting, ⁴⁴and the Lord spoke to Moses, saying, ⁴⁵"Get away from the midst of this congregation, that I may consume them in a moment." And they fell on their faces. ⁴⁶And Moses said to Aaron, "Take your censer, and put fire on it from off the altar and lay incense on it and carry it quickly to the congregation and make atonement for them,

---

¹ Ch 17:1 in Hebrew

for wrath has gone out from the LORD; the plague has begun." ⁴⁷So Aaron took it as Moses said and ran into the midst of the assembly. And behold, the plague had already begun among the people. And he put on the incense and made atonement for the people. ⁴⁸And he stood between the dead and the living, and the plague was stopped. ⁴⁹Now those who died in the plague were 14,700, besides those who died in the affair of Korah. ⁵⁰And Aaron returned to Moses at the entrance of the tent of meeting, when the plague was stopped.

17 ¹ The LORD spoke to Moses, saying, ²"Speak to the people of Israel, and get from them staffs, one for each fathers' house, from all their chiefs according to their fathers' houses, twelve staffs. Write each man's name on his staff, ³and write Aaron's name on the staff of Levi. For there shall be one staff for the head of each fathers' house. ⁴Then you shall deposit them in the tent of meeting before the testimony, where I meet with you. ⁵And the staff of the man whom I choose shall sprout. Thus I will make to cease from me the grumblings of the people of Israel, which they grumble against you." ⁶Moses spoke to the people of Israel. And all their chiefs gave him staffs, one for each chief, according to their fathers' houses, twelve staffs. And the staff of Aaron was among their staffs. ⁷And Moses deposited the staffs before the LORD in the tent of the testimony.

⁸On the next day Moses went into the tent of the testimony, and behold, the staff of Aaron for the house of Levi had sprouted and put forth buds and produced blossoms, and it bore ripe almonds. ⁹Then Moses brought out all the staffs from before the LORD to all the people of Israel. And they looked, and each man took his staff. ¹⁰And the LORD said to Moses, "Put back the staff of Aaron before the testimony, to be kept as a sign for the rebels, that you may make an end of their grumblings against me, lest they die." ¹¹Thus did Moses; as the LORD commanded him, so he did.

¹²And the people of Israel said to Moses, "Behold, we perish, we are undone, we are all undone. ¹³Everyone who comes near, who comes near to the tabernacle of the LORD, shall die. Are we all to perish?"

Law-giving interlude [chapters 18–19]. As in the previous law-giving interlude, the rhetorical form is the formula "the LORD spoke to Moses [or Aaron]." One obvious point in common between the narrative and instructional sections is the authority and sovereignty of God over the human race. Another theme that unifies the two is the motif of a covenant community that is required to do things in the manner that God prescribes. The necessity of obedience and the penalties of disobedience are yet another point of unity between the narrative and law-giving sections. The general topics covered in this interlude are laws governing priests and Levites (chapter 18) and rituals pertaining to purification of uncleanness (chapter 19). A good principle of interpretation for material like this is first to get the literal details straight and then ponder spiritual principles embodied in those details.

18 So the LORD said to Aaron, "You and your sons and your father's house with you shall bear iniquity connected with the sanctuary, and you and your sons with you shall bear iniquity connected with your priesthood. ²And with you bring your brothers also, the tribe of Levi, the tribe of your father, that they may join you and minister to you while you and your sons with you are before the tent of the testi-

¹ Ch 17:16 in Hebrew

mony. ³They shall keep guard over you and over the whole tent, but shall not come near to the vessels of the sanctuary or to the altar lest they, and you, die. ⁴They shall join you and keep guard over the tent of meeting for all the service of the tent, and no outsider shall come near you. ⁵And you shall keep guard over the sanctuary and over the altar, that there may never again be wrath on the people of Israel. ⁶And behold, I have taken your brothers the Levites from among the people of Israel. They are a gift to you, given to the Lᴏʀᴅ, to do the service of the tent of meeting. ⁷And you and your sons with you shall guard your priesthood for all that concerns the altar and that is within the veil; and you shall serve. I give your priesthood as a gift,¹ and any outsider who comes near shall be put to death."

⁸Then the Lᴏʀᴅ spoke to Aaron, "Behold, I have given you charge of the contributions made to me, all the consecrated things of the people of Israel. I have given them to you as a portion and to your sons as a perpetual due. ⁹This shall be yours of the most holy things, reserved from the fire: every offering of theirs, every grain offering of theirs and every sin offering of theirs and every guilt offering of theirs, which they render to me, shall be most holy to you and to your sons. ¹⁰In a most holy place shall you eat it. Every male may eat it; it is holy to you. ¹¹This also is yours: the contribution of their gift, all the wave offerings of the people of Israel. I have given them to you, and to your sons and daughters with you, as a perpetual due. Everyone who is clean in your house may eat it. ¹²All the best of the oil and all the best of the wine and of the grain, the firstfruits of what they give to the Lᴏʀᴅ, I give to you. ¹³The first ripe fruits of all that is in their land, which they bring to the Lᴏʀᴅ, shall be yours. Everyone who is clean in your house may eat it. ¹⁴Every devoted thing in Israel shall be yours. ¹⁵Everything that opens the womb of all flesh, whether man or beast, which they offer to the Lᴏʀᴅ, shall be yours. Nevertheless, the firstborn of man you shall redeem, and the firstborn of unclean animals you shall redeem. ¹⁶And their redemption price (at a month old you shall redeem them) you shall fix at five shekels² in silver, according to the shekel of the sanctuary, which is twenty gerahs. ¹⁷But the firstborn of a cow, or the firstborn of a sheep, or the firstborn of a goat, you shall not redeem; they are holy. You shall sprinkle their blood on the altar and shall burn their fat as a food offering, with a pleasing aroma to the Lᴏʀᴅ. ¹⁸But their flesh shall be yours, as the breast that is waved and as the right thigh are yours. ¹⁹All the holy contributions that the people of Israel present to the Lᴏʀᴅ I give to you, and to your sons and daughters with you, as a perpetual due. It is a covenant of salt forever before the Lᴏʀᴅ for you and for your offspring with you." ²⁰And the Lᴏʀᴅ said to Aaron, "You shall have no inheritance in their land, neither shall you have any portion among them. I am your portion and your inheritance among the people of Israel.

²¹"To the Levites I have given every tithe in Israel for an inheritance, in return for their service that they do, their service in the tent of meeting, ²²so that the people of Israel do not come near the tent of meeting, lest they bear sin and die. ²³But the Levites shall do the service of the tent of meeting, and they shall bear their iniquity. It shall be a perpetual statute throughout your generations, and among the people of Israel they shall have no inheritance. ²⁴For the tithe of the people of Israel, which they present as a contribution to the Lᴏʀᴅ, I have given to the Levites for an inheritance. Therefore I have said of them that they shall have no inheritance among the people of Israel."

²⁵And the Lᴏʀᴅ spoke to Moses, saying, ²⁶"Moreover, you shall speak and say to the

---

¹ Hebrew *service of gift* ² A *shekel* was about 2/5 ounce or 11 grams

Levites, 'When you take from the people of Israel the tithe that I have given you from them for your inheritance, then you shall present a contribution from it to the LORD, a tithe of the tithe. [27]And your contribution shall be counted to you as though it were the grain of the threshing floor, and as the fullness of the winepress. [28]So you shall also present a contribution to the LORD from all your tithes, which you receive from the people of Israel. And from it you shall give the LORD's contribution to Aaron the priest. [29]Out of all the gifts to you, you shall present every contribution due to the LORD; from each its best part is to be dedicated.' [30]Therefore you shall say to them, 'When you have offered from it the best of it, then the rest shall be counted to the Levites as produce of the threshing floor, and as produce of the winepress. [31]And you may eat it in any place, you and your households, for it is your reward in return for your service in the tent of meeting. [32]And you shall bear no sin by reason of it, when you have contributed the best of it. But you shall not profane the holy things of the people of Israel, lest you die.'"

19 Now the LORD spoke to Moses and to Aaron, saying, [2]"This is the statute of the law that the LORD has commanded: Tell the people of Israel to bring you a red heifer without defect, in which there is no blemish, and on which a yoke has never come. [3]And you shall give it to Eleazar the priest, and it shall be taken outside the camp and slaughtered before him. [4]And Eleazar the priest shall take some of its blood with his finger, and sprinkle some of its blood toward the front of the tent of meeting seven times. [5]And the heifer shall be burned in his sight. Its skin, its flesh, and its blood, with its dung, shall be burned. [6]And the priest shall take cedarwood and hyssop and scarlet yarn, and throw them into the fire burning the heifer. [7]Then the priest shall wash his clothes and bathe his body in water, and afterward he may come into the camp. But the priest shall be unclean until evening. [8]The one who burns the heifer shall wash his clothes in water and bathe his body in water and shall be unclean until evening. [9]And a man who is clean shall gather up the ashes of the heifer and deposit them outside the camp in a clean place. And they shall be kept for the water for impurity for the congregation of the people of Israel; it is a sin offering. [10]And the one who gathers the ashes of the heifer shall wash his clothes and be unclean until evening. And this shall be a perpetual statute for the people of Israel, and for the stranger who sojourns among them.

[11]"Whoever touches the dead body of any person shall be unclean seven days. [12]He shall cleanse himself with the water on the third day and on the seventh day, and so be clean. But if he does not cleanse himself on the third day and on the seventh day, he will not become clean. [13]Whoever touches a dead person, the body of anyone who has died, and does not cleanse himself, defiles the tabernacle of the LORD, and that person shall be cut off from Israel; because the water for impurity was not thrown on him, he shall be unclean. His uncleanness is still on him.

[14]"This is the law when someone dies in a tent: everyone who comes into the tent and everyone who is in the tent shall be unclean seven days. [15]And every open vessel that has no cover fastened on it is unclean. [16]Whoever in the open field touches someone who was killed with a sword or who died naturally, or touches a human bone or a grave, shall be unclean seven days. [17]For the unclean they shall take some ashes of the burnt sin offering, and fresh[1] water shall be added in a vessel. [18]Then a clean person shall take hyssop and dip it in the water and sprinkle it on the tent and

[1] Hebrew *living*

on all the furnishings and on the persons who were there and on whoever touched the bone, or the slain or the dead or the grave. ¹⁹And the clean person shall sprinkle it on the unclean on the third day and on the seventh day. Thus on the seventh day he shall cleanse him, and he shall wash his clothes and bathe himself in water, and at evening he shall be clean.

²⁰"If the man who is unclean does not cleanse himself, that person shall be cut off from the midst of the assembly, since he has defiled the sanctuary of the LORD. Because the water for impurity has not been thrown on him, he is unclean. ²¹And it shall be a statute forever for them. The one who sprinkles the water for impurity shall wash his clothes, and the one who touches the water for impurity shall be unclean until evening. ²²And whatever the unclean person touches shall be unclean, and anyone who touches it shall be unclean until evening."

Experiences of a nation on the march [chapters 20–21]. The narrative section that ensues is a minicollection of travel stories. The events mingle personal stories (the death of Miriam, the tragic failure of Moses when he strikes the rock, and the death of Aaron), stories of the murmuring and rebellion of the people (the bitter waters at Meribah, the plague of fiery serpents), and encounters and battles with other nations. With individual stories, the usual narrative questions provide the appropriate grid: What are the plot conflicts, and how are they resolved? How does the heroic leader figure into the action? What role does the setting play in the events that occur? What do we know about the characters, and what is the storyteller saying about life by means of them? In regard to characterization, the incident of Moses' striking the rock (20:10–13) is the tragic turning point of his life and needs to be explored for its latent but unexplained meanings.

20 And the people of Israel, the whole congregation, came into the wilderness of Zin in the first month, and the people stayed in Kadesh. And Miriam died there and was buried there.

²Now there was no water for the congregation. And they assembled themselves together against Moses and against Aaron. ³And the people quarreled with Moses and said, "Would that we had perished when our brothers perished before the LORD! ⁴Why have you brought the assembly of the LORD into this wilderness, that we should die here, both we and our cattle? ⁵And why have you made us come up out of Egypt to bring us to this evil place? It is no place for grain or figs or vines or pomegranates, and there is no water to drink." ⁶Then Moses and Aaron went from the presence of the assembly to the entrance of the tent of meeting and fell on their faces. And the glory of the LORD appeared to them, ⁷and the LORD spoke to Moses, saying, ⁸"Take the staff, and assemble the congregation, you and Aaron your brother, and tell the rock before their eyes to yield its water. So you shall bring water out of the rock for them and give drink to the congregation and their cattle." ⁹And Moses took the staff from before the LORD, as he commanded him.

¹⁰Then Moses and Aaron gathered the assembly together before the rock, and he said to them, "Hear now, you rebels: shall we bring water for you out of this rock?" ¹¹And Moses lifted up his hand and struck the rock with his staff twice, and water came out abundantly, and the congregation drank, and their livestock. ¹²And the LORD said to Moses and Aaron, "Because you did not believe in me, to uphold me as holy in the eyes of the people of Israel, therefore you shall not bring this assembly

into the land that I have given them." ¹³These are the waters of Meribah,¹ where the people of Israel quarreled with the LORD, and through them he showed himself holy.

¹⁴Moses sent messengers from Kadesh to the king of Edom: "Thus says your brother Israel: You know all the hardship that we have met: ¹⁵how our fathers went down to Egypt, and we lived in Egypt a long time. And the Egyptians dealt harshly with us and our fathers. ¹⁶And when we cried to the LORD, he heard our voice and sent an angel and brought us out of Egypt. And here we are in Kadesh, a city on the edge of your territory. ¹⁷Please let us pass through your land. We will not pass through field or vineyard, or drink water from a well. We will go along the King's Highway. We will not turn aside to the right hand or to the left until we have passed through your territory." ¹⁸But Edom said to him, "You shall not pass through, lest I come out with the sword against you." ¹⁹And the people of Israel said to him, "We will go up by the highway, and if we drink of your water, I and my livestock, then I will pay for it. Let me only pass through on foot, nothing more." ²⁰But he said, "You shall not pass through." And Edom came out against them with a large army and with a strong force. ²¹Thus Edom refused to give Israel passage through his territory, so Israel turned away from him.

²²And they journeyed from Kadesh, and the people of Israel, the whole congregation, came to Mount Hor. ²³And the LORD said to Moses and Aaron at Mount Hor, on the border of the land of Edom, ²⁴"Let Aaron be gathered to his people, for he shall not enter the land that I have given to the people of Israel, because you rebelled against my command at the waters of Meribah. ²⁵Take Aaron and Eleazar his son and bring them up to Mount Hor. ²⁶And strip Aaron of his garments and put them on Eleazar his son. And Aaron shall be gathered to his people and shall die there." ²⁷Moses did as the LORD commanded. And they went up Mount Hor in the sight of all the congregation. ²⁸And Moses stripped Aaron of his garments and put them on Eleazar his son. And Aaron died there on the top of the mountain. Then Moses and Eleazar came down from the mountain. ²⁹And when all the congregation saw that Aaron had perished, all the house of Israel wept for Aaron thirty days.

21 When the Canaanite, the king of Arad, who lived in the Negeb, heard that Israel was coming by the way of Atharim, he fought against Israel, and took some of them captive. ²And Israel vowed a vow to the LORD and said, "If you will indeed give this people into my hand, then I will devote their cities to destruction."² ³And the LORD heeded the voice of Israel and gave over the Canaanites, and they devoted them and their cities to destruction. So the name of the place was called Hormah.³

⁴From Mount Hor they set out by the way to the Red Sea, to go around the land of Edom. And the people became impatient on the way. ⁵And the people spoke against God and against Moses, "Why have you brought us up out of Egypt to die in the wilderness? For there is no food and no water, and we loathe this worthless food." ⁶Then the LORD sent fiery serpents among the people, and they bit the people, so that many people of Israel died. ⁷And the people came to Moses and said, "We have sinned, for we have spoken against the LORD and against you. Pray to the LORD, that he take away the serpents from us." So Moses prayed for the people. ⁸And the LORD said to Moses, "Make a fiery serpent and set it on a pole, and everyone who is bitten, when he sees it,

¹ *Meribah* means *quarreling* ² That is, set apart (devote) as an offering to the Lord (for destruction); also verse 3 ³ *Hormah* means *destruction*

shall live." ⁹So Moses made a bronze¹ serpent and set it on a pole. And if a serpent bit anyone, he would look at the bronze serpent and live.

¹⁰And the people of Israel set out and camped in Oboth. ¹¹And they set out from Oboth and camped at Iye-abarim, in the wilderness that is opposite Moab, toward the sunrise. ¹²From there they set out and camped in the Valley of Zered. ¹³From there they set out and camped on the other side of the Arnon, which is in the wilderness that extends from the border of the Amorites, for the Arnon is the border of Moab, between Moab and the Amorites. ¹⁴Therefore it is said in the Book of the Wars of the LORD,

> "Waheb in Suphah, and the valleys of the Arnon,
> ¹⁵ and the slope of the valleys
> that extends to the seat of Ar,
> and leans to the border of Moab."

¹⁶And from there they continued to Beer;² that is the well of which the LORD said to Moses, "Gather the people together, so that I may give them water." ¹⁷Then Israel sang this song:

> "Spring up, O well!—Sing to it!—
> ¹⁸ the well that the princes made,
> that the nobles of the people dug,
> with the scepter and with their staffs."

And from the wilderness they went on to Mattanah, ¹⁹and from Mattanah to Nahaliel, and from Nahaliel to Bamoth, ²⁰and from Bamoth to the valley lying in the region of Moab by the top of Pisgah that looks down on the desert.³

²¹Then Israel sent messengers to Sihon king of the Amorites, saying, ²²"Let me pass through your land. We will not turn aside into field or vineyard. We will not drink the water of a well. We will go by the King's Highway until we have passed through your territory." ²³But Sihon would not allow Israel to pass through his territory. He gathered all his people together and went out against Israel to the wilderness and came to Jahaz and fought against Israel. ²⁴And Israel defeated him with the edge of the sword and took possession of his land from the Arnon to the Jabbok, as far as to the Ammonites, for the border of the Ammonites was strong. ²⁵And Israel took all these cities, and Israel settled in all the cities of the Amorites, in Heshbon, and in all its villages. ²⁶For Heshbon was the city of Sihon the king of the Amorites, who had fought against the former king of Moab and taken all his land out of his hand, as far as the Arnon. ²⁷Therefore the ballad singers say,

> "Come to Heshbon, let it be built;
> let the city of Sihon be established.
> ²⁸ For fire came out from Heshbon,
> flame from the city of Sihon.
> It devoured Ar of Moab,
> and swallowed⁴ the heights of the Arnon.
> ²⁹ Woe to you, O Moab!
> You are undone, O people of Chemosh!
> He has made his sons fugitives,
> and his daughters captives,

¹Or copper ²Beer means well ³Or Jeshimon ⁴Septuagint; Hebrew the lords of

to an Amorite king, Sihon.
30 So we overthrew them;
    Heshbon, as far as Dibon, perished;
    and we laid waste as far as Nophah;
    fire spread as far as Medeba."[1]

[31]Thus Israel lived in the land of the Amorites. [32]And Moses sent to spy out Jazer, and they captured its villages and dispossessed the Amorites who were there. [33]Then they turned and went up by the way to Bashan. And Og the king of Bashan came out against them, he and all his people, to battle at Edrei. [34]But the Lord said to Moses, "Do not fear him, for I have given him into your hand, and all his people, and his land. And you shall do to him as you did to Sihon king of the Amorites, who lived at Heshbon." [35]So they defeated him and his sons and all his people, until he had no survivor left. And they possessed his land.

A prophet of God who degenerates into a hireling [chapter 22]. Three chapters narrate the prophetic career of Balaam in leisurely detail. The opening chapter provides the narrative backdrop to the prophecies that Balaam eventually pronounces. The narrative is rich in its portrayal of universal human experience, and it focuses on the contamination of an apparently good person through the desire for financial gain. The prologue to the eventual prophecies unfolds as a five-phase narrative. First we are alerted that the improbable story of prophecy that will ensue arises from an evil motivation, as the fearful Moabite king Balak desires to see God's people cursed (vv. 1–6). Second, Balaam's initial inquiry of God and rejection of Balak's overture seem to be exemplary but actually constitute an ironic false hope that is raised only to be dashed (vv. 7–14). Third, when Balak renews his request to Balaam, the prophet's weak will surfaces, as we learn that he secretly wants to perform the curse (vv. 15–20). Fourth, if we are surprised by God's granting of permission to Balaam to undertake his quest, we are quickly reassured by the extended narrative of Balaam's encounter with the angel of the Lord with a drawn sword in the middle of the path, accompanied by the famous incident of the donkey that talked (vv. 21–35), an event that elicits Balaam's temporary repentance (v. 34). Finally, Balaam arrives at the court of Balak, ready for prophetic action (vv. 36–40). By this point the story has become a classic suspense story, as we have been led to wonder what will happen.

22 Then the people of Israel set out and camped in the plains of Moab beyond the Jordan at Jericho. [2]And Balak the son of Zippor saw all that Israel had done to the Amorites. [3]And Moab was in great dread of the people, because they were many. Moab was overcome with fear of the people of Israel. [4]And Moab said to the elders of Midian, "This horde will now lick up all that is around us, as the ox licks up the grass of the field." So Balak the son of Zippor, who was king of Moab at that time, [5]sent messengers to Balaam the son of Beor at Pethor, which is near the River in the land of the people of Amaw,[2] to call him, saying, "Behold, a people has come out of Egypt. They cover the face of the earth, and they are dwelling opposite me. [6]Come now, curse this people for me, since they are too mighty for me. Perhaps I shall be able to defeat them and drive them from the land, for I know that he whom you bless is blessed, and he whom you curse is cursed."

[1] Compare Samaritan and Septuagint; Hebrew *and we laid waste as far as Nophah, which is as far as Medeba* [2] Or *his kindred*

⁷So the elders of Moab and the elders of Midian departed with the fees for divination in their hand. And they came to Balaam and gave him Balak's message. ⁸And he said to them, "Lodge here tonight, and I will bring back word to you, as the Lord speaks to me." So the princes of Moab stayed with Balaam. ⁹And God came to Balaam and said, "Who are these men with you?" ¹⁰And Balaam said to God, "Balak the son of Zippor, king of Moab, has sent to me, saying, ¹¹'Behold, a people has come out of Egypt, and it covers the face of the earth. Now come, curse them for me. Perhaps I shall be able to fight against them and drive them out.'" ¹²God said to Balaam, "You shall not go with them. You shall not curse the people, for they are blessed." ¹³So Balaam rose in the morning and said to the princes of Balak, "Go to your own land, for the Lord has refused to let me go with you." ¹⁴So the princes of Moab rose and went to Balak and said, "Balaam refuses to come with us."

¹⁵Once again Balak sent princes, more in number and more honorable than these. ¹⁶And they came to Balaam and said to him, "Thus says Balak the son of Zippor: 'Let nothing hinder you from coming to me, ¹⁷for I will surely do you great honor, and whatever you say to me I will do. Come, curse this people for me.'" ¹⁸But Balaam answered and said to the servants of Balak, "Though Balak were to give me his house full of silver and gold, I could not go beyond the command of the Lord my God to do less or more. ¹⁹So you, too, please stay here tonight, that I may know what more the Lord will say to me." ²⁰And God came to Balaam at night and said to him, "If the men have come to call you, rise, go with them; but only do what I tell you." ²¹So Balaam rose in the morning and saddled his donkey and went with the princes of Moab.

²²But God's anger was kindled because he went, and the angel of the Lord took his stand in the way as his adversary. Now he was riding on the donkey, and his two servants were with him. ²³And the donkey saw the angel of the Lord standing in the road, with a drawn sword in his hand. And the donkey turned aside out of the road and went into the field. And Balaam struck the donkey, to turn her into the road. ²⁴Then the angel of the Lord stood in a narrow path between the vineyards, with a wall on either side. ²⁵And when the donkey saw the angel of the Lord, she pushed against the wall and pressed Balaam's foot against the wall. So he struck her again. ²⁶Then the angel of the Lord went ahead and stood in a narrow place, where there was no way to turn either to the right or to the left. ²⁷When the donkey saw the angel of the Lord, she lay down under Balaam. And Balaam's anger was kindled, and he struck the donkey with his staff. ²⁸Then the Lord opened the mouth of the donkey, and she said to Balaam, "What have I done to you, that you have struck me these three times?" ²⁹And Balaam said to the donkey, "Because you have made a fool of me. I wish I had a sword in my hand, for then I would kill you." ³⁰And the donkey said to Balaam, "Am I not your donkey, on which you have ridden all your life long to this day? Is it my habit to treat you this way?" And he said, "No."

³¹Then the Lord opened the eyes of Balaam, and he saw the angel of the Lord standing in the way, with his drawn sword in his hand. And he bowed down and fell on his face. ³²And the angel of the Lord said to him, "Why have you struck your donkey these three times? Behold, I have come out to oppose you because your way is perverse¹ before me. ³³The donkey saw me and turned aside before me these three times. If she had not turned aside from me, surely just now I would have killed you and let her live." ³⁴Then Balaam said to the angel of the Lord, "I have sinned, for I did not know that you stood in the road against me. Now therefore, if it is evil in your

¹ Or reckless

sight, I will turn back." ³⁵And the angel of the LORD said to Balaam, "Go with the men, but speak only the word that I tell you." So Balaam went on with the princes of Balak.

³⁶When Balak heard that Balaam had come, he went out to meet him at the city of Moab, on the border formed by the Arnon, at the extremity of the border. ³⁷And Balak said to Balaam, "Did I not send to you to call you? Why did you not come to me? Am I not able to honor you?" ³⁸Balaam said to Balak, "Behold, I have come to you! Have I now any power of my own to speak anything? The word that God puts in my mouth, that must I speak." ³⁹Then Balaam went with Balak, and they came to Kiriath-huzoth. ⁴⁰And Balak sacrificed oxen and sheep, and sent for Balaam and for the princes who were with him.

⁴¹And in the morning Balak took Balaam and brought him up to Bamoth-baal, and from there he saw a fraction of the people.

Balaam's prophecies [chapters 23–24]. Two time-honored plot motifs are the dominant patterns. One is *poetic justice (virtue rewarded, vice punished or thwarted). Two ignominious experiments are thwarted—Balak's desire to see the Israelites cursed and Balaam's implied desire to land a prophesying gig that would yield honor and a handsome payment. The concluding verse of the section is a satiric jab at the failed experiment: "Then Balaam rose and went back to his place. And Balak also went his way," 24:25). The plot also rests on *reversal, a narrative situation in which an action produces the opposite of the effect intended: Balak and Balaam think that the prophet will utter a curse, and each time he announces an extravagant blessing. The three prophecies belong to the genre known as the *oracle of blessing, and they are couched in highly poetic form, a very touchstone of eloquence. The third oracle contains a famous messianic prophecy (24:17). The role of the interlude in which Balaam blesses Israel is to serve as a *foil to the negative picture of the Israelites that emerges from the narrative as a whole. The episode also has the mocking flavor that we associate with slave literature—literature that mocks a power figure who seeks to oppress the author's nation or group.

23 And Balaam said to Balak, "Build for me here seven altars, and prepare for me here seven bulls and seven rams." ²Balak did as Balaam had said. And Balak and Balaam offered on each altar a bull and a ram. ³And Balaam said to Balak, "Stand beside your burnt offering, and I will go. Perhaps the LORD will come to meet me, and whatever he shows me I will tell you." And he went to a bare height, ⁴and God met Balaam. And Balaam said to him, "I have arranged the seven altars and I have offered on each altar a bull and a ram." ⁵And the LORD put a word in Balaam's mouth and said, "Return to Balak, and thus you shall speak." ⁶And he returned to him, and behold, he and all the princes of Moab were standing beside his burnt offering. ⁷And Balaam took up his discourse and said,

"From Aram Balak has brought me,
    the king of Moab from the eastern mountains:
'Come, curse Jacob for me,
    and come, denounce Israel!'
⁸ How can I curse whom God has not cursed?
    How can I denounce whom the LORD has not denounced?

⁹   For from the top of the crags I see him,
         from the hills I behold him;
      behold, a people dwelling alone,
         and not counting itself among the nations!
¹⁰ Who can count the dust of Jacob
         or number the fourth part[1] of Israel?
      Let me die the death of the upright,
         and let my end be like his!"

¹¹And Balak said to Balaam, "What have you done to me? I took you to curse my enemies, and behold, you have done nothing but bless them." ¹²And he answered and said, "Must I not take care to speak what the LORD puts in my mouth?"

¹³And Balak said to him, "Please come with me to another place, from which you may see them. You shall see only a fraction of them and shall not see them all. Then curse them for me from there." ¹⁴And he took him to the field of Zophim, to the top of Pisgah, and built seven altars and offered a bull and a ram on each altar. ¹⁵Balaam said to Balak, "Stand here beside your burnt offering, while I meet the LORD over there." ¹⁶And the LORD met Balaam and put a word in his mouth and said, "Return to Balak, and thus shall you speak." ¹⁷And he came to him, and behold, he was standing beside his burnt offering, and the princes of Moab with him. And Balak said to him, "What has the LORD spoken?" ¹⁸And Balaam took up his discourse and said,

      "Rise, Balak, and hear;
         give ear to me, O son of Zippor:
¹⁹ God is not man, that he should lie,
         or a son of man, that he should change his mind.
      Has he said, and will he not do it?
         Or has he spoken, and will he not fulfill it?
²⁰ Behold, I received a command to bless:
         he has blessed, and I cannot revoke it.
²¹ He has not beheld misfortune in Jacob,
         nor has he seen trouble in Israel.
      The LORD their God is with them,
         and the shout of a king is among them.
²² God brings them out of Egypt
         and is for them like the horns of the wild ox.
²³ For there is no enchantment against Jacob,
         no divination against Israel;
      now it shall be said of Jacob and Israel,
         'What has God wrought!'
²⁴ Behold, a people! As a lioness it rises up
         and as a lion it lifts itself;
      it does not lie down until it has devoured the prey
         and drunk the blood of the slain."

²⁵And Balak said to Balaam, "Do not curse them at all, and do not bless them at all." ²⁶But Balaam answered Balak, "Did I not tell you, 'All that the LORD says, that I must do'?" ²⁷And Balak said to Balaam, "Come now, I will take you to another place. Perhaps

---

[1] Or dust clouds

it will please God that you may curse them for me from there." ²⁸So Balak took Balaam to the top of Peor, which overlooks the desert.¹ ²⁹And Balaam said to Balak, "Build for me here seven altars and prepare for me here seven bulls and seven rams." ³⁰And Balak did as Balaam had said, and offered a bull and a ram on each altar.

24 When Balaam saw that it pleased the Lord to bless Israel, he did not go, as at other times, to look for omens, but set his face toward the wilderness. ²And Balaam lifted up his eyes and saw Israel camping tribe by tribe. And the Spirit of God came upon him, ³and he took up his discourse and said,

"The oracle of Balaam the son of Beor,
    the oracle of the man whose eye is opened,²
⁴   the oracle of him who hears the words of God,
        who sees the vision of the Almighty,
        falling down with his eyes uncovered:
⁵   How lovely are your tents, O Jacob,
        your encampments, O Israel!
⁶   Like palm groves³ that stretch afar,
        like gardens beside a river,
    like aloes that the Lord has planted,
        like cedar trees beside the waters.
⁷   Water shall flow from his buckets,
        and his seed shall be in many waters;
    his king shall be higher than Agag,
        and his kingdom shall be exalted.
⁸   God brings him out of Egypt
        and is for him like the horns of the wild ox;
    he shall eat up the nations, his adversaries,
        and shall break their bones in pieces
        and pierce them through with his arrows.
⁹   He crouched, he lay down like a lion
        and like a lioness; who will rouse him up?
    Blessed are those who bless you,
        and cursed are those who curse you."

¹⁰And Balak's anger was kindled against Balaam, and he struck his hands together. And Balak said to Balaam, "I called you to curse my enemies, and behold, you have blessed them these three times. ¹¹Therefore now flee to your own place. I said, 'I will certainly honor you,' but the Lord has held you back from honor." ¹²And Balaam said to Balak, "Did I not tell your messengers whom you sent to me, ¹³'If Balak should give me his house full of silver and gold, I would not be able to go beyond the word of the Lord, to do either good or bad of my own will. What the Lord speaks, that will I speak'? ¹⁴And now, behold, I am going to my people. Come, I will let you know what this people will do to your people in the latter days."

¹⁵And he took up his discourse and said,

"The oracle of Balaam the son of Beor,
    the oracle of the man whose eye is opened,

¹ Or Jeshimon ² Or closed, or perfect; also verse 15 ³ Or valleys

¹⁶   the oracle of him who hears the words of God,
  and knows the knowledge of the Most High,
 who sees the vision of the Almighty,
  falling down with his eyes uncovered:
¹⁷   I see him, but not now;
  I behold him, but not near:
 a star shall come out of Jacob,
  and a scepter shall rise out of Israel;
 it shall crush the forehead¹ of Moab
  and break down all the sons of Sheth.
¹⁸   Edom shall be dispossessed;
  Seir also, his enemies, shall be dispossessed.
 Israel is doing valiantly.
¹⁹   And one from Jacob shall exercise dominion
  and destroy the survivors of cities!"

²⁰Then he looked on Amalek and took up his discourse and said,

"Amalek was the first among the nations,
 but its end is utter destruction."

²¹And he looked on the Kenite, and took up his discourse and said,

"Enduring is your dwelling place,
 and your nest is set in the rock.
²²   Nevertheless, Kain shall be burned
 when Asshur takes you away captive."

²³And he took up his discourse and said,

"Alas, who shall live when God does this?
²⁴ But ships shall come from Kittim
 and shall afflict Asshur and Eber;
  and he too shall come to utter destruction."

²⁵Then Balaam rose and went back to his place. And Balak also went his way.

Bowing to Baal, a spear in the stomach, and harassing the Midianites [chapter 25].
Whereas the Israelites' encounters with the countries or tribes through whose region they
travel usually produce conflict stories, chapter 25 begins with the opposite in the form
of an equally threatening accommodation to the Midianites. This excursion into idolatry
develops into a series of combat scenes, shocking to modern sensibilities but pleasing
to God. Since the biblical writers always presuppose that God is the norm of perfection,
a good interpretive strategy whenever we have doubts about God in the stories of the
Bible is to accept the writers' presuppositions of a good God and discover the logic of
God's actions and commands. In the present instance, the mainspring of what happens
is God's insistence that his chosen people be pure in their devotion to him instead of
worshiping idols.

---

¹ Hebrew *corners* [of the head]

25 While Israel lived in Shittim, the people began to whore with the daughters of Moab. ²These invited the people to the sacrifices of their gods, and the people ate and bowed down to their gods. ³So Israel yoked himself to Baal of Peor. And the anger of the LORD was kindled against Israel. ⁴And the LORD said to Moses, "Take all the chiefs of the people and hang¹ them in the sun before the LORD, that the fierce anger of the LORD may turn away from Israel." ⁵And Moses said to the judges of Israel, "Each of you kill those of his men who have yoked themselves to Baal of Peor."

⁶And behold, one of the people of Israel came and brought a Midianite woman to his family, in the sight of Moses and in the sight of the whole congregation of the people of Israel, while they were weeping in the entrance of the tent of meeting. ⁷When Phinehas the son of Eleazar, son of Aaron the priest, saw it, he rose and left the congregation and took a spear in his hand ⁸and went after the man of Israel into the chamber and pierced both of them, the man of Israel and the woman through her belly. Thus the plague on the people of Israel was stopped. ⁹Nevertheless, those who died by the plague were twenty-four thousand.

¹⁰And the LORD said to Moses, ¹¹"Phinehas the son of Eleazar, son of Aaron the priest, has turned back my wrath from the people of Israel, in that he was jealous with my jealousy among them, so that I did not consume the people of Israel in my jealousy. ¹²Therefore say, 'Behold, I give to him my covenant of peace, ¹³and it shall be to him and to his descendants after him the covenant of a perpetual priesthood, because he was jealous for his God and made atonement for the people of Israel.'"

¹⁴The name of the slain man of Israel, who was killed with the Midianite woman, was Zimri the son of Salu, chief of a father's house belonging to the Simeonites. ¹⁵And the name of the Midianite woman who was killed was Cozbi the daughter of Zur, who was the tribal head of a father's house in Midian.

¹⁶And the LORD spoke to Moses, saying, ¹⁷"Harass the Midianites and strike them down, ¹⁸for they have harassed you with their wiles, with which they beguiled you in the matter of Peor, and in the matter of Cozbi, the daughter of the chief of Midian, their sister, who was killed on the day of the plague on account of Peor."

Census figures [chapter 26]. After some sensational narrative material, the book now swings back to a section of civic records and religious regulations. Chapter 26, along with the first two chapters of Numbers, gives the book its name. We can account for the presence of a census list only by accepting the premise on which the book is based, that it is both a narrative and a book of records and laws. The conclusion of the list (vv. 63–65) gives an important interpretive slant to the census: in a story in which the older generation has ignominiously forfeited its opportunity to enter the Promised Land, the new census is a tabulation of the generation of promise.

---

26 After the plague, the LORD said to Moses and to Eleazar the son of Aaron, the priest, ²"Take a census of all the congregation of the people of Israel, from twenty years old and upward, by their fathers' houses, all in Israel who are able to go to war." ³And Moses and Eleazar the priest spoke with them in the plains of Moab by the Jordan at Jericho, saying, ⁴"Take a census of the people,² from twenty

---

¹ Or impale ² Take a census of the people is implied (compare verse 2)

years old and upward," as the Lord commanded Moses. The people of Israel who came out of the land of Egypt were:

⁵Reuben, the firstborn of Israel; the sons of Reuben: of Hanoch, the clan of the Hanochites; of Pallu, the clan of the Palluites; ⁶of Hezron, the clan of the Hezronites; of Carmi, the clan of the Carmites. ⁷These are the clans of the Reubenites, and those listed were 43,730. ⁸And the sons of Pallu: Eliab. ⁹The sons of Eliab: Nemuel, Dathan, and Abiram. These are the Dathan and Abiram, chosen from the congregation, who contended against Moses and Aaron in the company of Korah, when they contended against the Lord ¹⁰and the earth opened its mouth and swallowed them up together with Korah, when that company died, when the fire devoured 250 men, and they became a warning. ¹¹But the sons of Korah did not die.

¹²The sons of Simeon according to their clans: of Nemuel, the clan of the Nemuelites; of Jamin, the clan of the Jaminites; of Jachin, the clan of the Jachinites; ¹³of Zerah, the clan of the Zerahites; of Shaul, the clan of the Shaulites. ¹⁴These are the clans of the Simeonites, 22,200.

¹⁵The sons of Gad according to their clans: of Zephon, the clan of the Zephonites; of Haggi, the clan of the Haggites; of Shuni, the clan of the Shunites; ¹⁶of Ozni, the clan of the Oznites; of Eri, the clan of the Erites; ¹⁷of Arod, the clan of the Arodites; of Areli, the clan of the Arelites. ¹⁸These are the clans of the sons of Gad as they were listed, 40,500.

¹⁹The sons of Judah were Er and Onan; and Er and Onan died in the land of Canaan. ²⁰And the sons of Judah according to their clans were: of Shelah, the clan of the Shelanites; of Perez, the clan of the Perezites; of Zerah, the clan of the Zerahites. ²¹And the sons of Perez were: of Hezron, the clan of the Hezronites; of Hamul, the clan of the Hamulites. ²²These are the clans of Judah as they were listed, 76,500.

²³The sons of Issachar according to their clans: of Tola, the clan of the Tolaites; of Puvah, the clan of the Punites; ²⁴of Jashub, the clan of the Jashubites; of Shimron, the clan of the Shimronites. ²⁵These are the clans of Issachar as they were listed, 64,300.

²⁶The sons of Zebulun, according to their clans: of Sered, the clan of the Seredites; of Elon, the clan of the Elonites; of Jahleel, the clan of the Jahleelites. ²⁷These are the clans of the Zebulunites as they were listed, 60,500.

²⁸The sons of Joseph according to their clans: Manasseh and Ephraim. ²⁹The sons of Manasseh: of Machir, the clan of the Machirites; and Machir was the father of Gilead; of Gilead, the clan of the Gileadites. ³⁰These are the sons of Gilead: of Iezer, the clan of the Iezerites; of Helek, the clan of the Helekites; ³¹and of Asriel, the clan of the Asrielites; and of Shechem, the clan of the Shechemites; ³²and of Shemida, the clan of the Shemidaites; and of Hepher, the clan of the Hepherites. ³³Now Zelophehad the son of Hepher had no sons, but daughters. And the names of the daughters of Zelophehad were Mahlah, Noah, Hoglah, Milcah, and Tirzah. ³⁴These are the clans of Manasseh, and those listed were 52,700.

³⁵These are the sons of Ephraim according to their clans: of Shuthelah, the clan of the Shuthelahites; of Becher, the clan of the Becherites; of Tahan, the clan of the Tahanites. ³⁶And these are the sons of Shuthelah: of Eran, the clan of the Eranites. ³⁷These are the clans of the sons of Ephraim as they were listed, 32,500. These are the sons of Joseph according to their clans.

³⁸The sons of Benjamin according to their clans: of Bela, the clan of the Belaites; of Ashbel, the clan of the Ashbelites; of Ahiram, the clan of the Ahiramites; ³⁹of

Shephupham, the clan of the Shuphamites; of Hupham, the clan of the Huphamites. ⁴⁰And the sons of Bela were Ard and Naaman: of Ard, the clan of the Ardites; of Naaman, the clan of the Naamites. ⁴¹These are the sons of Benjamin according to their clans, and those listed were 45,600.

⁴²These are the sons of Dan according to their clans: of Shuham, the clan of the Shuhamites. These are the clans of Dan according to their clans. ⁴³All the clans of the Shuhamites, as they were listed, were 64,400.

⁴⁴The sons of Asher according to their clans: of Imnah, the clan of the Imnites; of Ishvi, the clan of the Ishvites; of Beriah, the clan of the Beriites. ⁴⁵Of the sons of Beriah: of Heber, the clan of the Heberites; of Malchiel, the clan of the Malchielites. ⁴⁶And the name of the daughter of Asher was Serah. ⁴⁷These are the clans of the sons of Asher as they were listed, 53,400.

⁴⁸The sons of Naphtali according to their clans: of Jahzeel, the clan of the Jahzeelites; of Guni, the clan of the Gunites; ⁴⁹of Jezer, the clan of the Jezerites; of Shillem, the clan of the Shillemites. ⁵⁰These are the clans of Naphtali according to their clans, and those listed were 45,400.

⁵¹This was the list of the people of Israel, 601,730.

⁵²The LORD spoke to Moses, saying, ⁵³"Among these the land shall be divided for inheritance according to the number of names. ⁵⁴To a large tribe you shall give a large inheritance, and to a small tribe you shall give a small inheritance; every tribe shall be given its inheritance in proportion to its list. ⁵⁵But the land shall be divided by lot. According to the names of the tribes of their fathers they shall inherit. ⁵⁶Their inheritance shall be divided according to lot between the larger and the smaller."

⁵⁷This was the list of the Levites according to their clans: of Gershon, the clan of the Gershonites; of Kohath, the clan of the Kohathites; of Merari, the clan of the Merarites. ⁵⁸These are the clans of Levi: the clan of the Libnites, the clan of the Hebronites, the clan of the Mahlites, the clan of the Mushites, the clan of the Korahites. And Kohath was the father of Amram. ⁵⁹The name of Amram's wife was Jochebed the daughter of Levi, who was born to Levi in Egypt. And she bore to Amram Aaron and Moses and Miriam their sister. ⁶⁰And to Aaron were born Nadab, Abihu, Eleazar, and Ithamar. ⁶¹But Nadab and Abihu died when they offered unauthorized fire before the LORD. ⁶²And those listed were 23,000, every male from a month old and upward. For they were not listed among the people of Israel, because there was no inheritance given to them among the people of Israel.

⁶³These were those listed by Moses and Eleazar the priest, who listed the people of Israel in the plains of Moab by the Jordan at Jericho. ⁶⁴But among these there was not one of those listed by Moses and Aaron the priest, who had listed the people of Israel in the wilderness of Sinai. ⁶⁵For the LORD had said of them, "They shall die in the wilderness." Not one of them was left, except Caleb the son of Jephunneh and Joshua the son of Nun.

A question of inheritance and an announced succession [chapter 27]. The common thread in the two units that make up chapter 27 is that both events involve passing something on from one generation to the next. In a story in which a new nation is partly feeling its way, the law governing the passing on of an inheritance to the daughters of a family where there is no male heir (vv. 5–11) is occasioned by a real-life situation

(vv. 1–4). The next incident, God's announcement of Moses' death and his appointment of Joshua as Moses' successor, has far-reaching implications for the future history of Israel. It is couched in overtones of the numinous and serves the narrative function of foreshadowing.

27 Then drew near the daughters of Zelophehad the son of Hepher, son of Gilead, son of Machir, son of Manasseh, from the clans of Manasseh the son of Joseph. The names of his daughters were: Mahlah, Noah, Hoglah, Milcah, and Tirzah. ²And they stood before Moses and before Eleazar the priest and before the chiefs and all the congregation, at the entrance of the tent of meeting, saying, ³"Our father died in the wilderness. He was not among the company of those who gathered themselves together against the LORD in the company of Korah, but died for his own sin. And he had no sons. ⁴Why should the name of our father be taken away from his clan because he had no son? Give to us a possession among our father's brothers."

⁵Moses brought their case before the LORD. ⁶And the LORD said to Moses, ⁷"The daughters of Zelophehad are right. You shall give them possession of an inheritance among their father's brothers and transfer the inheritance of their father to them. ⁸And you shall speak to the people of Israel, saying, 'If a man dies and has no son, then you shall transfer his inheritance to his daughter. ⁹And if he has no daughter, then you shall give his inheritance to his brothers. ¹⁰And if he has no brothers, then you shall give his inheritance to his father's brothers. ¹¹And if his father has no brothers, then you shall give his inheritance to the nearest kinsman of his clan, and he shall possess it. And it shall be for the people of Israel a statute and rule, as the LORD commanded Moses.'"

¹²The LORD said to Moses, "Go up into this mountain of Abarim and see the land that I have given to the people of Israel. ¹³When you have seen it, you also shall be gathered to your people, as your brother Aaron was, ¹⁴because you rebelled against my word in the wilderness of Zin when the congregation quarreled, failing to uphold me as holy at the waters before their eyes." (These are the waters of Meribah of Kadesh in the wilderness of Zin.) ¹⁵Moses spoke to the LORD, saying, ¹⁶"Let the LORD, the God of the spirits of all flesh, appoint a man over the congregation ¹⁷who shall go out before them and come in before them, who shall lead them out and bring them in, that the congregation of the LORD may not be as sheep that have no shepherd." ¹⁸So the LORD said to Moses, "Take Joshua the son of Nun, a man in whom is the Spirit, and lay your hand on him. ¹⁹Make him stand before Eleazar the priest and all the congregation, and you shall commission him in their sight. ²⁰You shall invest him with some of your authority, that all the congregation of the people of Israel may obey. ²¹And he shall stand before Eleazar the priest, who shall inquire for him by the judgment of the Urim before the LORD. At his word they shall go out, and at his word they shall come in, both he and all the people of Israel with him, the whole congregation." ²²And Moses did as the LORD commanded him. He took Joshua and made him stand before Eleazar the priest and the whole congregation, ²³and he laid his hands on him and commissioned him as the LORD directed through Moses.

Further laws and regulations [chapters 28–29]. The regulations in this block cover a range of offerings. The rules were of course important to the running of Israelite society, but their function in the narrative context of Numbers is to fill out our understanding of the society whose journey makes up the narrative sections of the book.

28 The LORD spoke to Moses, saying, ²"Command the people of Israel and say to them, 'My offering, my food for my food offerings, my pleasing aroma, you shall be careful to offer to me at its appointed time.' ³And you shall say to them, This is the food offering that you shall offer to the LORD: two male lambs a year old without blemish, day by day, as a regular offering. ⁴The one lamb you shall offer in the morning, and the other lamb you shall offer at twilight; ⁵also a tenth of an ephah¹ of fine flour for a grain offering, mixed with a quarter of a hin² of beaten oil. ⁶It is a regular burnt offering, which was ordained at Mount Sinai for a pleasing aroma, a food offering to the LORD. ⁷Its drink offering shall be a quarter of a hin for each lamb. In the Holy Place you shall pour out a drink offering of strong drink to the LORD. ⁸The other lamb you shall offer at twilight. Like the grain offering of the morning, and like its drink offering, you shall offer it as a food offering, with a pleasing aroma to the LORD.

⁹"On the Sabbath day, two male lambs a year old without blemish, and two tenths of an ephah of fine flour for a grain offering, mixed with oil, and its drink offering: ¹⁰this is the burnt offering of every Sabbath, besides the regular burnt offering and its drink offering.

¹¹"At the beginnings of your months, you shall offer a burnt offering to the LORD: two bulls from the herd, one ram, seven male lambs a year old without blemish; ¹²also three tenths of an ephah of fine flour for a grain offering, mixed with oil, for each bull, and two tenths of fine flour for a grain offering, mixed with oil, for the one ram; ¹³and a tenth of fine flour mixed with oil as a grain offering for every lamb; for a burnt offering with a pleasing aroma, a food offering to the LORD. ¹⁴Their drink offerings shall be half a hin of wine for a bull, a third of a hin for a ram, and a quarter of a hin for a lamb. This is the burnt offering of each month throughout the months of the year. ¹⁵Also one male goat for a sin offering to the LORD; it shall be offered besides the regular burnt offering and its drink offering.

¹⁶"On the fourteenth day of the first month is the LORD's Passover, ¹⁷and on the fifteenth day of this month is a feast. Seven days shall unleavened bread be eaten. ¹⁸On the first day there shall be a holy convocation. You shall not do any ordinary work, ¹⁹but offer a food offering, a burnt offering to the LORD: two bulls from the herd, one ram, and seven male lambs a year old; see that they are without blemish; ²⁰also their grain offering of fine flour mixed with oil; three tenths of an ephah shall you offer for a bull, and two tenths for a ram; ²¹a tenth shall you offer for each of the seven lambs; ²²also one male goat for a sin offering, to make atonement for you. ²³You shall offer these besides the burnt offering of the morning, which is for a regular burnt offering. ²⁴In the same way you shall offer daily, for seven days, the food of a food offering, with a pleasing aroma to the LORD. It shall be offered besides the regular burnt offering and its drink offering. ²⁵And on the seventh day you shall have a holy convocation. You shall not do any ordinary work.

²⁶"On the day of the firstfruits, when you offer a grain offering of new grain to the

---

¹ An *ephah* was about 3/5 bushel or 22 liters ² A *hin* was about 4 quarts or 3.5 liters

Lord at your Feast of Weeks, you shall have a holy convocation. You shall not do any ordinary work, ²⁷but offer a burnt offering, with a pleasing aroma to the Lord: two bulls from the herd, one ram, seven male lambs a year old; ²⁸also their grain offering of fine flour mixed with oil, three tenths of an ephah for each bull, two tenths for one ram, ²⁹a tenth for each of the seven lambs; ³⁰with one male goat, to make atonement for you. ³¹Besides the regular burnt offering and its grain offering, you shall offer them and their drink offering. See that they are without blemish.

29 "On the first day of the seventh month you shall have a holy convocation. You shall not do any ordinary work. It is a day for you to blow the trumpets, ²and you shall offer a burnt offering, for a pleasing aroma to the Lord: one bull from the herd, one ram, seven male lambs a year old without blemish; ³also their grain offering of fine flour mixed with oil, three tenths of an ephah[1] for the bull, two tenths for the ram, ⁴and one tenth for each of the seven lambs; ⁵with one male goat for a sin offering, to make atonement for you; ⁶besides the burnt offering of the new moon, and its grain offering, and the regular burnt offering and its grain offering, and their drink offering, according to the rule for them, for a pleasing aroma, a food offering to the Lord.

⁷"On the tenth day of this seventh month you shall have a holy convocation and afflict yourselves. You shall do no work, ⁸but you shall offer a burnt offering to the Lord, a pleasing aroma: one bull from the herd, one ram, seven male lambs a year old: see that they are without blemish. ⁹And their grain offering shall be of fine flour mixed with oil, three tenths of an ephah for the bull, two tenths for the one ram, ¹⁰a tenth for each of the seven lambs; ¹¹also one male goat for a sin offering, besides the sin offering of atonement, and the regular burnt offering and its grain offering, and their drink offerings.

¹²"On the fifteenth day of the seventh month you shall have a holy convocation. You shall not do any ordinary work, and you shall keep a feast to the Lord seven days. ¹³And you shall offer a burnt offering, a food offering, with a pleasing aroma to the Lord, thirteen bulls from the herd, two rams, fourteen male lambs a year old; they shall be without blemish; ¹⁴and their grain offering of fine flour mixed with oil, three tenths of an ephah for each of the thirteen bulls, two tenths for each of the two rams, ¹⁵and a tenth for each of the fourteen lambs; ¹⁶also one male goat for a sin offering, besides the regular burnt offering, its grain offering and its drink offering.

¹⁷"On the second day twelve bulls from the herd, two rams, fourteen male lambs a year old without blemish, ¹⁸with the grain offering and the drink offerings for the bulls, for the rams, and for the lambs, in the prescribed quantities; ¹⁹also one male goat for a sin offering, besides the regular burnt offering and its grain offering, and their drink offerings.

²⁰"On the third day eleven bulls, two rams, fourteen male lambs a year old without blemish, ²¹with the grain offering and the drink offerings for the bulls, for the rams, and for the lambs, in the prescribed quantities; ²²also one male goat for a sin offering, besides the regular burnt offering and its grain offering and its drink offering.

²³"On the fourth day ten bulls, two rams, fourteen male lambs a year old without blemish, ²⁴with the grain offering and the drink offerings for the bulls, for the rams, and for the lambs, in the prescribed quantities; ²⁵also one male goat for a sin offering, besides the regular burnt offering, its grain offering and its drink offering.

---

[1] An *ephah* was about 3/5 bushel or 22 liters

²⁶"On the fifth day nine bulls, two rams, fourteen male lambs a year old without blemish, ²⁷with the grain offering and the drink offerings for the bulls, for the rams, and for the lambs, in the prescribed quantities; ²⁸also one male goat for a sin offering; besides the regular burnt offering and its grain offering and its drink offering.

²⁹"On the sixth day eight bulls, two rams, fourteen male lambs a year old without blemish, ³⁰with the grain offering and the drink offerings for the bulls, for the rams, and for the lambs, in the prescribed quantities; ³¹also one male goat for a sin offering; besides the regular burnt offering, its grain offering, and its drink offerings.

³²"On the seventh day seven bulls, two rams, fourteen male lambs a year old without blemish, ³³with the grain offering and the drink offerings for the bulls, for the rams, and for the lambs, in the prescribed quantities; ³⁴also one male goat for a sin offering; besides the regular burnt offering, its grain offering, and its drink offering.

³⁵"On the eighth day you shall have a solemn assembly. You shall not do any ordinary work, ³⁶but you shall offer a burnt offering, a food offering, with a pleasing aroma to the LORD: one bull, one ram, seven male lambs a year old without blemish, ³⁷and the grain offering and the drink offerings for the bull, for the ram, and for the lambs, in the prescribed quantities; ³⁸also one male goat for a sin offering; besides the regular burnt offering and its grain offering and its drink offering.

³⁹"These you shall offer to the LORD at your appointed feasts, in addition to your vow offerings and your freewill offerings, for your burnt offerings, and for your grain offerings, and for your drink offerings, and for your peace offerings."

⁴⁰¹ So Moses told the people of Israel everything just as the LORD had commanded Moses.

Laws concerning vows [chapter 30]. Several things immediately impress themselves on us as we read this chapter. One is the remoteness and strangeness of the biblical world from our own world in many of its practices. A second is the often complicated nature of the rules that prevailed in ancient societies. By entering into these qualities of strangeness and complexity, we can ponder the nature of the OT world. For starters, this chapter shows the importance that ancient cultures (including Israel) placed on vows. However, this chapter does not deal with undifferentiated vows but mainly with how to handle vows that a woman has made before marriage when she comes to the time of her marriage. The various possibilities are difficult to disentangle, but a main distinction exists between vows made under a father's authority and those made under a husband's authority.

---

30 Moses spoke to the heads of the tribes of the people of Israel, saying, "This is what the LORD has commanded. ²If a man vows a vow to the LORD, or swears an oath to bind himself by a pledge, he shall not break his word. He shall do according to all that proceeds out of his mouth.

³"If a woman vows a vow to the LORD and binds herself by a pledge, while within her father's house in her youth, ⁴and her father hears of her vow and of her pledge by which she has bound herself and says nothing to her, then all her vows shall stand, and every pledge by which she has bound herself shall stand. ⁵But if her father opposes her on the day that he hears of it, no vow of hers, no pledge by which she has bound herself shall stand. And the LORD will forgive her, because her father opposed her.

---

¹ Ch 30:1 in Hebrew

[6]"If she marries a husband, while under her vows or any thoughtless utterance of her lips by which she has bound herself, [7]and her husband hears of it and says nothing to her on the day that he hears, then her vows shall stand, and her pledges by which she has bound herself shall stand. [8]But if, on the day that her husband comes to hear of it, he opposes her, then he makes void her vow that was on her, and the thoughtless utterance of her lips by which she bound herself. And the LORD will forgive her. [9](But any vow of a widow or of a divorced woman, anything by which she has bound herself, shall stand against her.) [10]And if she vowed in her husband's house or bound herself by a pledge with an oath, [11]and her husband heard of it and said nothing to her and did not oppose her, then all her vows shall stand, and every pledge by which she bound herself shall stand. [12]But if her husband makes them null and void on the day that he hears them, then whatever proceeds out of her lips concerning her vows or concerning her pledge of herself shall not stand. Her husband has made them void, and the LORD will forgive her. [13]Any vow and any binding oath to afflict herself, her husband may establish,[1] or her husband may make void. [14]But if her husband says nothing to her from day to day, then he establishes all her vows or all her pledges that are upon her. He has established them, because he said nothing to her on the day that he heard of them. [15]But if he makes them null and void after he has heard of them, then he shall bear her iniquity."

[16]These are the statutes that the LORD commanded Moses about a man and his wife and about a father and his daughter while she is in her youth within her father's house.

An epic battle story [chapter 31]. Narrative makes a return appearance in the form of an extended battle story. A number of conventional motifs are present, as follows: mustering of the army (vv. 1–5); dispatching the army to battle (v. 6); the battle itself (vv. 7–10); the taking of plunder (vv. 11–54). The unusual feature of the story is the long account of division of plunder, which in this case is an intricate series of events and rules.

31

The LORD spoke to Moses, saying, [2]"Avenge the people of Israel on the Midianites. Afterward you shall be gathered to your people." [3]So Moses spoke to the people, saying, "Arm men from among you for the war, that they may go against Midian to execute the LORD's vengeance on Midian. [4]You shall send a thousand from each of the tribes of Israel to the war." [5]So there were provided, out of the thousands of Israel, a thousand from each tribe, twelve thousand armed for war. [6]And Moses sent them to the war, a thousand from each tribe, together with Phinehas the son of Eleazar the priest, with the vessels of the sanctuary and the trumpets for the alarm in his hand. [7]They warred against Midian, as the LORD commanded Moses, and killed every male. [8]They killed the kings of Midian with the rest of their slain, Evi, Rekem, Zur, Hur, and Reba, the five kings of Midian. And they also killed Balaam the son of Beor with the sword. [9]And the people of Israel took captive the women of Midian and their little ones, and they took as plunder all their cattle, their flocks, and all their goods. [10]All their cities in the places where they lived, and all their encampments, they burned with fire, [11]and took all the spoil and all the plunder, both of man and of beast. [12]Then they brought the captives and the plunder and the spoil to Moses, and

---

[1] Or may allow to stand

to Eleazar the priest, and to the congregation of the people of Israel, at the camp on the plains of Moab by the Jordan at Jericho.

[13]Moses and Eleazar the priest and all the chiefs of the congregation went to meet them outside the camp. [14]And Moses was angry with the officers of the army, the commanders of thousands and the commanders of hundreds, who had come from service in the war. [15]Moses said to them, "Have you let all the women live? [16]Behold, these, on Balaam's advice, caused the people of Israel to act treacherously against the LORD in the incident of Peor, and so the plague came among the congregation of the LORD. [17]Now therefore, kill every male among the little ones, and kill every woman who has known man by lying with him. [18]But all the young girls who have not known man by lying with him keep alive for yourselves. [19]Encamp outside the camp seven days. Whoever of you has killed any person and whoever has touched any slain, purify yourselves and your captives on the third day and on the seventh day. [20]You shall purify every garment, every article of skin, all work of goats' hair, and every article of wood."

[21]Then Eleazar the priest said to the men in the army who had gone to battle: "This is the statute of the law that the LORD has commanded Moses: [22]only the gold, the silver, the bronze, the iron, the tin, and the lead, [23]everything that can stand the fire, you shall pass through the fire, and it shall be clean. Nevertheless, it shall also be purified with the water for impurity. And whatever cannot stand the fire, you shall pass through the water. [24]You must wash your clothes on the seventh day, and you shall be clean. And afterward you may come into the camp."

[25]The LORD said to Moses, [26]"Take the count of the plunder that was taken, both of man and of beast, you and Eleazar the priest and the heads of the fathers' houses of the congregation, [27]and divide the plunder into two parts between the warriors who went out to battle and all the congregation. [28]And levy for the LORD a tribute from the men of war who went out to battle, one out of five hundred, of the people and of the oxen and of the donkeys and of the flocks. [29]Take it from their half and give it to Eleazar the priest as a contribution to the LORD. [30]And from the people of Israel's half you shall take one drawn out of every fifty, of the people, of the oxen, of the donkeys, and of the flocks, of all the cattle, and give them to the Levites who keep guard over the tabernacle of the LORD." [31]And Moses and Eleazar the priest did as the LORD commanded Moses.

[32]Now the plunder remaining of the spoil that the army took was 675,000 sheep, [33]72,000 cattle, [34]61,000 donkeys, [35]and 32,000 persons in all, women who had not known man by lying with him. [36]And the half, the portion of those who had gone out in the army, numbered 337,500 sheep, [37]and the LORD's tribute of sheep was 675. [38]The cattle were 36,000, of which the LORD's tribute was 72. [39]The donkeys were 30,500, of which the LORD's tribute was 61. [40]The persons were 16,000, of which the LORD's tribute was 32 persons. [41]And Moses gave the tribute, which was the contribution for the LORD, to Eleazar the priest, as the LORD commanded Moses.

[42]From the people of Israel's half, which Moses separated from that of the men who had served in the army— [43]now the congregation's half was 337,500 sheep, [44]36,000 cattle, [45]and 30,500 donkeys, [46]and 16,000 persons— [47]from the people of Israel's half Moses took one of every 50, both of persons and of beasts, and gave them to the Levites who kept guard over the tabernacle of the LORD, as the LORD commanded Moses.

⁴⁸Then the officers who were over the thousands of the army, the commanders of thousands and the commanders of hundreds, came near to Moses ⁴⁹and said to Moses, "Your servants have counted the men of war who are under our command, and there is not a man missing from us. ⁵⁰And we have brought the LORD's offering, what each man found, articles of gold, armlets and bracelets, signet rings, earrings, and beads, to make atonement for ourselves before the LORD." ⁵¹And Moses and Eleazar the priest received from them the gold, all crafted articles. ⁵²And all the gold of the contribution that they presented to the LORD, from the commanders of thousands and the commanders of hundreds, was 16,750 shekels.¹ ⁵³(The men in the army had each taken plunder for himself.) ⁵⁴And Moses and Eleazar the priest received the gold from the commanders of thousands and of hundreds, and brought it into the tent of meeting, as a memorial for the people of Israel before the LORD.

> **Settlement of two-and-a-half tribes east of the Jordan River** [chapter 32]. We know that we are nearing the end of the journey story when we come to a chapter that narrates how two-and-a-half tribes decide to settle east of the Jordan River, on the condition that their warriors will help to conquer Canaan west of the Jordan before finally settling down in their allotted places.

32 Now the people of Reuben and the people of Gad had a very great number of livestock. And they saw the land of Jazer and the land of Gilead, and behold, the place was a place for livestock. ²So the people of Gad and the people of Reuben came and said to Moses and to Eleazar the priest and to the chiefs of the congregation, ³"Ataroth, Dibon, Jazer, Nimrah, Heshbon, Elealeh, Sebam, Nebo, and Beon, ⁴the land that the LORD struck down before the congregation of Israel, is a land for livestock, and your servants have livestock." ⁵And they said, "If we have found favor in your sight, let this land be given to your servants for a possession. Do not take us across the Jordan."

⁶But Moses said to the people of Gad and to the people of Reuben, "Shall your brothers go to the war while you sit here? ⁷Why will you discourage the heart of the people of Israel from going over into the land that the LORD has given them? ⁸Your fathers did this, when I sent them from Kadesh-barnea to see the land. ⁹For when they went up to the Valley of Eshcol and saw the land, they discouraged the heart of the people of Israel from going into the land that the LORD had given them. ¹⁰And the LORD's anger was kindled on that day, and he swore, saying, ¹¹'Surely none of the men who came up out of Egypt, from twenty years old and upward, shall see the land that I swore to give to Abraham, to Isaac, and to Jacob, because they have not wholly followed me, ¹²none except Caleb the son of Jephunneh the Kenizzite and Joshua the son of Nun, for they have wholly followed the LORD.' ¹³And the LORD's anger was kindled against Israel, and he made them wander in the wilderness forty years, until all the generation that had done evil in the sight of the LORD was gone. ¹⁴And behold, you have risen in your fathers' place, a brood of sinful men, to increase still more the fierce anger of the LORD against Israel! ¹⁵For if you turn away from following him, he will again abandon them in the wilderness, and you will destroy all this people."

¹⁶Then they came near to him and said, "We will build sheepfolds here for our livestock, and cities for our little ones, ¹⁷but we will take up arms, ready to go before the

¹ A *shekel* was about 2/5 ounce or 11 grams

people of Israel, until we have brought them to their place. And our little ones shall live in the fortified cities because of the inhabitants of the land. ¹⁸We will not return to our homes until each of the people of Israel has gained his inheritance. ¹⁹For we will not inherit with them on the other side of the Jordan and beyond, because our inheritance has come to us on this side of the Jordan to the east." ²⁰So Moses said to them, "If you will do this, if you will take up arms to go before the Lord for the war, ²¹and every armed man of you will pass over the Jordan before the Lord, until he has driven out his enemies from before him ²²and the land is subdued before the Lord; then after that you shall return and be free of obligation to the Lord and to Israel, and this land shall be your possession before the Lord. ²³But if you will not do so, behold, you have sinned against the Lord, and be sure your sin will find you out. ²⁴Build cities for your little ones and folds for your sheep, and do what you have promised." ²⁵And the people of Gad and the people of Reuben said to Moses, "Your servants will do as my lord commands. ²⁶Our little ones, our wives, our livestock, and all our cattle shall remain there in the cities of Gilead, ²⁷but your servants will pass over, every man who is armed for war, before the Lord to battle, as my lord orders."

²⁸So Moses gave command concerning them to Eleazar the priest and to Joshua the son of Nun and to the heads of the fathers' houses of the tribes of the people of Israel. ²⁹And Moses said to them, "If the people of Gad and the people of Reuben, every man who is armed to battle before the Lord, will pass with you over the Jordan and the land shall be subdued before you, then you shall give them the land of Gilead for a possession. ³⁰However, if they will not pass over with you armed, they shall have possessions among you in the land of Canaan." ³¹And the people of Gad and the people of Reuben answered, "What the Lord has said to your servants, we will do. ³²We will pass over armed before the Lord into the land of Canaan, and the possession of our inheritance shall remain with us beyond the Jordan."

³³And Moses gave to them, to the people of Gad and to the people of Reuben and to the half-tribe of Manasseh the son of Joseph, the kingdom of Sihon king of the Amorites and the kingdom of Og king of Bashan, the land and its cities with their territories, the cities of the land throughout the country. ³⁴And the people of Gad built Dibon, Ataroth, Aroer, ³⁵Atroth-shophan, Jazer, Jogbehah, ³⁶Beth-nimrah and Beth-haran, fortified cities, and folds for sheep. ³⁷And the people of Reuben built Heshbon, Elealeh, Kiriathaim, ³⁸Nebo, and Baal-meon (their names were changed), and Sibmah. And they gave other names to the cities that they built. ³⁹And the sons of Machir the son of Manasseh went to Gilead and captured it, and dispossessed the Amorites who were in it. ⁴⁰And Moses gave Gilead to Machir the son of Manasseh, and he settled in it. ⁴¹And Jair the son of Manasseh went and captured their villages, and called them Havvoth-jair.¹ ⁴²And Nobah went and captured Kenath and its villages, and called it Nobah, after his own name.

Review of the campsites of the journey [33:1–49]. Still more sense of closure emerges when, to our surprise, instead of giving us further journeying, the writer interrupts the progress of the story by recapping the campsites at which the nation has stayed on its wilderness journey.

¹ Havvoth-jair means the villages of Jair

33 These are the stages of the people of Israel, when they went out of the land of Egypt by their companies under the leadership of Moses and Aaron. [2]Moses wrote down their starting places, stage by stage, by command of the Lord, and these are their stages according to their starting places. [3]They set out from Rameses in the first month, on the fifteenth day of the first month. On the day after the Passover, the people of Israel went out triumphantly in the sight of all the Egyptians, [4]while the Egyptians were burying all their firstborn, whom the Lord had struck down among them. On their gods also the Lord executed judgments.

[5]So the people of Israel set out from Rameses and camped at Succoth. [6]And they set out from Succoth and camped at Etham, which is on the edge of the wilderness. [7]And they set out from Etham and turned back to Pi-hahiroth, which is east of Baal-zephon, and they camped before Migdol. [8]And they set out from before Hahiroth[1] and passed through the midst of the sea into the wilderness, and they went a three days' journey in the wilderness of Etham and camped at Marah. [9]And they set out from Marah and came to Elim; at Elim there were twelve springs of water and seventy palm trees, and they camped there. [10]And they set out from Elim and camped by the Red Sea. [11]And they set out from the Red Sea and camped in the wilderness of Sin. [12]And they set out from the wilderness of Sin and camped at Dophkah. [13]And they set out from Dophkah and camped at Alush. [14]And they set out from Alush and camped at Rephidim, where there was no water for the people to drink. [15]And they set out from Rephidim and camped in the wilderness of Sinai. [16]And they set out from the wilderness of Sinai and camped at Kibroth-hattaavah. [17]And they set out from Kibroth-hattaavah and camped at Hazeroth. [18]And they set out from Hazeroth and camped at Rithmah. [19]And they set out from Rithmah and camped at Rimmon-perez. [20]And they set out from Rimmon-perez and camped at Libnah. [21]And they set out from Libnah and camped at Rissah. [22]And they set out from Rissah and camped at Kehelathah. [23]And they set out from Kehelathah and camped at Mount Shepher. [24]And they set out from Mount Shepher and camped at Haradah. [25]And they set out from Haradah and camped at Makheloth. [26]And they set out from Makheloth and camped at Tahath. [27]And they set out from Tahath and camped at Terah. [28]And they set out from Terah and camped at Mithkah. [29]And they set out from Mithkah and camped at Hashmonah. [30]And they set out from Hashmonah and camped at Moseroth. [31]And they set out from Moseroth and camped at Bene-jaakan. [32]And they set out from Bene-jaakan and camped at Hor-haggidgad. [33]And they set out from Hor-haggidgad and camped at Jotbathah. [34]And they set out from Jotbathah and camped at Abronah. [35]And they set out from Abronah and camped at Ezion-geber. [36]And they set out from Ezion-geber and camped in the wilderness of Zin (that is, Kadesh). [37]And they set out from Kadesh and camped at Mount Hor, on the edge of the land of Edom.

[38]And Aaron the priest went up Mount Hor at the command of the Lord and died there, in the fortieth year after the people of Israel had come out of the land of Egypt, on the first day of the fifth month. [39]And Aaron was 123 years old when he died on Mount Hor.

[40]And the Canaanite, the king of Arad, who lived in the Negeb in the land of Canaan, heard of the coming of the people of Israel.

[41]And they set out from Mount Hor and camped at Zalmonah. [42]And they set out from Zalmonah and camped at Punon. [43]And they set out from Punon and camped at

---

[1] Some manuscripts and versions Pi-hahiroth

Oboth. ⁴⁴And they set out from Oboth and camped at Iye-abarim, in the territory of Moab. ⁴⁵And they set out from Iyim and camped at Dibon-gad. ⁴⁶And they set out from Dibon-gad and camped at Almon-diblathaim. ⁴⁷And they set out from Almon-diblathaim and camped in the mountains of Abarim, before Nebo. ⁴⁸And they set out from the mountains of Abarim and camped in the plains of Moab by the Jordan at Jericho; ⁴⁹they camped by the Jordan from Beth-jeshimoth as far as Abel-shittim in the plains of Moab.

> **Instructions for dividing the Promised Land** [33:50–34:29]. The final note of closure comes with a substantial settlement narrative (after the travel narrative). At the head of the unit, standing almost as a "theme verse," is a solemn exhortation from God to Moses that the Israelites must make the conquest of Canaan a complete conquest (33:50–56). The nation's failure to do so becomes a source of self-destruction for them at a later point in their history (see Judg. 1:22–2:23). Chapter 34 identifies the boundaries of the land (vv. 1–15) and narrates the choosing of the men to divide the land (vv. 16–29). The first item on our agenda is to relive the events, imagining ourselves present at the epoch-making formation of the nation in its land. Then we can ponder the symbolic meanings of God's covenant people's setting the boundaries of a long-promised land and preparing finally to parcel it out.

⁵⁰And the LORD spoke to Moses in the plains of Moab by the Jordan at Jericho, saying, ⁵¹"Speak to the people of Israel and say to them, When you pass over the Jordan into the land of Canaan, ⁵²then you shall drive out all the inhabitants of the land from before you and destroy all their figured stones and destroy all their metal images and demolish all their high places. ⁵³And you shall take possession of the land and settle in it, for I have given the land to you to possess it. ⁵⁴You shall inherit the land by lot according to your clans. To a large tribe you shall give a large inheritance, and to a small tribe you shall give a small inheritance. Wherever the lot falls for anyone, that shall be his. According to the tribes of your fathers you shall inherit. ⁵⁵But if you do not drive out the inhabitants of the land from before you, then those of them whom you let remain shall be as barbs in your eyes and thorns in your sides, and they shall trouble you in the land where you dwell. ⁵⁶And I will do to you as I thought to do to them."

34 The LORD spoke to Moses, saying, ²"Command the people of Israel, and say to them, When you enter the land of Canaan (this is the land that shall fall to you for an inheritance, the land of Canaan as defined by its borders), ³your south side shall be from the wilderness of Zin alongside Edom, and your southern border shall run from the end of the Salt Sea on the east. ⁴And your border shall turn south of the ascent of Akrabbim, and cross to Zin, and its limit shall be south of Kadesh-barnea. Then it shall go on to Hazar-addar, and pass along to Azmon. ⁵And the border shall turn from Azmon to the Brook of Egypt, and its limit shall be at the sea.

⁶"For the western border, you shall have the Great Sea and its¹ coast. This shall be your western border.

⁷"This shall be your northern border: from the Great Sea you shall draw a line to Mount Hor. ⁸From Mount Hor you shall draw a line to Lebo-hamath, and the limit of

¹ Syriac; Hebrew lacks *its*

the border shall be at Zedad. [9]Then the border shall extend to Ziphron, and its limit shall be at Hazar-enan. This shall be your northern border.

[10]"You shall draw a line for your eastern border from Hazar-enan to Shepham. [11]And the border shall go down from Shepham to Riblah on the east side of Ain. And the border shall go down and reach to the shoulder of the Sea of Chinnereth on the east. [12]And the border shall go down to the Jordan, and its limit shall be at the Salt Sea. This shall be your land as defined by its borders all around."

[13]Moses commanded the people of Israel, saying, "This is the land that you shall inherit by lot, which the LORD has commanded to give to the nine tribes and to the half-tribe. [14]For the tribe of the people of Reuben by fathers' houses and the tribe of the people of Gad by their fathers' houses have received their inheritance, and also the half-tribe of Manasseh. [15]The two tribes and the half-tribe have received their inheritance beyond the Jordan east of Jericho, toward the sunrise."

[16]The LORD spoke to Moses, saying, [17]"These are the names of the men who shall divide the land to you for inheritance: Eleazar the priest and Joshua the son of Nun. [18]You shall take one chief from every tribe to divide the land for inheritance. [19]These are the names of the men: Of the tribe of Judah, Caleb the son of Jephunneh. [20]Of the tribe of the people of Simeon, Shemuel the son of Ammihud. [21]Of the tribe of Benjamin, Elidad the son of Chislon. [22]Of the tribe of the people of Dan a chief, Bukki the son of Jogli. [23]Of the people of Joseph: of the tribe of the people of Manasseh a chief, Hanniel the son of Ephod. [24]And of the tribe of the people of Ephraim a chief, Kemuel the son of Shiphtan. [25]Of the tribe of the people of Zebulun a chief, Elizaphan the son of Parnach. [26]Of the tribe of the people of Issachar a chief, Paltiel the son of Azzan. [27]And of the tribe of the people of Asher a chief, Ahihud the son of Shelomi. [28]Of the tribe of the people of Naphtali a chief, Pedahel the son of Ammihud. [29]These are the men whom the LORD commanded to divide the inheritance for the people of Israel in the land of Canaan."

Instructions for life within the Promised Land [chapters 35–36]. We end the book of Numbers not with narrative material but with miscellaneous instructions for living within the Promised Land. By our standards this may seem anticlimactic, but this material signals the importance of law giving to the literary design of Numbers. In the author's mind, the instructions are as much a part of the story as the narrative events, and we can profitably ponder what this tells us about God and his design for his people. The sequence of instructions is as follows: the cities and pasturelands allotted to the Levites (35:1–8); the number of the cities of refuge, along with an outline of the ways in which they were to be used (35:9–34); laws concerning the marriage of female heirs (chapter 36). We can ponder what it says about God and biblical religion that this is the last word of the entire book; for starters, it shows the importance that God places on the commonplace and on ordinary people.

35 The LORD spoke to Moses in the plains of Moab by the Jordan at Jericho, saying, [2]"Command the people of Israel to give to the Levites some of the inheritance of their possession as cities for them to dwell in. And you shall give to the Levites pasturelands around the cities. [3]The cities shall be theirs to dwell in, and their pasturelands shall be for their cattle and for their livestock and for all their beasts. [4]The pasturelands of the cities, which you shall give to the Levites, shall reach from

the wall of the city outward a thousand cubits[1] all around. ⁵And you shall measure, outside the city, on the east side two thousand cubits, and on the south side two thousand cubits, and on the west side two thousand cubits, and on the north side two thousand cubits, the city being in the middle. This shall belong to them as pastureland for their cities.

⁶"The cities that you give to the Levites shall be the six cities of refuge, where you shall permit the manslayer to flee, and in addition to them you shall give forty-two cities. ⁷All the cities that you give to the Levites shall be forty-eight, with their pasturelands. ⁸And as for the cities that you shall give from the possession of the people of Israel, from the larger tribes you shall take many, and from the smaller tribes you shall take few; each, in proportion to the inheritance that it inherits, shall give of its cities to the Levites."

⁹And the LORD spoke to Moses, saying, ¹⁰"Speak to the people of Israel and say to them, When you cross the Jordan into the land of Canaan, ¹¹then you shall select cities to be cities of refuge for you, that the manslayer who kills any person without intent may flee there. ¹²The cities shall be for you a refuge from the avenger, that the manslayer may not die until he stands before the congregation for judgment. ¹³And the cities that you give shall be your six cities of refuge. ¹⁴You shall give three cities beyond the Jordan, and three cities in the land of Canaan, to be cities of refuge. ¹⁵These six cities shall be for refuge for the people of Israel, and for the stranger and for the sojourner among them, that anyone who kills any person without intent may flee there.

¹⁶"But if he struck him down with an iron object, so that he died, he is a murderer. The murderer shall be put to death. ¹⁷And if he struck him down with a stone tool that could cause death, and he died, he is a murderer. The murderer shall be put to death. ¹⁸Or if he struck him down with a wooden tool that could cause death, and he died, he is a murderer. The murderer shall be put to death. ¹⁹The avenger of blood shall himself put the murderer to death; when he meets him, he shall put him to death. ²⁰And if he pushed him out of hatred or hurled something at him, lying in wait, so that he died, ²¹or in enmity struck him down with his hand, so that he died, then he who struck the blow shall be put to death. He is a murderer. The avenger of blood shall put the murderer to death when he meets him.

²²"But if he pushed him suddenly without enmity, or hurled anything on him without lying in wait ²³or used a stone that could cause death, and without seeing him dropped it on him, so that he died, though he was not his enemy and did not seek his harm, ²⁴then the congregation shall judge between the manslayer and the avenger of blood, in accordance with these rules. ²⁵And the congregation shall rescue the manslayer from the hand of the avenger of blood, and the congregation shall restore him to his city of refuge to which he had fled, and he shall live in it until the death of the high priest who was anointed with the holy oil. ²⁶But if the manslayer shall at any time go beyond the boundaries of his city of refuge to which he fled, ²⁷and the avenger of blood finds him outside the boundaries of his city of refuge, and the avenger of blood kills the manslayer, he shall not be guilty of blood. ²⁸For he must remain in his city of refuge until the death of the high priest, but after the death of the high priest the manslayer may return to the land of his possession. ²⁹And these things shall be for a statute and rule for you throughout your generations in all your dwelling places.

---

[1] A *cubit* was about 18 inches or 45 centimeters

³⁰"If anyone kills a person, the murderer shall be put to death on the evidence of witnesses. But no person shall be put to death on the testimony of one witness. ³¹Moreover, you shall accept no ransom for the life of a murderer, who is guilty of death, but he shall be put to death. ³²And you shall accept no ransom for him who has fled to his city of refuge, that he may return to dwell in the land before the death of the high priest. ³³You shall not pollute the land in which you live, for blood pollutes the land, and no atonement can be made for the land for the blood that is shed in it, except by the blood of the one who shed it. ³⁴You shall not defile the land in which you live, in the midst of which I dwell, for I the LORD dwell in the midst of the people of Israel."

36 The heads of the fathers' houses of the clan of the people of Gilead the son of Machir, son of Manasseh, from the clans of the people of Joseph, came near and spoke before Moses and before the chiefs, the heads of the fathers' houses of the people of Israel. ²They said, "The LORD commanded my lord to give the land for inheritance by lot to the people of Israel, and my lord was commanded by the LORD to give the inheritance of Zelophehad our brother to his daughters. ³But if they are married to any of the sons of the other tribes of the people of Israel, then their inheritance will be taken from the inheritance of our fathers and added to the inheritance of the tribe into which they marry. So it will be taken away from the lot of our inheritance. ⁴And when the jubilee of the people of Israel comes, then their inheritance will be added to the inheritance of the tribe into which they marry, and their inheritance will be taken from the inheritance of the tribe of our fathers."

⁵And Moses commanded the people of Israel according to the word of the LORD, saying, "The tribe of the people of Joseph is right. ⁶This is what the LORD commands concerning the daughters of Zelophehad, 'Let them marry whom they think best, only they shall marry within the clan of the tribe of their father. ⁷The inheritance of the people of Israel shall not be transferred from one tribe to another, for every one of the people of Israel shall hold on to the inheritance of the tribe of his fathers. ⁸And every daughter who possesses an inheritance in any tribe of the people of Israel shall be wife to one of the clan of the tribe of her father, so that every one of the people of Israel may possess the inheritance of his fathers. ⁹So no inheritance shall be transferred from one tribe to another, for each of the tribes of the people of Israel shall hold on to its own inheritance.'"

¹⁰The daughters of Zelophehad did as the LORD commanded Moses, ¹¹for Mahlah, Tirzah, Hoglah, Milcah, and Noah, the daughters of Zelophehad, were married to sons of their father's brothers. ¹²They were married into the clans of the people of Manasseh the son of Joseph, and their inheritance remained in the tribe of their father's clan.

¹³These are the commandments and the rules that the LORD commanded through Moses to the people of Israel in the plains of Moab by the Jordan at Jericho.

DEUTERONOMY

The book at a glance. 34 chapters, 958 verses. The book of Deuteronomy can be subtitled "farewell instructions for a nation." The book records an extended oration by Moses to the nation that he has led for more than forty years and that he is about to relinquish to the leadership of Joshua as he stands on the verge of his own death. Two major events form the substance of Deuteronomy. First, the long speech that Moses delivers to his nation has the effect of a renewal of the covenant on the plains of Moab. Second, the leadership of the nation passes from Moses to Joshua during the course of the book. The original audience was the generation of Israelites who had been born in the wilderness and who were therefore not present at the first giving of the law at Mount Sinai. The title Deuteronomy means "second law." This book is only partly a recapitulation of earlier books of the Pentateuch; it also contains much new material for a nation poised at last to enter the Promised Land, and even the material repeated from earlier books appears in the new context of the nation's imminent entry into Canaan.

▌ Genres. The last four books of the Pentateuch are alike in their mingling of (1) *narrative and (2) instructions concerning the laws by which God wanted his covenant people to live. Despite this similarity of content, Deuteronomy differs from the preceding books by being cast into the form of a *farewell discourse in which Moses is pictured as speaking to the nation (the opening verse states that "these are the words that Moses spoke to all Israel beyond the Jordan"). The repeated formula in the preceding three books is "the LORD spoke to Moses," but in Deuteronomy the rhetorical stance is that Moses speaks to the people. Because the law giving is phrased as Moses' words to his nation, the effect is that of an extended exhortation to covenant faithfulness. Moses gives his followers a somber pep talk as they are about to enter the Promised Land. Deuteronomy contains less narrative material than the three preceding books, but occasionally the speeches of Moses are placed into their narrative context. Late in the book, two formal discourses are cast into poetic form: the "Song of Moses" and Moses' pronouncement of blessing on the nation. (For more information on items accompanied by an asterisk, see the glossary at the back of this Bible.)

▌ Unifying motifs. The most constant ingredient in the book is the lists of commands that Moses gives. Moses utters these commands in an implied situation of the nation's leader giving a farewell address to his followers, and this rhetorical situation unifies the book (as the book occasionally reminds us). The understood framework of all the laws is that they are an expression of the demands and obligations of the covenant. It is

Passage	Specific Content	Underlying Principles	Implications for the Nation
1:1–3:29	Moses rehearses Israel's past	Learning from the past	Israel's identity as God's people
4:1–49	Moses exhorts the nation about the future	Principles for future living in the Promised Land	
5:1–6:25	Moses states and explains the Ten Commandments		
7:1–26	Instructions to defeat the Canaanites		
8:1–11:32	Mingled history and rules for living		
12:1–13:18	Rules, chiefly prohibitions	Specific rules for living as God's covenant people in the Promised Land	Israel's behavior as God's people
14:1–29	Clean and unclean animals; tithe of produce		
15:1–18	Rules about the poor and slaves		
15:19–17:17	Ceremonial observances		
17:18–18:22	Judges, kings, priests, prophets		
19:1–20:20	Criminal laws (19); rules for warfare (20)		
21:1–26:19	Wide-ranging rules, chiefly moral		
27:1–28:68	Blessings and curses	Incentives to obey God's rules	Israel's covenant commitment
29:1–30:20	Moses' exhortations to keep the covenant		
31:1–29	Arrangement for Joshua to succeed Moses	Close of Moses' career as leader of his nation	Last words from a leader
31:30–33:29	Song of Moses and Moses' blessing of the nation		
34:1–12	Transfer of leadership		

possible that the literary form of the suzerainty treaty of the ancient Near East lurks in the background (in a suzerainty treaty, a king or suzerain rehearsed what he had done for his nation and stipulated what he required in response). There is also an incipient note of anticipation, as we understand that the instructions are being given to a people that is on the verge of setting up a *utopia in a Promised Land—a good society governed by identifiable institutions and practices.

▌**Tips for reading.** With so little interspersed narrative, Deuteronomy poses a distinct challenge, especially if read through from beginning to end in a short span of time. Later OT writers often refer back to Deuteronomy when assessing their culture's moral and spiritual state, and if we build bridges between the text and our own situation today, we can continue to find in Deuteronomy a measuring stick of personal and national life. Furthermore, we need to look beyond the rules to what they are intended to address—the hearts, souls, and attitudes of people, and not simply their external behavior. Even though the format of the book (lists of laws) seems to make it a story of unremitting obligation and thus a recipe for burdensome legalism, we should look for the ways in which the book also expresses God's grace. Finally, we need to stay on the alert to determine whether a given rule falls into the category of (a) OT ceremonial laws that ended with the coming of Christ, (b) civil laws for Israel (for the most part not intended for other nations), or (c) moral or spiritual laws that are God's permanent will for human relationships.

▌ Inferred literary intentions. The book is designed to achieve the following literary purposes:

- impress upon us the seriousness of our actions before a holy God

- prompt us to think about how specific rules given to God's chosen people long ago apply to us today

- indirectly portray the character of God through a detailed account of what pleases and displeases him

- catch the impressiveness of Moses' oratorical performance

- keep us continuously aware of the rhetorical situation of the farewell discourse

- transport us from our own time and place to the ancient world of the Israelites as they are poised to enter the Promised Land

▌ Theological themes. (1) The nature of God: the long lists of rules for living are an indirect portrait of God. (2) Morality: many of the rules direct people regarding how to relate to other people. (3) Holiness: the rules also outline how people can be holy rather than unholy in their actions and thoughts. (4) Covenant: the laws of Deuteronomy can be viewed as an expression of God's covenant expectations and his people's covenant obligations. (4) Obedience to God: throughout the book, the warnings, curses, and blessings that Moses announces are linked to obedience or disobedience to God.

▌ The book of Deuteronomy as a chapter in the master story of the Bible. The Bible tells the story of how God wants his people to live. This is exactly what the instructions in the book of Deuteronomy accomplish. Additionally, the overall story of the Bible is the story of the soul's choice, as individuals repeatedly make a choice for or against God. The book of Deuteronomy places the great choice before us. Deuteronomy also contributes to the story of salvation history: the rules and regulations were foreshadowings of the perfect obedience and sacrifice of Christ.

The beginning of the oration [chapter 1]. The form in which the book of Deuteronomy is cast is the farewell discourse or oration. One of the standard *motifs in that genre is a recollection of the past. Because the orator in this case is the leader of the nation, the recollection of the past is the nation's history during the leadership of the speaker.

The formality of the occasion is matched by the copiousness of the style in which Moses speaks, and we need to be receptive to the exhilaration of the dramatic situation and the grandness of the style. Here and in the next two chapters, we can theorize about why Moses chooses the incidents that he chooses for his rehearsal of history and also what spiritual messages are conveyed by that selectivity. For example, underlying the national and military events narrated in chapter 1 is a pattern of sin, punishment, and repentance.

1 These are the words that Moses spoke to all Israel beyond the Jordan in the wilderness, in the Arabah opposite Suph, between Paran and Tophel, Laban, Hazeroth, and Dizahab. ²It is eleven days' journey from Horeb by the way of Mount Seir to Kadesh-barnea. ³In the fortieth year, on the first day of the eleventh month, Moses spoke to the people of Israel according to all that the LORD had given him in commandment to them, ⁴after he had defeated Sihon the king of the Amorites, who lived in Heshbon, and Og the king of Bashan, who lived in Ashtaroth and in Edrei. ⁵Beyond the Jordan, in the land of Moab, Moses undertook to explain this law, saying, ⁶"The LORD our God said to us in Horeb, 'You have stayed long enough at this mountain. ⁷Turn and take your journey, and go to the hill country of the Amorites and to all their neighbors in the Arabah, in the hill country and in the lowland and in the Negeb and by the seacoast, the land of the Canaanites, and Lebanon, as far as the great river, the river Euphrates. ⁸See, I have set the land before you. Go in and take possession of the land that the LORD swore to your fathers, to Abraham, to Isaac, and to Jacob, to give to them and to their offspring after them.'

⁹"At that time I said to you, 'I am not able to bear you by myself. ¹⁰The LORD your God has multiplied you, and behold, you are today as numerous as the stars of heaven. ¹¹May the LORD, the God of your fathers, make you a thousand times as many as you are and bless you, as he has promised you! ¹²How can I bear by myself the weight and burden of you and your strife? ¹³Choose for your tribes wise, understanding, and experienced men, and I will appoint them as your heads.' ¹⁴And you answered me, 'The thing that you have spoken is good for us to do.' ¹⁵So I took the heads of your tribes, wise and experienced men, and set them as heads over you, commanders of thousands, commanders of hundreds, commanders of fifties, commanders of tens, and officers, throughout your tribes. ¹⁶And I charged your judges at that time, 'Hear the cases between your brothers, and judge righteously between a man and his brother or the alien who is with him. ¹⁷You shall not be partial in judgment. You shall hear the small and the great alike. You shall not be intimidated by anyone, for the judgment is God's. And the case that is too hard for you, you shall bring to me, and I will hear it.' ¹⁸And I commanded you at that time all the things that you should do.

¹⁹"Then we set out from Horeb and went through all that great and terrifying wilderness that you saw, on the way to the hill country of the Amorites, as the LORD our God commanded us. And we came to Kadesh-barnea. ²⁰And I said to you, 'You have come to the hill country of the Amorites, which the LORD our God is giving us. ²¹See, the LORD your God has set the land before you. Go up, take possession, as the LORD, the God of your fathers, has told you. Do not fear or be dismayed.' ²²Then all of you came near me and said, 'Let us send men before us, that they may explore the land

for us and bring us word again of the way by which we must go up and the cities into which we shall come.' ²³The thing seemed good to me, and I took twelve men from you, one man from each tribe. ²⁴And they turned and went up into the hill country, and came to the Valley of Eshcol and spied it out. ²⁵And they took in their hands some of the fruit of the land and brought it down to us, and brought us word again and said, 'It is a good land that the LORD our God is giving us.'

²⁶"Yet you would not go up, but rebelled against the command of the LORD your God. ²⁷And you murmured in your tents and said, 'Because the LORD hated us he has brought us out of the land of Egypt, to give us into the hand of the Amorites, to destroy us. ²⁸Where are we going up? Our brothers have made our hearts melt, saying, "The people are greater and taller than we. The cities are great and fortified up to heaven. And besides, we have seen the sons of the Anakim there."' ²⁹Then I said to you, 'Do not be in dread or afraid of them. ³⁰The LORD your God who goes before you will himself fight for you, just as he did for you in Egypt before your eyes, ³¹and in the wilderness, where you have seen how the LORD your God carried you, as a man carries his son, all the way that you went until you came to this place.' ³²Yet in spite of this word you did not believe the LORD your God, ³³who went before you in the way to seek you out a place to pitch your tents, in fire by night and in the cloud by day, to show you by what way you should go.

³⁴"And the LORD heard your words and was angered, and he swore, ³⁵'Not one of these men of this evil generation shall see the good land that I swore to give to your fathers, ³⁶except Caleb the son of Jephunneh. He shall see it, and to him and to his children I will give the land on which he has trodden, because he has wholly followed the LORD!' ³⁷Even with me the LORD was angry on your account and said, 'You also shall not go in there. ³⁸Joshua the son of Nun, who stands before you, he shall enter. Encourage him, for he shall cause Israel to inherit it. ³⁹And as for your little ones, who you said would become a prey, and your children, who today have no knowledge of good or evil, they shall go in there. And to them I will give it, and they shall possess it. ⁴⁰But as for you, turn, and journey into the wilderness in the direction of the Red Sea.'

⁴¹"Then you answered me, 'We have sinned against the LORD. We ourselves will go up and fight, just as the LORD our God commanded us.' And every one of you fastened on his weapons of war and thought it easy to go up into the hill country. ⁴²And the LORD said to me, 'Say to them, Do not go up or fight, for I am not in your midst, lest you be defeated before your enemies.' ⁴³So I spoke to you, and you would not listen; but you rebelled against the command of the LORD and presumptuously went up into the hill country. ⁴⁴Then the Amorites who lived in that hill country came out against you and chased you as bees do and beat you down in Seir as far as Hormah. ⁴⁵And you returned and wept before the LORD, but the LORD did not listen to your voice or give ear to you. ⁴⁶So you remained at Kadesh many days, the days that you remained there.

A leader's reminiscence [chapter 2]. The rehearsal of the nation's recent past continues in this chapter. It stands to reason that Moses the leader recalls the events that in retrospect were the landmark events of his tenure as leader. It is like a U.S. president's memoirs of his term in office. With that as a premise, we can assimilate the chapter in terms of what we infer about Moses' assessment of his political and religious career. Moses emerges as the archetypal leader, and what he remembers in chapter 2 are the military victories on which he led his nation, under the ultimate leadership of God (in this regard it is useful to go through the chapter looking at all the references to God). The specific events recalled in chapter 2 are as follows: God's command to purchase provisions from the Edomites instead of engaging them in military conflict (vv. 1–8); thirty-eight years of wandering in the wilderness (vv. 8–15); commencement of the march to Canaan (vv. 16–25); conquest of Sihon king of Heshbon (vv. 26–37).

2 "Then we turned and journeyed into the wilderness in the direction of the Red Sea, as the Lord told me. And for many days we traveled around Mount Seir. ²Then the Lord said to me, ³'You have been traveling around this mountain country long enough. Turn northward ⁴and command the people, "You are about to pass through the territory of your brothers, the people of Esau, who live in Seir; and they will be afraid of you. So be very careful. ⁵Do not contend with them, for I will not give you any of their land, no, not so much as for the sole of the foot to tread on, because I have given Mount Seir to Esau as a possession. ⁶You shall purchase food from them for money, that you may eat, and you shall also buy water of them for money, that you may drink. ⁷For the Lord your God has blessed you in all the work of your hands. He knows your going through this great wilderness. These forty years the Lord your God has been with you. You have lacked nothing."' ⁸So we went on, away from our brothers, the people of Esau, who live in Seir, away from the Arabah road from Elath and Ezion-geber.

"And we turned and went in the direction of the wilderness of Moab. ⁹And the Lord said to me, 'Do not harass Moab or contend with them in battle, for I will not give you any of their land for a possession, because I have given Ar to the people of Lot for a possession.' ¹⁰(The Emim formerly lived there, a people great and many, and tall as the Anakim. ¹¹Like the Anakim they are also counted as Rephaim, but the Moabites call them Emim. ¹²The Horites also lived in Seir formerly, but the people of Esau dispossessed them and destroyed them from before them and settled in their place, as Israel did to the land of their possession, which the Lord gave to them.) ¹³'Now rise up and go over the brook Zered.' So we went over the brook Zered. ¹⁴And the time from our leaving Kadesh-barnea until we crossed the brook Zered was thirty-eight years, until the entire generation, that is, the men of war, had perished from the camp, as the Lord had sworn to them. ¹⁵For indeed the hand of the Lord was against them, to destroy them from the camp, until they had perished.

¹⁶"So as soon as all the men of war had perished and were dead from among the people, ¹⁷the Lord said to me, ¹⁸'Today you are to cross the border of Moab at Ar. ¹⁹And when you approach the territory of the people of Ammon, do not harass them or contend with them, for I will not give you any of the land of the people of Ammon as a possession, because I have given it to the sons of Lot for a possession.' ²⁰(It is also counted as a land of Rephaim. Rephaim formerly lived there—but the Ammonites call them Zamzummim— ²¹a people great and many, and tall as the Anakim; but the Lord destroyed them before the Ammonites,¹ and they dispossessed them and settled in their place, ²²as he did for the people of Esau, who live in Seir, when he destroyed the Horites before them and they dispossessed them and settled in their place even to

¹ Hebrew them

this day. ²³As for the Avvim, who lived in villages as far as Gaza, the Caphtorim, who came from Caphtor, destroyed them and settled in their place.) ²⁴'Rise up, set out on your journey and go over the Valley of the Arnon. Behold, I have given into your hand Sihon the Amorite, king of Heshbon, and his land. Begin to take possession, and contend with him in battle. ²⁵This day I will begin to put the dread and fear of you on the peoples who are under the whole heaven, who shall hear the report of you and shall tremble and be in anguish because of you.'

²⁶"So I sent messengers from the wilderness of Kedemoth to Sihon the king of Heshbon, with words of peace, saying, ²⁷'Let me pass through your land. I will go only by the road; I will turn aside neither to the right nor to the left. ²⁸You shall sell me food for money, that I may eat, and give me water for money, that I may drink. Only let me pass through on foot, ²⁹as the sons of Esau who live in Seir and the Moabites who live in Ar did for me, until I go over the Jordan into the land that the LORD our God is giving to us.' ³⁰But Sihon the king of Heshbon would not let us pass by him, for the LORD your God hardened his spirit and made his heart obstinate, that he might give him into your hand, as he is this day. ³¹And the LORD said to me, 'Behold, I have begun to give Sihon and his land over to you. Begin to take possession, that you may occupy his land.' ³²Then Sihon came out against us, he and all his people, to battle at Jahaz. ³³And the LORD our God gave him over to us, and we defeated him and his sons and all his people. ³⁴And we captured all his cities at that time and devoted to destruction¹ every city, men, women, and children. We left no survivors. ³⁵Only the livestock we took as spoil for ourselves, with the plunder of the cities that we captured. ³⁶From Aroer, which is on the edge of the Valley of the Arnon, and from the city that is in the valley, as far as Gilead, there was not a city too high for us. The LORD our God gave all into our hands. ³⁷Only to the land of the sons of Ammon you did not draw near, that is, to all the banks of the river Jabbok and the cities of the hill country, whatever the LORD our God had forbidden us.

From history to the present moment [chapter 3]. As Moses brings his historical recollections to an end, he moves through the following sequence: events that happened on the march in the wilderness (vv. 1–11); the recent past in which two and a half tribes were allowed to settle east of the Jordan River (vv. 12–17); conditions under which those tribes were given permission to settle outside the regular boundary of the nation (vv. 18–20); Moses' instruction to his successor (vv. 21–22); God's refusal to allow Moses to enter the Promised Land, accompanied by God's command to transfer the leadership to Joshua (vv. 23–29). God is a conspicuous character in the account; we can assemble a portrait of God on the basis of these references. We also get an implied portrait of good leadership in the actions of Moses.

3 "Then we turned and went up the way to Bashan. And Og the king of Bashan came out against us, he and all his people, to battle at Edrei. ²But the LORD said to me, 'Do not fear him, for I have given him and all his people and his land into your hand. And you shall do to him as you did to Sihon the king of the Amorites, who lived at Heshbon.' ³So the LORD our God gave into our hand Og also, the king of Bashan, and all his people, and we struck him down until he had no survivor left. ⁴And we took all his cities at that time—there was not a city that we did not take from them—sixty cities, the whole region of Argob, the kingdom of Og in Bashan. ⁵All these were

¹ That is, set apart (devoted) as an offering to the Lord (for destruction)

cities fortified with high walls, gates, and bars, besides very many unwalled villages. [6]And we devoted them to destruction,[1] as we did to Sihon the king of Heshbon, devoting to destruction every city, men, women, and children. [7]But all the livestock and the spoil of the cities we took as our plunder. [8]So we took the land at that time out of the hand of the two kings of the Amorites who were beyond the Jordan, from the Valley of the Arnon to Mount Hermon [9](the Sidonians call Hermon Sirion, while the Amorites call it Senir), [10]all the cities of the tableland and all Gilead and all Bashan, as far as Salecah and Edrei, cities of the kingdom of Og in Bashan. [11](For only Og the king of Bashan was left of the remnant of the Rephaim. Behold, his bed was a bed of iron. Is it not in Rabbah of the Ammonites? Nine cubits[2] was its length, and four cubits its breadth, according to the common cubit.[3])

[12]"When we took possession of this land at that time, I gave to the Reubenites and the Gadites the territory beginning at Aroer, which is on the edge of the Valley of the Arnon, and half the hill country of Gilead with its cities. [13]The rest of Gilead, and all Bashan, the kingdom of Og, that is, all the region of Argob, I gave to the half-tribe of Manasseh. (All that portion of Bashan is called the land of Rephaim. [14]Jair the Manassite took all the region of Argob, that is, Bashan, as far as the border of the Geshurites and the Maacathites, and called the villages after his own name, Havvoth-jair, as it is to this day.) [15]To Machir I gave Gilead, [16]and to the Reubenites and the Gadites I gave the territory from Gilead as far as the Valley of the Arnon, with the middle of the valley as a border, as far over as the river Jabbok, the border of the Ammonites; [17]the Arabah also, with the Jordan as the border, from Chinnereth as far as the Sea of the Arabah, the Salt Sea, under the slopes of Pisgah on the east.

[18]"And I commanded you at that time, saying, 'The LORD your God has given you this land to possess. All your men of valor shall cross over armed before your brothers, the people of Israel. [19]Only your wives, your little ones, and your livestock (I know that you have much livestock) shall remain in the cities that I have given you, [20]until the LORD gives rest to your brothers, as to you, and they also occupy the land that the LORD your God gives them beyond the Jordan. Then each of you may return to his possession which I have given you.' [21]And I commanded Joshua at that time, 'Your eyes have seen all that the LORD your God has done to these two kings. So will the LORD do to all the kingdoms into which you are crossing. [22]You shall not fear them, for it is the LORD your God who fights for you.'

[23]"And I pleaded with the LORD at that time, saying, [24]'O Lord GOD, you have only begun to show your servant your greatness and your mighty hand. For what god is there in heaven or on earth who can do such works and mighty acts as yours? [25]Please let me go over and see the good land beyond the Jordan, that good hill country and Lebanon.' [26]But the LORD was angry with me because of you and would not listen to me. And the LORD said to me, 'Enough from you; do not speak to me of this matter again. [27]Go up to the top of Pisgah and lift up your eyes westward and northward and southward and eastward, and look at it with your eyes, for you shall not go over this Jordan. [28]But charge Joshua, and encourage and strengthen him, for he shall go over at the head of this people, and he shall put them in possession of the land that you shall see.' [29]So we remained in the valley opposite Beth-peor.

---

[1] That is, set apart (devoted) as an offering to the Lord (for destruction); twice in this verse   [2] A *cubit* was about 18 inches or 45 centimeters   [3] Hebrew *cubit of a man*

Exhortation to a nation [chapter 4]. The opening verse is a transition from recollection of the past to exhortation regarding the future. The rhetorical formulas interspersed throughout the passage suggest that the purpose is not primarily to inform but to move the listeners to obedience: "listen to" (v. 1); "keep them and do them" (v. 6); "only take care" (v. 9); "therefore watch yourselves" (v. 15); "therefore you shall keep his statutes and his commandments" (v. 40). The need to obey is the unifying theme of the chapter. Specific topics include the following: prologue (vv. 1–5); exhortation and motivation to obey (vv. 6–8); recollection of the glory of God's revelation at Mount Sinai (vv. 9–14); the need to refrain from idolatry and a prediction of what will happen if the nation disobeys that prohibition (vv. 15–31); a reminder of the special spiritual status of Israel (vv. 32–40); Moses' establishment of cities of refuge (vv. 41–43); description of the setting in which Moses delivered his oration that we know as the book of Deuteronomy (vv. 44–49).

4 "And now, O Israel, listen to the statutes and the rules[1] that I am teaching you, and do them, that you may live, and go in and take possession of the land that the LORD, the God of your fathers, is giving you. [2] You shall not add to the word that I command you, nor take from it, that you may keep the commandments of the LORD your God that I command you. [3] Your eyes have seen what the LORD did at Baal-peor, for the LORD your God destroyed from among you all the men who followed the Baal of Peor. [4] But you who held fast to the LORD your God are all alive today. [5] See, I have taught you statutes and rules, as the LORD my God commanded me, that you should do them in the land that you are entering to take possession of it. [6] Keep them and do them, for that will be your wisdom and your understanding in the sight of the peoples, who, when they hear all these statutes, will say, 'Surely this great nation is a wise and understanding people.' [7] For what great nation is there that has a god so near to it as the LORD our God is to us, whenever we call upon him? [8] And what great nation is there, that has statutes and rules so righteous as all this law that I set before you today?

[9] "Only take care, and keep your soul diligently, lest you forget the things that your eyes have seen, and lest they depart from your heart all the days of your life. Make them known to your children and your children's children— [10] how on the day that you stood before the LORD your God at Horeb, the LORD said to me, 'Gather the people to me, that I may let them hear my words, so that they may learn to fear me all the days that they live on the earth, and that they may teach their children so.' [11] And you came near and stood at the foot of the mountain, while the mountain burned with fire to the heart of heaven, wrapped in darkness, cloud, and gloom. [12] Then the LORD spoke to you out of the midst of the fire. You heard the sound of words, but saw no form; there was only a voice. [13] And he declared to you his covenant, which he commanded you to perform, that is, the Ten Commandments,[2] and he wrote them on two tablets of stone. [14] And the LORD commanded me at that time to teach you statutes and rules, that you might do them in the land that you are going over to possess.

[15] "Therefore watch yourselves very carefully. Since you saw no form on the day that the LORD spoke to you at Horeb out of the midst of the fire, [16] beware lest you act corruptly by making a carved image for yourselves, in the form of any figure, the likeness of male or female, [17] the likeness of any animal that is on the earth, the likeness of any winged bird that flies in the air, [18] the likeness of anything that creeps on the

---

[1] Or *just decrees*; also verses 5, 8, 14, 45   [2] Hebrew *words*

ground, the likeness of any fish that is in the water under the earth. [19]And beware lest you raise your eyes to heaven, and when you see the sun and the moon and the stars, all the host of heaven, you be drawn away and bow down to them and serve them, things that the LORD your God has allotted to all the peoples under the whole heaven. [20]But the LORD has taken you and brought you out of the iron furnace, out of Egypt, to be a people of his own inheritance, as you are this day. [21]Furthermore, the LORD was angry with me because of you, and he swore that I should not cross the Jordan, and that I should not enter the good land that the LORD your God is giving you for an inheritance. [22]For I must die in this land; I must not go over the Jordan. But you shall go over and take possession of that good land. [23]Take care, lest you forget the covenant of the LORD your God, which he made with you, and make a carved image, the form of anything that the LORD your God has forbidden you. [24]For the LORD your God is a consuming fire, a jealous God.

[25]"When you father children and children's children, and have grown old in the land, if you act corruptly by making a carved image in the form of anything, and by doing what is evil in the sight of the LORD your God, so as to provoke him to anger, [26]I call heaven and earth to witness against you today, that you will soon utterly perish from the land that you are going over the Jordan to possess. You will not live long in it, but will be utterly destroyed. [27]And the LORD will scatter you among the peoples, and you will be left few in number among the nations where the LORD will drive you. [28]And there you will serve gods of wood and stone, the work of human hands, that neither see, nor hear, nor eat, nor smell. [29]But from there you will seek the LORD your God and you will find him, if you search after him with all your heart and with all your soul. [30]When you are in tribulation, and all these things come upon you in the latter days, you will return to the LORD your God and obey his voice. [31]For the LORD your God is a merciful God. He will not leave you or destroy you or forget the covenant with your fathers that he swore to them.

[32]"For ask now of the days that are past, which were before you, since the day that God created man on the earth, and ask from one end of heaven to the other, whether such a great thing as this has ever happened or was ever heard of. [33]Did any people ever hear the voice of a god speaking out of the midst of the fire, as you have heard, and still live? [34]Or has any god ever attempted to go and take a nation for himself from the midst of another nation, by trials, by signs, by wonders, and by war, by a mighty hand and an outstretched arm, and by great deeds of terror, all of which the LORD your God did for you in Egypt before your eyes? [35]To you it was shown, that you might know that the LORD is God; there is no other besides him. [36]Out of heaven he let you hear his voice, that he might discipline you. And on earth he let you see his great fire, and you heard his words out of the midst of the fire. [37]And because he loved your fathers and chose their offspring after them[1] and brought you out of Egypt with his own presence, by his great power, [38]driving out before you nations greater and mightier than yourselves, to bring you in, to give you their land for an inheritance, as it is this day, [39]know therefore today, and lay it to your heart, that the LORD is God in heaven above and on the earth beneath; there is no other. [40]Therefore you shall keep his statutes and his commandments, which I command you today, that it may go well with you and with your children after you, and that you may prolong your days in the land that the LORD your God is giving you for all time."

[41]Then Moses set apart three cities in the east beyond the Jordan, [42]that the man-

---

[1] Hebrew *his offspring after him*

slayer might flee there, anyone who kills his neighbor unintentionally, without being
at enmity with him in time past; he may flee to one of these cities and save his life:
⁴³Bezer in the wilderness on the tableland for the Reubenites, Ramoth in Gilead for
the Gadites, and Golan in Bashan for the Manassites.

⁴⁴This is the law that Moses set before the people of Israel. ⁴⁵These are the testimonies, the statutes, and the rules, which Moses spoke to the people of Israel when they
came out of Egypt, ⁴⁶beyond the Jordan in the valley opposite Beth-peor, in the land of
Sihon the king of the Amorites, who lived at Heshbon, whom Moses and the people
of Israel defeated when they came out of Egypt. ⁴⁷And they took possession of his
land and the land of Og, the king of Bashan, the two kings of the Amorites, who lived
to the east beyond the Jordan; ⁴⁸from Aroer, which is on the edge of the Valley of the
Arnon, as far as Mount Sirion¹ (that is, Hermon), ⁴⁹together with all the Arabah on
the east side of the Jordan as far as the Sea of the Arabah, under the slopes of Pisgah.

> **Recollection of the law that God gave at Mount Sinai** [chapter 5]. The lead-in (vv.
> 1–5) informs us that in this unit Moses aims to rehearse the law that God gave the
> nation at Mount Sinai (vv. 6–21), along with a reminder of the events that transpired on
> that occasion (vv. 22–33). The restatement of the Ten Commandments reminds us that
> Deuteronomy is a "second law"—a book that partly restates laws recorded in earlier
> books of the Pentateuch. Throughout his farewell address, Moses keeps his rhetorical or
> persuasive purpose in mind—to move the people to obey the law that he rehearses (vv.
> 32–33).

5 And Moses summoned all Israel and said to them, "Hear, O Israel, the statutes
and the rules that I speak in your hearing today, and you shall learn them and be
careful to do them. ²The LORD our God made a covenant with us in Horeb. ³Not with
our fathers did the LORD make this covenant, but with us, who are all of us here alive
today. ⁴The LORD spoke with you face to face at the mountain, out of the midst of the
fire, ⁵while I stood between the LORD and you at that time, to declare to you the word
of the LORD. For you were afraid because of the fire, and you did not go up into the
mountain. He said:

⁶"'I am the LORD your God, who brought you out of the land of Egypt, out of the
house of slavery.

⁷"'You shall have no other gods before² me.

⁸"'You shall not make for yourself a carved image, or any likeness of anything that
is in heaven above, or that is on the earth beneath, or that is in the water under the
earth. ⁹You shall not bow down to them or serve them; for I the LORD your God am a
jealous God, visiting the iniquity of the fathers on the children to the third and fourth
generation of those who hate me, ¹⁰but showing steadfast love to thousands³ of those
who love me and keep my commandments.

¹¹"'You shall not take the name of the LORD your God in vain, for the LORD will not
hold him guiltless who takes his name in vain.

¹²"'Observe the Sabbath day, to keep it holy, as the LORD your God commanded
you. ¹³Six days you shall labor and do all your work, ¹⁴but the seventh day is a
Sabbath to the LORD your God. On it you shall not do any work, you or your son or
your daughter or your male servant or your female servant, or your ox or your donkey

---

¹ Syriac; Hebrew *Sion* ² Or *besides* ³ Or *to the thousandth generation*

or any of your livestock, or the sojourner who is within your gates, that your male servant and your female servant may rest as well as you. [15]You shall remember that you were a slave[1] in the land of Egypt, and the LORD your God brought you out from there with a mighty hand and an outstretched arm. Therefore the LORD your God commanded you to keep the Sabbath day.

[16]"'Honor your father and your mother, as the LORD your God commanded you, that your days may be long, and that it may go well with you in the land that the LORD your God is giving you.

[17]"'You shall not murder.[2]

[18]"'And you shall not commit adultery.

[19]"'And you shall not steal.

[20]"'And you shall not bear false witness against your neighbor.

[21]"'And you shall not covet your neighbor's wife. And you shall not desire your neighbor's house, his field, or his male servant, or his female servant, his ox, or his donkey, or anything that is your neighbor's.'

[22]"These words the LORD spoke to all your assembly at the mountain out of the midst of the fire, the cloud, and the thick darkness, with a loud voice; and he added no more. And he wrote them on two tablets of stone and gave them to me. [23]And as soon as you heard the voice out of the midst of the darkness, while the mountain was burning with fire, you came near to me, all the heads of your tribes, and your elders. [24]And you said, 'Behold, the LORD our God has shown us his glory and greatness, and we have heard his voice out of the midst of the fire. This day we have seen God speak with man, and man still live. [25]Now therefore why should we die? For this great fire will consume us. If we hear the voice of the LORD our God any more, we shall die. [26]For who is there of all flesh, that has heard the voice of the living God speaking out of the midst of fire as we have, and has still lived? [27]Go near and hear all that the LORD our God will say and speak to us all that the LORD our God will speak to you, and we will hear and do it.'

[28]"And the LORD heard your words, when you spoke to me. And the LORD said to me, 'I have heard the words of this people, which they have spoken to you. They are right in all that they have spoken. [29]Oh that they had such a mind as this always, to fear me and to keep all my commandments, that it might go well with them and with their descendants[3] forever! [30]Go and say to them, "Return to your tents." [31]But you, stand here by me, and I will tell you the whole commandment and the statutes and the rules that you shall teach them, that they may do them in the land that I am giving them to possess.' [32]You shall be careful therefore to do as the LORD your God has commanded you. You shall not turn aside to the right hand or to the left. [33]You shall walk in all the way that the LORD your God has commanded you, that you may live, and that it may go well with you, and that you may live long in the land that you shall possess.

What to do about the law that God gave [chapter 6]. This chapter may be a follow-up to the recollection of the Ten Commandments, though it is not implausible to see it as a general statement about how to view all of the laws that God gives. Three chief lessons are asserted: the need to obey God's law (vv. 1–3); the need to teach the law to children (vv. 4–9, 20–25); the need to obey only the true God as the prerequisite to living well in the Promised Land (vv. 10–19).

---

[1] Or *servant* [2] The Hebrew word also covers causing human death through carelessness or negligence [3] Or *sons*

6 "Now this is the commandment, the statutes and the rules[1] that the LORD your God commanded me to teach you, that you may do them in the land to which you are going over, to possess it, [2]that you may fear the LORD your God, you and your son and your son's son, by keeping all his statutes and his commandments, which I command you, all the days of your life, and that your days may be long. [3]Hear therefore, O Israel, and be careful to do them, that it may go well with you, and that you may multiply greatly, as the LORD, the God of your fathers, has promised you, in a land flowing with milk and honey.

[4]"Hear, O Israel: The LORD our God, the LORD is one.[2] [5]You shall love the LORD your God with all your heart and with all your soul and with all your might. [6]And these words that I command you today shall be on your heart. [7]You shall teach them diligently to your children, and shall talk of them when you sit in your house, and when you walk by the way, and when you lie down, and when you rise. [8]You shall bind them as a sign on your hand, and they shall be as frontlets between your eyes. [9]You shall write them on the doorposts of your house and on your gates.

[10]"And when the LORD your God brings you into the land that he swore to your fathers, to Abraham, to Isaac, and to Jacob, to give you—with great and good cities that you did not build, [11]and houses full of all good things that you did not fill, and cisterns that you did not dig, and vineyards and olive trees that you did not plant— and when you eat and are full, [12]then take care lest you forget the LORD, who brought you out of the land of Egypt, out of the house of slavery. [13]It is the LORD your God you shall fear. Him you shall serve and by his name you shall swear. [14]You shall not go after other gods, the gods of the peoples who are around you— [15]for the LORD your God in your midst is a jealous God—lest the anger of the LORD your God be kindled against you, and he destroy you from off the face of the earth.

[16]"You shall not put the LORD your God to the test, as you tested him at Massah. [17]You shall diligently keep the commandments of the LORD your God, and his testimonies and his statutes, which he has commanded you. [18]And you shall do what is right and good in the sight of the LORD, that it may go well with you, and that you may go in and take possession of the good land that the LORD swore to give to your fathers [19]by thrusting out all your enemies from before you, as the LORD has promised.

[20]"When your son asks you in time to come, 'What is the meaning of the testimonies and the statutes and the rules that the LORD our God has commanded you?' [21]then you shall say to your son, 'We were Pharaoh's slaves in Egypt. And the LORD brought us out of Egypt with a mighty hand. [22]And the LORD showed signs and wonders, great and grievous, against Egypt and against Pharaoh and all his household, before our eyes. [23]And he brought us out from there, that he might bring us in and give us the land that he swore to give to our fathers. [24]And the LORD commanded us to do all these statutes, to fear the LORD our God, for our good always, that he might preserve us alive, as we are this day. [25]And it will be righteousness for us, if we are careful to do all this commandment before the LORD our God, as he has commanded us.'

Dealing with the Canaanites [chapter 7]. This chapter contains Moses' instructions to the nation regarding how they must deal with the Canaanites when they enter the Promised Land. The rhetorical form is what we might call a game plan for an upcoming conflict. The game plan unfolds as follows: the need to destroy the Canaanites and not

---

[1] Or just decrees; also verse 20 [2] Or The LORD our God is one LORD; or The LORD is our God, the LORD is one; or The LORD is our God, the LORD alone

intermarry with them (vv. 1–5); the reason for that command, namely Israel's status as God's people, called to be pure in their loyalty to God (vv. 6–16); assurance that God will strengthen the Israelites for the task of destroying the Canaanites (vv. 17–24); reiteration of the need to avoid contamination in the form of idolatry (vv. 25–26). Among the themes that pervade these details are the following: the sovereignty of God (note the prominence of God as the chief agent in this chapter); God's call to his people to obey him and rely on him; God's call to holiness and his total repudiation of sin.

7 "When the Lord your God brings you into the land that you are entering to take possession of it, and clears away many nations before you, the Hittites, the Girgashites, the Amorites, the Canaanites, the Perizzites, the Hivites, and the Jebusites, seven nations more numerous and mightier than yourselves, ²and when the Lord your God gives them over to you, and you defeat them, then you must devote them to complete destruction.¹ You shall make no covenant with them and show no mercy to them. ³You shall not intermarry with them, giving your daughters to their sons or taking their daughters for your sons, ⁴for they would turn away your sons from following me, to serve other gods. Then the anger of the Lord would be kindled against you, and he would destroy you quickly. ⁵But thus shall you deal with them: you shall break down their altars and dash in pieces their pillars and chop down their Asherim and burn their carved images with fire.

⁶"For you are a people holy to the Lord your God. The Lord your God has chosen you to be a people for his treasured possession, out of all the peoples who are on the face of the earth. ⁷It was not because you were more in number than any other people that the Lord set his love on you and chose you, for you were the fewest of all peoples, ⁸but it is because the Lord loves you and is keeping the oath that he swore to your fathers, that the Lord has brought you out with a mighty hand and redeemed you from the house of slavery, from the hand of Pharaoh king of Egypt. ⁹Know therefore that the Lord your God is God, the faithful God who keeps covenant and steadfast love with those who love him and keep his commandments, to a thousand generations, ¹⁰and repays to their face those who hate him, by destroying them. He will not be slack with one who hates him. He will repay him to his face. ¹¹You shall therefore be careful to do the commandment and the statutes and the rules that I command you today.

¹²"And because you listen to these rules and keep and do them, the Lord your God will keep with you the covenant and the steadfast love that he swore to your fathers. ¹³He will love you, bless you, and multiply you. He will also bless the fruit of your womb and the fruit of your ground, your grain and your wine and your oil, the increase of your herds and the young of your flock, in the land that he swore to your fathers to give you. ¹⁴You shall be blessed above all peoples. There shall not be male or female barren among you or among your livestock. ¹⁵And the Lord will take away from you all sickness, and none of the evil diseases of Egypt, which you knew, will he inflict on you, but he will lay them on all who hate you. ¹⁶And you shall consume all the peoples that the Lord your God will give over to you. Your eye shall not pity them, neither shall you serve their gods, for that would be a snare to you.

¹⁷"If you say in your heart, 'These nations are greater than I. How can I dispossess them?' ¹⁸you shall not be afraid of them but you shall remember what the Lord your

¹ That is, set apart (devote) as an offering to the Lord (for destruction)

God did to Pharaoh and to all Egypt, [19]the great trials that your eyes saw, the signs, the wonders, the mighty hand, and the outstretched arm, by which the LORD your God brought you out. So will the LORD your God do to all the peoples of whom you are afraid. [20]Moreover, the LORD your God will send hornets among them, until those who are left and hide themselves from you are destroyed. [21]You shall not be in dread of them, for the LORD your God is in your midst, a great and awesome God. [22]The LORD your God will clear away these nations before you little by little. You may not make an end of them at once,[1] lest the wild beasts grow too numerous for you. [23]But the LORD your God will give them over to you and throw them into great confusion, until they are destroyed. [24]And he will give their kings into your hand, and you shall make their name perish from under heaven. No one shall be able to stand against you until you have destroyed them. [25]The carved images of their gods you shall burn with fire. You shall not covet the silver or the gold that is on them or take it for yourselves, lest you be ensnared by it, for it is an abomination to the LORD your God. [26]And you shall not bring an abominable thing into your house and become devoted to destruction[2] like it. You shall utterly detest and abhor it, for it is devoted to destruction.

How to enter the Promised Land [8:1–9:5]. The general drift of this unit is prospective, as Moses outlines the proper attitude for entering the Promised Land. The keynotes are as follows: the need for humble gratitude regarding God's past blessings (8:1–10); warning against pride and forgetfulness, accompanied by a prediction of divine judgment for those lapses (8:11–20); God's confidence-instilling promise that he will strengthen the Israelites for conquest (9:1–3); reasons that this should not lead the Israelites to think themselves inherently superior (9:4–5). Good ways to organize the passage include the following: note the references to the past and the future and the way Moses relates them to each other; organize the material into a list of positive commands and a corresponding list of prohibitions; generalize about how God wants believers to live in all circumstances on the basis of these specific commands to a specific nation at a specific time in history.

8 "The whole commandment that I command you today you shall be careful to do, that you may live and multiply, and go in and possess the land that the LORD swore to give to your fathers. [2]And you shall remember the whole way that the LORD your God has led you these forty years in the wilderness, that he might humble you, testing you to know what was in your heart, whether you would keep his commandments or not. [3]And he humbled you and let you hunger and fed you with manna, which you did not know, nor did your fathers know, that he might make you know that man does not live by bread alone, but man lives by every word[3] that comes from the mouth of the LORD. [4]Your clothing did not wear out on you and your foot did not swell these forty years. [5]Know then in your heart that, as a man disciplines his son, the LORD your God disciplines you. [6]So you shall keep the commandments of the LORD your God by walking in his ways and by fearing him. [7]For the LORD your God is bringing you into a good land, a land of brooks of water, of fountains and springs, flowing out in the valleys and hills, [8]a land of wheat and barley, of vines and fig trees and pomegranates, a land of olive trees and honey, [9]a land in which you will eat bread without scarcity, in which you will lack nothing, a land whose stones are iron,

---

[1] Or *quickly* [2] That is, set apart (devoted) as an offering to the Lord (for destruction); twice in this verse [3] Hebrew *by all*

and out of whose hills you can dig copper. ¹⁰And you shall eat and be full, and you shall bless the LORD your God for the good land he has given you.

¹¹"Take care lest you forget the LORD your God by not keeping his commandments and his rules and his statutes, which I command you today, ¹²lest, when you have eaten and are full and have built good houses and live in them, ¹³and when your herds and flocks multiply and your silver and gold is multiplied and all that you have is multiplied, ¹⁴then your heart be lifted up, and you forget the LORD your God, who brought you out of the land of Egypt, out of the house of slavery, ¹⁵who led you through the great and terrifying wilderness, with its fiery serpents and scorpions and thirsty ground where there was no water, who brought you water out of the flinty rock, ¹⁶who fed you in the wilderness with manna that your fathers did not know, that he might humble you and test you, to do you good in the end. ¹⁷Beware lest you say in your heart, 'My power and the might of my hand have gotten me this wealth.' ¹⁸You shall remember the LORD your God, for it is he who gives you power to get wealth, that he may confirm his covenant that he swore to your fathers, as it is this day. ¹⁹And if you forget the LORD your God and go after other gods and serve them and worship them, I solemnly warn you today that you shall surely perish. ²⁰Like the nations that the LORD makes to perish before you, so shall you perish, because you would not obey the voice of the LORD your God.

9 "Hear, O Israel: you are to cross over the Jordan today, to go in to dispossess nations greater and mightier than yourselves, cities great and fortified up to heaven, ²a people great and tall, the sons of the Anakim, whom you know, and of whom you have heard it said, 'Who can stand before the sons of Anak?' ³Know therefore today that he who goes over before you as a consuming fire is the LORD your God. He will destroy them and subdue them before you. So you shall drive them out and make them perish quickly, as the LORD has promised you.

⁴"Do not say in your heart, after the LORD your God has thrust them out before you, 'It is because of my righteousness that the LORD has brought me in to possess this land,' whereas it is because of the wickedness of these nations that the LORD is driving them out before you. ⁵Not because of your righteousness or the uprightness of your heart are you going in to possess their land, but because of the wickedness of these nations the LORD your God is driving them out from before you, and that he may confirm the word that the LORD swore to your fathers, to Abraham, to Isaac, and to Jacob.

History lesson [9:6–10:11]. Whereas the thrust of the previous unit was prospective, the stance in this passage is retrospective. Moses rehearses the national history of the exodus as a way of proving the thesis that has already been stated in the preceding unit and restated in 9:6—that God is not giving Israel the Promised Land because of meritorious behavior. On the contrary, Israel is "a stubborn people" that has been "rebellious against the LORD" from the deliverance out of Egypt to the present day (9:6–7). The entire remainder of the history lesson offers supporting proof for that thesis, as Moses gives a selective history of the exodus, with the events arranged chronologically as follows: the golden calf (9:8–17); Moses' heroic intercession for Israel on that occasion of sin (9:18–19); God's punishment of the idolaters at Mount Sinai (9:20–21); further rebellions against God during the exodus (9:22–24); further intercession by Moses for his people (9:25–29); replacement tables of the law (10:1–5, 10–11); details of the journey through the wilderness (10:6–9).

⁶"Know, therefore, that the LORD your God is not giving you this good land to possess because of your righteousness, for you are a stubborn people. ⁷Remember and do not forget how you provoked the LORD your God to wrath in the wilderness. From the day you came out of the land of Egypt until you came to this place, you have been rebellious against the LORD. ⁸Even at Horeb you provoked the LORD to wrath, and the LORD was so angry with you that he was ready to destroy you. ⁹When I went up the mountain to receive the tablets of stone, the tablets of the covenant that the LORD made with you, I remained on the mountain forty days and forty nights. I neither ate bread nor drank water. ¹⁰And the LORD gave me the two tablets of stone written with the finger of God, and on them were all the words that the LORD had spoken with you on the mountain out of the midst of the fire on the day of the assembly. ¹¹And at the end of forty days and forty nights the LORD gave me the two tablets of stone, the tablets of the covenant. ¹²Then the LORD said to me, 'Arise, go down quickly from here, for your people whom you have brought from Egypt have acted corruptly. They have turned aside quickly out of the way that I commanded them; they have made themselves a metal image.'

¹³"Furthermore, the LORD said to me, 'I have seen this people, and behold, it is a stubborn people. ¹⁴Let me alone, that I may destroy them and blot out their name from under heaven. And I will make of you a nation mightier and greater than they.' ¹⁵So I turned and came down from the mountain, and the mountain was burning with fire. And the two tablets of the covenant were in my two hands. ¹⁶And I looked, and behold, you had sinned against the LORD your God. You had made yourselves a golden[1] calf. You had turned aside quickly from the way that the LORD had commanded you. ¹⁷So I took hold of the two tablets and threw them out of my two hands and broke them before your eyes. ¹⁸Then I lay prostrate before the LORD as before, forty days and forty nights. I neither ate bread nor drank water, because of all the sin that you had committed, in doing what was evil in the sight of the LORD to provoke him to anger. ¹⁹For I was afraid of the anger and hot displeasure that the LORD bore against you, so that he was ready to destroy you. But the LORD listened to me that time also. ²⁰And the LORD was so angry with Aaron that he was ready to destroy him. And I prayed for Aaron also at the same time. ²¹Then I took the sinful thing, the calf that you had made, and burned it with fire and crushed it, grinding it very small, until it was as fine as dust. And I threw the dust of it into the brook that ran down from the mountain.

²²"At Taberah also, and at Massah and at Kibroth-hattaavah you provoked the LORD to wrath. ²³And when the LORD sent you from Kadesh-barnea, saying, 'Go up and take possession of the land that I have given you,' then you rebelled against the commandment of the LORD your God and did not believe him or obey his voice. ²⁴You have been rebellious against the LORD from the day that I knew you.

²⁵"So I lay prostrate before the LORD for these forty days and forty nights, because the LORD had said he would destroy you. ²⁶And I prayed to the LORD, 'O Lord GOD, do not destroy your people and your heritage, whom you have redeemed through your greatness, whom you have brought out of Egypt with a mighty hand. ²⁷Remember your servants, Abraham, Isaac, and Jacob. Do not regard the stubbornness of this

---

[1] Hebrew cast-metal

people, or their wickedness or their sin, ²⁸lest the land from which you brought us say, "Because the LORD was not able to bring them into the land that he promised them, and because he hated them, he has brought them out to put them to death in the wilderness." ²⁹For they are your people and your heritage, whom you brought out by your great power and by your outstretched arm.'

10 "At that time the LORD said to me, 'Cut for yourself two tablets of stone like the first, and come up to me on the mountain and make an ark of wood. ²And I will write on the tablets the words that were on the first tablets that you broke, and you shall put them in the ark.' ³So I made an ark of acacia wood, and cut two tablets of stone like the first, and went up the mountain with the two tablets in my hand. ⁴And he wrote on the tablets, in the same writing as before, the Ten Commandments[1] that the LORD had spoken to you on the mountain out of the midst of the fire on the day of the assembly. And the LORD gave them to me. ⁵Then I turned and came down from the mountain and put the tablets in the ark that I had made. And there they are, as the LORD commanded me."

⁶(The people of Israel journeyed from Beeroth Bene-jaakan[2] to Moserah. There Aaron died, and there he was buried. And his son Eleazar ministered as priest in his place. ⁷From there they journeyed to Gudgodah, and from Gudgodah to Jotbathah, a land with brooks of water. ⁸At that time the LORD set apart the tribe of Levi to carry the ark of the covenant of the LORD to stand before the LORD to minister to him and to bless in his name, to this day. ⁹Therefore Levi has no portion or inheritance with his brothers. The LORD is his inheritance, as the LORD your God said to him.)

¹⁰"I myself stayed on the mountain, as at the first time, forty days and forty nights, and the LORD listened to me that time also. The LORD was unwilling to destroy you. ¹¹And the LORD said to me, 'Arise, go on your journey at the head of the people, so that they may go in and possess the land, which I swore to their fathers to give them.'

Life's great choice [10:12–11:32]. As the book of Deuteronomy unfolds, it will survey a very large number of OT ceremonial and civil laws. As a portal to that code book, Moses lays out a framework within which to understand the multitude of specific rules. In this introductory panel, Moses asserts the need to obey God's law—not just the laws unique to Israel but also God's timeless moral law. The material is couched as a formal oratory that unfolds as follows: fear and obedience toward God as the great requirement in life (10:12–22); the command to love God, in an awareness of God's past acts of judgment against disobedience (11:1–7); keeping God's commandments as the requirement for living well in the Promised Land (11:8–12); another command to obey and love God, accompanied by a reminder of the blessings and misfortunes that will follow from obedience and disobedience (11:13–17); a command to be continuously aware of God's commands and to teach them in one's family (11:18–21); an incentive to obey (11:22–25); life's great either-or—obedience and blessing versus disobedience and a curse (11:26–32). The passage is built on an interrelated set of contrasts and opposites: God's actions toward Israel in the past as distinct from his promised dealings with them in the future; disobeying God versus obeying him; blessing versus curse.

¹²"And now, Israel, what does the LORD your God require of you, but to fear the LORD your God, to walk in all his ways, to love him, to serve the LORD your God with

---

[1] Hebrew *words* [2] Or *the wells of the Bene-jaakan*

all your heart and with all your soul, [13]and to keep the commandments and statutes of the LORD, which I am commanding you today for your good? [14]Behold, to the LORD your God belong heaven and the heaven of heavens, the earth with all that is in it. [15]Yet the LORD set his heart in love on your fathers and chose their offspring after them, you above all peoples, as you are this day. [16]Circumcise therefore the foreskin of your heart, and be no longer stubborn. [17]For the LORD your God is God of gods and Lord of lords, the great, the mighty, and the awesome God, who is not partial and takes no bribe. [18]He executes justice for the fatherless and the widow, and loves the sojourner, giving him food and clothing. [19]Love the sojourner, therefore, for you were sojourners in the land of Egypt. [20]You shall fear the LORD your God. You shall serve him and hold fast to him, and by his name you shall swear. [21]He is your praise. He is your God, who has done for you these great and terrifying things that your eyes have seen. [22]Your fathers went down to Egypt seventy persons, and now the LORD your God has made you as numerous as the stars of heaven.

11 "You shall therefore love the LORD your God and keep his charge, his statutes, his rules, and his commandments always. [2]And consider today (since I am not speaking to your children who have not known or seen it), consider the discipline[1] of the LORD your God, his greatness, his mighty hand and his outstretched arm, [3]his signs and his deeds that he did in Egypt to Pharaoh the king of Egypt and to all his land, [4]and what he did to the army of Egypt, to their horses and to their chariots, how he made the water of the Red Sea flow over them as they pursued after you, and how the LORD has destroyed them to this day, [5]and what he did to you in the wilderness, until you came to this place, [6]and what he did to Dathan and Abiram the sons of Eliab, son of Reuben, how the earth opened its mouth and swallowed them up, with their households, their tents, and every living thing that followed them, in the midst of all Israel. [7]For your eyes have seen all the great work of the LORD that he did.

[8]"You shall therefore keep the whole commandment that I command you today, that you may be strong, and go in and take possession of the land that you are going over to possess, [9]and that you may live long in the land that the LORD swore to your fathers to give to them and to their offspring, a land flowing with milk and honey. [10]For the land that you are entering to take possession of it is not like the land of Egypt, from which you have come, where you sowed your seed and irrigated it,[2] like a garden of vegetables. [11]But the land that you are going over to possess is a land of hills and valleys, which drinks water by the rain from heaven, [12]a land that the LORD your God cares for. The eyes of the LORD your God are always upon it, from the beginning of the year to the end of the year.

[13]"And if you will indeed obey my commandments that I command you today, to love the LORD your God, and to serve him with all your heart and with all your soul, [14]he[3] will give the rain for your land in its season, the early rain and the later rain, that you may gather in your grain and your wine and your oil. [15]And he will give grass in your fields for your livestock, and you shall eat and be full. [16]Take care lest your heart be deceived, and you turn aside and serve other gods and worship them; [17]then the anger of the LORD will be kindled against you, and he will shut up the heavens, so that there will be no rain, and the land will yield no fruit, and you will perish quickly off the good land that the LORD is giving you.

[18]"You shall therefore lay up these words of mine in your heart and in your soul,

---

[1] Or *instruction* [2] Hebrew *watered it with your feet* [3] Samaritan, Septuagint, Vulgate; Hebrew *I*; also verse 15

and you shall bind them as a sign on your hand, and they shall be as frontlets between your eyes. [19]You shall teach them to your children, talking of them when you are sitting in your house, and when you are walking by the way, and when you lie down, and when you rise. [20]You shall write them on the doorposts of your house and on your gates, [21]that your days and the days of your children may be multiplied in the land that the LORD swore to your fathers to give them, as long as the heavens are above the earth. [22]For if you will be careful to do all this commandment that I command you to do, loving the LORD your God, walking in all his ways, and holding fast to him, [23]then the LORD will drive out all these nations before you, and you will dispossess nations greater and mightier than yourselves. [24]Every place on which the sole of your foot treads shall be yours. Your territory shall be from the wilderness to[1] the Lebanon and from the River, the river Euphrates, to the western sea. [25]No one shall be able to stand against you. The LORD your God will lay the fear of you and the dread of you on all the land that you shall tread, as he promised you.

[26]"See, I am setting before you today a blessing and a curse: [27]the blessing, if you obey the commandments of the LORD your God, which I command you today, [28]and the curse, if you do not obey the commandments of the LORD your God, but turn aside from the way that I am commanding you today, to go after other gods that you have not known. [29]And when the LORD your God brings you into the land that you are entering to take possession of it, you shall set the blessing on Mount Gerizim and the curse on Mount Ebal. [30]Are they not beyond the Jordan, west of the road, toward the going down of the sun, in the land of the Canaanites who live in the Arabah, opposite Gilgal, beside the oak[2] of Moreh? [31]For you are to cross over the Jordan to go in to take possession of the land that the LORD your God is giving you. And when you possess it and live in it, [32]you shall be careful to do all the statutes and the rules that I am setting before you today.

Things to avoid [chapter 12]. The lead-in (v. 1) repeats the constant thesis of Deuteronomy—the need to obey God's commands after the nation has entered the Promised Land. Although the chapter moves in a predictable rhythm between positive commands regarding what to do and prohibitions regarding what not to do, the preponderance is toward the latter, and increasingly so in the second half of the chapter. The positive commands serve as antidotes to the conduct that is forbidden. The two main and interrelated topics are (1) proper worship and sacrifices and (2) rules regarding animal meat—eating it and offering it in sacrifice.

12 "These are the statutes and rules that you shall be careful to do in the land that the LORD, the God of your fathers, has given you to possess, all the days that you live on the earth. [2]You shall surely destroy all the places where the nations whom you shall dispossess served their gods, on the high mountains and on the hills and under every green tree. [3]You shall tear down their altars and dash in pieces their pillars and burn their Asherim with fire. You shall chop down the carved images of their gods and destroy their name out of that place. [4]You shall not worship the LORD your God in that way. [5]But you shall seek the place that the LORD your God will choose out of all your tribes to put his name and make his habitation[3] there. There you shall go, [6]and there you shall bring your burnt offerings and your sacrifices, your

---

[1] Hebrew *and* [2] Septuagint, Syriac; see Genesis 12:6. Hebrew *oaks*, or *terebinths* [3] Or *name as its habitation*

tithes and the contribution that you present, your vow offerings, your freewill offerings, and the firstborn of your herd and of your flock. ⁷And there you shall eat before
the Lord your God, and you shall rejoice, you and your households, in all that you
undertake, in which the Lord your God has blessed you.

⁸"You shall not do according to all that we are doing here today, everyone doing
whatever is right in his own eyes, ⁹for you have not as yet come to the rest and to the
inheritance that the Lord your God is giving you. ¹⁰But when you go over the Jordan
and live in the land that the Lord your God is giving you to inherit, and when he gives
you rest from all your enemies around, so that you live in safety, ¹¹then to the place
that the Lord your God will choose, to make his name dwell there, there you shall
bring all that I command you: your burnt offerings and your sacrifices, your tithes
and the contribution that you present, and all your finest vow offerings that you vow
to the Lord. ¹²And you shall rejoice before the Lord your God, you and your sons and
your daughters, your male servants and your female servants, and the Levite that is
within your towns, since he has no portion or inheritance with you. ¹³Take care that
you do not offer your burnt offerings at any place that you see, ¹⁴but at the place that
the Lord will choose in one of your tribes, there you shall offer your burnt offerings,
and there you shall do all that I am commanding you.

¹⁵"However, you may slaughter and eat meat within any of your towns, as much as
you desire, according to the blessing of the Lord your God that he has given you. The
unclean and the clean may eat of it, as of the gazelle and as of the deer. ¹⁶Only you
shall not eat the blood; you shall pour it out on the earth like water. ¹⁷You may not eat
within your towns the tithe of your grain or of your wine or of your oil, or the firstborn of your herd or of your flock, or any of your vow offerings that you vow, or your
freewill offerings or the contribution that you present, ¹⁸but you shall eat them before
the Lord your God in the place that the Lord your God will choose, you and your son
and your daughter, your male servant and your female servant, and the Levite who is
within your towns. And you shall rejoice before the Lord your God in all that you
undertake. ¹⁹Take care that you do not neglect the Levite as long as you live in your
land.

²⁰"When the Lord your God enlarges your territory, as he has promised you, and
you say, 'I will eat meat,' because you crave meat, you may eat meat whenever you
desire. ²¹If the place that the Lord your God will choose to put his name there is too
far from you, then you may kill any of your herd or your flock, which the Lord has
given you, as I have commanded you, and you may eat within your towns whenever
you desire. ²²Just as the gazelle or the deer is eaten, so you may eat of it. The unclean
and the clean alike may eat of it. ²³Only be sure that you do not eat the blood, for the
blood is the life, and you shall not eat the life with the flesh. ²⁴You shall not eat it; you
shall pour it out on the earth like water. ²⁵You shall not eat it, that all may go well with
you and with your children after you, when you do what is right in the sight of the
Lord. ²⁶But the holy things that are due from you, and your vow offerings, you shall
take, and you shall go to the place that the Lord will choose, ²⁷and offer your burnt
offerings, the flesh and the blood, on the altar of the Lord your God. The blood of
your sacrifices shall be poured out on the altar of the Lord your God, but the flesh
you may eat. ²⁸Be careful to obey all these words that I command you, that it may go
well with you and with your children after you forever, when you do what is good
and right in the sight of the Lord your God.

[29] "When the LORD your God cuts off before you the nations whom you go in to dispossess, and you dispossess them and dwell in their land, [30] take care that you be not ensnared to follow them, after they have been destroyed before you, and that you do not inquire about their gods, saying, 'How did these nations serve their gods?—that I also may do the same.' [31] You shall not worship the LORD your God in that way, for every abominable thing that the LORD hates they have done for their gods, for they even burn their sons and their daughters in the fire to their gods.

[32] [1] "Everything that I command you, you shall be careful to do. You shall not add to it or take from it.

More prohibitions [chapter 13]. The underlying topic is the need to remain loyal to God and his commands, accompanied by rules that need to be obeyed. There are three main variations on the central theme: the need to reject false prophets who try to lead people away from God (vv. 1–5); the need to destroy secret idolaters (vv. 6–11); the need to destroy cities that harbor preachers of idolatry (vv. 12–18).

13

"If a prophet or a dreamer of dreams arises among you and gives you a sign or a wonder, [2] and the sign or wonder that he tells you comes to pass, and if he says, 'Let us go after other gods,' which you have not known, 'and let us serve them,' [3] you shall not listen to the words of that prophet or that dreamer of dreams. For the LORD your God is testing you, to know whether you love the LORD your God with all your heart and with all your soul. [4] You shall walk after the LORD your God and fear him and keep his commandments and obey his voice, and you shall serve him and hold fast to him. [5] But that prophet or that dreamer of dreams shall be put to death, because he has taught rebellion against the LORD your God, who brought you out of the land of Egypt and redeemed you out of the house of slavery, to make you leave the way in which the LORD your God commanded you to walk. So you shall purge the evil[2] from your midst.

[6] "If your brother, the son of your mother, or your son or your daughter or the wife you embrace[3] or your friend who is as your own soul entices you secretly, saying, 'Let us go and serve other gods,' which neither you nor your fathers have known, [7] some of the gods of the peoples who are around you, whether near you or far off from you, from the one end of the earth to the other, [8] you shall not yield to him or listen to him, nor shall your eye pity him, nor shall you spare him, nor shall you conceal him. [9] But you shall kill him. Your hand shall be first against him to put him to death, and afterward the hand of all the people. [10] You shall stone him to death with stones, because he sought to draw you away from the LORD your God, who brought you out of the land of Egypt, out of the house of slavery. [11] And all Israel shall hear and fear and never again do any such wickedness as this among you.

[12] "If you hear in one of your cities, which the LORD your God is giving you to dwell there, [13] that certain worthless fellows have gone out among you and have drawn away the inhabitants of their city, saying, 'Let us go and serve other gods,' which you have not known, [14] then you shall inquire and make search and ask diligently. And behold, if it be true and certain that such an abomination has been done among you, [15] you shall surely put the inhabitants of that city to the sword, devoting it to destruction,[4] all who are in it and its cattle, with the edge of the sword. [16] You shall gather all

---

[1] Ch 13:1 in Hebrew [2] Or *evil person* [3] Hebrew *the wife of your bosom* [4] That is, setting apart (devoting) as an offering to the Lord (for destruction)

its spoil into the midst of its open square and burn the city and all its spoil with fire, as a whole burnt offering to the LORD your God. It shall be a heap forever. It shall not be built again. [17]None of the devoted things shall stick to your hand, that the LORD may turn from the fierceness of his anger and show you mercy and have compassion on you and multiply you, as he swore to your fathers, [18]if you obey the voice of the LORD your God, keeping all his commandments that I am commanding you today, and doing what is right in the sight of the LORD your God.

Rules governing animals and produce offerings [chapter 14]. The subject of this chapter is ceremonial laws. As we read the chapter, we are immersed in nitty-gritty details of earthly life. Verses 1–21 give detailed dietary lists of clean and unclean animals. Even though the religious significance is that Israel must be holy and set apart from surrounding cultures (vv. 1–2, 21), we are also to understand that hygienic and health issues were involved in the prohibitions related to unclean animals. Verses 22–29 shift the focus to tithes of crops and produce and deal specifically with the worship of God through offerings.

14 "You are the sons of the LORD your God. You shall not cut yourselves or make any baldness on your foreheads for the dead. [2]For you are a people holy to the LORD your God, and the LORD has chosen you to be a people for his treasured possession, out of all the peoples who are on the face of the earth.

[3]"You shall not eat any abomination. [4]These are the animals you may eat: the ox, the sheep, the goat, [5]the deer, the gazelle, the roebuck, the wild goat, the ibex,[i] the antelope, and the mountain sheep. [6]Every animal that parts the hoof and has the hoof cloven in two and chews the cud, among the animals, you may eat. [7]Yet of those that chew the cud or have the hoof cloven you shall not eat these: the camel, the hare, and the rock badger, because they chew the cud but do not part the hoof, are unclean for you. [8]And the pig, because it parts the hoof but does not chew the cud, is unclean for you. Their flesh you shall not eat, and their carcasses you shall not touch.

[9]"Of all that are in the waters you may eat these: whatever has fins and scales you may eat. [10]And whatever does not have fins and scales you shall not eat; it is unclean for you.

[11]"You may eat all clean birds. [12]But these are the ones that you shall not eat: the eagle,[2] the bearded vulture, the black vulture, [13]the kite, the falcon of any kind; [14]every raven of any kind; [15]the ostrich, the nighthawk, the sea gull, the hawk of any kind; [16]the little owl and the short-eared owl, the barn owl [17]and the tawny owl, the carrion vulture and the cormorant, [18]the stork, the heron of any kind; the hoopoe and the bat. [19]And all winged insects are unclean for you; they shall not be eaten. [20]All clean winged things you may eat.

[21]"You shall not eat anything that has died naturally. You may give it to the sojourner who is within your towns, that he may eat it, or you may sell it to a foreigner. For you are a people holy to the LORD your God.

"You shall not boil a young goat in its mother's milk.

[22]"You shall tithe all the yield of your seed that comes from the field year by year. [23]And before the LORD your God, in the place that he will choose, to make his name dwell there, you shall eat the tithe of your grain, of your wine, and of your oil, and the

---

[1] Or *addax* [2] The identity of many of these birds is uncertain

firstborn of your herd and flock, that you may learn to fear the LORD your God always. ²⁴And if the way is too long for you, so that you are not able to carry the tithe, when the LORD your God blesses you, because the place is too far from you, which the LORD your God chooses, to set his name there, ²⁵then you shall turn it into money and bind up the money in your hand and go to the place that the LORD your God chooses ²⁶and spend the money for whatever you desire—oxen or sheep or wine or strong drink, whatever your appetite craves. And you shall eat there before the LORD your God and rejoice, you and your household. ²⁷And you shall not neglect the Levite who is within your towns, for he has no portion or inheritance with you.

²⁸"At the end of every three years you shall bring out all the tithe of your produce in the same year and lay it up within your towns. ²⁹And the Levite, because he has no portion or inheritance with you, and the sojourner, the fatherless, and the widow, who are within your towns, shall come and eat and be filled, that the LORD your God may bless you in all the work of your hands that you do.

Rules protecting the rights of the poor and of slaves [15:1–18]. A main moral strand in OT laws is the protection of the rights of marginalized groups within Israelite society. This chapter accordingly outlines the obligations of the rank-and-file Israelite in regard to releasing debts (vv. 1–6), being generous toward the poor who need loans (vv. 7–11), and releasing slaves every seventh year (vv. 12–18).

15 "At the end of every seven years you shall grant a release. ²And this is the manner of the release: every creditor shall release what he has lent to his neighbor. He shall not exact it of his neighbor, his brother, because the LORD's release has been proclaimed. ³Of a foreigner you may exact it, but whatever of yours is with your brother your hand shall release. ⁴But there will be no poor among you; for the LORD will bless you in the land that the LORD your God is giving you for an inheritance to possess— ⁵if only you will strictly obey the voice of the LORD your God, being careful to do all this commandment that I command you today. ⁶For the LORD your God will bless you, as he promised you, and you shall lend to many nations, but you shall not borrow, and you shall rule over many nations, but they shall not rule over you.

⁷"If among you, one of your brothers should become poor, in any of your towns within your land that the LORD your God is giving you, you shall not harden your heart or shut your hand against your poor brother, ⁸but you shall open your hand to him and lend him sufficient for his need, whatever it may be. ⁹Take care lest there be an unworthy thought in your heart and you say, 'The seventh year, the year of release is near,' and your eye look grudgingly[1] on your poor brother, and you give him nothing, and he cry to the LORD against you, and you be guilty of sin. ¹⁰You shall give to him freely, and your heart shall not be grudging when you give to him, because for this the LORD your God will bless you in all your work and in all that you undertake. ¹¹For there will never cease to be poor in the land. Therefore I command you, 'You shall open wide your hand to your brother, to the needy and to the poor, in your land.'

¹²"If your brother, a Hebrew man or a Hebrew woman, is sold[2] to you, he shall serve you six years, and in the seventh year you shall let him go free from you. ¹³And when you let him go free from you, you shall not let him go empty-handed. ¹⁴You

---

[1] Or be evil; also verse 10 [2] Or sells himself

shall furnish him liberally out of your flock, out of your threshing floor, and out of your winepress. As the LORD your God has blessed you, you shall give to him. ¹⁵You shall remember that you were a slave in the land of Egypt, and the LORD your God redeemed you; therefore I command you this today. ¹⁶But if he says to you, 'I will not go out from you,' because he loves you and your household, since he is well-off with you, ¹⁷then you shall take an awl, and put it through his ear into the door, and he shall be your slave forever. And to your female slave you shall do the same. ¹⁸It shall not seem hard to you when you let him go free from you, for at half the cost of a hired servant he has served you six years. So the LORD your God will bless you in all that you do.

> **Ceremonial observances** [15:19–16:17]. The annual calendar of religious observances was the rhythm around which Israelite life was to be built. This unit outlines the ground rules for the three major annual feasts—the Passover (16:1–8), the Feast of Weeks (16:9–12), and the Feast of Tabernacles or Booths (16:13–15). Two short sections address the obligations surrounding these three feasts (16:16–17) and the issue of consecrating the firstborn of animals (15:19–23).

¹⁹"All the firstborn males that are born of your herd and flock you shall dedicate to the LORD your God. You shall do no work with the firstborn of your herd, nor shear the firstborn of your flock. ²⁰You shall eat it, you and your household, before the LORD your God year by year at the place that the LORD will choose. ²¹But if it has any blemish, if it is lame or blind or has any serious blemish whatever, you shall not sacrifice it to the LORD your God. ²²You shall eat it within your towns. The unclean and the clean alike may eat it, as though it were a gazelle or a deer. ²³Only you shall not eat its blood; you shall pour it out on the ground like water.

16 "Observe the month of Abib and keep the Passover to the LORD your God, for in the month of Abib the LORD your God brought you out of Egypt by night. ²And you shall offer the Passover sacrifice to the LORD your God, from the flock or the herd, at the place that the LORD will choose, to make his name dwell there. ³You shall eat no leavened bread with it. Seven days you shall eat it with unleavened bread, the bread of affliction—for you came out of the land of Egypt in haste—that all the days of your life you may remember the day when you came out of the land of Egypt. ⁴No leaven shall be seen with you in all your territory for seven days, nor shall any of the flesh that you sacrifice on the evening of the first day remain all night until morning. ⁵You may not offer the Passover sacrifice within any of your towns that the LORD your God is giving you, ⁶but at the place that the LORD your God will choose, to make his name dwell in it, there you shall offer the Passover sacrifice, in the evening at sunset, at the time you came out of Egypt. ⁷And you shall cook it and eat it at the place that the LORD your God will choose. And in the morning you shall turn and go to your tents. ⁸For six days you shall eat unleavened bread, and on the seventh day there shall be a solemn assembly to the LORD your God. You shall do no work on it.

⁹"You shall count seven weeks. Begin to count the seven weeks from the time the sickle is first put to the standing grain. ¹⁰Then you shall keep the Feast of Weeks to the LORD your God with the tribute of a freewill offering from your hand, which you shall give as the LORD your God blesses you. ¹¹And you shall rejoice before the LORD

your God, you and your son and your daughter, your male servant and your female servant, the Levite who is within your towns, the sojourner, the fatherless, and the widow who are among you, at the place that the LORD your God will choose, to make his name dwell there. ¹²You shall remember that you were a slave in Egypt; and you shall be careful to observe these statutes.

¹³"You shall keep the Feast of Booths seven days, when you have gathered in the produce from your threshing floor and your winepress. ¹⁴You shall rejoice in your feast, you and your son and your daughter, your male servant and your female servant, the Levite, the sojourner, the fatherless, and the widow who are within your towns. ¹⁵For seven days you shall keep the feast to the LORD your God at the place that the LORD will choose, because the LORD your God will bless you in all your produce and in all the work of your hands, so that you will be altogether joyful.

¹⁶"Three times a year all your males shall appear before the LORD your God at the place that he will choose: at the Feast of Unleavened Bread, at the Feast of Weeks, and at the Feast of Booths. They shall not appear before the LORD empty-handed. ¹⁷Every man shall give as he is able, according to the blessing of the LORD your God that he has given you.

Civil laws [16:18–17:20]. In addition to ceremonial laws that had to do with religious practices, the Mosaic law included civil laws, or what today we consider the domain of government. This unit belongs to that category. Specific offices and the duties attending them are as follows: judges (16:18–20); interjected rules prohibiting idolatry (16:21) and offering a defective animal in sacrifice (17:1); rules governing the witness required for determining whether someone is guilty of idolatry, along with the prescribed punishment for idolatry (17:2–7); courts of appeal and the duty of citizens to respect their decisions (17:8–13); rules governing kings (17:14–20).

¹⁸"You shall appoint judges and officers in all your towns that the LORD your God is giving you, according to your tribes, and they shall judge the people with righteous judgment. ¹⁹You shall not pervert justice. You shall not show partiality, and you shall not accept a bribe, for a bribe blinds the eyes of the wise and subverts the cause of the righteous. ²⁰Justice, and only justice, you shall follow, that you may live and inherit the land that the LORD your God is giving you.

²¹"You shall not plant any tree as an Asherah beside the altar of the LORD your God that you shall make. ²²And you shall not set up a pillar, which the LORD your God hates.

17 "You shall not sacrifice to the LORD your God an ox or a sheep in which is a blemish, any defect whatever, for that is an abomination to the LORD your God.

²"If there is found among you, within any of your towns that the LORD your God is giving you, a man or woman who does what is evil in the sight of the LORD your God, in transgressing his covenant, ³and has gone and served other gods and worshiped them, or the sun or the moon or any of the host of heaven, which I have forbidden, ⁴and it is told you and you hear of it, then you shall inquire diligently, and if it is true and certain that such an abomination has been done in Israel, ⁵then you shall bring out to your gates that man or woman who has done this evil thing, and you shall

stone that man or woman to death with stones. ⁶On the evidence of two witnesses or of three witnesses the one who is to die shall be put to death; a person shall not be put to death on the evidence of one witness. ⁷The hand of the witnesses shall be first against him to put him to death, and afterward the hand of all the people. So you shall purge¹ the evil² from your midst.

⁸"If any case arises requiring decision between one kind of homicide and another, one kind of legal right and another, or one kind of assault and another, any case within your towns that is too difficult for you, then you shall arise and go up to the place that the LORD your God will choose. ⁹And you shall come to the Levitical priests and to the judge who is in office in those days, and you shall consult them, and they shall declare to you the decision. ¹⁰Then you shall do according to what they declare to you from that place that the LORD will choose. And you shall be careful to do according to all that they direct you. ¹¹According to the instructions that they give you, and according to the decision which they pronounce to you, you shall do. You shall not turn aside from the verdict that they declare to you, either to the right hand or to the left. ¹²The man who acts presumptuously by not obeying the priest who stands to minister there before the LORD your God, or the judge, that man shall die. So you shall purge the evil from Israel. ¹³And all the people shall hear and fear and not act presumptuously again.

¹⁴"When you come to the land that the LORD your God is giving you, and you possess it and dwell in it and then say, 'I will set a king over me, like all the nations that are around me,' ¹⁵you may indeed set a king over you whom the LORD your God will choose. One from among your brothers you shall set as king over you. You may not put a foreigner over you, who is not your brother. ¹⁶Only he must not acquire many horses for himself or cause the people to return to Egypt in order to acquire many horses, since the LORD has said to you, 'You shall never return that way again.' ¹⁷And he shall not acquire many wives for himself, lest his heart turn away, nor shall he acquire for himself excessive silver and gold.

¹⁸"And when he sits on the throne of his kingdom, he shall write for himself in a book a copy of this law, approved by³ the Levitical priests. ¹⁹And it shall be with him, and he shall read in it all the days of his life, that he may learn to fear the LORD his God by keeping all the words of this law and these statutes, and doing them, ²⁰that his heart may not be lifted up above his brothers, and that he may not turn aside from the commandment, either to the right hand or to the left, so that he may continue long in his kingdom, he and his children, in Israel.

Priests and prophets [chapter 18]. The ceremonial system and the broader religious life of Israel required special groups to oversee them. This chapter delineates rules for two categories of religious leaders. One group is the priests and Levites (vv. 1–8). The section devoted to prophets divides into two sections: a command to avoid pagan practices that we would loosely label as the occult (vv. 9–14) and God's promise to send true prophets (vv. 15–22). Some of the latter section deals with prophets whom God sent throughout OT history, while other statements can plausibly be interpreted as messianic prophecies about Christ, the final prophet. At every point in the middle of Deuteronomy, we will benefit from keeping in mind the rhetorical situation—a national and religious leader addressing a nation that is on the verge of entering and settling into the Promised

Land—and the book's affinities with utopian literature, which presents a vision of the good society and of the institutions and practices that lead to such a society.

18 "The Levitical priests, all the tribe of Levi, shall have no portion or inheritance with Israel. They shall eat the Lord's food offerings[1] as their[2] inheritance. [2]They shall have no inheritance among their brothers; the Lord is their inheritance, as he promised them. [3]And this shall be the priests' due from the people, from those offering a sacrifice, whether an ox or a sheep: they shall give to the priest the shoulder and the two cheeks and the stomach. [4]The firstfruits of your grain, of your wine and of your oil, and the first fleece of your sheep, you shall give him. [5]For the Lord your God has chosen him out of all your tribes to stand and minister in the name of the Lord, him and his sons for all time.

[6]"And if a Levite comes from any of your towns out of all Israel, where he lives—and he may come when he desires[3]—to the place that the Lord will choose, [7]and ministers in the name of the Lord his God, like all his fellow Levites who stand to minister there before the Lord, [8]then he may have equal portions to eat, besides what he receives from the sale of his patrimony.[4]

[9]"When you come into the land that the Lord your God is giving you, you shall not learn to follow the abominable practices of those nations. [10]There shall not be found among you anyone who burns his son or his daughter as an offering,[5] anyone who practices divination or tells fortunes or interprets omens, or a sorcerer [11]or a charmer or a medium or a necromancer or one who inquires of the dead, [12]for whoever does these things is an abomination to the Lord. And because of these abominations the Lord your God is driving them out before you. [13]You shall be blameless before the Lord your God, [14]for these nations, which you are about to dispossess, listen to fortune-tellers and to diviners. But as for you, the Lord your God has not allowed you to do this.

[15]"The Lord your God will raise up for you a prophet like me from among you, from your brothers—it is to him you shall listen— [16]just as you desired of the Lord your God at Horeb on the day of the assembly, when you said, 'Let me not hear again the voice of the Lord my God or see this great fire any more, lest I die.' [17]And the Lord said to me, 'They are right in what they have spoken. [18]I will raise up for them a prophet like you from among their brothers. And I will put my words in his mouth, and he shall speak to them all that I command him. [19]And whoever will not listen to my words that he shall speak in my name, I myself will require it of him. [20]But the prophet who presumes to speak a word in my name that I have not commanded him to speak, or[6] who speaks in the name of other gods, that same prophet shall die.' [21]And if you say in your heart, 'How may we know the word that the Lord has not spoken?'— [22]when a prophet speaks in the name of the Lord, if the word does not come to pass or come true, that is a word that the Lord has not spoken; the prophet has spoken it presumptuously. You need not be afraid of him.

Criminal laws [chapter 19]. Moses next takes up the rules governing certain criminal offenses, especially types of murder. The sequence is as follows: a command to set aside

[1] Or the offerings by fire to the Lord [2] Hebrew his [3] Or lives—if he comes enthusiastically [4] The meaning of the Hebrew is uncertain [5] Hebrew makes his son or his daughter pass through the fire [6] Or and

three cities of refuge in the Promised Land (vv. 1–3), with the possible need eventually to set aside three more (vv. 8–10); conditions of eligibility to take refuge in these cities (vv. 4–7); punishment for murderers (vv. 11–13); prohibition of removing landmarks (v. 14); laws regarding witnesses (vv. 15–21).

19

"When the Lord your God cuts off the nations whose land the Lord your God is giving you, and you dispossess them and dwell in their cities and in their houses, ²you shall set apart three cities for yourselves in the land that the Lord your God is giving you to possess. ³You shall measure the distances¹ and divide into three parts the area of the land that the Lord your God gives you as a possession, so that any manslayer can flee to them.

⁴"This is the provision for the manslayer, who by fleeing there may save his life. If anyone kills his neighbor unintentionally without having hated him in the past— ⁵as when someone goes into the forest with his neighbor to cut wood, and his hand swings the axe to cut down a tree, and the head slips from the handle and strikes his neighbor so that he dies—he may flee to one of these cities and live, ⁶lest the avenger of blood in hot anger pursue the manslayer and overtake him, because the way is long, and strike him fatally, though the man did not deserve to die, since he had not hated his neighbor in the past. ⁷Therefore I command you, You shall set apart three cities. ⁸And if the Lord your God enlarges your territory, as he has sworn to your fathers, and gives you all the land that he promised to give to your fathers— ⁹provided you are careful to keep all this commandment, which I command you today, by loving the Lord your God and by walking ever in his ways—then you shall add three other cities to these three, ¹⁰lest innocent blood be shed in your land that the Lord your God is giving you for an inheritance, and so the guilt of bloodshed be upon you.

¹¹"But if anyone hates his neighbor and lies in wait for him and attacks him and strikes him fatally so that he dies, and he flees into one of these cities, ¹²then the elders of his city shall send and take him from there, and hand him over to the avenger of blood, so that he may die. ¹³Your eye shall not pity him, but you shall purge the guilt of innocent blood² from Israel, so that it may be well with you.

¹⁴"You shall not move your neighbor's landmark, which the men of old have set, in the inheritance that you will hold in the land that the Lord your God is giving you to possess.

¹⁵"A single witness shall not suffice against a person for any crime or for any wrong in connection with any offense that he has committed. Only on the evidence of two witnesses or of three witnesses shall a charge be established. ¹⁶If a malicious witness arises to accuse a person of wrongdoing, ¹⁷then both parties to the dispute shall appear before the Lord, before the priests and the judges who are in office in those days. ¹⁸The judges shall inquire diligently, and if the witness is a false witness and has accused his brother falsely, ¹⁹then you shall do to him as he had meant to do to his brother. So you shall purge the evil³ from your midst. ²⁰And the rest shall hear and fear, and shall never again commit any such evil among you. ²¹Your eye shall not pity. It shall be life for life, eye for eye, tooth for tooth, hand for hand, foot for foot.

---

¹ Hebrew *road* ² Or *the blood of the innocent* ³ Or *evil person*

Rules for holy warfare [chapter 20]. As the later historical books of the OT attest, warfare became a leading activity of the nation of Israel, both in the conquest of Canaan and in its defense after conquest. It is not surprising, therefore, to find a chapter laying down rules for conducting a just war. First Moses gives rules outlining who is exempt from military conscription (vv. 1–9). Then he lays out how to approach an enemy city, first offering terms of peace (vv. 10–11) and then conducting a siege according to pre-scribed rules (vv. 12–20). Good questions to ask are what the instructions tell us about God and what they tell us about his design for how he wants his people to live.

20 "When you go out to war against your enemies, and see horses and chariots and an army larger than your own, you shall not be afraid of them, for the LORD your God is with you, who brought you up out of the land of Egypt. ²And when you draw near to the battle, the priest shall come forward and speak to the people ³and shall say to them, 'Hear, O Israel, today you are drawing near for battle against your enemies: let not your heart faint. Do not fear or panic or be in dread of them, ⁴for the LORD your God is he who goes with you to fight for you against your enemies, to give you the victory.' ⁵Then the officers shall speak to the people, saying, 'Is there any man who has built a new house and has not dedicated it? Let him go back to his house, lest he die in the battle and another man dedicate it. ⁶And is there any man who has planted a vineyard and has not enjoyed its fruit? Let him go back to his house, lest he die in the battle and another man enjoy its fruit. ⁷And is there any man who has betrothed a wife and has not taken her? Let him go back to his house, lest he die in the battle and another man take her.' ⁸And the officers shall speak further to the people, and say, 'Is there any man who is fearful and fainthearted? Let him go back to his house, lest he make the heart of his fellows melt like his own.' ⁹And when the officers have finished speaking to the people, then commanders shall be appointed at the head of the people.

¹⁰"When you draw near to a city to fight against it, offer terms of peace to it. ¹¹And if it responds to you peaceably and it opens to you, then all the people who are found in it shall do forced labor for you and shall serve you. ¹²But if it makes no peace with you, but makes war against you, then you shall besiege it. ¹³And when the LORD your God gives it into your hand, you shall put all its males to the sword, ¹⁴but the women and the little ones, the livestock, and everything else in the city, all its spoil, you shall take as plunder for yourselves. And you shall enjoy the spoil of your enemies, which the LORD your God has given you. ¹⁵Thus you shall do to all the cities that are very far from you, which are not cities of the nations here. ¹⁶But in the cities of these peoples that the LORD your God is giving you for an inheritance, you shall save alive nothing that breathes, ¹⁷but you shall devote them to complete destruction,¹ the Hittites and the Amorites, the Canaanites and the Perizzites, the Hivites and the Jebusites, as the LORD your God has commanded, ¹⁸that they may not teach you to do according to all their abominable practices that they have done for their gods, and so you sin against the LORD your God.

¹⁹"When you besiege a city for a long time, making war against it in order to take it, you shall not destroy its trees by wielding an axe against them. You may eat from them, but you shall not cut them down. Are the trees in the field human, that they should be besieged by you? ²⁰Only the trees that you know are not trees for food you

¹ That is, set apart (devote) as an offering to the Lord (for destruction)

may destroy and cut down, that you may build siegeworks against the city that makes war with you, until it falls.

Miscellaneous rules [21:1–22:12]. Now begins a wide-ranging kaleidoscope of rules covering situations that may seem bewildering to a modern reader. A good strategy is to accept the strangeness or "otherness" of the world that we enter as we read the chapter and then ponder what corrective value it might hold to experience life from this new perspective. A loose outline of topics is as follows: how to process a murder when its circumstances are unknown (21:1–9); how to marry a captive woman (21:10–14); the inviolability of the inheritance rights of the firstborn son (21:15–17); prescription of the death penalty for a rebellious son (21:18–21); the need to bury a hanged criminal before nightfall (21:22–23); rules of neighborliness (22:1–4); miscellaneous rules (22:5–12).

21 "If in the land that the Lord your God is giving you to possess someone is found slain, lying in the open country, and it is not known who killed him, ²then your elders and your judges shall come out, and they shall measure the distance to the surrounding cities. ³And the elders of the city that is nearest to the slain man shall take a heifer that has never been worked and that has not pulled in a yoke. ⁴And the elders of that city shall bring the heifer down to a valley with running water, which is neither plowed nor sown, and shall break the heifer's neck there in the valley. ⁵Then the priests, the sons of Levi, shall come forward, for the Lord your God has chosen them to minister to him and to bless in the name of the Lord, and by their word every dispute and every assault shall be settled. ⁶And all the elders of that city nearest to the slain man shall wash their hands over the heifer whose neck was broken in the valley, ⁷and they shall testify, 'Our hands did not shed this blood, nor did our eyes see it shed. ⁸Accept atonement, O Lord, for your people Israel, whom you have redeemed, and do not set the guilt of innocent blood in the midst of your people Israel, so that their blood guilt be atoned for.' ⁹So you shall purge the guilt of innocent blood from your midst, when you do what is right in the sight of the Lord.

¹⁰"When you go out to war against your enemies, and the Lord your God gives them into your hand and you take them captive, ¹¹and you see among the captives a beautiful woman, and you desire to take her to be your wife, ¹²and you bring her home to your house, she shall shave her head and pare her nails. ¹³And she shall take off the clothes in which she was captured and shall remain in your house and lament her father and her mother a full month. After that you may go in to her and be her husband, and she shall be your wife. ¹⁴But if you no longer delight in her, you shall let her go where she wants. But you shall not sell her for money, nor shall you treat her as a slave, since you have humiliated her.

¹⁵"If a man has two wives, the one loved and the other unloved, and both the loved and the unloved have borne him children, and if the firstborn son belongs to the unloved,¹ ¹⁶then on the day when he assigns his possessions as an inheritance to his sons, he may not treat the son of the loved as the firstborn in preference to the son of the unloved, who is the firstborn, ¹⁷but he shall acknowledge the firstborn, the son of the unloved, by giving him a double portion of all that he has, for he is the firstfruits of his strength. The right of the firstborn is his.

¹⁸"If a man has a stubborn and rebellious son who will not obey the voice of his

¹ Or *hated*; also verses 16, 17

father or the voice of his mother, and, though they discipline him, will not listen to them, ¹⁹then his father and his mother shall take hold of him and bring him out to the elders of his city at the gate of the place where he lives, ²⁰and they shall say to the elders of his city, 'This our son is stubborn and rebellious; he will not obey our voice; he is a glutton and a drunkard.' ²¹Then all the men of the city shall stone him to death with stones. So you shall purge the evil from your midst, and all Israel shall hear, and fear.

²²"And if a man has committed a crime punishable by death and he is put to death, and you hang him on a tree, ²³his body shall not remain all night on the tree, but you shall bury him the same day, for a hanged man is cursed by God. You shall not defile your land that the Lord your God is giving you for an inheritance.

22 "You shall not see your brother's ox or his sheep going astray and ignore them. You shall take them back to your brother. ²And if he does not live near you and you do not know who he is, you shall bring it home to your house, and it shall stay with you until your brother seeks it. Then you shall restore it to him. ³And you shall do the same with his donkey or with his garment, or with any lost thing of your brother's, which he loses and you find; you may not ignore it. ⁴You shall not see your brother's donkey or his ox fallen down by the way and ignore them. You shall help him to lift them up again.

⁵"A woman shall not wear a man's garment, nor shall a man put on a woman's cloak, for whoever does these things is an abomination to the Lord your God.

⁶"If you come across a bird's nest in any tree or on the ground, with young ones or eggs and the mother sitting on the young or on the eggs, you shall not take the mother with the young. ⁷You shall let the mother go, but the young you may take for yourself, that it may go well with you, and that you may live long.

⁸"When you build a new house, you shall make a parapet for your roof, that you may not bring the guilt of blood upon your house, if anyone should fall from it.

⁹"You shall not sow your vineyard with two kinds of seed, lest the whole yield be forfeited,¹ the crop that you have sown and the yield of the vineyard. ¹⁰You shall not plow with an ox and a donkey together. ¹¹You shall not wear cloth of wool and linen mixed together.

¹²"You shall make yourself tassels on the four corners of the garment with which you cover yourself.

Sexual relationships [22:13–30]. The Bible takes the view that sexual behavior is important in the lives of individuals and societies, and it sometimes spells out the details of that conviction with a frankness that might surprise us. This unit outlines what is allowable and not allowable in regard to sexual relationships. Every society safeguards what it holds in highest value; the prohibitions that we read about in this unit are a partial explanation of how God's people were to safeguard the sanctity of married sexuality.

¹³"If any man takes a wife and goes in to her and then hates her ¹⁴and accuses her of misconduct and brings a bad name upon her, saying, 'I took this woman, and when I came near her, I did not find in her evidence of virginity,' ¹⁵then the father of the young woman and her mother shall take and bring out the evidence of her virginity

¹ Hebrew *become holy*

to the elders of the city in the gate. ¹⁶And the father of the young woman shall say to the elders, 'I gave my daughter to this man to marry, and he hates her; ¹⁷and behold, he has accused her of misconduct, saying, "I did not find in your daughter evidence of virginity." And yet this is the evidence of my daughter's virginity.' And they shall spread the cloak before the elders of the city. ¹⁸Then the elders of that city shall take the man and whip¹ him, ¹⁹and they shall fine him a hundred shekels² of silver and give them to the father of the young woman, because he has brought a bad name upon a virgin³ of Israel. And she shall be his wife. He may not divorce her all his days. ²⁰But if the thing is true, that evidence of virginity was not found in the young woman, ²¹then they shall bring out the young woman to the door of her father's house, and the men of her city shall stone her to death with stones, because she has done an outrageous thing in Israel by whoring in her father's house. So you shall purge the evil from your midst.

²²"If a man is found lying with the wife of another man, both of them shall die, the man who lay with the woman, and the woman. So you shall purge the evil from Israel.

²³"If there is a betrothed virgin, and a man meets her in the city and lies with her, ²⁴then you shall bring them both out to the gate of that city, and you shall stone them to death with stones, the young woman because she did not cry for help though she was in the city, and the man because he violated his neighbor's wife. So you shall purge the evil from your midst.

²⁵"But if in the open country a man meets a young woman who is betrothed, and the man seizes her and lies with her, then only the man who lay with her shall die. ²⁶But you shall do nothing to the young woman; she has committed no offense punishable by death. For this case is like that of a man attacking and murdering his neighbor, ²⁷because he met her in the open country, and though the betrothed young woman cried for help there was no one to rescue her.

²⁸"If a man meets a virgin who is not betrothed, and seizes her and lies with her, and they are found, ²⁹then the man who lay with her shall give to the father of the young woman fifty shekels of silver, and she shall be his wife, because he has violated her. He may not divorce her all his days.

³⁰⁴"A man shall not take his father's wife, so that he does not uncover his father's nakedness.⁵

Categories of people excluded from the Israelite community [23:1–14]. The motif of safeguarding the purity of the community extends into this unit as well. The passage is a list of exclusions from the Israelite camp. When the text uses the word assembly, it refers not primarily to a place or "sacred space" but rather to the people as a community.

23 "No one whose testicles are crushed or whose male organ is cut off shall enter the assembly of the LORD.

²"No one born of a forbidden union may enter the assembly of the LORD. Even to the tenth generation, none of his descendants may enter the assembly of the LORD.

³"No Ammonite or Moabite may enter the assembly of the LORD. Even to the tenth generation, none of them may enter the assembly of the LORD forever, ⁴because they did not meet you with bread and with water on the way, when you came out of Egypt, and because they hired against you Balaam the son of Beor from Pethor of

¹ Or discipline ² A *shekel* was about 2/5 ounce or 11 grams ³ Or *girl of marriageable age* ⁴ Ch 23:1 in Hebrew ⁵ Hebrew *uncover his father's skirt*

Mesopotamia, to curse you. [5]But the LORD your God would not listen to Balaam; instead the LORD your God turned the curse into a blessing for you, because the LORD your God loved you. [6]You shall not seek their peace or their prosperity all your days forever.

[7]"You shall not abhor an Edomite, for he is your brother. You shall not abhor an Egyptian, because you were a sojourner in his land. [8]Children born to them in the third generation may enter the assembly of the LORD.

[9]"When you are encamped against your enemies, then you shall keep yourself from every evil thing.

[10]"If any man among you becomes unclean because of a nocturnal emission, then he shall go outside the camp. He shall not come inside the camp, [11]but when evening comes, he shall bathe himself in water, and as the sun sets, he may come inside the camp.

[12]"You shall have a place outside the camp, and you shall go out to it. [13]And you shall have a trowel with your tools, and when you sit down outside, you shall dig a hole with it and turn back and cover up your excrement. [14]Because the LORD your God walks in the midst of your camp, to deliver you and to give up your enemies before you, therefore your camp must be holy, so that he may not see anything indecent among you and turn away from you.

Rules of the godly community [23:15–25:19]. This unit is a code book for the conduct of personal and community life. In the background is the utopian genre, which describes in detail how an ideal community conducts its affairs. One analytic grid to bring to the passage is to keep a running list of the areas of life that are covered, including the following: economic life and business practices; proper and improper worship; marriage and family; livelihood; legal and judicial life; warfare. A second grid is the relationships that are included: master and slave; lender and borrower; neighbors; husband and wife; owner and thief; parent and child; the haves and have-nots of society; combatants in war; seller and buyer.

[15]"You shall not give up to his master a slave who has escaped from his master to you. [16]He shall dwell with you, in your midst, in the place that he shall choose within one of your towns, wherever it suits him. You shall not wrong him.

[17]"None of the daughters of Israel shall be a cult prostitute, and none of the sons of Israel shall be a cult prostitute. [18]You shall not bring the fee of a prostitute or the wages of a dog[1] into the house of the LORD your God in payment for any vow, for both of these are an abomination to the LORD your God.

[19]"You shall not charge interest on loans to your brother, interest on money, interest on food, interest on anything that is lent for interest. [20]You may charge a foreigner interest, but you may not charge your brother interest, that the LORD your God may bless you in all that you undertake in the land that you are entering to take possession of it.

[21]"If you make a vow to the LORD your God, you shall not delay fulfilling it, for the LORD your God will surely require it of you, and you will be guilty of sin. [22]But if you refrain from vowing, you will not be guilty of sin. [23]You shall be careful to do what

---

[1] Or male prostitute

has passed your lips, for you have voluntarily vowed to the Lord your God what you have promised with your mouth.

²⁴"If you go into your neighbor's vineyard, you may eat your fill of grapes, as many as you wish, but you shall not put any in your bag. ²⁵If you go into your neighbor's standing grain, you may pluck the ears with your hand, but you shall not put a sickle to your neighbor's standing grain.

24

"When a man takes a wife and marries her, if then she finds no favor in his eyes because he has found some indecency in her, and he writes her a certificate of divorce and puts it in her hand and sends her out of his house, and she departs out of his house, ²and if she goes and becomes another man's wife, ³and the latter man hates her and writes her a certificate of divorce and puts it in her hand and sends her out of his house, or if the latter man dies, who took her to be his wife, ⁴then her former husband, who sent her away, may not take her again to be his wife, after she has been defiled, for that is an abomination before the Lord. And you shall not bring sin upon the land that the Lord your God is giving you for an inheritance.

⁵"When a man is newly married, he shall not go out with the army or be liable for any other public duty. He shall be free at home one year to be happy with his wife whom he has taken.

⁶"No one shall take a mill or an upper millstone in pledge, for that would be taking a life in pledge.

⁷"If a man is found stealing one of his brothers of the people of Israel, and if he treats him as a slave or sells him, then that thief shall die. So you shall purge the evil from your midst.

⁸"Take care, in a case of leprous¹ disease, to be very careful to do according to all that the Levitical priests shall direct you. As I commanded them, so you shall be careful to do. ⁹Remember what the Lord your God did to Miriam on the way as you came out of Egypt.

¹⁰"When you make your neighbor a loan of any sort, you shall not go into his house to collect his pledge. ¹¹You shall stand outside, and the man to whom you make the loan shall bring the pledge out to you. ¹²And if he is a poor man, you shall not sleep in his pledge. ¹³You shall restore to him the pledge as the sun sets, that he may sleep in his cloak and bless you. And it shall be righteousness for you before the Lord your God.

¹⁴"You shall not oppress a hired servant who is poor and needy, whether he is one of your brothers or one of the sojourners who are in your land within your towns. ¹⁵You shall give him his wages on the same day, before the sun sets (for he is poor and counts on it), lest he cry against you to the Lord, and you be guilty of sin.

¹⁶"Fathers shall not be put to death because of their children, nor shall children be put to death because of their fathers. Each one shall be put to death for his own sin.

¹⁷"You shall not pervert the justice due to the sojourner or to the fatherless, or take a widow's garment in pledge, ¹⁸but you shall remember that you were a slave in Egypt and the Lord your God redeemed you from there; therefore I command you to do this.

¹⁹"When you reap your harvest in your field and forget a sheaf in the field, you shall not go back to get it. It shall be for the sojourner, the fatherless, and the widow, that the Lord your God may bless you in all the work of your hands. ²⁰When you beat your olive trees, you shall not go over them again. It shall be for the sojourner, the

¹ *Leprosy* was a term for several skin diseases; see Leviticus 13

fatherless, and the widow. ²¹When you gather the grapes of your vineyard, you shall not strip it afterward. It shall be for the sojourner, the fatherless, and the widow. ²²You shall remember that you were a slave in the land of Egypt; therefore I command you to do this.

25 "If there is a dispute between men and they come into court and the judges decide between them, acquitting the innocent and condemning the guilty, ²then if the guilty man deserves to be beaten, the judge shall cause him to lie down and be beaten in his presence with a number of stripes in proportion to his offense. ³Forty stripes may be given him, but not more, lest, if one should go on to beat him with more stripes than these, your brother be degraded in your sight.

⁴"You shall not muzzle an ox when it is treading out the grain.

⁵"If brothers dwell together, and one of them dies and has no son, the wife of the dead man shall not be married outside the family to a stranger. Her husband's brother shall go in to her and take her as his wife and perform the duty of a husband's brother to her. ⁶And the first son whom she bears shall succeed to the name of his dead brother, that his name may not be blotted out of Israel. ⁷And if the man does not wish to take his brother's wife, then his brother's wife shall go up to the gate to the elders and say, 'My husband's brother refuses to perpetuate his brother's name in Israel; he will not perform the duty of a husband's brother to me.' ⁸Then the elders of his city shall call him and speak to him, and if he persists, saying, 'I do not wish to take her,' ⁹then his brother's wife shall go up to him in the presence of the elders and pull his sandal off his foot and spit in his face. And she shall answer and say, 'So shall it be done to the man who does not build up his brother's house.' ¹⁰And the name of his house¹ shall be called in Israel, 'The house of him who had his sandal pulled off.'

¹¹"When men fight with one another and the wife of the one draws near to rescue her husband from the hand of him who is beating him and puts out her hand and seizes him by the private parts, ¹²then you shall cut off her hand. Your eye shall have no pity.

¹³"You shall not have in your bag two kinds of weights, a large and a small. ¹⁴You shall not have in your house two kinds of measures, a large and a small. ¹⁵A full and fair² weight you shall have, a full and fair measure you shall have, that your days may be long in the land that the LORD your God is giving you. ¹⁶For all who do such things, all who act dishonestly, are an abomination to the LORD your God.

¹⁷"Remember what Amalek did to you on the way as you came out of Egypt, ¹⁸how he attacked you on the way when you were faint and weary, and cut off your tail, those who were lagging behind you, and he did not fear God. ¹⁹Therefore when the LORD your God has given you rest from all your enemies around you, in the land that the LORD your God is giving you for an inheritance to possess, you shall blot out the memory of Amalek from under heaven; you shall not forget.

Offerings to God [chapter 26]. This chapter brings closure to the middle of the book, with its multitude of specific rules. The rhetorical situation of Moses' address is restated in the opening verse, with its formula "when you come into the land that the LORD your God is giving you." The chapter outlines the procedure for the tithe of produce, accord-

---

¹ Hebrew *its name* ² Or *just*, or *righteous*; twice in this verse

ing to the following sequence: a command to take a tithe of the firstfruit of a crop to the priest, who was to lay it before the altar (vv. 2–4); the ritual speech (in the very touchstone of what is called the high style) that the bringer of the offering was to recite at the altar (vv. 5–10); worship and celebration before God (vv. 10–11); concluding prayer (also in a high, formal style) addressed to God after presenting the offering (vv. 12–15). In a summary statement at the end (vv. 16–19), Moses reiterates his main points—that the nation must keep God's commands, that Israel is God's own possession, and that the purpose of this chosen nation is to honor God.

26 "When you come into the land that the Lord your God is giving you for an inheritance and have taken possession of it and live in it, ²you shall take some of the first of all the fruit of the ground, which you harvest from your land that the Lord your God is giving you, and you shall put it in a basket, and you shall go to the place that the Lord your God will choose, to make his name to dwell there. ³And you shall go to the priest who is in office at that time and say to him, 'I declare today to the Lord your God that I have come into the land that the Lord swore to our fathers to give us.' ⁴Then the priest shall take the basket from your hand and set it down before the altar of the Lord your God.

⁵"And you shall make response before the Lord your God, 'A wandering Aramean was my father. And he went down into Egypt and sojourned there, few in number, and there he became a nation, great, mighty, and populous. ⁶And the Egyptians treated us harshly and humiliated us and laid on us hard labor. ⁷Then we cried to the Lord, the God of our fathers, and the Lord heard our voice and saw our affliction, our toil, and our oppression. ⁸And the Lord brought us out of Egypt with a mighty hand and an outstretched arm, with great deeds of terror,[1] with signs and wonders. ⁹And he brought us into this place and gave us this land, a land flowing with milk and honey. ¹⁰And behold, now I bring the first of the fruit of the ground, which you, O Lord, have given me.' And you shall set it down before the Lord your God and worship before the Lord your God. ¹¹And you shall rejoice in all the good that the Lord your God has given to you and to your house, you, and the Levite, and the sojourner who is among you.

¹²"When you have finished paying all the tithe of your produce in the third year, which is the year of tithing, giving it to the Levite, the sojourner, the fatherless, and the widow, so that they may eat within your towns and be filled, ¹³then you shall say before the Lord your God, 'I have removed the sacred portion out of my house, and moreover, I have given it to the Levite, the sojourner, the fatherless, and the widow, according to all your commandment that you have commanded me. I have not transgressed any of your commandments, nor have I forgotten them. ¹⁴I have not eaten of the tithe while I was mourning, or removed any of it while I was unclean, or offered any of it to the dead. I have obeyed the voice of the Lord my God. I have done according to all that you have commanded me. ¹⁵Look down from your holy habitation, from heaven, and bless your people Israel and the ground that you have given us, as you swore to our fathers, a land flowing with milk and honey.'

¹⁶"This day the Lord your God commands you to do these statutes and rules. You shall therefore be careful to do them with all your heart and with all your soul. ¹⁷You have declared today that the Lord is your God, and that you will walk in his ways,

[1] Hebrew *with great terror*

and keep his statutes and his commandments and his rules, and will obey his voice. [18]And the Lord has declared today that you are a people for his treasured possession, as he has promised you, and that you are to keep all his commandments, [19]and that he will set you in praise and in fame and in honor high above all nations that he has made, and that you shall be a people holy to the Lord your God, as he promised."

Moses prescribes a ceremonial renewal of the covenant [chapter 27]. The first half of the chapter (vv. 1–14) is in effect a narrative interlude in which we are placed in our imagination at the setting of the discourse that makes up the book of Deuteronomy. Verses 1, 9, and 11 variously ascribe the commands recorded in this brief unit to Moses, the elders, and the Levitical priests. Verses 9–10 command the people to obey what they are hearing "today." The rest of the commands, though, prescribe a future event, to occur after the nation enters Canaan. Moses prescribes a covenant renewal ceremony consisting of setting up a monument inscribed with the words of the law (vv. 2–4) and building an altar, also inscribed with the words of the law (vv. 6–8). Additionally, Moses prescribes an antiphonal reciting of the curses and blessings of the law from two mountains (Mount Gerizim and Mount Ebal, vv. 11–14). The rest of chapter 27 (vv. 15–26) lists the twelve curses that the Levites must recite from Mount Ebal, with each curse to be followed by the people's choral "Amen."

27 Now Moses and the elders of Israel commanded the people, saying, "Keep the whole commandment that I command you today. [2]And on the day you cross over the Jordan to the land that the Lord your God is giving you, you shall set up large stones and plaster them with plaster. [3]And you shall write on them all the words of this law, when you cross over to enter the land that the Lord your God is giving you, a land flowing with milk and honey, as the Lord, the God of your fathers, has promised you. [4]And when you have crossed over the Jordan, you shall set up these stones, concerning which I command you today, on Mount Ebal, and you shall plaster them with plaster. [5]And there you shall build an altar to the Lord your God, an altar of stones. You shall wield no iron tool on them; [6]you shall build an altar to the Lord your God of uncut[1] stones. And you shall offer burnt offerings on it to the Lord your God, [7]and you shall sacrifice peace offerings and shall eat there, and you shall rejoice before the Lord your God. [8]And you shall write on the stones all the words of this law very plainly."

[9]Then Moses and the Levitical priests said to all Israel, "Keep silence and hear, O Israel: this day you have become the people of the Lord your God. [10]You shall therefore obey the voice of the Lord your God, keeping his commandments and his statutes, which I command you today."

[11]That day Moses charged the people, saying, [12]"When you have crossed over the Jordan, these shall stand on Mount Gerizim to bless the people: Simeon, Levi, Judah, Issachar, Joseph, and Benjamin. [13]And these shall stand on Mount Ebal for the curse: Reuben, Gad, Asher, Zebulun, Dan, and Naphtali. [14]And the Levites shall declare to all the men of Israel in a loud voice:

[15]"'Cursed be the man who makes a carved or cast metal image, an abomination to the Lord, a thing made by the hands of a craftsman, and sets it up in secret.' And all the people shall answer and say, 'Amen.'

[1] Hebrew *whole*

16"'Cursed be anyone who dishonors his father or his mother.' And all the people shall say, 'Amen.'

17"'Cursed be anyone who moves his neighbor's landmark.' And all the people shall say, 'Amen.'

18"'Cursed be anyone who misleads a blind man on the road.' And all the people shall say, 'Amen.'

19"'Cursed be anyone who perverts the justice due to the sojourner, the fatherless, and the widow.' And all the people shall say, 'Amen.'

20"'Cursed be anyone who lies with his father's wife, because he has uncovered his father's nakedness.'[1] And all the people shall say, 'Amen.'

21"'Cursed be anyone who lies with any kind of animal.' And all the people shall say, 'Amen.'

22"'Cursed be anyone who lies with his sister, whether the daughter of his father or the daughter of his mother.' And all the people shall say, 'Amen.'

23"'Cursed be anyone who lies with his mother-in-law.' And all the people shall say, 'Amen.'

24"'Cursed be anyone who strikes down his neighbor in secret.' And all the people shall say, 'Amen.'

25"'Cursed be anyone who takes a bribe to shed innocent blood.' And all the people shall say, 'Amen.'

26"'Cursed be anyone who does not confirm the words of this law by doing them.' And all the people shall say, 'Amen.'

The blessings of obedience [28:1–14]. This unit continues the content of the covenant renewal ceremony that will take place. Its focus is on the blessings that God will shower on his people if they obey his commands. In effect it provides an incentive for obeying God's law. It is a brief and evocative picture of the good life of enjoying God's favor.

28 "And if you faithfully obey the voice of the LORD your God, being careful to do all his commandments that I command you today, the LORD your God will set you high above all the nations of the earth. ²And all these blessings shall come upon you and overtake you, if you obey the voice of the LORD your God. ³Blessed shall you be in the city, and blessed shall you be in the field. ⁴Blessed shall be the fruit of your womb and the fruit of your ground and the fruit of your cattle, the increase of your herds and the young of your flock. ⁵Blessed shall be your basket and your kneading bowl. ⁶Blessed shall you be when you come in, and blessed shall you be when you go out.

⁷"The LORD will cause your enemies who rise against you to be defeated before you. They shall come out against you one way and flee before you seven ways. ⁸The LORD will command the blessing on you in your barns and in all that you undertake. And he will bless you in the land that the LORD your God is giving you. ⁹The LORD will establish you as a people holy to himself, as he has sworn to you, if you keep the commandments of the LORD your God and walk in his ways. ¹⁰And all the peoples of the earth shall see that you are called by the name of the LORD, and they shall be afraid of you. ¹¹And the LORD will make you abound in prosperity, in the fruit of your

[1] Hebrew uncovered his father's skirt

womb and in the fruit of your livestock and in the fruit of your ground, within the land that the LORD swore to your fathers to give you. ¹²The LORD will open to you his good treasury, the heavens, to give the rain to your land in its season and to bless all the work of your hands. And you shall lend to many nations, but you shall not borrow. ¹³And the LORD will make you the head and not the tail, and you shall only go up and not down, if you obey the commandments of the LORD your God, which I command you today, being careful to do them, ¹⁴and if you do not turn aside from any of the words that I command you today, to the right hand or to the left, to go after other gods to serve them.

The curses of disobedience [28:15–68]. This unit completes the speeches that would be delivered from the two mountains at the covenant renewal ceremony enacted upon entry into the Promised Land. If the preceding list of blessings was a vision of the good life, this extended picture of curses is a *horror story—a vision of the archetypal bad life. The passage is so extended and relentless in its pictures of misfortune that no sane person would choose to live in disobedience if these are the results.

¹⁵"But if you will not obey the voice of the LORD your God or be careful to do all his commandments and his statutes that I command you today, then all these curses shall come upon you and overtake you. ¹⁶Cursed shall you be in the city, and cursed shall you be in the field. ¹⁷Cursed shall be your basket and your kneading bowl. ¹⁸Cursed shall be the fruit of your womb and the fruit of your ground, the increase of your herds and the young of your flock. ¹⁹Cursed shall you be when you come in, and cursed shall you be when you go out.

²⁰"The LORD will send on you curses, confusion, and frustration in all that you undertake to do, until you are destroyed and perish quickly on account of the evil of your deeds, because you have forsaken me. ²¹The LORD will make the pestilence stick to you until he has consumed you off the land that you are entering to take possession of it. ²²The LORD will strike you with wasting disease and with fever, inflammation and fiery heat, and with drought¹ and with blight and with mildew. They shall pursue you until you perish. ²³And the heavens over your head shall be bronze, and the earth under you shall be iron. ²⁴The LORD will make the rain of your land powder. From heaven dust shall come down on you until you are destroyed.

²⁵"The LORD will cause you to be defeated before your enemies. You shall go out one way against them and flee seven ways before them. And you shall be a horror to all the kingdoms of the earth. ²⁶And your dead body shall be food for all birds of the air and for the beasts of the earth, and there shall be no one to frighten them away. ²⁷The LORD will strike you with the boils of Egypt, and with tumors and scabs and itch, of which you cannot be healed. ²⁸The LORD will strike you with madness and blindness and confusion of mind, ²⁹and you shall grope at noonday, as the blind grope in darkness, and you shall not prosper in your ways.² And you shall be only oppressed and robbed continually, and there shall be no one to help you. ³⁰You shall betroth a wife, but another man shall ravish her. You shall build a house, but you shall not dwell in it. You shall plant a vineyard, but you shall not enjoy its fruit. ³¹Your ox shall be slaughtered before your eyes, but you shall not eat any of it. Your donkey shall be seized before your face, but shall not be restored to you. Your sheep shall be

¹ Or sword ² Or shall not succeed in finding your ways

given to your enemies, but there shall be no one to help you. ³²Your sons and your daughters shall be given to another people, while your eyes look on and fail with longing for them all day long, but you shall be helpless. ³³A nation that you have not known shall eat up the fruit of your ground and of all your labors, and you shall be only oppressed and crushed continually, ³⁴so that you are driven mad by the sights that your eyes see. ³⁵The Lord will strike you on the knees and on the legs with grievous boils of which you cannot be healed, from the sole of your foot to the crown of your head.

³⁶"The Lord will bring you and your king whom you set over you to a nation that neither you nor your fathers have known. And there you shall serve other gods of wood and stone. ³⁷And you shall become a horror, a proverb, and a byword among all the peoples where the Lord will lead you away. ³⁸You shall carry much seed into the field and shall gather in little, for the locust shall consume it. ³⁹You shall plant vineyards and dress them, but you shall neither drink of the wine nor gather the grapes, for the worm shall eat them. ⁴⁰You shall have olive trees throughout all your territory, but you shall not anoint yourself with the oil, for your olives shall drop off. ⁴¹You shall father sons and daughters, but they shall not be yours, for they shall go into captivity. ⁴²The cricket¹ shall possess all your trees and the fruit of your ground. ⁴³The sojourner who is among you shall rise higher and higher above you, and you shall come down lower and lower. ⁴⁴He shall lend to you, and you shall not lend to him. He shall be the head, and you shall be the tail.

⁴⁵"All these curses shall come upon you and pursue you and overtake you till you are destroyed, because you did not obey the voice of the Lord your God, to keep his commandments and his statutes that he commanded you. ⁴⁶They shall be a sign and a wonder against you and your offspring forever. ⁴⁷Because you did not serve the Lord your God with joyfulness and gladness of heart, because of the abundance of all things, ⁴⁸therefore you shall serve your enemies whom the Lord will send against you, in hunger and thirst, in nakedness, and lacking everything. And he will put a yoke of iron on your neck until he has destroyed you. ⁴⁹The Lord will bring a nation against you from far away, from the end of the earth, swooping down like the eagle, a nation whose language you do not understand, ⁵⁰a hard-faced nation who shall not respect the old or show mercy to the young. ⁵¹It shall eat the offspring of your cattle and the fruit of your ground, until you are destroyed; it also shall not leave you grain, wine, or oil, the increase of your herds or the young of your flock, until they have caused you to perish.

⁵²"They shall besiege you in all your towns, until your high and fortified walls, in which you trusted, come down throughout all your land. And they shall besiege you in all your towns throughout all your land, which the Lord your God has given you. ⁵³And you shall eat the fruit of your womb, the flesh of your sons and daughters, whom the Lord your God has given you, in the siege and in the distress with which your enemies shall distress you. ⁵⁴The man who is the most tender and refined among you will begrudge food to his brother, to the wife he embraces,² and to the last of the children whom he has left, ⁵⁵so that he will not give to any of them any of the flesh of his children whom he is eating, because he has nothing else left, in the siege and in the distress with which your enemy shall distress you in all your towns. ⁵⁶The most tender and refined woman among you, who would not venture to set the sole of her foot on the ground because she is so delicate and tender, will begrudge to the hus-

¹ Identity uncertain ² Hebrew *the wife of his bosom*

band she embraces,[1] to her son and to her daughter, [57]her afterbirth that comes out from between her feet and her children whom she bears, because lacking everything she will eat them secretly, in the siege and in the distress with which your enemy shall distress you in your towns.

[58]"If you are not careful to do all the words of this law that are written in this book, that you may fear this glorious and awesome name, the LORD your God, [59]then the LORD will bring on you and your offspring extraordinary afflictions, afflictions severe and lasting, and sicknesses grievous and lasting. [60]And he will bring upon you again all the diseases of Egypt, of which you were afraid, and they shall cling to you. [61]Every sickness also and every affliction that is not recorded in the book of this law, the LORD will bring upon you, until you are destroyed. [62]Whereas you were as numerous as the stars of heaven, you shall be left few in number, because you did not obey the voice of the LORD your God. [63]And as the LORD took delight in doing you good and multiplying you, so the LORD will take delight in bringing ruin upon you and destroying you. And you shall be plucked off the land that you are entering to take possession of it.

[64]"And the LORD will scatter you among all peoples, from one end of the earth to the other, and there you shall serve other gods of wood and stone, which neither you nor your fathers have known. [65]And among these nations you shall find no respite, and there shall be no resting place for the sole of your foot, but the LORD will give you there a trembling heart and failing eyes and a languishing soul. [66]Your life shall hang in doubt before you. Night and day you shall be in dread and have no assurance of your life. [67]In the morning you shall say, 'If only it were evening!' and at evening you shall say, 'If only it were morning!' because of the dread that your heart shall feel, and the sights that your eyes shall see. [68]And the LORD will bring you back in ships to Egypt, a journey that I promised that you should never make again; and there you shall offer yourselves for sale to your enemies as male and female slaves, but there will be no buyer."

Moses' follow-up exhortation [29:1–30:10]. The opening verse is a narrative closure to the script that Moses gave for reading at the covenant renewal ceremony. Then Moses recapitulates and interprets the covenant renewal ceremony that he has prescribed, expressed in the form of an extended exhortation. Moses wants his followers to understand the momentousness of what will happen at Mount Gerizim and Mount Ebal. First he reminds the Israelites of God's past acts of deliverance, ending with a command to behave in such a way as to elicit God's blessing (29:2–9). Then Moses stresses the solemnity of what is happening to the people on this day, the day of his oration, and not simply at the future covenant renewal (29:10–15). Next he warns his hearers that God will punish individuals who pay lip service to the covenant but secretly disregard it (29:16–29). The unit ends on a note that might well remind us of the prophetic *oracles of blessing (30:1–10). It is a vision of a future golden age in which God's benediction rests on his people in all areas of life, with primary emphasis on the spiritual aspects of life.

29 [2]These are the words of the covenant that the LORD commanded Moses to make with the people of Israel in the land of Moab, besides the covenant that he had made with them at Horeb.

---

[1] Hebrew *the husband of her bosom* [2] Ch 28:69 in Hebrew

²¹ And Moses summoned all Israel and said to them: "You have seen all that the LORD did before your eyes in the land of Egypt, to Pharaoh and to all his servants and to all his land, ³the great trials that your eyes saw, the signs, and those great wonders. ⁴But to this day the LORD has not given you a heart to understand or eyes to see or ears to hear. ⁵I have led you forty years in the wilderness. Your clothes have not worn out on you, and your sandals have not worn off your feet. ⁶You have not eaten bread, and you have not drunk wine or strong drink, that you may know that I am the LORD your God. ⁷And when you came to this place, Sihon the king of Heshbon and Og the king of Bashan came out against us to battle, but we defeated them. ⁸We took their land and gave it for an inheritance to the Reubenites, the Gadites, and the half-tribe of the Manassites. ⁹Therefore keep the words of this covenant and do them, that you may prosper² in all that you do.

¹⁰"You are standing today all of you before the LORD your God: the heads of your tribes,³ your elders, and your officers, all the men of Israel, ¹¹your little ones, your wives, and the sojourner who is in your camp, from the one who chops your wood to the one who draws your water, ¹²so that you may enter into the sworn covenant of the LORD your God, which the LORD your God is making with you today, ¹³that he may establish you today as his people, and that he may be your God, as he promised you, and as he swore to your fathers, to Abraham, to Isaac, and to Jacob. ¹⁴It is not with you alone that I am making this sworn covenant, ¹⁵but with whoever is standing here with us today before the LORD our God, and with whoever is not here with us today.

¹⁶"You know how we lived in the land of Egypt, and how we came through the midst of the nations through which you passed. ¹⁷And you have seen their detestable things, their idols of wood and stone, of silver and gold, which were among them. ¹⁸Beware lest there be among you a man or woman or clan or tribe whose heart is turning away today from the LORD our God to go and serve the gods of those nations. Beware lest there be among you a root bearing poisonous and bitter fruit, ¹⁹one who, when he hears the words of this sworn covenant, blesses himself in his heart, saying, 'I shall be safe, though I walk in the stubbornness of my heart.' This will lead to the sweeping away of moist and dry alike. ²⁰The LORD will not be willing to forgive him, but rather the anger of the LORD and his jealousy will smoke against that man, and the curses written in this book will settle upon him, and the LORD will blot out his name from under heaven. ²¹And the LORD will single him out from all the tribes of Israel for calamity, in accordance with all the curses of the covenant written in this Book of the Law. ²²And the next generation, your children who rise up after you, and the foreigner who comes from a far land, will say, when they see the afflictions of that land and the sicknesses with which the LORD has made it sick— ²³the whole land burned out with brimstone and salt, nothing sown and nothing growing, where no plant can sprout, an overthrow like that of Sodom and Gomorrah, Admah, and Zeboiim, which the LORD overthrew in his anger and wrath— ²⁴all the nations will say, 'Why has the LORD done thus to this land? What caused the heat of this great anger?' ²⁵Then people will say, 'It is because they abandoned the covenant of the LORD, the God of their fathers, which he made with them when he brought them out of the land of Egypt, ²⁶and went and served other gods and worshiped them, gods whom they had not known and whom he had not allotted to them. ²⁷Therefore the anger of the LORD was kindled against this land, bringing upon it all the curses writ-

---

¹ Ch 29:1 in Hebrew ² Or *deal wisely* ³ Septuagint, Syriac; Hebrew *your heads, your tribes*

ten in this book, [28] and the LORD uprooted them from their land in anger and fury and great wrath, and cast them into another land, as they are this day.'

[29] "The secret things belong to the LORD our God, but the things that are revealed belong to us and to our children forever, that we may do all the words of this law.

30

"And when all these things come upon you, the blessing and the curse, which I have set before you, and you call them to mind among all the nations where the LORD your God has driven you, [2] and return to the LORD your God, you and your children, and obey his voice in all that I command you today, with all your heart and with all your soul, [3] then the LORD your God will restore your fortunes and have compassion on you, and he will gather you again from all the peoples where the LORD your God has scattered you. [4] If your outcasts are in the uttermost parts of heaven, from there the LORD your God will gather you, and from there he will take you. [5] And the LORD your God will bring you into the land that your fathers possessed, that you may possess it. And he will make you more prosperous and numerous than your fathers. [6] And the LORD your God will circumcise your heart and the heart of your offspring, so that you will love the LORD your God with all your heart and with all your soul, that you may live. [7] And the LORD your God will put all these curses on your foes and enemies who persecuted you. [8] And you shall again obey the voice of the LORD and keep all his commandments that I command you today. [9] The LORD your God will make you abundantly prosperous in all the work of your hand, in the fruit of your womb and in the fruit of your cattle and in the fruit of your ground. For the LORD will again take delight in prospering you, as he took delight in your fathers, [10] when you obey the voice of the LORD your God, to keep his commandments and his statutes that are written in this Book of the Law, when you turn to the LORD your God with all your heart and with all your soul.

The great either-or stated a final time [30:11–20]. We now reach one of the most oratorical, eloquent, and awe-inspiring passages in the Bible. Employing the resources of the high style, Moses first asserts the closeness of God's word, so close that everyone can know it clearly (vv. 11–14). Then he places his audience in the position of needing to make the ultimate choice—the choice between life and death (vv. 15–20). Here is a memorable picture of individuals, families, and a nation at the great spiritual cross-roads of life.

[11] "For this commandment that I command you today is not too hard for you, neither is it far off. [12] It is not in heaven, that you should say, 'Who will ascend to heaven for us and bring it to us, that we may hear it and do it?' [13] Neither is it beyond the sea, that you should say, 'Who will go over the sea for us and bring it to us, that we may hear it and do it?' [14] But the word is very near you. It is in your mouth and in your heart, so that you can do it.

[15] "See, I have set before you today life and good, death and evil. [16] If you obey the commandments of the LORD your God[1] that I command you today, by loving the LORD your God, by walking in his ways, and by keeping his commandments and his statutes and his rules,[2] then you shall live and multiply, and the LORD your God will bless you in the land that you are entering to take possession of it. [17] But if your heart turns away, and you will not hear, but are drawn away to worship other gods and serve

---

[1] Septuagint; Hebrew lacks *If you obey the commandments of the LORD your God* [2] Or *his just decrees*

them, ¹⁸I declare to you today, that you shall surely perish. You shall not live long in the land that you are going over the Jordan to enter and possess. ¹⁹I call heaven and earth to witness against you today, that I have set before you life and death, blessing and curse. Therefore choose life, that you and your offspring may live, ²⁰loving the LORD your God, obeying his voice and holding fast to him, for he is your life and length of days, that you may dwell in the land that the LORD swore to your fathers, to Abraham, to Isaac, and to Jacob, to give them."

> **Succession rituals** [31:1–29]. The formal address to the nation is now over, and the text's attention shifts to various actions related to Moses' terminating his headship of the nation and transferring leadership to Joshua and the Levites. The sequence is as follows: Moses announces the end of his tenure and asserts again that God will strengthen the nation for the conquest of Canaan (vv. 1–6); Moses asserts the same encouragement to his chosen successor Joshua (vv. 7–8); Moses gives the law that he has articulated in the book of Deuteronomy to the priests and elders, along with instructions regarding when the law should be read to the nation (vv. 9–13); God convenes Moses and Joshua, reinforcing the end of Moses' tenure and commissioning Joshua as leader of the nation (vv. 14–23); Moses turns over the book of Deuteronomy to the Levites, instructs them to put it beside the ark of the covenant, and makes the surprising prediction that the nation will disobey what he has commanded them (vv. 24–29).

31 So Moses continued to speak these words to all Israel. ²And he said to them, "I am 120 years old today. I am no longer able to go out and come in. The LORD has said to me, 'You shall not go over this Jordan.' ³The LORD your God himself will go over before you. He will destroy these nations before you, so that you shall dispossess them, and Joshua will go over at your head, as the LORD has spoken. ⁴And the LORD will do to them as he did to Sihon and Og, the kings of the Amorites, and to their land, when he destroyed them. ⁵And the LORD will give them over to you, and you shall do to them according to the whole commandment that I have commanded you. ⁶Be strong and courageous. Do not fear or be in dread of them, for it is the LORD your God who goes with you. He will not leave you or forsake you."

⁷Then Moses summoned Joshua and said to him in the sight of all Israel, "Be strong and courageous, for you shall go with this people into the land that the LORD has sworn to their fathers to give them, and you shall put them in possession of it. ⁸It is the LORD who goes before you. He will be with you; he will not leave you or forsake you. Do not fear or be dismayed."

⁹Then Moses wrote this law and gave it to the priests, the sons of Levi, who carried the ark of the covenant of the LORD, and to all the elders of Israel. ¹⁰And Moses commanded them, "At the end of every seven years, at the set time in the year of release, at the Feast of Booths, ¹¹when all Israel comes to appear before the LORD your God at the place that he will choose, you shall read this law before all Israel in their hearing. ¹²Assemble the people, men, women, and little ones, and the sojourner within your towns, that they may hear and learn to fear the LORD your God, and be careful to do all the words of this law, ¹³and that their children, who have not known it, may hear and learn to fear the LORD your God, as long as you live in the land that you are going over the Jordan to possess."

¹⁴And the LORD said to Moses, "Behold, the days approach when you must die. Call

Joshua and present yourselves in the tent of meeting, that I may commission him." And Moses and Joshua went and presented themselves in the tent of meeting. [15]And the LORD appeared in the tent in a pillar of cloud. And the pillar of cloud stood over the entrance of the tent.

[16]And the LORD said to Moses, "Behold, you are about to lie down with your fathers. Then this people will rise and whore after the foreign gods among them in the land that they are entering, and they will forsake me and break my covenant that I have made with them. [17]Then my anger will be kindled against them in that day, and I will forsake them and hide my face from them, and they will be devoured. And many evils and troubles will come upon them, so that they will say in that day, 'Have not these evils come upon us because our God is not among us?' [18]And I will surely hide my face in that day because of all the evil that they have done, because they have turned to other gods.

[19]"Now therefore write this song and teach it to the people of Israel. Put it in their mouths, that this song may be a witness for me against the people of Israel. [20]For when I have brought them into the land flowing with milk and honey, which I swore to give to their fathers, and they have eaten and are full and grown fat, they will turn to other gods and serve them, and despise me and break my covenant. [21]And when many evils and troubles have come upon them, this song shall confront them as a witness (for it will live unforgotten in the mouths of their offspring). For I know what they are inclined to do even today, before I have brought them into the land that I swore to give." [22]So Moses wrote this song the same day and taught it to the people of Israel.

[23]And the LORD commissioned Joshua the son of Nun and said, "Be strong and courageous, for you shall bring the people of Israel into the land that I swore to give them. I will be with you."

[24]When Moses had finished writing the words of this law in a book to the very end, [25]Moses commanded the Levites who carried the ark of the covenant of the LORD, [26]"Take this Book of the Law and put it by the side of the ark of the covenant of the LORD your God, that it may be there for a witness against you. [27]For I know how rebellious and stubborn you are. Behold, even today while I am yet alive with you, you have been rebellious against the LORD. How much more after my death! [28]Assemble to me all the elders of your tribes and your officers, that I may speak these words in their ears and call heaven and earth to witness against them. [29]For I know that after my death you will surely act corruptly and turn aside from the way that I have commanded you. And in the days to come evil will befall you, because you will do what is evil in the sight of the LORD, provoking him to anger through the work of your hands."

The Song of Moses [31:30–32:47]. Moses ends the book of Deuteronomy with two poetic flourishes. The first is known as the Song of Moses. It is an *ode—an exalted *lyric poem written in the high style on a dignified subject. The order of sentiments follows the U-shaped pattern of literary *comedy, with a descent into *tragedy and a renascent to a happy ending. The sequence is as follows: a formal and exalted lead-in to the poem (32:1–3); a catalog of God's praiseworthy attributes and acts (32:4–14); a *foil in the form of disparise of Israel's faithlessness (32:15–18); a divine *soliloquy in which God asserts his judgment against the rebellious nation, ending with disparise of the pagan nations surrounding Israel (32:19–33); countermovement in the form of a divine soliloquy in which God predicts that he will punish the pagan nations and deliver Israel, ending with the poet's exclamation of praise of God's acts (32:34–43). The follow-up gives the narrative context of the song and Moses' admonishment to the nation to heed what he has said in it (32:44–47).

³⁰Then Moses spoke the words of this song until they were finished, in the ears of all the assembly of Israel:

32

"Give ear, O heavens, and I will speak,
   and let the earth hear the words of my mouth.
² May my teaching drop as the rain,
   my speech distill as the dew,
like gentle rain upon the tender grass,
   and like showers upon the herb.
³ For I will proclaim the name of the Lord;
   ascribe greatness to our God!

⁴ "The Rock, his work is perfect,
   for all his ways are justice.
A God of faithfulness and without iniquity,
   just and upright is he.
⁵ They have dealt corruptly with him;
   they are no longer his children because they are blemished;
   they are a crooked and twisted generation.
⁶ Do you thus repay the Lord,
   you foolish and senseless people?
Is not he your father, who created you,
   who made you and established you?
⁷ Remember the days of old;
   consider the years of many generations;
ask your father, and he will show you,
   your elders, and they will tell you.
⁸ When the Most High gave to the nations their inheritance,
   when he divided mankind,
he fixed the borders¹ of the peoples
   according to the number of the sons of God.²
⁹ But the Lord's portion is his people,
   Jacob his allotted heritage.

¹⁰ "He found him in a desert land,
   and in the howling waste of the wilderness;
he encircled him, he cared for him,
   he kept him as the apple of his eye.
¹¹ Like an eagle that stirs up its nest,
   that flutters over its young,
spreading out its wings, catching them,
   bearing them on its pinions,

¹ Or territories ² Compare Dead Sea Scroll, Septuagint; Masoretic Text Israel

12 the LORD alone guided him,
     no foreign god was with him.
13 He made him ride on the high places of the land,
     and he ate the produce of the field,
   and he suckled him with honey out of the rock,
     and oil out of the flinty rock.
14 Curds from the herd, and milk from the flock,
     with fat[1] of lambs,
   rams of Bashan and goats,
     with the very finest[2] of the wheat—
   and you drank foaming wine made from the blood of the grape.

15 "But Jeshurun grew fat, and kicked;
     you grew fat, stout, and sleek;
   then he forsook God who made him
     and scoffed at the Rock of his salvation.
16 They stirred him to jealousy with strange gods;
     with abominations they provoked him to anger.
17 They sacrificed to demons that were no gods,
     to gods they had never known,
   to new gods that had come recently,
     whom your fathers had never dreaded.
18 You were unmindful of the Rock that bore[3] you,
     and you forgot the God who gave you birth.

19 "The LORD saw it and spurned them,
     because of the provocation of his sons and his daughters.
20 And he said, 'I will hide my face from them;
     I will see what their end will be,
   For they are a perverse generation,
     children in whom is no faithfulness.
21 They have made me jealous with what is no god;
     they have provoked me to anger with their idols.
   So I will make them jealous with those who are no people;
     I will provoke them to anger with a foolish nation.
22 For a fire is kindled by my anger,
     and it burns to the depths of Sheol,
   devours the earth and its increase,
     and sets on fire the foundations of the mountains.

23 "'And I will heap disasters upon them;
     I will spend my arrows on them;
24 they shall be wasted with hunger,
     and devoured by plague
     and poisonous pestilence;
   I will send the teeth of beasts against them,
     with the venom of things that crawl in the dust.
25 Outdoors the sword shall bereave,

---

[1] That is, with the best [2] Hebrew *with the kidney fat* [3] Or *fathered*

and indoors terror,
    for young man and woman alike,
       the nursing child with the man of gray hairs.
26 I would have said, "I will cut them to pieces;
    I will wipe them from human memory,"
27 had I not feared provocation by the enemy,
    lest their adversaries should misunderstand,
    lest they should say, "Our hand is triumphant,
       it was not the Lord who did all this." '

28 "For they are a nation void of counsel,
    and there is no understanding in them.
29 If they were wise, they would understand this;
    they would discern their latter end!
30 How could one have chased a thousand,
    and two have put ten thousand to flight,
  unless their Rock had sold them,
    and the Lord had given them up?
31 For their rock is not as our Rock;
    our enemies are by themselves.
32 For their vine comes from the vine of Sodom
    and from the fields of Gomorrah;
  their grapes are grapes of poison;
    their clusters are bitter;
33 their wine is the poison of serpents
    and the cruel venom of asps.

34 " 'Is not this laid up in store with me,
    sealed up in my treasuries?
35 Vengeance is mine, and recompense,[1]
    for the time when their foot shall slip;
  for the day of their calamity is at hand,
    and their doom comes swiftly.'
36 For the Lord will vindicate[2] his people
    and have compassion on his servants,
  when he sees that their power is gone
    and there is none remaining, bond or free.
37 Then he will say, 'Where are their gods,
    the rock in which they took refuge,
38 who ate the fat of their sacrifices
    and drank the wine of their drink offering?
  Let them rise up and help you;
    let them be your protection!

39 " 'See now that I, even I, am he,
    and there is no god beside me;
  I kill and I make alive;
    I wound and I heal;

[1] Septuagint *and I will repay* [2] Septuagint *judge*

and there is none that can deliver out of my hand.

40 For I lift up my hand to heaven
        and swear, As I live forever,
41 if I sharpen my flashing sword[1]
        and my hand takes hold on judgment,
    I will take vengeance on my adversaries
        and will repay those who hate me.
42 I will make my arrows drunk with blood,
        and my sword shall devour flesh—
    with the blood of the slain and the captives,
        from the long-haired heads of the enemy.'

43 "Rejoice with him, O heavens;
        bow down to him, all gods,[2]
    for he avenges the blood of his children[3]
        and takes vengeance on his adversaries.
    He repays those who hate him[4]
        and cleanses[5] his people's land."[6]

[44] Moses came and recited all the words of this song in the hearing of the people, he and Joshua[7] the son of Nun. [45] And when Moses had finished speaking all these words to all Israel, [46] he said to them, "Take to heart all the words by which I am warning you today, that you may command them to your children, that they may be careful to do all the words of this law. [47] For it is no empty word for you, but your very life, and by this word you shall live long in the land that you are going over the Jordan to possess."

God summons Moses to die [32:48–52]. This narrative unit conveys an emotional voltage that is disproportionate to its brevity. God takes Moses to Mount Nebo, from which he can see the Promised Land that he disqualified himself from entering by his actions surrounding God's bringing water from the rock at Kadesh (Num. 20:10–13).

[48] That very day the Lord spoke to Moses, [49] "Go up this mountain of the Abarim, Mount Nebo, which is in the land of Moab, opposite Jericho, and view the land of Canaan, which I am giving to the people of Israel for a possession. [50] And die on the mountain which you go up, and be gathered to your people, as Aaron your brother died in Mount Hor and was gathered to his people, [51] because you broke faith with me in the midst of the people of Israel at the waters of Meribah-kadesh, in the wilderness of Zin, and because you did not treat me as holy in the midst of the people of Israel. [52] For you shall see the land before you, but you shall not go there, into the land that I am giving to the people of Israel."

Moses blesses a nation [chapter 33]. This chapter consists of another poem in the high style. The literary form is known as the *blessing and consists of pronouncements of specific blessings on specific tribes of Israel. Moses begins with the *theophany of

---

[1] Hebrew *the lightning of my sword* [2] Dead Sea Scroll, Septuagint; Masoretic Text *Rejoice his people, O nations* [3] Dead Sea Scroll, Septuagint; Masoretic Text *servants* [4] Dead Sea Scroll, Septuagint; Masoretic Text lacks *He repays those who hate him* [5] Or *atones for* [6] Septuagint, Vulgate; Hebrew *his land his people* [7] Septuagint, Syriac, Vulgate; Hebrew *Hoshea*

God as he appeared in his transcendence at Mount Sinai, giving the law and becoming king of a theocracy (vv. 2–6). Then Moses marches through the twelve tribes, pronouncing blessings unique to each one (vv. 7–25). Two poetic motifs or devices permeate the hymnic benedictions: (1) God is pictured as addressing the tribes directly (the rhetorical form is known as *apostrophe—addressing someone absent as though present and capable of hearing and responding); (2) the tribes are *personified and addressed as though they were individual persons. After the catalog of tribes, Moses branches out and addresses the entire nation as Jeshurun (v. 26), praising God for his praiseworthy acts and attributes (vv. 26–27), recalling Israel's safety under God's protection (v. 28), and pronouncing a benediction on the nation under God (v. 29).

33 This is the blessing with which Moses the man of God blessed the people of Israel before his death. ²He said,

"The LORD came from Sinai
　　and dawned from Seir upon us;[1]
　he shone forth from Mount Paran;
he came from the ten thousands of holy ones,
　　with flaming fire[2] at his right hand.
³　Yes, he loved his people,[3]
　　all his holy ones were in his[4] hand;
　so they followed[5] in your steps,
　　receiving direction from you,
⁴　when Moses commanded us a law,
　　as a possession for the assembly of Jacob.
⁵　Thus the LORD became king in Jeshurun,
　　when the heads of the people were gathered,
　　all the tribes of Israel together.

⁶　"Let Reuben live, and not die,
　　but let his men be few."

⁷And this he said of Judah:

　"Hear, O LORD, the voice of Judah,
　　and bring him in to his people.
　With your hands contend[6] for him,
　　and be a help against his adversaries."

⁸And of Levi he said,

　"Give to Levi[7] your Thummim,
　　and your Urim to your godly one,
　whom you tested at Massah,
　　with whom you quarreled at the waters of Meribah;
⁹　who said of his father and mother,
　　'I regard them not';
　he disowned his brothers

---

[1] Septuagint, Syriac, Vulgate; Hebrew *them* [2] The meaning of the Hebrew word is uncertain [3] Septuagint; Hebrew *peoples* [4] Hebrew *your* [5] The meaning of the Hebrew word is uncertain [6] Probable reading; Hebrew *With his hands he contended* [7] Dead Sea Scroll, Septuagint; Masoretic Text lacks *Give to Levi*

and ignored his children.
For they observed your word
  and kept your covenant.
¹⁰ They shall teach Jacob your rules
  and Israel your law;
they shall put incense before you
  and whole burnt offerings on your altar.
¹¹ Bless, O Lᴏʀᴅ, his substance,
    and accept the work of his hands;
crush the loins of his adversaries,
  of those who hate him, that they rise not again."

¹²Of Benjamin he said,

  "The beloved of the Lᴏʀᴅ dwells in safety.
  The High God¹ surrounds him all day long,
    and dwells between his shoulders."

¹³And of Joseph he said,

  "Blessed by the Lᴏʀᴅ be his land,
    with the choicest gifts of heaven above,²
    and of the deep that crouches beneath,
¹⁴ with the choicest fruits of the sun
    and the rich yield of the months,
¹⁵ with the finest produce of the ancient mountains
    and the abundance of the everlasting hills,
¹⁶ with the best gifts of the earth and its fullness
    and the favor of him who dwells in the bush.
May these rest on the head of Joseph,
  on the pate of him who is prince among his brothers.
¹⁷ A firstborn bull³—he has majesty,
    and his horns are the horns of a wild ox;
with them he shall gore the peoples,
  all of them, to the ends of the earth;
they are the ten thousands of Ephraim,
  and they are the thousands of Manasseh."

¹⁸And of Zebulun he said,

  "Rejoice, Zebulun, in your going out,
    and Issachar, in your tents.
¹⁹ They shall call peoples to their mountain;
    there they offer right sacrifices;
for they draw from the abundance of the seas
  and the hidden treasures of the sand."

²⁰And of Gad he said,

---

¹ Septuagint; Hebrew *dwells in safety by him. He* ² Two Hebrew manuscripts and Targum; Hebrew *with the dew* ³ Dead Sea Scroll, Septuagint, Samaritan; Masoretic Text *His firstborn bull*

"Blessed be he who enlarges Gad!
  Gad crouches like a lion;
  he tears off arm and scalp.
21 He chose the best of the land for himself,
  for there a commander's portion was reserved;
  and he came with the heads of the people,
  with Israel he executed the justice of the LORD,
  and his judgments for Israel."

22 And of Dan he said,

  "Dan is a lion's cub
  that leaps from Bashan."

23 And of Naphtali he said,

  "O Naphtali, sated with favor,
  and full of the blessing of the LORD,
  possess the lake[1] and the south."

24 And of Asher he said,

  "Most blessed of sons be Asher;
  let him be the favorite of his brothers,
  and let him dip his foot in oil.
25 Your bars shall be iron and bronze,
  and as your days, so shall your strength be.

26 "There is none like God, O Jeshurun,
  who rides through the heavens to your help,
  through the skies in his majesty.
27 The eternal God is your dwelling place,[2]
  and underneath are the everlasting arms.[3]
  And he thrust out the enemy before you
  and said, Destroy.
28 So Israel lived in safety,
  Jacob lived alone,[4]
  in a land of grain and wine,
  whose heavens drop down dew.
29 Happy are you, O Israel! Who is like you,
  a people saved by the LORD,
  the shield of your help,
  and the sword of your triumph!
  Your enemies shall come fawning to you,
  and you shall tread upon their backs."

Transfer of leadership [chapter 34]. The book of Deuteronomy ends with a narrative that recounts the transfer of leadership from Moses to Joshua. Two events make up the

---

[1] Or west [2] Or a dwelling place [3] Revocalization of verse 27 yields He subdues the ancient gods, and shatters the forces of old [4] Hebrew the abode of Jacob was alone

transfer—the death and burial of Moses (vv. 1–8), and endowment of his successor, Joshua (vv. 9–12). The first segment can be scrutinized to ascertain what aspects of Moses the writer chose to accentuate in his commemorative remarks about the leader's last moments. The second unit can be analyzed for what it implicitly says about the prerequisites for good leadership of Israel and, by implication, all believing communities.

34 Then Moses went up from the plains of Moab to Mount Nebo, to the top of Pisgah, which is opposite Jericho. And the LORD showed him all the land, Gilead as far as Dan, ²all Naphtali, the land of Ephraim and Manasseh, all the land of Judah as far as the western sea, ³the Negeb, and the Plain, that is, the Valley of Jericho the city of palm trees, as far as Zoar. ⁴And the LORD said to him, "This is the land of which I swore to Abraham, to Isaac, and to Jacob, 'I will give it to your offspring.' I have let you see it with your eyes, but you shall not go over there." ⁵So Moses the servant of the LORD died there in the land of Moab, according to the word of the LORD, ⁶and he buried him in the valley in the land of Moab opposite Beth-peor; but no one knows the place of his burial to this day. ⁷Moses was 120 years old when he died. His eye was undimmed, and his vigor unabated. ⁸And the people of Israel wept for Moses in the plains of Moab thirty days. Then the days of weeping and mourning for Moses were ended.

⁹And Joshua the son of Nun was full of the spirit of wisdom, for Moses had laid his hands on him. So the people of Israel obeyed him and did as the LORD had commanded Moses. ¹⁰And there has not arisen a prophet since in Israel like Moses, whom the LORD knew face to face, ¹¹none like him for all the signs and the wonders that the LORD sent him to do in the land of Egypt, to Pharaoh and to all his servants and to all his land, ¹²and for all the mighty power and all the great deeds of terror that Moses did in the sight of all Israel.

JOSHUA

The book at a glance. 24 chapters, 658 verses. The book of Joshua is a historical chronicle made up of individual stories and informational lists. Together these tell an overarching story of how the nation of Israel entered and conquered the Promised Land and parceled it out to the tribes and families. Individual units contribute their part to the overall story. As always, the procedure of literature is to embody the universal in the particular. The first item on our agenda as we work our way through the book of Joshua is to relive the literal events of the story. We need to take the concrete particulars seriously and use our imagination to enter the world of the text. Having done so, we must ponder the recognizable human experiences and the underlying principles, especially in the areas of leadership, community, and spiritual warfare.

▌**Genres.** Multiple *genres converge in the book of Joshua, making it a more complex book than its twenty-four chapters might suggest. The overall format is *narrative or story. The specific type of story is *epic—the story of a nation engaged in matters of state, including warfare. Epics always have a central hero, so we can also view the book of Joshua (whose name means "The Lord saves") as a *hero story. A feature of epics is the inclusion of epic catalogs (lists), and in the book of Joshua they are so extensive that the book becomes a historical chronicle in addition to an epic story. (For more information on items accompanied by an asterisk, see the glossary at the back of this Bible.)

▌**Challenges for the modern reader.** It is important to acknowledge the challenges that this book poses for modern readers. One challenge is that we need to understand and become interested in military strategy and tactics; the solution is to learn how ancient warfare was conducted. Second, as we read we need to accept the divinely ordained destruction of civilian populations in the war that this book records; doing so will be easier if we undertake the research that will tell us what kind of societies lived in Canaan (decadent societies guilty of evil perversions). The narrative thus becomes a story of God's holiness and justice. We also need to accept the premise that God's intention was to have his people occupy the Promised Land without any admixture of paganism. Third, as we read the book we need to deal with an abundance of unfamiliar geographic references; the solution is to use an atlas to locate the places about which we read.

▌**Tips for reading.** The best avenue toward enjoying and understanding this book is to immerse ourselves in the narrative world of the text. We need to imagine ourselves

Passage	Content	Contribution to the Story of the Promised Land	Type of Narrative
1:1–18	Joshua assumes leadership	Preparing to conquer the land	Conquest narrative
2:1–24	The two spies and Rahab		
3:1–5:15	Crossing the Jordan; stones of remembrance; ceremonial preparation		
6:1–27	Conquest of Jericho	Conquering the land	
7:1–8:35	Conquest of Ai		
9:1–27	The Gibeonites' deceit		
10:1–12:24	Conquest of assorted kings		
13:1–19:51	Parceling of land to the tribes	Dividing the land	Settlement narrative
20:1–21:45	Cities of refuge; cities of the Levites		
22:1–34	Joshua and the eastern tribes	Living in the land	
23:1–24:33	Joshua's last words and death		

present at the events and take the literal physical details seriously. We need to relish the suspense, the danger, the plot conflicts that the storyteller puts before us. An epic presents heightened images of good and evil, and all the more so with the implied holy war motif that we encounter in the OT. Along with the images of good and evil, we encounter images of heroism to admire and emulate. Finally, we should look not only *at* the world of the story and its characters but *through* that world to life as we know it. For all its apparent remoteness from us, the world of the book of Joshua is always at hand. One of the lessons that we learn is that God does not simply hand over the Promised Land as a gift; the nation needs to fight for it and claim it. Further, as we look closely at the story, we can see that the battle is as much spiritual as military and is won by faith as well as works.

▌**Inferred literary intentions.** The book is designed to achieve the following literary purposes:

- lead us to relive the physical battles that the Israelites conducted while conquering the Promised Land

- see a spiritual as well as military thread of action throughout the story

- admire the heroism of Joshua

- prompt us to look through the details of the stories and ponder the universal human experiences and underlying principles that apply to us

- challenge a common misconception that the Bible deals only with spiritual issues to the exclusion of real life in the world

▌**Theological themes.** (1) Divine sovereignty: the history of Israel is ultimately the story of God's designs for his people and his direction of history to preserve his chosen nation. (2) Human agency: even though God sometimes acts miraculously in the history that is narrated, his usual way of achieving his purposes is through the human actions and decisions of people. (3) Society and the state: the book of Joshua is about a whole society and its leaders, and it teaches important lessons about both. (4) The covenant: in conquering and settling the Promised Land, Joshua and the nation are fulfilling promises that God made as far back as Abraham. (5) Religious compromise: we repeatedly see the Israelites' inclination to be halfhearted in resisting the pagan culture that they confront in Canaan.

■ **The book of Joshua as a chapter in the master story of the Bible.** Through most of the OT, the story of salvation focuses on the history of a nation from which the Messiah would eventually be born. The book of Joshua narrates a crucial chapter in the history of Israel. The generation that enters Canaan, for all its faults, exhibits a faith that its forebears did not (and for lack of which they perished in the wilderness). The story of national deliverance and settlement about which we read in the book of Joshua is the story of God's saving purposes during that particular time in history. It also sets the pattern of holy warfare that culminates with Jesus Christ as the ultimate divine warrior who defeats sin, death, and the devil.

The introduction of the epic hero [chapter 1]. Epics focus on an epic hero, who ordinarily enters the story at the outset and is a unifying presence to the end of the story. The first chapter of Joshua introduces the titular hero of the book as a whole. A good way to organize our reading of chapter 1 is to analyze what the storyteller wants us to notice about Joshua when we first meet him in this book. The sequence of the chapter is as follows: God commissions and instructs Joshua (vv. 1–9); Joshua commands his officers to oversee preparation of the people for crossing the Jordan (vv. 10–11); Joshua negotiates with the two-and-a-half tribes that had secured permission from Moses to settle east of the Jordan (vv. 12–18).

1 After the death of Moses the servant of the Lord, the Lord said to Joshua the son of Nun, Moses' assistant, [2]"Moses my servant is dead. Now therefore arise, go over this Jordan, you and all this people, into the land that I am giving to them, to the people of Israel. [3]Every place that the sole of your foot will tread upon I have given to you, just as I promised to Moses. [4]From the wilderness and this Lebanon as far as the great river, the river Euphrates, all the land of the Hittites to the Great Sea toward the going down of the sun shall be your territory. [5]No man shall be able to stand before you all the days of your life. Just as I was with Moses, so I will be with you. I will not leave you or forsake you. [6]Be strong and courageous, for you shall cause this people to inherit the land that I swore to their fathers to give them. [7]Only be strong and very courageous, being careful to do according to all the law that Moses my servant commanded you. Do not turn from it to the right hand or to the left, that you may have good success[1] wherever you go. [8]This Book of the Law shall not depart from your mouth, but you shall meditate on it day and night, so that you may be careful to do according to all that is written in it. For then you will make your way prosperous, and then you will have good success. [9]Have I not commanded you? Be strong and coura-

---

[1] Or may act wisely

geous. Do not be frightened, and do not be dismayed, for the Lord your God is with you wherever you go."

[10]And Joshua commanded the officers of the people, [11]"Pass through the midst of the camp and command the people, 'Prepare your provisions, for within three days you are to pass over this Jordan to go in to take possession of the land that the Lord your God is giving you to possess.'"

[12]And to the Reubenites, the Gadites, and the half-tribe of Manasseh Joshua said, [13]"Remember the word that Moses the servant of the Lord commanded you, saying, 'The Lord your God is providing you a place of rest and will give you this land.' [14]Your wives, your little ones, and your livestock shall remain in the land that Moses gave you beyond the Jordan, but all the men of valor among you shall pass over armed before your brothers and shall help them, [15]until the Lord gives rest to your brothers as he has to you, and they also take possession of the land that the Lord your God is giving them. Then you shall return to the land of your possession and shall possess it, the land that Moses the servant of the Lord gave you beyond the Jordan toward the sunrise."

[16]And they answered Joshua, "All that you have commanded us we will do, and wherever you send us we will go. [17]Just as we obeyed Moses in all things, so we will obey you. Only may the Lord your God be with you, as he was with Moses! [18]Whoever rebels against your commandment and disobeys your words, whatever you command him, shall be put to death. Only be strong and courageous."

> **Rahab and the two spies** [chapter 2]. This story of danger, intrigue, and cleverness is one of the most famous stories in the OT. It is a favorite with children, and analyzing why this is so is a good initial avenue toward experiencing the narrative qualities of the episode. The story is told in leisurely detail, enabling us to relive it in our imagination. It ends with *poetic justice (virtue rewarded and vice thwarted).

2 And Joshua the son of Nun sent[1] two men secretly from Shittim as spies, saying, "Go, view the land, especially Jericho." And they went and came into the house of a prostitute whose name was Rahab and lodged there. [2]And it was told to the king of Jericho, "Behold, men of Israel have come here tonight to search out the land." [3]Then the king of Jericho sent to Rahab, saying, "Bring out the men who have come to you, who entered your house, for they have come to search out all the land." [4]But the woman had taken the two men and hidden them. And she said, "True, the men came to me, but I did not know where they were from. [5]And when the gate was about to be closed at dark, the men went out. I do not know where the men went. Pursue them quickly, for you will overtake them." [6]But she had brought them up to the roof and hid them with the stalks of flax that she had laid in order on the roof. [7]So the men pursued after them on the way to the Jordan as far as the fords. And the gate was shut as soon as the pursuers had gone out.

[8]Before the men[2] lay down, she came up to them on the roof [9]and said to the men, "I know that the Lord has given you the land, and that the fear of you has fallen upon us, and that all the inhabitants of the land melt away before you. [10]For we have heard how the Lord dried up the water of the Red Sea before you when you came out of Egypt, and what you did to the two kings of the Amorites who were beyond the

---

[1] Or *had sent* [2] Hebrew *they*

Jordan, to Sihon and Og, whom you devoted to destruction.[1] [11]And as soon as we heard it, our hearts melted, and there was no spirit left in any man because of you, for the LORD your God, he is God in the heavens above and on the earth beneath. [12]Now then, please swear to me by the LORD that, as I have dealt kindly with you, you also will deal kindly with my father's house, and give me a sure sign [13]that you will save alive my father and mother, my brothers and sisters, and all who belong to them, and deliver our lives from death." [14]And the men said to her, "Our life for yours even to death! If you do not tell this business of ours, then when the LORD gives us the land we will deal kindly and faithfully with you."

[15]Then she let them down by a rope through the window, for her house was built into the city wall, so that she lived in the wall. [16]And she said[2] to them, "Go into the hills, or the pursuers will encounter you, and hide there three days until the pursuers have returned. Then afterward you may go your way." [17]The men said to her, "We will be guiltless with respect to this oath of yours that you have made us swear. [18]Behold, when we come into the land, you shall tie this scarlet cord in the window through which you let us down, and you shall gather into your house your father and mother, your brothers, and all your father's household. [19]Then if anyone goes out of the doors of your house into the street, his blood shall be on his own head, and we shall be guiltless. But if a hand is laid on anyone who is with you in the house, his blood shall be on our head. [20]But if you tell this business of ours, then we shall be guiltless with respect to your oath that you have made us swear." [21]And she said, "According to your words, so be it." Then she sent them away, and they departed. And she tied the scarlet cord in the window.

[22]They departed and went into the hills and remained there three days until the pursuers returned, and the pursuers searched all along the way and found nothing. [23]Then the two men returned. They came down from the hills and passed over and came to Joshua the son of Nun, and they told him all that had happened to them. [24]And they said to Joshua, "Truly the LORD has given all the land into our hands. And also, all the inhabitants of the land melt away because of us."

> **Crossing the Jordan** [chapter 3]. This is the first *miracle story in an epic that will include many others (epics always feature what literary critics call simply "the marvelous"). Literary narratives are carefully structured by the storyteller, so it is important to relive the sequence of events as they are narrated. The general order of events in this chapter is as follows: preparations for the crossing (vv. 1–6); God's instructions to Joshua (and Joshua's to the people) about the religious significance of what is about to happen (vv. 7–13); the successful and miraculous crossing of the Jordan River (vv. 14–17). Crossing the Jordan River echoes the Israelites' crossing through the Red Sea at the time of the exodus, which is in a sense reenacted here.

3 Then Joshua rose early in the morning and they set out from Shittim. And they came to the Jordan, he and all the people of Israel, and lodged there before they passed over. [2]At the end of three days the officers went through the camp [3]and commanded the people, "As soon as you see the ark of the covenant of the LORD your God being carried by the Levitical priests, then you shall set out from your place and follow it. [4]Yet there shall be a distance between you and it, about 2,000 cubits[3] in length.

---

[1] That is, set apart (devoted) as an offering to the Lord (for destruction) [2] Or *had said* [3] A *cubit* was about 18 inches or 45 centimeters

Do not come near it, in order that you may know the way you shall go, for you have not passed this way before." ⁵Then Joshua said to the people, "Consecrate yourselves, for tomorrow the LORD will do wonders among you." ⁶And Joshua said to the priests, "Take up the ark of the covenant and pass on before the people." So they took up the ark of the covenant and went before the people.

⁷The LORD said to Joshua, "Today I will begin to exalt you in the sight of all Israel, that they may know that, as I was with Moses, so I will be with you. ⁸And as for you, command the priests who bear the ark of the covenant, 'When you come to the brink of the waters of the Jordan, you shall stand still in the Jordan.'" ⁹And Joshua said to the people of Israel, "Come here and listen to the words of the LORD your God." ¹⁰And Joshua said, "Here is how you shall know that the living God is among you and that he will without fail drive out from before you the Canaanites, the Hittites, the Hivites, the Perizzites, the Girgashites, the Amorites, and the Jebusites. ¹¹Behold, the ark of the covenant of the Lord of all the earth¹ is passing over before you into the Jordan. ¹²Now therefore take twelve men from the tribes of Israel, from each tribe a man. ¹³And when the soles of the feet of the priests bearing the ark of the LORD, the Lord of all the earth, shall rest in the waters of the Jordan, the waters of the Jordan shall be cut off from flowing, and the waters coming down from above shall stand in one heap."

¹⁴So when the people set out from their tents to pass over the Jordan with the priests bearing the ark of the covenant before the people, ¹⁵and as soon as those bearing the ark had come as far as the Jordan, and the feet of the priests bearing the ark were dipped in the brink of the water (now the Jordan overflows all its banks throughout the time of harvest), ¹⁶the waters coming down from above stood and rose up in a heap very far away, at Adam, the city that is beside Zarethan, and those flowing down toward the Sea of the Arabah, the Salt Sea, were completely cut off. And the people passed over opposite Jericho. ¹⁷Now the priests bearing the ark of the covenant of the LORD stood firmly on dry ground in the midst of the Jordan, and all Israel was passing over on dry ground until all the nation finished passing over the Jordan.

Twelve stones of remembrance [chapter 4]. Virtually everything that the Israelites will do in the book of Joshua is invested with religious and ceremonial significance. The pattern begins with this chapter. The process of collecting and erecting the twelve stones is narrated in unexpected detail, so it is obviously important that we get the facts of the event clearly registered in our imagination (a possible interpretation of v. 9 is that there were two separate monuments of stones erected to commemorate the event). Additionally, the storyteller gives us the information that we need in order to understand the ceremonial and symbolic meaning of the stones. We can ponder the application of the principle of "stones of remembrance" to our own lives, asking what God has done for us that deserves to be remembered.

4 When all the nation had finished passing over the Jordan, the LORD said to Joshua, ²"Take twelve men from the people, from each tribe a man, ³and command them, saying, 'Take twelve stones from here out of the midst of the Jordan, from the very place where the priests' feet stood firmly, and bring them over with you and lay them down in the place where you lodge tonight.'" ⁴Then Joshua called the twelve men from the people of Israel, whom he had appointed, a man from each tribe. ⁵And Joshua said to them, "Pass on before the ark of the LORD your God into the

¹ Hebrew *the ark of the covenant, the Lord of all the earth*

midst of the Jordan, and take up each of you a stone upon his shoulder, according to
the number of the tribes of the people of Israel, ⁶that this may be a sign among you.
When your children ask in time to come, 'What do those stones mean to you?' ⁷then
you shall tell them that the waters of the Jordan were cut off before the ark of the
covenant of the LORD. When it passed over the Jordan, the waters of the Jordan were
cut off. So these stones shall be to the people of Israel a memorial forever."

⁸And the people of Israel did just as Joshua commanded and took up twelve stones
out of the midst of the Jordan, according to the number of the tribes of the people of
Israel, just as the LORD told Joshua. And they carried them over with them to the place
where they lodged and laid them down¹ there. ⁹And Joshua set up twelve stones in the
midst of the Jordan, in the place where the feet of the priests bearing the ark of the
covenant had stood; and they are there to this day. ¹⁰For the priests bearing the ark
stood in the midst of the Jordan until everything was finished that the LORD commanded Joshua to tell the people, according to all that Moses had commanded Joshua.

The people passed over in haste. ¹¹And when all the people had finished passing
over, the ark of the LORD and the priests passed over before the people. ¹²The sons of
Reuben and the sons of Gad and the half-tribe of Manasseh passed over armed
before the people of Israel, as Moses had told them. ¹³About 40,000 ready for war
passed over before the LORD for battle, to the plains of Jericho. ¹⁴On that day the LORD
exalted Joshua in the sight of all Israel, and they stood in awe of him just as they had
stood in awe of Moses, all the days of his life.

¹⁵And the LORD said to Joshua, ¹⁶"Command the priests bearing the ark of the testimony to come up out of the Jordan." ¹⁷So Joshua commanded the priests, "Come up
out of the Jordan." ¹⁸And when the priests bearing the ark of the covenant of the LORD
came up from the midst of the Jordan, and the soles of the priests' feet were lifted up
on dry ground, the waters of the Jordan returned to their place and overflowed all its
banks, as before.

¹⁹The people came up out of the Jordan on the tenth day of the first month, and
they encamped at Gilgal on the east border of Jericho. ²⁰And those twelve stones,
which they took out of the Jordan, Joshua set up at Gilgal. ²¹And he said to the people
of Israel, "When your children ask their fathers in times to come, 'What do these
stones mean?' ²²then you shall let your children know, 'Israel passed over this Jordan
on dry ground.' ²³For the LORD your God dried up the waters of the Jordan for you
until you passed over, as the LORD your God did to the Red Sea, which he dried up for
us until we passed over, ²⁴so that all the peoples of the earth may know that the hand
of the LORD is mighty, that you may fear the LORD your God forever."²

Ceremonial preparations for the ensuing conquest [chapter 5]. As was true of the
exodus from Egypt, everything is carefully orchestrated in the events that are narrated
in the book of Joshua. The result is that the epic story becomes invested with an atmosphere of religious awe or the numinous. The two central sacraments of OT religion are
observed in the narrative of this chapter—circumcision (vv. 2–9) and the Passover, yet
another echo of the exodus (vv. 10–12). As bookends for these solemn events, we read
about the fear of the rival nations (v. 1) and Joshua's encounter with the angel of the
Lord (vv. 13–15).

¹ Or to rest ² Or all the days

5 As soon as all the kings of the Amorites who were beyond the Jordan to the west, and all the kings of the Canaanites who were by the sea, heard that the LORD had dried up the waters of the Jordan for the people of Israel until they had crossed over, their hearts melted and there was no longer any spirit in them because of the people of Israel.

²At that time the LORD said to Joshua, "Make flint knives and circumcise the sons of Israel a second time." ³So Joshua made flint knives and circumcised the sons of Israel at Gibeath-haaraloth.[1] ⁴And this is the reason why Joshua circumcised them: all the males of the people who came out of Egypt, all the men of war, had died in the wilderness on the way after they had come out of Egypt. ⁵Though all the people who came out had been circumcised, yet all the people who were born on the way in the wilderness after they had come out of Egypt had not been circumcised. ⁶For the people of Israel walked forty years in the wilderness, until all the nation, the men of war who came out of Egypt, perished, because they did not obey the voice of the LORD; the LORD swore to them that he would not let them see the land that the LORD had sworn to their fathers to give to us, a land flowing with milk and honey. ⁷So it was their children, whom he raised up in their place, that Joshua circumcised. For they were uncircumcised, because they had not been circumcised on the way.

⁸When the circumcising of the whole nation was finished, they remained in their places in the camp until they were healed. ⁹And the LORD said to Joshua, "Today I have rolled away the reproach of Egypt from you." And so the name of that place is called Gilgal[2] to this day.

¹⁰While the people of Israel were encamped at Gilgal, they kept the Passover on the fourteenth day of the month in the evening on the plains of Jericho. ¹¹And the day after the Passover, on that very day, they ate of the produce of the land, unleavened cakes and parched grain. ¹²And the manna ceased the day after they ate of the produce of the land. And there was no longer manna for the people of Israel, but they ate of the fruit of the land of Canaan that year.

¹³When Joshua was by Jericho, he lifted up his eyes and looked, and behold, a man was standing before him with his drawn sword in his hand. And Joshua went to him and said to him, "Are you for us, or for our adversaries?" ¹⁴And he said, "No; but I am the commander of the army of the LORD. Now I have come." And Joshua fell on his face to the earth and worshiped and said to him, "What does my lord say to his servant?" ¹⁵And the commander of the LORD's army said to Joshua, "Take off your sandals from your feet, for the place where you are standing is holy." And Joshua did so.

The conquest of Jericho [chapter 6]. This is a *battle story par excellence, and one in which surprise is a key narrative motif. Conquering a city is often a high point in the plot of an epic, and this is one of the most memorable stories in the book of Joshua. The element of surprise consists of multiple things—the procession of priests and warriors marching around the city on six consecutive days (with the people silent while the trumpets sound continuously); on the seventh day a climactic seven marches around the city, with the people shouting the last time; the fall of the city wall by an act of God rather than by military assault; the spoil saved for the treasury of God instead of being taken by the people. In addition to the motif of conquest, the story of the sparing of Rahab is a

---

[1] *Gibeath-haaraloth* means *the hill of the foreskins* [2] *Gilgal* sounds like the Hebrew for *to roll*

*rescue story, and to round out the heightened atmosphere of the story, at the end of the
chapter we observe Joshua lay a curse on the city.

6 Now Jericho was shut up inside and outside because of the people of Israel.
None went out, and none came in. ²And the Lord said to Joshua, "See, I have
given Jericho into your hand, with its king and mighty men of valor. ³You shall march
around the city, all the men of war going around the city once. Thus shall you do for
six days. ⁴Seven priests shall bear seven trumpets of rams' horns before the ark. On
the seventh day you shall march around the city seven times, and the priests shall
blow the trumpets. ⁵And when they make a long blast with the ram's horn, when you
hear the sound of the trumpet, then all the people shall shout with a great shout, and
the wall of the city will fall down flat,¹ and the people shall go up, everyone straight
before him." ⁶So Joshua the son of Nun called the priests and said to them, "Take up
the ark of the covenant and let seven priests bear seven trumpets of rams' horns
before the ark of the Lord." ⁷And he said to the people, "Go forward. March around
the city and let the armed men pass on before the ark of the Lord."

⁸And just as Joshua had commanded the people, the seven priests bearing the
seven trumpets of rams' horns before the Lord went forward, blowing the trumpets,
with the ark of the covenant of the Lord following them. ⁹The armed men were walking before the priests who were blowing the trumpets, and the rear guard was walking after the ark, while the trumpets blew continually. ¹⁰But Joshua commanded the
people, "You shall not shout or make your voice heard, neither shall any word go out
of your mouth, until the day I tell you to shout. Then you shall shout." ¹¹So he caused
the ark of the Lord to circle the city, going about it once. And they came into the
camp and spent the night in the camp.

¹²Then Joshua rose early in the morning, and the priests took up the ark of the
Lord. ¹³And the seven priests bearing the seven trumpets of rams' horns before the
ark of the Lord walked on, and they blew the trumpets continually. And the armed
men were walking before them, and the rear guard was walking after the ark of the
Lord, while the trumpets blew continually. ¹⁴And the second day they marched
around the city once, and returned into the camp. So they did for six days.

¹⁵On the seventh day they rose early, at the dawn of day, and marched around the
city in the same manner seven times. It was only on that day that they marched
around the city seven times. ¹⁶And at the seventh time, when the priests had blown
the trumpets, Joshua said to the people, "Shout, for the Lord has given you the city.
¹⁷And the city and all that is within it shall be devoted to the Lord for destruction.²
Only Rahab the prostitute and all who are with her in her house shall live, because
she hid the messengers whom we sent. ¹⁸But you, keep yourselves from the things
devoted to destruction, lest when you have devoted them you take any of the devoted
things and make the camp of Israel a thing for destruction and bring trouble upon it.
¹⁹But all silver and gold, and every vessel of bronze and iron, are holy to the Lord;
they shall go into the treasury of the Lord." ²⁰So the people shouted, and the trumpets
were blown. As soon as the people heard the sound of the trumpet, the people
shouted a great shout, and the wall fell down flat, so that the people went up into the
city, every man straight before him, and they captured the city. ²¹Then they devoted

---

¹ Hebrew *under itself*; also verse 20 ² That is, set apart (devoted) as an offering to the Lord (for destruction); also verses 18, 21

all in the city to destruction, both men and women, young and old, oxen, sheep, and donkeys, with the edge of the sword. ²²But to the two men who had spied out the land, Joshua said, "Go into the prostitute's house and bring out from there the woman and all who belong to her, as you swore to her." ²³So the young men who had been spies went in and brought out Rahab and her father and mother and brothers and all who belonged to her. And they brought all her relatives and put them outside the camp of Israel. ²⁴And they burned the city with fire, and everything in it. Only the silver and gold, and the vessels of bronze and of iron, they put into the treasury of the house of the Lord. ²⁵But Rahab the prostitute and her father's household and all who belonged to her, Joshua saved alive. And she has lived in Israel to this day, because she hid the messengers whom Joshua sent to spy out Jericho.

²⁶Joshua laid an oath on them at that time, saying, "Cursed before the Lord be the man who rises up and rebuilds this city, Jericho.

"At the cost of his firstborn shall he
    lay its foundation,
and at the cost of his youngest son
    shall he set up its gates."

²⁷So the Lord was with Joshua, and his fame was in all the land.

Achan's sin [chapter 7]. The next military event springs another surprise on us, as the Israelite army is unexpectedly defeated by the smaller army of the city of Ai. What started out as a battle story quickly turns into a story of crime and punishment—a detective story in which a process of investigation is conducted by means of divine lots that are cast on families. It is a story of search and discovery, and the suspense becomes nearly unbearable (especially for Achan) as the process of elimination unfolds. Of course all of this narrative richness does not exist only for the sake of telling an exciting story. The whole story is invested with ultimate spiritual meaning, phrased in terms of human sin and divine judgment. The two leading characters in the story are God and Achan, the archetypal sinner. Coming early in the nation's conquest of Canaan, the event served as an object lesson to the Israelites about the seriousness of sin. The same object lesson applies to us, as we are given to understand that holy war requires full obedience to the commands of God.

7 But the people of Israel broke faith in regard to the devoted things, for Achan the son of Carmi, son of Zabdi, son of Zerah, of the tribe of Judah, took some of the devoted things. And the anger of the Lord burned against the people of Israel.

²Joshua sent men from Jericho to Ai, which is near Beth-aven, east of Bethel, and said to them, "Go up and spy out the land." And the men went up and spied out Ai. ³And they returned to Joshua and said to him, "Do not have all the people go up, but let about two or three thousand men go up and attack Ai. Do not make the whole people toil up there, for they are few." ⁴So about 3,000 men went up there from the people. And they fled before the men of Ai, ⁵and the men of Ai killed about thirty-six of their men and chased them before the gate as far as Shebarim and struck them at the descent. And the hearts of the people melted and became as water.

⁶Then Joshua tore his clothes and fell to the earth on his face before the ark of the

Lord until the evening, he and the elders of Israel. And they put dust on their heads. [7]And Joshua said, "Alas, O Lord God, why have you brought this people over the Jordan at all, to give us into the hands of the Amorites, to destroy us? Would that we had been content to dwell beyond the Jordan! [8]O Lord, what can I say, when Israel has turned their backs before their enemies! [9]For the Canaanites and all the inhabitants of the land will hear of it and will surround us and cut off our name from the earth. And what will you do for your great name?"

[10]The Lord said to Joshua, "Get up! Why have you fallen on your face? [11]Israel has sinned; they have transgressed my covenant that I commanded them; they have taken some of the devoted things; they have stolen and lied and put them among their own belongings. [12]Therefore the people of Israel cannot stand before their enemies. They turn their backs before their enemies, because they have become devoted for destruction.[1] I will be with you no more, unless you destroy the devoted things from among you. [13]Get up! Consecrate the people and say, 'Consecrate yourselves for tomorrow; for thus says the Lord, God of Israel, "There are devoted things in your midst, O Israel. You cannot stand before your enemies until you take away the devoted things from among you." [14]In the morning therefore you shall be brought near by your tribes. And the tribe that the Lord takes by lot shall come near by clans. And the clan that the Lord takes shall come near by households. And the household that the Lord takes shall come near man by man. [15]And he who is taken with the devoted things shall be burned with fire, he and all that he has, because he has transgressed the covenant of the Lord, and because he has done an outrageous thing in Israel.'"

[16]So Joshua rose early in the morning and brought Israel near tribe by tribe, and the tribe of Judah was taken. [17]And he brought near the clans of Judah, and the clan of the Zerahites was taken. And he brought near the clan of the Zerahites man by man, and Zabdi was taken. [18]And he brought near his household man by man, and Achan the son of Carmi, son of Zabdi, son of Zerah, of the tribe of Judah, was taken. [19]Then Joshua said to Achan, "My son, give glory to the Lord God of Israel and give praise[2] to him. And tell me now what you have done; do not hide it from me." [20]And Achan answered Joshua, "Truly I have sinned against the Lord God of Israel, and this is what I did: [21]when I saw among the spoil a beautiful cloak from Shinar, and 200 shekels of silver, and a bar of gold weighing 50 shekels,[3] then I coveted them and took them. And see, they are hidden in the earth inside my tent, with the silver underneath."

[22]So Joshua sent messengers, and they ran to the tent; and behold, it was hidden in his tent with the silver underneath. [23]And they took them out of the tent and brought them to Joshua and to all the people of Israel. And they laid them down before the Lord. [24]And Joshua and all Israel with him took Achan the son of Zerah, and the silver and the cloak and the bar of gold, and his sons and daughters and his oxen and donkeys and sheep and his tent and all that he had. And they brought them up to the Valley of Achor. [25]And Joshua said, "Why did you bring trouble on us? The Lord brings trouble on you today." And all Israel stoned him with stones. They burned them with fire and stoned them with stones. [26]And they raised over him a great heap of stones that remains to this day. Then the Lord turned from his burning anger. Therefore, to this day the name of that place is called the Valley of Achor.[4]

[1] That is, set apart (devoted) as an offering to the Lord (for destruction) [2] Or *and make confession* [3] A *shekel* was about 2/5 ounce or 11 grams [4] *Achor* means *trouble*

The conquest of Ai [chapter 8]. As we progress through the book of Joshua, surprises are sprung on us at every turn. After the city of Jericho has been conquered by divine miracle, with the people's actions demonstrating anything but normal military strategy, Joshua 8 plunges us into a detailed account of battlefield strategy. A good way to experience the action is to imagine yourself present at the battle, taking time to piece together the specific steps of the battle that the author obviously thought to be important. This battle incorporates many of the details of battle protocol in the ancient world (for more, see the article on "battle stories" in the *Dictionary of Biblical Imagery* [Downers Grove, Ill.: InterVarsity Press, 1998]). The pervasive spiritual overtone of the epic of Joshua makes the story tug away from other epics, and we find a notable instance at the end of chapter 8. Ordinary epics would have ended the story at verse 29, with its account of the burial of the king of Ai, but in this story Joshua does a great deal more than reduce a city to ruins. He builds an altar, followed by an awe-inspiring recitation of the law of God, accompanied by its blessing and curse.

8 And the LORD said to Joshua, "Do not fear and do not be dismayed. Take all the fighting men with you, and arise, go up to Ai. See, I have given into your hand the king of Ai, and his people, his city, and his land. ²And you shall do to Ai and its king as you did to Jericho and its king. Only its spoil and its livestock you shall take as plunder for yourselves. Lay an ambush against the city, behind it."

³So Joshua and all the fighting men arose to go up to Ai. And Joshua chose 30,000 mighty men of valor and sent them out by night. ⁴And he commanded them, "Behold, you shall lie in ambush against the city, behind it. Do not go very far from the city, but all of you remain ready. ⁵And I and all the people who are with me will approach the city. And when they come out against us just as before, we shall flee before them. ⁶And they will come out after us, until we have drawn them away from the city. For they will say, 'They are fleeing from us, just as before.' So we will flee before them. ⁷Then you shall rise up from the ambush and seize the city, for the LORD your God will give it into your hand. ⁸And as soon as you have taken the city, you shall set the city on fire. You shall do according to the word of the LORD. See, I have commanded you." ⁹So Joshua sent them out. And they went to the place of ambush and lay between Bethel and Ai, to the west of Ai, but Joshua spent that night among the people.

¹⁰Joshua arose early in the morning and mustered the people and went up, he and the elders of Israel, before the people to Ai. ¹¹And all the fighting men who were with him went up and drew near before the city and encamped on the north side of Ai, with a ravine between them and Ai. ¹²He took about 5,000 men and set them in ambush between Bethel and Ai, to the west of the city. ¹³So they stationed the forces, the main encampment that was north of the city and its rear guard west of the city. But Joshua spent that night in the valley. ¹⁴And as soon as the king of Ai saw this, he and all his people, the men of the city, hurried and went out early to the appointed place[1] toward the Arabah to meet Israel in battle. But he did not know that there was an ambush against him behind the city. ¹⁵And Joshua and all Israel pretended to be beaten before them and fled in the direction of the wilderness. ¹⁶So all the people who were in the city were called together to pursue them, and as they pursued Joshua they were drawn away from the city. ¹⁷Not a man was left in Ai or Bethel who did not go out after Israel. They left the city open and pursued Israel.

[1] Hebrew *appointed time*

[18]Then the Lord said to Joshua, "Stretch out the javelin that is in your hand toward Ai, for I will give it into your hand." And Joshua stretched out the javelin that was in his hand toward the city. [19]And the men in the ambush rose quickly out of their place, and as soon as he had stretched out his hand, they ran and entered the city and captured it. And they hurried to set the city on fire. [20]So when the men of Ai looked back, behold, the smoke of the city went up to heaven, and they had no power to flee this way or that, for the people who fled to the wilderness turned back against the pursuers. [21]And when Joshua and all Israel saw that the ambush had captured the city, and that the smoke of the city went up, then they turned back and struck down the men of Ai. [22]And the others came out from the city against them, so they were in the midst of Israel, some on this side, and some on that side. And Israel struck them down, until there was left none that survived or escaped. [23]But the king of Ai they took alive, and brought him near to Joshua.

[24]When Israel had finished killing all the inhabitants of Ai in the open wilderness where they pursued them, and all of them to the very last had fallen by the edge of the sword, all Israel returned to Ai and struck it down with the edge of the sword. [25]And all who fell that day, both men and women, were 12,000, all the people of Ai. [26]But Joshua did not draw back his hand with which he stretched out the javelin until he had devoted all the inhabitants of Ai to destruction.[1] [27]Only the livestock and the spoil of that city Israel took as their plunder, according to the word of the Lord that he commanded Joshua. [28]So Joshua burned Ai and made it forever a heap of ruins, as it is to this day. [29]And he hanged the king of Ai on a tree until evening. And at sunset Joshua commanded, and they took his body down from the tree and threw it at the entrance of the gate of the city and raised over it a great heap of stones, which stands there to this day.

[30]At that time Joshua built an altar to the Lord, the God of Israel, on Mount Ebal, [31]just as Moses the servant of the Lord had commanded the people of Israel, as it is written in the Book of the Law of Moses, "an altar of uncut stones, upon which no man has wielded an iron tool." And they offered on it burnt offerings to the Lord and sacrificed peace offerings. [32]And there, in the presence of the people of Israel, he wrote on the stones a copy of the law of Moses, which he had written. [33]And all Israel, sojourner as well as native born, with their elders and officers and their judges, stood on opposite sides of the ark before the Levitical priests who carried the ark of the covenant of the Lord, half of them in front of Mount Gerizim and half of them in front of Mount Ebal, just as Moses the servant of the Lord had commanded at the first, to bless the people of Israel. [34]And afterward he read all the words of the law, the blessing and the curse, according to all that is written in the Book of the Law. [35]There was not a word of all that Moses commanded that Joshua did not read before all the assembly of Israel, and the women, and the little ones, and the sojourners who lived[2] among them.

The deceit of the Gibeonites [chapter 9]. The next episode of the prose epic of Joshua is not a battle story per se, but it does involve conflict between warring nations. It is a deception story on a grand scale. The narrative motif that most absorbs our attention is the cleverness of the Gibeonites' deception. The entire account is permeated with *dramatic irony, inasmuch as we know something that Joshua does not. We cringe as we

---

[1] That is, set apart (devoted) as an offering to the Lord (for destruction) [2] Or *traveled*

see Joshua make a terrible mistake. The response of the Israelites to their having been duped takes modern readers by surprise: instead of declaring the treaty void because it was obtained under false pretenses, the Israelites live up to the treaty, showing how inviolable for societies in the ancient world were such matters as covenants, treaties, vows, and one's word. The story ends with the epithets that became proverbial to cultures that know the Bible—"hewers of wood and drawers of water" (KJV).

9 As soon as all the kings who were beyond the Jordan in the hill country and in the lowland all along the coast of the Great Sea toward Lebanon, the Hittites, the Amorites, the Canaanites, the Perizzites, the Hivites, and the Jebusites, heard of this, ²they gathered together as one to fight against Joshua and Israel.

³But when the inhabitants of Gibeon heard what Joshua had done to Jericho and to Ai, ⁴they on their part acted with cunning and went and made ready provisions and took worn-out sacks for their donkeys, and wineskins, worn-out and torn and mended, ⁵with worn-out, patched sandals on their feet, and worn-out clothes. And all their provisions were dry and crumbly. ⁶And they went to Joshua in the camp at Gilgal and said to him and to the men of Israel, "We have come from a distant country, so now make a covenant with us." ⁷But the men of Israel said to the Hivites, "Perhaps you live among us; then how can we make a covenant with you?" ⁸They said to Joshua, "We are your servants." And Joshua said to them, "Who are you? And where do you come from?" ⁹They said to him, "From a very distant country your servants have come, because of the name of the LORD your God. For we have heard a report of him, and all that he did in Egypt, ¹⁰and all that he did to the two kings of the Amorites who were beyond the Jordan, to Sihon the king of Heshbon, and to Og king of Bashan, who lived in Ashtaroth. ¹¹So our elders and all the inhabitants of our country said to us, 'Take provisions in your hand for the journey and go to meet them and say to them, "We are your servants. Come now, make a covenant with us."' ¹²Here is our bread. It was still warm when we took it from our houses as our food for the journey on the day we set out to come to you, but now, behold, it is dry and crumbly. ¹³These wineskins were new when we filled them, and behold, they have burst. And these garments and sandals of ours are worn out from the very long journey." ¹⁴So the men took some of their provisions, but did not ask counsel from the LORD. ¹⁵And Joshua made peace with them and made a covenant with them, to let them live, and the leaders of the congregation swore to them.

¹⁶At the end of three days after they had made a covenant with them, they heard that they were their neighbors and that they lived among them. ¹⁷And the people of Israel set out and reached their cities on the third day. Now their cities were Gibeon, Chephirah, Beeroth, and Kiriath-jearim. ¹⁸But the people of Israel did not attack them, because the leaders of the congregation had sworn to them by the LORD, the God of Israel. Then all the congregation murmured against the leaders. ¹⁹But all the leaders said to all the congregation, "We have sworn to them by the LORD, the God of Israel, and now we may not touch them. ²⁰This we will do to them: let them live, lest wrath be upon us, because of the oath that we swore to them." ²¹And the leaders said to them, "Let them live." So they became cutters of wood and drawers of water for all the congregation, just as the leaders had said of them.

²²Joshua summoned them, and he said to them, "Why did you deceive us, saying,

'We are very far from you,' when you dwell among us? [23]Now therefore you are cursed, and some of you shall never be anything but servants, cutters of wood and drawers of water for the house of my God." [24]They answered Joshua, "Because it was told to your servants for a certainty that the LORD your God had commanded his servant Moses to give you all the land and to destroy all the inhabitants of the land from before you—so we feared greatly for our lives because of you and did this thing. [25]And now, behold, we are in your hand. Whatever seems good and right in your sight to do to us, do it." [26]So he did this to them and delivered them out of the hand of the people of Israel, and they did not kill them. [27]But Joshua made them that day cutters of wood and drawers of water for the congregation and for the altar of the LORD, to this day, in the place that he should choose.

Joshua's victories over assorted Canaanite kings [chapter 10]. Anyone who is familiar with epics like Homer's *Iliad*, Virgil's *Aeneid*, or the Old English epic *Beowulf* will know how to handle the material that the storyteller presents in the next three chapters. As in other epics, we move in a warrior's world. The preoccupations and life-and-death issues are not those of the office or home but those of the battlefield. The right way to absorb the material is to enter into the spirit and protocol of the military world that is portrayed. Stylistic features are the standard ones in epic literature: conspicuous and continuous use of *epithets (such as "the mighty men of valor" and "Horeb king of Gezer"); copia and fullness of expression to correspond to the grandeur of the action (for example, the piling up of synonyms when we read, "So Joshua struck the whole land, the hill country and the Negeb and the lowland and the slopes," v. 40); lists or catalogs; emphasis on geographic names and an expansive international scene of action. In addition to reliving the literal details of the history that is narrated, we can note these intermingled motifs and levels of meaning: (1) the continuous presence of God as a character in the story, so that we can piece together a portrait of what God is like just on the basis of these three chapters; (2) evidences of supernatural and miraculous events, so that the victories are more than merely human conquests (though we should not minimize or disparage the human heroism that is displayed); (3) images of human heroism; (4) the importance that strong leaders play in the life of a nation or group.

10

As soon as Adoni-zedek, king of Jerusalem, heard how Joshua had captured Ai and had devoted it to destruction,[1] doing to Ai and its king as he had done to Jericho and its king, and how the inhabitants of Gibeon had made peace with Israel and were among them, [2]he[2] feared greatly, because Gibeon was a great city, like one of the royal cities, and because it was greater than Ai, and all its men were warriors. [3]So Adoni-zedek king of Jerusalem sent to Hoham king of Hebron, to Piram king of Jarmuth, to Japhia king of Lachish, and to Debir king of Eglon, saying, [4]"Come up to me and help me, and let us strike Gibeon. For it has made peace with Joshua and with the people of Israel." [5]Then the five kings of the Amorites, the king of Jerusalem, the king of Hebron, the king of Jarmuth, the king of Lachish, and the king of Eglon, gathered their forces and went up with all their armies and encamped against Gibeon and made war against it.

[6]And the men of Gibeon sent to Joshua at the camp in Gilgal, saying, "Do not relax your hand from your servants. Come up to us quickly and save us and help us, for all

---

[1] That is, set apart (devoted) as an offering to the Lord (for destruction); also verses 28, 35, 37, 39, 40 [2] One Hebrew manuscript, Vulgate (compare Syriac); most Hebrew manuscripts *they*

the kings of the Amorites who dwell in the hill country are gathered against us." ⁷So Joshua went up from Gilgal, he and all the people of war with him, and all the mighty men of valor. ⁸And the LORD said to Joshua, "Do not fear them, for I have given them into your hands. Not a man of them shall stand before you." ⁹So Joshua came upon them suddenly, having marched up all night from Gilgal. ¹⁰And the LORD threw them into a panic before Israel, who[j] struck them with a great blow at Gibeon and chased them by the way of the ascent of Beth-horon and struck them as far as Azekah and Makkedah. ¹¹And as they fled before Israel, while they were going down the ascent of Beth-horon, the LORD threw down large stones from heaven on them as far as Azekah, and they died. There were more who died because of the hailstones than the sons of Israel killed with the sword.

¹²At that time Joshua spoke to the LORD in the day when the LORD gave the Amorites over to the sons of Israel, and he said in the sight of Israel,

> "Sun, stand still at Gibeon,
>   and moon, in the Valley of Aijalon."
> ¹³   And the sun stood still, and the moon stopped,
>   until the nation took vengeance on their enemies.

Is this not written in the Book of Jashar? The sun stopped in the midst of heaven and did not hurry to set for about a whole day. ¹⁴There has been no day like it before or since, when the LORD heeded the voice of a man, for the LORD fought for Israel.

¹⁵So Joshua returned, and all Israel with him, to the camp at Gilgal.

¹⁶These five kings fled and hid themselves in the cave at Makkedah. ¹⁷And it was told to Joshua, "The five kings have been found, hidden in the cave at Makkedah." ¹⁸And Joshua said, "Roll large stones against the mouth of the cave and set men by it to guard them, ¹⁹but do not stay there yourselves. Pursue your enemies; attack their rear guard. Do not let them enter their cities, for the LORD your God has given them into your hand." ²⁰When Joshua and the sons of Israel had finished striking them with a great blow until they were wiped out, and when the remnant that remained of them had entered into the fortified cities, ²¹then all the people returned safe to Joshua in the camp at Makkedah. Not a man moved his tongue against any of the people of Israel.

²²Then Joshua said, "Open the mouth of the cave and bring those five kings out to me from the cave." ²³And they did so, and brought those five kings out to him from the cave, the king of Jerusalem, the king of Hebron, the king of Jarmuth, the king of Lachish, and the king of Eglon. ²⁴And when they brought those kings out to Joshua, Joshua summoned all the men of Israel and said to the chiefs of the men of war who had gone with him, "Come near; put your feet on the necks of these kings." Then they came near and put their feet on their necks. ²⁵And Joshua said to them, "Do not be afraid or dismayed; be strong and courageous. For thus the LORD will do to all your enemies against whom you fight." ²⁶And afterward Joshua struck them and put them to death, and he hanged them on five trees. And they hung on the trees until evening. ²⁷But at the time of the going down of the sun, Joshua commanded, and they took them down from the trees and threw them into the cave where they had hidden themselves, and they set large stones against the mouth of the cave, which remain to this very day.

²⁸As for Makkedah, Joshua captured it on that day and struck it, and its king, with

---

¹ Or and he

the edge of the sword. He devoted to destruction every person in it; he left none remaining. And he did to the king of Makkedah just as he had done to the king of Jericho. ²⁹Then Joshua and all Israel with him passed on from Makkedah to Libnah and fought against Libnah. ³⁰And the LORD gave it also and its king into the hand of Israel. And he struck it with the edge of the sword, and every person in it; he left none remaining in it. And he did to its king as he had done to the king of Jericho. ³¹Then Joshua and all Israel with him passed on from Libnah to Lachish and laid siege to it and fought against it. ³²And the LORD gave Lachish into the hand of Israel, and he captured it on the second day and struck it with the edge of the sword, and every person in it, as he had done to Libnah. ³³Then Horam king of Gezer came up to help Lachish. And Joshua struck him and his people, until he left none remaining. ³⁴Then Joshua and all Israel with him passed on from Lachish to Eglon. And they laid siege to it and fought against it. ³⁵And they captured it on that day, and struck it with the edge of the sword. And he devoted every person in it to destruction that day, as he had done to Lachish. ³⁶Then Joshua and all Israel with him went up from Eglon to Hebron. And they fought against it ³⁷and captured it and struck it with the edge of the sword, and its king and its towns, and every person in it. He left none remaining, as he had done to Eglon, and devoted it to destruction and every person in it. ³⁸Then Joshua and all Israel with him turned back to Debir and fought against it ³⁹and he captured it with its king and all its towns. And they struck them with the edge of the sword and devoted to destruction every person in it; he left none remaining. Just as he had done to Hebron and to Libnah and its king, so he did to Debir and to its king. ⁴⁰So Joshua struck the whole land, the hill country and the Negeb and the lowland and the slopes, and all their kings. He left none remaining, but devoted to destruction all that breathed, just as the LORD God of Israel commanded. ⁴¹And Joshua struck them from Kadesh-barnea as far as Gaza, and all the country of Goshen, as far as Gibeon. ⁴²And Joshua captured all these kings and their land at one time, because the LORD God of Israel fought for Israel. ⁴³Then Joshua returned, and all Israel with him, to the camp at Gilgal.

Further conquests [chapters 11–12]. The ground rules for reading and interpreting these two chapters remain the same as were noted for chapter 10. We first need to relive the physical events to the degree to which the author gives us the facts of the battles. We need to be receptive of the epic grandeur of the account, including catalogs of defeated kings and epithets like "Jabin, king of Hazor." We need to note the role that God plays in the action and the heroism of Joshua as epic leader.

11 When Jabin, king of Hazor, heard of this, he sent to Jobab king of Madon, and to the king of Shimron, and to the king of Achshaph, ²and to the kings who were in the northern hill country, and in the Arabah south of Chinneroth, and in the lowland, and in Naphoth-dor on the west, ³to the Canaanites in the east and the west, the Amorites, the Hittites, the Perizzites, and the Jebusites in the hill country, and the

Hivites under Hermon in the land of Mizpah. ⁴And they came out with all their troops, a great horde, in number like the sand that is on the seashore, with very many horses and chariots. ⁵And all these kings joined their forces and came and encamped together at the waters of Merom to fight against Israel.

⁶And the Lord said to Joshua, "Do not be afraid of them, for tomorrow at this time I will give over all of them, slain, to Israel. You shall hamstring their horses and burn their chariots with fire." ⁷So Joshua and all his warriors came suddenly against them by the waters of Merom and fell upon them. ⁸And the Lord gave them into the hand of Israel, who struck them and chased them as far as Great Sidon and Misrephoth-maim, and eastward as far as the Valley of Mizpeh. And they struck them until he left none remaining. ⁹And Joshua did to them just as the Lord said to him: he hamstrung their horses and burned their chariots with fire.

¹⁰And Joshua turned back at that time and captured Hazor and struck its king with the sword, for Hazor formerly was the head of all those kingdoms. ¹¹And they struck with the sword all who were in it, devoting them to destruction;¹ there was none left that breathed. And he burned Hazor with fire. ¹²And all the cities of those kings, and all their kings, Joshua captured, and struck them with the edge of the sword, devoting them to destruction, just as Moses the servant of the Lord had commanded. ¹³But none of the cities that stood on mounds did Israel burn, except Hazor alone; that Joshua burned. ¹⁴And all the spoil of these cities and the livestock, the people of Israel took for their plunder. But every man they struck with the edge of the sword until they had destroyed them, and they did not leave any who breathed. ¹⁵Just as the Lord had commanded Moses his servant, so Moses commanded Joshua, and so Joshua did. He left nothing undone of all that the Lord had commanded Moses.

¹⁶So Joshua took all that land, the hill country and all the Negeb and all the land of Goshen and the lowland and the Arabah and the hill country of Israel and its lowland ¹⁷from Mount Halak, which rises toward Seir, as far as Baal-gad in the Valley of Lebanon below Mount Hermon. And he captured all their kings and struck them and put them to death. ¹⁸Joshua made war a long time with all those kings. ¹⁹There was not a city that made peace with the people of Israel except the Hivites, the inhabitants of Gibeon. They took them all in battle. ²⁰For it was the Lord's doing to harden their hearts that they should come against Israel in battle, in order that they should be devoted to destruction and should receive no mercy but be destroyed, just as the Lord commanded Moses.

²¹And Joshua came at that time and cut off the Anakim from the hill country, from Hebron, from Debir, from Anab, and from all the hill country of Judah, and from all the hill country of Israel. Joshua devoted them to destruction with their cities. ²²There was none of the Anakim left in the land of the people of Israel. Only in Gaza, in Gath, and in Ashdod did some remain. ²³So Joshua took the whole land, according to all that the Lord had spoken to Moses. And Joshua gave it for an inheritance to Israel according to their tribal allotments. And the land had rest from war.

12 Now these are the kings of the land whom the people of Israel defeated and took possession of their land beyond the Jordan toward the sunrise, from the Valley of the Arnon to Mount Hermon, with all the Arabah eastward: ²Sihon king of the Amorites who lived at Heshbon and ruled from Aroer, which is on the edge of the Valley of the Arnon, and from the middle of the valley as far as the river Jabbok, the

¹ That is, setting apart (devoting) as an offering to the Lord (for destruction); also verses 12, 20, 21

boundary of the Ammonites, that is, half of Gilead, ³and the Arabah to the Sea of Chinneroth eastward, and in the direction of Beth-jeshimoth, to the Sea of the Arabah, the Salt Sea, southward to the foot of the slopes of Pisgah; ⁴and Og¹ king of Bashan, one of the remnant of the Rephaim, who lived at Ashtaroth and at Edrei ⁵and ruled over Mount Hermon and Salecah and all Bashan to the boundary of the Geshurites and the Maacathites, and over half of Gilead to the boundary of Sihon king of Heshbon. ⁶Moses, the servant of the LORD, and the people of Israel defeated them. And Moses the servant of the LORD gave their land for a possession to the Reubenites and the Gadites and the half-tribe of Manasseh.

⁷And these are the kings of the land whom Joshua and the people of Israel defeated on the west side of the Jordan, from Baal-gad in the Valley of Lebanon to Mount Halak, that rises toward Seir (and Joshua gave their land to the tribes of Israel as a possession according to their allotments, ⁸in the hill country, in the lowland, in the Arabah, in the slopes, in the wilderness, and in the Negeb, the land of the Hittites, the Amorites, the Canaanites, the Perizzites, the Hivites, and the Jebusites): ⁹the king of Jericho, one; the king of Ai, which is beside Bethel, one; ¹⁰the king of Jerusalem, one; the king of Hebron, one; ¹¹the king of Jarmuth, one; the king of Lachish, one; ¹²the king of Eglon, one; the king of Gezer, one; ¹³the king of Debir, one; the king of Geder, one; ¹⁴the king of Hormah, one; the king of Arad, one; ¹⁵the king of Libnah, one; the king of Adullam, one; ¹⁶the king of Makkedah, one; the king of Bethel, one; ¹⁷the king of Tappuah, one; the king of Hepher, one; ¹⁸the king of Aphek, one; the king of Lasharon, one; ¹⁹the king of Madon, one; the king of Hazor, one; ²⁰the king of Shimron-meron, one; the king of Achshaph, one; ²¹the king of Taanach, one; the king of Megiddo, one; ²²the king of Kedesh, one; the king of Jokneam in Carmel, one; ²³the king of Dor in Naphath-dor, one; the king of Goiim in Galilee,² one; ²⁴the king of Tirzah, one: in all, thirty-one kings.

Dividing the land among the tribes [chapters 13–14]. Just as Virgil's *Aeneid* devotes six books to the journey motif and then six books to battle action, the epic of Joshua also divides the story material into halves. The first twelve chapters tell about the conquest of the Promised Land, and the next twelve are devoted to dividing the land and living in it. Chapters 13–19 belong to the genre of the historical chronicle. Although there is an underlying story line (as we picture Joshua parceling out plots of land day after day) and interspersed narrative sections, the bulk of the space is devoted to lists and data regarding real estate. A good way to relive these chapters is to imagine yourself present at the events as an interested party, wondering what land your tribe or family would be allotted and experiencing the excitement of surveying your piece of land for the first time. Things to note include these: (1) the heroic example of Caleb, still going strong at the age of eighty-five (14:6–15); (2) the picture of a well-ordered state, serving the interests of its citizens and deserving of respect from them; (3) the importance of a strong leader (Joshua) to preserve order in society; (4) evidences that the civil operations that we observe are at the same time religious events—outworkings of God's covenant dealings with his people and means through which the people are beneficiaries of God's generosity to them; (5) in keeping with that, hints that the principle of inheritance of the land within a family is of vital importance to the covenant people of God.

---

¹ Septuagint; Hebrew *the boundary of Og* ² Septuagint; Hebrew *Gilgal*

13 Now Joshua was old and advanced in years, and the LORD said to him, "You are old and advanced in years, and there remains yet very much land to possess. ²This is the land that yet remains: all the regions of the Philistines, and all those of the Geshurites ³(from the Shihor, which is east of Egypt, northward to the boundary of Ekron, it is counted as Canaanite; there are five rulers of the Philistines, those of Gaza, Ashdod, Ashkelon, Gath, and Ekron), and those of the Avvim, ⁴in the south, all the land of the Canaanites, and Mearah that belongs to the Sidonians, to Aphek, to the boundary of the Amorites, ⁵and the land of the Gebalites, and all Lebanon, toward the sunrise, from Baal-gad below Mount Hermon to Lebo-hamath, ⁶all the inhabitants of the hill country from Lebanon to Misrephoth-maim, even all the Sidonians. I myself will drive them out from before the people of Israel. Only allot the land to Israel for an inheritance, as I have commanded you. ⁷Now therefore divide this land for an inheritance to the nine tribes and half the tribe of Manasseh."

⁸With the other half of the tribe of Manasseh¹ the Reubenites and the Gadites received their inheritance, which Moses gave them, beyond the Jordan eastward, as Moses the servant of the LORD gave them: ⁹from Aroer, which is on the edge of the Valley of the Arnon, and the city that is in the middle of the valley, and all the tableland of Medeba as far as Dibon; ¹⁰and all the cities of Sihon king of the Amorites, who reigned in Heshbon, as far as the boundary of the Ammonites; ¹¹and Gilead, and the region of the Geshurites and Maacathites, and all Mount Hermon, and all Bashan to Salecah; ¹²all the kingdom of Og in Bashan, who reigned in Ashtaroth and in Edrei (he alone was left of the remnant of the Rephaim); these Moses had struck and driven out. ¹³Yet the people of Israel did not drive out the Geshurites or the Maacathites, but Geshur and Maacath dwell in the midst of Israel to this day.

¹⁴To the tribe of Levi alone Moses gave no inheritance. The offerings by fire to the LORD God of Israel are their inheritance, as he said to him.

¹⁵And Moses gave an inheritance to the tribe of the people of Reuben according to their clans. ¹⁶So their territory was from Aroer, which is on the edge of the Valley of the Arnon, and the city that is in the middle of the valley, and all the tableland by Medeba; ¹⁷with Heshbon, and all its cities that are in the tableland; Dibon, and Bamoth-baal, and Beth-baal-meon, ¹⁸and Jahaz, and Kedemoth, and Mephaath, ¹⁹and Kiriathaim, and Sibmah, and Zereth-shahar on the hill of the valley, ²⁰and Beth-peor, and the slopes of Pisgah, and Beth-jeshimoth, ²¹that is, all the cities of the tableland, and all the kingdom of Sihon king of the Amorites, who reigned in Heshbon, whom Moses defeated with the leaders of Midian, Evi and Rekem and Zur and Hur and Reba, the princes of Sihon, who lived in the land. ²²Balaam also, the son of Beor, the one who practiced divination, was killed with the sword by the people of Israel among the rest of their slain. ²³And the border of the people of Reuben was the Jordan as a boundary. This was the inheritance of the people of Reuben, according to their clans with their cities and villages.

²⁴Moses gave an inheritance also to the tribe of Gad, to the people of Gad, according to their clans. ²⁵Their territory was Jazer, and all the cities of Gilead, and half the land of the Ammonites, to Aroer, which is east of Rabbah, ²⁶and from Heshbon to Ramath-mizpeh and Betonim, and from Mahanaim to the territory of Debir,² ²⁷and in the valley Beth-haram, Beth-nimrah, Succoth, and Zaphon, the rest of the kingdom of Sihon king of Heshbon, having the Jordan as a boundary, to the lower end of the Sea

---

¹ Hebrew *With it* ² Septuagint, Syriac, Vulgate; Hebrew *Lidebir*

of Chinnereth, eastward beyond the Jordan. ²⁸This is the inheritance of the people of Gad according to their clans, with their cities and villages.

²⁹And Moses gave an inheritance to the half-tribe of Manasseh. It was allotted to the half-tribe of the people of Manasseh according to their clans. ³⁰Their region extended from Mahanaim, through all Bashan, the whole kingdom of Og king of Bashan, and all the towns of Jair, which are in Bashan, sixty cities, ³¹and half Gilead, and Ashtaroth, and Edrei, the cities of the kingdom of Og in Bashan. These were allotted to the people of Machir the son of Manasseh for the half of the people of Machir according to their clans.

³²These are the inheritances that Moses distributed in the plains of Moab, beyond the Jordan east of Jericho. ³³But to the tribe of Levi Moses gave no inheritance; the Lord God of Israel is their inheritance, just as he said to them.

14 These are the inheritances that the people of Israel received in the land of Canaan, which Eleazar the priest and Joshua the son of Nun and the heads of the fathers' houses of the tribes of the people of Israel gave them to inherit. ²Their inheritance was by lot, just as the Lord had commanded by the hand of Moses for the nine and one-half tribes. ³For Moses had given an inheritance to the two and one-half tribes beyond the Jordan, but to the Levites he gave no inheritance among them. ⁴For the people of Joseph were two tribes, Manasseh and Ephraim. And no portion was given to the Levites in the land, but only cities to dwell in, with their pasturelands for their livestock and their substance. ⁵The people of Israel did as the Lord commanded Moses; they allotted the land.

⁶Then the people of Judah came to Joshua at Gilgal. And Caleb the son of Jephunneh the Kenizzite said to him, "You know what the Lord said to Moses the man of God in Kadesh-barnea concerning you and me. ⁷I was forty years old when Moses the servant of the Lord sent me from Kadesh-barnea to spy out the land, and I brought him word again as it was in my heart. ⁸But my brothers who went up with me made the heart of the people melt; yet I wholly followed the Lord my God. ⁹And Moses swore on that day, saying, 'Surely the land on which your foot has trodden shall be an inheritance for you and your children forever, because you have wholly followed the Lord my God.' ¹⁰And now, behold, the Lord has kept me alive, just as he said, these forty-five years since the time that the Lord spoke this word to Moses, while Israel walked in the wilderness. And now, behold, I am this day eighty-five years old. ¹¹I am still as strong today as I was in the day that Moses sent me; my strength now is as my strength was then, for war and for going and coming. ¹²So now give me this hill country of which the Lord spoke on that day, for you heard on that day how the Anakim were there, with great fortified cities. It may be that the Lord will be with me, and I shall drive them out just as the Lord said."

¹³Then Joshua blessed him, and he gave Hebron to Caleb the son of Jephunneh for an inheritance. ¹⁴Therefore Hebron became the inheritance of Caleb the son of Jephunneh the Kenizzite to this day, because he wholly followed the Lord, the God of Israel. ¹⁵Now the name of Hebron formerly was Kiriath-arba.¹ (Arba² was the greatest man among the Anakim.) And the land had rest from war.

---

¹ *Kiriath-arba means the city of Arba* ² *Hebrew He*

Land allotted to the tribe of Judah [chapter 15]. The conventions of the historical chronicle dominate, as we mainly read lists of families and geographic areas. God obviously cares about the details of people's earthly well-being.

15 The allotment for the tribe of the people of Judah according to their clans reached southward to the boundary of Edom, to the wilderness of Zin at the farthest south. ²And their south boundary ran from the end of the Salt Sea, from the bay that faces southward. ³It goes out southward of the ascent of Akrabbim, passes along to Zin, and goes up south of Kadesh-barnea, along by Hezron, up to Addar, turns about to Karka, ⁴passes along to Azmon, goes out by the Brook of Egypt, and comes to its end at the sea. This shall be your south boundary. ⁵And the east boundary is the Salt Sea, to the mouth of the Jordan. And the boundary on the north side runs from the bay of the sea at the mouth of the Jordan. ⁶And the boundary goes up to Beth-hoglah and passes along north of Beth-arabah. And the boundary goes up to the stone of Bohan the son of Reuben. ⁷And the boundary goes up to Debir from the Valley of Achor, and so northward, turning toward Gilgal, which is opposite the ascent of Adummim, which is on the south side of the valley. And the boundary passes along to the waters of En-shemesh and ends at En-rogel. ⁸Then the boundary goes up by the Valley of the Son of Hinnom at the southern shoulder of the Jebusite (that is, Jerusalem). And the boundary goes up to the top of the mountain that lies over against the Valley of Hinnom, on the west, at the northern end of the Valley of Rephaim. ⁹Then the boundary extends from the top of the mountain to the spring of the waters of Nephtoah, and from there to the cities of Mount Ephron. Then the boundary bends around to Baalah (that is, Kiriath-jearim). ¹⁰And the boundary circles west of Baalah to Mount Seir, passes along to the northern shoulder of Mount Jearim (that is, Chesalon), and goes down to Beth-shemesh and passes along by Timnah. ¹¹The boundary goes out to the shoulder of the hill north of Ekron, then the boundary bends around to Shikkeron and passes along to Mount Baalah and goes out to Jabneel. Then the boundary comes to an end at the sea. ¹²And the west boundary was the Great Sea with its coastline. This is the boundary around the people of Judah according to their clans.

¹³According to the commandment of the Lᴏʀᴅ to Joshua, he gave to Caleb the son of Jephunneh a portion among the people of Judah, Kiriath-arba, that is, Hebron (Arba was the father of Anak). ¹⁴And Caleb drove out from there the three sons of Anak, Sheshai and Ahiman and Talmai, the descendants of Anak. ¹⁵And he went up from there against the inhabitants of Debir. Now the name of Debir formerly was Kiriath-sepher. ¹⁶And Caleb said, "Whoever strikes Kiriath-sepher and captures it, to him will I give Achsah my daughter as wife." ¹⁷And Othniel the son of Kenaz, the brother of Caleb, captured it. And he gave him Achsah his daughter as wife. ¹⁸When she came to him, she urged him to ask her father for a field. And she got off her donkey, and Caleb said to her, "What do you want?" ¹⁹She said to him, "Give me a blessing. Since you have given me the land of the Negeb, give me also springs of water." And he gave her the upper springs and the lower springs.

²⁰This is the inheritance of the tribe of the people of Judah according to their clans. ²¹The cities belonging to the tribe of the people of Judah in the extreme south, toward the boundary of Edom, were Kabzeel, Eder, Jagur, ²²Kinah, Dimonah, Adadah,

²³Kedesh, Hazor, Ithnan, ²⁴Ziph, Telem, Bealoth, ²⁵Hazor-hadattah, Kerioth-hezron (that is, Hazor), ²⁶Amam, Shema, Moladah, ²⁷Hazar-gaddah, Heshmon, Beth-pelet, ²⁸Hazar-shual, Beersheba, Biziothiah, ²⁹Baalah, Iim, Ezem, ³⁰Eltolad, Chesil, Hormah, ³¹Ziklag, Madmannah, Sansannah, ³²Lebaoth, Shilhim, Ain, and Rimmon: in all, twenty-nine cities with their villages.

³³And in the lowland, Eshtaol, Zorah, Ashnah, ³⁴Zanoah, En-gannim, Tappuah, Enam, ³⁵Jarmuth, Adullam, Socoh, Azekah, ³⁶Shaaraim, Adithaim, Gederah, Gederothaim: fourteen cities with their villages.

³⁷Zenan, Hadashah, Migdal-gad, ³⁸Dilean, Mizpeh, Joktheel, ³⁹Lachish, Bozkath, Eglon, ⁴⁰Cabbon, Lahmam, Chitlish, ⁴¹Gederoth, Beth-dagon, Naamah, and Makkedah: sixteen cities with their villages.

⁴²Libnah, Ether, Ashan, ⁴³Iphtah, Ashnah, Nezib, ⁴⁴Keilah, Achzib, and Mareshah: nine cities with their villages.

⁴⁵Ekron, with its towns and its villages; ⁴⁶from Ekron to the sea, all that were by the side of Ashdod, with their villages.

⁴⁷Ashdod, its towns and its villages; Gaza, its towns and its villages; to the Brook of Egypt, and the Great Sea with its coastline.

⁴⁸And in the hill country, Shamir, Jattir, Socoh, ⁴⁹Dannah, Kiriath-sannah (that is, Debir), ⁵⁰Anab, Eshtemoh, Anim, ⁵¹Goshen, Holon, and Giloh: eleven cities with their villages.

⁵²Arab, Dumah, Eshan, ⁵³Janim, Beth-tappuah, Aphekah, ⁵⁴Humtah, Kiriath-arba (that is, Hebron), and Zior: nine cities with their villages.

⁵⁵Maon, Carmel, Ziph, Juttah, ⁵⁶Jezreel, Jokdeam, Zanoah, ⁵⁷Kain, Gibeah, and Timnah: ten cities with their villages.

⁵⁸Halhul, Beth-zur, Gedor, ⁵⁹Maarath, Beth-anoth, and Eltekon: six cities with their villages.

⁶⁰Kiriath-baal (that is, Kiriath-jearim), and Rabbah: two cities with their villages.

⁶¹In the wilderness, Beth-arabah, Middin, Secacah, ⁶²Nibshan, the City of Salt, and Engedi: six cities with their villages.

⁶³But the Jebusites, the inhabitants of Jerusalem, the people of Judah could not drive out, so the Jebusites dwell with the people of Judah at Jerusalem to this day.

Parceling out land to the descendants of Joseph [chapters 16–17]. More lists unfold before us as we read, supplemented by the drama of the people of Joseph complaining about the inadequacy of their initial allotment (17:14–18).

16 The allotment of the people of Joseph went from the Jordan by Jericho, east of the waters of Jericho, into the wilderness, going up from Jericho into the hill country to Bethel. ²Then going from Bethel to Luz, it passes along to Ataroth, the territory of the Archites. ³Then it goes down westward to the territory of the Japhletites, as far as the territory of Lower Beth-horon, then to Gezer, and it ends at the sea.

⁴The people of Joseph, Manasseh and Ephraim, received their inheritance.

⁵The territory of the people of Ephraim by their clans was as follows: the boundary of their inheritance on the east was Ataroth-addar as far as Upper Beth-horon, ⁶and the boundary goes from there to the sea. On the north is Michmethath. Then on the

east the boundary turns around toward Taanath-shiloh and passes along beyond it on the east to Janoah, ⁷then it goes down from Janoah to Ataroth and to Naarah, and touches Jericho, ending at the Jordan. ⁸From Tappuah the boundary goes westward to the brook Kanah and ends at the sea. Such is the inheritance of the tribe of the people of Ephraim by their clans, ⁹together with the towns that were set apart for the people of Ephraim within the inheritance of the Manassites, all those towns with their villages. ¹⁰However, they did not drive out the Canaanites who lived in Gezer, so the Canaanites have lived in the midst of Ephraim to this day but have been made to do forced labor.

17 Then allotment was made to the people of Manasseh, for he was the firstborn of Joseph. To Machir the firstborn of Manasseh, the father of Gilead, were allotted Gilead and Bashan, because he was a man of war. ²And allotments were made to the rest of the people of Manasseh by their clans, Abiezer, Helek, Asriel, Shechem, Hepher, and Shemida. These were the male descendants of Manasseh the son of Joseph, by their clans.

³Now Zelophehad the son of Hepher, son of Gilead, son of Machir, son of Manasseh, had no sons, but only daughters, and these are the names of his daughters: Mahlah, Noah, Hoglah, Milcah, and Tirzah. ⁴They approached Eleazar the priest and Joshua the son of Nun and the leaders and said, "The LORD commanded Moses to give us an inheritance along with our brothers." So according to the mouth of the LORD he gave them an inheritance among the brothers of their father. ⁵Thus there fell to Manasseh ten portions, besides the land of Gilead and Bashan, which is on the other side of the Jordan, ⁶because the daughters of Manasseh received an inheritance along with his sons. The land of Gilead was allotted to the rest of the people of Manasseh.

⁷The territory of Manasseh reached from Asher to Michmethath, which is east of Shechem. Then the boundary goes along southward to the inhabitants of En-tappuah. ⁸The land of Tappuah belonged to Manasseh, but the town of Tappuah on the boundary of Manasseh belonged to the people of Ephraim. ⁹Then the boundary went down to the brook Kanah. These cities, to the south of the brook, among the cities of Manasseh, belong to Ephraim. Then the boundary of Manasseh goes on the north side of the brook and ends at the sea, ¹⁰the land to the south being Ephraim's and that to the north being Manasseh's, with the sea forming its boundary. On the north Asher is reached, and on the east Issachar. ¹¹Also in Issachar and in Asher Manasseh had Beth-shean and its villages, and Ibleam and its villages, and the inhabitants of Dor and its villages, and the inhabitants of En-dor and its villages, and the inhabitants of Taanach and its villages, and the inhabitants of Megiddo and its villages; the third is Naphath.¹ ¹²Yet the people of Manasseh could not take possession of those cities, but the Canaanites persisted in dwelling in that land. ¹³Now when the people of Israel grew strong, they put the Canaanites to forced labor, but did not utterly drive them out.

¹⁴Then the people of Joseph spoke to Joshua, saying, "Why have you given me but one lot and one portion as an inheritance, although I am a numerous people, since all along the LORD has blessed me?" ¹⁵And Joshua said to them, "If you are a numerous people, go up by yourselves to the forest, and there clear ground for yourselves in the land of the Perizzites and the Rephaim, since the hill country of Ephraim is too narrow for you." ¹⁶The people of Joseph said, "The hill country is not enough for us.

---

¹ The meaning of the Hebrew is uncertain

Yet all the Canaanites who dwell in the plain have chariots of iron, both those in Beth-shean and its villages and those in the Valley of Jezreel." ¹⁷Then Joshua said to the house of Joseph, to Ephraim and Manasseh, "You are a numerous people and have great power. You shall not have one allotment only, ¹⁸but the hill country shall be yours, for though it is a forest, you shall clear it and possess it to its farthest borders. For you shall drive out the Canaanites, though they have chariots of iron, and though they are strong."

Final allotments [chapters 18–19]. The drama of the allotment continues as we read about geographic regions and names of families. One way to assimilate the sheer abundance of details is to see in it the abundance of God's covenant blessings on his people.

18 Then the whole congregation of the people of Israel assembled at Shiloh and set up the tent of meeting there. The land lay subdued before them. ²There remained among the people of Israel seven tribes whose inheritance had not yet been apportioned. ³So Joshua said to the people of Israel, "How long will you put off going in to take possession of the land, which the LORD, the God of your fathers, has given you? ⁴Provide three men from each tribe, and I will send them out that they may set out and go up and down the land. They shall write a description of it with a view to their inheritances, and then come to me. ⁵They shall divide it into seven portions. Judah shall continue in his territory on the south, and the house of Joseph shall continue in their territory on the north. ⁶And you shall describe the land in seven divisions and bring the description here to me. And I will cast lots for you here before the LORD our God. ⁷The Levites have no portion among you, for the priesthood of the LORD is their heritage. And Gad and Reuben and half the tribe of Manasseh have received their inheritance beyond the Jordan eastward, which Moses the servant of the LORD gave them."

⁸So the men arose and went, and Joshua charged those who went to write the description of the land, saying, "Go up and down in the land and write a description and return to me. And I will cast lots for you here before the LORD in Shiloh." ⁹So the men went and passed up and down in the land and wrote in a book a description of it by towns in seven divisions. Then they came to Joshua to the camp at Shiloh, ¹⁰and Joshua cast lots for them in Shiloh before the LORD. And there Joshua apportioned the land to the people of Israel, to each his portion.

¹¹The lot of the tribe of the people of Benjamin according to its clans came up, and the territory allotted to it fell between the people of Judah and the people of Joseph. ¹²On the north side their boundary began at the Jordan. Then the boundary goes up to the shoulder north of Jericho, then up through the hill country westward, and it ends at the wilderness of Beth-aven. ¹³From there the boundary passes along southward in the direction of Luz, to the shoulder of Luz (that is, Bethel), then the boundary goes down to Ataroth-addar, on the mountain that lies south of Lower Beth-horon. ¹⁴Then the boundary goes in another direction, turning on the western side southward from the mountain that lies to the south, opposite Beth-horon, and it ends at Kiriath-baal (that is, Kiriath-jearim), a city belonging to the people of Judah. This forms the western side. ¹⁵And the southern side begins at the outskirts of Kiriath-jearim. And the boundary goes from there to Ephron,ʲ to the spring of the waters of

---

ʲ See 15:9; Hebrew *westward*

Nephtoah. [16]Then the boundary goes down to the border of the mountain that overlooks the Valley of the Son of Hinnom, which is at the north end of the Valley of Rephaim. And it then goes down the Valley of Hinnom, south of the shoulder of the Jebusites, and downward to En-rogel. [17]Then it bends in a northerly direction going on to En-shemesh, and from there goes to Geliloth, which is opposite the ascent of Adummim. Then it goes down to the stone of Bohan the son of Reuben, [18]and passing on to the north of the shoulder of Beth-arabah[1] it goes down to the Arabah. [19]Then the boundary passes on to the north of the shoulder of Beth-hoglah. And the boundary ends at the northern bay of the Salt Sea, at the south end of the Jordan: this is the southern border. [20]The Jordan forms its boundary on the eastern side. This is the inheritance of the people of Benjamin, according to their clans, boundary by boundary all around.

[21]Now the cities of the tribe of the people of Benjamin according to their clans were Jericho, Beth-hoglah, Emek-keziz, [22]Beth-arabah, Zemaraim, Bethel, [23]Avvim, Parah, Ophrah, [24]Chephar-ammoni, Ophni, Geba—twelve cities with their villages: [25]Gibeon, Ramah, Beeroth, [26]Mizpeh, Chephirah, Mozah, [27]Rekem, Irpeel, Taralah, [28]Zela, Haeleph, Jebus[2] (that is, Jerusalem), Gibeah[3] and Kiriath-jearim[4]—fourteen cities with their villages. This is the inheritance of the people of Benjamin according to its clans.

19

The second lot came out for Simeon, for the tribe of the people of Simeon, according to their clans, and their inheritance was in the midst of the inheritance of the people of Judah. [2]And they had for their inheritance Beersheba, Sheba, Moladah, [3]Hazar-shual, Balah, Ezem, [4]Eltolad, Bethul, Hormah, [5]Ziklag, Beth-marcaboth, Hazar-susah, [6]Beth-lebaoth, and Sharuhen—thirteen cities with their villages; [7]Ain, Rimmon, Ether, and Ashan—four cities with their villages, [8]together with all the villages around these cities as far as Baalath-beer, Ramah of the Negeb. This was the inheritance of the tribe of the people of Simeon according to their clans. [9]The inheritance of the people of Simeon formed part of the territory of the people of Judah. Because the portion of the people of Judah was too large for them, the people of Simeon obtained an inheritance in the midst of their inheritance.

[10]The third lot came up for the people of Zebulun, according to their clans. And the territory of their inheritance reached as far as Sarid. [11]Then their boundary goes up westward and on to Mareal and touches Dabbesheth, then the brook that is east of Jokneam. [12]From Sarid it goes in the other direction eastward toward the sunrise to the boundary of Chisloth-tabor. From there it goes to Daberath, then up to Japhia. [13]From there it passes along on the east toward the sunrise to Gath-hepher, to Ethkazin, and going on to Rimmon it bends toward Neah, [14]then on the north the boundary turns about to Hannathon, and it ends at the Valley of Iphtahel; [15]and Kattath, Nahalal, Shimron, Idalah, and Bethlehem—twelve cities with their villages. [16]This is the inheritance of the people of Zebulun, according to their clans—these cities with their villages.

[17]The fourth lot came out for Issachar, for the people of Issachar, according to their clans. [18]Their territory included Jezreel, Chesulloth, Shunem, [19]Hapharaim, Shion, Anaharath, [20]Rabbith, Kishion, Ebez, [21]Remeth, En-gannim, En-haddah, Beth-pazzez. [22]The boundary also touches Tabor, Shahazumah, and Beth-shemesh, and its bound-

---

[1] Septuagint; Hebrew *to the shoulder over against the Arabah* [2] Septuagint, Syriac, Vulgate; Hebrew *the Jebusite* [3] Hebrew *Gibeath* [4] Septuagint; Hebrew *Kiriath*

ary ends at the Jordan—sixteen cities with their villages. ²³This is the inheritance of the tribe of the people of Issachar, according to their clans—the cities with their villages.

²⁴The fifth lot came out for the tribe of the people of Asher according to their clans. ²⁵Their territory included Helkath, Hali, Beten, Achshaph, ²⁶Allammelech, Amad, and Mishal. On the west it touches Carmel and Shihor-libnath, ²⁷then it turns eastward, it goes to Beth-dagon, and touches Zebulun and the Valley of Iphtahel northward to Beth-emek and Neiel. Then it continues in the north to Cabul, ²⁸Ebron, Rehob, Hammon, Kanah, as far as Sidon the Great. ²⁹Then the boundary turns to Ramah, reaching to the fortified city of Tyre. Then the boundary turns to Hosah, and it ends at the sea; Mahalab,¹ Achzib, ³⁰Ummah, Aphek and Rehob—twenty-two cities with their villages. ³¹This is the inheritance of the tribe of the people of Asher according to their clans—these cities with their villages.

³²The sixth lot came out for the people of Naphtali, for the people of Naphtali, according to their clans. ³³And their boundary ran from Heleph, from the oak in Zaanannim, and Adami-nekeb, and Jabneel, as far as Lakkum, and it ended at the Jordan. ³⁴Then the boundary turns westward to Aznoth-tabor and goes from there to Hukkok, touching Zebulun at the south and Asher on the west and Judah on the east at the Jordan. ³⁵The fortified cities are Ziddim, Zer, Hammath, Rakkath, Chinnereth, ³⁶Adamah, Ramah, Hazor, ³⁷Kedesh, Edrei, En-hazor, ³⁸Yiron, Migdal-el, Horem, Beth-anath, and Beth-shemesh—nineteen cities with their villages. ³⁹This is the inheritance of the tribe of the people of Naphtali according to their clans—the cities with their villages.

⁴⁰The seventh lot came out for the tribe of the people of Dan, according to their clans. ⁴¹And the territory of its inheritance included Zorah, Eshtaol, Ir-shemesh, ⁴²Shaalabbin, Aijalon, Ithlah, ⁴³Elon, Timnah, Ekron, ⁴⁴Eltekeh, Gibbethon, Baalath, ⁴⁵Jehud, Bene-berak, Gath-rimmon, ⁴⁶and Me-jarkon and Rakkon with the territory over against Joppa. ⁴⁷When the territory of the people of Dan was lost to them, the people of Dan went up and fought against Leshem, and after capturing it and striking it with the sword they took possession of it and settled in it, calling Leshem, Dan, after the name of Dan their ancestor. ⁴⁸This is the inheritance of the tribe of the people of Dan, according to their clans—these cities with their villages.

⁴⁹When they had finished distributing the several territories of the land as inheritances, the people of Israel gave an inheritance among them to Joshua the son of Nun. ⁵⁰By command of the LORD they gave him the city that he asked, Timnath-serah in the hill country of Ephraim. And he rebuilt the city and settled in it.

⁵¹These are the inheritances that Eleazar the priest and Joshua the son of Nun and the heads of the fathers' houses of the tribes of the people of Israel distributed by lot at Shiloh before the LORD, at the entrance of the tent of meeting. So they finished dividing the land.

The cities of refuge [chapter 20]. In Numbers 35:9–34, God had given Moses detailed instructions about the cities of refuge, and here we see the implementation of the blueprint. The first thing to do with the narrative is to get the literal facts straight. Then we need to be responsive to the evocative concept of a city of refuge and ponder the moral

¹ Compare Septuagint; Hebrew *Mehebel*

and spiritual overtones of the institution, including thoughts on how God provides refuge from the enemies of God and us in our own situations.

20
Then the Lord said to Joshua, ²"Say to the people of Israel, 'Appoint the cities of refuge, of which I spoke to you through Moses, ³that the manslayer who strikes any person without intent or unknowingly may flee there. They shall be for you a refuge from the avenger of blood. ⁴He shall flee to one of these cities and shall stand at the entrance of the gate of the city and explain his case to the elders of that city. Then they shall take him into the city and give him a place, and he shall remain with them. ⁵And if the avenger of blood pursues him, they shall not give up the manslayer into his hand, because he struck his neighbor unknowingly, and did not hate him in the past. ⁶And he shall remain in that city until he has stood before the congregation for judgment, until the death of him who is high priest at the time. Then the manslayer may return to his own town and his own home, to the town from which he fled.'"

⁷So they set apart Kedesh in Galilee in the hill country of Naphtali, and Shechem in the hill country of Ephraim, and Kiriath-arba (that is, Hebron) in the hill country of Judah. ⁸And beyond the Jordan east of Jericho, they appointed Bezer in the wilderness on the tableland, from the tribe of Reuben, and Ramoth in Gilead, from the tribe of Gad, and Golan in Bashan, from the tribe of Manasseh. ⁹These were the cities designated for all the people of Israel and for the stranger sojourning among them, that anyone who killed a person without intent could flee there, so that he might not die by the hand of the avenger of blood, till he stood before the congregation.

The cities of the Levites [chapter 21]. Men of the tribe of Levi were the clerics of ancient Israel—professional religious leaders and servants. They were accordingly treated specially, in keeping with God's commands. We can read this chapter as giving us variations on the theme of the special spiritual and social status of the Levites. For example, the Levites were given cities but not regions of land. The lavishness of the provision comes through the mass of details, including repeated evocative references to pasturelands. At the end of this chapter (vv. 43–45) we find a grand summing up of the entire block of chapters devoted to the parceling of the land; we can profitably allow this summary to cast a retrospective light on the story of the division of the land and in fact to serve as an interpretive framework for the entire book of Joshua: the latent plot line of all that has been narrated is that God has kept his promises, as God's people are in possession of his land.

21
Then the heads of the fathers' houses of the Levites came to Eleazar the priest and to Joshua the son of Nun and to the heads of the fathers' houses of the tribes of the people of Israel. ²And they said to them at Shiloh in the land of Canaan, "The Lord commanded through Moses that we be given cities to dwell in, along with their pasturelands for our livestock." ³So by command of the Lord the people of Israel gave to the Levites the following cities and pasturelands out of their inheritance.

⁴The lot came out for the clans of the Kohathites. So those Levites who were

descendants of Aaron the priest received by lot from the tribes of Judah, Simeon, and Benjamin, thirteen cities.

⁵And the rest of the Kohathites received by lot from the clans of the tribe of Ephraim, from the tribe of Dan and the half-tribe of Manasseh, ten cities.

⁶The Gershonites received by lot from the clans of the tribe of Issachar, from the tribe of Asher, from the tribe of Naphtali, and from the half-tribe of Manasseh in Bashan, thirteen cities.

⁷The Merarites according to their clans received from the tribe of Reuben, the tribe of Gad, and the tribe of Zebulun, twelve cities.

⁸These cities and their pasturelands the people of Israel gave by lot to the Levites, as the LORD had commanded through Moses.

⁹Out of the tribe of the people of Judah and the tribe of the people of Simeon they gave the following cities mentioned by name, ¹⁰which went to the descendants of Aaron, one of the clans of the Kohathites who belonged to the people of Levi; since the lot fell to them first. ¹¹They gave them Kiriath-arba (Arba being the father of Anak), that is Hebron, in the hill country of Judah, along with the pasturelands around it. ¹²But the fields of the city and its villages had been given to Caleb the son of Jephunneh as his possession.

¹³And to the descendants of Aaron the priest they gave Hebron, the city of refuge for the manslayer, with its pasturelands, Libnah with its pasturelands, ¹⁴Jattir with its pasturelands, Eshtemoa with its pasturelands, ¹⁵Holon with its pasturelands, Debir with its pasturelands, ¹⁶Ain with its pasturelands, Juttah with its pasturelands, Beth-shemesh with its pasturelands—nine cities out of these two tribes; ¹⁷then out of the tribe of Benjamin, Gibeon with its pasturelands, Geba with its pasturelands, ¹⁸Anathoth with its pasturelands, and Almon with its pasturelands—four cities. ¹⁹The cities of the descendants of Aaron, the priests, were in all thirteen cities with their pasturelands.

²⁰As to the rest of the Kohathites belonging to the Kohathite clans of the Levites, the cities allotted to them were out of the tribe of Ephraim. ²¹To them were given Shechem, the city of refuge for the manslayer, with its pasturelands in the hill country of Ephraim, Gezer with its pasturelands, ²²Kibzaim with its pasturelands, Beth-horon with its pasturelands—four cities; ²³and out of the tribe of Dan, Elteke with its pasturelands, Gibbethon with its pasturelands, ²⁴Aijalon with its pasturelands, Gath-rimmon with its pasturelands—four cities; ²⁵and out of the half-tribe of Manasseh, Taanach with its pasturelands, and Gath-rimmon with its pasturelands—two cities. ²⁶The cities of the clans of the rest of the Kohathites were ten in all with their pasturelands.

²⁷And to the Gershonites, one of the clans of the Levites, were given out of the half-tribe of Manasseh, Golan in Bashan with its pasturelands, the city of refuge for the manslayer, and Beeshterah with its pasturelands—two cities; ²⁸and out of the tribe of Issachar, Kishion with its pasturelands, Daberath with its pasturelands, ²⁹Jarmuth with its pasturelands, En-gannim with its pasturelands—four cities; ³⁰and out of the tribe of Asher, Mishal with its pasturelands, Abdon with its pasturelands, ³¹Helkath with its pasturelands, and Rehob with its pasturelands—four cities; ³²and out of the tribe of Naphtali, Kedesh in Galilee with its pasturelands, the city of refuge for the manslayer, Hammoth-dor with its pasturelands, and Kartan with its pasturelands—three cities. ³³The cities of the several clans of the Gershonites were in all thirteen cities with their pasturelands.

³⁴And to the rest of the Levites, the Merarite clans, were given out of the tribe of Zebulun, Jokneam with its pasturelands, Kartah with its pasturelands, ³⁵Dimnah with its pasturelands, Nahalal with its pasturelands—four cities; ³⁶and out of the tribe of Reuben, Bezer with its pasturelands, Jahaz with its pasturelands, ³⁷Kedemoth with its pasturelands, and Mephaath with its pasturelands—four cities; ³⁸and out of the tribe of Gad, Ramoth in Gilead with its pasturelands, the city of refuge for the manslayer, Mahanaim with its pasturelands, ³⁹Heshbon with its pasturelands, Jazer with its pasturelands—four cities in all. ⁴⁰As for the cities of the several Merarite clans, that is, the remainder of the clans of the Levites, those allotted to them were in all twelve cities.

⁴¹The cities of the Levites in the midst of the possession of the people of Israel were in all forty-eight cities with their pasturelands. ⁴²These cities each had its pasturelands around it. So it was with all these cities.

⁴³Thus the LORD gave to Israel all the land that he swore to give to their fathers. And they took possession of it, and they settled there. ⁴⁴And the LORD gave them rest on every side just as he had sworn to their fathers. Not one of all their enemies had withstood them, for the LORD had given all their enemies into their hands. ⁴⁵Not one word of all the good promises that the LORD had made to the house of Israel had failed; all came to pass.

Civil war averted [chapter 22]. Just when we thought that the good life is about to envelop the nation, now cozily situated in the Promised Land, a story of conflict unexpectedly enters the epic. In the background is a long-standing agreement that two-and-a-half tribes had worked out with Moses (Numbers 32) and confirmed with Joshua (Josh. 1:12–18) stipulating that they could settle east of the Jordan River after helping the other tribes conquer Canaan. The sequence that unfolds in chapter 22 is as follows: Joshua gives the two-and-a-half tribes permission to go home beyond the Jordan (vv. 1–9); the returning tribes build an altar (v. 10); the western tribes are incensed by what they think the altar represents, and they prepare to wage war against the two-and-a-half tribes (vv. 11–12); before going to war, the incensed tribes send an envoy to voice formal charges of idolatry (vv. 13–20); in a highly formal and stylized speech, leaders of the two-and-a-half tribes defend their actions to the offended Israelites (vv. 21–29); the envoy is satisfied and returns with a positive report that is accepted (vv. 30–34). Coming through the narrative excitement of the event is an obvious preoccupation among the Israelites with avoiding idolatry and worshiping God only, and also the importance of unity among the people of God.

22 At that time Joshua summoned the Reubenites and the Gadites and the half-tribe of Manasseh, ²and said to them, "You have kept all that Moses the servant of the LORD commanded you and have obeyed my voice in all that I have commanded you. ³You have not forsaken your brothers these many days, down to this day, but have been careful to keep the charge of the LORD your God. ⁴And now the LORD your God has given rest to your brothers, as he promised them. Therefore turn and go to your tents in the land where your possession lies, which Moses the servant of the LORD gave you on the other side of the Jordan. ⁵Only be very careful to observe the commandment and the law that Moses the servant of the LORD commanded you, to love the LORD your God, and to walk in all his ways and to keep his commandments

and to cling to him and to serve him with all your heart and with all your soul." ⁶So Joshua blessed them and sent them away, and they went to their tents.

⁷Now to the one half of the tribe of Manasseh Moses had given a possession in Bashan, but to the other half Joshua had given a possession beside their brothers in the land west of the Jordan. And when Joshua sent them away to their homes and blessed them, ⁸he said to them, "Go back to your tents with much wealth and with very much livestock, with silver, gold, bronze, and iron, and with much clothing. Divide the spoil of your enemies with your brothers." ⁹So the people of Reuben and the people of Gad and the half-tribe of Manasseh returned home, parting from the people of Israel at Shiloh, which is in the land of Canaan, to go to the land of Gilead, their own land of which they had possessed themselves by command of the Lord through Moses.

¹⁰And when they came to the region of the Jordan that is in the land of Canaan, the people of Reuben and the people of Gad and the half-tribe of Manasseh built there an altar by the Jordan, an altar of imposing size. ¹¹And the people of Israel heard it said, "Behold, the people of Reuben and the people of Gad and the half-tribe of Manasseh have built the altar at the frontier of the land of Canaan, in the region about the Jordan, on the side that belongs to the people of Israel." ¹²And when the people of Israel heard of it, the whole assembly of the people of Israel gathered at Shiloh to make war against them.

¹³Then the people of Israel sent to the people of Reuben and the people of Gad and the half-tribe of Manasseh, in the land of Gilead, Phinehas the son of Eleazar the priest, ¹⁴and with him ten chiefs, one from each of the tribal families of Israel, every one of them the head of a family among the clans of Israel. ¹⁵And they came to the people of Reuben, the people of Gad, and the half-tribe of Manasseh, in the land of Gilead, and they said to them, ¹⁶"Thus says the whole congregation of the Lord, 'What is this breach of faith that you have committed against the God of Israel in turning away this day from following the Lord by building yourselves an altar this day in rebellion against the Lord? ¹⁷Have we not had enough of the sin at Peor from which even yet we have not cleansed ourselves, and for which there came a plague upon the congregation of the Lord, ¹⁸that you too must turn away this day from following the Lord? And if you too rebel against the Lord today then tomorrow he will be angry with the whole congregation of Israel. ¹⁹But now, if the land of your possession is unclean, pass over into the Lord's land where the Lord's tabernacle stands, and take for yourselves a possession among us. Only do not rebel against the Lord or make us as rebels by building for yourselves an altar other than the altar of the Lord our God. ²⁰Did not Achan the son of Zerah break faith in the matter of the devoted things, and wrath fell upon all the congregation of Israel? And he did not perish alone for his iniquity.'"

²¹Then the people of Reuben, the people of Gad, and the half-tribe of Manasseh said in answer to the heads of the families of Israel, ²²"The Mighty One, God, the Lord! The Mighty One, God, the Lord! He knows; and let Israel itself know! If it was in rebellion or in breach of faith against the Lord, do not spare us today ²³for building an altar to turn away from following the Lord. Or if we did so to offer burnt offerings or grain offerings or peace offerings on it, may the Lord himself take vengeance. ²⁴No, but we did it from fear that in time to come your children might say to our children, 'What have you to do with the Lord, the God of Israel? ²⁵For the Lord

has made the Jordan a boundary between us and you, you people of Reuben and people of Gad. You have no portion in the Lord.' So your children might make our children cease to worship the Lord. [26]Therefore we said, 'Let us now build an altar, not for burnt offering, nor for sacrifice, [27]but to be a witness between us and you, and between our generations after us, that we do perform the service of the Lord in his presence with our burnt offerings and sacrifices and peace offerings, so your children will not say to our children in time to come, "You have no portion in the Lord."' [28]And we thought, If this should be said to us or to our descendants in time to come, we should say, 'Behold, the copy of the altar of the Lord, which our fathers made, not for burnt offerings, nor for sacrifice, but to be a witness between us and you.' [29]Far be it from us that we should rebel against the Lord and turn away this day from following the Lord by building an altar for burnt offering, grain offering, or sacrifice, other than the altar of the Lord our God that stands before his tabernacle!"

[30]When Phinehas the priest and the chiefs of the congregation, the heads of the families of Israel who were with him, heard the words that the people of Reuben and the people of Gad and the people of Manasseh spoke, it was good in their eyes. [31]And Phinehas the son of Eleazar the priest said to the people of Reuben and the people of Gad and the people of Manasseh, "Today we know that the Lord is in our midst, because you have not committed this breach of faith against the Lord. Now you have delivered the people of Israel from the hand of the Lord."

[32]Then Phinehas the son of Eleazar the priest, and the chiefs, returned from the people of Reuben and the people of Gad in the land of Gilead to the land of Canaan, to the people of Israel, and brought back word to them. [33]And the report was good in the eyes of the people of Israel. And the people of Israel blessed God and spoke no more of making war against them to destroy the land where the people of Reuben and the people of Gad were settled. [34]The people of Reuben and the people of Gad called the altar Witness, "For," they said, "it is a witness between us that the Lord is God."

The epic leader's farewell discourse [23:1–24:28]. The literary genre of these chapters is the *farewell discourse by a famous leader. Moses had concluded his leadership with a formal farewell discourse (the book of Deuteronomy), and now his successor does the same. Chapter 23 is addressed to the nine-and-a-half tribes and chapter 24 to "all the tribes of Israel." The motifs that are woven into the tapestry of the discourse include the following: (1) Joshua's announcement that he is nearing the end of his earthly life; (2) recollection of past accomplishments as leader of the nation; (3) instructions regarding how the nation is to live after the leader's death; (4) challenges and exhortations to the nation to choose to remain faithful to God's covenant, accompanied by warnings of what will ensue if the nation is faithless to the covenant.

23 A long time afterward, when the Lord had given rest to Israel from all their surrounding enemies, and Joshua was old and well advanced in years, [2]Joshua summoned all Israel, its elders and heads, its judges and officers, and said to them, "I am now old and well advanced in years. [3]And you have seen all that the Lord your God has done to all these nations for your sake, for it is the Lord your God who has fought for you. [4]Behold, I have allotted to you as an inheritance for your tribes those nations that remain, along with all the nations that I have already cut off, from the Jordan to the Great Sea in the west. [5]The Lord your God will push them back before you and drive them out of your sight. And you shall possess their land, just as the Lord your God promised you. ⁶Therefore, be very strong to keep and to do all that is written in the Book of the Law of Moses, turning aside from it neither to the right hand nor to the left, ⁷that you may not mix with these nations remaining among you or make mention of the names of their gods or swear by them or serve them or bow down to them, ⁸but you shall cling to the Lord your God just as you have done to this day. ⁹For the Lord has driven out before you great and strong nations. And as for you, no man has been able to stand before you to this day. ¹⁰One man of you puts to flight a thousand, since it is the Lord your God who fights for you, just as he promised you. ¹¹Be very careful, therefore, to love the Lord your God. ¹²For if you turn back and cling to the remnant of these nations remaining among you and make marriages with them, so that you associate with them and they with you, ¹³know for certain that the Lord your God will no longer drive out these nations before you, but they shall be a snare and a trap for you, a whip on your sides and thorns in your eyes, until you perish from off this good ground that the Lord your God has given you.

¹⁴"And now I am about to go the way of all the earth, and you know in your hearts and souls, all of you, that not one word has failed of all the good things[1] that the Lord your God promised concerning you. All have come to pass for you; not one of them has failed. ¹⁵But just as all the good things that the Lord your God promised concerning you have been fulfilled for you, so the Lord will bring upon you all the evil things, until he has destroyed you from off this good land that the Lord your God has given you, ¹⁶if you transgress the covenant of the Lord your God, which he commanded you, and go and serve other gods and bow down to them. Then the anger of the Lord will be kindled against you, and you shall perish quickly from off the good land that he has given to you."

24 Joshua gathered all the tribes of Israel to Shechem and summoned the elders, the heads, the judges, and the officers of Israel. And they presented themselves before God. ²And Joshua said to all the people, "Thus says the Lord, the God of Israel, 'Long ago, your fathers lived beyond the Euphrates, Terah, the father of Abraham and of Nahor; and they served other gods. ³Then I took your father Abraham from beyond the River and led him through all the land of Canaan, and made his offspring many. I gave him Isaac. ⁴And to Isaac I gave Jacob and Esau. And I gave Esau the hill country of Seir to possess, but Jacob and his children went down to Egypt. ⁵And I sent Moses and Aaron, and I plagued Egypt with what I did in the midst of it, and afterward I brought you out.

⁶"'Then I brought your fathers out of Egypt, and you came to the sea. And the Egyptians pursued your fathers with chariots and horsemen to the Red Sea. ⁷And when they cried to the Lord, he put darkness between you and the Egyptians and made the sea come upon them and cover them; and your eyes saw what I did in Egypt. And you lived in the wilderness a long time. ⁸Then I brought you to the land of the Amorites, who lived on the other side of the Jordan. They fought with you, and I gave them into your hand, and you took possession of their land, and I destroyed them before you. ⁹Then Balak the son of Zippor, king of Moab, arose and fought against Israel. And he sent and invited Balaam the son of Beor to curse you, ¹⁰but I would not listen to Balaam. Indeed, he blessed you. So I delivered you out of his hand. ¹¹And you went over the Jordan and came to Jericho, and the leaders of Jericho fought

[1] Or *words*; also twice in verse 15

against you, and also the Amorites, the Perizzites, the Canaanites, the Hittites, the Girgashites, the Hivites, and the Jebusites. And I gave them into your hand. ¹²And I sent the hornet before you, which drove them out before you, the two kings of the Amorites; it was not by your sword or by your bow. ¹³I gave you a land on which you had not labored and cities that you had not built, and you dwell in them. You eat the fruit of vineyards and olive orchards that you did not plant.'

¹⁴"Now therefore fear the LORD and serve him in sincerity and in faithfulness. Put away the gods that your fathers served beyond the River and in Egypt, and serve the LORD. ¹⁵And if it is evil in your eyes to serve the LORD, choose this day whom you will serve, whether the gods your fathers served in the region beyond the River, or the gods of the Amorites in whose land you dwell. But as for me and my house, we will serve the LORD."

¹⁶Then the people answered, "Far be it from us that we should forsake the LORD to serve other gods, ¹⁷for it is the LORD our God who brought us and our fathers up from the land of Egypt, out of the house of slavery, and who did those great signs in our sight and preserved us in all the way that we went, and among all the peoples through whom we passed. ¹⁸And the LORD drove out before us all the peoples, the Amorites who lived in the land. Therefore we also will serve the LORD, for he is our God."

¹⁹But Joshua said to the people, "You are not able to serve the LORD, for he is a holy God. He is a jealous God; he will not forgive your transgressions or your sins. ²⁰If you forsake the LORD and serve foreign gods, then he will turn and do you harm and consume you, after having done you good." ²¹And the people said to Joshua, "No, but we will serve the LORD." ²²Then Joshua said to the people, "You are witnesses against yourselves that you have chosen the LORD, to serve him." And they said, "We are witnesses." ²³He said, "Then put away the foreign gods that are among you, and incline your heart to the LORD, the God of Israel." ²⁴And the people said to Joshua, "The LORD our God we will serve, and his voice we will obey." ²⁵So Joshua made a covenant with the people that day, and put in place statutes and rules for them at Shechem. ²⁶And Joshua wrote these words in the Book of the Law of God. And he took a large stone and set it up there under the terebinth that was by the sanctuary of the LORD. ²⁷And Joshua said to all the people, "Behold, this stone shall be a witness against us, for it has heard all the words of the LORD that he spoke to us. Therefore it shall be a witness against you, lest you deal falsely with your God." ²⁸So Joshua sent the people away, every man to his inheritance.

Burial of three heroes [24:29–33]. Epics customarily include accounts of burial rites for famous heroes. The prose epic of Joshua rounds out the epoch-making events that have been narrated with brief, understated accounts of the burials of three national heroes—a military and governmental leader, a patriarch from the past, and a high priest.

²⁹After these things Joshua the son of Nun, the servant of the LORD, died, being 110 years old. ³⁰And they buried him in his own inheritance at Timnath-serah, which is in the hill country of Ephraim, north of the mountain of Gaash.

³¹Israel served the LORD all the days of Joshua, and all the days of the elders who outlived Joshua and had known all the work that the LORD did for Israel.

³²As for the bones of Joseph, which the people of Israel brought up from Egypt, they buried them at Shechem, in the piece of land that Jacob bought from the sons of Hamor the father of Shechem for a hundred pieces of money.¹ It became an inheritance of the descendants of Joseph.

³³And Eleazar the son of Aaron died, and they buried him at Gibeah, the town of Phinehas his son, which had been given him in the hill country of Ephraim.

¹ Hebrew *for a hundred qesitah;* a unit of money of unknown value

JUDGES

The book at a glance. 21 chapters, 618 verses. In format, the book of Judges resembles the book of Genesis: it is mainly a collection of individual *hero stories that together form the history of Israel during a specific era. Like Genesis, too, Judges pictures a mixture of good and bad behavior. It is easy to get the balance between those two things wrong, so as readers we need to guard against either idealizing the judges unduly or, at the other extreme, looking for evidence everywhere that the picture is uniformly negative. The book of Judges covers a historical span of approximately three hundred years. The history primarily records events connected to religious and national leadership, and the organization in those spheres is so minimal and lacking in permanent structures that it often borders on chaos. The heroes about whom we read actually did not act as judges in the modern Western sense. They were charismatic military leaders whose chief function was to deliver the nation from its enemies. The Hebrew word rendered in our English Bibles as "judges" is variously translated by biblical scholars as "heroes," "leaders," "chieftains," "deliverers," or "warrior rulers."

▌**Genres.** The book of Judges is a hybrid, but the dominant *genre is hero story, and most readers remember the book for its stories of famous heroes called judges. Mingled with the hero stories are brief units of bare-bones historical facts about judges whose stories are not told in detail. The biographical material dealing with judges, in turn, is bracketed by sweeping historical material that deals with the background to the period of the judges (the opening two chapters) and a sequel to the period of the judges (chapters 17–21). *Poetry enters the book with the famous Song of Deborah (chapter 5). The story of Samson (chapters 13–16) meets the usual criteria of literary *tragedy. (For more information on items accompanied by an asterisk, see the glossary at the back of this Bible.)

▌**Format.** A pattern that is repeated numerous times (though it does not organize the entire book) is the following one: (1) the Israelites do what is evil in the sight of God; (2) God allows the nation to be conquered and oppressed by a neighboring nation; (3) the people cry to God; (4) God sends a judge to deliver the Israelites. Then the cycle repeats itself. A common misconception is that the people repent under their oppression, but the formula that the text uses is that they "cried out to the LORD," which indicates prayer but does not stipulate repentance. In addition to this repeated cycle, the book is structured on the premise of a double plot. The overall story is one of national descent into lawlessness and apostasy, as previewed by the author's comment

Passage	Content	Broad Time Span	Assessment
1:1–3:6	Incomplete conquest of Canaan	Before the judges	Failure
3:7–31	Ehud and two others	Period of the judges	Mingled failure and success
4:1–5:31	Deborah and Barak		
6:1–8:35	Gideon		
9:1–57	Abimelech		
10:1–12:15	Jephthah and five others		
13:1–16:31	Samson		
17:1–18:31	Micah's idols and fraudulent priest	After the judges	Failure
19:1–30	The Levite's concubine		
20:1–21:25	War against Benjamin		

in 2:19 that "whenever the judge died, they turned back and were more corrupt than their fathers." But placed within this outer story of the nation is a collection of hero stories that largely celebrate the exploits of heroic judges. Even though these judges had flaws, four of them are mentioned in the roll call of heroes of the faith in Hebrews 11, so we know that they were heroic as well as sinful.

▌**Key settings.** The main setting is not a place as such but consists rather of the nation of Israel, thereby producing a national arena for the events. The nation of Israel, in turn, is put into the larger international or intertribal sphere of neighboring nations. The most recurrent physical setting for the heroic exploits of the book is the battlefield, broadly defined to include any open space or field where individuals and armies engage in combat. Balancing that, some of the most memorable scenes occur in confined spaces: Eglon's chamber; the winepress where Gideon beats out wheat and is visited by an angel; the city wall from which a woman drops a millstone on the head of Abimelech; Delilah's inner chamber where the Philistines capture Samson; the threshold of the house where the Levite's concubine is abused and found dead the next morning.

▌**The cast of characters.** God is the main character, though that is established mainly by summary statements to the effect that "the Lᴏʀᴅ raised up for them a deliverer" (3:15), not by extensive scenes in which God is a participant in the action. The most conspicuous human characters are the judges, especially five of them—Ehud, Deborah, Gideon, Jephthah, and Samson. The nation itself assumes the quality of a corporate character and villain.

▌**Realism.** The literary technique of *realism permeates many parts of the Bible, but nowhere more obviously than in the book of Judges. Realism can be defined as the portrayal of life as it is in its combination of good and bad. The distinguishing feature of literary realism is its refusal to overlook the sordid side of life. As the book of Judges unfolds, we read shocking accounts of violence, sexual abuse, idolatry, and abuse of power. Before the book is over, we encounter gruesome scenes of bodily mutilation and dismemberment. As readers we need to brace ourselves to face the worst in regard to bad behavior, and we need to rest assured that the author of the book thought that such realism tells us something important that we need to know about life.

■ **Inferred literary intentions.** The book is designed to achieve the following literary purposes:

- give us models of heroism to admire

- shock us with vivid pictures of evil

- alternately inspire us with hope about human potential and disprove any illusions we might harbor about the goodness of the human race when left to its own resources

- prompt us to reflect that while history tells us what *happened*, literature tells us what *happens*, so that we can look through the historical details of the book to our life and times

- grip our imagination with sensational narrative events

- serve as an extended example story that shows how badly things go wrong when people do as they please

■ **Theological themes.** (1) Sin: the book is an expanded vision of human depravity— an anatomy of ways in which people can become grossly evil. (2) Divine grace: God repeatedly extends his mercy to his wayward people when they cry to him. (3) A view of history: history is viewed not primarily as dates and events but as human behavior seen from a theological perspective of God's favor toward nations that follow him and his judgment against nations that abandon him. (4) Apostasy: the book is a casebook of how individuals and a nation fall away from God after being temporarily restored to him.

■ **The book of Judges as a chapter in the master story of the Bible.** The master story of the Bible is the story of God's dealing with the human race, especially in the form of his covenant with his chosen people. In the OT, this is the history of the nation of Israel, and Judges records the history of Israel during a three-hundred-year period. More generally, the master story of the Bible is the story of individuals' choosing for or against God, and that is essentially the story line of the book of Judges. Additionally, the story of God's redemption of his people is a *rescue story, and the book of Judges shows the need for a deliverer.

> **Initiation into the book** [chapter 1]. The opening chapter of Judges is our initiation into the book and its world. The action of chapter 1 is mainly military in nature, and it falls into two main categories: places and tribes in Canaan that the tribes of Judah and Simeon capture (vv. 1–21) and a list of incomplete conquests by the other tribes, which we are to understand as a failure to obey God's command to take possession of the land (vv. 22–36). This chapter reads like a sequel to the book of Joshua, since the conquests and partial conquests listed in this chapter are part of the settlement of the Promised

Land. We need to begin by reliving the literal events and details of the story. Then we can list generalizations about the world that we enter as we read the opening chapter of the book—a military world, for example, and a world in which arrangement of societies by tribes and families is very important. Finally, in a chapter where conquest is the main *motif, we need to ponder the spiritual implications of the contrast that is drawn between complete conquests and incomplete conquests.

1 After the death of Joshua, the people of Israel inquired of the LORD, "Who shall go up first for us against the Canaanites, to fight against them?" ²The LORD said, "Judah shall go up; behold, I have given the land into his hand." ³And Judah said to Simeon his brother, "Come up with me into the territory allotted to me, that we may fight against the Canaanites. And I likewise will go with you into the territory allotted to you." So Simeon went with him. ⁴Then Judah went up and the LORD gave the Canaanites and the Perizzites into their hand, and they defeated 10,000 of them at Bezek. ⁵They found Adoni-bezek at Bezek and fought against him and defeated the Canaanites and the Perizzites. ⁶Adoni-bezek fled, but they pursued him and caught him and cut off his thumbs and his big toes. ⁷And Adoni-bezek said, "Seventy kings with their thumbs and their big toes cut off used to pick up scraps under my table. As I have done, so God has repaid me." And they brought him to Jerusalem, and he died there.

⁸And the men of Judah fought against Jerusalem and captured it and struck it with the edge of the sword and set the city on fire. ⁹And afterward the men of Judah went down to fight against the Canaanites who lived in the hill country, in the Negeb, and in the lowland. ¹⁰And Judah went against the Canaanites who lived in Hebron (now the name of Hebron was formerly Kiriath-arba), and they defeated Sheshai and Ahiman and Talmai.

¹¹From there they went against the inhabitants of Debir. The name of Debir was formerly Kiriath-sepher. ¹²And Caleb said, "He who attacks Kiriath-sepher and captures it, I will give him Achsah my daughter for a wife." ¹³And Othniel the son of Kenaz, Caleb's younger brother, captured it. And he gave him Achsah his daughter for a wife. ¹⁴When she came to him, she urged him to ask her father for a field. And she dismounted from her donkey, and Caleb said to her, "What do you want?" ¹⁵She said to him, "Give me a blessing. Since you have set me in the land of the Negeb, give me also springs of water." And Caleb gave her the upper springs and the lower springs.

¹⁶And the descendants of the Kenite, Moses' father-in-law, went up with the people of Judah from the city of palms into the wilderness of Judah, which lies in the Negeb near Arad, and they went and settled with the people. ¹⁷And Judah went with Simeon his brother, and they defeated the Canaanites who inhabited Zephath and devoted it to destruction. So the name of the city was called Hormah.¹ ¹⁸Judah also captured Gaza with its territory, and Ashkelon with its territory, and Ekron with its territory. ¹⁹And the LORD was with Judah, and he took possession of the hill country, but he could not drive out the inhabitants of the plain because they had chariots of iron. ²⁰And Hebron was given to Caleb, as Moses had said. And he drove out from it the three sons of Anak. ²¹But the people of Benjamin did not drive out the Jebusites who lived in Jerusalem, so the Jebusites have lived with the people of Benjamin in Jerusalem to this day.

---

¹ Hormah means utter destruction

²²The house of Joseph also went up against Bethel, and the LORD was with them. ²³And the house of Joseph scouted out Bethel. (Now the name of the city was formerly Luz.) ²⁴And the spies saw a man coming out of the city, and they said to him, "Please show us the way into the city, and we will deal kindly with you." ²⁵And he showed them the way into the city. And they struck the city with the edge of the sword, but they let the man and all his family go. ²⁶And the man went to the land of the Hittites and built a city and called its name Luz. That is its name to this day.

²⁷Manasseh did not drive out the inhabitants of Beth-shean and its villages, or Taanach and its villages, or the inhabitants of Dor and its villages, or the inhabitants of Ibleam and its villages, or the inhabitants of Megiddo and its villages, for the Canaanites persisted in dwelling in that land. ²⁸When Israel grew strong, they put the Canaanites to forced labor, but did not drive them out completely.

²⁹And Ephraim did not drive out the Canaanites who lived in Gezer, so the Canaanites lived in Gezer among them.

³⁰Zebulun did not drive out the inhabitants of Kitron, or the inhabitants of Nahalol, so the Canaanites lived among them, but became subject to forced labor.

³¹Asher did not drive out the inhabitants of Acco, or the inhabitants of Sidon or of Ahlab or of Achzib or of Helbah or of Aphik or of Rehob, ³²so the Asherites lived among the Canaanites, the inhabitants of the land, for they did not drive them out.

³³Naphtali did not drive out the inhabitants of Beth-shemesh, or the inhabitants of Beth-anath, so they lived among the Canaanites, the inhabitants of the land. Nevertheless, the inhabitants of Beth-shemesh and of Beth-anath became subject to forced labor for them.

³⁴The Amorites pressed the people of Dan back into the hill country, for they did not allow them to come down to the plain. ³⁵The Amorites persisted in dwelling in Mount Heres, in Aijalon, and in Shaalbim, but the hand of the house of Joseph rested heavily on them, and they became subject to forced labor. ³⁶And the border of the Amorites ran from the ascent of Akrabbim, from Sela and upward.

Preview of the rest of the book [2:1–3:6]. If the main narrative business of the opening chapter is to initiate us into the world of the book, the function of this unit is to preview what we will find in the rest of the book. This chapter provides an interpretive framework for the book as a whole. The keynotes are as follows: God's prediction that the Israelites will be thwarted by the remnants of the tribes that they did not subdue (2:1–5); the death of Joshua, accompanied by the ominous comment that the new generation "did not know the LORD or the work that he had done for Israel" (2:6–10); a summary account of how Israel's idolatrous apostasy resulted in its lack of military success (2:11–15); preview of the pattern that will ensue in the book of Judges—deliverance for the nation when God raises up individual judges, but apostasy and distress after a given judge dies (2:16–23); a list of the nations that God left unsubdued in order that the nation might learn warfare (3:1–6). We need to fix in our mind the principles that are established here (such as the evil of idolatry and God's demand of obedience) as reference points by which to measure what happens in the rest of the book.

2 Now the angel of the LORD went up from Gilgal to Bochim. And he said, "I brought you up from Egypt and brought you into the land that I swore to give to your fathers. I said, 'I will never break my covenant with you, ²and you shall make no

covenant with the inhabitants of this land; you shall break down their altars.' But you have not obeyed my voice. What is this you have done? ³So now I say, I will not drive them out before you, but they shall become thorns in your sides,¹ and their gods shall be a snare to you." ⁴As soon as the angel of the LORD spoke these words to all the people of Israel, the people lifted up their voices and wept. ⁵And they called the name of that place Bochim.² And they sacrificed there to the LORD.

⁶When Joshua dismissed the people, the people of Israel went each to his inheritance to take possession of the land. ⁷And the people served the LORD all the days of Joshua, and all the days of the elders who outlived Joshua, who had seen all the great work that the LORD had done for Israel. ⁸And Joshua the son of Nun, the servant of the LORD, died at the age of 110 years. ⁹And they buried him within the boundaries of his inheritance in Timnath-heres, in the hill country of Ephraim, north of the mountain of Gaash. ¹⁰And all that generation also were gathered to their fathers. And there arose another generation after them who did not know the LORD or the work that he had done for Israel.

¹¹And the people of Israel did what was evil in the sight of the LORD and served the Baals. ¹²And they abandoned the LORD, the God of their fathers, who had brought them out of the land of Egypt. They went after other gods, from among the gods of the peoples who were around them, and bowed down to them. And they provoked the LORD to anger. ¹³They abandoned the LORD and served the Baals and the Ashtaroth. ¹⁴So the anger of the LORD was kindled against Israel, and he gave them over to plunderers, who plundered them. And he sold them into the hand of their surrounding enemies, so that they could no longer withstand their enemies. ¹⁵Whenever they marched out, the hand of the LORD was against them for harm, as the LORD had warned, and as the LORD had sworn to them. And they were in terrible distress.

¹⁶Then the LORD raised up judges, who saved them out of the hand of those who plundered them. ¹⁷Yet they did not listen to their judges, for they whored after other gods and bowed down to them. They soon turned aside from the way in which their fathers had walked, who had obeyed the commandments of the LORD, and they did not do so. ¹⁸Whenever the LORD raised up judges for them, the LORD was with the judge, and he saved them from the hand of their enemies all the days of the judge. For the LORD was moved to pity by their groaning because of those who afflicted and oppressed them. ¹⁹But whenever the judge died, they turned back and were more corrupt than their fathers, going after other gods, serving them and bowing down to them. They did not drop any of their practices or their stubborn ways. ²⁰So the anger of the LORD was kindled against Israel, and he said, "Because this people has transgressed my covenant that I commanded their fathers and have not obeyed my voice, ²¹I will no longer drive out before them any of the nations that Joshua left when he died, ²²in order to test Israel by them, whether they will take care to walk in the way of the LORD as their fathers did, or not." ²³So the LORD left those nations, not driving them out quickly, and he did not give them into the hand of Joshua.

3 Now these are the nations that the LORD left, to test Israel by them, that is, all in Israel who had not experienced all the wars in Canaan. ²It was only in order that the generations of the people of Israel might know war, to teach war to those who had not known it before. ³These are the nations: the five lords of the Philistines and all the Canaanites and the Sidonians and the Hivites who lived on Mount Lebanon, from Mount Baal-hermon as far as Lebo-hamath. ⁴They were for the testing of Israel,

¹Vulgate, Old Latin (compare Septuagint); Hebrew *sides* ²*Bochim* means *weepers*

to know whether Israel would obey the commandments of the LORD, which he commanded their fathers by the hand of Moses. ⁵So the people of Israel lived among the Canaanites, the Hittites, the Amorites, the Perizzites, the Hivites, and the Jebusites. ⁶And their daughters they took to themselves for wives, and their own daughters they gave to their sons, and they served their gods.

> **The first wave of judges** [3:7–31]. This passage belongs mainly to Ehud, but the story of Ehud's assassination of Eglon is bracketed by summary accounts of the judgeships of Othniel (vv. 7–11) and Shamgar (v. 31). The story of Ehud is a classic hero story in the Bible. The lead-in tells us that "the LORD raised up for them a deliverer" (v. 15), and the main point of the story is to show exactly how God delivered them, namely, through human skill, resourcefulness, and giftedness. The story of Ehud is par excellence the story of a clever and resourceful hero. As a southpaw, Ehud carries his homemade sword on the unexpected right side, thereby evading detection. Once we are alerted to this disguise, virtually every detail in the story is a variation on the theme of the hero's resourcefulness. Ehud is clever in making and concealing a weapon (v. 16), arranging to be alone with his antagonist (vv. 17–19), tricking his victim (vv. 20–21), concealing the murder weapon in the original case of the disappearing sword (v. 22), making a getaway (vv. 23–25), and capitalizing on the assassination with a great military victory over the oppressive Moabites (vv. 26–30). The story is a *satire against an oppressive foreign king whose name means "calf," and when we note that this oppressive king is "a very fat man" (v. 17), we have the connotation of a fat calf being readied for slaughter. The story has the mocking tone of slave literature, a story told with relish at the expense of a foreign oppressor.

⁷And the people of Israel did what was evil in the sight of the LORD. They forgot the LORD their God and served the Baals and the Asheroth. ⁸Therefore the anger of the LORD was kindled against Israel, and he sold them into the hand of Cushan-rishathaim king of Mesopotamia. And the people of Israel served Cushan-rishathaim eight years. ⁹But when the people of Israel cried out to the LORD, the LORD raised up a deliverer for the people of Israel, who saved them, Othniel the son of Kenaz, Caleb's younger brother. ¹⁰The Spirit of the LORD was upon him, and he judged Israel. He went out to war, and the LORD gave Cushan-rishathaim king of Mesopotamia into his hand. And his hand prevailed over Cushan-rishathaim. ¹¹So the land had rest forty years. Then Othniel the son of Kenaz died.

¹²And the people of Israel again did what was evil in the sight of the LORD, and the LORD strengthened Eglon the king of Moab against Israel, because they had done what was evil in the sight of the LORD. ¹³He gathered to himself the Ammonites and the Amalekites, and went and defeated Israel. And they took possession of the city of palms. ¹⁴And the people of Israel served Eglon the king of Moab eighteen years.

¹⁵Then the people of Israel cried out to the LORD, and the LORD raised up for them a deliverer, Ehud, the son of Gera, the Benjaminite, a left-handed man. The people of Israel sent tribute by him to Eglon the king of Moab. ¹⁶And Ehud made for himself a sword with two edges, a cubit¹ in length, and he bound it on his right thigh under his clothes. ¹⁷And he presented the tribute to Eglon king of Moab. Now Eglon was a very fat man. ¹⁸And when Ehud had finished presenting the tribute, he sent away the people who carried the tribute. ¹⁹But he himself turned back at the idols near Gilgal and

---

¹ A *cubit* was about 18 inches or 45 centimeters

said, "I have a secret message for you, O king." And he commanded, "Silence." And all his attendants went out from his presence. ²⁰And Ehud came to him as he was sitting alone in his cool roof chamber. And Ehud said, "I have a message from God for you." And he arose from his seat. ²¹And Ehud reached with his left hand, took the sword from his right thigh, and thrust it into his belly. ²²And the hilt also went in after the blade, and the fat closed over the blade, for he did not pull the sword out of his belly; and the dung came out. ²³Then Ehud went out into the porch¹ and closed the doors of the roof chamber behind him and locked them.

²⁴When he had gone, the servants came, and when they saw that the doors of the roof chamber were locked, they thought, "Surely he is relieving himself in the closet of the cool chamber." ²⁵And they waited till they were embarrassed. But when he still did not open the doors of the roof chamber, they took the key and opened them, and there lay their lord dead on the floor.

²⁶Ehud escaped while they delayed, and he passed beyond the idols and escaped to Seirah. ²⁷When he arrived, he sounded the trumpet in the hill country of Ephraim. Then the people of Israel went down with him from the hill country, and he was their leader. ²⁸And he said to them, "Follow after me, for the LORD has given your enemies the Moabites into your hand." So they went down after him and seized the fords of the Jordan against the Moabites and did not allow anyone to pass over. ²⁹And they killed at that time about 10,000 of the Moabites, all strong, able-bodied men; not a man escaped. ³⁰So Moab was subdued that day under the hand of Israel. And the land had rest for eighty years.

³¹After him was Shamgar the son of Anath, who killed 600 of the Philistines with an oxgoad, and he also saved Israel.

The victory of Deborah and Barak over the Canaanites [chapter 4]. Biblical literature does not include many full-fledged stories of heroines, but this is one of the few. Deborah is one of the famous women of Israelite history—a woman who is called a prophetess (v. 4), who judges the nation (vv. 4–5), and who becomes a military leader (vv. 8–14). A second heroic woman also enters the story—Jael, the wife of Heber the Kenite, who assassinates Sisera, general of the king of Canaan's army (vv. 15–22). The narrative account, like Ehud's assassination of Eglon in the preceding chapter, enables us to relive the event in full realistic detail. Overall, the story is a *rescue story, as hinted in the last verse (v. 24).

4 And the people of Israel again did what was evil in the sight of the LORD after Ehud died. ²And the LORD sold them into the hand of Jabin king of Canaan, who reigned in Hazor. The commander of his army was Sisera, who lived in Harosheth-hagoyim. ³Then the people of Israel cried out to the LORD for help, for he had 900 chariots of iron and he oppressed the people of Israel cruelly for twenty years.

⁴Now Deborah, a prophetess, the wife of Lappidoth, was judging Israel at that time. ⁵She used to sit under the palm of Deborah between Ramah and Bethel in the hill country of Ephraim, and the people of Israel came up to her for judgment. ⁶She sent and summoned Barak the son of Abinoam from Kedesh-naphtali and said to him, "Has not the LORD, the God of Israel, commanded you, 'Go, gather your men at Mount Tabor, taking 10,000 from the people of Naphtali and the people of Zebulun. ⁷And I

---

¹ The meaning of the Hebrew word is uncertain

will draw out Sisera, the general of Jabin's army, to meet you by the river Kishon with his chariots and his troops, and I will give him into your hand'?" ⁸Barak said to her, "If you will go with me, I will go, but if you will not go with me, I will not go." ⁹And she said, "I will surely go with you. Nevertheless, the road on which you are going will not lead to your glory, for the LORD will sell Sisera into the hand of a woman." Then Deborah arose and went with Barak to Kedesh. ¹⁰And Barak called out Zebulun and Naphtali to Kedesh. And 10,000 men went up at his heels, and Deborah went up with him.

¹¹Now Heber the Kenite had separated from the Kenites, the descendants of Hobab the father-in-law of Moses, and had pitched his tent as far away as the oak in Zaanannim, which is near Kedesh.

¹²When Sisera was told that Barak the son of Abinoam had gone up to Mount Tabor, ¹³Sisera called out all his chariots, 900 chariots of iron, and all the men who were with him, from Harosheth-hagoyim to the river Kishon. ¹⁴And Deborah said to Barak, "Up! For this is the day in which the LORD has given Sisera into your hand. Does not the LORD go out before you?" So Barak went down from Mount Tabor with 10,000 men following him. ¹⁵And the LORD routed Sisera and all his chariots and all his army before Barak by the edge of the sword. And Sisera got down from his chariot and fled away on foot. ¹⁶And Barak pursued the chariots and the army to Harosheth-hagoyim, and all the army of Sisera fell by the edge of the sword; not a man was left.

¹⁷But Sisera fled away on foot to the tent of Jael, the wife of Heber the Kenite, for there was peace between Jabin the king of Hazor and the house of Heber the Kenite. ¹⁸And Jael came out to meet Sisera and said to him, "Turn aside, my lord; turn aside to me; do not be afraid." So he turned aside to her into the tent, and she covered him with a rug. ¹⁹And he said to her, "Please give me a little water to drink, for I am thirsty." So she opened a skin of milk and gave him a drink and covered him. ²⁰And he said to her, "Stand at the opening of the tent, and if any man comes and asks you, 'Is anyone here?' say, 'No.'" ²¹But Jael the wife of Heber took a tent peg, and took a hammer in her hand. Then she went softly to him and drove the peg into his temple until it went down into the ground while he was lying fast asleep from weariness. So he died. ²²And behold, as Barak was pursuing Sisera, Jael went out to meet him and said to him, "Come, and I will show you the man whom you are seeking." So he went in to her tent, and there lay Sisera dead, with the tent peg in his temple.

²³So on that day God subdued Jabin the king of Canaan before the people of Israel. ²⁴And the hand of the people of Israel pressed harder and harder against Jabin the king of Canaan, until they destroyed Jabin king of Canaan.

The Song of Deborah [chapter 5]. The story of military rescue that has just been narrated now receives poetic treatment. Since we have the historical facts of the matter as a reference point, we can work out a detailed comparison between prose narrative and poetic modes. When we do, it becomes obvious that the poet regularly resorts to hyperbole and other forms of poetic license. Further, the poet uses the technique of "leaping and lingering"—jumping from one vivid moment to another and elaborating it in detail but making no attempt to provide smooth narrative transitions between the selected scenes. The result is a series of impressionistic snapshots. In form, the poem is an *ode—an exalted lyric poem written in the high style on an impressive subject. For sheer exuberance, it is hard to surpass this poem.

5 Then sang Deborah and Barak the son of Abinoam on that day:

2 "That the leaders took the lead in Israel,
    that the people offered themselves willingly,
    bless the LORD!

3 "Hear, O kings; give ear, O princes;
    to the LORD I will sing;
    I will make melody to the LORD, the God of Israel.

4 "LORD, when you went out from Seir,
    when you marched from the region of Edom,
  the earth trembled
    and the heavens dropped,
    yes, the clouds dropped water.
5 The mountains quaked before the LORD,
    even Sinai before the LORD, the God of Israel.

6 "In the days of Shamgar, son of Anath,
    in the days of Jael, the highways were abandoned,
    and travelers kept to the byways.
7 The villagers ceased in Israel;
    they ceased to be until I arose;
    I, Deborah, arose as a mother in Israel.
8 When new gods were chosen,
    then war was in the gates.
  Was shield or spear to be seen
    among forty thousand in Israel?
9 My heart goes out to the commanders of Israel
    who offered themselves willingly among the people.
    Bless the LORD.

10 "Tell of it, you who ride on white donkeys,
    you who sit on rich carpets[1]
    and you who walk by the way.
11 To the sound of musicians[2] at the watering places,
    there they repeat the righteous triumphs of the LORD,
    the righteous triumphs of his villagers in Israel.

  "Then down to the gates marched the people of the LORD.

12 "Awake, awake, Deborah!
    Awake, awake, break out in a song!
  Arise, Barak, lead away your captives,
    O son of Abinoam.
13 Then down marched the remnant of the noble;

[1] The meaning of the Hebrew word is uncertain; it may connote *saddle blankets* [2] Or *archers*; the meaning of the Hebrew word is uncertain

the people of the Lord marched down for me against the mighty.
14 From Ephraim their root they marched down into the valley,[1]
   following you, Benjamin, with your kinsmen;
from Machir marched down the commanders,
   and from Zebulun those who bear the lieutenant's[2] staff;
15 the princes of Issachar came with Deborah,
   and Issachar faithful to Barak;
   into the valley they rushed at his heels.
Among the clans of Reuben
   there were great searchings of heart.
16 Why did you sit still among the sheepfolds,
   to hear the whistling for the flocks?
Among the clans of Reuben
   there were great searchings of heart.
17 Gilead stayed beyond the Jordan;
   and Dan, why did he stay with the ships?
Asher sat still at the coast of the sea,
   staying by his landings.
18 Zebulun is a people who risked their lives to the death;
   Naphtali, too, on the heights of the field.

19 "The kings came, they fought;
   then fought the kings of Canaan,
at Taanach, by the waters of Megiddo;
   they got no spoils of silver.
20 From heaven the stars fought,
   from their courses they fought against Sisera.
21 The torrent Kishon swept them away,
   the ancient torrent, the torrent Kishon.
   March on, my soul, with might!

22 "Then loud beat the horses' hoofs
   with the galloping, galloping of his steeds.

23 "Curse Meroz, says the angel of the Lord,
   curse its inhabitants thoroughly,
because they did not come to the help of the Lord,
   to the help of the Lord against the mighty.

24 "Most blessed of women be Jael,
   the wife of Heber the Kenite,
   of tent-dwelling women most blessed.
25 He asked water and she gave him milk;
   she brought him curds in a noble's bowl.
26 She sent her hand to the tent peg
   and her right hand to the workmen's mallet;
she struck Sisera;
   she crushed his head;

---

[1] Septuagint; Hebrew *in Amalek* [2] Hebrew *commander's*

she shattered and pierced his temple.
27   Between her feet
he sank, he fell, he lay still;
between her feet
he sank, he fell;
where he sank,
there he fell—dead.

28   "Out of the window she peered,
the mother of Sisera wailed through the lattice:
'Why is his chariot so long in coming?
Why tarry the hoofbeats of his chariots?'
29   Her wisest princesses answer,
indeed, she answers herself,
30   'Have they not found and divided the spoil?—
A womb or two for every man;
spoil of dyed materials for Sisera,
spoil of dyed materials embroidered,
two pieces of dyed work embroidered for the neck as spoil?'

31   "So may all your enemies perish, O LORD!
But your friends be like the sun as he rises in his might."

And the land had rest for forty years.

The reluctant hero [chapter 6]. The story of Gideon's conquest of the Midianites now gets three chapters. Literary heroes either display heroism from start to finish or achieve heroism as they develop during the course of the story. The story of Gideon is the story of the making of a hero. Virtually every detail in chapter 6 highlights Gideon's under-confidence and reluctance to act as a leader of Israel. The sequence unfolds as follows: the oppression of the Israelites by the Midianites (vv. 1–6); God's response to the nation's cry to him, first sending a prophet to rehearse the story of Israel's deliverance from Egypt by way of foreshadowing (vv. 7–10); dialogue in which God's angel seeks to instill confidence in Gideon, who repeatedly responds in a defeatist spirit (vv. 11–18); Gideon's dismay when he perceives that he has been speaking to the angel of God (vv. 19–24); countermovement in which Gideon acts decisively as a leader (vv. 25–35); back to a hesitant spirit as Gideon resorts to his fleece tests (vv. 36–40). In a story that will spring a series of surprises on us, this story begins with the spectacle of a future hero who conveys the impression of not wanting to be a hero.

6 The people of Israel did what was evil in the sight of the LORD, and the LORD gave them into the hand of Midian seven years. ²And the hand of Midian over-powered Israel, and because of Midian the people of Israel made for themselves the dens that are in the mountains and the caves and the strongholds. ³For whenever the Israelites planted crops, the Midianites and the Amalekites and the people of the East would come up against them. ⁴They would encamp against them and devour the produce of the land, as far as Gaza, and leave no sustenance in Israel and no sheep or ox or donkey. ⁵For they would come up with their livestock and their tents; they would

come like locusts in number—both they and their camels could not be counted—so that they laid waste the land as they came in. ⁶And Israel was brought very low because of Midian. And the people of Israel cried out for help to the Lord.

⁷When the people of Israel cried out to the Lord on account of the Midianites, ⁸the Lord sent a prophet to the people of Israel. And he said to them, "Thus says the Lord, the God of Israel: I led you up from Egypt and brought you out of the house of bondage. ⁹And I delivered you from the hand of the Egyptians and from the hand of all who oppressed you, and drove them out before you and gave you their land. ¹⁰And I said to you, 'I am the Lord your God; you shall not fear the gods of the Amorites in whose land you dwell.' But you have not obeyed my voice."

¹¹Now the angel of the Lord came and sat under the terebinth at Ophrah, which belonged to Joash the Abiezrite, while his son Gideon was beating out wheat in the winepress to hide it from the Midianites. ¹²And the angel of the Lord appeared to him and said to him, "The Lord is with you, O mighty man of valor." ¹³And Gideon said to him, "Please, sir,¹ if the Lord is with us, why then has all this happened to us? And where are all his wonderful deeds that our fathers recounted to us, saying, 'Did not the Lord bring us up from Egypt?' But now the Lord has forsaken us and given us into the hand of Midian." ¹⁴And the Lord² turned to him and said, "Go in this might of yours and save Israel from the hand of Midian; do not I send you?" ¹⁵And he said to him, "Please, Lord, how can I save Israel? Behold, my clan is the weakest in Manasseh, and I am the least in my father's house." ¹⁶And the Lord said to him, "But I will be with you, and you shall strike the Midianites as one man." ¹⁷And he said to him, "If now I have found favor in your eyes, then show me a sign that it is you who speak with me. ¹⁸Please do not depart from here until I come to you and bring out my present and set it before you." And he said, "I will stay till you return."

¹⁹So Gideon went into his house and prepared a young goat and unleavened cakes from an ephah³ of flour. The meat he put in a basket, and the broth he put in a pot, and brought them to him under the terebinth and presented them. ²⁰And the angel of God said to him, "Take the meat and the unleavened cakes, and put them on this rock, and pour the broth over them." And he did so. ²¹Then the angel of the Lord reached out the tip of the staff that was in his hand and touched the meat and the unleavened cakes. And fire sprang up from the rock and consumed the meat and the unleavened cakes. And the angel of the Lord vanished from his sight. ²²Then Gideon perceived that he was the angel of the Lord. And Gideon said, "Alas, O Lord God! For now I have seen the angel of the Lord face to face." ²³But the Lord said to him, "Peace be to you. Do not fear; you shall not die." ²⁴Then Gideon built an altar there to the Lord and called it, The Lord Is Peace. To this day it still stands at Ophrah, which belongs to the Abiezrites.

²⁵That night the Lord said to him, "Take your father's bull, and the second bull seven years old, and pull down the altar of Baal that your father has, and cut down the Asherah that is beside it ²⁶and build an altar to the Lord your God on the top of the stronghold here, with stones laid in due order. Then take the second bull and offer it as a burnt offering with the wood of the Asherah that you shall cut down." ²⁷So Gideon took ten men of his servants and did as the Lord had told him. But because he was too afraid of his family and the men of the town to do it by day, he did it by night.

²⁸When the men of the town rose early in the morning, behold, the altar of Baal

¹ Or Please, my Lord ² Septuagint the angel of the Lord; also verse 16 ³ An ephah was about 3/5 bushel or 22 liters

was broken down, and the Asherah beside it was cut down, and the second bull was offered on the altar that had been built. ²⁹And they said to one another, "Who has done this thing?" And after they had searched and inquired, they said, "Gideon the son of Joash has done this thing." ³⁰Then the men of the town said to Joash, "Bring out your son, that he may die, for he has broken down the altar of Baal and cut down the Asherah beside it." ³¹But Joash said to all who stood against him, "Will you contend for Baal? Or will you save him? Whoever contends for him shall be put to death by morning. If he is a god, let him contend for himself, because his altar has been broken down." ³²Therefore on that day Gideon[1] was called Jerubbaal, that is to say, "Let Baal contend against him," because he broke down his altar.

³³Now all the Midianites and the Amalekites and the people of the East came together, and they crossed the Jordan and encamped in the Valley of Jezreel. ³⁴But the Spirit of the LORD clothed Gideon, and he sounded the trumpet, and the Abiezrites were called out to follow him. ³⁵And he sent messengers throughout all Manasseh, and they too were called out to follow him. And he sent messengers to Asher, Zebulun, and Naphtali, and they went up to meet them.

³⁶Then Gideon said to God, "If you will save Israel by my hand, as you have said, ³⁷behold, I am laying a fleece of wool on the threshing floor. If there is dew on the fleece alone, and it is dry on all the ground, then I shall know that you will save Israel by my hand, as you have said." ³⁸And it was so. When he rose early next morning and squeezed the fleece, he wrung enough dew from the fleece to fill a bowl with water. ³⁹Then Gideon said to God, "Let not your anger burn against me; let me speak just once more. Please let me test just once more with the fleece. Please let it be dry on the fleece only, and on all the ground let there be dew." ⁴⁰And God did so that night; and it was dry on the fleece only, and on all the ground there was dew.

Gideon's transformation [chapter 7]. The middle chapter of the three devoted to Gideon portrays his turnaround, and the story surprises us repeatedly. After doing everything possible to instill confidence in a reluctant hero (the preceding chapter), God now undertakes a series of actions seemingly calculated to undermine Gideon's confidence. After successfully assembling an army, Gideon is directed through a sequence of actions that nearly take his army away from him, until he is left with an army of only three hundred soldiers (vv. 1–8). But then God sends him into the enemy camp to overhear a Midianite's dream and restore Gideon's confidence (vv. 9–14). Thereupon Gideon imparts battle strategy to his army (vv. 15–18) and successfully routs the Midianite army (vv. 19–25). Given that events in the first half of the chapter (vv. 2, 7) lead us to expect that God himself will deliver the nation much as he did at the Red Sea, we are surprised when God drops out of the story as a named character once the battle begins. In this story, God accomplishes his purposes through the actions of his people, even in their weakness.

7 Then Jerubbaal (that is, Gideon) and all the people who were with him rose early and encamped beside the spring of Harod. And the camp of Midian was north of them, by the hill of Moreh, in the valley.

²The LORD said to Gideon, "The people with you are too many for me to give the Midianites into their hand, lest Israel boast over me, saying, 'My own hand has saved me.' ³Now therefore proclaim in the ears of the people, saying, 'Whoever is fearful

[1] Hebrew *he*

and trembling, let him return home and hurry away from Mount Gilead.'" Then 22,000 of the people returned, and 10,000 remained.

⁴And the LORD said to Gideon, "The people are still too many. Take them down to the water, and I will test them for you there, and anyone of whom I say to you, 'This one shall go with you,' shall go with you, and anyone of whom I say to you, 'This one shall not go with you,' shall not go." ⁵So he brought the people down to the water. And the LORD said to Gideon, "Every one who laps the water with his tongue, as a dog laps, you shall set by himself. Likewise, every one who kneels down to drink." ⁶And the number of those who lapped, putting their hands to their mouths, was 300 men, but all the rest of the people knelt down to drink water. ⁷And the LORD said to Gideon, "With the 300 men who lapped I will save you and give the Midianites into your hand, and let all the others go every man to his home." ⁸So the people took provisions in their hands, and their trumpets. And he sent all the rest of Israel every man to his tent, but retained the 300 men. And the camp of Midian was below him in the valley.

⁹That same night the LORD said to him, "Arise, go down against the camp, for I have given it into your hand. ¹⁰But if you are afraid to go down, go down to the camp with Purah your servant. ¹¹And you shall hear what they say, and afterward your hands shall be strengthened to go down against the camp." Then he went down with Purah his servant to the outposts of the armed men who were in the camp. ¹²And the Midianites and the Amalekites and all the people of the East lay along the valley like locusts in abundance, and their camels were without number, as the sand that is on the seashore in abundance. ¹³When Gideon came, behold, a man was telling a dream to his comrade. And he said, "Behold, I dreamed a dream, and behold, a cake of barley bread tumbled into the camp of Midian and came to the tent and struck it so that it fell and turned it upside down, so that the tent lay flat." ¹⁴And his comrade answered, "This is no other than the sword of Gideon the son of Joash, a man of Israel; God has given into his hand Midian and all the camp."

¹⁵As soon as Gideon heard the telling of the dream and its interpretation, he worshiped. And he returned to the camp of Israel and said, "Arise, for the LORD has given the host of Midian into your hand." ¹⁶And he divided the 300 men into three companies and put trumpets into the hands of all of them and empty jars, with torches inside the jars. ¹⁷And he said to them, "Look at me, and do likewise. When I come to the outskirts of the camp, do as I do. ¹⁸When I blow the trumpet, I and all who are with me, then blow the trumpets also on every side of all the camp and shout, 'For the LORD and for Gideon.'"

¹⁹So Gideon and the hundred men who were with him came to the outskirts of the camp at the beginning of the middle watch, when they had just set the watch. And they blew the trumpets and smashed the jars that were in their hands. ²⁰Then the three companies blew the trumpets and broke the jars. They held in their left hands the torches, and in their right hands the trumpets to blow. And they cried out, "A sword for the LORD and for Gideon!" ²¹Every man stood in his place around the camp, and all the army ran. They cried out and fled. ²²When they blew the 300 trumpets, the LORD set every man's sword against his comrade and against all the army. And the army fled as far as Beth-shittah toward Zererah,¹ as far as the border of Abel-meholah, by Tabbath. ²³And the men of Israel were called out from Naphtali and from Asher and from all Manasseh, and they pursued after Midian.

²⁴Gideon sent messengers throughout all the hill country of Ephraim, saying,

¹ Some Hebrew manuscripts *Zeredah*

"Come down against the Midianites and capture the waters against them, as far as Beth-barah, and also the Jordan." So all the men of Ephraim were called out, and they captured the waters as far as Beth-barah, and also the Jordan. ²⁵And they captured the two princes of Midian, Oreb and Zeeb. They killed Oreb at the rock of Oreb, and Zeeb they killed at the winepress of Zeeb. Then they pursued Midian, and they brought the heads of Oreb and Zeeb to Gideon across the Jordan.

Rounding out a heroic life [chapter 8]. The story of Gideon is a full-fledged hero story in which we see the complete shape of the hero's life. Given Gideon's initial reluctance to be a hero, we are surprised in chapter 8 by his complete mastery of every obstacle that is put in his path during the war with the Midianites. He can even resolve a conflict with psychological warfare (vv. 1–3). When Gideon threatens the tribes who refuse to help him while he is pursuing the Midianites, his threats might well strike us as bravado (vv. 7–8), but after Gideon wins the battle, he returns to the intransigent tribes and makes good on his threats (v. 16). In ancient battle stories and *epic literature, the conventional reward for a warrior who leads his nation to victory is to become king, but the story of Gideon breaks the pattern when he refuses to accept the kingship that is offered to him (vv. 22–23). Then, in yet another unexpected turn of events, this idealized hero displays a disappointing flaw when he builds an idol that misleads his nation (vv. 24–27). The author refuses to enter into exposé journalism, however, and lets the hero's flaw rest with a mere mention. To complete the cycle that was predicted in 2:19, we end the chapter with an account of Israel's apostasy after Gideon's death (vv. 33–35).

8 Then the men of Ephraim said to him, "What is this that you have done to us, not to call us when you went to fight against Midian?" And they accused him fiercely. ²And he said to them, "What have I done now in comparison with you? Is not the gleaning of the grapes of Ephraim better than the grape harvest of Abiezer? ³God has given into your hands the princes of Midian, Oreb and Zeeb. What have I been able to do in comparison with you?" Then their anger[1] against him subsided when he said this.

⁴And Gideon came to the Jordan and crossed over, he and the 300 men who were with him, exhausted yet pursuing. ⁵So he said to the men of Succoth, "Please give loaves of bread to the people who follow me, for they are exhausted, and I am pursuing after Zebah and Zalmunna, the kings of Midian." ⁶And the officials of Succoth said, "Are the hands of Zebah and Zalmunna already in your hand, that we should give bread to your army?" ⁷So Gideon said, "Well then, when the LORD has given Zebah and Zalmunna into my hand, I will flail your flesh with the thorns of the wilderness and with briers." ⁸And from there he went up to Penuel, and spoke to them in the same way, and the men of Penuel answered him as the men of Succoth had answered. ⁹And he said to the men of Penuel, "When I come again in peace, I will break down this tower."

¹⁰Now Zebah and Zalmunna were in Karkor with their army, about 15,000 men, all who were left of all the army of the people of the East, for there had fallen 120,000 men who drew the sword. ¹¹And Gideon went up by the way of the tent dwellers east of Nobah and Jogbehah and attacked the army, for the army felt secure. ¹²And Zebah and Zalmunna fled, and he pursued them and captured the two kings of Midian, Zebah and Zalmunna, and he threw all the army into a panic.

[1] Hebrew *their spirit*

¹³Then Gideon the son of Joash returned from the battle by the ascent of Heres. ¹⁴And he captured a young man of Succoth and questioned him. And he wrote down for him the officials and elders of Succoth, seventy-seven men. ¹⁵And he came to the men of Succoth and said, "Behold Zebah and Zalmunna, about whom you taunted me, saying, 'Are the hands of Zebah and Zalmunna already in your hand, that we should give bread to your men who are exhausted?'" ¹⁶And he took the elders of the city, and he took thorns of the wilderness and briers and with them taught the men of Succoth a lesson. ¹⁷And he broke down the tower of Penuel and killed the men of the city.

¹⁸Then he said to Zebah and Zalmunna, "Where are the men whom you killed at Tabor?" They answered, "As you are, so were they. Every one of them resembled the son of a king." ¹⁹And he said, "They were my brothers, the sons of my mother. As the LORD lives, if you had saved them alive, I would not kill you." ²⁰So he said to Jether his firstborn, "Rise and kill them!" But the young man did not draw his sword, for he was afraid, because he was still a young man. ²¹Then Zebah and Zalmunna said, "Rise yourself and fall upon us, for as the man is, so is his strength." And Gideon arose and killed Zebah and Zalmunna, and he took the crescent ornaments that were on the necks of their camels.

²²Then the men of Israel said to Gideon, "Rule over us, you and your son and your grandson also, for you have saved us from the hand of Midian." ²³Gideon said to them, "I will not rule over you, and my son will not rule over you; the LORD will rule over you." ²⁴And Gideon said to them, "Let me make a request of you: every one of you give me the earrings from his spoil." (For they had golden earrings, because they were Ishmaelites.) ²⁵And they answered, "We will willingly give them." And they spread a cloak, and every man threw in it the earrings of his spoil. ²⁶And the weight of the golden earrings that he requested was 1,700 shekels¹ of gold, besides the crescent ornaments and the pendants and the purple garments worn by the kings of Midian, and besides the collars that were around the necks of their camels. ²⁷And Gideon made an ephod of it and put it in his city, in Ophrah. And all Israel whored after it there, and it became a snare to Gideon and to his family. ²⁸So Midian was subdued before the people of Israel, and they raised their heads no more. And the land had rest forty years in the days of Gideon.

²⁹Jerubbaal the son of Joash went and lived in his own house. ³⁰Now Gideon had seventy sons, his own offspring,² for he had many wives. ³¹And his concubine who was in Shechem also bore him a son, and he called his name Abimelech. ³²And Gideon the son of Joash died in a good old age and was buried in the tomb of Joash his father, at Ophrah of the Abiezrites.

³³As soon as Gideon died, the people of Israel turned again and whored after the Baals and made Baal-berith their god. ³⁴And the people of Israel did not remember the LORD their God, who had delivered them from the hand of all their enemies on every side, ³⁵and they did not show steadfast love to the family of Jerubbaal (that is, Gideon) in return for all the good that he had done to Israel.

An ill-fated judgeship [chapter 9]. This chapter is one of the oddest stories in the Bible—more sensational than a television drama. It records a troubled three-year rule by Gideon's son Abimelech. The action begins with the gruesome account of Abimelech's

---

¹ A *shekel* was about 2/5 ounce or 11 grams ² Hebrew *who came from his own loins*

execution of seventy of his brothers "on one stone" (v. 5). Abimelech was an ambitious politician who here tries to do what his father had refused, namely, set himself up as monarch (vv. 1–6). His surviving brother Jotham tells a parable in an attempt to get the populace to see how unwise they are in accepting Abimelech as king (vv. 7–21). The story in which Abimelech is forced to cope with Gaal's revolt (vv. 22–41) has touches of humor (vv. 34–38), but it ends as a story of violence (vv. 42–49). In yet another strange twist, Abimelech dies when a woman throws down a millstone from the top of a city wall, crushing his skull (vv. 50–57). In this chapter, truth seems stranger than fiction. The final lesson of the chapter is that human kingship, especially when it is not legitimate, fails; the implicit theme is that the nation needs God as king.

9 Now Abimelech the son of Jerubbaal went to Shechem to his mother's relatives and said to them and to the whole clan of his mother's family, ²"Say in the ears of all the leaders of Shechem, 'Which is better for you, that all seventy of the sons of Jerubbaal rule over you, or that one rule over you?' Remember also that I am your bone and your flesh."

³And his mother's relatives spoke all these words on his behalf in the ears of all the leaders of Shechem, and their hearts inclined to follow Abimelech, for they said, "He is our brother." ⁴And they gave him seventy pieces of silver out of the house of Baal-berith with which Abimelech hired worthless and reckless fellows, who followed him. ⁵And he went to his father's house at Ophrah and killed his brothers the sons of Jerubbaal, seventy men, on one stone. But Jotham the youngest son of Jerubbaal was left, for he hid himself. ⁶And all the leaders of Shechem came together, and all Beth-millo, and they went and made Abimelech king, by the oak of the pillar at Shechem.

⁷When it was told to Jotham, he went and stood on top of Mount Gerizim and cried aloud and said to them, "Listen to me, you leaders of Shechem, that God may listen to you. ⁸The trees once went out to anoint a king over them, and they said to the olive tree, 'Reign over us.' ⁹But the olive tree said to them, 'Shall I leave my abundance, by which gods and men are honored, and go hold sway over the trees?' ¹⁰And the trees said to the fig tree, 'You come and reign over us.' ¹¹But the fig tree said to them, 'Shall I leave my sweetness and my good fruit and go hold sway over the trees?' ¹²And the trees said to the vine, 'You come and reign over us.' ¹³But the vine said to them, 'Shall I leave my wine that cheers God and men and go hold sway over the trees?' ¹⁴Then all the trees said to the bramble, 'You come and reign over us.' ¹⁵And the bramble said to the trees, 'If in good faith you are anointing me king over you, then come and take refuge in my shade, but if not, let fire come out of the bramble and devour the cedars of Lebanon.'

¹⁶"Now therefore, if you acted in good faith and integrity when you made Abimelech king, and if you have dealt well with Jerubbaal and his house and have done to him as his deeds deserved— ¹⁷for my father fought for you and risked his life and delivered you from the hand of Midian, ¹⁸and you have risen up against my father's house this day and have killed his sons, seventy men on one stone, and have made Abimelech, the son of his female servant, king over the leaders of Shechem, because he is your relative— ¹⁹if you then have acted in good faith and integrity with Jerubbaal and with his house this day, then rejoice in Abimelech, and let him also

rejoice in you. ²⁰But if not, let fire come out from Abimelech and devour the leaders of Shechem and Beth-millo; and let fire come out from the leaders of Shechem and from Beth-millo and devour Abimelech." ²¹And Jotham ran away and fled and went to Beer and lived there, because of Abimelech his brother.

²²Abimelech ruled over Israel three years. ²³And God sent an evil spirit between Abimelech and the leaders of Shechem, and the leaders of Shechem dealt treacherously with Abimelech, ²⁴that the violence done to the seventy sons of Jerubbaal might come, and their blood be laid on Abimelech their brother, who killed them, and on the men of Shechem, who strengthened his hands to kill his brothers. ²⁵And the leaders of Shechem put men in ambush against him on the mountaintops, and they robbed all who passed by them along that way. And it was told to Abimelech.

²⁶And Gaal the son of Ebed moved into Shechem with his relatives, and the leaders of Shechem put confidence in him. ²⁷And they went out into the field and gathered the grapes from their vineyards and trod them and held a festival; and they went into the house of their god and ate and drank and reviled Abimelech. ²⁸And Gaal the son of Ebed said, "Who is Abimelech, and who are we of Shechem, that we should serve him? Is he not the son of Jerubbaal, and is not Zebul his officer? Serve the men of Hamor the father of Shechem; but why should we serve him? ²⁹Would that this people were under my hand! Then I would remove Abimelech. I would say¹ to Abimelech, 'Increase your army, and come out.'"

³⁰When Zebul the ruler of the city heard the words of Gaal the son of Ebed, his anger was kindled. ³¹And he sent messengers to Abimelech secretly,² saying, "Behold, Gaal the son of Ebed and his relatives have come to Shechem, and they are stirring up³ the city against you. ³²Now therefore, go by night, you and the people who are with you, and set an ambush in the field. ³³Then in the morning, as soon as the sun is up, rise early and rush upon the city. And when he and the people who are with him come out against you, you may do to them as your hand finds to do."

³⁴So Abimelech and all the men who were with him rose up by night and set an ambush against Shechem in four companies. ³⁵And Gaal the son of Ebed went out and stood in the entrance of the gate of the city, and Abimelech and the people who were with him rose from the ambush. ³⁶And when Gaal saw the people, he said to Zebul, "Look, people are coming down from the mountaintops!" And Zebul said to him, "You mistake⁴ the shadow of the mountains for men." ³⁷Gaal spoke again and said, "Look, people are coming down from the center of the land, and one company is coming from the direction of the Diviners' Oak." ³⁸Then Zebul said to him, "Where is your mouth now, you who said, 'Who is Abimelech, that we should serve him?' Are not these the people whom you despised? Go out now and fight with them." ³⁹And Gaal went out at the head of the leaders of Shechem and fought with Abimelech. ⁴⁰And Abimelech chased him, and he fled before him. And many fell wounded, up to the entrance of the gate. ⁴¹And Abimelech lived at Arumah, and Zebul drove out Gaal and his relatives, so that they could not dwell at Shechem.

⁴²On the following day, the people went out into the field, and Abimelech was told. ⁴³He took his people and divided them into three companies and set an ambush in the fields. And he looked and saw the people coming out of the city. So he rose against them and killed them. ⁴⁴Abimelech and the company that was with him rushed forward and stood at the entrance of the gate of the city, while the two companies rushed upon all who were in the field and killed them. ⁴⁵And Abimelech

---

¹ Septuagint; Hebrew *and he said* ² Or *at Tormah* ³ Hebrew *besieging, or closing up* ⁴ Hebrew *You see*

fought against the city all that day. He captured the city and killed the people who were in it, and he razed the city and sowed it with salt.

⁴⁶When all the leaders of the Tower of Shechem heard of it, they entered the stronghold of the house of El-berith. ⁴⁷Abimelech was told that all the leaders of the Tower of Shechem were gathered together. ⁴⁸And Abimelech went up to Mount Zalmon, he and all the people who were with him. And Abimelech took an axe in his hand and cut down a bundle of brushwood and took it up and laid it on his shoulder. And he said to the men who were with him, "What you have seen me do, hurry and do as I have done." ⁴⁹So every one of the people cut down his bundle and following Abimelech put it against the stronghold, and they set the stronghold on fire over them, so that all the people of the Tower of Shechem also died, about 1,000 men and women.

⁵⁰Then Abimelech went to Thebez and encamped against Thebez and captured it. ⁵¹But there was a strong tower within the city, and all the men and women and all the leaders of the city fled to it and shut themselves in, and they went up to the roof of the tower. ⁵²And Abimelech came to the tower and fought against it and drew near to the door of the tower to burn it with fire. ⁵³And a certain woman threw an upper millstone on Abimelech's head and crushed his skull. ⁵⁴Then he called quickly to the young man his armor-bearer and said to him, "Draw your sword and kill me, lest they say of me, 'A woman killed him.'" And his young man thrust him through, and he died. ⁵⁵And when the men of Israel saw that Abimelech was dead, everyone departed to his home. ⁵⁶Thus God returned the evil of Abimelech, which he committed against his father in killing his seventy brothers. ⁵⁷And God also made all the evil of the men of Shechem return on their heads, and upon them came the curse of Jotham the son of Jerubbaal.

> **Background for Jephthah's judgeship** [10:1–11:3]. Stories are built on a principle of moving back and forth between intense or sensational action and episodes of more relaxed action. Starting with the story of Ehud, virtually everything has been pitched at a high level of intensity. This unit brings us back to the ground. Two judgeships are reported in summary fashion (10:1–5). Then the cycle that recurs throughout the book kicks in: first "the people of Israel again did what was evil in the sight of the LORD" (10:6); then "the people of Israel cried out to the LORD" (10:10) and reformed their ways by turning away from idolatry (10:15–16). We subsequently read about a vacuum in leadership (10:17–18), after which we are given the unlikely background of the next judge, Jephthah, who is a prostitute's son exiled by his brothers (11:1–3). All of this material is the backdrop to the next story of deliverance.

10 After Abimelech there arose to save Israel Tola the son of Puah, son of Dodo, a man of Issachar, and he lived at Shamir in the hill country of Ephraim. ²And he judged Israel twenty-three years. Then he died and was buried at Shamir.

³After him arose Jair the Gileadite, who judged Israel twenty-two years. ⁴And he had thirty sons who rode on thirty donkeys, and they had thirty cities, called Havvoth-jair to this day, which are in the land of Gilead. ⁵And Jair died and was buried in Kamon.

⁶The people of Israel again did what was evil in the sight of the LORD and served the Baals and the Ashtaroth, the gods of Syria, the gods of Sidon, the gods of Moab, the gods of the Ammonites, and the gods of the Philistines. And they forsook the LORD and did not serve him. ⁷So the anger of the LORD was kindled against Israel, and

he sold them into the hand of the Philistines and into the hand of the Ammonites, ⁸and they crushed and oppressed the people of Israel that year. For eighteen years they oppressed all the people of Israel who were beyond the Jordan in the land of the Amorites, which is in Gilead. ⁹And the Ammonites crossed the Jordan to fight also against Judah and against Benjamin and against the house of Ephraim, so that Israel was severely distressed.

¹⁰And the people of Israel cried out to the LORD, saying, "We have sinned against you, because we have forsaken our God and have served the Baals." ¹¹And the LORD said to the people of Israel, "Did I not save you from the Egyptians and from the Amorites, from the Ammonites and from the Philistines? ¹²The Sidonians also, and the Amalekites and the Maonites oppressed you, and you cried out to me, and I saved you out of their hand. ¹³Yet you have forsaken me and served other gods; therefore I will save you no more. ¹⁴Go and cry out to the gods whom you have chosen; let them save you in the time of your distress." ¹⁵And the people of Israel said to the LORD, "We have sinned; do to us whatever seems good to you. Only please deliver us this day." ¹⁶So they put away the foreign gods from among them and served the LORD, and he became impatient over the misery of Israel.

¹⁷Then the Ammonites were called to arms, and they encamped in Gilead. And the people of Israel came together, and they encamped at Mizpah. ¹⁸And the people, the leaders of Gilead, said one to another, "Who is the man who will begin to fight against the Ammonites? He shall be head over all the inhabitants of Gilead."

11 Now Jephthah the Gileadite was a mighty warrior, but he was the son of a prostitute. Gilead was the father of Jephthah. ²And Gilead's wife also bore him sons. And when his wife's sons grew up, they drove Jephthah out and said to him, "You shall not have an inheritance in our father's house, for you are the son of another woman." ³Then Jephthah fled from his brothers and lived in the land of Tob, and worthless fellows collected around Jephthah and went out with him.

> **The judgeship of Jephthah** [11:4–40]. In contrast to judges whose judgeship is told only in summary fashion, the judges who receive full treatment emerge in our imagination as people whom we "get to know." Even though Jephthah is mentioned in the roll call of faith in Hebrews 11:32, the account that we read in this unit highlights his undesirable traits, especially his self-seeking and rashness. He is, however, "a mighty warrior" (Judges 11:1), and therefore the nation turns to him when it is oppressed by the Ammonites (vv. 4–8). Jephthah accepts the overture only as a bargaining ploy to become ruler (vv. 9–11). What follows is a detailed *battle story that requires careful analysis to piece together (vv. 12–28). The story of national conquest is then displaced by the personal and family tragedy that revolves around Jephthah's rash vow (vv. 29–33) leading to the execution of his daughter (vv. 34–40).

⁴After a time the Ammonites made war against Israel. ⁵And when the Ammonites made war against Israel, the elders of Gilead went to bring Jephthah from the land of Tob. ⁶And they said to Jephthah, "Come and be our leader, that we may fight against the Ammonites." ⁷But Jephthah said to the elders of Gilead, "Did you not hate me and drive me out of my father's house? Why have you come to me now when you are in distress?" ⁸And the elders of Gilead said to Jephthah, "That is why we have turned to

you now, that you may go with us and fight against the Ammonites and be our head over all the inhabitants of Gilead." ⁹Jephthah said to the elders of Gilead, "If you bring me home again to fight against the Ammonites, and the LORD gives them over to me, I will be your head." ¹⁰And the elders of Gilead said to Jephthah, "The LORD will be witness between us, if we do not do as you say." ¹¹So Jephthah went with the elders of Gilead, and the people made him head and leader over them. And Jephthah spoke all his words before the LORD at Mizpah.

¹²Then Jephthah sent messengers to the king of the Ammonites and said, "What do you have against me, that you have come to me to fight against my land?" ¹³And the king of the Ammonites answered the messengers of Jephthah, "Because Israel on coming up from Egypt took away my land, from the Arnon to the Jabbok and to the Jordan; now therefore restore it peaceably." ¹⁴Jephthah again sent messengers to the king of the Ammonites ¹⁵and said to him, "Thus says Jephthah: Israel did not take away the land of Moab or the land of the Ammonites, ¹⁶but when they came up from Egypt, Israel went through the wilderness to the Red Sea and came to Kadesh. ¹⁷Israel then sent messengers to the king of Edom, saying, 'Please let us pass through your land,' but the king of Edom would not listen. And they sent also to the king of Moab, but he would not consent. So Israel remained at Kadesh.

¹⁸"Then they journeyed through the wilderness and went around the land of Edom and the land of Moab and arrived on the east side of the land of Moab and camped on the other side of the Arnon. But they did not enter the territory of Moab, for the Arnon was the boundary of Moab. ¹⁹Israel then sent messengers to Sihon king of the Amorites, king of Heshbon, and Israel said to him, 'Please let us pass through your land to our country,' ²⁰but Sihon did not trust Israel to pass through his territory, so Sihon gathered all his people together and encamped at Jahaz and fought with Israel. ²¹And the LORD, the God of Israel, gave Sihon and all his people into the hand of Israel, and they defeated them. So Israel took possession of all the land of the Amorites, who inhabited that country. ²²And they took possession of all the territory of the Amorites from the Arnon to the Jabbok and from the wilderness to the Jordan. ²³So then the LORD, the God of Israel, dispossessed the Amorites from before his people Israel; and are you to take possession of them? ²⁴Will you not possess what Chemosh your god gives you to possess? And all that the LORD our God has dispossessed before us, we will possess. ²⁵Now are you any better than Balak the son of Zippor, king of Moab? Did he ever contend against Israel, or did he ever go to war with them? ²⁶While Israel lived in Heshbon and its villages, and in Aroer and its villages, and in all the cities that are on the banks of the Arnon, 300 years, why did you not deliver them within that time? ²⁷I therefore have not sinned against you, and you do me wrong by making war on me. The LORD, the Judge, decide this day between the people of Israel and the people of Ammon." ²⁸But the king of the Ammonites did not listen to the words of Jephthah that he sent to him.

²⁹Then the Spirit of the LORD was upon Jephthah, and he passed through Gilead and Manasseh and passed on to Mizpah of Gilead, and from Mizpah of Gilead he passed on to the Ammonites. ³⁰And Jephthah made a vow to the LORD and said, "If you will give the Ammonites into my hand, ³¹then whatever¹ comes out from the doors of my house to meet me when I return in peace from the Ammonites shall be the LORD's, and I will offer it² up for a burnt offering." ³²So Jephthah crossed over to the Ammonites to fight against them, and the LORD gave them into his hand. ³³And he

---

¹ Or whoever ² Or him

struck them from Aroer to the neighborhood of Minnith, twenty cities, and as far as Abel-keramim, with a great blow. So the Ammonites were subdued before the people of Israel. ³⁴Then Jephthah came to his home at Mizpah. And behold, his daughter came out to meet him with tambourines and with dances. She was his only child; besides her he had neither son nor daughter. ³⁵And as soon as he saw her, he tore his clothes and said, "Alas, my daughter! You have brought me very low, and you have become the cause of great trouble to me. For I have opened my mouth to the Lord, and I cannot take back my vow." ³⁶And she said to him, "My father, you have opened your mouth to the Lord; do to me according to what has gone out of your mouth, now that the Lord has avenged you on your enemies, on the Ammonites." ³⁷So she said to her father, "Let this thing be done for me: leave me alone two months, that I may go up and down on the mountains and weep for my virginity, I and my companions." ³⁸So he said, "Go." Then he sent her away for two months, and she departed, she and her companions, and wept for her virginity on the mountains. ³⁹And at the end of two months, she returned to her father, who did with her according to his vow that he had made. She had never known a man, and it became a custom in Israel ⁴⁰that the daughters of Israel went year by year to lament the daughter of Jephthah the Gileadite four days in the year.

The life and times of the judges [chapter 12]. Most of the stories in Judges are narrated objectively, with no help from the storyteller regarding distinguishing the good guys from the bad guys. The conflict narrated in verses 1–6 is a prime example. The tribe of Ephraim was an influential and self-important tribe with a track record for being belligerent when not asked to join a battle (8:1). Its leaders do an encore here (12:1). Gideon had placated the Ephraimites with soft talk (8:2–3), but this is not Jephthah's gift or preferred style (12:2–3). When the Ephraimites resort to trash talking (v. 4), Jephthah engages them in battle, killing a massive number at the fords of the Jordan River when they cannot pronounce the password without giving away their identity (vv. 4–6). The judgeship of Jephthah has been such a drastic downward spiral into violence that it is with relief that we see three judges handled in summary fashion (vv. 8–15).

12 The men of Ephraim were called to arms, and they crossed to Zaphon and said to Jephthah, "Why did you cross over to fight against the Ammonites and did not call us to go with you? We will burn your house over you with fire." ²And Jephthah said to them, "I and my people had a great dispute with the Ammonites, and when I called you, you did not save me from their hand. ³And when I saw that you would not save me, I took my life in my hand and crossed over against the Ammonites, and the Lord gave them into my hand. Why then have you come up to me this day to fight against me?" ⁴Then Jephthah gathered all the men of Gilead and fought with Ephraim. And the men of Gilead struck Ephraim, because they said, "You are fugitives of Ephraim, you Gileadites, in the midst of Ephraim and Manasseh." ⁵And the Gileadites captured the fords of the Jordan against the Ephraimites. And when any of the fugitives of Ephraim said, "Let me go over," the men of Gilead said to him, "Are you an Ephraimite?" When he said, "No," ⁶they said to him, "Then say Shibboleth," and he said, "Sibboleth," for he could not pronounce it right. Then they seized him and slaughtered him at the fords of the Jordan. At that time 42,000 of the Ephraimites fell.

⁷Jephthah judged Israel six years. Then Jephthah the Gileadite died and was buried in his city in Gilead.¹

⁸After him Ibzan of Bethlehem judged Israel. ⁹He had thirty sons, and thirty daughters he gave in marriage outside his clan, and thirty daughters he brought in from outside for his sons. And he judged Israel seven years. ¹⁰Then Ibzan died and was buried at Bethlehem.

¹¹After him Elon the Zebulunite judged Israel, and he judged Israel ten years. ¹²Then Elon the Zebulunite died and was buried at Aijalon in the land of Zebulun.

¹³After him Abdon the son of Hillel the Pirathonite judged Israel. ¹⁴He had forty sons and thirty grandsons, who rode on seventy donkeys, and he judged Israel eight years. ¹⁵Then Abdon the son of Hillel the Pirathonite died and was buried at Pirathon in the land of Ephraim, in the hill country of the Amalekites.

Most likely to succeed [chapter 13]. Samson gets the most space of all the judges. His story is a complex fusion of hero story and tragedy. In fact, we look at the very same episodes—his marriage to the woman of Timnah, for example, or his liaison with Delilah—from the opposite viewpoints of those two genres. Samson's personal life is a downward spiral into tragedy as he repeatedly violates his Nazirite vow and squanders God's gifts to him. But when viewed at a national level, the events of Samson's life are a story of superhuman strength used to deliver a nation. Tragedy presents an isolated hero, and among the judges, Samson is an isolated celebrity who is never shown leading an army but only engaged in personal crusades. Chapter 13 sketches out the heights from which Samson eventually fell. His birth is accompanied by miraculous signs—the appearance of an angel to a barren woman, the stipulation of his being a Nazirite from birth, and the reappearance of the angel to Manoah. To complete the "most likely to succeed" scenario, we read in the last verse that "the Spirit of the Lord began to stir him" (v. 25).

13 And the people of Israel again did what was evil in the sight of the Lord, so the Lord gave them into the hand of the Philistines for forty years.

²There was a certain man of Zorah, of the tribe of the Danites, whose name was Manoah. And his wife was barren and had no children. ³And the angel of the Lord appeared to the woman and said to her, "Behold, you are barren and have not borne children, but you shall conceive and bear a son. ⁴Therefore be careful and drink no wine or strong drink, and eat nothing unclean, ⁵for behold, you shall conceive and bear a son. No razor shall come upon his head, for the child shall be a Nazirite to God from the womb, and he shall begin to save Israel from the hand of the Philistines." ⁶Then the woman came and told her husband, "A man of God came to me, and his appearance was like the appearance of the angel of God, very awesome. I did not ask him where he was from, and he did not tell me his name, ⁷but he said to me, 'Behold, you shall conceive and bear a son. So then drink no wine or strong drink, and eat nothing unclean, for the child shall be a Nazirite to God from the womb to the day of his death.'"

⁸Then Manoah prayed to the Lord and said, "O Lord, please let the man of God whom you sent come again to us and teach us what we are to do with the child who

¹ Septuagint; Hebrew *in the cities of Gilead*

will be born." ⁹And God listened to the voice of Manoah, and the angel of God came again to the woman as she sat in the field. But Manoah her husband was not with her. ¹⁰So the woman ran quickly and told her husband, "Behold, the man who came to me the other day has appeared to me." ¹¹And Manoah arose and went after his wife and came to the man and said to him, "Are you the man who spoke to this woman?" And he said, "I am." ¹²And Manoah said, "Now when your words come true, what is to be the child's manner of life, and what is his mission?" ¹³And the angel of the LORD said to Manoah, "Of all that I said to the woman let her be careful. ¹⁴She may not eat of anything that comes from the vine, neither let her drink wine or strong drink, or eat any unclean thing. All that I commanded her let her observe."

¹⁵Manoah said to the angel of the LORD, "Please let us detain you and prepare a young goat for you." ¹⁶And the angel of the LORD said to Manoah, "If you detain me, I will not eat of your food. But if you prepare a burnt offering, then offer it to the LORD." (For Manoah did not know that he was the angel of the LORD.) ¹⁷And Manoah said to the angel of the LORD, "What is your name, so that, when your words come true, we may honor you?" ¹⁸And the angel of the LORD said to him, "Why do you ask my name, seeing it is wonderful?" ¹⁹So Manoah took the young goat with the grain offering, and offered it on the rock to the LORD, to the one who works¹ wonders, and Manoah and his wife were watching. ²⁰And when the flame went up toward heaven from the altar, the angel of the LORD went up in the flame of the altar. Now Manoah and his wife were watching, and they fell on their faces to the ground.

²¹The angel of the LORD appeared no more to Manoah and to his wife. Then Manoah knew that he was the angel of the LORD. ²²And Manoah said to his wife, "We shall surely die, for we have seen God." ²³But his wife said to him, "If the LORD had meant to kill us, he would not have accepted a burnt offering and a grain offering at our hands, or shown us all these things, or now announced to us such things as these." ²⁴And the woman bore a son and called his name Samson. And the young man grew, and the LORD blessed him. ²⁵And the Spirit of the LORD began to stir him in Mahaneh-dan, between Zorah and Eshtaol.

The hero goes down, down, down [chapter 14]. The first recorded event in Samson's adult life is an ill-fated, self-indulgent marriage to a Philistine woman. Already we see his pathetic search for emotional connectedness in the wrong places. First Samson commands his parents to arrange the marriage over their protest (vv. 1–4). Then he violates his Nazirite vow to avoid contact with corpses by scraping honey out of the carcass of a lion that he has killed (vv. 5–9). At the wedding feast Samson shows foolish arrogance and greed in posing his riddle, as well as a fatal inability to keep a secret from a pleading woman (vv. 10–18). His killing of thirty men to steal their garments to pay off his bet (vv. 19–20) is an abuse of his God-given strength. Our assessment of this adolescent behavior is suggested indirectly when four times in the chapter we read that Samson "went down" (vv. 1, 5, 7, 19); even though this is first of all a geographic descent, it metaphorically sums up his behavior as well. Yet this story of tragedy on a personal level is a part of a national rescue performed by a conquering hero (vv. 4, 19).

14 Samson went down to Timnah, and at Timnah he saw one of the daughters of the Philistines. ²Then he came up and told his father and mother, "I saw one of the daughters of the Philistines at Timnah. Now get her for me as my wife."

---

¹ Septuagint, Vulgate; Hebrew LORD, and working

³But his father and mother said to him, "Is there not a woman among the daughters of your relatives, or among all our people, that you must go to take a wife from the uncircumcised Philistines?" But Samson said to his father, "Get her for me, for she is right in my eyes."

⁴His father and mother did not know that it was from the Lᴏʀᴅ, for he was seeking an opportunity against the Philistines. At that time the Philistines ruled over Israel.

⁵Then Samson went down with his father and mother to Timnah, and they came to the vineyards of Timnah. And behold, a young lion came toward him roaring. ⁶Then the Spirit of the Lᴏʀᴅ rushed upon him, and although he had nothing in his hand, he tore the lion in pieces as one tears a young goat. But he did not tell his father or his mother what he had done. ⁷Then he went down and talked with the woman, and she was right in Samson's eyes.

⁸After some days he returned to take her. And he turned aside to see the carcass of the lion, and behold, there was a swarm of bees in the body of the lion, and honey. ⁹He scraped it out into his hands and went on, eating as he went. And he came to his father and mother and gave some to them, and they ate. But he did not tell them that he had scraped the honey from the carcass of the lion.

¹⁰His father went down to the woman, and Samson prepared a feast there, for so the young men used to do. ¹¹As soon as the people saw him, they brought thirty companions to be with him. ¹²And Samson said to them, "Let me now put a riddle to you. If you can tell me what it is, within the seven days of the feast, and find it out, then I will give you thirty linen garments and thirty changes of clothes, ¹³but if you cannot tell me what it is, then you shall give me thirty linen garments and thirty changes of clothes." And they said to him, "Put your riddle, that we may hear it." ¹⁴And he said to them,

> "Out of the eater came something to eat.
> Out of the strong came something sweet."

And in three days they could not solve the riddle.

¹⁵On the fourth¹ day they said to Samson's wife, "Entice your husband to tell us what the riddle is, lest we burn you and your father's house with fire. Have you invited us here to impoverish us?" ¹⁶And Samson's wife wept over him and said, "You only hate me; you do not love me. You have put a riddle to my people, and you have not told me what it is." And he said to her, "Behold, I have not told my father nor my mother, and shall I tell you?" ¹⁷She wept before him the seven days that their feast lasted, and on the seventh day he told her, because she pressed him hard. Then she told the riddle to her people. ¹⁸And the men of the city said to him on the seventh day before the sun went down,

> "What is sweeter than honey?
> What is stronger than a lion?"

And he said to them,

> "If you had not plowed with my heifer,
> you would not have found out my riddle."

¹⁹And the Spirit of the Lᴏʀᴅ rushed upon him, and he went down to Ashkelon and struck down thirty men of the town and took their spoil and gave the garments to

---

¹ Septuagint, Syriac; Hebrew *seventh*

those who had told the riddle. In hot anger he went back to his father's house. ²⁰And Samson's wife was given to his companion, who had been his best man.

> **Samson as national hero** [chapter 15]. This chapter, standing between chapters that narrate Samson's dealings with three Philistine women, is a momentary break in the tragedy of Samson, shifting the focus primarily to his career as the archetypal strong man. Samson belongs partly to the archetype of the trickster, and with his superior physical strength, the practical jokes that he plays on his opponents can be quite destructive. He catches three hundred foxes and sets the Philistines' grain fields on fire (vv. 1–7). Then, in an event rendered memorable by the aphoristic way in which the author expresses the situation, Samson "struck them hip and thigh" (v. 8). The next practical joke consists of Samson's allowing himself to be bound by his countrymen and delivered to his enemies (vv. 9–13), only to break the cords and kill a thousand enemies with the jawbone of a donkey (vv. 14–16), a heroic deliverance of God's people for which Samson is rewarded with the miracle of water springing from an unidentified "hollow place" (vv. 17–19). The concluding reminder that Samson ruled Israel for twenty years (v. 20; repeated in 16:31) alerts us that the tragic pattern that the storyteller imposes on the life of Samson is a distillation from a broader pool of data that was available.

15 After some days, at the time of wheat harvest, Samson went to visit his wife with a young goat. And he said, "I will go in to my wife in the chamber." But her father would not allow him to go in. ²And her father said, "I really thought that you utterly hated her, so I gave her to your companion. Is not her younger sister more beautiful than she? Please take her instead." ³And Samson said to them, "This time I shall be innocent in regard to the Philistines, when I do them harm." ⁴So Samson went and caught 300 foxes and took torches. And he turned them tail to tail and put a torch between each pair of tails. ⁵And when he had set fire to the torches, he let the foxes go into the standing grain of the Philistines and set fire to the stacked grain and the standing grain, as well as the olive orchards. ⁶Then the Philistines said, "Who has done this?" And they said, "Samson, the son-in-law of the Timnite, because he has taken his wife and given her to his companion." And the Philistines came up and burned her and her father with fire. ⁷And Samson said to them, "If this is what you do, I swear I will be avenged on you, and after that I will quit." ⁸And he struck them hip and thigh with a great blow, and he went down and stayed in the cleft of the rock of Etam.

⁹Then the Philistines came up and encamped in Judah and made a raid on Lehi. ¹⁰And the men of Judah said, "Why have you come up against us?" They said, "We have come up to bind Samson, to do to him as he did to us." ¹¹Then 3,000 men of Judah went down to the cleft of the rock of Etam, and said to Samson, "Do you not know that the Philistines are rulers over us? What then is this that you have done to us?" And he said to them, "As they did to me, so have I done to them." ¹²And they said to him, "We have come down to bind you, that we may give you into the hands of the Philistines." And Samson said to them, "Swear to me that you will not attack me yourselves." ¹³They said to him, "No; we will only bind you and give you into their hands. We will surely not kill you." So they bound him with two new ropes and brought him up from the rock.

¹⁴When he came to Lehi, the Philistines came shouting to meet him. Then the Spirit

of the LORD rushed upon him, and the ropes that were on his arms became as flax
that has caught fire, and his bonds melted off his hands. ¹⁵And he found a fresh jawbone of a donkey, and put out his hand and took it, and with it he struck 1,000 men.
¹⁶And Samson said,

> "With the jawbone of a donkey,
>   heaps upon heaps,
> with the jawbone of a donkey
>   have I struck down a thousand men."

¹⁷As soon as he had finished speaking, he threw away the jawbone out of his hand.
And that place was called Ramath-lehi.¹
   ¹⁸And he was very thirsty, and he called upon the LORD and said, "You have granted
this great salvation by the hand of your servant, and shall I now die of thirst and fall
into the hands of the uncircumcised?" ¹⁹And God split open the hollow place that is
at Lehi, and water came out from it. And when he drank, his spirit returned, and he
revived. Therefore the name of it was called En-hakkore;² it is at Lehi to this day.
²⁰And he judged Israel in the days of the Philistines twenty years.

The tragedy of Samson [chapter 16]. Samson is the archetypal strong man who could
defeat his enemies in battle but could not control his sensual appetites. Most tragic
heroes are afflicted by a single dominant flaw of character, but Samson exhibits multiple
flaws. We can bring them into focus by completing the formula "the dangers of . . .": the
dangers of self-reliance, physical strength, success, appetite, self-indulgence, overcon-
fidence, susceptibility to women of questionable character, religious complacency, recklessness, misplaced trust, squandered gifts from God, and broken vows. We catch hints
of these in the briefly narrated one-night stand with a prostitute at Gaza (vv. 1–3), but
the story in which they appear full-fledged is the story of Samson and Delilah (vv. 4–21).
It is a highly patterned story in which a common set of ingredients is repeated four
times, with a crucial difference introduced the fourth time (the so-called three-plus-one
motif). Samson thus comes to a tragic end, imprisoned and with his eyes gouged out,
but his life ends with intimations of renewed rapport with God (vv. 22–30). In terms of
his personal life, Samson's premature death is the final phase of a pattern of literary
tragedy, but it is also a heroic victory over Israel's enemies.

16 Samson went to Gaza, and there he saw a prostitute, and he went in to her.
²The Gazites were told, "Samson has come here." And they surrounded the
place and set an ambush for him all night at the gate of the city. They kept quiet all
night, saying, "Let us wait till the light of the morning; then we will kill him." ³But
Samson lay till midnight, and at midnight he arose and took hold of the doors of the
gate of the city and the two posts, and pulled them up, bar and all, and put them on
his shoulders and carried them to the top of the hill that is in front of Hebron.
   ⁴After this he loved a woman in the Valley of Sorek, whose name was Delilah. ⁵And
the lords of the Philistines came up to her and said to her, "Seduce him, and see
where his great strength lies, and by what means we may overpower him, that we
may bind him to humble him. And we will each give you 1,100 pieces of silver." ⁶So
Delilah said to Samson, "Please tell me where your great strength lies, and how you
might be bound, that one could subdue you."

¹ *Ramath-lehi means the hill of the jawbone* ² *En-hakkore means the spring of him who called*

[7]Samson said to her, "If they bind me with seven fresh bowstrings that have not been dried, then I shall become weak and be like any other man." [8]Then the lords of the Philistines brought up to her seven fresh bowstrings that had not been dried, and she bound him with them. [9]Now she had men lying in ambush in an inner chamber. And she said to him, "The Philistines are upon you, Samson!" But he snapped the bowstrings, as a thread of flax snaps when it touches the fire. So the secret of his strength was not known.

[10]Then Delilah said to Samson, "Behold, you have mocked me and told me lies. Please tell me how you might be bound." [11]And he said to her, "If they bind me with new ropes that have not been used, then I shall become weak and be like any other man." [12]So Delilah took new ropes and bound him with them and said to him, "The Philistines are upon you, Samson!" And the men lying in ambush were in an inner chamber. But he snapped the ropes off his arms like a thread.

[13]Then Delilah said to Samson, "Until now you have mocked me and told me lies. Tell me how you might be bound." And he said to her, "If you weave the seven locks of my head with the web and fasten it tight with the pin, then I shall become weak and be like any other man." [14]So while he slept, Delilah took the seven locks of his head and wove them into the web.[1] And she made them tight with the pin and said to him, "The Philistines are upon you, Samson!" But he awoke from his sleep and pulled away the pin, the loom, and the web.

[15]And she said to him, "How can you say, 'I love you,' when your heart is not with me? You have mocked me these three times, and you have not told me where your great strength lies." [16]And when she pressed him hard with her words day after day, and urged him, his soul was vexed to death. [17]And he told her all his heart, and said to her, "A razor has never come upon my head, for I have been a Nazirite to God from my mother's womb. If my head is shaved, then my strength will leave me, and I shall become weak and be like any other man."

[18]When Delilah saw that he had told her all his heart, she sent and called the lords of the Philistines, saying, "Come up again, for he has told me all his heart." Then the lords of the Philistines came up to her and brought the money in their hands. [19]She made him sleep on her knees. And she called a man and had him shave off the seven locks of his head. Then she began to torment him, and his strength left him. [20]And she said, "The Philistines are upon you, Samson!" And he awoke from his sleep and said, "I will go out as at other times and shake myself free." But he did not know that the LORD had left him. [21]And the Philistines seized him and gouged out his eyes and brought him down to Gaza and bound him with bronze shackles. And he ground at the mill in the prison. [22]But the hair of his head began to grow again after it had been shaved.

[23]Now the lords of the Philistines gathered to offer a great sacrifice to Dagon their god and to rejoice, and they said, "Our god has given Samson our enemy into our hand." [24]And when the people saw him, they praised their god. For they said, "Our god has given our enemy into our hand, the ravager of our country, who has killed many of us."[2] [25]And when their hearts were merry, they said, "Call Samson, that he may entertain us." So they called Samson out of the prison, and he entertained them. They made him stand between the pillars. [26]And Samson said to the young man who held him by the hand, "Let me feel the pillars on which the house rests, that I may lean against them." [27]Now the house was full of men and women. All the lords of the

---

[1] Compare Septuagint; Hebrew lacks *and fasten it tight . . . into the web* [2] Or *who has multiplied our slain*

Philistines were there, and on the roof there were about 3,000 men and women, who looked on while Samson entertained.

²⁸Then Samson called to the LORD and said, "O Lord GOD, please remember me and please strengthen me only this once, O God, that I may be avenged on the Philistines for my two eyes." ²⁹And Samson grasped the two middle pillars on which the house rested, and he leaned his weight against them, his right hand on the one and his left hand on the other. ³⁰And Samson said, "Let me die with the Philistines." Then he bowed with all his strength, and the house fell upon the lords and upon all the people who were in it. So the dead whom he killed at his death were more than those whom he had killed during his life. ³¹Then his brothers and all his family came down and took him and brought him up and buried him between Zorah and Eshtaol in the tomb of Manoah his father. He had judged Israel twenty years.

Bizarre happenings in a house in Ephraim [chapter 17]. We should note first that the last five chapters of Judges, starting here, are usually considered to be an appendix. Since there is no mention of judges in this material, and since we are told four times that the events happened when "there was no king in Israel" (17:6; 18:1; 19:1; 21:25), it is a plausible inference that these events happened after the period of the five major judges. There have been numerous strange and bizarre events narrated up to this point, but the material gets even more outrageous in this concluding unit. In chapter 17, a strange incident of a son's theft of money from his mother (vv. 1–2) leads to two more unexplained events—the mother's using the money to make an idol (vv. 3–6) and Micah's pressing an itinerant Levite to become his private priest (vv. 7–13). The author passes no judgment on the events that he narrates, but our intuitions tell us that this is bad behavior—an example of spiritual decline in a nation without a deliverer or ruler.

17 There was a man of the hill country of Ephraim, whose name was Micah. ²And he said to his mother, "The 1,100 pieces of silver that were taken from you, about which you uttered a curse, and also spoke it in my ears, behold, the silver is with me; I took it." And his mother said, "Blessed be my son by the LORD." ³And he restored the 1,100 pieces of silver to his mother. And his mother said, "I dedicate the silver to the LORD from my hand for my son, to make a carved image and a metal image. Now therefore I will restore it to you." ⁴So when he restored the money to his mother, his mother took 200 pieces of silver and gave it to the silversmith, who made it into a carved image and a metal image. And it was in the house of Micah. ⁵And the man Micah had a shrine, and he made an ephod and household gods, and ordained¹ one of his sons, who became his priest. ⁶In those days there was no king in Israel. Everyone did what was right in his own eyes.

⁷Now there was a young man of Bethlehem in Judah, of the family of Judah, who was a Levite, and he sojourned there. ⁸And the man departed from the town of Bethlehem in Judah to sojourn where he could find a place. And as he journeyed, he came to the hill country of Ephraim to the house of Micah. ⁹And Micah said to him, "Where do you come from?" And he said to him, "I am a Levite of Bethlehem in Judah, and I am going to sojourn where I may find a place." ¹⁰And Micah said to him, "Stay with me, and be to me a father and a priest, and I will give you ten pieces of silver a year and a suit of clothes and your living." And the Levite went in. ¹¹And the Levite was content to dwell with the man, and the young man became to him like one

¹ Hebrew *filled the hand of;* also verse 12

of his sons. [12]And Micah ordained the Levite, and the young man became his priest, and was in the house of Micah. [13]Then Micah said, "Now I know that the LORD will prosper me, because I have a Levite as priest."

Events stranger than fiction [chapter 18]. The incident involving Micah keeps expanding into more and more implausible territory. The sequence that unfolds in this chapter is as follows: expansionist Danites send out five spies, who happen upon the priest of Micah, who encourages them in their quest to find new territory (vv. 1–6); the Danites prepare for military invasion of the prosperous land of Laish (vv. 7–13); the five former spies revisit Micah's house and lure the priest to join them, accompanied by Micah's idols (vv. 14–20); Micah makes an unsuccessful attempt to retrieve his idols (vv. 21–26); the Danites conquer the utopia of Laish and set up Micah's idols as their mode of worship (vv. 27–31). The key to interpreting the behavior of the Danites is the authorial comment that "there was no king in Israel" (v. 1): we are expected to learn by negative example, repelled by the behavior of the Danites and also of a man who leads people into idolatry.

18 In those days there was no king in Israel. And in those days the tribe of the people of Dan was seeking for itself an inheritance to dwell in, for until then no inheritance among the tribes of Israel had fallen to them. [2]So the people of Dan sent five able men from the whole number of their tribe, from Zorah and from Eshtaol, to spy out the land and to explore it. And they said to them, "Go and explore the land." And they came to the hill country of Ephraim, to the house of Micah, and lodged there. [3]When they were by the house of Micah, they recognized the voice of the young Levite. And they turned aside and said to him, "Who brought you here? What are you doing in this place? What is your business here?" [4]And he said to them, "This is how Micah dealt with me: he has hired me, and I have become his priest." [5]And they said to him, "Inquire of God, please, that we may know whether the journey on which we are setting out will succeed." [6]And the priest said to them, "Go in peace. The journey on which you go is under the eye of the LORD."

[7]Then the five men departed and came to Laish and saw the people who were there, how they lived in security, after the manner of the Sidonians, quiet and unsuspecting, lacking[1] nothing that is in the earth and possessing wealth, and how they were far from the Sidonians and had no dealings with anyone. [8]And when they came to their brothers at Zorah and Eshtaol, their brothers said to them, "What do you report?" [9]They said, "Arise, and let us go up against them, for we have seen the land, and behold, it is very good. And will you do nothing? Do not be slow to go, to enter in and possess the land. [10]As soon as you go, you will come to an unsuspecting people. The land is spacious, for God has given it into your hands, a place where there is no lack of anything that is in the earth."

[11]So 600 men of the tribe of Dan, armed with weapons of war, set out from Zorah and Eshtaol, [12]and went up and encamped at Kiriath-jearim in Judah. On this account that place is called Mahaneh-dan[2] to this day; behold, it is west of Kiriath-jearim. [13]And they passed on from there to the hill country of Ephraim, and came to the house of Micah.

[14]Then the five men who had gone to scout out the country of Laish said to their brothers, "Do you know that in these houses there are an ephod, household gods, a

---

[1] Compare 18:10; the meaning of the Hebrew word is uncertain [2] Mahaneh-dan means camp of Dan

carved image, and a metal image? Now therefore consider what you will do." ¹⁵And they turned aside there and came to the house of the young Levite, at the home of Micah, and asked him about his welfare. ¹⁶Now the 600 men of the Danites, armed with their weapons of war, stood by the entrance of the gate. ¹⁷And the five men who had gone to scout out the land went up and entered and took the carved image, the ephod, the household gods, and the metal image, while the priest stood by the entrance of the gate with the 600 men armed with weapons of war. ¹⁸And when these went into Micah's house and took the carved image, the ephod, the household gods, and the metal image, the priest said to them, "What are you doing?" ¹⁹And they said to him, "Keep quiet; put your hand on your mouth and come with us and be to us a father and a priest. Is it better for you to be priest to the house of one man, or to be priest to a tribe and clan in Israel?" ²⁰And the priest's heart was glad. He took the ephod and the household gods and the carved image and went along with the people.

²¹So they turned and departed, putting the little ones and the livestock and the goods in front of them. ²²When they had gone a distance from the home of Micah, the men who were in the houses near Micah's house were called out, and they overtook the people of Dan. ²³And they shouted to the people of Dan, who turned around and said to Micah, "What is the matter with you, that you come with such a company?" ²⁴And he said, "You take my gods that I made and the priest, and go away, and what have I left? How then do you ask me, 'What is the matter with you?'" ²⁵And the people of Dan said to him, "Do not let your voice be heard among us, lest angry fellows fall upon you, and you lose your life with the lives of your household." ²⁶Then the people of Dan went their way. And when Micah saw that they were too strong for him, he turned and went back to his home.

²⁷But the people of Dan took what Micah had made, and the priest who belonged to him, and they came to Laish, to a people quiet and unsuspecting, and struck them with the edge of the sword and burned the city with fire. ²⁸And there was no deliverer because it was far from Sidon, and they had no dealings with anyone. It was in the valley that belongs to Beth-rehob. Then they rebuilt the city and lived in it. ²⁹And they named the city Dan, after the name of Dan their ancestor, who was born to Israel; but the name of the city was Laish at the first. ³⁰And the people of Dan set up the carved image for themselves, and Jonathan the son of Gershom, son of Moses,¹ and his sons were priests to the tribe of the Danites until the day of the captivity of the land. ³¹So they set up Micah's carved image that he made, as long as the house of God was at Shiloh.

From bad to worse [chapter 19]. This is the most gruesome piece of realism in the Bible. Again the interpretive clue lies in the first verse, with its claim that "there was no king in Israel," that is, no restraining influence of good government. The focus is on the concubine of a Levite. The first scenario narrates the vagaries of the Levite's relation with his concubine and with her father when the Levite goes to reclaim her (vv. 1–9). The second scenario involves a belated late-day journey that the Levite undertakes from his father-in-law's house, landing him and his concubine in the precarious position of sitting in the square Gibeah at nightfall, only to find that the law of hospitality has fallen into such disuse that no one invites them to spend the night (vv. 10–15). An old farmer's inviting the couple to spend the night is an ironic "false calm" before disaster

¹ Or Manasseh

(vv. 16–21). The fourth act in this sordid drama consists of the concubine's being thrust out of the safe home into the control of a mob of rapists (vv. 22–26). Act 5 unfolds when the Levite finds his concubine dead on the threshold the next morning, followed by his dismembering of her body into twelve parts and sending them throughout the country as a sign of protest against the moral rot that has taken control of Israel (vv. 27–30).

19 In those days, when there was no king in Israel, a certain Levite was sojourning in the remote parts of the hill country of Ephraim, who took to himself a concubine from Bethlehem in Judah. ²And his concubine was unfaithful to¹ him, and she went away from him to her father's house at Bethlehem in Judah, and was there some four months. ³Then her husband arose and went after her, to speak kindly to her and bring her back. He had with him his servant and a couple of donkeys. And she brought him into her father's house. And when the girl's father saw him, he came with joy to meet him. ⁴And his father-in-law, the girl's father, made him stay, and he remained with him three days. So they ate and drank and spent the night there. ⁵And on the fourth day they arose early in the morning, and he prepared to go, but the girl's father said to his son-in-law, "Strengthen your heart with a morsel of bread, and after that you may go." ⁶So the two of them sat and ate and drank together. And the girl's father said to the man, "Be pleased to spend the night, and let your heart be merry." ⁷And when the man rose up to go, his father-in-law pressed him, till he spent the night there again. ⁸And on the fifth day he arose early in the morning to depart. And the girl's father said, "Strengthen your heart and wait until the day declines." So they ate, both of them. ⁹And when the man and his concubine and his servant rose up to depart, his father-in-law, the girl's father, said to him, "Behold, now the day has waned toward evening. Please, spend the night. Behold, the day draws to its close. Lodge here and let your heart be merry, and tomorrow you shall arise early in the morning for your journey, and go home."

¹⁰But the man would not spend the night. He rose up and departed and arrived opposite Jebus (that is, Jerusalem). He had with him a couple of saddled donkeys, and his concubine was with him. ¹¹When they were near Jebus, the day was nearly over, and the servant said to his master, "Come now, let us turn aside to this city of the Jebusites and spend the night in it." ¹²And his master said to him, "We will not turn aside into the city of foreigners, who do not belong to the people of Israel, but we will pass on to Gibeah." ¹³And he said to his young man, "Come and let us draw near to one of these places and spend the night at Gibeah or at Ramah." ¹⁴So they passed on and went their way. And the sun went down on them near Gibeah, which belongs to Benjamin, ¹⁵and they turned aside there, to go in and spend the night at Gibeah. And he went in and sat down in the open square of the city, for no one took them into his house to spend the night.

¹⁶And behold, an old man was coming from his work in the field at evening. The man was from the hill country of Ephraim, and he was sojourning in Gibeah. The men of the place were Benjaminites. ¹⁷And he lifted up his eyes and saw the traveler in the open square of the city. And the old man said, "Where are you going? And where do you come from?" ¹⁸And he said to him, "We are passing from Bethlehem in Judah to the remote parts of the hill country of Ephraim, from which I come. I went to Bethlehem in Judah, and I am going to the house of the Lord,² but no one has taken

¹ Septuagint, Old Latin *became angry with* ² Septuagint *my home;* compare verse 29

me into his house. [19]We have straw and feed for our donkeys, with bread and wine for me and your female servant and the young man with your servants. There is no lack of anything." [20]And the old man said, "Peace be to you; I will care for all your wants. Only, do not spend the night in the square." [21]So he brought him into his house and gave the donkeys feed. And they washed their feet, and ate and drank.

[22]As they were making their hearts merry, behold, the men of the city, worthless fellows, surrounded the house, beating on the door. And they said to the old man, the master of the house, "Bring out the man who came into your house, that we may know him." [23]And the man, the master of the house, went out to them and said to them, "No, my brothers, do not act so wickedly; since this man has come into my house, do not do this vile thing. [24]Behold, here are my virgin daughter and his concubine. Let me bring them out now. Violate them and do with them what seems good to you, but against this man do not do this outrageous thing." [25]But the men would not listen to him. So the man seized his concubine and made her go out to them. And they knew her and abused her all night until the morning. And as the dawn began to break, they let her go. [26]And as morning appeared, the woman came and fell down at the door of the man's house where her master was, until it was light.

[27]And her master rose up in the morning, and when he opened the doors of the house and went out to go on his way, behold, there was his concubine lying at the door of the house, with her hands on the threshold. [28]He said to her, "Get up, let us be going." But there was no answer. Then he put her on the donkey, and the man rose up and went away to his home. [29]And when he entered his house, he took a knife, and taking hold of his concubine he divided her, limb by limb, into twelve pieces, and sent her throughout all the territory of Israel. [30]And all who saw it said, "Such a thing has never happened or been seen from the day that the people of Israel came up out of the land of Egypt until this day; consider it, take counsel, and speak."

Battle against Benjamin [chapter 20]. This unit is a full-fledged battle story, narrated in leisurely detail. The dismembered body of the concubine achieves its intended effect, as the chiefs of the entire nation hold an assembly to determine punishment for the tribe of Benjamin, whose city Gibeah was the scene of the concubine's gang rape and murder (vv. 1–7). The enraged people at the assembly resolve to attack Gibeah (vv. 8–11). The leaders of the tribe of Benjamin are given an opportunity to reform themselves, but they refuse (vv. 12–17). After initial victories by Benjamin (vv. 18–28), the aggressors carry off a rout by means of an ambush (vv. 29–48). We are intended to draw two conclusions from this realistic battle story: monstrous behavior deserves to be punished, and a society degenerates when it lacks civilized and God-sanctioned institutions for ordering its individual and communal life.

20 Then all the people of Israel came out, from Dan to Beersheba, including the land of Gilead, and the congregation assembled as one man to the LORD at Mizpah. [2]And the chiefs of all the people, of all the tribes of Israel, presented themselves in the assembly of the people of God, 400,000 men on foot that drew the sword. [3](Now the people of Benjamin heard that the people of Israel had gone up to Mizpah.) And the people of Israel said, "Tell us, how did this evil happen?" [4]And the Levite, the husband of the woman who was murdered, answered and said, "I came to Gibeah that belongs to Benjamin, I and my concubine, to spend the night. [5]And the leaders of Gibeah rose against me and surrounded the house against me by night. They meant to kill me, and they violated my concubine, and she is dead. ⁶So I took hold of my concubine and cut her in pieces and sent her throughout all the country of the inheritance of Israel, for they have committed abomination and outrage in Israel. ⁷Behold, you people of Israel, all of you, give your advice and counsel here."

⁸And all the people arose as one man, saying, "None of us will go to his tent, and none of us will return to his house. ⁹But now this is what we will do to Gibeah: we will go up against it by lot, ¹⁰and we will take ten men of a hundred throughout all the tribes of Israel, and a hundred of a thousand, and a thousand of ten thousand, to bring provisions for the people, that when they come they may repay Gibeah of Benjamin, for all the outrage that they have committed in Israel." ¹¹So all the men of Israel gathered against the city, united as one man.

¹²And the tribes of Israel sent men through all the tribe of Benjamin, saying, "What evil is this that has taken place among you? ¹³Now therefore give up the men, the worthless fellows in Gibeah, that we may put them to death and purge evil from Israel." But the Benjaminites would not listen to the voice of their brothers, the people of Israel. ¹⁴Then the people of Benjamin came together out of the cities to Gibeah to go out to battle against the people of Israel. ¹⁵And the people of Benjamin mustered out of their cities on that day 26,000 men who drew the sword, besides the inhabitants of Gibeah, who mustered 700 chosen men. ¹⁶Among all these were 700 chosen men who were left-handed; every one could sling a stone at a hair and not miss. ¹⁷And the men of Israel, apart from Benjamin, mustered 400,000 men who drew the sword; all these were men of war.

¹⁸The people of Israel arose and went up to Bethel and inquired of God, "Who shall go up first for us to fight against the people of Benjamin?" And the LORD said, "Judah shall go up first."

¹⁹Then the people of Israel rose in the morning and encamped against Gibeah. ²⁰And the men of Israel went out to fight against Benjamin, and the men of Israel drew up the battle line against them at Gibeah. ²¹The people of Benjamin came out of Gibeah and destroyed on that day 22,000 men of the Israelites. ²²But the people, the men of Israel, took courage, and again formed the battle line in the same place where they had formed it on the first day. ²³And the people of Israel went up and wept before the LORD until the evening. And they inquired of the LORD, "Shall we again draw near to fight against our brothers, the people of Benjamin?" And the LORD said, "Go up against them."

²⁴So the people of Israel came near against the people of Benjamin the second day. ²⁵And Benjamin went against them out of Gibeah the second day, and destroyed 18,000 men of the people of Israel. All these were men who drew the sword. ²⁶Then all the people of Israel, the whole army, went up and came to Bethel and wept. They sat there before the LORD and fasted that day until evening, and offered burnt offerings and peace offerings before the LORD. ²⁷And the people of Israel inquired of the LORD (for the ark of the covenant of God was there in those days, ²⁸and Phinehas the son of Eleazar, son of Aaron, ministered before it in those days), saying, "Shall we go out once more to battle against our brothers, the people of Benjamin, or shall we cease?" And the LORD said, "Go up, for tomorrow I will give them into your hand."

²⁹So Israel set men in ambush around Gibeah. ³⁰And the people of Israel went up against the people of Benjamin on the third day and set themselves in array against

Gibeah, as at other times. ³¹And the people of Benjamin went out against the people and were drawn away from the city. And as at other times they began to strike and kill some of the people in the highways, one of which goes up to Bethel and the other to Gibeah, and in the open country, about thirty men of Israel. ³²And the people of Benjamin said, "They are routed before us, as at the first." But the people of Israel said, "Let us flee and draw them away from the city to the highways." ³³And all the men of Israel rose up out of their place and set themselves in array at Baal-tamar, and the men of Israel who were in ambush rushed out of their place from Maareh-geba.¹ ³⁴And there came against Gibeah 10,000 chosen men out of all Israel, and the battle was hard, but the Benjaminites did not know that disaster was close upon them. ³⁵And the LORD defeated Benjamin before Israel, and the people of Israel destroyed 25,100 men of Benjamin that day. All these were men who drew the sword. ³⁶So the people of Benjamin saw that they were defeated.

The men of Israel gave ground to Benjamin, because they trusted the men in ambush whom they had set against Gibeah. ³⁷Then the men in ambush hurried and rushed against Gibeah; the men in ambush moved out and struck all the city with the edge of the sword. ³⁸Now the appointed signal between the men of Israel and the men in the main ambush was that when they made a great cloud of smoke rise up out of the city ³⁹the men of Israel should turn in battle. Now Benjamin had begun to strike and kill about thirty men of Israel. They said, "Surely they are defeated before us, as in the first battle." ⁴⁰But when the signal began to rise out of the city in a column of smoke, the Benjaminites looked behind them, and behold, the whole of the city went up in smoke to heaven. ⁴¹Then the men of Israel turned, and the men of Benjamin were dismayed, for they saw that disaster was close upon them. ⁴²Therefore they turned their backs before the men of Israel in the direction of the wilderness, but the battle overtook them. And those who came out of the cities were destroying them in their midst. ⁴³Surrounding the Benjaminites, they pursued them and trod them down from Nohah² as far as opposite Gibeah on the east. ⁴⁴Eighteen thousand men of Benjamin fell, all of them men of valor. ⁴⁵And they turned and fled toward the wilderness to the rock of Rimmon. Five thousand men of them were cut down in the highways. And they were pursued hard to Gidom, and 2,000 men of them were struck down. ⁴⁶So all who fell that day of Benjamin were 25,000 men who drew the sword, all of them men of valor. ⁴⁷But 600 men turned and fled toward the wilderness to the rock of Rimmon and remained at the rock of Rimmon four months. ⁴⁸And the men of Israel turned back against the people of Benjamin and struck them with the edge of the sword, the city, men and beasts and all that they found. And all the towns that they found they set on fire.

How one bad turn produces another [chapter 21]. This concluding chapter of the book of Judges is a sequel to the drastic defeat of the tribe of Benjamin. The opening event resembles what is called "dark comedy": the attackers of Benjamin had vowed not to give their daughters in marriage to the surviving Benjaminites, but having completed the slaughter, they sit down and weep because the tribe of Benjamin now has no means of perpetuating itself (vv. 1–7). After that the action gets so complicated that it is difficult to piece it together. The main motifs are murder, massacre, kidnapping, and abduction. The chaotic action mirrors the moral and spiritual state of the characters involved.

¹ Some Septuagint manuscripts *place west of Geba* ² Septuagint; Hebrew [at their] *resting place*

The concluding verse is an implied judgment on the whole sordid mess that has been narrated: "In those days there was no king in Israel. Everyone did what was right in his own eyes" (v. 25). We can understand these final five chapters of Judges as an anatomy of some specific ways in which the depravity of people expresses itself when unchecked by God's instituted restraints, which include the individual conscience.

21 Now the men of Israel had sworn at Mizpah, "No one of us shall give his daughter in marriage to Benjamin." ²And the people came to Bethel and sat there till evening before God, and they lifted up their voices and wept bitterly. ³And they said, "O LORD, the God of Israel, why has this happened in Israel, that today there should be one tribe lacking in Israel?" ⁴And the next day the people rose early and built there an altar and offered burnt offerings and peace offerings. ⁵And the people of Israel said, "Which of all the tribes of Israel did not come up in the assembly to the LORD?" For they had taken a great oath concerning him who did not come up to the LORD to Mizpah, saying, "He shall surely be put to death." ⁶And the people of Israel had compassion for Benjamin their brother and said, "One tribe is cut off from Israel this day. ⁷What shall we do for wives for those who are left, since we have sworn by the LORD that we will not give them any of our daughters for wives?"

⁸And they said, "What one is there of the tribes of Israel that did not come up to the LORD to Mizpah?" And behold, no one had come to the camp from Jabesh-gilead, to the assembly. ⁹For when the people were mustered, behold, not one of the inhabitants of Jabesh-gilead was there. ¹⁰So the congregation sent 12,000 of their bravest men there and commanded them, "Go and strike the inhabitants of Jabesh-gilead with the edge of the sword; also the women and the little ones. ¹¹This is what you shall do: every male and every woman that has lain with a male you shall devote to destruction." ¹²And they found among the inhabitants of Jabesh-gilead 400 young virgins who had not known a man by lying with him, and they brought them to the camp at Shiloh, which is in the land of Canaan.

¹³Then the whole congregation sent word to the people of Benjamin who were at the rock of Rimmon and proclaimed peace to them. ¹⁴And Benjamin returned at that time. And they gave them the women whom they had saved alive of the women of Jabesh-gilead, but they were not enough for them. ¹⁵And the people had compassion on Benjamin because the LORD had made a breach in the tribes of Israel.

¹⁶Then the elders of the congregation said, "What shall we do for wives for those who are left, since the women are destroyed out of Benjamin?" ¹⁷And they said, "There must be an inheritance for the survivors of Benjamin, that a tribe not be blotted out from Israel. ¹⁸Yet we cannot give them wives from our daughters." For the people of Israel had sworn, "Cursed be he who gives a wife to Benjamin." ¹⁹So they said, "Behold, there is the yearly feast of the LORD at Shiloh, which is north of Bethel, on the east of the highway that goes up from Bethel to Shechem, and south of Lebonah." ²⁰And they commanded the people of Benjamin, saying, "Go and lie in ambush in the vineyards ²¹and watch. If the daughters of Shiloh come out to dance in the dances, then come out of the vineyards and snatch each man his wife from the daughters of Shiloh, and go to the land of Benjamin. ²²And when their fathers or their brothers come to complain to us, we will say to them, 'Grant them graciously to us, because we did not take for each man of them his wife in battle, neither did you give them to

them, else you would now be guilty.'" ²³And the people of Benjamin did so and took their wives, according to their number, from the dancers whom they carried off. Then they went and returned to their inheritance and rebuilt the towns and lived in them. ²⁴And the people of Israel departed from there at that time, every man to his tribe and family, and they went out from there every man to his inheritance.

²⁵In those days there was no king in Israel. Everyone did what was right in his own eyes.

RUTH

The book at a glance. 4 chapters, 85 verses. In terms of storytelling technique, verse for verse, the book of Ruth is perhaps the greatest masterpiece of narrative art in the Bible. It is densely packed, yet the charm of the book is evident even to the most unsophisticated reader. Along with the Song of Solomon, the book of Ruth is the classic *love story of the Bible. Few stories in the Bible are told from a woman's viewpoint, but the story of Ruth is told from that perspective: not only is a woman the protagonist, but the world of the story is in major ways a woman's world, and the writer gives attention to feminine values and feelings. Of course Boaz in his role as kinsman-redeemer cuts a striking figure as a man who is a miniature figure of Christ. The story exalts virtuous womanhood and strong manhood.

▌**Genres.** The overall genre is *story or *narrative, but a host of further subtypes converge in the book of Ruth. The story of Ruth is a love story (see below). It is also an *idyll, which literary handbooks define as a brief story describing a simple, pleasant aspect of rural and domestic life. As that definition suggests, the story of Ruth has affinities with *pastoral (rural) literature, and in this case the idealized rural world provides an idealized setting in which the idealized romance of the book can take root and flourish. The story is also a *hero story built around the life of an exemplary heroine and featuring an idealized male hero as well. (For more information on items accompanied by an asterisk, see the glossary at the back of this Bible.)

Passage	Content	Human Experience Portrayed	Contribution to Ruth's Story
1:1–22	Background to the romance	Family loyalty	Ruth becomes a widow
2:1–23	Meeting and courtship	Hospitality to a stranger	Ruth receives kindness in a new home
3:1–18	Betrothal	The triumph of romantic love	Ruth finds a husband
4:1–22	Marriage	Married union and offspring	Ruth becomes a mother

▌**The conventions of a love story.** When we speak of a love story, we ordinarily mean a story of courtship leading to marriage. The ingredients of a happy love story, whether in real life or in literature, include the following: an eligible and idealized couple who are worthy of each other; background observers (including friends, family members, colleagues, and members of the community); a confidant(e) for each of the lovers; obstacles in love and marriage, including a rival; a matchmaker; certain archetypal events—first meeting, questioning others about the "eligible other," report of the first date to a confidante (more often than not one's mother), meetings and secret rendez-vous, good-bye scenes, the bestowing of favors, betrothal, and a "happily ever after" marriage as the climax. The story of Ruth, despite its brevity, contains all of these.

▌Organization and unity of the story. The *plot of the story of Ruth is a quest in which the stated goal is to find a home for Ruth (1:9; 3:1). The story follows the conventional U-shape of literary *comedy, with events first descending into potential tragedy and then rising to a happy ending as obstacles to fulfillment are gradually overcome. Each chapter of the book of Ruth makes its own contribution to the quest to find the fulfillment of marriage (see chart above). Women's concerns are a unifying element in the story. So is the rural world of the story, which is at one level a harvest celebration (accounting for the fact that this book has traditionally been read in the Jewish liturgical calendar during the Feast of Weeks, a harvest festival). Finally, the story is structured as an intricate web of references to the motif of emptiness versus fullness.

▌The cast of characters. The protagonist of the story is Ruth. Next to her in prominence are two family members who play major roles in her life—her mother-in-law, Naomi, and her eventual husband Boaz. In the next concentric ring are three people—Ruth's sister-in-law Orpah, her deceased first husband, and the unnamed rival whom Boaz outwits en route to marrying Ruth. On the fringe are the townspeople who witness the events and at the end pronounce their blessing on the married couple.

▌Inferred literary intentions. The book is designed to achieve the following literary purposes:

- draw us into the pleasures of a happy love story

- present an idealized heroine and hero for our admiration and emulation

- dazzle us with its storytelling technique

- celebrate the commonplace and assure us that God values it

- affirm domestic values and offer a picture of fulfilled womanhood

- prompt us to think about the theme of redemption on multiple levels

▌Theological themes. (1) Providence: God uses ordinary events and the tragedies of life to accomplish his redemptive purposes in people's lives; further, we infer that God's providential hand is behind all of the actions in the story. (2) Messianic history: not only is Ruth one of the few recorded non-Jews in OT times who was fully assimilated into the Jewish community, but she is actually in the messianic line. (3) Ethics: the generosity of Boaz to the sojourner Ruth is a casebook example of someone who practiced the ethics of covenant living as prescribed in the Mosaic law. (4) Redemption: Ruth's rescue and provision through the actions of a kinsman-redeemer are a human picture of God's redemption of his people.

▌The book of Ruth as a chapter in the master story of the Bible. One of the story lines of the Bible is the story of how God wants his people to live; the account of how

Ruth and Boaz acted contributes to that story line. Further, the very title that the text ascribes to Boaz—the Hebrew word *goel*, meaning "kinsman-redeemer"—signals that Boaz embodies qualities that belong preeminently to the ultimate kinsman-redeemer, Jesus Christ. Finally, the brief genealogy at the end of the book of Ruth identifies the book as a chapter in messianic history by tracing part of the lineage from which Jesus was born, with the grandson of Ruth and Boaz—David—as an early member of the line.

The crucible of suffering: foil to later action [chapter 1]. If we looked just at the story that is told in chapter 1, we would have no way of knowing that it is part of a love story. The chapter is structured as a downward spiral into greater and greater depths of domestic and personal loss, viewed from a woman's perspective. But this chapter is a foil to the eventual story of happy love that will emerge. Here we are introduced to the main characters (except for Boaz), and they form a pattern of contrasts or foils—the loyal and godly Ruth contrasted to her sister-in-law Orpah, and the courageous and youthful Ruth who undertakes a new phase of life versus the defeatism and bitterness of the older and now-barren Naomi. Finally, we can scrutinize the text for a systematic outworking of the contrast between emptiness and fullness (even though the apparent plot reflects emptiness, we can catch subtle hints of a countermovement toward full-ness). The most memorable passage of the opening chapter is Ruth's declaration of loyalty to Naomi, couched in parallel sentences and including a statement of commitment to Naomi's God (vv. 16–17).

1 In the days when the judges ruled there was a famine in the land, and a man of Bethlehem in Judah went to sojourn in the country of Moab, he and his wife and his two sons. ²The name of the man was Elimelech and the name of his wife Naomi, and the names of his two sons were Mahlon and Chilion. They were Ephrathites from Bethlehem in Judah. They went into the country of Moab and remained there. ³But Elimelech, the husband of Naomi, died, and she was left with her two sons. ⁴These took Moabite wives; the name of the one was Orpah and the name of the other Ruth. They lived there about ten years, ⁵and both Mahlon and Chilion died, so that the woman was left without her two sons and her husband.

⁶Then she arose with her daughters-in-law to return from the country of Moab, for she had heard in the fields of Moab that the LORD had visited his people and given them food. ⁷So she set out from the place where she was with her two daughters-in-law, and they went on the way to return to the land of Judah. ⁸But Naomi said to her two daughters-in-law, "Go, return each of you to her mother's house. May the LORD deal kindly with you, as you have dealt with the dead and with me. ⁹The LORD grant that you may find rest, each of you in the house of her husband!" Then she kissed them, and they lifted up their voices and wept. ¹⁰And they said to her, "No, we will return with you to your people." ¹¹But Naomi said, "Turn back, my daughters; why will you go with me? Have I yet sons in my womb that they may become your husbands? ¹²Turn back, my daughters; go your way, for I am too old to have a husband. If I should say I have hope, even if I should have a husband this night and should bear sons, ¹³would you therefore wait till they were grown? Would you therefore refrain from marrying? No, my daughters, for it is exceedingly bitter to me for your sake that

the hand of the Lord has gone out against me." [14]Then they lifted up their voices and wept again. And Orpah kissed her mother-in-law, but Ruth clung to her.

[15]And she said, "See, your sister-in-law has gone back to her people and to her gods; return after your sister-in-law." [16]But Ruth said, "Do not urge me to leave you or to return from following you. For where you go I will go, and where you lodge I will lodge. Your people shall be my people, and your God my God. [17]Where you die I will die, and there will I be buried. May the Lord do so to me and more also if anything but death parts me from you." [18]And when Naomi saw that she was determined to go with her, she said no more.

[19]So the two of them went on until they came to Bethlehem. And when they came to Bethlehem, the whole town was stirred because of them. And the women said, "Is this Naomi?" [20]She said to them, "Do not call me Naomi;[1] call me Mara,[2] for the Almighty has dealt very bitterly with me. [21]I went away full, and the Lord has brought me back empty. Why call me Naomi, when the Lord has testified against me and the Almighty has brought calamity upon me?"

[22]So Naomi returned, and Ruth the Moabite her daughter-in-law with her, who returned from the country of Moab. And they came to Bethlehem at the beginning of barley harvest.

The beginning of a courtship [chapter 2]. The central event of the chapter, the first meeting between Boaz and Ruth, is placed in the middle of the chapter, just as a painter puts the most important thing in the middle of a picture. The progress of the romance that emerges between the couple finds a metaphor in the progress of the grain harvest, whose beginning is noted at the outset (1:22) and whose end is named in the last verse of chapter 2 (v. 23). Fruitful analytic approaches to the chapter include the following: compiling character sketches of Boaz and Ruth, with emphasis on the things that make them idealized; identifying stages in the evolving romance, from first meeting to first love token to Ruth's account of the meeting to Naomi; entering in our imagination into the idealized pastoral (rustic) world the storyteller evokes; relishing the dramatic irony and humor at the end of the chapter, where Ruth and Naomi talk at cross-purposes (Ruth merely rehearses the facts of the day's events, while Naomi at once understands the potential for marriage when she hears that a kinsman is the one who has expressed an interest in Ruth).

2 Now Naomi had a relative of her husband's, a worthy man of the clan of Elimelech, whose name was Boaz. [2]And Ruth the Moabite said to Naomi, "Let me go to the field and glean among the ears of grain after him in whose sight I shall find favor." And she said to her, "Go, my daughter." [3]So she set out and went and gleaned in the field after the reapers, and she happened to come to the part of the field belonging to Boaz, who was of the clan of Elimelech. [4]And behold, Boaz came from Bethlehem. And he said to the reapers, "The Lord be with you!" And they answered, "The Lord bless you." [5]Then Boaz said to his young man who was in charge of the reapers, "Whose young woman is this?" [6]And the servant who was in charge of the reapers answered, "She is the young Moabite woman, who came back with Naomi from the country of Moab. [7]She said, 'Please let me glean and gather among the sheaves after the reapers.' So she came, and she has continued from early morning until now, except for a short rest."[3]

---

[1] Naomi means pleasant [2] Mara means bitter [3] Compare Septuagint, Vulgate; the meaning of the Hebrew phrase is uncertain

[8]Then Boaz said to Ruth, "Now, listen, my daughter, do not go to glean in another field or leave this one, but keep close to my young women. [9]Let your eyes be on the field that they are reaping, and go after them. Have I not charged the young men not to touch you? And when you are thirsty, go to the vessels and drink what the young men have drawn." [10]Then she fell on her face, bowing to the ground, and said to him, "Why have I found favor in your eyes, that you should take notice of me, since I am a foreigner?" [11]But Boaz answered her, "All that you have done for your mother-in-law since the death of your husband has been fully told to me, and how you left your father and mother and your native land and came to a people that you did not know before. [12]The Lord repay you for what you have done, and a full reward be given you by the Lord, the God of Israel, under whose wings you have come to take refuge!" [13]Then she said, "I have found favor in your eyes, my lord, for you have comforted me and spoken kindly to your servant, though I am not one of your servants."

[14]And at mealtime Boaz said to her, "Come here and eat some bread and dip your morsel in the wine." So she sat beside the reapers, and he passed to her roasted grain. And she ate until she was satisfied, and she had some left over. [15]When she rose to glean, Boaz instructed his young men, saying, "Let her glean even among the sheaves, and do not reproach her. [16]And also pull out some from the bundles for her and leave it for her to glean, and do not rebuke her."

[17]So she gleaned in the field until evening. Then she beat out what she had gleaned, and it was about an ephah[1] of barley. [18]And she took it up and went into the city. Her mother-in-law saw what she had gleaned. She also brought out and gave her what food she had left over after being satisfied. [19]And her mother-in-law said to her, "Where did you glean today? And where have you worked? Blessed be the man who took notice of you." So she told her mother-in-law with whom she had worked and said, "The man's name with whom I worked today is Boaz." [20]And Naomi said to her daughter-in-law, "May he be blessed by the Lord, whose kindness has not forsaken the living or the dead!" Naomi also said to her, "The man is a close relative of ours, one of our redeemers." [21]And Ruth the Moabite said, "Besides, he said to me, 'You shall keep close by my young men until they have finished all my harvest.'" [22]And Naomi said to Ruth, her daughter-in-law, "It is good, my daughter, that you go out with his young women, lest in another field you be assaulted." [23]So she kept close to the young women of Boaz, gleaning until the end of the barley and wheat harvests. And she lived with her mother-in-law.

An unusual way to become engaged [chapter 3]. In this chapter, an aggressive and clever woman (Naomi) comes up with a daring maneuver to secure Ruth's betrothal. Ruth dutifully carries out her mother-in-law's plan with stunning success, because Boaz, caught off guard by a midnight encounter with his beloved on the threshing floor, makes a splendid recovery and follows the promptings of his heart. The important motifs of the story as a whole here reach closure: the couple comes to a complete realization of what has been transpiring in their relationship, and the tension between emptiness and fullness is decisively resolved in the direction of fullness (as symbolized particularly in the huge amount of grain with which Boaz sends Ruth home). In regard to the title of kinsman-redeemer that is assigned to Boaz, the facts are as follows: (1) technically Boaz does not fit the criterion of the levirate marriage that stipulated that a man should

[1] An *ephah* was about 3/5 bushel or 22 liters

marry the childless widow of a brother (Deut. 25:5); (2) however, Boaz fulfills the spirit of levirate law because he is a relative (though not a brother) of Ruth's former husband; (3) in fulfilling the spirit of the levirate law, Boaz, paralleling Ruth's devotion to her mother-in-law, wins us with his magnanimous and gratuitous behavior, doing more than he was technically obligated to do.

3 Then Naomi her mother-in-law said to her, "My daughter, should I not seek rest for you, that it may be well with you? ²Is not Boaz our relative, with whose young women you were? See, he is winnowing barley tonight at the threshing floor. ³Wash therefore and anoint yourself, and put on your cloak and go down to the threshing floor, but do not make yourself known to the man until he has finished eating and drinking. ⁴But when he lies down, observe the place where he lies. Then go and uncover his feet and lie down, and he will tell you what to do." ⁵And she replied, "All that you say I will do."

⁶So she went down to the threshing floor and did just as her mother-in-law had commanded her. ⁷And when Boaz had eaten and drunk, and his heart was merry, he went to lie down at the end of the heap of grain. Then she came softly and uncovered his feet and lay down. ⁸At midnight the man was startled and turned over, and behold, a woman lay at his feet! ⁹He said, "Who are you?" And she answered, "I am Ruth, your servant. Spread your wings¹ over your servant, for you are a redeemer." ¹⁰And he said, "May you be blessed by the Lord, my daughter. You have made this last kindness greater than the first in that you have not gone after young men, whether poor or rich. ¹¹And now, my daughter, do not fear. I will do for you all that you ask, for all my fellow townsmen know that you are a worthy woman. ¹²And now it is true that I am a redeemer. Yet there is a redeemer nearer than I. ¹³Remain tonight, and in the morning, if he will redeem you, good; let him do it. But if he is not willing to redeem you, then, as the Lord lives, I will redeem you. Lie down until the morning."

¹⁴So she lay at his feet until the morning, but arose before one could recognize another. And he said, "Let it not be known that the woman came to the threshing floor." ¹⁵And he said, "Bring the garment you are wearing and hold it out." So she held it, and he measured out six measures of barley and put it on her. Then she went into the city. ¹⁶And when she came to her mother-in-law, she said, "How did you fare, my daughter?" Then she told her all that the man had done for her, ¹⁷saying, "These six measures of barley he gave to me, for he said to me, 'You must not go back empty-handed to your mother-in-law.'" ¹⁸She replied, "Wait, my daughter, until you learn how the matter turns out, for the man will not rest but will settle the matter today."

Celebration [chapter 4]. In the earlier betrothal scene, just when we had started to believe that the eligible couple was headed for marriage, the story became a suspense story because of the emergence of a rival who had a firmer claim to marry Ruth than Boaz did (3:12–13). Here in chapter 4, Boaz borrows a page from two aggressive women and in effect becomes his own matchmaker. The very next morning he overwhelms his rival (vv. 1–6) when he aggressively encounters him at the gate of the city, where legal actions were transacted. Boaz catches his rival off guard and stage-manages him throughout the encounter: he addresses him derisively as "friend" or "so and so" (v. 1); he pictures marriage to Ruth as entailing a heavy financial obligation, even though no

¹ Compare 2:12; the word for *wings* can also mean *corners of a garment*

one in Israelite society literally bought a bride (vv. 5–6); he uses a loaded term when he calls Ruth a Moabite (v. 5), and he fails to praise her as "a worthy woman," though he had done so earlier (3:11). With the final obstacle removed, the remainder of the story is devoted wholly to celebration and triumph: Boaz scrupulously adheres to the legal and public protocol for marrying Ruth (vv. 7–12); the storyteller returns to Naomi and pictures her fullness (vv. 13–17); and the genealogical addendum (vv. 18–22) links the offspring of Ruth and Boaz with the glorious patriotic figure of David, and beyond him, with the messianic line.

4 Now Boaz had gone up to the gate and sat down there. And behold, the redeemer, of whom Boaz had spoken, came by. So Boaz said, "Turn aside, friend; sit down here." And he turned aside and sat down. ²And he took ten men of the elders of the city and said, "Sit down here." So they sat down. ³Then he said to the redeemer, "Naomi, who has come back from the country of Moab, is selling the parcel of land that belonged to our relative Elimelech. ⁴So I thought I would tell you of it and say, 'Buy it in the presence of those sitting here and in the presence of the elders of my people.' If you will redeem it, redeem it. But if you[1] will not, tell me, that I may know, for there is no one besides you to redeem it, and I come after you." And he said, "I will redeem it." ⁵Then Boaz said, "The day you buy the field from the hand of Naomi, you also acquire Ruth[2] the Moabite, the widow of the dead, in order to perpetuate the name of the dead in his inheritance." ⁶Then the redeemer said, "I cannot redeem it for myself, lest I impair my own inheritance. Take my right of redemption yourself, for I cannot redeem it."

⁷Now this was the custom in former times in Israel concerning redeeming and exchanging: to confirm a transaction, the one drew off his sandal and gave it to the other, and this was the manner of attesting in Israel. ⁸So when the redeemer said to Boaz, "Buy it for yourself," he drew off his sandal. ⁹Then Boaz said to the elders and all the people, "You are witnesses this day that I have bought from the hand of Naomi all that belonged to Elimelech and all that belonged to Chilion and to Mahlon. ¹⁰Also Ruth the Moabite, the widow of Mahlon, I have bought to be my wife, to perpetuate the name of the dead in his inheritance, that the name of the dead may not be cut off from among his brothers and from the gate of his native place. You are witnesses this day." ¹¹Then all the people who were at the gate and the elders said, "We are witnesses. May the LORD make the woman, who is coming into your house, like Rachel and Leah, who together built up the house of Israel. May you act worthily in Ephrathah and be renowned in Bethlehem, ¹²and may your house be like the house of Perez, whom Tamar bore to Judah, because of the offspring that the LORD will give you by this young woman."

¹³So Boaz took Ruth, and she became his wife. And he went in to her, and the LORD gave her conception, and she bore a son. ¹⁴Then the women said to Naomi, "Blessed be the LORD, who has not left you this day without a redeemer, and may his name be renowned in Israel! ¹⁵He shall be to you a restorer of life and a nourisher of your old age, for your daughter-in-law who loves you, who is more to you than seven sons, has given birth to him." ¹⁶Then Naomi took the child and laid him on her lap and became his nurse. ¹⁷And the women of the neighborhood gave him a name, saying, "A son has

---

[1] Hebrew *he* [2] Masoretic Text *you also buy it from Ruth*

been born to Naomi." They named him Obed. He was the father of Jesse, the father of David.

[18]Now these are the generations of Perez: Perez fathered Hezron, [19]Hezron fathered Ram, Ram fathered Amminadab, [20]Amminadab fathered Nahshon, Nahshon fathered Salmon, [21]Salmon fathered Boaz, Boaz fathered Obed, [22]Obed fathered Jesse, and Jesse fathered David.

I SAMUEL

The book at a glance. 31 chapters, 810 verses. The immediate purpose of 1 Samuel was to record Israelite history from the time when it was a loose confederation of tribes ruled by a system of ad hoc judges to a constituted monarchy. The history recorded in the book does not primarily cover the life and times of ordinary people but the actions and decisions of national leaders. A second purpose of the book is to embody universal human experience as the means of teaching moral and spiritual lessons for all people at all times. Some of the lessons are individual and personal, involving (for example) the specific family situations of Eli, Saul, and David. But others apply to communities and nations, such as the lessons we learn about good and bad leadership for a people as seen in the conduct of Eli, Samuel, and Saul. Presented with such positive and negative examples, we can learn much about our daily lives by reading and pondering the book of 1 Samuel. Because the author is more interested in a few important figures than in groups and movements, we naturally remember the book partly by the characters who remain in our memory, especially Hannah, Eli, Samuel, Saul, Jonathan, and David.

▌**Genres.** The primary genre of 1 Samuel is *hero story. This is a way of saying that the author did not choose the usual method of OT historians in giving coverage to a broad span of people and events but instead focused primarily on three heroic leaders whose stories are elaborated at length—Samuel, Saul, and David. Three other characters are sufficiently prominent in the narrative that their stories are mini–hero stories—Hannah, Eli, and Jonathan. Within the species of hero story, the story of Saul is the only undisputed and fully elaborated literary *tragedy in the Bible. The story of David and Goliath is the prototypical *battle story in the Bible. The phase of David's life when he is the archetypal man on the run fits the narrative pattern of a fugitive story. Hannah's song of gratitude (2:1–10) is a *lyric poem in the specific form of a *praise psalm, and Samuel's last words to the nation (chapter 12) fit the genre of the *farewell discourse. (For more information on items accompanied by an asterisk, see the glossary at the back of this Bible.)

▌**Structure and format.** Labeling the book a collection of hero stories might make the format of the book look simpler than it really is. The first third of the book pits the decline of Eli and his sons against the rise of Samuel, so that we should picture these chapters in the form of an X (Eli's decline occurring simultaneously with Samuel's ascent). The remainder of the book is likewise an extended X in which the decline of Saul is played off against the rise of David. In this phase of the story, the stories of Saul

Passage	Content	History of Leadership	History of Israelite Government	Dominant Character
1:1–3:21	Birth and childhood of Samuel	Transition from Eli to Samuel	End of the era of the judges	Samuel
4:1–22	End of Eli's judgeship			
5:1–7:17	Samuel's judgeship			
8:1–22	The nation demands a king	Transition from Samuel to Saul	Beginning of the monarchy	Saul
9:1–11:15	Saul's appointment, coronation, and early success as king			
12:1–25	Samuel's farewell speech			
13:1–14:52	Saul's early reign	Saul's failure as a leader	A disillusioning start for the monarchy	
15:1–35	Saul's tragic choice			
16:1–23	David anointed king	Hope for a better leader is nurtured	The nation languishes while the future king bides his time	David
17:1–58	David and Goliath			
18:1–20:42	David endures Saul's hatred			
21:1–30:31	David's life as a fugitive			
31:1–13	Saul's tragic death	Saul's failure as leader highlighted	End of Saul's kingship	Saul

and David are intertwined, as we are kept up to date on the tragic decline of Saul and the life of the future king as a fugitive.

▌ **Tips for reading 1 Samuel.** This is a book of personalities, so paying close attention to characterization will pay big dividends. Similarly, the book is rich in universal, recognizable human experience, so that building bridges between the world of the text and our own experiences is an inviting approach to the book. Even though this book does not cover the vast spans of Israelite history that the other OT historical chronicles cover, it provides in-depth analyses of what makes for good and bad leadership. What is true for leaders, moreover, is true for all individuals in their choices for or against God.

▌ **Inferred literary intentions.** The book is designed to achieve the following literary purposes:

- exalt God as the great standard of goodness and sovereignty who transcends the struggles of the human race to manage its affairs

- enable readers to get to know a gallery of memorable characters

- draw us into gripping action, with all the attendant pleasures of literary narrative

- dazzle us with the writer's skill at character portrayal

■ lead us to ponder what constitutes success and failure in leaders and in every person's life

■ **Theological themes.** (1) Divine providence: despite all the emphasis on human endeavor, the book also shows that God is the sovereign deity who oversees human and national destiny. (2) Sin: the book shows us (especially in the figures of Eli and Saul) how people can destroy themselves and their families through sin. (3) Obedience to God: by way of positive and negative example, the book paints a picture of obedience to God as God's intended pattern for human life. (4) Kingship: the book gives us variations on the themes of divinely designated earthly kings and God as the only perfect King.

■ **1 Samuel as a chapter in the master story of the Bible.** The overall story of the Bible is how God worked out a plan to save the human race from sin and death. In the OT, this plan was nearly identical with the national history of God's chosen nation of Israel. First Samuel recounts the history of Israel at a very crucial stage of its existence. The crucial development in the nation was its unwillingness to have God as its only king. As we observe this phase of Israelite history, we are led to ponder what kind of rule we need and to conclude that only the eventual Son of David, Christ, is sufficient.

The birth of Samuel [1:1–2:11]. The protagonist of the opening unit of 1 Samuel is the heroine Hannah. Her antagonists are two insensitive men—her husband, Elkanah, and the priest Eli. The dominant action is the distress and triumph of Hannah. The story is a classic problem-solution story, with Hannah's barrenness the problem and the birth of Samuel through God's blessing its solution. In her triumph, Hannah is a model of godliness, especially in her gratitude to God for the gift of a son. Her song (2:1–10) is a praise psalm built around the motif of God's raising up the underdog and putting down the exalted. The psalm functions as an interpretive lens for the story that is narrated in chapter 1, inasmuch as both units assert God's intervening action on behalf of the oppressed and his disfavor toward authority figures who ignore the needs of people of humble status.

1 There was a certain man of Ramathaim-zophim of the hill country of Ephraim whose name was Elkanah the son of Jeroham, son of Elihu, son of Tohu, son of Zuph, an Ephrathite. ²He had two wives. The name of the one was Hannah, and the name of the other, Peninnah. And Peninnah had children, but Hannah had no children.

³Now this man used to go up year by year from his city to worship and to sacrifice to the LORD of hosts at Shiloh, where the two sons of Eli, Hophni and Phinehas, were priests of the LORD. ⁴On the day when Elkanah sacrificed, he would give portions to Peninnah his wife and to all her sons and daughters. ⁵But to Hannah he gave a double portion, because he loved her, though the LORD had closed her womb.¹ ⁶And her rival used to provoke her grievously to irritate her, because the LORD had closed her womb. ⁷So it went on year by year. As often as she went up to the house of the LORD, she used to provoke her. Therefore Hannah wept and would not eat. ⁸And Elkanah,

¹ Syriac; the meaning of the Hebrew is uncertain. Septuagint *And, although he loved Hannah, he would give Hannah only one portion, because the LORD had closed her womb*

her husband, said to her, "Hannah, why do you weep? And why do you not eat? And why is your heart sad? Am I not more to you than ten sons?"

[9]After they had eaten and drunk in Shiloh, Hannah rose. Now Eli the priest was sitting on the seat beside the doorpost of the temple of the LORD. [10]She was deeply distressed and prayed to the LORD and wept bitterly. [11]And she vowed a vow and said, "O LORD of hosts, if you will indeed look on the affliction of your servant and remember me and not forget your servant, but will give to your servant a son, then I will give him to the LORD all the days of his life, and no razor shall touch his head."

[12]As she continued praying before the LORD, Eli observed her mouth. [13]Hannah was speaking in her heart; only her lips moved, and her voice was not heard. Therefore Eli took her to be a drunken woman. [14]And Eli said to her, "How long will you go on being drunk? Put your wine away from you." [15]But Hannah answered, "No, my lord, I am a woman troubled in spirit. I have drunk neither wine nor strong drink, but I have been pouring out my soul before the LORD. [16]Do not regard your servant as a worthless woman, for all along I have been speaking out of my great anxiety and vexation." [17]Then Eli answered, "Go in peace, and the God of Israel grant your petition that you have made to him." [18]And she said, "Let your servant find favor in your eyes." Then the woman went her way and ate, and her face was no longer sad.

[19]They rose early in the morning and worshiped before the LORD; then they went back to their house at Ramah. And Elkanah knew Hannah his wife, and the LORD remembered her. [20]And in due time Hannah conceived and bore a son, and she called his name Samuel, for she said, "I have asked for him from the LORD."[1]

[21]The man Elkanah and all his house went up to offer to the LORD the yearly sacrifice and to pay his vow. [22]But Hannah did not go up, for she said to her husband, "As soon as the child is weaned, I will bring him, so that he may appear in the presence of the LORD and dwell there forever." [23]Elkanah her husband said to her, "Do what seems best to you; wait until you have weaned him; only, may the LORD establish his word." So the woman remained and nursed her son until she weaned him. [24]And when she had weaned him, she took him up with her, along with a three-year-old bull,[2] an ephah[3] of flour, and a skin of wine, and she brought him to the house of the LORD at Shiloh. And the child was young. [25]Then they slaughtered the bull, and they brought the child to Eli. [26]And she said, "Oh, my lord! As you live, my lord, I am the woman who was standing here in your presence, praying to the LORD. [27]For this child I prayed, and the LORD has granted me my petition that I made to him. [28]Therefore I have lent him to the LORD. As long as he lives, he is lent to the LORD."

And he worshiped the LORD there.

2 And Hannah prayed and said,

"My heart exults in the LORD;
    my strength[4] is exalted in the LORD.
My mouth derides my enemies,
    because I rejoice in your salvation.

[2] "There is none holy like the LORD;
    there is none besides you;
    there is no rock like our God.

---

[1] *Samuel* sounds like the Hebrew for *heard of God* [2] Septuagint, Syriac; Hebrew *three bulls* [3] An *ephah* was about 3/5 bushel or 22 liters [4] Hebrew *horn*

³ Talk no more so very proudly,
      let not arrogance come from your mouth;
   for the Lord is a God of knowledge,
      and by him actions are weighed.
⁴ The bows of the mighty are broken,
      but the feeble bind on strength.
⁵ Those who were full have hired themselves out for bread,
      but those who were hungry have ceased to hunger.
   The barren has borne seven,
      but she who has many children is forlorn.
⁶ The Lord kills and brings to life;
      he brings down to Sheol and raises up.
⁷ The Lord makes poor and makes rich;
      he brings low and he exalts.
⁸ He raises up the poor from the dust;
      he lifts the needy from the ash heap
   to make them sit with princes
      and inherit a seat of honor.
   For the pillars of the earth are the Lord's,
      and on them he has set the world.

⁹ "He will guard the feet of his faithful ones,
      but the wicked shall be cut off in darkness,
   for not by might shall a man prevail.
¹⁰ The adversaries of the Lord shall be broken to pieces;
      against them he will thunder in heaven.
   The Lord will judge the ends of the earth;
      he will give strength to his king
      and exalt the power[1] of his anointed."

¹¹Then Elkanah went home to Ramah. And the boy ministered to the Lord in the presence of Eli the priest.

The failure of Eli's family [2:12–36]. The book of 1 Samuel is structured as a series of risings and fallings. Hannah's story is shaped like a U: first we follow her downward spiral into greater and greater despair, then we ascend with her in her triumph as a mother. With that success story as a foil, the next unit fills us in on the corruption that has engulfed the family of Eli the priest. The story of scandal unfolds in three phases in this chapter: first we are told about the selfish behavior of Eil's two sons in regard to the sacrificial offerings brought by the laity (vv. 12–17); then we read about Eli's futile rebuke to his sons (vv. 22–25); finally we overhear a detailed *oracle of judgment that an unnamed "man of God" delivers to Eli, predicting that his metaphoric "house" will cease to be a priestly family in Israel (vv. 27–36). Inserted right into the middle of this material are two brief passages that idealize the youthful Samuel—one passage describing the "little robe" that Samuel's mother would annually bring to him in his place of service (vv. 18–21) and another simply telling us that, in contrast to the downward spiral of Eli's family, the young Samuel "continued to grow" in all possible ways (v. 26).

---

¹ Hebrew *horn*

¹²Now the sons of Eli were worthless men. They did not know the LORD. ¹³The custom of the priests with the people was that when any man offered sacrifice, the priest's servant¹ would come, while the meat was boiling, with a three-pronged fork in his hand, ¹⁴and he would thrust it into the pan or kettle or cauldron or pot. All that the fork brought up the priest would take for himself. This is what they did at Shiloh to all the Israelites who came there. ¹⁵Moreover, before the fat was burned, the priest's servant would come and say to the man who was sacrificing, "Give meat for the priest to roast, for he will not accept boiled meat from you but only raw." ¹⁶And if the man said to him, "Let them burn the fat first, and then take as much as you wish," he would say, "No, you must give it now, and if not, I will take it by force." ¹⁷Thus the sin of the young men was very great in the sight of the LORD, for the men treated the offering of the LORD with contempt.

¹⁸Samuel was ministering before the LORD, a boy clothed with a linen ephod. ¹⁹And his mother used to make for him a little robe and take it to him each year when she went up with her husband to offer the yearly sacrifice. ²⁰Then Eli would bless Elkanah and his wife, and say, "May the LORD give you children by this woman for the petition she asked of the LORD." So then they would return to their home. ²¹Indeed the LORD visited Hannah, and she conceived and bore three sons and two daughters. And the young man Samuel grew in the presence of the LORD.

²²Now Eli was very old, and he kept hearing all that his sons were doing to all Israel, and how they lay with the women who were serving at the entrance to the tent of meeting. ²³And he said to them, "Why do you do such things? For I hear of your evil dealings from all the people. ²⁴No, my sons; it is no good report that I hear the people of the LORD spreading abroad. ²⁵If someone sins against a man, God will mediate for him, but if someone sins against the LORD, who can intercede for him?" But they would not listen to the voice of their father, for it was the will of the LORD to put them to death.

²⁶Now the young man Samuel continued to grow both in stature and in favor with the LORD and also with man.

²⁷And there came a man of God to Eli and said to him, "Thus the LORD has said, 'Did I indeed reveal myself to the house of your father when they were in Egypt subject to the house of Pharaoh? ²⁸Did I choose him out of all the tribes of Israel to be my priest, to go up to my altar, to burn incense, to wear an ephod before me? I gave to the house of your father all my offerings by fire from the people of Israel. ²⁹Why then do you scorn² my sacrifices and my offerings that I commanded, and honor your sons above me by fattening yourselves on the choicest parts of every offering of my people Israel?' ³⁰Therefore the LORD, the God of Israel, declares: 'I promised that your house and the house of your father should go in and out before me forever,' but now the LORD declares: 'Far be it from me, for those who honor me I will honor, and those who despise me shall be lightly esteemed. ³¹Behold, the days are coming when I will cut off your strength and the strength of your father's house, so that there will not be an old man in your house. ³²Then in distress you will look with envious eye on all the prosperity that shall be bestowed on Israel, and there shall not be an old man in your house forever. ³³The only one of you whom I shall not cut off from my altar shall be spared to weep his³ eyes out to grieve his heart, and all the descendants⁴ of your house shall die by the sword of men.⁵ ³⁴And this that shall come upon your two sons,

---

¹ Hebrew *young man*; also verse 15 ² Septuagint; Hebrew *kick at* ³ Septuagint; Hebrew *your*; twice in this verse ⁴ Hebrew *increase* ⁵ Septuagint; Hebrew *die as men*

Hophni and Phinehas, shall be the sign to you: both of them shall die on the same day. ³⁵And I will raise up for myself a faithful priest, who shall do according to what is in my heart and in my mind. And I will build him a sure house, and he shall go in and out before my anointed forever. ³⁶And everyone who is left in your house shall come to implore him for a piece of silver or a loaf of bread and shall say, "Please put me in one of the priests' places, that I may eat a morsel of bread."'"

Samuel utters God's oracle of doom to Eli [chapter 3]. This story is a favorite with children, and analyzing why this is so is a good approach to the first half of the story. The story features a boy hero who undergoes experiences with which any child resonates—sleeping peacefully in the hallowed "temple of the LORD," being awakened by an unknown voice, tiptoeing through the dim light to the authority figure in his life, and being told to return to his bed. The suspense grows in intensity as the pattern is repeated. The overall pattern is well known in storytelling both within the Bible and beyond it; it is known as the three-plus-one pattern, meaning that a common set of events happens three times in an identical manner, and then a fourth time with a crucial change introduced. After Samuel receives the message from God the fourth time, he lies alone with the fearful message until daybreak, when Eli coaxes the message out of him. The concluding note recording Samuel's growing stature with God and society (vv. 19–21) alerts us that we are reading a transition story in which the leadership of the nation is passing from Eli to Samuel.

3 Now the young man Samuel was ministering to the LORD under Eli. And the word of the LORD was rare in those days; there was no frequent vision. ²At that time Eli, whose eyesight had begun to grow dim so that he could not see, was lying down in his own place. ³The lamp of God had not yet gone out, and Samuel was lying down in the temple of the LORD, where the ark of God was.

⁴Then the LORD called Samuel, and he said, "Here I am!" ⁵and ran to Eli and said, "Here I am, for you called me." But he said, "I did not call; lie down again." So he went and lay down.

⁶And the LORD called again, "Samuel!" and Samuel arose and went to Eli and said, "Here I am, for you called me." But he said, "I did not call, my son; lie down again." ⁷Now Samuel did not yet know the LORD, and the word of the LORD had not yet been revealed to him.

⁸And the LORD called Samuel again the third time. And he arose and went to Eli and said, "Here I am, for you called me." Then Eli perceived that the LORD was calling the young man. ⁹Therefore Eli said to Samuel, "Go, lie down, and if he calls you, you shall say, 'Speak, LORD, for your servant hears.'" So Samuel went and lay down in his place.

¹⁰And the LORD came and stood, calling as at other times, "Samuel! Samuel!" And Samuel said, "Speak, for your servant hears." ¹¹Then the LORD said to Samuel, "Behold, I am about to do a thing in Israel at which the two ears of everyone who hears it will tingle. ¹²On that day I will fulfill against Eli all that I have spoken concerning his house, from beginning to end. ¹³And I declare to him that I am about to punish his house forever, for the iniquity that he knew, because his sons were blaspheming God,¹ and he did not restrain them. ¹⁴Therefore I swear to the house of Eli that the iniquity of Eli's house shall not be atoned for by sacrifice or offering forever."

¹⁵Samuel lay until morning; then he opened the doors of the house of the LORD.

¹ Or blaspheming for themselves

And Samuel was afraid to tell the vision to Eli. ¹⁶But Eli called Samuel and said, "Samuel, my son." And he said, "Here I am." ¹⁷And Eli said, "What was it that he told you? Do not hide it from me. May God do so to you and more also if you hide anything from me of all that he told you." ¹⁸So Samuel told him everything and hid nothing from him. And he said, "It is the LORD. Let him do what seems good to him."

¹⁹And Samuel grew, and the LORD was with him and let none of his words fall to the ground. ²⁰And all Israel from Dan to Beersheba knew that Samuel was established as a prophet of the LORD. ²¹And the LORD appeared again at Shiloh, for the LORD revealed himself to Samuel at Shiloh by the word of the LORD.

> **Leadership taken from Eli** [chapter 4]. Following three chapters of literary narrative, the conventions of the historical chronicle dominate chapter 4. If we remember that the book of 1 Samuel tells the story of a nation at a time of crucial transitions, it is clear that the function of this chapter is to draw closure to the priestly career of Eli and his two sons. Eli had simply appeared as a commanding figure on the national stage in the opening chapter of the book, as though we already knew who he was. He was already an old man then, and he reaches his foredoomed end in this chapter, which unfolds as follows: defeat of the Israelite army by the Philistines and loss of the ark of the covenant in battle (vv. 1–11); the bearing of the tidings to Eli, who dies from a fall resulting from shock at the news (vv. 12–18); the birth to Eli's daughter-in-law of Ichabod, whose symbolic name "the glory is departed" summarizes the nation's poor spiritual health (vv. 19–22).

4 And the word of Samuel came to all Israel.

Now Israel went out to battle against the Philistines. They encamped at Ebenezer, and the Philistines encamped at Aphek. ²The Philistines drew up in line against Israel, and when the battle spread, Israel was defeated by the Philistines, who killed about four thousand men on the field of battle. ³And when the troops came to the camp, the elders of Israel said, "Why has the LORD defeated us today before the Philistines? Let us bring the ark of the covenant of the LORD here from Shiloh, that it may come among us and save us from the power of our enemies." ⁴So the people sent to Shiloh and brought from there the ark of the covenant of the LORD of hosts, who is enthroned on the cherubim. And the two sons of Eli, Hophni and Phinehas, were there with the ark of the covenant of God.

⁵As soon as the ark of the covenant of the LORD came into the camp, all Israel gave a mighty shout, so that the earth resounded. ⁶And when the Philistines heard the noise of the shouting, they said, "What does this great shouting in the camp of the Hebrews mean?" And when they learned that the ark of the LORD had come to the camp, ⁷the Philistines were afraid, for they said, "A god has come into the camp." And they said, "Woe to us! For nothing like this has happened before. ⁸Woe to us! Who can deliver us from the power of these mighty gods? These are the gods who struck the Egyptians with every sort of plague in the wilderness. ⁹Take courage, and be men, O Philistines, lest you become slaves to the Hebrews as they have been to you; be men and fight."

¹⁰So the Philistines fought, and Israel was defeated, and they fled, every man to his home. And there was a very great slaughter, for there fell of Israel thirty thousand

foot soldiers. [11] And the ark of God was captured, and the two sons of Eli, Hophni and Phinehas, died.

[12] A man of Benjamin ran from the battle line and came to Shiloh the same day, with his clothes torn and with dirt on his head. [13] When he arrived, Eli was sitting on his seat by the road watching, for his heart trembled for the ark of God. And when the man came into the city and told the news, all the city cried out. [14] When Eli heard the sound of the outcry, he said, "What is this uproar?" Then the man hurried and came and told Eli. [15] Now Eli was ninety-eight years old and his eyes were set so that he could not see. [16] And the man said to Eli, "I am he who has come from the battle; I fled from the battle today." And he said, "How did it go, my son?" [17] He who brought the news answered and said, "Israel has fled before the Philistines, and there has also been a great defeat among the people. Your two sons also, Hophni and Phinehas, are dead, and the ark of God has been captured." [18] As soon as he mentioned the ark of God, Eli fell over backward from his seat by the side of the gate, and his neck was broken and he died, for the man was old and heavy. He had judged Israel forty years.

[19] Now his daughter-in-law, the wife of Phinehas, was pregnant, about to give birth. And when she heard the news that the ark of God was captured, and that her father-in-law and her husband were dead, she bowed and gave birth, for her pains came upon her. [20] And about the time of her death the women attending her said to her, "Do not be afraid, for you have borne a son." But she did not answer or pay attention. [21] And she named the child Ichabod, saying, "The glory has departed[1] from Israel!" because the ark of God had been captured and because of her father-in-law and her husband. [22] And she said, "The glory has departed from Israel, for the ark of God has been captured."

Twenty very bad years [5:1–7:2]. This unit is devoted entirely to the exile of the ark of the covenant from its appointed place in Shiloh. Human leadership drops out of sight, and it is as though the ark of the covenant becomes the lost leader of Israel. The details of the successive events are told with leisurely fullness, according to the following sequence: the *satiric story of Dagon's falling down before the ark in the temple of Dagon (5:1–5); God's affliction of the Philistines with tumors, and the "summit" that the leaders call to determine what to do about the health crisis caused by the illicit possession of the ark of the covenant (5:6–12); the strange, elaborate rituals that the Philistines develop in the process of returning the ark to Israel (6:1–18); awe-inspiring events as the ark makes a partial return to its appointed place (6:19–7:2). The importance of the ark signifies the importance of the presence of God and the nature of his covenant relationship to Israel. The whole series of episodes involving the ark's exile and return shows that God is not to be trifled with and that his presence is dangerous. The story becomes a suspense story as we wonder if God's glory will ever return to Israel.

5 When the Philistines captured the ark of God, they brought it from Ebenezer to Ashdod. [2] Then the Philistines took the ark of God and brought it into the house of Dagon and set it up beside Dagon. [3] And when the people of Ashdod rose early the next day, behold, Dagon had fallen face downward on the ground before the ark of the LORD. So they took Dagon and put him back in his place. [4] But when they rose early on the next morning, behold, Dagon had fallen face downward on the ground before the ark of the LORD, and the head of Dagon and both his hands were lying cut

[1] Or *gone into exile*; also verse 22

off on the threshold. Only the trunk of Dagon was left to him. ⁵This is why the priests of Dagon and all who enter the house of Dagon do not tread on the threshold of Dagon in Ashdod to this day.

⁶The hand of the LORD was heavy against the people of Ashdod, and he terrified and afflicted them with tumors, both Ashdod and its territory. ⁷And when the men of Ashdod saw how things were, they said, "The ark of the God of Israel must not remain with us, for his hand is hard against us and against Dagon our god." ⁸So they sent and gathered together all the lords of the Philistines and said, "What shall we do with the ark of the God of Israel?" They answered, "Let the ark of the God of Israel be brought around to Gath." So they brought the ark of the God of Israel there. ⁹But after they had brought it around, the hand of the LORD was against the city, causing a very great panic, and he afflicted the men of the city, both young and old, so that tumors broke out on them. ¹⁰So they sent the ark of God to Ekron. But as soon as the ark of God came to Ekron, the people of Ekron cried out, "They have brought around to us the ark of the God of Israel to kill us and our people." ¹¹They sent therefore and gathered together all the lords of the Philistines and said, "Send away the ark of the God of Israel, and let it return to its own place, that it may not kill us and our people." For there was a deathly panic throughout the whole city. The hand of God was very heavy there. ¹²The men who did not die were struck with tumors, and the cry of the city went up to heaven.

6 The ark of the LORD was in the country of the Philistines seven months. ²And the Philistines called for the priests and the diviners and said, "What shall we do with the ark of the LORD? Tell us with what we shall send it to its place." ³They said, "If you send away the ark of the God of Israel, do not send it empty, but by all means return him a guilt offering. Then you will be healed, and it will be known to you why his hand does not turn away from you." ⁴And they said, "What is the guilt offering that we shall return to him?" They answered, "Five golden tumors and five golden mice, according to the number of the lords of the Philistines, for the same plague was on all of you and on your lords. ⁵So you must make images of your tumors and images of your mice that ravage the land, and give glory to the God of Israel. Perhaps he will lighten his hand from off you and your gods and your land. ⁶Why should you harden your hearts as the Egyptians and Pharaoh hardened their hearts? After he had dealt severely with them, did they not send the people away, and they departed? ⁷Now then, take and prepare a new cart and two milk cows on which there has never come a yoke, and yoke the cows to the cart, but take their calves home, away from them. ⁸And take the ark of the LORD and place it on the cart and put in a box at its side the figures of gold, which you are returning to him as a guilt offering. Then send it off and let it go its way ⁹and watch. If it goes up on the way to its own land, to Beth-shemesh, then it is he who has done us this great harm, but if not, then we shall know that it is not his hand that struck us; it happened to us by coincidence."

¹⁰The men did so, and took two milk cows and yoked them to the cart and shut up their calves at home. ¹¹And they put the ark of the LORD on the cart and the box with the golden mice and the images of their tumors. ¹²And the cows went straight in the direction of Beth-shemesh along one highway, lowing as they went. They turned neither to the right nor to the left, and the lords of the Philistines went after them as far as the border of Beth-shemesh. ¹³Now the people of Beth-shemesh were reaping their

wheat harvest in the valley. And when they lifted up their eyes and saw the ark, they rejoiced to see it. ¹⁴The cart came into the field of Joshua of Beth-shemesh and stopped there. A great stone was there. And they split up the wood of the cart and offered the cows as a burnt offering to the LORD. ¹⁵And the Levites took down the ark of the LORD and the box that was beside it, in which were the golden figures, and set them upon the great stone. And the men of Beth-shemesh offered burnt offerings and sacrificed sacrifices on that day to the LORD. ¹⁶And when the five lords of the Philistines saw it, they returned that day to Ekron.

¹⁷These are the golden tumors that the Philistines returned as a guilt offering to the LORD: one for Ashdod, one for Gaza, one for Ashkelon, one for Gath, one for Ekron, ¹⁸and the golden mice, according to the number of all the cities of the Philistines belonging to the five lords, both fortified cities and unwalled villages. The great stone beside which they set down the ark of the LORD is a witness to this day in the field of Joshua of Beth-shemesh.

¹⁹And he struck some of the men of Beth-shemesh, because they looked upon the ark of the LORD. He struck seventy men of them,¹ and the people mourned because the LORD had struck the people with a great blow. ²⁰Then the men of Beth-shemesh said, "Who is able to stand before the LORD, this holy God? And to whom shall he go up away from us?" ²¹So they sent messengers to the inhabitants of Kiriath-jearim, saying, "The Philistines have returned the ark of the LORD. Come down and take it up to you."

7 And the men of Kiriath-jearim came and took up the ark of the LORD and brought it to the house of Abinadab on the hill. And they consecrated his son Eleazar to have charge of the ark of the LORD. ²From the day that the ark was lodged at Kiriath-jearim, a long time passed, some twenty years, and all the house of Israel lamented after the LORD.

Samuel's judgeship [7:3–17]. Following the full literary embellishment of the preceding unit, the author now gives us a brief historical note on Samuel's career as the last judge of Israel. The sequence unfolds as follows: Samuel summons the nation to abandon its idolatry (vv. 3–4); Samuel intercedes for the nation as God delivers it from an attack by the Philistines (vv. 5–14); summary account of Samuel's judgeship (vv. 15–17). The heroic figure of Samuel is known to us chiefly through his life as a prophet. This unit gives us a picture of him as judge, and we need to remember that the judges of Israel did not primarily judge as we understand that role today. They were heroic deliverers, as Samuel is in this episode.

³And Samuel said to all the house of Israel, "If you are returning to the LORD with all your heart, then put away the foreign gods and the Ashtaroth from among you and direct your heart to the LORD and serve him only, and he will deliver you out of the hand of the Philistines." ⁴So the people of Israel put away the Baals and the Ashtaroth, and they served the LORD only.

⁵Then Samuel said, "Gather all Israel at Mizpah, and I will pray to the LORD for you." ⁶So they gathered at Mizpah and drew water and poured it out before the LORD and fasted on that day and said there, "We have sinned against the LORD." And Samuel judged the people of Israel at Mizpah. ⁷Now when the Philistines heard that

¹ Hebrew of the people seventy men, fifty thousand men

the people of Israel had gathered at Mizpah, the lords of the Philistines went up against Israel. And when the people of Israel heard of it, they were afraid of the Philistines. [8]And the people of Israel said to Samuel, "Do not cease to cry out to the LORD our God for us, that he may save us from the hand of the Philistines." [9]So Samuel took a nursing lamb and offered it as a whole burnt offering to the LORD. And Samuel cried out to the LORD for Israel, and the LORD answered him. [10]As Samuel was offering up the burnt offering, the Philistines drew near to attack Israel. But the LORD thundered with a mighty sound that day against the Philistines and threw them into confusion, and they were routed before Israel. [11]And the men of Israel went out from Mizpah and pursued the Philistines and struck them, as far as below Beth-car.

[12]Then Samuel took a stone and set it up between Mizpah and Shen[1] and called its name Ebenezer;[2] for he said, "Till now the LORD has helped us." [13]So the Philistines were subdued and did not again enter the territory of Israel. And the hand of the LORD was against the Philistines all the days of Samuel. [14]The cities that the Philistines had taken from Israel were restored to Israel, from Ekron to Gath, and Israel delivered their territory from the hand of the Philistines. There was peace also between Israel and the Amorites.

[15]Samuel judged Israel all the days of his life. [16]And he went on a circuit year by year to Bethel, Gilgal, and Mizpah. And he judged Israel in all these places. [17]Then he would return to Ramah, for his home was there, and there also he judged Israel. And he built there an altar to the LORD.

Israel demands a king [chapter 8]. The main subject of this chapter is monarchy, and we sense at once that we have entered a new phase of the history of Israel. Initially the nation had been led by two heroic leaders (Moses and Joshua) whom God directly appointed to lead the nation. That was followed by an ad hoc arrangement in which God raised up deliverers for very limited durations of time, without an institutionalized pattern of succession. As we now pass to the era of monarchy, national leadership has become institutionalized. Chapter 8 serves as a foreshadowing of future action in the book of 1 Samuel, and three motifs dominate: in verses 1–6, the people's desire for a king is ill-founded, a fact highlighted by their wish to be "like all the nations" (v. 20); God disapproves of the desire for a king because his own kingship should have been sufficient (vv. 7–9); human kingship is inherently flawed and doomed to fail in a fallen world (vv. 10–22). The ensuing story of Saul shows all of these predictions coming true.

8 When Samuel became old, he made his sons judges over Israel. [2]The name of his firstborn son was Joel, and the name of his second, Abijah; they were judges in Beersheba. [3]Yet his sons did not walk in his ways but turned aside after gain. They took bribes and perverted justice.

[4]Then all the elders of Israel gathered together and came to Samuel at Ramah [5]and said to him, "Behold, you are old and your sons do not walk in your ways. Now appoint for us a king to judge us like all the nations." [6]But the thing displeased Samuel when they said, "Give us a king to judge us." And Samuel prayed to the LORD. [7]And the LORD said to Samuel, "Obey the voice of the people in all that they say to you, for they have not rejected you, but they have rejected me from being king over them. [8]According to all the deeds that they have done, from the day I brought them up out of Egypt even to this day, forsaking me and serving other gods, so they are also

---

[1] Hebrew; Septuagint, Syriac *Jeshanah* [2] *Ebenezer* means *stone of help*

doing to you. ⁹Now then, obey their voice; only you shall solemnly warn them and show them the ways of the king who shall reign over them."

¹⁰So Samuel told all the words of the LORD to the people who were asking for a king from him. ¹¹He said, "These will be the ways of the king who will reign over you: he will take your sons and appoint them to his chariots and to be his horsemen and to run before his chariots. ¹²And he will appoint for himself commanders of thousands and commanders of fifties, and some to plow his ground and to reap his harvest, and to make his implements of war and the equipment of his chariots. ¹³He will take your daughters to be perfumers and cooks and bakers. ¹⁴He will take the best of your fields and vineyards and olive orchards and give them to his servants. ¹⁵He will take the tenth of your grain and of your vineyards and give it to his officers and to his servants. ¹⁶He will take your male servants and female servants and the best of your young men¹ and your donkeys, and put them to his work. ¹⁷He will take the tenth of your flocks, and you shall be his slaves. ¹⁸And in that day you will cry out because of your king, whom you have chosen for yourselves, but the LORD will not answer you in that day."

¹⁹But the people refused to obey the voice of Samuel. And they said, "No! But there shall be a king over us, ²⁰that we also may be like all the nations, and that our king may judge us and go out before us and fight our battles." ²¹And when Samuel had heard all the words of the people, he repeated them in the ears of the LORD. ²²And the LORD said to Samuel, "Obey their voice and make them a king." Samuel then said to the men of Israel, "Go every man to his city."

Saul anointed as king [9:1–10:16]. The story of Saul as told in 1 Samuel is the most extended and indisputable example of literary tragedy in the Bible. The first phase of a literary tragedy gives a glimpse of the exalted position from which the tragic hero eventually falls, and also the opening dilemma that faces the hero as he is drawn in two directions preceding his tragic choice. Three whole chapters idealize Saul, extending the opening phase far beyond conventional tragedy. The effect is to dispel any possible notion that Saul's tragedy is attributable to anything in the external situation in which he finds himself. In fact, a good way to organize our experience of chapters 9–10 is to move through them looking for the things that qualify Saul as being "most likely to succeed." The list includes the following: physical impressiveness (9:2); humility (9:21; 10:16, 22–23; see also 11:12–13); anointing by Samuel and God (10:1); a confirming sign of God's favor (the finding of the donkeys and related incidents) (10:1–5, 14–16); spiritual endowment by God (10:6–7, 9; see also 11:6); selection by lot (10:21); good advisers (10:26); decisive military leadership (see 11:1–11).

9 There was a man of Benjamin whose name was Kish, the son of Abiel, son of Zeror, son of Becorath, son of Aphiah, a Benjaminite, a man of wealth. ²And he had a son whose name was Saul, a handsome young man. There was not a man among the people of Israel more handsome than he. From his shoulders upward he was taller than any of the people.

³Now the donkeys of Kish, Saul's father, were lost. So Kish said to Saul his son, "Take one of the young men with you, and arise, go and look for the donkeys." ⁴And he passed through the hill country of Ephraim and passed through the land of Shalishah, but they did not find them. And they passed through the land of Shaalim,

¹ Septuagint *cattle*

but they were not there. Then they passed through the land of Benjamin, but did not find them.

⁵When they came to the land of Zuph, Saul said to his servant¹ who was with him, "Come, let us go back, lest my father cease to care about the donkeys and become anxious about us." ⁶But he said to him, "Behold, there is a man of God in this city, and he is a man who is held in honor; all that he says comes true. So now let us go there. Perhaps he can tell us the way we should go." ⁷Then Saul said to his servant, "But if we go, what can we bring the man? For the bread in our sacks is gone, and there is no present to bring to the man of God. What do we have?" ⁸The servant answered Saul again, "Here, I have with me a quarter of a shekel² of silver, and I will give it to the man of God to tell us our way." ⁹(Formerly in Israel, when a man went to inquire of God, he said, "Come, let us go to the seer," for today's "prophet" was formerly called a seer.) ¹⁰And Saul said to his servant, "Well said; come, let us go." So they went to the city where the man of God was.

¹¹As they went up the hill to the city, they met young women coming out to draw water and said to them, "Is the seer here?" ¹²They answered, "He is; behold, he is just ahead of you. Hurry. He has come just now to the city, because the people have a sacrifice today on the high place. ¹³As soon as you enter the city you will find him, before he goes up to the high place to eat. For the people will not eat till he comes, since he must bless the sacrifice; afterward those who are invited will eat. Now go up, for you will meet him immediately." ¹⁴So they went up to the city. As they were entering the city, they saw Samuel coming out toward them on his way up to the high place.

¹⁵Now the day before Saul came, the LORD had revealed to Samuel: ¹⁶"Tomorrow about this time I will send to you a man from the land of Benjamin, and you shall anoint him to be prince over my people Israel. He shall save my people from the hand of the Philistines. For I have seen³ my people, because their cry has come to me." ¹⁷When Samuel saw Saul, the LORD told him, "Here is the man of whom I spoke to you! He it is who shall restrain my people." ¹⁸Then Saul approached Samuel in the gate and said, "Tell me where is the house of the seer?" ¹⁹Samuel answered Saul, "I am the seer. Go up before me to the high place, for today you shall eat with me, and in the morning I will let you go and will tell you all that is on your mind. ²⁰As for your donkeys that were lost three days ago, do not set your mind on them, for they have been found. And for whom is all that is desirable in Israel? Is it not for you and for all your father's house?" ²¹Saul answered, "Am I not a Benjaminite, from the least of the tribes of Israel? And is not my clan the humblest of all the clans of the tribe of Benjamin? Why then have you spoken to me in this way?"

²²Then Samuel took Saul and his young man and brought them into the hall and gave them a place at the head of those who had been invited, who were about thirty persons. ²³And Samuel said to the cook, "Bring the portion I gave you, of which I said to you, 'Put it aside.'" ²⁴So the cook took up the leg and what was on it and set them before Saul. And Samuel said, "See, what was kept is set before you. Eat, because it was kept for you until the hour appointed, that you might eat with the guests."⁴

So Saul ate with Samuel that day. ²⁵And when they came down from the high place into the city, a bed was spread for Saul⁵ on the roof, and he lay down to sleep. ²⁶Then at the break of dawn⁶ Samuel called to Saul on the roof, "Up, that I may send you on your way." So Saul arose, and both he and Samuel went out into the street.

---

¹ Hebrew young man; also verses 7, 8, 10, 27 ² A shekel was about 2/5 ounce or 11 grams ³ Septuagint adds the affliction of ⁴ Hebrew appointed, saying, 'I have invited the people' ⁵ Septuagint; Hebrew and he spoke with Saul ⁶ Septuagint; Hebrew And they arose early and at the break of dawn

²⁷As they were going down to the outskirts of the city, Samuel said to Saul, "Tell the servant to pass on before us, and when he has passed on, stop here yourself for a while, that I may make known to you the word of God."

10 Then Samuel took a flask of oil and poured it on his head and kissed him and said, "Has not the Lᴏʀᴅ anointed you to be prince over his people Israel? And you shall reign over the people of the Lᴏʀᴅ and you will save them from the hand of their surrounding enemies. And this shall be the sign to you that the Lᴏʀᴅ has anointed you to be prince¹ over his heritage. ²When you depart from me today, you will meet two men by Rachel's tomb in the territory of Benjamin at Zelzah, and they will say to you, 'The donkeys that you went to seek are found, and now your father has ceased to care about the donkeys and is anxious about you, saying, "What shall I do about my son?"' ³Then you shall go on from there farther and come to the oak of Tabor. Three men going up to God at Bethel will meet you there, one carrying three young goats, another carrying three loaves of bread, and another carrying a skin of wine. ⁴And they will greet you and give you two loaves of bread, which you shall accept from their hand. ⁵After that you shall come to Gibeath-elohim,² where there is a garrison of the Philistines. And there, as soon as you come to the city, you will meet a group of prophets coming down from the high place with harp, tambourine, flute, and lyre before them, prophesying. ⁶Then the Spirit of the Lᴏʀᴅ will rush upon you, and you will prophesy with them and be turned into another man. ⁷Now when these signs meet you, do what your hand finds to do, for God is with you. ⁸Then go down before me to Gilgal. And behold, I am coming to you to offer burnt offerings and to sacrifice peace offerings. Seven days you shall wait, until I come to you and show you what you shall do."

⁹When he turned his back to leave Samuel, God gave him another heart. And all these signs came to pass that day. ¹⁰When they came to Gibeah,³ behold, a group of prophets met him, and the Spirit of God rushed upon him, and he prophesied among them. ¹¹And when all who knew him previously saw how he prophesied with the prophets, the people said to one another, "What has come over the son of Kish? Is Saul also among the prophets?" ¹²And a man of the place answered, "And who is their father?" Therefore it became a proverb, "Is Saul also among the prophets?" ¹³When he had finished prophesying, he came to the high place.

¹⁴Saul's uncle said to him and to his servant, "Where did you go?" And he said, "To seek the donkeys. And when we saw they were not to be found, we went to Samuel." ¹⁵And Saul's uncle said, "Please tell me what Samuel said to you." ¹⁶And Saul said to his uncle, "He told us plainly that the donkeys had been found." But about the matter of the kingdom, of which Samuel had spoken, he did not tell him anything.

Saul's coronation and first act as king [10:17–11:15]. The idealization of Saul continues in this unit, which is divided between Saul's coronation (10:17–27) and first decisive act as king, when he leads a successful military action against the Ammonites (chapter 11). In view of the interpretive framework provided earlier by chapter 8, and in view of Saul's eventual failure as king, the action in this phase is ironic—a misleading appearance or farce that will be replaced by a contrary reality when Saul shows his true colors.

¹ Septuagint; Hebrew lacks *over his people Israel? And you shall. . . . to be prince* ² *Gibeath-elohim* means *the hill of God* ³ *Gibeah* means *the hill*

¹⁷Now Samuel called the people together to the Lord at Mizpah. ¹⁸And he said to the people of Israel, "Thus says the Lord, the God of Israel, 'I brought up Israel out of Egypt, and I delivered you from the hand of the Egyptians and from the hand of all the kingdoms that were oppressing you.' ¹⁹But today you have rejected your God, who saves you from all your calamities and your distresses, and you have said to him, 'Set a king over us.' Now therefore present yourselves before the Lord by your tribes and by your thousands."

²⁰Then Samuel brought all the tribes of Israel near, and the tribe of Benjamin was taken by lot. ²¹He brought the tribe of Benjamin near by its clans, and the clan of the Matrites was taken by lot;¹ and Saul the son of Kish was taken by lot. But when they sought him, he could not be found. ²²So they inquired again of the Lord, "Is there a man still to come?" and the Lord said, "Behold, he has hidden himself among the baggage." ²³Then they ran and took him from there. And when he stood among the people, he was taller than any of the people from his shoulders upward. ²⁴And Samuel said to all the people, "Do you see him whom the Lord has chosen? There is none like him among all the people." And all the people shouted, "Long live the king!"

²⁵Then Samuel told the people the rights and duties of the kingship, and he wrote them in a book and laid it up before the Lord. Then Samuel sent all the people away, each one to his home. ²⁶Saul also went to his home at Gibeah, and with him went men of valor whose hearts God had touched. ²⁷But some worthless fellows said, "How can this man save us?" And they despised him and brought him no present. But he held his peace.

11 Then Nahash the Ammonite went up and besieged Jabesh-gilead, and all the men of Jabesh said to Nahash, "Make a treaty with us, and we will serve you." ²But Nahash the Ammonite said to them, "On this condition I will make a treaty with you, that I gouge out all your right eyes, and thus bring disgrace on all Israel." ³The elders of Jabesh said to him, "Give us seven days' respite that we may send messengers through all the territory of Israel. Then, if there is no one to save us, we will give ourselves up to you." ⁴When the messengers came to Gibeah of Saul, they reported the matter in the ears of the people, and all the people wept aloud.

⁵Now, behold, Saul was coming from the field behind the oxen. And Saul said, "What is wrong with the people, that they are weeping?" So they told him the news of the men of Jabesh. ⁶And the Spirit of God rushed upon Saul when he heard these words, and his anger was greatly kindled. ⁷He took a yoke of oxen and cut them in pieces and sent them throughout all the territory of Israel by the hand of messengers, saying, "Whoever does not come out after Saul and Samuel, so shall it be done to his oxen!" Then the dread of the Lord fell upon the people, and they came out as one man. ⁸When he mustered them at Bezek, the people of Israel were three hundred thousand, and the men of Judah thirty thousand. ⁹And they said to the messengers who had come, "Thus shall you say to the men of Jabesh-gilead: 'Tomorrow, by the time the sun is hot, you shall have deliverance.'" When the messengers came and told the men of Jabesh, they were glad. ¹⁰Therefore the men of Jabesh said, "Tomorrow we will give ourselves up to you, and you may do to us whatever seems good to you." ¹¹And the next day Saul put the people in three companies. And they came into the midst of the camp in the morning watch and struck down the Ammonites until the

---

¹ Septuagint adds *finally he brought the family of the Matrites near, man by man*

heat of the day. And those who survived were scattered, so that no two of them were left together.

¹²Then the people said to Samuel, "Who is it that said, 'Shall Saul reign over us?' Bring the men, that we may put them to death." ¹³But Saul said, "Not a man shall be put to death this day, for today the LORD has worked salvation in Israel." ¹⁴Then Samuel said to the people, "Come, let us go to Gilgal and there renew the kingdom." ¹⁵So all the people went to Gilgal, and there they made Saul king before the LORD in Gilgal. There they sacrificed peace offerings before the LORD, and there Saul and all the men of Israel rejoiced greatly.

Samuel's farewell address [chapter 12]. The formal address that Samuel delivers to the nation adheres to the conventions of the farewell address by a national leader to his followers as he relinquishes his position. A leading ingredient in such addresses is the leader's forecast of what will happen in the future, after he has departed the scene. In his formal and stately address, Samuel twice employs the rhetorical formula "but if" (vv. 14–15 and 25). By means of this formula, Samuel places the nation and its king in the position of having to choose between blessing and destruction—if the nation and its king obey God, they will be blessed, but if they disobey, they will be destroyed. In terms of the tragic pattern of Saul's life, Saul is now placed in the vulnerable position of needing to choose correctly and of facing a tragic penalty if he chooses wrongly. Intermingled with these motifs in chapter 12 is a moving story of national repentance and divine judgment. Of course the premise of literary narrative is that the specific events that happened to a particular group of people are universal in nature: we all need to choose for or against God.

12 And Samuel said to all Israel, "Behold, I have obeyed your voice in all that you have said to me and have made a king over you. ²And now, behold, the king walks before you, and I am old and gray; and behold, my sons are with you. I have walked before you from my youth until this day. ³Here I am; testify against me before the LORD and before his anointed. Whose ox have I taken? Or whose donkey have I taken? Or whom have I defrauded? Whom have I oppressed? Or from whose hand have I taken a bribe to blind my eyes with it? Testify against me¹ and I will restore it to you." ⁴They said, "You have not defrauded us or oppressed us or taken anything from any man's hand." ⁵And he said to them, "The LORD is witness against you, and his anointed is witness this day, that you have not found anything in my hand." And they said, "He is witness."

⁶And Samuel said to the people, "The LORD is witness,² who appointed Moses and Aaron and brought your fathers up out of the land of Egypt. ⁷Now therefore stand still that I may plead with you before the LORD concerning all the righteous deeds of the LORD that he performed for you and for your fathers. ⁸When Jacob went into Egypt, and the Egyptians oppressed them,³ then your fathers cried out to the LORD and the LORD sent Moses and Aaron, who brought your fathers out of Egypt and made them dwell in this place. ⁹But they forgot the LORD their God. And he sold them into the hand of Sisera, commander of the army of Hazor,⁴ and into the hand of the Philistines, and into the hand of the king of Moab. And they fought against them. ¹⁰And they cried out to the LORD and said, 'We have sinned, because we have for-

---

¹ Septuagint; Hebrew lacks *Testify against me* ² Septuagint; Hebrew lacks *is witness* ³ Septuagint; Hebrew lacks *and the Egyptians oppressed them* ⁴ Septuagint *the army of Jabin king of Hazor*

saken the LORD and have served the Baals and the Ashtaroth. But now deliver us out of the hand of our enemies, that we may serve you.' [1]And the LORD sent Jerubbaal and Barak[1] and Jephthah and Samuel and delivered you out of the hand of your enemies on every side, and you lived in safety. [12]And when you saw that Nahash the king of the Ammonites came against you, you said to me, 'No, but a king shall reign over us,' when the LORD your God was your king. [13]And now behold the king whom you have chosen, for whom you have asked; behold, the LORD has set a king over you. [14]If you will fear the LORD and serve him and obey his voice and not rebel against the commandment of the LORD, and if both you and the king who reigns over you will follow the LORD your God, it will be well. [15]But if you will not obey the voice of the LORD, but rebel against the commandment of the LORD, then the hand of the LORD will be against you and your king.[2] [16]Now therefore stand still and see this great thing that the LORD will do before your eyes. [17]Is it not wheat harvest today? I will call upon the LORD, that he may send thunder and rain. And you shall know and see that your wickedness is great, which you have done in the sight of the LORD, in asking for yourselves a king." [18]So Samuel called upon the LORD, and the LORD sent thunder and rain that day, and all the people greatly feared the LORD and Samuel.

[19]And all the people said to Samuel, "Pray for your servants to the LORD your God, that we may not die, for we have added to all our sins this evil, to ask for ourselves a king." [20]And Samuel said to the people, "Do not be afraid; you have done all this evil. Yet do not turn aside from following the LORD, but serve the LORD with all your heart. [21]And do not turn aside after empty things that cannot profit or deliver, for they are empty. [22]For the LORD will not forsake his people, for his great name's sake, because it has pleased the LORD to make you a people for himself. [23]Moreover, as for me, far be it from me that I should sin against the LORD by ceasing to pray for you, and I will instruct you in the good and the right way. [24]Only fear the LORD and serve him faithfully with all your heart. For consider what great things he has done for you. [25]But if you still do wickedly, you shall be swept away, both you and your king."

Prelude to tragedy [chapter 13]. Often in a literary tragedy we catch a glimpse of the hero's flaw before the scene in which he makes his decisive tragic choice. Chapter 13 serves that function in the story of Saul. Faced with the dilemma of needing to choose between (a) obeying the command to wait until Samuel arrives to perform offerings or (b) doing something to prevent his army from scattering, Saul does what is most immediately expedient and intrudes himself into the priestly office (in violation of the stipulation recorded in Num. 16:40). The same pattern of choosing to maintain his stature before the people instead of ruling in the strength of God and his commands will emerge in the major event of Saul's tragic career (chapter 15). The tragedy of Saul is given shape by four oracles that he receives from God through Samuel—an oracle of blessing when he is anointed king and three oracles of judgment that are increasingly specific and drastic. This time, Samuel announces that Saul's kingdom "shall not continue" (v. 14), meaning that it will not pass to Saul's son after his death, even though Saul personally still has a chance to make a success of his kingship.

13

Saul was ...[3] years old when he began to reign, and he reigned ... and two[4] years over Israel.

---

[1] Septuagint, Syriac; Hebrew *Bedan* [2] Septuagint; Hebrew *fathers* [3] The number is lacking in Hebrew and Septuagint [4] *Two* may not be the entire number; something may have dropped out

²Saul chose three thousand men of Israel. Two thousand were with Saul in Michmash and the hill country of Bethel, and a thousand were with Jonathan in Gibeah of Benjamin. The rest of the people he sent home, every man to his tent. ³Jonathan defeated the garrison of the Philistines that was at Geba, and the Philistines heard of it. And Saul blew the trumpet throughout all the land, saying, "Let the Hebrews hear." ⁴And all Israel heard it said that Saul had defeated the garrison of the Philistines, and also that Israel had become a stench to the Philistines. And the people were called out to join Saul at Gilgal.

⁵And the Philistines mustered to fight with Israel, thirty thousand chariots and six thousand horsemen and troops like the sand on the seashore in multitude. They came up and encamped in Michmash, to the east of Beth-aven. ⁶When the men of Israel saw that they were in trouble (for the people were hard pressed), the people hid themselves in caves and in holes and in rocks and in tombs and in cisterns, ⁷and some Hebrews crossed the fords of the Jordan to the land of Gad and Gilead. Saul was still at Gilgal, and all the people followed him trembling.

⁸He waited seven days, the time appointed by Samuel. But Samuel did not come to Gilgal, and the people were scattering from him. ⁹So Saul said, "Bring the burnt offering here to me, and the peace offerings." And he offered the burnt offering. ¹⁰As soon as he had finished offering the burnt offering, behold, Samuel came. And Saul went out to meet him and greet him. ¹¹Samuel said, "What have you done?" And Saul said, "When I saw that the people were scattering from me, and that you did not come within the days appointed, and that the Philistines had mustered at Michmash, ¹²I said, 'Now the Philistines will come down against me at Gilgal, and I have not sought the favor of the LORD.' So I forced myself, and offered the burnt offering." ¹³And Samuel said to Saul, "You have done foolishly. You have not kept the command of the LORD your God, with which he commanded you. For then the LORD would have established your kingdom over Israel forever. ¹⁴But now your kingdom shall not continue. The LORD has sought out a man after his own heart, and the LORD has commanded him to be prince over his people, because you have not kept what the LORD commanded you." ¹⁵And Samuel arose and went up from Gilgal. The rest of the people went up after Saul to meet the army; they went up from Gilgal¹ to Gibeah of Benjamin.

And Saul numbered the people who were present with him, about six hundred men. ¹⁶And Saul and Jonathan his son and the people who were present with them stayed in Geba of Benjamin, but the Philistines encamped in Michmash. ¹⁷And raiders came out of the camp of the Philistines in three companies. One company turned toward Ophrah, to the land of Shual; ¹⁸another company turned toward Beth-horon; and another company turned toward the border that looks down on the Valley of Zeboim toward the wilderness.

¹⁹Now there was no blacksmith to be found throughout all the land of Israel, for the Philistines said, "Lest the Hebrews make themselves swords or spears." ²⁰But every one of the Israelites went down to the Philistines to sharpen his plowshare, his mattock, his axe, or his sickle,² ²¹and the charge was two-thirds of a shekel³ for the plowshares and for the mattocks, and a third of a shekel⁴ for sharpening the axes and for setting the goads.⁵ ²²So on the day of the battle there was neither sword nor spear found in the hand of any of the people with Saul and Jonathan, but Saul and

---

¹ Septuagint; Hebrew lacks *The rest of the people . . . from Gilgal* ² Septuagint; Hebrew *plowshare* ³ Hebrew *was a pim* ⁴ A *shekel* was about 2/5 ounce or 11 grams ⁵ The meaning of the Hebrew verse is uncertain

Jonathan his son had them. [23]And the garrison of the Philistines went out to the pass of Michmash.

> **Saul's career as military leader** [chapter 14]. The large amount of space allotted to the incident in which Saul's son Jonathan unknowingly violates his father's edict that the soldiers refrain from eating on the day of battle signals its importance to the storyteller. Perhaps it was simply such a singular event that it became famous. Or maybe we are to see Saul's edict as a foolish and rash one and evidence of his weak leadership, which is the dominant pattern of his tragedy and a motif that we can profitably trace through this chapter. The event is handled in the manner of literary narrative, that is, in leisurely detail, so that there is a lot for us to relive in our imagination and ponder in terms of human significance.

14 One day Jonathan the son of Saul said to the young man who carried his armor, "Come, let us go over to the Philistine garrison on the other side." But he did not tell his father. [2]Saul was staying in the outskirts of Gibeah in the pomegranate cave[1] at Migron. The people who were with him were about six hundred men, [3]including Ahijah the son of Ahitub, Ichabod's brother, son of Phinehas, son of Eli, the priest of the LORD in Shiloh, wearing an ephod. And the people did not know that Jonathan had gone. [4]Within the passes, by which Jonathan sought to go over to the Philistine garrison, there was a rocky crag on the one side and a rocky crag on the other side. The name of the one was Bozez, and the name of the other Seneh. [5]The one crag rose on the north in front of Michmash, and the other on the south in front of Geba.

[6]Jonathan said to the young man who carried his armor, "Come, let us go over to the garrison of these uncircumcised. It may be that the LORD will work for us, for nothing can hinder the LORD from saving by many or by few." [7]And his armor-bearer said to him, "Do all that is in your heart. Do as you wish.[2] Behold, I am with you heart and soul." [8]Then Jonathan said, "Behold, we will cross over to the men, and we will show ourselves to them. [9]If they say to us, 'Wait until we come to you,' then we will stand still in our place, and we will not go up to them. [10]But if they say, 'Come up to us,' then we will go up, for the LORD has given them into our hand. And this shall be the sign to us." [11]So both of them showed themselves to the garrison of the Philistines. And the Philistines said, "Look, Hebrews are coming out of the holes where they have hidden themselves." [12]And the men of the garrison hailed Jonathan and his armor-bearer and said, "Come up to us, and we will show you a thing." And Jonathan said to his armor-bearer, "Come up after me, for the LORD has given them into the hand of Israel." [13]Then Jonathan climbed up on his hands and feet, and his armor-bearer after him. And they fell before Jonathan, and his armor-bearer killed them after him. [14]And that first strike, which Jonathan and his armor-bearer made, killed about twenty men within as it were half a furrow's length in an acre[3] of land. [15]And there was a panic in the camp, in the field, and among all the people. The garrison and even the raiders trembled, the earth quaked, and it became a very great panic.

[16]And the watchmen of Saul in Gibeah of Benjamin looked, and behold, the multitude was dispersing here and there.[4] [17]Then Saul said to the people who were with him, "Count and see who has gone from us." And when they had counted, behold,

---

[1] Or *under the pomegranate* [tree] [2] Septuagint *Do all that your mind inclines to* [3] Hebrew *a yoke* [4] Septuagint; Hebrew *they went here and there*

Jonathan and his armor-bearer were not there. ¹⁸So Saul said to Ahijah, "Bring the ark of God here." For the ark of God went at that time with the people¹ of Israel. ¹⁹Now while Saul was talking to the priest, the tumult in the camp of the Philistines increased more and more. So Saul said to the priest, "Withdraw your hand." ²⁰Then Saul and all the people who were with him rallied and went into the battle. And behold, every Philistine's sword was against his fellow, and there was very great confusion. ²¹Now the Hebrews who had been with the Philistines before that time and who had gone up with them into the camp, even they also turned to be with the Israelites who were with Saul and Jonathan. ²²Likewise, when all the men of Israel who had hidden themselves in the hill country of Ephraim heard that the Philistines were fleeing, they too followed hard after them in the battle. ²³So the LORD saved Israel that day. And the battle passed beyond Beth-aven.

²⁴And the men of Israel had been hard pressed that day, so Saul had laid an oath on the people, saying, "Cursed be the man who eats food until it is evening and I am avenged on my enemies." So none of the people had tasted food. ²⁵Now when all the people² came to the forest, behold, there was honey on the ground. ²⁶And when the people entered the forest, behold, the honey was dropping, but no one put his hand to his mouth, for the people feared the oath. ²⁷But Jonathan had not heard his father charge the people with the oath, so he put out the tip of the staff that was in his hand and dipped it in the honeycomb and put his hand to his mouth, and his eyes became bright. ²⁸Then one of the people said, "Your father strictly charged the people with an oath, saying, 'Cursed be the man who eats food this day.'" And the people were faint. ²⁹Then Jonathan said, "My father has troubled the land. See how my eyes have become bright because I tasted a little of this honey. ³⁰How much better if the people had eaten freely today of the spoil of their enemies that they found. For now the defeat among the Philistines has not been great."

³¹They struck down the Philistines that day from Michmash to Aijalon. And the people were very faint. ³²The people pounced on the spoil and took sheep and oxen and calves and slaughtered them on the ground. And the people ate them with the blood. ³³Then they told Saul, "Behold, the people are sinning against the LORD by eating with the blood." And he said, "You have dealt treacherously; roll a great stone to me here."³ ³⁴And Saul said, "Disperse yourselves among the people and say to them, 'Let every man bring his ox or his sheep and slaughter them here and eat, and do not sin against the LORD by eating with the blood.'" So every one of the people brought his ox with him that night and they slaughtered them there. ³⁵And Saul built an altar to the LORD; it was the first altar that he built to the LORD.

³⁶Then Saul said, "Let us go down after the Philistines by night and plunder them until the morning light; let us not leave a man of them." And they said, "Do whatever seems good to you." But the priest said, "Let us draw near to God here." ³⁷And Saul inquired of God, "Shall I go down after the Philistines? Will you give them into the hand of Israel?" But he did not answer him that day. ³⁸And Saul said, "Come here, all you leaders of the people, and know and see how this sin has arisen today. ³⁹For as the LORD lives who saves Israel, though it be in Jonathan my son, he shall surely die." But there was not a man among all the people who answered him. ⁴⁰Then he said to all Israel, "You shall be on one side, and I and Jonathan my son will be on the other side." And the people said to Saul, "Do what seems good to you." ⁴¹Therefore Saul said,

¹ Hebrew; Septuagint *"Bring the ephod."* For at that time he wore the ephod before the people ² Hebrew *land* ³ Septuagint; Hebrew *this day*

"O Lord God of Israel, why[1] have you not answered your servant this day? If this guilt is in me or in Jonathan my son, O Lord, God of Israel, give Urim. But if this guilt is in your people Israel, give Thummim." And Jonathan and Saul were taken, but the people escaped. [42]Then Saul said, "Cast the lot between me and my son Jonathan." And Jonathan was taken.

[43]Then Saul said to Jonathan, "Tell me what you have done." And Jonathan told him, "I tasted a little honey with the tip of the staff that was in my hand. Here I am; I will die." [44]And Saul said, "God do so to me and more also; you shall surely die, Jonathan." [45]Then the people said to Saul, "Shall Jonathan die, who has worked this great salvation in Israel? Far from it! As the Lord lives, there shall not one hair of his head fall to the ground, for he has worked with God this day." So the people ransomed Jonathan, so that he did not die. [46]Then Saul went up from pursuing the Philistines, and the Philistines went to their own place.

[47]When Saul had taken the kingship over Israel, he fought against all his enemies on every side, against Moab, against the Ammonites, against Edom, against the kings of Zobah, and against the Philistines. Wherever he turned he routed them. [48]And he did valiantly and struck the Amalekites and delivered Israel out of the hands of those who plundered them.

[49]Now the sons of Saul were Jonathan, Ishvi, and Malchi-shua. And the names of his two daughters were these: the name of the firstborn was Merab, and the name of the younger Michal. [50]And the name of Saul's wife was Ahinoam the daughter of Ahimaaz. And the name of the commander of his army was Abner the son of Ner, Saul's uncle. [51]Kish was the father of Saul, and Ner the father of Abner was the son of Abiel.

[52]There was hard fighting against the Philistines all the days of Saul. And when Saul saw any strong man, or any valiant man, he attached him to himself.

Saul's tragic choice [chapter 15]. This chapter contains the psychological and spiritual center of Saul's tragedy, and it will repay all of the attention that we can give it. When Saul buckles under the people's desire to save the best of the spoil and even the rival king's life (so that Agag can be brought back as a trophy), we see in him a tragedy of weak leadership. As always in biblical tragedy, the heart of the tragic choice consists of disobedience to what God has clearly commanded. Almost everything in this chapter is laden with tragic significance. When Samuel arrives to denounce Saul's act and offer an analysis of its tragic ingredients, we have the third oracle that he delivers to Saul, and this time the prediction is that the kingdom will be taken from Saul personally (v. 28).

15 And Samuel said to Saul, "The Lord sent me to anoint you king over his people Israel; now therefore listen to the words of the Lord. [2]Thus says the Lord of hosts, 'I have noted what Amalek did to Israel in opposing them on the way when they came up out of Egypt. [3]Now go and strike Amalek and devote to destruction[2] all that they have. Do not spare them, but kill both man and woman, child and infant, ox and sheep, camel and donkey.'"

[4]So Saul summoned the people and numbered them in Telaim, two hundred thousand men on foot, and ten thousand men of Judah. [5]And Saul came to the city of

[1] Vulgate (compare Septuagint); Hebrew *Saul said to the Lord, the God of Israel, "Why . . .* [2] That is, set apart (devote) as an offering to the Lord (for destruction); also verses 8, 9, 15, 18, 20, 21

Amalek and lay in wait in the valley. ⁶Then Saul said to the Kenites, "Go, depart; go down from among the Amalekites, lest I destroy you with them. For you showed kindness to all the people of Israel when they came up out of Egypt." So the Kenites departed from among the Amalekites. ⁷And Saul defeated the Amalekites from Havilah as far as Shur, which is east of Egypt. ⁸And he took Agag the king of the Amalekites alive and devoted to destruction all the people with the edge of the sword. ⁹But Saul and the people spared Agag and the best of the sheep and of the oxen and of the fattened calves¹ and the lambs, and all that was good, and would not utterly destroy them. All that was despised and worthless they devoted to destruction.

¹⁰The word of the Lord came to Samuel: ¹¹"I regret that I have made Saul king, for he has turned back from following me and has not performed my commandments." And Samuel was angry, and he cried to the Lord all night. ¹²And Samuel rose early to meet Saul in the morning. And it was told Samuel, "Saul came to Carmel, and behold, he set up a monument for himself and turned and passed on and went down to Gilgal." ¹³And Samuel came to Saul, and Saul said to him, "Blessed be you to the Lord. I have performed the commandment of the Lord." ¹⁴And Samuel said, "What then is this bleating of the sheep in my ears and the lowing of the oxen that I hear?" ¹⁵Saul said, "They have brought them from the Amalekites, for the people spared the best of the sheep and of the oxen to sacrifice to the Lord your God, and the rest we have devoted to destruction." ¹⁶Then Samuel said to Saul, "Stop! I will tell you what the Lord said to me this night." And he said to him, "Speak."

¹⁷And Samuel said, "Though you are little in your own eyes, are you not the head of the tribes of Israel? The Lord anointed you king over Israel. ¹⁸And the Lord sent you on a mission and said, 'Go, devote to destruction the sinners, the Amalekites, and fight against them until they are consumed.' ¹⁹Why then did you not obey the voice of the Lord? Why did you pounce on the spoil and do what was evil in the sight of the Lord?" ²⁰And Saul said to Samuel, "I have obeyed the voice of the Lord. I have gone on the mission on which the Lord sent me. I have brought Agag the king of Amalek, and I have devoted the Amalekites to destruction. ²¹But the people took of the spoil, sheep and oxen, the best of the things devoted to destruction, to sacrifice to the Lord your God in Gilgal." ²²And Samuel said,

"Has the Lord as great delight in burnt offerings and sacrifices,
    as in obeying the voice of the Lord?
Behold, to obey is better than sacrifice,
    and to listen than the fat of rams.
²³ For rebellion is as the sin of divination,
    and presumption is as iniquity and idolatry.
Because you have rejected the word of the Lord,
    he has also rejected you from being king."

²⁴Saul said to Samuel, "I have sinned, for I have transgressed the commandment of the Lord and your words, because I feared the people and obeyed their voice. ²⁵Now therefore, please pardon my sin and return with me that I may worship the Lord." ²⁶And Samuel said to Saul, "I will not return with you. For you have rejected the word of the Lord, and the Lord has rejected you from being king over Israel." ²⁷As Samuel turned to go away, Saul seized the skirt of his robe, and it tore. ²⁸And Samuel said to

¹ The meaning of the Hebrew term is uncertain

him, "The LORD has torn the kingdom of Israel from you this day and has given it to a neighbor of yours, who is better than you. ²⁹And also the Glory of Israel will not lie or have regret, for he is not a man, that he should have regret." ³⁰Then he said, "I have sinned; yet honor me now before the elders of my people and before Israel, and return with me, that I may bow before the LORD your God." ³¹So Samuel turned back after Saul, and Saul bowed before the LORD.

³²Then Samuel said, "Bring here to me Agag the king of the Amalekites." And Agag came to him cheerfully.¹ Agag said, "Surely the bitterness of death is past." ³³And Samuel said, "As your sword has made women childless, so shall your mother be childless among women." And Samuel hacked Agag to pieces before the LORD in Gilgal.

³⁴Then Samuel went to Ramah, and Saul went up to his house in Gibeah of Saul. ³⁵And Samuel did not see Saul again until the day of his death, but Samuel grieved over Saul. And the LORD regretted that he had made Saul king over Israel.

David anointed as Saul's successor [chapter 16]. With Saul's tragic choice now having occurred, the narrative takes a new direction as we read about the choosing and anointing of David as the next king. After the tragic decline of Saul, we sense a small ascent in the fortunes of the nation as David is selected by God to succeed him. Since Saul's kingship will last for as long as fifteen more years, the effect of David's immediate anointing as the next king is to suggest that God knows Saul to be an archetypal loser and can scarcely wait to get to a better king. The choice of the youngest son over his older brothers makes the story a favorite with children (who love a boy hero) as well as with adults (who share a universal sympathy for the worthy underdog). From this halfway point in the book to its end, David's ascending fortunes will be played off against Saul's tragic decline, and we get a foreshadowing of this in the second half of this chapter (vv. 14–23), with its account of Saul's depression and David's playing music to restore him to emotional equilibrium.

16 The LORD said to Samuel, "How long will you grieve over Saul, since I have rejected him from being king over Israel? Fill your horn with oil, and go. I will send you to Jesse the Bethlehemite, for I have provided for myself a king among his sons." ²And Samuel said, "How can I go? If Saul hears it, he will kill me." And the LORD said, "Take a heifer with you and say, 'I have come to sacrifice to the LORD.' ³And invite Jesse to the sacrifice, and I will show you what you shall do. And you shall anoint for me him whom I declare to you." ⁴Samuel did what the LORD commanded and came to Bethlehem. The elders of the city came to meet him trembling and said, "Do you come peaceably?" ⁵And he said, "Peaceably; I have come to sacrifice to the LORD. Consecrate yourselves, and come with me to the sacrifice." And he consecrated Jesse and his sons and invited them to the sacrifice.

⁶When they came, he looked on Eliab and thought, "Surely the LORD's anointed is before him." ⁷But the LORD said to Samuel, "Do not look on his appearance or on the height of his stature, because I have rejected him. For the LORD sees not as man sees: man looks on the outward appearance, but the LORD looks on the heart." ⁸Then Jesse called Abinadab and made him pass before Samuel. And he said, "Neither has the LORD chosen this one." ⁹Then Jesse made Shammah pass by. And he said, "Neither has the LORD chosen this one." ¹⁰And Jesse made seven of his sons pass before

¹ Or *haltingly* (compare Septuagint); the Hebrew is uncertain

Samuel. And Samuel said to Jesse, "The LORD has not chosen these." ¹¹Then Samuel said to Jesse, "Are all your sons here?" And he said, "There remains yet the youngest,¹ but behold, he is keeping the sheep." And Samuel said to Jesse, "Send and get him, for we will not sit down till he comes here." ¹²And he sent and brought him in. Now he was ruddy and had beautiful eyes and was handsome. And the LORD said, "Arise, anoint him, for this is he." ¹³Then Samuel took the horn of oil and anointed him in the midst of his brothers. And the Spirit of the LORD rushed upon David from that day forward. And Samuel rose up and went to Ramah.

¹⁴Now the Spirit of the LORD departed from Saul, and a harmful spirit from the LORD tormented him. ¹⁵And Saul's servants said to him, "Behold now, a harmful spirit from God is tormenting you. ¹⁶Let our lord now command your servants who are before you to seek out a man who is skillful in playing the lyre, and when the harmful spirit from God is upon you, he will play it, and you will be well." ¹⁷So Saul said to his servants, "Provide for me a man who can play well and bring him to me." ¹⁸One of the young men answered, "Behold, I have seen a son of Jesse the Bethlehemite, who is skillful in playing, a man of valor, a man of war, prudent in speech, and a man of good presence, and the LORD is with him." ¹⁹Therefore Saul sent messengers to Jesse and said, "Send me David your son, who is with the sheep." ²⁰And Jesse took a donkey laden with bread and a skin of wine and a young goat and sent them by David his son to Saul. ²¹And David came to Saul and entered his service. And Saul loved him greatly, and he became his armor-bearer. ²²And Saul sent to Jesse, saying, "Let David remain in my service, for he has found favor in my sight." ²³And whenever the harmful spirit from God was upon Saul, David took the lyre and played it with his hand. So Saul was refreshed and was well, and the harmful spirit departed from him.

David and Goliath [chapter 17]. Not only is this a favorite children's Bible story, featuring as it does a boy hero, but it is also the prototypical battle story in the Bible. It contains many of the conventions of the genre of the battle story and makes mention of rituals that ancient warriors and armies actually followed, including the following: the geographic details of a mountain as the place where armies gathered and the intervening valley as the place where the battle would take place (v. 3); the warrior's armor as an extension of his prowess (vv. 5–7); the prebattle ritual of a formal taunt directed by a champion against his enemy (vv. 10 and 43–44 from Goliath and vv. 45–47 from David); the challenge to single combat as a way of settling the conflict (vv. 8–9); the arming of the hero for battle (vv. 31–40); group scenes encircling the crucial central event of a single combat (vv. 41–49); postbattle rituals of a shout of triumph (v. 52) and claiming a trophy from the defeated enemy in the form of the enemy's head and armor (vv. 51, 54); flight of the defeated army and chase by the conquering army (vv. 52–53). While this story adheres to the general contours of the battle story, its effect is not primarily to elevate the hero as a great warrior but rather to praise God as a great deliverer. The David-Saul motif is advanced in this episode, as David steps in to do what Saul fails to do.

17 Now the Philistines gathered their armies for battle. And they were gathered at Socoh, which belongs to Judah, and encamped between Socoh and Azekah, in Ephes-dammim. ²And Saul and the men of Israel were gathered, and encamped in the Valley of Elah, and drew up in line of battle against the Philistines. ³And the

¹ Or smallest

Philistines stood on the mountain on the one side, and Israel stood on the mountain on the other side, with a valley between them. ⁴And there came out from the camp of the Philistines a champion named Goliath of Gath, whose height was six¹ cubits and a span. ⁵He had a helmet of bronze on his head, and he was armed with a coat of mail, and the weight of the coat was five thousand shekels² of bronze. ⁶And he had bronze armor on his legs, and a javelin of bronze slung between his shoulders. ⁷The shaft of his spear was like a weaver's beam, and his spear's head weighed six hundred shekels of iron. And his shield-bearer went before him. ⁸He stood and shouted to the ranks of Israel, "Why have you come out to draw up for battle? Am I not a Philistine, and are you not servants of Saul? Choose a man for yourselves, and let him come down to me. ⁹If he is able to fight with me and kill me, then we will be your servants. But if I prevail against him and kill him, then you shall be our servants and serve us." ¹⁰And the Philistine said, "I defy the ranks of Israel this day. Give me a man, that we may fight together." ¹¹When Saul and all Israel heard these words of the Philistine, they were dismayed and greatly afraid.

¹²Now David was the son of an Ephrathite of Bethlehem in Judah, named Jesse, who had eight sons. In the days of Saul the man was already old and advanced in years.³ ¹³The three oldest sons of Jesse had followed Saul to the battle. And the names of his three sons who went to the battle were Eliab the firstborn, and next to him Abinadab, and the third Shammah. ¹⁴David was the youngest. The three eldest followed Saul, ¹⁵but David went back and forth from Saul to feed his father's sheep at Bethlehem. ¹⁶For forty days the Philistine came forward and took his stand, morning and evening.

¹⁷And Jesse said to David his son, "Take for your brothers an ephah⁴ of this parched grain, and these ten loaves, and carry them quickly to the camp to your brothers. ¹⁸Also take these ten cheeses to the commander of their thousand. See if your brothers are well, and bring some token from them."

¹⁹Now Saul and they and all the men of Israel were in the Valley of Elah, fighting with the Philistines. ²⁰And David rose early in the morning and left the sheep with a keeper and took the provisions and went, as Jesse had commanded him. And he came to the encampment as the host was going out to the battle line, shouting the war cry. ²¹And Israel and the Philistines drew up for battle, army against army. ²²And David left the things in charge of the keeper of the baggage and ran to the ranks and went and greeted his brothers. ²³As he talked with them, behold, the champion, the Philistine of Gath, Goliath by name, came up out of the ranks of the Philistines and spoke the same words as before. And David heard him.

²⁴All the men of Israel, when they saw the man, fled from him and were much afraid. ²⁵And the men of Israel said, "Have you seen this man who has come up? Surely he has come up to defy Israel. And the king will enrich the man who kills him with great riches and will give him his daughter and make his father's house free in Israel." ²⁶And David said to the men who stood by him, "What shall be done for the man who kills this Philistine and takes away the reproach from Israel? For who is this uncircumcised Philistine, that he should defy the armies of the living God?" ²⁷And the people answered him in the same way, "So shall it be done to the man who kills him."

²⁸Now Eliab his eldest brother heard when he spoke to the men. And Eliab's anger

¹ Hebrew; Septuagint, Dead Sea Scroll and Josephus *four* ² A *shekel* was about 2/5 ounce or 11 grams ³ Septuagint, Syriac; Hebrew *years among men* ⁴ An *ephah* was about 3/5 bushel or 22 liters

was kindled against David, and he said, "Why have you come down? And with whom have you left those few sheep in the wilderness? I know your presumption and the evil of your heart, for you have come down to see the battle." ²⁹And David said, "What have I done now? Was it not but a word?" ³⁰And he turned away from him toward another, and spoke in the same way, and the people answered him again as before.

³¹When the words that David spoke were heard, they repeated them before Saul, and he sent for him. ³²And David said to Saul, "Let no man's heart fail because of him. Your servant will go and fight with this Philistine." ³³And Saul said to David, "You are not able to go against this Philistine to fight with him, for you are but a youth, and he has been a man of war from his youth." ³⁴But David said to Saul, "Your servant used to keep sheep for his father. And when there came a lion, or a bear, and took a lamb from the flock, ³⁵I went after him and struck him and delivered it out of his mouth. And if he arose against me, I caught him by his beard and struck him and killed him. ³⁶Your servant has struck down both lions and bears, and this uncircumcised Philistine shall be like one of them, for he has defied the armies of the living God." ³⁷And David said, "The Lᴏʀᴅ who delivered me from the paw of the lion and from the paw of the bear will deliver me from the hand of this Philistine." And Saul said to David, "Go, and the Lᴏʀᴅ be with you!"

³⁸Then Saul clothed David with his armor. He put a helmet of bronze on his head and clothed him with a coat of mail, ³⁹and David strapped his sword over his armor. And he tried in vain to go, for he had not tested them. Then David said to Saul, "I cannot go with these, for I have not tested them." So David put them off. ⁴⁰Then he took his staff in his hand and chose five smooth stones from the brook and put them in his shepherd's pouch. His sling was in his hand, and he approached the Philistine.

⁴¹And the Philistine moved forward and came near to David, with his shield-bearer in front of him. ⁴²And when the Philistine looked and saw David, he disdained him, for he was but a youth, ruddy and handsome in appearance. ⁴³And the Philistine said to David, "Am I a dog, that you come to me with sticks?" And the Philistine cursed David by his gods. ⁴⁴The Philistine said to David, "Come to me, and I will give your flesh to the birds of the air and to the beasts of the field." ⁴⁵Then David said to the Philistine, "You come to me with a sword and with a spear and with a javelin, but I come to you in the name of the Lᴏʀᴅ of hosts, the God of the armies of Israel, whom you have defied. ⁴⁶This day the Lᴏʀᴅ will deliver you into my hand, and I will strike you down and cut off your head. And I will give the dead bodies of the host of the Philistines this day to the birds of the air and to the wild beasts of the earth, that all the earth may know that there is a God in Israel, ⁴⁷and that all this assembly may know that the Lᴏʀᴅ saves not with sword and spear. For the battle is the Lᴏʀᴅ's, and he will give you into our hand."

⁴⁸When the Philistine arose and came and drew near to meet David, David ran quickly toward the battle line to meet the Philistine. ⁴⁹And David put his hand in his bag and took out a stone and slung it and struck the Philistine on his forehead. The stone sank into his forehead, and he fell on his face to the ground.

⁵⁰So David prevailed over the Philistine with a sling and with a stone, and struck the Philistine and killed him. There was no sword in the hand of David. ⁵¹Then David ran and stood over the Philistine and took his sword and drew it out of its sheath and killed him and cut off his head with it. When the Philistines saw that their champion was dead, they fled. ⁵²And the men of Israel and Judah rose with a shout and pursued

the Philistines as far as Gath[1] and the gates of Ekron, so that the wounded Philistines fell on the way from Shaaraim as far as Gath and Ekron. ⁵³And the people of Israel came back from chasing the Philistines, and they plundered their camp. ⁵⁴And David took the head of the Philistine and brought it to Jerusalem, but he put his armor in his tent.

⁵⁵As soon as Saul saw David go out against the Philistine, he said to Abner, the commander of the army, "Abner, whose son is this youth?" And Abner said, "As your soul lives, O king, I do not know." ⁵⁶And the king said, "Inquire whose son the boy is." ⁵⁷And as soon as David returned from the striking down of the Philistine, Abner took him, and brought him before Saul with the head of the Philistine in his hand. ⁵⁸And Saul said to him, "Whose son are you, young man?" And David answered, "I am the son of your servant Jesse the Bethlehemite."

The tangled relationship between Saul and David [chapter 18]. The overarching plot conflict for the rest of the book will be the conflict between Saul and David, with interspersed smaller conflicts. The central conflict is set in motion in chapter 18. The tension comes to a head when Saul and David return from battle and are greeted by women who sing of Saul's having slain "his thousands" and David his "ten thousands" (v. 7). Saul's pathologies surface with increasing clarity as the action unfolds; they include jealousy, insecurity, paranoia (as Saul incorrectly thinks that David intends to supplant him), and bipolar behavior (mood swings from the lows of depression to a gushing of goodwill when David spares his life).

18 As soon as he had finished speaking to Saul, the soul of Jonathan was knit to the soul of David, and Jonathan loved him as his own soul. ²And Saul took him that day and would not let him return to his father's house. ³Then Jonathan made a covenant with David, because he loved him as his own soul. ⁴And Jonathan stripped himself of the robe that was on him and gave it to David, and his armor, and even his sword and his bow and his belt. ⁵And David went out and was successful wherever Saul sent him, so that Saul set him over the men of war. And this was good in the sight of all the people and also in the sight of Saul's servants.

⁶As they were coming home, when David returned from striking down the Philistine, the women came out of all the cities of Israel, singing and dancing, to meet King Saul, with tambourines, with songs of joy, and with musical instruments.[2] ⁷And the women sang to one another as they celebrated,

"Saul has struck down his thousands,
    and David his ten thousands."

⁸And Saul was very angry, and this saying displeased him. He said, "They have ascribed to David ten thousands, and to me they have ascribed thousands, and what more can he have but the kingdom?" ⁹And Saul eyed David from that day on.

¹⁰The next day a harmful spirit from God rushed upon Saul, and he raved within his house while David was playing the lyre, as he did day by day. Saul had his spear in his hand. ¹¹And Saul hurled the spear, for he thought, "I will pin David to the wall." But David evaded him twice.

¹²Saul was afraid of David because the Lord was with him but had departed from

---

[1] Septuagint; Hebrew *Gai* [2] Or *triangles, or three-stringed instruments*

Saul. ¹³So Saul removed him from his presence and made him a commander of a thousand. And he went out and came in before the people. ¹⁴And David had success in all his undertakings, for the Lord was with him. ¹⁵And when Saul saw that he had great success, he stood in fearful awe of him. ¹⁶But all Israel and Judah loved David, for he went out and came in before them.

¹⁷Then Saul said to David, "Here is my elder daughter Merab. I will give her to you for a wife. Only be valiant for me and fight the Lord's battles." For Saul thought, "Let not my hand be against him, but let the hand of the Philistines be against him." ¹⁸And David said to Saul, "Who am I, and who are my relatives, my father's clan in Israel, that I should be son-in-law to the king?" ¹⁹But at the time when Merab, Saul's daughter, should have been given to David, she was given to Adriel the Meholathite for a wife.

²⁰Now Saul's daughter Michal loved David. And they told Saul, and the thing pleased him. ²¹Saul thought, "Let me give her to him, that she may be a snare for him and that the hand of the Philistines may be against him." Therefore Saul said to David a second time,¹ "You shall now be my son-in-law." ²²And Saul commanded his servants, "Speak to David in private and say, 'Behold, the king has delight in you, and all his servants love you. Now then become the king's son-in-law.'" ²³And Saul's servants spoke those words in the ears of David. And David said, "Does it seem to you a little thing to become the king's son-in-law, since I am a poor man and have no reputation?" ²⁴And the servants of Saul told him, "Thus and so did David speak." ²⁵Then Saul said, "Thus shall you say to David, 'The king desires no bride-price except a hundred foreskins of the Philistines, that he may be avenged of the king's enemies.'" Now Saul thought to make David fall by the hand of the Philistines. ²⁶And when his servants told David these words, it pleased David well to be the king's son-in-law. Before the time had expired, ²⁷David arose and went, along with his men, and killed two hundred of the Philistines. And David brought their foreskins, which were given in full number to the king, that he might become the king's son-in-law. And Saul gave him his daughter Michal for a wife. ²⁸But when Saul saw and knew that the Lord was with David, and that Michal, Saul's daughter, loved him, ²⁹Saul was even more afraid of David. So Saul was David's enemy continually.

³⁰Then the princes of the Philistines came out to battle, and as often as they came out David had more success than all the servants of Saul, so that his name was highly esteemed.

Saul's erratic behavior [chapter 19]. The literary impulse to show how events happened, and not simply record that certain things happened, is fully evident in a chapter such as this. The account is filled with specific realistic details. In a literary tragedy, the tragic hero becomes increasingly isolated from his society, and in this chapter we see Saul isolated from his own family as Jonathan and Michal help David to escape from their deranged and abusive father.

19 And Saul spoke to Jonathan his son and to all his servants, that they should kill David. But Jonathan, Saul's son, delighted much in David. ²And Jonathan told David, "Saul my father seeks to kill you. Therefore be on your guard in the morning. Stay in a secret place and hide yourself. ³And I will go out and stand beside my

¹ Hebrew *by two*

father in the field where you are, and I will speak to my father about you. And if I learn anything I will tell you." ⁴And Jonathan spoke well of David to Saul his father and said to him, "Let not the king sin against his servant David, because he has not sinned against you, and because his deeds have brought good to you. ⁵For he took his life in his hand and he struck down the Philistine, and the LORD worked a great salvation for all Israel. You saw it, and rejoiced. Why then will you sin against innocent blood by killing David without cause?" ⁶And Saul listened to the voice of Jonathan. Saul swore, "As the LORD lives, he shall not be put to death." ⁷And Jonathan called David, and Jonathan reported to him all these things. And Jonathan brought David to Saul, and he was in his presence as before.

⁸And there was war again. And David went out and fought with the Philistines and struck them with a great blow, so that they fled before him. ⁹Then a harmful spirit from the LORD came upon Saul, as he sat in his house with his spear in his hand. And David was playing the lyre. ¹⁰And Saul sought to pin David to the wall with the spear, but he eluded Saul, so that he struck the spear into the wall. And David fled and escaped that night.

¹¹Saul sent messengers to David's house to watch him, that he might kill him in the morning. But Michal, David's wife, told him, "If you do not escape with your life tonight, tomorrow you will be killed." ¹²So Michal let David down through the window, and he fled away and escaped. ¹³Michal took an image and laid it on the bed and put a pillow of goats' hair at its head and covered it with the clothes. ¹⁴And when Saul sent messengers to take David, she said, "He is sick." ¹⁵Then Saul sent the messengers to see David, saying, "Bring him up to me in the bed, that I may kill him." ¹⁶And when the messengers came in, behold, the image was in the bed, with the pillow of goats' hair at its head. ¹⁷Saul said to Michal, "Why have you deceived me thus and let my enemy go, so that he has escaped?" And Michal answered Saul, "He said to me, 'Let me go. Why should I kill you?'"

¹⁸Now David fled and escaped, and he came to Samuel at Ramah and told him all that Saul had done to him. And he and Samuel went and lived at Naioth. ¹⁹And it was told Saul, "Behold, David is at Naioth in Ramah." ²⁰Then Saul sent messengers to take David, and when they saw the company of the prophets prophesying, and Samuel standing as head over them, the Spirit of God came upon the messengers of Saul, and they also prophesied. ²¹When it was told Saul, he sent other messengers, and they also prophesied. And Saul sent messengers again the third time, and they also prophesied. ²²Then he himself went to Ramah and came to the great well that is in Secu. And he asked, "Where are Samuel and David?" And one said, "Behold, they are at Naioth in Ramah." ²³And he went there to Naioth in Ramah. And the Spirit of God came upon him also, and as he went he prophesied until he came to Naioth in Ramah. ²⁴And he too stripped off his clothes, and he too prophesied before Samuel and lay naked all that day and all that night. Thus it is said, "Is Saul also among the prophets?"

The friendship of David and Jonathan [chapter 20]. This is the classic story of male friendship in the Bible, just as the story of Ruth and Naomi is the classic story of female friendship. The detailed account of the relationship between David and Jonathan in this chapter is hardly necessary for purposes of the historical chronicle of a nation; it adheres instead to the literary impulse to present human experience for our understanding and celebration. Literature gives us forms for our experiences and feelings; in this chapter, our own experiences of friendship are given shape, as an ideal is set before us. At the level of plot, this chapter is a suspense story par excellence, topped off with a secret rendezvous. The events recorded here form the content of David's declaration in his elegy written in Jonathan's honor after his death, in which David claimed that he found Jonathan's love toward him to be distinctive, surpassing the love of women (2 Sam. 1:26). David was right: no woman in his life showed him the kind of devotion and loyalty that Jonathan did.

20 Then David fled from Naioth in Ramah and came and said before Jonathan, "What have I done? What is my guilt? And what is my sin before your father, that he seeks my life?" ²And he said to him, "Far from it! You shall not die. Behold, my father does nothing either great or small without disclosing it to me. And why should my father hide this from me? It is not so." ³But David vowed again, saying, "Your father knows well that I have found favor in your eyes, and he thinks, 'Do not let Jonathan know this, lest he be grieved.' But truly, as the LORD lives and as your soul lives, there is but a step between me and death." ⁴Then Jonathan said to David, "Whatever you say, I will do for you." ⁵David said to Jonathan, "Behold, tomorrow is the new moon, and I should not fail to sit at table with the king. But let me go, that I may hide myself in the field till the third day at evening. ⁶If your father misses me at all, then say, 'David earnestly asked leave of me to run to Bethlehem his city, for there is a yearly sacrifice there for all the clan.' ⁷If he says, 'Good!' it will be well with your servant, but if he is angry, then know that harm is determined by him. ⁸Therefore deal kindly with your servant, for you have brought your servant into a covenant of the LORD with you. But if there is guilt in me, kill me yourself, for why should you bring me to your father?" ⁹And Jonathan said, "Far be it from you! If I knew that it was determined by my father that harm should come to you, would I not tell you?" ¹⁰Then David said to Jonathan, "Who will tell me if your father answers you roughly?" ¹¹And Jonathan said to David, "Come, let us go out into the field." So they both went out into the field.

¹²And Jonathan said to David, "The LORD, the God of Israel, be witness!¹ When I have sounded out my father, about this time tomorrow, or the third day, behold, if he is well disposed toward David, shall I not then send and disclose it to you? ¹³But should it please my father to do you harm, the LORD do so to Jonathan and more also if I do not disclose it to you and send you away, that you may go in safety. May the LORD be with you, as he has been with my father. ¹⁴If I am still alive, show me the steadfast love of the LORD, that I may not die; ¹⁵and do not cut off² your steadfast love from my house forever, when the LORD cuts off every one of the enemies of David from the face of the earth." ¹⁶And Jonathan made a covenant with the house of David, saying, "May³ the LORD take vengeance on David's enemies." ¹⁷And Jonathan made David swear again by his love for him, for he loved him as he loved his own soul.

¹⁸Then Jonathan said to him, "Tomorrow is the new moon, and you will be missed, because your seat will be empty. ¹⁹On the third day go down quickly to the place where you hid yourself when the matter was in hand, and remain beside the stone heap.⁴ ²⁰And I will shoot three arrows to the side of it, as though I shot at a mark. ²¹And behold, I will send the young man, saying, 'Go, find the arrows.' If I say to the

---

¹ Hebrew lacks *be witness* ² Or *but if I die, do not cut off* ³ Septuagint *earth,* ⁴ *let not the name of Jonathan be cut off from the house of David. And may* ⁴ Septuagint; Hebrew *the stone Ezel*

young man, 'Look, the arrows are on this side of you, take them,' then you are to come, for, as the LORD lives, it is safe for you and there is no danger. [22]But if I say to the youth, 'Look, the arrows are beyond you,' then go, for the LORD has sent you away. [23]And as for the matter of which you and I have spoken, behold, the LORD is between you and me forever."

[24]So David hid himself in the field. And when the new moon came, the king sat down to eat food. [25]The king sat on his seat, as at other times, on the seat by the wall. Jonathan sat opposite,[1] and Abner sat by Saul's side, but David's place was empty. [26]Yet Saul did not say anything that day, for he thought, "Something has happened to him. He is not clean; surely he is not clean." [27]But on the second day, the day after the new moon, David's place was empty. And Saul said to Jonathan his son, "Why has not the son of Jesse come to the meal, either yesterday or today?" [28]Jonathan answered Saul, "David earnestly asked leave of me to go to Bethlehem. [29]He said, 'Let me go, for our clan holds a sacrifice in the city, and my brother has commanded me to be there. So now, if I have found favor in your eyes, let me get away and see my brothers.' For this reason he has not come to the king's table."

[30]Then Saul's anger was kindled against Jonathan, and he said to him, "You son of a perverse, rebellious woman, do I not know that you have chosen the son of Jesse to your own shame, and to the shame of your mother's nakedness? [31]For as long as the son of Jesse lives on the earth, neither you nor your kingdom shall be established. Therefore send and bring him to me, for he shall surely die." [32]Then Jonathan answered Saul his father, "Why should he be put to death? What has he done?" [33]But Saul hurled his spear at him to strike him. So Jonathan knew that his father was determined to put David to death. [34]And Jonathan rose from the table in fierce anger and ate no food the second day of the month, for he was grieved for David, because his father had disgraced him.

[35]In the morning Jonathan went out into the field to the appointment with David, and with him a little boy. [36]And he said to his boy, "Run and find the arrows that I shoot." As the boy ran, he shot an arrow beyond him. [37]And when the boy came to the place of the arrow that Jonathan had shot, Jonathan called after the boy and said, "Is not the arrow beyond you?" [38]And Jonathan called after the boy, "Hurry! Be quick! Do not stay!" So Jonathan's boy gathered up the arrows and came to his master. [39]But the boy knew nothing. Only Jonathan and David knew the matter. [40]And Jonathan gave his weapons to his boy and said to him, "Go and carry them to the city." [41]And as soon as the boy had gone, David rose from beside the stone heap[2] and fell on his face to the ground and bowed three times. And they kissed one another and wept with one another, David weeping the most. [42]Then Jonathan said to David, "Go in peace, because we have sworn both of us in the name of the LORD, saying, 'The LORD shall be between me and you, and between my offspring and your offspring, forever.'" And he rose and departed, and Jonathan went into the city.[3]

Man on the run [chapters 21–22]. As David flees from Saul, he begins a phase of his life in which we can see a number of important literary *archetypes converge. David is most obviously a fugitive or man on the run. He is also a king-in-waiting. The story frequently involves narrow escapes for David, and surely no one would deny the name *adventure story to this section of 1 Samuel. Further, what we read frequently adheres

---

[1] Compare Septuagint; Hebrew *stood up* [2] Septuagint; Hebrew *from beside the south* [3] This sentence is 21:1 in Hebrew

to the conventions of the battle story. There is little overt religious sentiment in what the storyteller chose to give us; perhaps the main pattern that we discern is God's providential protection of his chosen future king.

21 [1] Then David came to Nob to Ahimelech the priest. And Ahimelech came to meet David trembling and said to him, "Why are you alone, and no one with you?" [2]And David said to Ahimelech the priest, "The king has charged me with a matter and said to me, 'Let no one know anything of the matter about which I send you, and with which I have charged you.' I have made an appointment with the young men for such and such a place. [3]Now then, what do you have on hand? Give me five loaves of bread, or whatever is here." [4]And the priest answered David, "I have no common bread on hand, but there is holy bread—if the young men have kept themselves from women." [5]And David answered the priest, "Truly women have been kept from us as always when I go on an expedition. The vessels of the young men are holy even when it is an ordinary journey. How much more today will their vessels be holy?" [6]So the priest gave him the holy bread, for there was no bread there but the bread of the Presence, which is removed from before the Lord, to be replaced by hot bread on the day it is taken away.

[7]Now a certain man of the servants of Saul was there that day, detained before the Lord. His name was Doeg the Edomite, the chief of Saul's herdsmen.

[8]Then David said to Ahimelech, "Then have you not here a spear or a sword at hand? For I have brought neither my sword nor my weapons with me, because the king's business required haste." [9]And the priest said, "The sword of Goliath the Philistine, whom you struck down in the Valley of Elah, behold, it is here wrapped in a cloth behind the ephod. If you will take that, take it, for there is none but that here." And David said, "There is none like that; give it to me."

[10]And David rose and fled that day from Saul and went to Achish the king of Gath. [11]And the servants of Achish said to him, "Is not this David the king of the land? Did they not sing to one another of him in dances,

'Saul has struck down his thousands,
    and David his ten thousands'?"

[12]And David took these words to heart and was much afraid of Achish the king of Gath. [13]So he changed his behavior before them and pretended to be insane in their hands and made marks on the doors of the gate and let his spittle run down his beard. [14]Then Achish said to his servants, "Behold, you see the man is mad. Why then have you brought him to me? [15]Do I lack madmen, that you have brought this fellow to behave as a madman in my presence? Shall this fellow come into my house?"

22 David departed from there and escaped to the cave of Adullam. And when his brothers and all his father's house heard it, they went down there to him. [2]And everyone who was in distress, and everyone who was in debt, and everyone who was bitter in soul,[2] gathered to him. And he became captain over them. And there were with him about four hundred men.

[3]And David went from there to Mizpeh of Moab. And he said to the king of Moab, "Please let my father and my mother stay[3] with you, till I know what God will do for

---

[1] Ch 21:2 in Hebrew [2] Or *discontented* [3] Syriac, Vulgate; Hebrew *go out*

me." ⁴And he left them with the king of Moab, and they stayed with him all the time that David was in the stronghold. ⁵Then the prophet Gad said to David, "Do not remain in the stronghold; depart, and go into the land of Judah." So David departed and went into the forest of Hereth.

⁶Now Saul heard that David was discovered, and the men who were with him. Saul was sitting at Gibeah under the tamarisk tree on the height with his spear in his hand, and all his servants were standing about him. ⁷And Saul said to his servants who stood about him, "Hear now, people of Benjamin; will the son of Jesse give every one of you fields and vineyards, will he make you all commanders of thousands and commanders of hundreds, ⁸that all of you have conspired against me? No one discloses to me when my son makes a covenant with the son of Jesse. None of you is sorry for me or discloses to me that my son has stirred up my servant against me, to lie in wait, as at this day." ⁹Then answered Doeg the Edomite, who stood by the servants of Saul, "I saw the son of Jesse coming to Nob, to Ahimelech the son of Ahitub, ¹⁰and he inquired of the LORD for him and gave him provisions and gave him the sword of Goliath the Philistine."

¹¹Then the king sent to summon Ahimelech the priest, the son of Ahitub, and all his father's house, the priests who were at Nob, and all of them came to the king. ¹²And Saul said, "Hear now, son of Ahitub." And he answered, "Here I am, my lord." ¹³And Saul said to him, "Why have you conspired against me, you and the son of Jesse, in that you have given him bread and a sword and have inquired of God for him, so that he has risen against me, to lie in wait, as at this day?" ¹⁴Then Ahimelech answered the king, "And who among all your servants is so faithful as David, who is the king's son-in-law, and captain over[1] your bodyguard, and honored in your house? ¹⁵Is today the first time that I have inquired of God for him? No! Let not the king impute anything to his servant or to all the house of my father, for your servant has known nothing of all this, much or little." ¹⁶And the king said, "You shall surely die, Ahimelech, you and all your father's house." ¹⁷And the king said to the guard who stood about him, "Turn and kill the priests of the LORD, because their hand also is with David, and they knew that he fled and did not disclose it to me." But the servants of the king would not put out their hand to strike the priests of the LORD. ¹⁸Then the king said to Doeg, "You turn and strike the priests." And Doeg the Edomite turned and struck down the priests, and he killed on that day eighty-five persons who wore the linen ephod. ¹⁹And Nob, the city of the priests, he put to the sword; both man and woman, child and infant, ox, donkey and sheep, he put to the sword.

²⁰But one of the sons of Ahimelech the son of Ahitub, named Abiathar, escaped and fled after David. ²¹And Abiathar told David that Saul had killed the priests of the LORD. ²²And David said to Abiathar, "I knew on that day, when Doeg the Edomite was there, that he would surely tell Saul. I have occasioned the death of all the persons of your father's house. ²³Stay with me; do not be afraid, for he who seeks my life seeks your life. With me you shall be in safekeeping."

David and Saul in conflict [chapters 23–24]. The conflict between the deranged king and the king-in-waiting who lives in fear of death unfolds with lifelike twists and turns. The governing principle is the archetypal plot motif of chase and flight. The context in which that pattern unfolds is a struggle for the throne, since Saul is the ruling king

---

[1] Septuagint, Targum; Hebrew *and has turned aside to*

who knows that the kingship will be given to his neighbor (15:28), that is, David. There is also a conflict of generations here, with the older Saul trying to prevent the younger David from taking the kingship from him. As an additional overlay, as we read we are aware that this is the history of God's covenant nation Israel. As a chapter of covenant history, it is sordid, with the ruling king squandering his time hunting down a rival. Yet the quantity of details that the author gives us shows that he regards all of the action as important. When David spares Saul's life (24:1–7), it is obvious that Saul's paranoid fear that David is plotting to supplant him as king is the product of his own diseased mind. Saul's tragic decline is running its course, and his emotional instability is part of the pattern when he swings from murderous intent to gushing praise of David as being more worthy than he is (24:16–22). As for the development of David as a character, his magnanimity toward Saul proves his worthiness as the eventual king.

23 Now they told David, "Behold, the Philistines are fighting against Keilah and are robbing the threshing floors." ²Therefore David inquired of the LORD, "Shall I go and attack these Philistines?" And the LORD said to David, "Go and attack the Philistines and save Keilah." ³But David's men said to him, "Behold, we are afraid here in Judah; how much more then if we go to Keilah against the armies of the Philistines?" ⁴Then David inquired of the LORD again. And the LORD answered him, "Arise, go down to Keilah, for I will give the Philistines into your hand." ⁵And David and his men went to Keilah and fought with the Philistines and brought away their livestock and struck them with a great blow. So David saved the inhabitants of Keilah.

⁶When Abiathar the son of Ahimelech had fled to David to Keilah, he had come down with an ephod in his hand. ⁷Now it was told Saul that David had come to Keilah. And Saul said, "God has given him into my hand, for he has shut himself in by entering a town that has gates and bars." ⁸And Saul summoned all the people to war, to go down to Keilah, to besiege David and his men. ⁹David knew that Saul was plotting harm against him. And he said to Abiathar the priest, "Bring the ephod here." ¹⁰Then said David, "O LORD, the God of Israel, your servant has surely heard that Saul seeks to come to Keilah, to destroy the city on my account. ¹¹Will the men of Keilah surrender me into his hand? Will Saul come down, as your servant has heard? O LORD, the God of Israel, please tell your servant." And the LORD said, "He will come down." ¹²Then David said, "Will the men of Keilah surrender me and my men into the hand of Saul?" And the LORD said, "They will surrender you." ¹³Then David and his men, who were about six hundred, arose and departed from Keilah, and they went wherever they could go. When Saul was told that David had escaped from Keilah, he gave up the expedition. ¹⁴And David remained in the strongholds in the wilderness, in the hill country of the wilderness of Ziph. And Saul sought him every day, but God did not give him into his hand.

¹⁵David saw that Saul had come out to seek his life. David was in the wilderness of Ziph at Horesh. ¹⁶And Jonathan, Saul's son, rose and went to David at Horesh, and strengthened his hand in God. ¹⁷And he said to him, "Do not fear, for the hand of Saul my father shall not find you. You shall be king over Israel, and I shall be next to you. Saul my father also knows this." ¹⁸And the two of them made a covenant before the LORD. David remained at Horesh, and Jonathan went home.

¹⁹Then the Ziphites went up to Saul at Gibeah, saying, "Is not David hiding among us in the strongholds at Horesh, on the hill of Hachilah, which is south of Jeshimon? ²⁰Now come down, O king, according to all your heart's desire to come down, and our part shall be to surrender him into the king's hand." ²¹And Saul said, "May you be blessed by the LORD, for you have had compassion on me. ²²Go, make yet more sure. Know and see the place where his foot is, and who has seen him there, for it is told me that he is very cunning. ²³See therefore and take note of all the lurking places where he hides, and come back to me with sure information. Then I will go with you. And if he is in the land, I will search him out among all the thousands of Judah." ²⁴And they arose and went to Ziph ahead of Saul.

Now David and his men were in the wilderness of Maon, in the Arabah to the south of Jeshimon. ²⁵And Saul and his men went to seek him. And David was told, so he went down to the rock and lived in the wilderness of Maon. And when Saul heard that, he pursued after David in the wilderness of Maon. ²⁶Saul went on one side of the mountain, and David and his men on the other side of the mountain. And David was hurrying to get away from Saul. As Saul and his men were closing in on David and his men to capture them, ²⁷a messenger came to Saul, saying, "Hurry and come, for the Philistines have made a raid against the land." ²⁸So Saul returned from pursuing after David and went against the Philistines. Therefore that place was called the Rock of Escape.¹ ²⁹² And David went up from there and lived in the strongholds of Engedi.

24 ³ When Saul returned from following the Philistines, he was told, "Behold, David is in the wilderness of Engedi." ²Then Saul took three thousand chosen men out of all Israel and went to seek David and his men in front of the Wildgoats' Rocks. ³And he came to the sheepfolds by the way, where there was a cave, and Saul went in to relieve himself.⁴ Now David and his men were sitting in the innermost parts of the cave. ⁴And the men of David said to him, "Here is the day of which the LORD said to you, 'Behold, I will give your enemy into your hand, and you shall do to him as it shall seem good to you.'" Then David arose and stealthily cut off a corner of Saul's robe. ⁵And afterward David's heart struck him, because he had cut off a corner of Saul's robe. ⁶He said to his men, "The LORD forbid that I should do this thing to my lord, the LORD's anointed, to put out my hand against him, seeing he is the LORD's anointed." ⁷So David persuaded his men with these words and did not permit them to attack Saul. And Saul rose up and left the cave and went on his way.

⁸Afterward David also arose and went out of the cave, and called after Saul, "My lord the king!" And when Saul looked behind him, David bowed with his face to the earth and paid homage. ⁹And David said to Saul, "Why do you listen to the words of men who say, 'Behold, David seeks your harm'? ¹⁰Behold, this day your eyes have seen how the LORD gave you today into my hand in the cave. And some told me to kill you, but I spared you.⁵ I said, 'I will not put out my hand against my lord, for he is the LORD's anointed.' ¹¹See, my father, see the corner of your robe in my hand. For by the fact that I cut off the corner of your robe and did not kill you, you may know and see that there is no wrong or treason in my hands. I have not sinned against you, though you hunt my life to take it. ¹²May the LORD judge between me and you, may the LORD avenge me against you, but my hand shall not be against you. ¹³As the proverb of the ancients says, 'Out of the wicked comes wickedness.' But my hand shall not be against you. ¹⁴After whom has the king of Israel come out? After whom do you pur-

sue? After a dead dog! After a flea! ¹⁵May the LORD therefore be judge and give sentence between me and you, and see to it and plead my cause and deliver me from your hand."

¹⁶As soon as David had finished speaking these words to Saul, Saul said, "Is this your voice, my son David?" And Saul lifted up his voice and wept. ¹⁷He said to David, "You are more righteous than I, for you have repaid me good, whereas I have repaid you evil. ¹⁸And you have declared this day how you have dealt well with me, in that you did not kill me when the LORD put me into your hands. ¹⁹For if a man finds his enemy, will he let him go away safe? So may the LORD reward you with good for what you have done to me this day. ²⁰And now, behold, I know that you shall surely be king, and that the kingdom of Israel shall be established in your hand. ²¹Swear to me therefore by the LORD that you will not cut off my offspring after me, and that you will not destroy my name out of my father's house." ²²And David swore this to Saul. Then Saul went home, but David and his men went up to the stronghold.

> **David recognizes something good when he sees her** [chapter 25]. The tense public history of David and Saul, which is a nearly continuous narrow escape for David, takes a break with this chapter, which tells the story of David and Abigail. In its own way, it is a love story that springs from an unlikely set of circumstances. The key to grasping what happens in this chapter is to realize that it is the story of a heroine—a woman of worth named Abigail. Perhaps through no fault of her own, Abigail begins the story married to a "harsh and badly behaved" man (v. 3)—a man whose name, Nabal, is a pun on the Hebrew word meaning fool (as in our circles the name Bill is also a pun on the word for a payment that is due). The story gives us an interesting glimpse into what life was like for the fugitive David, and it unfolds according to these phases: because David's Robin Hood–style band has protected Nabal's sheep from raids, David legitimately requests food from Nabal during the time of sheep shearing (vv. 1–8); when the churlish Nabal responds by insulting David, David loses his temper and sets off immediately to attack him (vv. 9–13); Nabal's clever wife intercepts David with lavish provision of food, and she also speaks eloquently and sensibly to him (vv. 14–31); David is very impressed and immediately relents in his anger (vv. 32–35); after Nabal recovers from his drunken state, Abigail informs him of what she has done, and Nabal promptly experiences a heart-stopping moment and dies ten days later (vv. 36–38); David, who knew a good thing when he saw it, woos and marries Abigail (vv. 39–44).

25 Now Samuel died. And all Israel assembled and mourned for him, and they buried him in his house at Ramah.

Then David rose and went down to the wilderness of Paran. ²And there was a man in Maon whose business was in Carmel. The man was very rich; he had three thousand sheep and a thousand goats. He was shearing his sheep in Carmel. ³Now the name of the man was Nabal, and the name of his wife Abigail. The woman was discerning and beautiful, but the man was harsh and badly behaved; he was a Calebite. ⁴David heard in the wilderness that Nabal was shearing his sheep. ⁵So David sent ten young men. And David said to the young men, "Go up to Carmel, and go to Nabal and greet him in my name. ⁶And thus you shall greet him: 'Peace be to you, and peace be to your house, and peace be to all that you have. ⁷I hear that you have shearers. Now your shepherds have been with us, and we did them no harm, and they missed nothing all the time they were in Carmel. ⁸Ask your young men, and they will tell you. Therefore let my young men find favor in your eyes, for we come on a feast day. Please give whatever you have at hand to your servants and to your son David.'"

⁹When David's young men came, they said all this to Nabal in the name of David, and then they waited. ¹⁰And Nabal answered David's servants, "Who is David? Who is the son of Jesse? There are many servants these days who are breaking away from their masters. ¹¹Shall I take my bread and my water and my meat that I have killed for my shearers and give it to men who come from I do not know where?" ¹²So David's young men turned away and came back and told him all this. ¹³And David said to his men, "Every man strap on his sword!" And every man of them strapped on his sword. David also strapped on his sword. And about four hundred men went up after David, while two hundred remained with the baggage.

¹⁴But one of the young men told Abigail, Nabal's wife, "Behold, David sent messengers out of the wilderness to greet our master, and he railed at them. ¹⁵Yet the men were very good to us, and we suffered no harm, and we did not miss anything when we were in the fields, as long as we went with them. ¹⁶They were a wall to us both by night and by day, all the while we were with them keeping the sheep. ¹⁷Now therefore know this and consider what you should do, for harm is determined against our master and against all his house, and he is such a worthless man that one cannot speak to him."

¹⁸Then Abigail made haste and took two hundred loaves and two skins of wine and five sheep already prepared and five seahs[1] of parched grain and a hundred clusters of raisins and two hundred cakes of figs, and laid them on donkeys. ¹⁹And she said to her young men, "Go on before me; behold, I come after you." But she did not tell her husband Nabal. ²⁰And as she rode on the donkey and came down under cover of the mountain, behold, David and his men came down toward her, and she met them. ²¹Now David had said, "Surely in vain have I guarded all that this fellow has in the wilderness, so that nothing was missed of all that belonged to him, and he has returned me evil for good. ²²God do so to the enemies of David[2] and more also, if by morning I leave so much as one male of all who belong to him."

²³When Abigail saw David, she hurried and got down from the donkey and fell before David on her face and bowed to the ground. ²⁴She fell at his feet and said, "On me alone, my lord, be the guilt. Please let your servant speak in your ears, and hear the words of your servant. ²⁵Let not my lord regard this worthless fellow, Nabal, for as his name is, so is he. Nabal[3] is his name, and folly is with him. But I your servant did not see the young men of my lord, whom you sent. ²⁶Now then, my lord, as the Lord lives, and as your soul lives, because the Lord has restrained you from bloodguilt and from saving with your own hand, now then let your enemies and those who seek to do evil to my lord be as Nabal. ²⁷And now let this present that your servant has brought to my lord be given to the young men who follow my lord. ²⁸Please forgive the trespass of your servant. For the Lord will certainly make my lord a sure house, because my lord is fighting the battles of the Lord, and evil shall not be found in you so long as you live. ²⁹If men rise up to pursue you and to seek your life, the life of my lord shall be bound in the bundle of the living in the care of the Lord your God. And the lives of your enemies he shall sling out as from the hollow of a sling. ³⁰And when the Lord has done to my lord according to all the good that he has spoken concerning you and has appointed you prince over Israel, ³¹my lord shall have no cause of

---

[1] A *seah* was about 7 quarts or 7.3 liters [2] Septuagint *to David* [3] *Nabal* means *fool*

grief or pangs of conscience for having shed blood without cause or for my lord taking vengeance himself. And when the LORD has dealt well with my lord, then remember your servant."

³²And David said to Abigail, "Blessed be the LORD, the God of Israel, who sent you
this day to meet me! ³³Blessed be your discretion, and blessed be you, who have kept
me this day from bloodguilt and from avenging myself with my own hand! ³⁴For as
surely as the LORD, the God of Israel, lives, who has restrained me from hurting you,
unless you had hurried and come to meet me, truly by morning there had not been
left to Nabal so much as one male." ³⁵Then David received from her hand what she
had brought him. And he said to her, "Go up in peace to your house. See, I have
obeyed your voice, and I have granted your petition."

³⁶And Abigail came to Nabal, and behold, he was holding a feast in his house, like
the feast of a king. And Nabal's heart was merry within him, for he was very drunk.
So she told him nothing at all until the morning light. ³⁷In the morning, when the
wine had gone out of Nabal, his wife told him these things, and his heart died within
him, and he became as a stone. ³⁸And about ten days later the LORD struck Nabal, and
he died.

³⁹When David heard that Nabal was dead, he said, "Blessed be the LORD who has
avenged the insult I received at the hand of Nabal, and has kept back his servant
from wrongdoing. The LORD has returned the evil of Nabal on his own head." Then
David sent and spoke to Abigail, to take her as his wife. ⁴⁰When the servants of David
came to Abigail at Carmel, they said to her, "David has sent us to you to take you to
him as his wife." ⁴¹And she rose and bowed with her face to the ground and said,
"Behold, your handmaid is a servant to wash the feet of the servants of my lord."
⁴²And Abigail hurried and rose and mounted a donkey, and her five young women
attended her. She followed the messengers of David and became his wife.

⁴³David also took Ahinoam of Jezreel, and both of them became his wives. ⁴⁴Saul
had given Michal his daughter, David's wife, to Palti the son of Laish, who was of
Gallim.

Déjà vu in the story of Saul and David [chapter 26]. The text returns to the saga of
Saul's attempt to eliminate the person he wrongly thinks is a rival for the throne. The
second episode in which David spares Saul's life when he could easily have killed the
king is a virtual rerun of the event narrated two chapters earlier. This episode meets all
the requirements of an adventure story. The ingredients include chase and flight, hidden
moves in the darkness, close calls, tricks played on an unsuspecting person, and dramatic disclosure of secret events and identities.

26 Then the Ziphites came to Saul at Gibeah, saying, "Is not David hiding himself on the hill of Hachilah, which is on the east of Jeshimon?" ²So Saul arose
and went down to the wilderness of Ziph with three thousand chosen men of Israel
to seek David in the wilderness of Ziph. ³And Saul encamped on the hill of Hachilah,
which is beside the road on the east of Jeshimon. But David remained in the wilderness. When he saw that Saul came after him into the wilderness, ⁴David sent out
spies and learned that Saul had come. ⁵Then David rose and came to the place where
Saul had encamped. And David saw the place where Saul lay, with Abner the son of

Ner, the commander of his army. Saul was lying within the encampment, while the army was encamped around him.

⁶Then David said to Ahimelech the Hittite, and to Joab's brother Abishai the son of Zeruiah, "Who will go down with me into the camp to Saul?" And Abishai said, "I will go down with you." ⁷So David and Abishai went to the army by night. And there lay Saul sleeping within the encampment, with his spear stuck in the ground at his head, and Abner and the army lay around him. ⁸Then said Abishai to David, "God has given your enemy into your hand this day. Now please let me pin him to the earth with one stroke of the spear, and I will not strike him twice." ⁹But David said to Abishai, "Do not destroy him, for who can put out his hand against the Lord's anointed and be guiltless?" ¹⁰And David said, "As the Lord lives, the Lord will strike him, or his day will come to die, or he will go down into battle and perish. ¹¹The Lord forbid that I should put out my hand against the Lord's anointed. But take now the spear that is at his head and the jar of water, and let us go." ¹²So David took the spear and the jar of water from Saul's head, and they went away. No man saw it or knew it, nor did any awake, for they were all asleep, because a deep sleep from the Lord had fallen upon them.

¹³Then David went over to the other side and stood far off on the top of the hill, with a great space between them. ¹⁴And David called to the army, and to Abner the son of Ner, saying, "Will you not answer, Abner?" Then Abner answered, "Who are you who calls to the king?" ¹⁵And David said to Abner, "Are you not a man? Who is like you in Israel? Why then have you not kept watch over your lord the king? For one of the people came in to destroy the king your lord. ¹⁶This thing that you have done is not good. As the Lord lives, you deserve to die, because you have not kept watch over your lord, the Lord's anointed. And now see where the king's spear is and the jar of water that was at his head."

¹⁷Saul recognized David's voice and said, "Is this your voice, my son David?" And David said, "It is my voice, my lord, O king." ¹⁸And he said, "Why does my lord pursue after his servant? For what have I done? What evil is on my hands? ¹⁹Now therefore let my lord the king hear the words of his servant. If it is the Lord who has stirred you up against me, may he accept an offering, but if it is men, may they be cursed before the Lord, for they have driven me out this day that I should have no share in the heritage of the Lord, saying, 'Go, serve other gods.' ²⁰Now therefore, let not my blood fall to the earth away from the presence of the Lord, for the king of Israel has come out to seek a single flea like one who hunts a partridge in the mountains."

²¹Then Saul said, "I have sinned. Return, my son David, for I will no more do you harm, because my life was precious in your eyes this day. Behold, I have acted foolishly, and have made a great mistake." ²²And David answered and said, "Here is the spear, O king! Let one of the young men come over and take it. ²³The Lord rewards every man for his righteousness and his faithfulness, for the Lord gave you into my hand today, and I would not put out my hand against the Lord's anointed. ²⁴Behold, as your life was precious this day in my sight, so may my life be precious in the sight of the Lord, and may he deliver me out of all tribulation." ²⁵Then Saul said to David, "Blessed be you, my son David! You will do many things and will succeed in them." So David went his way, and Saul returned to his place.

David's career as fugitive and trickster [chapter 27]. David is still the king-in-waiting, and this is why the storyteller continues to trace his life. Chapter 27 deals with a
single phase of David's life as a fugitive: the era in which he is under the protection
of Achish, king of Gath. The chapter unfolds according to the following sequence: David
decides to pursue his fugitive life in the land of the Philistines, specifically in alliance
with Achish, king of Gath (vv. 1–4); David receives the town of Ziklag for as a residence
for himself and his band of six hundred warriors (vv. 5–7); David tricks Achish into thinking that he is conducting raids against the outposts of David's own nation, whereas he
is actually killing off the enemies of Israel (vv. 8–12). The author's tone is objective, and
we are left to our own intuitions regarding whether David's behavior is right or wrong.

27 Then David said in his heart, "Now I shall perish one day by the hand of
Saul. There is nothing better for me than that I should escape to the land of the
Philistines. Then Saul will despair of seeking me any longer within the borders of
Israel, and I shall escape out of his hand." ²So David arose and went over, he and the
six hundred men who were with him, to Achish the son of Maoch, king of Gath. ³And
David lived with Achish at Gath, he and his men, every man with his household, and
David with his two wives, Ahinoam of Jezreel, and Abigail of Carmel, Nabal's widow.
⁴And when it was told Saul that David had fled to Gath, he no longer sought him.

⁵Then David said to Achish, "If I have found favor in your eyes, let a place be given
me in one of the country towns, that I may dwell there. For why should your servant
dwell in the royal city with you?" ⁶So that day Achish gave him Ziklag. Therefore
Ziklag has belonged to the kings of Judah to this day. ⁷And the number of the days
that David lived in the country of the Philistines was a year and four months.

⁸Now David and his men went up and made raids against the Geshurites, the
Girzites, and the Amalekites, for these were the inhabitants of the land from of old,
as far as Shur, to the land of Egypt. ⁹And David would strike the land and would leave
neither man nor woman alive, but would take away the sheep, the oxen, the donkeys,
the camels, and the garments, and come back to Achish. ¹⁰When Achish asked,
"Where have you made a raid today?" David would say, "Against the Negeb of
Judah," or, "Against the Negeb of the Jerahmeelites," or, "Against the Negeb of the
Kenites." ¹¹And David would leave neither man nor woman alive to bring news to
Gath, thinking, "lest they should tell about us and say, 'So David has done.'" Such was
his custom all the while he lived in the country of the Philistines. ¹²And Achish
trusted David, thinking, "He has made himself an utter stench to his people Israel;
therefore he shall always be my servant."

The low point of Saul's tragic decline [chapter 28]. David's relative success as a
man on the run is now contrasted to Saul's increasingly desperate situation, which
reaches its nadir with his visit to the female medium at Endor. Saul has become the
archetypal secretive, superstitious, and sleazy political ruler. We relive the event in vivid
detail and are made to feel its tawdriness. The summoning of the spirit of the deceased
Samuel is the final oracle that Samuel delivers to Saul, and in keeping with the unfolding pattern, the word of judgment is now even more personal and immediate than the
previous oracles of judgment, as Samuel announces that Saul will die on the following
day (v. 19). In terms of the pattern of literary tragedy that has been unfolding, we should

note that Samuel reiterates Saul's tragic mistake in the war against the Amalekites as
the turning point of his life (v. 18).

28 In those days the Philistines gathered their forces for war, to fight against Israel. And Achish said to David, "Understand that you and your men are to go out with me in the army." ²David said to Achish, "Very well, you shall know what your servant can do." And Achish said to David, "Very well, I will make you my body-guard for life."

³Now Samuel had died, and all Israel had mourned for him and buried him in Ramah, his own city. And Saul had put the mediums and the necromancers out of the land. ⁴The Philistines assembled and came and encamped at Shunem. And Saul gathered all Israel, and they encamped at Gilboa. ⁵When Saul saw the army of the Philistines, he was afraid, and his heart trembled greatly. ⁶And when Saul inquired of the LORD, the LORD did not answer him, either by dreams, or by Urim, or by prophets. ⁷Then Saul said to his servants, "Seek out for me a woman who is a medium, that I may go to her and inquire of her." And his servants said to him, "Behold, there is a medium at En-dor."

⁸So Saul disguised himself and put on other garments and went, he and two men with him. And they came to the woman by night. And he said, "Divine for me by a spirit and bring up for me whomever I shall name to you." ⁹The woman said to him, "Surely you know what Saul has done, how he has cut off the mediums and the necromancers from the land. Why then are you laying a trap for my life to bring about my death?" ¹⁰But Saul swore to her by the LORD, "As the LORD lives, no punishment shall come upon you for this thing." ¹¹Then the woman said, "Whom shall I bring up for you?" He said, "Bring up Samuel for me." ¹²When the woman saw Samuel, she cried out with a loud voice. And the woman said to Saul, "Why have you deceived me? You are Saul." ¹³The king said to her, "Do not be afraid. What do you see?" And the woman said to Saul, "I see a god coming up out of the earth." ¹⁴He said to her, "What is his appearance?" And she said, "An old man is coming up, and he is wrapped in a robe." And Saul knew that it was Samuel, and he bowed with his face to the ground and paid homage.

¹⁵Then Samuel said to Saul, "Why have you disturbed me by bringing me up?" Saul answered, "I am in great distress, for the Philistines are warring against me, and God has turned away from me and answers me no more, either by prophets or by dreams. Therefore I have summoned you to tell me what I shall do." ¹⁶And Samuel said, "Why then do you ask me, since the LORD has turned from you and become your enemy? ¹⁷The LORD has done to you as he spoke by me, for the LORD has torn the kingdom out of your hand and given it to your neighbor, David. ¹⁸Because you did not obey the voice of the LORD and did not carry out his fierce wrath against Amalek, therefore the LORD has done this thing to you this day. ¹⁹Moreover, the LORD will give Israel also with you into the hand of the Philistines, and tomorrow you and your sons shall be with me. The LORD will give the army of Israel also into the hand of the Philistines."

²⁰Then Saul fell at once full length on the ground, filled with fear because of the words of Samuel. And there was no strength in him, for he had eaten nothing all day and all night. ²¹And the woman came to Saul, and when she saw that he was terrified, she said to him, "Behold, your servant has obeyed you. I have taken my life in my

hand and have listened to what you have said to me. ²²Now therefore, you also obey your servant. Let me set a morsel of bread before you; and eat, that you may have strength when you go on your way." ²³He refused and said, "I will not eat." But his servants, together with the woman, urged him, and he listened to their words. So he arose from the earth and sat on the bed. ²⁴Now the woman had a fattened calf in the house, and she quickly killed it, and she took flour and kneaded it and baked unleavened bread of it, ²⁵and she put it before Saul and his servants, and they ate. Then they rose and went away that night.

> **David as military conqueror** [chapters 29–30]. Increasingly as the story of 1 Samuel unfolds, David ceases to be a Robin Hood figure leading a merry band of outlaws and becomes a heroic warrior in the epic mold. The action in this unit focuses on a single battle. It began as a war of the Philistines against the Israelites, with David being dismissed from the Philistine army because the lords of the Philistines doubted his loyalty (chapter 21). When he arrives back at his town of Ziklag, he finds that it has been destroyed by the Amalekites and the families taken captive (30:1–6), whereupon he pursues and defeats the Amalekites (30:7–20). Dividing the spoils was a military ritual in epic literature and ancient cultures, and here it becomes amplified into a story laden with multiple significance (30:21–30).

29 Now the Philistines had gathered all their forces at Aphek. And the Israelites were encamped by the spring that is in Jezreel. ²As the lords of the Philistines were passing on by hundreds and by thousands, and David and his men were passing on in the rear with Achish, ³the commanders of the Philistines said, "What are these Hebrews doing here?" And Achish said to the commanders of the Philistines, "Is this not David, the servant of Saul, king of Israel, who has been with me now for days and years, and since he deserted to me I have found no fault in him to this day." ⁴But the commanders of the Philistines were angry with him. And the commanders of the Philistines said to him, "Send the man back, that he may return to the place to which you have assigned him. He shall not go down with us to battle, lest in the battle he become an adversary to us. For how could this fellow reconcile himself to his lord? Would it not be with the heads of the men here? ⁵Is not this David, of whom they sing to one another in dances,

'Saul has struck down his thousands,
  and David his ten thousands'?"

⁶Then Achish called David and said to him, "As the LORD lives, you have been honest, and to me it seems right that you should march out and in with me in the campaign. For I have found nothing wrong in you from the day of your coming to me to this day. Nevertheless, the lords do not approve of you. ⁷So go back now; and go peaceably, that you may not displease the lords of the Philistines." ⁸And David said to Achish, "But what have I done? What have you found in your servant from the day I entered your service until now, that I may not go and fight against the enemies of my lord the king?" ⁹And Achish answered David and said, "I know that you are as blameless in my sight as an angel of God. Nevertheless, the commanders of the Philistines have said, 'He shall not go up with us to the battle.' ¹⁰Now then rise early in the morn-

ing with the servants of your lord who came with you, and start early in the morning, and depart as soon as you have light." ¹¹So David set out with his men early in the morning to return to the land of the Philistines. But the Philistines went up to Jezreel.

30 Now when David and his men came to Ziklag on the third day, the Amalekites had made a raid against the Negeb and against Ziklag. They had overcome Ziklag and burned it with fire ²and taken captive the women and all¹ who were in it, both small and great. They killed no one, but carried them off and went their way. ³And when David and his men came to the city, they found it burned with fire, and their wives and sons and daughters taken captive. ⁴Then David and the people who were with him raised their voices and wept until they had no more strength to weep. ⁵David's two wives also had been taken captive, Ahinoam of Jezreel and Abigail the widow of Nabal of Carmel. ⁶And David was greatly distressed, for the people spoke of stoning him, because all the people were bitter in soul,² each for his sons and daughters. But David strengthened himself in the LORD his God.

⁷And David said to Abiathar the priest, the son of Ahimelech, "Bring me the ephod." So Abiathar brought the ephod to David. ⁸And David inquired of the LORD, "Shall I pursue after this band? Shall I overtake them?" He answered him, "Pursue, for you shall surely overtake and shall surely rescue." ⁹So David set out, and the six hundred men who were with him, and they came to the brook Besor, where those who were left behind stayed. ¹⁰But David pursued, he and four hundred men. Two hundred stayed behind, who were too exhausted to cross the brook Besor.

¹¹They found an Egyptian in the open country and brought him to David. And they gave him bread and he ate. They gave him water to drink, ¹²and they gave him a piece of a cake of figs and two clusters of raisins. And when he had eaten, his spirit revived, for he had not eaten bread or drunk water for three days and three nights. ¹³And David said to him, "To whom do you belong? And where are you from?" He said, "I am a young man of Egypt, servant to an Amalekite, and my master left me behind because I fell sick three days ago. ¹⁴We had made a raid against the Negeb of the Cherethites and against that which belongs to Judah and against the Negeb of Caleb, and we burned Ziklag with fire." ¹⁵And David said to him, "Will you take me down to this band?" And he said, "Swear to me by God that you will not kill me or deliver me into the hands of my master, and I will take you down to this band."

¹⁶And when he had taken him down, behold, they were spread abroad over all the land, eating and drinking and dancing, because of all the great spoil they had taken from the land of the Philistines and from the land of Judah. ¹⁷And David struck them down from twilight until the evening of the next day, and not a man of them escaped, except four hundred young men, who mounted camels and fled. ¹⁸David recovered all that the Amalekites had taken, and David rescued his two wives. ¹⁹Nothing was missing, whether small or great, sons or daughters, spoil or anything that had been taken. David brought back all. ²⁰David also captured all the flocks and herds, and the people drove the livestock before him,³ and said, "This is David's spoil."

²¹Then David came to the two hundred men who had been too exhausted to follow David, and who had been left at the brook Besor. And they went out to meet David and to meet the people who were with him. And when David came near to the people he greeted them. ²²Then all the wicked and worthless fellows among the men who had gone with David said, "Because they did not go with us, we will not give them any

---

¹ Septuagint; Hebrew lacks *and all* ² Compare 22:2 ³ The meaning of the Hebrew clause is uncertain

of the spoil that we have recovered, except that each man may lead away his wife and children, and depart." ²³But David said, "You shall not do so, my brothers, with what the LORD has given us. He has preserved us and given into our hand the band that came against us. ²⁴Who would listen to you in this matter? For as his share is who goes down into the battle, so shall his share be who stays by the baggage. They shall share alike." ²⁵And he made it a statute and a rule for Israel from that day forward to this day.

²⁶When David came to Ziklag, he sent part of the spoil to his friends, the elders of Judah, saying, "Here is a present for you from the spoil of the enemies of the LORD." ²⁷It was for those in Bethel, in Ramoth of the Negeb, in Jattir, ²⁸in Aroer, in Siphmoth, in Eshtemoa, ²⁹in Racal, in the cities of the Jerahmeelites, in the cities of the Kenites, ³⁰in Hormah, in Bor-ashan, in Athach, ³¹in Hebron, for all the places where David and his men had roamed.

The death of Saul [chapter 31]. The tragic end of Saul concludes the book of 1 Samuel, confirming that the dominant pattern in the book has been the tragedy of Saul. The action of this battle story is divided into the following events: the ignominious battlefield death of Saul by suicide (vv. 1–6); the flight of the Israelites before the Philistines (v. 7); the postbattle rituals of collecting the armor of the casualties and displaying the armor of vanquished leaders (vv. 8–10); the heroic retrieval of the bodies of Saul and his sons from gloating adversaries (vv. 12–13).

31 Now the Philistines fought against Israel, and the men of Israel fled before the Philistines and fell slain on Mount Gilboa. ²And the Philistines overtook Saul and his sons, and the Philistines struck down Jonathan and Abinadab and Malchi-shua, the sons of Saul. ³The battle pressed hard against Saul, and the archers found him, and he was badly wounded by the archers. ⁴Then Saul said to his armor-bearer, "Draw your sword, and thrust me through with it, lest these uncircumcised come and thrust me through, and mistreat me." But his armor-bearer would not, for he feared greatly. Therefore Saul took his own sword and fell upon it. ⁵And when his armor-bearer saw that Saul was dead, he also fell upon his sword and died with him. ⁶Thus Saul died, and his three sons, and his armor-bearer, and all his men, on the same day together. ⁷And when the men of Israel who were on the other side of the valley and those beyond the Jordan saw that the men of Israel had fled and that Saul and his sons were dead, they abandoned their cities and fled. And the Philistines came and lived in them.

⁸The next day, when the Philistines came to strip the slain, they found Saul and his three sons fallen on Mount Gilboa. ⁹So they cut off his head and stripped off his armor and sent messengers throughout the land of the Philistines, to carry the good news to the house of their idols and to the people. ¹⁰They put his armor in the temple of Ashtaroth, and they fastened his body to the wall of Beth-shan. ¹¹But when the inhabitants of Jabesh-gilead heard what the Philistines had done to Saul, ¹²all the valiant men arose and went all night and took the body of Saul and the bodies of his sons from the wall of Beth-shan, and they came to Jabesh and burned them there. ¹³And they took their bones and buried them under the tamarisk tree in Jabesh and fasted seven days.

2 SAMUEL

The book at a glance. 24 chapters, 695 verses. Like 1 Samuel, this book is a historical chronicle that uses literary resources for telling a nation's history. Considered in the ancient context that produced the book, it can be called court history, meaning that its chief subject matter is the history of what happened at court (where the king was the dominant figure), recorded by official court historians. Whereas 1 Samuel focused on several major characters, from start to finish 2 Samuel belongs to the central heroic figure of David. The author was obviously privy to personal information about David in addition to his actions in the public and political spheres. Throughout, we need to pay attention to the ways in which God is a leading actor in the story.

▌**Genres.** Set within the general framework of a historical chronicle, 2 Samuel is primarily the prose *epic of David, telling the story of a nation led by a heroic leader. It is at the same time a *hero story in which the protagonist, while not wholly idealized, is a largely exemplary and representative character who embodies the struggles and ideals of his society. While the story does not possess the single linear sequence of literary *tragedy, it meets the essential tragic criterion of locating the source of the hero's downfall in a single tragic choice. We should picture David's life as portrayed in 2 Samuel as a pyramid: the trajectory is positive until the Bathsheba/Uriah debacle, after which David's life goes into decline as tragic consequences work their poison. Of course the general *narrative grid of *plot, *character, and *setting are continuously operative as we progress through the individual episodes of the larger epic and tragedy. (For more information on items accompanied by an asterisk, see the glossary at the back of this Bible.)

▌**Unifying elements.** The presence of David as the engaging central character is the primary unifying focus of this collection of stories. The world of the story also unifies the book: it is a political and courtly world, a military world, a religious world, and a domestic world. Two threads of action make up the story of David's heroic life—the public life of a king and the personal life of a family man.

▌**Storytelling technique.** David is one of the most colorful characters in the Bible—a bigger-than-life figure of heroic accomplishments and passions. The strategy of the author of 2 Samuel is to build virtually everything around this heroic figure. The interpretation that he gives to David's life (not shared by the authors of Kings and Chronicles) falls into a tragic pattern, with David's decline traceable to a single point in his life, narrated in 2 Samuel 11. The test motif sums up a lot of what the author

Passage	Narrative Event	David's Life Story	Sphere of David's Rule	Time Frame
1:1–27	Death of Saul and Jonathan, and David's response	David gradually consolidates his political power	David rules Judah only, from Hebron	Seven-and-a-half years
2:1–4:12	David rules Judah and battles Israel			
5:1–25	David becomes king over all Israel			
6:1–23	David brings the ark to Jerusalem	David as worshiper	David rules all Israel from Jerusalem	33 years
7:1–29	David's desire to build a temple refused by God			
8:1–10:19	David's successes	David's early reign		
11:1–12:31	David, Bathsheba, and Uriah	David's tragic choice		
13:1–18:33	David's conflict with Absalom; civil war	The tragic consequences of David's sin		
19:1–21:22	David's further kingship	David's mixed record as king		
22:1–23:7	David's hymns of praise			
23:8–39	David's mighty men			
24:1–25	God's punishment of David for taking a census			

wished to say about life, as characters are repeatedly put into situations that test them. The technique of *realism permeates the book as the storyteller refuses to ignore either the good or bad aspects of the characters. The story is rich in recognizable human experiences. The dramatic impulse to present the actual words and dialogues of characters is continuous.

▌**Inferred literary intentions.** The book is designed to achieve the following literary purposes:

- tell the epic story of the nation of Israel under the kingship of David

- unify the action around the engaging central figure of David and thereby adhere to the conventions of the hero story

- lead us to see the literary pattern of tragedy in the life of David

- narrate the dual story of David's public and personal lives during his forty years as king

- show the failings as well as the virtues and successes of the protagonist

- tell the story with heavy reliance on the literary resources of drama (quoted speeches and dialogues) and realism

- capture the lives of other public figures beyond David, as well as lesser-known events in the lives of little-known characters

- deal with the historical data in such a way as to exemplify universal human experience

▌Theological themes. (1) The covenant: the kingship of David was central to God's plan to save the human race through a lineage that would culminate in the birth of Jesus. (2) Godly leadership: this is a story of a king and nation, and in it we see what constitutes good and bad leadership in the eyes of God. (3) Sin, repentance, and forgiveness: the central event of the story, David's sin and its aftermath, is a case study in how sin operates and what can and cannot be done about it after it has been committed. (4) Society: the social emphasis of 2 Samuel is on the inherently flawed nature and fragility of human institutions, including family and state.

▌2 Samuel as a chapter in the master story of the Bible. The story of redemptive history ascribes great importance to David. Jesus came from the line of David, and in the messianic prophecy of Ezekiel 34:22–23 Jesus is even called "my servant David." Along with 1 Chronicles, 2 Samuel is the "official biography" of David. Of particular importance is the so-called Davidic covenant that God establishes with David in 2 Samuel 7:11–16, with God's promise of an everlasting kingdom that is fulfilled in the kingship of Christ. We can also note an implied foil: Jesus is the perfect king who never meets the kind of tragic downfall that engulfed David as a result of his sins.

David's lament over the deaths of Saul and Jonathan [chapter 1]. The last chapter of 1 Samuel flows seamlessly into the opening chapter of 2 Samuel. The death of Saul was narrated in the previous book, and as 2 Samuel opens we overhear the announcement of the deaths of Saul and Jonathan to David. In a book that will be replete with recognizable human experiences, we meet this element already in the opening paragraph as we read about the archetypal opportunist in the form of a messenger who, in expectation of winning David's favor, fabricates a story of his having killed King Saul. The execution of the messenger on the command of David is reported objectively, with no hint as to how the storyteller thinks we should respond. This is typical of the storytelling technique in the Bible, where the writers narrate what happened but only occasionally explain or interpret it. David, we know, was a poet, and his emotional response to the deaths of Saul and Jonathan is expressed in a *lyric genre that has been important to literature generally but is present in the Bible only in this chapter. It is known as elegy—a poem about death occasioned by the passing of a specific person. In a conventional elegy, a poet expresses grief, celebrates the lost person, and comes to grips with the loss. David's brief elegy, written in the verse form of parallelism, laments the loss and celebrates the accomplishments of two deceased leaders of Israel, one of them David's closest friend (v. 26).

1 After the death of Saul, when David had returned from striking down the Amalekites, David remained two days in Ziklag. ²And on the third day, behold, a man came from Saul's camp, with his clothes torn and dirt on his head. And when he came to David, he fell to the ground and paid homage. ³David said to him, "Where do you come from?" And he said to him, "I have escaped from the camp of Israel." ⁴And David said to him, "How did it go? Tell me." And he answered, "The people fled from the battle, and also many of the people have fallen and are dead, and Saul and his son Jonathan are also dead." ⁵Then David said to the young man who told him, "How do you know that Saul and his son Jonathan are dead?" ⁶And the young man who told him said, "By chance I happened to be on Mount Gilboa, and there was Saul leaning on his spear, and behold, the chariots and the horsemen were close upon him. ⁷And when he looked behind him, he saw me, and called to me. And I answered, 'Here I am.' ⁸And he said to me, 'Who are you?' I answered him, 'I am an Amalekite.' ⁹And he said to me 'Stand beside me and kill me, for anguish has seized me, and yet my life still lingers.' ¹⁰So I stood beside him and killed him, because I was sure that he could not live after he had fallen. And I took the crown that was on his head and the armlet that was on his arm, and I have brought them here to my lord."

¹¹Then David took hold of his clothes and tore them, and so did all the men who were with him. ¹²And they mourned and wept and fasted until evening for Saul and for Jonathan his son and for the people of the Lᴏʀᴅ and for the house of Israel, because they had fallen by the sword. ¹³And David said to the young man who told him, "Where do you come from?" And he answered, "I am the son of a sojourner, an Amalekite." ¹⁴David said to him, "How is it you were not afraid to put out your hand to destroy the Lᴏʀᴅ's anointed?" ¹⁵Then David called one of the young men and said, "Go, execute him." And he struck him down so that he died. ¹⁶And David said to him, "Your blood be on your head, for your own mouth has testified against you, saying, 'I have killed the Lᴏʀᴅ's anointed.'"

¹⁷And David lamented with this lamentation over Saul and Jonathan his son, ¹⁸and he said it¹ should be taught to the people of Judah; behold, it is written in the Book of Jashar.² He said:

¹⁹ "Your glory, O Israel, is slain on your high places!
      How the mighty have fallen!
²⁰ Tell it not in Gath,
      publish it not in the streets of Ashkelon,
    lest the daughters of the Philistines rejoice,
    lest the daughters of the uncircumcised exult.

²¹ "You mountains of Gilboa,
      let there be no dew or rain upon you,
      nor fields of offerings!³
    For there the shield of the mighty was defiled,
      the shield of Saul, not anointed with oil.

²² "From the blood of the slain,
      from the fat of the mighty,
    the bow of Jonathan turned not back,
      and the sword of Saul returned not empty.

²³ "Saul and Jonathan, beloved and lovely!
      In life and in death they were not divided;

¹ Septuagint; Hebrew *the Bow*, which may be the name of the lament's tune ² Or *of the upright* ³ Septuagint *firstfruits*

they were swifter than eagles;
    they were stronger than lions.

24 "You daughters of Israel, weep over Saul,
    who clothed you luxuriously in scarlet,
    who put ornaments of gold on your apparel.

25 "How the mighty have fallen
    in the midst of the battle!

"Jonathan lies slain on your high places.
26   I am distressed for you, my brother Jonathan;
very pleasant have you been to me;
    your love to me was extraordinary,
    surpassing the love of women.

27 "How the mighty have fallen,
    and the weapons of war perished!"

David's difficult path to the kingship [chapter 2]. Chapters 2–4 tell the story of David's gradual ascent to the kingship over all Israel. Heretofore David has been a fugitive king-in-waiting. As 2 Samuel opens, David is not recognized as king by any segment of Israel, though he had long since been anointed king by the prophet Samuel in obedience to God's command (1 Sam. 16:6–13). The main plot line in chapters 2–4 is the difficulty that David encounters in dealing with the sympathizers of Saul after he has been anointed king of Judah. The story of that hostility begins in chapter 2, where the main events are as follows: David is anointed king over Judah (vv. 1–4a); David courts the favor of a segment of Saul's constituency (vv. 4b–7); Abner, cousin of Saul who had been commander of Saul's army, sets up Saul's son Ish-bosheth as a puppet king (vv. 8–11); Joab, David's nephew and military leader, pursues warfare with the followers of Abner and Ish-bosheth (vv. 12–23); Abner and Joab declare a truce (vv. 24–32). All of this fast-moving action assumes the quality of a suspense story, as we are led to wonder whether David will be able to secure the kingdom.

2 After this David inquired of the Lord, "Shall I go up into any of the cities of Judah?" And the Lord said to him, "Go up." David said, "To which shall I go up?" And he said, "To Hebron." ²So David went up there, and his two wives also, Ahinoam of Jezreel and Abigail the widow of Nabal of Carmel. ³And David brought up his men who were with him, everyone with his household, and they lived in the towns of Hebron. ⁴And the men of Judah came, and there they anointed David king over the house of Judah.

When they told David, "It was the men of Jabesh-gilead who buried Saul," ⁵David sent messengers to the men of Jabesh-gilead and said to them, "May you be blessed by the Lord, because you showed this loyalty to Saul your lord and buried him. ⁶Now may the Lord show steadfast love and faithfulness to you. And I will do good to you because you have done this thing. ⁷Now therefore let your hands be strong, and be valiant, for Saul your lord is dead, and the house of Judah has anointed me king over them."

[8]But Abner the son of Ner, commander of Saul's army, took Ish-bosheth the son of Saul and brought him over to Mahanaim, [9]and he made him king over Gilead and the Ashurites and Jezreel and Ephraim and Benjamin and all Israel. [10]Ish-bosheth, Saul's son, was forty years old when he began to reign over Israel, and he reigned two years. But the house of Judah followed David. [11]And the time that David was king in Hebron over the house of Judah was seven years and six months.

[12]Abner the son of Ner, and the servants of Ish-bosheth the son of Saul, went out from Mahanaim to Gibeon. [13]And Joab the son of Zeruiah and the servants of David went out and met them at the pool of Gibeon. And they sat down, the one on the one side of the pool, and the other on the other side of the pool. [14]And Abner said to Joab, "Let the young men arise and compete before us." And Joab said, "Let them arise." [15]Then they arose and passed over by number, twelve for Benjamin and Ish-bosheth the son of Saul, and twelve of the servants of David. [16]And each caught his opponent by the head and thrust his sword in his opponent's side, so they fell down together. Therefore that place was called Helkath-hazzurim,[1] which is at Gibeon. [17]And the battle was very fierce that day. And Abner and the men of Israel were beaten before the servants of David.

[18]And the three sons of Zeruiah were there, Joab, Abishai, and Asahel. Now Asahel was as swift of foot as a wild gazelle. [19]And Asahel pursued Abner, and as he went, he turned neither to the right hand nor to the left from following Abner. [20]Then Abner looked behind him and said, "Is it you, Asahel?" And he answered, "It is I." [21]Abner said to him, "Turn aside to your right hand or to your left, and seize one of the young men and take his spoil." But Asahel would not turn aside from following him. [22]And Abner said again to Asahel, "Turn aside from following me. Why should I strike you to the ground? How then could I lift up my face to your brother Joab?" [23]But he refused to turn aside. Therefore Abner struck him in the stomach with the butt of his spear, so that the spear came out at his back. And he fell there and died where he was. And all who came to the place where Asahel had fallen and died, stood still.

[24]But Joab and Abishai pursued Abner. And as the sun was going down they came to the hill of Ammah, which lies before Giah on the way to the wilderness of Gibeon. [25]And the people of Benjamin gathered themselves together behind Abner and became one group and took their stand on the top of a hill. [26]Then Abner called to Joab, "Shall the sword devour forever? Do you not know that the end will be bitter? How long will it be before you tell your people to turn from the pursuit of their brothers?" [27]And Joab said, "As God lives, if you had not spoken, surely the men would not have given up the pursuit of their brothers until the morning." [28]So Joab blew the trumpet, and all the men stopped and pursued Israel no more, nor did they fight anymore.

[29]And Abner and his men went all that night through the Arabah. They crossed the Jordan, and marching the whole morning, they came to Mahanaim. [30]Joab returned from the pursuit of Abner. And when he had gathered all the people together, there were missing from David's servants nineteen men besides Asahel. [31]But the servants of David had struck down of Benjamin 360 of Abner's men. [32]And they took up Asahel and buried him in the tomb of his father, which was at Bethlehem. And Joab and his men marched all night, and the day broke upon them at Hebron.

---

[1] Helkath-hazzurim means the field of sword-edges

The war runs its course [chapter 3]. The literary technique in this chapter and else-where in 2 Samuel is realism, which here takes the form of recording the good, the bad, and the ugly during a political and military struggle for power. In chapter 3, after an opening verse that summarizes the ascendancy of David over the house of Saul and a brief catalog of sons while David was king in Judah (vv. 2–5), the warfare pursues its course as follows: Abner transfers his loyalty to David after Ish-bosheth criticizes him (vv. 6–16); Joab kills Abner (vv. 17–30), to the great disapproval of David (vv. 31–39), though Joab survives the disfavor to become a key member of David's army and court in the remaining story of 2 Samuel. The best way to relish narrative material like this is to read it in the spirit of the huge body of ancient literature (and the OT) known as *battle stories. Additionally, the literary realism of material like this dispels a common miscon-ception that the Bible is a "nice" book, sanitized of what is sordid in human experience.

3 There was a long war between the house of Saul and the house of David. And David grew stronger and stronger, while the house of Saul became weaker and weaker.

²And sons were born to David at Hebron: his firstborn was Amnon, of Ahinoam of Jezreel; ³and his second, Chileab, of Abigail the widow of Nabal of Carmel; and the third, Absalom the son of Maacah the daughter of Talmai king of Geshur; ⁴and the fourth, Adonijah the son of Haggith; and the fifth, Shephatiah the son of Abital; ⁵and the sixth, Ithream, of Eglah, David's wife. These were born to David in Hebron.

⁶While there was war between the house of Saul and the house of David, Abner was making himself strong in the house of Saul. ⁷Now Saul had a concubine whose name was Rizpah, the daughter of Aiah. And Ish-bosheth said to Abner, "Why have you gone in to my father's concubine?" ⁸Then Abner was very angry over the words of Ish-bosheth and said, "Am I a dog's head of Judah? To this day I keep showing stead-fast love to the house of Saul your father, to his brothers, and to his friends, and have not given you into the hand of David. And yet you charge me today with a fault con-cerning a woman. ⁹God do so to Abner and more also, if I do not accomplish for David what the Lord has sworn to him, ¹⁰to transfer the kingdom from the house of Saul and set up the throne of David over Israel and over Judah, from Dan to Beersheba." ¹¹And Ish-bosheth could not answer Abner another word, because he feared him.

¹²And Abner sent messengers to David on his behalf,¹ saying, "To whom does the land belong? Make your covenant with me, and behold, my hand shall be with you to bring over all Israel to you." ¹³And he said, "Good; I will make a covenant with you. But one thing I require of you; that is, you shall not see my face unless you first bring Michal, Saul's daughter, when you come to see my face." ¹⁴Then David sent messen-gers to Ish-bosheth, Saul's son, saying, "Give me my wife Michal, for whom I paid the bridal price of a hundred foreskins of the Philistines." ¹⁵And Ish-bosheth sent and took her from her husband Paltiel the son of Laish. ¹⁶But her husband went with her, weeping after her all the way to Bahurim. Then Abner said to him, "Go, return." And he returned.

¹⁷And Abner conferred with the elders of Israel, saying, "For some time past you have been seeking David as king over you. ¹⁸Now then bring it about, for the Lord has promised David, saying, 'By the hand of my servant David I will save my people

¹ Or *where he was*; Septuagint *at Hebron*

Israel from the hand of the Philistines, and from the hand of all their enemies.'" [19]Abner also spoke to Benjamin. And then Abner went to tell David at Hebron all that Israel and the whole house of Benjamin thought good to do.

[20]When Abner came with twenty men to David at Hebron, David made a feast for Abner and the men who were with him. [21]And Abner said to David, "I will arise and go and will gather all Israel to my lord the king, that they may make a covenant with you, and that you may reign over all that your heart desires." So David sent Abner away, and he went in peace.

[22]Just then the servants of David arrived with Joab from a raid, bringing much spoil with them. But Abner was not with David at Hebron, for he had sent him away, and he had gone in peace. [23]When Joab and all the army that was with him came, it was told Joab, "Abner the son of Ner came to the king, and he has let him go, and he has gone in peace." [24]Then Joab went to the king and said, "What have you done? Behold, Abner came to you. Why is it that you have sent him away, so that he is gone? [25]You know that Abner the son of Ner came to deceive you and to know your going out and your coming in, and to know all that you are doing."

[26]When Joab came out from David's presence, he sent messengers after Abner, and they brought him back from the cistern of Sirah. But David did not know about it. [27]And when Abner returned to Hebron, Joab took him aside into the midst of the gate to speak with him privately, and there he struck him in the stomach, so that he died, for the blood of Asahel his brother. [28]Afterward, when David heard of it, he said, "I and my kingdom are forever guiltless before the LORD for the blood of Abner the son of Ner. [29]May it fall upon the head of Joab and upon all his father's house, and may the house of Joab never be without one who has a discharge or who is leprous or who holds a spindle or who falls by the sword or who lacks bread!" [30]So Joab and Abishai his brother killed Abner, because he had put their brother Asahel to death in the battle at Gibeon.

[31]Then David said to Joab and to all the people who were with him, "Tear your clothes and put on sackcloth and mourn before Abner." And King David followed the bier. [32]They buried Abner at Hebron. And the king lifted up his voice and wept at the grave of Abner, and all the people wept. [33]And the king lamented for Abner, saying,

> "Should Abner die as a fool dies?
> [34]   Your hands were not bound;
>   your feet were not fettered;
>   as one falls before the wicked
>   you have fallen."

And all the people wept again over him. [35]Then all the people came to persuade David to eat bread while it was yet day. But David swore, saying, "God do so to me and more also, if I taste bread or anything else till the sun goes down!" [36]And all the people took notice of it, and it pleased them, as everything that the king did pleased all the people. [37]So all the people and all Israel understood that day that it had not been the king's will to put to death Abner the son of Ner. [38]And the king said to his servants, "Do you not know that a prince and a great man has fallen this day in Israel? [39]And I was gentle today, though anointed king. These men, the sons of Zeruiah, are more severe than I. The LORD repay the evildoer according to his wickedness!"

David's opposition disintegrates [chapter 4]. The plot line of chapters 2–4 is the events that bring about David's ascent to the throne. Chapter 4 has little to do directly with David; its function is to show how the rival forces of Saul's sympathizers collapse, thereby preparing the way for David to become king of all Israel. The action in chapter 4 is gruesome and cruel. The main action in the chapter is the murder of the puppet king Ish-bosheth by two of his military captains, who hope to gain favor with David by presenting him with the head of his deceased rival, only to have David order their death and dismemberment. David will show similar unpredictable behavior after the death of family members before the story is complete. In fact, David's drastic mood swings and unpredictable emotional responses to events constitute a leading motif in the story and lead us to ponder the virtue of self-control as we see it violated in David's responses.

4 When Ish-bosheth, Saul's son, heard that Abner had died at Hebron, his courage failed, and all Israel was dismayed. ²Now Saul's son had two men who were captains of raiding bands; the name of the one was Baanah, and the name of the other Rechab, sons of Rimmon a man of Benjamin from Beeroth (for Beeroth also is counted part of Benjamin; ³the Beerothites fled to Gittaim and have been sojourners there to this day).

⁴Jonathan, the son of Saul, had a son who was crippled in his feet. He was five years old when the news about Saul and Jonathan came from Jezreel, and his nurse took him up and fled, and as she fled in her haste, he fell and became lame. And his name was Mephibosheth.

⁵Now the sons of Rimmon the Beerothite, Rechab and Baanah, set out, and about the heat of the day they came to the house of Ish-bosheth as he was taking his noonday rest. ⁶And they came into the midst of the house as if to get wheat, and they stabbed him in the stomach. Then Rechab and Baanah his brother escaped.[1] ⁷When they came into the house, as he lay on his bed in his bedroom, they struck him and put him to death and beheaded him. They took his head and went by the way of the Arabah all night, ⁸and brought the head of Ish-bosheth to David at Hebron. And they said to the king, "Here is the head of Ish-bosheth, the son of Saul, your enemy, who sought your life. The LORD has avenged my lord the king this day on Saul and on his offspring." ⁹But David answered Rechab and Baanah his brother, the sons of Rimmon the Beerothite, "As the LORD lives, who has redeemed my life out of every adversity, ¹⁰when one told me, 'Behold, Saul is dead,' and thought he was bringing good news, I seized him and killed him at Ziklag, which was the reward I gave him for his news. ¹¹How much more, when wicked men have killed a righteous man in his own house on his bed, shall I not now require his blood at your hand and destroy you from the earth?" ¹²And David commanded his young men, and they killed them and cut off their hands and feet and hanged them beside the pool at Hebron. But they took the head of Ish-bosheth and buried it in the tomb of Abner at Hebron.

David's coronation over all Israel [chapter 5]. After seven-and-a-half years of political and military struggle, at the age of thirty David has achieved sufficient political stature to prompt all the tribes of Israel to come to him at Hebron and declare their loyalty to him as king (vv. 1–5). David's first recorded highlights as king are to capture Jerusalem and make it his capital (vv. 6–10), build a palace (vv. 11–12), take wives and

[1] Septuagint *And behold, the doorkeeper of the house had been cleaning wheat, but she grew drowsy and slept. So Rechab and Baanah his brother slipped in*

father children (vv. 13–16), and defeat his national enemy the Philistines (vv. 17–25). The common thread in all of these events is that they were part and parcel of a kingly life in ancient cultures. As we end chapter 5, we see the king honored by his people's submission, secure in his royal capital, exalted in his royal palace, and powerful in defeating his enemies.

5 Then all the tribes of Israel came to David at Hebron and said, "Behold, we are your bone and flesh. ²In times past, when Saul was king over us, it was you who led out and brought in Israel. And the LORD said to you, 'You shall be shepherd of my people Israel, and you shall be prince over Israel.'" ³So all the elders of Israel came to the king at Hebron, and King David made a covenant with them at Hebron before the LORD, and they anointed David king over Israel. ⁴David was thirty years old when he began to reign, and he reigned forty years. ⁵At Hebron he reigned over Judah seven years and six months, and at Jerusalem he reigned over all Israel and Judah thirty-three years.¹

⁶And the king and his men went to Jerusalem against the Jebusites, the inhabitants of the land, who said to David, "You will not come in here, but the blind and the lame will ward you off"—thinking, "David cannot come in here." ⁷Nevertheless, David took the stronghold of Zion, that is, the city of David. ⁸And David said on that day, "Whoever would strike the Jebusites, let him get up the water shaft to attack 'the lame and the blind,' who are hated by David's soul." Therefore it is said, "The blind and the lame shall not come into the house." ⁹And David lived in the stronghold and called it the city of David. And David built the city all around from the Millo inward. ¹⁰And David became greater and greater, for the LORD, the God of hosts, was with him.

¹¹And Hiram king of Tyre sent messengers to David, and cedar trees, also carpenters and masons who built David a house. ¹²And David knew that the LORD had established him king over Israel, and that he had exalted his kingdom for the sake of his people Israel.

¹³And David took more concubines and wives from Jerusalem, after he came from Hebron, and more sons and daughters were born to David. ¹⁴And these are the names of those who were born to him in Jerusalem: Shammua, Shobab, Nathan, Solomon, ¹⁵Ibhar, Elishua, Nepheg, Japhia, ¹⁶Elishama, Eliada, and Eliphelet.

¹⁷When the Philistines heard that David had been anointed king over Israel, all the Philistines went up to search for David. But David heard of it and went down to the stronghold. ¹⁸Now the Philistines had come and spread out in the Valley of Rephaim. ¹⁹And David inquired of the LORD, "Shall I go up against the Philistines? Will you give them into my hand?" And the LORD said to David, "Go up, for I will certainly give the Philistines into your hand." ²⁰And David came to Baal-perazim, and David defeated them there. And he said, "The LORD has burst through my enemies before me like a bursting flood." Therefore the name of that place is called Baal-perazim.² ²¹And the Philistines left their idols there, and David and his men carried them away.

²²And the Philistines came up yet again and spread out in the Valley of Rephaim. ²³And when David inquired of the LORD, he said, "You shall not go up; go around to their rear, and come against them opposite the balsam trees. ²⁴And when you hear the sound of marching in the tops of the balsam trees, then rouse yourself, for then the

¹ Dead Sea Scroll lacks verses 4-5 ² *Baal-perazim* means *lord of bursting through*

LORD has gone out before you to strike down the army of the Philistines." ²⁵And David did as the LORD commanded him, and struck down the Philistines from Geba to Gezer.

David as worshiper [chapter 6]. No human character in the Bible is as many-sided as David. The roles that he fills cover a broad range. The picture of David that emerges from the first five chapters of 2 Samuel has left us unprepared for the totally different picture that emerges in chapter 6. Here we meet David the worshiper, a man whose religious passions are as strong as his military passions. The king emerges as a religious leader, balancing his political and military leadership as presented earlier. The celebration surrounding the transfer of the ark to Jerusalem is reckless in its abandon and even rowdy (vv. 5, 14–15). This, in turn, is balanced by the sense of the numinous that accompanies the journey of the ark to Jerusalem, seen especially in God's smiting of Uzzah for touching the ark, accompanied by David's fear (vv. 6–11). The story of David the public worshiper is then counterbalanced by the domestic scene of his unpleasantness with his wife Michal (vv. 20–23), whom he has reclaimed from her second husband in one of the truly heartrending scenes of 2 Samuel (3:14–16).

6 David again gathered all the chosen men of Israel, thirty thousand. ²And David arose and went with all the people who were with him from Baale-judah to bring up from there the ark of God, which is called by the name of the LORD of hosts who sits enthroned on the cherubim. ³And they carried the ark of God on a new cart and brought it out of the house of Abinadab, which was on the hill. And Uzzah and Ahio,¹ the sons of Abinadab, were driving the new cart,² ⁴with the ark of God, and Ahio went before the ark.

⁵And David and all the house of Israel were making merry before the LORD, with songs³ and lyres and harps and tambourines and castanets and cymbals. ⁶And when they came to the threshing floor of Nacon, Uzzah put out his hand to the ark of God and took hold of it, for the oxen stumbled. ⁷And the anger of the LORD was kindled against Uzzah, and God struck him down there because of his error, and he died there beside the ark of God. ⁸And David was angry because the LORD had burst forth against Uzzah. And that place is called Perez-uzzah,⁴ to this day. ⁹And David was afraid of the LORD that day, and he said, "How can the ark of the LORD come to me?" ¹⁰So David was not willing to take the ark of the LORD into the city of David. But David took it aside to the house of Obed-edom the Gittite. ¹¹And the ark of the LORD remained in the house of Obed-edom the Gittite three months, and the LORD blessed Obed-edom and all his household.

¹²And it was told King David, "The LORD has blessed the household of Obed-edom and all that belongs to him, because of the ark of God." So David went and brought up the ark of God from the house of Obed-edom to the city of David with rejoicing. ¹³And when those who bore the ark of the LORD had gone six steps, he sacrificed an ox and a fattened animal. ¹⁴And David danced before the LORD with all his might. And David was wearing a linen ephod. ¹⁵So David and all the house of Israel brought up the ark of the LORD with shouting and with the sound of the horn.

¹⁶As the ark of the LORD came into the city of David, Michal the daughter of Saul looked out of the window and saw King David leaping and dancing before the LORD, and she despised him in her heart. ¹⁷And they brought in the ark of the LORD and set

---

¹ Or *and his brother*; also verse 4 ² Compare Septuagint; Hebrew *the new cart, and brought it out of the house of Abinadab, which was on the hill* ³ Septuagint, 1 Chronicles 13:8; Hebrew *fir trees* ⁴ *Perez-uzzah* means *the bursting forth upon Uzzah*

it in its place, inside the tent that David had pitched for it. And David offered burnt offerings and peace offerings before the Lord. ¹⁸And when David had finished offering the burnt offerings and the peace offerings, he blessed the people in the name of the Lord of hosts ¹⁹and distributed among all the people, the whole multitude of Israel, both men and women, a cake of bread, a portion of meat,¹ and a cake of raisins to each one. Then all the people departed, each to his house.

²⁰And David returned to bless his household. But Michal the daughter of Saul came out to meet David and said, "How the king of Israel honored himself today, uncovering himself today before the eyes of his servants' female servants, as one of the vulgar fellows shamelessly uncovers himself!" ²¹And David said to Michal, "It was before the Lord, who chose me above your father and above all his house, to appoint me as prince over Israel, the people of the Lord—and I will make merry before the Lord. ²²I will make myself yet more contemptible than this, and I will be abased in your² eyes. But by the female servants of whom you have spoken, by them I shall be held in honor." ²³And Michal the daughter of Saul had no child to the day of her death.

David's desire to build a temple is thwarted by God [chapter 7]. The storyteller's implied idealization of David in the preceding chapter becomes much stronger in chapter 7, through the writer's selection of material. We have a whole chapter devoted to David's spiritual devotion to God, as seen in his desire to build a temple. Even though God (through the agency of the prophet Nathan) declines David's offer to build a temple, the rejection is couched in words of extreme approval of David (vv. 8–16). This speech includes the Davidic covenant in which God promises an eternal kingdom to David's house (v. 16), a prophecy fulfilled in Christ. This awe-inspiring speech is followed by David's equally eloquent and moving prayer (vv. 18–29), also couched in a formal and exalted style. Throughout the OT narratives, formal occasions elicit the lofty style from speakers, even when the surrounding narrative style is realistic.

7 Now when the king lived in his house and the Lord had given him rest from all his surrounding enemies, ²the king said to Nathan the prophet, "See now, I dwell in a house of cedar, but the ark of God dwells in a tent." ³And Nathan said to the king, "Go, do all that is in your heart, for the Lord is with you."

⁴But that same night the word of the Lord came to Nathan, ⁵"Go and tell my servant David, 'Thus says the Lord: Would you build me a house to dwell in? ⁶I have not lived in a house since the day I brought up the people of Israel from Egypt to this day, but I have been moving about in a tent for my dwelling. ⁷In all places where I have moved with all the people of Israel, did I speak a word with any of the judges³ of Israel, whom I commanded to shepherd my people Israel, saying, "Why have you not built me a house of cedar?"' ⁸Now, therefore, thus you shall say to my servant David, 'Thus says the Lord of hosts, I took you from the pasture, from following the sheep, that you should be prince over my people Israel. ⁹And I have been with you wherever you went and have cut off all your enemies from before you. And I will make for you a great name, like the name of the great ones of the earth. ¹⁰And I will appoint a place for my people Israel and will plant them, so that they may dwell in their own place and be disturbed no more. And violent men shall afflict them no more, as formerly, ¹¹from the time that I appointed judges over my people Israel. And I will give you rest from all your enemies. Moreover, the Lord declares to you that the Lord will make you a

¹ Vulgate; the meaning of the Hebrew term is uncertain ² Septuagint; Hebrew *my* ³ Compare 1 Chronicles 17:6; Hebrew *tribes*

house. [12]When your days are fulfilled and you lie down with your fathers, I will raise up your offspring after you, who shall come from your body, and I will establish his kingdom. [13]He shall build a house for my name, and I will establish the throne of his kingdom forever. [14]I will be to him a father, and he shall be to me a son. When he commits iniquity, I will discipline him with the rod of men, with the stripes of the sons of men, [15]but my steadfast love will not depart from him, as I took it from Saul, whom I put away from before you. [16]And your house and your kingdom shall be made sure forever before me.[1] Your throne shall be established forever.'" [17]In accordance with all these words, and in accordance with all this vision, Nathan spoke to David.

[18]Then King David went in and sat before the LORD and said, "Who am I, O Lord GOD, and what is my house, that you have brought me thus far? [19]And yet this was a small thing in your eyes, O Lord GOD. You have spoken also of your servant's house for a great while to come, and this is instruction for mankind, O Lord GOD! [20]And what more can David say to you? For you know your servant, O Lord GOD! [21]Because of your promise, and according to your own heart, you have brought about all this greatness, to make your servant know it. [22]Therefore you are great, O LORD God. For there is none like you, and there is no God besides you, according to all that we have heard with our ears. [23]And who is like your people Israel, the one nation on earth whom God went to redeem to be his people, making himself a name and doing for them[2] great and awesome things by driving out[3] before your people, whom you redeemed for yourself from Egypt, a nation and its gods? [24]And you established for yourself your people Israel to be your people forever. And you, O LORD, became their God. [25]And now, O LORD God, confirm forever the word that you have spoken concerning your servant and concerning his house, and do as you have spoken. [26]And your name will be magnified forever, saying, 'The LORD of hosts is God over Israel,' and the house of your servant David will be established before you. [27]For you, O LORD of hosts, the God of Israel, have made this revelation to your servant, saying, 'I will build you a house.' Therefore your servant has found courage to pray this prayer to you. [28]And now, O Lord GOD, you are God, and your words are true, and you have promised this good thing to your servant. [29]Now therefore may it please you to bless the house of your servant, so that it may continue forever before you. For you, O Lord GOD, have spoken, and with your blessing shall the house of your servant be blessed forever."

David's kingly power [chapter 8]. The storyteller's overall pattern in 2 Samuel is to trace an arc of increasing success in David's kingly life for ten chapters. Chapters 8–10 bring that arc to its highest point. We can infer that the court historian has recorded the decisive and extraordinary events in David's kingly life. Chapter 8 records David's military success against enemies. The literary form that the writer chooses to celebrate David as conqueror is lists of conquered kings, as well as kings who pay David tribute in the form of treasure and goods. After all the details, two summary statements speak volumes: "David made a name for himself" (v. 13) and "the LORD gave victory to David wherever he went" (v. 14). We can see here an index to the writer's worldview: human heroism is a possibility in the world, and yet God is the sovereign bestower of human giftedness who directs events in the world to their providential end.

8 After this David defeated the Philistines and subdued them, and David took Metheg-ammah out of the hand of the Philistines.

---

[1] Septuagint; Hebrew *you* [2] With a few Targums, Vulgate, Syriac; Hebrew *you* [3] Septuagint (compare 1 Chronicles 17:21); Hebrew *for your land*

²And he defeated Moab and he measured them with a line, making them lie down on the ground. Two lines he measured to be put to death, and one full line to be spared. And the Moabites became servants to David and brought tribute.

³David also defeated Hadadezer the son of Rehob, king of Zobah, as he went to restore his power at the river Euphrates. ⁴And David took from him 1,700 horsemen, and 20,000 foot soldiers. And David hamstrung all the chariot horses but left enough for 100 chariots. ⁵And when the Syrians of Damascus came to help Hadadezer king of Zobah, David struck down 22,000 men of the Syrians. ⁶Then David put garrisons in Aram of Damascus, and the Syrians became servants to David and brought tribute. And the LORD gave victory to David wherever he went. ⁷And David took the shields of gold that were carried by the servants of Hadadezer and brought them to Jerusalem. ⁸And from Betah and from Berothai, cities of Hadadezer, King David took very much bronze.

⁹When Toi king of Hamath heard that David had defeated the whole army of Hadadezer, ¹⁰Toi sent his son Joram to King David, to ask about his health and to bless him because he had fought against Hadadezer and defeated him, for Hadadezer had often been at war with Toi. And Joram brought with him articles of silver, of gold, and of bronze. ¹¹These also King David dedicated to the LORD, together with the silver and gold that he dedicated from all the nations he subdued, ¹²from Edom, Moab, the Ammonites, the Philistines, Amalek, and from the spoil of Hadadezer the son of Rehob, king of Zobah.

¹³And David made a name for himself when he returned from striking down 18,000 Edomites in the Valley of Salt. ¹⁴Then he put garrisons in Edom; throughout all Edom he put garrisons, and all the Edomites became David's servants. And the LORD gave victory to David wherever he went.

¹⁵So David reigned over all Israel. And David administered justice and equity to all his people. ¹⁶Joab the son of Zeruiah was over the army, and Jehoshaphat the son of Ahilud was recorder, ¹⁷and Zadok the son of Ahitub and Ahimelech the son of Abiathar were priests, and Seraiah was secretary, ¹⁸and Benaiah the son of Jehoiada was over¹ the Cherethites and the Pelethites, and David's sons were priests.

David's kingly compassion [chapter 9]. The storyteller chose material from David's life by two criteria—typical or representative events and decisive, once-only events. The previous chapter gave highlights from a sphere of David's life that was repeated many times—success on the battlefield. Chapter 9 balances that side of David's personality and experiences with an event from his personal life, one that demonstrates compassion rather than prowess in battle. The account narrates David's kindness to a son of Saul, whose supporters had made life miserable for David as he was moving toward kingship. David even elevates this crippled son of Saul, theoretically a potential rival to the throne, to a place at the royal table.

9 And David said, "Is there still anyone left of the house of Saul, that I may show him kindness for Jonathan's sake?" ²Now there was a servant of the house of Saul whose name was Ziba, and they called him to David. And the king said to him, "Are you Ziba?" And he said, "I am your servant." ³And the king said, "Is there not still someone of the house of Saul, that I may show the kindness of God to him?" Ziba

---

¹ Compare 20:23, 1 Chronicles 18:17, Syriac, Targum, Vulgate; Hebrew lacks *was over*

said to the king, "There is still a son of Jonathan; he is crippled in his feet." ⁴The king said to him, "Where is he?" And Ziba said to the king, "He is in the house of Machir the son of Ammiel, at Lo-debar." ⁵Then King David sent and brought him from the house of Machir the son of Ammiel, at Lo-debar. ⁶And Mephibosheth the son of Jonathan, son of Saul, came to David and fell on his face and paid homage. And David said, "Mephibosheth!" And he answered, "Behold, I am your servant." ⁷And David said to him, "Do not fear, for I will show you kindness for the sake of your father Jonathan, and I will restore to you all the land of Saul your father, and you shall eat at my table always." ⁸And he paid homage and said, "What is your servant, that you should show regard for a dead dog such as I?"

⁹Then the king called Ziba, Saul's servant, and said to him, "All that belonged to Saul and to all his house I have given to your master's grandson. ¹⁰And you and your sons and your servants shall till the land for him and shall bring in the produce, that your master's grandson may have bread to eat. But Mephibosheth your master's grandson shall always eat at my table." Now Ziba had fifteen sons and twenty servants. ¹¹Then Ziba said to the king, "According to all that my lord the king commands his servant, so will your servant do." So Mephibosheth ate at David's¹ table, like one of the king's sons. ¹²And Mephibosheth had a young son, whose name was Mica. And all who lived in Ziba's house became Mephibosheth's servants. ¹³So Mephibosheth lived in Jerusalem, for he ate always at the king's table. Now he was lame in both his feet.

David's kingly justice [chapter 10]. In the back-and-forth rhythm of the story, chapter 10 swings us back to the public and political sphere as David copes with a situation in which his envoy to the king of the Ammonites had been subjected to shame (vv. 1–5). David shows decisive leadership in exacting justice for the affront, according to the following sequence: Joab's clever tactics in defeating the two armies of the Ammonites and their cohorts the Syrians (vv. 6–14); David's defeat of the Syrians in a second battle (vv. 15–19).

10

After this the king of the Ammonites died, and Hanun his son reigned in his place. ²And David said, "I will deal loyally² with Hanun the son of Nahash, as his father dealt loyally with me." So David sent by his servants to console him concerning his father. And David's servants came into the land of the Ammonites. ³But the princes of the Ammonites said to Hanun their lord, "Do you think, because David has sent comforters to you, that he is honoring your father? Has not David sent his servants to you to search the city and to spy it out and to overthrow it?" ⁴So Hanun took David's servants and shaved off half the beard of each and cut off their garments in the middle, at their hips, and sent them away. ⁵When it was told David, he sent to meet them, for the men were greatly ashamed. And the king said, "Remain at Jericho until your beards have grown and then return."

⁶When the Ammonites saw that they had become a stench to David, the Ammonites sent and hired the Syrians of Beth-rehob, and the Syrians of Zobah, 20,000 foot soldiers, and the king of Maacah with 1,000 men, and the men of Tob, 12,000 men. ⁷And when David heard of it, he sent Joab and all the host of the mighty men. ⁸And the Ammonites came out and drew up in battle array at the entrance of

¹ Septuagint; Hebrew *my* ² Or *kindly*; twice in this verse

the gate, and the Syrians of Zobah and of Rehob and the men of Tob and Maacah were by themselves in the open country.

⁹When Joab saw that the battle was set against him both in front and in the rear, he chose some of the best men of Israel and arrayed them against the Syrians. ¹⁰The rest of his men he put in the charge of Abishai his brother, and he arrayed them against the Ammonites. ¹¹And he said, "If the Syrians are too strong for me, then you shall help me, but if the Ammonites are too strong for you, then I will come and help you. ¹²Be of good courage, and let us be courageous for our people, and for the cities of our God, and may the LORD do what seems good to him." ¹³So Joab and the people who were with him drew near to battle against the Syrians, and they fled before him. ¹⁴And when the Ammonites saw that the Syrians fled, they likewise fled before Abishai and entered the city. Then Joab returned from fighting against the Ammonites and came to Jerusalem.

¹⁵But when the Syrians saw that they had been defeated by Israel, they gathered themselves together. ¹⁶And Hadadezer sent and brought out the Syrians who were beyond the Euphrates.¹ They came to Helam, with Shobach the commander of the army of Hadadezer at their head. ¹⁷And when it was told David, he gathered all Israel together and crossed the Jordan and came to Helam. The Syrians arrayed themselves against David and fought with him. ¹⁸And the Syrians fled before Israel, and David killed of the Syrians the men of 700 chariots, and 40,000 horsemen, and wounded Shobach the commander of their army, so that he died there. ¹⁹And when all the kings who were servants of Hadadezer saw that they had been defeated by Israel, they made peace with Israel and became subject to them. So the Syrians were afraid to save the Ammonites anymore.

David's tragic choice [chapter 11]. The story of a leader's sexual sin followed by a cover-up is as up-to-date as the daily news. In the overall movement of the narrative of 2 Samuel, it is the turning point in David's personal and political life, the destructive choice through which the hero shows his tragic flaw of character. It is a story of sexual temptation and fall. In an understated rather than salacious style, the storyteller includes enough information to make the sex scene vivid and understandable (vv. 1–5), and this carries over into the attempted trickery of Uriah as well (vv. 6–13). As in real life, one sin leads to another, and David the adulterer becomes David the murderer (vv. 14–25). It is almost the perfect crime, but the parting shot in the chapter brings a divine perspective into the human drama that has been unfolding: "But the thing that David had done displeased the LORD" (v. 27). As the next chapter will show, it is God's perspective that matters. The literary principle that we need constantly to apply is that characters in a story are representative of people generally and of us as readers. All stories are at some level example stories, and interpretation begins when we ask of what they are examples.

11 In the spring of the year, the time when kings go out to battle, David sent Joab, and his servants with him, and all Israel. And they ravaged the Ammonites and besieged Rabbah. But David remained at Jerusalem.

²It happened, late one afternoon, when David arose from his couch and was walking on the roof of the king's house, that he saw from the roof a woman bathing; and the woman was very beautiful. ³And David sent and inquired about the woman. And

¹ Hebrew *the River*

one said, "Is not this Bathsheba, the daughter of Eliam, the wife of Uriah the Hittite?" ⁴So David sent messengers and took her, and she came to him, and he lay with her. (Now she had been purifying herself from her uncleanness.) Then she returned to her house. ⁵And the woman conceived, and she sent and told David, "I am pregnant."

⁶So David sent word to Joab, "Send me Uriah the Hittite." And Joab sent Uriah to David. ⁷When Uriah came to him, David asked how Joab was doing and how the people were doing and how the war was going. ⁸Then David said to Uriah, "Go down to your house and wash your feet." And Uriah went out of the king's house, and there followed him a present from the king. ⁹But Uriah slept at the door of the king's house with all the servants of his lord, and did not go down to his house. ¹⁰When they told David, "Uriah did not go down to his house," David said to Uriah, "Have you not come from a journey? Why did you not go down to your house?" ¹¹Uriah said to David, "The ark and Israel and Judah dwell in booths, and my lord Joab and the servants of my lord are camping in the open field. Shall I then go to my house, to eat and to drink and to lie with my wife? As you live, and as your soul lives, I will not do this thing." ¹²Then David said to Uriah, "Remain here today also, and tomorrow I will send you back." So Uriah remained in Jerusalem that day and the next. ¹³And David invited him, and he ate in his presence and drank, so that he made him drunk. And in the evening he went out to lie on his couch with the servants of his lord, but he did not go down to his house.

¹⁴In the morning David wrote a letter to Joab and sent it by the hand of Uriah. ¹⁵In the letter he wrote, "Set Uriah in the forefront of the hardest fighting, and then draw back from him, that he may be struck down, and die." ¹⁶And as Joab was besieging the city, he assigned Uriah to the place where he knew there were valiant men. ¹⁷And the men of the city came out and fought with Joab, and some of the servants of David among the people fell. Uriah the Hittite also died. ¹⁸Then Joab sent and told David all the news about the fighting. ¹⁹And he instructed the messenger, "When you have finished telling all the news about the fighting to the king, ²⁰then, if the king's anger rises, and if he says to you, 'Why did you go so near the city to fight? Did you not know that they would shoot from the wall? ²¹Who killed Abimelech the son of Jerubbesheth? Did not a woman cast an upper millstone on him from the wall, so that he died at Thebez? Why did you go so near the wall?' then you shall say, 'Your servant Uriah the Hittite is dead also.'"

²²So the messenger went and came and told David all that Joab had sent him to tell. ²³The messenger said to David, "The men gained an advantage over us and came out against us in the field, but we drove them back to the entrance of the gate. ²⁴Then the archers shot at your servants from the wall. Some of the king's servants are dead, and your servant Uriah the Hittite is dead also." ²⁵David said to the messenger, "Thus shall you say to Joab, 'Do not let this matter trouble you, for the sword devours now one and now another. Strengthen your attack against the city and overthrow it.' And encourage him."

²⁶When the wife of Uriah heard that Uriah her husband was dead, she lamented over her husband. ²⁷And when the mourning was over, David sent and brought her to his house, and she became his wife and bore him a son. But the thing that David had done displeased the LORD.

David as guilty criminal and ideal penitent [chapter 12]. It is important to note at the outset that in this chapter God becomes a character in the action much more directly than in the previous material. In a story in which the hero fills many roles, David enters new territory in the aftermath of his tragic sins. The action begins with an incident dripping with *dramatic irony: Nathan tells the king a fictional parable in such a way as to trick David into thinking that he is judging a civil case (vv. 1–6). With Nathan's famous one-liner, "You are the man!" (v. 7), David enters his career as convicted criminal. The charge against him (vv. 8–9) is immediately followed by sentencing (vv. 10–12) in a divine courtroom. David's formal reply to the sentence is an exemplary confession (v. 13a), and God's judgment is in a sense modified by David's repentant spirit (vv. 13b–14). The narrative intensity remains at a high pitch with the account of David's extreme anguish over the illness of his child by Bathsheba (vv. 15–19). Then the phenomenon of plot surprise enters the story when the child dies and, instead of being even more smitten by grief, David instantaneously returns to life as normal (vv. 20–23). Then, as if to get our attention off the tragic phase of David's life, the author includes the incidents of David and Bathsheba's second child (vv. 24–25) and a notable military triumph (vv. 26–31). The famous story told in this chapter is one of the clearest Old Testament pictures of God's forgiveness.

12 And the LORD sent Nathan to David. He came to him and said to him, "There were two men in a certain city, the one rich and the other poor. ²The rich man had very many flocks and herds, ³but the poor man had nothing but one little ewe lamb, which he had bought. And he brought it up, and it grew up with him and with his children. It used to eat of his morsel and drink from his cup and lie in his arms,¹ and it was like a daughter to him. ⁴Now there came a traveler to the rich man, and he was unwilling to take one of his own flock or herd to prepare for the guest who had come to him, but he took the poor man's lamb and prepared it for the man who had come to him." ⁵Then David's anger was greatly kindled against the man, and he said to Nathan, "As the LORD lives, the man who has done this deserves to die, ⁶and he shall restore the lamb fourfold, because he did this thing, and because he had no pity."

⁷Nathan said to David, "You are the man! Thus says the LORD, the God of Israel, 'I anointed you king over Israel, and I delivered you out of the hand of Saul. ⁸And I gave you your master's house and your master's wives into your arms and gave you the house of Israel and of Judah. And if this were too little, I would add to you as much more. ⁹Why have you despised the word of the LORD, to do what is evil in his sight? You have struck down Uriah the Hittite with the sword and have taken his wife to be your wife and have killed him with the sword of the Ammonites. ¹⁰Now therefore the sword shall never depart from your house, because you have despised me and have taken the wife of Uriah the Hittite to be your wife.' ¹¹Thus says the LORD, 'Behold, I will raise up evil against you out of your own house. And I will take your wives before your eyes and give them to your neighbor, and he shall lie with your wives in the sight of this sun. ¹²For you did it secretly, but I will do this thing before all Israel and before the sun.'" ¹³David said to Nathan, "I have sinned against the LORD." And Nathan said to David, "The LORD also has put away your sin; you shall not die. ¹⁴Nevertheless, because by this deed you have utterly scorned the LORD,² the child who is born to you shall die." ¹⁵Then Nathan went to his house.

And the LORD afflicted the child that Uriah's wife bore to David, and he became

¹ Hebrew *bosom*; also verse 8 ² Masoretic Text *the enemies of the LORD*; Dead Sea Scroll *the word of the LORD*

sick. ¹⁶David therefore sought God on behalf of the child. And David fasted and went in and lay all night on the ground. ¹⁷And the elders of his house stood beside him, to raise him from the ground, but he would not, nor did he eat food with them. ¹⁸On the seventh day the child died. And the servants of David were afraid to tell him that the child was dead, for they said, "Behold, while the child was yet alive, we spoke to him, and he did not listen to us. How then can we say to him the child is dead? He may do himself some harm." ¹⁹But when David saw that his servants were whispering together, David understood that the child was dead. And David said to his servants, "Is the child dead?" They said, "He is dead." ²⁰Then David arose from the earth and washed and anointed himself and changed his clothes. And he went into the house of the LORD and worshiped. He then went to his own house. And when he asked, they set food before him, and he ate. ²¹Then his servants said to him, "What is this thing that you have done? You fasted and wept for the child while he was alive; but when the child died, you arose and ate food." ²²He said, "While the child was still alive, I fasted and wept, for I said, 'Who knows whether the LORD will be gracious to me, that the child may live?' ²³But now he is dead. Why should I fast? Can I bring him back again? I shall go to him, but he will not return to me."

²⁴Then David comforted his wife, Bathsheba, and went in to her and lay with her, and she bore a son, and he called his name Solomon. And the LORD loved him ²⁵and sent a message by Nathan the prophet. So he called his name Jedidiah,¹ because of the LORD.

²⁶Now Joab fought against Rabbah of the Ammonites and took the royal city. ²⁷And Joab sent messengers to David and said, "I have fought against Rabbah; moreover, I have taken the city of waters. ²⁸Now then gather the rest of the people together and encamp against the city and take it, lest I take the city and it be called by my name." ²⁹So David gathered all the people together and went to Rabbah and fought against it and took it. ³⁰And he took the crown of their king from his head. The weight of it was a talent² of gold, and in it was a precious stone, and it was placed on David's head. And he brought out the spoil of the city, a very great amount. ³¹And he brought out the people who were in it and set them to labor with saws and iron picks and iron axes and made them toil at³ the brick kilns. And thus he did to all the cities of the Ammonites. Then David and all the people returned to Jerusalem.

David's predicted troubles begin [chapter 13]. The trajectory of David's life as told in 2 Samuel is a pyramid in which events build into a rising tide of success until the sordid chapter of David's sin with Bathsheba and Uriah. The trajectory after that is downward, in keeping with the tragic design of the story. In the conviction scene, God had predicted that "the sword shall never depart from your house" (12:10), and in chapter 13 we begin to see what that means. The story of Amnon's incestuous rape of Tamar is told in full realistic and sickening detail (vv. 1–19). The realistic mode continues with the story of Absalom's murder of Amnon (vv. 20–33). The scene of ritual lament by David and his sons (vv. 34–39) is familiar in ancient literature. David's story has now become a story of crime and punishment.

13

Now Absalom, David's son, had a beautiful sister, whose name was Tamar. And after a time Amnon, David's son, loved her. ²And Amnon was so tormented that he made himself ill because of his sister Tamar, for she was a virgin, and

¹ *Jedidiah* means *beloved of the LORD* ² A *talent* was about 75 pounds or 34 kilograms ³ Hebrew *pass through*

it seemed impossible to Amnon to do anything to her. ³But Amnon had a friend, whose name was Jonadab, the son of Shimeah, David's brother. And Jonadab was a very crafty man. ⁴And he said to him, "O son of the king, why are you so haggard morning after morning? Will you not tell me?" Amnon said to him, "I love Tamar, my brother Absalom's sister." ⁵Jonadab said to him, "Lie down on your bed and pretend to be ill. And when your father comes to see you, say to him, 'Let my sister Tamar come and give me bread to eat, and prepare the food in my sight, that I may see it and eat it from her hand.'" ⁶So Amnon lay down and pretended to be ill. And when the king came to see him, Amnon said to the king, "Please let my sister Tamar come and make a couple of cakes in my sight, that I may eat from her hand."

⁷Then David sent home to Tamar, saying, "Go to your brother Amnon's house and prepare food for him." ⁸So Tamar went to her brother Amnon's house, where he was lying down. And she took dough and kneaded it and made cakes in his sight and baked the cakes. ⁹And she took the pan and emptied it out before him, but he refused to eat. And Amnon said, "Send out everyone from me." So everyone went out from him. ¹⁰Then Amnon said to Tamar, "Bring the food into the chamber, that I may eat from your hand." And Tamar took the cakes she had made and brought them into the chamber to Amnon her brother. ¹¹But when she brought them near him to eat, he took hold of her and said to her, "Come, lie with me, my sister." ¹²She answered him, "No, my brother, do not violate¹ me, for such a thing is not done in Israel; do not do this outrageous thing. ¹³As for me, where could I carry my shame? And as for you, you would be as one of the outrageous fools in Israel. Now therefore, please speak to the king, for he will not withhold me from you." ¹⁴But he would not listen to her, and being stronger than she, he violated her and lay with her.

¹⁵Then Amnon hated her with very great hatred, so that the hatred with which he hated her was greater than the love with which he had loved her. And Amnon said to her, "Get up! Go!" ¹⁶But she said to him, "No, my brother, for this wrong in sending me away is greater than the other that you did to me."² But he would not listen to her. ¹⁷He called the young man who served him and said, "Put this woman out of my presence and bolt the door after her." ¹⁸Now she was wearing a long robe³ with sleeves, for thus were the virgin daughters of the king dressed. So his servant put her out and bolted the door after her. ¹⁹And Tamar put ashes on her head and tore the long robe that she wore. And she laid her hand on her head and went away, crying aloud as she went.

²⁰And her brother Absalom said to her, "Has Amnon your brother been with you? Now hold your peace, my sister. He is your brother; do not take this to heart." So Tamar lived, a desolate woman, in her brother Absalom's house. ²¹When King David heard of all these things, he was very angry.⁴ ²²But Absalom spoke to Amnon neither good nor bad, for Absalom hated Amnon, because he had violated his sister Tamar.

²³After two full years Absalom had sheepshearers at Baal-hazor, which is near Ephraim, and Absalom invited all the king's sons. ²⁴And Absalom came to the king and said, "Behold, your servant has sheepshearers. Please let the king and his servants go with your servant." ²⁵But the king said to Absalom, "No, my son, let us not all go, lest we be burdensome to you." He pressed him, but he would not go but gave him his blessing. ²⁶Then Absalom said, "If not, please let my brother Amnon go with us." And the king said to him, "Why should he go with you?" ²⁷But Absalom pressed him

---

¹ Or *humiliate*; also verses 14, 22, 32 ² Compare Septuagint, Vulgate; the meaning of the Hebrew is uncertain ³ Or *a robe of many colors* (compare Genesis 37:3); also verse 19 ⁴ Dead Sea Scroll, Septuagint add *But he would not punish his son Amnon, because he loved him, since he was his firstborn*

until he let Amnon and all the king's sons go with him. ²⁸Then Absalom commanded his servants, "Mark when Amnon's heart is merry with wine, and when I say to you, 'Strike Amnon,' then kill him. Do not fear; have I not commanded you? Be courageous and be valiant." ²⁹So the servants of Absalom did to Amnon as Absalom had commanded. Then all the king's sons arose, and each mounted his mule and fled.

³⁰While they were on the way, news came to David, "Absalom has struck down all the king's sons, and not one of them is left." ³¹Then the king arose and tore his garments and lay on the earth. And all his servants who were standing by tore their garments. ³²But Jonadab the son of Shimeah, David's brother, said, "Let not my lord suppose that they have killed all the young men, the king's sons, for Amnon alone is dead. For by the command of Absalom this has been determined from the day he violated his sister Tamar. ³³Now therefore let not my lord the king so take it to heart as to suppose that all the king's sons are dead, for Amnon alone is dead."

³⁴But Absalom fled. And the young man who kept the watch lifted up his eyes and looked, and behold, many people were coming from the road behind him¹ by the side of the mountain. ³⁵And Jonadab said to the king, "Behold, the king's sons have come; as your servant said, so it has come about." ³⁶And as soon as he had finished speaking, behold, the king's sons came and lifted up their voice and wept. And the king also and all his servants wept very bitterly.

³⁷But Absalom fled and went to Talmai the son of Ammihud, king of Geshur. And David mourned for his son day after day. ³⁸So Absalom fled and went to Geshur, and was there three years. ³⁹And the spirit of the king² longed to go out³ to Absalom, because he was comforted about Amnon, since he was dead.

Absalom's homecoming: prelude to disaster [14:1–24]. Chapter 14 is a bridge between Absalom's career as executioner and his career as usurper of the throne. It is a story of intrigue in which the machinations of Joab bring about the return of Absalom from exile to David's court.

14 Now Joab the son of Zeruiah knew that the king's heart went out to Absalom. ²And Joab sent to Tekoa and brought from there a wise woman and said to her, "Pretend to be a mourner and put on mourning garments. Do not anoint yourself with oil, but behave like a woman who has been mourning many days for the dead. ³Go to the king and speak thus to him." So Joab put the words in her mouth.

⁴When the woman of Tekoa came to the king, she fell on her face to the ground and paid homage and said, "Save me, O king." ⁵And the king said to her, "What is your trouble?" She answered, "Alas, I am a widow; my husband is dead. ⁶And your servant had two sons, and they quarreled with one another in the field. There was no one to separate them, and one struck the other and killed him. ⁷And now the whole clan has risen against your servant, and they say, 'Give up the man who struck his brother, that we may put him to death for the life of his brother whom he killed.' And so they would destroy the heir also. Thus they would quench my coal that is left and leave to my husband neither name nor remnant on the face of the earth."

⁸Then the king said to the woman, "Go to your house, and I will give orders concerning you." ⁹And the woman of Tekoa said to the king, "On me be the guilt, my lord the king, and on my father's house; let the king and his throne be guiltless." ¹⁰The king

---

¹ Septuagint *the Horonaim Road* ² Dead Sea Scroll, Septuagint; Hebrew *David* ³ Compare Vulgate *ceased to go out*

said, "If anyone says anything to you, bring him to me, and he shall never touch you again." [11]Then she said, "Please let the king invoke the Lord your God, that the avenger of blood kill no more, and my son be not destroyed." He said, "As the Lord lives, not one hair of your son shall fall to the ground."

[12]Then the woman said, "Please let your servant speak a word to my lord the king." He said, "Speak." [13]And the woman said, "Why then have you planned such a thing against the people of God? For in giving this decision the king convicts himself, inasmuch as the king does not bring his banished one home again. [14]We must all die; we are like water spilled on the ground, which cannot be gathered up again. But God will not take away life, and he devises means so that the banished one will not remain an outcast. [15]Now I have come to say this to my lord the king because the people have made me afraid, and your servant thought, 'I will speak to the king; it may be that the king will perform the request of his servant. [16]For the king will hear and deliver his servant from the hand of the man who would destroy me and my son together from the heritage of God.' [17]And your servant thought, 'The word of my lord the king will set me at rest,' for my lord the king is like the angel of God to discern good and evil. The Lord your God be with you!"

[18]Then the king answered the woman, "Do not hide from me anything I ask you." And the woman said, "Let my lord the king speak." [19]The king said, "Is the hand of Joab with you in all this?" The woman answered and said, "As surely as you live, my lord the king, one cannot turn to the right hand or to the left from anything that my lord the king has said. It was your servant Joab who commanded me; it was he who put all these words in the mouth of your servant. [20]In order to change the course of things your servant Joab did this. But my lord has wisdom like the wisdom of the angel of God to know all things that are on the earth."

[21]Then the king said to Joab, "Behold now, I grant this; go, bring back the young man Absalom." [22]And Joab fell on his face to the ground and paid homage and blessed the king. And Joab said, "Today your servant knows that I have found favor in your sight, my lord the king, in that the king has granted the request of his servant." [23]So Joab arose and went to Geshur and brought Absalom to Jerusalem. [24]And the king said, "Let him dwell apart in his own house; he is not to come into my presence." So Absalom lived apart in his own house and did not come into the king's presence.

Absalom's revolt [14:25–15:12]. Absalom becomes the archetypal villain of the story at this point. His roles are treacherous son and ambitious usurper. His personal style foreshadows that of Shakespeare's villain Iago: he is the charming and winsome villain without conscience. The right approach to the episode is to explore how skillfully the storyteller has selected details that make it possible to compile a portrait of Absalom. The main theme is the self-tempting nature of superior human endowment leading to self-seeking ambition.

[25]Now in all Israel there was no one so much to be praised for his handsome appearance as Absalom. From the sole of his foot to the crown of his head there was no blemish in him. [26]And when he cut the hair of his head (for at the end of every year he used to cut it; when it was heavy on him, he cut it), he weighed the hair of his

head, two hundred shekels[1] by the king's weight. [27]There were born to Absalom three sons, and one daughter whose name was Tamar. She was a beautiful woman.

[28]So Absalom lived two full years in Jerusalem, without coming into the king's presence. [29]Then Absalom sent for Joab, to send him to the king, but Joab would not come to him. And he sent a second time, but Joab would not come. [30]Then he said to his servants, "See, Joab's field is next to mine, and he has barley there; go and set it on fire." So Absalom's servants set the field on fire.[2] [31]Then Joab arose and went to Absalom at his house and said to him, "Why have your servants set my field on fire?" [32]Absalom answered Joab, "Behold, I sent word to you, 'Come here, that I may send you to the king, to ask, "Why have I come from Geshur? It would be better for me to be there still." Now therefore let me go into the presence of the king, and if there is guilt in me, let him put me to death.'" [33]Then Joab went to the king and told him, and he summoned Absalom. So he came to the king and bowed himself on his face to the ground before the king, and the king kissed Absalom.

15 After this Absalom got himself a chariot and horses, and fifty men to run before him. [2]And Absalom used to rise early and stand beside the way of the gate. And when any man had a dispute to come before the king for judgment, Absalom would call to him and say, "From what city are you?" And when he said, "Your servant is of such and such a tribe in Israel," [3]Absalom would say to him, "See, your claims are good and right, but there is no man designated by the king to hear you." [4]Then Absalom would say, "Oh that I were judge in the land! Then every man with a dispute or cause might come to me, and I would give him justice." [5]And whenever a man came near to pay homage to him, he would put out his hand and take hold of him and kiss him. [6]Thus Absalom did to all of Israel who came to the king for judgment. So Absalom stole the hearts of the men of Israel.

[7]And at the end of four[3] years Absalom said to the king, "Please let me go and pay my vow, which I have vowed to the LORD, in Hebron. [8]For your servant vowed a vow while I lived at Geshur in Aram, saying, 'If the LORD will indeed bring me back to Jerusalem, then I will offer worship to[4] the LORD.'" [9]The king said to him, "Go in peace." So he arose and went to Hebron. [10]But Absalom sent secret messengers throughout all the tribes of Israel, saying, "As soon as you hear the sound of the trumpet, then say, 'Absalom is king at Hebron!'" [11]With Absalom went two hundred men from Jerusalem who were invited guests, and they went in their innocence and knew nothing. [12]And while Absalom was offering the sacrifices, he sent for[5] Ahithophel the Gilonite, David's counselor, from his city Giloh. And the conspiracy grew strong, and the people with Absalom kept increasing.

David flees for his life [15:13–16:14]. The genius of the story told in this unit is the vividness with which it captures the confusion that characterized the event in real life. Everything happens in haste as David and his followers leave Jerusalem in a chaotic procession or march on foot. Impromptu decisions occur at breakneck speed. Realistic snapshots capture memorable moments: the king halting at the last house while his servants troop past him (15:18); the pathetic group walking on foot and weeping aloud as they press on into the wilderness (15:23); the Levites who are bearing the ark being sent back to Jerusalem (15:29); David weeping as he ascends the Mount of Olives,

[1] A *shekel* was about 2/5 ounce or 11 grams [2] Septuagint, Dead Sea Scroll add *So Joab's servants came to him with their clothes torn, and they said to him, "The servants of Absalom have set your field on fire."* [3] Septuagint, Syriac; Hebrew *forty* [4] Or *will serve* [5] Or *sent*

"barefoot and with his head covered" (15:30); Shimei walking along the hillside opposite David, cursing him persistently and throwing dust and stones at him (16:5, 6). Equally memorable is the gallery of characters who emerge as the account unfolds: the foreigner Ittai, who arrived "only yesterday" (15:20) and remains loyal to David even when urged to return to Jerusalem; the treacherous Ahithophel, David's adviser who turns against him; Hushai, loyal adviser to David who returns to Jerusalem hoping to counteract the counsel of Ahithophel; the opportunist Ziba, the servant of Mephibosheth who, hoping to gain Mephibosheth's estate, tells a lie about Mephibosheth's having turned traitor against David; the cantankerous Shimei, relative of Saul, who taunts David as he walks. The episode comes alive in our imagination as vividly as if we were watching a television drama.

[13]And a messenger came to David, saying, "The hearts of the men of Israel have gone after Absalom." [14]Then David said to all his servants who were with him at Jerusalem, "Arise, and let us flee, or else there will be no escape for us from Absalom. Go quickly, lest he overtake us quickly and bring down ruin on us and strike the city with the edge of the sword." [15]And the king's servants said to the king, "Behold, your servants are ready to do whatever my lord the king decides." [16]So the king went out, and all his household after him. And the king left ten concubines to keep the house. [17]And the king went out, and all the people after him. And they halted at the last house.

[18]And all his servants passed by him, and all the Cherethites, and all the Pelethites, and all the six hundred Gittites who had followed him from Gath, passed on before the king. [19]Then the king said to Ittai the Gittite, "Why do you also go with us? Go back and stay with the king, for you are a foreigner and also an exile from your home. [20]You came only yesterday, and shall I today make you wander about with us, since I go I know not where? Go back and take your brothers with you, and may the LORD show[1] steadfast love and faithfulness to you." [21]But Ittai answered the king, "As the LORD lives, and as my lord the king lives, wherever my lord the king shall be, whether for death or for life, there also will your servant be." [22]And David said to Ittai, "Go then, pass on." So Ittai the Gittite passed on with all his men and all the little ones who were with him. [23]And all the land wept aloud as all the people passed by, and the king crossed the brook Kidron, and all the people passed on toward the wilderness.

[24]And Abiathar came up, and behold, Zadok came also with all the Levites, bearing the ark of the covenant of God. And they set down the ark of God until the people had all passed out of the city. [25]Then the king said to Zadok, "Carry the ark of God back into the city. If I find favor in the eyes of the LORD, he will bring me back and let me see both it and his dwelling place. [26]But if he says, 'I have no pleasure in you,' behold, here I am, let him do to me what seems good to him." [27]The king also said to Zadok the priest, "Are you not a seer? Go back[2] to the city in peace, with your two sons, Ahimaaz your son, and Jonathan the son of Abiathar. [28]See, I will wait at the fords of the wilderness until word comes from you to inform me." [29]So Zadok and Abiathar carried the ark of God back to Jerusalem, and they remained there.

[30]But David went up the ascent of the Mount of Olives, weeping as he went, barefoot and with his head covered. And all the people who were with him covered their heads, and they went up, weeping as they went. [31]And it was told David, "Ahithophel

---

[1] Septuagint; Hebrew lacks *may the LORD show* [2] Septuagint *The king also said to Zadok the priest, "Look, go back*

is among the conspirators with Absalom." And David said, "O LORD, please turn the counsel of Ahithophel into foolishness."

[32] While David was coming to the summit, where God was worshiped, behold, Hushai the Archite came to meet him with his coat torn and dirt on his head. [33] David said to him, "If you go on with me, you will be a burden to me. [34] But if you return to the city and say to Absalom, 'I will be your servant, O king; as I have been your father's servant in time past, so now I will be your servant,' then you will defeat for me the counsel of Ahithophel. [35] Are not Zadok and Abiathar the priests with you there? So whatever you hear from the king's house, tell it to Zadok and Abiathar the priests. [36] Behold, their two sons are with them there, Ahimaaz, Zadok's son, and Jonathan, Abiathar's son, and by them you shall send to me everything you hear." [37] So Hushai, David's friend, came into the city, just as Absalom was entering Jerusalem.

16 When David had passed a little beyond the summit, Ziba the servant of Mephibosheth met him, with a couple of donkeys saddled, bearing two hundred loaves of bread, a hundred bunches of raisins, a hundred of summer fruits, and a skin of wine. [2] And the king said to Ziba, "Why have you brought these?" Ziba answered, "The donkeys are for the king's household to ride on, the bread and summer fruit for the young men to eat, and the wine for those who faint in the wilderness to drink." [3] And the king said, "And where is your master's son?" Ziba said to the king, "Behold, he remains in Jerusalem, for he said, 'Today the house of Israel will give me back the kingdom of my father.'" [4] Then the king said to Ziba, "Behold, all that belonged to Mephibosheth is now yours." And Ziba said, "I pay homage; let me ever find favor in your sight, my lord the king."

[5] When King David came to Bahurim, there came out a man of the family of the house of Saul, whose name was Shimei, the son of Gera, and as he came he cursed continually. [6] And he threw stones at David and at all the servants of King David, and all the people and all the mighty men were on his right hand and on his left. [7] And Shimei said as he cursed, "Get out, get out, you man of blood, you worthless man! [8] The LORD has avenged on you all the blood of the house of Saul, in whose place you have reigned, and the LORD has given the kingdom into the hand of your son Absalom. See, your evil is on you, for you are a man of blood."

[9] Then Abishai the son of Zeruiah said to the king, "Why should this dead dog curse my lord the king? Let me go over and take off his head." [10] But the king said, "What have I to do with you, you sons of Zeruiah? If he is cursing because the LORD has said to him, 'Curse David,' who then shall say, 'Why have you done so?'" [11] And David said to Abishai and to all his servants, "Behold, my own son seeks my life; how much more now may this Benjaminite! Leave him alone, and let him curse, for the LORD has told him to. [12] It may be that the LORD will look on the wrong done to me,[1] and that the LORD will repay me with good for his cursing today." [13] So David and his men went on the road, while Shimei went along on the hillside opposite him and cursed as he went and threw stones at him and flung dust. [14] And the king, and all the people who were with him, arrived weary at the Jordan.[2] And there he refreshed himself.

Absalom's rule in Jerusalem [16:15–17:23]. The scene now shifts from David in exile to his son Absalom as temporary ruler in Jerusalem. To our surprise, the story becomes

---

[1] Septuagint, Vulgate *will look upon my affliction* [2] Septuagint; Hebrew lacks *at the Jordan*

mainly a story of intrigue as Hushai, loyal to David but pretending loyalty to Absalom, competes with Ahithophel to influence Absalom's battle strategy. In this deception story, the villainous Absalom is outwitted by the cleverness of Hushai, with the narrator tipping his hand to influence our interpretation of the event (17:14).

[15]Now Absalom and all the people, the men of Israel, came to Jerusalem, and Ahithophel with him. [16]And when Hushai the Archite, David's friend, came to Absalom, Hushai said to Absalom, "Long live the king! Long live the king!" [17]And Absalom said to Hushai, "Is this your loyalty to your friend? Why did you not go with your friend?" [18]And Hushai said to Absalom, "No, for whom the LORD and this people and all the men of Israel have chosen, his I will be, and with him I will remain. [19]And again, whom should I serve? Should it not be his son? As I have served your father, so I will serve you."

[20]Then Absalom said to Ahithophel, "Give your counsel. What shall we do?" [21]Ahithophel said to Absalom, "Go in to your father's concubines, whom he has left to keep the house, and all Israel will hear that you have made yourself a stench to your father, and the hands of all who are with you will be strengthened." [22]So they pitched a tent for Absalom on the roof. And Absalom went in to his father's concubines in the sight of all Israel. [23]Now in those days the counsel that Ahithophel gave was as if one consulted the word of God; so was all the counsel of Ahithophel esteemed, both by David and by Absalom.

17 Moreover, Ahithophel said to Absalom, "Let me choose twelve thousand men, and I will arise and pursue David tonight. [2]I will come upon him while he is weary and discouraged and throw him into a panic, and all the people who are with him will flee. I will strike down only the king, [3]and I will bring all the people back to you as a bride comes home to her husband. You seek the life of only one man,[1] and all the people will be at peace." [4]And the advice seemed right in the eyes of Absalom and all the elders of Israel.

[5]Then Absalom said, "Call Hushai the Archite also, and let us hear what he has to say." [6]And when Hushai came to Absalom, Absalom said to him, "Thus has Ahithophel spoken; shall we do as he says? If not, you speak." [7]Then Hushai said to Absalom, "This time the counsel that Ahithophel has given is not good." [8]Hushai said, "You know that your father and his men are mighty men, and that they are enraged,[2] like a bear robbed of her cubs in the field. Besides, your father is expert in war; he will not spend the night with the people. [9]Behold, even now he has hidden himself in one of the pits or in some other place. And as soon as some of the people fall[3] at the first attack, whoever hears it will say, 'There has been a slaughter among the people who follow Absalom.' [10]Then even the valiant man, whose heart is like the heart of a lion, will utterly melt with fear, for all Israel knows that your father is a mighty man, and that those who are with him are valiant men. [11]But my counsel is that all Israel be gathered to you, from Dan to Beersheba, as the sand by the sea for multitude, and that you go to battle in person. [12]So we shall come upon him in some place where he is to be found, and we shall light upon him as the dew falls on the ground, and of him and all the men with him not one will be left. [13]If he withdraws into a city, then all Israel will bring ropes to that city, and we shall drag it into the valley, until not even a

---

[1] Septuagint; Hebrew *back to you. Like the return of the whole is the man whom you seek* [2] Hebrew *bitter of soul* [3] Or *And as he falls on them*

pebble is to be found there." [14]And Absalom and all the men of Israel said, "The coun-sel of Hushai the Archite is better than the counsel of Ahithophel." For the LORD had ordained[1] to defeat the good counsel of Ahithophel, so that the LORD might bring harm upon Absalom.

[15]Then Hushai said to Zadok and Abiathar the priests, "Thus and so did Ahithophel counsel Absalom and the elders of Israel, and thus and so have I coun-seled. [16]Now therefore send quickly and tell David, 'Do not stay tonight at the fords of the wilderness, but by all means pass over, lest the king and all the people who are with him be swallowed up.'" [17]Now Jonathan and Ahimaaz were waiting at En-rogel. A female servant was to go and tell them, and they were to go and tell King David, for they were not to be seen entering the city. [18]But a young man saw them and told Absalom. So both of them went away quickly and came to the house of a man at Bahurim, who had a well in his courtyard. And they went down into it. [19]And the woman took and spread a covering over the well's mouth and scattered grain on it, and nothing was known of it. [20]When Absalom's servants came to the woman at the house, they said, "Where are Ahimaaz and Jonathan?" And the woman said to them, "They have gone over the brook[2] of water." And when they had sought and could not find them, they returned to Jerusalem.

[21]After they had gone, the men came up out of the well, and went and told King David. They said to David, "Arise, and go quickly over the water, for thus and so has Ahithophel counseled against you." [22]Then David arose, and all the people who were with him, and they crossed the Jordan. By daybreak not one was left who had not crossed the Jordan.

[23]When Ahithophel saw that his counsel was not followed, he saddled his donkey and went off home to his own city. He set his house in order and hanged himself, and he died and was buried in the tomb of his father.

> **David at war with his son** [17:24–18:33]. The epic action of military combat now comes to dominate the story. It is not only a civil war but also a war between family members. The events are narrated in full, realistic detail, especially the circumstances of Absalom's death. The continuing love of David for his scoundrel son is the dominant emotional undertow, and it works at odds with David's need to defeat Absalom if he wishes to escape with his life. This loyalty to mortal enemies is characteristic of David. Thus he responds to his rescue from a son who tried to kill him by uncontrollably lament-ing the death of that son (18:33). As when Saul died, David's anger flashes only at those who announce the death with pleasure or seek to benefit from it.

[24]Then David came to Mahanaim. And Absalom crossed the Jordan with all the men of Israel. [25]Now Absalom had set Amasa over the army instead of Joab. Amasa was the son of a man named Ithra the Ishmaelite,[3] who had married Abigal the daughter of Nahash, sister of Zeruiah, Joab's mother. [26]And Israel and Absalom encamped in the land of Gilead.

[27]When David came to Mahanaim, Shobi the son of Nahash from Rabbah of the Ammonites, and Machir the son of Ammiel from Lo-debar, and Barzillai the Gileadite from Rogelim, [28]brought beds, basins, and earthen vessels, wheat, barley, flour, parched grain, beans and lentils,[4] [29]honey and curds and sheep and cheese from the

---

[1] Hebrew *commanded* [2] The meaning of the Hebrew word is uncertain [3] Compare 1 Chronicles 2:17; Hebrew *Israelite* [4] Hebrew adds *and parched grain*

herd, for David and the people with him to eat, for they said, "The people are hungry and weary and thirsty in the wilderness."

18 Then David mustered the men who were with him and set over them commanders of thousands and commanders of hundreds. ²And David sent out the army, one third under the command of Joab, one third under the command of Abishai the son of Zeruiah, Joab's brother, and one third under the command of Ittai the Gittite. And the king said to the men, "I myself will also go out with you." ³But the men said, "You shall not go out. For if we flee, they will not care about us. If half of us die, they will not care about us. But you are worth ten thousand of us. Therefore it is better that you send us help from the city." ⁴The king said to them, "Whatever seems best to you I will do." So the king stood at the side of the gate, while all the army marched out by hundreds and by thousands. ⁵And the king ordered Joab and Abishai and Ittai, "Deal gently for my sake with the young man Absalom." And all the people heard when the king gave orders to all the commanders about Absalom.

⁶So the army went out into the field against Israel, and the battle was fought in the forest of Ephraim. ⁷And the men of Israel were defeated there by the servants of David, and the loss there was great on that day, twenty thousand men. ⁸The battle spread over the face of all the country, and the forest devoured more people that day than the sword.

⁹And Absalom happened to meet the servants of David. Absalom was riding on his mule, and the mule went under the thick branches of a great oak,¹ and his head caught fast in the oak, and he was suspended between heaven and earth, while the mule that was under him went on. ¹⁰And a certain man saw it and told Joab, "Behold, I saw Absalom hanging in an oak." ¹¹Joab said to the man who told him, "What, you saw him! Why then did you not strike him there to the ground? I would have been glad to give you ten pieces of silver and a belt." ¹²But the man said to Joab, "Even if I felt in my hand the weight of a thousand pieces of silver, I would not reach out my hand against the king's son, for in our hearing the king commanded you and Abishai and Ittai, 'For my sake protect the young man Absalom.' ¹³On the other hand, if I had dealt treacherously against his life² (and there is nothing hidden from the king), then you yourself would have stood aloof." ¹⁴Joab said, "I will not waste time like this with you." And he took three javelins in his hand and thrust them into the heart of Absalom while he was still alive in the oak. ¹⁵And ten young men, Joab's armor-bearers, surrounded Absalom and struck him and killed him.

¹⁶Then Joab blew the trumpet, and the troops came back from pursuing Israel, for Joab restrained them. ¹⁷And they took Absalom and threw him into a great pit in the forest and raised over him a very great heap of stones. And all Israel fled every one to his own home. ¹⁸Now Absalom in his lifetime had taken and set up for himself the pillar that is in the King's Valley, for he said, "I have no son to keep my name in remembrance." He called the pillar after his own name, and it is called Absalom's monument³ to this day.

¹⁹Then Ahimaaz the son of Zadok said, "Let me run and carry news to the king that the LORD has delivered him from the hand of his enemies." ²⁰And Joab said to him, "You are not to carry news today. You may carry news another day, but today you shall carry no news, because the king's son is dead." ²¹Then Joab said to the Cushite, "Go, tell the king what you have seen." The Cushite bowed before Joab, and ran. ²²Then

---

¹ Or terebinth; also verses 10, 14 ² Or at the risk of my life ³ Or Absalom's hand

Ahimaaz the son of Zadok said again to Joab, "Come what may, let me also run after the Cushite." And Joab said, "Why will you run, my son, seeing that you will have no reward for the news?" [23]"Come what may," he said, "I will run." So he said to him, "Run." Then Ahimaaz ran by the way of the plain, and outran the Cushite.

[24]Now David was sitting between the two gates, and the watchman went up to the roof of the gate by the wall, and when he lifted up his eyes and looked, he saw a man running alone. [25]The watchman called out and told the king. And the king said, "If he is alone, there is news in his mouth." And he drew nearer and nearer. [26]The watchman saw another man running. And the watchman called to the gate and said, "See, another man running alone!" The king said, "He also brings news." [27]The watchman said, "I think the running of the first is like the running of Ahimaaz the son of Zadok." And the king said, "He is a good man and comes with good news."

[28]Then Ahimaaz cried out to the king, "All is well." And he bowed before the king with his face to the earth and said, "Blessed be the LORD your God, who has delivered up the men who raised their hand against my lord the king." [29]And the king said, "Is it well with the young man Absalom?" Ahimaaz answered, "When Joab sent the king's servant, your servant, I saw a great commotion, but I do not know what it was." [30]And the king said, "Turn aside and stand here." So he turned aside and stood still.

[31]And behold, the Cushite came, and the Cushite said, "Good news for my lord the king! For the LORD has delivered you this day from the hand of all who rose up against you." [32]The king said to the Cushite, "Is it well with the young man Absalom?" And the Cushite answered, "May the enemies of my lord the king and all who rise up against you for evil be like that young man." [33][1] And the king was deeply moved and went up to the chamber over the gate and wept. And as he went, he said, "O my son Absalom, my son, my son Absalom! Would I had died instead of you, O Absalom, my son, my son!"

A semblance of order is restored to the kingdom [chapter 19]. The action now turns to the immediate aftermath of Absalom's insurrection and the resulting civil war. The events that the chronicler chose to record are these: Joab's calling David to his senses in regard to his excessive mourning over the death of Absalom (vv. 1–8); the high priests' persuasion of the unsettled nation to invite David back to Jerusalem as king (vv. 9–15); Shimei's confession of wrongdoing and pardon by David (vv. 16–23); Mephibosheth's clearing his name of Ziba's earlier slander (vv. 24–30); David's encounter with a bene- factor from earlier in his life (vv. 31–40); an intertribal squabble about who has the most claim to the restored king (vv. 41–43). As we often find in OT narrative, the details here are too unlikely to be fictional. In this reestablishment of the kingdom, we catch echoes of David's earlier triumphs of power, mercy, and justice, but they occur on a less grand scale, and David emerges diminished in our estimation.

19

It was told Joab, "Behold, the king is weeping and mourning for Absalom." [2]So the victory that day was turned into mourning for all the people, for the people heard that day, "The king is grieving for his son." [3]And the people stole into the city that day as people steal in who are ashamed when they flee in battle. [4]The king covered his face, and the king cried with a loud voice, "O my son Absalom, O Absalom, my son, my son!" [5]Then Joab came into the house to the king and said, "You have today covered with shame the faces of all your servants, who have this day

[1] Ch 19:1 in Hebrew

saved your life and the lives of your sons and your daughters and the lives of your wives and your concubines, [6]because you love those who hate you and hate those who love you. For you have made it clear today that commanders and servants are nothing to you, for today I know that if Absalom were alive and all of us were dead today, then you would be pleased. [7]Now therefore arise, go out and speak kindly to your servants, for I swear by the LORD, if you do not go, not a man will stay with you this night, and this will be worse for you than all the evil that has come upon you from your youth until now." [8]Then the king arose and took his seat in the gate. And the people were all told, "Behold, the king is sitting in the gate." And all the people came before the king.

Now Israel had fled every man to his own home. [9]And all the people were arguing throughout all the tribes of Israel, saying, "The king delivered us from the hand of our enemies and saved us from the hand of the Philistines, and now he has fled out of the land from Absalom. [10]But Absalom, whom we anointed over us, is dead in battle. Now therefore why do you say nothing about bringing the king back?"

[11]And King David sent this message to Zadok and Abiathar the priests: "Say to the elders of Judah, 'Why should you be the last to bring the king back to his house, when the word of all Israel has come to the king?[1] [12]You are my brothers; you are my bone and my flesh. Why then should you be the last to bring back the king?' [13]And say to Amasa, 'Are you not my bone and my flesh? God do so to me and more also, if you are not commander of my army from now on in place of Joab.'" [14]And he swayed the heart of all the men of Judah as one man, so that they sent word to the king, "Return, both you and all your servants." [15]So the king came back to the Jordan, and Judah came to Gilgal to meet the king and to bring the king over the Jordan.

[16]And Shimei the son of Gera, the Benjaminite, from Bahurim, hurried to come down with the men of Judah to meet King David. [17]And with him were a thousand men from Benjamin. And Ziba the servant of the house of Saul, with his fifteen sons and his twenty servants, rushed down to the Jordan before the king, [18]and they crossed the ford to bring over the king's household and to do his pleasure. And Shimei the son of Gera fell down before the king, as he was about to cross the Jordan, [19]and said to the king, "Let not my lord hold me guilty or remember how your servant did wrong on the day my lord the king left Jerusalem. Do not let the king take it to heart. [20]For your servant knows that I have sinned. Therefore, behold, I have come this day, the first of all the house of Joseph to come down to meet my lord the king." [21]Abishai the son of Zeruiah answered, "Shall not Shimei be put to death for this, because he cursed the LORD's anointed?" [22]But David said, "What have I to do with you, you sons of Zeruiah, that you should this day be as an adversary to me? Shall anyone be put to death in Israel this day? For do I not know that I am this day king over Israel?" [23]And the king said to Shimei, "You shall not die." And the king gave him his oath.

[24]And Mephibosheth the son of Saul came down to meet the king. He had neither taken care of his feet nor trimmed his beard nor washed his clothes, from the day the king departed until the day he came back in safety. [25]And when he came to Jerusalem to meet the king, the king said to him, "Why did you not go with me, Mephibosheth?" [26]He answered, "My lord, O king, my servant deceived me, for your servant said to him, 'I will saddle a donkey for myself,[2] that I may ride on it and go with the king.' For your servant is lame. [27]He has slandered your servant to my lord the king. But my lord the king is like the angel of God; do therefore what seems good to you. [28]For all my

---

[1] Septuagint; Hebrew to the king, to his house [2] Septuagint, Syriac, Vulgate Saddle a donkey for me

father's house were but men doomed to death before my lord the king, but you set your servant among those who eat at your table. What further right have I, then, to cry to the king?" ²⁹And the king said to him, "Why speak any more of your affairs? I have decided: you and Ziba shall divide the land." ³⁰And Mephibosheth said to the king, "Oh, let him take it all, since my lord the king has come safely home."

³¹Now Barzillai the Gileadite had come down from Rogelim, and he went on with the king to the Jordan, to escort him over the Jordan. ³²Barzillai was a very aged man, eighty years old. He had provided the king with food while he stayed at Mahanaim, for he was a very wealthy man. ³³And the king said to Barzillai, "Come over with me, and I will provide for you with me in Jerusalem." ³⁴But Barzillai said to the king, "How many years have I still to live, that I should go up with the king to Jerusalem? ³⁵I am this day eighty years old. Can I discern what is pleasant and what is not? Can your servant taste what he eats or what he drinks? Can I still listen to the voice of singing men and singing women? Why then should your servant be an added burden to my lord the king? ³⁶Your servant will go a little way over the Jordan with the king. Why should the king repay me with such a reward? ³⁷Please let your servant return, that I may die in my own city near the grave of my father and my mother. But here is your servant Chimham. Let him go over with my lord the king, and do for him whatever seems good to you." ³⁸And the king answered, "Chimham shall go over with me, and I will do for him whatever seems good to you, and all that you desire of me I will do for you." ³⁹Then all the people went over the Jordan, and the king went over. And the king kissed Barzillai and blessed him, and he returned to his own home. ⁴⁰The king went on to Gilgal, and Chimham went on with him. All the people of Judah, and also half the people of Israel, brought the king on his way.

⁴¹Then all the men of Israel came to the king and said to the king, "Why have our brothers the men of Judah stolen you away and brought the king and his household over the Jordan, and all David's men with him?" ⁴²All the men of Judah answered the men of Israel, "Because the king is our close relative. Why then are you angry over this matter? Have we eaten at all at the king's expense? Or has he given us any gift?" ⁴³And the men of Israel answered the men of Judah, "We have ten shares in the king, and in David also we have more than you. Why then did you despise us? Were we not the first to speak of bringing back our king?" But the words of the men of Judah were fiercer than the words of the men of Israel.

Yet another revolt [chapter 20]. Just when we hoped the story would move toward a happy ending, we are frustrated by another revolt, this time by Sheba. The very weariness that we feel underscores the larger pattern that is unfolding: David's having to live with the consequences of his tragic act, as predicted by God. The story belongs to the genre of political intrigue, and the overall sequence is revolt, counteraction, quelling of the revolt. The narrative ingredient of surprise enters the story yet again as the "wise woman" of the city of Abel gets a hearing with the warlike Joab and convinces him not to destroy the city if the head of the rebel Sheba is thrown to him over the city wall; the woman makes good on her bargain, and the city is spared (vv. 14–22). As often in the realistic battle stories of the OT, the gruesome and shocking are treated matter-of-factly, as though they are all in a day's work.

20

Now there happened to be there a worthless man, whose name was Sheba, the son of Bichri, a Benjaminite. And he blew the trumpet and said,

"We have no portion in David,
and we have no inheritance in the son of Jesse;
every man to his tents, O Israel!"

²So all the men of Israel withdrew from David and followed Sheba the son of Bichri. But the men of Judah followed their king steadfastly from the Jordan to Jerusalem.

³And David came to his house at Jerusalem. And the king took the ten concubines whom he had left to care for the house and put them in a house under guard and provided for them, but did not go in to them. So they were shut up until the day of their death, living as if in widowhood.

⁴Then the king said to Amasa, "Call the men of Judah together to me within three days, and be here yourself." ⁵So Amasa went to summon Judah, but he delayed beyond the set time that had been appointed him. ⁶And David said to Abishai, "Now Sheba the son of Bichri will do us more harm than Absalom. Take your lord's servants and pursue him, lest he get himself to fortified cities and escape from us."[1] ⁷And there went out after him Joab's men and the Cherethites and the Pelethites, and all the mighty men. They went out from Jerusalem to pursue Sheba the son of Bichri. ⁸When they were at the great stone that is in Gibeon, Amasa came to meet them. Now Joab was wearing a soldier's garment, and over it was a belt with a sword in its sheath fastened on his thigh, and as he went forward it fell out. ⁹And Joab said to Amasa, "Is it well with you, my brother?" And Joab took Amasa by the beard with his right hand to kiss him. ¹⁰But Amasa did not observe the sword that was in Joab's hand. So Joab struck him with it in the stomach and spilled his entrails to the ground without striking a second blow, and he died.

Then Joab and Abishai his brother pursued Sheba the son of Bichri. ¹¹And one of Joab's young men took his stand by Amasa and said, "Whoever favors Joab, and whoever is for David, let him follow Joab." ¹²And Amasa lay wallowing in his blood in the highway. And anyone who came by, seeing him, stopped. And when the man saw that all the people stopped, he carried Amasa out of the highway into the field and threw a garment over him. ¹³When he was taken out of the highway, all the people went on after Joab to pursue Sheba the son of Bichri.

¹⁴And Sheba passed through all the tribes of Israel to Abel of Beth-maacah,[2] and all the Bichrites[3] assembled and followed him in. ¹⁵And all the men who were with Joab came and besieged him in Abel of Beth-maacah. They cast up a mound against the city, and it stood against the rampart, and they were battering the wall to throw it down. ¹⁶Then a wise woman called from the city, "Listen! Listen! Tell Joab, 'Come here, that I may speak to you.'" ¹⁷And he came near her, and the woman said, "Are you Joab?" He answered, "I am." Then she said to him, "Listen to the words of your servant." And he answered, "I am listening." ¹⁸Then she said, "They used to say in former times, 'Let them but ask counsel at Abel,' and so they settled a matter. ¹⁹I am one of those who are peaceable and faithful in Israel. You seek to destroy a city that is a mother in Israel. Why will you swallow up the heritage of the LORD?" ²⁰Joab answered, "Far be it from me, far be it, that I should swallow up or destroy! ²¹That is not true. But a man of the hill country of Ephraim, called Sheba the son of Bichri, has lifted up his

---

[1] Hebrew *and snatch away our eyes* [2] Compare 20:15; Hebrew *and Beth-maacah* [3] Hebrew *Berites*

hand against King David. Give up him alone, and I will withdraw from the city." And the woman said to Joab, "Behold, his head shall be thrown to you over the wall." ²²Then the woman went to all the people in her wisdom. And they cut off the head of Sheba the son of Bichri and threw it out to Joab. So he blew the trumpet, and they dispersed from the city, every man to his home. And Joab returned to Jerusalem to the king.

²³Now Joab was in command of all the army of Israel; and Benaiah the son of Jehoiada was in command of the Cherethites and the Pelethites; ²⁴and Adoram was in charge of the forced labor; and Jehoshaphat the son of Ahilud was the recorder; ²⁵and Sheva was secretary; and Zadok and Abiathar were priests; ²⁶and Ira the Jairite was also David's priest.

More violence in the story of David's reign [chapter 21]. No matter how much we long for things to improve in the life of the penitent and beleaguered David, the tragic consequences of his earlier sin continue to dog him; if we reflect on the matter, we can see that David is reaping the consequences of his murder of Uriah. In this chapter, the combat motif continues to dominate the narrative. In the main event of the chapter, David has to placate God (whose disfavor has been signaled by three years of drought) regarding Saul's guilt in relation to the Gibeonites (vv. 1–14). In a book where justice has been a major literary motif, this event reinforces that theme. The chapter ends with a brief account of David's further military victories, reminding us that despite all David's failings and all the people who wanted him removed, the story is a hero story.

21 Now there was a famine in the days of David for three years, year after year. And David sought the face of the LORD. And the LORD said, "There is blood-guilt on Saul and on his house, because he put the Gibeonites to death." ²So the king called the Gibeonites and spoke to them. Now the Gibeonites were not of the people of Israel but of the remnant of the Amorites. Although the people of Israel had sworn to spare them, Saul had sought to strike them down in his zeal for the people of Israel and Judah. ³And David said to the Gibeonites, "What shall I do for you? And how shall I make atonement, that you may bless the heritage of the LORD?" ⁴The Gibeonites said to him, "It is not a matter of silver or gold between us and Saul or his house; neither is it for us to put any man to death in Israel." And he said, "What do you say that I shall do for you?" ⁵They said to the king, "The man who consumed us and planned to destroy us, so that we should have no place in all the territory of Israel, ⁶let seven of his sons be given to us, so that we may hang them before the LORD at Gibeah of Saul, the chosen of the LORD." And the king said, "I will give them."

⁷But the king spared Mephibosheth, the son of Saul's son Jonathan, because of the oath of the LORD that was between them, between David and Jonathan the son of Saul. ⁸The king took the two sons of Rizpah the daughter of Aiah, whom she bore to Saul, Armoni and Mephibosheth; and the five sons of Merab¹ the daughter of Saul, whom she bore to Adriel the son of Barzillai the Meholathite; ⁹and he gave them into the hands of the Gibeonites, and they hanged them on the mountain before the LORD, and the seven of them perished together. They were put to death in the first days of harvest, at the beginning of barley harvest.

¹⁰Then Rizpah the daughter of Aiah took sackcloth and spread it for herself on the rock, from the beginning of harvest until rain fell upon them from the heavens. And

¹ Two Hebrew manuscripts, Septuagint; most Hebrew manuscripts *Michal*

she did not allow the birds of the air to come upon them by day, or the beasts of the field by night. ¹¹When David was told what Rizpah the daughter of Aiah, the concubine of Saul, had done, ¹²David went and took the bones of Saul and the bones of his son Jonathan from the men of Jabesh-gilead, who had stolen them from the public square of Beth-shan, where the Philistines had hanged them, on the day the Philistines killed Saul on Gilboa. ¹³And he brought up from there the bones of Saul and the bones of his son Jonathan; and they gathered the bones of those who were hanged. ¹⁴And they buried the bones of Saul and his son Jonathan in the land of Benjamin in Zela, in the tomb of Kish his father. And they did all that the king commanded. And after that God responded to the plea for the land.

¹⁵There was war again between the Philistines and Israel, and David went down together with his servants, and they fought against the Philistines. And David grew weary. ¹⁶And Ishbi-benob, one of the descendants of the giants, whose spear weighed three hundred shekels¹ of bronze, and who was armed with a new sword, thought to kill David. ¹⁷But Abishai the son of Zeruiah came to his aid and attacked the Philistine and killed him. Then David's men swore to him, "You shall no longer go out with us to battle, lest you quench the lamp of Israel."

¹⁸After this there was again war with the Philistines at Gob. Then Sibbecai the Hushathite struck down Saph, who was one of the descendants of the giants. ¹⁹And there was again war with the Philistines at Gob, and Elhanan the son of Jaare-oregim, the Bethlehemite, struck down Goliath the Gittite, the shaft of whose spear was like a weaver's beam.² ²⁰And there was again war at Gath, where there was a man of great stature, who had six fingers on each hand, and six toes on each foot, twenty-four in number, and he also was descended from the giants. ²¹And when he taunted Israel, Jonathan the son of Shimei, David's brother, struck him down. ²²These four were descended from the giants in Gath, and they fell by the hand of David and by the hand of his servants.

David's songs of praise [chapter 22]. The closest we come to a happy ending for 2 Samuel is two *lyric poems composed by David the poet (yet another role of David and facet of his character). The lead-in to the first of the two poems indicates that it was occasioned by events much earlier in David's life; the song is inserted at this late point in the narrative for the literary purpose of reaching closure on David's heroic life (the poem reappears as Psalm 18 in the Psalter). Its genre is *psalm of praise. The outline of the poem is as follows: opening ascription of praise to God for deliverance from enemies (22:2–4); hyperbolic and metaphoric rescue story of God's deliverance of the speaker (22:5–20); praise of God's covenant faithfulness to the upright speaker (22:21–31); a spiritualized version of the conventional arming of the hero in epic literature, combined with an equally familiar *boast (22:32–46); concluding praise of God (22:47–51). A good analytic lens through which to analyze the poem is to scrutinize the ways this psalm of praise shows itself to be the composition of a warrior-king.

22 And David spoke to the Lᴏʀᴅ the words of this song on the day when the Lᴏʀᴅ delivered him from the hand of all his enemies, and from the hand of Saul. ²He said,

"The LORD is my rock and my fortress and my deliverer,
3   my[1] God, my rock, in whom I take refuge,
my shield, and the horn of my salvation,
       my stronghold and my refuge,
       my savior; you save me from violence.
4   I call upon the LORD, who is worthy to be praised,
       and I am saved from my enemies.

5   "For the waves of death encompassed me,
       the torrents of destruction assailed me;[2]
6   the cords of Sheol entangled me;
       the snares of death confronted me.

7   "In my distress I called upon the LORD;
       to my God I called.
From his temple he heard my voice,
       and my cry came to his ears.

8   "Then the earth reeled and rocked;
       the foundations of the heavens trembled
       and quaked, because he was angry.
9   Smoke went up from his nostrils,[3]
       and devouring fire from his mouth;
       glowing coals flamed forth from him.
10   He bowed the heavens and came down;
       thick darkness was under his feet.
11   He rode on a cherub and flew;
       he was seen on the wings of the wind.
12   He made darkness around him his canopy,
       thick clouds, a gathering of water.
13   Out of the brightness before him
       coals of fire flamed forth.
14   The LORD thundered from heaven,
       and the Most High uttered his voice.
15   And he sent out arrows and scattered them;
       lightning, and routed them.
16   Then the channels of the sea were seen;
       the foundations of the world were laid bare,
at the rebuke of the LORD,
       at the blast of the breath of his nostrils.

17   "He sent from on high, he took me;
       he drew me out of many waters.
18   He rescued me from my strong enemy,
       from those who hated me,
       for they were too mighty for me.
19   They confronted me in the day of my calamity,
       but the LORD was my support.

---

[1] Septuagint (compare Psalm 18:2); Hebrew lacks *my*   [2] Or *terrified me*   [3] Or *in his wrath*

²⁰ He brought me out into a broad place;
  he rescued me, because he delighted in me.

²¹ "The Lord dealt with me according to my righteousness;
  according to the cleanness of my hands he rewarded me.
²² For I have kept the ways of the Lord
  and have not wickedly departed from my God.
²³ For all his rules were before me,
  and from his statutes I did not turn aside.
²⁴ I was blameless before him,
  and I kept myself from guilt.
²⁵ And the Lord has rewarded me according to my righteousness,
  according to my cleanness in his sight.

²⁶ "With the merciful you show yourself merciful;
  with the blameless man you show yourself blameless;
²⁷ with the purified you deal purely,
  and with the crooked you make yourself seem tortuous.
²⁸ You save a humble people,
  but your eyes are on the haughty to bring them down.
²⁹ For you are my lamp, O Lord,
  and my God lightens my darkness.
³⁰ For by you I can run against a troop,
  and by my God I can leap over a wall.
³¹ This God—his way is perfect;
  the word of the Lord proves true;
  he is a shield for all those who take refuge in him.

³² "For who is God, but the Lord?
  And who is a rock, except our God?
³³ This God is my strong refuge
  and has made my[1] way blameless.[2]
³⁴ He made my feet like the feet of a deer
  and set me secure on the heights.
³⁵ He trains my hands for war,
  so that my arms can bend a bow of bronze.
³⁶ You have given me the shield of your salvation,
  and your gentleness made me great.
³⁷ You gave a wide place for my steps under me,
  and my feet[3] did not slip;
³⁸ I pursued my enemies and destroyed them,
  and did not turn back until they were consumed.
³⁹ I consumed them; I thrust them through, so that they did not rise;
  they fell under my feet.
⁴⁰ For you equipped me with strength for the battle;
  you made those who rise against me sink under me.
⁴¹ You made my enemies turn their backs to me,[4]
  those who hated me, and I destroyed them.
⁴² They looked, but there was none to save;

---

[1] Or his; also verse 34 [2] Compare Psalm 18:32; Hebrew he has blamelessly set my way free, or he has made my way spring up blamelessly [3] Hebrew ankles
[4] Or You gave me my enemies' necks

they cried to the Lord, but he did not answer them.
43 I beat them fine as the dust of the earth;
   I crushed them and stamped them down like the mire of the streets.

44 "You delivered me from strife with my people;[1]
      you kept me as the head of the nations;
   people whom I had not known served me.
45 Foreigners came cringing to me;
      as soon as they heard of me, they obeyed me.
46 Foreigners lost heart
      and came trembling[2] out of their fortresses.

47 "The Lord lives, and blessed be my rock,
      and exalted be my God, the rock of my salvation,
48 the God who gave me vengeance
      and brought down peoples under me,
49 who brought me out from my enemies;
      you exalted me above those who rose against me;
      you delivered me from men of violence.

50 "For this I will praise you, O Lord, among the nations,
      and sing praises to your name.
51 Great salvation he brings[3] to his king,
      and shows steadfast love to his anointed,
      to David and his offspring forever."

Swan song [23:1–7]. We end 2 Samuel with a second song by David, which the historian labels his "last words" (v. 1). This brief lyric poem is a conventional psalm of praise. The lead-in contains one of the truly evocative epithets in the Bible when it calls David "the sweet psalmist of Israel" (v. 1).

23

Now these are the last words of David:

The oracle of David, the son of Jesse,
   the oracle of the man who was raised on high,
the anointed of the God of Jacob,
   the sweet psalmist of Israel:[4]

2 "The Spirit of the Lord speaks by me;
      his word is on my tongue.
3 The God of Israel has spoken;
      the Rock of Israel has said to me:
   When one rules justly over men,
      ruling in the fear of God,
4 he dawns on them like the morning light,
      like the sun shining forth on a cloudless morning,
      like rain[5] that makes grass to sprout from the earth.

[1] Septuagint with the peoples [2] Compare Psalm 18:45; Hebrew equipped themselves [3] Or He is a tower of salvation [4] Or the favorite of the songs of Israel [5] Hebrew from rain

5   "For does not my house stand so with God?
        For he has made with me an everlasting covenant,
        ordered in all things and secure.
    For will he not cause to prosper
        all my help and my desire?
6   But worthless men[1] are all like thorns that are thrown away,
        for they cannot be taken with the hand;
7   but the man who touches them
        arms himself with iron and the shaft of a spear,
        and they are utterly consumed with fire."[2]

Historical postscript [23:8–39]. Second Samuel ends with an appendix of historical data that the chronicler wanted to include in his court history for purposes of completeness. If the material seems anticlimactic, even that fits the writer's interpretation
of David's life, which was noteworthy in its achievements but fell far short of what
might have been; after great beginnings, David's kingship was anticlimactic. The list
of David's "mighty men" is an epic roll call of warriors. Even here the writer's storytelling instincts come through, with vivid snatches of narrative that leave us wishing for
more information—about the warrior who "wielded his spear against eight hundred" (v.
8); about Eleazar, whose battlefield intensity makes his hand cling to his sword; about
Shammah, who takes his stand against the Philistines in "a plot of ground full of lentils"
(vv. 9–11); about the three loyal soldiers who risked their lives to bring water from
Bethlehem to David, only to have David refuse to drink water that had been gathered
at such risk; about Benaiah, who "struck down a lion in a pit on a day when snow had
fallen" (vv. 16–20). In a narrative such as this we see an important tendency of biblical
narrative to regard individuals as important, coupled with an impulse to record the data
of real life. Named individuality is important in the Bible, which is concerned with ordinary people and seemingly mundane events as well as kings and extraordinary exploits.

---

[8] These are the names of the mighty men whom David had: Josheb-basshebeth a
Tahchemonite; he was chief of the three.[3] He wielded his spear[4] against eight hundred whom he killed at one time.

[9] And next to him among the three mighty men was Eleazar the son of Dodo, son of
Ahohi. He was with David when they defied the Philistines who were gathered there
for battle, and the men of Israel withdrew. [10] He rose and struck down the Philistines
until his hand was weary, and his hand clung to the sword. And the LORD brought
about a great victory that day, and the men returned after him only to strip the slain.

[11] And next to him was Shammah, the son of Agee the Hararite. The Philistines
gathered together at Lehi, where there was a plot of ground full of lentils, and the
men fled from the Philistines. [12] But he took his stand in the midst of the plot and
defended it and struck down the Philistines, and the LORD worked a great victory.

[13] And three of the thirty chief men went down and came about harvest time to
David at the cave of Adullam, when a band of Philistines was encamped in the Valley
of Rephaim. [14] David was then in the stronghold, and the garrison of the Philistines
was then at Bethlehem. [15] And David said longingly, "Oh, that someone would give me
water to drink from the well of Bethlehem that is by the gate!" [16] Then the three

---

[1] Hebrew *worthlessness* [2] Hebrew *consumed with fire in the sitting* [3] Or *of the captains* [4] 1 Chronicles 11:11; the meaning of the Hebrew expression is
uncertain

mighty men broke through the camp of the Philistines and drew water out of the well of Bethlehem that was by the gate and carried and brought it to David. But he would not drink of it. He poured it out to the LORD [17]and said, "Far be it from me, O LORD, that I should do this. Shall I drink the blood of the men who went at the risk of their lives?" Therefore he would not drink it. These things the three mighty men did.

[18]Now Abishai, the brother of Joab, the son of Zeruiah, was chief of the thirty.[1] And he wielded his spear against three hundred men[2] and killed them and won a name beside the three. [19]He was the most renowned of the thirty[3] and became their commander, but he did not attain to the three.

[20]And Benaiah the son of Jehoiada was a valiant man[4] of Kabzeel, a doer of great deeds. He struck down two ariels[5] of Moab. He also went down and struck down a lion in a pit on a day when snow had fallen. [21]And he struck down an Egyptian, a handsome man. The Egyptian had a spear in his hand, but Benaiah went down to him with a staff and snatched the spear out of the Egyptian's hand and killed him with his own spear. [22]These things did Benaiah the son of Jehoiada, and won a name beside the three mighty men. [23]He was renowned among the thirty, but he did not attain to the three. And David set him over his bodyguard.

[24]Asahel the brother of Joab was one of the thirty; Elhanan the son of Dodo of Bethlehem, [25]Shammah of Harod, Elika of Harod, [26]Helez the Paltite, Ira the son of Ikkesh of Tekoa, [27]Abiezer of Anathoth, Mebunnai the Hushathite, [28]Zalmon the Ahohite, Maharai of Netophah, [29]Heleb the son of Baanah of Netophah, Ittai the son of Ribai of Gibeah of the people of Benjamin, [30]Benaiah of Pirathon, Hiddai of the brooks of Gaash, [31]Abi-albon the Arbathite, Azmaveth of Bahurim, [32]Eliahba the Shaalbonite, the sons of Jashen, Jonathan, [33]Shammah the Hararite, Ahiam the son of Sharar the Hararite, [34]Eliphelet the son of Ahasbai of Maacah, Eliam the son of Ahithophel of Gilo, [35]Hezro[6] of Carmel, Paarai the Arbite, [36]Igal the son of Nathan of Zobah, Bani the Gadite, [37]Zelek the Ammonite, Naharai of Beeroth, the armorbearer of Joab the son of Zeruiah, [38]Ira the Ithrite, Gareb the Ithrite, [39]Uriah the Hittite: thirty-seven in all.

God's punishment of David for taking a census [chapter 24]. Like the previous unit, this long chapter devoted to a striking negative event in David's life is chronologically out of place and appears as an addendum. We are left to infer what the writer intends. The last chapter of any story is a consciously composed ending in which the storyteller reaches closure, often by some form of summary or reminder of what has preceded. Ordinarily the last chapter should be regarded as the writer's last word on the story as a whole. One way to make narrative sense of this chapter is to scrutinize it for echoes of motifs, events, and themes that have been present throughout the preceding book. The list of such echoes keeps expanding; here is a beginning list: God as the governing character in what happens; David the king as the chief human actor; the fate of the nation of Israel as the main story line; action carried out by military leaders; a notable blunder by David that incites God's anger and judgment; David as penitent and worshiper; supernatural or marvelous events (the angel of death who afflicts the land with pestilence); everyday realism (David's bargaining with Gad over the purchase of his threshing floor); a great spiritual lesson tucked into the story as just one detail among others (David's refusal to offer something to God that cost him nothing—v. 24).

---

[1] Two Hebrew manuscripts, Syriac; most Hebrew manuscripts *three* [2] Or *slain ones* [3] 1 Chronicles 11:25; Hebrew *Was he the most renowned of the three?* [4] Or *the son of Ishhai* [5] The meaning of the word *ariel* is unknown [6] Or *Hezrai*

24

Again the anger of the LORD was kindled against Israel, and he incited David against them, saying, "Go, number Israel and Judah." ²So the king said to Joab, the commander of the army,[1] who was with him, "Go through all the tribes of Israel, from Dan to Beersheba, and number the people, that I may know the number of the people." ³But Joab said to the king, "May the LORD your God add to the people a hundred times as many as they are, while the eyes of my lord the king still see it, but why does my lord the king delight in this thing?" ⁴But the king's word prevailed against Joab and the commanders of the army. So Joab and the commanders of the army went out from the presence of the king to number the people of Israel. ⁵They crossed the Jordan and began from Aroer,[2] and from the city that is in the middle of the valley, toward Gad and on to Jazer. ⁶Then they came to Gilead, and to Kadesh in the land of the Hittites;[3] and they came to Dan, and from Dan[4] they went around to Sidon, ⁷and came to the fortress of Tyre and to all the cities of the Hivites and Canaanites; and they went out to the Negeb of Judah at Beersheba. ⁸So when they had gone through all the land, they came to Jerusalem at the end of nine months and twenty days. ⁹And Joab gave the sum of the numbering of the people to the king: in Israel there were 800,000 valiant men who drew the sword, and the men of Judah were 500,000.

¹⁰But David's heart struck him after he had numbered the people. And David said to the LORD, "I have sinned greatly in what I have done. But now, O LORD, please take away the iniquity of your servant, for I have done very foolishly." ¹¹And when David arose in the morning, the word of the LORD came to the prophet Gad, David's seer, saying, ¹²"Go and say to David, 'Thus says the LORD, Three things I offer[5] you. Choose one of them, that I may do it to you.'" ¹³So Gad came to David and told him, and said to him, "Shall three[6] years of famine come to you in your land? Or will you flee three months before your foes while they pursue you? Or shall there be three days' pestilence in your land? Now consider, and decide what answer I shall return to him who sent me." ¹⁴Then David said to Gad, "I am in great distress. Let us fall into the hand of the LORD, for his mercy is great; but let me not fall into the hand of man."

¹⁵So the LORD sent a pestilence on Israel from the morning until the appointed time. And there died of the people from Dan to Beersheba 70,000 men. ¹⁶And when the angel stretched out his hand toward Jerusalem to destroy it, the LORD relented from the calamity and said to the angel who was working destruction among the people, "It is enough; now stay your hand." And the angel of the LORD was by the threshing floor of Araunah the Jebusite. ¹⁷Then David spoke to the LORD when he saw the angel who was striking the people, and said, "Behold, I have sinned, and I have done wickedly. But these sheep, what have they done? Please let your hand be against me and against my father's house."

¹⁸And Gad came that day to David and said to him, "Go up, raise an altar to the LORD on the threshing floor of Araunah the Jebusite." ¹⁹So David went up at Gad's word, as the LORD commanded. ²⁰And when Araunah looked down, he saw the king and his servants coming on toward him. And Araunah went out and paid homage to the king with his face to the ground. ²¹And Araunah said, "Why has my lord the king come to his servant?" David said, "To buy the threshing floor from you, in order to build an altar to the LORD, that the plague may be averted from the people." ²²Then Araunah said to David, "Let my lord the king take and offer up what seems good to

---

[1] Septuagint *to Joab and the commanders of the army* [2] Septuagint; Hebrew *encamped in Aroer* [3] Septuagint; Hebrew *to the land of Tahtim-hodshi* [4] Septuagint; Hebrew *they came to Dan-jaan and* [5] Or *hold over* [6] Compare 1 Chronicles 21:12, Septuagint; Hebrew *seven*

him. Here are the oxen for the burnt offering and the threshing sledges and the yokes of the oxen for the wood. ²³All this, O king, Araunah gives to the king." And Araunah said to the king, "May the Lord your God accept you." ²⁴But the king said to Araunah, "No, but I will buy it from you for a price. I will not offer burnt offerings to the Lord my God that cost me nothing." So David bought the threshing floor and the oxen for fifty shekels[1] of silver. ²⁵And David built there an altar to the Lord and offered burnt offerings and peace offerings. So the Lord responded to the plea for the land, and the plague was averted from Israel.

[1] A *shekel* was about 2/5 ounce or 11 grams

1 KINGS

> **The book at a glance.** 22 chapters, 816 verses. Together, 1 and 2 Kings record the history of God's people from the death of King David to the Babylonian captivity—a span of roughly four hundred years. As their traditional titles suggest, these books focus on the kings of Israel and Judah, although the prophets Elijah and Elisha also play a prominent role. The book of 1 Kings divides neatly into two halves. The first eleven chapters tell the story of the rise and fall of King Solomon: his succession to the throne of his father David, his superlative wisdom, his vast wealth, his two grand building projects of a temple and a palace, and his utter folly in taking foreign wives and worshiping foreign gods. The last eleven chapters tell the story of the divided kingdom. Solomon's sons and their rivals wage civil war, splitting the nation in two. Afterward, both the northern kingdom (Israel) and the southern kingdom (Judah) go into spiritual decline. Many of the same events are also recounted in 1 and 2 Chronicles, which offer a somewhat more positive portrayal of Solomon and the kings of Judah, emphasizing God's fulfillment of his promises to David. The two books of Kings fully expose royal sin as a warning not to worship any other gods. This is the main message of 1 Kings: turning away from the one true God is always a disaster, whether personally or nationally (or both).

▌**Genre.** The book of 1 Kings is written in the form of historical *narrative—specifically, a record of monarchical succession. As such, it gives basic factual information about the name of each king, what kingdom he ruled (Israel or Judah), the date of his accession to the throne, the length of his reign, his religious and other policies, the details of his death, and the name of his successor. However, the author is as much a theologian as he is a historian. It is not his intention to provide every historical detail, and on occasion he directs readers who want more information to consult other sources (e.g., 14:29). Rather, his intention is to interpret the history of Israel along theological lines, showing what happens when political and spiritual leaders foolishly choose to worship false gods instead of wisely choosing to worship the one true God. The subgenres of the book include *farewell address, list of government officials, building description, dedicatory prayer, inventory, curse, *miracle story, bet, *taunt, and *soliloquy. (For more information on items accompanied by an asterisk, see the glossary at the back of this Bible.)

▌**Unifying elements.** The formulaic succession of kings and the pervasive concern with events surrounding the royal court give 1 Kings its fundamental unity. The character of Solomon also exercises a dominant influence, and even the division of the

Passage	Content	Royal Succession	Political Situation	Capital
1:1–2:46	Solomon takes David's throne	Solomon	United Kingdom	Jerusalem
3:1–4:34	Solomon's wisdom and wealth			
5:1–8:66	Solomon builds and dedicates God's temple			
9:1–10:29	Solomon's rule and reputation			
11:1–43	Solomon's folly			
12:1–15	Rehoboam's folly	Rehoboam, Jeroboam	Divided Kingdom	Jerusalem and Samaria
12:16–13:34	Jeroboam's rebellion			
14:1–31	The death of Jeroboam and Rehoboam			
15:1–24	The decline of Judah	Abijam, Asa		
15:25–16:34	The decline of Israel	Nadab, Baasha, Elah, Zimri, Omri, Ahab		
17:1–24	Elijah and the famine	Ahab and Jezebel		
18:1–46	Elijah on the mountaintop			
19:1–21	Elijah in the wilderness			
20:1–22:40	The end of Ahab			
22:41–53	Two more kings	Jehoshaphat, Ahaziah		

kingdom after his death may be viewed as an outworking of some of the dysfunctional internal dynamics of his royal household. The book is also unified by the choice that each king (and the nation itself) has to make between following God and worshiping idols. The general movement of the book is from wisdom to folly, as Solomon's downfall is recapitulated in the choices of his sons and grandsons. The *archetype of the evil king dominates the book. Although King David makes only a brief appearance at the beginning of the narrative, his kingship is often used as the royal standard for his successors. Other unifying elements include the importance of true worship (including the proper location for worship, which is the temple in Jerusalem, not the "high places" in Samaria) and the power of prayer (Solomon's prayer of dedication at the temple is one of the normative prayers of the Old Testament, and Elijah's miraculous ministry as prophet is in large measure a ministry of prayer).

▮ **Inferred literary intentions.** The book is designed to achieve the following literary purposes:

- ▪ record the royal history of Israel and Judah
- ▪ use the resources of storytelling to make characters and events come alive in our imagination

- document the glories of Solomon's kingdom

- present a gallery of memorable characters

- explain how the kingdom came to be divided

- demonstrate the folly of turning away from the wisdom of God

- show the difference between doing "what is evil" and doing "what is pleasing" to God

- embody religious meaning in characters and their choices

- give us memorable examples of God's powerful presence in worship

- give us a notable example (namely, the prophet Elijah) of how to keep on following God when it seems as if everyone else has turned against him

▮ **Theological themes.** (1) Sin and judgment: God rewards kings and nations for obedience and punishes them for disobedience. (2) Prayer and worship: Solomon (at the temple in Jerusalem) and Elijah (on Mt. Carmel) show us how to do it right; Jeroboam and the prophets of Baal show us how to do it wrong (at the high places in Samaria). (3) Covenant: God continues to keep his promises to David, and his descendants are either blessed or cursed depending on their obedience or disobedience to the will of God. (4) Providence: God miraculously provides for Elijah and the needy people who were blessed by his ministry.

▮ **The book of 1 Kings as a chapter in the master story of the Bible.** The book of 1 Kings shows both the glory of a kingdom and the inevitable failure of any merely human form of government, and thus it prepares us for the coming kingdom of God. The splendors of Solomon give us a glimmer of the glories God has for us in his eternal kingdom—but only if our king is Christ, whom the New Testament calls "something greater than Solomon" (Matt. 12:42). In recording the royal line of David, 1 Kings gives us part of the "back story" for the birth of Jesus as the true king of Israel.

> **Two rivals seek the throne** [1:1–27]. David is in decline, and with the future of his dynasty hanging in the balance, the king's court has become a place of royal intrigue. The opening plot conflict of the book arises from Adonijah's ambition to usurp the throne—an ambition his father has allowed to go unchecked. Meanwhile, the prophet Nathan and queen Bathsheba are conspiring to have Solomon crowned as king. Who is David's choice in this *conflict story? More important, who is God's choice?

1 Now King David was old and advanced in years. And although they covered him with clothes, he could not get warm. ²Therefore his servants said to him, "Let a young woman be sought for my lord the king, and let her wait on the king and be in his service. Let her lie in your arms,¹ that my lord the king may be warm." ³So they sought for a beautiful young woman throughout all the territory of Israel, and found Abishag the Shunammite, and brought her to the king. ⁴The young woman was very

¹ Or *in your bosom*

beautiful, and she was of service to the king and attended to him, but the king knew her not.

⁵Now Adonijah the son of Haggith exalted himself, saying, "I will be king." And he prepared for himself chariots and horsemen, and fifty men to run before him. ⁶His father had never at any time displeased him by asking, "Why have you done thus and so?" He was also a very handsome man, and he was born next after Absalom. ⁷He conferred with Joab the son of Zeruiah and with Abiathar the priest. And they followed Adonijah and helped him. ⁸But Zadok the priest and Benaiah the son of Jehoiada and Nathan the prophet and Shimei and Rei and David's mighty men were not with Adonijah.

⁹Adonijah sacrificed sheep, oxen, and fattened cattle by the Serpent's Stone, which is beside En-rogel, and he invited all his brothers, the king's sons, and all the royal officials of Judah, ¹⁰but he did not invite Nathan the prophet or Benaiah or the mighty men or Solomon his brother.

¹¹Then Nathan said to Bathsheba the mother of Solomon, "Have you not heard that Adonijah the son of Haggith has become king and David our lord does not know it? ¹²Now therefore come, let me give you advice, that you may save your own life and the life of your son Solomon. ¹³Go in at once to King David, and say to him, 'Did you not, my lord the king, swear to your servant, saying, "Solomon your son shall reign after me, and he shall sit on my throne"? Why then is Adonijah king?' ¹⁴Then while you are still speaking with the king, I also will come in after you and confirm¹ your words."

¹⁵So Bathsheba went to the king in his chamber (now the king was very old, and Abishag the Shunammite was attending to the king). ¹⁶Bathsheba bowed and paid homage to the king, and the king said, "What do you desire?" ¹⁷She said to him, "My lord, you swore to your servant by the Lord your God, saying, 'Solomon your son shall reign after me, and he shall sit on my throne.' ¹⁸And now, behold, Adonijah is king, although you, my lord the king, do not know it. ¹⁹He has sacrificed oxen, fattened cattle, and sheep in abundance, and has invited all the sons of the king, Abiathar the priest, and Joab the commander of the army, but Solomon your servant he has not invited. ²⁰And now, my lord the king, the eyes of all Israel are on you, to tell them who shall sit on the throne of my lord the king after him. ²¹Otherwise it will come to pass, when my lord the king sleeps with his fathers, that I and my son Solomon will be counted offenders."

²²While she was still speaking with the king, Nathan the prophet came in. ²³And they told the king, "Here is Nathan the prophet." And when he came in before the king, he bowed before the king, with his face to the ground. ²⁴And Nathan said, "My lord the king, have you said, 'Adonijah shall reign after me, and he shall sit on my throne'? ²⁵For he has gone down this day and has sacrificed oxen, fattened cattle, and sheep in abundance, and has invited all the king's sons, the commanders² of the army, and Abiathar the priest. And behold, they are eating and drinking before him, and saying, 'Long live King Adonijah!' ²⁶But me, your servant, and Zadok the priest, and Benaiah the son of Jehoiada, and your servant Solomon he has not invited. ²⁷Has this thing been brought about by my lord the king and you have not told your servants who should sit on the throne of my lord the king after him?"

---

¹ Or *expand on* ² Hebrew; Septuagint *Joab the commander*

Solomon anointed as king [1:28–53]. David has sworn that Solomon will be his successor, and here he acts decisively to fulfill his promise. Solomon's legitimacy as Israel's rightful king is confirmed by the united support of Israel's prophet (Nathan), priest (Zadok), and king (David). There are signs throughout the narrative that this choice has been made for the honor of God and with his blessing. The succession narrative ends with Solomon's rival—Adonijah himself—paying homage to Solomon as king.

²⁸Then King David answered, "Call Bathsheba to me." So she came into the king's presence and stood before the king. ²⁹And the king swore, saying, "As the LORD lives, who has redeemed my soul out of every adversity, ³⁰as I swore to you by the LORD, the God of Israel, saying, 'Solomon your son shall reign after me, and he shall sit on my throne in my place,' even so will I do this day." ³¹Then Bathsheba bowed with her face to the ground and paid homage to the king and said, "May my lord King David live forever!"

³²King David said, "Call to me Zadok the priest, Nathan the prophet, and Benaiah the son of Jehoiada." So they came before the king. ³³And the king said to them, "Take with you the servants of your lord and have Solomon my son ride on my own mule, and bring him down to Gihon. ³⁴And let Zadok the priest and Nathan the prophet there anoint him king over Israel. Then blow the trumpet and say, 'Long live King Solomon!' ³⁵You shall then come up after him, and he shall come and sit on my throne, for he shall be king in my place. And I have appointed him to be ruler over Israel and over Judah." ³⁶And Benaiah the son of Jehoiada answered the king, "Amen! May the LORD, the God of my lord the king, say so. ³⁷As the LORD has been with my lord the king, even so may he be with Solomon, and make his throne greater than the throne of my lord King David."

³⁸So Zadok the priest, Nathan the prophet, and Benaiah the son of Jehoiada, and the Cherethites and the Pelethites went down and had Solomon ride on King David's mule and brought him to Gihon. ³⁹There Zadok the priest took the horn of oil from the tent and anointed Solomon. Then they blew the trumpet, and all the people said, "Long live King Solomon!" ⁴⁰And all the people went up after him, playing on pipes, and rejoicing with great joy, so that the earth was split by their noise.

⁴¹Adonijah and all the guests who were with him heard it as they finished feasting. And when Joab heard the sound of the trumpet, he said, "What does this uproar in the city mean?" ⁴²While he was still speaking, behold, Jonathan the son of Abiathar the priest came. And Adonijah said, "Come in, for you are a worthy man and bring good news." ⁴³Jonathan answered Adonijah, "No, for our lord King David has made Solomon king, ⁴⁴and the king has sent with him Zadok the priest, Nathan the prophet, and Benaiah the son of Jehoiada, and the Cherethites and the Pelethites. And they had him ride on the king's mule. ⁴⁵And Zadok the priest and Nathan the prophet have anointed him king at Gihon, and they have gone up from there rejoicing, so that the city is in an uproar. This is the noise that you have heard. ⁴⁶Solomon sits on the royal throne. ⁴⁷Moreover, the king's servants came to congratulate our lord King David, saying, 'May your God make the name of Solomon more famous than yours, and make his throne greater than your throne.' And the king bowed himself on the bed. ⁴⁸And the king also said, 'Blessed be the LORD, the God of Israel, who has granted someone¹ to sit on my throne this day, my own eyes seeing it.' "

¹ Septuagint *one of my offspring*

⁴⁹Then all the guests of Adonijah trembled and rose, and each went his own way. ⁵⁰And Adonijah feared Solomon. So he arose and went and took hold of the horns of the altar. ⁵¹Then it was told Solomon, "Behold, Adonijah fears King Solomon, for behold, he has laid hold of the horns of the altar, saying, 'Let King Solomon swear to me first that he will not put his servant to death with the sword.'" ⁵²And Solomon said, "If he will show himself a worthy man, not one of his hairs shall fall to the earth, but if wickedness is found in him, he shall die." ⁵³So King Solomon sent, and they brought him down from the altar. And he came and paid homage to King Solomon, and Solomon said to him, "Go to your house."

Solomon consolidates his kingdom [chapter 2]. With his dying words David tells his son how to be spiritually successful in ruling the people of God. A good king is faithful to God, heart and soul, and always follows God's Word—the criteria by which Solomon and all his successors will be judged. Following David's farewell discourse and a brief death scene, the rest of the chapter shows how Solomon secures his kingdom by taking just vengeance on the enemies of the house of David. The events of this *revenge story confirm the truth of the everlasting blessing that Solomon claims for David's throne at the end of the chapter (v. 45).

2 When David's time to die drew near, he commanded Solomon his son, saying, ²"I am about to go the way of all the earth. Be strong, and show yourself a man, ³and keep the charge of the LORD your God, walking in his ways and keeping his statutes, his commandments, his rules, and his testimonies, as it is written in the Law of Moses, that you may prosper in all that you do and wherever you turn, ⁴that the LORD may establish his word that he spoke concerning me, saying, 'If your sons pay close attention to their way, to walk before me in faithfulness with all their heart and with all their soul, you shall not lack¹ a man on the throne of Israel.'

⁵"Moreover, you also know what Joab the son of Zeruiah did to me, how he dealt with the two commanders of the armies of Israel, Abner the son of Ner, and Amasa the son of Jether, whom he killed, avenging² in time of peace for blood that had been shed in war, and putting the blood of war³ on the belt around his⁴ waist and on the sandals on his feet. ⁶Act therefore according to your wisdom, but do not let his gray head go down to Sheol in peace. ⁷But deal loyally with the sons of Barzillai the Gileadite, and let them be among those who eat at your table, for with such loyalty⁵ they met me when I fled from Absalom your brother. ⁸And there is also with you Shimei the son of Gera, the Benjaminite from Bahurim, who cursed me with a grievous curse on the day when I went to Mahanaim. But when he came down to meet me at the Jordan, I swore to him by the LORD, saying, 'I will not put you to death with the sword.' ⁹Now therefore do not hold him guiltless, for you are a wise man. You will know what you ought to do to him, and you shall bring his gray head down with blood to Sheol."

¹⁰Then David slept with his fathers and was buried in the city of David. ¹¹And the time that David reigned over Israel was forty years. He reigned seven years in Hebron and thirty-three years in Jerusalem. ¹²So Solomon sat on the throne of David his father, and his kingdom was firmly established.

¹³Then Adonijah the son of Haggith came to Bathsheba the mother of Solomon.

---

¹ Hebrew there shall not be cut off for you ² Septuagint; Hebrew placing ³ Septuagint innocent blood ⁴ Septuagint my; twice in this verse
⁵ Or steadfast love

And she said, "Do you come peacefully?" He said, "Peacefully." ¹⁴Then he said, "I have something to say to you." She said, "Speak." ¹⁵He said, "You know that the kingdom was mine, and that all Israel fully expected me to reign. However, the kingdom has turned about and become my brother's, for it was his from the LORD. ¹⁶And now I have one request to make of you; do not refuse me." She said to him, "Speak." ¹⁷And he said, "Please ask King Solomon—he will not refuse you—to give me Abishag the Shunammite as my wife." ¹⁸Bathsheba said, "Very well; I will speak for you to the king."

¹⁹So Bathsheba went to King Solomon to speak to him on behalf of Adonijah. And the king rose to meet her and bowed down to her. Then he sat on his throne and had a seat brought for the king's mother, and she sat on his right. ²⁰Then she said, "I have one small request to make of you; do not refuse me." And the king said to her, "Make your request, my mother, for I will not refuse you." ²¹She said, "Let Abishag the Shunammite be given to Adonijah your brother as his wife." ²²King Solomon answered his mother, "And why do you ask Abishag the Shunammite for Adonijah? Ask for him the kingdom also, for he is my older brother, and on his side are Abiathar[1] the priest and Joab the son of Zeruiah." ²³Then King Solomon swore by the LORD, saying, "God do so to me and more also if this word does not cost Adonijah his life! ²⁴Now therefore as the LORD lives, who has established me and placed me on the throne of David my father, and who has made me a house, as he promised, Adonijah shall be put to death today." ²⁵So King Solomon sent Benaiah the son of Jehoiada, and he struck him down, and he died.

²⁶And to Abiathar the priest the king said, "Go to Anathoth, to your estate, for you deserve death. But I will not at this time put you to death, because you carried the ark of the Lord GOD before David my father, and because you shared in all my father's affliction." ²⁷So Solomon expelled Abiathar from being priest to the LORD, thus fulfilling the word of the LORD that he had spoken concerning the house of Eli in Shiloh.

²⁸When the news came to Joab—for Joab had supported Adonijah although he had not supported Absalom—Joab fled to the tent of the LORD and caught hold of the horns of the altar. ²⁹And when it was told King Solomon, "Joab has fled to the tent of the LORD, and behold, he is beside the altar," Solomon sent Benaiah the son of Jehoiada, saying, "Go, strike him down." ³⁰So Benaiah came to the tent of the LORD and said to him, "The king commands, 'Come out.'" But he said, "No, I will die here." Then Benaiah brought the king word again, saying, "Thus said Joab, and thus he answered me." ³¹The king replied to him, "Do as he has said, strike him down and bury him, and thus take away from me and from my father's house the guilt for the blood that Joab shed without cause. ³²The LORD will bring back his bloody deeds on his own head, because, without the knowledge of my father David, he attacked and killed with the sword two men more righteous and better than himself, Abner the son of Ner, commander of the army of Israel, and Amasa the son of Jether, commander of the army of Judah. ³³So shall their blood come back on the head of Joab and on the head of his descendants forever. But for David and for his descendants and for his house and for his throne there shall be peace from the LORD forevermore." ³⁴Then Benaiah the son of Jehoiada went up and struck him down and put him to death. And he was buried in his own house in the wilderness. ³⁵The king put Benaiah the son of Jehoiada over the army in place of Joab, and the king put Zadok the priest in the place of Abiathar.

---

[1] Septuagint, Syriac, Vulgate; Hebrew *and for him and for Abiathar*

³⁶Then the king sent and summoned Shimei and said to him, "Build yourself a house in Jerusalem and dwell there, and do not go out from there to any place whatever. ³⁷For on the day you go out and cross the brook Kidron, know for certain that you shall die. Your blood shall be on your own head." ³⁸And Shimei said to the king, "What you say is good; as my lord the king has said, so will your servant do." So Shimei lived in Jerusalem many days.

³⁹But it happened at the end of three years that two of Shimei's servants ran away to Achish, son of Maacah, king of Gath. And when it was told Shimei, "Behold, your servants are in Gath," ⁴⁰Shimei arose and saddled a donkey and went to Gath to Achish to seek his servants. Shimei went and brought his servants from Gath. ⁴¹And when Solomon was told that Shimei had gone from Jerusalem to Gath and returned, ⁴²the king sent and summoned Shimei and said to him, "Did I not make you swear by the LORD and solemnly warn you, saying, 'Know for certain that on the day you go out and go to any place whatever, you shall die'? And you said to me, 'What you say is good; I will obey.' ⁴³Why then have you not kept your oath to the LORD and the commandment with which I commanded you?" ⁴⁴The king also said to Shimei, "You know in your own heart all the harm that you did to David my father. So the LORD will bring back your harm on your own head. ⁴⁵But King Solomon shall be blessed, and the throne of David shall be established before the LORD forever." ⁴⁶Then the king commanded Benaiah the son of Jehoiada, and he went out and struck him down, and he died.

So the kingdom was established in the hand of Solomon.

Solomon's wisdom [chapter 3]. The opening verses introduce two story lines that will become important in the rest of the narrative: Solomon's unholy alliances with foreign women and the need for a temple to serve as a divinely ordained location for the worship of God (replacing the "high places" that would so often tempt the Israelites to false worship). But the main emphasis of the passage is on Solomon's dream (a vision story) and his prayer for wisdom, which turns into a gift narrative (a story that focuses on the conferring of a gift). The new king is presented as a loving servant of God who wants, more than any other blessing that God can give, the understanding to govern his people wisely. God answers this prayer by doing more than Solomon asked or imagined, making him the wisest of men and crowning him with riches and honor. The case of the baby that Solomon threatens to divide in two is a world-famous demonstration of the king's extraordinary God-given gift of wisdom (vv. 16–28).

3 Solomon made a marriage alliance with Pharaoh king of Egypt. He took Pharaoh's daughter and brought her into the city of David until he had finished building his own house and the house of the LORD and the wall around Jerusalem. ²The people were sacrificing at the high places, however, because no house had yet been built for the name of the LORD.

³Solomon loved the LORD, walking in the statutes of David his father, only he sacrificed and made offerings at the high places. ⁴And the king went to Gibeon to sacrifice there, for that was the great high place. Solomon used to offer a thousand burnt offerings on that altar. ⁵At Gibeon the LORD appeared to Solomon in a dream by night, and God said, "Ask what I shall give you." ⁶And Solomon said, "You have shown great and steadfast love to your servant David my father, because he walked before you in faithfulness, in righteousness, and in uprightness of heart toward you.

And you have kept for him this great and steadfast love and have given him a son to sit on his throne this day. [7]And now, O LORD my God, you have made your servant king in place of David my father, although I am but a little child. I do not know how to go out or come in. [8]And your servant is in the midst of your people whom you have chosen, a great people, too many to be numbered or counted for multitude. [9]Give your servant therefore an understanding mind to govern your people, that I may discern between good and evil, for who is able to govern this your great people?"

[10]It pleased the Lord that Solomon had asked this. [11]And God said to him, "Because you have asked this, and have not asked for yourself long life or riches or the life of your enemies, but have asked for yourself understanding to discern what is right, [12]behold, I now do according to your word. Behold, I give you a wise and discerning mind, so that none like you has been before you and none like you shall arise after you. [13]I give you also what you have not asked, both riches and honor, so that no other king shall compare with you, all your days. [14]And if you will walk in my ways, keeping my statutes and my commandments, as your father David walked, then I will lengthen your days."

[15]And Solomon awoke, and behold, it was a dream. Then he came to Jerusalem and stood before the ark of the covenant of the Lord, and offered up burnt offerings and peace offerings, and made a feast for all his servants.

[16]Then two prostitutes came to the king and stood before him. [17]The one woman said, "Oh, my lord, this woman and I live in the same house, and I gave birth to a child while she was in the house. [18]Then on the third day after I gave birth, this woman also gave birth. And we were alone. There was no one else with us in the house; only we two were in the house. [19]And this woman's son died in the night, because she lay on him. [20]And she arose at midnight and took my son from beside me, while your servant slept, and laid him at her breast, and laid her dead son at my breast. [21]When I rose in the morning to nurse my child, behold, he was dead. But when I looked at him closely in the morning, behold, he was not the child that I had borne." [22]But the other woman said, "No, the living child is mine, and the dead child is yours." The first said, "No, the dead child is yours, and the living child is mine." Thus they spoke before the king.

[23]Then the king said, "The one says, 'This is my son that is alive, and your son is dead'; and the other says, 'No; but your son is dead, and my son is the living one.'" [24]And the king said, "Bring me a sword." So a sword was brought before the king. [25]And the king said, "Divide the living child in two, and give half to the one and half to the other." [26]Then the woman whose son was alive said to the king, because her heart yearned for her son, "Oh, my lord, give her the living child, and by no means put him to death." But the other said, "He shall be neither mine nor yours; divide him." [27]Then the king answered and said, "Give the living child to the first woman, and by no means put him to death; she is his mother." [28]And all Israel heard of the judgment that the king had rendered, and they stood in awe of the king, because they perceived that the wisdom of God was in him to do justice.

Solomon in all his glory [chapter 4]. This chapter is a factual summary of Solomon's kingship. The records of the king's court provide a royal inventory of his officials and their duties, the geographic boundaries of his kingdom, the wealth of his house and stables, and the international fame of his wisdom in all branches of human knowledge. By the blessing of God and for the joy of his people, Solomon has everything a king could ever need or want. This early picture of Solomon's prosperity and success becomes an important part of his identity in the rest of the story, as we are led to contemplate both the advantages and the dangers of such prosperity.

4 King Solomon was king over all Israel, ²and these were his high officials: Azariah the son of Zadok was the priest; ³Elihoreph and Ahijah the sons of Shisha were secretaries; Jehoshaphat the son of Ahilud was recorder; ⁴Benaiah the son of Jehoiada was in command of the army; Zadok and Abiathar were priests; ⁵Azariah the son of Nathan was over the officers; Zabud the son of Nathan was priest and king's friend; ⁶Ahishar was in charge of the palace; and Adoniram the son of Abda was in charge of the forced labor.

⁷Solomon had twelve officers over all Israel, who provided food for the king and his household. Each man had to make provision for one month in the year. ⁸These were their names: Ben-hur, in the hill country of Ephraim; ⁹Ben-deker, in Makaz, Shaalbim, Beth-shemesh, and Elonbeth-hanan; ¹⁰Ben-hesed, in Arubboth (to him belonged Socoh and all the land of Hepher); ¹¹Ben-abinadab, in all Naphath-dor (he had Taphath the daughter of Solomon as his wife); ¹²Baana the son of Ahilud, in Taanach, Megiddo, and all Beth-shean that is beside Zarethan below Jezreel, and from Beth-shean to Abel-meholah, as far as the other side of Jokmeam; ¹³Ben-geber, in Ramoth-gilead (he had the villages of Jair the son of Manasseh, which are in Gilead, and he had the region of Argob, which is in Bashan, sixty great cities with walls and bronze bars); ¹⁴Ahinadab the son of Iddo, in Mahanaim; ¹⁵Ahimaaz, in Naphtali (he had taken Basemath the daughter of Solomon as his wife); ¹⁶Baana the son of Hushai, in Asher and Bealoth; ¹⁷Jehoshaphat the son of Paruah, in Issachar; ¹⁸Shimei the son of Ela, in Benjamin; ¹⁹Geber the son of Uri, in the land of Gilead, the country of Sihon king of the Amorites and of Og king of Bashan. And there was one governor who was over the land.

²⁰Judah and Israel were as many as the sand by the sea. They ate and drank and were happy. ²¹ ¹ Solomon ruled over all the kingdoms from the Euphrates to the land of the Philistines and to the border of Egypt. They brought tribute and served Solomon all the days of his life.

²²Solomon's provision for one day was thirty cors² of fine flour and sixty cors of meal, ²³ten fat oxen, and twenty pasture-fed cattle, a hundred sheep, besides deer, gazelles, roebucks, and fattened fowl. ²⁴For he had dominion over all the region west of the Euphrates from Tiphsah to Gaza, over all the kings west of the Euphrates. And he had peace on all sides around him. ²⁵And Judah and Israel lived in safety, from Dan even to Beersheba, every man under his vine and under his fig tree, all the days of Solomon. ²⁶Solomon also had 40,000 stalls of horses for his chariots, and 12,000 horsemen. ²⁷And those officers supplied provisions for King Solomon, and for all who came to King Solomon's table, each one in his month. They let nothing be lacking. ²⁸Barley also and straw for the horses and swift steeds they brought to the place where it was required, each according to his duty.

²⁹And God gave Solomon wisdom and understanding beyond measure, and breadth of mind like the sand on the seashore, ³⁰so that Solomon's wisdom surpassed the

---

¹ Ch 5:1 in Hebrew ² A *cor* was about 6 bushels or 220 liters

wisdom of all the people of the east and all the wisdom of Egypt. ³¹For he was wiser than all other men, wiser than Ethan the Ezrahite, and Heman, Calcol, and Darda, the sons of Mahol, and his fame was in all the surrounding nations. ³²He also spoke 3,000 proverbs, and his songs were 1,005. ³³He spoke of trees, from the cedar that is in Lebanon to the hyssop that grows out of the wall. He spoke also of beasts, and of birds, and of reptiles, and of fish. ³⁴And people of all nations came to hear the wisdom of Solomon, and from all the kings of the earth, who had heard of his wisdom.

> **A house for God** [chapter 5]. As a man who was almost always at war, David was never permitted to build a temple for the worship of God. But Solomon rules a peaceable kingdom, and thus he decides to build the house God had promised that the son of David would build in his name. People often want to know the facts about a large or important building, and here the historian obliges by telling us how much timber and stone went into the temple, how much it cost, where it came from, and how large a labor force was used in the actual construction. A careful inventory like this is a common convention in literature of the court.

5 ¹ Now Hiram king of Tyre sent his servants to Solomon when he heard that they had anointed him king in place of his father, for Hiram always loved David. ²And Solomon sent word to Hiram, ³"You know that David my father could not build a house for the name of the LORD his God because of the warfare with which his enemies surrounded him, until the LORD put them under the soles of his feet. ⁴But now the LORD my God has given me rest on every side. There is neither adversary nor misfortune. ⁵And so I intend to build a house for the name of the LORD my God, as the LORD said to David my father, 'Your son, whom I will set on your throne in your place, shall build the house for my name.' ⁶Now therefore command that cedars of Lebanon be cut for me. And my servants will join your servants, and I will pay you for your servants such wages as you set, for you know that there is no one among us who knows how to cut timber like the Sidonians."

⁷As soon as Hiram heard the words of Solomon, he rejoiced greatly and said, "Blessed be the LORD this day, who has given to David a wise son to be over this great people." ⁸And Hiram sent to Solomon, saying, "I have heard the message that you have sent to me. I am ready to do all you desire in the matter of cedar and cypress timber. ⁹My servants shall bring it down to the sea from Lebanon, and I will make it into rafts to go by sea to the place you direct. And I will have them broken up there, and you shall receive it. And you shall meet my wishes by providing food for my household." ¹⁰So Hiram supplied Solomon with all the timber of cedar and cypress that he desired, ¹¹while Solomon gave Hiram 20,000 cors² of wheat as food for his household, and 20,000³ cors of beaten oil. Solomon gave this to Hiram year by year. ¹²And the LORD gave Solomon wisdom, as he promised him. And there was peace between Hiram and Solomon, and the two of them made a treaty.

¹³King Solomon drafted forced labor out of all Israel, and the draft numbered 30,000 men. ¹⁴And he sent them to Lebanon, 10,000 a month in shifts. They would be a month in Lebanon and two months at home. Adoniram was in charge of the draft. ¹⁵Solomon also had 70,000 burden-bearers and 80,000 stonecutters in the hill country, ¹⁶besides Solomon's 3,300 chief officers who were over the work, who had

---

¹ Ch 5:15 in Hebrew ² A *cor* was about 6 bushels or 220 liters ³ Septuagint; Hebrew *twenty*

charge of the people who carried on the work. ¹⁷At the king's command they quarried out great, costly stones in order to lay the foundation of the house with dressed stones. ¹⁸So Solomon's builders and Hiram's builders and the men of Gebal did the cutting and prepared the timber and the stone to build the house.

> **Solomon builds the temple** [chapter 6]. The court historian here gives another royal inventory. This time it is a complete formal description of the temple itself—its dimensions, its floor plan (clearly based on God's blueprint for the tabernacle Moses made in the wilderness), and the precious materials that go into its construction. As far as God is concerned, however, what is in Solomon's heart is more important than what Solomon does with his hands. The place where God most wants to dwell is with the people who keep his covenant (see vv. 11–13).

6 In the four hundred and eightieth year after the people of Israel came out of the land of Egypt, in the fourth year of Solomon's reign over Israel, in the month of Ziv, which is the second month, he began to build the house of the Lord. ²The house that King Solomon built for the Lord was sixty cubits¹ long, twenty cubits wide, and thirty cubits high. ³The vestibule in front of the nave of the house was twenty cubits long, equal to the width of the house, and ten cubits deep in front of the house. ⁴And he made for the house windows with recessed frames.² ⁵He also built a structure³ against the wall of the house, running around the walls of the house, both the nave and the inner sanctuary. And he made side chambers all around. ⁶The lowest story⁴ was five cubits broad, the middle one was six cubits broad, and the third was seven cubits broad. For around the outside of the house he made offsets on the wall in order that the supporting beams should not be inserted into the walls of the house.

⁷When the house was built, it was with stone prepared at the quarry, so that neither hammer nor axe nor any tool of iron was heard in the house while it was being built.

⁸The entrance for the lowest⁵ story was on the south side of the house, and one went up by stairs to the middle story, and from the middle story to the third. ⁹So he built the house and finished it, and he made the ceiling of the house of beams and planks of cedar. ¹⁰He built the structure against the whole house, five cubits high, and it was joined to the house with timbers of cedar.

¹¹Now the word of the Lord came to Solomon, ¹²"Concerning this house that you are building, if you will walk in my statutes and obey my rules and keep all my commandments and walk in them, then I will establish my word with you, which I spoke to David your father. ¹³And I will dwell among the children of Israel and will not forsake my people Israel."

¹⁴So Solomon built the house and finished it. ¹⁵He lined the walls of the house on the inside with boards of cedar. From the floor of the house to the walls of the ceiling, he covered them on the inside with wood, and he covered the floor of the house with boards of cypress. ¹⁶He built twenty cubits of the rear of the house with boards of cedar from the floor to the walls, and he built this within as an inner sanctuary, as the Most Holy Place. ¹⁷The house, that is, the nave in front of the inner sanctuary, was forty cubits long. ¹⁸The cedar within the house was carved in the form of gourds and open flowers. All was cedar; no stone was seen. ¹⁹The inner sanctuary he prepared in the innermost part of the house, to set there the ark of the covenant of the

---

¹ A *cubit* was about 18 inches or 45 centimeters ² Or *blocked lattice windows* ³ Or *platform*; also verse 10 ⁴ Septuagint; Hebrew *structure, or platform*
⁵ Septuagint, Targum; Hebrew *middle*

LORD. [20]The inner sanctuary[1] was twenty cubits long, twenty cubits wide, and twenty cubits high, and he overlaid it with pure gold. He also overlaid[2] an altar of cedar. [21]And Solomon overlaid the inside of the house with pure gold, and he drew chains of gold across, in front of the inner sanctuary, and overlaid it with gold. [22]And he overlaid the whole house with gold, until all the house was finished. Also the whole altar that belonged to the inner sanctuary he overlaid with gold.

[23]In the inner sanctuary he made two cherubim of olivewood, each ten cubits high. [24]Five cubits was the length of one wing of the cherub, and five cubits the length of the other wing of the cherub; it was ten cubits from the tip of one wing to the tip of the other. [25]The other cherub also measured ten cubits; both cherubim had the same measure and the same form. [26]The height of one cherub was ten cubits, and so was that of the other cherub. [27]He put the cherubim in the innermost part of the house. And the wings of the cherubim were spread out so that a wing of one touched the one wall, and a wing of the other cherub touched the other wall; their other wings touched each other in the middle of the house. [28]And he overlaid the cherubim with gold.

[29]Around all the walls of the house he carved engraved figures of cherubim and palm trees and open flowers, in the inner and outer rooms. [30]The floor of the house he overlaid with gold in the inner and outer rooms.

[31]For the entrance to the inner sanctuary he made doors of olivewood; the lintel and the doorposts were five-sided.[3] [32]He covered the two doors of olivewood with carvings of cherubim, palm trees, and open flowers. He overlaid them with gold and spread gold on the cherubim and on the palm trees.

[33]So also he made for the entrance to the nave doorposts of olivewood, in the form of a square, [34]and two doors of cypress wood. The two leaves of the one door were folding, and the two leaves of the other door were folding. [35]On them he carved cherubim and palm trees and open flowers, and he overlaid them with gold evenly applied on the carved work. [36]He built the inner court with three courses of cut stone and one course of cedar beams.

[37]In the fourth year the foundation of the house of the LORD was laid, in the month of Ziv. [38]And in the eleventh year, in the month of Bul, which is the eighth month, the house was finished in all its parts, and according to all its specifications. He was seven years in building it.

A house for Solomon [chapter 7]. In addition to the house that he built for God, Solomon built a house for himself—a royal palace (vv. 1–12). Court literature from the ancient past (including Homer's epic story *The Odyssey*) often lingers lovingly on the domestic lives of aristocratic characters, and that is what we find here. Underneath this ostensible success story is a counterstory, as careful reading of this building narrative reveals the troubling fact that Solomon's own house takes almost twice as long to build as the house he built for God, and it is almost twice as big. The rest of this chapter (vv. 13–51) gives a detailed description of the interior furnishings for the temple. Most of the objects mentioned in this priestly inventory were used in the worship of God: an altar for incense, basins for cleansing, lamp stands for light, utensils for tending the fires of sacrifice, and so forth. There is a concern here for form as well as function; each item is skillfully crafted and beautifully designed.

---

[1] Vulgate; Hebrew *and before the inner sanctuary* [2] Septuagint *made* [3] The meaning of the Hebrew phrase is uncertain

7 Solomon was building his own house thirteen years, and he finished his entire house.

²He built the House of the Forest of Lebanon. Its length was a hundred cubits[1] and its breadth fifty cubits and its height thirty cubits, and it was built on four[2] rows of cedar pillars, with cedar beams on the pillars. ³And it was covered with cedar above the chambers that were on the forty-five pillars, fifteen in each row. ⁴There were window frames in three rows, and window opposite window in three tiers. ⁵All the doorways and windows[3] had square frames, and window was opposite window in three tiers.

⁶And he made the Hall of Pillars; its length was fifty cubits, and its breadth thirty cubits. There was a porch in front with pillars, and a canopy in front of them.

⁷And he made the Hall of the Throne where he was to pronounce judgment, even the Hall of Judgment. It was finished with cedar from floor to rafters.[4]

⁸His own house where he was to dwell, in the other court back of the hall, was of like workmanship. Solomon also made a house like this hall for Pharaoh's daughter whom he had taken in marriage.

⁹All these were made of costly stones, cut according to measure, sawed with saws, back and front, even from the foundation to the coping, and from the outside to the great court. ¹⁰The foundation was of costly stones, huge stones, stones of eight and ten cubits. ¹¹And above were costly stones, cut according to measurement, and cedar. ¹²The great court had three courses of cut stone all around, and a course of cedar beams; so had the inner court of the house of the Lord and the vestibule of the house.

¹³And King Solomon sent and brought Hiram from Tyre. ¹⁴He was the son of a widow of the tribe of Naphtali, and his father was a man of Tyre, a worker in bronze. And he was full of wisdom, understanding, and skill for making any work in bronze. He came to King Solomon and did all his work.

¹⁵He cast two pillars of bronze. Eighteen cubits was the height of one pillar, and a line of twelve cubits measured its circumference. It was hollow, and its thickness was four fingers. The second pillar was the same.[5] ¹⁶He also made two capitals of cast bronze to set on the tops of the pillars. The height of the one capital was five cubits, and the height of the other capital was five cubits. ¹⁷There were lattices of checker work with wreaths of chain work for the capitals on the tops of the pillars, a lattice[6] for the one capital and a lattice for the other capital. ¹⁸Likewise he made pomegranates[7] in two rows around the one latticework to cover the capital that was on the top of the pillar, and he did the same with the other capital. ¹⁹Now the capitals that were on the tops of the pillars in the vestibule were of lily-work, four cubits. ²⁰The capitals were on the two pillars and also above the rounded projection which was beside the latticework. There were two hundred pomegranates in two rows all around, and so with the other capital. ²¹He set up the pillars at the vestibule of the temple. He set up the pillar on the south and called its name Jachin, and he set up the pillar on the north and called its name Boaz. ²²And on the tops of the pillars was lily-work. Thus the work of the pillars was finished.

²³Then he made the sea of cast metal. It was round, ten cubits from brim to brim, and five cubits high, and a line of thirty cubits measured its circumference. ²⁴Under its brim were gourds, for ten cubits, compassing the sea all around. The gourds were

---

[1] A *cubit* was about 18 inches or 45 centimeters [2] Septuagint *three* [3] Septuagint; Hebrew *posts* [4] Syriac, Vulgate; Hebrew *floor* [5] Targum, Syriac (compare Septuagint and Jeremiah 52:21); Hebrew *fingers. And a line of twelve cubits measured the circumference of the second pillar* [6] Septuagint; Hebrew *seven; twice in this verse* [7] Two manuscripts (compare Septuagint); Hebrew *pillars*

in two rows, cast with it when it was cast. ²⁵It stood on twelve oxen, three facing north, three facing west, three facing south, and three facing east. The sea was set on them, and all their rear parts were inward. ²⁶Its thickness was a handbreadth,¹ and its brim was made like the brim of a cup, like the flower of a lily. It held two thousand baths.²

²⁷He also made the ten stands of bronze. Each stand was four cubits long, four cubits wide, and three cubits high. ²⁸This was the construction of the stands: they had panels, and the panels were set in the frames, ²⁹and on the panels that were set in the frames were lions, oxen, and cherubim. On the frames, both above and below the lions and oxen, there were wreaths of beveled work. ³⁰Moreover, each stand had four bronze wheels and axles of bronze, and at the four corners were supports for a basin. The supports were cast with wreaths at the side of each. ³¹Its opening was within a crown that projected upward one cubit. Its opening was round, as a pedestal is made, a cubit and a half deep. At its opening there were carvings, and its panels were square, not round. ³²And the four wheels were underneath the panels. The axles of the wheels were of one piece with the stands, and the height of a wheel was a cubit and a half. ³³The wheels were made like a chariot wheel; their axles, their rims, their spokes, and their hubs were all cast. ³⁴There were four supports at the four corners of each stand. The supports were of one piece with the stands. ³⁵And on the top of the stand there was a round band half a cubit high; and on the top of the stand its stays and its panels were of one piece with it. ³⁶And on the surfaces of its stays and on its panels, he carved cherubim, lions, and palm trees, according to the space of each, with wreaths all around. ³⁷After this manner he made the ten stands. All of them were cast alike, of the same measure and the same form.

³⁸And he made ten basins of bronze. Each basin held forty baths, each basin measured four cubits, and there was a basin for each of the ten stands. ³⁹And he set the stands, five on the south side of the house, and five on the north side of the house. And he set the sea at the southeast corner of the house.

⁴⁰Hiram also made the pots, the shovels, and the basins. So Hiram finished all the work that he did for King Solomon on the house of the LORD: ⁴¹the two pillars, the two bowls of the capitals that were on the tops of the pillars, and the two latticeworks to cover the two bowls of the capitals that were on the tops of the pillars; ⁴²and the four hundred pomegranates for the two latticeworks, two rows of pomegranates for each latticework, to cover the two bowls of the capitals that were on the pillars; ⁴³the ten stands, and the ten basins on the stands; ⁴⁴and the one sea, and the twelve oxen underneath the sea.

⁴⁵Now the pots, the shovels, and the basins, all these vessels in the house of the LORD, which Hiram made for King Solomon, were of burnished bronze. ⁴⁶In the plain of the Jordan the king cast them, in the clay ground between Succoth and Zarethan. ⁴⁷And Solomon left all the vessels unweighed, because there were so many of them; the weight of the bronze was not ascertained.

⁴⁸So Solomon made all the vessels that were in the house of the LORD: the golden altar, the golden table for the bread of the Presence, ⁴⁹the lampstands of pure gold, five on the south side and five on the north, before the inner sanctuary; the flowers, the lamps, and the tongs, of gold; ⁵⁰the cups, snuffers, basins, dishes for incense, and fire pans, of pure gold; and the sockets of gold, for the doors of the innermost part of the house, the Most Holy Place, and for the doors of the nave of the temple.

⁵¹Thus all the work that King Solomon did on the house of the LORD was finished.

---

¹ A *handbreadth* was about 3 inches or 7.5 centimeters ² A *bath* was about 6 gallons or 22 liters

And Solomon brought in the things that David his father had dedicated, the silver, the gold, and the vessels, and stored them in the treasuries of the house of the LORD.

> **The entrance of the ark** [8:1–21]. The most important part of the temple was the ark of the covenant, which contained the tablets of the covenant God made with Moses and which signified that God was enthroned among his people. Once the temple was complete, Solomon had the ark brought up in formal procession with the elders and priests of Israel and placed in the Most Holy Place. This dedication story tells how God confers his blessing on what the king has done by filling the temple with the glory-cloud of his holy presence. Solomon's prayer of blessing for God and his people (vv. 12–21) rehearses the promises that God made to David—covenant promises that are fulfilled in the house that the king built in God's name.

8 Then Solomon assembled the elders of Israel and all the heads of the tribes, the leaders of the fathers' houses of the people of Israel, before King Solomon in Jerusalem, to bring up the ark of the covenant of the LORD out of the city of David, which is Zion. ²And all the men of Israel assembled to King Solomon at the feast in the month Ethanim, which is the seventh month. ³And all the elders of Israel came, and the priests took up the ark. ⁴And they brought up the ark of the LORD, the tent of meeting, and all the holy vessels that were in the tent; the priests and the Levites brought them up. ⁵And King Solomon and all the congregation of Israel, who had assembled before him, were with him before the ark, sacrificing so many sheep and oxen that they could not be counted or numbered. ⁶Then the priests brought the ark of the covenant of the LORD to its place in the inner sanctuary of the house, in the Most Holy Place, underneath the wings of the cherubim. ⁷For the cherubim spread out their wings over the place of the ark, so that the cherubim overshadowed the ark and its poles. ⁸And the poles were so long that the ends of the poles were seen from the Holy Place before the inner sanctuary; but they could not be seen from outside. And they are there to this day. ⁹There was nothing in the ark except the two tablets of stone that Moses put there at Horeb, where the LORD made a covenant with the people of Israel, when they came out of the land of Egypt. ¹⁰And when the priests came out of the Holy Place, a cloud filled the house of the LORD, ¹¹so that the priests could not stand to minister because of the cloud, for the glory of the LORD filled the house of the LORD.

¹²Then Solomon said, "The LORD[1] has said that he would dwell in thick darkness. ¹³I have indeed built you an exalted house, a place for you to dwell in forever." ¹⁴Then the king turned around and blessed all the assembly of Israel, while all the assembly of Israel stood. ¹⁵And he said, "Blessed be the LORD, the God of Israel, who with his hand has fulfilled what he promised with his mouth to David my father, saying, ¹⁶'Since the day that I brought my people Israel out of Egypt, I chose no city out of all the tribes of Israel in which to build a house, that my name might be there. But I chose David to be over my people Israel.' ¹⁷Now it was in the heart of David my father to build a house for the name of the LORD, the God of Israel. ¹⁸But the LORD said to David my father, 'Whereas it was in your heart to build a house for my name, you did well that it was in your heart. ¹⁹Nevertheless, you shall not build the house, but your son who shall be born to you shall build the house for my name.' ²⁰Now the LORD has

---

[1] Septuagint *The LORD has set the sun in the heavens, but*

fulfilled his promise that he made. For I have risen in the place of David my father, and sit on the throne of Israel, as the LORD promised, and I have built the house for the name of the LORD, the God of Israel. ²¹And there I have provided a place for the ark, in which is the covenant of the LORD that he made with our fathers, when he brought them out of the land of Egypt."

Solomon's prayer of dedication [8:22–66]. Solomon's prayer dedicating the temple for sacred worship is one of the high points of the Old Testament. The king gives exalted praise to God for the unique majesty of his sovereign being and for his steadfast faithfulness in keeping the covenant promises he made to David. Solomon acknowledges that Almighty God cannot be contained in any earthly house. Nevertheless, he intercedes for God's blessing, asking that God will condescend to dwell with his people and to hear the prayers they offer in his house. Many of the petitions he makes are conditional ("if a man sins," for example, or "if there is famine in the land," or "when a foreigner . . . comes and prays toward this house"). The king's prayer thus anticipates the kinds of troubles that the people of God are likely to face (often as the consequence of their own sin) and seeks in advance forgiveness or provision or whatever other divine blessing they will need. Later episodes in the history of Israel will show how God answers Solomon's prayer, including many episodes in 1 and 2 Kings (Elijah's prayer for forgiveness and the end of famine, for example, or Naaman the Syrian and his prayer for healing). Solomon's prayer even anticipates Israel's eventual exile and return (vv. 46–53). The worship service ends with *benediction and consecration: the king blesses the people (vv. 54–61) and offers more than 100,000 sacrifices to dedicate the temple for the worship of God (vv. 62–64). After seven days of feasting, the people go home rejoicing in the goodness of their God. Remembering that literature tells us what happens as well as what happened, we can see universal principles embodied in the historical particulars of the story: many of Solomon's requests for God's blessing are the prayers of believers in all ages.

²²Then Solomon stood before the altar of the LORD in the presence of all the assembly of Israel and spread out his hands toward heaven, ²³and said, "O LORD, God of Israel, there is no God like you, in heaven above or on earth beneath, keeping covenant and showing steadfast love to your servants who walk before you with all their heart, ²⁴who have kept with your servant David my father what you declared to him. You spoke with your mouth, and with your hand have fulfilled it this day. ²⁵Now therefore, O LORD, God of Israel, keep for your servant David my father what you have promised him, saying, 'You shall not lack a man to sit before me on the throne of Israel, if only your sons pay close attention to their way, to walk before me as you have walked before me.' ²⁶Now therefore, O God of Israel, let your word be confirmed, which you have spoken to your servant David my father.

²⁷"But will God indeed dwell on the earth? Behold, heaven and the highest heaven cannot contain you; how much less this house that I have built! ²⁸Yet have regard to the prayer of your servant and to his plea, O LORD my God, listening to the cry and to the prayer that your servant prays before you this day, ²⁹that your eyes may be open night and day toward this house, the place of which you have said, 'My name shall be there,' that you may listen to the prayer that your servant offers toward this place. ³⁰And listen to the plea of your servant and of your people Israel, when they pray

toward this place. And listen in heaven your dwelling place, and when you hear, forgive.

[31]"If a man sins against his neighbor and is made to take an oath and comes and swears his oath before your altar in this house, [32]then hear in heaven and act and judge your servants, condemning the guilty by bringing his conduct on his own head, and vindicating the righteous by rewarding him according to his righteousness.

[33]"When your people Israel are defeated before the enemy because they have sinned against you, and if they turn again to you and acknowledge your name and pray and plead with you in this house, [34]then hear in heaven and forgive the sin of your people Israel and bring them again to the land that you gave to their fathers.

[35]"When heaven is shut up and there is no rain because they have sinned against you, if they pray toward this place and acknowledge your name and turn from their sin, when you afflict them, [36]then hear in heaven and forgive the sin of your servants, your people Israel, when you teach them the good way in which they should walk, and grant rain upon your land, which you have given to your people as an inheritance.

[37]"If there is famine in the land, if there is pestilence or blight or mildew or locust or caterpillar, if their enemy besieges them in the land at their gates,[1] whatever plague, whatever sickness there is, [38]whatever prayer, whatever plea is made by any man or by all your people Israel, each knowing the affliction of his own heart and stretching out his hands toward this house, [39]then hear in heaven your dwelling place and forgive and act and render to each whose heart you know, according to all his ways (for you, you only, know the hearts of all the children of mankind), [40]that they may fear you all the days that they live in the land that you gave to our fathers.

[41]"Likewise, when a foreigner, who is not of your people Israel, comes from a far country for your name's sake [42](for they shall hear of your great name and your mighty hand, and of your outstretched arm), when he comes and prays toward this house, [43]hear in heaven your dwelling place and do according to all for which the foreigner calls to you, in order that all the peoples of the earth may know your name and fear you, as do your people Israel, and that they may know that this house that I have built is called by your name.

[44]"If your people go out to battle against their enemy, by whatever way you shall send them, and they pray to the LORD toward the city that you have chosen and the house that I have built for your name, [45]then hear in heaven their prayer and their plea, and maintain their cause.

[46]"If they sin against you—for there is no one who does not sin—and you are angry with them and give them to an enemy, so that they are carried away captive to the land of the enemy, far off or near, [47]yet if they turn their heart in the land to which they have been carried captive, and repent and plead with you in the land of their captors, saying, 'We have sinned and have acted perversely and wickedly,' [48]if they repent with all their mind and with all their heart in the land of their enemies, who carried them captive, and pray to you toward their land, which you gave to their fathers, the city that you have chosen, and the house that I have built for your name, [49]then hear in heaven your dwelling place their prayer and their plea, and maintain their cause [50]and forgive your people who have sinned against you, and all their transgressions that they have committed against you, and grant them compassion in the sight of those who carried them captive, that they may have compassion on them [51](for they are your people, and your heritage, which you brought out of Egypt, from

---

[1] Septuagint, Syriac *in any of their cities*

the midst of the iron furnace). ⁵²Let your eyes be open to the plea of your servant and to the plea of your people Israel, giving ear to them whenever they call to you. ⁵³For you separated them from among all the peoples of the earth to be your heritage, as you declared through Moses your servant, when you brought our fathers out of Egypt, O Lord GOD."

⁵⁴Now as Solomon finished offering all this prayer and plea to the LORD, he arose from before the altar of the LORD, where he had knelt with hands outstretched toward heaven. ⁵⁵And he stood and blessed all the assembly of Israel with a loud voice, saying, ⁵⁶"Blessed be the LORD who has given rest to his people Israel, according to all that he promised. Not one word has failed of all his good promise, which he spoke by Moses his servant. ⁵⁷The LORD our God be with us, as he was with our fathers. May he not leave us or forsake us, ⁵⁸that he may incline our hearts to him, to walk in all his ways and to keep his commandments, his statutes, and his rules, which he commanded our fathers. ⁵⁹Let these words of mine, with which I have pleaded before the LORD, be near to the LORD our God day and night, and may he maintain the cause of his servant and the cause of his people Israel, as each day requires, ⁶⁰that all the peoples of the earth may know that the LORD is God; there is no other. ⁶¹Let your heart therefore be wholly true to the LORD our God, walking in his statutes and keeping his commandments, as at this day."

⁶²Then the king, and all Israel with him, offered sacrifice before the LORD. ⁶³Solomon offered as peace offerings to the LORD 22,000 oxen and 120,000 sheep. So the king and all the people of Israel dedicated the house of the LORD. ⁶⁴The same day the king consecrated the middle of the court that was before the house of the LORD, for there he offered the burnt offering and the grain offering and the fat pieces of the peace offerings, because the bronze altar that was before the LORD was too small to receive the burnt offering and the grain offering and the fat pieces of the peace offerings.

⁶⁵So Solomon held the feast at that time, and all Israel with him, a great assembly, from Lebo-hamath to the Brook of Egypt, before the LORD our God, seven days.¹ ⁶⁶On the eighth day he sent the people away, and they blessed the king and went to their homes joyful and glad of heart for all the goodness that the LORD had shown to David his servant and to Israel his people.

Solomon meets with God [9:1–9]. God answers Solomon's prayers by consecrating the temple as his holy dwelling place. However, when Solomon has a second divine-human encounter, God reveals that his presence with his people is not unconditional. Once again, Solomon and his successors are confronted with a choice. If they keep the covenant, walking with God the way their father David did, then their throne will be established forever. However, if they turn away from God to worship other deities, then Israel will be cut off from the land, and the very temple that they built for God will be utterly destroyed. History records the tragic choices that they made, and as the historian records the splendors of the Solomonic age, he is setting the stage to show how even the greatest earthly glories are forfeited when people abandon the one true God.

9 As soon as Solomon had finished building the house of the LORD and the king's house and all that Solomon desired to build, ²the LORD appeared to Solomon a second time, as he had appeared to him at Gibeon. ³And the LORD said to him, "I have heard your prayer and your plea, which you have made before me. I have conse-

¹ Septuagint; Hebrew *seven days and seven days, fourteen days*

crated this house that you have built, by putting my name there forever. My eyes and my heart will be there for all time. [4]And as for you, if you will walk before me, as David your father walked, with integrity of heart and uprightness, doing according to all that I have commanded you, and keeping my statutes and my rules, [5]then I will establish your royal throne over Israel forever, as I promised David your father, saying, 'You shall not lack a man on the throne of Israel.' [6]But if you turn aside from following me, you or your children, and do not keep my commandments and my statutes that I have set before you, but go and serve other gods and worship them, [7]then I will cut off Israel from the land that I have given them, and the house that I have consecrated for my name I will cast out of my sight, and Israel will become a proverb and a byword among all peoples. [8]And this house will become a heap of ruins.[1] Everyone passing by it will be astonished and will hiss, and they will say, 'Why has the Lord done thus to this land and to this house?' [9]Then they will say, 'Because they abandoned the Lord their God who brought their fathers out of the land of Egypt and laid hold on other gods and worshiped them and served them. Therefore the Lord has brought all this disaster on them.'"

The golden age [9:10–10:29]. The historian shows Solomon at the height of his powers, beginning with an account of his international prominence by land and by sea (9:10–28). The king's famous diplomatic visit from the queen of Sheba, who is so amazed by what she sees in her royal audience that it leaves her breathless, serves to further enhance his reputation for wealth and wisdom (10:1–13). So do the factual details in the second half of chapter 10, which inventories the vast amount of gold in his treasury, the fabulous opulence of his palace, and the international renown of his royal counsel. This was Solomon's golden age, and editorial comments scattered throughout this passage remind us that everything he had was a gift from God.

[10]At the end of twenty years, in which Solomon had built the two houses, the house of the Lord and the king's house, [11]and Hiram king of Tyre had supplied Solomon with cedar and cypress timber and gold, as much as he desired, King Solomon gave to Hiram twenty cities in the land of Galilee. [12]But when Hiram came from Tyre to see the cities that Solomon had given him, they did not please him. [13]Therefore he said, "What kind of cities are these that you have given me, my brother?" So they are called the land of Cabul to this day. [14]Hiram had sent to the king 120 talents[2] of gold.

[15]And this is the account of the forced labor that King Solomon drafted to build the house of the Lord and his own house and the Millo and the wall of Jerusalem and Hazor and Megiddo and Gezer [16](Pharaoh king of Egypt had gone up and captured Gezer and burned it with fire, and had killed the Canaanites who lived in the city, and had given it as dowry to his daughter, Solomon's wife; [17]so Solomon rebuilt Gezer) and Lower Beth-horon [18]and Baalath and Tamar in the wilderness, in the land of Judah,[3] [19]and all the store cities that Solomon had, and the cities for his chariots, and the cities for his horsemen, and whatever Solomon desired to build in Jerusalem, in Lebanon, and in all the land of his dominion. [20]All the people who were left of the Amorites, the Hittites, the Perizzites, the Hivites, and the Jebusites, who were not of the people of Israel— [21]their descendants who were left after them in the land, whom the people of Israel were unable to devote to destruction[4]—these Solomon drafted to

---

[1] Syriac, Old Latin; Hebrew *will become high* [2] A *talent* was about 75 pounds or 34 kilograms [3] Hebrew lacks *of Judah* [4] That is, set apart (devote) as an offering to the Lord (for destruction)

be slaves, and so they are to this day. [22]But of the people of Israel Solomon made no slaves. They were the soldiers, they were his officials, his commanders, his captains, his chariot commanders and his horsemen.

[23]These were the chief officers who were over Solomon's work: 550 who had charge of the people who carried on the work.

[24]But Pharaoh's daughter went up from the city of David to her own house that Solomon had built for her. Then he built the Millo.

[25]Three times a year Solomon used to offer up burnt offerings and peace offerings on the altar that he built to the LORD, making offerings with it[1] before the LORD. So he finished the house.

[26]King Solomon built a fleet of ships at Ezion-geber, which is near Eloth on the shore of the Red Sea, in the land of Edom. [27]And Hiram sent with the fleet his servants, seamen who were familiar with the sea, together with the servants of Solomon. [28]And they went to Ophir and brought from there gold, 420 talents, and they brought it to King Solomon.

10

Now when the queen of Sheba heard of the fame of Solomon concerning the name of the LORD, she came to test him with hard questions. [2]She came to Jerusalem with a very great retinue, with camels bearing spices and very much gold and precious stones. And when she came to Solomon, she told him all that was on her mind. [3]And Solomon answered all her questions; there was nothing hidden from the king that he could not explain to her. [4]And when the queen of Sheba had seen all the wisdom of Solomon, the house that he had built, [5]the food of his table, the seating of his officials, and the attendance of his servants, their clothing, his cupbearers, and his burnt offerings that he offered at the house of the LORD, there was no more breath in her.

[6]And she said to the king, "The report was true that I heard in my own land of your words and of your wisdom, [7]but I did not believe the reports until I came and my own eyes had seen it. And behold, the half was not told me. Your wisdom and prosperity surpass the report that I heard. [8]Happy are your men! Happy are your servants, who continually stand before you and hear your wisdom! [9]Blessed be the LORD your God, who has delighted in you and set you on the throne of Israel! Because the LORD loved Israel forever, he has made you king, that you may execute justice and righteousness." [10]Then she gave the king 120 talents[2] of gold, and a very great quantity of spices and precious stones. Never again came such an abundance of spices as these that the queen of Sheba gave to King Solomon.

[11]Moreover, the fleet of Hiram, which brought gold from Ophir, brought from Ophir a very great amount of almug wood and precious stones. [12]And the king made of the almug wood supports for the house of the LORD and for the king's house, also lyres and harps for the singers. No such almug wood has come or been seen to this day.

[13]And King Solomon gave to the queen of Sheba all that she desired, whatever she asked besides what was given her by the bounty of King Solomon. So she turned and went back to her own land with her servants.

[14]Now the weight of gold that came to Solomon in one year was 666 talents of gold, [15]besides that which came from the explorers and from the business of the merchants, and from all the kings of the west and from the governors of the land. [16]King Solomon made 200 large shields of beaten gold; 600 shekels[3] of gold went into each

---

[1] Septuagint lacks *with it* [2] A *talent* was about 75 pounds or 34 kilograms [3] A *shekel* was about 2/5 ounce or 11 grams

shield. ¹⁷And he made 300 shields of beaten gold; three minas¹ of gold went into each shield. And the king put them in the House of the Forest of Lebanon. ¹⁸The king also made a great ivory throne and overlaid it with the finest gold. ¹⁹The throne had six steps, and at the back of the throne was a calf's head, and on each side of the seat were armrests and two lions standing beside the armrests, ²⁰while twelve lions stood there, one on each end of a step on the six steps. The like of it was never made in any kingdom. ²¹All King Solomon's drinking vessels were of gold, and all the vessels of the House of the Forest of Lebanon were of pure gold. None were of silver; silver was not considered as anything in the days of Solomon. ²²For the king had a fleet of ships of Tarshish at sea with the fleet of Hiram. Once every three years the fleet of ships of Tarshish used to come bringing gold, silver, ivory, apes, and peacocks.²

²³Thus King Solomon excelled all the kings of the earth in riches and in wisdom. ²⁴And the whole earth sought the presence of Solomon to hear his wisdom, which God had put into his mind. ²⁵Every one of them brought his present, articles of silver and gold, garments, myrrh, spices, horses, and mules, so much year by year.

²⁶And Solomon gathered together chariots and horsemen. He had 1,400 chariots and 12,000 horsemen, whom he stationed in the chariot cities and with the king in Jerusalem. ²⁷And the king made silver as common in Jerusalem as stone, and he made cedar as plentiful as the sycamore of the Shephelah. ²⁸And Solomon's import of horses was from Egypt and Kue, and the king's traders received them from Kue at a price. ²⁹A chariot could be imported from Egypt for 600 shekels of silver and a horse for 150, and so through the king's traders they were exported to all the kings of the Hittites and the kings of Syria.

Solomon's folly [chapter 11]. The opening verses of this scene of folly are ominous. In direct violation of the law of God, Solomon has taken many wives from many nations that do not worship the one true God (vv. 1–3). Even worse, in later years the king's heart turns to the worship of foreign gods (vv. 4–8). Solomon has done what is evil in God's sight, and given everything that 1 Kings has already said about the consequences of failing to obey the Word of God, we know that this can only mean disaster for the king and his kingdom, as proves to be the case. The curse God pronounces in the judgment speech in verses 11–13 is played out in the rest of 1 Kings. God will take away Solomon's kingdom. However, for the sake of David, this act of divine judgment will not occur until after Solomon dies, and even then one tribe (Judah) will remain to carry on David's legacy and fulfill God's covenant promise. Enemies rise up against Solomon (vv. 14–25), culminating with the uprising of Jeroboam (vv. 26–40), who receives Ahijah's prophecy that he will rule over the ten tribes of Israel to the north and that he will have God's blessing—provided that he obeys the word of God. The death of Solomon passes without evaluative comment, but we know that he did not end his kingship nearly as well as he began. The overall shape of Solomon's life falls into the pattern of literary *tragedy, as a great man falls into ruin through a series of choices that reveal the sinful flaws at the heart of his character.

11 Now King Solomon loved many foreign women, along with the daughter of Pharaoh: Moabite, Ammonite, Edomite, Sidonian, and Hittite women, ²from the nations concerning which the LORD had said to the people of Israel, "You shall not enter into marriage with them, neither shall they with you, for surely they will

---

¹ A *mina* was about 1 1/4 pounds or 0.6 kilogram ² Or *baboons*

turn away your heart after their gods." Solomon clung to these in love. ³He had 700 wives, princesses, and 300 concubines. And his wives turned away his heart. ⁴For when Solomon was old his wives turned away his heart after other gods, and his heart was not wholly true to the LORD his God, as was the heart of David his father. ⁵For Solomon went after Ashtoreth the goddess of the Sidonians, and after Milcom the abomination of the Ammonites. ⁶So Solomon did what was evil in the sight of the LORD and did not wholly follow the LORD, as David his father had done. ⁷Then Solomon built a high place for Chemosh the abomination of Moab, and for Molech the abomination of the Ammonites, on the mountain east of Jerusalem. ⁸And so he did for all his foreign wives, who made offerings and sacrificed to their gods.

⁹And the LORD was angry with Solomon, because his heart had turned away from the LORD, the God of Israel, who had appeared to him twice ¹⁰and had commanded him concerning this thing, that he should not go after other gods. But he did not keep what the LORD commanded. ¹¹Therefore the LORD said to Solomon, "Since this has been your practice and you have not kept my covenant and my statutes that I have commanded you, I will surely tear the kingdom from you and will give it to your servant. ¹²Yet for the sake of David your father I will not do it in your days, but I will tear it out of the hand of your son. ¹³However, I will not tear away all the kingdom, but I will give one tribe to your son, for the sake of David my servant and for the sake of Jerusalem that I have chosen."

¹⁴And the LORD raised up an adversary against Solomon, Hadad the Edomite. He was of the royal house in Edom. ¹⁵For when David was in Edom, and Joab the commander of the army went up to bury the slain, he struck down every male in Edom ¹⁶(for Joab and all Israel remained there six months, until he had cut off every male in Edom). ¹⁷But Hadad fled to Egypt, together with certain Edomites of his father's servants, Hadad still being a little child. ¹⁸They set out from Midian and came to Paran and took men with them from Paran and came to Egypt, to Pharaoh king of Egypt, who gave him a house and assigned him an allowance of food and gave him land. ¹⁹And Hadad found great favor in the sight of Pharaoh, so that he gave him in marriage the sister of his own wife, the sister of Tahpenes the queen. ²⁰And the sister of Tahpenes bore him Genubath his son, whom Tahpenes weaned in Pharaoh's house. And Genubath was in Pharaoh's house among the sons of Pharaoh. ²¹But when Hadad heard in Egypt that David slept with his fathers and that Joab the commander of the army was dead, Hadad said to Pharaoh, "Let me depart, that I may go to my own country." ²²But Pharaoh said to him, "What have you lacked with me that you are now seeking to go to your own country?" And he said to him, "Only let me depart."

²³God also raised up as an adversary to him, Rezon the son of Eliada, who had fled from his master Hadadezer king of Zobah. ²⁴And he gathered men about him and became leader of a marauding band, after the killing by David. And they went to Damascus and lived there and made him king in Damascus. ²⁵He was an adversary of Israel all the days of Solomon, doing harm as Hadad did. And he loathed Israel and reigned over Syria.

²⁶Jeroboam the son of Nebat, an Ephraimite of Zeredah, a servant of Solomon, whose mother's name was Zeruah, a widow, also lifted up his hand against the king. ²⁷And this was the reason why he lifted up his hand against the king. Solomon built the Millo, and closed up the breach of the city of David his father. ²⁸The man Jeroboam was very able, and when Solomon saw that the young man was industrious

he gave him charge over all the forced labor of the house of Joseph. [29]And at that time, when Jeroboam went out of Jerusalem, the prophet Ahijah the Shilonite found him on the road. Now Ahijah had dressed himself in a new garment, and the two of them were alone in the open country. [30]Then Ahijah laid hold of the new garment that was on him, and tore it into twelve pieces. [31]And he said to Jeroboam, "Take for yourself ten pieces, for thus says the LORD, the God of Israel, 'Behold, I am about to tear the kingdom from the hand of Solomon and will give you ten tribes [32](but he shall have one tribe, for the sake of my servant David and for the sake of Jerusalem, the city that I have chosen out of all the tribes of Israel), [33]because they have[1] forsaken me and worshiped Ashtoreth the goddess of the Sidonians, Chemosh the god of Moab, and Milcom the god of the Ammonites, and they have not walked in my ways, doing what is right in my sight and keeping my statutes and my rules, as David his father did. [34]Nevertheless, I will not take the whole kingdom out of his hand, but I will make him ruler all the days of his life, for the sake of David my servant whom I chose, who kept my commandments and my statutes. [35]But I will take the kingdom out of his son's hand and will give it to you, ten tribes. [36]Yet to his son I will give one tribe, that David my servant may always have a lamp before me in Jerusalem, the city where I have chosen to put my name. [37]And I will take you, and you shall reign over all that your soul desires, and you shall be king over Israel. [38]And if you will listen to all that I command you, and will walk in my ways, and do what is right in my eyes by keeping my statutes and my commandments, as David my servant did, I will be with you and will build you a sure house, as I built for David, and I will give Israel to you. [39]And I will afflict the offspring of David because of this, but not forever.'" [40]Solomon sought therefore to kill Jeroboam. But Jeroboam arose and fled into Egypt, to Shishak king of Egypt, and was in Egypt until the death of Solomon.

[41]Now the rest of the acts of Solomon, and all that he did, and his wisdom, are they not written in the Book of the Acts of Solomon? [42]And the time that Solomon reigned in Jerusalem over all Israel was forty years. [43]And Solomon slept with his fathers and was buried in the city of David his father. And Rehoboam his son reigned in his place.

Rehoboam's folly [12:1–15]. The genre of *succession story comes to dominate the book at this point. Rehoboam is the rightful heir to the throne of David and Solomon. Like them, he must choose between wisdom and folly, either following God's way or going his own way. The wise old men of Israel advise him to be a servant leader, but in this scene of folly Rehoboam senselessly follows the foolish advice of his peers and crudely threatens Israel with harsh servitude. The editorial comment in the last verse of this passage reminds us that God can use even human folly to fulfill his promise.

12

Rehoboam went to Shechem, for all Israel had come to Shechem to make him king. [2]And as soon as Jeroboam the son of Nebat heard of it (for he was still in Egypt, where he had fled from King Solomon), then Jeroboam returned from[2] Egypt. [3]And they sent and called him, and Jeroboam and all the assembly of Israel came and said to Rehoboam, [4]"Your father made our yoke heavy. Now therefore lighten the hard service of your father and his heavy yoke on us, and we will serve you." [5]He said to them, "Go away for three days, then come again to me." So the people went away.

[6]Then King Rehoboam took counsel with the old men, who had stood before

---

[1] Septuagint, Syriac, Vulgate *he has*; twice in this verse [2] Septuagint, Vulgate (compare 2 Chronicles 10:2); Hebrew *lived in*

Solomon his father while he was yet alive, saying, "How do you advise me to answer this people?" ⁷And they said to him, "If you will be a servant to this people today and serve them, and speak good words to them when you answer them, then they will be your servants forever." ⁸But he abandoned the counsel that the old men gave him and took counsel with the young men who had grown up with him and stood before him. ⁹And he said to them, "What do you advise that we answer this people who have said to me, 'Lighten the yoke that your father put on us'?" ¹⁰And the young men who had grown up with him said to him, "Thus shall you speak to this people who said to you, 'Your father made our yoke heavy, but you lighten it for us,' thus shall you say to them, 'My little finger is thicker than my father's thighs. ¹¹And now, whereas my father laid on you a heavy yoke, I will add to your yoke. My father disciplined you with whips, but I will discipline you with scorpions.'"

¹²So Jeroboam and all the people came to Rehoboam the third day, as the king said, "Come to me again the third day." ¹³And the king answered the people harshly, and forsaking the counsel that the old men had given him, ¹⁴he spoke to them according to the counsel of the young men, saying, "My father made your yoke heavy, but I will add to your yoke. My father disciplined you with whips, but I will discipline you with scorpions." ¹⁵So the king did not listen to the people, for it was a turn of affairs brought about by the LORD that he might fulfill his word, which the LORD spoke by Ahijah the Shilonite to Jeroboam the son of Nebat.

A house divided [12:16–33]. The unfolding action now expands into a story of revolt. The people instantly rebel against the new regime, and the kingdom is divided between north and south, Israel and Judah, Jeroboam and Rehoboam. Although in human terms this civil war is understandable and almost justifiable, the writer makes it clear that rebellion against the heir of David is rebellion against the house of God. Nevertheless, the divided kingdom is also God's act of judgment, and therefore the warriors of Judah may not fight to reclaim Israel (vv. 21–24). Rehoboam has been very foolish, but Jeroboam's rule will be even worse. In order to secure his political position and keep people in Israel from going to Judah, he sets up alternative worship services. With obvious contempt for temple worship in Jerusalem, with blatant disregard for the second commandment, and in apparent ignorance of what happened to Aaron earlier when he committed exactly the same sin (see Exodus 32), Jeroboam makes golden calves for people to worship in Bethel and Dan. He also sets up his own sacrifices, offered by his own priests, at his own high places, on his own feast days. In effect, Jeroboam has invented his own religion in a counterfeit kingdom, and as a result his kingship will become proverbial for rebellion against God.

¹⁶And when all Israel saw that the king did not listen to them, the people answered the king, "What portion do we have in David? We have no inheritance in the son of Jesse. To your tents, O Israel! Look now to your own house, David." So Israel went to their tents. ¹⁷But Rehoboam reigned over the people of Israel who lived in the cities of Judah. ¹⁸Then King Rehoboam sent Adoram, who was taskmaster over the forced labor, and all Israel stoned him to death with stones. And King Rehoboam hurried to mount his chariot to flee to Jerusalem. ¹⁹So Israel has been in rebellion against the house of David to this day. ²⁰And when all Israel heard that Jeroboam had returned,

they sent and called him to the assembly and made him king over all Israel. There was none that followed the house of David but the tribe of Judah only.

²¹ When Rehoboam came to Jerusalem, he assembled all the house of Judah and the tribe of Benjamin, 180,000 chosen warriors, to fight against the house of Israel, to restore the kingdom to Rehoboam the son of Solomon. ²² But the word of God came to Shemaiah the man of God: ²³ "Say to Rehoboam the son of Solomon, king of Judah, and to all the house of Judah and Benjamin, and to the rest of the people, ²⁴ 'Thus says the LORD, You shall not go up or fight against your relatives the people of Israel. Every man return to his home, for this thing is from me.'" So they listened to the word of the LORD and went home again, according to the word of the LORD.

²⁵ Then Jeroboam built Shechem in the hill country of Ephraim and lived there. And he went out from there and built Penuel. ²⁶ And Jeroboam said in his heart, "Now the kingdom will turn back to the house of David. ²⁷ If this people go up to offer sacrifices in the temple of the LORD at Jerusalem, then the heart of this people will turn again to their lord, to Rehoboam king of Judah, and they will kill me and return to Rehoboam king of Judah." ²⁸ So the king took counsel and made two calves of gold. And he said to the people, "You have gone up to Jerusalem long enough. Behold your gods, O Israel, who brought you up out of the land of Egypt." ²⁹ And he set one in Bethel, and the other he put in Dan. ³⁰ Then this thing became a sin, for the people went as far as Dan to be before one.[1] ³¹ He also made temples on high places and appointed priests from among all the people, who were not of the Levites. ³² And Jeroboam appointed a feast on the fifteenth day of the eighth month like the feast that was in Judah, and he offered sacrifices on the altar. So he did in Bethel, sacrificing to the calves that he made. And he placed in Bethel the priests of the high places that he had made. ³³ He went up to the altar that he had made in Bethel on the fifteenth day in the eighth month, in the month that he had devised from his own heart. And he instituted a feast for the people of Israel and went up to the altar to make offerings.

Jeroboam and the man of God [chapter 13]. This chapter begins with an unnamed man of God making a prophecy that reformation will come. On the very altar of Bethel where Jeroboam is poised to offer an unholy sacrifice, Josiah a descendant of David will put Jeroboam's wicked prophets to death. When Jeroboam angrily reaches out to seize the man of God, his hand instantly withers; however, when he prays for healing, his hand is restored. A curious episode follows, in which an old prophet in Bethel deceives the "man of God." This perversion of a hospitality story sets the stage for the judgment scene that follows. For his disobedience, the man of God is attacked and killed by a lion. As the prophet of Bethel collects the corpse, he tells us that despite his disobedience and death, the man's words of prophecy against Jeroboam will certainly come to pass. Jeroboam himself should take these strange events as a warning to obey the word of God, but the chapter ends by telling us that he will do no such thing. A pervasive *irony is present throughout 1 Kings, as one king after another perversely does the very things that we know he should avoid doing.

13

And behold, a man of God came out of Judah by the word of the LORD to Bethel. Jeroboam was standing by the altar to make offerings. ² And the man cried against the altar by the word of the LORD and said, "O altar, altar, thus says the LORD: 'Behold, a son shall be born to the house of David, Josiah by name, and he shall

---

[1] Septuagint *went to the one at Bethel and to the other as far as Dan*

1 KINGS 13:3484

sacrifice on you the priests of the high places who make offerings on you, and human bones shall be burned on you.'" ³And he gave a sign the same day, saying, "This is the sign that the Lord has spoken: 'Behold, the altar shall be torn down, and the ashes that are on it shall be poured out.'" ⁴And when the king heard the saying of the man of God, which he cried against the altar at Bethel, Jeroboam stretched out his hand from the altar, saying, "Seize him." And his hand, which he stretched out against him, dried up, so that he could not draw it back to himself. ⁵The altar also was torn down, and the ashes poured out from the altar, according to the sign that the man of God had given by the word of the Lord. ⁶And the king said to the man of God, "Entreat now the favor of the Lord your God, and pray for me, that my hand may be restored to me." And the man of God entreated the Lord, and the king's hand was restored to him and became as it was before. ⁷And the king said to the man of God, "Come home with me, and refresh yourself, and I will give you a reward." ⁸And the man of God said to the king, "If you give me half your house, I will not go in with you. And I will not eat bread or drink water in this place, ⁹for so was it commanded me by the word of the Lord, saying, 'You shall neither eat bread nor drink water nor return by the way that you came.'" ¹⁰So he went another way and did not return by the way that he came to Bethel.

¹¹Now an old prophet lived in Bethel. And his sons¹ came and told him all that the man of God had done that day in Bethel. They also told to their father the words that he had spoken to the king. ¹²And their father said to them, "Which way did he go?" And his sons showed him the way that the man of God who came from Judah had gone. ¹³And he said to his sons, "Saddle the donkey for me." So they saddled the donkey for him and he mounted it. ¹⁴And he went after the man of God and found him sitting under an oak. And he said to him, "Are you the man of God who came from Judah?" And he said, "I am." ¹⁵Then he said to him, "Come home with me and eat bread." ¹⁶And he said, "I may not return with you, or go in with you, neither will I eat bread nor drink water with you in this place, ¹⁷for it was said to me by the word of the Lord, 'You shall neither eat bread nor drink water there, nor return by the way that you came.'" ¹⁸And he said to him, "I also am a prophet as you are, and an angel spoke to me by the word of the Lord, saying, 'Bring him back with you into your house that he may eat bread and drink water.'" But he lied to him. ¹⁹So he went back with him and ate bread in his house and drank water.

²⁰And as they sat at the table, the word of the Lord came to the prophet who had brought him back. ²¹And he cried to the man of God who came from Judah, "Thus says the Lord, 'Because you have disobeyed the word of the Lord and have not kept the command that the Lord your God commanded you, ²²but have come back and have eaten bread and drunk water in the place of which he said to you, "Eat no bread and drink no water," your body shall not come to the tomb of your fathers.'" ²³And after he had eaten bread and drunk, he saddled the donkey for the prophet whom he had brought back. ²⁴And as he went away a lion met him on the road and killed him. And his body was thrown in the road, and the donkey stood beside it; the lion also stood beside the body. ²⁵And behold, men passed by and saw the body thrown in the road and the lion standing by the body. And they came and told it in the city where the old prophet lived.

²⁶And when the prophet who had brought him back from the way heard of it, he said, "It is the man of God who disobeyed the word of the Lord; therefore the Lord

---

¹ Septuagint, Syriac, Vulgate; Hebrew *son*

has given him to the lion, which has torn him and killed him, according to the word that the Lord spoke to him." ²⁷And he said to his sons, "Saddle the donkey for me." And they saddled it. ²⁸And he went and found his body thrown in the road, and the donkey and the lion standing beside the body. The lion had not eaten the body or torn the donkey. ²⁹And the prophet took up the body of the man of God and laid it on the donkey and brought it back to the city¹ to mourn and to bury him. ³⁰And he laid the body in his own grave. And they mourned over him, saying, "Alas, my brother!" ³¹And after he had buried him, he said to his sons, "When I die, bury me in the grave in which the man of God is buried; lay my bones beside his bones. ³²For the saying that he called out by the word of the Lord against the altar in Bethel and against all the houses of the high places that are in the cities of Samaria shall surely come to pass."

³³After this thing Jeroboam did not turn from his evil way, but made priests for the high places again from among all the people. Any who would, he ordained to be priests of the high places. ³⁴And this thing became sin to the house of Jeroboam, so as to cut it off and to destroy it from the face of the earth.

God's judgment against Jeroboam [14:1–20]. At the beginning of this deathbed scene, Jeroboam's son is sick, so the king sends his wife (in disguise) to the prophet Ahijah in order to see if the child will live. Ahijah sees through her disguise and gives her a terrible prophecy of doom for the house of Jeroboam. The king has not kept God's commandments the way that David did, but has provoked God's anger by worshiping other gods. As a result, every member of Jeroboam's family will die, and everything that belongs to him will perish. In fact, the very moment that Jeroboam's wife sets foot in her house, her son will die. Even worse, the prophet says that all Israel will be taken into captivity because Jeroboam has led the nation into idolatry. The prophecies in this judgment speech all come true, starting already in this passage with the deaths of Jeroboam's son and of Jeroboam himself.

14 At that time Abijah the son of Jeroboam fell sick. ²And Jeroboam said to his wife, "Arise, and disguise yourself, that it not be known that you are the wife of Jeroboam, and go to Shiloh. Behold, Ahijah the prophet is there, who said of me that I should be king over this people. ³Take with you ten loaves, some cakes, and a jar of honey, and go to him. He will tell you what shall happen to the child."

⁴Jeroboam's wife did so. She arose and went to Shiloh and came to the house of Ahijah. Now Ahijah could not see, for his eyes were dim because of his age. ⁵And the Lord said to Ahijah, "Behold, the wife of Jeroboam is coming to inquire of you concerning her son, for he is sick. Thus and thus shall you say to her."

When she came, she pretended to be another woman. ⁶But when Ahijah heard the sound of her feet, as she came in at the door, he said, "Come in, wife of Jeroboam. Why do you pretend to be another? For I am charged with unbearable news for you. ⁷Go, tell Jeroboam, 'Thus says the Lord, the God of Israel: "Because I exalted you from among the people and made you leader over my people Israel ⁸and tore the kingdom away from the house of David and gave it to you, and yet you have not been like my servant David, who kept my commandments and followed me with all his heart, doing only that which was right in my eyes, ⁹but you have done evil above all who were before you and have gone and made for yourself other gods and metal images, provoking me to anger, and have cast me behind your back, ¹⁰therefore behold, I will

¹ Septuagint; Hebrew *he came to the city of the old prophet*

bring harm upon the house of Jeroboam and will cut off from Jeroboam every male, both bond and free in Israel, and will burn up the house of Jeroboam, as a man burns up dung until it is all gone. [11]Anyone belonging to Jeroboam who dies in the city the dogs shall eat, and anyone who dies in the open country the birds of the heavens shall eat, for the LORD has spoken it."' [12]Arise therefore, go to your house. When your feet enter the city, the child shall die. [13]And all Israel shall mourn for him and bury him, for he only of Jeroboam shall come to the grave, because in him there is found something pleasing to the LORD, the God of Israel, in the house of Jeroboam. [14]Moreover, the LORD will raise up for himself a king over Israel who shall cut off the house of Jeroboam today. And henceforth, [15]the LORD will strike Israel as a reed is shaken in the water, and root up Israel out of this good land that he gave to their fathers and scatter them beyond the Euphrates, because they have made their Asherim, provoking the LORD to anger. [16]And he will give Israel up because of the sins of Jeroboam, which he sinned and made Israel to sin."

[17]Then Jeroboam's wife arose and departed and came to Tirzah. And as she came to the threshold of the house, the child died. [18]And all Israel buried him and mourned for him, according to the word of the LORD, which he spoke by his servant Ahijah the prophet.

[19]Now the rest of the acts of Jeroboam, how he warred and how he reigned, behold, they are written in the Book of the Chronicles of the Kings of Israel. [20]And the time that Jeroboam reigned was twenty-two years. And he slept with his fathers, and Nadab his son reigned in his place.

> **Three kings of Judah** [14:21–15:24]. Each of the first three kings of Judah is evaluated according to the will of God. First comes Rehoboam, who did what was evil in God's sight by leading his people into the debaucheries of pagan idolatry; he is plundered by the Egyptians, who carry off many of the treasures of Solomon. Next comes Rehoboam's son Abijam, who is nearly as wicked. Nevertheless, for the sake of David, God preserves Abijam's rule over Jerusalem. The third king is Asa, and he is blessed with a long and prosperous kingdom. Like his father David before him, Asa does what is right in the sight of God, and he is able to undo much of the damage that Rehoboam had done. There are undercurrents of Judah's ongoing civil war with Israel throughout this court narrative, with Asa's resistance to Baasha (15:16–22) showing God's favor on Judah as the kingdom of the true and rightful king.

[21]Now Rehoboam the son of Solomon reigned in Judah. Rehoboam was forty-one years old when he began to reign, and he reigned seventeen years in Jerusalem, the city that the LORD had chosen out of all the tribes of Israel, to put his name there. His mother's name was Naamah the Ammonite. [22]And Judah did what was evil in the sight of the LORD, and they provoked him to jealousy with their sins that they committed, more than all that their fathers had done. [23]For they also built for themselves high places and pillars and Asherim on every high hill and under every green tree, [24]and there were also male cult prostitutes in the land. They did according to all the abominations of the nations that the LORD drove out before the people of Israel.

[25]In the fifth year of King Rehoboam, Shishak king of Egypt came up against Jerusalem. [26]He took away the treasures of the house of the LORD and the treasures of the king's house. He took away everything. He also took away all the shields of gold

that Solomon had made, [27]and King Rehoboam made in their place shields of bronze, and committed them to the hands of the officers of the guard, who kept the door of the king's house. [28]And as often as the king went into the house of the LORD, the guard carried them and brought them back to the guardroom.

[29]Now the rest of the acts of Rehoboam and all that he did, are they not written in the Book of the Chronicles of the Kings of Judah? [30]And there was war between Rehoboam and Jeroboam continually. [31]And Rehoboam slept with his fathers and was buried with his fathers in the city of David. His mother's name was Naamah the Ammonite. And Abijam his son reigned in his place.

15

Now in the eighteenth year of King Jeroboam the son of Nebat, Abijam began to reign over Judah. [2]He reigned for three years in Jerusalem. His mother's name was Maacah the daughter of Abishalom. [3]And he walked in all the sins that his father did before him, and his heart was not wholly true to the LORD his God, as the heart of David his father. [4]Nevertheless, for David's sake the LORD his God gave him a lamp in Jerusalem, setting up his son after him, and establishing Jerusalem, [5]because David did what was right in the eyes of the LORD and did not turn aside from anything that he commanded him all the days of his life, except in the matter of Uriah the Hittite. [6]Now there was war between Rehoboam and Jeroboam all the days of his life. [7]The rest of the acts of Abijam and all that he did, are they not written in the Book of the Chronicles of the Kings of Judah? And there was war between Abijam and Jeroboam. [8]And Abijam slept with his fathers, and they buried him in the city of David. And Asa his son reigned in his place.

[9]In the twentieth year of Jeroboam king of Israel, Asa began to reign over Judah, [10]and he reigned forty-one years in Jerusalem. His mother's name was Maacah the daughter of Abishalom. [11]And Asa did what was right in the eyes of the LORD, as David his father had done. [12]He put away the male cult prostitutes out of the land and removed all the idols that his fathers had made. [13]He also removed Maacah his mother from being queen mother because she had made an abominable image for Asherah. And Asa cut down her image and burned it at the brook Kidron. [14]But the high places were not taken away. Nevertheless, the heart of Asa was wholly true to the LORD all his days. [15]And he brought into the house of the LORD the sacred gifts of his father and his own sacred gifts, silver, and gold, and vessels.

[16]And there was war between Asa and Baasha king of Israel all their days. [17]Baasha king of Israel went up against Judah and built Ramah, that he might permit no one to go out or come in to Asa king of Judah. [18]Then Asa took all the silver and the gold that were left in the treasures of the house of the LORD and the treasures of the king's house and gave them into the hands of his servants. And King Asa sent them to Benhadad the son of Tabrimmon, the son of Hezion, king of Syria, who lived in Damascus, saying, [19]"Let there be a covenant[1] between me and you, as there was between my father and your father. Behold, I am sending to you a present of silver and gold. Go, break your covenant with Baasha king of Israel, that he may withdraw from me." [20]And Ben-hadad listened to King Asa and sent the commanders of his armies against the cities of Israel and conquered Ijon, Dan, Abel-beth-maacah, and all Chinneroth, with all the land of Naphtali. [21]And when Baasha heard of it, he stopped building Ramah, and he lived in Tirzah. [22]Then King Asa made a proclamation to all Judah, none was exempt, and they carried away the stones of Ramah and

---

[1] Or treaty; twice in this verse

its timber, with which Baasha had been building, and with them King Asa built Geba of Benjamin and Mizpah. ²³Now the rest of all the acts of Asa, all his might, and all that he did, and the cities that he built, are they not written in the Book of the Chronicles of the Kings of Judah? But in his old age he was diseased in his feet. ²⁴And Asa slept with his fathers and was buried with his fathers in the city of David his father, and Jehoshaphat his son reigned in his place.

> **Six kings of Israel** [15:25–16:34]. In the early decades of the divided kingdom, things in Judah sometimes seem to get better spiritually, but things in Israel always seem to be getting worse. Each of the first six kings of Israel does what was evil in God's sight: Nadab (15:25–32), Baasha (15:33–16:7), Elah (16:8–14), Zimri (16:15–20), Omri (16:21–28), and Ahab (16:29–34). Ahab, we are told, does much more evil than any of his predecessors, especially by following his wife Jezebel in the worship of Baal and Asherah. Most of these kings take the throne by means of violence, and with *poetic justice many of them die by the same sword that brought them to power. Jeroboam's name is often mentioned in these succession narratives as the archetype of the evil king. It is his sins that are being repeated in Israel and judged by God.

²⁵Nadab the son of Jeroboam began to reign over Israel in the second year of Asa king of Judah, and he reigned over Israel two years. ²⁶He did what was evil in the sight of the LORD and walked in the way of his father, and in his sin which he made Israel to sin.

²⁷Baasha the son of Ahijah, of the house of Issachar, conspired against him. And Baasha struck him down at Gibbethon, which belonged to the Philistines, for Nadab and all Israel were laying siege to Gibbethon. ²⁸So Baasha killed him in the third year of Asa king of Judah and reigned in his place. ²⁹And as soon as he was king, he killed all the house of Jeroboam. He left to the house of Jeroboam not one that breathed, until he had destroyed it, according to the word of the LORD that he spoke by his servant Ahijah the Shilonite. ³⁰It was for the sins of Jeroboam that he sinned and that he made Israel to sin, and because of the anger to which he provoked the LORD, the God of Israel.

³¹Now the rest of the acts of Nadab and all that he did, are they not written in the Book of the Chronicles of the Kings of Israel? ³²And there was war between Asa and Baasha king of Israel all their days.

³³In the third year of Asa king of Judah, Baasha the son of Ahijah began to reign over all Israel at Tirzah, and he reigned twenty-four years. ³⁴He did what was evil in the sight of the LORD and walked in the way of Jeroboam and in his sin which he made Israel to sin.

16 And the word of the LORD came to Jehu the son of Hanani against Baasha, saying, ²"Since I exalted you out of the dust and made you leader over my people Israel, and you have walked in the way of Jeroboam and have made my people Israel to sin, provoking me to anger with their sins, ³behold, I will utterly sweep away Baasha and his house, and I will make your house like the house of Jeroboam the son of Nebat. ⁴Anyone belonging to Baasha who dies in the city the dogs shall eat, and anyone of his who dies in the field the birds of the heavens shall eat."

⁵Now the rest of the acts of Baasha and what he did, and his might, are they not

written in the Book of the Chronicles of the Kings of Israel? ⁶And Baasha slept with his fathers and was buried at Tirzah, and Elah his son reigned in his place. ⁷Moreover, the word of the LORD came by the prophet Jehu the son of Hanani against Baasha and his house, both because of all the evil that he did in the sight of the LORD, provoking him to anger with the work of his hands, in being like the house of Jeroboam, and also because he destroyed it.

⁸In the twenty-sixth year of Asa king of Judah, Elah the son of Baasha began to reign over Israel in Tirzah, and he reigned two years. ⁹But his servant Zimri, commander of half his chariots, conspired against him. When he was at Tirzah, drinking himself drunk in the house of Arza, who was over the household in Tirzah, ¹⁰Zimri came in and struck him down and killed him, in the twenty-seventh year of Asa king of Judah, and reigned in his place.

¹¹When he began to reign, as soon as he had seated himself on his throne, he struck down all the house of Baasha. He did not leave him a single male of his relatives or his friends. ¹²Thus Zimri destroyed all the house of Baasha, according to the word of the LORD, which he spoke against Baasha by Jehu the prophet, ¹³for all the sins of Baasha and the sins of Elah his son, which they sinned and which they made Israel to sin, provoking the LORD God of Israel to anger with their idols. ¹⁴Now the rest of the acts of Elah and all that he did, are they not written in the Book of the Chronicles of the Kings of Israel?

¹⁵In the twenty-seventh year of Asa king of Judah, Zimri reigned seven days in Tirzah. Now the troops were encamped against Gibbethon, which belonged to the Philistines, ¹⁶and the troops who were encamped heard it said, "Zimri has conspired, and he has killed the king." Therefore all Israel made Omri, the commander of the army, king over Israel that day in the camp. ¹⁷So Omri went up from Gibbethon, and all Israel with him, and they besieged Tirzah. ¹⁸And when Zimri saw that the city was taken, he went into the citadel of the king's house and burned the king's house over him with fire and died, ¹⁹because of his sins that he committed, doing evil in the sight of the LORD, walking in the way of Jeroboam, and for his sin which he committed, making Israel to sin. ²⁰Now the rest of the acts of Zimri, and the conspiracy that he made, are they not written in the Book of the Chronicles of the Kings of Israel?

²¹Then the people of Israel were divided into two parts. Half of the people followed Tibni the son of Ginath, to make him king, and half followed Omri. ²²But the people who followed Omri overcame the people who followed Tibni the son of Ginath. So Tibni died, and Omri became king. ²³In the thirty-first year of Asa king of Judah, Omri began to reign over Israel, and he reigned for twelve years; six years he reigned in Tirzah. ²⁴He bought the hill of Samaria from Shemer for two talents¹ of silver, and he fortified the hill and called the name of the city that he built Samaria, after the name of Shemer, the owner of the hill.

²⁵Omri did what was evil in the sight of the LORD, and did more evil than all who were before him. ²⁶For he walked in all the way of Jeroboam the son of Nebat, and in the sins that he made Israel to sin, provoking the LORD, the God of Israel, to anger by their idols. ²⁷Now the rest of the acts of Omri that he did, and the might that he showed, are they not written in the Book of the Chronicles of the Kings of Israel? ²⁸And Omri slept with his fathers and was buried in Samaria, and Ahab his son reigned in his place.

²⁹In the thirty-eighth year of Asa king of Judah, Ahab the son of Omri began to

---

¹ A *talent* was about 75 pounds or 34 kilograms

reign over Israel, and Ahab the son of Omri reigned over Israel in Samaria twenty-two years. ³⁰And Ahab the son of Omri did evil in the sight of the Lord, more than all who were before him. ³¹And as if it had been a light thing for him to walk in the sins of Jeroboam the son of Nebat, he took for his wife Jezebel the daughter of Ethbaal king of the Sidonians, and went and served Baal and worshiped him. ³²He erected an altar for Baal in the house of Baal, which he built in Samaria. ³³And Ahab made an Asherah. Ahab did more to provoke the Lord, the God of Israel, to anger than all the kings of Israel who were before him. ³⁴In his days Hiel of Bethel built Jericho. He laid its foundation at the cost of Abiram his firstborn, and set up its gates at the cost of his youngest son Segub, according to the word of the Lord, which he spoke by Joshua the son of Nun.

Elijah and the great drought [chapter 17]. The great prophet Elijah suddenly appears on the scene to announce to Ahab that there will be no rain in Israel—a judgment God had long ago revealed through Moses as the appropriate punishment for Israel's idolatry (Deut. 11:16–17). Elijah then goes into seclusion for a time of testing—the initiatory ordeal whereby he is prepared for his life as a prophet by learning to trust God for provision. While Israel suffers, God's faithful prophet drinks water from the brook Cherith and receives his daily bread, which is miraculously carried in twice a day by ravens (vv. 3–7). The prophet then proceeds to Zarephath, where he meets a widow who is preparing one last meal for her son before dying. By faith she receives a miraculous provision of flour and oil, which are promised to last as long as the drought (vv. 8–16). The main spiritual lesson in these two miracle stories (which are also stories of providence) is that even in times of trouble, God will provide for his faithful servants and for everyone who trusts in his word. When the woman's son later becomes ill and breathes his last, Elijah works yet another wonder and brings him back to life. The primary purpose of this miracle is explained in verse 24: it confirms that the prophet's word is true.

17 Now Elijah the Tishbite, of Tishbe¹ in Gilead, said to Ahab, "As the Lord, the God of Israel, lives, before whom I stand, there shall be neither dew nor rain these years, except by my word." ²And the word of the Lord came to him: ³"Depart from here and turn eastward and hide yourself by the brook Cherith, which is east of the Jordan. ⁴You shall drink from the brook, and I have commanded the ravens to feed you there." ⁵So he went and did according to the word of the Lord. He went and lived by the brook Cherith that is east of the Jordan. ⁶And the ravens brought him bread and meat in the morning, and bread and meat in the evening, and he drank from the brook. ⁷And after a while the brook dried up, because there was no rain in the land.

⁸Then the word of the Lord came to him, ⁹"Arise, go to Zarephath, which belongs to Sidon, and dwell there. Behold, I have commanded a widow there to feed you." ¹⁰So he arose and went to Zarephath. And when he came to the gate of the city, behold, a widow was there gathering sticks. And he called to her and said, "Bring me a little water in a vessel, that I may drink." ¹¹And as she was going to bring it, he called to her and said, "Bring me a morsel of bread in your hand." ¹²And she said, "As the Lord your God lives, I have nothing baked, only a handful of flour in a jar and a little oil in a jug. And now I am gathering a couple of sticks that I may go in and prepare it for myself and my son, that we may eat it and die." ¹³And Elijah said to her, "Do not fear;

¹ Septuagint; Hebrew *of the settlers*

go and do as you have said. But first make me a little cake of it and bring it to me, and afterward make something for yourself and your son. ¹⁴For thus says the LORD, the God of Israel, 'The jar of flour shall not be spent, and the jug of oil shall not be empty, until the day that the LORD sends rain upon the earth.'" ¹⁵And she went and did as Elijah said. And she and he and her household ate for many days. ¹⁶The jar of flour was not spent, neither did the jug of oil become empty, according to the word of the LORD that he spoke by Elijah.

¹⁷After this the son of the woman, the mistress of the house, became ill. And his illness was so severe that there was no breath left in him. ¹⁸And she said to Elijah, "What have you against me, O man of God? You have come to me to bring my sin to remembrance and to cause the death of my son!" ¹⁹And he said to her, "Give me your son." And he took him from her arms and carried him up into the upper chamber where he lodged, and laid him on his own bed. ²⁰And he cried to the LORD, "O LORD my God, have you brought calamity even upon the widow with whom I sojourn, by killing her son?" ²¹Then he stretched himself upon the child three times and cried to the LORD, "O LORD my God, let this child's life¹ come into him again." ²²And the LORD listened to the voice of Elijah. And the life of the child came into him again, and he revived. ²³And Elijah took the child and brought him down from the upper chamber into the house and delivered him to his mother. And Elijah said, "See, your son lives." ²⁴And the woman said to Elijah, "Now I know that you are a man of God, and that the word of the LORD in your mouth is truth."

Ahab confronts Elijah [18:1–19]. Desperate times call for desperate measures. Wicked Queen Jezebel has threatened to kill all of God's prophets, but faithful Obadiah has hidden them in caves and is secretly bringing them what little food he has left. Even King Ahab must be suffering from the famine, for he is out looking for a little grass and water for his animals. When Elijah comes looking for Ahab, Obadiah warns him to keep his distance because Ahab has put a bounty on the prophet's head. But the prophet is on a mission from God and insists on seeing the king. When Ahab finally has the chance to confront Elijah about the famine, he accuses him of being the "troubler of Israel" (v. 17). But who is the real troublemaker here? Elijah knows that the real trouble with Israel is the worship of Baal, which Ahab and his fathers have promoted. So this preliminary *encounter story ends with the prophet proposing a duel: he will challenge all 450 prophets of Baal, winner takes all. The stage is set for the most heroic of all Elijah's *hero stories.

18 After many days the word of the LORD came to Elijah, in the third year, saying, "Go, show yourself to Ahab, and I will send rain upon the earth." ²So Elijah went to show himself to Ahab. Now the famine was severe in Samaria. ³And Ahab called Obadiah, who was over the household. (Now Obadiah feared the LORD greatly, ⁴and when Jezebel cut off the prophets of the LORD, Obadiah took a hundred prophets and hid them by fifties in a cave and fed them with bread and water.) ⁵And Ahab said to Obadiah, "Go through the land to all the springs of water and to all the valleys. Perhaps we may find grass and save the horses and mules alive, and not lose some of the animals." ⁶So they divided the land between them to pass through it. Ahab went in one direction by himself, and Obadiah went in another direction by himself.

¹ Or *soul*; also verse 22

⁷And as Obadiah was on the way, behold, Elijah met him. And Obadiah recognized him and fell on his face and said, "Is it you, my lord Elijah?" ⁸And he answered him, "It is I. Go, tell your lord, 'Behold, Elijah is here.'" ⁹And he said, "How have I sinned, that you would give your servant into the hand of Ahab, to kill me? ¹⁰As the LORD your God lives, there is no nation or kingdom where my lord has not sent to seek you. And when they would say, 'He is not here,' he would take an oath of the kingdom or nation, that they had not found you. ¹¹And now you say, 'Go, tell your lord, "Behold, Elijah is here."' ¹²And as soon as I have gone from you, the Spirit of the LORD will carry you I know not where. And so, when I come and tell Ahab and he cannot find you, he will kill me, although I your servant have feared the LORD from my youth. ¹³Has it not been told my lord what I did when Jezebel killed the prophets of the LORD, how I hid a hundred men of the LORD's prophets by fifties in a cave and fed them with bread and water? ¹⁴And now you say, 'Go, tell your lord, "Behold, Elijah is here"'; and he will kill me." ¹⁵And Elijah said, "As the LORD of hosts lives, before whom I stand, I will surely show myself to him today." ¹⁶So Obadiah went to meet Ahab, and told him. And Ahab went to meet Elijah.

¹⁷When Ahab saw Elijah, Ahab said to him, "Is it you, you troubler of Israel?" ¹⁸And he answered, "I have not troubled Israel, but you have, and your father's house, because you have abandoned the commandments of the LORD and followed the Baals. ¹⁹Now therefore send and gather all Israel to me at Mount Carmel, and the 450 prophets of Baal and the 400 prophets of Asherah, who eat at Jezebel's table."

Elijah confronts the prophets of Baal [18:20–46]. The Israelites and all their prophets gather at Mount Carmel for the showdown, which is an archetypal bet or dare. Elijah begins by telling the people they have a spiritual choice to make. They cannot keep limping between two religious alternatives but must decide once and for all: will they worship the Lord God of Israel or bow down to Baal? The ensuing scene follows the usual conventions of a duel scene, complete with the following features: setting of the ground rules; selection of the field for battle; gathering of spectators in support of each contestant; assembling of the weapons to be used in the combat (in this case a sacrificial one); the contest itself; exchange of taunts; triumph of the victor; and dismissal of the vanquished from the field of combat. The terms of the duel are simple: the god who answers by fire is God. Thus the confrontation will be resolved by the power of prayer. Humanly speaking, the prophets of Baal have every advantage. Elijah sportingly allows them to choose their own bull and build their altar first; then he gives them all day to call on their gods. But it is all to no avail, and the more frenzied they become in their worship, the more scathing the prophet becomes in his satiric attack on Baal, who apparently is too "busy" to answer prayer. To prove the power of God, Elijah drenches his own altar with water. Then he utters a simple prayer, offered to the one true God and based on his covenant promise. When fire falls from heaven, God triumphs, Elijah exults, the people prostrate themselves in worship, and the prophets of Baal are put to the sword (an execution story). Now that the proper sacrifice has been offered to the proper God, God's blessing returns, and in further answer to Elijah's prayers, the drought in Israel ends with a downpour.

²⁰So Ahab sent to all the people of Israel and gathered the prophets together at Mount Carmel. ²¹And Elijah came near to all the people and said, "How long will you go limping between two different opinions? If the LORD is God, follow him; but if

Baal, then follow him." And the people did not answer him a word. ²²Then Elijah said to the people, "I, even I only, am left a prophet of the LORD, but Baal's prophets are 450 men. ²³Let two bulls be given to us, and let them choose one bull for themselves and cut it in pieces and lay it on the wood, but put no fire to it. And I will prepare the other bull and lay it on the wood and put no fire to it. ²⁴And you call upon the name of your god, and I will call upon the name of the LORD, and the God who answers by fire, he is God." And all the people answered, "It is well spoken." ²⁵Then Elijah said to the prophets of Baal, "Choose for yourselves one bull and prepare it first, for you are many, and call upon the name of your god, but put no fire to it." ²⁶And they took the bull that was given them, and they prepared it and called upon the name of Baal from morning until noon, saying, "O Baal, answer us!" But there was no voice, and no one answered. And they limped around the altar that they had made. ²⁷And at noon Elijah mocked them, saying, "Cry aloud, for he is a god. Either he is musing, or he is relieving himself, or he is on a journey, or perhaps he is asleep and must be awakened." ²⁸And they cried aloud and cut themselves after their custom with swords and lances, until the blood gushed out upon them. ²⁹And as midday passed, they raved on until the time of the offering of the oblation, but there was no voice. No one answered; no one paid attention.

³⁰Then Elijah said to all the people, "Come near to me." And all the people came near to him. And he repaired the altar of the LORD that had been thrown down. ³¹Elijah took twelve stones, according to the number of the tribes of the sons of Jacob, to whom the word of the LORD came, saying, "Israel shall be your name," ³²and with the stones he built an altar in the name of the LORD. And he made a trench about the altar, as great as would contain two seahs¹ of seed. ³³And he put the wood in order and cut the bull in pieces and laid it on the wood. And he said, "Fill four jars with water and pour it on the burnt offering and on the wood." ³⁴And he said, "Do it a second time." And they did it a second time. And he said, "Do it a third time." And they did it a third time. ³⁵And the water ran around the altar and filled the trench also with water.

³⁶And at the time of the offering of the oblation, Elijah the prophet came near and said, "O LORD, God of Abraham, Isaac, and Israel, let it be known this day that you are God in Israel, and that I am your servant, and that I have done all these things at your word. ³⁷Answer me, O LORD, answer me, that this people may know that you, O LORD, are God, and that you have turned their hearts back." ³⁸Then the fire of the LORD fell and consumed the burnt offering and the wood and the stones and the dust, and licked up the water that was in the trench. ³⁹And when all the people saw it, they fell on their faces and said, "The LORD, he is God; the LORD, he is God." ⁴⁰And Elijah said to them, "Seize the prophets of Baal; let not one of them escape." And they seized them. And Elijah brought them down to the brook Kishon and slaughtered them there.

⁴¹And Elijah said to Ahab, "Go up, eat and drink, for there is a sound of the rushing of rain." ⁴²So Ahab went up to eat and to drink. And Elijah went up to the top of Mount Carmel. And he bowed himself down on the earth and put his face between his knees. ⁴³And he said to his servant, "Go up now, look toward the sea." And he went up and looked and said, "There is nothing." And he said, "Go again," seven times. ⁴⁴And at the seventh time he said, "Behold, a little cloud like a man's hand is rising from the sea." And he said, "Go up, say to Ahab, 'Prepare your chariot and go down, lest the rain stop you.'" ⁴⁵And in a little while the heavens grew black with clouds and wind, and there was a great rain. And Ahab rode and went to Jezreel. ⁴⁶And the hand

¹ A *seah* was about 7 quarts or 7.3 liters

of the Lord was on Elijah, and he gathered up his garment and ran before Ahab to the entrance of Jezreel.

Elijah in the wilderness [chapter 19]. Elijah comes down from his famous victory on the mountaintop and descends into the valley of despair. Running for his life to escape from Jezebel's murderous pursuit, the prophet comes to the end of himself and asks the Lord to take his life (vv. 1–4). It is clear from his subsequent complaint (v. 14) that he is feeling more than a little sorry for himself, as if he were the only righteous man left in Israel! Yet the Lord reaches down to Elijah in mercy, giving him food and rest and whispering to him with a still, small voice (vv. 5–12). The *travel story that ended with a burnout scene gives way to a *rescue story that is also an encounter story. God still has work for Elijah to do—prophets and kings to anoint who will fulfill his plans for Israel (vv. 13–17). Nor is Elijah God's only man left; there are still seven thousand Israelites (the archetypal faithful remnant) who refuse to bow down to Baal (v. 18). The chapter ends with the call of Elisha to serve as Elijah's assistant. This *call narrative gives assurance that God's work will continue and that the prophet himself will have the help and encouragement he needs to be faithful in his ongoing ministry.

19 Ahab told Jezebel all that Elijah had done, and how he had killed all the prophets with the sword. ²Then Jezebel sent a messenger to Elijah, saying, "So may the gods do to me and more also, if I do not make your life as the life of one of them by this time tomorrow." ³Then he was afraid, and he arose and ran for his life and came to Beersheba, which belongs to Judah, and left his servant there.

⁴But he himself went a day's journey into the wilderness and came and sat down under a broom tree. And he asked that he might die, saying, "It is enough; now, O Lord, take away my life, for I am no better than my fathers." ⁵And he lay down and slept under a broom tree. And behold, an angel touched him and said to him, "Arise and eat." ⁶And he looked, and behold, there was at his head a cake baked on hot stones and a jar of water. And he ate and drank and lay down again. ⁷And the angel of the Lord came again a second time and touched him and said, "Arise and eat, for the journey is too great for you." ⁸And he arose and ate and drank, and went in the strength of that food forty days and forty nights to Horeb, the mount of God.

⁹There he came to a cave and lodged in it. And behold, the word of the Lord came to him, and he said to him, "What are you doing here, Elijah?" ¹⁰He said, "I have been very jealous for the Lord, the God of hosts. For the people of Israel have forsaken your covenant, thrown down your altars, and killed your prophets with the sword, and I, even I only, am left, and they seek my life, to take it away." ¹¹And he said, "Go out and stand on the mount before the Lord." And behold, the Lord passed by, and a great and strong wind tore the mountains and broke in pieces the rocks before the Lord, but the Lord was not in the wind. And after the wind an earthquake, but the Lord was not in the earthquake. ¹²And after the earthquake a fire, but the Lord was not in the fire. And after the fire the sound of a low whisper.¹ ¹³And when Elijah heard it, he wrapped his face in his cloak and went out and stood at the entrance of the cave. And behold, there came a voice to him and said, "What are you doing here, Elijah?" ¹⁴He said, "I have been very jealous for the Lord, the God of hosts. For the people of Israel have forsaken your covenant, thrown down your altars, and killed your prophets with the sword, and I, even I only, am left, and they seek my life, to take

¹ Or a sound, a thin silence

it away." ¹⁵And the LORD said to him, "Go, return on your way to the wilderness of Damascus. And when you arrive, you shall anoint Hazael to be king over Syria. ¹⁶And Jehu the son of Nimshi you shall anoint to be king over Israel, and Elisha the son of Shaphat of Abel-meholah you shall anoint to be prophet in your place. ¹⁷And the one who escapes from the sword of Hazael shall Jehu put to death, and the one who escapes from the sword of Jehu shall Elisha put to death. ¹⁸Yet I will leave seven thousand in Israel, all the knees that have not bowed to Baal, and every mouth that has not kissed him."

¹⁹So he departed from there and found Elisha the son of Shaphat, who was plowing with twelve yoke of oxen in front of him, and he was with the twelfth. Elijah passed by him and cast his cloak upon him. ²⁰And he left the oxen and ran after Elijah and said, "Let me kiss my father and my mother, and then I will follow you." And he said to him, "Go back again, for what have I done to you?" ²¹And he returned from following him and took the yoke of oxen and sacrificed them and boiled their flesh with the yokes of the oxen and gave it to the people, and they ate. Then he arose and went after Elijah and assisted him.

War between Israel and Syria [chapter 20]. The story of the kings continues with a conflict story recounting the warfare between Israel (under Ahab) and Syria (under Ben-hadad). The battle begins with Ahab and Ben-hadad exchanging threats and ultimatums, boasts and counterthreats, including Ahab's classic taunt, "Let not him who straps on his armor boast himself as he who takes it off" (v. 11). There are two battles, one up in the hills (vv. 13–21) and one down on the plain (vv. 22–30). In both cases a prophet promises that God will gain victory for his people in their holy war against his enemies (vv. 13–14, 22, 28). Ben-hadad is captured in battle and ought to be put to death, yet Ahab spares his life, making a covenant with a pagan king rather than keeping covenant with the God of Israel. Ahab's failure to take the appropriate and divinely ordained vengeance is paralleled in a strange encounter in the ministry of an unnamed prophet (vv. 35–41)—a real-life parable that sets the stage for Ahab's condemnation: because Ahab has let a man go whom the Lord had devoted to destruction, his own life will be forfeit (v. 42).

20 Ben-hadad the king of Syria gathered all his army together. Thirty-two kings were with him, and horses and chariots. And he went up and closed in on Samaria and fought against it. ²And he sent messengers into the city to Ahab king of Israel and said to him, "Thus says Ben-hadad: ³'Your silver and your gold are mine; your best wives and children also are mine.'" ⁴And the king of Israel answered, "As you say, my lord, O king, I am yours, and all that I have." ⁵The messengers came again and said, "Thus says Ben-hadad: 'I sent to you, saying, "Deliver to me your silver and your gold, your wives and your children." ⁶Nevertheless I will send my servants to you tomorrow about this time, and they shall search your house and the houses of your servants and lay hands on whatever pleases you and take it away.'"

⁷Then the king of Israel called all the elders of the land and said, "Mark, now, and see how this man is seeking trouble, for he sent to me for my wives and my children, and for my silver and my gold, and I did not refuse him." ⁸And all the elders and all the people said to him, "Do not listen or consent." ⁹So he said to the messengers of Ben-hadad, "Tell my lord the king, 'All that you first demanded of your servant I will

do, but this thing I cannot do.'" And the messengers departed and brought him word again. [10]Ben-hadad sent to him and said, "The gods do so to me and more also, if the dust of Samaria shall suffice for handfuls for all the people who follow me." [11]And the king of Israel answered, "Tell him, 'Let not him who straps on his armor boast himself as he who takes it off.'" [12]When Ben-hadad heard this message as he was drinking with the kings in the booths, he said to his men, "Take your positions." And they took their positions against the city.

[13]And behold, a prophet came near to Ahab king of Israel and said, "Thus says the Lord, Have you seen all this great multitude? Behold, I will give it into your hand this day, and you shall know that I am the Lord." [14]And Ahab said, "By whom?" He said, "Thus says the Lord, By the servants of the governors of the districts." Then he said, "Who shall begin the battle?" He answered, "You." [15]Then he mustered the servants of the governors of the districts, and they were 232. And after them he mustered all the people of Israel, seven thousand.

[16]And they went out at noon, while Ben-hadad was drinking himself drunk in the booths, he and the thirty-two kings who helped him. [17]The servants of the governors of the districts went out first. And Ben-hadad sent out scouts, and they reported to him, "Men are coming out from Samaria." [18]He said, "If they have come out for peace, take them alive. Or if they have come out for war, take them alive."

[19]So these went out of the city, the servants of the governors of the districts and the army that followed them. [20]And each struck down his man. The Syrians fled, and Israel pursued them, but Ben-hadad king of Syria escaped on a horse with horsemen. [21]And the king of Israel went out and struck the horses and chariots, and struck the Syrians with a great blow.

[22]Then the prophet came near to the king of Israel and said to him, "Come, strengthen yourself, and consider well what you have to do, for in the spring the king of Syria will come up against you."

[23]And the servants of the king of Syria said to him, "Their gods are gods of the hills, and so they were stronger than we. But let us fight against them in the plain, and surely we shall be stronger than they. [24]And do this: remove the kings, each from his post, and put commanders in their places, [25]and muster an army like the army that you have lost, horse for horse, and chariot for chariot. Then we will fight against them in the plain, and surely we shall be stronger than they." And he listened to their voice and did so.

[26]In the spring, Ben-hadad mustered the Syrians and went up to Aphek to fight against Israel. [27]And the people of Israel were mustered and were provisioned and went against them. The people of Israel encamped before them like two little flocks of goats, but the Syrians filled the country. [28]And a man of God came near and said to the king of Israel, "Thus says the Lord, 'Because the Syrians have said, "The Lord is a god of the hills but he is not a god of the valleys," therefore I will give all this great multitude into your hand, and you shall know that I am the Lord.'" [29]And they encamped opposite one another seven days. Then on the seventh day the battle was joined. And the people of Israel struck down of the Syrians 100,000 foot soldiers in one day. [30]And the rest fled into the city of Aphek, and the wall fell upon 27,000 men who were left.

Ben-hadad also fled and entered an inner chamber in the city. [31]And his servants said to him, "Behold now, we have heard that the kings of the house of Israel are merciful kings. Let us put sackcloth around our waists and ropes on our heads and go out to the king of Israel. Perhaps he will spare your life." ³²So they tied sackcloth around their waists and put ropes on their heads and went to the king of Israel and said, "Your servant Ben-hadad says, 'Please, let me live.'" And he said, "Does he still live? He is my brother." ³³Now the men were watching for a sign, and they quickly took it up from him and said, "Yes, your brother Ben-hadad." Then he said, "Go and bring him." Then Ben-hadad came out to him, and he caused him to come up into the chariot. ³⁴And Ben-hadad said to him, "The cities that my father took from your father I will restore, and you may establish bazaars for yourself in Damascus, as my father did in Samaria." And Ahab said, "I will let you go on these terms." So he made a covenant with him and let him go.

³⁵And a certain man of the sons of the prophets said to his fellow at the command of the LORD, "Strike me, please." But the man refused to strike him. ³⁶Then he said to him, "Because you have not obeyed the voice of the LORD, behold, as soon as you have gone from me, a lion shall strike you down." And as soon as he had departed from him, a lion met him and struck him down. ³⁷Then he found another man and said, "Strike me, please." And the man struck him—struck him and wounded him. ³⁸So the prophet departed and waited for the king by the way, disguising himself with a bandage over his eyes. ³⁹And as the king passed, he cried to the king and said, "Your servant went out into the midst of the battle, and behold, a soldier turned and brought a man to me and said, 'Guard this man; if by any means he is missing, your life shall be for his life, or else you shall pay a talent¹ of silver.' ⁴⁰And as your servant was busy here and there, he was gone." The king of Israel said to him, "So shall your judgment be; you yourself have decided it." ⁴¹Then he hurried to take the bandage away from his eyes, and the king of Israel recognized him as one of the prophets. ⁴²And he said to him, "Thus says the LORD, 'Because you have let go out of your hand the man whom I had devoted to destruction,² therefore your life shall be for his life, and your people for his people.'" ⁴³And the king of Israel went to his house vexed and sullen and came to Samaria.

The grapes of wrath [chapter 21]. The infamous incident of Ahab's theft of Naboth's vineyard epitomizes the whole spiritual situation in Israel during the days of Ahab and Jezebel. The murder story is told with such deft attention to detail that the characters come alive. Ahab is so keen to get Naboth's vineyard—a choice piece of property near the king's palace—that he is sick with envy. Naboth will not sell, because he knows that the land is a divine inheritance and thus he has a covenant obligation to keep it in the family. Domineering Jezebel steps in with a devious scheme to get her husband what he wants. Paid witnesses bring trumped-up charges against righteous Naboth, and he is wrongfully put to death. But the royal couple's crime will not go unpunished. With the perfect timing of poetic justice, Elijah arrives on the scene just as Ahab is taking possession of Naboth's vineyard. The prophet utters one of the most chilling condemnations anywhere in Scripture: Ahab and Jezebel will be completely cut off. They will not even have the dignity of a decent burial, for the dogs will lick their blood. Surprisingly, the chapter ends with a narrative reversal: Ahab repents in sackcloth and ashes, and the Lord responds by promising not to destroy Ahab's family until after the death of the man himself.

---

¹ A *talent* was about 75 pounds or 34 kilograms ²That is, set apart (devoted) as an offering to the Lord (for destruction)

21 Now Naboth the Jezreelite had a vineyard in Jezreel, beside the palace of Ahab king of Samaria. ²And after this Ahab said to Naboth, "Give me your vineyard, that I may have it for a vegetable garden, because it is near my house, and I will give you a better vineyard for it; or, if it seems good to you, I will give you its value in money." ³But Naboth said to Ahab, "The LORD forbid that I should give you the inheritance of my fathers." ⁴And Ahab went into his house vexed and sullen because of what Naboth the Jezreelite had said to him, for he had said, "I will not give you the inheritance of my fathers." And he lay down on his bed and turned away his face and would eat no food.

⁵But Jezebel his wife came to him and said to him, "Why is your spirit so vexed that you eat no food?" ⁶And he said to her, "Because I spoke to Naboth the Jezreelite and said to him, 'Give me your vineyard for money, or else, if it please you, I will give you another vineyard for it.' And he answered, 'I will not give you my vineyard.'" ⁷And Jezebel his wife said to him, "Do you now govern Israel? Arise and eat bread and let your heart be cheerful; I will give you the vineyard of Naboth the Jezreelite."

⁸So she wrote letters in Ahab's name and sealed them with his seal, and she sent the letters to the elders and the leaders who lived with Naboth in his city. ⁹And she wrote in the letters, "Proclaim a fast, and set Naboth at the head of the people. ¹⁰And set two worthless men opposite him, and let them bring a charge against him, saying, 'You have cursed¹ God and the king.' Then take him out and stone him to death." ¹¹And the men of his city, the elders and the leaders who lived in his city, did as Jezebel had sent word to them. As it was written in the letters that she had sent to them, ¹²they proclaimed a fast and set Naboth at the head of the people. ¹³And the two worthless men came in and sat opposite him. And the worthless men brought a charge against Naboth in the presence of the people, saying, "Naboth cursed God and the king." So they took him outside the city and stoned him to death with stones. ¹⁴Then they sent to Jezebel, saying, "Naboth has been stoned; he is dead."

¹⁵As soon as Jezebel heard that Naboth had been stoned and was dead, Jezebel said to Ahab, "Arise, take possession of the vineyard of Naboth the Jezreelite, which he refused to give you for money, for Naboth is not alive, but dead." ¹⁶And as soon as Ahab heard that Naboth was dead, Ahab arose to go down to the vineyard of Naboth the Jezreelite, to take possession of it.

¹⁷Then the word of the LORD came to Elijah the Tishbite, saying, ¹⁸"Arise, go down to meet Ahab king of Israel, who is in Samaria; behold, he is in the vineyard of Naboth, where he has gone to take possession. ¹⁹And you shall say to him, 'Thus says the LORD, "Have you killed and also taken possession?"' And you shall say to him, 'Thus says the LORD: "In the place where dogs licked up the blood of Naboth shall dogs lick your own blood."'"

²⁰Ahab said to Elijah, "Have you found me, O my enemy?" He answered, "I have found you, because you have sold yourself to do what is evil in the sight of the LORD. ²¹Behold, I will bring disaster upon you. I will utterly burn you up, and will cut off from Ahab every male, bond or free, in Israel. ²²And I will make your house like the house of Jeroboam the son of Nebat, and like the house of Baasha the son of Ahijah, for the anger to which you have provoked me, and because you have made Israel to sin. ²³And of Jezebel the LORD also said, 'The dogs shall eat Jezebel within the walls of Jezreel.' ²⁴Anyone belonging to Ahab who dies in the city the dogs shall eat, and anyone of his who dies in the open country the birds of the heavens shall eat."

---

¹ Hebrew *blessed*; also verse 13

²⁵(There was none who sold himself to do what was evil in the sight of the LORD like Ahab, whom Jezebel his wife incited. ²⁶He acted very abominably in going after idols, as the Amorites had done, whom the LORD cast out before the people of Israel.)

²⁷And when Ahab heard those words, he tore his clothes and put sackcloth on his flesh and fasted and lay in sackcloth and went about dejectedly. ²⁸And the word of the LORD came to Elijah the Tishbite, saying, ²⁹"Have you seen how Ahab has humbled himself before me? Because he has humbled himself before me, I will not bring the disaster in his days; but in his son's days I will bring the disaster upon his house."

The end of Ahab [22:1–40]. In this conflict story, Israel (under Ahab) and Judah (under Jehoshaphat) unite to fight their common enemy, the Syrians. Jehoshaphat is the more godly of the two kings, for he insists that they get a word from the Lord before going into battle and urges Ahab to show proper respect for prophets who speak a true word from God. There is a further contrast in this passage between Zedekiah and the false prophets, who prophesy victory, and Micaiah, who never says what Ahab wants to hear but always says what God tells him to say. Although Micaiah tells the kings to go to battle, he also prophesies that Israel's shepherd (i.e., Ahab) will be struck down. Violent conflict erupts between the prophets over who is telling the truth. Ahab angrily puts Micaiah in prison, but we already sense that all the prophet's words will come true. And they do come true. Although Ahab disguises himself during the ensuing battle, seeking to save himself by his own clever schemes, justice prevails. The king is struck dead by a random arrow, and the blood from his corpse is licked up by wild dogs, fulfilling the word of Micaiah and Elijah, which is also the Word of God.

22 For three years Syria and Israel continued without war. ²But in the third year Jehoshaphat the king of Judah came down to the king of Israel. ³And the king of Israel said to his servants, "Do you know that Ramoth-gilead belongs to us, and we keep quiet and do not take it out of the hand of the king of Syria?" ⁴And he said to Jehoshaphat, "Will you go with me to battle at Ramoth-gilead?" And Jehoshaphat said to the king of Israel, "I am as you are, my people as your people, my horses as your horses."

⁵And Jehoshaphat said to the king of Israel, "Inquire first for the word of the LORD." ⁶Then the king of Israel gathered the prophets together, about four hundred men, and said to them, "Shall I go to battle against Ramoth-gilead, or shall I refrain?" And they said, "Go up, for the Lord will give it into the hand of the king." ⁷But Jehoshaphat said, "Is there not here another prophet of the LORD of whom we may inquire?" ⁸And the king of Israel said to Jehoshaphat, "There is yet one man by whom we may inquire of the LORD, Micaiah the son of Imlah, but I hate him, for he never prophesies good concerning me, but evil." And Jehoshaphat said, "Let not the king say so." ⁹Then the king of Israel summoned an officer and said, "Bring quickly Micaiah the son of Imlah." ¹⁰Now the king of Israel and Jehoshaphat the king of Judah were sitting on their thrones, arrayed in their robes, at the threshing floor at the entrance of the gate of Samaria, and all the prophets were prophesying before them. ¹¹And Zedekiah the son of Chenaanah made for himself horns of iron and said, "Thus says the LORD, 'With these you shall push the Syrians until they are destroyed.'" ¹²And all the prophets prophesied so and said, "Go up to Ramoth-gilead and triumph; the LORD will give it into the hand of the king."

¹³And the messenger who went to summon Micaiah said to him, "Behold, the words of the prophets with one accord are favorable to the king. Let your word be like the word of one of them, and speak favorably." ¹⁴But Micaiah said, "As the LORD lives, what the LORD says to me, that I will speak." ¹⁵And when he had come to the king, the king said to him, "Micaiah, shall we go to Ramoth-gilead to battle, or shall we refrain?" And he answered him, "Go up and triumph; the LORD will give it into the hand of the king." ¹⁶But the king said to him, "How many times shall I make you swear that you speak to me nothing but the truth in the name of the LORD?" ¹⁷And he said, "I saw all Israel scattered on the mountains, as sheep that have no shepherd. And the LORD said, 'These have no master; let each return to his home in peace.'" ¹⁸And the king of Israel said to Jehoshaphat, "Did I not tell you that he would not prophesy good concerning me, but evil?" ¹⁹And Micaiah said, "Therefore hear the word of the LORD: I saw the LORD sitting on his throne, and all the host of heaven standing beside him on his right hand and on his left; ²⁰and the LORD said, 'Who will entice Ahab, that he may go up and fall at Ramoth-gilead?' And one said one thing, and another said another. ²¹Then a spirit came forward and stood before the LORD, saying, 'I will entice him.' ²²And the LORD said to him, 'By what means?' And he said, 'I will go out, and will be a lying spirit in the mouth of all his prophets.' And he said, 'You are to entice him, and you shall succeed; go out and do so.' ²³Now therefore behold, the LORD has put a lying spirit in the mouth of all these your prophets; the LORD has declared disaster for you."

²⁴Then Zedekiah the son of Chenaanah came near and struck Micaiah on the cheek and said, "How did the Spirit of the LORD go from me to speak to you?" ²⁵And Micaiah said, "Behold, you shall see on that day when you go into an inner chamber to hide yourself." ²⁶And the king of Israel said, "Seize Micaiah, and take him back to Amon the governor of the city and to Joash the king's son, ²⁷and say, 'Thus says the king, "Put this fellow in prison and feed him meager rations of bread and water, until I come in peace."'" ²⁸And Micaiah said, "If you return in peace, the LORD has not spoken by me." And he said, "Hear, all you peoples!"

²⁹So the king of Israel and Jehoshaphat the king of Judah went up to Ramoth-gilead. ³⁰And the king of Israel said to Jehoshaphat, "I will disguise myself and go into battle, but you wear your robes." And the king of Israel disguised himself and went into battle. ³¹Now the king of Syria had commanded the thirty-two captains of his chariots, "Fight with neither small nor great, but only with the king of Israel." ³²And when the captains of the chariots saw Jehoshaphat, they said, "It is surely the king of Israel." So they turned to fight against him. And Jehoshaphat cried out. ³³And when the captains of the chariots saw that it was not the king of Israel, they turned back from pursuing him. ³⁴But a certain man drew his bow at random¹ and struck the king of Israel between the scale armor and the breastplate. Therefore he said to the driver of his chariot, "Turn around and carry me out of the battle, for I am wounded." ³⁵And the battle continued that day, and the king was propped up in his chariot facing the Syrians, until at evening he died. And the blood of the wound flowed into the bottom of the chariot. ³⁶And about sunset a cry went through the army, "Every man to his city, and every man to his country!"

³⁷So the king died, and was brought to Samaria. And they buried the king in Samaria. ³⁸And they washed the chariot by the pool of Samaria, and the dogs licked up his blood, and the prostitutes washed themselves in it, according to the word of

¹ Hebrew *in his innocence*

the LORD that he had spoken. [39]Now the rest of the acts of Ahab and all that he did, and the ivory house that he built and all the cities that he built, are they not written in the Book of the Chronicles of the Kings of Israel? [40]So Ahab slept with his fathers, and Ahaziah his son reigned in his place.

Two more kings [22:41–53]. The book of 1 Kings comes to a close with brief court narratives of one more good king of Judah (Jehoshaphat, vv. 41–50) and one more bad king of Israel (Ahaziah, vv. 51–53). But the story of the two kingdoms will continue with the book of 2 Kings. This concluding unit is a helpful epitome of all that has preceded, comprising the following elements that have dominated the book as a whole: a court history of kings; coverage of both Judah and Israel; application of a spiritual criterion for kingly success, with kings judged as doing either right or wrong, either good or evil in the sight of the Lord.

[41]Jehoshaphat the son of Asa began to reign over Judah in the fourth year of Ahab king of Israel. [42]Jehoshaphat was thirty-five years old when he began to reign, and he reigned twenty-five years in Jerusalem. His mother's name was Azubah the daughter of Shilhi. [43]He walked in all the way of Asa his father. He did not turn aside from it, doing what was right in the sight of the LORD. Yet the high places were not taken away, and the people still sacrificed and made offerings on the high places. [44]Jehoshaphat also made peace with the king of Israel.

[45]Now the rest of the acts of Jehoshaphat, and his might that he showed, and how he warred, are they not written in the Book of the Chronicles of the Kings of Judah? [46]And from the land he exterminated the remnant of the male cult prostitutes who remained in the days of his father Asa.

[47]There was no king in Edom; a deputy was king. [48]Jehoshaphat made ships of Tarshish to go to Ophir for gold, but they did not go, for the ships were wrecked at Ezion-geber. [49]Then Ahaziah the son of Ahab said to Jehoshaphat, "Let my servants go with your servants in the ships," but Jehoshaphat was not willing. [50]And Jehoshaphat slept with his fathers and was buried with his fathers in the city of David his father, and Jehoram his son reigned in his place.

[51]Ahaziah the son of Ahab began to reign over Israel in Samaria in the seventeenth year of Jehoshaphat king of Judah, and he reigned two years over Israel. [52]He did what was evil in the sight of the LORD and walked in the way of his father and in the way of his mother and in the way of Jeroboam the son of Nebat, who made Israel to sin. [53]He served Baal and worshiped him and provoked the LORD, the God of Israel, to anger in every way that his father had done.

2 KINGS

The book at a glance. 25 chapters, 719 verses. The history in 2 Kings picks up where 1 Kings left off—in the middle of the account of the two kingdoms (Israel and Judah) that were formed when the united kingdom was divided after Solomon died. If 1 Kings was the decline of the divided kingdom, then 2 Kings is the fall, because by the end of the book both Israel and Judah are in captivity (to Assyria and Babylon, respectively). The book's lengthy cast of characters consists mainly of kings, as the title suggests, but there are also many prophets. The four main characters are the mighty prophet Elisha and three noble kings: Joash, Hezekiah, and Josiah. The spiritual leadership of these godly men alerts us to a recurring pattern in 1 and 2 Kings: formation, deformation, and reformation. The holy kingdom that was formed on the basis of God's covenant with David and the rest of his royal line is constantly deformed by wicked kings who lead the people of God into idolatry—the worship of other gods. From time to time, however, there is a countermovement in the direction of spiritual renewal, under the ministry of God's word and through the initiative of godly rulers who lead the people in faith and repentance. Nevertheless, the general movement of the book is a downward spiral toward spiritual decline, as the historian reports two national disasters: Israel's captivity and then Judah's. Like its prequel (the book of 1 Kings), the book of 2 Kings shows what happens when people, kings, and nations rebel against God.

▌**Genres.** Nearly everything that was said about 1 Kings as historical *narrative also applies to 2 Kings, for they are simply two volumes of one book. Second Kings is a record of monarchical succession in the divided kingdom, generally telling when and how each king came to the throne of Israel or Judah, explaining in more or less detail what happened during his reign, giving a spiritual assessment of his leadership, and indicating how he died. Since the general shape of the narrative is tragic, 2 Kings can be read as a national *tragedy: through its own sinful choices, a great nation falls into wrack and ruin. Some of the episodes in the book are narratives in their own right, and they fall into a number of subgenres, such as *confrontation narrative, medical case, *ascension story, *succession story, recovery story, *battle story, *hero story, *miracle story, *resurrection narrative, murder story, *revenge story, prayer, *prophecy (in the form of *poetry), *reformation story, and captivity narrative. Far from simply giving us the facts, the historian has told us what happened with a reporter's eye for the significant detail, a storyteller's flair for the dramatic, and a pastor's heart

Passage	Content	Political Situation	Prophetic Ministry
1:1–18	Elijah prophesies against Ahaziah	Divided Kingdom: Israel	Elisha succeeds Elijah
2:1–25	Elijah rides up into heaven		
3:1–27	Moab rebels against Israel		
4:1–8:15	Elisha works wonders		
8:16–29	Jehoram and Ahaziah (Judah)	Divided Kingdom: Israel and Judah	Elisha
9:1–10:36	Jehu's bloody reign (Israel)		
11:1–12:21	Joash repairs the temple (Judah)		
13:1–16:20	Twelve kings of Israel and Judah		
17:1–41	Assyria captures Israel		
18:1–20:21	Hezekiah's rescue and recovery	Continuing Kingdom: Judah	Isaiah and other prophets, as well as Huldah the prophetess
21:1–26	The worst kings of Judah		
22:1–23:30	Josiah's reformation		
23:31–24:20	The last free kings of Judah		
25:1–26	Babylon captures Judah		
25:27–30	Epilogue: David's son survives		

for teaching people the difference between right and wrong. (For more information on items accompanied by an asterisk, see the glossary at the back of this Bible.)

▋ **Unifying elements.** The book is mainly unified by its historical account of the kings and kingdoms of Israel and Judah, with their capital cities in Samaria and Jerusalem, respectively. Although the narrative sometimes switches from one kingdom to the other, the order is generally chronological, covering some three hundred years of royal history. Since there are nearly thirty kings in all, it is possible to get lost in the details. However, the general pattern of reformation, deformation, and decline gives a strong sense of unity to the narrative as a whole. The occasional ministry of prophets from Elijah to Elisha to Isaiah and others is another unifying element in the book. So is the obvious parallel between Israel's captivity by the Assyrians (chapter 17) and Judah's captivity by the Babylonians (chapters 24–25). Pairing these two national catastrophes in one book gives a heightened sense of tragic loss.

▋ **Inferred literary intentions.** The book is designed to achieve the following literary purposes:

- record the royal history of Israel and Judah

- explain (especially to the righteous remnant of the captives in Babylon) how both nations ended up in captivity, by documenting their rebellion against God

- encourage spiritual renewal by recounting the memorable ministries of wonder workers like Elisha and reformers like Josiah

- use the resources of storytelling to make the history of God's people come alive
- present a cast of characters who are memorable for their positive or negative response to God
- show the difference between turning to God and turning away from God in a time of medical or military crisis
- use positive and negative outcomes to help teach readers to make the right moral choices
- give hope that God will continue to keep his royal promise to David and all the people of God

Theological themes. (1) Sin and judgment: as in 1 Kings, God rewards obedience and punishes disobedience, with the captivities in Assyria and Babylon serving as warnings of the final judgment. (2) Repentance and faith: kings and other people who repent of their sins and trust in God will experience healing and blessing. (3) Revelation: the prophecies that God has revealed in his word by the prophets always come true. (4) Reformation: where his word is obeyed and his worship is honored, God brings new spiritual blessing to his people.

The book of 2 Kings as a chapter in the master story of the Bible. Second Kings records an important segment of the history of the people of God, giving special attention to the successes and failures of the OT kings. Whether by positive or negative example, the best and worst of kings point to the need for and the blessings of the kingship of Christ. In this respect, the ending of the book is especially significant because it shows that the royal line of David will continue, giving hope that God's covenant promise of an eternal kingdom will still be fulfilled.

Elijah curses Ahaziah on his deathbed [chapter 1]. The book begins with a mishap in the form of a house accident: Ahaziah, who was first introduced as an evil king of Israel at the end of 1 Kings, has fallen from the second story of his palace. Desperate to know whether he will live or die, the king sends messengers to consult one of the demon-gods of the Canaanites (vv. 1–2). With his usual and supernatural ability to be in the right place at the right time, Elijah meets the messengers on their way. In addition to telling them that Ahaziah will die, he condemns the king for going to a false god rather than consulting the true prophet in Israel (vv. 3–4). In a story that follows a familiar narrative pattern of threefold repetition, the king sends out three successive parties of fifty soldiers to seize Elijah and bring him back to the palace. The first two parties are consumed with fire before they can make the arrest (vv. 9–12), thereby proving that Elijah really is the prophet of God. But the third time proves to be the charm, because the third captain is wise enough to acknowledge Elijah as a mighty man of God and to beg for mercy (vv. 13–15). The effect of the episode as a whole is to confirm the power of Elijah as the prophet of God and to condemn Ahaziah or anyone else who tries to find out the future by any other means than the revealed word of God. In view of the link that the narrative draws between Ahaziah's nonrecovery from his accident and the sin of consulting a pagan god (v. 16), the entire story told in this chapter is an example of *poetic

justice (vice punished). *Irony pervades the episode as well: Ahaziah goes to drastic measures in order to get the message that he will die.

1 After the death of Ahab, Moab rebelled against Israel. ²Now Ahaziah fell through the lattice in his upper chamber in Samaria, and lay sick; so he sent messengers, telling them, "Go, inquire of Baal-zebub, the god of Ekron, whether I shall recover from this sickness." ³But the angel of the LORD said to Elijah the Tishbite, "Arise, go up to meet the messengers of the king of Samaria, and say to them, 'Is it because there is no God in Israel that you are going to inquire of Baal-zebub, the god of Ekron? ⁴Now therefore thus says the LORD, You shall not come down from the bed to which you have gone up, but you shall surely die.'" So Elijah went.

⁵The messengers returned to the king, and he said to them, "Why have you returned?" ⁶And they said to him, "There came a man to meet us, and said to us, 'Go back to the king who sent you, and say to him, Thus says the LORD, Is it because there is no God in Israel that you are sending to inquire of Baal-zebub, the god of Ekron? Therefore you shall not come down from the bed to which you have gone up, but you shall surely die.'" ⁷He said to them, "What kind of man was he who came to meet you and told you these things?" ⁸They answered him, "He wore a garment of hair, with a belt of leather about his waist." And he said, "It is Elijah the Tishbite."

⁹Then the king sent to him a captain of fifty men with his fifty. He went up to Elijah, who was sitting on the top of a hill, and said to him, "O man of God, the king says, 'Come down.'" ¹⁰But Elijah answered the captain of fifty, "If I am a man of God, let fire come down from heaven and consume you and your fifty." Then fire came down from heaven and consumed him and his fifty.

¹¹Again the king sent to him another captain of fifty men with his fifty. And he answered and said to him, "O man of God, this is the king's order, 'Come down quickly!'" ¹²But Elijah answered them, "If I am a man of God, let fire come down from heaven and consume you and your fifty." Then the fire of God came down from heaven and consumed him and his fifty.

¹³Again the king sent the captain of a third fifty with his fifty. And the third captain of fifty went up and came and fell on his knees before Elijah and entreated him, "O man of God, please let my life, and the life of these fifty servants of yours, be precious in your sight. ¹⁴Behold, fire came down from heaven and consumed the two former captains of fifty men with their fifties, but now let my life be precious in your sight." ¹⁵Then the angel of the LORD said to Elijah, "Go down with him; do not be afraid of him." So he arose and went down with him to the king ¹⁶and said to him, "Thus says the LORD, 'Because you have sent messengers to inquire of Baal-zebub, the god of Ekron—is it because there is no God in Israel to inquire of his word?—therefore you shall not come down from the bed to which you have gone up, but you shall surely die.'"

¹⁷So he died according to the word of the LORD that Elijah had spoken. Jehoram became king in his place in the second year of Jehoram the son of Jehoshaphat, king of Judah, because Ahaziah had no son. ¹⁸Now the rest of the acts of Ahaziah that he did, are they not written in the Book of the Chronicles of the Kings of Israel?

Chariots of fire [chapter 2]. This famous account is both an ascension narrative and a succession story. The story is built around the pattern of three-plus-one, as a common set of ingredients appears four times but with a crucial change introduced the fourth time (Elijah is taken to heaven in the fourth occurrence). The drama builds as successive groups of students from Elijah's seminary prophesy that the time has come for their master to go home to God (vv. 3, 5), which he does in a miraculous whirlwind of fire and angels (vv. 11–12). But the emphasis falls on Elisha as the man anointed to become Elijah's successor as a prophet in Israel: his commitment to stay by his master's side, his request for a full inheritance of his master's spirit, and his witness to his master's ascension (vv. 6–10). God proves that Elisha has inherited Elijah's mantle by enabling him to perform for his first miracle (see *miracle story in the glossary) the same sign that Elijah performed for his last miracle: the parting of the River Jordan. The validity of Elisha's ministry is further confirmed by the acclamation of the other prophets (vv. 15–18), by his miraculous sign of healing a spring of water (vv. 19–22), and by the revenge that God's two bears take on a gang of boys who dare to mock Elisha for his hair loss (vv. 23–25). In the Bible, miracles cluster in four crucial eras (the exodus, the prophets, the life of Christ, the early church); the spectacular events narrated in this chapter signal that the action occurs at an epoch-making moment in Israelite history.

2 Now when the LORD was about to take Elijah up to heaven by a whirlwind, Elijah and Elisha were on their way from Gilgal. ²And Elijah said to Elisha, "Please stay here, for the LORD has sent me as far as Bethel." But Elisha said, "As the LORD lives, and as you yourself live, I will not leave you." So they went down to Bethel. ³And the sons of the prophets who were in Bethel came out to Elisha and said to him, "Do you know that today the LORD will take away your master from over you?" And he said, "Yes, I know it; keep quiet."

⁴Elijah said to him, "Elisha, please stay here, for the LORD has sent me to Jericho." But he said, "As the LORD lives, and as you yourself live, I will not leave you." So they came to Jericho. ⁵The sons of the prophets who were at Jericho drew near to Elisha and said to him, "Do you know that today the LORD will take away your master from over you?" And he answered, "Yes, I know it; keep quiet."

⁶Then Elijah said to him, "Please stay here, for the LORD has sent me to the Jordan." But he said, "As the LORD lives, and as you yourself live, I will not leave you." So the two of them went on. ⁷Fifty men of the sons of the prophets also went and stood at some distance from them, as they both were standing by the Jordan. ⁸Then Elijah took his cloak and rolled it up and struck the water, and the water was parted to the one side and to the other, till the two of them could go over on dry ground.

⁹When they had crossed, Elijah said to Elisha, "Ask what I shall do for you, before I am taken from you." And Elisha said, "Please let there be a double portion of your spirit on me." ¹⁰And he said, "You have asked a hard thing; yet, if you see me as I am being taken from you, it shall be so for you, but if you do not see me, it shall not be so." ¹¹And as they still went on and talked, behold, chariots of fire and horses of fire separated the two of them. And Elijah went up by a whirlwind into heaven. ¹²And Elisha saw it and he cried, "My father, my father! The chariots of Israel and its horsemen!" And he saw him no more.

Then he took hold of his own clothes and tore them in two pieces. ¹³And he took up the cloak of Elijah that had fallen from him and went back and stood on the bank of the Jordan. ¹⁴Then he took the cloak of Elijah that had fallen from him and struck the water, saying, "Where is the LORD, the God of Elijah?" And when he had struck the water, the water was parted to the one side and to the other, and Elisha went over.

¹⁵Now when the sons of the prophets who were at Jericho saw him opposite them, they said, "The spirit of Elijah rests on Elisha." And they came to meet him and bowed to the ground before him. ¹⁶And they said to him, "Behold now, there are with your servants fifty strong men. Please let them go and seek your master. It may be that the Spirit of the LORD has caught him up and cast him upon some mountain or into some valley." And he said, "You shall not send." ¹⁷But when they urged him till he was ashamed, he said, "Send." They sent therefore fifty men. And for three days they sought him but did not find him. ¹⁸And they came back to him while he was staying at Jericho, and he said to them, "Did I not say to you, 'Do not go'?"

¹⁹Now the men of the city said to Elisha, "Behold, the situation of this city is pleasant, as my lord sees, but the water is bad, and the land is unfruitful." ²⁰He said, "Bring me a new bowl, and put salt in it." So they brought it to him. ²¹Then he went to the spring of water and threw salt in it and said, "Thus says the LORD, I have healed this water; from now on neither death nor miscarriage shall come from it." ²²So the water has been healed to this day, according to the word that Elisha spoke.

²³He went up from there to Bethel, and while he was going up on the way, some small boys came out of the city and jeered at him, saying, "Go up, you baldhead! Go up, you baldhead!" ²⁴And he turned around, and when he saw them, he cursed them in the name of the LORD. And two she-bears came out of the woods and tore forty-two of the boys. ²⁵From there he went on to Mount Carmel, and from there he returned to Samaria.

The Moabite rebellion [chapter 3]. Elisha's next appearance is on the international stage. When the Moabites rebel against Israel, they face the combined strength of Israel (under Jehoram) and Judah (under Jehoshaphat). To his credit, Jehoshaphat seeks the Lord's will for the battle (vv. 10–12). Serving as Elijah's successor, Elisha prophesies a miraculous flood, which the Moabites subsequently mistake for rivers of the blood of their enemies, to their own destruction. This episode is a battle story with a *reversal that results from a case of mistaken identity.

3 In the eighteenth year of Jehoshaphat king of Judah, Jehoram the son of Ahab became king over Israel in Samaria, and he reigned twelve years. ²He did what was evil in the sight of the LORD, though not like his father and mother, for he put away the pillar of Baal that his father had made. ³Nevertheless, he clung to the sin of Jeroboam the son of Nebat, which he made Israel to sin; he did not depart from it.

⁴Now Mesha king of Moab was a sheep breeder, and he had to deliver to the king of Israel 100,000 lambs and the wool of 100,000 rams. ⁵But when Ahab died, the king of Moab rebelled against the king of Israel. ⁶So King Jehoram marched out of Samaria at that time and mustered all Israel. ⁷And he went and sent word to Jehoshaphat king of Judah, "The king of Moab has rebelled against me. Will you go with me to battle against Moab?" And he said, "I will go. I am as you are, my people as your people, my horses as your horses." ⁸Then he said, "By which way shall we march?" Jehoram answered, "By the way of the wilderness of Edom."

⁹So the king of Israel went with the king of Judah and the king of Edom. And when they had made a circuitous march of seven days, there was no water for the army or for the animals that followed them. ¹⁰Then the king of Israel said, "Alas! The LORD has called these three kings to give them into the hand of Moab." ¹¹And Jehoshaphat said, "Is there no prophet of the LORD here, through whom we may inquire of the LORD?" Then one of the king of Israel's servants answered, "Elisha the son of Shaphat is here, who poured water on the hands of Elijah." ¹²And Jehoshaphat said, "The word of the LORD is with him." So the king of Israel and Jehoshaphat and the king of Edom went down to him.

¹³And Elisha said to the king of Israel, "What have I to do with you? Go to the prophets of your father and to the prophets of your mother." But the king of Israel said to him, "No; it is the LORD who has called these three kings to give them into the hand of Moab." ¹⁴And Elisha said, "As the LORD of hosts lives, before whom I stand, were it not that I have regard for Jehoshaphat the king of Judah, I would neither look at you nor see you. ¹⁵But now bring me a musician." And when the musician played, the hand of the LORD came upon him. ¹⁶And he said, "Thus says the LORD, 'I will make this dry streambed full of pools.' ¹⁷For thus says the LORD, 'You shall not see wind or rain, but that streambed shall be filled with water, so that you shall drink, you, your livestock, and your animals.' ¹⁸This is a light thing in the sight of the LORD. He will also give the Moabites into your hand, ¹⁹and you shall attack every fortified city and every choice city, and shall fell every good tree and stop up all springs of water and ruin every good piece of land with stones." ²⁰The next morning, about the time of offering the sacrifice, behold, water came from the direction of Edom, till the country was filled with water.

²¹When all the Moabites heard that the kings had come up to fight against them, all who were able to put on armor, from the youngest to the oldest, were called out and were drawn up at the border. ²²And when they rose early in the morning and the sun shone on the water, the Moabites saw the water opposite them as red as blood. ²³And they said, "This is blood; the kings have surely fought together and struck one another down. Now then, Moab, to the spoil!" ²⁴But when they came to the camp of Israel, the Israelites rose and struck the Moabites, till they fled before them. And they went forward, striking the Moabites as they went.¹ ²⁵And they overthrew the cities, and on every good piece of land every man threw a stone until it was covered. They stopped every spring of water and felled all the good trees, till only its stones were left in Kir-hareseth, and the slingers surrounded and attacked it. ²⁶When the king of Moab saw that the battle was going against him, he took with him 700 swordsmen to break through, opposite the king of Edom, but they could not. ²⁷Then he took his oldest son who was to reign in his place and offered him for a burnt offering on the wall. And there came great wrath against Israel. And they withdrew from him and returned to their own land.

The miracle worker [chapter 4]. The hero stories of Elisha continue with a series of miraculous signs: the widow's oil (vv. 1–7), the gift of a son for a barren Shunammite woman (vv. 8–17), the son brought back to life (vv. 18–37), the removal of death from a pot of stew (vv. 38–41), and the feeding of the one hundred (vv. 42–44). By performing the same kinds of miracles that his master once performed (provision, resurrection,

---

¹ Septuagint; the meaning of the Hebrew is uncertain

healing), Elisha confirms that he has indeed inherited the spirit of Elijah. This opens up a fruitful line of messianic interpretation. If Elijah serves as a type of John the Baptist (see Matt. 17:12; Luke 1:17)—the forerunner of the Christ—then Elisha's miracles point to the majesty of Jesus himself. Each miracle calls for a response of faith, and together these miracles confirm the truth of the word that God spoke through his servant Elisha.

4 Now the wife of one of the sons of the prophets cried to Elisha, "Your servant my husband is dead, and you know that your servant feared the LORD, but the creditor has come to take my two children to be his slaves." ²And Elisha said to her, "What shall I do for you? Tell me; what have you in the house?" And she said, "Your servant has nothing in the house except a jar of oil." ³Then he said, "Go outside, borrow vessels from all your neighbors, empty vessels and not too few. ⁴Then go in and shut the door behind yourself and your sons and pour into all these vessels. And when one is full, set it aside." ⁵So she went from him and shut the door behind herself and her sons. And as she poured they brought the vessels to her. ⁶When the vessels were full, she said to her son, "Bring me another vessel." And he said to her, "There is not another." Then the oil stopped flowing. ⁷She came and told the man of God, and he said, "Go, sell the oil and pay your debts, and you and your sons can live on the rest."

⁸One day Elisha went on to Shunem, where a wealthy woman lived, who urged him to eat some food. So whenever he passed that way, he would turn in there to eat food. ⁹And she said to her husband, "Behold now, I know that this is a holy man of God who is continually passing our way. ¹⁰Let us make a small room on the roof with walls and put there for him a bed, a table, a chair, and a lamp, so that whenever he comes to us, he can go in there."

¹¹One day he came there, and he turned into the chamber and rested there. ¹²And he said to Gehazi his servant, "Call this Shunammite." When he had called her, she stood before him. ¹³And he said to him, "Say now to her, 'See, you have taken all this trouble for us; what is to be done for you? Would you have a word spoken on your behalf to the king or to the commander of the army?'" She answered, "I dwell among my own people." ¹⁴And he said, "What then is to be done for her?" Gehazi answered, "Well, she has no son, and her husband is old." ¹⁵He said, "Call her." And when he had called her, she stood in the doorway. ¹⁶And he said, "At this season, about this time next year, you shall embrace a son." And she said, "No, my lord, O man of God; do not lie to your servant." ¹⁷But the woman conceived, and she bore a son about that time the following spring, as Elisha had said to her.

¹⁸When the child had grown, he went out one day to his father among the reapers. ¹⁹And he said to his father, "Oh, my head, my head!" The father said to his servant, "Carry him to his mother." ²⁰And when he had lifted him and brought him to his mother, the child sat on her lap till noon, and then he died. ²¹And she went up and laid him on the bed of the man of God and shut the door behind him and went out. ²²Then she called to her husband and said, "Send me one of the servants and one of the donkeys, that I may quickly go to the man of God and come back again." ²³And he said, "Why will you go to him today? It is neither new moon nor Sabbath." She said, "All is well." ²⁴Then she saddled the donkey, and she said to her servant, "Urge the

animal on; do not slacken the pace for me unless I tell you." ²⁵So she set out and came to the man of God at Mount Carmel.

When the man of God saw her coming, he said to Gehazi his servant, "Look, there is the Shunammite. ²⁶Run at once to meet her and say to her, 'Is all well with you? Is all well with your husband? Is all well with the child?'" And she answered, "All is well." ²⁷And when she came to the mountain to the man of God, she caught hold of his feet. And Gehazi came to push her away. But the man of God said, "Leave her alone, for she is in bitter distress, and the Lord has hidden it from me and has not told me." ²⁸Then she said, "Did I ask my lord for a son? Did I not say, 'Do not deceive me?'" ²⁹He said to Gehazi, "Tie up your garment and take my staff in your hand and go. If you meet anyone, do not greet him, and if anyone greets you, do not reply. And lay my staff on the face of the child." ³⁰Then the mother of the child said, "As the Lord lives and as you yourself live, I will not leave you." So he arose and followed her. ³¹Gehazi went on ahead and laid the staff on the face of the child, but there was no sound or sign of life. Therefore he returned to meet him and told him, "The child has not awakened."

³²When Elisha came into the house, he saw the child lying dead on his bed. ³³So he went in and shut the door behind the two of them and prayed to the Lord. ³⁴Then he went up and lay on the child, putting his mouth on his mouth, his eyes on his eyes, and his hands on his hands. And as he stretched himself upon him, the flesh of the child became warm. ³⁵Then he got up again and walked once back and forth in the house, and went up and stretched himself upon him. The child sneezed seven times, and the child opened his eyes. ³⁶Then he summoned Gehazi and said, "Call this Shunammite." So he called her. And when she came to him, he said, "Pick up your son." ³⁷She came and fell at his feet, bowing to the ground. Then she picked up her son and went out.

³⁸And Elisha came again to Gilgal when there was a famine in the land. And as the sons of the prophets were sitting before him, he said to his servant, "Set on the large pot, and boil stew for the sons of the prophets." ³⁹One of them went out into the field to gather herbs, and found a wild vine and gathered from it his lap full of wild gourds, and came and cut them up into the pot of stew, not knowing what they were. ⁴⁰And they poured out some for the men to eat. But while they were eating of the stew, they cried out, "O man of God, there is death in the pot!" And they could not eat it. ⁴¹He said, "Then bring flour." And he threw it into the pot and said, "Pour some out for the men, that they may eat." And there was no harm in the pot.

⁴²A man came from Baal-shalishah, bringing the man of God bread of the first-fruits, twenty loaves of barley and fresh ears of grain in his sack. And Elisha said, "Give to the men, that they may eat." ⁴³But his servant said, "How can I set this before a hundred men?" So he repeated, "Give them to the men, that they may eat, for thus says the Lord, 'They shall eat and have some left.'" ⁴⁴So he set it before them. And they ate and had some left, according to the word of the Lord.

A tale of two lepers [chapter 5]. The story of noble Naaman and greedy Gehazi is one of the Bible's small masterpieces, told in the grand style. The plot turns on poetic justice, as virtuous behavior is rewarded and evil behavior is punished. Desperate enough to act on a tip he receives from one of his Jewish slave girls, a Syrian general (Naaman) goes to Israel, looking to find the cure for his leprosy. Elisha tells the man to perform a simple rite of cleansing—so simple, in fact, that at first Naaman thinks it is beneath his dignity to bathe seven times in the Jordan River, as Elisha instructs. But in the end he complies, and his skin becomes as soft and pure as a baby's. The interethnic tensions that have been simmering throughout the passage boil to the surface when Elisha refuses to accept any remuneration for God's gracious work in the life of one Israel's traditional enemies. Greedy for gain, Elisha's servant Gehazi comes up with a clever scheme for getting something from the general before he goes back to Syria. But Elisha knows about the whole thing and, in an irony of ironies, curses Gehazi with the very disease that once ailed Naaman.

5 Naaman, commander of the army of the king of Syria, was a great man with his master and in high favor, because by him the LORD had given victory to Syria. He was a mighty man of valor, but he was a leper.[1] [2]Now the Syrians on one of their raids had carried off a little girl from the land of Israel, and she worked in the service of Naaman's wife. [3]She said to her mistress, "Would that my lord were with the prophet who is in Samaria! He would cure him of his leprosy." [4]So Naaman went in and told his lord, "Thus and so spoke the girl from the land of Israel." [5]And the king of Syria said, "Go now, and I will send a letter to the king of Israel."

So he went, taking with him ten talents of silver, six thousand shekels[2] of gold, and ten changes of clothing. [6]And he brought the letter to the king of Israel, which read, "When this letter reaches you, know that I have sent to you Naaman my servant, that you may cure him of his leprosy." [7]And when the king of Israel read the letter, he tore his clothes and said, "Am I God, to kill and to make alive, that this man sends word to me to cure a man of his leprosy? Only consider, and see how he is seeking a quarrel with me."

[8]But when Elisha the man of God heard that the king of Israel had torn his clothes, he sent to the king, saying, "Why have you torn your clothes? Let him come now to me, that he may know that there is a prophet in Israel." [9]So Naaman came with his horses and chariots and stood at the door of Elisha's house. [10]And Elisha sent a messenger to him, saying, "Go and wash in the Jordan seven times, and your flesh shall be restored, and you shall be clean." [11]But Naaman was angry and went away, saying, "Behold, I thought that he would surely come out to me and stand and call upon the name of the LORD his God, and wave his hand over the place and cure the leper. [12]Are not Abana[3] and Pharpar, the rivers of Damascus, better than all the waters of Israel? Could I not wash in them and be clean?" So he turned and went away in a rage. [13]But his servants came near and said to him, "My father, it is a great word the prophet has spoken to you; will you not do it? Has he actually said to you, 'Wash, and be clean'?" [14]So he went down and dipped himself seven times in the Jordan, according to the word of the man of God, and his flesh was restored like the flesh of a little child, and he was clean.

[15]Then he returned to the man of God, he and all his company, and he came and stood before him. And he said, "Behold, I know that there is no God in all the earth but in Israel; so accept now a present from your servant." [16]But he said, "As the LORD lives, before whom I stand, I will receive none." And he urged him to take it, but he refused. [17]Then Naaman said, "If not, please let there be given to your servant two mules' load

[1] *Leprosy* was a term for several skin diseases; see Leviticus 13 [2] A *talent* was about 75 pounds or 34 kilograms; a *shekel* was about 2/5 ounce or 11 grams [3] Or *Amana*

of earth, for from now on your servant will not offer burnt offering or sacrifice to any god but the LORD. ¹⁸In this matter may the LORD pardon your servant: when my master goes into the house of Rimmon to worship there, leaning on my arm, and I bow myself in the house of Rimmon, when I bow myself in the house of Rimmon, the LORD pardon your servant in this matter." ¹⁹He said to him, "Go in peace."

But when Naaman had gone from him a short distance, ²⁰Gehazi, the servant of Elisha the man of God, said, "See, my master has spared this Naaman the Syrian, in not accepting from his hand what he brought. As the LORD lives, I will run after him and get something from him." ²¹So Gehazi followed Naaman. And when Naaman saw someone running after him, he got down from the chariot to meet him and said, "Is all well?" ²²And he said, "All is well. My master has sent me to say, 'There have just now come to me from the hill country of Ephraim two young men of the sons of the prophets. Please give them a talent of silver and two changes of clothing.'" ²³And Naaman said, "Be pleased to accept two talents." And he urged him and tied up two talents of silver in two bags, with two changes of clothing, and laid them on two of his servants. And they carried them before Gehazi. ²⁴And when he came to the hill, he took them from their hand and put them in the house, and he sent the men away, and they departed. ²⁵He went in and stood before his master, and Elisha said to him, "Where have you been, Gehazi?" And he said, "Your servant went nowhere." ²⁶But he said to him, "Did not my heart go when the man turned from his chariot to meet you? Was it a time to accept money and garments, olive orchards and vineyards, sheep and oxen, male servants and female servants? ²⁷Therefore the leprosy of Naaman shall cling to you and to your descendants forever." So he went out from his presence a leper, like snow.

The invisible army [6:1–23]. The first episode in this unit is a short miracle story about the recovery of a valuable axe head (vv. 1–7). It is followed by the account of a miraculous deliverance that is one of the most famous *rescue stories in the Bible. Upon discovering that Elisha has been foiling his plans to capture the king of Israel, the king of Syria sends a large army to capture the prophet at Dothan. But Elisha's army turns out to be even bigger: he is surrounded by the horses and chariots of fiery angels. This *recognition story shows that God is on Elisha's side.

6 Now the sons of the prophets said to Elisha, "See, the place where we dwell under your charge is too small for us. ²Let us go to the Jordan and each of us get there a log, and let us make a place for us to dwell there." And he answered, "Go." ³Then one of them said, "Be pleased to go with your servants." And he answered, "I will go." ⁴So he went with them. And when they came to the Jordan, they cut down trees. ⁵But as one was felling a log, his axe head fell into the water, and he cried out, "Alas, my master! It was borrowed." ⁶Then the man of God said, "Where did it fall?" When he showed him the place, he cut off a stick and threw it in there and made the iron float. ⁷And he said, "Take it up." So he reached out his hand and took it.

⁸Once when the king of Syria was warring against Israel, he took counsel with his servants, saying, "At such and such a place shall be my camp." ⁹But the man of God sent word to the king of Israel, "Beware that you do not pass this place, for the Syrians are going down there." ¹⁰And the king of Israel sent to the place about which

the man of God told him. Thus he used to warn him, so that he saved himself there more than once or twice.

¹¹And the mind of the king of Syria was greatly troubled because of this thing, and he called his servants and said to them, "Will you not show me who of us is for the king of Israel?" ¹²And one of his servants said, "None, my lord, O king; but Elisha, the prophet who is in Israel, tells the king of Israel the words that you speak in your bedroom." ¹³And he said, "Go and see where he is, that I may send and seize him." It was told him, "Behold, he is in Dothan." ¹⁴So he sent there horses and chariots and a great army, and they came by night and surrounded the city.

¹⁵When the servant of the man of God rose early in the morning and went out, behold, an army with horses and chariots was all around the city. And the servant said, "Alas, my master! What shall we do?" ¹⁶He said, "Do not be afraid, for those who are with us are more than those who are with them." ¹⁷Then Elisha prayed and said, "O LORD, please open his eyes that he may see." So the LORD opened the eyes of the young man, and he saw, and behold, the mountain was full of horses and chariots of fire all around Elisha. ¹⁸And when the Syrians came down against him, Elisha prayed to the LORD and said, "Please strike this people with blindness." So he struck them with blindness in accordance with the prayer of Elisha. ¹⁹And Elisha said to them, "This is not the way, and this is not the city. Follow me, and I will bring you to the man whom you seek." And he led them to Samaria.

²⁰As soon as they entered Samaria, Elisha said, "O LORD, open the eyes of these men, that they may see." So the LORD opened their eyes and they saw, and behold, they were in the midst of Samaria. ²¹As soon as the king of Israel saw them, he said to Elisha, "My father, shall I strike them down? Shall I strike them down?" ²²He answered, "You shall not strike them down. Would you strike down those whom you have taken captive with your sword and with your bow? Set bread and water before them, that they may eat and drink and go to their master." ²³So he prepared for them a great feast, and when they had eaten and drunk, he sent them away, and they went to their master. And the Syrians did not come again on raids into the land of Israel.

The siege of Samaria [6:24–7:20]. This war story brings together several elements that are common in the Elisha narratives: conflict between Israel and Syria, miracles of provision and protection, surprising reversals, and an act of divine judgment so ironic that it qualifies as poetic justice. Israel's capital city, Samaria, is under siege, and the situation is so desperate that some Israelites have resorted to cannibalism in order to survive. Angry with God and overwhelmed with dread, the king threatens to murder God's prophet. But Elisha calmly informs him that by tomorrow food will be so plentiful in the city that it will be sold at a discount. When the captain of the king's army scoffs at the very idea, Elisha further prophesies that although the doubting captain will see this prophecy come true, he will not live long enough to taste any of the good food for himself. This prophecy comes true when the army of Syria hears the army of God and flees in terror, leaving all its provisions behind. Ironically, four lepers are the first to discover what has happened, and their revels in the camp that the Syrians abandoned make for one of the most memorable celebration scenes in the Bible. When the news gets back to the Israel's king, he thinks it is too good to be true. For one man the news *is* too good to be true: in the ensuing stampede, the doubting captain of the king's army gets trampled to death. For sheer narrative action, it is hard to beat a story like this.

²⁴Afterward Ben-hadad king of Syria mustered his entire army and went up and besieged Samaria. ²⁵And there was a great famine in Samaria, as they besieged it, until a donkey's head was sold for eighty shekels of silver, and the fourth part of a kab¹ of dove's dung for five shekels of silver. ²⁶Now as the king of Israel was passing by on the wall, a woman cried out to him, saying, "Help, my lord, O king!" ²⁷And he said, "If the LORD will not help you, how shall I help you? From the threshing floor, or from the winepress?" ²⁸And the king asked her, "What is your trouble?" She answered, "This woman said to me, 'Give your son, that we may eat him today, and we will eat my son tomorrow.' ²⁹So we boiled my son and ate him. And on the next day I said to her, 'Give your son, that we may eat him.' But she has hidden her son." ³⁰When the king heard the words of the woman, he tore his clothes—now he was passing by on the wall—and the people looked, and behold, he had sackcloth beneath on his body— ³¹and he said, "May God do so to me and more also, if the head of Elisha the son of Shaphat remains on his shoulders today."

³²Elisha was sitting in his house, and the elders were sitting with him. Now the king had dispatched a man from his presence, but before the messenger arrived Elisha said to the elders, "Do you see how this murderer has sent to take off my head? Look, when the messenger comes, shut the door and hold the door fast against him. Is not the sound of his master's feet behind him?" ³³And while he was still speaking with them, the messenger came down to him and said, "This trouble is from the LORD! Why should I wait for the LORD any longer?"

7 But Elisha said, "Hear the word of the LORD: thus says the LORD, Tomorrow about this time a seah² of fine flour shall be sold for a shekel,³ and two seahs of barley for a shekel, at the gate of Samaria." ²Then the captain on whose hand the king leaned said to the man of God, "If the LORD himself should make windows in heaven, could this thing be?" But he said, "You shall see it with your own eyes, but you shall not eat of it."

³Now there were four men who were lepers⁴ at the entrance to the gate. And they said to one another, "Why are we sitting here until we die? ⁴If we say, 'Let us enter the city,' the famine is in the city, and we shall die there. And if we sit here, we die also. So now come, let us go over to the camp of the Syrians. If they spare our lives we shall live, and if they kill us we shall but die." ⁵So they arose at twilight to go to the camp of the Syrians. But when they came to the edge of the camp of the Syrians, behold, there was no one there. ⁶For the Lord had made the army of the Syrians hear the sound of chariots and of horses, the sound of a great army, so that they said to one another, "Behold, the king of Israel has hired against us the kings of the Hittites and the kings of Egypt to come against us." ⁷So they fled away in the twilight and abandoned their tents, their horses, and their donkeys, leaving the camp as it was, and fled for their lives. ⁸And when these lepers came to the edge of the camp, they went into a tent and ate and drank, and they carried off silver and gold and clothing and went and hid them. Then they came back and entered another tent and carried off things from it and went and hid them.

¹ A *shekel* was about 2/5 ounce or 11 grams; a *kab* was about 1 quart or 1 liter ² A *seah* was about 7 quarts or 7.3 liters ³ A *shekel* was about 2/5 ounce or 11 grams ⁴ *Leprosy* was a term for several skin diseases; see Leviticus 13

⁹Then they said to one another, "We are not doing right. This day is a day of good news. If we are silent and wait until the morning light, punishment will overtake us. Now therefore come; let us go and tell the king's household." ¹⁰So they came and called to the gatekeepers of the city and told them, "We came to the camp of the Syrians, and behold, there was no one to be seen or heard there, nothing but the horses tied and the donkeys tied and the tents as they were." ¹¹Then the gatekeepers called out, and it was told within the king's household. ¹²And the king rose in the night and said to his servants, "I will tell you what the Syrians have done to us. They know that we are hungry. Therefore they have gone out of the camp to hide themselves in the open country, thinking, 'When they come out of the city, we shall take them alive and get into the city.'" ¹³And one of his servants said, "Let some men take five of the remaining horses, seeing that those who are left here will fare like the whole multitude of Israel who have already perished. Let us send and see." ¹⁴So they took two horsemen, and the king sent them after the army of the Syrians, saying, "Go and see." ¹⁵So they went after them as far as the Jordan, and behold, all the way was littered with garments and equipment that the Syrians had thrown away in their haste. And the messengers returned and told the king.

¹⁶Then the people went out and plundered the camp of the Syrians. So a seah of fine flour was sold for a shekel, and two seahs of barley for a shekel, according to the word of the LORD. ¹⁷Now the king had appointed the captain on whose hand he leaned to have charge of the gate. And the people trampled him in the gate, so that he died, as the man of God had said when the king came down to him. ¹⁸For when the man of God had said to the king, "Two seahs of barley shall be sold for a shekel, and a seah of fine flour for a shekel, about this time tomorrow in the gate of Samaria," ¹⁹the captain had answered the man of God, "If the LORD himself should make windows in heaven, could such a thing be?" And he had said, "You shall see it with your own eyes, but you shall not eat of it." ²⁰And so it happened to him, for the people trampled him in the gate and he died.

A chapter from court history [chapter 8]. The four episodes in this chapter—a king's restoration of land to a widow (vv. 1–6), a foreign king's assassination (vv. 7–15), the reign of Jehoram (vv. 16–24), the reign of Ahaziah (vv. 25–29)—all involve noteworthy events in the life of a king. The dominant literary technique is *realism, in multiple ways: the portrayal of real-life events (as illustrated by the wealth of named characters and places and such recognizable experiences as a widow's worry about her economic future, political revolt, and a visit to a sick person); refusal to sidestep violent action (an assassination and battle-inflicted wounds); the inclusion of concrete details (references to the ripping open of pregnant women and smothering a person with a bed cloth dipped in water). All of this down-to-earth realism is of course kept within a religious and moral framework. Hazael's murder of Syria's king, Ben-hadad, makes a tyrannical pagan king pay for his bullying. It also fulfills one of Elisha's prophecies and mirrors an analogous episode from the end of Elijah's ministry (see 1:1–18). Elisha has proven to be Elijah's successor in every aspect of his ministry. Jehoram and Ahaziah—the son and grandson of Ahab—are declared to have done "evil in the sight of the LORD" (although for the sake of his covenant with David, God spared the first of the two from destruction).

8 Now Elisha had said to the woman whose son he had restored to life, "Arise, and depart with your household, and sojourn wherever you can, for the LORD has called for a famine, and it will come upon the land for seven years." ²So the woman arose and did according to the word of the man of God. She went with her household and sojourned in the land of the Philistines seven years. ³And at the end of the seven years, when the woman returned from the land of the Philistines, she went to appeal to the king for her house and her land. ⁴Now the king was talking with Gehazi the servant of the man of God, saying, "Tell me all the great things that Elisha has done." ⁵And while he was telling the king how Elisha had restored the dead to life, behold, the woman whose son he had restored to life appealed to the king for her house and her land. And Gehazi said, "My lord, O king, here is the woman, and here is her son whom Elisha restored to life." ⁶And when the king asked the woman, she told him. So the king appointed an official for her, saying, "Restore all that was hers, together with all the produce of the fields from the day that she left the land until now."

⁷Now Elisha came to Damascus. Ben-hadad the king of Syria was sick. And when it was told him, "The man of God has come here," ⁸the king said to Hazael, "Take a present with you and go to meet the man of God, and inquire of the LORD through him, saying, 'Shall I recover from this sickness?'" ⁹So Hazael went to meet him, and took a present with him, all kinds of goods of Damascus, forty camel loads. When he came and stood before him, he said, "Your son Ben-hadad king of Syria has sent me to you, saying, 'Shall I recover from this sickness?'" ¹⁰And Elisha said to him, "Go, say to him, 'You shall certainly recover,' but the LORD has shown me that he shall certainly die." ¹¹And he fixed his gaze and stared at him, until he was embarrassed. And the man of God wept. ¹²And Hazael said, "Why does my lord weep?" He answered, "Because I know the evil that you will do to the people of Israel. You will set on fire their fortresses, and you will kill their young men with the sword and dash in pieces their little ones and rip open their pregnant women." ¹³And Hazael said, "What is your servant, who is but a dog, that he should do this great thing?" Elisha answered, "The LORD has shown me that you are to be king over Syria." ¹⁴Then he departed from Elisha and came to his master, who said to him, "What did Elisha say to you?" And he answered, "He told me that you would certainly recover." ¹⁵But the next day he took the bed cloth[1] and dipped it in water and spread it over his face, till he died. And Hazael became king in his place.

¹⁶In the fifth year of Joram the son of Ahab, king of Israel, when Jehoshaphat was king of Judah,[2] Jehoram the son of Jehoshaphat, king of Judah, began to reign. ¹⁷He was thirty-two years old when he became king, and he reigned eight years in Jerusalem. ¹⁸And he walked in the way of the kings of Israel, as the house of Ahab had done, for the daughter of Ahab was his wife. And he did what was evil in the sight of the LORD. ¹⁹Yet the LORD was not willing to destroy Judah, for the sake of David his servant, since he promised to give a lamp to him and to his sons forever.

²⁰In his days Edom revolted from the rule of Judah and set up a king of their own. ²¹Then Joram[3] passed over to Zair with all his chariots and rose by night, and he and his chariot commanders struck the Edomites who had surrounded him, but his army fled home. ²²So Edom revolted from the rule of Judah to this day. Then Libnah revolted at the same time. ²³Now the rest of the acts of Joram, and all that he did, are they not written in the Book of the Chronicles of the Kings of Judah? ²⁴So Joram slept

[1] The meaning of the Hebrew is uncertain [2] Septuagint, Syriac lack *when Jehoshaphat was king of Judah* [3] *Joram* is another spelling of *Jehoram* (the son of Jehoshaphat) as in verse 16; also verses 23, 24

with his fathers and was buried with his fathers in the city of David, and Ahaziah his son reigned in his place.

²⁵In the twelfth year of Joram the son of Ahab, king of Israel, Ahaziah the son of Jehoram, king of Judah, began to reign. ²⁶Ahaziah was twenty-two years old when he began to reign, and he reigned one year in Jerusalem. His mother's name was Athaliah; she was a granddaughter of Omri king of Israel. ²⁷He also walked in the way of the house of Ahab and did what was evil in the sight of the LORD, as the house of Ahab had done, for he was son-in-law to the house of Ahab.

²⁸He went with Joram the son of Ahab to make war against Hazael king of Syria at Ramoth-gilead, and the Syrians wounded Joram. ²⁹And King Joram returned to be healed in Jezreel of the wounds that the Syrians had given him at Ramah, when he fought against Hazael king of Syria. And Ahaziah the son of Jehoram king of Judah went down to see Joram the son of Ahab in Jezreel, because he was sick.

The fall of the house of Ahab [chapter 9]. Elisha sends one of his student-prophets to anoint Jehu king over Israel (vv. 1–13). This anointing brings the Elijah narratives to a close, because God has appointed Jehu to wreak vengeance on the house of Ahab, thus fulfilling Elijah's prophecies against that wicked king and all his descendants. Upon ascending to the throne, Jehu wastes little time in driving his chariot madly (see v. 20) to pursue Joram and Ahaziah to the death (vv. 14–29) and then to throw Jezebel down from her high boudoir to be devoured by dogs, just as Elijah promised (vv. 30–37; cf. 1 Kings 21:23)—another notable example of poetic justice. In terms of literary technique, this is the very touchstone of certain aspects of realism, especially the focus on violence.

9 Then Elisha the prophet called one of the sons of the prophets and said to him, "Tie up your garments, and take this flask of oil in your hand, and go to Ramoth-gilead. ²And when you arrive, look there for Jehu the son of Jehoshaphat, son of Nimshi. And go in and have him rise from among his fellows, and lead him to an inner chamber. ³Then take the flask of oil and pour it on his head and say, 'Thus says the LORD, I anoint you king over Israel.' Then open the door and flee; do not linger."

⁴So the young man, the servant of the prophet, went to Ramoth-gilead. ⁵And when he came, behold, the commanders of the army were in council. And he said, "I have a word for you, O commander." And Jehu said, "To which of us all?" And he said, "To you, O commander." ⁶So he arose and went into the house. And the young man poured the oil on his head, saying to him, "Thus says the LORD, the God of Israel, I anoint you king over the people of the LORD, over Israel. ⁷And you shall strike down the house of Ahab your master, so that I may avenge on Jezebel the blood of my servants the prophets, and the blood of all the servants of the LORD. ⁸For the whole house of Ahab shall perish, and I will cut off from Ahab every male, bond or free, in Israel. ⁹And I will make the house of Ahab like the house of Jeroboam the son of Nebat, and like the house of Baasha the son of Ahijah. ¹⁰And the dogs shall eat Jezebel in the territory of Jezreel, and none shall bury her." Then he opened the door and fled.

¹¹When Jehu came out to the servants of his master, they said to him, "Is all well? Why did this mad fellow come to you?" And he said to them, "You know the fellow and his talk." ¹²And they said, "That is not true; tell us now." And he said, "Thus and

so he spoke to me, saying, 'Thus says the Lord, I anoint you king over Israel.'" ¹³Then in haste every man of them took his garment and put it under him on the bare¹ steps, and they blew the trumpet and proclaimed, "Jehu is king."

¹⁴Thus Jehu the son of Jehoshaphat the son of Nimshi conspired against Joram. (Now Joram with all Israel had been on guard at Ramoth-gilead against Hazael king of Syria, ¹⁵but King Joram had returned to be healed in Jezreel of the wounds that the Syrians had given him, when he fought with Hazael king of Syria.) So Jehu said, "If this is your decision, then let no one slip out of the city to go and tell the news in Jezreel." ¹⁶Then Jehu mounted his chariot and went to Jezreel, for Joram lay there. And Ahaziah king of Judah had come down to visit Joram.

¹⁷Now the watchman was standing on the tower in Jezreel, and he saw the company of Jehu as he came and said, "I see a company." And Joram said, "Take a horseman and send to meet them, and let him say, 'Is it peace?'" ¹⁸So a man on horseback went to meet him and said, "Thus says the king, 'Is it peace?'" And Jehu said, "What do you have to do with peace? Turn around and ride behind me." And the watchman reported, saying, "The messenger reached them, but he is not coming back." ¹⁹Then he sent out a second horseman, who came to them and said, "Thus the king has said, 'Is it peace?'" And Jehu answered, "What do you have to do with peace? Turn around and ride behind me." ²⁰Again the watchman reported, "He reached them, but he is not coming back. And the driving is like the driving of Jehu the son of Nimshi, for he drives furiously."

²¹Joram said, "Make ready." And they made ready his chariot. Then Joram king of Israel and Ahaziah king of Judah set out, each in his chariot, and went to meet Jehu, and met him at the property of Naboth the Jezreelite. ²²And when Joram saw Jehu, he said, "Is it peace, Jehu?" He answered, "What peace can there be, so long as the whorings and the sorceries of your mother Jezebel are so many?" ²³Then Joram reined about and fled, saying to Ahaziah, "Treachery, O Ahaziah!" ²⁴And Jehu drew his bow with his full strength, and shot Joram between the shoulders, so that the arrow pierced his heart, and he sank in his chariot. ²⁵Jehu said to Bidkar his aide, "Take him up and throw him on the plot of ground belonging to Naboth the Jezreelite. For remember, when you and I rode side by side behind Ahab his father, how the Lord made this pronouncement against him: ²⁶'As surely as I saw yesterday the blood of Naboth and the blood of his sons—declares the Lord—I will repay you on this plot of ground.' Now therefore take him up and throw him on the plot of ground, in accordance with the word of the Lord."

²⁷When Ahaziah the king of Judah saw this, he fled in the direction of Beth-haggan. And Jehu pursued him and said, "Shoot him also." And they shot him² in the chariot at the ascent of Gur, which is by Ibleam. And he fled to Megiddo and died there. ²⁸His servants carried him in a chariot to Jerusalem, and buried him in his tomb with his fathers in the city of David.

²⁹In the eleventh year of Joram the son of Ahab, Ahaziah began to reign over Judah.

³⁰When Jehu came to Jezreel, Jezebel heard of it. And she painted her eyes and adorned her head and looked out of the window. ³¹And as Jehu entered the gate, she said, "Is it peace, you Zimri, murderer of your master?" ³²And he lifted up his face to the window and said, "Who is on my side? Who?" Two or three eunuchs looked out at him. ³³He said, "Throw her down." So they threw her down. And some of her blood spattered on the wall and on the horses, and they trampled on her. ³⁴Then he went in

¹ The meaning of the Hebrew word is uncertain ² Syriac, Vulgate (compare Septuagint); Hebrew lacks *and they shot him*

and ate and drank. And he said, "See now to this cursed woman and bury her, for she is a king's daughter." ³⁵But when they went to bury her, they found no more of her than the skull and the feet and the palms of her hands. ³⁶When they came back and told him, he said, "This is the word of the LORD, which he spoke by his servant Elijah the Tishbite, 'In the territory of Jezreel the dogs shall eat the flesh of Jezebel, ³⁷and the corpse of Jezebel shall be as dung on the face of the field in the territory of Jezreel, so that no one can say, This is Jezebel.'"

Full vengeance [chapter 10]. Realism continues in this story of an ever-expanding massacre. First Jehu fulfills Elijah's prophecy (see v. 10) and satisfies God's vengeance (see v. 30) against Ahab by putting all seventy of his sons to the sword (vv. 1–17) and killing all the remaining prophets of Baal (vv. 18–27). It is a story of total revenge and purging, executed with cunning trickery and deadly efficiency, for a righteous purpose. Yet for all his youthful zeal, Jehu perpetuates the sins of Jeroboam, with the result that Israel is still in spiritual (vv. 28–31) and political (vv. 32–36) decline.

10 Now Ahab had seventy sons in Samaria. So Jehu wrote letters and sent them to Samaria, to the rulers of the city,¹ to the elders, and to the guardians of the sons² of Ahab, saying, ²"Now then, as soon as this letter comes to you, seeing your master's sons are with you, and there are with you chariots and horses, fortified cities also, and weapons, ³select the best and fittest of your master's sons and set him on his father's throne and fight for your master's house." ⁴But they were exceedingly afraid and said, "Behold, the two kings could not stand before him. How then can we stand?" ⁵So he who was over the palace, and he who was over the city, together with the elders and the guardians, sent to Jehu, saying, "We are your servants, and we will do all that you tell us. We will not make anyone king. Do whatever is good in your eyes." ⁶Then he wrote to them a second letter, saying, "If you are on my side, and if you are ready to obey me, take the heads of your master's sons and come to me at Jezreel tomorrow at this time." Now the king's sons, seventy persons, were with the great men of the city, who were bringing them up. ⁷And as soon as the letter came to them, they took the king's sons and slaughtered them, seventy persons, and put their heads in baskets and sent them to him at Jezreel. ⁸When the messenger came and told him, "They have brought the heads of the king's sons," he said, "Lay them in two heaps at the entrance of the gate until the morning." ⁹Then in the morning, when he went out, he stood and said to all the people, "You are innocent. It was I who conspired against my master and killed him, but who struck down all these? ¹⁰Know then that there shall fall to the earth nothing of the word of the LORD, which the LORD spoke concerning the house of Ahab, for the LORD has done what he said by his servant Elijah." ¹¹So Jehu struck down all who remained of the house of Ahab in Jezreel, all his great men and his close friends and his priests, until he left him none remaining.

¹²Then he set out and went to Samaria. On the way, when he was at Beth-eked of the Shepherds, ¹³Jehu met the relatives of Ahaziah king of Judah, and he said, "Who are you?" And they answered, "We are the relatives of Ahaziah, and we came down to visit the royal princes and the sons of the queen mother." ¹⁴He said, "Take them

---

¹ Septuagint, Vulgate; Hebrew *rulers of Jezreel* ² Hebrew lacks *of the sons*

alive." And they took them alive and slaughtered them at the pit of Beth-eked, forty-two persons, and he spared none of them.

¹⁵And when he departed from there, he met Jehonadab the son of Rechab coming to meet him. And he greeted him and said to him, "Is your heart true to my heart as mine is to yours?" And Jehonadab answered, "It is." Jehu said,¹ "If it is, give me your hand." So he gave him his hand. And Jehu took him up with him into the chariot. ¹⁶And he said, "Come with me, and see my zeal for the LORD." So he² had him ride in his chariot. ¹⁷And when he came to Samaria, he struck down all who remained to Ahab in Samaria, till he had wiped them out, according to the word of the LORD that he spoke to Elijah.

¹⁸Then Jehu assembled all the people and said to them, "Ahab served Baal a little, but Jehu will serve him much. ¹⁹Now therefore call to me all the prophets of Baal, all his worshipers and all his priests. Let none be missing, for I have a great sacrifice to offer to Baal. Whoever is missing shall not live." But Jehu did it with cunning in order to destroy the worshipers of Baal. ²⁰And Jehu ordered, "Sanctify a solemn assembly for Baal." So they proclaimed it. ²¹And Jehu sent throughout all Israel, and all the worshipers of Baal came, so that there was not a man left who did not come. And they entered the house of Baal, and the house of Baal was filled from one end to the other. ²²He said to him who was in charge of the wardrobe, "Bring out the vestments for all the worshipers of Baal." So he brought out the vestments for them. ²³Then Jehu went into the house of Baal with Jehonadab the son of Rechab, and he said to the worshipers of Baal, "Search, and see that there is no servant of the LORD here among you, but only the worshipers of Baal." ²⁴Then they³ went in to offer sacrifices and burnt offerings.

Now Jehu had stationed eighty men outside and said, "The man who allows any of those whom I give into your hands to escape shall forfeit his life." ²⁵So as soon as he had made an end of offering the burnt offering, Jehu said to the guard and to the officers, "Go in and strike them down; let not a man escape." So when they put them to the sword, the guard and the officers cast them out and went into the inner room of the house of Baal, ²⁶and they brought out the pillar that was in the house of Baal and burned it. ²⁷And they demolished the pillar of Baal, and demolished the house of Baal, and made it a latrine to this day.

²⁸Thus Jehu wiped out Baal from Israel. ²⁹But Jehu did not turn aside from the sins of Jeroboam the son of Nebat, which he made Israel to sin—that is, the golden calves that were in Bethel and in Dan. ³⁰And the LORD said to Jehu, "Because you have done well in carrying out what is right in my eyes, and have done to the house of Ahab according to all that was in my heart, your sons of the fourth generation shall sit on the throne of Israel." ³¹But Jehu was not careful to walk in the law of the LORD, the God of Israel, with all his heart. He did not turn from the sins of Jeroboam, which he made Israel to sin.

³²In those days the LORD began to cut off parts of Israel. Hazael defeated them throughout the territory of Israel: ³³from the Jordan eastward, all the land of Gilead, the Gadites, and the Reubenites, and the Manassites, from Aroer, which is by the Valley of the Arnon, that is, Gilead and Bashan. ³⁴Now the rest of the acts of Jehu and all that he did, and all his might, are they not written in the Book of the Chronicles of the Kings of Israel? ³⁵So Jehu slept with his fathers, and they buried him in Samaria. And Jehoahaz his son reigned in his place. ³⁶The time that Jehu reigned over Israel in Samaria was twenty-eight years.

---

¹ Septuagint; Hebrew lacks *Jehu said* ² Septuagint, Syriac, Targum; Hebrew *they* ³ Septuagint *he* (compare verse 25)

The boy king of Judah [chapter 11]. Bloody Athaliah usurps the throne by deadly force, but righteous men and women (especially princess Jehosheba and Jehoiada the priest) act courageously and decisively to preserve the life of Judah's anointed, the baby Joash. The child grows up in hiding—the secret heir and future-king-in-hiding motif—until his guardians unveil his royal identity at the temple in Jerusalem and crown him as Judah's rightful king. Following the death of wicked Athaliah, Jehoiada leads the people of Judah in renewing their covenant with their God and their king. Thus the coronation of Joash marks the beginning of a reformation in Judah. After many years of royal disappointment, David finally has an heir of whom Judah can be proud. The overall story line is familiar in literature: the triumph of good over evil, rendered all the more appealing by that perennial narrative favorite, the boy hero.

11 Now when Athaliah the mother of Ahaziah saw that her son was dead, she arose and destroyed all the royal family. ²But Jehosheba, the daughter of King Joram, sister of Ahaziah, took Joash the son of Ahaziah and stole him away from among the king's sons who were being put to death, and she put[1] him and his nurse in a bedroom. Thus they[2] hid him from Athaliah, so that he was not put to death. ³And he remained with her six years, hidden in the house of the Lord, while Athaliah reigned over the land.

⁴But in the seventh year Jehoiada sent and brought the captains of the Carites and of the guards, and had them come to him in the house of the Lord. And he made a covenant with them and put them under oath in the house of the Lord, and he showed them the king's son. ⁵And he commanded them, "This is the thing that you shall do: one third of you, those who come off duty on the Sabbath and guard the king's house ⁶(another third being at the gate Sur and a third at the gate behind the guards) shall guard the palace.[3] ⁷And the two divisions of you, which come on duty in force on the Sabbath and guard the house of the Lord on behalf of the king, ⁸shall surround the king, each with his weapons in his hand. And whoever approaches the ranks is to be put to death. Be with the king when he goes out and when he comes in."

⁹The captains did according to all that Jehoiada the priest commanded, and they each brought his men who were to go off duty on the Sabbath, with those who were to come on duty on the Sabbath, and came to Jehoiada the priest. ¹⁰And the priest gave to the captains the spears and shields that had been King David's, which were in the house of the Lord. ¹¹And the guards stood, every man with his weapons in his hand, from the south side of the house to the north side of the house, around the altar and the house on behalf of the king. ¹²Then he brought out the king's son and put the crown on him and gave him the testimony. And they proclaimed him king and anointed him, and they clapped their hands and said, "Long live the king!"

¹³When Athaliah heard the noise of the guard and of the people, she went into the house of the Lord to the people. ¹⁴And when she looked, there was the king standing by the pillar, according to the custom, and the captains and the trumpeters beside the king, and all the people of the land rejoicing and blowing trumpets. And Athaliah tore her clothes and cried, "Treason! Treason!" ¹⁵Then Jehoiada the priest commanded the captains who were set over the army, "Bring her out between the ranks, and put to death with the sword anyone who follows her." For the priest said, "Let her

---

[1] Compare 2 Chronicles 22:11; Hebrew lacks *and she put* [2] Septuagint, Syriac, Vulgate (compare 2 Chronicles 22:11) *she* [3] The meaning of the Hebrew word is uncertain

not be put to death in the house of the LORD." ¹⁶So they laid hands on her; and she went through the horses' entrance to the king's house, and there she was put to death.

¹⁷And Jehoiada made a covenant between the LORD and the king and people, that they should be the LORD's people, and also between the king and the people. ¹⁸Then all the people of the land went to the house of Baal and tore it down; his altars and his images they broke in pieces, and they killed Mattan the priest of Baal before the altars. And the priest posted watchmen over the house of the LORD. ¹⁹And he took the captains, the Carites, the guards, and all the people of the land, and they brought the king down from the house of the LORD, marching through the gate of the guards to the king's house. And he took his seat on the throne of the kings. ²⁰So all the people of the land rejoiced, and the city was quiet after Athaliah had been put to death with the sword at the king's house.

²¹ ¹ Jehoash² was seven years old when he began to reign.

> **Joash repairs the temple** [chapter 12]. It is characteristic of the good kings of Judah that they have a passion for the public worship of God, and Joash is no exception. In this reformation story he begins his long reign over Judah by instructing the priests to make ongoing repairs to the house of God (vv. 1–5). When it is later discovered that the priests have been neglecting this sacred responsibility (vv. 6–8), Jehoiada devises a new and practical scheme for collecting and disbursing the necessary funds (vv. 9–16). This fundraising effort shows the importance of good stewardship in doing God's work. The way that Joash deals with a military threat from Syria (vv. 17–18) and the way he meets his demise (vv. 19–21) indicate that his kingship ended much less impressively than it began. The decline and fall of King Joash mirrors the spiritual decline of Judah.

12 In the seventh year of Jehu, Jehoash³ began to reign, and he reigned forty years in Jerusalem. His mother's name was Zibiah of Beersheba. ²And Jehoash did what was right in the eyes of the LORD all his days, because Jehoiada the priest instructed him. ³Nevertheless, the high places were not taken away; the people continued to sacrifice and make offerings on the high places.

⁴Jehoash said to the priests, "All the money of the holy things that is brought into the house of the LORD, the money for which each man is assessed—the money from the assessment of persons—and the money that a man's heart prompts him to bring into the house of the LORD, ⁵let the priests take, each from his donor, and let them repair the house wherever any need of repairs is discovered." ⁶But by the twenty-third year of King Jehoash, the priests had made no repairs on the house. ⁷Therefore King Jehoash summoned Jehoiada the priest and the other priests and said to them, "Why are you not repairing the house? Now therefore take no more money from your donors, but hand it over for the repair of the house." ⁸So the priests agreed that they should take no more money from the people, and that they should not repair the house.

⁹Then Jehoiada the priest took a chest and bored a hole in the lid of it and set it beside the altar on the right side as one entered the house of the LORD. And the priests who guarded the threshold put in it all the money that was brought into the house of the LORD. ¹⁰And whenever they saw that there was much money in the chest, the king's secretary and the high priest came up and they bagged and counted the

---

¹ Ch 12:1 in Hebrew ² *Jehoash* is another spelling of *Joash* (son of Ahaziah) as in verse 2 ³ *Jehoash* is another spelling of *Joash* (son of Ahaziah) as in 11:2; also verses 2, 4, 6, 7, 18

money that was found in the house of the LORD. ¹¹Then they would give the money
that was weighed out into the hands of the workmen who had the oversight of the
house of the LORD. And they paid it out to the carpenters and the builders who
worked on the house of the LORD, ¹²and to the masons and the stonecutters, as well as
to buy timber and quarried stone for making repairs on the house of the LORD, and
for any outlay for the repairs of the house. ¹³But there were not made for the house of
the LORD basins of silver, snuffers, bowls, trumpets, or any vessels of gold, or of silver,
from the money that was brought into the house of the LORD, ¹⁴for that was given to
the workmen who were repairing the house of the LORD with it. ¹⁵And they did not
ask an accounting from the men into whose hand they delivered the money to pay
out to the workmen, for they dealt honestly. ¹⁶The money from the guilt offerings and
the money from the sin offerings was not brought into the house of the LORD; it
belonged to the priests.

¹⁷At that time Hazael king of Syria went up and fought against Gath and took it.
But when Hazael set his face to go up against Jerusalem, ¹⁸Jehoash king of Judah took
all the sacred gifts that Jehoshaphat and Jehoram and Ahaziah his fathers, the kings
of Judah, had dedicated, and his own sacred gifts, and all the gold that was found in
the treasuries of the house of the LORD and of the king's house, and sent these to
Hazael king of Syria. Then Hazael went away from Jerusalem.

¹⁹Now the rest of the acts of Joash and all that he did, are they not written in the
Book of the Chronicles of the Kings of Judah? ²⁰His servants arose and made a conspiracy and struck down Joash in the house of Millo, on the way that goes down to
Silla. ²¹It was Jozacar the son of Shimeath and Jehozabad the son of Shomer, his servants, who struck him down, so that he died. And they buried him with his fathers in
the city of David, and Amaziah his son reigned in his place.

Jehoahaz and Jehoash [chapter 13]. In stories with double plot lines, storytellers swing back and forth between the two plots. While Joash was ruling in the south
(Judah), Jehoahaz and Jehoash were reigning in the north (Israel). These two lackluster
kings are described in similar terms. They both do what was evil in God's sight, following
in the sins of their father Jeroboam (meaning especially that they maintain high places
for false worship). Yet there are also some glimmers of hope. Jehoahaz later turns to the
Lord and escapes from the Syrians (vv. 4–5). And in fulfillment of Elisha's last prophecy—spoken from his deathbed—Jehoash (also called Joash) gains three victories over
the Syrians (although if the king had greater confidence in the word of God, his triumph
would have been even more comprehensive). As the biblical historian is careful to show,
God gives his people these victories because of his covenant love (see v. 23). Elisha's
final miracle may be the most remarkable: the bones in his grave bring a man back to
life (vv. 20–21). This posthumous miracle proves again the heroic nature of Elisha's ministry and points to the resurrection power of his God.

13 In the twenty-third year of Joash the son of Ahaziah, king of Judah, Jehoahaz
the son of Jehu began to reign over Israel in Samaria, and he reigned seventeen years. ²He did what was evil in the sight of the LORD and followed the sins of
Jeroboam the son of Nebat, which he made Israel to sin; he did not depart from them.
³And the anger of the LORD was kindled against Israel, and he gave them continually
into the hand of Hazael king of Syria and into the hand of Ben-hadad the son of

Hazael. ⁴Then Jehoahaz sought the favor of the LORD, and the LORD listened to him, for he saw the oppression of Israel, how the king of Syria oppressed them. ⁵(Therefore the LORD gave Israel a savior, so that they escaped from the hand of the Syrians, and the people of Israel lived in their homes as formerly. ⁶Nevertheless, they did not depart from the sins of the house of Jeroboam, which he made Israel to sin, but walked[1] in them; and the Asherah also remained in Samaria.) ⁷For there was not left to Jehoahaz an army of more than fifty horsemen and ten chariots and ten thousand footmen, for the king of Syria had destroyed them and made them like the dust at threshing. ⁸Now the rest of the acts of Jehoahaz and all that he did, and his might, are they not written in the Book of the Chronicles of the Kings of Israel? ⁹So Jehoahaz slept with his fathers, and they buried him in Samaria, and Joash his son reigned in his place.

¹⁰In the thirty-seventh year of Joash king of Judah, Jehoash[2] the son of Jehoahaz began to reign over Israel in Samaria, and he reigned sixteen years. ¹¹He also did what was evil in the sight of the LORD. He did not depart from all the sins of Jeroboam the son of Nebat, which he made Israel to sin, but he walked in them. ¹²Now the rest of the acts of Joash and all that he did, and the might with which he fought against Amaziah king of Judah, are they not written in the Book of the Chronicles of the Kings of Israel? ¹³So Joash slept with his fathers, and Jeroboam sat on his throne. And Joash was buried in Samaria with the kings of Israel.

¹⁴Now when Elisha had fallen sick with the illness of which he was to die, Joash king of Israel went down to him and wept before him, crying, "My father, my father! The chariots of Israel and its horsemen!" ¹⁵And Elisha said to him, "Take a bow and arrows." So he took a bow and arrows. ¹⁶Then he said to the king of Israel, "Draw the bow," and he drew it. And Elisha laid his hands on the king's hands. ¹⁷And he said, "Open the window eastward," and he opened it. Then Elisha said, "Shoot," and he shot. And he said, "The LORD's arrow of victory, the arrow of victory over Syria! For you shall fight the Syrians in Aphek until you have made an end of them." ¹⁸And he said, "Take the arrows," and he took them. And he said to the king of Israel, "Strike the ground with them." And he struck three times and stopped. ¹⁹Then the man of God was angry with him and said, "You should have struck five or six times; then you would have struck down Syria until you had made an end of it, but now you will strike down Syria only three times."

²⁰So Elisha died, and they buried him. Now bands of Moabites used to invade the land in the spring of the year. ²¹And as a man was being buried, behold, a marauding band was seen and the man was thrown into the grave of Elisha, and as soon as the man touched the bones of Elisha, he revived and stood on his feet.

²²Now Hazael king of Syria oppressed Israel all the days of Jehoahaz. ²³But the LORD was gracious to them and had compassion on them, and he turned toward them, because of his covenant with Abraham, Isaac, and Jacob, and would not destroy them, nor has he cast them from his presence until now.

²⁴When Hazael king of Syria died, Ben-hadad his son became king in his place. ²⁵Then Jehoash the son of Jehoahaz took again from Ben-hadad the son of Hazael the cities that he had taken from Jehoahaz his father in war. Three times Joash defeated him and recovered the cities of Israel.

---

[1] Septuagint, Syriac, Targum, Vulgate; Hebrew *he walked* [2] *Jehoash* is another spelling for *Joash* (son of Jehoahaz) as in verses 9, 12-14; also verse 25

Amaziah reigns in Judah [14:1–22]. In the back-and-forth movement between the two nations in the divided kingdom, the narrative returns to Judah, where Amaziah rules for many years, like his father Joash before him. From the spiritual point of view, Amaziah's reign is a mixed blessing, and there are signs of both faith and apostasy. In the broad sweep of 1 and 2 Kings, there can be little doubt that Judah and Israel are both in sharp decline. Things reach a new low in the civil war between Amaziah and Jehoash, when Israel plunders Judah and the temple of God (vv. 11–14).

14

In the second year of Joash the son of Joahaz, king of Israel, Amaziah the son of Joash, king of Judah, began to reign. [2] He was twenty-five years old when he began to reign, and he reigned twenty-nine years in Jerusalem. His mother's name was Jehoaddin of Jerusalem. [3] And he did what was right in the eyes of the Lord, yet not like David his father. He did in all things as Joash his father had done. [4] But the high places were not removed; the people still sacrificed and made offerings on the high places. [5] And as soon as the royal power was firmly in his hand, he struck down his servants who had struck down the king his father. [6] But he did not put to death the children of the murderers, according to what is written in the Book of the Law of Moses, where the Lord commanded, "Fathers shall not be put to death because of their children, nor shall children be put to death because of their fathers. But each one shall die for his own sin."

[7] He struck down ten thousand Edomites in the Valley of Salt and took Sela by storm, and called it Joktheel, which is its name to this day.

[8] Then Amaziah sent messengers to Jehoash[1] the son of Jehoahaz, son of Jehu, king of Israel, saying, "Come, let us look one another in the face." [9] And Jehoash king of Israel sent word to Amaziah king of Judah, "A thistle on Lebanon sent to a cedar on Lebanon, saying, 'Give your daughter to my son for a wife,' and a wild beast of Lebanon passed by and trampled down the thistle. [10] You have indeed struck down Edom, and your heart has lifted you up. Be content with your glory, and stay at home, for why should you provoke trouble so that you fall, you and Judah with you?"

[11] But Amaziah would not listen. So Jehoash king of Israel went up, and he and Amaziah king of Judah faced one another in battle at Beth-shemesh, which belongs to Judah. [12] And Judah was defeated by Israel, and every man fled to his home. [13] And Jehoash king of Israel captured Amaziah king of Judah, the son of Jehoash, son of Ahaziah, at Beth-shemesh, and came to Jerusalem and broke down the wall of Jerusalem for four hundred cubits,[2] from the Ephraim Gate to the Corner Gate. [14] And he seized all the gold and silver, and all the vessels that were found in the house of the Lord and in the treasuries of the king's house, also hostages, and he returned to Samaria.

[15] Now the rest of the acts of Jehoash that he did, and his might, and how he fought with Amaziah king of Judah, are they not written in the Book of the Chronicles of the Kings of Israel? [16] And Jehoash slept with his fathers and was buried in Samaria with the kings of Israel, and Jeroboam his son reigned in his place.

[17] Amaziah the son of Joash, king of Judah, lived fifteen years after the death of Jehoash son of Jehoahaz, king of Israel. [18] Now the rest of the deeds of Amaziah, are they not written in the Book of the Chronicles of the Kings of Judah? [19] And they made a conspiracy against him in Jerusalem, and he fled to Lachish. But they sent after him

---

[1] *Jehoash* is another spelling for *Joash* (son of Jehoahaz) as in 13:9, 12-14; also verses 9, 11-16 [2] A *cubit* was about 18 inches or 45 centimeters

to Lachish and put him to death there. ²⁰And they brought him on horses; and he was buried in Jerusalem with his fathers in the city of David. ²¹And all the people of Judah took Azariah, who was sixteen years old, and made him king instead of his father Amaziah. ²²He built Elath and restored it to Judah, after the king slept with his fathers.

> **Kings of Israel and Judah** [14:23–15:38]. Six kings of Israel—Jeroboam (14:23–29), Zechariah (15:8–12), Shallum (15:13–16), Menahem (15:17–22), Pekahiah (15:23–26), and Pekah (15:27–31)—are all described in negative terms, both for the general character of their kingship and for their specific misdeeds. Although some political and military information is included, the primary standard of evaluation in each case is the same standard that God applies to everyone: obedience to his revealed will. By contrast, Azariah (15:1–7) and Jotham (15:32–38)—both kings of Judah—receive some words of commendation. This is typical of the divided kingdom: whereas the kings of Israel were almost all bad, some of the kings of Judah tried to follow the Lord. In keeping with the literary nature of the material, even though the accounts of the kings are reviewed in summary fashion, the text never becomes purely abstract; it is filled with concrete details that appeal to our imagination.

²³In the fifteenth year of Amaziah the son of Joash, king of Judah, Jeroboam the son of Joash, king of Israel, began to reign in Samaria, and he reigned forty-one years. ²⁴And he did what was evil in the sight of the LORD. He did not depart from all the sins of Jeroboam the son of Nebat, which he made Israel to sin. ²⁵He restored the border of Israel from Lebo-hamath as far as the Sea of the Arabah, according to the word of the LORD, the God of Israel, which he spoke by his servant Jonah the son of Amittai, the prophet, who was from Gath-hepher. ²⁶For the LORD saw that the affliction of Israel was very bitter, for there was none left, bond or free, and there was none to help Israel. ²⁷But the LORD had not said that he would blot out the name of Israel from under heaven, so he saved them by the hand of Jeroboam the son of Joash.

²⁸Now the rest of the acts of Jeroboam and all that he did, and his might, how he fought, and how he restored Damascus and Hamath to Judah in Israel, are they not written in the Book of the Chronicles of the Kings of Israel? ²⁹And Jeroboam slept with his fathers, the kings of Israel, and Zechariah his son reigned in his place.

15 In the twenty-seventh year of Jeroboam king of Israel, Azariah the son of Amaziah, king of Judah, began to reign. ²He was sixteen years old when he began to reign, and he reigned fifty-two years in Jerusalem. His mother's name was Jecoliah of Jerusalem. ³And he did what was right in the eyes of the LORD, according to all that his father Amaziah had done. ⁴Nevertheless, the high places were not taken away. The people still sacrificed and made offerings on the high places. ⁵And the LORD touched the king, so that he was a leper¹ to the day of his death, and he lived in a separate house.² And Jotham the king's son was over the household, governing the people of the land. ⁶Now the rest of the acts of Azariah, and all that he did, are they not written in the Book of the Chronicles of the Kings of Judah? ⁷And Azariah slept with his fathers, and they buried him with his fathers in the city of David, and Jotham his son reigned in his place.

⁸In the thirty-eighth year of Azariah king of Judah, Zechariah the son of Jeroboam reigned over Israel in Samaria six months. ⁹And he did what was evil in the sight of

¹ *Leprosy* was a term for several skin diseases; see Leviticus 13 ² The meaning of the Hebrew word is uncertain

the Lord, as his fathers had done. He did not depart from the sins of Jeroboam the son of Nebat, which he made Israel to sin. ¹⁰Shallum the son of Jabesh conspired against him and struck him down at Ibleam and put him to death and reigned in his place. ¹¹Now the rest of the deeds of Zechariah, behold, they are written in the Book of the Chronicles of the Kings of Israel. ¹²(This was the promise of the Lord that he gave to Jehu, "Your sons shall sit on the throne of Israel to the fourth generation." And so it came to pass.)

¹³Shallum the son of Jabesh began to reign in the thirty-ninth year of Uzziah¹ king of Judah, and he reigned one month in Samaria. ¹⁴Then Menahem the son of Gadi came up from Tirzah and came to Samaria, and he struck down Shallum the son of Jabesh in Samaria and put him to death and reigned in his place. ¹⁵Now the rest of the deeds of Shallum, and the conspiracy that he made, behold, they are written in the Book of the Chronicles of the Kings of Israel. ¹⁶At that time Menahem sacked Tiphsah and all who were in it and its territory from Tirzah on, because they did not open it to him. Therefore he sacked it, and he ripped open all the women in it who were pregnant.

¹⁷In the thirty-ninth year of Azariah king of Judah, Menahem the son of Gadi began to reign over Israel, and he reigned ten years in Samaria. ¹⁸And he did what was evil in the sight of the Lord. He did not depart all his days from all the sins of Jeroboam the son of Nebat, which he made Israel to sin. ¹⁹Pul² the king of Assyria came against the land, and Menahem gave Pul a thousand talents³ of silver, that he might help him to confirm his hold on the royal power. ²⁰Menahem exacted the money from Israel, that is, from all the wealthy men, fifty shekels⁴ of silver from every man, to give to the king of Assyria. So the king of Assyria turned back and did not stay there in the land. ²¹Now the rest of the deeds of Menahem and all that he did, are they not written in the Book of the Chronicles of the Kings of Israel? ²²And Menahem slept with his fathers, and Pekahiah his son reigned in his place.

²³In the fiftieth year of Azariah king of Judah, Pekahiah the son of Menahem began to reign over Israel in Samaria, and he reigned two years. ²⁴And he did what was evil in the sight of the Lord. He did not turn away from the sins of Jeroboam the son of Nebat, which he made Israel to sin. ²⁵And Pekah the son of Remaliah, his captain, conspired against him with fifty men of the people of Gilead, and struck him down in Samaria, in the citadel of the king's house with Argob and Arieh; he put him to death and reigned in his place. ²⁶Now the rest of the deeds of Pekahiah and all that he did, behold, they are written in the Book of the Chronicles of the Kings of Israel.

²⁷In the fifty-second year of Azariah king of Judah, Pekah the son of Remaliah began to reign over Israel in Samaria, and he reigned twenty years. ²⁸And he did what was evil in the sight of the Lord. He did not depart from the sins of Jeroboam the son of Nebat, which he made Israel to sin. ²⁹In the days of Pekah king of Israel, Tiglath-pileser king of Assyria came and captured Ijon, Abel-beth-maacah, Janoah, Kedesh, Hazor, Gilead, and Galilee, all the land of Naphtali, and he carried the people captive to Assyria. ³⁰Then Hoshea the son of Elah made a conspiracy against Pekah the son of Remaliah and struck him down and put him to death and reigned in his place, in the twentieth year of Jotham the son of Uzziah. ³¹Now the rest of the acts of Pekah and all that he did, behold, they are written in the Book of the Chronicles of the Kings of Israel.

---

¹ Another name for *Azariah* ² Another name for *Tiglath-pileser III* (compare verse 29) ³ A *talent* was about 75 pounds or 34 kilograms ⁴ A *shekel* was about 2/5 ounce or 11 grams

³²In the second year of Pekah the son of Remaliah, king of Israel, Jotham the son of Uzziah, king of Judah, began to reign. ³³He was twenty-five years old when he began to reign, and he reigned sixteen years in Jerusalem. His mother's name was Jerusha the daughter of Zadok. ³⁴And he did what was right in the eyes of the LORD, according to all that his father Uzziah had done. ³⁵Nevertheless, the high places were not removed. The people still sacrificed and made offerings on the high places. He built the upper gate of the house of the LORD. ³⁶Now the rest of the acts of Jotham and all that he did, are they not written in the Book of the Chronicles of the Kings of Judah? ³⁷In those days the LORD began to send Rezin the king of Syria and Pekah the son of Remaliah against Judah. ³⁸Jotham slept with his fathers and was buried with his fathers in the city of David his father, and Ahaz his son reigned in his place.

Ahaz leads Judah astray [chapter 16]. Although the reign of king Ahaz is chronicled with customary reserve, anyone familiar with the biblical pattern for worship will know that what he does is nothing less than an abomination. From the outset we are told that Ahaz did not do what was right in Judah, like his ancestor David, but followed the wicked example of the evil kings of Israel to the north (vv. 2–3). In addition to forfeiting treasure from the house of God to make an unholy alliance with the Assyrians (vv. 5–9), Ahaz adopts the worship practices of the Syrians, rearranging the inside of the temple to accommodate their idolatry (vv. 10–20).

16 In the seventeenth year of Pekah the son of Remaliah, Ahaz the son of Jotham, king of Judah, began to reign. ²Ahaz was twenty years old when he began to reign, and he reigned sixteen years in Jerusalem. And he did not do what was right in the eyes of the LORD his God, as his father David had done, ³but he walked in the way of the kings of Israel. He even burned his son as an offering,¹ according to the despicable practices of the nations whom the LORD drove out before the people of Israel. ⁴And he sacrificed and made offerings on the high places and on the hills and under every green tree.

⁵Then Rezin king of Syria and Pekah the son of Remaliah, king of Israel, came up to wage war on Jerusalem, and they besieged Ahaz but could not conquer him. ⁶At that time Rezin the king of Syria recovered Elath for Syria and drove the men of Judah from Elath, and the Edomites came to Elath, where they dwell to this day. ⁷So Ahaz sent messengers to Tiglath-pileser king of Assyria, saying, "I am your servant and your son. Come up and rescue me from the hand of the king of Syria and from the hand of the king of Israel, who are attacking me." ⁸Ahaz also took the silver and gold that was found in the house of the LORD and in the treasures of the king's house and sent a present to the king of Assyria. ⁹And the king of Assyria listened to him. The king of Assyria marched up against Damascus and took it, carrying its people captive to Kir, and he killed Rezin.

¹⁰When King Ahaz went to Damascus to meet Tiglath-pileser king of Assyria, he saw the altar that was at Damascus. And King Ahaz sent to Uriah the priest a model of the altar, and its pattern, exact in all its details. ¹¹And Uriah the priest built the altar; in accordance with all that King Ahaz had sent from Damascus, so Uriah the priest made it, before King Ahaz arrived from Damascus. ¹²And when the king came from Damascus, the king viewed the altar. Then the king drew near to the altar and

¹ Or made his son pass through the fire

went up on it [13]and burned his burnt offering and his grain offering and poured his drink offering and threw the blood of his peace offerings on the altar. [14]And the bronze altar that was before the LORD he removed from the front of the house, from the place between his altar and the house of the LORD, and put it on the north side of his altar. [15]And King Ahaz commanded Uriah the priest, saying, "On the great altar burn the morning burnt offering and the evening grain offering and the king's burnt offering and his grain offering, with the burnt offering of all the people of the land, and their grain offering and their drink offering. And throw on it all the blood of the burnt offering and all the blood of the sacrifice, but the bronze altar shall be for me to inquire by." [16]Uriah the priest did all this, as King Ahaz commanded.

[17]And King Ahaz cut off the frames of the stands and removed the basin from them, and he took down the sea[1] from off the bronze oxen that were under it and put it on a stone pedestal. [18]And the covered way for the Sabbath that had been built inside the house and the outer entrance for the king he caused to go around the house of the LORD, because of the king of Assyria. [19]Now the rest of the acts of Ahaz that he did, are they not written in the Book of the Chronicles of the Kings of Judah? [20]And Ahaz slept with his fathers and was buried with his fathers in the city of David, and Hezekiah his son reigned in his place.

Israel goes into exile [17:1–23]. Although the northern and southern kingdoms are both in spiritual decline, Israel is the first to fall. The circumstances that precipitate Israel's invasion by the Assyrians involve a good deal of political folly on the part of King Hoshea. However, the careful historian who wrote 1 and 2 Kings was also an astute theologian, and he takes the time to explain that Israel's downfall was no less than the nation deserved for its many sins, especially in the area of false worship (vv. 7–23). This explanation is a good summary of what was happening in Israel spiritually from the exodus to the exile and also a clear warning for any nation that chooses to go its own way rather than God's way.

17 In the twelfth year of Ahaz king of Judah, Hoshea the son of Elah began to reign in Samaria over Israel, and he reigned nine years. [2]And he did what was evil in the sight of the LORD, yet not as the kings of Israel who were before him. [3]Against him came up Shalmaneser king of Assyria. And Hoshea became his vassal and paid him tribute. [4]But the king of Assyria found treachery in Hoshea, for he had sent messengers to So, king of Egypt, and offered no tribute to the king of Assyria, as he had done year by year. Therefore the king of Assyria shut him up and bound him in prison. [5]Then the king of Assyria invaded all the land and came to Samaria, and for three years he besieged it.

[6]In the ninth year of Hoshea, the king of Assyria captured Samaria, and he carried the Israelites away to Assyria and placed them in Halah, and on the Habor, the river of Gozan, and in the cities of the Medes.

[7]And this occurred because the people of Israel had sinned against the LORD their God, who had brought them up out of the land of Egypt from under the hand of Pharaoh king of Egypt, and had feared other gods [8]and walked in the customs of the nations whom the LORD drove out before the people of Israel, and in the customs that the kings of Israel had practiced. [9]And the people of Israel did secretly against the

---

[1] Compare 1 Kings 7:23

LORD their God things that were not right. They built for themselves high places in all their towns, from watchtower to fortified city. ¹⁰They set up for themselves pillars and Asherim on every high hill and under every green tree, ¹¹and there they made offerings on all the high places, as the nations did whom the LORD carried away before them. And they did wicked things, provoking the LORD to anger, ¹²and they served idols, of which the LORD had said to them, "You shall not do this." ¹³Yet the LORD warned Israel and Judah by every prophet and every seer, saying, "Turn from your evil ways and keep my commandments and my statutes, in accordance with all the Law that I commanded your fathers, and that I sent to you by my servants the prophets."

¹⁴But they would not listen, but were stubborn, as their fathers had been, who did not believe in the LORD their God. ¹⁵They despised his statutes and his covenant that he made with their fathers and the warnings that he gave them. They went after false idols and became false, and they followed the nations that were around them, concerning whom the LORD had commanded them that they should not do like them. ¹⁶And they abandoned all the commandments of the LORD their God, and made for themselves metal images of two calves; and they made an Asherah and worshiped all the host of heaven and served Baal. ¹⁷And they burned their sons and their daughters as offerings¹ and used divination and omens and sold themselves to do evil in the sight of the LORD, provoking him to anger. ¹⁸Therefore the LORD was very angry with Israel and removed them out of his sight. None was left but the tribe of Judah only.

¹⁹Judah also did not keep the commandments of the LORD their God, but walked in the customs that Israel had introduced. ²⁰And the LORD rejected all the descendants of Israel and afflicted them and gave them into the hand of plunderers, until he had cast them out of his sight.

²¹When he had torn Israel from the house of David, they made Jeroboam the son of Nebat king. And Jeroboam drove Israel from following the LORD and made them commit great sin. ²²The people of Israel walked in all the sins that Jeroboam did. They did not depart from them, ²³until the LORD removed Israel out of his sight, as he had spoken by all his servants the prophets. So Israel was exiled from their own land to Assyria until this day.

What happens in Samaria [17:24–41]. After the exile, the Assyrians resettle the northern kingdom with people from many nations who worship many gods. This *story of origins introduces us to the ancestors of the Samaritans whom we later meet in the NT. Not surprisingly, although some biblical forms for the true worship of God are retained, the region is dominated by religious pluralism and theological syncretism (vv. 24–33). Once again, the biblical historian evaluates this spiritual inconsistency according to the commandments of God and his covenant with Israel (vv. 34–41)—a consistent norm throughout 2 Kings.

²⁴And the king of Assyria brought people from Babylon, Cuthah, Avva, Hamath, and Sepharvaim, and placed them in the cities of Samaria instead of the people of Israel. And they took possession of Samaria and lived in its cities. ²⁵And at the beginning of their dwelling there, they did not fear the LORD. Therefore the LORD sent lions among them, which killed some of them. ²⁶So the king of Assyria was told, "The nations that you have carried away and placed in the cities of Samaria do not know

---

¹ Or made their sons and their daughters pass through the fire

the law of the god of the land. Therefore he has sent lions among them, and behold, they are killing them, because they do not know the law of the god of the land." [27]Then the king of Assyria commanded, "Send there one of the priests whom you carried away from there, and let him[1] go and dwell there and teach them the law of the god of the land." [28]So one of the priests whom they had carried away from Samaria came and lived in Bethel and taught them how they should fear the Lord.

[29]But every nation still made gods of its own and put them in the shrines of the high places that the Samaritans had made, every nation in the cities in which they lived. [30]The men of Babylon made Succoth-benoth, the men of Cuth made Nergal, the men of Hamath made Ashima, [31]and the Avvites made Nibhaz and Tartak; and the Sepharvites burned their children in the fire to Adrammelech and Anammelech, the gods of Sepharvaim. [32]They also feared the Lord and appointed from among themselves all sorts of people as priests of the high places, who sacrificed for them in the shrines of the high places. [33]So they feared the Lord but also served their own gods, after the manner of the nations from among whom they had been carried away.

[34]To this day they do according to the former manner. They do not fear the Lord, and they do not follow the statutes or the rules or the law or the commandment that the Lord commanded the children of Jacob, whom he named Israel. [35]The Lord made a covenant with them and commanded them, "You shall not fear other gods or bow yourselves to them or serve them or sacrifice to them, [36]but you shall fear the Lord, who brought you out of the land of Egypt with great power and with an outstretched arm. You shall bow yourselves to him, and to him you shall sacrifice. [37]And the statutes and the rules and the law and the commandment that he wrote for you, you shall always be careful to do. You shall not fear other gods, [38]and you shall not forget the covenant that I have made with you. You shall not fear other gods, [39]but you shall fear the Lord your God, and he will deliver you out of the hand of all your enemies." [40]However, they would not listen, but they did according to their former manner.

[41]So these nations feared the Lord and also served their carved images. Their children did likewise, and their children's children—as their fathers did, so they do to this day.

Hezekiah's crisis [chapter 18]. From this point on, the question becomes whether Judah will learn anything from Israel's lesson. Things look promising at the beginning. The story of Hezekiah slows down the ongoing action of 2 Kings; by way of analogy, it is like a two-hour season-ending special for a weekly television drama. The list of Hezekiah's kingly virtues and godly initiatives is impressive, especially the claim that he trusted God more than any king of Judah before or since (v. 5). At first the king is able to resist the army that carried Israel into exile (vv. 9–12). However, a decade later the Assyrians renew their threat under Sennacherib, capturing every city in Judah except Jerusalem. Although Hezekiah tries to buy the Assyrians off (vv. 14–16), they continue their advance, and when they reach the holy city, Rabshakeh taunts the king and his people—in their own language—with the claim that it is God's will for them to fall into the hands of the undefeated Assyrians (vv. 17–35). Will the Lord deliver his people or not?

---

[1] Syriac, Vulgate; Hebrew *them*

18 In the third year of Hoshea son of Elah, king of Israel, Hezekiah the son of Ahaz, king of Judah, began to reign. [2]He was twenty-five years old when he began to reign, and he reigned twenty-nine years in Jerusalem. His mother's name was Abi the daughter of Zechariah. [3]And he did what was right in the eyes of the LORD, according to all that David his father had done. [4]He removed the high places and broke the pillars and cut down the Asherah. And he broke in pieces the bronze serpent that Moses had made, for until those days the people of Israel had made offerings to it (it was called Nehushtan).[1] [5]He trusted in the LORD, the God of Israel, so that there was none like him among all the kings of Judah after him, nor among those who were before him. [6]For he held fast to the LORD. He did not depart from following him, but kept the commandments that the LORD commanded Moses. [7]And the LORD was with him; wherever he went out, he prospered. He rebelled against the king of Assyria and would not serve him. [8]He struck down the Philistines as far as Gaza and its territory, from watchtower to fortified city.

[9]In the fourth year of King Hezekiah, which was the seventh year of Hoshea son of Elah, king of Israel, Shalmaneser king of Assyria came up against Samaria and besieged it, [10]and at the end of three years he took it. In the sixth year of Hezekiah, which was the ninth year of Hoshea king of Israel, Samaria was taken. [11]The king of Assyria carried the Israelites away to Assyria and put them in Halah, and on the Habor, the river of Gozan, and in the cities of the Medes, [12]because they did not obey the voice of the LORD their God but transgressed his covenant, even all that Moses the servant of the LORD commanded. They neither listened nor obeyed.

[13]In the fourteenth year of King Hezekiah, Sennacherib king of Assyria came up against all the fortified cities of Judah and took them. [14]And Hezekiah king of Judah sent to the king of Assyria at Lachish, saying, "I have done wrong; withdraw from me. Whatever you impose on me I will bear." And the king of Assyria required of Hezekiah king of Judah three hundred talents[2] of silver and thirty talents of gold. [15]And Hezekiah gave him all the silver that was found in the house of the LORD and in the treasuries of the king's house. [16]At that time Hezekiah stripped the gold from the doors of the temple of the LORD and from the doorposts that Hezekiah king of Judah had overlaid and gave it to the king of Assyria. [17]And the king of Assyria sent the Tartan, the Rab-saris, and the Rabshakeh with a great army from Lachish to King Hezekiah at Jerusalem. And they went up and came to Jerusalem. When they arrived, they came and stood by the conduit of the upper pool, which is on the highway to the Washer's Field. [18]And when they called for the king, there came out to them Eliakim the son of Hilkiah, who was over the household, and Shebnah the secretary, and Joah the son of Asaph, the recorder.

[19]And the Rabshakeh said to them, "Say to Hezekiah, 'Thus says the great king, the king of Assyria: On what do you rest this trust of yours? [20]Do you think that mere words are strategy and power for war? In whom do you now trust, that you have rebelled against me? [21]Behold, you are trusting now in Egypt, that broken reed of a staff, which will pierce the hand of any man who leans on it. Such is Pharaoh king of Egypt to all who trust in him. [22]But if you say to me, "We trust in the LORD our God," is it not he whose high places and altars Hezekiah has removed, saying to Judah and to Jerusalem, "You shall worship before this altar in Jerusalem"? [23]Come now, make a wager with my master the king of Assyria: I will give you two thousand horses, if you are able on your part to set riders on them. [24]How then can you repulse a single cap-

---

[1] *Nehushtan* sounds like the Hebrew for both *bronze* and *serpent* [2] A *talent* was about 75 pounds or 34 kilograms

tain among the least of my master's servants, when you trust in Egypt for chariots and for horsemen? ²⁵Moreover, is it without the LORD that I have come up against this place to destroy it? The LORD said to me, Go up against this land, and destroy it.'"

²⁶Then Eliakim the son of Hilkiah, and Shebnah, and Joah, said to the Rabshakeh, "Please speak to your servants in Aramaic, for we understand it. Do not speak to us in the language of Judah within the hearing of the people who are on the wall." ²⁷But the Rabshakeh said to them, "Has my master sent me to speak these words to your master and to you, and not to the men sitting on the wall, who are doomed with you to eat their own dung and to drink their own urine?"

²⁸Then the Rabshakeh stood and called out in a loud voice in the language of Judah: "Hear the word of the great king, the king of Assyria! ²⁹Thus says the king: 'Do not let Hezekiah deceive you, for he will not be able to deliver you out of my¹ hand. ³⁰Do not let Hezekiah make you trust in the LORD by saying, The LORD will surely deliver us, and this city will not be given into the hand of the king of Assyria.' ³¹Do not listen to Hezekiah, for thus says the king of Assyria: 'Make your peace with me² and come out to me. Then each one of you will eat of his own vine, and each one of his own fig tree, and each one of you will drink the water of his own cistern, ³²until I come and take you away to a land like your own land, a land of grain and wine, a land of bread and vineyards, a land of olive trees and honey, that you may live, and not die. And do not listen to Hezekiah when he misleads you by saying, The LORD will deliver us. ³³Has any of the gods of the nations ever delivered his land out of the hand of the king of Assyria? ³⁴Where are the gods of Hamath and Arpad? Where are the gods of Sepharvaim, Hena, and Ivvah? Have they delivered Samaria out of my hand? ³⁵Who among all the gods of the lands have delivered their lands out of my hand, that the LORD should deliver Jerusalem out of my hand?'"

³⁶But the people were silent and answered him not a word, for the king's command was, "Do not answer him." ³⁷Then Eliakim the son of Hilkiah, who was over the household, and Shebna the secretary, and Joah the son of Asaph, the recorder, came to Hezekiah with their clothes torn and told him the words of the Rabshakeh.

Hezekiah's prayer for national deliverance [chapter 19]. In his distress, Hezekiah does not despair but wisely takes his nation's crisis to the Lord in prayer (vv. 1–4, 14–19) and seeks the counsel of God's prophet Isaiah (vv. 5–7). The king's prayer is a model of praise and petition, with a plea for deliverance that is based on an appeal for God to prove that he alone is God. Where there is life, there is hope—hope that the one true God may still have mercy on the remnant of his people. And God does have mercy. While the Assyrians continue to boast about their unbeaten streak (vv. 8–13)— a notable taunt scene—Isaiah assures Hezekiah that his prayers have been heard. He also prophesies that for the sake of God's covenant with David, the Assyrians will be prevented from ever entering Jerusalem and will go back home in defeat (vv. 20–34). Such proves to be the case, as the angel of the Lord strikes down tens of thousands of Assyrian soldiers in a famous rescue story (vv. 35–37).

19 As soon as King Hezekiah heard it, he tore his clothes and covered himself with sackcloth and went into the house of the LORD. ²And he sent Eliakim, who was over the household, and Shebna the secretary, and the senior priests, covered with sackcloth, to the prophet Isaiah the son of Amoz. ³They said to him, "Thus

¹ Hebrew his ² Hebrew Make a blessing with me

says Hezekiah, This day is a day of distress, of rebuke, and of disgrace; children have come to the point of birth, and there is no strength to bring them forth. ⁴It may be that the LORD your God heard all the words of the Rabshakeh, whom his master the king of Assyria has sent to mock the living God, and will rebuke the words that the LORD your God has heard; therefore lift up your prayer for the remnant that is left." ⁵When the servants of King Hezekiah came to Isaiah, ⁶Isaiah said to them, "Say to your master, 'Thus says the LORD: Do not be afraid because of the words that you have heard, with which the servants of the king of Assyria have reviled me. ⁷Behold, I will put a spirit in him, so that he shall hear a rumor and return to his own land, and I will make him fall by the sword in his own land.'"

⁸The Rabshakeh returned, and found the king of Assyria fighting against Libnah, for he heard that the king had left Lachish. ⁹Now the king heard concerning Tirhakah king of Cush, "Behold, he has set out to fight against you." So he sent messengers again to Hezekiah, saying, ¹⁰"Thus shall you speak to Hezekiah king of Judah: 'Do not let your God in whom you trust deceive you by promising that Jerusalem will not be given into the hand of the king of Assyria. ¹¹Behold, you have heard what the kings of Assyria have done to all lands, devoting them to destruction. And shall you be delivered? ¹²Have the gods of the nations delivered them, the nations that my fathers destroyed, Gozan, Haran, Rezeph, and the people of Eden who were in Telassar? ¹³Where is the king of Hamath, the king of Arpad, the king of the city of Sepharvaim, the king of Hena, or the king of Ivvah?'"

¹⁴Hezekiah received the letter from the hand of the messengers and read it; and Hezekiah went up to the house of the LORD and spread it before the LORD. ¹⁵And Hezekiah prayed before the LORD and said: "O LORD, the God of Israel, enthroned above the cherubim, you are the God, you alone, of all the kingdoms of the earth; you have made heaven and earth. ¹⁶Incline your ear, O LORD, and hear; open your eyes, O LORD, and see; and hear the words of Sennacherib, which he has sent to mock the living God. ¹⁷Truly, O LORD, the kings of Assyria have laid waste the nations and their lands ¹⁸and have cast their gods into the fire, for they were not gods, but the work of men's hands, wood and stone. Therefore they were destroyed. ¹⁹So now, O LORD our God, save us, please, from his hand, that all the kingdoms of the earth may know that you, O LORD, are God alone."

²⁰Then Isaiah the son of Amoz sent to Hezekiah, saying, "Thus says the LORD, the God of Israel: Your prayer to me about Sennacherib king of Assyria I have heard. ²¹This is the word that the LORD has spoken concerning him:

"She despises you, she scorns you—
    the virgin daughter of Zion;
she wags her head behind you—
    the daughter of Jerusalem.

²²   "Whom have you mocked and reviled?
        Against whom have you raised your voice
    and lifted your eyes to the heights?
        Against the Holy One of Israel!
²³   By your messengers you have mocked the Lord,
        and you have said, 'With my many chariots

I have gone up the heights of the mountains,
    to the far recesses of Lebanon;
I felled its tallest cedars,
    its choicest cypresses;
I entered its farthest lodging place,
    its most fruitful forest.
24 I dug wells
    and drank foreign waters,
and I dried up with the sole of my foot
    all the streams of Egypt.'

25 "Have you not heard
    that I determined it long ago?
I planned from days of old
    what now I bring to pass,
that you should turn fortified cities
    into heaps of ruins,
26 while their inhabitants, shorn of strength,
    are dismayed and confounded,
and have become like plants of the field
    and like tender grass,
like grass on the housetops,
    blighted before it is grown.

27 "But I know your sitting down
    and your going out and coming in,
    and your raging against me.
28 Because you have raged against me
    and your complacency has come into my ears,
I will put my hook in your nose
    and my bit in your mouth,
and I will turn you back on the way
    by which you came.

29 "And this shall be the sign for you: this year eat what grows of itself, and in the second year what springs of the same. Then in the third year sow and reap and plant vineyards, and eat their fruit. 30 And the surviving remnant of the house of Judah shall again take root downward and bear fruit upward. 31 For out of Jerusalem shall go a remnant, and out of Mount Zion a band of survivors. The zeal of the LORD will do this.

32 "Therefore thus says the LORD concerning the king of Assyria: He shall not come into this city or shoot an arrow there, or come before it with a shield or cast up a siege mound against it. 33 By the way that he came, by the same he shall return, and he shall not come into this city, declares the LORD. 34 For I will defend this city to save it, for my own sake and for the sake of my servant David."

35 And that night the angel of the LORD went out and struck down 185,000 in the camp of the Assyrians. And when people arose early in the morning, behold, these were all dead bodies. 36 Then Sennacherib king of Assyria departed and went home and lived at Nineveh. 37 And as he was worshiping in the house of Nisroch his god,

Adrammelech and Sharezer, his sons, struck him down with the sword and escaped into the land of Ararat. And Esarhaddon his son reigned in his place.

> **Hezekiah's prayer for personal healing** [chapter 20]. The second great crisis of Hezekiah's life is personal rather than national: at the same time the Assyrians are threatening his kingdom, the king becomes sick and is told by God's prophet that he has no chance of recovery. Once again Hezekiah prays, and Isaiah tells him that his prayers are answered, although this time the king seems more concerned about his own well-being than about the glory of God (see v. 3). His self-interest is even more apparent in his subsequent encounter with envoys from the rising power of Babylon. After Hezekiah foolishly shows them everything in his royal treasury (vv. 12–13), Isaiah prophesies that eventually the Babylonians will come and carry it all away, including the king's own sons (vv. 14–18). Far from repenting for what he has done, Hezekiah receives Isaiah's words of judgment as good news: after all, it won't happen during his lifetime (v. 19). The story of Hezekiah encapsulates the repeated pattern of 2 Kings: despite occasional flashes of godliness, the overwhelming bent of the kings is to end badly.

20 In those days Hezekiah became sick and was at the point of death. And Isaiah the prophet the son of Amoz came to him and said to him, "Thus says the LORD, 'Set your house in order, for you shall die; you shall not recover.'" ²Then Hezekiah turned his face to the wall and prayed to the LORD, saying, ³"Now, O LORD, please remember how I have walked before you in faithfulness and with a whole heart, and have done what is good in your sight." And Hezekiah wept bitterly. ⁴And before Isaiah had gone out of the middle court, the word of the LORD came to him: ⁵"Turn back, and say to Hezekiah the leader of my people, Thus says the LORD, the God of David your father: I have heard your prayer; I have seen your tears. Behold, I will heal you. On the third day you shall go up to the house of the LORD, ⁶and I will add fifteen years to your life. I will deliver you and this city out of the hand of the king of Assyria, and I will defend this city for my own sake and for my servant David's sake." ⁷And Isaiah said, "Bring a cake of figs. And let them take and lay it on the boil, that he may recover."

⁸And Hezekiah said to Isaiah, "What shall be the sign that the LORD will heal me, and that I shall go up to the house of the LORD on the third day?" ⁹And Isaiah said, "This shall be the sign to you from the LORD, that the LORD will do the thing that he has promised: shall the shadow go forward ten steps, or go back ten steps?" ¹⁰And Hezekiah answered, "It is an easy thing for the shadow to lengthen ten steps. Rather let the shadow go back ten steps." ¹¹And Isaiah the prophet called to the LORD, and he brought the shadow back ten steps, by which it had gone down on the steps of Ahaz.

¹²At that time Merodach-baladan the son of Baladan, king of Babylon, sent envoys with letters and a present to Hezekiah, for he heard that Hezekiah had been sick. ¹³And Hezekiah welcomed them, and he showed them all his treasure house, the silver, the gold, the spices, the precious oil, his armory, all that was found in his storehouses. There was nothing in his house or in all his realm that Hezekiah did not show them. ¹⁴Then Isaiah the prophet came to King Hezekiah, and said to him, "What did these men say? And from where did they come to you?" And Hezekiah said, "They have come from a far country, from Babylon." ¹⁵He said, "What have they seen

in your house?" And Hezekiah answered, "They have seen all that is in my house; there is nothing in my storehouses that I did not show them."

¹⁶Then Isaiah said to Hezekiah, "Hear the word of the LORD: ¹⁷Behold, the days are coming, when all that is in your house, and that which your fathers have stored up till this day, shall be carried to Babylon. Nothing shall be left, says the LORD. ¹⁸And some of your own sons, who shall be born to you, shall be taken away, and they shall be eunuchs in the palace of the king of Babylon." ¹⁹Then said Hezekiah to Isaiah, "The word of the LORD that you have spoken is good." For he thought, "Why not, if there will be peace and security in my days?"

²⁰The rest of the deeds of Hezekiah and all his might and how he made the pool and the conduit and brought water into the city, are they not written in the Book of the Chronicles of the Kings of Judah? ²¹And Hezekiah slept with his fathers, and Manasseh his son reigned in his place.

Manasseh and Amon [chapter 21]. One step forward, two steps back. After returning to God in many ways under King Hezekiah, Judah falls back into idolatry under Manasseh and Amon. Bloodthirsty Manasseh reigns for more than half a century, during which he leads the people of God into all the pagan and godless practices of the surrounding nations, defiling the temple that Solomon built (vv. 1–9, 16–18). As a result—say the prophets, using memorable images of destruction—Judah will go into exile, just like Israel (vv. 10–15). Mercifully, the reign of Manasseh's evil son Amon is much briefer (vv. 19–26).

21 Manasseh was twelve years old when he began to reign, and he reigned fifty-five years in Jerusalem. His mother's name was Hephzibah. ²And he did what was evil in the sight of the LORD, according to the despicable practices of the nations whom the LORD drove out before the people of Israel. ³For he rebuilt the high places that Hezekiah his father had destroyed, and he erected altars for Baal and made an Asherah, as Ahab king of Israel had done, and worshiped all the host of heaven and served them. ⁴And he built altars in the house of the LORD, of which the LORD had said, "In Jerusalem will I put my name." ⁵And he built altars for all the host of heaven in the two courts of the house of the LORD. ⁶And he burned his son as an offering[1] and used fortune-telling and omens and dealt with mediums and with necromancers. He did much evil in the sight of the LORD, provoking him to anger. ⁷And the carved image of Asherah that he had made he set in the house of which the LORD said to David and to Solomon his son, "In this house, and in Jerusalem, which I have chosen out of all the tribes of Israel, I will put my name forever. ⁸And I will not cause the feet of Israel to wander anymore out of the land that I gave to their fathers, if only they will be careful to do according to all that I have commanded them, and according to all the Law that my servant Moses commanded them." ⁹But they did not listen, and Manasseh led them astray to do more evil than the nations had done whom the LORD destroyed before the people of Israel.

¹⁰And the LORD said by his servants the prophets, ¹¹"Because Manasseh king of Judah has committed these abominations and has done things more evil than all that the Amorites did, who were before him, and has made Judah also to sin with his idols, ¹²therefore thus says the LORD, the God of Israel: Behold, I am bringing upon

---

[1] Hebrew *made his son pass through the fire*

Jerusalem and Judah such disaster[1] that the ears of everyone who hears of it will tingle. ¹³And I will stretch over Jerusalem the measuring line of Samaria, and the plumb line of the house of Ahab, and I will wipe Jerusalem as one wipes a dish, wiping it and turning it upside down. ¹⁴And I will forsake the remnant of my heritage and give them into the hand of their enemies, and they shall become a prey and a spoil to all their enemies, ¹⁵because they have done what is evil in my sight and have provoked me to anger, since the day their fathers came out of Egypt, even to this day."

¹⁶Moreover, Manasseh shed very much innocent blood, till he had filled Jerusalem from one end to another, besides the sin that he made Judah to sin so that they did what was evil in the sight of the LORD.

¹⁷Now the rest of the acts of Manasseh and all that he did, and the sin that he committed, are they not written in the Book of the Chronicles of the Kings of Judah? ¹⁸And Manasseh slept with his fathers and was buried in the garden of his house, in the garden of Uzza, and Amon his son reigned in his place.

¹⁹Amon was twenty-two years old when he began to reign, and he reigned two years in Jerusalem. His mother's name was Meshullemeth the daughter of Haruz of Jotbah. ²⁰And he did what was evil in the sight of the LORD, as Manasseh his father had done. ²¹He walked in all the way in which his father walked and served the idols that his father served and worshiped them. ²²He abandoned the LORD, the God of his fathers, and did not walk in the way of the LORD. ²³And the servants of Amon conspired against him and put the king to death in his house. ²⁴But the people of the land struck down all those who had conspired against King Amon, and the people of the land made Josiah his son king in his place. ²⁵Now the rest of the acts of Amon that he did, are they not written in the Book of the Chronicles of the Kings of Judah? ²⁶And he was buried in his tomb in the garden of Uzza, and Josiah his son reigned in his place.

Josiah's discovery [chapter 22]. Once again, a boy king comes to the throne to set Judah on the course to spiritual renewal. Like his forebear David, Josiah is careful to keep the law of the Lord (vv. 1–2); like Joash before him, he begins a building campaign to restore the temple (vv. 3–7; cf. 12:4–16). In the course of this campaign, Hilkiah the high priest rediscovers "the Book of the Law" (v. 8). In all likelihood, this was a copy of the book of Deuteronomy, which, like the temple in which it was found, had fallen into disuse. Upon hearing what the law demands, Josiah tears his garments, rightly fearing that Judah's disobedience merits the wrath of God (vv. 11–13). The words of Huldah the prophetess give hope to Josiah and to every penitent sinner: although judgment is coming, God will have mercy on people like Josiah, who truly repent of their sins (vv. 14–20). This chapter recounts one of the red-letter moments of OT history.

22 Josiah was eight years old when he began to reign, and he reigned thirty-one years in Jerusalem. His mother's name was Jedidah the daughter of Adaiah of Bozkath. ²And he did what was right in the eyes of the LORD and walked in all the way of David his father, and he did not turn aside to the right or to the left.

³In the eighteenth year of King Josiah, the king sent Shaphan the son of Azaliah, son of Meshullam, the secretary, to the house of the LORD, saying, ⁴"Go up to Hilkiah the high priest, that he may count the money that has been brought into the house of the LORD, which the keepers of the threshold have collected from the people. ⁵And let it be given into the hand of the workmen who have the oversight of the house of the

¹ Or evil

Lord, and let them give it to the workmen who are at the house of the Lord, repairing the house ⁶(that is, to the carpenters, and to the builders, and to the masons), and let them use it for buying timber and quarried stone to repair the house. ⁷But no accounting shall be asked from them for the money that is delivered into their hand, for they deal honestly."

⁸And Hilkiah the high priest said to Shaphan the secretary, "I have found the Book of the Law in the house of the Lord." And Hilkiah gave the book to Shaphan, and he read it. ⁹And Shaphan the secretary came to the king, and reported to the king, "Your servants have emptied out the money that was found in the house and have delivered it into the hand of the workmen who have the oversight of the house of the Lord." ¹⁰Then Shaphan the secretary told the king, "Hilkiah the priest has given me a book." And Shaphan read it before the king.

¹¹When the king heard the words of the Book of the Law, he tore his clothes. ¹²And the king commanded Hilkiah the priest, and Ahikam the son of Shaphan, and Achbor the son of Micaiah, and Shaphan the secretary, and Asaiah the king's servant, saying, ¹³"Go, inquire of the Lord for me, and for the people, and for all Judah, concerning the words of this book that has been found. For great is the wrath of the Lord that is kindled against us, because our fathers have not obeyed the words of this book, to do according to all that is written concerning us."

¹⁴So Hilkiah the priest, and Ahikam, and Achbor, and Shaphan, and Asaiah went to Huldah the prophetess, the wife of Shallum the son of Tikvah, son of Harhas, keeper of the wardrobe (now she lived in Jerusalem in the Second Quarter), and they talked with her. ¹⁵And she said to them, "Thus says the Lord, the God of Israel: 'Tell the man who sent you to me, ¹⁶Thus says the Lord, Behold, I will bring disaster upon this place and upon its inhabitants, all the words of the book that the king of Judah has read. ¹⁷Because they have forsaken me and have made offerings to other gods, that they might provoke me to anger with all the work of their hands, therefore my wrath will be kindled against this place, and it will not be quenched. ¹⁸But to the king of Judah, who sent you to inquire of the Lord, thus shall you say to him, Thus says the Lord, the God of Israel: Regarding the words that you have heard, ¹⁹because your heart was penitent, and you humbled yourself before the Lord, when you heard how I spoke against this place and against its inhabitants, that they should become a desolation and a curse, and you have torn your clothes and wept before me, I also have heard you, declares the Lord. ²⁰Therefore, behold, I will gather you to your fathers, and you shall be gathered to your grave in peace, and your eyes shall not see all the disaster that I will bring upon this place.'" And they brought back word to the king.

Josiah's reformation [23:1–30]. Under the reforming influence of God's Word (here called the Book of the Covenant), Josiah initiates a full restoration of God's worship. His notable reforms include restoring the reading of Scripture to its rightful place in Judah's worship (v. 2); renewing the covenant with Judah's God (v. 3); burning the implements of pagan idolatry (v. 4); deposing and executing the priests of false worship (vv. 5, 20); breaking down the altars for the worship of foreign gods, including places for ritual prostitution and child sacrifice (vv. 6–14); tearing down the high places of Jeroboam (vv. 15, 19); honoring the memory of God's true prophets (vv. 17–18); reinstituting the sacrament of Passover, which had long since fallen into neglect (vv. 21–23); and ridding

the nation of mediums, necromancers, and other idolaters (v. 24). The commendation
Josiah receives as a result is well deserved (v. 25). Nevertheless, the writer reminds us
that the sins of Manasseh will still bring judgment on Judah and Jerusalem (vv. 26–27).
Even at a time of reformation, deformation is never far away.

23 Then the king sent, and all the elders of Judah and Jerusalem were gathered
to him. ²And the king went up to the house of the LORD, and with him all the
men of Judah and all the inhabitants of Jerusalem and the priests and the prophets,
all the people, both small and great. And he read in their hearing all the words of the
Book of the Covenant that had been found in the house of the LORD. ³And the king
stood by the pillar and made a covenant before the LORD, to walk after the LORD and
to keep his commandments and his testimonies and his statutes with all his heart
and all his soul, to perform the words of this covenant that were written in this book.
And all the people joined in the covenant.

⁴And the king commanded Hilkiah the high priest and the priests of the second
order and the keepers of the threshold to bring out of the temple of the LORD all the
vessels made for Baal, for Asherah, and for all the host of heaven. He burned them
outside Jerusalem in the fields of the Kidron and carried their ashes to Bethel. ⁵And
he deposed the priests whom the kings of Judah had ordained to make offerings in
the high places at the cities of Judah and around Jerusalem; those also who burned
incense to Baal, to the sun and the moon and the constellations and all the host of
the heavens. ⁶And he brought out the Asherah from the house of the LORD, outside
Jerusalem, to the brook Kidron, and burned it at the brook Kidron and beat it to dust
and cast the dust of it upon the graves of the common people. ⁷And he broke down
the houses of the male cult prostitutes who were in the house of the LORD, where the
women wove hangings for the Asherah. ⁸And he brought all the priests out of the cities of Judah, and defiled the high places where the priests had made offerings, from
Geba to Beersheba. And he broke down the high places of the gates that were at the
entrance of the gate of Joshua the governor of the city, which were on one's left at the
gate of the city. ⁹However, the priests of the high places did not come up to the altar
of the LORD in Jerusalem, but they ate unleavened bread among their brothers. ¹⁰And
he defiled Topheth, which is in the Valley of the Son of Hinnom, that no one might
burn his son or his daughter as an offering to Molech.¹ ¹¹And he removed the horses
that the kings of Judah had dedicated to the sun, at the entrance to the house of the
LORD, by the chamber of Nathan-melech the chamberlain, which was in the pre-
cincts.² And he burned the chariots of the sun with fire. ¹²And the altars on the roof
of the upper chamber of Ahaz, which the kings of Judah had made, and the altars
that Manasseh had made in the two courts of the house of the LORD, he pulled down
and broke in pieces³ and cast the dust of them into the brook Kidron. ¹³And the king
defiled the high places that were east of Jerusalem, to the south of the mount of corruption, which Solomon the king of Israel had built for Ashtoreth the abomination of
the Sidonians, and for Chemosh the abomination of Moab, and for Milcom the
abomination of the Ammonites. ¹⁴And he broke in pieces the pillars and cut down the
Asherim and filled their places with the bones of men.

¹⁵Moreover, the altar at Bethel, the high place erected by Jeroboam the son of
Nebat, who made Israel to sin, that altar with the high place he pulled down and

¹ Hebrew might cause his son or daughter to pass through the fire for Molech ² The meaning of the Hebrew word is uncertain ³ Hebrew pieces from there

burned,[1] reducing it to dust. He also burned the Asherah. [16]And as Josiah turned, he saw the tombs there on the mount. And he sent and took the bones out of the tombs and burned them on the altar and defiled it, according to the word of the LORD that the man of God proclaimed, who had predicted these things. [17]Then he said, "What is that monument that I see?" And the men of the city told him, "It is the tomb of the man of God who came from Judah and predicted[2] these things that you have done against the altar at Bethel." [18]And he said, "Let him be; let no man move his bones." So they let his bones alone, with the bones of the prophet who came out of Samaria. [19]And Josiah removed all the shrines also of the high places that were in the cities of Samaria, which kings of Israel had made, provoking the LORD to anger. He did to them according to all that he had done at Bethel. [20]And he sacrificed all the priests of the high places who were there, on the altars, and burned human bones on them. Then he returned to Jerusalem.

[21]And the king commanded all the people, "Keep the Passover to the LORD your God, as it is written in this Book of the Covenant." [22]For no such Passover had been kept since the days of the judges who judged Israel, or during all the days of the kings of Israel or of the kings of Judah. [23]But in the eighteenth year of King Josiah this Passover was kept to the LORD in Jerusalem.

[24]Moreover, Josiah put away the mediums and the necromancers and the household gods and the idols and all the abominations that were seen in the land of Judah and in Jerusalem, that he might establish the words of the law that were written in the book that Hilkiah the priest found in the house of the LORD. [25]Before him there was no king like him, who turned to the LORD with all his heart and with all his soul and with all his might, according to all the Law of Moses, nor did any like him arise after him.

[26]Still the LORD did not turn from the burning of his great wrath, by which his anger was kindled against Judah, because of all the provocations with which Manasseh had provoked him. [27]And the LORD said, "I will remove Judah also out of my sight, as I have removed Israel, and I will cast off this city that I have chosen, Jerusalem, and the house of which I said, My name shall be there."

[28]Now the rest of the acts of Josiah and all that he did, are they not written in the Book of the Chronicles of the Kings of Judah? [29]In his days Pharaoh Neco king of Egypt went up to the king of Assyria to the river Euphrates. King Josiah went to meet him, and Pharaoh Neco killed him at Megiddo, as soon as he saw him. [30]And his servants carried him dead in a chariot from Megiddo and brought him to Jerusalem and buried him in his own tomb. And the people of the land took Jehoahaz the son of Josiah, and anointed him, and made him king in his father's place.

The last kings of Jerusalem [23:31–24:17]. The years leading up to the Babylonian exile are not happy ones for the kings of Judah, none of whom fear God. Jehoahaz is held captive in Egypt (23:31–34). Jehoiakim refuses to pay tribute to Nebuchadnezzar and suffers the wrath of Babylon (23:35–24:7). Jehoiachin fares even worse, for it is in his day that Nebuchadnezzar besieges Jerusalem and begins deporting its leaders to Babylon, including the king and his unfortunate family (24:8–17). The judgment that God has threatened for so long is finally starting to fall on Judah, as the glories of Solomon's

---

[1] Septuagint *broke in pieces its stones* [2] Hebrew *called*

kingdom are carried into captivity (see 24:13). The vivid images of defeat and decay at the end of 2 Kings reinforce the book's central motif of spiritual declension.

[31]Jehoahaz was twenty-three years old when he began to reign, and he reigned three months in Jerusalem. His mother's name was Hamutal the daughter of Jeremiah of Libnah. [32]And he did what was evil in the sight of the LORD, according to all that his fathers had done. [33]And Pharaoh Neco put him in bonds at Riblah in the land of Hamath, that he might not reign in Jerusalem, and laid on the land a tribute of a hundred talents[1] of silver and a talent of gold. [34]And Pharaoh Neco made Eliakim the son of Josiah king in the place of Josiah his father, and changed his name to Jehoiakim. But he took Jehoahaz away, and he came to Egypt and died there. [35]And Jehoiakim gave the silver and the gold to Pharaoh, but he taxed the land to give the money according to the command of Pharaoh. He exacted the silver and the gold of the people of the land, from everyone according to his assessment, to give it to Pharaoh Neco.

[36]Jehoiakim was twenty-five years old when he began to reign, and he reigned eleven years in Jerusalem. His mother's name was Zebidah the daughter of Pedaiah of Rumah. [37]And he did what was evil in the sight of the LORD, according to all that his fathers had done.

24 In his days, Nebuchadnezzar king of Babylon came up, and Jehoiakim became his servant three years. Then he turned and rebelled against him. [2]And the LORD sent against him bands of the Chaldeans and bands of the Syrians and bands of the Moabites and bands of the Ammonites, and sent them against Judah to destroy it, according to the word of the LORD that he spoke by his servants the prophets. [3]Surely this came upon Judah at the command of the LORD, to remove them out of his sight, for the sins of Manasseh, according to all that he had done, [4]and also for the innocent blood that he had shed. For he filled Jerusalem with innocent blood, and the LORD would not pardon. [5]Now the rest of the deeds of Jehoiakim and all that he did, are they not written in the Book of the Chronicles of the Kings of Judah? [6]So Jehoiakim slept with his fathers, and Jehoiachin his son reigned in his place. [7]And the king of Egypt did not come again out of his land, for the king of Babylon had taken all that belonged to the king of Egypt from the Brook of Egypt to the river Euphrates.

[8]Jehoiachin was eighteen years old when he became king, and he reigned three months in Jerusalem. His mother's name was Nehushta the daughter of Elnathan of Jerusalem. [9]And he did what was evil in the sight of the LORD, according to all that his father had done.

[10]At that time the servants of Nebuchadnezzar king of Babylon came up to Jerusalem, and the city was besieged. [11]And Nebuchadnezzar king of Babylon came to the city while his servants were besieging it, [12]and Jehoiachin the king of Judah gave himself up to the king of Babylon, himself and his mother and his servants and his officials and his palace officials. The king of Babylon took him prisoner in the eighth year of his reign [13]and carried off all the treasures of the house of the LORD and the treasures of the king's house, and cut in pieces all the vessels of gold in the temple of the LORD, which Solomon king of Israel had made, as the LORD had fore-

---

[1] A *talent* was about 75 pounds or 34 kilograms

told. ¹⁴He carried away all Jerusalem and all the officials and all the mighty men of valor, 10,000 captives, and all the craftsmen and the smiths. None remained, except the poorest people of the land. ¹⁵And he carried away Jehoiachin to Babylon. The king's mother, the king's wives, his officials, and the chief men of the land he took into captivity from Jerusalem to Babylon. ¹⁶And the king of Babylon brought captive to Babylon all the men of valor, 7,000, and the craftsmen and the metal workers, 1,000, all of them strong and fit for war. ¹⁷And the king of Babylon made Mattaniah, Jehoiachin's uncle, king in his place, and changed his name to Zedekiah.

The fall of Jerusalem [24:18–25:21]. The Babylonians appoint Zedekiah (who is related to Jehoiachin but is not David's rightful heir) to serve as their puppet king in Jerusalem. Like Jehoiachin, Zedekiah does what is evil in the sight of the Lord. He also commits the folly of rebelling against Nebuchadnezzar, and this is the proximate cause of Jerusalem's final destruction. The Babylonian siege lasts for more than a year, during which the citizens of Jerusalem endure a severe famine. When the city is finally over-run, there are scenes of unimaginable horror: Zedekiah's sons are slaughtered; the king himself is blinded and led off to Babylon in chains; the temple, the palace, and the city walls are burned to the ground; the golden treasures left at the temple are carried off to the treasuries of Nebuchadnezzar; Judah's priests are put to death; and almost everyone else is sent into exile. The devastation is total, God's judgment complete.

¹⁸Zedekiah was twenty-one years old when he became king, and he reigned eleven years in Jerusalem. His mother's name was Hamutal the daughter of Jeremiah of Libnah. ¹⁹And he did what was evil in the sight of the Lord, according to all that Jehoiakim had done. ²⁰For because of the anger of the Lord it came to the point in Jerusalem and Judah that he cast them out from his presence.

And Zedekiah rebelled against the king of Babylon.

25 And in the ninth year of his reign, in the tenth month, on the tenth day of the month, Nebuchadnezzar king of Babylon came with all his army against Jerusalem and laid siege to it. And they built siegeworks all around it. ²So the city was besieged till the eleventh year of King Zedekiah. ³On the ninth day of the fourth month the famine was so severe in the city that there was no food for the people of the land. ⁴Then a breach was made in the city, and all the men of war fled by night by the way of the gate between the two walls, by the king's garden, though the Chaldeans were around the city. And they went in the direction of the Arabah. ⁵But the army of the Chaldeans pursued the king and overtook him in the plains of Jericho, and all his army was scattered from him. ⁶Then they captured the king and brought him up to the king of Babylon at Riblah, and they passed sentence on him. ⁷They slaughtered the sons of Zedekiah before his eyes, and put out the eyes of Zedekiah and bound him in chains and took him to Babylon.

⁸In the fifth month, on the seventh day of the month—that was the nineteenth year of King Nebuchadnezzar, king of Babylon—Nebuzaradan, the captain of the body-guard, a servant of the king of Babylon, came to Jerusalem. ⁹And he burned the house of the Lord and the king's house and all the houses of Jerusalem; every great house he burned down. ¹⁰And all the army of the Chaldeans, who were with the captain of the guard, broke down the walls around Jerusalem. ¹¹And the rest of the people who

were left in the city and the deserters who had deserted to the king of Babylon, together with the rest of the multitude, Nebuzaradan the captain of the guard carried into exile. [12]But the captain of the guard left some of the poorest of the land to be vinedressers and plowmen.

[13]And the pillars of bronze that were in the house of the Lord, and the stands and the bronze sea that were in the house of the Lord, the Chaldeans broke in pieces and carried the bronze to Babylon. [14]And they took away the pots and the shovels and the snuffers and the dishes for incense and all the vessels of bronze used in the temple service, [15]the fire pans also and the bowls. What was of gold the captain of the guard took away as gold, and what was of silver, as silver. [16]As for the two pillars, the one sea, and the stands that Solomon had made for the house of the Lord, the bronze of all these vessels was beyond weight. [17]The height of the one pillar was eighteen cubits,[1] and on it was a capital of bronze. The height of the capital was three cubits. A latticework and pomegranates, all of bronze, were all around the capital. And the second pillar had the same, with the latticework.

[18]And the captain of the guard took Seraiah the chief priest and Zephaniah the second priest and the three keepers of the threshold, [19]and from the city he took an officer who had been in command of the men of war, and five men of the king's council who were found in the city, and the secretary of the commander of the army who mustered the people of the land, and sixty men of the people of the land who were found in the city. [20]And Nebuzaradan the captain of the guard took them and brought them to the king of Babylon at Riblah. [21]And the king of Babylon struck them down and put them to death at Riblah in the land of Hamath. So Judah was taken into exile out of its land.

After the fall [25:22–30]. The epilogue to 1 and 2 Kings has literary and theological significance. After a brief account of what happens back in Jerusalem (and also in Egypt, where many people fled, against the will of God) after the deportation (vv. 22–26), the historian shows us what is happening in Babylon, where Jehoiachin—the rightful king of Judah—has been released from prison to sit at the king's royal table. Although he is still in captivity, he is also still alive, and thus the promises God made to David have not failed. One day the exile will be over and the King will come again.

[22]And over the people who remained in the land of Judah, whom Nebuchadnezzar king of Babylon had left, he appointed Gedaliah the son of Ahikam, son of Shaphan, governor. [23]Now when all the captains and their men heard that the king of Babylon had appointed Gedaliah governor, they came with their men to Gedaliah at Mizpah, namely, Ishmael the son of Nethaniah, and Johanan the son of Kareah, and Seraiah the son of Tanhumeth the Netophathite, and Jaazaniah the son of the Maacathite. [24]And Gedaliah swore to them and their men, saying, "Do not be afraid because of the Chaldean officials. Live in the land and serve the king of Babylon, and it shall be well with you." [25]But in the seventh month, Ishmael the son of Nethaniah, son of Elishama, of the royal family, came with ten men and struck down Gedaliah and put him to death along with the Jews and the Chaldeans who were with him at Mizpah. [26]Then all the people, both small and great, and the captains of the forces arose and went to Egypt, for they were afraid of the Chaldeans.

[1] A *cubit* was about 18 inches or 45 centimeters

²⁷And in the thirty-seventh year of the exile of Jehoiachin king of Judah, in the twelfth month, on the twenty-seventh day of the month, Evil-merodach king of Babylon, in the year that he began to reign, graciously freed[1] Jehoiachin king of Judah from prison. ²⁸And he spoke kindly to him and gave him a seat above the seats of the kings who were with him in Babylon. ²⁹So Jehoiachin put off his prison garments. And every day of his life he dined regularly at the king's table, ³⁰and for his allowance, a regular allowance was given him by the king, according to his daily needs, as long as he lived.

---

[1] Hebrew *reign, lifted up the head of*

I CHRONICLES

The book at a glance. 29 chapters, 941 verses. First Chronicles is primarily a historical chronicle and only secondarily a work of literature. The main human character is King David, and the writer gives a highly idealized picture of him (largely omitting the tragic view of his life that the writer of 2 Samuel presents). Further, he presents Israelite history from a religious viewpoint, with emphasis on the temple. From the combined picture of an ideal monarch and detailed account of temple worship, we can build a picture of what the author regards as a good society. The providential theme is also important, as events are repeatedly ascribed to God. To this we can add that the history we read is a record of how God preserved the messianic line that eventually produced Jesus. One biblical scholar calls the author of the book the first OT theologian, and another scholar claims that the author implicitly agreed with the Greek writer Dionysius's claim that history is "philosophy teaching by examples," with the result that the book gives us spiritual models to copy or avoid.

▌Genres. The book is mainly a documentary historical chronicle, consisting of facts and figures from Israelite history during the reign of David. More specifically, the genre is court history: it centers on the king and the leaders of the nation. Because David is the protagonist, at times the writer veers away from historical chronicle toward biography, and at some points he narrates an event in sufficient detail that we find something resembling a *hero story. Specific forms of documentary writing include *genealogies, inventories, and summaries of events, such as lists of David's victories. We also find speeches or orations, prayers, and a *psalm of praise. (For more information on items accompanied by an asterisk, see the glossary at the back of this Bible.)

▌Cast of characters. God is the center of reference in the book—the one to whom all events and characters relate. The chief human character is David in his role as king. Two other kings bracket David's life as narrated in this book—Saul before him and Solomon after him. Groups of people also play prominent roles, including the Levites, the priests, others who assisted in worship at the temple, and military and civil officials. Finally, the nation, repeatedly called "all Israel," assumes the quality of a corporate character.

▌The story line. Even though the book is structured as a historical chronicle rather than a *narrative, the history does tell a story that can be called the story of God's

Passage	Content	The Story as It Relates to God	Literary Form	Type of History	Time Frame
1:1–9:44	The history of Israel before the monarchy	God's people	Genealogies	Straightforward factual history	Millennia
10:1–12:40	Beginning of David's kingship	God's anointed king	Narrative and lists		
13:1–14	Ark of the covenant				
14:1–17	David's military victories	The ark of God's covenant	Chiefly narrative		
15:1–16:43	Ark of the covenant			Interpretive history, mainly religious but also political	33 years
17:1–27	The Davidic covenant	God's covenant with David			
18:1–22:1	Political events	Armies of God's people	History and narrative		
22:2–26:28	Plans for the temple				
26:29–27:34	Political matters	God's temple and nation	Lists and narrative		
28:1–29:30	End of David's kingship				

covenant dealings with the human race. The main features of this story of covenant history are as follows: (1) it is a story of Israel from Adam to the beginning of the monarchy; (2) because this is Israelite history, it is the story of God's covenant dealings with the human race and then a specific nation; (3) David is depicted as the special ruler of Israelite history, and he becomes a type (foreshadowing) of Christ when God declares his covenant with David to be an eternal covenant; (4) because this is the story of God's covenant community, worship at the temple has a central place in the action.

▌ **Inferred literary intentions.** The book is designed to achieve the following literary purposes:

- give us a factual history of Israel during David's reign

- place that history in an interpretive religious framework

- evoke our admiration of David

- show us the importance of the temple in the covenant history of Israel

- prompt us to reflect on how the details of Israelite history during this era embody timeless spiritual principles

▌ **Theological themes.** (1) Covenant: the history narrated in this book is an account of God's dealings with his covenant people. (2) The nature of God: because God is prominent in the action, we receive a picture of who he is. (3) Worship: because of the emphasis on the temple, the book can be viewed partly as a worship manual.

■ **1 Chronicles as a chapter in the master story of the Bible.** The Bible presents the story of God's covenant dealings with the human race. In the OT, this was mainly the account of Israel's history. First Chronicles tells the story of God's dealings with Israel during a crucial stage of its history, and the king during that era, David, is a symbolic figure—a foreshadowing of the ultimate Davidic king, Christ. Because the opening genealogies in the book trace the human race from Adam through David, there is a sense in which 1 Chronicles is a summary of the master story of the Bible up to the day of the author.

The genealogies of Adam through Jacob [chapter 1]. First Chronicles starts with nine chapters of genealogies. Those in chapter 1 begin with Adam and take us through the era of the patriarchs. Overall, 1 Chronicles is a court history of the nation of Israel. When the Chronicler begins with Adam, he is making the point that the history of God's covenant people started at the beginning of human history.

1 [1] Adam, Seth, Enosh; [2] Kenan, Mahalalel, Jared; [3] Enoch, Methuselah, Lamech; [4] Noah, Shem, Ham, and Japheth.

[5] The sons of Japheth: Gomer, Magog, Madai, Javan, Tubal, Meshech, and Tiras. [6] The sons of Gomer: Ashkenaz, Riphath,[2] and Togarmah. [7] The sons of Javan: Elishah, Tarshish, Kittim, and Rodanim.

[8] The sons of Ham: Cush, Egypt, Put, and Canaan. [9] The sons of Cush: Seba, Havilah, Sabta, Raama, and Sabteca. The sons of Raamah: Sheba and Dedan. [10] Cush fathered Nimrod. He was the first on earth to be a mighty man.[3]

[11] Egypt fathered Ludim, Anamim, Lehabim, Naphtuhim, [12] Pathrusim, Casluhim (from whom the Philistines came), and Caphtorim.

[13] Canaan fathered Sidon his firstborn and Heth, [14] and the Jebusites, the Amorites, the Girgashites, [15] the Hivites, the Arkites, the Sinites, [16] the Arvadites, the Zemarites, and the Hamathites.

[17] The sons of Shem: Elam, Asshur, Arpachshad, Lud, and Aram. And the sons of Aram:[4] Uz, Hul, Gether, and Meshech. [18] Arpachshad fathered Shelah, and Shelah fathered Eber. [19] To Eber were born two sons: the name of the one was Peleg[5] (for in his days the earth was divided), and his brother's name was Joktan. [20] Joktan fathered Almodad, Sheleph, Hazarmaveth, Jerah, [21] Hadoram, Uzal, Diklah, [22] Obal,[6] Abimael, Sheba, [23] Ophir, Havilah, and Jobab; all these were the sons of Joktan.

[24] Shem, Arpachshad, Shelah; [25] Eber, Peleg, Reu; [26] Serug, Nahor, Terah; [27] Abram, that is, Abraham.

[28] The sons of Abraham: Isaac and Ishmael. [29] These are their genealogies: the firstborn of Ishmael, Nebaioth, and Kedar, Adbeel, Mibsam, [30] Mishma, Dumah, Massa, Hadad, Tema, [31] Jetur, Naphish, and Kedemah. These are the sons of Ishmael. [32] The sons of Keturah, Abraham's concubine: she bore Zimran, Jokshan, Medan, Midian, Ishbak, and Shuah. The sons of Jokshan: Sheba and Dedan. [33] The sons of Midian: Ephah, Epher, Hanoch, Abida, and Eldaah. All these were the descendants of Keturah.

---

[1] Many names in these genealogies are spelled differently in other biblical books [2] Septuagint; Hebrew *Diphath* [3] Or *He began to be a mighty man on the earth* [4] Septuagint; Hebrew lacks *And the sons of Aram* [5] *Peleg* means *division* [6] Septuagint, Syriac (compare Genesis 10:28); Hebrew *Ebal*

³⁴Abraham fathered Isaac. The sons of Isaac: Esau and Israel. ³⁵The sons of Esau: Eliphaz, Reuel, Jeush, Jalam, and Korah. ³⁶The sons of Eliphaz: Teman, Omar, Zepho, Gatam, Kenaz, and of Timna,¹ Amalek. ³⁷The sons of Reuel: Nahath, Zerah, Shammah, and Mizzah.

³⁸The sons of Seir: Lotan, Shobal, Zibeon, Anah, Dishon, Ezer, and Dishan. ³⁹The sons of Lotan: Hori and Hemam;² and Lotan's sister was Timna. ⁴⁰The sons of Shobal: Alvan,³ Manahath, Ebal, Shepho,⁴ and Onam. The sons of Zibeon: Aiah and Anah. ⁴¹The son⁵ of Anah: Dishon. The sons of Dishon: Hemdan,⁶ Eshban, Ithran, and Cheran. ⁴²The sons of Ezer: Bilhan, Zaavan, and Akan.⁷ The sons of Dishan: Uz and Aran.

⁴³These are the kings who reigned in the land of Edom before any king reigned over the people of Israel: Bela the son of Beor, the name of his city being Dinhabah. ⁴⁴Bela died, and Jobab the son of Zerah of Bozrah reigned in his place. ⁴⁵Jobab died, and Husham of the land of the Temanites reigned in his place. ⁴⁶Husham died, and Hadad the son of Bedad, who defeated Midian in the country of Moab, reigned in his place, the name of his city being Avith. ⁴⁷Hadad died, and Samlah of Masrekah reigned in his place. ⁴⁸Samlah died, and Shaul of Rehoboth on the Euphrates reigned in his place. ⁴⁹Shaul died, and Baal-hanan, the son of Achbor, reigned in his place. ⁵⁰Baal-hanan died, and Hadad reigned in his place, the name of his city being Pai; and his wife's name was Mehetabel, the daughter of Matred, the daughter of Mezahab. ⁵¹And Hadad died.

The chiefs of Edom were: chiefs Timna, Alvah, Jetheth, ⁵²Oholibamah, Elah, Pinon, ⁵³Kenaz, Teman, Mibzar, ⁵⁴Magdiel, and Iram; these are the chiefs of Edom.

The descendants of Judah [chapter 2]. The opening verse lists the sons of Jacob (the twelve tribes of Israel) and then gives a privileged position to Judah, through whose lineage the Messiah would be born, and traces it to David (an inference, inasmuch as the first verse of the next chapter begins "These are the sons of David"). Biblical genealogies always show that God's interest extends to individuals and that he takes human history seriously.

2 These are the sons of Israel: Reuben, Simeon, Levi, Judah, Issachar, Zebulun, ²Dan, Joseph, Benjamin, Naphtali, Gad, and Asher. ³The sons of Judah: Er, Onan and Shelah; these three Bath-shua the Canaanite bore to him. Now Er, Judah's firstborn, was evil in the sight of the LORD, and he put him to death. ⁴His daughter-in-law Tamar also bore him Perez and Zerah. Judah had five sons in all.

⁵The sons of Perez: Hezron and Hamul. ⁶The sons of Zerah: Zimri, Ethan, Heman, Calcol, and Dara, five in all. ⁷The son⁸ of Carmi: Achan, the troubler of Israel, who broke faith in the matter of the devoted thing; ⁸and Ethan's son was Azariah.

⁹The sons of Hezron that were born to him: Jerahmeel, Ram, and Chelubai. ¹⁰Ram fathered Amminadab, and Amminadab fathered Nahshon, prince of the sons of Judah. ¹¹Nahshon fathered Salmon,⁹ Salmon fathered Boaz, ¹²Boaz fathered Obed, Obed fathered Jesse. ¹³Jesse fathered Eliab his firstborn, Abinadab the second, Shimea the third, ¹⁴Nethanel the fourth, Raddai the fifth, ¹⁵Ozem the sixth, David the seventh. ¹⁶And their sisters were Zeruiah and Abigail. The sons of Zeruiah: Abishai,

¹ Septuagint (compare Genesis 36:12); Hebrew lacks *and of* ² Septuagint (compare Genesis 36:22); Hebrew *Homam* ³ Septuagint (compare Genesis 36:23); Hebrew *Alian* ⁴ Septuagint (compare Genesis 36:23); Hebrew *Shephi* ⁵ Hebrew *sons* ⁶ Septuagint (compare Genesis 36:26); Hebrew *Hamran* ⁷ Septuagint (compare Genesis 36:27); Hebrew *Jaakan* ⁸ Hebrew *sons* ⁹ Septuagint (compare Ruth 4:21); Hebrew *Salma*

Joab, and Asahel, three. ¹⁷Abigail bore Amasa, and the father of Amasa was Jether the Ishmaelite.

¹⁸Caleb the son of Hezron fathered children by his wife Azubah, and by Jerioth; and these were her sons: Jesher, Shobab, and Ardon. ¹⁹When Azubah died, Caleb married Ephrath, who bore him Hur. ²⁰Hur fathered Uri, and Uri fathered Bezalel.

²¹Afterward Hezron went in to the daughter of Machir the father of Gilead, whom he married when he was sixty years old, and she bore him Segub. ²²And Segub fathered Jair, who had twenty-three cities in the land of Gilead. ²³But Geshur and Aram took from them Havvoth-jair, Kenath, and its villages, sixty towns. All these were descendants of Machir, the father of Gilead. ²⁴After the death of Hezron, Caleb went in to Ephrathah,¹ the wife of Hezron his father, and she bore him Ashhur, the father of Tekoa.

²⁵The sons of Jerahmeel, the firstborn of Hezron: Ram, his firstborn, Bunah, Oren, Ozem, and Ahijah. ²⁶Jerahmeel also had another wife, whose name was Atarah; she was the mother of Onam. ²⁷The sons of Ram, the firstborn of Jerahmeel: Maaz, Jamin, and Eker. ²⁸The sons of Onam: Shammai and Jada. The sons of Shammai: Nadab and Abishur. ²⁹The name of Abishur's wife was Abihail, and she bore him Ahban and Molid. ³⁰The sons of Nadab: Seled and Appaim; and Seled died childless. ³¹The son² of Appaim: Ishi. The son of Ishi: Sheshan. The son of Sheshan: Ahlai. ³²The sons of Jada, Shammai's brother: Jether and Jonathan; and Jether died childless. ³³The sons of Jonathan: Peleth and Zaza. These were the descendants of Jerahmeel. ³⁴Now Sheshan had no sons, only daughters, but Sheshan had an Egyptian slave whose name was Jarha. ³⁵So Sheshan gave his daughter in marriage to Jarha his slave, and she bore him Attai. ³⁶Attai fathered Nathan, and Nathan fathered Zabad. ³⁷Zabad fathered Ephlal, and Ephlal fathered Obed. ³⁸Obed fathered Jehu, and Jehu fathered Azariah. ³⁹Azariah fathered Helez, and Helez fathered Eleasah. ⁴⁰Eleasah fathered Sismai, and Sismai fathered Shallum. ⁴¹Shallum fathered Jekamiah, and Jekamiah fathered Elishama.

⁴²The sons of Caleb the brother of Jerahmeel: Mareshah³ his firstborn, who fathered Ziph. The son⁴ of Mareshah: Hebron.⁵ ⁴³The sons of Hebron: Korah, Tappuah, Rekem and Shema. ⁴⁴Shema fathered Raham, the father of Jorkeam; and Rekem fathered Shammai. ⁴⁵The son of Shammai: Maon; and Maon fathered Beth-zur. ⁴⁶Ephah also, Caleb's concubine, bore Haran, Moza, and Gazez; and Haran fathered Gazez. ⁴⁷The sons of Jahdai: Regem, Jotham, Geshan, Pelet, Ephah, and Shaaph. ⁴⁸Maacah, Caleb's concubine, bore Sheber and Tirhanah. ⁴⁹She also bore Shaaph the father of Madmannah, Sheva the father of Machbenah and the father of Gibea; and the daughter of Caleb was Achsah. ⁵⁰These were the descendants of Caleb.

The sons⁶ of Hur the firstborn of Ephrathah: Shobal the father of Kiriath-jearim, ⁵¹Salma, the father of Bethlehem, and Hareph the father of Beth-gader. ⁵²Shobal the father of Kiriath-jearim had other sons: Haroeh, half of the Menuhoth. ⁵³And the clans of Kiriath-jearim: the Ithrites, the Puthites, the Shumathites, and the Mishraites; from these came the Zorathites and the Eshtaolites. ⁵⁴The sons of Salma: Bethlehem, the Netophathites, Atroth-beth-joab and half of the Manahathites, the Zorites. ⁵⁵The clans also of the scribes who lived at Jabez: the Tirathites, the Shimeathites and the Sucathites. These are the Kenites who came from Hammath, the father of the house of Rechab.

---

¹ Septuagint, Vulgate; Hebrew *in Caleb Ephrathah* ² Hebrew *sons*; three times in this verse ³ Septuagint; Hebrew *Mesha* ⁴ Hebrew *sons* ⁵ Hebrew *the father of Hebron* ⁶ Septuagint, Vulgate; Hebrew *son*

The descendants of David [chapter 3]. The bare listing of names continues, but this time we sense a special significance to the genealogy because it consists of the descendants of the mighty David. This is covenant history in capital letters, and one of the points to emerge is that covenant history is particularized, made up of ordinary people who lived their individual lives within the broader plan of God.

3 These are the sons of David who were born to him in Hebron: the firstborn, Amnon, by Ahinoam the Jezreelite; the second, Daniel, by Abigail the Carmelite, ²the third, Absalom, whose mother was Maacah, the daughter of Talmai, king of Geshur; the fourth, Adonijah, whose mother was Haggith; ³the fifth, Shephatiah, by Abital; the sixth, Ithream, by his wife Eglah; ⁴six were born to him in Hebron, where he reigned for seven years and six months. And he reigned thirty-three years in Jerusalem. ⁵These were born to him in Jerusalem: Shimea, Shobab, Nathan and Solomon, four by Bath-shua, the daughter of Ammiel; ⁶then Ibhar, Elishama, Eliphelet, ⁷Nogah, Nepheg, Japhia, ⁸Elishama, Eliada, and Eliphelet, nine. ⁹All these were David's sons, besides the sons of the concubines, and Tamar was their sister.

¹⁰The son of Solomon was Rehoboam, Abijah his son, Asa his son, Jehoshaphat his son, ¹¹Joram his son, Ahaziah his son, Joash his son, ¹²Amaziah his son, Azariah his son, Jotham his son, ¹³Ahaz his son, Hezekiah his son, Manasseh his son, ¹⁴Amon his son, Josiah his son. ¹⁵The sons of Josiah: Johanan the firstborn, the second Jehoiakim, the third Zedekiah, the fourth Shallum. ¹⁶The descendants of Jehoiakim: Jeconiah his son, Zedekiah his son; ¹⁷and the sons of Jeconiah, the captive: Shealtiel his son, ¹⁸Malchiram, Pedaiah, Shenazzar, Jekamiah, Hoshama and Nedabiah; ¹⁹and the sons of Pedaiah: Zerubbabel and Shimei; and the sons of Zerubbabel: Meshullam and Hananiah, and Shelomith was their sister; ²⁰and Hashubah, Ohel, Berechiah, Hasadiah, and Jushab-hesed, five. ²¹The sons of Hananiah: Pelatiah and Jeshaiah, his son[1] Rephaiah, his son Arnan, his son Obadiah, his son Shecaniah. ²²The son[2] of Shecaniah: Shemaiah. And the sons of Shemaiah: Hattush, Igal, Bariah, Neariah, and Shaphat, six. ²³The sons of Neariah: Elioenai, Hizkiah, and Azrikam, three. ²⁴The sons of Elioenai: Hodaviah, Eliashib, Pelaiah, Akkub, Johanan, Delaiah, and Anani, seven.

Descendants of Judah and Simeon [chapter 4]. Now it emerges that the lineage of David in chapter 3 was an insertion into the genealogies of the sons of Jacob. The families of Judah and Simeon are recorded in chapter 4. We get more than a mere listing of names in this chapter, though. From time to time the compiler adds hints of a story that tease us into wondering what the larger picture is.

4 The sons of Judah: Perez, Hezron, Carmi, Hur, and Shobal. ²Reaiah the son of Shobal fathered Jahath, and Jahath fathered Ahumai and Lahad. These were the clans of the Zorathites. ³These were the sons[3] of Etam: Jezreel, Ishma, and Idbash; and the name of their sister was Hazzelelponi, ⁴and Penuel fathered Gedor, and Ezer fathered Hushah. These were the sons of Hur, the firstborn of Ephrathah, the father of Bethlehem. ⁵Ashhur, the father of Tekoa, had two wives, Helah and Naarah; ⁶Naarah bore him Ahuzzam, Hepher, Temeni, and Haahashtari. These were the sons of Naarah. ⁷The sons of Helah: Zereth, Izhar, and Ethnan. ⁸Koz fathered Anub, Zobebah, and the clans of Aharhel, the son of Harum. ⁹Jabez was more honorable

---

[1] Septuagint (compare Syriac, Vulgate); Hebrew *sons of*; four times in this verse [2] Hebrew *sons* [3] Septuagint (compare Vulgate); Hebrew *father*

than his brothers; and his mother called his name Jabez, saying, "Because I bore him in pain."[1] [10]Jabez called upon the God of Israel, saying, "Oh that you would bless me and enlarge my border, and that your hand might be with me, and that you would keep me from harm[2] so that it might not bring me pain!" And God granted what he asked. [11]Chelub, the brother of Shuhah, fathered Mehir, who fathered Eshton. [12]Eshton fathered Beth-rapha, Paseah, and Tehinnah, the father of Ir-nahash. These are the men of Recah. [13]The sons of Kenaz: Othniel and Seraiah; and the sons of Othniel: Hathath and Meonothai.[3] [14]Meonothai fathered Ophrah; and Seraiah fathered Joab, the father of Ge-harashim,[4] so-called because they were craftsmen. [15]The sons of Caleb the son of Jephunneh: Iru, Elah, and Naam; and the son[5] of Elah: Kenaz. [16]The sons of Jehallelel: Ziph, Ziphah, Tiria, and Asarel. [17]The sons of Ezrah: Jether, Mered, Epher, and Jalon. These are the sons of Bithiah, the daughter of Pharaoh, whom Mered married;[6] and she conceived and bore[7] Miriam, Shammai, and Ishbah, the father of Eshtemoa. [18]And his Judahite wife bore Jered the father of Gedor, Heber the father of Soco, and Jekuthiel the father of Zanoah. [19]The sons of the wife of Hodiah, the sister of Naham, were the fathers of Keilah the Garmite and Eshtemoa the Maacathite. [20]The sons of Shimon: Amnon, Rinnah, Ben-hanan, and Tilon. The sons of Ishi: Zoheth and Ben-zoheth. [21]The sons of Shelah the son of Judah: Er the father of Lecah, Laadah the father of Mareshah, and the clans of the house of linen workers at Beth-ashbea; [22]and Jokim, and the men of Cozeba, and Joash, and Saraph, who ruled in Moab and returned to Lehem[8] (now the records[9] are ancient). [23]These were the potters who were inhabitants of Netaim and Gederah. They lived there in the king's service.

[24]The sons of Simeon: Nemuel, Jamin, Jarib, Zerah, Shaul; [25]Shallum was his son, Mibsam his son, Mishma his son. [26]The sons of Mishma: Hammuel his son, Zaccur his son, Shimei his son. [27]Shimei had sixteen sons and six daughters; but his brothers did not have many children, nor did all their clan multiply like the men of Judah. [28]They lived in Beersheba, Moladah, Hazar-shual, [29]Bilhah, Ezem, Tolad, [30]Bethuel, Hormah, Ziklag, [31]Beth-marcaboth, Hazar-susim, Beth-biri, and Shaaraim. These were their cities until David reigned. [32]And their villages were Etam, Ain, Rimmon, Tochen, and Ashan, five cities, [33]along with all their villages that were around these cities as far as Baal. These were their settlements, and they kept a genealogical record.

[34]Meshobab, Jamlech, Joshah the son of Amaziah, [35]Joel, Jehu the son of Joshibiah, son of Seraiah, son of Asiel, [36]Elioenai, Jaakobah, Jeshohaiah, Asaiah, Adiel, Jesimiel, Benaiah, [37]Ziza the son of Shiphi, son of Allon, son of Jedaiah, son of Shimri, son of Shemaiah— [38]these mentioned by name were princes in their clans, and their fathers' houses increased greatly. [39]They journeyed to the entrance of Gedor, to the east side of the valley, to seek pasture for their flocks, [40]where they found rich, good pasture, and the land was very broad, quiet, and peaceful, for the former inhabitants there belonged to Ham. [41]These, registered by name, came in the days of Hezekiah, king of Judah, and destroyed their tents and the Meunites who were found there, and marked them for destruction to this day, and settled in their place, because there was pasture there for their flocks. [42]And some of them, five hundred men of the Simeonites, went to Mount Seir, having as their leaders Pelatiah, Neariah, Rephaiah,

---

[1] *Jabez* sounds like the Hebrew for *pain* [2] Or *evil* [3] Septuagint, Vulgate; Hebrew lacks *Meonothai* [4] *Ge-harashim* means *valley of craftsmen* [5] Hebrew *sons* [6] The clause *These are . . . married* is transposed from verse 18 [7] Hebrew lacks *and bore* [8] Vulgate (compare Septuagint); Hebrew *and Jashubi-lahem* [9] Or *matters*

and Uzziel, the sons of Ishi. ⁴³And they defeated the remnant of the Amalekites who had escaped, and they have lived there to this day.

5 The sons of Reuben the firstborn of Israel (for he was the firstborn, but because he defiled his father's couch, his birthright was given to the sons of Joseph the son of Israel, so that he could not be enrolled as the oldest son; ²though Judah became strong among his brothers and a chief came from him, yet the birthright belonged to Joseph), ³the sons of Reuben, the firstborn of Israel: Hanoch, Pallu, Hezron, and Carmi. ⁴The sons of Joel: Shemaiah his son, Gog his son, Shimei his son, ⁵Micah his son, Reaiah his son, Baal his son, ⁶Beerah his son, whom Tiglath-pileser¹ king of Assyria carried away into exile; he was a chief of the Reubenites. ⁷And his kinsmen by their clans, when the genealogy of their generations was recorded: the chief, Jeiel, and Zechariah, ⁸and Bela the son of Azaz, son of Shema, son of Joel, who lived in Aroer, as far as Nebo and Baal-meon. ⁹He also lived to the east as far as the entrance of the desert this side of the Euphrates, because their livestock had multiplied in the land of Gilead. ¹⁰And in the days of Saul they waged war against the Hagrites, who fell into their hand. And they lived in their tents throughout all the region east of Gilead.

¹¹The sons of Gad lived over against them in the land of Bashan as far as Salecah: ¹²Joel the chief, Shapham the second, Janai, and Shaphat in Bashan. ¹³And their kinsmen according to their fathers' houses: Michael, Meshullam, Sheba, Jorai, Jacan, Zia and Eber, seven. ¹⁴These were the sons of Abihail the son of Huri, son of Jaroah, son of Gilead, son of Michael, son of Jeshishai, son of Jahdo, son of Buz. ¹⁵Ahi the son of Abdiel, son of Guni, was chief in their fathers' houses, ¹⁶and they lived in Gilead, in Bashan and in its towns, and in all the pasturelands of Sharon to their limits. ¹⁷All of these were recorded in genealogies in the days of Jotham king of Judah, and in the days of Jeroboam king of Israel.

¹⁸The Reubenites, the Gadites, and the half-tribe of Manasseh had valiant men who carried shield and sword, and drew the bow, expert in war, 44,760, able to go to war. ¹⁹They waged war against the Hagrites, Jetur, Naphish, and Nodab. ²⁰And when they prevailed over them, the Hagrites and all who were with them were given into their hands, for they cried out to God in the battle, and he granted their urgent plea because they trusted in him. ²¹They carried off their livestock: 50,000 of their camels, 250,000 sheep, 2,000 donkeys, and 100,000 men alive. ²²For many fell, because the war was of God. And they lived in their place until the exile.

²³The members of the half-tribe of Manasseh lived in the land. They were very numerous from Bashan to Baal-hermon, Senir, and Mount Hermon. ²⁴These were the heads of their fathers' houses: Epher,² Ishi, Eliel, Azriel, Jeremiah, Hodaviah, and Jahdiel, mighty warriors, famous men, heads of their fathers' houses. ²⁵But they broke faith with the God of their fathers, and whored after the gods of the peoples of the land, whom God had destroyed before them. ²⁶So the God of Israel stirred up the spirit of Pul king of Assyria, the spirit of Tiglath-pileser king of Assyria, and he took

¹ Hebrew *Tilgath-pilneser*; also verse 26 ² Septuagint, Vulgate; Hebrew *and Epher*

them into exile, namely, the Reubenites, the Gadites, and the half-tribe of Manasseh, and brought them to Halah, Habor, Hara, and the river Gozan, to this day.

The Levites [chapter 6]. The large amount of space (eighty-one verses) devoted to the Levites hints at their special status as the tribe that conducted the worship of the nation. In addition to the names of ancestors, we find snatches of the duties that some of the men performed and also of the places that they were allotted for living.

6 ¹ The sons of Levi: Gershon, Kohath, and Merari. ²The sons of Kohath: Amram, Izhar, Hebron, and Uzziel. ³The children of Amram: Aaron, Moses, and Miriam. The sons of Aaron: Nadab, Abihu, Eleazar, and Ithamar. ⁴Eleazar fathered Phinehas, Phinehas fathered Abishua, ⁵Abishua fathered Bukki, Bukki fathered Uzzi, ⁶Uzzi fathered Zerahiah, Zerahiah fathered Meraioth, ⁷Meraioth fathered Amariah, Amariah fathered Ahitub, ⁸Ahitub fathered Zadok, Zadok fathered Ahimaaz, ⁹Ahimaaz fathered Azariah, Azariah fathered Johanan, ¹⁰and Johanan fathered Azariah (it was he who served as priest in the house that Solomon built in Jerusalem). ¹¹Azariah fathered Amariah, Amariah fathered Ahitub, ¹²Ahitub fathered Zadok, Zadok fathered Shallum, ¹³Shallum fathered Hilkiah, Hilkiah fathered Azariah, ¹⁴Azariah fathered Seraiah, Seraiah fathered Jehozadak; ¹⁵and Jehozadak went into exile when the LORD sent Judah and Jerusalem into exile by the hand of Nebuchadnezzar.

¹⁶² The sons of Levi: Gershom, Kohath, and Merari. ¹⁷And these are the names of the sons of Gershom: Libni and Shimei. ¹⁸The sons of Kohath: Amram, Izhar, Hebron and Uzziel. ¹⁹The sons of Merari: Mahli and Mushi. These are the clans of the Levites according to their fathers. ²⁰Of Gershom: Libni his son, Jahath his son, Zimmah his son, ²¹Joah his son, Iddo his son, Zerah his son, Jeatherai his son. ²²The sons of Kohath: Amminadab his son, Korah his son, Assir his son, ²³Elkanah his son, Ebiasaph his son, Assir his son, ²⁴Tahath his son, Uriel his son, Uzziah his son, and Shaul his son. ²⁵The sons of Elkanah: Amasai and Ahimoth, ²⁶Elkanah his son, Zophai his son, Nahath his son, ²⁷Eliab his son, Jeroham his son, Elkanah his son. ²⁸The sons of Samuel: Joel³ his firstborn, the second Abijah.⁴ ²⁹The sons of Merari: Mahli, Libni his son, Shimei his son, Uzzah his son, ³⁰Shimea his son, Haggiah his son, and Asaiah his son.

³¹These are the men whom David put in charge of the service of song in the house of the LORD after the ark rested there. ³²They ministered with song before the tabernacle of the tent of meeting until Solomon built the house of the LORD in Jerusalem, and they performed their service according to their order. ³³These are the men who served and their sons. Of the sons of the Kohathites: Heman the singer the son of Joel, son of Samuel, ³⁴son of Elkanah, son of Jeroham, son of Eliel, son of Toah, ³⁵son of Zuph, son of Elkanah, son of Mahath, son of Amasai, ³⁶son of Elkanah, son of Joel, son of Azariah, son of Zephaniah, ³⁷son of Tahath, son of Assir, son of Ebiasaph, son of Korah, ³⁸son of Izhar, son of Kohath, son of Levi, son of Israel; ³⁹and his brother Asaph, who stood on his right hand, namely, Asaph the son of Berechiah, son of Shimea, ⁴⁰son of Michael, son of Baaseiah, son of Malchijah, ⁴¹son of Ethni, son of Zerah, son of Adaiah, ⁴²son of Ethan, son of Zimmah, son of Shimei, ⁴³son of Jahath, son of Gershom, son of Levi. ⁴⁴On the left hand were their brothers, the sons of

¹ Ch 5:27 in Hebrew ² Ch 6:1 in Hebrew ³ Septuagint, Syriac (compare verse 33 and 1 Samuel 8:2); Hebrew lacks *Joel* ⁴ Hebrew *and Abijah*

Merari: Ethan the son of Kishi, son of Abdi, son of Malluch, ⁴⁵son of Hashabiah, son of Amaziah, son of Hilkiah, ⁴⁶son of Amzi, son of Bani, son of Shemer, ⁴⁷son of Mahli, son of Mushi, son of Merari, son of Levi. ⁴⁸And their brothers the Levites were appointed for all the service of the tabernacle of the house of God.

⁴⁹But Aaron and his sons made offerings on the altar of burnt offering and on the altar of incense for all the work of the Most Holy Place, and to make atonement for Israel, according to all that Moses the servant of God had commanded. ⁵⁰These are the sons of Aaron: Eleazar his son, Phinehas his son, Abishua his son, ⁵¹Bukki his son, Uzzi his son, Zerahiah his son, ⁵²Meraioth his son, Amariah his son, Ahitub his son, ⁵³Zadok his son, Ahimaaz his son.

⁵⁴These are their dwelling places according to their settlements within their borders: to the sons of Aaron of the clans of Kohathites, for theirs was the first lot, ⁵⁵to them they gave Hebron in the land of Judah and its surrounding pasturelands, ⁵⁶but the fields of the city and its villages they gave to Caleb the son of Jephunneh. ⁵⁷To the sons of Aaron they gave the cities of refuge: Hebron, Libnah with its pasturelands, Jattir, Eshtemoa with its pasturelands, ⁵⁸Hilen with its pasturelands, Debir with its pasturelands, ⁵⁹Ashan with its pasturelands, and Beth-shemesh with its pasturelands; ⁶⁰and from the tribe of Benjamin, Gibeon,¹ Geba with its pasturelands, Alemeth with its pasturelands, and Anathoth with its pasturelands. All their cities throughout their clans were thirteen.

⁶¹To the rest of the Kohathites were given by lot out of the clan of the tribe, out of the half-tribe, the half of Manasseh, ten cities. ⁶²To the Gershomites according to their clans were allotted thirteen cities out of the tribes of Issachar, Asher, Naphtali and Manasseh in Bashan. ⁶³To the Merarites according to their clans were allotted twelve cities out of the tribes of Reuben, Gad, and Zebulun. ⁶⁴So the people of Israel gave the Levites the cities with their pasturelands. ⁶⁵They gave by lot out of the tribes of Judah, Simeon, and Benjamin these cities that are mentioned by name.

⁶⁶And some of the clans of the sons of Kohath had cities of their territory out of the tribe of Ephraim. ⁶⁷They were given the cities of refuge: Shechem with its pasturelands in the hill country of Ephraim, Gezer with its pasturelands, ⁶⁸Jokmeam with its pasturelands, Beth-horon with its pasturelands, ⁶⁹Aijalon with its pasturelands, Gath-rimmon with its pasturelands, ⁷⁰and out of the half-tribe of Manasseh, Aner with its pasturelands, and Bileam with its pasturelands, for the rest of the clans of the Kohathites.

⁷¹To the Gershomites were given out of the clan of the half-tribe of Manasseh: Golan in Bashan with its pasturelands and Ashtaroth with its pasturelands; ⁷²and out of the tribe of Issachar: Kedesh with its pasturelands, Daberath with its pasturelands, ⁷³Ramoth with its pasturelands, and Anem with its pasturelands; ⁷⁴out of the tribe of Asher: Mashal with its pasturelands, Abdon with its pasturelands, ⁷⁵Hukok with its pasturelands, and Rehob with its pasturelands; ⁷⁶and out of the tribe of Naphtali: Kedesh in Galilee with its pasturelands, Hammon with its pasturelands, and Kiriathaim with its pasturelands. ⁷⁷To the rest of the Merarites were allotted out of the tribe of Zebulun: Rimmono with its pasturelands, Tabor with its pasturelands, ⁷⁸and beyond the Jordan at Jericho, on the east side of the Jordan, out of the tribe of Reuben: Bezer in the wilderness with its pasturelands, Jahzah with its pasturelands, ⁷⁹Kedemoth with its pasturelands, and Mephaath with its pasturelands; ⁸⁰and out of the tribe of Gad: Ramoth in Gilead with its pasturelands, Mahanaim with its pasturelands, ⁸¹Heshbon with its pasturelands, and Jazer with its pasturelands.

---

¹ Septuagint, Syriac (compare Joshua 21:17); Hebrew lacks *Gibeon*

Five more tribes [chapter 7]. The staple of the account continues to be names of descendants, but there are interspersed references to the number of soldiers in a given clan, hints of stories, and places of settlement.

7 The sons[1] of Issachar: Tola, Puah, Jashub, and Shimron, four. [2]The sons of Tola: Uzzi, Rephaiah, Jeriel, Jahmai, Ibsam, and Shemuel, heads of their fathers' houses, namely of Tola, mighty warriors of their generations, their number in the days of David being 22,600. [3]The son[2] of Uzzi: Izrahiah. And the sons of Izrahiah: Michael, Obadiah, Joel, and Isshiah, all five of them were chief men. [4]And along with them, by their generations, according to their fathers' houses, were units of the army for war, 36,000, for they had many wives and sons. [5]Their kinsmen belonging to all the clans of Issachar were in all 87,000 mighty warriors, enrolled by genealogy.

[6]The sons of Benjamin: Bela, Becher, and Jediael, three. [7]The sons of Bela: Ezbon, Uzzi, Uzziel, Jerimoth, and Iri, five, heads of fathers' houses, mighty warriors. And their enrollment by genealogies was 22,034. [8]The sons of Becher: Zemirah, Joash, Eliezer, Elioenai, Omri, Jeremoth, Abijah, Anathoth, and Alemeth. All these were the sons of Becher. [9]And their enrollment by genealogies, according to their generations, as heads of their fathers' houses, mighty warriors, was 20,200. [10]The son of Jediael: Bilhan. And the sons of Bilhan: Jeush, Benjamin, Ehud, Chenaanah, Zethan, Tarshish, and Ahishahar. [11]All these were the sons of Jediael according to the heads of their fathers' houses, mighty warriors, 17,200, able to go to war. [12]And Shuppim and Huppim were the sons of Ir, Hushim the son of Aher.

[13]The sons of Naphtali: Jahziel, Guni, Jezer and Shallum, the descendants of Bilhah.

[14]The sons of Manasseh: Asriel, whom his Aramean concubine bore; she bore Machir the father of Gilead. [15]And Machir took a wife for Huppim and for Shuppim. The name of his sister was Maacah. And the name of the second was Zelophehad, and Zelophehad had daughters. [16]And Maacah the wife of Machir bore a son, and she called his name Peresh; and the name of his brother was Sheresh; and his sons were Ulam and Rakem. [17]The son of Ulam: Bedan. These were the sons of Gilead the son of Machir, son of Manasseh. [18]And his sister Hammolecheth bore Ishhod, Abiezer and Mahlah. [19]The sons of Shemida were Ahian, Shechem, Likhi, and Aniam.

[20]The sons of Ephraim: Shuthelah, and Bered his son, Tahath his son, Eleadah his son, Tahath his son, [21]Zabad his son, Shuthelah his son, and Ezer and Elead, whom the men of Gath who were born in the land killed, because they came down to raid their livestock. [22]And Ephraim their father mourned many days, and his brothers came to comfort him. [23]And Ephraim went in to his wife, and she conceived and bore a son. And he called his name Beriah, because disaster had befallen his house.[3] [24]His daughter was Sheerah, who built both Lower and Upper Beth-horon, and Uzzen-sheerah. [25]Rephah was his son, Resheph his son, Telah his son, Tahan his son, [26]Ladan his son, Ammihud his son, Elishama his son, [27]Nun[4] his son, Joshua his son. [28]Their possessions and settlements were Bethel and its towns, and to the east Naaran, and to the west Gezer and its towns, Shechem and its towns, and Ayyah and its towns; [29]also in possession of the Manassites, Beth-shean and its towns, Taanach and its towns, Megiddo and its towns, Dor and its towns. In these lived the sons of Joseph the son of Israel.

[30]The sons of Asher: Imnah, Ishvah, Ishvi, Beriah, and their sister Serah. [31]The sons

[1] Syriac (compare Vulgate); Hebrew *And to the sons* [2] Hebrew *sons*; also verses 10, 12, 17 [3] *Beriah* sounds like the Hebrew for *disaster* [4] Hebrew *Non*

of Beriah: Heber, and Malchiel, who fathered Birzaith. [32]Heber fathered Japhlet, Shomer, Hotham, and their sister Shua. [33]The sons of Japhlet: Pasach, Bimhal, and Ashvath. These are the sons of Japhlet. [34]The sons of Shemer his brother: Rohgah, Jehubbah, and Aram. [35]The sons of Helem his brother: Zophah, Imna, Shelesh, and Amal. [36]The sons of Zophah: Suah, Harnepher, Shual, Beri, Imrah. [37]Bezer, Hod, Shamma, Shilshah, Ithran, and Beera. [38]The sons of Jether: Jephunneh, Pispa, and Ara. [39]The sons of Ulla: Arah, Hanniel, and Rizia. [40]All of these were men of Asher, heads of fathers' houses, approved, mighty warriors, chiefs of the princes. Their number enrolled by genealogies, for service in war, was 26,000 men.

> **Offspring of Benjamin** [chapter 8]. Still more names. At this point we need to remind ourselves of the purposes of genealogies in the OT: they show the importance that Israelite society accorded to the family and to the continuity of generations; they demonstrate the importance that God places on the individual; they remind us that history is ultimately made up of individuals; they prove that God takes history seriously; they reveal that God protected the history of his covenant people and of the messianic line through the centuries. They also confirm the historicity of the Bible's master story.

8 Benjamin fathered Bela his firstborn, Ashbel the second, Aharah the third, [2]Nohah the fourth, and Rapha the fifth. [3]And Bela had sons: Addar, Gera, Abihud, [4]Abishua, Naaman, Ahoah, [5]Gera, Shephuphan, and Huram. [6]These are the sons of Ehud (they were heads of fathers' houses of the inhabitants of Geba, and they were carried into exile to Manahath): [7]Naaman,[1] Ahijah, and Gera, that is, Heglam,[2] who fathered Uzza and Ahihud. [8]And Shaharaim fathered sons in the country of Moab after he had sent away Hushim and Baara his wives. [9]He fathered sons by Hodesh his wife: Jobab, Zibia, Mesha, Malcam, [10]Jeuz, Sachia, and Mirmah. These were his sons, heads of fathers' houses. [11]He also fathered sons by Hushim: Abitub and Elpaal. [12]The sons of Elpaal: Eber, Misham, and Shemed, who built Ono and Lod with its towns, [13]and Beriah and Shema (they were heads of fathers' houses of the inhabitants of Aijalon, who caused the inhabitants of Gath to flee); [14]and Ahio, Shashak, and Jeremoth. [15]Zebadiah, Arad, Eder, [16]Michael, Ishpah, and Joha were sons of Beriah. [17]Zebadiah, Meshullam, Hizki, Heber, [18]Ishmerai, Izliah, and Jobab were the sons of Elpaal. [19]Jakim, Zichri, Zabdi, [20]Elienai, Zillethai, Eliel, [21]Adaiah, Beraiah, and Shimrath were the sons of Shimei. [22]Ishpan, Eber, Eliel, [23]Abdon, Zichri, Hanan, [24]Hananiah, Elam, Anthothijah, [25]Iphdeiah, and Penuel were the sons of Shashak. [26]Shamsherai, Shehariah, Athaliah, [27]Jaareshiah, Elijah, and Zichri were the sons of Jeroham. [28]These were the heads of fathers' houses, according to their generations, chief men. These lived in Jerusalem.

[29]Jeiel[3] the father of Gibeon lived in Gibeon, and the name of his wife was Maacah. [30]His firstborn son: Abdon, then Zur, Kish, Baal, Nadab, [31]Gedor, Ahio, Zecher, [32]and Mikloth (he fathered Shimeah). Now these also lived opposite their kinsmen in Jerusalem, with their kinsmen. [33]Ner was the father of Kish, Kish of Saul, Saul of Jonathan, Malchi-shua, Abinadab and Eshbaal; [34]and the son of Jonathan was Meribbaal; and Merib-baal was the father of Micah. [35]The sons of Micah: Pithon, Melech, Tarea, and Ahaz. [36]Ahaz fathered Jehoaddah, and Jehoaddah fathered Alemeth, Azmaveth, and Zimri. Zimri fathered Moza. [37]Moza fathered Binea; Raphah was his

---

[1] Hebrew *and Naaman* [2] Or *he carried them into exile* [3] Compare 9:35; Hebrew lacks *Jeiel*

son, Eleasah his son, Azel his son. [38]Azel had six sons, and these are their names: Azrikam, Bocheru, Ishmael, Sheariah, Obadiah, and Hanan. All these were the sons of Azel. [39]The sons of Eshek his brother: Ulam his firstborn, Jeush the second, and Eliphelet the third. [40]The sons of Ulam were men who were mighty warriors, bowmen, having many sons and grandsons, 150. All these were Benjaminites.

> **Lists of those who returned from exile** [chapter 9]. Suddenly the author fast-forwards to the time of the restoration after the exile in Babylon (v. 2). The opening verse, with its mention of how "all Israel was recorded in genealogies," alerts us to an additional interpretive framework for the genealogies of 1 Chronicles: they tell the story of corporate Israel, God's covenant nation. Verses 2–34 cover material similar to that found in the book of Nehemiah, and the categories are accordingly familiar to anyone who reads the corresponding section of Nehemiah—laity, priests, Levites, gatekeepers, those in charge of temple worship. This shows the author's interest in the institutions that made up his society and the groups who took leadership in it. The last unit in the chapter, verses 35–44, gives the genealogy of King Saul, thereby introducing the central part of the book, which deals with (a) the predecessor of David, (b) the kingship of David, and (c) the successor of David.

9 So all Israel was recorded in genealogies, and these are written in the Book of the Kings of Israel. And Judah was taken into exile in Babylon because of their breach of faith. [2]Now the first to dwell again in their possessions in their cities were Israel, the priests, the Levites, and the temple servants. [3]And some of the people of Judah, Benjamin, Ephraim, and Manasseh lived in Jerusalem: [4]Uthai the son of Ammihud, son of Omri, son of Imri, son of Bani, from the sons of Perez the son of Judah. [5]And of the Shilonites: Asaiah the firstborn, and his sons. [6]Of the sons of Zerah: Jeuel and their kinsmen, 690. [7]Of the Benjaminites: Sallu the son of Meshullam, son of Hodaviah, son of Hassenuah, [8]Ibneiah the son of Jeroham, Elah the son of Uzzi, son of Michri, and Meshullam the son of Shephatiah, son of Reuel, son of Ibnijah; [9]and their kinsmen according to their generations, 956. All these were heads of fathers' houses according to their fathers' houses.

[10]Of the priests: Jedaiah, Jehoiarib, Jachin, [11]and Azariah the son of Hilkiah, son of Meshullam, son of Zadok, son of Meraioth, son of Ahitub, the chief officer of the house of God; [12]and Adaiah the son of Jeroham, son of Pashhur, son of Malchijah, and Maasai the son of Adiel, son of Jahzerah, son of Meshullam, son of Meshillemith, son of Immer; [13]besides their kinsmen, heads of their fathers' houses, 1,760, mighty men for the work of the service of the house of God.

[14]Of the Levites: Shemaiah the son of Hasshub, son of Azrikam, son of Hashabiah, of the sons of Merari; [15]and Bakbakkar, Heresh, Galal and Mattaniah the son of Mica, son of Zichri, son of Asaph; [16]and Obadiah the son of Shemaiah, son of Galal, son of Jeduthun, and Berechiah the son of Asa, son of Elkanah, who lived in the villages of the Netophathites.

[17]The gatekeepers were Shallum, Akkub, Talmon, Ahiman, and their kinsmen (Shallum was the chief); [18]until then they were in the king's gate on the east side as the gatekeepers of the camps of the Levites. [19]Shallum the son of Kore, son of Ebiasaph, son of Korah, and his kinsmen of his fathers' house, the Korahites, were in charge of the work of the service, keepers of the thresholds of the tent, as their

fathers had been in charge of the camp of the LORD, keepers of the entrance. ²⁰And Phinehas the son of Eleazar was the chief officer over them in time past; the LORD was with him. ²¹Zechariah the son of Meshelemiah was gatekeeper at the entrance of the tent of meeting. ²²All these, who were chosen as gatekeepers at the thresholds, were 212. They were enrolled by genealogies in their villages. David and Samuel the seer established them in their office of trust. ²³So they and their sons were in charge of the gates of the house of the LORD, that is, the house of the tent, as guards. ²⁴The gatekeepers were on the four sides, east, west, north, and south. ²⁵And their kinsmen who were in their villages were obligated to come in every seven days, in turn, to be with these, ²⁶for the four chief gatekeepers, who were Levites, were entrusted to be over the chambers and the treasures of the house of God. ²⁷And they lodged around the house of God, for on them lay the duty of watching, and they had charge of opening it every morning.

²⁸Some of them had charge of the utensils of service, for they were required to count them when they were brought in and taken out. ²⁹Others of them were appointed over the furniture and over all the holy utensils, also over the fine flour, the wine, the oil, the incense, and the spices. ³⁰Others, of the sons of the priests, prepared the mixing of the spices, ³¹and Mattithiah, one of the Levites, the firstborn of Shallum the Korahite, was entrusted with making the flat cakes. ³²Also some of their kinsmen of the Kohathites had charge of the showbread, to prepare it every Sabbath.

³³Now these, the singers, the heads of fathers' houses of the Levites, were in the chambers of the temple free from other service, for they were on duty day and night. ³⁴These were heads of fathers' houses of the Levites, according to their generations, leaders. These lived in Jerusalem.

³⁵In Gibeon lived the father of Gibeon, Jeiel, and the name of his wife was Maacah, ³⁶and his firstborn son Abdon, then Zur, Kish, Baal, Ner, Nadab, ³⁷Gedor, Ahio, Zechariah, and Mikloth; ³⁸and Mikloth was the father of Shimeam; and these also lived opposite their kinsmen in Jerusalem, with their kinsmen. ³⁹Ner fathered Kish, Kish fathered Saul, Saul fathered Jonathan, Malchi-shua, Abinadab, and Eshbaal. ⁴⁰And the son of Jonathan was Merib-baal, and Merib-baal fathered Micah. ⁴¹The sons of Micah: Pithon, Melech, Tahrea, and Ahaz.ʲ ⁴²And Ahaz fathered Jarah, and Jarah fathered Alemeth, Azmaveth, and Zimri. And Zimri fathered Moza. ⁴³Moza fathered Binea, and Rephaiah was his son, Eleasah his son, Azel his son. ⁴⁴Azel had six sons and these are their names: Azrikam, Bocheru, Ishmael, Sheariah, Obadiah, and Hanan; these were the sons of Azel.

The story of Saul's end [chapter 10]. The tragic life of Saul is narrated in 1 Samuel. First Chronicles records only his death. Narrative makes a welcome introduction into the story after nine chapters of genealogies. In addition to giving the historical details surrounding the undignified death of Saul (vv. 1–12), the Chronicler makes an interpretive judgment as to why Saul met such a pathetic end: his rejection of God (vv. 13–14). The history of Saul thus participates in a pattern that we see throughout the OT: the authors' giving a moral and spiritual history as well as a national and political history.

¹ Compare 8:35; Hebrew lacks *and Ahaz*

10 Now the Philistines fought against Israel, and the men of Israel fled before the Philistines and fell slain on Mount Gilboa. ²And the Philistines overtook Saul and his sons, and the Philistines struck down Jonathan and Abinadab and Malchi-shua, the sons of Saul. ³The battle pressed hard against Saul, and the archers found him, and he was wounded by the archers. ⁴Then Saul said to his armor-bearer, "Draw your sword and thrust me through with it, lest these uncircumcised come and mistreat me." But his armor-bearer would not, for he feared greatly. Therefore Saul took his own sword and fell upon it. ⁵And when his armor-bearer saw that Saul was dead, he also fell upon his sword and died. ⁶Thus Saul died; he and his three sons and all his house died together. ⁷And when all the men of Israel who were in the valley saw that the army¹ had fled and that Saul and his sons were dead, they abandoned their cities and fled, and the Philistines came and lived in them.

⁸The next day, when the Philistines came to strip the slain, they found Saul and his sons fallen on Mount Gilboa. ⁹And they stripped him and took his head and his armor, and sent messengers throughout the land of the Philistines to carry the good news to their idols and to the people. ¹⁰And they put his armor in the temple of their gods and fastened his head in the temple of Dagon. ¹¹But when all Jabesh-gilead heard all that the Philistines had done to Saul, ¹²all the valiant men arose and took away the body of Saul and the bodies of his sons, and brought them to Jabesh. And they buried their bones under the oak in Jabesh and fasted seven days.

¹³So Saul died for his breach of faith. He broke faith with the LORD in that he did not keep the command of the LORD, and also consulted a medium, seeking guidance. ¹⁴He did not seek guidance from the LORD. Therefore the LORD put him to death and turned the kingdom over to David the son of Jesse.

David's accession to the throne [chapter 11]. Historical chronicle and narrative merge in this chapter, which gives us a picture of how David became king over "all Israel." The sequence of the chapter is as follows: the nation's request to David at Hebron that he become king over the country (vv. 1–3); David's conquest of Jerusalem, which is established as "the city of David" (vv. 4–9); the elite group of "mighty men" (v. 10) who constituted David's leadership core, along with brief accounts of their exploits (vv. 10–25); a further *epic catalog of "mighty men," that is, warriors (vv. 26–47). As always, it is legitimate to ask where we find edification in this passage. Many chapters of the OT historical chronicles, including this one, show what a human document the Bible is and correspondingly how important ordinary earthly activities are to God. Furthermore, we see the strength and legitimacy of David's kingship and the implied hand of God in his ascension to the royal throne.

11 Then all Israel gathered together to David at Hebron and said, "Behold, we are your bone and flesh. ²In times past, even when Saul was king, it was you who led out and brought in Israel. And the LORD your God said to you, 'You shall be shepherd of my people Israel, and you shall be prince over my people Israel.'" ³So all the elders of Israel came to the king at Hebron, and David made a covenant with them at Hebron before the LORD. And they anointed David king over Israel, according to the word of the LORD by Samuel.

⁴And David and all Israel went to Jerusalem, that is, Jebus, where the Jebusites were, the inhabitants of the land. ⁵The inhabitants of Jebus said to David, "You will

¹ Hebrew *they*

not come in here." Nevertheless, David took the stronghold of Zion, that is, the city of David. ⁶David said, "Whoever strikes the Jebusites first shall be chief and commander." And Joab the son of Zeruiah went up first, so he became chief. ⁷And David lived in the stronghold; therefore it was called the city of David. ⁸And he built the city all around from the Millo in complete circuit, and Joab repaired the rest of the city. ⁹And David became greater and greater, for the LORD of hosts was with him.

¹⁰Now these are the chiefs of David's mighty men, who gave him strong support in his kingdom, together with all Israel, to make him king, according to the word of the LORD concerning Israel. ¹¹This is an account of David's mighty men: Jashobeam, a Hachmonite, was chief of the three.ⁱ He wielded his spear against 300 whom he killed at one time.

¹²And next to him among the three mighty men was Eleazar the son of Dodo, the Ahohite. ¹³He was with David at Pas-dammim when the Philistines were gathered there for battle. There was a plot of ground full of barley, and the men fled from the Philistines. ¹⁴But he took his² stand in the midst of the plot and defended it and killed the Philistines. And the LORD saved them by a great victory.

¹⁵Three of the thirty chief men went down to the rock to David at the cave of Adullam, when the army of Philistines was encamped in the Valley of Rephaim. ¹⁶David was then in the stronghold, and the garrison of the Philistines was then at Bethlehem. ¹⁷And David said longingly, "Oh that someone would give me water to drink from the well of Bethlehem that is by the gate!" ¹⁸Then the three mighty men broke through the camp of the Philistines and drew water out of the well of Bethlehem that was by the gate and took it and brought it to David. But David would not drink it. He poured it out to the LORD ¹⁹and said, "Far be it from me before my God that I should do this. Shall I drink the lifeblood of these men? For at the risk of their lives they brought it." Therefore he would not drink it. These things did the three mighty men.

²⁰Now Abishai, the brother of Joab, was chief of the thirty.³ And he wielded his spear against 300 men and killed them and won a name beside the three. ²¹He was the most renowned⁴ of the thirty⁵ and became their commander, but he did not attain to the three.

²²And Benaiah the son of Jehoiada was a valiant man⁶ of Kabzeel, a doer of great deeds. He struck down two heroes of Moab. He also went down and struck down a lion in a pit on a day when snow had fallen. ²³And he struck down an Egyptian, a man of great stature, five cubits⁷ tall. The Egyptian had in his hand a spear like a weaver's beam, but Benaiah went down to him with a staff and snatched the spear out of the Egyptian's hand and killed him with his own spear. ²⁴These things did Benaiah the son of Jehoiada and won a name beside the three mighty men. ²⁵He was renowned among the thirty, but he did not attain to the three. And David set him over his bodyguard.

²⁶The mighty men were Asahel the brother of Joab, Elhanan the son of Dodo of Bethlehem, ²⁷Shammoth of Harod,⁸ Helez the Pelonite, ²⁸Ira the son of Ikkesh of Tekoa, Abiezer of Anathoth, ²⁹Sibbecai the Hushathite, Ilai the Ahohite, ³⁰Maharai of Netophah, Heled the son of Baanah of Netophah, ³¹Ithai the son of Ribai of Gibeah of the people of Benjamin, Benaiah of Pirathon, ³²Hurai of the brooks of Gaash, Abiel

¹ Compare 2 Samuel 23:8; Hebrew *thirty*, or *captains* ² Compare 2 Samuel 23:12; Hebrew *they . . . their* ³ Syriac; Hebrew *three* ⁴ Compare 2 Samuel 23:19; Hebrew *more renowned among the two* ⁵ Syriac; Hebrew *three* ⁶ Syriac; Hebrew *the son of a valiant man* ⁷ A cubit was about 18 inches or 45 centimeters ⁸ Compare 2 Samuel 23:25; Hebrew *the Harorite*

the Arbathite, ³³Azmaveth of Baharum, Eliahba the Shaalbonite, ³⁴Hashem¹ the Gizonite, Jonathan the son of Shagee the Hararite, ³⁵Ahiam the son of Sachar the Hararite, Eliphal the son of Ur, ³⁶Hepher the Mecherathite, Ahijah the Pelonite, ³⁷Hezro of Carmel, Naarai the son of Ezbai, ³⁸Joel the brother of Nathan, Mibhar the son of Hagri, ³⁹Zelek the Ammonite, Naharai of Beeroth, the armor-bearer of Joab the son of Zeruiah, ⁴⁰Ira the Ithrite, Gareb the Ithrite, ⁴¹Uriah the Hittite, Zabad the son of Ahlai, ⁴²Adina the son of Shiza the Reubenite, a leader of the Reubenites, and thirty with him, ⁴³Hanan the son of Maacah, and Joshaphat the Mithnite, ⁴⁴Uzzia the Ashterathite, Shama and Jeiel the sons of Hotham the Aroerite, ⁴⁵Jediael the son of Shimri, and Joha his brother, the Tizite, ⁴⁶Eliel the Mahavite, and Jeribai, and Joshaviah, the sons of Elnaam, and Ithmah the Moabite, ⁴⁷Eliel, and Obed, and Jaasiel the Mezobaite.

Lists of David's supporters [chapter 12]. Following the list of mighty men in the preceding chapter, chapter 12 is in effect a narrative flashback that fills in the picture of David's supporters while he was king over Judah, before he became king over all Israel. Even though the primary form of the unit is the catalog or list, there are interspersed hints of narrative or human interest, such as the ambidextrous bowmen and shooters with the sling (v. 2).

12 Now these are the men who came to David at Ziklag, while he could not move about freely because of Saul the son of Kish. And they were among the mighty men who helped him in war. ²They were bowmen and could shoot arrows and sling stones with either the right or the left hand; they were Benjaminites, Saul's kinsmen. ³The chief was Ahiezer, then Joash, both sons of Shemaah of Gibeah; also Jeziel and Pelet, the sons of Azmaveth; Beracah, Jehu of Anathoth, ⁴Ishmaiah of Gibeon, a mighty man among the thirty and a leader over the thirty; Jeremiah,² Jahaziel, Johanan, Jozabad of Gederah, ⁵Eluzai,³ Jerimoth, Bealiah, Shemariah, Shephatiah the Haruphite; ⁶Elkanah, Isshiah, Azarel, Joezer, and Jashobeam, the Korahites; ⁷And Joelah and Zebadiah, the sons of Jeroham of Gedor.

⁸From the Gadites there went over to David at the stronghold in the wilderness mighty and experienced warriors, expert with shield and spear, whose faces were like the faces of lions and who were swift as gazelles upon the mountains: ⁹Ezer the chief, Obadiah second, Eliab third, ¹⁰Mishmannah fourth, Jeremiah fifth, ¹¹Attai sixth, Eliel seventh, ¹²Johanan eighth, Elzabad ninth, ¹³Jeremiah tenth, Machbannai eleventh. ¹⁴These Gadites were officers of the army; the least was a match for a hundred men and the greatest for a thousand. ¹⁵These are the men who crossed the Jordan in the first month, when it was overflowing all its banks, and put to flight all those in the valleys, to the east and to the west.

¹⁶And some of the men of Benjamin and Judah came to the stronghold to David. ¹⁷David went out to meet them and said to them, "If you have come to me in friendship to help me, my heart will be joined to you; but if to betray me to my adversaries, although there is no wrong in my hands, then may the God of our fathers see and rebuke you." ¹⁸Then the Spirit clothed Amasai, chief of the thirty, and he said,

"We are yours, O David,
    and with you, O son of Jesse!

¹ Compare Septuagint and 2 Samuel 23:32; Hebrew *the sons of Hashem* ² Hebrew verse 5 ³ Hebrew verse 6

> Peace, peace to you,
>   and peace to your helpers!
> For your God helps you."

Then David received them and made them officers of his troops.

[19]Some of the men of Manasseh deserted to David when he came with the Philistines for the battle against Saul. (Yet he did not help them, for the rulers of the Philistines took counsel and sent him away, saying, "At peril to our heads he will desert to his master Saul.") [20]As he went to Ziklag, these men of Manasseh deserted to him: Adnah, Jozabad, Jediael, Michael, Jozabad, Elihu, and Zillethai, chiefs of thousands in Manasseh. [21]They helped David against the band of raiders, for they were all mighty men of valor and were commanders in the army. [22]For from day to day men came to David to help him, until there was a great army, like an army of God.

[23]These are the numbers of the divisions of the armed troops who came to David in Hebron to turn the kingdom of Saul over to him, according to the word of the LORD. [24]The men of Judah bearing shield and spear were 6,800 armed troops. [25]Of the Simeonites, mighty men of valor for war, 7,100. [26]Of the Levites 4,600. [27]The prince Jehoiada, of the house of Aaron, and with him 3,700. [28]Zadok, a young man mighty in valor, and twenty-two commanders from his own fathers' house. [29]Of the Benjaminites, the kinsmen of Saul, 3,000, of whom the majority had to that point kept their allegiance to the house of Saul. [30]Of the Ephraimites 20,800, mighty men of valor, famous men in their fathers' houses. [31]Of the half-tribe of Manasseh 18,000, who were expressly named to come and make David king. [32]Of Issachar, men who had understanding of the times, to know what Israel ought to do, 200 chiefs, and all their kinsmen under their command. [33]Of Zebulun 50,000 seasoned troops, equipped for battle with all the weapons of war, to help David[1] with singleness of purpose. [34]Of Naphtali 1,000 commanders with whom were 37,000 men armed with shield and spear. [35]Of the Danites 28,600 men equipped for battle. [36]Of Asher 40,000 seasoned troops ready for battle. [37]Of the Reubenites and Gadites and the half-tribe of Manasseh from beyond the Jordan, 120,000 men armed with all the weapons of war.

[38]All these, men of war, arrayed in battle order, came to Hebron with full intent to make David king over all Israel. Likewise, all the rest of Israel were of a single mind to make David king. [39]And they were there with David for three days, eating and drinking, for their brothers had made preparation for them. [40]And also their relatives, from as far as Issachar and Zebulun and Naphtali, came bringing food on donkeys and on camels and on mules and on oxen, abundant provisions of flour, cakes of figs, clusters of raisins, and wine and oil, oxen and sheep, for there was joy in Israel.

Transporting the ark of the covenant [chapter 13]. The story of the changing fortunes of the ark of the covenant is central to the religious history of OT Israel. The transfer of the ark from its place of neglect dating back to Saul's reign (v. 3) is a major event in the history of the ark. The sequence of chapter 13 is as follows: the nation's dedication to the project of bringing the ark back to Jerusalem (vv. 1–4); the fetching of the ark and the beginning of a procession to transfer it, amid celebration (vv. 5–8); the mysterious action of God in striking Uzzah dead for touching the ark to keep if from toppling when one of the oxen carrying it stumbles (vv. 9–10); David's resulting anger and fear

---

[1] Septuagint; Hebrew lacks *David*

> (vv. 11–12); a three-month interruption of the procession (vv. 13–14). The narrator gives us no explanatory help, so we are left to ponder what the meaning of these events is. We sense a mingling of joy and fear, appropriate to the majesty and holiness of God.

13 David consulted with the commanders of thousands and of hundreds, with every leader. ²And David said to all the assembly of Israel, "If it seems good to you and from the LORD our God, let us send abroad to our brothers who remain in all the lands of Israel, as well as to the priests and Levites in the cities that have pasture-lands, that they may be gathered to us. ³Then let us bring again the ark of our God to us, for we did not seek it¹ in the days of Saul." ⁴All the assembly agreed to do so, for the thing was right in the eyes of all the people.

⁵So David assembled all Israel from the Nile² of Egypt to Lebo-hamath, to bring the ark of God from Kiriath-jearim. ⁶And David and all Israel went up to Baalah, that is, to Kiriath-jearim that belongs to Judah, to bring up from there the ark of God, which is called by the name of the LORD who sits enthroned above the cherubim. ⁷And they carried the ark of God on a new cart, from the house of Abinadab, and Uzzah and Ahio³ were driving the cart. ⁸And David and all Israel were rejoicing before God with all their might, with song and lyres and harps and tambourines and cymbals and trumpets.

⁹And when they came to the threshing floor of Chidon, Uzzah put out his hand to take hold of the ark, for the oxen stumbled. ¹⁰And the anger of the LORD was kindled against Uzzah, and he struck him down because he put out his hand to the ark, and he died there before God. ¹¹And David was angry because the LORD had broken out against Uzzah. And that place is called Perez-uzza⁴ to this day. ¹²And David was afraid of God that day, and he said, "How can I bring the ark of God home to me?" ¹³So David did not take the ark home into the city of David, but took it aside to the house of Obed-edom the Gittite. ¹⁴And the ark of God remained with the household of Obed-edom in his house three months. And the LORD blessed the household of Obed-edom and all that he had.

David's success as king [chapter 14]. This brief summary of David's early successes as king of all Israel is a typical specimen of court history. It is the king, specifically, whose life is recalled, and because of that focus, the court history shades off into the genre of hero story at this point. The chronicle of success shows David doing what ancient kings were expected to do—he builds a palace when he realizes that his kingship is stable (vv. 1–2); he marries multiple wives and fathers multiple children (vv. 3–7); he leads the army in conquest of national adversaries (vv. 8–17). We can scrutinize the text for how the court historian wants us to interpret David's success in a religious light. The book of Deuteronomy forms a helpful background as well: David's victory over the nation's enemies is a sign of God's blessing for obedience, but David's multiplication of wives is a sign that something is awry, inasmuch as Deuteronomy 17:17 records God's prohibition of that practice.

---

¹ Or him ² Hebrew *Shihor* ³ Or *and his brother* ⁴ *Perez-uzza* means *the breaking out against Uzzah*

14 And Hiram king of Tyre sent messengers to David, and cedar trees, also masons and carpenters to build a house for him. [2] And David knew that the LORD had established him as king over Israel, and that his kingdom was highly exalted for the sake of his people Israel.

[3] And David took more wives in Jerusalem, and David fathered more sons and daughters. [4] These are the names of the children born to him in Jerusalem: Shammua, Shobab, Nathan, Solomon, [5] Ibhar, Elishua, Elpelet, [6] Nogah, Nepheg, Japhia, [7] Elishama, Beeliada and Eliphelet.

[8] When the Philistines heard that David had been anointed king over all Israel, all the Philistines went up to search for David. But David heard of it and went out against them. [9] Now the Philistines had come and made a raid in the Valley of Rephaim. [10] And David inquired of God, "Shall I go up against the Philistines? Will you give them into my hand?" And the LORD said to him, "Go up, and I will give them into your hand." [11] And he went up to Baal-perazim, and David struck them down there. And David said, "God has broken through[1] my enemies by my hand, like a bursting flood." Therefore the name of that place is called Baal-perazim. [12] And they left their gods there, and David gave command, and they were burned.

[13] And the Philistines yet again made a raid in the valley. [14] And when David again inquired of God, God said to him, "You shall not go up after them; go around and come against them opposite the balsam trees. [15] And when you hear the sound of marching in the tops of the balsam trees, then go out to battle, for God has gone out before you to strike down the army of the Philistines." [16] And David did as God commanded him, and they struck down the Philistine army from Gibeon to Gezer. [17] And the fame of David went out into all lands, and the LORD brought the fear of him upon all nations.

Establishment of religious worship in Jerusalem [15:1–16:3]. In contrast to the chronicler of 2 Samuel, who cast the life of David in a tragic pattern, the author of 1 Chronicles largely idealizes him. A major part of this idealization focuses on David's concern for the formal worship of God, whether at the tabernacle (15:1 and 16:1) or in the preparations for an eventual temple. The sequence of 15:1–16:3 is as follows: preparations to complete the transfer of the ark of the covenant from an outlying region to Jerusalem (15:1–15); David's instructions regarding the music that should accompany the moving of the ark, along with a long list of musicians (15:16–24); narrative account of David's ecstatic behavior on the occasion of the ark's transfer (15:25–29); the offerings that are performed when the ark enters Jerusalem (16:1–3). The events recorded here are a high point of 1 Chronicles, since they represent God's presence with his people, confirming his blessing on the monarchy.

---

15 David[2] built houses for himself in the city of David. And he prepared a place for the ark of God and pitched a tent for it. [2] Then David said that no one but the Levites may carry the ark of God, for the LORD had chosen them to carry the ark of the LORD and to minister to him forever. [3] And David assembled all Israel at Jerusalem to bring up the ark of the LORD to its place, which he had prepared for it. [4] And David gathered together the sons of Aaron and the Levites: [5] of the sons of Kohath, Uriel the chief, with 120 of his brothers; [6] of the sons of Merari, Asaiah the chief, with 220 of his brothers; [7] of the sons of Gershom, Joel the chief, with 130 of his

---

[1] *Baal-perazim means Lord of breaking through* [2] Hebrew *He*

brothers; [8]of the sons of Elizaphan, Shemaiah the chief, with 200 of his brothers; [9]of the sons of Hebron, Eliel the chief, with 80 of his brothers; [10]of the sons of Uzziel, Amminadab the chief, with 112 of his brothers. [11]Then David summoned the priests Zadok and Abiathar, and the Levites Uriel, Asaiah, Joel, Shemaiah, Eliel, and Amminadab, [12]and said to them, "You are the heads of the fathers' houses of the Levites. Consecrate yourselves, you and your brothers, so that you may bring up the ark of the LORD, the God of Israel, to the place that I have prepared for it. [13]Because you did not carry it the first time, the LORD our God broke out against us, because we did not seek him according to the rule." [14]So the priests and the Levites consecrated themselves to bring up the ark of the LORD, the God of Israel. [15]And the Levites carried the ark of God on their shoulders with the poles, as Moses had commanded according to the word of the LORD.

[16]David also commanded the chiefs of the Levites to appoint their brothers as the singers who should play loudly on musical instruments, on harps and lyres and cymbals, to raise sounds of joy. [17]So the Levites appointed Heman the son of Joel; and of his brothers Asaph the son of Berechiah; and of the sons of Merari, their brothers, Ethan the son of Kushaiah; [18]and with them their brothers of the second order, Zechariah, Jaaziel, Shemiramoth, Jehiel, Unni, Eliab, Benaiah, Maaseiah, Mattithiah, Eliphelehu, and Mikneiah, and the gatekeepers Obed-edom and Jeiel. [19]The singers, Heman, Asaph, and Ethan, were to sound bronze cymbals; [20]Zechariah, Aziel, Shemiramoth, Jehiel, Unni, Eliab, Maaseiah, and Benaiah were to play harps according to Alamoth; [21]but Mattithiah, Eliphelehu, Mikneiah, Obed-edom, Jeiel, and Azaziah were to lead with lyres according to the Sheminith. [22]Chenaniah, leader of the Levites in music, should direct the music, for he understood it. [23]Berechiah and Elkanah were to be gatekeepers for the ark. [24]Shebaniah, Joshaphat, Nethanel, Amasai, Zechariah, Benaiah, and Eliezer, the priests, should blow the trumpets before the ark of God. Obed-edom and Jehiah were to be gatekeepers for the ark.

[25]So David and the elders of Israel and the commanders of thousands went to bring up the ark of the covenant of the LORD from the house of Obed-edom with rejoicing. [26]And because God helped the Levites who were carrying the ark of the covenant of the LORD, they sacrificed seven bulls and seven rams. [27]David was clothed with a robe of fine linen, as also were all the Levites who were carrying the ark, and the singers and Chenaniah the leader of the music of the singers. And David wore a linen ephod. [28]So all Israel brought up the ark of the covenant of the LORD with shouting, to the sound of the horn, trumpets, and cymbals, and made loud music on harps and lyres.

[29]And as the ark of the covenant of the LORD came to the city of David, Michal the daughter of Saul looked out of the window and saw King David dancing and rejoicing, and she despised him in her heart.

16

And they brought in the ark of God and set it inside the tent that David had pitched for it, and they offered burnt offerings and peace offerings before God. [2]And when David had finished offering the burnt offerings and the peace offerings, he blessed the people in the name of the LORD [3]and distributed to all Israel, both men and women, to each a loaf of bread, a portion of meat,[1] and a cake of raisins.

[1] Compare Septuagint, Syriac, Vulgate; the meaning of the Hebrew is uncertain

Institution of musical and poetic worship [16:4–43]. With the ark of the covenant now safely established in Jerusalem, the king sets about to ensure that proper worship rituals will take place around it. Music figures prominently in David's design. He appoints permanent worship leaders and musicians to perform their functions at the ark (vv. 4–6). The climax of the day of celebration when the ark arrives in Jerusalem is a psalm of thanksgiving (vv. 8–36) that David "on that day . . . first appointed" to be sung (v. 7). The poem has all the usual ingredients of a *praise psalm, but with individualizing touches. The conventional call to praise God occurs not only at the beginning (vv. 8–13), but again at two interspersed places (vv. 23–24, 28–34). This means that half of the poem consists of calls to praise, with the effect being a heightened sense of excitement. The rest of the psalm consists of brief lists of God's praiseworthy acts and attributes (vv. 14–22, 25–27), a prayer for God to deliver and save his people (v. 35), and a concluding benediction (v. 36). The chapter ends with a narrative account of the end of the day of celebration (vv. 37–43). First Chronicles ranges widely over the political history of David's reign; this chapter highlights the spiritual keynote of the history, especially the centrality of God in it.

⁴Then he appointed some of the Levites as ministers before the ark of the LORD, to invoke, to thank, and to praise the LORD, the God of Israel. ⁵Asaph was the chief, and second to him were Zechariah, Jeiel, Shemiramoth, Jehiel, Mattithiah, Eliab, Benaiah, Obed-edom, and Jeiel, who were to play harps and lyres; Asaph was to sound the cymbals, ⁶and Benaiah and Jahaziel the priests were to blow trumpets regularly before the ark of the covenant of God. ⁷Then on that day David first appointed that thanksgiving be sung to the LORD by Asaph and his brothers.

⁸   Oh give thanks to the LORD; call upon his name;
       make known his deeds among the peoples!
⁹   Sing to him; sing praises to him;
       tell of all his wondrous works!
¹⁰   Glory in his holy name;
       let the hearts of those who seek the LORD rejoice!
¹¹   Seek the LORD and his strength;
       seek his presence continually!
¹²   Remember the wondrous works that he has done,
       his miracles and the judgments he uttered,
¹³   O offspring of Israel his servant,
       sons of Jacob, his chosen ones!

¹⁴   He is the LORD our God;
       his judgments are in all the earth.
¹⁵   Remember his covenant forever,
       the word that he commanded, for a thousand generations,
¹⁶   the covenant that he made with Abraham,
       his sworn promise to Isaac,
¹⁷   which he confirmed as a statute to Jacob,
       as an everlasting covenant to Israel,

18 saying, "To you I will give the land of Canaan,
    as your portion for an inheritance."

19 When you were few in number,
    and of little account, and sojourners in it,
20 wandering from nation to nation,
    from one kingdom to another people,
21 he allowed no one to oppress them;
    he rebuked kings on their account,
22 saying, "Touch not my anointed ones,
    do my prophets no harm!"

23 Sing to the LORD, all the earth!
    Tell of his salvation from day to day.
24 Declare his glory among the nations,
    his marvelous works among all the peoples!
25 For great is the LORD, and greatly to be praised,
    and he is to be held in awe above all gods.
26 For all the gods of the peoples are idols,
    but the LORD made the heavens.
27 Splendor and majesty are before him;
    strength and joy are in his place.

28 Ascribe to the LORD, O clans of the peoples,
    ascribe to the LORD glory and strength!
29 Ascribe to the LORD the glory due his name;
    bring an offering and come before him!
    Worship the LORD in the splendor of holiness;[1]
30   tremble before him, all the earth;
    yes, the world is established; it shall never be moved.
31 Let the heavens be glad, and let the earth rejoice,
    and let them say among the nations, "The LORD reigns!"
32 Let the sea roar, and all that fills it;
    let the field exult, and everything in it!
33 Then shall the trees of the forest sing for joy
    before the LORD, for he comes to judge the earth.
34 Oh give thanks to the LORD, for he is good;
    for his steadfast love endures forever!

35 Say also:

    "Save us, O God of our salvation,
        and gather and deliver us from among the nations,
    that we may give thanks to your holy name,
        and glory in your praise.
36 Blessed be the LORD, the God of Israel,
        from everlasting to everlasting!"

Then all the people said, "Amen!" and praised the LORD.

---

[1] Or *in holy attire*

³⁷So David left Asaph and his brothers there before the ark of the covenant of the LORD to minister regularly before the ark as each day required, ³⁸and also Obed-edom and his¹ sixty-eight brothers, while Obed-edom, the son of Jeduthun, and Hosah were to be gatekeepers. ³⁹And he left Zadok the priest and his brothers the priests before the tabernacle of the LORD in the high place that was at Gibeon ⁴⁰to offer burnt offerings to the LORD on the altar of burnt offering regularly morning and evening, to do all that is written in the Law of the LORD that he commanded Israel. ⁴¹With them were Heman and Jeduthun and the rest of those chosen and expressly named to give thanks to the LORD, for his steadfast love endures forever. ⁴²Heman and Jeduthun had trumpets and cymbals for the music and instruments for sacred song. The sons of Jeduthun were appointed to the gate.

⁴³Then all the people departed each to his house, and David went home to bless his household.

David's thwarted desire to build a temple [chapter 17]. A large part of the Chronicler's partiality toward David is evidenced in his inclusion of material surrounding David's desire to build a temple and his gathering of the materials for the building project. Chapter 17 recounts one of the high points of OT Israelite history, even though the action occurs in the privacy of David's room. The cast of characters numbers three—David, the prophet Nathan, and God. The sequence unfolds as follows: temporary approval of David's desire to build a temple (vv. 1–2); a long and stately speech (vv. 3–14) from God to Nathan (subsequently reported to David, v. 15) in which God vetoes David's plan, providing reasons for that verdict (vv. 4–10) and a compensating blessing on David and his house (vv. 10–14); David's prayer of submission (vv. 16–27). Two of the peaks of the OT are present in this chapter—the Davidic covenant that is also a messianic promise (vv. 11–14) and David's exalted prayer extolling God, one of the greatest prayers recorded in the Bible.

17 Now when David lived in his house, David said to Nathan the prophet, "Behold, I dwell in a house of cedar, but the ark of the covenant of the LORD is under a tent." ²And Nathan said to David, "Do all that is in your heart, for God is with you."

³But that same night the word of the LORD came to Nathan, ⁴"Go and tell my servant David, 'Thus says the LORD: It is not you who will build me a house to dwell in. ⁵For I have not lived in a house since the day I brought up Israel to this day, but I have gone from tent to tent and from dwelling to dwelling. ⁶In all places where I have moved with all Israel, did I speak a word with any of the judges of Israel, whom I commanded to shepherd my people, saying, "Why have you not built me a house of cedar?"' ⁷Now, therefore, thus shall you say to my servant David, 'Thus says the LORD of hosts, I took you from the pasture, from following the sheep, to be prince over my people Israel, ⁸and I have been with you wherever you have gone and have cut off all your enemies from before you. And I will make for you a name, like the name of the great ones of the earth. ⁹And I will appoint a place for my people Israel and will plant them, that they may dwell in their own place and be disturbed no more. And violent men shall waste them no more, as formerly, ¹⁰from the time that I appointed judges over my people Israel. And I will subdue all your enemies. Moreover, I declare to you that the LORD will build you a house. ¹¹When your days are fulfilled to walk with your

¹ Hebrew *their*

fathers, I will raise up your offspring after you, one of your own sons, and I will establish his kingdom. ¹²He shall build a house for me, and I will establish his throne forever. ¹³I will be to him a father, and he shall be to me a son. I will not take my steadfast love from him, as I took it from him who was before you, ¹⁴but I will confirm him in my house and in my kingdom forever, and his throne shall be established forever.'" ¹⁵In accordance with all these words, and in accordance with all this vision, Nathan spoke to David.

¹⁶Then King David went in and sat before the LORD and said, "Who am I, O LORD God, and what is my house, that you have brought me thus far? ¹⁷And this was a small thing in your eyes, O God. You have also spoken of your servant's house for a great while to come, and have shown me future generations,¹ O LORD God! ¹⁸And what more can David say to you for honoring your servant? For you know your servant. ¹⁹For your servant's sake, O LORD, and according to your own heart, you have done all this greatness, in making known all these great things. ²⁰There is none like you, O LORD, and there is no God besides you, according to all that we have heard with our ears. ²¹And who is like your people Israel, the one² nation on earth whom God went to redeem to be his people, making for yourself a name for great and awesome things, in driving out nations before your people whom you redeemed from Egypt? ²²And you made your people Israel to be your people forever, and you, O LORD, became their God. ²³And now, O LORD, let the word that you have spoken concerning your servant and concerning his house be established forever, and do as you have spoken, ²⁴and your name will be established and magnified forever, saying, 'The LORD of hosts, the God of Israel, is Israel's God,' and the house of your servant David will be established before you. ²⁵For you, my God, have revealed to your servant that you will build a house for him. Therefore your servant has found courage to pray before you. ²⁶And now, O LORD, you are God, and you have promised this good thing to your servant. ²⁷Now you have been pleased to bless the house of your servant, that it may continue forever before you, for it is you, O LORD, who have blessed, and it is blessed forever."

The king's military victories [chapters 18–20]. The Chronicler has two main contexts for praising his hero—the religious and the military/political. With this unit the focus returns to the second of these spheres of David's success. Its main function is to idealize David as king and military genius. The material is consonant with what we find in court chronicles of ancient literate societies. Although the account falls mainly into the genre of military records, it is possible to find other threads as well—David's administrative practices, for example (18:14–17), and stories of human interest (19:1–5).

18 After this David defeated the Philistines and subdued them, and he took Gath and its villages out of the hand of the Philistines.

²And he defeated Moab, and the Moabites became servants to David and brought tribute.

³David also defeated Hadadezer king of Zobah-Hamath, as he went to set up his monument³ at the river Euphrates. ⁴And David took from him 1,000 chariots, 7,000 horsemen, and 20,000 foot soldiers. And David hamstrung all the chariot horses, but left enough for 100 chariots. ⁵And when the Syrians of Damascus came to help Hadadezer king of Zobah, David struck down 22,000 men of the Syrians. ⁶Then

---

¹ The meaning of the Hebrew is uncertain ² Septuagint, Vulgate *other* ³ Hebrew *hand*

David put garrisons[1] in Syria of Damascus, and the Syrians became servants to David and brought tribute. And the LORD gave victory to David[2] wherever he went. ⁷And David took the shields of gold that were carried by the servants of Hadadezer and brought them to Jerusalem. ⁸And from Tibhath and from Cun, cities of Hadadezer, David took a large amount of bronze. With it Solomon made the bronze sea and the pillars and the vessels of bronze.

⁹When Tou king of Hamath heard that David had defeated the whole army of Hadadezer, king of Zobah, ¹⁰he sent his son Hadoram to King David, to ask about his health and to bless him because he had fought against Hadadezer and defeated him; for Hadadezer had often been at war with Tou. And he sent all sorts of articles of gold, of silver, and of bronze. ¹¹These also King David dedicated to the LORD, together with the silver and gold that he had carried off from all the nations, from Edom, Moab, the Ammonites, the Philistines, and Amalek.

¹²And Abishai, the son of Zeruiah, killed 18,000 Edomites in the Valley of Salt. ¹³Then he put garrisons in Edom, and all the Edomites became David's servants. And the LORD gave victory to David wherever he went.

¹⁴So David reigned over all Israel, and he administered justice and equity to all his people. ¹⁵And Joab the son of Zeruiah was over the army; and Jehoshaphat the son of Ahilud was recorder; ¹⁶and Zadok the son of Ahitub and Ahimelech the son of Abiathar were priests; and Shavsha was secretary; ¹⁷and Benaiah the son of Jehoiada was over the Cherethites and the Pelethites; and David's sons were the chief officials in the service of the king.

19 Now after this Nahash the king of the Ammonites died, and his son reigned in his place. ²And David said, "I will deal kindly with Hanun the son of Nahash, for his father dealt kindly with me." So David sent messengers to console him concerning his father. And David's servants came to the land of the Ammonites to Hanun to console him. ³But the princes of the Ammonites said to Hanun, "Do you think, because David has sent comforters to you, that he is honoring your father? Have not his servants come to you to search and to overthrow and to spy out the land?" ⁴So Hanun took David's servants and shaved them and cut off their garments in the middle, at their hips, and sent them away; ⁵and they departed. When David was told concerning the men, he sent messengers to meet them, for the men were greatly ashamed. And the king said, "Remain at Jericho until your beards have grown and then return."

⁶When the Ammonites saw that they had become a stench to David, Hanun and the Ammonites sent 1,000 talents[3] of silver to hire chariots and horsemen from Mesopotamia, from Aram-maacah, and from Zobah. ⁷They hired 32,000 chariots and the king of Maacah with his army, who came and encamped before Medeba. And the Ammonites were mustered from their cities and came to battle. ⁸When David heard of it, he sent Joab and all the army of the mighty men. ⁹And the Ammonites came out and drew up in battle array at the entrance of the city, and the kings who had come were by themselves in the open country.

¹⁰When Joab saw that the battle was set against him both in front and in the rear, he chose some of the best men of Israel and arrayed them against the Syrians. ¹¹The rest of his men he put in the charge of Abishai his brother, and they were arrayed

---

[1] Septuagint, Vulgate, 2 Samuel 8:6 (compare Syriac); Hebrew lacks *garrisons* [2] Hebrew *the LORD saved David*; also verse 13 [3] A *talent* was about 75 pounds or 34 kilograms

against the Ammonites. ¹²And he said, "If the Syrians are too strong for me, then you shall help me, but if the Ammonites are too strong for you, then I will help you. ¹³Be strong, and let us use our strength for our people and for the cities of our God, and may the LORD do what seems good to him." ¹⁴So Joab and the people who were with him drew near before the Syrians for battle, and they fled before him. ¹⁵And when the Ammonites saw that the Syrians fled, they likewise fled before Abishai, Joab's brother, and entered the city. Then Joab came to Jerusalem.

¹⁶But when the Syrians saw that they had been defeated by Israel, they sent messengers and brought out the Syrians who were beyond the Euphrates, with Shophach the commander of the army of Hadadezer at their head. ¹⁷And when it was told to David, he gathered all Israel together and crossed the Jordan and came to them and drew up his forces against them. And when David set the battle in array against the Syrians, they fought with him. ¹⁸And the Syrians fled before Israel, and David killed of the Syrians the men of 7,000 chariots and 40,000 foot soldiers, and put to death also Shophach the commander of their army. ¹⁹And when the servants of Hadadezer saw that they had been defeated by Israel, they made peace with David and became subject to him. So the Syrians were not willing to save the Ammonites anymore.

20 In the spring of the year, the time when kings go out to battle, Joab led out the army and ravaged the country of the Ammonites and came and besieged Rabbah. But David remained at Jerusalem. And Joab struck down Rabbah and overthrew it. ²And David took the crown of their king from his head. He found that it weighed a talent¹ of gold, and in it was a precious stone. And it was placed on David's head. And he brought out the spoil of the city, a very great amount. ³And he brought out the people who were in it and set them to labor² with saws and iron picks and axes.³ And thus David did to all the cities of the Ammonites. Then David and all the people returned to Jerusalem.

⁴And after this there arose war with the Philistines at Gezer. Then Sibbecai the Hushathite struck down Sippai, who was one of the descendants of the giants, and the Philistines were subdued. ⁵And there was again war with the Philistines, and Elhanan the son of Jair struck down Lahmi the brother of Goliath the Gittite, the shaft of whose spear was like a weaver's beam. ⁶And there was again war at Gath, where there was a man of great stature, who had six fingers on each hand and six toes on each foot, twenty-four in number, and he also was descended from the giants. ⁷And when he taunted Israel, Jonathan the son of Shimea, David's brother, struck him down. ⁸These were descended from the giants in Gath, and they fell by the hand of David and by the hand of his servants.

Census and plague [21:1–17]. Chapter 21 springs some surprises on us. After numerous chapters idealizing David, the events recorded in this unit expose a notable failing. Satan enters the cast of characters (v. 1), and the entire episode has a heavily supernatural aura, as God appears directly and a mysterious angel of God is a major actor in the drama. Additionally, we have the awe-inspiring ingredients of a divinely sent plague and a propitiatory sacrifice that brings the plague to an end. The sequence is as follows: Satan incites David to take a census (v. 1); David overrides the objections of his adviser Joab and insists on taking it (vv. 2–6); God punishes David for his action with a

¹ A *talent* was about 75 pounds or 34 kilograms ² Compare 2 Samuel 12:31; Hebrew *he sawed* ³ Compare 2 Samuel 12:31; Hebrew *saws*

plague in the land (vv. 7–17). Our chief interpretive task is to ponder the nature of God as he emerges in the events and, as part of that, to infer why God objected so strongly to David's taking the census (for example, David's quest for success as measured in earthly terms and his proud ambition).

21 Then Satan stood against Israel and incited David to number Israel. ²So David said to Joab and the commanders of the army, "Go, number Israel, from Beersheba to Dan, and bring me a report, that I may know their number." ³But Joab said, "May the Lord add to his people a hundred times as many as they are! Are they not, my lord the king, all of them my lord's servants? Why then should my lord require this? Why should it be a cause of guilt for Israel?" ⁴But the king's word prevailed against Joab. So Joab departed and went throughout all Israel and came back to Jerusalem. ⁵And Joab gave the sum of the numbering of the people to David. In all Israel there were 1,100,000 men who drew the sword, and in Judah 470,000 who drew the sword. ⁶But he did not include Levi and Benjamin in the numbering, for the king's command was abhorrent to Joab.

⁷But God was displeased with this thing, and he struck Israel. ⁸And David said to God, "I have sinned greatly in that I have done this thing. But now, please take away the iniquity of your servant, for I have acted very foolishly." ⁹And the Lord spoke to Gad, David's seer, saying, ¹⁰"Go and say to David, 'Thus says the Lord, Three things I offer you; choose one of them, that I may do it to you.'" ¹¹So Gad came to David and said to him, "Thus says the Lord, 'Choose what you will: ¹²either three years of famine, or three months of devastation by your foes while the sword of your enemies overtakes you, or else three days of the sword of the Lord, pestilence on the land, with the angel of the Lord destroying throughout all the territory of Israel.' Now decide what answer I shall return to him who sent me." ¹³Then David said to Gad, "I am in great distress. Let me fall into the hand of the Lord, for his mercy is very great, but do not let me fall into the hand of man."

¹⁴So the Lord sent a pestilence on Israel, and 70,000 men of Israel fell. ¹⁵And God sent the angel to Jerusalem to destroy it, but as he was about to destroy it, the Lord saw, and he relented from the calamity. And he said to the angel who was working destruction, "It is enough; now stay your hand." And the angel of the Lord was standing by the threshing floor of Ornan the Jebusite. ¹⁶And David lifted his eyes and saw the angel of the Lord standing between earth and heaven, and in his hand a drawn sword stretched out over Jerusalem. Then David and the elders, clothed in sackcloth, fell upon their faces. ¹⁷And David said to God, "Was it not I who gave command to number the people? It is I who have sinned and done great evil. But these sheep, what have they done? Please let your hand, O Lord my God, be against me and against my father's house. But do not let the plague be on your people."

David's preparations for building the temple [21:18–22:19]. The shocking events surrounding David's census are followed by a scene of worship and sacrifice (21:18–30), ending with David's announcement that the threshing floor of Ornan will be the site of the temple (22:1). On the heels of that, the Chronicler turns his attention to David's preparations for Solomon's building of the temple. The author chose to include the following material: David's gathering of building materials (22:2–5); David's formally instructing his son and successor Solomon, explaining his own thwarted desire to build a temple (22:6–11), commanding him to be a godly ruler (22:12–13), and reminding him of the building materials (including craftsmen) that are at his disposal (22:14–16); David's parallel charge to the nation's leaders to follow through on the temple venture (22:17–19). While the main subject is worship and the need to honor God with a sanctuary dedicated to his presence, with implied lessons that are timeless, we can also catch glimpses of godly leadership and a godly society.

[18]Now the angel of the LORD had commanded Gad to say to David that David should go up and raise an altar to the LORD on the threshing floor of Ornan the Jebusite. [19]So David went up at Gad's word, which he had spoken in the name of the LORD. [20]Now Ornan was threshing wheat. He turned and saw the angel, and his four sons who were with him hid themselves. [21]As David came to Ornan, Ornan looked and saw David and went out from the threshing floor and paid homage to David with his face to the ground. [22]And David said to Ornan, "Give me the site of the threshing floor that I may build on it an altar to the LORD—give it to me at its full price—that the plague may be averted from the people." [23]Then Ornan said to David, "Take it, and let my lord the king do what seems good to him. See, I give the oxen for burnt offerings and the threshing sledges for the wood and the wheat for a grain offering; I give it all." [24]But King David said to Ornan, "No, but I will buy them for the full price. I will not take for the LORD what is yours, nor offer burnt offerings that cost me nothing." [25]So David paid Ornan 600 shekels[1] of gold by weight for the site. [26]And David built there an altar to the LORD and presented burnt offerings and peace offerings and called on the LORD, and the LORD[2] answered him with fire from heaven upon the altar of burnt offering. [27]Then the LORD commanded the angel, and he put his sword back into its sheath.

[28]At that time, when David saw that the LORD had answered him at the threshing floor of Ornan the Jebusite, he sacrificed there. [29]For the tabernacle of the LORD, which Moses had made in the wilderness, and the altar of burnt offering were at that time in the high place at Gibeon, [30]but David could not go before it to inquire of God, for he was afraid of the sword of the angel of the LORD.

22 Then David said, "Here shall be the house of the LORD God and here the altar of burnt offering for Israel."

[2]David commanded to gather together the resident aliens who were in the land of Israel, and he set stonecutters to prepare dressed stones for building the house of God. [3]David also provided great quantities of iron for nails for the doors of the gates and for clamps, as well as bronze in quantities beyond weighing, [4]and cedar timbers without number, for the Sidonians and Tyrians brought great quantities of cedar to David. [5]For David said, "Solomon my son is young and inexperienced, and the house that is to be built for the LORD must be exceedingly magnificent, of fame and glory throughout all lands. I will therefore make preparation for it." So David provided materials in great quantity before his death.

[6]Then he called for Solomon his son and charged him to build a house for the LORD, the God of Israel. [7]David said to Solomon, "My son, I had it in my heart to build a house to the name of the LORD my God. [8]But the word of the LORD came to me, saying, 'You have shed much blood and have waged great wars. You shall not build a house to my name, because you have shed so much blood before me on the earth. [9]Behold, a

---

[1] A *shekel* was about 2/5 ounce or 11 grams [2] Hebrew *he*

son shall be born to you who shall be a man of rest. I will give him rest from all his surrounding enemies. For his name shall be Solomon, and I will give peace and quiet to Israel in his days. [10]He shall build a house for my name. He shall be my son, and I will be his father, and I will establish his royal throne in Israel forever.'

[11]"Now, my son, the LORD be with you, so that you may succeed in building the house of the LORD your God, as he has spoken concerning you. [12]Only, may the LORD grant you discretion and understanding, that when he gives you charge over Israel you may keep the law of the LORD your God. [13]Then you will prosper if you are careful to observe the statutes and the rules that the LORD commanded Moses for Israel. Be strong and courageous. Fear not; do not be dismayed. [14]With great pains I have provided for the house of the LORD 100,000 talents[1] of gold, a million talents of silver, and bronze and iron beyond weighing, for there is so much of it; timber and stone, too, I have provided. To these you must add. [15]You have an abundance of workmen: stonecutters, masons, carpenters, and all kinds of craftsmen without number, skilled in working [16]gold, silver, bronze, and iron. Arise and work! The LORD be with you!"

[17]David also commanded all the leaders of Israel to help Solomon his son, saying, [18]"Is not the LORD your God with you? And has he not given you peace on every side? For he has delivered the inhabitants of the land into my hand, and the land is subdued before the LORD and his people. [19]Now set your mind and heart to seek the LORD your God. Arise and build the sanctuary of the LORD God, so that the ark of the covenant of the LORD and the holy vessels of God may be brought into a house built for the name of the LORD."

Instructions for Levites and priests [chapters 23–24]. The remainder of the book of 1 Chronicles is devoted to David's last acts as a king on the verge of handing over the kingdom to those who will succeed him. These chapters have the nature of a *farewell discourse (23:27 uses the formula "the last words of David"). The parting instructions that the writer chose to include reflect his own conception of what matters most in a well-ordered nation, and doubtless the material reflects David's thinking along the same lines, with a focus on worship and the leadership of it. This unit unfolds as follows: David's organization of the Levites, followed by a list of names (23:1–23); David's final instructions regarding the duties of the Levites (23:24–32); a list of the divisions of the priests (chapter 24).

23 When David was old and full of days, he made Solomon his son king over Israel.

[2]David[2] assembled all the leaders of Israel and the priests and the Levites. [3]The Levites, thirty years old and upward, were numbered, and the total was 38,000 men. [4]"Twenty-four thousand of these," David said,[3] "shall have charge of the work in the house of the LORD, 6,000 shall be officers and judges, [5]4,000 gatekeepers, and 4,000 shall offer praises to the LORD with the instruments that I have made for praise." [6]And David organized them in divisions corresponding to the sons of Levi: Gershon, Kohath, and Merari.

[7]The sons of Gershon[4] were Ladan and Shimei. [8]The sons of Ladan: Jehiel the chief, and Zetham, and Joel, three. [9]The sons of Shimei: Shelomoth, Haziel, and Haran, three. These were the heads of the fathers' houses of Ladan. [10]And the sons of

---

[1] A talent was about 75 pounds or 34 kilograms [2] Hebrew He [3] Hebrew lacks David said [4] Vulgate (compare Septuagint, Syriac); Hebrew to the Gershonite

Shimei: Jahath, Zina, and Jeush and Beriah. These four were the sons of Shimei. [11]Jahath was the chief, and Zizah the second; but Jeush and Beriah did not have many sons, therefore they became counted as a single father's house.

[12]The sons of Kohath: Amram, Izhar, Hebron, and Uzziel, four. [13]The sons of Amram: Aaron and Moses. Aaron was set apart to dedicate the most holy things, that he and his sons forever should make offerings before the LORD and minister to him and pronounce blessings in his name forever. [14]But the sons of Moses the man of God were named among the tribe of Levi. [15]The sons of Moses: Gershom and Eliezer. [16]The sons of Gershom: Shebuel the chief. [17]The sons of Eliezer: Rehabiah the chief. Eliezer had no other sons, but the sons of Rehabiah were very many. [18]The sons of Izhar: Shelomith the chief. [19]The sons of Hebron: Jeriah the chief, Amariah the second, Jahaziel the third, and Jekameam the fourth. [20]The sons of Uzziel: Micah the chief and Isshiah the second.

[21]The sons of Merari: Mahli and Mushi. The sons of Mahli: Eleazar and Kish. [22]Eleazar died having no sons, but only daughters; their kinsmen, the sons of Kish, married them. [23]The sons of Mushi: Mahli, Eder, and Jeremoth, three.

[24]These were the sons of Levi by their fathers' houses, the heads of fathers' houses as they were listed according to the number of the names of the individuals from twenty years old and upward who were to do the work for the service of the house of the LORD. [25]For David said, "The LORD, the God of Israel, has given rest to his people, and he dwells in Jerusalem forever. [26]And so the Levites no longer need to carry the tabernacle or any of the things for its service." [27]For by the last words of David the sons of Levi were numbered from twenty years old and upward. [28]For their duty was to assist the sons of Aaron for the service of the house of the LORD, having the care of the courts and the chambers, the cleansing of all that is holy, and any work for the service of the house of God. [29]Their duty was also to assist with the showbread, the flour for the grain offering, the wafers of unleavened bread, the baked offering, the offering mixed with oil, and all measures of quantity or size. [30]And they were to stand every morning, thanking and praising the LORD, and likewise at evening, [31]and whenever burnt offerings were offered to the LORD on Sabbaths, new moons, and feast days, according to the number required of them, regularly before the LORD. [32]Thus they were to keep charge of the tent of meeting and the sanctuary, and to attend the sons of Aaron, their brothers, for the service of the house of the LORD.

24 The divisions of the sons of Aaron were these. The sons of Aaron: Nadab, Abihu, Eleazar, and Ithamar. [2]But Nadab and Abihu died before their father and had no children, so Eleazar and Ithamar became the priests. [3]With the help of Zadok of the sons of Eleazar, and Ahimelech of the sons of Ithamar, David organized them according to the appointed duties in their service. [4]Since more chief men were found among the sons of Eleazar than among the sons of Ithamar, they organized them under sixteen heads of fathers' houses of the sons of Eleazar, and eight of the sons of Ithamar. [5]They divided them by lot, all alike, for there were sacred officers and officers of God among both the sons of Eleazar and the sons of Ithamar. [6]And the scribe Shemaiah, the son of Nethanel, a Levite, recorded them in the presence of the king and the princes and Zadok the priest and Ahimelech the son of Abiathar and the heads of the fathers' houses of the priests and of the Levites, one father's house being chosen for Eleazar and one chosen for Ithamar.

⁷The first lot fell to Jehoiarib, the second to Jedaiah, ⁸the third to Harim, the fourth to Seorim, ⁹the fifth to Malchijah, the sixth to Mijamin, ¹⁰the seventh to Hakkoz, the eighth to Abijah, ¹¹the ninth to Jeshua, the tenth to Shecaniah, ¹²the eleventh to Eliashib, the twelfth to Jakim, ¹³the thirteenth to Huppah, the fourteenth to Jeshebeab, ¹⁴the fifteenth to Bilgah, the sixteenth to Immer, ¹⁵the seventeenth to Hezir, the eighteenth to Happizzez, ¹⁶the nineteenth to Pethahiah, the twentieth to Jehezkel, ¹⁷the twenty-first to Jachin, the twenty-second to Gamul, ¹⁸the twenty-third to Delaiah, the twenty-fourth to Maaziah. ¹⁹These had as their appointed duty in their service to come into the house of the Lord according to the procedure established for them by Aaron their father, as the Lord God of Israel had commanded him.

²⁰And of the rest of the sons of Levi: of the sons of Amram, Shubael; of the sons of Shubael, Jehdeiah. ²¹Of Rehabiah: of the sons of Rehabiah, Isshiah the chief. ²²Of the Izharites, Shelomoth; of the sons of Shelomoth, Jahath. ²³The sons of Hebron:¹ Jeriah the chief,² Amariah the second, Jahaziel the third, Jekameam the fourth. ²⁴The sons of Uzziel, Micah; of the sons of Micah, Shamir. ²⁵The brother of Micah, Isshiah; of the sons of Isshiah, Zechariah. ²⁶The sons of Merari: Mahli and Mushi. The sons of Jaaziah: Beno.³ ²⁷The sons of Merari: of Jaaziah, Beno, Shoham, Zaccur, and Ibri. ²⁸Of Mahli: Eleazar, who had no sons. ²⁹Of Kish, the sons of Kish: Jerahmeel. ³⁰The sons of Mushi: Mahli, Eder, and Jerimoth. These were the sons of the Levites according to their fathers' houses. ³¹These also, the head of each father's house and his younger brother alike, cast lots, just as their brothers the sons of Aaron, in the presence of King David, Zadok, Ahimelech, and the heads of fathers' houses of the priests and of the Levites.

Temple musicians [chapter 25]. This chapter lists the musicians who are enlisted to perform at the temple (vv. 1–7), followed by the casting of lots to determine the order in which the respective groups of musicians will perform their part of the service at the temple (vv. 8–31). In addition to demonstrating once again that named individuality is important in the Bible and therefore to God, we see (a) the importance of music in worship and (b) the ideal of a well-ordered community.

25 David and the chiefs of the service also set apart for the service the sons of Asaph, and of Heman, and of Jeduthun, who prophesied with lyres, with harps, and with cymbals. The list of those who did the work and of their duties was: ²Of the sons of Asaph: Zaccur, Joseph, Nethaniah, and Asharelah, sons of Asaph, under the direction of Asaph, who prophesied under the direction of the king. ³Of Jeduthun, the sons of Jeduthun: Gedaliah, Zeri, Jeshaiah, Shimei,⁴ Hashabiah, and Mattithiah, six, under the direction of their father Jeduthun, who prophesied with the lyre in thanksgiving and praise to the Lord. ⁴Of Heman, the sons of Heman: Bukkiah, Mattaniah, Uzziel, Shebuel and Jerimoth, Hananiah, Hanani, Eliathah, Giddalti, and Romamti-ezer, Joshbekashah, Mallothi, Hothir, Mahazioth. ⁵All these were the sons of Heman the king's seer, according to the promise of God to exalt him, for God had given Heman fourteen sons and three daughters. ⁶They were all under the direction of their father in the music in the house of the Lord with cymbals, harps, and lyres for the service of the house of God. Asaph, Jeduthun, and Heman were under the

¹ Compare 23:19; Hebrew lacks *Hebron* ² Compare 23:19; Hebrew lacks *the chief* ³ Or *his son*; also verse 27 ⁴ One Hebrew manuscript, Septuagint; most Hebrew manuscripts lack *Shimei*

order of the king. [7]The number of them along with their brothers, who were trained in singing to the LORD, all who were skillful, was 288. [8]And they cast lots for their duties, small and great, teacher and pupil alike.

[9]The first lot fell for Asaph to Joseph; the second to Gedaliah, to him and his brothers and his sons, twelve; [10]the third to Zaccur, his sons and his brothers, twelve; [11]the fourth to Izri, his sons and his brothers, twelve; [12]the fifth to Nethaniah, his sons and his brothers, twelve; [13]the sixth to Bukkiah, his sons and his brothers, twelve; [14]the seventh to Jesharelah, his sons and his brothers, twelve; [15]the eighth to Jeshaiah, his sons and his brothers, twelve; [16]the ninth to Mattaniah, his sons and his brothers, twelve; [17]the tenth to Shimei, his sons and his brothers, twelve; [18]the eleventh to Azarel, his sons and his brothers, twelve; [19]the twelfth to Hashabiah, his sons and his brothers, twelve; [20]to the thirteenth, Shubael, his sons and his brothers, twelve; [21]to the fourteenth, Mattithiah, his sons and his brothers, twelve; [22]to the fifteenth, to Jeremoth, his sons and his brothers, twelve; [23]to the sixteenth, to Hananiah, his sons and his brothers, twelve; [24]to the seventeenth, to Joshbekashah, his sons and his brothers, twelve; [25]to the eighteenth, to Hanani, his sons and his brothers, twelve; [26]to the nineteenth, to Mallothi, his sons and his brothers, twelve; [27]to the twentieth, to Eliathah, his sons and his brothers, twelve; [28]to the twenty-first, to Hothir, his sons and his brothers, twelve; [29]to the twenty-second, to Giddalti, his sons and his brothers, twelve; [30]to the twenty-third, to Mahazioth, his sons and his brothers, twelve; [31]to the twenty-fourth, to Romamti-ezer, his sons and his brothers, twelve.

The appointment of additional temple workers [chapter 26]. The professional staff that David wants to man the temple keeps expanding. In this chapter we find lists of gatekeepers (vv. 1–19), treasurers (vv. 20–28), and "officers and judges" (vv. 29–32). At the very least, we can see God's view that in the worshiping community "all things should be done decently and in order" (1 Cor. 14:40).

26 As for the divisions of the gatekeepers: of the Korahites, Meshelemiah the son of Kore, of the sons of Asaph. [2]And Meshelemiah had sons: Zechariah the firstborn, Jediael the second, Zebadiah the third, Jathniel the fourth, [3]Elam the fifth, Jehohanan the sixth, Eliehoenai the seventh. [4]And Obed-edom had sons: Shemaiah the firstborn, Jehozabad the second, Joah the third, Sachar the fourth, Nethanel the fifth, [5]Ammiel the sixth, Issachar the seventh, Peullethai the eighth, for God blessed him. [6]Also to his son Shemaiah were sons born who were rulers in their fathers' houses, for they were men of great ability. [7]The sons of Shemaiah: Othni, Rephael, Obed and Elzabad, whose brothers were able men, Elihu and Semachiah. [8]All these were of the sons of Obed-edom with their sons and brothers, able men qualified for the service; sixty-two of Obed-edom. [9]And Meshelemiah had sons and brothers, able men, eighteen. [10]And Hosah, of the sons of Merari, had sons: Shimri the chief (for though he was not the firstborn, his father made him chief), [11]Hilkiah the second, Tebaliah the third, Zechariah the fourth: all the sons and brothers of Hosah were thirteen.

[12]These divisions of the gatekeepers, corresponding to their chief men, had duties, just as their brothers did, ministering in the house of the LORD. [13]And they cast lots by fathers' houses, small and great alike, for their gates. [14]The lot for the east fell to

Shelemiah. They cast lots also for his son Zechariah, a shrewd counselor, and his lot came out for the north. ¹⁵Obed-edom's came out for the south, and to his sons was allotted the gatehouse. ¹⁶For Shuppim and Hosah it came out for the west, at the gate of Shallecheth on the road that goes up. Watch corresponded to watch. ¹⁷On the east there were six each day,¹ on the north four each day, on the south four each day, as well as two and two at the gatehouse. ¹⁸And for the colonnade² on the west there were four at the road and two at the colonnade. ¹⁹These were the divisions of the gatekeepers among the Korahites and the sons of Merari.

²⁰And of the Levites, Ahijah had charge of the treasuries of the house of God and the treasuries of the dedicated gifts. ²¹The sons of Ladan, the sons of the Gershonites belonging to Ladan, the heads of the fathers' houses belonging to Ladan the Gershonite: Jehieli.³

²²The sons of Jehieli, Zetham, and Joel his brother, were in charge of the treasuries of the house of the LORD. ²³Of the Amramites, the Izharites, the Hebronites, and the Uzzielites— ²⁴and Shebuel the son of Gershom, son of Moses, was chief officer in charge of the treasuries. ²⁵His brothers: from Eliezer were his son Rehabiah, and his son Jeshaiah, and his son Joram, and his son Zichri, and his son Shelomoth. ²⁶This Shelomoth and his brothers were in charge of all the treasuries of the dedicated gifts that David the king and the heads of the fathers' houses and the officers of the thousands and the hundreds and the commanders of the army had dedicated. ²⁷From spoil won in battles they dedicated gifts for the maintenance of the house of the LORD. ²⁸Also all that Samuel the seer and Saul the son of Kish and Abner the son of Ner and Joab the son of Zeruiah had dedicated—all dedicated gifts were in the care of Shelomoth⁴ and his brothers.

²⁹Of the Izharites, Chenaniah and his sons were appointed to external duties for Israel, as officers and judges. ³⁰Of the Hebronites, Hashabiah and his brothers, 1,700 men of ability, had the oversight of Israel westward of the Jordan for all the work of the LORD and for the service of the king. ³¹Of the Hebronites, Jerijah was chief of the Hebronites of whatever genealogy or fathers' houses. (In the fortieth year of David's reign search was made and men of great ability among them were found at Jazer in Gilead.) ³²King David appointed him and his brothers, 2,700 men of ability, heads of fathers' houses, to have the oversight of the Reubenites, the Gadites and the half-tribe of the Manassites for everything pertaining to God and for the affairs of the king.

Appointment of military and civil officials [chapter 27]. With the assignment of temple duties having been covered, an additional chapter is now devoted to military and civil leaders and officers. More specifically, we find lists of military commanders and groups that were on duty by the months of the year (vv. 1–15), leaders over the tribes (vv. 16–24), treasurers (vv. 25–31), and counselors, including Joab, the commander of the king's army (vv. 32–34).

27 This is the number of the people of Israel, the heads of fathers' houses, the commanders of thousands and hundreds, and their officers who served the king in all matters concerning the divisions that came and went, month after month throughout the year, each division numbering 24,000:

¹ Septuagint; Hebrew *six Levites* ² Or *court*; Hebrew *parbar* (meaning unknown); twice in this verse ³ The Hebrew of verse 21 is uncertain ⁴ Hebrew *Shelomith*

²Jashobeam the son of Zabdiel was in charge of the first division in the first month; in his division were 24,000. ³He was a descendant of Perez and was chief of all the commanders. He served for the first month. ⁴Dodai the Ahohite¹ was in charge of the division of the second month; in his division were 24,000. ⁵The third commander, for the third month, was Benaiah, the son of Jehoiada the chief priest; in his division were 24,000. ⁶This is the Benaiah who was a mighty man of the thirty and in command of the thirty; Ammizabad his son was in charge of his division.² ⁷Asahel the brother of Joab was fourth, for the fourth month, and his son Zebadiah after him; in his division were 24,000. ⁸The fifth commander, for the fifth month, was Shamhuth the Izrahite; in his division were 24,000. ⁹Sixth, for the sixth month, was Ira, the son of Ikkesh the Tekoite; in his division were 24,000. ¹⁰Seventh, for the seventh month, was Helez the Pelonite, of the sons of Ephraim; in his division were 24,000. ¹¹Eighth, for the eighth month, was Sibbecai the Hushathite, of the Zerahites; in his division were 24,000. ¹²Ninth, for the ninth month, was Abiezer of Anathoth, a Benjaminite; in his division were 24,000. ¹³Tenth, for the tenth month, was Maharai of Netophah, of the Zerahites; in his division were 24,000. ¹⁴Eleventh, for the eleventh month, was Benaiah of Pirathon, of the sons of Ephraim; in his division were 24,000. ¹⁵Twelfth, for the twelfth month, was Heldai the Netophathite, of Othniel; in his division were 24,000.

¹⁶Over the tribes of Israel, for the Reubenites, Eliezer the son of Zichri was chief officer; for the Simeonites, Shephatiah the son of Maacah; ¹⁷for Levi, Hashabiah the son of Kemuel; for Aaron, Zadok; ¹⁸for Judah, Elihu, one of David's brothers; for Issachar, Omri the son of Michael; ¹⁹for Zebulun, Ishmaiah the son of Obadiah; for Naphtali, Jeremoth the son of Azriel; ²⁰for the Ephraimites, Hoshea the son of Azaziah; for the half-tribe of Manasseh, Joel the son of Pedaiah; ²¹for the half-tribe of Manasseh in Gilead, Iddo the son of Zechariah; for Benjamin, Jaasiel the son of Abner; ²²for Dan, Azarel the son of Jeroham. These were the leaders of the tribes of Israel. ²³David did not count those below twenty years of age, for the LORD had promised to make Israel as many as the stars of heaven. ²⁴Joab the son of Zeruiah began to count, but did not finish. Yet wrath came upon Israel for this, and the number was not entered in the chronicles of King David.

²⁵Over the king's treasuries was Azmaveth the son of Adiel; and over the treasuries in the country, in the cities, in the villages, and in the towers, was Jonathan the son of Uzziah; ²⁶and over those who did the work of the field for tilling the soil was Ezri the son of Chelub; ²⁷and over the vineyards was Shimei the Ramathite; and over the produce of the vineyards for the wine cellars was Zabdi the Shiphmite. ²⁸Over the olive and sycamore trees in the Shephelah was Baal-hanan the Gederite; and over the stores of oil was Joash. ²⁹Over the herds that pastured in Sharon was Shitrai the Sharonite; over the herds in the valleys was Shaphat the son of Adlai. ³⁰Over the camels was Obil the Ishmaelite; and over the donkeys was Jehdeiah the Meronothite. Over the flocks was Jaziz the Hagrite. ³¹All these were stewards of King David's property.

³²Jonathan, David's uncle, was a counselor, being a man of understanding and a scribe. He and Jehiel the son of Hachmoni attended the king's sons. ³³Ahithophel was the king's counselor, and Hushai the Archite was the king's friend. ³⁴Ahithophel was

---

¹ Septuagint; Hebrew *Ahohite and his division and Mikloth the chief officer* ² Septuagint, Vulgate; Hebrew *was his division*

succeeded by Jehoiada the son of Benaiah, and Abiathar. Joab was commander of the king's army.

David's farewell discourse [chapter 28]. A leader's farewell discourse is an important biblical genre. Chapter 28 reports David's farewell discourse. The speech represents David's final words of wisdom, and they are as relevant to us today as they were to the first assembled audience of national leaders. Verse 1 establishes the situation in which David speaks. Then David rehearses how God refused his intention to build a temple and gave that duty to Solomon instead (vv. 2–8), after which David commissions Solomon to perform the task of building the temple (vv. 9–10, 20–21), with an interspersed narrative telling how David hands over to Solomon the blueprint for the temple and its furnishings (vv. 11–19).

28 David assembled at Jerusalem all the officials of Israel, the officials of the tribes, the officers of the divisions that served the king, the commanders of thousands, the commanders of hundreds, the stewards of all the property and livestock of the king and his sons, together with the palace officials, the mighty men and all the seasoned warriors. ²Then King David rose to his feet and said: "Hear me, my brothers and my people. I had it in my heart to build a house of rest for the ark of the covenant of the LORD and for the footstool of our God, and I made preparations for building. ³But God said to me, 'You may not build a house for my name, for you are a man of war and have shed blood.' ⁴Yet the LORD God of Israel chose me from all my father's house to be king over Israel forever. For he chose Judah as leader, and in the house of Judah my father's house, and among my father's sons he took pleasure in me to make me king over all Israel. ⁵And of all my sons (for the LORD has given me many sons) he has chosen Solomon my son to sit on the throne of the kingdom of the LORD over Israel. ⁶He said to me, 'It is Solomon your son who shall build my house and my courts, for I have chosen him to be my son, and I will be his father. ⁷I will establish his kingdom forever if he continues strong in keeping my commandments and my rules, as he is today.' ⁸Now therefore in the sight of all Israel, the assembly of the LORD, and in the hearing of our God, observe and seek out all the commandments of the LORD your God, that you may possess this good land and leave it for an inheritance to your children after you forever.

⁹"And you, Solomon my son, know the God of your father and serve him with a whole heart and with a willing mind, for the LORD searches all hearts and understands every plan and thought. If you seek him, he will be found by you, but if you forsake him, he will cast you off forever. ¹⁰Be careful now, for the LORD has chosen you to build a house for the sanctuary; be strong and do it."

¹¹Then David gave Solomon his son the plan of the vestibule of the temple,ʲ and of its houses, its treasuries, its upper rooms, and its inner chambers, and of the room for the mercy seat; ¹²and the plan of all that he had in mind for the courts of the house of the LORD, all the surrounding chambers, the treasuries of the house of God, and the treasuries for dedicated gifts; ¹³for the divisions of the priests and of the Levites, and all the work of the service in the house of the LORD; for all the vessels for the service in the house of the LORD, ¹⁴the weight of gold for all golden vessels for each service, the weight of silver vessels for each service, ¹⁵the weight of the golden lampstands and their lamps, the weight of gold for each lampstand and its lamps, the weight of silver for a lampstand and its lamps, according to the use of each lampstand in the

¹ Hebrew lacks *of the temple*

service, ¹⁶the weight of gold for each table for the showbread, the silver for the silver tables, ¹⁷and pure gold for the forks, the basins and the cups; for the golden bowls and the weight of each; for the silver bowls and the weight of each; ¹⁸for the altar of incense made of refined gold, and its weight; also his plan for the golden chariot of the cherubim that spread their wings and covered the ark of the covenant of the LORD. ¹⁹"All this he made clear to me in writing from the hand of the LORD, all the work to be done according to the plan."

²⁰Then David said to Solomon his son, "Be strong and courageous and do it. Do not be afraid and do not be dismayed, for the LORD God, even my God, is with you. He will not leave you or forsake you, until all the work for the service of the house of the LORD is finished. ²¹And behold the divisions of the priests and the Levites for all the service of the house of God; and with you in all the work will be every willing man who has skill for any kind of service; also the officers and all the people will be wholly at your command."

Contributions to the building project of the temple [29:1–22a]. With all of the officials of the kingdom assembled at Jerusalem to hear David's final words (28:1), David uses the occasion to solicit contributions to the temple building project. The unit unfolds as follows: David's appeal to the nation to contribute toward the cost of the temple (vv. 1–5), followed by a narrative account of how the people make their offerings (vv. 6–9); David's grand prayer (vv. 10–19), followed by the worship and offerings of the people to celebrate the successful conclusion of a phase of the building project (vv. 20–22a). In the climactic summoning of the nation (chapters 28–29), we get a picture of what things mattered most to David as a godly ruler and accordingly what should matter most to the people of God, including the need to offer the best of oneself and one's resources to God.

29 And David the king said to all the assembly, "Solomon my son, whom alone God has chosen, is young and inexperienced, and the work is great, for the palace will not be for man but for the LORD God. ²So I have provided for the house of my God, so far as I was able, the gold for the things of gold, the silver for the things of silver, and the bronze for the things of bronze, the iron for the things of iron, and wood for the things of wood, besides great quantities of onyx and stones for setting, antimony, colored stones, all sorts of precious stones and marble. ³Moreover, in addition to all that I have provided for the holy house, I have a treasure of my own of gold and silver, and because of my devotion to the house of my God I give it to the house of my God: ⁴3,000 talents¹ of gold, of the gold of Ophir, and 7,000 talents of refined silver, for overlaying the walls of the house,² ⁵and for all the work to be done by craftsmen, gold for the things of gold and silver for the things of silver. Who then will offer willingly, consecrating himself³ today to the LORD?"

⁶Then the leaders of fathers' houses made their freewill offerings, as did also the leaders of the tribes, the commanders of thousands and of hundreds, and the officers over the king's work. ⁷They gave for the service of the house of God 5,000 talents and 10,000 darics⁴ of gold, 10,000 talents of silver, 18,000 talents of bronze and 100,000 talents of iron. ⁸And whoever had precious stones gave them to the treasury of the house of the LORD, in the care of Jehiel the Gershonite. ⁹Then the people rejoiced because they had given willingly, for with a whole heart they had offered freely to the LORD. David the king also rejoiced greatly.

¹ A *talent* was about 75 pounds or 34 kilograms ² Septuagint; Hebrew *houses* ³ Or *ordaining himself*; Hebrew *filling his hand* ⁴ A *daric* was a coin weighing about 1/4 ounce or 8.5 grams

¹⁰Therefore David blessed the LORD in the presence of all the assembly. And David said: "Blessed are you, O LORD, the God of Israel our father, forever and ever. ¹¹Yours, O LORD, is the greatness and the power and the glory and the victory and the majesty, for all that is in the heavens and in the earth is yours. Yours is the kingdom, O LORD, and you are exalted as head above all. ¹²Both riches and honor come from you, and you rule over all. In your hand are power and might, and in your hand it is to make great and to give strength to all. ¹³And now we thank you, our God, and praise your glorious name.

¹⁴"But who am I, and what is my people, that we should be able thus to offer willingly? For all things come from you, and of your own have we given you. ¹⁵For we are strangers before you and sojourners, as all our fathers were. Our days on the earth are like a shadow, and there is no abiding.¹ ¹⁶O LORD our God, all this abundance that we have provided for building you a house for your holy name comes from your hand and is all your own. ¹⁷I know, my God, that you test the heart and have pleasure in uprightness. In the uprightness of my heart I have freely offered all these things, and now I have seen your people, who are present here, offering freely and joyously to you. ¹⁸O LORD, the God of Abraham, Isaac, and Israel, our fathers, keep forever such purposes and thoughts in the hearts of your people, and direct their hearts toward you. ¹⁹Grant to Solomon my son a whole heart that he may keep your commandments, your testimonies, and your statutes, performing all, and that he may build the palace for which I have made provision."

²⁰Then David said to all the assembly, "Bless the LORD your God." And all the assembly blessed the LORD, the God of their fathers, and bowed their heads and paid homage to the LORD and to the king. ²¹And they offered sacrifices to the LORD, and on the next day offered burnt offerings to the LORD, 1,000 bulls, 1,000 rams, and 1,000 lambs, with their drink offerings, and sacrifices in abundance for all Israel. ²²And they ate and drank before the LORD on that day with great gladness.

Succession narrative [29:22b–30]. The life of David reaches closure with two brief narrative units—the elevation of Solomon to the kingship (vv. 22b–25) and the death and accomplishments of David (vv. 26–30). The brief list of other historical chronicles where the author of 1 Chronicles invites his readers to read more about David's kingship hints at his importance as a national hero.

And they made Solomon the son of David king the second time, and they anointed him as prince for the LORD, and Zadok as priest. ²³Then Solomon sat on the throne of the LORD as king in place of David his father. And he prospered, and all Israel obeyed him. ²⁴All the leaders and the mighty men, and also all the sons of King David, pledged their allegiance to King Solomon. ²⁵And the LORD made Solomon very great in the sight of all Israel and bestowed on him such royal majesty as had not been on any king before him in Israel.

²⁶Thus David the son of Jesse reigned over all Israel. ²⁷The time that he reigned over Israel was forty years. He reigned seven years in Hebron and thirty-three years in Jerusalem. ²⁸Then he died at a good age, full of days, riches, and honor. And Solomon his son reigned in his place. ²⁹Now the acts of King David, from first to last,

¹ Septuagint, Vulgate; Hebrew *hope*, or *prospect*

are written in the Chronicles of Samuel the seer, and in the Chronicles of Nathan the prophet, and in the Chronicles of Gad the seer, [30]with accounts of all his rule and his might and of the circumstances that came upon him and upon Israel and upon all the kingdoms of the countries.

2 CHRONICLES

The book at a glance. 36 chapters, 822 verses. Second Chronicles records the history of a nation over a span of about four hundred years, yet the focus is so thoroughly on individual kings that the book seems less like the history of a nation than an anthology of brief biographies. Sometimes the compiler focuses on individual events, giving us information equivalent to what a modern television crew might film on site. But this is supplemented by factual data that resembles material that the writer of a feature article might uncover in the national archives. The incidents about which we read are representative of the spiritual flavor of the nation and its kings. While the original audience had a patriotic or nationalistic interest in the facts and characters the historian put before them, our interest is in the timeless principles that come through the particulars. The writer makes the latter task easy by keeping the facts of national history within a strong interpretive framework in which people and events are regarded in spiritual terms. Political and religious history mingle with biographical sketches. The primary literary impulse is to give us positive examples to emulate and negative examples to avoid.

▌**Genres.** The main genre is court history—the history of a nation as embodied in the actions of its kings. Because of the magnitude of the action—four hundred years of a nation's history—the book is in a loose sense a prose *epic, though without the usual glorification of the writer's nation. Some of the stories of individual kings are told in sufficient detail that history moves in the direction of biography and even *hero story. The stories of many of the kings and their disappointing downfalls have affinities with literary *tragedy, and the pictures of national life under the good kings are brief *utopian visions of a good society. (For more information on items accompanied by an asterisk, see the glossary at the back of this Bible.)

▌**The author's philosophy of history.** Things will fall into place if we take time to summarize the author's view of history, since it determines the content of his book (the details chosen for inclusion and the interpretive slant given to them). First, the compiler of 2 Chronicles believes that rulers and especially kings essentially determine the spiritual and political destiny of a nation. Kings, in turn, are subject mainly to a single criterion, spiritual in nature: they do what is either good or evil in the sight of God. Further, blessing is the predictable effect of godly rule, whereas a nation languishes when its king abandons God. Additionally the history of a king and nation consists of two main ingredients—the spiritual sphere and the political/military sphere. The literary

Passage	Content	Era of National History
1:1–17	Beginning of Solomon's reign	Reign of Solomon over the united monarchy
2:1–7:22	Building and dedication of the temple	
8:1–9:31	Solomon's reign	
10:1–11:17	Division of the kingdom into Israel and Judah	End of the united monarchy
11:18–12:16	Reign of Rehoboam	History of the monarchy of Judah during the divided kingdom
13:1–22	Reign of Abijah	
14:1–16:14	Reign of Asa	
17:1–20:37	Reign of Jehoshaphat	
21:1–22:12	Three bad leaders: Jehoram, Ahaziah, Athaliah	
23:1–21	The high priest Jehoiada's coup	
24:1–28:27	Five kings: Joash, Amaziah, Uzziah, Jotham, Ahaz	
29:1–32:33	Reign of Hezekiah	
33:1–25	Reigns of Manasseh and Amon	
34:1–35:27	Reign of Josiah	
36:1–16	Last four kings	
36:17–23	Captivity and return of Judah	End of the monarchy of Judah

principle of outcome is very important, moreover: the way the story of a given king ends is our interpretive key for ascertaining the main meaning of that king's life.

▍ **The primary personal lessons.** What was true for the kings of Judah is true in every person's life: obedience to God and true worship of him bring blessing, while the flouting of God and resorting to substitute gods bring death. Even more striking, perhaps, is the lesson we learn about how hard it is to finish life well spiritually, especially after earlier success. Time after time our hearts sink as we read about the disappointing end of kings who began well.

▍ **Format of the book.** Even though the book is primarily a historical chronicle, its format has more in common with the flow of a *story than with that of a history book. Stories are based on a principle of back-and-forth rhythm, and 2 Chronicles obeys this rule of narrative construction. As we read, the pendulum swings back and forth between good and bad rulers and between God's blessing and punishment. We also move back and forth between religious happenings and more "secular" political or military happenings (with some of the material resembling what we might encounter in *any* book of ancient history). Just as we remember a story partly as a gallery of memorable characters, so, too, 2 Chronicles remains in our memories as a collection of imposing kings with impressive-sounding names. Further, the succession of these names and kings gives the book a sense of progressive movement such as a story possesses. Finally, the author alternates between relatively brief accounts of evil kings and more extended accounts of good kings.

▍The cast of characters. The chief actor in the national drama is God. As in other ancient epics, the deity in this account initiates action, expresses his divine will, and determines the outcome of human history. Second in importance are the kings of Judah (with five of them getting the most space—Solomon, Asa, Jehoshaphat, Hezekiah, and Josiah). Individual prophets like Nathan, Micaiah, Elijah, and Isaiah also play important roles. The nation, referred to approximately twenty times as "all Israel," assumes a corporate identity.

▍Inferred literary intentions. The book is designed to achieve the following literary purposes:

- embody national history in the form of the stories of the individual kings of the nation

- present the stories of the good kings as hero stories

- tell two stories—the religious stances of the kings (the religious history of the nation) and their political successes and failures

- set up a back-and-forth rhythm between good and evil conduct in the national rulers

- make the key characters and events come alive in our imagination so that we relive the characters and events

- inspire us to want to follow God and end well

- impress on us how difficult it is to end well

- expose the evil and self-destructiveness of self-reliance and self-will

▍Theological themes. (1) The sovereignty of God: God is the main character in the book, and from his extended portrait we get a picture of what he is like. (2) Sin and its judgment: despite the presence of occasional good kings, the book gives an anatomy of human sinfulness and of God's judgment against it. (3) Human responsibility: the kings are continuously shown in the act of choosing either good or evil, sending the message that life is a choice for or against God. (4) Providence: through all the byways of human agency—some good, some bad—God directs and protects the kingly line from which the Messiah would be eventually born.

▍2 Chronicles as a chapter in the master story of the Bible. This book contributes to the master story of the Bible in two chief ways. First, the master story of the Bible is the story of salvation history, and a large part of that story is the history of the covenant nation from which the Messiah was born. Nearly four hundred years of that history are covered in 2 Chronicles. Second, the master story of the Bible is also the story of the battle between good and evil in the life of every individual and nation, and 2 Chronicles also tells the story of that perennial conflict.

> **The auspicious start of Solomon's reign** [chapter 1]. After the mighty reign of
> Israel's greatest king (David), how could his son possibly fill his father's shoes? That
> is our natural question as we begin to read the court record known as 2 Chronicles. The
> first chapter gives us hope that Solomon will pull it off. The opening summary verse
> tells us that God made Solomon great. Solomon's first public act is one of worship at
> the appropriate place (vv. 2–6). Even more impressive is God's appearance to Solomon
> in a night vision, in which Solomon asks for wisdom to rule well and is given an added
> promise of wealth and honor (vv. 7–13). The third phase in the opening triptych is a
> summary of Solomon's regal splendor (vv. 14–17). The writer of 1 Kings also gave full
> coverage to Solomon's success, but he included a closing chapter that traced Solomon's
> tragic decline into apostasy; the writer of 2 Chronicles chose not to include that negative
> material and gives us a wholly idealized portrait of Solomon instead.

1 Solomon the son of David established himself in his kingdom, and the LORD his God was with him and made him exceedingly great.

²Solomon spoke to all Israel, to the commanders of thousands and of hundreds, to the judges, and to all the leaders in all Israel, the heads of fathers' houses. ³And Solomon, and all the assembly with him, went to the high place that was at Gibeon, for the tent of meeting of God, which Moses the servant of the LORD had made in the wilderness, was there. ⁴(But David had brought up the ark of God from Kiriath-jearim to the place that David had prepared for it, for he had pitched a tent for it in Jerusalem.) ⁵Moreover, the bronze altar that Bezalel the son of Uri, son of Hur, had made, was there before the tabernacle of the LORD. And Solomon and the assembly sought it[1] out. ⁶And Solomon went up there to the bronze altar before the LORD, which was at the tent of meeting, and offered a thousand burnt offerings on it.

⁷In that night God appeared to Solomon, and said to him, "Ask what I shall give you." ⁸And Solomon said to God, "You have shown great and steadfast love to David my father, and have made me king in his place. ⁹O LORD God, let your word to David my father be now fulfilled, for you have made me king over a people as numerous as the dust of the earth. ¹⁰Give me now wisdom and knowledge to go out and come in before this people, for who can govern this people of yours, which is so great?" ¹¹God answered Solomon, "Because this was in your heart, and you have not asked possessions, wealth, honor, or the life of those who hate you, and have not even asked long life, but have asked wisdom and knowledge for yourself that you may govern my people over whom I have made you king, ¹²wisdom and knowledge are granted to you. I will also give you riches, possessions, and honor, such as none of the kings had who were before you, and none after you shall have the like." ¹³So Solomon came from[2] the high place at Gibeon, from before the tent of meeting, to Jerusalem. And he reigned over Israel.

¹⁴Solomon gathered together chariots and horsemen. He had 1,400 chariots and 12,000 horsemen, whom he stationed in the chariot cities and with the king in Jerusalem. ¹⁵And the king made silver and gold as common in Jerusalem as stone, and he made cedar as plentiful as the sycamore of the Shephelah. ¹⁶And Solomon's import of horses was from Egypt and Kue, and the king's traders would buy them from Kue for a price. ¹⁷They imported a chariot from Egypt for 600 shekels[3] of silver, and a

---

[1] Or *him* [2] Septuagint, Vulgate; Hebrew *to* [3] A *shekel* was about 2/5 ounce or 11 grams

horse for 150. Likewise through them these were exported to all the kings of the Hittites and the kings of Syria.

> **Preparations for building the temple** [chapter 2]. To idealize Solomon still further, the Chronicler devotes six whole chapters to his oversight of the building of the temple. Chapter 2 catalogs the materials that Solomon collected for the building project, along with the names and numbers of personnel who were gathered to perform various aspects of the work. As always in biblical narrative, our first task is to imagine ourselves present at the exciting events that are re-created for us by the writers. Then we need to reflect on why this particular building deserves such elaborate attention.

2 [1] Now Solomon purposed to build a temple for the name of the LORD, and a royal palace for himself. [22] And Solomon assigned 70,000 men to bear burdens and 80,000 to quarry in the hill country, and 3,600 to oversee them. [3]And Solomon sent word to Hiram the king of Tyre: "As you dealt with David my father and sent him cedar to build himself a house to dwell in, so deal with me. [4]Behold, I am about to build a house for the name of the LORD my God and dedicate it to him for the burning of incense of sweet spices before him, and for the regular arrangement of the showbread, and for burnt offerings morning and evening, on the Sabbaths and the new moons and the appointed feasts of the LORD our God, as ordained forever for Israel. [5]The house that I am to build will be great, for our God is greater than all gods. [6]But who is able to build him a house, since heaven, even highest heaven, cannot contain him? Who am I to build a house for him, except as a place to make offerings before him? [7]So now send me a man skilled to work in gold, silver, bronze, and iron, and in purple, crimson, and blue fabrics, trained also in engraving, to be with the skilled workers who are with me in Judah and Jerusalem, whom David my father provided. [8]Send me also cedar, cypress, and algum timber from Lebanon, for I know that your servants know how to cut timber in Lebanon. And my servants will be with your servants, [9]to prepare timber for me in abundance, for the house I am to build will be great and wonderful. [10]I will give for your servants, the woodsmen who cut timber, 20,000 cors[3] of crushed wheat, 20,000 cors of barley, 20,000 baths[4] of wine, and 20,000 baths of oil."

[11]Then Hiram the king of Tyre answered in a letter that he sent to Solomon, "Because the LORD loves his people, he has made you king over them." [12]Hiram also said, "Blessed be the LORD God of Israel, who made heaven and earth, who has given King David a wise son, who has discretion and understanding, who will build a temple for the LORD and a royal palace for himself.

[13]"Now I have sent a skilled man, who has understanding, Huram-abi, [14]the son of a woman of the daughters of Dan, and his father was a man of Tyre. He is trained to work in gold, silver, bronze, iron, stone, and wood, and in purple, blue, and crimson fabrics and fine linen, and to do all sorts of engraving and execute any design that may be assigned him, with your craftsmen, the craftsmen of my lord, David your father. [15]Now therefore the wheat and barley, oil and wine, of which my lord has spoken, let him send to his servants. [16]And we will cut whatever timber you need from Lebanon and bring it to you in rafts by sea to Joppa, so that you may take it up to Jerusalem."

[17]Then Solomon counted all the resident aliens who were in the land of Israel, after

---

[1] Ch 1:18 in Hebrew [2] Ch 2:1 in Hebrew [3] A *cor* was about 6 bushels or 220 liters [4] A *bath* was about 6 gallons or 22 liters

the census of them that David his father had taken, and there were found 153,600. [18]Seventy thousand of them he assigned to bear burdens, 80,000 to quarry in the hill country, and 3,600 as overseers to make the people work.

> **The building of the temple** [chapter 3]. With the materials in place, the building project moves to the construction phase. A visual reconstruction of the final building can doubtless help us understand what we read in chapter 3, but even without that aid, we can catch a glimpse of the splendor and visual beauty of the building. While some of the art present in the temple was purely aesthetic, existing for the sake of beauty alone, other details (such as cherubim and stately pillars) were spiritual symbols that spoke of the holiness of the place and the attributes of God.

3 Then Solomon began to build the house of the LORD in Jerusalem on Mount Moriah, where the LORD[1] had appeared to David his father, at the place that David had appointed, on the threshing floor of Ornan the Jebusite. [2]He began to build in the second month of the fourth year of his reign. [3]These are Solomon's measurements[2] for building the house of God: the length, in cubits[3] of the old standard, was sixty cubits, and the breadth twenty cubits. [4]The vestibule in front of the nave of the house was twenty cubits long, equal to the width of the house,[4] and its height was 120 cubits. He overlaid it on the inside with pure gold. [5]The nave he lined with cypress and covered it with fine gold and made palms and chains on it. [6]He adorned the house with settings of precious stones. The gold was gold of Parvaim. [7]So he lined the house with gold—its beams, its thresholds, its walls, and its doors—and he carved cherubim on the walls.

[8]And he made the Most Holy Place. Its length, corresponding to the breadth of the house, was twenty cubits, and its breadth was twenty cubits. He overlaid it with 600 talents[5] of fine gold. [9]The weight of gold for the nails was fifty shekels.[6] And he overlaid the upper chambers with gold.

[10]In the Most Holy Place he made two cherubim of wood[7] and overlaid[8] them with gold. [11]The wings of the cherubim together extended twenty cubits: one wing of the one, of five cubits, touched the wall of the house, and its other wing, of five cubits, touched the wing of the other cherub; [12]and of this cherub, one wing, of five cubits, touched the wall of the house, and the other wing, also of five cubits, was joined to the wing of the first cherub. [13]The wings of these cherubim extended twenty cubits. The cherubim[9] stood on their feet, facing the nave. [14]And he made the veil of blue and purple and crimson fabrics and fine linen, and he worked cherubim on it.

[15]In front of the house he made two pillars thirty-five cubits high, with a capital of five cubits on the top of each. [16]He made chains like a necklace[10] and put them on the tops of the pillars, and he made a hundred pomegranates and put them on the chains. [17]He set up the pillars in front of the temple, one on the south, the other on the north; that on the south he called Jachin, and that on the north Boaz.

> **The furnishings of the temple** [chapter 4]. In this chapter, even more than the preceding one, the sheer quantity of details makes a symbolic statement about the beauty,

---

[1] Septuagint; Hebrew lacks *the LORD* [2] Syriac; Hebrew *foundations* [3] A *cubit* was about 18 inches or 45 centimeters [4] Compare 1 Kings 6:3; the meaning of the Hebrew is uncertain [5] A *talent* was about 75 pounds or 34 kilograms [6] A *shekel* was about 2/5 ounce or 11 grams [7] Septuagint; the meaning of the Hebrew is uncertain [8] Hebrew *they overlaid* [9] Hebrew *they* [10] Hebrew *chains in the inner sanctuary*

abundance, and transcendence of worshiping God in this sacred place. The wealth of detail implies a spiritual opulence as well as a feast for the senses. We can also catch a sense of the excitement of the building process itself. Of course some of the furnishings were functional as well as aesthetic, and we can ponder the spiritual functions of the utensils—an altar for sacrifice, basins for ritual cleansings, and utensils for burning incense symbolic of the ascent of prayers to God.

4 He made an altar of bronze, twenty cubits[1] long and twenty cubits wide and ten cubits high. [2]Then he made the sea of cast metal. It was round, ten cubits from brim to brim, and five cubits high, and a line of thirty cubits measured its circumference. [3]Under it were figures of gourds,[2] for ten cubits, compassing the sea all around. The gourds were in two rows, cast with it when it was cast. [4]It stood on twelve oxen, three facing north, three facing west, three facing south, and three facing east. The sea was set on them, and all their rear parts were inward. [5]Its thickness was a handbreadth.[3] And its brim was made like the brim of a cup, like the flower of a lily. It held 3,000 baths.[4] [6]He also made ten basins in which to wash, and set five on the south side, and five on the north side. In these they were to rinse off what was used for the burnt offering, and the sea was for the priests to wash in.

[7]And he made ten golden lampstands as prescribed, and set them in the temple, five on the south side and five on the north. [8]He also made ten tables and placed them in the temple, five on the south side and five on the north. And he made a hundred basins of gold. [9]He made the court of the priests and the great court and doors for the court and overlaid their doors with bronze. [10]And he set the sea at the southeast corner of the house.

[11]Hiram also made the pots, the shovels, and the basins. So Hiram finished the work that he did for King Solomon on the house of God: [12]the two pillars, the bowls, and the two capitals on the top of the pillars; and the two latticeworks to cover the two bowls of the capitals that were on the top of the pillars; [13]and the 400 pomegranates for the two latticeworks, two rows of pomegranates for each latticework, to cover the two bowls of the capitals that were on the pillars. [14]He made the stands also, and the basins on the stands, [15]and the one sea, and the twelve oxen underneath it. [16]The pots, the shovels, the forks, and all the equipment for these Huram-abi made of burnished bronze for King Solomon for the house of the LORD. [17]In the plain of the Jordan the king cast them, in the clay ground between Succoth and Zeredah.[5] [18]Solomon made all these things in great quantities, for the weight of the bronze was not sought.

[19]So Solomon made all the vessels that were in the house of God: the golden altar, the tables for the bread of the Presence, [20]the lampstands and their lamps of pure gold to burn before the inner sanctuary, as prescribed; [21]the flowers, the lamps, and the tongs, of purest gold; [22]the snuffers, basins, dishes for incense, and fire pans, of pure gold, and the sockets[6] of the temple, for the inner doors to the Most Holy Place and for the doors of the nave of the temple were of gold.

The bringing of the ark to the temple [chapter 5]. Things build to a crescendo as the block of five chapters devoted to the temple construction unfolds. The ark of the

---

[1] A *cubit* was about 18 inches or 45 centimeters [2] Compare 1 Kings 7:24; Hebrew *oxen*; twice in this verse [3] A *handbreadth* was about 3 inches or 7.5 centimeters [4] A *bath* was about 6 gallons or 22 liters [5] Spelled *Zarethan* in 1 Kings 7:46 [6] Compare 1 Kings 7:50; Hebrew *the entrance of the house*

covenant was the most holy physical object in the nation of Israel—the visible symbol of God's presence with his people. In this chapter we read about its transfer from temporary quarters in Jerusalem to which David had earlier brought it (see 2 Sam. 6:17) to the temple. The climax of the ark's journey is the presence of God filling the temple, so that the priests cannot remain in it (vv. 13–14).

5 Thus all the work that Solomon did for the house of the LORD was finished. And Solomon brought in the things that David his father had dedicated, and stored the silver, the gold, and all the vessels in the treasuries of the house of God. ²Then Solomon assembled the elders of Israel and all the heads of the tribes, the leaders of the fathers' houses of the people of Israel, in Jerusalem, to bring up the ark of the covenant of the LORD out of the city of David, which is Zion. ³And all the men of Israel assembled before the king at the feast that is in the seventh month. ⁴And all the elders of Israel came, and the Levites took up the ark. ⁵And they brought up the ark, the tent of meeting, and all the holy vessels that were in the tent; the Levitical priests brought them up. ⁶And King Solomon and all the congregation of Israel, who had assembled before him, were before the ark, sacrificing so many sheep and oxen that they could not be counted or numbered. ⁷Then the priests brought the ark of the covenant of the LORD to its place, in the inner sanctuary of the house, in the Most Holy Place, underneath the wings of the cherubim. ⁸The cherubim spread out their wings over the place of the ark, so that the cherubim made a covering above the ark and its poles. ⁹And the poles were so long that the ends of the poles were seen from the Holy Place before the inner sanctuary, but they could not be seen from outside. And they are¹ there to this day. ¹⁰There was nothing in the ark except the two tablets that Moses put there at Horeb, where the LORD made a covenant with the people of Israel, when they came out of Egypt. ¹¹And when the priests came out of the Holy Place (for all the priests who were present had consecrated themselves, without regard to their divisions, ¹²and all the Levitical singers, Asaph, Heman, and Jeduthun, their sons and kinsmen, arrayed in fine linen, with cymbals, harps, and lyres, stood east of the altar with 120 priests who were trumpeters; ¹³and it was the duty of the trumpeters and singers to make themselves heard in unison in praise and thanksgiving to the LORD), and when the song was raised, with trumpets and cymbals and other musical instruments, in praise to the LORD,

"For he is good,
    for his steadfast love endures forever,"

the house, the house of the LORD, was filled with a cloud, ¹⁴so that the priests could not stand to minister because of the cloud, for the glory of the LORD filled the house of God.

The dedication of the temple [chapter 6]. There is no grander chapter in the Bible than this one. Solomon the king, as representative of the nation, conducts himself with a stateliness and speaks with a formality that the occasion demands. Who would not want a ruler who can speak as Solomon does in this chapter? First Solomon pronounces a blessing on God for the temple—a blessing that chiefly recalls his father David's inter-

¹ Hebrew *it is*

actions with God about a future temple and God's promises regarding the temple (vv. 1–11). Then Solomon prays the prayer of dedication, a highly patterned and rhetorically embellished prayer replete with repeated formulas (such as "if . . . , then"). The pattern underlying the parallel statements is a petition to God that if the nation sins or an external calamity like famine or invasion happens, then God will hear the prayers that are uttered from the temple. The prayer is a petitionary prayer in its most exalted mode. The principle underlying this exalted prayer still applies: when God's people are in distress, they can pray to God to hear and answer their petitions. Additionally, Solomon's prayer shows the range of things for which believers can pray.

6 Then Solomon said, "The LORD has said that he would dwell in thick darkness. ²But I have built you an exalted house, a place for you to dwell in forever." ³Then the king turned around and blessed all the assembly of Israel, while all the assembly of Israel stood. ⁴And he said, "Blessed be the LORD, the God of Israel, who with his hand has fulfilled what he promised with his mouth to David my father, saying, ⁵'Since the day that I brought my people out of the land of Egypt, I chose no city out of all the tribes of Israel in which to build a house, that my name might be there, and I chose no man as prince over my people Israel; ⁶but I have chosen Jerusalem that my name may be there, and I have chosen David to be over my people Israel.' ⁷Now it was in the heart of David my father to build a house for the name of the LORD, the God of Israel. ⁸But the LORD said to David my father, 'Whereas it was in your heart to build a house for my name, you did well that it was in your heart. ⁹Nevertheless, it is not you who shall build the house, but your son who shall be born to you shall build the house for my name.' ¹⁰Now the LORD has fulfilled his promise that he made. For I have risen in the place of David my father and sit on the throne of Israel, as the LORD promised, and I have built the house for the name of the LORD, the God of Israel. ¹¹And there I have set the ark, in which is the covenant of the LORD that he made with the people of Israel."

¹²Then Solomon stood before the altar of the LORD in the presence of all the assembly of Israel and spread out his hands. ¹³Solomon had made a bronze platform five cubits[1] long, five cubits wide, and three cubits high, and had set it in the court, and he stood on it. Then he knelt on his knees in the presence of all the assembly of Israel, and spread out his hands toward heaven, ¹⁴and said, "O LORD, God of Israel, there is no God like you, in heaven or on earth, keeping covenant and showing steadfast love to your servants who walk before you with all their heart, ¹⁵who have kept with your servant David my father what you declared to him. You spoke with your mouth, and with your hand have fulfilled it this day. ¹⁶Now therefore, O LORD, God of Israel, keep for your servant David my father what you have promised him, saying, 'You shall not lack a man to sit before me on the throne of Israel, if only your sons pay close attention to their way, to walk in my law as you have walked before me.' ¹⁷Now therefore, O LORD, God of Israel, let your word be confirmed, which you have spoken to your servant David.

¹⁸"But will God indeed dwell with man on the earth? Behold, heaven and the highest heaven cannot contain you, how much less this house that I have built! ¹⁹Yet have regard to the prayer of your servant and to his plea, O LORD my God, listening to the cry and to the prayer that your servant prays before you, ²⁰that your eyes may be open

[1] A *cubit* was about 18 inches or 45 centimeters

day and night toward this house, the place where you have promised to set your name, that you may listen to the prayer that your servant offers toward this place. ²¹And listen to the pleas of your servant and of your people Israel, when they pray toward this place. And listen from heaven your dwelling place, and when you hear, forgive.

²²"If a man sins against his neighbor and is made to take an oath and comes and swears his oath before your altar in this house, ²³then hear from heaven and act and judge your servants, repaying the guilty by bringing his conduct on his own head, and vindicating the righteous by rewarding him according to his righteousness.

²⁴"If your people Israel are defeated before the enemy because they have sinned against you, and they turn again and acknowledge your name and pray and plead with you in this house, ²⁵then hear from heaven and forgive the sin of your people Israel and bring them again to the land that you gave to them and to their fathers.

²⁶"When heaven is shut up and there is no rain because they have sinned against you, if they pray toward this place and acknowledge your name and turn from their sin, when you afflict¹ them, ²⁷then hear in heaven and forgive the sin of your servants, your people Israel, when you teach them the good way² in which they should walk, and grant rain upon your land, which you have given to your people as an inheritance.

²⁸"If there is famine in the land, if there is pestilence or blight or mildew or locust or caterpillar, if their enemies besiege them in the land at their gates, whatever plague, whatever sickness there is, ²⁹whatever prayer, whatever plea is made by any man or by all your people Israel, each knowing his own affliction and his own sorrow and stretching out his hands toward this house, ³⁰then hear from heaven your dwelling place and forgive and render to each whose heart you know, according to all his ways, for you, you only, know the hearts of the children of mankind, ³¹that they may fear you and walk in your ways all the days that they live in the land that you gave to our fathers.

³²"Likewise, when a foreigner, who is not of your people Israel, comes from a far country for the sake of your great name and your mighty hand and your outstretched arm, when he comes and prays toward this house, ³³hear from heaven your dwelling place and do according to all for which the foreigner calls to you, in order that all the peoples of the earth may know your name and fear you, as do your people Israel, and that they may know that this house that I have built is called by your name.

³⁴"If your people go out to battle against their enemies, by whatever way you shall send them, and they pray to you toward this city that you have chosen and the house that I have built for your name, ³⁵then hear from heaven their prayer and their plea, and maintain their cause.

³⁶"If they sin against you—for there is no one who does not sin—and you are angry with them and give them to an enemy, so that they are carried away captive to a land far or near, ³⁷yet if they turn their heart in the land to which they have been carried captive, and repent and plead with you in the land of their captivity, saying, 'We have sinned and have acted perversely and wickedly,' ³⁸if they repent with all their mind and with all their heart in the land of their captivity to which they were carried captive, and pray toward their land, which you gave to their fathers, the city that you have chosen and the house that I have built for your name, ³⁹then hear from heaven your dwelling place their prayer and their pleas, and maintain their cause and forgive your

¹ Septuagint, Vulgate; Hebrew *answer* ² Septuagint, Syriac, Vulgate (compare 1 Kings 8:36); Hebrew *toward the good way*

people who have sinned against you. ⁴⁰Now, O my God, let your eyes be open and your ears attentive to the prayer of this place.

⁴¹ "And now arise, O LORD God, and go to your resting place,
　　　you and the ark of your might.
　　Let your priests, O LORD God, be clothed with salvation,
　　　and let your saints rejoice in your goodness.
⁴² 　O LORD God, do not turn away the face of your anointed one!
　　　Remember your steadfast love for David your servant."

God's response to Solomon's prayer [chapter 7]. The successive chapters devoted to the temple are like waves coming on to the shore, with each wave higher than the preceding one. The momentous events narrated in this chapter unfold in the following sequence: God's fire comes down and consumes the offering, and the people bow before his presence (vv. 1–3); the priests perform the ceremonies of worship (vv. 4–6); Solomon consecrates the middle court, oversees sacrificial offerings, and holds a seven-day national feast (vv. 7–10); God appears to Solomon in a night vision and promises blessing for obedience (vv. 11–18) and judgment for disobedience (vv. 19–22).

7 As soon as Solomon finished his prayer, fire came down from heaven and consumed the burnt offering and the sacrifices, and the glory of the LORD filled the temple. ²And the priests could not enter the house of the LORD, because the glory of the LORD filled the LORD's house. ³When all the people of Israel saw the fire come down and the glory of the LORD on the temple, they bowed down with their faces to the ground on the pavement and worshiped and gave thanks to the LORD, saying, "For he is good, for his steadfast love endures forever."

⁴Then the king and all the people offered sacrifice before the LORD. ⁵King Solomon offered as a sacrifice 22,000 oxen and 120,000 sheep. So the king and all the people dedicated the house of God. ⁶The priests stood at their posts; the Levites also, with the instruments for music to the LORD that King David had made for giving thanks to the LORD—for his steadfast love endures forever—whenever David offered praises by their ministry;¹ opposite them the priests sounded trumpets, and all Israel stood.

⁷And Solomon consecrated the middle of the court that was before the house of the LORD, for there he offered the burnt offering and the fat of the peace offerings, because the bronze altar Solomon had made could not hold the burnt offering and the grain offering and the fat.

⁸At that time Solomon held the feast for seven days, and all Israel with him, a very great assembly, from Lebo-hamath to the Brook of Egypt. ⁹And on the eighth day they held a solemn assembly, for they had kept the dedication of the altar seven days and the feast seven days. ¹⁰On the twenty-third day of the seventh month he sent the people away to their homes, joyful and glad of heart for the prosperity that the LORD had granted to David and to Solomon and to Israel his people.

¹¹Thus Solomon finished the house of the LORD and the king's house. All that Solomon had planned to do in the house of the LORD and in his own house he successfully accomplished. ¹²Then the LORD appeared to Solomon in the night and said to him: "I have heard your prayer and have chosen this place for myself as a house of sacrifice. ¹³When I shut up the heavens so that there is no rain, or command the

¹ Hebrew *by their hand*

locust to devour the land, or send pestilence among my people, ¹⁴if my people who are called by my name humble themselves, and pray and seek my face and turn from their wicked ways, then I will hear from heaven and will forgive their sin and heal their land. ¹⁵Now my eyes will be open and my ears attentive to the prayer that is made in this place. ¹⁶For now I have chosen and consecrated this house that my name may be there forever. My eyes and my heart will be there for all time. ¹⁷And as for you, if you will walk before me as David your father walked, doing according to all that I have commanded you and keeping my statutes and my rules, ¹⁸then I will establish your royal throne, as I covenanted with David your father, saying, 'You shall not lack a man to rule Israel.'

¹⁹"But if you¹ turn aside and forsake my statutes and my commandments that I have set before you, and go and serve other gods and worship them, ²⁰then I will pluck you² up from my land that I have given you, and this house that I have consecrated for my name, I will cast out of my sight, and I will make it a proverb and a byword among all peoples. ²¹And at this house, which was exalted, everyone passing by will be astonished and say, 'Why has the LORD done thus to this land and to this house?' ²²Then they will say, 'Because they abandoned the LORD, the God of their fathers who brought them out of the land of Egypt and laid hold on other gods and worshiped them and served them. Therefore he has brought all this disaster on them.'"

Solomon's regal success [chapter 8]. The biography of Solomon continues to be a success story in this chapter. First we read about Solomon's grand building projects (vv. 1–11), after which the Chronicler returns to Solomon's care for the public worship of God at the temple (vv. 12–16). A concluding note about Solomon's fetching of gold from Ophir (vv. 17–18) suddenly reminds us that we are reading court history: anything that struck the court chronicler as important found its way into the official records. This was Israel's golden age, literally and figuratively.

8 At the end of twenty years, in which Solomon had built the house of the LORD and his own house, ²Solomon rebuilt the cities that Hiram had given to him, and settled the people of Israel in them.

³And Solomon went to Hamath-zobah and took it. ⁴He built Tadmor in the wilderness and all the store cities that he built in Hamath. ⁵He also built Upper Beth-horon and Lower Beth-horon, fortified cities with walls, gates, and bars, ⁶and Baalath, and all the store cities that Solomon had and all the cities for his chariots and the cities for his horsemen, and whatever Solomon desired to build in Jerusalem, in Lebanon, and in all the land of his dominion. ⁷All the people who were left of the Hittites, the Amorites, the Perizzites, the Hivites, and the Jebusites, who were not of Israel, ⁸from their descendants who were left after them in the land, whom the people of Israel had not destroyed—these Solomon drafted as forced labor, and so they are to this day. ⁹But of the people of Israel Solomon made no slaves for his work; they were soldiers, and his officers, the commanders of his chariots, and his horsemen. ¹⁰And these were the chief officers of King Solomon, 250, who exercised authority over the people.

¹¹Solomon brought Pharaoh's daughter up from the city of David to the house that he had built for her, for he said, "My wife shall not live in the house of David king of Israel, for the places to which the ark of the LORD has come are holy."

¹ The Hebrew for *you* is plural here ² Hebrew *them;* twice in this verse

¹²Then Solomon offered up burnt offerings to the Lord on the altar of the Lord that he had built before the vestibule, ¹³as the duty of each day required, offering according to the commandment of Moses for the Sabbaths, the new moons, and the three annual feasts—the Feast of Unleavened Bread, the Feast of Weeks, and the Feast of Booths. ¹⁴According to the ruling of David his father, he appointed the divisions of the priests for their service, and the Levites for their offices of praise and ministry before the priests as the duty of each day required, and the gatekeepers in their divisions at each gate, for so David the man of God had commanded. ¹⁵And they did not turn aside from what the king had commanded the priests and Levites concerning any matter and concerning the treasuries.

¹⁶Thus was accomplished all the work of Solomon from¹ the day the foundation of the house of the Lord was laid until it was finished. So the house of the Lord was completed.

¹⁷Then Solomon went to Ezion-geber and Eloth on the shore of the sea, in the land of Edom. ¹⁸And Hiram sent to him by the hand of his servants ships and servants familiar with the sea, and they went to Ophir together with the servants of Solomon and brought from there 450 talents² of gold and brought it to King Solomon.

Final tributes to Solomon's regal greatness [chapter 9]. We have already had abundant reason to marvel at Solomon's kingship, but this chapter tops the preceding ones. The famous visit of the queen of Sheba (vv. 1–12) never loses its grip on our imagination, with the queen's praise of Solomon's court standing as the last word of human commendation of his kingship (vv. 5–8). Solomon has made Israel great among the nations. The ensuing inventory of Solomon's treasures (vv. 13–28) is so extravagant that we can hardly imagine it. A concluding note on the king's death (vv. 29–31) ends the account with no hint of the tragic dimension that the author of 1 Kings found in Solomon's life. The author has chosen to see the good in Solomon in order to emphasize God's blessing on his kingship.

9 Now when the queen of Sheba heard of the fame of Solomon, she came to Jerusalem to test him with hard questions, having a very great retinue and camels bearing spices and very much gold and precious stones. And when she came to Solomon, she told him all that was on her mind. ²And Solomon answered all her questions. There was nothing hidden from Solomon that he could not explain to her. ³And when the queen of Sheba had seen the wisdom of Solomon, the house that he had built, ⁴the food of his table, the seating of his officials, and the attendance of his servants, and their clothing, his cupbearers, and their clothing, and his burnt offerings that he offered at the house of the Lord, there was no more breath in her.

⁵And she said to the king, "The report was true that I heard in my own land of your words and of your wisdom, ⁶but I did not believe the³ reports until I came and my own eyes had seen it. And behold, half the greatness of your wisdom was not told me; you surpass the report that I heard. ⁷Happy are your wives!⁴ Happy are these your servants, who continually stand before you and hear your wisdom! ⁸Blessed be the Lord your God, who has delighted in you and set you on his throne as king for the Lord your God! Because your God loved Israel and would establish them forever, he has made you king over them, that you may execute justice and righteousness." ⁹Then

---

¹ Septuagint, Syriac, Vulgate; Hebrew *to* ² A *talent* was about 75 pounds or 34 kilograms ³ Hebrew *their* ⁴ Septuagint (compare 1 Kings 10:8); Hebrew *men*

she gave the king 120 talents[1] of gold, and a very great quantity of spices, and precious stones. There were no spices such as those that the queen of Sheba gave to King Solomon.

[10]Moreover, the servants of Hiram and the servants of Solomon, who brought gold from Ophir, brought algum wood and precious stones. [11]And the king made from the algum wood supports for the house of the LORD and for the king's house, lyres also and harps for the singers. There never was seen the like of them before in the land of Judah.

[12]And King Solomon gave to the queen of Sheba all that she desired, whatever she asked besides what she had brought to the king. So she turned and went back to her own land with her servants.

[13]Now the weight of gold that came to Solomon in one year was 666 talents of gold, [14]besides that which the explorers and merchants brought. And all the kings of Arabia and the governors of the land brought gold and silver to Solomon. [15]King Solomon made 200 large shields of beaten gold; 600 shekels[2] of beaten gold went into each shield. [16]And he made 300 shields of beaten gold; 300 shekels of gold went into each shield; and the king put them in the House of the Forest of Lebanon. [17]The king also made a great ivory throne and overlaid it with pure gold. [18]The throne had six steps and a footstool of gold, which were attached to the throne, and on each side of the seat were armrests and two lions standing beside the armrests, [19]while twelve lions stood there, one on each end of a step on the six steps. Nothing like it was ever made for any kingdom. [20]All King Solomon's drinking vessels were of gold, and all the vessels of the House of the Forest of Lebanon were of pure gold. Silver was not considered as anything in the days of Solomon. [21]For the king's ships went to Tarshish with the servants of Hiram. Once every three years the ships of Tarshish used to come bringing gold, silver, ivory, apes, and peacocks.[3]

[22]Thus King Solomon excelled all the kings of the earth in riches and in wisdom. [23]And all the kings of the earth sought the presence of Solomon to hear his wisdom, which God had put into his mind. [24]Every one of them brought his present, articles of silver and of gold, garments, myrrh, spices, horses, and mules, so much year by year. [25]And Solomon had 4,000 stalls for horses and chariots, and 12,000 horsemen, whom he stationed in the chariot cities and with the king in Jerusalem. [26]And he ruled over all the kings from the Euphrates to the land of the Philistines and to the border of Egypt. [27]And the king made silver as common in Jerusalem as stone, and he made cedar as plentiful as the sycamore of the Shephelah. [28]And horses were imported for Solomon from Egypt and from all lands.

[29]Now the rest of the acts of Solomon, from first to last, are they not written in the history of Nathan the prophet, and in the prophecy of Ahijah the Shilonite, and in the visions of Iddo the seer concerning Jeroboam the son of Nebat? [30]Solomon reigned in Jerusalem over all Israel forty years. [31]And Solomon slept with his fathers and was buried in the city of David his father, and Rehoboam his son reigned in his place.

The division of the kingdom [chapter 10]. Perhaps the quickness with which the unity of the nation dissolves after Solomon's death is a hint of the disaffection that Solomon's luxurious lifestyle had generated among the populace (see v. 4), but it is equally possible that the division of the kingdom was almost entirely the result of the folly and arro-

---

[1] A *talent* was about 75 pounds or 34 kilograms [2] A *shekel* was about 2/5 ounce or 11 grams [3] Or *baboons*

gance of Solomon's son Rehoboam. In any case, chapter 10 is a satiric exposure of bad counsel and youthful folly. The rest of 2 Chronicles will be filled with famous vignettes from the history of Judah, and the series begins with the famous three-day summit meeting that Rehoboam undertakes (vv. 5–11). The conflict between old counselors who encourage kindness toward citizens and young counselors who favor bullying of the citizenry belongs to an archetypal pattern known as the conflict of generations. It is also an example of bad counsel, which Dante consigns to one of the lowest circles of Hell. The folly of Rehoboam shows itself immediately when it splits the nation (vv. 12–19).

10 Rehoboam went to Shechem, for all Israel had come to Shechem to make him king. ²And as soon as Jeroboam the son of Nebat heard of it (for he was in Egypt, where he had fled from King Solomon), then Jeroboam returned from Egypt. ³And they sent and called him. And Jeroboam and all Israel came and said to Rehoboam, ⁴"Your father made our yoke heavy. Now therefore lighten the hard service of your father and his heavy yoke on us, and we will serve you." ⁵He said to them, "Come to me again in three days." So the people went away.

⁶Then King Rehoboam took counsel with the old men,[1] who had stood before Solomon his father while he was yet alive, saying, "How do you advise me to answer this people?" ⁷And they said to him, "If you will be good to this people and please them and speak good words to them, then they will be your servants forever." ⁸But he abandoned the counsel that the old men gave him, and took counsel with the young men who had grown up with him and stood before him. ⁹And he said to them, "What do you advise that we answer this people who have said to me, 'Lighten the yoke that your father put on us'?" ¹⁰And the young men who had grown up with him said to him, "Thus shall you speak to the people who said to you, 'Your father made our yoke heavy, but you lighten it for us'; thus shall you say to them, 'My little finger is thicker than my father's thighs. ¹¹And now, whereas my father laid on you a heavy yoke, I will add to your yoke. My father disciplined you with whips, but I will discipline you with scorpions.'"

¹²So Jeroboam and all the people came to Rehoboam the third day, as the king said, "Come to me again the third day." ¹³And the king answered them harshly; and forsaking the counsel of the old men, ¹⁴King Rehoboam spoke to them according to the counsel of the young men, saying, "My father made your yoke heavy, but I will add to it. My father disciplined you with whips, but I will discipline you with scorpions." ¹⁵So the king did not listen to the people, for it was a turn of affairs brought about by God that the LORD might fulfill his word, which he spoke by Ahijah the Shilonite to Jeroboam the son of Nebat.

¹⁶And when all Israel saw that the king did not listen to them, the people answered the king, "What portion have we in David? We have no inheritance in the son of Jesse. Each of you to your tents, O Israel! Look now to your own house, David." So all Israel went to their tents. ¹⁷But Rehoboam reigned over the people of Israel who lived in the cities of Judah. ¹⁸Then King Rehoboam sent Hadoram,[2] who was taskmaster over the forced labor, and the people of Israel stoned him to death with stones. And King Rehoboam quickly mounted his chariot to flee to Jerusalem. ¹⁹So Israel has been in rebellion against the house of David to this day.

---

[1] Or *the elders*; also verses 8, 13 [2] Spelled *Adoram* in 1 Kings 12:18

Rehoboam begins his reign over Judah [chapter 11]. The previous chapter ended with the foolish young king Rehoboam's flight for his life in his chariot after his forced-labor taskmaster was stoned to death by the indignant Israelites (10:18). Chapter 11 shows Rehoboam setting up shop as king, now within the limited sphere of just the two southern tribes instead of twelve. What did godless kings of the ancient world do when they came to power? They did what Rehoboam does here: raise an army to protect the king's interests (vv. 1–4); create a defensive system of fortresses and weapons (vv. 5–12); establish an eclectic network of religious practices (vv. 13–17); contract multiple marriages; father multiple children; and look out for the political interests of the king's family and intended heir (vv. 18–23). We can profitably contrast this to the conspicuous priority that David and Solomon had given to the public worship of God. Still, the picture of Rehoboam's first three years is not uniformly bad: he listens to the prophet of God when counseled not to attack the ten tribes of Israel (vv. 3–4); he successfully protects his nation (v. 12); he allows for the correct worship of God in Jerusalem in addition to setting up his own priests (vv. 15–17); and he distributes power among his sons in such a way as to produce a harmonious situation (v. 23).

11 When Rehoboam came to Jerusalem, he assembled the house of Judah and Benjamin, 180,000 chosen warriors, to fight against Israel, to restore the kingdom to Rehoboam. ²But the word of the Lord came to Shemaiah the man of God: ³"Say to Rehoboam the son of Solomon, king of Judah, and to all Israel in Judah and Benjamin, ⁴'Thus says the Lord, You shall not go up or fight against your relatives. Return every man to his home, for this thing is from me.'" So they listened to the word of the Lord and returned and did not go against Jeroboam.

⁵Rehoboam lived in Jerusalem, and he built cities for defense in Judah. ⁶He built Bethlehem, Etam, Tekoa, ⁷Beth-zur, Soco, Adullam, ⁸Gath, Mareshah, Ziph, ⁹Adoraim, Lachish, Azekah, ¹⁰Zorah, Aijalon, and Hebron, fortified cities that are in Judah and in Benjamin. ¹¹He made the fortresses strong, and put commanders in them, and stores of food, oil, and wine. ¹²And he put shields and spears in all the cities and made them very strong. So he held Judah and Benjamin.

¹³And the priests and the Levites who were in all Israel presented themselves to him from all places where they lived. ¹⁴For the Levites left their common lands and their holdings and came to Judah and Jerusalem, because Jeroboam and his sons cast them out from serving as priests of the Lord, ¹⁵and he appointed his own priests for the high places and for the goat idols and for the calves that he had made. ¹⁶And those who had set their hearts to seek the Lord God of Israel came after them from all the tribes of Israel to Jerusalem to sacrifice to the Lord, the God of their fathers. ¹⁷They strengthened the kingdom of Judah, and for three years they made Rehoboam the son of Solomon secure, for they walked for three years in the way of David and Solomon.

¹⁸Rehoboam took as wife Mahalath the daughter of Jerimoth the son of David, and of Abihail the daughter of Eliab the son of Jesse, ¹⁹and she bore him sons, Jeush, Shemariah, and Zaham. ²⁰After her he took Maacah the daughter of Absalom, who bore him Abijah, Attai, Ziza, and Shelomith. ²¹Rehoboam loved Maacah the daughter of Absalom above all his wives and concubines (he took eighteen wives and sixty concubines, and fathered twenty-eight sons and sixty daughters). ²²And Rehoboam appointed Abijah the son of Maacah as chief prince among his brothers, for he intended to make him king. ²³And he dealt wisely and distributed some of his sons

through all the districts of Judah and Benjamin, in all the fortified cities, and he gave them abundant provisions and procured wives for them.[1]

> **The negative final verdict on Rehoboam** [chapter 12]. The temporary success of Rehoboam narrated in chapter 12 was the archetypal false dawn before the storm. The opening verse of chapter 12 gives the Chronicler's negative assessment of Rehoboam's reign. This is repeated at the end of the chapter in the author's summary of Rehoboam's reign (vv. 13–16). We should note the Chronicler's view of history. He is not primarily interested in political and military history (though he records it) but in the spiritual history of the individal kings and in the influence that this has on the whole nation. Yet the events of Rehoboam's reign that are recorded in verses 2–12 are an ambiguous mixture of success and failure, leading to partial but not total destruction (vv. 7, 12). From this point on, we need to be ready to see the positive and negative examples of kings' behavior as adding up to models of action for us, too, to follow or reject.

12 When the rule of Rehoboam was established and he was strong, he abandoned the law of the LORD, and all Israel with him. ²In the fifth year of King Rehoboam, because they had been unfaithful to the LORD, Shishak king of Egypt came up against Jerusalem ³with 1,200 chariots and 60,000 horsemen. And the people were without number who came with him from Egypt—Libyans, Sukkiim, and Ethiopians. ⁴And he took the fortified cities of Judah and came as far as Jerusalem. ⁵Then Shemaiah the prophet came to Rehoboam and to the princes of Judah, who had gathered at Jerusalem because of Shishak, and said to them, "Thus says the LORD, 'You abandoned me, so I have abandoned you to the hand of Shishak.'" ⁶Then the princes of Israel and the king humbled themselves and said, "The LORD is righteous." ⁷When the LORD saw that they humbled themselves, the word of the LORD came to Shemaiah: "They have humbled themselves. I will not destroy them, but I will grant them some deliverance, and my wrath shall not be poured out on Jerusalem by the hand of Shishak. ⁸Nevertheless, they shall be servants to him, that they may know my service and the service of the kingdoms of the countries."

⁹So Shishak king of Egypt came up against Jerusalem. He took away the treasures of the house of the LORD and the treasures of the king's house. He took away everything. He also took away the shields of gold that Solomon had made, ¹⁰and King Rehoboam made in their place shields of bronze and committed them to the hands of the officers of the guard, who kept the door of the king's house. ¹¹And as often as the king went into the house of the LORD, the guard came and carried them and brought them back to the guardroom. ¹²And when he humbled himself the wrath of the LORD turned from him, so as not to make a complete destruction. Moreover, conditions were good[2] in Judah.

¹³So King Rehoboam grew strong in Jerusalem and reigned. Rehoboam was forty-one years old when he began to reign, and he reigned seventeen years in Jerusalem, the city that the LORD had chosen out of all the tribes of Israel to put his name there. His mother's name was Naamah the Ammonite. ¹⁴And he did evil, for he did not set his heart to seek the LORD.

¹⁵Now the acts of Rehoboam, from first to last, are they not written in the chronicles of Shemaiah the prophet and of Iddo the seer?[3] There were continual wars

---

[1] Hebrew *and sought a multitude of wives* [2] Hebrew *good things were found* [3] After *seer*, Hebrew adds *according to genealogy*

between Rehoboam and Jeroboam. ¹⁶And Rehoboam slept with his fathers and was buried in the city of David, and Abijah¹ his son reigned in his place.

The reign of Abijah [chapter 13]. This chapter exemplifies the format into which the Chronicler will now cast the individual reigns of kings. Three primary ingredients enter the record for Abijah in this chapter: (1) summary facts and assessments of his reign, including how long he reigned, whom he married, that he died, and where to find further information about him; (2) a record of how the official practice of religion under the priests and Levites fared during his reign; (3) one or more key political or military events that were crucial in his reign. Most of chapter 13 deals with one decisive event, narrated in relatively full detail: the successful defense of Judah against an invasion from Israel under its king, Jeroboam. We can glean edification from the chapter by noting the verses that tell us why Judah was victorious: its faithfulness to God.

13 In the eighteenth year of King Jeroboam, Abijah began to reign over Judah. ²He reigned for three years in Jerusalem. His mother's name was Micaiah² the daughter of Uriel of Gibeah.

Now there was war between Abijah and Jeroboam. ³Abijah went out to battle, having an army of valiant men of war, 400,000 chosen men. And Jeroboam drew up his line of battle against him with 800,000 chosen mighty warriors. ⁴Then Abijah stood up on Mount Zemaraim that is in the hill country of Ephraim and said, "Hear me, O Jeroboam and all Israel! ⁵Ought you not to know that the LORD God of Israel gave the kingship over Israel forever to David and his sons by a covenant of salt? ⁶Yet Jeroboam the son of Nebat, a servant of Solomon the son of David, rose up and rebelled against his lord, ⁷and certain worthless scoundrels gathered about him and defied Rehoboam the son of Solomon, when Rehoboam was young and irresolute³ and could not withstand them.

⁸"And now you think to withstand the kingdom of the LORD in the hand of the sons of David, because you are a great multitude and have with you the golden calves that Jeroboam made you for gods. ⁹Have you not driven out the priests of the LORD, the sons of Aaron, and the Levites, and made priests for yourselves like the peoples of other lands? Whoever comes for ordination⁴ with a young bull or seven rams becomes a priest of what are no gods. ¹⁰But as for us, the LORD is our God, and we have not forsaken him. We have priests ministering to the LORD who are sons of Aaron, and Levites for their service. ¹¹They offer to the LORD every morning and every evening burnt offerings and incense of sweet spices, set out the showbread on the table of pure gold, and care for the golden lampstand that its lamps may burn every evening. For we keep the charge of the LORD our God, but you have forsaken him. ¹²Behold, God is with us at our head, and his priests with their battle trumpets to sound the call to battle against you. O sons of Israel, do not fight against the LORD, the God of your fathers, for you cannot succeed."

¹³Jeroboam had sent an ambush around to come upon them from behind. Thus his troops⁵ were in front of Judah, and the ambush was behind them. ¹⁴And when Judah looked, behold, the battle was in front of and behind them. And they cried to the LORD, and the priests blew the trumpets. ¹⁵Then the men of Judah raised the battle shout. And when the men of Judah shouted, God defeated Jeroboam and all Israel before Abijah and Judah. ¹⁶The men of Israel fled before Judah, and God gave them

¹ Spelled *Abijam* in 1 Kings 14:31 ² Spelled *Maacah* in 1 Kings 15:2 ³ Hebrew *soft of heart* ⁴ Hebrew *to fill his hand* ⁵ Hebrew *they*

into their hand. [17]Abijah and his people struck them with great force, so there fell slain of Israel 500,000 chosen men. [18]Thus the men of Israel were subdued at that time, and the men of Judah prevailed, because they relied on the LORD, the God of their fathers. [19]And Abijah pursued Jeroboam and took cities from him, Bethel with its villages and Jeshanah with its villages and Ephron[1] with its villages. [20]Jeroboam did not recover his power in the days of Abijah. And the LORD struck him down, and he died. [21]But Abijah grew mighty. And he took fourteen wives and had twenty-two sons and sixteen daughters. [22]The rest of the acts of Abijah, his ways and his sayings, are written in the story of the prophet Iddo.

> **What King Asa does well** [chapter 14]. The portraits of the kings range on a continuum of brief sketches to relatively full records of a reign. King Asa gets three whole chapters, and each one has its own agenda. The Chronicler is our traveling companion through his history, and we can trust him to give us the right interpretive clues. In this case, he tells us at once that "Asa did what was good and right in the eyes of the LORD his God" (v. 2). Then we get the details: removal of places of idol worship (vv. 3–5); fortification of key cities with able warriors (vv. 6–8), with the king's confidence based on the fact that "we have sought the LORD our God" (v. 7); God's defeat of the Ethiopian army as a reward for faithfulness (vv. 9–15).

14

[2] Abijah slept with his fathers, and they buried him in the city of David. And Asa his son reigned in his place. In his days the land had rest for ten years. [2][3] And Asa did what was good and right in the eyes of the LORD his God. [3]He took away the foreign altars and the high places and broke down the pillars and cut down the Asherim [4]and commanded Judah to seek the LORD, the God of their fathers, and to keep the law and the commandment. [5]He also took out of all the cities of Judah the high places and the incense altars. And the kingdom had rest under him. [6]He built fortified cities in Judah, for the land had rest. He had no war in those years, for the LORD gave him peace. [7]And he said to Judah, "Let us build these cities and surround them with walls and towers, gates and bars. The land is still ours, because we have sought the LORD our God. We have sought him, and he has given us peace on every side." So they built and prospered. [8]And Asa had an army of 300,000 from Judah, armed with large shields and spears, and 280,000 men from Benjamin that carried shields and drew bows. All these were mighty men of valor.

[9]Zerah the Ethiopian came out against them with an army of a million men and 300 chariots, and came as far as Mareshah. [10]And Asa went out to meet him, and they drew up their lines of battle in the Valley of Zephathah at Mareshah. [11]And Asa cried to the LORD his God, "O LORD, there is none like you to help, between the mighty and the weak. Help us, O LORD our God, for we rely on you, and in your name we have come against this multitude. O LORD, you are our God; let not man prevail against you." [12]So the LORD defeated the Ethiopians before Asa and before Judah, and the Ethiopians fled. [13]Asa and the people who were with him pursued them as far as Gerar, and the Ethiopians fell until none remained alive, for they were broken before the LORD and his army. The men of Judah[4] carried away very much spoil. [14]And they attacked all the cities around Gerar, for the fear of the LORD was upon them. They plundered all the cities, for there was much plunder in them. [15]And they struck down

---

[1] Or *Ephrain* [2] Ch 13:23 in Hebrew [3] Ch 14:1 in Hebrew [4] Hebrew *they*

the tents of those who had livestock and carried away sheep in abundance and camels. Then they returned to Jerusalem.

Asa's religious reforms [chapter 15]. The promising beginning of Asa's reign gets even better in this chapter, with its account of reforms that Asa instituted in the religious life of his nation. The sequence unfolds as follows: a prophet encourages Asa to continue on his godly path, secure in the knowledge that God will reward him if he does so (vv. 1–7); Asa responds by repairing the altar at the temple, reinstituting the sacrificial system, and leading the nation in making an oath to serve God (vv. 8–15); Asa removes part of the idolatry from the land and honors God (vv. 16–18). The key to extracting the edification of the chapter is to trace the references to God and observe what God desires and rewards in human behavior, especially toward him. The last verse of chapter 15 brings in a time line and draws a boundary around the first thirty-five years of Asa's reign. This is important because the next six years of his reign will be a decline from the heights about which we have read for two chapters.

15 The Spirit of God came upon Azariah the son of Oded, ²and he went out to meet Asa and said to him, "Hear me, Asa, and all Judah and Benjamin: The LORD is with you while you are with him. If you seek him, he will be found by you, but if you forsake him, he will forsake you. ³For a long time Israel was without the true God, and without a teaching priest and without law, ⁴but when in their distress they turned to the LORD, the God of Israel, and sought him, he was found by them. ⁵In those times there was no peace to him who went out or to him who came in, for great disturbances afflicted all the inhabitants of the lands. ⁶They were broken in pieces. Nation was crushed by nation and city by city, for God troubled them with every sort of distress. ⁷But you, take courage! Do not let your hands be weak, for your work shall be rewarded."

⁸As soon as Asa heard these words, the prophecy of Azariah the son of Oded, he took courage and put away the detestable idols from all the land of Judah and Benjamin and from the cities that he had taken in the hill country of Ephraim, and he repaired the altar of the LORD that was in front of the vestibule of the house of the LORD.[1] ⁹And he gathered all Judah and Benjamin, and those from Ephraim, Manasseh, and Simeon who were residing with them, for great numbers had deserted to him from Israel when they saw that the LORD his God was with him. ¹⁰They were gathered at Jerusalem in the third month of the fifteenth year of the reign of Asa. ¹¹They sacrificed to the LORD on that day from the spoil that they had brought 700 oxen and 7,000 sheep. ¹²And they entered into a covenant to seek the LORD, the God of their fathers, with all their heart and with all their soul, ¹³but that whoever would not seek the LORD, the God of Israel, should be put to death, whether young or old, man or woman. ¹⁴They swore an oath to the LORD with a loud voice and with shouting and with trumpets and with horns. ¹⁵And all Judah rejoiced over the oath, for they had sworn with all their heart and had sought him with their whole desire, and he was found by them, and the LORD gave them rest all around.

¹⁶Even Maacah, his mother, King Asa removed from being queen mother because she had made a detestable image for Asherah. Asa cut down her image, crushed it, and burned it at the brook Kidron. ¹⁷But the high places were not taken out of Israel. Nevertheless, the heart of Asa was wholly true all his days. ¹⁸And he brought into the

---

[1] Hebrew *the vestibule of the LORD*

house of God the sacred gifts of his father and his own sacred gifts, silver, and gold, and vessels. ¹⁹And there was no more war until the thirty-fifth year of the reign of Asa.

> **Asa's disappointing end** [chapter 16]. The stories recorded in 2 Chronicles are example stories—stories that hold up positive and negative examples for us to contemplate and learn from. As the last six years of Asa's life pass before us, he becomes an example of the tragedy of not finishing well. The first thirty-five years, as recorded in the preceding two chapters, had been a nearly complete spiritual and political triumph. Now Asa drifts from his spiritual moorings. The details unfold as follows: Asa successfully counters a threat from Israel (the northern kingdom) through an alliance with Ben-hadad king of Syria (vv. 1–6); when Asa's alliance is denounced by a prophet, Asa loses his temper and becomes cruel (vv. 7–10); when Asa becomes ill, he trusts in physicians instead of God (vv. 11–12); summary account of Asa's death (vv. 13–14). Usually the Chronicler accompanies the obituary for a given king with an assessment of spiritual success or failure; its absence here may signal the author's disappointment that a king whose reign was exemplary for decades slid into failure in his declining years.

16 In the thirty-sixth year of the reign of Asa, Baasha king of Israel went up against Judah and built Ramah, that he might permit no one to go out or come in to Asa king of Judah. ²Then Asa took silver and gold from the treasures of the house of the LORD and the king's house and sent them to Ben-hadad king of Syria, who lived in Damascus, saying, ³"There is a covenant¹ between me and you, as there was between my father and your father. Behold, I am sending to you silver and gold. Go, break your covenant with Baasha king of Israel, that he may withdraw from me." ⁴And Ben-hadad listened to King Asa and sent the commanders of his armies against the cities of Israel, and they conquered Ijon, Dan, Abel-maim, and all the store cities of Naphtali. ⁵And when Baasha heard of it, he stopped building Ramah and let his work cease. ⁶Then King Asa took all Judah, and they carried away the stones of Ramah and its timber, with which Baasha had been building, and with them he built Geba and Mizpah.

⁷At that time Hanani the seer came to Asa king of Judah and said to him, "Because you relied on the king of Syria, and did not rely on the LORD your God, the army of the king of Syria has escaped you. ⁸Were not the Ethiopians and the Libyans a huge army with very many chariots and horsemen? Yet because you relied on the LORD, he gave them into your hand. ⁹For the eyes of the LORD run to and fro throughout the whole earth, to give strong support to those whose heart is blameless toward him. You have done foolishly in this, for from now on you will have wars." ¹⁰Then Asa was angry with the seer and put him in the stocks in prison, for he was in a rage with him because of this. And Asa inflicted cruelties upon some of the people at the same time.

¹¹The acts of Asa, from first to last, are written in the Book of the Kings of Judah and Israel. ¹²In the thirty-ninth year of his reign Asa was diseased in his feet, and his disease became severe. Yet even in his disease he did not seek the LORD, but sought help from physicians. ¹³And Asa slept with his fathers, dying in the forty-first year of his reign. ¹⁴They buried him in the tomb that he had cut for himself in the city of David. They laid him on a bier that had been filled with various kinds of spices prepared by the perfumer's art, and they made a very great fire in his honor.

---

¹ Or *treaty*; twice in this verse

Jehoshaphat's good beginning [chapter 17]. Jehoshaphat gets four whole chapters, resulting in an even more complete hero story than the story of Asa his father. Chapter 17 is a success story for us to admire and emulate, unfolding according to the following sequence: Jehoshaphat fortifies the nation, elicits the loyalty of his people, and resists idolatry (vv. 1–6); the king firmly establishes a system of teaching God's law throughout the land (vv. 7–9); Jehoshaphat's high esteem among surrounding nations and his military and financial success (vv. 10–19). Two intertwined stories are told: the human story of a good king and the religious story of what constitutes a godly commonwealth.

17 Jehoshaphat his son reigned in his place and strengthened himself against Israel. ²He placed forces in all the fortified cities of Judah and set garrisons in the land of Judah, and in the cities of Ephraim that Asa his father had captured. ³The Lord was with Jehoshaphat, because he walked in the earlier ways of his father David. He did not seek the Baals, ⁴but sought the God of his father and walked in his commandments, and not according to the practices of Israel. ⁵Therefore the Lord established the kingdom in his hand. And all Judah brought tribute to Jehoshaphat, and he had great riches and honor. ⁶His heart was courageous in the ways of the Lord. And furthermore, he took the high places and the Asherim out of Judah.

⁷In the third year of his reign he sent his officials, Ben-hail, Obadiah, Zechariah, Nethanel, and Micaiah, to teach in the cities of Judah; ⁸and with them the Levites, Shemaiah, Nethaniah, Zebadiah, Asahel, Shemiramoth, Jehonathan, Adonijah, Tobijah, and Tobadonijah; and with these Levites, the priests Elishama and Jehoram. ⁹And they taught in Judah, having the Book of the Law of the Lord with them. They went about through all the cities of Judah and taught among the people.

¹⁰And the fear of the Lord fell upon all the kingdoms of the lands that were around Judah, and they made no war against Jehoshaphat. ¹¹Some of the Philistines brought Jehoshaphat presents and silver for tribute, and the Arabians also brought him 7,700 rams and 7,700 goats. ¹²And Jehoshaphat grew steadily greater. He built in Judah fortresses and store cities, ¹³and he had large supplies in the cities of Judah. He had soldiers, mighty men of valor, in Jerusalem. ¹⁴This was the muster of them by fathers' houses: Of Judah, the commanders of thousands: Adnah the commander, with 300,000 mighty men of valor; ¹⁵and next to him Jehohanan the commander, with 280,000; ¹⁶and next to him Amasiah the son of Zichri, a volunteer for the service of the Lord, with 200,000 mighty men of valor. ¹⁷Of Benjamin: Eliada, a mighty man of valor, with 200,000 men armed with bow and shield; ¹⁸and next to him Jehozabad with 180,000 armed for war. ¹⁹These were in the service of the king, besides those whom the king had placed in the fortified cities throughout all Judah.

A regrettable lapse [18:1–19:3]. This unit is a full-fledged *battle story, narrated in leisurely detail so that we can relive the events in our imagination. The sequence is as follows: Ahab entices Jehoshaphat to join him in a war effort (18:1–3); upon second thought, Jehoshaphat requests that Ahab inquire whether the intended battle has God's approval, and although four hundred false prophets predict victory, Jehoshaphat holds out for an additional prophet (18:4–11); the true prophet Micaiah prophesies doom for Ahab, who responds in anger and puts Micaiah in prison (18:12–27); the alliance is defeated and Ahab is killed in battle, with Jehoshaphat barely escaping (18:28–34);

the prophet Jehu denounces Jehoshaphat for his foolish alliance with Ahab (19:1–3). The story stands as an example of the bad effects of unholy alliances and any venture that does not have God's approval.

18

Now Jehoshaphat had great riches and honor, and he made a marriage alliance with Ahab. ²After some years he went down to Ahab in Samaria. And Ahab killed an abundance of sheep and oxen for him and for the people who were with him, and induced him to go up against Ramoth-gilead. ³Ahab king of Israel said to Jehoshaphat king of Judah, "Will you go with me to Ramoth-gilead?" He answered him, "I am as you are, my people as your people. We will be with you in the war."

⁴And Jehoshaphat said to the king of Israel, "Inquire first for the word of the Lᴏʀᴅ." ⁵Then the king of Israel gathered the prophets together, four hundred men, and said to them, "Shall we go to battle against Ramoth-gilead, or shall I refrain?" And they said, "Go up, for God will give it into the hand of the king." ⁶But Jehoshaphat said, "Is there not here another prophet of the Lᴏʀᴅ of whom we may inquire?" ⁷And the king of Israel said to Jehoshaphat, "There is yet one man by whom we may inquire of the Lᴏʀᴅ, Micaiah the son of Imlah; but I hate him, for he never prophesies good concerning me, but always evil." And Jehoshaphat said, "Let not the king say so." ⁸Then the king of Israel summoned an officer and said, "Bring quickly Micaiah the son of Imlah." ⁹Now the king of Israel and Jehoshaphat the king of Judah were sitting on their thrones, arrayed in their robes. And they were sitting at the threshing floor at the entrance of the gate of Samaria, and all the prophets were prophesying before them. ¹⁰And Zedekiah the son of Chenaanah made for himself horns of iron and said, "Thus says the Lᴏʀᴅ, 'With these you shall push the Syrians until they are destroyed.'" ¹¹And all the prophets prophesied so and said, "Go up to Ramoth-gilead and triumph. The Lᴏʀᴅ will give it into the hand of the king."

¹²And the messenger who went to summon Micaiah said to him, "Behold, the words of the prophets with one accord are favorable to the king. Let your word be like the word of one of them, and speak favorably." ¹³But Micaiah said, "As the Lᴏʀᴅ lives, what my God says, that I will speak." ¹⁴And when he had come to the king, the king said to him, "Micaiah, shall we go to Ramoth-gilead to battle, or shall I refrain?" And he answered, "Go up and triumph; they will be given into your hand." ¹⁵But the king said to him, "How many times shall I make you swear that you speak to me nothing but the truth in the name of the Lᴏʀᴅ?" ¹⁶And he said, "I saw all Israel scattered on the mountains, as sheep that have no shepherd. And the Lᴏʀᴅ said, 'These have no master; let each return to his home in peace.'" ¹⁷And the king of Israel said to Jehoshaphat, "Did I not tell you that he would not prophesy good concerning me, but evil?" ¹⁸And Micaiah said, "Therefore hear the word of the Lᴏʀᴅ: I saw the Lᴏʀᴅ sitting on his throne, and all the host of heaven standing on his right hand and on his left. ¹⁹And the Lᴏʀᴅ said, 'Who will entice Ahab the king of Israel, that he may go up and fall at Ramoth-gilead?' And one said one thing, and another said another. ²⁰Then a spirit came forward and stood before the Lᴏʀᴅ, saying, 'I will entice him.' And the Lᴏʀᴅ said to him, 'By what means?' ²¹And he said, 'I will go out, and will be a lying spirit in the mouth of all his prophets.' And he said, 'You are to entice him, and you shall succeed; go out and do so.' ²²Now therefore behold, the Lᴏʀᴅ has put a lying

spirit in the mouth of these your prophets. The LORD has declared disaster concerning you."

²³Then Zedekiah the son of Chenaanah came near and struck Micaiah on the cheek and said, "Which way did the Spirit of the LORD go from me to speak to you?" ²⁴And Micaiah said, "Behold, you shall see on that day when you go into an inner chamber to hide yourself." ²⁵And the king of Israel said, "Seize Micaiah and take him back to Amon the governor of the city and to Joash the king's son, ²⁶and say, 'Thus says the king, Put this fellow in prison and feed him with meager rations of bread and water until I return in peace.'" ²⁷And Micaiah said, "If you return in peace, the LORD has not spoken by me." And he said, "Hear, all you peoples!"

²⁸So the king of Israel and Jehoshaphat the king of Judah went up to Ramoth-gilead. ²⁹And the king of Israel said to Jehoshaphat, "I will disguise myself and go into battle, but you wear your robes." And the king of Israel disguised himself, and they went into battle. ³⁰Now the king of Syria had commanded the captains of his chariots, "Fight with neither small nor great, but only with the king of Israel." ³¹As soon as the captains of the chariots saw Jehoshaphat, they said, "It is the king of Israel." So they turned to fight against him. And Jehoshaphat cried out, and the LORD helped him; God drew them away from him. ³²For as soon as the captains of the chariots saw that it was not the king of Israel, they turned back from pursuing him. ³³But a certain man drew his bow at random[1] and struck the king of Israel between the scale armor and the breastplate. Therefore he said to the driver of his chariot, "Turn around and carry me out of the battle, for I am wounded." ³⁴And the battle continued that day, and the king of Israel was propped up in his chariot facing the Syrians until evening. Then at sunset he died.

19 Jehoshaphat the king of Judah returned in safety to his house in Jerusalem. ²But Jehu the son of Hanani the seer went out to meet him and said to King Jehoshaphat, "Should you help the wicked and love those who hate the LORD? Because of this, wrath has gone out against you from the LORD. ³Nevertheless, some good is found in you, for you destroyed the Asherahs out of the land, and have set your heart to seek God."

> **Further godly reforms** [19:4–11]. After the narrative of the ill-fated alliance with Ahab, this unit returns to a summary of policies that Jehoshaphat instituted in Judah. The result is a utopian glimpse into a good society based on judicial orderliness and fairness.

⁴Jehoshaphat lived at Jerusalem. And he went out again among the people, from Beersheba to the hill country of Ephraim, and brought them back to the LORD, the God of their fathers. ⁵He appointed judges in the land in all the fortified cities of Judah, city by city, ⁶and said to the judges, "Consider what you do, for you judge not for man but for the LORD. He is with you in giving judgment. ⁷Now then, let the fear of the LORD be upon you. Be careful what you do, for there is no injustice with the LORD our God, or partiality or taking bribes."

⁸Moreover, in Jerusalem Jehoshaphat appointed certain Levites and priests and heads of families of Israel, to give judgment for the LORD and to decide disputed cases. They had their seat at Jerusalem. ⁹And he charged them: "Thus you shall do in

---

[1] Hebrew *in his innocence*

the fear of the LORD, in faithfulness, and with your whole heart: ¹⁰whenever a case comes to you from your brothers who live in their cities, concerning bloodshed, law or commandment, statutes or rules, then you shall warn them, that they may not incur guilt before the LORD and wrath may not come upon you and your brothers. Thus you shall do, and you will not incur guilt. ¹¹And behold, Amariah the chief priest is over you in all matters of the LORD; and Zebadiah the son of Ishmael, the governor of the house of Judah, in all the king's matters, and the Levites will serve you as officers. Deal courageously, and may the LORD be with the upright!"[1]

> **Another battle story** [chapter 20]. The appearance of another battle story narrated in full detail alerts us that 2 Chronicles is court history—a history of what happened at the nation's court, with the emphasis on what the ruling monarch did. A lot of the attention of an ancient king was taken up with battles, and that is what we find here. The sequence is as follows: preamble to battle (vv. 1–4); the king prays to God for deliverance in a public assembly (vv. 5–12); Jahaziel delivers a battle address to the people (vv. 13–19); the army marches to battle singing God's praise, and God defeats the enemy (vv. 20–30). This textbook example of the holy war motif is followed by a summary of Jehoshaphat's reign, mixed in its verdict (vv. 31–37). The kingly career of Jehoshaphat stands open to view, and it is easy to discern in it what we ourselves should do and avoid.

20 After this the Moabites and Ammonites, and with them some of the Meunites,[2] came against Jehoshaphat for battle. ²Some men came and told Jehoshaphat, "A great multitude is coming against you from Edom,[3] from beyond the sea; and, behold, they are in Hazazon-tamar" (that is, Engedi). ³Then Jehoshaphat was afraid and set his face to seek the LORD, and proclaimed a fast throughout all Judah. ⁴And Judah assembled to seek help from the LORD; from all the cities of Judah they came to seek the LORD.

⁵And Jehoshaphat stood in the assembly of Judah and Jerusalem, in the house of the LORD, before the new court, ⁶and said, "O LORD, God of our fathers, are you not God in heaven? You rule over all the kingdoms of the nations. In your hand are power and might, so that none is able to withstand you. ⁷Did you not, our God, drive out the inhabitants of this land before your people Israel, and give it forever to the descendants of Abraham your friend? ⁸And they have lived in it and have built for you in it a sanctuary for your name, saying, ⁹'If disaster comes upon us, the sword, judgment,[4] or pestilence, or famine, we will stand before this house and before you—for your name is in this house—and cry out to you in our affliction, and you will hear and save.' ¹⁰And now behold, the men of Ammon and Moab and Mount Seir, whom you would not let Israel invade when they came from the land of Egypt, and whom they avoided and did not destroy— ¹¹behold, they reward us by coming to drive us out of your possession, which you have given us to inherit. ¹²O our God, will you not execute judgment on them? For we are powerless against this great horde that is coming against us. We do not know what to do, but our eyes are on you."

¹³Meanwhile all Judah stood before the LORD, with their little ones, their wives, and their children. ¹⁴And the Spirit of the LORD came upon Jahaziel the son of Zechariah, son of Benaiah, son of Jeiel, son of Mattaniah, a Levite of the sons of Asaph, in the midst of the assembly. ¹⁵And he said, "Listen, all Judah and inhabitants of Jerusalem

---

[1] Hebrew *the good* [2] Compare 26:7; Hebrew *Ammonites* [3] One Hebrew manuscript; most Hebrew manuscripts *Aram* (Syria) [4] Or *the sword of judgment*

and King Jehoshaphat: Thus says the LORD to you, 'Do not be afraid and do not be dismayed at this great horde, for the battle is not yours but God's. [16]Tomorrow go down against them. Behold, they will come up by the ascent of Ziz. You will find them at the end of the valley, east of the wilderness of Jeruel. [17]You will not need to fight in this battle. Stand firm, hold your position, and see the salvation of the LORD on your behalf, O Judah and Jerusalem.' Do not be afraid and do not be dismayed. Tomorrow go out against them, and the LORD will be with you."

[18]Then Jehoshaphat bowed his head with his face to the ground, and all Judah and the inhabitants of Jerusalem fell down before the LORD, worshiping the LORD. [19]And the Levites, of the Kohathites and the Korahites, stood up to praise the LORD, the God of Israel, with a very loud voice.

[20]And they rose early in the morning and went out into the wilderness of Tekoa. And when they went out, Jehoshaphat stood and said, "Hear me, Judah and inhabitants of Jerusalem! Believe in the LORD your God, and you will be established; believe his prophets, and you will succeed." [21]And when he had taken counsel with the people, he appointed those who were to sing to the LORD and praise him in holy attire, as they went before the army, and say,

"Give thanks to the LORD,
    for his steadfast love endures forever."

[22]And when they began to sing and praise, the LORD set an ambush against the men of Ammon, Moab, and Mount Seir, who had come against Judah, so that they were routed. [23]For the men of Ammon and Moab rose against the inhabitants of Mount Seir, devoting them to destruction, and when they had made an end of the inhabitants of Seir, they all helped to destroy one another.

[24]When Judah came to the watchtower of the wilderness, they looked toward the horde, and behold, there[1] were dead bodies lying on the ground; none had escaped. [25]When Jehoshaphat and his people came to take their spoil, they found among them, in great numbers, goods, clothing, and precious things, which they took for themselves until they could carry no more. They were three days in taking the spoil, it was so much. [26]On the fourth day they assembled in the Valley of Beracah,[2] for there they blessed the LORD. Therefore the name of that place has been called the Valley of Beracah to this day. [27]Then they returned, every man of Judah and Jerusalem, and Jehoshaphat at their head, returning to Jerusalem with joy, for the LORD had made them rejoice over their enemies. [28]They came to Jerusalem with harps and lyres and trumpets, to the house of the LORD. [29]And the fear of God came on all the kingdoms of the countries when they heard that the LORD had fought against the enemies of Israel. [30]So the realm of Jehoshaphat was quiet, for his God gave him rest all around.

[31]Thus Jehoshaphat reigned over Judah. He was thirty-five years old when he began to reign, and he reigned twenty-five years in Jerusalem. His mother's name was Azubah the daughter of Shilhi. [32]He walked in the way of Asa his father and did not turn aside from it, doing what was right in the sight of the LORD. [33]The high places, however, were not taken away; the people had not yet set their hearts upon the God of their fathers.

[34]Now the rest of the acts of Jehoshaphat, from first to last, are written in the chronicles of Jehu the son of Hanani, which are recorded in the Book of the Kings of Israel.

---

[1] Hebrew *they* [2] *Beracah* means *blessing*

³⁵After this Jehoshaphat king of Judah joined with Ahaziah king of Israel, who acted wickedly. ³⁶He joined him in building ships to go to Tarshish, and they built the ships in Ezion-geber. ³⁷Then Eliezer the son of Dodavahu of Mareshah prophesied against Jehoshaphat, saying, "Because you have joined with Ahaziah, the LORD will destroy what you have made." And the ships were wrecked and were not able to go to Tarshish.

> **The bad reign of Jehoram** [chapter 21]. The reigns of Asa and Jehoshaphat were predominantly good, and both kings were given multichapter treatment. Jehoram was a bad king, and he gets only one chapter. The sequence is as follows: the facts of Jehoram's accession to the throne and a summary verdict that he was a wicked king like the kings of Israel (vv. 1–7); Jehoram attempts to deal with rebellious groups (vv. 8–10); Jehoram establishes the worship of idols and receives a letter from the prophet Elijah predicting that he will come to a bad end (vv. 11–15); Elijah's prophecy comes true, as Jehoram dies of a horrible illness (vv. 16–20). A sardonic understatement marks him as the archetypal example of how not to live one's life: "he departed with no one's regret" (v. 20).

21 Jehoshaphat slept with his fathers and was buried with his fathers in the city of David, and Jehoram his son reigned in his place. ²He had brothers, the sons of Jehoshaphat: Azariah, Jehiel, Zechariah, Azariah, Michael, and Shephatiah; all these were the sons of Jehoshaphat king of Israel.¹ ³Their father gave them great gifts of silver, gold, and valuable possessions, together with fortified cities in Judah, but he gave the kingdom to Jehoram, because he was the firstborn. ⁴When Jehoram had ascended the throne of his father and was established, he killed all his brothers with the sword, and also some of the princes of Israel. ⁵Jehoram was thirty-two years old when he became king, and he reigned eight years in Jerusalem. ⁶And he walked in the way of the kings of Israel, as the house of Ahab had done, for the daughter of Ahab was his wife. And he did what was evil in the sight of the LORD. ⁷Yet the LORD was not willing to destroy the house of David, because of the covenant that he had made with David, and since he had promised to give a lamp to him and to his sons forever.

⁸In his days Edom revolted from the rule of Judah and set up a king of their own. ⁹Then Jehoram passed over with his commanders and all his chariots, and he rose by night and struck the Edomites who had surrounded him and his chariot commanders. ¹⁰So Edom revolted from the rule of Judah to this day. At that time Libnah also revolted from his rule, because he had forsaken the LORD, the God of his fathers.

¹¹Moreover, he made high places in the hill country of Judah and led the inhabitants of Jerusalem into whoredom and made Judah go astray. ¹²And a letter came to him from Elijah the prophet, saying, "Thus says the LORD, the God of David your father, 'Because you have not walked in the ways of Jehoshaphat your father, or in the ways of Asa king of Judah, ¹³but have walked in the way of the kings of Israel and have enticed Judah and the inhabitants of Jerusalem into whoredom, as the house of Ahab led Israel into whoredom, and also you have killed your brothers, of your father's house, who were better than yourself, ¹⁴behold, the LORD will bring a great plague on your people, your children, your wives, and all your possessions, ¹⁵and you yourself will have a severe sickness with a disease of your bowels, until your bowels come out because of the disease, day by day.'"

¹ That is, Judah

¹⁶And the LORD stirred up against Jehoram the anger¹ of the Philistines and of the Arabians who are near the Ethiopians. ¹⁷And they came up against Judah and invaded it and carried away all the possessions they found that belonged to the king's house, and also his sons and his wives, so that no son was left to him except Jehoahaz, his youngest son. ¹⁸And after all this the LORD struck him in his bowels with an incurable disease. ¹⁹In the course of time, at the end of two years, his bowels came out because of the disease, and he died in great agony. His people made no fire in his honor, like the fires made for his fathers. ²⁰He was thirty-two years old when he began to reign, and he reigned eight years in Jerusalem. And he departed with no one's regret. They buried him in the city of David, but not in the tombs of the kings.

More bad news for the kingdom [chapter 22]. While most mothers portrayed in the Bible are good mothers, a few haunt our memories, and the mother whose "name was Athaliah" (v. 2) is one of these. Her son Ahaziah reigns only one year because of his foolish military alliance with the king of Israel (vv. 1–9). In the ensuing power vaccum, Athaliah kills the claimants to the throne (except for one son of King Ahaziah who escapes), seizes the throne, and becomes ruling queen (vv. 10–12).

22 And the inhabitants of Jerusalem made Ahaziah, his youngest son, king in his place, for the band of men that came with the Arabians to the camp had killed all the older sons. So Ahaziah the son of Jehoram king of Judah reigned. ²Ahaziah was twenty-two years old when he began to reign, and he reigned one year in Jerusalem. His mother's name was Athaliah, the granddaughter of Omri. ³He also walked in the ways of the house of Ahab, for his mother was his counselor in doing wickedly. ⁴He did what was evil in the sight of the LORD, as the house of Ahab had done. For after the death of his father they were his counselors, to his undoing. ⁵He even followed their counsel and went with Jehoram the son of Ahab king of Israel to make war against Hazael king of Syria at Ramoth-gilead. And the Syrians wounded Joram, ⁶and he returned to be healed in Jezreel of the wounds that he had received at Ramah, when he fought against Hazael king of Syria. And Ahaziah the son of Jehoram king of Judah went down to see Joram the son of Ahab in Jezreel, because he was wounded.

⁷But it was ordained by God that the downfall of Ahaziah should come about through his going to visit Joram. For when he came there, he went out with Jehoram to meet Jehu the son of Nimshi, whom the LORD had anointed to destroy the house of Ahab. ⁸And when Jehu was executing judgment on the house of Ahab, he met the princes of Judah and the sons of Ahaziah's brothers, who attended Ahaziah, and he killed them. ⁹He searched for Ahaziah, and he was captured while hiding in Samaria, and he was brought to Jehu and put to death. They buried him, for they said, "He is the grandson of Jehoshaphat, who sought the LORD with all his heart." And the house of Ahaziah had no one able to rule the kingdom.

¹⁰Now when Athaliah the mother of Ahaziah saw that her son was dead, she arose and destroyed all the royal family of the house of Judah. ¹¹But Jehoshabeath,² the daughter of the king, took Joash the son of Ahaziah and stole him away from among the king's sons who were about to be put to death, and she put him and his nurse in a

¹ Hebrew *spirit* ² Spelled *Jehosheba* in 2 Kings 11:2

bedroom. Thus Jehoshabeath, the daughter of King Jehoram and wife of Jehoiada the priest, because she was a sister of Ahaziah, hid him[1] from Athaliah, so that she did not put him to death. [12]And he remained with them six years, hidden in the house of God, while Athaliah reigned over the land.

A priest engineers a coup [chapter 23]. For sheer narrative excitement, this chapter is a high point in 2 Chronicles. The preceding chapter ended with a reference to the fact that the priest Jehoiada concealed the very young son of the previous king during the six years that Athaliah ruled (22:11–12). Chapter 23 narrates, blow by blow, how Jehoiada makes his move to establish seven-year-old Joash as king and depose the wicked queen. Jehoiada stage-manages the entire drama, which is narrated with such vividness that we readily relive it in our imagination. It is a story of the defeat of evil and the triumph of good.

23 But in the seventh year Jehoiada took courage and entered into a covenant with the commanders of hundreds, Azariah the son of Jeroham, Ishmael the son of Jehohanan, Azariah the son of Obed, Maaseiah the son of Adaiah, and Elishaphat the son of Zichri. [2]And they went about through Judah and gathered the Levites from all the cities of Judah, and the heads of fathers' houses of Israel, and they came to Jerusalem. [3]And all the assembly made a covenant with the king in the house of God. And Jehoiada[2] said to them, "Behold, the king's son! Let him reign, as the LORD spoke concerning the sons of David. [4]This is the thing that you shall do: of you priests and Levites who come off duty on the Sabbath, one third shall be gate-keepers, [5]and one third shall be at the king's house and one third at the Gate of the Foundation. And all the people shall be in the courts of the house of the LORD. [6]Let no one enter the house of the LORD except the priests and ministering Levites. They may enter, for they are holy, but all the people shall keep the charge of the LORD. [7]The Levites shall surround the king, each with his weapons in his hand. And whoever enters the house shall be put to death. Be with the king when he comes in and when he goes out."

[8]The Levites and all Judah did according to all that Jehoiada the priest com-manded, and they each brought his men, who were to go off duty on the Sabbath, with those who were to come on duty on the Sabbath, for Jehoiada the priest did not dismiss the divisions. [9]And Jehoiada the priest gave to the captains the spears and the large and small shields that had been King David's, which were in the house of God. [10]And he set all the people as a guard for the king, every man with his weapon in his hand, from the south side of the house to the north side of the house, around the altar and the house. [11]Then they brought out the king's son and put the crown on him and gave him the testimony. And they proclaimed him king, and Jehoiada and his sons anointed him, and they said, "Long live the king."

[12]When Athaliah heard the noise of the people running and praising the king, she went into the house of the LORD to the people. [13]And when she looked, there was the king standing by his pillar at the entrance, and the captains and the trumpeters beside the king, and all the people of the land rejoicing and blowing trumpets, and the singers with their musical instruments leading in the celebration. And Athaliah tore her clothes and cried, "Treason! Treason!" [14]Then Jehoiada the priest brought out

---

[1] That is, Joash [2] Hebrew *he*

the captains who were set over the army, saying to them, "Bring her out between the ranks, and anyone who follows her is to be put to death with the sword." For the priest said, "Do not put her to death in the house of the LORD." ¹⁵So they laid hands on her,[1] and she went into the entrance of the horse gate of the king's house, and they put her to death there.

¹⁶And Jehoiada made a covenant between himself and all the people and the king that they should be the LORD's people. ¹⁷Then all the people went to the house of Baal and tore it down; his altars and his images they broke in pieces, and they killed Mattan the priest of Baal before the altars. ¹⁸And Jehoiada posted watchmen for the house of the LORD under the direction of the Levitical priests and the Levites whom David had organized to be in charge of the house of the LORD, to offer burnt offerings to the LORD, as it is written in the Law of Moses, with rejoicing and with singing, according to the order of David. ¹⁹He stationed the gatekeepers at the gates of the house of the LORD so that no one should enter who was in any way unclean. ²⁰And he took the captains, the nobles, the governors of the people, and all the people of the land, and they brought the king down from the house of the LORD, marching through the upper gate to the king's house. And they set the king on the royal throne. ²¹So all the people of the land rejoiced, and the city was quiet after Athaliah had been put to death with the sword.

Joash's reign [chapter 24]. As we move through the succession of kings, the Chronicler generally relieves us of any suspense regarding the next king's reign. We learn from the start that Joash "did what was right in the eyes of the LORD all the days of Jehoiada the priest" (vv. 1–3). This cuts two ways: Joash's reign is good up to a certain point, but as the chapter unfolds it becomes clear that a now-familiar pattern is reenacted in his life. The good part of Joash's reign is an inspiring picture of the repair of the temple, including the collection of money for its cost (vv. 4–14). The turning point of Joash's rule comes with the death of the remarkable priest Jehoiada (vv. 15–16). The rest is all downhill: Joash listens to his princes and disregards the prophets (vv. 17–19), kills the godly son of Jehoiada (vv. 20–22), falls in battle against the Syrians (vv. 23–24), and is killed by his own servants as he lies battle-wounded in his bed (vv. 25–27). To extract the message of this story and the others of 2 Chronicles, we need to pay attention to our responses as we read: no one would wish to make the mistakes and come to the end that Joash did.

24 Joash[2] was seven years old when he began to reign, and he reigned forty years in Jerusalem. His mother's name was Zibiah of Beersheba. ²And Joash did what was right in the eyes of the LORD all the days of Jehoiada the priest. ³Jehoiada got for him two wives, and he had sons and daughters.

⁴After this Joash decided to restore the house of the LORD. ⁵And he gathered the priests and the Levites and said to them, "Go out to the cities of Judah and gather from all Israel money to repair the house of your God from year to year, and see that you act quickly." But the Levites did not act quickly. ⁶So the king summoned Jehoiada the chief and said to him, "Why have you not required the Levites to bring in from Judah and Jerusalem the tax levied by Moses, the servant of the LORD, and the congregation of Israel for the tent of testimony?" ⁷For the sons of Athaliah, that wicked

---

[1] Or *they made a passage for her* [2] Spelled *Jehoash* in 2 Kings 12:1

woman, had broken into the house of God, and had also used all the dedicated things of the house of the LORD for the Baals.

⁸So the king commanded, and they made a chest and set it outside the gate of the house of the LORD. ⁹And proclamation was made throughout Judah and Jerusalem to bring in for the LORD the tax that Moses the servant of God laid on Israel in the wilderness. ¹⁰And all the princes and all the people rejoiced and brought their tax and dropped it into the chest until they had finished.¹ ¹¹And whenever the chest was brought to the king's officers by the Levites, when they saw that there was much money in it, the king's secretary and the officer of the chief priest would come and empty the chest and take it and return it to its place. Thus they did day after day, and collected money in abundance. ¹²And the king and Jehoiada gave it to those who had charge of the work of the house of the LORD, and they hired masons and carpenters to restore the house of the LORD, and also workers in iron and bronze to repair the house of the LORD. ¹³So those who were engaged in the work labored, and the repairing went forward in their hands, and they restored the house of God to its proper condition and strengthened it. ¹⁴And when they had finished, they brought the rest of the money before the king and Jehoiada, and with it were made utensils for the house of the LORD, both for the service and for the burnt offerings, and dishes for incense and vessels of gold and silver. And they offered burnt offerings in the house of the LORD regularly all the days of Jehoiada.

¹⁵But Jehoiada grew old and full of days, and died. He was 130 years old at his death. ¹⁶And they buried him in the city of David among the kings, because he had done good in Israel, and toward God and his house.

¹⁷Now after the death of Jehoiada the princes of Judah came and paid homage to the king. Then the king listened to them. ¹⁸And they abandoned the house of the LORD, the God of their fathers, and served the Asherim and the idols. And wrath came upon Judah and Jerusalem for this guilt of theirs. ¹⁹Yet he sent prophets among them to bring them back to the LORD. These testified against them, but they would not pay attention.

²⁰Then the Spirit of God clothed Zechariah the son of Jehoiada the priest, and he stood above the people, and said to them, "Thus says God, 'Why do you break the commandments of the LORD, so that you cannot prosper? Because you have forsaken the LORD, he has forsaken you.'" ²¹But they conspired against him, and by command of the king they stoned him with stones in the court of the house of the LORD. ²²Thus Joash the king did not remember the kindness that Jehoiada, Zechariah's father, had shown him, but killed his son. And when he was dying, he said, "May the LORD see and avenge!"²

²³At the end of the year the army of the Syrians came up against Joash. They came to Judah and Jerusalem and destroyed all the princes of the people from among the people and sent all their spoil to the king of Damascus. ²⁴Though the army of the Syrians had come with few men, the LORD delivered into their hand a very great army, because Judah³ had forsaken the LORD, the God of their fathers. Thus they executed judgment on Joash.

²⁵When they had departed from him, leaving him severely wounded, his servants conspired against him because of the blood of the son⁴ of Jehoiada the priest, and killed him on his bed. So he died, and they buried him in the city of David, but they did not bury him in the tombs of the kings. ²⁶Those who conspired against him were

---

¹ Or until it was full ² Hebrew and seek ³ Hebrew they ⁴ Septuagint, Vulgate; Hebrew sons

Zabad the son of Shimeath the Ammonite, and Jehozabad the son of Shimrith the Moabite. ²⁷Accounts of his sons and of the many oracles against him and of the rebuilding¹ of the house of God are written in the Story of the Book of the Kings. And Amaziah his son reigned in his place.

Amaziah's mixed review [chapter 25]. By this point in our progress through 2 Chronicles, it is obvious that the main motif is that a good man is hard to find. Even with the good kings, there is a fly in the ointment—a flaw in the royal throne. The ambiguity of Amaziah's reign is captured right at the outset: "he did what was right in the eyes of the LORD, yet not with a whole heart" (v. 2). The rest of the chapter shows what this means. On the positive side, Amaziah exacts justice regarding the murder of his father (vv. 1–4) and defeats the Edomites by following the counsel of a prophet who has told him not to go to battle allied with the army of Israel (vv. 5–13). But the bad conduct of Amaziah seems to outweigh the good: he sets up idol worship and silences a prophet who objects (vv. 14–16); he is defeated in an ill-advised battle against Israel (vv. 17–24); and he is assassinated by conspirators (vv. 25–28). The story shows where the sin of double-mindedness leads.

25 Amaziah was twenty-five years old when he began to reign, and he reigned twenty-nine years in Jerusalem. His mother's name was Jehoaddan of Jerusalem. ²And he did what was right in the eyes of the LORD, yet not with a whole heart. ³And as soon as the royal power was firmly his, he killed his servants who had struck down the king his father. ⁴But he did not put their children to death, according to what is written in the Law, in the Book of Moses, where the LORD commanded, "Fathers shall not die because of their children, nor children die because of their fathers, but each one shall die for his own sin."

⁵Then Amaziah assembled the men of Judah and set them by fathers' houses under commanders of thousands and of hundreds for all Judah and Benjamin. He mustered those twenty years old and upward, and found that they were 300,000 choice men, fit for war, able to handle spear and shield. ⁶He hired also 100,000 mighty men of valor from Israel for 100 talents² of silver. ⁷But a man of God came to him and said, "O king, do not let the army of Israel go with you, for the LORD is not with Israel, with all these Ephraimites. ⁸But go, act, be strong for the battle. Why should you suppose that God will cast you down before the enemy? For God has power to help or to cast down." ⁹And Amaziah said to the man of God, "But what shall we do about the hundred talents that I have given to the army of Israel?" The man of God answered, "The LORD is able to give you much more than this." ¹⁰Then Amaziah discharged the army that had come to him from Ephraim to go home again. And they became very angry with Judah and returned home in fierce anger. ¹¹But Amaziah took courage and led out his people and went to the Valley of Salt and struck down 10,000 men of Seir. ¹²The men of Judah captured another 10,000 alive and took them to the top of a rock and threw them down from the top of the rock, and they were all dashed to pieces. ¹³But the men of the army whom Amaziah sent back, not letting them go with him to battle, raided the cities of Judah, from Samaria to Beth-horon, and struck down 3,000 people in them and took much spoil.

¹⁴After Amaziah came from striking down the Edomites, he brought the gods of the men of Seir and set them up as his gods and worshiped them, making offerings to

---

¹ Hebrew *founding* ² A *talent* was about 75 pounds or 34 kilograms

them. [15]Therefore the LORD was angry with Amaziah and sent to him a prophet, who said to him, "Why have you sought the gods of a people who did not deliver their own people from your hand?" [16]But as he was speaking, the king said to him, "Have we made you a royal counselor? Stop! Why should you be struck down?" So the prophet stopped, but said, "I know that God has determined to destroy you, because you have done this and have not listened to my counsel."

[17]Then Amaziah king of Judah took counsel and sent to Joash the son of Jehoahaz, son of Jehu, king of Israel, saying, "Come, let us look one another in the face." [18]And Joash the king of Israel sent word to Amaziah king of Judah, "A thistle on Lebanon sent to a cedar on Lebanon, saying, 'Give your daughter to my son for a wife,' and a wild beast of Lebanon passed by and trampled down the thistle. [19]You say, 'See, I[1] have struck down Edom,' and your heart has lifted you up in boastfulness. But now stay at home. Why should you provoke trouble so that you fall, you and Judah with you?"

[20]But Amaziah would not listen, for it was of God, in order that he might give them into the hand of their enemies, because they had sought the gods of Edom. [21]So Joash king of Israel went up, and he and Amaziah king of Judah faced one another in battle at Beth-shemesh, which belongs to Judah. [22]And Judah was defeated by Israel, and every man fled to his home. [23]And Joash king of Israel captured Amaziah king of Judah, the son of Joash, son of Ahaziah, at Beth-shemesh, and brought him to Jerusalem and broke down the wall of Jerusalem for 400 cubits,[2] from the Ephraim Gate to the Corner Gate. [24]And he seized all the gold and silver, and all the vessels that were found in the house of God, in the care of Obed-edom. He seized also the treasuries of the king's house, also hostages, and he returned to Samaria.

[25]Amaziah the son of Joash, king of Judah, lived fifteen years after the death of Joash the son of Jehoahaz, king of Israel. [26]Now the rest of the deeds of Amaziah, from first to last, are they not written in the Book of the Kings of Judah and Israel? [27]From the time when he turned away from the LORD they made a conspiracy against him in Jerusalem, and he fled to Lachish. But they sent after him to Lachish and put him to death there. [28]And they brought him upon horses, and he was buried with his fathers in the city of David.[3]

Uzziah repeats the pattern [chapter 26]. The opening announcement that Uzziah "was sixteen years old when he began to reign" (v. 3) alerts us to a repeated occurrence: many of the kings of Judah came to the throne at what is by modern standards a very young age. By now, too, we should have picked up on the Chronicler's distinctive way of conducting his history. Thus when he tells us that Uzziah "did what was right in the eyes of the LORD, according to all that his father Amaziah had done" (v. 4), we should read that as code that means Uzziah was a combination of good and bad. The history of his rule as recorded by the Chronicler is as follows: the facts of his accession to the throne, along with an assessment that ends with the riddling claim that "as long as he sought the LORD, God made him prosper" (vv. 1–5); details about Uzziah's military resources (vv. 6–15); Uzziah's pride, resulting in God's making him a leper when he attempts to burn incense in the temple (vv. 16–21); obituary-style summing up of his kingship (vv. 22–23).

26 And all the people of Judah took Uzziah, who was sixteen years old, and made him king instead of his father Amaziah. [2]He built Eloth and restored it to Judah, after the king slept with his fathers. [3]Uzziah was sixteen years old when he

---

[1] Hebrew *you* [2] A *cubit* was about 18 inches or 45 centimeters [3] Hebrew *of Judah*

began to reign, and he reigned fifty-two years in Jerusalem. His mother's name was Jecoliah of Jerusalem. [4]And he did what was right in the eyes of the LORD, according to all that his father Amaziah had done. [5]He set himself to seek God in the days of Zechariah, who instructed him in the fear of God, and as long as he sought the LORD, God made him prosper.

[6]He went out and made war against the Philistines and broke through the wall of Gath and the wall of Jabneh and the wall of Ashdod, and he built cities in the territory of Ashdod and elsewhere among the Philistines. [7]God helped him against the Philistines and against the Arabians who lived in Gurbaal and against the Meunites. [8]The Ammonites paid tribute to Uzziah, and his fame spread even to the border of Egypt, for he became very strong. [9]Moreover, Uzziah built towers in Jerusalem at the Corner Gate and at the Valley Gate and at the Angle, and fortified them. [10]And he built towers in the wilderness and cut out many cisterns, for he had large herds, both in the Shephelah and in the plain, and he had farmers and vinedressers in the hills and in the fertile lands, for he loved the soil. [11]Moreover, Uzziah had an army of soldiers, fit for war, in divisions according to the numbers in the muster made by Jeiel the secretary and Maaseiah the officer, under the direction of Hananiah, one of the king's commanders. [12]The whole number of the heads of fathers' houses of mighty men of valor was 2,600. [13]Under their command was an army of 307,500, who could make war with mighty power, to help the king against the enemy. [14]And Uzziah prepared for all the army shields, spears, helmets, coats of mail, bows, and stones for slinging. [15]In Jerusalem he made engines, invented by skillful men, to be on the towers and the corners, to shoot arrows and great stones. And his fame spread far, for he was marvelously helped, till he was strong.

[16]But when he was strong, he grew proud, to his destruction. For he was unfaithful to the LORD his God and entered the temple of the LORD to burn incense on the altar of incense. [17]But Azariah the priest went in after him, with eighty priests of the LORD who were men of valor, [18]and they withstood King Uzziah and said to him, "It is not for you, Uzziah, to burn incense to the LORD, but for the priests, the sons of Aaron, who are consecrated to burn incense. Go out of the sanctuary, for you have done wrong, and it will bring you no honor from the LORD God." [19]Then Uzziah was angry. Now he had a censer in his hand to burn incense, and when he became angry with the priests, leprosy[1] broke out on his forehead in the presence of the priests in the house of the LORD, by the altar of incense. [20]And Azariah the chief priest and all the priests looked at him, and behold, he was leprous in his forehead! And they rushed him out quickly, and he himself hurried to go out, because the LORD had struck him. [21]And King Uzziah was a leper to the day of his death, and being a leper lived in a separate house, for he was excluded from the house of the LORD. And Jotham his son was over the king's household, governing the people of the land.

[22]Now the rest of the acts of Uzziah, from first to last, Isaiah the prophet the son of Amoz wrote. [23]And Uzziah slept with his fathers, and they buried him with his fathers in the burial field that belonged to the kings, for they said, "He is a leper." And Jotham his son reigned in his place.

The reign of Jotham [chapter 27]. The brief nine-verse summary of Jotham's reign teases us into wishing that we knew more. It is primarily a story of political success, but

---

[1] *Leprosy* was a term for several skin diseases; see Leviticus 13

that success is placed within a religious framework of the king's doing "what was right in the eyes of the LORD" (v. 2) and ordering "his ways before the LORD his God" (v. 6). The Chronicler chose not to elaborate on the summary statement that "the people still followed corrupt practices" (v. 2).

27 Jotham was twenty-five years old when he began to reign, and he reigned sixteen years in Jerusalem. His mother's name was Jerushah the daughter of Zadok. ²And he did what was right in the eyes of the LORD according to all that his father Uzziah had done, except he did not enter the temple of the LORD. But the people still followed corrupt practices. ³He built the upper gate of the house of the LORD and did much building on the wall of Ophel. ⁴Moreover, he built cities in the hill country of Judah, and forts and towers on the wooded hills. ⁵He fought with the king of the Ammonites and prevailed against them. And the Ammonites gave him that year 100 talents¹ of silver, and 10,000 cors² of wheat and 10,000 of barley. The Ammonites paid him the same amount in the second and the third years. ⁶So Jotham became mighty, because he ordered his ways before the LORD his God. ⁷Now the rest of the acts of Jotham, and all his wars and his ways, behold, they are written in the Book of the Kings of Israel and Judah. ⁸He was twenty-five years old when he began to reign, and he reigned sixteen years in Jerusalem. ⁹And Jotham slept with his fathers, and they buried him in the city of David, and Ahaz his son reigned in his place.

The rule of Ahaz [chapter 28]. At the outset of the chapter the Chronicler lets us know that Ahaz was an evil ruler (vv. 1–4). According to the author, the great either-or that determined the success or failure of rulers was their spiritual stance toward God. Ahaz's governing trait was his idolatry (vv. 1–4). The failure of his rule unfolds as a litany of military defeats—to Syria (vv. 5–7); to Israel (vv. 8–15); to the Edomites and Assyrians (vv. 16–21). The concluding paragraph (vv. 22–27) is a tissue of warnings to us regarding our religious actions, and a new development is that whereas most of the kings who are recorded as having failed did so when their initial success led them to disregard God, this time the Chronicler marvels that even "in the time of his distress he became yet more faithless to the LORD" (v. 22).

28 Ahaz was twenty years old when he began to reign, and he reigned sixteen years in Jerusalem. And he did not do what was right in the eyes of the LORD, as his father David had done, ²but he walked in the ways of the kings of Israel. He even made metal images for the Baals, ³and he made offerings in the Valley of the Son of Hinnom and burned his sons as an offering,³ according to the abominations of the nations whom the LORD drove out before the people of Israel. ⁴And he sacrificed and made offerings on the high places and on the hills and under every green tree.

⁵Therefore the LORD his God gave him into the hand of the king of Syria, who defeated him and took captive a great number of his people and brought them to Damascus. He was also given into the hand of the king of Israel, who struck him with great force. ⁶For Pekah the son of Remaliah killed 120,000 from Judah in one day, all of them men of valor, because they had forsaken the LORD, the God of their fathers.

---

¹ A *talent* was about 75 pounds or 34 kilograms ² A *cor* was about 6 bushels or 220 liters ³ Hebrew *made his sons pass through the fire*

[7]And Zichri, a mighty man of Ephraim, killed Maaseiah the king's son and Azrikam the commander of the palace and Elkanah the next in authority to the king. [8]The men of Israel took captive 200,000 of their relatives, women, sons, and daughters. They also took much spoil from them and brought the spoil to Samaria. [9]But a prophet of the LORD was there, whose name was Oded, and he went out to meet the army that came to Samaria and said to them, "Behold, because the LORD, the God of your fathers, was angry with Judah, he gave them into your hand, but you have killed them in a rage that has reached up to heaven. [10]And now you intend to subjugate the people of Judah and Jerusalem, male and female, as your slaves. Have you not sins of your own against the LORD your God? [11]Now hear me, and send back the captives from your relatives whom you have taken, for the fierce wrath of the LORD is upon you."

[12]Certain chiefs also of the men of Ephraim, Azariah the son of Johanan, Berechiah the son of Meshillemoth, Jehizkiah the son of Shallum, and Amasa the son of Hadlai, stood up against those who were coming from the war [13]and said to them, "You shall not bring the captives in here, for you propose to bring upon us guilt against the LORD in addition to our present sins and guilt. For our guilt is already great, and there is fierce wrath against Israel." [14]So the armed men left the captives and the spoil before the princes and all the assembly. [15]And the men who have been mentioned by name rose and took the captives, and with the spoil they clothed all who were naked among them. They clothed them, gave them sandals, provided them with food and drink, and anointed them, and carrying all the feeble among them on donkeys, they brought them to their kinsfolk at Jericho, the city of palm trees. Then they returned to Samaria.

[16]At that time King Ahaz sent to the king[1] of Assyria for help. [17]For the Edomites had again invaded and defeated Judah and carried away captives. [18]And the Philistines had made raids on the cities in the Shephelah and the Negeb of Judah, and had taken Beth-shemesh, Aijalon, Gederoth, Soco with its villages, Timnah with its villages, and Gimzo with its villages. And they settled there. [19]For the LORD humbled Judah because of Ahaz king of Israel, for he had made Judah act sinfully[2] and had been very unfaithful to the LORD. [20]So Tiglath-pileser[3] king of Assyria came against him and afflicted him instead of strengthening him. [21]For Ahaz took a portion from the house of the LORD and the house of the king and of the princes, and gave tribute to the king of Assyria, but it did not help him.

[22]In the time of his distress he became yet more faithless to the LORD—this same King Ahaz. [23]For he sacrificed to the gods of Damascus that had defeated him and said, "Because the gods of the kings of Syria helped them, I will sacrifice to them that they may help me." But they were the ruin of him and of all Israel. [24]And Ahaz gathered together the vessels of the house of God and cut in pieces the vessels of the house of God, and he shut up the doors of the house of the LORD, and he made himself altars in every corner of Jerusalem. [25]In every city of Judah he made high places to make offerings to other gods, provoking to anger the LORD, the God of his fathers. [26]Now the rest of his acts and all his ways, from first to last, behold, they are written in the Book of the Kings of Judah and Israel. [27]And Ahaz slept with his fathers, and they buried him in the city, in Jerusalem, for they did not bring him into the tombs of the kings of Israel. And Hezekiah his son reigned in his place.

---

[1] Septuagint, Syriac, Vulgate (compare 2 Kings 16:7); Hebrew *kings* [2] Or *wildly* [3] Hebrew *Tilgath-pilneser*

Hezekiah, king of reforms [chapter 29]. A rhythm has emerged in which the Chronicler usually gives more space to the good kings than to the bad ones. At this point in our progress through 2 Chronicles we have come to long for something positive to break the string of bad kings. We get it with Hezekiah. The first of four chapters devoted to King Hezekiah is a detailed account of the feats that Hezekiah performed in regard to the temple. The catalog includes the following: the king commands the reopening and cleansing of the temple (vv. 1–11); the Levites perform the cleansing (vv. 12–19); the temple is consecrated with music and sacrificial offerings (vv. 20–30); the people bring their sacrificial offerings to the temple amidst rejoicing (vv. 31–36). This is a utopian interlude—a picture of the good society based on the worship of God as the center of the community's life.

29 Hezekiah began to reign when he was twenty-five years old, and he reigned twenty-nine years in Jerusalem. His mother's name was Abijah[1] the daughter of Zechariah. [2]And he did what was right in the eyes of the LORD, according to all that David his father had done.

[3]In the first year of his reign, in the first month, he opened the doors of the house of the LORD and repaired them. [4]He brought in the priests and the Levites and assembled them in the square on the east [5]and said to them, "Hear me, Levites! Now consecrate yourselves, and consecrate the house of the LORD, the God of your fathers, and carry out the filth from the Holy Place. [6]For our fathers have been unfaithful and have done what was evil in the sight of the LORD our God. They have forsaken him and have turned away their faces from the habitation of the LORD and turned their backs. [7]They also shut the doors of the vestibule and put out the lamps and have not burned incense or offered burnt offerings in the Holy Place to the God of Israel. [8]Therefore the wrath of the LORD came on Judah and Jerusalem, and he has made them an object of horror, of astonishment, and of hissing, as you see with your own eyes. [9]For behold, our fathers have fallen by the sword, and our sons and our daughters and our wives are in captivity for this. [10]Now it is in my heart to make a covenant with the LORD, the God of Israel, in order that his fierce anger may turn away from us. [11]My sons, do not now be negligent, for the LORD has chosen you to stand in his presence, to minister to him and to be his ministers and make offerings to him."

[12]Then the Levites arose, Mahath the son of Amasai, and Joel the son of Azariah, of the sons of the Kohathites; and of the sons of Merari, Kish the son of Abdi, and Azariah the son of Jehallelel; and of the Gershonites, Joah the son of Zimmah, and Eden the son of Joah; [13]and of the sons of Elizaphan, Shimri and Jeuel; and of the sons of Asaph, Zechariah and Mattaniah; [14]and of the sons of Heman, Jehuel and Shimei; and of the sons of Jeduthun, Shemaiah and Uzziel. [15]They gathered their brothers and consecrated themselves and went in as the king had commanded, by the words of the LORD, to cleanse the house of the LORD. [16]The priests went into the inner part of the house of the LORD to cleanse it, and they brought out all the uncleanness that they found in the temple of the LORD into the court of the house of the LORD. And the Levites took it and carried it out to the brook Kidron. [17]They began to consecrate on the first day of the first month, and on the eighth day of the month they came to the vestibule of the LORD. Then for eight days they consecrated the house of the LORD, and on the sixteenth day of the first month they finished. [18]Then

---

[1] Spelled *Abi* in 2 Kings 18:2

they went in to Hezekiah the king and said, "We have cleansed all the house of the Lord, the altar of burnt offering and all its utensils, and the table for the showbread and all its utensils. [19]All the utensils that King Ahaz discarded in his reign when he was faithless, we have made ready and consecrated, and behold, they are before the altar of the Lord."

[20]Then Hezekiah the king rose early and gathered the officials of the city and went up to the house of the Lord. [21]And they brought seven bulls, seven rams, seven lambs, and seven male goats for a sin offering for the kingdom and for the sanctuary and for Judah. And he commanded the priests, the sons of Aaron, to offer them on the altar of the Lord. [22]So they slaughtered the bulls, and the priests received the blood and threw it against the altar. And they slaughtered the rams, and their blood was thrown against the altar. And they slaughtered the lambs, and their blood was thrown against the altar. [23]Then the goats for the sin offering were brought to the king and the assembly, and they laid their hands on them, [24]and the priests slaughtered them and made a sin offering with their blood on the altar, to make atonement for all Israel. For the king commanded that the burnt offering and the sin offering should be made for all Israel.

[25]And he stationed the Levites in the house of the Lord with cymbals, harps, and lyres, according to the commandment of David and of Gad the king's seer and of Nathan the prophet, for the commandment was from the Lord through his prophets. [26]The Levites stood with the instruments of David, and the priests with the trumpets. [27]Then Hezekiah commanded that the burnt offering be offered on the altar. And when the burnt offering began, the song to the Lord began also, and the trumpets, accompanied by the instruments of David king of Israel. [28]The whole assembly worshiped, and the singers sang, and the trumpeters sounded. All this continued until the burnt offering was finished. [29]When the offering was finished, the king and all who were present with him bowed themselves and worshiped. [30]And Hezekiah the king and the officials commanded the Levites to sing praises to the Lord with the words of David and of Asaph the seer. And they sang praises with gladness, and they bowed down and worshiped.

[31]Then Hezekiah said, "You have now consecrated yourselves to[1] the Lord. Come near; bring sacrifices and thank offerings to the house of the Lord." And the assembly brought sacrifices and thank offerings, and all who were of a willing heart brought burnt offerings. [32]The number of the burnt offerings that the assembly brought was 70 bulls, 100 rams, and 200 lambs; all these were for a burnt offering to the Lord. [33]And the consecrated offerings were 600 bulls and 3,000 sheep. [34]But the priests were too few and could not flay all the burnt offerings, so until other priests had consecrated themselves, their brothers the Levites helped them, until the work was finished—for the Levites were more upright in heart than the priests in consecrating themselves. [35]Besides the great number of burnt offerings, there was the fat of the peace offerings, and there were the drink offerings for the burnt offerings. Thus the service of the house of the Lord was restored. [36]And Hezekiah and all the people rejoiced because God had prepared for the people, for the thing came about suddenly.

The Passover is celebrated [chapter 30]. The story of Hezekiah's godly rule keeps getting better and better. In this chapter the Passover is celebrated, apparently after

---

[1] Hebrew *filled your hand for*

a long period of neglect. The story begins with Hezekiah sending letters throughout the land summoning people to Jerusalem to celebrate the Passover (vv. 1–12); the people respond and commemorate the Passover according to the rules (vv. 13–22); the celebration is extended for another week (vv. 23–27). The account allows us to relive the excitement of this event and share the joy of its spiritual meaning. The key to the interpretation of the chapter is to pay attention to the references to God and the people's actions as they are oriented toward their purification before God. We can read the account with a view toward answering the question, What attitudes and actions please God? Secondarily, How should people relate to God? This chapter, too, narrates a utopian story of a blessed commonwealth.

30 Hezekiah sent to all Israel and Judah, and wrote letters also to Ephraim and Manasseh, that they should come to the house of the Lord at Jerusalem to keep the Passover to the Lord, the God of Israel. ²For the king and his princes and all the assembly in Jerusalem had taken counsel to keep the Passover in the second month— ³for they could not keep it at that time because the priests had not consecrated themselves in sufficient number, nor had the people assembled in Jerusalem— ⁴and the plan seemed right to the king and all the assembly. ⁵So they decreed to make a proclamation throughout all Israel, from Beersheba to Dan, that the people should come and keep the Passover to the Lord, the God of Israel, at Jerusalem, for they had not kept it as often as prescribed. ⁶So couriers went throughout all Israel and Judah with letters from the king and his princes, as the king had commanded, saying, "O people of Israel, return to the Lord, the God of Abraham, Isaac, and Israel, that he may turn again to the remnant of you who have escaped from the hand of the kings of Assyria. ⁷Do not be like your fathers and your brothers, who were faithless to the Lord God of their fathers, so that he made them a desolation, as you see. ⁸Do not now be stiff-necked as your fathers were, but yield yourselves to the Lord and come to his sanctuary, which he has consecrated forever, and serve the Lord your God, that his fierce anger may turn away from you. ⁹For if you return to the Lord, your brothers and your children will find compassion with their captors and return to this land. For the Lord your God is gracious and merciful and will not turn away his face from you, if you return to him."

¹⁰So the couriers went from city to city through the country of Ephraim and Manasseh, and as far as Zebulun, but they laughed them to scorn and mocked them. ¹¹However, some men of Asher, of Manasseh, and of Zebulun humbled themselves and came to Jerusalem. ¹²The hand of God was also on Judah to give them one heart to do what the king and the princes commanded by the word of the Lord.

¹³And many people came together in Jerusalem to keep the Feast of Unleavened Bread in the second month, a very great assembly. ¹⁴They set to work and removed the altars that were in Jerusalem, and all the altars for burning incense they took away and threw into the Kidron Valley. ¹⁵And they slaughtered the Passover lamb on the fourteenth day of the second month. And the priests and the Levites were ashamed, so that they consecrated themselves and brought burnt offerings into the house of the Lord. ¹⁶They took their accustomed posts according to the Law of Moses the man of God. The priests threw the blood that they received from the hand of the Levites. ¹⁷For there were many in the assembly who had not consecrated themselves.

Therefore the Levites had to slaughter the Passover lamb for everyone who was not clean, to consecrate it to the LORD. [18]For a majority of the people, many of them from Ephraim, Manasseh, Issachar, and Zebulun, had not cleansed themselves, yet they ate the Passover otherwise than as prescribed. For Hezekiah had prayed for them, saying, "May the good LORD pardon everyone [19]who sets his heart to seek God, the LORD, the God of his fathers, even though not according to the sanctuary's rules of cleanness."[1] [20]And the LORD heard Hezekiah and healed the people. [21]And the people of Israel who were present at Jerusalem kept the Feast of Unleavened Bread seven days with great gladness, and the Levites and the priests praised the LORD day by day, singing with all their might[2] to the LORD. [22]And Hezekiah spoke encouragingly to all the Levites who showed good skill in the service of the LORD. So they ate the food of the festival for seven days, sacrificing peace offerings and giving thanks to the LORD, the God of their fathers.

[23]Then the whole assembly agreed together to keep the feast for another seven days. So they kept it for another seven days with gladness. [24]For Hezekiah king of Judah gave the assembly 1,000 bulls and 7,000 sheep for offerings, and the princes gave the assembly 1,000 bulls and 10,000 sheep. And the priests consecrated themselves in great numbers. [25]The whole assembly of Judah, and the priests and the Levites, and the whole assembly that came out of Israel, and the sojourners who came out of the land of Israel, and the sojourners who lived in Judah, rejoiced. [26]So there was great joy in Jerusalem, for since the time of Solomon the son of David king of Israel there had been nothing like this in Jerusalem. [27]Then the priests and the Levites arose and blessed the people, and their voice was heard, and their prayer came to his holy habitation in heaven.

Further religious reforms [chapter 31]. Literature that discusses what makes a ruler good and that portrays good and bad rulers is so extensive that it could make up a whole section of a library. The story of King Hezekiah fits into that literary tradition. Chapter 31 extends the fully elaborated story of Hezekiah's reform of temple worship that began in the preceding chapter. The sequence is as follows: Hezekiah oversees the dismantling of the shrines of idols (v. 1); the priests and Levites are reestablished in their roles as the leaders of worship (v. 2); contributions are collected for the support of those who serve at the temple (vv. 3–10); the priests and Levites are reorganized to enable them to conduct worship at the temple (vv. 11–19); summary statement of Hezekiah's religious reforms (vv. 20–21).

31 Now when all this was finished, all Israel who were present went out to the cities of Judah and broke in pieces the pillars and cut down the Asherim and broke down the high places and the altars throughout all Judah and Benjamin, and in Ephraim and Manasseh, until they had destroyed them all. Then all the people of Israel returned to their cities, every man to his possession.

[2]And Hezekiah appointed the divisions of the priests and of the Levites, division by division, each according to his service, the priests and the Levites, for burnt offerings and peace offerings, to minister in the gates of the camp of the LORD and to give thanks and praise. [3]The contribution of the king from his own possessions was for the burnt offerings: the burnt offerings of morning and evening, and the burnt offerings for the Sabbaths, the new moons, and the appointed feasts, as it is written in the

Law of the LORD. ⁴And he commanded the people who lived in Jerusalem to give the portion due to the priests and the Levites, that they might give themselves to the Law of the LORD. ⁵As soon as the command was spread abroad, the people of Israel gave in abundance the firstfruits of grain, wine, oil, honey, and of all the produce of the field. And they brought in abundantly the tithe of everything. ⁶And the people of Israel and Judah who lived in the cities of Judah also brought in the tithe of cattle and sheep, and the tithe of the dedicated things that had been dedicated to the LORD their God, and laid them in heaps. ⁷In the third month they began to pile up the heaps, and finished them in the seventh month. ⁸When Hezekiah and the princes came and saw the heaps, they blessed the LORD and his people Israel. ⁹And Hezekiah questioned the priests and the Levites about the heaps. ¹⁰Azariah the chief priest, who was of the house of Zadok, answered him, "Since they began to bring the contributions into the house of the LORD, we have eaten and had enough and have plenty left, for the LORD has blessed his people, so that we have this large amount left."

¹¹Then Hezekiah commanded them to prepare chambers in the house of the LORD, and they prepared them. ¹²And they faithfully brought in the contributions, the tithes, and the dedicated things. The chief officer in charge of them was Conaniah the Levite, with Shimei his brother as second, ¹³while Jehiel, Azaziah, Nahath, Asahel, Jerimoth, Jozabad, Eliel, Ismachiah, Mahath, and Benaiah were overseers assisting Conaniah and Shimei his brother, by the appointment of Hezekiah the king and Azariah the chief officer of the house of God. ¹⁴And Kore the son of Imnah the Levite, keeper of the east gate, was over the freewill offerings to God, to apportion the contribution reserved for the LORD and the most holy offerings. ¹⁵Eden, Miniamin, Jeshua, Shemaiah, Amariah, and Shecaniah were faithfully assisting him in the cities of the priests, to distribute the portions to their brothers, old and young alike, by divisions, ¹⁶except those enrolled by genealogy, males from three years old and upward—all who entered the house of the LORD as the duty of each day required—for their service according to their offices, by their divisions. ¹⁷The enrollment of the priests was according to their fathers' houses; that of the Levites from twenty years old and upward was according to their offices, by their divisions. ¹⁸They were enrolled with all their little children, their wives, their sons, and their daughters, the whole assembly, for they were faithful in keeping themselves holy. ¹⁹And for the sons of Aaron, the priests, who were in the fields of common land belonging to their cities, there were men in the several cities who were designated by name to distribute portions to every male among the priests and to everyone among the Levites who was enrolled.

²⁰Thus Hezekiah did throughout all Judah, and he did what was good and right and faithful before the LORD his God. ²¹And every work that he undertook in the service of the house of God and in accordance with the law and the commandments, seeking his God, he did with all his heart, and prospered.

Hezekiah deals with a military threat [chapter 32]. The story narrated in this chapter is one of the memorable stories of the OT. The story follows a classic problem-solution format. The problem comes in the form of Sennacherib's invasion of Judah (v. 1). Hezekiah's immediate response is to fortify Jerusalem (vv. 2–8). Sennacherib king of Assyria responds to that by sending letters to the populace of Jerusalem urging them to defect from Hezekiah and surrender to him (vv. 9–19); God responds to Hezekiah's prayer for deliverance by killing the army of Sennacherib (vv. 20–23). The battle story is followed by the personal story of Hezekiah's illness, pride, and repentance (vv. 24–26). We then get a summary of Hezekiah's prosperity (vv. 27–30) and a very truncated account (v. 31) of an event recorded at greater length in 2 Kings 20:12–19 concerning Hezekiah's folly in showing off his treasures to the emissaries of the king of Babylon. The customary formulas are used to record the death of Hezekiah and succession of the throne (vv. 32–33).

32 After these things and these acts of faithfulness, Sennacherib king of Assyria came and invaded Judah and encamped against the fortified cities, thinking to win them for himself. ²And when Hezekiah saw that Sennacherib had come and intended to fight against Jerusalem, ³he planned with his officers and his mighty men to stop the water of the springs that were outside the city; and they helped him. ⁴A great many people were gathered, and they stopped all the springs and the brook that flowed through the land, saying, "Why should the kings of Assyria come and find much water?" ⁵He set to work resolutely and built up all the wall that was broken down and raised towers upon it,¹ and outside it he built another wall, and he strengthened the Millo in the city of David. He also made weapons and shields in abundance. ⁶And he set combat commanders over the people and gathered them together to him in the square at the gate of the city and spoke encouragingly to them, saying, ⁷"Be strong and courageous. Do not be afraid or dismayed before the king of Assyria and all the horde that is with him, for there are more with us than with him. ⁸With him is an arm of flesh, but with us is the Lᴏʀᴅ our God, to help us and to fight our battles." And the people took confidence from the words of Hezekiah king of Judah.

⁹After this, Sennacherib king of Assyria, who was besieging Lachish with all his forces, sent his servants to Jerusalem to Hezekiah king of Judah and to all the people of Judah who were in Jerusalem, saying, ¹⁰"Thus says Sennacherib king of Assyria, 'On what are you trusting, that you endure the siege in Jerusalem? ¹¹Is not Hezekiah misleading you, that he may give you over to die by famine and by thirst, when he tells you, "The Lᴏʀᴅ our God will deliver us from the hand of the king of Assyria"? ¹²Has not this same Hezekiah taken away his high places and his altars and commanded Judah and Jerusalem, "Before one altar you shall worship, and on it you shall burn your sacrifices"? ¹³Do you not know what I and my fathers have done to all the peoples of other lands? Were the gods of the nations of those lands at all able to deliver their lands out of my hand? ¹⁴Who among all the gods of those nations that my fathers devoted to destruction was able to deliver his people from my hand, that your God should be able to deliver you from my hand? ¹⁵Now, therefore, do not let Hezekiah deceive you or mislead you in this fashion, and do not believe him, for no god of any nation or kingdom has been able to deliver his people from my hand or from the hand of my fathers. How much less will your God deliver you out of my hand!'"

¹⁶And his servants said still more against the Lᴏʀᴅ God and against his servant Hezekiah. ¹⁷And he wrote letters to cast contempt on the Lᴏʀᴅ, the God of Israel, and to speak against him, saying, "Like the gods of the nations of the lands who have not delivered their people from my hands, so the God of Hezekiah will not deliver his people from my hand." ¹⁸And they shouted it with a loud voice in the language of

¹ Vulgate; Hebrew *and raised upon the towers*

Judah to the people of Jerusalem who were on the wall, to frighten and terrify them, in order that they might take the city. ¹⁹And they spoke of the God of Jerusalem as they spoke of the gods of the peoples of the earth, which are the work of men's hands.

²⁰Then Hezekiah the king and Isaiah the prophet, the son of Amoz, prayed because of this and cried to heaven. ²¹And the Lord sent an angel, who cut off all the mighty warriors and commanders and officers in the camp of the king of Assyria. So he returned with shame of face to his own land. And when he came into the house of his god, some of his own sons struck him down there with the sword. ²²So the Lord saved Hezekiah and the inhabitants of Jerusalem from the hand of Sennacherib king of Assyria and from the hand of all his enemies, and he provided for them on every side. ²³And many brought gifts to the Lord to Jerusalem and precious things to Hezekiah king of Judah, so that he was exalted in the sight of all nations from that time onward.

²⁴In those days Hezekiah became sick and was at the point of death, and he prayed to the Lord, and he answered him and gave him a sign. ²⁵But Hezekiah did not make return according to the benefit done to him, for his heart was proud. Therefore wrath came upon him and Judah and Jerusalem. ²⁶But Hezekiah humbled himself for the pride of his heart, both he and the inhabitants of Jerusalem, so that the wrath of the Lord did not come upon them in the days of Hezekiah.

²⁷And Hezekiah had very great riches and honor, and he made for himself treasuries for silver, for gold, for precious stones, for spices, for shields, and for all kinds of costly vessels; ²⁸storehouses also for the yield of grain, wine, and oil; and stalls for all kinds of cattle, and sheepfolds. ²⁹He likewise provided cities for himself, and flocks and herds in abundance, for God had given him very great possessions. ³⁰This same Hezekiah closed the upper outlet of the waters of Gihon and directed them down to the west side of the city of David. And Hezekiah prospered in all his works. ³¹And so in the matter of the envoys of the princes of Babylon, who had been sent to him to inquire about the sign that had been done in the land, God left him to himself, in order to test him and to know all that was in his heart.

³²Now the rest of the acts of Hezekiah and his good deeds, behold, they are written in the vision of Isaiah the prophet the son of Amoz, in the Book of the Kings of Judah and Israel. ³³And Hezekiah slept with his fathers, and they buried him in the upper part of the tombs of the sons of David, and all Judah and the inhabitants of Jerusalem did him honor at his death. And Manasseh his son reigned in his place.

"Good with bad expect to hear" [chapter 33]. The vision of fallen human history that concludes Milton's epic Paradise Lost is governed by the formula "good with bad expect to hear." Chapter 33 reenacts this same rhythm. It records the facts surrounding the reigns of two evil kings. Manasseh totally misleads the nation into the worst idol worship that can be imagined (vv. 1–9). But in keeping with the ambivalent behavior of most of the kings about whom we read in 2 Chronicles, when Manasseh is captured by the king of Assyria, he repents and is restored to his kingship (vv. 10–13). Thereafter he destroys the idols in the land and restores the true worship of God (vv. 14–20), reversing the pattern elsewhere in 2 Chronicles by being a king who ends better than he began. Amon is the archetypal evil king who is assassinated by his own servants (vv. 21–25).

33 Manasseh was twelve years old when he began to reign, and he reigned fifty-five years in Jerusalem. [2]And he did what was evil in the sight of the Lord, according to the abominations of the nations whom the Lord drove out before the people of Israel. [3]For he rebuilt the high places that his father Hezekiah had broken down, and he erected altars to the Baals, and made Asherahs, and worshiped all the host of heaven and served them. [4]And he built altars in the house of the Lord, of which the Lord had said, "In Jerusalem shall my name be forever." [5]And he built altars for all the host of heaven in the two courts of the house of the Lord. [6]And he burned his sons as an offering in the Valley of the Son of Hinnom, and used fortune-telling and omens and sorcery, and dealt with mediums and with necromancers. He did much evil in the sight of the Lord, provoking him to anger. [7]And the carved image of the idol that he had made he set in the house of God, of which God said to David and to Solomon his son, "In this house, and in Jerusalem, which I have chosen out of all the tribes of Israel, I will put my name forever, [8]and I will no more remove the foot of Israel from the land that I appointed for your fathers, if only they will be careful to do all that I have commanded them, all the law, the statutes, and the rules given through Moses." [9]Manasseh led Judah and the inhabitants of Jerusalem astray, to do more evil than the nations whom the Lord destroyed before the people of Israel.

[10]The Lord spoke to Manasseh and to his people, but they paid no attention. [11]Therefore the Lord brought upon them the commanders of the army of the king of Assyria, who captured Manasseh with hooks and bound him with chains of bronze and brought him to Babylon. [12]And when he was in distress, he entreated the favor of the Lord his God and humbled himself greatly before the God of his fathers. [13]He prayed to him, and God was moved by his entreaty and heard his plea and brought him again to Jerusalem into his kingdom. Then Manasseh knew that the Lord was God.

[14]Afterward he built an outer wall for the city of David west of Gihon, in the valley, and for the entrance into the Fish Gate, and carried it around Ophel, and raised it to a very great height. He also put commanders of the army in all the fortified cities in Judah. [15]And he took away the foreign gods and the idol from the house of the Lord, and all the altars that he had built on the mountain of the house of the Lord and in Jerusalem, and he threw them outside of the city. [16]He also restored the altar of the Lord and offered on it sacrifices of peace offerings and of thanksgiving, and he commanded Judah to serve the Lord, the God of Israel. [17]Nevertheless, the people still sacrificed at the high places, but only to the Lord their God.

[18]Now the rest of the acts of Manasseh, and his prayer to his God, and the words of the seers who spoke to him in the name of the Lord, the God of Israel, behold, they are in the Chronicles of the Kings of Israel. [19]And his prayer, and how God was moved by his entreaty, and all his sin and his faithlessness, and the sites on which he built high places and set up the Asherim and the images, before he humbled himself, behold, they are written in the Chronicles of the Seers.[1] [20]So Manasseh slept with his fathers, and they buried him in his house, and Amon his son reigned in his place.

[21]Amon was twenty-two years old when he began to reign, and he reigned two years in Jerusalem. [22]And he did what was evil in the sight of the Lord, as Manasseh his father had done. Amon sacrificed to all the images that Manasseh his father had made, and served them. [23]And he did not humble himself before the Lord, as Manasseh his father had humbled himself, but this Amon incurred guilt more and

---

[1] One Hebrew manuscript, Septuagint; most Hebrew manuscripts *of Hozai*

more. ²⁴And his servants conspired against him and put him to death in his house. ²⁵But the people of the land struck down all those who had conspired against King Amon. And the people of the land made Josiah his son king in his place.

The pendulum swings [chapter 34]. Second Chronicles is based on a back-and-forth movement between good kings and bad kings. With Josiah we return to the positive mode, and Josiah accordingly gets extended treatment. In a book famous for its striking moments, this chapter contains the account of the discovery of the Book of the Law in the temple. The sequence is as follows: Josiah comes to the throne at the age of eight and in the eighth year of his reign removes pagan altars from the land (vv. 1–7); Josiah initiates the repair of the temple (vv. 8–13); the Book of the Law is discovered in the temple (vv. 14–18); Josiah is devastated by the content of the law as it is read to him, and he commands his servant to inquire of a prophetess what the implications of non-compliance with the law will be (vv. 19–21); the prophetess confirms that God's anger rests on people who ignore his law, but she adds that because Josiah is penitent he will escape the judgment that God will send on Judah (vv. 22–28); Josiah orchestrates a national covenant with God to obey the law (vv. 29–33). The mainspring of the action is a discovery story and a repentance story, both pointing us to the theme that the Word of God brings reformation and renewal to a kingdom whose king honors that Word.

34

Josiah was eight years old when he began to reign, and he reigned thirty-one years in Jerusalem. ²And he did what was right in the eyes of the LORD, and walked in the ways of David his father; and he did not turn aside to the right hand or to the left. ³For in the eighth year of his reign, while he was yet a boy, he began to seek the God of David his father, and in the twelfth year he began to purge Judah and Jerusalem of the high places, the Asherim, and the carved and the metal images. ⁴And they chopped down the altars of the Baals in his presence, and he cut down the incense altars that stood above them. And he broke in pieces the Asherim and the carved and the metal images, and he made dust of them and scattered it over the graves of those who had sacrificed to them. ⁵He also burned the bones of the priests on their altars and cleansed Judah and Jerusalem. ⁶And in the cities of Manasseh, Ephraim, and Simeon, and as far as Naphtali, in their ruins¹ all around, ⁷he broke down the altars and beat the Asherim and the images into powder and cut down all the incense altars throughout all the land of Israel. Then he returned to Jerusalem.

⁸Now in the eighteenth year of his reign, when he had cleansed the land and the house, he sent Shaphan the son of Azaliah, and Maaseiah the governor of the city, and Joah the son of Joahaz, the recorder, to repair the house of the LORD his God. ⁹They came to Hilkiah the high priest and gave him the money that had been brought into the house of God, which the Levites, the keepers of the threshold, had collected from Manasseh and Ephraim and from all the remnant of Israel and from all Judah and Benjamin and from the inhabitants of Jerusalem. ¹⁰And they gave it to the workmen who were working in the house of the LORD. And the workmen who were working in the house of the LORD gave it for repairing and restoring the house. ¹¹They gave it to the carpenters and the builders to buy quarried stone, and timber for binders and beams for the buildings that the kings of Judah had let go to ruin. ¹²And the men did the work faithfully. Over them were set Jahath and Obadiah the Levites, of the sons of Merari, and Zechariah and Meshullam, of the sons of the Kohathites, to have

---

¹ The meaning of the Hebrew is uncertain

oversight. The Levites, all who were skillful with instruments of music, [13]were over the burden-bearers and directed all who did work in every kind of service, and some of the Levites were scribes and officials and gatekeepers.

[14]While they were bringing out the money that had been brought into the house of the LORD, Hilkiah the priest found the Book of the Law of the LORD given through Moses. [15]Then Hilkiah answered and said to Shaphan the secretary, "I have found the Book of the Law in the house of the LORD." And Hilkiah gave the book to Shaphan. [16]Shaphan brought the book to the king, and further reported to the king, "All that was committed to your servants they are doing. [17]They have emptied out the money that was found in the house of the LORD and have given it into the hand of the overseers and the workmen." [18]Then Shaphan the secretary told the king, "Hilkiah the priest has given me a book." And Shaphan read from it before the king.

[19]And when the king heard the words of the Law, he tore his clothes. [20]And the king commanded Hilkiah, Ahikam the son of Shaphan, Abdon the son of Micah, Shaphan the secretary, and Asaiah the king's servant, saying, [21]"Go, inquire of the LORD for me and for those who are left in Israel and in Judah, concerning the words of the book that has been found. For great is the wrath of the LORD that is poured out on us, because our fathers have not kept the word of the LORD, to do according to all that is written in this book."

[22]So Hilkiah and those whom the king had sent[1] went to Huldah the prophetess, the wife of Shallum the son of Tokhath, son of Hasrah, keeper of the wardrobe (now she lived in Jerusalem in the Second Quarter) and spoke to her to that effect. [23]And she said to them, "Thus says the LORD, the God of Israel: 'Tell the man who sent you to me, [24]Thus says the LORD, Behold, I will bring disaster upon this place and upon its inhabitants, all the curses that are written in the book that was read before the king of Judah. [25]Because they have forsaken me and have made offerings to other gods, that they might provoke me to anger with all the works of their hands, therefore my wrath will be poured out on this place and will not be quenched. [26]But to the king of Judah, who sent you to inquire of the LORD, thus shall you say to him, Thus says the LORD, the God of Israel: Regarding the words that you have heard, [27]because your heart was tender and you humbled yourself before God when you heard his words against this place and its inhabitants, and you have humbled yourself before me and have torn your clothes and wept before me, I also have heard you, declares the LORD. [28]Behold, I will gather you to your fathers, and you shall be gathered to your grave in peace, and your eyes shall not see all the disaster that I will bring upon this place and its inhabitants.'" And they brought back word to the king.

[29]Then the king sent and gathered together all the elders of Judah and Jerusalem. [30]And the king went up to the house of the LORD, with all the men of Judah and the inhabitants of Jerusalem and the priests and the Levites, all the people both great and small. And he read in their hearing all the words of the Book of the Covenant that had been found in the house of the LORD. [31]And the king stood in his place and made a covenant before the LORD, to walk after the LORD and to keep his commandments and his testimonies and his statutes, with all his heart and all his soul, to perform the words of the covenant that were written in this book. [32]Then he made all who were present in Jerusalem and in Benjamin join in it. And the inhabitants of Jerusalem did according to the covenant of God, the God of their fathers. [33]And Josiah took away all the abominations from all the territory that belonged to the people of Israel and

---

[1] Syriac, Vulgate; Hebrew lacks *had sent*

made all who were present in Israel serve the LORD their God. All his days they did not turn away from following the LORD, the God of their fathers.

Reinstitution of the Passover [35:1–19]. Second Chronicles is a court history in which we hear almost nothing about the personal and domestic lives of the kings. What we hear about is their practice or nonpractice of public religion and their successes and failures on the battlefield. This unit continues the idealized record of Josiah's restoration of the religious life of the covenant people of God. The main action is the reinstitution of the Passover. The quantity of details signals the importance of what happened—a picture of the priority of worship in the ideal community.

35 Josiah kept a Passover to the LORD in Jerusalem. And they slaughtered the Passover lamb on the fourteenth day of the first month. ²He appointed the priests to their offices and encouraged them in the service of the house of the LORD. ³And he said to the Levites who taught all Israel and who were holy to the LORD, "Put the holy ark in the house that Solomon the son of David, king of Israel, built. You need not carry it on your shoulders. Now serve the LORD your God and his people Israel. ⁴Prepare yourselves according to your fathers' houses by your divisions, as prescribed in the writing of David king of Israel and the document of Solomon his son. ⁵And stand in the Holy Place according to the groupings of the fathers' houses of your brothers the lay people, and according to the division of the Levites by fathers' household. ⁶And slaughter the Passover lamb, and consecrate yourselves, and prepare for your brothers, to do according to the word of the LORD by Moses."

⁷Then Josiah contributed to the lay people, as Passover offerings for all who were present, lambs and young goats from the flock to the number of 30,000, and 3,000 bulls; these were from the king's possessions. ⁸And his officials contributed willingly to the people, to the priests, and to the Levites. Hilkiah, Zechariah, and Jehiel, the chief officers of the house of God, gave to the priests for the Passover offerings 2,600 Passover lambs and 300 bulls. ⁹Conaniah also, and Shemaiah and Nethanel his brothers, and Hashabiah and Jeiel and Jozabad, the chiefs of the Levites, gave to the Levites for the Passover offerings 5,000 lambs and young goats and 500 bulls.

¹⁰When the service had been prepared for, the priests stood in their place, and the Levites in their divisions according to the king's command. ¹¹And they slaughtered the Passover lamb, and the priests threw the blood that they received from them while the Levites flayed the sacrifices. ¹²And they set aside the burnt offerings that they might distribute them according to the groupings of the fathers' houses of the lay people, to offer to the LORD, as it is written in the Book of Moses. And so they did with the bulls. ¹³And they roasted the Passover lamb with fire according to the rule; and they boiled the holy offerings in pots, in cauldrons, and in pans, and carried them quickly to all the lay people. ¹⁴And afterward they prepared for themselves and for the priests, because the priests, the sons of Aaron, were offering the burnt offerings and the fat parts until night; so the Levites prepared for themselves and for the priests, the sons of Aaron. ¹⁵The singers, the sons of Asaph, were in their place according to the command of David, and Asaph, and Heman, and Jeduthun the king's seer; and the gatekeepers were at each gate. They did not need to depart from their service, for their brothers the Levites prepared for them.

¹⁶So all the service of the LORD was prepared that day, to keep the Passover and to offer burnt offerings on the altar of the LORD, according to the command of King Josiah. ¹⁷And the people of Israel who were present kept the Passover at that time, and the Feast of Unleavened Bread seven days. ¹⁸No Passover like it had been kept in Israel since the days of Samuel the prophet. None of the kings of Israel had kept such a Passover as was kept by Josiah, and the priests and the Levites, and all Judah and Israel who were present, and the inhabitants of Jerusalem. ¹⁹In the eighteenth year of the reign of Josiah this Passover was kept.

Josiah's end [35:20–27]. Given the previous accounts of kings who began well and ended badly, the foregoing story of Josiah's reign might well seem too good to be true. It wasn't, but our suspicions that there must be something negative in Josiah's kingly career turn out to be true. Josiah pays a heavy price—his own death—for foolishly engaging the king of Egypt in battle (vv. 20–24a). But the Chronicler refuses to elaborate the negative aspect of Josiah's rule, and the concluding formulaic summary of his career accentuates the positive, as we even hear a reference to Jeremiah's uttering a lament for Josiah (vv. 24b–27).

²⁰After all this, when Josiah had prepared the temple, Neco king of Egypt went up to fight at Carchemish on the Euphrates, and Josiah went out to meet him. ²¹But he sent envoys to him, saying, "What have we to do with each other, king of Judah? I am not coming against you this day, but against the house with which I am at war. And God has commanded me to hurry. Cease opposing God, who is with me, lest he destroy you." ²²Nevertheless, Josiah did not turn away from him, but disguised himself in order to fight with him. He did not listen to the words of Neco from the mouth of God, but came to fight in the plain of Megiddo. ²³And the archers shot King Josiah. And the king said to his servants, "Take me away, for I am badly wounded." ²⁴So his servants took him out of the chariot and carried him in his second chariot and brought him to Jerusalem. And he died and was buried in the tombs of his fathers. All Judah and Jerusalem mourned for Josiah. ²⁵Jeremiah also uttered a lament for Josiah; and all the singing men and singing women have spoken of Josiah in their laments to this day. They made these a rule in Israel; behold, they are written in the Laments. ²⁶Now the rest of the acts of Josiah, and his good deeds according to what is written in the Law of the LORD, ²⁷and his acts, first and last, behold, they are written in the Book of the Kings of Israel and Judah.

The end of a nation [chapter 36]. The keynote of the last chapter is captivity. It is as though the final kings of Judah whiz past us here at the end of the book. Three successive kings are taken captive by enemies—Jehoahaz by Egypt (vv. 1–4), Jehoiakim by Babylon (vv. 5–8), and Jehoiachin by Babylon (vv. 9–10). The accounts are brief, but there are enough concrete particulars to hint at stories of tragedy (such as the fetters in which Jehoiakim is taken to Babylon). Given the potential of the nation to be blessed by God (as we have glimpses of it with the accounts of good kings), its decline into repudiation of God and his prophets finally becomes sickening to read (vv. 11–16). It is with a sense of justice satisfied that we read about the decisive end that Babylon made of the nation (vv. 17–21). The overall national history of 2 Chronicles follows the same pattern that we see in most of the kings: it is a story in which early promise ends in spiritual defeat. In an unexpected coda (vv. 22–23), the book fast-forwards to the time of the return of a remnant from Persia back to Jerusalem. The narrative principle of "end stress" should not escape us here: the final word of 2 Chronicles is not defeat but renewal, as God's redemptive plan is stronger than human failure.

36

The people of the land took Jehoahaz the son of Josiah and made him king in his father's place in Jerusalem. ²Jehoahaz was twenty-three years old when he began to reign, and he reigned three months in Jerusalem. ³Then the king of Egypt deposed him in Jerusalem and laid on the land a tribute of a hundred talents of silver and a talent¹ of gold. ⁴And the king of Egypt made Eliakim his brother king over Judah and Jerusalem, and changed his name to Jehoiakim. But Neco took Jehoahaz his brother and carried him to Egypt.

⁵Jehoiakim was twenty-five years old when he began to reign, and he reigned eleven years in Jerusalem. He did what was evil in the sight of the LORD his God. ⁶Against him came up Nebuchadnezzar king of Babylon and bound him in chains to take him to Babylon. ⁷Nebuchadnezzar also carried part of the vessels of the house of the LORD to Babylon and put them in his palace in Babylon. ⁸Now the rest of the acts of Jehoiakim, and the abominations that he did, and what was found against him, behold, they are written in the Book of the Kings of Israel and Judah. And Jehoiachin his son reigned in his place.

⁹Jehoiachin was eighteen² years old when he became king, and he reigned three months and ten days in Jerusalem. He did what was evil in the sight of the LORD. ¹⁰In the spring of the year King Nebuchadnezzar sent and brought him to Babylon, with the precious vessels of the house of the LORD, and made his brother Zedekiah king over Judah and Jerusalem.

¹¹Zedekiah was twenty-one years old when he began to reign, and he reigned eleven years in Jerusalem. ¹²He did what was evil in the sight of the LORD his God. He did not humble himself before Jeremiah the prophet, who spoke from the mouth of the LORD. ¹³He also rebelled against King Nebuchadnezzar, who had made him swear by God. He stiffened his neck and hardened his heart against turning to the LORD, the God of Israel. ¹⁴All the officers of the priests and the people likewise were exceedingly unfaithful, following all the abominations of the nations. And they polluted the house of the LORD that he had made holy in Jerusalem.

¹⁵The LORD, the God of their fathers, sent persistently to them by his messengers, because he had compassion on his people and on his dwelling place. ¹⁶But they kept mocking the messengers of God, despising his words and scoffing at his prophets, until the wrath of the LORD rose against his people, until there was no remedy.

¹⁷Therefore he brought up against them the king of the Chaldeans, who killed their young men with the sword in the house of their sanctuary and had no compassion on young man or virgin, old man or aged. He gave them all into his hand. ¹⁸And all the vessels of the house of God, great and small, and the treasures of the house of the LORD, and the treasures of the king and of his princes, all these he brought to Babylon. ¹⁹And they burned the house of God and broke down the wall of Jerusalem and burned all its palaces with fire and destroyed all its precious vessels. ²⁰He took into exile in Babylon those who had escaped from the sword, and they became ser-

¹ A *talent* was about 75 pounds or 34 kilograms ² Septuagint (compare 2 Kings 24:8); most Hebrew manuscripts *eight*

vants to him and to his sons until the establishment of the kingdom of Persia, [21]to fulfill the word of the Lord by the mouth of Jeremiah, until the land had enjoyed its Sabbaths. All the days that it lay desolate it kept Sabbath, to fulfill seventy years.

[22]Now in the first year of Cyrus king of Persia, that the word of the Lord by the mouth of Jeremiah might be fulfilled, the Lord stirred up the spirit of Cyrus king of Persia, so that he made a proclamation throughout all his kingdom and also put it in writing: [23]"Thus says Cyrus king of Persia, 'The Lord, the God of heaven, has given me all the kingdoms of the earth, and he has charged me to build him a house at Jerusalem, which is in Judah. Whoever is among you of all his people, may the Lord his God be with him. Let him go up.'"

EZRA

The book at a glance. 10 chapters, 280 verses. The book of Ezra is a *return story that recounts the events that made up the first and second returns to the land of Israel by a remnant of Jews who survived the Babylonian captivity of Judah. By means of this particular historical situation, we are intended to learn how people in the believing community can conduct their lives in a way that pleases God. More than half a century separated the two returns narrated in this book. The primary impulse of the author is documentary: to record the historical facts surrounding the two returns to Palestine—sometimes in the form of lists and inventories, sometimes in the form of *narrative or story. However, this documentary aim is combined with a religious impulse to choose events from the era that teach lessons about God's covenant faithfulness and the need for his people to maintain high standards of holiness in their communal and personal lives. The book is named after the protagonist and likely author of the book, whose priestly ministry provided spiritual leadership for the returning remnant of the people of God.

▌**Genres.** The primary form is historical narrative, in the specific form of a return story that narrates the return of groups of people to their homeland after exile (a pattern made famous in ancient Greek literature by Homer's *Odyssey*). But the flow of the story is interrupted by a variety of documentary material—lists of people and supplies, transcripts of official documents, the *genealogy of Ezra, royal and other official letters, memoirs, and prayers. Sometimes the material tells a story; at other times it resembles the daily newspaper or archived material. (For more information on items accompanied by an asterisk, see the glossary at the back of this Bible.)

▌**The story line and key characters.** The overall story has to do with the return of exiles from captivity in Babylon. The opening verse of the book makes it clear that the two returns narrated in the book of Ezra were a fulfillment of earlier prophecies that a remnant would return after seventy years of captivity (relevant passages include Isa. 45:1–5, 13 and Jer. 5:11–12; 29:10). Upon their return, the settlers did what settlers always do—they restored life along the lines of what it had been like before the exile. We get a picture of covenant life starting over again, in keeping with the priorities that this particular nation had always been commanded to follow. The central character in this story of starting over is Ezra. He is a decisive character whose arrival with the second wave of returnees causes sparks to fly. Characters of secondary importance include three Persian kings (Cyrus, Darius, and Artaxerxes), Zerubbabel (who leads the

Passage	Content	Story Line	Main Action
1:1–11	Preparations for the return	First return	
2:1–70	Lists of those who returned		
3:1–13	Beginning of the rebuilding of the temple		Restoration under Zerubbabel
4:1–5:17	The rebuilding halted by a hostile challenge	Rebuilding the temple	
6:1–22	Rebuilding permitted and completed		
7:1–28	Royal permission for a remnant of Jews to return	Second return	
8:1–36	Return of the remnant		Reform under Ezra
9:1–10:44	Ezra puts a decisive end to intermarriage	Reforming the life of the community	

first return and the rebuilding of the temple), the workers who rebuild the temple, and ignominious Israelites who have married foreign women with pagan worship practices.

Unifying motifs. (1) The atmosphere of new beginnings—of institutional life being revived along old and established lines. (2) The writer's preoccupation with the reporting of facts. (3) The prominent role of strong leaders. (4) The centrality of religious concerns such as worship, obedience to God's law, and prayer in the life of the believing community.

Inferred literary intentions. The book is designed to achieve the following literary purposes:

- captivate us with the excitement of life starting over in the homeland after exile
- allow us to relive events of the two returns and resettlement in the old country
- show by the events in the story that God is displeased when his people do not take his commands seriously
- relish such narrative qualities as conflict, suspense, and ordeal
- activate us to see what is universal about the historical particulars

Theological themes. (1) Providence: the story is an account of how God directed events to a favorable conclusion for his chosen nation. (2) Holiness: especially in the second half of the book, we see the need for God's people to remain spiritually separate from unbelief. (3) Covenant: the events highlight that the history being recounted is the history of the covenant nation of Israel, whose covenant with God is renewed and restored.

The book of Ezra as a chapter in the master story of the Bible. In the OT, the story of redemptive history that spans the entire Bible focuses on the specific nation of Israel (both the people and their land). The return of the exiles to their homeland is an important phase in the national history of Israel, and it entwines with another important thread in the master story of the Bible: how God wants his people to live and how he wants them *not* to live.

Preparations for the return of a remnant [chapter 1]. The opening chapter gets the return story started with an account of events that eventually lead to the return. The outline is as follows: an edict from Cyrus, king of Persia, invites Jews to return to Jerusalem to build a temple (vv. 1–4); a remnant responds with willingness to return (vv. 5–6); an inventory of treasures of the earlier temple that Cyrus dispatches with the returnees (vv. 7–11). We should read the chapter in the spirit of anticipation that the events inspired in the people about whom we read.

---

1 In the first year of Cyrus king of Persia, that the word of the LORD by the mouth of Jeremiah might be fulfilled, the LORD stirred up the spirit of Cyrus king of Persia, so that he made a proclamation throughout all his kingdom and also put it in writing:

²"Thus says Cyrus king of Persia: The LORD, the God of heaven, has given me all the kingdoms of the earth, and he has charged me to build him a house at Jerusalem, which is in Judah. ³Whoever is among you of all his people, may his God be with him, and let him go up to Jerusalem, which is in Judah, and rebuild the house of the LORD, the God of Israel—he is the God who is in Jerusalem. ⁴And let each survivor, in whatever place he sojourns, be assisted by the men of his place with silver and gold, with goods and with beasts, besides freewill offerings for the house of God that is in Jerusalem."

⁵Then rose up the heads of the fathers' houses of Judah and Benjamin, and the priests and the Levites, everyone whose spirit God had stirred to go up to rebuild the house of the LORD that is in Jerusalem. ⁶And all who were about them aided them with vessels of silver, with gold, with goods, with beasts, and with costly wares, besides all that was freely offered. ⁷Cyrus the king also brought out the vessels of the house of the LORD that Nebuchadnezzar had carried away from Jerusalem and placed in the house of his gods. ⁸Cyrus king of Persia brought these out in the charge of Mithredath the treasurer, who counted them out to Sheshbazzar the prince of Judah. ⁹And this was the number of them: 30 basins of gold, 1,000 basins of silver, 29 censers, ¹⁰30 bowls of gold, 410 bowls of silver, and 1,000 other vessels; ¹¹all the vessels of gold and of silver were 5,400. All these did Sheshbazzar bring up, when the exiles were brought up from Babylonia to Jerusalem.

Lists of those who returned [chapter 2]. Ezra was both a priest and a scribe (7:11), and the temperament of a scribe or recorder is fully evident in Ezra 2. The most obvious lesson that we learn from these lists of names is that the Bible is a historical document in which real events and real people are shown to matter to God and to the writers of the Bible. Although many of the names are unfamiliar to us, they serve to remind us that we, too, are known by God and that one day God will bring us home too.

2 Now these were the people of the province who came up out of the captivity of those exiles whom Nebuchadnezzar the king of Babylon had carried captive to Babylonia. They returned to Jerusalem and Judah, each to his own town. ²They came with Zerubbabel, Jeshua, Nehemiah, Seraiah, Reelaiah, Mordecai, Bilshan, Mispar, Bigvai, Rehum, and Baanah.

The number of the men of the people of Israel: ³the sons of Parosh, 2,172. ⁴The sons of Shephatiah, 372. ⁵The sons of Arah, 775. ⁶The sons of Pahath-moab, namely the sons of Jeshua and Joab, 2,812. ⁷The sons of Elam, 1,254. ⁸The sons of Zattu, 945. ⁹The sons of Zaccai, 760. ¹⁰The sons of Bani, 642. ¹¹The sons of Bebai, 623. ¹²The sons of Azgad, 1,222. ¹³The sons of Adonikam, 666. ¹⁴The sons of Bigvai, 2,056. ¹⁵The sons of Adin, 454. ¹⁶The sons of Ater, namely of Hezekiah, 98. ¹⁷The sons of Bezai, 323. ¹⁸The sons of Jorah, 112. ¹⁹The sons of Hashum, 223. ²⁰The sons of Gibbar, 95. ²¹The sons of Bethlehem, 123. ²²The men of Netophah, 56. ²³The men of Anathoth, 128. ²⁴The sons of Azmaveth, 42. ²⁵The sons of Kiriath-arim, Chephirah, and Beeroth, 743. ²⁶The sons of Ramah and Geba, 621. ²⁷The men of Michmas, 122. ²⁸The men of Bethel and Ai, 223. ²⁹The sons of Nebo, 52. ³⁰The sons of Magbish, 156. ³¹The sons of the other Elam, 1,254. ³²The sons of Harim, 320. ³³The sons of Lod, Hadid, and Ono, 725. ³⁴The sons of Jericho, 345. ³⁵The sons of Senaah, 3,630.

³⁶The priests: the sons of Jedaiah, of the house of Jeshua, 973. ³⁷The sons of Immer, 1,052. ³⁸The sons of Pashhur, 1,247. ³⁹The sons of Harim, 1,017.

⁴⁰The Levites: the sons of Jeshua and Kadmiel, of the sons of Hodaviah, 74. ⁴¹The singers: the sons of Asaph, 128. ⁴²The sons of the gatekeepers: the sons of Shallum, the sons of Ater, the sons of Talmon, the sons of Akkub, the sons of Hatita, and the sons of Shobai, in all 139.

⁴³The temple servants: the sons of Ziha, the sons of Hasupha, the sons of Tabbaoth, ⁴⁴the sons of Keros, the sons of Siaha, the sons of Padon, ⁴⁵the sons of Lebanah, the sons of Hagabah, the sons of Akkub, ⁴⁶the sons of Hagab, the sons of Shamlai, the sons of Hanan, ⁴⁷the sons of Giddel, the sons of Gahar, the sons of Reaiah, ⁴⁸the sons of Rezin, the sons of Nekoda, the sons of Gazzam, ⁴⁹the sons of Uzza, the sons of Paseah, the sons of Besai, ⁵⁰the sons of Asnah, the sons of Meunim, the sons of Nephisim, ⁵¹the sons of Bakbuk, the sons of Hakupha, the sons of Harhur, ⁵²the sons of Bazluth, the sons of Mehida, the sons of Harsha, ⁵³the sons of Barkos, the sons of Sisera, the sons of Temah, ⁵⁴the sons of Neziah, and the sons of Hatipha.

⁵⁵The sons of Solomon's servants: the sons of Sotai, the sons of Hassophereth, the sons of Peruda, ⁵⁶the sons of Jaalah, the sons of Darkon, the sons of Giddel, ⁵⁷the sons of Shephatiah, the sons of Hattil, the sons of Pochereth-hazzebaim, and the sons of Ami.

⁵⁸All the temple servants and the sons of Solomon's servants were 392.

⁵⁹The following were those who came up from Tel-melah, Tel-harsha, Cherub, Addan, and Immer, though they could not prove their fathers' houses or their descent, whether they belonged to Israel: ⁶⁰the sons of Delaiah, the sons of Tobiah, and the sons of Nekoda, 652. ⁶¹Also, of the sons of the priests: the sons of Habaiah, the sons of Hakkoz, and the sons of Barzillai (who had taken a wife from the daughters of Barzillai the Gileadite, and was called by their name). ⁶²These sought their registration among those enrolled in the genealogies, but they were not found there, and so they were excluded from the priesthood as unclean. ⁶³The governor told them that

they were not to partake of the most holy food, until there should be a priest to consult Urim and Thummim.

⁶⁴The whole assembly together was 42,360, ⁶⁵besides their male and female servants, of whom there were 7,337, and they had 200 male and female singers. ⁶⁶Their horses were 736, their mules were 245, ⁶⁷their camels were 435, and their donkeys were 6,720.

⁶⁸Some of the heads of families, when they came to the house of the Lord that is in Jerusalem, made freewill offerings for the house of God, to erect it on its site. ⁶⁹According to their ability they gave to the treasury of the work 61,000 darics¹ of gold, 5,000 minas² of silver, and 100 priests' garments.

⁷⁰Now the priests, the Levites, some of the people, the singers, the gatekeepers, and the temple servants lived in their towns, and all the rest of Israel³ in their towns.

The rebuilding of the temple begins [chapter 3]. The historical impulse to record the facts of the matter continues to dominate, but it takes a narrative turn in the sense that the author tells us what happens in the returning community once the people arrive in Jerusalem. The sequence in the chapter is as follows: the priests reinstitute the system of offerings (vv. 1–6a); materials are gathered for rebuilding the temple (vv. 6b–7); the rebuilding of the temple begins (vv. 8–9); a ceremony is performed when the foundations of the temple are laid (vv. 10–11), accompanied by mingled praise and weeping in response to the shape the new temple is taking (vv. 12–13). All of these events are momentous and dramatic; we need to picture ourselves present. Having done that, we can ponder (1) the priestly preoccupation with formal worship of God and (2) the experience of unmet expectations mingled with nostalgia for better days as the result of disobedience of God (the experience of the returned exiles).

3 When the seventh month came, and the children of Israel were in the towns, the people gathered as one man to Jerusalem. ²Then arose Jeshua the son of Jozadak, with his fellow priests, and Zerubbabel the son of Shealtiel with his kinsmen, and they built the altar of the God of Israel, to offer burnt offerings on it, as it is written in the Law of Moses the man of God. ³They set the altar in its place, for fear was on them because of the peoples of the lands, and they offered burnt offerings on it to the Lord, burnt offerings morning and evening. ⁴And they kept the Feast of Booths, as it is written, and offered the daily burnt offerings by number according to the rule, as each day required, ⁵and after that the regular burnt offerings, the offerings at the new moon and at all the appointed feasts of the Lord, and the offerings of everyone who made a freewill offering to the Lord. ⁶From the first day of the seventh month they began to offer burnt offerings to the Lord. But the foundation of the temple of the Lord was not yet laid. ⁷So they gave money to the masons and the carpenters, and food, drink, and oil to the Sidonians and the Tyrians to bring cedar trees from Lebanon to the sea, to Joppa, according to the grant that they had from Cyrus king of Persia.

⁸Now in the second year after their coming to the house of God at Jerusalem, in the second month, Zerubbabel the son of Shealtiel and Jeshua the son of Jozadak made a beginning, together with the rest of their kinsmen, the priests and the Levites and all who had come to Jerusalem from the captivity. They appointed the Levites, from twenty years old and upward, to supervise the work of the house of the Lord. ⁹And

¹ A *daric* was a coin weighing about 1/4 ounce or 8.5 grams ² A *mina* was about 1 1/4 pounds or 0.6 kilogram ³ Hebrew *all Israel*

Jeshua with his sons and his brothers, and Kadmiel and his sons, the sons of Judah, together supervised the workmen in the house of God, along with the sons of Henadad and the Levites, their sons and brothers.

¹⁰And when the builders laid the foundation of the temple of the LORD, the priests in their vestments came forward with trumpets, and the Levites, the sons of Asaph, with cymbals, to praise the LORD, according to the directions of David king of Israel. ¹¹And they sang responsively, praising and giving thanks to the LORD,

"For he is good,
    for his steadfast love endures forever toward Israel."

And all the people shouted with a great shout when they praised the LORD, because the foundation of the house of the LORD was laid. ¹²But many of the priests and Levites and heads of fathers' houses, old men who had seen the first house, wept with a loud voice when they saw the foundation of this house being laid, though many shouted aloud for joy, ¹³so that the people could not distinguish the sound of the joyful shout from the sound of the people's weeping, for the people shouted with a great shout, and the sound was heard far away.

The rebuilding is halted [chapter 4]. Literary narrative now takes over as the story becomes a *conflict story with significant intrigue. The action is rather complicated and unfolds as follows: adversaries of the Jews offer to help rebuild the temple, but the offer is refused (vv. 1–3); the enemies resort to various forms of pressure to discourage the people of Judah in their rebuilding project (vv. 4–6); the adversaries write a formal letter to King Artaxerxes slandering the Jews and misrepresenting their cause (vv. 7–16); the king replies with an order that the Jews desist (vv. 17–22); the letter is relayed to the leaders of the Jews, and work stops (vv. 23–24). By now the story has become a full-fledged conflict story, and a suspense story as well, as we are led to wonder whether and how the temple will be rebuilt.

4 Now when the adversaries of Judah and Benjamin heard that the returned exiles were building a temple to the LORD, the God of Israel, ²they approached Zerubbabel and the heads of fathers' houses and said to them, "Let us build with you, for we worship your God as you do, and we have been sacrificing to him ever since the days of Esarhaddon king of Assyria who brought us here." ³But Zerubbabel, Jeshua, and the rest of the heads of fathers' houses in Israel said to them, "You have nothing to do with us in building a house to our God; but we alone will build to the LORD, the God of Israel, as King Cyrus the king of Persia has commanded us."

⁴Then the people of the land discouraged the people of Judah and made them afraid to build ⁵and bribed counselors against them to frustrate their purpose, all the days of Cyrus king of Persia, even until the reign of Darius king of Persia.

⁶And in the reign of Ahasuerus, in the beginning of his reign, they wrote an accusation against the inhabitants of Judah and Jerusalem.

⁷In the days of Artaxerxes, Bishlam and Mithredath and Tabeel and the rest of their associates wrote to Artaxerxes king of Persia. The letter was written in Aramaic and translated.¹ ⁸Rehum the commander and Shimshai the scribe wrote a letter against Jerusalem to Artaxerxes the king as follows: ⁹Rehum the commander,

---

¹ Hebrew *written in Aramaic and translated in Aramaic*, indicating that 4:8–6:18 is in Aramaic; another interpretation is *The letter was written in the Aramaic script and set forth in the Aramaic language*

Shimshai the scribe, and the rest of their associates, the judges, the governors, the officials, the Persians, the men of Erech, the Babylonians, the men of Susa, that is, the Elamites, ¹⁰and the rest of the nations whom the great and noble Osnappar deported and settled in the cities of Samaria and in the rest of the province Beyond the River. ¹¹(This is a copy of the letter that they sent.) "To Artaxerxes the king: Your servants, the men of the province Beyond the River, send greeting. And now ¹²be it known to the king that the Jews who came up from you to us have gone to Jerusalem. They are rebuilding that rebellious and wicked city. They are finishing the walls and repairing the foundations. ¹³Now be it known to the king that if this city is rebuilt and the walls finished, they will not pay tribute, custom, or toll, and the royal revenue will be impaired. ¹⁴Now because we eat the salt of the palace and it is not fitting for us to witness the king's dishonor, therefore we send and inform the king, ¹⁵in order that search may be made in the book of the records of your fathers. You will find in the book of the records and learn that this city is a rebellious city, hurtful to kings and provinces, and that sedition was stirred up in it from of old. That was why this city was laid waste. ¹⁶We make known to the king that if this city is rebuilt and its walls finished, you will then have no possession in the province Beyond the River."

¹⁷The king sent an answer: "To Rehum the commander and Shimshai the scribe and the rest of their associates who live in Samaria and in the rest of the province Beyond the River, greeting. And now ¹⁸the letter that you sent to us has been plainly read before me. ¹⁹And I made a decree, and search has been made, and it has been found that this city from of old has risen against kings, and that rebellion and sedition have been made in it. ²⁰And mighty kings have been over Jerusalem, who ruled over the whole province Beyond the River, to whom tribute, custom, and toll were paid. ²¹Therefore make a decree that these men be made to cease, and that this city be not rebuilt, until a decree is made by me. ²²And take care not to be slack in this matter. Why should damage grow to the hurt of the king?"

²³Then, when the copy of King Artaxerxes' letter was read before Rehum and Shimshai the scribe and their associates, they went in haste to the Jews at Jerusalem and by force and power made them cease. ²⁴Then the work on the house of God that is in Jerusalem stopped, and it ceased until the second year of the reign of Darius king of Persia.

Further complications [chapter 5]. When the Jews restart the building project (vv. 1–2) and are again challenged by hostile forces (vv. 3–4), the governor has the good sense and fair-mindedness to let the Jews continue their work while his formal letter of inquiry is sent to King Darius (vv. 5–17). The suspense continues, as we are led to wonder how the opposition and inquiry will turn out.

5 Now the prophets, Haggai and Zechariah the son of Iddo, prophesied to the Jews who were in Judah and Jerusalem, in the name of the God of Israel who was over them. ²Then Zerubbabel the son of Shealtiel and Jeshua the son of Jozadak arose and began to rebuild the house of God that is in Jerusalem, and the prophets of God were with them, supporting them.

³At the same time Tattenai the governor of the province Beyond the River and Shethar-bozenai and their associates came to them and spoke to them thus: "Who

gave you a decree to build this house and to finish this structure?" [4]They[1] also asked them this: "What are the names of the men who are building this building?" [5]But the eye of their God was on the elders of the Jews, and they did not stop them until the report should reach Darius and then an answer be returned by letter concerning it.

[6]This is a copy of the letter that Tattenai the governor of the province Beyond the River and Shethar-bozenai and his associates, the governors who were in the province Beyond the River, sent to Darius the king. [7]They sent him a report, in which was written as follows: "To Darius the king, all peace. [8]Be it known to the king that we went to the province of Judah, to the house of the great God. It is being built with huge stones, and timber is laid in the walls. This work goes on diligently and prospers in their hands. [9]Then we asked those elders and spoke to them thus: 'Who gave you a decree to build this house and to finish this structure?' [10]We also asked them their names, for your information, that we might write down the names of their leaders.[2] [11]And this was their reply to us: 'We are the servants of the God of heaven and earth, and we are rebuilding the house that was built many years ago, which a great king of Israel built and finished. [12]But because our fathers had angered the God of heaven, he gave them into the hand of Nebuchadnezzar king of Babylon, the Chaldean, who destroyed this house and carried away the people to Babylonia. [13]However, in the first year of Cyrus king of Babylon, Cyrus the king made a decree that this house of God should be rebuilt. [14]And the gold and silver vessels of the house of God, which Nebuchadnezzar had taken out of the temple that was in Jerusalem and brought into the temple of Babylon, these Cyrus the king took out of the temple of Babylon, and they were delivered to one whose name was Sheshbazzar, whom he had made governor; [15]and he said to him, "Take these vessels, go and put them in the temple that is in Jerusalem, and let the house of God be rebuilt on its site." [16]Then this Sheshbazzar came and laid the foundations of the house of God that is in Jerusalem, and from that time until now it has been in building, and it is not yet finished.' [17]Therefore, if it seems good to the king, let search be made in the royal archives there in Babylon, to see whether a decree was issued by Cyrus the king for the rebuilding of this house of God in Jerusalem. And let the king send us his pleasure in this matter."

The rebuilding completed [chapter 6]. The suspense story winds its way to a happy ending: Darius searches the royal archives and discovers the decree of his predecessor Cyrus allowing the Jews to rebuild the temple (vv. 1–5); Darius commands the governor not only to allow the rebuilding but to pay for it (vv. 6–12); the governor complies and the temple is completed (vv. 13–15); the temple is dedicated and the sacrificial system is reinstated (vv. 16–22). In the central importance that the people gave to rebuilding the temple we can see the priorities around which God wants his people to order their personal and communal lives. Poetic justice enters the story when the Jews' enemies are required to pay for the rebuilding project.

6 Then Darius the king made a decree, and search was made in Babylonia, in the house of the archives where the documents were stored. [2]And in Ecbatana, the capital that is in the province of Media, a scroll was found on which this was written: "A record. [3]In the first year of Cyrus the king, Cyrus the king issued a decree:

[1] Septuagint, Syriac; Aramaic We [2] Aramaic of the men at their heads

Concerning the house of God at Jerusalem, let the house be rebuilt, the place where sacrifices were offered, and let its foundations be retained. Its height shall be sixty cubits[1] and its breadth sixty cubits, ⁴with three layers of great stones and one layer of timber. Let the cost be paid from the royal treasury. ⁵And also let the gold and silver vessels of the house of God, which Nebuchadnezzar took out of the temple that is in Jerusalem and brought to Babylon, be restored and brought back to the temple that is in Jerusalem, each to its place. You shall put them in the house of God."

⁶"Now therefore, Tattenai, governor of the province Beyond the River, Shethar-bozenai, and your associates the governors who are in the province Beyond the River, keep away. ⁷Let the work on this house of God alone. Let the governor of the Jews and the elders of the Jews rebuild this house of God on its site. ⁸Moreover, I make a decree regarding what you shall do for these elders of the Jews for the rebuilding of this house of God. The cost is to be paid to these men in full and without delay from the royal revenue, the tribute of the province from Beyond the River. ⁹And whatever is needed—bulls, rams, or sheep for burnt offerings to the God of heaven, wheat, salt, wine, or oil, as the priests at Jerusalem require—let that be given to them day by day without fail, ¹⁰that they may offer pleasing sacrifices to the God of heaven and pray for the life of the king and his sons. ¹¹Also I make a decree that if anyone alters this edict, a beam shall be pulled out of his house, and he shall be impaled on it, and his house shall be made a dunghill. ¹²May the God who has caused his name to dwell there overthrow any king or people who shall put out a hand to alter this, or to destroy this house of God that is in Jerusalem. I Darius make a decree; let it be done with all diligence."

¹³Then, according to the word sent by Darius the king, Tattenai, the governor of the province Beyond the River, Shethar-bozenai, and their associates did with all diligence what Darius the king had ordered. ¹⁴And the elders of the Jews built and prospered through the prophesying of Haggai the prophet and Zechariah the son of Iddo. They finished their building by decree of the God of Israel and by decree of Cyrus and Darius and Artaxerxes king of Persia; ¹⁵and this house was finished on the third day of the month of Adar, in the sixth year of the reign of Darius the king.

¹⁶And the people of Israel, the priests and the Levites, and the rest of the returned exiles, celebrated the dedication of this house of God with joy. ¹⁷They offered at the dedication of this house of God 100 bulls, 200 rams, 400 lambs, and as a sin offering for all Israel 12 male goats, according to the number of the tribes of Israel. ¹⁸And they set the priests in their divisions and the Levites in their divisions, for the service of God at Jerusalem, as it is written in the Book of Moses.

¹⁹On the fourteenth day of the first month, the returned exiles kept the Passover. ²⁰For the priests and the Levites had purified themselves together; all of them were clean. So they slaughtered the Passover lamb for all the returned exiles, for their fellow priests, and for themselves. ²¹It was eaten by the people of Israel who had returned from exile, and also by every one who had joined them and separated himself from the uncleanness of the peoples of the land to worship the LORD, the God of Israel. ²²And they kept the Feast of Unleavened Bread seven days with joy, for the LORD had made them joyful and had turned the heart of the king of Assyria to them, so that he aided them in the work of the house of God, the God of Israel.

[1] A *cubit* was about 18 inches or 45 centimeters

Preparations for a second group of returnees [chapter 7]. We now begin a rerun of the action that greeted us at the outset of the book. Again a Persian king shows favor to a valued Jewish employee of the Persian court in response to his desire to return to his homeland (vv. 1–6); other influential Jewish leaders also return to Jerusalem (vv. 7–10); a royal decree provides an extensive inventory of the goods and privileges to which the returning Jews are entitled (vv. 11–24) and also the rights of governing to which Ezra is entitled (vv. 25–26); Ezra expresses gratitude for all of these events (vv. 27–28). Ezra is said to be "a man learned in matters of the commandments of the LORD" (v. 11); the importance of his return to Jerusalem is that now the people have someone to teach them the Word of God.

7 Now after this, in the reign of Artaxerxes king of Persia, Ezra the son of Seraiah, son of Azariah, son of Hilkiah, ²son of Shallum, son of Zadok, son of Ahitub, ³son of Amariah, son of Azariah, son of Meraioth, ⁴son of Zerahiah, son of Uzzi, son of Bukki, ⁵son of Abishua, son of Phinehas, son of Eleazar, son of Aaron the chief priest— ⁶this Ezra went up from Babylonia. He was a scribe skilled in the Law of Moses that the LORD, the God of Israel, had given, and the king granted him all that he asked, for the hand of the LORD his God was on him.

⁷And there went up also to Jerusalem, in the seventh year of Artaxerxes the king, some of the people of Israel, and some of the priests and Levites, the singers and gate-keepers, and the temple servants. ⁸And Ezra¹ came to Jerusalem in the fifth month, which was in the seventh year of the king. ⁹For on the first day of the first month he began to go up from Babylonia, and on the first day of the fifth month he came to Jerusalem, for the good hand of his God was on him. ¹⁰For Ezra had set his heart to study the Law of the LORD, and to do it and to teach his statutes and rules in Israel.

¹¹This is a copy of the letter that King Artaxerxes gave to Ezra the priest, the scribe, a man learned in matters of the commandments of the LORD and his statutes for Israel: ¹²"Artaxerxes, king of kings, to Ezra the priest, the scribe of the Law of the God of heaven. Peace.² And now ¹³I make a decree that anyone of the people of Israel or their priests or Levites in my kingdom, who freely offers to go to Jerusalem, may go with you. ¹⁴For you are sent by the king and his seven counselors to make inquiries about Judah and Jerusalem according to the Law of your God, which is in your hand, ¹⁵and also to carry the silver and gold that the king and his counselors have freely offered to the God of Israel, whose dwelling is in Jerusalem, ¹⁶with all the silver and gold that you shall find in the whole province of Babylonia, and with the freewill offerings of the people and the priests, vowed willingly for the house of their God that is in Jerusalem. ¹⁷With this money, then, you shall with all diligence buy bulls, rams, and lambs, with their grain offerings and their drink offerings, and you shall offer them on the altar of the house of your God that is in Jerusalem. ¹⁸Whatever seems good to you and your brothers to do with the rest of the silver and gold, you may do, according to the will of your God. ¹⁹The vessels that have been given you for the service of the house of your God, you shall deliver before the God of Jerusalem. ²⁰And whatever else is required for the house of your God, which it falls to you to provide, you may provide it out of the king's treasury.

²¹"And I, Artaxerxes the king, make a decree to all the treasurers in the province Beyond the River: Whatever Ezra the priest, the scribe of the Law of the God of heaven, requires of you, let it be done with all diligence, ²²up to 100 talents³ of silver,

---

¹ Aramaic *he* ² Aramaic *Perfect* (probably a greeting) ³ A *talent* was about 75 pounds or 34 kilograms

100 cors[1] of wheat, 100 baths[2] of wine, 100 baths of oil, and salt without prescribing how much. [23]Whatever is decreed by the God of heaven, let it be done in full for the house of the God of heaven, lest his wrath be against the realm of the king and his sons. [24]We also notify you that it shall not be lawful to impose tribute, custom, or toll on anyone of the priests, the Levites, the singers, the doorkeepers, the temple servants, or other servants of this house of God.

[25]"And you, Ezra, according to the wisdom of your God that is in your hand, appoint magistrates and judges who may judge all the people in the province Beyond the River, all such as know the laws of your God. And those who do not know them, you shall teach. [26]Whoever will not obey the law of your God and the law of the king, let judgment be strictly executed on him, whether for death or for banishment or for confiscation of his goods or for imprisonment."

[27]Blessed be the LORD, the God of our fathers, who put such a thing as this into the heart of the king, to beautify the house of the LORD that is in Jerusalem, [28]and who extended to me his steadfast love before the king and his counselors, and before all the king's mighty officers. I took courage, for the hand of the LORD my God was on me, and I gathered leading men from Israel to go up with me.

The return journey [chapter 8]. This chapter is a full-fledged return story, replete with an account of the journey from Babylon to Jerusalem (making the passage fall into the genre of *travel story). First the author assembles the cast of characters for the ensuing journey (vv. 1–14). At a three-day encampment on the journey, Ezra ascertains that the group does not include Levites, so he sends an emissary of officials to Casiphia to enlist a group of temple servants (vv. 15–20). Subsequent events on the return journey include a fast to seek God for safe passage (vv. 21–23); dispatching of the priests with the treasures designed for use at the temple (vv. 24–30); first activities upon arriving in Jerusalem (vv. 31–36). It is a story of divine providence, faith in God for personal safety, and giving priority to the worship of God.

8 These are the heads of their fathers' houses, and this is the genealogy of those who went up with me from Babylonia, in the reign of Artaxerxes the king: [2]Of the sons of Phinehas, Gershom. Of the sons of Ithamar, Daniel. Of the sons of David, Hattush. [3]Of the sons of Shecaniah, who was of the sons of Parosh, Zechariah, with whom were registered 150 men. [4]Of the sons of Pahath-moab, Eliehoenai the son of Zerahiah, and with him 200 men. [5]Of the sons of Zattu,[3] Shecaniah the son of Jahaziel, and with him 300 men. [6]Of the sons of Adin, Ebed the son of Jonathan, and with him 50 men. [7]Of the sons of Elam, Jeshaiah the son of Athaliah, and with him 70 men. [8]Of the sons of Shephatiah, Zebadiah the son of Michael, and with him 80 men. [9]Of the sons of Joab, Obadiah the son of Jehiel, and with him 218 men. [10]Of the sons of Bani,[4] Shelomith the son of Josiphiah, and with him 160 men. [11]Of the sons of Bebai, Zechariah, the son of Bebai, and with him 28 men. [12]Of the sons of Azgad, Johanan the son of Hakkatan, and with him 110 men. [13]Of the sons of Adonikam, those who came later, their names being Eliphelet, Jeuel, and Shemaiah, and with them 60 men. [14]Of the sons of Bigvai, Uthai and Zaccur, and with them 70 men.

[15]I gathered them to the river that runs to Ahava, and there we camped three days. As I reviewed the people and the priests, I found there none of the sons of Levi. [16]Then I sent for Eliezer, Ariel, Shemaiah, Elnathan, Jarib, Elnathan, Nathan,

---

[1] A *cor* was about 6 bushels or 220 liters   [2] A *bath* was about 6 gallons or 22 liters   [3] Septuagint; Hebrew lacks *of Zattu*   [4] Septuagint; Hebrew lacks *Bani*

Zechariah, and Meshullam, leading men, and for Joiarib and Elnathan, who were men of insight, [17]and sent them to Iddo, the leading man at the place Casiphia, telling them what to say to Iddo and his brothers and[1] the temple servants at the place Casiphia, namely, to send us ministers for the house of our God. [18]And by the good hand of our God on us, they brought us a man of discretion, of the sons of Mahli the son of Levi, son of Israel, namely Sherebiah with his sons and kinsmen, 18; [19]also Hashabiah, and with him Jeshaiah of the sons of Merari, with his kinsmen and their sons, 20; [20]besides 220 of the temple servants, whom David and his officials had set apart to attend the Levites. These were all mentioned by name.

[21]Then I proclaimed a fast there, at the river Ahava, that we might humble ourselves before our God, to seek from him a safe journey for ourselves, our children, and all our goods. [22]For I was ashamed to ask the king for a band of soldiers and horsemen to protect us against the enemy on our way, since we had told the king, "The hand of our God is for good on all who seek him, and the power of his wrath is against all who forsake him." [23]So we fasted and implored our God for this, and he listened to our entreaty.

[24]Then I set apart twelve of the leading priests: Sherebiah, Hashabiah, and ten of their kinsmen with them. [25]And I weighed out to them the silver and the gold and the vessels, the offering for the house of our God that the king and his counselors and his lords and all Israel there present had offered. [26]I weighed out into their hand 650 talents[2] of silver, and silver vessels worth 200 talents,[3] and 100 talents of gold, [27]20 bowls of gold worth 1,000 darics,[4] and two vessels of fine bright bronze as precious as gold. [28]And I said to them, "You are holy to the LORD, and the vessels are holy, and the silver and the gold are a freewill offering to the LORD, the God of your fathers. [29]Guard them and keep them until you weigh them before the chief priests and the Levites and the heads of fathers' houses in Israel at Jerusalem, within the chambers of the house of the LORD." [30]So the priests and the Levites took over the weight of the silver and the gold and the vessels, to bring them to Jerusalem, to the house of our God.

[31]Then we departed from the river Ahava on the twelfth day of the first month, to go to Jerusalem. The hand of our God was on us, and he delivered us from the hand of the enemy and from ambushes by the way. [32]We came to Jerusalem, and there we remained three days. [33]On the fourth day, within the house of our God, the silver and the gold and the vessels were weighed into the hands of Meremoth the priest, son of Uriah, and with him was Eleazar the son of Phinehas, and with them were the Levites, Jozabad the son of Jeshua and Noadiah the son of Binnui. [34]The whole was counted and weighed, and the weight of everything was recorded.

[35]At that time those who had come from captivity, the returned exiles, offered burnt offerings to the God of Israel, twelve bulls for all Israel, ninety-six rams, seventy-seven lambs, and as a sin offering twelve male goats. All this was a burnt offering to the LORD. [36]They also delivered the king's commissions to the king's satraps[5] and to the governors of the province Beyond the River, and they aided the people and the house of God.

The problem of mixed marriages [chapter 9]. Once Ezra takes stock of the state of the nation in Palestine, he is appalled by the problem of mixed marriage that had become an established social pattern in Israel. The sequence of the action is as follows:

[1] Hebrew lacks and [2] A *talent* was about 75 pounds or 34 kilograms [3] Revocalization; the number is missing in the Masoretic Text [4] A *daric* was a coin weighing about 1/4 ounce or 8.5 grams [5] A *satrap* was a Persian official

Ezra learns about the intermarriage problem and responds with extravagant gestures of personal distress (vv. 1–4); Ezra offers a formal prayer of confession to God (vv. 5–15). Ezra's extreme behavior in this chapter is the clue to the meaning of the intermarriage: it is a flagrant violation of the covenant obligation of God's people to remain separate from sin. The specific social situation embodies a profound spiritual principle that is the foundation for our understanding what happens in the next chapter. The principle involved is not racial or ethnic but religious (a rejection of idolatry).

9 After these things had been done, the officials approached me and said, "The people of Israel and the priests and the Levites have not separated themselves from the peoples of the lands with their abominations, from the Canaanites, the Hittites, the Perizzites, the Jebusites, the Ammonites, the Moabites, the Egyptians, and the Amorites. [2] For they have taken some of their daughters to be wives for themselves and for their sons, so that the holy race[1] has mixed itself with the peoples of the lands. And in this faithlessness the hand of the officials and chief men has been foremost." [3] As soon as I heard this, I tore my garment and my cloak and pulled hair from my head and beard and sat appalled. [4] Then all who trembled at the words of the God of Israel, because of the faithlessness of the returned exiles, gathered around me while I sat appalled until the evening sacrifice. [5] And at the evening sacrifice I rose from my fasting, with my garment and my cloak torn, and fell upon my knees and spread out my hands to the LORD my God, [6] saying:

"O my God, I am ashamed and blush to lift my face to you, my God, for our iniquities have risen higher than our heads, and our guilt has mounted up to the heavens. [7] From the days of our fathers to this day we have been in great guilt. And for our iniquities we, our kings, and our priests have been given into the hand of the kings of the lands, to the sword, to captivity, to plundering, and to utter shame, as it is today. [8] But now for a brief moment favor has been shown by the LORD our God, to leave us a remnant and to give us a secure hold[2] within his holy place, that our God may brighten our eyes and grant us a little reviving in our slavery. [9] For we are slaves. Yet our God has not forsaken us in our slavery, but has extended to us his steadfast love before the kings of Persia, to grant us some reviving to set up the house of our God, to repair its ruins, and to give us protection[3] in Judea and Jerusalem.

[10] "And now, O our God, what shall we say after this? For we have forsaken your commandments, [11] which you commanded by your servants the prophets, saying, 'The land that you are entering, to take possession of it, is a land impure with the impurity of the peoples of the lands, with their abominations that have filled it from end to end with their uncleanness. [12] Therefore do not give your daughters to their sons, neither take their daughters for your sons, and never seek their peace or prosperity, that you may be strong and eat the good of the land and leave it for an inheritance to your children forever.' [13] And after all that has come upon us for our evil deeds and for our great guilt, seeing that you, our God, have punished us less than our iniquities deserved and have given us such a remnant as this, [14] shall we break your commandments again and intermarry with the peoples who practice these abominations? Would you not be angry with us until you consumed us, so that there should be no remnant, nor any to escape? [15] O LORD, the God of Israel, you are just, for we are left a remnant that has escaped, as it is today. Behold, we are before you in our guilt, for none can stand before you because of this."

---

[1] Hebrew *offspring* [2] Hebrew *nail*, or *tent-pin* [3] Hebrew *a wall*

Ezra's reform movement [chapter 10]. The events of the preceding chapter were a prelude to what happens in this chapter. The action begins when Ezra's anguish produces a similar attitude of confession and resolve in the nation at large, with the result that the men take an oath to divorce the foreign wives they have taken and the children they have fathered with them (vv. 1–5). After Ezra spends a night fasting in a temple room (v. 6), he sends a proclamation summoning the exiles to a meeting at the temple (vv. 7–8). When the assembly convenes, representatives of the people are named to consider the issue of intermarriage (vv. 9–17). This narrative is followed by a list of men who had married foreign wives (vv. 18–44). The implication is that these men subsequently divorce their foreign wives. We must interpret these wholesale divorces as a onetime event that show in a graphic way the need for God's covenant community to keep separate from evil and to protect the covenant by maintaining spiritual and marital purity.

10 While Ezra prayed and made confession, weeping and casting himself down before the house of God, a very great assembly of men, women, and children, gathered to him out of Israel, for the people wept bitterly. ²And Shecaniah the son of Jehiel, of the sons of Elam, addressed Ezra: "We have broken faith with our God and have married foreign women from the peoples of the land, but even now there is hope for Israel in spite of this. ³Therefore let us make a covenant with our God to put away all these wives and their children, according to the counsel of my lord¹ and of those who tremble at the commandment of our God, and let it be done according to the Law. ⁴Arise, for it is your task, and we are with you; be strong and do it." ⁵Then Ezra arose and made the leading priests and Levites and all Israel take oath that they would do as had been said. So they took the oath.

⁶Then Ezra withdrew from before the house of God and went to the chamber of Jehohanan the son of Eliashib, where he spent the night,² neither eating bread nor drinking water, for he was mourning over the faithlessness of the exiles. ⁷And a proclamation was made throughout Judah and Jerusalem to all the returned exiles that they should assemble at Jerusalem, ⁸and that if anyone did not come within three days, by order of the officials and the elders all his property should be forfeited, and he himself banned from the congregation of the exiles.

⁹Then all the men of Judah and Benjamin assembled at Jerusalem within the three days. It was the ninth month, on the twentieth day of the month. And all the people sat in the open square before the house of God, trembling because of this matter and because of the heavy rain. ¹⁰And Ezra the priest stood up and said to them, "You have broken faith and married foreign women, and so increased the guilt of Israel. ¹¹Now then make confession to the LORD, the God of your fathers and do his will. Separate yourselves from the peoples of the land and from the foreign wives." ¹²Then all the assembly answered with a loud voice, "It is so; we must do as you have said. ¹³But the people are many, and it is a time of heavy rain; we cannot stand in the open. Nor is this a task for one day or for two, for we have greatly transgressed in this matter. ¹⁴Let our officials stand for the whole assembly. Let all in our cities who have taken foreign wives come at appointed times, and with them the elders and judges of every city, until the fierce wrath of our God over this matter is turned away from us." ¹⁵Only Jonathan the son of Asahel and Jahzeiah the son of Tikvah opposed this, and Meshullam and Shabbethai the Levite supported them.

¹⁶Then the returned exiles did so. Ezra the priest selected men,³ heads of fathers'

---

¹ Or of the Lord ² Probable reading; Hebrew *where he went* ³ Syriac; Hebrew *And there were selected Ezra . . .*

houses, according to their fathers' houses, each of them designated by name. On the first day of the tenth month they sat down to examine the matter; [17]and by the first day of the first month they had come to the end of all the men who had married foreign women.

[18]Now there were found some of the sons of the priests who had married foreign women: Maaseiah, Eliezer, Jarib, and Gedaliah, some of the sons of Jeshua the son of Jozadak and his brothers. [19]They pledged themselves to put away their wives, and their guilt offering was a ram of the flock for their guilt.[1] [20]Of the sons of Immer: Hanani and Zebadiah. [21]Of the sons of Harim: Maaseiah, Elijah, Shemaiah, Jehiel, and Uzziah. [22]Of the sons of Pashhur: Elioenai, Maaseiah, Ishmael, Nethanel, Jozabad, and Elasah.

[23]Of the Levites: Jozabad, Shimei, Kelaiah (that is, Kelita), Pethahiah, Judah, and Eliezer. [24]Of the singers: Eliashib. Of the gatekeepers: Shallum, Telem, and Uri.

[25]And of Israel: of the sons of Parosh: Ramiah, Izziah, Malchijah, Mijamin, Eleazar, Hashabiah,[2] and Benaiah. [26]Of the sons of Elam: Mattaniah, Zechariah, Jehiel, Abdi, Jeremoth, and Elijah. [27]Of the sons of Zattu: Elioenai, Eliashib, Mattaniah, Jeremoth, Zabad, and Aziza. [28]Of the sons of Bebai were Jehohanan, Hananiah, Zabbai, and Athlai. [29]Of the sons of Bani were Meshullam, Malluch, Adaiah, Jashub, Sheal, and Jeremoth. [30]Of the sons of Pahath-moab: Adna, Chelal, Benaiah, Maaseiah, Mattaniah, Bezalel, Binnui, and Manasseh. [31]Of the sons of Harim: Eliezer, Isshijah, Malchijah, Shemaiah, Shimeon, [32]Benjamin, Malluch, and Shemariah. [33]Of the sons of Hashum: Mattenai, Mattattah, Zabad, Eliphelet, Jeremai, Manasseh, and Shimei. [34]Of the sons of Bani: Maadai, Amram, Uel, [35]Benaiah, Bedeiah, Cheluhi, [36]Vaniah, Meremoth, Eliashib, [37]Mattaniah, Mattenai, Jaasu. [38]Of the sons of Binnui:[3] Shimei, [39]Shelemiah, Nathan, Adaiah, [40]Machnadebai, Shashai, Sharai, [41]Azarel, Shelemiah, Shemariah, [42]Shallum, Amariah, and Joseph. [43]Of the sons of Nebo: Jeiel, Mattithiah, Zabad, Zebina, Jaddai, Joel, and Benaiah. [44]All these had married foreign women, and some of the women had even borne children.[4]

---

[1] Or as their reparation [2] Septuagint; Hebrew Malchijah [3] Septuagint; Hebrew Bani, Binnui [4] Or and they put them away with their children

NEHEMIAH

The book at a glance. 13 chapters, 406 verses. The book of Nehemiah has been called one of the liveliest pieces of writing in the Bible. It is a sequel to the book of Ezra, which records the stories of the first two remnants that returned from exile to Jerusalem. The book of Nehemiah tells the story of what befell the third wave of returnees, some thirteen years after the second group had returned. Two main actions occur—the rebuilding of the wall of Jerusalem and the recommitment of the returned exiles to fulfill their covenant obligations. There is something for virtually everyone in this book, which is a general's diary, a governor's report, a civil record, a management handbook, and a memoir all in one short book. The events covered in this historical chronicle and collection of hero stories span approximately fifteen years. Part of the liveliness of the book stems from the striking character of Nehemiah, who emerges from the pages as a godly and decisive leader.

▌ Genres. The book of Nehemiah displays the same mixture of *narrative and documentary material (lists, inventories, *genealogies) that the book of Ezra contains, but it possesses a stronger narrative flair. The rebuilding of the city wall becomes a full-fledged *conflict story, replete with suspense and heroism. The covenant renewal ceremony (chapters 8–9) is one of the grand dramas in the Bible. The title character, Nehemiah, is such a commanding figure that the overall story is also a *hero story. However, documentary material regularly interrupts the flow of the narrative, showing the historical impulse of the author. The broader circle of stories into which the book of Nehemiah falls is the *return story. Since much of the book is cast as a first-person narrative, the book also has the flavor of a memoir. (For more information on items accompanied by an asterisk, see the glossary at the back of this Bible.)

▌ A companion story to Ezra. The book of Nehemiah invites comparison to its predecessor, Ezra. The careers of Ezra and Nehemiah overlapped, and the book of Nehemiah completes the action that began with the book of Ezra. The book of Ezra deals with two main events—the movement to rebuild the temple and a reform movement based on a return to the law of the covenant. The book of Nehemiah follows the same pattern: as in the book of Ezra, the first half is a rebuilding story (the rebuilding of the city wall), and the second half is a story of reform (a return to obeying God's covenant rules). The division of duties between Nehemiah and Ezra are complementary: Nehemiah's leadership is governmental and administrative, while Ezra's leadership is priestly and liturgical.

Passage	Content	Story Line	Focus	Arena of Activity	Community Sphere
1:1–2:20	Planning for the rebuilding of the city wall				
3:1–6:19	Rebuilding the wall amidst conflict without and within	Rebuilding the wall	Work	The wall of Jerusalem	Civil life of the community
7:1–73	List of those who returned				
8:1–18	The law read and explained				
9:1–10:39	Covenant renewal ceremony	Reforming the people	Spiritual renewal and rectitude	God's law	Religious life of the community
11:1–12:47	Resettling of Jerusalem				
13:1–31	Reforms of Nehemiah				

▌**The sense of place.** Nehemiah is a book in which we are seldom allowed to lose sight of where events are happening. The main setting is the city of Jerusalem. The story of Nehemiah's riding on horseback through the ruined city by night is one of the most vivid and haunting stories in the Bible. The main events of the book—rebuilding the wall, public renewal of the covenant, dedication of the city wall—are situated in specific settings that come alive in our imagination.

▌**The cast of characters.** If the book of Nehemiah is memorable for its settings, we also remember its vivid cast of characters. Foremost is the heroic leader Nehemiah, the governor. The priest and scribe Ezra plays a key role in the covenant renewal ceremony. Beyond that, we encounter the names of hundreds of other people, showing how important individuals are in God's sight. Many of the groups of characters are identified by their vocation, such as priest, builder, gatekeeper, singer, and so forth, making the book of Nehemiah a sourcebook for the idea of vocation.

▌**Inferred literary intentions.** The book is designed to achieve the following literary purposes:

■ record the historical facts of the events that the author chose to include in his account

■ allow us to relive the events in our imagination

■ grip us with the drama of the key events

■ admire the heroic leaders Nehemiah and Ezra

■ give us glimpses of a *utopian society

■ embody the content of the book in the usual narrative forms of plot, setting, and character

▌Theological themes. (1) Covenant: the book of Nehemiah is a handbook for how God's OT people lived under the covenant. (2) Worship: the restoration of correct worship in Jerusalem is shown to be central to the life of God's covenant people. (3) Leadership: the story shows how the success of the restoration of a nation depended on the agency of decisive and godly leaders. (4) Obedience: from start to finish we see that individuals and groups of believers need continually to choose to obey God if they wish to live well.

▌The book of Nehemiah as a chapter in the master story of the Bible. Like the book of Ezra, the book of Nehemiah records an important phase of the national history of God's OT covenant nation. In this history we can see how God wants his people to live and worship, and this is a main strand in the master story of the Bible. Furthermore, rebuilding the city of God, literally and symbolically, is a key biblical theme.

> **The humble beginnings of a return movement** [chapter 1]. The opening page of any narrative is an initiation into the characters and world of the story that is to follow. Right from the start we notice the first-person point of view, as Nehemiah speaks in his own person ("I was in Susa the capital"). In view of the major movement that Nehemiah will inspire and oversee, we cannot help but be surprised by the modest beginnings of the movement. It all begins with the report to Nehemiah, living in exile in Persia, that the wall of Jerusalem remains in ruins nearly a hundred years after the first return (vv. 1–3). This is followed by Nehemiah's private mourning and prayer of intercession for his nation. Nehemiah is a man who embraces the cause of God's people in his own soul, longing for the rebirth of his nation.

1 The words of Nehemiah the son of Hacaliah.

Now it happened in the month of Chislev, in the twentieth year, as I was in Susa the capital,[1] ²that Hanani, one of my brothers, came with certain men from Judah. And I asked them concerning the Jews who escaped, who had survived the exile, and concerning Jerusalem. ³And they said to me, "The remnant there in the province who had survived the exile is in great trouble and shame. The wall of Jerusalem is broken down, and its gates are destroyed by fire."

⁴As soon as I heard these words I sat down and wept and mourned for days, and I continued fasting and praying before the God of heaven. ⁵And I said, "O LORD God of heaven, the great and awesome God who keeps covenant and steadfast love with those who love him and keep his commandments, ⁶let your ear be attentive and your eyes open, to hear the prayer of your servant that I now pray before you day and night for the people of Israel your servants, confessing the sins of the people of Israel, which we have sinned against you. Even I and my father's house have sinned. ⁷We have acted very corruptly against you and have not kept the commandments, the statutes, and the rules that you commanded your servant Moses. ⁸Remember the word that you commanded your servant Moses, saying, 'If you are unfaithful, I will scatter you among the peoples, ⁹but if you return to me and keep my commandments and do them, though your outcasts are in the uttermost parts of heaven, from there I will gather them and bring them to the place that I have chosen, to make my name dwell there.' ¹⁰They are your servants and your people, whom you have redeemed by

---

¹ Or the fortified city

your great power and by your strong hand. ¹¹O Lord, let your ear be attentive to the prayer of your servant, and to the prayer of your servants who delight to fear your name, and give success to your servant today, and grant him mercy in the sight of this man."

Now I was cupbearer to the king.

A leader springs into action [chapter 2]. We now learn that Nehemiah is cupbearer to the king of Persia (v. 1), and from this seemingly unimportant situation a whole string of providential consequences unfolds: Nehemiah's sadness is noted by the king and results in Nehemiah's request to return to his homeland to rebuild the city of Jerusalem (vv. 2–8); Nehemiah travels to Jerusalem and examines the state of its disrepair (vv. 9–16); Nehemiah challenges the leaders of the covenant community to rebuild the wall of Jerusalem (vv. 17–20). For high drama in the narratives of the Bible, it is hard to beat the account of Nehemiah secretly examining the fallen city on horseback by night. Further, Nehemiah emerges as a heroic figure whose courage and resolve are an example to us, along with his impulse toward protection of his community.

2 In the month of Nisan, in the twentieth year of King Artaxerxes, when wine was before him, I took up the wine and gave it to the king. Now I had not been sad in his presence. ²And the king said to me, "Why is your face sad, seeing you are not sick? This is nothing but sadness of the heart." Then I was very much afraid. ³I said to the king, "Let the king live forever! Why should not my face be sad, when the city, the place of my fathers' graves, lies in ruins, and its gates have been destroyed by fire?" ⁴Then the king said to me, "What are you requesting?" So I prayed to the God of heaven. ⁵And I said to the king, "If it pleases the king, and if your servant has found favor in your sight, that you send me to Judah, to the city of my fathers' graves, that I may rebuild it." ⁶And the king said to me (the queen sitting beside him), "How long will you be gone, and when will you return?" So it pleased the king to send me when I had given him a time. ⁷And I said to the king, "If it pleases the king, let letters be given me to the governors of the province Beyond the River, that they may let me pass through until I come to Judah, ⁸and a letter to Asaph, the keeper of the king's forest, that he may give me timber to make beams for the gates of the fortress of the temple, and for the wall of the city, and for the house that I shall occupy." And the king granted me what I asked, for the good hand of my God was upon me.

⁹Then I came to the governors of the province Beyond the River and gave them the king's letters. Now the king had sent with me officers of the army and horsemen. ¹⁰But when Sanballat the Horonite and Tobiah the Ammonite servant heard this, it displeased them greatly that someone had come to seek the welfare of the people of Israel.

¹¹So I went to Jerusalem and was there three days. ¹²Then I arose in the night, I and a few men with me. And I told no one what my God had put into my heart to do for Jerusalem. There was no animal with me but the one on which I rode. ¹³I went out by night by the Valley Gate to the Dragon Spring and to the Dung Gate, and I inspected the walls of Jerusalem that were broken down and its gates that had been destroyed by fire. ¹⁴Then I went on to the Fountain Gate and to the King's Pool, but there was no room for the animal that was under me to pass. ¹⁵Then I went up in the night by the valley and inspected the wall, and I turned back and entered by the Valley Gate, and

so returned. [16]And the officials did not know where I had gone or what I was doing, and I had not yet told the Jews, the priests, the nobles, the officials, and the rest who were to do the work.

[17]Then I said to them, "You see the trouble we are in, how Jerusalem lies in ruins with its gates burned. Come, let us build the wall of Jerusalem, that we may no longer suffer derision." [18]And I told them of the hand of my God that had been upon me for good, and also of the words that the king had spoken to me. And they said, "Let us rise up and build." So they strengthened their hands for the good work. [19]But when Sanballat the Horonite and Tobiah the Ammonite servant and Geshem the Arab heard of it, they jeered at us and despised us and said, "What is this thing that you are doing? Are you rebelling against the king?" [20]Then I replied to them, "The God of heaven will make us prosper, and we his servants will arise and build, but you have no portion or right or claim[1] in Jerusalem."

The rebuilding project begins [chapter 3]. Narrative now gives way to the documentary impulse to record names. This chapter is, in fact, a civil record of personnel and materials that will go into the rebuilding of the wall and gates of the city. A good way to relive the rebuilding project is to imagine oneself present. A sense of ceaseless community work emerges from the lists that are recorded. The whole scene comes alive as we read the names of specific physical places that were rebuilt—the Sheep Gate, the Tower of the Hundred, the Fish Gate, and dozens of other evocative architectural features on the building site. An implied theme is a community's need for good organization.

3 Then Eliashib the high priest rose up with his brothers the priests, and they built the Sheep Gate. They consecrated it and set its doors. They consecrated it as far as the Tower of the Hundred, as far as the Tower of Hananel. [2]And next to him the men of Jericho built. And next to them[2] Zaccur the son of Imri built.

[3]The sons of Hassenaah built the Fish Gate. They laid its beams and set its doors, its bolts, and its bars. [4]And next to them Meremoth the son of Uriah, son of Hakkoz repaired. And next to them Meshullam the son of Berechiah, son of Meshezabel repaired. And next to them Zadok the son of Baana repaired. [5]And next to them the Tekoites repaired, but their nobles would not stoop to serve their Lord.[3]

[6]Joiada the son of Paseah and Meshullam the son of Besodeiah repaired the Gate of Yeshanah.[4] They laid its beams and set its doors, its bolts, and its bars. [7]And next to them repaired Melatiah the Gibeonite and Jadon the Meronothite, the men of Gibeon and of Mizpah, the seat of the governor of the province Beyond the River. [8]Next to them Uzziel the son of Harhaiah, goldsmiths, repaired. Next to him Hananiah, one of the perfumers, repaired, and they restored Jerusalem as far as the Broad Wall. [9]Next to them Rephaiah the son of Hur, ruler of half the district of[5] Jerusalem, repaired. [10]Next to them Jedaiah the son of Harumaph repaired opposite his house. And next to him Hattush the son of Hashabneiah repaired. [11]Malchijah the son of Harim and Hasshub the son of Pahath-moab repaired another section and the Tower of the Ovens. [12]Next to him Shallum the son of Hallohesh, ruler of half the district of Jerusalem, repaired, he and his daughters.

[13]Hanun and the inhabitants of Zanoah repaired the Valley Gate. They rebuilt it

---

[1] Or memorial [2] Hebrew him [3] Or lords [4] Or of the old city [5] Or foreman of half the portion assigned to; also verses 12, 14, 15, 16, 17, 18

and set its doors, its bolts, and its bars, and repaired a thousand cubits[1] of the wall, as far as the Dung Gate.

[14]Malchijah the son of Rechab, ruler of the district of Beth-haccherem, repaired the Dung Gate. He rebuilt it and set its doors, its bolts, and its bars.

[15]And Shallum the son of Col-hozeh, ruler of the district of Mizpah, repaired the Fountain Gate. He rebuilt it and covered it and set its doors, its bolts, and its bars. And he built the wall of the Pool of Shelah of the king's garden, as far as the stairs that go down from the city of David. [16]After him Nehemiah the son of Azbuk, ruler of half the district of Beth-zur, repaired to a point opposite the tombs of David, as far as the artificial pool, and as far as the house of the mighty men. [17]After him the Levites repaired: Rehum the son of Bani. Next to him Hashabiah, ruler of half the district of Keilah, repaired for his district. [18]After him their brothers repaired: Bavvai the son of Henadad, ruler of half the district of Keilah. [19]Next to him Ezer the son of Jeshua, ruler of Mizpah, repaired another section opposite the ascent to the armory at the buttress.[2] [20]After him Baruch the son of Zabbai repaired another section from the buttress to the door of the house of Eliashib the high priest. [21]After him Meremoth the son of Uriah, son of Hakkoz repaired another section from the door of the house of Eliashib to the end of the house of Eliashib. [22]After him the priests, the men of the surrounding area, repaired. [23]After them Benjamin and Hasshub repaired opposite their house. After them Azariah the son of Maaseiah, son of Ananiah repaired beside his own house. [24]After him Binnui the son of Henadad repaired another section, from the house of Azariah to the buttress [25]and to the corner. Palal the son of Uzai repaired opposite the buttress and the tower projecting from the upper house of the king at the court of the guard. After him Pedaiah the son of Parosh [26]and the temple servants living on Ophel repaired to a point opposite the Water Gate on the east and the projecting tower. [27]After him the Tekoites repaired another section opposite the great projecting tower as far as the wall of Ophel.

[28]Above the Horse Gate the priests repaired, each one opposite his own house. [29]After them Zadok the son of Immer repaired opposite his own house. After him Shemaiah the son of Shecaniah, the keeper of the East Gate, repaired. [30]After him Hananiah the son of Shelemiah and Hanun the sixth son of Zalaph repaired another section. After him Meshullam the son of Berechiah repaired opposite his chamber. [31]After him Malchijah, one of the goldsmiths, repaired as far as the house of the temple servants and of the merchants, opposite the Muster Gate,[3] and to the upper chamber of the corner. [32]And between the upper chamber of the corner and the Sheep Gate the goldsmiths and the merchants repaired.

Plot and counterplot [chapter 4]. What began simply as a story that has gripped us with its picture of industriousness, efficiency of organization, and engineering and architectural expertise now becomes a conflict story, as the Jews' neighbors display hostility to them and their rebuilding of the city wall. The conflict unfolds as a plot by the Jews' enemies and a counterplot by the Jews. The sequence is as follows: Sanballat and Tobiah taunt the Jews (vv. 1–3); the Jews pray to God for deliverance and continue to build the wall (vv. 4–6); a confederation of enemies plans a secret attack on the Jews, who respond with prayer and stationing of armed defenders at the wall (vv. 7–14); the Jews continue to build the wall with a strategy of half of the men building the wall and half of them standing guard (vv. 15–20), along with a scheme of alternating nighttime watch

[1] A *cubit* was about 18 inches or 45 centimeters [2] Or *corner*; also verses 20, 24, 25 [3] Or *Hammiphkad Gate*

and daytime work (vv. 21–23). Good ways to read this chapter include the following: follow the plot conflict between the Jews and their enemies; note the specific ingredient-sof human ingenuity in the actions of the Jews; observe the references to God—both the people's expression of faith in God and the introduction of God as an actor in the story. The archetype at work is the triumph of the godly underdog.

4 [1] Now when Sanballat heard that we were building the wall, he was angry and greatly enraged, and he jeered at the Jews. [2]And he said in the presence of his brothers and of the army of Samaria, "What are these feeble Jews doing? Will they restore it for themselves?[2] Will they sacrifice? Will they finish up in a day? Will they revive the stones out of the heaps of rubbish, and burned ones at that?" [3]Tobiah the Ammonite was beside him, and he said, "Yes, what they are building—if a fox goes up on it he will break down their stone wall!" [4]Hear, O our God, for we are despised. Turn back their taunt on their own heads and give them up to be plundered in a land where they are captives. [5]Do not cover their guilt, and let not their sin be blotted out from your sight, for they have provoked you to anger in the presence of the builders.

[6]So we built the wall. And all the wall was joined together to half its height, for the people had a mind to work.

[7][3] But when Sanballat and Tobiah and the Arabs and the Ammonites and the Ashdodites heard that the repairing of the walls of Jerusalem was going forward and that the breaches were beginning to be closed, they were very angry. [8]And they all plotted together to come and fight against Jerusalem and to cause confusion in it. [9]And we prayed to our God and set a guard as a protection against them day and night.

[10]In Judah it was said,[4] "The strength of those who bear the burdens is failing. There is too much rubble. By ourselves we will not be able to rebuild the wall." [11]And our enemies said, "They will not know or see till we come among them and kill them and stop the work." [12]At that time the Jews who lived near them came from all directions and said to us ten times, "You must return to us."[5] [13]So in the lowest parts of the space behind the wall, in open places, I stationed the people by their clans, with their swords, their spears, and their bows. [14]And I looked and arose and said to the nobles and to the officials and to the rest of the people, "Do not be afraid of them. Remember the Lord, who is great and awesome, and fight for your brothers, your sons, your daughters, your wives, and your homes."

[15]When our enemies heard that it was known to us and that God had frustrated their plan, we all returned to the wall, each to his work. [16]From that day on, half of my servants worked on construction, and half held the spears, shields, bows, and coats of mail. And the leaders stood behind the whole house of Judah, [17]who were building on the wall. Those who carried burdens were loaded in such a way that each labored on the work with one hand and held his weapon with the other. [18]And each of the builders had his sword strapped at his side while he built. The man who sounded the trumpet was beside me. [19]And I said to the nobles and to the officials and to the rest of the people, "The work is great and widely spread, and we are separated on the wall, far from one another. [20]In the place where you hear the sound of the trumpet, rally to us there. Our God will fight for us."

[21]So we labored at the work, and half of them held the spears from the break of

---

[1] Ch 3:33 in Hebrew [2] Or *Will they commit themselves to God?* [3] Ch 4:1 in Hebrew [4] Hebrew *Judah said* [5] The meaning of the Hebrew is uncertain

dawn until the stars came out. ²²I also said to the people at that time, "Let every man and his servant pass the night within Jerusalem, that they may be a guard for us by night and may labor by day." ²³So neither I nor my brothers nor my servants nor the men of the guard who followed me, none of us took off our clothes; each kept his weapon at his right hand.¹

> **Trouble from within** [chapter 5]. The story now takes a surprising twist. For the first time we read about obstacles to success from within the godly community itself. The chapter unfolds as follows: it emerges that the builders of the wall have undergone unconscionable financial hardship while doing the work of state in rebuilding the wall (vv. 1–5); Nehemiah takes decisive action against the exploiters (vv. 6–13); Nehemiah catalogs the sacrifices that he himself has made on behalf of the nation and asks God to reward him for his sacrifices (vv. 14–19). As we read, we can (a) relive the very human story that unfolds, (b) observe negative examples of behavior to avoid, and (c) admire the heroic courage and generosity of the leader Nehemiah, who emerges as one of the fully developed characters of the Bible.

5 Now there arose a great outcry of the people and of their wives against their Jewish brothers. ²For there were those who said, "With our sons and our daughters, we are many. So let us get grain, that we may eat and keep alive." ³There were also those who said, "We are mortgaging our fields, our vineyards, and our houses to get grain because of the famine." ⁴And there were those who said, "We have borrowed money for the king's tax on our fields and our vineyards. ⁵Now our flesh is as the flesh of our brothers, our children are as their children. Yet we are forcing our sons and our daughters to be slaves, and some of our daughters have already been enslaved, but it is not in our power to help it, for other men have our fields and our vineyards."

⁶I was very angry when I heard their outcry and these words. ⁷I took counsel with myself, and I brought charges against the nobles and the officials. I said to them, "You are exacting interest, each from his brother." And I held a great assembly against them ⁸and said to them, "We, as far as we are able, have bought back our Jewish brothers who have been sold to the nations, but you even sell your brothers that they may be sold to us!" They were silent and could not find a word to say. ⁹So I said, "The thing that you are doing is not good. Ought you not to walk in the fear of our God to prevent the taunts of the nations our enemies? ¹⁰Moreover, I and my brothers and my servants are lending them money and grain. Let us abandon this exacting of interest. ¹¹Return to them this very day their fields, their vineyards, their olive orchards, and their houses, and the percentage of money, grain, wine, and oil that you have been exacting from them." ¹²Then they said, "We will restore these and require nothing from them. We will do as you say." And I called the priests and made them swear to do as they had promised. ¹³I also shook out the fold² of my garment and said, "So may God shake out every man from his house and from his labor who does not keep this promise. So may he be shaken out and emptied." And all the assembly said "Amen" and praised the Lord. And the people did as they had promised.

¹⁴Moreover, from the time that I was appointed to be their governor in the land of Judah, from the twentieth year to the thirty-second year of Artaxerxes the king, twelve years, neither I nor my brothers ate the food allowance of the governor. ¹⁵The former

---

¹ Probable reading; Hebrew *each his weapon the water* ² Hebrew *bosom*

governors who were before me laid heavy burdens on the people and took from them for their daily ration[1] forty shekels[2] of silver. Even their servants lorded it over the people. But I did not do so, because of the fear of God. [16]I also persevered in the work on this wall, and we acquired no land, and all my servants were gathered there for the work. [17]Moreover, there were at my table 150 men, Jews and officials, besides those who came to us from the nations that were around us. [18]Now what was prepared at my expense[3] for each day was one ox and six choice sheep and birds, and every ten days all kinds of wine in abundance. Yet for all this I did not demand the food allowance of the governor, because the service was too heavy on this people. [19]Remember for my good, O my God, all that I have done for this people.

Standing firm against enemies [chapter 6]. The story now swings back to the external threats to the building project. The heroic actions of Nehemiah unfold as follows: Nehemiah stands up to the intended trickery and the bullying tactics of Sanballat and Tobiah (vv. 1–9); Nehemiah also rejects the intended trickery of false prophets planted by the enemies in the Jewish community (vv. 10–14); the wall is completed as Nehemiah endures still more efforts to harm him (vv. 15–19). Again we can see an abundance of recognizable human experience in all of this action, such as the scheming minds of envious people and the benefits of being cautious and clever as the need arises. Two other patterns to trace are the cleverness of Nehemiah and the appeals that he makes to God to help and vindicate him.

6 Now when Sanballat and Tobiah and Geshem the Arab and the rest of our enemies heard that I had built the wall and that there was no breach left in it (although up to that time I had not set up the doors in the gates), [2]Sanballat and Geshem sent to me, saying, "Come and let us meet together at Hakkephirim in the plain of Ono." But they intended to do me harm. [3]And I sent messengers to them, saying, "I am doing a great work and I cannot come down. Why should the work stop while I leave it and come down to you?" [4]And they sent to me four times in this way, and I answered them in the same manner. [5]In the same way Sanballat for the fifth time sent his servant to me with an open letter in his hand. [6]In it was written, "It is reported among the nations, and Geshem[4] also says it, that you and the Jews intend to rebel; that is why you are building the wall. And according to these reports you wish to become their king. [7]And you have also set up prophets to proclaim concerning you in Jerusalem, 'There is a king in Judah.' And now the king will hear of these reports. So now come and let us take counsel together." [8]Then I sent to him, saying, "No such things as you say have been done, for you are inventing them out of your own mind." [9]For they all wanted to frighten us, thinking, "Their hands will drop from the work, and it will not be done." But now, O God,[5] strengthen my hands.

[10]Now when I went into the house of Shemaiah the son of Delaiah, son of Mehetabel, who was confined to his home, he said, "Let us meet together in the house of God, within the temple. Let us close the doors of the temple, for they are coming to kill you. They are coming to kill you by night." [11]But I said, "Should such a man as I run away? And what man such as I could go into the temple and live?[6] I will not go in." [12]And I understood and saw that God had not sent him, but he had pronounced the prophecy against me because Tobiah and Sanballat had hired him. [13]For this pur-

---

[1] Compare Vulgate; Hebrew *took from them with food and wine afterward* [2] A *shekel* was about 2/5 ounce or 11 grams [3] Or *prepared for me* [4] Hebrew *Gashmu* [5] Hebrew lacks *O God* [6] Or *would go into the temple to save his life*

pose he was hired, that I should be afraid and act in this way and sin, and so they could give me a bad name in order to taunt me. [14]Remember Tobiah and Sanballat, O my God, according to these things that they did, and also the prophetess Noadiah and the rest of the prophets who wanted to make me afraid.

[15]So the wall was finished on the twenty-fifth day of the month Elul, in fifty-two days. [16]And when all our enemies heard of it, all the nations around us were afraid and fell greatly in their own esteem, for they perceived that this work had been accomplished with the help of our God. [17]Moreover, in those days the nobles of Judah sent many letters to Tobiah, and Tobiah's letters came to them. [18]For many in Judah were bound by oath to him, because he was the son-in-law of Shecaniah the son of Arah: and his son Jehohanan had taken the daughter of Meshullam the son of Berechiah as his wife. [19]Also they spoke of his good deeds in my presence and reported my words to him. And Tobiah sent letters to make me afraid.

Life returns to normal [chapter 7]. Chapter 7 draws a boundary around the narrative of the building of the wall of Jerusalem. As we read about the stipulations that Nehemiah sets up in connection with guarding the gates of the completed wall (vv. 1–4), it dawns on us that never has there been a more famous wall in the history of the world than this storied wall of the rebuilt Jerusalem. The bulk of the chapter (vv. 6–69) is devoted to lists of names and tabulation of numbers of those who returned to Jerusalem from exile in Babylon. As the lists keep expanding, we begin to get caught up in the excitement and magnitude of the event. At the end of the chapter we catch hints of a story with the description of what the leaders and populace gave to the building project (vv. 70–72), along with a summary of the influential professional groups that enabled the nation once again to live in their towns (v. 73). A strong sense of community cooperation emerges, giving us a picture of what it takes to build the city of God.

7 Now when the wall had been built and I had set up the doors, and the gatekeepers, the singers, and the Levites had been appointed, [2]I gave my brother Hanani and Hananiah the governor of the castle charge over Jerusalem, for he was a more faithful and God-fearing man than many. [3]And I said to them, "Let not the gates of Jerusalem be opened until the sun is hot. And while they are still standing guard, let them shut and bar the doors. Appoint guards from among the inhabitants of Jerusalem, some at their guard posts and some in front of their own homes." [4]The city was wide and large, but the people within it were few, and no houses had been rebuilt.

[5]Then my God put it into my heart to assemble the nobles and the officials and the people to be enrolled by genealogy. And I found the book of the genealogy of those who came up at the first, and I found written in it:

[6]These were the people of the province who came up out of the captivity of those exiles whom Nebuchadnezzar the king of Babylon had carried into exile. They returned to Jerusalem and Judah, each to his town. [7]They came with Zerubbabel, Jeshua, Nehemiah, Azariah, Raamiah, Nahamani, Mordecai, Bilshan, Mispereth, Bigvai, Nehum, Baanah.

The number of the men of the people of Israel: [8]the sons of Parosh, 2,172. [9]The sons of Shephatiah, 372. [10]The sons of Arah, 652. [11]The sons of Pahath-moab, namely the sons of Jeshua and Joab, 2,818. [12]The sons of Elam, 1,254. [13]The sons of Zattu, 845.

[14]The sons of Zaccai, 760. [15]The sons of Binnui, 648. [16]The sons of Bebai, 628. [17]The sons of Azgad, 2,322. [18]The sons of Adonikam, 667. [19]The sons of Bigvai, 2,067. [20]The sons of Adin, 655. [21]The sons of Ater, namely of Hezekiah, 98. [22]The sons of Hashum, 328. [23]The sons of Bezai, 324. [24]The sons of Hariph, 112. [25]The sons of Gibeon, 95. [26]The men of Bethlehem and Netophah, 188. [27]The men of Anathoth, 128. [28]The men of Beth-azmaveth, 42. [29]The men of Kiriath-jearim, Chephirah, and Beeroth, 743. [30]The men of Ramah and Geba, 621. [31]The men of Michmas, 122. [32]The men of Bethel and Ai, 123. [33]The men of the other Nebo, 52. [34]The sons of the other Elam, 1,254. [35]The sons of Harim, 320. [36]The sons of Jericho, 345. [37]The sons of Lod, Hadid, and Ono, 721. [38]The sons of Senaah, 3,930.

[39]The priests: the sons of Jedaiah, namely the house of Jeshua, 973. [40]The sons of Immer, 1,052. [41]The sons of Pashhur, 1,247. [42]The sons of Harim, 1,017.

[43]The Levites: the sons of Jeshua, namely of Kadmiel of the sons of Hodevah, 74. [44]The singers: the sons of Asaph, 148. [45]The gatekeepers: the sons of Shallum, the sons of Ater, the sons of Talmon, the sons of Akkub, the sons of Hatita, the sons of Shobai, 138.

[46]The temple servants: the sons of Ziha, the sons of Hasupha, the sons of Tabbaoth, [47]the sons of Keros, the sons of Sia, the sons of Padon, [48]the sons of Lebana, the sons of Hagaba, the sons of Shalmai, [49]the sons of Hanan, the sons of Giddel, the sons of Gahar, [50]the sons of Reaiah, the sons of Rezin, the sons of Nekoda, [51]the sons of Gazzam, the sons of Uzza, the sons of Paseah, [52]the sons of Besai, the sons of Meunim, the sons of Nephushesim, [53]the sons of Bakbuk, the sons of Hakupha, the sons of Harhur, [54]the sons of Bazlith, the sons of Mehida, the sons of Harsha, [55]the sons of Barkos, the sons of Sisera, the sons of Temah, [56]the sons of Neziah, the sons of Hatipha.

[57]The sons of Solomon's servants: the sons of Sotai, the sons of Sophereth, the sons of Perida, [58]the sons of Jaala, the sons of Darkon, the sons of Giddel, [59]the sons of Shephatiah, the sons of Hattil, the sons of Pochereth-hazzebaim, the sons of Amon.

[60]All the temple servants and the sons of Solomon's servants were 392.

[61]The following were those who came up from Tel-melah, Tel-harsha, Cherub, Addon, and Immer, but they could not prove their fathers' houses nor their descent, whether they belonged to Israel: [62]the sons of Delaiah, the sons of Tobiah, the sons of Nekoda, 642. [63]Also, of the priests: the sons of Hobaiah, the sons of Hakkoz, the sons of Barzillai (who had taken a wife of the daughters of Barzillai the Gileadite and was called by their name). [64]These sought their registration among those enrolled in the genealogies, but it was not found there, so they were excluded from the priesthood as unclean. [65]The governor told them that they were not to partake of the most holy food until a priest with Urim and Thummim should arise.

[66]The whole assembly together was 42,360, [67]besides their male and female servants, of whom there were 7,337. And they had 245 singers, male and female. [68]Their horses were 736, their mules 245,[1] [69]their camels 435, and their donkeys 6,720.

[70]Now some of the heads of fathers' houses gave to the work. The governor gave to the treasury 1,000 darics[2] of gold, 50 basins, 30 priests' garments and 500 minas[3] of silver.[4] [71]And some of the heads of fathers' houses gave into the treasury of the work 20,000 darics of gold and 2,200 minas of silver. [72]And what the rest of the people gave was 20,000 darics of gold, 2,000 minas of silver, and 67 priests' garments.

---

[1] Ezra 2:66 and the margins of some Hebrew manuscripts; Hebrew lacks *Their horses . . . 245* [2] A *daric* was a coin weighing about 1/4 ounce or 8.5 grams [3] A *mina* was about 1 1/4 pounds or 0.6 kilogram [4] Probable reading; Hebrew lacks *minas of silver*

⁷³So the priests, the Levites, the gatekeepers, the singers, some of the people, the temple servants, and all Israel, lived in their towns.

And when the seventh month had come, the people of Israel were in their towns.

> **The law reinstituted** [chapter 8]. Chapter 8 begins a three-chapter block that is one of the great stories in the Bible. Much of the action is dramatized through recorded speeches by speakers and audiences that are placed in a specific setting. Chapter 8 is divided into two episodes. In the first unit (vv. 1–12) we read about the gathering of the people in the city square to hear Ezra read the law. The event unfolds as a ceremonial observance filled with ritual and formal protocol. The story is rich with principles relating to the centrality of God's law in the life of the believing community, the need to have the law interpreted by teachers educated in it, the responsibility of laypeople to be receptive to God's Word. The event unfolds as a drama in miniature. The second half of the chapter (vv. 13–18) narrates how the people renew their observance of the Feast of Booths in keeping with what they read in the law regarding it. Important motifs are the people's sorrow for their sin and Ezra's famous exhortation to joy in verse 10.

8 And all the people gathered as one man into the square before the Water Gate. And they told Ezra the scribe to bring the Book of the Law of Moses that the LORD had commanded Israel. ²So Ezra the priest brought the Law before the assembly, both men and women and all who could understand what they heard, on the first day of the seventh month. ³And he read from it facing the square before the Water Gate from early morning until midday, in the presence of the men and the women and those who could understand. And the ears of all the people were attentive to the Book of the Law. ⁴And Ezra the scribe stood on a wooden platform that they had made for the purpose. And beside him stood Mattithiah, Shema, Anaiah, Uriah, Hilkiah, and Maaseiah on his right hand, and Pedaiah, Mishael, Malchijah, Hashum, Hashbaddanah, Zechariah, and Meshullam on his left hand. ⁵And Ezra opened the book in the sight of all the people, for he was above all the people, and as he opened it all the people stood. ⁶And Ezra blessed the LORD, the great God, and all the people answered, "Amen, Amen," lifting up their hands. And they bowed their heads and worshiped the LORD with their faces to the ground. ⁷Also Jeshua, Bani, Sherebiah, Jamin, Akkub, Shabbethai, Hodiah, Maaseiah, Kelita, Azariah, Jozabad, Hanan, Pelaiah, the Levites,¹ helped the people to understand the Law, while the people remained in their places. ⁸They read from the book, from the Law of God, clearly,² and they gave the sense, so that the people understood the reading.

⁹And Nehemiah, who was the governor, and Ezra the priest and scribe, and the Levites who taught the people said to all the people, "This day is holy to the LORD your God; do not mourn or weep." For all the people wept as they heard the words of the Law. ¹⁰Then he said to them, "Go your way. Eat the fat and drink sweet wine and send portions to anyone who has nothing ready, for this day is holy to our Lord. And do not be grieved, for the joy of the LORD is your strength." ¹¹So the Levites calmed all the people, saying, "Be quiet, for this day is holy; do not be grieved." ¹²And all the people went their way to eat and drink and to send portions and to make great rejoicing, because they had understood the words that were declared to them.

¹³On the second day the heads of fathers' houses of all the people, with the priests and the Levites, came together to Ezra the scribe in order to study the words of the

---

¹Vulgate; Hebrew *and the Levites* ²Or *with interpretation,* or *paragraph by paragraph*

Law. [14]And they found it written in the Law that the LORD had commanded by Moses that the people of Israel should dwell in booths[1] during the feast of the seventh month, [15]and that they should proclaim it and publish it in all their towns and in Jerusalem, "Go out to the hills and bring branches of olive, wild olive, myrtle, palm, and other leafy trees to make booths, as it is written." [16]So the people went out and brought them and made booths for themselves, each on his roof, and in their courts and in the courts of the house of God, and in the square at the Water Gate and in the square at the Gate of Ephraim. [17]And all the assembly of those who had returned from the captivity made booths and lived in the booths, for from the days of Jeshua the son of Nun to that day the people of Israel had not done so. And there was very great rejoicing. [18]And day by day, from the first day to the last day, he read from the Book of the Law of God. They kept the feast seven days, and on the eighth day there was a solemn assembly, according to the rule.

> **Ezra's address to God at the covenant renewal ceremony** [chapter 9]. The renewal of the covenant begins with a narrative account of the religious assembly of the people and their leaders (vv. 1–5). Then we get a full account of a formal and embellished address by Ezra to God. The rhetorical stance of direct address to God makes the oration read like a prayer, though the concluding statement that "we make a firm covenant in writing" (v. 38) resembles a formal speech at a ceremony more than a prayer. To render the situation even more complex, Ezra's rehearsal of national history in the address is for the benefit of the human audience more than for God's benefit and gives the speech the flavor of a sermon. The keynotes of the speech are as follows: exaltation of God for his greatness and for his acts of deliverance in the history of Israel; God's giving of his law and the nation's disobedience of that law; a penitential note as Ezra confesses the sins of a nation; vindication of God in his punishment of the nation for its disobedience.

9 Now on the twenty-fourth day of this month the people of Israel were assembled with fasting and in sackcloth, and with earth on their heads. [2]And the Israelites separated themselves from all foreigners and stood and confessed their sins and the iniquities of their fathers. [3]And they stood up in their place and read from the Book of the Law of the LORD their God for a quarter of the day; for another quarter of it they made confession and worshiped the LORD their God. [4]On the stairs of the Levites stood Jeshua, Bani, Kadmiel, Shebaniah, Bunni, Sherebiah, Bani, and Chenani; and they cried with a loud voice to the LORD their God. [5]Then the Levites, Jeshua, Kadmiel, Bani, Hashabneiah, Sherebiah, Hodiah, Shebaniah, and Pethahiah, said, "Stand up and bless the LORD your God from everlasting to everlasting. Blessed be your glorious name, which is exalted above all blessing and praise.

[6][2] "You are the LORD, you alone. You have made heaven, the heaven of heavens, with all their host, the earth and all that is on it, the seas and all that is in them; and you preserve all of them; and the host of heaven worships you. [7]You are the LORD, the God who chose Abram and brought him out of Ur of the Chaldeans and gave him the name Abraham. [8]You found his heart faithful before you, and made with him the covenant to give to his offspring the land of the Canaanite, the Hittite, the Amorite, the Perizzite, the Jebusite, and the Girgashite. And you have kept your promise, for you are righteous.

[9]"And you saw the affliction of our fathers in Egypt and heard their cry at the Red

---

[1] Or temporary shelters [2] Septuagint adds And Ezra said

Sea, [10]and performed signs and wonders against Pharaoh and all his servants and all the people of his land, for you knew that they acted arrogantly against our fathers. And you made a name for yourself, as it is to this day. [11]And you divided the sea before them, so that they went through the midst of the sea on dry land, and you cast their pursuers into the depths, as a stone into mighty waters. [12]By a pillar of cloud you led them in the day, and by a pillar of fire in the night to light for them the way in which they should go. [13]You came down on Mount Sinai and spoke with them from heaven and gave them right rules and true laws, good statutes and commandments, [14]and you made known to them your holy Sabbath and commanded them commandments and statutes and a law by Moses your servant. [15]You gave them bread from heaven for their hunger and brought water for them out of the rock for their thirst, and you told them to go in to possess the land that you had sworn to give them.

[16]"But they and our fathers acted presumptuously and stiffened their neck and did not obey your commandments. [17]They refused to obey and were not mindful of the wonders that you performed among them, but they stiffened their neck and appointed a leader to return to their slavery in Egypt. But you are a God ready to forgive, gracious and merciful, slow to anger and abounding in steadfast love, and did not forsake them. [18]Even when they had made for themselves a golden[1] calf and said, 'This is your God who brought you up out of Egypt,' and had committed great blasphemies, [19]you in your great mercies did not forsake them in the wilderness. The pillar of cloud to lead them in the way did not depart from them by day, nor the pillar of fire by night to light for them the way by which they should go. [20]You gave your good Spirit to instruct them and did not withhold your manna from their mouth and gave them water for their thirst. [21]Forty years you sustained them in the wilderness, and they lacked nothing. Their clothes did not wear out and their feet did not swell.

[22]"And you gave them kingdoms and peoples and allotted to them every corner. So they took possession of the land of Sihon king of Heshbon and the land of Og king of Bashan. [23]You multiplied their children as the stars of heaven, and you brought them into the land that you had told their fathers to enter and possess. [24]So the descendants went in and possessed the land, and you subdued before them the inhabitants of the land, the Canaanites, and gave them into their hand, with their kings and the peoples of the land, that they might do with them as they would. [25]And they captured fortified cities and a rich land, and took possession of houses full of all good things, cisterns already hewn, vineyards, olive orchards and fruit trees in abundance. So they ate and were filled and became fat and delighted themselves in your great goodness.

[26]"Nevertheless, they were disobedient and rebelled against you and cast your law behind their back and killed your prophets, who had warned them in order to turn them back to you, and they committed great blasphemies. [27]Therefore you gave them into the hand of their enemies, who made them suffer. And in the time of their suffering they cried out to you and you heard them from heaven, and according to your great mercies you gave them saviors who saved them from the hand of their enemies. [28]But after they had rest they did evil again before you, and you abandoned them to the hand of their enemies, so that they had dominion over them. Yet when they turned and cried to you, you heard from heaven, and many times you delivered them according to your mercies. [29]And you warned them in order to turn them back to your law. Yet they acted presumptuously and did not obey your commandments, but sinned against your rules, which if a person does them, he shall live by them, and

---

[1] Hebrew *metal*

they turned a stubborn shoulder and stiffened their neck and would not obey. [30]Many years you bore with them and warned them by your Spirit through your prophets. Yet they would not give ear. Therefore you gave them into the hand of the peoples of the lands. [31]Nevertheless, in your great mercies you did not make an end of them or forsake them, for you are a gracious and merciful God.

[32]"Now, therefore, our God, the great, the mighty, and the awesome God, who keeps covenant and steadfast love, let not all the hardship seem little to you that has come upon us, upon our kings, our princes, our priests, our prophets, our fathers, and all your people, since the time of the kings of Assyria until this day. [33]Yet you have been righteous in all that has come upon us, for you have dealt faithfully and we have acted wickedly. [34]Our kings, our princes, our priests, and our fathers have not kept your law or paid attention to your commandments and your warnings that you gave them. [35]Even in their own kingdom, and amid your great goodness that you gave them, and in the large and rich land that you set before them, they did not serve you or turn from their wicked works. [36]Behold, we are slaves this day; in the land that you gave to our fathers to enjoy its fruit and its good gifts, behold, we are slaves. [37]And its rich yield goes to the kings whom you have set over us because of our sins. They rule over our bodies and over our livestock as they please, and we are in great distress. [38][1] "Because of all this we make a firm covenant in writing; on the sealed document are the names of[2] our princes, our Levites, and our priests.

The renewal of the covenant [chapter 10]. This chapter provides the content of the covenant that the nation signed at the renewal ceremony. First we get a list of the names of the leaders who sign the covenant (vv. 1–27). The rest of the passage is an inventory of the things that the people and their leaders commit themselves to refraining from doing (vv. 28–31) and the obligations that they accept as part of living God's law (vv. 32–39). As we read about specific practices that believers in the NT dispensation no longer continue, we need to ponder the enduring spiritual principles underlying them.

10

[3] "On the seals are the names of[4] Nehemiah the governor, the son of Hacaliah, Zedekiah, [2]Seraiah, Azariah, Jeremiah, [3]Pashhur, Amariah, Malchijah, [4]Hattush, Shebaniah, Malluch, [5]Harim, Meremoth, Obadiah, [6]Daniel, Ginnethon, Baruch, [7]Meshullam, Abijah, Mijamin, [8]Maaziah, Bilgai, Shemaiah; these are the priests. [9]And the Levites: Jeshua the son of Azaniah, Binnui of the sons of Henadad, Kadmiel; [10]and their brothers, Shebaniah, Hodiah, Kelita, Pelaiah, Hanan, [11]Mica, Rehob, Hashabiah, [12]Zaccur, Sherebiah, Shebaniah, [13]Hodiah, Bani, Beninu. [14]The chiefs of the people: Parosh, Pahath-moab, Elam, Zattu, Bani, [15]Bunni, Azgad, Bebai, [16]Adonijah, Bigvai, Adin, [17]Ater, Hezekiah, Azzur, [18]Hodiah, Hashum, Bezai, [19]Hariph, Anathoth, Nebai, [20]Magpiash, Meshullam, Hezir, [21]Meshezabel, Zadok, Jaddua, [22]Pelatiah, Hanan, Anaiah, [23]Hoshea, Hananiah, Hasshub, [24]Hallohesh, Pilha, Shobek, [25]Rehum, Hashabnah, Maaseiah, [26]Ahiah, Hanan, Anan, [27]Malluch, Harim, Baanah.

[28]"The rest of the people, the priests, the Levites, the gatekeepers, the singers, the temple servants, and all who have separated themselves from the peoples of the lands to the Law of God, their wives, their sons, their daughters, all who have knowledge and understanding, [29]join with their brothers, their nobles, and enter into a curse and an oath to walk in God's Law that was given by Moses the servant of God,

[1] Ch 10:1 in Hebrew [2] Hebrew lacks *the names of* [3] Ch 10:2 in Hebrew [4] Hebrew lacks *the names of*

and to observe and do all the commandments of the LORD our Lord and his rules and his statutes. [30]We will not give our daughters to the peoples of the land or take their daughters for our sons. [31]And if the peoples of the land bring in goods or any grain on the Sabbath day to sell, we will not buy from them on the Sabbath or on a holy day. And we will forego the crops of the seventh year and the exaction of every debt.

[32]"We also take on ourselves the obligation to give yearly a third part of a shekel[1] for the service of the house of our God: [33]for the showbread, the regular grain offering, the regular burnt offering, the Sabbaths, the new moons, the appointed feasts, the holy things, and the sin offerings to make atonement for Israel, and for all the work of the house of our God. [34]We, the priests, the Levites, and the people, have likewise cast lots for the wood offering, to bring it into the house of our God, according to our fathers' houses, at times appointed, year by year, to burn on the altar of the LORD our God, as it is written in the Law. [35]We obligate ourselves to bring the firstfruits of our ground and the firstfruits of all fruit of every tree, year by year, to the house of the LORD; [36]also to bring to the house of our God, to the priests who minister in the house of our God, the firstborn of our sons and of our cattle, as it is written in the Law, and the firstborn of our herds and of our flocks; [37]and to bring the first of our dough, and our contributions, the fruit of every tree, the wine and the oil, to the priests, to the chambers of the house of our God; and to bring to the Levites the tithes from our ground, for it is the Levites who collect the tithes in all our towns where we labor. [38]And the priest, the son of Aaron, shall be with the Levites when the Levites receive the tithes. And the Levites shall bring up the tithe of the tithes to the house of our God, to the chambers of the storehouse. [39]For the people of Israel and the sons of Levi shall bring the contribution of grain, wine, and oil to the chambers, where the vessels of the sanctuary are, as well as the priests who minister, and the gatekeepers and the singers. We will not neglect the house of our God."

The resettlement of Jerusalem and its suburbs [11:1–12:26]. The book of Nehemiah has affinities with utopian literature, which portrays a good society and highlights the institutional key that makes the society good. The renewing of the covenant in the preceding chapters pictures the institutional key that underlies the good society that Ezra and Nehemiah help to reestablish. The lists of clan leaders who repeopled Jerusalem and the surrounding territory in this present unit build up a cumulative picture of a well-ordered society. As we look at the categories of people who are named, it is obvious that the author regards the religious leaders (such as priests and Levites) as having special prominence in this holy commonwealth.

11 Now the leaders of the people lived in Jerusalem. And the rest of the people cast lots to bring one out of ten to live in Jerusalem the holy city, while nine out of ten[2] remained in the other towns. [2]And the people blessed all the men who willingly offered to live in Jerusalem.

[3]These are the chiefs of the province who lived in Jerusalem; but in the towns of Judah everyone lived on his property in their towns: Israel, the priests, the Levites, the temple servants, and the descendants of Solomon's servants. [4]And in Jerusalem lived certain of the sons of Judah and of the sons of Benjamin. Of the sons of Judah: Athaiah the son of Uzziah, son of Zechariah, son of Amariah, son of Shephatiah, son

[1] A *shekel* was about 2/5 ounce or 11 grams [2] Hebrew *nine hands*

of Mahalalel, of the sons of Perez; [5]and Maaseiah the son of Baruch, son of Colhozeh, son of Hazaiah, son of Adaiah, son of Joiarib, son of Zechariah, son of the Shilonite. [6]All the sons of Perez who lived in Jerusalem were 468 valiant men.

[7]And these are the sons of Benjamin: Sallu the son of Meshullam, son of Joed, son of Pedaiah, son of Kolaiah, son of Maaseiah, son of Ithiel, son of Jeshaiah, [8]and his brothers, men of valor, 928.[1] [9]Joel the son of Zichri was their overseer; and Judah the son of Hassenuah was second over the city.

[10]Of the priests: Jedaiah the son of Joiarib, Jachin, [11]Seraiah the son of Hilkiah, son of Meshullam, son of Zadok, son of Meraioth, son of Ahitub, ruler of the house of God, [12]and their brothers who did the work of the house, 822; and Adaiah the son of Jeroham, son of Pelaliah, son of Amzi, son of Zechariah, son of Pashhur, son of Malchijah, [13]and his brothers, heads of fathers' houses, 242; and Amashsai, the son of Azarel, son of Ahzai, son of Meshillemoth, son of Immer, [14]and their brothers, mighty men of valor, 128; their overseer was Zabdiel the son of Haggedolim.

[15]And of the Levites: Shemaiah the son of Hasshub, son of Azrikam, son of Hashabiah, son of Bunni; [16]and Shabbethai and Jozabad, of the chiefs of the Levites, who were over the outside work of the house of God; [17]and Mattaniah the son of Mica, son of Zabdi, son of Asaph, who was the leader of the praise,[2] who gave thanks, and Bakbukiah, the second among his brothers; and Abda the son of Shammua, son of Galal, son of Jeduthun. [18]All the Levites in the holy city were 284.

[19]The gatekeepers, Akkub, Talmon and their brothers, who kept watch at the gates, were 172. [20]And the rest of Israel, and of the priests and the Levites, were in all the towns of Judah, every one in his inheritance. [21]But the temple servants lived on Ophel; and Ziha and Gishpa were over the temple servants.

[22]The overseer of the Levites in Jerusalem was Uzzi the son of Bani, son of Hashabiah, son of Mattaniah, son of Mica, of the sons of Asaph, the singers, over the work of the house of God. [23]For there was a command from the king concerning them, and a fixed provision for the singers, as every day required. [24]And Pethahiah the son of Meshezabel, of the sons of Zerah the son of Judah, was at the king's side[3] in all matters concerning the people.

[25]And as for the villages, with their fields, some of the people of Judah lived in Kiriath-arba and its villages, and in Dibon and its villages, and in Jekabzeel and its villages, [26]and in Jeshua and in Moladah and Beth-pelet, [27]in Hazar-shual, in Beersheba and its villages, [28]in Ziklag, in Meconah and its villages, [29]in En-rimmon, in Zorah, in Jarmuth, [30]Zanoah, Adullam, and their villages, Lachish and its fields, and Azekah and its villages. So they encamped from Beersheba to the Valley of Hinnom. [31]The people of Benjamin also lived from Geba onward, at Michmash, Aija, Bethel and its villages, [32]Anathoth, Nob, Ananiah, [33]Hazor, Ramah, Gittaim, [34]Hadid, Zeboim, Neballat, [35]Lod, and Ono, the valley of craftsmen. [36]And certain divisions of the Levites in Judah were assigned to Benjamin.

12

These are the priests and the Levites who came up with Zerubbabel the son of Shealtiel, and Jeshua: Seraiah, Jeremiah, Ezra, [2]Amariah, Malluch, Hattush, [3]Shecaniah, Rehum, Meremoth, [4]Iddo, Ginnethoi, Abijah, [5]Mijamin, Maadiah, Bilgah, [6]Shemaiah, Joiarib, Jedaiah, [7]Sallu, Amok, Hilkiah, Jedaiah. These were the chiefs of the priests and of their brothers in the days of Jeshua.

[8]And the Levites: Jeshua, Binnui, Kadmiel, Sherebiah, Judah, and Mattaniah, who

---

[1] Compare Septuagint; Hebrew *Jeshaiah, and after him Gabbai, Sallai, 928* [2] Compare Septuagint, Vulgate; Hebrew *beginning* [3] Hebrew *hand*

with his brothers was in charge of the songs of thanksgiving. ⁹And Bakbukiah and Unni and their brothers stood opposite them in the service. ¹⁰And Jeshua was the father of Joiakim, Joiakim the father of Eliashib, Eliashib the father of Joiada, ¹¹Joiada the father of Jonathan, and Jonathan the father of Jaddua.

¹²And in the days of Joiakim were priests, heads of fathers' houses: of Seraiah, Meraiah; of Jeremiah, Hananiah; ¹³of Ezra, Meshullam; of Amariah, Jehohanan; ¹⁴of Malluchi, Jonathan; of Shebaniah, Joseph; ¹⁵of Harim, Adna; of Meraioth, Helkai; ¹⁶of Iddo, Zechariah; of Ginnethon, Meshullam; ¹⁷of Abijah, Zichri; of Miniamin, of Moadiah, Piltai; ¹⁸of Bilgah, Shammua; of Shemaiah, Jehonathan; ¹⁹of Joiarib, Mattenai; of Jedaiah, Uzzi; ²⁰of Sallai, Kallai; of Amok, Eber; ²¹of Hilkiah, Hashabiah; of Jedaiah, Nethanel.

²²In the days of Eliashib, Joiada, Johanan, and Jaddua, the Levites were recorded as heads of fathers' houses; so too were the priests in the reign of Darius the Persian. ²³As for the sons of Levi, their heads of fathers' houses were written in the Book of the Chronicles until the days of Johanan the son of Eliashib. ²⁴And the chiefs of the Levites: Hashabiah, Sherebiah, and Jeshua the son of Kadmiel, with their brothers who stood opposite them, to praise and to give thanks, according to the commandment of David the man of God, watch by watch. ²⁵Mattaniah, Bakbukiah, Obadiah, Meshullam, Talmon, and Akkub were gatekeepers standing guard at the storehouses of the gates. ²⁶These were in the days of Joiakim the son of Jeshua son of Jozadak, and in the days of Nehemiah the governor and of Ezra, the priest and scribe.

Dedication of the city walls [12:27–47]. The establishment of the fledgling utopia had begun with an epic feat of rebuilding the wall of Jerusalem amid opposition and difficulty. After intervening information about the society that reinhabits the city, we return to the storied wall with an account of its dedication. A good way to progress through the chapter is to imagine oneself present at the events. The exaltation of the ceremony is breathtaking, and we should note the conspicuous attention to evocative place-names like the Water Gate, the Tower of the Ovens and the Broad Wall. Equally compelling is the detail "the joy of Jerusalem was heard far away" (v. 43). The concluding paragraph further delineates the ways in which ancient worship practices are reinstituted (vv. 44–47).

²⁷And at the dedication of the wall of Jerusalem they sought the Levites in all their places, to bring them to Jerusalem to celebrate the dedication with gladness, with thanksgivings and with singing, with cymbals, harps, and lyres. ²⁸And the sons of the singers gathered together from the district surrounding Jerusalem and from the villages of the Netophathites; ²⁹also from Beth-gilgal and from the region of Geba and Azmaveth, for the singers had built for themselves villages around Jerusalem. ³⁰And the priests and the Levites purified themselves, and they purified the people and the gates and the wall.

³¹Then I brought the leaders of Judah up onto the wall and appointed two great choirs that gave thanks. One went to the south on the wall to the Dung Gate. ³²And after them went Hoshaiah and half of the leaders of Judah, ³³and Azariah, Ezra, Meshullam, ³⁴Judah, Benjamin, Shemaiah, and Jeremiah, ³⁵and certain of the priests' sons with trumpets: Zechariah the son of Jonathan, son of Shemaiah, son of Mattaniah, son of Micaiah, son of Zaccur, son of Asaph; ³⁶and his relatives,

Shemaiah, Azarel, Milalai, Gilalai, Maai, Nethanel, Judah, and Hanani, with the musical instruments of David the man of God. And Ezra the scribe went before them. [37]At the Fountain Gate they went up straight before them by the stairs of the city of David, at the ascent of the wall, above the house of David, to the Water Gate on the east.

[38]The other choir of those who gave thanks went to the north, and I followed them with half of the people, on the wall, above the Tower of the Ovens, to the Broad Wall, [39]and above the Gate of Ephraim, and by the Gate of Yeshanah,[1] and by the Fish Gate and the Tower of Hananel and the Tower of the Hundred, to the Sheep Gate; and they came to a halt at the Gate of the Guard. [40]So both choirs of those who gave thanks stood in the house of God, and I and half of the officials with me; [41]and the priests Eliakim, Maaseiah, Miniamin, Micaiah, Elioenai, Zechariah, and Hananiah, with trumpets; [42]and Maaseiah, Shemaiah, Eleazar, Uzzi, Jehohanan, Malchijah, Elam, and Ezer. And the singers sang with Jezrahiah as their leader. [43]And they offered great sacrifices that day and rejoiced, for God had made them rejoice with great joy; the women and children also rejoiced. And the joy of Jerusalem was heard far away.

[44]On that day men were appointed over the storerooms, the contributions, the first-fruits, and the tithes, to gather into them the portions required by the Law for the priests and for the Levites according to the fields of the towns, for Judah rejoiced over the priests and the Levites who ministered. [45]And they performed the service of their God and the service of purification, as did the singers and the gatekeepers, according to the command of David and his son Solomon. [46]For long ago in the days of David and Asaph there were directors of the singers, and there were songs[2] of praise and thanksgiving to God. [47]And all Israel in the days of Zerubbabel and in the days of Nehemiah gave the daily portions for the singers and the gatekeepers; and they set apart that which was for the Levites; and the Levites set apart that which was for the sons of Aaron.

Nehemiah's reforms [chapter 13]. The exaltation of the covenant renewal ceremony and the dedication of the walls gives way to some glimpses of unholy behavior in the community at the end of the book. The keynote of this chapter is the same as that of the earlier ceremonial sections of the book: to show that a good society is one that knows and obeys God's law. The sequence is as follows: a reading of the law leads the people to separate themselves from foreigners (vv. 1–3); Nehemiah cleanses the temple of the desecration represented by allowing a pagan (Tobiah) to have his residence in it (vv. 4–9); Nehemiah also needs to reinstitute the financial support of the Levites so they can do their appointed work in the temple (vv. 10–14); Nehemiah calls a halt to various types of Sabbath breaking (vv. 15–22); Nehemiah stands up to men who had married pagan women (vv. 23–29); summary statement by Nehemiah regarding his reforms (v. 30).

13 On that day they read from the Book of Moses in the hearing of the people. And in it was found written that no Ammonite or Moabite should ever enter the assembly of God, [2]for they did not meet the people of Israel with bread and water, but hired Balaam against them to curse them—yet our God turned the curse into a blessing. [3]As soon as the people heard the law, they separated from Israel all those of foreign descent.

[4]Now before this, Eliashib the priest, who was appointed over the chambers of the

[1] Or of the old city [2] Or leaders

house of our God, and who was related to Tobiah, [5]prepared for Tobiah a large chamber where they had previously put the grain offering, the frankincense, the vessels, and the tithes of grain, wine, and oil, which were given by commandment to the Levites, singers, and gatekeepers, and the contributions for the priests. [6]While this was taking place, I was not in Jerusalem, for in the thirty-second year of Artaxerxes king of Babylon I went to the king. And after some time I asked leave of the king [7]and came to Jerusalem, and I then discovered the evil that Eliashib had done for Tobiah, preparing for him a chamber in the courts of the house of God. [8]And I was very angry, and I threw all the household furniture of Tobiah out of the chamber. [9]Then I gave orders, and they cleansed the chambers, and I brought back there the vessels of the house of God, with the grain offering and the frankincense.

[10]I also found out that the portions of the Levites had not been given to them, so that the Levites and the singers, who did the work, had fled each to his field. [11]So I confronted the officials and said, "Why is the house of God forsaken?" And I gathered them together and set them in their stations. [12]Then all Judah brought the tithe of the grain, wine, and oil into the storehouses. [13]And I appointed as treasurers over the storehouses Shelemiah the priest, Zadok the scribe, and Pedaiah of the Levites, and as their assistant Hanan the son of Zaccur, son of Mattaniah, for they were considered reliable, and their duty was to distribute to their brothers. [14]Remember me, O my God, concerning this, and do not wipe out my good deeds that I have done for the house of my God and for his service.

[15]In those days I saw in Judah people treading winepresses on the Sabbath, and bringing in heaps of grain and loading them on donkeys, and also wine, grapes, figs, and all kinds of loads, which they brought into Jerusalem on the Sabbath day. And I warned them on the day when they sold food. [16]Tyrians also, who lived in the city, brought in fish and all kinds of goods and sold them on the Sabbath to the people of Judah, in Jerusalem itself! [17]Then I confronted the nobles of Judah and said to them, "What is this evil thing that you are doing, profaning the Sabbath day? [18]Did not your fathers act in this way, and did not our God bring all this disaster[1] on us and on this city? Now you are bringing more wrath on Israel by profaning the Sabbath."

[19]As soon as it began to grow dark at the gates of Jerusalem before the Sabbath, I commanded that the doors should be shut and gave orders that they should not be opened until after the Sabbath. And I stationed some of my servants at the gates, that no load might be brought in on the Sabbath day. [20]Then the merchants and sellers of all kinds of wares lodged outside Jerusalem once or twice. [21]But I warned them and said to them, "Why do you lodge outside the wall? If you do so again, I will lay hands on you." From that time on they did not come on the Sabbath. [22]Then I commanded the Levites that they should purify themselves and come and guard the gates, to keep the Sabbath day holy. Remember this also in my favor, O my God, and spare me according to the greatness of your steadfast love.

[23]In those days also I saw the Jews who had married women of Ashdod, Ammon, and Moab. [24]And half of their children spoke the language of Ashdod, and they could not speak the language of Judah, but only the language of each people. [25]And I confronted them and cursed them and beat some of them and pulled out their hair. And I made them take oath in the name of God, saying, "You shall not give your daughters to their sons, or take their daughters for your sons or for yourselves. [26]Did not Solomon king of Israel sin on account of such women? Among the many nations

---

[1] The Hebrew word can mean *evil*, *harm*, or *disaster*, depending on the context

there was no king like him, and he was beloved by his God, and God made him king over all Israel. Nevertheless, foreign women made even him to sin. [27] Shall we then listen to you and do all this great evil and act treacherously against our God by marrying foreign women?"

[28] And one of the sons of Jehoiada, the son of Eliashib the high priest, was the son-in-law of Sanballat the Horonite. Therefore I chased him from me. [29] Remember them, O my God, because they have desecrated the priesthood and the covenant of the priesthood and the Levites.

[30] Thus I cleansed them from everything foreign, and I established the duties of the priests and Levites, each in his work; [31] and I provided for the wood offering at appointed times, and for the firstfruits.

Remember me, O my God, for good.

ESTHER

The book at a glance. 10 chapters, 167 verses. The book of Esther is a story
par excellence. It has virtually all of the ingredients that people through the
ages have most loved in a story—a beautiful and courageous heroine, a
romantic love thread, a dire threat to the good characters, an ideally villainous
villain, suspense, *dramatic irony, evocative descriptions of exotic places,
sudden *reversal of action, *poetic justice, and a happy ending. God does not
enter the action as a named character, but he is the understood presence
behind the "seen." The ostensible purpose of the story is to explain how the
annual Jewish celebration of the Feast of Purim began, but the religious
meaning of the story is universal. It is a story of divine providence and of the
need to resist evil in reliance on God. The book also presents a model for
maintaining one's spiritual identity instead of giving in to cultural pressures
when they are ungodly.

❚ Genres. The book of Esther is first of all a *hero story. As a *narrative, it fulfills all of
the demands of storytelling (see "The Book at a Glance"). As a hero story, specifically,
the action is constructed around the engaging central figure of a heroine whose
Persian name, Esther, means "star." But the story is also a patriotic story of national
history—a *rescue story in which a whole nation is delivered from destruction. The U-
shaped descent into potential *tragedy and ascent to a happy ending is a plot pattern
known as *comedy. (For more information on items accompanied by an asterisk, see
the glossary at the back of this Bible.)

❚ Satire. The genre of *satire (the exposure of vice or folly) in Esther focuses on the
leading male characters. King Ahasuerus is a bumbling, inept figure whose perverse
values are evident already in chapter 1 when he throws a stag party. Haman is a totally
villainous person—narcissistic and vengeful. Through the centuries in Jewish circles,
when the story of Esther is read at the annual Feast of Purim, it has been a custom to
boo, hiss, and use noisemakers whenever the name Haman is mentioned. A man
(Mordecai) manages to put his whole nation at risk by his behavior, and only a woman
can get the nation out of its fix.

❚ The heroine. Esther is a developing character, not a character who displays
admirable qualities right from the start. In her early days in the harem, she fits right
into the pagan lifestyle that prevails among the young women who spend a whole year
enhancing themselves in a beauty spa. People in the harem do not even know that
Esther is a religious person. She has two names, hinting at the identity crisis that she

Passage	Content	The Story of the Nation	The Story of the Heroine
1:1–22	How the Persian king comes to need a new queen	The Jews are threatened	Esther takes the path of least resistance
2:1–23	Esther becomes queen		
3:1–15	How Haman plots the destruction of the Jews		
4:1–17	Mordecai pressures Esther to help her nation	The Jews are rescued and victorious	Esther heroically identifies with God's people
5:1–14	Haman's plot and Esther's counterplot		
6:1–7:10	Esther and Mordecai thwart Haman's plot		
8:1–10:3	The Jews defeat their enemies and celebrate their victory		

undergoes when she hits the big time in Persian society. But Esther becomes heroic when she is transformed by the ordeal of taking great risks to save her nation.

▌ Numbers that count in the book of Esther. In the book of Esther there are: 250 appearances of the Hebrew word for "king" or "to rule"; 37 references to Esther by name; 10 banquets or feasts; 3 key references to the Persian court chronicles; 3 important man-woman pairings (Ahasuerus and Vashti, Mordecai and Esther, Haman and Zeresh); 2 fasts; 0 references to God.

▌ Inferred literary intentions. The book is designed to achieve the following literary purposes:

- captivate us with its wealth of good storytelling content and technique

- adhere to the conventions of storytelling

- present a gallery of memorable characters

- make the world of the Persian court come alive in our imagination

- elicit strong reader sympathy for Esther and the Jews and antipathy to the villain Haman

- prompt us to see that even though God is not explicitly mentioned in the story, the striking coincidences that lead to the deliverance of the Jews must be the result of God's hidden providence

▌ Theological themes. (1) Providence: the book embodies the theme of providence in the action itself. (2) Human heroism: we see in the behavior of Esther that heroism is a possibility even in a sinful and pagan world. (3) The covenant: it is not just any nation whose story is told but specifically the covenant nation of Israel, and we are led to see that the survival of the covenant nation was carefully orchestrated by God. (4) Sin and judgment: the story of the villainous Haman shows that sinners reap what they sow.

▌ The book of Esther as a chapter in the master story of the Bible. In the OT, the story of salvation history is largely the history of a specific nation, Israel. The nation is nearly rendered extinct in the events that are narrated in the book of Esther, and we are led to feel how miraculously God protected the messianic line until Jesus was born.

Anatomy of a bad decision [chapter 1]. The opening paragraph of the book is one of the most vivid pieces of descriptive writing in the Bible, as we look in on a picture of decadent luxury and indulgence (vv. 1–9). With that as a backdrop, our heart sinks as we watch a drunken king make a shameful request of his wife to put herself on display in front of a hall full of drunken men (vv. 10–11). Vashti emerges a moral foil to such decadence by her courageous refusal to put herself on display (v. 12). The remainder of the chapter is devoted to a satiric portrayal of weak men who are so threatened by the behavior of Vashti that they set into motion the entire communication system of the nation to send an edict that all wives must honor their husbands! If the moral degradation were not so offensive, this would be the material of dark comedy, and in fact the story of Esther has the mocking tone of slave literature.

1 Now in the days of Ahasuerus, the Ahasuerus who reigned from India to Ethiopia over 127 provinces, [2]in those days when King Ahasuerus sat on his royal throne in Susa, the capital,[1] [3]in the third year of his reign he gave a feast for all his officials and servants. The army of Persia and Media and the nobles and governors of the provinces were before him, [4]while he showed the riches of his royal glory and the splendor and pomp of his greatness for many days, 180 days. [5]And when these days were completed, the king gave for all the people present in Susa, the citadel, both great and small, a feast lasting for seven days in the court of the garden of the king's palace. [6]There were white cotton curtains and violet hangings fastened with cords of fine linen and purple to silver rods[2] and marble pillars, and also couches of gold and silver on a mosaic pavement of porphyry, marble, mother-of-pearl and precious stones. [7]Drinks were served in golden vessels, vessels of different kinds, and the royal wine was lavished according to the bounty of the king. [8]And drinking was according to this edict: "There is no compulsion." For the king had given orders to all the staff of his palace to do as each man desired. [9]Queen Vashti also gave a feast for the women in the palace that belonged to King Ahasuerus.

[10]On the seventh day, when the heart of the king was merry with wine, he commanded Mehuman, Biztha, Harbona, Bigtha and Abagtha, Zethar and Carkas, the seven eunuchs who served in the presence of King Ahasuerus, [11]to bring Queen Vashti before the king with her royal crown,[3] in order to show the peoples and the princes her beauty, for she was lovely to look at. [12]But Queen Vashti refused to come at the king's command delivered by the eunuchs. At this the king became enraged, and his anger burned within him.

[13]Then the king said to the wise men who knew the times (for this was the king's procedure toward all who were versed in law and judgment, [14]the men next to him being Carshena, Shethar, Admatha, Tarshish, Meres, Marsena, and Memucan, the seven princes of Persia and Media, who saw the king's face, and sat first in the kingdom): [15]"According to the law, what is to be done to Queen Vashti, because she has not performed the command of King Ahasuerus delivered by the eunuchs?" [16]Then

[1] Or the fortified city [2] Or rings [3] Or headdress

Memucan said in the presence of the king and the officials, "Not only against the king has Queen Vashti done wrong, but also against all the officials and all the peoples who are in all the provinces of King Ahasuerus. ¹⁷For the queen's behavior will be made known to all women, causing them to look at their husbands with contempt, since they will say, 'King Ahasuerus commanded Queen Vashti to be brought before him, and she did not come.' ¹⁸This very day the noble women of Persia and Media who have heard of the queen's behavior will say the same to all the king's officials, and there will be contempt and wrath in plenty. ¹⁹If it please the king, let a royal order go out from him, and let it be written among the laws of the Persians and the Medes so that it may not be repealed, that Vashti is never again to come before King Ahasuerus. And let the king give her royal position to another who is better than she. ²⁰So when the decree made by the king is proclaimed throughout all his kingdom, for it is vast, all women will give honor to their husbands, high and low alike." ²¹This advice pleased the king and the princes, and the king did as Memucan proposed. ²²He sent letters to all the royal provinces, to every province in its own script and to every people in its own language, that every man be master in his own household and speak according to the language of his people.

> **Esther's big chance?** [chapter 2]. The satiric portrait of King Ahasuerus continues in this chapter. After the king sobers up, he faces the need to find a new wife. Esther becomes a key player in the action, but she is hardly idealized: she fits right into the pagan lifestyle of the harem; she does not maintain Jewish dietary rules; although she is glamorous in the eyes of a pagan society, even to the point of receiving the queen's crown and her own feast, she so completely conceals her religious and ethnic identity that people do not have a clue about her Jewishness. The concluding paragraph of the chapter (vv. 19–23) introduces two important motifs into the story that do not deal personally with Esther: the courtier Mordecai, Esther's cousin, is introduced, and in a notable coincidence, he manages to spare the king's life by uncovering a plot against the king.

2 After these things, when the anger of King Ahasuerus had abated, he remembered Vashti and what she had done and what had been decreed against her. ²Then the king's young men who attended him said, "Let beautiful young virgins be sought out for the king. ³And let the king appoint officers in all the provinces of his kingdom to gather all the beautiful young virgins to the harem in Susa the capital, under custody of Hegai, the king's eunuch, who is in charge of the women. Let their cosmetics be given them. ⁴And let the young woman who pleases the king be queen instead of Vashti." This pleased the king, and he did so.

⁵Now there was a Jew in Susa the citadel whose name was Mordecai, the son of Jair, son of Shimei, son of Kish, a Benjaminite, ⁶who had been carried away from Jerusalem among the captives carried away with Jeconiah king of Judah, whom Nebuchadnezzar king of Babylon had carried away. ⁷He was bringing up Hadassah, that is Esther, the daughter of his uncle, for she had neither father nor mother. The young woman had a beautiful figure and was lovely to look at, and when her father and her mother died, Mordecai took her as his own daughter. ⁸So when the king's order and his edict were proclaimed, and when many young women were gathered in Susa the citadel in custody of Hegai, Esther also was taken into the king's palace

and put in custody of Hegai, who had charge of the women. ⁹And the young woman pleased him and won his favor. And he quickly provided her with her cosmetics and her portion of food, and with seven chosen young women from the king's palace, and advanced her and her young women to the best place in the harem. ¹⁰Esther had not made known her people or kindred, for Mordecai had commanded her not to make it known. ¹¹And every day Mordecai walked in front of the court of the harem to learn how Esther was and what was happening to her.

¹²Now when the turn came for each young woman to go in to King Ahasuerus, after being twelve months under the regulations for the women, since this was the regular period of their beautifying, six months with oil of myrrh and six months with spices and ointments for women— ¹³when the young woman went in to the king in this way, she was given whatever she desired to take with her from the harem to the king's palace. ¹⁴In the evening she would go in, and in the morning she would return to the second harem in custody of Shaashgaz, the king's eunuch, who was in charge of the concubines. She would not go in to the king again, unless the king delighted in her and she was summoned by name.

¹⁵When the turn came for Esther the daughter of Abihail the uncle of Mordecai, who had taken her as his own daughter, to go in to the king, she asked for nothing except what Hegai the king's eunuch, who had charge of the women, advised. Now Esther was winning favor in the eyes of all who saw her. ¹⁶And when Esther was taken to King Ahasuerus, into his royal palace, in the tenth month, which is the month of Tebeth, in the seventh year of his reign, ¹⁷the king loved Esther more than all the women, and she won grace and favor in his sight more than all the virgins, so that he set the royal crown¹ on her head and made her queen instead of Vashti. ¹⁸Then the king gave a great feast for all his officials and servants; it was Esther's feast. He also granted a remission of taxes to the provinces and gave gifts with royal generosity.

¹⁹Now when the virgins were gathered together the second time, Mordecai was sitting at the king's gate. ²⁰Esther had not made known her kindred or her people, as Mordecai had commanded her, for Esther obeyed Mordecai just as when she was brought up by him. ²¹In those days, as Mordecai was sitting at the king's gate, Bigthan and Teresh, two of the king's eunuchs, who guarded the threshold, became angry and sought to lay hands on King Ahasuerus. ²²And this came to the knowledge of Mordecai, and he told it to Queen Esther, and Esther told the king in the name of Mordecai. ²³When the affair was investigated and found to be so, the men were both hanged on the gallows.² And it was recorded in the book of the chronicles in the presence of the king.

Enter Haman [chapter 3]. The book of Esther tells two stories—the national story of Israel in exile and the personal hero story of Esther. Chapter 3 shifts the focus from Esther to the nation, and the plot line features Haman, one of the famous villains in the pages of the Bible. The inciting moment in this half of the story is Mordecai's refusal to bow before Haman. We are not told why. There are numerous instances of faithful people bowing before authority figures in the OT, so there was no religious principle involved. Mordecai's refusal was probably based on his estimate of Haman's unworthiness. The satiric portrayal of Haman is advanced by his extreme and irrational anger against Mordecai, extended to the whole nation of the Jews, and the satiric portrayal of Ahasuerus continues when we see how easily hoodwinked he is by Haman's intrigue.

---

¹ Or *headdress* ² Or *suspended on a stake*

3 After these things King Ahasuerus promoted Haman the Agagite, the son of Hammedatha, and advanced him and set his throne above all the officials who were with him. ²And all the king's servants who were at the king's gate bowed down and paid homage to Haman, for the king had so commanded concerning him. But Mordecai did not bow down or pay homage. ³Then the king's servants who were at the king's gate said to Mordecai, "Why do you transgress the king's command?" ⁴And when they spoke to him day after day and he would not listen to them, they told Haman, in order to see whether Mordecai's words would stand, for he had told them that he was a Jew. ⁵And when Haman saw that Mordecai did not bow down or pay homage to him, Haman was filled with fury. ⁶But he disdained to lay hands on Mordecai alone. So, as they had made known to him the people of Mordecai, Haman sought to destroy all the Jews, the people of Mordecai, throughout the whole kingdom of Ahasuerus.

⁷In the first month, which is the month of Nisan, in the twelfth year of King Ahasuerus, they cast Pur (that is, they cast lots) before Haman day after day; and they cast it month after month till the twelfth month, which is the month of Adar. ⁸Then Haman said to King Ahasuerus, "There is a certain people scattered abroad and dispersed among the peoples in all the provinces of your kingdom. Their laws are different from those of every other people, and they do not keep the king's laws, so that it is not to the king's profit to tolerate them. ⁹If it please the king, let it be decreed that they be destroyed, and I will pay 10,000 talents[1] of silver into the hands of those who have charge of the king's business, that they may put it into the king's treasuries." ¹⁰So the king took his signet ring from his hand and gave it to Haman the Agagite, the son of Hammedatha, the enemy of the Jews. ¹¹And the king said to Haman, "The money is given to you, the people also, to do with them as it seems good to you."

¹²Then the king's scribes were summoned on the thirteenth day of the first month, and an edict, according to all that Haman commanded, was written to the king's satraps and to the governors over all the provinces and to the officials of all the peoples, to every province in its own script and every people in its own language. It was written in the name of King Ahasuerus and sealed with the king's signet ring. ¹³Letters were sent by couriers to all the king's provinces with instruction to destroy, to kill, and to annihilate all Jews, young and old, women and children, in one day, the thirteenth day of the twelfth month, which is the month of Adar, and to plunder their goods. ¹⁴A copy of the document was to be issued as a decree in every province by proclamation to all the peoples to be ready for that day. ¹⁵The couriers went out hurriedly by order of the king, and the decree was issued in Susa the citadel. And the king and Haman sat down to drink, but the city of Susa was thrown into confusion.

Esther's great moment [chapter 4]. Up to this point, Esther has taken the path of least resistance, and when Mordecai first informs her of the Jews' plight, her first response is to avoid personal risk (vv. 10–11). But Mordecai puts extreme pressure on his cousin (vv. 13–14), in the process uttering the immortal sentiment "Who knows whether you have not come to the kingdom for such a time as this?" (v. 14). Esther has a change of heart and utters her own immortal sentiment when she says, "Go, gather all the Jews to be found in Susa, and hold a fast on my behalf. . . . Then I will go to the king, . . . and if I perish, I perish" (v. 16).

[1] A *talent* was about 75 pounds or 34 kilograms

4 When Mordecai learned all that had been done, Mordecai tore his clothes and put on sackcloth and ashes, and went out into the midst of the city, and he cried out with a loud and bitter cry. ²He went up to the entrance of the king's gate, for no one was allowed to enter the king's gate clothed in sackcloth. ³And in every province, wherever the king's command and his decree reached, there was great mourning among the Jews, with fasting and weeping and lamenting, and many of them lay in sackcloth and ashes.

⁴When Esther's young women and her eunuchs came and told her, the queen was deeply distressed. She sent garments to clothe Mordecai, so that he might take off his sackcloth, but he would not accept them. ⁵Then Esther called for Hathach, one of the king's eunuchs, who had been appointed to attend her, and ordered him to go to Mordecai to learn what this was and why it was. ⁶Hathach went out to Mordecai in the open square of the city in front of the king's gate, ⁷and Mordecai told him all that had happened to him, and the exact sum of money that Haman had promised to pay into the king's treasuries for the destruction of the Jews. ⁸Mordecai also gave him a copy of the written decree issued in Susa for their destruction, that he might show it to Esther and explain it to her and command her to go to the king to beg his favor and plead with him on behalf of her people. ⁹And Hathach went and told Esther what Mordecai had said. ¹⁰Then Esther spoke to Hathach and commanded him to go to Mordecai and say, ¹¹"All the king's servants and the people of the king's provinces know that if any man or woman goes to the king inside the inner court without being called, there is but one law—to be put to death, except the one to whom the king holds out the golden scepter so that he may live. But as for me, I have not been called to come in to the king these thirty days."

¹²And they told Mordecai what Esther had said. ¹³Then Mordecai told them to reply to Esther, "Do not think to yourself that in the king's palace you will escape any more than all the other Jews. ¹⁴For if you keep silent at this time, relief and deliverance will rise for the Jews from another place, but you and your father's house will perish. And who knows whether you have not come to the kingdom for such a time as this?" ¹⁵Then Esther told them to reply to Mordecai, ¹⁶"Go, gather all the Jews to be found in Susa, and hold a fast on my behalf, and do not eat or drink for three days, night or day. I and my young women will also fast as you do. Then I will go to the king, though it is against the law, and if I perish, I perish." ¹⁷Mordecai then went away and did everything as Esther had ordered him.

Esther intervenes for her nation [chapter 5]. The book of Esther is written in an embellished style, with scenes and speeches presented in full detail. In this chapter, this technique yields the famous picture of Esther appearing unsummoned before the king, who extends his scepter toward the queen. Esther invites the king to two banquets, perhaps weakening at the first one when the king asks what she wants (v. 8) and in any case increasing the suspense of the story. The storyteller does not tell us why Esther also invites Haman, but it may have been part of a strategy to force the king into making a decision on the spot when at the second banquet Esther makes her accusation. But we are a long way from that moment when Haman returns from the first banquet "joyful and glad of heart" (v. 9) and bragging to his wife and friends (vv. 10–13). The construction of the gallows that Haman intends for Mordecai shows him to be the archetypal over-reacher—the person whose personal ambition is too excessive to succeed.

5 On the third day Esther put on her royal robes and stood in the inner court of the king's palace, in front of the king's quarters, while the king was sitting on his royal throne inside the throne room opposite the entrance to the palace. ²And when the king saw Queen Esther standing in the court, she won favor in his sight, and he held out to Esther the golden scepter that was in his hand. Then Esther approached and touched the tip of the scepter. ³And the king said to her, "What is it, Queen Esther? What is your request? It shall be given you, even to the half of my kingdom." ⁴And Esther said, "If it please the king, let the king and Haman come today to a feast that I have prepared for the king." ⁵Then the king said, "Bring Haman quickly, so that we may do as Esther has asked." So the king and Haman came to the feast that Esther had prepared. ⁶And as they were drinking wine after the feast, the king said to Esther, "What is your wish? It shall be granted you. And what is your request? Even to the half of my kingdom, it shall be fulfilled." ⁷Then Esther answered, "My wish and my request is: ⁸If I have found favor in the sight of the king, and if it please the king to grant my wish and fulfill my request, let the king and Haman come to the feast that I will prepare for them, and tomorrow I will do as the king has said."

⁹And Haman went out that day joyful and glad of heart. But when Haman saw Mordecai in the king's gate, that he neither rose nor trembled before him, he was filled with wrath against Mordecai. ¹⁰Nevertheless, Haman restrained himself and went home, and he sent and brought his friends and his wife Zeresh. ¹¹And Haman recounted to them the splendor of his riches, the number of his sons, all the promotions with which the king had honored him, and how he had advanced him above the officials and the servants of the king. ¹²Then Haman said, "Even Queen Esther let no one but me come with the king to the feast she prepared. And tomorrow also I am invited by her together with the king. ¹³Yet all this is worth nothing to me, so long as I see Mordecai the Jew sitting at the king's gate." ¹⁴Then his wife Zeresh and all his friends said to him, "Let a gallows¹ fifty cubits² high be made, and in the morning tell the king to have Mordecai hanged upon it. Then go joyfully with the king to the feast." This idea pleased Haman, and he had the gallows made.

Haman's comeuppance [chapter 6]. The sudden turning of the tables on a villainous character is a stock moment in stories, and in this chapter we see a memorable example of it. The most original act of the bungling King Ahasuerus is to have a sleepless night (v. 1). By means of this coincidence, the king comes to have the chronicles of his "memorable deeds" read to him, which in turn uncovers that he has done nothing to honor the man who saved his life (vv. 1–3). Haman's early arrival at court shows his eagerness to execute Mordecai (vv. 4–5). But Haman's overweening pride (what the Greek tragedians called hubris) is his undoing when, thinking that the king cannot possibly want to honor anyone more highly than him, he prescribes a litany of honors that he is immediately commanded to perform for his mortal enemy Mordecai. Again a note of satiric humor dominates the story.

6 On that night the king could not sleep. And he gave orders to bring the book of memorable deeds, the chronicles, and they were read before the king. ²And it was found written how Mordecai had told about Bigthana and Teresh, two of the king's eunuchs, who guarded the threshold, and who had sought to lay hands on King Ahasuerus. ³And the king said, "What honor or distinction has been bestowed

¹ Or *stake*; twice in this verse ² A *cubit* was about 18 inches or 45 centimeters

on Mordecai for this?" The king's young men who attended him said, "Nothing has been done for him." ⁴And the king said, "Who is in the court?" Now Haman had just entered the outer court of the king's palace to speak to the king about having Mordecai hanged on the gallows[1] that he had prepared for him. ⁵And the king's young men told him, "Haman is there, standing in the court." And the king said, "Let him come in." ⁶So Haman came in, and the king said to him, "What should be done to the man whom the king delights to honor?" And Haman said to himself, "Whom would the king delight to honor more than me?" ⁷And Haman said to the king, "For the man whom the king delights to honor, ⁸let royal robes be brought, which the king has worn, and the horse that the king has ridden, and on whose head a royal crown[2] is set. ⁹And let the robes and the horse be handed over to one of the king's most noble officials. Let them dress the man whom the king delights to honor, and let them lead him on the horse through the square of the city, proclaiming before him: 'Thus shall it be done to the man whom the king delights to honor.'" ¹⁰Then the king said to Haman, "Hurry; take the robes and the horse, as you have said, and do so to Mordecai the Jew, who sits at the king's gate. Leave out nothing that you have mentioned." ¹¹So Haman took the robes and the horse, and he dressed Mordecai and led him through the square of the city, proclaiming before him, "Thus shall it be done to the man whom the king delights to honor."

¹²Then Mordecai returned to the king's gate. But Haman hurried to his house, mourning and with his head covered. ¹³And Haman told his wife Zeresh and all his friends everything that had happened to him. Then his wise men and his wife Zeresh said to him, "If Mordecai, before whom you have begun to fall, is of the Jewish people, you will not overcome him but will surely fall before him."

¹⁴While they were yet talking with him, the king's eunuchs arrived and hurried to bring Haman to the feast that Esther had prepared.

The rescue of the nation [chapter 7]. The second banquet that Esther stages for the king and Haman brings the plot against the Jews to defeat. Speaking briefly but courageously, Esther acquaints the king with the plot against her nation and makes an accusation against Haman (vv. 3–6). The inept king's most decisive act results from misinterpreting Haman's intention when he sees Haman falling on the queen's couch to plead for his life (vv. 7–8). The downfall of the villain is climaxed with poetic justice when Haman is hanged on the gallows that he had prepared for Mordecai.

7 So the king and Haman went in to feast with Queen Esther. ²And on the second day, as they were drinking wine after the feast, the king again said to Esther, "What is your wish, Queen Esther? It shall be granted you. And what is your request? Even to the half of my kingdom, it shall be fulfilled." ³Then Queen Esther answered, "If I have found favor in your sight, O king, and if it please the king, let my life be granted me for my wish, and my people for my request. ⁴For we have been sold, I and my people, to be destroyed, to be killed, and to be annihilated. If we had been sold merely as slaves, men and women, I would have been silent, for our affliction is not to be compared with the loss to the king." ⁵Then King Ahasuerus said to Queen Esther, "Who is he, and where is he, who has dared[3] to do this?" ⁶And Esther said, "A foe and

[1] Or suspended on a stake [2] Or headdress [3] Hebrew whose heart has filled him

enemy! This wicked Haman!" Then Haman was terrified before the king and the queen.

⁷And the king arose in his wrath from the wine-drinking and went into the palace garden, but Haman stayed to beg for his life from Queen Esther, for he saw that harm was determined against him by the king. ⁸And the king returned from the palace garden to the place where they were drinking wine, as Haman was falling on the couch where Esther was. And the king said, "Will he even assault the queen in my presence, in my own house?" As the word left the mouth of the king, they covered Haman's face. ⁹Then Harbona, one of the eunuchs in attendance on the king, said, "Moreover, the gallows¹ that Haman has prepared for Mordecai, whose word saved the king, is standing at Haman's house, fifty cubits² high." ¹⁰And the king said, "Hang him on that." So they hanged Haman on the gallows that he had prepared for Mordecai. Then the wrath of the king abated.

The counterplot gains momentum [chapter 8]. Merely eliminating Haman from the scene is not sufficient to save the Jewish nation, because the unchangeable "law of the Medes and Persians" stipulating the destruction of the Jews cannot be revoked. So the Persian postal system is set into motion again with a decree (written in the high style, as is everything in book of Esther) that allows the Jews to defend themselves on the fateful day of their planned demise. That story is bracketed by references to the elevation of Mordecai to a place of prominence in the kingdom (vv. 1–2, 15).

8 On that day King Ahasuerus gave to Queen Esther the house of Haman, the enemy of the Jews. And Mordecai came before the king, for Esther had told what he was to her. ²And the king took off his signet ring, which he had taken from Haman, and gave it to Mordecai. And Esther set Mordecai over the house of Haman.

³Then Esther spoke again to the king. She fell at his feet and wept and pleaded with him to avert the evil plan of Haman the Agagite and the plot that he had devised against the Jews. ⁴When the king held out the golden scepter to Esther, ⁵Esther rose and stood before the king. And she said, "If it please the king, and if I have found favor in his sight, and if the thing seems right before the king, and I am pleasing in his eyes, let an order be written to revoke the letters devised by Haman the Agagite, the son of Hammedatha, which he wrote to destroy the Jews who are in all the provinces of the king. ⁶For how can I bear to see the calamity that is coming to my people? Or how can I bear to see the destruction of my kindred?" ⁷Then King Ahasuerus said to Queen Esther and to Mordecai the Jew, "Behold, I have given Esther the house of Haman, and they have hanged him on the gallows,³ because he intended to lay hands on the Jews. ⁸But you may write as you please with regard to the Jews, in the name of the king, and seal it with the king's ring, for an edict written in the name of the king and sealed with the king's ring cannot be revoked."

⁹The king's scribes were summoned at that time, in the third month, which is the month of Sivan, on the twenty-third day. And an edict was written, according to all that Mordecai commanded concerning the Jews, to the satraps and the governors and the officials of the provinces from India to Ethiopia, 127 provinces, to each province in its own script and to each people in its own language, and also to the Jews in their script and their language. ¹⁰And he wrote in the name of King Ahasuerus and sealed

---

¹ Or *stake*; also verse 10 ² A *cubit* was about 18 inches or 45 centimeters ³ Or *stake*

it with the king's signet ring. Then he sent the letters by mounted couriers riding on swift horses that were used in the king's service, bred from the royal stud, ¹¹saying that the king allowed the Jews who were in every city to gather and defend their lives, to destroy, to kill, and to annihilate any armed force of any people or province that might attack them, children and women included, and to plunder their goods, ¹²on one day throughout all the provinces of King Ahasuerus, on the thirteenth day of the twelfth month, which is the month of Adar. ¹³A copy of what was written was to be issued as a decree in every province, being publicly displayed to all peoples, and the Jews were to be ready on that day to take vengeance on their enemies. ¹⁴So the couriers, mounted on their swift horses that were used in the king's service, rode out hurriedly, urged by the king's command. And the decree was issued in Susa the citadel.

¹⁵Then Mordecai went out from the presence of the king in royal robes of blue and white, with a great golden crown¹ and a robe of fine linen and purple, and the city of Susa shouted and rejoiced. ¹⁶The Jews had light and gladness and joy and honor. ¹⁷And in every province and in every city, wherever the king's command and his edict reached, there was gladness and joy among the Jews, a feast and a holiday. And many from the peoples of the country declared themselves Jews, for fear of the Jews had fallen on them.

The Jews conquer their enemies [chapters 9–10]. All of the foregoing plot and counterplot now reaches its climax in a *battle story that recounts the Jews' successful defense of themselves against outbreaks of Persian hostility. A comic U-shaped plot ordinarily ends with either a wedding or a feast, and we get the latter in this chapter (9:16–19). The first festivity then expands outward into an extended explanation of how the first festival of deliverance became the basis for the annual Feast of Purim (9:20–32). A coda at the end of the book summarizes the fame that Mordecai achieved in the Persian court (chapter 10).

9 Now in the twelfth month, which is the month of Adar, on the thirteenth day of the same, when the king's command and edict were about to be carried out, on the very day when the enemies of the Jews hoped to gain the mastery over them, the reverse occurred: the Jews gained mastery over those who hated them. ²The Jews gathered in their cities throughout all the provinces of King Ahasuerus to lay hands on those who sought their harm. And no one could stand against them, for the fear of them had fallen on all peoples. ³All the officials of the provinces and the satraps and the governors and the royal agents also helped the Jews, for the fear of Mordecai had fallen on them. ⁴For Mordecai was great in the king's house, and his fame spread throughout all the provinces, for the man Mordecai grew more and more powerful. ⁵The Jews struck all their enemies with the sword, killing and destroying them, and did as they pleased to those who hated them. ⁶In Susa the citadel itself the Jews killed and destroyed 500 men, ⁷and also killed Parshandatha and Dalphon and Aspatha ⁸and Poratha and Adalia and Aridatha ⁹and Parmashta and Arisai and Aridai and Vaizatha, ¹⁰the ten sons of Haman the son of Hammedatha, the enemy of the Jews, but they laid no hand on the plunder.

¹¹That very day the number of those killed in Susa the citadel was reported to the king. ¹²And the king said to Queen Esther, "In Susa the citadel the Jews have killed

¹ Or headdress

and destroyed 500 men and also the ten sons of Haman. What then have they done in the rest of the king's provinces! Now what is your wish? It shall be granted you. And what further is your request? It shall be fulfilled." [13]And Esther said, "If it please the king, let the Jews who are in Susa be allowed tomorrow also to do according to this day's edict. And let the ten sons of Haman be hanged on the gallows."[1] [14]So the king commanded this to be done. A decree was issued in Susa, and the ten sons of Haman were hanged. [15]The Jews who were in Susa gathered also on the fourteenth day of the month of Adar and they killed 300 men in Susa, but they laid no hands on the plunder.

[16]Now the rest of the Jews who were in the king's provinces also gathered to defend their lives, and got relief from their enemies and killed 75,000 of those who hated them, but they laid no hands on the plunder. [17]This was on the thirteenth day of the month of Adar, and on the fourteenth day they rested and made that a day of feasting and gladness. [18]But the Jews who were in Susa gathered on the thirteenth day and on the fourteenth, and rested on the fifteenth day, making that a day of feasting and gladness. [19]Therefore the Jews of the villages, who live in the rural towns, hold the fourteenth day of the month of Adar as a day for gladness and feasting, as a holiday, and as a day on which they send gifts of food to one another.

[20]And Mordecai recorded these things and sent letters to all the Jews who were in all the provinces of King Ahasuerus, both near and far, [21]obliging them to keep the fourteenth day of the month Adar and also the fifteenth day of the same, year by year, [22]as the days on which the Jews got relief from their enemies, and as the month that had been turned for them from sorrow into gladness and from mourning into a holiday; that they should make them days of feasting and gladness, days for sending gifts of food to one another and gifts to the poor.

[23]So the Jews accepted what they had started to do, and what Mordecai had written to them. [24]For Haman the Agagite, the son of Hammedatha, the enemy of all the Jews, had plotted against the Jews to destroy them, and had cast Pur (that is, cast lots), to crush and to destroy them. [25]But when it came before the king, he gave orders in writing that his evil plan that he had devised against the Jews should return on his own head, and that he and his sons should be hanged on the gallows.[2] [26]Therefore they called these days Purim, after the term Pur. Therefore, because of all that was written in this letter, and of what they had faced in this matter, and of what had happened to them, [27]the Jews firmly obligated themselves and their offspring and all who joined them, that without fail they would keep these two days according to what was written and at the time appointed every year, [28]that these days should be remembered and kept throughout every generation, in every clan, province, and city, and that these days of Purim should never fall into disuse among the Jews, nor should the commemoration of these days cease among their descendants.

[29]Then Queen Esther, the daughter of Abihail, and Mordecai the Jew gave full written authority, confirming this second letter about Purim. [30]Letters were sent to all the Jews, to the 127 provinces of the kingdom of Ahasuerus, in words of peace and truth, [31]that these days of Purim should be observed at their appointed seasons, as Mordecai the Jew and Queen Esther obligated them, and as they had obligated themselves and their offspring, with regard to their fasts and their lamenting. [32]The command of Queen Esther confirmed these practices of Purim, and it was recorded in writing.

---

[1] Or stake [2] Or suspended on a stake

10

King Ahasuerus imposed tax on the land and on the coastlands of the sea. ²And all the acts of his power and might, and the full account of the high honor of Mordecai, to which the king advanced him, are they not written in the Book of the Chronicles of the kings of Media and Persia? ³For Mordecai the Jew was second in rank to King Ahasuerus, and he was great among the Jews and popular with the multitude of his brothers, for he sought the welfare of his people and spoke peace to all his people.

JOB

> **The book at a glance.** 42 chapters, 1,070 verses. The book of Job is the classic study in the Bible and beyond it to deal with the problem of undeserved suffering. It raises the question not simply why people in general suffer but specifically why the righteous suffer. Philosophers and theologians call this "the problem of evil," and the attempt to offer a satisfactory solution to the problem is called *theodicy*. On the literary level, the book of Job aims to be truthful to the human experience of suffering. A second level at which the book operates is to have various human characters offer their perspectives on the spectacle of exceptional calamity and suffering. There is also a polemical (argumentative) level of the discourse: in the thinking of the OT Israelites (and really the viewpoint is perennial), there exists an automatic correspondence between good behavior and prosperity, a viewpoint that the book of Job decisively refutes with its portrayal of a blameless man who suffers greatly. Finally, there is a divine perspective on human suffering that takes the form of God's interaction with Job in the voice from the whirlwind.

▌**Genres.** The story begins and ends with a *narrative frame in which the author tells the story of the fall and restoration of the protagonist Job. Within those bookends, though, the primary form is *drama, as we are presented with the speeches and dialogues of the actors in the story. The form in which these speeches are cast is *poetry. The long poetic speeches are examples of oratory. So much of the material falls into the form of *aphoristic *proverbs that the book is sometimes said to be an example of *wisdom literature. The overall U-shaped movement of the story makes it a literary *comedy. Even though it is therefore not a true *tragedy, it nonetheless incorporates certain features of literary tragedy—a story of exceptional calamity, the spectacle of extraordinary suffering, an exalted *hero who undergoes a great fall from prosperity, the onset of the hero's difficulties at a specific point, evocation of the tragic emotions of pity and fear, a moment of tragic perception, and the theme of wisdom through suffering. The book also resembles a form of modern drama known as the problem play, in which a problem is posed (in the case of the book of Job, why the righteous suffer) and various characters then discuss the problem in an attempt to find a solution. (For more information on items accompanied by an asterisk, see the glossary at the back of this Bible.)

▌**Keys to enjoying and understanding the book of Job.** (1) We need to relish the Hebrew poetry (including *imagery and *parallelism) of the book and to respect the leisurely pace that this produces. (2) Subtle *dramatic irony pervades the book:

Passage	Content	Job in Relation to Others	Literary Form	The Problem of Evil	Job's Behavior
1:1–2:13	Prologue set in heaven	Job is tested by Satan	Prose narrative	The problem is posed in the form of an example	Job is patient
3:1–26	Job's speech of despair				
4:1–14:22	First cycle of speeches				
15:1–21:34	Second cycle of speeches	Job is counseled by "friends"	Poetic drama	Human wisdom fails to solve the problem of undeserved suffering	Job is initially defiant but gradually softens his statements
22:1–27:23	Third cycle of speeches				
28:1–31:40	Job's concluding speeches: poem in praise of wisdom, summary of Job's life, great oath of innocence				
32:1–37:24	Elihu's speeches	Job is counseled by Elihu	Poetic monologue		
38:1–42:6	The voice from the whirlwind	Job is questioned by God	Poetic drama	God's answer to the problem of suffering	Job is silent and repents
42:7–17	Epilogue	Job is vindicated by God	Prose narrative	God's reward to the sufferer	Job prospers

the friends' orthodoxy is ironic because it does not accurately apply to Job's situation, and Job in his rebelliousness utters many sentiments (including accusations against God) that we know from the prologue set in heaven are untrue. (3) The line of argument is not intricate and detailed but simple, as the friends keep repeating a few ideas (suffering is punitive; God is just; Job needs to confess his wrongdoing and God will restore him), and Job keeps protesting his innocence and God's unfairness; the format is not that of philosophic inquiry but a drama in which characters become more and more angry with each other.

▌ How to avoid misinterpreting the book.
Although Job's behavior in the prose prologue (chapters 1–2) is exemplary, after that his behavior degenerates into defiance toward God. This can be proved by God's rebuke of Job in his speeches from the whirlwind and equally from Job's two responses to the voice from the whirlwind. In the first response (40:1–3), Job applies God's rebuke to himself, humbles himself, and resolves to stop talking (and we might note that it was Job's words that got him into trouble in his speeches of defiance). In the second response (42:1–6), Job again applies God's rebuke to himself, admits that he has spoken untruth, and repents for his

misconduct. All of this material proves that we should not idealize Job's behavior after the first two chapters.

■ **Unifying frameworks.** (1) The outline of the story, which possesses the usual narrative features of beginning-middle-end shapeliness; conflict among characters leading to resolution; such plot *motifs as progression, *quest, testing, and a moment of *epiphany near the end (the voice from the whirlwind and the insight that Job attains in response). (2) The cycles of the speeches, arranged symmetrically (see chart above). (3) The ironic discrepancy between what we as readers know on the basis of the prologue set in heaven and the sentiments uttered by the human characters. (4) The obtuseness of the friends, which is like background static to the progress that Job makes. (5) The intellectual and spiritual progress of Job. (6) The intellectual or philosophic problem of how to make sense of the suffering of the righteous.

■ **Inferred literary intentions.** The book is designed to achieve the following literary purposes:

- set a group of characters into action in an attempt to solve an intellectual problem that is posed at the outset

- catch us up in such narrative patterns as quest, conflict, and movement toward a moment of epiphany

- embody truth in the literary technique of irony

- involve us in the character clashes that make up the dramatic format of the book

- embody the content in the form of poetry

- be truthful to such universal human experiences as suffering, defiance, and submission to God

- use the resources of high art to analyze the question of why the righteous suffer

■ **Theological themes.** (1) The sovereignty of God: God's management of the universe is seen in latent form in the prologue set in heaven and becomes the dominant theme in the speeches from the whirlwind. (2) Suffering: the book poses the question of why the righteous suffer in the specific example of Job. (3) Theodicy: the book belongs to the branch of philosophy that attempts to reconcile God's goodness and sovereignty on the one hand and the fact of evil and suffering in the world on the other hand. (4) The nature of God: during the course of the speeches and dialogue, the characters in the book express a wide-ranging series of ideas about God.

■ **The book of Job as a chapter in the master story of the Bible.** The master story of the Bible tells us what God is like and how people should relate to him. The book of Job takes a particular approach to that purpose, showing through a specific example how people should relate to God by means of their suffering.

The prologue set in heaven [chapter 1]. The first two chapters are devoted to the same narrative material—a prologue to the book set in heaven, with similar events unfolding in two waves in the respective chapters. Taking both chapters together, we learn the important things that serve as a frame of reference against which we measure how wide of the mark the speeches that follow are. In chapter 1 these key revelations include the following: God is allowing but not causing the suffering of Job; God has not relinquished his providential control over Job's life (v. 12); Job is blameless and not guilty of any sin that might account for his suffering (vv. 1, 5, 8, 22); Job's suffering is a test of his faith, not a punishment for his sin. Chapter 1 unfolds according to the following sequence: an opening portrait of the good life as OT believers conceived it (vv. 1–5); God accepts Satan's archetypal bet or dare (vv. 6–12); exceptional calamity befalls Job as his children and fortune are taken from him (vv. 13–19); Job responds with exemplary patience and piety (vv. 20–22).

1 There was a man in the land of Uz whose name was Job, and that man was blameless and upright, one who feared God and turned away from evil. ²There were born to him seven sons and three daughters. ³He possessed 7,000 sheep, 3,000 camels, 500 yoke of oxen, and 500 female donkeys, and very many servants, so that this man was the greatest of all the people of the east. ⁴His sons used to go and hold a feast in the house of each one on his day, and they would send and invite their three sisters to eat and drink with them. ⁵And when the days of the feast had run their course, Job would send and consecrate them, and he would rise early in the morning and offer burnt offerings according to the number of them all. For Job said, "It may be that my children have sinned, and cursed[1] God in their hearts." Thus Job did continually.

⁶Now there was a day when the sons of God came to present themselves before the LORD, and Satan[2] also came among them. ⁷The LORD said to Satan, "From where have you come?" Satan answered the LORD and said, "From going to and fro on the earth, and from walking up and down on it." ⁸And the LORD said to Satan, "Have you considered my servant Job, that there is none like him on the earth, a blameless and upright man, who fears God and turns away from evil?" ⁹Then Satan answered the LORD and said, "Does Job fear God for no reason? ¹⁰Have you not put a hedge around him and his house and all that he has, on every side? You have blessed the work of his hands, and his possessions have increased in the land. ¹¹But stretch out your hand and touch all that he has, and he will curse you to your face." ¹²And the LORD said to Satan, "Behold, all that he has is in your hand. Only against him do not stretch out your hand." So Satan went out from the presence of the LORD.

¹³Now there was a day when his sons and daughters were eating and drinking wine in their oldest brother's house, ¹⁴and there came a messenger to Job and said, "The oxen were plowing and the donkeys feeding beside them, ¹⁵and the Sabeans fell upon them and took them and struck down the servants[3] with the edge of the sword, and I alone have escaped to tell you." ¹⁶While he was yet speaking, there came another and said, "The fire of God fell from heaven and burned up the sheep and the servants and consumed them, and I alone have escaped to tell you." ¹⁷While he was yet speaking, there came another and said, "The Chaldeans formed three groups and made a raid on the camels and took them and struck down the servants with the edge

[1] The Hebrew word *bless* is used euphemistically for *curse* in 1:5, 11; 2:5, 9 [2] Hebrew *the Adversary*; so throughout chapters 1–2 [3] Hebrew *the young men*; also verses 16, 17

of the sword, and I alone have escaped to tell you." [18]While he was yet speaking, there came another and said, "Your sons and daughters were eating and drinking wine in their oldest brother's house, [19]and behold, a great wind came across the wilderness and struck the four corners of the house, and it fell upon the young people, and they are dead, and I alone have escaped to tell you."

[20]Then Job arose and tore his robe and shaved his head and fell on the ground and worshiped. [21]And he said, "Naked I came from my mother's womb, and naked shall I return. The LORD gave, and the LORD has taken away; blessed be the name of the LORD."

[22]In all this Job did not sin or charge God with wrong.

> **Prologue, part 2** [chapter 2]. Chapter 2 is a companion to chapter 1, built on the artistic principle of "the same in the other," meaning that we retread the same motifs in a different form. The effect of literary repetition like this is to accentuate all of the issues that are presented, in this case the complete innocence of Job, the exceptional nature of his calamity, and the respective roles of God and Satan in Job's suffering. The background premises are reestablished: God is allowing but not causing the suffering of Job; God has not relinquished his providential control over Job's life (v. 6); Job is blameless and not guilty of any sin that might account for his suffering (vv. 3, 10); Job's suffering is a test of his faith, not a punishment for his sin. Even the action reads like a rerun: a heavenly council scene (vv. 1–2); God accepts Satan's wager (vv. 3–6); Job is afflicted (vv. 7–8); Job exhibits exemplary patience and piety (vv. 9–10). Adding to the dramatic effect is the arrival and silence of Job's three friends (vv. 11–13).

2 Again there was a day when the sons of God came to present themselves before the LORD, and Satan also came among them to present himself before the LORD. [2]And the LORD said to Satan, "From where have you come?" Satan answered the LORD and said, "From going to and fro on the earth, and from walking up and down on it." [3]And the LORD said to Satan, "Have you considered my servant Job, that there is none like him on the earth, a blameless and upright man, who fears God and turns away from evil? He still holds fast his integrity, although you incited me against him to destroy him without reason." [4]Then Satan answered the LORD and said, "Skin for skin! All that a man has he will give for his life. [5]But stretch out your hand and touch his bone and his flesh, and he will curse you to your face." [6]And the LORD said to Satan, "Behold, he is in your hand; only spare his life."

[7]So Satan went out from the presence of the LORD and struck Job with loathsome sores from the sole of his foot to the crown of his head. [8]And he took a piece of broken pottery with which to scrape himself while he sat in the ashes.

[9]Then his wife said to him, "Do you still hold fast your integrity? Curse God and die." [10]But he said to her, "You speak as one of the foolish women would speak. Shall we receive good from God, and shall we not receive evil?"[1] In all this Job did not sin with his lips.

[11]Now when Job's three friends heard of all this evil that had come upon him, they came each from his own place, Eliphaz the Temanite, Bildad the Shuhite, and Zophar the Naamathite. They made an appointment together to come to show him sympathy and comfort him. [12]And when they saw him from a distance, they did not recognize him. And they raised their voices and wept, and they tore their robes and sprinkled

---

[1] Or *disaster*; also verse 11

dust on their heads toward heaven. ¹³And they sat with him on the ground seven days and seven nights, and no one spoke a word to him, for they saw that his suffering was very great.

> **Job's lament** [chapter 3]. Job now undergoes a sudden fall in the form of a complete loss of patience. The irony of Job's behavior is that it is not what God had intended when he had agreed to Satan's torment of him. Job's descent into despair unfolds according to the following pattern: Job utters a formal curse on the day of his birth, phrased as a desire for darkness to replace light as Job attempts to reverse the order of creation (vv. 1–10); Job expresses a death wish (vv. 11–23); Job laments his condition (vv. 24–26). Literature is the voice of authentic human experience, and in this chapter we listen to the voice of human suffering.

3 After this Job opened his mouth and cursed the day of his birth. ²And Job said:

³ "Let the day perish on which I was born,
  and the night that said,
  'A man is conceived.'
⁴ Let that day be darkness!
  May God above not seek it,
  nor light shine upon it.
⁵ Let gloom and deep darkness claim it.
  Let clouds dwell upon it;
  let the blackness of the day terrify it.
⁶ That night—let thick darkness seize it!
  Let it not rejoice among the days of the year;
  let it not come into the number of the months.
⁷ Behold, let that night be barren;
  let no joyful cry enter it.
⁸ Let those curse it who curse the day,
  who are ready to rouse up Leviathan.
⁹ Let the stars of its dawn be dark;
  let it hope for light, but have none,
  nor see the eyelids of the morning,
¹⁰ because it did not shut the doors of my mother's womb,
  nor hide trouble from my eyes.

¹¹ "Why did I not die at birth,
  come out from the womb and expire?
¹² Why did the knees receive me?
  Or why the breasts, that I should nurse?
¹³ For then I would have lain down and been quiet;
  I would have slept; then I would have been at rest,
¹⁴ with kings and counselors of the earth
  who rebuilt ruins for themselves,
¹⁵ or with princes who had gold,
  who filled their houses with silver.

16 Or why was I not as a hidden stillborn child,
        as infants who never see the light?
17 There the wicked cease from troubling,
        and there the weary are at rest.
18 There the prisoners are at ease together;
        they hear not the voice of the taskmaster.
19 The small and the great are there,
        and the slave is free from his master.

20 "Why is light given to him who is in misery,
        and life to the bitter in soul,
21 who long for death, but it comes not,
        and dig for it more than for hidden treasures,
22 who rejoice exceedingly
        and are glad when they find the grave?
23 Why is light given to a man whose way is hidden,
        whom God has hedged in?
24 For my sighing comes instead of¹ my bread,
        and my groanings are poured out like water.
25 For the thing that I fear comes upon me,
        and what I dread befalls me.
26 I am not at ease, nor am I quiet;
        I have no rest, but trouble comes."

Eliphaz's first speech [chapters 4–5]. The first cycle of speeches now begins. Eliphaz begins by addressing Job gently (4:1–6), and then he expounds on his favorite sermon topics—people reap what they sow (4:7–21); if people suffer, this is evidence of their sinfulness (5:1–7); God's on his throne, all's right with the world (5:8–16); if Job will repent, God will bless him (5:17–27). Our verdict on Eliphaz's speech should be as follows: he has spoken theoretic truth; he has spoken in a spirit of gentle reproof; his theoretic truth and intended reproof are wide of the mark, however, because they do not fit Job's situation: Job is not suffering because he has done wrong but for the opposite reason—because he is righteous.

4 Then Eliphaz the Temanite answered and said:

2 "If one ventures a word with you, will you be impatient?
        Yet who can keep from speaking?
3 Behold, you have instructed many,
        and you have strengthened the weak hands.
4 Your words have upheld him who was stumbling,
        and you have made firm the feeble knees.
5 But now it has come to you, and you are impatient;
        it touches you, and you are dismayed.
6 Is not your fear of God² your confidence,
        and the integrity of your ways your hope?

---

¹ Or *like*; Hebrew *before* ² Hebrew lacks *of God*

7 "Remember: who that was innocent ever perished?
　　Or where were the upright cut off?
8 As I have seen, those who plow iniquity
　　and sow trouble reap the same.
9 By the breath of God they perish,
　　and by the blast of his anger they are consumed.
10 The roar of the lion, the voice of the fierce lion,
　　the teeth of the young lions are broken.
11 The strong lion perishes for lack of prey,
　　and the cubs of the lioness are scattered.

12 "Now a word was brought to me stealthily;
　　my ear received the whisper of it.
13 Amid thoughts from visions of the night,
　　when deep sleep falls on men,
14 dread came upon me, and trembling,
　　which made all my bones shake.
15 A spirit glided past my face;
　　the hair of my flesh stood up.
16 It stood still,
　　but I could not discern its appearance.
　A form was before my eyes;
　　there was silence, then I heard a voice:
17 'Can mortal man be in the right before[1] God?
　　Can a man be pure before his Maker?
18 Even in his servants he puts no trust,
　　and his angels he charges with error;
19 how much more those who dwell in houses of clay,
　　whose foundation is in the dust,
　　who are crushed like the moth.
20 Between morning and evening they are beaten to pieces;
　　they perish forever without anyone regarding it.
21 Is not their tent-cord plucked up within them,
　　do they not die, and that without wisdom?'

5 "Call now; is there anyone who will answer you?
　　To which of the holy ones will you turn?
2 Surely vexation kills the fool,
　　and jealousy slays the simple.
3 I have seen the fool taking root,
　　but suddenly I cursed his dwelling.
4 His children are far from safety;
　　they are crushed in the gate,
　　and there is no one to deliver them.
5 The hungry eat his harvest,
　　and he takes it even out of thorns,[2]
　　and the thirsty pant[3] after his[4] wealth.

---

[1] Or more than; twice in this verse [2] The meaning of the Hebrew is uncertain [3] Aquila, Symmachus, Syriac, Vulgate; Hebrew could be read as and the snare pants [4] Hebrew their

⁶   For affliction does not come from the dust,
     nor does trouble sprout from the ground,
⁷   but man is born to trouble
     as the sparks fly upward.

⁸   "As for me, I would seek God,
     and to God would I commit my cause,
⁹   who does great things and unsearchable,
     marvelous things without number:
¹⁰   he gives rain on the earth
     and sends waters on the fields;
¹¹   he sets on high those who are lowly,
     and those who mourn are lifted to safety.
¹²   He frustrates the devices of the crafty,
     so that their hands achieve no success.
¹³   He catches the wise in their own craftiness,
     and the schemes of the wily are brought to a quick end.
¹⁴   They meet with darkness in the daytime
     and grope at noonday as in the night.
¹⁵   But he saves the needy from the sword of their mouth
     and from the hand of the mighty.
¹⁶   So the poor have hope,
     and injustice shuts her mouth.

¹⁷   "Behold, blessed is the one whom God reproves;
     therefore despise not the discipline of the Almighty.
¹⁸   For he wounds, but he binds up;
     he shatters, but his hands heal.
¹⁹   He will deliver you from six troubles;
     in seven no evil¹ shall touch you.
²⁰   In famine he will redeem you from death,
     and in war from the power of the sword.
²¹   You shall be hidden from the lash of the tongue,
     and shall not fear destruction when it comes.
²²   At destruction and famine you shall laugh,
     and shall not fear the beasts of the earth.
²³   For you shall be in league with the stones of the field,
     and the beasts of the field shall be at peace with you.
²⁴   You shall know that your tent is at peace,
     and you shall inspect your fold and miss nothing.
²⁵   You shall know also that your offspring shall be many,
     and your descendants as the grass of the earth.
²⁶   You shall come to your grave in ripe old age,
     like a sheaf gathered up in its season.
²⁷   Behold, this we have searched out; it is true.
     Hear, and know it for your good."²

---

¹ Or *disaster* ² Hebrew *for yourself*

6 Then Job answered and said:

2 "Oh that my vexation were weighed,
     and all my calamity laid in the balances!
3 For then it would be heavier than the sand of the sea;
     therefore my words have been rash.
4 For the arrows of the Almighty are in me;
     my spirit drinks their poison;
     the terrors of God are arrayed against me.
5 Does the wild donkey bray when he has grass,
     or the ox low over his fodder?
6 Can that which is tasteless be eaten without salt,
     or is there any taste in the juice of the mallow?[1]
7 My appetite refuses to touch them;
     they are as food that is loathsome to me.[2]

8 "Oh that I might have my request,
     and that God would fulfill my hope,
9 that it would please God to crush me,
     that he would let loose his hand and cut me off!
10 This would be my comfort;
     I would even exult[3] in pain unsparing,
     for I have not denied the words of the Holy One.
11 What is my strength, that I should wait?
     And what is my end, that I should be patient?
12 Is my strength the strength of stones, or is my flesh bronze?
13 Have I any help in me,
     when resource is driven from me?

14 "He who withholds[4] kindness from a friend
     forsakes the fear of the Almighty.
15 My brothers are treacherous as a torrent-bed,
     as torrential streams that pass away,
16 which are dark with ice,
     and where the snow hides itself.
17 When they melt, they disappear;
     when it is hot, they vanish from their place.
18 The caravans turn aside from their course;
     they go up into the waste and perish.
19 The caravans of Tema look,
     the travelers of Sheba hope.
20 They are ashamed because they were confident;

---

[1] The meaning of the Hebrew word is uncertain [2] The meaning of the Hebrew is uncertain [3] The meaning of the Hebrew word is uncertain [4] Syriac, Vulgate (compare Targum); the meaning of the Hebrew word is uncertain

they come there and are disappointed.
21 For you have now become nothing;
    you see my calamity and are afraid.
22 Have I said, 'Make me a gift'?
    Or, 'From your wealth offer a bribe for me'?
23 Or, 'Deliver me from the adversary's hand'?
    Or, 'Redeem me from the hand of the ruthless'?

24 "Teach me, and I will be silent;
    make me understand how I have gone astray.
25 How forceful are upright words!
    But what does reproof from you reprove?
26 Do you think that you can reprove words,
    when the speech of a despairing man is wind?
27 You would even cast lots over the fatherless,
    and bargain over your friend.

28 "But now, be pleased to look at me,
    for I will not lie to your face.
29 Please turn; let no injustice be done.
    Turn now; my vindication is at stake.
30 Is there any injustice on my tongue?
    Cannot my palate discern the cause of calamity?

7 "Has not man a hard service on earth,
    and are not his days like the days of a hired hand?
2 Like a slave who longs for the shadow,
    and like a hired hand who looks for his wages,
3 so I am allotted months of emptiness,
    and nights of misery are apportioned to me.
4 When I lie down I say, 'When shall I arise?'
    But the night is long,
    and I am full of tossing till the dawn.
5 My flesh is clothed with worms and dirt;
    my skin hardens, then breaks out afresh.
6 My days are swifter than a weaver's shuttle
    and come to their end without hope.

7 "Remember that my life is a breath;
    my eye will never again see good.
8 The eye of him who sees me will behold me no more;
    while your eyes are on me, I shall be gone.
9 As the cloud fades and vanishes,
    so he who goes down to Sheol does not come up;
10 he returns no more to his house,
    nor does his place know him anymore.

11 "Therefore I will not restrain my mouth;
    I will speak in the anguish of my spirit;

I will complain in the bitterness of my soul.
12 Am I the sea, or a sea monster,
      that you set a guard over me?
13 When I say, 'My bed will comfort me,
      my couch will ease my complaint,'
14 then you scare me with dreams
      and terrify me with visions,
15 so that I would choose strangling
      and death rather than my bones.
16 I loathe my life; I would not live forever.
      Leave me alone, for my days are a breath.
17 What is man, that you make so much of him,
      and that you set your heart on him,
18 visit him every morning
      and test him every moment?
19 How long will you not look away from me,
      nor leave me alone till I swallow my spit?
20 If I sin, what do I do to you, you watcher of mankind?
      Why have you made me your mark?
      Why have I become a burden to you?
21 Why do you not pardon my transgression
      and take away my iniquity?
      For now I shall lie in the earth;
      you will seek me, but I shall not be."

Bildad's first speech [chapter 8]. Starting here, the lead-ins to the speeches retain none of the gentleness of Eliphaz's opening words (4:1–6). Bildad is rude and accusing toward Job. His speech repeats arguments that Eliphaz has already asserted: God is just; Job should repent as a prerequisite to God's blessing him; evildoers will perish. The irony of all this is that it does not fit Job's situation.

8 Then Bildad the Shuhite answered and said:
2 "How long will you say these things,
      and the words of your mouth be a great wind?
3 Does God pervert justice?
      Or does the Almighty pervert the right?
4 If your children have sinned against him,
      he has delivered them into the hand of their transgression.
5 If you will seek God
      and plead with the Almighty for mercy,
6 if you are pure and upright,
      surely then he will rouse himself for you
      and restore your rightful habitation.
7 And though your beginning was small,
      your latter days will be very great.

8   "For inquire, please, of bygone ages,
     and consider what the fathers have searched out.
9   For we are but of yesterday and know nothing,
     for our days on earth are a shadow.
10   Will they not teach you and tell you
     and utter words out of their understanding?

11   "Can papyrus grow where there is no marsh?
     Can reeds flourish where there is no water?
12   While yet in flower and not cut down,
     they wither before any other plant.
13   Such are the paths of all who forget God;
     the hope of the godless shall perish.
14   His confidence is severed,
     and his trust is a spider's web.[1]
15   He leans against his house, but it does not stand;
     he lays hold of it, but it does not endure.
16   He is a lush plant before the sun,
     and his shoots spread over his garden.
17   His roots entwine the stone heap;
     he looks upon a house of stones.
18   If he is destroyed from his place,
     then it will deny him, saying, 'I have never seen you.'
19   Behold, this is the joy of his way,
     and out of the soil others will spring.

20   "Behold, God will not reject a blameless man,
     nor take the hand of evildoers.
21   He will yet fill your mouth with laughter,
     and your lips with shouting.
22   Those who hate you will be clothed with shame,
     and the tent of the wicked will be no more."

Job's reply to Bildad [chapters 9–10]. In chapter 9 Job elaborates on the subject of God's transcendence and omniscience. But instead of this being a cause for reassurance, as in the *psalms of praise, Job adduces it as a reason to despair—God is so transcendent over the earthly and human scene that he pays no attention to it. Chapter 10 restates Job's despair in his suffering.

9 Then Job answered and said:

2   "Truly I know that it is so:
     But how can a man be in the right before God?
3   If one wished to contend with him,
     one could not answer him once in a thousand times.
4   He is wise in heart and mighty in strength
     —who has hardened himself against him, and succeeded?—

---

[1] Hebrew *house*

5   he who removes mountains, and they know it not,
        when he overturns them in his anger,
6   who shakes the earth out of its place,
        and its pillars tremble;
7   who commands the sun, and it does not rise;
        who seals up the stars;
8   who alone stretched out the heavens
        and trampled the waves of the sea;
9   who made the Bear and Orion,
        the Pleiades and the chambers of the south;
10 who does great things beyond searching out,
        and marvelous things beyond number.
11 Behold, he passes by me, and I see him not;
        he moves on, but I do not perceive him.
12 Behold, he snatches away; who can turn him back?
        Who will say to him, 'What are you doing?'

13 "God will not turn back his anger;
        beneath him bowed the helpers of Rahab.
14 How then can I answer him,
        choosing my words with him?
15 Though I am in the right, I cannot answer him;
        I must appeal for mercy to my accuser.[1]
16 If I summoned him and he answered me,
        I would not believe that he was listening to my voice.
17 For he crushes me with a tempest
        and multiplies my wounds without cause;
18 he will not let me get my breath,
        but fills me with bitterness.
19 If it is a contest of strength, behold, he is mighty!
        If it is a matter of justice, who can summon him?[2]
20 Though I am in the right, my own mouth would condemn me;
        though I am blameless, he would prove me perverse.
21 I am blameless; I regard not myself;
        I loathe my life.
22 It is all one; therefore I say,
        He destroys both the blameless and the wicked.
23 When disaster brings sudden death,
        he mocks at the calamity[3] of the innocent.
24 The earth is given into the hand of the wicked;
        he covers the faces of its judges—
        if it is not he, who then is it?

25 "My days are swifter than a runner;
        they flee away; they see no good.
26 They go by like skiffs of reed,
        like an eagle swooping on the prey.

---

[1] Or to my judge [2] Compare Septuagint; Hebrew me [3] The meaning of the Hebrew word is uncertain

²⁷ If I say, 'I will forget my complaint,
     I will put off my sad face, and be of good cheer,'
²⁸ I become afraid of all my suffering,
     for I know you will not hold me innocent.
²⁹ I shall be condemned;
     why then do I labor in vain?
³⁰ If I wash myself with snow
     and cleanse my hands with lye,
³¹ yet you will plunge me into a pit,
     and my own clothes will abhor me.
³² For he is not a man, as I am, that I might answer him,
     that we should come to trial together.
³³ There is no¹ arbiter between us,
     who might lay his hand on us both.
³⁴ Let him take his rod away from me,
     and let not dread of him terrify me.
³⁵ Then I would speak without fear of him,
     for I am not so in myself.

10 "I loathe my life;
     I will give free utterance to my complaint;
     I will speak in the bitterness of my soul.
² I will say to God, Do not condemn me;
     let me know why you contend against me.
³ Does it seem good to you to oppress,
     to despise the work of your hands
     and favor the designs of the wicked?
⁴ Have you eyes of flesh?
     Do you see as man sees?
⁵ Are your days as the days of man,
     or your years as a man's years,
⁶ that you seek out my iniquity
     and search for my sin,
⁷ although you know that I am not guilty,
     and there is none to deliver out of your hand?
⁸ Your hands fashioned and made me,
     and now you have destroyed me altogether.
⁹ Remember that you have made me like clay;
     and will you return me to the dust?
¹⁰ Did you not pour me out like milk
     and curdle me like cheese?
¹¹ You clothed me with skin and flesh,
     and knit me together with bones and sinews.
¹² You have granted me life and steadfast love,
     and your care has preserved my spirit.
¹³ Yet these things you hid in your heart;
     I know that this was your purpose.

---

¹ Or Would that there were an

¹⁴ If I sin, you watch me
      and do not acquit me of my iniquity.
¹⁵ If I am guilty, woe to me!
      If I am in the right, I cannot lift up my head,
      for I am filled with disgrace
      and look on my affliction.
¹⁶ And were my head lifted up,¹ you would hunt me like a lion
      and again work wonders against me.
¹⁷ You renew your witnesses against me
      and increase your vexation toward me;
      you bring fresh troops against me.

¹⁸ "Why did you bring me out from the womb?
      Would that I had died before any eye had seen me
¹⁹ and were as though I had not been,
      carried from the womb to the grave.
²⁰ Are not my days few?
      Then cease, and leave me alone, that I may find a little cheer
²¹ before I go—and I shall not return—
      to the land of darkness and deep shadow,
²² the land of gloom like thick darkness,
      like deep shadow without any order,
      where light is as thick darkness."

Zophar's first speech [chapter 11]. The anger thermometer continues to rise as Zophar begins by attacking Job (vv. 1–6). Then he repeats the same ideas that his friends had voiced—God judges "worthless men" (v. 11); if Job will repent, God will bless him.

11 Then Zophar the Naamathite answered and said:

² "Should a multitude of words go unanswered,
      and a man full of talk be judged right?
³ Should your babble silence men,
      and when you mock, shall no one shame you?
⁴ For you say, 'My doctrine is pure,
      and I am clean in God's² eyes.'
⁵ But oh, that God would speak
      and open his lips to you,
⁶ and that he would tell you the secrets of wisdom!
      For he is manifold in understanding.³
      Know then that God exacts of you less than your guilt deserves.

⁷ "Can you find out the deep things of God?
      Can you find out the limit of the Almighty?
⁸ It is higher than heaven⁴—what can you do?
      Deeper than Sheol—what can you know?
⁹ Its measure is longer than the earth

---

¹ Hebrew lacks *my head* ² Hebrew *your* ³ The meaning of the Hebrew is uncertain ⁴ Hebrew *The heights of heaven*

and broader than the sea.

¹⁰ If he passes through and imprisons
and summons the court, who can turn him back?

¹¹ For he knows worthless men;
when he sees iniquity, will he not consider it?

¹² But a stupid man will get understanding
when a wild donkey's colt is born a man!

¹³ "If you prepare your heart,
you will stretch out your hands toward him.

¹⁴ If iniquity is in your hand, put it far away,
and let not injustice dwell in your tents.

¹⁵ Surely then you will lift up your face without blemish;
you will be secure and will not fear.

¹⁶ You will forget your misery;
you will remember it as waters that have passed away.

¹⁷ And your life will be brighter than the noonday;
its darkness will be like the morning.

¹⁸ And you will feel secure, because there is hope;
you will look around and take your rest in security.

¹⁹ You will lie down, and none will make you afraid;
many will court your favor.

²⁰ But the eyes of the wicked will fail;
all way of escape will be lost to them,
and their hope is to breathe their last."

Job's reply to Zophar [chapter 12]. The first cycle of speeches ends with a long speech by Job that lasts for three chapters. Chapter 12 begins with one of the masterpieces of sarcasm in the Bible (v. 2). After that, Job retorts sharply to Zophar, and the key passage of that retort is verses 13–25. These verses are a catalog of the sovereign acts of God, as in the praise psalms. The twist is that all of God's actions in the catalog are acts of disaster. This is a bitter man's creed, praising a sadistic God.

---

12 Then Job answered and said:

² "No doubt you are the people,
and wisdom will die with you.

³ But I have understanding as well as you;
I am not inferior to you.
Who does not know such things as these?

⁴ I am a laughingstock to my friends;
I, who called to God and he answered me,
a just and blameless man, am a laughingstock.

⁵ In the thought of one who is at ease there is contempt for misfortune;
it is ready for those whose feet slip.

⁶ The tents of robbers are at peace,

and those who provoke God are secure,
    who bring their god in their hand.[1]

7 "But ask the beasts, and they will teach you;
    the birds of the heavens, and they will tell you;
8 or the bushes of the earth,[2] and they will teach you;
    and the fish of the sea will declare to you.
9 Who among all these does not know
    that the hand of the LORD has done this?
10 In his hand is the life of every living thing
    and the breath of all mankind.
11 Does not the ear test words
    as the palate tastes food?
12 Wisdom is with the aged,
    and understanding in length of days.

13 "With God[3] are wisdom and might;
    he has counsel and understanding.
14 If he tears down, none can rebuild;
    if he shuts a man in, none can open.
15 If he withholds the waters, they dry up;
    if he sends them out, they overwhelm the land.
16 With him are strength and sound wisdom;
    the deceived and the deceiver are his.
17 He leads counselors away stripped,
    and judges he makes fools.
18 He looses the bonds of kings
    and binds a waistcloth on their hips.
19 He leads priests away stripped
    and overthrows the mighty.
20 He deprives of speech those who are trusted
    and takes away the discernment of the elders.
21 He pours contempt on princes
    and loosens the belt of the strong.
22 He uncovers the deeps out of darkness
    and brings deep darkness to light.
23 He makes nations great, and he destroys them;
    he enlarges nations, and leads them away.
24 He takes away understanding from the chiefs of the people of the earth
    and makes them wander in a pathless waste.
25 They grope in the dark without light,
    and he makes them stagger like a drunken man.

Job's defense of himself [chapter 13]. The middle chapter of Job's final speech in the first cycle begins as a put-down of his counselors (vv. 1–12), but after that the focus is on Job's defense of his innocence and integrity (vv. 13–28).

---

[1] The meaning of the Hebrew is uncertain [2] Or *speak to the earth* [3] Hebrew *him*

13 "Behold, my eye has seen all this,
       my ear has heard and understood it.

2 What you know, I also know;
       I am not inferior to you.

3 But I would speak to the Almighty,
       and I desire to argue my case with God.

4 As for you, you whitewash with lies;
       worthless physicians are you all.

5 Oh that you would keep silent,
       and it would be your wisdom!

6 Hear now my argument
       and listen to the pleadings of my lips.

7 Will you speak falsely for God
       and speak deceitfully for him?

8 Will you show partiality toward him?
       Will you plead the case for God?

9 Will it be well with you when he searches you out?
       Or can you deceive him, as one deceives a man?

10 He will surely rebuke you
       if in secret you show partiality.

11 Will not his majesty terrify you,
       and the dread of him fall upon you?

12 Your maxims are proverbs of ashes;
       your defenses are defenses of clay.

13 "Let me have silence, and I will speak,
       and let come on me what may.

14 Why should I take my flesh in my teeth
       and put my life in my hand?

15 Though he slay me, I will hope in him;[1]
       yet I will argue my ways to his face.

16 This will be my salvation,
       that the godless shall not come before him.

17 Keep listening to my words,
       and let my declaration be in your ears.

18 Behold, I have prepared my case;
       I know that I shall be in the right.

19 Who is there who will contend with me?
       For then I would be silent and die.

20 Only grant me two things,
       then I will not hide myself from your face:

21 withdraw your hand far from me,
       and let not dread of you terrify me.

22 Then call, and I will answer;
       or let me speak, and you reply to me.

23 How many are my iniquities and my sins?
       Make me know my transgression and my sin.

---

[1] Or *Behold, he will slay me; I have no hope*

²⁴ Why do you hide your face
    and count me as your enemy?
²⁵ Will you frighten a driven leaf
    and pursue dry chaff?
²⁶ For you write bitter things against me
    and make me inherit the iniquities of my youth.
²⁷ You put my feet in the stocks
    and watch all my paths;
    you set a limit for¹ the soles of my feet.
²⁸ Man² wastes away like a rotten thing,
    like a garment that is moth-eaten.

Job's complaint [chapter 14]. The speeches in the book of Job do not cover just one topic but are to some extent *stream-of-consciousness in their movement, pursuing thoughts as they actually appear when a person is thinking through an issue. The general thrust of chapter 14 is Job's lament regarding his suffering and frustrated dreams. As we thus end the first cycle of speeches, we can summarize what has happened as follows: (1) Job's counselors have asserted that God is just and Job guilty; (2) Job has asserted that he is innocent and God unjust. Neither of these viewpoints is accurate, as we know from the prologue set in heaven.

14
¹ "Man who is born of a woman
    is few of days and full of trouble.
² He comes out like a flower and withers;
    he flees like a shadow and continues not.
³ And do you open your eyes on such a one
    and bring me into judgment with you?
⁴ Who can bring a clean thing out of an unclean?
    There is not one.
⁵ Since his days are determined,
    and the number of his months is with you,
    and you have appointed his limits that he cannot pass,
⁶ look away from him and leave him alone,³
    that he may enjoy, like a hired hand, his day.

⁷ "For there is hope for a tree,
    if it be cut down, that it will sprout again,
    and that its shoots will not cease.
⁸ Though its root grow old in the earth,
    and its stump die in the soil,
⁹ yet at the scent of water it will bud
    and put out branches like a young plant.
¹⁰ But a man dies and is laid low;
    man breathes his last, and where is he?
¹¹ As waters fail from a lake
    and a river wastes away and dries up,
¹² so a man lies down and rises not again;

---

¹ Or *you marked* ² Hebrew *He* ³ Probable reading; Hebrew *look away from him, that he may cease*

till the heavens are no more he will not awake
  or be roused out of his sleep.
¹³ Oh that you would hide me in Sheol,
    that you would conceal me until your wrath be past,
    that you would appoint me a set time, and remember me!
¹⁴ If a man dies, shall he live again?
    All the days of my service I would wait,
      till my renewal[1] should come.
¹⁵ You would call, and I would answer you;
    you would long for the work of your hands.
¹⁶ For then you would number my steps;
    you would not keep watch over my sin;
¹⁷ my transgression would be sealed up in a bag,
    and you would cover over my iniquity.

¹⁸ "But the mountain falls and crumbles away,
    and the rock is removed from its place;
¹⁹ the waters wear away the stones;
    the torrents wash away the soil of the earth;
    so you destroy the hope of man.
²⁰ You prevail forever against him, and he passes;
    you change his countenance, and send him away.
²¹ His sons come to honor, and he does not know it;
    they are brought low, and he perceives it not.
²² He feels only the pain of his own body,
    and he mourns only for himself."

Eliphaz's second speech [chapter 15]. As the second cycle unfolds, it is as though Job and his friends have not even listened to each other. The friends, in particular, make no progress whatsoever in their thinking. In Eliphaz's second speech, he reiterates the viewpoint that God is just and Job guilty, with the conclusion that Job needs to repent. Eliphaz reaches a climax of oratorical eloquence in verses 20–35, where he paints a detailed picture of the destruction that comes upon a wicked person. By assuming Job's guilt, the three friends completely miss the specific question that Job's experience raises, namely, why do the righteous suffer?

15 Then Eliphaz the Temanite answered and said:
² "Should a wise man answer with windy knowledge,
    and fill his belly with the east wind?
³ Should he argue in unprofitable talk,
    or in words with which he can do no good?
⁴ But you are doing away with the fear of God[2]
    and hindering meditation before God.
⁵ For your iniquity teaches your mouth,
    and you choose the tongue of the crafty.

[1] Or relief [2] Hebrew lacks of God

⁶   Your own mouth condemns you, and not I;
      your own lips testify against you.

⁷   "Are you the first man who was born?
      Or were you brought forth before the hills?
⁸   Have you listened in the council of God?
      And do you limit wisdom to yourself?
⁹   What do you know that we do not know?
      What do you understand that is not clear to us?
¹⁰ Both the gray-haired and the aged are among us,
      older than your father.
¹¹ Are the comforts of God too small for you,
      or the word that deals gently with you?
¹² Why does your heart carry you away,
      and why do your eyes flash,
¹³ that you turn your spirit against God
      and bring such words out of your mouth?
¹⁴ What is man, that he can be pure?
      Or he who is born of a woman, that he can be righteous?
¹⁵ Behold, God¹ puts no trust in his holy ones,
       and the heavens are not pure in his sight;
¹⁶ how much less one who is abominable and corrupt,
      a man who drinks injustice like water!

¹⁷ "I will show you; hear me,
      and what I have seen I will declare
¹⁸ (what wise men have told,
      without hiding it from their fathers,
¹⁹ to whom alone the land was given,
      and no stranger passed among them).
²⁰ The wicked man writhes in pain all his days,
      through all the years that are laid up for the ruthless.
²¹ Dreadful sounds are in his ears;
      in prosperity the destroyer will come upon him.
²² He does not believe that he will return out of darkness,
      and he is marked for the sword.
²³ He wanders abroad for bread, saying, 'Where is it?'
      He knows that a day of darkness is ready at his hand;
²⁴ distress and anguish terrify him;
      they prevail against him, like a king ready for battle.
²⁵ Because he has stretched out his hand against God
      and defies the Almighty,
²⁶ running stubbornly against him
      with a thickly bossed shield;
²⁷ because he has covered his face with his fat
      and gathered fat upon his waist
²⁸ and has lived in desolate cities,

¹ Hebrew *he*

in houses that none should inhabit,
  which were ready to become heaps of ruins;
29 he will not be rich, and his wealth will not endure,
  nor will his possessions spread over the earth;[1]
30 he will not depart from darkness;
  the flame will dry up his shoots,
  and by the breath of his mouth he will depart.
31 Let him not trust in emptiness, deceiving himself,
  for emptiness will be his payment.
32 It will be paid in full before his time,
  and his branch will not be green.
33 He will shake off his unripe grape like the vine,
  and cast off his blossom like the olive tree.
34 For the company of the godless is barren,
  and fire consumes the tents of bribery.
35 They conceive trouble and give birth to evil,
  and their womb prepares deceit."

Job's reply to Eliphaz [chapters 16–17]. Job makes as little progress as Eliphaz does in his thinking in these two chapters. After a *satiric put-down of his counselors (16:1–5), Job perpetuates his defiant accusations against God (e.g., 16:6–17). There is also self-pity mixed in, yet an authentic note of human suffering is sounded.

16 Then Job answered and said:

2 "I have heard many such things;
  miserable comforters are you all.
3 Shall windy words have an end?
  Or what provokes you that you answer?
4 I also could speak as you do,
  if you were in my place;
  I could join words together against you
  and shake my head at you.
5 I could strengthen you with my mouth,
  and the solace of my lips would assuage your pain.

6 "If I speak, my pain is not assuaged,
  and if I forbear, how much of it leaves me?
7 Surely now God has worn me out;
  he has[2] made desolate all my company.
8 And he has shriveled me up,
  which is a witness against me,
  and my leanness has risen up against me;
  it testifies to my face.
9 He has torn me in his wrath and hated me;
  he has gnashed his teeth at me;
  my adversary sharpens his eyes against me.

---

[1] Or nor will his produce bend down to the earth [2] Hebrew you have; also verse 8

10 Men have gaped at me with their mouth;
    they have struck me insolently on the cheek;
    they mass themselves together against me.
11 God gives me up to the ungodly
    and casts me into the hands of the wicked.
12 I was at ease, and he broke me apart;
    he seized me by the neck and dashed me to pieces;
    he set me up as his target;
13   his archers surround me.
He slashes open my kidneys and does not spare;
    he pours out my gall on the ground.
14 He breaks me with breach upon breach;
    he runs upon me like a warrior.
15 I have sewed sackcloth upon my skin
    and have laid my strength in the dust.
16 My face is red with weeping,
    and on my eyelids is deep darkness,
17 although there is no violence in my hands,
    and my prayer is pure.

18 "O earth, cover not my blood,
    and let my cry find no resting place.
19 Even now, behold, my witness is in heaven,
    and he who testifies for me is on high.
20 My friends scorn me;
    my eye pours out tears to God,
21 that he would argue the case of a man with God,
    as[1] a son of man does with his neighbor.
22 For when a few years have come
    I shall go the way from which I shall not return.

17

"My spirit is broken; my days are extinct;
    the graveyard is ready for me.
2 Surely there are mockers about me,
    and my eye dwells on their provocation.

3 "Lay down a pledge for me with yourself;
    who is there who will put up security for me?
4 Since you have closed their hearts to understanding,
    therefore you will not let them triumph.
5 He who informs against his friends to get a share of their property—
    the eyes of his children will fail.

6 "He has made me a byword of the peoples,
    and I am one before whom men spit.
7 My eye has grown dim from vexation,
    and all my members are like a shadow.
8 The upright are appalled at this,

[1] Hebrew *and*

and the innocent stirs himself up against the godless.
9   Yet the righteous holds to his way,
       and he who has clean hands grows stronger and stronger.
10   But you, come on again, all of you,
       and I shall not find a wise man among you.
11   My days are past; my plans are broken off,
       the desires of my heart.
12   They make night into day:
       'The light,' they say, 'is near to the darkness.'[1]
13   If I hope for Sheol as my house,
       if I make my bed in darkness,
14   if I say to the pit, 'You are my father,'
       and to the worm, 'My mother,' or 'My sister,'
15   where then is my hope?
       Who will see my hope?
16   Will it go down to the bars of Sheol?
       Shall we descend together into the dust?"

> **Bildad's second speech** [chapter 18]. The friends are becoming increasingly tactless in portraying the bad end of the wicked, with the implication that Job's suffering is an example of such. In fact, we can scrutinize this chapter for hints that Bildad is rubbing salt into Job's wounds with specific references to his calamity.

18 Then Bildad the Shuhite answered and said:

2   "How long will you hunt for words?
       Consider, and then we will speak.
3   Why are we counted as cattle?
       Why are we stupid in your sight?
4   You who tear yourself in your anger,
         shall the earth be forsaken for you,
         or the rock be removed out of its place?

5   "Indeed, the light of the wicked is put out,
       and the flame of his fire does not shine.
6   The light is dark in his tent,
       and his lamp above him is put out.
7   His strong steps are shortened,
       and his own schemes throw him down.
8   For he is cast into a net by his own feet,
       and he walks on its mesh.
9   A trap seizes him by the heel;
       a snare lays hold of him.
10   A rope is hidden for him in the ground,
       a trap for him in the path.
11   Terrors frighten him on every side,
       and chase him at his heels.

---
[1] The meaning of the Hebrew is uncertain

¹² His strength is famished,
  and calamity is ready for his stumbling.
¹³ It consumes the parts of his skin;
  the firstborn of death consumes his limbs.
¹⁴ He is torn from the tent in which he trusted
  and is brought to the king of terrors.
¹⁵ In his tent dwells that which is none of his;
  sulfur is scattered over his habitation.
¹⁶ His roots dry up beneath,
  and his branches wither above.
¹⁷ His memory perishes from the earth,
  and he has no name in the street.
¹⁸ He is thrust from light into darkness,
  and driven out of the world.
¹⁹ He has no posterity or progeny among his people,
  and no survivor where he used to live.
²⁰ They of the west are appalled at his day,
  and horror seizes them of the east.
²¹ Surely such are the dwellings of the unrighteous,
  such is the place of him who knows not God."

Job's reply to Bildad [chapter 19]. Job continues to make false accusations against God, but he also makes intellectual progress in this speech. We might note in passing that there have been scattered brief statements in Job's earlier speeches that contain the seeds of his recovery, but since they are such isolated brief statements, it is hard to attribute genuine progress to them. But in the present chapter, Job's great affirmation of the resurrection (vv. 23–27) represents a genuine advance in his thinking, inasmuch as it lifts the gaze beyond the earthly sphere to the heavenly sphere. If there is to be a satisfactory solution to the problem of suffering, it will need to incorporate a supernatural perspective.

19 Then Job answered and said:

² "How long will you torment me
  and break me in pieces with words?
³ These ten times you have cast reproach upon me;
  are you not ashamed to wrong me?
⁴ And even if it be true that I have erred,
  my error remains with myself.
⁵ If indeed you magnify yourselves against me
  and make my disgrace an argument against me,
⁶ know then that God has put me in the wrong
  and closed his net about me.
⁷ Behold, I cry out, 'Violence!' but I am not answered;
  I call for help, but there is no justice.
⁸ He has walled up my way, so that I cannot pass,

and he has set darkness upon my paths.
⁹   He has stripped from me my glory
      and taken the crown from my head.
¹⁰ He breaks me down on every side, and I am gone,
      and my hope has he pulled up like a tree.
¹¹ He has kindled his wrath against me
      and counts me as his adversary.
¹² His troops come on together;
      they have cast up their siege ramp¹ against me
      and encamp around my tent.

¹³ "He has put my brothers far from me,
      and those who knew me are wholly estranged from me.
¹⁴ My relatives have failed me,
      my close friends have forgotten me.
¹⁵ The guests in my house and my maidservants count me as a stranger;
      I have become a foreigner in their eyes.
¹⁶ I call to my servant, but he gives me no answer;
      I must plead with him with my mouth for mercy.
¹⁷ My breath is strange to my wife,
      and I am a stench to the children of my own mother.
¹⁸ Even young children despise me;
      when I rise they talk against me.
¹⁹ All my intimate friends abhor me,
      and those whom I loved have turned against me.
²⁰ My bones stick to my skin and to my flesh,
      and I have escaped by the skin of my teeth.
²¹ Have mercy on me, have mercy on me, O you my friends,
      for the hand of God has touched me!
²² Why do you, like God, pursue me?
      Why are you not satisfied with my flesh?

²³ "Oh that my words were written!
      Oh that they were inscribed in a book!
²⁴ Oh that with an iron pen and lead
      they were engraved in the rock forever!
²⁵ For I know that my Redeemer lives,
      and at the last he will stand upon the earth.²
²⁶ And after my skin has been thus destroyed,
      yet in³ my flesh I shall see God,
²⁷ whom I shall see for myself,
      and my eyes shall behold, and not another.
      My heart faints within me!
²⁸ If you say, 'How we will pursue him!'
      and, 'The root of the matter is found in him,'
²⁹ be afraid of the sword,

---

¹ Hebrew *their way* ² Hebrew *dust* ³ Or *without*

for wrath brings the punishment of the sword,
    that you may know there is a judgment."

Zophar's second speech [chapter 20]. The best that Zophar can produce is an extended portrait of the destruction of the rich evildoer, and again we catch the hint of an attack on Job, specifically.

20 Then Zophar the Naamathite answered and said:

2   "Therefore my thoughts answer me,
    because of my haste within me.
3   I hear censure that insults me,
    and out of my understanding a spirit answers me.
4   Do you not know this from of old,
    since man was placed on earth,
5   that the exulting of the wicked is short,
    and the joy of the godless but for a moment?
6   Though his height mount up to the heavens,
    and his head reach to the clouds,
7   he will perish forever like his own dung;
    those who have seen him will say, 'Where is he?'
8   He will fly away like a dream and not be found;
    he will be chased away like a vision of the night.
9   The eye that saw him will see him no more,
    nor will his place any more behold him.
10   His children will seek the favor of the poor,
    and his hands will give back his wealth.
11   His bones are full of his youthful vigor,
    but it will lie down with him in the dust.

12   "Though evil is sweet in his mouth,
    though he hides it under his tongue,
13   though he is loath to let it go
    and holds it in his mouth,
14   yet his food is turned in his stomach;
    it is the venom of cobras within him.
15   He swallows down riches and vomits them up again;
    God casts them out of his belly.
16   He will suck the poison of cobras;
    the tongue of a viper will kill him.
17   He will not look upon the rivers,
    the streams flowing with honey and curds.
18   He will give back the fruit of his toil
    and will not swallow it down;
  from the profit of his trading
    he will get no enjoyment.

¹⁹   For he has crushed and abandoned the poor;
    he has seized a house that he did not build.

²⁰   "Because he knew no contentment in his belly,
    he will not let anything in which he delights escape him.
²¹   There was nothing left after he had eaten;
    therefore his prosperity will not endure.
²²   In the fullness of his sufficiency he will be in distress;
    the hand of everyone in misery will come against him.
²³   To fill his belly to the full,
    God[1] will send his burning anger against him
    and rain it upon him into his body.
²⁴   He will flee from an iron weapon;
    a bronze arrow will strike him through.
²⁵   It is drawn forth and comes out of his body;
    the glittering point comes out of his gallbladder;
    terrors come upon him.
²⁶   Utter darkness is laid up for his treasures;
    a fire not fanned will devour him;
    what is left in his tent will be consumed.
²⁷   The heavens will reveal his iniquity,
    and the earth will rise up against him.
²⁸   The possessions of his house will be carried away,
    dragged off in the day of God's[2] wrath.
²⁹   This is the wicked man's portion from God,
    the heritage decreed for him by God."

Breakthrough [chapter 21]. If Job's vision of the resurrection in 19:23–27 represented an important but fleeting advance, chapter 21 represents a more major breakthrough. In this speech, Job decisively refutes his friends' claims that the wicked are punished. After a heartrending cry of suffering (vv. 1–6), Job presents extensive evidence that not only do the wicked not suffer—they actually prosper. They even get prominent funerals (vv. 32–33). It is easy to miss what has happened here, but Job decisively dissociates suffering from the fact of sin or guilt on the part of the sufferer. While this does not solve the problem of innocent suffering, it refutes a false solution to the problem.

21   Then Job answered and said:

²   "Keep listening to my words,
    and let this be your comfort.
³   Bear with me, and I will speak,
    and after I have spoken, mock on.
⁴   As for me, is my complaint against man?
    Why should I not be impatient?
⁵   Look at me and be appalled,
    and lay your hand over your mouth.
⁶   When I remember, I am dismayed,
    and shuddering seizes my flesh.

[1] Hebrew *he* [2] Hebrew *his*

7   Why do the wicked live,
       reach old age, and grow mighty in power?
8   Their offspring are established in their presence,
       and their descendants before their eyes.
9   Their houses are safe from fear,
       and no rod of God is upon them.
10 Their bull breeds without fail;
       their cow calves and does not miscarry.
11 They send out their little boys like a flock,
       and their children dance.
12 They sing to the tambourine and the lyre
       and rejoice to the sound of the pipe.
13 They spend their days in prosperity,
       and in peace they go down to Sheol.
14 They say to God, 'Depart from us!
       We do not desire the knowledge of your ways.
15 What is the Almighty, that we should serve him?
       And what profit do we get if we pray to him?'
16 Behold, is not their prosperity in their hand?
       The counsel of the wicked is far from me.

17 "How often is it that the lamp of the wicked is put out?
       That their calamity comes upon them?
       That God[1] distributes pains in his anger?
18 That they are like straw before the wind,
       and like chaff that the storm carries away?
19 You say, 'God stores up their iniquity for their children.'
       Let him pay it out to them, that they may know it.
20 Let their own eyes see their destruction,
       and let them drink of the wrath of the Almighty.
21 For what do they care for their houses after them,
       when the number of their months is cut off?
22 Will any teach God knowledge,
       seeing that he judges those who are on high?
23 One dies in his full vigor,
       being wholly at ease and secure,
24 his pails[2] full of milk
       and the marrow of his bones moist.
25 Another dies in bitterness of soul,
       never having tasted of prosperity.
26 They lie down alike in the dust,
       and the worms cover them.

27 "Behold, I know your thoughts
       and your schemes to wrong me.
28 For you say, 'Where is the house of the prince?
       Where is the tent in which the wicked lived?'

---

[1] Hebrew *he* [2] The meaning of the Hebrew word is uncertain

²⁹   Have you not asked those who travel the roads,
        and do you not accept their testimony
³⁰   that the evil man is spared in the day of calamity,
        that he is rescued in the day of wrath?
³¹   Who declares his way to his face,
        and who repays him for what he has done?
³²   When he is carried to the grave,
        watch is kept over his tomb.
³³   The clods of the valley are sweet to him;
        all mankind follows after him,
        and those who go before him are innumerable.
³⁴   How then will you comfort me with empty nothings?
        There is nothing left of your answers but falsehood."

Eliphaz's third speech [chapter 22]. As previewed by the chart for this book (see introduction to the book, p. 684), the exchanges between Job and his counselors unfold in three largely symmetrical cycles, and the third cycle starts with chapter 22. In this chapter, Eliphaz repeats his familiar themes, but they are now couched in the most direct attack on Job that has yet occurred.

22 Then Eliphaz the Temanite answered and said:

²   "Can a man be profitable to God?
        Surely he who is wise is profitable to himself.
³   Is it any pleasure to the Almighty if you are in the right,
        or is it gain to him if you make your ways blameless?
⁴   Is it for your fear of him that he reproves you
        and enters into judgment with you?
⁵   Is not your evil abundant?
        There is no end to your iniquities.
⁶   For you have exacted pledges of your brothers for nothing
        and stripped the naked of their clothing.
⁷   You have given no water to the weary to drink,
        and you have withheld bread from the hungry.
⁸   The man with power possessed the land,
        and the favored man lived in it.
⁹   You have sent widows away empty,
        and the arms of the fatherless were crushed.
¹⁰   Therefore snares are all around you,
        and sudden terror overwhelms you,
¹¹   or darkness, so that you cannot see,
        and a flood of water covers you.

¹²   "Is not God high in the heavens?
        See the highest stars, how lofty they are!
¹³   But you say, 'What does God know?
        Can he judge through the deep darkness?

¹⁴ Thick clouds veil him, so that he does not see,
and he walks on the vault of heaven.'
¹⁵ Will you keep to the old way
that wicked men have trod?
¹⁶ They were snatched away before their time;
their foundation was washed away.
¹⁷ They said to God, 'Depart from us,'
and 'What can the Almighty do to us?'[1]
¹⁸ Yet he filled their houses with good things—
but the counsel of the wicked is far from me.
¹⁹ The righteous see it and are glad;
the innocent one mocks at them,
²⁰ saying, 'Surely our adversaries are cut off,
and what they left the fire has consumed.'

²¹ "Agree with God, and be at peace;
thereby good will come to you.
²² Receive instruction from his mouth,
and lay up his words in your heart.
²³ If you return to the Almighty you will be built up;
if you remove injustice far from your tents,
²⁴ if you lay gold in the dust,
and gold of Ophir among the stones of the torrent-bed,
²⁵ then the Almighty will be your gold
and your precious silver.
²⁶ For then you will delight yourself in the Almighty
and lift up your face to God.
²⁷ You will make your prayer to him, and he will hear you,
and you will pay your vows.
²⁸ You will decide on a matter, and it will be established for you,
and light will shine on your ways.
²⁹ For when they are humbled you say, 'It is because of pride';[2]
but he saves the lowly.
³⁰ He delivers even the one who is not innocent,[3]
who will be delivered through the cleanness of your hands."

Job's reply to Eliphaz [chapters 23–24]. At this point we need to realize that in each of the three cycles of speeches, Job makes intellectual and spiritual progress. In the third cycle, he utters a preponderance of truth, even though his defiance and wrong thinking about God's character and actions toward him continue. In chapter 23, Job expresses a new confidence that he can trust God's integrity. By comparison, chapter 24 represents a reversion to Job's former thinking that God prospers the wicked.

23

Then Job answered and said:

² "Today also my complaint is bitter;[4]
my hand is heavy on account of my groaning.

---

[1] Hebrew *them* [2] Or *you say, 'It is exaltation'* [3] Septuagint, Syriac, Vulgate; Hebrew *him that is not innocent* [4] Or *defiant*

³   Oh, that I knew where I might find him,
        that I might come even to his seat!
⁴   I would lay my case before him
        and fill my mouth with arguments.
⁵   I would know what he would answer me
        and understand what he would say to me.
⁶   Would he contend with me in the greatness of his power?
        No; he would pay attention to me.
⁷   There an upright man could argue with him,
        and I would be acquitted forever by my judge.

⁸   "Behold, I go forward, but he is not there,
        and backward, but I do not perceive him;
⁹   on the left hand when he is working, I do not behold him;
        he turns to the right hand, but I do not see him.
¹⁰   But he knows the way that I take;
        when he has tried me, I shall come out as gold.
¹¹   My foot has held fast to his steps;
        I have kept his way and have not turned aside.
¹²   I have not departed from the commandment of his lips;
        I have treasured the words of his mouth more than my portion of food.
¹³   But he is unchangeable,[1] and who can turn him back?
        What he desires, that he does.
¹⁴   For he will complete what he appoints for me,
        and many such things are in his mind.
¹⁵   Therefore I am terrified at his presence;
        when I consider, I am in dread of him.
¹⁶   God has made my heart faint;
        the Almighty has terrified me;
¹⁷   yet I am not silenced because of the darkness,
        nor because thick darkness covers my face.

24

    "Why are not times of judgment kept by the Almighty,
        and why do those who know him never see his days?
²   Some move landmarks;
        they seize flocks and pasture them.
³   They drive away the donkey of the fatherless;
        they take the widow's ox for a pledge.
⁴   They thrust the poor off the road;
        the poor of the earth all hide themselves.
⁵   Behold, like wild donkeys in the desert
        the poor[2] go out to their toil, seeking game;
        the wasteland yields food for their children.
⁶   They gather their[3] fodder in the field,
        and they glean the vineyard of the wicked man.
⁷   They lie all night naked, without clothing,
        and have no covering in the cold.

---

[1] Or one [2] Hebrew they [3] Hebrew his

8 They are wet with the rain of the mountains
    and cling to the rock for lack of shelter.
9 (There are those who snatch the fatherless child from the breast,
    and they take a pledge against the poor.)
10 They go about naked, without clothing;
    hungry, they carry the sheaves;
11 among the olive rows of the wicked[1] they make oil;
    they tread the winepresses, but suffer thirst.
12 From out of the city the dying groan,
    and the soul of the wounded cries for help;
    yet God charges no one with wrong.

13 "There are those who rebel against the light,
    who are not acquainted with its ways,
    and do not stay in its paths.
14 The murderer rises before it is light,
    that he may kill the poor and needy,
    and in the night he is like a thief.
15 The eye of the adulterer also waits for the twilight,
    saying, 'No eye will see me';
    and he veils his face.
16 In the dark they dig through houses;
    by day they shut themselves up;
    they do not know the light.
17 For deep darkness is morning to all of them;
    for they are friends with the terrors of deep darkness.

18 "You say, 'Swift are they on the face of the waters;
    their portion is cursed in the land;
    no treader turns toward their vineyards.
19 Drought and heat snatch away the snow waters;
    so does Sheol those who have sinned.
20 The womb forgets them;
    the worm finds them sweet;
they are no longer remembered,
    so wickedness is broken like a tree.'

21 "They wrong the barren, childless woman,
    and do no good to the widow.
22 Yet God[2] prolongs the life of the mighty by his power;
    they rise up when they despair of life.
23 He gives them security, and they are supported,
    and his eyes are upon their ways.
24 They are exalted a little while, and then are gone;
    they are brought low and gathered up like all others;
    they are cut off like the heads of grain.
25 If it is not so, who will prove me a liar
    and show that there is nothing in what I say?"

[1] Hebrew their olive rows [2] Hebrew he

Final exchange between Bildad and Job [chapters 25–26]. A truncated speech by Bildad reverts to Job's earlier speech that portrayed God as being so transcendent that a human stands no chance of a fair hearing with him (chapter 25). In a speech that anticipates the voice from the whirlwind, Job extols the transcendence of God over the world of nature (chapter 26), ending with the conclusion that God's ways are mysterious and unknowable to people (26:14).

25 Then Bildad the Shuhite answered and said:

2 "Dominion and fear are with God;[1]
    he makes peace in his high heaven.
3 Is there any number to his armies?
    Upon whom does his light not arise?
4 How then can man be in the right before God?
    How can he who is born of woman be pure?
5 Behold, even the moon is not bright,
    and the stars are not pure in his eyes;
6 how much less man, who is a maggot,
    and the son of man, who is a worm!"

26 Then Job answered and said:

2 "How you have helped him who has no power!
    How you have saved the arm that has no strength!
3 How you have counseled him who has no wisdom,
    and plentifully declared sound knowledge!
4 With whose help have you uttered words,
    and whose breath has come out from you?
5 The dead tremble
    under the waters and their inhabitants.
6 Sheol is naked before God,[2]
    and Abaddon has no covering.
7 He stretches out the north over the void
    and hangs the earth on nothing.
8 He binds up the waters in his thick clouds,
    and the cloud is not split open under them.
9 He covers the face of the full moon[3]
    and spreads over it his cloud.
10 He has inscribed a circle on the face of the waters
    at the boundary between light and darkness.
11 The pillars of heaven tremble
    and are astounded at his rebuke.
12 By his power he stilled the sea;
    by his understanding he shattered Rahab.
13 By his wind the heavens were made fair;
    his hand pierced the fleeing serpent.
14 Behold, these are but the outskirts of his ways,

---

[1] Hebrew *him* [2] Hebrew *him* [3] Or *his throne*

and how small a whisper do we hear of him!
But the thunder of his power who can understand?"

27 And Job again took up his discourse, and said:

2 "As God lives, who has taken away my right,
    and the Almighty, who has made my soul bitter,
3 as long as my breath is in me,
    and the spirit of God is in my nostrils,
4 my lips will not speak falsehood,
    and my tongue will not utter deceit.
5 Far be it from me to say that you are right;
    till I die I will not put away my integrity from me.
6 I hold fast my righteousness and will not let it go;
    my heart does not reproach me for any of my days.

7 "Let my enemy be as the wicked,
    and let him who rises up against me be as the unrighteous.
8 For what is the hope of the godless when God cuts him off,
    when God takes away his life?
9 Will God hear his cry
    when distress comes upon him?
10 Will he take delight in the Almighty?
    Will he call upon God at all times?
11 I will teach you concerning the hand of God;
    what is with the Almighty I will not conceal.
12 Behold, all of you have seen it yourselves;
    why then have you become altogether vain?

13 "This is the portion of a wicked man with God,
    and the heritage that oppressors receive from the Almighty:
14 If his children are multiplied, it is for the sword,
    and his descendants have not enough bread.
15 Those who survive him the pestilence buries,
    and his widows do not weep.
16 Though he heap up silver like dust,
    and pile up clothing like clay,
17 he may pile it up, but the righteous will wear it,
    and the innocent will divide the silver.

¹⁸   He builds his house like a moth's,
      like a booth that a watchman makes.
¹⁹   He goes to bed rich, but will do so no more;
      he opens his eyes, and his wealth is gone.
²⁰   Terrors overtake him like a flood;
      in the night a whirlwind carries him off.
²¹   The east wind lifts him up and he is gone;
      it sweeps him out of his place.
²²   It[1] hurls at him without pity;
      he flees from its[2] power in headlong flight.
²³   It claps its hands at him
      and hisses at him from its place.

Poem in praise of wisdom [chapter 28]. Just as the cycles of speeches were preceded by a speech by Job standing outside the cycles (chapter 3), here at the end we also get speeches from Job that succeed the cycles instead of being a part of them. All of Job's speeches in this unit are oratorical masterpieces. Chapter 28 is an *ode in praise of wisdom. It unfolds in three movements: the marvel of human skill or wisdom that can find every secret thing, as symbolized by the ability to find minerals and jewels in the earth (vv. 1–11); but in answer to the question of where wisdom can be found (v. 12), the poem next asserts that there is one thing—wisdom—that human ingenuity cannot find (vv. 13–22); the solution to the problem is that God understands the way to wisdom (vv. 23–28). While the poem can thus be read as a freestanding poem in praise of God's superior wisdom, if we place it into the larger context of the book of Job, we can see it as expressing a new humility on the part of Job to answer the ultimate mysteries of human existence (such as the problem of suffering) and a new appreciation for transcendence as opposed to human knowledge. It may even foreshadow the voice from the whirlwind.

---

28 ¹   "Surely there is a mine for silver,
      and a place for gold that they refine.
²   Iron is taken out of the earth,
      and copper is smelted from the ore.
³   Man puts an end to darkness
      and searches out to the farthest limit
      the ore in gloom and deep darkness.
⁴   He opens shafts in a valley away from where anyone lives;
      they are forgotten by travelers;
      they hang in the air, far away from mankind; they swing to and fro.
⁵   As for the earth, out of it comes bread,
      but underneath it is turned up as by fire.
⁶   Its stones are the place of sapphires,[3]
      and it has dust of gold.

⁷   "That path no bird of prey knows,
      and the falcon's eye has not seen it.
⁸   The proud beasts have not trodden it;
      the lion has not passed over it.

---

[1] Or *He* (that is, God); also verse 23 [2] Or *his*; also verse 23 [3] Or *lapis lazuli*; also verse 16

⁹ "Man puts his hand to the flinty rock
       and overturns mountains by the roots.
¹⁰ He cuts out channels in the rocks,
       and his eye sees every precious thing.
¹¹ He dams up the streams so that they do not trickle,
       and the thing that is hidden he brings out to light.

¹² "But where shall wisdom be found?
       And where is the place of understanding?
¹³ Man does not know its worth,
       and it is not found in the land of the living.
¹⁴ The deep says, 'It is not in me,'
       and the sea says, 'It is not with me.'
¹⁵ It cannot be bought for gold,
       and silver cannot be weighed as its price.
¹⁶ It cannot be valued in the gold of Ophir,
       in precious onyx or sapphire.
¹⁷ Gold and glass cannot equal it,
       nor can it be exchanged for jewels of fine gold.
¹⁸ No mention shall be made of coral or of crystal;
       the price of wisdom is above pearls.
¹⁹ The topaz of Ethiopia cannot equal it,
       nor can it be valued in pure gold.

²⁰ "From where, then, does wisdom come?
       And where is the place of understanding?
²¹ It is hidden from the eyes of all living
       and concealed from the birds of the air.
²² Abaddon and Death say,
       'We have heard a rumor of it with our ears.'

²³ "God understands the way to it,
       and he knows its place.
²⁴ For he looks to the ends of the earth
       and sees everything under the heavens.
²⁵ When he gave to the wind its weight
       and apportioned the waters by measure,
²⁶ when he made a decree for the rain
       and a way for the lightning of the thunder,
²⁷ then he saw it and declared it;
       he established it, and searched it out.
²⁸ And he said to man,
       'Behold, the fear of the Lord, that is wisdom,
           and to turn away from evil is understanding.'"

Job's self-portrait: past prosperity [chapter 29]. In chapters 29–30, Job takes stock of his situation. In the first half of the unit (chapter 29) he paints an idealized portrait of his life before his suffering came upon him. It is a picture of the proverbial man on top of the world.

29
And Job again took up his discourse, and said:

2 "Oh, that I were as in the months of old,
   as in the days when God watched over me,
3 when his lamp shone upon my head,
   and by his light I walked through darkness,
4 as I was in my prime,[1]
   when the friendship of God was upon my tent,
5 when the Almighty was yet with me,
   when my children were all around me,
6 when my steps were washed with butter,
   and the rock poured out for me streams of oil!
7 When I went out to the gate of the city,
   when I prepared my seat in the square,
8 the young men saw me and withdrew,
   and the aged rose and stood;
9 the princes refrained from talking
   and laid their hand on their mouth;
10 the voice of the nobles was hushed,
   and their tongue stuck to the roof of their mouth.
11 When the ear heard, it called me blessed,
   and when the eye saw, it approved,
12 because I delivered the poor who cried for help,
   and the fatherless who had none to help him.
13 The blessing of him who was about to perish came upon me,
   and I caused the widow's heart to sing for joy.
14 I put on righteousness, and it clothed me;
   my justice was like a robe and a turban.
15 I was eyes to the blind
   and feet to the lame.
16 I was a father to the needy,
   and I searched out the cause of him whom I did not know.
17 I broke the fangs of the unrighteous
   and made him drop his prey from his teeth.
18 Then I thought, 'I shall die in my nest,
   and I shall multiply my days as the sand,
19 my roots spread out to the waters,
   with the dew all night on my branches,
20 my glory fresh with me,
   and my bow ever new in my hand.'

21 "Men listened to me and waited
   and kept silence for my counsel.
22 After I spoke they did not speak again,

[1] Hebrew *my autumn days*

and my word dropped upon them.
23 They waited for me as for the rain,
      and they opened their mouths as for the spring rain.
24 I smiled on them when they had no confidence,
      and the light of my face they did not cast down.
25 I chose their way and sat as chief,
      and I lived like a king among his troops,
      like one who comforts mourners.

Job's self-portrait: present suffering and abasement [chapter 30]. As Job now turns from the past to the present, his abasement is as heightened as his earlier success had been. The voice of human suffering and isolation has never been more poignantly sounded.

30 "But now they laugh at me,
        men who are younger than I,
    whose fathers I would have disdained
      to set with the dogs of my flock.
2   What could I gain from the strength of their hands,
      men whose vigor is gone?
3   Through want and hard hunger
      they gnaw the dry ground by night in waste and desolation;
4   they pick saltwort and the leaves of bushes,
      and the roots of the broom tree for their food.[1]
5   They are driven out from human company;
      they shout after them as after a thief.
6   In the gullies of the torrents they must dwell,
      in holes of the earth and of the rocks.
7   Among the bushes they bray;
      under the nettles they huddle together.
8   A senseless, a nameless brood,
      they have been whipped out of the land.

9   "And now I have become their song;
      I am a byword to them.
10 They abhor me; they keep aloof from me;
      they do not hesitate to spit at the sight of me.
11 Because God has loosed my cord and humbled me,
      they have cast off restraint[2] in my presence.
12 On my right hand the rabble rise;
      they push away my feet;
      they cast up against me their ways of destruction.
13 They break up my path;
      they promote my calamity;
      they need no one to help them.
14 As through a wide breach they come;
      amid the crash they roll on.

[1] Or *warmth* [2] Hebrew *the bridle*

15   Terrors are turned upon me;
         my honor is pursued as by the wind,
         and my prosperity has passed away like a cloud.

16   "And now my soul is poured out within me;
         days of affliction have taken hold of me.
17   The night racks my bones,
         and the pain that gnaws me takes no rest.
18   With great force my garment is disfigured;
         it binds me about like the collar of my tunic.
19   God[1] has cast me into the mire,
         and I have become like dust and ashes.
20   I cry to you for help and you do not answer me;
         I stand, and you only look at me.
21   You have turned cruel to me;
         with the might of your hand you persecute me.
22   You lift me up on the wind; you make me ride on it,
         and you toss me about in the roar of the storm.
23   For I know that you will bring me to death
         and to the house appointed for all living.

24   "Yet does not one in a heap of ruins stretch out his hand,
         and in his disaster cry for help?[2]
25   Did not I weep for him whose day was hard?
         Was not my soul grieved for the needy?
26   But when I hoped for good, evil came,
         and when I waited for light, darkness came.
27   My inward parts are in turmoil and never still;
         days of affliction come to meet me.
28   I go about darkened, but not by the sun;
         I stand up in the assembly and cry for help.
29   I am a brother of jackals
         and a companion of ostriches.
30   My skin turns black and falls from me,
         and my bones burn with heat.
31   My lyre is turned to mourning,
         and my pipe to the voice of those who weep.

Job's great oath of innocence [chapter 31]. Job now rounds out his oratorical fire-works with a great oath of innocence. The rhetorical format that occurs fifteen times is the formula "if I have . . ." followed by naming immoral behavior. Then Job adds a curse if he has been guilty of the practice just named. The curses that he stipulates are heightened and even violent, the effect being to magnify Job's confidence in his inno-cence of the evil that he hypothetically evokes.

---

[1] Hebrew He [2] The meaning of the Hebrew is uncertain

31

"I have made a covenant with my eyes;
   how then could I gaze at a virgin?
2 What would be my portion from God above
      and my heritage from the Almighty on high?
3 Is not calamity for the unrighteous,
      and disaster for the workers of iniquity?
4 Does not he see my ways
      and number all my steps?

5 "If I have walked with falsehood
      and my foot has hastened to deceit;
6 (Let me be weighed in a just balance,
      and let God know my integrity!)
7 if my step has turned aside from the way
      and my heart has gone after my eyes,
      and if any spot has stuck to my hands,
8 then let me sow, and another eat,
      and let what grows for me[1] be rooted out.

9 "If my heart has been enticed toward a woman,
      and I have lain in wait at my neighbor's door,
10 then let my wife grind for another,
       and let others bow down on her.
11 For that would be a heinous crime;
       that would be an iniquity to be punished by the judges;
12 for that would be a fire that consumes as far as Abaddon,
       and it would burn to the root all my increase.

13 "If I have rejected the cause of my manservant or my maidservant,
       when they brought a complaint against me,
14 what then shall I do when God rises up?
       When he makes inquiry, what shall I answer him?
15 Did not he who made me in the womb make him?
       And did not one fashion us in the womb?

16 "If I have withheld anything that the poor desired,
       or have caused the eyes of the widow to fail,
17 or have eaten my morsel alone,
       and the fatherless has not eaten of it
18 (for from my youth the fatherless[2] grew up with me as with a father,
       and from my mother's womb I guided the widow[3]),
19 if I have seen anyone perish for lack of clothing,
       or the needy without covering,
20 if his body has not blessed me,[4]
       and if he was not warmed with the fleece of my sheep,
21 if I have raised my hand against the fatherless,
       because I saw my help in the gate,
22 then let my shoulder blade fall from my shoulder,

---

[1] Or let my descendants [2] Hebrew he [3] Hebrew her [4] Hebrew if his loins have not blessed me

and let my arm be broken from its socket.

23 For I was in terror of calamity from God,
      and I could not have faced his majesty.

24 "If I have made gold my trust
      or called fine gold my confidence,
25 if I have rejoiced because my wealth was abundant
      or because my hand had found much,
26 if I have looked at the sun[1] when it shone,
      or the moon moving in splendor,
27 and my heart has been secretly enticed,
      and my mouth has kissed my hand,
28 this also would be an iniquity to be punished by the judges,
      for I would have been false to God above.

29 "If I have rejoiced at the ruin of him who hated me,
      or exulted when evil overtook him
30 (I have not let my mouth sin
      by asking for his life with a curse),
31 if the men of my tent have not said,
      'Who is there that has not been filled with his meat?'
32 (the sojourner has not lodged in the street;
      I have opened my doors to the traveler),
33 if I have concealed my transgressions as others do[2]
      by hiding my iniquity in my bosom,
34 because I stood in great fear of the multitude,
      and the contempt of families terrified me,
      so that I kept silence, and did not go out of doors—
35 Oh, that I had one to hear me!
      (Here is my signature! Let the Almighty answer me!)
      Oh, that I had the indictment written by my adversary!
36 Surely I would carry it on my shoulder;
      I would bind it on me as a crown;
37 I would give him an account of all my steps;
      like a prince I would approach him.

38 "If my land has cried out against me
      and its furrows have wept together,
39 if I have eaten its yield without payment
      and made its owners breathe their last,
40 let thorns grow instead of wheat,
      and foul weeds instead of barley."

The words of Job are ended.

Elihu arrives [chapter 32]. Elihu is one of the unattractive minor characters in the Bible. Whatever we might say in partial mitigation of his negative characteristics, he is an arrogant young man. In terms of the ongoing story, though, Elihu infuses a new

---

[1] Hebrew *the light* [2] Or *as Adam did*

energy into the action at a point when Job's interaction with his three friends has run its course and run out of steam (v. 1). As an agent of conflict, Elihu declares that he disagrees with all of the participants in the earlier dialogue—the three friends as well as Job (vv. 2–3). Chapter 32 is a formal introduction of Elihu into the action, and inasmuch as he does all the speaking, what we are given is a self-portrait. The keynotes are as follows: Elihu is the archetypal angry young man (vv. 4–10); he correctly observes that Job's three friends have failed to articulate wisdom (vv. 11–15); he wants to enter the discussion for less than valid reasons (vv. 16–22), chiefly that he is "full of words" (v. 18) and needs to speak to "find relief" (v. 20). The effect of the lead-in is to generate suspense, as we are led to wonder whether Elihu will accomplish more than the three friends have accomplished.

32 So these three men ceased to answer Job, because he was righteous in his own eyes. ²Then Elihu the son of Barachel the Buzite, of the family of Ram, burned with anger. He burned with anger at Job because he justified himself rather than God. ³He burned with anger also at Job's three friends because they had found no answer, although they had declared Job to be in the wrong. ⁴Now Elihu had waited to speak to Job because they were older than he. ⁵And when Elihu saw that there was no answer in the mouth of these three men, he burned with anger.

⁶And Elihu the son of Barachel the Buzite answered and said:

"I am young in years,
  and you are aged;
therefore I was timid and afraid
  to declare my opinion to you.
⁷ I said, 'Let days speak,
  and many years teach wisdom.'
⁸ But it is the spirit in man,
  the breath of the Almighty, that makes him understand.
⁹ It is not the old[1] who are wise,
  nor the aged who understand what is right.
¹⁰ Therefore I say, 'Listen to me;
  let me also declare my opinion.'

¹¹ "Behold, I waited for your words,
  I listened for your wise sayings,
  while you searched out what to say.
¹² I gave you my attention,
  and, behold, there was none among you who refuted Job
  or who answered his words.
¹³ Beware lest you say, 'We have found wisdom;
  God may vanquish him, not a man.'
¹⁴ He has not directed his words against me,
  and I will not answer him with your speeches.

¹⁵ "They are dismayed; they answer no more;
  they have not a word to say.
¹⁶ And shall I wait, because they do not speak,

[1] Hebrew *many* [in years]

because they stand there, and answer no more?

17 I also will answer with my share;
   I also will declare my opinion.
18 For I am full of words;
   the spirit within me constrains me.
19 Behold, my belly is like wine that has no vent;
   like new wineskins ready to burst.
20 I must speak, that I may find relief;
   I must open my lips and answer.
21 I will not show partiality to any man
   or use flattery toward any person.
22 For I do not know how to flatter,
   else my Maker would soon take me away.

Déjà vu [chapter 33]. The suspense regarding whether Elihu will raise the debate to a new level is quickly answered when it is obvious that Elihu, despite his earlier put-down of the three friends' thinking, repeats their arguments. The sequence of Elihu's topics is as follows: a bombastic address to Job that ends with an ironic reassurance that, even though Elihu is about to be extremely impressive, Job need not be afraid of him, since he is just a fellow mortal (vv. 1–7); Job is incorrect in protesting his innocence (vv. 8–12a); God is transcendent over humans (vv. 12b–14); God sends human suffering as a warning and discipline to people, so that people who have been afflicted should confess their sin to God (vv. 15–30); Job should repent in Elihu's presence (vv. 31–33). All of these ideas have already been advanced multiple times. Like the friends, Elihu asserts God's justice but fails to show that it applies to Job's situation, and in declaring that suffering is punishment for sin he overlooks that the purpose might instead be that God wishes to reveal himself in human suffering.

33

"But now, hear my speech, O Job,
   and listen to all my words.
2 Behold, I open my mouth;
   the tongue in my mouth speaks.
3 My words declare the uprightness of my heart,
   and what my lips know they speak sincerely.
4 The Spirit of God has made me,
   and the breath of the Almighty gives me life.
5 Answer me, if you can;
   set your words in order before me; take your stand.
6 Behold, I am toward God as you are;
   I too was pinched off from a piece of clay.
7 Behold, no fear of me need terrify you;
   my pressure will not be heavy upon you.

8 "Surely you have spoken in my ears,
   and I have heard the sound of your words.
9 You say, 'I am pure, without transgression;
   I am clean, and there is no iniquity in me.

10   Behold, he finds occasions against me,
         he counts me as his enemy,
11   he puts my feet in the stocks
         and watches all my paths.'

12   "Behold, in this you are not right. I will answer you,
         for God is greater than man.
13   Why do you contend against him,
         saying, 'He will answer none of man's[1] words'?[2]
14   For God speaks in one way,
         and in two, though man does not perceive it.
15   In a dream, in a vision of the night,
         when deep sleep falls on men,
         while they slumber on their beds,
16   then he opens the ears of men
         and terrifies them with warnings,
17   that he may turn man aside from his deed
         and conceal pride from a man;
18   he keeps back his soul from the pit,
         his life from perishing by the sword.

19   "Man is also rebuked with pain on his bed
         and with continual strife in his bones,
20   so that his life loathes bread,
         and his appetite the choicest food.
21   His flesh is so wasted away that it cannot be seen,
         and his bones that were not seen stick out.
22   His soul draws near the pit,
         and his life to those who bring death.
23   If there be for him an angel,
         a mediator, one of the thousand,
         to declare to man what is right for him,
24   and he is merciful to him, and says,
         'Deliver him from going down into the pit;
         I have found a ransom;
25   let his flesh become fresh with youth;
         let him return to the days of his youthful vigor';
26   then man[3] prays to God, and he accepts him;
         he sees his face with a shout of joy,
         and he restores to man his righteousness.
27   He sings before men and says:
         'I sinned and perverted what was right,
         and it was not repaid to me.
28   He has redeemed my soul from going down into the pit,
         and my life shall look upon the light.'

29   "Behold, God does all these things,
         twice, three times, with a man,

---

[1] Hebrew his [2] Or He will not answer for any of his own words [3] Hebrew he

30 to bring back his soul from the pit,
    that he may be lighted with the light of life.
31 Pay attention, O Job, listen to me;
    be silent, and I will speak.
32 If you have any words, answer me;
    speak, for I desire to justify you.
33 If not, listen to me;
    be silent, and I will teach you wisdom."

More attacks from Elihu [chapters 34–35]. When Elihu forewarned Job that he was "full of words" (32:18), he spoke the truth. He offers a semblance of something new, but not much substance of it. Having given up on Job, Elihu begins this unit by forming a committee with the three friends to "know among ourselves what is good" (34:1–4). The attack on Job is vehement in this unit, but we have seen similar acrimony in some of the friends' earlier speeches as well. The actual topics covered are old: God is sovereign; suffering is punitive; Job is guilty. It is possible to see a new wrinkle, though, if we interpret the following statements as referring not to Job's spiritual state before Satan afflicted him but instead to Job's words of rebellion after his initial state: "he adds rebellion to his sin" and "multiples his words against God" (34:37); "he multiplies words without knowledge" (35:16).

34 Then Elihu answered and said:

2 "Hear my words, you wise men,
    and give ear to me, you who know;
3 for the ear tests words
    as the palate tastes food.
4 Let us choose what is right;
    let us know among ourselves what is good.
5 For Job has said, 'I am in the right,
    and God has taken away my right;
6 in spite of my right I am counted a liar;
    my wound is incurable, though I am without transgression.'
7 What man is like Job,
    who drinks up scoffing like water,
8 who travels in company with evildoers
    and walks with wicked men?
9 For he has said, 'It profits a man nothing
    that he should take delight in God.'

10 "Therefore, hear me, you men of understanding:
    far be it from God that he should do wickedness,
    and from the Almighty that he should do wrong.
11 For according to the work of a man he will repay him,
    and according to his ways he will make it befall him.
12 Of a truth, God will not do wickedly,
    and the Almighty will not pervert justice.

13 Who gave him charge over the earth,
and who laid on him[1] the whole world?
14 If he should set his heart to it
and gather to himself his spirit and his breath,
15 all flesh would perish together,
and man would return to dust.

16 "If you have understanding, hear this;
listen to what I say.
17 Shall one who hates justice govern?
Will you condemn him who is righteous and mighty,
18 who says to a king, 'Worthless one,'
and to nobles, 'Wicked man,'
19 who shows no partiality to princes,
nor regards the rich more than the poor,
for they are all the work of his hands?
20 In a moment they die;
at midnight the people are shaken and pass away,
and the mighty are taken away by no human hand.

21 "For his eyes are on the ways of a man,
and he sees all his steps.
22 There is no gloom or deep darkness
where evildoers may hide themselves.
23 For God[2] has no need to consider a man further,
that he should go before God in judgment.
24 He shatters the mighty without investigation
and sets others in their place.
25 Thus, knowing their works,
he overturns them in the night, and they are crushed.
26 He strikes them for their wickedness
in a place for all to see,
27 because they turned aside from following him
and had no regard for any of his ways,
28 so that they caused the cry of the poor to come to him,
and he heard the cry of the afflicted—
29 When he is quiet, who can condemn?
When he hides his face, who can behold him,
whether it be a nation or a man?—
30 that a godless man should not reign,
that he should not ensnare the people.

31 "For has anyone said to God,
'I have borne punishment; I will not offend any more;
32 teach me what I do not see;
if I have done iniquity, I will do it no more'?
33 Will he then make repayment to suit you,
because you reject it?

For you must choose, and not I;
  therefore declare what you know.[1]
34 Men of understanding will say to me,
  and the wise man who hears me will say:
35 'Job speaks without knowledge;
  his words are without insight.'
36 Would that Job were tried to the end,
  because he answers like wicked men.
37 For he adds rebellion to his sin;
  he claps his hands among us
  and multiplies his words against God."

35

And Elihu answered and said:

2 "Do you think this to be just?
  Do you say, 'It is my right before God,'
3 that you ask, 'What advantage have I?
  How am I better off than if I had sinned?'
4 I will answer you
  and your friends with you.
5 Look at the heavens, and see;
  and behold the clouds, which are higher than you.
6 If you have sinned, what do you accomplish against him?
  And if your transgressions are multiplied, what do you do to him?
7 If you are righteous, what do you give to him?
  Or what does he receive from your hand?
8 Your wickedness concerns a man like yourself,
  and your righteousness a son of man.

9 "Because of the multitude of oppressions people cry out;
  they call for help because of the arm of the mighty.[2]
10 But none says, 'Where is God my Maker,
  who gives songs in the night,
11 who teaches us more than the beasts of the earth
  and makes us wiser than the birds of the heavens?'
12 There they cry out, but he does not answer,
  because of the pride of evil men.
13 Surely God does not hear an empty cry,
  nor does the Almighty regard it.
14 How much less when you say that you do not see him,
  that the case is before him, and you are waiting for him!
15 And now, because his anger does not punish,
  and he does not take much note of transgression,[3]
16 Job opens his mouth in empty talk;
  he multiplies words without knowledge."

[1] The meaning of the Hebrew in verses 29-33 is uncertain [2] Or the many [3] Theodotion, Symmachus (compare Vulgate); the meaning of the Hebrew word is uncertain

Still more from Elihu [36:1–21]. Elihu is, indeed, inexhaustible in his supply of words. As he conceitedly speaks "on God's behalf" (v. 2), he covers well-worn territory—God is mighty; God favors the righteous and punishes the wicked; people who are suffering need to repent. As we ponder the effect of this repetition, we can accurately conclude that our frustration as readers rises to a breaking point, in effect preparing the way for God's counter-statements from the whirlwind.

36 And Elihu continued, and said:

2 "Bear with me a little, and I will show you,
    for I have yet something to say on God's behalf.
3 I will get my knowledge from afar
    and ascribe righteousness to my Maker.
4 For truly my words are not false;
    one who is perfect in knowledge is with you.

5 "Behold, God is mighty, and does not despise any;
    he is mighty in strength of understanding.
6 He does not keep the wicked alive,
    but gives the afflicted their right.
7 He does not withdraw his eyes from the righteous,
    but with kings on the throne
    he sets them forever, and they are exalted.
8 And if they are bound in chains
    and caught in the cords of affliction,
9 then he declares to them their work
    and their transgressions, that they are behaving arrogantly.
10 He opens their ears to instruction
    and commands that they return from iniquity.
11 If they listen and serve him,
    they complete their days in prosperity,
    and their years in pleasantness.
12 But if they do not listen, they perish by the sword
    and die without knowledge.

13 "The godless in heart cherish anger;
    they do not cry for help when he binds them.
14 They die in youth,
    and their life ends among the cult prostitutes.
15 He delivers the afflicted by their affliction
    and opens their ear by adversity.
16 He also allured you out of distress
    into a broad place where there was no cramping,
    and what was set on your table was full of fatness.

17 "But you are full of the judgment on the wicked;
    judgment and justice seize you.
18 Beware lest wrath entice you into scoffing,

and let not the greatness of the ransom turn you aside.
¹⁹ Will your cry for help avail to keep you from distress,
    or all the force of your strength?
²⁰ Do not long for the night,
    when peoples vanish in their place.
²¹ Take care; do not turn to iniquity,
    for this you have chosen rather than affliction.

A poem in praise of God's transcendence [36:22–37:24]. Elihu partly redeems himself in our estimation with his concluding ode in praise of God's transcendent power and majesty. Elihu adduces his evidence for God's power from the forces of nature, and by means of this technique he foreshadows the speeches of the voice from the whirlwind in chapters 38–41. But Elihu's parting shot is self-incriminating: God "does not regard any who are wise in their own conceit" (37:24).

---

²² Behold, God is exalted in his power;
    who is a teacher like him?
²³ Who has prescribed for him his way,
    or who can say, 'You have done wrong'?
²⁴ "Remember to extol his work,
    of which men have sung.
²⁵ All mankind has looked on it;
    man beholds it from afar.
²⁶ Behold, God is great, and we know him not;
    the number of his years is unsearchable.
²⁷ For he draws up the drops of water;
    they distill his mist in rain,
²⁸ which the skies pour down
    and drop on mankind abundantly.
²⁹ Can anyone understand the spreading of the clouds,
    the thunderings of his pavilion?
³⁰ Behold, he scatters his lightning about him
    and covers the roots of the sea.
³¹ For by these he judges peoples;
    he gives food in abundance.
³² He covers his hands with the lightning
    and commands it to strike the mark.
³³ Its crashing declares his presence;[1]
    the cattle also declare that he rises.

37 "At this also my heart trembles
    and leaps out of its place.
² Keep listening to the thunder of his voice
    and the rumbling that comes from his mouth.
³ Under the whole heaven he lets it go,
    and his lightning to the corners of the earth.
⁴ After it his voice roars;

---

[1] Hebrew *declares concerning him*

he thunders with his majestic voice,
and he does not restrain the lightnings[1] when his voice is heard.
⁵ God thunders wondrously with his voice;
he does great things that we cannot comprehend.
⁶ For to the snow he says, 'Fall on the earth,'
likewise to the downpour, his mighty downpour.
⁷ He seals up the hand of every man,
that all men whom he made may know it.
⁸ Then the beasts go into their lairs,
and remain in their dens.
⁹ From its chamber comes the whirlwind,
and cold from the scattering winds.
¹⁰ By the breath of God ice is given,
and the broad waters are frozen fast.
¹¹ He loads the thick cloud with moisture;
the clouds scatter his lightning.
¹² They turn around and around by his guidance,
to accomplish all that he commands them
on the face of the habitable world.
¹³ Whether for correction or for his land
or for love, he causes it to happen.

¹⁴ "Hear this, O Job;
stop and consider the wondrous works of God.
¹⁵ Do you know how God lays his command upon them
and causes the lightning of his cloud to shine?
¹⁶ Do you know the balancings[2] of the clouds,
the wondrous works of him who is perfect in knowledge,
¹⁷ you whose garments are hot
when the earth is still because of the south wind?
¹⁸ Can you, like him, spread out the skies,
hard as a cast metal mirror?
¹⁹ Teach us what we shall say to him;
we cannot draw up our case because of darkness.
²⁰ Shall it be told him that I would speak?
Did a man ever wish that he would be swallowed up?

²¹ "And now no one looks on the light
when it is bright in the skies,
when the wind has passed and cleared them.
²² Out of the north comes golden splendor;
God is clothed with awesome majesty.
²³ The Almighty—we cannot find him;
he is great in power;
justice and abundant righteousness he will not violate.
²⁴ Therefore men fear him;
he does not regard any who are wise in their own conceit."[3]

[1] Hebrew *them* [2] Or *hoverings* [3] Hebrew *in heart*

God begins his first speech from the whirlwind [chapter 38]. The two voices from the whirlwind are the climax of the book. The question of innocent suffering is finally resolved, though not fully answered. The plot motif of reversal is fully evident, in the following ways: after God's silence all through the deliberations among Job and his counselors, God finally speaks; Job had attempted to bring God to question, and now God questions Job; instead of answering Job's questions, God asks a series of counter-questions; although God speaks, he does not (as we surely expected) answer Job's questions.

As we start to read God's first speech, we are overwhelmed by the rhetorical force of what pours forth from God. It is as though God sends Job (and us) reeling with a seemingly endless barrage of *rhetorical questions (questions asked to elicit assent rather than information). All of the questions concern the mysteries of nature in the two areas of the origin of various natural phenomena and the providence that directs and sustains them. Since the implied answer to the questions is that only God knows and does these things, the catalog of questions is a demonstration of God's superior knowledge and power.

38 Then the LORD answered Job out of the whirlwind and said:

2 "Who is this that darkens counsel by words without knowledge?
3 Dress for action[1] like a man;
      I will question you, and you make it known to me.

4 "Where were you when I laid the foundation of the earth?
      Tell me, if you have understanding.
5 Who determined its measurements—surely you know!
      Or who stretched the line upon it?
6 On what were its bases sunk,
      or who laid its cornerstone,
7 when the morning stars sang together
      and all the sons of God shouted for joy?

8 "Or who shut in the sea with doors
      when it burst out from the womb,
9 when I made clouds its garment
      and thick darkness its swaddling band,
10 and prescribed limits for it
      and set bars and doors,
11 and said, 'Thus far shall you come, and no farther,
      and here shall your proud waves be stayed'?

12 "Have you commanded the morning since your days began,
      and caused the dawn to know its place,
13 that it might take hold of the skirts of the earth,
      and the wicked be shaken out of it?
14 It is changed like clay under the seal,
      and its features stand out like a garment.
15 From the wicked their light is withheld,
      and their uplifted arm is broken.

---

[1] Hebrew *Gird up your loins*

16   "Have you entered into the springs of the sea,
         or walked in the recesses of the deep?
17   Have the gates of death been revealed to you,
         or have you seen the gates of deep darkness?
18   Have you comprehended the expanse of the earth?
         Declare, if you know all this.

19   "Where is the way to the dwelling of light,
         and where is the place of darkness,
20   that you may take it to its territory
         and that you may discern the paths to its home?
21   You know, for you were born then,
         and the number of your days is great!

22   "Have you entered the storehouses of the snow,
         or have you seen the storehouses of the hail,
23   which I have reserved for the time of trouble,
         for the day of battle and war?
24   What is the way to the place where the light is distributed,
         or where the east wind is scattered upon the earth?

25   "Who has cleft a channel for the torrents of rain
         and a way for the thunderbolt,
26   to bring rain on a land where no man is,
         on the desert in which there is no man,
27   to satisfy the waste and desolate land,
         and to make the ground sprout with grass?

28   "Has the rain a father,
         or who has begotten the drops of dew?
29   From whose womb did the ice come forth,
         and who has given birth to the frost of heaven?
30   The waters become hard like stone,
         and the face of the deep is frozen.

31   "Can you bind the chains of the Pleiades
         or loose the cords of Orion?
32   Can you lead forth the Mazzaroth[1] in their season,
         or can you guide the Bear with its children?
33   Do you know the ordinances of the heavens?
         Can you establish their rule on the earth?

34   "Can you lift up your voice to the clouds,
         that a flood of waters may cover you?
35   Can you send forth lightnings, that they may go
         and say to you, 'Here we are'?
36   Who has put wisdom in the inward parts[2]
         or given understanding to the mind?[3]
37   Who can number the clouds by wisdom?

---

[1] Probably the name of a constellation [2] Or *in the ibis* [3] Or *rooster*

Or who can tilt the waterskins of the heavens,
38   when the dust runs into a mass
        and the clods stick fast together?

39   "Can you hunt the prey for the lion,
        or satisfy the appetite of the young lions,
40   when they crouch in their dens
        or lie in wait in their thicket?
41   Who provides for the raven its prey,
        when its young ones cry to God for help,
        and wander about for lack of food?

God completes his first speech, and Job responds [39:1–40:5]. As God continues, his exalted science quiz would seem to be irrelevant to the question of human suffering, so we are pushed to see that the speech is relevant to the announced topic, though it approaches the topic in an indirect way. Here are good points to keep in mind while unpacking chapters 38–39: (1) If Job cannot even pass a biology test, how can he hope to solve such an ultimate question as why the righteous suffer? (2) Ostensibly the speech demonstrates God's transcendent power and knowledge, since obviously only God can control nature as the questions portray him as doing. (3) But since the questions show God's closeness to his creation, they also prove his immanence (his presence in creation). (4) Furthermore, God's speech shows his marvelous management of, and providence over, even the small parts of nature, so that the effect is that of a rhetorical "how much more"—if God is this intimately concerned for the nonhuman forces of nature, will he not much more take care of his human creatures? Job's response to God's speech (40:1–5) shows his submission to God's superior knowledge and power.

---

39   "Do you know when the mountain goats give birth?
        Do you observe the calving of the does?
2   Can you number the months that they fulfill,
        and do you know the time when they give birth,
3   when they crouch, bring forth their offspring,
        and are delivered of their young?
4   Their young ones become strong; they grow up in the open;
        they go out and do not return to them.

5   "Who has let the wild donkey go free?
        Who has loosed the bonds of the swift donkey,
6   to whom I have given the arid plain for his home
        and the salt land for his dwelling place?
7   He scorns the tumult of the city;
        he hears not the shouts of the driver.
8   He ranges the mountains as his pasture,
        and he searches after every green thing.

9   "Is the wild ox willing to serve you?
        Will he spend the night at your manger?
10   Can you bind him in the furrow with ropes,

or will he harrow the valleys after you?
11 Will you depend on him because his strength is great,
      and will you leave to him your labor?
12 Do you have faith in him that he will return your grain
      and gather it to your threshing floor?

13 "The wings of the ostrich wave proudly,
      but are they the pinions and plumage of love?[1]
14 For she leaves her eggs to the earth
      and lets them be warmed on the ground,
15 forgetting that a foot may crush them
      and that the wild beast may trample them.
16 She deals cruelly with her young, as if they were not hers;
      though her labor be in vain, yet she has no fear,
17 because God has made her forget wisdom
      and given her no share in understanding.
18 When she rouses herself to flee,[2]
      she laughs at the horse and his rider.

19 "Do you give the horse his might?
      Do you clothe his neck with a mane?
20 Do you make him leap like the locust?
      His majestic snorting is terrifying.
21 He paws[3] in the valley and exults in his strength;
      he goes out to meet the weapons.
22 He laughs at fear and is not dismayed;
      he does not turn back from the sword.
23 Upon him rattle the quiver,
      the flashing spear, and the javelin.
24 With fierceness and rage he swallows the ground;
      he cannot stand still at the sound of the trumpet.
25 When the trumpet sounds, he says 'Aha!'
      He smells the battle from afar,
      the thunder of the captains, and the shouting.

26 "Is it by your understanding that the hawk soars
      and spreads his wings toward the south?
27 Is it at your command that the eagle mounts up
      and makes his nest on high?
28 On the rock he dwells and makes his home,
      on the rocky crag and stronghold.
29 From there he spies out the prey;
      his eyes behold it from far away.
30 His young ones suck up blood,
      and where the slain are, there is he."

---

[1] The meaning of the Hebrew is uncertain [2] The meaning of the Hebrew is uncertain [3] Hebrew *They paw*

40 And the LORD said to Job:

2 "Shall a faultfinder contend with the Almighty?
     He who argues with God, let him answer it."

3 Then Job answered the LORD and said:

4 "Behold, I am of small account; what shall I answer you?
     I lay my hand on my mouth.
5 I have spoken once, and I will not answer;
     twice, but I will proceed no further."

God's second speech from the whirlwind [40:6–42:6]. God continues to appeal to nature for the terms of his discourse, but instead of taking a wide-angle view, he now concentrates on two awesome creatures. The pictures of both are imaginative masterpieces. First God implicitly rebukes Job for Job's earlier accusations against God's character (40:6–14). Then comes the exalted description of Behemoth (40:15–24), probably an imaginatively embellished hippopotamus. That is followed by an even more extravagant picture of Leviathan, probably a mythological version of a crocodile (chapter 41). The general movement of chapter 41 is as follows: general commentary on the beast's awesome power and terror (41:1–12); a description of the beast's head, teeth, and impenetrable armor of scales (41:13–24); a picture of the beast's rising up and brushing off attacks and then demolishing his assailants (41:25–32); a final comment on his supremacy and power (41:33–34). In response to the first speech from the whirlwind, Job had decided to stop talking (40:4–5), but his response this time (42:1–6) goes well beyond that, as Job recants what he had said and repents for having misspoken in regard to God's character. Here, too, we can see an indirect tie-in to the question of human suffering; even though the intellectual problem of why the righteous suffer has not been answered, Job the sufferer has grown spiritually as his suffering has been the means of his relating to God in a fuller way.

6 Then the LORD answered Job out of the whirlwind and said:

7 "Dress for action[1] like a man;
     I will question you, and you make it known to me.
8 Will you even put me in the wrong?
     Will you condemn me that you may be in the right?
9 Have you an arm like God,
     and can you thunder with a voice like his?

10 "Adorn yourself with majesty and dignity;
     clothe yourself with glory and splendor.
11 Pour out the overflowings of your anger,
     and look on everyone who is proud and abase him.
12 Look on everyone who is proud and bring him low
     and tread down the wicked where they stand.
13 Hide them all in the dust together;
     bind their faces in the world below.[2]

---

[1] Hebrew *Gird up your loins* [2] Hebrew *in the hidden place*

¹⁴ Then will I also acknowledge to you
     that your own right hand can save you.

¹⁵ "Behold, Behemoth,¹
     which I made as I made you;
     he eats grass like an ox.
¹⁶ Behold, his strength in his loins,
     and his power in the muscles of his belly.
¹⁷ He makes his tail stiff like a cedar;
     the sinews of his thighs are knit together.
¹⁸ His bones are tubes of bronze,
     his limbs like bars of iron.

¹⁹ "He is the first of the works² of God;
     let him who made him bring near his sword!
²⁰ For the mountains yield food for him
     where all the wild beasts play.
²¹ Under the lotus plants he lies,
     in the shelter of the reeds and in the marsh.
²² For his shade the lotus trees cover him;
     the willows of the brook surround him.
²³ Behold, if the river is turbulent he is not frightened;
     he is confident though Jordan rushes against his mouth.
²⁴ Can one take him by his eyes,³
     or pierce his nose with a snare?

41 ⁴ "Can you draw out Leviathan⁵ with a fishhook
     or press down his tongue with a cord?
² Can you put a rope in his nose
     or pierce his jaw with a hook?
³ Will he make many pleas to you?
     Will he speak to you soft words?
⁴ Will he make a covenant with you
     to take him for your servant forever?
⁵ Will you play with him as with a bird,
     or will you put him on a leash for your girls?
⁶ Will traders bargain over him?
     Will they divide him up among the merchants?
⁷ Can you fill his skin with harpoons
     or his head with fishing spears?
⁸ Lay your hands on him;
     remember the battle—you will not do it again!
⁹ ⁶ Behold, the hope of a man is false;
     he is laid low even at the sight of him.
¹⁰ No one is so fierce that he dares to stir him up.
     Who then is he who can stand before me?

¹ A large animal, exact identity unknown ² Hebrew *ways* ³ Or *in his sight* ⁴ Ch 40:25 in Hebrew ⁵ A large sea animal, exact identity unknown ⁶ Ch 41:1 in Hebrew

¹¹   Who has first given to me, that I should repay him?
       Whatever is under the whole heaven is mine.

¹²   "I will not keep silence concerning his limbs,
       or his mighty strength, or his goodly frame.
¹³   Who can strip off his outer garment?
       Who would come near him with a bridle?
¹⁴   Who can open the doors of his face?
       Around his teeth is terror.
¹⁵   His back is made of¹ rows of shields,
       shut up closely as with a seal.
¹⁶   One is so near to another
       that no air can come between them.
¹⁷   They are joined one to another;
       they clasp each other and cannot be separated.
¹⁸   His sneezings flash forth light,
       and his eyes are like the eyelids of the dawn.
¹⁹   Out of his mouth go flaming torches;
       sparks of fire leap forth.
²⁰   Out of his nostrils comes forth smoke,
       as from a boiling pot and burning rushes.
²¹   His breath kindles coals,
       and a flame comes forth from his mouth.
²²   In his neck abides strength,
       and terror dances before him.
²³   The folds of his flesh stick together,
       firmly cast on him and immovable.
²⁴   His heart is hard as a stone,
       hard as the lower millstone.
²⁵   When he raises himself up the mighty² are afraid;
       at the crashing they are beside themselves.
²⁶   Though the sword reaches him, it does not avail,
       nor the spear, the dart, or the javelin.
²⁷   He counts iron as straw,
       and bronze as rotten wood.
²⁸   The arrow cannot make him flee;
       for him sling stones are turned to stubble.
²⁹   Clubs are counted as stubble;
       he laughs at the rattle of javelins.
³⁰   His underparts are like sharp potsherds;
       he spreads himself like a threshing sledge on the mire.
³¹   He makes the deep boil like a pot;
       he makes the sea like a pot of ointment.
³²   Behind him he leaves a shining wake;
       one would think the deep to be white-haired.
³³   On earth there is not his like,
       a creature without fear.

¹ Or *His pride is in his* ² Or *gods*

³⁴   He sees everything that is high;
     he is king over all the sons of pride."

42 Then Job answered the LORD and said:

²   "I know that you can do all things,
     and that no purpose of yours can be thwarted.
³   'Who is this that hides counsel without knowledge?'
     Therefore I have uttered what I did not understand,
     things too wonderful for me, which I did not know.
⁴   'Hear, and I will speak;
     I will question you, and you make it known to me.'
⁵   I had heard of you by the hearing of the ear,
     but now my eye sees you;
⁶   therefore I despise myself,
     and repent[1] in dust and ashes."

> **Epilogue** [42:7–17]. In the prologue, Job's fortunes were stripped from him. In the epilogue, his fortunes are restored. The governing literary principle of the epilogue is *poetic justice, as virtue is rewarded and vice rebuked. The specific manifestations of that are as follows: (1) Satan is not even mentioned, having been implicitly defeated by the triumph of faith that Job attains at the end of the story; (2) God affirms Job and rebukes Job's friends (vv. 7–9); (3) God restores the external fortunes of Job (vv. 10–17).

⁷After the LORD had spoken these words to Job, the LORD said to Eliphaz the Temanite: "My anger burns against you and against your two friends, for you have not spoken of me what is right, as my servant Job has. ⁸Now therefore take seven bulls and seven rams and go to my servant Job and offer up a burnt offering for yourselves. And my servant Job shall pray for you, for I will accept his prayer not to deal with you according to your folly. For you have not spoken of me what is right, as my servant Job has." ⁹So Eliphaz the Temanite and Bildad the Shuhite and Zophar the Naamathite went and did what the LORD had told them, and the LORD accepted Job's prayer.

¹⁰And the LORD restored the fortunes of Job, when he had prayed for his friends. And the LORD gave Job twice as much as he had before. ¹¹Then came to him all his brothers and sisters and all who had known him before, and ate bread with him in his house. And they showed him sympathy and comforted him for all the evil[2] that the LORD had brought upon him. And each of them gave him a piece of money[3] and a ring of gold.

¹²And the LORD blessed the latter days of Job more than his beginning. And he had 14,000 sheep, 6,000 camels, 1,000 yoke of oxen, and 1,000 female donkeys. ¹³He had also seven sons and three daughters. ¹⁴And he called the name of the first daughter Jemimah, and the name of the second Keziah, and the name of the third Keren-happuch. ¹⁵And in all the land there were no women so beautiful as Job's daughters. And their father gave them an inheritance among their brothers. ¹⁶And after this Job lived 140 years, and saw his sons, and his sons' sons, four generations. ¹⁷And Job died, an old man, and full of days.

---

¹ Or *and am comforted* ² Or *disaster* ³ Hebrew *a qesitah*; a unit of money of unknown value

THE PSALMS

The book at a glance. 150 chapters, 2,461 verses. The book of Psalms is a collection of *lyric poems. Since these poems were originally also sung and recited liturgically, we can view the Psalter (the title given to the collection of 150 poems) as Israel's hymnbook. Further, since the *psalms were particularly associated with worship in the temple in Jerusalem, we can view them as "largely a Temple collection" (C. S. Lewis). The thing that the psalms do best is express a full range of feelings and reflections of the believing soul. John Calvin was so impressed by this aspect of the psalms that he famously called the Psalter "an anatomy of all the parts of the soul," adding that "there is not an emotion of which any one can be conscious that is not here represented as in a mirror." The psalms are self-contained compositions, meant to be read individually. Although there is no progressive structure to the Psalms as a whole, there are some groupings within it. The chart that follows should not be taken to imply that the poems that appear in the various groupings all match each other in tone or theme.

▌ Genres. The one constant is that all 150 poems are *lyrics. Lyrics are either emotional or reflective, meaning that the dominant content is a series of feelings or a series of thoughts. A lyric poet ordinarily speaks in the personal, first-person mode (both singular and plural), and the result is a subjective expression of experience. This being the case, a good strategy for reading any lyric poem is to regard the poet as sharing more and more information about the chosen topic or experience. Because the content of these poems is expressed in a poetic idiom, we need to be ready to interpret such staples of *poetry as *image, *metaphor, *simile, *personification, *hyperbole, and *apostrophe. (For more information on items accompanied by an asterisk, see the glossary at the back of this Bible.)

▌ Verse form. All of the psalms are written in the verse form of *parallelism. The main types of parallelism are *synonymous parallelism (in which the second line repeats the content of the first in different images but similar grammatical form); *antithetic parallelism (in which the second line states a contrast to the first); *climactic parallelism (in which the second line repeats part of the preceding line and then adds to it); *synthetic ("growing" or "progressing") parallelism (in which strictly speaking there is no parallelism but the second line completes the thought of the first, so that, as in the other forms of parallelism, the two lines form a unit).

▌ Lyric as the leading poetic genre in the Psalms. Here are six useful things to know

Division in the Hebrew Psalter	General Content	Dominant Lyric Genres
Psalms 1–41	Wide-ranging experiences: the voice of suffering dominates, but not by a wide margin, over praise and reflection regarding the blessings of God in the poets' lives	Lament psalms; praise psalms; reflective lyrics; nature poems
Psalms 42–72	As in the first book of the Psalms, the note of suffering and human sinfulness dominates, but praise of God for his greatness comes in a close second, and the experience of worship is definitely introduced	In order of decreasing frequency: lament, praise psalm, worship psalm, lyric of personal experience, assorted forms that appear only once
Psalms 73–89	More emphasis on the communal life of the nation and believing community than in the two previous books	Laments and praise psalms dominate, but there are so many additional genres that the unit is actually a poetic miscellany
Psalms 90–106	The primary focus is on God's acts and attributes	The praise psalm dominates by a wide margin
Psalms 107–150	Because this is such a large unit within the Psalter, its content ranges over all of life. Prominent topics include the praise of God; worship; the vicissitudes of life (in the lament psalms); God's Word or law; all of life. Psalms 120–134 are songs of ascent, pilgrim songs sung or recited on the pilgrimage to Jerusalem	Praise psalms dominate; numerous lament psalms; a wide range of other lyric subtypes

about lyric poems such as we find in the Psalter: (1) Lyric poems are unified around a central idea, feeling, or *motif. (2) The unity of a poem can be formulated as a series of variations on the central theme/motif. (3) Lyric poems do not ordinarily tell a story, although often a life experience provides the occasion for a lyric. (4) Lyric poems usually fall into two categories based on the predominant subject matter: the poet presents either feelings or reflections. (5) Lyrics have an overall three-part structure, consisting of introduction–development–conclusion or closure. (6) In the middle part, the poet develops the theme using as many as four techniques: repetition, listing or catalog, contrast, and association (in which the poet branches out from an initial idea to a related idea).

▌ **The two main subcategories.** *Lament psalms (also called complaints) and *praise psalms are the most numerous categories in the Psalter. The characteristics of the lament psalm are as follows: (1) There are five main ingredients, which may appear in any order and may appear more than once in a psalm: invocation or cry to God; the lament, or definition of the crisis; petition; statement of confidence in God; vow to praise God. (2) Laments are *occasional poems arising out of a specific event or situation in the poet's or nation's life. (3) The poet in a lament psalm typically does these things: he undertakes a quest to master a crisis and find peace in the midst of it;

he paints a heightened and often figurative picture of the crisis; he protests about the situation to God and perhaps to himself and his readers; he attempts to persuade God to act; he finds a satisfactory solution to the problem. Praise psalms have the following traits: (1) They praise God (poems in praise of people go by other names). (2) They have three main parts: a call to praise (which may occur more than once in the poem), list of the praiseworthy acts and attributes of God, and a note of resolution (such as a concluding prayer or wish).

▌**Other subgenres.** *Worship psalms (also called songs of Zion); *nature poems; *royal psalms (dealing with the king); meditative poems; thanksgiving psalms; *encomium (a poem praising either a general character type or an abstract quality); penitential psalms (dealing with confession and forgiveness of sin); poems of personal testimony; *epithalamion (wedding poem, with Psalm 45 as the sole example).

▌**Tips for reading the Psalms.** Things that we should *not* do with the Psalms include these: try to read psalms as stories; speculate unduly about the details of the life situation that may underlie a given psalm; regard the individual poems as chapters in an ongoing sequence; ignore the images and figures of speech and quickly translate them into a series of ideas; operate on the premise that a psalm is like an essay in being structured as a logical sequence of ideas with clear transitions between units; read a psalm as a collection of individual verses with little connection among them. The positive counterparts of those futile ways of reading include the following: anticipate a flow of feelings and/or reflections rather than narrative events; instead of viewing yourself as undertaking a journey through a series of events (as in narrative), begin with the premise that the poet will share more and more information about his feelings and/or his reflections; accept that poems are self-contained compositions, not chapters in an ongoing sequence; be ready for sudden movement from one topic or feeling to another (C. S. Lewis spoke of "the emotional rather than logical connections" in the psalms); begin with the premise that poets think in images rather than abstractions and that they prefer the figurative or nonliteral to the literal.

▌**Inferred literary intentions.** The book is designed to achieve the following literary purposes:

- give expression to the emotional and reflective side of religious experience

- express truth by means of images and figures of speech

- package the content in highly artistic poetry, so that the beauty of expression is an important part of the total effect

- do things with words that we do not ordinarily do with them (seen chiefly in the use of figurative language)

- be truthful to human experience and portray its nuances accurately

- exalt God and his creation

- provide the materials for private and public worship (including worship in song)

- record human *responses to* God and the experiences of life

- showcase literary beauty

▌Theological themes. (1) The nature of God: no book of the Bible offers a more comprehensive survey of the acts and attributes of God. (2) The nature of people: because every psalm is at some level a personal statement by a poet, Psalms is also an index to what people are like, both good and bad. (3) Nature and the physical creation: the psalms say and imply many things about the external world that God made and sustains. (4) Worship: the psalms are used in worship, and many of them talk about worship. (5) Suffering: the many lament psalms yield a theology of suffering.

▌The Psalms as a chapter in the master story of the Bible. The master story of the Bible is a record of what God does and what people do in history. The psalms assert directly, and imply indirectly, what God does in the three arenas of nature or creation, history, and the personal lives of people. The primary actions of God that the psalms record are his acts of creation, providence, judgment, and redemption/rescue. Psalms also tells the story of what people do in history (including within that the individual poets' testimonies to their own experiences). Additionally, many of the psalms express messianic expectations.

The blessed man: an encomium in praise of the godly person [Psalm 1]. An *encomium is a poem or prose piece that praises either an abstract quality or a general character type by means of a set of established conventions and motifs. Psalm 1 praises the godly person in the standard terms of the genre, as follows: an introduction to the subject of praise (in the form of an opening *beatitude); catalog of the praiseworthy acts and qualities of the subject; the superiority motif (showing the superiority of the subject by contrasting it to its opposite); awakening of the desire to emulate the subject and thus share his destiny. Additionally Psalm 1 uses the technique of the character sketch or portrait and heightens the effect by means of a *foil (a contrast that sets off the subject).

BOOK ONE

1 Blessed is the man[1]
who walks not in the counsel of the wicked,
nor stands in the way of sinners,
   nor sits in the seat of scoffers;
[2] but his delight is in the law[2] of the LORD,
   and on his law he meditates day and night.

[3] He is like a tree
   planted by streams of water
that yields its fruit in its season,
   and its leaf does not wither.
In all that he does, he prospers.

[1] The singular Hebrew word for *man* (*ish*) is used here to portray a representative example of a godly person; see preface [2] Or *instruction*

4   The wicked are not so,
        but are like chaff that the wind drives away.

5   Therefore the wicked will not stand in the judgment,
        nor sinners in the congregation of the righteous;
6   for the LORD knows the way of the righteous,
        but the way of the wicked will perish.

Why do the nations rage? The futility of conspiring against God [Psalm 2]. Psalm 2 uses *rhetorical question, description, dramatized speeches, and *apostrophe to make us feel the futility of conspiracy against God. The units are as follows: the theme announced (v. 1); the spectacle of rebellion against God (vv. 2–3); God's scornful defeat of such conspiracy (vv. 4–6); God's decree giving his anointed power over the conspiring nations (vv. 7–9); admonition warning the conspirators (vv. 10–11); concluding benediction on those who take refuge in the God who can foil conspirators (last line).

---

2   Why do the nations rage[1]
        and the peoples plot in vain?
2   The kings of the earth set themselves,
        and the rulers take counsel together,
        against the LORD and against his Anointed, saying,
3   "Let us burst their bonds apart
        and cast away their cords from us."

4   He who sits in the heavens laughs;
        the Lord holds them in derision.
5   Then he will speak to them in his wrath,
        and terrify them in his fury, saying,
6   "As for me, I have set my King
        on Zion, my holy hill."

7   I will tell of the decree:
     The LORD said to me, "You are my Son;
        today I have begotten you.
8   Ask of me, and I will make the nations your heritage,
        and the ends of the earth your possession.
9   You shall break[2] them with a rod of iron
        and dash them in pieces like a potter's vessel."

10   Now therefore, O kings, be wise;
        be warned, O rulers of the earth.
11   Serve the LORD with fear,
        and rejoice with trembling.
12   Kiss the Son,
        lest he be angry, and you perish in the way,
        for his wrath is quickly kindled.
     Blessed are all who take refuge in him.

---

[1] Or *nations noisily assemble* [2] Revocalization yields (compare Septuagint) *You shall rule*

How many are my foes: a lament [Psalm 3]. This is the first appearance of one of the two most numerous categories in the Psalter, namely, the *lament or complaint. Psalm 3 is a simplified version of the form: definition of the crisis (vv. 1–2); statement of confidence in God (vv. 3–6); petition to God for help (v. 7); concluding praise of God (v. 8).

3 A PSALM OF DAVID, WHEN HE FLED FROM ABSALOM HIS SON.
O LORD, how many are my foes!
   Many are rising against me;
2 many are saying of my soul,
   there is no salvation for him in God.   *Selah*[1]

3 But you, O LORD, are a shield about me,
   my glory, and the lifter of my head.
4 I cried aloud to the LORD,
   and he answered me from his holy hill.   *Selah*

5 I lay down and slept;
   I woke again, for the LORD sustained me.
6 I will not be afraid of many thousands of people
   who have set themselves against me all around.

7 Arise, O LORD!
   Save me, O my God!
For you strike all my enemies on the cheek;
   you break the teeth of the wicked.

8 Salvation belongs to the LORD;
   your blessing be on your people!   *Selah*

Lament in a time of crisis [Psalm 4]. The point of unity of this disjointed poem is that throughout the poem the speaker is responding to a crisis, perhaps slander. The "big idea" is how to cope with people who attack or doubt the faith. The units are as follows: call to God for help (v. 1); retort (in the form of *apostrophe) to evil people who abuse the psalmist with their slander (vv. 2–3); exhortation to right conduct, addressed to those who are misbehaving, or possibly to the speaker himself (vv. 4–5); a lament that the crisis described earlier is leading observers to doubt the faith (v. 6); assertion of the speaker's joy in God (vv. 7–8).

4 TO THE CHOIRMASTER: WITH STRINGED INSTRUMENTS. A PSALM OF DAVID.
Answer me when I call, O God of my righteousness!
   You have given me relief when I was in distress.
   Be gracious to me and hear my prayer!

2 O men,[2] how long shall my honor be turned into shame?
   How long will you love vain words and seek after lies?   *Selah*
3 But know that the LORD has set apart the godly for himself;
   the LORD hears when I call to him.

---

[1] The meaning of the Hebrew word *Selah*, used frequently in the Psalms, is uncertain. It may be a musical or liturgical direction [2] Or *O men of rank*

⁴   Be angry,¹ and do not sin;
      ponder in your own hearts on your beds, and be silent.   *Selah*
⁵   Offer right sacrifices,
      and put your trust in the LORD.

⁶   There are many who say, "Who will show us some good?
      Lift up the light of your face upon us, O LORD!"
⁷   You have put more joy in my heart
      than they have when their grain and wine abound.

⁸   In peace I will both lie down and sleep;
      for you alone, O LORD, make me dwell in safety.

Consider my groaning: a prayer for deliverance from enemies [Psalm 5]. This
psalm has affinities with the lament psalm but does not fit that form exactly. The poet's
opening invocation (vv. 1–3) specifying the time as morning leads commentators to label
the psalm a morning prayer. After the invocation, the movement of the poet's thought is
as follows: statement of confidence in God (vv. 4–7); petition for deliverance (v. 8); combination of accusation of slanderers and petition that God will punish them (vv. 9–10);
praise of God for his defense of the righteous (vv. 11–12).

---

5   TO THE CHOIRMASTER: FOR THE FLUTES. A PSALM OF DAVID.
      Give ear to my words, O LORD;
         consider my groaning.
²   Give attention to the sound of my cry,
         my King and my God,
      for to you do I pray.
³   O LORD, in the morning you hear my voice;
      in the morning I prepare a sacrifice for you² and watch.

⁴   For you are not a God who delights in wickedness;
         evil may not dwell with you.
⁵   The boastful shall not stand before your eyes;
         you hate all evildoers.
⁶   You destroy those who speak lies;
         the LORD abhors the bloodthirsty and deceitful man.

⁷   But I, through the abundance of your steadfast love,
         will enter your house.
      I will bow down toward your holy temple
         in the fear of you.
⁸   Lead me, O LORD, in your righteousness
         because of my enemies;
         make your way straight before me.

⁹   For there is no truth in their mouth;
         their inmost self is destruction;
      their throat is an open grave;
         they flatter with their tongue.

---

¹ Or *Be agitated* ² Or *I direct my prayer to you*

¹⁰   Make them bear their guilt, O God;
        let them fall by their own counsels;
      because of the abundance of their transgressions cast them out,
        for they have rebelled against you.

¹¹   But let all who take refuge in you rejoice;
        let them ever sing for joy,
      and spread your protection over them,
        that those who love your name may exult in you.
¹²   For you bless the righteous, O Lᴏʀᴅ;
        you cover him with favor as with a shield.

Rebuke me not in your anger: a penitential psalm [Psalm 6]. This is one of the seven
*penitential psalms of Christian tradition (the others being 32, 38, 51, 102, 130, and
143). The poem is a pleading with God not to abandon the speaker in his distress (v. 1).
The psychology of the poem flows from this stance of the speaker's awareness of his low
estate before God and people. The movement of thought and feeling unfolds as follows:
description of the speaker's spiritual and physical distress (vv. 2–3); prayer to God for
deliverance from the distress (vv. 4–5); further hyperbolic description of the speaker's
physical and spiritual desolation (vv. 6–7); combined statement of confidence in God
and repudiation of the speaker's enemies (vv. 8–10).

6 Tᴏ ᴛʜᴇ ᴄʜᴏɪʀᴍᴀsᴛᴇʀ: ᴡɪᴛʜ sᴛʀɪɴɢᴇᴅ ɪɴsᴛʀᴜᴍᴇɴᴛs; ᴀᴄᴄᴏʀᴅɪɴɢ ᴛᴏ Tʜᴇ Sʜᴇᴍɪɴɪᴛʜ.¹
A Psᴀʟᴍ ᴏғ Dᴀᴠɪᴅ.

¹   O Lᴏʀᴅ, rebuke me not in your anger,
        nor discipline me in your wrath.
²   Be gracious to me, O Lᴏʀᴅ, for I am languishing;
        heal me, O Lᴏʀᴅ, for my bones are troubled.
³   My soul also is greatly troubled.
        But you, O Lᴏʀᴅ—how long?

⁴   Turn, O Lᴏʀᴅ, deliver my life;
        save me for the sake of your steadfast love.
⁵   For in death there is no remembrance of you;
        in Sheol who will give you praise?

⁶   I am weary with my moaning;
        every night I flood my bed with tears;
        I drench my couch with my weeping.
⁷   My eye wastes away because of grief;
        it grows weak because of all my foes.

⁸   Depart from me, all you workers of evil,
        for the Lᴏʀᴅ has heard the sound of my weeping.
⁹   The Lᴏʀᴅ has heard my plea;
        the Lᴏʀᴅ accepts my prayer.
¹⁰   All my enemies shall be ashamed and greatly troubled;
        they shall turn back and be put to shame in a moment.

¹ Probably a musical or liturgical term

Save me from all my pursuers: a prayer for vindication [Psalm 7]. While having affinities with the lament psalm, this poem is more precisely a lyric expression of sentiments felt by someone falsely accused. The sequence is as follows: invocation and petition asking God to protect the speaker from attackers (vv. 1–2); the speaker's protestation of innocence, using the rhetorical format "if . . . , let . . ." (vv. 3–5); appeal to God to take up the speaker's defense against his enemies (vv. 6–9); statement of trust in God (vv. 10–11); assertion that evil people are subject to God's judgment (vv. 12–16); the speaker's praise of God (v. 17).

7

A SHIGGAION[1] OF DAVID, WHICH HE SANG TO THE LORD CONCERNING THE WORDS OF CUSH, A BENJAMINITE.

1   O LORD my God, in you do I take refuge;
        save me from all my pursuers and deliver me,
2   lest like a lion they tear my soul apart,
        rending it in pieces, with none to deliver.

3   O LORD my God, if I have done this,
        if there is wrong in my hands,
4   if I have repaid my friend[2] with evil
        or plundered my enemy without cause,
5   let the enemy pursue my soul and overtake it,
        and let him trample my life to the ground
        and lay my glory in the dust.   *Selah*

6   Arise, O LORD, in your anger;
        lift yourself up against the fury of my enemies;
        awake for me; you have appointed a judgment.
7   Let the assembly of the peoples be gathered about you;
        over it return on high.

8   The LORD judges the peoples;
        judge me, O LORD, according to my righteousness
        and according to the integrity that is in me.
9   Oh, let the evil of the wicked come to an end,
        and may you establish the righteous—
    you who test the minds and hearts,[3]
        O righteous God!
10 My shield is with God,
        who saves the upright in heart.
11 God is a righteous judge,
        and a God who feels indignation every day.

12 If a man[4] does not repent, God[5] will whet his sword;
        he has bent and readied his bow;
13 he has prepared for him his deadly weapons,
        making his arrows fiery shafts.
14 Behold, the wicked man conceives evil
        and is pregnant with mischief

---

[1] Probably a musical or liturgical term [2] Hebrew *the one at peace with me* [3] Hebrew *the hearts and kidneys* [4] Hebrew *he* [5] Hebrew *he*

and gives birth to lies.
15 He makes a pit, digging it out,
        and falls into the hole that he has made.
16 His mischief returns upon his own head,
        and on his own skull his violence descends.

17 I will give to the LORD the thanks due to his righteousness,
        and I will sing praise to the name of the LORD, the Most High.

How majestic is your name in all the earth: nature poem [Psalm 8]. Psalm 8 is one of five nature psalms (the others being 19, 29, 104, and 148). Its specific focus within that genre is to celebrate the place of man (men and women) in the scale of creation. In that vein, the poem is built around the central paradox of man's simultaneous smallness and greatness in the order of nature. The sequence of ideas is as follows: ascription of praise to God, repeated in the last verse, giving the poem an envelope structure (vv. 1, 9); assertion that God's glory in the creation silences his detractors (vv. 1–2); human smallness in relation to the immensity of the heavenly bodies (vv. 3–4); celebration of man's greatness in having been made only a little lower than the angels and given dominion over the natural creation (vv. 5–8).

8

To the choirmaster: according to The Gittith.[1] A Psalm of David.
O LORD, our Lord,
    how majestic is your name in all the earth!
You have set your glory above the heavens.
2   Out of the mouth of babies and infants,
    you have established strength because of your foes,
        to still the enemy and the avenger.

3   When I look at your heavens, the work of your fingers,
        the moon and the stars, which you have set in place,
4   what is man that you are mindful of him,
        and the son of man that you care for him?

5   Yet you have made him a little lower than the heavenly beings[2]
        and crowned him with glory and honor.
6   You have given him dominion over the works of your hands;
        you have put all things under his feet,
7   all sheep and oxen,
        and also the beasts of the field,
8   the birds of the heavens, and the fish of the sea,
        whatever passes along the paths of the seas.

9   O LORD, our Lord,
        how majestic is your name in all the earth!

I will give thanks to the LORD: a modified praise psalm [Psalm 9]. The conventional call to praise consists of a simple assertion by the poet that he will give thanks to God (vv. 1–2). This is followed by a catalog of God's acts of deliverance (vv. 3–6) and praise

---

[1] Probably a musical or liturgical term [2] Or *than God*; Septuagint *than the angels*

of God for his attributes of eternity and justice, as well as his role as the one who provides safety for those who trust in his eternity and justice (vv. 7–9). This section of praise is followed by a call to praise (vv. 11–12); a prayer to God to be gracious (vv. 13–14); praise of God for executing justice (vv. 15–18); and a concluding prayer for God to assert his justice (vv. 19–20).

9 [1] TO THE CHOIRMASTER: ACCORDING TO MUTH-LABBEN.[2] A PSALM OF DAVID.
I will give thanks to the LORD with my whole heart;
I will recount all of your wonderful deeds.

[2] I will be glad and exult in you;
I will sing praise to your name, O Most High.

[3] When my enemies turn back,
they stumble and perish before[3] your presence.

[4] For you have maintained my just cause;
you have sat on the throne, giving righteous judgment.

[5] You have rebuked the nations; you have made the wicked perish;
you have blotted out their name forever and ever.

[6] The enemy came to an end in everlasting ruins;
their cities you rooted out;
the very memory of them has perished.

[7] But the LORD sits enthroned forever;
he has established his throne for justice,

[8] and he judges the world with righteousness;
he judges the peoples with uprightness.

[9] The LORD is a stronghold for the oppressed,
a stronghold in times of trouble.

[10] And those who know your name put their trust in you,
for you, O LORD, have not forsaken those who seek you.

[11] Sing praises to the LORD, who sits enthroned in Zion!
Tell among the peoples his deeds!

[12] For he who avenges blood is mindful of them;
he does not forget the cry of the afflicted.

[13] Be gracious to me, O LORD!
See my affliction from those who hate me,
O you who lift me up from the gates of death,

[14] that I may recount all your praises,
that in the gates of the daughter of Zion
I may rejoice in your salvation.

[15] The nations have sunk in the pit that they made;
in the net that they hid, their own foot has been caught.

[16] The LORD has made himself known; he has executed judgment;
the wicked are snared in the work of their own hands.   *Higgaion.*[4] *Selah*

---

[1] Psalms 9 and 10 together follow an acrostic pattern, each stanza beginning with the successive letters of the Hebrew alphabet. In the Septuagint they form one psalm [2] Probably a musical or liturgical term [3] Or *because of* [4] Probably a musical or liturgical term

¹⁷ The wicked shall return to Sheol,
all the nations that forget God.

¹⁸ For the needy shall not always be forgotten,
and the hope of the poor shall not perish forever.

¹⁹ Arise, O Lᴏʀᴅ! Let not man prevail;
let the nations be judged before you!
²⁰ Put them in fear, O Lᴏʀᴅ!
Let the nations know that they are but men! *Selah*

Why do you hide yourself? A lament psalm [Psalm 10]. Psalm 10 presents the conventional motifs of the lament psalm in the following order: invocation (v. 1); the lament or definition of the crisis (vv. 2–11); mingled petition to God to act and statement of confidence that God can be trusted to act (vv. 12–18). The portrait of the wicked oppressors and their innocent victims comes alive through the portraiture techniques of *epithet, hyperbole, metaphor, and images.

10
Why, O Lᴏʀᴅ, do you stand far away?
Why do you hide yourself in times of trouble?

² In arrogance the wicked hotly pursue the poor;
let them be caught in the schemes that they have devised.
³ For the wicked boasts of the desires of his soul,
and the one greedy for gain curses¹ and renounces the Lᴏʀᴅ.
⁴ In the pride of his face² the wicked does not seek him;³
all his thoughts are, "There is no God."
⁵ His ways prosper at all times;
your judgments are on high, out of his sight;
as for all his foes, he puffs at them.
⁶ He says in his heart, "I shall not be moved;
throughout all generations I shall not meet adversity."
⁷ His mouth is filled with cursing and deceit and oppression;
under his tongue are mischief and iniquity.
⁸ He sits in ambush in the villages;
in hiding places he murders the innocent.
His eyes stealthily watch for the helpless;
⁹ he lurks in ambush like a lion in his thicket;
he lurks that he may seize the poor;
he seizes the poor when he draws him into his net.
¹⁰ The helpless are crushed, sink down,
and fall by his might.
¹¹ He says in his heart, "God has forgotten,
he has hidden his face, he will never see it."

¹² Arise, O Lᴏʀᴅ; O God, lift up your hand;
forget not the afflicted.
¹³ Why does the wicked renounce God

¹ Or *and he blesses the one greedy for gain* ² Or *of his anger* ³ Or *the wicked says, "He will not call to account"*

and say in his heart, "You will not call to account"?

14 But you do see, for you note mischief and vexation,
   that you may take it into your hands;
   to you the helpless commits himself;
   you have been the helper of the fatherless.

15 Break the arm of the wicked and evildoer;
   call his wickedness to account till you find none.

16 The LORD is king forever and ever;
   the nations perish from his land.

17 O LORD, you hear the desire of the afflicted;
   you will strengthen their heart; you will incline your ear

18 to do justice to the fatherless and the oppressed,
   so that man who is of the earth may strike terror no more.

In the LORD I take refuge: lyric meditation on God's sovereignty [Psalm 11]. The opening line announces the unifying theme or focus: the speaker's confidence in God as refuge. The variations on the theme of God's reliable protection are as follows: description of the speaker's detractors who occasioned the poem (vv. 2–3); catalog of God's acts of deliverance for the righteous who are oppressed (vv. 4–7). The question that the poet asks in verse 3 is answered in the rest of the poem: when the foundations of a just society are threatened by evil forces, God can be trusted to enforce justice toward the righteous.

11

TO THE CHOIRMASTER. OF DAVID.
   In the LORD I take refuge;
how can you say to my soul,
   "Flee like a bird to your mountain,

2 for behold, the wicked bend the bow;
   they have fitted their arrow to the string
   to shoot in the dark at the upright in heart;

3 if the foundations are destroyed,
   what can the righteous do?"[1]

4 The LORD is in his holy temple;
   the LORD's throne is in heaven;
   his eyes see, his eyelids test the children of man.

5 The LORD tests the righteous,
   but his soul hates the wicked and the one who loves violence.

6 Let him rain coals on the wicked;
   fire and sulfur and a scorching wind shall be the portion of their cup.

7 For the LORD is righteous;
he loves righteous deeds;
   the upright shall behold his face.

On every side the wicked prowl: plea for protection from a godless society [Psalm 12]. The theme of this lament psalm is announced in verse 7: God will guard believers

[1] Or for the foundations will be destroyed; what has the righteous done?

as they live in a godless society. The variations on that theme are as follows: portrait of a godless society (vv. 1–2); a wish for God to act in judgment against such a society (vv. 3–4); God's reliable promise to act on behalf of the oppressed (vv. 5–6); assertion of the unifying theme that God will guard his own as they live in a wicked society (vv. 7–8).

12

To the choirmaster: according to The Sheminith.[1] A Psalm of David.
Save, O Lord, for the godly one is gone;
  for the faithful have vanished from among the children of man.
2 Everyone utters lies to his neighbor;
  with flattering lips and a double heart they speak.

3 May the Lord cut off all flattering lips,
  the tongue that makes great boasts,
4 those who say, "With our tongue we will prevail,
  our lips are with us; who is master over us?"

5 "Because the poor are plundered, because the needy groan,
  I will now arise," says the Lord;
  "I will place him in the safety for which he longs."
6 The words of the Lord are pure words,
  like silver refined in a furnace on the ground,
  purified seven times.

7 You, O Lord, will keep them;
  you will guard us[2] from this generation forever.
8 On every side the wicked prowl,
  as vileness is exalted among the children of man.

Forget me not: prayer for deliverance [Psalm 13]. The genre of Psalm 13 is the prayer for rescue. Everything in the poem relates to that: a questioning of God built around the motif of "how long" the speaker's crisis will endure (vv. 1–2); a petition to God to rescue the speaker from his enemies (vv. 3–4); statement of confidence in God (v. 5a); vow to praise God (vv. 5b–6).

13

To the choirmaster. A Psalm of David.
How long, O Lord? Will you forget me forever?
  How long will you hide your face from me?
2 How long must I take counsel in my soul
  and have sorrow in my heart all the day?
  How long shall my enemy be exalted over me?

3 Consider and answer me, O Lord my God;
  light up my eyes, lest I sleep the sleep of death,
4 lest my enemy say, "I have prevailed over him,"
  lest my foes rejoice because I am shaken.

5 But I have trusted in your steadfast love;
  my heart shall rejoice in your salvation.

---

[1] Probably a musical or liturgical term [2] Or *guard him*

⁶   I will sing to the LORD,
        because he has dealt bountifully with me.

> **They have all turned aside: a satiric psalm** [Psalm 14]. The format that explains the poem is *satire—an attack on human vice and folly. Variations on the satiric theme are as follows: a very brief portrait of the fool who denies the existence of God (v. 1a); a put-down of corrupt humanity (vv. 1b-4); a scornful repudiation of the supposed power of the wicked against the righteous (vv. 5–6); statement of longing that God would save his people from the morass that the poem has described (v. 7).

14 TO THE CHOIRMASTER. OF DAVID.
        The fool says in his heart, "There is no God."
    They are corrupt, they do abominable deeds,
        there is none who does good.

²   The LORD looks down from heaven on the children of man,
        to see if there are any who understand,¹
        who seek after God.

³   They have all turned aside; together they have become corrupt;
        there is none who does good,
            not even one.

⁴   Have they no knowledge, all the evildoers
        who eat up my people as they eat bread
        and do not call upon the LORD?

⁵   There they are in great terror,
        for God is with the generation of the righteous.
⁶   You would shame the plans of the poor,
        but² the LORD is his refuge.

⁷   Oh, that salvation for Israel would come out of Zion!
        When the LORD restores the fortunes of his people,
        let Jacob rejoice, let Israel be glad.

> **Dwelling on God's holy hill: the ideal worshiper** [Psalm 15]. The format of Psalm 15 is simplicity personified: an opening question regarding who can worship God acceptably (v. 1) is followed by a portrait of the ideal worshiper (vv. 2–5). We can ponder the specific virtues that make up the portrait of the ideal worshiper.

15 A PSALM OF DAVID.
        O LORD, who shall sojourn in your tent?
    Who shall dwell on your holy hill?

²   He who walks blamelessly and does what is right
        and speaks truth in his heart;
³   who does not slander with his tongue
        and does no evil to his neighbor,

¹ Or that act wisely ² Or for

nor takes up a reproach against his friend;
4 in whose eyes a vile person is despised,
      but who honors those who fear the LORD;
    who swears to his own hurt and does not change;
5 who does not put out his money at interest
      and does not take a bribe against the innocent.
    He who does these things shall never be moved.

Pleasures forevermore: a praise psalm [Psalm 16]. Although the opening petition may lead us to expect a lament psalm, in fact the content places this poem into the category of praise psalm. The specific motifs are as follows: statement of personal devotion to God (v. 2); praise of the godly (v. 3); foil in the form of a brief description of those who pursue another god (v. 4); catalog of God's blessings in the speaker's life (vv. 5–8); expression of joy (v. 9); further catalog of God's blessings to the speaker (vv. 10–11).

16

A MIKTAM[1] OF DAVID.
   Preserve me, O God, for in you I take refuge.
2 I say to the LORD, "You are my Lord;
      I have no good apart from you."

3 As for the saints in the land, they are the excellent ones,
      in whom is all my delight.[2]

4 The sorrows of those who run after[3] another god shall multiply;
      their drink offerings of blood I will not pour out
      or take their names on my lips.

5 The LORD is my chosen portion and my cup;
      you hold my lot.
6 The lines have fallen for me in pleasant places;
      indeed, I have a beautiful inheritance.

7 I bless the LORD who gives me counsel;
      in the night also my heart instructs me.[4]
8 I have set the LORD always before me;
      because he is at my right hand, I shall not be shaken.

9 Therefore my heart is glad, and my whole being[5] rejoices;
      my flesh also dwells secure.
10 For you will not abandon my soul to Sheol,
      or let your holy one see corruption.[6]

11 You make known to me the path of life;
      in your presence there is fullness of joy;
      at your right hand are pleasures forevermore.

Hear a just cause, O LORD: a lament psalm [Psalm 17]. The conventional motifs of the lament psalm unfold as follows: opening cry to God (vv. 1–2); protestation of inno-

---

[1] Probably a musical or liturgical term [2] Or To the saints in the land, the excellent in whom is all my delight, I say: [3] Or who acquire [4] Hebrew my kidneys instruct me [5] Hebrew my glory [6] Or see the pit

cence (vv. 3–5); petition that God will protect the righteous who call on him (vv. 6–9); description of the wicked oppressors (vv. 10–12); second petitionary section—a plea to be delivered from people whose world view is earthbound (vv. 13–14); statement of confidence that the speaker will see God in life and in the afterlife (v. 15). The imagery of the first half is that of a courtroom trial, but this underlying metaphor does not persist to the end.

17

A Prayer of David.

Hear a just cause, O Lord; attend to my cry!
  Give ear to my prayer from lips free of deceit!
2 From your presence let my vindication come!
  Let your eyes behold the right!

3 You have tried my heart, you have visited me by night,
    you have tested me, and you will find nothing;
    I have purposed that my mouth will not transgress.
4 With regard to the works of man, by the word of your lips
    I have avoided the ways of the violent.
5 My steps have held fast to your paths;
    my feet have not slipped.

6 I call upon you, for you will answer me, O God;
    incline your ear to me; hear my words.
7 Wondrously show[1] your steadfast love,
    O Savior of those who seek refuge
    from their adversaries at your right hand.

8 Keep me as the apple of your eye;
    hide me in the shadow of your wings,
9 from the wicked who do me violence,
    my deadly enemies who surround me.

10 They close their hearts to pity;
    with their mouths they speak arrogantly.
11 They have now surrounded our steps;
    they set their eyes to cast us to the ground.
12 He is like a lion eager to tear,
    as a young lion lurking in ambush.

13 Arise, O Lord! Confront him, subdue him!
    Deliver my soul from the wicked by your sword,
14 from men by your hand, O Lord,
    from men of the world whose portion is in this life.[2]
  You fill their womb with treasure;[3]
    they are satisfied with children,
    and they leave their abundance to their infants.

15 As for me, I shall behold your face in righteousness;
    when I awake, I shall be satisfied with your likeness.

---

[1] Or *Distinguish me by* [2] Or *from men whose portion in life is of the world* [3] Or *As for your treasured ones, you fill their womb*

David's song of victory [Psalm 18]. The *song of victory was a familiar genre of war-faring nations in the ancient world. Such songs were cast in the form of battlefield celebrations. This genre explains why military imagery dominates in Psalm 18, as both the speaker and God appear in the role of warrior. Although most psalms of praise use a catalog technique, a few, including this one, use a portrait technique: the poet paints a metaphoric picture of God. The sequence is as follows: opening statement of praise to God as a warrior who has rescued the speaker (vv. 1–3); metaphoric description of the crisis in which the speaker found himself (vv. 4–6); metaphoric portrait of God in his action of battlefield rescuer (vv. 7–19); the speaker's statement of his own innocence that qualified him for God's rescue, branching out to a general statement of God's mercy toward the blameless (vv. 20–30); praise of God as the one who arms the warrior, a theocentric version of the *epic motif of the arming of the *hero (vv. 31–45); concluding statements of praise (vv. 46–50).

18

To the choirmaster. A Psalm of David, the servant of the Lord, who addressed the words of this song to the Lord on the day when the Lord rescued him from the hand of all his enemies, and from the hand of Saul. He said:

1   I love you, O Lord, my strength.
2   The Lord is my rock and my fortress and my deliverer,
        my God, my rock, in whom I take refuge,
        my shield, and the horn of my salvation, my stronghold.
3   I call upon the Lord, who is worthy to be praised,
        and I am saved from my enemies.

4   The cords of death encompassed me;
        the torrents of destruction assailed me;[1]
5   the cords of Sheol entangled me;
        the snares of death confronted me.

6   In my distress I called upon the Lord;
        to my God I cried for help.
    From his temple he heard my voice,
        and my cry to him reached his ears.

7   Then the earth reeled and rocked;
        the foundations also of the mountains trembled
        and quaked, because he was angry.
8   Smoke went up from his nostrils,[2]
        and devouring fire from his mouth;
        glowing coals flamed forth from him.
9   He bowed the heavens and came down;
        thick darkness was under his feet.
10 He rode on a cherub and flew;
        he came swiftly on the wings of the wind.
11 He made darkness his covering, his canopy around him,
        thick clouds dark with water.
12 Out of the brightness before him
        hailstones and coals of fire broke through his clouds.

---

[1] Or terrified me [2] Or in his wrath

¹³ The Lᴏʀᴅ also thundered in the heavens,
   and the Most High uttered his voice,
   hailstones and coals of fire.
¹⁴ And he sent out his arrows and scattered them;
   he flashed forth lightnings and routed them.
¹⁵ Then the channels of the sea were seen,
   and the foundations of the world were laid bare
at your rebuke, O Lᴏʀᴅ,
   at the blast of the breath of your nostrils.
¹⁶ He sent from on high, he took me;
   he drew me out of many waters.
¹⁷ He rescued me from my strong enemy
   and from those who hated me,
   for they were too mighty for me.
¹⁸ They confronted me in the day of my calamity,
   but the Lᴏʀᴅ was my support.
¹⁹ He brought me out into a broad place;
   he rescued me, because he delighted in me.

²⁰ The Lᴏʀᴅ dealt with me according to my righteousness;
   according to the cleanness of my hands he rewarded me.
²¹ For I have kept the ways of the Lᴏʀᴅ,
   and have not wickedly departed from my God.
²² For all his rules¹ were before me,
   and his statutes I did not put away from me.
²³ I was blameless before him,
   and I kept myself from my guilt.
²⁴ So the Lᴏʀᴅ has rewarded me according to my righteousness,
   according to the cleanness of my hands in his sight.

²⁵ With the merciful you show yourself merciful;
   with the blameless man you show yourself blameless;
²⁶ with the purified you show yourself pure;
   and with the crooked you make yourself seem tortuous.
²⁷ For you save a humble people,
   but the haughty eyes you bring down.
²⁸ For it is you who light my lamp;
   the Lᴏʀᴅ my God lightens my darkness.
²⁹ For by you I can run against a troop,
   and by my God I can leap over a wall.
³⁰ This God—his way is perfect;²
   the word of the Lᴏʀᴅ proves true;
   he is a shield for all those who take refuge in him.

³¹ For who is God, but the Lᴏʀᴅ?
   And who is a rock, except our God?—
³² the God who equipped me with strength

---

¹ Or just decrees ² Or blameless

and made my way blameless.
³³ He made my feet like the feet of a deer
and set me secure on the heights.
³⁴ He trains my hands for war,
so that my arms can bend a bow of bronze.
³⁵ You have given me the shield of your salvation,
and your right hand supported me,
and your gentleness made me great.
³⁶ You gave a wide place for my steps under me,
and my feet did not slip.
³⁷ I pursued my enemies and overtook them,
and did not turn back till they were consumed.
³⁸ I thrust them through, so that they were not able to rise;
they fell under my feet.
³⁹ For you equipped me with strength for the battle;
you made those who rise against me sink under me.
⁴⁰ You made my enemies turn their backs to me,[1]
and those who hated me I destroyed.
⁴¹ They cried for help, but there was none to save;
they cried to the Lord, but he did not answer them.
⁴² I beat them fine as dust before the wind;
I cast them out like the mire of the streets.

⁴³ You delivered me from strife with the people;
you made me the head of the nations;
people whom I had not known served me.
⁴⁴ As soon as they heard of me they obeyed me;
foreigners came cringing to me.
⁴⁵ Foreigners lost heart
and came trembling out of their fortresses.

⁴⁶ The Lord lives, and blessed be my rock,
and exalted be the God of my salvation—
⁴⁷ the God who gave me vengeance
and subdued peoples under me,
⁴⁸ who delivered me from my enemies;
yes, you exalted me above those who rose against me;
you rescued me from the man of violence.

⁴⁹ For this I will praise you, O Lord, among the nations,
and sing to your name.
⁵⁰ Great salvation he brings to his king,
and shows steadfast love to his anointed,
to David and his offspring forever.

Praise of God's revelation [Psalm 19]. The first half of the poem makes this the second of five nature psalms in the Psalter. The unifying theme is God's excellent revelation of himself—in nature and in his law, in world and Word. As one of the most patterned

[1] Or You gave me my enemies' necks

poems in the Psalter, this poem is breathtaking in its symmetry: God's revelation of himself in nature falls into the complementary halves of the heavenly bodies in general (vv. 1–4a) and the sun specifically (vv. 4b–6). God's revelation of himself in his law falls into the complementary halves of a section that praises the law for its perfections and effects (vv. 7–11) and a section that petitions God to keep the speaker from transgressing the law (vv. 12–14).

19

To the choirmaster. A Psalm of David.

The heavens declare the glory of God,
  and the sky above[1] proclaims his handiwork.
2 Day to day pours out speech,
  and night to night reveals knowledge.
3 There is no speech, nor are there words,
  whose voice is not heard.
4 Their voice[2] goes out through all the earth,
  and their words to the end of the world.
In them he has set a tent for the sun,
5   which comes out like a bridegroom leaving his chamber,
  and, like a strong man, runs its course with joy.
6 Its rising is from the end of the heavens,
  and its circuit to the end of them,
  and there is nothing hidden from its heat.

7 The law of the Lord is perfect,[3]
  reviving the soul;
the testimony of the Lord is sure,
  making wise the simple;
8 the precepts of the Lord are right,
  rejoicing the heart;
the commandment of the Lord is pure,
  enlightening the eyes;
9 the fear of the Lord is clean,
  enduring forever;
the rules[4] of the Lord are true,
  and righteous altogether.
10 More to be desired are they than gold,
  even much fine gold;
sweeter also than honey
  and drippings of the honeycomb.
11 Moreover, by them is your servant warned;
  in keeping them there is great reward.

12 Who can discern his errors?
  Declare me innocent from hidden faults.
13 Keep back your servant also from presumptuous sins;
  let them not have dominion over me!

---

[1] Hebrew *the expanse*; compare Genesis 1:6-8   [2] Or *Their measuring line*   [3] Or *blameless*   [4] Or *just decrees*

Then I shall be blameless,
and innocent of great transgression.

¹⁴ Let the words of my mouth and the meditation of my heart
be acceptable in your sight,
O LORD, my rock and my redeemer.

> **God save the king: a prayer for victory** [Psalm 20]. The imagery of battle and victory,
> coupled with the wish expressed in the last verse that the Lord will save the king, makes
> it plausible to put this psalm into the category of royal psalm—a poem that focuses on
> the king, in this case the king as he prepares to enter battle. But we need to avoid tying
> a poem like this so closely to an inferred original occasion that we miss the fact that
> the sentiments it expresses are appropriate for any believer in God in any situation in
> life. The sequence is as follows: a litany of wishes for the victory of the king, using the
> "may . . ." formula (vv. 1–5); assertion that victory comes from trusting in God, not from
> military resources (vv. 6–8); prayer to God to save the king (v. 9).

20
To THE CHOIRMASTER. A PSALM OF DAVID.
May the LORD answer you in the day of trouble!
May the name of the God of Jacob protect you!

² May he send you help from the sanctuary
and give you support from Zion!

³ May he remember all your offerings
and regard with favor your burnt sacrifices!   *Selah*

⁴ May he grant you your heart's desire
and fulfill all your plans!

⁵ May we shout for joy over your salvation,
and in the name of our God set up our banners!
May the LORD fulfill all your petitions!

⁶ Now I know that the LORD saves his anointed;
he will answer him from his holy heaven
with the saving might of his right hand.

⁷ Some trust in chariots and some in horses,
but we trust in the name of the LORD our God.

⁸ They collapse and fall,
but we rise and stand upright.

⁹ O LORD, save the king!
May he answer us when we call.

> **God saved the king: a song of victory** [Psalm 21]. Whereas the preceding psalm
> prays for the king's deliverance, this psalm celebrates the king's deliverance. The poem
> falls into three parts: praise to God for his blessings on the king (vv. 1–7); apostro-
> phe (direct address) to the king, predicting his future success against his enemies (vv.
> 8–12); ascription of praise to God (v. 13).

21

To the choirmaster. A Psalm of David.

O Lord, in your strength the king rejoices,
and in your salvation how greatly he exults!

2 You have given him his heart's desire
and have not withheld the request of his lips. *Selah*

3 For you meet him with rich blessings;
you set a crown of fine gold upon his head.

4 He asked life of you; you gave it to him,
length of days forever and ever.

5 His glory is great through your salvation;
splendor and majesty you bestow on him.

6 For you make him most blessed forever;[1]
you make him glad with the joy of your presence.

7 For the king trusts in the Lord,
and through the steadfast love of the Most High he shall not be moved.

8 Your hand will find out all your enemies;
your right hand will find out those who hate you.

9 You will make them as a blazing oven
when you appear.
The Lord will swallow them up in his wrath,
and fire will consume them.

10 You will destroy their descendants from the earth,
and their offspring from among the children of man.

11 Though they plan evil against you,
though they devise mischief, they will not succeed.

12 For you will put them to flight;
you will aim at their faces with your bows.

13 Be exalted, O Lord, in your strength!
We will sing and praise your power.

My God, my God, why have you forsaken me? The song of the sufferer [Psalm 22].
This poem is a memorable expression of the suffering soul. The poem speaks in universal terms that all people in distress can echo as expressing their feelings. But this is also a poem of "second meanings" in which many of the sentiments were preeminently true of the Messiah in the sacrificial sufferings of his passion and death (see, for example, Matt. 27:46). The sequence of feelings is as follows: opening cry of distress to God (vv. 1–2); foil—God's deliverance of his people in the past (vv. 3–5); return to the present: the speaker's extreme suffering and rejection (vv. 6–18); petition that God deliver the speaker (vv. 19–21a); praise of God for his deliverance (vv. 21b–31). It is evident that while the first half of the poem belongs to the genre of the lament psalm, the conventions of the praise psalm dominate the second half.

22

To the choirmaster: according to The Doe of the Dawn. A Psalm of David.

My God, my God, why have you forsaken me?
Why are you so far from saving me, from the words of my groaning?

---

[1] Or make him a source of blessing forever

2   O my God, I cry by day, but you do not answer,
        and by night, but I find no rest.

3   Yet you are holy,
        enthroned on the praises[1] of Israel.
4   In you our fathers trusted;
        they trusted, and you delivered them.
5   To you they cried and were rescued;
        in you they trusted and were not put to shame.

6   But I am a worm and not a man,
        scorned by mankind and despised by the people.
7   All who see me mock me;
        they make mouths at me; they wag their heads;
8   "He trusts in the LORD; let him deliver him;
        let him rescue him, for he delights in him!"

9   Yet you are he who took me from the womb;
        you made me trust you at my mother's breasts.
10 On you was I cast from my birth,
        and from my mother's womb you have been my God.
11 Be not far from me,
        for trouble is near,
        and there is none to help.

12 Many bulls encompass me;
        strong bulls of Bashan surround me;
13 they open wide their mouths at me,
        like a ravening and roaring lion.

14 I am poured out like water,
        and all my bones are out of joint;
    my heart is like wax;
        it is melted within my breast;
15 my strength is dried up like a potsherd,
        and my tongue sticks to my jaws;
        you lay me in the dust of death.

16 For dogs encompass me;
        a company of evildoers encircles me;
    they have pierced my hands and feet[2]—
17 I can count all my bones—
        they stare and gloat over me;
18 they divide my garments among them,
        and for my clothing they cast lots.

19 But you, O LORD, do not be far off!
        O you my help, come quickly to my aid!
20 Deliver my soul from the sword,
        my precious life from the power of the dog!

---

[1] Or *dwelling in the praises* [2] Some Hebrew manuscripts, Septuagint, Vulgate, Syriac; most Hebrew manuscripts *like a lion* [they are at] *my hands and feet*

21   Save me from the mouth of the lion!
      You have rescued[1] me from the horns of the wild oxen!

22   I will tell of your name to my brothers;
          in the midst of the congregation I will praise you:
23   You who fear the LORD, praise him!
          All you offspring of Jacob, glorify him,
          and stand in awe of him, all you offspring of Israel!
24   For he has not despised or abhorred
          the affliction of the afflicted,
      and he has not hidden his face from him,
          but has heard, when he cried to him.

25   From you comes my praise in the great congregation;
          my vows I will perform before those who fear him.
26   The afflicted[2] shall eat and be satisfied;
          those who seek him shall praise the LORD!
          May your hearts live forever!

27   All the ends of the earth shall remember
          and turn to the LORD,
      and all the families of the nations
          shall worship before you.
28   For kingship belongs to the LORD,
          and he rules over the nations.

29   All the prosperous of the earth eat and worship;
          before him shall bow all who go down to the dust,
          even the one who could not keep himself alive.
30   Posterity shall serve him;
          it shall be told of the Lord to the coming generation;
31   they shall come and proclaim his righteousness to a people yet unborn,
          that he has done it.

The LORD is my shepherd: the world's greatest lyric [Psalm 23]. Psalm 23 is a *pastoral poem built around the motif of the daily acts of provision that a good shepherd performs for his sheep. The sheep-shepherd relationship, in turn, is a metaphor for the providence that God extends to his followers. At the sheep-shepherd level, the sequence of provisions is as follows: the controlling metaphor and theme established (v. 1); midday resting in an oasis, after morning feeding and drinking (vv. 2–3a); guidance in safe paths (v. 3b) and protection through dangerous parts of the journey over the path (v. 4); provision of grazing (v. 5a); caring for injured sheep in the sheepfold at the end of the day (v. 5b); prediction that the sheep are always assured of returning to the sheepfold at the end of the day (v. 6). When we carry over the meanings of these provisions to the human level, we luxuriate in the comprehensiveness of God's provision for those who follow him.

---

[1] Hebrew *answered* [2] Or *The meek*

23

A Psalm of David.
The Lord is my shepherd; I shall not want.
2   He makes me lie down in green pastures.
He leads me beside still waters.[1]
3   He restores my soul.
He leads me in paths of righteousness[2]
    for his name's sake.

4   Even though I walk through the valley of the shadow of death,[3]
    I will fear no evil,
for you are with me;
    your rod and your staff,
    they comfort me.

5   You prepare a table before me
    in the presence of my enemies;
you anoint my head with oil;
    my cup overflows.
6   Surely[4] goodness and mercy[5] shall follow me
    all the days of my life,
and I shall dwell[6] in the house of the Lord
    forever.[7]

Lift up your heads, O gates: a psalm of worship [Psalm 24]. Speculation among scholars has been extravagant about a possible occasion for this psalm. Our safest interpretive stance is to see the sentiments as universal—applicable to any occasion of public worship of God or to any grand occasion when we enter into the worship of God. The opening verse establishes a very general context for what follows: God's supremacy in the earth that he created (vv. 1–2). Then in an abrupt shift, the poet asks who can worship such a holy God acceptably (v. 3). This is followed by an answer to the question, giving us a brief portrait of the lifestyle of the ideal worshiper (vv. 4–6). With the worship situation now firmly established, the rest of the poem pictures an actual scene of divine exaltation at a physical structure with gates by which the victor enters, either city gates or the gates of the temple (vv. 7–10). High drama pervades the question-and-answer dialogue of these latter verses. Apostrophe and personification are standard ways by which poets express strong feeling, and we have examples here in the poet's address to the gates (vv. 7, 9) and an imaginary questioner (vv. 8, 10).

24

A Psalm of David.
The earth is the Lord's and the fullness thereof,[8]
    the world and those who dwell therein,
2   for he has founded it upon the seas
    and established it upon the rivers.

3   Who shall ascend the hill of the Lord?
    And who shall stand in his holy place?
4   He who has clean hands and a pure heart,

---

[1] Hebrew *beside waters of rest* [2] Or *in right paths* [3] Or *the valley of deep darkness* [4] Or *Only* [5] Or *steadfast love* [6] Or *shall return to dwell* [7] Hebrew *for length of days* [8] Or *and all that fills it*

who does not lift up his soul to what is false
and does not swear deceitfully.
⁵ He will receive blessing from the LORD
and righteousness from the God of his salvation.
⁶ Such is the generation of those who seek him,
who seek the face of the God of Jacob.¹   *Selah*

⁷ Lift up your heads, O gates!
And be lifted up, O ancient doors,
that the King of glory may come in.
⁸ Who is this King of glory?
The LORD, strong and mighty,
the LORD, mighty in battle!
⁹ Lift up your heads, O gates!
And lift them up, O ancient doors,
that the King of glory may come in.
¹⁰ Who is this King of glory?
The LORD of hosts,
he is the King of glory!   *Selah*

An alphabet of petition and praise [Psalm 25]. Many of the psalms are not tightly unified and do not fit completely into such conventional genres as lament and praise psalm. Psalm 25 illustrates this lack of tidiness. The poem is mainly a petitionary prayer addressed to God, but verses 8–10 and 12–15 are declarative rather than petitionary (and v. 3, though addressed to God, is also declarative). Furthermore, although many of the petitions hint at specific crises in the life of the speaker, this poem lacks the conventional parts of the lament psalm other than the petitionary section. The sequence is as follows: opening expression of trust in God's goodness (vv. 1–3); the speaker's personal petition for God's forgiveness of his sins (vv. 6–7); general assertions of God's perfections (vv. 8–10); a second petition for forgiveness (v. 11); a sketch of the type of person who qualifies for God's favor (vv. 12–15); a concluding petitionary section (vv. 16–22). This psalm is an *acrostic poem in which the successive verses begin with the consecutive letters of the Hebrew alphabet.

25 ² OF DAVID.
To you, O LORD, I lift up my soul.
² O my God, in you I trust;
let me not be put to shame;
let not my enemies exult over me.
³ Indeed, none who wait for you shall be put to shame;
they shall be ashamed who are wantonly treacherous.

⁴ Make me to know your ways, O LORD;
teach me your paths.
⁵ Lead me in your truth and teach me,
for you are the God of my salvation;
for you I wait all the day long.

¹ Septuagint, Syriac, and two Hebrew manuscripts; Masoretic Text *Jacob, who seek your face* ² This psalm is an acrostic poem, each verse beginning with the successive letters of the Hebrew alphabet

6   Remember your mercy, O Lord, and your steadfast love,
        for they have been from of old.
7   Remember not the sins of my youth or my transgressions;
        according to your steadfast love remember me,
        for the sake of your goodness, O Lord!

8   Good and upright is the Lord;
        therefore he instructs sinners in the way.
9   He leads the humble in what is right,
        and teaches the humble his way.
10 All the paths of the Lord are steadfast love and faithfulness,
        for those who keep his covenant and his testimonies.

11 For your name's sake, O Lord,
        pardon my guilt, for it is great.
12 Who is the man who fears the Lord?
        Him will he instruct in the way that he should choose.
13 His soul shall abide in well-being,
        and his offspring shall inherit the land.
14 The friendship[1] of the Lord is for those who fear him,
        and he makes known to them his covenant.
15 My eyes are ever toward the Lord,
        for he will pluck my feet out of the net.

16 Turn to me and be gracious to me,
        for I am lonely and afflicted.
17 The troubles of my heart are enlarged;
        bring me out of my distresses.
18 Consider my affliction and my trouble,
        and forgive all my sins.

19 Consider how many are my foes,
        and with what violent hatred they hate me.
20 Oh, guard my soul, and deliver me!
        Let me not be put to shame, for I take refuge in you.
21 May integrity and uprightness preserve me,
        for I wait for you.

22 Redeem Israel, O God,
        out of all his troubles.

Vindicate me, O Lord: a poet's protestation of innocence [Psalm 26]. Although the poem begins with a prayer that God vindicate or approve the speaker, thereby raising expectations of a lament psalm (vv. 1–2), the entire remainder of the poem is a self-portrait of the speaker's innocence—a confession of his faith in God and desire to serve him. A good analytic approach is to note the specific elements that make up a godly person.

---

[1] Or *The secret counsel*

26

OF DAVID.
Vindicate me, O LORD,
for I have walked in my integrity,
and I have trusted in the LORD without wavering.
2 Prove me, O LORD, and try me;
test my heart and my mind.[1]
3 For your steadfast love is before my eyes,
and I walk in your faithfulness.

4 I do not sit with men of falsehood,
nor do I consort with hypocrites.
5 I hate the assembly of evildoers,
and I will not sit with the wicked.

6 I wash my hands in innocence
and go around your altar, O LORD,
7 proclaiming thanksgiving aloud,
and telling all your wondrous deeds.

8 O LORD, I love the habitation of your house
and the place where your glory dwells.
9 Do not sweep my soul away with sinners,
nor my life with bloodthirsty men,
10 in whose hands are evil devices,
and whose right hands are full of bribes.

11 But as for me, I shall walk in my integrity;
redeem me, and be gracious to me.
12 My foot stands on level ground;
in the great assembly I will bless the LORD.

The LORD is my light and my salvation: what it means to trust in God [Psalm 27]. The key to this psalm is to know that it combines two separate genres—the song of victory (thanksgiving for a battlefield deliverance) and a worship psalm. The opening line declares that the Lord is the speaker's salvation; the rest of the poem can be analyzed on the basis of what this saving relationship means. Trusting in God for one's salvation means that a person is confident in God and free from fear (v. 1); has confidence against enemies (vv. 2–3, 5); longs to worship God and have communion with him (vv. 4, 6–8); prays to God as a lasting refuge (vv. 9–10); relies on God for help against enemies (vv. 11–12); has confidence in God and waits for him (vv. 13–14).

27

OF DAVID.
The LORD is my light and my salvation;
whom shall I fear?
The LORD is the stronghold[2] of my life;
of whom shall I be afraid?

2 When evildoers assail me
to eat up my flesh,

[1] Hebrew test my kidneys and my heart [2] Or refuge

my adversaries and foes,
   it is they who stumble and fall.

3 Though an army encamp against me,
   my heart shall not fear;
  though war arise against me,
   yet[1] I will be confident.

4 One thing have I asked of the Lord,
   that will I seek after:
  that I may dwell in the house of the Lord
   all the days of my life,
  to gaze upon the beauty of the Lord
   and to inquire[2] in his temple.

5 For he will hide me in his shelter
   in the day of trouble;
  he will conceal me under the cover of his tent;
   he will lift me high upon a rock.

6 And now my head shall be lifted up
   above my enemies all around me,
  and I will offer in his tent
   sacrifices with shouts of joy;
  I will sing and make melody to the Lord.

7 Hear, O Lord, when I cry aloud;
   be gracious to me and answer me!
8 You have said, "Seek[3] my face."
  My heart says to you,
   "Your face, Lord, do I seek."[4]
9 Hide not your face from me.
  Turn not your servant away in anger,
   O you who have been my help.
  Cast me not off; forsake me not,
   O God of my salvation!
10 For my father and my mother have forsaken me,
   but the Lord will take me in.

11 Teach me your way, O Lord,
   and lead me on a level path
   because of my enemies.
12 Give me not up to the will of my adversaries;
   for false witnesses have risen against me,
   and they breathe out violence.

13 I believe[5] that I shall look upon the goodness of the Lord
   in the land of the living!
14 Wait for the Lord;

---

[1] Or in this [2] Or meditate [3] The command (seek) is addressed to more than one person [4] The meaning of the Hebrew verse is uncertain [5] Other Hebrew manuscripts Oh! Had I not believed

be strong, and let your heart take courage;
     wait for the LORD!

To you, O LORD, I call [Psalm 28]. The standard motifs of the lament psalm appear as follows: introductory call to God (vv. 1–2); petition for deliverance (v. 3); the "complaint" or definition of the crisis (vv. 3–5); statement of confidence in God, combined with praise of God for answered prayer (vv. 6–8); concluding petition (v. 9). Often psalms that have been individual and personal in focus turn to a communal focus at the end; the concluding verse here is an example. (Earlier psalms in this pattern include 3, 5, 14, and 25.)

28
OF DAVID.
     To you, O LORD, I call;
       my rock, be not deaf to me,
     lest, if you be silent to me,
       I become like those who go down to the pit.
2   Hear the voice of my pleas for mercy,
       when I cry to you for help,
     when I lift up my hands
       toward your most holy sanctuary.[1]

3   Do not drag me off with the wicked,
       with the workers of evil,
     who speak peace with their neighbors
       while evil is in their hearts.
4   Give to them according to their work
       and according to the evil of their deeds;
     give to them according to the work of their hands;
       render them their due reward.
5   Because they do not regard the works of the LORD
       or the work of his hands,
     he will tear them down and build them up no more.

6   Blessed be the LORD!
       For he has heard the voice of my pleas for mercy.
7   The LORD is my strength and my shield;
       in him my heart trusts, and I am helped;
     my heart exults,
       and with my song I give thanks to him.

8   The LORD is the strength of his people;[2]
       he is the saving refuge of his anointed.
9   Oh, save your people and bless your heritage!
       Be their shepherd and carry them forever.

Song of the thunderstorm [Psalm 29]. This is the third nature poem in the Psalter, and it is a parody of Canaanite poems based on the Baal myth. Baal was the Canaanite god of the rainstorm and therefore of fertility and crops. In the myth that grew up around his worship, there was an annual battle between Baal and the god of death and the salt

---

[1] Hebrew *your innermost sanctuary* [2] Some Hebrew manuscripts, Septuagint, Syriac; most Hebrew manuscripts *is their strength*

sea. In the myth, Baal would annually defeat his foe (symbolized by the Mediterranean Sea) and move eastward to land (i.e., the annual rains would come), where he built a palace for himself and was enthroned as god. Psalm 29 is polemical or argumentative, ascribing to God all the power that the pagans typically ascribed to Baal. The motifs are the same as those in the Baal poems: ascription of praise to deity (vv. 1–2); the storm arising in the sea (vv. 3–4); the storm moving onto land (vv. 5–9); enthronement and worship of God by his people (vv. 10–11).

29

A PSALM OF DAVID.
Ascribe to the LORD, O heavenly beings,[1]
ascribe to the LORD glory and strength.
2 Ascribe to the LORD the glory due his name;
worship the LORD in the splendor of holiness.[2]

3 The voice of the LORD is over the waters;
the God of glory thunders,
the LORD, over many waters.
4 The voice of the LORD is powerful;
the voice of the LORD is full of majesty.

5 The voice of the LORD breaks the cedars;
the LORD breaks the cedars of Lebanon.
6 He makes Lebanon to skip like a calf,
and Sirion like a young wild ox.

7 The voice of the LORD flashes forth flames of fire.
8 The voice of the LORD shakes the wilderness;
the LORD shakes the wilderness of Kadesh.

9 The voice of the LORD makes the deer give birth[3]
and strips the forests bare,
and in his temple all cry, "Glory!"

10 The LORD sits enthroned over the flood;
the LORD sits enthroned as king forever.
11 May the LORD give strength to his people!
May the LORD bless[4] his people with peace!

Joy comes with the morning [Psalm 30]. This psalm praises God for rescue from a life-threatening crisis of which we catch only glimpses. The sequence is as follows: the poet's praise of God for deliverance from a life-threatening illness (vv. 1–3); call to the community of believers to praise God (vv. 4–5); recollection of the speaker's ill-founded self-confidence before his crisis (vv. 6–7); petition to God to save the speaker's life (vv. 8–10); praise of God for deliverance (vv. 11–12).

30

A PSALM OF DAVID. A SONG AT THE DEDICATION OF THE TEMPLE.
I will extol you, O LORD, for you have drawn me up
and have not let my foes rejoice over me.
2 O LORD my God, I cried to you for help,

[1] Hebrew sons of God, or sons of might [2] Or in holy attire [3] Revocalization yields makes the oaks to shake [4] Or The LORD will give … The LORD will bless

and you have healed me.
³ O Lord, you have brought up my soul from Sheol;
   you restored me to life from among those who go down to the pit.[1]

⁴ Sing praises to the Lord, O you his saints,
   and give thanks to his holy name.[2]
⁵ For his anger is but for a moment,
   and his favor is for a lifetime.[3]
Weeping may tarry for the night,
   but joy comes with the morning.

⁶ As for me, I said in my prosperity,
   "I shall never be moved."
⁷ By your favor, O Lord,
   you made my mountain stand strong;
you hid your face;
   I was dismayed.

⁸ To you, O Lord, I cry,
   and to the Lord I plead for mercy:
⁹ "What profit is there in my death,[4]
   if I go down to the pit?[5]
Will the dust praise you?
   Will it tell of your faithfulness?
¹⁰ Hear, O Lord, and be merciful to me!
   O Lord, be my helper!"

¹¹ You have turned for me my mourning into dancing;
   you have loosed my sackcloth
   and clothed me with gladness,
¹² that my glory may sing your praise and not be silent.
   O Lord my God, I will give thanks to you forever!

You have set my feet in a broad place: a combined lament and praise psalm [Psalm 31]. Psalm 31 mingles elements of the lament and the praise psalm in approximately equal quantities. The poem unfolds as follows: opening petition that God rescue the speaker (vv. 1–2); praise of God for deliverance from affliction (vv. 3–8); petition for deliverance (vv. 9–10); description of the speaker's crisis (vv. 11–13); statement of trust in God (vv. 14–15); petition for deliverance (vv. 16–18); catalog of God's praiseworthy acts (vv. 19–22); expansion outward to the community of believers in a call to faith (vv. 23–24).

31 To the choirmaster. A Psalm of David.
   In you, O Lord, do I take refuge;
   let me never be put to shame;
   in your righteousness deliver me!
² Incline your ear to me;
   rescue me speedily!

---

[1] Or to life, that I should not go down to the pit [2] Hebrew to the memorial of his holiness (see Exodus 3:15) [3] Or and in his favor is life [4] Hebrew in my blood [5] Or to corruption

Be a rock of refuge for me,
    a strong fortress to save me!

3 For you are my rock and my fortress;
    and for your name's sake you lead me and guide me;
4 you take me out of the net they have hidden for me,
    for you are my refuge.
5 Into your hand I commit my spirit;
    you have redeemed me, O LORD, faithful God.

6 I hate[1] those who pay regard to worthless idols,
    but I trust in the LORD.
7 I will rejoice and be glad in your steadfast love,
    because you have seen my affliction;
    you have known the distress of my soul,
8 and you have not delivered me into the hand of the enemy;
    you have set my feet in a broad place.

9 Be gracious to me, O LORD, for I am in distress;
    my eye is wasted from grief;
    my soul and my body also.
10 For my life is spent with sorrow,
    and my years with sighing;
my strength fails because of my iniquity,
    and my bones waste away.

11 Because of all my adversaries I have become a reproach,
    especially to my neighbors,
and an object of dread to my acquaintances;
    those who see me in the street flee from me.
12 I have been forgotten like one who is dead;
    I have become like a broken vessel.
13 For I hear the whispering of many—
    terror on every side!—
as they scheme together against me,
    as they plot to take my life.

14 But I trust in you, O LORD;
    I say, "You are my God."
15 My times are in your hand;
    rescue me from the hand of my enemies and from my persecutors!
16 Make your face shine on your servant;
    save me in your steadfast love!
17 O LORD, let me not be put to shame,
    for I call upon you;
let the wicked be put to shame;
    let them go silently to Sheol.
18 Let the lying lips be mute,

[1] Masoretic Text; one Hebrew manuscript, Septuagint, Syriac, Jerome *You hate*

which speak insolently against the righteous
   in pride and contempt.

19 Oh, how abundant is your goodness,
   which you have stored up for those who fear you
and worked for those who take refuge in you,
   in the sight of the children of mankind!
20 In the cover of your presence you hide them
   from the plots of men;
you store them in your shelter
   from the strife of tongues.

21 Blessed be the LORD,
   for he has wondrously shown his steadfast love to me
   when I was in a besieged city.
22 I had said in my alarm,[1]
   "I am cut off from your sight."
But you heard the voice of my pleas for mercy
   when I cried to you for help.

23 Love the LORD, all you his saints!
   The LORD preserves the faithful
   but abundantly repays the one who acts in pride.
24 Be strong, and let your heart take courage,
   all you who wait for the LORD!

The supreme psalm of forgiveness [Psalm 32]. This is the second of the traditional seven penitential psalms. It is a partly narrative poem in which the speaker recalls his crisis of guilt stemming from sin. The sequence is as follows: two beatitudes that assert the blessedness of being forgiven by God (vv. 1–2); recollection of guilt (vv. 3–4); recollection of how the speaker's guilt was relieved by God's forgiveness (v. 5); the poet's universalizing on the basis of his own experience that God is merciful to all who call on him (vv. 6–7); instruction by the speaker to his readers regarding God's goodness (vv. 8–11).

32 A MASKIL[2] OF DAVID.
   Blessed is the one whose transgression is forgiven,
   whose sin is covered.
2 Blessed is the man against whom the LORD counts no iniquity,
   and in whose spirit there is no deceit.

3 For when I kept silent, my bones wasted away
   through my groaning all day long.
4 For day and night your hand was heavy upon me;
   my strength was dried up[3] as by the heat of summer.   *Selah*

5 I acknowledged my sin to you,
   and I did not cover my iniquity;

[1] Or *in my haste* [2] Probably a musical or liturgical term [3] Hebrew *my vitality was changed*

I said, "I will confess my transgressions to the LORD,"
and you forgave the iniquity of my sin.   *Selah*

⁶ Therefore let everyone who is godly
offer prayer to you at a time when you may be found;
surely in the rush of great waters,
they shall not reach him.
⁷ You are a hiding place for me;
you preserve me from trouble;
you surround me with shouts of deliverance.   *Selah*

⁸ I will instruct you and teach you in the way you should go;
I will counsel you with my eye upon you.
⁹ Be not like a horse or a mule, without understanding,
which must be curbed with bit and bridle,
or it will not stay near you.

¹⁰ Many are the sorrows of the wicked,
but steadfast love surrounds the one who trusts in the LORD.
¹¹ Be glad in the LORD, and rejoice, O righteous,
and shout for joy, all you upright in heart!

Praise befits the upright [Psalm 33]. Psalm 33 is the prototypical praise psalm—a specimen where we see the essential traits of the genre highlighted. The focus is on two aspects of God's activity—his word and his work (editorialized in v. 4). The conventional motifs of the praise psalm unfold as follows: formal call to praise, including the command to praise, the recipient of the command, and mode of praise to be used (vv. 1–3); praise of God for his character and attributes (vv. 4–5); praise of God for his creation of the earth (vv. 6–9); praise of God for his frustrating the "counsel of the nations," that is, his omnipotence in the events of nations (vv. 10–12); praise of God for his omniscience (vv. 13–15); praise of God for his ability to save or deliver (vv. 16–19, with the inability of human resources in vv. 16–17 serving as a foil to the main assertion); statement of trust in this praiseworthy God (vv. 20–22).

33
Shout for joy in the LORD, O you righteous!
Praise befits the upright.
² Give thanks to the LORD with the lyre;
make melody to him with the harp of ten strings!
³ Sing to him a new song;
play skillfully on the strings, with loud shouts.

⁴ For the word of the LORD is upright,
and all his work is done in faithfulness.
⁵ He loves righteousness and justice;
the earth is full of the steadfast love of the LORD.

⁶ By the word of the LORD the heavens were made,
and by the breath of his mouth all their host.

7   He gathers the waters of the sea as a heap;
     he puts the deeps in storehouses.

8   Let all the earth fear the LORD;
     let all the inhabitants of the world stand in awe of him!
9   For he spoke, and it came to be;
     he commanded, and it stood firm.

10   The LORD brings the counsel of the nations to nothing;
     he frustrates the plans of the peoples.
11   The counsel of the LORD stands forever,
     the plans of his heart to all generations.
12   Blessed is the nation whose God is the LORD,
     the people whom he has chosen as his heritage!

13   The LORD looks down from heaven;
     he sees all the children of man;
14   from where he sits enthroned he looks out
     on all the inhabitants of the earth,
15   he who fashions the hearts of them all
     and observes all their deeds.
16   The king is not saved by his great army;
     a warrior is not delivered by his great strength.
17   The war horse is a false hope for salvation,
     and by its great might it cannot rescue.

18   Behold, the eye of the LORD is on those who fear him,
     on those who hope in his steadfast love,
19   that he may deliver their soul from death
     and keep them alive in famine.

20   Our soul waits for the LORD;
     he is our help and our shield.
21   For our heart is glad in him,
     because we trust in his holy name.
22   Let your steadfast love, O LORD, be upon us,
     even as we hope in you.

Oh, taste and see that the LORD is good [Psalm 34]. The theme of this praise psalm is laid out in the concluding verse: "the LORD redeems the life of his servants" (v. 22). The variations on that theme of praise are as follows: introductory call to praise (vv. 1–3); personal narrative of deliverance (vv. 4–6); a general assertion that God delivers his people (vv. 7–10); a portrait of what it means to be God's servant and therefore receive God's redemption (vv. 11–14); catalog of God's praiseworthy acts on behalf of his servants (vv. 15–21); concluding statement of theme (v. 22). This psalm is an acrostic poem in which the first letters of the verses follow the order of letters in the Hebrew alphabet.

34 [1] Of David, when he changed his behavior before Abimelech, so that he drove him out, and he went away.

1 I will bless the Lord at all times;
   his praise shall continually be in my mouth.
2 My soul makes its boast in the Lord;
   let the humble hear and be glad.
3 Oh, magnify the Lord with me,
   and let us exalt his name together!

4 I sought the Lord, and he answered me
   and delivered me from all my fears.
5 Those who look to him are radiant,
   and their faces shall never be ashamed.
6 This poor man cried, and the Lord heard him
   and saved him out of all his troubles.
7 The angel of the Lord encamps
   around those who fear him, and delivers them.

8 Oh, taste and see that the Lord is good!
   Blessed is the man who takes refuge in him!
9 Oh, fear the Lord, you his saints,
   for those who fear him have no lack!
10 The young lions suffer want and hunger;
   but those who seek the Lord lack no good thing.

11 Come, O children, listen to me;
   I will teach you the fear of the Lord.
12 What man is there who desires life
   and loves many days, that he may see good?
13 Keep your tongue from evil
   and your lips from speaking deceit.
14 Turn away from evil and do good;
   seek peace and pursue it.

15 The eyes of the Lord are toward the righteous
   and his ears toward their cry.
16 The face of the Lord is against those who do evil,
   to cut off the memory of them from the earth.
17 When the righteous cry for help, the Lord hears
   and delivers them out of all their troubles.
18 The Lord is near to the brokenhearted
   and saves the crushed in spirit.

19 Many are the afflictions of the righteous,
   but the Lord delivers him out of them all.
20 He keeps all his bones;
   not one of them is broken.
21 Affliction will slay the wicked,

[1] This psalm is an acrostic poem, each verse beginning with the successive letters of the Hebrew alphabet

and those who hate the righteous will be condemned.
²² The LORD redeems the life of his servants;
   none of those who take refuge in him will be condemned.

O Lord, be not far from me: an expanded lament psalm [Psalm 35]. Psalm 35 is a long lament psalm that employs the standard motifs, as follows: opening cry to God (v. 1); petitions that God will act on the speaker's behalf to deliver him (vv. 2–8); vow to praise God (vv. 9–10); the complaint or definition of the crisis (vv. 11–16); another section of petition (vv. 17–19); further description of the enemies who constitute the speaker's problem (vv. 20–21); further petition (vv. 22–26); statement of confidence in God (v. 27), merging into a vow to praise God (v. 28). All the lament psalms embody a strategy by which the speaker confronts and conquers his crisis. The variations on the main theme (that is, the conventional motifs of the lament psalm) are the specific means by which the speaker accomplishes that twofold task: as the poet invokes God, defines his crisis, petitions God, expresses his confidence in God, and vows to praise God, he is both confronting and conquering his crisis.

35

OF DAVID.

Contend, O LORD, with those who contend with me;
   fight against those who fight against me!
² Take hold of shield and buckler
   and rise for my help!
³ Draw the spear and javelin[1]
   against my pursuers!
Say to my soul,
   "I am your salvation!"

⁴ Let them be put to shame and dishonor
   who seek after my life!
Let them be turned back and disappointed
   who devise evil against me!
⁵ Let them be like chaff before the wind,
   with the angel of the LORD driving them away!
⁶ Let their way be dark and slippery,
   with the angel of the LORD pursuing them!

⁷ For without cause they hid their net for me;
   without cause they dug a pit for my life.[2]
⁸ Let destruction come upon him when he does not know it!
And let the net that he hid ensnare him;
   let him fall into it—to his destruction!

⁹ Then my soul will rejoice in the LORD,
   exulting in his salvation.
¹⁰ All my bones shall say,
   "O LORD, who is like you,
   delivering the poor

---

[1] Or and close the way [2] The word pit is transposed from the preceding line; Hebrew For without cause they hid the pit of their net for me; without cause they dug for my life

from him who is too strong for him,
the poor and needy from him who robs him?"
11 Malicious[1] witnesses rise up;
they ask me of things that I do not know.
12 They repay me evil for good;
my soul is bereft.[2]
13 But I, when they were sick—
I wore sackcloth;
I afflicted myself with fasting;
I prayed with head bowed[3] on my chest.
14   I went about as though I grieved for my friend or my brother;
as one who laments his mother,
I bowed down in mourning.

15 But at my stumbling they rejoiced and gathered;
they gathered together against me;
wretches whom I did not know
tore at me without ceasing;
16 like profane mockers at a feast,[4]
they gnash at me with their teeth.

17 How long, O Lord, will you look on?
Rescue me from their destruction,
my precious life from the lions!
18 I will thank you in the great congregation;
in the mighty throng I will praise you.

19 Let not those rejoice over me
who are wrongfully my foes,
and let not those wink the eye
who hate me without cause.
20 For they do not speak peace,
but against those who are quiet in the land
they devise words of deceit.
21 They open wide their mouths against me;
they say, "Aha, Aha!
Our eyes have seen it!"

22 You have seen, O Lord; be not silent!
O Lord, be not far from me!
23 Awake and rouse yourself for my vindication,
for my cause, my God and my Lord!
24 Vindicate me, O Lord, my God,
according to your righteousness,
and let them not rejoice over me!
25 Let them not say in their hearts,
"Aha, our heart's desire!"
Let them not say, "We have swallowed him up."

[1] Or Violent [2] Hebrew it is bereavement to my soul [3] Or my prayer shall turn back [4] The meaning of the Hebrew phrase is uncertain

²⁶ Let them be put to shame and disappointed altogether
    who rejoice at my calamity!
Let them be clothed with shame and dishonor
    who magnify themselves against me!

²⁷ Let those who delight in my righteousness
    shout for joy and be glad
    and say evermore,
"Great is the LORD,
    who delights in the welfare of his servant!"
²⁸ Then my tongue shall tell of your righteousness
    and of your praise all the day long.

> **Taking refuge in the shadow of God's wings** [Psalm 36]. In the opening section of this combined lament and praise psalm, the poet casts his utterance in the direction of a lament psalm, as he at once paints a portrait of the wicked person (vv. 1–4). Just when we expect a petitionary section, though, the poet gives us the standard content of a praise psalm, as he extols God for his attributes (vv. 5–7) and favor to people (vv. 8–9). That, in turn, modulates back in the direction of a lament when the poet prays that God will rescue the righteous from the hand of the wicked (vv. 10–12).

36

TO THE CHOIRMASTER. OF DAVID, THE SERVANT OF THE LORD.
Transgression speaks to the wicked
    deep in his heart;[1]
there is no fear of God
    before his eyes.
² For he flatters himself in his own eyes
    that his iniquity cannot be found out and hated.
³ The words of his mouth are trouble and deceit;
    he has ceased to act wisely and do good.
⁴ He plots trouble while on his bed;
    he sets himself in a way that is not good;
    he does not reject evil.

⁵ Your steadfast love, O LORD, extends to the heavens,
    your faithfulness to the clouds.
⁶ Your righteousness is like the mountains of God;
    your judgments are like the great deep;
    man and beast you save, O LORD.

⁷ How precious is your steadfast love, O God!
    The children of mankind take refuge in the shadow of your wings.
⁸ They feast on the abundance of your house,
    and you give them drink from the river of your delights.
⁹ For with you is the fountain of life;
    in your light do we see light.

[1] Some Hebrew manuscripts, Syriac, Jerome (compare Septuagint); most Hebrew manuscripts *in my heart*

¹⁰ Oh, continue your steadfast love to those who know you,
        and your righteousness to the upright of heart!
¹¹ Let not the foot of arrogance come upon me,
        nor the hand of the wicked drive me away.
¹² There the evildoers lie fallen;
        they are thrust down, unable to rise.

The mouth of the righteous utters wisdom: a wisdom psalm [Psalm 37]. This long psalm represents a new lyric genre in the ongoing progress of the book of Psalms. It is cast into the form of an extended discourse of instruction. This at once reminds us of OT *wisdom literature, and if we then note the miscellaneous structure of the psalm, we realize that its format is a collection of proverbs, an effect reinforced by the large number of commands in the psalm. The implied situation is that of the lament psalms—the righteous being afflicted by the wicked. Within this situation of combat, the speaker in the poem offers advice for coping with the situation just described. Only a loose outline of topics can be suggested: a command not to be overly concerned about the temporary conduct of the wicked (vv. 1–2); commands regarding how to relate to God in trying situations (vv. 3–7); a return to advice concerning how to respond with self-control toward the wicked, whose prosperity is transient (vv. 8–11); an extended passage that elaborates the theme of how the wicked are ultimately helpless before God (vv. 12–22); as an extension of that, a portrait of the benefits that the righteous experience from serving God (vv. 23–34); a merging of the two main emphases of the psalm, as the blessings of the righteous and the fall of the wicked are mingled in a concluding note of resolution to the poet's meditation (vv. 35–40).

37 ¹ OF DAVID.
    Fret not yourself because of evildoers;
        be not envious of wrongdoers!
² For they will soon fade like the grass
        and wither like the green herb.

³ Trust in the LORD, and do good;
        dwell in the land and befriend faithfulness.²
⁴ Delight yourself in the LORD,
        and he will give you the desires of your heart.

⁵ Commit your way to the LORD;
        trust in him, and he will act.
⁶ He will bring forth your righteousness as the light,
        and your justice as the noonday.

⁷ Be still before the LORD and wait patiently for him;
        fret not yourself over the one who prospers in his way,
        over the man who carries out evil devices!

⁸ Refrain from anger, and forsake wrath!
        Fret not yourself; it tends only to evil.

¹ This psalm is an acrostic poem, each stanza beginning with the successive letters of the Hebrew alphabet ² Or *and feed on faithfulness*, or *and find safe pasture*

⁹ For the evildoers shall be cut off,
      but those who wait for the Lᴏʀᴅ shall inherit the land.

¹⁰ In just a little while, the wicked will be no more;
      though you look carefully at his place, he will not be there.
¹¹ But the meek shall inherit the land
      and delight themselves in abundant peace.

¹² The wicked plots against the righteous
      and gnashes his teeth at him,
¹³ but the Lord laughs at the wicked,
      for he sees that his day is coming.

¹⁴ The wicked draw the sword and bend their bows
      to bring down the poor and needy,
      to slay those whose way is upright;
¹⁵ their sword shall enter their own heart,
      and their bows shall be broken.

¹⁶ Better is the little that the righteous has
      than the abundance of many wicked.
¹⁷ For the arms of the wicked shall be broken,
      but the Lᴏʀᴅ upholds the righteous.

¹⁸ The Lᴏʀᴅ knows the days of the blameless,
      and their heritage will remain forever;
¹⁹ they are not put to shame in evil times;
      in the days of famine they have abundance.

²⁰ But the wicked will perish;
      the enemies of the Lᴏʀᴅ are like the glory of the pastures;
      they vanish—like smoke they vanish away.

²¹ The wicked borrows but does not pay back,
      but the righteous is generous and gives;
²² for those blessed by the Lᴏʀᴅ[1] shall inherit the land,
      but those cursed by him shall be cut off.

²³ The steps of a man are established by the Lᴏʀᴅ,
      when he delights in his way;
²⁴ though he fall, he shall not be cast headlong,
      for the Lᴏʀᴅ upholds his hand.

²⁵ I have been young, and now am old,
      yet I have not seen the righteous forsaken
      or his children begging for bread.
²⁶ He is ever lending generously,
      and his children become a blessing.

²⁷ Turn away from evil and do good;
      so shall you dwell forever.

---

[1] Hebrew *by him*

28 For the Lord loves justice;
    he will not forsake his saints.
They are preserved forever,
    but the children of the wicked shall be cut off.
29 The righteous shall inherit the land
    and dwell upon it forever.

30 The mouth of the righteous utters wisdom,
    and his tongue speaks justice.
31 The law of his God is in his heart;
    his steps do not slip.

32 The wicked watches for the righteous
    and seeks to put him to death.
33 The Lord will not abandon him to his power
    or let him be condemned when he is brought to trial.

34 Wait for the Lord and keep his way,
    and he will exalt you to inherit the land;
    you will look on when the wicked are cut off.

35 I have seen a wicked, ruthless man,
    spreading himself like a green laurel tree.[1]
36 But he passed away,[2] and behold, he was no more;
    though I sought him, he could not be found.

37 Mark the blameless and behold the upright,
    for there is a future for the man of peace.
38 But transgressors shall be altogether destroyed;
    the future of the wicked shall be cut off.

39 The salvation of the righteous is from the Lord;
    he is their stronghold in the time of trouble.
40 The Lord helps them and delivers them;
    he delivers them from the wicked and saves them,
    because they take refuge in him.

I confess my iniquity [Psalm 38]. This is the third of the church's traditional penitential psalms. Penitential psalms are a variation on the conventional lament psalm. In them, the poet defines a dire crisis and asks for God's deliverance. But the twists on the lament form are these: the speaker's antagonist is not an external enemy but himself; the threat is not physical threat or slander but spiritual guilt; the petition is to be delivered not from a threat to life or political oppression but from peril of soul. The outline is as follows: introductory cry to God (v. 1); definition of the crisis, a highly metaphoric portrayal of the effects of guilt, including physical symptoms (vv. 2–10); as an extension of the crisis, a picture of the isolation of the speaker from others, in a manner reminiscent of the more customary lament psalms (vv. 11–14); statement of confidence in God (vv. 15–16); confession of sin (vv. 17–18); a return to the portrait of the speaker's enemies (vv. 19–20); prayer to God for deliverance (vv. 21–22).

---

[1] The identity of this tree is uncertain   [2] Or *But one passed by*

38

A PSALM OF DAVID, FOR THE MEMORIAL OFFERING.
O LORD, rebuke me not in your anger,
   nor discipline me in your wrath!
2 For your arrows have sunk into me,
   and your hand has come down on me.

3 There is no soundness in my flesh
      because of your indignation;
   there is no health in my bones
      because of my sin.
4 For my iniquities have gone over my head;
      like a heavy burden, they are too heavy for me.

5 My wounds stink and fester
      because of my foolishness,
6 I am utterly bowed down and prostrate;
      all the day I go about mourning.
7 For my sides are filled with burning,
      and there is no soundness in my flesh.
8 I am feeble and crushed;
      I groan because of the tumult of my heart.

9 O Lord, all my longing is before you;
      my sighing is not hidden from you.
10 My heart throbs; my strength fails me,
      and the light of my eyes—it also has gone from me.
11 My friends and companions stand aloof from my plague,
      and my nearest kin stand far off.

12 Those who seek my life lay their snares;
      those who seek my hurt speak of ruin
      and meditate treachery all day long.

13 But I am like a deaf man; I do not hear,
      like a mute man who does not open his mouth.
14 I have become like a man who does not hear,
      and in whose mouth are no rebukes.

15 But for you, O LORD, do I wait;
      it is you, O Lord my God, who will answer.
16 For I said, "Only let them not rejoice over me,
      who boast against me when my foot slips!"

17 For I am ready to fall,
      and my pain is ever before me.
18 I confess my iniquity;
      I am sorry for my sin.
19 But my foes are vigorous, they are mighty,
      and many are those who hate me wrongfully.

20   Those who render me evil for good
          accuse me because I follow after good.

21   Do not forsake me, O LORD!
          O my God, be not far from me!
22   Make haste to help me,
          O Lord, my salvation!

Deliver me from all my transgressions [Psalm 39]. Although not normally classified as a penitential psalm, Psalm 39 nonetheless has the essential qualities of that form. The crisis from which the poet seeks relief is God's discipline of him for his sins. The conventions of the lament psalm unfold as follows: an opening description of personal distress (vv. 1–3); petition to God (v. 4); lament about the human plight of mutability (vv. 5–6); statement of confidence in God (v. 7); an extended petitionary section in which the speaker prays that God restore him to divine favor (vv. 8–13).

39

TO THE CHOIRMASTER: TO JEDUTHUN. A PSALM OF DAVID.
          I said, "I will guard my ways,
       that I may not sin with my tongue;
    I will guard my mouth with a muzzle,
       so long as the wicked are in my presence."
2   I was mute and silent;
          I held my peace to no avail,
    and my distress grew worse.
3   My heart became hot within me.
    As I mused, the fire burned;
          then I spoke with my tongue:

4   "O LORD, make me know my end
          and what is the measure of my days;
          let me know how fleeting I am!
5   Behold, you have made my days a few handbreadths,
          and my lifetime is as nothing before you.
    Surely all mankind stands as a mere breath!   *Selah*
6   Surely a man goes about as a shadow!
    Surely for nothing[1] they are in turmoil;
          man heaps up wealth and does not know who will gather!

7   "And now, O Lord, for what do I wait?
          My hope is in you.
8   Deliver me from all my transgressions.
          Do not make me the scorn of the fool!
9   I am mute; I do not open my mouth,
          for it is you who have done it.
10   Remove your stroke from me;
          I am spent by the hostility of your hand.
11   When you discipline a man
          with rebukes for sin,

---

[1] Hebrew *Surely as a breath*

you consume like a moth what is dear to him;
    surely all mankind is a mere breath!   *Selah*

12 "Hear my prayer, O Lᴏʀᴅ,
    and give ear to my cry;
    hold not your peace at my tears!
For I am a sojourner with you,
    a guest, like all my fathers.
13 Look away from me, that I may smile again,
    before I depart and am no more!"

I waited patiently for the Lᴏʀᴅ: a combined praise psalm and lament [Psalm 40].
Psalm 40 begins with a catalog of God's praiseworthy acts, as in the conventional praise psalm (vv. 1–5). In a variation on the praise motif, the speaker then gives a brief narrative of his own delight in obeying God (vv. 6–8) and his testimony to God's goodness in the congregation (vv. 9–10). This is followed by material that fits the lament psalm, as the poet combines petitions to God to deliver him with a description of enemies who threaten him (vv. 11–15). The poem ends in the general vein of the standard vow to praise God combined with a statement of confidence in God (vv. 16–17).

---

40 Tᴏ ᴛʜᴇ ᴄʜᴏɪʀᴍᴀsᴛᴇʀ. A Psᴀʟᴍ ᴏꜰ Dᴀᴠɪᴅ.
    I waited patiently for the Lᴏʀᴅ;
    he inclined to me and heard my cry.
2 He drew me up from the pit of destruction,
    out of the miry bog,
and set my feet upon a rock,
    making my steps secure.
3 He put a new song in my mouth,
    a song of praise to our God.
Many will see and fear,
    and put their trust in the Lᴏʀᴅ.

4 Blessed is the man who makes
    the Lᴏʀᴅ his trust,
who does not turn to the proud,
    to those who go astray after a lie!
5 You have multiplied, O Lᴏʀᴅ my God,
    your wondrous deeds and your thoughts toward us;
    none can compare with you!
I will proclaim and tell of them,
    yet they are more than can be told.

6 In sacrifice and offering you have not delighted,
    but you have given me an open ear.[1]
Burnt offering and sin offering
    you have not required.
7 Then I said, "Behold, I have come;
    in the scroll of the book it is written of me:

---

[1] Hebrew *ears you have dug for me*

8   I delight to do your will, O my God;
       your law is within my heart."

9   I have told the glad news of deliverance[1]
       in the great congregation;
     behold, I have not restrained my lips,
       as you know, O LORD.
10   I have not hidden your deliverance within my heart;
       I have spoken of your faithfulness and your salvation;
     I have not concealed your steadfast love and your faithfulness
       from the great congregation.

11   As for you, O LORD, you will not restrain
       your mercy from me;
     your steadfast love and your faithfulness will
       ever preserve me!
12   For evils have encompassed me
       beyond number;
     my iniquities have overtaken me,
       and I cannot see;
     they are more than the hairs of my head;
       my heart fails me.

13   Be pleased, O LORD, to deliver me!
       O LORD, make haste to help me!
14   Let those be put to shame and disappointed altogether
       who seek to snatch away my life;
     let those be turned back and brought to dishonor
       who delight in my hurt!
15   Let those be appalled because of their shame
       who say to me, "Aha, Aha!"

16   But may all who seek you
       rejoice and be glad in you;
     may those who love your salvation
       say continually, "Great is the LORD!"
17   As for me, I am poor and needy,
       but the Lord takes thought for me.
     You are my help and my deliverer;
       do not delay, O my God!

Lament psalm [Psalm 41]. A standard lament psalm rounds out the first book of Psalms in the Hebrew Psalter. The sequence is as follows: statement of confidence in God's help to those who conduct themselves in a godly manner toward the poor or weak (vv. 1–3); recollection of a time when the poet prayed to God for forgiveness (v. 4); description of the speaker's present suffering at the hands of enemies (vv. 5–9); prayer to God for help (v. 10); praise of God for deliverance (vv. 11–13). By being a *doxology, verse 13 rounds out the first of five sections of the Psalter on a note of closure.

---

[1] Hebrew *righteousness*; also verse 10

41

To the choirmaster. A Psalm of David.
Blessed is the one who considers the poor![1]
In the day of trouble the LORD delivers him;
2   the LORD protects him and keeps him alive;
he is called blessed in the land;
you do not give him up to the will of his enemies.
3   The LORD sustains him on his sickbed;
in his illness you restore him to full health.[2]

4   As for me, I said, "O LORD, be gracious to me;
heal me,[3] for I have sinned against you!"
5   My enemies say of me in malice,
"When will he die, and his name perish?"
6   And when one comes to see me, he utters empty words,
while his heart gathers iniquity;
when he goes out, he tells it abroad.
7   All who hate me whisper together about me;
they imagine the worst for me.[4]

8   They say, "A deadly thing is poured out[5] on him;
he will not rise again from where he lies."
9   Even my close friend in whom I trusted,
who ate my bread, has lifted his heel against me.
10   But you, O LORD, be gracious to me,
and raise me up, that I may repay them!

11   By this I know that you delight in me:
my enemy will not shout in triumph over me.
12   But you have upheld me because of my integrity,
and set me in your presence forever.

13   Blessed be the LORD, the God of Israel,
from everlasting to everlasting!
Amen and Amen.

Let them bring me to your holy hill [Psalms 42–43]. The case is overwhelming that these two poems actually constitute a single worship psalm. This composite poem is composed of three movements of feeling that end with an identical refrain (42:5, 11; 43:5). The content of the poem falls into place if we reconstruct the poem's context from hints that the poet gives us: the speaker is living in exile and is taunted by his pagan neighbors, while he is prevented from carrying out his regular worship of God in the temple in Jerusalem. The poem is thus an expression of sorrow about the speaker's inability to worship God as he wishes (and recalls) and his longing to experience such worship. The sequence is as follows: longing to worship God (42:1–12); sorrow over inability to worship God (42:3); recollection of past worship in the temple (42:4); self-rebuke and the poet's command to himself to hope (42:5); the despair of the speaker as he endures the taunts of his pagan neighbors (42:6–10); refrain in which the poet again rebukes himself for depression and enjoins himself to hope (42:11); prayer to God for deliver-

---

[1] Or weak [2] Hebrew you turn all his bed [3] Hebrew my soul [4] Or they devise evil against me [5] Or has fastened

ance from oppressive taunts and for a restoration of his worship in Jerusalem (43:1–4);
refrain, now repeated for the last time (43:5).

BOOK TWO

42

To the choirmaster. A Maskil[1] of the Sons of Korah.
As a deer pants for flowing streams,
so pants my soul for you, O God.
2 My soul thirsts for God,
for the living God.
When shall I come and appear before God?[2]
3 My tears have been my food
day and night,
while they say to me all the day long,
"Where is your God?"
4 These things I remember,
as I pour out my soul:
how I would go with the throng
and lead them in procession to the house of God
with glad shouts and songs of praise,
a multitude keeping festival.

5 Why are you cast down, O my soul,
and why are you in turmoil within me?
Hope in God; for I shall again praise him,
my salvation[3] 6and my God.

My soul is cast down within me;
therefore I remember you
from the land of Jordan and of Hermon,
from Mount Mizar.
7 Deep calls to deep
at the roar of your waterfalls;
all your breakers and your waves
have gone over me.
8 By day the LORD commands his steadfast love,
and at night his song is with me,
a prayer to the God of my life.
9 I say to God, my rock:
"Why have you forgotten me?
Why do I go mourning
because of the oppression of the enemy?"
10 As with a deadly wound in my bones,
my adversaries taunt me,
while they say to me all the day long,
"Where is your God?"

---

[1] Probably a musical or liturgical term [2] Revocalization yields *and see the face of God* [3] Hebrew *the salvation of my face*; also verse 11 and 43:5

11 Why are you cast down, O my soul,
    and why are you in turmoil within me?
  Hope in God; for I shall again praise him,
    my salvation and my God.

43 Vindicate me, O God, and defend my cause
      against an ungodly people,
  from the deceitful and unjust man
    deliver me!
2 For you are the God in whom I take refuge;
    why have you rejected me?
  Why do I go about mourning
    because of the oppression of the enemy?

3 Send out your light and your truth;
    let them lead me;
  let them bring me to your holy hill
    and to your dwelling!
4 Then I will go to the altar of God,
    to God my exceeding joy,
  and I will praise you with the lyre,
    O God, my God.

5 Why are you cast down, O my soul,
    and why are you in turmoil within me?
  Hope in God; for I shall again praise him,
    my salvation and my God.

Our soul is bowed down to the dust: a communal lament [Psalm 44]. All of the laments thus far in the Psalter have been personal laments, built around the poet's personal crisis. Psalm 44 is a community lament built around a national defeat. The poem begins with a foil that contrasts the past to the present crisis—a recollection of God's past acts of victory on behalf of his covenant nation (vv. 1–8). Verse 9 begins a countermovement in which the poet paints an extended portrait of defeat, a variation on the standard lament convention of describing the present crisis in detail (vv. 9–16). The element of protest is always just below the surface in lament psalms, and here it takes the form of the poet's protest that calamity has come upon his nation even though the nation has remained faithful to God (vv. 17–22). The poem ends with the conventional petition to God to deliver, and it makes use of the sleeping God motif (vv. 23–26).

44 To the choirmaster. A Maskil[1] of the Sons of Korah.
     O God, we have heard with our ears,
  our fathers have told us,
  what deeds you performed in their days,
    in the days of old:
2 you with your own hand drove out the nations,
    but them you planted;
  you afflicted the peoples,

---

[1] Probably a musical or liturgical term

but them you set free;
3   for not by their own sword did they win the land,
      nor did their own arm save them,
    but your right hand and your arm,
      and the light of your face,
      for you delighted in them.

4   You are my King, O God;
      ordain salvation for Jacob!
5   Through you we push down our foes;
      through your name we tread down those who rise up against us.
6   For not in my bow do I trust,
      nor can my sword save me.
7   But you have saved us from our foes
      and have put to shame those who hate us.
8   In God we have boasted continually,
      and we will give thanks to your name forever.   *Selah*

9   But you have rejected us and disgraced us
      and have not gone out with our armies.
10 You have made us turn back from the foe,
      and those who hate us have gotten spoil.
11 You have made us like sheep for slaughter
      and have scattered us among the nations.
12 You have sold your people for a trifle,
      demanding no high price for them.
13 You have made us the taunt of our neighbors,
      the derision and scorn of those around us.
14 You have made us a byword among the nations,
      a laughingstock[1] among the peoples.
15 All day long my disgrace is before me,
      and shame has covered my face
16 at the sound of the taunter and reviler,
      at the sight of the enemy and the avenger.

17 All this has come upon us,
      though we have not forgotten you,
      and we have not been false to your covenant.
18 Our heart has not turned back,
      nor have our steps departed from your way;
19 yet you have broken us in the place of jackals
      and covered us with the shadow of death.
20 If we had forgotten the name of our God
      or spread out our hands to a foreign god,
21 would not God discover this?
      For he knows the secrets of the heart.
22 Yet for your sake we are killed all the day long;
      we are regarded as sheep to be slaughtered.

---

[1] Hebrew *a shaking of the head*

23   Awake! Why are you sleeping, O Lord?
       Rouse yourself! Do not reject us forever!
24   Why do you hide your face?
       Why do you forget our affliction and oppression?
25   For our soul is bowed down to the dust;
       our belly clings to the ground.
26   Rise up; come to our help!
       Redeem us for the sake of your steadfast love!

With joy and gladness they are led along: celebration of a royal wedding [Psalm 45].
Psalm 45 springs a pleasant surprise on us by being a wedding poem, known in literary terms as an *epithalamion. We infer that the occasion is a royal wedding (of which
there were many in ancient courts, we need to remind ourselves). An epithalamion was
ordinarily written by a court poet, and this is what we find here. The fact that there are
possible messianic overtones should not lead us to minimize the primary human level.
Hyperbole abounds in love poetry, so we should not be quick to turn statements in the
direction of messianic prophecy simply because they exceed the literal facts of a human
wedding. The poem unfolds as follows: the court poet generates a sense of anticipation
regarding the exalted sentiments that will follow (v. 1); praise of the kingly bridegroom
(vv. 2–9); praise of the chosen bride (vv. 10–17). An epithalamion always celebrates
the wedding day, and not simply the institution of marriage, so in this poem we catch
glimpses of the exalted splendor of this particular royal wedding.

45   To the choirmaster: according to Lilies. A Maskil[1] of the Sons of Korah;
       a love song.

1   My heart overflows with a pleasing theme;
       I address my verses to the king;
       my tongue is like the pen of a ready scribe.

2   You are the most handsome of the sons of men;
       grace is poured upon your lips;
       therefore God has blessed you forever.
3   Gird your sword on your thigh, O mighty one,
       in your splendor and majesty!

4   In your majesty ride out victoriously
       for the cause of truth and meekness and righteousness;
       let your right hand teach you awesome deeds!
5   Your arrows are sharp
       in the heart of the king's enemies;
       the peoples fall under you.

6   Your throne, O God, is forever and ever.
       The scepter of your kingdom is a scepter of uprightness;
7   you have loved righteousness and hated wickedness.
       Therefore God, your God, has anointed you
       with the oil of gladness beyond your companions;

---

[1] Probably a musical or liturgical term

8   your robes are all fragrant with myrrh and aloes and cassia.
     From ivory palaces stringed instruments make you glad;
9   daughters of kings are among your ladies of honor;
       at your right hand stands the queen in gold of Ophir.

10   Hear, O daughter, and consider, and incline your ear:
       forget your people and your father's house,
11   and the king will desire your beauty.
     Since he is your lord, bow to him.
12   The people[1] of Tyre will seek your favor with gifts,
       the richest of the people.[2]

13   All glorious is the princess in her chamber, with robes interwoven with gold.
14   In many-colored robes she is led to the king,
       with her virgin companions following behind her.
15   With joy and gladness they are led along
       as they enter the palace of the king.

16   In place of your fathers shall be your sons;
       you will make them princes in all the earth.
17   I will cause your name to be remembered in all generations;
       therefore nations will praise you forever and ever.

A mighty fortress [Psalm 46]. This famous praise psalm falls neatly into three sections. The main theme is articulated three times (vv. 1, 7, 11) and consists of the certainty of God's presence in troubling times. The central motif is a catalog of God's acts of protection. The three main movements are as follows: God's presence amid natural disaster (vv. 1–3); God's miraculous protection of his holy city and, by metaphoric extension, his protection of his people in all times and places (vv. 4–7); God's final assertion of his authority over warring nations (vv. 8–11). The imagery is continuously evocative and emotional. The poem instills the very calm that the poet asserts. An eschatological, end-times interpretation of the poem is appropriate, not only because of the terminal imagery in verses 8–9 but also in view of the natural upheaval in verses 2–3, reminiscent of the imagery of cataclysmic disruption of nature in the eschatological visions of the NT.

46 To the choirmaster. Of the Sons of Korah. According to Alamoth.[3] A Song.
     God is our refuge and strength,
       a very present[4] help in trouble.
2   Therefore we will not fear though the earth gives way,
       though the mountains be moved into the heart of the sea,
3   though its waters roar and foam,
       though the mountains tremble at its swelling.   *Selah*

4   There is a river whose streams make glad the city of God,
       the holy habitation of the Most High.
5   God is in the midst of her; she shall not be moved;
       God will help her when morning dawns.

[1] Hebrew *daughter* [2] Or *The daughter of Tyre is here with gifts, the richest of people seek your favor* [3] Probably a musical or liturgical term [4] Or *well proved*

⁶   The nations rage, the kingdoms totter;
    he utters his voice, the earth melts.
⁷   The LORD of hosts is with us;
    the God of Jacob is our fortress.   *Selah*

⁸   Come, behold the works of the LORD,
    how he has brought desolations on the earth.
⁹   He makes wars cease to the end of the earth;
    he breaks the bow and shatters the spear;
    he burns the chariots with fire.
¹⁰ "Be still, and know that I am God.
    I will be exalted among the nations,
    I will be exalted in the earth!"
¹¹ The LORD of hosts is with us;
    the God of Jacob is our fortress.   *Selah*

God sits on his holy throne: a praise psalm [Psalm 47]. Psalm 47 praises God as King, and the statement that he "has gone up with a shout" (v. 5) is similar to phrases in other praise psalms, requiring no speculation about annual enthronement rituals for God. The sequence is as follows: call to praise (v. 1), repeated in verses 6–7; catalog of God's praiseworthy acts of triumph over the nations of the earth (vv. 2–5); assertions that God reigns over the nations of the earth (vv. 7–9). The underlying narrative is God's conquest (vv. 1–5) followed by his subsequent rule (vv. 6–9).

47

TO THE CHOIRMASTER. A PSALM OF THE SONS OF KORAH.
    Clap your hands, all peoples!
    Shout to God with loud songs of joy!
²   For the LORD, the Most High, is to be feared,
    a great king over all the earth.
³   He subdued peoples under us,
    and nations under our feet.
⁴   He chose our heritage for us,
    the pride of Jacob whom he loves.   *Selah*

⁵   God has gone up with a shout,
    the LORD with the sound of a trumpet.
⁶   Sing praises to God, sing praises!
    Sing praises to our King, sing praises!
⁷   For God is the King of all the earth;
    sing praises with a psalm![1]

⁸   God reigns over the nations;
    God sits on his holy throne.
⁹   The princes of the peoples gather
    as the people of the God of Abraham.
    For the shields of the earth belong to God;
    he is highly exalted!

---

[1] Hebrew *maskil*

Let Mount Zion be glad: a worship psalm [Psalm 48]. Because of the specific references to worshiping God in the temple, it is plausible to place this poem in the category
of worship psalm, also called song of Zion. In the first three verses, the pilgrim catches
glimpses of Jerusalem and the temple and is led to exclaim about the privileged nature
of the site where God's visible glory dwells in the temple. Verses 4–6 narrate a metaphoric divine protection of God's holy city. Verses 8–11 branch out from that narrative
to general feelings of praise as the speaker worships in Jerusalem. In the concluding
movement, the speaker either addresses himself or apostrophizes his fellow worshipers
to luxuriate in the physical details of worshiping God in the temple (vv. 12–14).

48

A Song. A Psalm of the Sons of Korah.
Great is the LORD and greatly to be praised
   in the city of our God!
His holy mountain, ²beautiful in elevation,
   is the joy of all the earth,
Mount Zion, in the far north,
   the city of the great King.
³ Within her citadels God
   has made himself known as a fortress.

⁴ For behold, the kings assembled;
   they came on together.
⁵ As soon as they saw it, they were astounded;
   they were in panic; they took to flight.
⁶ Trembling took hold of them there,
   anguish as of a woman in labor.
⁷ By the east wind you shattered
   the ships of Tarshish.
⁸ As we have heard, so have we seen
   in the city of the LORD of hosts,
   in the city of our God,
   which God will establish forever.   *Selah*

⁹ We have thought on your steadfast love, O God,
   in the midst of your temple.
¹⁰ As your name, O God,
   so your praise reaches to the ends of the earth.
   Your right hand is filled with righteousness.
¹¹   Let Mount Zion be glad!
Let the daughters of Judah rejoice
   because of your judgments!

¹² Walk about Zion, go around her,
   number her towers,
¹³ consider well her ramparts,
   go through her citadels,
that you may tell the next generation
¹⁴   that this is God,

our God forever and ever.
   He will guide us forever.[1]

My mouth shall speak wisdom: a poetic sermon on what money can't buy [Psalm 49]. The rhetorical format of this poem is that of the admonition to a nation or congregation. Everything in the poem relates to this rhetorical situation. The speaker begins with a summons to listen, as is common in OT wisdom literature (vv. 1–3). The main subject of the poetic oration is the wealthy, and the interpretive slant is highlighted in a refrain that is repeated almost verbatim (vv. 12, 20): wealth is fleeting, and all people are mortal (including the wealthy), so it is futile to trust in riches for salvation. The poem has a strongly repetitive structure, as the speaker keeps repeating the ideas that money is fleeting, that people cannot save their lives through wealth, that people who trust in money to save them are therefore foolish, and that God alone can save a person.

49

To the choirmaster. A Psalm of the Sons of Korah.
   Hear this, all peoples!
Give ear, all inhabitants of the world,
² both low and high,
      rich and poor together!
³ My mouth shall speak wisdom;
      the meditation of my heart shall be understanding.
⁴ I will incline my ear to a proverb;
      I will solve my riddle to the music of the lyre.

⁵ Why should I fear in times of trouble,
      when the iniquity of those who cheat me surrounds me,
⁶ those who trust in their wealth
      and boast of the abundance of their riches?
⁷ Truly no man can ransom another,
      or give to God the price of his life,
⁸ for the ransom of their life is costly
      and can never suffice,
⁹ that he should live on forever
      and never see the pit.

¹⁰ For he sees that even the wise die;
      the fool and the stupid alike must perish
      and leave their wealth to others.
¹¹ Their graves are their homes forever,[2]
      their dwelling places to all generations,
      though they called lands by their own names.
¹² Man in his pomp will not remain;
      he is like the beasts that perish.

¹³ This is the path of those who have foolish confidence;
      yet after them people approve of their boasts.[3]   Selah
¹⁴ Like sheep they are appointed for Sheol;

---

[1] Septuagint; another reading is (compare Jerome, Syriac) *He will guide us beyond death* [2] Septuagint, Syriac, Targum; Hebrew *Their inward thought was that their homes were forever* [3] Or *and of those after them who approve of their boasts*

death shall be their shepherd,
and the upright shall rule over them in the morning.
Their form shall be consumed in Sheol, with no place to dwell.

15 But God will ransom my soul from the power of Sheol,
for he will receive me.   *Selah*

16 Be not afraid when a man becomes rich,
when the glory of his house increases.
17 For when he dies he will carry nothing away;
his glory will not go down after him.
18 For though, while he lives, he counts himself blessed
—and though you get praise when you do well for yourself—
19 his soul will go to the generation of his fathers,
who will never again see light.
20 Man in his pomp yet without understanding is like the beasts that perish.

God himself is judge [Psalm 50]. Whereas in Psalm 49 a priestly or prophetic representative of God admonished the congregation, in Psalm 50 God himself is pictured as uttering the exhortation (vv. 1–6). The first theme in God's rebuke to his people is an assertion that people have been wrong to think that God somehow needed their sacrifices to sustain himself; that is a pagan way of thinking (vv. 7–13). This is followed by the antidote to this wrong way of viewing sacrifices; the antidote consists of viewing sacrifices spiritually as an expression of thanksgiving (vv. 14–15). Whereas the preceding rebuke had been directed against God's covenant people (v. 7), the second rebuke is directed against "the wicked" and focuses on people's living in blatant disobedience to God's moral commands (vv. 16–21). God's exhortation ends with a warning to the wicked and a promise of salvation to people who live rightly before him (vv. 22–23).

50

A Psalm of Asaph.
The Mighty One, God the Lord,
speaks and summons the earth
from the rising of the sun to its setting.
2 Out of Zion, the perfection of beauty,
God shines forth.

3 Our God comes; he does not keep silence;[1]
before him is a devouring fire,
around him a mighty tempest.
4 He calls to the heavens above
and to the earth, that he may judge his people:
5 "Gather to me my faithful ones,
who made a covenant with me by sacrifice!"
6 The heavens declare his righteousness,
for God himself is judge!   *Selah*

7 "Hear, O my people, and I will speak;
O Israel, I will testify against you.
I am God, your God.

---

[1] Or *May our God come, and not keep silence*

8   Not for your sacrifices do I rebuke you;
      your burnt offerings are continually before me.
9   I will not accept a bull from your house
      or goats from your folds.
10 For every beast of the forest is mine,
      the cattle on a thousand hills.
11 I know all the birds of the hills,
      and all that moves in the field is mine.

12 "If I were hungry, I would not tell you,
      for the world and its fullness are mine.
13 Do I eat the flesh of bulls
      or drink the blood of goats?
14 Offer to God a sacrifice of thanksgiving,[1]
      and perform your vows to the Most High,
15 and call upon me in the day of trouble;
      I will deliver you, and you shall glorify me."

16 But to the wicked God says:
      "What right have you to recite my statutes
      or take my covenant on your lips?
17 For you hate discipline,
      and you cast my words behind you.
18 If you see a thief, you are pleased with him,
      and you keep company with adulterers.

19 "You give your mouth free rein for evil,
      and your tongue frames deceit.
20 You sit and speak against your brother;
      you slander your own mother's son.
21 These things you have done, and I have been silent;
      you thought that I[2] was one like yourself.
      But now I rebuke you and lay the charge before you.

22 "Mark this, then, you who forget God,
      lest I tear you apart, and there be none to deliver!
23 The one who offers thanksgiving as his sacrifice glorifies me;
      to one who orders his way rightly
      I will show the salvation of God!"

Create in me a clean heart, O God: the sinner's prayer [Psalm 51]. This is the most famous of the seven penitential psalms and is a classic on the subject of sin, guilt, confession, and forgiveness. According to the headnote, the occasion of the poem is David's conviction of sin after the prophet Nathan had confronted him regarding David's adultery with Bathsheba and murder of her husband (2 Sam. 12:1–15). Within this penitential format, the poem follows the conventions of the traditional lament psalm. The crisis from which the speaker requires deliverance is inner and spiritual, namely, his guilt before God (vv. 1–6). This is followed by a moving section of petition for forgiveness (vv. 7–12). The conventional vow to praise God is phrased partly as a petition that God

---

[1] Or *Make thanksgiving your sacrifice to God* [2] Or *that the I AM*

will enable the speaker to praise him appropriately and even teach others to praise him
(vv. 13–15), followed by an unexpected piece of reflection regarding how the appropriate sacrifice is a contrite heart, not merely external offerings (vv. 16–17). The last two
verses (vv. 18–19) are an addendum in which the poet shows that even though he had
earlier asserted the superiority of inner contriteness over external sacrifices (vv. 16–17),
he knows that God's ideal is "right sacrifices" at the divinely appointed place of worship,
combining a contrite heart and the prescribed sacrifices administered by priests.

51

To the choirmaster. A Psalm of David, when Nathan the prophet went to him,
after he had gone in to Bathsheba.

1   Have mercy on me,[1] O God,
        according to your steadfast love;
    according to your abundant mercy
        blot out my transgressions.
2   Wash me thoroughly from my iniquity,
        and cleanse me from my sin!

3   For I know my transgressions,
        and my sin is ever before me.
4   Against you, you only, have I sinned
        and done what is evil in your sight,
    so that you may be justified in your words
        and blameless in your judgment.
5   Behold, I was brought forth in iniquity,
        and in sin did my mother conceive me.
6   Behold, you delight in truth in the inward being,
        and you teach me wisdom in the secret heart.

7   Purge me with hyssop, and I shall be clean;
        wash me, and I shall be whiter than snow.
8   Let me hear joy and gladness;
        let the bones that you have broken rejoice.
9   Hide your face from my sins,
        and blot out all my iniquities.
10 Create in me a clean heart, O God,
        and renew a right[2] spirit within me.
11 Cast me not away from your presence,
        and take not your Holy Spirit from me.
12 Restore to me the joy of your salvation,
        and uphold me with a willing spirit.

13 Then I will teach transgressors your ways,
        and sinners will return to you.
14 Deliver me from bloodguiltiness, O God,
        O God of my salvation,
        and my tongue will sing aloud of your righteousness.
15 O Lord, open my lips,

[1] Or Be gracious to me [2] Or steadfast

and my mouth will declare your praise.
¹⁶ For you will not delight in sacrifice, or I would give it;
   you will not be pleased with a burnt offering.
¹⁷ The sacrifices of God are a broken spirit;
   a broken and contrite heart, O God, you will not despise.

¹⁸ Do good to Zion in your good pleasure;
   build up the walls of Jerusalem;
¹⁹ then will you delight in right sacrifices,
   in burnt offerings and whole burnt offerings;
   then bulls will be offered on your altar.

I trust in the steadfast love of God: a modified lament psalm [Psalm 52]. Implicitly underlying this psalm is the standard situation of the lament psalm: the speaker is besieged by hostile people. But the usual motifs appear in somewhat unconventional form. At the outset, the poet addresses his adversaries directly as part of a statement of confidence in God (v. 1). This is followed by the conventional portrait of the evil oppressors, addressed, however, directly to the oppressors rather than to God (vv. 2–5). The subsequent statement of confidence pictures the anticipated taunt of the righteous over the speaker's oppressors (vv. 6–7). In another variation on a conventional motif, the vow to praise God contrasts the destruction of the wealthy who trusted in their riches (the taunt in v. 7) with the eternal nature of the rewards that righteous persons will receive because they trusted in God (vv. 8–9).

52

TO THE CHOIRMASTER. A MASKIL[1] OF DAVID, WHEN DOEG, THE EDOMITE, CAME AND TOLD SAUL, "DAVID HAS COME TO THE HOUSE OF AHIMELECH."

¹ Why do you boast of evil, O mighty man?
   The steadfast love of God endures all the day.
² Your tongue plots destruction,
   like a sharp razor, you worker of deceit.
³ You love evil more than good,
   and lying more than speaking what is right.   *Selah*
⁴ You love all words that devour,
   O deceitful tongue.

⁵ But God will break you down forever;
   he will snatch and tear you from your tent;
   he will uproot you from the land of the living.   *Selah*
⁶ The righteous shall see and fear,
   and shall laugh at him, saying,
⁷ "See the man who would not make
   God his refuge,
   but trusted in the abundance of his riches
   and sought refuge in his own destruction!"[2]

⁸ But I am like a green olive tree
   in the house of God.

---

¹ Probably a musical or liturgical term ² Or *in his work of destruction*

I trust in the steadfast love of God
  forever and ever.
9 I will thank you forever,
    because you have done it.
  I will wait for your name, for it is good,
    in the presence of the godly.

There is none who does good: a satiric psalm [Psalm 53]. Psalm 53 is almost identical to Psalm 14. The basic stance is satiric, as the poem exposes the folly and sinfulness of a certain type of person. The outline is as follows; a very brief portrait of the fool as someone who says that there is no God (v. 1a); a put-down of corrupt humanity (vv. 1b–4); a scornful repudiation of the supposed power of the wicked against the righteous (v. 5); statement of longing that God would save his people from the spiritual and moral morass that the poem has described (v. 6).

53

To the choirmaster: according to Mahalath. A Maskil[1] of David.
  The fool says in his heart, "There is no God."
  They are corrupt, doing abominable iniquity;
    there is none who does good.

2 God looks down from heaven
    on the children of man
  to see if there are any who understand,[2]
    who seek after God.

3 They have all fallen away;
    together they have become corrupt;
  there is none who does good,
    not even one.

4 Have those who work evil no knowledge,
    who eat up my people as they eat bread,
    and do not call upon God?

5 There they are, in great terror,
    where there is no terror!
  For God scatters the bones of him who encamps against you;
    you put them to shame, for God has rejected them.

6 Oh, that salvation for Israel would come out of Zion!
    When God restores the fortunes of his people,
    let Jacob rejoice, let Israel be glad.

Behold, God is my helper [Psalm 54]. This is one of the briefest lament psalms. It has all the conventional motifs, though: combined cry to God and petition for deliverance (vv. 1–2); description of the crisis (v. 3); statement of confidence in God (vv. 4–5); vow to praise God (vv. 6–7).

[1] Probably musical or liturgical terms [2] Or *who act wisely*

54
To the choirmaster: with stringed instruments. A Maskil[1] of David, when the Ziphites went and told Saul, "Is not David hiding among us?"

1 O God, save me by your name,
    and vindicate me by your might.
2 O God, hear my prayer;
    give ear to the words of my mouth.

3 For strangers[2] have risen against me;
    ruthless men seek my life;
    they do not set God before themselves.   *Selah*

4 Behold, God is my helper;
    the Lord is the upholder of my life.
5 He will return the evil to my enemies;
    in your faithfulness put an end to them.

6 With a freewill offering I will sacrifice to you;
    I will give thanks to your name, O Lord, for it is good.
7 For he has delivered me from every trouble,
    and my eye has looked in triumph on my enemies.

A lament of someone betrayed [Psalm 55]. Using the standard motifs of the lament psalm, the speaker in this poem responds to the specific crisis of betrayal by a friend. The sequence is as follows: introductory cry to God to hear (vv. 1–3a); description of the crisis (vv. 3b–8); brief petition to God to help (v. 9); further description of the oppressive situation that requires a solution (vv. 10–14); brief petition for redress (v. 15); statement of confidence in God (vv. 16–19); brief return to the treason under which the speaker chafes (vv. 20–21); statement of confidence in God (vv. 22–23).

55
To the choirmaster: with stringed instruments. A Maskil[3] of David.
    Give ear to my prayer, O God,
    and hide not yourself from my plea for mercy!
2 Attend to me, and answer me;
    I am restless in my complaint and I moan,
3 because of the noise of the enemy,
    because of the oppression of the wicked.
For they drop trouble upon me,
    and in anger they bear a grudge against me.

4 My heart is in anguish within me;
    the terrors of death have fallen upon me.
5 Fear and trembling come upon me,
    and horror overwhelms me.
6 And I say, "Oh, that I had wings like a dove!
    I would fly away and be at rest;
7 yes, I would wander far away;
    I would lodge in the wilderness;   *Selah*

---

[1] Probably a musical or liturgical term [2] Some Hebrew manuscripts and Targum *insolent men* (compare Psalm 86:14) [3] Probably a musical or liturgical term

8   I would hurry to find a shelter
        from the raging wind and tempest."

9   Destroy, O Lord, divide their tongues;
        for I see violence and strife in the city.
10 Day and night they go around it
        on its walls,
    and iniquity and trouble are within it;
11   ruin is in its midst;
    oppression and fraud
        do not depart from its marketplace.

12 For it is not an enemy who taunts me—
        then I could bear it;
    it is not an adversary who deals insolently with me—
        then I could hide from him.
13 But it is you, a man, my equal,
        my companion, my familiar friend.
14 We used to take sweet counsel together;
        within God's house we walked in the throng.
15 Let death steal over them;
        let them go down to Sheol alive;
        for evil is in their dwelling place and in their heart.

16 But I call to God,
        and the LORD will save me.
17 Evening and morning and at noon
        I utter my complaint and moan,
        and he hears my voice.
18 He redeems my soul in safety
        from the battle that I wage,
        for many are arrayed against me.
19 God will give ear and humble them,
        he who is enthroned from of old,   *Selah*
    because they do not change
        and do not fear God.

20 My companion[1] stretched out his hand against his friends;
        he violated his covenant.
21 His speech was smooth as butter,
        yet war was in his heart;
    his words were softer than oil,
        yet they were drawn swords.

22 Cast your burden on the LORD,
        and he will sustain you;
    he will never permit
        the righteous to be moved.

[1] Hebrew *He*

²³ But you, O God, will cast them down
     into the pit of destruction;
  men of blood and treachery
     shall not live out half their days.
  But I will trust in you.

What can man do to me? [Psalm 56]. This lament psalm unfolds as follows: opening cry to God combined with petition to God to help (vv. 1–2); statement of confidence
in God (vv. 3–4); definition of the crisis (vv. 5–7); statement of confidence in God (vv.
6–11); vow to praise God (vv. 12–13). The inner logic of all lament psalms is that the
speaker confronts and conquers his crisis by naming it, by praying to God to act, and by
expressing trust in God.

56

To THE CHOIRMASTER: ACCORDING TO THE DOVE ON FAR-OFF TEREBINTHS. A MIKTAM[1]
OF DAVID, WHEN THE PHILISTINES SEIZED HIM IN GATH.

¹ Be gracious to me, O God, for man tramples on me;
     all day long an attacker oppresses me;
² my enemies trample on me all day long,
     for many attack me proudly.
³ When I am afraid,
     I put my trust in you.
⁴ In God, whose word I praise,
     in God I trust; I shall not be afraid.
     What can flesh do to me?

⁵ All day long they injure my cause;[2]
     all their thoughts are against me for evil.
⁶ They stir up strife, they lurk;
     they watch my steps,
     as they have waited for my life.
⁷ For their crime will they escape?
     In wrath cast down the peoples, O God!

⁸ You have kept count of my tossings;[3]
     put my tears in your bottle.
     Are they not in your book?
⁹ Then my enemies will turn back
     in the day when I call.
     This I know, that[4] God is for me.
¹⁰ In God, whose word I praise,
     in the LORD, whose word I praise,
¹¹ in God I trust; I shall not be afraid.
     What can man do to me?

¹² I must perform my vows to you, O God;
     I will render thank offerings to you.
¹³ For you have delivered my soul from death,

---

¹ Probably a musical or liturgical term ² Or *they twist my words* ³ Or *wanderings* ⁴ Or *because*

yes, my feet from falling,
that I may walk before God
in the light of life.

Till the storms of destruction pass by [Psalm 57]. The conventional lament motifs appear in the following form: introductory cry to God (vv. 1–2); statement of confidence in God (v. 3); definition of the crisis (v. 4); petition (a refrain appearing in vv. 5 and 11); definition of the crisis (v. 6); vow to praise God (vv. 7–10). Lament psalms are minitheodicies: they find a solution to the problem of evil by asserting that God will judge evildoers and rescue their victims.

57
TO THE CHOIRMASTER: ACCORDING TO DO NOT DESTROY. A MIKTAM[1] OF DAVID, WHEN HE FLED FROM SAUL, IN THE CAVE.

1   Be merciful to me, O God, be merciful to me,
      for in you my soul takes refuge;
   in the shadow of your wings I will take refuge,
      till the storms of destruction pass by.
2   I cry out to God Most High,
      to God who fulfills his purpose for me.
3   He will send from heaven and save me;
      he will put to shame him who tramples on me.   *Selah*
   God will send out his steadfast love and his faithfulness!

4   My soul is in the midst of lions;
      I lie down amid fiery beasts—
   the children of man, whose teeth are spears and arrows,
      whose tongues are sharp swords.

5   Be exalted, O God, above the heavens!
      Let your glory be over all the earth!

6   They set a net for my steps;
      my soul was bowed down.
   They dug a pit in my way,
      but they have fallen into it themselves.   *Selah*
7   My heart is steadfast, O God,
      my heart is steadfast!
   I will sing and make melody!
8   Awake, my glory![2]
   Awake, O harp and lyre!
      I will awake the dawn!
9   I will give thanks to you, O Lord, among the peoples;
      I will sing praises to you among the nations.
10 For your steadfast love is great to the heavens,
      your faithfulness to the clouds.

11 Be exalted, O God, above the heavens!
      Let your glory be over all the earth!

[1] Probably a musical or liturgical term [2] Or *my whole being*

O God, break the teeth in their mouths [Psalm 58]. The general drift of this satiric psalm is to disparage the wicked and wish them ill. The poem opens with a taunt addressed directly to the powerful wicked of the earth, using the technique of apostrophe (vv. 1–2). In an extension of this satiric attack, verses 3–5 assert the utter depravity of the people addressed earlier. Taken one step further, the satiric portrait becomes a prayer to God to destroy the wicked (vv. 6–9). The antidote or satiric norm is the righteous pictured in verses 10–11.

58

To the choirmaster: according to Do Not Destroy. A Miktam[1] of David.

Do you indeed decree what is right, you gods?[2]
   Do you judge the children of man uprightly?
² No, in your hearts you devise wrongs;
   your hands deal out violence on earth.

³ The wicked are estranged from the womb;
   they go astray from birth, speaking lies.
⁴ They have venom like the venom of a serpent,
   like the deaf adder that stops its ear,
⁵ so that it does not hear the voice of charmers
   or of the cunning enchanter.

⁶ O God, break the teeth in their mouths;
   tear out the fangs of the young lions, O Lord!
⁷ Let them vanish like water that runs away;
   when he aims his arrows, let them be blunted.
⁸ Let them be like the snail that dissolves into slime,
   like the stillborn child who never sees the sun.
⁹ Sooner than your pots can feel the heat of thorns,
   whether green or ablaze, may he sweep them away![3]

¹⁰ The righteous will rejoice when he sees the vengeance;
   he will bathe his feet in the blood of the wicked.
¹¹ Mankind will say, "Surely there is a reward for the righteous;
   surely there is a God who judges on earth."

Deliver me from my enemies, O my God [Psalm 59]. The occasion underlying this lament psalm is stated in the headnote: David is surrounded in his house by Saul's soldiers. The standard motifs weave in and out of the poem: introductory cry to God to deliver (vv. 1–2); definition of the crisis (vv. 3–4a); petition to God to help (vv. 4b–5); further definition of the crisis (vv. 6–7); statement of confidence in God (vv. 8–10); petitions for deliverance from enemies (vv. 11–13); further description of the crisis that needs a solution (vv. 14–15); vow to praise God (vv. 16–17).

59

To the choirmaster: according to Do Not Destroy. A Miktam[4] of David, when Saul sent men to watch his house in order to kill him.

¹ Deliver me from my enemies, O my God;
   protect me from those who rise up against me;

---

[1] Probably a musical or liturgical term [2] Or *mighty lords* (by revocalization; Hebrew *in silence*) [3] The meaning of the Hebrew verse is uncertain [4] Probably a musical or liturgical term

²   deliver me from those who work evil,
      and save me from bloodthirsty men.

³   For behold, they lie in wait for my life;
      fierce men stir up strife against me.
    For no transgression or sin of mine, O LORD,
⁴   for no fault of mine, they run and make ready.
    Awake, come to meet me, and see!
⁵   You, LORD God of hosts, are God of Israel.
    Rouse yourself to punish all the nations;
      spare none of those who treacherously plot evil.   *Selah*

⁶   Each evening they come back,
      howling like dogs
      and prowling about the city.
⁷   There they are, bellowing with their mouths
      with swords in their lips—
      for "Who," they think,¹ "will hear us?"

⁸   But you, O LORD, laugh at them;
      you hold all the nations in derision.
⁹   O my Strength, I will watch for you,
      for you, O God, are my fortress.
¹⁰ My God in his steadfast love² will meet me;
      God will let me look in triumph on my enemies.

¹¹ Kill them not, lest my people forget;
      make them totter³ by your power and bring them down,
      O Lord, our shield!
¹² For the sin of their mouths, the words of their lips,
      let them be trapped in their pride.
    For the cursing and lies that they utter,
¹³   consume them in wrath;
      consume them till they are no more,
    that they may know that God rules over Jacob
      to the ends of the earth.   *Selah*

¹⁴ Each evening they come back,
      howling like dogs
      and prowling about the city.
¹⁵ They wander about for food
      and growl if they do not get their fill.

¹⁶ But I will sing of your strength;
      I will sing aloud of your steadfast love in the morning.
    For you have been to me a fortress
      and a refuge in the day of my distress.
¹⁷ O my Strength, I will sing praises to you,

---

¹ Hebrew lacks *they think* ² Or *The God who shows me steadfast love* ³ Or *wander*

for you, O God, are my fortress,
the God who shows me steadfast love.

Lament of the defeated [Psalm 60]. This communal lament presents variations on the standard motifs of the lament psalm. All of the lament psalms are *occasional poems, and this one was occasioned by a national defeat in battle. The poem opens with a description of the crisis represented by God's abandonment of his people in battle (vv. 1–3); verses 4–8 are a statement of confidence in God as the one who will revive his chosen nation; verses 9–10 revisit the defeat of the nation; verse 11 petitions God to help; verse 12 is a statement of confidence in God.

60
To the choirmaster: according to Shushan Eduth. A Miktam[1] of David; for instruction; when he strove with Aram-naharaim and with Aram-zobah, and when Joab on his return struck down twelve thousand of Edom in the Valley of Salt.

1   O God, you have rejected us, broken our defenses;
        you have been angry; oh, restore us.
2   You have made the land to quake; you have torn it open;
        repair its breaches, for it totters.
3   You have made your people see hard things;
        you have given us wine to drink that made us stagger.

4   You have set up a banner for those who fear you,
        that they may flee to it from the bow.[2]   *Selah*
5   That your beloved ones may be delivered,
        give salvation by your right hand and answer us!

6   God has spoken in his holiness:[3]
        "With exultation I will divide up Shechem
        and portion out the Vale of Succoth.
7   Gilead is mine; Manasseh is mine;
        Ephraim is my helmet;
        Judah is my scepter.
8   Moab is my washbasin;
        upon Edom I cast my shoe;
        over Philistia I shout in triumph."[4]

9   Who will bring me to the fortified city?
        Who will lead me to Edom?
10 Have you not rejected us, O God?
        You do not go forth, O God, with our armies.
11 Oh, grant us help against the foe,
        for vain is the salvation of man!
12 With God we shall do valiantly;
        it is he who will tread down our foes.

---

[1] Probably musical or liturgical terms [2] Or *that it may be displayed because of truth* [3] Or *sanctuary* [4] Revocalization (compare Psalm 108:10); Masoretic Text *over me, O Philistia, shout in triumph*

The rock that is higher: a petitionary psalm [Psalm 61]. The backbone of this poem is a string of petitions to God expressed as a prayer. The petitions are enclosed within a call to God to hear the prayer (v. 1) and a vow to praise God (v. 8). Some of the petitions are personal, while others are prayers for the king.

61

To the choirmaster: with stringed instruments. Of David.

Hear my cry, O God,
  listen to my prayer;
2 from the end of the earth I call to you
  when my heart is faint.
Lead me to the rock
  that is higher than I,
3 for you have been my refuge,
  a strong tower against the enemy.

4 Let me dwell in your tent forever!
  Let me take refuge under the shelter of your wings!   *Selah*
5 For you, O God, have heard my vows;
  you have given me the heritage of those who fear your name.

6 Prolong the life of the king;
  may his years endure to all generations!
7 May he be enthroned forever before God;
  appoint steadfast love and faithfulness to watch over him!

8 So will I ever sing praises to your name,
  as I perform my vows day after day.

He only is my rock and my salvation: a lyric of trust in God [Psalm 62]. In the background lie the ingredients of a lament psalm, but the expression of trust that forms a standard part of that genre is so highlighted that the remaining motifs are present only in latent form. The sequence is as follows: assertion of trust in God (vv. 1–2); description (in the mode of the lament psalm) of oppressors (vv. 3–4); trust in God restated (vv. 5–7); address to the reader to trust in God (vv. 8–10); concluding resolution in the form of a reiteration of God's power that should logically elicit submission to him (vv. 11–12).

62

To the choirmaster: according to Jeduthun. A Psalm of David.

For God alone my soul waits in silence;
  from him comes my salvation.
2 He only is my rock and my salvation,
  my fortress; I shall not be greatly shaken.

3 How long will all of you attack a man
  to batter him,
  like a leaning wall, a tottering fence?
4 They only plan to thrust him down from his high position.
  They take pleasure in falsehood.

They bless with their mouths,
  but inwardly they curse.   *Selah*

⁵ For God alone, O my soul, wait in silence,
  for my hope is from him.
⁶ He only is my rock and my salvation,
  my fortress; I shall not be shaken.
⁷ On God rests my salvation and my glory;
  my mighty rock, my refuge is God.

⁸ Trust in him at all times, O people;
  pour out your heart before him;
  God is a refuge for us.   *Selah*

⁹ Those of low estate are but a breath;
  those of high estate are a delusion;
in the balances they go up;
  they are together lighter than a breath.
¹⁰ Put no trust in extortion;
  set no vain hopes on robbery;
  if riches increase, set not your heart on them.

¹¹ Once God has spoken;
  twice have I heard this:
that power belongs to God,
¹² and that to you, O Lord, belongs steadfast love.
For you will render to a man
  according to his work.

My mouth will praise you [Psalm 63]. This lyric of personal trust follows the same contour as the preceding psalm: underlying it is the situation of the conventional lament psalm occasioned by a distressing situation, but the poem is a prayer of trust addressed to God. The sequence is as follows: opening invocation to God expressing the speaker's longing for God (v. 1); mingled statements of the speaker's satisfaction in God, devotion to God, and past benefits received from God (vv. 2–8); statement of confidence that the speaker will be delivered from his enemies (vv. 9–10); vow to praise God in the future (v. 11).

---

63 A PSALM OF DAVID, WHEN HE WAS IN THE WILDERNESS OF JUDAH.
O God, you are my God; earnestly I seek you;
  my soul thirsts for you;
my flesh faints for you,
  as in a dry and weary land where there is no water.
² So I have looked upon you in the sanctuary,
  beholding your power and glory.
³ Because your steadfast love is better than life,
  my lips will praise you.

⁴ So I will bless you as long as I live;
   in your name I will lift up my hands.

⁵ My soul will be satisfied as with fat and rich food,
   and my mouth will praise you with joyful lips,
⁶ when I remember you upon my bed,
   and meditate on you in the watches of the night;
⁷ for you have been my help,
   and in the shadow of your wings I will sing for joy.
⁸ My soul clings to you;
   your right hand upholds me.

⁹ But those who seek to destroy my life
   shall go down into the depths of the earth;
¹⁰ they shall be given over to the power of the sword;
   they shall be a portion for jackals.
¹¹ But the king shall rejoice in God;
   all who swear by him shall exult,
   for the mouths of liars will be stopped.

Hear my voice, O God, in my complaint [Psalm 64]. Psalm 64 is the prototypical lament psalm—the specimen in which the conventional elements stand out highlighted, as follows: introductory cry to God (v. 1a); petitions for deliverance (vv. 1b–2); definition of the crisis (vv. 3–6); statement of confidence in God (vv. 7–8); prediction that people will praise God (vv. 9–10). This sequence is elaborated with vivid poetic texture and memorable imagery.

64

To the choirmaster. A Psalm of David.
Hear my voice, O God, in my complaint;
   preserve my life from dread of the enemy.
² Hide me from the secret plots of the wicked,
   from the throng of evildoers,
³ who whet their tongues like swords,
   who aim bitter words like arrows,
⁴ shooting from ambush at the blameless,
   shooting at him suddenly and without fear.
⁵ They hold fast to their evil purpose;
   they talk of laying snares secretly,
thinking, "Who can see them?"
⁶   They search out injustice,
saying, "We have accomplished a diligent search."
   For the inward mind and heart of a man are deep!

⁷ But God shoots his arrow at them;
   they are wounded suddenly.
⁸ They are brought to ruin, with their own tongues turned against them;
   all who see them will wag their heads.
⁹ Then all mankind fears;

they tell what God has brought about
and ponder what he has done.

10 Let the righteous one rejoice in the Lord
and take refuge in him!
Let all the upright in heart exult!

> **Praise is due to you, O God, in Zion** [Psalm 65]. The conventional motifs of the praise
> psalm unfold as follows: formal call to praise God (vv. 1–2); catalog of God's praisewor-
> thy acts, ranging from forgiveness of sins (v. 3) to satisfying his people as they worship
> him (v. 4) to acts of rescue (v. 5) to his creating the world (vv. 6–8) to acts of provi-
> dence in nature now (vv. 9–13). The poem contains some of the most memorable nature
> imagery in the entire Psalter, with personification figuring prominently in the last two
> verses.

65

To the choirmaster. A Psalm of David. A Song.
Praise is due to you,[1] O God, in Zion,
and to you shall vows be performed.
2 O you who hear prayer,
to you shall all flesh come.
3 When iniquities prevail against me,
you atone for our transgressions.
4 Blessed is the one you choose and bring near,
to dwell in your courts!
We shall be satisfied with the goodness of your house,
the holiness of your temple!

5 By awesome deeds you answer us with righteousness,
O God of our salvation,
the hope of all the ends of the earth
and of the farthest seas;
6 the one who by his strength established the mountains,
being girded with might;
7 who stills the roaring of the seas,
the roaring of their waves,
the tumult of the peoples,
8 so that those who dwell at the ends of the earth are in awe at your signs.
You make the going out of the morning and the evening to shout for joy.

9 You visit the earth and water it;[2]
you greatly enrich it;
the river of God is full of water;
you provide their grain,
for so you have prepared it.
10 You water its furrows abundantly,
settling its ridges,
softening it with showers,
and blessing its growth.

[1] Or *Praise waits for you in silence* [2] Or *and make it overflow*

11   You crown the year with your bounty;
      your wagon tracks overflow with abundance.
12   The pastures of the wilderness overflow,
      the hills gird themselves with joy,
13   the meadows clothe themselves with flocks,
      the valleys deck themselves with grain,
      they shout and sing together for joy.

Come and see what God has done [Psalm 66]. This poem behaves true to the form of the praise psalm: formal call to praise (vv. 1–5); catalog of praiseworthy acts (vv. 6–7); brief interruption of the catalog with another call to praise (v. 8); return to the catalog of acts for which God is to be praised (vv. 9–12); linking of the praise with acts of worship (vv. 13–15); another call to praise (v. 16); personal testimony of God's praiseworthy acts (vv. 17–19); concluding note of resolution in the form of a beatitude (v. 20). A good approach to the poem is to note the spheres in which God's praiseworthy acts occur.

66 To the choirmaster. A Song. A Psalm.
Shout for joy to God, all the earth;
2   sing the glory of his name;
     give to him glorious praise!
3   Say to God, "How awesome are your deeds!
     So great is your power that your enemies come cringing to you.
4   All the earth worships you
     and sings praises to you;
     they sing praises to your name."   *Selah*

5   Come and see what God has done:
     he is awesome in his deeds toward the children of man.
6   He turned the sea into dry land;
     they passed through the river on foot.
     There did we rejoice in him,
7   who rules by his might forever,
   whose eyes keep watch on the nations—
     let not the rebellious exalt themselves.   *Selah*

8   Bless our God, O peoples;
     let the sound of his praise be heard,
9   who has kept our soul among the living
     and has not let our feet slip.
10 For you, O God, have tested us;
     you have tried us as silver is tried.
11 You brought us into the net;
     you laid a crushing burden on our backs;
12 you let men ride over our heads;
     we went through fire and through water;
     yet you have brought us out to a place of abundance.

13   I will come into your house with burnt offerings;
       I will perform my vows to you,
14   that which my lips uttered
       and my mouth promised when I was in trouble.
15   I will offer to you burnt offerings of fattened animals,
       with the smoke of the sacrifice of rams;
    I will make an offering of bulls and goats.   *Selah*

16   Come and hear, all you who fear God,
       and I will tell what he has done for my soul.
17   I cried to him with my mouth,
       and high praise was on[1] my tongue.[2]
18   If I had cherished iniquity in my heart,
       the Lord would not have listened.
19   But truly God has listened;
       he has attended to the voice of my prayer.

20   Blessed be God,
       because he has not rejected my prayer
       or removed his steadfast love from me!

Let the peoples praise you, O God [Psalm 67]. While not following the standard form of the praise psalm, Psalm 67 nonetheless contains the right ingredients to be classified as such: a prayer that God's blessings will be upon the speaker's nation (vv. 1–2); ascription of praise to God, using the "let" formula five times (vv. 3–5); concluding sentiments of praise, including a mention of harvest (vv. 6–7). This poem has an international or global focus, and we might call it a missionary psalm.

67   To the choirmaster: with stringed instruments. A Psalm. A Song.
      May God be gracious to us and bless us
      and make his face to shine upon us,   *Selah*
2   that your way may be known on earth,
       your saving power among all nations.
3   Let the peoples praise you, O God;
       let all the peoples praise you!

4   Let the nations be glad and sing for joy,
       for you judge the peoples with equity
       and guide the nations upon earth.   *Selah*
5   Let the peoples praise you, O God;
       let all the peoples praise you!

6   The earth has yielded its increase;
       God, our God, shall bless us.
7   God shall bless us;
       let all the ends of the earth fear him!

[1] Hebrew under [2] Or and he was exalted with my tongue

Exult before him [Psalm 68]. After a succession of relatively brief praise psalms, Psalm 68 gives us an exalted version of the genre in the high style. The sequence is as follows: opening praise of God for his power to judge evil and bless the righteous (vv. 1–3); call to praise (v. 4); catalog of God's praiseworthy acts (vv. 5–14); praise of God's dwelling place in Zion, expressed in a highly figurative manner (vv. 15–16); praise of God using the motif of God as a conquering warrior and king returning from battle in triumph and accepting tribute from conquered kings (vv. 17–31); concluding section of calls to praise (vv. 32–35). The exuberance of the poem is obvious. The primary motif is God as a conquering warrior who rides triumphantly into a capital city.

68

To the choirmaster. A Psalm of David. A Song.

God shall arise, his enemies shall be scattered;
  and those who hate him shall flee before him!
2 As smoke is driven away, so you shall drive them away;
    as wax melts before fire,
    so the wicked shall perish before God!
3 But the righteous shall be glad;
    they shall exult before God;
    they shall be jubilant with joy!

4 Sing to God, sing praises to his name;
    lift up a song to him who rides through the deserts;
  his name is the Lord;
    exult before him!
5 Father of the fatherless and protector of widows
    is God in his holy habitation.
6 God settles the solitary in a home;
    he leads out the prisoners to prosperity,
    but the rebellious dwell in a parched land.

7 O God, when you went out before your people,
    when you marched through the wilderness,   *Selah*
8 the earth quaked, the heavens poured down rain,
    before God, the One of Sinai,
    before God, the God of Israel.
9 Rain in abundance, O God, you shed abroad;
    you restored your inheritance as it languished;
10 your flock[1] found a dwelling in it;
    in your goodness, O God, you provided for the needy.

11 The Lord gives the word;
    the women who announce the news are a great host:
12 "The kings of the armies—they flee, they flee!"
  The women at home divide the spoil—
13   though you men lie among the sheepfolds—
  the wings of a dove covered with silver,
    its pinions with shimmering gold.

---

[1] Or *your congregation*

14 When the Almighty scatters kings there,
      let snow fall on Zalmon.

15 O mountain of God, mountain of Bashan;
      O many-peaked[1] mountain, mountain of Bashan!
16 Why do you look with hatred, O many-peaked mountain,
      at the mount that God desired for his abode,
      yes, where the LORD will dwell forever?
17 The chariots of God are twice ten thousand,
      thousands upon thousands;
      the Lord is among them; Sinai is now in the sanctuary.
18 You ascended on high,
      leading a host of captives in your train
      and receiving gifts among men,
    even among the rebellious, that the LORD God may dwell there.

19 Blessed be the Lord,
      who daily bears us up;
      God is our salvation.   *Selah*
20 Our God is a God of salvation,
      and to GOD, the Lord, belong deliverances from death.
21 But God will strike the heads of his enemies,
      the hairy crown of him who walks in his guilty ways.
22 The Lord said,
      "I will bring them back from Bashan,
    I will bring them back from the depths of the sea,
23 that you may strike your feet in their blood,
      that the tongues of your dogs may have their portion from the foe."

24 Your procession is[2] seen, O God,
      the procession of my God, my King, into the sanctuary—
25 the singers in front, the musicians last,
      between them virgins playing tambourines:
26 "Bless God in the great congregation,
      the LORD, O you[3] who are of Israel's fountain!"
27 There is Benjamin, the least of them, in the lead,
      the princes of Judah in their throng,
      the princes of Zebulun, the princes of Naphtali.

28 Summon your power, O God,[4]
      the power, O God, by which you have worked for us.
29 Because of your temple at Jerusalem
      kings shall bear gifts to you.
30 Rebuke the beasts that dwell among the reeds,
      the herd of bulls with the calves of the peoples.
    Trample underfoot those who lust after tribute;
      scatter the peoples who delight in war.[5]

---

[1] Or *hunch-backed*; also verse 16   [2] Or *has been*   [3] The Hebrew for *you* is plural here   [4] Probable reading; Hebrew *Your God has summoned your power*
[5] The meaning of the Hebrew verse is uncertain

³¹ Nobles shall come from Egypt;
    Cush shall hasten to stretch out her hands to God.

³² O kingdoms of the earth, sing to God;
    sing praises to the Lord,   *Selah*
³³ to him who rides in the heavens, the ancient heavens;
    behold, he sends out his voice, his mighty voice.
³⁴ Ascribe power to God,
    whose majesty is over Israel,
    and whose power is in the skies.
³⁵ Awesome is God from his¹ sanctuary;
    the God of Israel—he is the one who gives power and strength to his people.
Blessed be God!

The Lord hears the needy [Psalm 69]. The elaborate praise psalm preceding this poem is now complemented by an equally elaborate psalm of lament. It unfolds as follows: a brief introductory cry to God (v. 1); description of the speaker's situation of distress (vv. 1–12); petitions to God to act (vv. 13–18); a return to the narrative of the things that threaten the speaker (vv. 19–21); petition that the speaker's oppressors receive what they have inflicted on the speaker (vv. 22–28); petition (v. 29); vow to praise (vv. 30–33); brief call to praise (v. 34); statement of confidence in God (vv. 35–36).

69

To the choirmaster: according to Lilies. Of David.
    Save me, O God!
    For the waters have come up to my neck.²
² I sink in deep mire,
    where there is no foothold;
I have come into deep waters,
    and the flood sweeps over me.
³ I am weary with my crying out;
    my throat is parched.
My eyes grow dim
    with waiting for my God.

⁴ More in number than the hairs of my head
    are those who hate me without cause;
mighty are those who would destroy me,
    those who attack me with lies.
What I did not steal
    must I now restore?
⁵ O God, you know my folly;
    the wrongs I have done are not hidden from you.

⁶ Let not those who hope in you be put to shame through me,
    O Lord God of hosts;
let not those who seek you be brought to dishonor through me,
    O God of Israel.
⁷ For it is for your sake that I have borne reproach,

¹ Septuagint; Hebrew *your* ² Or *waters threaten my life*

that dishonor has covered my face.
⁸ I have become a stranger to my brothers,
    an alien to my mother's sons.

⁹ For zeal for your house has consumed me,
    and the reproaches of those who reproach you have fallen on me.
¹⁰ When I wept and humbled¹ my soul with fasting,
    it became my reproach.
¹¹ When I made sackcloth my clothing,
    I became a byword to them.
¹² I am the talk of those who sit in the gate,
    and the drunkards make songs about me.

¹³ But as for me, my prayer is to you, O Lord.
    At an acceptable time, O God,
    in the abundance of your steadfast love answer me in your saving faithfulness.
¹⁴ Deliver me
    from sinking in the mire;
  let me be delivered from my enemies
    and from the deep waters.
¹⁵ Let not the flood sweep over me,
    or the deep swallow me up,
    or the pit close its mouth over me.

¹⁶ Answer me, O Lord, for your steadfast love is good;
    according to your abundant mercy, turn to me.
¹⁷ Hide not your face from your servant;
    for I am in distress; make haste to answer me.
¹⁸ Draw near to my soul, redeem me;
    ransom me because of my enemies!

¹⁹ You know my reproach,
    and my shame and my dishonor;
    my foes are all known to you.
²⁰ Reproaches have broken my heart,
    so that I am in despair.
  I looked for pity, but there was none,
    and for comforters, but I found none.
²¹ They gave me poison for food,
    and for my thirst they gave me sour wine to drink.

²² Let their own table before them become a snare;
    and when they are at peace, let it become a trap.²
²³ Let their eyes be darkened, so that they cannot see,
    and make their loins tremble continually.
²⁴ Pour out your indignation upon them,
    and let your burning anger overtake them.
²⁵ May their camp be a desolation;
    let no one dwell in their tents.

¹ Hebrew lacks and humbled ² Hebrew; a slight revocalization yields (compare Septuagint, Syriac, Jerome) a snare, and retribution and a trap

26 For they persecute him whom you have struck down,
      and they recount the pain of those you have wounded.
27 Add to them punishment upon punishment;
      may they have no acquittal from you.[1]
28 Let them be blotted out of the book of the living;
      let them not be enrolled among the righteous.

29 But I am afflicted and in pain;
      let your salvation, O God, set me on high!

30 I will praise the name of God with a song;
      I will magnify him with thanksgiving.
31 This will please the Lord more than an ox
      or a bull with horns and hoofs.
32 When the humble see it they will be glad;
      you who seek God, let your hearts revive.
33 For the Lord hears the needy
      and does not despise his own people who are prisoners.

34 Let heaven and earth praise him,
      the seas and everything that moves in them.
35 For God will save Zion
      and build up the cities of Judah,
   and people shall dwell there and possess it;
36   the offspring of his servants shall inherit it,
      and those who love his name shall dwell in it.

Make haste to help me: an abbreviated lament [Psalm 70]. The standard ingredients of the lament psalm appear in condensed form, as follows: introductory cry to God (v. 1); petitions to God to deliver the speaker, combined with a picture of the crisis (vv. 2–3); instead of a vow to praise, a wish or prayer that God will be praised (v. 4); mingled petitions and statement of confidence in God (v. 5). As the lament psalms accumulate, it becomes obvious that the poets who composed the Psalter were frequently threatened by the vicissitudes of life. God emerges as the only reliable hope in an uncertain world.

70
To the choirmaster. Of David, for the memorial offering.
Make haste, O God, to deliver me!
   O Lord, make haste to help me!
2 Let them be put to shame and confusion
      who seek my life!
   Let them be turned back and brought to dishonor
      who delight in my hurt!
3 Let them turn back because of their shame
      who say, "Aha, Aha!"

4 May all who seek you
      rejoice and be glad in you!
   May those who love your salvation

[1] Hebrew *may they not come into your righteousness*

say evermore, "God is great!"
5   But I am poor and needy;
        hasten to me, O God!
    You are my help and my deliverer;
        O LORD, do not delay!

You, O Lord, are my hope [Psalm 71]. No lament psalm follows exactly the same format as the others; every one has its individualizing traits, despite the constancy of the five main elements. In Psalm 71 the stock ingredients unfold as follows: petitions to God to deliver the speaker from his crisis (vv. 1–4); praise (vv. 5–8); petition (v. 9); definition of crisis (vv. 10–11); petition (vv. 12–13); a very extended vow to praise God that eventually makes the psalm feel like a praise psalm (vv. 12–24).

---

71 In you, O LORD, do I take refuge;
        let me never be put to shame!
2   In your righteousness deliver me and rescue me;
        incline your ear to me, and save me!
3   Be to me a rock of refuge,
        to which I may continually come;
    you have given the command to save me,
        for you are my rock and my fortress.

4   Rescue me, O my God, from the hand of the wicked,
        from the grasp of the unjust and cruel man.
5   For you, O Lord, are my hope,
        my trust, O LORD, from my youth.
6   Upon you I have leaned from before my birth;
        you are he who took me from my mother's womb.
    My praise is continually of you.

7   I have been as a portent to many,
        but you are my strong refuge.
8   My mouth is filled with your praise,
        and with your glory all the day.
9   Do not cast me off in the time of old age;
        forsake me not when my strength is spent.
10 For my enemies speak concerning me;
        those who watch for my life consult together
11 and say, "God has forsaken him;
        pursue and seize him,
        for there is none to deliver him."

12 O God, be not far from me;
        O my God, make haste to help me!
13 May my accusers be put to shame and consumed;
        with scorn and disgrace may they be covered
        who seek my hurt.
14 But I will hope continually

and will praise you yet more and more.
15 My mouth will tell of your righteous acts,
   of your deeds of salvation all the day,
   for their number is past my knowledge.
16 With the mighty deeds of the Lord GOD I will come;
   I will remind them of your righteousness, yours alone.

17 O God, from my youth you have taught me,
   and I still proclaim your wondrous deeds.
18 So even to old age and gray hairs,
   O God, do not forsake me,
   until I proclaim your might to another generation,
   your power to all those to come.
19 Your righteousness, O God,
   reaches the high heavens.
   You who have done great things,
   O God, who is like you?
20 You who have made me see many troubles and calamities
   will revive me again;
   from the depths of the earth
   you will bring me up again.
21 You will increase my greatness
   and comfort me again.

22 I will also praise you with the harp
   for your faithfulness, O my God;
   I will sing praises to you with the lyre,
   O Holy One of Israel.
23 My lips will shout for joy,
   when I sing praises to you;
   my soul also, which you have redeemed.
24 And my tongue will talk of your righteous help all the day long,
   for they have been put to shame and disappointed
   who sought to do me hurt.

> **Give the king your justice, O God** [Psalm 72]. This royal psalm is primarily a peti-
> tionary prayer on behalf of the king. Using the formula "may he . . . ," the poet lists the
> things that he wants God to grant to the king. We can compile a list of the things that in
> the poet's mind and imagination add up to a picture of the blessed kingdom. As is cus-
> tomary in the psalms, at the end the poet moves from his main topic to a statement of
> blessing toward God (vv. 18–19). The concluding statement in verse 20 reminds us that
> Psalm 72 marks the end of the second section of the Psalter in its Hebrew version.

72 OF SOLOMON.
   Give the king your justice, O God,
   and your righteousness to the royal son!
2 May he judge your people with righteousness,

and your poor with justice!

³ Let the mountains bear prosperity for the people,
   and the hills, in righteousness!
⁴ May he defend the cause of the poor of the people,
   give deliverance to the children of the needy,
   and crush the oppressor!

⁵ May they fear you¹ while the sun endures,
   and as long as the moon, throughout all generations!
⁶ May he be like rain that falls on the mown grass,
   like showers that water the earth!
⁷ In his days may the righteous flourish,
   and peace abound, till the moon be no more!

⁸ May he have dominion from sea to sea,
   and from the River² to the ends of the earth!
⁹ May desert tribes bow down before him,
   and his enemies lick the dust!
¹⁰ May the kings of Tarshish and of the coastlands
    render him tribute;
   may the kings of Sheba and Seba
    bring gifts!
¹¹ May all kings fall down before him,
    all nations serve him!

¹² For he delivers the needy when he calls,
    the poor and him who has no helper.
¹³ He has pity on the weak and the needy,
    and saves the lives of the needy.
¹⁴ From oppression and violence he redeems their life,
    and precious is their blood in his sight.

¹⁵ Long may he live;
    may gold of Sheba be given to him!
   May prayer be made for him continually,
    and blessings invoked for him all the day!
¹⁶ May there be abundance of grain in the land;
    on the tops of the mountains may it wave;
    may its fruit be like Lebanon;
   and may people blossom in the cities
    like the grass of the field!
¹⁷ May his name endure forever,
    his fame continue as long as the sun!
   May people be blessed in him,
    all nations call him blessed!

¹⁸ Blessed be the LORD, the God of Israel,
    who alone does wondrous things.
¹⁹ Blessed be his glorious name forever;

---

¹ Septuagint *He shall endure* ² That is, the Euphrates

may the whole earth be filled with his glory!
Amen and Amen!

20   The prayers of David, the son of Jesse, are ended.

Personal testimony of spiritual deliverance [Psalm 73]. Psalm 73 is a high point of
the Psalms and a poem with great contemporary relevance. The poem is cast in the form
of a retrospective narrative in which the speaker recalls his existential crisis of faith
when he envied the prosperous wicked. The opening sequence is as follows: a statement
of the safe position at which the speaker landed at the end—a victory speech at the
finish line to prevent possible misunderstanding regarding what is to follow (v. 1); a preview of the crisis (vv. 2–3); a portrait of the prosperous wicked as they are in themselves
(vv. 4–9) and as viewed by the culture at large (vv. 10–12); the speaker's self-pity
and discontent over having lived a godly life of self-denial while the wicked prospered
(vv. 13–15). Right in the middle of the poem we have the reversal: the speaker's recovery of a right view of God and life when he worshiped God in the temple (vv. 16–17). In
the second half of the poem, we revisit the topics that we traversed in the first half, as
follows: a second view of the prosperous wicked—the reason the speaker changed his
attitude (vv. 18–20); the speaker's retrospective put-down of his earlier ungodly attitude when he envied the wicked (vv. 21–22); a second view of the godly life—a spiritual
inventory of what the speaker possesses in God and now perceives to be better than the
temporary earthly prosperity of the wicked (vv. 23–26); a summary of the twofold movement of the psalm, which has contrasted the temporary nature of the wicked's earthly
success (v. 27) and the implicitly unending rewards of the godly (v. 28).

BOOK THREE

73   A PSALM OF ASAPH.
Truly God is good to Israel,
    to those who are pure in heart.
2   But as for me, my feet had almost stumbled,
    my steps had nearly slipped.
3   For I was envious of the arrogant
    when I saw the prosperity of the wicked.

4   For they have no pangs until death;
    their bodies are fat and sleek.
5   They are not in trouble as others are;
    they are not stricken like the rest of mankind.
6   Therefore pride is their necklace;
    violence covers them as a garment.
7   Their eyes swell out through fatness;
    their hearts overflow with follies.
8   They scoff and speak with malice;
    loftily they threaten oppression.
9   They set their mouths against the heavens,
    and their tongue struts through the earth.
10 Therefore his people turn back to them,
    and find no fault in them.[1]

[1] Probable reading; Hebrew *the waters of a full cup are drained by them*

11   And they say, "How can God know?
          Is there knowledge in the Most High?"
12   Behold, these are the wicked;
          always at ease, they increase in riches.
13   All in vain have I kept my heart clean
          and washed my hands in innocence.
14   For all the day long I have been stricken
          and rebuked every morning.
15   If I had said, "I will speak thus,"
          I would have betrayed the generation of your children.

16   But when I thought how to understand this,
          it seemed to me a wearisome task,
17   until I went into the sanctuary of God;
          then I discerned their end.

18   Truly you set them in slippery places;
          you make them fall to ruin.
19   How they are destroyed in a moment,
          swept away utterly by terrors!
20   Like a dream when one awakes,
          O Lord, when you rouse yourself, you despise them as phantoms.
21   When my soul was embittered,
          when I was pricked in heart,
22   I was brutish and ignorant;
          I was like a beast toward you.

23   Nevertheless, I am continually with you;
          you hold my right hand.
24   You guide me with your counsel,
          and afterward you will receive me to glory.
25   Whom have I in heaven but you?
          And there is nothing on earth that I desire besides you.
26   My flesh and my heart may fail,
          but God is the strength[1] of my heart and my portion forever.

27   For behold, those who are far from you shall perish;
          you put an end to everyone who is unfaithful to you.
28   But for me it is good to be near God;
          I have made the Lord GOD my refuge,
          that I may tell of all your works.

Remember your congregation: a communal lament [Psalm 74]. The poem unfolds according to the standard conventions of the lament psalm, though the crisis is public and national rather than personal: opening cry to God (v. 1); petition to God for deliverance (vv. 2–3); description of the occasion of the poem, including the destruction of the temple (vv. 4–11); statement of confidence in God—a rehearsal of God's acts in the mode of praise psalms (vv. 12–17); petitions for deliverance (vv. 18–23). A theme that

---

[1] Hebrew rock

is woven throughout the poem is lament over the way in which God's name has been dishonored by the scoffing of Israel's enemies.

74

A Maskil[1] of Asaph.

O God, why do you cast us off forever?
    Why does your anger smoke against the sheep of your pasture?
2 Remember your congregation, which you have purchased of old,
    which you have redeemed to be the tribe of your heritage!
    Remember Mount Zion, where you have dwelt.
3 Direct your steps to the perpetual ruins;
    the enemy has destroyed everything in the sanctuary!

4 Your foes have roared in the midst of your meeting place;
    they set up their own signs for signs.
5 They were like those who swing axes
    in a forest of trees.[2]
6 And all its carved wood
    they broke down with hatchets and hammers.
7 They set your sanctuary on fire;
    they profaned the dwelling place of your name,
    bringing it down to the ground.
8 They said to themselves, "We will utterly subdue them";
    they burned all the meeting places of God in the land.

9 We do not see our signs;
    there is no longer any prophet,
    and there is none among us who knows how long.
10 How long, O God, is the foe to scoff?
    Is the enemy to revile your name forever?
11 Why do you hold back your hand, your right hand?
    Take it from the fold of your garment[3] and destroy them!

12 Yet God my King is from of old,
    working salvation in the midst of the earth.
13 You divided the sea by your might;
    you broke the heads of the sea monsters[4] on the waters.
14 You crushed the heads of Leviathan;
    you gave him as food for the creatures of the wilderness.
15 You split open springs and brooks;
    you dried up ever-flowing streams.
16 Yours is the day, yours also the night;
    you have established the heavenly lights and the sun.
17 You have fixed all the boundaries of the earth;
    you have made summer and winter.

18 Remember this, O Lord, how the enemy scoffs,
    and a foolish people reviles your name.

---

[1] Probably a musical or liturgical term [2] The meaning of the Hebrew is uncertain [3] Hebrew *from your bosom* [4] Or *the great sea creatures*

19 Do not deliver the soul of your dove to the wild beasts;
     do not forget the life of your poor forever.

20 Have regard for the covenant,
     for the dark places of the land are full of the habitations of violence.
21 Let not the downtrodden turn back in shame;
     let the poor and needy praise your name.

22 Arise, O God, defend your cause;
     remember how the foolish scoff at you all the day!
23 Do not forget the clamor of your foes,
     the uproar of those who rise against you, which goes up continually!

It is God who executes judgment [Psalm 75]. Most praise psalms extol God for a range of acts and attributes. Psalm 75 zeroes in primarily on one of God's acts—his acts of judgment against evil. The sequence is as follows: formal introduction to the praise (v. 1); a quoted speech in which God asserts his intention to judge the earth (vv. 2–5); the poet's follow-up in which he praises God for his acts of judgment (vv. 6–10).

75

TO THE CHOIRMASTER: ACCORDING TO DO NOT DESTROY. A PSALM OF ASAPH. A SONG.
   We give thanks to you, O God;
   we give thanks, for your name is near.
   We[1] recount your wondrous deeds.

2 "At the set time that I appoint
     I will judge with equity.
3 When the earth totters, and all its inhabitants,
     it is I who keep steady its pillars.   *Selah*
4 I say to the boastful, 'Do not boast,'
     and to the wicked, 'Do not lift up your horn;
5 do not lift up your horn on high,
     or speak with haughty neck.'"

6 For not from the east or from the west
     and not from the wilderness comes lifting up,
7 but it is God who executes judgment,
     putting down one and lifting up another.
8 For in the hand of the LORD there is a cup
     with foaming wine, well mixed,
   and he pours out from it,
     and all the wicked of the earth
     shall drain it down to the dregs.

9 But I will declare it forever;
     I will sing praises to the God of Jacob.
10 All the horns of the wicked I will cut off,
     but the horns of the righteous shall be lifted up.

---

[1] Hebrew *They*

His name is great in Israel [Psalm 76]. As is true of the lament psalms also, each praise psalm is unique, even though a common store of motifs makes up the basic rubric. While Psalm 76 exhibits the conventional categories of the praise psalm, the details constitute the original element in the poem, as follows: an assertion, partly by metaphoric means, of God's exalted greatness and splendor (vv. 1–3); an apostrophe (direct address) to God extolling him as a victorious divine warrior (vv. 4–6); while shuttling back and forth between direct address to God and third-person narrative of God's acts, the poet presents further evidence that God is praiseworthy (vv. 7–10); a sudden apostrophe to the believing community to make its vows to this exalted God (vv. 11–12). As we move through the lament and praise psalms, we move between the expected and the original.

76

To the choirmaster: with stringed instruments. A Psalm of Asaph. A Song.
In Judah God is known;
 his name is great in Israel.
² His abode has been established in Salem,
 his dwelling place in Zion.
³ There he broke the flashing arrows,
 the shield, the sword, and the weapons of war.   *Selah*

⁴ Glorious are you, more majestic
 than the mountains of prey.
⁵ The stouthearted were stripped of their spoil;
 they sank into sleep;
all the men of war
 were unable to use their hands.
⁶ At your rebuke, O God of Jacob,
 both rider and horse lay stunned.

⁷ But you, you are to be feared!
 Who can stand before you
 when once your anger is roused?
⁸ From the heavens you uttered judgment;
 the earth feared and was still,
⁹ when God arose to establish judgment,
 to save all the humble of the earth.   *Selah*

¹⁰ Surely the wrath of man shall praise you;
 the remnant¹ of wrath you will put on like a belt.
¹¹ Make your vows to the Lᴏʀᴅ your God and perform them;
 let all around him bring gifts
 to him who is to be feared,
¹² who cuts off the spirit of princes,
 who is to be feared by the kings of the earth.

I will remember the deeds of the Lᴏʀᴅ [Psalm 77]. The psalm begins as a lament poem, with the conventional cry to God to help at the outset (vv. 1–2), followed by complaint itself (vv. 3–10). The speaker's anguish is heightened when he contrasts God's

---

¹ Or extremity

past acts of favor with the present absence of God's blessing. Then, in a sudden shift, the speaker returns to the theme of God's past mighty deeds (vv. 11–12) and elaborates those meditations in a full-fledged praise psalm (vv. 13–20) in which the main data and imagery come from the exodus of Israel from Egypt.

77

To the choirmaster: according to Jeduthun. A Psalm of Asaph.

I cry aloud to God,
aloud to God, and he will hear me.

2 In the day of my trouble I seek the Lord;
    in the night my hand is stretched out without wearying;
    my soul refuses to be comforted.

3 When I remember God, I moan;
    when I meditate, my spirit faints.   *Selah*

4 You hold my eyelids open;
    I am so troubled that I cannot speak.

5 I consider the days of old,
    the years long ago.

6 I said,[1] "Let me remember my song in the night;
    let me meditate in my heart."
    Then my spirit made a diligent search:

7 "Will the Lord spurn forever,
    and never again be favorable?

8 Has his steadfast love forever ceased?
    Are his promises at an end for all time?

9 Has God forgotten to be gracious?
    Has he in anger shut up his compassion?"   *Selah*

10 Then I said, "I will appeal to this,
     to the years of the right hand of the Most High."[2]

11 I will remember the deeds of the LORD;
     yes, I will remember your wonders of old.

12 I will ponder all your work,
     and meditate on your mighty deeds.

13 Your way, O God, is holy.
     What god is great like our God?

14 You are the God who works wonders;
     you have made known your might among the peoples.

15 You with your arm redeemed your people,
     the children of Jacob and Joseph.   *Selah*

16 When the waters saw you, O God,
     when the waters saw you, they were afraid;
     indeed, the deep trembled.

17 The clouds poured out water;
     the skies gave forth thunder;
     your arrows flashed on every side.

---

[1] Hebrew lacks *I said* [2] Or *This is my grief: that the right hand of the Most High has changed*

18 The crash of your thunder was in the whirlwind;
        your lightnings lighted up the world;
        the earth trembled and shook.
19 Your way was through the sea,
        your path through the great waters;
        yet your footprints were unseen.[1]
20 You led your people like a flock
        by the hand of Moses and Aaron.

> **The glorious deeds of the Lord: a historical psalm** [Psalm 78]. This long psalm is a
> rehearsal of Israelite history, viewed through the interpretive lens of Israel's disloyalty to
> God. The sequence is as follows: an orienting section in which the speaker summons his
> audience to listen, as in the mode of OT wisdom teachers (vv. 1–4); a section in which
> the speaker announces his purpose in rehearsing history—that God's works will be
> passed from one generation to the next and that God's covenant people will not perpetu-
> ate the rebelliousness of the exodus generation (vv. 5–8); a litany of national ignominies
> during the wilderness journey of the exodus (vv. 9–55); still more apostasy after the
> nation entered the Promised Land (vv. 56–58); God's anger displayed against the nation
> (vv. 59–66); God's choice of Judah and David as his people's last best hope (vv. 67–72).

78
A Maskil[2] of Asaph.
    Give ear, O my people, to my teaching;
        incline your ears to the words of my mouth!
2   I will open my mouth in a parable;
        I will utter dark sayings from of old,
3   things that we have heard and known,
        that our fathers have told us.
4   We will not hide them from their children,
        but tell to the coming generation
    the glorious deeds of the Lord, and his might,
        and the wonders that he has done.

5   He established a testimony in Jacob
        and appointed a law in Israel,
    which he commanded our fathers
        to teach to their children,
6   that the next generation might know them,
        the children yet unborn,
    and arise and tell them to their children,
7   so that they should set their hope in God
    and not forget the works of God,
        but keep his commandments;
8   and that they should not be like their fathers,
        a stubborn and rebellious generation,
    a generation whose heart was not steadfast,
        whose spirit was not faithful to God.

[1] Hebrew *unknown* [2] Probably a musical or liturgical term

⁹ The Ephraimites, armed with¹ the bow,
  turned back on the day of battle.
¹⁰ They did not keep God's covenant,
  but refused to walk according to his law.
¹¹ They forgot his works
  and the wonders that he had shown them.
¹² In the sight of their fathers he performed wonders
  in the land of Egypt, in the fields of Zoan.
¹³ He divided the sea and let them pass through it,
  and made the waters stand like a heap.
¹⁴ In the daytime he led them with a cloud,
  and all the night with a fiery light.
¹⁵ He split rocks in the wilderness
  and gave them drink abundantly as from the deep.
¹⁶ He made streams come out of the rock
  and caused waters to flow down like rivers.

¹⁷ Yet they sinned still more against him,
  rebelling against the Most High in the desert.
¹⁸ They tested God in their heart
  by demanding the food they craved.
¹⁹ They spoke against God, saying,
  "Can God spread a table in the wilderness?
²⁰ He struck the rock so that water gushed out
  and streams overflowed.
  Can he also give bread
  or provide meat for his people?"

²¹ Therefore, when the LORD heard, he was full of wrath;
  a fire was kindled against Jacob;
  his anger rose against Israel,
²² because they did not believe in God
  and did not trust his saving power.
²³ Yet he commanded the skies above
  and opened the doors of heaven,
²⁴ and he rained down on them manna to eat
  and gave them the grain of heaven.
²⁵ Man ate of the bread of the angels;
  he sent them food in abundance.
²⁶ He caused the east wind to blow in the heavens,
  and by his power he led out the south wind;
²⁷ he rained meat on them like dust,
  winged birds like the sand of the seas;
²⁸ he let them fall in the midst of their camp,
  all around their dwellings.
²⁹ And they ate and were well filled,
  for he gave them what they craved.

¹ Hebrew *armed and shooting*

30 But before they had satisfied their craving,
        while the food was still in their mouths,
31 the anger of God rose against them,
        and he killed the strongest of them
        and laid low the young men of Israel.

32 In spite of all this, they still sinned;
        despite his wonders, they did not believe.
33 So he made their days vanish like[1] a breath,[2]
        and their years in terror.
34 When he killed them, they sought him;
        they repented and sought God earnestly.
35 They remembered that God was their rock,
        the Most High God their redeemer.
36 But they flattered him with their mouths;
        they lied to him with their tongues.
37 Their heart was not steadfast toward him;
        they were not faithful to his covenant.
38 Yet he, being compassionate,
        atoned for their iniquity
        and did not destroy them;
    he restrained his anger often
        and did not stir up all his wrath.
39 He remembered that they were but flesh,
        a wind that passes and comes not again.
40 How often they rebelled against him in the wilderness
        and grieved him in the desert!
41 They tested God again and again
        and provoked the Holy One of Israel.
42 They did not remember his power[3]
        or the day when he redeemed them from the foe,
43 when he performed his signs in Egypt
        and his marvels in the fields of Zoan.
44 He turned their rivers to blood,
        so that they could not drink of their streams.
45 He sent among them swarms of flies, which devoured them,
        and frogs, which destroyed them.
46 He gave their crops to the destroying locust
        and the fruit of their labor to the locust.
47 He destroyed their vines with hail
        and their sycamores with frost.
48 He gave over their cattle to the hail
        and their flocks to thunderbolts.
49 He let loose on them his burning anger,
        wrath, indignation, and distress,
        a company of destroying angels.
50 He made a path for his anger;

[1] Hebrew in [2] Or vapor [3] Hebrew hand

he did not spare them from death,
but gave their lives over to the plague.
51 He struck down every firstborn in Egypt,
the firstfruits of their strength in the tents of Ham.
52 Then he led out his people like sheep
and guided them in the wilderness like a flock.
53 He led them in safety, so that they were not afraid,
but the sea overwhelmed their enemies.
54 And he brought them to his holy land,
to the mountain which his right hand had won.
55 He drove out nations before them;
he apportioned them for a possession
and settled the tribes of Israel in their tents.

56 Yet they tested and rebelled against the Most High God
and did not keep his testimonies,
57 but turned away and acted treacherously like their fathers;
they twisted like a deceitful bow.
58 For they provoked him to anger with their high places;
they moved him to jealousy with their idols.
59 When God heard, he was full of wrath,
and he utterly rejected Israel.
60 He forsook his dwelling at Shiloh,
the tent where he dwelt among mankind,
61 and delivered his power to captivity,
his glory to the hand of the foe.
62 He gave his people over to the sword
and vented his wrath on his heritage.
63 Fire devoured their young men,
and their young women had no marriage song.
64 Their priests fell by the sword,
and their widows made no lamentation.
65 Then the Lord awoke as from sleep,
like a strong man shouting because of wine.
66 And he put his adversaries to rout;
he put them to everlasting shame.

67 He rejected the tent of Joseph;
he did not choose the tribe of Ephraim,
68 but he chose the tribe of Judah,
Mount Zion, which he loves.
69 He built his sanctuary like the high heavens,
like the earth, which he has founded forever.
70 He chose David his servant
and took him from the sheepfolds;
71 from following the nursing ewes he brought him
to shepherd Jacob his people,

Israel his inheritance.
72 With upright heart he shepherded them
    and guided them with his skillful hand.

They have laid Jerusalem in ruins: a communal lament [Psalm 79]. This psalm incorporates three of the conventional five parts of the lament psalm—an immediate and vivid description of the crisis, namely, the destruction of Jerusalem and the temple (vv. 1–4); an expanded section of petitions to God to act on behalf of the nation (vv. 5–12); a concluding vow to give thanks to God forever, from generation to generation (v. 13).

79

A PSALM OF ASAPH.
    O God, the nations have come into your inheritance;
    they have defiled your holy temple;
    they have laid Jerusalem in ruins.
2   They have given the bodies of your servants
    to the birds of the heavens for food,
    the flesh of your faithful to the beasts of the earth.
3   They have poured out their blood like water
    all around Jerusalem,
    and there was no one to bury them.
4   We have become a taunt to our neighbors,
    mocked and derided by those around us.

5   How long, O LORD? Will you be angry forever?
    Will your jealousy burn like fire?
6   Pour out your anger on the nations
    that do not know you,
    and on the kingdoms
    that do not call upon your name!
7   For they have devoured Jacob
    and laid waste his habitation.

8   Do not remember against us our former iniquities;[1]
    let your compassion come speedily to meet us,
    for we are brought very low.
9   Help us, O God of our salvation,
    for the glory of your name;
    deliver us, and atone for our sins,
    for your name's sake!
10 Why should the nations say,
    "Where is their God?"
    Let the avenging of the outpoured blood of your servants
    be known among the nations before our eyes!

11 Let the groans of the prisoners come before you;
    according to your great power, preserve those doomed to die!
12 Return sevenfold into the lap of our neighbors
    the taunts with which they have taunted you, O Lord!

[1] Or the iniquities of former generations

¹³ But we your people, the sheep of your pasture,
      will give thanks to you forever;
      from generation to generation we will recount your praise.

Restore us, O God [Psalm 80]. The standard motifs in this communal lament unfold as follows: introductory cry to God (vv. 1–2a); petition (vv. 2b–3); brief definition of the crisis (vv. 4–6); petition (v. 7); expanded portrayal of the crisis (vv. 8–13); petitions for restoration (vv. 14–19). The dominant motif is a wished-for return to a previous state of God's favor on his chosen nation. The controlling image patterns are those of restoration and the nation as a vine planted by God.

---

80 TO THE CHOIRMASTER: ACCORDING TO LILIES. A TESTIMONY. OF ASAPH, A PSALM.
      Give ear, O Shepherd of Israel,
      you who lead Joseph like a flock!
   You who are enthroned upon the cherubim, shine forth.
²   Before Ephraim and Benjamin and Manasseh,
   stir up your might
      and come to save us!

³ Restore us,¹ O God;
      let your face shine, that we may be saved!

⁴ O LORD God of hosts,
      how long will you be angry with your people's prayers?
⁵ You have fed them with the bread of tears
      and given them tears to drink in full measure.
⁶ You make us an object of contention for our neighbors,
      and our enemies laugh among themselves.

⁷ Restore us, O God of hosts;
      let your face shine, that we may be saved!

⁸ You brought a vine out of Egypt;
      you drove out the nations and planted it.
⁹ You cleared the ground for it;
      it took deep root and filled the land.
¹⁰ The mountains were covered with its shade,
      the mighty cedars with its branches.
¹¹ It sent out its branches to the sea
      and its shoots to the River.²
¹² Why then have you broken down its walls,
      so that all who pass along the way pluck its fruit?
¹³ The boar from the forest ravages it,
      and all that move in the field feed on it.

¹⁴ Turn again, O God of hosts!
      Look down from heaven, and see;
   have regard for this vine,
¹⁵   the stock that your right hand planted,

---

¹ Or *Turn us again;* also verses 7, 19 ² That is, the Euphrates

and for the son whom you made strong for yourself.
¹⁶ They have burned it with fire; they have cut it down;
   may they perish at the rebuke of your face!
¹⁷ But let your hand be on the man of your right hand,
   the son of man whom you have made strong for yourself!
¹⁸ Then we shall not turn back from you;
   give us life, and we will call upon your name!

¹⁹ Restore us, O Lᴏʀᴅ God of hosts!
   Let your face shine, that we may be saved!

Hear, O my people: a poetic oracle [Psalm 81]. The psalm begins as a typical praise psalm with an introductory call to praise (vv. 1–5a). But then a mysterious reference to an unknown language (v. 5) serves as a lead-in to an oracle from God, presented in the rhetorical form of a quoted speech or dramatic monologue to the nation (vv. 6–16). The divine oracle develops the following specific topics: brief list of God's acts in the life of Israel (vv. 6–7); God's demand of exclusive loyalty asserted and invited (vv. 8–10); brief account of God's judgment against Israel for not listening to God's voice (vv. 11–12); God's longing to deliver and bless his people in exchange for obedience (vv. 13–16).

81

Tᴏ ᴛʜᴇ ᴄʜᴏɪʀᴍᴀsᴛᴇʀ: ᴀᴄᴄᴏʀᴅɪɴɢ ᴛᴏ Tʜᴇ Gɪᴛᴛɪᴛʜ.¹ Oғ Asᴀᴘʜ.
   Sing aloud to God our strength;
   shout for joy to the God of Jacob!
² Raise a song; sound the tambourine,
   the sweet lyre with the harp.
³ Blow the trumpet at the new moon,
   at the full moon, on our feast day.

⁴ For it is a statute for Israel,
   a rule² of the God of Jacob.
⁵ He made it a decree in Joseph
   when he went out over³ the land of Egypt.
I hear a language I had not known:
⁶ "I relieved your⁴ shoulder of the burden;
   your hands were freed from the basket.
⁷ In distress you called, and I delivered you;
   I answered you in the secret place of thunder;
   I tested you at the waters of Meribah.   *Selah*
⁸ Hear, O my people, while I admonish you!
   O Israel, if you would but listen to me!
⁹ There shall be no strange god among you;
   you shall not bow down to a foreign god.
¹⁰ I am the Lᴏʀᴅ your God,
   who brought you up out of the land of Egypt.
   Open your mouth wide, and I will fill it.

¹¹ "But my people did not listen to my voice;
   Israel would not submit to me.

¹ Probably a musical or liturgical term ² Or *just decree* ³ Or *against* ⁴ Hebrew *his*; also next line

¹² So I gave them over to their stubborn hearts,
    to follow their own counsels.
¹³ Oh, that my people would listen to me,
    that Israel would walk in my ways!
¹⁴ I would soon subdue their enemies
    and turn my hand against their foes.
¹⁵ Those who hate the LORD would cringe toward him,
    and their fate would last forever.
¹⁶ But he would feed you¹ with the finest of the wheat,
    and with honey from the rock I would satisfy you."

> **God has taken his place in the divine council** [Psalm 82]. The underlying situation in the poem is the poet's disillusionment with earthly rulership. The format in which this disillusionment is packaged is an imaginary divine council of gods in which God takes his preeminent place and from which he speaks (v. 1). The gods may be either supernatural powers or earthly rulers metaphorically called gods. The ensuing poem shuttles back and forth between statements from God and from the poet, as follows: God commands an unspecified audience (the gods?) to execute justice and compassion in society (vv. 2–4); the poet's satiric put-down of misguided people, perhaps the same gods or rulers whom God has just addressed (v. 5); an unspecified voice (God's?) divests the gods of their powers (vv. 6–7); the poet prays that God himself will compensate for the failure of the gods or rulers described earlier by coming as judge of the nations (v. 8).

82

A PSALM OF ASAPH.
    God has taken his place in the divine council;
    in the midst of the gods he holds judgment:
² "How long will you judge unjustly
    and show partiality to the wicked?   *Selah*
³ Give justice to the weak and the fatherless;
    maintain the right of the afflicted and the destitute.
⁴ Rescue the weak and the needy;
    deliver them from the hand of the wicked."

⁵ They have neither knowledge nor understanding,
    they walk about in darkness;
    all the foundations of the earth are shaken.

⁶ I said, "You are gods,
    sons of the Most High, all of you;
⁷ nevertheless, like men you shall die,
    and fall like any prince."²

⁸ Arise, O God, judge the earth;
    for you shall inherit all the nations!

> **Let them perish in disgrace: a communal lament** [Psalm 83]. All lament psalms are occasional poems that refer to a specific situation in either the personal life of the poet or the public life of his nation. The occasion of this poem is a military threat against

¹ That is, Israel; Hebrew *him* ² Or *fall as one man, O princes*

Israel by a coalition of enemies. A further context is the holy war motif in which Israel is God's nation and the enemies of Israel are also the enemies of God. When faced with a national crisis, OT poets turned naturally to the lament psalm as the best literary form by which to express their feelings. The poem unfolds according to the following sequence: introductory cry to God to act (v. 1); description of the crisis (vv. 2–8); petition, which in this case is also an imprecation or calling down of a curse on the enemies (vv. 9–18).

83

A SONG. A PSALM OF ASAPH.

O God, do not keep silence;
do not hold your peace or be still, O God!
2 For behold, your enemies make an uproar;
those who hate you have raised their heads.
3 They lay crafty plans against your people;
they consult together against your treasured ones.
4 They say, "Come, let us wipe them out as a nation;
let the name of Israel be remembered no more!"
5 For they conspire with one accord;
against you they make a covenant—
6 the tents of Edom and the Ishmaelites,
Moab and the Hagrites,
7 Gebal and Ammon and Amalek,
Philistia with the inhabitants of Tyre;
8 Asshur also has joined them;
they are the strong arm of the children of Lot.   *Selah*

9 Do to them as you did to Midian,
as to Sisera and Jabin at the river Kishon,
10 who were destroyed at En-dor,
who became dung for the ground.
11 Make their nobles like Oreb and Zeeb,
all their princes like Zebah and Zalmunna,
12 who said, "Let us take possession for ourselves
of the pastures of God."

13 O my God, make them like whirling dust,[1]
like chaff before the wind.
14 As fire consumes the forest,
as the flame sets the mountains ablaze,
15 so may you pursue them with your tempest
and terrify them with your hurricane!
16 Fill their faces with shame,
that they may seek your name, O LORD.
17 Let them be put to shame and dismayed forever;
let them perish in disgrace,
18 that they may know that you alone,

---

[1] Or like a tumbleweed

whose name is the LORD,
    are the Most High over all the earth.

How lovely is your dwelling place [Psalm 84]. Psalm 84 is the prototypical worship psalm (also called song of Zion) in the Psalter. The overall strategy of a worship psalm is to express longing to worship God and to celebrate the joy of worshiping him. Worship psalms are occasional poems in which the speaker relives the details of worshiping God in the temple in Jerusalem. In Psalm 84, these ingredients produce the following sequence: statement of theme—the loveliness of worshiping God in the temple (v. 1); feelings of anticipation and initial responses to the temple upon arrival (vv. 2–4); celebration of the joy of the pilgrimage to Jerusalem (vv. 5–7); a prayer for the anointed king, uttered in the temple (vv. 8–9); assertion of the supreme value that the poet places on the worship of God (v. 10); concluding feelings of the worshiper, ending with a beatitude (vv. 11–12).

84
To the choirmaster: according to The Gittith.[1] A Psalm of the Sons of Korah.

1 How lovely is your dwelling place,
    O LORD of hosts!
2 My soul longs, yes, faints
        for the courts of the LORD;
    my heart and flesh sing for joy
        to the living God.

3 Even the sparrow finds a home,
        and the swallow a nest for herself,
        where she may lay her young,
    at your altars, O LORD of hosts,
        my King and my God.
4 Blessed are those who dwell in your house,
        ever singing your praise!   *Selah*

5 Blessed are those whose strength is in you,
        in whose heart are the highways to Zion.[2]
6 As they go through the Valley of Baca
        they make it a place of springs;
        the early rain also covers it with pools.
7 They go from strength to strength;
        each one appears before God in Zion.

8 O LORD God of hosts, hear my prayer;
        give ear, O God of Jacob!   *Selah*
9 Behold our shield, O God;
        look on the face of your anointed!

10 For a day in your courts is better
        than a thousand elsewhere.
    I would rather be a doorkeeper in the house of my God

---

[1] Probably a musical or liturgical term [2] Hebrew lacks *to Zion*

than dwell in the tents of wickedness.
11 For the LORD God is a sun and shield;
the LORD bestows favor and honor.
No good thing does he withhold
from those who walk uprightly.
12 O LORD of hosts,
blessed is the one who trusts in you!

Restore us again [Psalm 85]. This communal lament psalm does not come right out and state the standard "complaint"; instead it hints at it in the first three verses, in which the poet recalls God's past favor toward his people (from whom we infer that God has withdrawn his favor in the present). The rest of the poem then falls into the standard sections: petition for God to solve the problem that has been defined (vv. 4–7); statement of confidence that the loving and faithful God will act (vv. 8–13).

85 TO THE CHOIRMASTER. A PSALM OF THE SONS OF KORAH.
LORD, you were favorable to your land;
you restored the fortunes of Jacob.
2 You forgave the iniquity of your people;
you covered all their sin. *Selah*
3 You withdrew all your wrath;
you turned from your hot anger.

4 Restore us again, O God of our salvation,
and put away your indignation toward us!
5 Will you be angry with us forever?
Will you prolong your anger to all generations?
6 Will you not revive us again,
that your people may rejoice in you?
7 Show us your steadfast love, O LORD,
and grant us your salvation.

8 Let me hear what God the LORD will speak,
for he will speak peace to his people, to his saints;
but let them not turn back to folly.
9 Surely his salvation is near to those who fear him,
that glory may dwell in our land.

10 Steadfast love and faithfulness meet;
righteousness and peace kiss each other.
11 Faithfulness springs up from the ground,
and righteousness looks down from the sky.
12 Yes, the LORD will give what is good,
and our land will yield its increase.
13 Righteousness will go before him
and make his footsteps a way.

You alone are God [Psalm 86]. Psalm 86 combines features of the lament and the praise psalm. As in the standard lament, the poet begins with a cry to God to hear his prayer (v. 1) and a series of petitions (vv. 2–7). There follows a section of praise constructed in the usual mode of a praise psalm as a series of assertions of God's praise-worthy acts and character (vv. 8–13, with v. 11 constituting a one-verse petition in the middle of the unit). The poem ends with a return to the lament format: description of the poet's crisis (v. 14); statement of confidence in God (v. 15); petition (vv. 16–17a); further statement of confidence (v. 17b).

86

A PRAYER OF DAVID.
Incline your ear, O LORD, and answer me,
   for I am poor and needy.
2 Preserve my life, for I am godly;
   save your servant, who trusts in you—you are my God.
3 Be gracious to me, O Lord,
   for to you do I cry all the day.
4 Gladden the soul of your servant,
   for to you, O Lord, do I lift up my soul.
5 For you, O Lord, are good and forgiving,
   abounding in steadfast love to all who call upon you.
6 Give ear, O LORD, to my prayer;
   listen to my plea for grace.
7 In the day of my trouble I call upon you,
   for you answer me.

8 There is none like you among the gods, O Lord,
   nor are there any works like yours.
9 All the nations you have made shall come
   and worship before you, O Lord,
   and shall glorify your name.
10 For you are great and do wondrous things;
   you alone are God.
11 Teach me your way, O LORD,
   that I may walk in your truth;
   unite my heart to fear your name.
12 I give thanks to you, O Lord my God, with my whole heart,
   and I will glorify your name forever.
13 For great is your steadfast love toward me;
   you have delivered my soul from the depths of Sheol.

14 O God, insolent men have risen up against me;
   a band of ruthless men seeks my life,
   and they do not set you before them.
15 But you, O Lord, are a God merciful and gracious,
   slow to anger and abounding in steadfast love and faithfulness.
16 Turn to me and be gracious to me;
   give your strength to your servant,
   and save the son of your maidservant.

¹⁷ Show me a sign of your favor,
  that those who hate me may see and be put to shame
  because you, LORD, have helped me and comforted me.

Glorious things of you are spoken, O city of God [Psalm 87]. This brief song of Zion praises the worship of God by praising the city of Jerusalem and everyone who lives in it. The subject of the first two verses, God's presence in his temple in Jerusalem, is the stimulus to the lyric response that follows. With Jerusalem's favored position thus established, the rest of this evocative poem praises the city of God by describing the exalted status that the city enjoys among people of many nations who know it. The Psalms are the songbook of a specific nation and believing community, but when we look closely at the declarations that the poets make, we often find the motif of the universal kingship and salvation of God, extending beyond all national boundaries to all nations and the whole earth.

---

87 A PSALM OF THE SONS OF KORAH. A SONG.
  On the holy mount stands the city he founded;
² the LORD loves the gates of Zion
    more than all the dwelling places of Jacob.
³ Glorious things of you are spoken,
    O city of God.   *Selah*

⁴ Among those who know me I mention Rahab and Babylon;
    behold, Philistia and Tyre, with Cush¹—
    "This one was born there," they say.
⁵ And of Zion it shall be said,
    "This one and that one were born in her";
    for the Most High himself will establish her.
⁶ The LORD records as he registers the peoples,
    "This one was born there."   *Selah*

⁷ Singers and dancers alike say,
    "All my springs are in you."

Afflicted and close to death [Psalm 88]. The lament motifs unfold as follows: introductory cry to God to hear the psalmist's prayer (vv. 1–2); description of the speaker's crisis, in which the poet uses the imagery of death and the pit to picture his distress as something that God has placed upon him (vv. 3–9); an unexpected insertion of rhetorical questions that indirectly obligate God to rescue the speaker so he can continue to serve God in the land of the living (vv. 10–12); petition to God to act (vv. 13–14); a return to a portrayal of the speaker's distress (vv. 15–18). This lament psalm stands out from the others in not including a statement of confidence in God or vow to praise him.

---

88 A SONG. A PSALM OF THE SONS OF KORAH. TO THE CHOIRMASTER: ACCORDING TO
  MAHALATH LEANNOTH. A MASKIL² OF HEMAN THE EZRAHITE.

¹ O LORD, God of my salvation;
    I cry out day and night before you.

---

¹ Probably *Nubia* ² Probably musical or liturgical terms

2   Let my prayer come before you;
     incline your ear to my cry!

3   For my soul is full of troubles,
     and my life draws near to Sheol.
4   I am counted among those who go down to the pit;
     I am a man who has no strength,
5   like one set loose among the dead,
     like the slain that lie in the grave,
   like those whom you remember no more,
     for they are cut off from your hand.
6   You have put me in the depths of the pit,
     in the regions dark and deep.
7   Your wrath lies heavy upon me,
     and you overwhelm me with all your waves.   *Selah*

8   You have caused my companions to shun me;
     you have made me a horror[1] to them.
   I am shut in so that I cannot escape;
9   my eye grows dim through sorrow.
   Every day I call upon you, O Lord;
     I spread out my hands to you.
10   Do you work wonders for the dead?
     Do the departed rise up to praise you?   *Selah*
11   Is your steadfast love declared in the grave,
     or your faithfulness in Abaddon?
12   Are your wonders known in the darkness,
     or your righteousness in the land of forgetfulness?

13   But I, O Lord, cry to you;
     in the morning my prayer comes before you.
14   O Lord, why do you cast my soul away?
     Why do you hide your face from me?
15   Afflicted and close to death from my youth up,
     I suffer your terrors; I am helpless.[2]
16   Your wrath has swept over me;
     your dreadful assaults destroy me.
17   They surround me like a flood all day long;
     they close in on me together.
18   You have caused my beloved and my friend to shun me;
     my companions have become darkness.[3]

Your faithfulness you swore to David: a prayer of the covenant [Psalm 89]. This poem will fall into place if we are aware of its context: the covenant promise that God made to David to establish his kingdom forever (2 Sam. 7:4), a promise ultimately fulfilled in Christ. The opening four verses allude to this covenant promise. After that, the poem ranges rather widely, but always within the understood context of the Davidic covenant. The units are as follows: catalog of God's praiseworthy acts in creation and

---

[1] Or *an abomination* [2] The meaning of the Hebrew word is uncertain [3] Or *darkness has become my only companion*

redemption, in the mode of praise psalms (vv. 5–18); an embellished poetic version of the Davidic covenant (vv. 19–37); a description of the current low estate of the nation and seeming abandonment of the Lord's anointed king, in the mode of the conventional lament psalm (vv. 38–45); an appeal to God to remedy the nation's distress, again in motifs reminiscent of the lament psalm, including questions directed to God (vv. 46–51); concluding benediction and amen, bringing book 3 of the Psalter to a close (v. 52).

89

A Maskil[1] of Ethan the Ezrahite.
I will sing of the steadfast love of the Lord, forever;
with my mouth I will make known your faithfulness to all generations.
2   For I said, "Steadfast love will be built up forever;
in the heavens you will establish your faithfulness."
3   You have said, "I have made a covenant with my chosen one;
I have sworn to David my servant:
4   'I will establish your offspring forever,
and build your throne for all generations.'"   *Selah*

5   Let the heavens praise your wonders, O Lord,
your faithfulness in the assembly of the holy ones!
6   For who in the skies can be compared to the Lord?
Who among the heavenly beings[2] is like the Lord,
7   a God greatly to be feared in the council of the holy ones,
and awesome above all who are around him?
8   O Lord God of hosts,
who is mighty as you are, O Lord,
with your faithfulness all around you?
9   You rule the raging of the sea;
when its waves rise, you still them.
10   You crushed Rahab like a carcass;
you scattered your enemies with your mighty arm.
11   The heavens are yours; the earth also is yours;
the world and all that is in it, you have founded them.
12   The north and the south, you have created them;
Tabor and Hermon joyously praise your name.
13   You have a mighty arm;
strong is your hand, high your right hand.
14   Righteousness and justice are the foundation of your throne;
steadfast love and faithfulness go before you.
15   Blessed are the people who know the festal shout,
who walk, O Lord, in the light of your face,
16   who exult in your name all the day
and in your righteousness are exalted.
17   For you are the glory of their strength;
by your favor our horn is exalted.
18   For our shield belongs to the Lord,
our king to the Holy One of Israel.

---

[1] Probably a musical or liturgical term [2] Hebrew *the sons of God,* or *the sons of might*

¹⁹ Of old you spoke in a vision to your godly one,¹ and said:
    "I have granted help to one who is mighty;
    I have exalted one chosen from the people.
²⁰ I have found David, my servant;
    with my holy oil I have anointed him,
²¹ so that my hand shall be established with him;
    my arm also shall strengthen him.
²² The enemy shall not outwit him;
    the wicked shall not humble him.
²³ I will crush his foes before him
    and strike down those who hate him.
²⁴ My faithfulness and my steadfast love shall be with him,
    and in my name shall his horn be exalted.
²⁵ I will set his hand on the sea
    and his right hand on the rivers.
²⁶ He shall cry to me, 'You are my Father,
    my God, and the Rock of my salvation.'
²⁷ And I will make him the firstborn,
    the highest of the kings of the earth.
²⁸ My steadfast love I will keep for him forever,
    and my covenant will stand firm² for him.
²⁹ I will establish his offspring forever
    and his throne as the days of the heavens.
³⁰ If his children forsake my law
    and do not walk according to my rules,³
³¹ if they violate my statutes
    and do not keep my commandments,
³² then I will punish their transgression with the rod
    and their iniquity with stripes,
³³ but I will not remove from him my steadfast love
    or be false to my faithfulness.
³⁴ I will not violate my covenant
    or alter the word that went forth from my lips.
³⁵ Once for all I have sworn by my holiness;
    I will not lie to David.
³⁶ His offspring shall endure forever,
    his throne as long as the sun before me.
³⁷ Like the moon it shall be established forever,
    a faithful witness in the skies."   *Selah*

³⁸ But now you have cast off and rejected;
    you are full of wrath against your anointed.
³⁹ You have renounced the covenant with your servant;
    you have defiled his crown in the dust.
⁴⁰ You have breached all his walls;
    you have laid his strongholds in ruins.
⁴¹ All who pass by plunder him;

---

¹ Some Hebrew manuscripts *godly ones* ² Or *will remain faithful* ³ Or *my just decrees*

he has become the scorn of his neighbors.
42 You have exalted the right hand of his foes;
    you have made all his enemies rejoice.
43 You have also turned back the edge of his sword,
    and you have not made him stand in battle.
44 You have made his splendor to cease
    and cast his throne to the ground.
45 You have cut short the days of his youth;
    you have covered him with shame.   *Selah*

46 How long, O Lᴏʀᴅ? Will you hide yourself forever?
    How long will your wrath burn like fire?
47 Remember how short my time is!
    For what vanity you have created all the children of man!
48 What man can live and never see death?
    Who can deliver his soul from the power of Sheol?   *Selah*

49 Lord, where is your steadfast love of old,
    which by your faithfulness you swore to David?
50 Remember, O Lord, how your servants are mocked,
    and how I bear in my heart the insults[1] of all the many nations,
51 with which your enemies mock, O Lᴏʀᴅ,
    with which they mock the footsteps of your anointed.

52 Blessed be the Lᴏʀᴅ forever!
                   Amen and Amen.

Teach us to number our days [Psalm 90]. Psalm 90 is a famous poem on the subject of human mutability and mortality, which in turn are related to human sinfulness. The units unfold as follows: an optimistic assertion of God's eternity (vv. 1–2); a foil established: the eternal God easily brings mortals to their individual ends (vv. 3–6); the poet asserts that God enforces human mortality as a punishment for human sinfulness (vv. 7–12); a prayer of petition that God will have pity on his mortal creatures (vv. 13–17).

BOOK FOUR

90

A Pʀᴀʏᴇʀ ᴏf Mᴏsᴇs, ᴛʜᴇ ᴍᴀɴ ᴏf Gᴏᴅ.
    Lord, you have been our dwelling place[2]
in all generations.
2 Before the mountains were brought forth,
    or ever you had formed the earth and the world,
    from everlasting to everlasting you are God.

3 You return man to dust
    and say, "Return, O children of man!"[3]
4 For a thousand years in your sight
    are but as yesterday when it is past,
    or as a watch in the night.

---

[1] Hebrew lacks *the insults* [2] Some Hebrew manuscripts (compare Septuagint) *our refuge* [3] Or *of Adam*

⁵ You sweep them away as with a flood; they are like a dream,
     like grass that is renewed in the morning:
⁶ in the morning it flourishes and is renewed;
     in the evening it fades and withers.

⁷ For we are brought to an end by your anger;
     by your wrath we are dismayed.
⁸ You have set our iniquities before you,
     our secret sins in the light of your presence.

⁹ For all our days pass away under your wrath;
     we bring our years to an end like a sigh.
¹⁰ The years of our life are seventy,
     or even by reason of strength eighty;
     yet their span¹ is but toil and trouble;
     they are soon gone, and we fly away.
¹¹ Who considers the power of your anger,
     and your wrath according to the fear of you?

¹² So teach us to number our days
     that we may get a heart of wisdom.
¹³ Return, O Lᴏʀᴅ! How long?
     Have pity on your servants!
¹⁴ Satisfy us in the morning with your steadfast love,
     that we may rejoice and be glad all our days.
¹⁵ Make us glad for as many days as you have afflicted us,
     and for as many years as we have seen evil.
¹⁶ Let your work be shown to your servants,
     and your glorious power to their children.
¹⁷ Let the favor² of the Lord our God be upon us,
     and establish the work of our hands upon us;
     yes, establish the work of our hands!

A psalm of trust in the God who protects [Psalm 91]. This poem has affinities with the psalm of praise, but the format of the poem does not fit that traditional genre. The opening verse identifies the subject of the poem (the person who trusts in God), and the second verse narrows that topic down to a theme (the confidence that comes to the person who trusts in God). The reason for this confidence is then given in the form of the catalog of God's praiseworthy acts of protection (vv. 3–13). The poet chooses examples that give us heightened pictures of danger and deliverance, and together they show the total range of God's protection. At the end, God is pictured as confirming that he will protect the person who trusts in him (vv. 14–16).

91 He who dwells in the shelter of the Most High
     will abide in the shadow of the Almighty.
² I will say³ to the Lᴏʀᴅ, "My refuge and my fortress,
     my God, in whom I trust."

¹ Or pride ² Or beauty ³ Septuagint He will say

3   For he will deliver you from the snare of the fowler
        and from the deadly pestilence.
4   He will cover you with his pinions,
        and under his wings you will find refuge;
        his faithfulness is a shield and buckler.
5   You will not fear the terror of the night,
        nor the arrow that flies by day,
6   nor the pestilence that stalks in darkness,
        nor the destruction that wastes at noonday.

7   A thousand may fall at your side,
        ten thousand at your right hand,
        but it will not come near you.
8   You will only look with your eyes
        and see the recompense of the wicked.

9   Because you have made the Lord your dwelling place—
        the Most High, who is my refuge[1]—
10 no evil shall be allowed to befall you,
        no plague come near your tent.

11 For he will command his angels concerning you
        to guard you in all your ways.
12 On their hands they will bear you up,
        lest you strike your foot against a stone.
13 You will tread on the lion and the adder;
        the young lion and the serpent you will trample underfoot.

14 "Because he holds fast to me in love, I will deliver him;
        I will protect him, because he knows my name.
15 When he calls to me, I will answer him;
        I will be with him in trouble;
        I will rescue him and honor him.
16 With long life I will satisfy him
        and show him my salvation."

It is good to give thanks to the Lord [Psalm 92]. This poem follows the usual order of a psalm of praise: formal call to praise (vv. 1–4); description of how the wicked who cannot praise God will perish, an implied foil to the poet who is about to praise God (vv. 5–9); in contrast to the wicked people just described, the poet praises God for his many blessings (vv. 10–15).

92   A Psalm. A Song for the Sabbath.

     It is good to give thanks to the Lord,
        to sing praises to your name, O Most High;
2   to declare your steadfast love in the morning,
        and your faithfulness by night,
3   to the music of the lute and the harp,

---

[1] Or For you, O Lord, are my refuge! You have made the Most High your dwelling place

to the melody of the lyre.

4 For you, O Lord, have made me glad by your work;
   at the works of your hands I sing for joy.

5 How great are your works, O Lord!
   Your thoughts are very deep!
6 The stupid man cannot know;
   the fool cannot understand this:
7 that though the wicked sprout like grass
   and all evildoers flourish,
they are doomed to destruction forever;
8   but you, O Lord, are on high forever.
9 For behold, your enemies, O Lord,
   for behold, your enemies shall perish;
   all evildoers shall be scattered.

10 But you have exalted my horn like that of the wild ox;
   you have poured over me[1] fresh oil.
11 My eyes have seen the downfall of my enemies;
   my ears have heard the doom of my evil assailants.

12 The righteous flourish like the palm tree
   and grow like a cedar in Lebanon.
13 They are planted in the house of the Lord;
   they flourish in the courts of our God.
14 They still bear fruit in old age;
   they are ever full of sap and green,
15 to declare that the Lord is upright;
   he is my rock, and there is no unrighteousness in him.

The Lord is robed in majesty [Psalm 93]. This brief praise psalm is unified by the motif of God's kingly rule. Every unit contributes to this motif in its own way, as follows: God described as a majestic king (v. 1); God's creation of the world makes it the sphere that he rules from his throne (vv. 1–2); God's might is declared to be even greater than the power of "many waters," perhaps meaning the primal forces of chaos (vv. 3–4); generalized praise of God, with the motif of God's decrees linking the verse to the theme of universal rule (v. 5).

93 The Lord reigns; he is robed in majesty;
   the Lord is robed; he has put on strength as his belt.
Yes, the world is established; it shall never be moved.
2 Your throne is established from of old;
   you are from everlasting.

3 The floods have lifted up, O Lord,
   the floods have lifted up their voice;
   the floods lift up their roaring.
4 Mightier than the thunders of many waters,

[1] Compare Syriac; the meaning of the Hebrew is uncertain

mightier than the waves of the sea,
the LORD on high is mighty!

5   Your decrees are very trustworthy;
     holiness befits your house,
     O LORD, forevermore.

Justice will return to the righteous [Psalm 94]. The unifying theme is God's justice
in its two dimensions of favor toward the righteous and judgment against the wicked.
From start to finish, God is pictured as divine judge. This content is packaged in the
traditional form of the lament, as follows: introductory cry to God to judge the earth
(vv. 1–2); portrait of the evil, presented as the problem that requires the solution represented by God's justice (vv. 3–7); satiric put-down of the wicked (vv. 8–11) for thinking
that the judge does not know what they are doing (see v. 7), an implied variation on
the conventional motif of confidence in God; statement of confidence in God to judge on
behalf of the righteous (vv. 12–15); in place of the customary vow to praise God, a section that actually praises God, in the mode of the praise psalms (vv. 16–23).

94

O LORD, God of vengeance,
O God of vengeance, shine forth!
2   Rise up, O judge of the earth;
     repay to the proud what they deserve!
3   O LORD, how long shall the wicked,
     how long shall the wicked exult?
4   They pour out their arrogant words;
     all the evildoers boast.
5   They crush your people, O LORD,
     and afflict your heritage.
6   They kill the widow and the sojourner,
     and murder the fatherless;
7   and they say, "The LORD does not see;
     the God of Jacob does not perceive."

8   Understand, O dullest of the people!
     Fools, when will you be wise?
9   He who planted the ear, does he not hear?
     He who formed the eye, does he not see?
10   He who disciplines the nations, does he not rebuke?
     He who teaches man knowledge—
11   the LORD—knows the thoughts of man,
         that they are but a breath.[1]

12   Blessed is the man whom you discipline, O LORD,
     and whom you teach out of your law,
13   to give him rest from days of trouble,
     until a pit is dug for the wicked.
14   For the LORD will not forsake his people;
     he will not abandon his heritage;

---

[1] Septuagint *they are futile*

¹⁵   for justice will return to the righteous,
         and all the upright in heart will follow it.

¹⁶   Who rises up for me against the wicked?
         Who stands up for me against evildoers?
¹⁷   If the LORD had not been my help,
         my soul would soon have lived in the land of silence.
¹⁸   When I thought, "My foot slips,"
         your steadfast love, O LORD, held me up.
¹⁹   When the cares of my heart are many,
         your consolations cheer my soul.
²⁰   Can wicked rulers be allied with you,
         those who frame injustice by statute?
²¹   They band together against the life of the righteous
         and condemn the innocent to death.¹
²²   But the LORD has become my stronghold,
         and my God the rock of my refuge.
²³   He will bring back on them their iniquity
         and wipe them out for their wickedness;
         the LORD our God will wipe them out.

Let us sing to the LORD [Psalm 95]. Many of the psalms are innovative modifications of either the lament psalm or the praise psalm. Psalm 95 is a praise psalm that springs surprises on us, including such a distinct shift halfway through that we seem to have two distinct poems. The formal call to praise (vv. 1–2, 6) reads like a priestly call to worship. The so-called motivatory sections ("for . . .") that follow these two calls to praise are exactly what we expect in a praise psalm, praising God for his creation of the world and his covenant with his people (vv. 3–5, 7a). But the poem ends with a wholly unexpected denunciation of the nation from the voice of God, who reaches back to the exodus wanderings for evidence of his people's faithlessness (vv. 7b–11).

95

Oh come, let us sing to the LORD;
         let us make a joyful noise to the rock of our salvation!
²   Let us come into his presence with thanksgiving;
         let us make a joyful noise to him with songs of praise!
³   For the LORD is a great God,
         and a great King above all gods.
⁴   In his hand are the depths of the earth;
         the heights of the mountains are his also.
⁵   The sea is his, for he made it,
         and his hands formed the dry land.

⁶   Oh come, let us worship and bow down;
         let us kneel before the LORD, our Maker!
⁷   For he is our God,
         and we are the people of his pasture,
         and the sheep of his hand.

¹ Hebrew *condemn innocent blood*

Today, if you hear his voice,
8   do not harden your hearts, as at Meribah,
      as on the day at Massah in the wilderness,
9   when your fathers put me to the test
      and put me to the proof, though they had seen my work.
10 For forty years I loathed that generation
      and said, "They are a people who go astray in their heart,
      and they have not known my ways."
11 Therefore I swore in my wrath,
      "They shall not enter my rest."

Sing to the Lord a new song [Psalm 96]. The conventional motifs of the praise psalm unfold as follows: formal call to praise, issuing a command to praise, giving the mode of praise (song), and identifying the group to whom the call is issued (all the earth; vv. 1–3); brief catalog of God's praiseworthy acts and qualities (vv. 4–6); exalted call to praise (vv. 7–9); brief dramatized script of what the poet wants the people to say (v. 10); a command to various forces of nature to praise God, using the rhetorical formula "let . . ." (vv. 11–12a); prediction that God will come to judge the earth (vv. 12b –13). Again the praise overflows national concerns to call on all the nations (vv. 3, 5, 6, 10, 13). Despite the repeated formulas in the fixed forms of the Psalter, every individual example is unique.

96

      Oh sing to the Lord a new song;
      sing to the Lord, all the earth!
2   Sing to the Lord, bless his name;
      tell of his salvation from day to day.
3   Declare his glory among the nations,
      his marvelous works among all the peoples!
4   For great is the Lord, and greatly to be praised;
      he is to be feared above all gods.
5   For all the gods of the peoples are worthless idols,
      but the Lord made the heavens.
6   Splendor and majesty are before him;
      strength and beauty are in his sanctuary.

7   Ascribe to the Lord, O families of the peoples,
      ascribe to the Lord glory and strength!
8   Ascribe to the Lord the glory due his name;
      bring an offering, and come into his courts!
9   Worship the Lord in the splendor of holiness;[1]
      tremble before him, all the earth!

10 Say among the nations, "The Lord reigns!
      Yes, the world is established; it shall never be moved;
      he will judge the peoples with equity."

11 Let the heavens be glad, and let the earth rejoice;
      let the sea roar, and all that fills it;

---

[1] Or *in holy attire*

12   let the field exult, and everything in it!
        Then shall all the trees of the forest sing for joy
13   before the Lord, for he comes,
            for he comes to judge the earth.
        He will judge the world in righteousness,
            and the peoples in his faithfulness.

> **Rejoice in the Lord** [Psalm 97]. Setting the tone for the entire poem, the poet starts
> his praise psalm by asserting that "the Lord reigns" and listing the recipients of the call
> to praise as natural phenomena (the earth and coastlands, v. 1). The first unit of actual
> praise focuses on forces of nature, used to paint a metaphoric and hyperbolic portrait
> of God as the God of the storm (vv. 2–5). From that point the units are as follows: an
> assertion that the heavens proclaim God's glory and people observe it (v. 6); God's supe-
> riority to pagan idols (v. 7); an assertion that Zion and Judah rejoice because of God's
> judgments (v. 8); further catalog of God's exaltation and praiseworthy acts (vv. 9–11);
> command to rejoice in God and give thanks to him (v. 12).

97

The Lord reigns, let the earth rejoice;
        let the many coastlands be glad!
2   Clouds and thick darkness are all around him;
        righteousness and justice are the foundation of his throne.
3   Fire goes before him
        and burns up his adversaries all around.
4   His lightnings light up the world;
        the earth sees and trembles.
5   The mountains melt like wax before the Lord,
        before the Lord of all the earth.

6   The heavens proclaim his righteousness,
        and all the peoples see his glory.
7   All worshipers of images are put to shame,
        who make their boast in worthless idols;
        worship him, all you gods!

8   Zion hears and is glad,
        and the daughters of Judah rejoice,
        because of your judgments, O Lord.
9   For you, O Lord, are most high over all the earth;
        you are exalted far above all gods.

10 O you who love the Lord, hate evil!
        He preserves the lives of his saints;
        he delivers them from the hand of the wicked.
11 Light is sown[1] for the righteous,
        and joy for the upright in heart.
12 Rejoice in the Lord, O you righteous,
        and give thanks to his holy name!

---

[1] Most Hebrew manuscripts; one Hebrew manuscript, Septuagint, Syriac, Jerome *Light dawns*

Let the sea roar [Psalm 98]. The format of this praise psalm is as follows: call to praise (v. 1); catalog of praiseworthy acts on behalf of Israel and the nations (vv. 1–3); call to people to praise God (vv. 4–6); call to the forces of nature to praise, using the "let . . ." formula (vv. 7–8); concluding motivatory section ("for. . ."), with the focus on God's coming as judge of the earth (v. 9). Imagery of festive sounds is the dominant image pattern.

98

A Psalm.

Oh sing to the Lord a new song,
for he has done marvelous things!
His right hand and his holy arm
have worked salvation for him.
2 The Lord has made known his salvation;
he has revealed his righteousness in the sight of the nations.
3 He has remembered his steadfast love and faithfulness
to the house of Israel.
All the ends of the earth have seen
the salvation of our God.

4 Make a joyful noise to the Lord, all the earth;
break forth into joyous song and sing praises!
5 Sing praises to the Lord with the lyre,
with the lyre and the sound of melody!
6 With trumpets and the sound of the horn
make a joyful noise before the King, the Lord!

7 Let the sea roar, and all that fills it;
the world and those who dwell in it!
8 Let the rivers clap their hands;
let the hills sing for joy together
9 before the Lord, for he comes
to judge the earth.
He will judge the world with righteousness,
and the peoples with equity.

Praise psalm [Psalm 99]. This is a streamlined praise psalm that employs the following motifs: opening assertion that God reigns (vv. 1–2); mingled praise and call to praise (vv. 3–5); catalog of God's praiseworthy acts (vv. 6–8); call to praise (v. 9). Two image patterns dominate: God's enthronement and kingly exaltation, and the worship of God, including priestly references.

99

The Lord reigns; let the peoples tremble!
He sits enthroned upon the cherubim; let the earth quake!
2 The Lord is great in Zion;
he is exalted over all the peoples.
3 Let them praise your great and awesome name!
Holy is he!

⁴ The King in his might loves justice.¹
    You have established equity;
  you have executed justice
    and righteousness in Jacob.
⁵ Exalt the LORD our God;
    worship at his footstool!
  Holy is he!

⁶ Moses and Aaron were among his priests,
    Samuel also was among those who called upon his name.
  They called to the LORD, and he answered them.
⁷ In the pillar of the cloud he spoke to them;
    they kept his testimonies
    and the statute that he gave them.

⁸ O LORD our God, you answered them;
    you were a forgiving God to them,
    but an avenger of their wrongdoings.
⁹ Exalt the LORD our God,
    and worship at his holy mountain;
    for the LORD our God is holy!

Enter his gates with thanksgiving [Psalm 100]. Psalm 100 combines features of the praise psalm and the worship psalm. The first four verses use the imperative form of the verb and thereby command people to perform a range of acts of praise, including worship in the temple (vv. 1–4); the last verse praises God for specific attributes (v. 5).

100

A PSALM FOR GIVING THANKS.
Make a joyful noise to the LORD, all the earth!
² Serve the LORD with gladness!
    Come into his presence with singing!

³ Know that the LORD, he is God!
    It is he who made us, and we are his;²
  we are his people, and the sheep of his pasture.

⁴ Enter his gates with thanksgiving,
    and his courts with praise!
  Give thanks to him; bless his name!

⁵ For the LORD is good;
    his steadfast love endures forever,
    and his faithfulness to all generations.

I will ponder the way that is blameless: a godly man's list of resolutions [Psalm 101]. It is customary to call this psalm one of the royal psalms, expressing a king's sentiments, specifically. But except for one or two references, the pledge that the speaker voices in this psalm can be any godly person's list of resolutions. The structure of the poem is strongly repetitive, with the principle of choosing to act virtuously maintained

¹ Or *The might of the King loves justice* ² Or *and not we ourselves*

in different forms. A good analytic grid is to note the things that the speaker refuses to do in regard to the wicked and that he determines positively to do regarding the godly and virtuous. Additionally, we can note the spheres of life in which the speaker's actions occur.

101

A PSALM OF DAVID.
I will sing of steadfast love and justice;
  to you, O LORD, I will make music.
2 I will ponder the way that is blameless.
    Oh when will you come to me?
  I will walk with integrity of heart
    within my house;
3 I will not set before my eyes
    anything that is worthless.
  I hate the work of those who fall away;
    it shall not cling to me.
4 A perverse heart shall be far from me;
    I will know nothing of evil.

5 Whoever slanders his neighbor secretly
    I will destroy.
  Whoever has a haughty look and an arrogant heart
    I will not endure.

6 I will look with favor on the faithful in the land,
    that they may dwell with me;
  he who walks in the way that is blameless
    shall minister to me.

7 No one who practices deceit
    shall dwell in my house;
  no one who utters lies
    shall continue before my eyes.

8 Morning by morning I will destroy
    all the wicked in the land,
  cutting off all the evildoers
    from the city of the LORD.

I wither away like grass [Psalm 102]. As the headnote hints, this is one of the most intense personal laments in the Psalter. It is also the fifth of the seven penitential psalms, though there is little in the psalm to link it specifically with God's judgment against the speaker for sin. The motifs unfold as follows: introductory cry to God (vv. 1–2); extended metaphoric and hyperbolic portrait of the personal desolation of the speaker (vv. 3–11); extended statement of confidence in God—so extended that it becomes a catalog of God's acts in the mode of the praise psalms (vv. 12–22); brief return to the speaker's crisis (v. 23); petition to God to act (v. 24); praise to God for being eternal, in contrast to the mortal speaker (vv. 25–27); statement of confidence in God (v. 28).

102

A Prayer of one afflicted, when he is faint and pours out his complaint before the Lord.

¹ Hear my prayer, O Lord;
  let my cry come to you!
² Do not hide your face from me
    in the day of my distress!
  Incline your ear to me;
    answer me speedily in the day when I call!

³ For my days pass away like smoke,
    and my bones burn like a furnace.
⁴ My heart is struck down like grass and has withered;
    I forget to eat my bread.
⁵ Because of my loud groaning
    my bones cling to my flesh.
⁶ I am like a desert owl of the wilderness,
    like an owl¹ of the waste places;
⁷ I lie awake;
    I am like a lonely sparrow on the housetop.
⁸ All the day my enemies taunt me;
    those who deride me use my name for a curse.
⁹ For I eat ashes like bread
    and mingle tears with my drink,
¹⁰ because of your indignation and anger;
    for you have taken me up and thrown me down.
¹¹ My days are like an evening shadow;
    I wither away like grass.

¹² But you, O Lord, are enthroned forever;
    you are remembered throughout all generations.
¹³ You will arise and have pity on Zion;
    it is the time to favor her;
    the appointed time has come.
¹⁴ For your servants hold her stones dear
    and have pity on her dust.
¹⁵ Nations will fear the name of the Lord,
    and all the kings of the earth will fear your glory.
¹⁶ For the Lord builds up Zion;
    he appears in his glory;
¹⁷ he regards the prayer of the destitute
    and does not despise their prayer.
¹⁸ Let this be recorded for a generation to come,
    so that a people yet to be created may praise the Lord:

¹ The precise identity of these birds is uncertain

19   that he looked down from his holy height;
      from heaven the Lord looked at the earth,
20   to hear the groans of the prisoners,
      to set free those who were doomed to die,
21   that they may declare in Zion the name of the Lord,
      and in Jerusalem his praise,
22   when peoples gather together,
      and kingdoms, to worship the Lord.

23   He has broken my strength in midcourse;
      he has shortened my days.
24   "O my God," I say, "take me not away
      in the midst of my days—
  you whose years endure
      throughout all generations!"

25   Of old you laid the foundation of the earth,
      and the heavens are the work of your hands.
26   They will perish, but you will remain;
      they will all wear out like a garment.
  You will change them like a robe, and they will pass away,
27   but you are the same, and your years have no end.
28   The children of your servants shall dwell secure;
      their offspring shall be established before you.

Bless the Lord, O my soul [Psalm 103]. Psalm 103 is a high point among the praise psalms. It is so exalted in scope and language that it ranks as an *ode—the most elevated member of the lyric family. The poem unfolds as follows: a call to praise, directed inward to the poet himself and consisting of a threefold call to "bless" God (vv. 1–2); a catalog of six great acts of God, with the first five expressed in strictly parallel form, "who . . ." (vv. 3–5); a brief catalog of God's general acts (v. 6) and his acts in the history of Israel (v. 7); praise of four attributes of God (v. 8), balanced by a catalog of four corresponding acts of God (vv. 9–10); three parallel similes that praise God's attributes (vv. 11–13); praise of the permanent love of God (vv. 17–18) set over against the foil of the transience of people (vv. 14–16); following a verse that sets up the motif of God's universal kingship (v. 19), a climax of four doxologies (commands to praise) that work out of the details of God's universal kingship (vv. 20–22).

103   Of David.
    Bless the Lord, O my soul,
      and all that is within me,
      bless his holy name!
2   Bless the Lord, O my soul,
      and forget not all his benefits,
3   who forgives all your iniquity,
      who heals all your diseases,
4   who redeems your life from the pit,
      who crowns you with steadfast love and mercy,

⁵ who satisfies you with good
   so that your youth is renewed like the eagle's.

⁶ The LORD works righteousness
   and justice for all who are oppressed.
⁷ He made known his ways to Moses,
   his acts to the people of Israel.
⁸ The LORD is merciful and gracious,
   slow to anger and abounding in steadfast love.
⁹ He will not always chide,
   nor will he keep his anger forever.
¹⁰ He does not deal with us according to our sins,
   nor repay us according to our iniquities.
¹¹ For as high as the heavens are above the earth,
   so great is his steadfast love toward those who fear him;
¹² as far as the east is from the west,
   so far does he remove our transgressions from us.
¹³ As a father shows compassion to his children,
   so the LORD shows compassion to those who fear him.
¹⁴ For he knows our frame;[1]
   he remembers that we are dust.

¹⁵ As for man, his days are like grass;
   he flourishes like a flower of the field;
¹⁶ for the wind passes over it, and it is gone,
   and its place knows it no more.
¹⁷ But the steadfast love of the LORD is from everlasting to everlasting on those who
           fear him,
   and his righteousness to children's children,
¹⁸ to those who keep his covenant
   and remember to do his commandments.
¹⁹ The LORD has established his throne in the heavens,
   and his kingdom rules over all.

²⁰ Bless the LORD, O you his angels,
   you mighty ones who do his word,
   obeying the voice of his word!
²¹ Bless the LORD, all his hosts,
   his ministers, who do his will!
²² Bless the LORD, all his works,
   in all places of his dominion.
   Bless the LORD, O my soul!

Ode to nature and the God of nature [Psalm 104]. This is the fourth of five nature poems in the Psalter, and it is so exalted and long that it ranks as an ode. The poem unfolds as follows: opening ascription of praise to the God of nature (v. 1); the function of nature (to serve God), expressed in highly metaphoric language (vv. 1–4); the origin of nature (a mini–creation story), again highly figurative in expression (vv. 5–9); God's

---

[1] Or knows how we are formed

provision for nature and through nature at the level of the earth—nature at ground level (vv. 10–18); the provision that nature supplies at the level of the heavenly bodies, which give us time (vv. 19–23); emotional interlude (v. 24); the provision that nature supplies in the ocean (vv. 25–26); summary statement about God's provisions in nature, with a strongly theocentric view of nature emerging (vv. 27–30); concluding praise section in which the poet expresses the wish that the God of nature will be appropriately honored and detractors of that glory subdued (vv. 31–35).

104

Bless the LORD, O my soul!
O LORD my God, you are very great!
You are clothed with splendor and majesty,
2   covering yourself with light as with a garment,
    stretching out the heavens like a tent.
3   He lays the beams of his chambers on the waters;
    he makes the clouds his chariot;
        he rides on the wings of the wind;
4   he makes his messengers winds,
        his ministers a flaming fire.

5   He set the earth on its foundations,
        so that it should never be moved.
6   You covered it with the deep as with a garment;
        the waters stood above the mountains.
7   At your rebuke they fled;
        at the sound of your thunder they took to flight.
8   The mountains rose, the valleys sank down
        to the place that you appointed for them.
9   You set a boundary that they may not pass,
        so that they might not again cover the earth.

10   You make springs gush forth in the valleys;
        they flow between the hills;
11   they give drink to every beast of the field;
        the wild donkeys quench their thirst.
12   Beside them the birds of the heavens dwell;
        they sing among the branches.
13   From your lofty abode you water the mountains;
        the earth is satisfied with the fruit of your work.

14   You cause the grass to grow for the livestock
        and plants for man to cultivate,
    that he may bring forth food from the earth
15   and wine to gladden the heart of man,
    oil to make his face shine
        and bread to strengthen man's heart.

16   The trees of the LORD are watered abundantly,
        the cedars of Lebanon that he planted.

¹⁷ In them the birds build their nests;
    the stork has her home in the fir trees.
¹⁸ The high mountains are for the wild goats;
    the rocks are a refuge for the rock badgers.

¹⁹ He made the moon to mark the seasons;¹
    the sun knows its time for setting.
²⁰ You make darkness, and it is night,
    when all the beasts of the forest creep about.
²¹ The young lions roar for their prey,
    seeking their food from God.
²² When the sun rises, they steal away
    and lie down in their dens.
²³ Man goes out to his work
    and to his labor until the evening.

²⁴ O Lord, how manifold are your works!
    In wisdom have you made them all;
    the earth is full of your creatures.
²⁵ Here is the sea, great and wide,
    which teems with creatures innumerable,
    living things both small and great.
²⁶ There go the ships,
    and Leviathan, which you formed to play in it.²

²⁷ These all look to you,
    to give them their food in due season.
²⁸ When you give it to them, they gather it up;
    when you open your hand, they are filled with good things.
²⁹ When you hide your face, they are dismayed;
    when you take away their breath, they die
    and return to their dust.
³⁰ When you send forth your Spirit,³ they are created,
    and you renew the face of the ground.

³¹ May the glory of the Lord endure forever;
    may the Lord rejoice in his works,
³² who looks on the earth and it trembles,
    who touches the mountains and they smoke!
³³ I will sing to the Lord as long as I live;
    I will sing praise to my God while I have being.
³⁴ May my meditation be pleasing to him,
    for I rejoice in the Lord.
³⁵ Let sinners be consumed from the earth,
    and let the wicked be no more!
Bless the Lord, O my soul!
Praise the Lord!

---

[1] Or *the appointed times* (compare Genesis 1:14) [2] Or *you formed to play with* [3] Or *breath*

The song of Israel's salvation [Psalm 105]. Every praise psalm has its own finger-print, and this one's distinctive feature is that it is a long historical poem as well as a praise psalm. The formal call to praise is extended over six verses (vv. 1–6). Thereafter the poet rehearses in poetic and verse form the following phases of Israelite history: the patriarchal origins of the nation (vv. 7–15); rescue in the time of Joseph (vv. 16–22); deliverance from bondage in Egypt (vv. 23–38); provision in the wilderness wanderings (vv. 39–42); settlement in the Promised Land (vv. 43–45).

105

Oh give thanks to the Lord; call upon his name;
make known his deeds among the peoples!

2 Sing to him, sing praises to him;
tell of all his wondrous works!

3 Glory in his holy name;
let the hearts of those who seek the Lord rejoice!

4 Seek the Lord and his strength;
seek his presence continually!

5 Remember the wondrous works that he has done,
his miracles, and the judgments he uttered,

6 O offspring of Abraham, his servant,
children of Jacob, his chosen ones!

7 He is the Lord our God;
his judgments are in all the earth.

8 He remembers his covenant forever,
the word that he commanded, for a thousand generations,

9 the covenant that he made with Abraham,
his sworn promise to Isaac,

10 which he confirmed to Jacob as a statute,
to Israel as an everlasting covenant,

11 saying, "To you I will give the land of Canaan
as your portion for an inheritance."

12 When they were few in number,
of little account, and sojourners in it,

13 wandering from nation to nation,
from one kingdom to another people,

14 he allowed no one to oppress them;
he rebuked kings on their account,

15 saying, "Touch not my anointed ones,
do my prophets no harm!"

16 When he summoned a famine on the land
and broke all supply[1] of bread,

17 he had sent a man ahead of them,
Joseph, who was sold as a slave.

18 His feet were hurt with fetters;
his neck was put in a collar of iron;

19 until what he had said came to pass,

[1] Hebrew *staff*

the word of the LORD tested him.
20 The king sent and released him;
the ruler of the peoples set him free;
21 he made him lord of his house
and ruler of all his possessions,
22 to bind[1] his princes at his pleasure
and to teach his elders wisdom.

23 Then Israel came to Egypt;
Jacob sojourned in the land of Ham.
24 And the LORD made his people very fruitful
and made them stronger than their foes.
25 He turned their hearts to hate his people,
to deal craftily with his servants.

26 He sent Moses, his servant,
and Aaron, whom he had chosen.
27 They performed his signs among them
and miracles in the land of Ham.
28 He sent darkness, and made the land dark;
they did not rebel[2] against his words.
29 He turned their waters into blood
and caused their fish to die.
30 Their land swarmed with frogs,
even in the chambers of their kings.
31 He spoke, and there came swarms of flies,
and gnats throughout their country.
32 He gave them hail for rain,
and fiery lightning bolts through their land.
33 He struck down their vines and fig trees,
and shattered the trees of their country.
34 He spoke, and the locusts came,
young locusts without number,
35 which devoured all the vegetation in their land
and ate up the fruit of their ground.
36 He struck down all the firstborn in their land,
the firstfruits of all their strength.

37 Then he brought out Israel with silver and gold,
and there was none among his tribes who stumbled.
38 Egypt was glad when they departed,
for dread of them had fallen upon it.

39 He spread a cloud for a covering,
and fire to give light by night.
40 They asked, and he brought quail,
and gave them bread from heaven in abundance.
41 He opened the rock, and water gushed out;

---

[1] Septuagint, Syriac, Jerome instruct [2] Septuagint, Syriac omit not

it flowed through the desert like a river.
⁴² For he remembered his holy promise,
and Abraham, his servant.

⁴³ So he brought his people out with joy,
his chosen ones with singing.
⁴⁴ And he gave them the lands of the nations,
and they took possession of the fruit of the peoples' toil,
⁴⁵ that they might keep his statutes
and observe his laws.
Praise the LORD!

Both we and our fathers have sinned [Psalm 106]. Like the preceding psalm, Psalm 106 is a long poetic rehearsal of Israelite history, with such a strong emphasis on the sinfulness of the nation that the poem takes on the character of a confession. Some sections are a catalog of God's praiseworthy acts, in the mode of praise psalms; other sections expose Israel's failings and fall into the genre of satire. The poem begins with a call to praise (vv. 1–2), followed by an unexpected beatitude on virtuous people (v. 3) and the speaker's personal prayer for the prosperity of his nation (vv. 4–5). Thereafter the motifs unfold as follows: praise of God's mercy on his sinful people at the time of the exodus (vv. 6–12); satiric litany of the nation's ignominious behaviors in the wilderness (vv. 13–23) and in the Promised Land (vv. 24–39); recollection of God's anger toward an apostate people during the Babylonian captivity (vv. 40–43); recollection of God's subsequent relenting from his anger on the basis of his covenant love (vv. 44–46); prayer for God's salvation (v. 47); beatitude toward God, plus an amen (v. 48). Literature is a concrete universal; by means of these specific references to OT Israel we can perceive truth about God and his people in all eras. This psalm ends the fourth unit in the Hebrew Psalter.

106

Praise the LORD!
Oh give thanks to the LORD, for he is good,
for his steadfast love endures forever!
² Who can utter the mighty deeds of the LORD,
or declare all his praise?
³ Blessed are they who observe justice,
who do righteousness at all times!

⁴ Remember me, O LORD, when you show favor to your people;
help me when you save them,¹
⁵ that I may look upon the prosperity of your chosen ones,
that I may rejoice in the gladness of your nation,
that I may glory with your inheritance.

⁶ Both we and our fathers have sinned;
we have committed iniquity; we have done wickedness.
⁷ Our fathers, when they were in Egypt,
did not consider your wondrous works;
they did not remember the abundance of your steadfast love,

¹ Or Remember me, O LORD, with the favor you show to your people; help me with your salvation

but rebelled by the sea, at the Red Sea.
8 Yet he saved them for his name's sake,
    that he might make known his mighty power.
9 He rebuked the Red Sea, and it became dry,
    and he led them through the deep as through a desert.
10 So he saved them from the hand of the foe
    and redeemed them from the power of the enemy.
11 And the waters covered their adversaries;
    not one of them was left.
12 Then they believed his words;
    they sang his praise.

13 But they soon forgot his works;
    they did not wait for his counsel.
14 But they had a wanton craving in the wilderness,
    and put God to the test in the desert;
15 he gave them what they asked,
    but sent a wasting disease among them.

16 When men in the camp were jealous of Moses
    and Aaron, the holy one of the LORD,
17 the earth opened and swallowed up Dathan,
    and covered the company of Abiram.
18 Fire also broke out in their company;
    the flame burned up the wicked.

19 They made a calf in Horeb
    and worshiped a metal image.
20 They exchanged the glory of God
    for the image of an ox that eats grass.
21 They forgot God, their Savior,
    who had done great things in Egypt,
22 wondrous works in the land of Ham,
    and awesome deeds by the Red Sea.
23 Therefore he said he would destroy them—
    had not Moses, his chosen one,
    stood in the breach before him,
    to turn away his wrath from destroying them.

24 Then they despised the pleasant land,
    having no faith in his promise.
25 They murmured in their tents,
    and did not obey the voice of the LORD.
26 Therefore he raised his hand and swore to them
    that he would make them fall in the wilderness,
27 and would make their offspring fall among the nations,
    scattering them among the lands.

28   Then they yoked themselves to the Baal of Peor,
        and ate sacrifices offered to the dead;
29   they provoked the Lord to anger with their deeds,
        and a plague broke out among them.
30   Then Phinehas stood up and intervened,
        and the plague was stayed.
31   And that was counted to him as righteousness
        from generation to generation forever.

32   They angered him at the waters of Meribah,
        and it went ill with Moses on their account,
33   for they made his spirit bitter,[1]
        and he spoke rashly with his lips.

34   They did not destroy the peoples,
        as the Lord commanded them,
35   but they mixed with the nations
        and learned to do as they did.
36   They served their idols,
        which became a snare to them.
37   They sacrificed their sons
        and their daughters to the demons;
38   they poured out innocent blood,
        the blood of their sons and daughters,
     whom they sacrificed to the idols of Canaan,
        and the land was polluted with blood.
39   Thus they became unclean by their acts,
        and played the whore in their deeds.

40   Then the anger of the Lord was kindled against his people,
        and he abhorred his heritage;
41   he gave them into the hand of the nations,
        so that those who hated them ruled over them.
42   Their enemies oppressed them,
        and they were brought into subjection under their power.
43   Many times he delivered them,
        but they were rebellious in their purposes
        and were brought low through their iniquity.

44   Nevertheless, he looked upon their distress,
        when he heard their cry.
45   For their sake he remembered his covenant,
        and relented according to the abundance of his steadfast love.
46   He caused them to be pitied
        by all those who held them captive.

47   Save us, O Lord our God,
        and gather us from among the nations,

---

[1] Or *they rebelled against God's Spirit*

that we may give thanks to your holy name
and glory in your praise.

[48] Blessed be the LORD, the God of Israel,
from everlasting to everlasting!
And let all the people say, "Amen!"
Praise the LORD!

He delivered them from their distress [Psalm 107]. This praise poem begins with a call to praise (vv. 1–3), after which it divides into two distinct movements. Verses 4–32 praise God by narrating four parallel rescues that God performed—to people lost in the desert (vv. 4–9); people in prison (vv. 10–16); people suffering from disease (vv. 17–22); people threatened on the stormy sea (vv. 23–32). Each of these four ministries follows the same pattern: presenting a group in distress; the refrain that "then they cried to the LORD in their trouble," followed by the refrain that "he delivered them from their distress"; a narrative of blessing that exactly reverses the preceding distress, concluded with the refrain command "Let them thank the LORD for his steadfast love, for his wondrous works to the children of man." The second main unit praises God for his power over his creatures, as seen in his ability to reverse an existing situation. First we observe how God turns something positive into something desolate (vv. 33–34), then something desolate into something fruitful (vv. 35–38). In a parallel reversal, God raises the low (vv. 39, 41) and brings down the exalted (v. 40). The poem ends on the positive note of asserting that the upright delight in what God does (v. 42), accompanied by an exhortation to readers or hearers of the psalm to attend to what the poet has said.

BOOK FIVE

107

Oh give thanks to the LORD, for he is good,
for his steadfast love endures forever!
[2] Let the redeemed of the LORD say so,
whom he has redeemed from trouble[1]
[3] and gathered in from the lands,
from the east and from the west,
from the north and from the south.

[4] Some wandered in desert wastes,
finding no way to a city to dwell in;
[5] hungry and thirsty,
their soul fainted within them.
[6] Then they cried to the LORD in their trouble,
and he delivered them from their distress.
[7] He led them by a straight way
till they reached a city to dwell in.
[8] Let them thank the LORD for his steadfast love,
for his wondrous works to the children of man!
[9] For he satisfies the longing soul,
and the hungry soul he fills with good things.

[1] Or from the hand of the foe

¹⁰ Some sat in darkness and in the shadow of death,
    prisoners in affliction and in irons,
¹¹ for they had rebelled against the words of God,
    and spurned the counsel of the Most High.
¹² So he bowed their hearts down with hard labor;
    they fell down, with none to help.
¹³ Then they cried to the Lord in their trouble,
    and he delivered them from their distress.
¹⁴ He brought them out of darkness and the shadow of death,
    and burst their bonds apart.
¹⁵ Let them thank the Lord for his steadfast love,
    for his wondrous works to the children of man!
¹⁶ For he shatters the doors of bronze
    and cuts in two the bars of iron.

¹⁷ Some were fools through their sinful ways,
    and because of their iniquities suffered affliction;
¹⁸ they loathed any kind of food,
    and they drew near to the gates of death.
¹⁹ Then they cried to the Lord in their trouble,
    and he delivered them from their distress.
²⁰ He sent out his word and healed them,
    and delivered them from their destruction.
²¹ Let them thank the Lord for his steadfast love,
    for his wondrous works to the children of man!
²² And let them offer sacrifices of thanksgiving,
    and tell of his deeds in songs of joy!

²³ Some went down to the sea in ships,
    doing business on the great waters;
²⁴ they saw the deeds of the Lord,
    his wondrous works in the deep.
²⁵ For he commanded and raised the stormy wind,
    which lifted up the waves of the sea.
²⁶ They mounted up to heaven; they went down to the depths;
    their courage melted away in their evil plight;
²⁷ they reeled and staggered like drunken men
    and were at their wits' end.[1]
²⁸ Then they cried to the Lord in their trouble,
    and he delivered them from their distress.
²⁹ He made the storm be still,
    and the waves of the sea were hushed.
³⁰ Then they were glad that the waters[2] were quiet,
    and he brought them to their desired haven.
³¹ Let them thank the Lord for his steadfast love,
    for his wondrous works to the children of man!

---

[1] Hebrew *and all their wisdom was swallowed up*   [2] Hebrew *they*

³² Let them extol him in the congregation of the people,
    and praise him in the assembly of the elders.

³³ He turns rivers into a desert,
    springs of water into thirsty ground,
³⁴ a fruitful land into a salty waste,
    because of the evil of its inhabitants.
³⁵ He turns a desert into pools of water,
    a parched land into springs of water.
³⁶ And there he lets the hungry dwell,
    and they establish a city to live in;
³⁷ they sow fields and plant vineyards
    and get a fruitful yield.
³⁸ By his blessing they multiply greatly,
    and he does not let their livestock diminish.

³⁹ When they are diminished and brought low
    through oppression, evil, and sorrow,
⁴⁰ he pours contempt on princes
    and makes them wander in trackless wastes;
⁴¹ but he raises up the needy out of affliction
    and makes their families like flocks.
⁴² The upright see it and are glad,
    and all wickedness shuts its mouth.

⁴³ Whoever is wise, let him attend to these things;
    let them consider the steadfast love of the LORD.

With God we shall do valiantly [Psalm 108]. This combined praise and lament psalm begins with a conventional call to praise (vv. 1–3). Then the poet assembles the rationale for that call, in the following sequence: praise of God's attributes (vv. 4–6); praise of God's promise to exalt Israel and defeat its enemies (vv. 7–9). But in the very mention of that promise we can infer (with an anticipation in v. 6) that the nation is in distress and needs God's promised rescue, because at the end of the poem the conventions of the lament take over, as follows: definition of a national crisis (vv. 10–11); petition for God to rescue (v. 12); statement of confidence in God in the face of the crisis (v. 13).

108

A SONG. A PSALM OF DAVID.
    My heart is steadfast, O God!
    I will sing and make melody with all my being!¹
² Awake, O harp and lyre!
    I will awake the dawn!
³ I will give thanks to you, O LORD, among the peoples;
    I will sing praises to you among the nations.
⁴ For your steadfast love is great above the heavens;
    your faithfulness reaches to the clouds.

---

¹ Hebrew *with my glory*

5   Be exalted, O God, above the heavens!
       Let your glory be over all the earth!
6   That your beloved ones may be delivered,
       give salvation by your right hand and answer me!

7   God has promised in his holiness:[1]
       "With exultation I will divide up Shechem
       and portion out the Valley of Succoth.
8   Gilead is mine; Manasseh is mine;
       Ephraim is my helmet,
       Judah my scepter.
9   Moab is my washbasin;
       upon Edom I cast my shoe;
       over Philistia I shout in triumph."

10 Who will bring me to the fortified city?
       Who will lead me to Edom?
11 Have you not rejected us, O God?
       You do not go out, O God, with our armies.
12 Oh grant us help against the foe,
       for vain is the salvation of man!
13 With God we shall do valiantly;
       it is he who will tread down our foes.

Let curses come upon him [Psalm 109]. Although it is customary to speak of "the imprecatory psalms" (with Psalms 69 and 109 considered the major ones), strictly speaking no psalm is devoted entirely to calling down curses on one's enemies. In Psalms 69 and 109, the element of imprecation is enclosed in the familiar contours of the lament psalm, and we need to keep that framework in view if we wish to avoid distorting the poems. Psalm 109 combines expected and unexpected features when we approach it under the rubric of the lament psalm: introductory cry to God (v. 1); definition of the crisis, implied to be slander directed against the speaker (vv. 2–5); petitionary section in the rare form of an imprecation (calling down a curse on one's enemies), using the rhetorical format "let . . ." (vv. 6–15); restatement of the indictment against the oppressors (vv. 16–18a); return to the imprecation (vv. 18b–20); return to the complaint (definition of crisis), beginning with a cry to God to help (vv. 21–25); petition to God to help (vv. 26–29); vow to praise God (vv. 30–31). Three ingredients within the psalm serve to mitigate the starkness of the speaker's imprecations: the speaker's self-portrait as a person abused by his enemies (vv. 2–5, 22–25); the speaker's reliance on God as the one who will administer justice (vv. 1, 21, 26–27, 31, along with the continuous rhetorical stance of asking God to perform the justice); a continuous interspersed rehearsal of the atrocities that the speaker's enemies have perpetrated.

109 To the choirmaster. A Psalm of David.
       Be not silent, O God of my praise!
2   For wicked and deceitful mouths are opened against me,
       speaking against me with lying tongues.
3   They encircle me with words of hate,

[1] Or sanctuary

and attack me without cause.
⁴ In return for my love they accuse me,
    but I give myself to prayer.¹
⁵ So they reward me evil for good,
    and hatred for my love.

⁶ Appoint a wicked man against him;
    let an accuser stand at his right hand.
⁷ When he is tried, let him come forth guilty;
    let his prayer be counted as sin!
⁸ May his days be few;
    may another take his office!
⁹ May his children be fatherless
    and his wife a widow!
¹⁰ May his children wander about and beg,
    seeking food far from the ruins they inhabit!
¹¹ May the creditor seize all that he has;
    may strangers plunder the fruits of his toil!
¹² Let there be none to extend kindness to him,
    nor any to pity his fatherless children!
¹³ May his posterity be cut off;
    may his name be blotted out in the second generation!
¹⁴ May the iniquity of his fathers be remembered before the LORD,
    and let not the sin of his mother be blotted out!
¹⁵ Let them be before the LORD continually,
    that he may cut off the memory of them from the earth!

¹⁶ For he did not remember to show kindness,
    but pursued the poor and needy
    and the brokenhearted, to put them to death.
¹⁷ He loved to curse; let curses come² upon him!
    He did not delight in blessing; may it be far³ from him!
¹⁸ He clothed himself with cursing as his coat;
    may it soak⁴ into his body like water,
    like oil into his bones!
¹⁹ May it be like a garment that he wraps around him,
    like a belt that he puts on every day!
²⁰ May this be the reward of my accusers from the LORD,
    of those who speak evil against my life!

²¹ But you, O GOD my Lord,
    deal on my behalf for your name's sake;
    because your steadfast love is good, deliver me!
²² For I am poor and needy,
    and my heart is stricken within me.
²³ I am gone like a shadow at evening;
    I am shaken off like a locust.

---

¹ Hebrew *but I am prayer* ² Revocalization; Masoretic Text *curses have come* ³ Revocalization; Masoretic Text *it is far* ⁴ Revocalization; Masoretic Text *it has soaked*

24 My knees are weak through fasting;
        my body has become gaunt, with no fat.
25 I am an object of scorn to my accusers;
        when they see me, they wag their heads.

26 Help me, O Lord my God!
        Save me according to your steadfast love!
27 Let them know that this is your hand;
        you, O Lord, have done it!
28 Let them curse, but you will bless!
        They arise and are put to shame, but your servant will be glad!
29 May my accusers be clothed with dishonor;
        may they be wrapped in their own shame as in a cloak!

30 With my mouth I will give great thanks to the Lord;
        I will praise him in the midst of the throng.
31 For he stands at the right hand of the needy one,
        to save him from those who condemn his soul to death.

Sit at my right hand: a royal psalm [Psalm 110]. The focus is on the godly king, with the implied double meaning that the ultimate embodiment of this ideal is Christ. The poem begins with a quotation from God exalting the king (v. 1) and a snatch of narrative in which God gives the king a scepter (v. 2). This is followed by a list of triumphs of the king, with the poet addressing the king (viewed additionally as a priest in v. 4) directly in apostrophe (vv. 2–4). In the last movement, the triumphs of the king take the form of a list of things that God does in his role as warrior, with the implication that the triumphs of the king and of God are synonymous (vv. 5–7). This is the most frequently quoted psalm in the NT, showing its strong messianic undertones.

110

A Psalm of David.
The Lord says to my Lord:
    "Sit at my right hand,
until I make your enemies your footstool."

2 The Lord sends forth from Zion
        your mighty scepter.
        Rule in the midst of your enemies!
3 Your people will offer themselves freely
        on the day of your power,[1]
        in holy garments;[2]
    from the womb of the morning,
        the dew of your youth will be yours.[3]
4 The Lord has sworn
        and will not change his mind,
    "You are a priest forever
        after the order of Melchizedek."

[1] Or on the day you lead your forces [2] Masoretic Text; some Hebrew manuscripts and Jerome on the holy mountains [3] The meaning of the Hebrew is uncertain

5   The Lord is at your right hand;
       he will shatter kings on the day of his wrath.
6   He will execute judgment among the nations,
       filling them with corpses;
    he will shatter chiefs[1]
       over the wide earth.
7   He will drink from the brook by the way;
       therefore he will lift up his head.

Praising the Lord from A to Z [Psalm 111]. In this acrostic praise psalm, the lines begin with the consecutive letters of the Hebrew alphabet, and the units unfold as follows: call to praise (v. 1); catalog of God's praiseworthy attributes and acts of provision (vv. 2–9); a note of resolution in the form of declaring that the beginning of wisdom is to fear this praiseworthy God (v. 10).

111 [2] Praise the Lord!
       I will give thanks to the Lord with my whole heart,
    in the company of the upright, in the congregation.
2   Great are the works of the Lord,
       studied by all who delight in them.
3   Full of splendor and majesty is his work,
       and his righteousness endures forever.
4   He has caused his wondrous works to be remembered;
       the Lord is gracious and merciful.
5   He provides food for those who fear him;
       he remembers his covenant forever.
6   He has shown his people the power of his works,
       in giving them the inheritance of the nations.
7   The works of his hands are faithful and just;
       all his precepts are trustworthy;
8   they are established forever and ever,
       to be performed with faithfulness and uprightness.
9   He sent redemption to his people;
       he has commanded his covenant forever.
       Holy and awesome is his name!
10 The fear of the Lord is the beginning of wisdom;
       all those who practice it have a good understanding.
       His praise endures forever!

Encomium in praise of the godly person [Psalm 112]. The successive half-verses follow the sequence of letters in the Hebrew alphabet, making this an acrostic poem. Although the poem begins with a line that ascribes praise to God, this psalm is not a praise psalm but an encomium that praises the godly person. The conventional motifs are as follows: introduction to the subject that will be praised, in the form of a beatitude (v. 1b); in a variation of the customary motif of praising the subject's distinguished ancestry, a prediction that the godly person's offspring will be mighty and blessed (v. 2);

---

[1] Or *the head* [2] This psalm is an acrostic poem, each line beginning with the successive letters of the Hebrew alphabet

catalog of the superior acts and rewards of the person being praised, especially his generosity and stability (vv. 3–9); the superiority of godliness heightened by being contrasted to a foil, the wicked (v. 10).

112

[1] Praise the LORD!
Blessed is the man who fears the LORD,
who greatly delights in his commandments!

2 His offspring will be mighty in the land;
the generation of the upright will be blessed.

3 Wealth and riches are in his house,
and his righteousness endures forever.

4 Light dawns in the darkness for the upright;
he is gracious, merciful, and righteous.

5 It is well with the man who deals generously and lends;
who conducts his affairs with justice.

6 For the righteous will never be moved;
he will be remembered forever.

7 He is not afraid of bad news;
his heart is firm, trusting in the LORD.

8 His heart is steady; he will not be afraid,
until he looks in triumph on his adversaries.

9 He has distributed freely; he has given to the poor;
his righteousness endures forever;
his horn is exalted in honor.

10 The wicked man sees it and is angry;
he gnashes his teeth and melts away;
the desire of the wicked will perish!

Praise the LORD [Psalm 113]. This psalm epitomizes the genre of the simple (as distinct from elaborate) praise psalm. In keeping with its simple beauty, the poem has an envelope structure that begins and ends with the refrain "praise the LORD," and this, too, prevails in a number of psalms. The poem unfolds as follows: call to praise (v. 1); catalog of the God's praiseworthy acts and attributes, beginning with a beatitude (vv. 2–9); repetition of the call to praise (last line). The dominant image pattern is directional imagery (high, above, raises, lifts), and the main action for which God is praised is his elevation of the lowly.

113

Praise the LORD!
Praise, O servants of the LORD,
praise the name of the LORD!

2 Blessed be the name of the LORD
from this time forth and forevermore!

3 From the rising of the sun to its setting,
the name of the LORD is to be praised!

---

[1] This psalm is an acrostic poem, each line beginning with the successive letters of the Hebrew alphabet

4   The Lord is high above all nations,
        and his glory above the heavens!
5   Who is like the Lord our God,
        who is seated on high,
6   who looks far down
        on the heavens and the earth?
7   He raises the poor from the dust
        and lifts the needy from the ash heap,
8   to make them sit with princes,
        with the princes of his people.
9   He gives the barren woman a home,
        making her the joyous mother of children.
    Praise the Lord!

When Israel went out from Egypt [Psalm 114]. There is no better example in the entire Psalter of how Hebrew parallelism works and of the beauty that attends it. The poem also makes notable use of personification and apostrophe. By means of those poetic devices, the poet recreates the excitement of the miraculous deliverance of Israel at the Red Sea.

114

When Israel went out from Egypt,
    the house of Jacob from a people of strange language,
2   Judah became his sanctuary,
        Israel his dominion.

3   The sea looked and fled;
        Jordan turned back.
4   The mountains skipped like rams,
        the hills like lambs.

5   What ails you, O sea, that you flee?
        O Jordan, that you turn back?
6   O mountains, that you skip like rams?
        O hills, like lambs?

7   Tremble, O earth, at the presence of the Lord,
        at the presence of the God of Jacob,
8   who turns the rock into a pool of water,
        the flint into a spring of water.

We will bless the Lord [Psalm 115]. There are differentiating features to this poem considered as a praise psalm, but that genre nonetheless dominates the development: ascription of praise to God (v. 1); a retort to pagans who ask where the God of the Israelites is (vv. 2–3); a satiric put-down of the pagan worshipers of lifeless idols—an indirect way of praising the true and living God (vv. 4–8); a highly patterned unit in which three groups are addressed directly and told to "trust in the Lord," accompanied by the refrain "He is their help and their shield" (vv. 9–11); another highly patterned unit of promises that God will bless various groups (vv. 12–13); a unit in which the poet addresses his fellow believers and prays for God's blessing on them (vv. 14–15); concluding praise of God (vv. 16–18).

115

Not to us, O Lord, not to us, but to your name give glory,
for the sake of your steadfast love and your faithfulness!

2   Why should the nations say,
       "Where is their God?"
3   Our God is in the heavens;
       he does all that he pleases.

4   Their idols are silver and gold,
       the work of human hands.
5   They have mouths, but do not speak;
       eyes, but do not see.
6   They have ears, but do not hear;
       noses, but do not smell.
7   They have hands, but do not feel;
       feet, but do not walk;
       and they do not make a sound in their throat.
8   Those who make them become like them;
       so do all who trust in them.

9   O Israel,[i] trust in the Lord!
       He is their help and their shield.
10 O house of Aaron, trust in the Lord!
       He is their help and their shield.
11 You who fear the Lord, trust in the Lord!
       He is their help and their shield.

12 The Lord has remembered us; he will bless us;
       he will bless the house of Israel;
       he will bless the house of Aaron;
13 he will bless those who fear the Lord,
       both the small and the great.

14 May the Lord give you increase,
       you and your children!
15 May you be blessed by the Lord,
       who made heaven and earth!

16 The heavens are the Lord's heavens,
       but the earth he has given to the children of man.
17 The dead do not praise the Lord,
       nor do any who go down into silence.
18 But we will bless the Lord
       from this time forth and forevermore.
    Praise the Lord!

---

[i] Masoretic Text; many Hebrew manuscripts, Septuagint, Syriac *O house of Israel*

What shall I render to the LORD? [Psalm 116]. Instead of beginning with a call to praise, the poet asserts his personal love and loyalty to God (vv. 1–2). Then the usual praise motifs appear in the following form: personal narrative praising God's rescue of the speaker from death (vv. 3–4); praise of God for his attributes and acts of rescue in general (vv. 5–6a); return to the speaker's personal testimony (vv. 6b–11); vow to praise God and worship him (vv. 12–19). It is obvious that this praise psalm highlights the speaker's personal experience and that it expands the vow to praise God beyond the norm.

116

I love the LORD, because he has heard
my voice and my pleas for mercy.
2 Because he inclined his ear to me,
therefore I will call on him as long as I live.
3 The snares of death encompassed me;
the pangs of Sheol laid hold on me;
I suffered distress and anguish.
4 Then I called on the name of the LORD:
"O LORD, I pray, deliver my soul!"

5 Gracious is the LORD, and righteous;
our God is merciful.
6 The LORD preserves the simple;
when I was brought low, he saved me.
7 Return, O my soul, to your rest;
for the LORD has dealt bountifully with you.

8 For you have delivered my soul from death,
my eyes from tears,
my feet from stumbling;
9 I will walk before the LORD
in the land of the living.

10 I believed, even when[1] I spoke,
"I am greatly afflicted";
11 I said in my alarm,
"All mankind are liars."

12 What shall I render to the LORD
for all his benefits to me?
13 I will lift up the cup of salvation
and call on the name of the LORD,
14 I will pay my vows to the LORD
in the presence of all his people.

15 Precious in the sight of the LORD
is the death of his saints.
16 O LORD, I am your servant;
I am your servant, the son of your maidservant.
You have loosed my bonds.

[1] Or believed, indeed; Septuagint believed, therefore

¹⁷ I will offer to you the sacrifice of thanksgiving
    and call on the name of the Lord.
¹⁸ I will pay my vows to the Lord
    in the presence of all his people,
¹⁹ in the courts of the house of the Lord,
    in your midst, O Jerusalem.
Praise the Lord!

Extol him, all peoples [Psalm 117]. This shortest psalm unfolds with a pleasing simplicity: call for all nations to praise God (v. 1); praise of God's attributes (v. 2); call to praise (last line).

117
Praise the Lord, all nations!
    Extol him, all peoples!
² For great is his steadfast love toward us,
    and the faithfulness of the Lord endures forever.
Praise the Lord!

The right hand of the Lord does valiantly [Psalm 118]. This poem begins and ends with a repeated refrain that is a call to give thanks (vv. 1, 29). The second half of the refrain, moreover, is picked up in a threefold unit in which various members of the believing community are commanded to praise God, using the rhetorical format "let . . . say" (vv. 2–4). Thereafter the main units of praise are as follows: personal narrative of deliverance by God, in the mode of the military song of victory after a battlefield triumph (vv. 5–18); introduction of a procession motif in which the righteous enter through metaphoric or literal gates (vv. 19–24); brief prayer for success (v. 25); a return to the procession motif as the one who comes in the name of God is praised (vv. 26–27); vow to praise God (v. 28); call to praise (v. 29). The military motifs of rescue from enemies and a procession of triumph dominate the poem.

118
Oh give thanks to the Lord, for he is good;
    for his steadfast love endures forever!

² Let Israel say,
    "His steadfast love endures forever."
³ Let the house of Aaron say,
    "His steadfast love endures forever."
⁴ Let those who fear the Lord say,
    "His steadfast love endures forever."

⁵ Out of my distress I called on the Lord;
    the Lord answered me and set me free.
⁶ The Lord is on my side; I will not fear.
    What can man do to me?
⁷ The Lord is on my side as my helper;
    I shall look in triumph on those who hate me.

⁸ It is better to take refuge in the LORD
   than to trust in man.
⁹ It is better to take refuge in the LORD
   than to trust in princes.

¹⁰ All nations surrounded me;
   in the name of the LORD I cut them off!
¹¹ They surrounded me, surrounded me on every side;
   in the name of the LORD I cut them off!
¹² They surrounded me like bees;
   they went out like a fire among thorns;
   in the name of the LORD I cut them off!
¹³ I was pushed hard,[1] so that I was falling,
   but the LORD helped me.

¹⁴ The LORD is my strength and my song;
   he has become my salvation.
¹⁵ Glad songs of salvation
   are in the tents of the righteous:
"The right hand of the LORD does valiantly,
¹⁶   the right hand of the LORD exalts,
   the right hand of the LORD does valiantly!"

¹⁷ I shall not die, but I shall live,
   and recount the deeds of the LORD.
¹⁸ The LORD has disciplined me severely,
   but he has not given me over to death.

¹⁹ Open to me the gates of righteousness,
   that I may enter through them
   and give thanks to the LORD.
²⁰ This is the gate of the LORD;
   the righteous shall enter through it.
²¹ I thank you that you have answered me
   and have become my salvation.
²² The stone that the builders rejected
   has become the cornerstone.[2]
²³ This is the LORD's doing;
   it is marvelous in our eyes.
²⁴ This is the day that the LORD has made;
   let us rejoice and be glad in it.

²⁵ Save us, we pray, O LORD!
   O LORD, we pray, give us success!

²⁶ Blessed is he who comes in the name of the LORD!
   We bless you from the house of the LORD.
²⁷ The LORD is God,
   and he has made his light to shine upon us.

---

[1] Hebrew *You* (that is, the enemy) *pushed me hard* [2] Hebrew *the head of the corner*

Bind the festal sacrifice with cords,
 up to the horns of the altar!

²⁸ You are my God, and I will give thanks to you;
 you are my God; I will extol you.
²⁹ Oh give thanks to the Lord, for he is good;
 for his steadfast love endures forever!

I will delight in your statutes: an encomium in praise of God's Word [119:1–88].
Psalm 119, as everyone knows, is "the big one." Its subject is God's law, that is, God's revealed Word, and the genre is the encomium, with the pattern of elevating the subject, listing its praiseworthy acts and qualities, showing its superiority over other things, listing the rewards that attend it, and encouraging the reader to imitate this superior thing (God's law). Additionally, the poem is an elaborate acrostic in which twenty-two units follow the order of the Hebrew alphabet, with the effect heightened by the fact that each of the eight verses within a unit begins with the letter of the alphabet that is featured in the unit. The overall effect of the poem is like turning a prism in the light: as we progress through the psalm, we contemplate various facets of God's revealed Word. The rhetorical format involves continuous address to God, which lends an aura of prayer to the entire collection of individual poems. There is no continuous line of thought, even within the eight-verse units (though some of them have thematic unity). The best way to read the psalm, therefore, is as a collection of individual proverbs on the subject of God's Word.

Aleph

119
¹ Blessed are those whose way is blameless,
 who walk in the law of the Lord!
² Blessed are those who keep his testimonies,
 who seek him with their whole heart,
³ who also do no wrong,
 but walk in his ways!
⁴ You have commanded your precepts
 to be kept diligently.
⁵ Oh that my ways may be steadfast
 in keeping your statutes!
⁶ Then I shall not be put to shame,
 having my eyes fixed on all your commandments.
⁷ I will praise you with an upright heart,
 when I learn your righteous rules.[2]
⁸ I will keep your statutes;
 do not utterly forsake me!

Beth

⁹ How can a young man keep his way pure?
 By guarding it according to your word.
¹⁰ With my whole heart I seek you;
 let me not wander from your commandments!

---

[1] This psalm is an acrostic poem of twenty-two stanzas, following the letters of the Hebrew alphabet; within a stanza, each verse begins with the same Hebrew letter [2] Or *your just and righteous decrees*; also verses 62, 106, 160, 164

¹¹ I have stored up your word in my heart,
     that I might not sin against you.
¹² Blessed are you, O LORD;
     teach me your statutes!
¹³ With my lips I declare
     all the rules[1] of your mouth.
¹⁴ In the way of your testimonies I delight
     as much as in all riches.
¹⁵ I will meditate on your precepts
     and fix my eyes on your ways.
¹⁶ I will delight in your statutes;
     I will not forget your word.

GIMEL

¹⁷ Deal bountifully with your servant,
     that I may live and keep your word.
¹⁸ Open my eyes, that I may behold
     wondrous things out of your law.
¹⁹ I am a sojourner on the earth;
     hide not your commandments from me!
²⁰ My soul is consumed with longing
     for your rules[2] at all times.
²¹ You rebuke the insolent, accursed ones,
     who wander from your commandments.
²² Take away from me scorn and contempt,
     for I have kept your testimonies.
²³ Even though princes sit plotting against me,
     your servant will meditate on your statutes.
²⁴ Your testimonies are my delight;
     they are my counselors.

DALETH

²⁵ My soul clings to the dust;
     give me life according to your word!
²⁶ When I told of my ways, you answered me;
     teach me your statutes!
²⁷ Make me understand the way of your precepts,
     and I will meditate on your wondrous works.
²⁸ My soul melts away for sorrow;
     strengthen me according to your word!
²⁹ Put false ways far from me
     and graciously teach me your law!
³⁰ I have chosen the way of faithfulness;
     I set your rules before me.
³¹ I cling to your testimonies, O LORD;
     let me not be put to shame!

---

[1] Or *all the just decrees* [2] Or *your just decrees*; also verses 30, 39, 43, 52, 75, 102, 108, 137, 156, 175

³² I will run in the way of your commandments
        when you enlarge my heart!¹

HE

³³ Teach me, O LORD, the way of your statutes;
        and I will keep it to the end.²
³⁴ Give me understanding, that I may keep your law
        and observe it with my whole heart.
³⁵ Lead me in the path of your commandments,
        for I delight in it.
³⁶ Incline my heart to your testimonies,
        and not to selfish gain!
³⁷ Turn my eyes from looking at worthless things;
        and give me life in your ways.
³⁸ Confirm to your servant your promise,
        that you may be feared.
³⁹ Turn away the reproach that I dread,
        for your rules are good.
⁴⁰ Behold, I long for your precepts;
        in your righteousness give me life!

WAW

⁴¹ Let your steadfast love come to me, O LORD,
        your salvation according to your promise;
⁴² then shall I have an answer for him who taunts me,
        for I trust in your word.
⁴³ And take not the word of truth utterly out of my mouth,
        for my hope is in your rules.
⁴⁴ I will keep your law continually,
        forever and ever,
⁴⁵ and I shall walk in a wide place,
        for I have sought your precepts.
⁴⁶ I will also speak of your testimonies before kings
        and shall not be put to shame,
⁴⁷ for I find my delight in your commandments,
        which I love.
⁴⁸ I will lift up my hands toward your commandments, which I love,
        and I will meditate on your statutes.

ZAYIN

⁴⁹ Remember your word to your servant,
        in which you have made me hope.
⁵⁰ This is my comfort in my affliction,
        that your promise gives me life.
⁵¹ The insolent utterly deride me,
        but I do not turn away from your law.
⁵² When I think of your rules from of old,
        I take comfort, O LORD.

---

¹ Or for you set my heart free ² Or keep it as my reward

53 Hot indignation seizes me because of the wicked,
    who forsake your law.
54 Your statutes have been my songs
    in the house of my sojourning.
55 I remember your name in the night, O LORD,
    and keep your law.
56 This blessing has fallen to me,
    that I have kept your precepts.

HETH

57 The LORD is my portion;
    I promise to keep your words.
58 I entreat your favor with all my heart;
    be gracious to me according to your promise.
59 When I think on my ways,
    I turn my feet to your testimonies;
60 I hasten and do not delay
    to keep your commandments.
61 Though the cords of the wicked ensnare me,
    I do not forget your law.
62 At midnight I rise to praise you,
    because of your righteous rules.
63 I am a companion of all who fear you,
    of those who keep your precepts.
64 The earth, O LORD, is full of your steadfast love;
    teach me your statutes!

TETH

65 You have dealt well with your servant,
    O LORD, according to your word.
66 Teach me good judgment and knowledge,
    for I believe in your commandments.
67 Before I was afflicted I went astray,
    but now I keep your word.
68 You are good and do good;
    teach me your statutes.
69 The insolent smear me with lies,
    but with my whole heart I keep your precepts;
70 their heart is unfeeling like fat,
    but I delight in your law.
71 It is good for me that I was afflicted,
    that I might learn your statutes.
72 The law of your mouth is better to me
    than thousands of gold and silver pieces.

YODH

73 Your hands have made and fashioned me;
    give me understanding that I may learn your commandments.

74 Those who fear you shall see me and rejoice,
    because I have hoped in your word.
75 I know, O LORD, that your rules are righteous,
    and that in faithfulness you have afflicted me.
76 Let your steadfast love comfort me
    according to your promise to your servant.
77 Let your mercy come to me, that I may live;
    for your law is my delight.
78 Let the insolent be put to shame,
    because they have wronged me with falsehood;
    as for me, I will meditate on your precepts.
79 Let those who fear you turn to me,
    that they may know your testimonies.
80 May my heart be blameless in your statutes,
    that I may not be put to shame!

                    KAPH
81 My soul longs for your salvation;
    I hope in your word.
82 My eyes long for your promise;
    I ask, "When will you comfort me?"
83 For I have become like a wineskin in the smoke,
    yet I have not forgotten your statutes.
84 How long must your servant endure?[1]
    When will you judge those who persecute me?
85 The insolent have dug pitfalls for me;
    they do not live according to your law.
86 All your commandments are sure;
    they persecute me with falsehood; help me!
87 They have almost made an end of me on earth,
    but I have not forsaken your precepts.
88 In your steadfast love give me life,
    that I may keep the testimonies of your mouth.

Meditations on God's Word [119:89–176]. A good analytic exercise is to note the following things: (1) the range of terms by which the law of God is named; (2) the superior qualities that the poet ascribes to God's Word; (3) the range of exemplary responses and uses that the poet encourages in regard to God's law; (4) the rewards that come from responding to God's law in those ways; (5) the range of ways in which the poet relates to God by means of God's Word or law; (6) the personal benefits that the poet claims to have received from God's Word (so that the poem takes on the qualities of a personal testimony). In regard to the terms by which God's Word is named, eight key synonyms appear in the original Hebrew text and are translated by such English words as law, word, rules, statutes, testimonies, commandments, precepts, and so forth. These eight synonyms appear 178 times in 176 verses and are present in some form in all but five verses.

---

[1] Hebrew *How many are the days of your servant?*

Lamedh

⁸⁹ Forever, O Lᴏʀᴅ, your word
    is firmly fixed in the heavens.
⁹⁰ Your faithfulness endures to all generations;
    you have established the earth, and it stands fast.
⁹¹ By your appointment they stand this day,
    for all things are your servants.
⁹² If your law had not been my delight,
    I would have perished in my affliction.
⁹³ I will never forget your precepts,
    for by them you have given me life.
⁹⁴ I am yours; save me,
    for I have sought your precepts.
⁹⁵ The wicked lie in wait to destroy me,
    but I consider your testimonies.
⁹⁶ I have seen a limit to all perfection,
    but your commandment is exceedingly broad.

Mem

⁹⁷ Oh how I love your law!
    It is my meditation all the day.
⁹⁸ Your commandment makes me wiser than my enemies,
    for it is ever with me.
⁹⁹ I have more understanding than all my teachers,
    for your testimonies are my meditation.
¹⁰⁰ I understand more than the aged,[1]
    for I keep your precepts.
¹⁰¹ I hold back my feet from every evil way,
    in order to keep your word.
¹⁰² I do not turn aside from your rules,
    for you have taught me.
¹⁰³ How sweet are your words to my taste,
    sweeter than honey to my mouth!
¹⁰⁴ Through your precepts I get understanding;
    therefore I hate every false way.

Nun

¹⁰⁵ Your word is a lamp to my feet
    and a light to my path.
¹⁰⁶ I have sworn an oath and confirmed it,
    to keep your righteous rules.
¹⁰⁷ I am severely afflicted;
    give me life, O Lᴏʀᴅ, according to your word!
¹⁰⁸ Accept my freewill offerings of praise, O Lᴏʀᴅ,
    and teach me your rules.
¹⁰⁹ I hold my life in my hand continually,
    but I do not forget your law.

---

[1] Or the elders

¹¹⁰ The wicked have laid a snare for me,
　　but I do not stray from your precepts.
¹¹¹ Your testimonies are my heritage forever,
　　for they are the joy of my heart.
¹¹² I incline my heart to perform your statutes
　　forever, to the end.¹

SAMEKH

¹¹³ I hate the double-minded,
　　but I love your law.
¹¹⁴ You are my hiding place and my shield;
　　I hope in your word.
¹¹⁵ Depart from me, you evildoers,
　　that I may keep the commandments of my God.
¹¹⁶ Uphold me according to your promise, that I may live,
　　and let me not be put to shame in my hope!
¹¹⁷ Hold me up, that I may be safe
　　and have regard for your statutes continually!
¹¹⁸ You spurn all who go astray from your statutes,
　　for their cunning is in vain.
¹¹⁹ All the wicked of the earth you discard like dross,
　　therefore I love your testimonies.
¹²⁰ My flesh trembles for fear of you,
　　and I am afraid of your judgments.

AYIN

¹²¹ I have done what is just and right;
　　do not leave me to my oppressors.
¹²² Give your servant a pledge of good;
　　let not the insolent oppress me.
¹²³ My eyes long for your salvation
　　and for the fulfillment of your righteous promise.
¹²⁴ Deal with your servant according to your steadfast love,
　　and teach me your statutes.
¹²⁵ I am your servant; give me understanding,
　　that I may know your testimonies!
¹²⁶ It is time for the LORD to act,
　　for your law has been broken.
¹²⁷ Therefore I love your commandments
　　above gold, above fine gold.
¹²⁸ Therefore I consider all your precepts to be right;
　　I hate every false way.

PE

¹²⁹ Your testimonies are wonderful;
　　therefore my soul keeps them.
¹³⁰ The unfolding of your words gives light;
　　it imparts understanding to the simple.

---

¹ Or *statutes; the reward is eternal*

¹³¹ I open my mouth and pant,
     because I long for your commandments.
¹³² Turn to me and be gracious to me,
     as is your way with those who love your name.
¹³³ Keep steady my steps according to your promise,
     and let no iniquity get dominion over me.
¹³⁴ Redeem me from man's oppression,
     that I may keep your precepts.
¹³⁵ Make your face shine upon your servant,
     and teach me your statutes.
¹³⁶ My eyes shed streams of tears,
     because people do not keep your law.

Tsadhe

¹³⁷ Righteous are you, O Lord,
     and right are your rules.
¹³⁸ You have appointed your testimonies in righteousness
     and in all faithfulness.
¹³⁹ My zeal consumes me,
     because my foes forget your words.
¹⁴⁰ Your promise is well tried,
     and your servant loves it.
¹⁴¹ I am small and despised,
     yet I do not forget your precepts.
¹⁴² Your righteousness is righteous forever,
     and your law is true.
¹⁴³ Trouble and anguish have found me out,
     but your commandments are my delight.
¹⁴⁴ Your testimonies are righteous forever;
     give me understanding that I may live.

Qoph

¹⁴⁵ With my whole heart I cry; answer me, O Lord!
     I will keep your statutes.
¹⁴⁶ I call to you; save me,
     that I may observe your testimonies.
¹⁴⁷ I rise before dawn and cry for help;
     I hope in your words.
¹⁴⁸ My eyes are awake before the watches of the night,
     that I may meditate on your promise.
¹⁴⁹ Hear my voice according to your steadfast love;
     O Lord, according to your justice give me life.
¹⁵⁰ They draw near who persecute me with evil purpose;
     they are far from your law.
¹⁵¹ But you are near, O Lord,
     and all your commandments are true.

¹⁵² Long have I known from your testimonies
    that you have founded them forever.

Resh

¹⁵³ Look on my affliction and deliver me,
    for I do not forget your law.
¹⁵⁴ Plead my cause and redeem me;
    give me life according to your promise!
¹⁵⁵ Salvation is far from the wicked,
    for they do not seek your statutes.
¹⁵⁶ Great is your mercy, O Lord;
    give me life according to your rules.
¹⁵⁷ Many are my persecutors and my adversaries,
    but I do not swerve from your testimonies.
¹⁵⁸ I look at the faithless with disgust,
    because they do not keep your commands.
¹⁵⁹ Consider how I love your precepts!
    Give me life according to your steadfast love.
¹⁶⁰ The sum of your word is truth,
    and every one of your righteous rules endures forever.

Sin and Shin

¹⁶¹ Princes persecute me without cause,
    but my heart stands in awe of your words.
¹⁶² I rejoice at your word
    like one who finds great spoil.
¹⁶³ I hate and abhor falsehood,
    but I love your law.
¹⁶⁴ Seven times a day I praise you
    for your righteous rules.
¹⁶⁵ Great peace have those who love your law;
    nothing can make them stumble.
¹⁶⁶ I hope for your salvation, O Lord,
    and I do your commandments.
¹⁶⁷ My soul keeps your testimonies;
    I love them exceedingly.
¹⁶⁸ I keep your precepts and testimonies,
    for all my ways are before you.

Taw

¹⁶⁹ Let my cry come before you, O Lord;
    give me understanding according to your word!
¹⁷⁰ Let my plea come before you;
    deliver me according to your word.
¹⁷¹ My lips will pour forth praise,
    for you teach me your statutes.
¹⁷² My tongue will sing of your word,
    for all your commandments are right.

¹⁷³ Let your hand be ready to help me,
        for I have chosen your precepts.
¹⁷⁴ I long for your salvation, O Lᴏʀᴅ,
        and your law is my delight.
¹⁷⁵ Let my soul live and praise you,
        and let your rules help me.
¹⁷⁶ I have gone astray like a lost sheep; seek your servant,
        for I do not forget your commandments.

I am for peace, but they are for war [Psalm 120]. Psalm 120 is the first of fifteen consecutive psalms that bear the common heading "A song of Ascents," meaning that these poems were sung or recited on pilgrimages as people went "up" to Jerusalem to worship in the temple. What is remarkable about the collection is the range of thoughts and sentiments that passed through the pilgrims' minds as they recited these psalms, which do not deal single-mindedly with worship but instead cover virtually all of life. Psalm 120, for example, surprises us by being a lament psalm that unfolds in the following sequence: narrative lead-in in which the speaker recalls that he called on God, who delivered him (v. 1); an actual prayer to God in the present tense to deliver the speaker from his current crisis (v. 2); a sudden apostrophe to the speaker's enemies, on whom the speaker wishes disaster (vv. 3–4); the speaker's lament that he lives in exile amid pagan enemies (vv. 5–7). This is an occasional poem in which the pilgrim who speaks is living as an alien in a foreign land (in this regard the poem invites comparison with Psalms 42–43).

120
A Sᴏɴɢ ᴏғ Aꜱᴄᴇɴᴛꜱ.
In my distress I called to the Lᴏʀᴅ,
        and he answered me.
² Deliver me, O Lᴏʀᴅ,
        from lying lips,
        from a deceitful tongue.

³ What shall be given to you,
        and what more shall be done to you,
        you deceitful tongue?
⁴ A warrior's sharp arrows,
        with glowing coals of the broom tree!

⁵ Woe to me, that I sojourn in Meshech,
        that I dwell among the tents of Kedar!
⁶ Too long have I had my dwelling
        among those who hate peace.
⁷ I am for peace,
        but when I speak, they are for war!

I lift up my eyes to the hills: the traveler's psalm [Psalm 121]. To this day, Psalm 121 is the psalm of choice for people ready to set out on a journey. The poem is firmly rooted in the physical experiences of the pilgrims who traveled to Jerusalem: the pilgrim catches sight of the mountains, which represent the dangers of travel to him, leading

---

him to assert to himself that God is the one who unceasingly protects the traveler on the perilous journey (vv. 1–2); catalog of God's acts of protection for the traveler (vv. 3–6); summary of the preceding catalog, possibly branching out from the physical pilgrimage to the metaphoric journey of life (v. 7); prediction that God's protection extends beyond the pilgrimage to a believer's entire life and throughout all time (v. 8).

121

A Song of Ascents.

I lift up my eyes to the hills.
From where does my help come?
2 My help comes from the Lord,
who made heaven and earth.

3 He will not let your foot be moved;
he who keeps you will not slumber.
4 Behold, he who keeps Israel
will neither slumber nor sleep.

5 The Lord is your keeper;
the Lord is your shade on your right hand.
6 The sun shall not strike you by day,
nor the moon by night.

7 The Lord will keep you from all evil;
he will keep your life.
8 The Lord will keep
your going out and your coming in
from this time forth and forevermore.

I was glad when they said to me, "Let us go to the house of the Lord" [Psalm 122]. Since the temple in Jerusalem was the center of the religious life of the Israelite nation, the city of Jerusalem itself is prominent in the worship psalms. This underlies Psalm 122, which is a series of exclamations and brief prayers regarding the holy city of Jerusalem and those who live and worship there. The poem is highly charged emotionally.

122

A Song of Ascents. Of David.

I was glad when they said to me,
"Let us go to the house of the Lord!"
2 Our feet have been standing
within your gates, O Jerusalem!

3 Jerusalem—built as a city
that is bound firmly together,
4 to which the tribes go up,
the tribes of the Lord,
as was decreed for[1] Israel,
to give thanks to the name of the Lord.
5 There thrones for judgment were set,
the thrones of the house of David.

[1] Or as a testimony for

⁶   Pray for the peace of Jerusalem!
      "May they be secure who love you!
⁷   Peace be within your walls
      and security within your towers!"
⁸   For my brothers and companions' sake
      I will say, "Peace be within you!"
⁹   For the sake of the house of the LORD our God,
      I will seek your good.

As the eyes of a maidservant [Psalm 123]. With Psalm 123 we are still early in the series of fifteen psalms that bear the superscription "A song of Ascents." In this poem the thoughts of the pilgrim turn to God, in the following order: invocation of the transcendent God (v. 1); twin similes by which the speaker expresses the bent of his being to look to God as the one from whom his blessings flow (v. 2); prayer to God for deliverance from the scorn of unbelievers (vv. 3–4).

123
A SONG OF ASCENTS.
      To you I lift up my eyes,
      O you who are enthroned in the heavens!
²   Behold, as the eyes of servants
      look to the hand of their master,
   as the eyes of a maidservant
      to the hand of her mistress,
   so our eyes look to the LORD our God,
      till he has mercy upon us.

³   Have mercy upon us, O LORD, have mercy upon us,
      for we have had more than enough of contempt.
⁴   Our soul has had more than enough
      of the scorn of those who are at ease,
      of the contempt of the proud.

If it had not been the LORD who was on our side: a thanksgiving psalm [Psalm 124]. The poet begins by imagining the calamity that would have engulfed his nation if God had not delivered it (vv. 1–5). Then he expresses thanks to God for the deliverance (vv. 6–7), with the lyric rounded out with a concluding assertion that God is the one in whom the nation trusts (v. 8).

124
A SONG OF ASCENTS. OF DAVID.
      If it had not been the LORD who was on our side—
      let Israel now say—
²   if it had not been the LORD who was on our side
      when people rose up against us,
³   then they would have swallowed us up alive,
      when their anger was kindled against us;
⁴   then the flood would have swept us away,
      the torrent would have gone over us;

⁵ then over us would have gone
    the raging waters.

⁶ Blessed be the LORD,
    who has not given us
    as prey to their teeth!
⁷ We have escaped like a bird
    from the snare of the fowlers;
the snare is broken,
    and we have escaped!

⁸ Our help is in the name of the LORD,
    who made heaven and earth.

Those who trust in the LORD are like Mount Zion [Psalm 125]. The template on which the poem is built is the contrast between the godly and the wicked. Within that rubric, the poem unfolds as follows: comparison of the godly to Mount Zion in their stability (v. 1) and to Jerusalem surrounded by mountains in their enclosure by God (v. 2); in a sudden shift of thought, an assertion that wicked rulers (foreigners?) need to be rooted out of the land or the godly might be corrupted (v. 3); prayer that God will bless the godly (v. 4); assertion that God will defeat evildoers (v. 5a); concluding prayer for peace on Israel (v. 5b). The physical location of the speaker is the outskirts of Jerusalem, and in keeping with the fact that Jerusalem was the capital city as well as the center of religious worship, there is a patriotic undercurrent to the poem.

125 A SONG OF ASCENTS.
Those who trust in the LORD are like Mount Zion,
    which cannot be moved, but abides forever.
² As the mountains surround Jerusalem,
    so the LORD surrounds his people,
    from this time forth and forevermore.
³ For the scepter of wickedness shall not rest
    on the land allotted to the righteous,
lest the righteous stretch out
    their hands to do wrong.
⁴ Do good, O LORD, to those who are good,
    and to those who are upright in their hearts!
⁵ But those who turn aside to their crooked ways
    the LORD will lead away with evildoers!
    Peace be upon Israel!

Combined praise psalm and lament [Psalm 126]. In another song of ascents, the poet begins in the mode of a praise psalm by recalling a past occasion of national deliverance by God (vv. 1–3). The element of lament enters in veiled fashion: when the poet prays that God will restore the fortunes of the nation (v. 4), we can infer that the nation is in distress and needs to be rescued, while the comment that those who sow in tears will reap in joy (vv. 5–6) is a variation on the theme in lament psalms of confidence in God.

126

A Song of Ascents.
When the Lord restored the fortunes of Zion,
we were like those who dream.
² Then our mouth was filled with laughter,
and our tongue with shouts of joy;
then they said among the nations,
"The Lord has done great things for them."
³ The Lord has done great things for us;
we are glad.

⁴ Restore our fortunes, O Lord,
like streams in the Negeb!
⁵ Those who sow in tears
shall reap with shouts of joy!
⁶ He who goes out weeping,
bearing the seed for sowing,
shall come home with shouts of joy,
bringing his sheaves with him.

A psalm of the household [Psalm 127]. The range of topics that ran through the minds of the pilgrims on their way to Jerusalem as recorded in the songs of ascent is extensive. In this reflective lyric, the pilgrim meditates on two topics taken from everyday life. The first is the need for God to labor with people as they work, since purely human labor is futile and even such a commonplace experience as sleep is a gift from God (vv. 1–3). In a second experience taken from everyday life, the poet reflects on the blessings that children represent (vv. 3–5). The theme of the household unifies the two parts.

127

A Song of Ascents. Of Solomon.
Unless the Lord builds the house,
those who build it labor in vain.
Unless the Lord watches over the city,
the watchman stays awake in vain.
² It is in vain that you rise up early
and go late to rest,
eating the bread of anxious toil;
for he gives to his beloved sleep.

³ Behold, children are a heritage from the Lord,
the fruit of the womb a reward.
⁴ Like arrows in the hand of a warrior
are the children[1] of one's youth.
⁵ Blessed is the man
who fills his quiver with them!
He shall not be put to shame
when he speaks with his enemies in the gate.[2]

---

[1] Or sons [2] Or They shall not be put to shame when they speak with their enemies in the gate

The blessed man: an encomium [Psalm 128]. This poem praising a general character type begins by introducing the subject: the blessedness of the person who reveres God (v. 1). The superior quality of such a person is first praised through a description of the domestic blessings and rewards that come to such a person (vv. 2–4). The further motif is a prayer for the blessing of the godly person being praised, with the conventional praise of distinguished ancestry taking the form of a prayer for posterity (vv. 5–6). References to Jerusalem and Zion tie the poem to the pilgrimage motif of the songs of ascent.

128 A Song of Ascents.
Blessed is everyone who fears the Lord,
who walks in his ways!

2   You shall eat the fruit of the labor of your hands;
you shall be blessed, and it shall be well with you.

3   Your wife will be like a fruitful vine
within your house;
your children will be like olive shoots
around your table.

4   Behold, thus shall the man be blessed
who fears the Lord.

5   The Lord bless you from Zion!
May you see the prosperity of Jerusalem
all the days of your life!

6   May you see your children's children!
Peace be upon Israel!

Greatly have they afflicted me [Psalm 129]. It might surprise us to find lament psalms in the songs of the pilgrims traveling to Jerusalem, but we find them in Psalms 129–130, right in the middle of the songs of ascent. The lament motifs in Psalm 129 unfold as follows: description of the speaker's distress—the problem that requires a solution, as in all lament psalms (vv. 1–3); statement of confidence in God (v. 4); petition for deliverance (vv. 5–8a); concluding statement of blessing (v. 8b).

129 A Song of Ascents.
"Greatly[1] have they afflicted me from my youth"—
let Israel now say—

2   "Greatly have they afflicted me from my youth,
yet they have not prevailed against me.

3   The plowers plowed upon my back;
they made long their furrows."

4   The Lord is righteous;
he has cut the cords of the wicked.

5   May all who hate Zion
be put to shame and turned backward!

6   Let them be like the grass on the housetops,

[1] Or Often; also verse 2

which withers before it grows up,
⁷ with which the reaper does not fill his hand
    nor the binder of sheaves his arms,
⁸ nor do those who pass by say,
    "The blessing of the LORD be upon you!
    We bless you in the name of the LORD!"

Out of the depths I cry to you, O LORD [Psalm 130]. In labeling this a penitential psalm (the sixth of seven), we should note that the penitential psalms are variations on the conventional lament psalm. The modification is that the enemy is not external but internal, taking the form of the speaker's guilt before God. The variations on the central theme of a guilt that needs to be forgiven are as follows: opening cry to God to hear the speaker's prayer for mercy (vv. 1–2); brief statement of the problem that requires a solution, namely, the plight of a guilty sinner before a holy God (v. 3); an extended statement of confidence in God (vv. 4–8). The poem is governed by the vocabulary and experience of sin, hope in God, forgiveness, and redemption. At the conclusion of the poem, the motif of forgiveness expands outward from the speaker to Israel.

130
A SONG OF ASCENTS.
Out of the depths I cry to you, O LORD!
² O Lord, hear my voice!
Let your ears be attentive
    to the voice of my pleas for mercy!

³ If you, O LORD, should mark iniquities,
    O Lord, who could stand?
⁴ But with you there is forgiveness,
    that you may be feared.

⁵ I wait for the LORD, my soul waits,
    and in his word I hope;
⁶ my soul waits for the Lord
    more than watchmen for the morning,
    more than watchmen for the morning.

⁷ O Israel, hope in the LORD!
    For with the LORD there is steadfast love,
    and with him is plentiful redemption.
⁸ And he will redeem Israel
    from all his iniquities.

Prayer of the humble soul [Psalm 131]. This simple poem is mainly addressed as a prayer to God. In it, the speaker asserts his humility before God (vv. 1–2), rounding off his meditation with an apostrophe to a personified Israel to hope in the Lord forever (v. 3). The controlling image is that of a weaned infant who can rest against a mother's breast without searching for milk.

131

A Song of Ascents. Of David.
O Lord, my heart is not lifted up;
my eyes are not raised too high;
I do not occupy myself with things
    too great and too marvelous for me.
2   But I have calmed and quieted my soul,
        like a weaned child with its mother;
        like a weaned child is my soul within me.

3   O Israel, hope in the Lord
        from this time forth and forevermore.

God's promises to David [Psalm 132]. Because the kingship motif is so prominent in this poem, some have called it a royal psalm, but the more important focus is the covenant that God established with David to establish his son on an eternal throne and to make Jerusalem his dwelling place. This poem is one of the songs of ascent, and as the speaker approaches the temple he ponders the covenant that God established with David and through David to his people. Fitting in with the pilgrimage context are the references the poet makes to David's desire to build a temple and to the temple that was eventually built. The poem can be read partly as a poetic recollection or summary of the event recorded in 2 Samuel 7:1–17, combining David's desire to build a temple and God's asserting in place of that an eternal covenant with David's lineage. The poem unfolds as follows: a prayer for God to honor David's intense desire to build the temple (vv. 1–5); the pilgrim's response to the summons to travel to the temple for worship (vv. 6–7), followed by a prayer that God would go in an imagined festal procession to the temple (vv. 8–9); another recollection of the covenant that God made to David—a promise ultimately fulfilled in Christ (vv. 10–12); a poetic embellishment of the covenant promise in which God confers blessings on his covenant nation (vv. 13–18). The poem is unified by the motif of God's blessings on his covenant nation as those blessings crystallize around the Davidic covenant.

132

A Song of Ascents.
Remember, O Lord, in David's favor,
all the hardships he endured,
2   how he swore to the Lord
        and vowed to the Mighty One of Jacob,
3   "I will not enter my house
        or get into my bed,
4   I will not give sleep to my eyes
        or slumber to my eyelids,
5   until I find a place for the Lord,
        a dwelling place for the Mighty One of Jacob."

6   Behold, we heard of it in Ephrathah;
        we found it in the fields of Jaar.
7   "Let us go to his dwelling place;
        let us worship at his footstool!"

8   Arise, O Lord, and go to your resting place,
         you and the ark of your might.
9   Let your priests be clothed with righteousness,
         and let your saints shout for joy.
10   For the sake of your servant David,
         do not turn away the face of your anointed one.

11   The Lord swore to David a sure oath
         from which he will not turn back:
     "One of the sons of your body[1]
         I will set on your throne.
12   If your sons keep my covenant
         and my testimonies that I shall teach them,
     their sons also forever
         shall sit on your throne."

13   For the Lord has chosen Zion;
         he has desired it for his dwelling place:
14   "This is my resting place forever;
         here I will dwell, for I have desired it.
15   I will abundantly bless her provisions;
         I will satisfy her poor with bread.
16   Her priests I will clothe with salvation,
         and her saints will shout for joy.
17   There I will make a horn to sprout for David;
         I have prepared a lamp for my anointed.
18   His enemies I will clothe with shame,
         but on him his crown will shine."

When brothers dwell in unity [Psalm 133]. The topic (the joys of spiritually like-minded people enjoying worship together) is not unexpected in a collection of psalms that center on traveling to worship God in the temple. The opening verse introduces the subject of praise (believers' dwelling in unity) and declares the experience to be good. This is followed by two similes (each built around evocative allusions) that require us to unpack the ways in which fellowship is like the two things to which it is compared: the oil that ran down Aaron's body is not only an image of totally covering something but also had a sacramental and unique quality (inasmuch as the oil was a mixture for the sole purpose of anointing Aaron, with no one other than priests allowed to mix it), while the dew of Hermon likewise totally covers an area and in addition brings refreshment. The concluding lines comment on the blessed nature of the fellowship that has been described.

133

A Song of Ascents. Of David.
Behold, how good and pleasant it is
    when brothers dwell in unity![2]
2   It is like the precious oil on the head,
         running down on the beard,
     on the beard of Aaron,

---

[1] Hebrew *of your fruit of the womb* [2] Or *dwell together*

running down on the collar of his robes!
3   It is like the dew of Hermon,
    which falls on the mountains of Zion!
For there the LORD has commanded the blessing,
    life forevermore.

You servants who stand by night in the house of the LORD [Psalm 134]. The function of this last song of ascents is to state concluding sentiments about the worship experience itself and to round out the fifteen songs of ascent on a note a closure. The first two verses may have been spoken as a liturgical recitation by departing worshipers to the priests as they left the temple, with a priest responding with the blessing stated in verse 3. The three lyric sentiments unfold as follows: a call for the "servants of the LORD" to bless God (v. 1); a command to lift up hands and bless God in the holy place (v. 2); a benediction conferring God's blessing on worshipers (v. 3).

134

A SONG OF ASCENTS.
Come, bless the LORD, all you servants of the LORD,
    who stand by night in the house of the LORD!
2   Lift up your hands to the holy place
    and bless the LORD!

3   May the LORD bless you from Zion,
    he who made heaven and earth!

Praise the LORD, for the LORD is good [Psalm 135]. The standard motifs of praise unfold as follows: an opening call to praise, directed to either priests or worshipers at the temple (vv. 1–3); catalog of God's praiseworthy acts and attributes in creation, judgment, and salvation (vv. 4–14), including an inserted address directly to God (v. 13); a foil to God's greatness in the form of a satiric put-down of pagan idols (vv. 15–18); concluding call to praise God (vv. 19–21), giving the poem an envelope structure.

135

Praise the LORD!
Praise the name of the LORD,
    give praise, O servants of the LORD,
2   who stand in the house of the LORD,
    in the courts of the house of our God!
3   Praise the LORD, for the LORD is good;
    sing to his name, for it is pleasant![1]
4   For the LORD has chosen Jacob for himself,
    Israel as his own possession.

5   For I know that the LORD is great,
    and that our Lord is above all gods.
6   Whatever the LORD pleases, he does,
    in heaven and on earth,
    in the seas and all deeps.
7   He it is who makes the clouds rise at the end of the earth,

---

[1] Or for he is beautiful

who makes lightnings for the rain
  and brings forth the wind from his storehouses.

⁸ He it was who struck down the firstborn of Egypt,
  both of man and of beast;
⁹ who in your midst, O Egypt,
  sent signs and wonders
  against Pharaoh and all his servants;
¹⁰ who struck down many nations
  and killed mighty kings,
¹¹ Sihon, king of the Amorites,
  and Og, king of Bashan,
  and all the kingdoms of Canaan,
¹² and gave their land as a heritage,
  a heritage to his people Israel.

¹³ Your name, O LORD, endures forever,
  your renown,¹ O LORD, throughout all ages.
¹⁴ For the LORD will vindicate his people
  and have compassion on his servants.

¹⁵ The idols of the nations are silver and gold,
  the work of human hands.
¹⁶ They have mouths, but do not speak;
  they have eyes, but do not see;
¹⁷ they have ears, but do not hear,
  nor is there any breath in their mouths.
¹⁸ Those who make them become like them,
  so do all who trust in them!

¹⁹ O house of Israel, bless the LORD!
  O house of Aaron, bless the LORD!
²⁰ O house of Levi, bless the LORD!
  You who fear the LORD, bless the LORD!
²¹ Blessed be the LORD from Zion,
  he who dwells in Jerusalem!
Praise the LORD!

His steadfast love endures forever: an antiphonal psalm [Psalm 136]. The most distinctive feature of Psalm 136 is that it is the famous example of an antiphonal poem in the Psalter: each verse consists of an assertion made by a speaker or group, followed by a response in the form of a refrain from another speaker or group. The effect is that of a main melodic line that carries the thrust of thought forward and a refrain that balances the first half of each verse. Each verse is thus a combination of something new (an action of God that is named) and something repeated. The main melodic line is a conventional praise psalm that begins with a call to praise (vv. 1–3), is followed by a catalog of God's praiseworthy acts (vv. 4–25), and ends with a concluding call to thanks (v. 26). The praiseworthy acts of God are drawn from three arenas—God's creation

---

¹ Or remembrance

of the world (vv. 4–9), his acts of providence and deliverance during the exodus (vv. 10–22), and his general acts of deliverance and providence (vv. 23–25).

136
Give thanks to the LORD, for he is good,
  for his steadfast love endures forever.
2 Give thanks to the God of gods,
    for his steadfast love endures forever.
3 Give thanks to the Lord of lords,
    for his steadfast love endures forever;

4 to him who alone does great wonders,
    for his steadfast love endures forever;
5 to him who by understanding made the heavens,
    for his steadfast love endures forever;
6 to him who spread out the earth above the waters,
    for his steadfast love endures forever;
7 to him who made the great lights,
    for his steadfast love endures forever;
8 the sun to rule over the day,
    for his steadfast love endures forever;
9 the moon and stars to rule over the night,
    for his steadfast love endures forever;

10 to him who struck down the firstborn of Egypt,
    for his steadfast love endures forever;
11 and brought Israel out from among them,
    for his steadfast love endures forever;
12 with a strong hand and an outstretched arm,
    for his steadfast love endures forever;
13 to him who divided the Red Sea in two,
    for his steadfast love endures forever;
14 and made Israel pass through the midst of it,
    for his steadfast love endures forever;
15 but overthrew[1] Pharaoh and his host in the Red Sea,
    for his steadfast love endures forever;
16 to him who led his people through the wilderness,
    for his steadfast love endures forever;

17 to him who struck down great kings,
    for his steadfast love endures forever;
18 and killed mighty kings,
    for his steadfast love endures forever;
19 Sihon, king of the Amorites,
    for his steadfast love endures forever;
20 and Og, king of Bashan,
    for his steadfast love endures forever;
21 and gave their land as a heritage,
    for his steadfast love endures forever;

[1] Hebrew *shook off*

²² a heritage to Israel his servant,
>   for his steadfast love endures forever.

²³ It is he who remembered us in our low estate,
>   for his steadfast love endures forever;
²⁴ and rescued us from our foes,
>   for his steadfast love endures forever;
²⁵ he who gives food to all flesh,
>   for his steadfast love endures forever.

²⁶ Give thanks to the God of heaven,
>   for his steadfast love endures forever.

By the waters of Babylon [Psalm 137]. The context of this poem is the nation of Judah's exile in Babylon. The poem begins with a remembrance of a specific moment in the exile: the Israelites' sitting down by a stream, perhaps on their march to Babylon, and being taunted by their captors with a request to "sing us one of the songs of Zion" (vv. 1–3). The force of that moment is then captured in the form a rhetorical question (v. 4) and a vow to prize Jerusalem (a patriotic reference but also a reference to worship of God in the temple) above all other things, an implied protest against the taunting request that the Hebrews sing a psalm (vv. 5–6). The force of the poet's previously stated feelings is so strong that the poem ends with an imprecation, or calling down of misfortune on one's enemies (vv. 7–9).

137

By the waters of Babylon,
>   there we sat down and wept,
>   when we remembered Zion.
²   On the willows¹ there
>   we hung up our lyres.
³   For there our captors
>   required of us songs,
>   and our tormentors, mirth, saying,
>   "Sing us one of the songs of Zion!"

⁴   How shall we sing the Lord's song
>   in a foreign land?
⁵   If I forget you, O Jerusalem,
>   let my right hand forget its skill!
⁶   Let my tongue stick to the roof of my mouth,
>   if I do not remember you,
>   if I do not set Jerusalem
>   above my highest joy!

⁷   Remember, O Lord, against the Edomites
>   the day of Jerusalem,
>   how they said, "Lay it bare, lay it bare,
>   down to its foundations!"
⁸   O daughter of Babylon, doomed to be destroyed,

¹ Or poplars

blessed shall he be who repays you
with what you have done to us!
9 Blessed shall he be who takes your little ones
and dashes them against the rock!

A song of thanksgiving [Psalm 138]. The keynote of thanks is sounded in the first two verses, which establish the mode of thanksgiving in a manner parallel to the call to praise in the praise psalms. After this introduction, the motifs unfold as follows: personal narrative of deliverance (v. 3); generalized statement that all kings of the earth will give thanks to God (vv. 4–5), along with the reason for that thanks (v. 6); return to the first-person mode, as the poet narrates God's present deliverance (v. 7) and ends by predicting God's blessing, asserting God's eternal love, and praying for God's presence (v. 8).

138

OF DAVID.
I give you thanks, O LORD, with my whole heart;
before the gods I sing your praise;
2 I bow down toward your holy temple
and give thanks to your name for your steadfast love and your faithfulness,
for you have exalted above all things
your name and your word.[1]
3 On the day I called, you answered me;
my strength of soul you increased.[2]

4 All the kings of the earth shall give you thanks, O LORD,
for they have heard the words of your mouth,
5 and they shall sing of the ways of the LORD,
for great is the glory of the LORD.
6 For though the LORD is high, he regards the lowly,
but the haughty he knows from afar.

7 Though I walk in the midst of trouble,
you preserve my life;
you stretch out your hand against the wrath of my enemies,
and your right hand delivers me.
8 The LORD will fulfill his purpose for me;
your steadfast love, O LORD, endures forever.
Do not forsake the work of your hands.

An ode in praise of God [Psalm 139]. Psalm 139 is one of the poetic triumphs of the Psalter. It is a praise psalm that exalts God's greatness. The poem consists of four six-verse units, each governed by its own theme: God's omniscience (vv. 1–6); God's omnipresence (vv. 7–12); God's omnificence (quality of being all-creating; vv. 13–18); God's holiness, a theme elaborated with the motif of purging the wicked way (vv. 19–24). Each unit is developed with its own intricate techniques, including parallelism, repetition, word patterns and image patterns, and metaphors.

---

[1] Or you have exalted your word above all your name [2] Hebrew you made me bold in my soul with strength

139
<small>To the choirmaster. A Psalm of David.</small>
O Lord, you have searched me and known me!
² You know when I sit down and when I rise up;
   you discern my thoughts from afar.
³ You search out my path and my lying down
   and are acquainted with all my ways.
⁴ Even before a word is on my tongue,
   behold, O Lord, you know it altogether.
⁵ You hem me in, behind and before,
   and lay your hand upon me.
⁶ Such knowledge is too wonderful for me;
   it is high; I cannot attain it.

⁷ Where shall I go from your Spirit?
   Or where shall I flee from your presence?
⁸ If I ascend to heaven, you are there!
   If I make my bed in Sheol, you are there!
⁹ If I take the wings of the morning
   and dwell in the uttermost parts of the sea,
¹⁰ even there your hand shall lead me,
   and your right hand shall hold me.
¹¹ If I say, "Surely the darkness shall cover me,
   and the light about me be night,"
¹² even the darkness is not dark to you;
   the night is bright as the day,
   for darkness is as light with you.

¹³ For you formed my inward parts;
   you knitted me together in my mother's womb.
¹⁴ I praise you, for I am fearfully and wonderfully made.[1]
   Wonderful are your works;
   my soul knows it very well.
¹⁵ My frame was not hidden from you,
   when I was being made in secret,
   intricately woven in the depths of the earth.
¹⁶ Your eyes saw my unformed substance;
   in your book were written, every one of them,
   the days that were formed for me,
   when as yet there was none of them.

¹⁷ How precious to me are your thoughts, O God!
   How vast is the sum of them!
¹⁸ If I would count them, they are more than the sand.
   I awake, and I am still with you.

¹⁹ Oh that you would slay the wicked, O God!
   O men of blood, depart from me!
²⁰ They speak against you with malicious intent;

[1] Or for I am fearfully set apart

your enemies take your name in vain![1]
21 Do I not hate those who hate you, O Lord?
      And do I not loathe those who rise up against you?
22 I hate them with complete hatred;
      I count them my enemies.

23 Search me, O God, and know my heart!
      Try me and know my thoughts![2]
24 And see if there be any grievous way in me,
      and lead me in the way everlasting![3]

Preserve me from violent men [Psalm 140]. The opening verse is a typical lead-in for a lament psalm, combining a cry to God and specific petitions to God. Thereafter the motifs unfold in standard lament psalm form, as follows: definition of the speaker's crisis, involving the schemes of violent people (vv. 2–3); petition (v. 4); another description of the crisis (v. 5); statement of confidence in God (vv. 6–7); petition in the form of an imprecation (vv. 8–11); statement of confidence in God (v. 12); vow to praise to God (v. 13).

140

To the choirmaster. A Psalm of David.
  Deliver me, O Lord, from evil men;
    preserve me from violent men,
2   who plan evil things in their heart
      and stir up wars continually.
3   They make their tongue sharp as a serpent's,
      and under their lips is the venom of asps.   *Selah*

4   Guard me, O Lord, from the hands of the wicked;
      preserve me from violent men,
      who have planned to trip up my feet.
5   The arrogant have hidden a trap for me,
      and with cords they have spread a net;[4]
      beside the way they have set snares for me.   *Selah*

6   I say to the Lord, You are my God;
      give ear to the voice of my pleas for mercy, O Lord!
7   O Lord, my Lord, the strength of my salvation,
      you have covered my head in the day of battle.
8   Grant not, O Lord, the desires of the wicked;
      do not further their[5] evil plot, or they will be exalted!   *Selah*

9   As for the head of those who surround me,
      let the mischief of their lips overwhelm them!
10 Let burning coals fall upon them!
      Let them be cast into fire,
      into miry pits, no more to rise!
11 Let not the slanderer be established in the land;
      let evil hunt down the violent man speedily!

---

[1] Hebrew lacks *your name* [2] Or *cares* [3] Or *in the ancient way* (compare Jeremiah 6:16) [4] Or *they have spread cords as a net* [5] Hebrew *his*

¹² I know that the LORD will maintain the cause of the afflicted,
        and will execute justice for the needy.
¹³ Surely the righteous shall give thanks to your name;
        the upright shall dwell in your presence.

A prayer to be kept from evil [Psalm 141]. Psalm 141 is a godly person's prayer to be kept from evil both within and without. The opening invocation (vv. 1–2) is general in its content and could appear at the beginning of many a psalm. In verses 3–4 the speaker prays that he himself will be kept from evil. In the obscure following unit, the poet distances himself from the company of the evil (vv. 5–7). After asserting that his trust is in God (v. 8), the poet ends by praying that God will keep him from the snares of evil people who plot against him (last line of v. 8 to the end of the psalm).

141 A PSALM OF DAVID.
O LORD, I call upon you; hasten to me!
Give ear to my voice when I call to you!
² Let my prayer be counted as incense before you,
        and the lifting up of my hands as the evening sacrifice!

³ Set a guard, O LORD, over my mouth;
        keep watch over the door of my lips!
⁴ Do not let my heart incline to any evil,
        to busy myself with wicked deeds
in company with men who work iniquity,
        and let me not eat of their delicacies!

⁵ Let a righteous man strike me—it is a kindness;
        let him rebuke me—it is oil for my head;
        let my head not refuse it.
Yet my prayer is continually against their evil deeds.
⁶ When their judges are thrown over the cliff,[1]
        then they shall hear my words, for they are pleasant.
⁷ As when one plows and breaks up the earth,
        so shall our bones be scattered at the mouth of Sheol.[2]

⁸ But my eyes are toward you, O GOD, my Lord;
        in you I seek refuge; leave me not defenseless![3]
⁹ Keep me from the trap that they have laid for me
        and from the snares of evildoers!
¹⁰ Let the wicked fall into their own nets,
        while I pass by safely.

I pour out my complaint [Psalm 142]. The poet identifies the genre of this psalm when he calls it a complaint (v. 2). When he adds that his complaint is poured out, we catch the essential nature of the lament psalms—poems about a distressing situation uttered without inhibition. The poem unfolds according to the conventional motifs of the lament psalm: opening cry to God (vv. 1–3a); description of the speaker's crisis (vv. 3b–4); statement of confidence in God (v. 5); petition (vv. 6–7a); concluding statement of

---

[1] Or *When their judges fall into the hands of the Rock* [2] The meaning of the Hebrew in verses 6, 7 is uncertain [3] Hebrew *refuge; do not pour out my life!*

confidence in God (v. 7b). The imagery of the poem clusters around a contrast between
danger (paths with hidden traps; persecutors; prison) and safety (refuge; a "portion in
the land of the living"; a surrounding company of the righteous).

142
A MASKIL[1] OF DAVID, WHEN HE WAS IN THE CAVE. A PRAYER.
With my voice I cry out to the LORD;
with my voice I plead for mercy to the LORD.
2 I pour out my complaint before him;
I tell my trouble before him.

3 When my spirit faints within me,
you know my way!
In the path where I walk
they have hidden a trap for me.
4 Look to the right and see:
there is none who takes notice of me;
no refuge remains to me;
no one cares for my soul.

5 I cry to you, O LORD;
I say, "You are my refuge,
my portion in the land of the living."
6 Attend to my cry,
for I am brought very low!
Deliver me from my persecutors,
for they are too strong for me!
7 Bring me out of prison,
that I may give thanks to your name!
The righteous will surround me,
for you will deal bountifully with me.

Give ear to my pleas for mercy [Psalm 143]. This is the last of the seven penitential
psalms of church tradition. The only basis for that classification, though, is the first two
verses, which identify the speaker's crisis as a need for mercy (v. 1) and then ask God
to withhold judgment against him (v. 2). The poem is basically a lament psalm in the
conventional mode, unfolding as follows: introductory cry to God to hear the speaker's
prayer (v. 1); petition (v. 2); definition of the speaker's crisis—attacks directed against
him by enemies (vv. 3–4); statement of confidence in God (vv. 5–6); petition (vv. 7–12).
The distinctive feature of the psalm is that the poet devotes half of the poem to petition.

143
A PSALM OF DAVID.
Hear my prayer, O LORD;
give ear to my pleas for mercy!
In your faithfulness answer me, in your righteousness!
2 Enter not into judgment with your servant,
for no one living is righteous before you.

[1] Probably a musical or liturgical term

3 For the enemy has pursued my soul;
  he has crushed my life to the ground;
  he has made me sit in darkness like those long dead.
4 Therefore my spirit faints within me;
  my heart within me is appalled.

5 I remember the days of old;
  I meditate on all that you have done;
  I ponder the work of your hands.
6 I stretch out my hands to you;
  my soul thirsts for you like a parched land. *Selah*

7 Answer me quickly, O LORD!
  My spirit fails!
Hide not your face from me,
  lest I be like those who go down to the pit.
8 Let me hear in the morning of your steadfast love,
  for in you I trust.
Make me know the way I should go,
  for to you I lift up my soul.

9 Deliver me from my enemies, O LORD!
  I have fled to you for refuge![1]
10 Teach me to do your will,
  for you are my God!
Let your good Spirit lead me
  on level ground!

11 For your name's sake, O LORD, preserve my life!
  In your righteousness bring my soul out of trouble!
12 And in your steadfast love you will cut off my enemies,
  and you will destroy all the adversaries of my soul,
  for I am your servant.

God who gives victory to kings: a royal psalm [Psalm 144]. Because the speaker is obviously the king of a nation, this poem is a royal psalm—a king's testimony (vv. 1–2, 9–11) and desire for himself as military leader (vv. 5–8) and for his nation of followers (vv. 12–14). The motifs unfold as follows: opening statement exalting God (v. 1); a spiritualized version of the epic motif of the arming of the hero, as David ascribes his military prowess to endowment from God (vv. 1–2); interlude in which the poet wonders why God would elevate a person in this way (v. 3), with an additional meditation on human transience (v. 4); still in the mode of war poetry, prayer that God will appear as storm god and divine warrior to rescue the speaker from the threat of foreign powers (vv. 5–8); return to the praise of God as the one who gives victory to his chosen king (vv. 9–10); return to the petitionary mode as the speaker asks God to rescue him from foreigners (v. 11); in a shift of focus, prayer for the earthly welfare of the king's subjects (vv. 12–14); concluding beatitudes that highlight the privileged status of a nation under a God who blesses his people as the poet has just described (v. 15).

---

[1] One Hebrew manuscript, Septuagint; most Hebrew manuscripts *To you I have covered*

144 Of David.
Blessed be the Lord, my rock,
who trains my hands for war,
and my fingers for battle;
² he is my steadfast love and my fortress,
my stronghold and my deliverer,
my shield and he in whom I take refuge,
who subdues peoples[1] under me.

³ O Lord, what is man that you regard him,
or the son of man that you think of him?
⁴ Man is like a breath;
his days are like a passing shadow.

⁵ Bow your heavens, O Lord, and come down!
Touch the mountains so that they smoke!
⁶ Flash forth the lightning and scatter them;
send out your arrows and rout them!
⁷ Stretch out your hand from on high;
rescue me and deliver me from the many waters,
from the hand of foreigners,
⁸ whose mouths speak lies
and whose right hand is a right hand of falsehood.

⁹ I will sing a new song to you, O God;
upon a ten-stringed harp I will play to you,
¹⁰ who gives victory to kings,
who rescues David his servant from the cruel sword.
¹¹ Rescue me and deliver me
from the hand of foreigners,
whose mouths speak lies
and whose right hand is a right hand of falsehood.

¹² May our sons in their youth
be like plants full grown,
our daughters like corner pillars
cut for the structure of a palace;
¹³ may our granaries be full,
providing all kinds of produce;
may our sheep bring forth thousands
and ten thousands in our fields;
¹⁴ may our cattle be heavy with young,
suffering no mishap or failure in bearing;[2]
may there be no cry of distress in our streets!
¹⁵ Blessed are the people to whom such blessings fall!
Blessed are the people whose God is the Lord!

[1] Many Hebrew manuscripts, Dead Sea Scroll, Jerome, Syriac, Aquila; most Hebrew manuscripts *subdues my people* [2] Hebrew *with no breaking in or going out*

> **Every day I will bless you** [Psalm 145]. This exalted praise psalm is an acrostic poem in which the successive verses begin with the letters of the Hebrew alphabet in consecutive order. The motifs of praise unfold as follows: opening statement of the poet's intention to praise God (vv. 1–3); description of how God's praise is passed on from generation to generation among the godly (vv. 4–7); praise of God's attributes (vv. 8–9); direct address to God, praising him for his works and power (vv. 10–13a); praise of God's acts (vv. 13b–14); praise directed to God (vv. 15–16); catalog of God's praiseworthy acts (vv. 17–20); the poet's resolve to praise God forever (v. 21).

145

[1] A Song of Praise. Of David.

I will extol you, my God and King,
and bless your name forever and ever.
[2] Every day I will bless you
and praise your name forever and ever.
[3] Great is the Lord, and greatly to be praised,
and his greatness is unsearchable.

[4] One generation shall commend your works to another,
and shall declare your mighty acts.
[5] On the glorious splendor of your majesty,
and on your wondrous works, I will meditate.
[6] They shall speak of the might of your awesome deeds,
and I will declare your greatness.
[7] They shall pour forth the fame of your abundant goodness
and shall sing aloud of your righteousness.

[8] The Lord is gracious and merciful,
slow to anger and abounding in steadfast love.
[9] The Lord is good to all,
and his mercy is over all that he has made.

[10] All your works shall give thanks to you, O Lord,
and all your saints shall bless you!
[11] They shall speak of the glory of your kingdom
and tell of your power,
[12] to make known to the children of man your[2] mighty deeds,
and the glorious splendor of your kingdom.
[13] Your kingdom is an everlasting kingdom,
and your dominion endures throughout all generations.

[The Lord is faithful in all his words
and kind in all his works.][3]
[14] The Lord upholds all who are falling
and raises up all who are bowed down.
[15] The eyes of all look to you,
and you give them their food in due season.
[16] You open your hand;
you satisfy the desire of every living thing.

---

[1] This psalm is an acrostic poem, each verse beginning with the successive letters of the Hebrew alphabet   [2] Hebrew *his*; also next line   [3] These two lines are supplied by one Hebrew manuscript, Septuagint, Syriac (compare Dead Sea Scroll)

17 The LORD is righteous in all his ways
     and kind in all his works.
18 The LORD is near to all who call on him,
     to all who call on him in truth.
19 He fulfills the desire of those who fear him;
     he also hears their cry and saves them.
20 The LORD preserves all who love him,
     but all the wicked he will destroy.

21 My mouth will speak the praise of the LORD,
     and let all flesh bless his holy name forever and ever.

I will sing praises to my God while I have my being [Psalm 146]. The customary units of the praise psalm appear in the following order: call to praise (vv. 1–2); a foil to the praise of God in the form of dispraise of trusting in human rulers (vv. 3–4); catalog of God's praiseworthy acts in creation and in behalf of the weak of the earth (vv. 5–10); repetition of the refrain that started the poem (last line).

146
Praise the LORD!
Praise the LORD, O my soul!
2 I will praise the LORD as long as I live;
     I will sing praises to my God while I have my being.

3 Put not your trust in princes,
     in a son of man, in whom there is no salvation.
4 When his breath departs, he returns to the earth;
     on that very day his plans perish.

5 Blessed is he whose help is the God of Jacob,
     whose hope is in the LORD his God,
6 who made heaven and earth,
     the sea, and all that is in them,
who keeps faith forever;
7   who executes justice for the oppressed,
     who gives food to the hungry.

The LORD sets the prisoners free;
8   the LORD opens the eyes of the blind.
The LORD lifts up those who are bowed down;
     the LORD loves the righteous.
9 The LORD watches over the sojourners;
     he upholds the widow and the fatherless,
     but the way of the wicked he brings to ruin.

10 The LORD will reign forever,
     your God, O Zion, to all generations.
Praise the LORD!

Great is our Lord [Psalm 147]. Like many praise psalms, this one begins and ends with the formula "praise the LORD" (vv. 1, 20). Within this envelope, the poem alternates between commands to praise God (vv. 1, 7, 12) and catalogs of God's praiseworthy acts (vv. 2–6, 8–11, 13–20). All three units of praise alternate between God's acts in the human community and in nature. Whereas the first two units are generalized, extending to believers in all places and times, the focus of the third unit is specifically on OT Israel, as the call to praise already signals (v. 12) and as the concluding reference to God's revelation highlights (vv. 19–20). As we near the end of the Psalter, it becomes obvious that the book is structured as moving toward a final crescendo of praise.

147

Praise the LORD!
For it is good to sing praises to our God;
   for it is pleasant,[1] and a song of praise is fitting.
2 The LORD builds up Jerusalem;
   he gathers the outcasts of Israel.
3 He heals the brokenhearted
   and binds up their wounds.
4 He determines the number of the stars;
   he gives to all of them their names.
5 Great is our Lord, and abundant in power;
   his understanding is beyond measure.
6 The LORD lifts up the humble;[2]
   he casts the wicked to the ground.

7 Sing to the LORD with thanksgiving;
   make melody to our God on the lyre!
8 He covers the heavens with clouds;
   he prepares rain for the earth;
   he makes grass grow on the hills.
9 He gives to the beasts their food,
   and to the young ravens that cry.
10 His delight is not in the strength of the horse,
   nor his pleasure in the legs of a man,
11 but the LORD takes pleasure in those who fear him,
   in those who hope in his steadfast love.

12 Praise the LORD, O Jerusalem!
   Praise your God, O Zion!
13 For he strengthens the bars of your gates;
   he blesses your children within you.
14 He makes peace in your borders;
   he fills you with the finest of the wheat.
15 He sends out his command to the earth;
   his word runs swiftly.
16 He gives snow like wool;
   he scatters hoarfrost like ashes.
17 He hurls down his crystals of ice like crumbs;
   who can stand before his cold?

---

[1] Or for he is beautiful   [2] Or afflicted

¹⁸   He sends out his word, and melts them;
       he makes his wind blow and the waters flow.
¹⁹   He declares his word to Jacob,
       his statutes and rules[1] to Israel.
²⁰   He has not dealt thus with any other nation;
       they do not know his rules.[2]
   Praise the LORD!

Praise him, sun and moon: a nature poem [Psalm 148]. This is the fifth nature poem in the Psalter. As in the other nature poems, the poet handles the material in such a way as to deflect the ultimate praise to God. The poem is a chain of doxologies (commands to praise God) and also a catalog of apostrophes (direct addresses to phenomena that are absent but treated as if they were present and could hear and respond). The poem's arrangement is highly artistic. There are three general movements, as creatures are successively commanded to praise God "from the heavens" (vv. 1–5), "from the earth," meaning nonhuman earthly creatures (vv. 7–10), and "all peoples" (vv. 11–13). Even though the third movement focuses on people rather than what we ordinarily think of as nature, in the biblical view people are part of nature. Twice the string of doxologies and apostrophes is interrupted as the poet states a reason for commanding creatures to praise God, beginning with the connective word *for* (vv. 5, 13). In the first of these two units, the poet offers God's creation of the whole world as the reason for creatures to praise God (vv. 5–6). In the second motivatory section (vv. 13–14), addressed specifically to people, the proposed reason for praising God is his redemption of his people, as signaled by the word pattern of "raised up a horn," "his people," "all his saints," "the people of Israel who are near to him."

148
   Praise the LORD!
   Praise the LORD from the heavens;
       praise him in the heights!
²   Praise him, all his angels;
       praise him, all his hosts!

³   Praise him, sun and moon,
       praise him, all you shining stars!
⁴   Praise him, you highest heavens,
       and you waters above the heavens!

⁵   Let them praise the name of the LORD!
       For he commanded and they were created.
⁶   And he established them forever and ever;
       he gave a decree, and it shall not pass away.[3]

⁷   Praise the LORD from the earth,
       you great sea creatures and all deeps,
⁸   fire and hail, snow and mist,
       stormy wind fulfilling his word!

⁹   Mountains and all hills,
       fruit trees and all cedars!

---

[1] Or *and just decrees* [2] Or *his just decrees* [3] Or *it shall not be transgressed*

¹⁰ Beasts and all livestock,
   creeping things and flying birds!

¹¹ Kings of the earth and all peoples,
   princes and all rulers of the earth!
¹² Young men and maidens together,
   old men and children!

¹³ Let them praise the name of the LORD,
   for his name alone is exalted;
   his majesty is above earth and heaven.
¹⁴ He has raised up a horn for his people,
   praise for all his saints,
   for the people of Israel who are near to him.
Praise the LORD!

Let the godly exult [Psalm 149]. The conventional motifs of the praise psalm unfold as follows: formal call to praise, including the command itself, the audience to whom the command is directed, and the modes of praise (vocal and instrumental music and dancing; vv. 1–3); the reason for the command, namely, the praiseworthy acts of God (v. 4); a return to the commands to praise (vv. 5–6); in an unexpected development, a call to wield weapons against the enemies of God (vv. 6–9).

149
Praise the LORD!
   Sing to the LORD a new song,
his praise in the assembly of the godly!
² Let Israel be glad in his Maker;
   let the children of Zion rejoice in their King!
³ Let them praise his name with dancing,
   making melody to him with tambourine and lyre!
⁴ For the LORD takes pleasure in his people;
   he adorns the humble with salvation.
⁵ Let the godly exult in glory;
   let them sing for joy on their beds.
⁶ Let the high praises of God be in their throats
   and two-edged swords in their hands,
⁷ to execute vengeance on the nations
   and punishments on the peoples,
⁸ to bind their kings with chains
   and their nobles with fetters of iron,
⁹ to execute on them the judgment written!
   This is honor for all his godly ones.
Praise the LORD!

Let everything that has breath praise the LORD [Psalm 150]. Psalm 150 is to the Psalter what the climax of sound is at the end of an animated symphony performance. Its unique feature is that it consists entirely of the conventional call to praise. The variations on the theme are as follows: the command to praise (opening and closing lines); who must praise God, and where (v. 1); what God should be praised for (v. 2); the modes of praise, all of them musical instruments (vv. 3–5); a restatement of who should praise God (v. 6).

150

Praise the LORD!
Praise God in his sanctuary;
    praise him in his mighty heavens![1]

[2] Praise him for his mighty deeds;
    praise him according to his excellent greatness!

[3] Praise him with trumpet sound;
    praise him with lute and harp!
[4] Praise him with tambourine and dance;
    praise him with strings and pipe!
[5] Praise him with sounding cymbals;
    praise him with loud clashing cymbals!
[6] Let everything that has breath praise the LORD!
    Praise the LORD!

---

[1] Hebrew *expanse* (compare Genesis 1:6-8)

PROVERBS

The book at a glance. 31 chapters, 915 verses. The book of Proverbs is what the title implies—a collection or anthology of individual *proverbs. At the beginning and end of the book the proverbs are arranged into topical clusters, but in the middle the organization consists of a random collection of individual units. In ancient cultures, proverbs were a form of instruction for young people—the equivalent of our school classroom. Writings produced by the wise men of ancient cultures are known as *wisdom literature. Wise men or teachers were one of the three categories of OT religious leaders, with prophets and priests being the other two (Jer. 18:18 refers to all three groups). In biblical thinking, wisdom is skill for living. The wise men of ancient cultures possessed four chief traits: (1) they were careful observers of the human condition; (2) they were teachers; (3) they were masters of a particular kind of discourse (the proverb); (4) they were authority figures who asserted their wisdom without apology or reservation.

▋**Genres.** The overall category is *wisdom literature, which is a designation of subject matter more than of form. Wisdom literature is the literature produced by wise men, and the form in which that wisdom comes to us is the *proverb. A proverb is a concise, memorable statement of truth. Some of the proverbs are phrased as straightforward declarative "sayings," while others are phrased as imperative exhortations. Additionally, the book of Proverbs is *poetry, with the result that we need to apply what we know about interpreting such staples of poetry as *image, *metaphor, and *simile. The verse form of this poetry is called *parallelism, and most of the book of Proverbs consists of two-line units that require the second line to complete the thought of the first, by way of repetition, contrast, or comparison. Other techniques include analogy ("the fruit of the righteous is a tree of life," 11:30), the brief portrait (such as the portrait of the drunkard in 23:29–35), and numerical listings (such as the list of four mysterious things in 30:18–19). (For more information on items accompanied by an asterisk, see the glossary at the back of this Bible.)

▋**The proverb as a literary form.** Proverbs are concise, memorable sayings. They strip away extraneous material and focus on a single aspect of experience. They state principles that extend to a whole category of similar experiences; for example, the proverb "Righteousness exalts a nation" (Prov. 14:34) states a principle that accurately applies to nations at all points in history. A good proverb not only states an insight but actually compels insight. Many proverbs are both particular and universal: for example, the proverb "In the place where the tree falls, there it will lie" (Eccles. 11:3) paints a

Passage	Content	Textual Heading	Literary Techniques
1:1–9:18	The claims of Wisdom and Folly in their appeal to the young man	The Proverbs of Solomon	Proverbs couched in couplets using various types of parallelism; antithesis; comparison; portrait; dramatic monologue; brief narrative; *encomium; an array of conventional wisdom literature formulas
10:1–29:27	Anthology of proverbs	The Proverbs of Solomon	Proverbs embodied in the form of parallel constructions, especially antithetic parallelism; the resources of poetry
30:1–33	Proverb clusters	The Words of Agur	Proverbs grouped by topics or numerical schemes
31:1–31	Proverb clusters: a mother's words to her son, and praise of the virtuous wife	The Words of Lemuel	Proverb cluster, plus an encomium arranged as an acrostic poem

concrete picture, but that picture is a symbol or metaphor of the universal principle of finality that attends many events in life. Proverbs often gain their impact by virtue of the poetry in which they are expressed, such as *image, *metaphor, and *simile. Proverbs are observations regarding the repeatable situations of life, but an observation should not necessarily be construed as a promise. Thus the proverb "Train up a child in the way he should go; even when he is old he will not depart from it" (Prov. 22:6) is an observation about what usually happens, not a promise that it will always happen. The most powerful context for a proverb is the everyday situation in life where it applies. Finally, the deeper meanings of a proverb, including a proverb that is observational in format, will emerge if we apply the following grid to it: What virtue does this proverb enjoin? What vice does it denounce? What value does it affirm?

▌**The biblical concept of wisdom.** Wisdom is skill for living. In the OT, wisdom is not so much a systematic philosophy or theology as a sense of life and a worldview that builds up gradually from the specific examples that are provided. In other words, the approach to life is inductive. Some leading assumptions of that worldview include the following: there are standards by which we can differentiate between good conduct and bad conduct; actions invariably produce consequences; life requires us to make choices between good and bad options; the good life requires active choice and strenuous moral effort; all of life is momentous; the ultimate choice that people need to make is to choose to obey God's rules for living.

▌**The story that the proverbs tell.** Although the book of Proverbs is an anthology of proverbs rather than a narrative, it is possible to view these proverbs as telling a story. The overall *plot line is the quest for the good life. This quest occurs in an implied context of a plot conflict between good and evil, wisdom and folly. Within the book itself, the person who undertakes the quest is the pupil, usually referred to as "my son." But this son is the representative of us as readers, so it is actually we who are being instructed regarding how to achieve the good life. Several other characters fill out the cast of characters: the speaker or narrator, who is an authoritative voice that commands our attention and belief; two personified women named Wisdom and Folly; a virtuous wife who is praised at the end of the book; and a host of individuals whose actions show them to be either wise or foolish. While seeming to be a collection of proverbs, this book is also a gallery of characters.

▌**Tips for reading.** Except in the first nine chapters and the *encomium on the good wife at the end of the book, it would be futile to look for structural coherence and continuity as we read. The book is mainly a repository of individual proverbs. Individual proverbs need first to be contemplated all by themselves, as if we were turning a prism in the light to catch the nuances of light. Then we need to be aware that the real context for an individual proverb is not its position in a literary anthology but the experiences of real life. So having understood what a proverb is asserting, we need to think of real-life applications or proofs that confirm it. The proverb thus becomes a lens that brings a tiny aspect of life into an exact focus. Although the proverbs in the book of Proverbs are not generally arranged in topical clusters, it is possible to peruse the book looking for proverbs on a topic and compose one's own proverb cluster. When we are contemplating a given proverb, good questions to ask include these: When in life do I confront this particular experience or choice? When have I seen or been in this situation? Whose life in my circle of acquaintances illustrates this type of wisdom or folly?

▌**Inferred literary intentions.** The book is designed to achieve the following literary purposes:

- be artistic with words and syntax (the gift of aphorism)
- make the abstractions wisdom and folly concrete to our imagination
- express wisdom in the specific form of proverbs and poetry
- show that all areas of life require us to make moral and spiritual choices
- convince us that the choices that we make have momentous consequences
- persuade and move us to choose wisdom rather than folly as we live our daily life
- use the resources of the poetic idiom to embody truth and render the statements aphoristic
- make continuous appeals to everyday life as a way of showing us that this is where the religious life is lived, not in some ethereal "other" world

▌**Theological themes.** (1) Wisdom and folly: although these two concepts do not make it into our books of systematic theology, this would surprise the ancient wise men, since much of what they wanted us to know about God and people was summed up in these two categories. (2) Ethics: a majority of the proverbs deal with the relations of people to each other. (3) The view of God: the book of Proverbs is a detailed outline of what God likes and dislikes, values and regards as worthless, and as we contemplate those things, we come to an understanding of God. (4) The view of the person: the book keeps a focus on what people are like and what they ought to be like.

▌The book of Proverbs as a chapter in the master story of the Bible. From start to finish, the story of the Bible is how God wants us to live in a world that is a cosmic battleground between good and evil and in which people must choose between them. Every individual proverb in the book of Proverbs is a tiny moment in that story. Just as God is the protagonist of the Bible's master story, so, too, in the book of Proverbs God is the one who sets the rules that he wants people to obey. Additionally, when the NT connects Jesus to wisdom (as in the statement of Col. 2:3 that in Christ "are hidden all the treasures of wisdom"), it is drawing on what the OT says about wisdom.

Prologue [1:1–7]. Few books of the Bible have such an explicit opening identification of the author (v. 1), the purpose (vv. 2–6), and the main theme (v. 7) as the book of Proverbs does. It is useful to know that the first nine chapters of Proverbs are a highly unified block, unlike the rest of the book. In these chapters we find an implied dramatic situation of a wise man or parent addressing a "son"; a unifying plot conflict between wisdom and folly, putting the listener in a position of needing to choose one over the other; personifications of Wisdom and Folly as enticing and impressive women; clustering of proverbs to form a series of individual compositions; controlling image patterns (including the path or way, jewel imagery, and sexual references).

1 The proverbs of Solomon, son of David, king of Israel:

² To know wisdom and instruction,
    to understand words of insight,
³ to receive instruction in wise dealing,
    in righteousness, justice, and equity;
⁴ to give prudence to the simple,
    knowledge and discretion to the youth—
⁵ Let the wise hear and increase in learning,
    and the one who understands obtain guidance,
⁶ to understand a proverb and a saying,
    the words of the wise and their riddles.

⁷ The fear of the LORD is the beginning of knowledge;
    fools despise wisdom and instruction.

Opening exhortation to the son [1:8–19]. In form, the unit is a *dramatic monologue in which a parent addresses a son. After a summons to listen followed by an assertion of the rewards for doing so, the passage gets the book off to a semisensational start with its lurid picture of people who get gain through violence, accompanied by a warning to steer clear of such people and such violence.

⁸ Hear, my son, your father's instruction,
    and forsake not your mother's teaching,

⁹   for they are a graceful garland for your head
      and pendants for your neck.

¹⁰ My son, if sinners entice you,
      do not consent.

¹¹ If they say, "Come with us, let us lie in wait for blood;
      let us ambush the innocent without reason;

¹² like Sheol let us swallow them alive,
      and whole, like those who go down to the pit;

¹³ we shall find all precious goods,
      we shall fill our houses with plunder;

¹⁴ throw in your lot among us;
      we will all have one purse"—

¹⁵ my son, do not walk in the way with them;
      hold back your foot from their paths,

¹⁶ for their feet run to evil,
      and they make haste to shed blood.

¹⁷ For in vain is a net spread
      in the sight of any bird,

¹⁸ but these men lie in wait for their own blood;
      they set an ambush for their own lives.

¹⁹ Such are the ways of everyone who is greedy for unjust gain;
      it takes away the life of its possessors.

A street oration by an imposing woman [1:20–33]. Throughout the first nine chapters wisdom and folly are personified as women who clamor for allegiance. In this unit Wisdom takes a formal stand in the ancient equivalent of the public square (vv. 20–21) and then utters a formal oration to the public, like a Sunday-afternoon orator on the Speakers' Corner in Hyde Park, London. The gist of her appeal to the public is an exhortation to give heed to her words and (even more) a warning of the dire effects of neglecting her.

²⁰ Wisdom cries aloud in the street,
      in the markets she raises her voice;

²¹ at the head of the noisy streets she cries out;
      at the entrance of the city gates she speaks:

²² "How long, O simple ones, will you love being simple?
      How long will scoffers delight in their scoffing
         and fools hate knowledge?

²³ If you turn at my reproof,[1]
      behold, I will pour out my spirit to you;
      I will make my words known to you.

²⁴ Because I have called and you refused to listen,
      have stretched out my hand and no one has heeded,

²⁵ because you have ignored all my counsel
      and would have none of my reproof,

²⁶ I also will laugh at your calamity;

---

[1] Or *Will you turn away at my reproof?*

I will mock when terror strikes you,
27   when terror strikes you like a storm
      and your calamity comes like a whirlwind,
      when distress and anguish come upon you.
28   Then they will call upon me, but I will not answer;
      they will seek me diligently but will not find me.
29   Because they hated knowledge
      and did not choose the fear of the LORD,
30   would have none of my counsel
      and despised all my reproof,
31   therefore they shall eat the fruit of their way,
      and have their fill of their own devices.
32   For the simple are killed by their turning away,
      and the complacency of fools destroys them;
33   but whoever listens to me will dwell secure
      and will be at ease, without dread of disaster."

Dramatic monologue: teacher and pupil as father and son [chapter 2]. The literary density of the first nine chapters now appears in full force. The subject is an exhortation to heed wisdom, accompanied by reasons for doing so (one of the reasons being the rewards that come from following wisdom rather than folly). Techniques for which to look include the following: jewel imagery, as a way of expressing the value and desirability of wisdom; metaphor and simile; the verse form of parallelism in its varied forms; the image of the path or way; heightened contrast between wisdom and folly; the evocative catalog of the rewards of wisdom in verses 10–22.

2   My son, if you receive my words
      and treasure up my commandments with you,
2   making your ear attentive to wisdom
      and inclining your heart to understanding;
3   yes, if you call out for insight
      and raise your voice for understanding,
4   if you seek it like silver
      and search for it as for hidden treasures,
5   then you will understand the fear of the LORD
      and find the knowledge of God.
6   For the LORD gives wisdom;
      from his mouth come knowledge and understanding;
7   he stores up sound wisdom for the upright;
      he is a shield to those who walk in integrity,
8   guarding the paths of justice
      and watching over the way of his saints.
9   Then you will understand righteousness and justice
      and equity, every good path;
10   for wisdom will come into your heart,
      and knowledge will be pleasant to your soul;

11 discretion will watch over you,
    understanding will guard you,
12 delivering you from the way of evil,
    from men of perverted speech,
13 who forsake the paths of uprightness
    to walk in the ways of darkness,
14 who rejoice in doing evil
    and delight in the perverseness of evil,
15 men whose paths are crooked,
    and who are devious in their ways.

16 So you will be delivered from the forbidden[1] woman,
    from the adulteress[2] with her smooth words,
17 who forsakes the companion of her youth
    and forgets the covenant of her God;
18 for her house sinks down to death,
    and her paths to the departed;[3]
19 none who go to her come back,
    nor do they regain the paths of life.

20 So you will walk in the way of the good
    and keep to the paths of the righteous.
21 For the upright will inhabit the land,
    and those with integrity will remain in it,
22 but the wicked will be cut off from the land,
    and the treacherous will be rooted out of it.

The great contrast [3:1–12]. This is a highly stylized passage based on a single technique—a regular rhythm of command followed by the reward that will come from obeying the command. With one exception (vv. 5–6), the command gets a verse and then the reward gets a verse.

3 My son, do not forget my teaching,
    but let your heart keep my commandments,
2 for length of days and years of life
    and peace they will add to you.

3 Let not steadfast love and faithfulness forsake you;
    bind them around your neck;
    write them on the tablet of your heart.
4 So you will find favor and good success[4]
    in the sight of God and man.

5 Trust in the LORD with all your heart,
    and do not lean on your own understanding.
6 In all your ways acknowledge him,
    and he will make straight your paths.
7 Be not wise in your own eyes;

[1] Hebrew strange [2] Hebrew foreign woman [3] Hebrew to the Rephaim [4] Or repute

fear the LORD, and turn away from evil.
8 It will be healing to your flesh[1]
    and refreshment[2] to your bones.

9 Honor the LORD with your wealth
    and with the firstfruits of all your produce;
10 then your barns will be filled with plenty,
    and your vats will be bursting with wine.

11 My son, do not despise the LORD's discipline
    or be weary of his reproof,
12 for the LORD reproves him whom he loves,
    as a father the son in whom he delights.

An encomium in praise of wisdom [3:13–20]. An *encomium is a poem or prose piece that praises either a general character type (as in Ps. 1) or an abstract quality (as here). This short poem uses the conventional motifs of the encomium: introduction of the subject of praise (v. 13); the superiority of the subject over its rivals (vv. 14–15); the praiseworthy acts and qualities of the subject (vv. 16–18); the distinguished ancestry and (where relevant) the ancientness of the subject being praised (vv. 19–20).

13 Blessed is the one who finds wisdom,
    and the one who gets understanding,
14 for the gain from her is better than gain from silver
    and her profit better than gold.
15 She is more precious than jewels,
    and nothing you desire can compare with her.
16 Long life is in her right hand;
    in her left hand are riches and honor.
17 Her ways are ways of pleasantness,
    and all her paths are peace.
18 She is a tree of life to those who lay hold of her;
    those who hold her fast are called blessed.

19 The LORD by wisdom founded the earth;
    by understanding he established the heavens;
20 by his knowledge the deeps broke open,
    and the clouds drop down the dew.

Momentous advice to a son [3:21–35]. This dramatic monologue is somewhat miscellaneous in content and technique. Here are things for which to look: the command formula that directs the listener what to do and avoid; expression in the form of imagery (jewelry, pathway, house); urgency of tone; antithesis.

21 My son, do not lose sight of these—
    keep sound wisdom and discretion,
22 and they will be life for your soul

---

[1] Hebrew *navel* [2] Or *medicine*

and adornment for your neck.
²³ Then you will walk on your way securely,
and your foot will not stumble.
²⁴ If you lie down, you will not be afraid;
when you lie down, your sleep will be sweet.
²⁵ Do not be afraid of sudden terror
or of the ruin[1] of the wicked, when it comes,
²⁶ for the LORD will be your confidence
and will keep your foot from being caught.
²⁷ Do not withhold good from those to whom it is due,[2]
when it is in your power to do it.

²⁸ Do not say to your neighbor, "Go, and come again,
tomorrow I will give it"—when you have it with you.
²⁹ Do not plan evil against your neighbor,
who dwells trustingly beside you.
³⁰ Do not contend with a man for no reason,
when he has done you no harm.
³¹ Do not envy a man of violence
and do not choose any of his ways,
³² for the devious person is an abomination to the LORD,
but the upright are in his confidence.
³³ The LORD's curse is on the house of the wicked,
but he blesses the dwelling of the righteous.
³⁴ Toward the scorners he is scornful,
but to the humble he gives favor.[3]
³⁵ The wise will inherit honor,
but fools get[4] disgrace.

Further admonitions [chapter 4]. The opening nine verses are a set piece of some familiar formulas of wisdom literature: (1) a summons to listen (v. 1); (2) motivation (vv. 2–4a); (3) admonitions (vv. 4b–6a, 7b–8); (4) consequences of choosing wisdom (vv. 6, 8, 9). Verses 10–13 use the imagery of romantic love, in effect urging the listener to have a love affair with wisdom. Verses 14–19 use vivid figures of speech and the command formula to denounce the way of folly. Verses 20–27 are generalized exhortations, and they introduce an image that will be important in this part of the book: the conduct of life as a spring of water that flows from a reliable source (v. 23).

4 Hear, O sons, a father's instruction,
and be attentive, that you may gain[5] insight,
² for I give you good precepts;
do not forsake my teaching.
³ When I was a son with my father,
tender, the only one in the sight of my mother,
⁴ he taught me and said to me,
"Let your heart hold fast my words;
keep my commandments, and live.

---

[1] Hebrew *storm* [2] Hebrew *Do not withhold good from its owners* [3] Or *grace* [4] The meaning of the Hebrew word is uncertain [5] Hebrew *know*

⁵ Get wisdom; get insight;
   do not forget, and do not turn away from the words of my mouth.
⁶ Do not forsake her, and she will keep you;
   love her, and she will guard you.
⁷ The beginning of wisdom is this: Get wisdom,
   and whatever you get, get insight.
⁸ Prize her highly, and she will exalt you;
   she will honor you if you embrace her.
⁹ She will place on your head a graceful garland;
   she will bestow on you a beautiful crown."

¹⁰ Hear, my son, and accept my words,
   that the years of your life may be many.
¹¹ I have taught you the way of wisdom;
   I have led you in the paths of uprightness.
¹² When you walk, your step will not be hampered,
   and if you run, you will not stumble.
¹³ Keep hold of instruction; do not let go;
   guard her, for she is your life.
¹⁴ Do not enter the path of the wicked,
   and do not walk in the way of the evil.
¹⁵ Avoid it; do not go on it;
   turn away from it and pass on.
¹⁶ For they cannot sleep unless they have done wrong;
   they are robbed of sleep unless they have made someone stumble.
¹⁷ For they eat the bread of wickedness
   and drink the wine of violence.
¹⁸ But the path of the righteous is like the light of dawn,
   which shines brighter and brighter until full day.
¹⁹ The way of the wicked is like deep darkness;
   they do not know over what they stumble.

²⁰ My son, be attentive to my words;
   incline your ear to my sayings.
²¹ Let them not escape from your sight;
   keep them within your heart.
²² For they are life to those who find them,
   and healing to all their¹ flesh.
²³ Keep your heart with all vigilance,
   for from it flow the springs of life.
²⁴ Put away from you crooked speech,
   and put devious talk far from you.
²⁵ Let your eyes look directly forward,
   and your gaze be straight before you.
²⁶ Ponder² the path of your feet;
   then all your ways will be sure.

---

¹ Hebrew *his* ² Or *Make level*

²⁷   Do not swerve to the right or to the left;
          turn your foot away from evil.

Plain talk on sex [chapter 5]. Sometimes the first nine chapters use sexual imagery in a metaphoric sense (partly because of the introduction of the personified women Wisdom and Folly), while at other times the sexual references are literal. Chapter 5 is an example of the latter. In its original setting, wisdom literature was partly a form of instruction to young courtiers, with a view toward training good princes or leaders. That may partly explain the importance that the book of Proverbs gives to steering clear of sexual sin. Chapter 5 is an extended warning against succumbing to enticing women. The imagery and metaphors pack part of the punch, as do the imperative verbs. The warnings of what to avoid are set over against one of the most evocative affirmations of married sexual love in the Bible, with emphasis on the privacy of the sexual relationship as God intended it (vv. 15, 17–19). The concluding verse, even though its specific function is to bring closure to the brief dissertation on sexual sin, is an apt summary of a main thrust of the book of Proverbs as a whole: "He dies for lack of discipline."

---

5   My son, be attentive to my wisdom;
          incline your ear to my understanding,
²   that you may keep discretion,
          and your lips may guard knowledge.
³   For the lips of a forbidden¹ woman drip honey,
          and her speech² is smoother than oil,
⁴   but in the end she is bitter as wormwood,
          sharp as a two-edged sword.
⁵   Her feet go down to death;
          her steps follow the path to³ Sheol;
⁶   she does not ponder the path of life;
          her ways wander, and she does not know it.

⁷   And now, O sons, listen to me,
          and do not depart from the words of my mouth.
⁸   Keep your way far from her,
          and do not go near the door of her house,
⁹   lest you give your honor to others
          and your years to the merciless,
¹⁰   lest strangers take their fill of your strength,
          and your labors go to the house of a foreigner,
¹¹   and at the end of your life you groan,
          when your flesh and body are consumed,
¹²   and you say, "How I hated discipline,
          and my heart despised reproof!
¹³   I did not listen to the voice of my teachers
          or incline my ear to my instructors.
¹⁴   I am at the brink of utter ruin
          in the assembled congregation."

---

¹ Hebrew *strange*; also verse 20 ² Hebrew *palate* ³ Hebrew *lay hold of*

¹⁵ Drink water from your own cistern,
    flowing water from your own well.
¹⁶ Should your springs be scattered abroad,
    streams of water in the streets?
¹⁷ Let them be for yourself alone,
    and not for strangers with you.
¹⁸ Let your fountain be blessed,
    and rejoice in the wife of your youth,
¹⁹ a lovely deer, a graceful doe.
Let her breasts fill you at all times with delight;
    be intoxicated[1] always in her love.
²⁰ Why should you be intoxicated, my son, with a forbidden woman
    and embrace the bosom of an adulteress?[2]
²¹ For a man's ways are before the eyes of the LORD,
    and he ponders[3] all his paths.
²² The iniquities of the wicked ensnare him,
    and he is held fast in the cords of his sin.
²³ He dies for lack of discipline,
    and because of his great folly he is led astray.

Four proverb clusters [6:1–19]. The first nine chapters of Proverbs differ from most of the remainder of the book by the molding of the material into larger units than the individual proverb, and we see that in this unit. In successive units, we find the following arrangement of the material: warning not to put up security (become a pledge) for a neighbor (vv. 1–5); a classic minidiscourse of the wise ant and the ignominious sluggard (vv. 6–11); portrait of a person who sows discord (vv. 12–15); satire on seven vices (vv. 16–19).

6 My son, if you have put up security for your neighbor,
    have given your pledge for a stranger,
² if you are snared in the words of your mouth,
    caught in the words of your mouth,
³ then do this, my son, and save yourself,
    for you have come into the hand of your neighbor:
    go, hasten,[4] and plead urgently with your neighbor.
⁴ Give your eyes no sleep
    and your eyelids no slumber;
⁵ save yourself like a gazelle from the hand of the hunter,[5]
    like a bird from the hand of the fowler.

⁶ Go to the ant, O sluggard;
    consider her ways, and be wise.
⁷ Without having any chief,
    officer, or ruler,
⁸ she prepares her bread in summer
    and gathers her food in harvest.
⁹ How long will you lie there, O sluggard?

[1] Hebrew be led astray; also verse 20 [2] Hebrew a foreign woman [3] Or makes level [4] Or humble yourself [5] Hebrew lacks of the hunter

When will you arise from your sleep?
10 A little sleep, a little slumber,
    a little folding of the hands to rest,
11 and poverty will come upon you like a robber,
    and want like an armed man.

12 A worthless person, a wicked man,
    goes about with crooked speech,
13 winks with his eyes, signals[1] with his feet,
    points with his finger,
14 with perverted heart devises evil,
    continually sowing discord;
15 therefore calamity will come upon him suddenly;
    in a moment he will be broken beyond healing.

16 There are six things that the LORD hates,
    seven that are an abomination to him:
17 haughty eyes, a lying tongue,
    and hands that shed innocent blood,
18 a heart that devises wicked plans,
    feet that make haste to run to evil,
19 a false witness who breathes out lies,
    and one who sows discord among brothers.

Second warning against the wiles of an adulterous woman [6:20–35]. The opening summons to listen (vv. 20–23) is very general in nature and could fit into a collection of proverbs at any point, but in the context of what follows it lends urgency to the real subject of the unit, namely, the need for a man to steer clear of sexual temptation (vv. 24–35). The lure is captured partly with poetic concreteness, with pictures of a smooth tongue (v. 24) and enticing eyelashes (v. 25). Verses 27–29 employ a frequent technique of OT wisdom literature—a list of rhetorical questions that lead up to the actual topic under consideration as the last item in the list. In this case, the questions also use analogies from nature, another strategy of the wise men. The final movement emphasizes the self-defeating outcome of any excursion into sexual amours with another man's wife (vv. 32–35).

20 My son, keep your father's commandment,
    and forsake not your mother's teaching.
21 Bind them on your heart always;
    tie them around your neck.
22 When you walk, they[2] will lead you;
    when you lie down, they will watch over you;
    and when you awake, they will talk with you.
23 For the commandment is a lamp and the teaching a light,
    and the reproofs of discipline are the way of life,
24 to preserve you from the evil woman,[3]
    from the smooth tongue of the adulteress.[4]

---

[1] Hebrew *scrapes* [2] Hebrew *it*; three times in this verse [3] Revocalization (compare Septuagint) yields *from the wife of a neighbor* [4] Hebrew *the foreign woman*

²⁵ Do not desire her beauty in your heart,
  and do not let her capture you with her eyelashes;
²⁶ for the price of a prostitute is only a loaf of bread,[1]
  but a married woman[2] hunts down a precious life.
²⁷ Can a man carry fire next to his chest
  and his clothes not be burned?
²⁸ Or can one walk on hot coals
  and his feet not be scorched?
²⁹ So is he who goes in to his neighbor's wife;
  none who touches her will go unpunished.
³⁰ People do not despise a thief if he steals
  to satisfy his appetite when he is hungry,
³¹ but if he is caught, he will pay sevenfold;
  he will give all the goods of his house.
³² He who commits adultery lacks sense;
  he who does it destroys himself.
³³ He will get wounds and dishonor,
  and his disgrace will not be wiped away.
³⁴ For jealousy makes a man furious,
  and he will not spare when he takes revenge.
³⁵ He will accept no compensation;
  he will refuse though you multiply gifts.

A temptation story [chapter 7]. Chapter 7 begins with the usual summons to obey (vv. 1–3) and commands to embrace wisdom (v. 4), but the generic material quickly narrows to the subject of sexual sin (v. 5). Then follows one of the most impressive passages in the book of Proverbs, as the writer abandons the technique of the collection of proverbs and composes a vivid temptation story (vv. 6–23). The principal actors are "a young man lacking sense" (v. 7) and the archetypal "forbidden woman" (v. 5)—not a literal prostitute but a married woman acting promiscuously like a prostitute (v. 10). The temptation story is a triumph of vividness. Instead of handling the experience of sexual sin as a modern writer would, the author here displays an evocative reticence and gives us vivid metaphors of what the event means in terms of destruction of one's soul (vv. 22–23). After the narrative is complete, the author offers a concluding warning to his listener to avoid what he has just observed by way of fictional narrative (vv. 24–25), and in a masterstroke, giving in to sexual temptation suddenly becomes magnified into losing an epic battle (v. 26) and inviting oneself to the chambers of death (v. 27).

7 My son, keep my words
  and treasure up my commandments with you;
² keep my commandments and live;
  keep my teaching as the apple of your eye;
³ bind them on your fingers;
  write them on the tablet of your heart.
⁴ Say to wisdom, "You are my sister,"
  and call insight your intimate friend,

---

[1] Or (compare Septuagint, Syriac, Vulgate) *for a prostitute leaves a man with nothing but a loaf of bread* [2] Hebrew *a man's wife*

⁵   to keep you from the forbidden[1] woman,
     from the adulteress[2] with her smooth words.

⁶   For at the window of my house
     I have looked out through my lattice,
⁷   and I have seen among the simple,
     I have perceived among the youths,
     a young man lacking sense,
⁸   passing along the street near her corner,
     taking the road to her house
⁹   in the twilight, in the evening,
     at the time of night and darkness.

¹⁰   And behold, the woman meets him,
     dressed as a prostitute, wily of heart.[3]
¹¹   She is loud and wayward;
     her feet do not stay at home;
¹²   now in the street, now in the market,
     and at every corner she lies in wait.
¹³   She seizes him and kisses him,
     and with bold face she says to him,
¹⁴   "I had to offer sacrifices,[4]
     and today I have paid my vows;
¹⁵   so now I have come out to meet you,
     to seek you eagerly, and I have found you.
¹⁶   I have spread my couch with coverings,
     colored linens from Egyptian linen;
¹⁷   I have perfumed my bed with myrrh,
     aloes, and cinnamon.
¹⁸   Come, let us take our fill of love till morning;
     let us delight ourselves with love.
¹⁹   For my husband is not at home;
     he has gone on a long journey;
²⁰   he took a bag of money with him;
     at full moon he will come home."

²¹   With much seductive speech she persuades him;
     with her smooth talk she compels him.
²²   All at once he follows her,
     as an ox goes to the slaughter,
     or as a stag is caught fast[5]
²³   till an arrow pierces its liver;
     as a bird rushes into a snare;
     he does not know that it will cost him his life.

²⁴   And now, O sons, listen to me,
     and be attentive to the words of my mouth.
²⁵   Let not your heart turn aside to her ways;

---

[1] Hebrew *strange* [2] Hebrew *the foreign woman* [3] Hebrew *guarded in heart* [4] Hebrew *peace offerings* [5] Probable reading (compare Septuagint, Vulgate, Syriac); Hebrew *as an anklet for the discipline of a fool*

do not stray into her paths,
26   for many a victim has she laid low,
    and all her slain are a mighty throng.
27   Her house is the way to Sheol,
    going down to the chambers of death.

Wisdom's self-characterization [chapter 8]. Chapter 8 is an even longer self-contained unit. On the surface, it is a speech of self-characterization and self-advertisement by the personified woman Wisdom. But after the lead-in to the speech (vv. 1–3), the content of the speech of Wisdom about herself actually falls into the usual formulas of the encomium, as follows: the desirable qualities of Wisdom (vv. 6–9); the superiority of Wisdom to other things (vv. 10–11); a catalog of the rewards that Wisdom offers and the acts that she performs (vv. 12–21); the distinguished ancestry of Wisdom (vv. 22–31); the call to emulate (vv. 32–36). As always in the book of Proverbs, the texture of the speech is the very touchstone of poetry.

8 Does not wisdom call?
  Does not understanding raise her voice?
2   On the heights beside the way,
    at the crossroads she takes her stand;
3   beside the gates in front of the town,
    at the entrance of the portals she cries aloud:
4   "To you, O men, I call,
    and my cry is to the children of man.
5   O simple ones, learn prudence;
    O fools, learn sense.
6   Hear, for I will speak noble things,
    and from my lips will come what is right,
7   for my mouth will utter truth;
    wickedness is an abomination to my lips.
8   All the words of my mouth are righteous;
    there is nothing twisted or crooked in them.
9   They are all straight to him who understands,
    and right to those who find knowledge.
10   Take my instruction instead of silver,
    and knowledge rather than choice gold,
11   for wisdom is better than jewels,
    and all that you may desire cannot compare with her.

12   "I, wisdom, dwell with prudence,
    and I find knowledge and discretion.
13   The fear of the Lord is hatred of evil.
  Pride and arrogance and the way of evil
    and perverted speech I hate.
14   I have counsel and sound wisdom;
    I have insight; I have strength.
15   By me kings reign,

and rulers decree what is just;

16 by me princes rule,
   and nobles, all who govern justly.[1]

17 I love those who love me,
   and those who seek me diligently find me.

18 Riches and honor are with me,
   enduring wealth and righteousness.

19 My fruit is better than gold, even fine gold,
   and my yield than choice silver.

20 I walk in the way of righteousness,
   in the paths of justice,

21 granting an inheritance to those who love me,
   and filling their treasuries.

22 "The Lord possessed[2] me at the beginning of his work,[3]
   the first of his acts of old.

23 Ages ago I was set up,
   at the first, before the beginning of the earth.

24 When there were no depths I was brought forth,
   when there were no springs abounding with water.

25 Before the mountains had been shaped,
   before the hills, I was brought forth,

26 before he had made the earth with its fields,
   or the first of the dust of the world.

27 When he established the heavens, I was there;
   when he drew a circle on the face of the deep,

28 when he made firm the skies above,
   when he established[4] the fountains of the deep,

29 when he assigned to the sea its limit,
   so that the waters might not transgress his command,
   when he marked out the foundations of the earth,

30 then I was beside him, like a master workman,
   and I was daily his[5] delight,
   rejoicing before him always,

31 rejoicing in his inhabited world
   and delighting in the children of man.

32 "And now, O sons, listen to me:
   blessed are those who keep my ways.

33 Hear instruction and be wise,
   and do not neglect it.

34 Blessed is the one who listens to me,
   watching daily at my gates,
   waiting beside my doors.

35 For whoever finds me finds life
   and obtains favor from the Lord,

---

[1] Most Hebrew manuscripts; many Hebrew manuscripts, Septuagint *govern the earth* [2] Or *fathered*; Septuagint *created* [3] Hebrew *way* [4] The meaning of the Hebrew is uncertain [5] Or *daily filled with*

³⁶ but he who fails to find me injures himself;
     all who hate me love death."

> **Invitation to a banquet** [chapter 9]. The first nine chapters of Proverbs are a tour de force that is aptly climaxed by chapter 9, which is a set piece of literary contrast. Wisdom and Folly both prepare a banquet and invite the listener to it. In the middle of the chapter we find an interlude consisting of miscellaneous proverbs (vv. 7–12). This is mainly a dividing wall between the two contrasting banquets, one prepared by Wisdom (vv. 1–6) and the other by Folly (vv. 13–18). It is useful to draw lines between details in the first six verses that are echoed in verses 13–18.

9 Wisdom has built her house;
     she has hewn her seven pillars.
² She has slaughtered her beasts; she has mixed her wine;
     she has also set her table.
³ She has sent out her young women to call
     from the highest places in the town,
⁴ "Whoever is simple, let him turn in here!"
     To him who lacks sense she says,
⁵ "Come, eat of my bread
     and drink of the wine I have mixed.
⁶ Leave your simple ways,[1] and live,
     and walk in the way of insight."

⁷ Whoever corrects a scoffer gets himself abuse,
     and he who reproves a wicked man incurs injury.
⁸ Do not reprove a scoffer, or he will hate you;
     reprove a wise man, and he will love you.
⁹ Give instruction[2] to a wise man, and he will be still wiser;
     teach a righteous man, and he will increase in learning.
¹⁰ The fear of the LORD is the beginning of wisdom,
     and the knowledge of the Holy One is insight.
¹¹ For by me your days will be multiplied,
     and years will be added to your life.
¹² If you are wise, you are wise for yourself;
     if you scoff, you alone will bear it.

¹³ The woman Folly is loud;
     she is seductive[3] and knows nothing.
¹⁴ She sits at the door of her house;
     she takes a seat on the highest places of the town,
¹⁵ calling to those who pass by,
     who are going straight on their way,
¹⁶ "Whoever is simple, let him turn in here!"
     And to him who lacks sense she says,
¹⁷ "Stolen water is sweet,
     and bread eaten in secret is pleasant."

---

[1] Or *Leave the company of the simple* [2] Hebrew lacks *instruction* [3] Or *full of simpleness*

¹⁸   But he does not know that the dead¹ are there,
    that her guests are in the depths of Sheol.

Collected proverbs [chapter 10]. With the unified composition of the first nine chapters behind us, chapter 10 is our initiation into the kind of material that will govern the remainder of the book. To make reading the material inviting, we need to accept right from the start the fragmented nature of what we are reading. Chapter 10 is a collection of individual, one-verse proverbs. Each one of them falls into the form of a thought couplet in which the two lines belong together, and in chapter 10 the relationship is one of antithesis. We see the great conflict that exists in life between the good and the bad, the wise and foolish, with the further thought that it is to our advantage to choose the one over the other. In addition to assimilating the random list of proverbs as representing the mixed nature of life as we live it, we can work through the passage looking for groupings, in effect arranging our own proverb clusters (either for this chapter or among a block of chapters). For example, selected proverbs in chapter 10 talk about our dealings with other people, with possessions, with lifestyle, and with words or speech.

10   The proverbs of Solomon.

A wise son makes a glad father,
    but a foolish son is a sorrow to his mother.
²   Treasures gained by wickedness do not profit,
    but righteousness delivers from death.
³   The Lord does not let the righteous go hungry,
    but he thwarts the craving of the wicked.
⁴   A slack hand causes poverty,
    but the hand of the diligent makes rich.
⁵   He who gathers in summer is a prudent son,
    but he who sleeps in harvest is a son who brings shame.
⁶   Blessings are on the head of the righteous,
    but the mouth of the wicked conceals violence.
⁷   The memory of the righteous is a blessing,
    but the name of the wicked will rot.
⁸   The wise of heart will receive commandments,
    but a babbling fool will come to ruin.
⁹   Whoever walks in integrity walks securely,
    but he who makes his ways crooked will be found out.
¹⁰ Whoever winks the eye causes trouble,
    but a babbling fool will come to ruin.
¹¹ The mouth of the righteous is a fountain of life,
    but the mouth of the wicked conceals violence.
¹² Hatred stirs up strife,
    but love covers all offenses.
¹³ On the lips of him who has understanding, wisdom is found,
    but a rod is for the back of him who lacks sense.
¹⁴ The wise lay up knowledge,
    but the mouth of a fool brings ruin near.

¹ Hebrew *Rephaim*

15 A rich man's wealth is his strong city;
       the poverty of the poor is their ruin.
16 The wage of the righteous leads to life,
       the gain of the wicked to sin.
17 Whoever heeds instruction is on the path to life,
       but he who rejects reproof leads others astray.
18 The one who conceals hatred has lying lips,
       and whoever utters slander is a fool.
19 When words are many, transgression is not lacking,
       but whoever restrains his lips is prudent.
20 The tongue of the righteous is choice silver;
       the heart of the wicked is of little worth.
21 The lips of the righteous feed many,
       but fools die for lack of sense.
22 The blessing of the LORD makes rich,
       and he adds no sorrow with it.[1]
23 Doing wrong is like a joke to a fool,
       but wisdom is pleasure to a man of understanding.
24 What the wicked dreads will come upon him,
       but the desire of the righteous will be granted.
25 When the tempest passes, the wicked is no more,
       but the righteous is established forever.
26 Like vinegar to the teeth and smoke to the eyes,
       so is the sluggard to those who send him.
27 The fear of the LORD prolongs life,
       but the years of the wicked will be short.
28 The hope of the righteous brings joy,
       but the expectation of the wicked will perish.
29 The way of the LORD is a stronghold to the blameless,
       but destruction to evildoers.
30 The righteous will never be removed,
       but the wicked will not dwell in the land.
31 The mouth of the righteous brings forth wisdom,
       but the perverse tongue will be cut off.
32 The lips of the righteous know what is acceptable,
       but the mouth of the wicked, what is perverse.

The great either-or [chapters 11–12]. Antithetic parallelism dominates these two chapters as well, as the two sentences that make up each individual verse set one thing against its opposite. It is fruitful to ponder what sense of life and worldview emerge from this dialectical rhetoric. A large part of the meaning of these two chapters is embodied in the *epithets that recur: "the humble," "the upright," "the righteous," "the wicked," "the treacherous," "the godless man," etc. Another analytic grid for the material is to note the categories of human experience that the chapters cover—economic life, society, future reward and punishment, the good life, relations with others, domestic life, etc.

---

[1] Or and toil adds nothing to it

11

A false balance is an abomination to the Lord,
   but a just weight is his delight.
2 When pride comes, then comes disgrace,
   but with the humble is wisdom.
3 The integrity of the upright guides them,
   but the crookedness of the treacherous destroys them.
4 Riches do not profit in the day of wrath,
   but righteousness delivers from death.
5 The righteousness of the blameless keeps his way straight,
   but the wicked falls by his own wickedness.
6 The righteousness of the upright delivers them,
   but the treacherous are taken captive by their lust.
7 When the wicked dies, his hope will perish,
   and the expectation of wealth[1] perishes too.
8 The righteous is delivered from trouble,
   and the wicked walks into it instead.
9 With his mouth the godless man would destroy his neighbor,
   but by knowledge the righteous are delivered.
10 When it goes well with the righteous, the city rejoices,
   and when the wicked perish there are shouts of gladness.
11 By the blessing of the upright a city is exalted,
   but by the mouth of the wicked it is overthrown.
12 Whoever belittles his neighbor lacks sense,
   but a man of understanding remains silent.
13 Whoever goes about slandering reveals secrets,
   but he who is trustworthy in spirit keeps a thing covered.
14 Where there is no guidance, a people falls,
   but in an abundance of counselors there is safety.
15 Whoever puts up security for a stranger will surely suffer harm,
   but he who hates striking hands in pledge is secure.
16 A gracious woman gets honor,
   and violent men get riches.
17 A man who is kind benefits himself,
   but a cruel man hurts himself.
18 The wicked earns deceptive wages,
   but one who sows righteousness gets a sure reward.
19 Whoever is steadfast in righteousness will live,
   but he who pursues evil will die.
20 Those of crooked heart are an abomination to the Lord,
   but those of blameless ways are his delight.
21 Be assured, an evil person will not go unpunished,
   but the offspring of the righteous will be delivered.
22 Like a gold ring in a pig's snout
   is a beautiful woman without discretion.
23 The desire of the righteous ends only in good;
   the expectation of the wicked in wrath.
24 One gives freely, yet grows all the richer;

---

[1] Or of his strength, or of iniquity

another withholds what he should give, and only suffers want.
²⁵ Whoever brings blessing will be enriched,
  and one who waters will himself be watered.
²⁶ The people curse him who holds back grain,
  but a blessing is on the head of him who sells it.
²⁷ Whoever diligently seeks good seeks favor,[1]
  but evil comes to him who searches for it.
²⁸ Whoever trusts in his riches will fall,
  but the righteous will flourish like a green leaf.
²⁹ Whoever troubles his own household will inherit the wind,
  and the fool will be servant to the wise of heart.
³⁰ The fruit of the righteous is a tree of life,
  and whoever captures souls is wise.
³¹ If the righteous is repaid on earth,
  how much more the wicked and the sinner!

12 Whoever loves discipline loves knowledge,
  but he who hates reproof is stupid.
² A good man obtains favor from the LORD,
  but a man of evil devices he condemns.
³ No one is established by wickedness,
  but the root of the righteous will never be moved.
⁴ An excellent wife is the crown of her husband,
  but she who brings shame is like rottenness in his bones.
⁵ The thoughts of the righteous are just;
  the counsels of the wicked are deceitful.
⁶ The words of the wicked lie in wait for blood,
  but the mouth of the upright delivers them.
⁷ The wicked are overthrown and are no more,
  but the house of the righteous will stand.
⁸ A man is commended according to his good sense,
  but one of twisted mind is despised.
⁹ Better to be lowly and have a servant
  than to play the great man and lack bread.
¹⁰ Whoever is righteous has regard for the life of his beast,
  but the mercy of the wicked is cruel.
¹¹ Whoever works his land will have plenty of bread,
  but he who follows worthless pursuits lacks sense.
¹² Whoever is wicked covets the spoil of evildoers,
  but the root of the righteous bears fruit.
¹³ An evil man is ensnared by the transgression of his lips,
  but the righteous escapes from trouble.
¹⁴ From the fruit of his mouth a man is satisfied with good,
  and the work of a man's hand comes back to him.
¹⁵ The way of a fool is right in his own eyes,
  but a wise man listens to advice.
¹⁶ The vexation of a fool is known at once,

[1] Or *acceptance*

but the prudent ignores an insult.
17 Whoever speaks[1] the truth gives honest evidence,
   but a false witness utters deceit.
18 There is one whose rash words are like sword thrusts,
   but the tongue of the wise brings healing.
19 Truthful lips endure forever,
   but a lying tongue is but for a moment.
20 Deceit is in the heart of those who devise evil,
   but those who plan peace have joy.
21 No ill befalls the righteous,
   but the wicked are filled with trouble.
22 Lying lips are an abomination to the LORD,
   but those who act faithfully are his delight.
23 A prudent man conceals knowledge,
   but the heart of fools proclaims folly.
24 The hand of the diligent will rule,
   while the slothful will be put to forced labor.
25 Anxiety in a man's heart weighs him down,
   but a good word makes him glad.
26 One who is righteous is a guide to his neighbor,[2]
   but the way of the wicked leads them astray.
27 Whoever is slothful will not roast his game,
   but the diligent man will get precious wealth.[3]
28 In the path of righteousness is life,
   and in its pathway there is no death.

Learning to value what God values [chapters 13–14]. Antithetic parallelism continues to be the dominant rhetorical mode of individual proverbs, and the organization continues to be random. We can appreciate this randomness as giving expression to the mixed nature of our daily life, which also has many facets that defy tidy patterns. Proverbs express a sense of values, and we can read these two chapters as "notes" toward an understanding of what God values. The life of godliness consists of coming to value the things that God values. Individual proverbs also embody a moral scheme of virtues to be emulated and vices to be avoided. For most of the verses in these two chapters, we can tease out an implied virtue and an implied vice.

13 A wise son hears his father's instruction,
   but a scoffer does not listen to rebuke.
2 From the fruit of his mouth a man eats what is good,
   but the desire of the treacherous is for violence.
3 Whoever guards his mouth preserves his life;
   he who opens wide his lips comes to ruin.
4 The soul of the sluggard craves and gets nothing,
   while the soul of the diligent is richly supplied.
5 The righteous hates falsehood,
   but the wicked brings shame[4] and disgrace.

[1] Hebrew *breathes out* [2] Or *The righteous chooses his friends carefully* [3] Or *but diligence is precious wealth* [4] Or *stench*

⁶ Righteousness guards him whose way is blameless,
   but sin overthrows the wicked.
⁷ One pretends to be rich, yet has nothing;
   another pretends to be poor, yet has great wealth.
⁸ The ransom of a man's life is his wealth,
   but a poor man hears no threat.
⁹ The light of the righteous rejoices,
   but the lamp of the wicked will be put out.
¹⁰ By insolence comes nothing but strife,
   but with those who take advice is wisdom.
¹¹ Wealth gained hastily[1] will dwindle,
   but whoever gathers little by little will increase it.
¹² Hope deferred makes the heart sick,
   but a desire fulfilled is a tree of life.
¹³ Whoever despises the word brings destruction on himself,
   but he who reveres the commandment will be rewarded.
¹⁴ The teaching of the wise is a fountain of life,
   that one may turn away from the snares of death.
¹⁵ Good sense wins favor,
   but the way of the treacherous is their ruin.[2]
¹⁶ In everything the prudent acts with knowledge,
   but a fool flaunts his folly.
¹⁷ A wicked messenger falls into trouble,
   but a faithful envoy brings healing.
¹⁸ Poverty and disgrace come to him who ignores instruction,
   but whoever heeds reproof is honored.
¹⁹ A desire fulfilled is sweet to the soul,
   but to turn away from evil is an abomination to fools.
²⁰ Whoever walks with the wise becomes wise,
   but the companion of fools will suffer harm.
²¹ Disaster[3] pursues sinners,
   but the righteous are rewarded with good.
²² A good man leaves an inheritance to his children's children,
   but the sinner's wealth is laid up for the righteous.
²³ The fallow ground of the poor would yield much food,
   but it is swept away through injustice.
²⁴ Whoever spares the rod hates his son,
   but he who loves him is diligent to discipline him.[4]
²⁵ The righteous has enough to satisfy his appetite,
   but the belly of the wicked suffers want.

14

The wisest of women builds her house,
   but folly with her own hands tears it down.
² Whoever walks in uprightness fears the LORD,
   but he who is devious in his ways despises him.
³ By the mouth of a fool comes a rod for his back,[5]

---

[1] Or *by fraud* [2] Probable reading (compare Septuagint, Syriac, Vulgate); Hebrew *is rugged,* or *is an enduring rut* [3] Or *Evil* [4] Or *who loves him disciplines him early* [5] Or *In the mouth of a fool is a rod of pride*

but the lips of the wise will preserve them.
4 Where there are no oxen, the manger is clean,
       but abundant crops come by the strength of the ox.
5 A faithful witness does not lie,
       but a false witness breathes out lies.
6 A scoffer seeks wisdom in vain,
       but knowledge is easy for a man of understanding.
7 Leave the presence of a fool,
       for there you do not meet words of knowledge.
8 The wisdom of the prudent is to discern his way,
       but the folly of fools is deceiving.
9 Fools mock at the guilt offering,
       but the upright enjoy acceptance.[1]
10 The heart knows its own bitterness,
       and no stranger shares its joy.
11 The house of the wicked will be destroyed,
       but the tent of the upright will flourish.
12 There is a way that seems right to a man,
       but its end is the way to death.[2]
13 Even in laughter the heart may ache,
       and the end of joy may be grief.
14 The backslider in heart will be filled with the fruit of his ways,
       and a good man will be filled with the fruit of his ways.
15 The simple believes everything,
       but the prudent gives thought to his steps.
16 One who is wise is cautious[3] and turns away from evil,
       but a fool is reckless and careless.
17 A man of quick temper acts foolishly,
       and a man of evil devices is hated.
18 The simple inherit folly,
       but the prudent are crowned with knowledge.
19 The evil bow down before the good,
       the wicked at the gates of the righteous.
20 The poor is disliked even by his neighbor,
       but the rich has many friends.
21 Whoever despises his neighbor is a sinner,
       but blessed is he who is generous to the poor.
22 Do they not go astray who devise evil?
       Those who devise good meet[4] steadfast love and faithfulness.
23 In all toil there is profit,
       but mere talk tends only to poverty.
24 The crown of the wise is their wealth,
       but the folly of fools brings folly.
25 A truthful witness saves lives,
       but one who breathes out lies is deceitful.
26 In the fear of the LORD one has strong confidence,
       and his children will have a refuge.

---

[1] Hebrew but among the upright is acceptance [2] Hebrew ways of death [3] Or fears [the LORD] [4] Or show

²⁷ The fear of the Lord is a fountain of life,
    that one may turn away from the snares of death.
²⁸ In a multitude of people is the glory of a king,
    but without people a prince is ruined.
²⁹ Whoever is slow to anger has great understanding,
    but he who has a hasty temper exalts folly.
³⁰ A tranquil[1] heart gives life to the flesh,
    but envy[2] makes the bones rot.
³¹ Whoever oppresses a poor man insults his Maker,
    but he who is generous to the needy honors him.
³² The wicked is overthrown through his evildoing,
    but the righteous finds refuge in his death.
³³ Wisdom rests in the heart of a man of understanding,
    but it makes itself known even in the midst of fools.[3]
³⁴ Righteousness exalts a nation,
    but sin is a reproach to any people.
³⁵ A servant who deals wisely has the king's favor,
    but his wrath falls on one who acts shamefully.

Wisdom and folly: variations on a theme [chapters 15–16]. The patterning continues to be random, and the formatting the same (a series of two-line aphorisms, most but not all them based on the principle of contrast). This is a good point at which to remind ourselves that in the mind of the wise man, all that he has to say falls into two categories that seemed so natural to the ancient mind but that people today may struggle to fill with content. Those two concepts are wisdom and folly. In addition to noting the usual considerations of values, virtues, and vices, we can profitably analyze the data with a view toward coming up with definitions of wisdom and folly ("skill for living" is one legitimate interpretive slant on the concept of wisdom, but there are others).

---

15 A soft answer turns away wrath,
    but a harsh word stirs up anger.
² The tongue of the wise commends knowledge,
    but the mouths of fools pour out folly.
³ The eyes of the Lord are in every place,
    keeping watch on the evil and the good.
⁴ A gentle[4] tongue is a tree of life,
    but perverseness in it breaks the spirit.
⁵ A fool despises his father's instruction,
    but whoever heeds reproof is prudent.
⁶ In the house of the righteous there is much treasure,
    but trouble befalls the income of the wicked.
⁷ The lips of the wise spread knowledge;
    not so the hearts of fools.[5]
⁸ The sacrifice of the wicked is an abomination to the Lord,
    but the prayer of the upright is acceptable to him.
⁹ The way of the wicked is an abomination to the Lord,

---

[1] Or *healing* [2] Or *jealousy* [3] Or *Wisdom rests quietly in the heart of a man of understanding, but makes itself known in the midst of fools* [4] Or *healing* [5] Or *the hearts of fools are not steadfast*

but he loves him who pursues righteousness.

¹⁰ There is severe discipline for him who forsakes the way;
　　whoever hates reproof will die.

¹¹ Sheol and Abaddon lie open before the LORD;
　　how much more the hearts of the children of man!

¹² A scoffer does not like to be reproved;
　　he will not go to the wise.

¹³ A glad heart makes a cheerful face,
　　but by sorrow of heart the spirit is crushed.

¹⁴ The heart of him who has understanding seeks knowledge,
　　but the mouths of fools feed on folly.

¹⁵ All the days of the afflicted are evil,
　　but the cheerful of heart has a continual feast.

¹⁶ Better is a little with the fear of the LORD
　　than great treasure and trouble with it.

¹⁷ Better is a dinner of herbs where love is
　　than a fattened ox and hatred with it.

¹⁸ A hot-tempered man stirs up strife,
　　but he who is slow to anger quiets contention.

¹⁹ The way of a sluggard is like a hedge of thorns,
　　but the path of the upright is a level highway.

²⁰ A wise son makes a glad father,
　　but a foolish man despises his mother.

²¹ Folly is a joy to him who lacks sense,
　　but a man of understanding walks straight ahead.

²² Without counsel plans fail,
　　but with many advisers they succeed.

²³ To make an apt answer is a joy to a man,
　　and a word in season, how good it is!

²⁴ The path of life leads upward for the prudent,
　　that he may turn away from Sheol beneath.

²⁵ The LORD tears down the house of the proud
　　but maintains the widow's boundaries.

²⁶ The thoughts of the wicked are an abomination to the LORD,
　　but gracious words are pure.

²⁷ Whoever is greedy for unjust gain troubles his own household,
　　but he who hates bribes will live.

²⁸ The heart of the righteous ponders how to answer,
　　but the mouth of the wicked pours out evil things.

²⁹ The LORD is far from the wicked,
　　but he hears the prayer of the righteous.

³⁰ The light of the eyes rejoices the heart,
　　and good news refreshes[1] the bones.

³¹ The ear that listens to life-giving reproof
　　will dwell among the wise.

³² Whoever ignores instruction despises himself,
　　but he who listens to reproof gains intelligence.

---

[1] Hebrew *makes fat*

³³ The fear of the LORD is instruction in wisdom,
  and humility comes before honor.

16 The plans of the heart belong to man,
  but the answer of the tongue is from the LORD.
² All the ways of a man are pure in his own eyes,
  but the LORD weighs the spirit.
³ Commit your work to the LORD,
  and your plans will be established.
⁴ The LORD has made everything for its purpose,
  even the wicked for the day of trouble.
⁵ Everyone who is arrogant in heart is an abomination to the LORD;
  be assured, he will not go unpunished.
⁶ By steadfast love and faithfulness iniquity is atoned for,
  and by the fear of the LORD one turns away from evil.
⁷ When a man's ways please the LORD,
  he makes even his enemies to be at peace with him.
⁸ Better is a little with righteousness
  than great revenues with injustice.
⁹ The heart of man plans his way,
  but the LORD establishes his steps.
¹⁰ An oracle is on the lips of a king;
  his mouth does not sin in judgment.
¹¹ A just balance and scales are the LORD's;
  all the weights in the bag are his work.
¹² It is an abomination to kings to do evil,
  for the throne is established by righteousness.
¹³ Righteous lips are the delight of a king,
  and he loves him who speaks what is right.
¹⁴ A king's wrath is a messenger of death,
  and a wise man will appease it.
¹⁵ In the light of a king's face there is life,
  and his favor is like the clouds that bring the spring rain.
¹⁶ How much better to get wisdom than gold!
  To get understanding is to be chosen rather than silver.
¹⁷ The highway of the upright turns aside from evil;
  whoever guards his way preserves his life.
¹⁸ Pride goes before destruction,
  and a haughty spirit before a fall.
¹⁹ It is better to be of a lowly spirit with the poor
  than to divide the spoil with the proud.
²⁰ Whoever gives thought to the word¹ will discover good,
  and blessed is he who trusts in the LORD.
²¹ The wise of heart is called discerning,
  and sweetness of speech increases persuasiveness.
²² Good sense is a fountain of life to him who has it,
  but the instruction of fools is folly.

¹ Or *to a matter*

23 The heart of the wise makes his speech judicious
　　and adds persuasiveness to his lips.
24 Gracious words are like a honeycomb,
　　sweetness to the soul and health to the body.
25 There is a way that seems right to a man,
　　but its end is the way to death.[1]
26 A worker's appetite works for him;
　　his mouth urges him on.
27 A worthless man plots evil,
　　and his speech[2] is like a scorching fire.
28 A dishonest man spreads strife,
　　and a whisperer separates close friends.
29 A man of violence entices his neighbor
　　and leads him in a way that is not good.
30 Whoever winks his eyes plans[3] dishonest things;
　　he who purses his lips brings evil to pass.
31 Gray hair is a crown of glory;
　　it is gained in a righteous life.
32 Whoever is slow to anger is better than the mighty,
　　and he who rules his spirit than he who takes a city.
33 The lot is cast into the lap,
　　but its every decision is from the LORD.

How to succeed in life by really trying [chapters 17–18]. While "thought couplets" continue to be the basic format of these chapters, we move away from the nearly exclusive use of antithetical parallelism in favor of other kinds of parallelism, such as *synonymous parallelism and *synthetic (growing) parallelism (as in "The name of the LORD is a strong tower; the righteous man runs into it and is safe," 18:10). As we assimilate the individual proverbs, we continue to get a sense that the good life requires active choice and strenuous effort. We can scrutinize these chapters for evidence that the writers of wisdom literature conceive of the moral life not as something into which people drift by natural inclination but as something that requires a metaphoric swimming against the tide. Another useful strategy is to apply the grid of values/virtues/vices not simply to individual proverbs but to the whole book of Proverbs. Chapters 17–18 can be taken as a microcosm: According to these chapters, what does God value most? What virtues does God want people to cultivate? What vices does he want them to avoid? The broad categories of generosity, speech, and relating to other people are leading topics in these two chapters.

17

　　Better is a dry morsel with quiet
　　than a house full of feasting[4] with strife.
2 A servant who deals wisely will rule over a son who acts shamefully
　　and will share the inheritance as one of the brothers.
3 The crucible is for silver, and the furnace is for gold,
　　and the LORD tests hearts.
4 An evildoer listens to wicked lips,
　　and a liar gives ear to a mischievous tongue.

---

[1] Hebrew *ways of death* [2] Hebrew *what is on his lips* [3] Hebrew *to plan* [4] Hebrew *sacrifices*

⁵ Whoever mocks the poor insults his Maker;
    he who is glad at calamity will not go unpunished.
⁶ Grandchildren are the crown of the aged,
    and the glory of children is their fathers.
⁷ Fine speech is not becoming to a fool;
    still less is false speech to a prince.
⁸ A bribe is like a magic stone in the eyes of the one who gives it;
    wherever he turns he prospers.
⁹ Whoever covers an offense seeks love,
    but he who repeats a matter separates close friends.
¹⁰ A rebuke goes deeper into a man of understanding
    than a hundred blows into a fool.
¹¹ An evil man seeks only rebellion,
    and a cruel messenger will be sent against him.
¹² Let a man meet a she-bear robbed of her cubs
    rather than a fool in his folly.
¹³ If anyone returns evil for good,
    evil will not depart from his house.
¹⁴ The beginning of strife is like letting out water,
    so quit before the quarrel breaks out.
¹⁵ He who justifies the wicked and he who condemns the righteous
    are both alike an abomination to the LORD.
¹⁶ Why should a fool have money in his hand to buy wisdom
    when he has no sense?
¹⁷ A friend loves at all times,
    and a brother is born for adversity.
¹⁸ One who lacks sense gives a pledge
    and puts up security in the presence of his neighbor.
¹⁹ Whoever loves transgression loves strife;
    he who makes his door high seeks destruction.
²⁰ A man of crooked heart does not discover good,
    and one with a dishonest tongue falls into calamity.
²¹ He who sires a fool gets himself sorrow,
    and the father of a fool has no joy.
²² A joyful heart is good medicine,
    but a crushed spirit dries up the bones.
²³ The wicked accepts a bribe in secret[1]
    to pervert the ways of justice.
²⁴ The discerning sets his face toward wisdom,
    but the eyes of a fool are on the ends of the earth.
²⁵ A foolish son is a grief to his father
    and bitterness to her who bore him.
²⁶ To impose a fine on a righteous man is not good,
    nor to strike the noble for their uprightness.
²⁷ Whoever restrains his words has knowledge,
    and he who has a cool spirit is a man of understanding.
²⁸ Even a fool who keeps silent is considered wise;
    when he closes his lips, he is deemed intelligent.

[1] Hebrew *a bribe from the bosom*

18

Whoever isolates himself seeks his own desire;
he breaks out against all sound judgment.

2 A fool takes no pleasure in understanding,
but only in expressing his opinion.

3 When wickedness comes, contempt comes also,
and with dishonor comes disgrace.

4 The words of a man's mouth are deep waters;
the fountain of wisdom is a bubbling brook.

5 It is not good to be partial to[1] the wicked
or to deprive the righteous of justice.

6 A fool's lips walk into a fight,
and his mouth invites a beating.

7 A fool's mouth is his ruin,
and his lips are a snare to his soul.

8 The words of a whisperer are like delicious morsels;
they go down into the inner parts of the body.

9 Whoever is slack in his work
is a brother to him who destroys.

10 The name of the LORD is a strong tower;
the righteous man runs into it and is safe.

11 A rich man's wealth is his strong city,
and like a high wall in his imagination.

12 Before destruction a man's heart is haughty,
but humility comes before honor.

13 If one gives an answer before he hears,
it is his folly and shame.

14 A man's spirit will endure sickness,
but a crushed spirit who can bear?

15 An intelligent heart acquires knowledge,
and the ear of the wise seeks knowledge.

16 A man's gift makes room for him
and brings him before the great.

17 The one who states his case first seems right,
until the other comes and examines him.

18 The lot puts an end to quarrels
and decides between powerful contenders.

19 A brother offended is more unyielding than a strong city,
and quarreling is like the bars of a castle.

20 From the fruit of a man's mouth his stomach is satisfied;
he is satisfied by the yield of his lips.

21 Death and life are in the power of the tongue,
and those who love it will eat its fruits.

22 He who finds a wife finds a good thing
and obtains favor from the LORD.

23 The poor use entreaties,

---

[1] Hebrew *to lift the face of*

but the rich answer roughly.
²⁴ A man of many companions may come to ruin,
   but there is a friend who sticks closer than a brother.

How to fail in life [chapters 19–20]. If the proverbs yield an extended blueprint for
how to succeed in life, they also yield a picture of how to fail. We can scrutinize these
two chapters as an extended description of how to fail at life—a composite portrait of
the archetypal loser. The positive commands are an extended *foil and antidote to the
negative picture. As part of such an exploration, we can start to compile a gallery of
archetypal character types—all of them villains—such as the cheater, the sluggard
(lazy person), the scoffer, the drunkard, and the gossip. While most of the proverbs
describe human action, some of them state specifically what God does; we can comb
these proverbs for a composite portrait of God.

19

Better is a poor person who walks in his integrity
than one who is crooked in speech and is a fool.
² Desire¹ without knowledge is not good,
   and whoever makes haste with his feet misses his way.
³ When a man's folly brings his way to ruin,
   his heart rages against the LORD.
⁴ Wealth brings many new friends,
   but a poor man is deserted by his friend.
⁵ A false witness will not go unpunished,
   and he who breathes out lies will not escape.
⁶ Many seek the favor of a generous man,²
   and everyone is a friend to a man who gives gifts.
⁷ All a poor man's brothers hate him;
   how much more do his friends go far from him!
   He pursues them with words, but does not have them.³
⁸ Whoever gets sense loves his own soul;
   he who keeps understanding will discover good.
⁹ A false witness will not go unpunished,
   and he who breathes out lies will perish.
¹⁰ It is not fitting for a fool to live in luxury,
   much less for a slave to rule over princes.
¹¹ Good sense makes one slow to anger,
   and it is his glory to overlook an offense.
¹² A king's wrath is like the growling of a lion,
   but his favor is like dew on the grass.
¹³ A foolish son is ruin to his father,
   and a wife's quarreling is a continual dripping of rain.
¹⁴ House and wealth are inherited from fathers,
   but a prudent wife is from the LORD.
¹⁵ Slothfulness casts into a deep sleep,
   and an idle person will suffer hunger.
¹⁶ Whoever keeps the commandment keeps his life;

---

¹ Or *A soul* ² Or *of a noble* ³ The meaning of the Hebrew sentence is uncertain

he who despises his ways will die.

17 Whoever is generous to the poor lends to the LORD,
  and he will repay him for his deed.
18 Discipline your son, for there is hope;
  do not set your heart on putting him to death.
19 A man of great wrath will pay the penalty,
  for if you deliver him, you will only have to do it again.
20 Listen to advice and accept instruction,
  that you may gain wisdom in the future.
21 Many are the plans in the mind of a man,
  but it is the purpose of the LORD that will stand.
22 What is desired in a man is steadfast love,
  and a poor man is better than a liar.
23 The fear of the LORD leads to life,
  and whoever has it rests satisfied;
  he will not be visited by harm.
24 The sluggard buries his hand in the dish
  and will not even bring it back to his mouth.
25 Strike a scoffer, and the simple will learn prudence;
  reprove a man of understanding, and he will gain knowledge.
26 He who does violence to his father and chases away his mother
  is a son who brings shame and reproach.
27 Cease to hear instruction, my son,
  and you will stray from the words of knowledge.
28 A worthless witness mocks at justice,
  and the mouth of the wicked devours iniquity.
29 Condemnation is ready for scoffers,
  and beating for the backs of fools.

20 Wine is a mocker, strong drink a brawler,
  and whoever is led astray by it is not wise.[1]
2 The terror of a king is like the growling of a lion;
  whoever provokes him to anger forfeits his life.
3 It is an honor for a man to keep aloof from strife,
  but every fool will be quarreling.
4 The sluggard does not plow in the autumn;
  he will seek at harvest and have nothing.
5 The purpose in a man's heart is like deep water,
  but a man of understanding will draw it out.
6 Many a man proclaims his own steadfast love,
  but a faithful man who can find?
7 The righteous who walks in his integrity—
  blessed are his children after him!
8 A king who sits on the throne of judgment
  winnows all evil with his eyes.
9 Who can say, "I have made my heart pure;
  I am clean from my sin"?

---

[1] Or will not become wise

10   Unequal[1] weights and unequal measures
      are both alike an abomination to the LORD.

11   Even a child makes himself known by his acts,
      by whether his conduct is pure and upright.[2]

12   The hearing ear and the seeing eye,
      the LORD has made them both.

13   Love not sleep, lest you come to poverty;
      open your eyes, and you will have plenty of bread.

14   "Bad, bad," says the buyer,
      but when he goes away, then he boasts.

15   There is gold and abundance of costly stones,
      but the lips of knowledge are a precious jewel.

16   Take a man's garment when he has put up security for a stranger,
      and hold it in pledge when he puts up security for foreigners.[3]

17   Bread gained by deceit is sweet to a man,
      but afterward his mouth will be full of gravel.

18   Plans are established by counsel;
      by wise guidance wage war.

19   Whoever goes about slandering reveals secrets;
      therefore do not associate with a simple babbler.[4]

20   If one curses his father or his mother,
      his lamp will be put out in utter darkness.

21   An inheritance gained hastily in the beginning
      will not be blessed in the end.

22   Do not say, "I will repay evil";
      wait for the LORD, and he will deliver you.

23   Unequal weights are an abomination to the LORD,
      and false scales are not good.

24   A man's steps are from the LORD;
      how then can man understand his way?

25   It is a snare to say rashly, "It is holy,"
      and to reflect only after making vows.

26   A wise king winnows the wicked
      and drives the wheel over them.

27   The spirit[5] of man is the lamp of the LORD,
      searching all his innermost parts.

28   Steadfast love and faithfulness preserve the king,
      and by steadfast love his throne is upheld.

29   The glory of young men is their strength,
      but the splendor of old men is their gray hair.

30   Blows that wound cleanse away evil;
      strokes make clean the innermost parts.

Living God's law [chapters 21–22]. When we think of God's law, we think most naturally of the books of law in the Pentateuch or the commands of Jesus or the *paraenesis sections of the NT epistles. But the proverbs also constitute God's law. Some of them are

---

[1] Or *Two kinds of*; also verse 23   [2] Or *Even a child can dissemble in his actions, though his conduct seems pure and upright*   [3] Or *for an adulteress* (compare 27:13)   [4] Hebrew *with one who is simple in his lips*   [5] Hebrew *breath*

phrased as commands: "Train up a child in the way he should go" (22:6); "Drive out a scoffer" (22:10); "Do not rob the poor" (22:22). But even when a proverb is expressed in a descriptive rather than prescriptive format, it embodies God's law for living and contains an implied command. A good analytic grid for the proverbs in these two chapters is to ponder how each one is an explicit or implicit rule for life.

21

The king's heart is a stream of water in the hand of the LORD;
　　he turns it wherever he will.
2　Every way of a man is right in his own eyes,
　　but the LORD weighs the heart.
3　To do righteousness and justice
　　is more acceptable to the LORD than sacrifice.
4　Haughty eyes and a proud heart,
　　the lamp[1] of the wicked, are sin.
5　The plans of the diligent lead surely to abundance,
　　but everyone who is hasty comes only to poverty.
6　The getting of treasures by a lying tongue
　　is a fleeting vapor and a snare of death.[2]
7　The violence of the wicked will sweep them away,
　　because they refuse to do what is just.
8　The way of the guilty is crooked,
　　but the conduct of the pure is upright.
9　It is better to live in a corner of the housetop
　　than in a house shared with a quarrelsome wife.
10　The soul of the wicked desires evil;
　　his neighbor finds no mercy in his eyes.
11　When a scoffer is punished, the simple becomes wise;
　　when a wise man is instructed, he gains knowledge.
12　The Righteous One observes the house of the wicked;
　　he throws the wicked down to ruin.
13　Whoever closes his ear to the cry of the poor
　　will himself call out and not be answered.
14　A gift in secret averts anger,
　　and a concealed bribe,[3] strong wrath.
15　When justice is done, it is a joy to the righteous
　　but terror to evildoers.
16　One who wanders from the way of good sense
　　will rest in the assembly of the dead.
17　Whoever loves pleasure will be a poor man;
　　he who loves wine and oil will not be rich.
18　The wicked is a ransom for the righteous,
　　and the traitor for the upright.
19　It is better to live in a desert land
　　than with a quarrelsome and fretful woman.
20　Precious treasure and oil are in a wise man's dwelling,
　　but a foolish man devours it.

[1] Or *the plowing*　[2] Some Hebrew manuscripts, Septuagint, Latin; most Hebrew manuscripts *vapor for those who seek death*　[3] Hebrew *a bribe in the bosom*

21 Whoever pursues righteousness and kindness
   will find life, righteousness, and honor.
22 A wise man scales the city of the mighty
   and brings down the stronghold in which they trust.
23 Whoever keeps his mouth and his tongue
   keeps himself out of trouble.
24 "Scoffer" is the name of the arrogant, haughty man
   who acts with arrogant pride.
25 The desire of the sluggard kills him,
   for his hands refuse to labor.
26 All day long he craves and craves,
   but the righteous gives and does not hold back.
27 The sacrifice of the wicked is an abomination;
   how much more when he brings it with evil intent.
28 A false witness will perish,
   but the word of a man who hears will endure.
29 A wicked man puts on a bold face,
   but the upright gives thought to[1] his ways.
30 No wisdom, no understanding, no counsel
   can avail against the Lord.
31 The horse is made ready for the day of battle,
   but the victory belongs to the Lord.

22 A good name is to be chosen rather than great riches,
   and favor is better than silver or gold.
2 The rich and the poor meet together;
   the Lord is the maker of them all.
3 The prudent sees danger and hides himself,
   but the simple go on and suffer for it.
4 The reward for humility and fear of the Lord
   is riches and honor and life.[2]
5 Thorns and snares are in the way of the crooked;
   whoever guards his soul will keep far from them.
6 Train up a child in the way he should go;
   even when he is old he will not depart from it.
7 The rich rules over the poor,
   and the borrower is the slave of the lender.
8 Whoever sows injustice will reap calamity,
   and the rod of his fury will fail.
9 Whoever has a bountiful[3] eye will be blessed,
   for he shares his bread with the poor.
10 Drive out a scoffer, and strife will go out,
   and quarreling and abuse will cease.
11 He who loves purity of heart,
   and whose speech is gracious, will have the king as his friend.
12 The eyes of the Lord keep watch over knowledge,
   but he overthrows the words of the traitor.

---

[1] Or establishes [2] Or The reward for humility is the fear of the Lord, riches and honor and life [3] Hebrew good

¹³   The sluggard says, "There is a lion outside!
       I shall be killed in the streets!"
¹⁴   The mouth of forbidden¹ women is a deep pit;
       he with whom the LORD is angry will fall into it.
¹⁵   Folly is bound up in the heart of a child,
       but the rod of discipline drives it far from him.
¹⁶   Whoever oppresses the poor to increase his own wealth,
       or gives to the rich, will only come to poverty.

¹⁷   Incline your ear, and hear the words of the wise,
       and apply your heart to my knowledge,
¹⁸   for it will be pleasant if you keep them within you,
       if all of them are ready on your lips.
¹⁹   That your trust may be in the LORD,
       I have made them known to you today, even to you.
²⁰   Have I not written for you thirty sayings
       of counsel and knowledge,
²¹   to make you know what is right and true,
       that you may give a true answer to those who sent you?

²²   Do not rob the poor, because he is poor,
       or crush the afflicted at the gate,
²³   for the LORD will plead their cause
       and rob of life those who rob them.
²⁴   Make no friendship with a man given to anger,
       nor go with a wrathful man,
²⁵   lest you learn his ways
       and entangle yourself in a snare.
²⁶   Be not one of those who give pledges,
       who put up security for debts.
²⁷   If you have nothing with which to pay,
       why should your bed be taken from under you?
²⁸   Do not move the ancient landmark
       that your fathers have set.
²⁹   Do you see a man skillful in his work?
       He will stand before kings;
       he will not stand before obscure men.

A list of things better left undone [chapters 23–24]. While the format continues to be the miscellaneous collection of proverbs extending to many areas of life, one thing that distinguishes these two chapters is that they have a lot to say about what not to do: do not toil to acquire wealth, for example (23:4–5), and do not withhold discipline from a child (23:13). Even the positive pictures (as of a wise son [23:15–16] and a wise man [24:5]) are an implied contrast to the bad actions addressed in most of these two chapters. At the level of literary form, we can notice some proverb clusters: prudent behavior when dining with a ruler (23:1–3); similar advice about not eating with a stingy person (23:6–8); a famous portrait of the drunkard (23:29–35); praise of wisdom (24:3–7); vignette of a sluggard (24:30–34). Many other two-verse units are also present.

¹ Hebrew *strange*

23

When you sit down to eat with a ruler,
　　observe carefully what[1] is before you,
2　and put a knife to your throat
　　　if you are given to appetite.
3　Do not desire his delicacies,
　　　for they are deceptive food.
4　Do not toil to acquire wealth;
　　　be discerning enough to desist.
5　When your eyes light on it, it is gone,
　　　for suddenly it sprouts wings,
　　　flying like an eagle toward heaven.
6　Do not eat the bread of a man who is stingy;[2]
　　　do not desire his delicacies,
7　for he is like one who is inwardly calculating.[3]
　　　"Eat and drink!" he says to you,
　　　but his heart is not with you.
8　You will vomit up the morsels that you have eaten,
　　　and waste your pleasant words.
9　Do not speak in the hearing of a fool,
　　　for he will despise the good sense of your words.
10　Do not move an ancient landmark
　　　or enter the fields of the fatherless,
11　for their Redeemer is strong;
　　　he will plead their cause against you.
12　Apply your heart to instruction
　　　and your ear to words of knowledge.
13　Do not withhold discipline from a child;
　　　if you strike him with a rod, he will not die.
14　If you strike him with the rod,
　　　you will save his soul from Sheol.
15　My son, if your heart is wise,
　　　my heart too will be glad.
16　My inmost being[4] will exult
　　　when your lips speak what is right.
17　Let not your heart envy sinners,
　　　but continue in the fear of the LORD all the day.
18　Surely there is a future,
　　　and your hope will not be cut off.

19　Hear, my son, and be wise,
　　　and direct your heart in the way.
20　Be not among drunkards[5]
　　　or among gluttonous eaters of meat,
21　for the drunkard and the glutton will come to poverty,
　　　and slumber will clothe them with rags.

---

[1] Or who　[2] Hebrew whose eye is evil　[3] Or for as he calculates in his soul, so is he　[4] Hebrew My kidneys　[5] Hebrew those who drink too much wine

²²   Listen to your father who gave you life,
      and do not despise your mother when she is old.
²³   Buy truth, and do not sell it;
      buy wisdom, instruction, and understanding.
²⁴   The father of the righteous will greatly rejoice;
      he who fathers a wise son will be glad in him.
²⁵   Let your father and mother be glad;
      let her who bore you rejoice.

²⁶   My son, give me your heart,
      and let your eyes observe[1] my ways.
²⁷   For a prostitute is a deep pit;
      an adulteress[2] is a narrow well.
²⁸   She lies in wait like a robber
      and increases the traitors among mankind.

²⁹   Who has woe? Who has sorrow?
      Who has strife? Who has complaining?
    Who has wounds without cause?
      Who has redness of eyes?
³⁰   Those who tarry long over wine;
      those who go to try mixed wine.
³¹   Do not look at wine when it is red,
      when it sparkles in the cup
      and goes down smoothly.
³²   In the end it bites like a serpent
      and stings like an adder.
³³   Your eyes will see strange things,
      and your heart utter perverse things.
³⁴   You will be like one who lies down in the midst of the sea,
      like one who lies on the top of a mast.[3]
³⁵   "They struck me," you will say,[4] "but I was not hurt;
      they beat me, but I did not feel it.
    When shall I awake?
      I must have another drink."

24   Be not envious of evil men,
      nor desire to be with them,
²   for their hearts devise violence,
      and their lips talk of trouble.

³   By wisdom a house is built,
      and by understanding it is established;
⁴   by knowledge the rooms are filled
      with all precious and pleasant riches.
⁵   A wise man is full of strength,
      and a man of knowledge enhances his might,
⁶   for by wise guidance you can wage your war,

---

[1] Or delight in [2] Hebrew a foreign woman [3] Or of the rigging [4] Hebrew lacks you will say

and in abundance of counselors there is victory.
⁷ Wisdom is too high for a fool;
  in the gate he does not open his mouth.

⁸ Whoever plans to do evil
  will be called a schemer.
⁹ The devising¹ of folly is sin,
  and the scoffer is an abomination to mankind.

¹⁰ If you faint in the day of adversity,
  your strength is small.
¹¹ Rescue those who are being taken away to death;
  hold back those who are stumbling to the slaughter.
¹² If you say, "Behold, we did not know this,"
  does not he who weighs the heart perceive it?
  Does not he who keeps watch over your soul know it,
  and will he not repay man according to his work?

¹³ My son, eat honey, for it is good,
  and the drippings of the honeycomb are sweet to your taste.
¹⁴ Know that wisdom is such to your soul;
  if you find it, there will be a future,
  and your hope will not be cut off.

¹⁵ Lie not in wait as a wicked man against the dwelling of the righteous;
  do no violence to his home;
¹⁶ for the righteous falls seven times and rises again,
  but the wicked stumble in times of calamity.

¹⁷ Do not rejoice when your enemy falls,
  and let not your heart be glad when he stumbles,
¹⁸ lest the Lᴏʀᴅ see it and be displeased,
  and turn away his anger from him.

¹⁹ Fret not yourself because of evildoers,
  and be not envious of the wicked,
²⁰ for the evil man has no future;
  the lamp of the wicked will be put out.

²¹ My son, fear the Lᴏʀᴅ and the king,
  and do not join with those who do otherwise,
²² for disaster will arise suddenly from them,
  and who knows the ruin that will come from them both?

²³These also are sayings of the wise.

  Partiality in judging is not good.
²⁴ Whoever says to the wicked, "You are in the right,"
  will be cursed by peoples, abhorred by nations,
²⁵ but those who rebuke the wicked will have delight,
  and a good blessing will come upon them.

¹ Or scheming

26   Whoever gives an honest answer
       kisses the lips.

27   Prepare your work outside;
       get everything ready for yourself in the field,
       and after that build your house.

28   Be not a witness against your neighbor without cause,
       and do not deceive with your lips.

29   Do not say, "I will do to him as he has done to me;
       I will pay the man back for what he has done."

30   I passed by the field of a sluggard,
       by the vineyard of a man lacking sense,

31   and behold, it was all overgrown with thorns;
       the ground was covered with nettles,
       and its stone wall was broken down.

32   Then I saw and considered it;
       I looked and received instruction.

33   A little sleep, a little slumber,
       a little folding of the hands to rest,

34   and poverty will come upon you like a robber,
       and want like an armed man.

The rhetoric of the wise man [chapters 25–26]. A literary approach to the Bible is interested in the "how" of an utterance as well as the "what." These two chapters can be explored for the techniques that composers of proverbs typically use. The basic mode is poetry, with the usual array of imagery, metaphors, and similes. The impulse toward concretion is a good thing to observe. The aim of a proverb is to be striking and memorable, and a useful bit of initial analysis is to theorize about what makes a given proverb different from ordinary, forgettable assertions. The fact that proverbs are expressed in a language and syntax that remove them from everyday discourse should not obscure the ways in which they are consistently rooted in everyday, universal human experience. Once we observe that, we can ponder our own experiences and observations of life that illustrate a given proverb. "Like cold water to a thirsty soul, so is good news from a far country" (25:25): how has that been true in our own life? With all of the appeals to real life, a latent note of humor is always capable of entering the picture (as in 26:13–19).

25 These also are proverbs of Solomon which the men of Hezekiah king of Judah copied.

2   It is the glory of God to conceal things,
       but the glory of kings is to search things out.

3   As the heavens for height, and the earth for depth,
       so the heart of kings is unsearchable.

4   Take away the dross from the silver,
       and the smith has material for a vessel;

5   take away the wicked from the presence of the king,

and his throne will be established in righteousness.
6 Do not put yourself forward in the king's presence
    or stand in the place of the great,
7 for it is better to be told, "Come up here,"
    than to be put lower in the presence of a noble.

What your eyes have seen
8   do not hastily bring into court,
for[1] what will you do in the end,
    when your neighbor puts you to shame?
9 Argue your case with your neighbor himself,
    and do not reveal another's secret,
10 lest he who hears you bring shame upon you,
    and your ill repute have no end.

11 A word fitly spoken
    is like apples of gold in a setting of silver.
12 Like a gold ring or an ornament of gold
    is a wise reprover to a listening ear.
13 Like the cold of snow in the time of harvest
    is a faithful messenger to those who send him;
    he refreshes the soul of his masters.
14 Like clouds and wind without rain
    is a man who boasts of a gift he does not give.

15 With patience a ruler may be persuaded,
    and a soft tongue will break a bone.
16 If you have found honey, eat only enough for you,
    lest you have your fill of it and vomit it.
17 Let your foot be seldom in your neighbor's house,
    lest he have his fill of you and hate you.
18 A man who bears false witness against his neighbor
    is like a war club, or a sword, or a sharp arrow.
19 Trusting in a treacherous man in time of trouble
    is like a bad tooth or a foot that slips.
20 Whoever sings songs to a heavy heart
    is like one who takes off a garment on a cold day,
    and like vinegar on soda.
21 If your enemy is hungry, give him bread to eat,
    and if he is thirsty, give him water to drink,
22 for you will heap burning coals on his head,
    and the Lord will reward you.
23 The north wind brings forth rain,
    and a backbiting tongue, angry looks.
24 It is better to live in a corner of the housetop
    than in a house shared with a quarrelsome wife.
25 Like cold water to a thirsty soul,
    so is good news from a far country.

---

[1] Hebrew or else

²⁶ Like a muddied spring or a polluted fountain
   is a righteous man who gives way before the wicked.
²⁷ It is not good to eat much honey,
   nor is it glorious to seek one's own glory.[1]
²⁸ A man without self-control
   is like a city broken into and left without walls.

26

Like snow in summer or rain in harvest,
   so honor is not fitting for a fool.
² Like a sparrow in its flitting, like a swallow in its flying,
   a curse that is causeless does not alight.
³ A whip for the horse, a bridle for the donkey,
   and a rod for the back of fools.
⁴ Answer not a fool according to his folly,
   lest you be like him yourself.
⁵ Answer a fool according to his folly,
   lest he be wise in his own eyes.
⁶ Whoever sends a message by the hand of a fool
   cuts off his own feet and drinks violence.
⁷ Like a lame man's legs, which hang useless,
   is a proverb in the mouth of fools.
⁸ Like one who binds the stone in the sling
   is one who gives honor to a fool.
⁹ Like a thorn that goes up into the hand of a drunkard
   is a proverb in the mouth of fools.
¹⁰ Like an archer who wounds everyone
   is one who hires a passing fool or drunkard.[2]
¹¹ Like a dog that returns to his vomit
   is a fool who repeats his folly.
¹² Do you see a man who is wise in his own eyes?
   There is more hope for a fool than for him.
¹³ The sluggard says, "There is a lion in the road!
   There is a lion in the streets!"
¹⁴ As a door turns on its hinges,
   so does a sluggard on his bed.
¹⁵ The sluggard buries his hand in the dish;
   it wears him out to bring it back to his mouth.
¹⁶ The sluggard is wiser in his own eyes
   than seven men who can answer sensibly.
¹⁷ Whoever meddles in a quarrel not his own
   is like one who takes a passing dog by the ears.
¹⁸ Like a madman who throws firebrands, arrows, and death
¹⁹ is the man who deceives his neighbor
   and says, "I am only joking!"
²⁰ For lack of wood the fire goes out,
   and where there is no whisperer, quarreling ceases.
²¹ As charcoal to hot embers and wood to fire,

---

[1] The meaning of the Hebrew line is uncertain [2] Or *hires a fool or passersby*

so is a quarrelsome man for kindling strife.

22 The words of a whisperer are like delicious morsels;
      they go down into the inner parts of the body.
23 Like the glaze[1] covering an earthen vessel
      are fervent lips with an evil heart.
24 Whoever hates disguises himself with his lips
      and harbors deceit in his heart;
25 when he speaks graciously, believe him not,
      for there are seven abominations in his heart;
26 though his hatred be covered with deception,
      his wickedness will be exposed in the assembly.
27 Whoever digs a pit will fall into it,
      and a stone will come back on him who starts it rolling.
28 A lying tongue hates its victims,
      and a flattering mouth works ruin.

Snapshots of life [chapters 27–28]. The wise men have been compared to photographers. They are gifted observers of the human scene, and they have the ability to bring vast areas of human experience into focus, as with a camera click. We can read chapters 27–28 with an eye to the immense range of life that gets covered, as well as the wise man's skill in bringing it into focus. Often it is the poetic form of a proverb that achieves the effect: "Like a bird that strays from its nest / is a man who strays from his home" (27:8); "the righteous are bold as a lion" (28:1).

27

Do not boast about tomorrow,
      for you do not know what a day may bring.
2 Let another praise you, and not your own mouth;
      a stranger, and not your own lips.
3 A stone is heavy, and sand is weighty,
      but a fool's provocation is heavier than both.
4 Wrath is cruel, anger is overwhelming,
      but who can stand before jealousy?
5 Better is open rebuke
      than hidden love.
6 Faithful are the wounds of a friend;
      profuse are the kisses of an enemy.
7 One who is full loathes honey,
      but to one who is hungry everything bitter is sweet.
8 Like a bird that strays from its nest
      is a man who strays from his home.
9 Oil and perfume make the heart glad,
      and the sweetness of a friend comes from his earnest counsel.[2]
10 Do not forsake your friend and your father's friend,
      and do not go to your brother's house in the day of your calamity.
      Better is a neighbor who is near
      than a brother who is far away.

---

[1] By revocalization; Hebrew *silver of dross* [2] Or *and so does the sweetness of a friend that comes from his earnest counsel*

¹¹ Be wise, my son, and make my heart glad,
    that I may answer him who reproaches me.
¹² The prudent sees danger and hides himself,
    but the simple go on and suffer for it.
¹³ Take a man's garment when he has put up security for a stranger,
    and hold it in pledge when he puts up security for an adulteress.¹
¹⁴ Whoever blesses his neighbor with a loud voice,
    rising early in the morning,
    will be counted as cursing.
¹⁵ A continual dripping on a rainy day
    and a quarrelsome wife are alike;
¹⁶ to restrain her is to restrain the wind
    or to grasp² oil in one's right hand.
¹⁷ Iron sharpens iron,
    and one man sharpens another.³
¹⁸ Whoever tends a fig tree will eat its fruit,
    and he who guards his master will be honored.
¹⁹ As in water face reflects face,
    so the heart of man reflects the man.
²⁰ Sheol and Abaddon are never satisfied,
    and never satisfied are the eyes of man.
²¹ The crucible is for silver, and the furnace is for gold,
    and a man is tested by his praise.
²² Crush a fool in a mortar with a pestle
    along with crushed grain,
    yet his folly will not depart from him.

²³ Know well the condition of your flocks,
    and give attention to your herds,
²⁴ for riches do not last forever;
    and does a crown endure to all generations?
²⁵ When the grass is gone and the new growth appears
    and the vegetation of the mountains is gathered,
²⁶ the lambs will provide your clothing,
    and the goats the price of a field.
²⁷ There will be enough goats' milk for your food,
    for the food of your household
    and maintenance for your girls.

28

The wicked flee when no one pursues,
    but the righteous are bold as a lion.
² When a land transgresses, it has many rulers,
    but with a man of understanding and knowledge,
    its stability will long continue.
³ A poor man who oppresses the poor
    is a beating rain that leaves no food.
⁴ Those who forsake the law praise the wicked,

---

¹ Hebrew *a foreign woman*; a slight emendation yields (compare Vulgate; see also 20:16) *foreigners* ² Hebrew *to meet with* ³ Hebrew *sharpens the face of another*

but those who keep the law strive against them.
5 Evil men do not understand justice,
      but those who seek the Lord understand it completely.
6 Better is a poor man who walks in his integrity
      than a rich man who is crooked in his ways.
7 The one who keeps the law is a son with understanding,
      but a companion of gluttons shames his father.
8 Whoever multiplies his wealth by interest and profit[1]
      gathers it for him who is generous to the poor.
9 If one turns away his ear from hearing the law,
      even his prayer is an abomination.
10 Whoever misleads the upright into an evil way
      will fall into his own pit,
      but the blameless will have a goodly inheritance.
11 A rich man is wise in his own eyes,
      but a poor man who has understanding will find him out.
12 When the righteous triumph, there is great glory,
      but when the wicked rise, people hide themselves.
13 Whoever conceals his transgressions will not prosper,
      but he who confesses and forsakes them will obtain mercy.
14 Blessed is the one who fears the Lord always,
      but whoever hardens his heart will fall into calamity.
15 Like a roaring lion or a charging bear
      is a wicked ruler over a poor people.
16 A ruler who lacks understanding is a cruel oppressor,
      but he who hates unjust gain will prolong his days.
17 If one is burdened with the blood of another,
      he will be a fugitive until death;[2]
      let no one help him.
18 Whoever walks in integrity will be delivered,
      but he who is crooked in his ways will suddenly fall.
19 Whoever works his land will have plenty of bread,
      but he who follows worthless pursuits will have plenty of poverty.
20 A faithful man will abound with blessings,
      but whoever hastens to be rich will not go unpunished.
21 To show partiality is not good,
      but for a piece of bread a man will do wrong.
22 A stingy man[3] hastens after wealth
      and does not know that poverty will come upon him.
23 Whoever rebukes a man will afterward find more favor
      than he who flatters with his tongue.
24 Whoever robs his father or his mother
      and says, "That is no transgression,"
      is a companion to a man who destroys.
25 A greedy man stirs up strife,
      but the one who trusts in the Lord will be enriched.
26 Whoever trusts in his own mind is a fool,

---

[1] That is, profit that comes from charging interest to the poor [2] Hebrew *until the pit* [3] Hebrew *A man whose eye is evil*

but he who walks in wisdom will be delivered.
²⁷ Whoever gives to the poor will not want,
  but he who hides his eyes will get many a curse.
²⁸ When the wicked rise, people hide themselves,
  but when they perish, the righteous increase.

The book of Proverbs in microcosm [chapter 29]. The content and format of chapter 29 are similar to what we find in the preceding chapters, but as we near the end of the book as a whole, we can view this chapter as summing up what has happened in the book at the levels of form and content. The keynotes include the following: thought couplets as the basic unit; wide-ranging subject matter, all joined, however, by the fact that the author is differentiating between wisdom and folly for our benefit; the verse form of parallelism in its various types; vignettes of real life; the embodiment of a system of values, virtues, and vices.

29
He who is often reproved, yet stiffens his neck,
  will suddenly be broken beyond healing.
² When the righteous increase, the people rejoice,
  but when the wicked rule, the people groan.
³ He who loves wisdom makes his father glad,
  but a companion of prostitutes squanders his wealth.
⁴ By justice a king builds up the land,
  but he who exacts gifts¹ tears it down.
⁵ A man who flatters his neighbor
  spreads a net for his feet.
⁶ An evil man is ensnared in his transgression,
  but a righteous man sings and rejoices.
⁷ A righteous man knows the rights of the poor;
  a wicked man does not understand such knowledge.
⁸ Scoffers set a city aflame,
  but the wise turn away wrath.
⁹ If a wise man has an argument with a fool,
  the fool only rages and laughs, and there is no quiet.
¹⁰ Bloodthirsty men hate one who is blameless
  and seek the life of the upright.²
¹¹ A fool gives full vent to his spirit,
  but a wise man quietly holds it back.
¹² If a ruler listens to falsehood,
  all his officials will be wicked.
¹³ The poor man and the oppressor meet together;
  the LORD gives light to the eyes of both.
¹⁴ If a king faithfully judges the poor,
  his throne will be established forever.
¹⁵ The rod and reproof give wisdom,
  but a child left to himself brings shame to his mother.
¹⁶ When the wicked increase, transgression increases,
  but the righteous will look upon their downfall.

¹ Or who taxes heavily ² Or but the upright seek his soul

17   Discipline your son, and he will give you rest;
         he will give delight to your heart.
18   Where there is no prophetic vision the people cast off restraint,[1]
         but blessed is he who keeps the law.
19   By mere words a servant is not disciplined,
         for though he understands, he will not respond.
20   Do you see a man who is hasty in his words?
         There is more hope for a fool than for him.
21   Whoever pampers his servant from childhood
         will in the end find him his heir.[2]
22   A man of wrath stirs up strife,
         and one given to anger causes much transgression.
23   One's pride will bring him low,
         but he who is lowly in spirit will obtain honor.
24   The partner of a thief hates his own life;
         he hears the curse, but discloses nothing.
25   The fear of man lays a snare,
         but whoever trusts in the Lord is safe.
26   Many seek the face of a ruler,
         but it is from the Lord that a man gets justice.
27   An unjust man is an abomination to the righteous,
         but one whose way is straight is an abomination to the wicked.

Proverb clusters [30:1–31:9]. The wise man continues to survey all of life in this section, but a distinctive feature is the presence of proverb clusters and other special techniques, including the following: humility in realizing the limitation of human knowledge when compared to God's knowledge (30:1–6); two requests (30:7–9); proverbs on misuse of words (30:10–14); numerical proverbs (30:15–31); more bad behavior to avoid (30:32–33); proverbs that a king learned from his mother (31:1–9).

30

The words of Agur son of Jakeh. The oracle.[3]

The man declares, I am weary, O God;
         I am weary, O God, and worn out.[4]
2   Surely I am too stupid to be a man.
         I have not the understanding of a man.
3   I have not learned wisdom,
         nor have I knowledge of the Holy One.
4   Who has ascended to heaven and come down?
         Who has gathered the wind in his fists?
      Who has wrapped up the waters in a garment?
         Who has established all the ends of the earth?
      What is his name, and what is his son's name?
         Surely you know!

---

[1] Or *the people are discouraged* [2] The meaning of the Hebrew word rendered *his heir* is uncertain [3] Or *Jakeh, the man of Massa* [4] Revocalization; Hebrew *The man declares to Ithiel, to Ithiel and Ucal*

⁵ Every word of God proves true;
    he is a shield to those who take refuge in him.
⁶ Do not add to his words,
    lest he rebuke you and you be found a liar.

⁷ Two things I ask of you;
    deny them not to me before I die:
⁸ Remove far from me falsehood and lying;
    give me neither poverty nor riches;
    feed me with the food that is needful for me,
⁹ lest I be full and deny you
    and say, "Who is the LORD?"
or lest I be poor and steal
    and profane the name of my God.

¹⁰ Do not slander a servant to his master,
    lest he curse you, and you be held guilty.

¹¹ There are those¹ who curse their fathers
    and do not bless their mothers.
¹² There are those who are clean in their own eyes
    but are not washed of their filth.
¹³ There are those—how lofty are their eyes,
    how high their eyelids lift!
¹⁴ There are those whose teeth are swords,
    whose fangs are knives,
to devour the poor from off the earth,
    the needy from among mankind.

¹⁵ The leech has two daughters:
    Give and Give.²
Three things are never satisfied;
    four never say, "Enough":
¹⁶ Sheol, the barren womb,
    the land never satisfied with water,
    and the fire that never says, "Enough."

¹⁷ The eye that mocks a father
    and scorns to obey a mother
will be picked out by the ravens of the valley
    and eaten by the vultures.

¹⁸ Three things are too wonderful for me;
    four I do not understand:
¹⁹ the way of an eagle in the sky,
    the way of a serpent on a rock,
the way of a ship on the high seas,
    and the way of a man with a virgin.

---

¹ Hebrew *There is a generation;* also verses 12, 13, 14 ² Or *"Give, give,"* they cry

20 This is the way of an adulteress:
        she eats and wipes her mouth
        and says, "I have done no wrong."

21 Under three things the earth trembles;
        under four it cannot bear up:
22 a slave when he becomes king,
        and a fool when he is filled with food;
23 an unloved woman when she gets a husband,
        and a maidservant when she displaces her mistress.

24 Four things on earth are small,
        but they are exceedingly wise:
25 the ants are a people not strong,
        yet they provide their food in the summer;
26 the rock badgers are a people not mighty,
        yet they make their homes in the cliffs;
27 the locusts have no king,
        yet all of them march in rank;
28 the lizard you can take in your hands,
        yet it is in kings' palaces.

29 Three things are stately in their tread;
        four are stately in their stride:
30 the lion, which is mightiest among beasts
        and does not turn back before any;
31 the strutting rooster,[1] the he-goat,
        and a king whose army is with him.[2]

32 If you have been foolish, exalting yourself,
        or if you have been devising evil,
        put your hand on your mouth.
33 For pressing milk produces curds,
        pressing the nose produces blood,
        and pressing anger produces strife.

31

The words of King Lemuel. An oracle that his mother taught him:

2   What are you doing, my son?[3] What are you doing, son of my womb?
        What are you doing, son of my vows?
3   Do not give your strength to women,
        your ways to those who destroy kings.
4   It is not for kings, O Lemuel,
        it is not for kings to drink wine,
        or for rulers to take strong drink,
5   lest they drink and forget what has been decreed
        and pervert the rights of all the afflicted.
6   Give strong drink to the one who is perishing,
        and wine to those in bitter distress;[4]

---

[1] Or the magpie, or the greyhound; Hebrew girt-of-loins [2] Or against whom there is no rising up [3] Hebrew What, my son? [4] Hebrew those bitter in soul

⁷ let them drink and forget their poverty
and remember their misery no more.
⁸ Open your mouth for the mute,
for the rights of all who are destitute.¹
⁹ Open your mouth, judge righteously,
defend the rights of the poor and needy.

The portrait of the virtuous wife [31:10–31]. We end the book of Proverbs with the most impressive literary performance of all. The genre of the portrait of the virtuous wife is the *encomium—a poem praising a general character type (as here) or an abstract quality like love or faith. To heighten the effect, the author composed an *acrostic poem in which the successive verses begin with the consecutive letter of the Hebrew alphabet. The opening verse introduces the subject ("an excellent wife") and asserts its supreme value, thereby introducing the superiority motif (using the technique of comparison) that is standard in encomia. What follows is a catalog of the praiseworthy acts and qualities of the virtuous wife, arranged as an ever-widening context of activity: relation to husband (vv. 11–12); the domestic sphere, with emphasis of providing for the physical needs of the household (vv. 13–19); and the social and economic life of the community (vv. 20–26). Then, because the subject of the poem is a woman in her role of wife, the catalog ends by returning to the sphere of the family (vv. 27–29). But verse 30 raises the pitch even higher, moving from the domestic to the realm. The reward motif is important in encomia, and here it takes the form of a concluding wish that the virtuous wife receive what she deserves for her excellence (v. 31).

¹⁰² An excellent wife who can find?
She is far more precious than jewels.
¹¹ The heart of her husband trusts in her,
and he will have no lack of gain.
¹² She does him good, and not harm,
all the days of her life.
¹³ She seeks wool and flax,
and works with willing hands.
¹⁴ She is like the ships of the merchant;
she brings her food from afar.
¹⁵ She rises while it is yet night
and provides food for her household
and portions for her maidens.
¹⁶ She considers a field and buys it;
with the fruit of her hands she plants a vineyard.
¹⁷ She dresses herself³ with strength
and makes her arms strong.
¹⁸ She perceives that her merchandise is profitable.
Her lamp does not go out at night.
¹⁹ She puts her hands to the distaff,
and her hands hold the spindle.
²⁰ She opens her hand to the poor

¹ Hebrew *are sons of passing away* ² Verses 10-31 are an acrostic poem, each verse beginning with the successive letters of the Hebrew alphabet ³ Hebrew *She girds her loins*

and reaches out her hands to the needy.
21   She is not afraid of snow for her household,
       for all her household are clothed in scarlet.[1]
22   She makes bed coverings for herself;
       her clothing is fine linen and purple.
23   Her husband is known in the gates
       when he sits among the elders of the land.
24   She makes linen garments and sells them;
       she delivers sashes to the merchant.
25   Strength and dignity are her clothing,
       and she laughs at the time to come.
26   She opens her mouth with wisdom,
       and the teaching of kindness is on her tongue.
27   She looks well to the ways of her household
       and does not eat the bread of idleness.
28   Her children rise up and call her blessed;
       her husband also, and he praises her:
29   "Many women have done excellently,
       but you surpass them all."
30   Charm is deceitful, and beauty is vain,
       but a woman who fears the LORD is to be praised.
31   Give her of the fruit of her hands,
       and let her works praise her in the gates.

---

[1] Or *in double thickness*

ECCLESIASTES

> **The book at a glance.** 12 chapters, 222 verses. Herman Melville called it "the truest of all books," and his fellow American novelist Thomas Wolfe described it as "the highest flower of poetry, eloquence, and truth." Despite the attempts of biblical scholars and others to make the book seem problematical and inaccessible, it is an easy book to read and grasp. The viewpoint espoused by the author is a virtual summary of the biblical worldview: life lived by purely human and earthly standards is empty, while life with God at the center is fulfilling. The author tells us near the end of the book (12:9-10) exactly how he went about his task, and in the same passage provides his self-characterization: he is a teacher, a collector and careful arranger of proverbs, a stylist and wordsmith, and a person in quest of the truth. The book of Ecclesiastes has been aptly called the most contemporary or modern book in the Bible.

▌**Format.** Although Ecclesiastes is a collection of proverbs, it does not read like a typical collection of proverbs. This is because the proverbs are molded into clusters and furthermore because there is a unifying plot line that holds the units together. The units fall into the three categories of recollections, reflections, and mood pieces. All of these are expressed by a single narrator, who in effect tells the story of his quest to find satisfaction in life. This quest is reconstructed from the safe position of someone whose quest ended satisfactorily. The transitions between units often keep the quest in view: "so I turned to consider," "again I saw," "then I saw," etc. As we watch the quest unfold, we are continuously aware of the discrepancy between the narrator's present outlook and his futile search undertaken in the past. In effect, the speaker recalls the labyrinth of dead ends that he pursued, recreating his restless past with full vividness but not representing it as his mature outlook. Along with the narrative thread, the observational format of much of the material gives the book a meditative cast.

▌**The book's dialectical structure.** Ecclesiastes is organized as a prolonged contrast between two viewpoints. In terms of space, the major theme is the emptiness of life under the sun, that is, life lived by merely human and earthly values. The counterpart, which is intertwined and does not (contrary to a common misconception) surface only at the end, asserts an alternative to life at ground level. We might call it life above the sun—a God-centered view that opens the door to finding meaning in the earthly sphere. The book shuttles back and forth between negative and positive sections. The key to interpreting the parts of the book accurately is to note into which of the two contexts a passage falls. The writer himself gives us hints in this regard. The phrase "under the sun" or an equivalent appears conspicuously in the negative sections. The

Passage	Subject Matter	Dominant Mood	Literary Forms and Motifs
1:1–3	Introduction to author and theme	Negative	Superscription
1:4–2:23	Life under the sun: meaningless cycles; pursuit of knowledge, pleasure, wealth, work	Negative	Lyric meditation; brief narrative; quest motif
2:24–26	Life above the sun: the God-centered life	Positive	Declarations by the wise man
3:1–22	Two views of time	Positive	Lyric meditation; declarations by the wise man
4:1–5:17	Life under the sun: how life fails to satisfy	Negative	Catalog of observations; commands to the reader
5:18–20	Life above the sun: the God-centered life	Positive	Declarations by the wise man
6:1–9:6	Life under the sun: the disappointments and disillusionments of life	Negative	Observations and exhortations by the wise man
9:7–10	The enjoyment of life	Positive	Commands
9:11–10:20	Life under the sun: disillusionment and folly	Negative	Observations by the wise man
11:1–12:8	How to live well despite the limitations that are inevitable parts of life	Positive	Commands by the wise man
12:9–14	Wrap-up: concluding thoughts	Positive	Rituals of closure

positive sections, which are briefer than the negative ones (like a breath of fresh air), refer conspicuously to God. The negative passages tell us the truth just as thoroughly as the positive sections do: they tell us the truth about life without God.

▌ **Unifying image patterns and motifs.** The phrase "under the sun" or its equivalent occurs more than thirty times. The word translated "vanity" appears as the word for vapor or breath in the original Hebrew text; it appears thirty-one times and suggests the fleetingness and emptiness of life lived without God at the center. To keep us rooted in real life, the author repeatedly uses imagery of eating, drinking, toil, sleep, death, and the cycles of nature. The book of Ecclesiastes has a flavor all its own; we recognize it instantly when we read or hear a passage, and no other book is quite the same.

▌ **The rhetoric of the book.** The book of Ecclesiastes has a strong persuasive cast, as the author attempts to persuade us of the futility of life under the sun and the glory of life above the sun. However, the Hebrew way of conducting an argument is not to lay out a logical sequence of arguments. Instead, the author of Ecclesiastes keeps repeating his claims so often that we come to agree with him. His appeal is to observable human experience, and his persuasive purpose is gained by getting us to feel the truthfulness of his viewpoint.

▌Genres. The *proverb is the basic building block of the book. Although the book is not primarily structured like a story, the underlying *quest motif gives it a *narrative effect—an effect heightened by the continuous presence of a first-person narrator. Many of the negative, under-the-sun passages are voiced as a protest, so that the genre of protest literature comes into play. While all wisdom literature tends to make use of the resources of *poetry, including the verse form of *parallelism, the book of Ecclesiastes flaunts its poetic medium much more than ordinary wisdom literature does. The author is a master of *image, *metaphor, and *simile. (For more information on items accompanied by an asterisk, see the glossary at the back of this Bible.)

▌Tips for reading Ecclesiastes. Individual passages need to be read in light of the dialectical structure of the book as a whole. Assertions made in the "under the sun" passages do not represent the author's final viewpoint, whereas those that appear in the positive passages do. The book is partly observational and descriptive in format; we need to approach such passages in a meditative way, reflecting on our own experiences of the phenomena that the author describes. The book is also very affective, so we need to be receptive of the moods that it seeks to instill. Proverbs rely on real life as their best context, so we need to illustrate them from our own observations and experiences. Additionally, we will do justice to the book of Ecclesiastes only if we are receptive to the poetic medium in which it is couched.

▌Inferred literary intentions. The book is designed to achieve the following literary purposes:

- make the reader feel the emptiness of life lived by purely human and earthly values

- lead the reader to feel the exaltation of a God-centered life

- be truthful to human experience

- appeal to our emotions and imagination as well as our reason

- express truth in the form of poetry and proverb

- lead us to share the author's quest to find satisfaction in life

- unify the individual proverbs and clusters around a central conflict between negative and positive viewpoints, as well as around a unifying quest motif

- embody much of the meaning of the work in image patterns

▌Theological themes. (1) The nature of people: the book of Ecclesiastes presents authentic human experience and excels in showing essential human nature. (2) The good life: by means of its quest motif, the book shows by negative and positive example how to live well and the restlessness of the human soul until it rests in God. (3) The nature of God: God is implicitly shown to be creator, judge, and provider, as well as the all-sufficient goal of human longing. (4) The Fall: behind the restlessness of the speaker's futile quest to find meaning apart from God lies the story of Genesis 3 (see 7:29 for confirmation).

■ Ecclesiastes as a chapter in the master story of the Bible. The purpose of the Bible's master story is to lead the reader to faith in God and in Christ as the supreme sacrifice. Whatever the particular slant of a given book of the Bible, the overall purpose is the same. The book of Ecclesiastes has been called a Christ-shaped vacuum. Its contribution to the story line of the Bible is to record the longing of the human soul to find satisfaction and to point us toward the satisfaction of that longing in a Christ-centered experience of life. Jesus is the meaning of life, and if he is not at the center of our daily experience, we will find only futility and frustration.

Prologue [1:1–3]. The forthrightness of the author (identified as King Solomon) is one of his most attractive traits. He tells us at once who he is and the keynote of his book. The word translated as "vanity" appears thirty-one times in the book and in the original Hebrew is a concrete image—vapor or breath. We need to turn that metaphor like a prism in the light, teasing out how it relates to the overall effect of Ecclesiastes.

1

The words of the Preacher,[1] the son of David, king in Jerusalem.

² Vanity[2] of vanities, says the Preacher,
   vanity of vanities! All is vanity.
³ What does man gain by all the toil
   at which he toils under the sun?

Meditation on the futile cycles of life [1:4–11]. The author's first meditation on the emptiness of life under the sun is a mood piece in which he gives example after example of the cycles of nature (vv. 4–7) and the corresponding cycles in human experience (vv. 8–11). The common denominator in all of the cycles that are portrayed is that there is repetition but no progress. The first half of the poem is a tissue of contrasts—between the changing generations and the unchanging earth, the sun's rising and setting (east vs. west), the wind's blowing to the south and the north (opposites) but always returning, and streams running to the sea but returning to the place of origin. As a pivot between the two halves of the poem stands the statement of theme: "All things are full of weariness" (v. 8). Then the poet shifts the focus from nature to people, still with a view toward getting us to feel how futile our repeated actions in life are. He records a litany of failures—failure to find satisfaction in seeing and hearing (v. 8), failure to introduce genuine progress or change into human history (vv. 9–10), failure of memory, resulting in oblivion to the individual (v. 11). Verse 8 uses the formula "not satisfied," and one of the distinguishing features of Ecclesiastes is that the voice of unsatisfied desire runs strong.

---

⁴ A generation goes, and a generation comes,
   but the earth remains forever.
⁵ The sun rises, and the sun goes down,
   and hastens[3] to the place where it rises.
⁶ The wind blows to the south
   and goes around to the north;
   around and around goes the wind,

---

¹ Or *Convener*, or *Collector*; Hebrew *Qoheleth* (so throughout Ecclesiastes) ² Hebrew *vapor* (so throughout Ecclesiastes) ³ Or *and returns panting*

and on its circuits the wind returns.
7   All streams run to the sea,
         but the sea is not full;
      to the place where the streams flow,
         there they flow again.
8   All things are full of weariness;
         a man cannot utter it;
      the eye is not satisfied with seeing,
         nor the ear filled with hearing.
9   What has been is what will be,
         and what has been done is what will be done,
         and there is nothing new under the sun.
10   Is there a thing of which it is said,
         "See, this is new"?
      It has been already
         in the ages before us.
11   There is no remembrance of former things,[1]
         nor will there be any remembrance
      of later things[2] yet to be
         among those who come after.

> **The futile quest to find meaning in knowledge** [1:12–18]. This unit is a mininarra-
> tive—an abbreviated quest story in which the speaker pictures himself as the arche-
> typal quester who speaks of applying his heart (vv. 13, 17), seeking and searching (v.
> 13), seeing everything (v. 14), and acquiring great wisdom (v. 16). We should note the
> following things about the quest: (1) it was a humanistic quest that the speaker under-
> took by himself (vv. 13, 16, 17); (2) it was a comprehensive quest (vv. 13, 14, 16); (3)
> it was an unsuccessful quest (vv. 13, 14, 15, 17); (4) it was a self-centered quest. This
> passage records one of the dead ends that the speaker pursued in this quest to find
> meaning in life.

¹²I the Preacher have been king over Israel in Jerusalem. ¹³And I applied my heart[3] to seek and to search out by wisdom all that is done under heaven. It is an unhappy business that God has given to the children of man to be busy with. ¹⁴I have seen everything that is done under the sun, and behold, all is vanity and a striving after wind.[4]

15   What is crooked cannot be made straight,
         and what is lacking cannot be counted.

¹⁶I said in my heart, "I have acquired great wisdom, surpassing all who were over Jerusalem before me, and my heart has had great experience of wisdom and knowl-edge." ¹⁷And I applied my heart to know wisdom and to know madness and folly. I perceived that this also is but a striving after wind.

18   For in much wisdom is much vexation,
         and he who increases knowledge increases sorrow.

---

¹ Or *former people* ² Or *later people* ³ The Hebrew term denotes the center of one's inner life, including mind, will, and emotions ⁴ Or *a feeding on wind*; compare Hosea 12:1 (so throughout Ecclesiastes)

The futile quest to find meaning in pleasure [2:1–11]. The nature of the speaker's quest in the next mini-narrative is editorialized for us right at the outset: "I said in my heart, 'Come now, I will test you with pleasure; enjoy yourself'" (v. 1). In a book that has been called the most contemporary (that is, modern or even postmodern) book in the Bible, the speaker takes us on a guided tour of the mad urge to acquire that we see in our culture and our own lives. The passage gives us a catalog of acquisitions and attempted avenues of pleasure. Even as we observe a courtly version of the acquisitive lifestyle, it is easy for us to see real-life applications: a fancy house and yard (vv. 5–6); possessions (v. 7); money, entertainment, and sex (v. 8). The passage asserts the paradox of hedonism: the more one searches for pleasure, the less of it one finds. To clinch the point, verses 9–10 warn us that the speaker had a superlative amount of wealth with which to pursue the hedonistic life, so that if even he came up short (v. 11), we are no more likely to succeed in the same experiment in living. The speaker's quest did not fail because he lacked money but because pleasure in itself cannot satisfy.

2 I said in my heart, "Come now, I will test you with pleasure; enjoy yourself." But behold, this also was vanity. ²I said of laughter, "It is mad," and of pleasure, "What use is it?" ³I searched with my heart how to cheer my body with wine—my heart still guiding me with wisdom—and how to lay hold on folly, till I might see what was good for the children of man to do under heaven during the few days of their life. ⁴I made great works. I built houses and planted vineyards for myself. ⁵I made myself gardens and parks, and planted in them all kinds of fruit trees. ⁶I made myself pools from which to water the forest of growing trees. ⁷I bought male and female slaves, and had slaves who were born in my house. I had also great possessions of herds and flocks, more than any who had been before me in Jerusalem. ⁸I also gathered for myself silver and gold and the treasure of kings and provinces. I got singers, both men and women, and many concubines,¹ the delight of the children of man.

⁹So I became great and surpassed all who were before me in Jerusalem. Also my wisdom remained with me. ¹⁰And whatever my eyes desired I did not keep from them. I kept my heart from no pleasure, for my heart found pleasure in all my toil, and this was my reward for all my toil. ¹¹Then I considered all that my hands had done and the toil I had expended in doing it, and behold, all was vanity and a striving after wind, and there was nothing to be gained under the sun.

The futile quest to find meaning in permanent achievement [2:12–17]. We need to tease the meaning out of the next unit without help from the narrator. The passage is phrased as a protest, and upon analysis it turns out that the writer is protesting the inability of a person to achieve something that will survive him and become permanent. The narrator wanted to produce an enduring legacy but found that "there is no enduring remembrance" (v. 16). As elsewhere in the book, the image that sums up the futility of life under the sun is chasing after the wind (v. 17).

¹²So I turned to consider wisdom and madness and folly. For what can the man do who comes after the king? Only what has already been done. ¹³Then I saw that there is more gain in wisdom than in folly, as there is more gain in light than in darkness. ¹⁴The wise person has his eyes in his head, but the fool walks in darkness. And yet I perceived that the same event happens to all of them. ¹⁵Then I said in my heart,

¹ The meaning of the Hebrew word is uncertain

"What happens to the fool will happen to me also. Why then have I been so very wise?" And I said in my heart that this also is vanity. ¹⁶For of the wise as of the fool there is no enduring remembrance, seeing that in the days to come all will have been long forgotten. How the wise dies just like the fool! ¹⁷So I hated life, because what is done under the sun was grievous to me, for all is vanity and a striving after wind.

The futile quest to find meaning in work [2:18–23]. The writer has one more barrage of futility before he presents his first positive passage in the book. This time we look at the life of a workaholic who fails to find satisfaction in work. Word patterns count for a lot of the literary effect of Ecclesiastes, and this passage is a prime illustration: "toil" (vv. 18, 20, 21, 22), "toiled" (vv. 19, 21), "toils" (v. 22), "labors" (v. 20).

¹⁸I hated all my toil in which I toil under the sun, seeing that I must leave it to the man who will come after me, ¹⁹and who knows whether he will be wise or a fool? Yet he will be master of all for which I toiled and used my wisdom under the sun. This also is vanity. ²⁰So I turned about and gave my heart up to despair over all the toil of my labors under the sun, ²¹because sometimes a person who has toiled with wisdom and knowledge and skill must leave everything to be enjoyed by someone who did not toil for it. This also is vanity and a great evil. ²²What has a man from all the toil and striving of heart with which he toils beneath the sun? ²³For all his days are full of sorrow, and his work is a vexation. Even in the night his heart does not rest. This also is vanity.

The God-centered alternative [2:24–26]. The first positive passage is over as quickly as it starts, alerting us that the positive passages are shorter than the melancholy brooding of the negative passages. This brief passage flatly contradicts what the previous units have asserted. Up to now, the narrator has denied the possibility of finding satisfaction in life; now he suddenly asserts the very possibility that he has denied. We should note that the spheres in which he finds such satisfaction are the same as in the negative passages—eating, drinking, toiling, knowledge. This means that the book of Ecclesiastes is not escapist. It does not find satisfaction in some ethereal other world but instead brings the otherworldly perspective down into earthly pursuits. The reason the author can assert the possibility of enjoyment in the very areas where he had earlier denied it lies in the God-centered perspective of the passage: "from the hand of God" (v. 24); "apart from him who can . . . ?" (v. 25); "God has given" (v. 26). What spoiled work, pleasure, and wisdom in the earlier units was the attempt to get more out of them than they can offer in themselves; once God is placed at the center, things fall into place.

²⁴There is nothing better for a person than that he should eat and drink and find enjoyment¹ in his toil. This also, I saw, is from the hand of God, ²⁵for apart from him² who can eat or who can have enjoyment? ²⁶For to the one who pleases him God has given wisdom and knowledge and joy, but to the sinner he has given the business of gathering and collecting, only to give to one who pleases God. This also is vanity and a striving after wind.

---

¹ Or *and make his soul see good* ² Some Hebrew manuscripts, Septuagint, Syriac; most Hebrew manuscripts *apart from me*

The world's most famous poem on the subject of time [3:1–8]. The poem on time is a poetic tour de force. The subject is the problem of time, as the world has called it; the theme (interpretive slant) is announced at the outset, as the poem asserts that there is a time for everything. It is one of the most oratorical passages in the Bible, and the specific techniques include the following: strict parallelism within verses, so that the second line gives an example of an experience similar to that in the first line (being born and planting something in v. 2, for example); antithesis (pairing of opposites, such as weeping and laughing in v. 4); an identical grammatical structure to each line, consisting of (a) the formula "a time to," (b) naming a human action, (c) the contrasting formula "and a time to," and (d) naming a second human action that is antithetical to the first action; evocation of elemental, universal human experiences; concreteness (time ceases to be an abstraction as the examples accumulate). There is no overall progression in the passage, but generally the two lines of each verse deal with a similar experience, and the verses alternate between naming the positive experiences first (being born and planting in v. 2) and the negative experiences first (killing and breaking down in v. 3). The poem illustrates the haunting and cumulative effect of Hebrew poetry: by the time we finish the poem, we are emotionally convinced that there is, indeed, a time for everything. In terms of the rhythm of the book of Ecclesiastes, the poem is positive in mood: within the given that we cannot control the events of life, the poem (a) implies that life is as much good as bad, (b) embodies a spirit of calm resignation rather than protest in regard to the time-bound nature of human life, (c) affirms an order to human life, and (d) asserts the positive theme of timeliness (if we cannot control time, we can plug into its flow). Additionally, three later statements on the theme of "a time for everything" give the idea a strongly positive meaning (3:11, 17; 7:14).

3 For everything there is a season, and a time for every matter under heaven:

2   a time to be born, and a time to die;
a time to plant, and a time to pluck up what is planted;
3   a time to kill, and a time to heal;
a time to break down, and a time to build up;
4   a time to weep, and a time to laugh;
a time to mourn, and a time to dance;
5   a time to cast away stones, and a time to gather stones together;
a time to embrace, and a time to refrain from embracing;
6   a time to seek, and a time to lose;
a time to keep, and a time to cast away;
7   a time to tear, and a time to sew;
a time to keep silence, and a time to speak;
8   a time to love, and a time to hate;
a time for war, and a time for peace.

God's view of time [3:9–22]. This is a somewhat elusive passage, but it will fall into place if we view it as giving us further variations on the subject of time that was introduced earlier in the chapter. The poem on "a time for everything" views time from a human perspective; the rest of the chapter looks at time from a transcendent perspective. In sequence, here are the assertions that the passage makes: God is the one who gives time and life (vv. 9–10); all that happens is part of God's beautiful order (v. 11a); people have a capacity for transcendence—for something beyond time (v. 11b); we must accept time as God's gift to be enjoyed (vv. 12–13); God has placed people under the limitations of time so they will revere him (v. 14); God can salvage what from a human point of view are the losses of time (v. 15); time is the arena within which God tests people (vv. 16–17); God controls time (v. 18); because of the limited duration of time, people should make the most of it while they have it (vv. 20–22).

⁹What gain has the worker from his toil? ¹⁰I have seen the business that God has given to the children of man to be busy with. ¹¹He has made everything beautiful in its time. Also, he has put eternity into man's heart, yet so that he cannot find out what God has done from the beginning to the end. ¹²I perceived that there is nothing better for them than to be joyful and to do good as long as they live; ¹³also that everyone should eat and drink and take pleasure in all his toil—this is God's gift to man.

¹⁴I perceived that whatever God does endures forever; nothing can be added to it, nor anything taken from it. God has done it, so that people fear before him. ¹⁵That which is, already has been; that which is to be, already has been; and God seeks what has been driven away.¹

¹⁶Moreover, I saw under the sun that in the place of justice, even there was wickedness, and in the place of righteousness, even there was wickedness. ¹⁷I said in my heart, God will judge the righteous and the wicked, for there is a time for every matter and for every work. ¹⁸I said in my heart with regard to the children of man that God is testing them that they may see that they themselves are but beasts. ¹⁹For what happens to the children of man and what happens to the beasts is the same; as one dies, so dies the other. They all have the same breath, and man has no advantage over the beasts, for all is vanity. ²⁰All go to one place. All are from the dust, and to dust all return. ²¹Who knows whether the spirit of man goes upward and the spirit of the beast goes down into the earth? ²²So I saw that there is nothing better than that a man should rejoice in his work, for that is his lot. Who can bring him to see what will be after him?

A melancholy survey of life under the sun [chapter 4]. The quest motif is kept alive in our awareness by the narrative lead-ins: "again I saw" (v. 1); "then I saw" (v. 4); "again, I saw" (v. 7). The refrain "under the sun" appears four times (vv. 1, 3, 7, 15) to remind us that the observations that the speaker records in this chapter deal with life at ground level—life lived without God at the center. The dominant mood is unsatisfied desire, as signaled by the phrase "never satisfied" in verse 7. The spheres of life that are surveyed are as follows: the weak who are oppressed by the strong (vv. 1–3); social groupings based on attitudes toward work—the "keeping up with the Joneses" syndrome (v. 4), the dropout (v. 5), and the golden mean between extremes (v. 6); the compulsive moneymaker (vv. 7–8); and the transitoriness of fame and popularity (vv. 13–16). Although the dominant mood is negative, verses 9–12 offer a modified antidote in the form of human companionship and marriage.

4 Again I saw all the oppressions that are done under the sun. And behold, the tears of the oppressed, and they had no one to comfort them! On the side of their oppressors there was power, and there was no one to comfort them. ²And I

¹ Hebrew *what has been pursued*

thought the dead who are already dead more fortunate than the living who are still alive. ³But better than both is he who has not yet been and has not seen the evil deeds that are done under the sun.

⁴Then I saw that all toil and all skill in work come from a man's envy of his neighbor. This also is vanity and a striving after wind.

⁵The fool folds his hands and eats his own flesh.

⁶Better is a handful of quietness than two hands full of toil and a striving after wind.

⁷Again, I saw vanity under the sun: ⁸one person who has no other, either son or brother, yet there is no end to all his toil, and his eyes are never satisfied with riches, so that he never asks, "For whom am I toiling and depriving myself of pleasure?" This also is vanity and an unhappy business.

⁹Two are better than one, because they have a good reward for their toil. ¹⁰For if they fall, one will lift up his fellow. But woe to him who is alone when he falls and has not another to lift him up! ¹¹Again, if two lie together, they keep warm, but how can one keep warm alone? ¹²And though a man might prevail against one who is alone, two will withstand him—a threefold cord is not quickly broken.

¹³Better was a poor and wise youth than an old and foolish king who no longer knew how to take advice. ¹⁴For he went from prison to the throne, though in his own kingdom he had been born poor. ¹⁵I saw all the living who move about under the sun, along with that¹ youth who was to stand in the king's² place. ¹⁶There was no end of all the people, all of whom he led. Yet those who come later will not rejoice in him. Surely this also is vanity and a striving after wind.

> **Worship of God as an avenue toward satisfaction [5:1–7].** These seven verses demonstrate at once three traits that set the positive passages of Ecclesiastes off from the negative passages: it is brief; it elevates God to the center; it replaces the mode of melancholy survey with the rhetoric of commands (so that we are left with the impression that something can be made of life if we follow the correct path). The positive advice is to worship God properly (with a satiric undertone that criticizes inappropriate worship, including insincerity of vows and the multiplying of empty words in worship). Verse 2 is one of the key verses in Ecclesiastes, setting out a two-tiered view of life that is implied throughout: "God is in heaven and you are on earth."

5 ³ Guard your steps when you go to the house of God. To draw near to listen is better than to offer the sacrifice of fools, for they do not know that they are doing evil. ²⁴ Be not rash with your mouth, nor let your heart be hasty to utter a word before God, for God is in heaven and you are on earth. Therefore let your words be few. ³For a dream comes with much business, and a fool's voice with many words.

⁴When you vow a vow to God, do not delay paying it, for he has no pleasure in fools. Pay what you vow. ⁵It is better that you should not vow than that you should vow and not pay. ⁶Let not your mouth lead you⁵ into sin, and do not say before the messenger⁶ that it was a mistake. Why should God be angry at your voice and destroy the work of your hands? ⁷For when dreams increase and words grow many, there is vanity;⁷ but God is the one you must fear.

---

¹ Hebrew *the second* ² Hebrew *his* ³ Ch 4:17 in Hebrew ⁴ Ch 5:1 in Hebrew ⁵ Hebrew *your flesh* ⁶ Or *angel* ⁷ Or *For when dreams and vanities increase, words also grow many*

Satire against wealth [5:8–17]. These verses are a condensed miniessay on the evils and futility that attend a devotion to making money. The variations on that theme are as follows: the futility of greed among public officials (vv. 8–9); the inability of wealth to satisfy the deepest human longings and to do so permanently (v. 10); the relative uselessness of money (v. 11); the anxieties that attend wealth (v. 12); the self-destructiveness that money can bring into a person's life (v. 13); the fleeting nature of money and the danger of losing one's possessions (vv. 14–15); a memorable portrait of the workaholic (vv. 16–17).

⁸If you see in a province the oppression of the poor and the violation of justice and righteousness, do not be amazed at the matter, for the high official is watched by a higher, and there are yet higher ones over them. ⁹But this is gain for a land in every way: a king committed to cultivated fields.¹

¹⁰He who loves money will not be satisfied with money, nor he who loves wealth with his income; this also is vanity. ¹¹When goods increase, they increase who eat them, and what advantage has their owner but to see them with his eyes? ¹²Sweet is the sleep of a laborer, whether he eats little or much, but the full stomach of the rich will not let him sleep.

¹³There is a grievous evil that I have seen under the sun: riches were kept by their owner to his hurt, ¹⁴and those riches were lost in a bad venture. And he is father of a son, but he has nothing in his hand. ¹⁵As he came from his mother's womb he shall go again, naked as he came, and shall take nothing for his toil that he may carry away in his hand. ¹⁶This also is a grievous evil: just as he came, so shall he go, and what gain is there to him who toils for the wind? ¹⁷Moreover, all his days he eats in darkness in much vexation and sickness and anger.

The human quest satisfied [5:18–20]. This passage has all the hallmarks of the positive sections of Ecclesiastes: it aggressively brings God into the picture (every verse); it offers the possibility of enjoyment in place of the defeatism of the negative sections (vv. 18–19); it encourages contentment with one's daily lot instead of searching madly to find satisfaction elsewhere (vv. 18–19); it asserts that enjoyment and contentment can be found in the very spheres of eating, drinking, and work that in the negative passages are disparaged as not satisfying the human heart (vv. 18–19). To climax the passage, the writer gives us another of the key principles of this book: it speaks of the paradox of being diverted from life (which has just been described in totally positive terms) by God's joy in one's heart (v. 20).

¹⁸Behold, what I have seen to be good and fitting is to eat and drink and find enjoyment² in all the toil with which one toils under the sun the few days of his life that God has given him, for this is his lot. ¹⁹Everyone also to whom God has given wealth and possessions and power to enjoy them, and to accept his lot and rejoice in his toil—this is the gift of God. ²⁰For he will not much remember the days of his life because God keeps him occupied with joy in his heart.

More melancholy observations [chapter 6]. The author next unloads a series of observations on us that receive their keynote from the envelope structure of the passage, with the theme phrase "under the sun" appearing in the opening and closing

---

¹ The meaning of the Hebrew verse is uncertain ² Or *and see good*

verses. For the author, the supreme tragedy is not being able to enjoy life (vv. 2, 3, 6; note that these verses, which speak of not enjoying life, are the exact antithesis to the preceding unit, which had conspicuously raised the possibility of finding enjoyment). The voice of unsatisfied desire is again editorialized for us: "his appetite is not satisfied" (v. 7), buttressed by the evocative formula "the wandering of the appetite" (v. 9).

6 There is an evil that I have seen under the sun, and it lies heavy on mankind: ²a man to whom God gives wealth, possessions, and honor, so that he lacks nothing of all that he desires, yet God does not give him power to enjoy them, but a stranger enjoys them. This is vanity; it is a grievous evil. ³If a man fathers a hundred children and lives many years, so that the days of his years are many, but his soul is not satisfied with life's good things, and he also has no burial, I say that a stillborn child is better off than he. ⁴For it comes in vanity and goes in darkness, and in darkness its name is covered. ⁵Moreover, it has not seen the sun or known anything, yet it finds rest rather than he. ⁶Even though he should live a thousand years twice over, yet enjoy¹ no good—do not all go to the one place?

⁷All the toil of man is for his mouth, yet his appetite is not satisfied.² ⁸For what advantage has the wise man over the fool? And what does the poor man have who knows how to conduct himself before the living? ⁹Better is the sight of the eyes than the wandering of the appetite: this also is vanity and a striving after wind.

¹⁰Whatever has come to be has already been named, and it is known what man is, and that he is not able to dispute with one stronger than he. ¹¹The more words, the more vanity, and what is the advantage to man? ¹²For who knows what is good for man while he lives the few days of his vain life, which he passes like a shadow? For who can tell man what will be after him under the sun?

The wisdom of seeing life as mainly tragic [7:1–14]. This unit is not starkly negative, and in fact the case can be made that it has a positive undertow. The passage begins (vv. 1–8) with eight comparative proverbs asserting that a feature of life that we would ordinarily think to be negative is "better" than its counterpart. Verse 3 can perhaps be taken as a summary: "Sorrow is better than laughter." The author is protesting against any frivolous affirmation of life, and this opens the way toward seeing the passage as less negative than it would otherwise appear, since it leaves open the possibility of a more realistic affirmation of life. This positive tinge becomes even more evident in the follow-up passage (vv. 9–14), where the author tells us how to assimilate the truths that he has just uttered. Even though life is inherently tragic, we should not rage against that fact (v. 9) nor indulge in a fit of nostalgia (v. 10), but rather allow wisdom to protect us (vv. 11–12) with a balanced view of life (vv. 13–14).

7 A good name is better than precious ointment,
    and the day of death than the day of birth.
² It is better to go to the house of mourning
    than to go to the house of feasting,
for this is the end of all mankind,
    and the living will lay it to heart.
³ Sorrow is better than laughter,
    for by sadness of face the heart is made glad.

¹ Or see ² Hebrew filled

⁴ The heart of the wise is in the house of mourning,
      but the heart of fools is in the house of mirth.
⁵ It is better for a man to hear the rebuke of the wise
      than to hear the song of fools.
⁶ For as the crackling of thorns under a pot,
      so is the laughter of the fools;
      this also is vanity.
⁷ Surely oppression drives the wise into madness,
      and a bribe corrupts the heart.
⁸ Better is the end of a thing than its beginning,
      and the patient in spirit is better than the proud in spirit.
⁹ Be not quick in your spirit to become angry,
      for anger lodges in the bosom of fools.
¹⁰ Say not, "Why were the former days better than these?"
      For it is not from wisdom that you ask this.
¹¹ Wisdom is good with an inheritance,
      an advantage to those who see the sun.
¹² For the protection of wisdom is like the protection of money,
      and the advantage of knowledge is that wisdom preserves the life of him who
         has it.
¹³ Consider the work of God:
      who can make straight what he has made crooked?

¹⁴In the day of prosperity be joyful, and in the day of adversity consider: God has made the one as well as the other, so that man may not find out anything that will be after him.

Disillusionment with life under the sun [7:15–29]. The overall narrative cast of the book is kept alive as the writer reminds us of the underlying quest motif: "I have seen" (v. 15); "I have tested" (v. 23); "I turned . . . to search out and to seek" (v. 25); "has sought repeatedly" (v. 28); "I found . . . I have not found" (vv. 27–29). There is no unifying topical arrangement, just a series of observations covering many areas of life. The organization of Ecclesiastes requires us to keep on our toes continuously, and one evidence of this is the way in which even in this predominantly negative section the author drops a positive aside into the mix (vv. 18–19). At the end (vv. 26–29), though, we have a summary statement. On the surface, this is an antifeminist passage in which a famous lover in the ancient world refers to his seven hundred wives and three hundred concubines (v. 28). We might note in passing that in this verse men are declared to be only one-tenth of one percent better than women. In the antifeminist context of the passage, the claim that "God made man upright, but they have sought out many schemes" (v. 29) is a comment on the deviousness of women. But the passage is also an allusion to Genesis 1–3, asserting that God is not to blame for the miseries of human experience as we contemplate them in the book of Ecclesiastes. The implied logic of the statement is that as a human race we live "under the sun" because we have refused to live under God.

---

¹⁵In my vain life I have seen everything. There is a righteous man who perishes in his righteousness, and there is a wicked man who prolongs his life in his evildoing.

[16] Be not overly righteous, and do not make yourself too wise. Why should you destroy yourself? [17] Be not overly wicked, neither be a fool. Why should you die before your time? [18] It is good that you should take hold of this, and from that withhold not your hand, for the one who fears God shall come out from both of them.

[19] Wisdom gives strength to the wise man more than ten rulers who are in a city.

[20] Surely there is not a righteous man on earth who does good and never sins.

[21] Do not take to heart all the things that people say, lest you hear your servant cursing you. [22] Your heart knows that many times you yourself have cursed others.

[23] All this I have tested by wisdom. I said, "I will be wise," but it was far from me. [24] That which has been is far off, and deep, very deep; who can find it out?

[25] I turned my heart to know and to search out and to seek wisdom and the scheme of things, and to know the wickedness of folly and the foolishness that is madness. [26] And I find something more bitter than death: the woman whose heart is snares and nets, and whose hands are fetters. He who pleases God escapes her, but the sinner is taken by her. [27] Behold, this is what I found, says the Preacher, while adding one thing to another to find the scheme of things— [28] which my soul has sought repeatedly, but I have not found. One man among a thousand I found, but a woman among all these I have not found. [29] See, this alone I found, that God made man upright, but they have sought out many schemes.

Negative observations, chiefly about power structures [chapter 8]. Compared to the first half of the book, the trend in the second half of Ecclesiastes until the final chapter is in the direction of an increasingly miscellaneous collection of diffuse proverbs. With a little streamlining, though, chapter 8 is unified by the motif of observations about living with the authorities in one's life. The keynote is sounded at the end of verse 9, with its theme of the human power to hurt those who are subject to that power (in the mode of William Wordsworth's lament about "what man has made of man"). The variations on the theme include the following: living in subjection to the king (vv. 1–9); the seeming but illusory exemption of the powerful from judgment (vv. 10–13); how life is sometimes unfair, and how to live with that fact (vv. 14–15); a generalized comment on the inability of people to understand human history by their own wisdom (vv. 16–17).

8 Who is like the wise?
And who knows the interpretation of a thing?
A man's wisdom makes his face shine,
and the hardness of his face is changed.

[2] I say:[1] Keep the king's command, because of God's oath to him.[2] [3] Be not hasty to go from his presence. Do not take your stand in an evil cause, for he does whatever he pleases. [4] For the word of the king is supreme, and who may say to him, "What are you doing?" [5] Whoever keeps a command will know no evil thing, and the wise heart will know the proper time and the just way. [6] For there is a time and a way for everything, although man's trouble[3] lies heavy on him. [7] For he does not know what is to be, for who can tell him how it will be? [8] No man has power to retain the spirit, or power over the day of death. There is no discharge from war, nor will wickedness deliver those who are given to it. [9] All this I observed while applying my heart to all that is done under the sun, when man had power over man to his hurt.

[1] Hebrew lacks say [2] Or because of your oath to God [3] Or evil

¹⁰Then I saw the wicked buried. They used to go in and out of the holy place and were praised¹ in the city where they had done such things. This also is vanity. ¹¹Because the sentence against an evil deed is not executed speedily, the heart of the children of man is fully set to do evil. ¹²Though a sinner does evil a hundred times and prolongs his life, yet I know that it will be well with those who fear God, because they fear before him. ¹³But it will not be well with the wicked, neither will he prolong his days like a shadow, because he does not fear before God.

¹⁴There is a vanity that takes place on earth, that there are righteous people to whom it happens according to the deeds of the wicked, and there are wicked people to whom it happens according to the deeds of the righteous. I said that this also is vanity. ¹⁵And I commend joy, for man has no good thing under the sun but to eat and drink and be joyful, for this will go with him in his toil through the days of his life that God has given him under the sun.

¹⁶When I applied my heart to know wisdom, and to see the business that is done on earth, how neither day nor night do one's eyes see sleep, ¹⁷then I saw all the work of God, that man cannot find out the work that is done under the sun. However much man may toil in seeking, he will not find it out. Even though a wise man claims to know, he cannot find it out.

A protest against death [9:1–6]. One reason the book of Ecclesiastes seems familiar to the modern sensibility is that much of it is couched in the mode of protest literature, which is the dominant mode of modern literature. The first paragraph of chapter 9 is an implied protest against death, with emphasis on how death comes equally to the righteous and the evil and how it brings people to oblivion (vv. 5–6).

9 But all this I laid to heart, examining it all, how the righteous and the wise and their deeds are in the hand of God. Whether it is love or hate, man does not know; both are before him. ²It is the same for all, since the same event happens to the righteous and the wicked, to the good and the evil,² to the clean and the unclean, to him who sacrifices and him who does not sacrifice. As the good one is, so is the sinner, and he who swears is as he who shuns an oath. ³This is an evil in all that is done under the sun, that the same event happens to all. Also, the hearts of the children of man are full of evil, and madness is in their hearts while they live, and after that they go to the dead. ⁴But he who is joined with all the living has hope, for a living dog is better than a dead lion. ⁵For the living know that they will die, but the dead know nothing, and they have no more reward, for the memory of them is forgotten. ⁶Their love and their hate and their envy have already perished, and forever they have no more share in all that is done under the sun.

An affirmation of enlightened hedonism [9:7–10]. Just when we feel a sense of suffocation from the seemingly endless survey of life under the sun, the writer comes through with one of his patented positive passages. It is a rapid-fire sequence of commands to enjoy earthly life with zest. Verse 8 embodies this spirit in traditional images of joy (white garments and fragrant oil).

---

¹ Some Hebrew manuscripts, Septuagint, Vulgate; most Hebrew manuscripts *forgotten* ² Septuagint, Syriac, Vulgate; Hebrew lacks *and the evil*

⁷Go, eat your bread with joy, and drink your wine with a merry heart, for God has already approved what you do.

⁸Let your garments be always white. Let not oil be lacking on your head.

⁹Enjoy life with the wife whom you love, all the days of your vain life that he has given you under the sun, because that is your portion in life and in your toil at which you toil under the sun. ¹⁰Whatever your hand finds to do, do it with your might,¹ for there is no work or thought or knowledge or wisdom in Sheol, to which you are going.

Still more depressing observations [9:11–18]. The quest motif continues with the formulas "again I saw" (v. 11) and "I have also seen" (v. 13). Specific observations include the following: the lack of a cause-effect connection between superior talent and success in life (v. 11); people's susceptibility to sudden calamity (v. 12); the lack of reward for wise people (vv. 13–15). Yet the passage ends with a paradoxical affirmation of wisdom even when it is unrewarded in life (vv. 16–18).

¹¹Again I saw that under the sun the race is not to the swift, nor the battle to the strong, nor bread to the wise, nor riches to the intelligent, nor favor to those with knowledge, but time and chance happen to them all. ¹²For man does not know his time. Like fish that are taken in an evil net, and like birds that are caught in a snare, so the children of man are snared at an evil time, when it suddenly falls upon them.

¹³I have also seen this example of wisdom under the sun, and it seemed great to me. ¹⁴There was a little city with few men in it, and a great king came against it and besieged it, building great siegeworks against it. ¹⁵But there was found in it a poor, wise man, and he by his wisdom delivered the city. Yet no one remembered that poor man. ¹⁶But I say that wisdom is better than might, though the poor man's wisdom is despised and his words are not heard.

¹⁷The words of the wise heard in quiet are better than the shouting of a ruler among fools. ¹⁸Wisdom is better than weapons of war, but one sinner destroys much good.

A collection of proverbs [chapter 10]. The book of Ecclesiastes becomes increasingly miscellaneous until the very end. Chapter 10 is a collection of individual proverbs. The main motif is yet another survey of observations about life under the sun. The general import of the proverbs is hinted in verse 10: "wisdom helps one to succeed." Some specific topics include the following: brief snapshots of folly (vv. 1–3); observations about power structures and rulers (vv. 4–7); satiric snapshots of people who do not use their head or take adequate precautions, accompanied by latent humor (vv. 8–11); the importance of words (vv. 12–15); political observations (vv. 16–17); laziness made vivid (v. 18); a cynical observation about living high on the hog (v. 19); not criticizing one's superior (v. 20).

10 Dead flies make the perfumer's ointment give off a stench;
so a little folly outweighs wisdom and honor.
² A wise man's heart inclines him to the right,
but a fool's heart to the left.
³ Even when the fool walks on the road, he lacks sense,
and he says to everyone that he is a fool.

---

¹ Or *finds to do with your might, do it*

⁴   If the anger of the ruler rises against you, do not leave your place,
       for calmness[1] will lay great offenses to rest.

⁵There is an evil that I have seen under the sun, as it were an error proceeding from the ruler: ⁶folly is set in many high places, and the rich sit in a low place. ⁷I have seen slaves on horses, and princes walking on the ground like slaves.

⁸   He who digs a pit will fall into it,
       and a serpent will bite him who breaks through a wall.
⁹   He who quarries stones is hurt by them,
       and he who splits logs is endangered by them.
¹⁰ If the iron is blunt, and one does not sharpen the edge,
       he must use more strength,
       but wisdom helps one to succeed.[2]
¹¹ If the serpent bites before it is charmed,
       there is no advantage to the charmer.

¹² The words of a wise man's mouth win him favor,[3]
       but the lips of a fool consume him.
¹³ The beginning of the words of his mouth is foolishness,
       and the end of his talk is evil madness.
¹⁴ A fool multiplies words,
       though no man knows what is to be,
       and who can tell him what will be after him?
¹⁵ The toil of a fool wearies him,
       for he does not know the way to the city.

¹⁶ Woe to you, O land, when your king is a child,
       and your princes feast in the morning!
¹⁷ Happy are you, O land, when your king is the son of the nobility,
       and your princes feast at the proper time,
       for strength, and not for drunkenness!
¹⁸ Through sloth the roof sinks in,
       and through indolence the house leaks.
¹⁹ Bread is made for laughter,
       and wine gladdens life,
       and money answers everything.
²⁰ Even in your thoughts, do not curse the king,
       nor in your bedroom curse the rich,
     for a bird of the air will carry your voice,
       or some winged creature tell the matter.

Living zestfully in a less-than-perfect world [11:1–8]. In this passage we proceed by a pattern of pairs of verses. In each case, the wise man does two things: he acknowledges the limitations that inevitably influence the outcome of human action, and he urges us to grab the opportunities of life despite this potentially negative context. Specifically, the wise man tells us to (a) be generous and/or diversify our investments abroad and at home (vv. 1–2); (b) not allow the fact that we cannot predict what

---

[1] Hebrew *healing* [2] Or *wisdom is an advantage for success* [3] Or *are gracious*

will succeed to inhibit us from enthusiastically throwing ourselves into our ventures (vv. 3–4, 5–6); (c) enjoy the commonplaces of life when we can, because we do not know how long we will be able to do so (vv. 7–8).

11

Cast your bread upon the waters,
   for you will find it after many days.
2 Give a portion to seven, or even to eight,
      for you know not what disaster may happen on earth.
3 If the clouds are full of rain,
      they empty themselves on the earth,
   and if a tree falls to the south or to the north,
      in the place where the tree falls, there it will lie.
4 He who observes the wind will not sow,
      and he who regards the clouds will not reap.

5As you do not know the way the spirit comes to the bones in the womb[1] of a woman with child, so you do not know the work of God who makes everything.

6In the morning sow your seed, and at evening withhold not your hand, for you do not know which will prosper, this or that, or whether both alike will be good.

7Light is sweet, and it is pleasant for the eyes to see the sun.

8So if a person lives many years, let him rejoice in them all; but let him remember that the days of darkness will be many. All that comes is vanity.

Summing up [11:9–12:8]. The customary way for a writer to structure a narrative work is to move toward a climactic moment of *epiphany (revelation or heightened insight) near the end. We have a version of that technique in this unit late in Ecclesiastes. The gist of the advice is to live life joyfully (11:9–10; implied in 12:1), and we might note that the rhetorical situation is that of a mature wise man addressing young people (11:9; 12:1). We should live life to the full in a double awareness—of God as Creator (12:1) and as Judge (11:9), as beginning and end, alpha and omega. To give urgency to this advice to live life zestfully, the writer paints a haunting portrait of the physiological decays that accompany old age, and the passage actually runs away with the section (12:2–5). The mode is highly metaphorical, as various physical symptoms of old age are described figuratively (lost teeth referred to as grinders that have ceased, for example). The only way to do justice to the passage is to figure out what parts of the body and their functions are being described. The catalog ends with a conceptual summary: "desire fails" (v. 5). Then, after the poet has detailed the trials of old age, we get a picture of the actual cessation of earthly life (vv. 6–8). To render the passage even richer, the author overlays the individual metaphors with general image patterns: storm imagery (v. 2); a disintegrating house (vv. 3–4); a catalog of failed human functions (vv. 4–5); broken household objects (v. 6); separation of body and soul (v. 7).

9Rejoice, O young man, in your youth, and let your heart cheer you in the days of your youth. Walk in the ways of your heart and the sight of your eyes. But know that for all these things God will bring you into judgment.

10Remove vexation from your heart, and put away pain[2] from your body, for youth and the dawn of life are vanity.

---

[1] Some Hebrew manuscripts, Targum; most Hebrew manuscripts *As you do not know the way of the wind, or how the bones grow in the womb* [2] Or *evil*

12 Remember also your Creator in the days of your youth, before the evil days come and the years draw near of which you will say, "I have no pleasure in them"; [2] before the sun and the light and the moon and the stars are darkened and the clouds return after the rain, [3] in the day when the keepers of the house tremble, and the strong men are bent, and the grinders cease because they are few, and those who look through the windows are dimmed, [4] and the doors on the street are shut—when the sound of the grinding is low, and one rises up at the sound of a bird, and all the daughters of song are brought low— [5] they are afraid also of what is high, and terrors are in the way; the almond tree blossoms, the grasshopper drags itself along,[1] and desire fails, because man is going to his eternal home, and the mourners go about the streets— [6] before the silver cord is snapped, or the golden bowl is broken, or the pitcher is shattered at the fountain, or the wheel broken at the cistern, [7] and the dust returns to the earth as it was, and the spirit returns to God who gave it. [8] Vanity of vanities, says the Preacher; all is vanity.

> **Enactment of some literary rituals of conclusion** [12:9–14]. At the end, the speaker steps out of his role as narrator of a personal quest and stands back and looks at the work of literature that he has created. In effect, he conducts a fireside chat with his readers, taking us into his confidence (the ancient equivalent of the modern genre of the interview with the author). In the most complete statement of authorial intention in the entire Bible, the author engages in a bit of self-characterization and statement of purpose (vv. 9–10). Then he comments on the value of the kind of literature he has composed, namely, the collection of proverbs (v. 11). He also asserts the adequacy of what he has composed on his chosen subject and cries on his reader's shoulders about the trials of the writing life (v. 12). Then, with the quest motif fully in our awareness, the writer asserts the goal of the quest that he has shared, with the image of "the end of the matter" (v. 13a) serving as the punch line. The writer ends by summing up the goal of his quest (vv. 13b–14), leaving the reader with a clear sense of choice between good and evil as the final note. This is the end toward which the book of Ecclesiastes has tended from the very beginning.

[9] Besides being wise, the Preacher also taught the people knowledge, weighing and studying and arranging many proverbs with great care. [10] The Preacher sought to find words of delight, and uprightly he wrote words of truth.

[11] The words of the wise are like goads, and like nails firmly fixed are the collected sayings; they are given by one Shepherd. [12] My son, beware of anything beyond these. Of making many books there is no end, and much study is a weariness of the flesh.

[13] The end of the matter; all has been heard. Fear God and keep his commandments, for this is the whole duty of man.[2] [14] For God will bring every deed into judgment, with[3] every secret thing, whether good or evil.

---

[1] Or is a burden [2] Or the duty of all mankind [3] Or into the judgment on

THE SONG OF SOLOMON

The book at a glance. 8 chapters, 117 verses. The Song of Solomon is a small anthology of love lyrics. For people who relish poetry in general and love poetry specifically, this is a high point in the Bible. For many readers, however, the book is something of an embarrassment because it is so unrestrained about romantic passion and physical attractiveness. That is a great pity, because God is the one who gave the gift of poetry to the human race, and romantic love is one of the most universal and deeply felt human emotions. To relish reading the Song of Solomon, we need to get rid of our inhibitions about extravagant expressions of romantic passion. Further, we need to forget about prose literalism and take flight on the wings of the fantastic and poetic imagination. The writer of the Song of Solomon is a poet who pulls out all the stops. The genius of intense poetry like this is that the poet is our representative, saying what we want said, too, only saying it much better than we can.

Poetic Fragments: Falling in Love (1:1–8)
Love Poems (Courtship Overtones) (1:9–2:7)
Wedding Poems (2:8–5:1)
Love Poems (Marriage Overtones) (5:2–7:13)
Poetic Fragments: Falling in Love (8:1–14)

■ **Structure of the book.** The chart shows at a glance that the Song of Solomon is structured on the principle of what literary critics call ring composition. In such an arrangement, as we progress through the poem from beginning to end, in the second half of the book we encounter the same topics through which we traveled in the first half, but now in the reverse order. It is like making our way through a series of concentric rings. A modern poet would not end a collection of love poems with the same experience of falling in love that was present at the beginning, but ancient authors were fond of this rhetorical pattern, which biblical scholars call chiasm (crossing). Counteracting the formality of ring composition is the presence of a technique that we usually assume modern authors invented—*stream of conscious-ness, in which the organization follows the random flow of a person's thought instead of a logical progression. In the Song of Solomon, we observe a kaleidoscopic jumping from one image or thought to another. Additionally, even though the individual units are self-contained, we can see that they are united by a quest motif: the two lovers are in a quest to find satisfaction in love.

▌Genres. The complexity of this brief collection of *poems and *lyric fragments emerges when we start to name the *genres that converge in it. The largest label we can give the book is *love poetry. Furthermore, it is *pastoral love poetry in which the lovers are shepherd and shepherdess, and the setting is an ideally flowery and fruitful rural landscape. If a love poem or collection of love poems celebrates the occasion of a specific wedding, it is called an *epithalamion, and that is what we have here. (For more information on items accompanied by an asterisk, see the glossary at the back of this Bible.)

▌Love poetry. Love poetry exists to portray the feelings and experiences of romantic passion. It tends toward the highly figurative and is at the opposite end of the spectrum from literal realism. Here are things that love poets from time immemorial have done: they portray the emotions of romantic love in heightened form; they situate idealized love in an idealized rural or natural setting; they compare either the beloved or the romance to the best things in nature (the beloved is like a garden, for example, and the delights of a couple's being together are like eating fruit in the shade of a tree); they portray typical moments in a courtship or romance (a kiss, a walk, a parting, a wedding). Common subgenres in love poetry include the following: dialogue (in which the lovers express their feelings to each other); *emblematic blazon (praising the beloved by cataloging the physical features of the beloved and comparing them to objects in nature); *invitation to love (which in pastoral poetry takes the form of inviting the beloved to go on a walk in nature); *lyric outpouring of romantic feelings. Love poets have also often pictured events in a romance as a dream or vision rather than a direct narrative.

▌Pastoral poetry. Pastoral poetry is so called because the surface details come from the shepherd's life. The characters are shepherds and shepherdesses. The action consists partly of the activities customarily done by shepherds. The setting is an idealized world of natural beauty. The imagery comes from nature. Pastoral literature evokes an idealized good life and good place, and often the shepherds and shepherd-esses are a thin disguise for real people (in the Song of Solomon, these are Solomon and a Shulammite woman). As an extension of that fictional situation, most pastoral poetry through the centuries has been written by city or court poets, so that the actual court residence of the "shepherd" and "shepherdess" often shows through the rural facade.

▌The comparisons in the Song of Solomon. The Song of Solomon is most remem-bered for its extravagant comparisons—the woman compared to a horse in Pharaoh's court, for example, and her hair to a flock of goats. The conventions within which the ancient poet wrote yield these ground rules for interpreting the comparisons: (1) the primary correspondence is not visual—indeed most of the time there is no visual correspondence at all; (2) the comparisons are figurative rather than literal; (3) what the beloved and the creature or thing to which he or she is compared have in common is a certain quality—usually the quality of excellence, or of being the best of its kind; (4) additionally, the carryover is the value of the two things that are compared (the woman is like a mare among Pharaoh's chariots in being the best that it is possible to be).

❚ **The poet as observer.** Poets are by the very nature of their craft careful observers of life. In the case of Song of Solomon, we will benefit from listing the things that this particular poet observed closely, because it brings to awareness things that might be overlooked. The poet who composed Song of Solomon was a close observer of people in love; nature; the conventions of love poetry; women and feminine beauty; birds; body parts; the rituals of romance; wedding protocol; the heightened moods that accompany being in love; sexual behavior.

❚ **Inferred literary intentions.** The book is designed to achieve the following literary purposes:

- express the feelings of romantic love in the most heightened form possible

- enable us to experience the poet as our representative, expressing our romantic feelings and experiences more aptly and eloquently than we can

- give a truthful rendition of the experiences of romantic love

- dazzle us with the poet's expertise in an impressive range of poetic genres

- lift our imagination far above the mundane level of literal reality

- awaken us to the ideas and attitudes that make up the biblical ethic of wedded romantic love

- leave us convinced that God approves of physical, sexual love

❚ **Theological themes.** (1) The ethics of romantic love and marriage: this book gives us a picture of how God intends people to live as sexual and romantic creatures. (2) Creation: nature is so continuously present in the this anthology of love poems that we can deduce a doctrine of nature from the book. (3) The divine-human relationship: the Bible regularly uses imagery of sex and marriage to portray the relationship between God and his people, and thus this extended portrayal of love and marriage in its idealized form gives us a norm by which to understand the Bible's metaphoric picture of God's relationship to his people.

❚ **The Song of Solomon as a chapter in the master story of the Bible.** The Bible is partly the human race's testimony to its own experience. In the Song of Solomon, the poet records the human race's experience of romantic passion. In the Bible, the story of what people do and feel is always intertwined with the story of how God wants people to live, not simply how they do live. The Song of Solomon tells the story of how God wants men and women in love to relate to each other. It also sets a pattern for love that finds its highest expression in the soul's love for God, and God's love for his people in Jesus Christ.

> **Introduction to the book** [1:1–8]. The opening eight verses introduce us to the following things: (1) the two lead characters in the romance; (2) the setting; (3) the action or underlying plot (the quest for satisfaction in love); (4) the style, which can be characterized as passionate, sensuous (sensory, having to do with the senses), metaphoric,

hyperbolic, and pastoral. Only by a conscious effort can we disentangle these threads (and it is important that we do so); the poet mingles them together in an organization that can only be called stream-of-consciousness.

1 The Song of Songs, which is Solomon's.

SHE[1]

2 Let him kiss me with the kisses of his mouth!
   For your love is better than wine;
3   your anointing oils are fragrant;
   your name is oil poured out;
       therefore virgins love you.
4 Draw me after you; let us run.
   The king has brought me into his chambers.

OTHERS

We will exult and rejoice in you;
   we will extol your love more than wine;
   rightly do they love you.

SHE

5 I am very dark, but lovely,
   O daughters of Jerusalem,
like the tents of Kedar,
   like the curtains of Solomon.
6 Do not gaze at me because I am dark,
   because the sun has looked upon me.
My mother's sons were angry with me;
   they made me keeper of the vineyards,
   but my own vineyard I have not kept!
7 Tell me, you whom my soul loves,
   where you pasture your flock,
   where you make it lie down at noon;
for why should I be like one who veils herself
   beside the flocks of your companions?

HE

8 If you do not know,
   O most beautiful among women,
follow in the tracks of the flock,
   and pasture your young goats
   beside the shepherds' tents.

The lovers' dialogue [1:9–2:7]. This lyric passage, too, is structured as a fluid flow of thought and images. We even shift without transition from one speaker to another. For this reason, as readers we need to be constantly alert to the kaleidoscopic sequence that unfolds before us. The main subject of the lyric fragments that we overhear is the value and delight that the lovers find in each other and their romantic relationship. The style is highly metaphoric, and this places on us the obligation of interpreting how A is

---
[1] The translators have added speaker identifications based on the gender and number of the Hebrew words

like B—how the beloved's eyes are like doves and how the beloved is like a rose or an apple tree, for example.

HE

⁹ I compare you, my love,
    to a mare among Pharaoh's chariots.
¹⁰ Your cheeks are lovely with ornaments,
    your neck with strings of jewels.

OTHERS

¹¹ We will make for you¹ ornaments of gold,
    studded with silver.

SHE

¹² While the king was on his couch,
    my nard gave forth its fragrance.
¹³ My beloved is to me a sachet of myrrh
    that lies between my breasts.
¹⁴ My beloved is to me a cluster of henna blossoms
    in the vineyards of Engedi.

HE

¹⁵ Behold, you are beautiful, my love;
    behold, you are beautiful;
    your eyes are doves.

SHE

¹⁶ Behold, you are beautiful, my beloved, truly delightful.
Our couch is green;
¹⁷   the beams of our house are cedar;
    our rafters are pine.

2 I am a rose² of Sharon,
    a lily of the valleys.

HE

² As a lily among brambles,
    so is my love among the young women.

SHE

³ As an apple tree among the trees of the forest,
    so is my beloved among the young men.
With great delight I sat in his shadow,
    and his fruit was sweet to my taste.
⁴ He brought me to the banqueting house,³
    and his banner over me was love.
⁵ Sustain me with raisins;
    refresh me with apples,
    for I am sick with love.
⁶ His left hand is under my head,
    and his right hand embraces me!

¹ The Hebrew for *you* is feminine singular ² Probably a bulb, such as a crocus, asphodel, or narcissus ³ Hebrew *the house of wine*

⁷   I adjure you,¹ O daughters of Jerusalem,
         by the gazelles or the does of the field,
     that you not stir up or awaken love
             until it pleases.

Anticipated arrival of the groom for the wedding [2:8–17]. The middle of the Song of Solomon gives us a highly metaphoric and hyperbolic reenactment of familiar wedding rituals. In this unit, the woman fantasizes about what the groom's arrival for the wedding will be like. The invitation to love that the groom is portrayed as uttering (vv. 10–13) is a conventional pastoral genre; in effect, the invitation to go for a walk in the spring landscape is a metaphoric invitation to marriage. Coming through all of the poetic flights are the emotions that all lovers feel as their wedding approaches.

SHE

⁸   The voice of my beloved!
         Behold, he comes,
     leaping over the mountains,
         bounding over the hills.
⁹   My beloved is like a gazelle
         or a young stag.
     Behold, there he stands
         behind our wall,
     gazing through the windows,
         looking through the lattice.
¹⁰   My beloved speaks and says to me:
     "Arise, my love, my beautiful one,
         and come away,
¹¹   for behold, the winter is past;
         the rain is over and gone.
¹²   The flowers appear on the earth,
         the time of singing² has come,
     and the voice of the turtledove
         is heard in our land.
¹³   The fig tree ripens its figs,
         and the vines are in blossom;
         they give forth fragrance.
     Arise, my love, my beautiful one,
         and come away.
¹⁴   O my dove, in the clefts of the rock,
         in the crannies of the cliff,
     let me see your face,
         let me hear your voice,
     for your voice is sweet,
         and your face is lovely.
¹⁵   Catch the foxes³ for us,
         the little foxes

---

¹ That is, I put you on oath; so throughout the Song ² Or *pruning* ³ Or *jackals*

that spoil the vineyards,
 for our vineyards are in blossom."

16 My beloved is mine, and I am his;
 he grazes[1] among the lilies.
17 Until the day breathes
 and the shadows flee,
turn, my beloved, be like a gazelle
 or a young stag on cleft mountains.[2]

The groom's arrival [chapter 3]. We get two versions of the groom's actual arrival. The first version is the woman's dream or fantasy of the event (vv. 1–5), in which the narrative motif is seeking and finding. Bringing her beloved into her parental home (v. 4) is what it will mean to be married. The woman's dream version of Solomon's arrival is followed by a description of the king's actual arrival in full processional splendor (vv. 6–11).

SHE

3 On my bed by night
 I sought him whom my soul loves;
 I sought him, but found him not.
2 I will rise now and go about the city,
 in the streets and in the squares;
I will seek him whom my soul loves.
 I sought him, but found him not.
3 The watchmen found me
 as they went about in the city.
"Have you seen him whom my soul loves?"
4 Scarcely had I passed them
 when I found him whom my soul loves.
I held him, and would not let him go
 until I had brought him into my mother's house,
 and into the chamber of her who conceived me.
5 I adjure you, O daughters of Jerusalem,
 by the gazelles or the does of the field,
that you not stir up or awaken love
 until it pleases.

6 What is that coming up from the wilderness
 like columns of smoke,
perfumed with myrrh and frankincense,
 with all the fragrant powders of a merchant?
7 Behold, it is the litter[3] of Solomon!
Around it are sixty mighty men,
 some of the mighty men of Israel,
8 all of them wearing swords
 and expert in war,
each with his sword at his thigh,

---

[1] Or *he pastures his flock* [2] Or *mountains of Bether* [3] That is, the couch on which servants carry a king

against terror by night.
⁹ King Solomon made himself a carriage¹
    from the wood of Lebanon.
¹⁰ He made its posts of silver,
    its back of gold, its seat of purple;
  its interior was inlaid with love
    by the daughters of Jerusalem.
¹¹ Go out, O daughters of Zion,
    and look upon King Solomon,
  with the crown with which his mother crowned him
    on the day of his wedding,
    on the day of the gladness of his heart.

The perfection of feminine beauty [4:1–8]. This is the first of four *emblematic blazons in the Song of Solomon—three of them praising the bride and one the groom. A blazon is a love poem that praises the beloved by listing his or her desirable physical features and/or virtues. An emblematic blazon conducts the praise by comparing the beloved's physical features to objects or "emblems" in nature. In this particular blazon, the poet begins and ends with conceptual summaries (vv. 1, 7), and between these bookends he conducts the catalog of excellencies by moving downward from the woman's eyes to her breasts. The comparisons are not primarily visual (and usually not visual at all). The things that the woman's physical features have in common with the things to which they are compared are as follows: (1) the emotional satisfaction that both convey; (2) the superlative value of both (a tower of David is a tower par excellence, for example); (3) certain qualities that both have in common. An example of the latter is the comparison of the woman's teeth to lambs in verse 2: on the strength of the comparison, we can experience the qualities of whiteness, wetness, symmetry, and completeness.

HE

4 Behold, you are beautiful, my love,
    behold, you are beautiful!
  Your eyes are doves
    behind your veil.
  Your hair is like a flock of goats
    leaping down the slopes of Gilead.
² Your teeth are like a flock of shorn ewes
    that have come up from the washing,
  all of which bear twins,
    and not one among them has lost its young.
³ Your lips are like a scarlet thread,
    and your mouth is lovely.
  Your cheeks are like halves of a pomegranate
    behind your veil.
⁴ Your neck is like the tower of David,
    built in rows of stone;²
  on it hang a thousand shields,
    all of them shields of warriors.

---

¹ Or *sedan chair* ² The meaning of the Hebrew word is uncertain

5   Your two breasts are like two fawns,
         twins of a gazelle,
         that graze among the lilies.
6   Until the day breathes
         and the shadows flee,
     I will go away to the mountain of myrrh
         and the hill of frankincense.
7   You are altogether beautiful, my love;
         there is no flaw in you.
8   Come with me from Lebanon, my bride;
         come with me from Lebanon.
     Depart[1] from the peak of Amana,
         from the peak of Senir and Hermon,
     from the dens of lions,
         from the mountains of leopards.

Consummation of the love [4:9–5:1]. Starting with the poems that deal with the arrival of the groom for the wedding, the poems in the middle of the Song of Solomon make the collection an *epithalamion (literally "upon the wedding chamber"), or wedding poem. The wedding lyrics in the Song of Solomon culminate in a poem that uses the reticence of symbolism to picture the physical consummation of the love. Except for 4:16, in which the bride expresses a wish that she be desirable to her husband, and 5:1b, which is a choral comment by attenders at the wedding addressed to the couple, the passage represents the groom as addressing his bride. The rhetorical mode is decorous and indirect, as the woman is compared to a garden. The lushness of sensory imagery is a symbol of the intoxication of sexual passion. The final effect of the passage is to leave us assured that in claiming sexual love as their possession, the couple is claiming something of great value.

                 HE

9   You have captivated my heart, my sister, my bride;
         you have captivated my heart with one glance of your eyes,
         with one jewel of your necklace.
10   How beautiful is your love, my sister, my bride!
         How much better is your love than wine,
         and the fragrance of your oils than any spice!
11   Your lips drip nectar, my bride;
         honey and milk are under your tongue;
         the fragrance of your garments is like the fragrance of Lebanon.
12   A garden locked is my sister, my bride,
         a spring locked, a fountain sealed.
13   Your shoots are an orchard of pomegranates
         with all choicest fruits,
         henna with nard,
14   nard and saffron, calamus and cinnamon,
         with all trees of frankincense,
     myrrh and aloes,

---

[1] Or Look

with all choice spices—
¹⁵ a garden fountain, a well of living water,
and flowing streams from Lebanon.

¹⁶ Awake, O north wind,
and come, O south wind!
Blow upon my garden,
let its spices flow.

SHE

Let my beloved come to his garden,
and eat its choicest fruits.

HE

5 I came to my garden, my sister, my bride,
I gathered my myrrh with my spice,
I ate my honeycomb with my honey,
I drank my wine with my milk.

OTHERS

Eat, friends, drink,
and be drunk with love!

A song of separation [5:2–9]. The wedding poems are the center of the concentric
rings around which the collection of poems is constructed. The wedding poems were preceded by the songs of two people in love (1:9–2:7). The implied context was courtship.
Here, on the other side of the wedding poems, we have more songs of two people in love,
with marriage as the implied context. The frustration of the experience of temporary
separation of the newlyweds is expressed as a fantasy or dream in which the woman
pictures herself as traveling about the city in quest for her beloved and not finding him.

SHE

² I slept, but my heart was awake.
A sound! My beloved is knocking.
"Open to me, my sister, my love,
my dove, my perfect one,
for my head is wet with dew,
my locks with the drops of the night."
³ I had put off my garment;
how could I put it on?
I had bathed my feet;
how could I soil them?
⁴ My beloved put his hand to the latch,
and my heart was thrilled within me.
⁵ I arose to open to my beloved,
and my hands dripped with myrrh,
my fingers with liquid myrrh,
on the handles of the bolt.

6   I opened to my beloved,
    but my beloved had turned and gone.
  My soul failed me when he spoke.
  I sought him, but found him not;
    I called him, but he gave no answer.
7   The watchmen found me
    as they went about in the city;
  they beat me, they bruised me,
    they took away my veil,
    those watchmen of the walls.
8   I adjure you, O daughters of Jerusalem,
    if you find my beloved,
  that you tell him
    I am sick with love.

OTHERS

9   What is your beloved more than another beloved,
    O most beautiful among women?
  What is your beloved more than another beloved,
    that you thus adjure us?

Masculine attractiveness perfected [5:10–6:3]. This passage is an emblematic blazon in praise of the male *hero of the Song of Solomon. All of the rules noted above apply to our interpretation of this poem in praise of the woman's beloved. The blazon is followed by a brief bit of imagined dialogue in which the question of the onlookers of the romance (6:1) allows the bride to assert yet again her satisfaction in love (6:2–3).

SHE

10   My beloved is radiant and ruddy,
    distinguished among ten thousand.
11   His head is the finest gold;
    his locks are wavy,
    black as a raven.
12   His eyes are like doves
    beside streams of water,
  bathed in milk,
    sitting beside a full pool.[1]
13   His cheeks are like beds of spices,
    mounds of sweet-smelling herbs.
  His lips are lilies,
    dripping liquid myrrh.
14   His arms are rods of gold,
    set with jewels.
  His body is polished ivory,[2]
    bedecked with sapphires.[3]
15   His legs are alabaster columns,
    set on bases of gold.

[1] The meaning of the Hebrew is uncertain [2] The meaning of the Hebrew word is uncertain [3] Hebrew *lapis lazuli*

His appearance is like Lebanon,
 choice as the cedars.
16 His mouth[1] is most sweet,
 and he is altogether desirable.
This is my beloved and this is my friend,
 O daughters of Jerusalem.

OTHERS

6 Where has your beloved gone,
 O most beautiful among women?
Where has your beloved turned,
 that we may seek him with you?

SHE

2 My beloved has gone down to his garden
 to the beds of spices,
to graze[2] in the gardens
 and to gather lilies.
3 I am my beloved's and my beloved is mine;
 he grazes among the lilies.

Emblematic blazon in praise of the woman [6:4–12]. Now it is the woman's turn to be praised in another emblematic blazon. A mysterious narrative fragment (vv. 11–12) follows the blazon; it may be the woman's fantasy of what it is like to be with her beloved.

HE

4 You are beautiful as Tirzah, my love,
 lovely as Jerusalem,
 awesome as an army with banners.
5 Turn away your eyes from me,
 for they overwhelm me—
Your hair is like a flock of goats
 leaping down the slopes of Gilead.
6 Your teeth are like a flock of ewes
 that have come up from the washing;
all of them bear twins;
 not one among them has lost its young.
7 Your cheeks are like halves of a pomegranate
 behind your veil.
8 There are sixty queens and eighty concubines,
 and virgins without number.
9 My dove, my perfect one, is the only one,
 the only one of her mother,
 pure to her who bore her.
The young women saw her and called her blessed;
 the queens and concubines also, and they praised her.

---

[1] Hebrew *palate* [2] Or *to pasture his flock*; also verse 3

¹⁰ "Who is this who looks down like the dawn,
   beautiful as the moon, bright as the sun,
   awesome as an army with banners?"

SHE

¹¹ I went down to the nut orchard
   to look at the blossoms of the valley,
to see whether the vines had budded,
   whether the pomegranates were in bloom.
¹² Before I was aware, my desire set me
   among the chariots of my kinsman, a prince.¹

Feminine beauty affirmed again [6:13–7:9]. This is the fourth emblematic blazon in the collection. Although the modest woman feels as self-conscious as a lover performing a ritual dance in front of onlookers (6:13), probably the entire poem of praise should be understood as spoken by the husband. This time the catalog of excellencies moves up from the feet to the hair.

OTHERS

^{13 2} Return, return, O Shulammite,
   return, return, that we may look upon you.

HE

Why should you look upon the Shulammite,
   as upon a dance before two armies?³

7 How beautiful are your feet in sandals,
   O noble daughter!
Your rounded thighs are like jewels,
   the work of a master hand.
² Your navel is a rounded bowl
   that never lacks mixed wine.
Your belly is a heap of wheat,
   encircled with lilies.
³ Your two breasts are like two fawns,
   twins of a gazelle.
⁴ Your neck is like an ivory tower.
Your eyes are pools in Heshbon,
   by the gate of Bath-rabbim.
Your nose is like a tower of Lebanon,
   which looks toward Damascus.
⁵ Your head crowns you like Carmel,
   and your flowing locks are like purple;
   a king is held captive in the tresses.

⁶ How beautiful and pleasant you are,
   O loved one, with all your delights!⁴
⁷ Your stature is like a palm tree,
   and your breasts are like its clusters.

¹ Or chariots of Ammi-Nadib ² Ch 7:1 in Hebrew ³ Or dance of Mahanaim ⁴ Or among delights

⁸   I say I will climb the palm tree
       and lay hold of its fruit.
    Oh may your breasts be like clusters of the vine,
       and the scent of your breath like apples,
⁹   and your mouth¹ like the best wine.

SHE

    It goes down smoothly for my beloved,
       gliding over lips and teeth.²

> **Pastoral invitation to love** [7:10–13]. Earlier (2:10–15) the eager bride-to-be had
> pictured her fiancé as inviting her to go on a walk in nature. Now the bride utters her
> pastoral invitation to love. Our sentiment for nature is aroused and then transferred to
> romantic sentiment. More generally, pastoral love poetry is based on the premise of hav-
> ing an idealized natural setting (an ideally flowery and fruitful landscape) as the appro-
> priate setting for an idealized romance.

SHE

¹⁰ I am my beloved's,
       and his desire is for me.

¹¹ Come, my beloved,
          let us go out into the fields
          and lodge in the villages;³
¹² let us go out early to the vineyards
          and see whether the vines have budded,
       whether the grape blossoms have opened
          and the pomegranates are in bloom.
       There I will give you my love.
¹³ The mandrakes give forth fragrance,
          and beside our doors are all choice fruits,
       new as well as old,
          which I have laid up for you, O my beloved.

> **Falling in love, part 2** [8:1–5]. We end the Song of Solomon where we began it—with
> the couple falling in love all over again. This is part of the ring composition of the book.
> There are some curious and mysterious details in chapter 8, ending the collection on
> a somewhat anticlimactic mood after the titanic passions that have preceded. In this
> unit, we traverse the following sentiments: the woman's desire to be able to express
> her affection in public without raising anyone's eyebrows (v. 1) and her desire to have
> her beloved accepted in her parental home (v. 2); the woman's exclamation of passion
> in wishing that her beloved would embrace her right now (v. 3); the refrain (which also
> appears in 2:7 and 5:8) that appears in contexts of the woman's nearly uncontrollable
> passion and that is a self-rebuke in which the woman acknowledges her need to let love
> run its course (v. 4); a flashback that recalls the scene of falling in love (v. 5).

¹ Hebrew *palate* ² Septuagint, Syriac, Vulgate; Hebrew *causing the lips of sleepers to speak* ³ Or *among the henna plants*

8 Oh that you were like a brother to me
     who nursed at my mother's breasts!
If I found you outside, I would kiss you,
     and none would despise me.
2 I would lead you and bring you
     into the house of my mother—
     she who used to teach me.
I would give you spiced wine to drink,
     the juice of my pomegranate.
3 His left hand is under my head,
     and his right hand embraces me!
4 I adjure you, O daughters of Jerusalem,
     that you not stir up or awaken love
     until it pleases.

5 Who is that coming up from the wilderness,
     leaning on her beloved?

Under the apple tree I awakened you.
There your mother was in labor with you;
     there she who bore you was in labor.

The moment of epiphany to which the whole book moves [8:6–7]. The most customary way to structure a major work of literature is to move it toward some climactic *moment of epiphany late in the book. These two verses serve that function in the Song of Solomon. They express the woman's request for permanence in love (v. 6), followed by descriptions of the all-conquering power of love. This is the kind of love that the collection as a whole has celebrated. The image of the seal in verse 6 rests on the ancient practice of carrying a seal (used to generate an official signature that had the effect of claiming possession of something) either on a chain around one's neck or on one's finger ("arm"). The import is double, as the woman wants her beloved to claim her as his possession and to be always near her (the proximity motif). The remaining metaphors assert the ability of love to conquer anything that challenges it and end with a comment on its supreme value.

SHE

6 Set me as a seal upon your heart,
     as a seal upon your arm,
for love is strong as death,
     jealousy[1] is fierce as the grave.[2]
Its flashes are flashes of fire,
     the very flame of the LORD.
7 Many waters cannot quench love,
     neither can floods drown it.
If a man offered for love
     all the wealth of his house,
     he[3] would be utterly despised.

---

[1] Or ardor [2] Hebrew as Sheol [3] Or it

Concluding sentiments [8:8–14]. We end the Song of Solomon in a subdued mood. Keeping in mind that the sentiments are those that accompany the experience of falling in love, we begin with the following sequence: the woman's brothers deliberate the fate of their sister (v. 8), deciding that if she is chaste they will honor her but that if she is morally loose, they will protect her (v. 9); the woman asserts her chastity and ability to attract her own husband without her brothers' help (v. 10). Verses 11–12 play with the garden imagery that has been prominent in the collection, as the woman contrasts Solomon's royal multiplicity of vineyards (v. 11) to the way in which her beloved is her only and sufficient vineyard (v. 12). Finally, Solomon asks to hear the voice of his beloved (who is evocatively called the one who dwells "in the gardens" [v. 13]), and the woman responds with a plea that her beloved not be gone long (echoing earlier imagery of gazelle and young stag [v. 14]).

OTHERS

8 We have a little sister,
   and she has no breasts.
What shall we do for our sister
   on the day when she is spoken for?
9 If she is a wall,
   we will build on her a battlement of silver,
but if she is a door,
   we will enclose her with boards of cedar.

SHE

10 I was a wall,
    and my breasts were like towers;
then I was in his eyes
    as one who finds[1] peace.

11 Solomon had a vineyard at Baal-hamon;
    he let out the vineyard to keepers;
    each one was to bring for its fruit a thousand pieces of silver.
12 My vineyard, my very own, is before me;
    you, O Solomon, may have the thousand,
    and the keepers of the fruit two hundred.

HE

13 O you who dwell in the gardens,
    with companions listening for your voice;
    let me hear it.

SHE

14 Make haste, my beloved,
    and be like a gazelle
or a young stag
    on the mountains of spices.

[1] Or brings out

ISAIAH

The book at a glance. 66 chapters, 1,292 verses. The most obvious feature of the book of Isaiah is its massiveness. Its sheer length generates an immense scope of genres and themes. For these reasons, the book of Isaiah has been labeled "a Bible within the Bible" and "a miniature Bible." It has also been called "the centerpiece of the story of Israel" and "the Romans of the Old Testament," because it sets forth God's case against sinners and outlines a way of salvation for them. If in addition to these descriptions of the content of the book we add the claim that Isaiah was "the most sublime of all poets," we have a good portal by which to enter the prophetic book of Isaiah. Although the original audience was Judah before it was carried off to Babylon, the book's message is timeless and applies to all people who sin and need a Savior. It is useful to know from the beginning of our reading of this book that the personality and life story of the prophet do not emerge with the fullness with which the stories of Jeremiah and Daniel allow us to know those two prophets.

▌**Prophecy as the dominant genre.** The overall *genre of the book is *prophecy, which is a very comprehensive form. Although biblical prophets primarily *tell forth* God's message in their contemporary situation and only occasionally *foretell* the future, the last third of Isaiah is an exception in being mainly predictive of the future. The opening movement, though, is more of a warning against sin than a blueprint for the future. As Isaiah looks at his world, he does three things: he depicts its evil, denounces that evil, and predicts God's imminent judgment against that evil. All three of these ingredients are typically couched in the form of the *oracle of judgment—a divine indictment of present evil. Additionally, biblical prophets intermingle, and end their books with, visions of God's restored favor to his people; these visions are couched in the form of the *oracle of redemption (also called oracle of salvation) and *oracle of blessing.

▌**Other genres.** The oracles of judgment need to be approached as examples of *satire: they have an object of attack, a vehicle in which the attack is embodied, a stated or implied norm by which the criticism is conducted, and a prevailing tone of either ridicule or disgust. Because much of the book of Isaiah envisions things that either have not yet happened or do not literally happen in the symbolic form in which they are portrayed, the genre of *visionary writing is continuously operative in the book of Isaiah (the author *envisions* something that does not literally exist or that has not yet happened). A preponderance of the book is cast in the form of *poetry, with the result that we need to apply all that we know about such staples of poetry as *imagery, *metaphor, *simile, *apostrophe, and *hyperbole. Many of the visions of redemption in

Chapters	Content	Prophetic Genre	Dominant Mood	Main Time Frame
1–12	Prophecies to Judah	Oracle of judgment; oracle of salvation		
13–24	Prophecies to the nations	Oracle of judgment		The present; the immediate and intermediate future
25–27	Prophecies of deliverance	Oracle of judgment	Warning	
28–35	Prophecies of both judgment and salvation	Oracle of judgment; oracle of salvation		
36–39	The story of King Hezekiah	Narrative	Admiration of a heroic example	Contemporary with the prophet
40–66	Prophecies mainly of salvation	Oracle of salvation	Consolation and hope	Intermediate and eschatological future

the last third of Isaiah are *lyric in form and effect. *Apocalyptic writing appears prominently in chapters 40–66. Because the agents who interact with God are often nations rather than individuals, and because the forces of nature are also sometimes actors, the label *cosmic drama* is a helpful concept. Finally, in this book that encompasses such a diversity of material, we even have a full-fledged hero story involving King Hezekiah and the prophet Isaiah (chapters 36–39). (For more information on items accompanied by an asterisk, see the glossary at the back of this Bible.)

▌Format. A book this large and lacking a narrative line must be viewed as an anthology or collection of individual compositions. Literary scholars also speak of a book like this as being encyclopedic in scope and structure. It is futile to look for a smooth flow from one unit to the next. The book swings back and forth between oracles of judgment and oracles of salvation. The general movement of the book of Isaiah is from an emphasis on evil and judgment to rapturous visions of a coming redemption—a movement from bad news to good news. But this is only a general pattern that should not lead us to distort the smaller swings, which persist to the very last verses of the book, between evil/judgment and redemption/restoration. A further important thing to know about the arrangement of the material is that the treatment of time in biblical prophecy is very complex. The time frame often telescopes the timeless, the present, the intermediate future, and eschatological (end times) future. For example, a vision of a coming golden age might be (a) a highly metaphoric picture of God's favor, either on a specific OT occasion like the restoration after the exile or generally, at any time in history; and/or (b) a symbolic messianic prophecy that would be fulfilled in Christ's incarnation and sacrifice; and/or (c) a symbolic picture of the final, eschatological salvation of God's people.

▌Tips for reading and interpreting Isaiah. We should not look for a continuous narrative flow; the book is an anthology of separate, predominantly brief units. In the first thirty-nine chapters, much of the material is highly topical, meaning that Isaiah describes specific events and nations of his own time; the best way to deal with this topicality is to go for what is timeless and universal embodied within the time-bound. If we do not look *through* the historical particulars to our own world, we are left with a museum of dated prophecies about long-gone nations. Because time is telescoped in Isaiah's predictions of the future, we need to trust our own intuitions in regard to whether a given prophecy is predicting something in the immediate future (e.g., the fall of a nation mentioned by Isaiah), the intermediate future (a messianic prophecy fulfilled when Christ became incarnate), or the eschatological future (the end of history). Finally, Isaiah is both a poet and a visionary prophet; he regularly makes use of *poetic license and resorts to *fantasy as his medium. This does not mean that what he portrays does not deal with real persons and events; it only means that these real persons and events are not portrayed literally. For example, if we put the following prediction into its context, it is a prophecy of the impending destruction of Babylon: "I will make the heavens tremble, / and the earth will be shaken out of its place" (13:13). Babylon was, in fact, destroyed, but it did not literally happen as Isaiah's prophetic vision portrayed it.

▌Inferred literary intentions. The book is designed to achieve the following literary purposes:

- present a grand panorama of God's acts of judgment and salvation as they affect nations and individuals

- paint a detailed picture of what God approves and disapproves

- give a general outline of what God intended to do from the time of Isaiah to the end of history

- move readers to reject sin and flee to God for salvation

- use the resources of visionary writing and poetry to present reality in a manner that is often nonliteral

- embody truth chiefly in the prophetic genres of oracles of judgment, oracles of salvation/redemption, and oracles of blessing

- satirize evil

- embody truth in poetic form

- appeal to a reader's imagination as a vehicle for truth

- awaken longing for a coming Savior

▌Theological themes. (1) The nature of God: the book of Isaiah is a one-volume book of theology, with emphasis on God's sovereignty, judgment against evil, and mercy. (2) Sin: the book of Isaiah is also a one-volume anatomy of the sins of the human race. (3) Judgment: the book of Isaiah explores why and how God plans to judge people and nations for their evil. (4) Salvation: the book of Isaiah gives numerous assertions and metaphoric pictures of how God saves people, and as part of that it includes key passages on the atoning sacrifice of Christ. (5) Eschatology: Isaiah is a major repository of pictures of what the end of history will be like, and eternity ever after.

▌ **Isaiah as a chapter in the master story of the Bible.** The whole master story of the Bible gets told in capsule form in Isaiah. If we piece together the individual visions into a composite story, it is a story of (a) the fall of the human race into sin, (b) its perpetuation of that sin through its corrupt actions and rebellion against God, (c) God's judgment of human evil but also provision of a way of escape from that judgment through a Savior, and (d) God's plan to bring human history to an end with a final destruction of evil and the glorification of believers in a new heaven and a new earth.

Initiation into the world of the book of Isaiah [chapter 1]. The opening chapter is our initiation into the content and form of the book as a whole. The first thing we notice is that the material is fluid and mixed. The right rubric by which to negotiate this organization is what in modern literature is called stream of consciousness, meaning that the material unfolds according to the thought processes of human psychology rather than topically and logically. Tidy outlines would likely confuse us once we start our journey through the material. In chapter 1, we move without transition from the opening prologue (v. 1) to an *apostrophe to the heavens and earth (vv. 2–3), to multiple apostrophes to the nation of Israel, denounced for its evil (vv. 4–15), and thence to appeals to Israel to reform (vv. 16–19), then back to a satiric exposure of the sinfulness of Israel, personified as a city (vv. 20–25), then, without transition, to an oracle of salvation (vv. 26–27), and finally back to a vision of judgment (vv. 28–31). The only safe rule for reading is to trust what we see as we gaze at the text and accept stream of consciousness as the organizing pattern. Chapter 1 epitomizes not only the content and organization of the book as a whole but also many of its stylistic techniques, including the following: a highly poetic idiom, replete with poetic license; apostrophe as a staple ("Ah, sinful nation"; "Hear the word of the LORD, you rulers of Sodom"); symbolism (e.g., sin as red, the city as a harlot, God's judgment as a garden without water); nations and cities as characters; satire. We should also note the fluid movement back and forth between present-tense descriptions and future-tense predictions, and even occasionally the common prophetic practice of narrating events that will yet occur as though they have already happened (e.g., vv. 7–9).

1 The vision of Isaiah the son of Amoz, which he saw concerning Judah and Jerusalem in the days of Uzziah, Jotham, Ahaz, and Hezekiah, kings of Judah.

2   Hear, O heavens, and give ear, O earth;
        for the LORD has spoken:
    "Children[1] have I reared and brought up,
        but they have rebelled against me.
3   The ox knows its owner,
        and the donkey its master's crib,
    but Israel does not know,
        my people do not understand."

4   Ah, sinful nation,
        a people laden with iniquity,
    offspring of evildoers,
        children who deal corruptly!
    They have forsaken the LORD,

---

[1] Or Sons; also verse 4

they have despised the Holy One of Israel,
they are utterly estranged.

5   Why will you still be struck down?
        Why will you continue to rebel?
    The whole head is sick,
        and the whole heart faint.
6   From the sole of the foot even to the head,
        there is no soundness in it,
    but bruises and sores
        and raw wounds;
    they are not pressed out or bound up
        or softened with oil.

7   Your country lies desolate;
        your cities are burned with fire;
    in your very presence
        foreigners devour your land;
        it is desolate, as overthrown by foreigners.
8   And the daughter of Zion is left
        like a booth in a vineyard,
    like a lodge in a cucumber field,
        like a besieged city.

9   If the LORD of hosts
        had not left us a few survivors,
    we should have been like Sodom,
        and become like Gomorrah.

10 Hear the word of the LORD,
        you rulers of Sodom!
    Give ear to the teaching[1] of our God,
        you people of Gomorrah!
11 "What to me is the multitude of your sacrifices?
        says the LORD;
    I have had enough of burnt offerings of rams
        and the fat of well-fed beasts;
    I do not delight in the blood of bulls,
        or of lambs, or of goats.

12 "When you come to appear before me,
        who has required of you
        this trampling of my courts?
13 Bring no more vain offerings;
        incense is an abomination to me.
    New moon and Sabbath and the calling of convocations—
        I cannot endure iniquity and solemn assembly.
14 Your new moons and your appointed feasts
        my soul hates;

1 Or law

they have become a burden to me;
    I am weary of bearing them.
¹⁵ When you spread out your hands,
    I will hide my eyes from you;
even though you make many prayers,
    I will not listen;
    your hands are full of blood.
¹⁶ Wash yourselves; make yourselves clean;
    remove the evil of your deeds from before my eyes;
cease to do evil,
¹⁷   learn to do good;
seek justice,
    correct oppression;
bring justice to the fatherless,
    plead the widow's cause.

¹⁸ "Come now, let us reason[1] together, says the LORD:
    though your sins are like scarlet,
        they shall be as white as snow;
though they are red like crimson,
        they shall become like wool.
¹⁹ If you are willing and obedient,
    you shall eat the good of the land;
²⁰ but if you refuse and rebel,
    you shall be eaten by the sword;
    for the mouth of the LORD has spoken."

²¹ How the faithful city
    has become a whore,[2]
    she who was full of justice!
Righteousness lodged in her,
    but now murderers.
²² Your silver has become dross,
    your best wine mixed with water.
²³ Your princes are rebels
    and companions of thieves.
Everyone loves a bribe
    and runs after gifts.
They do not bring justice to the fatherless,
    and the widow's cause does not come to them.

²⁴ Therefore the Lord declares,
    the LORD of hosts,
    the Mighty One of Israel:
"Ah, I will get relief from my enemies
    and avenge myself on my foes.
²⁵ I will turn my hand against you
    and will smelt away your dross as with lye

---

[1] Or *dispute* [2] Or *become unchaste*

and remove all your alloy.
26 And I will restore your judges as at the first,
      and your counselors as at the beginning.
   Afterward you shall be called the city of righteousness,
      the faithful city."

27 Zion shall be redeemed by justice,
      and those in her who repent, by righteousness.
28 But rebels and sinners shall be broken together,
      and those who forsake the LORD shall be consumed.
29 For they[1] shall be ashamed of the oaks
      that you desired;
   and you shall blush for the gardens
      that you have chosen.
30 For you shall be like an oak
      whose leaf withers,
      and like a garden without water.
31 And the strong shall become tinder,
      and his work a spark,
   and both of them shall burn together,
      with none to quench them.

Preview of things to come [chapter 2]. Chapter 2 gives us further signposts regarding the form and content of the book that is to come. It begins with a glorious vision of what God will do redemptively in "the latter days" (vv. 1–5). The remainder of the chapter is a vision of God's fearful judgment against sinners. The poetic impulse to render everything concretely is something we need to embrace from the start of the book.

---

2 The word that Isaiah the son of Amoz saw concerning Judah and Jerusalem.

2   It shall come to pass in the latter days
      that the mountain of the house of the LORD
   shall be established as the highest of the mountains,
      and shall be lifted up above the hills;
   and all the nations shall flow to it,
3   and many peoples shall come, and say:
   "Come, let us go up to the mountain of the LORD,
      to the house of the God of Jacob,
   that he may teach us his ways
      and that we may walk in his paths."
   For out of Zion shall go the law,[2]
      and the word of the LORD from Jerusalem.
4   He shall judge between the nations,
      and shall decide disputes for many peoples;
   and they shall beat their swords into plowshares,
      and their spears into pruning hooks;

---

[1] Some Hebrew manuscripts *you* [2] Or *teaching*

nation shall not lift up sword against nation,
   neither shall they learn war anymore.

5 O house of Jacob,
   come, let us walk
     in the light of the LORD.

6 For you have rejected your people,
   the house of Jacob,
because they are full of things from the east
   and of fortune-tellers like the Philistines,
   and they strike hands with the children of foreigners.
7 Their land is filled with silver and gold,
   and there is no end to their treasures;
their land is filled with horses,
   and there is no end to their chariots.
8 Their land is filled with idols;
   they bow down to the work of their hands,
   to what their own fingers have made.
9 So man is humbled,
   and each one is brought low—
   do not forgive them!
10 Enter into the rock
   and hide in the dust
from before the terror of the LORD,
   and from the splendor of his majesty.
11 The haughty looks of man shall be brought low,
   and the lofty pride of men shall be humbled,
and the LORD alone will be exalted in that day.

12 For the LORD of hosts has a day
   against all that is proud and lofty,
   against all that is lifted up—and it shall be brought low;
13 against all the cedars of Lebanon,
   lofty and lifted up;
   and against all the oaks of Bashan;
14 against all the lofty mountains,
   and against all the uplifted hills;
15 against every high tower,
   and against every fortified wall;
16 against all the ships of Tarshish,
   and against all the beautiful craft.
17 And the haughtiness of man shall be humbled,
   and the lofty pride of men shall be brought low,
   and the LORD alone will be exalted in that day.
18 And the idols shall utterly pass away.
19 And people shall enter the caves of the rocks
   and the holes of the ground,[1]

[1] Hebrew *dust*

from before the terror of the LORD,
>   and from the splendor of his majesty,
>   when he rises to terrify the earth.

20   In that day mankind will cast away
>   their idols of silver and their idols of gold,
>   which they made for themselves to worship,
>   to the moles and to the bats,
21   to enter the caverns of the rocks
>   and the clefts of the cliffs,
>   from before the terror of the LORD,
>   and from the splendor of his majesty,
>   when he rises to terrify the earth.
22   Stop regarding man
>   in whose nostrils is breath,
>   for of what account is he?

Oracles of judgment and salvation [chapters 3–4]. Most of this section consists of a satiric exposé of Judah's evil (with 3:16–26 serving as a particularly memorable example). Accordingly we should compile a running list of the objects of satiric attack, noting that God himself is the norm by which these things are seen to be deficient. But in keeping with the tendency of prophetic discourse to move from judgment to blessing without transition, we end the unit with a golden age vision of a perfect society, a vision that is partly messianic and partly *apocalyptic (end-times; 4:2–6).

3   For behold, the Lord GOD of hosts
>   is taking away from Jerusalem and from Judah
>   support and supply,[1]
>   all support of bread,
>   and all support of water;
2   the mighty man and the soldier,
>   the judge and the prophet,
>   the diviner and the elder,
3   the captain of fifty
>   and the man of rank,
>   the counselor and the skillful magician
>   and the expert in charms.
4   And I will make boys their princes,
>   and infants[2] shall rule over them.
5   And the people will oppress one another,
>   every one his fellow
>   and every one his neighbor;
>   the youth will be insolent to the elder,
>   and the despised to the honorable.

6   For a man will take hold of his brother
>   in the house of his father, saying:

---

[1] Hebrew *staff* [2] Or *caprice*

"You have a cloak;
 you shall be our leader,
 and this heap of ruins
  shall be under your rule";
7 in that day he will speak out, saying:
 "I will not be a healer;[1]
  in my house there is neither bread nor cloak;
 you shall not make me
  leader of the people."
8 For Jerusalem has stumbled,
  and Judah has fallen,
 because their speech and their deeds are against the Lord,
  defying his glorious presence.[2]

9 For the look on their faces bears witness against them;
  they proclaim their sin like Sodom;
  they do not hide it.
 Woe to them!
  For they have brought evil on themselves.
10 Tell the righteous that it shall be well with them,
  for they shall eat the fruit of their deeds.
11 Woe to the wicked! It shall be ill with him,
  for what his hands have dealt out shall be done to him.
12 My people—infants are their oppressors,
  and women rule over them.
 O my people, your guides mislead you
  and they have swallowed up[3] the course of your paths.

13 The Lord has taken his place to contend;
  he stands to judge peoples.
14 The Lord will enter into judgment
  with the elders and princes of his people:
 "It is you who have devoured[4] the vineyard,
  the spoil of the poor is in your houses.
15 What do you mean by crushing my people,
  by grinding the face of the poor?"
       declares the Lord God of hosts.

16 The Lord said:
 Because the daughters of Zion are haughty
  and walk with outstretched necks,
  glancing wantonly with their eyes,
 mincing along as they go,
  tinkling with their feet,
17 therefore the Lord will strike with a scab
  the heads of the daughters of Zion,
  and the Lord will lay bare their secret parts.

---

[1] Hebrew binder of wounds [2] Hebrew the eyes of his glory [3] Or they have confused [4] Or grazed over; compare Exodus 22:5

¹⁸In that day the Lord will take away the finery of the anklets, the headbands, and the crescents; ¹⁹the pendants, the bracelets, and the scarves; ²⁰the headdresses, the armlets, the sashes, the perfume boxes, and the amulets; ²¹the signet rings and nose rings; ²²the festal robes, the mantles, the cloaks, and the handbags; ²³the mirrors, the linen garments, the turbans, and the veils.

²⁴   Instead of perfume there will be rottenness;
         and instead of a belt, a rope;
     and instead of well-set hair, baldness;
         and instead of a rich robe, a skirt of sackcloth;
         and branding instead of beauty.
²⁵   Your men shall fall by the sword
         and your mighty men in battle.
²⁶   And her gates shall lament and mourn;
         empty, she shall sit on the ground.

4 And seven women shall take hold of one man in that day, saying, "We will eat our own bread and wear our own clothes, only let us be called by your name; take away our reproach."

²In that day the branch of the LORD shall be beautiful and glorious, and the fruit of the land shall be the pride and honor of the survivors of Israel. ³And he who is left in Zion and remains in Jerusalem will be called holy, everyone who has been recorded for life in Jerusalem, ⁴when the Lord shall have washed away the filth of the daughters of Zion and cleansed the bloodstains of Jerusalem from its midst by a spirit of judgment and by a spirit of burning.¹ ⁵Then the LORD will create over the whole site of Mount Zion and over her assemblies a cloud by day, and smoke and the shining of a flaming fire by night; for over all the glory there will be a canopy. ⁶There will be a booth for shade by day from the heat, and for a refuge and a shelter from the storm and rain.

Satire against Judah [chapter 5]. The general content remains the same—an exposé of Judah's evil and assurances of God's coming judgment against it. In terms of technique, though, it is possible to see the chapter as a self-contained literary unit. We begin with an extended metaphor (what literary critics call a "conceit" or "little idea") in which Judah is portrayed as God's vineyard (vv. 1–7). This is followed by a sixfold exhibit of the familiar "woe" formula of prophetic satire, with the woes naming specific moral sins (vv. 8–23). A final surrealistic vision portrays the nation as it will be under God's judgment (vv. 24–30).

5 Let me sing for my beloved
     my love song concerning his vineyard:
   My beloved had a vineyard
       on a very fertile hill.
² He dug it and cleared it of stones,
       and planted it with choice vines;
   he built a watchtower in the midst of it,
       and hewed out a wine vat in it;

¹ Or purging

and he looked for it to yield grapes,
    but it yielded wild grapes.

³ And now, O inhabitants of Jerusalem
    and men of Judah,
judge between me and my vineyard.
⁴ What more was there to do for my vineyard,
    that I have not done in it?
When I looked for it to yield grapes,
    why did it yield wild grapes?

⁵ And now I will tell you
    what I will do to my vineyard.
I will remove its hedge,
    and it shall be devoured;¹
I will break down its wall,
    and it shall be trampled down.
⁶ I will make it a waste;
    it shall not be pruned or hoed,
    and briers and thorns shall grow up;
I will also command the clouds
    that they rain no rain upon it.

⁷ For the vineyard of the LORD of hosts
    is the house of Israel,
and the men of Judah
    are his pleasant planting;
and he looked for justice,
    but behold, bloodshed;²
for righteousness,
    but behold, an outcry!³

⁸ Woe to those who join house to house,
    who add field to field,
until there is no more room,
    and you are made to dwell alone
    in the midst of the land.
⁹ The LORD of hosts has sworn in my hearing:
"Surely many houses shall be desolate,
    large and beautiful houses, without inhabitant.
¹⁰ For ten acres⁴ of vineyard shall yield but one bath,
    and a homer of seed shall yield but an ephah."⁵

¹¹ Woe to those who rise early in the morning,
    that they may run after strong drink,
who tarry late into the evening
    as wine inflames them!
¹² They have lyre and harp,

---

¹ Or *grazed over*; compare Exodus 22:5 ² The Hebrew words for *justice* and *bloodshed* sound alike ³ The Hebrew words for *righteous* and *outcry* sound alike ⁴ Hebrew *ten yoke*, the area ten yoke of oxen can plow in a day ⁵ A *bath* was about 6 gallons or 22 liters; a *homer* was about 6 bushels or 220 liters; an *ephah* was about 3/5 bushel or 22 liters

tambourine and flute and wine at their feasts,
but they do not regard the deeds of the LORD,
   or see the work of his hands.

13   Therefore my people go into exile
      for lack of knowledge;[1]
   their honored men go hungry,[2]
      and their multitude is parched with thirst.
14   Therefore Sheol has enlarged its appetite
      and opened its mouth beyond measure,
   and the nobility of Jerusalem[3] and her multitude will go down,
      her revelers and he who exults in her.
15   Man is humbled, and each one is brought low,
      and the eyes of the haughty[4] are brought low.
16   But the LORD of hosts is exalted[5] in justice,
      and the Holy God shows himself holy in righteousness.
17   Then shall the lambs graze as in their pasture,
      and nomads shall eat among the ruins of the rich.

18   Woe to those who draw iniquity with cords of falsehood,
      who draw sin as with cart ropes,
19   who say: "Let him be quick,
      let him speed his work
      that we may see it;
   let the counsel of the Holy One of Israel draw near,
      and let it come, that we may know it!"
20   Woe to those who call evil good
      and good evil,
   who put darkness for light
      and light for darkness,
   who put bitter for sweet
      and sweet for bitter!
21   Woe to those who are wise in their own eyes,
      and shrewd in their own sight!
22   Woe to those who are heroes at drinking wine,
      and valiant men in mixing strong drink,
23   who acquit the guilty for a bribe,
      and deprive the innocent of his right!

24   Therefore, as the tongue of fire devours the stubble,
      and as dry grass sinks down in the flame,
   so their root will be as rottenness,
      and their blossom go up like dust;
   for they have rejected the law of the LORD of hosts,
      and have despised the word of the Holy One of Israel.
25   Therefore the anger of the LORD was kindled against his people,
      and he stretched out his hand against them and struck them,
      and the mountains quaked;

---

[1] Or *without their knowledge* [2] Or *die of hunger* [3] Hebrew *her nobility* [4] Hebrew *high* [5] Hebrew *high*

and their corpses were as refuse
  in the midst of the streets.
For all this his anger has not turned away,
  and his hand is stretched out still.

²⁶ He will raise a signal for nations far away,
    and whistle for them from the ends of the earth;
  and behold, quickly, speedily they come!
²⁷ None is weary, none stumbles,
    none slumbers or sleeps,
  not a waistband is loose,
    not a sandal strap broken;
²⁸ their arrows are sharp,
    all their bows bent,
  their horses' hoofs seem like flint,
    and their wheels like the whirlwind.
²⁹ Their roaring is like a lion,
    like young lions they roar;
  they growl and seize their prey;
    they carry it off, and none can rescue.
³⁰ They will growl over it on that day,
    like the growling of the sea.
  And if one looks to the land,
    behold, darkness and distress;
  and the light is darkened by its clouds.

The call of the prophet [chapter 6]. God's call of the prophet is an archetype in the Bible's prophetic literature (meaning that it is a repeated event composed of common elements). The call of Isaiah gives us a particularly full scenario, in the following sequence: situating the prophet in a specific time (v. 1a); a vision of the transcendent God in a heavenly setting (vv. 1b–4); the prophet's confession of his own sinfulness and inadequacy to perform the prophetic task (v. 5); the equipping of the prophet for his task by atonement and forgiveness (vv. 6–7); commissioning from God (v. 8a); the prophet's acceptance of God's call to the prophetic task of proclamation (v. 8b); the message that is entrusted to the prophet to proclaim (vv. 9–13). When Isaiah says "Woe is me!" (v. 5), this is the seventh and climactic "woe" in the series that started in the preceding chapter.

6 In the year that King Uzziah died I saw the Lord sitting upon a throne, high and lifted up; and the train¹ of his robe filled the temple. ²Above him stood the seraphim. Each had six wings: with two he covered his face, and with two he covered his feet, and with two he flew. ³And one called to another and said:

  "Holy, holy, holy is the LORD of hosts;
    the whole earth is full of his glory!"²

⁴And the foundations of the thresholds shook at the voice of him who called, and the house was filled with smoke. ⁵And I said: "Woe is me! For I am lost; for I am a man of

¹ Or hem ² Or may his glory fill the whole earth

unclean lips, and I dwell in the midst of a people of unclean lips; for my eyes have seen the King, the LORD of hosts!"

⁶Then one of the seraphim flew to me, having in his hand a burning coal that he had taken with tongs from the altar. ⁷And he touched my mouth and said: "Behold, this has touched your lips; your guilt is taken away, and your sin atoned for."

⁸And I heard the voice of the Lord saying, "Whom shall I send, and who will go for us?" Then I said, "Here am I! Send me." ⁹And he said, "Go, and say to this people:

"'Keep on hearing,¹ but do not understand;
keep on seeing,² but do not perceive.'
¹⁰   Make the heart of this people dull,³
        and their ears heavy,
        and blind their eyes;
    lest they see with their eyes,
        and hear with their ears,
    and understand with their hearts,
        and turn and be healed."
¹¹   Then I said, "How long, O Lord?"
    And he said:
    "Until cities lie waste
        without inhabitant,
    and houses without people,
        and the land is a desolate waste,
¹²   and the LORD removes people far away,
        and the forsaken places are many in the midst of the land.
¹³   And though a tenth remain in it,
        it will be burned⁴ again,
    like a terebinth or an oak,
        whose stump remains
        when it is felled."
    The holy seed⁵ is its stump.

Messages of warning to Judah [chapters 7–8]. This unit is rooted in a specific historical situation involving enticements to King Ahaz to join a military alliance with Israel and Syria against Assyria. The gist of Isaiah's prophecies in this unit is to dissuade Ahaz from joining the alliance and call him instead to trust in God. The unit begins with narrative hints of the historical situation (7:1–9). Set over against the alliance is a sign of Immanuel ("God with us") designed to instill trust in God's deliverance (vv. 10–17); while this had a specific meaning and fulfillment in the days of Ahaz and Isaiah, we can see in the passage the literary phenomenon of "second meanings," inasmuch as the imagery also has messianic overtones. The remainder of the unit consists of oracles of judgment. Sometimes the mode is fantasy: God did not literally shave the head of Assyria with a razor (7:20), nor did the military invasion of Assyria take the form of the Euphrates River flooding Judah (8:7–8). Nevertheless, these fantastic images are symbolic of God's actual judgments in history.

---

¹ Or *Hear indeed* ² Or *see indeed* ³ Hebrew *fat* ⁴ Or *purged* ⁵ Or *offspring*

7 In the days of Ahaz the son of Jotham, son of Uzziah, king of Judah, Rezin the king of Syria and Pekah the son of Remaliah the king of Israel came up to Jerusalem to wage war against it, but could not yet mount an attack against it. [2]When the house of David was told, "Syria is in league with[1] Ephraim," the heart of Ahaz[2] and the heart of his people shook as the trees of the forest shake before the wind.

[3]And the Lord said to Isaiah, "Go out to meet Ahaz, you and Shear-jashub[3] your son, at the end of the conduit of the upper pool on the highway to the Washer's Field. [4]And say to him, 'Be careful, be quiet, do not fear, and do not let your heart be faint because of these two smoldering stumps of firebrands, at the fierce anger of Rezin and Syria and the son of Remaliah. [5]Because Syria, with Ephraim and the son of Remaliah, has devised evil against you, saying, [6]"Let us go up against Judah and terrify it, and let us conquer it[4] for ourselves, and set up the son of Tabeel as king in the midst of it," [7]thus says the Lord God:

"'It shall not stand,
     and it shall not come to pass.
[8] For the head of Syria is Damascus,
     and the head of Damascus is Rezin.
And within sixty-five years
     Ephraim will be shattered from being a people.
[9] And the head of Ephraim is Samaria,
     and the head of Samaria is the son of Remaliah.
If you[5] are not firm in faith,
     you will not be firm at all.'"

[10]Again the Lord spoke to Ahaz, [11]"Ask a sign of the Lord your[6] God; let it be deep as Sheol or high as heaven." [12]But Ahaz said, "I will not ask, and I will not put the Lord to the test." [13]And he[7] said, "Hear then, O house of David! Is it too little for you to weary men, that you weary my God also? [14]Therefore the Lord himself will give you a sign. Behold, the virgin shall conceive and bear a son, and shall call his name Immanuel.[8] [15]He shall eat curds and honey when he knows how to refuse the evil and choose the good. [16]For before the boy knows how to refuse the evil and choose the good, the land whose two kings you dread will be deserted. [17]The Lord will bring upon you and upon your people and upon your father's house such days as have not come since the day that Ephraim departed from Judah—the king of Assyria."

[18]In that day the Lord will whistle for the fly that is at the end of the streams of Egypt, and for the bee that is in the land of Assyria. [19]And they will all come and settle in the steep ravines, and in the clefts of the rocks, and on all the thornbushes, and on all the pastures.[9]

[20]In that day the Lord will shave with a razor that is hired beyond the River—with the king of Assyria—the head and the hair of the feet, and it will sweep away the beard also.

[21]In that day a man will keep alive a young cow and two sheep, [22]and because of the abundance of milk that they give, he will eat curds, for everyone who is left in the land will eat curds and honey.

[23]In that day every place where there used to be a thousand vines, worth a thou-

---

[1] Hebrew *Syria has rested upon* [2] Hebrew *his heart* [3] *Shear-jashub* means *A remnant shall return* [4] Hebrew *let us split it open* [5] The Hebrew for *you* is plural in verses 9, 13, 14 [6] The Hebrew for *you* and *your* is singular in verses 11, 16, 17 [7] That is, Isaiah [8] *Immanuel* means *God is with us* [9] Or *watering holes,* or *brambles*

sand shekels[1] of silver, will become briers and thorns. [24]With bow and arrows a man will come there, for all the land will be briers and thorns. [25]And as for all the hills that used to be hoed with a hoe, you will not come there for fear of briers and thorns, but they will become a place where cattle are let loose and where sheep tread.

8 Then the LORD said to me, "Take a large tablet and write on it in common characters,[2] 'Belonging to Maher-shalal-hash-baz.'[3] [2]And I will get reliable witnesses, Uriah the priest and Zechariah the son of Jeberechiah, to attest for me."

[3]And I went to the prophetess, and she conceived and bore a son. Then the LORD said to me, "Call his name Maher-shalal-hash-baz; [4]for before the boy knows how to cry 'My father' or 'My mother,' the wealth of Damascus and the spoil of Samaria will be carried away before the king of Assyria."

[5]The LORD spoke to me again: [6]"Because this people has refused the waters of Shiloah that flow gently, and rejoice over Rezin and the son of Remaliah, [7]therefore, behold, the Lord is bringing up against them the waters of the River, mighty and many, the king of Assyria and all his glory. And it will rise over all its channels and go over all its banks, [8]and it will sweep on into Judah, it will overflow and pass on, reaching even to the neck, and its outspread wings will fill the breadth of your land, O Immanuel."

[9]   Be broken,[4] you peoples, and be shattered;[5]
            give ear, all you far countries;
         strap on your armor and be shattered;
            strap on your armor and be shattered.
[10]   Take counsel together, but it will come to nothing;
            speak a word, but it will not stand,
         for God is with us.[6]

[11]For the LORD spoke thus to me with his strong hand upon me, and warned me not to walk in the way of this people, saying: [12]"Do not call conspiracy all that this people calls conspiracy, and do not fear what they fear, nor be in dread. [13]But the LORD of hosts, him you shall honor as holy. Let him be your fear, and let him be your dread. [14]And he will become a sanctuary and a stone of offense and a rock of stumbling to both houses of Israel, a trap and a snare to the inhabitants of Jerusalem. [15]And many shall stumble on it. They shall fall and be broken; they shall be snared and taken."

[16]Bind up the testimony; seal the teaching[7] among my disciples. [17]I will wait for the LORD, who is hiding his face from the house of Jacob, and I will hope in him. [18]Behold, I and the children whom the LORD has given me are signs and portents in Israel from the LORD of hosts, who dwells on Mount Zion. [19]And when they say to you, "Inquire of the mediums and the necromancers who chirp and mutter," should not a people inquire of their God? Should they inquire of the dead on behalf of the living? [20]To the teaching and to the testimony! If they will not speak according to this word, it is because they have no dawn. [21]They will pass through the land,[8] greatly distressed and hungry. And when they are hungry, they will be enraged and will speak contemptuously against[9] their king and their God, and turn their faces upward. [22]And they will look to the earth, but behold, distress and darkness, the gloom of anguish. And they will be thrust into thick darkness.

---

[1] A *shekel* was about 2/5 ounce or 11 grams [2] Hebrew *with a man's stylus* [3] *Maher-shalal-hash-baz* means *The spoil speeds, the prey hastens* [4] Or *Be evil* [5] Or *dismayed* [6] The Hebrew for *God is with us* is *Immanuel* [7] Or *law*; also verse 20 [8] Hebrew *it* [9] Or *speak contemptuously by*

A famous messianic prophecy [9:1–7]. Set in the middle of the prevailing visions of judgment against Judah is a vision of the coming Messiah. The poetry accounts for much of the literary power of the passage, along with a list of evocative epithets in verse 6.

9 ¹ But there will be no gloom for her who was in anguish. In the former time he brought into contempt the land of Zebulun and the land of Naphtali, but in the latter time he has made glorious the way of the sea, the land beyond the Jordan, Galilee of the nations.²

²³ The people who walked in darkness
        have seen a great light;
    those who dwelt in a land of deep darkness,
        on them has light shined.
³   You have multiplied the nation;
        you have increased its joy;
    they rejoice before you
        as with joy at the harvest,
        as they are glad when they divide the spoil.
⁴   For the yoke of his burden,
        and the staff for his shoulder,
        the rod of his oppressor,
        you have broken as on the day of Midian.
⁵   For every boot of the tramping warrior in battle tumult
        and every garment rolled in blood
        will be burned as fuel for the fire.
⁶   For to us a child is born,
        to us a son is given;
    and the government shall be upon⁴ his shoulder,
        and his name shall be called⁵
    Wonderful Counselor, Mighty God,
        Everlasting Father, Prince of Peace.
⁷   Of the increase of his government and of peace
        there will be no end,
    on the throne of David and over his kingdom,
        to establish it and to uphold it
    with justice and with righteousness
        from this time forth and forevermore.
    The zeal of the LORD of hosts will do this.

Visions of things to come [9:8–10:34]. The rhetorical/persuasive strategy of this unit remains the same as with earlier oracles of judgment, as Isaiah seeks to warn his nation that God will judge it if it rejects him and that God will also judge the surrounding nations, so trusting them is a futile venture. As we negotiate all of the topical references, we need to get a grip on the literary principle that writers tell us not only what happened but also what happens, so that Isaiah's message to his own society still applies today. The names have changed, but the spiritual principles remain the same: seeking satisfaction and security in earthly things will bring us to ruin.

¹ Ch 8:23 in Hebrew ² Or *of the Gentiles* ³ Ch 9:1 in Hebrew ⁴ Or *is upon* ⁵ Or *is called*

8   The Lord has sent a word against Jacob,
      and it will fall on Israel;
9   and all the people will know,
      Ephraim and the inhabitants of Samaria,
      who say in pride and in arrogance of heart:
10   "The bricks have fallen,
      but we will build with dressed stones;
    the sycamores have been cut down,
      but we will put cedars in their place."
11   But the LORD raises the adversaries of Rezin against him,
      and stirs up his enemies.
12   The Syrians on the east and the Philistines on the west
      devour Israel with open mouth.
    For all this his anger has not turned away,
      and his hand is stretched out still.

13   The people did not turn to him who struck them,
      nor inquire of the LORD of hosts.
14   So the LORD cut off from Israel head and tail,
      palm branch and reed in one day—
15   the elder and honored man is the head,
      and the prophet who teaches lies is the tail;
16   for those who guide this people have been leading them astray,
      and those who are guided by them are swallowed up.
17   Therefore the Lord does not rejoice over their young men,
      and has no compassion on their fatherless and widows;
    for everyone is godless and an evildoer,
      and every mouth speaks folly.[1]
    For all this his anger has not turned away,
      and his hand is stretched out still.

18   For wickedness burns like a fire;
      it consumes briers and thorns;
    it kindles the thickets of the forest,
      and they roll upward in a column of smoke.
19   Through the wrath of the LORD of hosts
      the land is scorched,
    and the people are like fuel for the fire;
      no one spares another.
20   They slice meat on the right, but are still hungry,
      and they devour on the left, but are not satisfied;
    each devours the flesh of his own arm,
21   Manasseh devours Ephraim, and Ephraim devours Manasseh;
      together they are against Judah.
    For all this his anger has not turned away,
      and his hand is stretched out still.

---

[1] Or speaks disgraceful things

10

Woe to those who decree iniquitous decrees,
and the writers who keep writing oppression,
² to turn aside the needy from justice
and to rob the poor of my people of their right,
that widows may be their spoil,
and that they may make the fatherless their prey!
³ What will you do on the day of punishment,
in the ruin that will come from afar?
To whom will you flee for help,
and where will you leave your wealth?
⁴ Nothing remains but to crouch among the prisoners
or fall among the slain.
For all this his anger has not turned away,
and his hand is stretched out still.

⁵ Ah, Assyria, the rod of my anger;
the staff in their hands is my fury!
⁶ Against a godless nation I send him,
and against the people of my wrath I command him,
to take spoil and seize plunder,
and to tread them down like the mire of the streets.
⁷ But he does not so intend,
and his heart does not so think;
but it is in his heart to destroy,
and to cut off nations not a few;
⁸ for he says:
"Are not my commanders all kings?
⁹ Is not Calno like Carchemish?
Is not Hamath like Arpad?
Is not Samaria like Damascus?
¹⁰ As my hand has reached to the kingdoms of the idols,
whose carved images were greater than those of Jerusalem and Samaria,
¹¹ shall I not do to Jerusalem and her idols
as I have done to Samaria and her images?"

¹²When the Lord has finished all his work on Mount Zion and on Jerusalem, he[1] will punish the speech of the arrogant heart of the king of Assyria and the boastful look in his eyes. ¹³For he says:

"By the strength of my hand I have done it,
and by my wisdom, for I have understanding;
I remove the boundaries of peoples,
and plunder their treasures;
like a bull I bring down those who sit on thrones.
¹⁴ My hand has found like a nest
the wealth of the peoples;
and as one gathers eggs that have been forsaken,
so I have gathered all the earth;

[1] Hebrew I

and there was none that moved a wing
   or opened the mouth or chirped."

¹⁵ Shall the axe boast over him who hews with it,
   or the saw magnify itself against him who wields it?
As if a rod should wield him who lifts it,
   or as if a staff should lift him who is not wood!

¹⁶ Therefore the Lord God of hosts
   will send wasting sickness among his stout warriors,
and under his glory a burning will be kindled,
   like the burning of fire.

¹⁷ The light of Israel will become a fire,
   and his Holy One a flame,
and it will burn and devour
   his thorns and briers in one day.

¹⁸ The glory of his forest and of his fruitful land
   the Lord will destroy, both soul and body,
   and it will be as when a sick man wastes away.

¹⁹ The remnant of the trees of his forest will be so few
   that a child can write them down.

²⁰In that day the remnant of Israel and the survivors of the house of Jacob will no more lean on him who struck them, but will lean on the Lord, the Holy One of Israel, in truth. ²¹A remnant will return, the remnant of Jacob, to the mighty God. ²²For though your people Israel be as the sand of the sea, only a remnant of them will return. Destruction is decreed, overflowing with righteousness. ²³For the Lord God of hosts will make a full end, as decreed, in the midst of all the earth.

²⁴Therefore thus says the Lord God of hosts: "O my people, who dwell in Zion, be not afraid of the Assyrians when they strike with the rod and lift up their staff against you as the Egyptians did. ²⁵For in a very little while my fury will come to an end, and my anger will be directed to their destruction. ²⁶And the Lord of hosts will wield against them a whip, as when he struck Midian at the rock of Oreb. And his staff will be over the sea, and he will lift it as he did in Egypt. ²⁷And in that day his burden will depart from your shoulder, and his yoke from your neck; and the yoke will be broken because of the fat."[1]

²⁸ He has come to Aiath;
   he has passed through Migron;
   at Michmash he stores his baggage;

²⁹ they have crossed over the pass;
   at Geba they lodge for the night;
Ramah trembles;
   Gibeah of Saul has fled.

³⁰ Cry aloud, O daughter of Gallim!
   Give attention, O Laishah!
   O poor Anathoth!

³¹ Madmenah is in flight;
   the inhabitants of Gebim flee for safety.

---

[1] The meaning of the Hebrew is uncertain

³² This very day he will halt at Nob;
>   he will shake his fist
>   at the mount of the daughter of Zion,
>   the hill of Jerusalem.

³³ Behold, the Lord GOD of hosts
>   will lop the boughs with terrifying power;
> the great in height will be hewn down,
>   and the lofty will be brought low.
³⁴ He will cut down the thickets of the forest with an axe,
>   and Lebanon will fall by the Majestic One.

Oracles of redemption: visions of the coming Messiah [chapters 11–12]. As an antidote to the false promises of deliverance by earthly kingdoms, we receive a famous messianic prophecy of the branch of Jesse (chapter 11). As the chapter unfolds, we confront the mysteries of prophetic time: some of the references point to what Jesus accomplished by his incarnation (vv. 1–5), but those fulfillments telescope into pictures of a golden age that seem to fit the coming millennium and eschaton (vv. 6–16). In any event, the mode is visionary rather than literal. Chapter 12 is a *psalm of praise, imagined as being uttered by beneficiaries of God's salvation as just named ("you will say in that day"—v. 1).

11

There shall come forth a shoot from the stump of Jesse,
>   and a branch from his roots shall bear fruit.
² And the Spirit of the LORD shall rest upon him,
>   the Spirit of wisdom and understanding,
>   the Spirit of counsel and might,
>   the Spirit of knowledge and the fear of the LORD.
³ And his delight shall be in the fear of the LORD.
> He shall not judge by what his eyes see,
>   or decide disputes by what his ears hear,
⁴ but with righteousness he shall judge the poor,
>   and decide with equity for the meek of the earth;
> and he shall strike the earth with the rod of his mouth,
>   and with the breath of his lips he shall kill the wicked.
⁵ Righteousness shall be the belt of his waist,
>   and faithfulness the belt of his loins.

⁶ The wolf shall dwell with the lamb,
>   and the leopard shall lie down with the young goat,
> and the calf and the lion and the fattened calf together;
>   and a little child shall lead them.
⁷ The cow and the bear shall graze;
>   their young shall lie down together;
>   and the lion shall eat straw like the ox.
⁸ The nursing child shall play over the hole of the cobra,
>   and the weaned child shall put his hand on the adder's den.

⁹ They shall not hurt or destroy
       in all my holy mountain;
   for the earth shall be full of the knowledge of the LORD
       as the waters cover the sea.

¹⁰In that day the root of Jesse, who shall stand as a signal for the peoples—of him shall the nations inquire, and his resting place shall be glorious.

¹¹In that day the Lord will extend his hand yet a second time to recover the remnant that remains of his people, from Assyria, from Egypt, from Pathros, from Cush,[1] from Elam, from Shinar, from Hamath, and from the coastlands of the sea.

¹² He will raise a signal for the nations
       and will assemble the banished of Israel,
   and gather the dispersed of Judah
       from the four corners of the earth.
¹³ The jealousy of Ephraim shall depart,
       and those who harass Judah shall be cut off;
   Ephraim shall not be jealous of Judah,
       and Judah shall not harass Ephraim.
¹⁴ But they shall swoop down on the shoulder of the Philistines in the west,
       and together they shall plunder the people of the east.
   They shall put out their hand against Edom and Moab,
       and the Ammonites shall obey them.
¹⁵ And the LORD will utterly destroy[2]
       the tongue of the Sea of Egypt,
   and will wave his hand over the River
       with his scorching breath,[3]
   and strike it into seven channels,
       and he will lead people across in sandals.
¹⁶ And there will be a highway from Assyria
       for the remnant that remains of his people,
   as there was for Israel
       when they came up from the land of Egypt.

12 You[4] will say in that day:
   "I will give thanks to you, O LORD,
       for though you were angry with me,
   your anger turned away,
       that you might comfort me.

²   "Behold, God is my salvation;
       I will trust, and will not be afraid;
   for the LORD GOD[5] is my strength and my song,
       and he has become my salvation."

³With joy you[6] will draw water from the wells of salvation. ⁴And you will say in that day:

---

[1] Probably *Nubia* [2] Hebrew *devote to destruction* [3] Or *wind* [4] The Hebrew for *you* is singular in verse 1 [5] Hebrew *for Yah, the LORD* [6] The Hebrew for *you* is plural in verses 3, 4

"Give thanks to the LORD,
    call upon his name,
make known his deeds among the peoples,
    proclaim that his name is exalted.

⁵ "Sing praises to the LORD, for he has done gloriously;
    let this be made known[1] in all the earth.
⁶ Shout, and sing for joy, O inhabitant of Zion,
    for great in your[2] midst is the Holy One of Israel."

The doom of Assyria and Babylon predicted [chapters 13–14]. After twelve chapters in which the focus has been on the prophet's own nation of Judah, we now enter an extended unit in which the main message is judgment against various surrounding nations. The dominant world power of the day, Assyria (also called Babylon), gets the most space. Chapter 13 dispenses with pictures of social evil and goes right to the kill in the form of vivid pictures of coming destruction. In chapter 14, verses 1–21 constitute a *taunt song addressed to the king of Babylon, who is pictured as already deceased. The unit ends with brief predictions of the coming destruction of Assyria (14:22–27), with a concluding address warning Philistia not to become smug just because its tormentor Assyria will fall (14:28–32).

---

13 The oracle concerning Babylon which Isaiah the son of Amoz saw.

² On a bare hill raise a signal;
    cry aloud to them;
wave the hand for them to enter
    the gates of the nobles.
³ I myself have commanded my consecrated ones,
    and have summoned my mighty men to execute my anger,
    my proudly exulting ones.[3]

⁴ The sound of a tumult is on the mountains
    as of a great multitude!
The sound of an uproar of kingdoms,
    of nations gathering together!
The LORD of hosts is mustering
    a host for battle.
⁵ They come from a distant land,
    from the end of the heavens,
the LORD and the weapons of his indignation,
    to destroy the whole land.[4]

⁶ Wail, for the day of the LORD is near;
    as destruction from the Almighty[5] it will come!
⁷ Therefore all hands will be feeble,
    and every human heart will melt.
⁸ They will be dismayed:

---

[1] Or *this is made known* [2] The Hebrew for *your* in verse 6 is singular, referring to the *inhabitant of Zion* [3] Or *those who exult in my majesty* [4] Or *earth*; also verse 9 [5] The Hebrew words for *destruction* and *almighty* sound alike

pangs and agony will seize them;
>> they will be in anguish like a woman in labor.
They will look aghast at one another;
>> their faces will be aflame.

9 Behold, the day of the LORD comes,
>> cruel, with wrath and fierce anger,
to make the land a desolation
>> and to destroy its sinners from it.
10 For the stars of the heavens and their constellations
>> will not give their light;
the sun will be dark at its rising,
>> and the moon will not shed its light.
11 I will punish the world for its evil,
>> and the wicked for their iniquity;
I will put an end to the pomp of the arrogant,
>> and lay low the pompous pride of the ruthless.
12 I will make people more rare than fine gold,
>> and mankind than the gold of Ophir.
13 Therefore I will make the heavens tremble,
>> and the earth will be shaken out of its place,
at the wrath of the LORD of hosts
>> in the day of his fierce anger.
14 And like a hunted gazelle,
>> or like sheep with none to gather them,
each will turn to his own people,
>> and each will flee to his own land.
15 Whoever is found will be thrust through,
>> and whoever is caught will fall by the sword.
16 Their infants will be dashed in pieces
>> before their eyes;
their houses will be plundered
>> and their wives ravished.

17 Behold, I am stirring up the Medes against them,
>> who have no regard for silver
>> and do not delight in gold.
18 Their bows will slaughter[1] the young men;
>> they will have no mercy on the fruit of the womb;
>> their eyes will not pity children.
19 And Babylon, the glory of kingdoms,
>> the splendor and pomp of the Chaldeans,
will be like Sodom and Gomorrah
>> when God overthrew them.
20 It will never be inhabited
>> or lived in for all generations;
no Arab will pitch his tent there;

---

[1] Hebrew *dash in pieces*

no shepherds will make their flocks lie down there.
21 But wild animals will lie down there,
 and their houses will be full of howling creatures;
there ostriches[1] will dwell,
 and there wild goats will dance.
22 Hyenas[2] will cry in its towers,
 and jackals in the pleasant palaces;
its time is close at hand
 and its days will not be prolonged.

14 For the LORD will have compassion on Jacob and will again choose Israel, and will set them in their own land, and sojourners will join them and will attach themselves to the house of Jacob. ²And the peoples will take them and bring them to their place, and the house of Israel will possess them in the LORD's land as male and female slaves. They will take captive those who were their captors, and rule over those who oppressed them.

³When the LORD has given you rest from your pain and turmoil and the hard service with which you were made to serve, ⁴you will take up this taunt against the king of Babylon:

"How the oppressor has ceased,
 the insolent fury[3] ceased!
5 The LORD has broken the staff of the wicked,
 the scepter of rulers,
6 that struck the peoples in wrath
 with unceasing blows,
that ruled the nations in anger
 with unrelenting persecution.
7 The whole earth is at rest and quiet;
 they break forth into singing.
8 The cypresses rejoice at you,
 the cedars of Lebanon, saying,
'Since you were laid low,
 no woodcutter comes up against us.'
9 Sheol beneath is stirred up
 to meet you when you come;
it rouses the shades to greet you,
 all who were leaders of the earth;
it raises from their thrones
 all who were kings of the nations.
10 All of them will answer
 and say to you:
'You too have become as weak as we!
 You have become like us!'
11 Your pomp is brought down to Sheol,
 the sound of your harps;
maggots are laid as a bed beneath you,
 and worms are your covers.

---

[1] Or owls [2] Or foxes [3] Dead Sea Scroll (compare Septuagint, Syriac, Vulgate); the meaning of the word in the Masoretic Text is uncertain

12 "How you are fallen from heaven,
        O Day Star, son of Dawn!
    How you are cut down to the ground,
        you who laid the nations low!
13 You said in your heart,
        'I will ascend to heaven;
    above the stars of God
        I will set my throne on high;
    I will sit on the mount of assembly
        in the far reaches of the north;[1]
14 I will ascend above the heights of the clouds;
        I will make myself like the Most High.'
15 But you are brought down to Sheol,
        to the far reaches of the pit.
16 Those who see you will stare at you
        and ponder over you:
    'Is this the man who made the earth tremble,
        who shook kingdoms,
17 who made the world like a desert
        and overthrew its cities,
        who did not let his prisoners go home?'
18 All the kings of the nations lie in glory,
        each in his own tomb;[2]
19 but you are cast out, away from your grave,
        like a loathed branch,
    clothed with the slain, those pierced by the sword,
        who go down to the stones of the pit,
        like a dead body trampled underfoot.
20 You will not be joined with them in burial,
        because you have destroyed your land,
        you have slain your people.

    "May the offspring of evildoers
        nevermore be named!
21 Prepare slaughter for his sons
        because of the guilt of their fathers,
    lest they rise and possess the earth,
        and fill the face of the world with cities."

    22"I will rise up against them," declares the Lord of hosts, "and will cut off from Babylon name and remnant, descendants and posterity," declares the Lord. 23"And I will make it a possession of the hedgehog,[3] and pools of water, and I will sweep it with the broom of destruction," declares the Lord of hosts.

24   The Lord of hosts has sworn:
    "As I have planned,
        so shall it be,
    and as I have purposed,

---

[1] Or in the remote parts of Zaphon [2] Hebrew house [3] Possibly porcupine, or owl

so shall it stand,

25   that I will break the Assyrian in my land,
      and on my mountains trample him underfoot;
and his yoke shall depart from them,
      and his burden from their shoulder."

26   This is the purpose that is purposed
      concerning the whole earth,
and this is the hand that is stretched out
      over all the nations.

27   For the LORD of hosts has purposed,
      and who will annul it?
His hand is stretched out,
      and who will turn it back?

28 In the year that King Ahaz died came this oracle:

29   Rejoice not, O Philistia, all of you,
      that the rod that struck you is broken,
for from the serpent's root will come forth an adder,
      and its fruit will be a flying fiery serpent.

30   And the firstborn of the poor will graze,
      and the needy lie down in safety;
but I will kill your root with famine,
      and your remnant it will slay.

31   Wail, O gate; cry out, O city;
      melt in fear, O Philistia, all of you!
For smoke comes out of the north,
      and there is no straggler in his ranks.

32   What will one answer the messengers of the nation?
      "The LORD has founded Zion,
      and in her the afflicted of his people find refuge."

Prediction of doom for Moab [chapters 15–16]. The motif of God's judgment of the
nations continues with this extended vision of the coming downfall of Moab. We can
scrutinize the passage for intermingled elements of satire and prediction of coming
doom (pictured as having already happened).

15   An oracle concerning Moab.

Because Ar of Moab is laid waste in a night,
      Moab is undone;
because Kir of Moab is laid waste in a night,
      Moab is undone.

2   He has gone up to the temple,[1] and to Dibon,
      to the high places[2] to weep;
over Nebo and over Medeba

---

[1] Hebrew the house [2] Or temple, even Dibon to the high places

Moab wails.
On every head is baldness;
    every beard is shorn;
3   in the streets they wear sackcloth;
    on the housetops and in the squares
    everyone wails and melts in tears.
4   Heshbon and Elealeh cry out;
    their voice is heard as far as Jahaz;
therefore the armed men of Moab cry aloud;
    his soul trembles.
5   My heart cries out for Moab;
    her fugitives flee to Zoar,
    to Eglath-shelishiyah.
For at the ascent of Luhith
    they go up weeping;
on the road to Horonaim
    they raise a cry of destruction;
6   the waters of Nimrim
    are a desolation;
the grass is withered, the vegetation fails,
    the greenery is no more.
7   Therefore the abundance they have gained
    and what they have laid up
they carry away
    over the Brook of the Willows.
8   For a cry has gone
    around the land of Moab;
her wailing reaches to Eglaim;
    her wailing reaches to Beer-elim.
9   For the waters of Dibon[1] are full of blood;
    for I will bring upon Dibon even more,
a lion for those of Moab who escape,
    for the remnant of the land.

16 Send the lamb to the ruler of the land,
    from Sela, by way of the desert,
    to the mount of the daughter of Zion.
2   Like fleeing birds,
    like a scattered nest,
so are the daughters of Moab
    at the fords of the Arnon.

3   "Give counsel;
    grant justice;
make your shade like night
    at the height of noon;
    shelter the outcasts;

---

[1] Dead Sea Scroll, Vulgate (compare Syriac); Masoretic Text *Dimon* (twice in this verse)

do not reveal the fugitive;

4   let the outcasts of Moab
      sojourn among you;
  be a shelter to them[1]
      from the destroyer.
When the oppressor is no more,
    and destruction has ceased,
and he who tramples underfoot has vanished from the land,

5   then a throne will be established in steadfast love,
      and on it will sit in faithfulness
      in the tent of David
one who judges and seeks justice
    and is swift to do righteousness."

6   We have heard of the pride of Moab—
      how proud he is!—
of his arrogance, his pride, and his insolence;
    in his idle boasting he is not right.

7   Therefore let Moab wail for Moab,
      let everyone wail.
Mourn, utterly stricken,
    for the raisin cakes of Kir-hareseth.

8   For the fields of Heshbon languish,
      and the vine of Sibmah;
the lords of the nations
    have struck down its branches,
which reached to Jazer
    and strayed to the desert;
its shoots spread abroad
    and passed over the sea.

9   Therefore I weep with the weeping of Jazer
      for the vine of Sibmah;
I drench you with my tears,
    O Heshbon and Elealeh;
for over your summer fruit and your harvest
    the shout has ceased.

10   And joy and gladness are taken away from the fruitful field,
    and in the vineyards no songs are sung,
      no cheers are raised;
no treader treads out wine in the presses;
    I have put an end to the shouting.

11   Therefore my inner parts moan like a lyre for Moab,
    and my inmost self for Kir-hareseth.

[12]And when Moab presents himself, when he wearies himself on the high place, when he comes to his sanctuary to pray, he will not prevail. [13]This is the word that the Lord spoke concerning Moab in the past. [14]But now the

---

[1] Some Hebrew manuscripts, Septuagint, Syriac; Masoretic Text *let my outcasts sojourn among you; as for Moab, be a shelter to them*

Lord has spoken, saying, "In three years, like the years of a hired worker, the glory of Moab will be brought into contempt, in spite of all his great multitude, and those who remain will be very few and feeble."

Judgment of Damascus and Samaria [chapters 17–18]. By now it is apparent that the oracles against the nations are a mini-anthology in the larger scheme of the book; Isaiah is a prophet to the nations. As the pageant of doomed nations unfolds before our gaze, if we place the names into a context of OT history the list reads like a roll call of the degraded—a list of losers. The scope of this cosmic drama is international. At a literary level, we can relish the poetry and visionary qualities of the writing. At the level of content, we need to assimilate the message that the presently powerful people and nations of the earth are ultimately powerless before God.

17 An oracle concerning Damascus.

Behold, Damascus will cease to be a city
    and will become a heap of ruins.
2 The cities of Aroer are deserted;
      they will be for flocks,
      which will lie down, and none will make them afraid.
3 The fortress will disappear from Ephraim,
      and the kingdom from Damascus;
  and the remnant of Syria will be
      like the glory of the children of Israel,
                    declares the Lord of hosts.

4 And in that day the glory of Jacob will be brought low,
      and the fat of his flesh will grow lean.
5 And it shall be as when the reaper gathers standing grain
      and his arm harvests the ears,
  and as when one gleans the ears of grain
      in the Valley of Rephaim.
6 Gleanings will be left in it,
      as when an olive tree is beaten—
  two or three berries
      in the top of the highest bough,
  four or five
      on the branches of a fruit tree,
                    declares the Lord God of Israel.

7 In that day man will look to his Maker, and his eyes will look on the Holy One of Israel. 8 He will not look to the altars, the work of his hands, and he will not look on what his own fingers have made, either the Asherim or the altars of incense.

9 In that day their strong cities will be like the deserted places of the wooded heights and the hilltops, which they deserted because of the children of Israel, and there will be desolation.

¹⁰ For you have forgotten the God of your salvation
       and have not remembered the Rock of your refuge;
   therefore, though you plant pleasant plants
       and sow the vine-branch of a stranger,
¹¹ though you make them grow¹ on the day that you plant them,
       and make them blossom in the morning that you sow,
   yet the harvest will flee away²
       in a day of grief and incurable pain.

¹² Ah, the thunder of many peoples;
       they thunder like the thundering of the sea!
   Ah, the roar of nations;
       they roar like the roaring of mighty waters!
¹³ The nations roar like the roaring of many waters,
       but he will rebuke them, and they will flee far away,
   chased like chaff on the mountains before the wind
       and whirling dust before the storm.
¹⁴ At evening time, behold, terror!
       Before morning, they are no more!
   This is the portion of those who loot us,
       and the lot of those who plunder us.

18

   Ah, land of whirring wings
       that is beyond the rivers of Cush,³
² which sends ambassadors by the sea,
       in vessels of papyrus on the waters!
   Go, you swift messengers,
       to a nation, tall and smooth,
   to a people feared near and far,
       a nation mighty and conquering,
       whose land the rivers divide.

³ All you inhabitants of the world,
       you who dwell on the earth,
   when a signal is raised on the mountains, look!
       When a trumpet is blown, hear!
⁴ For thus the LORD said to me:
   "I will quietly look from my dwelling
       like clear heat in sunshine,
       like a cloud of dew in the heat of harvest."
⁵ For before the harvest, when the blossom is over,
       and the flower becomes a ripening grape,
   he cuts off the shoots with pruning hooks,
       and the spreading branches he lops off and clears away.
⁶ They shall all of them be left
       to the birds of prey of the mountains
       and to the beasts of the earth.

---

¹ Or though you carefully fence them ² Or will be a heap ³ Probably Nubia

And the birds of prey will summer on them,
>   and all the beasts of the earth will winter on them.

7At that time tribute will be brought to the LORD of hosts

from a people tall and smooth,
>   from a people feared near and far,
a nation mighty and conquering,
>   whose land the rivers divide,

to Mount Zion, the place of the name of the LORD of hosts.

> **Egypt also gets its comeuppance** [chapters 19–20]. The movement of God's engine of
> judgment through the eastern Mediterranean region continues with an extended proph-
> ecy against Egypt. Verses 19–25 of chapter 19, which picture a conversion of people
> within Egypt, set up a momentary countermovement, but when that particular prophecy
> will be fulfilled remains mysterious. As we read the oracles against the nations, at the
> level of content and application we need to look beyond the specific historical references
> to what is universal—to an analysis of what things displease God and how God deals
> with the things that offend his holiness.

19 An oracle concerning Egypt.

Behold, the LORD is riding on a swift cloud
>   and comes to Egypt;
and the idols of Egypt will tremble at his presence,
>   and the heart of the Egyptians will melt within them.
2   And I will stir up Egyptians against Egyptians,
>   and they will fight, each against another
>   and each against his neighbor,
>   city against city, kingdom against kingdom;
3   and the spirit of the Egyptians within them will be emptied out,
>   and I will confound[1] their counsel;
>   and they will inquire of the idols and the sorcerers,
>   and the mediums and the necromancers;
4   and I will give over the Egyptians
>   into the hand of a hard master,
>   and a fierce king will rule over them,
>   declares the Lord GOD of hosts.

5   And the waters of the sea will be dried up,
>   and the river will be dry and parched,
6   and its canals will become foul,
>   and the branches of Egypt's Nile will diminish and dry up,
>   reeds and rushes will rot away.
7   There will be bare places by the Nile,
>   on the brink of the Nile,
>   and all that is sown by the Nile will be parched,

---

1 Or I will swallow up

will be driven away, and will be no more.

8   The fishermen will mourn and lament,
        all who cast a hook in the Nile;
      and they will languish
        who spread nets on the water.
9   The workers in combed flax will be in despair,
        and the weavers of white cotton.
10   Those who are the pillars of the land will be crushed,
        and all who work for pay will be grieved.

11   The princes of Zoan are utterly foolish;
        the wisest counselors of Pharaoh give stupid counsel.
      How can you say to Pharaoh,
        "I am a son of the wise,
        a son of ancient kings"?
12   Where then are your wise men?
        Let them tell you
        that they might know what the Lord of hosts has purposed against Egypt.
13   The princes of Zoan have become fools,
        and the princes of Memphis are deluded;
      those who are the cornerstones of her tribes
        have made Egypt stagger.
14   The Lord has mingled within her a spirit of confusion,
        and they will make Egypt stagger in all its deeds,
        as a drunken man staggers in his vomit.
15   And there will be nothing for Egypt
        that head or tail, palm branch or reed, may do.

¹⁶In that day the Egyptians will be like women, and tremble with fear before the hand that the Lord of hosts shakes over them. ¹⁷And the land of Judah will become a terror to the Egyptians. Everyone to whom it is mentioned will fear because of the purpose that the Lord of hosts has purposed against them.

¹⁸In that day there will be five cities in the land of Egypt that speak the language of Canaan and swear allegiance to the Lord of hosts. One of these will be called the City of Destruction.¹

¹⁹In that day there will be an altar to the Lord in the midst of the land of Egypt, and a pillar to the Lord at its border. ²⁰It will be a sign and a witness to the Lord of hosts in the land of Egypt. When they cry to the Lord because of oppressors, he will send them a savior and defender, and deliver them. ²¹And the Lord will make himself known to the Egyptians, and the Egyptians will know the Lord in that day and worship with sacrifice and offering, and they will make vows to the Lord and perform them. ²²And the Lord will strike Egypt, striking and healing, and they will return to the Lord, and he will listen to their pleas for mercy and heal them.

²³In that day there will be a highway from Egypt to Assyria, and Assyria will come into Egypt, and Egypt into Assyria, and the Egyptians will worship with the Assyrians.

²⁴In that day Israel will be the third with Egypt and Assyria, a blessing in the midst

---

¹ Dead Sea Scroll and some other manuscripts *City of the Sun*

of the earth, ²⁵whom the LORD of hosts has blessed, saying, "Blessed be Egypt my people, and Assyria the work of my hands, and Israel my inheritance."

20

In the year that the commander in chief, who was sent by Sargon the king of Assyria, came to Ashdod and fought against it and captured it— ²at that time the LORD spoke by Isaiah the son of Amoz, saying, "Go, and loose the sackcloth from your waist and take off your sandals from your feet," and he did so, walking naked and barefoot.

³Then the LORD said, "As my servant Isaiah has walked naked and barefoot for three years as a sign and a portent against Egypt and Cush,¹ ⁴so shall the king of Assyria lead away the Egyptian captives and the Cushite exiles, both the young and the old, naked and barefoot, with buttocks uncovered, the nakedness of Egypt. ⁵Then they shall be dismayed and ashamed because of Cush their hope and of Egypt their boast. ⁶And the inhabitants of this coastland will say in that day, 'Behold, this is what has happened to those in whom we hoped and to whom we fled for help to be delivered from the king of Assyria! And we, how shall we escape?'"

Still more losers [chapter 21]. The material is cut from the same cloth as the previous chapters and consists of visions of coming destruction for additional nations of the eastern Mediterranean world—Babylon, Dumah (Edom), and Arabia. We can look for variations on the following themes: (1) the evil that nations and civilizations perpetrate; (2) God's disapproval of such evil; (3) God's plan to destroy evil nations.

21

The oracle concerning the wilderness of the sea.

As whirlwinds in the Negeb sweep on,
  it comes from the wilderness,
  from a terrible land.
² A stern vision is told to me;
  the traitor betrays,
  and the destroyer destroys.
Go up, O Elam;
  lay siege, O Media;
all the sighing she has caused
  I bring to an end.
³ Therefore my loins are filled with anguish;
  pangs have seized me,
  like the pangs of a woman in labor;
I am bowed down so that I cannot hear;
  I am dismayed so that I cannot see.
⁴ My heart staggers; horror has appalled me;
  the twilight I longed for
  has been turned for me into trembling.
⁵ They prepare the table,
  they spread the rugs,²
  they eat, they drink.
Arise, O princes;

¹ Probably *Nubia* ² Or *they set the watchman*

oil the shield!
6   For thus the Lord said to me:
"Go, set a watchman;
     let him announce what he sees.
7   When he sees riders, horsemen in pairs,
       riders on donkeys, riders on camels,
     let him listen diligently,
       very diligently."
8   Then he who saw cried out:[1]
"Upon a watchtower I stand, O Lord,
     continually by day,
   and at my post I am stationed
     whole nights.
9   And behold, here come riders,
       horsemen in pairs!"
   And he answered,
     "Fallen, fallen is Babylon;
   and all the carved images of her gods
     he has shattered to the ground."
10   O my threshed and winnowed one,
       what I have heard from the LORD of hosts,
       the God of Israel, I announce to you.

11 The oracle concerning Dumah.

   One is calling to me from Seir,
     "Watchman, what time of the night?
     Watchman, what time of the night?"
12   The watchman says:
   "Morning comes, and also the night.
     If you will inquire, inquire;
     come back again."

13 The oracle concerning Arabia.

   In the thickets in Arabia you will lodge,
     O caravans of Dedanites.
14   To the thirsty bring water;
       meet the fugitive with bread,
       O inhabitants of the land of Tema.
15   For they have fled from the swords,
       from the drawn sword,
     from the bent bow,
       and from the press of battle.

16 For thus the Lord said to me, "Within a year, according to the years of a hired worker, all the glory of Kedar will come to an end. 17 And the remainder of the archers of the mighty men of the sons of Kedar will be few, for the LORD, the God of Israel, has spoken."

---

[1] Dead Sea Scroll, Syriac; Masoretic Text *Then a lion cried out,* or *Then he cried out like a lion*

Judgment of Jerusalem [chapter 22]. While the technique remains the same (visions of judgment), we need to take note that the covenant nation of Judah appears in the list of evil and godless nations that will come within the sweep of God's engine of judgment. This is bad company for the covenant nation.

22

The oracle concerning the valley of vision.

What do you mean that you have gone up,
    all of you, to the housetops,
² you who are full of shoutings,
    tumultuous city, exultant town?
Your slain are not slain with the sword
    or dead in battle.
³ All your leaders have fled together;
    without the bow they were captured.
All of you who were found were captured,
    though they had fled far away.
⁴ Therefore I said:
"Look away from me;
    let me weep bitter tears;
do not labor to comfort me
    concerning the destruction of the daughter of my people."

⁵ For the Lord GOD of hosts has a day
    of tumult and trampling and confusion
    in the valley of vision,
a battering down of walls
    and a shouting to the mountains.
⁶ And Elam bore the quiver
    with chariots and horsemen,
    and Kir uncovered the shield.
⁷ Your choicest valleys were full of chariots,
    and the horsemen took their stand at the gates.
⁸ He has taken away the covering of Judah.

In that day you looked to the weapons of the House of the Forest, ⁹and you saw that the breaches of the city of David were many. You collected the waters of the lower pool, ¹⁰and you counted the houses of Jerusalem, and you broke down the houses to fortify the wall. ¹¹You made a reservoir between the two walls for the water of the old pool. But you did not look to him who did it, or see him who planned it long ago.

¹² In that day the Lord GOD of hosts
    called for weeping and mourning,
    for baldness and wearing sackcloth;
¹³ and behold, joy and gladness,
    killing oxen and slaughtering sheep,
    eating flesh and drinking wine.
"Let us eat and drink,

for tomorrow we die."
¹⁴ The LORD of hosts has revealed himself in my ears:
"Surely this iniquity will not be atoned for you until you die,"
says the Lord GOD of hosts.

¹⁵Thus says the Lord GOD of hosts, "Come, go to this steward, to Shebna, who is over the household, and say to him: ¹⁶What have you to do here, and whom have you here, that you have cut out here a tomb for yourself, you who cut out a tomb on the height and carve a dwelling for yourself in the rock? ¹⁷Behold, the LORD will hurl you away violently, O you strong man. He will seize firm hold on you ¹⁸and whirl you around and around, and throw you like a ball into a wide land. There you shall die, and there shall be your glorious chariots, you shame of your master's house. ¹⁹I will thrust you from your office, and you will be pulled down from your station. ²⁰In that day I will call my servant Eliakim the son of Hilkiah, ²¹and I will clothe him with your robe, and will bind your sash on him, and will commit your authority to his hand. And he shall be a father to the inhabitants of Jerusalem and to the house of Judah. ²²And I will place on his shoulder the key of the house of David. He shall open, and none shall shut; and he shall shut, and none shall open. ²³And I will fasten him like a peg in a secure place, and he will become a throne of honor to his father's house. ²⁴And they will hang on him the whole honor of his father's house, the offspring and issue, every small vessel, from the cups to all the flagons. ²⁵In that day, declares the LORD of hosts, the peg that was fastened in a secure place will give way, and it will be cut down and fall, and the load that was on it will be cut off, for the LORD has spoken."

Doom song for Tyre [chapter 23]. Tyre also receives special treatment, in the form of a *doom song—a poem that prophetically laments the fall of a king or nation still in power at the time of the poem's composition. The doom song is followed by a brief prediction of Tyre's restoration after seventy years (vv. 15–23).

23
The oracle concerning Tyre.

Wail, O ships of Tarshish,
for Tyre is laid waste, without house or harbor!
From the land of Cyprus¹
it is revealed to them.
² Be still, O inhabitants of the coast;
the merchants of Sidon, who cross the sea, have filled you.
³ And on many waters
your revenue was the grain of Shihor,
the harvest of the Nile;
you were the merchant of the nations.
⁴ Be ashamed, O Sidon, for the sea has spoken,
the stronghold of the sea, saying:
"I have neither labored nor given birth,
I have neither reared young men
nor brought up young women."
⁵ When the report comes to Egypt,

¹ Hebrew *Kittim*; also verse 12

they will be in anguish¹ over the report about Tyre.
6   Cross over to Tarshish;
        wail, O inhabitants of the coast!
7   Is this your exultant city
        whose origin is from days of old,
    whose feet carried her
        to settle far away?
8   Who has purposed this
        against Tyre, the bestower of crowns,
    whose merchants were princes,
        whose traders were the honored of the earth?
9   The Lord of hosts has purposed it,
        to defile the pompous pride of all glory,²
        to dishonor all the honored of the earth.
10 Cross over your land like the Nile,
        O daughter of Tarshish;
        there is no restraint anymore.
11 He has stretched out his hand over the sea;
        he has shaken the kingdoms;
    the Lord has given command concerning Canaan
        to destroy its strongholds.
12 And he said:
    "You will no more exult,
        O oppressed virgin daughter of Sidon;
    arise, cross over to Cyprus,
        even there you will have no rest."

¹³Behold the land of the Chaldeans! This is the people that was not;³ Assyria destined it for wild beasts. They erected their siege towers, they stripped her palaces bare, they made her a ruin.

14 Wail, O ships of Tarshish,
        for your stronghold is laid waste.

¹⁵In that day Tyre will be forgotten for seventy years, like the days⁴ of one king. At the end of seventy years, it will happen to Tyre as in the song of the prostitute:

16 "Take a harp;
        go about the city,
        O forgotten prostitute!
    Make sweet melody;
        sing many songs,
        that you may be remembered."

¹⁷At the end of seventy years, the Lord will visit Tyre, and she will return to her wages and will prostitute herself with all the kingdoms of the world on the face of the earth. ¹⁸Her merchandise and her wages will be holy to the Lord. It will not be stored or hoarded, but her merchandise will supply abundant food and fine clothing for those who dwell before the Lord.

---

¹ Hebrew *they will have labor pains* ² The Hebrew words for *glory* and *hosts* sound alike ³ Or *that has become nothing* ⁴ Or *lifetime*

Summary [chapter 24]. After the extended block of oracles of judgment connected to specific nations, chapter 24 moves to an overview—an apocalyptic vision of God's judgment of the whole earth. The chapter is a vivid and terrifying vision of cosmic destruction. Intermingled are brief glimpses of salvation (vv. 14–16; 23b).

24 Behold, the LORD will empty the earth[1] and make it desolate,
and he will twist its surface and scatter its inhabitants.
2 And it shall be, as with the people, so with the priest;
as with the slave, so with his master;
as with the maid, so with her mistress;
as with the buyer, so with the seller;
as with the lender, so with the borrower;
as with the creditor, so with the debtor.
3 The earth shall be utterly empty and utterly plundered;
for the LORD has spoken this word.

4 The earth mourns and withers;
the world languishes and withers;
the highest people of the earth languish.
5 The earth lies defiled
under its inhabitants;
for they have transgressed the laws,
violated the statutes,
broken the everlasting covenant.
6 Therefore a curse devours the earth,
and its inhabitants suffer for their guilt;
therefore the inhabitants of the earth are scorched,
and few men are left.
7 The wine mourns,
the vine languishes,
all the merry-hearted sigh.
8 The mirth of the tambourines is stilled,
the noise of the jubilant has ceased,
the mirth of the lyre is stilled.
9 No more do they drink wine with singing;
strong drink is bitter to those who drink it.
10 The wasted city is broken down;
every house is shut up so that none can enter.
11 There is an outcry in the streets for lack of wine;
all joy has grown dark;
the gladness of the earth is banished.
12 Desolation is left in the city;
the gates are battered into ruins.
13 For thus it shall be in the midst of the earth
among the nations,
as when an olive tree is beaten,
as at the gleaning when the grape harvest is done.

---

[1] Or *land*; also throughout this chapter

14 They lift up their voices, they sing for joy;
        over the majesty of the LORD they shout from the west.[1]
15 Therefore in the east[2] give glory to the LORD;
        in the coastlands of the sea, give glory to the name of the LORD, the God of Israel.
16 From the ends of the earth we hear songs of praise,
        of glory to the Righteous One.
    But I say, "I waste away,
        I waste away. Woe is me!
    For the traitors have betrayed,
        with betrayal the traitors have betrayed."

17 Terror and the pit and the snare[3]
        are upon you, O inhabitant of the earth!
18 He who flees at the sound of the terror
        shall fall into the pit,
    and he who climbs out of the pit
        shall be caught in the snare.
    For the windows of heaven are opened,
        and the foundations of the earth tremble.
19 The earth is utterly broken,
        the earth is split apart,
        the earth is violently shaken.
20 The earth staggers like a drunken man;
        it sways like a hut;
    its transgression lies heavy upon it,
        and it falls, and will not rise again.

21 On that day the LORD will punish
        the host of heaven, in heaven,
        and the kings of the earth, on the earth.
22 They will be gathered together
        as prisoners in a pit;
    they will be shut up in a prison,
        and after many days they will be punished.
23 Then the moon will be confounded
        and the sun ashamed,
    for the LORD of hosts reigns
        on Mount Zion and in Jerusalem,
    and his glory will be before his elders.

A vision of restoration [chapter 25]. After the terrifying visions of God's judgment against the evil nations, this vision of God's plan for deliverance comes as a breath of fresh air in the ongoing progress of the book of Isaiah. The specific forms in which given units of Isaiah are expressed is quite varied, from the impersonal formula "The oracle concerning . . . ," to statements by the prophet in his own person, to the report formula "The LORD said to me . . ." The first half of chapter 25 (vv. 1–5) is a prayer expressed by a speaker directly to God, while the second half is a straightforward narrative of what will happen in the future.

---

[1] Hebrew *from the sea* [2] Hebrew *in the realm of light* [3] The Hebrew words for *terror, pit,* and *snare* sound alike

25

O LORD, you are my God;
I will exalt you; I will praise your name,
for you have done wonderful things,
plans formed of old, faithful and sure.

2 For you have made the city a heap,
the fortified city a ruin;
the foreigners' palace is a city no more;
it will never be rebuilt.

3 Therefore strong peoples will glorify you;
cities of ruthless nations will fear you.

4 For you have been a stronghold to the poor,
a stronghold to the needy in his distress,
a shelter from the storm and a shade from the heat;
for the breath of the ruthless is like a storm against a wall,

5 like heat in a dry place.
You subdue the noise of the foreigners;
as heat by the shade of a cloud,
so the song of the ruthless is put down.

6 On this mountain the LORD of hosts will make for all peoples
a feast of rich food, a feast of well-aged wine,
of rich food full of marrow, of aged wine well refined.

7 And he will swallow up on this mountain
the covering that is cast over all peoples,
the veil that is spread over all nations.

8 He will swallow up death forever;
and the Lord GOD will wipe away tears from all faces,
and the reproach of his people he will take away from all the earth,
for the LORD has spoken.

9 It will be said on that day,
"Behold, this is our God; we have waited for him, that he might save us.
This is the LORD; we have waited for him;
let us be glad and rejoice in his salvation."

10 For the hand of the LORD will rest on this mountain,
and Moab shall be trampled down in his place,
as straw is trampled down in a dunghill.[1]

11 And he will spread out his hands in the midst of it
as a swimmer spreads his hands out to swim,
but the LORD will lay low his pompous pride together with the skill[2] of his hands.

12 And the high fortifications of his walls he will bring down,
lay low, and cast to the ground, to the dust.

Oracles of salvation [chapters 26–27]. Both chapters are couched in the formula of what will happen "in that day" (26:1; 27:1, 2, 12, 13) or "in days to come" (27:6), signaling future action as the subject. Whereas in much prophetic literature the "day of the LORD" motif announces judgment and destruction, in these two chapters the motif involves God's coming in saving grace. In poetry such as we find here, the images and

---

[1] The Hebrew words for *dunghill* and for the Moabite town *Madmen* (Jeremiah 48:2) sound alike   [2] Or *in spite of the skill*

metaphors are what pack the punch, so we need to ponder what images make up the good life of God's blessing.

26

In that day this song will be sung in the land of Judah:

"We have a strong city;
    he sets up salvation
    as walls and bulwarks.
2 Open the gates,
    that the righteous nation that keeps faith may enter in.
3 You keep him in perfect peace
    whose mind is stayed on you,
    because he trusts in you.
4 Trust in the LORD forever,
    for the LORD GOD is an everlasting rock.
5 For he has humbled
    the inhabitants of the height,
    the lofty city.
He lays it low, lays it low to the ground,
    casts it to the dust.
6 The foot tramples it,
    the feet of the poor,
    the steps of the needy."

7 The path of the righteous is level;
    you make level the way of the righteous.
8 In the path of your judgments,
    O LORD, we wait for you;
your name and remembrance
    are the desire of our soul.
9 My soul yearns for you in the night;
    my spirit within me earnestly seeks you.
For when your judgments are in the earth,
    the inhabitants of the world learn righteousness.
10 If favor is shown to the wicked,
    he does not learn righteousness;
in the land of uprightness he deals corruptly
    and does not see the majesty of the LORD.
11 O LORD, your hand is lifted up,
    but they do not see it.
Let them see your zeal for your people, and be ashamed.
    Let the fire for your adversaries consume them.
12 O LORD, you will ordain peace for us,
    for you have indeed done for us all our works.
13 O LORD our God,
    other lords besides you have ruled over us,
    but your name alone we bring to remembrance.

14   They are dead, they will not live;
            they are shades, they will not arise;
        to that end you have visited them with destruction
            and wiped out all remembrance of them.
15   But you have increased the nation, O LORD,
            you have increased the nation; you are glorified;
            you have enlarged all the borders of the land.

16   O LORD, in distress they sought you;
            they poured out a whispered prayer
            when your discipline was upon them.
17   Like a pregnant woman
            who writhes and cries out in her pangs
            when she is near to giving birth,
        so were we because of you, O LORD;
18   we were pregnant, we writhed,
            but we have given birth to wind.
        We have accomplished no deliverance in the earth,
            and the inhabitants of the world have not fallen.
19   Your dead shall live; their bodies shall rise.
            You who dwell in the dust, awake and sing for joy!
        For your dew is a dew of light,
            and the earth will give birth to the dead.

20   Come, my people, enter your chambers,
            and shut your doors behind you;
        hide yourselves for a little while
            until the fury has passed by.
21   For behold, the LORD is coming out from his place
            to punish the inhabitants of the earth for their iniquity,
        and the earth will disclose the blood shed on it,
            and will no more cover its slain.

27

In that day the LORD with his hard and great and strong sword will punish Leviathan the fleeing serpent, Leviathan the twisting serpent, and he will slay the dragon that is in the sea.

2   In that day,
        "A pleasant vineyard,[1] sing of it!
3   I, the LORD, am its keeper;
            every moment I water it.
            Lest anyone punish it,
        I keep it night and day;
4   I have no wrath.
        Would that I had thorns and briers to battle!
            I would march against them,
            I would burn them up together.
5   Or let them lay hold of my protection,

---
[1] Many Hebrew manuscripts *A vineyard of wine*

> let them make peace with me,
> let them make peace with me."

⁶ In days to come¹ Jacob shall take root,
   Israel shall blossom and put forth shoots
   and fill the whole world with fruit.

⁷ Has he struck them as he struck those who struck them?
   Or have they been slain as their slayers were slain?
⁸ Measure by measure,² by exile you contended with them;
   he removed them with his fierce breath³ in the day of the east wind.
⁹ Therefore by this the guilt of Jacob will be atoned for,
   and this will be the full fruit of the removal of his sin:⁴
when he makes all the stones of the altars
   like chalkstones crushed to pieces,
   no Asherim or incense altars will remain standing.
¹⁰ For the fortified city is solitary,
   a habitation deserted and forsaken, like the wilderness;
there the calf grazes;
   there it lies down and strips its branches.
¹¹ When its boughs are dry, they are broken;
   women come and make a fire of them.
For this is a people without discernment;
   therefore he who made them will not have compassion on them;
   he who formed them will show them no favor.

¹²In that day from the river Euphrates to the Brook of Egypt the Lᴏʀᴅ will thresh out the grain, and you will be gleaned one by one, O people of Israel. ¹³And in that day a great trumpet will be blown, and those who were lost in the land of Assyria and those who were driven out to the land of Egypt will come and worship the Lᴏʀᴅ on the holy mountain at Jerusalem.

Back to judgment [chapter 28]. In the back-and-forth rhythm of the book as a whole, the pendulum now swings back to visions of judgment. Chapter 28 has three distinct subjects—pronouncement of woe to drunkards of Ephraim (vv. 1–8), prediction of judgment for the scoffers of Jerusalem (vv. 9–22), and an analogy of the type we find in *wisdom literature that asserts that God's judgment will be measured and reasonable (vv. 23–29).

28   Ah, the proud crown of the drunkards of Ephraim,
   and the fading flower of its glorious beauty,
   which is on the head of the rich valley of those overcome with wine!
² Behold, the Lord has one who is mighty and strong;
   like a storm of hail, a destroying tempest,
like a storm of mighty, overflowing waters,
   he casts down to the earth with his hand.
³ The proud crown of the drunkards of Ephraim

¹ Hebrew *In those to come* ² Or *By driving her away*; the meaning of the Hebrew word is uncertain ³ Or *wind* ⁴ Septuagint *and this is the blessing when I take away his sin*

will be trodden underfoot;
⁴ and the fading flower of its glorious beauty,
   which is on the head of the rich valley,
  will be like a first-ripe fig before the summer:
   when someone sees it, he swallows it
   as soon as it is in his hand.

⁵ In that day the LORD of hosts will be a crown of glory,[1]
   and a diadem of beauty, to the remnant of his people,
⁶ and a spirit of justice to him who sits in judgment,
   and strength to those who turn back the battle at the gate.

⁷ These also reel with wine
   and stagger with strong drink;
  the priest and the prophet reel with strong drink,
   they are swallowed by[2] wine,
   they stagger with strong drink,
  they reel in vision,
   they stumble in giving judgment.
⁸ For all tables are full of filthy vomit,
   with no space left.

⁹ "To whom will he teach knowledge,
   and to whom will he explain the message?
  Those who are weaned from the milk,
   those taken from the breast?
¹⁰ For it is precept upon precept, precept upon precept,
   line upon line, line upon line,
   here a little, there a little."

¹¹ For by people of strange lips
   and with a foreign tongue
  the LORD will speak to this people,
¹²   to whom he has said,
  "This is rest;
   give rest to the weary;
  and this is repose";
   yet they would not hear.
¹³ And the word of the LORD will be to them
  precept upon precept, precept upon precept,
   line upon line, line upon line,
   here a little, there a little,
  that they may go, and fall backward,
   and be broken, and snared, and taken.

¹⁴ Therefore hear the word of the LORD, you scoffers,
   who rule this people in Jerusalem!
¹⁵ Because you have said, "We have made a covenant with death,
   and with Sheol we have an agreement,

---

[1] The Hebrew words for glory and hosts sound alike [2] Or confused by

when the overwhelming whip passes through
    it will not come to us,
for we have made lies our refuge,
    and in falsehood we have taken shelter";
16 therefore thus says the Lord God,
  "Behold, I am the one who has laid[1] as a foundation in Zion,
    a stone, a tested stone,
  a precious cornerstone, of a sure foundation:
    'Whoever believes will not be in haste.'
17 And I will make justice the line,
    and righteousness the plumb line;
  and hail will sweep away the refuge of lies,
    and waters will overwhelm the shelter."
18 Then your covenant with death will be annulled,
    and your agreement with Sheol will not stand;
  when the overwhelming scourge passes through,
    you will be beaten down by it.
19 As often as it passes through it will take you;
    for morning by morning it will pass through,
    by day and by night;
  and it will be sheer terror to understand the message.
20 For the bed is too short to stretch oneself on,
    and the covering too narrow to wrap oneself in.
21 For the Lord will rise up as on Mount Perazim;
    as in the Valley of Gibeon he will be roused;
  to do his deed—strange is his deed!
    and to work his work—alien is his work!
22 Now therefore do not scoff,
    lest your bonds be made strong;
  for I have heard a decree of destruction
    from the Lord God of hosts against the whole land.

23 Give ear, and hear my voice;
    give attention, and hear my speech.
24 Does he who plows for sowing plow continually?
    Does he continually open and harrow his ground?
25 When he has leveled its surface,
    does he not scatter dill, sow cumin,
  and put in wheat in rows
    and barley in its proper place,
    and emmer[2] as the border?
26 For he is rightly instructed;
    his God teaches him.

27 Dill is not threshed with a threshing sledge,
    nor is a cart wheel rolled over cumin,
  but dill is beaten out with a stick,

---

[1] Dead Sea Scroll *I am laying* [2] A type of wheat

and cumin with a rod.
28   Does one crush grain for bread?
          No, he does not thresh it forever;[1]
      when he drives his cart wheel over it
          with his horses, he does not crush it.
29   This also comes from the LORD of hosts;
          he is wonderful in counsel
          and excellent in wisdom.

> **Oracles of judgment** [29:1–30:17]. Two further chapters extend the message of judgment. One way to assimilate the material is to be alert to echoes of themes and techniques from earlier parts of the book. In this unit, nations are still doing their evil, God is still predicting that he will punish them, the prophet is still denouncing alliances with foreign nations, and trusting in God for deliverance is still offered as the only safe course (29:5–8, 17–24).

29
Ah, Ariel, Ariel,
      the city where David encamped!
Add year to year;
      let the feasts run their round.
2   Yet I will distress Ariel,
          and there shall be moaning and lamentation,
          and she shall be to me like an Ariel.[2]
3   And I will encamp against you all around,
          and will besiege you with towers
          and I will raise siegeworks against you.
4   And you will be brought low; from the earth you shall speak,
          and from the dust your speech will be bowed down;
      your voice shall come from the ground like the voice of a ghost,
          and from the dust your speech shall whisper.

5   But the multitude of your foreign foes shall be like small dust,
          and the multitude of the ruthless like passing chaff.
      And in an instant, suddenly,
6   you will be visited by the LORD of hosts
      with thunder and with earthquake and great noise,
          with whirlwind and tempest, and the flame of a devouring fire.
7   And the multitude of all the nations that fight against Ariel,
          all that fight against her and her stronghold and distress her,
          shall be like a dream, a vision of the night.
8   As when a hungry man dreams he is eating
          and awakes with his hunger not satisfied,
      or as when a thirsty man dreams he is drinking
          and awakes faint, with his thirst not quenched,
      so shall the multitude of all the nations be
          that fight against Mount Zion.

[1] Or *Grain is crushed for bread; he will surely thresh it, but not forever* [2] *Ariel* could mean *lion of God*, or *hero* (2 Samuel 23:20), or *altar hearth* (Ezekiel 43:15-16).

9   Astonish yourselves[1] and be astonished;
         blind yourselves and be blind!
     Be drunk, but not with wine;
         stagger, but not with strong drink!
10   For the LORD has poured out upon you
         a spirit of deep sleep,
     and has closed your eyes (the prophets),
         and covered your heads (the seers).

[11]And the vision of all this has become to you like the words of a book that is sealed. When men give it to one who can read, saying, "Read this," he says, "I cannot, for it is sealed." [12]And when they give the book to one who cannot read, saying, "Read this," he says, "I cannot read."

13   And the Lord said:
     "Because this people draw near with their mouth
         and honor me with their lips,
         while their hearts are far from me,
     and their fear of me is a commandment taught by men,
14   therefore, behold, I will again
         do wonderful things with this people,
         with wonder upon wonder;
     and the wisdom of their wise men shall perish,
         and the discernment of their discerning men shall be hidden."

15   Ah, you who hide deep from the LORD your counsel,
         whose deeds are in the dark,
         and who say, "Who sees us? Who knows us?"
16   You turn things upside down!
     Shall the potter be regarded as the clay,
     that the thing made should say of its maker,
         "He did not make me";
     or the thing formed say of him who formed it,
         "He has no understanding"?

17   Is it not yet a very little while
         until Lebanon shall be turned into a fruitful field,
         and the fruitful field shall be regarded as a forest?
18   In that day the deaf shall hear
         the words of a book,
     and out of their gloom and darkness
         the eyes of the blind shall see.
19   The meek shall obtain fresh joy in the LORD,
         and the poor among mankind shall exult in the Holy One of Israel.
20   For the ruthless shall come to nothing
         and the scoffer cease,
         and all who watch to do evil shall be cut off,
21   who by a word make a man out to be an offender,

---

[1] Or *Linger awhile*

and lay a snare for him who reproves in the gate,
and with an empty plea turn aside him who is in the right.

[22]Therefore thus says the LORD, who redeemed Abraham, concerning the house of Jacob:

"Jacob shall no more be ashamed,
no more shall his face grow pale.
[23]   For when he sees his children,
the work of my hands, in his midst,
they will sanctify my name;
they will sanctify the Holy One of Jacob
and will stand in awe of the God of Israel.
[24]   And those who go astray in spirit will come to understanding,
and those who murmur will accept instruction."

30 "Ah, stubborn children," declares the LORD,
"who carry out a plan, but not mine,
and who make an alliance,[1] but not of my Spirit,
that they may add sin to sin;
[2]   who set out to go down to Egypt,
without asking for my direction,
to take refuge in the protection of Pharaoh
and to seek shelter in the shadow of Egypt!
[3]   Therefore shall the protection of Pharaoh turn to your shame,
and the shelter in the shadow of Egypt to your humiliation.
[4]   For though his officials are at Zoan
and his envoys reach Hanes,
[5]   everyone comes to shame
through a people that cannot profit them,
that brings neither help nor profit,
but shame and disgrace."

[6]An oracle on the beasts of the Negeb.

Through a land of trouble and anguish,
from where come the lioness and the lion,
the adder and the flying fiery serpent,
they carry their riches on the backs of donkeys,
and their treasures on the humps of camels,
to a people that cannot profit them.
[7]   Egypt's help is worthless and empty;
therefore I have called her
"Rahab who sits still."

[8]   And now, go, write it before them on a tablet
and inscribe it in a book,
that it may be for the time to come
as a witness forever.[2]

---

[1] Hebrew *who weave a web* [2] Some Hebrew manuscripts, Syriac, Targum, Vulgate, and Greek versions; Masoretic Text *forever and ever*

⁹ For they are a rebellious people,
    lying children,
    children unwilling to hear
      the instruction of the LORD;
¹⁰ who say to the seers, "Do not see,"
    and to the prophets, "Do not prophesy to us what is right;
    speak to us smooth things,
      prophesy illusions,
¹¹ leave the way, turn aside from the path,
    let us hear no more about the Holy One of Israel."
¹² Therefore thus says the Holy One of Israel,
    "Because you despise this word
      and trust in oppression and perverseness
      and rely on them,
¹³ therefore this iniquity shall be to you
      like a breach in a high wall, bulging out, and about to collapse,
      whose breaking comes suddenly, in an instant;
¹⁴ and its breaking is like that of a potter's vessel
      that is smashed so ruthlessly
    that among its fragments not a shard is found
      with which to take fire from the hearth,
      or to dip up water out of the cistern."

¹⁵ For thus said the Lord GOD, the Holy One of Israel,
    "In returning¹ and rest you shall be saved;
      in quietness and in trust shall be your strength."
    But you were unwilling, ¹⁶and you said,
    "No! We will flee upon horses";
      therefore you shall flee away;
    and, "We will ride upon swift steeds";
      therefore your pursuers shall be swift.
¹⁷ A thousand shall flee at the threat of one;
      at the threat of five you shall flee,
    till you are left
      like a flagstaff on the top of a mountain,
      like a signal on a hill.

Oracles of salvation [30:18–32:20]. In yet another mood swing, the prophet shifts his focus to assurances and pictures of God's restoration of his people (despite a brief fragment of judgment in 31:1–3). The first thing to do is simply to be receptive to the effect of the images and pictures. Then we can begin to analyze the specific images and techniques by which the text instills those feelings. An additional analytic grid is to look for a dialectical dialogue between the oracles of judgment and redemption—ways in which the oracles of redemption reverse or are opposites to the oracles of judgment.

¹⁸ Therefore the LORD waits to be gracious to you,
      and therefore he exalts himself to show mercy to you.

¹ Or repentance

> For the Lord is a God of justice;
> blessed are all those who wait for him.

[19] For a people shall dwell in Zion, in Jerusalem; you shall weep no more. He will surely be gracious to you at the sound of your cry. As soon as he hears it, he answers you. [20] And though the Lord give you the bread of adversity and the water of affliction, yet your Teacher will not hide himself anymore, but your eyes shall see your Teacher. [21] And your ears shall hear a word behind you, saying, "This is the way, walk in it," when you turn to the right or when you turn to the left. [22] Then you will defile your carved idols overlaid with silver and your gold-plated metal images. You will scatter them as unclean things. You will say to them, "Be gone!"

[23] And he will give rain for the seed with which you sow the ground, and bread, the produce of the ground, which will be rich and plenteous. In that day your livestock will graze in large pastures, [24] and the oxen and the donkeys that work the ground will eat seasoned fodder, which has been winnowed with shovel and fork. [25] And on every lofty mountain and every high hill there will be brooks running with water, in the day of the great slaughter, when the towers fall. [26] Moreover, the light of the moon will be as the light of the sun, and the light of the sun will be sevenfold, as the light of seven days, in the day when the Lord binds up the brokenness of his people, and heals the wounds inflicted by his blow.

[27]   Behold, the name of the Lord comes from afar,
> burning with his anger, and in thick rising smoke;[1]
> his lips are full of fury,
> and his tongue is like a devouring fire;
[28]   his breath is like an overflowing stream
> that reaches up to the neck;
> to sift the nations with the sieve of destruction,
> and to place on the jaws of the peoples a bridle that leads astray.

[29] You shall have a song as in the night when a holy feast is kept, and gladness of heart, as when one sets out to the sound of the flute to go to the mountain of the Lord, to the Rock of Israel. [30] And the Lord will cause his majestic voice to be heard and the descending blow of his arm to be seen, in furious anger and a flame of devouring fire, with a cloudburst and storm and hailstones. [31] The Assyrians will be terror-stricken at the voice of the Lord, when he strikes with his rod. [32] And every stroke of the appointed staff that the Lord lays on them will be to the sound of tambourines and lyres. Battling with brandished arm, he will fight with them. [33] For a burning place[2] has long been prepared; indeed, for the king it is made ready, its pyre made deep and wide, with fire and wood in abundance; the breath of the Lord, like a stream of sulfur, kindles it.

31

Woe to those who go down to Egypt for help
and rely on horses,
> who trust in chariots because they are many
> and in horsemen because they are very strong,
> but do not look to the Holy One of Israel
> or consult the Lord!

---

[1] Hebrew *in weight of uplifted clouds* [2] Or *For Topheth*

² And yet he is wise and brings disaster;
  he does not call back his words,
but will arise against the house of the evildoers
  and against the helpers of those who work iniquity.
³ The Egyptians are man, and not God,
  and their horses are flesh, and not spirit.
When the Lᴏʀᴅ stretches out his hand,
  the helper will stumble, and he who is helped will fall,
  and they will all perish together.

⁴ For thus the Lᴏʀᴅ said to me,
  "As a lion or a young lion growls over his prey,
  and when a band of shepherds is called out against him
he is not terrified by their shouting
  or daunted at their noise,
so the Lᴏʀᴅ of hosts will come down
  to fight[1] on Mount Zion and on its hill.
⁵ Like birds hovering, so the Lᴏʀᴅ of hosts
  will protect Jerusalem;
he will protect and deliver it;
  he will spare and rescue it."

⁶Turn to him from whom people[2] have deeply revolted, O children of Israel. ⁷For in that day everyone shall cast away his idols of silver and his idols of gold, which your hands have sinfully made for you.

⁸ "And the Assyrian shall fall by a sword, not of man;
  and a sword, not of man, shall devour him;
and he shall flee from the sword,
  and his young men shall be put to forced labor.
⁹ His rock shall pass away in terror,
  and his officers desert the standard in panic,"
declares the Lᴏʀᴅ, whose fire is in Zion,
  and whose furnace is in Jerusalem.

32
Behold, a king will reign in righteousness,
  and princes will rule in justice.
² Each will be like a hiding place from the wind,
  a shelter from the storm,
like streams of water in a dry place,
  like the shade of a great rock in a weary land.
³ Then the eyes of those who see will not be closed,
  and the ears of those who hear will give attention.
⁴ The heart of the hasty will understand and know,
  and the tongue of the stammerers will hasten to speak distinctly.
⁵ The fool will no more be called noble,
  nor the scoundrel said to be honorable.
⁶ For the fool speaks folly,

---

[1] The Hebrew words for *hosts* and *to fight* sound alike [2] Hebrew *they*

and his heart is busy with iniquity,
    to practice ungodliness,
        to utter error concerning the LORD,
    to leave the craving of the hungry unsatisfied,
        and to deprive the thirsty of drink.
7 As for the scoundrel—his devices are evil;
        he plans wicked schemes
    to ruin the poor with lying words,
        even when the plea of the needy is right.
8 But he who is noble plans noble things,
        and on noble things he stands.

9 Rise up, you women who are at ease, hear my voice;
        you complacent daughters, give ear to my speech.
10 In little more than a year
        you will shudder, you complacent women;
    for the grape harvest fails,
        the fruit harvest will not come.
11 Tremble, you women who are at ease,
        shudder, you complacent ones;
    strip, and make yourselves bare,
        and tie sackcloth around your waist.
12 Beat your breasts for the pleasant fields,
        for the fruitful vine,
13 for the soil of my people
        growing up in thorns and briers,
    yes, for all the joyous houses
        in the exultant city.
14 For the palace is forsaken,
        the populous city deserted;
    the hill and the watchtower
        will become dens forever,
    a joy of wild donkeys,
        a pasture of flocks;
15 until the Spirit is poured upon us from on high,
        and the wilderness becomes a fruitful field,
        and the fruitful field is deemed a forest.
16 Then justice will dwell in the wilderness,
        and righteousness abide in the fruitful field.
17 And the effect of righteousness will be peace,
        and the result of righteousness, quietness and trust[1] forever.
18 My people will abide in a peaceful habitation,
        in secure dwellings, and in quiet resting places.
19 And it will hail when the forest falls down,
        and the city will be utterly laid low.
20 Happy are you who sow beside all waters,
        who let the feet of the ox and the donkey range free.

---

[1] Or security

Recapitulation [chapters 33–34]. In the ongoing flow of the book of Isaiah, we are here reaching the end of the predominantly negative section of the prophecy. With the foregoing visions of evil and judgment as a context, we can read these two chapters as a summing up of God's judicial case against sinful humanity and his blueprint for action against it. The objects of satiric attack are the literary vehicle by which the prophet shows us the things of which God disapproves. The emerging portrait of God as judge is reconfirmed in these chapters. And to remind us of how fluid the structure of the book is—how thoroughly it uses the technique of stream of consciousness—right in the middle of the visions of judgment is a messianic and/or eschatological vision of a coming golden age (33:17–24).

33

Ah, you destroyer,
who yourself have not been destroyed,
you traitor,
whom none has betrayed!
When you have ceased to destroy,
you will be destroyed;
and when you have finished betraying,
they will betray you.

2 O Lord, be gracious to us; we wait for you.
Be our arm every morning,
our salvation in the time of trouble.
3 At the tumultuous noise peoples flee;
when you lift yourself up, nations are scattered,
4 and your spoil is gathered as the caterpillar gathers;
as locusts leap, it is leapt upon.

5 The Lord is exalted, for he dwells on high;
he will fill Zion with justice and righteousness,
6 and he will be the stability of your times,
abundance of salvation, wisdom, and knowledge;
the fear of the Lord is Zion's[1] treasure.

7 Behold, their heroes cry in the streets;
the envoys of peace weep bitterly.
8 The highways lie waste;
the traveler ceases.
Covenants are broken;
cities[2] are despised;
there is no regard for man.
9 The land mourns and languishes;
Lebanon is confounded and withers away;
Sharon is like a desert,
and Bashan and Carmel shake off their leaves.

10 "Now I will arise," says the Lord,
"now I will lift myself up;
now I will be exalted.

[1] Hebrew his [2] Masoretic Text; Dead Sea Scroll *witnesses*

¹¹ You conceive chaff; you give birth to stubble;
  your breath is a fire that will consume you.
¹² And the peoples will be as if burned to lime,
  like thorns cut down, that are burned in the fire."

¹³ Hear, you who are far off, what I have done;
  and you who are near, acknowledge my might.
¹⁴ The sinners in Zion are afraid;
  trembling has seized the godless:
 "Who among us can dwell with the consuming fire?
  Who among us can dwell with everlasting burnings?"
¹⁵ He who walks righteously and speaks uprightly,
  who despises the gain of oppressions,
 who shakes his hands, lest they hold a bribe,
  who stops his ears from hearing of bloodshed
  and shuts his eyes from looking on evil,
¹⁶ he will dwell on the heights;
  his place of defense will be the fortresses of rocks;
  his bread will be given him; his water will be sure.

¹⁷ Your eyes will behold the king in his beauty;
  they will see a land that stretches afar.
¹⁸ Your heart will muse on the terror:
 "Where is he who counted, where is he who weighed the tribute?
  Where is he who counted the towers?"
¹⁹ You will see no more the insolent people,
  the people of an obscure speech that you cannot comprehend,
  stammering in a tongue that you cannot understand.
²⁰ Behold Zion, the city of our appointed feasts!
  Your eyes will see Jerusalem,
  an untroubled habitation, an immovable tent,
 whose stakes will never be plucked up,
  nor will any of its cords be broken.
²¹ But there the Lᴏʀᴅ in majesty will be for us
  a place of broad rivers and streams,
 where no galley with oars can go,
  nor majestic ship can pass.
²² For the Lᴏʀᴅ is our judge; the Lᴏʀᴅ is our lawgiver;
  the Lᴏʀᴅ is our king; he will save us.

²³ Your cords hang loose;
  they cannot hold the mast firm in its place
  or keep the sail spread out.
 Then prey and spoil in abundance will be divided;
  even the lame will take the prey.
²⁴ And no inhabitant will say, "I am sick";
  the people who dwell there will be forgiven their iniquity.

34

Draw near, O nations, to hear,
   and give attention, O peoples!
Let the earth hear, and all that fills it;
   the world, and all that comes from it.
2   For the LORD is enraged against all the nations,
      and furious against all their host;
   he has devoted them to destruction,[1] has given them over for slaughter.
3   Their slain shall be cast out,
      and the stench of their corpses shall rise;
   the mountains shall flow with their blood.
4   All the host of heaven shall rot away,
      and the skies roll up like a scroll.
   All their host shall fall,
      as leaves fall from the vine,
      like leaves falling from the fig tree.

5   For my sword has drunk its fill in the heavens;
      behold, it descends for judgment upon Edom,
      upon the people I have devoted to destruction.
6   The LORD has a sword; it is sated with blood;
      it is gorged with fat,
      with the blood of lambs and goats,
      with the fat of the kidneys of rams.
   For the LORD has a sacrifice in Bozrah,
      a great slaughter in the land of Edom.
7   Wild oxen shall fall with them,
      and young steers with the mighty bulls.
   Their land shall drink its fill of blood,
      and their soil shall be gorged with fat.

8   For the LORD has a day of vengeance,
      a year of recompense for the cause of Zion.
9   And the streams of Edom[2] shall be turned into pitch,
      and her soil into sulfur;
      her land shall become burning pitch.
10 Night and day it shall not be quenched;
      its smoke shall go up forever.
   From generation to generation it shall lie waste;
      none shall pass through it forever and ever.
11 But the hawk and the porcupine[3] shall possess it,
      the owl and the raven shall dwell in it.
   He shall stretch the line of confusion[4] over it,
      and the plumb line of emptiness.
12 Its nobles—there is no one there to call it a kingdom,
      and all its princes shall be nothing.

---

[1] That is, set apart (devoted) as an offering to the Lord (for destruction); also verse 5 [2] Hebrew *her streams* [3] The identity of the animals rendered *hawk* and *porcupine* is uncertain [4] Hebrew *formlessness*

13 Thorns shall grow over its strongholds,
    nettles and thistles in its fortresses.
  It shall be the haunt of jackals,
    an abode for ostriches.[1]
14 And wild animals shall meet with hyenas;
    the wild goat shall cry to his fellow;
  indeed, there the night bird[2] settles
    and finds for herself a resting place.
15 There the owl nests and lays
    and hatches and gathers her young in her shadow;
  indeed, there the hawks are gathered,
    each one with her mate.
16 Seek and read from the book of the LORD:
    Not one of these shall be missing;
    none shall be without her mate.
  For the mouth of the LORD has commanded,
    and his Spirit has gathered them.
17 He has cast the lot for them;
    his hand has portioned it out to them with the line;
  they shall possess it forever;
    from generation to generation they shall dwell in it.

A famous golden age prophecy [chapter 35]. The first block of oracles ends not with judgment but with an oracle of salvation. It is such a famous poem that virtually every line is a household proverb in the family of the faithful. The vision is a prime example of what literary scholars call ambiguity or open-ended metaphor, meaning that the poetic texture can legitimately be taken to refer to multiple things at the same time. The images of a coming golden age in this chapter can be interpreted as a vision of (a) God's blessings on all who believe in him and follow his ways, (b) the salvation and blessings that descended on the human race when Christ came to earth and earned its salvation, and (c) the future, eschatological state of the millennium and/or eternity in heaven.

35 The wilderness and the dry land shall be glad;
    the desert shall rejoice and blossom like the crocus;
2 it shall blossom abundantly
    and rejoice with joy and singing.
  The glory of Lebanon shall be given to it,
    the majesty of Carmel and Sharon.
  They shall see the glory of the LORD,
    the majesty of our God.

3 Strengthen the weak hands,
    and make firm the feeble knees.
4 Say to those who have an anxious heart,
    "Be strong; fear not!
  Behold, your God

---

[1] Or owls [2] Identity uncertain

will come with vengeance,
    with the recompense of God.
    He will come and save you."

5   Then the eyes of the blind shall be opened,
        and the ears of the deaf unstopped;
6   then shall the lame man leap like a deer,
        and the tongue of the mute sing for joy.
    For waters break forth in the wilderness,
        and streams in the desert;
7   the burning sand shall become a pool,
        and the thirsty ground springs of water;
    in the haunt of jackals, where they lie down,
        the grass shall become reeds and rushes.

8   And a highway shall be there,
        and it shall be called the Way of Holiness;
    the unclean shall not pass over it.
        It shall belong to those who walk on the way;
        even if they are fools, they shall not go astray.[1]
9   No lion shall be there,
        nor shall any ravenous beast come up on it;
    they shall not be found there,
        but the redeemed shall walk there.
10 And the ransomed of the LORD shall return
        and come to Zion with singing;
    everlasting joy shall be upon their heads;
        they shall obtain gladness and joy,
        and sorrow and sighing shall flee away.

Narrative interlude [chapters 36–37]. The author now springs a surprise on us. It is not unexpected to find snatches of narrative in prophetic books, but chapters 36–39 of Isaiah are transported right out of a historical chronicle (2 Kings 18–20) and dropped into the middle of Isaiah's anthology of prophetic oracles. The status of the encyclopedic book of Isaiah as an anthology makes it easier for us to assimilate this unexpected development. The tie-in with the prophetic material is obvious: Isaiah was a prophet who served in the time of King Hezekiah. Chapters 36–37 are the first movement of the narrative. They are part of a war chronicle in which the big bully on the block, Assyria, sends threatening demands to the small nation of Judah. This potential horror story unfolds in five successive waves: the king of Assyria sends a missive to the populace of Judah demanding that they ignore King Hezekiah and surrender (chapter 36); Hezekiah receives encouragement from his advisers and from Isaiah that God will protect his kingdom (37:1–7); an Assyrian emissary returns with a new taunt (37:8–13); in a matchless story, Hezekiah spreads out the threatening letter before God in the temple (37:14–20) and is rewarded for his faith by an oracle from Isaiah predicting God's defeat of Assyria (37:21–35); the Assyrian army is demolished by an angel of God (37:36–38). It is a *rescue story par excellence. Inasmuch as the narrative is placed in the middle of the prophetic book of Isaiah, fruitful tie-ins can be made between the story and the

---

[1] Or if they are fools, they shall not wander in it

prophetic oracles of chapters 1–35. The story stands as proof that when God's people resist the temptation to misplace their trust in something besides God, they will be saved.

36 In the fourteenth year of King Hezekiah, Sennacherib king of Assyria came up against all the fortified cities of Judah and took them. ²And the king of Assyria sent the Rabshakeh¹ from Lachish to King Hezekiah at Jerusalem, with a great army. And he stood by the conduit of the upper pool on the highway to the Washer's Field. ³And there came out to him Eliakim the son of Hilkiah, who was over the household, and Shebna the secretary, and Joah the son of Asaph, the recorder.

⁴And the Rabshakeh said to them, "Say to Hezekiah, 'Thus says the great king, the king of Assyria: On what do you rest this trust of yours? ⁵Do you think that mere words are strategy and power for war? In whom do you now trust, that you have rebelled against me? ⁶Behold, you are trusting in Egypt, that broken reed of a staff, which will pierce the hand of any man who leans on it. Such is Pharaoh king of Egypt to all who trust in him. ⁷But if you say to me, "We trust in the Lord our God," is it not he whose high places and altars Hezekiah has removed, saying to Judah and to Jerusalem, "You shall worship before this altar"? ⁸Come now, make a wager with my master the king of Assyria: I will give you two thousand horses, if you are able on your part to set riders on them. ⁹How then can you repulse a single captain among the least of my master's servants, when you trust in Egypt for chariots and for horsemen? ¹⁰Moreover, is it without the Lord that I have come up against this land to destroy it? The Lord said to me, Go up against this land and destroy it.'"

¹¹Then Eliakim, Shebna, and Joah said to the Rabshakeh, "Please speak to your servants in Aramaic, for we understand it. Do not speak to us in the language of Judah within the hearing of the people who are on the wall." ¹²But the Rabshakeh said, "Has my master sent me to speak these words to your master and to you, and not to the men sitting on the wall, who are doomed with you to eat their own dung and drink their own urine?"

¹³Then the Rabshakeh stood and called out in a loud voice in the language of Judah: "Hear the words of the great king, the king of Assyria! ¹⁴Thus says the king: 'Do not let Hezekiah deceive you, for he will not be able to deliver you. ¹⁵Do not let Hezekiah make you trust in the Lord by saying, "The Lord will surely deliver us. This city will not be given into the hand of the king of Assyria." ¹⁶Do not listen to Hezekiah. For thus says the king of Assyria: Make your peace with me² and come out to me. Then each one of you will eat of his own vine, and each one of his own fig tree, and each one of you will drink the water of his own cistern, ¹⁷until I come and take you away to a land like your own land, a land of grain and wine, a land of bread and vineyards. ¹⁸Beware lest Hezekiah mislead you by saying, "The Lord will deliver us." Has any of the gods of the nations delivered his land out of the hand of the king of Assyria? ¹⁹Where are the gods of Hamath and Arpad? Where are the gods of Sepharvaim? Have they delivered Samaria out of my hand? ²⁰Who among all the gods of these lands have delivered their lands out of my hand, that the Lord should deliver Jerusalem out of my hand?'"

²¹But they were silent and answered him not a word, for the king's command was, "Do not answer him." ²²Then Eliakim the son of Hilkiah, who was over the household,

---

¹ *Rabshakeh* is the title of a high-ranking Assyrian military officer ² Hebrew *Make a blessing with me*

and Shebna the secretary, and Joah the son of Asaph, the recorder, came to Hezekiah with their clothes torn, and told him the words of the Rabshakeh.

37 As soon as King Hezekiah heard it, he tore his clothes and covered himself with sackcloth and went into the house of the LORD. [2]And he sent Eliakim, who was over the household, and Shebna the secretary, and the senior priests, covered with sackcloth, to the prophet Isaiah the son of Amoz. [3]They said to him, "Thus says Hezekiah, 'This day is a day of distress, of rebuke, and of disgrace; children have come to the point of birth, and there is no strength to bring them forth. [4]It may be that the LORD your God will hear the words of the Rabshakeh, whom his master the king of Assyria has sent to mock the living God, and will rebuke the words that the LORD your God has heard; therefore lift up your prayer for the remnant that is left.'"

[5]When the servants of King Hezekiah came to Isaiah, [6]Isaiah said to them, "Say to your master, 'Thus says the LORD: Do not be afraid because of the words that you have heard, with which the young men of the king of Assyria have reviled me. [7]Behold, I will put a spirit in him, so that he shall hear a rumor and return to his own land, and I will make him fall by the sword in his own land.'"

[8]The Rabshakeh returned, and found the king of Assyria fighting against Libnah, for he had heard that the king had left Lachish. [9]Now the king heard concerning Tirhakah king of Cush,[1] "He has set out to fight against you." And when he heard it, he sent messengers to Hezekiah, saying, [10]"Thus shall you speak to Hezekiah king of Judah: 'Do not let your God in whom you trust deceive you by promising that Jerusalem will not be given into the hand of the king of Assyria. [11]Behold, you have heard what the kings of Assyria have done to all lands, devoting them to destruction. And shall you be delivered? [12]Have the gods of the nations delivered them, the nations that my fathers destroyed, Gozan, Haran, Rezeph, and the people of Eden who were in Telassar? [13]Where is the king of Hamath, the king of Arpad, the king of the city of Sepharvaim, the king of Hena, or the king of Ivvah?'"

[14]Hezekiah received the letter from the hand of the messengers, and read it; and Hezekiah went up to the house of the LORD, and spread it before the LORD. [15]And Hezekiah prayed to the LORD: [16]"O LORD of hosts, God of Israel, enthroned above the cherubim, you are the God, you alone, of all the kingdoms of the earth; you have made heaven and earth. [17]Incline your ear, O LORD, and hear; open your eyes, O LORD, and see; and hear all the words of Sennacherib, which he has sent to mock the living God. [18]Truly, O LORD, the kings of Assyria have laid waste all the nations and their lands, [19]and have cast their gods into the fire. For they were no gods, but the work of men's hands, wood and stone. Therefore they were destroyed. [20]So now, O LORD our God, save us from his hand, that all the kingdoms of the earth may know that you alone are the LORD."

[21]Then Isaiah the son of Amoz sent to Hezekiah, saying, "Thus says the LORD, the God of Israel: Because you have prayed to me concerning Sennacherib king of Assyria, [22]this is the word that the LORD has spoken concerning him:

"'She despises you, she scorns you—
    the virgin daughter of Zion;
she wags her head behind you—
    the daughter of Jerusalem.

---

[1] Probably *Nubia*

²³ "'Whom have you mocked and reviled?
    Against whom have you raised your voice
  and lifted your eyes to the heights?
    Against the Holy One of Israel!
²⁴ By your servants you have mocked the Lord,
    and you have said, With my many chariots
  I have gone up the heights of the mountains,
    to the far recesses of Lebanon,
  to cut down its tallest cedars,
    its choicest cypresses,
  to come to its remotest height,
    its most fruitful forest.
²⁵ I dug wells
    and drank waters,
  to dry up with the sole of my foot
    all the streams of Egypt.

²⁶ "'Have you not heard
    that I determined it long ago?
  I planned from days of old
    what now I bring to pass,
  that you should make fortified cities
    crash into heaps of ruins,
²⁷ while their inhabitants, shorn of strength,
    are dismayed and confounded,
  and have become like plants of the field
    and like tender grass,
  like grass on the housetops,
    blighted¹ before it is grown.

²⁸ "'I know your sitting down
    and your going out and coming in,
    and your raging against me.
²⁹ Because you have raged against me
    and your complacency has come to my ears,
  I will put my hook in your nose
    and my bit in your mouth,
  and I will turn you back on the way
    by which you came.'

³⁰ "And this shall be the sign for you: this year you shall eat what grows of itself, and in the second year what springs from that. Then in the third year sow and reap, and plant vineyards, and eat their fruit. ³¹And the surviving remnant of the house of Judah shall again take root downward and bear fruit upward. ³²For out of Jerusalem shall go a remnant, and out of Mount Zion a band of survivors. The zeal of the LORD of hosts will do this.

³³"Therefore thus says the LORD concerning the king of Assyria: He shall not come into this city or shoot an arrow there or come before it with a shield or cast up a siege

¹ Some Hebrew manuscripts and 2 Kings 19:26; most Hebrew manuscripts *like a field*

mound against it. [34] By the way that he came, by the same he shall return, and he shall not come into this city, declares the LORD. [35] For I will defend this city to save it, for my own sake and for the sake of my servant David."

[36] And the angel of the LORD went out and struck down a hundred and eighty-five thousand in the camp of the Assyrians. And when people arose early in the morning, behold, these were all dead bodies. [37] Then Sennacherib king of Assyria departed and returned home and lived at Nineveh. [38] And as he was worshiping in the house of Nisroch his god, Adrammelech and Sharezer, his sons, struck him down with the sword. And after they escaped into the land of Ararat, Esarhaddon his son reigned in his place.

Hezekiah's illness and recovery [chapter 38]. Hezekiah goes on to a second triumph of faith in an event that was personal rather than national. In a richly human story, Hezekiah falls terminally ill (v. 1a), receives a message from Isaiah to put his house in order (v. 1b), prays to God (vv. 2–3), and receives a reprieve from death (vv. 4–6), accompanied by a confirming sign (vv. 7–8) and a prescription of medicine (vv. 21–22). To top off this feel-good story, Hezekiah turns poet and composes a beautiful psalm of praise (vv. 9–20) built around the motif of God's rescue of a terminally ill patient from death.

38 In those days Hezekiah became sick and was at the point of death. And Isaiah the prophet the son of Amoz came to him, and said to him, "Thus says the LORD: Set your house in order, for you shall die, you shall not recover."[1] [2] Then Hezekiah turned his face to the wall and prayed to the LORD, [3] and said, "Please, O LORD, remember how I have walked before you in faithfulness and with a whole heart, and have done what is good in your sight." And Hezekiah wept bitterly.

[4] Then the word of the LORD came to Isaiah: [5] "Go and say to Hezekiah, Thus says the LORD, the God of David your father: I have heard your prayer; I have seen your tears. Behold, I will add fifteen years to your life.[2] [6] I will deliver you and this city out of the hand of the king of Assyria, and will defend this city.

[7] "This shall be the sign to you from the LORD, that the LORD will do this thing that he has promised: [8] Behold, I will make the shadow cast by the declining sun on the dial of Ahaz turn back ten steps." So the sun turned back on the dial the ten steps by which it had declined.[3]

[9] A writing of Hezekiah king of Judah, after he had been sick and had recovered from his sickness:

[10]   I said, In the middle[4] of my days
         I must depart;
     I am consigned to the gates of Sheol
         for the rest of my years.
[11]   I said, I shall not see the LORD,
             the LORD in the land of the living;
     I shall look on man no more
         among the inhabitants of the world.
[12]   My dwelling is plucked up and removed from me
             like a shepherd's tent;

---

[1] Or *live*; also verses 9, 21 [2] Hebrew *to your days* [3] The meaning of the Hebrew verse is uncertain [4] Or *In the quiet*

like a weaver I have rolled up my life;
>   he cuts me off from the loom;
> from day to night you bring me to an end;
13   I calmed myself[1] until morning;
> like a lion he breaks all my bones;
>   from day to night you bring me to an end.

14   Like a swallow or a crane I chirp;
>   I moan like a dove.
> My eyes are weary with looking upward.
>   O Lord, I am oppressed; be my pledge of safety!
15   What shall I say? For he has spoken to me,
>   and he himself has done it.
> I walk slowly all my years
>   because of the bitterness of my soul.

16   O Lord, by these things men live,
>   and in all these is the life of my spirit.
>   Oh restore me to health and make me live!
17   Behold, it was for my welfare
>   that I had great bitterness;
> but in love you have delivered my life
>   from the pit of destruction,
> for you have cast all my sins
>   behind your back.
18   For Sheol does not thank you;
>   death does not praise you;
> those who go down to the pit do not hope
>   for your faithfulness.
19   The living, the living, he thanks you,
>   as I do this day;
> the father makes known to the children
>   your faithfulness.

20   The LORD will save me,
>   and we will play my music on stringed instruments
> all the days of our lives,
>   at the house of the LORD.

[21] Now Isaiah had said, "Let them take a cake of figs and apply it to the boil, that he may recover." [22] Hezekiah also had said, "What is the sign that I shall go up to the house of the LORD?"

Postscript on Hezekiah: letdown of the year [chapter 39]. Before the story of Hezekiah ends, the king descends from the heights and becomes a huge spiritual disappointment. Having lost the humility that he had voiced in his lyric poem of deliverance, he shows off his wealth to visiting emissaries from Babylon (vv. 1–2), is called to account for having done so by Isaiah (vv. 3–7), and selfishly disengages himself from

---

[1] Or (with Targum) *I cried for help*

the prophecy that his own family will one day be carried into exile by taking refuge in the thought that at least he will be dead by the time of the calamity (v. 8). Whereas Hezekiah had earlier been a model of faith to be emulated, he ends in the ignominious camp known by literary scholars as "negative example"—showing us how not to live after having been rescued by God.

39 At that time Merodach-baladan the son of Baladan, king of Babylon, sent envoys with letters and a present to Hezekiah, for he heard that he had been sick and had recovered. ²And Hezekiah welcomed them gladly. And he showed them his treasure house, the silver, the gold, the spices, the precious oil, his whole armory, all that was found in his storehouses. There was nothing in his house or in all his realm that Hezekiah did not show them. ³Then Isaiah the prophet came to King Hezekiah, and said to him, "What did these men say? And from where did they come to you?" Hezekiah said, "They have come to me from a far country, from Babylon." ⁴He said, "What have they seen in your house?" Hezekiah answered, "They have seen all that is in my house. There is nothing in my storehouses that I did not show them."

⁵Then Isaiah said to Hezekiah, "Hear the word of the LORD of hosts: ⁶Behold, the days are coming, when all that is in your house, and that which your fathers have stored up till this day, shall be carried to Babylon. Nothing shall be left, says the LORD. ⁷And some of your own sons, who will come from you, whom you will father, shall be taken away, and they shall be eunuchs in the palace of the king of Babylon." ⁸Then said Hezekiah to Isaiah, "The word of the LORD that you have spoken is good." For he thought, "There will be peace and security in my days."

First wave of oracles of redemption [chapter 40]. Despite the interspersed oracles of salvation in the first thirty-five chapters of Isaiah, nothing in that material fully prepares us for the final long movement of the book. Chapters 40–66 are mainly cut from the same cloth and may be compared to the orchestral crescendo during the final movement of a symphony. One literary critic has identified this material as constituting a brand new genre that he calls the rhapsody (the same critic entitled chapters 40–66 Rhapsody of Zion Redeemed). Chapter 40 is our initiation into this new mode, and it includes one of the high points of biblical poetry. Four brief prefatory units lead up to this famous poem: an opening command by God to comfort his people (vv. 1–2); an unidentified "voice" that announces a preparation for the coming glory of the Lord (vv. 3–5); another "voice" that asserts human mutability as contrasted to the eternal word of God (vv. 6–8); a command to announce the coming of God (vv. 9–11). We know on the basis of NT references to this material that its primary import is messianic prophecy. Then comes the exalted *ode that praises the transcendence of God (vv. 12–26), followed by an assertion that the transcendent power of God is a cause for people to trust in God's empowerment (vv. 27–31). The imagery and metaphors are awe inspiring. The primary rhetorical mode in the poem praising God's transcendence is twofold: the poet adduces the huge forces of nature as evidence of the Creator's superior power, and he introduces examples of weakness (nations, idols, people) as a foil to set off God's transcendent greatness. In the follow-up to the praise (vv. 27–31), the poet in effect applies God's superior power to the lives of his followers, asserting that God's power is available to people who wait for him.

40

Comfort, comfort my people, says your God.
² Speak tenderly to Jerusalem,
  and cry to her
that her warfare¹ is ended,
  that her iniquity is pardoned,
that she has received from the LORD's hand
  double for all her sins.

³ A voice cries:²
"In the wilderness prepare the way of the LORD;
  make straight in the desert a highway for our God.
⁴ Every valley shall be lifted up,
  and every mountain and hill be made low;
the uneven ground shall become level,
  and the rough places a plain.
⁵ And the glory of the LORD shall be revealed,
  and all flesh shall see it together,
for the mouth of the LORD has spoken."

⁶ A voice says, "Cry!"
  And I said,³ "What shall I cry?"
All flesh is grass,
  and all its beauty⁴ is like the flower of the field.
⁷ The grass withers, the flower fades
  when the breath of the LORD blows on it;
  surely the people are grass.
⁸ The grass withers, the flower fades,
  but the word of our God will stand forever.

⁹ Get you up to a high mountain,
  O Zion, herald of good news;⁵
lift up your voice with strength,
  O Jerusalem, herald of good news;⁶
  lift it up, fear not;
say to the cities of Judah,
  "Behold your God!"
¹⁰ Behold, the Lord GOD comes with might,
  and his arm rules for him;
behold, his reward is with him,
  and his recompense before him.
¹¹ He will tend his flock like a shepherd;
  he will gather the lambs in his arms;
he will carry them in his bosom,
  and gently lead those that are with young.

¹² Who has measured the waters in the hollow of his hand
  and marked off the heavens with a span,

---

¹ Or time of service ² Or A voice of one crying ³ Revocalization based on Dead Sea Scroll, Septuagint, Vulgate; Masoretic Text And someone says ⁴ Or all its constancy ⁵ Or O herald of good news to Zion ⁶ Or O herald of good news to Jerusalem

enclosed the dust of the earth in a measure
    and weighed the mountains in scales
    and the hills in a balance?
13 Who has measured[1] the Spirit of the LORD,
    or what man shows him his counsel?
14 Whom did he consult,
    and who made him understand?
Who taught him the path of justice,
    and taught him knowledge,
    and showed him the way of understanding?
15 Behold, the nations are like a drop from a bucket,
    and are accounted as the dust on the scales;
    behold, he takes up the coastlands like fine dust.
16 Lebanon would not suffice for fuel,
    nor are its beasts enough for a burnt offering.
17 All the nations are as nothing before him,
    they are accounted by him as less than nothing and emptiness.

18 To whom then will you liken God,
    or what likeness compare with him?
19 An idol! A craftsman casts it,
    and a goldsmith overlays it with gold
    and casts for it silver chains.
20 He who is too impoverished for an offering
    chooses wood[2] that will not rot;
he seeks out a skillful craftsman
    to set up an idol that will not move.

21 Do you not know? Do you not hear?
    Has it not been told you from the beginning?
    Have you not understood from the foundations of the earth?
22 It is he who sits above the circle of the earth,
    and its inhabitants are like grasshoppers;
who stretches out the heavens like a curtain,
    and spreads them like a tent to dwell in;
23 who brings princes to nothing,
    and makes the rulers of the earth as emptiness.

24 Scarcely are they planted, scarcely sown,
    scarcely has their stem taken root in the earth,
when he blows on them, and they wither,
    and the tempest carries them off like stubble.

25 To whom then will you compare me,
    that I should be like him? says the Holy One.
26 Lift up your eyes on high and see:
    who created these?
He who brings out their host by number,

---

[1] Or *has directed* [2] Or *He chooses valuable wood*

calling them all by name,
    by the greatness of his might,
    and because he is strong in power
    not one is missing.

27 Why do you say, O Jacob,
    and speak, O Israel,
  "My way is hidden from the LORD,
    and my right is disregarded by my God"?
28 Have you not known? Have you not heard?
  The LORD is the everlasting God,
    the Creator of the ends of the earth.
  He does not faint or grow weary;
    his understanding is unsearchable.
29 He gives power to the faint,
    and to him who has no might he increases strength.
30 Even youths shall faint and be weary,
    and young men shall fall exhausted;
31 but they who wait for the LORD shall renew their strength;
    they shall mount up with wings like eagles;
  they shall run and not be weary;
    they shall walk and not faint.

Oracles of redemption [chapter 41]. This chapter is a collection of individual oracles. By a variety of means, the prophet offers messages of consolation and hope to God's people.

41 Listen to me in silence,
    O coastlands;
  let the peoples renew their strength;
  let them approach, then let them speak;
    let us together draw near for judgment.

2 Who stirred up one from the east
    whom victory meets at every step?[1]
  He gives up nations before him,
    so that he tramples kings underfoot;
  he makes them like dust with his sword,
    like driven stubble with his bow.
3 He pursues them and passes on safely,
    by paths his feet have not trod.
4 Who has performed and done this,
    calling the generations from the beginning?
  I, the LORD, the first,
    and with the last; I am he.

5 The coastlands have seen and are afraid;
    the ends of the earth tremble;

---

[1] Or whom righteousness calls to follow?

they have drawn near and come.
⁶ Everyone helps his neighbor
    and says to his brother, "Be strong!"
⁷ The craftsman strengthens the goldsmith,
    and he who smooths with the hammer him who strikes the anvil,
saying of the soldering, "It is good";
    and they strengthen it with nails so that it cannot be moved.

⁸ But you, Israel, my servant,
    Jacob, whom I have chosen,
    the offspring of Abraham, my friend;
⁹ you whom I took from the ends of the earth,
    and called from its farthest corners,
saying to you, "You are my servant,
    I have chosen you and not cast you off";
¹⁰ fear not, for I am with you;
    be not dismayed, for I am your God;
I will strengthen you, I will help you,
    I will uphold you with my righteous right hand.

¹¹ Behold, all who are incensed against you
    shall be put to shame and confounded;
those who strive against you
    shall be as nothing and shall perish.
¹² You shall seek those who contend with you,
    but you shall not find them;
those who war against you
    shall be as nothing at all.
¹³ For I, the LORD your God,
    hold your right hand;
it is I who say to you, "Fear not,
    I am the one who helps you."

¹⁴ Fear not, you worm Jacob,
    you men of Israel!
I am the one who helps you, declares the LORD;
    your Redeemer is the Holy One of Israel.
¹⁵ Behold, I make of you a threshing sledge,
    new, sharp, and having teeth;
you shall thresh the mountains and crush them,
    and you shall make the hills like chaff;
¹⁶ you shall winnow them, and the wind shall carry them away,
    and the tempest shall scatter them.
And you shall rejoice in the LORD;
    in the Holy One of Israel you shall glory.

¹⁷ When the poor and needy seek water,
    and there is none,

and their tongue is parched with thirst,
  I the Lord will answer them;
    I the God of Israel will not forsake them.
18 I will open rivers on the bare heights,
    and fountains in the midst of the valleys.
  I will make the wilderness a pool of water,
    and the dry land springs of water.
19 I will put in the wilderness the cedar,
    the acacia, the myrtle, and the olive.
  I will set in the desert the cypress,
    the plane and the pine together,
20 that they may see and know,
    may consider and understand together,
  that the hand of the Lord has done this,
    the Holy One of Israel has created it.

21 Set forth your case, says the Lord;
    bring your proofs, says the King of Jacob.
22 Let them bring them, and tell us
    what is to happen.
  Tell us the former things, what they are,
    that we may consider them,
  that we may know their outcome;
    or declare to us the things to come.
23 Tell us what is to come hereafter,
    that we may know that you are gods;
  do good, or do harm,
    that we may be dismayed and terrified.[1]
24 Behold, you are nothing,
    and your work is less than nothing;
    an abomination is he who chooses you.

25 I stirred up one from the north, and he has come,
    from the rising of the sun, and he shall call upon my name;
  he shall trample on rulers as on mortar,
    as the potter treads clay.
26 Who declared it from the beginning, that we might know,
    and beforehand, that we might say, "He is right"?
  There was none who declared it, none who proclaimed,
    none who heard your words.
27 I was the first to say[2] to Zion, "Behold, here they are!"
    and I give to Jerusalem a herald of good news.
28 But when I look, there is no one;
    among these there is no counselor
  who, when I ask, gives an answer.
29 Behold, they are all a delusion;

---

[1] Or that we may both be dismayed and see [2] Or Formerly I said

their works are nothing;
   their metal images are empty wind.

Messages from God, mainly hopeful [chapter 42]. The preceding two chapters began a pattern that continues in chapter 42 as God speaks directly to his people. The effect is a divine conversation with covenant Israel, but it extends beyond the Israelites to us as readers—a high privilege indeed. Specific topics include a description of God's chosen servant (Christ; vv. 1–4); an oracle of restoration (vv. 5–9); a lyric of praise by the prophet himself (vv. 10–13); God's prediction of future deliverance (vv. 14–17); an oracle of judgment against faithless Israel (vv. 18–25).

42

Behold my servant, whom I uphold,
   my chosen, in whom my soul delights;
I have put my Spirit upon him;
   he will bring forth justice to the nations.
2 He will not cry aloud or lift up his voice,
   or make it heard in the street;
3 a bruised reed he will not break,
   and a faintly burning wick he will not quench;
   he will faithfully bring forth justice.
4 He will not grow faint or be discouraged[1]
   till he has established justice in the earth;
   and the coastlands wait for his law.

5 Thus says God, the Lord,
   who created the heavens and stretched them out,
   who spread out the earth and what comes from it,
who gives breath to the people on it
   and spirit to those who walk in it:
6 "I am the Lord; I have called you in righteousness;
   I will take you by the hand and keep you;
I will give you as a covenant for the people,
   a light for the nations,
7   to open the eyes that are blind,
to bring out the prisoners from the dungeon,
   from the prison those who sit in darkness.
8 I am the Lord; that is my name;
   my glory I give to no other,
   nor my praise to carved idols.
9 Behold, the former things have come to pass,
   and new things I now declare;
before they spring forth
   I tell you of them."

10 Sing to the Lord a new song,
   his praise from the end of the earth,
   you who go down to the sea, and all that fills it,

---

[1] Or bruised

the coastlands and their inhabitants.
11 Let the desert and its cities lift up their voice,
the villages that Kedar inhabits;
let the habitants of Sela sing for joy,
let them shout from the top of the mountains.
12 Let them give glory to the LORD,
and declare his praise in the coastlands.
13 The LORD goes out like a mighty man,
like a man of war he stirs up his zeal;
he cries out, he shouts aloud,
he shows himself mighty against his foes.

14 For a long time I have held my peace;
I have kept still and restrained myself;
now I will cry out like a woman in labor;
I will gasp and pant.
15 I will lay waste mountains and hills,
and dry up all their vegetation;
I will turn the rivers into islands,¹
and dry up the pools.
16 And I will lead the blind
in a way that they do not know,
in paths that they have not known
I will guide them.
I will turn the darkness before them into light,
the rough places into level ground.
These are the things I do,
and I do not forsake them.
17 They are turned back and utterly put to shame,
who trust in carved idols,
who say to metal images,
"You are our gods."

18 Hear, you deaf,
and look, you blind, that you may see!
19 Who is blind but my servant,
or deaf as my messenger whom I send?
Who is blind as my dedicated one,²
or blind as the servant of the LORD?
20 He sees many things, but does not observe them;
his ears are open, but he does not hear.
21 The LORD was pleased, for his righteousness' sake,
to magnify his law and make it glorious.
22 But this is a people plundered and looted;
they are all of them trapped in holes
and hidden in prisons;
they have become plunder with none to rescue,

¹ Or *into coastlands* ² Or *as the one at peace with me*

spoil with none to say, "Restore!"
23 Who among you will give ear to this,
will attend and listen for the time to come?
24 Who gave up Jacob to the looter,
and Israel to the plunderers?
Was it not the LORD, against whom we have sinned,
in whose ways they would not walk,
and whose law they would not obey?
25 So he poured on him the heat of his anger
and the might of battle;
it set him on fire all around, but he did not understand;
it burned him up, but he did not take it to heart.

Apostrophes from God: what God will do to redeem his people [43:1–44:5]. The structure is a collage of brief segments, and attempts to divide such material topically are fairly useless. The dominant technique is the apostrophe—direct addresses to people and personified groups as though they were present and could hear, even though the listeners are not literally present to hear the messages reported through the prophet. The general drift of the material is God's declaration of the redemptive acts that he will perform for a personified Israel. The messages are all messages of consolation (43:22–24 is an indictment of sinful Israel, but it sets up the statement of forgiveness that follows immediately).

43 But now thus says the LORD,
he who created you, O Jacob,
he who formed you, O Israel:
"Fear not, for I have redeemed you;
I have called you by name, you are mine.
2 When you pass through the waters, I will be with you;
and through the rivers, they shall not overwhelm you;
when you walk through fire you shall not be burned,
and the flame shall not consume you.
3 For I am the LORD your God,
the Holy One of Israel, your Savior.
I give Egypt as your ransom,
Cush and Seba in exchange for you.
4 Because you are precious in my eyes,
and honored, and I love you,
I give men in return for you,
peoples in exchange for your life.
5 Fear not, for I am with you;
I will bring your offspring from the east,
and from the west I will gather you.
6 I will say to the north, Give up,
and to the south, Do not withhold;
bring my sons from afar

and my daughters from the end of the earth,

7   everyone who is called by my name,
    whom I created for my glory,
    whom I formed and made."

8   Bring out the people who are blind, yet have eyes,
    who are deaf, yet have ears!
9   All the nations gather together,
    and the peoples assemble.
Who among them can declare this,
    and show us the former things?
Let them bring their witnesses to prove them right,
    and let them hear and say, It is true.
10 "You are my witnesses," declares the LORD,
    "and my servant whom I have chosen,
that you may know and believe me
    and understand that I am he.
Before me no god was formed,
    nor shall there be any after me.
11 I, I am the LORD,
    and besides me there is no savior.
12 I declared and saved and proclaimed,
    when there was no strange god among you;
    and you are my witnesses," declares the LORD, "and I am God.
13 Also henceforth I am he;
    there is none who can deliver from my hand;
    I work, and who can turn it back?"

14 Thus says the LORD,
    your Redeemer, the Holy One of Israel:
"For your sake I send to Babylon
    and bring them all down as fugitives,
    even the Chaldeans, in the ships in which they rejoice.
15 I am the LORD, your Holy One,
    the Creator of Israel, your King."

16 Thus says the LORD,
    who makes a way in the sea,
    a path in the mighty waters,
17 who brings forth chariot and horse,
    army and warrior;
they lie down, they cannot rise,
    they are extinguished, quenched like a wick:
18 "Remember not the former things,
    nor consider the things of old.
19 Behold, I am doing a new thing;
    now it springs forth, do you not perceive it?
I will make a way in the wilderness

and rivers in the desert.
20 The wild beasts will honor me,
the jackals and the ostriches,
for I give water in the wilderness,
rivers in the desert,
to give drink to my chosen people,
21 the people whom I formed for myself
that they might declare my praise.

22 "Yet you did not call upon me, O Jacob;
but you have been weary of me, O Israel!
23 You have not brought me your sheep for burnt offerings,
or honored me with your sacrifices.
I have not burdened you with offerings,
or wearied you with frankincense.
24 You have not bought me sweet cane with money,
or satisfied me with the fat of your sacrifices.
But you have burdened me with your sins;
you have wearied me with your iniquities.

25 "I, I am he
who blots out your transgressions for my own sake,
and I will not remember your sins.
26 Put me in remembrance; let us argue together;
set forth your case, that you may be proved right.
27 Your first father sinned,
and your mediators transgressed against me.
28 Therefore I will profane the princes of the sanctuary,
and deliver Jacob to utter destruction
and Israel to reviling.

44 "But now hear, O Jacob my servant,
Israel whom I have chosen!
2 Thus says the Lord who made you,
who formed you from the womb and will help you:
Fear not, O Jacob my servant,
Jeshurun whom I have chosen.
3 For I will pour water on the thirsty land,
and streams on the dry ground;
I will pour my Spirit upon your offspring,
and my blessing on your descendants.
4 They shall spring up among the grass
like willows by flowing streams.
5 This one will say, 'I am the Lord's,'
another will call on the name of Jacob,
and another will write on his hand, 'The Lord's,'
and name himself by the name of Israel."

A celebration of God's superiority to idols [44:6–28]. Any division of the material in the last main section of Isaiah is somewhat arbitrary, but chapter 44 holds together as a contrast between the true God and idols. Verses 9–20 are an extended satiric ridicule of people who fashion physical idols and worship them. The surrounding material can be read as a foil to such folly. These verses praise a transcendent God who is without comparison (vv. 6–8), who has redeemed his people (vv. 21–23), and who is sovereign over all things (vv. 24–28).

⁶   Thus says the LORD, the King of Israel
     and his Redeemer, the LORD of hosts:
  "I am the first and I am the last;
    besides me there is no god.
⁷   Who is like me? Let him proclaim it.[1]
    Let him declare and set it before me,
  since I appointed an ancient people.
    Let them declare what is to come, and what will happen.
⁸   Fear not, nor be afraid;
    have I not told you from of old and declared it?
    And you are my witnesses!
  Is there a God besides me?
    There is no Rock; I know not any."

⁹All who fashion idols are nothing, and the things they delight in do not profit. Their witnesses neither see nor know, that they may be put to shame. ¹⁰Who fashions a god or casts an idol that is profitable for nothing? ¹¹Behold, all his companions shall be put to shame, and the craftsmen are only human. Let them all assemble, let them stand forth. They shall be terrified; they shall be put to shame together.

¹²The ironsmith takes a cutting tool and works it over the coals. He fashions it with hammers and works it with his strong arm. He becomes hungry, and his strength fails; he drinks no water and is faint. ¹³The carpenter stretches a line; he marks it out with a pencil. He shapes it with planes and marks it with a compass. He shapes it into the figure of a man, with the beauty of a man, to dwell in a house. ¹⁴He cuts down cedars, or he chooses a cypress tree or an oak and lets it grow strong among the trees of the forest. He plants a cedar and the rain nourishes it. ¹⁵Then it becomes fuel for a man. He takes a part of it and warms himself; he kindles a fire and bakes bread. Also he makes a god and worships it; he makes it an idol and falls down before it. ¹⁶Half of it he burns in the fire. Over the half he eats meat; he roasts it and is satisfied. Also he warms himself and says, "Aha, I am warm, I have seen the fire!" ¹⁷And the rest of it he makes into a god, his idol, and falls down to it and worships it. He prays to it and says, "Deliver me, for you are my god!"

¹⁸They know not, nor do they discern, for he has shut their eyes, so that they cannot see, and their hearts, so that they cannot understand. ¹⁹No one considers, nor is there knowledge or discernment to say, "Half of it I burned in the fire; I also baked bread on its coals; I roasted meat and have eaten. And shall I make the rest of it an abomination? Shall I fall down before a block of wood?" ²⁰He feeds on ashes; a deluded heart has led him astray, and he cannot deliver himself or say, "Is there not a lie in my right hand?"

---

[1] Or *Who like me can proclaim it?*

21 Remember these things, O Jacob,
    and Israel, for you are my servant;
  I formed you; you are my servant;
    O Israel, you will not be forgotten by me.
22 I have blotted out your transgressions like a cloud
    and your sins like mist;
  return to me, for I have redeemed you.

23 Sing, O heavens, for the Lord has done it;
    shout, O depths of the earth;
  break forth into singing, O mountains,
    O forest, and every tree in it!
  For the Lord has redeemed Jacob,
    and will be glorified[1] in Israel.

24 Thus says the Lord, your Redeemer,
    who formed you from the womb:
  "I am the Lord, who made all things,
    who alone stretched out the heavens,
    who spread out the earth by myself,
25 who frustrates the signs of liars
    and makes fools of diviners,
  who turns wise men back
    and makes their knowledge foolish,
26 who confirms the word of his servant
    and fulfills the counsel of his messengers,
  who says of Jerusalem, 'She shall be inhabited,'
    and of the cities of Judah, 'They shall be built,
    and I will raise up their ruins';
27 who says to the deep, 'Be dry;
    I will dry up your rivers';
28 who says of Cyrus, 'He is my shepherd,
    and he shall fulfill all my purpose';
  saying of Jerusalem, 'She shall be built,'
    and of the temple, 'Your foundation shall be laid.'"

God's intention to save Israel [chapter 45]. The rhetorical mode is suggested by the formula "thus says the Lord" (vv. 1, 11, 14, 18): the prophet is reporting what God has said. The material is wide ranging, but the general drift is to outline a program of redemption for God's covenant people. Since God is the chief actor, a good approach to the material is to note what the chapter tells us about God and his grace.

45 Thus says the Lord to his anointed, to Cyrus,
    whose right hand I have grasped,
  to subdue nations before him
    and to loose the belts of kings,
  to open doors before him

[1] Or *will display his beauty*

that gates may not be closed:
² "I will go before you
    and level the exalted places,¹
I will break in pieces the doors of bronze
    and cut through the bars of iron,
³ I will give you the treasures of darkness
    and the hoards in secret places,
that you may know that it is I, the Lord,
    the God of Israel, who call you by your name.
⁴ For the sake of my servant Jacob,
    and Israel my chosen,
I call you by your name,
    I name you, though you do not know me.
⁵ I am the Lord, and there is no other,
    besides me there is no God;
    I equip you, though you do not know me,
⁶ that people may know, from the rising of the sun
    and from the west, that there is none besides me;
    I am the Lord, and there is no other.
⁷ I form light and create darkness,
    I make well-being and create calamity,
    I am the Lord, who does all these things.

⁸ "Shower, O heavens, from above,
    and let the clouds rain down righteousness;
let the earth open, that salvation and righteousness may bear fruit;
    let the earth cause them both to sprout;
    I the Lord have created it.

⁹ "Woe to him who strives with him who formed him,
    a pot among earthen pots!
Does the clay say to him who forms it, 'What are you making?'
    or 'Your work has no handles'?
¹⁰ Woe to him who says to a father, 'What are you begetting?'
    or to a woman, 'With what are you in labor?'"

¹¹ Thus says the Lord,
    the Holy One of Israel, and the one who formed him:
"Ask me of things to come;
    will you command me concerning my children and the work of my hands?²
¹² I made the earth
    and created man on it;
it was my hands that stretched out the heavens,
    and I commanded all their host.
¹³ I have stirred him up in righteousness,
    and I will make all his ways level;
he shall build my city

---

¹ Masoretic Text; Dead Sea Scroll, Septuagint *level the mountains* ² A slight emendation yields *will you question me about my children, or command me concerning the work of my hands?*

and set my exiles free,
    not for price or reward,"
        says the LORD of hosts.

¹⁴   Thus says the LORD:
    "The wealth of Egypt and the merchandise of Cush,
        and the Sabeans, men of stature,
    shall come over to you and be yours;
        they shall follow you;
        they shall come over in chains and bow down to you.
    They will plead with you, saying:
        'Surely God is in you, and there is no other,
        no god besides him.'"

¹⁵   Truly, you are a God who hides himself,
        O God of Israel, the Savior.
¹⁶   All of them are put to shame and confounded;
        the makers of idols go in confusion together.
¹⁷   But Israel is saved by the LORD
        with everlasting salvation;
    you shall not be put to shame or confounded
        to all eternity.

¹⁸   For thus says the LORD,
    who created the heavens
        (he is God!),
    who formed the earth and made it
        (he established it;
    he did not create it empty,
        he formed it to be inhabited!):
    "I am the LORD, and there is no other.
¹⁹   I did not speak in secret,
        in a land of darkness;
    I did not say to the offspring of Jacob,
        'Seek me in vain.'¹
    I the LORD speak the truth;
        I declare what is right.

²⁰   "Assemble yourselves and come;
        draw near together,
        you survivors of the nations!
    They have no knowledge
        who carry about their wooden idols,
    and keep on praying to a god
        that cannot save.
²¹   Declare and present your case;
        let them take counsel together!
    Who told this long ago?

¹ Hebrew *in emptiness*

Who declared it of old?
Was it not I, the LORD?
And there is no other god besides me,
a righteous God and a Savior;
there is none besides me.

²² "Turn to me and be saved,
all the ends of the earth!
For I am God, and there is no other.
²³ By myself I have sworn;
from my mouth has gone out in righteousness
a word that shall not return:
'To me every knee shall bow,
every tongue shall swear allegiance.'[1]

²⁴ "Only in the LORD, it shall be said of me,
are righteousness and strength;
to him shall come and be ashamed
all who were incensed against him.
²⁵ In the LORD all the offspring of Israel
shall be justified and shall glory."

God asserts his sovereignty over the nations [chapters 46–47]. The format continues to be a shifting sequence of brief units. The rhetorical mode is a series of declarations from God regarding what he intends to do in the time just ahead, along with statements about his divine power. There is a general focus on nations, and we can discern the following loose (but not strict) division of subjects: God's superiority to pagan idols (chapter 46); a satiric oracle predicting Babylon's destruction (chapter 47).

46

Bel bows down; Nebo stoops;
their idols are on beasts and livestock;
these things you carry are borne
as burdens on weary beasts.
² They stoop; they bow down together;
they cannot save the burden,
but themselves go into captivity.

³ "Listen to me, O house of Jacob,
all the remnant of the house of Israel,
who have been borne by me from before your birth,
carried from the womb;
⁴ even to your old age I am he,
and to gray hairs I will carry you.
I have made, and I will bear;
I will carry and will save.

⁵ "To whom will you liken me and make me equal,
and compare me, that we may be alike?

[1] Septuagint *every tongue shall confess to God*

6   Those who lavish gold from the purse,
        and weigh out silver in the scales,
    hire a goldsmith, and he makes it into a god;
        then they fall down and worship!
7   They lift it to their shoulders, they carry it,
        they set it in its place, and it stands there;
        it cannot move from its place.
    If one cries to it, it does not answer
        or save him from his trouble.

8   "Remember this and stand firm,
        recall it to mind, you transgressors,
9   remember the former things of old;
    for I am God, and there is no other;
        I am God, and there is none like me,
10 declaring the end from the beginning
        and from ancient times things not yet done,
    saying, 'My counsel shall stand,
        and I will accomplish all my purpose,'
11 calling a bird of prey from the east,
        the man of my counsel from a far country.
    I have spoken, and I will bring it to pass;
        I have purposed, and I will do it.

12 "Listen to me, you stubborn of heart,
        you who are far from righteousness:
13 I bring near my righteousness; it is not far off,
        and my salvation will not delay;
    I will put salvation in Zion,
        for Israel my glory."

47 Come down and sit in the dust,
        O virgin daughter of Babylon;
    sit on the ground without a throne,
        O daughter of the Chaldeans!
    For you shall no more be called
        tender and delicate.
2   Take the millstones and grind flour,
        put off your veil,
    strip off your robe, uncover your legs,
        pass through the rivers.
3   Your nakedness shall be uncovered,
        and your disgrace shall be seen.
    I will take vengeance,
        and I will spare no one.
4   Our Redeemer—the Lord of hosts is his name—
        is the Holy One of Israel.

⁵ Sit in silence, and go into darkness,
   O daughter of the Chaldeans;
for you shall no more be called
   the mistress of kingdoms.
⁶ I was angry with my people;
   I profaned my heritage;
I gave them into your hand;
   you showed them no mercy;
on the aged you made your yoke exceedingly heavy.
⁷ You said, "I shall be mistress forever,"
   so that you did not lay these things to heart
   or remember their end.

⁸ Now therefore hear this, you lover of pleasures,
   who sit securely,
who say in your heart,
   "I am, and there is no one besides me;
I shall not sit as a widow
   or know the loss of children":
⁹ These two things shall come to you
   in a moment, in one day;
the loss of children and widowhood
   shall come upon you in full measure,
in spite of your many sorceries
   and the great power of your enchantments.

¹⁰ You felt secure in your wickedness,
    you said, "No one sees me";
your wisdom and your knowledge led you astray,
and you said in your heart,
    "I am, and there is no one besides me."
¹¹ But evil shall come upon you,
    which you will not know how to charm away;
disaster shall fall upon you,
    for which you will not be able to atone;
and ruin shall come upon you suddenly,
    of which you know nothing.

¹² Stand fast in your enchantments
    and your many sorceries,
    with which you have labored from your youth;
perhaps you may be able to succeed;
    perhaps you may inspire terror.
¹³ You are wearied with your many counsels;
    let them stand forth and save you,
those who divide the heavens,
    who gaze at the stars,

who at the new moons make known
    what shall come upon you.

14 Behold, they are like stubble;
    the fire consumes them;
they cannot deliver themselves
    from the power of the flame.
No coal for warming oneself is this,
    no fire to sit before!
15 Such to you are those with whom you have labored,
    who have done business with you from your youth;
they wander about, each in his own direction;
    there is no one to save you.

Oracles of deliverance [chapters 48–49]. God continues to speak a series of messages that the prophet reports. The audience is God's covenant people, who are called
by a range of names (Jacob, Israel, Judah, "my servant," etc.). The messages are predominantly God's rehearsal of his acts of deliverance, with an undertow of God's judgment against the wicked and unbelieving.

48

Hear this, O house of Jacob,
    who are called by the name of Israel,
    and who came from the waters of Judah,
who swear by the name of the LORD
    and confess the God of Israel,
    but not in truth or right.
2 For they call themselves after the holy city,
    and stay themselves on the God of Israel;
    the LORD of hosts is his name.

3 "The former things I declared of old;
    they went out from my mouth, and I announced them;
    then suddenly I did them, and they came to pass.
4 Because I know that you are obstinate,
    and your neck is an iron sinew
    and your forehead brass,
5 I declared them to you from of old,
    before they came to pass I announced them to you,
lest you should say, 'My idol did them,
    my carved image and my metal image commanded them.'

6 "You have heard; now see all this;
    and will you not declare it?
From this time forth I announce to you new things,
    hidden things that you have not known.
7 They are created now, not long ago;
    before today you have never heard of them,
    lest you should say, 'Behold, I knew them.'

8   You have never heard, you have never known,
        from of old your ear has not been opened.
    For I knew that you would surely deal treacherously,
        and that from before birth you were called a rebel.

9   "For my name's sake I defer my anger,
        for the sake of my praise I restrain it for you,
        that I may not cut you off.
10 Behold, I have refined you, but not as silver;
        I have tried[1] you in the furnace of affliction.
11 For my own sake, for my own sake, I do it,
        for how should my name[2] be profaned?
        My glory I will not give to another.

12 "Listen to me, O Jacob,
        and Israel, whom I called!
    I am he; I am the first,
        and I am the last.
13 My hand laid the foundation of the earth,
        and my right hand spread out the heavens;
    when I call to them,
        they stand forth together.

14 "Assemble, all of you, and listen!
        Who among them has declared these things?
    The LORD loves him;
        he shall perform his purpose on Babylon,
        and his arm shall be against the Chaldeans.
15 I, even I, have spoken and called him;
        I have brought him, and he will prosper in his way.
16 Draw near to me, hear this:
        from the beginning I have not spoken in secret,
        from the time it came to be I have been there."
    And now the Lord GOD has sent me, and his Spirit.

17 Thus says the LORD,
        your Redeemer, the Holy One of Israel:
    "I am the LORD your God,
        who teaches you to profit,
        who leads you in the way you should go.
18 Oh that you had paid attention to my commandments!
        Then your peace would have been like a river,
        and your righteousness like the waves of the sea;
19 your offspring would have been like the sand,
        and your descendants like its grains;
    their name would never be cut off
        or destroyed from before me."

---

[1] Or I have chosen [2] Hebrew lacks my name

20   Go out from Babylon, flee from Chaldea,
     declare this with a shout of joy, proclaim it,
 send it out to the end of the earth;
     say, "The LORD has redeemed his servant Jacob!"
21   They did not thirst when he led them through the deserts;
     he made water flow for them from the rock;
 he split the rock and the water gushed out.

22   "There is no peace," says the LORD, "for the wicked."

49

Listen to me, O coastlands,
     and give attention, you peoples from afar.
The LORD called me from the womb,
     from the body of my mother he named my name.
2   He made my mouth like a sharp sword;
     in the shadow of his hand he hid me;
 he made me a polished arrow;
     in his quiver he hid me away.
3   And he said to me, "You are my servant,
     Israel, in whom I will be glorified."[1]
4   But I said, "I have labored in vain;
     I have spent my strength for nothing and vanity;
 yet surely my right is with the LORD,
     and my recompense with my God."

5   And now the LORD says,
     he who formed me from the womb to be his servant,
 to bring Jacob back to him;
     and that Israel might be gathered to him—
 for I am honored in the eyes of the LORD,
     and my God has become my strength—
6   he says:
 "It is too light a thing that you should be my servant
     to raise up the tribes of Jacob
     and to bring back the preserved of Israel;
 I will make you as a light for the nations,
     that my salvation may reach to the end of the earth."

7   Thus says the LORD,
     the Redeemer of Israel and his Holy One,
 to one deeply despised, abhorred by the nation,
     the servant of rulers:
 "Kings shall see and arise;
     princes, and they shall prostrate themselves;
 because of the LORD, who is faithful,
     the Holy One of Israel, who has chosen you."

8   Thus says the LORD:
 "In a time of favor I have answered you;

---

[1] Or *I will display my beauty*

in a day of salvation I have helped you;
I will keep you and give you
    as a covenant to the people,
to establish the land,
    to apportion the desolate heritages,
9   saying to the prisoners, 'Come out,'
    to those who are in darkness, 'Appear.'
They shall feed along the ways;
    on all bare heights shall be their pasture;
10 they shall not hunger or thirst,
    neither scorching wind nor sun shall strike them,
for he who has pity on them will lead them,
    and by springs of water will guide them.
11 And I will make all my mountains a road,
    and my highways shall be raised up.
12 Behold, these shall come from afar,
    and behold, these from the north and from the west,[1]
    and these from the land of Syene."[2]

13 Sing for joy, O heavens, and exult, O earth;
    break forth, O mountains, into singing!
For the LORD has comforted his people
    and will have compassion on his afflicted.

14 But Zion said, "The LORD has forsaken me;
    my Lord has forgotten me."

15 "Can a woman forget her nursing child,
    that she should have no compassion on the son of her womb?
Even these may forget,
    yet I will not forget you.
16 Behold, I have engraved you on the palms of my hands;
    your walls are continually before me.
17 Your builders make haste;[3]
    your destroyers and those who laid you waste go out from you.
18 Lift up your eyes around and see;
    they all gather, they come to you.
As I live, declares the LORD,
    you shall put them all on as an ornament;
    you shall bind them on as a bride does.

19 "Surely your waste and your desolate places
    and your devastated land—
surely now you will be too narrow for your inhabitants,
    and those who swallowed you up will be far away.
20 The children of your bereavement
    will yet say in your ears:
'The place is too narrow for me;

---

[1] Hebrew *from the sea* [2] Dead Sea Scroll; Masoretic Text *Sinim* [3] Dead Sea Scroll; Masoretic Text *Your children make haste*

make room for me to dwell in.'
21   Then you will say in your heart:
        'Who has borne me these?
     I was bereaved and barren,
        exiled and put away,
        but who has brought up these?
     Behold, I was left alone;
        from where have these come?' "

22   Thus says the Lord God:
     "Behold, I will lift up my hand to the nations,
        and raise my signal to the peoples;
     and they shall bring your sons in their bosom,
        and your daughters shall be carried on their shoulders.
23   Kings shall be your foster fathers,
        and their queens your nursing mothers.
     With their faces to the ground they shall bow down to you,
        and lick the dust of your feet.
     Then you will know that I am the Lord;
        those who wait for me shall not be put to shame."

24   Can the prey be taken from the mighty,
        or the captives of a tyrant[1] be rescued?
25   For thus says the Lord:
     "Even the captives of the mighty shall be taken,
        and the prey of the tyrant be rescued,
     for I will contend with those who contend with you,
        and I will save your children.
26   I will make your oppressors eat their own flesh,
        and they shall be drunk with their own blood as with wine.
     Then all flesh shall know
        that I am the Lord your Savior,
        and your Redeemer, the Mighty One of Jacob."

Miscellany of oracles [chapter 50]. In this interlude, the material becomes even more mixed. The general sequence is as follows: God's power to judge sin (vv. 1–3); the obedience of God's servant (vv. 4–9); exhortation to trust in God and abandon evil (vv. 10–11).

50   Thus says the Lord:
     "Where is your mother's certificate of divorce,
        with which I sent her away?
     Or which of my creditors is it
        to whom I have sold you?
     Behold, for your iniquities you were sold,
        and for your transgressions your mother was sent away.
2   Why, when I came, was there no man;
        why, when I called, was there no one to answer?

---

[1] Dead Sea Scroll, Syriac, Vulgate (see also verse 25); Masoretic Text *of a righteous man*

Is my hand shortened, that it cannot redeem?
　Or have I no power to deliver?
Behold, by my rebuke I dry up the sea,
　I make the rivers a desert;
their fish stink for lack of water
　and die of thirst.
³　I clothe the heavens with blackness
　　and make sackcloth their covering."

⁴　The Lord God has given me
　　the tongue of those who are taught,
that I may know how to sustain with a word
　him who is weary.
Morning by morning he awakens;
　he awakens my ear
　to hear as those who are taught.
⁵　The Lord God has opened my ear,
　　and I was not rebellious;
　　I turned not backward.
⁶　I gave my back to those who strike,
　　and my cheeks to those who pull out the beard;
I hid not my face
　from disgrace and spitting.

⁷　But the Lord God helps me;
　　therefore I have not been disgraced;
therefore I have set my face like a flint,
　and I know that I shall not be put to shame.
⁸　He who vindicates me is near.
Who will contend with me?
　Let us stand up together.
Who is my adversary?
　Let him come near to me.
⁹　Behold, the Lord God helps me;
　who will declare me guilty?
Behold, all of them will wear out like a garment;
　the moth will eat them up.

¹⁰　Who among you fears the Lord
　　and obeys the voice of his servant?
Let him who walks in darkness
　and has no light
trust in the name of the Lord
　and rely on his God.
¹¹　Behold, all you who kindle a fire,
　　who equip yourselves with burning torches!
Walk by the light of your fire,
　and by the torches that you have kindled!

This you have from my hand:
you shall lie down in torment.

51

"Listen to me, you who pursue righteousness,
    you who seek the LORD:
look to the rock from which you were hewn,
    and to the quarry from which you were dug.
2 Look to Abraham your father
    and to Sarah who bore you;
for he was but one when I called him,
    that I might bless him and multiply him.
3 For the LORD comforts Zion;
    he comforts all her waste places
and makes her wilderness like Eden,
    her desert like the garden of the LORD;
joy and gladness will be found in her,
    thanksgiving and the voice of song.

4 "Give attention to me, my people,
    and give ear to me, my nation;
for a law[1] will go out from me,
    and I will set my justice for a light to the peoples.
5 My righteousness draws near,
    my salvation has gone out,
    and my arms will judge the peoples;
the coastlands hope for me,
    and for my arm they wait.
6 Lift up your eyes to the heavens,
    and look at the earth beneath;
for the heavens vanish like smoke,
    the earth will wear out like a garment,
    and they who dwell in it will die in like manner;[2]
but my salvation will be forever,
    and my righteousness will never be dismayed.

7 "Listen to me, you who know righteousness,
    the people in whose heart is my law;
fear not the reproach of man,
    nor be dismayed at their revilings.
8 For the moth will eat them up like a garment,

---

[1] Or for teaching; also verse 7   [2] Or will die like gnats

and the worm will eat them like wool;
   but my righteousness will be forever,
      and my salvation to all generations."

9   Awake, awake, put on strength,
      O arm of the LORD;
   awake, as in days of old,
      the generations of long ago.
   Was it not you who cut Rahab in pieces,
      who pierced the dragon?
10   Was it not you who dried up the sea,
      the waters of the great deep,
   who made the depths of the sea a way
      for the redeemed to pass over?
11   And the ransomed of the LORD shall return
      and come to Zion with singing;
   everlasting joy shall be upon their heads;
      they shall obtain gladness and joy,
      and sorrow and sighing shall flee away.

12   "I, I am he who comforts you;
      who are you that you are afraid of man who dies,
      of the son of man who is made like grass,
13   and have forgotten the LORD, your Maker,
      who stretched out the heavens
      and laid the foundations of the earth,
   and you fear continually all the day
      because of the wrath of the oppressor,
   when he sets himself to destroy?
      And where is the wrath of the oppressor?
14   He who is bowed down shall speedily be released;
      he shall not die and go down to the pit,
      neither shall his bread be lacking.
15   I am the LORD your God,
      who stirs up the sea so that its waves roar—
      the LORD of hosts is his name.
16   And I have put my words in your mouth
      and covered you in the shadow of my hand,
   establishing[1] the heavens
      and laying the foundations of the earth,
      and saying to Zion, 'You are my people.'"

17   Wake yourself, wake yourself,
      stand up, O Jerusalem,
   you who have drunk from the hand of the LORD
      the cup of his wrath,
   who have drunk to the dregs
      the bowl, the cup of staggering.

[1] Or planting

18   There is none to guide her
         among all the sons she has borne;
      there is none to take her by the hand
         among all the sons she has brought up.
19   These two things have happened to you—
         who will console you?—
      devastation and destruction, famine and sword;
         who will comfort you?[1]
20   Your sons have fainted;
         they lie at the head of every street
         like an antelope in a net;
      they are full of the wrath of the Lord,
         the rebuke of your God.

21   Therefore hear this, you who are afflicted,
         who are drunk, but not with wine:
22   Thus says your Lord, the Lord,
         your God who pleads the cause of his people:
      "Behold, I have taken from your hand the cup of staggering;
         the bowl of my wrath you shall drink no more;
23   and I will put it into the hand of your tormentors,
         who have said to you,
         'Bow down, that we may pass over';
      and you have made your back like the ground
         and like the street for them to pass over."

52 Awake, awake,
       put on your strength, O Zion;
    put on your beautiful garments,
       O Jerusalem, the holy city;
    for there shall no more come into you
       the uncircumcised and the unclean.
2   Shake yourself from the dust and arise;
       be seated, O Jerusalem;
    loose the bonds from your neck,
       O captive daughter of Zion.

³For thus says the Lord: "You were sold for nothing, and you shall be redeemed without money." ⁴For thus says the Lord God: "My people went down at the first into Egypt to sojourn there, and the Assyrian oppressed them for nothing. ⁵Now therefore what have I here," declares the Lord, "seeing that my people are taken away for nothing? Their rulers wail," declares the Lord, "and continually all the day my name is despised. ⁶Therefore my people shall know my name. Therefore in that day they shall know that it is I who speak; here am I."

7   How beautiful upon the mountains
       are the feet of him who brings good news,
    who publishes peace, who brings good news of happiness,

---

[1] Dead Sea Scroll, Septuagint, Syriac, Vulgate; Masoretic Text *how shall I comfort you*

who publishes salvation,
who says to Zion, "Your God reigns."
[8] The voice of your watchmen—they lift up their voice;
together they sing for joy;
for eye to eye they see
the return of the LORD to Zion.
[9] Break forth together into singing,
you waste places of Jerusalem,
for the LORD has comforted his people;
he has redeemed Jerusalem.
[10] The LORD has bared his holy arm
before the eyes of all the nations,
and all the ends of the earth shall see
the salvation of our God.

[11] Depart, depart, go out from there;
touch no unclean thing;
go out from the midst of her; purify yourselves,
you who bear the vessels of the LORD.
[12] For you shall not go out in haste,
and you shall not go in flight,
for the LORD will go before you,
and the God of Israel will be your rear guard.

Praise of the suffering servant [52:13–53:12]. This is one of the most famous passages in Isaiah and one of the most famous messianic prophecies in the Bible. In its format, this poem is an *encomium—a poem that praises its subject with such formulas as a formal introduction to the subject, the distinguished ancestry of the subject, a catalog of praiseworthy acts and attributes, the superiority of the subject to all rivals, and a conclusion urging the reader to emulate the person or quality being praised. This song of the suffering servant is actually a *parody of the conventional encomium: although it praises the subject with the conventional categories, it inverts them and praises him for what the world at large would regard as unpraiseworthy qualities. A lead-in promises to praise the subject in standard terms (52:13), but the suffering servant is then praised for being marred beyond parallel (52:14–15), for being of undistinguished ancestry and social standing (53:1–2), for acts that by conventional standards would render him contemptible (53:3–6), and for a life's conclusion that is the opposite of a conventional success story (53:7–9). Verses 3–6 stress the subject's redemptive actions, and verses 7–9 highlight their tragic nature when judged by ordinary standards of success. The concluding section reads more like a standard encomium, as the suffering servant is praised for what his suffering has accomplished (53:10–12). Even here there are reversals and paradoxes, as the suffering servant triumphs not because he defeated his enemies in open combat for personal benefit but because he gave his life for others.

[13] Behold, my servant shall act wisely;[1]
he shall be high and lifted up,
and shall be exalted.

---

[1] Or shall prosper

14 As many were astonished at you—
    his appearance was so marred, beyond human semblance,
    and his form beyond that of the children of mankind—
15 so shall he sprinkle[1] many nations;
    kings shall shut their mouths because of him;
for that which has not been told them they see,
    and that which they have not heard they understand.

53 Who has believed what he has heard from us?[2]
    And to whom has the arm of the LORD been revealed?
2 For he grew up before him like a young plant,
    and like a root out of dry ground;
he had no form or majesty that we should look at him,
    and no beauty that we should desire him.
3 He was despised and rejected[3] by men;
    a man of sorrows,[4] and acquainted with[5] grief;[6]
and as one from whom men hide their faces[7]
    he was despised, and we esteemed him not.

4 Surely he has borne our griefs
    and carried our sorrows;
yet we esteemed him stricken,
    smitten by God, and afflicted.
5 But he was wounded for our transgressions;
    he was crushed for our iniquities;
upon him was the chastisement that brought us peace,
    and with his stripes we are healed.
6 All we like sheep have gone astray;
    we have turned—every one—to his own way;
and the LORD has laid on him
    the iniquity of us all.

7 He was oppressed, and he was afflicted,
    yet he opened not his mouth;
like a lamb that is led to the slaughter,
    and like a sheep that before its shearers is silent,
    so he opened not his mouth.
8 By oppression and judgment he was taken away;
    and as for his generation, who considered
that he was cut off out of the land of the living,
    stricken for the transgression of my people?
9 And they made his grave with the wicked
    and with a rich man in his death,
although he had done no violence,
    and there was no deceit in his mouth.

10 Yet it was the will of the LORD to crush him;
    he has put him to grief;[8]

---

[1] Or startle [2] Or Who has believed what we have heard? [3] Or forsaken [4] Or pains; also verse 4 [5] Or and knowing [6] Or sickness; also verse 4 [7] Or as one who hides his face from us [8] Or he has made him sick

when his soul makes[1] an offering for guilt,
   he shall see his offspring; he shall prolong his days;
the will of the Lord shall prosper in his hand.
[11] Out of the anguish of his soul he shall see[2] and be satisfied;
   by his knowledge shall the righteous one, my servant,
     make many to be accounted righteous,
     and he shall bear their iniquities.
[12] Therefore I will divide him a portion with the many,[3]
   and he shall divide the spoil with the strong,[4]
because he poured out his soul to death
   and was numbered with the transgressors;
yet he bore the sin of many,
   and makes intercession for the transgressors.

God's blessings toward his people [chapter 54]. The rapturous tone continues, as does the miscellaneous structure of the ideas and feelings that pour out. The general format is the oracle of blessing. The rhetorical pattern is the catalog of blessings. The dominant poetic device is apostrophe—direct addresses to people and groups imagined to be present and listening but not literally present. Apostrophe is a standard way of expressing strong feeling in poetry and serves that purpose here.

54

"Sing, O barren one, who did not bear;
   break forth into singing and cry aloud,
   you who have not been in labor!
For the children of the desolate one will be more
   than the children of her who is married," says the Lord.
[2] "Enlarge the place of your tent,
   and let the curtains of your habitations be stretched out;
do not hold back; lengthen your cords
   and strengthen your stakes.
[3] For you will spread abroad to the right and to the left,
   and your offspring will possess the nations
   and will people the desolate cities.

[4] "Fear not, for you will not be ashamed;
   be not confounded, for you will not be disgraced;
for you will forget the shame of your youth,
   and the reproach of your widowhood you will remember no more.
[5] For your Maker is your husband,
   the Lord of hosts is his name;
and the Holy One of Israel is your Redeemer,
   the God of the whole earth he is called.
[6] For the Lord has called you
   like a wife deserted and grieved in spirit,
like a wife of youth when she is cast off,
   says your God.
[7] For a brief moment I deserted you,

---

[1] Or *when you make his soul* [2] Masoretic Text; Dead Sea Scroll *he shall see light* [3] Or *with the great* [4] Or *with the numerous*

but with great compassion I will gather you.
8   In overflowing anger for a moment
        I hid my face from you,
    but with everlasting love I will have compassion on you,"
        says the LORD, your Redeemer.

9   "This is like the days of Noah[1] to me:
        as I swore that the waters of Noah
        should no more go over the earth,
    so I have sworn that I will not be angry with you,
        and will not rebuke you.
10 For the mountains may depart
        and the hills be removed,
    but my steadfast love shall not depart from you,
        and my covenant of peace shall not be removed,"
        says the LORD, who has compassion on you.

11 "O afflicted one, storm-tossed and not comforted,
        behold, I will set your stones in antimony,
        and lay your foundations with sapphires.[2]
12 I will make your pinnacles of agate,[3]
        your gates of carbuncles,[4]
        and all your wall of precious stones.
13 All your children shall be taught by the LORD,
        and great shall be the peace of your children.
14 In righteousness you shall be established;
        you shall be far from oppression, for you shall not fear;
        and from terror, for it shall not come near you.
15 If anyone stirs up strife,
        it is not from me;
    whoever stirs up strife with you
        shall fall because of you.
16 Behold, I have created the smith
        who blows the fire of coals
        and produces a weapon for its purpose.
    I have also created the ravager to destroy;
17   no weapon that is fashioned against you shall succeed,
        and you shall confute every tongue that rises against you in judgment.
    This is the heritage of the servants of the LORD
        and their vindication[5] from me, declares the LORD."

Divine invitation [chapter 55]. God continues to speak to his people in terms of love and blessing. The rhetorical pattern is an exalted invitation (vv. 1–3a and 6–7), accompanied by promises of blessings that make acceptance of the invitation the only suitable response (vv. 3b–5, 8–11). The individual units are so aphoristic and familiar that many of them have long since been taken out of the context of this particular chapter.

[1] Some manuscripts *For this is as the waters of Noah* [2] Or *lapis lazuli* [3] Or *jasper, or ruby* [4] Or *crystal* [5] Or *righteousness*

55
"Come, everyone who thirsts,
    come to the waters;
and he who has no money,
    come, buy and eat!
Come, buy wine and milk
    without money and without price.
2 Why do you spend your money for that which is not bread,
    and your labor for that which does not satisfy?
Listen diligently to me, and eat what is good,
    and delight yourselves in rich food.
3 Incline your ear, and come to me;
    hear, that your soul may live;
and I will make with you an everlasting covenant,
    my steadfast, sure love for David.
4 Behold, I made him a witness to the peoples,
    a leader and commander for the peoples.
5 Behold, you shall call a nation that you do not know,
    and a nation that did not know you shall run to you,
because of the Lord your God, and of the Holy One of Israel,
    for he has glorified you.

6 "Seek the Lord while he may be found;
    call upon him while he is near;
7 let the wicked forsake his way,
    and the unrighteous man his thoughts;
let him return to the Lord, that he may have compassion on him,
    and to our God, for he will abundantly pardon.
8 For my thoughts are not your thoughts,
    neither are your ways my ways, declares the Lord.
9 For as the heavens are higher than the earth,
    so are my ways higher than your ways
    and my thoughts than your thoughts.

10 "For as the rain and the snow come down from heaven
    and do not return there but water the earth,
making it bring forth and sprout,
    giving seed to the sower and bread to the eater,
11 so shall my word be that goes out from my mouth;
    it shall not return to me empty,
but it shall accomplish that which I purpose,
    and shall succeed in the thing for which I sent it.

12 "For you shall go out in joy
    and be led forth in peace;
the mountains and the hills before you
    shall break forth into singing,
    and all the trees of the field shall clap their hands.
13 Instead of the thorn shall come up the cypress;

instead of the brier shall come up the myrtle;
and it shall make a name for the Lord,
    an everlasting sign that shall not be cut off."

Exhortations and warnings from God [chapters 56–57]. To some extent this block of material sets up a countermovement to the rapturous addresses from God that have preceded it. Although there are continued promises of blessing to those who qualify through obedience to God (56:1–8) and repentance (57:14–21), the dominant motif is denunciation of those who reject God, couched in the rhetoric of oracles of judgment.

56

Thus says the Lord:
"Keep justice, and do righteousness,
for soon my salvation will come,
    and my deliverance be revealed.
2   Blessed is the man who does this,
        and the son of man who holds it fast,
    who keeps the Sabbath, not profaning it,
        and keeps his hand from doing any evil."

3   Let not the foreigner who has joined himself to the Lord say,
        "The Lord will surely separate me from his people";
    and let not the eunuch say,
        "Behold, I am a dry tree."
4   For thus says the Lord:
    "To the eunuchs who keep my Sabbaths,
        who choose the things that please me
        and hold fast my covenant,
5   I will give in my house and within my walls
        a monument and a name
        better than sons and daughters;
    I will give them an everlasting name
        that shall not be cut off.

6   "And the foreigners who join themselves to the Lord,
        to minister to him, to love the name of the Lord,
        and to be his servants,
    everyone who keeps the Sabbath and does not profane it,
        and holds fast my covenant—
7   these I will bring to my holy mountain,
        and make them joyful in my house of prayer;
    their burnt offerings and their sacrifices
        will be accepted on my altar;
    for my house shall be called a house of prayer
        for all peoples."
8   The Lord God,
        who gathers the outcasts of Israel, declares,

"I will gather yet others to him
　　besides those already gathered."

⁹　All you beasts of the field, come to devour—
　　all you beasts in the forest.
¹⁰　His watchmen are blind;
　　they are all without knowledge;
　they are all silent dogs;
　　they cannot bark,
　dreaming, lying down,
　　loving to slumber.
¹¹　The dogs have a mighty appetite;
　　they never have enough.
　But they are shepherds who have no understanding;
　　they have all turned to their own way,
　　each to his own gain, one and all.
¹²　"Come," they say, "let me get wine;
　　let us fill ourselves with strong drink;
　and tomorrow will be like this day,
　　great beyond measure."

57 The righteous man perishes,
　　and no one lays it to heart;
　devout men are taken away,
　　while no one understands.
　For the righteous man is taken away from calamity;
²　　he enters into peace;
　they rest in their beds
　　who walk in their uprightness.
³　But you, draw near,
　　sons of the sorceress,
　　offspring of the adulterer and the loose woman.
⁴　Whom are you mocking?
　　Against whom do you open your mouth wide
　　and stick out your tongue?
　Are you not children of transgression,
　　the offspring of deceit,
⁵　you who burn with lust among the oaks,¹
　　under every green tree,
　who slaughter your children in the valleys,
　　under the clefts of the rocks?
⁶　Among the smooth stones of the valley is your portion;
　　they, they, are your lot;
　to them you have poured out a drink offering,
　　you have brought a grain offering.
　　Shall I relent for these things?
⁷　On a high and lofty mountain

---

¹ Or among the terebinths

you have set your bed,
and there you went up to offer sacrifice.
⁸ Behind the door and the doorpost
you have set up your memorial;
for, deserting me, you have uncovered your bed,
you have gone up to it,
you have made it wide;
and you have made a covenant for yourself with them,
you have loved their bed,
you have looked on nakedness.¹
⁹ You journeyed to the king with oil
and multiplied your perfumes;
you sent your envoys far off,
and sent down even to Sheol.
¹⁰ You were wearied with the length of your way,
but you did not say, "It is hopeless";
you found new life for your strength,
and so you were not faint.²

¹¹ Whom did you dread and fear,
so that you lied,
and did not remember me,
did not lay it to heart?
Have I not held my peace, even for a long time,
and you do not fear me?
¹² I will declare your righteousness and your deeds,
but they will not profit you.
¹³ When you cry out, let your collection of idols deliver you!
The wind will carry them off,
a breath will take them away.
But he who takes refuge in me shall possess the land
and shall inherit my holy mountain.

¹⁴ And it shall be said,
"Build up, build up, prepare the way,
remove every obstruction from my people's way."
¹⁵ For thus says the One who is high and lifted up,
who inhabits eternity, whose name is Holy:
"I dwell in the high and holy place,
and also with him who is of a contrite and lowly spirit,
to revive the spirit of the lowly,
and to revive the heart of the contrite.
¹⁶ For I will not contend forever,
nor will I always be angry;
for the spirit would grow faint before me,
and the breath of life that I made.
¹⁷ Because of the iniquity of his unjust gain I was angry,

¹ Or on a monument (see 56:5); Hebrew on a hand ² Hebrew and so you were not sick

I struck him; I hid my face and was angry,
    but he went on backsliding in the way of his own heart.
18   I have seen his ways, but I will heal him;
    I will lead him and restore comfort to him and his mourners,
19   creating the fruit of the lips.
   Peace, peace, to the far and to the near," says the Lord,
    "and I will heal him.
20   But the wicked are like the tossing sea;
    for it cannot be quiet,
    and its waters toss up mire and dirt.
21   There is no peace," says my God, "for the wicked."

> **The blessings of true fasting, morality, and Sabbath keeping** [chapter 58]. The general drift of the chapter is to instill a desire to worship God properly and sincerely. God continues to address his people through the agency of the prophet Isaiah. After an opening rebuke for insincere fasting (vv. 1–5), the chapter unfolds in this sequence: the kind of fasting that God requires, along with the blessings that come from it (vv. 6–9a); God's blessings on a moral society (vv. 9b–12); God's blessing for keeping the Sabbath (vv. 13–14).

58 "Cry aloud; do not hold back;
    lift up your voice like a trumpet;
  declare to my people their transgression,
    to the house of Jacob their sins.
2   Yet they seek me daily
    and delight to know my ways,
  as if they were a nation that did righteousness
    and did not forsake the judgment of their God;
  they ask of me righteous judgments;
    they delight to draw near to God.
3   'Why have we fasted, and you see it not?
    Why have we humbled ourselves, and you take no knowledge of it?'
  Behold, in the day of your fast you seek your own pleasure,[1]
    and oppress all your workers.
4   Behold, you fast only to quarrel and to fight
    and to hit with a wicked fist.
  Fasting like yours this day
    will not make your voice to be heard on high.
5   Is such the fast that I choose,
    a day for a person to humble himself?
  Is it to bow down his head like a reed,
    and to spread sackcloth and ashes under him?
  Will you call this a fast,
    and a day acceptable to the Lord?

6   "Is not this the fast that I choose:
    to loose the bonds of wickedness,

---

[1] Or pursue your own business

   to undo the straps of the yoke,
 to let the oppressed[1] go free,
   and to break every yoke?
7 Is it not to share your bread with the hungry
   and bring the homeless poor into your house;
 when you see the naked, to cover him,
   and not to hide yourself from your own flesh?
8 Then shall your light break forth like the dawn,
   and your healing shall spring up speedily;
 your righteousness shall go before you;
   the glory of the LORD shall be your rear guard.
9 Then you shall call, and the LORD will answer;
   you shall cry, and he will say, 'Here I am.'
 If you take away the yoke from your midst,
   the pointing of the finger, and speaking wickedness,
10 if you pour yourself out for the hungry
   and satisfy the desire of the afflicted,
 then shall your light rise in the darkness
   and your gloom be as the noonday.
11 And the LORD will guide you continually
   and satisfy your desire in scorched places
   and make your bones strong;
 and you shall be like a watered garden,
   like a spring of water,
   whose waters do not fail.
12 And your ancient ruins shall be rebuilt;
   you shall raise up the foundations of many generations;
 you shall be called the repairer of the breach,
   the restorer of streets to dwell in.

13 "If you turn back your foot from the Sabbath,
   from doing your pleasure[2] on my holy day,
 and call the Sabbath a delight
   and the holy day of the LORD honorable;
 if you honor it, not going your own ways,
   or seeking your own pleasure,[3] or talking idly;[4]
14 then you shall take delight in the LORD,
   and I will make you ride on the heights of the earth;[5]
 I will feed you with the heritage of Jacob your father,
   for the mouth of the LORD has spoken."

National sin, confession, and salvation [chapter 59]. The rhetorical mode continues to be God's address to a nation. Three movements make up the chapter: God indicts Israel for sins of injustice and violence (vv. 1–8); the nation confesses and repents (vv. 9–15a); God intervenes to redeem Zion (vv. 15b–21).

---

[1] Or *bruised* [2] Or *business* [3] Or *pursuing your own business* [4] Hebrew *or speaking a word* [5] Or *of the land*

59

Behold, the Lᴏʀᴅ's hand is not shortened, that it cannot save,
   or his ear dull, that it cannot hear;
² but your iniquities have made a separation
      between you and your God,
   and your sins have hidden his face from you
      so that he does not hear.
³ For your hands are defiled with blood
      and your fingers with iniquity;
   your lips have spoken lies;
      your tongue mutters wickedness.
⁴ No one enters suit justly;
      no one goes to law honestly;
   they rely on empty pleas, they speak lies,
      they conceive mischief and give birth to iniquity.
⁵ They hatch adders' eggs;
      they weave the spider's web;
   he who eats their eggs dies,
      and from one that is crushed a viper is hatched.
⁶ Their webs will not serve as clothing;
      men will not cover themselves with what they make.
   Their works are works of iniquity,
      and deeds of violence are in their hands.
⁷ Their feet run to evil,
      and they are swift to shed innocent blood;
   their thoughts are thoughts of iniquity;
      desolation and destruction are in their highways.
⁸ The way of peace they do not know,
      and there is no justice in their paths;
   they have made their roads crooked;
      no one who treads on them knows peace.

⁹ Therefore justice is far from us,
      and righteousness does not overtake us;
   we hope for light, and behold, darkness,
      and for brightness, but we walk in gloom.
¹⁰ We grope for the wall like the blind;
      we grope like those who have no eyes;
   we stumble at noon as in the twilight,
      among those in full vigor we are like dead men.
¹¹ We all growl like bears;
      we moan and moan like doves;
   we hope for justice, but there is none;
      for salvation, but it is far from us.
¹² For our transgressions are multiplied before you,
      and our sins testify against us;
   for our transgressions are with us,
      and we know our iniquities:

13 transgressing, and denying the LORD,
      and turning back from following our God,
    speaking oppression and revolt,
      conceiving and uttering from the heart lying words.
14 Justice is turned back,
      and righteousness stands far away;
    for truth has stumbled in the public squares,
      and uprightness cannot enter.
15 Truth is lacking,
      and he who departs from evil makes himself a prey.

    The LORD saw it, and it displeased him[1]
      that there was no justice.
16 He saw that there was no man,
      and wondered that there was no one to intercede;
    then his own arm brought him salvation,
      and his righteousness upheld him.
17 He put on righteousness as a breastplate,
      and a helmet of salvation on his head;
    he put on garments of vengeance for clothing,
      and wrapped himself in zeal as a cloak.
18 According to their deeds, so will he repay,
      wrath to his adversaries, repayment to his enemies;
    to the coastlands he will render repayment.
19 So they shall fear the name of the LORD from the west,
      and his glory from the rising of the sun;
    for he will come like a rushing stream,[2]
      which the wind of the LORD drives.

20   "And a Redeemer will come to Zion,
      to those in Jacob who turn from transgression," declares the LORD.

[21]"And as for me, this is my covenant with them," says the LORD: "My Spirit that is
upon you, and my words that I have put in your mouth, shall not depart out of your
mouth, or out of the mouth of your offspring, or out of the mouth of your children's
offspring," says the LORD, "from this time forth and forevermore."

> **A vision of Zion restored** [chapter 60]. With this chapter we begin the final ascent of
> the rhapsody of Zion redeemed. The material is organized as a litany of the blessings
> that God promises to bestow on his people, called Zion. It is the first of multiple golden
> age prophecies at the end of Isaiah. The key interpretive question is to what the pictures
> refer. Four possibilities exist, and they are not mutually exclusive: the material might
> be (a) a metaphoric and hyperbolic picture of the restoration of Judah to its homeland
> after the exile in Babylon, and/or (b) a metaphoric picture of the blessings that come to
> the redeemed anytime, anywhere, and/or (c) a messianic prophecy of the blessings that
> Christ brought with his incarnation, atonement, and resurrection, and/or (d) a vision of
> the coming eschaton (either the millennium or heaven, or both).

---

[1] Hebrew *and it was evil in his eyes* [2] Hebrew *a narrow river*

60

Arise, shine, for your light has come,
    and the glory of the Lord has risen upon you.
2 For behold, darkness shall cover the earth,
    and thick darkness the peoples;
but the Lord will arise upon you,
    and his glory will be seen upon you.
3 And nations shall come to your light,
    and kings to the brightness of your rising.

4 Lift up your eyes all around, and see;
    they all gather together, they come to you;
your sons shall come from afar,
    and your daughters shall be carried on the hip.
5 Then you shall see and be radiant;
    your heart shall thrill and exult,[1]
because the abundance of the sea shall be turned to you,
    the wealth of the nations shall come to you.
6 A multitude of camels shall cover you,
    the young camels of Midian and Ephah;
    all those from Sheba shall come.
They shall bring gold and frankincense,
    and shall bring good news, the praises of the Lord.
7 All the flocks of Kedar shall be gathered to you;
    the rams of Nebaioth shall minister to you;
they shall come up with acceptance on my altar,
    and I will beautify my beautiful house.

8 Who are these that fly like a cloud,
    and like doves to their windows?
9 For the coastlands shall hope for me,
    the ships of Tarshish first,
to bring your children from afar,
    their silver and gold with them,
for the name of the Lord your God,
    and for the Holy One of Israel,
    because he has made you beautiful.

10 Foreigners shall build up your walls,
    and their kings shall minister to you;
for in my wrath I struck you,
    but in my favor I have had mercy on you.
11 Your gates shall be open continually;
    day and night they shall not be shut,
that people may bring to you the wealth of the nations,
    with their kings led in procession.
12 For the nation and kingdom
    that will not serve you shall perish;
    those nations shall be utterly laid waste.

---

[1] Hebrew *your heart shall tremble and grow wide*

¹³   The glory of Lebanon shall come to you,
         the cypress, the plane, and the pine,
     to beautify the place of my sanctuary,
         and I will make the place of my feet glorious.
¹⁴   The sons of those who afflicted you
         shall come bending low to you,
     and all who despised you
         shall bow down at your feet;
     they shall call you the City of the Lᴏʀᴅ,
         the Zion of the Holy One of Israel.

¹⁵   Whereas you have been forsaken and hated,
         with no one passing through,
     I will make you majestic forever,
         a joy from age to age.
¹⁶   You shall suck the milk of nations;
         you shall nurse at the breast of kings;
     and you shall know that I, the Lᴏʀᴅ, am your Savior
         and your Redeemer, the Mighty One of Jacob.

¹⁷   Instead of bronze I will bring gold,
         and instead of iron I will bring silver;
     instead of wood, bronze,
         instead of stones, iron.
     I will make your overseers peace
         and your taskmasters righteousness.
¹⁸   Violence shall no more be heard in your land,
         devastation or destruction within your borders;
     you shall call your walls Salvation,
         and your gates Praise.

¹⁹   The sun shall be no more
         your light by day,
     nor for brightness shall the moon
         give you light;[1]
     but the Lᴏʀᴅ will be your everlasting light,
         and your God will be your glory.[2]
²⁰   Your sun shall no more go down,
         nor your moon withdraw itself;
     for the Lᴏʀᴅ will be your everlasting light,
         and your days of mourning shall be ended.
²¹   Your people shall all be righteous;
         they shall possess the land forever,
     the branch of my planting, the work of my hands,
         that I might be glorified.[3]
²²   The least one shall become a clan,
         and the smallest one a mighty nation;

---

[1] Masoretic Text; Dead Sea Scroll, Septuagint, Targum add *by night* [2] Or *your beauty* [3] Or *that I might display my beauty*

I am the LORD;
   in its time I will hasten it.

> **More good news for God's people** [chapters 61–62]. The visionary mode continues
> as the prophet pictures the restoration of a symbolic city called Zion, the city of God.
> In a stream-of-consciousness pattern, we move from one subject to another and from
> the prophet as speaker to God as speaker. The image of the holy city dominates the sec-
> tion, and even though it is given the physical properties of the actual city of Jerusalem,
> its future restoration and glory make it more symbolic than literal. The best approach
> is probably to see all four levels at work in this chapter (see headnote to chapter 60,
> above).

61

The Spirit of the Lord GOD is upon me,
   because the LORD has anointed me
to bring good news to the poor;[1]
   he has sent me to bind up the brokenhearted,
to proclaim liberty to the captives,
   and the opening of the prison to those who are bound;[2]
2 to proclaim the year of the LORD's favor,
   and the day of vengeance of our God;
     to comfort all who mourn;
3 to grant to those who mourn in Zion—
     to give them a beautiful headdress instead of ashes,
the oil of gladness instead of mourning,
     the garment of praise instead of a faint spirit;
that they may be called oaks of righteousness,
     the planting of the LORD, that he may be glorified.[3]
4 They shall build up the ancient ruins;
   they shall raise up the former devastations;
they shall repair the ruined cities,
   the devastations of many generations.

5 Strangers shall stand and tend your flocks;
   foreigners shall be your plowmen and vinedressers;
6 but you shall be called the priests of the LORD;
   they shall speak of you as the ministers of our God;
you shall eat the wealth of the nations,
   and in their glory you shall boast.
7 Instead of your shame there shall be a double portion;
   instead of dishonor they shall rejoice in their lot;
therefore in their land they shall possess a double portion;
   they shall have everlasting joy.

8 For I the LORD love justice;
   I hate robbery and wrong;[4]
I will faithfully give them their recompense,
   and I will make an everlasting covenant with them.

---

[1] Or afflicted [2] Or the opening [of the eyes] to those who are blind; Septuagint and recovery of sight to the blind [3] Or that he may display his beauty
[4] Or robbery with a burnt offering

⁹ Their offspring shall be known among the nations,
    and their descendants in the midst of the peoples;
all who see them shall acknowledge them,
    that they are an offspring the Lord has blessed.

¹⁰ I will greatly rejoice in the Lord;
    my soul shall exult in my God,
for he has clothed me with the garments of salvation;
    he has covered me with the robe of righteousness,
as a bridegroom decks himself like a priest with a beautiful headdress,
    and as a bride adorns herself with her jewels.

¹¹ For as the earth brings forth its sprouts,
    and as a garden causes what is sown in it to sprout up,
so the Lord God will cause righteousness and praise
    to sprout up before all the nations.

62

For Zion's sake I will not keep silent,
    and for Jerusalem's sake I will not be quiet,
until her righteousness goes forth as brightness,
    and her salvation as a burning torch.

² The nations shall see your righteousness,
    and all the kings your glory,
and you shall be called by a new name
    that the mouth of the Lord will give.

³ You shall be a crown of beauty in the hand of the Lord,
    and a royal diadem in the hand of your God.

⁴ You shall no more be termed Forsaken,[1]
    and your land shall no more be termed Desolate,[2]
but you shall be called My Delight Is in Her,[3]
    and your land Married;[4]
for the Lord delights in you,
    and your land shall be married.

⁵ For as a young man marries a young woman,
    so shall your sons marry you,
and as the bridegroom rejoices over the bride,
    so shall your God rejoice over you.

⁶ On your walls, O Jerusalem,
    I have set watchmen;
all the day and all the night
    they shall never be silent.
You who put the Lord in remembrance,
    take no rest,

⁷ and give him no rest
    until he establishes Jerusalem
    and makes it a praise in the earth.

⁸ The Lord has sworn by his right hand
    and by his mighty arm:

---

[1] Hebrew *Azubah* [2] Hebrew *Shemamah* [3] Hebrew *Hephzibah* [4] Hebrew *Beulah*

"I will not again give your grain
    to be food for your enemies,
and foreigners shall not drink your wine
    for which you have labored;
⁹ but those who garner it shall eat it
    and praise the Lord,
and those who gather it shall drink it
    in the courts of my sanctuary."[1]

¹⁰ Go through, go through the gates;
    prepare the way for the people;
build up, build up the highway;
    clear it of stones;
    lift up a signal over the peoples.
¹¹ Behold, the Lord has proclaimed
    to the end of the earth:
Say to the daughter of Zion,
  "Behold, your salvation comes;
behold, his reward is with him,
    and his recompense before him."
¹² And they shall be called The Holy People,
    The Redeemed of the Lord;
and you shall be called Sought Out,
    A City Not Forsaken.

Israel's prayer for deliverance from its enemies [chapters 63–64]. This material, too, is partly a counterpoint to the general plot line of Isaiah 40–66. With an opening vision of God's judgment to set the tone (63:1–6), we move through this sequence: the prophet's recollection of God's love (63:7–9) and Israel's rebelliousness in the time of Moses (63:10–14); an appeal to God to restore Israel (63:15–64:4); confession of sin (64:5–7); asking God to deliver (64:8–12).

63 Who is this who comes from Edom,
    in crimsoned garments from Bozrah,
he who is splendid in his apparel,
    marching in the greatness of his strength?
"It is I, speaking in righteousness,
    mighty to save."

² Why is your apparel red,
    and your garments like his who treads in the winepress?

³ "I have trodden the winepress alone,
    and from the peoples no one was with me;
I trod them in my anger
    and trampled them in my wrath;
their lifeblood[2] spattered on my garments,
    and stained all my apparel.

[1] Or in my holy courts [2] Or their juice; also verse 6

⁴   For the day of vengeance was in my heart,
        and my year of redemption¹ had come.
⁵   I looked, but there was no one to help;
        I was appalled, but there was no one to uphold;
    so my own arm brought me salvation,
        and my wrath upheld me.
⁶   I trampled down the peoples in my anger;
        I made them drunk in my wrath,
        and I poured out their lifeblood on the earth."

⁷   I will recount the steadfast love of the LORD,
        the praises of the LORD,
    according to all that the LORD has granted us,
        and the great goodness to the house of Israel
    that he has granted them according to his compassion,
        according to the abundance of his steadfast love.
⁸   For he said, "Surely they are my people,
        children who will not deal falsely."
    And he became their Savior.
⁹   In all their affliction he was afflicted,²
        and the angel of his presence saved them;
    in his love and in his pity he redeemed them;
        he lifted them up and carried them all the days of old.

¹⁰   But they rebelled
        and grieved his Holy Spirit;
    therefore he turned to be their enemy,
        and himself fought against them.
¹¹   Then he remembered the days of old,
        of Moses and his people.³
    Where is he who brought them up out of the sea
        with the shepherds of his flock?
    Where is he who put in the midst of them
        his Holy Spirit,
¹²   who caused his glorious arm
        to go at the right hand of Moses,
    who divided the waters before them
        to make for himself an everlasting name,
¹³   who led them through the depths?
    Like a horse in the desert,
        they did not stumble.
¹⁴   Like livestock that go down into the valley,
        the Spirit of the LORD gave them rest.
    So you led your people,
        to make for yourself a glorious name.

¹⁵   Look down from heaven and see,
        from your holy and beautiful⁴ habitation.

---

¹ Or the year of my redeemed ² Or he did not afflict ³ Or Then his people remembered the days of old, of Moses ⁴ Or holy and glorious

Where are your zeal and your might?
> The stirring of your inner parts and your compassion
> are held back from me.

16 For you are our Father,
> though Abraham does not know us,
> and Israel does not acknowledge us;
> you, O Lord, are our Father,
> our Redeemer from of old is your name.

17 O Lord, why do you make us wander from your ways
> and harden our heart, so that we fear you not?
> Return for the sake of your servants,
> the tribes of your heritage.

18 Your holy people held possession for a little while;[1]
> our adversaries have trampled down your sanctuary.

19 We have become like those over whom you have never ruled,
> like those who are not called by your name.

64 Oh that you would rend the heavens and come down,
> that the mountains might quake at your presence—

2 2 as when fire kindles brushwood
> and the fire causes water to boil—
> to make your name known to your adversaries,
> and that the nations might tremble at your presence!

3 When you did awesome things that we did not look for,
> you came down, the mountains quaked at your presence.

4 From of old no one has heard
> or perceived by the ear,
> no eye has seen a God besides you,
> who acts for those who wait for him.

5 You meet him who joyfully works righteousness,
> those who remember you in your ways.
> Behold, you were angry, and we sinned;
> in our sins we have been a long time, and shall we be saved?[3]

6 We have all become like one who is unclean,
> and all our righteous deeds are like a polluted garment.
> We all fade like a leaf,
> and our iniquities, like the wind, take us away.

7 There is no one who calls upon your name,
> who rouses himself to take hold of you;
> for you have hidden your face from us,
> and have made us melt in[4] the hand of our iniquities.

8 But now, O Lord, you are our Father;
> we are the clay, and you are our potter;
> we are all the work of your hand.

9 Be not so terribly angry, O Lord,
> and remember not iniquity forever.

---

[1] Or They have dispossessed your holy people for a little while [2] Ch 64:1 in Hebrew [3] Or in your ways is continuance, that we might be saved [4] Masoretic Text; Septuagint, Syriac, Targum have delivered us into

Behold, please look, we are all your people.
10   Your holy cities have become a wilderness;
        Zion has become a wilderness,
     Jerusalem a desolation.
11   Our holy and beautiful¹ house,
        where our fathers praised you,
     has been burned by fire,
        and all our pleasant places have become ruins.
12   Will you restrain yourself at these things, O LORD?
     Will you keep silent, and afflict us so terribly?

God's reply to Israel [chapter 65]. The first half of the chapter (vv. 1–16) has the effect of God's answering the prayer for deliverance that has immediately preceded. The reply is a mixed message, as God's disapproval of those who forsake him is mingled with forgiveness to the penitent and faithful. In fact, verses 13–16 are a formal separation of God's "servants" from the disobedient, with blessing coming to the former and judgment to the latter. The second half of the chapter (vv. 17–25) is a famous golden age prophecy in which the immediate future (return after exile), the intermediate future (the messianic age), and the eschatological future flow together.

---

65 I was ready to be sought by those who did not ask for me;
        I was ready to be found by those who did not seek me.
     I said, "Here am I, here am I,"
        to a nation that was not called by² my name.
2   I spread out my hands all the day
        to a rebellious people,
     who walk in a way that is not good,
        following their own devices;
3   a people who provoke me
        to my face continually,
     sacrificing in gardens
        and making offerings on bricks;
4   who sit in tombs,
        and spend the night in secret places;
     who eat pig's flesh,
        and broth of tainted meat is in their vessels;
5   who say, "Keep to yourself,
        do not come near me, for I am too holy for you."
     These are a smoke in my nostrils,
        a fire that burns all the day.
6   Behold, it is written before me:
        "I will not keep silent, but I will repay;
     I will indeed repay into their bosom
7   both your iniquities and your fathers' iniquities together,
                        says the LORD;
     because they made offerings on the mountains

---

¹ Or holy and glorious ² Or that did not call upon

and insulted me on the hills,
I will measure into their bosom
    payment for their former deeds."[1]

8   Thus says the LORD:
"As the new wine is found in the cluster,
    and they say, 'Do not destroy it,
    for there is a blessing in it,'
so I will do for my servants' sake,
    and not destroy them all.
9   I will bring forth offspring from Jacob,
    and from Judah possessors of my mountains;
my chosen shall possess it,
    and my servants shall dwell there.
10 Sharon shall become a pasture for flocks,
    and the Valley of Achor a place for herds to lie down,
for my people who have sought me.
11 But you who forsake the LORD,
    who forget my holy mountain,
who set a table for Fortune
    and fill cups of mixed wine for Destiny,
12 I will destine you to the sword,
    and all of you shall bow down to the slaughter,
because, when I called, you did not answer;
    when I spoke, you did not listen,
but you did what was evil in my eyes
    and chose what I did not delight in."

13 Therefore thus says the Lord GOD:
"Behold, my servants shall eat,
    but you shall be hungry;
behold, my servants shall drink,
    but you shall be thirsty;
behold, my servants shall rejoice,
    but you shall be put to shame;
14 behold, my servants shall sing for gladness of heart,
    but you shall cry out for pain of heart
    and shall wail for breaking of spirit.
15 You shall leave your name to my chosen for a curse,
    and the Lord GOD will put you to death,
    but his servants he will call by another name.
16 So that he who blesses himself in the land
    shall bless himself by the God of truth,
and he who takes an oath in the land
    shall swear by the God of truth;
because the former troubles are forgotten
    and are hidden from my eyes.

---

[1] Or I will first measure their payment into their bosom

17   "For behold, I create new heavens
         and a new earth,
     and the former things shall not be remembered
         or come into mind.
18   But be glad and rejoice forever
         in that which I create;
     for behold, I create Jerusalem to be a joy,
         and her people to be a gladness.
19   I will rejoice in Jerusalem
         and be glad in my people;
     no more shall be heard in it the sound of weeping
         and the cry of distress.
20   No more shall there be in it
         an infant who lives but a few days,
         or an old man who does not fill out his days,
     for the young man shall die a hundred years old,
         and the sinner a hundred years old shall be accursed.
21   They shall build houses and inhabit them;
         they shall plant vineyards and eat their fruit.
22   They shall not build and another inhabit;
         they shall not plant and another eat;
     for like the days of a tree shall the days of my people be,
         and my chosen shall long enjoy[1] the work of their hands.
23   They shall not labor in vain
         or bear children for calamity,[2]
     for they shall be the offspring of the blessed of the LORD,
         and their descendants with them.
24   Before they call I will answer;
         while they are yet speaking I will hear.
25   The wolf and the lamb shall graze together;
         the lion shall eat straw like the ox,
         and dust shall be the serpent's food.
     They shall not hurt or destroy
         in all my holy mountain,"
                         says the LORD.

Closure [chapter 66]. A good way to ponder the concluding chapter is to read it in an awareness of how it sums up and recapitulates the form and message of the book as a whole. The twin motifs of judgment against sinners (vv. 1–4; 15–17; 24) and blessing on the faithful (the rest of the chapter) govern the material. The great either-or is set before the reader one last time. At the very end, the prophet's vision of heaven is set against his vision of hell (vv. 22–24).

66   Thus says the LORD:
     "Heaven is my throne,
         and the earth is my footstool;

[1] Hebrew *shall wear out* [2] Or *for sudden terror*

what is the house that you would build for me,
  and what is the place of my rest?
² All these things my hand has made,
  and so all these things came to be,
                declares the LORD.
  But this is the one to whom I will look:
    he who is humble and contrite in spirit
    and trembles at my word.

³ "He who slaughters an ox is like one who kills a man;
    he who sacrifices a lamb, like one who breaks a dog's neck;
  he who presents a grain offering, like one who offers pig's blood;
    he who makes a memorial offering of frankincense, like one who blesses an idol.
  These have chosen their own ways,
    and their soul delights in their abominations;
⁴ I also will choose harsh treatment for them
    and bring their fears upon them,
  because when I called, no one answered,
    when I spoke, they did not listen;
  but they did what was evil in my eyes
    and chose that in which I did not delight."

⁵ Hear the word of the LORD,
    you who tremble at his word:
  "Your brothers who hate you
    and cast you out for my name's sake
  have said, 'Let the LORD be glorified,
    that we may see your joy';
    but it is they who shall be put to shame.

⁶ "The sound of an uproar from the city!
    A sound from the temple!
  The sound of the LORD,
    rendering recompense to his enemies!

⁷ "Before she was in labor
    she gave birth;
  before her pain came upon her
    she delivered a son.
⁸ Who has heard such a thing?
    Who has seen such things?
  Shall a land be born in one day?
    Shall a nation be brought forth in one moment?
  For as soon as Zion was in labor
    she brought forth her children.
⁹ Shall I bring to the point of birth and not cause to bring forth?"
    says the LORD;

"shall I, who cause to bring forth, shut the womb?"
    says your God.

10 "Rejoice with Jerusalem, and be glad for her,
    all you who love her;
  rejoice with her in joy,
    all you who mourn over her;
11 that you may nurse and be satisfied
    from her consoling breast;
  that you may drink deeply with delight
    from her glorious abundance."[1]

12 For thus says the LORD:
  "Behold, I will extend peace to her like a river,
    and the glory of the nations like an overflowing stream;
  and you shall nurse, you shall be carried upon her hip,
    and bounced upon her knees.
13 As one whom his mother comforts,
    so I will comfort you;
  you shall be comforted in Jerusalem.
14 You shall see, and your heart shall rejoice;
    your bones shall flourish like the grass;
  and the hand of the LORD shall be known to his servants,
    and he shall show his indignation against his enemies.

15 "For behold, the LORD will come in fire,
    and his chariots like the whirlwind,
  to render his anger in fury,
    and his rebuke with flames of fire.
16 For by fire will the LORD enter into judgment,
    and by his sword, with all flesh;
  and those slain by the LORD shall be many.

17 "Those who sanctify and purify themselves to go into the gardens, following one in the midst, eating pig's flesh and the abomination and mice, shall come to an end together, declares the LORD.

18 "For I know[2] their works and their thoughts, and the time is coming[3] to gather all nations and tongues. And they shall come and shall see my glory, 19and I will set a sign among them. And from them I will send survivors to the nations, to Tarshish, Pul, and Lud, who draw the bow, to Tubal and Javan, to the coastlands far away, that have not heard my fame or seen my glory. And they shall declare my glory among the nations. 20And they shall bring all your brothers from all the nations as an offering to the LORD, on horses and in chariots and in litters and on mules and on dromedaries, to my holy mountain Jerusalem, says the LORD, just as the Israelites bring their grain offering in a clean vessel to the house of the LORD. 21And some of them also I will take for priests and for Levites, says the LORD.

---

[1] Or breast [2] Septuagint, Syriac; Hebrew lacks know [3] Hebrew and it is coming

²² "For as the new heavens and the new earth
   that I make
shall remain before me, says the Lord,
   so shall your offspring and your name remain.
²³   From new moon to new moon,
   and from Sabbath to Sabbath,
all flesh shall come to worship before me,
declares the Lord.

²⁴"And they shall go out and look on the dead bodies of the men who have rebelled against me. For their worm shall not die, their fire shall not be quenched, and they shall be an abhorrence to all flesh."

JEREMIAH

The book at a glance. 52 chapters, 1,364 verses. The book of Jeremiah is a prophetic tour de force that documents the spiritual decline and tragic downfall of Jerusalem, as viewed from the divinely ordained perspective of Jeremiah, the weeping prophet. The wide sweep of the book takes in nearly fifty years of salvation history—the last decades before the fall of Jerusalem and Judah's exile to Babylon. In addition to giving words of warning to the people of God, Jeremiah prophesies judgment against many other nations. Through stories, object lessons, social commentary, and prophecies of doom, Jeremiah shows what happens to a culture that has lost its way spiritually and what suffering results when people forget their God. Yet the book also shows what comfort God has for his people in times of persecution and exile and what hope we have for the future in the promises of God. The preponderance of judgment gives the book of Jeremiah a somber tone. However, the dark backdrop of divine judgment also makes the promises of God's saving grace and Jeremiah's own indomitable faithfulness shine with more brilliant intensity.

▌**Genres.** Jeremiah is an anthology or collection of writings drawn from an entire lifetime in prophetic ministry. The *narrative sections scattered throughout the book are loosely structured around the main events of Jeremiah's life in ministry, which themselves were shaped by Judah's decline, fall, and exile in Babylon. But a majority of the material in the book is prophetic, much of it in the form of *poetry. This material does not always follow a historical sequence; the logic of its arrangement is sometimes topical rather than chronological. It may be helpful to think of the book of Jeremiah as a notebook or scrapbook of things written by the prophet and about his ministry. Jeremiah includes enough "news clippings" to piece together the story of his life, but just as important are the prophetic poems he wrote to address the spiritual needs of his generation and to express the emotions of his suffering soul. The list of subgenres shows how diverse the anthology is: *call narrative, covenant lawsuit, jeremiad (a long recitation of mournful complaints), *doom poem, *satire, sermon, *oracle of judgment, *oracle of salvation, memoir, *lament or complaint, *soliloquy, prophetic object lesson, restoration *prophecy, messianic prophecy, *epistle, prayer, royal audience, *rescue narrative, murder story, and judgment narrative. (For more information on the items accompanied by an asterisk, see the glossary at the back of this Bible.)

▌**Unifying elements.** The two main unifying elements in the book are the person of Jeremiah himself and the city that he loved: Jerusalem. As we read the book of Jeremiah, we watch the prophet in action, following the broad contours of his biogra-

Passage	Content	Subject Matter	Time Frame
1:1–19	The call of the prophet	Prologue	Before the fall of Jerusalem
2:1–4:4	God files for divorce	Jeremiah's first public sermons	
4:5–6:30	Predictions of judgment against Judah		
7–10	Temple sermon; predicted judgment		
11–17	Prophecies and dialogues with God	Jeremiah's experiences as a prophet	
18–19	At the potter's house		
20:1–18	Jeremiah's dark night of the soul		
21–23	Prophecies against Judah		
24–25	Predictions of captivity	Prophecies about the coming captivity	
26:1–24	Jeremiah tried and acquitted		
27–28	Predictions of captivity		
29:1–32	Letter of hope to the exiles		
30–31	Return from captivity; the new covenant	Book of consolation	
32:1–44	Jeremiah buys a house in Jerusalem		
33:1–26	Prediction of Jerusalem restored		
34–35	Zedekiah's treachery; the Rechabites' faithfulness	Siege and fall of Jerusalem	The fall of Jerusalem
36:1–32	Jehoiakim burns Jeremiah's scroll		
37–38	Jeremiah in prison and in a cistern		
39:1–18	The fall of Jerusalem		
40–41	The governor assassinated; Jeremiah released	God's judgment against the nations	After the fall of Jerusalem
42–44	Bad news for those who escaped to Egypt		
45:1–5	God's message to Jeremiah's secretary Baruch		
46–49	Woe to Egypt and seven other nations		
50–51	Destruction for Babylon		
52:1–34	The fall of Jerusalem retold	Epilogue	

phy in the years leading up to and following the cataclysmic fall of Jerusalem (to trace the prophet's story line, see especially chapters 1, 4, 7, 11–13, 18–20, 24–29, 32, 34–43). At the same time, we see through windows into the prophet's soul and witness the grief that he suffered in watching the people he loved persist in sin and finally fall under the judgment of God. The many minor characters in the book—especially the rebellious kings, lying prophets, and unruly priests who constantly oppose the prophet's ministry, as well as the handful of his faithful supporters—are all seen in relationship to Jeremiah. Viewed as a *story, the book of Jeremiah has a unifying *plot conflict: will Jeremiah's hearers listen to God's warnings and repent of their sin, or will they reject the message of God's prophet and be destroyed? The city of Jerusalem also has a strong unifying presence in the book. Various neighborhoods throughout the city provide a locus for the book's narrative action, and the fall of the city is the major event that dominates the book, which begins with Jerusalem's destiny hanging in the balance and ends with the city meeting the doom it deserves at the hands of the Babylonians.

▌**Inferred literary intentions.** The book is designed to achieve the following literary purposes:

- introduce us to the man Jeremiah and tell us the inside story of his ministry as a suffering servant

- use the resources of narrative to document the prophet's experiences and the resources of poetry to reveal his interior life

- embody the prophetic message of the book in poetic images and figurative language

- intermingle narrative sections and visionary sections

- give us an example of faithfulness in ministry during a time of spiritual decline

- vindicate God's justice by documenting the sins that led to Judah's downfall

- show us what happens when people fall out of love with God

- record oracles of hope and prophecies of doom

- give vivid images of a fallen city, both before and after it is destroyed by enemies

- present a memorable cast of minor characters who make good and bad choices in times of spiritual conflict

- warn godless nations that they too will fall under judgment

- inspire confidence in the authority and reliability of God's Word—both its promises and its threats

- assure us that God still has plans for the hope and future of his people

▌**Theological themes.** (1) Sin: as much as any of the prophets, Jeremiah exposes the cold affections and hypocritical deceptions of the human heart, as well as the social devastation that comes from sins like materialism, violence, injustice, pagan idolatry, goddess worship, sexual immorality, and infanticide. (2) Repentance: Jeremiah repeatedly calls people to turn back to the God they have forsaken. (3) Divine judgment: the book is full of prophecies of God's judgment against people's sin, as well as examples of that judgment in the history of Jerusalem and Babylon. (4) God's sovereignty: God rules over the nations the way that a potter shapes clay, and God has a plan of saving mercy for his wayward people. (5) Revelation: Jeremiah's ongoing conflict with Judah's false prophets and godless kings centers on the question of who truly speaks for God. (6) Covenant: the book of Jeremiah is famous for God's covenant lawsuit against his people and for prophecies of the new covenant that God will establish through David's royal son.

▌Jeremiah as a chapter in the master story of the Bible. Like most of the prophets, Jeremiah shows the basic pattern of sin, judgment, and grace in the relationship of fallen humanity to a holy and merciful God. He does this by documenting one of the main acts of judgment in the OT: Judah's exile to Babylon. In various ways the book also anticipates the coming of redemption in Christ. Jeremiah himself is a suffering servant who endures intense persecution for his faithfulness to God; it is not surprising that people later wondered whether Jesus might be the second coming of this prophet (see Matt. 16:14). Jeremiah also makes important messianic predictions about the restoration of the people of God—promises that all find their ultimate fulfillment in Jesus Christ.

> **Jeremiah's call as prophet [1:1–10].** After a brief introduction that situates Jeremiah in space and time, the prophet tells us how he was called to the ministry. A man was not qualified to serve as an OT prophet unless he received God's message the way that Jeremiah received it: directly from God himself. Various features of Jeremiah's call narrative are familiar from the stories of Moses, Isaiah, and other prophets. The Lord speaks a word that the prophet can hear, calling him into ministry. The man immediately protests that he is unfit for the calling—in Jeremiah's case because he is too young to be a prophet. The Lord then touches his mouth to give him the gift of prophetic utterance. Jeremiah is given the specific commission to speak words of destruction and construction. This call narrative anticipates the main themes and conflicts that follow, as the words of the prophet break down and build up Israel and the nations (see 1:10).

1 The words of Jeremiah, the son of Hilkiah, one of the priests who were in Anathoth in the land of Benjamin, ²to whom the word of the LORD came in the days of Josiah the son of Amon, king of Judah, in the thirteenth year of his reign. ³It came also in the days of Jehoiakim the son of Josiah, king of Judah, and until the end of the eleventh year of Zedekiah, the son of Josiah, king of Judah, until the captivity of Jerusalem in the fifth month.

⁴Now the word of the LORD came to me, saying,

⁵ "Before I formed you in the womb I knew you,
    and before you were born I consecrated you;
    I appointed you a prophet to the nations."

⁶Then I said, "Ah, Lord GOD! Behold, I do not know how to speak, for I am only a youth." ⁷But the LORD said to me,

    "Do not say, 'I am only a youth';
    for to all to whom I send you, you shall go,
    and whatever I command you, you shall speak.

8   Do not be afraid of them,
       for I am with you to deliver you,
                       declares the LORD."

9Then the LORD put out his hand and touched my mouth. And the LORD said to me,

    "Behold, I have put my words in your mouth.
10   See, I have set you this day over nations and over kingdoms,
       to pluck up and to break down,
       to destroy and to overthrow,
       to build and to plant."

The almond branch and the boiling pot [1:11–19]. Already in his first two prophetic visions Jeremiah foresees the dreadful act of divine judgment that is the main action of the book: the siege and fall of Jerusalem. The *metaphors of the almond branch and the boiling pot also tell him why judgment must come and how much opposition he will suffer as a result of his calling. Although Jeremiah had a unique ministry, the story of his call serves to remind us of our own divine calling. Our situation is similar to Jeremiah's: we have been known by God from our mother's womb; we have been given gifts that God wants us to use for building up the church; we are living in a society that is destined for judgment; we must suffer for the sake of Christ, but God has promised to be with us always and to deliver us in the end.

11And the word of the LORD came to me, saying, "Jeremiah, what do you see?" And I said, "I see an almond[1] branch." 12Then the LORD said to me, "You have seen well, for I am watching over my word to perform it."

13The word of the LORD came to me a second time, saying, "What do you see?" And I said, "I see a boiling pot, facing away from the north." 14Then the LORD said to me, "Out of the north disaster[2] shall be let loose upon all the inhabitants of the land. 15For behold, I am calling all the tribes of the kingdoms of the north, declares the LORD, and they shall come, and every one shall set his throne at the entrance of the gates of Jerusalem, against all its walls all around and against all the cities of Judah. 16And I will declare my judgments against them, for all their evil in forsaking me. They have made offerings to other gods and worshiped the works of their own hands. 17But you, dress yourself for work;[3] arise, and say to them everything that I command you. Do not be dismayed by them, lest I dismay you before them. 18And I, behold, I make you this day a fortified city, an iron pillar, and bronze walls, against the whole land, against the kings of Judah, its officials, its priests, and the people of the land. 19They will fight against you, but they shall not prevail against you, for I am with you, declares the LORD, to deliver you."

God files for divorce [2:1–3:5]. Jeremiah's first long speech comes in the form of a covenant lawsuit in which God legally files for separation from his people. The premise of the passage is that God's covenant relationship with his people is like a broken marriage in which a wife has been unfaithful to her husband. God's basic charge is the only legitimate biblical grounds for divorce, namely, adultery. In this case the adultery is spiritual: God's people are consorting with other gods. However, some of Jeremiah's

---

[1] *Almond* sounds like the Hebrew for *watching* (compare verse 12) [2] The Hebrew word can mean *evil, harm,* or *disaster,* depending on the context; so throughout Jeremiah [3] Hebrew *gird up your loins*

language has sexual overtones because one common form of religious unfaithfulness in those days was Canaanite idol worship, with its orgiastic rituals. After briefly recounting the honeymoon period of his relationship with his people, including their deliverance from Egypt and survival in the wilderness, God provides mounting evidence of their spiritual unfaithfulness. The key to reading this passage is to take careful note of the *images and metaphors that Jeremiah uses to describe Judah's spiritual condition (e.g. broken cisterns, wild vines, donkeys and camels in heat) and to consider what it is like when people fall out of love with God.

2 The word of the LORD came to me, saying, [2]"Go and proclaim in the hearing of Jerusalem, Thus says the LORD,

"I remember the devotion of your youth,
>   your love as a bride,
how you followed me in the wilderness,
>   in a land not sown.
[3]   Israel was holy to the LORD,
>   the firstfruits of his harvest.
All who ate of it incurred guilt;
>   disaster came upon them,
>   declares the LORD."

[4]Hear the word of the LORD, O house of Jacob, and all the clans of the house of Israel. [5]Thus says the LORD:

"What wrong did your fathers find in me
>   that they went far from me,
and went after worthlessness, and became worthless?
[6]   They did not say, 'Where is the LORD
>   who brought us up from the land of Egypt,
who led us in the wilderness,
>   in a land of deserts and pits,
in a land of drought and deep darkness,
>   in a land that none passes through,
>   where no man dwells?'
[7]   And I brought you into a plentiful land
>   to enjoy its fruits and its good things.
But when you came in, you defiled my land
>   and made my heritage an abomination.
[8]   The priests did not say, 'Where is the LORD?'
>   Those who handle the law did not know me;
the shepherds[1] transgressed against me;
>   the prophets prophesied by Baal
>   and went after things that do not profit.

[9]   "Therefore I still contend with you,
>   declares the LORD,
>   and with your children's children I will contend.

---

[1] Or rulers

10   For cross to the coasts of Cyprus and see,
         or send to Kedar and examine with care;
         see if there has been such a thing.
11   Has a nation changed its gods,
         even though they are no gods?
      But my people have changed their glory
         for that which does not profit.
12   Be appalled, O heavens, at this;
         be shocked, be utterly desolate,
                              declares the Lord,
13   for my people have committed two evils:
      they have forsaken me,
         the fountain of living waters,
      and hewed out cisterns for themselves,
         broken cisterns that can hold no water.

14   "Is Israel a slave? Is he a homeborn servant?
         Why then has he become a prey?
15   The lions have roared against him;
         they have roared loudly.
      They have made his land a waste;
         his cities are in ruins, without inhabitant.
16   Moreover, the men of Memphis and Tahpanhes
         have shaved[1] the crown of your head.
17   Have you not brought this upon yourself
         by forsaking the Lord your God,
         when he led you in the way?
18   And now what do you gain by going to Egypt
         to drink the waters of the Nile?
      Or what do you gain by going to Assyria
         to drink the waters of the Euphrates?
19   Your evil will chastise you,
         and your apostasy will reprove you.
      Know and see that it is evil and bitter
         for you to forsake the Lord your God;
         the fear of me is not in you,
                    declares the Lord God of hosts.

20   "For long ago I broke your yoke
         and burst your bonds;
         but you said, 'I will not serve.'
      Yes, on every high hill
         and under every green tree
         you bowed down like a whore.
21   Yet I planted you a choice vine,
         wholly of pure seed.
      How then have you turned degenerate

---

[1] Hebrew *grazed*

and become a wild vine?

²² Though you wash yourself with lye
and use much soap,
the stain of your guilt is still before me,
declares the Lord God.

²³ How can you say, 'I am not unclean,
I have not gone after the Baals'?
Look at your way in the valley;
know what you have done—
a restless young camel running here and there,

²⁴ a wild donkey used to the wilderness,
in her heat sniffing the wind!
Who can restrain her lust?
None who seek her need weary themselves;
in her month they will find her.

²⁵ Keep your feet from going unshod
and your throat from thirst.
But you said, 'It is hopeless,
for I have loved foreigners,
and after them I will go.'

²⁶ "As a thief is shamed when caught,
so the house of Israel shall be shamed:
they, their kings, their officials,
their priests, and their prophets,

²⁷ who say to a tree, 'You are my father,'
and to a stone, 'You gave me birth.'
For they have turned their back to me,
and not their face.
But in the time of their trouble they say,
'Arise and save us!'

²⁸ But where are your gods
that you made for yourself?
Let them arise, if they can save you,
in your time of trouble;
for as many as your cities
are your gods, O Judah.

²⁹ "Why do you contend with me?
You have all transgressed against me,
declares the LORD.

³⁰ In vain have I struck your children;
they took no correction;
your own sword devoured your prophets
like a ravening lion.

³¹ And you, O generation, behold the word of the LORD.
Have I been a wilderness to Israel,

or a land of thick darkness?
Why then do my people say, 'We are free,
  we will come no more to you'?
³² Can a virgin forget her ornaments,
  or a bride her attire?
Yet my people have forgotten me
  days without number.

³³ "How well you direct your course
  to seek love!
So that even to wicked women
  you have taught your ways.
³⁴ Also on your skirts is found
  the lifeblood of the guiltless poor;
you did not find them breaking in.
  Yet in spite of all these things
³⁵ you say, 'I am innocent;
  surely his anger has turned from me.'
Behold, I will bring you to judgment
  for saying, 'I have not sinned.'
³⁶ How much you go about,
  changing your way!
You shall be put to shame by Egypt
  as you were put to shame by Assyria.
³⁷ From it too you will come away
  with your hands on your head,
for the LORD has rejected those in whom you trust,
  and you will not prosper by them.

3 "If[1] a man divorces his wife
  and she goes from him
and becomes another man's wife,
  will he return to her?
Would not that land be greatly polluted?
You have played the whore with many lovers;
  and would you return to me?
              declares the LORD.
² Lift up your eyes to the bare heights, and see!
  Where have you not been ravished?
By the waysides you have sat awaiting lovers
  like an Arab in the wilderness.
You have polluted the land
  with your vile whoredom.
³ Therefore the showers have been withheld,
  and the spring rain has not come;
yet you have the forehead of a whore;
  you refuse to be ashamed.

---

[1] Septuagint, Syriac; Hebrew *Saying, "If*

⁴ Have you not just now called to me,
　　'My father, you are the friend of my youth—
⁵ will he be angry forever,
　　will he be indignant to the end?'
Behold, you have spoken,
　　but you have done all the evil that you could."

The unfaithful called to repent [3:6–4:4]. Judah (the southern kingdom, the tribes of Judah and Benjamin) is not the only adulteress. Her sister Israel (the northern kingdom, the other ten tribes of Israel) has been just as faithless to God. However, there seems to be some hope of reconciliation. God continues to call his people to repent and return. He offers them mercy, promising that he will not be angry forever. Using metaphors of marriage and adultery, he continues to identify himself as Israel's husband. He pledges to provide his people with faithful leaders to serve as their spiritual shepherds. He promises to restore Jerusalem as his royal city, the place of his own personal presence and the seat of his power over the nations. The question is, Will Israel and Judah repent of their sins and return to the Lord as their Father, their Husband, their Savior, and their God? And will we return to God from our own spiritual unfaithfulness?

---

⁶The LORD said to me in the days of King Josiah: "Have you seen what she did, that faithless one, Israel, how she went up on every high hill and under every green tree, and there played the whore? ⁷And I thought, 'After she has done all this she will return to me,' but she did not return, and her treacherous sister Judah saw it. ⁸She saw that for all the adulteries of that faithless one, Israel, I had sent her away with a decree of divorce. Yet her treacherous sister Judah did not fear, but she too went and played the whore. ⁹Because she took her whoredom lightly, she polluted the land, committing adultery with stone and tree. ¹⁰Yet for all this her treacherous sister Judah did not return to me with her whole heart, but in pretense, declares the LORD."

¹¹And the LORD said to me, "Faithless Israel has shown herself more righteous than treacherous Judah. ¹²Go, and proclaim these words toward the north, and say,

"'Return, faithless Israel,
　　　　　　　　declares the LORD.
　I will not look on you in anger,
　　for I am merciful,
　　　　　　　　declares the LORD;
　I will not be angry forever.
¹³ Only acknowledge your guilt,
　　that you rebelled against the LORD your God
　and scattered your favors among foreigners under every green tree,
　　and that you have not obeyed my voice,
　　　　　　　　declares the LORD.
¹⁴ Return, O faithless children,
　　　　　　　　declares the LORD;
　　for I am your master;
　I will take you, one from a city and two from a family,
　　and I will bring you to Zion.

¹⁵"'And I will give you shepherds after my own heart, who will feed you with knowledge and understanding. ¹⁶And when you have multiplied and increased in the land, in those days, declares the LORD, they shall no more say, "The ark of the covenant of the LORD." It shall not come to mind or be remembered or missed; it shall not be made again. ¹⁷At that time Jerusalem shall be called the throne of the LORD, and all nations shall gather to it, to the presence of the LORD in Jerusalem, and they shall no more stubbornly follow their own evil heart. ¹⁸In those days the house of Judah shall join the house of Israel, and together they shall come from the land of the north to the land that I gave your fathers for a heritage.

¹⁹ "'I said,

How I would set you among my sons,
    and give you a pleasant land,
        a heritage most beautiful of all nations.
And I thought you would call me, My Father,
    and would not turn from following me.
²⁰ Surely, as a treacherous wife leaves her husband,
    so have you been treacherous to me, O house of Israel,
                    declares the LORD.'"

²¹ A voice on the bare heights is heard,
    the weeping and pleading of Israel's sons
because they have perverted their way;
    they have forgotten the LORD their God.
²² "Return, O faithless sons;
    I will heal your faithlessness."
"Behold, we come to you,
    for you are the LORD our God.
²³ Truly the hills are a delusion,
    the orgies¹ on the mountains.
Truly in the LORD our God
    is the salvation of Israel.

²⁴"But from our youth the shameful thing has devoured all for which our fathers labored, their flocks and their herds, their sons and their daughters. ²⁵Let us lie down in our shame, and let our dishonor cover us. For we have sinned against the LORD our God, we and our fathers, from our youth even to this day, and we have not obeyed the voice of the LORD our God."

4 "If you return, O Israel,
                declares the LORD,
    to me you should return.
If you remove your detestable things from my presence,
    and do not waver,
² and if you swear, 'As the LORD lives,'
    in truth, in justice, and in righteousness,
then nations shall bless themselves in him,
    and in him shall they glory."

¹ Hebrew commotion

³For thus says the LORD to the men of Judah and Jerusalem:

"Break up your fallow ground,
   and sow not among thorns.
⁴   Circumcise yourselves to the LORD;
      remove the foreskin of your hearts,
      O men of Judah and inhabitants of Jerusalem;
   lest my wrath go forth like fire,
      and burn with none to quench it,
      because of the evil of your deeds."

First prophecy of Jerusalem's fall [4:5–31]. With many vivid images of terrible destruction, Jeremiah prophesies the overthrow of Jerusalem by an enemy from the north (Babylon). Although this doom poem is a predictive prophecy, it is presented as an eyewitness account, which gives the whole scene an intense immediacy; we can almost see the siege of city and hear the sounds of its devastation. Beginning in verse 10, Jeremiah's personal emotional response to this prophecy is intense anguish. As the prophet makes his lament, in the form of a soliloquy, he is doing something more than telling us what will happen to Jerusalem; he is showing us what it feels like for sinners to fall into the hands of an angry God.

⁵Declare in Judah, and proclaim in Jerusalem, and say,

"Blow the trumpet through the land;
   cry aloud and say,
'Assemble, and let us go
   into the fortified cities!'
⁶   Raise a standard toward Zion,
      flee for safety, stay not,
   for I bring disaster from the north,
      and great destruction.
⁷   A lion has gone up from his thicket,
      a destroyer of nations has set out;
      he has gone out from his place
   to make your land a waste;
      your cities will be ruins
      without inhabitant.
⁸   For this put on sackcloth,
      lament and wail,
   for the fierce anger of the LORD
      has not turned back from us."

⁹"In that day, declares the LORD, courage shall fail both king and officials. The priests shall be appalled and the prophets astounded." ¹⁰Then I said, "Ah, Lord GOD, surely you have utterly deceived this people and Jerusalem, saying, 'It shall be well with you,' whereas the sword has reached their very life."

¹¹At that time it will be said to this people and to Jerusalem, "A hot wind from the bare heights in the desert toward the daughter of my people, not to winnow or

cleanse, [12]a wind too full for this comes for me. Now it is I who speak in judgment upon them."

13   Behold, he comes up like clouds;
         his chariots like the whirlwind;
      his horses are swifter than eagles—
         woe to us, for we are ruined!
14   O Jerusalem, wash your heart from evil,
         that you may be saved.
      How long shall your wicked thoughts
         lodge within you?
15   For a voice declares from Dan
         and proclaims trouble from Mount Ephraim.
16   Warn the nations that he is coming;
         announce to Jerusalem,
      "Besiegers come from a distant land;
         they shout against the cities of Judah.
17   Like keepers of a field are they against her all around,
         because she has rebelled against me,
                                declares the LORD.
18   Your ways and your deeds
         have brought this upon you.
      This is your doom, and it is bitter;
         it has reached your very heart."

19   My anguish, my anguish! I writhe in pain!
         Oh the walls of my heart!
      My heart is beating wildly;
         I cannot keep silent,
      for I hear the sound of the trumpet,
         the alarm of war.
20   Crash follows hard on crash;
         the whole land is laid waste.
      Suddenly my tents are laid waste,
         my curtains in a moment.
21   How long must I see the standard
         and hear the sound of the trumpet?

22   "For my people are foolish;
         they know me not;
      they are stupid children;
         they have no understanding.
      They are 'wise'—in doing evil!
         But how to do good they know not."

23   I looked on the earth, and behold, it was without form and void;
         and to the heavens, and they had no light.
24   I looked on the mountains, and behold, they were quaking,

and all the hills moved to and fro.
25 I looked, and behold, there was no man,
   and all the birds of the air had fled.
26 I looked, and behold, the fruitful land was a desert,
   and all its cities were laid in ruins
   before the LORD, before his fierce anger.

27 For thus says the LORD, "The whole land shall be a desolation; yet I will not make a full end.

28 "For this the earth shall mourn,
   and the heavens above be dark;
   for I have spoken; I have purposed;
   I have not relented, nor will I turn back."

29 At the noise of horseman and archer
   every city takes to flight;
   they enter thickets; they climb among rocks;
   all the cities are forsaken,
   and no man dwells in them.
30 And you, O desolate one,
   what do you mean that you dress in scarlet,
   that you adorn yourself with ornaments of gold,
   that you enlarge your eyes with paint?
   In vain you beautify yourself.
   Your lovers despise you;
   they seek your life.
31 For I heard a cry as of a woman in labor,
   anguish as of one giving birth to her first child,
   the cry of the daughter of Zion gasping for breath,
   stretching out her hands,
   "Woe is me! I am fainting before murderers."

A good man is hard to find [chapter 5]. This chapter is presented as a quest: Jeremiah goes through the city, neighborhood by neighborhood, looking for one righteous man. But all have sinned, and as a result, all will fall under the judgment of God. In addition to imagery of spiritual adultery and further prophecies of judgment from the north, this passage includes themes that will become prominent elements in Jeremiah's satiric critique: lying prophets, greedy priests, and all the people who love to follow their lead. The prophet uses a series of unflattering metaphors and similes to describe these groups of people and their characteristic sins.

5 Run to and fro through the streets of Jerusalem,
  look and take note!
  Search her squares to see
    if you can find a man,
  one who does justice

and seeks truth,
that I may pardon her.
2 Though they say, "As the LORD lives,"
yet they swear falsely.
3 O LORD, do not your eyes look for truth?
You have struck them down,
but they felt no anguish;
you have consumed them,
but they refused to take correction.
They have made their faces harder than rock;
they have refused to repent.

4 Then I said, "These are only the poor;
they have no sense;
for they do not know the way of the LORD,
the justice of their God.
5 I will go to the great
and will speak to them,
for they know the way of the LORD,
the justice of their God."
But they all alike had broken the yoke;
they had burst the bonds.

6 Therefore a lion from the forest shall strike them down;
a wolf from the desert shall devastate them.
A leopard is watching their cities;
everyone who goes out of them shall be torn in pieces,
because their transgressions are many,
their apostasies are great.

7 "How can I pardon you?
Your children have forsaken me
and have sworn by those who are no gods.
When I fed them to the full,
they committed adultery
and trooped to the houses of whores.
8 They were well-fed, lusty stallions,
each neighing for his neighbor's wife.
9 Shall I not punish them for these things?
declares the LORD;
and shall I not avenge myself
on a nation such as this?

10 "Go up through her vine rows and destroy,
but make not a full end;
strip away her branches,
for they are not the LORD's.
11 For the house of Israel and the house of Judah

have been utterly treacherous to me,
       declares the LORD.
12 They have spoken falsely of the LORD
       and have said, 'He will do nothing;
    no disaster will come upon us,
       nor shall we see sword or famine.
13 The prophets will become wind;
       the word is not in them.
    Thus shall it be done to them!'"

14 Therefore thus says the LORD, the God of hosts:
    "Because you have spoken this word,
       behold, I am making my words in your mouth a fire,
       and this people wood, and the fire shall consume them.
15 Behold, I am bringing against you
       a nation from afar, O house of Israel,
              declares the LORD.
    It is an enduring nation;
       it is an ancient nation,
    a nation whose language you do not know,
       nor can you understand what they say.
16 Their quiver is like an open tomb;
       they are all mighty warriors.
17 They shall eat up your harvest and your food;
       they shall eat up your sons and your daughters;
    they shall eat up your flocks and your herds;
       they shall eat up your vines and your fig trees;
    your fortified cities in which you trust
       they shall beat down with the sword."

18"But even in those days, declares the LORD, I will not make a full end of you. 19And
when your people say, 'Why has the LORD our God done all these things to us?' you
shall say to them, 'As you have forsaken me and served foreign gods in your land, so
you shall serve foreigners in a land that is not yours.'"

20 Declare this in the house of Jacob;
       proclaim it in Judah:
21 "Hear this, O foolish and senseless people,
       who have eyes, but see not,
       who have ears, but hear not.
22 Do you not fear me? declares the LORD.
       Do you not tremble before me?
    I placed the sand as the boundary for the sea,
       a perpetual barrier that it cannot pass;
    though the waves toss, they cannot prevail;
       though they roar, they cannot pass over it.
23 But this people has a stubborn and rebellious heart;
       they have turned aside and gone away.

24 They do not say in their hearts,
       'Let us fear the LORD our God,
   who gives the rain in its season,
       the autumn rain and the spring rain,
   and keeps for us
       the weeks appointed for the harvest.'
25 Your iniquities have turned these away,
       and your sins have kept good from you.
26 For wicked men are found among my people;
       they lurk like fowlers lying in wait.[1]
   They set a trap;
       they catch men.
27 Like a cage full of birds,
       their houses are full of deceit;
   therefore they have become great and rich;
28   they have grown fat and sleek.
   They know no bounds in deeds of evil;
       they judge not with justice
   the cause of the fatherless, to make it prosper,
       and they do not defend the rights of the needy.
29 Shall I not punish them for these things?
                       declares the LORD,
       and shall I not avenge myself
   on a nation such as this?"

30 An appalling and horrible thing
       has happened in the land:
31 the prophets prophesy falsely,
       and the priests rule at their direction;
   my people love to have it so,
       but what will you do when the end comes?

At the crossroads [chapter 6]. The effect of Jeremiah's oracles of judgment is cumulative. Each prediction of foreign invasion, each image of military disaster, each scene of urban devastation, each accusation of shameless sin, and each prophecy of divine wrath adds to the sense of Jerusalem's imminent doom and the total devastation that will follow the coming of God's judgment. The prophet achieves his dramatic rhetorical effect in part by making direct address to the people of God, their invading enemies, and the natural world. God's people are at a spiritual crossroads: Will they listen to Jeremiah's prophecy and repent or ignore their God and be destroyed?

6 Flee for safety, O people of Benjamin,
       from the midst of Jerusalem!
   Blow the trumpet in Tekoa,
       and raise a signal on Beth-haccherem,
   for disaster looms out of the north,
       and great destruction.

[1] The meaning of the Hebrew is uncertain

²   The lovely and delicately bred I will destroy,
the daughter of Zion.[1]

³   Shepherds with their flocks shall come against her;
they shall pitch their tents around her;
they shall pasture, each in his place.

⁴   "Prepare war against her;
arise, and let us attack at noon!
Woe to us, for the day declines,
for the shadows of evening lengthen!

⁵   Arise, and let us attack by night
and destroy her palaces!"

⁶   For thus says the Lᴏʀᴅ of hosts:
"Cut down her trees;
cast up a siege mound against Jerusalem.
This is the city that must be punished;
there is nothing but oppression within her.

⁷   As a well keeps its water fresh,
so she keeps fresh her evil;
violence and destruction are heard within her;
sickness and wounds are ever before me.

⁸   Be warned, O Jerusalem,
lest I turn from you in disgust,
lest I make you a desolation,
an uninhabited land."

⁹   Thus says the Lᴏʀᴅ of hosts:
"They shall glean thoroughly as a vine
the remnant of Israel;
like a grape-gatherer pass your hand again
over its branches."

¹⁰   To whom shall I speak and give warning,
that they may hear?
Behold, their ears are uncircumcised,
they cannot listen;
behold, the word of the Lᴏʀᴅ is to them an object of scorn;
they take no pleasure in it.

¹¹   Therefore I am full of the wrath of the Lᴏʀᴅ;
I am weary of holding it in.
"Pour it out upon the children in the street,
and upon the gatherings of young men, also;
both husband and wife shall be taken,
the elderly and the very aged.

¹²   Their houses shall be turned over to others,
their fields and wives together,
for I will stretch out my hand

---

[1] Or *I have likened the daughter of Zion to the loveliest pasture*

against the inhabitants of the land,"
           declares the LORD.
13 "For from the least to the greatest of them,
   everyone is greedy for unjust gain;
and from prophet to priest,
   everyone deals falsely.
14 They have healed the wound of my people lightly,
   saying, 'Peace, peace,'
when there is no peace.
15 Were they ashamed when they committed abomination?
   No, they were not at all ashamed;
they did not know how to blush.
Therefore they shall fall among those who fall;
   at the time that I punish them, they shall be overthrown,"
           says the LORD.

16 Thus says the LORD:
"Stand by the roads, and look,
   and ask for the ancient paths,
where the good way is; and walk in it,
   and find rest for your souls.
But they said, 'We will not walk in it.'
17 I set watchmen over you, saying,
   'Pay attention to the sound of the trumpet!'
But they said, 'We will not pay attention.'
18 Therefore hear, O nations,
   and know, O congregation, what will happen to them.
19 Hear, O earth; behold, I am bringing disaster upon this people,
   the fruit of their devices,
because they have not paid attention to my words;
   and as for my law, they have rejected it.
20 What use to me is frankincense that comes from Sheba,
   or sweet cane from a distant land?
Your burnt offerings are not acceptable,
   nor your sacrifices pleasing to me.
21 Therefore thus says the LORD:
'Behold, I will lay before this people
   stumbling blocks against which they shall stumble;
fathers and sons together,
   neighbor and friend shall perish.'"

22 Thus says the LORD:
"Behold, a people is coming from the north country,
   a great nation is stirring from the farthest parts of the earth.
23 They lay hold on bow and javelin;
   they are cruel and have no mercy;
the sound of them is like the roaring sea;

they ride on horses,
   set in array as a man for battle,
   against you, O daughter of Zion!"
²⁴ We have heard the report of it;
   our hands fall helpless;
anguish has taken hold of us,
   pain as of a woman in labor.
²⁵ Go not out into the field,
   nor walk on the road,
for the enemy has a sword;
   terror is on every side.
²⁶ O daughter of my people, put on sackcloth,
   and roll in ashes;
make mourning as for an only son,
   most bitter lamentation,
for suddenly the destroyer
   will come upon us.

²⁷ "I have made you a tester of metals among my people,
   that you may know and test their ways.
²⁸ They are all stubbornly rebellious,
   going about with slanders;
they are bronze and iron;
   all of them act corruptly.
²⁹ The bellows blow fiercely;
   the lead is consumed by the fire;
in vain the refining goes on,
   for the wicked are not removed.
³⁰ Rejected silver they are called,
   for the LORD has rejected them."

Jeremiah's temple sermon [7:1–8:3]. This chapter gives a transcript of the famous reformation sermon that Jeremiah preached on the steps of the temple in Jerusalem during one of Israel's major religious festivals. The prophet's main homiletical theme is hypocrisy: religious observance without moral obedience cannot save. Although the people are still going through the motions of worship, their hearts are far from God. Jeremiah proves this by giving a lengthy catalog of their sins. They have broken nearly all of the Ten Commandments and committed the vile sins of goddess worship and ritual infanticide in the dreadful Valley of Slaughter. The prophet's mode is satiric, his tone accusatory.

7 The word that came to Jeremiah from the LORD: ²"Stand in the gate of the LORD's house, and proclaim there this word, and say, Hear the word of the LORD, all you men of Judah who enter these gates to worship the LORD. ³Thus says the LORD of hosts, the God of Israel: Amend your ways and your deeds, and I will let you dwell in this place. ⁴Do not trust in these deceptive words: 'This is the temple of the LORD, the temple of the LORD, the temple of the LORD.'

⁵"For if you truly amend your ways and your deeds, if you truly execute justice one with another, ⁶if you do not oppress the sojourner, the fatherless, or the widow, or shed innocent blood in this place, and if you do not go after other gods to your own harm, ⁷then I will let you dwell in this place, in the land that I gave of old to your fathers forever.

⁸"Behold, you trust in deceptive words to no avail. ⁹Will you steal, murder, commit adultery, swear falsely, make offerings to Baal, and go after other gods that you have not known, ¹⁰and then come and stand before me in this house, which is called by my name, and say, 'We are delivered!'—only to go on doing all these abominations? ¹¹Has this house, which is called by my name, become a den of robbers in your eyes? Behold, I myself have seen it, declares the Lord. ¹²Go now to my place that was in Shiloh, where I made my name dwell at first, and see what I did to it because of the evil of my people Israel. ¹³And now, because you have done all these things, declares the Lord, and when I spoke to you persistently you did not listen, and when I called you, you did not answer, ¹⁴therefore I will do to the house that is called by my name, and in which you trust, and to the place that I gave to you and to your fathers, as I did to Shiloh. ¹⁵And I will cast you out of my sight, as I cast out all your kinsmen, all the offspring of Ephraim.

¹⁶"As for you, do not pray for this people, or lift up a cry or prayer for them, and do not intercede with me, for I will not hear you. ¹⁷Do you not see what they are doing in the cities of Judah and in the streets of Jerusalem? ¹⁸The children gather wood, the fathers kindle fire, and the women knead dough, to make cakes for the queen of heaven. And they pour out drink offerings to other gods, to provoke me to anger. ¹⁹Is it I whom they provoke? declares the Lord. Is it not themselves, to their own shame? ²⁰Therefore thus says the Lord God: behold, my anger and my wrath will be poured out on this place, upon man and beast, upon the trees of the field and the fruit of the ground; it will burn and not be quenched."

²¹Thus says the Lord of hosts, the God of Israel: "Add your burnt offerings to your sacrifices, and eat the flesh. ²²For in the day that I brought them out of the land of Egypt, I did not speak to your fathers or command them concerning burnt offerings and sacrifices. ²³But this command I gave them: 'Obey my voice, and I will be your God, and you shall be my people. And walk in all the way that I command you, that it may be well with you.' ²⁴But they did not obey or incline their ear, but walked in their own counsels and the stubbornness of their evil hearts, and went backward and not forward. ²⁵From the day that your fathers came out of the land of Egypt to this day, I have persistently sent all my servants the prophets to them, day after day. ²⁶Yet they did not listen to me or incline their ear, but stiffened their neck. They did worse than their fathers.

²⁷"So you shall speak all these words to them, but they will not listen to you. You shall call to them, but they will not answer you. ²⁸And you shall say to them, 'This is the nation that did not obey the voice of the Lord their God, and did not accept discipline; truth has perished; it is cut off from their lips.'

²⁹ "'Cut off your hair and cast it away;
    raise a lamentation on the bare heights,
  for the Lord has rejected and forsaken
    the generation of his wrath.'

[30]"For the sons of Judah have done evil in my sight, declares the LORD. They have set their detestable things in the house that is called by my name, to defile it. [31]And they have built the high places of Topheth, which is in the Valley of the Son of Hinnom, to burn their sons and their daughters in the fire, which I did not command, nor did it come into my mind. [32]Therefore, behold, the days are coming, declares the LORD, when it will no more be called Topheth, or the Valley of the Son of Hinnom, but the Valley of Slaughter; for they will bury in Topheth, because there is no room elsewhere. [33]And the dead bodies of this people will be food for the birds of the air, and for the beasts of the earth, and none will frighten them away. [34]And I will silence in the cities of Judah and in the streets of Jerusalem the voice of mirth and the voice of gladness, the voice of the bridegroom and the voice of the bride, for the land shall become a waste.

8 "At that time, declares the LORD, the bones of the kings of Judah, the bones of its officials, the bones of the priests, the bones of the prophets, and the bones of the inhabitants of Jerusalem shall be brought out of their tombs. [2]And they shall be spread before the sun and the moon and all the host of heaven, which they have loved and served, which they have gone after, and which they have sought and worshiped. And they shall not be gathered or buried. They shall be as dung on the surface of the ground. [3]Death shall be preferred to life by all the remnant that remains of this evil family in all the places where I have driven them, declares the LORD of hosts.

> **Jeremiah weeps** [8:4–9:22]. After further prophecies of death and destruction (8:1–17)—brought about in large part because Jerusalem listened to the deceptive words of lying prophets—the prophet offers a lament for the people he loves. He also calls others to join his jeremiad (9:17–22), knowing that tears of sadness are one godly response to the coming judgment of a deceitful and abusive society. Who will weep for the lost and their sufferings?

[4]   "You shall say to them, Thus says the LORD:
>   When men fall, do they not rise again?
>   If one turns away, does he not return?
[5]   Why then has this people turned away
>   in perpetual backsliding?
>   They hold fast to deceit;
>   they refuse to return.
[6]   I have paid attention and listened,
>   but they have not spoken rightly;
>   no man relents of his evil,
>   saying, 'What have I done?'
>   Everyone turns to his own course,
>   like a horse plunging headlong into battle.
[7]   Even the stork in the heavens
>   knows her times,
>   and the turtledove, swallow, and crane[1]
>   keep the time of their coming,

---
[1] The meaning of the Hebrew word is uncertain

but my people know not
   the rules[1] of the Lord.

8 "How can you say, 'We are wise,
   and the law of the Lord is with us'?
But behold, the lying pen of the scribes
   has made it into a lie.
9 The wise men shall be put to shame;
   they shall be dismayed and taken;
behold, they have rejected the word of the Lord,
   so what wisdom is in them?
10 Therefore I will give their wives to others
   and their fields to conquerors,
because from the least to the greatest
   everyone is greedy for unjust gain;
from prophet to priest,
   everyone deals falsely.
11 They have healed the wound of my people lightly,
   saying, 'Peace, peace,'
   when there is no peace.
12 Were they ashamed when they committed abomination?
   No, they were not at all ashamed;
   they did not know how to blush.
Therefore they shall fall among the fallen;
   when I punish them, they shall be overthrown,
        says the Lord.
13 When I would gather them, declares the Lord,
   there are no grapes on the vine,
   nor figs on the fig tree;
even the leaves are withered,
   and what I gave them has passed away from them."[2]

14 Why do we sit still?
Gather together; let us go into the fortified cities
   and perish there,
for the Lord our God has doomed us to perish
   and has given us poisoned water to drink,
because we have sinned against the Lord.
15 We looked for peace, but no good came;
   for a time of healing, but behold, terror.

16 "The snorting of their horses is heard from Dan;
   at the sound of the neighing of their stallions
   the whole land quakes.
They come and devour the land and all that fills it,
   the city and those who dwell in it.
17 For behold, I am sending among you serpents,

---

[1] Or just decrees [2] The meaning of the Hebrew is uncertain

adders that cannot be charmed,
   and they shall bite you,"
                   declares the LORD.

¹⁸   My joy is gone; grief is upon me;[1]
     my heart is sick within me.
¹⁹   Behold, the cry of the daughter of my people
     from the length and breadth of the land:
  "Is the LORD not in Zion?
    Is her King not in her?"
  "Why have they provoked me to anger with their carved images
    and with their foreign idols?"
²⁰   "The harvest is past, the summer is ended,
     and we are not saved."
²¹   For the wound of the daughter of my people is my heart wounded;
     I mourn, and dismay has taken hold on me.

²²   Is there no balm in Gilead?
     Is there no physician there?
   Why then has the health of the daughter of my people
     not been restored?

9
² Oh that my head were waters,
    and my eyes a fountain of tears,
  that I might weep day and night
    for the slain of the daughter of my people!
²³   Oh that I had in the desert
    a travelers' lodging place,
  that I might leave my people
    and go away from them!
  For they are all adulterers,
    a company of treacherous men.
³   They bend their tongue like a bow;
    falsehood and not truth has grown strong[4] in the land;
  for they proceed from evil to evil,
    and they do not know me, declares the LORD.

⁴   Let everyone beware of his neighbor,
    and put no trust in any brother,
  for every brother is a deceiver,
    and every neighbor goes about as a slanderer.
⁵   Everyone deceives his neighbor,
    and no one speaks the truth;
  they have taught their tongue to speak lies;
    they weary themselves committing iniquity.
⁶   Heaping oppression upon oppression, and deceit upon deceit,
    they refuse to know me, declares the LORD.

---

[1] Compare Septuagint; the meaning of the Hebrew is uncertain [2] Ch 8:23 in Hebrew [3] Ch 9:1 in Hebrew [4] Septuagint; Hebrew *and not for truth they have grown strong*

7   Therefore thus says the Lord of hosts:
    "Behold, I will refine them and test them,
        for what else can I do, because of my people?
8   Their tongue is a deadly arrow;
        it speaks deceitfully;
    with his mouth each speaks peace to his neighbor,
        but in his heart he plans an ambush for him.
9   Shall I not punish them for these things? declares the Lord,
        and shall I not avenge myself
        on a nation such as this?

10 "I will take up weeping and wailing for the mountains,
        and a lamentation for the pastures of the wilderness,
    because they are laid waste so that no one passes through,
        and the lowing of cattle is not heard;
    both the birds of the air and the beasts
        have fled and are gone.
11 I will make Jerusalem a heap of ruins,
        a lair of jackals,
    and I will make the cities of Judah a desolation,
        without inhabitant."

¹²Who is the man so wise that he can understand this? To whom has the mouth of the Lord spoken, that he may declare it? Why is the land ruined and laid waste like a wilderness, so that no one passes through? ¹³And the Lord says: "Because they have forsaken my law that I set before them, and have not obeyed my voice or walked in accord with it, ¹⁴but have stubbornly followed their own hearts and have gone after the Baals, as their fathers taught them. ¹⁵Therefore thus says the Lord of hosts, the God of Israel: Behold, I will feed this people with bitter food, and give them poisonous water to drink. ¹⁶I will scatter them among the nations whom neither they nor their fathers have known, and I will send the sword after them, until I have consumed them."

17 Thus says the Lord of hosts:
    "Consider, and call for the mourning women to come;
        send for the skillful women to come;
18 let them make haste and raise a wailing over us,
        that our eyes may run down with tears
        and our eyelids flow with water.
19 For a sound of wailing is heard from Zion:
        'How we are ruined!
        We are utterly shamed,
    because we have left the land,
        because they have cast down our dwellings.'"

20 Hear, O women, the word of the Lord,
        and let your ear receive the word of his mouth;
    teach to your daughters a lament,

and each to her neighbor a dirge.

21 For death has come up into our windows;
　　it has entered our palaces,
cutting off the children from the streets
　　and the young men from the squares.
22 Speak, "Thus declares the Lord:
'The dead bodies of men shall fall
　　like dung upon the open field,
like sheaves after the reaper,
　　and none shall gather them.'"

> **Something to boast about** [9:23–10:25]. What Jeremiah says about boasting ("Let
> not the wise man boast in his wisdom, let not the mighty man boast in his might," and
> so forth; see 9:23–24) is one of the most famous parts of his prophecy. The context for
> these words is significant, for the prophet proceeds to contrast the idols of the nations
> (which are nothing to boast about) with the power and the wisdom of God (who alone is
> worthy of our boasting). The satiric tone of Jeremiah's *diatribe against idol worshipers
> and the impotence of their handmade gods is reminiscent of similar polemics in Isaiah
> and the Psalms.

23 Thus says the Lord: "Let not the wise man boast in his wisdom, let not the mighty man boast in his might, let not the rich man boast in his riches, 24 but let him who boasts boast in this, that he understands and knows me, that I am the Lord who practices steadfast love, justice, and righteousness in the earth. For in these things I delight, declares the Lord."

25 "Behold, the days are coming, declares the Lord, when I will punish all those who are circumcised merely in the flesh— 26 Egypt, Judah, Edom, the sons of Ammon, Moab, and all who dwell in the desert who cut the corners of their hair, for all these nations are uncircumcised, and all the house of Israel are uncircumcised in heart."

10 Hear the word that the Lord speaks to you, O house of Israel. 2 Thus says the Lord:

"Learn not the way of the nations,
　　nor be dismayed at the signs of the heavens
　　because the nations are dismayed at them,
3 for the customs of the peoples are vanity.[1]
A tree from the forest is cut down
　　and worked with an axe by the hands of a craftsman.
4 They decorate it with silver and gold;
　　they fasten it with hammer and nails
　　so that it cannot move.
5 Their idols[2] are like scarecrows in a cucumber field,
　　and they cannot speak;
they have to be carried,
　　for they cannot walk.
Do not be afraid of them,

---

[1] Or *vapor, or mist* [2] Hebrew *They*

for they cannot do evil,
neither is it in them to do good."

6   There is none like you, O LORD;
you are great, and your name is great in might.
7   Who would not fear you, O King of the nations?
For this is your due;
for among all the wise ones of the nations
and in all their kingdoms
there is none like you.
8   They are both stupid and foolish;
the instruction of idols is but wood!
9   Beaten silver is brought from Tarshish,
and gold from Uphaz.
They are the work of the craftsman and of the hands of the goldsmith;
their clothing is violet and purple;
they are all the work of skilled men.
10   But the LORD is the true God;
he is the living God and the everlasting King.
At his wrath the earth quakes,
and the nations cannot endure his indignation.

11 Thus shall you say to them: "The gods who did not make the heavens and the earth shall perish from the earth and from under the heavens." [1]

12   It is he who made the earth by his power,
who established the world by his wisdom,
and by his understanding stretched out the heavens.
13   When he utters his voice, there is a tumult of waters in the heavens,
and he makes the mist rise from the ends of the earth.
He makes lightning for the rain,
and he brings forth the wind from his storehouses.
14   Every man is stupid and without knowledge;
every goldsmith is put to shame by his idols,
for his images are false,
and there is no breath in them.
15   They are worthless, a work of delusion;
at the time of their punishment they shall perish.
16   Not like these is he who is the portion of Jacob,
for he is the one who formed all things,
and Israel is the tribe of his inheritance;
the LORD of hosts is his name.

17   Gather up your bundle from the ground,
O you who dwell under siege!
18   For thus says the LORD:
"Behold, I am slinging out the inhabitants of the land
at this time,

[1] This verse is in Aramaic

and I will bring distress on them,
    that they may feel it."

19 Woe is me because of my hurt!
    My wound is grievous.
  But I said, "Truly this is an affliction,
    and I must bear it."
20 My tent is destroyed,
    and all my cords are broken;
  my children have gone from me,
    and they are not;
  there is no one to spread my tent again
    and to set up my curtains.
21 For the shepherds are stupid
    and do not inquire of the LORD;
  therefore they have not prospered,
    and all their flock is scattered.

22 A voice, a rumor! Behold, it comes!—
    a great commotion out of the north country
  to make the cities of Judah a desolation,
    a lair of jackals.

23 I know, O LORD, that the way of man is not in himself,
    that it is not in man who walks to direct his steps.
24 Correct me, O LORD, but in justice;
    not in your anger, lest you bring me to nothing.

25 Pour out your wrath on the nations that know you not,
    and on the peoples that call not on your name,
  for they have devoured Jacob;
    they have devoured him and consumed him,
    and have laid waste his habitation.

A broken relationship [11:1–17]. In this prophecy, which takes the literary form of a lawsuit, Jeremiah summarizes how the people of Jerusalem have broken covenant with God and what will happen as a result. Somewhat surprisingly, the prophet is forbidden to intercede for their deliverance. If God says that judgment will come, then judgment will come, and not even prayer can stop it now.

11 The word that came to Jeremiah from the LORD: ²"Hear the words of this covenant, and speak to the men of Judah and the inhabitants of Jerusalem. ³You shall say to them, Thus says the LORD, the God of Israel: Cursed be the man who does not hear the words of this covenant ⁴that I commanded your fathers when I brought them out of the land of Egypt, from the iron furnace, saying, Listen to my voice, and do all that I command you. So shall you be my people, and I will be your God, ⁵that I may confirm the oath that I swore to your fathers, to give them a land flowing with milk and honey, as at this day." Then I answered, "So be it, LORD."

⁶And the Lord said to me, "Proclaim all these words in the cities of Judah and in the streets of Jerusalem: Hear the words of this covenant and do them. ⁷For I solemnly warned your fathers when I brought them up out of the land of Egypt, warning them persistently, even to this day, saying, Obey my voice. ⁸Yet they did not obey or incline their ear, but everyone walked in the stubbornness of his evil heart. Therefore I brought upon them all the words of this covenant, which I commanded them to do, but they did not."

⁹Again the Lord said to me, "A conspiracy exists among the men of Judah and the inhabitants of Jerusalem. ¹⁰They have turned back to the iniquities of their forefathers, who refused to hear my words. They have gone after other gods to serve them. The house of Israel and the house of Judah have broken my covenant that I made with their fathers. ¹¹Therefore, thus says the Lord, Behold, I am bringing disaster upon them that they cannot escape. Though they cry to me, I will not listen to them. ¹²Then the cities of Judah and the inhabitants of Jerusalem will go and cry to the gods to whom they make offerings, but they cannot save them in the time of their trouble. ¹³For your gods have become as many as your cities, O Judah, and as many as the streets of Jerusalem are the altars you have set up to shame, altars to make offerings to Baal.

¹⁴"Therefore do not pray for this people, or lift up a cry or prayer on their behalf, for I will not listen when they call to me in the time of their trouble. ¹⁵What right has my beloved in my house, when she has done many vile deeds? Can even sacrificial flesh avert your doom? Can you then exult? ¹⁶The Lord once called you 'a green olive tree, beautiful with good fruit.' But with the roar of a great tempest he will set fire to it, and its branches will be consumed. ¹⁷The Lord of hosts, who planted you, has decreed disaster against you, because of the evil that the house of Israel and the house of Judah have done, provoking me to anger by making offerings to Baal."

The complaint of a persecuted prophet [11:18–12:17]. It is evident from the closing verses of chapter 11 that Jeremiah has enemies in his own hometown—religious leaders who hate his preaching on sin, repentance, and judgment and who therefore are plotting to kill him. Troubled by this spiritual opposition, especially in its contrast to the apparent prosperity of the wicked, Jeremiah complains to God about his persecutions (12:1–4). God responds with yet another prophecy of judgment, replete with stark images of destruction; like Jeremiah, his people will suffer from their enemies (12:5–13). Yet the prophecy ends with a promise of grace: God's people will be rescued from their enemies and returned to their land, and even the godless nations can be saved by faith and repentance (12:14–17).

¹⁸   The Lord made it known to me and I knew;
        then you showed me their deeds.
¹⁹   But I was like a gentle lamb
        led to the slaughter.
      I did not know it was against me
        they devised schemes, saying,
      "Let us destroy the tree with its fruit,
        let us cut him off from the land of the living,
        that his name be remembered no more."

20   But, O Lord of hosts, who judges righteously,
        who tests the heart and the mind,
      let me see your vengeance upon them,
        for to you have I committed my cause.

²¹Therefore thus says the Lord concerning the men of Anathoth, who seek your life, and say, "Do not prophesy in the name of the Lord, or you will die by our hand"— ²²therefore thus says the Lord of hosts: "Behold, I will punish them. The young men shall die by the sword, their sons and their daughters shall die by famine, ²³and none of them shall be left. For I will bring disaster upon the men of Anathoth, the year of their punishment."

12 Righteous are you, O Lord,
        when I complain to you;
      yet I would plead my case before you.
      Why does the way of the wicked prosper?
        Why do all who are treacherous thrive?
2   You plant them, and they take root;
        they grow and produce fruit;
      you are near in their mouth
        and far from their heart.
3   But you, O Lord, know me;
        you see me, and test my heart toward you.
      Pull them out like sheep for the slaughter,
        and set them apart for the day of slaughter.
4   How long will the land mourn
        and the grass of every field wither?
      For the evil of those who dwell in it
        the beasts and the birds are swept away,
        because they said, "He will not see our latter end."

5   "If you have raced with men on foot, and they have wearied you,
        how will you compete with horses?
      And if in a safe land you are so trusting,
        what will you do in the thicket of the Jordan?
6   For even your brothers and the house of your father,
        even they have dealt treacherously with you;
        they are in full cry after you;
      do not believe them,
        though they speak friendly words to you."

7   "I have forsaken my house;
        I have abandoned my heritage;
      I have given the beloved of my soul
        into the hands of her enemies.
8   My heritage has become to me
        like a lion in the forest;
      she has lifted up her voice against me;

therefore I hate her.
9   Is my heritage to me like a hyena's lair?
     Are the birds of prey against her all around?
    Go, assemble all the wild beasts;
      bring them to devour.
10   Many shepherds have destroyed my vineyard;
     they have trampled down my portion;
    they have made my pleasant portion
     a desolate wilderness.
11   They have made it a desolation;
     desolate, it mourns to me.
    The whole land is made desolate,
     but no man lays it to heart.
12   Upon all the bare heights in the desert
     destroyers have come,
    for the sword of the Lord devours
     from one end of the land to the other;
     no flesh has peace.
13   They have sown wheat and have reaped thorns;
     they have tired themselves out but profit nothing.
    They shall be ashamed of their[1] harvests
     because of the fierce anger of the Lord."

[14]Thus says the Lord concerning all my evil neighbors who touch the heritage that I have given my people Israel to inherit: "Behold, I will pluck them up from their land, and I will pluck up the house of Judah from among them. [15]And after I have plucked them up, I will again have compassion on them, and I will bring them again each to his heritage and each to his land. [16]And it shall come to pass, if they will diligently learn the ways of my people, to swear by my name, 'As the Lord lives,' even as they taught my people to swear by Baal, then they shall be built up in the midst of my people. [17]But if any nation will not listen, then I will utterly pluck it up and destroy it, declares the Lord."

When the best becomes the worst [chapter 13]. As a prophetic sign of impending judgment, Jeremiah buries a linen undergarment somewhere near Babylon. When he returns to dig it up again, it is good for nothing. The meaning of this object lesson is that God will bring similar ruin to his sinful people Israel. In the prophecies that follow, some of the best things in life—things like wine, women, and royalty—become corrupted by sin and fall under the judgment of God.

13 Thus says the Lord to me, "Go and buy a linen loincloth and put it around your waist, and do not dip it in water." [2]So I bought a loincloth according to the word of the Lord, and put it around my waist. [3]And the word of the Lord came to me a second time, [4]"Take the loincloth that you have bought, which is around your waist, and arise, go to the Euphrates and hide it there in a cleft of the rock." [5]So I went and hid it by the Euphrates, as the Lord commanded me. [6]And after many days the Lord said to me, "Arise, go to the Euphrates, and take from there the loincloth that I

---

[1] Hebrew *your*

commanded you to hide there." ⁷Then I went to the Euphrates, and dug, and I took the loincloth from the place where I had hidden it. And behold, the loincloth was spoiled; it was good for nothing.

⁸Then the word of the LORD came to me: ⁹"Thus says the LORD: Even so will I spoil the pride of Judah and the great pride of Jerusalem. ¹⁰This evil people, who refuse to hear my words, who stubbornly follow their own heart and have gone after other gods to serve them and worship them, shall be like this loincloth, which is good for nothing. ¹¹For as the loincloth clings to the waist of a man, so I made the whole house of Israel and the whole house of Judah cling to me, declares the LORD, that they might be for me a people, a name, a praise, and a glory, but they would not listen.

¹²"You shall speak to them this word: 'Thus says the LORD, the God of Israel, "Every jar shall be filled with wine."' And they will say to you, 'Do we not indeed know that every jar will be filled with wine?' ¹³Then you shall say to them, 'Thus says the LORD: Behold, I will fill with drunkenness all the inhabitants of this land: the kings who sit on David's throne, the priests, the prophets, and all the inhabitants of Jerusalem. ¹⁴And I will dash them one against another, fathers and sons together, declares the LORD. I will not pity or spare or have compassion, that I should not destroy them.'"

¹⁵   Hear and give ear; be not proud,
      for the LORD has spoken.
¹⁶   Give glory to the LORD your God
      before he brings darkness,
   before your feet stumble
      on the twilight mountains,
   and while you look for light
      he turns it into gloom
      and makes it deep darkness.
¹⁷   But if you will not listen,
      my soul will weep in secret for your pride;
   my eyes will weep bitterly and run down with tears,
      because the LORD's flock has been taken captive.

¹⁸   Say to the king and the queen mother:
      "Take a lowly seat,
   for your beautiful crown
      has come down from your head."
¹⁹   The cities of the Negeb are shut up,
      with none to open them;
   all Judah is taken into exile,
      wholly taken into exile.
²⁰   "Lift up your eyes and see
      those who come from the north.
   Where is the flock that was given you,
      your beautiful flock?
²¹   What will you say when they set as head over you
      those whom you yourself have taught to be friends to you?

Will not pangs take hold of you
  like those of a woman in labor?
22 And if you say in your heart,
  'Why have these things come upon me?'
it is for the greatness of your iniquity
  that your skirts are lifted up
  and you suffer violence.
23 Can the Ethiopian change his skin
  or the leopard his spots?
Then also you can do good
  who are accustomed to do evil.
24 I will scatter you[1] like chaff
  driven by the wind from the desert.
25 This is your lot,
  the portion I have measured out to you, declares the Lord,
because you have forgotten me
  and trusted in lies.
26 I myself will lift up your skirts over your face,
  and your shame will be seen.
27 I have seen your abominations,
  your adulteries and neighings, your lewd whorings,
  on the hills in the field.
Woe to you, O Jerusalem!
  How long will it be before you are made clean?"

Without a prayer [14:1–15:9]. Jeremiah uses images of thirst to show that judgment is beginning to fall on Judah in the form of famine (14:1–10). When he points out that many of the other prophets are still preaching prosperity, God reassures him that his own message is the true one and that the lying prophets themselves will come under judgment. But this is small comfort to Jeremiah, who is distressed by the sufferings of God's people and seeks to pray on their behalf, even to make confession for their sins (14:18–22). This will be to no avail, for God is determined to bring them to judgment, here cataloged as a series of disasters (15:1–9).

14

The word of the Lord that came to Jeremiah concerning the drought:

2 "Judah mourns,
  and her gates languish;
her people lament on the ground,
  and the cry of Jerusalem goes up.
3 Her nobles send their servants for water;
  they come to the cisterns;
they find no water;
  they return with their vessels empty;
they are ashamed and confounded
  and cover their heads.

---

[1] Hebrew them

⁴   Because of the ground that is dismayed,
       since there is no rain on the land,
    the farmers are ashamed;
       they cover their heads.
⁵   Even the doe in the field forsakes her newborn fawn
       because there is no grass.
⁶   The wild donkeys stand on the bare heights;
       they pant for air like jackals;
    their eyes fail
       because there is no vegetation.

⁷   "Though our iniquities testify against us,
       act, O Lord, for your name's sake;
    for our backslidings are many;
       we have sinned against you.
⁸   O you hope of Israel,
       its savior in time of trouble,
    why should you be like a stranger in the land,
       like a traveler who turns aside to tarry for a night?
⁹   Why should you be like a man confused,
       like a mighty warrior who cannot save?
    Yet you, O Lord, are in the midst of us,
       and we are called by your name;
       do not leave us."

¹⁰   Thus says the Lord concerning this people:
     "They have loved to wander thus;
       they have not restrained their feet;
    therefore the Lord does not accept them;
       now he will remember their iniquity
       and punish their sins."

¹¹The Lord said to me: "Do not pray for the welfare of this people. ¹²Though they fast, I will not hear their cry, and though they offer burnt offering and grain offering, I will not accept them. But I will consume them by the sword, by famine, and by pestilence."

¹³Then I said: "Ah, Lord God, behold, the prophets say to them, 'You shall not see the sword, nor shall you have famine, but I will give you assured peace in this place.'" ¹⁴And the Lord said to me: "The prophets are prophesying lies in my name. I did not send them, nor did I command them or speak to them. They are prophesying to you a lying vision, worthless divination, and the deceit of their own minds. ¹⁵Therefore thus says the Lord concerning the prophets who prophesy in my name although I did not send them, and who say, 'Sword and famine shall not come upon this land': By sword and famine those prophets shall be consumed. ¹⁶And the people to whom they prophesy shall be cast out in the streets of Jerusalem, victims of famine and sword, with none to bury them—them, their wives, their sons, and their daughters. For I will pour out their evil upon them.

¹⁷ "You shall say to them this word:
'Let my eyes run down with tears night and day,
    and let them not cease,
for the virgin daughter of my people is shattered with a great wound,
    with a very grievous blow.
¹⁸ If I go out into the field,
    behold, those pierced by the sword!
And if I enter the city,
    behold, the diseases of famine!
For both prophet and priest ply their trade through the land
    and have no knowledge.'"

¹⁹ Have you utterly rejected Judah?
    Does your soul loathe Zion?
Why have you struck us down
    so that there is no healing for us?
We looked for peace, but no good came;
    for a time of healing, but behold, terror.
²⁰ We acknowledge our wickedness, O LORD,
    and the iniquity of our fathers,
    for we have sinned against you.
²¹ Do not spurn us, for your name's sake;
    do not dishonor your glorious throne;
    remember and do not break your covenant with us.
²² Are there any among the false gods of the nations that can bring rain?
    Or can the heavens give showers?
Are you not he, O LORD our God?
    We set our hope on you,
    for you do all these things.

15 Then the LORD said to me, "Though Moses and Samuel stood before me, yet my heart would not turn toward this people. Send them out of my sight, and let them go! ²And when they ask you, 'Where shall we go?' you shall say to them, 'Thus says the LORD:

"'Those who are for pestilence, to pestilence,
    and those who are for the sword, to the sword;
those who are for famine, to famine,
    and those who are for captivity, to captivity.'

³I will appoint over them four kinds of destroyers, declares the LORD: the sword to kill, the dogs to tear, and the birds of the air and the beasts of the earth to devour and destroy. ⁴And I will make them a horror to all the kingdoms of the earth because of what Manasseh the son of Hezekiah, king of Judah, did in Jerusalem.

⁵ "Who will have pity on you, O Jerusalem,
    or who will grieve for you?
Who will turn aside
    to ask about your welfare?

6   You have rejected me, declares the LORD;
        you keep going backward,
    so I have stretched out my hand against you and destroyed you—
        I am weary of relenting.
7   I have winnowed them with a winnowing fork
        in the gates of the land;
    I have bereaved them; I have destroyed my people;
        they did not turn from their ways.
8   I have made their widows more in number
        than the sand of the seas;
    I have brought against the mothers of young men
        a destroyer at noonday;
    I have made anguish and terror
        fall upon them suddenly.
9   She who bore seven has grown feeble;
        she has fainted away;
    her sun went down while it was yet day;
        she has been shamed and disgraced.
    And the rest of them I will give to the sword
        before their enemies,
                        declares the LORD."

Jeremiah the pariah [15:10–16:21]. The prophet's ministry itself was an object lesson—a real-life parable about God's judgment against Judah's sin. As a sign of the
coming destruction, Jeremiah was forbidden to marry, have children, attend a funeral,
celebrate a wedding, or sit down to a feast (16:5–13). This was to show that when
Jerusalem fell, there would be no more weddings or feasts or funerals. These strictures
only added to the prophet's sufferings and the sense of isolation he felt from his own
people. In this section of his prophecy (which is partly a soliloquy) we hear further words
of Jeremiah's lament—the sufferings of an anguished soul who loves God and is faithful
to his ministry, yet sometimes finds it hard to understand or even accept God's plan for
his people. We also see some promises of God's salvation: for Jeremiah himself (15:19–
21), for his people Israel (16:14–15), and for the nations (16:16–21). This is the message
of the book in microcosm: sorrow for the destruction that God will bring in judgment, but
not without hope in his saving mercy.

¹⁰Woe is me, my mother, that you bore me, a man of strife and contention to the
whole land! I have not lent, nor have I borrowed, yet all of them curse me. ¹¹The LORD
said, "Have I not¹ set you free for their good? Have I not pleaded for you before the
enemy in the time of trouble and in the time of distress? ¹²Can one break iron, iron
from the north, and bronze?

¹³"Your wealth and your treasures I will give as spoil, without price, for all your
sins, throughout all your territory. ¹⁴I will make you serve your enemies in a land that
you do not know, for in my anger a fire is kindled that shall burn forever."

15   O LORD, you know;
        remember me and visit me,

¹ The meaning of the Hebrew is uncertain

and take vengeance for me on my persecutors.
In your forbearance take me not away;
   know that for your sake I bear reproach.
¹⁶ Your words were found, and I ate them,
   and your words became to me a joy
    and the delight of my heart,
for I am called by your name,
   O Lord, God of hosts.
¹⁷ I did not sit in the company of revelers,
   nor did I rejoice;
I sat alone, because your hand was upon me,
   for you had filled me with indignation.
¹⁸ Why is my pain unceasing,
   my wound incurable,
   refusing to be healed?
Will you be to me like a deceitful brook,
   like waters that fail?

¹⁹ Therefore thus says the Lord:
"If you return, I will restore you,
   and you shall stand before me.
If you utter what is precious, and not what is worthless,
   you shall be as my mouth.
They shall turn to you,
   but you shall not turn to them.
²⁰ And I will make you to this people
   a fortified wall of bronze;
they will fight against you,
   but they shall not prevail over you,
for I am with you
   to save you and deliver you,
                declares the Lord.
²¹ I will deliver you out of the hand of the wicked,
   and redeem you from the grasp of the ruthless."

16 The word of the Lord came to me: ²"You shall not take a wife, nor shall you have sons or daughters in this place. ³For thus says the Lord concerning the sons and daughters who are born in this place, and concerning the mothers who bore them and the fathers who fathered them in this land: ⁴They shall die of deadly diseases. They shall not be lamented, nor shall they be buried. They shall be as dung on the surface of the ground. They shall perish by the sword and by famine, and their dead bodies shall be food for the birds of the air and for the beasts of the earth.

⁵"For thus says the Lord: Do not enter the house of mourning, or go to lament or grieve for them, for I have taken away my peace from this people, my steadfast love and mercy, declares the Lord. ⁶Both great and small shall die in this land. They shall not be buried, and no one shall lament for them or cut himself or make himself bald for them. ⁷No one shall break bread for the mourner, to comfort him for the dead, nor

shall anyone give him the cup of consolation to drink for his father or his mother. ⁸You shall not go into the house of feasting to sit with them, to eat and drink. ⁹For thus says the LORD of hosts, the God of Israel: Behold, I will silence in this place, before your eyes and in your days, the voice of mirth and the voice of gladness, the voice of the bridegroom and the voice of the bride.

¹⁰"And when you tell this people all these words, and they say to you, 'Why has the LORD pronounced all this great evil against us? What is our iniquity? What is the sin that we have committed against the LORD our God?' ¹¹then you shall say to them: 'Because your fathers have forsaken me, declares the LORD, and have gone after other gods and have served and worshiped them, and have forsaken me and have not kept my law, ¹²and because you have done worse than your fathers, for behold, every one of you follows his stubborn, evil will, refusing to listen to me. ¹³Therefore I will hurl you out of this land into a land that neither you nor your fathers have known, and there you shall serve other gods day and night, for I will show you no favor.'

¹⁴"Therefore, behold, the days are coming, declares the LORD, when it shall no longer be said, 'As the LORD lives who brought up the people of Israel out of the land of Egypt,' ¹⁵but 'As the LORD lives who brought up the people of Israel out of the north country and out of all the countries where he had driven them.' For I will bring them back to their own land that I gave to their fathers.

¹⁶"Behold, I am sending for many fishers, declares the LORD, and they shall catch them. And afterward I will send for many hunters, and they shall hunt them from every mountain and every hill, and out of the clefts of the rocks. ¹⁷For my eyes are on all their ways. They are not hidden from me, nor is their iniquity concealed from my eyes. ¹⁸But first I will doubly repay their iniquity and their sin, because they have polluted my land with the carcasses of their detestable idols, and have filled my inheritance with their abominations."

¹⁹   O LORD, my strength and my stronghold,
        my refuge in the day of trouble,
    to you shall the nations come
        from the ends of the earth and say:
    "Our fathers have inherited nothing but lies,
        worthless things in which there is no profit.
²⁰   Can man make for himself gods?
        Such are not gods!"

²¹"Therefore, behold, I will make them know, this once I will make them know my power and my might, and they shall know that my name is the LORD."

From the prophet's notebook [chapter 17]. The book of Jeremiah is an anthology or collection of writings from a lifetime in ministry. In keeping with this format, the material in this chapter is rather diverse: an accusation regarding Judah's sin, with yet another prophecy of judgment (vv. 1–4); a poetic, psalm-like comparison between God's curse on those who trust in themselves and God's blessing on those who trust in him (vv. 5–13); a prophet's prayer for personal healing and deliverance from persecution (vv. 14–18); and a short sermon on God's blessings and curses for a city that either keeps or fails to keep God's holy Sabbath (vv. 19–27). Although this material is not strongly unified by any obvious principle of logical arrangement, it helps to complete the portrait of Jeremiah as the weeping prophet and to document some of the main burdens of his ministry.

17

"The sin of Judah is written with a pen of iron; with a point of diamond it is engraved on the tablet of their heart, and on the horns of their altars, ²while their children remember their altars and their Asherim, beside every green tree and on the high hills, ³on the mountains in the open country. Your wealth and all your treasures I will give for spoil as the price of your high places for sin throughout all your territory. ⁴You shall loosen your hand from your heritage that I gave to you, and I will make you serve your enemies in a land that you do not know, for in my anger a fire is kindled that shall burn forever."

⁵   Thus says the LORD:
"Cursed is the man who trusts in man
    and makes flesh his strength,[1]
    whose heart turns away from the LORD.
⁶   He is like a shrub in the desert,
    and shall not see any good come.
He shall dwell in the parched places of the wilderness,
    in an uninhabited salt land.

⁷   "Blessed is the man who trusts in the LORD,
    whose trust is the LORD.
⁸   He is like a tree planted by water,
    that sends out its roots by the stream,
and does not fear when heat comes,
    for its leaves remain green,
and is not anxious in the year of drought,
    for it does not cease to bear fruit."

⁹   The heart is deceitful above all things,
    and desperately sick;
    who can understand it?
¹⁰ "I the LORD search the heart
    and test the mind,[2]
to give every man according to his ways,
    according to the fruit of his deeds."

¹¹ Like the partridge that gathers a brood that she did not hatch,
    so is he who gets riches but not by justice;
in the midst of his days they will leave him,
    and at his end he will be a fool.

¹² A glorious throne set on high from the beginning
    is the place of our sanctuary.
¹³ O LORD, the hope of Israel,
    all who forsake you shall be put to shame;
those who turn away from you[3] shall be written in the earth,
    for they have forsaken the LORD, the fountain of living water.

[1] Hebrew arm [2] Hebrew kidneys [3] Hebrew me

¹⁴   Heal me, O Lᴏʀᴅ, and I shall be healed;
        save me, and I shall be saved,
        for you are my praise.
¹⁵   Behold, they say to me,
        "Where is the word of the Lᴏʀᴅ?
        Let it come!"
¹⁶   I have not run away from being your shepherd,
        nor have I desired the day of sickness.
     You know what came out of my lips;
        it was before your face.
¹⁷   Be not a terror to me;
        you are my refuge in the day of disaster.
¹⁸   Let those be put to shame who persecute me,
        but let me not be put to shame;
     let them be dismayed,
        but let me not be dismayed;
     bring upon them the day of disaster;
        destroy them with double destruction!

¹⁹Thus said the Lᴏʀᴅ to me: "Go and stand in the People's Gate, by which the kings of Judah enter and by which they go out, and in all the gates of Jerusalem, ²⁰and say: 'Hear the word of the Lᴏʀᴅ, you kings of Judah, and all Judah, and all the inhabitants of Jerusalem, who enter by these gates. ²¹Thus says the Lᴏʀᴅ: Take care for the sake of your lives, and do not bear a burden on the Sabbath day or bring it in by the gates of Jerusalem. ²²And do not carry a burden out of your houses on the Sabbath or do any work, but keep the Sabbath day holy, as I commanded your fathers. ²³Yet they did not listen or incline their ear, but stiffened their neck, that they might not hear and receive instruction.

²⁴"But if you listen to me, declares the Lᴏʀᴅ, and bring in no burden by the gates of this city on the Sabbath day, but keep the Sabbath day holy and do no work on it, ²⁵then there shall enter by the gates of this city kings and princes who sit on the throne of David, riding in chariots and on horses, they and their officials, the men of Judah and the inhabitants of Jerusalem. And this city shall be inhabited forever. ²⁶And people shall come from the cities of Judah and the places around Jerusalem, from the land of Benjamin, from the Shephelah, from the hill country, and from the Negeb, bringing burnt offerings and sacrifices, grain offerings and frankincense, and bringing thank offerings to the house of the Lᴏʀᴅ. ²⁷But if you do not listen to me, to keep the Sabbath day holy, and not to bear a burden and enter by the gates of Jerusalem on the Sabbath day, then I will kindle a fire in its gates, and it shall devour the palaces of Jerusalem and shall not be quenched.'"

At the potter's house [chapter 18]. In yet another one of his prophetic object lessons, Jeremiah goes down to the potter's house for a prophetic field trip. There he sees an artisan shaping and then reshaping a flawed clay pot. This is a symbol of God's absolute sovereignty over his people Israel (or anyone else, for that matter). God will shape and reshape in judgment and mercy, always doing whatever he thinks is best. In response to this prophecy, the people dismiss God's word and begin to plot against Jeremiah (see

18:18). The prophet's vindictive prayer at the end of the chapter seems to betray more zeal for God's vengeance than passion for God's mercy (18:19–23).

18

The word that came to Jeremiah from the LORD: [2]"Arise, and go down to the potter's house, and there I will let you hear my words." [3]So I went down to the potter's house, and there he was working at his wheel. [4]And the vessel he was making of clay was spoiled in the potter's hand, and he reworked it into another vessel, as it seemed good to the potter to do.

[5]Then the word of the LORD came to me: [6]"O house of Israel, can I not do with you as this potter has done? declares the LORD. Behold, like the clay in the potter's hand, so are you in my hand, O house of Israel. [7]If at any time I declare concerning a nation or a kingdom, that I will pluck up and break down and destroy it, [8]and if that nation, concerning which I have spoken, turns from its evil, I will relent of the disaster that I intended to do to it. [9]And if at any time I declare concerning a nation or a kingdom that I will build and plant it, [10]and if it does evil in my sight, not listening to my voice, then I will relent of the good that I had intended to do to it. [11]Now, therefore, say to the men of Judah and the inhabitants of Jerusalem: 'Thus says the LORD, Behold, I am shaping disaster against you and devising a plan against you. Return, every one from his evil way, and amend your ways and your deeds.'

[12]"But they say, 'That is in vain! We will follow our own plans, and will every one act according to the stubbornness of his evil heart.'

[13] "Therefore thus says the LORD:
Ask among the nations,
    Who has heard the like of this?
The virgin Israel
    has done a very horrible thing.
[14] Does the snow of Lebanon leave
    the crags of Sirion?[1]
Do the mountain waters run dry,[2]
    the cold flowing streams?
[15] But my people have forgotten me;
    they make offerings to false gods;
they made them stumble in their ways,
    in the ancient roads,
and to walk into side roads,
    not the highway,
[16] making their land a horror,
    a thing to be hissed at forever.
Everyone who passes by it is horrified
    and shakes his head.
[17] Like the east wind I will scatter them
    before the enemy.
I will show them my back, not my face,
    in the day of their calamity."

---

[1] Hebrew *of the field* [2] Hebrew *Are foreign waters plucked up*

¹⁸Then they said, "Come, let us make plots against Jeremiah, for the law shall not perish from the priest, nor counsel from the wise, nor the word from the prophet. Come, let us strike him with the tongue, and let us not pay attention to any of his words."

19   Hear me, O LORD,
            and listen to the voice of my adversaries.
20   Should good be repaid with evil?
            Yet they have dug a pit for my life.
        Remember how I stood before you
            to speak good for them,
            to turn away your wrath from them.
21   Therefore deliver up their children to famine;
            give them over to the power of the sword;
        let their wives become childless and widowed.
            May their men meet death by pestilence,
            their youths be struck down by the sword in battle.
22   May a cry be heard from their houses,
            when you bring the plunderer suddenly upon them!
        For they have dug a pit to take me
            and laid snares for my feet.
23   Yet you, O LORD, know
            all their plotting to kill me.
        Forgive not their iniquity,
            nor blot out their sin from your sight.
        Let them be overthrown before you;
            deal with them in the time of your anger.

Clay in the hands of an angry potter [chapter 19]. Jeremiah is told to buy one of the potter's clay pots, take it out to the Valley of Slaughter, and smash it on the ground as a sign of God's judgment against Jerusalem for offering child sacrifices and committing other heinous sins. The prophet's dramatic actions in this narrative speak as loudly as his prophetic words of judgment, which the people refuse to hear.

19 Thus says the LORD, "Go, buy a potter's earthenware flask, and take some of the elders of the people and some of the elders of the priests, ²and go out to the Valley of the Son of Hinnom at the entry of the Potsherd Gate, and proclaim there the words that I tell you. ³You shall say, 'Hear the word of the LORD, O kings of Judah and inhabitants of Jerusalem. Thus says the LORD of hosts, the God of Israel: Behold, I am bringing such disaster upon this place that the ears of everyone who hears of it will tingle. ⁴Because the people have forsaken me and have profaned this place by making offerings in it to other gods whom neither they nor their fathers nor the kings of Judah have known; and because they have filled this place with the blood of innocents, ⁵and have built the high places of Baal to burn their sons in the fire as burnt offerings to Baal, which I did not command or decree, nor did it come into my mind— ⁶therefore, behold, days are coming, declares the LORD, when this place shall no more be called Topheth, or the Valley of the Son of Hinnom, but the Valley of Slaughter.

⁷And in this place I will make void the plans of Judah and Jerusalem, and will cause their people to fall by the sword before their enemies, and by the hand of those who seek their life. I will give their dead bodies for food to the birds of the air and to the beasts of the earth. ⁸And I will make this city a horror, a thing to be hissed at. Everyone who passes by it will be horrified and will hiss because of all its wounds. ⁹And I will make them eat the flesh of their sons and their daughters, and everyone shall eat the flesh of his neighbor in the siege and in the distress, with which their enemies and those who seek their life afflict them.'

¹⁰"Then you shall break the flask in the sight of the men who go with you, ¹¹and shall say to them, 'Thus says the Lord of hosts: So will I break this people and this city, as one breaks a potter's vessel, so that it can never be mended. Men shall bury in Topheth because there will be no place else to bury. ¹²Thus will I do to this place, declares the Lord, and to its inhabitants, making this city like Topheth. ¹³The houses of Jerusalem and the houses of the kings of Judah—all the houses on whose roofs offerings have been offered to all the host of heaven, and drink offerings have been poured out to other gods—shall be defiled like the place of Topheth.'"

¹⁴Then Jeremiah came from Topheth, where the Lord had sent him to prophesy, and he stood in the court of the Lord's house and said to all the people: ¹⁵"Thus says the Lord of hosts, the God of Israel, behold, I am bringing upon this city and upon all its towns all the disaster that I have pronounced against it, because they have stiffened their neck, refusing to hear my words."

Postcard from prison [chapter 20]. A brief prison narrative tells how Jeremiah was beaten and thrown in prison by Pashhur, the chief of the temple police. Apparently the prophet's words of judgment against Jerusalem were regarded as treasonous blasphemy. Undaunted in public, Jeremiah makes an explicit prophecy of Babylonian captivity for Pashhur and almost everyone else in Jerusalem. But when he is alone in his prison cell, the prophet is despondent. This is his dark night of the soul—the time of spiritual darkness when he regrets ever agreeing to serve the Lord in ministry and seems to despair of life itself, cursing the day he was born. If only he did not have to speak God's word of judgment or hear the taunts of his many enemies! After a short interlude of praise, Jeremiah's soliloquy ends with a question: Why is God letting all these things happen to him? No answer is forthcoming, as is often the case when people question what God is doing in their lives. However, there are answers to be found in the total context of the prophet's ministry and in the larger story of God's salvation, of which Jeremiah is one small but important part.

20 Now Pashhur the priest, the son of Immer, who was chief officer in the house of the Lord, heard Jeremiah prophesying these things. ²Then Pashhur beat Jeremiah the prophet, and put him in the stocks that were in the upper Benjamin Gate of the house of the Lord. ³The next day, when Pashhur released Jeremiah from the stocks, Jeremiah said to him, "The Lord does not call your name Pashhur, but Terror On Every Side. ⁴For thus says the Lord: Behold, I will make you a terror to yourself and to all your friends. They shall fall by the sword of their enemies while you look on. And I will give all Judah into the hand of the king of Babylon. He shall carry them captive to Babylon, and shall strike them down with the sword. ⁵Moreover, I will give all the wealth of the city, all its gains, all its prized belongings, and all the treasures of the kings of Judah into the hand of their enemies, who shall plunder them and seize them and carry them to Babylon. ⁶And you, Pashhur, and all who dwell in your house, shall go into captivity. To Babylon you shall go, and there you shall die, and there you shall be buried, you and all your friends, to whom you have prophesied falsely."

⁷   O Lord, you have deceived me,
    and I was deceived;
  you are stronger than I,
    and you have prevailed.
  I have become a laughingstock all the day;
    everyone mocks me.
⁸   For whenever I speak, I cry out,
    I shout, "Violence and destruction!"
  For the word of the Lord has become for me
    a reproach and derision all day long.
⁹   If I say, "I will not mention him,
    or speak any more in his name,"
  there is in my heart as it were a burning fire
    shut up in my bones,
  and I am weary with holding it in,
    and I cannot.
¹⁰ For I hear many whispering.
    Terror is on every side!
  "Denounce him! Let us denounce him!"
    say all my close friends,
      watching for my fall.
  "Perhaps he will be deceived;
    then we can overcome him
    and take our revenge on him."
¹¹ But the Lord is with me as a dread warrior;
    therefore my persecutors will stumble;
    they will not overcome me.
  They will be greatly shamed,
    for they will not succeed.
  Their eternal dishonor
    will never be forgotten.
¹² O Lord of hosts, who tests the righteous,
    who sees the heart and the mind,¹
  let me see your vengeance upon them,
    for to you have I committed my cause.

¹³ Sing to the Lord;
    praise the Lord!
  For he has delivered the life of the needy
    from the hand of evildoers.

¹⁴ Cursed be the day
    on which I was born!

---

¹ Hebrew *kidneys*

> The day when my mother bore me,
> let it not be blessed!
> ¹⁵ Cursed be the man who brought the news to my father,
> "A son is born to you,"
> making him very glad.
> ¹⁶ Let that man be like the cities
> that the LORD overthrew without pity;
> let him hear a cry in the morning
> and an alarm at noon,
> ¹⁷ because he did not kill me in the womb;
> so my mother would have been my grave,
> and her womb forever great.
> ¹⁸ Why did I come out from the womb
> to see toil and sorrow,
> and spend my days in shame?

A message for King Zedekiah [chapter 21]. This oracle of judgment was given at the time when Babylon was besieging Jerusalem. Weak-willed Zedekiah wanted to know: would the Lord save his holy city (21:1–2)? No, because the Lord himself was bringing this judgment against Jerusalem. Nevertheless, there was one way to survive the onslaught. If Zedekiah would surrender to the Babylonians, the lives of his people would be spared (albeit as captives of war). God was giving the king and his people one final opportunity to listen to his prophet Jeremiah and repent of their many sins before being utterly destroyed.

21 This is the word that came to Jeremiah from the LORD, when King Zedekiah sent to him Pashhur the son of Malchiah and Zephaniah the priest, the son of Maaseiah, saying, ²"Inquire of the LORD for us, for Nebuchadnezzar[1] king of Babylon is making war against us. Perhaps the LORD will deal with us according to all his wonderful deeds and will make him withdraw from us."

³Then Jeremiah said to them: ⁴"Thus you shall say to Zedekiah, 'Thus says the LORD, the God of Israel: Behold, I will turn back the weapons of war that are in your hands and with which you are fighting against the king of Babylon and against the Chaldeans who are besieging you outside the walls. And I will bring them together into the midst of this city. ⁵I myself will fight against you with outstretched hand and strong arm, in anger and in fury and in great wrath. ⁶And I will strike down the inhabitants of this city, both man and beast. They shall die of a great pestilence. ⁷Afterward, declares the LORD, I will give Zedekiah king of Judah and his servants and the people in this city who survive the pestilence, sword, and famine into the hand of Nebuchadnezzar king of Babylon and into the hand of their enemies, into the hand of those who seek their lives. He shall strike them down with the edge of the sword. He shall not pity them or spare them or have compassion.'

⁸"And to this people you shall say: 'Thus says the LORD: Behold, I set before you the way of life and the way of death. ⁹He who stays in this city shall die by the sword, by famine, and by pestilence, but he who goes out and surrenders to the Chaldeans who are besieging you shall live and shall have his life as a prize of war. ¹⁰For I have set

---

[1] Hebrew *Nebuchadrezzar*, another spelling for *Nebuchadnezzar* (king of Babylon) occurring frequently from Jeremiah 21–52; this latter spelling is used throughout Jeremiah for consistency

my face against this city for harm and not for good, declares the LORD: it shall be given into the hand of the king of Babylon, and he shall burn it with fire.'

¹¹"And to the house of the king of Judah say, 'Hear the word of the LORD, ¹²O house of David! Thus says the LORD:

"'Execute justice in the morning,
        and deliver from the hand of the oppressor
    him who has been robbed,
lest my wrath go forth like fire,
    and burn with none to quench it,
    because of your evil deeds.'"

¹³   "Behold, I am against you, O inhabitant of the valley,
        O rock of the plain,
                            declares the LORD;
    you who say, 'Who shall come down against us,
        or who shall enter our habitations?'
¹⁴   I will punish you according to the fruit of your deeds,
                            declares the LORD;
    I will kindle a fire in her forest,
    and it shall devour all that is around her."

A royal disaster, a righteous hope [22:1–23:8]. Since the kings mentioned in this passage (Shallum and Jehoiakim) preceded Zedekiah on the throne, Jeremiah must have given this prophecy sometime earlier in his ministry (as an anthology, the book of Jeremiah is not always arranged chronologically). Chapter 22 is an extended attack on the sins of the royal house of Judah and an explanation of the harsh punishment these kings deserve. There are images here of self-indulgence, injustice, and impending judgment. By way of negative example, a portrait emerges of godly leadership—the kind of spiritual shepherding God promises at the beginning of chapter 23. The famous messianic prophecy of a righteous Branch from the house of David brings hope of justice, righteousness, and salvation (23:1–8). At the same time he was predicting Judah's captivity, Jeremiah was also promising Judah's return and restoration.

22 Thus says the LORD: "Go down to the house of the king of Judah and speak there this word, ²and say, 'Hear the word of the LORD, O king of Judah, who sits on the throne of David, you, and your servants, and your people who enter these gates. ³Thus says the LORD: Do justice and righteousness, and deliver from the hand of the oppressor him who has been robbed. And do no wrong or violence to the resident alien, the fatherless, and the widow, nor shed innocent blood in this place. ⁴For if you will indeed obey this word, then there shall enter the gates of this house kings who sit on the throne of David, riding in chariots and on horses, they and their servants and their people. ⁵But if you will not obey these words, I swear by myself, declares the LORD, that this house shall become a desolation. ⁶For thus says the LORD concerning the house of the king of Judah:

"'You are like Gilead to me,
    like the summit of Lebanon,

yet surely I will make you a desert,
    an uninhabited city.[j]

7 I will prepare destroyers against you,
    each with his weapons,
  and they shall cut down your choicest cedars
    and cast them into the fire.

8 "And many nations will pass by this city, and every man will say to his neighbor, "Why has the Lord dealt thus with this great city?" 9And they will answer, "Because they have forsaken the covenant of the Lord their God and worshiped other gods and served them." ' "

10 Weep not for him who is dead,
    nor grieve for him,
  but weep bitterly for him who goes away,
    for he shall return no more
    to see his native land.

11For thus says the Lord concerning Shallum the son of Josiah, king of Judah, who reigned instead of Josiah his father, and who went away from this place: "He shall return here no more, 12but in the place where they have carried him captive, there shall he die, and he shall never see this land again."

13 "Woe to him who builds his house by unrighteousness,
    and his upper rooms by injustice,
  who makes his neighbor serve him for nothing
    and does not give him his wages,
14 who says, 'I will build myself a great house
    with spacious upper rooms,'
  who cuts out windows for it,
    paneling it with cedar
    and painting it with vermilion.
15 Do you think you are a king
    because you compete in cedar?
  Did not your father eat and drink
    and do justice and righteousness?
    Then it was well with him.
16 He judged the cause of the poor and needy;
    then it was well.
  Is not this to know me?
    declares the Lord.
17 But you have eyes and heart
    only for your dishonest gain,
  for shedding innocent blood,
    and for practicing oppression and violence."

18Therefore thus says the Lord concerning Jehoiakim the son of Josiah, king of Judah:

[1] Hebrew *cities*

"They shall not lament for him, saying,
    'Ah, my brother!' or 'Ah, sister!'
They shall not lament for him, saying,
    'Ah, lord!' or 'Ah, his majesty!'
¹⁹ With the burial of a donkey he shall be buried,
    dragged and dumped beyond the gates of Jerusalem."

²⁰ "Go up to Lebanon, and cry out,
    and lift up your voice in Bashan;
cry out from Abarim,
    for all your lovers are destroyed.
²¹ I spoke to you in your prosperity,
    but you said, 'I will not listen.'
This has been your way from your youth,
    that you have not obeyed my voice.
²² The wind shall shepherd all your shepherds,
    and your lovers shall go into captivity;
then you will be ashamed and confounded
    because of all your evil.
²³ O inhabitant of Lebanon,
    nested among the cedars,
how you will be pitied when pangs come upon you,
    pain as of a woman in labor!"

²⁴"As I live, declares the LORD, though Coniah the son of Jehoiakim, king of Judah, were the signet ring on my right hand, yet I would tear you off ²⁵and give you into the hand of those who seek your life, into the hand of those of whom you are afraid, even into the hand of Nebuchadnezzar king of Babylon and into the hand of the Chaldeans. ²⁶I will hurl you and the mother who bore you into another country, where you were not born, and there you shall die. ²⁷But to the land to which they will long to return, there they shall not return."

²⁸ Is this man Coniah a despised, broken pot,
    a vessel no one cares for?
Why are he and his children hurled and cast
    into a land that they do not know?
²⁹ O land, land, land,
    hear the word of the LORD!
³⁰ Thus says the LORD:
"Write this man down as childless,
    a man who shall not succeed in his days,
for none of his offspring shall succeed
    in sitting on the throne of David
    and ruling again in Judah."

23 "Woe to the shepherds who destroy and scatter the sheep of my pasture!" declares the LORD. ²Therefore thus says the LORD, the God of Israel, concerning the shepherds who care for my people: "You have scattered my flock and have driven them away, and you have not attended to them. Behold, I will attend to you for your evil deeds, declares the LORD. ³Then I will gather the remnant of my flock out of all the countries where I have driven them, and I will bring them back to their fold, and they shall be fruitful and multiply. ⁴I will set shepherds over them who will care for them, and they shall fear no more, nor be dismayed, neither shall any be missing, declares the LORD.

⁵"Behold, the days are coming, declares the LORD, when I will raise up for David a righteous Branch, and he shall reign as king and deal wisely, and shall execute justice and righteousness in the land. ⁶In his days Judah will be saved, and Israel will dwell securely. And this is the name by which he will be called: 'The LORD is our righteousness.'

⁷"Therefore, behold, the days are coming, declares the LORD, when they shall no longer say, 'As the LORD lives who brought up the people of Israel out of the land of Egypt,' ⁸but 'As the LORD lives who brought up and led the offspring of the house of Israel out of the north country and out of all the countries where he¹ had driven them.' Then they shall dwell in their own land."

Truth or consequences [23:9–40]. The prophets were as bad as the kings. Unlike Jeremiah, who received his prophecies from the Lord, the lying prophets were saying things that came only from their own fertile and fanciful imaginations. Their repeated predictions of peace and prosperity were vain hopes; their so-called visions were empty dreams; their false prophecies serve only as a foil for the truth of God's prophet. The only true words of knowledge come from God himself, and any prophet (then or now) who falsely claims to have received personal divine revelation will fall under the judgment of God.

⁹Concerning the prophets:

My heart is broken within me;
    all my bones shake;
I am like a drunken man,
    like a man overcome by wine,
because of the LORD
    and because of his holy words.
¹⁰ For the land is full of adulterers;
    because of the curse the land mourns,
    and the pastures of the wilderness are dried up.
Their course is evil,
    and their might is not right.
¹¹ "Both prophet and priest are ungodly;
    even in my house I have found their evil,
            declares the LORD.
¹² Therefore their way shall be to them
    like slippery paths in the darkness,
    into which they shall be driven and fall,
for I will bring disaster upon them

---

¹ Septuagint; Hebrew *I*

in the year of their punishment,
      declares the LORD.
¹³ In the prophets of Samaria
    I saw an unsavory thing:
  they prophesied by Baal
    and led my people Israel astray.
¹⁴ But in the prophets of Jerusalem
    I have seen a horrible thing:
  they commit adultery and walk in lies;
    they strengthen the hands of evildoers,
    so that no one turns from his evil;
  all of them have become like Sodom to me,
    and its inhabitants like Gomorrah."
¹⁵ Therefore thus says the LORD of hosts concerning the prophets:
  "Behold, I will feed them with bitter food
    and give them poisoned water to drink,
  for from the prophets of Jerusalem
    ungodliness has gone out into all the land."

¹⁶Thus says the LORD of hosts: "Do not listen to the words of the prophets who prophesy to you, filling you with vain hopes. They speak visions of their own minds, not from the mouth of the LORD. ¹⁷They say continually to those who despise the word of the LORD, 'It shall be well with you'; and to everyone who stubbornly follows his own heart, they say, 'No disaster shall come upon you.'"

¹⁸ For who among them has stood in the council of the LORD
    to see and to hear his word,
    or who has paid attention to his word and listened?
¹⁹ Behold, the storm of the LORD!
    Wrath has gone forth,
  a whirling tempest;
    it will burst upon the head of the wicked.
²⁰ The anger of the LORD will not turn back
    until he has executed and accomplished
    the intents of his heart.
  In the latter days you will understand it clearly.

²¹ "I did not send the prophets,
    yet they ran;
  I did not speak to them,
    yet they prophesied.
²² But if they had stood in my council,
    then they would have proclaimed my words to my people,
  and they would have turned them from their evil way,
    and from the evil of their deeds.

²³"Am I a God at hand, declares the LORD, and not a God far away? ²⁴Can a man hide himself in secret places so that I cannot see him? declares the LORD. Do I not fill

heaven and earth? declares the LORD. ²⁵I have heard what the prophets have said who prophesy lies in my name, saying, 'I have dreamed, I have dreamed!' ²⁶How long shall there be lies in the heart of the prophets who prophesy lies, and who prophesy the deceit of their own heart, ²⁷who think to make my people forget my name by their dreams that they tell one another, even as their fathers forgot my name for Baal? ²⁸Let the prophet who has a dream tell the dream, but let him who has my word speak my word faithfully. What has straw in common with wheat? declares the LORD. ²⁹Is not my word like fire, declares the LORD, and like a hammer that breaks the rock in pieces? ³⁰Therefore, behold, I am against the prophets, declares the LORD, who steal my words from one another. ³¹Behold, I am against the prophets, declares the LORD, who use their tongues and declare, 'declares the LORD.' ³²Behold, I am against those who prophesy lying dreams, declares the LORD, and who tell them and lead my people astray by their lies and their recklessness, when I did not send them or charge them. So they do not profit this people at all, declares the LORD.

³³"When one of this people, or a prophet or a priest asks you, 'What is the burden of the LORD?' you shall say to them, 'You are the burden,¹ and I will cast you off, declares the LORD.' ³⁴And as for the prophet, priest, or one of the people who says, 'The burden of the LORD,' I will punish that man and his household. ³⁵Thus shall you say, every one to his neighbor and every one to his brother, 'What has the LORD answered?' or 'What has the LORD spoken?' ³⁶But 'the burden of the LORD' you shall mention no more, for the burden is every man's own word, and you pervert the words of the living God, the LORD of hosts, our God. ³⁷Thus you shall say to the prophet, 'What has the LORD answered you?' or 'What has the LORD spoken?' ³⁸But if you say, 'The burden of the LORD,' thus says the LORD, 'Because you have said these words, "The burden of the LORD," when I sent to you, saying, "You shall not say, 'The burden of the LORD,'" ³⁹therefore, behold, I will surely lift you up and cast you away from my presence, you and the city that I gave to you and your fathers. ⁴⁰And I will bring upon you everlasting reproach and perpetual shame, which shall not be forgotten.'"

Two baskets of figs [chapter 24]. By this point in the story, the Babylonians had begun to carry some of God's people off into captivity. The first wave of exiles included King Jeconiah and other leading citizens of Jerusalem, leaving mainly poor people behind, including Jeremiah. In another of his famous object lessons, the prophet compares these two groups of people—the exiles in Babylon and the refugees in Jerusalem—to two baskets of figs that he sees at the temple. Strangely enough, the good figs represent the people in Babylon, whom God promises to bless during their exile. The bad figs represent the people who have stayed behind, for God had told his people to surrender to the Babylonians rather than trying to resist his judgment for their sins; the people who stayed behind will perish.

24 After Nebuchadnezzar king of Babylon had taken into exile from Jerusalem Jeconiah the son of Jehoiakim, king of Judah, together with the officials of Judah, the craftsmen, and the metal workers, and had brought them to Babylon, the LORD showed me this vision: behold, two baskets of figs placed before the temple of the LORD. ²One basket had very good figs, like first-ripe figs, but the other basket had very bad figs, so bad that they could not be eaten. ³And the LORD said to me, "What do you see, Jeremiah?" I said, "Figs, the good figs very good, and the bad figs very bad, so bad that they cannot be eaten."

⁴Then the word of the LORD came to me: ⁵"Thus says the LORD, the God of Israel: Like these good figs, so I will regard as good the exiles from Judah, whom I have sent away from this place to the land of the Chaldeans. ⁶I will set my eyes on them for good, and I will bring them back to this land. I will build them up, and not tear them down; I will plant them, and not uproot them. ⁷I will give them a heart to know that I am the LORD, and they shall be my people and I will be their God, for they shall return to me with their whole heart.

⁸"But thus says the LORD: Like the bad figs that are so bad they cannot be eaten, so will I treat Zedekiah the king of Judah, his officials, the remnant of Jerusalem who remain in this land, and those who dwell in the land of Egypt. ⁹I will make them a horror¹ to all the kingdoms of the earth, to be a reproach, a byword, a taunt, and a curse in all the places where I shall drive them. ¹⁰And I will send sword, famine, and pestilence upon them, until they shall be utterly destroyed from the land that I gave to them and their fathers."

Seventy years of captivity [25:1–14]. In this prophecy, which dates back to the reign of Jeconiah's father Jehoiakim, Jeremiah makes an explicit prediction about the timing of Israel's captivity, which is further specified to take place in Babylon. After seventy years in exile, the remnant of God's people will be restored to the Promised Land. Whereas most of Jeremiah's prophecies use highly figurative language, this oracle of judgment is more prosaic in its predictions.

25 The word that came to Jeremiah concerning all the people of Judah, in the fourth year of Jehoiakim the son of Josiah, king of Judah (that was the first year of Nebuchadnezzar king of Babylon), ²which Jeremiah the prophet spoke to all the people of Judah and all the inhabitants of Jerusalem: ³"For twenty-three years, from the thirteenth year of Josiah the son of Amon, king of Judah, to this day, the word of the LORD has come to me, and I have spoken persistently to you, but you have not listened. ⁴You have neither listened nor inclined your ears to hear, although the LORD persistently sent to you all his servants the prophets, ⁵saying, 'Turn now, every one of you, from his evil way and evil deeds, and dwell upon the land that the LORD has given to you and your fathers from of old and forever. ⁶Do not go after other gods to serve and worship them, or provoke me to anger with the work of your hands. Then I will do you no harm.' ⁷Yet you have not listened to me, declares the LORD, that you might provoke me to anger with the work of your hands to your own harm.

⁸"Therefore thus says the LORD of hosts: Because you have not obeyed my words, ⁹behold, I will send for all the tribes of the north, declares the LORD, and for Nebuchadnezzar the king of Babylon, my servant, and I will bring them against this land and its inhabitants, and against all these surrounding nations. I will devote them to destruction, and make them a horror, a hissing, and an everlasting desolation. ¹⁰Moreover, I will banish from them the voice of mirth and the voice of gladness, the voice of the bridegroom and the voice of the bride, the grinding of the millstones and the light of the lamp. ¹¹This whole land shall become a ruin and a waste, and these nations shall serve the king of Babylon seventy years. ¹²Then after seventy years

¹ Compare Septuagint; Hebrew *horror for evil*

are completed, I will punish the king of Babylon and that nation, the land of the Chaldeans, for their iniquity, declares the LORD, making the land an everlasting waste. [13]I will bring upon that land all the words that I have uttered against it, everything written in this book, which Jeremiah prophesied against all the nations. [14]For many nations and great kings shall make slaves even of them, and I will recompense them according to their deeds and the work of their hands."

The cup of God's wrath [25:15–38]. Jeremiah often prophesies that God will punish his people for their sins and that he will use godless nations like Babylon to do the punishing. However, the people of these nations should not think that they are somehow superior to the people of Israel or that they are under God's blessing. On the contrary, eventually they too will be punished for their sins. The prophecy in this chapter—with its lengthy catalog of foreign nations and vivid imagery of destruction—uses a cup of strong drink as a governing metaphor for the judgment that will fall not only on Judah and Jerusalem but also on the whole international community of God's enemies.

[15]Thus the LORD, the God of Israel, said to me: "Take from my hand this cup of the wine of wrath, and make all the nations to whom I send you drink it. [16]They shall drink and stagger and be crazed because of the sword that I am sending among them."

[17]So I took the cup from the LORD's hand, and made all the nations to whom the LORD sent me drink it: [18]Jerusalem and the cities of Judah, its kings and officials, to make them a desolation and a waste, a hissing and a curse, as at this day; [19]Pharaoh king of Egypt, his servants, his officials, all his people, [20]and all the mixed tribes among them; all the kings of the land of Uz and all the kings of the land of the Philistines (Ashkelon, Gaza, Ekron, and the remnant of Ashdod); [21]Edom, Moab, and the sons of Ammon; [22]all the kings of Tyre, all the kings of Sidon, and the kings of the coastland across the sea; [23]Dedan, Tema, Buz, and all who cut the corners of their hair; [24]all the kings of Arabia and all the kings of the mixed tribes who dwell in the desert; [25]all the kings of Zimri, all the kings of Elam, and all the kings of Media; [26]all the kings of the north, far and near, one after another, and all the kingdoms of the world that are on the face of the earth. And after them the king of Babylon[1] shall drink.

[27]"Then you shall say to them, 'Thus says the LORD of hosts, the God of Israel: Drink, be drunk and vomit, fall and rise no more, because of the sword that I am sending among you.'

[28]"And if they refuse to accept the cup from your hand to drink, then you shall say to them, 'Thus says the LORD of hosts: You must drink! [29]For behold, I begin to work disaster at the city that is called by my name, and shall you go unpunished? You shall not go unpunished, for I am summoning a sword against all the inhabitants of the earth, declares the LORD of hosts.'

[30]"You, therefore, shall prophesy against them all these words, and say to them:

"'The LORD will roar from on high,
        and from his holy habitation utter his voice;
    he will roar mightily against his fold,
        and shout, like those who tread grapes,
    against all the inhabitants of the earth.

---

[1] Hebrew *Sheshach*, a code name for Babylon

³¹   The clamor will resound to the ends of the earth,
> for the LORD has an indictment against the nations;
> he is entering into judgment with all flesh,
>   and the wicked he will put to the sword,
>   declares the LORD.'

³²   "Thus says the LORD of hosts:
> Behold, disaster is going forth
>   from nation to nation,
> and a great tempest is stirring
> from the farthest parts of the earth!

³³ "And those pierced by the LORD on that day shall extend from one end of the earth to the other. They shall not be lamented, or gathered, or buried; they shall be dung on the surface of the ground.

³⁴   "Wail, you shepherds, and cry out,
>   and roll in ashes, you lords of the flock,
> for the days of your slaughter and dispersion have come,
>   and you shall fall like a choice vessel.

³⁵   No refuge will remain for the shepherds,
>   nor escape for the lords of the flock.

³⁶   A voice—the cry of the shepherds,
>   and the wail of the lords of the flock!
> For the LORD is laying waste their pasture,

³⁷   and the peaceful folds are devastated
>   because of the fierce anger of the LORD.

³⁸   Like a lion he has left his lair,
>   for their land has become a waste
> because of the sword of the oppressor,
>   and because of his fierce anger."

The temple sermon and its aftermath [chapter 26]. The message Jeremiah gives at the beginning of this chapter appears to be the same message he preached back in chapter 7—his temple sermon. Here the story is brought to completion with an account of the death threats the prophet received afterward for saying that Jerusalem and its temple will be destroyed (26:7–11, 16). The narrative is full of vivid details that convey the climate of public opinion during the troubled years leading up to the fall of Jerusalem. The conflict between Jeremiah's supporters and the people who considered him public enemy number one highlights a central concern of the book as a whole: Is Jeremiah telling the truth about the coming judgment, or not? In the end, the people agree to wait and see, sparing the prophet's life for the time being.

26 In the beginning of the reign of Jehoiakim the son of Josiah, king of Judah, this word came from the LORD: ²"Thus says the LORD: Stand in the court of the LORD's house, and speak to all the cities of Judah that come to worship in the house of the LORD all the words that I command you to speak to them; do not hold back a word. ³It may be they will listen, and every one turn from his evil way, that I may relent of the disaster that I intend to do to them because of their evil deeds. ⁴You shall say to them, 'Thus says the LORD: If you will not listen to me, to walk in my law that I have set before you, ⁵and to listen to the words of my servants the prophets whom I send to you urgently, though you have not listened, ⁶then I will make this house like Shiloh, and I will make this city a curse for all the nations of the earth.'"

⁷The priests and the prophets and all the people heard Jeremiah speaking these words in the house of the LORD. ⁸And when Jeremiah had finished speaking all that the LORD had commanded him to speak to all the people, then the priests and the prophets and all the people laid hold of him, saying, "You shall die! ⁹Why have you prophesied in the name of the LORD, saying, 'This house shall be like Shiloh, and this city shall be desolate, without inhabitant'?" And all the people gathered around Jeremiah in the house of the LORD.

¹⁰When the officials of Judah heard these things, they came up from the king's house to the house of the LORD and took their seat in the entry of the New Gate of the house of the LORD. ¹¹Then the priests and the prophets said to the officials and to all the people, "This man deserves the sentence of death, because he has prophesied against this city, as you have heard with your own ears."

¹²Then Jeremiah spoke to all the officials and all the people, saying, "The LORD sent me to prophesy against this house and this city all the words you have heard. ¹³Now therefore mend your ways and your deeds, and obey the voice of the LORD your God, and the LORD will relent of the disaster that he has pronounced against you. ¹⁴But as for me, behold, I am in your hands. Do with me as seems good and right to you. ¹⁵Only know for certain that if you put me to death, you will bring innocent blood upon yourselves and upon this city and its inhabitants, for in truth the LORD sent me to you to speak all these words in your ears."

¹⁶Then the officials and all the people said to the priests and the prophets, "This man does not deserve the sentence of death, for he has spoken to us in the name of the LORD our God." ¹⁷And certain of the elders of the land arose and spoke to all the assembled people, saying, ¹⁸"Micah of Moresheth prophesied in the days of Hezekiah king of Judah, and said to all the people of Judah: 'Thus says the LORD of hosts,

"'Zion shall be plowed as a field;
    Jerusalem shall become a heap of ruins,
    and the mountain of the house a wooded height.'

¹⁹Did Hezekiah king of Judah and all Judah put him to death? Did he not fear the LORD and entreat the favor of the LORD, and did not the LORD relent of the disaster that he had pronounced against them? But we are about to bring great disaster upon ourselves."

²⁰There was another man who prophesied in the name of the LORD, Uriah the son of Shemaiah from Kiriath-jearim. He prophesied against this city and against this land in words like those of Jeremiah. ²¹And when King Jehoiakim, with all his warriors and all the officials, heard his words, the king sought to put him to death. But when Uriah heard of it, he was afraid and fled and escaped to Egypt. ²²Then King Jehoiakim sent to Egypt certain men, Elnathan the son of Achbor and others with him, ²³and they took Uriah from Egypt and brought him to King Jehoiakim, who

struck him down with the sword and dumped his dead body into the burial place of the common people.

²⁴But the hand of Ahikam the son of Shaphan was with Jeremiah so that he was not given over to the people to be put to death.

Under the yoke of Babylon [chapters 27–28]. Diplomats from foreign nations have descended on Jerusalem to persuade King Zedekiah to join their alliance or else suffer the consequences. To make another one of his famous prophetic object lessons, Jeremiah puts a wooden yoke around his neck, such as a team of oxen might wear. His point is that God has ordained for Judah to come under the yoke of Babylonian rule and therefore any nation that does not submit to King Nebuchadnezzar will suffer famine, sword, and pestilence (27:4–8). This message is in direct contradiction to what foolish Hananiah and the other false prophets are saying, namely, that God will break the Babylonian yoke and restore the first wave of exiles to the land (28:1–4). Once again, the plot conflict hinges on who is telling the truth. The only true prophet is someone who has a message from God, as Hananiah will discover when he falls under the wrath of God.

---

27 In the beginning of the reign of Zedekiah¹ the son of Josiah, king of Judah, this word came to Jeremiah from the LORD. ²Thus the LORD said to me: "Make yourself straps and yoke-bars, and put them on your neck. ³Send word² to the king of Edom, the king of Moab, the king of the sons of Ammon, the king of Tyre, and the king of Sidon by the hand of the envoys who have come to Jerusalem to Zedekiah king of Judah. ⁴Give them this charge for their masters: 'Thus says the LORD of hosts, the God of Israel: This is what you shall say to your masters: ⁵"It is I who by my great power and my outstretched arm have made the earth, with the men and animals that are on the earth, and I give it to whomever it seems right to me. ⁶Now I have given all these lands into the hand of Nebuchadnezzar, the king of Babylon, my servant, and I have given him also the beasts of the field to serve him. ⁷All the nations shall serve him and his son and his grandson, until the time of his own land comes. Then many nations and great kings shall make him their slave.

⁸"'But if any nation or kingdom will not serve this Nebuchadnezzar king of Babylon, and put its neck under the yoke of the king of Babylon, I will punish that nation with the sword, with famine, and with pestilence, declares the LORD, until I have consumed it by his hand. ⁹So do not listen to your prophets, your diviners, your dreamers, your fortune-tellers, or your sorcerers, who are saying to you, 'You shall not serve the king of Babylon.' ¹⁰For it is a lie that they are prophesying to you, with the result that you will be removed far from your land, and I will drive you out, and you will perish. ¹¹But any nation that will bring its neck under the yoke of the king of Babylon and serve him, I will leave on its own land, to work it and dwell there, declares the LORD."'"

¹²To Zedekiah king of Judah I spoke in like manner: "Bring your necks under the yoke of the king of Babylon, and serve him and his people and live. ¹³Why will you and your people die by the sword, by famine, and by pestilence, as the LORD has spoken concerning any nation that will not serve the king of Babylon? ¹⁴Do not listen to the words of the prophets who are saying to you, 'You shall not serve the king of Babylon,' for it is a lie that they are prophesying to you. ¹⁵I have not sent them, declares the LORD,

---

¹ Or Jehoiakim ² Hebrew Send them

but they are prophesying falsely in my name, with the result that I will drive you out and you will perish, you and the prophets who are prophesying to you."

[16]Then I spoke to the priests and to all this people, saying, "Thus says the LORD: Do not listen to the words of your prophets who are prophesying to you, saying, 'Behold, the vessels of the LORD's house will now shortly be brought back from Babylon,' for it is a lie that they are prophesying to you. [17]Do not listen to them; serve the king of Babylon and live. Why should this city become a desolation? [18]If they are prophets, and if the word of the LORD is with them, then let them intercede with the LORD of hosts, that the vessels that are left in the house of the LORD, in the house of the king of Judah, and in Jerusalem may not go to Babylon. [19]For thus says the LORD of hosts concerning the pillars, the sea, the stands, and the rest of the vessels that are left in this city, [20]which Nebuchadnezzar king of Babylon did not take away, when he took into exile from Jerusalem to Babylon Jeconiah the son of Jehoiakim, king of Judah, and all the nobles of Judah and Jerusalem— [21]thus says the LORD of hosts, the God of Israel, concerning the vessels that are left in the house of the LORD, in the house of the king of Judah, and in Jerusalem: [22]They shall be carried to Babylon and remain there until the day when I visit them, declares the LORD. Then I will bring them back and restore them to this place."

28 In that same year, at the beginning of the reign of Zedekiah king of Judah, in the fifth month of the fourth year, Hananiah the son of Azzur, the prophet from Gibeon, spoke to me in the house of the LORD, in the presence of the priests and all the people, saying, [2]"Thus says the LORD of hosts, the God of Israel: I have broken the yoke of the king of Babylon. [3]Within two years I will bring back to this place all the vessels of the LORD's house, which Nebuchadnezzar king of Babylon took away from this place and carried to Babylon. [4]I will also bring back to this place Jeconiah the son of Jehoiakim, king of Judah, and all the exiles from Judah who went to Babylon, declares the LORD, for I will break the yoke of the king of Babylon."

[5]Then the prophet Jeremiah spoke to Hananiah the prophet in the presence of the priests and all the people who were standing in the house of the LORD, [6]and the prophet Jeremiah said, "Amen! May the LORD do so; may the LORD make the words that you have prophesied come true, and bring back to this place from Babylon the vessels of the house of the LORD, and all the exiles. [7]Yet hear now this word that I speak in your hearing and in the hearing of all the people. [8]The prophets who preceded you and me from ancient times prophesied war, famine, and pestilence against many countries and great kingdoms. [9]As for the prophet who prophesies peace, when the word of that prophet comes to pass, then it will be known that the LORD has truly sent the prophet."

[10]Then the prophet Hananiah took the yoke-bars from the neck of Jeremiah the prophet and broke them. [11]And Hananiah spoke in the presence of all the people, saying, "Thus says the LORD: Even so will I break the yoke of Nebuchadnezzar king of Babylon from the neck of all the nations within two years." But Jeremiah the prophet went his way.

[12]Sometime after the prophet Hananiah had broken the yoke-bars from off the neck of Jeremiah the prophet, the word of the LORD came to Jeremiah: [13]"Go, tell Hananiah, 'Thus says the LORD: You have broken wooden bars, but you have made in their place bars of iron. [14]For thus says the LORD of hosts, the God of Israel: I have put

upon the neck of all these nations an iron yoke to serve Nebuchadnezzar king of Babylon, and they shall serve him, for I have given to him even the beasts of the field.' ¹⁵And Jeremiah the prophet said to the prophet Hananiah, "Listen, Hananiah, the LORD has not sent you, and you have made this people trust in a lie. ¹⁶Therefore thus says the LORD: 'Behold, I will remove you from the face of the earth. This year you shall die, because you have uttered rebellion against the LORD.'"

¹⁷In that same year, in the seventh month, the prophet Hananiah died.

> **A letter from home** [chapter 29]. Although Jeremiah is still in Jerusalem, King Jeconiah and most of Judah's leaders have already been carried off to Babylon in the first wave of exiles. Jeremiah is still their prophet, and in this epistle he tells the exiles not to escape but to make themselves at home in Babylon—pursuing the peace and prosperity of that great city—because God's good plans for their future blessing include seven decades of spiritual growth in captivity before they come back home (29:4–14). Yet again, the prophet has to confront his naysayers—lying prophets like Shemaiah, who deny that Jeremiah speaks for God (29:24–32).

29 These are the words of the letter that Jeremiah the prophet sent from Jerusalem to the surviving elders of the exiles, and to the priests, the prophets, and all the people, whom Nebuchadnezzar had taken into exile from Jerusalem to Babylon. ²This was after King Jeconiah and the queen mother, the eunuchs, the officials of Judah and Jerusalem, the craftsmen, and the metal workers had departed from Jerusalem. ³The letter was sent by the hand of Elasah the son of Shaphan and Gemariah the son of Hilkiah, whom Zedekiah king of Judah sent to Babylon to Nebuchadnezzar king of Babylon. It said: ⁴"Thus says the LORD of hosts, the God of Israel, to all the exiles whom I have sent into exile from Jerusalem to Babylon: ⁵Build houses and live in them; plant gardens and eat their produce. ⁶Take wives and have sons and daughters; take wives for your sons, and give your daughters in marriage, that they may bear sons and daughters; multiply there, and do not decrease. ⁷But seek the welfare of the city where I have sent you into exile, and pray to the LORD on its behalf, for in its welfare you will find your welfare. ⁸For thus says the LORD of hosts, the God of Israel: Do not let your prophets and your diviners who are among you deceive you, and do not listen to the dreams that they dream,¹ ⁹for it is a lie that they are prophesying to you in my name; I did not send them, declares the LORD.

¹⁰"For thus says the LORD: When seventy years are completed for Babylon, I will visit you, and I will fulfill to you my promise and bring you back to this place. ¹¹For I know the plans I have for you, declares the LORD, plans for welfare² and not for evil, to give you a future and a hope. ¹²Then you will call upon me and come and pray to me, and I will hear you. ¹³You will seek me and find me, when you seek me with all your heart. ¹⁴I will be found by you, declares the LORD, and I will restore your fortunes and gather you from all the nations and all the places where I have driven you, declares the LORD, and I will bring you back to the place from which I sent you into exile.

¹⁵"Because you have said, 'The LORD has raised up prophets for us in Babylon,' ¹⁶thus says the LORD concerning the king who sits on the throne of David, and concerning all the people who dwell in this city, your kinsmen who did not go out with

¹ Hebrew your dreams, which you cause to dream ² Or peace

you into exile: [17]'Thus says the LORD of hosts, behold, I am sending on them sword, famine, and pestilence, and I will make them like vile figs that are so rotten they cannot be eaten. [18]I will pursue them with sword, famine, and pestilence, and will make them a horror to all the kingdoms of the earth, to be a curse, a terror, a hissing, and a reproach among all the nations where I have driven them, [19]because they did not pay attention to my words, declares the LORD, that I persistently sent to you by my servants the prophets, but you would not listen, declares the LORD.' [20]Hear the word of the LORD, all you exiles whom I sent away from Jerusalem to Babylon: [21]'Thus says the LORD of hosts, the God of Israel, concerning Ahab the son of Kolaiah and Zedekiah the son of Maaseiah, who are prophesying a lie to you in my name: Behold, I will deliver them into the hand of Nebuchadnezzar king of Babylon, and he shall strike them down before your eyes. [22]Because of them this curse shall be used by all the exiles from Judah in Babylon: "The LORD make you like Zedekiah and Ahab, whom the king of Babylon roasted in the fire," [23]because they have done an outrageous thing in Israel, they have committed adultery with their neighbors' wives, and they have spoken in my name lying words that I did not command them. I am the one who knows, and I am witness, declares the LORD.'"

[24]To Shemaiah of Nehelam you shall say: [25]"Thus says the LORD of hosts, the God of Israel: You have sent letters in your name to all the people who are in Jerusalem, and to Zephaniah the son of Maaseiah the priest, and to all the priests, saying, [26]'The LORD has made you priest instead of Jehoiada the priest, to have charge in the house of the LORD over every madman who prophesies, to put him in the stocks and neck irons. [27]Now why have you not rebuked Jeremiah of Anathoth who is prophesying to you? [28]For he has sent to us in Babylon, saying, "Your exile will be long; build houses and live in them, and plant gardens and eat their produce."'"

[29]Zephaniah the priest read this letter in the hearing of Jeremiah the prophet. [30]Then the word of the LORD came to Jeremiah: [31]"Send to all the exiles, saying, 'Thus says the LORD concerning Shemaiah of Nehelam: Because Shemaiah had prophesied to you when I did not send him, and has made you trust in a lie, [32]therefore thus says the LORD: Behold, I will punish Shemaiah of Nehelam and his descendants. He shall not have anyone living among this people, and he shall not see the good that I will do to my people, declares the LORD, for he has spoken rebellion against the LORD.'"

From sorrow to hope [chapter 30]. Here we begin "The Book of Consolation"—a concentrated section of hopeful prophecies about the full salvation of Israel and Judah. After the exile, there will be a return; God will restore his people. Many images from earlier in the book—an incurable wound, for example, and a forgotten lover—recur in these prophecies. What was lost will be found; what was abandoned will be recovered; what was wounded will be healed; what was wicked will be destroyed.

30 The word that came to Jeremiah from the LORD: [2]"Thus says the LORD, the God of Israel: Write in a book all the words that I have spoken to you. [3]For behold, days are coming, declares the LORD, when I will restore the fortunes of my people, Israel and Judah, says the LORD, and I will bring them back to the land that I gave to their fathers, and they shall take possession of it."

[4]These are the words that the LORD spoke concerning Israel and Judah:

⁵　"Thus says the LORD:
We have heard a cry of panic,
　of terror, and no peace.
⁶　Ask now, and see,
　can a man bear a child?
Why then do I see every man
　with his hands on his stomach like a woman in labor?
　Why has every face turned pale?
⁷　Alas! That day is so great
　there is none like it;
it is a time of distress for Jacob;
　yet he shall be saved out of it.

⁸"And it shall come to pass in that day, declares the LORD of hosts, that I will break his yoke from off your neck, and I will burst your bonds, and foreigners shall no more make a servant of him.¹ ⁹But they shall serve the LORD their God and David their king, whom I will raise up for them.

¹⁰　"Then fear not, O Jacob my servant, declares the LORD,
　　nor be dismayed, O Israel;
for behold, I will save you from far away,
　and your offspring from the land of their captivity.
Jacob shall return and have quiet and ease,
　and none shall make him afraid.
¹¹　For I am with you to save you,
　　　　　　　declares the LORD;
I will make a full end of all the nations
　among whom I scattered you,
　but of you I will not make a full end.
I will discipline you in just measure,
　and I will by no means leave you unpunished.

¹²　"For thus says the LORD:
Your hurt is incurable,
　and your wound is grievous.
¹³　There is none to uphold your cause,
　no medicine for your wound,
　no healing for you.
¹⁴　All your lovers have forgotten you;
　they care nothing for you;
for I have dealt you the blow of an enemy,
　the punishment of a merciless foe,
because your guilt is great,
　because your sins are flagrant.
¹⁵　Why do you cry out over your hurt?
　Your pain is incurable.
Because your guilt is great,
　because your sins are flagrant,

---

¹ Or serve him

I have done these things to you.
16 Therefore all who devour you shall be devoured,
    and all your foes, every one of them, shall go into captivity;
those who plunder you shall be plundered,
    and all who prey on you I will make a prey.
17 For I will restore health to you,
    and your wounds I will heal,
                  declares the LORD,
because they have called you an outcast:
    'It is Zion, for whom no one cares!'

18 "Thus says the LORD:
Behold, I will restore the fortunes of the tents of Jacob
    and have compassion on his dwellings;
the city shall be rebuilt on its mound,
    and the palace shall stand where it used to be.
19 Out of them shall come songs of thanksgiving,
    and the voices of those who celebrate.
I will multiply them, and they shall not be few;
    I will make them honored, and they shall not be small.
20 Their children shall be as they were of old,
    and their congregation shall be established before me,
    and I will punish all who oppress them.
21 Their prince shall be one of themselves;
    their ruler shall come out from their midst;
I will make him draw near, and he shall approach me,
    for who would dare of himself to approach me?
                  declares the LORD.
22 And you shall be my people,
    and I will be your God."

23 Behold the storm of the LORD!
    Wrath has gone forth,
a whirling tempest;
    it will burst upon the head of the wicked.
24 The fierce anger of the LORD will not turn back
    until he has executed and accomplished
    the intentions of his mind.
In the latter days you will understand this.

The new covenant [chapter 31]. Jeremiah's famous promise of a new covenant comes at the end of this chapter, but the chapter also begins with the promise that is at the very heart of the covenant: God will be the God of his people. In this chapter many sad images of exile, loss, grief, curse, and judgment are reversed by happier images of return, recovery, joy, blessing, and grace. This is a poetic depiction of the good life, almost a *utopia: a worshiping community living in a beautiful city, set in a bountiful countryside, under the love of an ever-faithful God. Even after all his prophecies of woe and doom, Jeremiah testifies that happy days will come again.

31

"At that time, declares the Lord, I will be the God of all the clans of Israel, and they shall be my people."

2   Thus says the Lord:
"The people who survived the sword
    found grace in the wilderness;
when Israel sought for rest,
3   the Lord appeared to him[1] from far away.
I have loved you with an everlasting love;
    therefore I have continued my faithfulness to you.
4   Again I will build you, and you shall be built,
    O virgin Israel!
Again you shall adorn yourself with tambourines
    and shall go forth in the dance of the merrymakers.
5   Again you shall plant vineyards
    on the mountains of Samaria;
the planters shall plant
    and shall enjoy the fruit.
6   For there shall be a day when watchmen will call
    in the hill country of Ephraim:
'Arise, and let us go up to Zion,
    to the Lord our God.'"

7   For thus says the Lord:
"Sing aloud with gladness for Jacob,
    and raise shouts for the chief of the nations;
proclaim, give praise, and say,
    'O Lord, save your people,
    the remnant of Israel.'
8   Behold, I will bring them from the north country
    and gather them from the farthest parts of the earth,
among them the blind and the lame,
    the pregnant woman and she who is in labor, together;
    a great company, they shall return here.
9   With weeping they shall come,
    and with pleas for mercy I will lead them back,
I will make them walk by brooks of water,
    in a straight path in which they shall not stumble,
for I am a father to Israel,
    and Ephraim is my firstborn.

10   "Hear the word of the Lord, O nations,
    and declare it in the coastlands far away;
say, 'He who scattered Israel will gather him,
    and will keep him as a shepherd keeps his flock.'
11   For the Lord has ransomed Jacob
    and has redeemed him from hands too strong for him.
12   They shall come and sing aloud on the height of Zion,

---

[1] Septuagint; Hebrew *me*

and they shall be radiant over the goodness of the LORD,
   over the grain, the wine, and the oil,
      and over the young of the flock and the herd;
   their life shall be like a watered garden,
      and they shall languish no more.
13 Then shall the young women rejoice in the dance,
      and the young men and the old shall be merry.
   I will turn their mourning into joy;
      I will comfort them, and give them gladness for sorrow.
14 I will feast the soul of the priests with abundance,
      and my people shall be satisfied with my goodness,
                    declares the LORD."

15 Thus says the LORD:
   "A voice is heard in Ramah,
      lamentation and bitter weeping.
   Rachel is weeping for her children;
      she refuses to be comforted for her children,
      because they are no more."

16 Thus says the LORD:
   "Keep your voice from weeping,
      and your eyes from tears,
   for there is a reward for your work,
                    declares the LORD,
      and they shall come back from the land of the enemy.
17 There is hope for your future,
                    declares the LORD,
      and your children shall come back to their own country.
18 I have heard Ephraim grieving,
   'You have disciplined me, and I was disciplined,
      like an untrained calf;
   bring me back that I may be restored,
      for you are the LORD my God.
19 For after I had turned away, I relented,
      and after I was instructed, I struck my thigh;
   I was ashamed, and I was confounded,
      because I bore the disgrace of my youth.'
20 Is Ephraim my dear son?
      Is he my darling child?
   For as often as I speak against him,
      I do remember him still.
   Therefore my heart[1] yearns for him;
      I will surely have mercy on him,
                    declares the LORD.

21 "Set up road markers for yourself;
      make yourself guideposts;

---

[1] Hebrew *bowels*

consider well the highway,
>   the road by which you went.
Return, O virgin Israel,
>   return to these your cities.
²² How long will you waver,
>   O faithless daughter?
For the Lord has created a new thing on the earth:
>   a woman encircles a man."

²³ Thus says the Lord of hosts, the God of Israel: "Once more they shall use these words in the land of Judah and in its cities, when I restore their fortunes:

> "'The Lord bless you, O habitation of righteousness,
> >   O holy hill!'

²⁴ And Judah and all its cities shall dwell there together, and the farmers and those who wander with their flocks. ²⁵ For I will satisfy the weary soul, and every languishing soul I will replenish."

²⁶ At this I awoke and looked, and my sleep was pleasant to me.

²⁷ "Behold, the days are coming, declares the Lord, when I will sow the house of Israel and the house of Judah with the seed of man and the seed of beast. ²⁸ And it shall come to pass that as I have watched over them to pluck up and break down, to overthrow, destroy, and bring harm, so I will watch over them to build and to plant, declares the Lord. ²⁹ In those days they shall no longer say:

> "'The fathers have eaten sour grapes,
> >   and the children's teeth are set on edge.'

³⁰ But everyone shall die for his own sin. Each man who eats sour grapes, his teeth shall be set on edge.

³¹ "Behold, the days are coming, declares the Lord, when I will make a new covenant with the house of Israel and the house of Judah, ³² not like the covenant that I made with their fathers on the day when I took them by the hand to bring them out of the land of Egypt, my covenant that they broke, though I was their husband, declares the Lord. ³³ But this is the covenant that I will make with the house of Israel after those days, declares the Lord: I will put my law within them, and I will write it on their hearts. And I will be their God, and they shall be my people. ³⁴ And no longer shall each one teach his neighbor and each his brother, saying, 'Know the Lord,' for they shall all know me, from the least of them to the greatest, declares the Lord. For I will forgive their iniquity, and I will remember their sin no more."

³⁵ Thus says the Lord,
>   who gives the sun for light by day
> >   and the fixed order of the moon and the stars for light by night,
>   who stirs up the sea so that its waves roar—
> >   the Lord of hosts is his name:
³⁶ "If this fixed order departs
>   from before me, declares the Lord,

then shall the offspring of Israel cease
   from being a nation before me forever.'"

37   Thus says the LORD:
"If the heavens above can be measured,
   and the foundations of the earth below can be explored,
then I will cast off all the offspring of Israel
   for all that they have done,
                declares the LORD."

   38"Behold, the days are coming, declares the LORD, when the city shall be rebuilt for the LORD from the Tower of Hananel to the Corner Gate. 39And the measuring line shall go out farther, straight to the hill Gareb, and shall then turn to Goah. 40The whole valley of the dead bodies and the ashes, and all the fields as far as the brook Kidron, to the corner of the Horse Gate toward the east, shall be sacred to the LORD. It shall not be uprooted or overthrown anymore forever."

> **Buyer's market** [chapter 32]. In order to honor God's promise of land for his people, yet against every rational principle of real estate acquisition, Jeremiah negotiates with his fast-talking cousin Hanamel to purchase a piece of property and thus keep it in the family. The property lies outside Jerusalem, and thus at the time of closing (described here in careful detail) it is in enemy territory, occupied by the besieging Babylonians. Jeremiah's bold investment is a prophetic sign that after seventy years of captivity God will once again restore his people to their land. Although Jeremiah has the faith to make this investment, banking on the promises of God, he seems to have second thoughts afterward and seeks understanding through prayer. After praising God for the perfections of his character and his saving grace in history, the prophet asks God for some further explanation and perhaps also for some reassurance that he has done the right thing (vv. 16–25). God's lengthy answer looks beyond the judgment that already surrounded Jerusalem to the consoling promises of his everlasting covenant. In many ways this chapter summarizes the book of Jeremiah, showing the faith of the prophet, the coming of judgment, and the future grace of God.

32 The word that came to Jeremiah from the LORD in the tenth year of Zedekiah king of Judah, which was the eighteenth year of Nebuchadnezzar. 2At that time the army of the king of Babylon was besieging Jerusalem, and Jeremiah the prophet was shut up in the court of the guard that was in the palace of the king of Judah. 3For Zedekiah king of Judah had imprisoned him, saying, "Why do you prophesy and say, 'Thus says the LORD: Behold, I am giving this city into the hand of the king of Babylon, and he shall capture it; 4Zedekiah king of Judah shall not escape out of the hand of the Chaldeans, but shall surely be given into the hand of the king of Babylon, and shall speak with him face to face and see him eye to eye. 5And he shall take Zedekiah to Babylon, and there he shall remain until I visit him, declares the LORD. Though you fight against the Chaldeans, you shall not succeed'?"

   6Jeremiah said, "The word of the LORD came to me: 7Behold, Hanamel the son of Shallum your uncle will come to you and say, 'Buy my field that is at Anathoth, for the right of redemption by purchase is yours.' 8Then Hanamel my cousin came to me in the court of the guard, in accordance with the word of the LORD, and said to me,

'Buy my field that is at Anathoth in the land of Benjamin, for the right of possession and redemption is yours; buy it for yourself.' Then I knew that this was the word of the Lord.

⁹"And I bought the field at Anathoth from Hanamel my cousin, and weighed out the money to him, seventeen shekels of silver. ¹⁰I signed the deed, sealed it, got witnesses, and weighed the money on scales. ¹¹Then I took the sealed deed of purchase, containing the terms and conditions and the open copy. ¹²And I gave the deed of purchase to Baruch the son of Neriah son of Mahseiah, in the presence of Hanamel my cousin, in the presence of the witnesses who signed the deed of purchase, and in the presence of all the Judeans who were sitting in the court of the guard. ¹³I charged Baruch in their presence, saying, ¹⁴"Thus says the Lord of hosts, the God of Israel: Take these deeds, both this sealed deed of purchase and this open deed, and put them in an earthenware vessel, that they may last for a long time. ¹⁵For thus says the Lord of hosts, the God of Israel: Houses and fields and vineyards shall again be bought in this land.'

¹⁶"After I had given the deed of purchase to Baruch the son of Neriah, I prayed to the Lord, saying: ¹⁷'Ah, Lord God! It is you who have made the heavens and the earth by your great power and by your outstretched arm! Nothing is too hard for you. ¹⁸You show steadfast love to thousands, but you repay the guilt of fathers to their children after them, O great and mighty God, whose name is the Lord of hosts, ¹⁹great in counsel and mighty in deed, whose eyes are open to all the ways of the children of man, rewarding each one according to his ways and according to the fruit of his deeds. ²⁰You have shown signs and wonders in the land of Egypt, and to this day in Israel and among all mankind, and have made a name for yourself, as at this day. ²¹You brought your people Israel out of the land of Egypt with signs and wonders, with a strong hand and outstretched arm, and with great terror. ²²And you gave them this land, which you swore to their fathers to give them, a land flowing with milk and honey. ²³And they entered and took possession of it. But they did not obey your voice or walk in your law. They did nothing of all you commanded them to do. Therefore you have made all this disaster come upon them. ²⁴Behold, the siege mounds have come up to the city to take it, and because of sword and famine and pestilence the city is given into the hands of the Chaldeans who are fighting against it. What you spoke has come to pass, and behold, you see it. ²⁵Yet you, O Lord God, have said to me, "Buy the field for money and get witnesses"—though the city is given into the hands of the Chaldeans.'"

²⁶The word of the Lord came to Jeremiah: ²⁷"Behold, I am the Lord, the God of all flesh. Is anything too hard for me? ²⁸Therefore, thus says the Lord: Behold, I am giving this city into the hands of the Chaldeans and into the hand of Nebuchadnezzar king of Babylon, and he shall capture it. ²⁹The Chaldeans who are fighting against this city shall come and set this city on fire and burn it, with the houses on whose roofs offerings have been made to Baal and drink offerings have been poured out to other gods, to provoke me to anger. ³⁰For the children of Israel and the children of Judah have done nothing but evil in my sight from their youth. The children of Israel have done nothing but provoke me to anger by the work of their hands, declares the Lord. ³¹This city has aroused my anger and wrath, from the day it was built to this day, so that I will remove it from my sight ³²because of all the evil of the children of Israel and the children of Judah that they did to provoke me to anger—their kings

and their officials, their priests and their prophets, the men of Judah and the inhabitants of Jerusalem. ³³They have turned to me their back and not their face. And though I have taught them persistently, they have not listened to receive instruction. ³⁴They set up their abominations in the house that is called by my name, to defile it. ³⁵They built the high places of Baal in the Valley of the Son of Hinnom, to offer up their sons and daughters to Molech, though I did not command them, nor did it enter into my mind, that they should do this abomination, to cause Judah to sin.

³⁶"Now therefore thus says the Lᴏʀᴅ, the God of Israel, concerning this city of which you say, 'It is given into the hand of the king of Babylon by sword, by famine, and by pestilence': ³⁷Behold, I will gather them from all the countries to which I drove them in my anger and my wrath and in great indignation. I will bring them back to this place, and I will make them dwell in safety. ³⁸And they shall be my people, and I will be their God. ³⁹I will give them one heart and one way, that they may fear me forever, for their own good and the good of their children after them. ⁴⁰I will make with them an everlasting covenant, that I will not turn away from doing good to them. And I will put the fear of me in their hearts, that they may not turn from me. ⁴¹I will rejoice in doing them good, and I will plant them in this land in faithfulness, with all my heart and all my soul.

⁴²"For thus says the Lᴏʀᴅ: Just as I have brought all this great disaster upon this people, so I will bring upon them all the good that I promise them. ⁴³Fields shall be bought in this land of which you are saying, 'It is a desolation, without man or beast; it is given into the hand of the Chaldeans.' ⁴⁴Fields shall be bought for money, and deeds shall be signed and sealed and witnessed, in the land of Benjamin, in the places about Jerusalem, and in the cities of Judah, in the cities of the hill country, in the cities of the Shephelah, and in the cities of the Negeb; for I will restore their fortunes, declares the Lᴏʀᴅ."

The best of all promises [chapter 33]. "The Book of Consolation" ends with further promises for the hope and future of Israel and Judah. Although Jerusalem is about to be destroyed, in coming days it will be fully restored to become the City of God. The project of urban renewal described in this oracle of restoration is bound up with the messianic promise of the coming king—the Branch of David, the Lord our righteousness—who by the promise of the everlasting covenant will reign on God's throne forever (33:12–18). The covenant promise of eternal salvation is just as certain as all Jeremiah's prophecies of judgment against Jerusalem.

33 The word of the Lᴏʀᴅ came to Jeremiah a second time, while he was still shut up in the court of the guard: ²"Thus says the Lᴏʀᴅ who made the earth,¹ the Lᴏʀᴅ who formed it to establish it—the Lᴏʀᴅ is his name: ³Call to me and I will answer you, and will tell you great and hidden things that you have not known. ⁴For thus says the Lᴏʀᴅ, the God of Israel, concerning the houses of this city and the houses of the kings of Judah that were torn down to make a defense against the siege mounds and against the sword: ⁵They are coming in to fight against the Chaldeans and to fill them² with the dead bodies of men whom I shall strike down in my anger and my wrath, for I have hidden my face from this city because of all their evil. ⁶Behold, I will bring to it health and healing, and I will heal them and reveal to them

¹ Septuagint; Hebrew *it* ² That is, the torn-down houses

abundance of prosperity and security. ⁷I will restore the fortunes of Judah and the fortunes of Israel, and rebuild them as they were at first. ⁸I will cleanse them from all the guilt of their sin against me, and I will forgive all the guilt of their sin and rebellion against me. ⁹And this city¹ shall be to me a name of joy, a praise and a glory before all the nations of the earth who shall hear of all the good that I do for them. They shall fear and tremble because of all the good and all the prosperity I provide for it.

¹⁰"Thus says the LORD: In this place of which you say, 'It is a waste without man or beast,' in the cities of Judah and the streets of Jerusalem that are desolate, without man or inhabitant or beast, there shall be heard again ¹¹the voice of mirth and the voice of gladness, the voice of the bridegroom and the voice of the bride, the voices of those who sing, as they bring thank offerings to the house of the LORD:

"'Give thanks to the LORD of hosts,
   for the LORD is good,
   for his steadfast love endures forever!'

For I will restore the fortunes of the land as at first, says the LORD.

¹²"Thus says the LORD of hosts: In this place that is waste, without man or beast, and in all of its cities, there shall again be habitations of shepherds resting their flocks. ¹³In the cities of the hill country, in the cities of the Shephelah, and in the cities of the Negeb, in the land of Benjamin, the places about Jerusalem, and in the cities of Judah, flocks shall again pass under the hands of the one who counts them, says the LORD.

¹⁴"Behold, the days are coming, declares the LORD, when I will fulfill the promise I made to the house of Israel and the house of Judah. ¹⁵In those days and at that time I will cause a righteous Branch to spring up for David, and he shall execute justice and righteousness in the land. ¹⁶In those days Judah will be saved, and Jerusalem will dwell securely. And this is the name by which it will be called: 'The LORD is our righteousness.'

¹⁷"For thus says the LORD: David shall never lack a man to sit on the throne of the house of Israel, ¹⁸and the Levitical priests shall never lack a man in my presence to offer burnt offerings, to burn grain offerings, and to make sacrifices forever."

¹⁹The word of the LORD came to Jeremiah: ²⁰"Thus says the LORD: If you can break my covenant with the day and my covenant with the night, so that day and night will not come at their appointed time, ²¹then also my covenant with David my servant may be broken, so that he shall not have a son to reign on his throne, and my covenant with the Levitical priests my ministers. ²²As the host of heaven cannot be numbered and the sands of the sea cannot be measured, so I will multiply the offspring of David my servant, and the Levitical priests who minister to me."

²³The word of the LORD came to Jeremiah: ²⁴"Have you not observed that these people are saying, 'The LORD has rejected the two clans that he chose'? Thus they have despised my people so that they are no longer a nation in their sight. ²⁵Thus says the LORD: If I have not established my covenant with day and night and the fixed order of heaven and earth, ²⁶then I will reject the offspring of Jacob and David my servant and will not choose one of his offspring to rule over the offspring of Abraham, Isaac, and Jacob. For I will restore their fortunes and will have mercy on them."

¹ Hebrew *And it*

Emancipation revocation [chapter 34]. The main action of the narrative continues with a prophetic dialogue between Jeremiah and Zedekiah, whom the Babylonians have installed as their puppet king in Jerusalem. The prophet condemns Zedekiah for his faithlessness in first proclaiming liberty for Judah's slaves and then later putting them back under the yoke of slavery. By violating God's protections for slaves and the biblical provisions for their ultimate freedom, the king has broken covenant with God. As a result, he will be taken captive by the Babylonians. A story about a divinely appointed leader's failure to follow through on his God-given responsibility becomes a story of judgment on a national scale.

34 The word that came to Jeremiah from the Lord, when Nebuchadnezzar king of Babylon and all his army and all the kingdoms of the earth under his dominion and all the peoples were fighting against Jerusalem and all of its cities: ²"Thus says the Lord, the God of Israel: Go and speak to Zedekiah king of Judah and say to him, 'Thus says the Lord: Behold, I am giving this city into the hand of the king of Babylon, and he shall burn it with fire. ³You shall not escape from his hand but shall surely be captured and delivered into his hand. You shall see the king of Babylon eye to eye and speak with him face to face. And you shall go to Babylon.' ⁴Yet hear the word of the Lord, O Zedekiah king of Judah! Thus says the Lord concerning you: 'You shall not die by the sword. ⁵You shall die in peace. And as spices were burned for your fathers, the former kings who were before you, so people shall burn spices for you and lament for you, saying, "Alas, lord!"' For I have spoken the word, declares the Lord."

⁶Then Jeremiah the prophet spoke all these words to Zedekiah king of Judah, in Jerusalem, ⁷when the army of the king of Babylon was fighting against Jerusalem and against all the cities of Judah that were left, Lachish and Azekah, for these were the only fortified cities of Judah that remained.

⁸The word that came to Jeremiah from the Lord, after King Zedekiah had made a covenant with all the people in Jerusalem to make a proclamation of liberty to them, ⁹that everyone should set free his Hebrew slaves, male and female, so that no one should enslave a Jew, his brother. ¹⁰And they obeyed, all the officials and all the people who had entered into the covenant that everyone would set free his slave, male or female, so that they would not be enslaved again. They obeyed and set them free. ¹¹But afterward they turned around and took back the male and female slaves they had set free, and brought them into subjection as slaves. ¹²The word of the Lord came to Jeremiah from the Lord: ¹³"Thus says the Lord, the God of Israel: I myself made a covenant with your fathers when I brought them out of the land of Egypt, out of the house of bondage, saying, ¹⁴'At the end of seven years each of you must set free the fellow Hebrew who has been sold to you and has served you six years; you must set him free from your service.' But your fathers did not listen to me or incline their ears to me. ¹⁵You recently repented and did what was right in my eyes by proclaiming liberty, each to his neighbor, and you made a covenant before me in the house that is called by my name, ¹⁶but then you turned around and profaned my name when each of you took back his male and female slaves, whom you had set free according to their desire, and you brought them into subjection to be your slaves.

¹⁷"Therefore, thus says the Lord: You have not obeyed me by proclaiming liberty, every one to his brother and to his neighbor; behold, I proclaim to you liberty to the

sword, to pestilence, and to famine, declares the LORD. I will make you a horror to all the kingdoms of the earth. [18]And the men who transgressed my covenant and did not keep the terms of the covenant that they made before me, I will make them like[1] the calf that they cut in two and passed between its parts— [19]the officials of Judah, the officials of Jerusalem, the eunuchs, the priests, and all the people of the land who passed between the parts of the calf. [20]And I will give them into the hand of their enemies and into the hand of those who seek their lives. Their dead bodies shall be food for the birds of the air and the beasts of the earth. [21]And Zedekiah king of Judah and his officials I will give into the hand of their enemies and into the hand of those who seek their lives, into the hand of the army of the king of Babylon which has withdrawn from you. [22]Behold, I will command, declares the LORD, and will bring them back to this city. And they will fight against it and take it and burn it with fire. I will make the cities of Judah a desolation without inhabitant."

Promise keepers [chapter 35]. The faithlessness of nearly everyone in Jerusalem (not least King Zedekiah) stands in sharp contrast to the Rechabites, who steadfastly keep their pious vow not to drink any wine as a voluntary sign of their devotion to God. In narrative terms, the Rechabites are a foil to Judah's unfaithfulness and thus serve as an example of the life that is pleasing to God.

35 The word that came to Jeremiah from the LORD in the days of Jehoiakim the son of Josiah, king of Judah: [2]"Go to the house of the Rechabites and speak with them and bring them to the house of the LORD, into one of the chambers; then offer them wine to drink." [3]So I took Jaazaniah the son of Jeremiah, son of Habazziniah and his brothers and all his sons and the whole house of the Rechabites. [4]I brought them to the house of the LORD into the chamber of the sons of Hanan the son of Igdaliah, the man of God, which was near the chamber of the officials, above the chamber of Maaseiah the son of Shallum, keeper of the threshold. [5]Then I set before the Rechabites pitchers full of wine, and cups, and I said to them, "Drink wine." [6]But they answered, "We will drink no wine, for Jonadab the son of Rechab, our father, commanded us, 'You shall not drink wine, neither you nor your sons forever. [7]You shall not build a house; you shall not sow seed; you shall not plant or have a vineyard; but you shall live in tents all your days, that you may live many days in the land where you sojourn.' [8]We have obeyed the voice of Jonadab the son of Rechab, our father, in all that he commanded us, to drink no wine all our days, ourselves, our wives, our sons, or our daughters, [9]and not to build houses to dwell in. We have no vineyard or field or seed, [10]but we have lived in tents and have obeyed and done all that Jonadab our father commanded us. [11]But when Nebuchadnezzar king of Babylon came up against the land, we said, 'Come, and let us go to Jerusalem for fear of the army of the Chaldeans and the army of the Syrians.' So we are living in Jerusalem."

[12]Then the word of the LORD came to Jeremiah: [13]"Thus says the LORD of hosts, the God of Israel: Go and say to the people of Judah and the inhabitants of Jerusalem, Will you not receive instruction and listen to my words? declares the LORD. [14]The command that Jonadab the son of Rechab gave to his sons, to drink no wine, has been kept, and they drink none to this day, for they have obeyed their father's command. I have spoken to you persistently, but you have not listened to me. [15]I have sent

---

[1] Hebrew lacks *them like*

to you all my servants the prophets, sending them persistently, saying, 'Turn now every one of you from his evil way, and amend your deeds, and do not go after other gods to serve them, and then you shall dwell in the land that I gave to you and your fathers.' But you did not incline your ear or listen to me. ¹⁶The sons of Jonadab the son of Rechab have kept the command that their father gave them, but this people has not obeyed me. ¹⁷Therefore, thus says the LORD, the God of hosts, the God of Israel: Behold, I am bringing upon Judah and all the inhabitants of Jerusalem all the disaster that I have pronounced against them, because I have spoken to them and they have not listened, I have called to them and they have not answered."

¹⁸But to the house of the Rechabites Jeremiah said, "Thus says the LORD of hosts, the God of Israel: Because you have obeyed the command of Jonadab your father and kept all his precepts and done all that he commanded you, ¹⁹therefore thus says the LORD of hosts, the God of Israel: Jonadab the son of Rechab shall never lack a man to stand before me."

Book burning [chapter 36]. In another narrative flashback, Jeremiah recounts one of the most shocking episodes in the entire OT. To his own damnation, and in rash defiance of the living God, King Jehoiakim burns the first edition of Jeremiah's writing, using it as fuel for his wintertime fire. The story is told in sufficient detail to show the character contrast between two kinds of men, who have two very different attitudes toward the Word of God. Their dispute is central to the plot conflict of the book of Jeremiah as a whole: will people listen to the word of God's prophet or not? Most of Jehoiakim's advisers are compliant with the king's attempt to destroy Jeremiah's written prophecies, which is actually an attempt to censor God's Word. But Baruch, Micaiah, Elishama, Delaiah, and Gemariah all seek to honor Jeremiah's scriptures by having them read aloud, with the intent of seeing them obeyed. The chapter ends with the triumph of the Word, as God inspires Jeremiah to dictate a new and longer edition of his prophecy. The outcome of the narrative—namely the preservation of Jeremiah's writings—proves that he is God's prophet.

36 In the fourth year of Jehoiakim the son of Josiah, king of Judah, this word came to Jeremiah from the LORD: ²"Take a scroll and write on it all the words that I have spoken to you against Israel and Judah and all the nations, from the day I spoke to you, from the days of Josiah until today. ³It may be that the house of Judah will hear all the disaster that I intend to do to them, so that every one may turn from his evil way, and that I may forgive their iniquity and their sin."

⁴Then Jeremiah called Baruch the son of Neriah, and Baruch wrote on a scroll at the dictation of Jeremiah all the words of the LORD that he had spoken to him. ⁵And Jeremiah ordered Baruch, saying, "I am banned from going to the house of the LORD, ⁶so you are to go, and on a day of fasting in the hearing of all the people in the LORD's house you shall read the words of the LORD from the scroll that you have written at my dictation. You shall read them also in the hearing of all the men of Judah who come out of their cities. ⁷It may be that their plea for mercy will come before the LORD, and that every one will turn from his evil way, for great is the anger and wrath that the LORD has pronounced against this people." ⁸And Baruch the son of Neriah did all that Jeremiah the prophet ordered him about reading from the scroll the words of the LORD in the LORD's house.

⁹In the fifth year of Jehoiakim the son of Josiah, king of Judah, in the ninth month, all the people in Jerusalem and all the people who came from the cities of Judah to Jerusalem proclaimed a fast before the LORD. ¹⁰Then, in the hearing of all the people, Baruch read the words of Jeremiah from the scroll, in the house of the LORD, in the chamber of Gemariah the son of Shaphan the secretary, which was in the upper court, at the entry of the New Gate of the LORD's house.

¹¹When Micaiah the son of Gemariah, son of Shaphan, heard all the words of the LORD from the scroll, ¹²he went down to the king's house, into the secretary's chamber, and all the officials were sitting there: Elishama the secretary, Delaiah the son of Shemaiah, Elnathan the son of Achbor, Gemariah the son of Shaphan, Zedekiah the son of Hananiah, and all the officials. ¹³And Micaiah told them all the words that he had heard, when Baruch read the scroll in the hearing of the people. ¹⁴Then all the officials sent Jehudi the son of Nethaniah, son of Shelemiah, son of Cushi, to say to Baruch, "Take in your hand the scroll that you read in the hearing of the people, and come." So Baruch the son of Neriah took the scroll in his hand and came to them. ¹⁵And they said to him, "Sit down and read it." So Baruch read it to them. ¹⁶When they heard all the words, they turned one to another in fear. And they said to Baruch, "We must report all these words to the king." ¹⁷Then they asked Baruch, "Tell us, please, how did you write all these words? Was it at his dictation?" ¹⁸Baruch answered them, "He dictated all these words to me, while I wrote them with ink on the scroll." ¹⁹Then the officials said to Baruch, "Go and hide, you and Jeremiah, and let no one know where you are."

²⁰So they went into the court to the king, having put the scroll in the chamber of Elishama the secretary, and they reported all the words to the king. ²¹Then the king sent Jehudi to get the scroll, and he took it from the chamber of Elishama the secretary. And Jehudi read it to the king and all the officials who stood beside the king. ²²It was the ninth month, and the king was sitting in the winter house, and there was a fire burning in the fire pot before him. ²³As Jehudi read three or four columns, the king would cut them off with a knife and throw them into the fire in the fire pot, until the entire scroll was consumed in the fire that was in the fire pot. ²⁴Yet neither the king nor any of his servants who heard all these words was afraid, nor did they tear their garments. ²⁵Even when Elnathan and Delaiah and Gemariah urged the king not to burn the scroll, he would not listen to them. ²⁶And the king commanded Jerahmeel the king's son and Seraiah the son of Azriel and Shelemiah the son of Abdeel to seize Baruch the secretary and Jeremiah the prophet, but the LORD hid them.

²⁷Now after the king had burned the scroll with the words that Baruch wrote at Jeremiah's dictation, the word of the LORD came to Jeremiah: ²⁸"Take another scroll and write on it all the former words that were in the first scroll, which Jehoiakim the king of Judah has burned. ²⁹And concerning Jehoiakim king of Judah you shall say, 'Thus says the LORD, You have burned this scroll, saying, "Why have you written in it that the king of Babylon will certainly come and destroy this land, and will cut off from it man and beast?" ³⁰Therefore thus says the LORD concerning Jehoiakim king of Judah: He shall have none to sit on the throne of David, and his dead body shall be cast out to the heat by day and the frost by night. ³¹And I will punish him and his offspring and his servants for their iniquity. I will bring upon them and upon the inhabitants of Jerusalem and upon the people of Judah all the disaster that I have pronounced against them, but they would not hear.' "

³²Then Jeremiah took another scroll and gave it to Baruch the scribe, the son of Neriah, who wrote on it at the dictation of Jeremiah all the words of the scroll that Jehoiakim king of Judah had burned in the fire. And many similar words were added to them.

> **Benedict Jeremiah?** [chapter 37]. Here the narrative action returns to the time of Zedekiah's reign. It is important to bear in mind that Jeremiah's anthology is not always arranged chronologically but sometimes thematically. Zedekiah is now in revolt against Babylonian domination. In this arrest narrative, Babylon is besieging Jerusalem, and Jeremiah has been spotted going back and forth between the city and enemy-occupied territory, presumably on some prophetic mission from God. By this point the religious leaders have long since tired of listening to Jeremiah's message of judgment against Jerusalem and are only too happy to have the prophet beaten and thrown into prison—despite his protests—on suspicion of conspiracy. There Jeremiah receives his daily rations, until there is no bread left in the city.

37 Zedekiah the son of Josiah, whom Nebuchadnezzar king of Babylon made king in the land of Judah, reigned instead of Coniah the son of Jehoiakim. ²But neither he nor his servants nor the people of the land listened to the words of the LORD that he spoke through Jeremiah the prophet.

³King Zedekiah sent Jehucal the son of Shelemiah, and Zephaniah the priest, the son of Maaseiah, to Jeremiah the prophet, saying, "Please pray for us to the LORD our God." ⁴Now Jeremiah was still going in and out among the people, for he had not yet been put in prison. ⁵The army of Pharaoh had come out of Egypt. And when the Chaldeans who were besieging Jerusalem heard news about them, they withdrew from Jerusalem.

⁶Then the word of the LORD came to Jeremiah the prophet: ⁷"Thus says the LORD, God of Israel: Thus shall you say to the king of Judah who sent you to me to inquire of me, 'Behold, Pharaoh's army that came to help you is about to return to Egypt, to its own land. ⁸And the Chaldeans shall come back and fight against this city. They shall capture it and burn it with fire. ⁹Thus says the LORD, Do not deceive yourselves, saying, "The Chaldeans will surely go away from us," for they will not go away. ¹⁰For even if you should defeat the whole army of Chaldeans who are fighting against you, and there remained of them only wounded men, every man in his tent, they would rise up and burn this city with fire.'"

¹¹Now when the Chaldean army had withdrawn from Jerusalem at the approach of Pharaoh's army, ¹²Jeremiah set out from Jerusalem to go to the land of Benjamin to receive his portion there among the people. ¹³When he was at the Benjamin Gate, a sentry there named Irijah the son of Shelemiah, son of Hananiah, seized Jeremiah the prophet, saying, "You are deserting to the Chaldeans." ¹⁴And Jeremiah said, "It is a lie; I am not deserting to the Chaldeans." But Irijah would not listen to him, and seized Jeremiah and brought him to the officials. ¹⁵And the officials were enraged at Jeremiah, and they beat him and imprisoned him in the house of Jonathan the secretary, for it had been made a prison.

¹⁶When Jeremiah had come to the dungeon cells and remained there many days, ¹⁷King Zedekiah sent for him and received him. The king questioned him secretly in his house and said, "Is there any word from the LORD?" Jeremiah said, "There is."

Then he said, "You shall be delivered into the hand of the king of Babylon." [18]Jeremiah also said to King Zedekiah, "What wrong have I done to you or your servants or this people, that you have put me in prison? [19]Where are your prophets who prophesied to you, saying, 'The king of Babylon will not come against you and against this land'? [20]Now hear, please, O my lord the king: let my humble plea come before you and do not send me back to the house of Jonathan the secretary, lest I die there." [21]So King Zedekiah gave orders, and they committed Jeremiah to the court of the guard. And a loaf of bread was given him daily from the bakers' street, until all the bread of the city was gone. So Jeremiah remained in the court of the guard.

In and out of the cistern [chapter 38]. Preaching from prison, Jeremiah remains faithful to his calling and continues to prophesy that Jerusalem will fall to the Babylonians. Not surprisingly, his opponents view this as seditious speech and seek to have the prophet killed by throwing him to the bottom of a muddy cistern—the low point of his ministry. But in this rescue story Jeremiah is saved by loyal servants of the Word of God, including the Ethiopian servant Ebed-melech, who is one of the small heroes of the OT. No sooner is the prophet delivered from death than he is summoned to a secret audience with the king. Jeremiah's message has not changed: in this instance, obedience to God means surrendering to the Babylonians; military resistance will only end in fiery destruction, not simply for the city as a whole but also for Zedekiah and his family (38:17–23).

38 Now Shephatiah the son of Mattan, Gedaliah the son of Pashhur, Jucal the son of Shelemiah, and Pashhur the son of Malchiah heard the words that Jeremiah was saying to all the people, [2]"Thus says the LORD: He who stays in this city shall die by the sword, by famine, and by pestilence, but he who goes out to the Chaldeans shall live. He shall have his life as a prize of war, and live. [3]Thus says the LORD: This city shall surely be given into the hand of the army of the king of Babylon and be taken." [4]Then the officials said to the king, "Let this man be put to death, for he is weakening the hands of the soldiers who are left in this city, and the hands of all the people, by speaking such words to them. For this man is not seeking the welfare of this people, but their harm." [5]King Zedekiah said, "Behold, he is in your hands, for the king can do nothing against you." [6]So they took Jeremiah and cast him into the cistern of Malchiah, the king's son, which was in the court of the guard, letting Jeremiah down by ropes. And there was no water in the cistern, but only mud, and Jeremiah sank in the mud.

[7]When Ebed-melech the Ethiopian, a eunuch who was in the king's house, heard that they had put Jeremiah into the cistern—the king was sitting in the Benjamin Gate— [8]Ebed-melech went from the king's house and said to the king, [9]"My lord the king, these men have done evil in all that they did to Jeremiah the prophet by casting him into the cistern, and he will die there of hunger, for there is no bread left in the city." [10]Then the king commanded Ebed-melech the Ethiopian, "Take thirty men with you from here, and lift Jeremiah the prophet out of the cistern before he dies." [11]So Ebed-melech took the men with him and went to the house of the king, to a wardrobe in the storehouse, and took from there old rags and worn-out clothes, which he let down to Jeremiah in the cistern by ropes. [12]Then Ebed-melech the Ethiopian said to Jeremiah, "Put the rags and clothes between your armpits and the ropes." Jeremiah

did so. ¹³Then they drew Jeremiah up with ropes and lifted him out of the cistern. And Jeremiah remained in the court of the guard.

¹⁴King Zedekiah sent for Jeremiah the prophet and received him at the third entrance of the temple of the LORD. The king said to Jeremiah, "I will ask you a question; hide nothing from me." ¹⁵Jeremiah said to Zedekiah, "If I tell you, will you not surely put me to death? And if I give you counsel, you will not listen to me." ¹⁶Then King Zedekiah swore secretly to Jeremiah, "As the LORD lives, who made our souls, I will not put you to death or deliver you into the hand of these men who seek your life."

¹⁷Then Jeremiah said to Zedekiah, "Thus says the LORD, the God of hosts, the God of Israel: If you will surrender to the officials of the king of Babylon, then your life shall be spared, and this city shall not be burned with fire, and you and your house shall live. ¹⁸But if you do not surrender to the officials of the king of Babylon, then this city shall be given into the hand of the Chaldeans, and they shall burn it with fire, and you shall not escape from their hand." ¹⁹King Zedekiah said to Jeremiah, "I am afraid of the Judeans who have deserted to the Chaldeans, lest I be handed over to them and they deal cruelly with me." ²⁰Jeremiah said, "You shall not be given to them. Obey now the voice of the LORD in what I say to you, and it shall be well with you, and your life shall be spared. ²¹But if you refuse to surrender, this is the vision which the LORD has shown to me: ²²Behold, all the women left in the house of the king of Judah were being led out to the officials of the king of Babylon and were saying,

"'Your trusted friends have deceived you
    and prevailed against you;
now that your feet are sunk in the mud,
    they turn away from you.'

²³All your wives and your sons shall be led out to the Chaldeans, and you yourself shall not escape from their hand, but shall be seized by the king of Babylon, and this city shall be burned with fire."

²⁴Then Zedekiah said to Jeremiah, "Let no one know of these words, and you shall not die. ²⁵If the officials hear that I have spoken with you and come to you and say to you, 'Tell us what you said to the king and what the king said to you; hide nothing from us and we will not put you to death,' ²⁶then you shall say to them, 'I made a humble plea to the king that he would not send me back to the house of Jonathan to die there.'" ²⁷Then all the officials came to Jeremiah and asked him, and he answered them as the king had instructed him. So they stopped speaking with him, for the conversation had not been overheard. ²⁸And Jeremiah remained in the court of the guard until the day that Jerusalem was taken.

Jerusalem falls [chapter 39]. Jeremiah's judgment narrative of the last days of Jerusalem continues with the long-expected and frequently prophesied fall of the city. The prophet's words have come true; his ministry is thoroughly vindicated. Zedekiah sees his family brutally slaughtered before his own eyes, which are then put out by the Babylonians. Yet the lives of Jeremiah and his servant Ebed-melech are spared—a rescue story (39:11–18). In stories, actions are often judged by outcomes, and here the truth of God's judgment and grace is brought down to the individual level: those who deny the Word of God fall under his wrath, while those who trust in him are snatched from the fire.

39 In the ninth year of Zedekiah king of Judah, in the tenth month, Nebuchadnezzar king of Babylon and all his army came against Jerusalem and besieged it. ²In the eleventh year of Zedekiah, in the fourth month, on the ninth day of the month, a breach was made in the city. ³Then all the officials of the king of Babylon came and sat in the middle gate: Nergal-sar-ezer, Samgar-nebu, Sar-sekim the Rab-saris, Nergal-sar-ezer the Rab-mag, with all the rest of the officers of the king of Babylon. ⁴When Zedekiah king of Judah and all the soldiers saw them, they fled, going out of the city at night by way of the king's garden through the gate between the two walls; and they went toward the Arabah. ⁵But the army of the Chaldeans pursued them and overtook Zedekiah in the plains of Jericho. And when they had taken him, they brought him up to Nebuchadnezzar king of Babylon, at Riblah, in the land of Hamath; and he passed sentence on him. ⁶The king of Babylon slaughtered the sons of Zedekiah at Riblah before his eyes, and the king of Babylon slaughtered all the nobles of Judah. ⁷He put out the eyes of Zedekiah and bound him in chains to take him to Babylon. ⁸The Chaldeans burned the king's house and the house of the people, and broke down the walls of Jerusalem. ⁹Then Nebuzaradan, the captain of the guard, carried into exile to Babylon the rest of the people who were left in the city, those who had deserted to him, and the people who remained. ¹⁰Nebuzaradan, the captain of the guard, left in the land of Judah some of the poor people who owned nothing, and gave them vineyards and fields at the same time.

¹¹Nebuchadnezzar king of Babylon gave command concerning Jeremiah through Nebuzaradan, the captain of the guard, saying, ¹²"Take him, look after him well, and do him no harm, but deal with him as he tells you." ¹³So Nebuzaradan the captain of the guard, Nebushazban the Rab-saris, Nergal-sar-ezer the Rab-mag, and all the chief officers of the king of Babylon ¹⁴sent and took Jeremiah from the court of the guard. They entrusted him to Gedaliah the son of Ahikam, son of Shaphan, that he should take him home. So he lived among the people.

¹⁵The word of the LORD came to Jeremiah while he was shut up in the court of the guard: ¹⁶"Go, and say to Ebed-melech the Ethiopian, 'Thus says the LORD of hosts, the God of Israel: Behold, I will fulfill my words against this city for harm and not for good, and they shall be accomplished before you on that day. ¹⁷But I will deliver you on that day, declares the LORD, and you shall not be given into the hand of the men of whom you are afraid. ¹⁸For I will surely save you, and you shall not fall by the sword, but you shall have your life as a prize of war, because you have put your trust in me, declares the LORD.'"

The surviving remnant [chapters 40–41]. This episode begins in Ramah, the refugee transit camp where the Babylonians organized their defeated enemies for deportation. Given the freedom either to stay back home or to go in exile to Babylon, Jeremiah chooses to stay with the surviving remnant in Judah, under the leadership of Gedaliah as governor (see 40:2–6). Although Gedaliah wisely urges the people to submit to Babylonian rule as God's will for their lives, he is killed by Ishmael, who continues his murderous ways with the brutal slaughter of seventy holy men. The function of this assassination narrative is to set up the fateful choice that the remnant will make in chapters 42–43. Part of its purpose in salvation history is to show how God preserves a remnant of his people and provides for their needs, even in desperate situations of apparent defeat.

40 The word that came to Jeremiah from the LORD after Nebuzaradan the captain of the guard had let him go from Ramah, when he took him bound in chains along with all the captives of Jerusalem and Judah who were being exiled to Babylon. ²The captain of the guard took Jeremiah and said to him, "The LORD your God pronounced this disaster against this place. ³The LORD has brought it about, and has done as he said. Because you sinned against the LORD and did not obey his voice, this thing has come upon you. ⁴Now, behold, I release you today from the chains on your hands. If it seems good to you to come with me to Babylon, come, and I will look after you well, but if it seems wrong to you to come with me to Babylon, do not come. See, the whole land is before you; go wherever you think it good and right to go. ⁵If you remain,¹ then return to Gedaliah the son of Ahikam, son of Shaphan, whom the king of Babylon appointed governor of the cities of Judah, and dwell with him among the people. Or go wherever you think it right to go." So the captain of the guard gave him an allowance of food and a present, and let him go. ⁶Then Jeremiah went to Gedaliah the son of Ahikam, at Mizpah, and lived with him among the people who were left in the land.

⁷When all the captains of the forces in the open country and their men heard that the king of Babylon had appointed Gedaliah the son of Ahikam governor in the land and had committed to him men, women, and children, those of the poorest of the land who had not been taken into exile to Babylon, ⁸they went to Gedaliah at Mizpah—Ishmael the son of Nethaniah, Johanan the son of Kareah, Seraiah the son of Tanhumeth, the sons of Ephai the Netophathite, Jezaniah the son of the Maacathite, they and their men. ⁹Gedaliah the son of Ahikam, son of Shaphan, swore to them and their men, saying, "Do not be afraid to serve the Chaldeans. Dwell in the land and serve the king of Babylon, and it shall be well with you. ¹⁰As for me, I will dwell at Mizpah, to represent you before the Chaldeans who will come to us. But as for you, gather wine and summer fruits and oil, and store them in your vessels, and dwell in your cities that you have taken." ¹¹Likewise, when all the Judeans who were in Moab and among the Ammonites and in Edom and in other lands heard that the king of Babylon had left a remnant in Judah and had appointed Gedaliah the son of Ahikam, son of Shaphan, as governor over them, ¹²then all the Judeans returned from all the places to which they had been driven and came to the land of Judah, to Gedaliah at Mizpah. And they gathered wine and summer fruits in great abundance.

¹³Now Johanan the son of Kareah and all the leaders of the forces in the open country came to Gedaliah at Mizpah ¹⁴and said to him, "Do you know that Baalis the king of the Ammonites has sent Ishmael the son of Nethaniah to take your life?" But Gedaliah the son of Ahikam would not believe them. ¹⁵Then Johanan the son of Kareah spoke secretly to Gedaliah at Mizpah, "Please let me go and strike down Ishmael the son of Nethaniah, and no one will know it. Why should he take your life, so that all the Judeans who are gathered about you would be scattered, and the remnant of Judah would perish?" ¹⁶But Gedaliah the son of Ahikam said to Johanan the son of Kareah, "You shall not do this thing, for you are speaking falsely of Ishmael."

41 In the seventh month, Ishmael the son of Nethaniah, son of Elishama, of the royal family, one of the chief officers of the king, came with ten men to Gedaliah the son of Ahikam, at Mizpah. As they ate bread together there at Mizpah, ²Ishmael the son of Nethaniah and the ten men with him rose up and struck down

---

¹ Syriac; the meaning of the Hebrew phrase is uncertain

Gedaliah the son of Ahikam, son of Shaphan, with the sword, and killed him, whom the king of Babylon had appointed governor in the land. ³Ishmael also struck down all the Judeans who were with Gedaliah at Mizpah, and the Chaldean soldiers who happened to be there.

⁴On the day after the murder of Gedaliah, before anyone knew of it, ⁵eighty men arrived from Shechem and Shiloh and Samaria, with their beards shaved and their clothes torn, and their bodies gashed, bringing grain offerings and incense to present at the temple of the LORD. ⁶And Ishmael the son of Nethaniah came out from Mizpah to meet them, weeping as he came. As he met them, he said to them, "Come in to Gedaliah the son of Ahikam." ⁷When they came into the city, Ishmael the son of Nethaniah and the men with him slaughtered them and cast them into a cistern. ⁸But there were ten men among them who said to Ishmael, "Do not put us to death, for we have stores of wheat, barley, oil, and honey hidden in the fields." So he refrained and did not put them to death with their companions.

⁹Now the cistern into which Ishmael had thrown all the bodies of the men whom he had struck down along with[1] Gedaliah was the large cistern that King Asa had made for defense against Baasha king of Israel; Ishmael the son of Nethaniah filled it with the slain. ¹⁰Then Ishmael took captive all the rest of the people who were in Mizpah, the king's daughters and all the people who were left at Mizpah, whom Nebuzaradan, the captain of the guard, had committed to Gedaliah the son of Ahikam. Ishmael the son of Nethaniah took them captive and set out to cross over to the Ammonites.

¹¹But when Johanan the son of Kareah and all the leaders of the forces with him heard of all the evil that Ishmael the son of Nethaniah had done, ¹²they took all their men and went to fight against Ishmael the son of Nethaniah. They came upon him at the great pool that is in Gibeon. ¹³And when all the people who were with Ishmael saw Johanan the son of Kareah and all the leaders of the forces with him, they rejoiced. ¹⁴So all the people whom Ishmael had carried away captive from Mizpah turned around and came back, and went to Johanan the son of Kareah. ¹⁵But Ishmael the son of Nethaniah escaped from Johanan with eight men, and went to the Ammonites. ¹⁶Then Johanan the son of Kareah and all the leaders of the forces with him took from Mizpah all the rest of the people whom he had recovered from Ishmael the son of Nethaniah, after he had struck down Gedaliah the son of Ahikam—soldiers, women, children, and eunuchs, whom Johanan brought back from Gibeon. ¹⁷And they went and stayed at Geruth Chimham near Bethlehem, intending to go to Egypt ¹⁸because of the Chaldeans. For they were afraid of them, because Ishmael the son of Nethaniah had struck down Gedaliah the son of Ahikam, whom the king of Babylon had made governor over the land.

A fatal mistake [chapters 42–43]. After witnessing the tragic fall of Jerusalem and the terrible murder of governor Gedaliah, the small surviving remnant of Judah is tempted to leave the Promised Land altogether and go back to Egypt, in the hope of finding protection there from the Babylonians. In fact, the group is already making its way to Egypt when their emerging leaders stop and ask Jeremiah for his opinion. Should they stay in Judah or go to Egypt? The decision is critical and the prophet's answer is unequivocal: It is God's will for the remnant of his people to remain in Judah. If they stay, they will have God's full blessing; if they go, they will fall under his deadly curse (42:9–22). In the end,

---

[1] Hebrew *by the hand of*

the leaders of the remnant reject Jeremiah's counsel and decide to go back to the land of Egypt, the house of bondage. They go their own way instead of God's way, wrongly concluding that what Jeremiah says to them is only the word of man, not the Word of God. This flight narrative is a case study in not listening to God's word, not trusting God's plan, and not making a wise spiritual decision—problems that plague God's people throughout this book. The story ends with another object lesson, as Jeremiah digs up part of the pavement in front of one of Pharaoh's palaces and predicts that the king of Babylon will set up his throne on the very spot (43:10). The people who have gone down to Egypt will not escape the Babylonians after all. Nor will they escape the judgment of God.

42 Then all the commanders of the forces, and Johanan the son of Kareah and Jezaniah the son of Hoshaiah, and all the people from the least to the greatest, came near ²and said to Jeremiah the prophet, "Let our plea for mercy come before you, and pray to the LORD your God for us, for all this remnant—because we are left with but a few, as your eyes see us— ³that the LORD your God may show us the way we should go, and the thing that we should do." ⁴Jeremiah the prophet said to them, "I have heard you. Behold, I will pray to the LORD your God according to your request, and whatever the LORD answers you I will tell you. I will keep nothing back from you." ⁵Then they said to Jeremiah, "May the LORD be a true and faithful witness against us if we do not act according to all the word with which the LORD your God sends you to us. ⁶Whether it is good or bad, we will obey the voice of the LORD our God to whom we are sending you, that it may be well with us when we obey the voice of the LORD our God."

⁷At the end of ten days the word of the LORD came to Jeremiah. ⁸Then he summoned Johanan the son of Kareah and all the commanders of the forces who were with him, and all the people from the least to the greatest, ⁹and said to them, "Thus says the LORD, the God of Israel, to whom you sent me to present your plea for mercy before him: ¹⁰If you will remain in this land, then I will build you up and not pull you down; I will plant you, and not pluck you up; for I relent of the disaster that I did to you. ¹¹Do not fear the king of Babylon, of whom you are afraid. Do not fear him, declares the LORD, for I am with you, to save you and to deliver you from his hand. ¹²I will grant you mercy, that he may have mercy on you and let you remain in your own land. ¹³But if you say, 'We will not remain in this land,' disobeying the voice of the LORD your God ¹⁴and saying, 'No, we will go to the land of Egypt, where we shall not see war or hear the sound of the trumpet or be hungry for bread, and we will dwell there,' ¹⁵then hear the word of the LORD, O remnant of Judah. Thus says the LORD of hosts, the God of Israel: If you set your faces to enter Egypt and go to live there, ¹⁶then the sword that you fear shall overtake you there in the land of Egypt, and the famine of which you are afraid shall follow close after you to Egypt, and there you shall die. ¹⁷All the men who set their faces to go to Egypt to live there shall die by the sword, by famine, and by pestilence. They shall have no remnant or survivor from the disaster that I will bring upon them.

¹⁸"For thus says the LORD of hosts, the God of Israel: As my anger and my wrath were poured out on the inhabitants of Jerusalem, so my wrath will be poured out on you when you go to Egypt. You shall become an execration, a horror, a curse, and a taunt. You shall see this place no more. ¹⁹The LORD has said to you, O remnant of

Judah, 'Do not go to Egypt.' Know for a certainty that I have warned you this day [20]that you have gone astray at the cost of your lives. For you sent me to the Lord your God, saying, 'Pray for us to the Lord our God, and whatever the Lord our God says declare to us and we will do it.' [21]And I have this day declared it to you, but you have not obeyed the voice of the Lord your God in anything that he sent me to tell you. [22]Now therefore know for a certainty that you shall die by the sword, by famine, and by pestilence in the place where you desire to go to live."

43 When Jeremiah finished speaking to all the people all these words of the Lord their God, with which the Lord their God had sent him to them, [2]Azariah the son of Hoshaiah and Johanan the son of Kareah and all the insolent men said to Jeremiah, "You are telling a lie. The Lord our God did not send you to say, 'Do not go to Egypt to live there,' [3]but Baruch the son of Neriah has set you against us, to deliver us into the hand of the Chaldeans, that they may kill us or take us into exile in Babylon." [4]So Johanan the son of Kareah and all the commanders of the forces and all the people did not obey the voice of the Lord, to remain in the land of Judah. [5]But Johanan the son of Kareah and all the commanders of the forces took all the remnant of Judah who had returned to live in the land of Judah from all the nations to which they had been driven— [6]the men, the women, the children, the princesses, and every person whom Nebuzaradan the captain of the guard had left with Gedaliah the son of Ahikam, son of Shaphan; also Jeremiah the prophet and Baruch the son of Neriah. [7]And they came into the land of Egypt, for they did not obey the voice of the Lord. And they arrived at Tahpanhes.

[8]Then the word of the Lord came to Jeremiah in Tahpanhes: [9]"Take in your hands large stones and hide them in the mortar in the pavement that is at the entrance to Pharaoh's palace in Tahpanhes, in the sight of the men of Judah, [10]and say to them, 'Thus says the Lord of hosts, the God of Israel: Behold, I will send and take Nebuchadnezzar the king of Babylon, my servant, and I will set his throne above these stones that I have hidden, and he will spread his royal canopy over them. [11]He shall come and strike the land of Egypt, giving over to the pestilence those who are doomed to the pestilence, to captivity those who are doomed to captivity, and to the sword those who are doomed to the sword. [12]I shall kindle a fire in the temples of the gods of Egypt, and he shall burn them and carry them away captive. And he shall clean the land of Egypt as a shepherd cleans his cloak of vermin, and he shall go away from there in peace. [13]He shall break the obelisks of Heliopolis, which is in the land of Egypt, and the temples of the gods of Egypt he shall burn with fire.'"

Queen of the Nile [chapters 44–45]. Chapter 44 contains the words of the last prophetic oracle Jeremiah pronounced before he died. Speaking to the remnant in Egypt, he reminds them of the terrible things that God's people suffered in the fall of Jerusalem. He also reminds them why they suffered these things: because they rejected the message of God's true prophets and worshiped other gods. Now the people are in danger of repeating the same mistake again, this time by practicing goddess worship (see 44:15–19). Led by their wives, Jewish families have been making offerings to the "queen of heaven." Will God's people never learn to turn away from idolatry? Rejecting the one true God will end in deadly disaster, and only a remnant of the remnant will survive. This section ends with a flashback to a short prophecy Jeremiah gave to his secretary Baruch at a time when he was discouraged in his life and ministry (45:1–5). Rather than seeking great things for himself, Baruch needed to do his own small duty in supporting the larger purposes of God—a calling he faithfully fulfilled, as the book of Jeremiah shows.

44 The word that came to Jeremiah concerning all the Judeans who lived in the land of Egypt, at Migdol, at Tahpanhes, at Memphis, and in the land of Pathros, ²"Thus says the LORD of hosts, the God of Israel: You have seen all the disaster that I brought upon Jerusalem and upon all the cities of Judah. Behold, this day they are a desolation, and no one dwells in them, ³because of the evil that they committed, provoking me to anger, in that they went to make offerings and serve other gods that they knew not, neither they, nor you, nor your fathers. ⁴Yet I persistently sent to you all my servants the prophets, saying, 'Oh, do not do this abomination that I hate!' ⁵But they did not listen or incline their ear, to turn from their evil and make no offerings to other gods. ⁶Therefore my wrath and my anger were poured out and kindled in the cities of Judah and in the streets of Jerusalem, and they became a waste and a desolation, as at this day. ⁷And now thus says the LORD God of hosts, the God of Israel: Why do you commit this great evil against yourselves, to cut off from you man and woman, infant and child, from the midst of Judah, leaving you no remnant? ⁸Why do you provoke me to anger with the works of your hands, making offerings to other gods in the land of Egypt where you have come to live, so that you may be cut off and become a curse and a taunt among all the nations of the earth? ⁹Have you forgotten the evil of your fathers, the evil of the kings of Judah, the evil of their¹ wives, your own evil, and the evil of your wives, which they committed in the land of Judah and in the streets of Jerusalem? ¹⁰They have not humbled themselves even to this day, nor have they feared, nor walked in my law and my statutes that I set before you and before your fathers.

¹¹"Therefore thus says the LORD of hosts, the God of Israel: Behold, I will set my face against you for harm, to cut off all Judah. ¹²I will take the remnant of Judah who have set their faces to come to the land of Egypt to live, and they shall all be consumed. In the land of Egypt they shall fall; by the sword and by famine they shall be consumed. From the least to the greatest, they shall die by the sword and by famine, and they shall become an oath, a horror, a curse, and a taunt. ¹³I will punish those who dwell in the land of Egypt, as I have punished Jerusalem, with the sword, with famine, and with pestilence, ¹⁴so that none of the remnant of Judah who have come to live in the land of Egypt shall escape or survive or return to the land of Judah, to which they desire to return to dwell there. For they shall not return, except some fugitives."

¹⁵Then all the men who knew that their wives had made offerings to other gods, and all the women who stood by, a great assembly, all the people who lived in Pathros in the land of Egypt, answered Jeremiah: ¹⁶"As for the word that you have spoken to us in the name of the LORD, we will not listen to you. ¹⁷But we will do everything that we have vowed, make offerings to the queen of heaven and pour out drink offerings to her, as we did, both we and our fathers, our kings and our officials, in the cities of Judah and in the streets of Jerusalem. For then we had plenty of food, and prospered, and saw no disaster. ¹⁸But since we left off making offerings to the queen of heaven and pouring out drink offerings to her, we have lacked everything and have been consumed by the sword and by famine." ¹⁹And the women said,² "When we made

¹ Hebrew *his* ² Compare Syriac; Hebrew lacks *And the women said*

offerings to the queen of heaven and poured out drink offerings to her, was it without our husbands' approval that we made cakes for her bearing her image and poured out drink offerings to her?"

²⁰Then Jeremiah said to all the people, men and women, all the people who had given him this answer: ²¹"As for the offerings that you offered in the cities of Judah and in the streets of Jerusalem, you and your fathers, your kings and your officials, and the people of the land, did not the Lord remember them? Did it not come into his mind? ²²The Lord could no longer bear your evil deeds and the abominations that you committed. Therefore your land has become a desolation and a waste and a curse, without inhabitant, as it is this day. ²³It is because you made offerings and because you sinned against the Lord and did not obey the voice of the Lord or walk in his law and in his statutes and in his testimonies that this disaster has happened to you, as at this day."

²⁴Jeremiah said to all the people and all the women, "Hear the word of the Lord, all you of Judah who are in the land of Egypt. ²⁵Thus says the Lord of hosts, the God of Israel: You and your wives have declared with your mouths, and have fulfilled it with your hands, saying, 'We will surely perform our vows that we have made, to make offerings to the queen of heaven and to pour out drink offerings to her.' Then confirm your vows and perform your vows! ²⁶Therefore hear the word of the Lord, all you of Judah who dwell in the land of Egypt: Behold, I have sworn by my great name, says the Lord, that my name shall no more be invoked by the mouth of any man of Judah in all the land of Egypt, saying, 'As the Lord God lives.' ²⁷Behold, I am watching over them for disaster and not for good. All the men of Judah who are in the land of Egypt shall be consumed by the sword and by famine, until there is an end of them. ²⁸And those who escape the sword shall return from the land of Egypt to the land of Judah, few in number; and all the remnant of Judah, who came to the land of Egypt to live, shall know whose word will stand, mine or theirs. ²⁹This shall be the sign to you, declares the Lord, that I will punish you in this place, in order that you may know that my words will surely stand against you for harm: ³⁰Thus says the Lord, Behold, I will give Pharaoh Hophra king of Egypt into the hand of his enemies and into the hand of those who seek his life, as I gave Zedekiah king of Judah into the hand of Nebuchadnezzar king of Babylon, who was his enemy and sought his life."

45 The word that Jeremiah the prophet spoke to Baruch the son of Neriah, when he wrote these words in a book at the dictation of Jeremiah, in the fourth year of Jehoiakim the son of Josiah, king of Judah: ²"Thus says the Lord, the God of Israel, to you, O Baruch: ³You said, 'Woe is me! For the Lord has added sorrow to my pain. I am weary with my groaning, and I find no rest.' ⁴Thus shall you say to him, Thus says the Lord: Behold, what I have built I am breaking down, and what I have planted I am plucking up—that is, the whole land. ⁵And do you seek great things for yourself? Seek them not, for behold, I am bringing disaster upon all flesh, declares the Lord. But I will give you your life as a prize of war in all places to which you may go."

God's judgment on Egypt and the Philistines [chapters 46–47]. The last main section of the book presents Jeremiah's "Oracles against the Nations." These prophecies of judgment address most of the nations around Israel. God is not just the God of Israel but of all nations, and thus Jeremiah is a "prophet to the nations" (see 1:5). Based on the facts at the beginning of this chapter, Jeremiah's prophecy against Egypt was the first of his international oracles. It depicts the famous battle of Carchemish, where King Nebuchadnezzar of Babylon defeated Pharaoh Neco of Egypt. Each oracle shows extensive knowledge of each country's geographic features, political alliances, military capabilities, religious worship, and besetting sins. What were these people like? How are they like us? What were the wages of their sins? Since Egypt and the other nations were ancient enemies of the people of God, these prophecies may also be considered a form of protest literature. Israel's enemies will not go unpunished but will get the justice they deserve. Therefore, these grim promises of judgment are good news for the people of God, as we see in the comforting promises of Jeremiah 46:27–28.

46
The word of the Lord that came to Jeremiah the prophet concerning the nations.

²About Egypt. Concerning the army of Pharaoh Neco, king of Egypt, which was by the river Euphrates at Carchemish and which Nebuchadnezzar king of Babylon defeated in the fourth year of Jehoiakim the son of Josiah, king of Judah:

³ "Prepare buckler and shield,
    and advance for battle!
⁴ Harness the horses;
    mount, O horsemen!
Take your stations with your helmets,
    polish your spears,
    put on your armor!
⁵ Why have I seen it?
They are dismayed
    and have turned backward.
Their warriors are beaten down
    and have fled in haste;
they look not back—
    terror on every side!
                    declares the Lord.

⁶ "The swift cannot flee away,
    nor the warrior escape;
in the north by the river Euphrates
    they have stumbled and fallen.

⁷ "Who is this, rising like the Nile,
    like rivers whose waters surge?
⁸ Egypt rises like the Nile,
    like rivers whose waters surge.
He said, 'I will rise, I will cover the earth,
    I will destroy cities and their inhabitants.'
⁹ Advance, O horses,
    and rage, O chariots!
Let the warriors go out:

men of Cush and Put who handle the shield,
men of Lud, skilled in handling the bow.
¹⁰ That day is the day of the Lord God of hosts,
a day of vengeance,
to avenge himself on his foes.
The sword shall devour and be sated
and drink its fill of their blood.
For the Lord God of hosts holds a sacrifice
in the north country by the river Euphrates.
¹¹ Go up to Gilead, and take balm,
O virgin daughter of Egypt!
In vain you have used many medicines;
there is no healing for you.
¹² The nations have heard of your shame,
and the earth is full of your cry;
for warrior has stumbled against warrior;
they have both fallen together."

¹³The word that the Lord spoke to Jeremiah the prophet about the coming of
Nebuchadnezzar king of Babylon to strike the land of Egypt:

¹⁴ "Declare in Egypt, and proclaim in Migdol;
proclaim in Memphis and Tahpanhes;
say, 'Stand ready and be prepared,
for the sword shall devour around you.'
¹⁵ Why are your mighty ones face down?
They do not stand¹
because the Lord thrust them down.
¹⁶ He made many stumble, and they fell,
and they said one to another,
'Arise, and let us go back to our own people
and to the land of our birth,
because of the sword of the oppressor.'
¹⁷ Call the name of Pharaoh, king of Egypt,
'Noisy one who lets the hour go by.'

¹⁸ "As I live, declares the King,
whose name is the Lord of hosts,
like Tabor among the mountains
and like Carmel by the sea, shall one come.
¹⁹ Prepare yourselves baggage for exile,
O inhabitants of Egypt!
For Memphis shall become a waste,
a ruin, without inhabitant.

²⁰ "A beautiful heifer is Egypt,
but a biting fly from the north has come upon her.
²¹ Even her hired soldiers in her midst

---

¹ Hebrew *He does not stand*

are like fattened calves;
yes, they have turned and fled together;
   they did not stand,
for the day of their calamity has come upon them,
   the time of their punishment.

²² "She makes a sound like a serpent gliding away;
   for her enemies march in force
and come against her with axes
   like those who fell trees.
²³   They shall cut down her forest,
             declares the LORD,
   though it is impenetrable,
because they are more numerous than locusts;
   they are without number.
²⁴   The daughter of Egypt shall be put to shame;
   she shall be delivered into the hand of a people from the north."

²⁵The LORD of hosts, the God of Israel, said: "Behold, I am bringing punishment upon Amon of Thebes, and Pharaoh and Egypt and her gods and her kings, upon Pharaoh and those who trust in him. ²⁶I will deliver them into the hand of those who seek their life, into the hand of Nebuchadnezzar king of Babylon and his officers. Afterward Egypt shall be inhabited as in the days of old, declares the LORD.

²⁷ "But fear not, O Jacob my servant,
   nor be dismayed, O Israel,
for behold, I will save you from far away,
   and your offspring from the land of their captivity.
Jacob shall return and have quiet and ease,
   and none shall make him afraid.
²⁸   Fear not, O Jacob my servant,
             declares the LORD,
   for I am with you.
I will make a full end of all the nations
   to which I have driven you,
   but of you I will not make a full end.
I will discipline you in just measure,
   and I will by no means leave you unpunished."

47 The word of the LORD that came to Jeremiah the prophet concerning the Philistines, before Pharaoh struck down Gaza.

² "Thus says the LORD:
Behold, waters are rising out of the north,
   and shall become an overflowing torrent;
they shall overflow the land and all that fills it,
   the city and those who dwell in it.
Men shall cry out,
   and every inhabitant of the land shall wail.

³ At the noise of the stamping of the hoofs of his stallions,
      at the rushing of his chariots, at the rumbling of their wheels,
the fathers look not back to their children,
      so feeble are their hands,
⁴ because of the day that is coming to destroy
      all the Philistines,
to cut off from Tyre and Sidon
      every helper that remains.
For the LORD is destroying the Philistines,
      the remnant of the coastland of Caphtor.
⁵ Baldness has come upon Gaza;
      Ashkelon has perished.
O remnant of their valley,
      how long will you gash yourselves?
⁶ Ah, sword of the LORD!
      How long till you are quiet?
Put yourself into your scabbard;
      rest and be still!
⁷ How can it¹ be quiet
      when the LORD has given it a charge?
Against Ashkelon and against the seashore
      he has appointed it."

God's judgment on Moab [chapter 48]. Like his prophecies against Egypt and the Philistines, Jeremiah's prophecy against Moab takes us to the battlefront and gives a vivid poetic portrayal of armies at war. The battles these oracles describe were real military conflicts that are also recorded in other ancient documents—in Moab's case, a bitter defeat at the hand of the Babylonians. But Jeremiah is giving us a spiritual perspective on these events in human history. The main point of his international oracles is that God holds every nation accountable and will judge the whole world for its sins. Jeremiah's prophecy uses poetic imagery to identify many sins of the Moabites—rebellion, mockery, drunkenness, idolatry, self-righteousness, greed—but their main sin is pride (see vv. 29–30). In keeping with his identity as "the weeping prophet," Jeremiah's tone throughout this prophecy is mournful; the prophet weeps for his lost cousins, the Moabites (e.g. vv. 31–32). Happily, his last word to them is more hopeful: a promise that God will later restore their fortunes (v. 47).

48
Concerning Moab.
Thus says the LORD of hosts, the God of Israel:

"Woe to Nebo, for it is laid waste!
      Kiriathaim is put to shame, it is taken;
the fortress is put to shame and broken down;
²   the renown of Moab is no more.
In Heshbon they planned disaster against her:
      'Come, let us cut her off from being a nation!'

¹ Septuagint, Vulgate; Hebrew you

You also, O Madmen, shall be brought to silence;
    the sword shall pursue you.

3 "A voice! A cry from Horonaim,
    'Desolation and great destruction!'
4 Moab is destroyed;
    her little ones have made a cry.
5 For at the ascent of Luhith
    they go up weeping;[1]
  for at the descent of Horonaim
    they have heard the distressed cry[2] of destruction.
6 Flee! Save yourselves!
    You will be like a juniper in the desert!
7 For, because you trusted in your works and your treasures,
    you also shall be taken;
  and Chemosh shall go into exile
    with his priests and his officials.
8 The destroyer shall come upon every city,
    and no city shall escape;
  the valley shall perish,
    and the plain shall be destroyed,
    as the Lᴏʀᴅ has spoken.

9 "Give wings to Moab,
    for she would fly away;
  her cities shall become a desolation,
    with no inhabitant in them.

10"Cursed is he who does the work of the Lᴏʀᴅ with slackness, and cursed is he who keeps back his sword from bloodshed.

11 "Moab has been at ease from his youth
    and has settled on his dregs;
  he has not been emptied from vessel to vessel,
    nor has he gone into exile;
  so his taste remains in him,
    and his scent is not changed.

12"Therefore, behold, the days are coming, declares the Lᴏʀᴅ, when I shall send to him pourers who will pour him, and empty his vessels and break his[3] jars in pieces. 13Then Moab shall be ashamed of Chemosh, as the house of Israel was ashamed of Bethel, their confidence.

14 "How do you say, 'We are heroes
    and mighty men of war'?
15 The destroyer of Moab and his cities has come up,
    and the choicest of his young men have gone down to slaughter,
    declares the King, whose name is the Lᴏʀᴅ of hosts.
16 The calamity of Moab is near at hand,

---

[1] Hebrew *weeping goes up with weeping* [2] Septuagint (compare Isaiah 15:5) *heard the cry* [3] Septuagint, Aquila; Hebrew *their*

and his affliction hastens swiftly.

¹⁷ Grieve for him, all you who are around him,
    and all who know his name;
say, 'How the mighty scepter is broken,
    the glorious staff.'

¹⁸ "Come down from your glory,
    and sit on the parched ground,
      O inhabitant of Dibon!
For the destroyer of Moab has come up against you;
    he has destroyed your strongholds.

¹⁹ Stand by the way and watch,
    O inhabitant of Aroer!
Ask him who flees and her who escapes;
    say, 'What has happened?'

²⁰ Moab is put to shame, for it is broken;
    wail and cry!
Tell it beside the Arnon,
    that Moab is laid waste.

²¹ "Judgment has come upon the tableland, upon Holon, and Jahzah, and Mephaath, ²² and Dibon, and Nebo, and Beth-diblathaim, ²³ and Kiriathaim, and Beth-gamul, and Beth-meon, ²⁴ and Kerioth, and Bozrah, and all the cities of the land of Moab, far and near. ²⁵ The horn of Moab is cut off, and his arm is broken, declares the LORD.

²⁶ "Make him drunk, because he magnified himself against the LORD, so that Moab shall wallow in his vomit, and he too shall be held in derision. ²⁷ Was not Israel a derision to you? Was he found among thieves, that whenever you spoke of him you wagged your head?

²⁸ "Leave the cities, and dwell in the rock,
    O inhabitants of Moab!
Be like the dove that nests
    in the sides of the mouth of a gorge.

²⁹ We have heard of the pride of Moab—
    he is very proud—
of his loftiness, his pride, and his arrogance,
    and the haughtiness of his heart.

³⁰ I know his insolence, declares the LORD;
    his boasts are false,
    his deeds are false.

³¹ Therefore I wail for Moab;
    I cry out for all Moab;
    for the men of Kir-hareseth I mourn.

³² More than for Jazer I weep for you,
    O vine of Sibmah!
Your branches passed over the sea,
    reached to the Sea of Jazer;
on your summer fruits and your grapes

the destroyer has fallen.
33 Gladness and joy have been taken away
      from the fruitful land of Moab;
    I have made the wine cease from the winepresses;
      no one treads them with shouts of joy;
      the shouting is not the shout of joy.

³⁴"From the outcry at Heshbon even to Elealeh, as far as Jahaz they utter their voice, from Zoar to Horonaim and Eglath-shelishiyah. For the waters of Nimrim also have become desolate. ³⁵And I will bring to an end in Moab, declares the LORD, him who offers sacrifice in the high place and makes offerings to his god. ³⁶Therefore my heart moans for Moab like a flute, and my heart moans like a flute for the men of Kir-hareseth. Therefore the riches they gained have perished.

³⁷"For every head is shaved and every beard cut off. On all the hands are gashes, and around the waist is sackcloth. ³⁸On all the housetops of Moab and in the squares there is nothing but lamentation, for I have broken Moab like a vessel for which no one cares, declares the LORD. ³⁹How it is broken! How they wail! How Moab has turned his back in shame! So Moab has become a derision and a horror to all that are around him."

40 For thus says the LORD:
    "Behold, one shall fly swiftly like an eagle
      and spread his wings against Moab;
41 the cities shall be taken
      and the strongholds seized.
    The heart of the warriors of Moab shall be in that day
      like the heart of a woman in her birth pains;
42 Moab shall be destroyed and be no longer a people,
      because he magnified himself against the LORD.
43 Terror, pit, and snare
      are before you, O inhabitant of Moab!
                        declares the LORD.
44 He who flees from the terror
      shall fall into the pit,
    and he who climbs out of the pit
      shall be caught in the snare.
    For I will bring these things upon Moab,
      the year of their punishment,
                        declares the LORD.

45 "In the shadow of Heshbon
      fugitives stop without strength,
    for fire came out from Heshbon,
      flame from the house of Sihon;
    it has destroyed the forehead of Moab,
      the crown of the sons of tumult.
46 Woe to you, O Moab!
      The people of Chemosh are undone,

for your sons have been taken captive,
    and your daughters into captivity.
⁴⁷   Yet I will restore the fortunes of Moab
    in the latter days, declares the LORD."
Thus far is the judgment on Moab.

God's judgment on other nations [chapter 49]. Jeremiah's oracles of judgment continue with prophecies against Ammon, Edom, Syria, Kedar, Hazor, and Elam. The inclusion of these nations confirms that God is the Lord of all nations. Each people-group has its characteristic sins (e.g., the greed of the Ammonites or the militarism of the Elamites) and receives the destruction it deserves as a result. One good way to make practical connections from this passage is to consider in what ways we are tempted to trust in our financial prosperity, intellectual accomplishments, and military superiority rather than to trust in God. It is also important to notice the occasional glimmers of grace that show God has a plan for all nations and not just Israel (e.g., the promise in v. 39 that Elam will be restored in the latter days—a promise fulfilled at Pentecost; see Acts 2:9).

49

Concerning the Ammonites.
Thus says the LORD:

"Has Israel no sons?
    Has he no heir?
Why then has Milcom dispossessed Gad,
    and his people settled in its cities?
²   Therefore, behold, the days are coming,
    declares the LORD,
when I will cause the battle cry to be heard
    against Rabbah of the Ammonites;
it shall become a desolate mound,
    and its villages shall be burned with fire;
then Israel shall dispossess those who dispossessed him,
    says the LORD.

³   "Wail, O Heshbon, for Ai is laid waste!
    Cry out, O daughters of Rabbah!
Put on sackcloth,
    lament, and run to and fro among the hedges!
For Milcom shall go into exile,
    with his priests and his officials.
⁴   Why do you boast of your valleys,¹
    O faithless daughter,
who trusted in her treasures, saying,
    'Who will come against me?'
⁵   Behold, I will bring terror upon you,
    declares the Lord GOD of hosts,
    from all who are around you,

---

¹ Hebrew *boast of your valleys, your valley flows*

and you shall be driven out, every man straight before him,
  with none to gather the fugitives.

⁶"But afterward I will restore the fortunes of the Ammonites, declares the LORD."
⁷Concerning Edom.

Thus says the LORD of hosts:

"Is wisdom no more in Teman?
    Has counsel perished from the prudent?
    Has their wisdom vanished?
⁸ Flee, turn back, dwell in the depths,
    O inhabitants of Dedan!
  For I will bring the calamity of Esau upon him,
    the time when I punish him.
⁹ If grape-gatherers came to you,
    would they not leave gleanings?
  If thieves came by night,
    would they not destroy only enough for themselves?
¹⁰ But I have stripped Esau bare;
    I have uncovered his hiding places,
    and he is not able to conceal himself.
  His children are destroyed, and his brothers,
    and his neighbors; and he is no more.
¹¹ Leave your fatherless children; I will keep them alive;
    and let your widows trust in me."

¹²For thus says the LORD: "If those who did not deserve to drink the cup must drink it, will you go unpunished? You shall not go unpunished, but you must drink. ¹³For I have sworn by myself, declares the LORD, that Bozrah shall become a horror, a taunt, a waste, and a curse, and all her cities shall be perpetual wastes."

¹⁴ I have heard a message from the LORD,
    and an envoy has been sent among the nations:
  "Gather yourselves together and come against her,
    and rise up for battle!
¹⁵ For behold, I will make you small among the nations,
    despised among mankind.
¹⁶ The horror you inspire has deceived you,
    and the pride of your heart,
  you who live in the clefts of the rock,¹
    who hold the height of the hill.
  Though you make your nest as high as the eagle's,
    I will bring you down from there,
                    declares the LORD.

¹⁷"Edom shall become a horror. Everyone who passes by it will be horrified and will hiss because of all its disasters. ¹⁸As when Sodom and Gomorrah and their neighboring cities were overthrown, says the LORD, no man shall dwell there, no man shall sojourn in her. ¹⁹Behold, like a lion coming up from the jungle of the Jordan against a

¹ Or of Sela

perennial pasture, I will suddenly make him[1] run away from her. And I will appoint over her whomever I choose. For who is like me? Who will summon me? What shepherd can stand before me? [20]Therefore hear the plan that the LORD has made against Edom and the purposes that he has formed against the inhabitants of Teman: Even the little ones of the flock shall be dragged away. Surely their fold shall be appalled at their fate. [21]At the sound of their fall the earth shall tremble; the sound of their cry shall be heard at the Red Sea. [22]Behold, one shall mount up and fly swiftly like an eagle and spread his wings against Bozrah, and the heart of the warriors of Edom shall be in that day like the heart of a woman in her birth pains."

[23]Concerning Damascus:

"Hamath and Arpad are confounded,
 for they have heard bad news;
they melt in fear,
 they are troubled like the sea that cannot be quiet.
[24] Damascus has become feeble, she turned to flee,
  and panic seized her;
 anguish and sorrows have taken hold of her,
  as of a woman in labor.
[25] How is the famous city not forsaken,
  the city of my joy?
[26] Therefore her young men shall fall in her squares,
  and all her soldiers shall be destroyed in that day,
    declares the LORD of hosts.
[27] And I will kindle a fire in the wall of Damascus,
  and it shall devour the strongholds of Ben-hadad."

[28]Concerning Kedar and the kingdoms of Hazor that Nebuchadnezzar king of Babylon struck down.

Thus says the LORD:
"Rise up, advance against Kedar!
 Destroy the people of the east!
[29] Their tents and their flocks shall be taken,
  their curtains and all their goods;
 their camels shall be led away from them,
  and men shall cry to them: 'Terror on every side!'
[30] Flee, wander far away, dwell in the depths,
  O inhabitants of Hazor!
    declares the LORD.
 For Nebuchadnezzar king of Babylon
  has made a plan against you
  and formed a purpose against you.

[31] "Rise up, advance against a nation at ease,
  that dwells securely,
    declares the LORD,
 that has no gates or bars,

---

[1] Septuagint, Syriac *them*

that dwells alone.
³² Their camels shall become plunder,
their herds of livestock a spoil.
I will scatter to every wind
those who cut the corners of their hair,
and I will bring their calamity
from every side of them,
declares the LORD.
³³ Hazor shall become a haunt of jackals,
an everlasting waste;
no man shall dwell there;
no man shall sojourn in her."

³⁴The word of the LORD that came to Jeremiah the prophet concerning Elam, in the beginning of the reign of Zedekiah king of Judah. ³⁵Thus says the LORD of hosts: "Behold, I will break the bow of Elam, the mainstay of their might. ³⁶And I will bring upon Elam the four winds from the four quarters of heaven. And I will scatter them to all those winds, and there shall be no nation to which those driven out of Elam shall not come. ³⁷I will terrify Elam before their enemies and before those who seek their life. I will bring disaster upon them, my fierce anger, declares the LORD. I will send the sword after them, until I have consumed them, ³⁸and I will set my throne in Elam and destroy their king and officials, declares the LORD. ³⁹"But in the latter days I will restore the fortunes of Elam, declares the LORD."

God's judgment on Babylon [chapter 50]. The fall of Jerusalem is the climax of Jeremiah—the main event that dominates the action of the book. God's judgment against Babylon is part of the denouement—the tidying up of loose ends that brings a sense of closure to the book. As such, it is essential to the book's total message. Babylon serves as the instrument of God's judgment against Judah, but the Babylonians too will be judged. Given all the terrible things that they did to God's people, it is only right that their judgment should come at the end of Jeremiah's oracles against the nations and that the doom of their destruction should be prophesied in the most careful detail. Once again, Jeremiah gives a poetic description of a nation's last battle, punctuated with imperatives and staccato rhythms that convey a sense of urgent desperation (e.g., vv. 35–37). This time, though, there seems to be a particular note of triumph, as the prophet celebrates the defeat of one of God's worst enemies and one of the OT's main archetypes of evil (e.g. v. 2; cf. 51:48). There are signs that Babylon, ironically, will suffer the same kind of defeat that it so often inflicted on others, not least the city of Jerusalem (e.g., Babylon too is attacked from the north and is surrounded by a siege). Jeremiah's prophecy also includes instructions and promises that God gives to his people Israel (e.g. vv. 4–8, 20); Babylon's defeat is their deliverance.

50 The word that the LORD spoke concerning Babylon, concerning the land of the Chaldeans, by Jeremiah the prophet:

² "Declare among the nations and proclaim,
set up a banner and proclaim,

conceal it not, and say:
'Babylon is taken,
   Bel is put to shame,
   Merodach is dismayed.
Her images are put to shame,
   her idols are dismayed.'

³"For out of the north a nation has come up against her, which shall make her land a desolation, and none shall dwell in it; both man and beast shall flee away.

⁴"In those days and in that time, declares the Lᴏʀᴅ, the people of Israel and the people of Judah shall come together, weeping as they come, and they shall seek the Lᴏʀᴅ their God. ⁵They shall ask the way to Zion, with faces turned toward it, saying, 'Come, let us join ourselves to the Lᴏʀᴅ in an everlasting covenant that will never be forgotten.'

⁶"My people have been lost sheep. Their shepherds have led them astray, turning them away on the mountains. From mountain to hill they have gone. They have forgotten their fold. ⁷All who found them have devoured them, and their enemies have said, 'We are not guilty, for they have sinned against the Lᴏʀᴅ, their habitation of righteousness, the Lᴏʀᴅ, the hope of their fathers.'

⁸"Flee from the midst of Babylon, and go out of the land of the Chaldeans, and be as male goats before the flock. ⁹For behold, I am stirring up and bringing against Babylon a gathering of great nations, from the north country. And they shall array themselves against her. From there she shall be taken. Their arrows are like a skilled warrior who does not return empty-handed. ¹⁰Chaldea shall be plundered; all who plunder her shall be sated, declares the Lᴏʀᴅ.

11   "Though you rejoice, though you exult,
     O plunderers of my heritage,
   though you frolic like a heifer in the pasture,
     and neigh like stallions,
12   your mother shall be utterly shamed,
     and she who bore you shall be disgraced.
  Behold, she shall be the last of the nations,
     a wilderness, a dry land, and a desert.
13   Because of the wrath of the Lᴏʀᴅ she shall not be inhabited
     but shall be an utter desolation;
  everyone who passes by Babylon shall be appalled,
     and hiss because of all her wounds.
14   Set yourselves in array against Babylon all around,
     all you who bend the bow;
  shoot at her, spare no arrows,
     for she has sinned against the Lᴏʀᴅ.
15   Raise a shout against her all around;
     she has surrendered;
     her bulwarks have fallen;

her walls are thrown down.
For this is the vengeance of the LORD:
  take vengeance on her;
  do to her as she has done.
16 Cut off from Babylon the sower,
    and the one who handles the sickle in time of harvest;
  because of the sword of the oppressor,
    every one shall turn to his own people,
    and every one shall flee to his own land.

17 "Israel is a hunted sheep driven away by lions. First the king of Assyria devoured him, and now at last Nebuchadnezzar king of Babylon has gnawed his bones. 18 Therefore, thus says the LORD of hosts, the God of Israel: Behold, I am bringing punishment on the king of Babylon and his land, as I punished the king of Assyria. 19 I will restore Israel to his pasture, and he shall feed on Carmel and in Bashan, and his desire shall be satisfied on the hills of Ephraim and in Gilead. 20 In those days and in that time, declares the LORD, iniquity shall be sought in Israel, and there shall be none, and sin in Judah, and none shall be found, for I will pardon those whom I leave as a remnant.

21 "Go up against the land of Merathaim,[1]
    and against the inhabitants of Pekod.[2]
  Kill, and devote them to destruction,[3]
              declares the LORD,
    and do all that I have commanded you.
22 The noise of battle is in the land,
    and great destruction!
23 How the hammer of the whole earth
    is cut down and broken!
  How Babylon has become
    a horror among the nations!
24 I set a snare for you and you were taken, O Babylon,
    and you did not know it;
  you were found and caught,
    because you opposed the LORD.
25 The LORD has opened his armory
    and brought out the weapons of his wrath,
  for the Lord GOD of hosts has a work to do
    in the land of the Chaldeans.
26 Come against her from every quarter;
    open her granaries;
  pile her up like heaps of grain, and devote her to destruction;
    let nothing be left of her.
27 Kill all her bulls;
    let them go down to the slaughter.
  Woe to them, for their day has come,
    the time of their punishment.

[1] Merathaim means double rebellion [2] Pekod means punishment [3] That is, set apart (devote) as an offering to the Lord (for destruction)

²⁸"A voice! They flee and escape from the land of Babylon, to declare in Zion the vengeance of the LORD our God, vengeance for his temple.

²⁹"Summon archers against Babylon, all those who bend the bow. Encamp around her; let no one escape. Repay her according to her deeds; do to her according to all that she has done. For she has proudly defied the LORD, the Holy One of Israel. ³⁰Therefore her young men shall fall in her squares, and all her soldiers shall be destroyed on that day, declares the LORD.

³¹   "Behold, I am against you, O proud one,
            declares the Lord GOD of hosts,
        for your day has come,
            the time when I will punish you.
³²   The proud one shall stumble and fall,
            with none to raise him up,
        and I will kindle a fire in his cities,
            and it will devour all that is around him.

³³"Thus says the LORD of hosts: The people of Israel are oppressed, and the people of Judah with them. All who took them captive have held them fast; they refuse to let them go. ³⁴Their Redeemer is strong; the LORD of hosts is his name. He will surely plead their cause, that he may give rest to the earth, but unrest to the inhabitants of Babylon.

³⁵   "A sword against the Chaldeans, declares the LORD,
            and against the inhabitants of Babylon,
            and against her officials and her wise men!
³⁶   A sword against the diviners,
            that they may become fools!
        A sword against her warriors,
            that they may be destroyed!
³⁷   A sword against her horses and against her chariots,
            and against all the foreign troops in her midst,
            that they may become women!
        A sword against all her treasures,
            that they may be plundered!
³⁸   A drought against her waters,
            that they may be dried up!
        For it is a land of images,
            and they are mad over idols.

³⁹"Therefore wild beasts shall dwell with hyenas in Babylon, and ostriches shall dwell in her. She shall never again have people, nor be inhabited for all generations. ⁴⁰As when God overthrew Sodom and Gomorrah and their neighboring cities, declares the LORD, so no man shall dwell there, and no son of man shall sojourn in her.

⁴¹   "Behold, a people comes from the north;
            a mighty nation and many kings
            are stirring from the farthest parts of the earth.

42 They lay hold of bow and spear;
    they are cruel and have no mercy.
The sound of them is like the roaring of the sea;
    they ride on horses,
arrayed as a man for battle
    against you, O daughter of Babylon!

43 "The king of Babylon heard the report of them,
    and his hands fell helpless;
anguish seized him,
    pain as of a woman in labor.

44 "Behold, like a lion coming up from the thicket of the Jordan against a perennial pasture, I will suddenly make them run away from her, and I will appoint over her whomever I choose. For who is like me? Who will summon me? What shepherd can stand before me? 45 Therefore hear the plan that the Lord has made against Babylon, and the purposes that he has formed against the land of the Chaldeans: Surely the little ones of their flock shall be dragged away; surely their fold shall be appalled at their fate. 46 At the sound of the capture of Babylon the earth shall tremble, and her cry shall be heard among the nations."

Babylon destroyed [chapter 51]. Jeremiah's prophecy continues with more words of judgment. Babylon will be suddenly attacked and utterly destroyed, after which it will become a total and archetypical wasteland. The very length of this oracle is a sign that Babylon's defeat will be complete. At the time, of course, no one could imagine the Babylonian empire's ever coming to an end, but the precision of the prophecy serves as an encouragement to faith. In addition to what it says about the sins of Babylon, the prophecy says many things about the character of God—his justice, his power, his faithfulness to answer prayer. The oracle ends with Jeremiah's last object lesson. The prophet sends a copy of his words against Babylon to the city itself, with the instructions that after the scroll of his prophecy is read, it is to be tied with a heavy stone and thrown to the bottom of the Euphrates River. So it will be for Babylon: the city will sink to the depths and never resurface.

51 Thus says the Lord:
    "Behold, I will stir up the spirit of a destroyer
      against Babylon,
    against the inhabitants of Leb-kamai,[1]
2   and I will send to Babylon winnowers,
      and they shall winnow her,
    and they shall empty her land,
      when they come against her from every side
      on the day of trouble.
3   Let not the archer bend his bow,
      and let him not stand up in his armor.
    Spare not her young men;
      devote to destruction[2] all her army.
4   They shall fall down slain in the land of the Chaldeans,

and wounded in her streets.
⁵ For Israel and Judah have not been forsaken
     by their God, the Lᴏʀᴅ of hosts,
   but the land of the Chaldeans¹ is full of guilt
     against the Holy One of Israel.

⁶ "Flee from the midst of Babylon;
     let every one save his life!
   Be not cut off in her punishment,
     for this is the time of the Lᴏʀᴅ's vengeance,
     the repayment he is rendering her.
⁷ Babylon was a golden cup in the Lᴏʀᴅ's hand,
     making all the earth drunken;
   the nations drank of her wine;
     therefore the nations went mad.
⁸ Suddenly Babylon has fallen and been broken;
     wail for her!
   Take balm for her pain;
     perhaps she may be healed.
⁹ We would have healed Babylon,
     but she was not healed.
   Forsake her, and let us go
     each to his own country,
   for her judgment has reached up to heaven
     and has been lifted up even to the skies.
¹⁰ The Lᴏʀᴅ has brought about our vindication;
     come, let us declare in Zion
     the work of the Lᴏʀᴅ our God.

¹¹ "Sharpen the arrows!
     Take up the shields!

The Lᴏʀᴅ has stirred up the spirit of the kings of the Medes, because his purpose
concerning Babylon is to destroy it, for that is the vengeance of the Lᴏʀᴅ, the vengeance for his temple.

¹² "Set up a standard against the walls of Babylon;
      make the watch strong;
    set up watchmen;
      prepare the ambushes;
    for the Lᴏʀᴅ has both planned and done
      what he spoke concerning the inhabitants of Babylon.
¹³ O you who dwell by many waters,
      rich in treasures,
    your end has come;
      the thread of your life is cut.
¹⁴ The Lᴏʀᴅ of hosts has sworn by himself:

---

¹ Hebrew *their land*

Surely I will fill you with men, as many as locusts,
　　and they shall raise the shout of victory over you.

15 "It is he who made the earth by his power,
　　who established the world by his wisdom,
　and by his understanding stretched out the heavens.
16 When he utters his voice there is a tumult of waters in the heavens,
　　and he makes the mist rise from the ends of the earth.
　He makes lightning for the rain,
　　and he brings forth the wind from his storehouses.
17 Every man is stupid and without knowledge;
　　every goldsmith is put to shame by his idols,
　for his images are false,
　　and there is no breath in them.
18 They are worthless, a work of delusion;
　　at the time of their punishment they shall perish.
19 Not like these is he who is the portion of Jacob,
　　for he is the one who formed all things,
　and Israel is the tribe of his inheritance;
　　the Lord of hosts is his name.

20 "You are my hammer and weapon of war:
　with you I break nations in pieces;
　　with you I destroy kingdoms;
21 with you I break in pieces the horse and his rider;
　　with you I break in pieces the chariot and the charioteer;
22 with you I break in pieces man and woman;
　　with you I break in pieces the old man and the youth;
　with you I break in pieces the young man and the young woman;
23 　with you I break in pieces the shepherd and his flock;
　with you I break in pieces the farmer and his team;
　　with you I break in pieces governors and commanders.

24 "I will repay Babylon and all the inhabitants of Chaldea before your very eyes for all the evil that they have done in Zion, declares the Lord.

25 "Behold, I am against you, O destroying mountain,
　　　　　　　　declares the Lord,
　which destroys the whole earth;
　I will stretch out my hand against you,
　　and roll you down from the crags,
　　and make you a burnt mountain.
26 No stone shall be taken from you for a corner
　　and no stone for a foundation,
　but you shall be a perpetual waste,
　　declares the Lord.

27 "Set up a standard on the earth;
　　blow the trumpet among the nations;

prepare the nations for war against her;
  summon against her the kingdoms,
  Ararat, Minni, and Ashkenaz;
appoint a marshal against her;
  bring up horses like bristling locusts.
28 Prepare the nations for war against her,
  the kings of the Medes, with their governors and deputies,
  and every land under their dominion.
29 The land trembles and writhes in pain,
  for the LORD's purposes against Babylon stand,
to make the land of Babylon a desolation,
  without inhabitant.
30 The warriors of Babylon have ceased fighting;
  they remain in their strongholds;
their strength has failed;
  they have become women;
her dwellings are on fire;
  her bars are broken.
31 One runner runs to meet another,
  and one messenger to meet another,
to tell the king of Babylon
  that his city is taken on every side;
32 the fords have been seized,
  the marshes are burned with fire,
  and the soldiers are in panic.
33 For thus says the LORD of hosts, the God of Israel:
The daughter of Babylon is like a threshing floor
  at the time when it is trodden;
yet a little while
  and the time of her harvest will come."

34 "Nebuchadnezzar the king of Babylon has devoured me;
  he has crushed me;
he has made me an empty vessel;
  he has swallowed me like a monster;
he has filled his stomach with my delicacies;
  he has rinsed me out.[1]
35 The violence done to me and to my kinsmen be upon Babylon,"
  let the inhabitant of Zion say.
"My blood be upon the inhabitants of Chaldea,"
  let Jerusalem say.
36 Therefore thus says the LORD:
"Behold, I will plead your cause
  and take vengeance for you.
I will dry up her sea
  and make her fountain dry,

[1] Or he has expelled me

³⁷   and Babylon shall become a heap of ruins,
>   the haunt of jackals,
>   a horror and a hissing,
>   without inhabitant.

³⁸   "They shall roar together like lions;
>   they shall growl like lions' cubs.
³⁹   While they are inflamed I will prepare them a feast
>   and make them drunk, that they may become merry,
>   then sleep a perpetual sleep
>   and not wake, declares the Lord.
⁴⁰   I will bring them down like lambs to the slaughter,
>   like rams and male goats.

⁴¹   "How Babylon[1] is taken,
>   the praise of the whole earth seized!
>   How Babylon has become
>   a horror among the nations!
⁴²   The sea has come up on Babylon;
>   she is covered with its tumultuous waves.
⁴³   Her cities have become a horror,
>   a land of drought and a desert,
>   a land in which no one dwells,
>   and through which no son of man passes.
⁴⁴   And I will punish Bel in Babylon,
>   and take out of his mouth what he has swallowed.
>   The nations shall no longer flow to him;
>   the wall of Babylon has fallen.

⁴⁵   "Go out of the midst of her, my people!
>   Let every one save his life
>   from the fierce anger of the Lord!
⁴⁶   Let not your heart faint, and be not fearful
>   at the report heard in the land,
>   when a report comes in one year
>   and afterward a report in another year,
>   and violence is in the land,
>   and ruler is against ruler.

⁴⁷   "Therefore, behold, the days are coming
>   when I will punish the images of Babylon;
>   her whole land shall be put to shame,
>   and all her slain shall fall in the midst of her.
⁴⁸   Then the heavens and the earth,
>   and all that is in them,
>   shall sing for joy over Babylon,
>   for the destroyers shall come against them out of the north,
>   declares the Lord.

---

[1] Hebrew *Sheshach*, a code name for Babylon

⁴⁹   Babylon must fall for the slain of Israel,
          just as for Babylon have fallen the slain of all the earth.

⁵⁰   "You who have escaped from the sword,
          go, do not stand still!
      Remember the LORD from far away,
          and let Jerusalem come into your mind:
⁵¹   'We are put to shame, for we have heard reproach;
          dishonor has covered our face,
      for foreigners have come
          into the holy places of the LORD's house.'

⁵²   "Therefore, behold, the days are coming, declares the LORD,
          when I will execute judgment upon her images,
      and through all her land
          the wounded shall groan.
⁵³   Though Babylon should mount up to heaven,
          and though she should fortify her strong height,
      yet destroyers would come from me against her,
          declares the LORD.

⁵⁴   "A voice! A cry from Babylon!
          The noise of great destruction from the land of the Chaldeans!
⁵⁵   For the LORD is laying Babylon waste
          and stilling her mighty voice.
      Their waves roar like many waters;
          the noise of their voice is raised,
⁵⁶   for a destroyer has come upon her,
          upon Babylon;
      her warriors are taken;
          their bows are broken in pieces,
      for the LORD is a God of recompense;
          he will surely repay.
⁵⁷   I will make drunk her officials and her wise men,
          her governors, her commanders, and her warriors;
      they shall sleep a perpetual sleep and not wake,
          declares the King, whose name is the LORD of hosts.

⁵⁸   "Thus says the LORD of hosts:
      The broad wall of Babylon
          shall be leveled to the ground,
      and her high gates
          shall be burned with fire.
      The peoples labor for nothing,
          and the nations weary themselves only for fire."

⁵⁹The word that Jeremiah the prophet commanded Seraiah the son of Neriah, son of Mahseiah, when he went with Zedekiah king of Judah to Babylon, in the fourth year of his reign. Seraiah was the quartermaster. ⁶⁰Jeremiah wrote in a book all the disaster

that should come upon Babylon, all these words that are written concerning Babylon. ⁶¹And Jeremiah said to Seraiah: "When you come to Babylon, see that you read all these words, ⁶²and say, 'O Lᴏʀᴅ, you have said concerning this place that you will cut it off, so that nothing shall dwell in it, neither man nor beast, and it shall be desolate forever.' ⁶³When you finish reading this book, tie a stone to it and cast it into the midst of the Euphrates, ⁶⁴and say, 'Thus shall Babylon sink, to rise no more, because of the disaster that I am bringing upon her, and they shall become exhausted.'"

Thus far are the words of Jeremiah.

Final report of the fall of Jerusalem [chapter 52]. The book of Jeremiah ends with a postscript, possibly written by Jeremiah's secretary Baruch or someone else with a journalist's eye for detail. Unlike Jeremiah, who often expressed his own deep feelings about what he witnessed, the author is dispassionate in recounting the rebellion of Zedekiah, the siege of Jerusalem, the ensuing famine, the fall of the city, the looting and burning of the temple, and the deportation to Babylon, beginning seventy long years of exile. His aim is to record these events for posterity as accurately as possible and to confirm that all of Jeremiah's prophecies came true. Although the whole account is given rather matter-of-factly, the beginning and the end have special significance—the beginning because it explains why these things happened (see v. 3) and the end because it gives a hint as to what will happen next in God's plan for the salvation of the world. King Jehoiachin of Judah is in Babylon, where he has been released from prison and given a place of honor at the royal table. Even after everything the people of God have suffered and lost, the heir of David lives, giving hope that God's promise of salvation will still come true.

52 Zedekiah was twenty-one years old when he became king; and he reigned eleven years in Jerusalem. His mother's name was Hamutal the daughter of Jeremiah of Libnah. ²And he did what was evil in the sight of the Lᴏʀᴅ, according to all that Jehoiakim had done. ³For because of the anger of the Lᴏʀᴅ things came to the point in Jerusalem and Judah that he cast them out from his presence.

And Zedekiah rebelled against the king of Babylon. ⁴And in the ninth year of his reign, in the tenth month, on the tenth day of the month, Nebuchadnezzar king of Babylon came with all his army against Jerusalem, and laid siege to it. And they built siegeworks all around it. ⁵So the city was besieged till the eleventh year of King Zedekiah. ⁶On the ninth day of the fourth month the famine was so severe in the city that there was no food for the people of the land. ⁷Then a breach was made in the city, and all the men of war fled and went out from the city by night by the way of a gate between the two walls, by the king's garden, while the Chaldeans were around the city. And they went in the direction of the Arabah. ⁸But the army of the Chaldeans pursued the king and overtook Zedekiah in the plains of Jericho. And all his army was scattered from him. ⁹Then they captured the king and brought him up to the king of Babylon at Riblah in the land of Hamath, and he passed sentence on him. ¹⁰The king of Babylon slaughtered the sons of Zedekiah before his eyes, and also slaughtered all the officials of Judah at Riblah. ¹¹He put out the eyes of Zedekiah, and bound him in chains, and the king of Babylon took him to Babylon, and put him in prison till the day of his death.

¹²In the fifth month, on the tenth day of the month—that was the nineteenth year of King Nebuchadnezzar, king of Babylon—Nebuzaradan the captain of the body-

guard, who served the king of Babylon, entered Jerusalem. [13]And he burned the house of the LORD, and the king's house and all the houses of Jerusalem; every great house he burned down. [14]And all the army of the Chaldeans, who were with the captain of the guard, broke down all the walls around Jerusalem. [15]And Nebuzaradan the captain of the guard carried away captive some of the poorest of the people and the rest of the people who were left in the city and the deserters who had deserted to the king of Babylon, together with the rest of the artisans. [16]But Nebuzaradan the captain of the guard left some of the poorest of the land to be vinedressers and plowmen.

[17]And the pillars of bronze that were in the house of the LORD, and the stands and the bronze sea that were in the house of the LORD, the Chaldeans broke in pieces, and carried all the bronze to Babylon. [18]And they took away the pots and the shovels and the snuffers and the basins and the dishes for incense and all the vessels of bronze used in the temple service; [19]also the small bowls and the fire pans and the basins and the pots and the lampstands and the dishes for incense and the bowls for drink offerings. What was of gold the captain of the guard took away as gold, and what was of silver, as silver. [20]As for the two pillars, the one sea, the twelve bronze bulls that were under the sea,[1] and the stands, which Solomon the king had made for the house of the LORD, the bronze of all these things was beyond weight. [21]As for the pillars, the height of the one pillar was eighteen cubits,[2] its circumference was twelve cubits, and its thickness was four fingers, and it was hollow. [22]On it was a capital of bronze. The height of the one capital was five cubits. A network and pomegranates, all of bronze, were around the capital. And the second pillar had the same, with pomegranates. [23]There were ninety-six pomegranates on the sides; all the pomegranates were a hundred upon the network all around.

[24]And the captain of the guard took Seraiah the chief priest, and Zephaniah the second priest, and the three keepers of the threshold; [25]and from the city he took an officer who had been in command of the men of war, and seven men of the king's council, who were found in the city; and the secretary of the commander of the army who mustered the people of the land; and sixty men of the people of the land, who were found in the midst of the city. [26]And Nebuzaradan the captain of the guard took them and brought them to the king of Babylon at Riblah. [27]And the king of Babylon struck them down, and put them to death at Riblah in the land of Hamath. So Judah was taken into exile out of its land.

[28]This is the number of the people whom Nebuchadnezzar carried away captive: in the seventh year, 3,023 Judeans; [29]in the eighteenth year of Nebuchadnezzar he carried away captive from Jerusalem 832 persons; [30]in the twenty-third year of Nebuchadnezzar, Nebuzaradan the captain of the guard carried away captive of the Judeans 745 persons; all the persons were 4,600.

[31]And in the thirty-seventh year of the exile of Jehoiachin king of Judah, in the twelfth month, on the twenty-fifth day of the month, Evil-merodach king of Babylon, in the year that he became king, graciously freed[3] Jehoiachin king of Judah and brought him out of prison. [32]And he spoke kindly to him, and gave him a seat above the seats of the kings who were with him in Babylon. [33]So Jehoiachin put off his prison garments. And every day of his life he dined regularly at the king's table, [34]and for his allowance, a regular allowance was given him by the king according to his daily need, until the day of his death, as long as he lived.

---

[1] Hebrew lacks *the sea* [2] A *cubit* was about 18 inches or 45 centimeters [3] Hebrew *king, lifted up the head of*

LAMENTATIONS

The book at a glance. 5 chapters, 154 verses. During and after Babylon's terrible destruction of Jerusalem, the writer (traditionally and probably correctly identified as the prophet Jeremiah; see 2 Chron. 35:25) laments the tragic fall of the city he loved. Lamentations is unique in the Scriptures for its mood of almost unremitting gloom. The author has witnessed such terrible suffering—famine, murder, rape, cannibalism, and other unspeakable horrors—that the only appropriate response is to give voice to this suffering by raising a cry of woe. Whereas the book of Job deals with the problem of undeserved suffering at the personal level, Lamentations struggles with the issues raised by a community that is suffering exactly what it deserves—God has judged Jerusalem for its sins, to the loss and lamentation of all its citizens. In his anguish and distress, the poet wants to know: What is the meaning of all this suffering?

▋**Genre.** As the title indicates, the book of Lamentations is a collection of *laments, or melancholy dirges for a ruined society. The *poems in the book could also be termed *elegies or funeral orations, in which the author expresses deep personal and communal grief for the dead and for all of the suffering that surrounds their loss. In terms of structure, the first four poems are *acrostics—poems in which each verse starts with a successive letter of the Hebrew alphabet. This structure matches the poet's intent, which is to give full expression to the suffering of his people and the sorrows of his own soul—in effect, to offer a lament "from A to Z" (or *aleph* to *taw*). The highly structured form of the acrostic is also an attempt to impose some sense of order on a tragic situation that is chaotic beyond what anyone can bear. Lamentations is not an emotional outburst but a formal expression of grief in a high literary style. However, each lament moves rapidly from one topic to the next, revealing that the writer's soul is still in turmoil. Like most elegies, the *lyrics in Lamentations deal with profound loss by recollecting past glories and cataloging what is now gone forever, lamenting the finality of their loss while at the same time seeking to find consolation in present sorrows and some hope for the future. (For more information on items accompanied by an asterisk, see the glossary at the back of this Bible.)

▋**Unifying elements.** From its opening line to its final question, Lamentations is strongly unified by its almost unrelenting atmosphere of grief. The verse form of the acrostic also gives the book a strong sense of structural unity; even the last lament, which is not an acrostic, balances the book by dividing neatly into twenty-two verses. Each poem is complete in itself, with its own theme and structure; typically each

Passage	Poem	Theme	Structure
1:1–22	First lament	A city mourns its afflictions	Acrostic
2:1–22	Second lament	God is the source of Jerusalem's affliction	Acrostic
3:1–66	Third lament	Mercy for the afflicted from a faithful God	Triple acrostic
4:1–22	Fourth lament	Sin is the cause of the city's affliction	Acrostic
5:1–22	Fifth lament	After affliction, a prayer for God's mercy	Free verse

lament ends with a prayer or some other form of direct address to God. Yet the five laments also stand together as a full expression of Jerusalem's sorrow. The longest lament is in the middle—a triple acrostic with three verses for each letter of the Hebrew alphabet instead of just one—and expresses the heart of the book's message.

▌ Inferred literary intentions. The book is designed to achieve the following literary purposes:

- give artistic expression to the sorrows of the author's soul

- offer spiritual perspective on a national disaster

- demonstrate the justice of God in bringing his people to judgment

- depict the painful realities of that judgment in the effect that it has on individuals and the community

- cry for mercy by calling attention to the plight of God's suffering people

- offer hope to the grieving by reminding them of the faithfulness of God

- explore the purposes of God in a time of tragedy

- arrange all of this material in a highly artistic format

- embody the emotional meaning of the book in the form of lyric poetry

▌ Theological themes. (1) Sin: Lamentations makes it clear that Jerusalem is suffering for its sins, many of which are described in dramatic images. (2) Judgment: the sufferings of the book are all occasioned by the fact that God has condemned his people for their sins. (3) Mercy: the book at least hints at the consolation that weary sufferers may find in the tender mercies of a faithful God, which are new every morning.

▌ The book of Lamentations as a chapter in the master story of the Bible.
Lamentations is a book that touches the heart by showing the suffering that comes from falling under the judgment that sin deserves. Although Lamentations does not contain any specifically messianic prophecies, it eloquently anticipates the rejection and derision that Jesus suffered for his people. It also finds an echo in the lament that

Jesus offered for the very same city of Jerusalem (and for essentially the same reason) on the eve of his crucifixion (see Matt. 23:37-38).

Jerusalem in her desolation [chapter 1]. First the prophet (vv. 1–11) and then the city itself (vv. 12–22) lament the destruction that Jerusalem has suffered. There is a strong sense that they are eyewitnesses of the suffering they describe. Although the occasion of the city's suffering is not mentioned explicitly, it can only be the fall of Jerusalem after its long siege by the Babylonians. The main literary device is *personification: the poet portrays the city as a weeping woman—a royal princess—who has lost her children and become a slave. The *images all convey a sense of abandonment, loss, isolation, and grief. There are clear indications of what has happened to Jerusalem: siege, famine, invasion, death, defeat, looting, destruction, and deportation. The lyric also explains why all these things have happened: "the LORD has afflicted her for the multitude of her transgressions" (v. 5). Appropriately, then, the lament includes confession of sin (e.g., v. 20).

1 How lonely sits the city
    that was full of people!
How like a widow has she become,
    she who was great among the nations!
She who was a princess among the provinces
    has become a slave.

2 She weeps bitterly in the night,
    with tears on her cheeks;
among all her lovers
    she has none to comfort her;
all her friends have dealt treacherously with her;
    they have become her enemies.

3 Judah has gone into exile because of affliction
    and hard servitude;
she dwells now among the nations,
    but finds no resting place;
her pursuers have all overtaken her
    in the midst of her distress.[1]

4 The roads to Zion mourn,
    for none come to the festival;
all her gates are desolate;
    her priests groan;
her virgins have been afflicted,[2]
    and she herself suffers bitterly.

5 Her foes have become the head;
    her enemies prosper,
because the LORD has afflicted her
    for the multitude of her transgressions;

[1] Or in the narrow passes [2] Septuagint, Old Latin dragged away

her children have gone away,
  captives before the foe.

6   From the daughter of Zion
  all her majesty has departed.
Her princes have become like deer
  that find no pasture;
they fled without strength
  before the pursuer.

7   Jerusalem remembers
  in the days of her affliction and wandering
all the precious things
  that were hers from days of old.
When her people fell into the hand of the foe,
  and there was none to help her,
her foes gloated over her;
  they mocked at her downfall.

8   Jerusalem sinned grievously;
  therefore she became filthy;
all who honored her despise her,
  for they have seen her nakedness;
she herself groans
  and turns her face away.

9   Her uncleanness was in her skirts;
  she took no thought of her future;[1]
therefore her fall is terrible;
  she has no comforter.
"O Lord, behold my affliction,
  for the enemy has triumphed!"

10   The enemy has stretched out his hands
  over all her precious things;
for she has seen the nations
  enter her sanctuary,
those whom you forbade
  to enter your congregation.

11   All her people groan
  as they search for bread;
they trade their treasures for food
  to revive their strength.
"Look, O Lord, and see,
  for I am despised."

12   "Is it nothing to you, all you who pass by?
  Look and see
if there is any sorrow like my sorrow,

---

[1] Or end

which was brought upon me,
which the LORD inflicted
on the day of his fierce anger.

13 "From on high he sent fire;
into my bones[1] he made it descend;
he spread a net for my feet;
he turned me back;
he has left me stunned,
faint all the day long.

14 "My transgressions were bound[2] into a yoke;
by his hand they were fastened together;
they were set upon my neck;
he caused my strength to fail;
the Lord gave me into the hands
of those whom I cannot withstand.

15 "The Lord rejected
all my mighty men in my midst;
he summoned an assembly against me
to crush my young men;
the Lord has trodden as in a winepress
the virgin daughter of Judah.

16 "For these things I weep;
my eyes flow with tears;
for a comforter is far from me,
one to revive my spirit;
my children are desolate,
for the enemy has prevailed."

17 Zion stretches out her hands,
but there is none to comfort her;
the LORD has commanded against Jacob
that his neighbors should be his foes;
Jerusalem has become
a filthy thing among them.

18 "The LORD is in the right,
for I have rebelled against his word;
but hear, all you peoples,
and see my suffering;
my young women and my young men
have gone into captivity.

19 "I called to my lovers,
but they deceived me;
my priests and elders
perished in the city,

[1] Septuagint; Hebrew *bones and* [2] The meaning of the Hebrew is uncertain

while they sought food
    to revive their strength.

20 "Look, O LORD, for I am in distress;
    my stomach churns;
my heart is wrung within me,
    because I have been very rebellious.
In the street the sword bereaves;
    in the house it is like death.

21 "They heard[1] my groaning,
    yet there is no one to comfort me.
All my enemies have heard of my trouble;
    they are glad that you have done it.
You have brought[2] the day you announced;
    now let them be as I am.

22 "Let all their evildoing come before you,
    and deal with them
as you have dealt with me
    because of all my transgressions;
for my groans are many,
    and my heart is faint."

The desolation caused by divine judgment [chapter 2]. Jeremiah's second lament deals with many of the same sufferings as the first, with a deep sense of loss for all the things that are gone and will never come again. The prophet is not turning away from the sufferings of his people but continuing to lament them until he has given full expression to his grief and gained the understanding he seeks. The emphasis in the opening verses is on the anger of the Lord: he is the one who has brought all this suffering on Jerusalem, and thus he is portrayed as an enemy to his own people (see v. 5). The poet proceeds to document how this divine opposition has brought suffering to every member of society, from the king himself down to the littlest child dying in his mother's arms. A full recounting of woe is characteristic of the elegy as a literary form. Jeremiah ends by crying out to the Lord in prayer, hardly knowing how to intercede for his people but knowing that he must go to God with his distress. Although God is the one who has afflicted his people, he is also the only one who can help them.

2 How the Lord in his anger
    has set the daughter of Zion under a cloud!
He has cast down from heaven to earth
    the splendor of Israel;
he has not remembered his footstool
    in the day of his anger.

2 The Lord has swallowed up without mercy
    all the habitations of Jacob;
in his wrath he has broken down

---

[1] Septuagint, Syriac *Hear* [2] Syriac *Bring*

the strongholds of the daughter of Judah;
he has brought down to the ground in dishonor
the kingdom and its rulers.

³ He has cut down in fierce anger
all the might of Israel;
he has withdrawn from them his right hand
in the face of the enemy;
he has burned like a flaming fire in Jacob,
consuming all around.

⁴ He has bent his bow like an enemy,
with his right hand set like a foe;
and he has killed all who were delightful in our eyes
in the tent of the daughter of Zion;
he has poured out his fury like fire.

⁵ The Lord has become like an enemy;
he has swallowed up Israel;
he has swallowed up all its palaces;
he has laid in ruins its strongholds,
and he has multiplied in the daughter of Judah
mourning and lamentation.

⁶ He has laid waste his booth like a garden,
laid in ruins his meeting place;
the Lord has made Zion forget
festival and Sabbath,
and in his fierce indignation has spurned king and priest.

⁷ The Lord has scorned his altar,
disowned his sanctuary;
he has delivered into the hand of the enemy
the walls of her palaces;
they raised a clamor in the house of the Lord
as on the day of festival.

⁸ The Lord determined to lay in ruins
the wall of the daughter of Zion;
he stretched out the measuring line;
he did not restrain his hand from destroying;
he caused rampart and wall to lament;
they languished together.

⁹ Her gates have sunk into the ground;
he has ruined and broken her bars;
her king and princes are among the nations;
the law is no more,
and her prophets find
no vision from the Lord.

¹⁰ The elders of the daughter of Zion
    sit on the ground in silence;
they have thrown dust on their heads
    and put on sackcloth;
the young women of Jerusalem
    have bowed their heads to the ground.

¹¹ My eyes are spent with weeping;
    my stomach churns;
my bile is poured out to the ground
    because of the destruction of the daughter of my people,
because infants and babies faint
    in the streets of the city.

¹² They cry to their mothers,
    "Where is bread and wine?"
as they faint like a wounded man
    in the streets of the city,
as their life is poured out
    on their mothers' bosom.

¹³ What can I say for you, to what compare you,
    O daughter of Jerusalem?
What can I liken to you, that I may comfort you,
    O virgin daughter of Zion?
For your ruin is vast as the sea;
    who can heal you?

¹⁴ Your prophets have seen for you
    false and deceptive visions;
they have not exposed your iniquity
    to restore your fortunes,
but have seen for you oracles
    that are false and misleading.

¹⁵ All who pass along the way
    clap their hands at you;
they hiss and wag their heads
    at the daughter of Jerusalem:
"Is this the city that was called
    the perfection of beauty,
    the joy of all the earth?"

¹⁶ All your enemies
    rail against you;
they hiss, they gnash their teeth,
    they cry: "We have swallowed her!
Ah, this is the day we longed for;
    now we have it; we see it!"

17 The LORD has done what he purposed;
        he has carried out his word,
    which he commanded long ago;
        he has thrown down without pity;
    he has made the enemy rejoice over you
        and exalted the might of your foes.

18 Their heart cried to the Lord.
        O wall of the daughter of Zion,
    let tears stream down like a torrent
        day and night!
    Give yourself no rest,
        your eyes no respite!

19 "Arise, cry out in the night,
        at the beginning of the night watches!
    Pour out your heart like water
        before the presence of the Lord!
    Lift your hands to him
        for the lives of your children,
    who faint for hunger
        at the head of every street."

20 Look, O LORD, and see!
        With whom have you dealt thus?
    Should women eat the fruit of their womb,
        the children of their tender care?
    Should priest and prophet be killed
        in the sanctuary of the Lord?

21 In the dust of the streets
        lie the young and the old;
    my young women and my young men
        have fallen by the sword;
    you have killed them in the day of your anger,
        slaughtering without pity.

22 You summoned as if to a festival day
        my terrors on every side,
    and on the day of the anger of the LORD
        no one escaped or survived;
    those whom I held and raised
        my enemy destroyed.

From sorrow to hope [chapter 3]. This triple acrostic (three verses for each successive letter of the Hebrew alphabet, rather than just one) is longer than the other chapters and stands at the center of the book's message. Whereas the other laments express
the sorrows of the community as a whole, the third lament is intensely personal. From
the very first word it is apparent that in the context of the sufferings of his wider com-

munity, Jeremiah also wants to express his own personal woe: "I am the man who has seen affliction" (v. 1). While many of the circumstances described in this chapter could apply generally to Jerusalem, they closely match many of the experiences of the prophet himself (for comparison, see the book of Jeremiah), such as the Lord's refusal to hear his prayers (v. 8), the mockery he suffered from his contemporaries (v. 14), and his imprisonment in a cistern (vv. 52–54). The turning point in this lament and in Lamentations as a whole comes in verses 21–23, where the prophet begins to remember the steadfast love of his covenant God, whose mercies never come to an end. This well-known passage on the great faithfulness of God speaks with the greatest power when it is considered in its proper biblical context. Jeremiah experienced the morning-by-morning mercies of God while he was enduring the most excruciating sufferings that almost anyone can imagine. In remembering his God, the prophet gains a clearer and more complete understanding of God's sovereign purposes for the suffering of his people. In the verses that follow, therefore, he testifies to the mercy and justice of God and calls on his people to confess their sins, before calling on God to execute vengeance on his enemies.

3   I am the man who has seen affliction
       under the rod of his wrath;
2   he has driven and brought me
       into darkness without any light;
3   surely against me he turns his hand
       again and again the whole day long.

4   He has made my flesh and my skin waste away;
       he has broken my bones;
5   he has besieged and enveloped me
       with bitterness and tribulation;
6   he has made me dwell in darkness
       like the dead of long ago.

7   He has walled me about so that I cannot escape;
       he has made my chains heavy;
8   though I call and cry for help,
       he shuts out my prayer;
9   he has blocked my ways with blocks of stones;
       he has made my paths crooked.

10   He is a bear lying in wait for me,
       a lion in hiding;
11   he turned aside my steps and tore me to pieces;
       he has made me desolate;
12   he bent his bow and set me
       as a target for his arrow.

13   He drove into my kidneys
       the arrows of his quiver;
14   I have become the laughingstock of all peoples,
       the object of their taunts all day long.

15   He has filled me with bitterness;
       he has sated me with wormwood.

16   He has made my teeth grind on gravel,
       and made me cower in ashes;
17   my soul is bereft of peace;
       I have forgotten what happiness[1] is;
18   so I say, "My endurance has perished;
       so has my hope from the LORD."

19   Remember my affliction and my wanderings,
       the wormwood and the gall!
20   My soul continually remembers it
       and is bowed down within me.
21   But this I call to mind,
       and therefore I have hope:

22   The steadfast love of the LORD never ceases;[2]
       his mercies never come to an end;
23   they are new every morning;
       great is your faithfulness.
24   "The LORD is my portion," says my soul,
       "therefore I will hope in him."

25   The LORD is good to those who wait for him,
       to the soul who seeks him.
26   It is good that one should wait quietly
       for the salvation of the LORD.
27   It is good for a man that he bear
       the yoke in his youth.

28   Let him sit alone in silence
       when it is laid on him;
29   let him put his mouth in the dust—
       there may yet be hope;
30   let him give his cheek to the one who strikes,
       and let him be filled with insults.

31   For the Lord will not
       cast off forever,
32   but, though he cause grief, he will have compassion
       according to the abundance of his steadfast love;
33   for he does not willingly afflict
       or grieve the children of men.

34   To crush underfoot
       all the prisoners of the earth,
35   to deny a man justice
       in the presence of the Most High,

---

[1] Hebrew good [2] Syriac, Targum; Hebrew *Because of the steadfast love of the LORD, we are not cut off*

³⁶   to subvert a man in his lawsuit,
        the Lord does not approve.

³⁷   Who has spoken and it came to pass,
        unless the Lord has commanded it?
³⁸   Is it not from the mouth of the Most High
        that good and bad come?
³⁹   Why should a living man complain,
        a man, about the punishment of his sins?

⁴⁰   Let us test and examine our ways,
        and return to the LORD!
⁴¹   Let us lift up our hearts and hands
        to God in heaven:
⁴²   "We have transgressed and rebelled,
        and you have not forgiven.

⁴³   "You have wrapped yourself with anger and pursued us,
        killing without pity;
⁴⁴   you have wrapped yourself with a cloud
        so that no prayer can pass through.
⁴⁵   You have made us scum and garbage
        among the peoples.

⁴⁶   "All our enemies
        open their mouths against us;
⁴⁷   panic and pitfall have come upon us,
        devastation and destruction;
⁴⁸   my eyes flow with rivers of tears
        because of the destruction of the daughter of my people.

⁴⁹   "My eyes will flow without ceasing,
        without respite,
⁵⁰   until the LORD from heaven
        looks down and sees;
⁵¹   my eyes cause me grief
        at the fate of all the daughters of my city.

⁵²   "I have been hunted like a bird
        by those who were my enemies without cause;
⁵³   they flung me alive into the pit
        and cast stones on me;
⁵⁴   water closed over my head;
        I said, 'I am lost.'

⁵⁵   "I called on your name, O LORD,
        from the depths of the pit;
⁵⁶   you heard my plea, 'Do not close
        your ear to my cry for help!'

⁵⁷   You came near when I called on you;
        you said, 'Do not fear!'

⁵⁸   "You have taken up my cause, O Lord;
        you have redeemed my life.
⁵⁹   You have seen the wrong done to me, O Lᴏʀᴅ;
        judge my cause.
⁶⁰   You have seen all their vengeance,
        all their plots against me.

⁶¹   "You have heard their taunts, O Lᴏʀᴅ,
        all their plots against me.
⁶²   The lips and thoughts of my assailants
        are against me all the day long.
⁶³   Behold their sitting and their rising;
        I am the object of their taunts.

⁶⁴   "You will repay them,¹ O Lᴏʀᴅ,
        according to the work of their hands.
⁶⁵   You will give them² dullness of heart;
        your curse will be³ on them.
⁶⁶   You will pursue them⁴ in anger and destroy them
        from under your heavens, O Lᴏʀᴅ."⁵

The desolation brought by Judah's sin [chapter 4]. Once again the prophet takes up a lament, grieving that Jerusalem's gold has become dim. The fourth lament is notable for its horrific poetic description of famine in the streets of the city (vv. 3–10). Once again, the cause of this suffering is identified as the sin of God's people (e.g., vv. 11, 22). Here the blame is laid squarely at the feet of Judah's leaders: its prophets and priests (vv. 12–16) and also its kings, who vainly tried to save the nation by establishing unholy alliances with godless nations (vv. 17–20). The chapter ends with one of the book's few signs of hope: Judah's exile will not last forever; one day it will come to an end (v. 22).

---

4   How the gold has grown dim,
        how the pure gold is changed!
    The holy stones lie scattered
        at the head of every street.

²   The precious sons of Zion,
        worth their weight in fine gold,
    how they are regarded as earthen pots,
        the work of a potter's hands!

³   Even jackals offer the breast;
        they nurse their young,
    but the daughter of my people has become cruel,
        like the ostriches in the wilderness.

---

¹ Or *Repay them* ² Or *Give them* ³ Or *place your curse* ⁴ Or *Pursue them* ⁵ Syriac (compare Septuagint, Vulgate); Hebrew *the heavens of the Lᴏʀᴅ*

4 The tongue of the nursing infant sticks
        to the roof of its mouth for thirst;
    the children beg for food,
        but no one gives to them.

5 Those who once feasted on delicacies
        perish in the streets;
    those who were brought up in purple
        embrace ash heaps.

6 For the chastisement[1] of the daughter of my people has been greater
        than the punishment[2] of Sodom,
    which was overthrown in a moment,
        and no hands were wrung for her.[3]

7 Her princes were purer than snow,
        whiter than milk;
    their bodies were more ruddy than coral,
        the beauty of their form[4] was like sapphire.[5]

8 Now their face is blacker than soot;
        they are not recognized in the streets;
    their skin has shriveled on their bones;
        it has become as dry as wood.

9 Happier were the victims of the sword
        than the victims of hunger,
    who wasted away, pierced
        by lack of the fruits of the field.

10 The hands of compassionate women
        have boiled their own children;
    they became their food
        during the destruction of the daughter of my people.

11 The Lord gave full vent to his wrath;
        he poured out his hot anger,
    and he kindled a fire in Zion
        that consumed its foundations.

12 The kings of the earth did not believe,
        nor any of the inhabitants of the world,
    that foe or enemy could enter
        the gates of Jerusalem.

13 This was for the sins of her prophets
        and the iniquities of her priests,
    who shed in the midst of her
        the blood of the righteous.

---

[1] Or *iniquity* [2] Or *sin* [3] The meaning of the Hebrew is uncertain [4] The meaning of the Hebrew is uncertain [5] Hebrew *lapis lazuli*

14 They wandered, blind, through the streets;
      they were so defiled with blood
    that no one was able to touch
      their garments.

15 "Away! Unclean!" people cried at them.
      "Away! Away! Do not touch!"
    So they became fugitives and wanderers;
      people said among the nations,
      "They shall stay with us no longer."

16 The LORD himself[1] has scattered them;
      he will regard them no more;
    no honor was shown to the priests,
      no favor to the elders.

17 Our eyes failed, ever watching
      vainly for help;
    in our watching we watched
      for a nation which could not save.

18 They dogged our steps
      so that we could not walk in our streets;
    our end drew near; our days were numbered,
      for our end had come.

19 Our pursuers were swifter
      than the eagles in the heavens;
    they chased us on the mountains;
      they lay in wait for us in the wilderness.

20 The breath of our nostrils, the LORD's anointed,
      was captured in their pits,
    of whom we said, "Under his shadow
      we shall live among the nations."

21 Rejoice and be glad, O daughter of Edom,
      you who dwell in the land of Uz;
    but to you also the cup shall pass;
      you shall become drunk and strip yourself bare.

22 The punishment of your iniquity, O daughter of Zion, is accomplished;
      he will keep you in exile no longer;[2]
    but your iniquity, O daughter of Edom, he will punish;
      he will uncover your sins.

A desperate cry for mercy [chapter 5]. Unlike the other poems in Lamentations, the last lament is not an acrostic. Perhaps this is a sign that in his sorrow Jeremiah has lost some of his composure. Unable or unwilling to complete the formal literary composition he originally intended, he can only pour out his soul to God in prayer, interceding

---

[1] Hebrew *The face of the LORD* [2] Or *he will not exile you again*

for restoration and renewal. The seeming disorder of the lament mirrors the distress of the poet's own soul and the disaster that has befallen the city he loves. Here is a prayer of desperation—a cry for God's mercy when every other source of help has failed. The writer appeals for God to remember his people and then soberly recounts all of the woes they have suffered: military occupation, bereavement, dehydration, starvation, poverty, slavery, rape, and every other imaginable humiliation (vv. 2–13). With poignant images of loss, he describes the lonely, empty, joyless city that is left behind (vv. 14–18). He again acknowledges that all of this suffering is fully deserved: "Woe to us, for we have sinned!" (v. 16). Yet Jeremiah hopes against hope that God will not forget his people forever. His lamentations end with an unresolved question that can be answered only in the full context of Scripture: Has God utterly rejected his people, or will he again show mercy?

5 Remember, O Lord, what has befallen us;
   look, and see our disgrace!
2 Our inheritance has been turned over to strangers,
      our homes to foreigners.
3 We have become orphans, fatherless;
      our mothers are like widows.
4 We must pay for the water we drink;
      the wood we get must be bought.
5 Our pursuers are at our necks;[1]
      we are weary; we are given no rest.
6 We have given the hand to Egypt, and to Assyria,
      to get bread enough.
7 Our fathers sinned, and are no more;
      and we bear their iniquities.
8 Slaves rule over us;
      there is none to deliver us from their hand.
9 We get our bread at the peril of our lives,
      because of the sword in the wilderness.
10 Our skin is hot as an oven
      with the burning heat of famine.
11 Women are raped in Zion,
      young women in the towns of Judah.
12 Princes are hung up by their hands;
      no respect is shown to the elders.
13 Young men are compelled to grind at the mill,
      and boys stagger under loads of wood.
14 The old men have left the city gate,
      the young men their music.
15 The joy of our hearts has ceased;
      our dancing has been turned to mourning.
16 The crown has fallen from our head;
      woe to us, for we have sinned!
17 For this our heart has become sick,
      for these things our eyes have grown dim,

[1] Symmachus With a yoke on our necks

¹⁸   for Mount Zion which lies desolate;
        jackals prowl over it.
¹⁹   But you, O LORD, reign forever;
        your throne endures to all generations.
²⁰   Why do you forget us forever,
        why do you forsake us for so many days?
²¹   Restore us to yourself, O LORD, that we may be restored!
        Renew our days as of old—
²²   unless you have utterly rejected us,
        and you remain exceedingly angry with us.

EZEKIEL

The book at a glance. 48 chapters, 1,273 verses. The two most important things that we need to know about the book of Ezekiel are that it is *visionary writing and that it is an anthology of numerous individual units. Despite the far-flung fantasies of the author's visions, it would be wrong to conclude that the book is unrelated to real life. Its author was a real-life person—a married man (24:15–18) living in a house of his own (3:24; 8:1). He was both a priest and a prophet. In 597 B.C. he was exiled to Babylon, where he received his prophetic call (1:1–3) and composed the anthology that became the Old Testament book that bears his name. Ezekiel was about the same age as Daniel, and as a teenager he would have witnessed Jeremiah's impressive career as a prophet in Jerusalem. The book that Ezekiel wrote often baffles modern readers, but the keys that will unlock its conventions are readily available, and in fact the kaleidoscope of visions is reminiscent of special effects in modern movies and other video productions.

▌**Format.** The book of Ezekiel is one of the most complex books in the Bible because so many different *genres converge in it. It is important to grasp right at the start that this book is an anthology (collection) of separate pieces of writing. There is no single story line; the unity is simply that of a collection. The general arrangement of the material in the anthology is one that several other OT prophetic books also follow—a general movement from (1) oracles of judgment against the prophet's own nation of Judah (usually called Israel in the text), through (2) oracles of judgment against the surrounding pagan nations, to (3) oracles of future eschatological blessing on those who believe in God (called Israel in the text, but we need to remember that in the NT era God's promises to Israel find their fulfillment in the church as the Israel of God).

▌**Genres.** A good starting point is *visionary writing, which transports us to a world of the imagination where the rules of reality in our world are obviously suspended in favor of *fantasy. To understand and relish the book of Ezekiel, we often need to abandon expectations of realism. Second, Ezekiel employs a technique known as *symbolic reality, which occurs when a writer consistently transports us to a world of the imagination where the most important ingredients are symbols—for example, a vine or a boiling pot or a valley with dry bones. Third, *prophecy is itself a genre, made up of oracles (pronouncements from God through the agency of a prophet) that fall into two main categories—*oracles of judgment and *oracles of blessing. Oracles of judgment are ordinarily examples of *satire, and in the prophetic satire of Ezekiel we find three motifs: (1) description of evil, (2) denunciation of this evil, and 3) warnings and

Passage	Content	Timeline in Future History	Prophetic Scope	Type of Oracle	Time in National History
1:1–3:27	Call of the prophet				
4:1–7:27	Coming siege of Jerusalem	Present and imminent events	Fate of Judah	Visions of judgment	Before the fall of Jerusalem
8:1–11:25	Visions of the evil of Jerusalem				
12:1–24:27	Oracles of judgment				
25:1–32:32	Judgment against seven neighboring nations	Events somewhat in the future	Fate of the nations	Visions of judgment	After the fall of Jerusalem
33:1–39:29	Israel's restoration				
40:1–47:12	Visions of a new temple and worship	Final, end-times events	Future destiny of God's people	Visions of blessing	
47:13–48:35	Resettling of the Promised Land				

predictions that God will judge the evil. Prophecy often merges with *apocalyptic writing, which portrays eschatological events at the end of history. Finally, we should not overlook the obvious—the prophet Ezekiel expresses himself in the form of *poetry. (For more information on items accompanied by an asterisk, see the glossary at the back of this Bible.)

▌**Unifying elements.** God is the central character of the book. His authoritative voice lies behind the visions and oracles. He is the one who exercises judgment and blessing. The main human character is the mediator-prophet Ezekiel, who emerges as a vivid character in his own right. The story behind the oracles is that of a great conflict between good and evil and the final triumph of good and defeat of evil. The setting for the action is the region that surrounds the eastern half of the Mediterranean Sea. In the first half of the book, Judah's capital city Jerusalem is the main setting, while in the middle of the book the scope becomes international.

▌**Tips for reading Ezekiel.** As already hinted, the first prerequisite for understanding what is happening in Ezekiel is to abandon all expectations of realism. We should give ourselves to the sheer strangeness of what is presented. Ezekiel talks about real, historical events, but much of the time he does not portray these events in literal terms. Instead he prefers the fantastic as his mode. Additionally, we need to be ready for a kaleidoscope of details, always shifting and never in focus for very long. The best approach to the oracles of judgment is to analyze them according to the usual rules of satire.

▌**Inferred literary intentions.** The book is designed to achieve the following literary purposes:

- transport us to a world of the imagination that often uses the techniques of fantasy rather than literal realism

- satirically attack vice and evil

- embody much of the meaning in symbols

- employ the "strange world" motif (techniques of dislocation) as a way of subverting our complacency and our assumption that life as we experience it is normal or good

- warn us of God's judgment against sin

- instill hope in those who heed the prophet's call to repentance and obedience

▌**Theological themes.** (1) Human sinfulness, both individual and corporate: the first half of the book is an ever-expanding picture of evil, accompanied by "program notes" that state what God intends to do about the situation. (2) Judgment: prophetic books are always a delineation of God's pending judgment against evil. (3) Covenant: the implied context for both the judgment against Judah/Israel and its future restoration is the covenant relationship that God has with his people. (4) Salvation, including final redemption at the end of history: God is shown to be a God whose ultimate desire is to redeem those who trust in him. (5) Eschatology: the final fourth of the book gives us images of the end times.

▌**Ezekiel as a chapter in the master story of the Bible.** OT history is the history of a nation. There were many crucial milestones in the history of that nation, including the exile of Judah in Babylon. The book of Ezekiel is one of many prophetic books that tell the story of that exile—its causes, the events that led up to it, the destruction of Jerusalem, the life of the exiles in Babylon, and the hope for eventual restoration to the homeland. This covenant history takes place within the arena of a great conflict between good and evil for the soul of a nation and individuals. Further, the "big story" of the Bible as a whole has an *eschaton* or end, and the final movement of the book of Ezekiel tells the story of the end times. Additionally, a book as large as Ezekiel naturally includes numerous messianic prophecies.

Ezekiel's vision of a divine chariot [chapter 1]. This chapter is one of the imaginative flourishes of the Bible. The vision that the prophet shares with us uses the techniques of fantasy to whisk us away to a strange world that we imagine rather than visit in person. Following a narrative lead-in that situates the prophet in an actual place in Babylon (vv. 1–3), we are dazzled with a detailed description of a supernatural chariot. At the same time, we are initiated into the technique of symbolic reality. In this technique, the phenomena that the writer places before us are not realistic or lifelike but rather symbolic objects, such as creatures and a chariot that cannot even be fully pictured but that symbolize something (in this case, divine presence). The overall reality that is portrayed with a wealth of fantastic details is God's supernatural presence, majesty, and power. The individual details contribute toward the general sense of the supernatural mystery of God's being and should probably not be pressed into the service of specific meanings. It is the general effect of the vision that matters.

1 In the thirtieth year, in the fourth month, on the fifth day of the month, as I was among the exiles by the Chebar canal, the heavens were opened, and I saw visions of God.[1] [2]On the fifth day of the month (it was the fifth year of the exile of King Jehoiachin), [3]the word of the LORD came to Ezekiel the priest, the son of Buzi, in the land of the Chaldeans by the Chebar canal, and the hand of the LORD was upon him there.

[4]As I looked, behold, a stormy wind came out of the north, and a great cloud, with brightness around it, and fire flashing forth continually, and in the midst of the fire, as it were gleaming metal.[2] [5]And from the midst of it came the likeness of four living creatures. And this was their appearance: they had a human likeness, [6]but each had four faces, and each of them had four wings. [7]Their legs were straight, and the soles of their feet were like the sole of a calf's foot. And they sparkled like burnished bronze. [8]Under their wings on their four sides they had human hands. And the four had their faces and their wings thus: [9]their wings touched one another. Each one of them went straight forward, without turning as they went. [10]As for the likeness of their faces, each had a human face. The four had the face of a lion on the right side, the four had the face of an ox on the left side, and the four had the face of an eagle. [11]Such were their faces. And their wings were spread out above. Each creature had two wings, each of which touched the wing of another, while two covered their bodies. [12]And each went straight forward. Wherever the spirit would go, they went, without turning as they went. [13]As for the likeness of the living creatures, their appearance was like burning coals of fire, like the appearance of torches moving to and fro among the living creatures. And the fire was bright, and out of the fire went forth lightning. [14]And the living creatures darted to and fro, like the appearance of a flash of lightning.

[15]Now as I looked at the living creatures, I saw a wheel on the earth beside the living creatures, one for each of the four of them.[3] [16]As for the appearance of the wheels and their construction: their appearance was like the gleaming of beryl. And the four had the same likeness, their appearance and construction being as it were a wheel within a wheel. [17]When they went, they went in any of their four directions[4] without turning as they went. [18]And their rims were tall and awesome, and the rims of all four were full of eyes all around. [19]And when the living creatures went, the wheels went beside them; and when the living creatures rose from the earth, the wheels rose. [20]Wherever the spirit wanted to go, they went, and the wheels rose along with them, for the spirit of the living creatures[5] was in the wheels. [21]When those went, these went; and when those stood, these stood; and when those rose from the earth, the wheels rose along with them, for the spirit of the living creatures was in the wheels.

[22]Over the heads of the living creatures there was the likeness of an expanse, shining like awe-inspiring crystal, spread out above their heads. [23]And under the expanse their wings were stretched out straight, one toward another. And each creature had two wings covering its body. [24]And when they went, I heard the sound of their wings like the sound of many waters, like the sound of the Almighty, a sound of tumult like the sound of an army. When they stood still, they let down their wings. [25]And there

---

[1] Or from God [2] Or amber; also verse 27 [3] Hebrew of their faces [4] Hebrew on their four sides [5] Or the spirit of life; also verse 21

came a voice from above the expanse over their heads. When they stood still, they let down their wings.

²⁶And above the expanse over their heads there was the likeness of a throne, in appearance like sapphire;¹ and seated above the likeness of a throne was a likeness with a human appearance. ²⁷And upward from what had the appearance of his waist I saw as it were gleaming metal, like the appearance of fire enclosed all around. And downward from what had the appearance of his waist I saw as it were the appearance of fire, and there was brightness around him.² ²⁸Like the appearance of the bow that is in the cloud on the day of rain, so was the appearance of the brightness all around.

Such was the appearance of the likeness of the glory of the LORD. And when I saw it, I fell on my face, and I heard the voice of one speaking.

The call of the prophet [chapters 2–3]. The call of the prophet is an important OT genre, and we experience a notable example in these two chapters. The prophetic books often have an important biographical element in them, and we find biographical material in the story of the commissioning of Ezekiel to his prophetic vocation. The chief ingredients of this calling story are as follows: God's command to Ezekiel to be his fearless spokesman (2:1–7); the prophet's eating of a scroll, symbolic of his full acceptance of God's message on the scroll, which is a message of judgment (2:8–3:3); God's command to Ezekiel to proclaim his word to the house of Israel in exile, along with the effect that this had on the prophet (3:4–15); specific directives from God regarding the content and delivery of Ezekiel's prophetic message (3:16–21); the prophet's enforced silence as an external symbol of Israel's refusal to heed God's word (3:22–27). At this early point, we are still being initiated into the book, as we are introduced to such things as the visionary and symbolic mode of the book, the character of the prophet (especially his role as God's spokesman), the world that the prophet inhabits, and the nature and content of the prophet's mission to his nation. We should note the evidences of God's initiative in what is happening in the narrative and the ways in which our ordinary assumptions about reality are continuously subverted by the heavily supernatural and miraculous nature of the world that we enter as we read.

2 And he said to me, "Son of man,³ stand on your feet, and I will speak with you." ²And as he spoke to me, the Spirit entered into me and set me on my feet, and I heard him speaking to me. ³And he said to me, "Son of man, I send you to the people of Israel, to nations of rebels, who have rebelled against me. They and their fathers have transgressed against me to this very day. ⁴The descendants also are impudent and stubborn: I send you to them, and you shall say to them, 'Thus says the Lord GOD.' ⁵And whether they hear or refuse to hear (for they are a rebellious house) they will know that a prophet has been among them. ⁶And you, son of man, be not afraid of them, nor be afraid of their words, though briers and thorns are with you and you sit on scorpions.⁴ Be not afraid of their words, nor be dismayed at their looks, for they are a rebellious house. ⁷And you shall speak my words to them, whether they hear or refuse to hear, for they are a rebellious house.

⁸"But you, son of man, hear what I say to you. Be not rebellious like that rebellious house; open your mouth and eat what I give you." ⁹And when I looked, behold, a hand was stretched out to me, and behold, a scroll of a book was in it. ¹⁰And he

---

¹ Or lapis lazuli ² Or it ³ Or Son of Adam; so throughout Ezekiel ⁴ Or on scorpion plants

spread it before me. And it had writing on the front and on the back, and there were written on it words of lamentation and mourning and woe.

3 And he said to me, "Son of man, eat whatever you find here. Eat this scroll, and go, speak to the house of Israel." ²So I opened my mouth, and he gave me this scroll to eat. ³And he said to me, "Son of man, feed your belly with this scroll that I give you and fill your stomach with it." Then I ate it, and it was in my mouth as sweet as honey.

⁴And he said to me, "Son of man, go to the house of Israel and speak with my words to them. ⁵For you are not sent to a people of foreign speech and a hard language, but to the house of Israel— ⁶not to many peoples of foreign speech and a hard language, whose words you cannot understand. Surely, if I sent you to such, they would listen to you. ⁷But the house of Israel will not be willing to listen to you, for they are not willing to listen to me: because all the house of Israel have a hard forehead and a stubborn heart. ⁸Behold, I have made your face as hard as their faces, and your forehead as hard as their foreheads. ⁹Like emery harder than flint have I made your forehead. Fear them not, nor be dismayed at their looks, for they are a rebellious house." ¹⁰Moreover, he said to me, "Son of man, all my words that I shall speak to you receive in your heart, and hear with your ears. ¹¹And go to the exiles, to your people, and speak to them and say to them, 'Thus says the Lord God,' whether they hear or refuse to hear."

¹²Then the Spirit[1] lifted me up, and I heard behind me the voice[2] of a great earthquake: "Blessed be the glory of the Lord from its place!" ¹³It was the sound of the wings of the living creatures as they touched one another, and the sound of the wheels beside them, and the sound of a great earthquake. ¹⁴The Spirit lifted me up and took me away, and I went in bitterness in the heat of my spirit, the hand of the Lord being strong upon me. ¹⁵And I came to the exiles at Tel-abib, who were dwelling by the Chebar canal, and I sat where they were dwelling.[3] And I sat there overwhelmed among them seven days.

¹⁶And at the end of seven days, the word of the Lord came to me: ¹⁷"Son of man, I have made you a watchman for the house of Israel. Whenever you hear a word from my mouth, you shall give them warning from me. ¹⁸If I say to the wicked, 'You shall surely die,' and you give him no warning, nor speak to warn the wicked from his wicked way, in order to save his life, that wicked person shall die for[4] his iniquity, but his blood I will require at your hand. ¹⁹But if you warn the wicked, and he does not turn from his wickedness, or from his wicked way, he shall die for his iniquity, but you will have delivered your soul. ²⁰Again, if a righteous person turns from his righteousness and commits injustice, and I lay a stumbling block before him, he shall die. Because you have not warned him, he shall die for his sin, and his righteous deeds that he has done shall not be remembered, but his blood I will require at your hand. ²¹But if you warn the righteous person not to sin, and he does not sin, he shall surely live, because he took warning, and you will have delivered your soul."

²²And the hand of the Lord was upon me there. And he said to me, "Arise, go out into the valley,[5] and there I will speak with you." ²³So I arose and went out into the valley, and behold, the glory of the Lord stood there, like the glory that I had seen by the Chebar canal, and I fell on my face. ²⁴But the Spirit entered into me and set me on my feet, and he spoke with me and said to me, "Go, shut yourself within your house. ²⁵And

---

[1] Or the wind; also verse 14 [2] Or sound [3] Or Chebar, and to where they dwelt [4] Or in; also verses 19, 20 [5] Or plain; also verse 23

you, O son of man, behold, cords will be placed upon you, and you shall be bound with them, so that you cannot go out among the people. ²⁶And I will make your tongue cling to the roof of your mouth, so that you shall be mute and unable to reprove them, for they are a rebellious house. ²⁷But when I speak with you, I will open your mouth, and you shall say to them, 'Thus says the Lord GOD.' He who will hear, let him hear; and he who will refuse to hear, let him refuse, for they are a rebellious house.

> **Symbolic acts of the prophet** [4:1–5:4]. Ezekiel's initial prophetic tasks are strangeness personified, consisting of a series of symbolic or parabolic acts that God tells him to perform. We should relive the events in our imagination and then ponder what interpretation Ezekiel and his neighbors might have given to the strange behavior. Additionally, we should note that that the common denominator of Ezekiel's actions is that they pertain to an impending siege and destruction of Jerusalem, which in this context is a symbolic city representing the whole nation of Judah, and beyond that sinful humanity as it exists anytime, anywhere.

4 "And you, son of man, take a brick and lay it before you, and engrave on it a city, even Jerusalem. ²And put siegeworks against it, and build a siege wall against it, and cast up a mound against it. Set camps also against it, and plant battering rams against it all around. ³And you, take an iron griddle, and place it as an iron wall between you and the city; and set your face toward it, and let it be in a state of siege, and press the siege against it. This is a sign for the house of Israel.

⁴"Then lie on your left side, and place the punishment¹ of the house of Israel upon it. For the number of the days that you lie on it, you shall bear their punishment. ⁵For I assign to you a number of days, 390 days, equal to the number of the years of their punishment. So long shall you bear the punishment of the house of Israel. ⁶And when you have completed these, you shall lie down a second time, but on your right side, and bear the punishment of the house of Judah. Forty days I assign you, a day for each year. ⁷And you shall set your face toward the siege of Jerusalem, with your arm bared, and you shall prophesy against the city. ⁸And behold, I will place cords upon you, so that you cannot turn from one side to the other, till you have completed the days of your siege.

⁹"And you, take wheat and barley, beans and lentils, millet and emmer,² and put them into a single vessel and make your bread from them. During the number of days that you lie on your side, 390 days, you shall eat it. ¹⁰And your food that you eat shall be by weight, twenty shekels³ a day; from day to day⁴ you shall eat it. ¹¹And water you shall drink by measure, the sixth part of a hin;⁵ from day to day you shall drink. ¹²And you shall eat it as a barley cake, baking it in their sight on human dung." ¹³And the LORD said, "Thus shall the people of Israel eat their bread unclean, among the nations where I will drive them." ¹⁴Then I said, "Ah, Lord GOD! Behold, I have never defiled myself.⁶ From my youth up till now I have never eaten what died of itself or was torn by beasts, nor has tainted meat come into my mouth." ¹⁵Then he said to me, "See, I assign to you cow's dung instead of human dung, on which you may prepare your bread." ¹⁶Moreover, he said to me, "Son of man, behold, I will break the supply⁷ of bread in Jerusalem. They shall eat bread by weight and with anxiety, and they shall drink water by measure and in dismay. ¹⁷I will do this that they may

---

¹ Or *iniquity*; also verses 5, 6, 17 ² A type of wheat ³ A *shekel* was about 2/5 ounce or 11 grams ⁴ Or *at a set time daily*; also verse 11 ⁵ A *hin* was about 4 quarts or 3.5 liters ⁶ Hebrew *my soul* (or *throat*) *has never been made unclean* ⁷ Hebrew *staff*

lack bread and water, and look at one another in dismay, and rot away because of their punishment.

5 "And you, O son of man, take a sharp sword. Use it as a barber's razor and pass it over your head and your beard. Then take balances for weighing and divide the hair. ²A third part you shall burn in the fire in the midst of the city, when the days of the siege are completed. And a third part you shall take and strike with the sword all around the city. And a third part you shall scatter to the wind, and I will unsheathe the sword after them. ³And you shall take from these a small number and bind them in the skirts of your robe. ⁴And of these again you shall take some and cast them into the midst of the fire and burn them in the fire. From there a fire will come out into all the house of Israel.

God's word of judgment [5:5–17]. After the series of symbolic prophetic acts, God now pronounces his judgment in the form of words. Surprisingly, God does not tell Ezekiel to pronounce this judgment to the public. Rather, here God is treating his prophet as a confidant. God's address to Ezekiel mingles two subjects—the punishment that he is about to send on Judah and brief descriptions of the offenses that are being punished.

⁵"Thus says the Lord God: This is Jerusalem. I have set her in the center of the nations, with countries all around her. ⁶And she has rebelled against my rules by doing wickedness more than the nations, and against my statutes more than the countries all around her; for they have rejected my rules and have not walked in my statutes. ⁷Therefore thus says the Lord God: Because you are more turbulent than the nations that are all around you, and have not walked in my statutes or obeyed my rules, and have not[1] even acted according to the rules of the nations that are all around you, ⁸therefore thus says the Lord God: Behold, I, even I, am against you. And I will execute judgments[2] in your midst in the sight of the nations. ⁹And because of all your abominations I will do with you what I have never yet done, and the like of which I will never do again. ¹⁰Therefore fathers shall eat their sons in your midst, and sons shall eat their fathers. And I will execute judgments on you, and any of you who survive I will scatter to all the winds. ¹¹Therefore, as I live, declares the Lord God, surely, because you have defiled my sanctuary with all your detestable things and with all your abominations, therefore I will withdraw.[3] My eye will not spare, and I will have no pity. ¹²A third part of you shall die of pestilence and be consumed with famine in your midst; a third part shall fall by the sword all around you; and a third part I will scatter to all the winds and will unsheathe the sword after them.

¹³"Thus shall my anger spend itself, and I will vent my fury upon them and satisfy myself. And they shall know that I am the Lord—that I have spoken in my jealousy— when I spend my fury upon them. ¹⁴Moreover, I will make you a desolation and an object of reproach among the nations all around you and in the sight of all who pass by. ¹⁵You shall be[4] a reproach and a taunt, a warning and a horror, to the nations all around you, when I execute judgments on you in anger and fury, and with furious rebukes—I am the Lord; I have spoken— ¹⁶when I send against you[5] the deadly arrows of famine, arrows for destruction, which I will send to destroy you, and when

---

[1] Some Hebrew manuscripts and Syriac lack *not* [2] The same Hebrew expression can mean *obey rules*, or *execute judgments*, depending on the context [3] Some Hebrew manuscripts *I will cut you down* [4] Dead Sea Scroll, Septuagint, Syriac, Vulgate, Targum; Masoretic Text *And it shall be* [5] Hebrew *them*

I bring more and more famine upon you and break your supply[1] of bread. [17]I will send famine and wild beasts against you, and they will rob you of your children. Pestilence and blood shall pass through you, and I will bring the sword upon you. I am the LORD; I have spoken."

An oracle of judgment [chapter 6]. Beginning with the stock prophetic formula "The word of the LORD came to me" (v. 1), this chapter records three oracles that God "says" (vv. 3, 11) to the prophet, as follows: a prediction of how God will destroy Judah's idolatrous high places and the people who worship there (vv. 3–7); God's prediction that he will save a remnant who will remember God in exile (vv. 8–10); a repetition of the prediction of calamity that is about to occur (vv. 11–14). Whereas usually the reason for God's judgment in the prophetic books is the people's sinfulness, in this passage the reason that is stated four times is that the people "shall know that I am the LORD" (vv. 7, 10, 13, 14).

6 The word of the LORD came to me: [2]"Son of man, set your face toward the mountains of Israel, and prophesy against them, [3]and say, You mountains of Israel, hear the word of the Lord GOD! Thus says the Lord GOD to the mountains and the hills, to the ravines and the valleys: Behold, I, even I, will bring a sword upon you, and I will destroy your high places. [4]Your altars shall become desolate, and your incense altars shall be broken, and I will cast down your slain before your idols. [5]And I will lay the dead bodies of the people of Israel before their idols, and I will scatter your bones around your altars. [6]Wherever you dwell, the cities shall be waste and the high places ruined, so that your altars will be waste and ruined,[2] your idols broken and destroyed, your incense altars cut down, and your works wiped out. [7]And the slain shall fall in your midst, and you shall know that I am the LORD.

[8]"Yet I will leave some of you alive. When you have among the nations some who escape the sword, and when you are scattered through the countries, [9]then those of you who escape will remember me among the nations where they are carried captive, how I have been broken over their whoring heart that has departed from me and over their eyes that go whoring after their idols. And they will be loathsome in their own sight for the evils that they have committed, for all their abominations. [10]And they shall know that I am the LORD. I have not said in vain that I would do this evil to them."

[11]Thus says the Lord GOD: "Clap your hands and stamp your foot and say, Alas, because of all the evil abominations of the house of Israel, for they shall fall by the sword, by famine, and by pestilence. [12]He who is far off shall die of pestilence, and he who is near shall fall by the sword, and he who is left and is preserved shall die of famine. Thus I will spend my fury upon them. [13]And you shall know that I am the LORD, when their slain lie among their idols around their altars, on every high hill, on all the mountaintops, under every green tree, and under every leafy oak, wherever they offered pleasing aroma to all their idols. [14]And I will stretch out my hand against them and make the land desolate and waste, in all their dwelling places, from the wilderness to Riblah.[3] Then they will know that I am the LORD."

A climactic oracle of judgment [chapter 7]. The brief predictions of coming disaster in the preceding two chapters now expand into a horror story of vivid pictures of a day

---

[1] Hebrew *staff* [2] Or *and punished* [3] Some Hebrew manuscripts; most Hebrew manuscripts *Diblah*

of tumult (v. 7) and a day of doom (v. 10). As we read the chapter, we relive a future-tense story of the complete collapse of a nation under God's wrath and external assaults (v. 15 speaks aphoristically of the sword without and pestilence and famine within). Intermingled with the dominant motif of pictures of destruction are brief indictments explaining what has activated God's judgment. We need to let the pictures sink into our imagination and ponder what meanings the pictures and symbols embody, along with application to our own situation.

7 The word of the LORD came to me: ²"And you, O son of man, thus says the Lord GOD to the land of Israel: An end! The end has come upon the four corners of the land.¹ ³Now the end is upon you, and I will send my anger upon you; I will judge you according to your ways, and I will punish you for all your abominations. ⁴And my eye will not spare you, nor will I have pity, but I will punish you for your ways, while your abominations are in your midst. Then you will know that I am the LORD.

⁵"Thus says the Lord GOD: Disaster after disaster!² Behold, it comes. ⁶An end has come; the end has come; it has awakened against you. Behold, it comes. ⁷Your doom³ has come to you, O inhabitant of the land. The time has come; the day is near, a day of tumult, and not of joyful shouting on the mountains. ⁸Now I will soon pour out my wrath upon you, and spend my anger against you, and judge you according to your ways, and I will punish you for all your abominations. ⁹And my eye will not spare, nor will I have pity. I will punish you according to your ways, while your abominations are in your midst. Then you will know that I am the LORD, who strikes.

¹⁰"Behold, the day! Behold, it comes! Your doom has come; the rod has blossomed; pride has budded. ¹¹Violence has grown up into a rod of wickedness. None of them shall remain, nor their abundance, nor their wealth; neither shall there be preeminence among them.⁴ ¹²The time has come; the day has arrived. Let not the buyer rejoice, nor the seller mourn, for wrath is upon all their multitude.⁵ ¹³For the seller shall not return to what he has sold, while they live. For the vision concerns all their multitude; it shall not turn back; and because of his iniquity, none can maintain his life.⁶

¹⁴"They have blown the trumpet and made everything ready, but none goes to battle, for my wrath is upon all their multitude. ¹⁵The sword is without; pestilence and famine are within. He who is in the field dies by the sword, and him who is in the city famine and pestilence devour. ¹⁶And if any survivors escape, they will be on the mountains, like doves of the valleys, all of them moaning, each one over his iniquity. ¹⁷All hands are feeble, and all knees turn to water. ¹⁸They put on sackcloth, and horror covers them. Shame is on all faces, and baldness on all their heads. ¹⁹They cast their silver into the streets, and their gold is like an unclean thing. Their silver and gold are not able to deliver them in the day of the wrath of the LORD. They cannot satisfy their hunger or fill their stomachs with it. For it was the stumbling block of their iniquity. ²⁰His beautiful ornament they used for pride, and they made their abominable images and their detestable things of it. Therefore I make it an unclean thing to them. ²¹And I will give it into the hands of foreigners for prey, and to the wicked of the earth for spoil, and they shall profane it. ²²I will turn my face from them, and they shall profane my treasured⁷ place. Robbers shall enter and profane it.

¹ Or earth ² Some Hebrew manuscripts (compare Syriac, Targum); most Hebrew manuscripts *Disaster! A unique disaster!* ³ The meaning of the Hebrew word is uncertain; also verse 10 ⁴ The meaning of this last Hebrew sentence is uncertain ⁵ Or *abundance*; also verses 13, 14 ⁶ The meaning of this last Hebrew sentence is uncertain ⁷ Or *secret*

[23]"Forge a chain![1] For the land is full of bloody crimes and the city is full of violence. [24]I will bring the worst of the nations to take possession of their houses. I will put an end to the pride of the strong, and their holy places[2] shall be profaned. [25]When anguish comes, they will seek peace, but there shall be none. [26]Disaster comes upon disaster; rumor follows rumor. They seek a vision from the prophet, while the law[3] perishes from the priest and counsel from the elders. [27]The king mourns, the prince is wrapped in despair, and the hands of the people of the land are paralyzed by terror. According to their way I will do to them, and according to their judgments I will judge them, and they shall know that I am the LORD."

A surrealistic vision of corruption in the temple [chapter 8]. The visionary mode takes over in earnest as Ezekiel reveals a vision of what is happening in the temple. What he sees is far different from what a person would literally have seen in Ezekiel's day, when temple worship had become routine rather than genuine. Ezekiel's vision is a picture of what he calls abominations in the temple. The specific images and pictures are (a) poetic discourse in which we need to experience the images and their horrors and (b) a symbolic rather than literal account of what was happening in temple worship, so we need to interpret what the symbols communicate about the state of Ezekiel's nation and religious leaders. For example, there were not literally loathsome animals and idols in the temple (v. 10). Satire is also present in the scene, inasmuch as certain people and practices are held up to derision.

8 In the sixth year, in the sixth month, on the fifth day of the month, as I sat in my house, with the elders of Judah sitting before me, the hand of the Lord GOD fell upon me there. [2]Then I looked, and behold, a form that had the appearance of a man.[4] Below what appeared to be his waist was fire, and above his waist was something like the appearance of brightness, like gleaming metal.[5] [3]He put out the form of a hand and took me by a lock of my head, and the Spirit lifted me up between earth and heaven and brought me in visions of God to Jerusalem, to the entrance of the gateway of the inner court that faces north, where was the seat of the image of jealousy, which provokes to jealousy. [4]And behold, the glory of the God of Israel was there, like the vision that I saw in the valley.

[5]Then he said to me, "Son of man, lift up your eyes now toward the north." So I lifted up my eyes toward the north, and behold, north of the altar gate, in the entrance, was this image of jealousy. [6]And he said to me, "Son of man, do you see what they are doing, the great abominations that the house of Israel are committing here, to drive me far from my sanctuary? But you will see still greater abominations."

[7]And he brought me to the entrance of the court, and when I looked, behold, there was a hole in the wall. [8]Then he said to me, "Son of man, dig in the wall." So I dug in the wall, and behold, there was an entrance. [9]And he said to me, "Go in, and see the vile abominations that they are committing here." [10]So I went in and saw. And there, engraved on the wall all around, was every form of creeping things and loathsome beasts, and all the idols of the house of Israel. [11]And before them stood seventy men of the elders of the house of Israel, with Jaazaniah the son of Shaphan standing among them. Each had his censer in his hand, and the smoke of the cloud of incense went up. [12]Then he said to me, "Son of man, have you seen what the elders of the

---

[1] Probably refers to an instrument of captivity   [2] By revocalization (compare Septuagint); Hebrew *and those who sanctify them*   [3] Or *instruction*
[4] By revocalization (compare Septuagint); Hebrew *of fire*   [5] Or *amber*

house of Israel are doing in the dark, each in his room of pictures? For they say, 'The LORD does not see us, the LORD has forsaken the land.'" ¹³He said also to me, "You will see still greater abominations that they commit."

¹⁴Then he brought me to the entrance of the north gate of the house of the LORD, and behold, there sat women weeping for Tammuz. ¹⁵Then he said to me, "Have you seen this, O son of man? You will see still greater abominations than these."

¹⁶And he brought me into the inner court of the house of the LORD. And behold, at the entrance of the temple of the LORD, between the porch and the altar, were about twenty-five men, with their backs to the temple of the LORD, and their faces toward the east, worshiping the sun toward the east. ¹⁷Then he said to me, "Have you seen this, O son of man? Is it too light a thing for the house of Judah to commit the abominations that they commit here, that they should fill the land with violence and provoke me still further to anger? Behold, they put the branch to their¹ nose. ¹⁸Therefore I will act in wrath. My eye will not spare, nor will I have pity. And though they cry in my ears with a loud voice, I will not hear them."

Visions of judgment [chapter 9]. The focus now shifts from the temple to the city of Jerusalem (symbolic of the nation), but the literary mode remains the same. It is a visionary rather than literal account of what was happening on the streets of Jerusalem. Here, too, the prophet uses a pictorial approach, and the pictures, in turn, are symbols of certain realities, such as rampant evil and God's judgment of it. The story line of this piece of fantasy writing is that God sends executioners into the city to kill idolaters. In short, this is another horror story with spiritual meanings.

9 Then he cried in my ears with a loud voice, saying, "Bring near the executioners of the city, each with his destroying weapon in his hand." ²And behold, six men came from the direction of the upper gate, which faces north, each with his weapon for slaughter in his hand, and with them was a man clothed in linen, with a writing case at his waist. And they went in and stood beside the bronze altar.

³Now the glory of the God of Israel had gone up from the cherub on which it rested to the threshold of the house. And he called to the man clothed in linen, who had the writing case at his waist. ⁴And the LORD said to him, "Pass through the city, through Jerusalem, and put a mark on the foreheads of the men who sigh and groan over all the abominations that are committed in it." ⁵And to the others he said in my hearing, "Pass through the city after him, and strike. Your eye shall not spare, and you shall show no pity. ⁶Kill old men outright, young men and maidens, little children and women, but touch no one on whom is the mark. And begin at my sanctuary." So they began with the elders who were before the house. ⁷Then he said to them, "Defile the house, and fill the courts with the slain. Go out." So they went out and struck in the city. ⁸And while they were striking, and I was left alone, I fell upon my face, and cried, "Ah, Lord GOD! Will you destroy all the remnant of Israel in the outpouring of your wrath on Jerusalem?"

⁹Then he said to me, "The guilt of the house of Israel and Judah is exceedingly great. The land is full of blood, and the city full of injustice. For they say, 'The LORD has forsaken the land, and the LORD does not see.' ¹⁰As for me, my eye will not spare, nor will I have pity; I will bring their deeds upon their heads."

¹ Or my

¹¹And behold, the man clothed in linen, with the writing case at his waist, brought back word, saying, "I have done as you commanded me."

Visions of divine abandonment of Jerusalem [10:1–11:13]. In a return to the opening chapters of the book, Ezekiel again pictures whirling wheels and fantastic "creatures" (symbolic of God's presence and activity). By means of these visionary devices, the satiric attack on national and religious evil continues its onslaught on our imagination. The story line is that God departs from the wicked city (chapter 10 and 11:22–25) and predicts coming judgment on it (11:1–12). The feelings evoked by the pictures are primitive and universal; visionary and satiric writing like this requires readers to take stock of the feelings that are evoked.

10 Then I looked, and behold, on the expanse that was over the heads of the cherubim there appeared above them something like a sapphire,¹ in appearance like a throne. ²And he said to the man clothed in linen, "Go in among the whirling wheels underneath the cherubim. Fill your hands with burning coals from between the cherubim, and scatter them over the city."

And he went in before my eyes. ³Now the cherubim were standing on the south side of the house, when the man went in, and a cloud filled the inner court. ⁴And the glory of the Lord went up from the cherub to the threshold of the house, and the house was filled with the cloud, and the court was filled with the brightness of the glory of the Lord. ⁵And the sound of the wings of the cherubim was heard as far as the outer court, like the voice of God Almighty when he speaks.

⁶And when he commanded the man clothed in linen, "Take fire from between the whirling wheels, from between the cherubim," he went in and stood beside a wheel. ⁷And a cherub stretched out his hand from between the cherubim to the fire that was between the cherubim, and took some of it and put it into the hands of the man clothed in linen, who took it and went out. ⁸The cherubim appeared to have the form of a human hand under their wings.

⁹And I looked, and behold, there were four wheels beside the cherubim, one beside each cherub, and the appearance of the wheels was like sparkling beryl. ¹⁰And as for their appearance, the four had the same likeness, as if a wheel were within a wheel. ¹¹When they went, they went in any of their four directions² without turning as they went, but in whatever direction the front wheel³ faced, the others followed without turning as they went. ¹²And their whole body, their rims, and their spokes, their wings,⁴ and the wheels were full of eyes all around—the wheels that the four of them had. ¹³As for the wheels, they were called in my hearing "the whirling wheels." ¹⁴And every one had four faces: the first face was the face of the cherub, and the second face was a human face, and the third the face of a lion, and the fourth the face of an eagle.

¹⁵And the cherubim mounted up. These were the living creatures that I saw by the Chebar canal. ¹⁶And when the cherubim went, the wheels went beside them. And when the cherubim lifted up their wings to mount up from the earth, the wheels did not turn from beside them. ¹⁷When they stood still, these stood still, and when they mounted up, these mounted up with them, for the spirit of the living creatures⁵ was in them.

¹⁸Then the glory of the Lord went out from the threshold of the house, and stood

---

¹ Or *lapis lazuli* ² Hebrew *to their four sides* ³ Hebrew *the head* ⁴ Or *their whole body, their backs, their hands, and their wings* ⁵ Or *spirit of life*

over the cherubim. ¹⁹And the cherubim lifted up their wings and mounted up from the earth before my eyes as they went out, with the wheels beside them. And they stood at the entrance of the east gate of the house of the LORD, and the glory of the God of Israel was over them.

²⁰These were the living creatures that I saw underneath the God of Israel by the Chebar canal; and I knew that they were cherubim. ²¹Each had four faces, and each four wings, and underneath their wings the likeness of human hands. ²²And as for the likeness of their faces, they were the same faces whose appearance I had seen by the Chebar canal. Each one of them went straight forward.

11 The Spirit lifted me up and brought me to the east gate of the house of the LORD, which faces east. And behold, at the entrance of the gateway there were twenty-five men. And I saw among them Jaazaniah the son of Azzur, and Pelatiah the son of Benaiah, princes of the people. ²And he said to me, "Son of man, these are the men who devise iniquity and who give wicked counsel in this city; ³who say, 'The time is not near¹ to build houses. This city is the cauldron, and we are the meat.' ⁴Therefore prophesy against them, prophesy, O son of man."

⁵And the Spirit of the LORD fell upon me, and he said to me, "Say, Thus says the LORD: So you think, O house of Israel. For I know the things that come into your mind. ⁶You have multiplied your slain in this city and have filled its streets with the slain. ⁷Therefore thus says the Lord GOD: Your slain whom you have laid in the midst of it, they are the meat, and this city is the cauldron, but you shall be brought out of the midst of it. ⁸You have feared the sword, and I will bring the sword upon you, declares the Lord GOD. ⁹And I will bring you out of the midst of it, and give you into the hands of foreigners, and execute judgments upon you. ¹⁰You shall fall by the sword. I will judge you at the border of Israel, and you shall know that I am the LORD. ¹¹This city shall not be your cauldron, nor shall you be the meat in the midst of it. I will judge you at the border of Israel, ¹²and you shall know that I am the LORD. For you have not walked in my statutes, nor obeyed my rules, but have acted according to the rules of the nations that are around you."

¹³And it came to pass, while I was prophesying, that Pelatiah the son of Benaiah died. Then I fell down on my face and cried out with a loud voice and said, "Ah, Lord GOD! Will you make a full end of the remnant of Israel?"

Oracle of blessing [11:14–25]. As horrible as the future prospects of the nation are, tucked into the predominantly negative picture of the early parts of the book of Ezekiel is this unit that promises blessing and restoration for a remnant of the exiles. Especially famous and evocative is God's promise to replace the people's stony heart with a heart of flesh (vv. 17–20). Verses 22–25 are a summary of the entire block of preceding oracles.

---

¹⁴And the word of the LORD came to me: ¹⁵"Son of man, your brothers, even your brothers, your kinsmen,² the whole house of Israel, all of them, are those of whom the inhabitants of Jerusalem have said, 'Go far from the LORD; to us this land is given for a possession.' ¹⁶Therefore say, 'Thus says the Lord GOD: Though I removed them far off among the nations, and though I scattered them among the countries, yet I have been a sanctuary to them for a while³ in the countries where they have gone.'

---

¹ Or Is not the time near...? ² Hebrew the men of your redemption ³ Or in small measure

[17]Therefore say, 'Thus says the Lord GOD: I will gather you from the peoples and assemble you out of the countries where you have been scattered, and I will give you the land of Israel.' [18]And when they come there, they will remove from it all its detestable things and all its abominations. [19]And I will give them one heart, and a new spirit I will put within them. I will remove the heart of stone from their flesh and give them a heart of flesh, [20]that they may walk in my statutes and keep my rules and obey them. And they shall be my people, and I will be their God. [21]But as for those whose heart goes after their detestable things and their abominations, I will[1] bring their deeds upon their own heads, declares the Lord GOD."

[22]Then the cherubim lifted up their wings, with the wheels beside them, and the glory of the God of Israel was over them. [23]And the glory of the LORD went up from the midst of the city and stood on the mountain that is on the east side of the city. [24]And the Spirit lifted me up and brought me in the vision by the Spirit of God into Chaldea, to the exiles. Then the vision that I had seen went up from me. [25]And I told the exiles all the things that the LORD had shown me.

> **A picture of coming exile** [chapter 12]. At this point in the book we are still solidly in the predictive phase that covers the life of the nation before its being carried into captivity in Babylon. But the dominant atmosphere is that of an impending siege of the city and enforced exile. The main symbol of this chapter—the prophet's baggage packed for travel—drives the point home, and other details in the prophet's vision in this chapter are variations on the theme of the coming exile of the nation.

12 The word of the LORD came to me: [2]"Son of man, you dwell in the midst of a rebellious house, who have eyes to see, but see not, who have ears to hear, but hear not, for they are a rebellious house. [3]As for you, son of man, prepare for yourself an exile's baggage, and go into exile by day in their sight. You shall go like an exile from your place to another place in their sight. Perhaps they will understand, though[2] they are a rebellious house. [4]You shall bring out your baggage by day in their sight, as baggage for exile, and you shall go out yourself at evening in their sight, as those do who must go into exile. [5]In their sight dig through the wall, and bring your baggage out through it. [6]In their sight you shall lift the baggage upon your shoulder and carry it out at dusk. You shall cover your face that you may not see the land, for I have made you a sign for the house of Israel."

[7]And I did as I was commanded. I brought out my baggage by day, as baggage for exile, and in the evening I dug through the wall with my own hands. I brought out my baggage at dusk, carrying it on my shoulder in their sight.

[8]In the morning the word of the LORD came to me: [9]"Son of man, has not the house of Israel, the rebellious house, said to you, 'What are you doing?' [10]Say to them, 'Thus says the Lord GOD: This oracle concerns[3] the prince in Jerusalem and all the house of Israel who are in it.'[4] [11]Say, 'I am a sign for you: as I have done, so shall it be done to them. They shall go into exile, into captivity.' [12]And the prince who is among them shall lift his baggage upon his shoulder at dusk, and shall go out. They shall dig through the wall to bring him out through it. He shall cover his face, that he may not see the land with his eyes. [13]And I will spread my net over him, and he shall be taken in my snare. And I will bring him to Babylon, the land of the Chaldeans, yet he shall

---

[1] Hebrew *To the heart of their detestable things and their abominations their heart goes; I will* [2] Or *will see that* [3] Or *This burden is* [4] Hebrew *in the midst of them*

not see it, and he shall die there. ¹⁴And I will scatter toward every wind all who are around him, his helpers and all his troops, and I will unsheathe the sword after them. ¹⁵And they shall know that I am the Lᴏʀᴅ, when I disperse them among the nations and scatter them among the countries. ¹⁶But I will let a few of them escape from the sword, from famine and pestilence, that they may declare all their abominations among the nations where they go, and may know that I am the Lᴏʀᴅ."

¹⁷And the word of the Lᴏʀᴅ came to me: ¹⁸"Son of man, eat your bread with quaking, and drink water with trembling and with anxiety. ¹⁹And say to the people of the land, Thus says the Lord Gᴏᴅ concerning the inhabitants of Jerusalem in the land of Israel: They shall eat their bread with anxiety, and drink water in dismay. In this way her land will be stripped of all it contains, on account of the violence of all those who dwell in it. ²⁰And the inhabited cities shall be laid waste, and the land shall become a desolation; and you shall know that I am the Lᴏʀᴅ."

²¹And the word of the Lᴏʀᴅ came to me: ²²"Son of man, what is this proverb that you¹ have about the land of Israel, saying, 'The days grow long, and every vision comes to nothing'? ²³Tell them therefore, 'Thus says the Lord Gᴏᴅ: I will put an end to this proverb, and they shall no more use it as a proverb in Israel.' But say to them, The days are near, and the fulfillment² of every vision. ²⁴For there shall be no more any false vision or flattering divination within the house of Israel. ²⁵For I am the Lᴏʀᴅ; I will speak the word that I will speak, and it will be performed. It will no longer be delayed, but in your days, O rebellious house, I will speak the word and perform it, declares the Lord Gᴏᴅ."

²⁶And the word of the Lᴏʀᴅ came to me: ²⁷"Son of man, behold, they of the house of Israel say, 'The vision that he sees is for many days from now, and he prophesies of times far off.' ²⁸Therefore say to them, Thus says the Lord Gᴏᴅ: None of my words will be delayed any longer, but the word that I speak will be performed, declares the Lord Gᴏᴅ."

Denunciation of false prophets [chapter 13]. Two common rhetorical/stylistic features of the book up to this point have been the narrative thread in which the prophet states that "the word of the Lᴏʀᴅ came to me" and the formula with which God addresses the prophet—"son of man." We get more of the same in this chapter, which is a satire denouncing false prophets and prophetesses, especially those who prophesy peace when God is actually about to bring judgment.

13 The word of the Lᴏʀᴅ came to me: ²"Son of man, prophesy against the prophets of Israel, who are prophesying, and say to those who prophesy from their own hearts: 'Hear the word of the Lᴏʀᴅ!' ³Thus says the Lord Gᴏᴅ, Woe to the foolish prophets who follow their own spirit, and have seen nothing! ⁴Your prophets have been like jackals among ruins, O Israel. ⁵You have not gone up into the breaches, or built up a wall for the house of Israel, that it might stand in battle in the day of the Lᴏʀᴅ. ⁶They have seen false visions and lying divinations. They say, 'Declares the Lᴏʀᴅ,' when the Lᴏʀᴅ has not sent them, and yet they expect him to fulfill their word. ⁷Have you not seen a false vision and uttered a lying divination, whenever you have said, 'Declares the Lᴏʀᴅ,' although I have not spoken?"

⁸Therefore thus says the Lord Gᴏᴅ: "Because you have uttered falsehood and seen

¹ The Hebrew for *you* is plural ² Hebrew *word*

lying visions, therefore behold, I am against you, declares the Lord GOD. [9]My hand will be against the prophets who see false visions and who give lying divinations. They shall not be in the council of my people, nor be enrolled in the register of the house of Israel, nor shall they enter the land of Israel. And you shall know that I am the Lord GOD. [10]Precisely because they have misled my people, saying, 'Peace,' when there is no peace, and because, when the people build a wall, these prophets smear it with whitewash,[1] [11]say to those who smear it with whitewash that it shall fall! There will be a deluge of rain, and you, O great hailstones, will fall, and a stormy wind break out. [12]And when the wall falls, will it not be said to you, 'Where is the coating with which you smeared it?' [13]Therefore thus says the Lord GOD: I will make a stormy wind break out in my wrath, and there shall be a deluge of rain in my anger, and great hailstones in wrath to make a full end. [14]And I will break down the wall that you have smeared with whitewash, and bring it down to the ground, so that its foundation will be laid bare. When it falls, you shall perish in the midst of it, and you shall know that I am the LORD. [15]Thus will I spend my wrath upon the wall and upon those who have smeared it with whitewash, and I will say to you, The wall is no more, nor those who smeared it, [16]the prophets of Israel who prophesied concerning Jerusalem and saw visions of peace for her, when there was no peace, declares the Lord GOD.

[17]"And you, son of man, set your face against the daughters of your people, who prophesy out of their own minds. Prophesy against them [18]and say, Thus says the Lord GOD: Woe to the women who sew magic bands upon all wrists, and make veils for the heads of persons of every stature, in the hunt for souls! Will you hunt down souls belonging to my people and keep your own souls alive? [19]You have profaned me among my people for handfuls of barley and for pieces of bread, putting to death souls who should not die and keeping alive souls who should not live, by your lying to my people, who listen to lies.

[20]"Therefore thus says the Lord GOD: Behold, I am against your magic bands with which you hunt the souls like birds, and I will tear them from your arms, and I will let the souls whom you hunt go free, the souls like birds. [21]Your veils also I will tear off and deliver my people out of your hand, and they shall be no more in your hand as prey, and you shall know that I am the LORD. [22]Because you have disheartened the righteous falsely, although I have not grieved him, and you have encouraged the wicked, that he should not turn from his evil way to save his life, [23]therefore you shall no more see false visions nor practice divination. I will deliver my people out of your hand. And you shall know that I am the LORD."

More bad news [chapters 14–15]. Ezekiel is an anthology—a kaleidoscope of quickly shifting visions. The structure is cumulative and repetitive rather than linear and progressive. This way of proceeding anticipated a leading technique of modern literature known as stream of consciousness, in which we move through a series of loosely related fragments without clear transition between units. Chapters 14–15 fall into this pattern that characterizes the book as a whole. The unit begins with a narrative account: The elders of Israel sit down in front of the prophet (14:1). As Ezekiel looks at them, the word of God comes to him, declaring that the elders have enshrined idols in their hearts (14:2–3), followed by God's denunciation of such idolatry and prediction that he will punish it (14:4–11). From this the voice of God moves to visions of judgment and calam-

[1] Or *plaster*; also verses 11, 14, 15

ity that he will bring against the nation (14:12–23). Chapter 15 then offers the symbol of the charred wood of a vine as a picture of the destruction that is coming to a faithless nation. The vine is a common archetype for the nation in prophetic literature.

14 Then certain of the elders of Israel came to me and sat before me. [2]And the word of the LORD came to me: [3]"Son of man, these men have taken their idols into their hearts, and set the stumbling block of their iniquity before their faces. Should I indeed let myself be consulted by them? [4]Therefore speak to them and say to them, Thus says the Lord GOD: Any one of the house of Israel who takes his idols into his heart and sets the stumbling block of his iniquity before his face, and yet comes to the prophet, I the LORD will answer him as he comes with the multitude of his idols, [5]that I may lay hold of the hearts of the house of Israel, who are all estranged from me through their idols.

[6]"Therefore say to the house of Israel, Thus says the Lord GOD: Repent and turn away from your idols, and turn away your faces from all your abominations. [7]For any one of the house of Israel, or of the strangers who sojourn in Israel, who separates himself from me, taking his idols into his heart and putting the stumbling block of his iniquity before his face, and yet comes to a prophet to consult me through him, I the LORD will answer him myself. [8]And I will set my face against that man; I will make him a sign and a byword and cut him off from the midst of my people, and you shall know that I am the LORD. [9]And if the prophet is deceived and speaks a word, I, the LORD, have deceived that prophet, and I will stretch out my hand against him and will destroy him from the midst of my people Israel. [10]And they shall bear their punishment[1]—the punishment of the prophet and the punishment of the inquirer shall be alike— [11]that the house of Israel may no more go astray from me, nor defile themselves anymore with all their transgressions, but that they may be my people and I may be their God, declares the Lord GOD."

[12]And the word of the LORD came to me: [13]"Son of man, when a land sins against me by acting faithlessly, and I stretch out my hand against it and break its supply[2] of bread and send famine upon it, and cut off from it man and beast, [14]even if these three men, Noah, Daniel, and Job, were in it, they would deliver but their own lives by their righteousness, declares the Lord GOD.

[15]"If I cause wild beasts to pass through the land, and they ravage it, and it be made desolate, so that no one may pass through because of the beasts, [16]even if these three men were in it, as I live, declares the Lord GOD, they would deliver neither sons nor daughters. They alone would be delivered, but the land would be desolate.

[17]"Or if I bring a sword upon that land and say, Let a sword pass through the land, and I cut off from it man and beast, [18]though these three men were in it, as I live, declares the Lord GOD, they would deliver neither sons nor daughters, but they alone would be delivered.

[19]"Or if I send a pestilence into that land and pour out my wrath upon it with blood, to cut off from it man and beast, [20]even if Noah, Daniel, and Job were in it, as I live, declares the Lord GOD, they would deliver neither son nor daughter. They would deliver but their own lives by their righteousness.

[21]"For thus says the Lord GOD: How much more when I send upon Jerusalem my four disastrous acts of judgment, sword, famine, wild beasts, and pestilence, to cut off

---

[1] Or *iniquity*; three times in this verse [2] Hebrew *staff*

from it man and beast! ²²But behold, some survivors will be left in it, sons and daughters who will be brought out; behold, when they come out to you, and you see their
ways and their deeds, you will be consoled for the disaster that I have brought upon
Jerusalem, for all that I have brought upon it. ²³They will console you, when you see
their ways and their deeds, and you shall know that I have not done without cause all
that I have done in it, declares the Lord GOD."

15 And the word of the LORD came to me: ²"Son of man, how does the wood of
the vine surpass any wood, the vine branch that is among the trees of the forest? ³Is wood taken from it to make anything? Do people take a peg from it to hang
any vessel on it? ⁴Behold, it is given to the fire for fuel. When the fire has consumed
both ends of it, and the middle of it is charred, is it useful for anything? ⁵Behold,
when it was whole, it was used for nothing. How much less, when the fire has consumed it and it is charred, can it ever be used for anything! ⁶Therefore thus says the
Lord GOD: Like the wood of the vine among the trees of the forest, which I have given
to the fire for fuel, so have I given up the inhabitants of Jerusalem. ⁷And I will set my
face against them. Though they escape from the fire, the fire shall yet consume them,
and you will know that I am the LORD, when I set my face against them. ⁸And I will
make the land desolate, because they have acted faithlessly, declares the Lord GOD."

A foundling child turned prostitute [chapter 16]. Satire and symbolism continue to
dominate in chapter 16, which is an extended vision built around a sexual metaphor of
Israel's spiritual apostasy and faithlessness. We should read the passage at an emotional or affective level as expressing the loathsomeness of such rejection of God. Then
we need to interpret the extended metaphor as we interpret all metaphors—first by getting the picture at "level A" (in this case the behavior of a sexually loose woman) and
then carrying over the meanings to "level B" (spiritual rejection of God). As we do that,
we need to codify the exact nature of the charges that God through his prophet is making about the religious state of the nation. Yet even this vision of repulsive behavior
ends with God's promise of restitution (vv. 53–54, 59–63).

16 Again the word of the LORD came to me: ²"Son of man, make known to
Jerusalem her abominations, ³and say, Thus says the Lord GOD to Jerusalem:
Your origin and your birth are of the land of the Canaanites; your father was an
Amorite and your mother a Hittite. ⁴And as for your birth, on the day you were born
your cord was not cut, nor were you washed with water to cleanse you, nor rubbed
with salt, nor wrapped in swaddling cloths. ⁵No eye pitied you, to do any of these
things to you out of compassion for you, but you were cast out on the open field, for
you were abhorred, on the day that you were born.

⁶"And when I passed by you and saw you wallowing in your blood, I said to you in
your blood, 'Live!' I said to you in your blood, 'Live!' ⁷I made you flourish like a plant
of the field. And you grew up and became tall and arrived at full adornment. Your
breasts were formed, and your hair had grown; yet you were naked and bare.

⁸"When I passed by you again and saw you, behold, you were at the age for love,
and I spread the corner of my garment over you and covered your nakedness; I made
my vow to you and entered into a covenant with you, declares the Lord GOD, and you
became mine. ⁹Then I bathed you with water and washed off your blood from you

and anointed you with oil. ¹⁰I clothed you also with embroidered cloth and shod you with fine leather. I wrapped you in fine linen and covered you with silk.ᴵ ¹¹And I adorned you with ornaments and put bracelets on your wrists and a chain on your neck. ¹²And I put a ring on your nose and earrings in your ears and a beautiful crown on your head. ¹³Thus you were adorned with gold and silver, and your clothing was of fine linen and silk and embroidered cloth. You ate fine flour and honey and oil. You grew exceedingly beautiful and advanced to royalty. ¹⁴And your renown went forth among the nations because of your beauty, for it was perfect through the splendor that I had bestowed on you, declares the Lord GOD.

¹⁵"But you trusted in your beauty and played the whore² because of your renown and lavished your whorings³ on any passerby; your beauty⁴ became his. ¹⁶You took some of your garments and made for yourself colorful shrines, and on them played the whore. The like has never been, nor ever shall be.⁵ ¹⁷You also took your beautiful jewels of my gold and of my silver, which I had given you, and made for yourself images of men, and with them played the whore. ¹⁸And you took your embroidered garments to cover them, and set my oil and my incense before them. ¹⁹Also my bread that I gave you—I fed you with fine flour and oil and honey—you set before them for a pleasing aroma; and so it was, declares the Lord GOD. ²⁰And you took your sons and your daughters, whom you had borne to me, and these you sacrificed to them to be devoured. Were your whorings so small a matter ²¹that you slaughtered my children and delivered them up as an offering by fire to them? ²²And in all your abominations and your whorings you did not remember the days of your youth, when you were naked and bare, wallowing in your blood.

²³"And after all your wickedness (woe, woe to you! declares the Lord GOD), ²⁴you built yourself a vaulted chamber and made yourself a lofty place in every square. ²⁵At the head of every street you built your lofty place and made your beauty an abomination, offering yourself⁶ to any passerby and multiplying your whoring. ²⁶You also played the whore with the Egyptians, your lustful neighbors, multiplying your whoring, to provoke me to anger. ²⁷Behold, therefore, I stretched out my hand against you and diminished your allotted portion and delivered you to the greed of your enemies, the daughters of the Philistines, who were ashamed of your lewd behavior. ²⁸You played the whore also with the Assyrians, because you were not satisfied; yes, you played the whore with them, and still you were not satisfied. ²⁹You multiplied your whoring also with the trading land of Chaldea, and even with this you were not satisfied.

³⁰"How sick is your heart,⁷ declares the Lord GOD, because you did all these things, the deeds of a brazen prostitute, ³¹building your vaulted chamber at the head of every street, and making your lofty place in every square. Yet you were not like a prostitute, because you scorned payment. ³²Adulterous wife, who receives strangers instead of her husband! ³³Men give gifts to all prostitutes, but you gave your gifts to all your lovers, bribing them to come to you from every side with your whorings. ³⁴So you were different from other women in your whorings. No one solicited you to play the whore, and you gave payment, while no payment was given to you; therefore you were different.

³⁵"Therefore, O prostitute, hear the word of the LORD: ³⁶Thus says the Lord GOD, Because your lust was poured out and your nakedness uncovered in your whorings

¹Or with rich fabric ²Or were unfaithful; also verses 16, 17, 26, 28 ³Or unfaithfulness; also verses 20, 22, 25, 26, 29, 33, 34, 36 ⁴Hebrew it ⁵The meaning of this Hebrew sentence is uncertain ⁶Hebrew spreading your legs ⁷Revocalization yields How I am filled with anger against you

with your lovers, and with all your abominable idols, and because of the blood of your children that you gave to them, [37]therefore, behold, I will gather all your lovers with whom you took pleasure, all those you loved and all those you hated. I will gather them against you from every side and will uncover your nakedness to them, that they may see all your nakedness. [38]And I will judge you as women who commit adultery and shed blood are judged, and bring upon you the blood of wrath and jealousy. [39]And I will give you into their hands, and they shall throw down your vaulted chamber and break down your lofty places. They shall strip you of your clothes and take your beautiful jewels and leave you naked and bare. [40]They shall bring up a crowd against you, and they shall stone you and cut you to pieces with their swords. [41]And they shall burn your houses and execute judgments upon you in the sight of many women. I will make you stop playing the whore, and you shall also give payment no more. [42]So will I satisfy my wrath on you, and my jealousy shall depart from you. I will be calm and will no more be angry. [43]Because you have not remembered the days of your youth, but have enraged me with all these things, therefore, behold, I have returned your deeds upon your head, declares the Lord God. Have you not committed lewdness in addition to all your abominations?

[44]"Behold, everyone who uses proverbs will use this proverb about you: 'Like mother, like daughter.' [45]You are the daughter of your mother, who loathed her husband and her children; and you are the sister of your sisters, who loathed their husbands and their children. Your mother was a Hittite and your father an Amorite. [46]And your elder sister is Samaria, who lived with her daughters to the north of you; and your younger sister, who lived to the south of you, is Sodom with her daughters. [47]Not only did you walk in their ways and do according to their abominations; within a very little time you were more corrupt than they in all your ways. [48]As I live, declares the Lord God, your sister Sodom and her daughters have not done as you and your daughters have done. [49]Behold, this was the guilt of your sister Sodom: she and her daughters had pride, excess of food, and prosperous ease, but did not aid the poor and needy. [50]They were haughty and did an abomination before me. So I removed them, when I saw it. [51]Samaria has not committed half your sins. You have committed more abominations than they, and have made your sisters appear righteous by all the abominations that you have committed. [52]Bear your disgrace, you also, for you have intervened on behalf of your sisters. Because of your sins in which you acted more abominably than they, they are more in the right than you. So be ashamed, you also, and bear your disgrace, for you have made your sisters appear righteous.

[53]"I will restore their fortunes, both the fortunes of Sodom and her daughters, and the fortunes of Samaria and her daughters, and I will restore your own fortunes in their midst, [54]that you may bear your disgrace and be ashamed of all that you have done, becoming a consolation to them. [55]As for your sisters, Sodom and her daughters shall return to their former state, and Samaria and her daughters shall return to their former state, and you and your daughters shall return to your former state. [56]Was not your sister Sodom a byword in your mouth in the day of your pride, [57]before your wickedness was uncovered? Now you have become an object of reproach for the daughters of Syria[1] and all those around her, and for the daughters of the Philistines, those all around who despise you. [58]You bear the penalty of your lewdness and your abominations, declares the Lord.

[59]"For thus says the Lord God: I will deal with you as you have done, you who have

---

[1] Some manuscripts (compare Syriac) *of Edom*

despised the oath in breaking the covenant, ⁶⁰yet I will remember my covenant with you in the days of your youth, and I will establish for you an everlasting covenant. ⁶¹Then you will remember your ways and be ashamed when you take your sisters, both your elder and your younger, and I give them to you as daughters, but not on account of[1] the covenant with you. ⁶²I will establish my covenant with you, and you shall know that I am the Lᴏʀᴅ, ⁶³that you may remember and be confounded, and never open your mouth again because of your shame, when I atone for you for all that you have done, declares the Lord Gᴏᴅ."

Two eagles, a cedar tree, and a vine [chapter 17]. The prophecy continues to rely on great symbols as the means of embodying and conveying truth. The first six verses narrate how an imaginary eagle transplanted the top of a cedar tree in a foreign land, where it took root as a spreading vine. Verses 7–10 narrate how the spreading vine then reached out in the direction of a second great eagle. In verses 11–21, God interprets the details of these symbolic actions as representing the actions of various kings and nations. The main story line is Judah's being carried into exile by Nebuchadnezzar (vv. 11–14), an attempt by the king of Judah to secure an alliance with the king of Egypt (v. 15), and God's repudiation of that attempt to rely on a human alliance instead of God (vv. 16–21). In the final movement of the chapter (vv. 22–24), and still in the mode of symbolism, God pictures himself as taking the sprig from the top of a cedar tree and planting it on a mountaintop, where it becomes a tree of refuge for birds; this is an oracle of redemption predicting the return of God's favor to his people.

17 The word of the Lᴏʀᴅ came to me: ²"Son of man, propound a riddle, and speak a parable to the house of Israel; ³say, Thus says the Lord Gᴏᴅ: A great eagle with great wings and long pinions, rich in plumage of many colors, came to Lebanon and took the top of the cedar. ⁴He broke off the topmost of its young twigs and carried it to a land of trade and set it in a city of merchants. ⁵Then he took of the seed of the land and planted it in fertile soil.[2] He placed it beside abundant waters. He set it like a willow twig, ⁶and it sprouted and became a low spreading vine, and its branches turned toward him, and its roots remained where it stood. So it became a vine and produced branches and put out boughs.

⁷"And there was another great eagle with great wings and much plumage, and behold, this vine bent its roots toward him and shot forth its branches toward him from the bed where it was planted, that he might water it. ⁸It had been planted on good soil by abundant waters, that it might produce branches and bear fruit and become a noble vine.

⁹"Say, Thus says the Lord Gᴏᴅ: Will it thrive? Will he not pull up its roots and cut off its fruit, so that it withers, so that all its fresh sprouting leaves wither? It will not take a strong arm or many people to pull it from its roots. ¹⁰Behold, it is planted; will it thrive? Will it not utterly wither when the east wind strikes it—wither away on the bed where it sprouted?"

¹¹Then the word of the Lᴏʀᴅ came to me: ¹²"Say now to the rebellious house, Do you not know what these things mean? Tell them, behold, the king of Babylon came to Jerusalem, and took her king and her princes and brought them to him to Babylon. ¹³And he took one of the royal offspring[3] and made a covenant with him, putting him under oath (the chief men of the land he had taken away), ¹⁴that the kingdom might

[1] Or *not apart from* [2] Hebrew *in a field of seed* [3] Hebrew *seed*

be humble and not lift itself up, and keep his covenant that it might stand. ¹⁵But he rebelled against him by sending his ambassadors to Egypt, that they might give him horses and a large army. Will he thrive? Can one escape who does such things? Can he break the covenant and yet escape?

¹⁶"As I live, declares the Lord GOD, surely in the place where the king dwells who made him king, whose oath he despised, and whose covenant with him he broke, in Babylon he shall die. ¹⁷Pharaoh with his mighty army and great company will not help him in war, when mounds are cast up and siege walls built to cut off many lives. ¹⁸He despised the oath in breaking the covenant, and behold, he gave his hand and did all these things; he shall not escape. ¹⁹Therefore thus says the Lord GOD: As I live, surely it is my oath that he despised, and my covenant that he broke. I will return it upon his head. ²⁰I will spread my net over him, and he shall be taken in my snare, and I will bring him to Babylon and enter into judgment with him there for the treachery he has committed against me. ²¹And all the pick¹ of his troops shall fall by the sword, and the survivors shall be scattered to every wind, and you shall know that I am the LORD; I have spoken."

²²Thus says the Lord GOD: "I myself will take a sprig from the lofty top of the cedar and will set it out. I will break off from the topmost of its young twigs a tender one, and I myself will plant it on a high and lofty mountain. ²³On the mountain height of Israel will I plant it, that it may bear branches and produce fruit and become a noble cedar. And under it will dwell every kind of bird; in the shade of its branches birds of every sort will nest. ²⁴And all the trees of the field shall know that I am the LORD; I bring low the high tree, and make high the low tree, dry up the green tree, and make the dry tree flourish. I am the LORD; I have spoken, and I will do it."

Case studies [chapter 18]. This chapter is a gallery of case studies of possible behavior toward God. The rhetorical formula is "If a man . . . ," followed by the hypothetical behavior of that person. The two possible actions are righteous and repentant obedience of God or rebellion against God. The main points of these test cases are stated at the beginning and end of the chapter: every person is individually responsible for his or her sins (v. 4), and people should repent before God and thereby be saved from his judgment (vv. 30–32).

18 The word of the LORD came to me: ²"What do you² mean by repeating this proverb concerning the land of Israel, 'The fathers have eaten sour grapes, and the children's teeth are set on edge'? ³As I live, declares the Lord GOD, this proverb shall no more be used by you in Israel. ⁴Behold, all souls are mine; the soul of the father as well as the soul of the son is mine: the soul who sins shall die.

⁵"If a man is righteous and does what is just and right— ⁶if he does not eat upon the mountains or lift up his eyes to the idols of the house of Israel, does not defile his neighbor's wife or approach a woman in her time of menstrual impurity, ⁷does not oppress anyone, but restores to the debtor his pledge, commits no robbery, gives his bread to the hungry and covers the naked with a garment, ⁸does not lend at interest or take any profit,³ withholds his hand from injustice, executes true justice between man and man, ⁹walks in my statutes, and keeps my rules by acting faithfully—he is righteous; he shall surely live, declares the Lord GOD.

¹ Some Hebrew manuscripts, Syriac, Targum; most Hebrew manuscripts *all the fugitives* ² The Hebrew for *you* is plural ³ That is, profit that comes from charging interest to the poor; also verses 13, 17 (compare Leviticus 25:36)

¹⁰"If he fathers a son who is violent, a shedder of blood, who does any of these things ¹¹(though he himself did none of these things), who even eats upon the mountains, defiles his neighbor's wife, ¹²oppresses the poor and needy, commits robbery, does not restore the pledge, lifts up his eyes to the idols, commits abomination, ¹³lends at interest, and takes profit; shall he then live? He shall not live. He has done all these abominations; he shall surely die; his blood shall be upon himself.

¹⁴"Now suppose this man fathers a son who sees all the sins that his father has done; he sees, and does not do likewise: ¹⁵he does not eat upon the mountains or lift up his eyes to the idols of the house of Israel, does not defile his neighbor's wife, ¹⁶does not oppress anyone, exacts no pledge, commits no robbery, but gives his bread to the hungry and covers the naked with a garment, ¹⁷withholds his hand from iniquity,¹ takes no interest or profit, obeys my rules, and walks in my statutes; he shall not die for his father's iniquity; he shall surely live. ¹⁸As for his father, because he practiced extortion, robbed his brother, and did what is not good among his people, behold, he shall die for his iniquity.

¹⁹"Yet you say, 'Why should not the son suffer for the iniquity of the father?' When the son has done what is just and right, and has been careful to observe all my statutes, he shall surely live. ²⁰The soul who sins shall die. The son shall not suffer for the iniquity of the father, nor the father suffer for the iniquity of the son. The righteousness of the righteous shall be upon himself, and the wickedness of the wicked shall be upon himself.

²¹"But if a wicked person turns away from all his sins that he has committed and keeps all my statutes and does what is just and right, he shall surely live; he shall not die. ²²None of the transgressions that he has committed shall be remembered against him; for the righteousness that he has done he shall live. ²³Have I any pleasure in the death of the wicked, declares the Lord God, and not rather that he should turn from his way and live? ²⁴But when a righteous person turns away from his righteousness and does injustice and does the same abominations that the wicked person does, shall he live? None of the righteous deeds that he has done shall be remembered; for the treachery of which he is guilty and the sin he has committed, for them he shall die.

²⁵"Yet you say, 'The way of the Lord is not just.' Hear now, O house of Israel: Is my way not just? Is it not your ways that are not just? ²⁶When a righteous person turns away from his righteousness and does injustice, he shall die for it; for the injustice that he has done he shall die. ²⁷Again, when a wicked person turns away from the wickedness he has committed and does what is just and right, he shall save his life. ²⁸Because he considered and turned away from all the transgressions that he had committed, he shall surely live; he shall not die. ²⁹Yet the house of Israel says, 'The way of the Lord is not just.' O house of Israel, are my ways not just? Is it not your ways that are not just?

³⁰"Therefore I will judge you, O house of Israel, every one according to his ways, declares the Lord God. Repent and turn from all your transgressions, lest iniquity be your ruin.² ³¹Cast away from you all the transgressions that you have committed, and make yourselves a new heart and a new spirit! Why will you die, O house of Israel? ³²For I have no pleasure in the death of anyone, declares the Lord God; so turn, and live."

---

¹ Septuagint; Hebrew *from the poor* ² Or *lest iniquity be your stumbling block*

Elegy for fallen kings [chapter 19]. Chapter 19 introduces a new genre into the mix. It is lament or *elegy—a funeral poem, in this case for three kings of Judah. The manner of speaking is highly metaphoric (with the nation, for example, called a mother lion and a vineyard). The main point is still satiric, as evil kings are held up to rebuke and subjected to God's judgment.

19

And you, take up a lamentation for the princes of Israel, ²and say:

What was your mother? A lioness!
    Among lions she crouched;
in the midst of young lions
    she reared her cubs.
³ And she brought up one of her cubs;
    he became a young lion,
and he learned to catch prey;
    he devoured men.
⁴ The nations heard about him;
    he was caught in their pit,
and they brought him with hooks
    to the land of Egypt.
⁵ When she saw that she waited in vain,
    that her hope was lost,
she took another of her cubs
    and made him a young lion.
⁶ He prowled among the lions;
    he became a young lion,
and he learned to catch prey;
    he devoured men,
⁷ and seized[1] their widows.
    He laid waste their cities,
and the land was appalled and all who were in it
    at the sound of his roaring.
⁸ Then the nations set against him
    from provinces on every side;
they spread their net over him;
    he was taken in their pit.
⁹ With hooks they put him in a cage[2]
    and brought him to the king of Babylon;
    they brought him into custody,
that his voice should no more be heard
    on the mountains of Israel.

¹⁰ Your mother was like a vine in a vineyard[3]
    planted by the water,
fruitful and full of branches
    by reason of abundant water.
¹¹ Its strong stems became

---

¹ Hebrew *knew* ² Or *in a wooden collar* ³ Some Hebrew manuscripts; most Hebrew manuscripts *in your blood*

rulers' scepters;
it towered aloft
   among the thick boughs;[1]
it was seen in its height
   with the mass of its branches.
12 But the vine was plucked up in fury,
      cast down to the ground;
   the east wind dried up its fruit;
      they were stripped off and withered.
   As for its strong stem,
      fire consumed it.
13 Now it is planted in the wilderness,
      in a dry and thirsty land.
14 And fire has gone out from the stem of its shoots,
      has consumed its fruit,
   so that there remains in it no strong stem,
      no scepter for ruling.

This is a lamentation and has become a lamentation.

History lesson [chapter 20]. This long chapter ranks as a small anthology of oracles all by itself. The main story line of the chapter is a history of Israel, beginning with the exodus from Egypt and set within a framework of God's judgment of the nation for its waywardness, as is announced right at the outset (vv. 1–4). The perspective of the history lesson is satiric, as the sins of Israel are cataloged and denounced (vv. 5–39 and 45–49), but there is an inserted oracle of redemption (vv. 40–44).

20 In the seventh year, in the fifth month, on the tenth day of the month, certain of the elders of Israel came to inquire of the LORD, and sat before me. ²And the word of the LORD came to me: ³"Son of man, speak to the elders of Israel, and say to them, Thus says the Lord GOD, Is it to inquire of me that you come? As I live, declares the Lord GOD, I will not be inquired of by you. ⁴Will you judge them, son of man, will you judge them? Let them know the abominations of their fathers, ⁵and say to them, Thus says the Lord GOD: On the day when I chose Israel, I swore[2] to the offspring of the house of Jacob, making myself known to them in the land of Egypt; I swore to them, saying, I am the LORD your God. ⁶On that day I swore to them that I would bring them out of the land of Egypt into a land that I had searched out for them, a land flowing with milk and honey, the most glorious of all lands. ⁷And I said to them, Cast away the detestable things your eyes feast on, every one of you, and do not defile yourselves with the idols of Egypt; I am the LORD your God. ⁸But they rebelled against me and were not willing to listen to me. None of them cast away the detestable things their eyes feasted on, nor did they forsake the idols of Egypt.

"Then I said I would pour out my wrath upon them and spend my anger against them in the midst of the land of Egypt. ⁹But I acted for the sake of my name, that it should not be profaned in the sight of the nations among whom they lived, in whose sight I made myself known to them in bringing them out of the land of Egypt. ¹⁰So I led them out of the land of Egypt and brought them into the wilderness. ¹¹I gave them

---

[1] Or *the clouds* [2] Hebrew *I lifted my hand*; twice in this verse; also verses 6, 15, 23, 28, 42

my statutes and made known to them my rules, by which, if a person does them, he shall live. [12]Moreover, I gave them my Sabbaths, as a sign between me and them, that they might know that I am the LORD who sanctifies them. [13]But the house of Israel rebelled against me in the wilderness. They did not walk in my statutes but rejected my rules, by which, if a person does them, he shall live; and my Sabbaths they greatly profaned.

"Then I said I would pour out my wrath upon them in the wilderness, to make a full end of them. [14]But I acted for the sake of my name, that it should not be profaned in the sight of the nations, in whose sight I had brought them out. [15]Moreover, I swore to them in the wilderness that I would not bring them into the land that I had given them, a land flowing with milk and honey, the most glorious of all lands, [16]because they rejected my rules and did not walk in my statutes, and profaned my Sabbaths; for their heart went after their idols. [17]Nevertheless, my eye spared them, and I did not destroy them or make a full end of them in the wilderness.

[18]"And I said to their children in the wilderness, Do not walk in the statutes of your fathers, nor keep their rules, nor defile yourselves with their idols. [19]I am the LORD your God; walk in my statutes, and be careful to obey my rules, [20]and keep my Sabbaths holy that they may be a sign between me and you, that you may know that I am the LORD your God. [21]But the children rebelled against me. They did not walk in my statutes and were not careful to obey my rules, by which, if a person does them, he shall live; they profaned my Sabbaths.

"Then I said I would pour out my wrath upon them and spend my anger against them in the wilderness. [22]But I withheld my hand and acted for the sake of my name, that it should not be profaned in the sight of the nations, in whose sight I had brought them out. [23]Moreover, I swore to them in the wilderness that I would scatter them among the nations and disperse them through the countries, [24]because they had not obeyed my rules, but had rejected my statutes and profaned my Sabbaths, and their eyes were set on their fathers' idols. [25]Moreover, I gave them statutes that were not good and rules by which they could not have life, [26]and I defiled them through their very gifts in their offering up all their firstborn, that I might devastate them. I did it that they might know that I am the LORD.

[27]"Therefore, son of man, speak to the house of Israel and say to them, Thus says the Lord GOD: In this also your fathers blasphemed me, by dealing treacherously with me. [28]For when I had brought them into the land that I swore to give them, then wherever they saw any high hill or any leafy tree, there they offered their sacrifices and there they presented the provocation of their offering; there they sent up their pleasing aromas, and there they poured out their drink offerings. [29](I said to them, What is the high place to which you go? So its name is called Bamah[1] to this day.)

[30]"Therefore say to the house of Israel, Thus says the Lord GOD: Will you defile yourselves after the manner of your fathers and go whoring after their detestable things? [31]When you present your gifts and offer up your children in fire,[2] you defile yourselves with all your idols to this day. And shall I be inquired of by you, O house of Israel? As I live, declares the Lord GOD, I will not be inquired of by you.

[32]"What is in your mind shall never happen—the thought, 'Let us be like the nations, like the tribes of the countries, and worship wood and stone.'

[33]"As I live, declares the Lord GOD, surely with a mighty hand and an outstretched arm and with wrath poured out I will be king over you. [34]I will bring you out from the

---

[1] Bamah means high place [2] Hebrew and make your children pass through the fire

peoples and gather you out of the countries where you are scattered, with a mighty hand and an outstretched arm, and with wrath poured out. ³⁵And I will bring you into the wilderness of the peoples, and there I will enter into judgment with you face to face. ³⁶As I entered into judgment with your fathers in the wilderness of the land of Egypt, so I will enter into judgment with you, declares the Lord GOD. ³⁷I will make you pass under the rod, and I will bring you into the bond of the covenant. ³⁸I will purge out the rebels from among you, and those who transgress against me. I will bring them out of the land where they sojourn, but they shall not enter the land of Israel. Then you will know that I am the LORD.

³⁹"As for you, O house of Israel, thus says the Lord GOD: Go serve every one of you his idols, now and hereafter, if you will not listen to me; but my holy name you shall no more profane with your gifts and your idols.

⁴⁰"For on my holy mountain, the mountain height of Israel, declares the Lord GOD, there all the house of Israel, all of them, shall serve me in the land. There I will accept them, and there I will require your contributions and the choicest of your gifts, with all your sacred offerings. ⁴¹As a pleasing aroma I will accept you, when I bring you out from the peoples and gather you out of the countries where you have been scattered. And I will manifest my holiness among you in the sight of the nations. ⁴²And you shall know that I am the LORD, when I bring you into the land of Israel, the country that I swore to give to your fathers. ⁴³And there you shall remember your ways and all your deeds with which you have defiled yourselves, and you shall loathe yourselves for all the evils that you have committed. ⁴⁴And you shall know that I am the LORD, when I deal with you for my name's sake, not according to your evil ways, nor according to your corrupt deeds, O house of Israel, declares the Lord GOD."

⁴⁵¹ And the word of the LORD came to me: ⁴⁶"Son of man, set your face toward the southland;² preach against the south, and prophesy against the forest land in the Negeb. ⁴⁷Say to the forest of the Negeb, Hear the word of the LORD: Thus says the Lord GOD, Behold, I will kindle a fire in you, and it shall devour every green tree in you and every dry tree. The blazing flame shall not be quenched, and all faces from south to north shall be scorched by it. ⁴⁸All flesh shall see that I the LORD have kindled it; it shall not be quenched." ⁴⁹Then I said, "Ah, Lord GOD! They are saying of me, 'Is he not a maker of parables?'"

The vision of the drawn sword [chapter 21]. Chapter 21 is unified by the image of the drawn sword of God, a symbol of God's judgment against sin. The oracle of judgment against Judah (vv. 1–27) is mainly a prediction of the impending invasion by Babylon. At the end of the chapter, we find an oracle of judgment against the Ammonites (vv. 28–32).

21 ³ The word of the LORD came to me: ²"Son of man, set your face toward Jerusalem and preach against the sanctuaries.⁴ Prophesy against the land of Israel ³and say to the land of Israel, Thus says the LORD: Behold, I am against you and will draw my sword from its sheath and will cut off from you both righteous and wicked. ⁴Because I will cut off from you both righteous and wicked, therefore my sword shall be drawn from its sheath against all flesh from south to north. ⁵And all flesh shall know that I am the LORD. I have drawn my sword from its sheath; it shall not be sheathed again.

¹ Ch 21:1 in Hebrew ² Or *toward Teman* ³ Ch 21:6 in Hebrew ⁴ Some Hebrew manuscripts, compare Septuagint, Syriac *against their sanctuary*

⁶"As for you, son of man, groan; with breaking heart and bitter grief, groan before their eyes. ⁷And when they say to you, 'Why do you groan?' you shall say, 'Because of the news that it is coming. Every heart will melt, and all hands will be feeble; every spirit will faint, and all knees will be weak as water. Behold, it is coming, and it will be fulfilled,'" declares the Lord GOD.

⁸And the word of the LORD came to me: ⁹"Son of man, prophesy and say, Thus says the Lord, say:

"A sword, a sword is sharpened
    and also polished,
¹⁰   sharpened for slaughter,
    polished to flash like lightning!

(Or shall we rejoice? You have despised the rod, my son, with everything of wood.)¹ ¹¹So the sword is given to be polished, that it may be grasped in the hand. It is sharpened and polished to be given into the hand of the slayer. ¹²Cry out and wail, son of man, for it is against my people. It is against all the princes of Israel. They are delivered over to the sword with my people. Strike therefore upon your thigh. ¹³For it will not be a testing—what could it do if you despise the rod?"² declares the Lord GOD.

¹⁴"As for you, son of man, prophesy. Clap your hands and let the sword come down twice, yes, three times,³ the sword for those to be slain. It is the sword for the great slaughter, which surrounds them, ¹⁵that their hearts may melt, and many stumble.⁴ At all their gates I have given the glittering sword. Ah, it is made like lightning; it is taken up⁵ for slaughter. ¹⁶Cut sharply to the right; set yourself to the left, wherever your face is directed. ¹⁷I also will clap my hands, and I will satisfy my fury; I the LORD have spoken."

¹⁸The word of the LORD came to me again: ¹⁹"As for you, son of man, mark two ways for the sword of the king of Babylon to come. Both of them shall come from the same land. And make a signpost; make it at the head of the way to a city. ²⁰Mark a way for the sword to come to Rabbah of the Ammonites and to Judah, into Jerusalem the fortified. ²¹For the king of Babylon stands at the parting of the way, at the head of the two ways, to use divination. He shakes the arrows; he consults the teraphim;⁶ he looks at the liver. ²²Into his right hand comes the divination for Jerusalem, to set battering rams, to open the mouth with murder, to lift up the voice with shouting, to set battering rams against the gates, to cast up mounds, to build siege towers. ²³But to them it will seem like a false divination. They have sworn solemn oaths, but he brings their guilt to remembrance, that they may be taken.

²⁴"Therefore thus says the Lord GOD: Because you have made your guilt to be remembered, in that your transgressions are uncovered, so that in all your deeds your sins appear—because you have come to remembrance, you shall be taken in hand. ²⁵And you, O profane⁷ wicked one, prince of Israel, whose day has come, the time of your final punishment, ²⁶thus says the Lord GOD: Remove the turban and take off the crown. Things shall not remain as they are. Exalt that which is low, and bring low that which is exalted. ²⁷A ruin, ruin, ruin I will make it. This also shall not be, until he comes, the one to whom judgment belongs, and I will give it to him.

²⁸"And you, son of man, prophesy, and say, Thus says the Lord GOD concerning the

---

¹ Probable reading; Hebrew *The rod of my son despises everything of wood* ² Or *For it is a testing; and what if even the rod despises? It shall not be!*
³ Hebrew *its third* ⁴ Hebrew *many stumbling blocks* ⁵ The meaning of the Hebrew word rendered *taken up* is uncertain ⁶ Or *household idols* ⁷ Or *slain;*
also verse 29

Ammonites and concerning their reproach; say, A sword, a sword is drawn for the slaughter. It is polished to consume and to flash like lightning— ²⁹while they see for you false visions, while they divine lies for you—to place you on the necks of the profane wicked, whose day has come, the time of their final punishment. ³⁰Return it to its sheath. In the place where you were created, in the land of your origin, I will judge you. ³¹And I will pour out my indignation upon you; I will blow upon you with the fire of my wrath, and I will deliver you into the hands of brutish men, skillful to destroy. ³²You shall be fuel for the fire. Your blood shall be in the midst of the land. You shall be no more remembered, for I the LORD have spoken."

The vision of the bloody city [chapter 22]. This oracle of judgment is addressed to Jerusalem as representative of the nation. The main principle underlying the chapter is the satiric list of vices, accompanied by declarations of the wrath of God that these sins deserve.

22 And the word of the LORD came to me, saying, ²"And you, son of man, will you judge, will you judge the bloody city? Then declare to her all her abominations. ³You shall say, Thus says the Lord GOD: A city that sheds blood in her midst, so that her time may come, and that makes idols to defile herself! ⁴You have become guilty by the blood that you have shed, and defiled by the idols that you have made, and you have brought your days near, the appointed time of¹ your years has come. Therefore I have made you a reproach to the nations, and a mockery to all the countries. ⁵Those who are near and those who are far from you will mock you; your name is defiled; you are full of tumult.

⁶"Behold, the princes of Israel in you, every one according to his power, have been bent on shedding blood. ⁷Father and mother are treated with contempt in you; the sojourner suffers extortion in your midst; the fatherless and the widow are wronged in you. ⁸You have despised my holy things and profaned my Sabbaths. ⁹There are men in you who slander to shed blood, and people in you who eat on the mountains; they commit lewdness in your midst. ¹⁰In you men uncover their fathers' nakedness; in you they violate women who are unclean in their menstrual impurity. ¹¹One commits abomination with his neighbor's wife; another lewdly defiles his daughter-in-law; another in you violates his sister, his father's daughter. ¹²In you they take bribes to shed blood; you take interest and profit² and make gain of your neighbors by extortion; but me you have forgotten, declares the Lord GOD.

¹³"Behold, I strike my hand at the dishonest gain that you have made, and at the blood that has been in your midst. ¹⁴Can your courage endure, or can your hands be strong, in the days that I shall deal with you? I the LORD have spoken, and I will do it. ¹⁵I will scatter you among the nations and disperse you through the countries, and I will consume your uncleanness out of you. ¹⁶And you shall be profaned by your own doing in the sight of the nations, and you shall know that I am the LORD."

¹⁷And the word of the LORD came to me: ¹⁸"Son of man, the house of Israel has become dross to me; all of them are bronze and tin and iron and lead in the furnace; they are dross of silver. ¹⁹Therefore thus says the Lord GOD: Because you have all become dross, therefore, behold, I will gather you into the midst of Jerusalem. ²⁰As one gathers silver and bronze and iron and lead and tin into a furnace, to blow the

---

¹ Some Hebrew manuscripts, Septuagint, Syriac, Vulgate, Targum; most Hebrew manuscripts *until* ² That is, profit that comes from charging interest to the poor (compare Leviticus 25:36)

fire on it in order to melt it, so I will gather you in my anger and in my wrath, and I will put you in and melt you. ²¹I will gather you and blow on you with the fire of my wrath, and you shall be melted in the midst of it. ²²As silver is melted in a furnace, so you shall be melted in the midst of it, and you shall know that I am the LORD; I have poured out my wrath upon you."

²³And the word of the LORD came to me: ²⁴"Son of man, say to her, You are a land that is not cleansed or rained upon in the day of indignation. ²⁵The conspiracy of her prophets in her midst is like a roaring lion tearing the prey; they have devoured human lives; they have taken treasure and precious things; they have made many widows in her midst. ²⁶Her priests have done violence to my law and have profaned my holy things. They have made no distinction between the holy and the common, neither have they taught the difference between the unclean and the clean, and they have disregarded my Sabbaths, so that I am profaned among them. ²⁷Her princes in her midst are like wolves tearing the prey, shedding blood, destroying lives to get dishonest gain. ²⁸And her prophets have smeared whitewash for them, seeing false visions and divining lies for them, saying, 'Thus says the Lord GOD,' when the LORD has not spoken. ²⁹The people of the land have practiced extortion and committed robbery. They have oppressed the poor and needy, and have extorted from the sojourner without justice. ³⁰And I sought for a man among them who should build up the wall and stand in the breach before me for the land, that I should not destroy it, but I found none. ³¹Therefore I have poured out my indignation upon them. I have consumed them with the fire of my wrath. I have returned their way upon their heads, declares the Lord GOD."

Vision of the adulterous sisters [chapter 23]. The visionary and satiric modes continue to dominate, as does the technique of symbolism. The chapter narrates the history of two sisters and prostitutes named Oholah and Oholibah, symbolic of Samaria and Jerusalem (Judah). The sequence is as follows: the lewd behavior of the two metaphoric sisters (vv. 1–21); an oracle predicting destruction for Oholibah (vv. 22–35); an oracle of judgment against both sisters (vv. 36–49). A chapter such as this asks us first to look at its message for the original audience but then to look beyond that to what is universal in this story of sin and judgment. The metaphoric approach to the subject makes it easy to see what is universal in the situation.

23 The word of the LORD came to me: ²"Son of man, there were two women, the daughters of one mother. ³They played the whore in Egypt; they played the whore in their youth; there their breasts were pressed and their virgin bosoms¹ handled. ⁴Oholah was the name of the elder and Oholibah the name of her sister. They became mine, and they bore sons and daughters. As for their names, Oholah is Samaria, and Oholibah is Jerusalem.

⁵"Oholah played the whore while she was mine, and she lusted after her lovers the Assyrians, warriors ⁶clothed in purple, governors and commanders, all of them desirable young men, horsemen riding on horses. ⁷She bestowed her whoring upon them, the choicest men of Assyria all of them, and she defiled herself with all the idols of everyone after whom she lusted. ⁸She did not give up her whoring that she had begun in Egypt; for in her youth men had lain with her and handled her virgin bosom and

¹ Hebrew *nipples*; also verses 8, 21

poured out their whoring lust upon her. [9]Therefore I delivered her into the hands of her lovers, into the hands of the Assyrians, after whom she lusted. [10]These uncovered her nakedness; they seized her sons and her daughters; and as for her, they killed her with the sword; and she became a byword among women, when judgment had been executed on her.

[11]"Her sister Oholibah saw this, and she became more corrupt than her sister[1] in her lust and in her whoring, which was worse than that of her sister. [12]She lusted after the Assyrians, governors and commanders, warriors clothed in full armor, horsemen riding on horses, all of them desirable young men. [13]And I saw that she was defiled; they both took the same way. [14]But she carried her whoring further. She saw men portrayed on the wall, the images of the Chaldeans portrayed in vermilion, [15]wearing belts on their waists, with flowing turbans on their heads, all of them having the appearance of officers, a likeness of Babylonians whose native land was Chaldea. [16]When she saw them, she lusted after them and sent messengers to them in Chaldea. [17]And the Babylonians came to her into the bed of love, and they defiled her with their whoring lust. And after she was defiled by them, she turned from them in disgust. [18]When she carried on her whoring so openly and flaunted her nakedness, I turned in disgust from her, as I had turned in disgust from her sister. [19]Yet she increased her whoring, remembering the days of her youth, when she played the whore in the land of Egypt [20]and lusted after her paramours there, whose members were like those of donkeys, and whose issue was like that of horses. [21]Thus you longed for the lewdness of your youth, when the Egyptians handled your bosom and pressed[2] your young breasts."

[22]Therefore, O Oholibah, thus says the Lord God: "Behold, I will stir up against you your lovers from whom you turned in disgust, and I will bring them against you from every side: [23]the Babylonians and all the Chaldeans, Pekod and Shoa and Koa, and all the Assyrians with them, desirable young men, governors and commanders all of them, officers and men of renown, all of them riding on horses. [24]And they shall come against you from the north[3] with chariots and wagons and a host of peoples. They shall set themselves against you on every side with buckler, shield, and helmet; and I will commit the judgment to them, and they shall judge you according to their judgments. [25]And I will direct my jealousy against you, that they may deal with you in fury. They shall cut off your nose and your ears, and your survivors shall fall by the sword. They shall seize your sons and your daughters, and your survivors shall be devoured by fire. [26]They shall also strip you of your clothes and take away your beautiful jewels. [27]Thus I will put an end to your lewdness and your whoring begun in the land of Egypt, so that you shall not lift up your eyes to them or remember Egypt anymore.

[28]"For thus says the Lord God: Behold, I will deliver you into the hands of those whom you hate, into the hands of those from whom you turned in disgust, [29]and they shall deal with you in hatred and take away all the fruit of your labor and leave you naked and bare, and the nakedness of your whoring shall be uncovered. Your lewdness and your whoring [30]have brought this upon you, because you played the whore with the nations and defiled yourself with their idols. [31]You have gone the way of your sister; therefore I will give her cup into your hand. [32]Thus says the Lord God:

"You shall drink your sister's cup
    that is deep and large;

---

[1] Hebrew *than she* [2] Vulgate, Syriac; Hebrew *bosom for the sake of* [3] Septuagint; the meaning of the Hebrew word is unknown

you shall be laughed at and held in derision,
     for it contains much;
³³ you will be filled with drunkenness and sorrow.
A cup of horror and desolation,
     the cup of your sister Samaria;
³⁴ you shall drink it and drain it out,
     and gnaw its shards,
     and tear your breasts;

for I have spoken, declares the Lord GOD. ³⁵Therefore thus says the Lord GOD: Because you have forgotten me and cast me behind your back, you yourself must bear the consequences of your lewdness and whoring."

³⁶The LORD said to me: "Son of man, will you judge Oholah and Oholibah? Declare to them their abominations. ³⁷For they have committed adultery, and blood is on their hands. With their idols they have committed adultery, and they have even offered up[1] to them for food the children whom they had borne to me. ³⁸Moreover, this they have done to me: they have defiled my sanctuary on the same day and profaned my Sabbaths. ³⁹For when they had slaughtered their children in sacrifice to their idols, on the same day they came into my sanctuary to profane it. And behold, this is what they did in my house. ⁴⁰They even sent for men to come from afar, to whom a messenger was sent; and behold, they came. For them you bathed yourself, painted your eyes, and adorned yourself with ornaments. ⁴¹You sat on a stately couch, with a table spread before it on which you had placed my incense and my oil. ⁴²The sound of a carefree multitude was with her; and with men of the common sort, drunkards[2] were brought from the wilderness; and they put bracelets on the hands of the women, and beautiful crowns on their heads.

⁴³"Then I said of her who was worn out by adultery, Now they will continue to use her for a whore, even her![3] ⁴⁴For they have gone in to her, as men go in to a prostitute. Thus they went in to Oholah and to Oholibah, lewd women! ⁴⁵But righteous men shall pass judgment on them with the sentence of adulteresses, and with the sentence of women who shed blood, because they are adulteresses, and blood is on their hands."

⁴⁶For thus says the Lord GOD: "Bring up a vast host against them, and make them an object of terror and a plunder. ⁴⁷And the host shall stone them and cut them down with their swords. They shall kill their sons and their daughters, and burn up their houses. ⁴⁸Thus will I put an end to lewdness in the land, that all women may take warning and not commit lewdness as you have done. ⁴⁹And they shall return your lewdness upon you, and you shall bear the penalty for your sinful idolatry, and you shall know that I am the Lord GOD."

The vision of the boiling pot [chapter 24]. We continue to move in a symbolic world in this chapter, where the first half is devoted to a vision of a boiling pot in which an animal is cooked, symbolic of God's judgment against Jerusalem/Judah (vv. 1–14). A piece of biographical data—the death of Ezekiel's wife (vv. 15–18)—is followed by more predictions of judgment (vv. 19–27).

---

[1] Or have even made pass through the fire [2] Or Sabeans [3] The meaning of the Hebrew verse is uncertain

24

In the ninth year, in the tenth month, on the tenth day of the month, the word of the LORD came to me: ²"Son of man, write down the name of this day, this very day. The king of Babylon has laid siege to Jerusalem this very day. ³And utter a parable to the rebellious house and say to them, Thus says the Lord GOD:

"Set on the pot, set it on;
    pour in water also;
4   put in it the pieces of meat,
        all the good pieces, the thigh and the shoulder;
        fill it with choice bones.
5   Take the choicest one of the flock;
        pile the logs¹ under it;
    boil it well;
        seethe also its bones in it.

⁶"Therefore thus says the Lord GOD: Woe to the bloody city, to the pot whose corrosion is in it, and whose corrosion has not gone out of it! Take out of it piece after piece, without making any choice.² ⁷For the blood she has shed is in her midst; she put it on the bare rock; she did not pour it out on the ground to cover it with dust. ⁸To rouse my wrath, to take vengeance, I have set on the bare rock the blood she has shed, that it may not be covered. ⁹Therefore thus says the Lord GOD: Woe to the bloody city! I also will make the pile great. ¹⁰Heap on the logs, kindle the fire, boil the meat well, mix in the spices,³ and let the bones be burned up. ¹¹Then set it empty upon the coals, that it may become hot, and its copper may burn, that its uncleanness may be melted in it, its corrosion consumed. ¹²She has wearied herself with toil;⁴ its abundant corrosion does not go out of it. Into the fire with its corrosion! ¹³On account of your unclean lewdness, because I would have cleansed you and you were not cleansed from your uncleanness, you shall not be cleansed anymore till I have satisfied my fury upon you. ¹⁴I am the LORD. I have spoken; it shall come to pass; I will do it. I will not go back; I will not spare; I will not relent; according to your ways and your deeds you will be judged, declares the Lord GOD."

¹⁵The word of the LORD came to me: ¹⁶"Son of man, behold, I am about to take the delight of your eyes away from you at a stroke; yet you shall not mourn or weep, nor shall your tears run down. ¹⁷Sigh, but not aloud; make no mourning for the dead. Bind on your turban, and put your shoes on your feet; do not cover your lips, nor eat the bread of men." ¹⁸So I spoke to the people in the morning, and at evening my wife died. And on the next morning I did as I was commanded.

¹⁹And the people said to me, "Will you not tell us what these things mean for us, that you are acting thus?" ²⁰Then I said to them, "The word of the LORD came to me: ²¹'Say to the house of Israel, Thus says the Lord GOD: Behold, I will profane my sanctuary, the pride of your power, the delight of your eyes, and the yearning of your soul, and your sons and your daughters whom you left behind shall fall by the sword. ²²And you shall do as I have done; you shall not cover your lips, nor eat the bread of men. ²³Your turbans shall be on your heads and your shoes on your feet; you shall not mourn or weep, but you shall rot away in your iniquities and groan to one another. ²⁴Thus shall Ezekiel be to you a sign; according to all that he has done you shall do. When this comes, then you will know that I am the Lord GOD.'

¹ Compare verse 10; Hebrew *the bones* ² Hebrew *no lot has fallen upon it* ³ Or *empty out the broth* ⁴ The meaning of the Hebrew is uncertain

²⁵"As for you, son of man, surely on the day when I take from them their strong-hold, their joy and glory, the delight of their eyes and their soul's desire, and also their sons and daughters, ²⁶on that day a fugitive will come to you to report to you the news. ²⁷On that day your mouth will be opened to the fugitive, and you shall speak and be no longer mute. So you will be a sign to them, and they will know that I am the LORD."

> **Oracles of judgment against four surrounding nations** [chapter 25]. The focus of the book thus far has been the covenant nation of Judah. Chapter 25 initiates an eight-chapter block of prophecies directed against neighboring pagan nations. The rhetorical modes remain the familiar ones—satiric lists of abuses and predictions of coming destruction. God remains the authoritative speaker and judge.

25 The word of the LORD came to me: ²"Son of man, set your face toward the Ammonites and prophesy against them. ³Say to the Ammonites, Hear the word of the Lord GOD: Thus says the Lord GOD, Because you said, 'Aha!' over my sanctuary when it was profaned, and over the land of Israel when it was made deso-late, and over the house of Judah when they went into exile, ⁴therefore behold, I am handing you over to the people of the East for a possession, and they shall set their encampments among you and make their dwellings in your midst. They shall eat your fruit, and they shall drink your milk. ⁵I will make Rabbah a pasture for camels and Ammon¹ a fold for flocks. Then you will know that I am the LORD. ⁶For thus says the Lord GOD: Because you have clapped your hands and stamped your feet and rejoiced with all the malice within your soul against the land of Israel, ⁷therefore, behold, I have stretched out my hand against you, and will hand you over as plunder to the nations. And I will cut you off from the peoples and will make you perish out of the countries; I will destroy you. Then you will know that I am the LORD.

⁸"Thus says the Lord GOD: Because Moab and Seir² said, 'Behold, the house of Judah is like all the other nations,' ⁹therefore I will lay open the flank of Moab from the cities, from its cities on its frontier, the glory of the country, Beth-jeshimoth, Baal-meon, and Kiriathaim. ¹⁰I will give it along with the Ammonites to the people of the East as a possession, that the Ammonites may be remembered no more among the nations, ¹¹and I will execute judgments upon Moab. Then they will know that I am the LORD.

¹²"Thus says the Lord GOD: Because Edom acted revengefully against the house of Judah and has grievously offended in taking vengeance on them, ¹³therefore thus says the Lord GOD, I will stretch out my hand against Edom and cut off from it man and beast. And I will make it desolate; from Teman even to Dedan they shall fall by the sword. ¹⁴And I will lay my vengeance upon Edom by the hand of my people Israel, and they shall do in Edom according to my anger and according to my wrath, and they shall know my vengeance, declares the Lord GOD.

¹⁵"Thus says the Lord GOD: Because the Philistines acted revengefully and took vengeance with malice of soul to destroy in never-ending enmity, ¹⁶therefore thus says the Lord GOD, Behold, I will stretch out my hand against the Philistines, and I will cut off the Cherethites and destroy the rest of the seacoast. ¹⁷I will execute great

¹ Hebrew and the Ammonites ² Septuagint lacks and Seir

vengeance on them with wrathful rebukes. Then they will know that I am the LORD, when I lay my vengeance upon them."

> **Prediction of the fall of Tyre** [chapter 26]. The symbolic history of Tyre in Ezekiel 26–28 is one of the best known prophetic sections in the OT. The opening chapter of the three devoted to Tyre follows this sequence: prophecy of doom for Tyre (vv. 1–6); a specific prediction that Nebuchadnezzar king of Babylon will invade and capture Tyre (vv. 7–14); a picture of how the nations will look on in fear as Tyre is destroyed (vv. 15–18); concluding prediction by God that he will send Tyre down to a place with the evocative designation "the pit" (vv. 19–21).

26 In the eleventh year, on the first day of the month, the word of the LORD came to me: ²"Son of man, because Tyre said concerning Jerusalem, 'Aha, the gate of the peoples is broken; it has swung open to me. I shall be replenished, now that she is laid waste,' ³therefore thus says the Lord GOD: Behold, I am against you, O Tyre, and will bring up many nations against you, as the sea brings up its waves. ⁴They shall destroy the walls of Tyre and break down her towers, and I will scrape her soil from her and make her a bare rock. ⁵She shall be in the midst of the sea a place for the spreading of nets, for I have spoken, declares the Lord GOD. And she shall become plunder for the nations, ⁶and her daughters on the mainland shall be killed by the sword. Then they will know that I am the LORD.

⁷"For thus says the Lord GOD: Behold, I will bring against Tyre from the north Nebuchadnezzar[1] king of Babylon, king of kings, with horses and chariots, and with horsemen and a host of many soldiers. ⁸He will kill with the sword your daughters on the mainland. He will set up a siege wall against you and throw up a mound against you, and raise a roof of shields against you. ⁹He will direct the shock of his battering rams against your walls, and with his axes he will break down your towers. ¹⁰His horses will be so many that their dust will cover you. Your walls will shake at the noise of the horsemen and wagons and chariots, when he enters your gates as men enter a city that has been breached. ¹¹With the hoofs of his horses he will trample all your streets. He will kill your people with the sword, and your mighty pillars will fall to the ground. ¹²They will plunder your riches and loot your merchandise. They will break down your walls and destroy your pleasant houses. Your stones and timber and soil they will cast into the midst of the waters. ¹³And I will stop the music of your songs, and the sound of your lyres shall be heard no more. ¹⁴I will make you a bare rock. You shall be a place for the spreading of nets. You shall never be rebuilt, for I am the LORD; I have spoken, declares the Lord GOD.

¹⁵"Thus says the Lord GOD to Tyre: Will not the coastlands shake at the sound of your fall, when the wounded groan, when slaughter is made in your midst? ¹⁶Then all the princes of the sea will step down from their thrones and remove their robes and strip off their embroidered garments. They will clothe themselves with trembling; they will sit on the ground and tremble every moment and be appalled at you. ¹⁷And they will raise a lamentation over you and say to you,

"'How you have perished,
     you who were inhabited from the seas,
   O city renowned,

---

[1] Hebrew *Nebuchadrezzar*, so throughout Ezekiel

> who was mighty on the sea;
> she and her inhabitants imposed their terror
>   on all her inhabitants!
> ¹⁸ Now the coastlands tremble
>   on the day of your fall,
> and the coastlands that are on the sea
>   are dismayed at your passing.'

¹⁹"For thus says the Lord GOD: When I make you a city laid waste, like the cities that are not inhabited, when I bring up the deep over you, and the great waters cover you, ²⁰then I will make you go down with those who go down to the pit, to the people of old, and I will make you to dwell in the world below, among ruins from of old, with those who go down to the pit, so that you will not be inhabited; but I will set beauty in the land of the living. ²¹I will bring you to a dreadful end, and you shall be no more. Though you be sought for, you will never be found again, declares the Lord GOD."

Doom song over the destruction of Tyre [chapter 27]. A prophetic *doom song is a poetic lament or elegy over the demise of a nation (which might be represented by its king). Often a future destruction of the nation is pictured as having already occurred, hence the funeral rites for the nation that we find in the doom song. Here in chapter 27 we find a continued use of imagery and symbolism, as real-life places and people are pictured in metaphoric rather than literal terms. The genre of satire also helps to explain what we find in this chapter. The sequence is as follows: an extended picture of Tyre's prosperity, especially the success of its famous trade (vv. 1–25); a projected picture, expressed in evocative poetry, of the coming destruction of Tyre (vv. 26–36). Because Tyre was an island city, images of water and trade dominate the second poem.

27 The word of the LORD came to me: ²"Now you, son of man, raise a lamentation over Tyre, ³and say to Tyre, who dwells at the entrances to the sea, merchant of the peoples to many coastlands, thus says the Lord GOD:

> "O Tyre, you have said,
>   'I am perfect in beauty.'
> ⁴ Your borders are in the heart of the seas;
>   your builders made perfect your beauty.
> ⁵ They made all your planks
>   of fir trees from Senir;
> they took a cedar from Lebanon
>   to make a mast for you.
> ⁶ Of oaks of Bashan
>   they made your oars;
> they made your deck of pines
>   from the coasts of Cyprus,
>   inlaid with ivory.
> ⁷ Of fine embroidered linen from Egypt
>   was your sail,
>   serving as your banner;

blue and purple from the coasts of Elishah
   was your awning.
8   The inhabitants of Sidon and Arvad
   were your rowers;
your skilled men, O Tyre, were in you;
   they were your pilots.
9   The elders of Gebal and her skilled men were in you,
   caulking your seams;
all the ships of the sea with their mariners were in you
   to barter for your wares.

¹⁰"Persia and Lud and Put were in your army as your men of war. They hung the shield and helmet in you; they gave you splendor. ¹¹Men of Arvad and Helech were on your walls all around, and men of Gamad were in your towers. They hung their shields on your walls all around; they made perfect your beauty. ¹²"Tarshish did business with you because of your great wealth of every kind; silver, iron, tin, and lead they exchanged for your wares. ¹³Javan, Tubal, and Meshech traded with you; they exchanged human beings and vessels of bronze for your merchandise. ¹⁴From Beth-togarmah they exchanged horses, war horses, and mules for your wares. ¹⁵The men of Dedan¹ traded with you. Many coastlands were your own special markets; they brought you in payment ivory tusks and ebony. ¹⁶Syria did business with you because of your abundant goods; they exchanged for your wares emeralds, purple, embroidered work, fine linen, coral, and ruby. ¹⁷Judah and the land of Israel traded with you; they exchanged for your merchandise wheat of Minnith, meal,² honey, oil, and balm. ¹⁸Damascus did business with you for your abundant goods, because of your great wealth of every kind; wine of Helbon and wool of Sahar ¹⁹and casks of wine³ from Uzal they exchanged for your wares; wrought iron, cassia, and calamus were bartered for your merchandise. ²⁰Dedan traded with you in saddlecloths for riding. ²¹Arabia and all the princes of Kedar were your favored dealers in lambs, rams, and goats; in these they did business with you. ²²The traders of Sheba and Raamah traded with you; they exchanged for your wares the best of all kinds of spices and all precious stones and gold. ²³Haran, Canneh, Eden, traders of Sheba, Asshur, and Chilmad traded with you. ²⁴In your market these traded with you in choice garments, in clothes of blue and embroidered work, and in carpets of colored material, bound with cords and made secure. ²⁵The ships of Tarshish traveled for you with your merchandise. So you were filled and heavily laden in the heart of the seas.

26   "Your rowers have brought you out
   into the high seas.
The east wind has wrecked you
   in the heart of the seas.
27   Your riches, your wares, your merchandise,
   your mariners and your pilots,
your caulkers, your dealers in merchandise,
   and all your men of war who are in you,
with all your crew

---

¹ Hebrew; Septuagint *Rhodes* ² The meaning of the Hebrew word is unknown ³ Probable reading; Hebrew *wool of Sahar, Vedan, and Javan*

that is in your midst,
  sink into the heart of the seas
    on the day of your fall.
28 At the sound of the cry of your pilots
      the countryside shakes,
29 and down from their ships
      come all who handle the oar.
  The mariners and all the pilots of the sea
      stand on the land
30 and shout aloud over you
      and cry out bitterly.
  They cast dust on their heads
      and wallow in ashes;
31 they make themselves bald for you
      and put sackcloth on their waist,
  and they weep over you in bitterness of soul,
      with bitter mourning.
32 In their wailing they raise a lamentation for you
      and lament over you:
  'Who is like Tyre,
      like one destroyed in the midst of the sea?
33 When your wares came from the seas,
      you satisfied many peoples;
  with your abundant wealth and merchandise
      you enriched the kings of the earth.
34 Now you are wrecked by the seas,
      in the depths of the waters;
  your merchandise and all your crew in your midst
      have sunk with you.
35 All the inhabitants of the coastlands
      are appalled at you,
  and the hair of their kings bristles with horror;
      their faces are convulsed.
36 The merchants among the peoples hiss at you;
      you have come to a dreadful end
      and shall be no more forever.'"

Further oracles against Tyre [chapter 28]. Two more prophetic poems round out the impressive section devoted to Tyre—a list of indictments against the prince of Tyre, along with a prediction that he will be destroyed (vv. 1–10), and another doom song in which the fall of the prince of Tyre is treated as though it had already happened (vv. 11–19). The imagery and motifs that Ezekiel uses to develop his theme are so heightened that they have satanic overtones (especially in vv. 13–17). A brief oracle of judgment against Tyre's companion city Sidon (vv. 20–23) and an oracle of restoration for Israel (vv. 24–26) round out the chapter.

28

The word of the LORD came to me: [2]"Son of man, say to the prince of Tyre, Thus says the Lord GOD:

"Because your heart is proud,
   and you have said, 'I am a god,
I sit in the seat of the gods,
   in the heart of the seas,'
yet you are but a man, and no god,
   though you make your heart like the heart of a god—
[3]   you are indeed wiser than Daniel;
   no secret is hidden from you;
[4]   by your wisdom and your understanding
   you have made wealth for yourself,
and have gathered gold and silver
   into your treasuries;
[5]   by your great wisdom in your trade
   you have increased your wealth,
and your heart has become proud in your wealth—
[6]   therefore thus says the Lord GOD:
Because you make your heart
   like the heart of a god,
[7]   therefore, behold, I will bring foreigners upon you,
   the most ruthless of the nations;
and they shall draw their swords against the beauty of your wisdom
   and defile your splendor.
[8]   They shall thrust you down into the pit,
   and you shall die the death of the slain
   in the heart of the seas.
[9]   Will you still say, 'I am a god,'
   in the presence of those who kill you,
though you are but a man, and no god,
   in the hands of those who slay you?
[10]   You shall die the death of the uncircumcised
   by the hand of foreigners;
   for I have spoken, declares the Lord GOD."

[11]Moreover, the word of the LORD came to me: [12]"Son of man, raise a lamentation over the king of Tyre, and say to him, Thus says the Lord GOD:

"You were the signet of perfection,[1]
   full of wisdom and perfect in beauty.
[13]   You were in Eden, the garden of God;
   every precious stone was your covering,
sardius, topaz, and diamond,
   beryl, onyx, and jasper,
sapphire,[2] emerald, and carbuncle;
   and crafted in gold were your settings
   and your engravings.[3]

---

[1] The meaning of the Hebrew phrase is uncertain [2] Or *lapis lazuli* [3] The meaning of the Hebrew phrase is uncertain

On the day that you were created
   they were prepared.
[14] You were an anointed guardian cherub.
   I placed you;[1] you were on the holy mountain of God;
   in the midst of the stones of fire you walked.
[15] You were blameless in your ways
   from the day you were created,
   till unrighteousness was found in you.
[16] In the abundance of your trade
   you were filled with violence in your midst, and you sinned;
   so I cast you as a profane thing from the mountain of God,
   and I destroyed you,[2] O guardian cherub,
   from the midst of the stones of fire.
[17] Your heart was proud because of your beauty;
   you corrupted your wisdom for the sake of your splendor.
   I cast you to the ground;
   I exposed you before kings,
   to feast their eyes on you.
[18] By the multitude of your iniquities,
   in the unrighteousness of your trade
   you profaned your sanctuaries;
   so I brought fire out from your midst;
   it consumed you,
   and I turned you to ashes on the earth
   in the sight of all who saw you.
[19] All who know you among the peoples
   are appalled at you;
   you have come to a dreadful end
   and shall be no more forever."

[20]The word of the LORD came to me: [21]"Son of man, set your face toward Sidon, and prophesy against her [22]and say, Thus says the Lord GOD:

"Behold, I am against you, O Sidon,
   and I will manifest my glory in your midst.
And they shall know that I am the LORD
   when I execute judgments in her
   and manifest my holiness in her;
[23] for I will send pestilence into her,
   and blood into her streets;
and the slain shall fall in her midst,
   by the sword that is against her on every side.
Then they will know that I am the LORD.

[24]"And for the house of Israel there shall be no more a brier to prick or a thorn to hurt them among all their neighbors who have treated them with contempt. Then they will know that I am the Lord GOD.

[25]"Thus says the Lord GOD: When I gather the house of Israel from the peoples

---

[1] The meaning of the Hebrew phrase is uncertain [2] Or *banished you*

among whom they are scattered, and manifest my holiness in them in the sight of the nations, then they shall dwell in their own land that I gave to my servant Jacob. [26]And they shall dwell securely in it, and they shall build houses and plant vineyards. They shall dwell securely, when I execute judgments upon all their neighbors who have treated them with contempt. Then they will know that I am the LORD their God."

Oracles against Egypt [chapters 29–30]. The nation of Egypt now gets a whopping four chapters devoted to its predicted destruction. The subject and rhetorical forms remain constant, consisting of lists of indictments and predictions of destruction. Thematically these oracles assert the authority of God over nations. We can also note the rhetorical pattern of alternating poetry and prose (which carries into the next two chapters as well).

29 In the tenth year, in the tenth month, on the twelfth day of the month, the word of the LORD came to me: [2]"Son of man, set your face against Pharaoh king of Egypt, and prophesy against him and against all Egypt; [3]speak, and say, Thus says the Lord GOD:

"Behold, I am against you,
    Pharaoh king of Egypt,
the great dragon that lies
    in the midst of his streams,
that says, 'My Nile is my own;
    I made it for myself.'
[4] I will put hooks in your jaws,
    and make the fish of your streams stick to your scales;
and I will draw you up out of the midst of your streams,
    with all the fish of your streams
    that stick to your scales.
[5] And I will cast you out into the wilderness,
    you and all the fish of your streams;
you shall fall on the open field,
    and not be brought together or gathered.
To the beasts of the earth and to the birds of the heavens
    I give you as food.

[6]Then all the inhabitants of Egypt shall know that I am the LORD.

"Because you[1] have been a staff of reed to the house of Israel, [7]when they grasped you with the hand, you broke and tore all their shoulders; and when they leaned on you, you broke and made all their loins to shake.[2] [8]Therefore thus says the Lord GOD: Behold, I will bring a sword upon you, and will cut off from you man and beast, [9]and the land of Egypt shall be a desolation and a waste. Then they will know that I am the LORD.

"Because you[3] said, 'The Nile is mine, and I made it,' [10]therefore, behold, I am against you and against your streams, and I will make the land of Egypt an utter waste and desolation, from Migdol to Syene, as far as the border of Cush. [11]No foot of man shall pass through it, and no foot of beast shall pass through it; it shall be unin-

---

[1] Hebrew *they* [2] Syriac (compare Psalm 69:23); Hebrew *to stand* [3] Hebrew *he*

habited forty years. ¹²And I will make the land of Egypt a desolation in the midst of desolated countries, and her cities shall be a desolation forty years among cities that are laid waste. I will scatter the Egyptians among the nations, and disperse them through the countries.

¹³"For thus says the Lord GOD: At the end of forty years I will gather the Egyptians from the peoples among whom they were scattered, ¹⁴and I will restore the fortunes of Egypt and bring them back to the land of Pathros, the land of their origin, and there they shall be a lowly kingdom. ¹⁵It shall be the most lowly of the kingdoms, and never again exalt itself above the nations. And I will make them so small that they will never again rule over the nations. ¹⁶And it shall never again be the reliance of the house of Israel, recalling their iniquity, when they turn to them for aid. Then they will know that I am the Lord GOD."

¹⁷In the twenty-seventh year, in the first month, on the first day of the month, the word of the LORD came to me: ¹⁸"Son of man, Nebuchadnezzar king of Babylon made his army labor hard against Tyre. Every head was made bald, and every shoulder was rubbed bare, yet neither he nor his army got anything from Tyre to pay for the labor that he had performed against her. ¹⁹Therefore thus says the Lord GOD: Behold, I will give the land of Egypt to Nebuchadnezzar king of Babylon; and he shall carry off its wealth¹ and despoil it and plunder it; and it shall be the wages for his army. ²⁰I have given him the land of Egypt as his payment for which he labored, because they worked for me, declares the Lord GOD.

²¹"On that day I will cause a horn to spring up for the house of Israel, and I will open your lips among them. Then they will know that I am the LORD."

30

The word of the LORD came to me: ²"Son of man, prophesy, and say, Thus says the Lord GOD:

"Wail, 'Alas for the day!'
³   For the day is near,
       the day of the LORD is near;
    it will be a day of clouds,
       a time of doom for² the nations.
⁴   A sword shall come upon Egypt,
       and anguish shall be in Cush,
    when the slain fall in Egypt,
       and her wealth³ is carried away,
       and her foundations are torn down.

⁵Cush, and Put, and Lud, and all Arabia, and Libya,⁴ and the people of the land that is in league,⁵ shall fall with them by the sword.

⁶ "Thus says the LORD:
    Those who support Egypt shall fall,
       and her proud might shall come down;
    from Migdol to Syene
       they shall fall within her by the sword,
    declares the Lord GOD.
⁷   And they shall be desolated in the midst of desolated countries,

---

¹ Or multitude ² Hebrew lacks doom for ³ Or multitude; also verse 10 ⁴ With Septuagint; Hebrew Cub ⁵ Hebrew and the sons of the land of the covenant

and their cities shall be in the midst of cities that are laid waste.
8   Then they will know that I am the LORD,
      when I have set fire to Egypt,
      and all her helpers are broken.

9 "On that day messengers shall go out from me in ships to terrify the unsuspecting people of Cush, and anguish shall come upon them on the day of Egypt's doom;[1] for, behold, it comes!
    10 "Thus says the Lord GOD:

"I will put an end to the wealth of Egypt,
      by the hand of Nebuchadnezzar king of Babylon.
11   He and his people with him, the most ruthless of nations,
      shall be brought in to destroy the land,
      and they shall draw their swords against Egypt
      and fill the land with the slain.
12   And I will dry up the Nile
      and will sell the land into the hand of evildoers;
      I will bring desolation upon the land and everything in it,
      by the hand of foreigners;
      I am the LORD; I have spoken.

    13 "Thus says the Lord GOD:

"I will destroy the idols
      and put an end to the images in Memphis;
      there shall no longer be a prince from the land of Egypt;
      so I will put fear in the land of Egypt.
14   I will make Pathros a desolation
      and will set fire to Zoan
      and will execute judgments on Thebes.
15   And I will pour out my wrath on Pelusium,
      the stronghold of Egypt,
      and cut off the multitude[2] of Thebes.
16   And I will set fire to Egypt;
      Pelusium shall be in great agony;
      Thebes shall be breached,
      and Memphis shall face enemies[3] by day.
17   The young men of On and of Pi-beseth shall fall by the sword,
      and the women[4] shall go into captivity.
18   At Tehaphnehes the day shall be dark,
      when I break there the yoke bars of Egypt,
      and her proud might shall come to an end in her;
      she shall be covered by a cloud,
      and her daughters shall go into captivity.
19   Thus I will execute judgments on Egypt.
      Then they will know that I am the LORD."

    20 In the eleventh year, in the first month, on the seventh day of the month, the word of the LORD came to me: 21 "Son of man, I have broken the arm of Pharaoh king of

---

[1] Hebrew *the day of Egypt* [2] Or *wealth* [3] Or *distress* [4] Or *the cities*; Hebrew *they*

Egypt, and behold, it has not been bound up, to heal it by binding it with a bandage, so that it may become strong to wield the sword. ²²Therefore thus says the Lord GOD: Behold, I am against Pharaoh king of Egypt and will break his arms, both the strong arm and the one that was broken, and I will make the sword fall from his hand. ²³I will scatter the Egyptians among the nations and disperse them through the countries. ²⁴And I will strengthen the arms of the king of Babylon and put my sword in his hand, but I will break the arms of Pharaoh, and he will groan before him like a man mortally wounded. ²⁵I will strengthen the arms of the king of Babylon, but the arms of Pharaoh shall fall. Then they shall know that I am the LORD, when I put my sword into the hand of the king of Babylon and he stretches it out against the land of Egypt. ²⁶And I will scatter the Egyptians among the nations and disperse them throughout the countries. Then they will know that I am the LORD."

> **The symbolic history of a great cedar** [chapter 31]. With this chapter we return to the mode of symbolic reality, meaning that we enter a world of the imagination where the main entities are symbols rather than literal facts (this is not to deny that real-life Egypt is what is being portrayed). This time Ezekiel returns to the symbol of a great cedar tree, and again it represents a nation. The chapter begins with a poetic and descriptive flourish in which a more-than-earthly cedar tree is portrayed (vv. 1–9). Then God announces the judgment that he intends to bring against the cedar tree (vv. 10–18). Despite all the historical particulars in the chapter, the vision is as up to date as the latest newspaper, especially if we pay attention to how prominent the charge of pride is in God's charges against the nations.

31 In the eleventh year, in the third month, on the first day of the month, the word of the LORD came to me: ²"Son of man, say to Pharaoh king of Egypt and to his multitude:

"Whom are you like in your greatness?
³   Behold, Assyria was a cedar in Lebanon,
    with beautiful branches and forest shade,
        and of towering height,
        its top among the clouds.¹
⁴   The waters nourished it;
        the deep made it grow tall,
    making its rivers flow
        around the place of its planting,
    sending forth its streams
        to all the trees of the field.
⁵   So it towered high
        above all the trees of the field;
    its boughs grew large
        and its branches long
        from abundant water in its shoots.
⁶   All the birds of the heavens
        made their nests in its boughs;

---

¹ Or *its top went through the thick boughs*; also verses 10, 14

under its branches all the beasts of the field
  gave birth to their young,
and under its shadow
  lived all great nations.
7 It was beautiful in its greatness,
  in the length of its branches;
for its roots went down
  to abundant waters.
8 The cedars in the garden of God could not rival it,
  nor the fir trees equal its boughs;
neither were the plane trees
  like its branches;
no tree in the garden of God
  was its equal in beauty.
9 I made it beautiful
  in the mass of its branches,
and all the trees of Eden envied it,
  that were in the garden of God.

10 "Therefore thus says the Lord God: Because it[1] towered high and set its top among the clouds, and its heart was proud of its height, 11 I will give it into the hand of a mighty one of the nations. He shall surely deal with it as its wickedness deserves. I have cast it out. 12 Foreigners, the most ruthless of nations, have cut it down and left it. On the mountains and in all the valleys its branches have fallen, and its boughs have been broken in all the ravines of the land, and all the peoples of the earth have gone away from its shadow and left it. 13 On its fallen trunk dwell all the birds of the heavens, and on its branches are all the beasts of the field. 14 All this is in order that no trees by the waters may grow to towering height or set their tops among the clouds, and that no trees that drink water may reach up to them in height. For they are all given over to death, to the world below, among the children of man,[2] with those who go down to the pit.

15 "Thus says the Lord God: On the day the cedar[3] went down to Sheol I caused mourning; I closed the deep over it, and restrained its rivers, and many waters were stopped. I clothed Lebanon in gloom for it, and all the trees of the field fainted because of it. 16 I made the nations quake at the sound of its fall, when I cast it down to Sheol with those who go down to the pit. And all the trees of Eden, the choice and best of Lebanon, all that drink water, were comforted in the world below. 17 They also went down to Sheol with it, to those who are slain by the sword; yes, those who were its arm, who lived under its shadow among the nations.

18 "Whom are you thus like in glory and in greatness among the trees of Eden? You shall be brought down with the trees of Eden to the world below. You shall lie among the uncircumcised, with those who are slain by the sword.

"This is Pharaoh and all his multitude, declares the Lord God."

Funeral rites for a nation [chapter 32]. The extended chapter 32 brings the case against Egypt to closure. We find a prediction directed specifically against Pharaoh (vv. 1–8), followed by an oracle of judgment against the entire nation (vv. 9–16). Then we

---

[1] Syriac, Vulgate; Hebrew *you* [2] Or *of Adam* [3] Hebrew *it*

get one of the really striking passages in the book of Ezekiel: in a manner anticipatory of Dante's *Inferno*, God sends a message via Ezekiel to a personified Egypt to visit "the world below, . . . the pit" (32:18), where Pharaoh and his army will find the corpses of notorious sinners and nations of the ancient world (32:17–30). In a wry concluding touch, God says that Pharaoh "will be comforted" by his trip to hell (v. 31), before being laid to rest there himself (v. 32).

32 In the twelfth year, in the twelfth month, on the first day of the month, the word of the LORD came to me: ²"Son of man, raise a lamentation over Pharaoh king of Egypt and say to him:

"You consider yourself a lion of the nations,
> but you are like a dragon in the seas;
you burst forth in your rivers,
> trouble the waters with your feet,
> and foul their rivers.
³ Thus says the Lord GOD:
> I will throw my net over you
> with a host of many peoples,
> and they will haul you up in my dragnet.
⁴ And I will cast you on the ground;
> on the open field I will fling you,
and will cause all the birds of the heavens to settle on you,
> and I will gorge the beasts of the whole earth with you.
⁵ I will strew your flesh upon the mountains
> and fill the valleys with your carcass.¹
⁶ I will drench the land even to the mountains
> with your flowing blood,
> and the ravines will be full of you.
⁷ When I blot you out, I will cover the heavens
> and make their stars dark;
I will cover the sun with a cloud,
> and the moon shall not give its light.
⁸ All the bright lights of heaven
> will I make dark over you,
> and put darkness on your land,
> > declares the Lord GOD.

⁹"I will trouble the hearts of many peoples, when I bring your destruction among the nations, into the countries that you have not known. ¹⁰I will make many peoples appalled at you, and the hair of their kings shall bristle with horror because of you, when I brandish my sword before them. They shall tremble every moment, every one for his own life, on the day of your downfall.

¹¹"For thus says the Lord GOD: The sword of the king of Babylon shall come upon you. ¹²I will cause your multitude to fall by the swords of mighty ones, all of them most ruthless of nations.

¹ Hebrew *your height*

"They shall bring to ruin the pride of Egypt,
    and all its multitude[1] shall perish.
13   I will destroy all its beasts
    from beside many waters;
    and no foot of man shall trouble them anymore,
      nor shall the hoofs of beasts trouble them.
14   Then I will make their waters clear,
    and cause their rivers to run like oil,
                  declares the Lord God.
15   When I make the land of Egypt desolate,
    and when the land is desolate of all that fills it,
  when I strike down all who dwell in it,
    then they will know that I am the Lord.

16 This is a lamentation that shall be chanted; the daughters of the nations shall chant it; over Egypt, and over all her multitude, shall they chant it, declares the Lord God."

17 In the twelfth year, in the twelfth month,[2] on the fifteenth day of the month, the word of the Lord came to me: 18 "Son of man, wail over the multitude of Egypt, and send them down, her and the daughters of majestic nations, to the world below, to those who have gone down to the pit:

19   'Whom do you surpass in beauty?
    Go down and be laid to rest with the uncircumcised.'

20 They shall fall amid those who are slain by the sword. Egypt[3] is delivered to the sword; drag her away, and all her multitudes. 21 The mighty chiefs shall speak of them, with their helpers, out of the midst of Sheol: 'They have come down, they lie still, the uncircumcised, slain by the sword.'

22 "Assyria is there, and all her company, its graves all around it, all of them slain, fallen by the sword, 23 whose graves are set in the uttermost parts of the pit; and her company is all around her grave, all of them slain, fallen by the sword, who spread terror in the land of the living.

24 "Elam is there, and all her multitude around her grave; all of them slain, fallen by the sword, who went down uncircumcised into the world below, who spread their terror in the land of the living; and they bear their shame with those who go down to the pit. 25 They have made her a bed among the slain with all her multitude, her graves all around it, all of them uncircumcised, slain by the sword; for terror of them was spread in the land of the living, and they bear their shame with those who go down to the pit; they are placed among the slain.

26 "Meshech-Tubal is there, and all her multitude, her graves all around it, all of them uncircumcised, slain by the sword; for they spread their terror in the land of the living. 27 And they do not lie with the mighty, the fallen from among the uncircumcised, who went down to Sheol with their weapons of war, whose swords were laid under their heads, and whose iniquities are upon their bones; for the terror of the mighty men was in the land of the living. 28 But as for you, you shall be broken and lie among the uncircumcised, with those who are slain by the sword.

29 "Edom is there, her kings and all her princes, who for all their might are laid with

---

[1] Or wealth   [2] Hebrew lacks in the twelfth month   [3] Hebrew She

those who are killed by the sword; they lie with the uncircumcised, with those who go down to the pit.

³⁰"The princes of the north are there, all of them, and all the Sidonians, who have gone down in shame with the slain, for all the terror that they caused by their might; they lie uncircumcised with those who are slain by the sword, and bear their shame with those who go down to the pit.

³¹"When Pharaoh sees them, he will be comforted for all his multitude, Pharaoh and all his army, slain by the sword, declares the Lord GOD. ³²For I spread terror in the land of the living; and he shall be laid to rest among the uncircumcised, with those who are slain by the sword, Pharaoh and all his multitude, declares the Lord GOD."

> **Turning point** [chapter 33]. Chapter 33 marks the beginning of a gradual transition from the bad news part of the book of Ezekiel to the good news part. The chapter begins as a recommissioning of the prophet, as God declares Ezekiel to be "a watchman for the house of Israel" (v. 7). This is followed by an outline of the behavior that God desires (in place of the earlier indictments of the bad behavior that God despises), and the keynote is repentance (vv. 10–20). In the middle of the chapter Ezekiel receives the news that Jerusalem has fallen (vv. 21–22). The rest of the chapter (vv. 23–33) is a flashback in which God summarizes his case against wayward Jerusalem/Judah and a vindication of Ezekiel for having spoken the truth.

33 The word of the LORD came to me: ²"Son of man, speak to your people and say to them, If I bring the sword upon a land, and the people of the land take a man from among them, and make him their watchman, ³and if he sees the sword coming upon the land and blows the trumpet and warns the people, ⁴then if anyone who hears the sound of the trumpet does not take warning, and the sword comes and takes him away, his blood shall be upon his own head. ⁵He heard the sound of the trumpet and did not take warning; his blood shall be upon himself. But if he had taken warning, he would have saved his life. ⁶But if the watchman sees the sword coming and does not blow the trumpet, so that the people are not warned, and the sword comes and takes any one of them, that person is taken away in his iniquity, but his blood I will require at the watchman's hand.

⁷"So you, son of man, I have made a watchman for the house of Israel. Whenever you hear a word from my mouth, you shall give them warning from me. ⁸If I say to the wicked, O wicked one, you shall surely die, and you do not speak to warn the wicked to turn from his way, that wicked person shall die in his iniquity, but his blood I will require at your hand. ⁹But if you warn the wicked to turn from his way, and he does not turn from his way, that person shall die in his iniquity, but you will have delivered your soul.

¹⁰"And you, son of man, say to the house of Israel, Thus have you said: 'Surely our transgressions and our sins are upon us, and we rot away because of them. How then can we live?' ¹¹Say to them, As I live, declares the Lord GOD, I have no pleasure in the death of the wicked, but that the wicked turn from his way and live; turn back, turn back from your evil ways, for why will you die, O house of Israel?

¹²"And you, son of man, say to your people, The righteousness of the righteous shall not deliver him when he transgresses, and as for the wickedness of the wicked, he

shall not fall by it when he turns from his wickedness, and the righteous shall not be able to live by his righteousness[1] when he sins. [13]Though I say to the righteous that he shall surely live, yet if he trusts in his righteousness and does injustice, none of his righteous deeds shall be remembered, but in his injustice that he has done he shall die. [14]Again, though I say to the wicked, 'You shall surely die,' yet if he turns from his sin and does what is just and right, [15]if the wicked restores the pledge, gives back what he has taken by robbery, and walks in the statutes of life, not doing injustice, he shall surely live; he shall not die. [16]None of the sins that he has committed shall be remembered against him. He has done what is just and right; he shall surely live.

[17]"Yet your people say, 'The way of the Lord is not just,' when it is their own way that is not just. [18]When the righteous turns from his righteousness and does injustice, he shall die for it. [19]And when the wicked turns from his wickedness and does what is just and right, he shall live by this. [20]Yet you say, 'The way of the Lord is not just.' O house of Israel, I will judge each of you according to his ways."

[21]In the twelfth year of our exile, in the tenth month, on the fifth day of the month, a fugitive from Jerusalem came to me and said, "The city has been struck down." [22]Now the hand of the LORD had been upon me the evening before the fugitive came; and he had opened my mouth by the time the man came to me in the morning, so my mouth was opened, and I was no longer mute.

[23]The word of the LORD came to me: [24]"Son of man, the inhabitants of these waste places in the land of Israel keep saying, 'Abraham was only one man, yet he got possession of the land; but we are many; the land is surely given us to possess.' [25]Therefore say to them, Thus says the Lord GOD: You eat flesh with the blood and lift up your eyes to your idols and shed blood; shall you then possess the land? [26]You rely on the sword, you commit abominations, and each of you defiles his neighbor's wife; shall you then possess the land? [27]Say this to them, Thus says the Lord GOD: As I live, surely those who are in the waste places shall fall by the sword, and whoever is in the open field I will give to the beasts to be devoured, and those who are in strongholds and in caves shall die by pestilence. [28]And I will make the land a desolation and a waste, and her proud might shall come to an end, and the mountains of Israel shall be so desolate that none will pass through. [29]Then they will know that I am the LORD, when I have made the land a desolation and a waste because of all their abominations that they have committed.

[30]"As for you, son of man, your people who talk together about you by the walls and at the doors of the houses, say to one another, each to his brother, 'Come, and hear what the word is that comes from the LORD.' [31]And they come to you as people come, and they sit before you as my people, and they hear what you say but they will not do it; for with lustful talk in their mouths they act; their heart is set on their gain. [32]And behold, you are to them like one who sings lustful songs with a beautiful voice and plays[2] well on an instrument, for they hear what you say, but they will not do it. [33]When this comes—and come it will!—then they will know that a prophet has been among them."

Pastoral satire [chapter 34]. Ezekiel 34 is one of the famous chapters of the Bible. Its mode is *pastoral—literature set in a shepherd's milieu, with shepherds as characters and the actions those typically done by shepherds. Often these pastoral details are

---

[1] Hebrew *by it* [2] Hebrew *like the singing of lustful songs with a beautiful voice and one who plays*

metaphors for real-life people and situations, and that is what we find here. Religious leaders are pictured as shepherds and the rank-and-file Israelites as sheep. Bad religious leaders are portrayed metaphorically as bad shepherds; this aspect of the chapter keeps the negative satiric theme before us. But the vision also promises the coming of a good shepherd (metaphoric of Christ), who is identified as "my servant David" (v. 23), a reference to Christ's royal and Davidic lineage. This good shepherd will salvage the sheep that have been neglected and will exercise judgment, and he will even "make with them a covenant of peace and banish wild beasts from the land, so that they may dwell securely" (v. 25). The overall thrust of the chapter is to promise a coming consolation, even though the satiric attack on evil shepherds is an important part of the picture.

34 The word of the LORD came to me: [2]"Son of man, prophesy against the shepherds of Israel; prophesy, and say to them, even to the shepherds, Thus says the Lord GOD: Ah, shepherds of Israel who have been feeding yourselves! Should not shepherds feed the sheep? [3]You eat the fat, you clothe yourselves with the wool, you slaughter the fat ones, but you do not feed the sheep. [4]The weak you have not strengthened, the sick you have not healed, the injured you have not bound up, the strayed you have not brought back, the lost you have not sought, and with force and harshness you have ruled them. [5]So they were scattered, because there was no shepherd, and they became food for all the wild beasts. [6]My sheep were scattered; they wandered over all the mountains and on every high hill. My sheep were scattered over all the face of the earth, with none to search or seek for them.

[7]"Therefore, you shepherds, hear the word of the LORD: [8]As I live, declares the Lord GOD, surely because my sheep have become a prey, and my sheep have become food for all the wild beasts, since there was no shepherd, and because my shepherds have not searched for my sheep, but the shepherds have fed themselves, and have not fed my sheep, [9]therefore, you shepherds, hear the word of the LORD: [10]Thus says the Lord GOD, Behold, I am against the shepherds, and I will require my sheep at their hand and put a stop to their feeding the sheep. No longer shall the shepherds feed themselves. I will rescue my sheep from their mouths, that they may not be food for them.

[11]"For thus says the Lord GOD: Behold, I, I myself will search for my sheep and will seek them out. [12]As a shepherd seeks out his flock when he is among his sheep that have been scattered, so will I seek out my sheep, and I will rescue them from all places where they have been scattered on a day of clouds and thick darkness. [13]And I will bring them out from the peoples and gather them from the countries, and will bring them into their own land. And I will feed them on the mountains of Israel, by the ravines, and in all the inhabited places of the country. [14]I will feed them with good pasture, and on the mountain heights of Israel shall be their grazing land. There they shall lie down in good grazing land, and on rich pasture they shall feed on the mountains of Israel. [15]I myself will be the shepherd of my sheep, and I myself will make them lie down, declares the Lord GOD. [16]I will seek the lost, and I will bring back the strayed, and I will bind up the injured, and I will strengthen the weak, and the fat and the strong I will destroy.[j] I will feed them in justice.

[17]"As for you, my flock, thus says the Lord GOD: Behold, I judge between sheep and sheep, between rams and male goats. [18]Is it not enough for you to feed on the good pasture, that you must tread down with your feet the rest of your pasture; and to drink of clear water, that you must muddy the rest of the water with your feet? [19]And

---

[j] Septuagint, Syriac, Vulgate *I will watch over*

must my sheep eat what you have trodden with your feet, and drink what you have muddied with your feet?

²⁰"Therefore, thus says the Lord God to them: Behold, I, I myself will judge between the fat sheep and the lean sheep. ²¹Because you push with side and shoulder, and thrust at all the weak with your horns, till you have scattered them abroad, ²²I will rescue¹ my flock; they shall no longer be a prey. And I will judge between sheep and sheep. ²³And I will set up over them one shepherd, my servant David, and he shall feed them: he shall feed them and be their shepherd. ²⁴And I, the Lord, will be their God, and my servant David shall be prince among them. I am the Lord; I have spoken.

²⁵"I will make with them a covenant of peace and banish wild beasts from the land, so that they may dwell securely in the wilderness and sleep in the woods. ²⁶And I will make them and the places all around my hill a blessing, and I will send down the showers in their season; they shall be showers of blessing. ²⁷And the trees of the field shall yield their fruit, and the earth shall yield its increase, and they shall be secure in their land. And they shall know that I am the Lord, when I break the bars of their yoke, and deliver them from the hand of those who enslaved them. ²⁸They shall no more be a prey to the nations, nor shall the beasts of the land devour them. They shall dwell securely, and none shall make them afraid. ²⁹And I will provide for them renowned plantations so that they shall no more be consumed with hunger in the land, and no longer suffer the reproach of the nations. ³⁰And they shall know that I am the Lord their God with them, and that they, the house of Israel, are my people, declares the Lord God. ³¹And you are my sheep, human sheep of my pasture, and I am your God, declares the Lord God."

Oracle of judgment against one more oppressive neighbor [chapter 35]. There is one more pause before the redemptive surge of the final chapters of Ezekiel kicks in. It takes the form of an oracle of judgment against Edom (v. 15), which is called Mount Seir throughout the chapter. While the satiric mode is the same as that of the first part of the book of Ezekiel, the fact that the judgment is leveled against an oppressor of Israel makes its effect consolatory to the people of God.

35 The word of the Lord came to me: ²"Son of man, set your face against Mount Seir, and prophesy against it, ³and say to it, Thus says the Lord God: Behold, I am against you, Mount Seir, and I will stretch out my hand against you, and I will make you a desolation and a waste. ⁴I will lay your cities waste, and you shall become a desolation, and you shall know that I am the Lord. ⁵Because you cherished perpetual enmity and gave over the people of Israel to the power of the sword at the time of their calamity, at the time of their final punishment, ⁶therefore, as I live, declares the Lord God, I will prepare you for blood, and blood shall pursue you; because you did not hate bloodshed, therefore blood shall pursue you. ⁷I will make Mount Seir a waste and a desolation, and I will cut off from it all who come and go. ⁸And I will fill its mountains with the slain. On your hills and in your valleys and in all your ravines those slain with the sword shall fall. ⁹I will make you a perpetual desolation, and your cities shall not be inhabited. Then you will know that I am the Lord.

¹⁰"Because you said, 'These two nations and these two countries shall be mine, and we will take possession of them'—although the Lord was there— ¹¹therefore, as I live,

¹ Or save

declares the Lord GOD, I will deal with you according to the anger and envy that you showed because of your hatred against them. And I will make myself known among them, when I judge you. ¹²And you shall know that I am the LORD.

"I have heard all the revilings that you uttered against the mountains of Israel, saying, 'They are laid desolate; they are given us to devour.' ¹³And you magnified yourselves against me with your mouth, and multiplied your words against me; I heard it. ¹⁴Thus says the Lord GOD: While the whole earth rejoices, I will make you desolate. ¹⁵As you rejoiced over the inheritance of the house of Israel, because it was desolate, so I will deal with you; you shall be desolate, Mount Seir, and all Edom, all of it. Then they will know that I am the LORD.

> **Reversal** [chapter 36]. The tone in this chapter is frequently *lyric as the prophet delivers God's oracles of restoration to Israel. The earlier catalogs of evil and indictments now give way to lists of blessings, and one way to organize the material is to note the good things that God promises to carry out. The reversal motif is also prominent, as some of the same categories (the land, worship, the city) appear in a manner that is opposite to the earlier visions of destruction. The imagery of rebuilding appears as a controlling metaphor for the main message of the passage.

36 "And you, son of man, prophesy to the mountains of Israel, and say, O mountains of Israel, hear the word of the LORD. ²Thus says the Lord GOD: Because the enemy said of you, 'Aha!' and, 'The ancient heights have become our possession,' ³therefore prophesy, and say, Thus says the Lord GOD: Precisely because they made you desolate and crushed you from all sides, so that you became the possession of the rest of the nations, and you became the talk and evil gossip of the people, ⁴therefore, O mountains of Israel, hear the word of the Lord GOD: Thus says the Lord GOD to the mountains and the hills, the ravines and the valleys, the desolate wastes and the deserted cities, which have become a prey and derision to the rest of the nations all around, ⁵therefore thus says the Lord GOD: Surely I have spoken in my hot jealousy against the rest of the nations and against all Edom, who gave my land to themselves as a possession with wholehearted joy and utter contempt, that they might make its pasturelands a prey. ⁶Therefore prophesy concerning the land of Israel, and say to the mountains and hills, to the ravines and valleys, Thus says the Lord GOD: Behold, I have spoken in my jealous wrath, because you have suffered the reproach of the nations. ⁷Therefore thus says the Lord GOD: I swear that the nations that are all around you shall themselves suffer reproach.

⁸"But you, O mountains of Israel, shall shoot forth your branches and yield your fruit to my people Israel, for they will soon come home. ⁹For behold, I am for you, and I will turn to you, and you shall be tilled and sown. ¹⁰And I will multiply people on you, the whole house of Israel, all of it. The cities shall be inhabited and the waste places rebuilt. ¹¹And I will multiply on you man and beast, and they shall multiply and be fruitful. And I will cause you to be inhabited as in your former times, and will do more good to you than ever before. Then you will know that I am the LORD. ¹²I will let people walk on you, even my people Israel. And they shall possess you, and you shall be their inheritance, and you shall no longer bereave them of children. ¹³Thus says the Lord GOD: Because they say to you, 'You devour people, and you bereave your

nation of children,' [14]therefore you shall no longer devour people and no longer bereave your nation of children, declares the Lord God. [15]And I will not let you hear anymore the reproach of the nations, and you shall no longer bear the disgrace of the peoples and no longer cause your nation to stumble, declares the Lord God."

[16]The word of the LORD came to me: [17]"Son of man, when the house of Israel lived in their own land, they defiled it by their ways and their deeds. Their ways before me were like the uncleanness of a woman in her menstrual impurity. [18]So I poured out my wrath upon them for the blood that they had shed in the land, for the idols with which they had defiled it. [19]I scattered them among the nations, and they were dispersed through the countries. In accordance with their ways and their deeds I judged them. [20]But when they came to the nations, wherever they came, they profaned my holy name, in that people said of them, 'These are the people of the LORD, and yet they had to go out of his land.' [21]But I had concern for my holy name, which the house of Israel had profaned among the nations to which they came.

[22]"Therefore say to the house of Israel, Thus says the Lord God: It is not for your sake, O house of Israel, that I am about to act, but for the sake of my holy name, which you have profaned among the nations to which you came. [23]And I will vindicate the holiness of my great name, which has been profaned among the nations, and which you have profaned among them. And the nations will know that I am the LORD, declares the Lord God, when through you I vindicate my holiness before their eyes. [24]I will take you from the nations and gather you from all the countries and bring you into your own land. [25]I will sprinkle clean water on you, and you shall be clean from all your uncleannesses, and from all your idols I will cleanse you. [26]And I will give you a new heart, and a new spirit I will put within you. And I will remove the heart of stone from your flesh and give you a heart of flesh. [27]And I will put my Spirit within you, and cause you to walk in my statutes and be careful to obey my rules.[1] [28]You shall dwell in the land that I gave to your fathers, and you shall be my people, and I will be your God. [29]And I will deliver you from all your uncleannesses. And I will summon the grain and make it abundant and lay no famine upon you. [30]I will make the fruit of the tree and the increase of the field abundant, that you may never again suffer the disgrace of famine among the nations. [31]Then you will remember your evil ways, and your deeds that were not good, and you will loathe yourselves for your iniquities and your abominations. [32]It is not for your sake that I will act, declares the Lord God; let that be known to you. Be ashamed and confounded for your ways, O house of Israel.

[33]"Thus says the Lord God: On the day that I cleanse you from all your iniquities, I will cause the cities to be inhabited, and the waste places shall be rebuilt. [34]And the land that was desolate shall be tilled, instead of being the desolation that it was in the sight of all who passed by. [35]And they will say, 'This land that was desolate has become like the garden of Eden, and the waste and desolate and ruined cities are now fortified and inhabited.' [36]Then the nations that are left all around you shall know that I am the LORD; I have rebuilt the ruined places and replanted that which was desolate. I am the LORD; I have spoken, and I will do it.

[37]"Thus says the Lord God: This also I will let the house of Israel ask me to do for them: to increase their people like a flock. [38]Like the flock for sacrifices,[2] like the flock at Jerusalem during her appointed feasts, so shall the waste cities be filled with flocks of people. Then they will know that I am the LORD."

---

[1] Or my just decrees [2] Hebrew flock of holy things

The valley of dry bones and the two sticks [chapter 37]. The vision that begins this chapter is so famous that even people with little acquaintance with the book of Ezekiel are likely to have heard about the valley of dry bones. It is one of the grandest rebirth stories in all of literature. What happens to the dry bones is symbolic of the salvation that God promises to bring. It is one of the Bible's most memorable pictures of redemption and new life, meant to be experienced at a deep and primitive level of our being. The vision of the two sticks being joined into one is a metaphor of reconciliation. Since no such union between Joseph and Israel ever occurred politically, we have an early signal that the concluding chapters of Ezekiel, for all their Israelite specificity, need to be interpreted metaphorically and symbolically, as dealing with a spiritual "nation" of believers, not primarily a political nation of Israel.

37

The hand of the LORD was upon me, and he brought me out in the Spirit of the LORD and set me down in the middle of the valley;[1] it was full of bones. [2]And he led me around among them, and behold, there were very many on the surface of the valley, and behold, they were very dry. [3]And he said to me, "Son of man, can these bones live?" And I answered, "O Lord GOD, you know." [4]Then he said to me, "Prophesy over these bones, and say to them, O dry bones, hear the word of the LORD. [5]Thus says the Lord GOD to these bones: Behold, I will cause breath[2] to enter you, and you shall live. [6]And I will lay sinews upon you, and will cause flesh to come upon you, and cover you with skin, and put breath in you, and you shall live, and you shall know that I am the LORD."

[7]So I prophesied as I was commanded. And as I prophesied, there was a sound, and behold, a rattling,[3] and the bones came together, bone to its bone. [8]And I looked, and behold, there were sinews on them, and flesh had come upon them, and skin had covered them. But there was no breath in them. [9]Then he said to me, "Prophesy to the breath; prophesy, son of man, and say to the breath, Thus says the Lord GOD: Come from the four winds, O breath, and breathe on these slain, that they may live." [10]So I prophesied as he commanded me, and the breath came into them, and they lived and stood on their feet, an exceedingly great army.

[11]Then he said to me, "Son of man, these bones are the whole house of Israel. Behold, they say, 'Our bones are dried up, and our hope is lost; we are indeed cut off.' [12]Therefore prophesy, and say to them, Thus says the Lord GOD: Behold, I will open your graves and raise you from your graves, O my people. And I will bring you into the land of Israel. [13]And you shall know that I am the LORD, when I open your graves, and raise you from your graves, O my people. [14]And I will put my Spirit within you, and you shall live, and I will place you in your own land. Then you shall know that I am the LORD; I have spoken, and I will do it, declares the LORD."

[15]The word of the LORD came to me: [16]"Son of man, take a stick[4] and write on it, 'For Judah, and the people of Israel associated with him'; then take another stick and write on it, 'For Joseph (the stick of Ephraim) and all the house of Israel associated with him.' [17]And join them one to another into one stick, that they may become one in your hand. [18]And when your people say to you, 'Will you not tell us what you mean by these?' [19]say to them, Thus says the Lord GOD: Behold, I am about to take the stick of Joseph (that is in the hand of Ephraim) and the tribes of Israel associated with him. And I will join with it the stick of Judah,[5] and make them one stick, that they may be

---

[1] Or plain; also verse 2 [2] Or spirit; also verses 6, 9, 10 [3] Or an earthquake (compare 3:12, 13) [4] Or one piece of wood; also verses 17, 19, 20 [5] Hebrew And I will place them on it, the stick of Judah

one in my hand. ²⁰When the sticks on which you write are in your hand before their eyes, ²¹then say to them, Thus says the Lord GOD: Behold, I will take the people of Israel from the nations among which they have gone, and will gather them from all around, and bring them to their own land. ²²And I will make them one nation in the land, on the mountains of Israel. And one king shall be king over them all, and they shall be no longer two nations, and no longer divided into two kingdoms. ²³They shall not defile themselves anymore with their idols and their detestable things, or with any of their transgressions. But I will save them from all the backslidings¹ in which they have sinned, and will cleanse them; and they shall be my people, and I will be their God.

²⁴"My servant David shall be king over them, and they shall all have one shepherd. They shall walk in my rules and be careful to obey my statutes. ²⁵They shall dwell in the land that I gave to my servant Jacob, where your fathers lived. They and their children and their children's children shall dwell there forever, and David my servant shall be their prince forever. ²⁶I will make a covenant of peace with them. It shall be an everlasting covenant with them. And I will set them in their land² and multiply them, and will set my sanctuary in their midst forevermore. ²⁷My dwelling place shall be with them, and I will be their God, and they shall be my people. ²⁸Then the nations will know that I am the LORD who sanctifies Israel, when my sanctuary is in their midst forevermore."

The last battle [chapters 38–39]. If we take time to cast a retrospective look over the preceding parts of the book, it is obvious that the element of conflict has run strong. The story behind the satiric and prophetic visions has been a conflict between good and evil, between a righteous God and wayward humanity. Further, it is an understood rule of storytelling that a story is not over until the issues that have been introduced are resolved. Although we have seen many instances of God's taking his stand against evil and making promises to set things right, we have not yet seen a final conquest of evil. The unexpected battle of chapters 38–39 gives us this resolution. The best framework within which to experience this story of slaughter is *epic literature, with its heightened pictures of warfare conducted by nations. The imagery of weapons and slaughter is similar to what we find in Homer and Virgil. Of course the picture is heightened beyond literal battles. It belongs to a visionary and symbolic mode. The spiritual symbolism is what raises this epic battle above merely fictional ones: this is a picture of God's total defeat of evil as part of his final redemption of his people. For all its gruesomeness, this battle story is a vision of deliverance and consolation to those who are on the side of God. We should also see *apocalyptic overtones in the battle, which pictures the final conquest of evil at the end of the age.

38 The word of the LORD came to me: ²"Son of man, set your face toward Gog, of the land of Magog, the chief prince of Meshech³ and Tubal, and prophesy against him ³and say, Thus says the Lord GOD: Behold, I am against you, O Gog, chief prince of Meshech⁴ and Tubal. ⁴And I will turn you about and put hooks into your jaws, and I will bring you out, and all your army, horses and horsemen, all of them clothed in full armor, a great host, all of them with buckler and shield, wielding swords. ⁵Persia, Cush, and Put are with them, all of them with shield and helmet;

¹ Many Hebrew manuscripts; other Hebrew manuscripts *dwellings* ² Hebrew lacks *in their land* ³ Or *Magog, the prince of Rosh, Meshech* ⁴ Or *Gog, prince of Rosh, Meshech*

⁶Gomer and all his hordes; Beth-togarmah from the uttermost parts of the north with all his hordes—many peoples are with you.

⁷"Be ready and keep ready, you and all your hosts that are assembled about you, and be a guard for them. ⁸After many days you will be mustered. In the latter years you will go against the land that is restored from war, the land whose people were gathered from many peoples upon the mountains of Israel, which had been a continual waste. Its people were brought out from the peoples and now dwell securely, all of them. ⁹You will advance, coming on like a storm. You will be like a cloud covering the land, you and all your hordes, and many peoples with you.

¹⁰"Thus says the Lord GOD: On that day, thoughts will come into your mind, and you will devise an evil scheme ¹¹and say, 'I will go up against the land of unwalled villages. I will fall upon the quiet people who dwell securely, all of them dwelling without walls, and having no bars or gates,' ¹²to seize spoil and carry off plunder, to turn your hand against the waste places that are now inhabited, and the people who were gathered from the nations, who have acquired livestock and goods, who dwell at the center of the earth. ¹³Sheba and Dedan and the merchants of Tarshish and all its leaders¹ will say to you, 'Have you come to seize spoil? Have you assembled your hosts to carry off plunder, to carry away silver and gold, to take away livestock and goods, to seize great spoil?'

¹⁴"Therefore, son of man, prophesy, and say to Gog, Thus says the Lord GOD: On that day when my people Israel are dwelling securely, will you not know it? ¹⁵You will come from your place out of the uttermost parts of the north, you and many peoples with you, all of them riding on horses, a great host, a mighty army. ¹⁶You will come up against my people Israel, like a cloud covering the land. In the latter days I will bring you against my land, that the nations may know me, when through you, O Gog, I vindicate my holiness before their eyes.

¹⁷"Thus says the Lord GOD: Are you he of whom I spoke in former days by my servants the prophets of Israel, who in those days prophesied for years that I would bring you against them? ¹⁸But on that day, the day that Gog shall come against the land of Israel, declares the Lord GOD, my wrath will be roused in my anger. ¹⁹For in my jealousy and in my blazing wrath I declare, On that day there shall be a great earthquake in the land of Israel. ²⁰The fish of the sea and the birds of the heavens and the beasts of the field and all creeping things that creep on the ground, and all the people who are on the face of the earth, shall quake at my presence. And the mountains shall be thrown down, and the cliffs shall fall, and every wall shall tumble to the ground. ²¹I will summon a sword against Gog² on all my mountains, declares the Lord GOD. Every man's sword will be against his brother. ²²With pestilence and bloodshed I will enter into judgment with him, and I will rain upon him and his hordes and the many peoples who are with him torrential rains and hailstones, fire and sulfur. ²³So I will show my greatness and my holiness and make myself known in the eyes of many nations. Then they will know that I am the LORD.

39 "And you, son of man, prophesy against Gog and say, Thus says the Lord GOD: Behold, I am against you, O Gog, chief prince of Meshech³ and Tubal. ²And I will turn you about and drive you forward, and bring you up from the uttermost parts of the north, and lead you against the mountains of Israel. ³Then I will strike your bow from your left hand, and will make your arrows drop out of your

---

¹ Hebrew young lions ² Hebrew against him ³ Or Gog, prince of Rosh, Meshech

right hand. ⁴You shall fall on the mountains of Israel, you and all your hordes and the peoples who are with you. I will give you to birds of prey of every sort and to the beasts of the field to be devoured. ⁵You shall fall in the open field, for I have spoken, declares the Lord God. ⁶I will send fire on Magog and on those who dwell securely in the coastlands, and they shall know that I am the Lord.

⁷"And my holy name I will make known in the midst of my people Israel, and I will not let my holy name be profaned anymore. And the nations shall know that I am the Lord, the Holy One in Israel. ⁸Behold, it is coming and it will be brought about, declares the Lord God. That is the day of which I have spoken.

⁹"Then those who dwell in the cities of Israel will go out and make fires of the weapons and burn them, shields and bucklers, bow and arrows, clubs¹ and spears; and they will make fires of them for seven years, ¹⁰so that they will not need to take wood out of the field or cut down any out of the forests, for they will make their fires of the weapons. They will seize the spoil of those who despoiled them, and plunder those who plundered them, declares the Lord God.

¹¹"On that day I will give to Gog a place for burial in Israel, the Valley of the Travelers, east of the sea. It will block the travelers, for there Gog and all his multitude will be buried. It will be called the Valley of Hamon-gog.² ¹²For seven months the house of Israel will be burying them, in order to cleanse the land. ¹³All the people of the land will bury them, and it will bring them renown on the day that I show my glory, declares the Lord God. ¹⁴They will set apart men to travel through the land regularly and bury those travelers remaining on the face of the land, so as to cleanse it. At³ the end of seven months they will make their search. ¹⁵And when these travel through the land and anyone sees a human bone, then he shall set up a sign by it, till the buriers have buried it in the Valley of Hamon-gog. ¹⁶(Hamonah⁴ is also the name of the city.) Thus shall they cleanse the land.

¹⁷"As for you, son of man, thus says the Lord God: Speak to the birds of every sort and to all beasts of the field, 'Assemble and come, gather from all around to the sacrificial feast that I am preparing for you, a great sacrificial feast on the mountains of Israel, and you shall eat flesh and drink blood. ¹⁸You shall eat the flesh of the mighty, and drink the blood of the princes of the earth—of rams, of lambs, and of he-goats, of bulls, all of them fat beasts of Bashan. ¹⁹And you shall eat fat till you are filled, and drink blood till you are drunk, at the sacrificial feast that I am preparing for you. ²⁰And you shall be filled at my table with horses and charioteers, with mighty men and all kinds of warriors,' declares the Lord God.

²¹"And I will set my glory among the nations, and all the nations shall see my judgment that I have executed, and my hand that I have laid on them. ²²The house of Israel shall know that I am the Lord their God, from that day forward. ²³And the nations shall know that the house of Israel went into captivity for their iniquity, because they dealt so treacherously with me that I hid my face from them and gave them into the hand of their adversaries, and they all fell by the sword. ²⁴I dealt with them according to their uncleanness and their transgressions, and hid my face from them.

²⁵"Therefore thus says the Lord God: Now I will restore the fortunes of Jacob and have mercy on the whole house of Israel, and I will be jealous for my holy name. ²⁶They shall forget their shame and all the treachery they have practiced against me, when they dwell securely in their land with none to make them afraid, ²⁷when I have brought them back from the peoples and gathered them from their enemies' lands,

---

¹ Or javelins ² Hamon-gog means the multitude of Gog ³ Or Until ⁴ Hamonah means multitude

and through them have vindicated my holiness in the sight of many nations. ²⁸Then they shall know that I am the LORD their God, because I sent them into exile among the nations and then assembled them into their own land. I will leave none of them remaining among the nations anymore. ²⁹And I will not hide my face anymore from them, when I pour out my Spirit upon the house of Israel, declares the Lord GOD."

Vision of a restored temple [chapter 40]. Ezekiel has sprung a lot of surprises on us up to this point, but nothing could have prepared us for what we find here. For nearly eight chapters, Ezekiel gives us a detailed physical and architectural account of a new temple in Jerusalem. There is no good alternative to going with the flow and picturing in our imagination what is being described. It is a rule of literature that readers need to take seriously what the author takes seriously. But once we have done that, we are left with a serious crux that demands interpretive wisdom. Any thought that God wants Christians to return to OT temple practices must be rejected at once; the book of Hebrews makes it clear that OT temple worship has been permanently terminated by the sacrifice of Christ. The book of Ezekiel has used symbolism throughout, so it is a safe conclusion that the temple is a symbolic entity. What it symbolizes is the presence of God. The NT metaphor of Christians as God's temple (1 Cor. 3:16; 2 Cor. 6:16) is a good interpretive guide. Additionally, the temple here might well be an eschatological reality—a picture of the glorious saints of God in heaven with the Lamb at the center of their worship. Chapter 40 opens this unit by describing the gates and outer places of the temple.

40 In the twenty-fifth year of our exile, at the beginning of the year, on the tenth day of the month, in the fourteenth year after the city was struck down, on that very day, the hand of the LORD was upon me, and he brought me to the city.¹ ²In visions of God he brought me to the land of Israel, and set me down on a very high mountain, on which was a structure like a city to the south. ³When he brought me there, behold, there was a man whose appearance was like bronze, with a linen cord and a measuring reed in his hand. And he was standing in the gateway. ⁴And the man said to me, "Son of man, look with your eyes, and hear with your ears, and set your heart upon all that I shall show you, for you were brought here in order that I might show it to you. Declare all that you see to the house of Israel."

⁵And behold, there was a wall all around the outside of the temple area, and the length of the measuring reed in the man's hand was six long cubits, each being a cubit and a handbreadth² in length. So he measured the thickness of the wall, one reed; and the height, one reed. ⁶Then he went into the gateway facing east, going up its steps, and measured the threshold of the gate, one reed deep.³ ⁷And the side rooms, one reed long and one reed broad; and the space between the side rooms, five cubits; and the threshold of the gate by the vestibule of the gate at the inner end, one reed. ⁸Then he measured the vestibule of the gateway, on the inside, one reed. ⁹Then he measured the vestibule of the gateway, eight cubits; and its jambs, two cubits; and the vestibule of the gate was at the inner end. ¹⁰And there were three side rooms on either side of the east gate. The three were of the same size, and the jambs on either side were of the same size. ¹¹Then he measured the width of the opening of the gateway, ten cubits; and the length of the gateway, thirteen cubits. ¹²There was a barrier before

the side rooms, one cubit on either side. And the side rooms were six cubits on either side. [13]Then he measured the gate from the ceiling of the one side room to the ceiling of the other, a breadth of twenty-five cubits; the openings faced each other. [14]He measured also the vestibule, twenty cubits. And around the vestibule of the gateway was the court.[1] [15]From the front of the gate at the entrance to the front of the inner vestibule of the gate was fifty cubits. [16]And the gateway had windows all around, narrowing inwards toward the side rooms and toward their jambs, and likewise the vestibule had windows all around inside, and on the jambs were palm trees.

[17]Then he brought me into the outer court. And behold, there were chambers and a pavement, all around the court. Thirty chambers faced the pavement. [18]And the pavement ran along the side of the gates, corresponding to the length of the gates. This was the lower pavement. [19]Then he measured the distance from the inner front of the lower gate to the outer front of the inner court,[2] a hundred cubits on the east side and on the north side.[3]

[20]As for the gate that faced toward the north, belonging to the outer court, he measured its length and its breadth. [21]Its side rooms, three on either side, and its jambs and its vestibule were of the same size as those of the first gate. Its length was fifty cubits, and its breadth twenty-five cubits. [22]And its windows, its vestibule, and its palm trees were of the same size as those of the gate that faced toward the east. And by seven steps people would go up to it, and find its vestibule before them. [23]And opposite the gate on the north, as on the east, was a gate to the inner court. And he measured from gate to gate, a hundred cubits.

[24]And he led me toward the south, and behold, there was a gate on the south. And he measured its jambs and its vestibule; they had the same size as the others. [25]Both it and its vestibule had windows all around, like the windows of the others. Its length was fifty cubits, and its breadth twenty-five cubits. [26]And there were seven steps leading up to it, and its vestibule was before them, and it had palm trees on its jambs, one on either side. [27]And there was a gate on the south of the inner court. And he measured from gate to gate toward the south, a hundred cubits.

[28]Then he brought me to the inner court through the south gate, and he measured the south gate. It was of the same size as the others. [29]Its side rooms, its jambs, and its vestibule were of the same size as the others, and both it and its vestibule had windows all around. Its length was fifty cubits, and its breadth twenty-five cubits. [30]And there were vestibules all around, twenty-five cubits long and five cubits broad. [31]Its vestibule faced the outer court, and palm trees were on its jambs, and its stairway had eight steps.

[32]Then he brought me to the inner court on the east side, and he measured the gate. It was of the same size as the others. [33]Its side rooms, its jambs, and its vestibule were of the same size as the others, and both it and its vestibule had windows all around. Its length was fifty cubits, and its breadth twenty-five cubits. [34]Its vestibule faced the outer court, and it had palm trees on its jambs, on either side, and its stairway had eight steps.

[35]Then he brought me to the north gate, and he measured it. It had the same size as the others. [36]Its side rooms, its jambs, and its vestibule were of the same size as the others,[4] and it had windows all around. Its length was fifty cubits, and its breadth

---

[1] Text uncertain; Hebrew And he made the jambs sixty cubits, and to the jamb of the court was the gateway all around [2] Hebrew distance from before the low gate before the inner court to the outside [3] Or cubits. So far the eastern gate; now to the northern gate. [4] One manuscript (compare verses 29 and 33); most manuscripts lack were of the same size as the others

twenty-five cubits. [37]Its vestibule[1] faced the outer court, and it had palm trees on its jambs, on either side, and its stairway had eight steps.

[38]There was a chamber with its door in the vestibule of the gate,[2] where the burnt offering was to be washed. [39]And in the vestibule of the gate were two tables on either side, on which the burnt offering and the sin offering and the guilt offering were to be slaughtered. [40]And off to the side, on the outside as one goes up to the entrance of the north gate, were two tables; and off to the other side of the vestibule of the gate were two tables. [41]Four tables were on either side of the gate, eight tables, on which to slaughter. [42]And there were four tables of hewn stone for the burnt offering, a cubit and a half long, and a cubit and a half broad, and one cubit high, on which the instruments were to be laid with which the burnt offerings and the sacrifices were slaughtered. [43]And hooks,[3] a handbreadth long, were fastened all around within. And on the tables the flesh of the offering was to be laid.

[44]On the outside of the inner gateway there were two chambers[4] in the inner court, one[5] at the side of the north gate facing south, the other at the side of the south[6] gate facing north. [45]And he said to me, This chamber that faces south is for the priests who have charge of the temple, [46]and the chamber that faces north is for the priests who have charge of the altar. These are the sons of Zadok, who alone[7] among the sons of Levi may come near to the LORD to minister to him. [47]And he measured the court, a hundred cubits long and a hundred cubits broad, a square. And the altar was in front of the temple.

[48]Then he brought me to the vestibule of the temple and measured the jambs of the vestibule, five cubits on either side. And the breadth of the gate was fourteen cubits, and the sidewalls of the gate[8] were three cubits on either side. [49]The length of the vestibule was twenty cubits, and the breadth twelve[9] cubits, and people would go up to it by ten steps.[10] And there were pillars beside the jambs, one on either side.

The temple itself [chapters 41–42]. With these chapter we move from the temple area to the temple proper. We assimilate a barrage of architectural measurements and descriptions as we proceed through the chapters. These are best interpreted as symbolic of the wealth and perfection of the place where God is worshiped. At this point it is useful to codify what we know about Ezekiel himself: he is a symbolist who often expresses himself in great symbols rather than literal facts, and he is a priest as well as a prophet (1:3). It was natural that a priest who lived and breathed the temple would turn to the temple for a symbol of God's presence and glory.

41 Then he brought me to the nave and measured the jambs. On each side six cubits[11] was the breadth of the jambs.[12] [2]And the breadth of the entrance was ten cubits, and the sidewalls of the entrance were five cubits on either side. And he measured the length of the nave,[13] forty cubits, and its breadth, twenty cubits. [3]Then he went into the inner room and measured the jambs of the entrance, two cubits; and the entrance, six cubits; and the sidewalls on either side[14] of the entrance, seven cubits. [4]And he measured the length of the room, twenty cubits, and its breadth, twenty cubits, across the nave. And he said to me, "This is the Most Holy Place."

[5]Then he measured the wall of the temple, six cubits thick, and the breadth of the

[1] Septuagint, Vulgate (compare verses 26, 31, 34); Hebrew jambs [2] Hebrew at the jambs, the gates [3] Or shelves [4] Septuagint; Hebrew were chambers for singers [5] Hebrew lacks one [6] Septuagint; Hebrew east [7] Hebrew lacks alone [8] Septuagint; Hebrew lacks was fourteen cubits, and the sidewalls of the gate [9] Septuagint; Hebrew eleven [10] Septuagint; Hebrew and by steps that would go up to it [11] A cubit was about 18 inches or 45 centimeters [12] Compare Septuagint; Hebrew tent [13] Hebrew its length [14] Septuagint; Hebrew and the breadth

side chambers, four cubits, all around the temple. ⁶And the side chambers were in three stories, one over another, thirty in each story. There were offsets¹ all around the wall of the temple to serve as supports for the side chambers, so that they should not be supported by the wall of the temple. ⁷And it became broader as it wound upward to the side chambers, because the temple was enclosed upward all around the temple. Thus the temple had a broad area upward, and so one went up from the lowest story to the top story through the middle story. ⁸I saw also that the temple had a raised platform all around; the foundations of the side chambers measured a full reed of six long cubits. ⁹The thickness of the outer wall of the side chambers was five cubits. The free space between the side chambers of the temple and the ¹⁰other chambers was a breadth of twenty cubits all around the temple on every side. ¹¹And the doors of the side chambers opened on the free space, one door toward the north, and another door toward the south. And the breadth of the free space was five cubits all around.

¹²The building that was facing the separate yard on the west side was seventy cubits broad, and the wall of the building was five cubits thick all around, and its length ninety cubits.

¹³Then he measured the temple, a hundred cubits long; and the yard and the building with its walls, a hundred cubits long; ¹⁴also the breadth of the east front of the temple and the yard, a hundred cubits.

¹⁵Then he measured the length of the building facing the yard that was at the back and its galleries² on either side, a hundred cubits.

The inside of the nave and the vestibules of the court, ¹⁶the thresholds and the narrow windows and the galleries all around the three of them, opposite the threshold, were paneled with wood all around, from the floor up to the windows (now the windows were covered), ¹⁷to the space above the door, even to the inner room, and on the outside. And on all the walls all around, inside and outside, was a measured pattern.³ ¹⁸It was carved of cherubim and palm trees, a palm tree between cherub and cherub. Every cherub had two faces: ¹⁹a human face toward the palm tree on the one side, and the face of a young lion toward the palm tree on the other side. They were carved on the whole temple all around. ²⁰From the floor to above the door, cherubim and palm trees were carved; similarly the wall of the nave.

²¹The doorposts of the nave were squared, and in front of the Holy Place was something resembling ²²an altar of wood, three cubits high, two cubits long, and two cubits broad.⁴ Its corners, its base,⁵ and its walls were of wood. He said to me, "This is the table that is before the Lord." ²³The nave and the Holy Place had each a double door. ²⁴The double doors had two leaves apiece, two swinging leaves for each door. ²⁵And on the doors of the nave were carved cherubim and palm trees, such as were carved on the walls. And there was a canopy⁶ of wood in front of the vestibule outside. ²⁶And there were narrow windows and palm trees on either side, on the sidewalls of the vestibule, the side chambers of the temple, and the canopies.

42 Then he led me out into the outer court, toward the north, and he brought me to the chambers that were opposite the separate yard and opposite the building on the north. ²The length of the building whose door faced north was a hundred cubits,⁷ and the breadth fifty cubits. ³Facing the twenty cubits that belonged to

¹ Septuagint, compare 1 Kings 6:6; the meaning of the Hebrew word is uncertain ² The meaning of the Hebrew term is unknown; also verse 16 ³ Hebrew were measurements ⁴ Septuagint; Hebrew lacks two cubits broad ⁵ Septuagint; Hebrew length ⁶ The meaning of the Hebrew word is unknown; also verse 26 ⁷ A cubit was about 18 inches or 45 centimeters

the inner court, and facing the pavement that belonged to the outer court, was gallery[1] against gallery in three stories. [4]And before the chambers was a passage inward, ten cubits wide and a hundred cubits long,[2] and their doors were on the north. [5]Now the upper chambers were narrower, for the galleries took more away from them than from the lower and middle chambers of the building. [6]For they were in three stories, and they had no pillars like the pillars of the courts. Thus the upper chambers were set back from the ground more than the lower and the middle ones. [7]And there was a wall outside parallel to the chambers, toward the outer court, opposite the chambers, fifty cubits long. [8]For the chambers on the outer court were fifty cubits long, while those opposite the nave[3] were a hundred cubits long. [9]Below these chambers was an entrance on the east side, as one enters them from the outer court.

[10]In the thickness of the wall of the court, on the south[4] also, opposite the yard and opposite the building, there were chambers [11]with a passage in front of them. They were similar to the chambers on the north, of the same length and breadth, with the same exits[5] and arrangements and doors, [12]as were the entrances of the chambers on the south. There was an entrance at the beginning of the passage, the passage before the corresponding wall on the east as one enters them.[6]

[13]Then he said to me, "The north chambers and the south chambers opposite the yard are the holy chambers, where the priests who approach the LORD shall eat the most holy offerings. There they shall put the most holy offerings—the grain offering, the sin offering, and the guilt offering—for the place is holy. [14]When the priests enter the Holy Place, they shall not go out of it into the outer court without laying there the garments in which they minister, for these are holy. They shall put on other garments before they go near to that which is for the people."

[15]Now when he had finished measuring the interior of the temple area, he led me out by the gate that faced east, and measured the temple area all around. [16]He measured the east side with the measuring reed, 500 cubits by the measuring reed all around. [17]He measured the north side, 500 cubits by the measuring reed all around. [18]He measured the south side, 500 cubits by the measuring reed. [19]Then he turned to the west side and measured, 500 cubits by the measuring reed. [20]He measured it on the four sides. It had a wall around it, 500 cubits long and 500 cubits broad, to make a separation between the holy and the common.

God's glory returns to the temple [chapter 43]. Just as the visible glory of God descended on the tabernacle and temple at their dedication, in this vision of a restored temple God's glory appears (vv. 1–5), accompanied by a message to Ezekiel (vv. 6–12). The chapter is completed by God's instructions to Ezekiel regarding the altar for burnt offerings (vv. 13–17) and consecration of the altar (vv. 18–27). Perhaps this is the climax of the whole book. Additionally, as we proceed through these chapters that portray the glorious purity of the visionary temple, we might well remember visions earlier in the book of a corrupted temple filled with abominations.

43 Then he led me to the gate, the gate facing east. [2]And behold, the glory of the God of Israel was coming from the east. And the sound of his coming was like the sound of many waters, and the earth shone with his glory. [3]And the vision I saw was just like the vision that I had seen when he[7] came to destroy the city,

---

[1] The meaning of the Hebrew word is unknown; also verse 5 [2] Septuagint, Syriac; Hebrew *and a way of one cubit* [3] Or *temple* [4] Septuagint; Hebrew *east* [5] Hebrew *and all their exits* [6] The meaning of the Hebrew verse is uncertain [7] Some Hebrew manuscripts and Vulgate; most Hebrew manuscripts *when I*

and just like the vision that I had seen by the Chebar canal. And I fell on my face. [4]As the glory of the LORD entered the temple by the gate facing east, [5]the Spirit lifted me up and brought me into the inner court; and behold, the glory of the LORD filled the temple.

[6]While the man was standing beside me, I heard one speaking to me out of the temple, [7]and he said to me, "Son of man, this is the place of my throne and the place of the soles of my feet, where I will dwell in the midst of the people of Israel forever. And the house of Israel shall no more defile my holy name, neither they, nor their kings, by their whoring and by the dead bodies[1] of their kings at their high places,[2] [8]by setting their threshold by my threshold and their doorposts beside my doorposts, with only a wall between me and them. They have defiled my holy name by their abominations that they have committed, so I have consumed them in my anger. [9]Now let them put away their whoring and the dead bodies of their kings far from me, and I will dwell in their midst forever.

[10]"As for you, son of man, describe to the house of Israel the temple, that they may be ashamed of their iniquities; and they shall measure the plan. [11]And if they are ashamed of all that they have done, make known to them the design of the temple, its arrangement, its exits and its entrances, that is, its whole design; and make known to them as well all its statutes and its whole design and all its laws, and write it down in their sight, so that they may observe all its laws and all its statutes and carry them out. [12]This is the law of the temple: the whole territory on the top of the mountain all around shall be most holy. Behold, this is the law of the temple.

[13]"These are the measurements of the altar by cubits (the cubit being a cubit and a handbreadth):[3] its base shall be one cubit high[4] and one cubit broad, with a rim of one span[5] around its edge. And this shall be the height of the altar: [14]from the base on the ground to the lower ledge, two cubits, with a breadth of one cubit; and from the smaller ledge to the larger ledge, four cubits, with a breadth of one cubit; [15]and the altar hearth, four cubits; and from the altar hearth projecting upward, four horns. [16]The altar hearth shall be square, twelve cubits long by twelve broad. [17]The ledge also shall be square, fourteen cubits long by fourteen broad, with a rim around it half a cubit broad, and its base one cubit all around. The steps of the altar shall face east."

[18]And he said to me, "Son of man, thus says the Lord GOD: These are the ordinances for the altar: On the day when it is erected for offering burnt offerings upon it and for throwing blood against it, [19]you shall give to the Levitical priests of the family of Zadok, who draw near to me to minister to me, declares the Lord GOD, a bull from the herd for a sin offering. [20]And you shall take some of its blood and put it on the four horns of the altar and on the four corners of the ledge and upon the rim all around. Thus you shall purify the altar and make atonement for it. [21]You shall also take the bull of the sin offering, and it shall be burned in the appointed place belonging to the temple, outside the sacred area. [22]And on the second day you shall offer a male goat without blemish for a sin offering; and the altar shall be purified, as it was purified with the bull. [23]When you have finished purifying it, you shall offer a bull from the herd without blemish and a ram from the flock without blemish. [24]You shall present them before the LORD, and the priests shall sprinkle salt on them and offer them up as a burnt offering to the LORD. [25]For seven days you shall provide daily a male goat for a sin offering; also, a bull from the herd and a ram from the flock, without blem-

---

[1] Or the monuments; also verse 9 [2] Or at their deaths [3] A cubit was about 18 inches or 45 centimeters; a handbreadth was about 3 inches or 7.5 centimeters [4] Or its gutter shall be one cubit deep [5] A span was about 9 inches or 22 centimeters

ish, shall be provided. [26]Seven days shall they make atonement for the altar and cleanse it, and so consecrate it.[1] [27]And when they have completed these days, then from the eighth day onward the priests shall offer on the altar your burnt offerings and your peace offerings, and I will accept you, declares the Lord GOD."

> **Rules governing worship in the temple** [chapter 44]. With the temple itself having been described, Ezekiel's vision of a restored temple now outlines the rules governing those who will minister in the temple and the offerings that they will perform. In keeping with the symbolic mode of these temple chapters, our safest interpretation is to ponder the symbolic meanings that are embodied in the details—meanings like the holiness that God desires in his people; the primacy of pure religion in a society; the need to distinguish between the common and the holy; the need for atonement.

44 Then he brought me back to the outer gate of the sanctuary, which faces east. And it was shut. [2]And the LORD said to me, "This gate shall remain shut; it shall not be opened, and no one shall enter by it, for the LORD, the God of Israel, has entered by it. Therefore it shall remain shut. [3]Only the prince may sit in it to eat bread before the LORD. He shall enter by way of the vestibule of the gate, and shall go out by the same way."

[4]Then he brought me by way of the north gate to the front of the temple, and I looked, and behold, the glory of the LORD filled the temple of the LORD. And I fell on my face. [5]And the LORD said to me, "Son of man, mark well, see with your eyes, and hear with your ears all that I shall tell you concerning all the statutes of the temple of the LORD and all its laws. And mark well the entrance to the temple and all the exits from the sanctuary. [6]And say to the rebellious house,[2] to the house of Israel, Thus says the Lord GOD: O house of Israel, enough of all your abominations, [7]in admitting foreigners, uncircumcised in heart and flesh, to be in my sanctuary, profaning my temple, when you offer to me my food, the fat and the blood. You[3] have broken my covenant, in addition to all your abominations. [8]And you have not kept charge of my holy things, but you have set others to keep my charge for you in my sanctuary.

[9]"Thus says the Lord GOD: No foreigner, uncircumcised in heart and flesh, of all the foreigners who are among the people of Israel, shall enter my sanctuary. [10]But the Levites who went far from me, going astray from me after their idols when Israel went astray, shall bear their punishment.[4] [11]They shall be ministers in my sanctuary, having oversight at the gates of the temple and ministering in the temple. They shall slaughter the burnt offering and the sacrifice for the people, and they shall stand before the people, to minister to them. [12]Because they ministered to them before their idols and became a stumbling block of iniquity to the house of Israel, therefore I have sworn concerning them, declares the Lord GOD, and they shall bear their punishment. [13]They shall not come near to me, to serve me as priest, nor come near any of my holy things and the things that are most holy, but they shall bear their shame and the abominations that they have committed. [14]Yet I will appoint them to keep charge of the temple, to do all its service and all that is to be done in it.

[15]"But the Levitical priests, the sons of Zadok, who kept the charge of my sanctuary when the people of Israel went astray from me, shall come near to me to minister to me. And they shall stand before me to offer me the fat and the blood, declares the

---

[1] Hebrew *fill its hand* [2] Septuagint; Hebrew lacks *house* [3] Septuagint, Syriac, Vulgate; Hebrew *They* [4] Or *iniquity*; also verse 12

Lord God. ¹⁶They shall enter my sanctuary, and they shall approach my table, to minister to me, and they shall keep my charge. ¹⁷When they enter the gates of the inner court, they shall wear linen garments. They shall have nothing of wool on them, while they minister at the gates of the inner court, and within. ¹⁸They shall have linen turbans on their heads, and linen undergarments around their waists. They shall not bind themselves with anything that causes sweat. ¹⁹And when they go out into the outer court to the people, they shall put off the garments in which they have been ministering and lay them in the holy chambers. And they shall put on other garments, lest they transmit holiness to the people with their garments. ²⁰They shall not shave their heads or let their locks grow long; they shall surely trim the hair of their heads. ²¹No priest shall drink wine when he enters the inner court. ²²They shall not marry a widow or a divorced woman, but only virgins of the offspring of the house of Israel, or a widow who is the widow of a priest. ²³They shall teach my people the difference between the holy and the common, and show them how to distinguish between the unclean and the clean. ²⁴In a dispute, they shall act as judges, and they shall judge it according to my judgments. They shall keep my laws and my statutes in all my appointed feasts, and they shall keep my Sabbaths holy. ²⁵They shall not defile themselves by going near to a dead person. However, for father or mother, for son or daughter, for brother or unmarried sister they may defile themselves. ²⁶After he has become clean, they shall count seven days for him. ²⁷And on the day that he goes into the Holy Place, into the inner court, to minister in the Holy Place, he shall offer his sin offering, declares the Lord God.

²⁸"This shall be their inheritance: I am their inheritance: and you shall give them no possession in Israel; I am their possession. ²⁹They shall eat the grain offering, the sin offering, and the guilt offering, and every devoted thing in Israel shall be theirs. ³⁰And the first of all the firstfruits of all kinds, and every offering of all kinds from all your offerings, shall belong to the priests. You shall also give to the priests the first of your dough, that a blessing may rest on your house. ³¹The priests shall not eat of anything, whether bird or beast, that has died of itself or is torn by wild animals.

A holy commonwealth [chapter 45]. Chapter 45 sustains both the content and the style of the preceding chapter. In effect we look at a blueprint for a future ideal kingdom, in a manner reminiscent of the rules that God gave through Moses in the Pentateuch. Thus we read about parceling out of the land (vv. 1–8); rules governing social ethics (vv. 9–12); types of offerings and sacred seasons associated with them (vv. 13–25). Our safest interpretation is to regard the blueprint as describing a symbolic holy commonwealth that exists in our imaginations and souls rather than as a prediction of a coming literal and political realm.

45 "When you allot the land as an inheritance, you shall set apart for the Lord a portion of the land as a holy district, 25,000 cubits¹ long and 20,000² cubits broad. It shall be holy throughout its whole extent. ²Of this a square plot of 500 by 500 cubits shall be for the sanctuary, with fifty cubits for an open space around it. ³And from this measured district you shall measure off a section 25,000 cubits long and 10,000 broad, in which shall be the sanctuary, the Most Holy Place. ⁴It shall be the holy portion of the land. It shall be for the priests, who minister in the

¹ A *cubit* was about 18 inches or 45 centimeters ² Septuagint; Hebrew *ten*

sanctuary and approach the LORD to minister to him, and it shall be a place for their houses and a holy place for the sanctuary. ⁵Another section, 25,000 cubits long and 10,000 cubits broad, shall be for the Levites who minister at the temple, as their possession for cities to live in.¹

⁶"Alongside the portion set apart as the holy district you shall assign for the property of the city an area 5,000 cubits broad and 25,000 cubits long. It shall belong to the whole house of Israel.

⁷"And to the prince shall belong the land on both sides of the holy district and the property of the city, alongside the holy district and the property of the city, on the west and on the east, corresponding in length to one of the tribal portions, and extending from the western to the eastern boundary ⁸of the land. It is to be his property in Israel. And my princes shall no more oppress my people, but they shall let the house of Israel have the land according to their tribes.

⁹"Thus says the Lord GOD: Enough, O princes of Israel! Put away violence and oppression, and execute justice and righteousness. Cease your evictions of my people, declares the Lord GOD.

¹⁰"You shall have just balances, a just ephah, and a just bath.² ¹¹The ephah and the bath shall be of the same measure, the bath containing one tenth of a homer,³ and the ephah one tenth of a homer; the homer shall be the standard measure. ¹²The shekel shall be twenty gerahs;⁴ twenty shekels plus twenty-five shekels plus fifteen shekels shall be your mina.⁵

¹³"This is the offering that you shall make: one sixth of an ephah from each homer of wheat, and one sixth of an ephah from each homer of barley, ¹⁴and as the fixed portion of oil, measured in baths, one tenth of a bath from each cor⁶ (the cor, like the homer, contains ten baths).⁷ ¹⁵And one sheep from every flock of two hundred, from the watering places of Israel for grain offering, burnt offering, and peace offerings, to make atonement for them, declares the Lord GOD. ¹⁶All the people of the land shall be obliged to give this offering to the prince in Israel. ¹⁷It shall be the prince's duty to furnish the burnt offerings, grain offerings, and drink offerings, at the feasts, the new moons, and the Sabbaths, all the appointed feasts of the house of Israel: he shall provide the sin offerings, grain offerings, burnt offerings, and peace offerings, to make atonement on behalf of the house of Israel.

¹⁸"Thus says the Lord GOD: In the first month, on the first day of the month, you shall take a bull from the herd without blemish, and purify the sanctuary. ¹⁹The priest shall take some of the blood of the sin offering and put it on the doorposts of the temple, the four corners of the ledge of the altar, and the posts of the gate of the inner court. ²⁰You shall do the same on the seventh day of the month for anyone who has sinned through error or ignorance; so you shall make atonement for the temple.

²¹"In the first month, on the fourteenth day of the month, you shall celebrate the Feast of the Passover, and for seven days unleavened bread shall be eaten. ²²On that day the prince shall provide for himself and all the people of the land a young bull for a sin offering. ²³And on the seven days of the festival he shall provide as a burnt offering to the LORD seven young bulls and seven rams without blemish, on each of the seven days; and a male goat daily for a sin offering. ²⁴And he shall provide as a grain offering an ephah for each bull, an ephah for each ram, and a hin⁸ of oil to

---

¹ Septuagint; Hebrew *as their possession, twenty chambers* ² An *ephah* was about 3/5 of a bushel or 22 liters; a *bath* was about 6 gallons or 22 liters ³ A *homer* was about 6 bushels or 220 liters ⁴ A *shekel* was about 2/5 ounce or 11 grams; a *gerah* was about 1/50 ounce or 0.6 gram ⁵ A *mina* was about 1 1/4 pounds or 0.6 kilogram ⁶ A *cor* was about 6 bushels or 220 liters ⁷ See Vulgate; Hebrew *(ten baths are a homer, for ten baths are a homer)* ⁸ A *hin* was about 4 quarts or 3.5 liters

each ephah. ²⁵In the seventh month, on the fifteenth day of the month and for the seven days of the feast, he shall make the same provision for sin offerings, burnt offerings, and grain offerings, and for the oil.

A vision of holiness [chapter 46]. In terms of the surface details and rhetorical mode, this chapter, like the preceding one, transports us to the world of Leviticus and Numbers, with their multitude of regulations governing offerings and sacrifices. We should let our imagination be awakened by the physical details that are placed before us as we read. Having done so, we need to turn the details to symbolic account as expressing spiritual worship of God.

46 "Thus says the Lord God: The gate of the inner court that faces east shall be shut on the six working days, but on the Sabbath day it shall be opened, and on the day of the new moon it shall be opened. ²The prince shall enter by the vestibule of the gate from outside, and shall take his stand by the post of the gate. The priests shall offer his burnt offering and his peace offerings, and he shall worship at the threshold of the gate. Then he shall go out, but the gate shall not be shut until evening. ³The people of the land shall bow down at the entrance of that gate before the Lord on the Sabbaths and on the new moons. ⁴The burnt offering that the prince offers to the Lord on the Sabbath day shall be six lambs without blemish and a ram without blemish. ⁵And the grain offering with the ram shall be an ephah,¹ and the grain offering with the lambs shall be as much as he is able, together with a hin² of oil to each ephah. ⁶On the day of the new moon he shall offer a bull from the herd without blemish, and six lambs and a ram, which shall be without blemish. ⁷As a grain offering he shall provide an ephah with the bull and an ephah with the ram, and with the lambs as much as he is able, together with a hin of oil to each ephah. ⁸When the prince enters, he shall enter by the vestibule of the gate, and he shall go out by the same way.

⁹"When the people of the land come before the Lord at the appointed feasts, he who enters by the north gate to worship shall go out by the south gate, and he who enters by the south gate shall go out by the north gate: no one shall return by way of the gate by which he entered, but each shall go out straight ahead. ¹⁰When they enter, the prince shall enter with them, and when they go out, he shall go out.

¹¹"At the feasts and the appointed festivals, the grain offering with a young bull shall be an ephah, and with a ram an ephah, and with the lambs as much as one is able to give, together with a hin of oil to an ephah. ¹²When the prince provides a freewill offering, either a burnt offering or peace offerings as a freewill offering to the Lord, the gate facing east shall be opened for him. And he shall offer his burnt offering or his peace offerings as he does on the Sabbath day. Then he shall go out, and after he has gone out the gate shall be shut.

¹³"You shall provide a lamb a year old without blemish for a burnt offering to the Lord daily; morning by morning you shall provide it. ¹⁴And you shall provide a grain offering with it morning by morning, one sixth of an ephah, and one third of a hin of oil to moisten the flour, as a grain offering to the Lord. This is a perpetual statute. ¹⁵Thus the lamb and the meal offering and the oil shall be provided, morning by morning, for a regular burnt offering.

---

¹ An *ephah* was about 3/5 bushel or 22 liters ² A *hin* was about 4 quarts or 3.5 liters

[16]"Thus says the Lord God: If the prince makes a gift to any of his sons as his inheritance, it shall belong to his sons. It is their property by inheritance. [17]But if he makes a gift out of his inheritance to one of his servants, it shall be his to the year of liberty. Then it shall revert to the prince; surely it is his inheritance—it shall belong to his sons. [18]The prince shall not take any of the inheritance of the people, thrusting them out of their property. He shall give his sons their inheritance out of his own property, so that none of my people shall be scattered from his property."

[19]Then he brought me through the entrance, which was at the side of the gate, to the north row of the holy chambers for the priests, and behold, a place was there at the extreme western end of them. [20]And he said to me, "This is the place where the priests shall boil the guilt offering and the sin offering, and where they shall bake the grain offering, in order not to bring them out into the outer court and so transmit holiness to the people."

[21]Then he brought me out to the outer court and led me around to the four corners of the court. And behold, in each corner of the court there was another court— [22]in the four corners of the court were small[1] courts, forty cubits[2] long and thirty broad; the four were of the same size. [23]On the inside, around each of the four courts was a row of masonry, with hearths made at the bottom of the rows all around. [24]Then he said to me, "These are the kitchens where those who minister at the temple shall boil the sacrifices of the people."

The river flowing from the temple [47:1–12]. At the climax of the description of the new temple and worship is this vision of an archetypal life-giving river flowing out of the temple, with images of abundance evoking our deepest longings. This is paradise regained, a vision of a golden age that pictures the good life of belief in God and the coming glory of heaven.

47 Then he brought me back to the door of the temple, and behold, water was issuing from below the threshold of the temple toward the east (for the temple faced east). The water was flowing down from below the south end of the threshold of the temple, south of the altar. [2]Then he brought me out by way of the north gate and led me around on the outside to the outer gate that faces toward the east; and behold, the water was trickling out on the south side.

[3]Going on eastward with a measuring line in his hand, the man measured a thousand cubits,[3] and then led me through the water, and it was ankle-deep. [4]Again he measured a thousand, and led me through the water, and it was knee-deep. Again he measured a thousand, and led me through the water, and it was waist-deep. [5]Again he measured a thousand, and it was a river that I could not pass through, for the water had risen. It was deep enough to swim in, a river that could not be passed through. [6]And he said to me, "Son of man, have you seen this?"

Then he led me back to the bank of the river. [7]As I went back, I saw on the bank of the river very many trees on the one side and on the other. [8]And he said to me, "This water flows toward the eastern region and goes down into the Arabah, and enters the sea;[4] when the water flows into the sea, the water will become fresh.[5] [9]And wherever the river goes,[6] every living creature that swarms will live, and there will be very many

---

[1] Septuagint, Syriac, Vulgate; the meaning of the Hebrew word is uncertain [2] A *cubit* was about 18 inches or 45 centimeters [3] A *cubit* was about 18 inches or 45 centimeters [4] That is, the Dead Sea [5] Hebrew *will be healed*; also verses 9, 11 [6] Septuagint, Syriac, Vulgate, Targum; Hebrew *the two rivers go*

fish. For this water goes there, that the waters of the sea[1] may become fresh; so everything will live where the river goes. [10]Fishermen will stand beside the sea. From Engedi to Eneglaim it will be a place for the spreading of nets. Its fish will be of very many kinds, like the fish of the Great Sea.[2] [11]But its swamps and marshes will not become fresh; they are to be left for salt. [12]And on the banks, on both sides of the river, there will grow all kinds of trees for food. Their leaves will not wither, nor their fruit fail, but they will bear fresh fruit every month, because the water for them flows from the sanctuary. Their fruit will be for food, and their leaves for healing."

Dividing the Promised Land all over again [47:13–48:35]. Ezekiel has one more trick up his sleeve—one more surprise in a book that has specialized in the literary motif of surprise. Not only have we relived the construction and dedication of the temple (chapters 40–47), but now we are asked to relive in our imagination the settling of the Promised Land, replete with the division of the land among the Israelite tribes. It is a rule of literary interpretation that we know that we need to interpret something symbolically if it is impossible to interpret it literally. That rule is in force here. Our best option is to interpret this imaginary taking possession of a Promised Land as a metaphoric picture of entering the ultimate, eschatological Promised Land—heaven. We might well remember the concluding block of chapters in Ezekiel as summarizing in an eschatological mode the spiritual aspirations of the entire OT with its themes of God's people, God's place, the perfection of worship in the presence of God, the return to a garden city from a wilderness of exile.

[13]Thus says the Lord GOD: "This is the boundary[3] by which you shall divide the land for inheritance among the twelve tribes of Israel. Joseph shall have two portions. [14]And you shall divide equally what I swore to give to your fathers. This land shall fall to you as your inheritance.

[15]"This shall be the boundary of the land: On the north side, from the Great Sea by way of Hethlon to Lebo-hamath, and on to Zedad,[4] [16]Berothah, Sibraim (which lies on the border between Damascus and Hamath), as far as Hazer-hatticon, which is on the border of Hauran. [17]So the boundary shall run from the sea to Hazar-enan, which is on the northern border of Damascus, with the border of Hamath to the north.[5] This shall be the north side.[6]

[18]"On the east side, the boundary shall run between Hauran and Damascus; along the Jordan between Gilead and the land of Israel; to the eastern sea and as far as Tamar.[7] This shall be the east side.

[19]"On the south side, it shall run from Tamar as far as the waters of Meribah-kadesh, from there along the Brook of Egypt[8] to the Great Sea. This shall be the south side.

[20]"On the west side, the Great Sea shall be the boundary to a point opposite Lebo-hamath. This shall be the west side.

[21]"So you shall divide this land among you according to the tribes of Israel. [22]You shall allot it as an inheritance for yourselves and for the sojourners who reside among you and have had children among you. They shall be to you as native-born children of Israel. With you they shall be allotted an inheritance among the tribes of

[1] Hebrew lacks *the waters of the sea* [2] That is, the Mediterranean Sea; also verses 15, 19, 20 [3] Probable reading; Hebrew *The valley of the boundary*
[4] Septuagint; Hebrew *the entrance of Zedad, Hamath* [5] The meaning of the Hebrew is uncertain [6] Probable reading; Hebrew *and as for the north side*
[7] Compare Syriac; Hebrew *to the eastern sea you shall measure* [8] Hebrew lacks *of Egypt*

Israel. ²³In whatever tribe the sojourner resides, there you shall assign him his inheritance, declares the Lord GOD.

48 "These are the names of the tribes: Beginning at the northern extreme, beside the way of Hethlon to Lebo-hamath, as far as Hazar-enan (which is on the northern border of Damascus over against Hamath), and¹ extending from the east side to the west,² Dan, one portion. ²Adjoining the territory of Dan, from the east side to the west, Asher, one portion. ³Adjoining the territory of Asher, from the east side to the west, Naphtali, one portion. ⁴Adjoining the territory of Naphtali, from the east side to the west, Manasseh, one portion. ⁵Adjoining the territory of Manasseh, from the east side to the west, Ephraim, one portion. ⁶Adjoining the territory of Ephraim, from the east side to the west, Reuben, one portion. ⁷Adjoining the territory of Reuben, from the east side to the west, Judah, one portion.

⁸"Adjoining the territory of Judah, from the east side to the west, shall be the portion which you shall set apart, 25,000 cubits³ in breadth, and in length equal to one of the tribal portions, from the east side to the west, with the sanctuary in the midst of it. ⁹The portion that you shall set apart for the LORD shall be 25,000 cubits in length, and 20,000⁴ in breadth. ¹⁰These shall be the allotments of the holy portion: the priests shall have an allotment measuring 25,000 cubits on the northern side, 10,000 cubits in breadth on the western side, 10,000 in breadth on the eastern side, and 25,000 in length on the southern side, with the sanctuary of the LORD in the midst of it. ¹¹This shall be for the consecrated priests, the sons of Zadok, who kept my charge, who did not go astray when the people of Israel went astray, as the Levites did. ¹²And it shall belong to them as a special portion from the holy portion of the land, a most holy place, adjoining the territory of the Levites. ¹³And alongside the territory of the priests, the Levites shall have an allotment 25,000 cubits in length and 10,000 in breadth. The whole length shall be 25,000 cubits and the breadth 20,000.⁵ ¹⁴They shall not sell or exchange any of it. They shall not alienate this choice portion of the land, for it is holy to the LORD.

¹⁵"The remainder, 5,000 cubits in breadth and 25,000 in length, shall be for common use for the city, for dwellings and for open country. In the midst of it shall be the city, ¹⁶and these shall be its measurements: the north side 4,500 cubits, the south side 4,500, the east side 4,500, and the west side 4,500. ¹⁷And the city shall have open land: on the north 250 cubits, on the south 250, on the east 250, and on the west 250. ¹⁸The remainder of the length alongside the holy portion shall be 10,000 cubits to the east, and 10,000 to the west, and it shall be alongside the holy portion. Its produce shall be food for the workers of the city. ¹⁹And the workers of the city, from all the tribes of Israel, shall till it. ²⁰The whole portion that you shall set apart shall be 25,000 cubits square, that is, the holy portion together with the property of the city.

²¹"What remains on both sides of the holy portion and of the property of the city shall belong to the prince. Extending from the 25,000 cubits of the holy portion to the east border, and westward from the 25,000 cubits to the west border, parallel to the tribal portions, it shall belong to the prince. The holy portion with the sanctuary of the temple shall be in its midst. ²²It shall be separate from the property of the Levites and the property of the city, which are in the midst of that which belongs to

¹ Probable reading; Hebrew *and they shall be his* ² Septuagint (compare verses 2-8); Hebrew *the east side the west* ³ A *cubit* was about 18 inches or 45 centimeters ⁴ Compare 45:1; Hebrew *ten* ⁵ Septuagint; Hebrew *10,000*

the prince. The portion of the prince shall lie between the territory of Judah and the territory of Benjamin.

²³"As for the rest of the tribes: from the east side to the west, Benjamin, one portion. ²⁴Adjoining the territory of Benjamin, from the east side to the west, Simeon, one portion. ²⁵Adjoining the territory of Simeon, from the east side to the west, Issachar, one portion. ²⁶Adjoining the territory of Issachar, from the east side to the west, Zebulun, one portion. ²⁷Adjoining the territory of Zebulun, from the east side to the west, Gad, one portion. ²⁸And adjoining the territory of Gad to the south, the boundary shall run from Tamar to the waters of Meribah-kadesh, from there along the Brook of Egypt[1] to the Great Sea.[2] ²⁹This is the land that you shall allot as an inheritance among the tribes of Israel, and these are their portions, declares the Lord GOD.

³⁰"These shall be the exits of the city: On the north side, which is to be 4,500 cubits by measure, ³¹three gates, the gate of Reuben, the gate of Judah, and the gate of Levi, the gates of the city being named after the tribes of Israel. ³²On the east side, which is to be 4,500 cubits, three gates, the gate of Joseph, the gate of Benjamin, and the gate of Dan. ³³On the south side, which is to be 4,500 cubits by measure, three gates, the gate of Simeon, the gate of Issachar, and the gate of Zebulun. ³⁴On the west side, which is to be 4,500 cubits, three gates,[3] the gate of Gad, the gate of Asher, and the gate of Naphtali. ³⁵The circumference of the city shall be 18,000 cubits. And the name of the city from that time on shall be, The LORD Is There."

---

[1] Hebrew lacks *of Egypt* [2] That is, the Mediterranean Sea [3] One Hebrew manuscript, Syriac (compare Septuagint); most Hebrew manuscripts *their gates three*

DANIEL

The book at a glance. 12 chapters, 357 verses. Although listed among the four major prophets of the OT, Daniel does not resemble the others because of its preponderance of narrative and apocalyptic material. Its length of twelve chapters is actually more similar to some of the minor prophets. The book is half *narrative (chapters 1–6) and half *visionary and *apocalyptic writing (chapters 7–12). The narrative section tells stories about the Jewish community as it lived in exile in Babylon and Persia. The book revolves primarily around one of these exiles, Daniel, as we read about his career as a trusted adviser to three famous kings (Nebuchadnezzar, Belshazzar, and Darius). The visions of the future relate a double history—political history stretching from the time of Daniel through the Roman Empire and a more generalized, universal history recounting the struggle between forces of good and evil until the end of time. The issues with which the two halves of the book deal are universal, especially the following questions: How can followers of God maintain their loyalty to him while living in cultures that are hostile to biblical religion? What does the future hold, and how will history end?

▌Genres. No book in the Bible falls so decisively into two completely different *genres as Daniel does. The first six chapters are *hero stories composed of six distinct ordeals. The last six chapters are a series of visions that partly employ the literary techniques of *fantasy to portray vast stretches of political and spiritual history. The visions that deal with the end times are apocalyptic visions. The techniques of *symbolic reality figure prominently in all of the dreams and visions, including those in the first six chapters; in symbolic reality, the world that we enter as we read consists largely of great symbols instead of literal characters and places. (For more information on items accompanied by an asterisk, see the glossary at the back of this Bible.)

▌Unifying elements. In a book as heterogeneous as the book of Daniel, we naturally look for points of unity that will see us through from beginning to end. The prophet Daniel provides the greatest point of unity, since he figures in most of the separate episodes in the narrative half of the book and is the first-person narrator of the visions in the second half. The sovereignty of God is a unifying element in the plot and theme. The "world" of the story is constant, and its main features include the political and courtly arena of action (a world of courts and kings); supernatural and miraculous happenings and characters; the presence of dreams and visions; striking and famous images (the fiery furnace; a disembodied hand that writes on the wall; a lions' den; a gigantic statue of a man composed of various minerals).

Passage	Content	Foreign King Involved	Genre	Time Frame
1:1–21	Daniel and his three friends tested	Nebuchadnezzar	Narrative, with interspersed dreams	Mainly occurring in Daniel's present situation
2:1–49	Nebuchadnezzar's dream			
3:1–30	The fiery furnace			
4:1–37	Nebuchadnezzar's insanity and recovery			
5:1–31	The writing on the wall	Belshazzar		
6:1–28	Daniel in the lions' den	Darius		
7:1–28	Vision of the four beasts	Belshazzar	Dreams, with interspersed narrative	Mainly predictive of the future
8:1–27	Vision of the ram and goat			
9:1–27	Daniel's prayer and vision of the future	Darius		
10:1–12:13	Vision of the future and the last days	Cyrus		

▌**Inferred literary intentions.** The book is designed to achieve the following literary purposes:

- inspire us with images of heroism that dare us to be a Daniel
- captivate us with exciting narrative action and characters
- embody norms of behavior in heroic examples
- activate our imagination as we experience visions of future history
- awaken our sense of mystery about supernatural reality
- acknowledge the sovereign power and design of God

▌**Theological themes.** (1) The sovereignty of God: God is repeatedly demonstrated to be the ruler of the universe and the heavenly realm. (2) Godliness: the behavior of Daniel and his three friends embodies a godly ideal. (3) Eschatology: the concluding chapters are a vision of the end times.

▌**The book of Daniel as a chapter in the master story of the Bible.** The two halves of the book contribute to the master story of the Bible in complementary ways. The first six chapters show us how God wants us to live in a world that goes against everything he stands for. The last six chapters tell the story of God's sovereign rule over the nations.

Keeping the faith at the University of Babylon [chapter 1]. The story of Daniel and his three friends provides models of heroism. Chapter 1 is a story of testing. The test revolves around a conflict between lifestyles and religious values. As always, small things (questions of diet) gesture toward larger issues (paganism versus loyalty to

God). Faced with the challenge to their loyalty to God, the young men ask to be tested (v. 12). The outcome of the test embodies *poetic justice (virtue is rewarded) and makes the story a favorite with children, as the young men are rewarded by God (we infer) by emerging as ten times better than their pagan rivals.

1 In the third year of the reign of Jehoiakim king of Judah, Nebuchadnezzar king of Babylon came to Jerusalem and besieged it. ²And the Lord gave Jehoiakim king of Judah into his hand, with some of the vessels of the house of God. And he brought them to the land of Shinar, to the house of his god, and placed the vessels in the treasury of his god. ³Then the king commanded Ashpenaz, his chief eunuch, to bring some of the people of Israel, both of the royal family¹ and of the nobility, ⁴youths without blemish, of good appearance and skillful in all wisdom, endowed with knowledge, understanding learning, and competent to stand in the king's palace, and to teach them the literature and language of the Chaldeans. ⁵The king assigned them a daily portion of the food that the king ate, and of the wine that he drank. They were to be educated for three years, and at the end of that time they were to stand before the king. ⁶Among these were Daniel, Hananiah, Mishael, and Azariah of the tribe of Judah. ⁷And the chief of the eunuchs gave them names: Daniel he called Belteshazzar, Hananiah he called Shadrach, Mishael he called Meshach, and Azariah he called Abednego.

⁸But Daniel resolved that he would not defile himself with the king's food, or with the wine that he drank. Therefore he asked the chief of the eunuchs to allow him not to defile himself. ⁹And God gave Daniel favor and compassion in the sight of the chief of the eunuchs, ¹⁰and the chief of the eunuchs said to Daniel, "I fear my lord the king, who assigned your food and your drink; for why should he see that you were in worse condition than the youths who are of your own age? So you would endanger my head with the king." ¹¹Then Daniel said to the steward whom the chief of the eunuchs had assigned over Daniel, Hananiah, Mishael, and Azariah, ¹²"Test your servants for ten days; let us be given vegetables to eat and water to drink. ¹³Then let our appearance and the appearance of the youths who eat the king's food be observed by you, and deal with your servants according to what you see." ¹⁴So he listened to them in this matter, and tested them for ten days. ¹⁵At the end of ten days it was seen that they were better in appearance and fatter in flesh than all the youths who ate the king's food. ¹⁶So the steward took away their food and the wine they were to drink, and gave them vegetables.

¹⁷As for these four youths, God gave them learning and skill in all literature and wisdom, and Daniel had understanding in all visions and dreams. ¹⁸At the end of the time, when the king had commanded that they should be brought in, the chief of the eunuchs brought them in before Nebuchadnezzar. ¹⁹And the king spoke with them, and among all of them none was found like Daniel, Hananiah, Mishael, and Azariah. Therefore they stood before the king. ²⁰And in every matter of wisdom and understanding about which the king inquired of them, he found them ten times better than all the magicians and enchanters that were in all his kingdom. ²¹And Daniel was there until the first year of King Cyrus.

Nebuchadnezzar's dream [chapter 2]. Each of the first six chapters consists of a self-contained ordeal story. In chapter 2, Daniel's ability to describe and interpret the king's

---

¹ Hebrew *of the seed of the kingdom*

dream is tested. The style becomes an *epic style, with events narrated in full detail and with stately and embellished speeches included. The pattern that unfolds is as follows: the magicians are unable to describe and interpret Nebuchanezzar's dream (vv. 1–13); God reveals the content and meaning of the dream to Daniel, who responds with a psalm of thanksgiving (vv. 14–24); Daniel appears before the king to describe what the king saw in his dream (vv. 25–35) and then to interpret its meaning (vv. 36–45); Daniel is rewarded by being elevated (along with his three friends) in the kingdom (vv. 46–49). The conventions of the hero story are operating at full force in all of these happenings. The content, symbolic mode, and political meaning of Nebuchadnezzar's dream foreshadow the visions of the second half of the book.

2 In the second year of the reign of Nebuchadnezzar, Nebuchadnezzar had dreams; his spirit was troubled, and his sleep left him. ²Then the king commanded that the magicians, the enchanters, the sorcerers, and the Chaldeans be summoned to tell the king his dreams. So they came in and stood before the king. ³And the king said to them, "I had a dream, and my spirit is troubled to know the dream." ⁴Then the Chaldeans said to the king in Aramaic,¹ "O king, live forever! Tell your servants the dream, and we will show the interpretation." ⁵The king answered and said to the Chaldeans, "The word from me is firm: if you do not make known to me the dream and its interpretation, you shall be torn limb from limb, and your houses shall be laid in ruins. ⁶But if you show the dream and its interpretation, you shall receive from me gifts and rewards and great honor. Therefore show me the dream and its interpretation." ⁷They answered a second time and said, "Let the king tell his servants the dream, and we will show its interpretation." ⁸The king answered and said, "I know with certainty that you are trying to gain time, because you see that the word from me is firm— ⁹if you do not make the dream known to me, there is but one sentence for you. You have agreed to speak lying and corrupt words before me till the times change. Therefore tell me the dream, and I shall know that you can show me its interpretation." ¹⁰The Chaldeans answered the king and said, "There is not a man on earth who can meet the king's demand, for no great and powerful king has asked such a thing of any magician or enchanter or Chaldean. ¹¹The thing that the king asks is difficult, and no one can show it to the king except the gods, whose dwelling is not with flesh."

¹²Because of this the king was angry and very furious, and commanded that all the wise men of Babylon be destroyed. ¹³So the decree went out, and the wise men were about to be killed; and they sought Daniel and his companions, to kill them. ¹⁴Then Daniel replied with prudence and discretion to Arioch, the captain of the king's guard, who had gone out to kill the wise men of Babylon. ¹⁵He declared² to Arioch, the king's captain, "Why is the decree of the king so urgent?" Then Arioch made the matter known to Daniel. ¹⁶And Daniel went in and requested the king to appoint him a time, that he might show the interpretation to the king.

¹⁷Then Daniel went to his house and made the matter known to Hananiah, Mishael, and Azariah, his companions, ¹⁸and told them to seek mercy from the God of heaven concerning this mystery, so that Daniel and his companions might not be destroyed with the rest of the wise men of Babylon. ¹⁹Then the mystery was revealed to Daniel in a vision of the night. Then Daniel blessed the God of heaven. ²⁰Daniel answered and said:

---

¹ The text from this point to the end of chapter 7 is in Aramaic ² Aramaic *answered and said*; also verse 26

"Blessed be the name of God forever and ever,
    to whom belong wisdom and might.
²¹ He changes times and seasons;
    he removes kings and sets up kings;
    he gives wisdom to the wise
    and knowledge to those who have understanding;
²² he reveals deep and hidden things;
    he knows what is in the darkness,
    and the light dwells with him.
²³ To you, O God of my fathers,
    I give thanks and praise,
    for you have given me wisdom and might,
    and have now made known to me what we asked of you,
    for you have made known to us the king's matter."

²⁴Therefore Daniel went in to Arioch, whom the king had appointed to destroy the wise men of Babylon. He went and said thus to him: "Do not destroy the wise men of Babylon; bring me in before the king, and I will show the king the interpretation." ²⁵Then Arioch brought in Daniel before the king in haste and said thus to him: "I have found among the exiles from Judah a man who will make known to the king the interpretation." ²⁶The king declared to Daniel, whose name was Belteshazzar, "Are you able to make known to me the dream that I have seen and its interpretation?" ²⁷Daniel answered the king and said, "No wise men, enchanters, magicians, or astrologers can show to the king the mystery that the king has asked, ²⁸but there is a God in heaven who reveals mysteries, and he has made known to King Nebuchadnezzar what will be in the latter days. Your dream and the visions of your head as you lay in bed are these: ²⁹To you, O king, as you lay in bed came thoughts of what would be after this, and he who reveals mysteries made known to you what is to be. ³⁰But as for me, this mystery has been revealed to me, not because of any wisdom that I have more than all the living, but in order that the interpretation may be made known to the king, and that you may know the thoughts of your mind.

³¹"You saw, O king, and behold, a great image. This image, mighty and of exceeding brightness, stood before you, and its appearance was frightening. ³²The head of this image was of fine gold, its chest and arms of silver, its middle and thighs of bronze, ³³its legs of iron, its feet partly of iron and partly of clay. ³⁴As you looked, a stone was cut out by no human hand, and it struck the image on its feet of iron and clay, and broke them in pieces. ³⁵Then the iron, the clay, the bronze, the silver, and the gold, all together were broken in pieces, and became like the chaff of the summer threshing floors; and the wind carried them away, so that not a trace of them could be found. But the stone that struck the image became a great mountain and filled the whole earth.

³⁶"This was the dream. Now we will tell the king its interpretation. ³⁷You, O king, the king of kings, to whom the God of heaven has given the kingdom, the power, and the might, and the glory, ³⁸and into whose hand he has given, wherever they dwell, the children of man, the beasts of the field, and the birds of the heavens, making you rule over them all—you are the head of gold. ³⁹Another kingdom inferior to you shall arise after you, and yet a third kingdom of bronze, which shall rule over all the earth. ⁴⁰And

there shall be a fourth kingdom, strong as iron, because iron breaks to pieces and shatters all things. And like iron that crushes, it shall break and crush all these. ⁴¹And as you saw the feet and toes, partly of potter's clay and partly of iron, it shall be a divided kingdom, but some of the firmness of iron shall be in it, just as you saw iron mixed with the soft clay. ⁴²And as the toes of the feet were partly iron and partly clay, so the kingdom shall be partly strong and partly brittle. ⁴³As you saw the iron mixed with soft clay, so they will mix with one another in marriage,¹ but they will not hold together, just as iron does not mix with clay. ⁴⁴And in the days of those kings the God of heaven will set up a kingdom that shall never be destroyed, nor shall the kingdom be left to another people. It shall break in pieces all these kingdoms and bring them to an end, and it shall stand forever, ⁴⁵just as you saw that a stone was cut from a mountain by no human hand, and that it broke in pieces the iron, the bronze, the clay, the silver, and the gold. A great God has made known to the king what shall be after this. The dream is certain, and its interpretation sure."

⁴⁶Then King Nebuchadnezzar fell upon his face and paid homage to Daniel, and commanded that an offering and incense be offered up to him. ⁴⁷The king answered and said to Daniel, "Truly, your God is God of gods and Lord of kings, and a revealer of mysteries, for you have been able to reveal this mystery." ⁴⁸Then the king gave Daniel high honors and many great gifts, and made him ruler over the whole province of Babylon and chief prefect over all the wise men of Babylon. ⁴⁹Daniel made a request of the king, and he appointed Shadrach, Meshach, and Abednego over the affairs of the province of Babylon. But Daniel remained at the king's court.

The ordeal of the fiery furnace [chapter 3]. Daniel drops out of the story momentarily as the action shifts to Daniel's three friends. The story revolves around the plot *motifs of testing, conflict, threat, rescue, and virtue rewarded. The three friends show their heroism in choosing God in the face of death (vv. 16–18) and are vindicated by the appearance of God in the furnace to rescue them (vv. 24–25). The style of the chapter is the high style, filled with lists of synonyms to name related items of a class of objects ("the satraps, the prefects, and the governors, the counselors, the treasurers, the justices, the magistrates, and all the officials of the provinces"). The episode is a paradigm of Israel's experience in exile: God is with them in the furnace, where they are called to faithfulness.

3 King Nebuchadnezzar made an image of gold, whose height was sixty cubits² and its breadth six cubits. He set it up on the plain of Dura, in the province of Babylon. ²Then King Nebuchadnezzar sent to gather the satraps, the prefects, and the governors, the counselors, the treasurers, the justices, the magistrates, and all the officials of the provinces to come to the dedication of the image that King Nebuchadnezzar had set up. ³Then the satraps, the prefects, and the governors, the counselors, the treasurers, the justices, the magistrates, and all the officials of the provinces gathered for the dedication of the image that King Nebuchadnezzar had set up. And they stood before the image that Nebuchadnezzar had set up. ⁴And the herald proclaimed aloud, "You are commanded, O peoples, nations, and languages, ⁵that when you hear the sound of the horn, pipe, lyre, trigon, harp, bagpipe, and every kind of music, you are to fall down and worship the golden image that King Nebuchadnezzar has set up. ⁶And whoever does not fall down and worship shall

¹ Aramaic *by the seed of men* ² A *cubit* was about 18 inches or 45 centimeters

immediately be cast into a burning fiery furnace." ⁷Therefore, as soon as all the peoples heard the sound of the horn, pipe, lyre, trigon, harp, bagpipe, and every kind of music, all the peoples, nations, and languages fell down and worshiped the golden image that King Nebuchadnezzar had set up.

⁸Therefore at that time certain Chaldeans came forward and maliciously accused the Jews. ⁹They declared¹ to King Nebuchadnezzar, "O king, live forever! ¹⁰You, O king, have made a decree, that every man who hears the sound of the horn, pipe, lyre, trigon, harp, bagpipe, and every kind of music, shall fall down and worship the golden image. ¹¹And whoever does not fall down and worship shall be cast into a burning fiery furnace. ¹²There are certain Jews whom you have appointed over the affairs of the province of Babylon: Shadrach, Meshach, and Abednego. These men, O king, pay no attention to you; they do not serve your gods or worship the golden image that you have set up."

¹³Then Nebuchadnezzar in furious rage commanded that Shadrach, Meshach, and Abednego be brought. So they brought these men before the king. ¹⁴Nebuchadnezzar answered and said to them, "Is it true, O Shadrach, Meshach, and Abednego, that you do not serve my gods or worship the golden image that I have set up? ¹⁵Now if you are ready when you hear the sound of the horn, pipe, lyre, trigon, harp, bagpipe, and every kind of music, to fall down and worship the image that I have made, well and good.² But if you do not worship, you shall immediately be cast into a burning fiery furnace. And who is the god who will deliver you out of my hands?"

¹⁶Shadrach, Meshach, and Abednego answered and said to the king, "O Nebuchadnezzar, we have no need to answer you in this matter. ¹⁷If this be so, our God whom we serve is able to deliver us from the burning fiery furnace, and he will deliver us out of your hand, O king.³ ¹⁸But if not, be it known to you, O king, that we will not serve your gods or worship the golden image that you have set up."

¹⁹Then Nebuchadnezzar was filled with fury, and the expression of his face was changed against Shadrach, Meshach, and Abednego. He ordered the furnace heated seven times more than it was usually heated. ²⁰And he ordered some of the mighty men of his army to bind Shadrach, Meshach, and Abednego, and to cast them into the burning fiery furnace. ²¹Then these men were bound in their cloaks, their tunics,⁴ their hats, and their other garments, and they were thrown into the burning fiery furnace. ²²Because the king's order was urgent and the furnace overheated, the flame of the fire killed those men who took up Shadrach, Meshach, and Abednego. ²³And these three men, Shadrach, Meshach, and Abednego, fell bound into the burning fiery furnace.

²⁴Then King Nebuchadnezzar was astonished and rose up in haste. He declared to his counselors, "Did we not cast three men bound into the fire?" They answered and said to the king, "True, O king." ²⁵He answered and said, "But I see four men unbound, walking in the midst of the fire, and they are not hurt; and the appearance of the fourth is like a son of the gods."

²⁶Then Nebuchadnezzar came near to the door of the burning fiery furnace; he declared, "Shadrach, Meshach, and Abednego, servants of the Most High God, come out, and come here!" Then Shadrach, Meshach, and Abednego came out from the fire. ²⁷And the satraps, the prefects, the governors, and the king's counselors gathered together and saw that the fire had not had any power over the bodies of those men.

¹ Aramaic *answered and said*; also verses 24, 26 ² Aramaic lacks *well and good* ³ Or *If our God whom we serve is able to deliver us, he will deliver us from the burning fiery furnace and out of your hand, O king.* ⁴ The meaning of the Aramaic words rendered *cloaks* and *tunics* is uncertain; also verse 27

The hair of their heads was not singed, their cloaks were not harmed, and no smell of fire had come upon them. [28]Nebuchadnezzar answered and said, "Blessed be the God of Shadrach, Meshach, and Abednego, who has sent his angel and delivered his servants, who trusted in him, and set aside[1] the king's command, and yielded up their bodies rather than serve and worship any god except their own God. [29]Therefore I make a decree: Any people, nation, or language that speaks anything against the God of Shadrach, Meshach, and Abednego shall be torn limb from limb, and their houses laid in ruins, for there is no other god who is able to rescue in this way." [30]Then the king promoted Shadrach, Meshach, and Abednego in the province of Babylon.

The fall and rise of Nebuchadnezzar [chapter 4]. The story of Nebuchadnezzar is a minitragedy in the literary sense of *tragedy. Nebuchadnezzar is afflicted by the overweening pride that characterizes the tragic heroes of Greek tragedy. Tragedy is the spectacle of exceptional calamity, and Nebuchadnezzar's political stature makes his fall exceptional, as does the extreme humiliation to which he descends. But the story has a surprise ending that turns the tragedy into a U-shaped *comic plot, as the king humbly praises God and is rewarded by a return to his kingly honor (vv. 34–37). The heroism of Daniel again lies in his ability to interpret dreams. The motif of divine sovereignty is important in the entire book of Daniel, and in this chapter a pagan king learns who is sovereign.

4 [2] King Nebuchadnezzar to all peoples, nations, and languages, that dwell in all the earth: Peace be multiplied to you! [2]It has seemed good to me to show the signs and wonders that the Most High God has done for me.

[3]   How great are his signs,
        how mighty his wonders!
His kingdom is an everlasting kingdom,
        and his dominion endures from generation to generation.

[4][3] I, Nebuchadnezzar, was at ease in my house and prospering in my palace. [5]I saw a dream that made me afraid. As I lay in bed the fancies and the visions of my head alarmed me. [6]So I made a decree that all the wise men of Babylon should be brought before me, that they might make known to me the interpretation of the dream. [7]Then the magicians, the enchanters, the Chaldeans, and the astrologers came in, and I told them the dream, but they could not make known to me its interpretation. [8]At last Daniel came in before me—he who was named Belteshazzar after the name of my god, and in whom is the spirit of the holy gods[4]—and I told him the dream, saying, [9]"O Belteshazzar, chief of the magicians, because I know that the spirit of the holy gods is in you and that no mystery is too difficult for you, tell me the visions of my dream that I saw and their interpretation. [10]The visions of my head as I lay in bed were these: I saw, and behold, a tree in the midst of the earth, and its height was great. [11]The tree grew and became strong, and its top reached to heaven, and it was visible to the end of the whole earth. [12]Its leaves were beautiful and its fruit abundant, and in it was food for all. The beasts of the field found shade under it, and the birds of the heavens lived in its branches, and all flesh was fed from it. [13]"I saw in the visions of my head as I lay in bed, and behold, a watcher, a holy one,

---

[1] Aramaic *and changed* [2] Ch 3:31 in Aramaic [3] Ch 4:1 in Aramaic [4] Or *Spirit of the holy God*; also verses 9, 18

came down from heaven. [14]He proclaimed aloud and said thus: 'Chop down the tree and lop off its branches, strip off its leaves and scatter its fruit. Let the beasts flee from under it and the birds from its branches. [15]But leave the stump of its roots in the earth, bound with a band of iron and bronze, amid the tender grass of the field. Let him be wet with the dew of heaven. Let his portion be with the beasts in the grass of the earth. [16]Let his mind be changed from a man's, and let a beast's mind be given to him; and let seven periods of time pass over him. [17]The sentence is by the decree of the watchers, the decision by the word of the holy ones, to the end that the living may know that the Most High rules the kingdom of men and gives it to whom he will and sets over it the lowliest of men.' [18]This dream I, King Nebuchadnezzar, saw. And you, O Belteshazzar, tell me the interpretation, because all the wise men of my kingdom are not able to make known to me the interpretation, but you are able, for the spirit of the holy gods is in you."

[19]Then Daniel, whose name was Belteshazzar, was dismayed for a while, and his thoughts alarmed him. The king answered and said, "Belteshazzar, let not the dream or the interpretation alarm you." Belteshazzar answered and said, "My lord, may the dream be for those who hate you and its interpretation for your enemies! [20]The tree you saw, which grew and became strong, so that its top reached to heaven, and it was visible to the end of the whole earth, [21]whose leaves were beautiful and its fruit abundant, and in which was food for all, under which beasts of the field found shade, and in whose branches the birds of the heavens lived— [22]it is you, O king, who have grown and become strong. Your greatness has grown and reaches to heaven, and your dominion to the ends of the earth. [23]And because the king saw a watcher, a holy one, coming down from heaven and saying, 'Chop down the tree and destroy it, but leave the stump of its roots in the earth, bound with a band of iron and bronze, in the tender grass of the field, and let him be wet with the dew of heaven, and let his portion be with the beasts of the field, till seven periods of time pass over him,' [24]this is the interpretation, O king: It is a decree of the Most High, which has come upon my lord the king, [25]that you shall be driven from among men, and your dwelling shall be with the beasts of the field. You shall be made to eat grass like an ox, and you shall be wet with the dew of heaven, and seven periods of time shall pass over you, till you know that the Most High rules the kingdom of men and gives it to whom he will. [26]And as it was commanded to leave the stump of the roots of the tree, your kingdom shall be confirmed for you from the time that you know that Heaven rules. [27]Therefore, O king, let my counsel be acceptable to you: break off your sins by practicing righteousness, and your iniquities by showing mercy to the oppressed, that there may perhaps be a lengthening of your prosperity."

[28]All this came upon King Nebuchadnezzar. [29]At the end of twelve months he was walking on the roof of the royal palace of Babylon, [30]and the king answered and said, "Is not this great Babylon, which I have built by my mighty power as a royal residence and for the glory of my majesty?" [31]While the words were still in the king's mouth, there fell a voice from heaven, "O King Nebuchadnezzar, to you it is spoken: The kingdom has departed from you, [32]and you shall be driven from among men, and your dwelling shall be with the beasts of the field. And you shall be made to eat grass like an ox, and seven periods of time shall pass over you, until you know that the Most High rules the kingdom of men and gives it to whom he will." [33]Immediately the word was fulfilled against Nebuchadnezzar. He was driven from among men and ate

grass like an ox, and his body was wet with the dew of heaven till his hair grew as long as eagles' feathers, and his nails were like birds' claws.

³⁴At the end of the days I, Nebuchadnezzar, lifted my eyes to heaven, and my reason returned to me, and I blessed the Most High, and praised and honored him who lives forever,

> for his dominion is an everlasting dominion,
>   and his kingdom endures from generation to generation;
> ³⁵ all the inhabitants of the earth are accounted as nothing,
>   and he does according to his will among the host of heaven
>   and among the inhabitants of the earth;
> and none can stay his hand
>   or say to him, "What have you done?"

³⁶At the same time my reason returned to me, and for the glory of my kingdom, my majesty and splendor returned to me. My counselors and my lords sought me, and I was established in my kingdom, and still more greatness was added to me. ³⁷Now I, Nebuchadnezzar, praise and extol and honor the King of heaven, for all his works are right and his ways are just; and those who walk in pride he is able to humble.

The handwriting on the wall [chapter 5]. Daniel appears again as the heroic interpreter of dreams for a Babylonian king. In an episode rich in atmosphere, the scene of action is the luxurious and decadent court of Belshazzar, with the decadence rendered all the more abhorrent by the desecration of the vessels that had been plundered from the temple in Jerusalem (vv. 2–4). The episode turns into a phantasmagoria of shocking events, beginning with a disembodied hand that writes a mysterious message on the wall. Daniel steps into the horror with his characteristic confidence and charisma, interpreting the dream and announcing God's judgment against the evil king. In one of the most ironic events recorded in the Bible, Belshazzar responds to the message of doom by elevating Daniel to the position of third ruler in the kingdom that very night, but that night the kingdom falls to Darius the Mede.

5 King Belshazzar made a great feast for a thousand of his lords and drank wine in front of the thousand. ²Belshazzar, when he tasted the wine, commanded that the vessels of gold and of silver that Nebuchadnezzar his father¹ had taken out of the temple in Jerusalem be brought, that the king and his lords, his wives, and his concubines might drink from them. ³Then they brought in the golden vessels that had been taken out of the temple, the house of God in Jerusalem, and the king and his lords, his wives, and his concubines drank from them. ⁴They drank wine and praised the gods of gold and silver, bronze, iron, wood, and stone.

⁵Immediately the fingers of a human hand appeared and wrote on the plaster of the wall of the king's palace, opposite the lampstand. And the king saw the hand as it wrote. ⁶Then the king's color changed, and his thoughts alarmed him; his limbs gave way, and his knees knocked together. ⁷The king called loudly to bring in the enchanters, the Chaldeans, and the astrologers. The king declared² to the wise men of Babylon, "Whoever reads this writing, and shows me its interpretation, shall be

---

¹ Or *predecessor*; also verses 11, 13, 18 ² Aramaic *answered and said*; also verse 10

clothed with purple and have a chain of gold around his neck and shall be the third ruler in the kingdom." ⁸Then all the king's wise men came in, but they could not read the writing or make known to the king the interpretation. ⁹Then King Belshazzar was greatly alarmed, and his color changed, and his lords were perplexed.

¹⁰The queen,¹ because of the words of the king and his lords, came into the banqueting hall, and the queen declared, "O king, live forever! Let not your thoughts alarm you or your color change. ¹¹There is a man in your kingdom in whom is the spirit of the holy gods.² In the days of your father, light and understanding and wisdom like the wisdom of the gods were found in him, and King Nebuchadnezzar, your father—your father the king—made him chief of the magicians, enchanters, Chaldeans, and astrologers, ¹²because an excellent spirit, knowledge, and understanding to interpret dreams, explain riddles, and solve problems were found in this Daniel, whom the king named Belteshazzar. Now let Daniel be called, and he will show the interpretation."

¹³Then Daniel was brought in before the king. The king answered and said to Daniel, "You are that Daniel, one of the exiles of Judah, whom the king my father brought from Judah. ¹⁴I have heard of you that the spirit of the gods³ is in you, and that light and understanding and excellent wisdom are found in you. ¹⁵Now the wise men, the enchanters, have been brought in before me to read this writing and make known to me its interpretation, but they could not show the interpretation of the matter. ¹⁶But I have heard that you can give interpretations and solve problems. Now if you can read the writing and make known to me its interpretation, you shall be clothed with purple and have a chain of gold around your neck and shall be the third ruler in the kingdom."

¹⁷Then Daniel answered and said before the king, "Let your gifts be for yourself, and give your rewards to another. Nevertheless, I will read the writing to the king and make known to him the interpretation. ¹⁸O king, the Most High God gave Nebuchadnezzar your father kingship and greatness and glory and majesty. ¹⁹And because of the greatness that he gave him, all peoples, nations, and languages trembled and feared before him. Whom he would, he killed, and whom he would, he kept alive; whom he would, he raised up, and whom he would, he humbled. ²⁰But when his heart was lifted up and his spirit was hardened so that he dealt proudly, he was brought down from his kingly throne, and his glory was taken from him. ²¹He was driven from among the children of mankind, and his mind was made like that of a beast, and his dwelling was with the wild donkeys. He was fed grass like an ox, and his body was wet with the dew of heaven, until he knew that the Most High God rules the kingdom of mankind and sets over it whom he will. ²²And you his son,⁴ Belshazzar, have not humbled your heart, though you knew all this, ²³but you have lifted up yourself against the Lord of heaven. And the vessels of his house have been brought in before you, and you and your lords, your wives, and your concubines have drunk wine from them. And you have praised the gods of silver and gold, of bronze, iron, wood, and stone, which do not see or hear or know, but the God in whose hand is your breath, and whose are all your ways, you have not honored.

²⁴"Then from his presence the hand was sent, and this writing was inscribed. ²⁵And this is the writing that was inscribed: MENE, MENE, TEKEL, and PARSIN. ²⁶This is the interpretation of the matter: MENE, God has numbered⁵ the days of your kingdom and

¹ Or queen mother; twice in this verse ² Or Spirit of the holy God ³ Or Spirit of God ⁴ Or successor ⁵ MENE sounds like the Aramaic for numbered

brought it to an end; [27]TEKEL, you have been weighed[1] in the balances and found wanting; [28]PERES, your kingdom is divided and given to the Medes and Persians."[2]

[29]Then Belshazzar gave the command, and Daniel was clothed with purple, a chain of gold was put around his neck, and a proclamation was made about him, that he should be the third ruler in the kingdom.

[30]That very night Belshazzar the Chaldean king was killed. [31][3] And Darius the Mede received the kingdom, being about sixty-two years old.

Daniel in the lions' den [chapter 6]. It is obvious that the storyteller has selected the most spectacular events in Daniel's life for inclusion in his minianthology of hero stories. Chapter 6 is perhaps the most striking event in Daniel's life. The scene shifts forward to the rule of yet another great king of the ancient world, the Persian king Darius. Daniel is again presented as a hero of loyalty to God in the face of testing that comes in the form (again) of compulsory emperor worship. The specifics belong to an ancient world, but the principles involved are as close as our daily experience. The story of testing ends as a *rescue story and a story of virtue rewarded and vice punished (the slanderers are destroyed [v. 24]).

---

6 It pleased Darius to set over the kingdom 120 satraps, to be throughout the whole kingdom; [2]and over them three presidents, of whom Daniel was one, to whom these satraps should give account, so that the king might suffer no loss. [3]Then this Daniel became distinguished above all the other presidents and satraps, because an excellent spirit was in him. And the king planned to set him over the whole kingdom. [4]Then the presidents and the satraps sought to find a ground for complaint against Daniel with regard to the kingdom, but they could find no ground for complaint or any fault, because he was faithful, and no error or fault was found in him. [5]Then these men said, "We shall not find any ground for complaint against this Daniel unless we find it in connection with the law of his God."

[6]Then these presidents and satraps came by agreement[4] to the king and said to him, "O King Darius, live forever! [7]All the presidents of the kingdom, the prefects and the satraps, the counselors and the governors are agreed that the king should establish an ordinance and enforce an injunction, that whoever makes petition to any god or man for thirty days, except to you, O king, shall be cast into the den of lions. [8]Now, O king, establish the injunction and sign the document, so that it cannot be changed, according to the law of the Medes and the Persians, which cannot be revoked." [9]Therefore King Darius signed the document and injunction.

[10]When Daniel knew that the document had been signed, he went to his house where he had windows in his upper chamber open toward Jerusalem. He got down on his knees three times a day and prayed and gave thanks before his God, as he had done previously. [11]Then these men came by agreement and found Daniel making petition and plea before his God. [12]Then they came near and said before the king, concerning the injunction, "O king! Did you not sign an injunction, that anyone who makes petition to any god or man within thirty days except to you, O king, shall be cast into the den of lions?" The king answered and said, "The thing stands fast, according to the law of the Medes and Persians, which cannot be revoked." [13]Then they answered and said before the king, "Daniel, who is one of the exiles from Judah,

---

[1] TEKEL sounds like the Aramaic for *weighed* [2] PERES (the singular of *Parsin*) sounds like the Aramaic for *divided* and for *Persia* [3] Ch 6:1 in Aramaic
[4] Or *came thronging;* also verses 11, 15

pays no attention to you, O king, or the injunction you have signed, but makes his petition three times a day."

¹⁴Then the king, when he heard these words, was much distressed and set his mind to deliver Daniel. And he labored till the sun went down to rescue him. ¹⁵Then these men came by agreement to the king and said to the king, "Know, O king, that it is a law of the Medes and Persians that no injunction or ordinance that the king establishes can be changed."

¹⁶Then the king commanded, and Daniel was brought and cast into the den of lions. The king declared¹ to Daniel, "May your God, whom you serve continually, deliver you!" ¹⁷And a stone was brought and laid on the mouth of the den, and the king sealed it with his own signet and with the signet of his lords, that nothing might be changed concerning Daniel. ¹⁸Then the king went to his palace and spent the night fasting; no diversions were brought to him, and sleep fled from him.

¹⁹Then, at break of day, the king arose and went in haste to the den of lions. ²⁰As he came near to the den where Daniel was, he cried out in a tone of anguish. The king declared to Daniel, "O Daniel, servant of the living God, has your God, whom you serve continually, been able to deliver you from the lions?" ²¹Then Daniel said to the king, "O king, live forever! ²²My God sent his angel and shut the lions' mouths, and they have not harmed me, because I was found blameless before him; and also before you, O king, I have done no harm." ²³Then the king was exceedingly glad, and commanded that Daniel be taken up out of the den. So Daniel was taken up out of the den, and no kind of harm was found on him, because he had trusted in his God. ²⁴And the king commanded, and those men who had maliciously accused Daniel were brought and cast into the den of lions—they, their children, and their wives. And before they reached the bottom of the den, the lions overpowered them and broke all their bones in pieces.

²⁵Then King Darius wrote to all the peoples, nations, and languages that dwell in all the earth: "Peace be multiplied to you. ²⁶I make a decree, that in all my royal dominion people are to tremble and fear before the God of Daniel,

for he is the living God,
enduring forever;
his kingdom shall never be destroyed,
and his dominion shall be to the end.
²⁷He delivers and rescues;
he works signs and wonders
in heaven and on earth,
he who has saved Daniel
from the power of the lions."

²⁸So this Daniel prospered during the reign of Darius and the reign of Cyrus the Persian.

The vision of the four beasts [chapter 7]. The book of Daniel shifts into an entirely different mode with this chapter, as we enter a visionary world in which the primary phenomena are symbols rather than people and events such as we encounter in daily life. As we enter the second half of the book, we face a basic choice as to the level at which

¹ Aramaic *answered and said*; also verse 20

we intend to read. One level is political allegory, in which various symbols are identified as representing kings and kingdoms of ancient history. If we read at this level, the
four beasts of verses 1–8 are symbols of four great empires—Babylon, Persia, Greece,
and Rome. At the same time, or as an alternate level at which we can assimilate the
visions, we can allow the symbols to be a generalized picture of the empires and powers
of the world throughout history. This is rendered easy to do because intermingled with
the political thread are symbolic pictures of the messianic rule of Christ as it exists at
any point in history—as in verses 9–14 and 26–27 (with the latter passage also lending
itself to an eschatological interpretation).

7 In the first year of Belshazzar king of Babylon, Daniel saw a dream and visions
of his head as he lay in his bed. Then he wrote down the dream and told the sum
of the matter. ²Daniel declared,[1] "I saw in my vision by night, and behold, the four
winds of heaven were stirring up the great sea. ³And four great beasts came up out of
the sea, different from one another. ⁴The first was like a lion and had eagles' wings.
Then as I looked its wings were plucked off, and it was lifted up from the ground and
made to stand on two feet like a man, and the mind of a man was given to it. ⁵And
behold, another beast, a second one, like a bear. It was raised up on one side. It had
three ribs in its mouth between its teeth; and it was told, 'Arise, devour much flesh.'
⁶After this I looked, and behold, another, like a leopard, with four wings of a bird on
its back. And the beast had four heads, and dominion was given to it. ⁷After this I saw
in the night visions, and behold, a fourth beast, terrifying and dreadful and exceedingly strong. It had great iron teeth; it devoured and broke in pieces and stamped
what was left with its feet. It was different from all the beasts that were before it, and
it had ten horns. ⁸I considered the horns, and behold, there came up among them
another horn, a little one, before which three of the first horns were plucked up by
the roots. And behold, in this horn were eyes like the eyes of a man, and a mouth
speaking great things.
    ⁹"As I looked,

        thrones were placed,
            and the Ancient of Days took his seat;
        his clothing was white as snow,
            and the hair of his head like pure wool;
        his throne was fiery flames;
            its wheels were burning fire.
¹⁰   A stream of fire issued
            and came out from before him;
        a thousand thousands served him,
            and ten thousand times ten thousand stood before him;
        the court sat in judgment,
            and the books were opened.

    ¹¹"I looked then because of the sound of the great words that the horn was speak-
ing. And as I looked, the beast was killed, and its body destroyed and given over to be
burned with fire. ¹²As for the rest of the beasts, their dominion was taken away, but
their lives were prolonged for a season and a time.
    ¹³"I saw in the night visions,

---

[1] Aramaic *answered and said*

and behold, with the clouds of heaven
   there came one like a son of man,
and he came to the Ancient of Days
   and was presented before him.
14 And to him was given dominion
      and glory and a kingdom,
   that all peoples, nations, and languages
      should serve him;
   his dominion is an everlasting dominion,
      which shall not pass away,
   and his kingdom one
      that shall not be destroyed.

¹⁵"As for me, Daniel, my spirit within me¹ was anxious, and the visions of my head alarmed me. ¹⁶I approached one of those who stood there and asked him the truth concerning all this. So he told me and made known to me the interpretation of the things. ¹⁷'These four great beasts are four kings who shall arise out of the earth. ¹⁸But the saints of the Most High shall receive the kingdom and possess the kingdom forever, forever and ever.'

¹⁹"Then I desired to know the truth about the fourth beast, which was different from all the rest, exceedingly terrifying, with its teeth of iron and claws of bronze, and which devoured and broke in pieces and stamped what was left with its feet, ²⁰and about the ten horns that were on its head, and the other horn that came up and before which three of them fell, the horn that had eyes and a mouth that spoke great things, and that seemed greater than its companions. ²¹As I looked, this horn made war with the saints and prevailed over them, ²²until the Ancient of Days came, and judgment was given for the saints of the Most High, and the time came when the saints possessed the kingdom.

²³"Thus he said: 'As for the fourth beast,

   there shall be a fourth kingdom on earth,
      which shall be different from all the kingdoms,
   and it shall devour the whole earth,
      and trample it down, and break it to pieces.
24 As for the ten horns,
   out of this kingdom ten kings shall arise,
      and another shall arise after them;
   he shall be different from the former ones,
      and shall put down three kings.
25 He shall speak words against the Most High,
      and shall wear out the saints of the Most High,
      and shall think to change the times and the law;
   and they shall be given into his hand
      for a time, times, and half a time.
26 But the court shall sit in judgment,
      and his dominion shall be taken away,
         to be consumed and destroyed to the end.

¹ Aramaic *within its sheath*

²⁷   And the kingdom and the dominion
         and the greatness of the kingdoms under the whole heaven
         shall be given to the people of the saints of the Most High;
      their kingdom shall be an everlasting kingdom,
      and all dominions shall serve and obey them."[1]

²⁸"Here is the end of the matter. As for me, Daniel, my thoughts greatly alarmed me, and my color changed, but I kept the matter in my heart."

The vision of the ram and goat [chapter 8]. Symbolic and visionary modes continue in this chapter. No matter how we interpret the references, we cannot avoid having our imagination pierced with the mystery of what is presented to us, so that we understand that in prophetic literature the future is only partly revealed to us. One approach to the material is to consult a study Bible and see how scholars have interpreted the material as political allegory. A more literary approach simply assimilates the symbols as representative of universal principles, chiefly the spectacle of earthly powers presuming to be great but actually being subject to the sovereign rule of God. With either approach, we need to be receptive to the imaginative power of the images and symbols that fill the visions.

8 In the third year of the reign of King Belshazzar a vision appeared to me, Daniel, after that which appeared to me at the first. ²And I saw in the vision; and when I saw, I was in Susa the capital,[2] which is in the province of Elam. And I saw in the vision, and I was at the Ulai canal. ³I raised my eyes and saw, and behold, a ram standing on the bank of the canal. It had two horns, and both horns were high, but one was higher than the other, and the higher one came up last. ⁴I saw the ram charging westward and northward and southward. No beast could stand before him, and there was no one who could rescue from his power. He did as he pleased and became great.

⁵As I was considering, behold, a male goat came from the west across the face of the whole earth, without touching the ground. And the goat had a conspicuous horn between his eyes. ⁶He came to the ram with the two horns, which I had seen standing on the bank of the canal, and he ran at him in his powerful wrath. ⁷I saw him come close to the ram, and he was enraged against him and struck the ram and broke his two horns. And the ram had no power to stand before him, but he cast him down to the ground and trampled on him. And there was no one who could rescue the ram from his power. ⁸Then the goat became exceedingly great, but when he was strong, the great horn was broken, and instead of it there came up four conspicuous horns toward the four winds of heaven.

⁹Out of one of them came a little horn, which grew exceedingly great toward the south, toward the east, and toward the glorious land. ¹⁰It grew great, even to the host of heaven. And some of the host and some[3] of the stars it threw down to the ground and trampled on them. ¹¹It became great, even as great as the Prince of the host. And the regular burnt offering was taken away from him, and the place of his sanctuary was overthrown. ¹²And a host will be given over to it together with the regular burnt offering because of transgression,[4] and it will throw truth to the ground, and it will

---

[1] Or his kingdom shall be an everlasting kingdom, and all dominions shall serve and obey him [2] Or the fortified city [3] Or host, that is, some [4] Or in an act of rebellion

act and prosper. ¹³Then I heard a holy one speaking, and another holy one said to the one who spoke, "For how long is the vision concerning the regular burnt offering, the transgression that makes desolate, and the giving over of the sanctuary and host to be trampled underfoot?" ¹⁴And he said to me,¹ "For 2,300 evenings and mornings. Then the sanctuary shall be restored to its rightful state."

¹⁵When I, Daniel, had seen the vision, I sought to understand it. And behold, there stood before me one having the appearance of a man. ¹⁶And I heard a man's voice between the banks of the Ulai, and it called, "Gabriel, make this man understand the vision." ¹⁷So he came near where I stood. And when he came, I was frightened and fell on my face. But he said to me, "Understand, O son of man, that the vision is for the time of the end."

¹⁸And when he had spoken to me, I fell into a deep sleep with my face to the ground. But he touched me and made me stand up. ¹⁹He said, "Behold, I will make known to you what shall be at the latter end of the indignation, for it refers to the appointed time of the end. ²⁰As for the ram that you saw with the two horns, these are the kings of Media and Persia. ²¹And the goat² is the king of Greece. And the great horn between his eyes is the first king. ²²As for the horn that was broken, in place of which four others arose, four kingdoms shall arise from his³ nation, but not with his power. ²³And at the latter end of their kingdom, when the transgressors have reached their limit, a king of bold face, one who understands riddles, shall arise. ²⁴His power shall be great—but not by his own power; and he shall cause fearful destruction and shall succeed in what he does, and destroy mighty men and the people who are the saints. ²⁵By his cunning he shall make deceit prosper under his hand, and in his own mind he shall become great. Without warning he shall destroy many. And he shall even rise up against the Prince of princes, and he shall be broken—but by no human hand. ²⁶The vision of the evenings and the mornings that has been told is true, but seal up the vision, for it refers to many days from now."

²⁷And I, Daniel, was overcome and lay sick for some days. Then I rose and went about the king's business, but I was appalled by the vision and did not understand it.

> **Daniel as intercessor** [chapter 9]. This chapter contains one of the famous prayers of the Bible. The lead-in gives the narrative context of Daniel's prayer, namely, his realization that Jeremiah's prophecy of a seventy-year exile is coming to an end. The prayer that ensues contains the standard motifs of prayer: humility of approach to God (v. 3); invocation ascribing honor to God (v. 4); confession of sin (vv. 5–15); petition (vv. 16–19). Daniel's prayer is a covenant prayer on behalf of the nation. The prayer is followed by a moment of high drama, as the angel Gabriel appears, having been dispatched from heaven as Daniel began his prayer (vv. 20–23). Interpreters do not agree on how to handle Gabriel's vision of the future (vv. 24–27), but whatever historical references the vision might contain, we will not go wrong if we give the vision an eschatological, end-times interpretation.

9 In the first year of Darius the son of Ahasuerus, by descent a Mede, who was made king over the realm of the Chaldeans— ²in the first year of his reign, I, Daniel, perceived in the books the number of years that, according to the word of the Lᴏʀᴅ to Jeremiah the prophet, must pass before the end of the desolations of Jerusalem, namely, seventy years.

---

¹ Hebrew; Septuagint, Theodotion, Vulgate *to him* ² Or *the shaggy goat* ³ Theodotion, Septuagint, Vulgate; Hebrew *the*

³Then I turned my face to the Lord God, seeking him by prayer and pleas for mercy with fasting and sackcloth and ashes. ⁴I prayed to the LORD my God and made confession, saying, "O Lord, the great and awesome God, who keeps covenant and steadfast love with those who love him and keep his commandments, ⁵we have sinned and done wrong and acted wickedly and rebelled, turning aside from your commandments and rules. ⁶We have not listened to your servants the prophets, who spoke in your name to our kings, our princes, and our fathers, and to all the people of the land. ⁷To you, O Lord, belongs righteousness, but to us open shame, as at this day, to the men of Judah, to the inhabitants of Jerusalem, and to all Israel, those who are near and those who are far away, in all the lands to which you have driven them, because of the treachery that they have committed against you. ⁸To us, O LORD, belongs open shame, to our kings, to our princes, and to our fathers, because we have sinned against you. ⁹To the Lord our God belong mercy and forgiveness, for we have rebelled against him ¹⁰and have not obeyed the voice of the LORD our God by walking in his laws, which he set before us by his servants the prophets. ¹¹All Israel has transgressed your law and turned aside, refusing to obey your voice. And the curse and oath that are written in the Law of Moses the servant of God have been poured out upon us, because we have sinned against him. ¹²He has confirmed his words, which he spoke against us and against our rulers who ruled us,¹ by bringing upon us a great calamity. For under the whole heaven there has not been done anything like what has been done against Jerusalem. ¹³As it is written in the Law of Moses, all this calamity has come upon us; yet we have not entreated the favor of the LORD our God, turning from our iniquities and gaining insight by your truth. ¹⁴Therefore the LORD has kept ready the calamity and has brought it upon us, for the LORD our God is righteous in all the works that he has done, and we have not obeyed his voice. ¹⁵And now, O Lord our God, who brought your people out of the land of Egypt with a mighty hand, and have made a name for yourself, as at this day, we have sinned, we have done wickedly.

¹⁶"O Lord, according to all your righteous acts, let your anger and your wrath turn away from your city Jerusalem, your holy hill, because for our sins, and for the iniquities of our fathers, Jerusalem and your people have become a byword among all who are around us. ¹⁷Now therefore, O our God, listen to the prayer of your servant and to his pleas for mercy, and for your own sake, O Lord,² make your face to shine upon your sanctuary, which is desolate. ¹⁸O my God, incline your ear and hear. Open your eyes and see our desolations, and the city that is called by your name. For we do not present our pleas before you because of our righteousness, but because of your great mercy. ¹⁹O Lord, hear; O Lord, forgive. O Lord, pay attention and act. Delay not, for your own sake, O my God, because your city and your people are called by your name."

²⁰While I was speaking and praying, confessing my sin and the sin of my people Israel, and presenting my plea before the LORD my God for the holy hill of my God, ²¹while I was speaking in prayer, the man Gabriel, whom I had seen in the vision at the first, came to me in swift flight at the time of the evening sacrifice. ²²He made me understand, speaking with me and saying, "O Daniel, I have now come out to give you insight and understanding. ²³At the beginning of your pleas for mercy a word went out, and I have come to tell it to you, for you are greatly loved. Therefore consider the word and understand the vision.

²⁴"Seventy weeks³ are decreed about your people and your holy city, to finish the

---

¹ Or *our judges who judged us* ² Hebrew *for the Lord's sake* ³ Or *sevens;* also twice in verse 25 and once in verse 26

transgression, to put an end to sin, and to atone for iniquity, to bring in everlasting righteousness, to seal both vision and prophet, and to anoint a most holy place.[1] ²⁵Know therefore and understand that from the going out of the word to restore and build Jerusalem to the coming of an anointed one, a prince, there shall be seven weeks. Then for sixty-two weeks it shall be built again with squares and moat, but in a troubled time. ²⁶And after the sixty-two weeks, an anointed one shall be cut off and shall have nothing. And the people of the prince who is to come shall destroy the city and the sanctuary. Its[2] end shall come with a flood, and to the end there shall be war. Desolations are decreed. ²⁷And he shall make a strong covenant with many for one week,[3] and for half of the week he shall put an end to sacrifice and offering. And on the wing of abominations shall come one who makes desolate, until the decreed end is poured out on the desolator."

A divine-human encounter [10:1–11:1]. Visionary literature like Dante's *Divine Comedy* and Milton's *Paradise Lost* is filled with encounters between a supernatural being and either the narrator of the work or a character in the story. Chapter 10 enacts this famous motif. The action begins with the placing of the prophet Daniel in a specific time and place (vv. 1–4). The second phase is the appearance of an angelic being, so dazzling that the prophet falls into a deep sleep with his face on the ground (vv. 5–9). In an atmosphere suffused with the supernatural and numinous, further exchanges between Daniel and supernatural beings occur, the general effect being to encourage Daniel (vv. 10–20). Daniel's experience here is paradigmatic of the experience of the OT prophets: he encounters God directly and is overwhelmed by the transcendent glory of God. The narrative function of this chapter in the book of Daniel is to serve as a prelude to the ensuing visions of the future.

10

In the third year of Cyrus king of Persia a word was revealed to Daniel, who was named Belteshazzar. And the word was true, and it was a great conflict.[4] And he understood the word and had understanding of the vision.

²In those days I, Daniel, was mourning for three weeks. ³I ate no delicacies, no meat or wine entered my mouth, nor did I anoint myself at all, for the full three weeks. ⁴On the twenty-fourth day of the first month, as I was standing on the bank of the great river (that is, the Tigris) ⁵I lifted up my eyes and looked, and behold, a man clothed in linen, with a belt of fine gold from Uphaz around his waist. ⁶His body was like beryl, his face like the appearance of lightning, his eyes like flaming torches, his arms and legs like the gleam of burnished bronze, and the sound of his words like the sound of a multitude. ⁷And I, Daniel, alone saw the vision, for the men who were with me did not see the vision, but a great trembling fell upon them, and they fled to hide themselves. ⁸So I was left alone and saw this great vision, and no strength was left in me. My radiant appearance was fearfully changed,[5] and I retained no strength. ⁹Then I heard the sound of his words, and as I heard the sound of his words, I fell on my face in deep sleep with my face to the ground.

¹⁰And behold, a hand touched me and set me trembling on my hands and knees. ¹¹And he said to me, "O Daniel, man greatly loved, understand the words that I speak to you, and stand upright, for now I have been sent to you." And when he had spoken this word to me, I stood up trembling. ¹²Then he said to me, "Fear not, Daniel, for from the first day that you set your heart to understand and humbled yourself before your

---

[1] Or *thing, or one* [2] Or *His* [3] Or *seven;* twice in this verse [4] Or *and it was about a great conflict* [5] Hebrew *My splendor was changed to ruin*

God, your words have been heard, and I have come because of your words. [13]The prince of the kingdom of Persia withstood me twenty-one days, but Michael, one of the chief princes, came to help me, for I was left there with the kings of Persia, [14]and came to make you understand what is to happen to your people in the latter days. For the vision is for days yet to come."

[15]When he had spoken to me according to these words, I turned my face toward the ground and was mute. [16]And behold, one in the likeness of the children of man touched my lips. Then I opened my mouth and spoke. I said to him who stood before me, "O my lord, by reason of the vision pains have come upon me, and I retain no strength. [17]How can my lord's servant talk with my lord? For now no strength remains in me, and no breath is left in me."

[18]Again one having the appearance of a man touched me and strengthened me. [19]And he said, "O man greatly loved, fear not, peace be with you; be strong and of good courage." And as he spoke to me, I was strengthened and said, "Let my lord speak, for you have strengthened me." [20]Then he said, "Do you know why I have come to you? But now I will return to fight against the prince of Persia; and when I go out, behold, the prince of Greece will come. [21]But I will tell you what is inscribed in the book of truth: there is none who contends by my side against these except Michael, your prince.

11 "And as for me, in the first year of Darius the Mede, I stood up to confirm and strengthen him.

> **Apocalyptic visions of the future** [11:2–45]. The rhetoric of this chapter is visionary, meaning that we are bombarded with a host of details regarding what will happen in the future and that are envisioned in the imagination, since they have not yet happened. The details, moreover, appear in a kaleidoscopic and phantasmagoric pattern, and the effect is that we are reading something in code. Consulting a study Bible will show that it is possible to interpret the details as political allegory, but for many readers that produces a more bewildering picture than does reading the visions as a symbolic and apocalyptic account of history. If we read at a symbolic level, it is obvious that the main ingredients of the vision—the rise and fall of empires, international warfare, an endless succession of nations and rulers that have their day and then vanish—constitute a pattern that is always in the process of being fulfilled in earthly history.

[2]"And now I will show you the truth. Behold, three more kings shall arise in Persia, and a fourth shall be far richer than all of them. And when he has become strong through his riches, he shall stir up all against the kingdom of Greece. [3]Then a mighty king shall arise, who shall rule with great dominion and do as he wills. [4]And as soon as he has arisen, his kingdom shall be broken and divided toward the four winds of heaven, but not to his posterity, nor according to the authority with which he ruled, for his kingdom shall be plucked up and go to others besides these.

[5]"Then the king of the south shall be strong, but one of his princes shall be stronger than he and shall rule, and his authority shall be a great authority. [6]After some years they shall make an alliance, and the daughter of the king of the south shall come to the king of the north to make an agreement. But she shall not retain the

strength of her arm, and he and his arm shall not endure, but she shall be given up, and her attendants, he who fathered her, and he who supported[1] her in those times.

[7]"And from a branch from her roots one shall arise in his place. He shall come against the army and enter the fortress of the king of the north, and he shall deal with them and shall prevail. [8]He shall also carry off to Egypt their gods with their metal images and their precious vessels of silver and gold, and for some years he shall refrain from attacking the king of the north. [9]Then the latter shall come into the realm of the king of the south but shall return to his own land.

[10]"His sons shall wage war and assemble a multitude of great forces, which shall keep coming and overflow and pass through, and again shall carry the war as far as his fortress. [11]Then the king of the south, moved with rage, shall come out and fight against the king of the north. And he shall raise a great multitude, but it shall be given into his hand. [12]And when the multitude is taken away, his heart shall be exalted, and he shall cast down tens of thousands, but he shall not prevail. [13]For the king of the north shall again raise a multitude, greater than the first. And after some years[2] he shall come on with a great army and abundant supplies.

[14]"In those times many shall rise against the king of the south, and the violent among your own people shall lift themselves up in order to fulfill the vision, but they shall fail. [15]Then the king of the north shall come and throw up siegeworks and take a well-fortified city. And the forces of the south shall not stand, or even his best troops, for there shall be no strength to stand. [16]But he who comes against him shall do as he wills, and none shall stand before him. And he shall stand in the glorious land, with destruction in his hand. [17]He shall set his face to come with the strength of his whole kingdom, and he shall bring terms of an agreement and perform them. He shall give him the daughter of women to destroy the kingdom,[3] but it shall not stand or be to his advantage. [18]Afterward he shall turn his face to the coastlands and shall capture many of them, but a commander shall put an end to his insolence. Indeed,[4] he shall turn his insolence back upon him. [19]Then he shall turn his face back toward the fortresses of his own land, but he shall stumble and fall, and shall not be found.

[20]"Then shall arise in his place one who shall send an exactor of tribute for the glory of the kingdom. But within a few days he shall be broken, neither in anger nor in battle. [21]In his place shall arise a contemptible person to whom royal majesty has not been given. He shall come in without warning and obtain the kingdom by flatteries. [22]Armies shall be utterly swept away before him and broken, even the prince of the covenant. [23]And from the time that an alliance is made with him he shall act deceitfully, and he shall become strong with a small people. [24]Without warning he shall come into the richest parts[5] of the province, and he shall do what neither his fathers nor his fathers' fathers have done, scattering among them plunder, spoil, and goods. He shall devise plans against strongholds, but only for a time. [25]And he shall stir up his power and his heart against the king of the south with a great army. And the king of the south shall wage war with an exceedingly great and mighty army, but he shall not stand, for plots shall be devised against him. [26]Even those who eat his food shall break him. His army shall be swept away, and many shall fall down slain. [27]And as for the two kings, their hearts shall be bent on doing evil. They shall speak lies at the same table, but to no avail, for the end is yet to be at the time appointed. [28]And he shall return to his land with great wealth, but his heart shall be set against the holy covenant. And he shall work his will and return to his own land.

---

[1] Or obtained [2] Hebrew at the end of the times [3] Hebrew her, or it [4] The meaning of the Hebrew is uncertain [5] Or among the richest men

²⁹"At the time appointed he shall return and come into the south, but it shall not be this time as it was before. ³⁰For ships of Kittim shall come against him, and he shall be afraid and withdraw, and shall turn back and be enraged and take action against the holy covenant. He shall turn back and pay attention to those who forsake the holy covenant. ³¹Forces from him shall appear and profane the temple and fortress, and shall take away the regular burnt offering. And they shall set up the abomination that makes desolate. ³²He shall seduce with flattery those who violate the covenant, but the people who know their God shall stand firm and take action. ³³And the wise among the people shall make many understand, though for some days they shall stumble by sword and flame, by captivity and plunder. ³⁴When they stumble, they shall receive a little help. And many shall join themselves to them with flattery, ³⁵and some of the wise shall stumble, so that they may be refined, purified, and made white, until the time of the end, for it still awaits the appointed time.

³⁶"And the king shall do as he wills. He shall exalt himself and magnify himself above every god, and shall speak astonishing things against the God of gods. He shall prosper till the indignation is accomplished; for what is decreed shall be done. ³⁷He shall pay no attention to the gods of his fathers, or to the one beloved by women. He shall not pay attention to any other god, for he shall magnify himself above all. ³⁸He shall honor the god of fortresses instead of these. A god whom his fathers did not know he shall honor with gold and silver, with precious stones and costly gifts. ³⁹He shall deal with the strongest fortresses with the help of a foreign god. Those who acknowledge him he shall load with honor. He shall make them rulers over many and shall divide the land for a price.¹

⁴⁰"At the time of the end, the king of the south shall attack² him, but the king of the north shall rush upon him like a whirlwind, with chariots and horsemen, and with many ships. And he shall come into countries and shall overflow and pass through. ⁴¹He shall come into the glorious land. And tens of thousands shall fall, but these shall be delivered out of his hand: Edom and Moab and the main part of the Ammonites. ⁴²He shall stretch out his hand against the countries, and the land of Egypt shall not escape. ⁴³He shall become ruler of the treasures of gold and of silver, and all the precious things of Egypt, and the Libyans and the Cushites shall follow in his train. ⁴⁴But news from the east and the north shall alarm him, and he shall go out with great fury to destroy and devote many to destruction. ⁴⁵And he shall pitch his palatial tents between the sea and the glorious holy mountain. Yet he shall come to his end, with none to help him.

Visions of the end [chapter 12]. If the preceding chapter has allowed for an apocalyptic reading of the visions, the final chapter of the book requires us to read it in that manner. The chief motifs are as follows: (1) the ushering in of eternal bliss for the righteous; (2) details that lift the veil just a little to reveal a supernatural reality that transcends the earthly sphere; (3) conflict between good and evil and the need for the righteous to remain pure from the wicked; (4) the need to wait for the promised end.

12 "At that time shall arise Michael, the great prince who has charge of your people. And there shall be a time of trouble, such as never has been since there was a nation till that time. But at that time your people shall be delivered, every-

---

¹ Or *land as payment* ² Hebrew *thrust at*

one whose name shall be found written in the book. ²And many of those who sleep in the dust of the earth shall awake, some to everlasting life, and some to shame and everlasting contempt. ³And those who are wise shall shine like the brightness of the sky above;¹ and those who turn many to righteousness, like the stars forever and ever. ⁴But you, Daniel, shut up the words and seal the book, until the time of the end. Many shall run to and fro, and knowledge shall increase."

⁵Then I, Daniel, looked, and behold, two others stood, one on this bank of the stream and one on that bank of the stream. ⁶And someone said to the man clothed in linen, who was above the waters of the stream,² "How long shall it be till the end of these wonders?" ⁷And I heard the man clothed in linen, who was above the waters of the stream; he raised his right hand and his left hand toward heaven and swore by him who lives forever that it would be for a time, times, and half a time, and that when the shattering of the power of the holy people comes to an end all these things would be finished. ⁸I heard, but I did not understand. Then I said, "O my lord, what shall be the outcome of these things?" ⁹He said, "Go your way, Daniel, for the words are shut up and sealed until the time of the end. ¹⁰Many shall purify themselves and make themselves white and be refined, but the wicked shall act wickedly. And none of the wicked shall understand, but those who are wise shall understand. ¹¹And from the time that the regular burnt offering is taken away and the abomination that makes desolate is set up, there shall be 1,290 days. ¹²Blessed is he who waits and arrives at the 1,335 days. ¹³But go your way till the end. And you shall rest and shall stand in your allotted place at the end of the days."

---

¹ Hebrew *the expanse*; compare Genesis 1:6-8 ² Or *who was upstream*; also verse 7

HOSEA

The book at a glance. 14 chapters, 197 verses. The thing everyone remembers about the book of Hosea is that God tells the prophet to marry a prostitute. This is, indeed, a shocking but true premise. Throughout the entire Bible, marital and sexual imagery is regularly used as a metaphor for the relationship between God and those who believe in him. Believers who are true to God are a chaste bride; those who are apostate are an adulterous prostitute. The book of Hosea turns that metaphor into a living reality, though the reality of course is intended as a metaphor for the faithless covenant people of Israel (the northern kingdom). Although the marriage of Hosea and Gomer provides the narrative framework for the book, the forms and content of the book mainly resemble the typical prophetic genre of the OT, with its characteristic oracles, prophetic denunciations, and exhortations.

▌**Genres.** The main form of the book is *prophecy, and within that rubric, most of the book consists of *oracles of judgment, with only interspersed *oracles of salvation. The main literary form of the book is *satire, with the usual ingredients of objects of attack, a vehicle in which the exposure is embodied, a satiric norm by which the criticism is conducted, and a prevailing tone (in this case, sharp and bitter). Virtually all of the book is embodied in *poetry. The overall format is that of a legal or judicial indictment, as God presents a detailed case against his covenant people. (For more information on items accompanied by an asterisk, see the glossary at the back of this Bible.)

▌**Format and distinguishing features.** The vividness of the poetry and figurative language is a striking feature of the book, as God's people (for example) are pictured as an oven or a stubborn heifer or wild grapes. Even though the failed and restored marriage of Hosea and Gomer is present only in the first three chapters, the controlling metaphor of covenant Israel as an unfaithful wife exerts an implied presence through-out the book. The multiple lists of indictments that God brings against Israel also make the implied metaphor of a divine lawsuit a continuous presence. The frame of reference throughout the book is the covenant (the reciprocal relationship between God and Israel as delineated throughout the OT). Recurrent themes around which we can organize our reading of the book are as follows: (1) the unfolding list of acts and attitudes that disappoint God; (2) a picture of what people who reject God can expect to receive from him; (3) evidences of God's love and grace toward people who do not deserve them.

Passage	Content	Prophetic Genre	Main Focus
1:1–2:1	God's instructions to Hosea regarding his wife and children (vv. 1–9), and an oracle of redemption (1:10–2:1)	Narrative and oracle	The family life of Hosea as prophetic symbol
2:2–23	God's prophecies of judgment and restoration of Israel	Poetic oracles of judgment and restoration	
3:1–5	Hosea reclaims Gomer as his wife	Narrative	
4:1–7:16	God's indictment of Israel for unfaithfulness	Oracles of judgment; satire	Israel's apostasy
8:1–10:15	God's intent to punish Israel's unfaithfulness	Oracles of judgment	
11:1–11	God's mingled love and judgment toward Israel	Narrative of past covenant history; prediction of future events	
11:12–13:16	God's judgment against Judah	Oracles of judgment	
14:1–9	God's restoration of his people	Oracle of salvation	God's restoration of Israel

▌ **Inferred literary intentions.** The book is designed to achieve the following literary purposes:

- shock us into understanding the loathsomeness of sin in God's eyes
- shame the original audience and us as well for our rejection of God's affections
- use the format of satire to express the themes of the book
- appeal to our imagination with poetic vividness
- prompt readers to repentance and reformation of their lives

▌ **Theological themes.** (1) Human sinfulness: in OT Israel we can see an anatomy of the perverse human tendency to reject God and true religion. (2) The justice of God: the book presents a complete picture of how God judges human sinfulness. (3) The love of God: the book shows that God does not abandon his people but is a pursuing and persevering lover—an incurable romantic in a metaphoric sense.

▌ **The book of Hosea as a chapter in the master story of the Bible.** The master story of the Bible is the story of God's dealings with the human race and especially his covenant people. This is exactly what the book of Hosea is about, with emphasis on how God deals with his people when they reject him. The unique angle that the book of Hosea takes toward the covenant theme is that it presents God's relationship to his people as a divine-human love story. Further, the ignominy of Israel (symbolic of people generally) is that Israel looks for love in all the wrong places instead of finding it in God.

History of a family [1:1–2:1]. The first three chapters of Hosea are mixed in content and fluid in arrangement, so we need to be alert as we proceed through the material. Following an inscription for the book (v. 1), the central thrust of chapter 1 is the history of Hosea's marriage to Gomer, including the birth of children. We need to discern two threads of action—(1) the literal facts regarding the marriage and births of children and (2) hints that these are intended as a metaphor of the relationship between God and his covenant people. As we read the narrative, therefore, we need to ask what we learn about God and ourselves from Hosea's relationship with Gomer.

1 The word of the LORD that came to Hosea, the son of Beeri, in the days of Uzziah, Jotham, Ahaz, and Hezekiah, kings of Judah, and in the days of Jeroboam the son of Joash, king of Israel.

²When the LORD first spoke through Hosea, the LORD said to Hosea, "Go, take to yourself a wife of whoredom and have children of whoredom, for the land commits great whoredom by forsaking the LORD." ³So he went and took Gomer, the daughter of Diblaim, and she conceived and bore him a son.

⁴And the LORD said to him, "Call his name Jezreel, for in just a little while I will punish the house of Jehu for the blood of Jezreel, and I will put an end to the kingdom of the house of Israel. ⁵And on that day I will break the bow of Israel in the Valley of Jezreel."

⁶She conceived again and bore a daughter. And the LORD said to him, "Call her name No Mercy,¹ for I will no more have mercy on the house of Israel, to forgive them at all. ⁷But I will have mercy on the house of Judah, and I will save them by the LORD their God. I will not save them by bow or by sword or by war or by horses or by horsemen."

⁸When she had weaned No Mercy, she conceived and bore a son. ⁹And the LORD said, "Call his name Not My People,² for you are not my people, and I am not your God."³

¹⁰⁴ Yet the number of the children of Israel shall be like the sand of the sea, which cannot be measured or numbered. And in the place where it was said to them, "You are not my people," it shall be said to them, "Children⁵ of the living God." ¹¹And the children of Judah and the children of Israel shall be gathered together, and they shall appoint for themselves one head. And they shall go up from the land, for great shall be the day of Jezreel.

2 ⁶ Say to your brothers, "You are my people,"⁷ and to your sisters, "You have received mercy."⁸

Israel's waywardness [2:2–23]. With the metaphors of marriage and sexual promiscuity having been established as a frame of reference, chapter 2 allows the story of Hosea and Gomer largely to drop out of sight. The imagery of marriage, prostitution, and family continues to form the content of the prophet's message, but in place of Hosea and Gomer we have God and his wayward bride Israel. The passage unfolds as follows: the adulterous misconduct of Israel-as-wife (vv. 2–5); God's punishment of this wayward wife (vv. 6–13); God's promise to restore his wife (vv. 14–23). The key to assimilating the chapter is to be receptive to the evocative poetic imagery and metaphors and

---

¹ Hebrew *Lo-ruhama*, which means *she has not received mercy* ² Hebrew *Lo-ammi*, which means *not my people* ³ Hebrew *I am not yours* ⁴ Ch 2:1 in Hebrew ⁵ Or *Sons* ⁶ Ch 2:3 in Hebrew ⁷ Hebrew *ammi*, which means *my people* ⁸ Hebrew *ruhama*, which means *she has received mercy*

then to carry over the meanings from the wayward wife motif to the believer's relationship to God.

² "Plead with your mother, plead—
    for she is not my wife,
    and I am not her husband—
that she put away her whoring from her face,
    and her adultery from between her breasts;
³ lest I strip her naked
    and make her as in the day she was born,
and make her like a wilderness,
    and make her like a parched land,
    and kill her with thirst.
⁴ Upon her children also I will have no mercy,
    because they are children of whoredom.
⁵ For their mother has played the whore;
    she who conceived them has acted shamefully.
For she said, 'I will go after my lovers,
    who give me my bread and my water,
    my wool and my flax, my oil and my drink.'
⁶ Therefore I will hedge up her¹ way with thorns,
    and I will build a wall against her,
    so that she cannot find her paths.
⁷ She shall pursue her lovers
    but not overtake them,
and she shall seek them
    but shall not find them.
Then she shall say,
    'I will go and return to my first husband,
    for it was better for me then than now.'
⁸ And she did not know
    that it was I who gave her
    the grain, the wine, and the oil,
and who lavished on her silver and gold,
    which they used for Baal.
⁹ Therefore I will take back
    my grain in its time,
    and my wine in its season,
and I will take away my wool and my flax,
    which were to cover her nakedness.
¹⁰ Now I will uncover her lewdness
    in the sight of her lovers,
    and no one shall rescue her out of my hand.
¹¹ And I will put an end to all her mirth,
    her feasts, her new moons, her Sabbaths,
    and all her appointed feasts.

¹ Hebrew *your*

¹²   And I will lay waste her vines and her fig trees,
     of which she said,
  'These are my wages,
     which my lovers have given me.'
  I will make them a forest,
     and the beasts of the field shall devour them.
¹³   And I will punish her for the feast days of the Baals
     when she burned offerings to them
  and adorned herself with her ring and jewelry,
     and went after her lovers
     and forgot me, declares the LORD.

¹⁴   "Therefore, behold, I will allure her,
     and bring her into the wilderness,
     and speak tenderly to her.
¹⁵   And there I will give her her vineyards
     and make the Valley of Achor[1] a door of hope.
  And there she shall answer as in the days of her youth,
     as at the time when she came out of the land of Egypt.

¹⁶"And in that day, declares the LORD, you will call me 'My Husband,' and no longer will you call me 'My Baal.' ¹⁷For I will remove the names of the Baals from her mouth, and they shall be remembered by name no more. ¹⁸And I will make for them a covenant on that day with the beasts of the field, the birds of the heavens, and the creeping things of the ground. And I will abolish[2] the bow, the sword, and war from the land, and I will make you lie down in safety. ¹⁹And I will betroth you to me forever. I will betroth you to me in righteousness and in justice, in steadfast love and in mercy. ²⁰I will betroth you to me in faithfulness. And you shall know the LORD.

²¹   "And in that day I will answer, declares the LORD,
     I will answer the heavens,
     and they shall answer the earth,
²²   and the earth shall answer the grain, the wine, and the oil,
     and they shall answer Jezreel,[3]
²³   and I will sow her for myself in the land.
  And I will have mercy on No Mercy,[4]
     and I will say to Not My People,[5] 'You are my people';
     and he shall say, 'You are my God.'"

Hosea reclaims his wife [chapter 3]. With this brief chapter the narrative returns to the literal marriage of the couple that had been introduced to us in the opening chapter. The text itself pushes us to see metaphoric and spiritual meanings in the restored marriage. As we explore the symbolic level of the literal facts, we are led to see how extraordinary God's love is, as Hosea's relationship to Gomer goes against ordinary human expectations. Gomer is a prostitute, but instead of giving up on her, Hosea is called to love her tenderly, even to his own humiliation. In this situation we can see what kind of lover God is.

[1] Achor means *trouble*; compare Joshua 7:26 [2] Hebrew *break* [3] *Jezreel* means *God will sow* [4] Hebrew *Lo-ruhama* [5] Hebrew *Lo-ammi*

3 And the LORD said to me, "Go again, love a woman who is loved by another man and is an adulteress, even as the LORD loves the children of Israel, though they turn to other gods and love cakes of raisins." ²So I bought her for fifteen shekels of silver and a homer and a lethech¹ of barley. ³And I said to her, "You must dwell as mine for many days. You shall not play the whore, or belong to another man; so will I also be to you." ⁴For the children of Israel shall dwell many days without king or prince, without sacrifice or pillar, without ephod or household gods. ⁵Afterward the children of Israel shall return and seek the LORD their God, and David their king, and they shall come in fear to the LORD and to his goodness in the latter days.

> **God's controversy with Israel** [chapters 4–5]. After the shocking opening scenario of Hosea's marriage to a prostitute, the book now settles down to the customary forms of OT prophecy. The content of chapters 4–5 is God's formal "controversy" (4:1) with his covenant people. The form in which the accusations are couched is the familiar prophetic list of accusations against a guilty party. Common rhetorical features that appear include a formal summons to "hear" (4:1; 5:1); concrete images and pictures that render the misconduct vivid to our imagination; mingling of description of a present situation and predictions of future events; direct address to the people or nation ("O Israel," "O priest," "O Benjamin"). The use of *epithets or titles (e.g., "house of Israel," "house of Judah") is common in OT prophetic literature, but a distinctive epithet in Hosea is Ephraim as a name for the nation (nearly forty occurrences), probably because Ephraim was Israel's largest tribe.

4 Hear the word of the LORD, O children of Israel,
　　for the LORD has a controversy with the inhabitants of the land.
There is no faithfulness or steadfast love,
　　and no knowledge of God in the land;
² there is swearing, lying, murder, stealing, and committing adultery;
　　they break all bounds, and bloodshed follows bloodshed.
³ Therefore the land mourns,
　　and all who dwell in it languish,
and also the beasts of the field
　　and the birds of the heavens,
　　and even the fish of the sea are taken away.

⁴ Yet let no one contend,
　　and let none accuse,
　　for with you is my contention, O priest.²
⁵ You shall stumble by day;
　　the prophet also shall stumble with you by night;
　　and I will destroy your mother.
⁶ My people are destroyed for lack of knowledge;
　　because you have rejected knowledge,
　　I reject you from being a priest to me.
And since you have forgotten the law of your God,
　　I also will forget your children.

---

¹ A *shekel* was about 2/5 ounce or 11 grams; a *homer* was about 6 bushels or 220 liters; a *lethech* was about 3 bushels or 110 liters   ² Or *for your people are like those who contend with the priest*

7 The more they increased,
       the more they sinned against me;
     I will change their glory into shame.
8 They feed on the sin[1] of my people;
       they are greedy for their iniquity.
9 And it shall be like people, like priest;
     I will punish them for their ways
       and repay them for their deeds.
10 They shall eat, but not be satisfied;
       they shall play the whore, but not multiply,
     because they have forsaken the LORD
       to cherish [11]whoredom, wine, and new wine,
     which take away the understanding.
12 My people inquire of a piece of wood,
       and their walking staff gives them oracles.
     For a spirit of whoredom has led them astray,
       and they have left their God to play the whore.
13 They sacrifice on the tops of the mountains
       and burn offerings on the hills,
     under oak, poplar, and terebinth,
       because their shade is good.
     Therefore your daughters play the whore,
       and your brides commit adultery.
14 I will not punish your daughters when they play the whore,
       nor your brides when they commit adultery;
     for the men themselves go aside with prostitutes
       and sacrifice with cult prostitutes,
     and a people without understanding shall come to ruin.

15 Though you play the whore, O Israel,
       let not Judah become guilty.
     Enter not into Gilgal,
       nor go up to Beth-aven,
       and swear not, "As the LORD lives."
16 Like a stubborn heifer,
       Israel is stubborn;
     can the LORD now feed them
       like a lamb in a broad pasture?

17 Ephraim is joined to idols;
       leave him alone.
18 When their drink is gone, they give themselves to whoring;
       their rulers[2] dearly love shame.
19 A wind has wrapped them[3] in its wings,
       and they shall be ashamed because of their sacrifices.

---

[1] Or sin offering [2] Hebrew shields [3] Hebrew her

5 Hear this, O priests!
Pay attention, O house of Israel!
Give ear, O house of the king!
    For the judgment is for you;
for you have been a snare at Mizpah
    and a net spread upon Tabor.
² And the revolters have gone deep into slaughter,
    but I will discipline all of them.

³ I know Ephraim,
    and Israel is not hidden from me;
for now, O Ephraim, you have played the whore;
    Israel is defiled.
⁴ Their deeds do not permit them
    to return to their God.
For the spirit of whoredom is within them,
    and they know not the Lord.

⁵ The pride of Israel testifies to his face;[1]
    Israel and Ephraim shall stumble in his guilt;
    Judah also shall stumble with them.
⁶ With their flocks and herds they shall go
    to seek the Lord,
but they will not find him;
    he has withdrawn from them.
⁷ They have dealt faithlessly with the Lord;
    for they have borne alien children.
Now the new moon shall devour them with their fields.

⁸ Blow the horn in Gibeah,
    the trumpet in Ramah.
Sound the alarm at Beth-aven;
    we follow you,[2] O Benjamin!
⁹ Ephraim shall become a desolation
    in the day of punishment;
among the tribes of Israel
    I make known what is sure.
¹⁰ The princes of Judah have become
    like those who move the landmark;
upon them I will pour out
    my wrath like water.
¹¹ Ephraim is oppressed, crushed in judgment,
    because he was determined to go after filth.[3]
¹² But I am like a moth to Ephraim,
    and like dry rot to the house of Judah.

¹³ When Ephraim saw his sickness,
    and Judah his wound,

---

[1] Or in his presence [2] Or after you [3] Or to follow human precepts

then Ephraim went to Assyria,
> and sent to the great king.[1]
But he is not able to cure you
> or heal your wound.

14 For I will be like a lion to Ephraim,
> and like a young lion to the house of Judah.
I, even I, will tear and go away;
> I will carry off, and no one shall rescue.

15 I will return again to my place,
> until they acknowledge their guilt and seek my face,
> and in their distress earnestly seek me.

A further list of indictments [chapters 6–7]. Except for a brief dramatization of the nation's return to God at the outset of the passage (6:1–3), the material continues in the same vein as the preceding two chapters—an expanding list of God's accusations of misconduct. We need to let the images and metaphors penetrate our mind and emotions and then reflect on the universality and contemporary relevance of what God is saying through his prophet Hosea.

6 "Come, let us return to the LORD;
> for he has torn us, that he may heal us;
> he has struck us down, and he will bind us up.
2 After two days he will revive us;
> on the third day he will raise us up,
> that we may live before him.
3 Let us know; let us press on to know the LORD;
> his going out is sure as the dawn;
he will come to us as the showers,
> as the spring rains that water the earth."

4 What shall I do with you, O Ephraim?
> What shall I do with you, O Judah?
Your love is like a morning cloud,
> like the dew that goes early away.
5 Therefore I have hewn them by the prophets;
> I have slain them by the words of my mouth,
> and my judgment goes forth as the light.
6 For I desire steadfast love[2] and not sacrifice,
> the knowledge of God rather than burnt offerings.

7 But like Adam they transgressed the covenant;
> there they dealt faithlessly with me.
8 Gilead is a city of evildoers,
> tracked with blood.
9 As robbers lie in wait for a man,
> so the priests band together;
they murder on the way to Shechem;

---

[1] Or to King Jareb [2] Septuagint mercy

they commit villainy.
¹⁰ In the house of Israel I have seen a horrible thing;
Ephraim's whoredom is there; Israel is defiled.

¹¹ For you also, O Judah, a harvest is appointed,
when I restore the fortunes of my people.

7 When I would heal Israel,
the iniquity of Ephraim is revealed,
and the evil deeds of Samaria;
for they deal falsely;
the thief breaks in,
and the bandits raid outside.
² But they do not consider
that I remember all their evil.
Now their deeds surround them;
they are before my face.
³ By their evil they make the king glad,
and the princes by their treachery.
⁴ They are all adulterers;
they are like a heated oven
whose baker ceases to stir the fire,
from the kneading of the dough
until it is leavened.
⁵ On the day of our king, the princes
became sick with the heat of wine;
he stretched out his hand with mockers.
⁶ For with hearts like an oven they approach their intrigue;
all night their anger smolders;
in the morning it blazes like a flaming fire.
⁷ All of them are hot as an oven,
and they devour their rulers.
All their kings have fallen,
and none of them calls upon me.

⁸ Ephraim mixes himself with the peoples;
Ephraim is a cake not turned.
⁹ Strangers devour his strength,
and he knows it not;
gray hairs are sprinkled upon him,
and he knows it not.
¹⁰ The pride of Israel testifies to his face;[1]
yet they do not return to the LORD their God,
nor seek him, for all this.

¹¹ Ephraim is like a dove,
silly and without sense,
calling to Egypt, going to Assyria.

[1] Or *in his presence*

¹²   As they go, I will spread over them my net;
      I will bring them down like birds of the heavens;
      I will discipline them according to the report made to their congregation.
¹³   Woe to them, for they have strayed from me!
      Destruction to them, for they have rebelled against me!
   I would redeem them,
      but they speak lies against me.

¹⁴   They do not cry to me from the heart,
      but they wail upon their beds;
   for grain and wine they gash themselves;
      they rebel against me.
¹⁵   Although I trained and strengthened their arms,
      yet they devise evil against me.
¹⁶   They return, but not upward;[1]
      they are like a treacherous bow;
   their princes shall fall by the sword
      because of the insolence of their tongue.
   This shall be their derision in the land of Egypt.

From accusation to sentencing [chapter 8]. Now that God has presented his divine lawsuit against Israel, we move to the sentencing phase of the trial. Statements of God's intention to punish the guilty are mingled with continued reminders of why he is doing it.

8 Set the trumpet to your lips!
    One like a vulture is over the house of the LORD,
   because they have transgressed my covenant
      and rebelled against my law.
²   To me they cry,
      "My God, we—Israel—know you."
³   Israel has spurned the good;
      the enemy shall pursue him.

⁴   They made kings, but not through me.
      They set up princes, but I knew it not.
   With their silver and gold they made idols
      for their own destruction.
⁵   I have[2] spurned your calf, O Samaria.
      My anger burns against them.
   How long will they be incapable of innocence?
⁶   For it is from Israel;
   a craftsman made it;
      it is not God.
   The calf of Samaria
      shall be broken to pieces.[3]

⁷   For they sow the wind,
      and they shall reap the whirlwind.

[1] Or to the Most High [2] Hebrew He has [3] Or shall go up in flames

The standing grain has no heads;
　　it shall yield no flour;
if it were to yield,
　　strangers would devour it.
8　Israel is swallowed up;
　　already they are among the nations
　　as a useless vessel.
9　For they have gone up to Assyria,
　　a wild donkey wandering alone;
　　Ephraim has hired lovers.
10　Though they hire allies among the nations,
　　I will soon gather them up.
And the king and princes shall soon writhe
　　because of the tribute.

11　Because Ephraim has multiplied altars for sinning,
　　they have become to him altars for sinning.
12　Were I to write for him my laws by the ten thousands,
　　they would be regarded as a strange thing.
13　As for my sacrificial offerings,
　　they sacrifice meat and eat it,
　　but the LORD does not accept them.
Now he will remember their iniquity
　　and punish their sins;
　　they shall return to Egypt.
14　For Israel has forgotten his Maker
　　and built palaces,
and Judah has multiplied fortified cities;
　　so I will send a fire upon his cities,
　　and it shall devour her strongholds.

Punishments announced [chapter 9]. The keynote of the chapter is sounded in verse 7: "the days of punishment have come." Again we find an intermingling of (1) accusations of misconduct and (2) predictions of coming punishment.

9 Rejoice not, O Israel!
　　Exult not like the peoples;
for you have played the whore, forsaking your God.
　　You have loved a prostitute's wages
　　on all threshing floors.
2　Threshing floor and wine vat shall not feed them,
　　and the new wine shall fail them.
3　They shall not remain in the land of the LORD,
　　but Ephraim shall return to Egypt,
　　and they shall eat unclean food in Assyria.

4   They shall not pour drink offerings of wine to the Lord,
         and their sacrifices shall not please him.
     It shall be like mourners' bread to them;
         all who eat of it shall be defiled;
     for their bread shall be for their hunger only;
         it shall not come to the house of the Lord.

5   What will you do on the day of the appointed festival,
         and on the day of the feast of the Lord?
6   For behold, they are going away from destruction;
         but Egypt shall gather them;
         Memphis shall bury them.
     Nettles shall possess their precious things of silver;
         thorns shall be in their tents.

7   The days of punishment have come;
         the days of recompense have come;
         Israel shall know it.
     The prophet is a fool;
         the man of the spirit is mad,
     because of your great iniquity
         and great hatred.
8   The prophet is the watchman of Ephraim with my God;
         yet a fowler's snare is on all his ways,
         and hatred in the house of his God.
9   They have deeply corrupted themselves
         as in the days of Gibeah:
     he will remember their iniquity;
         he will punish their sins.

10   Like grapes in the wilderness,
         I found Israel.
     Like the first fruit on the fig tree
         in its first season,
         I saw your fathers.
     But they came to Baal-peor
         and consecrated themselves to the thing of shame,
         and became detestable like the thing they loved.
11   Ephraim's glory shall fly away like a bird—
         no birth, no pregnancy, no conception!
12   Even if they bring up children,
         I will bereave them till none is left.
     Woe to them
         when I depart from them!
13   Ephraim, as I have seen, was like a young palm[1] planted in a meadow;
         but Ephraim must lead his children out to slaughter.[2]
14   Give them, O Lord—
         what will you give?

---

[1] Or like Tyre [2] Hebrew to him who slaughters

Give them a miscarrying womb
 and dry breasts.

15 Every evil of theirs is in Gilgal;
 there I began to hate them.
Because of the wickedness of their deeds
 I will drive them out of my house.
I will love them no more;
 all their princes are rebels.

16 Ephraim is stricken;
 their root is dried up;
 they shall bear no fruit.
Even though they give birth,
 I will put their beloved children to death.

17 My God will reject them
 because they have not listened to him;
 they shall be wanderers among the nations.

Final verdict [chapter 10]. Chapter 10 is the third panel in a triptych that began with chapter 8. The rhetorical forms and content remain the same: nations and tribes and cities as the chief actors; occasional direct addresses to these *personified entities in the form of *apostrophe (e.g., "O Israel"; "sow for yourselves righteousness"; "you have plowed iniquity"); poetic images and figures of speech as the vehicles for the message; mingling of accusations of misconduct and predictions of coming calamity.

10

Israel is a luxuriant vine
 that yields its fruit.
The more his fruit increased,
 the more altars he built;
as his country improved,
 he improved his pillars.

2 Their heart is false;
 now they must bear their guilt.
The LORD[1] will break down their altars
 and destroy their pillars.

3 For now they will say:
 "We have no king,
for we do not fear the LORD;
 and a king—what could he do for us?"

4 They utter mere words;
 with empty oaths they make covenants;
so judgment springs up like poisonous weeds
 in the furrows of the field.

5 The inhabitants of Samaria tremble
 for the calf[2] of Beth-aven.
Its people mourn for it, and so do its idolatrous priests—

---

[1] Hebrew *He* [2] Or *calves*

those who rejoiced over it and over its glory—
for it has departed[1] from them.
⁶ The thing itself shall be carried to Assyria
as tribute to the great king.[2]
Ephraim shall be put to shame,
and Israel shall be ashamed of his idol.[3]

⁷ Samaria's king shall perish
like a twig on the face of the waters.
⁸ The high places of Aven, the sin of Israel,
shall be destroyed.
Thorn and thistle shall grow up
on their altars,
and they shall say to the mountains, "Cover us,"
and to the hills, "Fall on us."

⁹ From the days of Gibeah, you have sinned, O Israel;
there they have continued.
Shall not the war against the unjust[4] overtake them in Gibeah?
¹⁰ When I please, I will discipline them,
and nations shall be gathered against them
when they are bound up for their double iniquity.

¹¹ Ephraim was a trained calf
that loved to thresh,
and I spared her fair neck;
but I will put Ephraim to the yoke;
Judah must plow;
Jacob must harrow for himself.
¹² Sow for yourselves righteousness;
reap steadfast love;
break up your fallow ground,
for it is the time to seek the LORD,
that he may come and rain righteousness upon you.

¹³ You have plowed iniquity;
you have reaped injustice;
you have eaten the fruit of lies.
Because you have trusted in your own way
and in the multitude of your warriors,
¹⁴ therefore the tumult of war shall arise among your people,
and all your fortresses shall be destroyed,
as Shalman destroyed Beth-arbel on the day of battle;
mothers were dashed in pieces with their children.
¹⁵ Thus it shall be done to you, O Bethel,
because of your great evil.
At dawn the king of Israel
shall be utterly cut off.

[1] Or has gone into exile [2] Or to King Jareb [3] Or counsel [4] Hebrew the children of injustice

God's mixed feelings toward his beloved [11:1–11]. The onslaught of accusation and punishment has a temporary respite in this unit. The voice of judgment is still present (vv. 5–7), but it is preceded by expressions of divine parental love (vv. 1–4) and God's compassionate feelings, which result in a decision to restore Israel (vv. 8–11). God emerges in this unit as a thoroughly *anthropomorphic God, possessing the feelings of a human parent toward a wayward child.

11
When Israel was a child, I loved him,
    and out of Egypt I called my son.
2 The more they were called,
    the more they went away;
  they kept sacrificing to the Baals
    and burning offerings to idols.

3 Yet it was I who taught Ephraim to walk;
    I took them up by their arms,
  but they did not know that I healed them.
4 I led them with cords of kindness,[1]
    with the bands of love,
  and I became to them as one who eases the yoke on their jaws,
    and I bent down to them and fed them.

5 They shall not[2] return to the land of Egypt,
    but Assyria shall be their king,
  because they have refused to return to me.
6 The sword shall rage against their cities,
    consume the bars of their gates,
  and devour them because of their own counsels.
7 My people are bent on turning away from me,
    and though they call out to the Most High,
    he shall not raise them up at all.

8 How can I give you up, O Ephraim?
    How can I hand you over, O Israel?
  How can I make you like Admah?
    How can I treat you like Zeboiim?
  My heart recoils within me;
    my compassion grows warm and tender.
9 I will not execute my burning anger;
    I will not again destroy Ephraim;
  for I am God and not a man,
    the Holy One in your midst,
    and I will not come in wrath.[3]

10 They shall go after the Lord;
    he will roar like a lion;
  when he roars,
    his children shall come trembling from the west;

---

[1] Or *humaneness;* Hebrew *man* [2] Or *surely* [3] Or *into the city*

¹¹   they shall come trembling like birds from Egypt,
　　　and like doves from the land of Assyria,
　　　and I will return them to their homes, declares the Lord.

Final words of judgment [11:12–13:16]. An extended oracle of judgment brings to a climax the theme of justice in the book of Hosea. One more time we observe (1) God's indictments against his chosen nation; (2) predictions that he will punish the guilty; (3) poetic vividness; (4) direct addresses to the nation and its people.

^{12 1}   Ephraim has surrounded me with lies,
　　　and the house of Israel with deceit,
　　but Judah still walks with God
　　　and is faithful to the Holy One.

12   Ephraim feeds on the wind
　　　and pursues the east wind all day long;
　　they multiply falsehood and violence;
　　　they make a covenant with Assyria,
　　　and oil is carried to Egypt.

²   The Lord has an indictment against Judah
　　　and will punish Jacob according to his ways;
　　　he will repay him according to his deeds.
³   In the womb he took his brother by the heel,
　　　and in his manhood he strove with God.
⁴   He strove with the angel and prevailed;
　　　he wept and sought his favor.
　　He met God² at Bethel,
　　　and there God spoke with us—
⁵   the Lord, the God of hosts,
　　　the Lord is his memorial name:
⁶   "So you, by the help of your God, return,
　　　hold fast to love and justice,
　　　and wait continually for your God."

⁷   A merchant, in whose hands are false balances,
　　　he loves to oppress.
⁸   Ephraim has said, "Ah, but I am rich;
　　　I have found wealth for myself;
　　in all my labors they cannot find in me iniquity or sin."
⁹   I am the Lord your God
　　　from the land of Egypt;
　　I will again make you dwell in tents,
　　　as in the days of the appointed feast.

¹⁰   I spoke to the prophets;
　　　it was I who multiplied visions,
　　　and through the prophets gave parables.
¹¹   If there is iniquity in Gilead,

¹ Ch 12:1 in Hebrew ² Hebrew *him*

they shall surely come to nothing:
in Gilgal they sacrifice bulls;
    their altars also are like stone heaps
    on the furrows of the field.
¹² Jacob fled to the land of Aram;
    there Israel served for a wife,
    and for a wife he guarded sheep.
¹³ By a prophet the Lord brought Israel up from Egypt,
    and by a prophet he was guarded.
¹⁴ Ephraim has given bitter provocation;
    so his Lord will leave his bloodguilt on him
    and will repay him for his disgraceful deeds.

13

When Ephraim spoke, there was trembling;
    he was exalted in Israel,
but he incurred guilt through Baal and died.
² And now they sin more and more,
    and make for themselves metal images,
idols skillfully made of their silver,
    all of them the work of craftsmen.
It is said of them,
    "Those who offer human sacrifice kiss calves!"
³ Therefore they shall be like the morning mist
    or like the dew that goes early away,
like the chaff that swirls from the threshing floor
    or like smoke from a window.

⁴ But I am the Lord your God
    from the land of Egypt;
you know no God but me,
    and besides me there is no savior.
⁵ It was I who knew you in the wilderness,
    in the land of drought;
⁶ but when they had grazed,¹ they became full,
    they were filled, and their heart was lifted up;
    therefore they forgot me.
⁷ So I am to them like a lion;
    like a leopard I will lurk beside the way.
⁸ I will fall upon them like a bear robbed of her cubs;
    I will tear open their breast,
and there I will devour them like a lion,
    as a wild beast would rip them open.

⁹ He destroys² you, O Israel,
    for you are against me, against your helper.
¹⁰ Where now is your king, to save you in all your cities?
    Where are all your rulers—
those of whom you said,

---

¹ Hebrew *according to their pasture* ² Or *I will destroy*

"Give me a king and princes"?
11   I gave you a king in my anger,
       and I took him away in my wrath.

12   The iniquity of Ephraim is bound up;
       his sin is kept in store.
13   The pangs of childbirth come for him,
       but he is an unwise son,
     for at the right time he does not present himself
       at the opening of the womb.

14   Shall I ransom them from the power of Sheol?
       Shall I redeem them from Death?
     O Death, where are your plagues?
       O Sheol, where is your sting?
     Compassion is hidden from my eyes.

15   Though he may flourish among his brothers,
       the east wind, the wind of the LORD, shall come,
       rising from the wilderness,
     and his fountain shall dry up;
       his spring shall be parched;
     it shall strip his treasury
       of every precious thing.
16 1 Samaria shall bear her guilt,
       because she has rebelled against her God;
     they shall fall by the sword;
       their little ones shall be dashed in pieces,
       and their pregnant women ripped open.

Restoration of God's people [chapter 14]. Virtually all OT prophetic books end with a vision of blessing for the covenant people of God, and that is what we find here. First the prophet himself enjoins Israel to return to God (vv. 1–2a), followed by an imagined prayer of repentance by the nation (vv. 2b–3). Then God voices a promise of blessing (vv. 4–8). A postscript by the prophet appeals to his audience to heed his wisdom (v. 9).

14   Return, O Israel, to the LORD your God,
       for you have stumbled because of your iniquity.
2   Take with you words
       and return to the LORD;
     say to him,
       "Take away all iniquity;
     accept what is good,
       and we will pay with bulls
       the vows² of our lips.
3   Assyria shall not save us;
       we will not ride on horses;
     and we will say no more, 'Our God,'

---

    to the work of our hands.
     In you the orphan finds mercy."

4   I will heal their apostasy;
     I will love them freely,
      for my anger has turned from them.
5   I will be like the dew to Israel;
     he shall blossom like the lily;
     he shall take root like the trees of Lebanon;
6   his shoots shall spread out;
     his beauty shall be like the olive,
     and his fragrance like Lebanon.
7   They shall return and dwell beneath my[1] shadow;
     they shall flourish like the grain;
  they shall blossom like the vine;
     their fame shall be like the wine of Lebanon.

8   O Ephraim, what have I to do with idols?
     It is I who answer and look after you.[2]
  I am like an evergreen cypress;
     from me comes your fruit.

9   Whoever is wise, let him understand these things;
     whoever is discerning, let him know them;
  for the ways of the Lord are right,
     and the upright walk in them,
     but transgressors stumble in them.

---

[1] Hebrew *his* [2] Hebrew *him*

JOEL

The book at a glance. 3 chapters, 73 verses. Most of the so-called minor prophets of the OT are rendered memorable by some distinctive characteristic or action. For the prophecy of Hosea, we remember that the prophet married a prostitute. We remember Jonah for the giantesque *motif and Malachi for its question-and-answer format. We remember the book of Joel for its motif of the attack of the killer locusts. We infer that Joel's prophecy was occasioned by a plague of locusts that engulfed Judah. In Joel's prophetic imagination, the locusts become amplified into images of horror—pictures of God's judgment against human sinfulness. Of course Joel's images are timeless and universal, and so is the horror that the book evokes regarding God's punishment of human evil.

▮ **Genres and format.** Being a work of *prophecy, the book of Joel relies on the staples of the *oracle of judgment and *oracle of salvation. *Poetry counts for a lot in the book of Joel, whose author is particularly adept at description. By the time Joel's imagination amplifies the killer locusts into more-than-literal creatures, the book of Joel emerges as a horror story. The technique of *apostrophe (direct address to entities that are literally absent but treated as though they can hear and respond) is prominent in the first two chapters. Even though the writer is a prophet rather than a nature writer, there are so many pictures of nature in the book that it does rank as nature writing, in a prophetic mode. (For more information on items accompanied by an asterisk, see the glossary at the back of this Bible.)

Passage	Content	Prophetic Genre	Time Frame	The Speaker
1:1–20	Vision of a plague of locusts and drought	Oracle of judgment	Immediate "day of the LORD" (1:15)	The prophet speaks
2:1–17	Vision of an invading army	Oracle of judgment	Imminent "day of the LORD" (2:1)	
2:18–27	God's promise to restore his people	Oracle of salvation	A more remote future time	God speaks
2:28–3:21	God's promise of final, eschatological blessing	Oracle of salvation	Final, ultimate "day of the LORD" (3:14)	

▮ **Inferred literary intentions.** The book is designed to achieve the following literary purposes:

- appeal to our imagination with its vivid poetry and description, especially in regard to the forces of nature

- terrify us with images of helplessness in the face of assault (whether from locusts or an invading army)

- use nature imagery to evoke fear of God's judgment

- balance the terrifying pictures of God's judgment with winsome pictures of his blessing, with a view toward instilling repentance in the readers of the book

▌ Theological themes. (1) Judgment: the book demonstrates God's intention to punish people who reject his rules for living. (2) Repentance: an implied theme of the book of Joel is that repentance is the means by which sinful people can have fellowship with God. (3) Redemption: Joel devotes proportionately more space to pictures of God's restored favor than do the other minor prophets.

▌ The book of Joel as a chapter in the master story of the Bible. The Bible tells two stories simultaneously—what God does and what the human race does. The book of Joel advances both plot lines. It shows that humanity behaves so sinfully that it is subject to God's punishment, but along with that we see the possibility of relating to God by means of repentance. The divine story that the book of Joel tells is that God is displeased with human sinfulness and is intent on punishing it, but equally that he is a God of mercy who extends undeserved favor to his people. Also, the book of Joel gives us foreshadowings of the eschatological final chapter of human history.

The plague of locusts [chapter 1]. The opening chapter of Joel is an oracle of judgment in the customary prophetic mode. Following an inscription (v. 1) and a summons to listen (vv. 2–3), Joel uses as a launching pad for his vision of woe a description of the locusts that invaded the land (v. 4), and together these references constitute an image of terror for an agrarian society. The vision of the plague of locusts then expands outward into a generalized vision of drought and blight (vv. 5–20). The prophet leaves no doubt about the connection between the sins of his society and the natural devastation that has descended on the land. The rhetorical mode moves back and forth between direct address to various groups in Israelite society and descriptions of calamity.

1 The word of the LORD that came to Joel, the son of Pethuel:

2 Hear this, you elders;
  give ear, all inhabitants of the land!
Has such a thing happened in your days,
  or in the days of your fathers?
3 Tell your children of it,
  and let your children tell their children,
  and their children to another generation.

4 What the cutting locust left,
  the swarming locust has eaten.
What the swarming locust left,
  the hopping locust has eaten,

and what the hopping locust left,
 the destroying locust has eaten.

5   Awake, you drunkards, and weep,
 and wail, all you drinkers of wine,
because of the sweet wine,
 for it is cut off from your mouth.
6   For a nation has come up against my land,
 powerful and beyond number;
its teeth are lions' teeth,
 and it has the fangs of a lioness.
7   It has laid waste my vine
 and splintered my fig tree;
it has stripped off their bark and thrown it down;
 their branches are made white.

8   Lament like a virgin[1] wearing sackcloth
 for the bridegroom of her youth.
9   The grain offering and the drink offering are cut off
 from the house of the Lord.
The priests mourn,
 the ministers of the Lord.
10   The fields are destroyed,
 the ground mourns,
because the grain is destroyed,
 the wine dries up,
 the oil languishes.

11   Be ashamed,[2] O tillers of the soil;
 wail, O vinedressers,
for the wheat and the barley,
 because the harvest of the field has perished.
12   The vine dries up;
 the fig tree languishes.
Pomegranate, palm, and apple,
 all the trees of the field are dried up,
and gladness dries up
 from the children of man.

13   Put on sackcloth and lament, O priests;
 wail, O ministers of the altar.
Go in, pass the night in sackcloth,
 O ministers of my God!
Because grain offering and drink offering
 are withheld from the house of your God.

14   Consecrate a fast;
 call a solemn assembly.
Gather the elders

---

[1] Or young woman [2] The Hebrew words for dry up and be ashamed in verses 10-12, 17 sound alike

and all the inhabitants of the land
to the house of the Lord your God,
and cry out to the Lord.

¹⁵ Alas for the day!
For the day of the Lord is near,
and as destruction from the Almighty¹ it comes.
¹⁶ Is not the food cut off
before our eyes,
joy and gladness
from the house of our God?

¹⁷ The seed shrivels under the clods;²
the storehouses are desolate;
the granaries are torn down
because the grain has dried up.
¹⁸ How the beasts groan!
The herds of cattle are perplexed
because there is no pasture for them;
even the flocks of sheep suffer.³

¹⁹ To you, O Lord, I call.
For fire has devoured
the pastures of the wilderness,
and flame has burned
all the trees of the field.
²⁰ Even the beasts of the field pant for you
because the water brooks are dried up,
and fire has devoured
the pastures of the wilderness.

Attack of the killer locusts [2:1–17]. The summary of categories of locusts in 1:4 now becomes expanded into a full-scale metaphoric and/or hyperbolic narrative of their invasion. In keeping with how an invasion of locusts is experienced by people and locales, Joel pictures the arrival and destruction of the locusts as the actions of an army (vv. 1–11). It is one of the nightmare visions of the Bible. Yet a door of escape opens in the form of a follow-up call to repentance (vv. 12–17).

2 Blow a trumpet in Zion;
sound an alarm on my holy mountain!
Let all the inhabitants of the land tremble,
for the day of the Lord is coming; it is near,
² a day of darkness and gloom,
a day of clouds and thick darkness!
Like blackness there is spread upon the mountains
a great and powerful people;
their like has never been before,

---

¹ *Destruction* sounds like the Hebrew for *Almighty* ² The meaning of the Hebrew line is uncertain ³ Or *are made desolate*

nor will be again after them
through the years of all generations.

3   Fire devours before them,
      and behind them a flame burns.
The land is like the garden of Eden before them,
      but behind them a desolate wilderness,
      and nothing escapes them.

4   Their appearance is like the appearance of horses,
      and like war horses they run.
5   As with the rumbling of chariots,
      they leap on the tops of the mountains,
like the crackling of a flame of fire
      devouring the stubble,
like a powerful army
      drawn up for battle.

6   Before them peoples are in anguish;
      all faces grow pale.
7   Like warriors they charge;
      like soldiers they scale the wall.
They march each on his way;
      they do not swerve from their paths.
8   They do not jostle one another;
      each marches in his path;
they burst through the weapons
      and are not halted.
9   They leap upon the city,
      they run upon the walls,
they climb up into the houses,
      they enter through the windows like a thief.

10 The earth quakes before them;
      the heavens tremble.
The sun and the moon are darkened,
      and the stars withdraw their shining.
11 The Lord utters his voice
      before his army,
for his camp is exceedingly great;
      he who executes his word is powerful.
For the day of the Lord is great and very awesome;
      who can endure it?

12 "Yet even now," declares the Lord,
      "return to me with all your heart,
with fasting, with weeping, and with mourning;
13   and rend your hearts and not your garments."
Return to the Lord your God,

for he is gracious and merciful,
  slow to anger, and abounding in steadfast love;
  and he relents over disaster.
¹⁴ Who knows whether he will not turn and relent,
  and leave a blessing behind him,
a grain offering and a drink offering
  for the LORD your God?

¹⁵ Blow the trumpet in Zion;
  consecrate a fast;
call a solemn assembly;
¹⁶ gather the people.
Consecrate the congregation;
  assemble the elders;
gather the children,
  even nursing infants.
Let the bridegroom leave his room,
  and the bride her chamber.

¹⁷ Between the vestibule and the altar
  let the priests, the ministers of the LORD, weep
and say, "Spare your people, O LORD,
  and make not your heritage a reproach,
  a byword among the nations.¹
Why should they say among the peoples,
  'Where is their God?'"

Oracle of restoration [2:18–27]. At this halfway point the book reaches a pivot in which oracles of judgment are replaced by oracles of restoration. This first unit of the second half of the book uses extravagant images of abundance (especially natural abundance) to picture the return of Israel to God's favor. Since such a restoration to the land was never fully realized by Israel as a nation, we naturally move in the direction of interpreting the details as a symbolic vision of God's favor to his people whenever they trust in God and obey him.

¹⁸ Then the LORD became jealous for his land
  and had pity on his people.
¹⁹ The LORD answered and said to his people,
"Behold, I am sending to you
  grain, wine, and oil,
  and you will be satisfied;
and I will no more make you
  a reproach among the nations.

²⁰ "I will remove the northerner far from you,
  and drive him into a parched and desolate land,
his vanguard² into the eastern sea,
  and his rear guard³ into the western sea;

¹ Or reproach, that the nations should rule over them ² Hebrew face ³ Hebrew his end

the stench and foul smell of him will rise,
  for he has done great things.

21 "Fear not, O land;
    be glad and rejoice,
  for the LORD has done great things!
22 Fear not, you beasts of the field,
    for the pastures of the wilderness are green;
  the tree bears its fruit;
    the fig tree and vine give their full yield.

23 "Be glad, O children of Zion,
    and rejoice in the LORD your God,
  for he has given the early rain for your vindication;
    he has poured down for you abundant rain,
    the early and the latter rain, as before.

24 "The threshing floors shall be full of grain;
    the vats shall overflow with wine and oil.
25 I will restore to you the years
    that the swarming locust has eaten,
  the hopper, the destroyer, and the cutter,
    my great army, which I sent among you.

26 "You shall eat in plenty and be satisfied,
    and praise the name of the LORD your God,
  who has dealt wondrously with you.
  And my people shall never again be put to shame.
27 You shall know that I am in the midst of Israel,
    and that I am the LORD your God and there is none else.
  And my people shall never again be put to shame.

A vision of the last days [2:28–3:21]. The book ends by zooming to the distant future. The opening verses (2:28–29) were said by Peter on Pentecost to have been fulfilled on that very day (Acts 2:14–21), though imagery like this may have more than just one fulfillment or application. In the remainder of the book, the imagery and motifs belong to the realm of *apocalyptic visions of the end times. The main motifs are as follows: (1) a gathering of God's people to one place; (2) rebuke of pagan nations; (3) the battle motif; (4) harvest; (5) transformation (especially as encapsulated in the famous picture of swords being beaten into plowshares and spears into pruning hooks, v. 10); (6) abundance of bliss; (7) God as judge pronouncing destruction on evildoers.

28 1 "And it shall come to pass afterward,
    that I will pour out my Spirit on all flesh;
  your sons and your daughters shall prophesy,
    your old men shall dream dreams,
    and your young men shall see visions.

¹ Ch 3:1 in Hebrew

²⁹   Even on the male and female servants
    in those days I will pour out my Spirit.

³⁰ "And I will show wonders in the heavens and on the earth, blood and fire and columns of smoke. ³¹ The sun shall be turned to darkness, and the moon to blood, before the great and awesome day of the LORD comes. ³² And it shall come to pass that everyone who calls on the name of the LORD shall be saved. For in Mount Zion and in Jerusalem there shall be those who escape, as the LORD has said, and among the survivors shall be those whom the LORD calls.

3 ¹ "For behold, in those days and at that time, when I restore the fortunes of Judah and Jerusalem, ²I will gather all the nations and bring them down to the Valley of Jehoshaphat. And I will enter into judgment with them there, on behalf of my people and my heritage Israel, because they have scattered them among the nations and have divided up my land, ³ and have cast lots for my people, and have traded a boy for a prostitute, and have sold a girl for wine and have drunk it.

⁴ "What are you to me, O Tyre and Sidon, and all the regions of Philistia? Are you paying me back for something? If you are paying me back, I will return your payment on your own head swiftly and speedily. ⁵ For you have taken my silver and my gold, and have carried my rich treasures into your temples.² ⁶ You have sold the people of Judah and Jerusalem to the Greeks in order to remove them far from their own border. ⁷ Behold, I will stir them up from the place to which you have sold them, and I will return your payment on your own head. ⁸ I will sell your sons and your daughters into the hand of the people of Judah, and they will sell them to the Sabeans, to a nation far away, for the LORD has spoken."

⁹   Proclaim this among the nations:
    Consecrate for war;³
      stir up the mighty men.
    Let all the men of war draw near;
      let them come up.
¹⁰   Beat your plowshares into swords,
      and your pruning hooks into spears;
      let the weak say, "I am a warrior."

¹¹   Hasten and come,
      all you surrounding nations,
      and gather yourselves there.
    Bring down your warriors, O LORD.
¹²   Let the nations stir themselves up
      and come up to the Valley of Jehoshaphat;
    for there I will sit to judge
      all the surrounding nations.

¹³   Put in the sickle,
      for the harvest is ripe.
    Go in, tread,
      for the winepress is full.

---

¹ Ch 4:1 in Hebrew ² Or *palaces* ³ Or *Consecrate a war*

The vats overflow,
    for their evil is great.

14 Multitudes, multitudes,
    in the valley of decision!
For the day of the Lord is near
    in the valley of decision.

15 The sun and the moon are darkened,
    and the stars withdraw their shining.

16 The Lord roars from Zion,
    and utters his voice from Jerusalem,
    and the heavens and the earth quake.
But the Lord is a refuge to his people,
    a stronghold to the people of Israel.

17 "So you shall know that I am the Lord your God,
    who dwells in Zion, my holy mountain.
And Jerusalem shall be holy,
    and strangers shall never again pass through it.

18 "And in that day
the mountains shall drip sweet wine,
    and the hills shall flow with milk,
and all the streambeds of Judah
    shall flow with water;
and a fountain shall come forth from the house of the Lord
    and water the Valley of Shittim.

19 "Egypt shall become a desolation
    and Edom a desolate wilderness,
for the violence done to the people of Judah,
    because they have shed innocent blood in their land.

20 But Judah shall be inhabited forever,
    and Jerusalem to all generations.

21 I will avenge their blood,
    blood I have not avenged,[1]
    for the Lord dwells in Zion."

---

[1] Or I will acquit their bloodguilt that I have not acquitted

AMOS

The book at a glance. 9 chapters, 146 verses. The prophecy of Amos covers so much territory, and with such a range of prophetic techniques and motifs, that it is in effect a minianthology of prophetic writings all by itself. The prophet himself emerges as one of the most forceful characters in the Bible, so that we feel as though he is one of our closest acquaintances, even though we have spent only half an hour in his presence. Although the northern kingdom of Israel is the original audience of the book, Amos manages to incorporate Judah and the surrounding pagan nations as well. Amos characterizes himself as a plainspoken *satirist (7:14–15), but he is in fact a master of literary technique and rhetoric, seen especially in his management of small units of discourse. Amos is not a private observer but the spokesman for the oppressed of his society.

▌**Genres and rhetorical forms.** The umbrella under which everything fits is *prophecy, with its attendant *oracles of judgment and a concluding *oracle of redemption. But the dominant literary form is satire, with the usual elements of objects of attack, a satiric vehicle (very multiple in this book, such as catalogs of woe formulas and brief vignettes of bad behavior), a satiric norm or standard by which the criticism is conducted, and a prevailing satiric tone (in this case, biting and sarcastic). In addition to these big literary forms, Amos is a master of smaller forms such as *metaphor and *simile, *epithet ("you cows of Bashan"), *parallelism, *rhetorical questions, and *parody (in which a conventional literary or rhetorical form such as the priestly call to worship [4:4] is echoed with new or inverted effect relative to its usual meaning). Other genres that find a place in the book include *saying or *proverb, *doom song, the woe formula, and *visionary writing. (For more information on items accompanied by an asterisk, see the glossary at the back of this Bible.)

▌**Satire in the book of Amos.** The object of satiric attack in the book of Amos is public and institutional evil. Amos himself is the advocate of the oppressed, so he attacks the wealthy and privileged classes within his society and institutions such as organized religion and the judicial system. A multitude of satiric ripples circle out from the main objects of attack (the social and religious "establishment"), giving us a detailed picture of a corrupt and immoral society. The satiric norm is the character of God and his law, and references to them regularly punctuate the book.

Passage	Content	Prophetic Genre	Sphere of Action	Prophetic Mood
1:1–2:3	Visions of judgment against the pagan nations surrounding Judah	Oracle of judgment; satire	Pagan nations	Doom, hopelessness
2:4–5	Vision of judgment against Judah	Oracle of judgment	Judah	
2:6–6:14	Visions of judgment against Israel, the main subject of the prophecy	Oracle of judgment; satire	Israel	
7:1–9:10	Five visions of judgment	Prophetic vision	Israel	
9:11–15	God's promise to restore and bless his people	Oracle of salvation	God's universal kingdom	Hope

▌Inferred literary intentions. The book is designed to achieve the following literary purposes:

- subject its readers to a shock treatment in regard to their complicity with evil

- expose the public and institutionalized forms of corruption, including the corruption of the wealthy and privileged classes within society

- use small literary and rhetorical forms as part of a literary collage

- dazzle us with the imaginative energy and inventiveness of the author

▌Theological themes. (1) Moral responsibility: the book demonstrates that God has a standard of right and wrong and that he holds individuals and societies responsible to obey that standard. (2) Sin: the book of Amos is a small manual on how many ways a society can find to corrupt itself. (3) Divine judgment: by means of its satiric genre, the book of Amos asserts God's intention to judge people who ignore his moral standards of compassion and concern for the marginalized. (4) Social ethics: the book's vision of virtues and vices deals with groups and therefore implies a social (and not simply individual) view of the ethical life.

▌The book of Amos as a chapter in the master story of the Bible. The master story of the Bible is an account of how God demands that human beings live before him in holiness and righteousness. The approach of the book of Amos to that subject is to show us by means of an extended exposé how God does *not* want people to live. A distinctive slant that this book gives to the godly life is its emphasis on the responsibility of individuals to their community.

Oracles against the nations [1:1–2:5]. Following the inscription to the book, including a statement of theme (God as roaring lion [vv. 1–2]), Amos unfolds one of the most elaborately patterned passages in the Bible. Oracles of judgment against the surrounding pagan nations plus Judah are arranged in a highly artistic and repetitive design. The oracles all follow the same pattern, as follows: (1) an opening formula, "Thus says the Lord"; (2) a balanced pair of phrases, "for three transgressions of _____, and for four"; (3) a set formula for judgment that reads "I will not revoke the punishment"; (4) a statement of charges, with only one of the four sins named; (5) a list of judgments, beginning with the formula "So I will send a fire upon _____." Locating the successive nations on a map, we see that they form a circle around Israel and Judah, in effect setting a trap for the complacent covenant people of God, as suddenly Judah and then Israel appear in the company of evil nations. The activities that are held up to satiric exposure in these oracles all involve military atrocities, including excessive cruelty in warfare, stealing people for slave trade, and desecration of the dead. Right from the outset, Amos packs a punch with mastery of the resources of poetry and metaphor.

1 The words of Amos, who was among the shepherds[1] of Tekoa, which he saw concerning Israel in the days of Uzziah king of Judah and in the days of Jeroboam the son of Joash, king of Israel, two years[2] before the earthquake.
[2]And he said:

"The LORD roars from Zion
    and utters his voice from Jerusalem;
the pastures of the shepherds mourn,
    and the top of Carmel withers."

[3]Thus says the LORD:

"For three transgressions of Damascus,
    and for four, I will not revoke the punishment,[3]
because they have threshed Gilead
    with threshing sledges of iron.
[4] So I will send a fire upon the house of Hazael,
    and it shall devour the strongholds of Ben-hadad.
[5] I will break the gate-bar of Damascus,
    and cut off the inhabitants from the Valley of Aven,[4]
and him who holds the scepter from Beth-eden;
    and the people of Syria shall go into exile to Kir,"
                    says the LORD.

[6]Thus says the LORD:

"For three transgressions of Gaza,
    and for four, I will not revoke the punishment,
because they carried into exile a whole people
    to deliver them up to Edom.
[7] So I will send a fire upon the wall of Gaza,
    and it shall devour her strongholds.
[8] I will cut off the inhabitants from Ashdod,
    and him who holds the scepter from Ashkelon;
I will turn my hand against Ekron,
    and the remnant of the Philistines shall perish,"
                    says the Lord GOD.

[9]Thus says the LORD:

"For three transgressions of Tyre,
    and for four, I will not revoke the punishment,
because they delivered up a whole people to Edom,

---

[1] Or sheep breeders [2] Or during two years [3] Hebrew I will not turn it back; also verses 6, 9, 11, 13 [4] Or On

and did not remember the covenant of brotherhood.
10   So I will send a fire upon the wall of Tyre,
       and it shall devour her strongholds."

¹¹Thus says the LORD:

   "For three transgressions of Edom,
       and for four, I will not revoke the punishment,
    because he pursued his brother with the sword
       and cast off all pity,
    and his anger tore perpetually,
       and he kept his wrath forever.
¹²   So I will send a fire upon Teman,
       and it shall devour the strongholds of Bozrah."

¹³Thus says the LORD:

   "For three transgressions of the Ammonites,
       and for four, I will not revoke the punishment,
    because they have ripped open pregnant women in Gilead,
       that they might enlarge their border.
¹⁴   So I will kindle a fire in the wall of Rabbah,
       and it shall devour her strongholds,
    with shouting on the day of battle,
       with a tempest in the day of the whirlwind;
¹⁵   and their king shall go into exile,
       he and his princes[1] together,"
                         says the LORD.

2 Thus says the LORD:

   "For three transgressions of Moab,
       and for four, I will not revoke the punishment,[2]
    because he burned to lime
       the bones of the king of Edom.
²   So I will send a fire upon Moab,
       and it shall devour the strongholds of Kerioth,
    and Moab shall die amid uproar,
       amid shouting and the sound of the trumpet;
³   I will cut off the ruler from its midst,
       and will kill all its princes[3] with him,"
                         says the LORD.

⁴Thus says the LORD:

   "For three transgressions of Judah,
       and for four, I will not revoke the punishment,
    because they have rejected the law of the LORD,
       and have not kept his statutes,
    but their lies have led them astray,

¹ Or officials ² Hebrew I will not turn it back; also verses 4, 6 ³ Or officials

those after which their fathers walked.

5   So I will send a fire upon Judah,
    and it shall devour the strongholds of Jerusalem."

The opening volley against Israel [2:6–16]. The first oracle directed against Israel begins just as the preceding oracles had begun: "For three transgressions of Israel, and for four . . ." (v. 6). But the list of charges against God's covenant people is much longer and more expansive than the earlier indictments had been. The implied point is probably that God holds his own people to a higher standard than he expects from pagan nations. The only adequate way to deal with this opening oracle of judgment against Israel is to identify the objects of attack, which are often stated in a manner so oblique as to constitute a code language. For example, to "sell the righteous for silver" (v. 6) is a hyperbolic picture of oppression of the weak by the wealthy and powerful, while "turn aside the way of the afflicted" (v. 7) may refer to a corrupt judicial system. At the end of the unit (vv. 13–16), the prediction of punishment is our first example of parody in the book: in ancient *epic literature, the hero's superior strength in battle is the mainspring of the action, while in these verses the warrior is in effect deheroized, becoming the opposite of what an epic hero is supposed to be and do.

6Thus says the LORD:

"For three transgressions of Israel,
    and for four, I will not revoke the punishment,
because they sell the righteous for silver,
    and the needy for a pair of sandals—
7   those who trample the head of the poor into the dust of the earth
    and turn aside the way of the afflicted;
a man and his father go in to the same girl,
    so that my holy name is profaned;
8   they lay themselves down beside every altar
    on garments taken in pledge,
and in the house of their God they drink
    the wine of those who have been fined.

9   "Yet it was I who destroyed the Amorite before them,
    whose height was like the height of the cedars
    and who was as strong as the oaks;
I destroyed his fruit above
    and his roots beneath.
10 Also it was I who brought you up out of the land of Egypt
    and led you forty years in the wilderness,
    to possess the land of the Amorite.
11 And I raised up some of your sons for prophets,
    and some of your young men for Nazirites.
    Is it not indeed so, O people of Israel?"
                        declares the LORD.

12   "But you made the Nazirites drink wine,
        and commanded the prophets,
           saying, 'You shall not prophesy.'

13   "Behold, I will press you down in your place,
        as a cart full of sheaves presses down.
14   Flight shall perish from the swift,
        and the strong shall not retain his strength,
           nor shall the mighty save his life;
15   he who handles the bow shall not stand,
        and he who is swift of foot shall not save himself,
           nor shall he who rides the horse save his life;
16   and he who is stout of heart among the mighty
        shall flee away naked in that day,"
                                    declares the LORD.

Judgment against Israel [chapter 3]. We should note that the extended passage that expresses God's judgment against Israel (2:6–6:14) is a collection of diverse fragments, with the author moving in fluid manner from one fragment to the next without concern to provide transitions. To proceed chapter by chapter is a convenience, but the material is not arranged by chapter divisions. In sequence, chapter 3 unfolds as follows: an opening summons in which God explains that he intends to punish Israel precisely because it is his privileged nation (vv. 1–2); a poetic and stylized passage in which God claims personal responsibility for the calamity that is about to befall Israel (vv. 3–8); a catalog of the punitive acts that God will perform (vv. 9–15). Verses 3–6 use a common rhetorical formula of OT wisdom literature in which the author asks a series of rhetorical questions that ends with the actual topic of the discourse. At the end of the chapter, we again need to pick up on the shorthand message of the prophet: a reference to the altar (v. 14) implies a satiric attack on corrupt priests and worshipers, while references to winter house and summer house and houses of ivory (v. 15) refer to the wealthy classes of society.

3   Hear this word that the LORD has spoken against you, O people of Israel, against
    the whole family that I brought up out of the land of Egypt:

2   "You only have I known
        of all the families of the earth;
     therefore I will punish you
        for all your iniquities.

3   "Do two walk together,
        unless they have agreed to meet?
4   Does a lion roar in the forest,
        when he has no prey?
     Does a young lion cry out from his den,
        if he has taken nothing?
5   Does a bird fall in a snare on the earth,
        when there is no trap for it?
     Does a snare spring up from the ground,

when it has taken nothing?
⁶ Is a trumpet blown in a city,
  and the people are not afraid?
Does disaster come to a city,
  unless the Lᴏʀᴅ has done it?

⁷ "For the Lord Gᴏᴅ does nothing
  without revealing his secret
  to his servants the prophets.
⁸ The lion has roared;
  who will not fear?
The Lord Gᴏᴅ has spoken;
  who can but prophesy?"

⁹ Proclaim to the strongholds in Ashdod
  and to the strongholds in the land of Egypt,
and say, "Assemble yourselves on the mountains of Samaria,
  and see the great tumults within her,
  and the oppressed in her midst."
¹⁰ "They do not know how to do right," declares the Lᴏʀᴅ,
  "those who store up violence and robbery in their strongholds."

¹¹Therefore thus says the Lord Gᴏᴅ:

"An adversary shall surround the land
  and bring down¹ your defenses from you,
  and your strongholds shall be plundered."

¹²Thus says the Lᴏʀᴅ: "As the shepherd rescues from the mouth of the lion two legs, or a piece of an ear, so shall the people of Israel who dwell in Samaria be rescued, with the corner of a couch and part² of a bed.

¹³ "Hear, and testify against the house of Jacob,"
  declares the Lord Gᴏᴅ, the God of hosts,
¹⁴ "that on the day I punish Israel for his transgressions,
  I will punish the altars of Bethel,
and the horns of the altar shall be cut off
  and fall to the ground.
¹⁵ I will strike the winter house along with the summer house,
  and the houses of ivory shall perish,
and the great houses³ shall come to an end,"
  declares the Lᴏʀᴅ.

Satiric attack on the guilty [chapter 4]. The plainspoken satirist does not hesitate to resort to vituperation (speaking rudely and insultingly), and Amos gives us one of the most famous examples on record when he calls the wealthy women of Samaria "you cows of Bashan" (v. 1). The import of these opening verses (vv. 1–3) is to condemn the wealthy and indifferent of society. In the next unit (vv. 4–5) Amos turns his attention to the priestly class, and he shocks his readers by giving a parody of the priestly exhorta-

¹ Hebrew An adversary, one who surrounds the land—he shall bring down ² The meaning of the Hebrew word is uncertain ³ Or and many houses

tion to worship. The priestly exhortation was "come to Bethel and worship," but Amos makes it read "come to Bethel, and transgress" (v. 4). In an equally inventive parody, Amos lists God's mighty acts of power, as in the conventional *psalm of praise (vv. 6–11). The twist is that this particular catalog is a list of disasters. God claims that he sent these disasters in an attempt to induce the Israelites to repent and reform their lives, but the futility of the effort is captured in a formula that occurs five times: "yet you did not return to me." Because of the nation's hardheartedness, God asserts that he will once again send judgment (vv. 12–13).

4 "Hear this word, you cows of Bashan,
  who are on the mountain of Samaria,
who oppress the poor, who crush the needy,
  who say to your husbands, 'Bring, that we may drink!'
2 The Lord GOD has sworn by his holiness
  that, behold, the days are coming upon you,
when they shall take you away with hooks,
  even the last of you with fishhooks.
3 And you shall go out through the breaches,
  each one straight ahead;
and you shall be cast out into Harmon,"
          declares the LORD.

4 "Come to Bethel, and transgress;
  to Gilgal, and multiply transgression;
bring your sacrifices every morning,
  your tithes every three days;
5 offer a sacrifice of thanksgiving of that which is leavened,
  and proclaim freewill offerings, publish them;
  for so you love to do, O people of Israel!"
          declares the Lord GOD.

6 "I gave you cleanness of teeth in all your cities,
  and lack of bread in all your places,
yet you did not return to me,"
          declares the LORD.

7 "I also withheld the rain from you
  when there were yet three months to the harvest;
I would send rain on one city,
  and send no rain on another city;
one field would have rain,
  and the field on which it did not rain would wither;
8 so two or three cities would wander to another city
  to drink water, and would not be satisfied;
yet you did not return to me,"
          declares the LORD.

⁹ "I struck you with blight and mildew;
    your many gardens and your vineyards,
    your fig trees and your olive trees the locust devoured;
  yet you did not return to me,"
                  declares the LORD.

¹⁰ "I sent among you a pestilence after the manner of Egypt;
    I killed your young men with the sword,
  and carried away your horses,¹
    and I made the stench of your camp go up into your nostrils;
  yet you did not return to me,"
                  declares the LORD.

¹¹ "I overthrew some of you,
    as when God overthrew Sodom and Gomorrah,
    and you were as a brand² plucked out of the burning;
  yet you did not return to me,"
                  declares the LORD.

¹² "Therefore thus I will do to you, O Israel;
    because I will do this to you,
    prepare to meet your God, O Israel!"

¹³ For behold, he who forms the mountains and creates the wind,
    and declares to man what is his thought,
  who makes the morning darkness,
    and treads on the heights of the earth—
  the LORD, the God of hosts, is his name!

Another bad news passage [chapter 5]. The imaginative and satiric energy of Amos keeps intensifying in this chapter, which is a collection of fragments. There is no topical flow. To assimilate this chapter, we need to take the time to identify (1) the specific objects of satiric attack; (2) passages that assert the standard by which the prophet is conducting his attack, namely, the character and law of God (vv. 4, 6, 8–9, 14–15); and the predictions of imminent punishment. Again we need to be alert to the shorthand rhetoric of the prophet, so that we understand that the reference to hating the person who speaks truth "in the gate" (v. 10) refers to dislike of truth in politics, while "turning aside the needy in the gate" (v. 12) refers to a corrupt judicial system.

5 Hear this word that I take up over you in lamentation, O house of Israel:

² "Fallen, no more to rise,
    is the virgin Israel;
  forsaken on her land,
    with none to raise her up."

³ For thus says the Lord GOD:

  "The city that went out a thousand
    shall have a hundred left,

---

¹ Hebrew *along with the captivity of your horses* ² That is, a burning stick

and that which went out a hundred
   shall have ten left
   to the house of Israel."

⁴For thus says the LORD to the house of Israel:

"Seek me and live;
⁵   but do not seek Bethel,
and do not enter into Gilgal
   or cross over to Beersheba;
for Gilgal shall surely go into exile,
   and Bethel shall come to nothing."

⁶   Seek the LORD and live,
   lest he break out like fire in the house of Joseph,
   and it devour, with none to quench it for Bethel,
⁷   O you who turn justice to wormwood[1]
   and cast down righteousness to the earth!

⁸   He who made the Pleiades and Orion,
   and turns deep darkness into the morning
   and darkens the day into night,
who calls for the waters of the sea
   and pours them out on the surface of the earth,
the LORD is his name;
⁹   who makes destruction flash forth against the strong,
   so that destruction comes upon the fortress.

¹⁰   They hate him who reproves in the gate,
   and they abhor him who speaks the truth.
¹¹   Therefore because you trample on[2] the poor
   and you exact taxes of grain from him,
you have built houses of hewn stone,
   but you shall not dwell in them;
you have planted pleasant vineyards,
   but you shall not drink their wine.
¹²   For I know how many are your transgressions
   and how great are your sins—
you who afflict the righteous, who take a bribe,
   and turn aside the needy in the gate.
¹³   Therefore he who is prudent will keep silent in such a time,
   for it is an evil time.

¹⁴   Seek good, and not evil,
   that you may live;
and so the LORD, the God of hosts, will be with you,
   as you have said.
¹⁵   Hate evil, and love good,
   and establish justice in the gate;

¹ Or to bitter fruit ² Or you tax

it may be that the Lord, the God of hosts,
    will be gracious to the remnant of Joseph.

[16] Therefore thus says the Lord, the God of hosts, the Lord:

    "In all the squares there shall be wailing,
        and in all the streets they shall say, 'Alas! Alas!'
    They shall call the farmers to mourning
        and to wailing those who are skilled in lamentation,
[17]   and in all vineyards there shall be wailing,
        for I will pass through your midst,"
                     says the Lord.

[18]   Woe to you who desire the day of the Lord!
        Why would you have the day of the Lord?
    It is darkness, and not light,
[19]   as if a man fled from a lion,
    and a bear met him,
  or went into the house and leaned his hand against the wall,
    and a serpent bit him.
[20]   Is not the day of the Lord darkness, and not light,
    and gloom with no brightness in it?

[21]   "I hate, I despise your feasts,
    and I take no delight in your solemn assemblies.
[22]   Even though you offer me your burnt offerings and grain offerings,
    I will not accept them;
  and the peace offerings of your fattened animals,
    I will not look upon them.
[23]   Take away from me the noise of your songs;
    to the melody of your harps I will not listen.
[24]   But let justice roll down like waters,
    and righteousness like an ever-flowing stream.

[25] "Did you bring to me sacrifices and offerings during the forty years in the wilderness, O house of Israel? [26] You shall take up Sikkuth your king, and Kiyyun your star-god—your images that you made for yourselves, [27] and I will send you into exile beyond Damascus," says the Lord, whose name is the God of hosts.

Climax of the satire against Israel [chapter 6]. This chapter is as fluid in its movement from one topic to the next as the preceding chapters have been. The *aphoristic flair of Amos is one of his literary achievements, as in the famous proverb attacking complacency: "Woe to those who are at ease in Zion" (v. 1). Three common ingredients continue to appear: a running list of abuses (objects of attack); appeals to God himself as the standard to which people need to return as an antidote to the abuses; predictions of coming judgment.

6

"Woe to those who are at ease in Zion,
   and to those who feel secure on the mountain of Samaria,
the notable men of the first of the nations,
   to whom the house of Israel comes!

2 Pass over to Calneh, and see,
     and from there go to Hamath the great;
     then go down to Gath of the Philistines.
   Are you better than these kingdoms?
     Or is their territory greater than your territory,
3   O you who put far away the day of disaster
     and bring near the seat of violence?

4 "Woe to those who lie on beds of ivory
     and stretch themselves out on their couches,
   and eat lambs from the flock
     and calves from the midst of the stall,
5 who sing idle songs to the sound of the harp
     and like David invent for themselves instruments of music,
6 who drink wine in bowls
     and anoint themselves with the finest oils,
     but are not grieved over the ruin of Joseph!
7 Therefore they shall now be the first of those who go into exile,
     and the revelry of those who stretch themselves out shall pass away."

8 The Lord God has sworn by himself, declares the Lord, the God of hosts:

   "I abhor the pride of Jacob
     and hate his strongholds,
     and I will deliver up the city and all that is in it."

9 And if ten men remain in one house, they shall die. 10 And when one's relative, the one who anoints him for burial, shall take him up to bring the bones out of the house, and shall say to him who is in the innermost parts of the house, "Is there still anyone with you?" he shall say, "No"; and he shall say, "Silence! We must not mention the name of the Lord."

11   For behold, the Lord commands,
       and the great house shall be struck down into fragments,
       and the little house into bits.
12   Do horses run on rocks?
       Does one plow there[1] with oxen?
     But you have turned justice into poison
       and the fruit of righteousness into wormwood[2]—
13   you who rejoice in Lo-debar,[3]
       who say, "Have we not by our own strength
       captured Karnaim[4] for ourselves?"
14   "For behold, I will raise up against you a nation,
       O house of Israel," declares the Lord, the God of hosts;

---

[1] Or the sea [2] Or into bitter fruit [3] Lo-debar means nothing [4] Karnaim means horns (a symbol of strength)

"and they shall oppress you from Lebo-hamath
    to the Brook of the Arabah."

> **Four visions and a prophetic narrative** [chapters 7–8]. The diffuse organizational
> pattern that has preceded now becomes focused into a series of prophetic visions, with
> each of the visions in this unit preceded by the prophet's formula "This is what the Lord
> Gᴏᴅ showed me" (7:1, 4, 7; 8:1). The general drift of each of these four symbolic visions
> is that God's judgment is inevitable. The visions are, in sequence, a plague of locusts
> (7:1–3); a fire that devours the ocean (7:4–6); a plumb line used to measure the nation
> (7:7–9); a basket of summer fruit that expands into an extensive list of vices and a sur-
> realistic vision of punishment (chapter 8). Stuck into the middle of this unit (7:10–17) is
> a conflict narrative in which the priest Amaziah attempts to silence Amos, who responds
> with a patented prediction of coming woe.

7 This is what the Lord Gᴏᴅ showed me: behold, he was forming locusts when the
latter growth was just beginning to sprout, and behold, it was the latter growth
after the king's mowings. ²When they had finished eating the grass of the land, I said,

"O Lord Gᴏᴅ, please forgive!
    How can Jacob stand?
    He is so small!"
³   The Lᴏʀᴅ relented concerning this:
    "It shall not be," said the Lᴏʀᴅ.

⁴This is what the Lord Gᴏᴅ showed me: behold, the Lord Gᴏᴅ was calling for a judgment by fire, and it devoured the great deep and was eating up the land. ⁵Then I said,

"O Lord Gᴏᴅ, please cease!
    How can Jacob stand?
    He is so small!"
⁶   The Lᴏʀᴅ relented concerning this:
    "This also shall not be," said the Lord Gᴏᴅ.

⁷This is what he showed me: behold, the Lord was standing beside a wall built with
a plumb line, with a plumb line in his hand. ⁸And the Lᴏʀᴅ said to me, "Amos, what
do you see?" And I said, "A plumb line." Then the Lord said,

"Behold, I am setting a plumb line
    in the midst of my people Israel;
    I will never again pass by them;
⁹   the high places of Isaac shall be made desolate,
        and the sanctuaries of Israel shall be laid waste,
        and I will rise against the house of Jeroboam with the sword."

¹⁰Then Amaziah the priest of Bethel sent to Jeroboam king of Israel, saying, "Amos
has conspired against you in the midst of the house of Israel. The land is not able to
bear all his words. ¹¹For thus Amos has said,

"'Jeroboam shall die by the sword,
　　and Israel must go into exile
　　away from his land.'"

[12]And Amaziah said to Amos, "O seer, go, flee away to the land of Judah, and eat bread there, and prophesy there, [13]but never again prophesy at Bethel, for it is the king's sanctuary, and it is a temple of the kingdom."

[14]Then Amos answered and said to Amaziah, "I was[1] no prophet, nor a prophet's son, but I was a herdsman and a dresser of sycamore figs. [15]But the LORD took me from following the flock, and the LORD said to me, 'Go, prophesy to my people Israel.' [16]Now therefore hear the word of the LORD.

"You say, 'Do not prophesy against Israel,
　　and do not preach against the house of Isaac.'

[17]Therefore thus says the LORD:

"'Your wife shall be a prostitute in the city,
　　and your sons and your daughters shall fall by the sword,
　　and your land shall be divided up with a measuring line;
you yourself shall die in an unclean land,
　　and Israel shall surely go into exile away from its land.'"

8 This is what the Lord GOD showed me: behold, a basket of summer fruit. [2]And he said, "Amos, what do you see?" And I said, "A basket of summer fruit." Then the LORD said to me,

"The end[2] has come upon my people Israel;
　　I will never again pass by them.
[3]　The songs of the temple[3] shall become wailings[4] in that day,"
　　　　　　　　　　　declares the Lord GOD.
"So many dead bodies!"
"They are thrown everywhere!"
"Silence!"

[4]　Hear this, you who trample on the needy
　　　and bring the poor of the land to an end,
[5]　saying, "When will the new moon be over,
　　　that we may sell grain?
And the Sabbath,
　　that we may offer wheat for sale,
that we may make the ephah small and the shekel[5] great
　　and deal deceitfully with false balances,
[6]　that we may buy the poor for silver
　　　and the needy for a pair of sandals
　　　and sell the chaff of the wheat?"

[7]　The LORD has sworn by the pride of Jacob:
　　"Surely I will never forget any of their deeds.
[8]　Shall not the land tremble on this account,

---

[1] Or am; twice in this verse [2] The Hebrew words for end and summer fruit sound alike [3] Or palace [4] Or The singing women of the palace shall wail
[5] An ephah was about 3/5 bushel or 22 liters; a shekel was about 2/5 ounce or 11 grams

and everyone mourn who dwells in it,
  and all of it rise like the Nile,
    and be tossed about and sink again, like the Nile of Egypt?"

⁹ "And on that day," declares the Lord GOD,
    "I will make the sun go down at noon
      and darken the earth in broad daylight.
¹⁰ I will turn your feasts into mourning
      and all your songs into lamentation;
    I will bring sackcloth on every waist
      and baldness on every head;
    I will make it like the mourning for an only son
      and the end of it like a bitter day.

¹¹ "Behold, the days are coming," declares the Lord GOD,
      "when I will send a famine on the land—
    not a famine of bread, nor a thirst for water,
      but of hearing the words of the LORD.
¹² They shall wander from sea to sea,
      and from north to east;
    they shall run to and fro, to seek the word of the LORD,
      but they shall not find it.

¹³ "In that day the lovely virgins and the young men
      shall faint for thirst.
¹⁴ Those who swear by the Guilt of Samaria,
      and say, 'As your god lives, O Dan,'
    and, 'As the Way of Beersheba lives,'
      they shall fall, and never rise again."

The fifth vision [9:1–10]. The sequence of prophetic visions ends with a vision of God standing beside the altar, promising to exert his divine power with a display of judgment that cannot be avoided.

9 I saw the Lord standing beside¹ the altar, and he said:

"Strike the capitals until the thresholds shake,
    and shatter them on the heads of all the people;²
  and those who are left of them I will kill with the sword;
    not one of them shall flee away;
    not one of them shall escape.

² "If they dig into Sheol,
      from there shall my hand take them;
    if they climb up to heaven,
      from there I will bring them down.
³ If they hide themselves on the top of Carmel,
      from there I will search them out and take them;

---

¹ Or *on* ² Hebrew *all of them*

and if they hide from my sight at the bottom of the sea,
    there I will command the serpent, and it shall bite them.
4 And if they go into captivity before their enemies,
    there I will command the sword, and it shall kill them;
  and I will fix my eyes upon them
    for evil and not for good."

5 The Lord GOD of hosts,
  he who touches the earth and it melts,
    and all who dwell in it mourn,
  and all of it rises like the Nile,
    and sinks again, like the Nile of Egypt;
6 who builds his upper chambers in the heavens
    and founds his vault upon the earth;
  who calls for the waters of the sea
    and pours them out upon the surface of the earth—
  the LORD is his name.

7 "Are you not like the Cushites to me,
    O people of Israel?" declares the LORD.
  "Did I not bring up Israel from the land of Egypt,
    and the Philistines from Caphtor and the Syrians from Kir?
8 Behold, the eyes of the Lord GOD are upon the sinful kingdom,
    and I will destroy it from the surface of the ground,
      except that I will not utterly destroy the house of Jacob,"
               declares the LORD.

9 "For behold, I will command,
    and shake the house of Israel among all the nations
  as one shakes with a sieve,
    but no pebble shall fall to the earth.
10 All the sinners of my people shall die by the sword,
    who say, 'Disaster shall not overtake or meet us.'

Israel restored [9:11–15]. If we are familiar with the structure of the OT prophetic books, as we enter the late phase of the book we expect to find the conventional apocalyptic vision of a perfected world. In Amos these oracles of blessing are not prepared for but are sprung on us as sudden good news after a very heavy dose of bad news. Here the apocalyptic vision is only five verses long, but the poetry of the passage is so evocative that we do not feel cheated. Verse 11, with its picture of the ruins of David restored, was quoted by James at the Jerusalem council as proof that the inclusion of Gentiles in the NT church was in accord with OT prophecy (Acts 15:16–17). With that as a clue, our best interpretation of this *golden age prophecy is to see it as ultimately fulfilled in what the NT calls the latter days, which began with the coming of Christ.

11 "In that day I will raise up
    the booth of David that is fallen
  and repair its breaches,

and raise up its ruins
and rebuild it as in the days of old,
[12] that they may possess the remnant of Edom
and all the nations who are called by my name,"[1]
declares the LORD who does this.

[13] "Behold, the days are coming," declares the LORD,
"when the plowman shall overtake the reaper
and the treader of grapes him who sows the seed;
the mountains shall drip sweet wine,
and all the hills shall flow with it.
[14] I will restore the fortunes of my people Israel,
and they shall rebuild the ruined cities and inhabit them;
they shall plant vineyards and drink their wine,
and they shall make gardens and eat their fruit.
[15] I will plant them on their land,
and they shall never again be uprooted
out of the land that I have given them,"
says the LORD your God.

[1] Hebrew; Septuagint (compare Acts 15:17) *that the remnant of mankind and all the nations who are called by my name may seek the Lord*

OBADIAH

The book at a glance. One chapter, 21 verses. Obadiah is the shortest book in the OT. It is unique among OT prophetic books in being directed against a foreign nation, without any oracles of judgment against either Israel or Judah. The object of *satiric attack is the nation of Edom (descendants of Esau). The predicted defeat of Edom is, in turn, offered as an encouragement to the Israelites, who had been the victims of Edom's hostility and looting.

▌Genres. The primary *genre is *prophecy, and as is customary in prophecy, predictions of the future are couched in *oracles of judgment and an *oracle of salvation or deliverance. The oracles of judgment against Edom are examples of *satire, with discernible objects of attack and a satiric norm by which Edom and other nations are criticized. (For more information on items accompanied by an asterisk, see the glossary at the back of this Bible.)

Passage	Content	Prophetic Genre
1–9	Prediction of Edom's destruction	Oracle of judgment
10–14	Catalog of Edom's sins	Satire
15–16	Prediction that God will judge all nations for their evil deeds	Oracle of judgment
17–21	Golden age prophecy promising blessing for God's people	Oracle of salvation or deliverance

▌Historical backdrop. The book of Obadiah presupposes that we know the history that lies behind it. There are hints in the book of the following events from the past: the Edomites were descendants of Esau, so that the hostility between them and the Israelites goes back ultimately to the sibling rivalry of Jacob and Esau; when the Israelites were devastated by foreign armies, the Edomites did not feel any sympathy toward the Israelites because of their blood ties but instead gloated over their defeat and looted them. Psalm 137 catches the flavor of the hostility between Edom and Israel.

▌Inferred literary intentions. The book is designed to achieve the following literary purposes:

- impress upon us that God will judge nations and individuals who do terrible things
- instill fear in us regarding God's judgment against sinners

- lead us to vow not to behave as the Edomites did

- cause us to be thankful for God's promised deliverance and to resolve to be among the people whom God will raise up as his cherished possession

■ Theological themes. (1) The sovereignty of God: God announces what he will do in the world, and there is no doubt that he will do it. (2) The justice of God: the plain message of the first sixteen verses is that God will judge sinful nations and individuals. (3) The mercy of God: the concluding oracle of salvation announces the blessings of God, which are in no way merited by God's people.

■ The book of Obadiah as a chapter in the master story of the Bible. The master story of the Bible is the story of God's acts of judgment and mercy toward the human race. The book of Obadiah zeroes in on those two actions of God. Because this prophetic book is directed to a non-Jewish nation, moreover, we are led to see that the Bible is not just for the Jews but for everyone.

Prediction of destruction for Edom [verses 1–9]. The prophet begins by labeling his prophecy a vision, denoting that he will picture something that has not yet happened but is merely envisioned. The opening oracle of judgment predicts the fall of Edom. Things to look for include the following: what Edom will look like in the near future; the contrast of this imminent downfall to Edom's past prominence; hints of the genre of the *doom song, in which the future destruction of a nation is pictured as though it were past history.

¹The vision of Obadiah.

Thus says the Lord GOD concerning Edom:
We have heard a report from the LORD,
    and a messenger has been sent among the nations:
"Rise up! Let us rise against her for battle!"
²   Behold, I will make you small among the nations;
    you shall be utterly despised.¹
³   The pride of your heart has deceived you,
    you who live in the clefts of the rock,²
    in your lofty dwelling,
who say in your heart,
    "Who will bring me down to the ground?"
⁴   Though you soar aloft like the eagle,
    though your nest is set among the stars,
    from there I will bring you down,
               declares the LORD.

⁵   If thieves came to you,
    if plunderers came by night—
    how you have been destroyed!—
    would they not steal only enough for themselves?

¹ Or Behold, I have made you small among the nations; you are utterly despised ² Or Sela

If grape gatherers came to you,
　　would they not leave gleanings?
6　How Esau has been pillaged,
　　his treasures sought out!
7　All your allies have driven you to your border;
　　those at peace with you have deceived you;
　they have prevailed against you;
　　those who eat your bread[1] have set a trap beneath you—
　　you have[2] no understanding.

8　Will I not on that day, declares the LORD,
　　destroy the wise men out of Edom,
　　and understanding out of Mount Esau?
9　And your mighty men shall be dismayed, O Teman,
　　so that every man from Mount Esau will be cut off by slaughter.

The things that Edom should have left undone [verses 10–14]. This satiric passage is mainly a catalog of the things Edom should not have done. In strict parallelism, the prophet repeatedly uses the formula "do not . . ." On the basis of these declarations, we gradually get a full picture of a violent and vengeful nation. Also, if the catalog is a satiric attack on specific abuses, we can ponder the opposites of the actions that are denounced to compile a picture of behavior of which God approves.

10　Because of the violence done to your brother Jacob,
　　shame shall cover you,
　　and you shall be cut off forever.
11　On the day that you stood aloof,
　　on the day that strangers carried off his wealth
　and foreigners entered his gates
　　and cast lots for Jerusalem,
　　you were like one of them.
12　But do not gloat over the day of your brother
　　in the day of his misfortune;
　do not rejoice over the people of Judah
　　in the day of their ruin;
　do not boast[3]
　　in the day of distress.
13　Do not enter the gate of my people
　　in the day of their calamity;
　do not gloat over his disaster
　　in the day of his calamity;
　do not loot his wealth
　　in the day of his calamity.
14　Do not stand at the crossroads
　　to cut off his fugitives;
　do not hand over his survivors
　　in the day of distress.

---

[1] Hebrew lacks *those who eat* [2] Hebrew *he has* [3] Hebrew *do not enlarge your mouth*

The day of the Lord predicted [verses 15–16]. An archetype of OT prophetic literature is the day-of-the-Lord motif, which predicts and describes a coming day in which God will act decisively and on a cosmic scale. Usually "the day of the LORD" implies judgment, and that is its primary meaning here. But the day of the Lord will also be a day of deliverance for believers in God. The lead-in to the oracle of salvation that follows may be intended to link the promised salvation with the day of the Lord, inasmuch as it contrasts what God will do to all the nations with what will happen on Mount Zion.

15 For the day of the LORD is near upon all the nations.
  As you have done, it shall be done to you;
    your deeds shall return on your own head.
16 For as you have drunk on my holy mountain,
    so all the nations shall drink continually;
  they shall drink and swallow,
    and shall be as though they had never been.

A coming golden age [verses 17–21]. In the OT, a coming golden age—whether it is the restoration of God's people after exile, or a coming millennium, or the eschaton at the end of history—is often pictured in specific geographic terms. Israel triumphant is pictured as a physical kingdom in a specific land, even though the details may ultimately be symbolic rather than foretelling something that literally happened in the form in which the prophet pictures it. The ultimate fulfillment of this *golden age prophecy is the kingdom of Christ.

17 But in Mount Zion there shall be those who escape,
    and it shall be holy,
  and the house of Jacob shall possess their own possessions.
18 The house of Jacob shall be a fire,
    and the house of Joseph a flame,
    and the house of Esau stubble;
  they shall burn them and consume them,
    and there shall be no survivor for the house of Esau,
      for the LORD has spoken.

19 Those of the Negeb shall possess Mount Esau,
    and those of the Shephelah shall possess the land of the Philistines;
  they shall possess the land of Ephraim and the land of Samaria,
    and Benjamin shall possess Gilead.
20 The exiles of this host of the people of Israel
    shall possess the land of the Canaanites as far as Zarephath,
  and the exiles of Jerusalem who are in Sepharad
    shall possess the cities of the Negeb.
21 Saviors shall go up to Mount Zion
    to rule Mount Esau,
    and the kingdom shall be the LORD's.

JONAH

The book at a glance. 4 chapters, 48 verses. The story of Jonah is one of the best-known stories of the Bible. The book that tells this story is a missionary manual on the subject of the universal (as opposed to single-group) scope of God's salvation. The two main themes of the book support this missionary theme, as the book (1) exposes the sins of bigotry and ethnocentrism that seek to make God the possession of one's own nation or group and (2) demonstrates by a striking example that the saving love of God extends across national and cultural boundaries. The *protagonist Jonah is a prophet by vocation, and yet the *satiric book that bears his name is a short manual on how *not* to be a prophet.

▌Genres. The main *genre of the book is satire—the exposure of human vice or folly. Four things call for attention in a satire, as follows: (1) the *object of attack* is Jonah and what he represents—a bigotry and ethnocentrism that regarded God as the exclusive property of the believing community (in the OT, the nation of Israel); (2) the *satiric vehicle* is narrative or story (see below); (3) the *satiric norm* or standard by which Jonah's bad attitudes are judged is the character of God, who is portrayed as a God of universal mercy in the sense that his mercy is not limited by national boundaries; (4) the *satiric tone* is humorous, with Jonah emerging as a laughable figure—someone who runs away from God and is caught by a fish, and a childish and pouting prophet who prefers death to the loss of his shade tree. (For more information on items accompanied by an asterisk, see the glossary at the back of this Bible.)

Passage	Action	Setting	Most Memorable Scene/Event
1:1–17	Jonah's flight	The great sea	The great storm
2:1–10	Jonah's rescue	The belly of the great fish	Jonah inside the belly of the great fish
3:1–10	Jonah's sermon	Inside the great city	The great repentance of the people of Nineveh
4:1–11	Jonah's complaint	Outskirts of the great city	Jonah's defiance toward God as he sits under his shriveled shade plant

▌The story line. The external shape of the story neatly follows the division into four chapters, as follows: Jonah's commissioning and flight (chapter 1); Jonah's rescue and prayer of gratitude (chapter 2): Jonah's sermon and its astonishing success (chapter 3); Jonah's resentment over God's mercy (chapter 4). The protagonist in the story is Jonah, and the plot conflicts all center on him, as Jonah is shown to be in conflict with God, with elemental nature, with his prophetic calling, with the enemy city of Nineveh (that is, with unbelievers), and ultimately with himself (spiritually speaking, he is his own worst enemy).

▌Characterization and setting. The two main characters in the story are Jonah and God, and the main lesson of the story can be determined by compiling an ongoing portrait of a disobedient prophet and a merciful and saving God. Beyond the two main characters are two groups—the pagan sailors who end up fearing God (1:16) and the city of Nineveh, a large, undifferentiated group that repents. Two settings dominate the story, and both are images of terror: (1) elemental nature in its threatening form, whether a stormy ocean or the hot, arid countryside outside of Nineveh, and (2) the dread city of Nineveh, capital city of a world empire known for its cruelty in battle.

▌Stylistic features. (1) The giantesque motif—the motif of the unexpectedly large (extending, for example, to the magnitude of the task assigned to Jonah, of the fish that swallows him, and of the repentance that Jonah's eight-word sermon accomplishes). (2) A pervasive irony—for example, the ironic discrepancy between Jonah's prophetic vocation and his ignominious behavior, and the ironic impossibility of fleeing from the presence of God. (3) Humor, as Jonah's behavior is not only ignominious but also ridiculous.

▌Inferred literary intentions. The book is designed to achieve the following literary purposes:

- use the literary form of satire to expose the sins of bigotry and ethnocentrism

- embody those sins in the attitudes and actions of Jonah the prophet

- pack a wealth of action and characterization into one of the most condensed stories on record

- evoke praise to God for extending his salvation to all nations and groups

- captivate us with the giantesque nature of the events

▌Theological themes. (1) Salvation: specifically, this book deals with the scope of God's saving love, which is shown to be available to people of all races and nations. (2) Morality: the book shows that bigotry and ethnocentrism are sinful and that God's judgment stands against them. (3) Repentance: God's desire is for everyone to repent of sin. (4) The nature of faith: the book shows that an intellectual grasp of correct theology is not enough; one's actions and attitudes must match one's theology.

▌The book of Jonah as a chapter in the master story of the Bible. The book of Jonah makes a twofold contribution to the story of the Bible. It fits into the story of redemptive history by showing the nature of God's redemption—extending across national and cultural boundaries, requiring repentance, and based on the compassionate character of God. Second, the Bible reveals how God wants his people to live in the world, which we learn in this book by way of negative example as the behavior of Jonah shows us how *not* to live in regard to the unbelieving world. Additionally, Jonah's three-day descent into the water foreshadows the death and resurrection of Christ.

Jonah's commissioning and flight [chapter 1]. The opening chapter of Jonah introduces the narrative—its characters, its two main settings (the ocean and the city), and the plot (Jonah's mission to preach to Nineveh). It also introduces the satiric motif of the ignominious prophet, as every action of Jonah in the opening chapter exposes his failures. In fact, Jonah undertakes an impossible anti-quest (as Ps. 139:7–12 asserts, no one can flee from the presence of God). Jonah's statement about God in verse 9 is a theological formula that appears repeatedly in the Bible, showing that Jonah has a grasp of orthodox theology; his behavior, however, directly contradicts his theological assertion that he fears God, "who made the sea and the dry land." God's sparing of the sailors and their coming to "fear" God already shows that God's mercy extends beyond any racial or national boundary. Also, to highlight the ignominy of Jonah's behavior, the writer uses the technique of foil, as we observe the ways in which the pagan sailors behave more honorably than Jonah does.

---

1 Now the word of the LORD came to Jonah the son of Amittai, saying, ²"Arise, go to Nineveh, that great city, and call out against it, for their evil¹ has come up before me." ³But Jonah rose to flee to Tarshish from the presence of the LORD. He went down to Joppa and found a ship going to Tarshish. So he paid the fare and went on board, to go with them to Tarshish, away from the presence of the LORD.

⁴But the LORD hurled a great wind upon the sea, and there was a mighty tempest on the sea, so that the ship threatened to break up. ⁵Then the mariners were afraid, and each cried out to his god. And they hurled the cargo that was in the ship into the sea to lighten it for them. But Jonah had gone down into the inner part of the ship and had lain down and was fast asleep. ⁶So the captain came and said to him, "What do you mean, you sleeper? Arise, call out to your god! Perhaps the god will give a thought to us, that we may not perish."

⁷And they said to one another, "Come, let us cast lots, that we may know on whose account this evil has come upon us." So they cast lots, and the lot fell on Jonah. ⁸Then they said to him, "Tell us on whose account this evil has come upon us. What is your occupation? And where do you come from? What is your country? And of what people are you?" ⁹And he said to them, "I am a Hebrew, and I fear the LORD, the God of heaven, who made the sea and the dry land." ¹⁰Then the men were exceedingly afraid and said to him, "What is this that you have done!" For the men knew that he was fleeing from the presence of the LORD, because he had told them.

¹¹Then they said to him, "What shall we do to you, that the sea may quiet down for us?" For the sea grew more and more tempestuous. ¹²He said to them, "Pick me up and hurl me into the sea; then the sea will quiet down for you, for I know it is because of me that this great tempest has come upon you." ¹³Nevertheless, the men rowed hard² to get back to dry land, but they could not, for the sea grew more and more tempestuous against them. ¹⁴Therefore they called out to the LORD, "O LORD, let us not perish for this man's life, and lay not on us innocent blood, for you, O LORD, have done as it pleased you." ¹⁵So they picked up Jonah and hurled him into the sea, and

---

¹ The same Hebrew word can mean *evil* or *disaster*, depending on the context; so throughout Jonah ² Hebrew *the men dug in* [their oars]

the sea ceased from its raging. ¹⁶Then the men feared the LORD exceedingly, and they offered a sacrifice to the LORD and made vows.

¹⁷ ¹ And the LORD appointed² a great fish to swallow up Jonah. And Jonah was in the belly of the fish three days and three nights.

> **Jonah's rescue and prayer of gratitude** [chapter 2]. *Lyric poetry replaces prose narrative in chapter 2. The effect is that we are taken inside the very thinking and feeling of the protagonist at his moment of crisis. Just as Jonah twice in the story speaks well-worn theological statements, he here utters a psalm of praise that would be right at home in the Psalter. It is phrased in the verse form of *parallelism and recounts God's acts of deliverance (as Psalm 30 does, for example). Although this lyric prayer shows Jonah in the most favorable light in which we see him, chapter 2 fits into the satiric plan of the story in at least two ways: (1) it suggests the temporary and self-seeking nature of Jonah's repentance, since he does not change his hostile attitude toward non-Jews after his deliverance, and (2) the extravagant mercy that Jonah receives from God renders all the more reprehensible his rejection of that mercy when it is extended to others.

2 Then Jonah prayed to the LORD his God from the belly of the fish, ²saying,

"I called out to the LORD, out of my distress,
    and he answered me;
out of the belly of Sheol I cried,
    and you heard my voice.
³ For you cast me into the deep,
    into the heart of the seas,
    and the flood surrounded me;
all your waves and your billows
    passed over me.
⁴ Then I said, 'I am driven away
    from your sight;
yet I shall again look
    upon your holy temple.'
⁵ The waters closed in over me to take my life;
    the deep surrounded me;
weeds were wrapped about my head
⁶   at the roots of the mountains.
I went down to the land
    whose bars closed upon me forever;
yet you brought up my life from the pit,
    O LORD my God.
⁷ When my life was fainting away,
    I remembered the LORD,
and my prayer came to you,
    into your holy temple.
⁸ Those who pay regard to vain idols
    forsake their hope of steadfast love.
⁹ But I with the voice of thanksgiving

¹ Ch 2:1 in Hebrew ² Or had appointed

will sacrifice to you;
   what I have vowed I will pay.
      Salvation belongs to the Lord!"

¹⁰And the Lord spoke to the fish, and it vomited Jonah out upon the dry land.

> **The most effective short sermon on record** [chapter 3]. The opening verses take us
> back to the beginning of the story, confirming the futility of Jonah's attempt to run away
> from God and his mission. In effect, we begin this chapter with the recommissioning of
> the prophet. The giantesque motif governs chapter 3, reaching to such features as the
> enormous size of the city (probably the city-state) of Nineveh, the unprecedented suc-
> cess of Jonah's eight-word sermon, and the totally unexpected extent of the repentance
> of the people of Nineveh. The motif of God's expansive mercy likewise makes a repeat
> appearance.

3 Then the word of the Lord came to Jonah the second time, saying, ²"Arise, go to
   Nineveh, that great city, and call out against it the message that I tell you." ³So
Jonah arose and went to Nineveh, according to the word of the Lord. Now Nineveh
was an exceedingly great city,¹ three days' journey in breadth.² ⁴Jonah began to go
into the city, going a day's journey. And he called out, "Yet forty days, and Nineveh
shall be overthrown!" ⁵And the people of Nineveh believed God. They called for a fast
and put on sackcloth, from the greatest of them to the least of them.

⁶The word reached³ the king of Nineveh, and he arose from his throne, removed
his robe, covered himself with sackcloth, and sat in ashes. ⁷And he issued a proclamation and published through Nineveh, "By the decree of the king and his nobles:
Let neither man nor beast, herd nor flock, taste anything. Let them not feed or drink
water, ⁸but let man and beast be covered with sackcloth, and let them call out mightily to God. Let everyone turn from his evil way and from the violence that is in his
hands. ⁹Who knows? God may turn and relent and turn from his fierce anger, so that
we may not perish."

¹⁰When God saw what they did, how they turned from their evil way, God relented
of the disaster that he had said he would do to them, and he did not do it.

> **The final ignominy in Jonah's prophetic career** [chapter 4]. In a story that has fea-
> tured reversals and surprises (such as Jonah's unexpected betrayal of his prophetic
> office, his reversal of attitude in the fish's belly, and the surprising repentance of the
> Ninevites), the closing chapter springs yet another surprise on us: Jonah is angry at the
> success of his sermon and at God's mercy! Chapter 4 brings the strands of the story
> to their completion. First, the satiric characterization of Jonah reaches closure, as
> Jonah appears in the most petty light of all. Second, God's universal mercy (universal
> in the sense of transcending national boundaries) is brought to fulfillment, highlighted
> in the evocative final phrase "and also much cattle," a demonstration that God's con-
> cern extends beyond nations to creation itself. The liturgical cliché that Jonah mouths in
> verse 2 has a dozen parallels in the Bible, showing again that Jonah not only possesses
> correct theology but even expresses it in orthodox terms. The satiric point of the story
> is clinched when Jonah expresses revulsion against the very theology that he professes
> and against the very character of the God he claims to serve.

---

¹ Hebrew *a great city to God* ² Or *a visit was a three days' journey* ³ Or *had reached*

4 But it displeased Jonah exceedingly,[1] and he was angry. [2]And he prayed to the Lord and said, "O Lord, is not this what I said when I was yet in my country? That is why I made haste to flee to Tarshish; for I knew that you are a gracious God and merciful, slow to anger and abounding in steadfast love, and relenting from disaster. [3]Therefore now, O Lord, please take my life from me, for it is better for me to die than to live." [4]And the Lord said, "Do you do well to be angry?"

[5]Jonah went out of the city and sat to the east of the city and made a booth for himself there. He sat under it in the shade, till he should see what would become of the city. [6]Now the Lord God appointed a plant[2] and made it come up over Jonah, that it might be a shade over his head, to save him from his discomfort.[3] So Jonah was exceedingly glad because of the plant. [7]But when dawn came up the next day, God appointed a worm that attacked the plant, so that it withered. [8]When the sun rose, God appointed a scorching east wind, and the sun beat down on the head of Jonah so that he was faint. And he asked that he might die and said, "It is better for me to die than to live." [9]But God said to Jonah, "Do you do well to be angry for the plant?" And he said, "Yes, I do well to be angry, angry enough to die." [10]And the Lord said, "You pity the plant, for which you did not labor, nor did you make it grow, which came into being in a night and perished in a night. [11]And should not I pity Nineveh, that great city, in which there are more than 120,000 persons who do not know their right hand from their left, and also much cattle?"

---

[1] Hebrew *it was exceedingly evil to Jonah* [2] Hebrew *qiqayon*, probably the castor oil plant; also verses 7, 9, 10 [3] Or *his evil*

MICAH

The book at a glance. 7 chapters, 105 verses. The main subject of the prophetic book of Micah is how God deals with sinful humanity. Micah speaks as God's spokesman to Israel and Judah, his dual audience. Of course the NT successor of OT Israel and Judah is the believers who make up the church. The implied audience of the book is people with a conscience who want to be saved and work toward a righteous society. The implied purpose of Micah the prophet is to warn all people, especially God's people, that God does not tolerate sin and, along with that, to instill an attitude of repentance. Micah assumes that the information that the human race most needs is a double message—the bad news that the human race is headed for disaster if left to its own inclinations and the good news that God offers salvation.

▌**Genres.** The overall genre is *prophecy, which is itself a very comprehensive genre. The two basic forms are the *oracle of judgment and the *oracle of salvation or redemption. The oracles of judgment follow the rules of *satire: they have one or more objects of attack, a vehicle in which the attack is given expression, a stated or implied norm in reference to which the criticism is leveled, and a prevailing tone that is either biting or laughing. Some of the oracles of salvation picture a future golden age. These are either messianic visions of the first coming of Christ or *apocalyptic visions of Christ's second coming. Much of the content of the book is in the form of *poetry, requiring us to unpack the meanings of *images and figures of speech like *metaphor and *simile. (For more information on items accompanied by an asterisk, see the glossary at the back of this Bible.)

▌**Structure and format.** The basic plan of the book is an alternation back and forth between oracles of judgment and oracles of salvation. There are no clear transitions between the two types of material. Three times we read the prophet's call to "hear" (1:2; 3:1; 6:1). If we view these as signaling three major divisions, we can say that each one begins with visions of judgment and then moves to visions of redemption. The oracles of judgment mingle two motifs without transitions between them—a description of the evil that is occurring in Israel and Judah, and predictions and portrayals of God's punishment of those who practice evil. A distinctive rhetorical feature of the book is the prevalence of direct addresses to the audience: "Hear, you peoples" (1:2); "Make yourselves bald" (1:16); "Hear, you heads of Jacob" (3:1).

Passage	Content	Prophetic Genre	Sequence of Units
1:1–2:11	Descriptions of evil in Israel and Judah; predictions of judgment	Oracle of judgment	First collection, beginning, "Hear, you peoples" (1:2)
2:12–13	God's promise to redeem a remnant of his covenant people	Oracle of salvation	
3:1–12	God's prediction of judgment against the leaders of Israel	Oracle of judgment	Second collection, beginning, "Hear, you heads of Jacob" (3:1)
4:1–5:15	A golden age prophecy of God's blessings "in the latter days" (4:1)	Oracle of salvation	
6:1–7:13	Prophetic indictment of God's people and description of their punishment	Oracle of judgment	Third collection, beginning, "Hear what the LORD says" (6:1)
7:14–20	Pictures of Israel restored, and praise of God for his mercy in forgiving sin	Oracle of salvation	

▌**Inferred literary intentions.** The book is designed to achieve the following literary purposes:

- shock us into taking stock of the extent of evil in human society, including its presence among the people of God

- employ literary satire to convey a warning

- use the resources of poetry to embody the prophet's vision

- fire our imagination and hope with visions of a coming golden age and a redeemed society

- prompt us to build bridges between the situations pictured in the text and the form that those realities take in our own time and place

▌**Theological themes.** (1) Sin and judgment: the book shows that God takes sin very seriously and teaches that people must reflect his priorities by dealing justly with one another and the oppressed. (2) God's sovereignty: God has the power to judge sinners and also to save them through his promised Messiah. (3) Eschatology: the book contains apocalyptic visions of a future golden age.

▌**The book of Micah as a chapter in the master story of the Bible.** The master story of the Bible is the story of how God deals with the sinfulness of the human race. The book of Micah shows God acting in judgment against sin but also as having a plan to save those who believe in his promised Messiah.

Oracle of judgment against Judah and Samaria [chapters 1–2]. The opening verse sets the framework for the book as a whole: God has given his message to the prophet, who in turn announces the message to God's intended audience. The rhetorical stance of the opening oracle of judgment is direct address (*apostrophe), as Micah repeatedly speaks to the citizens of Judah (usually denoted by its capital city, Jerusalem) and Samaria as though they were present. Often the addresses are commands to do something. The literary form is satire, and thus we need to compile a running list of the things for which the recipients of the prophecy are being criticized. We also need to pay attention to poetic elements like imagery, metaphor, and *hyperbole. In keeping with customary prophetic procedure, Micah both describes the evil of society and predicts God's judgment against it. At the end of the unit, without transition, the prophet inserts a brief vision of God's restoration of Judah (2:12–13).

1 The word of the LORD that came to Micah of Moresheth in the days of Jotham, Ahaz, and Hezekiah, kings of Judah, which he saw concerning Samaria and Jerusalem.

² Hear, you peoples, all of you;[1]
    pay attention, O earth, and all that is in it,
and let the Lord GOD be a witness against you,
    the Lord from his holy temple.
³ For behold, the LORD is coming out of his place,
    and will come down and tread upon the high places of the earth.
⁴ And the mountains will melt under him,
    and the valleys will split open,
like wax before the fire,
    like waters poured down a steep place.
⁵ All this is for the transgression of Jacob
    and for the sins of the house of Israel.
What is the transgression of Jacob?
    Is it not Samaria?
And what is the high place of Judah?
    Is it not Jerusalem?
⁶ Therefore I will make Samaria a heap in the open country,
    a place for planting vineyards,
and I will pour down her stones into the valley
    and uncover her foundations.
⁷ All her carved images shall be beaten to pieces,
    all her wages shall be burned with fire,
    and all her idols I will lay waste,
for from the fee of a prostitute she gathered them,
    and to the fee of a prostitute they shall return.

⁸ For this I will lament and wail;
    I will go stripped and naked;
I will make lamentation like the jackals,
    and mourning like the ostriches.
⁹ For her wound is incurable,
    and it has come to Judah;
it has reached to the gate of my people,
    to Jerusalem.

[1] Hebrew *all of them*

10   Tell it not in Gath;
      weep not at all;
   in Beth-le-aphrah
      roll yourselves in the dust.
11   Pass on your way,
      inhabitants of Shaphir,
      in nakedness and shame;
   the inhabitants of Zaanan
      do not come out;
   the lamentation of Beth-ezel
      shall take away from you its standing place.
12   For the inhabitants of Maroth
      wait anxiously for good,
   because disaster has come down from the LORD
      to the gate of Jerusalem.
13   Harness the steeds to the chariots,
      inhabitants of Lachish;
   it was the beginning of sin
      to the daughter of Zion,
   for in you were found
      the transgressions of Israel.
14   Therefore you shall give parting gifts[1]
      to Moresheth-gath;
   the houses of Achzib shall be a deceitful thing
      to the kings of Israel.
15   I will again bring a conqueror to you,
      inhabitants of Mareshah;
   the glory of Israel
      shall come to Adullam.
16   Make yourselves bald and cut off your hair,
      for the children of your delight;
   make yourselves as bald as the eagle,
      for they shall go from you into exile.

2   Woe to those who devise wickedness
      and work evil on their beds!
   When the morning dawns, they perform it,
      because it is in the power of their hand.
2   They covet fields and seize them,
      and houses, and take them away;
   they oppress a man and his house,
      a man and his inheritance.
3   Therefore thus says the LORD:
   behold, against this family I am devising disaster,[2]
      from which you cannot remove your necks,
   and you shall not walk haughtily,
      for it will be a time of disaster.
4   In that day they shall take up a taunt song against you
      and moan bitterly,

---

[1] Or give dowry [2] The same Hebrew word can mean evil or disaster, depending on the context

and say, "We are utterly ruined;
    he changes the portion of my people;
how he removes it from me!
    To an apostate he allots our fields."
⁵ Therefore you will have none to cast the line by lot
    in the assembly of the Lᴏʀᴅ.

⁶ "Do not preach"—thus they preach—
    "one should not preach of such things;
    disgrace will not overtake us."
⁷ Should this be said, O house of Jacob?
    Has the Lᴏʀᴅ grown impatient?[1]
    Are these his deeds?
Do not my words do good
    to him who walks uprightly?
⁸ But lately my people have risen up as an enemy;
    you strip the rich robe from those who pass by trustingly
    with no thought of war.[2]
⁹ The women of my people you drive out
    from their delightful houses;
from their young children you take away
    my splendor forever.
¹⁰ Arise and go,
    for this is no place to rest,
because of uncleanness that destroys
    with a grievous destruction.
¹¹ If a man should go about and utter wind and lies,
    saying, "I will preach to you of wine and strong drink,"
    he would be the preacher for this people!
¹² I will surely assemble all of you, O Jacob;
    I will gather the remnant of Israel;
I will set them together
    like sheep in a fold,
like a flock in its pasture,
    a noisy multitude of men.
¹³ He who opens the breach goes up before them;
    they break through and pass the gate,
    going out by it.
Their king passes on before them,
    the Lᴏʀᴅ at their head.

Satire against the leaders of society [chapter 3]. The literary forms are the same as in the opening unit: direct address (apostrophe), satiric attack, a catalog of evil, and predictions of divine judgment. But the objects of satiric attack are the leaders of Jewish society—rulers, false prophets, priests.

[1] Hebrew *Has the spirit of the Lᴏʀᴅ grown short?* [2] Or *returning from war*

3 And I said:
Hear, you heads of Jacob
and rulers of the house of Israel!
Is it not for you to know justice?—
2   you who hate the good and love the evil,
who tear the skin from off my people[1]
and their flesh from off their bones,
3   who eat the flesh of my people,
and flay their skin from off them,
and break their bones in pieces
and chop them up like meat in a pot,
like flesh in a cauldron.

4   Then they will cry to the LORD,
but he will not answer them;
he will hide his face from them at that time,
because they have made their deeds evil.

5   Thus says the LORD concerning the prophets
who lead my people astray,
who cry "Peace"
when they have something to eat,
but declare war against him
who puts nothing into their mouths.
6   Therefore it shall be night to you, without vision,
and darkness to you, without divination.
The sun shall go down on the prophets,
and the day shall be black over them;
7   the seers shall be disgraced,
and the diviners put to shame;
they shall all cover their lips,
for there is no answer from God.
8   But as for me, I am filled with power,
with the Spirit of the LORD,
and with justice and might,
to declare to Jacob his transgression
and to Israel his sin.

9   Hear this, you heads of the house of Jacob
and rulers of the house of Israel,
who detest justice
and make crooked all that is straight,
10   who build Zion with blood
and Jerusalem with iniquity.
11   Its heads give judgment for a bribe;
its priests teach for a price;
its prophets practice divination for money;
yet they lean on the LORD and say,

[1] Hebrew *from off them*

"Is not the LORD in the midst of us?
No disaster shall come upon us."
12 Therefore because of you
Zion shall be plowed as a field;
Jerusalem shall become a heap of ruins,
and the mountain of the house a wooded height.

A golden age prophecy [chapter 4]. The book now presents an extended oracle of salvation that takes up two whole chapters. The lead-in (v. 1) states that the golden age that the prophet envisions will occur "in the latter days." The details that make up the content of the visions suggest both the blessings that came with the life and atoning death of the promised Messiah and an apocalyptic vision of the end times. The first thing we need to do when reading the OT *golden age prophecies is to be receptive of the exalted pictures that fill our imagination and the feelings that they evoke. This is affective poetry first of all. Then we need to ponder the specific types of blessings and experiences that will make up life in the age of perfection. Additionally, we should note that the vision is really a story of what God will do, so we need to compile a picture of God from it and be moved to appropriate worship.

---

4 It shall come to pass in the latter days
that the mountain of the house of the LORD
shall be established as the highest of the mountains,
and it shall be lifted up above the hills;
and peoples shall flow to it,
2   and many nations shall come, and say:
"Come, let us go up to the mountain of the LORD,
to the house of the God of Jacob,
that he may teach us his ways
and that we may walk in his paths."
For out of Zion shall go forth the law,[1]
and the word of the LORD from Jerusalem.
3 He shall judge between many peoples,
and shall decide for strong nations far away;
and they shall beat their swords into plowshares,
and their spears into pruning hooks;
nation shall not lift up sword against nation,
neither shall they learn war anymore;
4 but they shall sit every man under his vine and under his fig tree,
and no one shall make them afraid,
for the mouth of the LORD of hosts has spoken.
5 For all the peoples walk
each in the name of its god,
but we will walk in the name of the LORD our God
forever and ever.

6 In that day, declares the LORD,
I will assemble the lame

---

[1] Or teaching

and gather those who have been driven away
   and those whom I have afflicted;
[7] and the lame I will make the remnant,
   and those who were cast off, a strong nation;
and the LORD will reign over them in Mount Zion
   from this time forth and forevermore.

[8] And you, O tower of the flock,
   hill of the daughter of Zion,
to you shall it come,
   the former dominion shall come,
   kingship for the daughter of Jerusalem.

[9] Now why do you cry aloud?
   Is there no king in you?
Has your counselor perished,
   that pain seized you like a woman in labor?
[10] Writhe and groan,[1] O daughter of Zion,
   like a woman in labor,
for now you shall go out from the city
   and dwell in the open country;
   you shall go to Babylon.
There you shall be rescued;
   there the LORD will redeem you
   from the hand of your enemies.

[11] Now many nations
   are assembled against you,
saying, "Let her be defiled,
   and let our eyes gaze upon Zion."
[12] But they do not know
   the thoughts of the LORD;
they do not understand his plan,
   that he has gathered them as sheaves to the threshing floor.
[13] Arise and thresh,
   O daughter of Zion,
for I will make your horn iron,
   and I will make your hoofs bronze;
you shall beat in pieces many peoples;
   and shall devote[2] their gain to the LORD,
   their wealth to the Lord of the whole earth.

More blessings envisioned [chapter 5]. Chapter 5 is cut from the same cloth as the preceding chapter. The new element is a more overtly messianic emphasis (vv. 2–5). Verses 10–15 are couched in the rhetoric of predicted judgments and destruction, reminding us of oracles of judgment, but the context is that these acts of divine judgment are positive in the sense of purging the chosen nation of evil and protecting it against enemies.

---

[1] Or *push* [2] Hebrew *devote to destruction*

5 [1] Now muster your troops, O daughter[2] of troops;
        siege is laid against us;
    with a rod they strike the judge of Israel
        on the cheek.
[2][3] But you, O Bethlehem Ephrathah,
        who are too little to be among the clans of Judah,
    from you shall come forth for me
        one who is to be ruler in Israel,
    whose coming forth is from of old,
        from ancient days.
[3] Therefore he shall give them up until the time
        when she who is in labor has given birth;
    then the rest of his brothers shall return
        to the people of Israel.
[4] And he shall stand and shepherd his flock in the strength of the LORD,
        in the majesty of the name of the LORD his God.
    And they shall dwell secure, for now he shall be great
        to the ends of the earth.
[5] And he shall be their peace.

    When the Assyrian comes into our land
        and treads in our palaces,
    then we will raise against him seven shepherds
        and eight princes of men;
[6] they shall shepherd the land of Assyria with the sword,
        and the land of Nimrod at its entrances;
    and he shall deliver us from the Assyrian
        when he comes into our land
        and treads within our border.

[7] Then the remnant of Jacob shall be
        in the midst of many peoples
    like dew from the LORD,
        like showers on the grass,
    which delay not for a man
        nor wait for the children of man.
[8] And the remnant of Jacob shall be among the nations,
        in the midst of many peoples,
    like a lion among the beasts of the forest,
        like a young lion among the flocks of sheep,
    which, when it goes through, treads down
        and tears in pieces, and there is none to deliver.
[9] Your hand shall be lifted up over your adversaries,
        and all your enemies shall be cut off.

[10] And in that day, declares the LORD,
        I will cut off your horses from among you
        and will destroy your chariots;

---

[1] Ch 4:14 in Hebrew [2] That is, city [3] Ch 5:1 in Hebrew

¹¹ and I will cut off the cities of your land
    and throw down all your strongholds;
¹² and I will cut off sorceries from your hand,
    and you shall have no more tellers of fortunes;
¹³ and I will cut off your carved images
    and your pillars from among you,
and you shall bow down no more
    to the work of your hands;
¹⁴ and I will root out your Asherah images from among you
    and destroy your cities.
¹⁵ And in anger and wrath I will execute vengeance
    on the nations that did not obey.

An oracle of judgment [chapter 6]. In the back-and-forth rhythm of the book of Micah, the prophet now returns to the catalog of vices and predictions of God's judgment against them. A good way to discern the writer's organizing framework is to note the objects of satiric attack.

6 Hear what the Lᴏʀᴅ says:
    Arise, plead your case before the mountains,
    and let the hills hear your voice.
² Hear, you mountains, the indictment of the Lᴏʀᴅ,
    and you enduring foundations of the earth,
for the Lᴏʀᴅ has an indictment against his people,
    and he will contend with Israel.

³ "O my people, what have I done to you?
    How have I wearied you? Answer me!
⁴ For I brought you up from the land of Egypt
    and redeemed you from the house of slavery,
and I sent before you Moses,
    Aaron, and Miriam.
⁵ O my people, remember what Balak king of Moab devised,
    and what Balaam the son of Beor answered him,
and what happened from Shittim to Gilgal,
    that you may know the saving acts of the Lᴏʀᴅ."

⁶ "With what shall I come before the Lᴏʀᴅ,
    and bow myself before God on high?
Shall I come before him with burnt offerings,
    with calves a year old?
⁷ Will the Lᴏʀᴅ be pleased with[1] thousands of rams,
    with ten thousands of rivers of oil?
Shall I give my firstborn for my transgression,
    the fruit of my body for the sin of my soul?"
⁸ He has told you, O man, what is good;
    and what does the Lᴏʀᴅ require of you

---

[1] Or Will the Lᴏʀᴅ accept

but to do justice, and to love kindness,[1]
and to walk humbly with your God?

9 The voice of the LORD cries to the city—
and it is sound wisdom to fear your name:
"Hear of the rod and of him who appointed it![2]
10 Can I forget any longer the treasures[3] of wickedness in the house of the wicked,
and the scant measure that is accursed?
11 Shall I acquit the man with wicked scales
and with a bag of deceitful weights?
12 Your[4] rich men are full of violence;
your inhabitants speak lies,
and their tongue is deceitful in their mouth.
13 Therefore I strike you with a grievous blow,
making you desolate because of your sins.
14 You shall eat, but not be satisfied,
and there shall be hunger within you;
you shall put away, but not preserve,
and what you preserve I will give to the sword.
15 You shall sow, but not reap;
you shall tread olives, but not anoint yourselves with oil;
you shall tread grapes, but not drink wine.
16 For you have kept the statutes of Omri,[5]
and all the works of the house of Ahab;
and you have walked in their counsels,
that I may make you a desolation, and your[6] inhabitants a hissing;
so you shall bear the scorn of my people."

Visions of a decadent society [7:1–13]. The prophet continues to give us a phantasmagoria of snapshots of evil and impending destruction. The geographic names are foreign to us, but the experiences are timeless and always up to date.

7 Woe is me! For I have become
as when the summer fruit has been gathered,
as when the grapes have been gleaned:
there is no cluster to eat,
no first-ripe fig that my soul desires.
2 The godly has perished from the earth,
and there is no one upright among mankind;
they all lie in wait for blood,
and each hunts the other with a net.
3 Their hands are on what is evil, to do it well;
the prince and the judge ask for a bribe,
and the great man utters the evil desire of his soul;
thus they weave it together.
4 The best of them is like a brier,

---

[1] Or steadfast love [2] The meaning of the Hebrew is uncertain [3] Or Are there still treasures [4] Hebrew whose [5] Hebrew For the statutes of Omri are kept
[6] Hebrew its

    the most upright of them a thorn hedge.
  The day of your watchmen, of your punishment, has come;
    now their confusion is at hand.
⁵ Put no trust in a neighbor;
    have no confidence in a friend;
  guard the doors of your mouth
    from her who lies in your arms;[1]
⁶ for the son treats the father with contempt,
    the daughter rises up against her mother,
  the daughter-in-law against her mother-in-law;
    a man's enemies are the men of his own house.
⁷ But as for me, I will look to the LORD;
    I will wait for the God of my salvation;
    my God will hear me.

⁸ Rejoice not over me, O my enemy;
    when I fall, I shall rise;
  when I sit in darkness,
    the LORD will be a light to me.
⁹ I will bear the indignation of the LORD
    because I have sinned against him,
  until he pleads my cause
    and executes judgment for me.
  He will bring me out to the light;
    I shall look upon his vindication.
¹⁰ Then my enemy will see,
    and shame will cover her who said to me,
    "Where is the LORD your God?"
  My eyes will look upon her;
    now she will be trampled down
    like the mire of the streets.

¹¹ A day for the building of your walls!
    In that day the boundary shall be far extended.
¹² In that day they[2] will come to you,
    from Assyria and the cities of Egypt,
  and from Egypt to the River,
    from sea to sea and from mountain to mountain.
¹³ But the earth will be desolate
    because of its inhabitants,
    for the fruit of their deeds.

An oracle of God's mercy [7:14–20]. The OT prophetic books nearly always end with a vision of restoration and a future golden age. Here at the end of the book of Micah, this takes the form of the prophet's prayer addressed to God, highlighting God's forgiveness and compassion.

---

[1] Hebrew *bosom* [2] Hebrew *he*

¹⁴ Shepherd your people with your staff,
    the flock of your inheritance,
who dwell alone in a forest
    in the midst of a garden land;[1]
let them graze in Bashan and Gilead
    as in the days of old.
¹⁵ As in the days when you came out of the land of Egypt,
    I will show them[2] marvelous things.
¹⁶ The nations shall see and be ashamed of all their might;
they shall lay their hands on their mouths;
    their ears shall be deaf;
¹⁷ they shall lick the dust like a serpent,
    like the crawling things of the earth;
they shall come trembling out of their strongholds;
    they shall turn in dread to the Lᴏʀᴅ our God,
    and they shall be in fear of you.

¹⁸ Who is a God like you, pardoning iniquity
    and passing over transgression
    for the remnant of his inheritance?
He does not retain his anger forever,
    because he delights in steadfast love.
¹⁹ He will again have compassion on us;
    he will tread our iniquities underfoot.
You will cast all our[3] sins
    into the depths of the sea.
²⁰ You will show faithfulness to Jacob
    and steadfast love to Abraham,
as you have sworn to our fathers
    from the days of old.

---

[1] Hebrew *of Carmel* [2] Hebrew *him* [3] Hebrew *their*

NAHUM

The book at a glance. 3 chapters, 47 verses. While most OT prophetic books predict God's judgment against Israel and Judah, the prophecy in Nahum is directed against Nineveh, capital city and representative of the nation of Assyria. Because Assyria was a wicked nation, noted especially for its cruelty in warfare, the prophet makes no apology for predicting its destruction. He throws himself into his denunciation of Nineveh with enthusiasm and a taunting tone. Of course literature portrays the universal through the particular, so that what Nahum utters against Nineveh is God's message to all evil nations. Although most OT prophetic books end with a vision of blessing, the book of Nahum omits that conventional ending.

▌**Genres.** The overarching genre is *prophecy, which itself is a multiple form. The book of Nahum consists entirely of *oracles of judgment, with no appearance of an *oracle of redemption or blessing. In the second half of the book we find such genres as the *taunt, the pronouncement of woe (the woe formula), and vivid *narratives of destruction. There is a sense in which the whole book is an extended taunt, and since the imagery and *motifs are consistently military (with God pictured as a divine warrior), we can profitably consider the book war *poetry. (For more information on items accompanied by an asterisk, see the glossary at the back of this Bible.)

Passage	Content	Prophetic Genre	Time Frame
1:1–15	Preview to battle: vision of God as divine warrior about to rescue Judah from Nineveh	Visionary portrait	Anticipation of coming battle
2:1–3:4	Narrative of the coming sack of the city of Nineveh	Visionary narrative	Present-tense narrative of a future event
3:5–19	Postmortem taunting of the fallen city of Nineveh	Taunt song	Present- and future-tense account of a coming event

▌**Format.** The book of Nahum is constructed on a simple two-part plan. Chapter 1 is a prelude to battle. Chapters 2–3 move from preview to actual battle, pictured as a series of oracles of judgment against Nineveh and vivid pictures of its destruction (narrated as if by an eyewitness reporter). Chapter 2 is a present-tense narrative of the coming sack of Nineveh, while chapter 3 is mainly a taunting of a soon-to-be-destroyed enemy and an explanation of why the city deserves the punishment that will engulf it.

▌Inferred literary intentions. The book is designed to achieve the following literary purposes:

- picture God's judgment against an evil and cruel nation

- embody that message of judgment in the genres and motifs of ancient war literature

- evoke a sense of terror at God's judgment of evil

- use the resources of poetry to awaken our imagination

▌Theological themes. (1) The justice of God: the main thrust of the book is to assert God's anger against evil. (2) The moral responsibility of nations: in this book, God holds a nation responsible for its terrorism and cruelty against enemies. (3) The omnipotence of God: we are led to see that God can execute justice against nations as well as individuals.

▌Nahum as a chapter in the master story of the Bible. The master story of the Bible tells the truth about the evil of the human race and God's ways of dealing with that evil. In the book of Nahum, God deals with evil by punishing it in his holy wrath.

A divine warrior prepares to rescue his people from Nineveh [chapter 1]. The focus of chapter 1 is on God, who is portrayed indirectly by means of an oracle pronounced by the prophet Nahum. From start to finish, Nahum uses the resources of poetry to express his message, with the result that we must interpret the images and metaphors individually and reflectively as the poet puts them before us—images like whirlwind and fire and flood. What is chiefly communicated by these images in chapter 1 is the power of God. In chapter 1, the end to which God intends to put his power is judgment against his adversaries, that is, the Assyrians. As an implied plot unfolds, moreover, we learn in verses 12–15 that the prophesied judgment against Nineveh will be a *rescue story so far as Judah is concerned.

---

1 An oracle concerning Nineveh. The book of the vision of Nahum of Elkosh.

² The LORD is a jealous and avenging God;
  the LORD is avenging and wrathful;
the LORD takes vengeance on his adversaries
  and keeps wrath for his enemies.
³ The LORD is slow to anger and great in power,
  and the LORD will by no means clear the guilty.
His way is in whirlwind and storm,
  and the clouds are the dust of his feet.
⁴ He rebukes the sea and makes it dry;
  he dries up all the rivers;
Bashan and Carmel wither;
  the bloom of Lebanon withers.
⁵ The mountains quake before him;

the hills melt;
the earth heaves before him,
the world and all who dwell in it.

⁶ Who can stand before his indignation?
Who can endure the heat of his anger?
His wrath is poured out like fire,
and the rocks are broken into pieces by him.

⁷ The Lord is good,
a stronghold in the day of trouble;
he knows those who take refuge in him.

⁸ But with an overflowing flood
he will make a complete end of the adversaries,[1]
and will pursue his enemies into darkness.

⁹ What do you plot against the Lord?
He will make a complete end;
trouble will not rise up a second time.

¹⁰ For they are like entangled thorns,
like drunkards as they drink;
they are consumed like stubble fully dried.

¹¹ From you came one
who plotted evil against the Lord,
a worthless counselor.

¹² Thus says the Lord,
"Though they are at full strength and many,
they will be cut down and pass away.
Though I have afflicted you,
I will afflict you no more.

¹³ And now I will break his yoke from off you
and will burst your bonds apart."

¹⁴ The Lord has given commandment about you:
"No more shall your name be perpetuated;
from the house of your gods I will cut off
the carved image and the metal image.
I will make your grave, for you are vile."

¹⁵² Behold, upon the mountains, the feet of him
who brings good news,
who publishes peace!
Keep your feasts, O Judah;
fulfill your vows,
for never again shall the worthless pass through you;
he is utterly cut off.

The predicted siege and sack of Nineveh [2:1–3:4]. Prophecy makes extensive use of the rhetorical device of *reversal, and in this chapter the prophet speaks of Nineveh

---

[1] Hebrew *of her place* [2] Ch 2:1 in Hebrew

(a city still at its height as Nahum wrote) as already undergoing siege and destruction. The mode continues to be poetry, so we need to take the time to unpack the images and metaphors. The chapter evokes the actual terror of an attack and defeat.

2 The scatterer has come up against you.
Man the ramparts;
  watch the road;
dress for battle;[1]
  collect all your strength.

[2] For the LORD is restoring the majesty of Jacob
  as the majesty of Israel,
for plunderers have plundered them
  and ruined their branches.

[3] The shield of his mighty men is red;
  his soldiers are clothed in scarlet.
The chariots come with flashing metal
  on the day he musters them;
  the cypress spears are brandished.
[4] The chariots race madly through the streets;
  they rush to and fro through the squares;
they gleam like torches;
  they dart like lightning.
[5] He remembers his officers;
  they stumble as they go,
they hasten to the wall;
  the siege tower[2] is set up.
[6] The river gates are opened;
  the palace melts away;
[7] its mistress[3] is stripped;[4] she is carried off,
  her slave girls lamenting,
moaning like doves
  and beating their breasts.
[8] Nineveh is like a pool
  whose waters run away.[5]
"Halt! Halt!" they cry,
  but none turns back.
[9] Plunder the silver,
  plunder the gold!
There is no end of the treasure
  or of the wealth of all precious things.

[10] Desolate! Desolation and ruin!
  Hearts melt and knees tremble;
anguish is in all loins;
  all faces grow pale!

[1] Hebrew *gird your loins* [2] Or *the mantelet* [3] The meaning of the Hebrew word rendered *its mistress* is uncertain [4] Or *exiled* [5] Compare Septuagint; the meaning of the Hebrew is uncertain

¹¹ Where is the lions' den,
    the feeding place of the young lions,
    where the lion and lioness went,
    where his cubs were, with none to disturb?
¹² The lion tore enough for his cubs
    and strangled prey for his lionesses;
    he filled his caves with prey
    and his dens with torn flesh.

¹³Behold, I am against you, declares the Lord of hosts, and I will burn your¹ chariots in smoke, and the sword shall devour your young lions. I will cut off your prey from the earth, and the voice of your messengers shall no longer be heard.

3 Woe to the bloody city,
    all full of lies and plunder—
    no end to the prey!
² The crack of the whip, and rumble of the wheel,
    galloping horse and bounding chariot!
³ Horsemen charging,
    flashing sword and glittering spear,
hosts of slain,
    heaps of corpses,
dead bodies without end—
    they stumble over the bodies!
⁴ And all for the countless whorings of the prostitute,
    graceful and of deadly charms,
who betrays nations with her whorings,
    and peoples with her charms.

Explanation for Nineveh's defeat [3:5–19]. There is progression from the narrative account of the siege and fall of Nineveh in the preceding unit to a postmortem taunting of Nineveh. The explanation begins with an assertion from God himself that he is against Nineveh (v. 5). After that, three ingredients are mingled together—prediction of the destruction that God will orchestrate against Nineveh, taunting of Nineveh (with the writer implicitly celebrating the bad things that will happen to Nineveh), and intermittent hints of the justice of what will befall Nineveh (vv. 8–10, 16, end of 19). Once again, the vividness of the poetry is what gives the passage much of its power.

⁵ Behold, I am against you,
    declares the Lord of hosts,
    and will lift up your skirts over your face;
and I will make nations look at your nakedness
    and kingdoms at your shame.
⁶ I will throw filth at you
    and treat you with contempt
    and make you a spectacle.
⁷ And all who look at you will shrink from you and say,

¹ Hebrew *her*

Wasted is Nineveh; who will grieve for her?
Where shall I seek comforters for you?

⁸ Are you better than Thebes[1]
    that sat by the Nile,
with water around her,
    her rampart a sea,
    and water her wall?
⁹ Cush was her strength;
    Egypt too, and that without limit;
    Put and the Libyans were her[2] helpers.

¹⁰ Yet she became an exile;
    she went into captivity;
her infants were dashed in pieces
    at the head of every street;
for her honored men lots were cast,
    and all her great men were bound in chains.
¹¹ You also will be drunken;
    you will go into hiding;
you will seek a refuge from the enemy.
¹² All your fortresses are like fig trees
    with first-ripe figs—
if shaken they fall
    into the mouth of the eater.
¹³ Behold, your troops
    are women in your midst.
The gates of your land
    are wide open to your enemies;
    fire has devoured your bars.

¹⁴ Draw water for the siege;
    strengthen your forts;
go into the clay;
    tread the mortar;
    take hold of the brick mold!
¹⁵ There will the fire devour you;
    the sword will cut you off.
    It will devour you like the locust.
Multiply yourselves like the locust;
    multiply like the grasshopper!
¹⁶ You increased your merchants
    more than the stars of the heavens.
    The locust spreads its wings and flies away.

¹⁷ Your princes are like grasshoppers,
    your scribes[3] like clouds of locusts
settling on the fences

---

¹ Hebrew No-amon ² Hebrew your ³ Or marshals

in a day of cold—
  when the sun rises, they fly away;
    no one knows where they are.

¹⁸ Your shepherds are asleep,
    O king of Assyria;
      your nobles slumber.
  Your people are scattered on the mountains
    with none to gather them.
¹⁹ There is no easing your hurt;
    your wound is grievous.
  All who hear the news about you
    clap their hands over you.
  For upon whom has not come
    your unceasing evil?

HABAKKUK

The book at a glance. 3 chapters, 56 verses. All of the so-called twelve minor prophets of the OT have their distinctive features, so there is no sense of monotony as we move from one to the next. Habakkuk is the prophet who asked two questions that God answered at length and who then responded with a great prayer testifying to his faith in God. More specifically, the prophet expresses questions and doubts regarding God's justice and management of the world. The book of Habakkuk has affinities with the branch of philosophy known as theodicy (reconciling God's goodness toward the human race and his omnipotence, considered within a context of evil and suffering), inasmuch as the prophet's response of faith in the third chapter demonstrates that for him the power and goodness of God have been satisfactorily reconciled with the evil and suffering that he sees in the world. The most famous part of the book is the prophet's great testimony that he will maintain faith in God even if his external situation becomes disastrous (3:17–19).

▌Genres and format. In general, the book of Habakkuk does not follow the familiar contours of OT prophecy. The exception is that God's two answers to Habakkuk's questions (1:5–11; 2:2–20) fall into the genre known as *oracle of judgment. But other forms dominate our overall impression. The first two chapters fall into the dramatic format of dialogue; more specifically, they are question-and-answer exchanges between the prophet and God. The prophet's vision of God's appearance (3:3–15) is a *visionary *theophany, and it is followed by a personal testimony (3:17–19). Overall, the first-person format of the dialogue, the visionary theophany, and the testimony make the book read like a personal diary or journal. (For more information on items accompanied by an asterisk, see the glossary at the back of this Bible.)

▌Additional patterns. The prophet complains twice, listens to God twice, and prays once (chapter 3). There are two oracles from God (1:5–11; 2:2–20) and one vision of God (3:3–15). In the first two chapters, the prophet's faith is troubled; in chapter 3, it is triumphant. Two chapters tells us what God is doing, followed by a chapter that demonstrates who God is.

▌Inferred literary intentions. The book is designed to achieve the following literary purposes:

- give an account of God's design for the world in the form of a question-and-answer dialogue

Passage	Content	Prophetic Genre	Scene of Action
1:1–4	Habakkuk asks God his first question	Formal complaint	The prophet's own nation of Judah
1:5–11	God's reply	Oracle of judgment	
1:12–2:1	Habakkuk asks God his second question	Formal complaint	The world empire of Chaldea
2:2–20	God's reply to Habakkuk's question	Oracle of judgment using a fivefold woe formula	
3:1–15	Habakkuk's vision of God's power and sovereignty	Psalm of praise	The whole earth
3:16–19	Habakkuk's confession of faith in God in all circumstances	Personal testimony	The prophet's own soul

■ express the prophet's thoughts and feelings in a first-person format

■ express the content in highly poetic manner

■ move us to share the author's submission to God and his sovereign purpose

▌**Theological themes.** (1) The nature of God: in all the diverse genres of the book, we are led to contemplate God's justice, sovereignty, and trustworthiness. (2) Human sinfulness: the oracles of judgment are a typical prophetic anatomy of the evil of people and nations. (3) The nature of faith: the prophet's final statement of faith occupies the climactic position in the book and as such represents the correct response to the declarations and vision of God that have preceded it.

▌**The book of Habakkuk as a chapter in the master story of the Bible.** The master story of the Bible is the story of what God does. In the book of Habakkuk, God himself declares part of his grand design in the specific form of managing the world in justice. The corresponding human story in the Bible is how people should respond to this great God, and the concluding verses of Habakkuk tell part of that story.

> **The first question and answer** [1:1–11]. The prophet's opening question (vv. 1–4) is why God does not do something about the violence that is going on in his own society. The reply of God (vv. 5–11) is an oracle of judgment in which God reveals that he plans to use the nation of Chaldea or Babylon to punish Judah for its violence.

1 The oracle that Habakkuk the prophet saw.

2 O Lord, how long shall I cry for help,
   and you will not hear?
Or cry to you "Violence!"
   and you will not save?
3 Why do you make me see iniquity,
   and why do you idly look at wrong?
Destruction and violence are before me;

strife and contention arise.
4 So the law is paralyzed,
   and justice never goes forth.
For the wicked surround the righteous;
   so justice goes forth perverted.

5 "Look among the nations, and see;
   wonder and be astounded.
For I am doing a work in your days
   that you would not believe if told.
6 For behold, I am raising up the Chaldeans,
   that bitter and hasty nation,
who march through the breadth of the earth,
   to seize dwellings not their own.
7 They are dreaded and fearsome;
   their justice and dignity go forth from themselves.
8 Their horses are swifter than leopards,
   more fierce than the evening wolves;
   their horsemen press proudly on.
Their horsemen come from afar;
   they fly like an eagle swift to devour.
9 They all come for violence,
   all their faces forward.
They gather captives like sand.
10 At kings they scoff,
   and at rulers they laugh.
They laugh at every fortress,
   for they pile up earth and take it.
11 Then they sweep by like the wind and go on,
   guilty men, whose own might is their god!"

The second question and answer [1:12–2:20]. The prophet's second question (1:12–2:1) is why God would use an even more violent nation than Judah to punish Judah. God's answer is an oracle of judgment in which he predicts that eventually he will judge Babylon also. A main rhetorical feature of God's reply is a fivefold appearance of the common "woe" formula of biblical prophecy.

12 Are you not from everlasting,
   O Lᴏʀᴅ my God, my Holy One?
   We shall not die.
O Lᴏʀᴅ, you have ordained them as a judgment,
   and you, O Rock, have established them for reproof.
13 You who are of purer eyes than to see evil
   and cannot look at wrong,
why do you idly look at traitors
   and remain silent when the wicked swallows up
   the man more righteous than he?

14 You make mankind like the fish of the sea,
　　like crawling things that have no ruler.
15 He brings all of them up with a hook;
　　he drags them out with his net;
　he gathers them in his dragnet;
　　so he rejoices and is glad.
16 Therefore he sacrifices to his net
　　and makes offerings to his dragnet;
　for by them he lives in luxury,[1]
　　and his food is rich.
17 Is he then to keep on emptying his net
　　and mercilessly killing nations forever?

2 I will take my stand at my watchpost
　　and station myself on the tower,
　and look out to see what he will say to me,
　　and what I will answer concerning my complaint.

²And the Lord answered me:

"Write the vision;
　　make it plain on tablets,
　　so he may run who reads it.
3 For still the vision awaits its appointed time;
　　it hastens to the end—it will not lie.
　If it seems slow, wait for it;
　　it will surely come; it will not delay.

4 "Behold, his soul is puffed up; it is not upright within him,
　　but the righteous shall live by his faith.[2]

5 "Moreover, wine[3] is a traitor,
　　an arrogant man who is never at rest.[4]
　His greed is as wide as Sheol;
　　like death he has never enough.
　He gathers for himself all nations
　　and collects as his own all peoples."

⁶Shall not all these take up their taunt against him, with scoffing and riddles for him, and say,

"Woe to him who heaps up what is not his own—
　　for how long?—
　　and loads himself with pledges!"
7 Will not your debtors suddenly arise,
　　and those awake who will make you tremble?
　　Then you will be spoil for them.
8 Because you have plundered many nations,
　　all the remnant of the peoples shall plunder you,

---

[1] Hebrew *his portion is fat* [2] Or *faithfulness* [3] Masoretic Text; Dead Sea Scroll *wealth* [4] The meaning of the Hebrew of these two lines is uncertain

for the blood of man and violence to the earth,
     to cities and all who dwell in them.

9   "Woe to him who gets evil gain for his house,
     to set his nest on high,
     to be safe from the reach of harm!
10   You have devised shame for your house
     by cutting off many peoples;
     you have forfeited your life.
11   For the stone will cry out from the wall,
     and the beam from the woodwork respond.

12   "Woe to him who builds a town with blood
     and founds a city on iniquity!
13   Behold, is it not from the Lord of hosts
     that peoples labor merely for fire,
     and nations weary themselves for nothing?
14   For the earth will be filled
     with the knowledge of the glory of the Lord
     as the waters cover the sea.

15   "Woe to him who makes his neighbors drink—
     you pour out your wrath and make them drunk,
     in order to gaze at their nakedness!
16   You will have your fill of shame instead of glory.
     Drink, yourself, and show your uncircumcision!
     The cup in the Lord's right hand
     will come around to you,
     and utter shame will come upon your glory!
17   The violence done to Lebanon will overwhelm you,
     as will the destruction of the beasts that terrified them,
     for the blood of man and violence to the earth,
     to cities and all who dwell in them.

18   "What profit is an idol
     when its maker has shaped it,
     a metal image, a teacher of lies?
     For its maker trusts in his own creation
     when he makes speechless idols!
19   Woe to him who says to a wooden thing, Awake;
     to a silent stone, Arise!
     Can this teach?
     Behold, it is overlaid with gold and silver,
     and there is no breath at all in it.
20   But the Lord is in his holy temple;
     let all the earth keep silence before him."

A vision of God, followed by the prophet's response [chapter 3]. We should note at the outset that this chapter is the very touchstone of *poetry, which means that we need to take time to unpack the meanings of the images and figures of speech. The vision of God (vv. 3–15) is an imagined theophany that parallels some of the portraits of God in the Psalms (e.g., Ps. 18:7–15). The poet's response consists of two parts—a narrative of his reverence and submission to God (v. 16) and his personal testimony of faith (vv. 17–19).

3

A prayer of Habakkuk the prophet, according to Shigionoth.

² O LORD, I have heard the report of you,
  and your work, O LORD, do I fear.
In the midst of the years revive it;
  in the midst of the years make it known;
  in wrath remember mercy.

³ God came from Teman,
  and the Holy One from Mount Paran.
His splendor covered the heavens,
  and the earth was full of his praise.   *Selah*

⁴ His brightness was like the light;
  rays flashed from his hand;
  and there he veiled his power.

⁵ Before him went pestilence,
  and plague followed at his heels.[1]

⁶ He stood and measured the earth;
  he looked and shook the nations;
then the eternal mountains were scattered;
  the everlasting hills sank low.
  His were the everlasting ways.

⁷ I saw the tents of Cushan in affliction;
  the curtains of the land of Midian did tremble.

⁸ Was your wrath against the rivers, O LORD?
  Was your anger against the rivers,
  or your indignation against the sea,
when you rode on your horses,
  on your chariot of salvation?

⁹ You stripped the sheath from your bow,
  calling for many arrows.[2]   *Selah*
  You split the earth with rivers.

¹⁰ The mountains saw you and writhed;
  the raging waters swept on;
the deep gave forth its voice;
  it lifted its hands on high.

¹¹ The sun and moon stood still in their place
  at the light of your arrows as they sped,
  at the flash of your glittering spear.

¹² You marched through the earth in fury;

---

[1] Hebrew *feet* [2] The meaning of the Hebrew line is uncertain

you threshed the nations in anger.
¹³ You went out for the salvation of your people,
    for the salvation of your anointed.
You crushed the head of the house of the wicked,
    laying him bare from thigh to neck.[1]   *Selah*
¹⁴ You pierced with his own arrows the heads of his warriors,
    who came like a whirlwind to scatter me,
    rejoicing as if to devour the poor in secret.
¹⁵ You trampled the sea with your horses,
    the surging of mighty waters.

¹⁶ I hear, and my body trembles;
    my lips quiver at the sound;
rottenness enters into my bones;
    my legs tremble beneath me.
Yet I will quietly wait for the day of trouble
    to come upon people who invade us.

¹⁷ Though the fig tree should not blossom,
    nor fruit be on the vines,
the produce of the olive fail
    and the fields yield no food,
the flock be cut off from the fold
    and there be no herd in the stalls,
¹⁸ yet I will rejoice in the LORD;
    I will take joy in the God of my salvation.
¹⁹ GOD, the Lord, is my strength;
    he makes my feet like the deer's;
    he makes me tread on my high places.

To the choirmaster: with stringed[2] instruments.

---

[1] The meaning of the Hebrew line is uncertain [2] Hebrew *my stringed*

ZEPHANIAH

The book at a glance. 3 chapters, 53 verses. The purpose of this prophetic book is to predict the coming judgment of God against Judah and against surrounding pagan nations, with a complementary vision of God's restoration of a remnant of his people at the end of the book. The distinctive feature of the book of Zephaniah is that this vision of judgment is couched in the *motif of a coming "day of the LORD." As the variations on this theme accumulate, it becomes evident that there is a specific and immediate day of the Lord coming for Judah but also intermediate days of the Lord that will occur later in history, as well as an ultimate, eschatological day of the Lord that will occur at the end of human history. The certainty of God's favor to those trust in him for salvation climaxes the book and brings it to conclusion.

▌Genres. In format, the book of Zephaniah is a typical work of *prophecy, but with distinctive features woven into the tapestry. The primary genre within this prophetic book is the *oracle of judgment, with an *oracle of salvation coming at the expected place: the end. Whereas most OT prophetic books intermingle descriptions and denunciations of a nation's vices with predictions of judgment against them, Zephaniah largely dispenses with social critique and simply predicts a coming day of the Lord. The medium is *poetry, with its universalizing tendency, in place of contemporary historical references. (For more information on items accompanied by an asterisk, see the glossary at the back of this Bible.)

Passage	Content	Prophetic Genre	Scene of Action
1:1–18	Prediction of divine judgment against Judah	Oracle of judgment	Nation of Judah
2:1–3	Call to repentance	Formal summons	
2:4–15	Prediction of God's judgment against the nations	Oracle of judgment	Surrounding pagan nations
3:1–8	Pronouncement of woe against Jerusalem	Oracle of judgment	Jerusalem (and by extension Judah)
3:9–20	God's promise to restore the fortunes of his people	Oracle of salvation; golden age prophecy	Christ's kingdom, now and in the eschaton

▌Inferred literary intentions. The book is designed to achieve the following literary purposes:

- picture God's judgment of sin by means of the motif of a coming day of the Lord

- use the resources of poetry to paint vivid word-pictures of the coming judgment

- evoke fear of the coming judgment with a view to awakening repentance

- convey the possibility of God's blessing through a concluding oracle of restored favor with God

Theological themes. (1) God's anger: one of God's attributes is his anger against sin, and the book of Zephaniah is a primary text on that subject. (2) Repentance: intermingled with the visions of judgment are explicit or implied calls to repentance as the desired response to the pictures of doom. (3) Redemption: at the end we see that God's intention is to save a remnant.

The book of Zephaniah as a chapter in the master story of the Bible. The master story of the Bible tells what God does about the sinfulness of the human race. In the book of Zephaniah we see the double thread in that story—God's judgment against sin coupled with his call to people to repent and the salvation that comes when they do repent.

Oracle of judgment against evil Judah [1:1–2:3]. Following an inscription that gives us the author and date of the prophecy, Zephaniah launches at once into an oracle of judgment against his own nation. The poetic images and metaphors tumble onto the page in a crescendo of energetic predictions of destruction. It is the equivalent of a *horror story—a hunting down of a victim by an omnipotent judge. But just when there seems to be no possibility of escape, a door opens in the form of a formal summons to repent and be kept from harm on the day of the Lord (2:1–3).

1 The word of the LORD that came to Zephaniah the son of Cushi, son of Gedaliah, son of Amariah, son of Hezekiah, in the days of Josiah the son of Amon, king of Judah.

2 "I will utterly sweep away everything
    from the face of the earth," declares the LORD.
3 "I will sweep away man and beast;
    I will sweep away the birds of the heavens
    and the fish of the sea,
  and the rubble[1] with the wicked.
    I will cut off mankind
    from the face of the earth," declares the LORD.
4 "I will stretch out my hand against Judah
    and against all the inhabitants of Jerusalem;
  and I will cut off from this place the remnant of Baal
    and the name of the idolatrous priests along with the priests,
5 those who bow down on the roofs
    to the host of the heavens,
  those who bow down and swear to the LORD
    and yet swear by Milcom,

---

[1] Or *stumbling blocks* (that is, idols)

⁶ those who have turned back from following the LORD,
    who do not seek the LORD or inquire of him."

⁷ Be silent before the Lord GOD!
    For the day of the LORD is near;
  the LORD has prepared a sacrifice
    and consecrated his guests.
⁸ And on the day of the LORD's sacrifice—
  "I will punish the officials and the king's sons
    and all who array themselves in foreign attire.
⁹ On that day I will punish
    everyone who leaps over the threshold,
  and those who fill their master's¹ house
    with violence and fraud.

¹⁰ "On that day," declares the LORD,
    "a cry will be heard from the Fish Gate,
  a wail from the Second Quarter,
    a loud crash from the hills.
¹¹ Wail, O inhabitants of the Mortar!
    For all the traders² are no more;
  all who weigh out silver are cut off.
¹² At that time I will search Jerusalem with lamps,
    and I will punish the men
  who are complacent,³
    those who say in their hearts,
  'The LORD will not do good,
    nor will he do ill.'
¹³ Their goods shall be plundered,
    and their houses laid waste.
  Though they build houses,
    they shall not inhabit them;
  though they plant vineyards,
    they shall not drink wine from them."

¹⁴ The great day of the LORD is near,
    near and hastening fast;
  the sound of the day of the LORD is bitter;
    the mighty man cries aloud there.
¹⁵ A day of wrath is that day,
    a day of distress and anguish,
  a day of ruin and devastation,
    a day of darkness and gloom,
  a day of clouds and thick darkness,
¹⁶   a day of trumpet blast and battle cry
  against the fortified cities
    and against the lofty battlements.

---

¹ Or their Lord's ² Or all the people of Canaan ³ Hebrew are thickening on the dregs [of their wine]

17 I will bring distress on mankind,
    so that they shall walk like the blind,
    because they have sinned against the LORD;
their blood shall be poured out like dust,
    and their flesh like dung.
18 Neither their silver nor their gold
    shall be able to deliver them
    on the day of the wrath of the LORD.
In the fire of his jealousy,
    all the earth shall be consumed;
for a full and sudden end
    he will make of all the inhabitants of the earth.

2 Gather together, yes, gather,
    O shameless nation,
2 before the decree takes effect[1]
    —before the day passes away like chaff—
before there comes upon you
    the burning anger of the LORD,
before there comes upon you
    the day of the anger of the LORD.
3 Seek the LORD, all you humble of the land,
    who do his just commands;[2]
seek righteousness; seek humility;
    perhaps you may be hidden
    on the day of the anger of the LORD.

Oracle of judgment against surrounding pagan nations [2:4–15]. The names of the guilty change in this section, but the rhetoric remains the same—a series of oracles of judgment against nations.

4 For Gaza shall be deserted,
    and Ashkelon shall become a desolation;
Ashdod's people shall be driven out at noon,
    and Ekron shall be uprooted.

5 Woe to you inhabitants of the seacoast,
    you nation of the Cherethites!
The word of the LORD is against you,
    O Canaan, land of the Philistines;
    and I will destroy you until no inhabitant is left.
6 And you, O seacoast, shall be pastures,
    with meadows[3] for shepherds
    and folds for flocks.
7 The seacoast shall become the possession
    of the remnant of the house of Judah,
    on which they shall graze,
and in the houses of Ashkelon

---

[1] Hebrew *gives birth* [2] Or *who carry out his judgment* [3] Or *caves*

they shall lie down at evening.
For the Lord their God will be mindful of them
  and restore their fortunes.

8 "I have heard the taunts of Moab
    and the revilings of the Ammonites,
how they have taunted my people
  and made boasts against their territory.

9 Therefore, as I live," declares the Lord of hosts,
    the God of Israel,
"Moab shall become like Sodom,
  and the Ammonites like Gomorrah,
a land possessed by nettles and salt pits,
  and a waste forever.
The remnant of my people shall plunder them,
  and the survivors of my nation shall possess them."

10 This shall be their lot in return for their pride,
    because they taunted and boasted
  against the people of the Lord of hosts.

11 The Lord will be awesome against them;
    for he will famish all the gods of the earth,
and to him shall bow down,
    each in its place,
    all the lands of the nations.

12 You also, O Cushites,
    shall be slain by my sword.

13 And he will stretch out his hand against the north
    and destroy Assyria,
and he will make Nineveh a desolation,
  a dry waste like the desert.

14 Herds shall lie down in her midst,
    all kinds of beasts;[1]
even the owl and the hedgehog[2]
  shall lodge in her capitals;
a voice shall hoot in the window;
  devastation will be on the threshold;
  for her cedar work will be laid bare.

15 This is the exultant city
    that lived securely,
that said in her heart,
  "I am, and there is no one else."
What a desolation she has become,
  a lair for wild beasts!
Everyone who passes by her
  hisses and shakes his fist.

---

[1] Hebrew *beasts of every nation* [2] The identity of the animals rendered *owl* and *hedgehog* is uncertain

3 Woe to her who is rebellious and defiled,
    the oppressing city!
2 She listens to no voice;
    she accepts no correction.
She does not trust in the Lord;
    she does not draw near to her God.

3 Her officials within her
    are roaring lions;
her judges are evening wolves
    that leave nothing till the morning.
4 Her prophets are fickle, treacherous men;
her priests profane what is holy;
    they do violence to the law.
5 The Lord within her is righteous;
    he does no injustice;
every morning he shows forth his justice;
    each dawn he does not fail;
    but the unjust knows no shame.

6 "I have cut off nations;
    their battlements are in ruins;
I have laid waste their streets
    so that no one walks in them;
their cities have been made desolate,
    without a man, without an inhabitant.
7 I said, 'Surely you will fear me;
    you will accept correction.
Then your[1] dwelling would not be cut off
    according to all that I have appointed against you.'[2]
But all the more they were eager
    to make all their deeds corrupt.

8 "Therefore wait for me," declares the Lord,
    "for the day when I rise up to seize the prey.
For my decision is to gather nations,
    to assemble kingdoms,
to pour out upon them my indignation,
    all my burning anger;
for in the fire of my jealousy
    all the earth shall be consumed.

---

[1] Hebrew *her* [2] Hebrew *her*

pictured as bringing their tribute specifically to Israel/Jerusalem/Zion, the open-ended nature of the blessings portrayed in this vision makes it plausible to believe that it is intended as a symbolic or metaphoric picture of God's blessings to the redeemed in the eschaton and in heaven.

9　"For at that time I will change the speech of the peoples
　　　to a pure speech,
　　that all of them may call upon the name of the LORD
　　　and serve him with one accord.
10　From beyond the rivers of Cush
　　　my worshipers, the daughter of my dispersed ones,
　　　shall bring my offering.

11　"On that day you shall not be put to shame
　　　because of the deeds by which you have rebelled against me;
　　for then I will remove from your midst
　　　your proudly exultant ones,
　　and you shall no longer be haughty
　　　in my holy mountain.
12　But I will leave in your midst
　　　a people humble and lowly.
　　They shall seek refuge in the name of the LORD,
13　　　those who are left in Israel;
　　they shall do no injustice
　　　and speak no lies,
　　nor shall there be found in their mouth
　　　a deceitful tongue.
　　For they shall graze and lie down,
　　　and none shall make them afraid."

14　Sing aloud, O daughter of Zion;
　　　shout, O Israel!
　　Rejoice and exult with all your heart,
　　　O daughter of Jerusalem!
15　The LORD has taken away the judgments against you;
　　　he has cleared away your enemies.
　　The King of Israel, the LORD, is in your midst;
　　　you shall never again fear evil.
16　On that day it shall be said to Jerusalem:
　　"Fear not, O Zion;
　　　let not your hands grow weak.
17　The LORD your God is in your midst,
　　　a mighty one who will save;
　　he will rejoice over you with gladness;
　　　he will quiet you by his love;
　　he will exult over you with loud singing.
18　I will gather those of you who mourn for the festival,

so that you will no longer suffer reproach.[1]

19 Behold, at that time I will deal
    with all your oppressors.
And I will save the lame
    and gather the outcast,
and I will change their shame into praise
    and renown in all the earth.
20 At that time I will bring you in,
    at the time when I gather you together;
for I will make you renowned and praised
    among all the peoples of the earth,
when I restore your fortunes
    before your eyes," says the LORD.

---

[1] The meaning of the Hebrew is uncertain

HAGGAI

The book at a glance. 2 chapters, 38 verses. Whereas most OT prophetic books predict a coming exile for either Israel or Judah, the book of Haggai springs a surprise on us: it is addressed to exiles of Judah who have returned to Palestine after the Babylonian captivity. The prophecy has a specific occasion—the returned exiles' procrastination regarding the task of rebuilding the temple. Underlying the prophet's oracles is a cause-effect principle: the nation's depressed fortunes are linked to disobedience in regard to the rebuilding of the temple, while the restoration of their fortunes is linked to obedience in the matter. Because Zerubbabel was the ruler in charge of the nation at the time (see Ezra 1–6 for the details), the book is addressed to Zerubbabel instead of to the nation.

▌Genres and format.

Although the book of Haggai falls under the general rubric of *prophecy, it does not strike us as a typical prophetic book. It is written in prose instead of the customary *poetry. Although there are predictions of promised blessing, there are no *oracles of judgment in the usual sense. Instead, God simply calls the nation's attention to its low ebb, as though judgment had already occurred. We also find intermittent *golden age visions, as well as a *narrative episode (1:12–15). (For more information on items accompanied by an asterisk, see the glossary at the back of this Bible.)

Passage	Content	Prophetic Genre	Prevailing Mood	Story Line
1:1–11	A problem defined: the nation's lack of prosperity, linked to its failure to rebuild the temple	Prophetic rebuke	Languishing	Completion of the temple
1:12–15	The rebuilding of the temple	Narrative	Industriousness	
2:1–9	Reward for rebuilding the temple	Oracle of blessing	Encouragement	The glory of the temple
2:10–19	Promise of blessing for rebuilding the temple	Oracle of blessing	Hope and anticipation	Present blessing for obedience
2:20–23	Prophetic vision of evil defeated and God's ruler triumphant	Oracle of salvation, both messianic and apocalyptic	Longing	Promise of future blessing

▌A book about priorities. Though focusing on a specific instance (the rebuilding of the temple), Haggai is a relevant and timeless book on the need to put God's work first in our lives. For the prophet's society, rebuilding the temple was the visible sign of the people's determination to put God first; for us, the signs of supreme allegiance are other things. Because the book links the nation's blessing to its rebuilding of the temple, the theme is established that God's people cannot expect to enjoy his blessings without commitment to him.

▌Inferred literary intention. The book is designed to achieve the following literary purposes:

- allow us to relive a specific instance of the contrast between putting God second in life and putting him first

- paint vivid pictures of a nation languishing and a nation prospering

- give us a blueprint for living in a way that results in God's blessing

- express truth in striking *aphorisms

▌Theological themes. (1) The sovereignty of God: the book of Haggai exemplifies a view of history in which a people's blessing or misery is the result of their obedience or disobedience to God. (2) Worship: inasmuch as the rebuilding of the temple is the crucial test of the people's loyalty to God in this book, we can infer that God places supreme importance on worship of him.

▌The book of Haggai as a chapter in the master story of the Bible. The story of the Bible is partly the story of God's dealings with his covenant people. The covenant people in the book of Haggai are a remnant who returned to Palestine after the Babylonian captivity. God's dealings with them in judgment and blessing are a microcosm of how he deals with his people universally. Additionally, in the OT the temple was the special place of God's presence with his people, and the emphasis on the temple in Haggai fits with that understanding.

Rebuilding the temple [chapter 1]. The organization of the chapter follows a classic problem-solution format. The problem that is set forth is as follows: a reporting of the procrastination of the remnant in rebuilding the temple (vv. 1–2); a message from God asking the people simply to observe their languishing under God's judgment (vv. 3–11); a narrative of the rebuilding the temple (vv. 12–15). The rhetorical format of the message from God is the prophet's report of it.

---

1 In the second year of Darius the king, in the sixth month, on the first day of the month, the word of the LORD came by the hand of Haggai the prophet to Zerubbabel the son of Shealtiel, governor of Judah, and to Joshua the son of Jehozadak, the high priest: ²"Thus says the LORD of hosts: These people say the time has not yet come to rebuild the house of the LORD." ³Then the word of the LORD came by the hand of Haggai the prophet, ⁴"Is it a time for you yourselves to dwell in your

paneled houses, while this house lies in ruins? ⁵Now, therefore, thus says the Lᴏʀᴅ of hosts: Consider your ways. ⁶You have sown much, and harvested little. You eat, but you never have enough; you drink, but you never have your fill. You clothe your-selves, but no one is warm. And he who earns wages does so to put them into a bag with holes.

⁷"Thus says the Lᴏʀᴅ of hosts: Consider your ways. ⁸Go up to the hills and bring wood and build the house, that I may take pleasure in it and that I may be glorified, says the Lᴏʀᴅ. ⁹You looked for much, and behold, it came to little. And when you brought it home, I blew it away. Why? declares the Lᴏʀᴅ of hosts. Because of my house that lies in ruins, while each of you busies himself with his own house. ¹⁰Therefore the heavens above you have withheld the dew, and the earth has with-held its produce. ¹¹And I have called for a drought on the land and the hills, on the grain, the new wine, the oil, on what the ground brings forth, on man and beast, and on all their labors."

¹²Then Zerubbabel the son of Shealtiel, and Joshua the son of Jehozadak, the high priest, with all the remnant of the people, obeyed the voice of the Lᴏʀᴅ their God, and the words of Haggai the prophet, as the Lᴏʀᴅ their God had sent him. And the people feared the Lᴏʀᴅ. ¹³Then Haggai, the messenger of the Lᴏʀᴅ, spoke to the people with the Lᴏʀᴅ's message, "I am with you, declares the Lᴏʀᴅ." ¹⁴And the Lᴏʀᴅ stirred up the spirit of Zerubbabel the son of Shealtiel, governor of Judah, and the spirit of Joshua the son of Jehozadak, the high priest, and the spirit of all the remnant of the people. And they came and worked on the house of the Lᴏʀᴅ of hosts, their God, ¹⁵on the twenty-fourth day of the month, in the sixth month, in the second year of Darius the king.

Three visions of blessing [chapter 2]. This unit falls into two similar visions of God's blessing on the remnant, plus a messianic and apocalyptic vision of blessing in the remote future. The first vision of blessing (vv. 1–9) is couched as God's present blessing on the people as a reward for their having been obedient in rebuilding the temple. Part of the vision is a famous and evocative prediction that "the latter glory of this house shall be greater than the former" (v. 9). The second vision (vv. 10–18) is cut from the same cloth as the previous vision, but it is framed as a promise of future blessing, "from this day on" (v. 19). The last vision (vv. 20–23) is a messianic vision that was partly fulfilled with the coming of Christ but also has overtones of an end-times *apocalyptic vision. There is a mystery at work in the vision in the sense that the coming Messiah is called "Zerubbabel my servant" (v. 23).

2 In the seventh month, on the twenty-first day of the month, the word of the Lᴏʀᴅ came by the hand of Haggai the prophet, ²"Speak now to Zerubbabel the son of Shealtiel, governor of Judah, and to Joshua the son of Jehozadak, the high priest, and to all the remnant of the people, and say, ³'Who is left among you who saw this house in its former glory? How do you see it now? Is it not as nothing in your eyes? ⁴Yet now be strong, O Zerubbabel, declares the Lᴏʀᴅ. Be strong, O Joshua, son of Jehozadak, the high priest. Be strong, all you people of the land, declares the Lᴏʀᴅ. Work, for I am with you, declares the Lᴏʀᴅ of hosts, ⁵according to the covenant that I made with you when you came out of Egypt. My Spirit remains in your midst. Fear not. ⁶For thus says the Lᴏʀᴅ of hosts: Yet once more, in a little while, I will shake the heavens and

the earth and the sea and the dry land. ⁷And I will shake all nations, so that the treasures of all nations shall come in, and I will fill this house with glory, says the Lord of hosts. ⁸The silver is mine, and the gold is mine, declares the Lord of hosts. ⁹The latter glory of this house shall be greater than the former, says the Lord of hosts. And in this place I will give peace, declares the Lord of hosts.'"

¹⁰On the twenty-fourth day of the ninth month, in the second year of Darius, the word of the Lord came by Haggai the prophet, ¹¹"Thus says the Lord of hosts: Ask the priests about the law: ¹²'If someone carries holy meat in the fold of his garment and touches with his fold bread or stew or wine or oil or any kind of food, does it become holy?'" The priests answered and said, "No." ¹³Then Haggai said, "If someone who is unclean by contact with a dead body touches any of these, does it become unclean?" The priests answered and said, "It does become unclean." ¹⁴Then Haggai answered and said, "So is it with this people, and with this nation before me, declares the Lord, and so with every work of their hands. And what they offer there is unclean. ¹⁵Now then, consider from this day onward.¹ Before stone was placed upon stone in the temple of the Lord, ¹⁶how did you fare? When² one came to a heap of twenty measures, there were but ten. When one came to the wine vat to draw fifty measures, there were but twenty. ¹⁷I struck you and all the products of your toil with blight and with mildew and with hail, yet you did not turn to me, declares the Lord. ¹⁸Consider from this day onward, from the twenty-fourth day of the ninth month. Since the day that the foundation of the Lord's temple was laid, consider: ¹⁹Is the seed yet in the barn? Indeed, the vine, the fig tree, the pomegranate, and the olive tree have yielded nothing. But from this day on I will bless you."

²⁰The word of the Lord came a second time to Haggai on the twenty-fourth day of the month, ²¹"Speak to Zerubbabel, governor of Judah, saying, I am about to shake the heavens and the earth, ²²and to overthrow the throne of kingdoms. I am about to destroy the strength of the kingdoms of the nations, and overthrow the chariots and their riders. And the horses and their riders shall go down, every one by the sword of his brother. ²³On that day, declares the Lord of hosts, I will take you, O Zerubbabel my servant, the son of Shealtiel, declares the Lord, and make you like a³ signet ring, for I have chosen you, declares the Lord of hosts."

---

¹ Or *backward*; also verse 18 ² Probable reading (compare Septuagint); Hebrew *Lord, since they were. When* ³ Hebrew *the*

ZECHARIAH

The book at a glance. 14 chapters, 211 verses. In terms of length and
complexity, the *prophecy of Zechariah is the major book among what the
ancient Hebrew rabbis called The Twelve (the minor prophets). The original
audience of the book was (as with the book of Haggai) the remnant who had
returned from Babylonian exile. Because of its *visionary and *symbolic modes
and its futuristic orientation, the book of Zechariah (along with the book of
Daniel) is often considered to be the OT parallel to the NT book of Revelation.
Except for the prophecy of Isaiah, Zechariah is the most messianic prophetic
book of the OT. Because of the prevalence of symbolism rather than literal
statement, combined with the telescoping of time that is a common feature of
OT prophetic writing, a leading interpretive task is to disentangle the time
scheme of the book's prophecies. Three time frames are operative—the
imminent future, the intermediate (messianic) future, and the *apocalyptic or
*eschatological future.

▌**Genres.** The main *genre is futuristic prophecy, predicting events that will happen
later in history. Although there are some conventional *oracles of judgment and
*oracles of redemption in the second half of the book, in the first half the preferred
medium is visions that embody in symbolic form what God plans to do. This part of the
book needs to be approached as we approach the NT book of Revelation, that is, by
first allowing the images and symbols to activate our imagination and then exploring
what those details symbolize. Visions and oracles of salvation predominate over ones of
judgment. Because some of the visions are end-times visions, the genre of apocalyptic
vision is important in the book. (For more information on items accompanied by an
asterisk, see the glossary at the back of this Bible.)

▌**Format.** Like other prophetic books, Zechariah is a collection of individual units. In
keeping with its dream format of momentary pictures that follow each other quickly and
partly disjointedly, little *narrative continuity emerges. The nine visions that open the
book are organized like a succession of visual pageants. The oracles that make up the
second half of the book are equally kaleidoscopic in their arrangement, though they are
unified by the *motif of what God will do in blessing his people.

▌**Time frame of the visions.** Prophetic writing often mingles the following time tables:
the time contemporary with the prophet himself; the immediate or near future; the
intermediate future, especially the incarnation and earthly life of Christ; the remote
(end-times) future. The book of Zechariah exemplifies this mingling of times. For

Passage	Content	Prophetic Genre	Time Frame
1:1–6	Introduction to the book	Call of the prophet	
1:7–17	Horsemen's patrol		
1:18–21	Four horns		
2:1–13	Measuring line of Jerusalem		
3:1–10	High priest's garments		Immediate and
4:1–14	Lampstand and olive trees	Prophetic visions	messianic future
5:1–4	Flying scroll		
5:5–11	Woman in the container		
6:1–8	Four chariots		
6:9–15	The branch		
7:1–14	Messages of judgment	Prophetic messages	Messages for
8:1–23	A golden age prophecy		contemporary Judah
9:1–10:12	Visions of future blessing	Oracle of salvation	
11:1–17	Judgment against those who reject God's shepherd	Oracle of judgment	The messianic and eschatological future
12:1–14:21	Visions of ultimate blessing and the triumph of God	Oracle of salvation; golden age prophecy; apocalyptic vision	

example, the opening sequence of nine visions (chapters 1–6) will fall into place more readily if we begin with the prophet's situation, namely, the recent return of exiles to Jerusalem, as they rebuilt the temple and set about to restore the covenant life of the community. The first six chapters are filled with references to the temple and the reinstitution of worship there. In other ways, too, these visions send a message of encouragement to the exiles and their leaders that God is present with them as they start life over in Jerusalem. But as we read we are continuously aware that the *imagery, motifs, and vocabulary reach out beyond the immediate situation to the Messiah and the salvation that he brought with his redeeming death and resurrection, and also to end-times prophecies.

▌ **Inferred literary intentions.** The book is designed to achieve the following literary purposes:

- reveal future events (for the original audience) by means of symbols and visions

- awaken our imagination as a vehicle for assimilating truth

- embody truth in concrete images more than in abstractions, and in symbols more than by direct statement

- awaken a sense of mystery as well as clarity about future events

▌ **Theological themes.** (1) The nature of God: in a book that reveals much about God's actions, we can infer what God is like. (2) Salvation: the book predicts many events in redemptive history. (3) Eschatology: the latter parts of the book reveal what will happen at the end of human history. (4) Holiness: the vision of the change of robe for the high priest (3:1–10) is so striking that it naturally becomes an important picture of holiness that we carry away from the book, as is also true of the famous concluding picture (14:20–21) of the horses' bells and "every pot in Jerusalem and Judah" being holy.

■ **The book of Zechariah as a chapter in the master story of the Bible.** The Bible tells about God's unfolding plan to save a people for himself and to punish those who reject him. This is the basic content of the visions and oracles that make up the book of Zechariah. The book also promises the restoration of a godly king and a holy priesthood for the people of God—promises that find their fulfillment in the ministry of Christ as Priest and King.

> **Introduction and vision of the horse patrol** [1:1–17]. The book opens with a difficult introduction (1:1–6) that has as its main meaning that the nation of Judah must return to the ways of God. This is followed by the memorable vision of a man riding through a grove of myrtle trees on a red horse by night (vv. 7–17). As the strange details unfold, we see other colored horses and hear an angel reassure the rider that "we have patrolled the earth" (v. 11) and that God will restore the fortunes of Jerusalem. At this point we need to consider the context in which the prophet utters his vision: the return of the remnant to Jerusalem to set up a covenant life there. The vision of the horse patrol functions as a vision of God's blessing and favor to his people in their restored society in Jerusalem. But references to Zion quickly telescope beyond the immediate situation to a picture of God's protection of his people in all ages.

1 In the eighth month, in the second year of Darius, the word of the LORD came to the prophet Zechariah, the son of Berechiah, son of Iddo, saying, ²"The LORD was very angry with your fathers. ³Therefore say to them, Thus declares the LORD of hosts: Return to me, says the LORD of hosts, and I will return to you, says the LORD of hosts. ⁴Do not be like your fathers, to whom the former prophets cried out, 'Thus says the LORD of hosts, Return from your evil ways and from your evil deeds.' But they did not hear or pay attention to me, declares the LORD. ⁵Your fathers, where are they? And the prophets, do they live forever? ⁶But my words and my statutes, which I commanded my servants the prophets, did they not overtake your fathers? So they repented and said, As the LORD of hosts purposed to deal with us for our ways and deeds, so has he dealt with us."

⁷On the twenty-fourth day of the eleventh month, which is the month of Shebat, in the second year of Darius, the word of the LORD came to the prophet Zechariah, the son of Berechiah, son of Iddo, saying, ⁸"I saw in the night, and behold, a man riding on a red horse! He was standing among the myrtle trees in the glen, and behind him were red, sorrel, and white horses. ⁹Then I said, 'What are these, my lord?' The angel who talked with me said to me, 'I will show you what they are.' ¹⁰So the man who was standing among the myrtle trees answered, 'These are they whom the LORD has sent to patrol the earth.' ¹¹And they answered the angel of the LORD who was standing among the myrtle trees, and said, 'We have patrolled the earth, and behold, all the earth remains at rest.' ¹²Then the angel of the LORD said, 'O LORD of hosts, how long will you have no mercy on Jerusalem and the cities of Judah, against which you have

been angry these seventy years?' ¹³And the Lord answered gracious and comforting words to the angel who talked with me. ¹⁴So the angel who talked with me said to me, 'Cry out, Thus says the Lord of hosts: I am exceedingly jealous for Jerusalem and for Zion. ¹⁵And I am exceedingly angry with the nations that are at ease; for while I was angry but a little, they furthered the disaster. ¹⁶Therefore, thus says the Lord, I have returned to Jerusalem with mercy; my house shall be built in it, declares the Lord of hosts, and the measuring line shall be stretched out over Jerusalem. ¹⁷Cry out again, Thus says the Lord of hosts: My cities shall again overflow with prosperity, and the Lord will again comfort Zion and again choose Jerusalem.'"

Visions of the horns and smiths, and of the measuring line [1:18–2:13]. The visionary mode continues with a mysterious picture of four horns (symbolic of the nations that had scattered Judah) and four craftsmen (symbolic of the power that will now protect Jerusalem from those nations). Similarly, the visionary act of measuring Jerusalem (chapter 2) symbolizes God's protection of his nation and his restoration of his people in the land to which they have returned. As the vision of blessing unfolds, though, it expands outward from the immediate situation to messianic and eschatological ages, especially in the picture of God's dwelling with his people (2:11).

¹⁸ ¹ And I lifted my eyes and saw, and behold, four horns! ¹⁹And I said to the angel who talked with me, "What are these?" And he said to me, "These are the horns that have scattered Judah, Israel, and Jerusalem." ²⁰Then the Lord showed me four craftsmen. ²¹And I said, "What are these coming to do?" He said, "These are the horns that scattered Judah, so that no one raised his head. And these have come to terrify them, to cast down the horns of the nations who lifted up their horns against the land of Judah to scatter it."

2 ² And I lifted my eyes and saw, and behold, a man with a measuring line in his hand! ²Then I said, "Where are you going?" And he said to me, "To measure Jerusalem, to see what is its width and what is its length." ³And behold, the angel who talked with me came forward, and another angel came forward to meet him ⁴and said to him, "Run, say to that young man, 'Jerusalem shall be inhabited as villages without walls, because of the multitude of people and livestock in it. ⁵And I will be to her a wall of fire all around, declares the Lord, and I will be the glory in her midst.'"

⁶Up! Up! Flee from the land of the north, declares the Lord. For I have spread you abroad as the four winds of the heavens, declares the Lord. ⁷Up! Escape to Zion, you who dwell with the daughter of Babylon. ⁸For thus said the Lord of hosts, after his glory sent me³ to the nations who plundered you, for he who touches you touches the apple of his eye: ⁹"Behold, I will shake my hand over them, and they shall become plunder for those who served them. Then you will know that the Lord of hosts has sent me. ¹⁰Sing and rejoice, O daughter of Zion, for behold, I come and I will dwell in your midst, declares the Lord. ¹¹And many nations shall join themselves to the Lord in that day, and shall be my people. And I will dwell in your midst, and you shall know that the Lord of hosts has sent me to you. ¹²And the Lord will inherit Judah as his portion in the holy land, and will again choose Jerusalem."

¹³Be silent, all flesh, before the Lord, for he has roused himself from his holy dwelling.

¹ Ch 2:1 in Hebrew ² Ch 2:5 in Hebrew ³ Or *he sent me after glory*

The high priest's garments [chapter 3]. This brief visionary narrative is one of the high points of OT prophetic literature. Three main characters make up the cast of characters—the high priest Joshua, the sovereign God, and the accuser Satan. The priest is partly a representative figure here—the one in whom God's people as a whole stand before God, with the related question of whether they will have an acceptable mediator. The main action is the reclothing of the high priest, as his dirty garments are removed and replaced with clean ones (vv. 3–5). This symbolic transformation is a picture of forgiveness and new life—a mini–conversion story. It is followed by God's command to Joshua to walk in his ways and thereby rule God's house honorably. In the prophet's immediate context, the vision assured the returned exiles that God would reestablish the priesthood in the rebuilt temple. But verses 6–10 expand the scope beyond that and present us with a messianic prophecy about God's "servant the Branch." Within this messianic prophecy, moreover, we have a picture of Christ's atonement with the statement that God "will remove the iniquity of this land in a single day" (v. 9), a prophecy fulfilled on the day of Christ's crucifixion.

3 Then he showed me Joshua the high priest standing before the angel of the Lord, and Satan[1] standing at his right hand to accuse him. [2]And the Lord said to Satan, "The Lord rebuke you, O Satan! The Lord who has chosen Jerusalem rebuke you! Is not this a brand[2] plucked from the fire?" [3]Now Joshua was standing before the angel, clothed with filthy garments. [4]And the angel said to those who were standing before him, "Remove the filthy garments from him." And to him he said, "Behold, I have taken your iniquity away from you, and I will clothe you with pure vestments." [5]And I said, "Let them put a clean turban on his head." So they put a clean turban on his head and clothed him with garments. And the angel of the Lord was standing by.

[6]And the angel of the Lord solemnly assured Joshua, [7]"Thus says the Lord of hosts: If you will walk in my ways and keep my charge, then you shall rule my house and have charge of my courts, and I will give you the right of access among those who are standing here. [8]Hear now, O Joshua the high priest, you and your friends who sit before you, for they are men who are a sign: behold, I will bring my servant the Branch. [9]For behold, on the stone that I have set before Joshua, on a single stone with seven eyes,[3] I will engrave its inscription, declares the Lord of hosts, and I will remove the iniquity of this land in a single day. [10]In that day, declares the Lord of hosts, every one of you will invite his neighbor to come under his vine and under his fig tree."

The lampstand and two olive trees [chapter 4]. We continue to observe a pageant of symbolic visions as we read. The rhetorical format of the chapter is a dialogue between the prophet and an angel. There is mingled mystery and clarity in the vision of the lampstand (symbolizing God's Spirit) and two olive trees (symbolizing "two anointed ones" [v. 14] who are not further identified). There is a narrative thread interwoven with these symbolic details, and it tells the story of Zerubbabel's rebuilding of the temple. In their immediate context, the lampstand and oil-producing olive trees might be accoutrements of the temple and therefore a symbolic picture of God's presence in the reconstituted temple worship in the rebuilt Jerusalem. But the details continually press outward from that and become a picture of the perpetual supply of God's Spirit in "the whole earth" (v. 14).

[1] Satan means *the accuser* [2] That is, a burning stick [3] Or *facets*

4 And the angel who talked with me came again and woke me, like a man who is awakened out of his sleep. ²And he said to me, "What do you see?" I said, "I see, and behold, a lampstand all of gold, with a bowl on the top of it, and seven lamps on it, with seven lips on each of the lamps that are on the top of it. ³And there are two olive trees by it, one on the right of the bowl and the other on its left." ⁴And I said to the angel who talked with me, "What are these, my lord?" ⁵Then the angel who talked with me answered and said to me, "Do you not know what these are?" I said, "No, my lord." ⁶Then he said to me, "This is the word of the LORD to Zerubbabel: Not by might, nor by power, but by my Spirit, says the LORD of hosts. ⁷Who are you, O great mountain? Before Zerubbabel you shall become a plain. And he shall bring forward the top stone amid shouts of 'Grace, grace to it!'"

⁸Then the word of the LORD came to me, saying, ⁹"The hands of Zerubbabel have laid the foundation of this house; his hands shall also complete it. Then you will know that the LORD of hosts has sent me to you. ¹⁰For whoever has despised the day of small things shall rejoice, and shall see the plumb line in the hand of Zerubbabel.

"These seven are the eyes of the LORD, which range through the whole earth." ¹¹Then I said to him, "What are these two olive trees on the right and the left of the lampstand?" ¹²And a second time I answered and said to him, "What are these two branches of the olive trees, which are beside the two golden pipes from which the golden oil¹ is poured out?" ¹³He said to me, "Do you not know what these are?" I said, "No, my lord." ¹⁴Then he said, "These are the two anointed ones² who stand by the Lord of the whole earth."

The flying scroll and the woman in a measuring container [chapter 5]. The format continues to be the pageant of visions, and the visions, in turn, are made up of symbols, not literal characters and scenes from everyday life. In fact, *fantasy is an accurate label for the literary form that is employed. Two visions in this chapter are a flying scroll, thirty feet long and fifteen feet wide, which destroys the houses of thieves and false witnesses (5:1–4), and a personified woman named Wickedness, sitting inside a basket that is carried to a distant country (vv. 5–11). The question is what these visionary symbols mean, and the answer is that they symbolize God's judgment against evil (the flying scroll) and God's removal of evil from his people (the woman in the basket).

5 Again I lifted my eyes and saw, and behold, a flying scroll! ²And he said to me, "What do you see?" I answered, "I see a flying scroll. Its length is twenty cubits, and its width ten cubits."³ ³Then he said to me, "This is the curse that goes out over the face of the whole land. For everyone who steals shall be cleaned out according to what is on one side, and everyone who swears falsely⁴ shall be cleaned out according to what is on the other side. ⁴I will send it out, declares the LORD of hosts, and it shall enter the house of the thief, and the house of him who swears falsely by my name. And it shall remain in his house and consume it, both timber and stones."

⁵Then the angel who talked with me came forward and said to me, "Lift your eyes and see what this is that is going out." ⁶And I said, "What is it?" He said, "This is the basket⁵ that is going out." And he said, "This is their iniquity⁶ in all the land." ⁷And behold, the leaden cover was lifted, and there was a woman sitting in the basket!

¹ Hebrew lacks oil ² Hebrew two sons of new oil ³ A cubit was about 18 inches or 45 centimeters ⁴ Hebrew lacks falsely (supplied from verse 4) ⁵ Hebrew ephah; also verses 7-11. An ephah was about 3/5 bushel or 22 liters ⁶ One Hebrew manuscript, Septuagint, Syriac; most Hebrew manuscripts eye

⁸And he said, "This is Wickedness." And he thrust her back into the basket, and thrust down the leaden weight on its opening.

⁹Then I lifted my eyes and saw, and behold, two women coming forward! The wind was in their wings. They had wings like the wings of a stork, and they lifted up the basket between earth and heaven. ¹⁰Then I said to the angel who talked with me, "Where are they taking the basket?" ¹¹He said to me, "To the land of Shinar, to build a house for it. And when this is prepared, they will set the basket down there on its base."

Visions of the four chariots and the Branch [chapter 6]. The section of nine visions is rounded out with visions of four chariots of divine judgment sent out to patrol the earth (vv. 1–8) and a further vision or prophecy of the Branch (vv. 9–15). The patrols are symbolic of God's protection of his people. The vision of the Branch is a prophecy of the future coming of the Messiah.

6 Again I lifted my eyes and saw, and behold, four chariots came out from between two mountains. And the mountains were mountains of bronze. ²The first chariot had red horses, the second black horses, ³the third white horses, and the fourth chariot dappled horses—all of them strong.[1] ⁴Then I answered and said to the angel who talked with me, "What are these, my lord?" ⁵And the angel answered and said to me, "These are going out to the four winds of heaven, after presenting themselves before the Lord of all the earth. ⁶The chariot with the black horses goes toward the north country, the white ones go after them, and the dappled ones go toward the south country." ⁷When the strong horses came out, they were impatient to go and patrol the earth. And he said, "Go, patrol the earth." So they patrolled the earth. ⁸Then he cried to me, "Behold, those who go toward the north country have set my Spirit at rest in the north country."

⁹And the word of the Lord came to me: ¹⁰"Take from the exiles Heldai, Tobijah, and Jedaiah, who have arrived from Babylon, and go the same day to the house of Josiah, the son of Zephaniah. ¹¹Take from them silver and gold, and make a crown, and set it on the head of Joshua, the son of Jehozadak, the high priest. ¹²And say to him, 'Thus says the Lord of hosts, "Behold, the man whose name is the Branch: for he shall branch out from his place, and he shall build the temple of the Lord. ¹³It is he who shall build the temple of the Lord and shall bear royal honor, and shall sit and rule on his throne. And there shall be a priest on his throne, and the counsel of peace shall be between them both."' ¹⁴And the crown shall be in the temple of the Lord as a reminder to Helem,[2] Tobijah, Jedaiah, and Hen the son of Zephaniah.

¹⁵"And those who are far off shall come and help to build the temple of the Lord. And you shall know that the Lord of hosts has sent me to you. And this shall come to pass, if you will diligently obey the voice of the Lord your God."

Messages of judgment [chapter 7]. With the pageant of visions now over, the book of Zechariah turns to more customary prophetic forms and content. An opening question about whether the people should fast (vv. 1–3) leads to a series of statements of judgment from God. The general tenor of this sermonic material is that Judah was punished

---

[1] Or and the fourth chariot strong dappled horses [2] An alternate spelling of Heldai (verse 10)

by God (vv. 13–14) for its hypocritical practice of religious observances (vv. 4–7) and its immoral behavior (vv. 8–12).

7 In the fourth year of King Darius, the word of the LORD came to Zechariah on the fourth day of the ninth month, which is Chislev. ²Now the people of Bethel had sent Sharezer and Regem-melech and their men to entreat the favor of the LORD, ³saying to the priests of the house of the LORD of hosts and the prophets, "Should I weep and abstain in the fifth month, as I have done for so many years?"

⁴Then the word of the LORD of hosts came to me: ⁵"Say to all the people of the land and the priests, When you fasted and mourned in the fifth month and in the seventh, for these seventy years, was it for me that you fasted? ⁶And when you eat and when you drink, do you not eat for yourselves and drink for yourselves? ⁷Were not these the words that the LORD proclaimed by the former prophets, when Jerusalem was inhabited and prosperous, with her cities around her, and the South and the lowland were inhabited?"

⁸And the word of the LORD came to Zechariah, saying, ⁹"Thus says the LORD of hosts, Render true judgments, show kindness and mercy to one another, ¹⁰do not oppress the widow, the fatherless, the sojourner, or the poor, and let none of you devise evil against another in your heart." ¹¹But they refused to pay attention and turned a stubborn shoulder and stopped their ears that they might not hear.[1] ¹²They made their hearts diamond-hard lest they should hear the law and the words that the LORD of hosts had sent by his Spirit through the former prophets. Therefore great anger came from the LORD of hosts. ¹³"As I[2] called, and they would not hear, so they called, and I would not hear," says the LORD of hosts, ¹⁴"and I scattered them with a whirlwind among all the nations that they had not known. Thus the land they left was desolate, so that no one went to and fro, and the pleasant land was made desolate."

A golden age prophecy [chapter 8]. The sermonic material carries over from the preceding chapter, and it is again couched in prose rather than the customary poetry. The messages of judgment in chapter 7 are now balanced by messages of blessing. The chapter is an extended *golden age prophecy that pictures an ideal society blessed by God. When we move to interpreting the details, we can legitimately begin with the prophet's immediate situation and see in the vision a *hyperbolic and symbolic picture of the returned exiles setting up life in restored Jerusalem. But once again, the imagery and vocabulary bring to mind the blessings of the messianic kingdom that Christ brought during his life, death, and resurrection and, further, the coming glory of eternity (pictured as finding its center in Jerusalem as the place of salvation for the world). A good way to assimilate the chapter is to compile a running list of the categories and specific pictures that make up the good life that is pictured. The rhetorical form in which the visions are packaged is the formula "Thus says the LORD" or "The word of the LORD came to me, saying . . ."

8 And the word of the LORD of hosts came, saying, ²"Thus says the LORD of hosts: I am jealous for Zion with great jealousy, and I am jealous for her with great wrath. ³Thus says the LORD: I have returned to Zion and will dwell in the midst of Jerusalem, and Jerusalem shall be called the faithful city, and the mountain of the LORD of hosts, the holy mountain. ⁴Thus says the LORD of hosts: Old men and old

---

¹ Hebrew and made their ears too heavy to hear ² Hebrew he

women shall again sit in the streets of Jerusalem, each with staff in hand because of great age. ⁵And the streets of the city shall be full of boys and girls playing in its streets. ⁶Thus says the LORD of hosts: If it is marvelous in the sight of the remnant of this people in those days, should it also be marvelous in my sight, declares the LORD of hosts? ⁷Thus says the LORD of hosts: behold, I will save my people from the east country and from the west country, ⁸and I will bring them to dwell in the midst of Jerusalem. And they shall be my people, and I will be their God, in faithfulness and in righteousness."

⁹Thus says the LORD of hosts: "Let your hands be strong, you who in these days have been hearing these words from the mouth of the prophets who were present on the day that the foundation of the house of the LORD of hosts was laid, that the temple might be built. ¹⁰For before those days there was no wage for man or any wage for beast, neither was there any safety from the foe for him who went out or came in, for I set every man against his neighbor. ¹¹But now I will not deal with the remnant of this people as in the former days, declares the LORD of hosts. ¹²For there shall be a sowing of peace. The vine shall give its fruit, and the ground shall give its produce, and the heavens shall give their dew. And I will cause the remnant of this people to possess all these things. ¹³And as you have been a byword of cursing among the nations, O house of Judah and house of Israel, so will I save you, and you shall be a blessing. Fear not, but let your hands be strong."

¹⁴For thus says the LORD of hosts: "As I purposed to bring disaster to you when your fathers provoked me to wrath, and I did not relent, says the LORD of hosts, ¹⁵so again have I purposed in these days to bring good to Jerusalem and to the house of Judah; fear not. ¹⁶These are the things that you shall do: Speak the truth to one another; render in your gates judgments that are true and make for peace; ¹⁷do not devise evil in your hearts against one another, and love no false oath, for all these things I hate, declares the LORD."

¹⁸And the word of the LORD of hosts came to me, saying, ¹⁹"Thus says the LORD of hosts: The fast of the fourth month and the fast of the fifth and the fast of the seventh and the fast of the tenth shall be to the house of Judah seasons of joy and gladness and cheerful feasts. Therefore love truth and peace.

²⁰"Thus says the LORD of hosts: Peoples shall yet come, even the inhabitants of many cities. ²¹The inhabitants of one city shall go to another, saying, 'Let us go at once to entreat the favor of the LORD and to seek the LORD of hosts; I myself am going.' ²²Many peoples and strong nations shall come to seek the LORD of hosts in Jerusalem and to entreat the favor of the LORD. ²³Thus says the LORD of hosts: In those days ten men from the nations of every tongue shall take hold of the robe of a Jew, saying, 'Let us go with you, for we have heard that God is with you.' "

Vision of a coming king [chapter 9]. The motif of a coming golden age carries over from chapter 8, as does the messianic content of the vision. The book of Zechariah as a whole combines priestly and kingly motifs. The priestly motif has dominated thus far, but with chapter 9 the kingly motif is established. The structure of the material is fluid, but we can discern the following general outline: God's promise to protect Judah from its enemies (vv. 1–8); the triumphant arrival of Zion's gentle king to save his precious people (vv. 9–17). The mode is poetic and symbolic; the fulfillment is messianic.

9 The burden of the word of the LORD is against the land of Hadrach
    and Damascus is its resting place.
For the LORD has an eye on mankind
    and on all the tribes of Israel,[1]
2 and on Hamath also, which borders on it,
    Tyre and Sidon, though they are very wise.
3 Tyre has built herself a rampart
    and heaped up silver like dust,
    and fine gold like the mud of the streets.
4 But behold, the Lord will strip her of her possessions
    and strike down her power on the sea,
    and she shall be devoured by fire.

5 Ashkelon shall see it, and be afraid;
    Gaza too, and shall writhe in anguish;
    Ekron also, because its hopes are confounded.
The king shall perish from Gaza;
    Ashkelon shall be uninhabited;
6 a mixed people[2] shall dwell in Ashdod,
    and I will cut off the pride of Philistia.
7 I will take away its blood from its mouth,
    and its abominations from between its teeth;
it too shall be a remnant for our God;
    it shall be like a clan in Judah,
    and Ekron shall be like the Jebusites.
8 Then I will encamp at my house as a guard,
    so that none shall march to and fro;
no oppressor shall again march over them,
    for now I see with my own eyes.

9 Rejoice greatly, O daughter of Zion!
    Shout aloud, O daughter of Jerusalem!
Behold, your king is coming to you;
    righteous and having salvation is he,
humble and mounted on a donkey,
    on a colt, the foal of a donkey.
10 I will cut off the chariot from Ephraim
    and the war horse from Jerusalem;
and the battle bow shall be cut off,
    and he shall speak peace to the nations;
his rule shall be from sea to sea,
    and from the River to the ends of the earth.
11 As for you also, because of the blood of my covenant with you,
    I will set your prisoners free from the waterless pit.
12 Return to your stronghold, O prisoners of hope;
    today I declare that I will restore to you double.
13 For I have bent Judah as my bow;

---

[1] A slight emendation yields *For to the LORD belongs the capital of Syria and all the tribes of Israel* [2] Or *a foreign people*; Hebrew *a bastard*

I have made Ephraim its arrow.
I will stir up your sons, O Zion,
     against your sons, O Greece,
     and wield you like a warrior's sword.

[14] Then the LORD will appear over them,
     and his arrow will go forth like lightning;
the Lord GOD will sound the trumpet
     and will march forth in the whirlwinds of the south.
[15] The LORD of hosts will protect them,
     and they shall devour, and tread down the sling stones,
and they shall drink and roar as if drunk with wine,
     and be full like a bowl,
     drenched like the corners of the altar.

[16] On that day the LORD their God will save them,
     as the flock of his people;
for like the jewels of a crown
     they shall shine on his land.
[17] For how great is his goodness, and how great his beauty!
     Grain shall make the young men flourish,
     and new wine the young women.

Golden age prophecy [chapter 10]. With the king's having arrived, the prophet now turns to an expanded vision of the blessings of his rule. On a good day, the returned exiles might have seen the details as a hyperbolic and *metaphoric account of their life in the old land, but the more obvious application of the details is messianic and eschatological. The affective or emotional level of meaning is important in OT golden age prophecies, so we need to be receptive to the feelings and mood that this material awakens in us.

10

Ask rain from the LORD
     in the season of the spring rain,
from the LORD who makes the storm clouds,
     and he will give them showers of rain,
     to everyone the vegetation in the field.
[2] For the household gods utter nonsense,
     and the diviners see lies;
they tell false dreams
     and give empty consolation.
Therefore the people wander like sheep;
     they are afflicted for lack of a shepherd.

[3] "My anger is hot against the shepherds,
     and I will punish the leaders;[1]
for the LORD of hosts cares for his flock, the house of Judah,
     and will make them like his majestic steed in battle.
[4] From him shall come the cornerstone,

---

[1] Hebrew *the male goats*

    from him the tent peg,
    from him the battle bow,
       from him every ruler—all of them together.
⁵ They shall be like mighty men in battle,
       trampling the foe in the mud of the streets;
    they shall fight because the LORD is with them,
       and they shall put to shame the riders on horses.

⁶ "I will strengthen the house of Judah,
       and I will save the house of Joseph.
    I will bring them back because I have compassion on them,
       and they shall be as though I had not rejected them,
       for I am the LORD their God and I will answer them.
⁷ Then Ephraim shall become like a mighty warrior,
       and their hearts shall be glad as with wine.
    Their children shall see it and be glad;
       their hearts shall rejoice in the LORD.

⁸ "I will whistle for them and gather them in,
       for I have redeemed them,
       and they shall be as many as they were before.
⁹ Though I scattered them among the nations,
       yet in far countries they shall remember me,
       and with their children they shall live and return.
¹⁰ I will bring them home from the land of Egypt,
       and gather them from Assyria,
    and I will bring them to the land of Gilead and to Lebanon,
       till there is no room for them.
¹¹ He shall pass through the sea of troubles
       and strike down the waves of the sea,
    and all the depths of the Nile shall be dried up.
    The pride of Assyria shall be laid low,
       and the scepter of Egypt shall depart.
¹² I will make them strong in the LORD,
       and they shall walk in his name,"
              declares the LORD.

Oracle of judgment [chapter 11]. The messianic thread continues in this chapter, but changes are introduced as well. The format of visions gives way to an *allegorical narrative involving shepherds and sheep. After a lead-in announcing doom (vv. 1–3), the prophet pictures himself as undertaking the task of being a good shepherd to the flock of the Lord. The unfolding action is mysterious, but we are helped in piecing together the main action if we realize that the story that is told is a rejection story: the prophet, in his role as good shepherd, fails to be accepted by the flock and therefore abandons his attempt to shepherd the flock. There is a messianic dimension to these prophecies: the good shepherd is Christ; the rejection of the good shepherd is a metaphoric picture of what happened to Christ during his earthly life, including his atoning death; the shepherd's rejection of the sheep and annulment of the covenant (vv. 8–11) is God's temporary withdrawal of blessing from his wayward people, as when Israel and Judah were carried into captivity; the annulling of brotherhood between Judah and Israel (v. 14) refers to the division of the kingdom.

11

Open your doors, O Lebanon,
that the fire may devour your cedars!
² Wail, O cypress, for the cedar has fallen,
for the glorious trees are ruined!
Wail, oaks of Bashan,
for the thick forest has been felled!
³ The sound of the wail of the shepherds,
for their glory is ruined!
The sound of the roar of the lions,
for the thicket of the Jordan is ruined!

⁴Thus said the LORD my God: "Become shepherd of the flock doomed to slaughter. ⁵Those who buy them slaughter them and go unpunished, and those who sell them say, 'Blessed be the LORD, I have become rich,' and their own shepherds have no pity on them. ⁶For I will no longer have pity on the inhabitants of this land, declares the LORD. Behold, I will cause each of them to fall into the hand of his neighbor, and each into the hand of his king, and they shall crush the land, and I will deliver none from their hand."

⁷So I became the shepherd of the flock doomed to be slaughtered by the sheep traders. And I took two staffs, one I named Favor, the other I named Union. And I tended the sheep. ⁸In one month I destroyed the three shepherds. But I became impatient with them, and they also detested me. ⁹So I said, "I will not be your shepherd. What is to die, let it die. What is to be destroyed, let it be destroyed. And let those who are left devour the flesh of one another." ¹⁰And I took my staff Favor, and I broke it, annulling the covenant that I had made with all the peoples. ¹¹So it was annulled on that day, and the sheep traders, who were watching me, knew that it was the word of the LORD. ¹²Then I said to them, "If it seems good to you, give me my wages; but if not, keep them." And they weighed out as my wages thirty pieces of silver. ¹³Then the LORD said to me, "Throw it to the potter"—the lordly price at which I was priced by them. So I took the thirty pieces of silver and threw them into the house of the LORD, to the potter. ¹⁴Then I broke my second staff Union, annulling the brotherhood between Judah and Israel.

¹⁵Then the LORD said to me, "Take once more the equipment of a foolish shepherd. ¹⁶For behold, I am raising up in the land a shepherd who does not care for those being destroyed, or seek the young or heal the maimed or nourish the healthy, but devours the flesh of the fat ones, tearing off even their hoofs.

¹⁷   "Woe to my worthless shepherd,
who deserts the flock!
May the sword strike his arm
and his right eye!
Let his arm be wholly withered,
his right eye utterly blinded!"

Oracles of salvation [chapters 12–13]. We need to acknowledge at the outset of the concluding unit of the book of Zechariah that the oracles of redemption in biblical prophecy employ a metaphoric and symbolic mode that is open-ended in its potential applications. Language and imagery are often identical for the following three types of prophecy: (1) predictions of military and political events that are on the verge of happening; (2) predictions of an intermediate future from the time perspective of the prophet that were fulfilled with the coming of Christ; (3) eschatological, apocalyptic visions of the end of history and the ushering in of eternity. Often our intuition tells us that it is one of these rather than the others (or simultaneously with the others), but we may find it difficult to prove beyond doubt that our identification is true. A further consideration is that if certain lavish promises of restoration and blessing were not fulfilled in the history of Israel or Judah, we can probably take that as warrant to give those visions a messianic and/or eschatological interpretation. With those ground rules before us, we can probably see in these two chapters symbolic renditions of (1) the blessings of salvation in Christ (e.g., 12:10; 13:1) and (2) premonitions of events surrounding God's final conquest of evil and establishing of his kingdom in the eschaton. Again, we need to allow the poetic medium to pierce our imagination and emotions.

12 The burden of the word of the Lord concerning Israel: Thus declares the Lord, who stretched out the heavens and founded the earth and formed the spirit of man within him: ²"Behold, I am about to make Jerusalem a cup of staggering to all the surrounding peoples. The siege of Jerusalem will also be against Judah. ³On that day I will make Jerusalem a heavy stone for all the peoples. All who lift it will surely hurt themselves. And all the nations of the earth will gather against it. ⁴On that day, declares the Lord, I will strike every horse with panic, and its rider with madness. But for the sake of the house of Judah I will keep my eyes open, when I strike every horse of the peoples with blindness. ⁵Then the clans of Judah shall say to themselves, 'The inhabitants of Jerusalem have strength through the Lord of hosts, their God.'

⁶"On that day I will make the clans of Judah like a blazing pot in the midst of wood, like a flaming torch among sheaves. And they shall devour to the right and to the left all the surrounding peoples, while Jerusalem shall again be inhabited in its place, in Jerusalem.

⁷"And the Lord will give salvation to the tents of Judah first, that the glory of the house of David and the glory of the inhabitants of Jerusalem may not surpass that of Judah. ⁸On that day the Lord will protect the inhabitants of Jerusalem, so that the feeblest among them on that day shall be like David, and the house of David shall be like God, like the angel of the Lord, going before them. ⁹And on that day I will seek to destroy all the nations that come against Jerusalem.

¹⁰"And I will pour out on the house of David and the inhabitants of Jerusalem a spirit of grace and pleas for mercy, so that, when they look on me, on him whom they have pierced, they shall mourn for him, as one mourns for an only child, and weep bitterly over him, as one weeps over a firstborn. ¹¹On that day the mourning in Jerusalem will be as great as the mourning for Hadad-rimmon in the plain of Megiddo. ¹²The land shall mourn, each family¹ by itself: the family of the house of David by itself, and their wives by themselves; the family of the house of Nathan by itself, and their wives by themselves; ¹³the family of the house of Levi by itself, and their wives by themselves;

¹ Or *clan*; also verses 13, 14

the family of the Shimeites by itself, and their wives by themselves; [14]and all the families that are left, each by itself, and their wives by themselves.

13

"On that day there shall be a fountain opened for the house of David and the inhabitants of Jerusalem, to cleanse them from sin and uncleanness.

[2]"And on that day, declares the LORD of hosts, I will cut off the names of the idols from the land, so that they shall be remembered no more. And also I will remove from the land the prophets and the spirit of uncleanness. [3]And if anyone again prophesies, his father and mother who bore him will say to him, 'You shall not live, for you speak lies in the name of the LORD.' And his father and mother who bore him shall pierce him through when he prophesies.

[4]"On that day every prophet will be ashamed of his vision when he prophesies. He will not put on a hairy cloak in order to deceive, [5]but he will say, 'I am no prophet, I am a worker of the soil, for a man sold me in my youth.'[1] [6]And if one asks him, 'What are these wounds on your back?'[2] he will say, 'The wounds I received in the house of my friends.'

[7]   "Awake, O sword, against my shepherd,
         against the man who stands next to me,"
                          declares the LORD of hosts.

"Strike the shepherd, and the sheep will be scattered;
    I will turn my hand against the little ones.
[8] In the whole land, declares the LORD,
        two thirds shall be cut off and perish,
        and one third shall be left alive.
[9] And I will put this third into the fire,
        and refine them as one refines silver,
        and test them as gold is tested.
They will call upon my name,
    and I will answer them.
I will say, 'They are my people';
    and they will say, 'The LORD is my God.'"

The apocalypse of Zechariah [chapter 14]. As the prophetic visions of Zechariah have kept expanding outward from the immediate situation of the returned exiles of Judah, the frame of reference has moved imperceptibly through messianic history to the final consummation of history. We will not go wrong with the last chapter of Zechariah if we assimilate it as apocalyptic vision of the final defeat of evil and the attainment of perfection in heaven. The main motifs are as follows: the finality of the events that are narrated; battle (a climactic conflict between good and evil); images of perfection and the good life; the absence of negative features of human experience (the "no more" motif); images of abundance and luxurious fullness; the transformation of common experiences into something numinous and holy (especially in vv. 20–21); "the day of the LORD" as the time when all of these events will converge; the holiness that pervades all of reality in the coming redemption.

[1] Or for the land has been my possession since my youth [2] Or on your chest; Hebrew wounds between your hands

14 Behold, a day is coming for the Lord, when the spoil taken from you will be divided in your midst. ²For I will gather all the nations against Jerusalem to battle, and the city shall be taken and the houses plundered and the women raped. Half of the city shall go out into exile, but the rest of the people shall not be cut off from the city. ³Then the Lord will go out and fight against those nations as when he fights on a day of battle. ⁴On that day his feet shall stand on the Mount of Olives that lies before Jerusalem on the east, and the Mount of Olives shall be split in two from east to west by a very wide valley, so that one half of the Mount shall move northward, and the other half southward. ⁵And you shall flee to the valley of my mountains, for the valley of the mountains shall reach to Azal. And you shall flee as you fled from the earthquake in the days of Uzziah king of Judah. Then the Lord my God will come, and all the holy ones with him.

⁶On that day there shall be no light, cold, or frost.¹ ⁷And there shall be a unique² day, which is known to the Lord, neither day nor night, but at evening time there shall be light.

⁸On that day living waters shall flow out from Jerusalem, half of them to the eastern sea³ and half of them to the western sea.⁴ It shall continue in summer as in winter.

⁹And the Lord will be king over all the earth. On that day the Lord will be one and his name one.

¹⁰The whole land shall be turned into a plain from Geba to Rimmon south of Jerusalem. But Jerusalem shall remain aloft on its site from the Gate of Benjamin to the place of the former gate, to the Corner Gate, and from the Tower of Hananel to the king's winepresses. ¹¹And it shall be inhabited, for there shall never again be a decree of utter destruction.⁵ Jerusalem shall dwell in security.

¹²And this shall be the plague with which the Lord will strike all the peoples that wage war against Jerusalem: their flesh will rot while they are still standing on their feet, their eyes will rot in their sockets, and their tongues will rot in their mouths.

¹³And on that day a great panic from the Lord shall fall on them, so that each will seize the hand of another, and the hand of the one will be raised against the hand of the other. ¹⁴Even Judah will fight at Jerusalem. And the wealth of all the surrounding nations shall be collected, gold, silver, and garments in great abundance. ¹⁵And a plague like this plague shall fall on the horses, the mules, the camels, the donkeys, and whatever beasts may be in those camps.

¹⁶Then everyone who survives of all the nations that have come against Jerusalem shall go up year after year to worship the King, the Lord of hosts, and to keep the Feast of Booths. ¹⁷And if any of the families of the earth do not go up to Jerusalem to worship the King, the Lord of hosts, there will be no rain on them. ¹⁸And if the family of Egypt does not go up and present themselves, then on them there shall be no rain;⁶ there shall be the plague with which the Lord afflicts the nations that do not go up to keep the Feast of Booths. ¹⁹This shall be the punishment to Egypt and the punishment to all the nations that do not go up to keep the Feast of Booths.

²⁰And on that day there shall be inscribed on the bells of the horses, "Holy to the Lord." And the pots in the house of the Lord shall be as the bowls before the altar. ²¹And every pot in Jerusalem and Judah shall be holy to the Lord of hosts, so that all who sacrifice may come and take of them and boil the meat of the sacrifice in them. And there shall no longer be a trader⁷ in the house of the Lord of hosts on that day.

¹ Compare Septuagint, Syriac, Vulgate, Targum; the meaning of the Hebrew is uncertain ² Hebrew *one* ³ That is, the Dead Sea ⁴ That is, the Mediterranean Sea ⁵ The Hebrew term rendered *decree of utter destruction* refers to things devoted (or set apart) to the Lord (or by the Lord) for destruction ⁶ Hebrew lacks *rain* ⁷ Or *Canaanite*

MALACHI

The book at a glance. 4 chapters, 55 verses. With the book of Malachi, the OT comes to an end. The book therefore has an incipient quality of being a transition from the old covenant to the new covenant, which is still four hundred years off. The dominant note is judgment, as the book informs us regarding what happens when God's people ignore God's rules. The author's implied goal is to lead his readers to reform their lives. This goal is pursued by the prophet's warning his readers about God's impending judgment against sin, and equally by his painting such attractive pictures of God's blessings on those who obey his rules for living that anyone should want to do things God's way. Malachi writes to a backslidden covenant people for whom the life of faith has become a wearisome burden.

▌**Genres.** Each one of the twelve "minor" prophets is distinctive. The content of the book of Malachi places the book into the category of prophecy, but the form in which that content is packaged is out of the norm for OT prophecy. The book is written entirely in prose. Further, the material is not embodied in the conventional format of oracles of judgment and salvation. The dominant *genre is *satire—an attack on vice in a discernible literary form and with a satiric norm according to which the criticism is conducted. The object of attack is halfhearted and negligent religious service, which in the prophet's day took multiple forms (for example, inappropriate offerings, untruth promoted by priests, and the prevalence of divorce). The satiric norm is God's law. The primary vehicle in which the satire is conveyed is a *rhetoric of question and answer, as the people of Judah are pictured as asking a series of questions that God answers in an accusatory and condemning way. (For more information on items accompanied by an asterisk, see the glossary at the back of this Bible.)

Passage	Content	Prophetic Genre
1:1–5	God's judgment announced against apostate Israel	Oracle of judgment
1:6–2:9	Sins of the priests	Oracle of judgment
2:10–17	Sins of the people	Oracle of judgment
3:1–5	Sudden appearance of a judging God	Oracle of judgment
3:6–12	Sins of the tithe	Oracle of judgment
3:13–4:6	Predictions of mingled judgment and blessing	Oracle of judgment; oracle of salvation

▌Organization and format. The movement of the book is very fluid. The author shuttles back and forth between indictments from God and, without transition, promises from God to bless his people. Some of God's accusations are specific (for example, the ones dealing with divorce and the tithe), while others are very general in nature. One of the organizing patterns is an accumulating litany of attitudes and actions that are offensive to God. Another is an expanding portrait of the coming Messiah and the blessings that he will bring. Finally, a common pattern that is repeated is as follows: (1) God voices an indictment of his people for bad behavior; (2) the people are pictured as asking God how his charge is true; (3) God replies to the question, in the process of which he expands the charge. God's indictments are sometimes phrased as *rhetorical questions (e.g., 1:6, 8; 2:10, 15).

▌A relevant and contemporary book. The entire Bible is a mirror in which we see ourselves, but the book of Malachi is so preeminently. Even though Malachi writes to a nation that had been living in the rebuilt Jerusalem for nearly a century after the first exiles had returned, the pictures that he paints of halfhearted religion should strike us as very contemporaneous with our own situation. We can see "the sins of the saints" laid out to view. Further, the book deals with issues that are common to us—money, marriage, family, contributing to God's work, and many more.

▌Inferred literary intentions. The book is designed to achieve the following literary purposes:

- shock its readers out of their religious complacency

- use the resources of satire to raise our awareness regarding things that God considers offensive

- paint vivid word-pictures of the practices that God through the prophet denounces

- impress on us the seriousness of sin

- provide a double incentive to reform our lives in areas where we are lax—the threat of God's judgment and the promise of God's blessing (including messianic blessing) for obedience

▌Theological themes. (1) Sin: the book is a categorizing of sins, especially those that involve laxity in the religious and moral lives of those who profess to be God's people. (2) Divine judgment: the book demonstrates God's disapproval of his covenant people's taking his demands lightly. (3) Covenant: the book is a selective manual of covenant stipulations first outlined in the Pentateuch.

▌Malachi as a chapter in the master story of the Bible. The story of the Bible is the story of God's covenant dealings with his people. That covenant includes commands that God expects his people to obey. The book of Malachi shows what happens when God's people do not take God's demands seriously. It also anticipates the coming of the Messiah, who will turn the hearts of people back to God.

Sins of the priests [1:1–2:9]. The first five verses of the book are a backdrop to the ensuing lists of offenses. Using the question-and-answer format that is a distinctive feature of the book, verses 1–5 assert God's favor toward his people as seen in the defeat of Edom. With this established, the rest of the unit outlines the laxity of the priests of Judah in two areas—the performance of sacrifices (1:6–14) and teaching (2:1–9). As we work our way through the passage, we can codify (1) the exact nature of the offenses and (2) the interspersed response of God to these abuses.

1 The oracle of the word of the Lord to Israel by Malachi.[1]
²"I have loved you," says the Lord. But you say, "How have you loved us?" "Is not Esau Jacob's brother?" declares the Lord. "Yet I have loved Jacob ³but Esau I have hated. I have laid waste his hill country and left his heritage to jackals of the desert." ⁴If Edom says, "We are shattered but we will rebuild the ruins," the Lord of hosts says, "They may build, but I will tear down, and they will be called 'the wicked country,' and 'the people with whom the Lord is angry forever.'" ⁵Your own eyes shall see this, and you shall say, "Great is the Lord beyond the border of Israel!"

⁶"A son honors his father, and a servant his master. If then I am a father, where is my honor? And if I am a master, where is my fear? says the Lord of hosts to you, O priests, who despise my name. But you say, 'How have we despised your name?' ⁷By offering polluted food upon my altar. But you say, 'How have we polluted you?' By saying that the Lord's table may be despised. ⁸When you offer blind animals in sacrifice, is that not evil? And when you offer those that are lame or sick, is that not evil? Present that to your governor; will he accept you or show you favor? says the Lord of hosts. ⁹And now entreat the favor of God, that he may be gracious to us. With such a gift from your hand, will he show favor to any of you? says the Lord of hosts. ¹⁰Oh that there were one among you who would shut the doors, that you might not kindle fire on my altar in vain! I have no pleasure in you, says the Lord of hosts, and I will not accept an offering from your hand. ¹¹For from the rising of the sun to its setting my name will be[2] great among the nations, and in every place incense will be offered to my name, and a pure offering. For my name will be great among the nations, says the Lord of hosts. ¹²But you profane it when you say that the Lord's table is polluted, and its fruit, that is, its food may be despised. ¹³But you say, 'What a weariness this is,' and you snort at it, says the Lord of hosts. You bring what has been taken by violence or is lame or sick, and this you bring as your offering! Shall I accept that from your hand? says the Lord. ¹⁴Cursed be the cheat who has a male in his flock, and vows it, and yet sacrifices to the Lord what is blemished. For I am a great King, says the Lord of hosts, and my name will be feared among the nations.

2 "And now, O priests, this command is for you. ²If you will not listen, if you will not take it to heart to give honor to my name, says the Lord of hosts, then I will send the curse upon you and I will curse your blessings. Indeed, I have already cursed them, because you do not lay it to heart. ³Behold, I will rebuke your offspring,[3] and spread dung on your faces, the dung of your offerings, and you shall be taken away with it.[4] ⁴So shall you know that I have sent this command to you, that my covenant with Levi may stand, says the Lord of hosts. ⁵My covenant with him was one of life and peace, and I gave them to him. It was a covenant of fear, and he feared me.

---

[1] *Malachi* means *my messenger* [2] Or *is* (three times in verse 11; also verse 14) [3] Hebrew *seed* [4] Or *to it*

He stood in awe of my name. [6]True instruction[1] was in his mouth, and no wrong was found on his lips. He walked with me in peace and uprightness, and he turned many from iniquity. [7]For the lips of a priest should guard knowledge, and people[2] should seek instruction from his mouth, for he is the messenger of the LORD of hosts. [8]But you have turned aside from the way. You have caused many to stumble by your instruction. You have corrupted the covenant of Levi, says the LORD of hosts, [9]and so I make you despised and abased before all the people, inasmuch as you do not keep my ways but show partiality in your instruction."

> **Sins of the people** [2:10–17]. The sins of the laity are chiefly abuses in the institution of marriage. The specific charges concern marriage to idolaters (vv. 10–12) and divorce (vv. 13–16), with an addendum on the complaint that God's justice is a myth (v. 17). This passage establishes a covenantal basis for the permanence of marriage and shows one of the primary purposes of marriage: the procreation of godly offspring (v. 15).

[10]Have we not all one Father? Has not one God created us? Why then are we faithless to one another, profaning the covenant of our fathers? [11]Judah has been faithless, and abomination has been committed in Israel and in Jerusalem. For Judah has profaned the sanctuary of the LORD, which he loves, and has married the daughter of a foreign god. [12]May the LORD cut off from the tents of Jacob any descendant[3] of the man who does this, who brings an offering to the LORD of hosts!

[13]And this second thing you do. You cover the LORD's altar with tears, with weeping and groaning because he no longer regards the offering or accepts it with favor from your hand. [14]But you say, "Why does he not?" Because the LORD was witness between you and the wife of your youth, to whom you have been faithless, though she is your companion and your wife by covenant. [15]Did he not make them one, with a portion of the Spirit in their union?[4] And what was the one God[5] seeking?[6] Godly offspring. So guard yourselves[7] in your spirit, and let none of you be faithless to the wife of your youth. [16]"For the man who does not love his wife but divorces her,[8] says the LORD, the God of Israel, covers[9] his garment with violence, says the LORD of hosts. So guard yourselves in your spirit, and do not be faithless."

[17]You have wearied the LORD with your words. But you say, "How have we wearied him?" By saying, "Everyone who does evil is good in the sight of the LORD, and he delights in them." Or by asking, "Where is the God of justice?"

> **Oracles of judgment** [3:1–12]. This unit falls into two parts—a prophecy of the sudden appearance of a judging God, a messianic prophecy (vv. 1–5), and an indictment of the people for being negligent in their tithes, accompanied by a promise of lavish blessing for obedience in tithing (vv. 6–12). The image of the refining fire (v. 2) highlights a unifying thrust of the whole book: the refining of God's people to purify them of what is corrupt.

3 "Behold, I send my messenger, and he will prepare the way before me. And the Lord whom you seek will suddenly come to his temple; and the messenger of the covenant in whom you delight, behold, he is coming, says the LORD of hosts. [2]But who can endure the day of his coming, and who can stand when he appears? For he

---

[1] Or law; also verses 7, 8, 9 [2] Hebrew they [3] Hebrew any who wakes and answers [4] Hebrew in it [5] Hebrew the one [6] Or And not one has done this who has a portion of the Spirit. And what was that one seeking? [7] Or So take care; also verse 16 [8] Hebrew who hates and divorces [9] Probable meaning (compare Septuagint and Deuteronomy 24:1-4); or "The LORD, the God of Israel, says that he hates divorce, and him who covers

is like a refiner's fire and like fullers' soap. ³He will sit as a refiner and purifier of silver, and he will purify the sons of Levi and refine them like gold and silver, and they will bring offerings in righteousness to the Lord.¹ ⁴Then the offering of Judah and Jerusalem will be pleasing to the Lord as in the days of old and as in former years.

⁵"Then I will draw near to you for judgment. I will be a swift witness against the sorcerers, against the adulterers, against those who swear falsely, against those who oppress the hired worker in his wages, the widow and the fatherless, against those who thrust aside the sojourner, and do not fear me, says the Lord of hosts.

⁶"For I the Lord do not change; therefore you, O children of Jacob, are not consumed. ⁷From the days of your fathers you have turned aside from my statutes and have not kept them. Return to me, and I will return to you, says the Lord of hosts. But you say, 'How shall we return?' ⁸Will man rob God? Yet you are robbing me. But you say, 'How have we robbed you?' In your tithes and contributions. ⁹You are cursed with a curse, for you are robbing me, the whole nation of you. ¹⁰Bring the full tithe into the storehouse, that there may be food in my house. And thereby put me to the test, says the Lord of hosts, if I will not open the windows of heaven for you and pour down for you a blessing until there is no more need. ¹¹I will rebuke the devourer² for you, so that it will not destroy the fruits of your soil, and your vine in the field shall not fail to bear, says the Lord of hosts. ¹²Then all nations will call you blessed, for you will be a land of delight, says the Lord of hosts.

> **Mingled judgment and blessing** [3:13–4:6]. This unit is mixed in content. As we read, we need to differentiate verses that (1) continue to denounce Judah for perverting the demands of the covenant, (2) state commands from God to his people, and (3) predict the coming of the Messiah to accomplish redemption—a coming "day of the Lord."

¹³"Your words have been hard against me, says the Lord. But you say, 'How have we spoken against you?' ¹⁴You have said, 'It is vain to serve God. What is the profit of our keeping his charge or of walking as in mourning before the Lord of hosts? ¹⁵And now we call the arrogant blessed. Evildoers not only prosper but they put God to the test and they escape.'"

¹⁶Then those who feared the Lord spoke with one another. The Lord paid attention and heard them, and a book of remembrance was written before him of those who feared the Lord and esteemed his name. ¹⁷"They shall be mine, says the Lord of hosts, in the day when I make up my treasured possession, and I will spare them as a man spares his son who serves him. ¹⁸Then once more you shall see the distinction between the righteous and the wicked, between one who serves God and one who does not serve him.

4 ³ "For behold, the day is coming, burning like an oven, when all the arrogant and all evildoers will be stubble. The day that is coming shall set them ablaze, says the Lord of hosts, so that it will leave them neither root nor branch. ²But for you who fear my name, the sun of righteousness shall rise with healing in its wings. You shall go out leaping like calves from the stall. ³And you shall tread down the wicked, for

¹ Or *and they will belong to the* Lord, *bringers of an offering in righteousness* ² Probably a name for some crop-destroying pest or pests ³ Ch 4:1-6 is ch 3:19-24 in the Hebrew

they will be ashes under the soles of your feet, on the day when I act, says the LORD of hosts.

[4]"Remember the law of my servant Moses, the statutes and rules[1] that I commanded him at Horeb for all Israel.

[5]"Behold, I will send you Elijah the prophet before the great and awesome day of the LORD comes. [6]And he will turn the hearts of fathers to their children and the hearts of children to their fathers, lest I come and strike the land with a decree of utter destruction."[2]

---

[1] Or *and just decrees* [2] The Hebrew term rendered *decree of utter destruction* refers to things devoted (or set apart) to the Lord (or by the Lord) for destruction

The

NEW TESTAMENT

MATTHEW

The book at a glance. 28 chapters, 1,071 verses. The author was one of Jesus' disciples, and his *Gospel is the longest by chapter count. The result is that even though Matthew's Gospel has the advantage of coming first in the NT, it may initially seem more formidable than the others. Happily, there are things that make it very manageable once we are alerted to them (see below). All four Gospels have their own interpretive slant on the life of Jesus, and Matthew's emphasis is easy to discern. As a Jew writing to fellow Jews, Matthew sets out to prove that Jesus' life and atonement are the fulfillment of OT prophecies regarding the coming Messiah. Further, he is preoccupied with the motif of Jesus as King and with the nature of discipleship for those who follow Christ.

▌**Genres.** The primary genre is Gospel, and the organizing framework of all four Gospels is *narrative or story. However, within the narrative framework of Matthew's Gospel, a major amount of space is devoted to Jesus' *discourses. Beyond that, we find the usual array of subtypes: *birth stories, *calling or vocation stories, *miracle stories, *parables, *pronouncement stories, *encounter stories, *passion stories, and *resurrection stories. (For more information on items accompanied by an asterisk, see the glossary at the back of this Bible.)

▌**Format.** The chart below shows at a glance how substantial and complex the Gospel of Matthew is, but once we are alerted to the alternating pattern around which the book is organized, it falls neatly into place. Matthew was a tax collector and therefore a book-keeper by profession, and he displays his penchant for orderly arrangement in his account of Jesus' life. The material in Matthew's Gospel is based on a rhythmic, back-and-forth movement between blocks of narrative material and blocks of discourse material. There are five passages of discourse, corresponding to the five digits on our hand—a handy mnemonic device. In fact, we can remember the five sections of discourse if we list the questions that Jesus in effect answers in each unit: How are citizens of the kingdom to live (chapters 5–7)? How are traveling disciples to conduct themselves on their evangelistic journeys (chapter 10)? What parables did Jesus tell (chapter 13)? What warnings did Jesus give about not hindering entrance into the kingdom and on forgiveness (chapter 18)? How will human history end (chapters 24–25)? Matthew even uses a set formula to signal these units, ending each with a statement to the effect of "when Jesus had finished these sayings" (7:28; 11:1; 13:53; 19:1; 26:1).

▌**The story line.** Matthew and Luke are the only two Gospel writers who begin with the birth and childhood of Jesus, thereby signaling that they are writing with the genre of

Passage	Content	Literary Form	Geographic Region	Phase of Jesus' Life
1–2	Genealogy, nativity, flight into Egypt	Narrative	Bethlehem and Egypt	Birth of Jesus and inauguration of his ministry
3–4	Jesus' baptism, temptation, calling of the disciples	Narrative	Wilderness of Judea and Galilee	
5–7	Sermon on the Mount	Discourse	Galilee	
8–9	Chiefly miracles	Narrative		
10	Commissioning of the disciples	Discourse		
11–12	Conflict stories	Narrative		The public years: Jesus' life as an itinerant teacher and miracle worker
13	Parables	Discourse	Galilee	
14–17	A kaleidoscope of varied events	Narrative		
18	Warnings about not hindering entrance into the kingdom, and about forgiveness	Discourse		
19–20	Multiple events	Narrative	Judea	
21–23	Jesus vs. the religious leaders: events leading to the crucifixion	Narrative	Jerusalem	Conclusion of Jesus' earthly ministry
24–25	Olivet Discourse	Discourse		
26–28	Jesus' trial, crucifixion, and resurrection	Narrative		

*biography in mind. With the nativity stories serving as the prologue, Matthew then proceeds to tell the story of Jesus' public years in approximately chronological sequence, with Jesus' discourses collected into the interspersed sections of speeches. Like the other Gospels, Matthew's Gospel moves toward the climax of Jesus' death and resurrection. Key transitions are flagged by Matthew: "From that time Jesus began to preach" (4:17); "Jesus began to show his disciples that he must . . . be killed" (16:21).

▌**How to visualize the book.** At the center of the action is Jesus. Around him in concentric rings we find, in order of increasing prominence, (1) the disciples, (2) the religious establishment (usually called the Pharisees, or the scribes and Pharisees), and (3) ordinary people, sometimes consisting of individuals and more often consisting of a crowd of onlookers. Additionally, inasmuch as the Gospels are *travel stories, we must always have in mind that Jesus was an itinerant and that his two main activities in his travels were teaching and performing miracles (especially healing). The cast of leading characters includes Jesus, Mary and Joseph, John the Baptist, the disciples, the Jewish religious leaders, and the two political leaders who conduct the trial of Jesus (Caiaphas the high priest and the Roman governor Pontius Pilate). As always, a good strategy for reading a story is to regard yourself as an observant traveling companion of the *protagonist.

▌**Rhetorical and stylistic features.** All four Gospels have as their *rhetorical purpose to persuade readers to believe what the writers say about Jesus, and in particular to place their faith in Jesus as Savior and Lord of their lives. More specifically, Matthew's persuasive purpose is to convince (1) his Jewish readers that Jesus is the Messiah promised in the OT and (2) his non-Jewish Gentile readers that Jesus is the Messiah of the whole world (see the Great Commission in 28:19–20). The stylistic features that distinguish Matthew's Gospel include recurrent quotation and citation from the OT and an emphasis on Jesus as being kingly or royal (even the opening genealogy places Jesus' father Joseph in the Davidic line). Additionally, Matthew is fond of the epithet "Son of David" as a title for Christ, statements to the effect of "this was done that it might be fulfilled as the prophets had said," and the formula "the kingdom of heaven is like . . ."

▌**Inferred literary intentions.** The book is designed to achieve the following literary purposes:

- enable us to relive key events of Jesus' life, death, and resurrection

- allow us to listen to some of Jesus' famous speeches and dialogues

- inform us of the facts of Jesus' life and teaching

- persuade us that Jesus is the prophesied Messiah and a divine king

- show us how to enter God's heavenly kingdom and live as citizens of it

- elevate Jesus as the supreme hero

▌**Theological themes.** (1) Christology: the story tells what Jesus taught and did, with emphasis on the ways in which Jesus is the prophesied Messiah. (2) The way of salvation: the Gospel of Matthew shows how people can be saved from their sin through faith in Jesus. (3) The kingdom of God (also called kingdom of heaven): the book explains how people can enter this kingdom (the doctrine of salvation) and how they should live as citizens of it (ethics). (4) Eschatology: on the strength of the Olivet Discourse in chapters 24–25, Matthew's Gospel is a leading NT source of information on the last things.

▌**The Gospel of Matthew as a chapter in the master story of the Bible.** The Gospel of Matthew is our gateway into the NT. It is a grand *initiation story that introduces us to many things—the NT itself, the Gospel as a genre, the person and work of Jesus as the fulfillment of OT prophecies and foreshadowings. The centerpiece of the Bible's master story is the atonement of Christ, and if we are reading the books of the Bible in their canonical order, Matthew is the first storyteller within the Bible to record the centerpiece.

The genealogy of Jesus [1:1–17]. The biographical impulse is in full force as Matthew begins with the ancestry of the story's *hero. Matthew gives the human genealogy of Jesus on his father's side, representing the legal and royal lineage. It is a selective (nonexhaustive) and artistically arranged genealogy, clustered symmetrically into three groups of fourteen ancestors. Many of the names are unfamiliar, but we can profitably ponder the significance of the names that we do recognize as members of the messianic line. In particular, notice some surprising inclusions, some of which stress the Messiah's immersion in the gritty and even seamy side of fallen history—foreigners, women whose stories might raise eyebrows, and kings of dubious moral character.

1 The book of the genealogy of Jesus Christ, the son of David, the son of Abraham. ²Abraham was the father of Isaac, and Isaac the father of Jacob, and Jacob the father of Judah and his brothers, ³and Judah the father of Perez and Zerah by Tamar, and Perez the father of Hezron, and Hezron the father of Ram,¹ ⁴and Ram the father of Amminadab, and Amminadab the father of Nahshon, and Nahshon the father of Salmon, ⁵and Salmon the father of Boaz by Rahab, and Boaz the father of Obed by Ruth, and Obed the father of Jesse, ⁶and Jesse the father of David the king.

And David was the father of Solomon by the wife of Uriah, ⁷and Solomon the father of Rehoboam, and Rehoboam the father of Abijah, and Abijah the father of Asaph,² ⁸and Asaph the father of Jehoshaphat, and Jehoshaphat the father of Joram, and Joram the father of Uzziah, ⁹and Uzziah the father of Jotham, and Jotham the father of Ahaz, and Ahaz the father of Hezekiah, ¹⁰and Hezekiah the father of Manasseh, and Manasseh the father of Amos,³ and Amos the father of Josiah, ¹¹and Josiah the father of Jechoniah and his brothers, at the time of the deportation to Babylon.

¹²And after the deportation to Babylon: Jechoniah was the father of Shealtiel,⁴ and Shealtiel the father of Zerubbabel, ¹³and Zerubbabel the father of Abiud, and Abiud the father of Eliakim, and Eliakim the father of Azor, ¹⁴and Azor the father of Zadok, and Zadok the father of Achim, and Achim the father of Eliud, ¹⁵and Eliud the father of Eleazar, and Eleazar the father of Matthan, and Matthan the father of Jacob, ¹⁶and Jacob the father of Joseph the husband of Mary, of whom Jesus was born, who is called Christ.

¹⁷So all the generations from Abraham to David were fourteen generations, and from David to the deportation to Babylon fourteen generations, and from the deportation to Babylon to the Christ fourteen generations.

The nativity story [1:18–2:12]. Matthew chose to include two events of the birth of Jesus—the virgin birth (1:18–25) and the adoration of the wise men (2:1–12). Fruitful avenues to understanding these two events include (1) the heroism of Joseph and the wise men in following God's call, (2) the ways in which the human birth of Jesus is bathed in supernatural and miraculous happenings, (3) early evidence of Matthew's persuasive purpose to prove that Jesus is the prophesied Messiah, and (4) the kingship of Christ acknowledged by some of the wealthy and wise of the world.

¹⁸Now the birth of Jesus Christ⁵ took place in this way. When his mother Mary had been betrothed⁶ to Joseph, before they came together she was found to be with child from the Holy Spirit. ¹⁹And her husband Joseph, being a just man and unwilling to put her to shame, resolved to divorce her quietly. ²⁰But as he considered these things, behold, an angel of the Lord appeared to him in a dream, saying, "Joseph, son of

---

¹ Greek Aram; also verse 4 ² Asaph is probably an alternate spelling for Asa; some manuscripts read Asa; also verse 8 ³ Amos is probably an alternate spelling for Amon; some manuscripts read Amon; twice in this verse ⁴ Greek Salathiel; twice in this verse ⁵ Some manuscripts of the Christ ⁶ That is, legally pledged to be married

David, do not fear to take Mary as your wife, for that which is conceived in her is from the Holy Spirit. ²¹She will bear a son, and you shall call his name Jesus, for he will save his people from their sins." ²²All this took place to fulfill what the Lord had spoken by the prophet:

²³ ᵃ"Behold, the virgin shall conceive and bear a son,
    and they shall call his name Immanuel"

(which means, God with us). ²⁴When Joseph woke from sleep, he did as the angel of the Lord commanded him: he took his wife, ²⁵but knew her not until she had given birth to a son. And he called his name Jesus.

2 Now after Jesus was born in Bethlehem of Judea in the days of Herod the king, behold, wise men¹ from the east came to Jerusalem, ²saying, "Where is he who has been born king of the Jews? For we saw his star when it rose² and have come to worship him." ³When Herod the king heard this, he was troubled, and all Jerusalem with him; ⁴and assembling all the chief priests and scribes of the people, he inquired of them where the Christ was to be born. ⁵They told him, "In Bethlehem of Judea, for so it is written by the prophet:

⁶ᵇ"'And you, O Bethlehem, in the land of Judah,
    are by no means least among the rulers of Judah;
  for from you shall come a ruler
    who will shepherd my people Israel.'"

⁷Then Herod summoned the wise men secretly and ascertained from them what time the star had appeared. ⁸And he sent them to Bethlehem, saying, "Go and search diligently for the child, and when you have found him, bring me word, that I too may come and worship him." ⁹After listening to the king, they went on their way. And behold, the star that they had seen when it rose went before them until it came to rest over the place where the child was. ¹⁰When they saw the star, they rejoiced exceedingly with great joy. ¹¹And going into the house they saw the child with Mary his mother, and they fell down and worshiped him. Then, opening their treasures, they offered him gifts, gold and frankincense and myrrh. ¹²And being warned in a dream not to return to Herod, they departed to their own country by another way.

The flight into Egypt, the murder of the innocents, and the return to Nazareth
[2:13–23]. The incipient idealization that permeated the previous unit of the story now gives way to such narrative ingredients as danger, conflict, intrigue (Herod's machinations, which began in the previous unit with his pretended desire to worship the newborn king), atrocity, and narrow escape. It is important to reflect on what this surrounding context of extreme evil contributes to the story of Jesus. Equally, though, we can find evidences of divine providence and protection (the positive counterpart to the story of evil), with that providence encompassing Matthew's metanarrative of the life of Jesus as the fulfillment of OT messianic prophecy.

¹³Now when they had departed, behold, an angel of the Lord appeared to Joseph in a dream and said, "Rise, take the child and his mother, and flee to Egypt, and remain there until I tell you, for Herod is about to search for the child, to destroy him." ¹⁴And

---

¹ Greek *magi*; also verses 7, 16 ² Or *in the east*; also verse 9 ᵃ Isa. 7:14 ᵇ Mic. 5:2

he rose and took the child and his mother by night and departed to Egypt [15]and remained there until the death of Herod. This was to fulfill what the Lord had spoken by the prophet, [a]"Out of Egypt I called my son."

[16]Then Herod, when he saw that he had been tricked by the wise men, became furious, and he sent and killed all the male children in Bethlehem and in all that region who were two years old or under, according to the time that he had ascertained from the wise men. [17]Then was fulfilled what was spoken by the prophet Jeremiah:

[18] [b]"A voice was heard in Ramah,
       weeping and loud lamentation,
    Rachel weeping for her children;
       she refused to be comforted, because they are no more."

[19]But when Herod died, behold, an angel of the Lord appeared in a dream to Joseph in Egypt, [20]saying, "Rise, take the child and his mother and go to the land of Israel, for those who sought the child's life are dead." [21]And he rose and took the child and his mother and went to the land of Israel. [22]But when he heard that Archelaus was reigning over Judea in place of his father Herod, he was afraid to go there, and being warned in a dream he withdrew to the district of Galilee. [23]And he went and lived in a city called Nazareth, that what was spoken by the prophets might be fulfilled: "He shall be called a Nazarene."

John the Baptist, forerunner [chapter 3]. Matthew the storyteller now shifts the focus from Jesus to the primary auxiliary character of the early part of his narrative. It is always a good reading strategy to get to know all of the characters in a story as fully as possible, compiling a portrait of every one about whom we are given enough information to compile such a sketch. While other Gospel writers give us additional information about John the Baptist, we need to read Matthew's account on the premise that he has told us as much about John as we need to know for his purposes. In Matthew 3, John fills the roles of preacher of repentance, prophetic denouncer of his society and caller to reform, the one who prepares the way for Jesus, and finally baptizer of Jesus. We can profitably assimilate the chapter by imagining ourselves as a newspaper reporter covering the events. Another good angle is to scrutinize what John the Baptist teaches us about Jesus, either directly or indirectly.

3 [c]In those days John the Baptist came preaching in the wilderness of Judea, [2]"Repent, for the kingdom of heaven is at hand." [3]For this is he who was spoken of by the prophet Isaiah when he said,

   [d]"The voice of one crying in the wilderness:
    'Prepare[1] the way of the Lord;
       make his paths straight.'"

[4]Now John wore a garment of camel's hair and a leather belt around his waist, and his food was locusts and wild honey. [5]Then Jerusalem and all Judea and all the region about the Jordan were going out to him, [6]and they were baptized by him in the river Jordan, confessing their sins.

[7]But when he saw many of the Pharisees and Sadducees coming to his baptism, he

---

[1] Or crying: *Prepare in the wilderness* [a] Hos. 11:1 [b] Jer. 31:15 [c] For 3:1-12 see parallels Mark 1:2-8; Luke 3:1-17 [d] Isa. 40:3

said to them, "You brood of vipers! Who warned you to flee from the wrath to come? [8]Bear fruit in keeping with repentance. [9]And do not presume to say to yourselves, 'We have Abraham as our father,' for I tell you, God is able from these stones to raise up children for Abraham. [10]Even now the axe is laid to the root of the trees. Every tree therefore that does not bear good fruit is cut down and thrown into the fire.

[11]"I baptize you with water for repentance, but he who is coming after me is mightier than I, whose sandals I am not worthy to carry. He will baptize you with the Holy Spirit and fire. [12]His winnowing fork is in his hand, and he will clear his threshing floor and gather his wheat into the barn, but the chaff he will burn with unquenchable fire."

[13a]Then Jesus came from Galilee to the Jordan to John, to be baptized by him. [14]John would have prevented him, saying, "I need to be baptized by you, and do you come to me?" [15]But Jesus answered him, "Let it be so now, for thus it is fitting for us to fulfill all righteousness." Then he consented. [16]And when Jesus was baptized, immediately he went up from the water, and behold, the heavens were opened to him,[1] and he saw the Spirit of God descending like a dove and coming to rest on him; [17]and behold, a voice from heaven said, "This is my beloved Son,[2] with whom I am well pleased."

The temptation of Jesus [4:1–11]. It is a convention of storytelling that the hero and other characters along the way are put into situations that test them. In this *temptation story, standing at the very beginning of Jesus' ministry, Satan tries to lure Jesus from his innocence. Stories from time immemorial have featured the element of single combat, and that is what we find here. After responding to the literal details of the conflict between Jesus and Satan, we can profitably reflect on the larger symbolic meanings of the respective temptations (each one of which tempts Jesus to do God's will in Satan's supposedly easier way) and of Jesus' way of conquering the temptations by an appeal to the OT Scriptures. At every point as we read the Gospels, we need to remember that they are *hero stories that exist to exalt the protagonist of the story. The temptation story belongs to an esteemed literary and theological tradition known as Christus victor—Christ the victor over Satan and evil.

4 [b]Then Jesus was led up by the Spirit into the wilderness to be tempted by the devil. [2]And after fasting forty days and forty nights, he was hungry. [3]And the tempter came and said to him, "If you are the Son of God, command these stones to become loaves of bread." [4]But he answered, "It is written,

[c]"'Man shall not live by bread alone,
    but by every word that comes from the mouth of God.'"

[5]Then the devil took him to the holy city and set him on the pinnacle of the temple [6]and said to him, "If you are the Son of God, throw yourself down, for it is written,

[d]"'He will command his angels concerning you,'

and

"'On their hands they will bear you up,
    lest you strike your foot against a stone.'"

---

[1] Some manuscripts omit *to him* [2] Or *my Son, my (or the) Beloved* [a] For 3:13-17 see parallels Mark 1:9-11; Luke 3:21, 22 [b] For 4:1-11 see parallels Mark 1:12, 13; Luke 4:1-13 [c] Deut. 8:3 [d] Ps. 91:11, 12

⁷Jesus said to him, "Again it is written, ᵃ'You shall not put the Lord your God to the test.'" ⁸Again, the devil took him to a very high mountain and showed him all the kingdoms of the world and their glory. ⁹And he said to him, "All these I will give you, if you will fall down and worship me." ¹⁰Then Jesus said to him, "Be gone, Satan! For it is written,

ᵇ"'You shall worship the Lord your God
and him only shall you serve.'"

¹¹Then the devil left him, and behold, angels came and were ministering to him.

> **Initiation into ministry [4:12–25].** The latent initiatory motif in the temptation story becomes dominant in the rest of chapter 4, as Matthew gives us preliminary glimpses into three main aspects of Jesus' life as recorded in the Gospels—preaching in the countryside and villages (vv. 12–17), leading a band of followers known as disciples (vv. 18–22), and performing miracles of healing (vv. 23–25). The important thing to analyze is what we learn about Jesus on the basis of what Matthew records him as doing and saying and of people's responses to him.

¹²Now when he heard that John had been arrested, he withdrew into Galilee. ¹³And leaving Nazareth he went and lived in Capernaum by the sea, in the territory of Zebulun and Naphtali, ¹⁴so that what was spoken by the prophet Isaiah might be fulfilled:

¹⁵ ᶜ"The land of Zebulun and the land of Naphtali,
the way of the sea, beyond the Jordan, Galilee of the Gentiles—
¹⁶ the people dwelling in darkness
have seen a great light,
and for those dwelling in the region and shadow of death,
on them a light has dawned."

¹⁷From that time Jesus began to preach, saying, "Repent, for the kingdom of heaven is at hand."

¹⁸ᵈWhile walking by the Sea of Galilee, he saw two brothers, Simon (who is called Peter) and Andrew his brother, casting a net into the sea, for they were fishermen. ¹⁹And he said to them, "Follow me, and I will make you fishers of men." ²⁰Immediately they left their nets and followed him. ²¹And going on from there he saw two other brothers, James the son of Zebedee and John his brother, in the boat with Zebedee their father, mending their nets, and he called them. ²²Immediately they left the boat and their father and followed him.

²³And he went throughout all Galilee, teaching in their synagogues and proclaiming the gospel of the kingdom and healing every disease and every affliction among the people. ²⁴So his fame spread throughout all Syria, and they brought him all the sick, those afflicted with various diseases and pains, those oppressed by demons, epileptics, and paralytics, and he healed them. ²⁵And great crowds followed him from Galilee and the Decapolis, and from Jerusalem and Judea, and from beyond the Jordan.

ᵃDeut. 6:16 ᵇDeut. 6:13 ᶜIsa. 9:1, 2 ᵈFor 4:18-22 see parallel Mark 1:16-20

The beginning of Jesus' most famous sermon: prologue and portrait of the ideal Christian [5:1–16]. Jesus' Sermon on the Mount, placed in Matthew's Gospel as his first major discourse, has the nature of an inauguration speech. The Sermon on the Mount also has affinities to utopian literature, inasmuch as it gives a blueprint for a good society. Jesus outlines the life that is required of those who would follow him in the kingdom of heaven. Unlike conventional utopias, which provide an institutional key to the good society, Jesus says nothing about institutions and instead locates virtue in the individual human soul in obedience to God and under his blessing. The outline of this introductory unit is threefold: a prologue that gives us the setting and audience (vv. 1–2), the famous *beatitudes (vv. 2–12), and two *metaphors that characterize the true Christian (salt and light—vv. 13–16). The beatitudes are one of the most patterned passages in the entire New Testament. They follow the Hebrew verse form of *parallelism: in each beatitude, Jesus (a) pronounces a blessing on a group of people, (b) names the group according to their essential trait, and (c) offers a reason (which is at the same time a promise) for their condition of blessedness. The promised rewards are spiritual in nature and have an eschatological as well as temporal application. The literary technique was known in ancient literature as "the character" (we call it a "character sketch").

5 Seeing the crowds, he went up on the mountain, and when he sat down, his disciples came to him. ²And he opened his mouth and taught them, saying:

³"Blessed are the poor in spirit, for theirs is the kingdom of heaven.

⁴"Blessed are those who mourn, for they shall be comforted.

⁵"Blessed are the meek, for they shall inherit the earth.

⁶"Blessed are those who hunger and thirst for righteousness, for they shall be satisfied.

⁷"Blessed are the merciful, for they shall receive mercy.

⁸"Blessed are the pure in heart, for they shall see God.

⁹"Blessed are the peacemakers, for they shall be called sons[1] of God.

¹⁰"Blessed are those who are persecuted for righteousness' sake, for theirs is the kingdom of heaven.

¹¹"Blessed are you when others revile you and persecute you and utter all kinds of evil against you falsely on my account. ¹²Rejoice and be glad, for your reward is great in heaven, for so they persecuted the prophets who were before you.

¹³"You are the salt of the earth, but if salt has lost its taste, how shall its saltiness be restored? It is no longer good for anything except to be thrown out and trampled under people's feet.

¹⁴"You are the light of the world. A city set on a hill cannot be hidden. ¹⁵Nor do people light a lamp and put it under a basket, but on a stand, and it gives light to all in the house. ¹⁶In the same way, let your light shine before others, so that they may see your good works and give glory to your Father who is in heaven.

Jesus' interpretation of the OT law [5:17–48]. As the promised Messiah who is in the process of inaugurating a spiritual kingdom, Jesus next provides an amplified explanation of the role of the OT law in the messianic kingdom. As Moses received God's law on Mount Sinai, Jesus as the second Moses here delivers the law on a mountain. Overall,

---

[1] Greek huioi; see preface

Jesus clarifies the meaning of the OT law and intensifies its application. First Jesus declares the principle that he himself is the fulfillment of the law (vv. 17–19). Then, in a preview of the rest of his remarks on the law, Jesus states that his followers must apply the law much more fully than the Pharisees do (v. 20). With this principle as the foundation, Jesus then applies the principle of exceeding the righteousness of the Pharisees in the areas of murder and anger (vv. 21–26), lust (vv. 27–30), divorce (vv. 31–32), oaths (vv. 33–37), retaliation (vv. 38–42), and relating to enemies (vv. 43–48). The rhetorical pattern revolves around "you have heard that it was said . . . but I say to you . . ." In each case, Jesus extends true obedience beyond an external or legalistic level to a spiritual principle, in effect contrasting the letter of the law as it was conventionally understood and the spirit of the law as God intended it. The last verse summarizes the thrust of what Jesus demands: "You therefore must be perfect, as your heavenly Father is perfect" (v. 48).

[17] "Do not think that I have come to abolish the Law or the Prophets; I have not come to abolish them but to fulfill them. [18] For truly, I say to you, until heaven and earth pass away, not an iota, not a dot, will pass from the Law until all is accomplished. [19] Therefore whoever relaxes one of the least of these commandments and teaches others to do the same will be called least in the kingdom of heaven, but whoever does them and teaches them will be called great in the kingdom of heaven. [20] For I tell you, unless your righteousness exceeds that of the scribes and Pharisees, you will never enter the kingdom of heaven.

[21] "You have heard that it was said to those of old, [a]'You shall not murder; and whoever murders will be liable to judgment.' [22] But I say to you that everyone who is angry with his brother[1] will be liable to judgment; whoever insults[2] his brother will be liable to the council; and whoever says, 'You fool!' will be liable to the hell[3] of fire. [23] So if you are offering your gift at the altar and there remember that your brother has something against you, [24] leave your gift there before the altar and go. First be reconciled to your brother, and then come and offer your gift. [25] Come to terms quickly with your accuser while you are going with him to court, lest your accuser hand you over to the judge, and the judge to the guard, and you be put in prison. [26] Truly, I say to you, you will never get out until you have paid the last penny.[4]

[27] "You have heard that it was said, [b]'You shall not commit adultery.' [28] But I say to you that everyone who looks at a woman with lustful intent has already committed adultery with her in his heart. [29] If your right eye causes you to sin, tear it out and throw it away. For it is better that you lose one of your members than that your whole body be thrown into hell. [30] And if your right hand causes you to sin, cut it off and throw it away. For it is better that you lose one of your members than that your whole body go into hell.

[31] "It was also said, [c]'Whoever divorces his wife, let him give her a certificate of divorce.' [32] But I say to you that everyone who divorces his wife, except on the ground of sexual immorality, makes her commit adultery, and whoever marries a divorced woman commits adultery.

[33] "Again you have heard that it was said to those of old, 'You shall not swear falsely, but shall perform to the Lord what you have sworn.' [34] But I say to you, Do not take an oath at all, either by heaven, for it is the throne of God, [35] or by the earth, for it

---

[1] Some manuscripts insert *without cause* [2] Greek says *Raca* to (a term of abuse) [3] Greek *Gehenna*; also verses 29, 30 [4] Greek *kodrantes*, Roman copper coin (Latin *quadrans*) worth about 1/64 of a *denarius* (which was a day's wage for a laborer) [a] Ex. 20:13; Deut. 5:17 [b] Ex. 20:14; Deut. 5:18 [c] Deut. 24:1

is his footstool, or by Jerusalem, for it is the city of the great King. [36]And do not take an oath by your head, for you cannot make one hair white or black. [37]Let what you say be simply 'Yes' or 'No'; anything more than this comes from evil.[1]

[38]"You have heard that it was said, [a]'An eye for an eye and a tooth for a tooth.' [39]But I say to you, Do not resist the one who is evil. But [b]if anyone slaps you on the right cheek, turn to him the other also. [40]And if anyone would sue you and take your tunic,[2] let him have your cloak as well. [41]And if anyone forces you to go one mile, go with him two miles. [42]Give to the one who begs from you, and do not refuse the one who would borrow from you.

[43]"You have heard that it was said, [c]'You shall love your neighbor and hate your enemy.' [44]But I say to you, Love your enemies and pray for those who persecute you, [45]so that you may be sons of your Father who is in heaven. For he makes his sun rise on the evil and on the good, and sends rain on the just and on the unjust. [46]For if you love those who love you, what reward do you have? Do not even the tax collectors do the same? [47]And if you greet only your brothers,[3] what more are you doing than others? Do not even the Gentiles do the same? [48]You therefore must be perfect, as your heavenly Father is perfect.

Instructions on three religious practices [6:1–18]. Again Jesus states a principle and then applies it to specific situations. The principle is not to be ostentatious about external acts of piety (v. 1). Jesus proceeds to apply the principle of secret and inner piety to the three spheres of giving offerings in public worship (vv. 2–4), praying (vv. 5–15), and fasting (vv. 16–18). The so-called Lord's Prayer is highly patterned: it falls into the rhetorical pattern of parallelism; it follows a movement from invocation or preface to petitions to a concluding doxology; the underlying movement is from God's glory to human good. Additionally, note that the pronouns are plural rather than singular, so that the prayer is not primarily a private prayer for the individual believer but a family prayer for the people of God.

---

6 "Beware of practicing your righteousness before other people in order to be seen by them, for then you will have no reward from your Father who is in heaven.

[2]"Thus, when you give to the needy, sound no trumpet before you, as the hypocrites do in the synagogues and in the streets, that they may be praised by others. Truly, I say to you, they have received their reward. [3]But when you give to the needy, do not let your left hand know what your right hand is doing, [4]so that your giving may be in secret. And your Father who sees in secret will reward you.

[5]"And when you pray, you must not be like the hypocrites. For they love to stand and pray in the synagogues and at the street corners, that they may be seen by others. Truly, I say to you, they have received their reward. [6]But when you pray, go into your room and shut the door and pray to your Father who is in secret. And your Father who sees in secret will reward you.

[7]"And when you pray, do not heap up empty phrases as the Gentiles do, for they think that they will be heard for their many words. [8]Do not be like them, for your Father knows what you need before you ask him. [9]Pray then like this:

---

[1] Or the evil one [2] Greek chiton, a long garment worn under the cloak next to the skin [3] Or brothers and sisters. The plural Greek word adelphoi (translated "brothers") refers to siblings in a family. In New Testament usage, depending on the context, adelphoi may refer either to brothers or to brothers and sisters [a] Ex. 21:24; Lev. 24:20; Deut. 19:21 [b] For 5:39-42 see parallel Luke 6:29, 30 [c] Lev. 19:18

> "Our Father in heaven,
>   hallowed be your name.[1]
> [10] Your kingdom come,
>   your will be done,[2]
>   on earth as it is in heaven.
> [11] Give us this day our daily bread,[3]
> [12] and forgive us our debts,
>   as we also have forgiven our debtors.
> [13] And lead us not into temptation,
>   but deliver us from evil.[4]

[14]For if you forgive others their trespasses, your heavenly Father will also forgive you, [15]but if you do not forgive others their trespasses, neither will your Father forgive your trespasses.

[16]"And when you fast, do not look gloomy like the hypocrites, for they disfigure their faces that their fasting may be seen by others. Truly, I say to you, they have received their reward. [17]But when you fast, anoint your head and wash your face, [18]that your fasting may not be seen by others but by your Father who is in secret. And your Father who sees in secret will reward you.

> **A threefold exhortation to choose right values** [6:19–24]. Already it is evident that the Sermon on the Mount is a triumph of artistic patterning. Patterns of three are prominent. The three religious practices in the preceding unit are now supplemented by a threefold command about choosing right values—choosing heavenly rather than earthly treasure (vv. 19–21), being full of light rather than darkness (vv. 22–23), and serving God rather than money (v. 24).

[19]"Do not lay up for yourselves treasures on earth, where moth and rust[5] destroy and where thieves break in and steal, [20]but lay up for yourselves treasures in heaven, where neither moth nor rust destroys and where thieves do not break in and steal. [21]For where your treasure is, there your heart will be also.

[22]"The eye is the lamp of the body. So, if your eye is healthy, your whole body will be full of light, [23]but if your eye is bad, your whole body will be full of darkness. If then the light in you is darkness, how great is the darkness!

[24]"No one can serve two masters, for either he will hate the one and love the other, or he will be devoted to the one and despise the other. You cannot serve God and money.[6]

> **Jesus' discourse against anxiety** [6:25–34]. This passage is a prose poem and is so suffused with parallel constructions that it could be printed as a poem. It is a mood piece in which the combination of commands, imagery, and logic actually instills the freedom from worry that the passage prescribes. Jesus awakens our sentiment for nature and then turns that imagery into a "how much more" argument. The passage is also highly rhetorical or persuasive: Jesus (a) uses interspersed *rhetorical questions as a persuasive device, (b) issues direct commands, and (c) employs a subtle logic in his

---

[1] Or Let your name be kept holy, or Let your name be treated with reverence [2] Or Let your kingdom come, let your will be done [3] Or our bread for tomorrow [4] Or the evil one; some manuscripts add For yours is the kingdom and the power and the glory, forever. Amen [5] Or worm; also verse 20 [6] Greek mammon, a Semitic word for money or possessions

argument (leading us to see that worrying is both useless and evidence of lack of faith in God).

²⁵ ᵃ"Therefore I tell you, do not be anxious about your life, what you will eat or what you will drink, nor about your body, what you will put on. Is not life more than food, and the body more than clothing? ²⁶Look at the birds of the air: they neither sow nor reap nor gather into barns, and yet your heavenly Father feeds them. Are you not of more value than they? ²⁷And which of you by being anxious can add a single hour to his span of life?¹ ²⁸And why are you anxious about clothing? Consider the lilies of the field, how they grow: they neither toil nor spin, ²⁹yet I tell you, even Solomon in all his glory was not arrayed like one of these. ³⁰But if God so clothes the grass of the field, which today is alive and tomorrow is thrown into the oven, will he not much more clothe you, O you of little faith? ³¹Therefore do not be anxious, saying, 'What shall we eat?' or 'What shall we drink?' or 'What shall we wear?' ³²For the Gentiles seek after all these things, and your heavenly Father knows that you need them all. ³³But seek first the kingdom of God and his righteousness, and all these things will be added to you.

³⁴"Therefore do not be anxious about tomorrow, for tomorrow will be anxious for itself. Sufficient for the day is its own trouble.

Instruction on four practices [7:1–12]. After an extended discourse on a single subject, Jesus returns to a series of rapid-fire topics. He issues commands on not judging others without attention to our own faults (vv. 1–5), not profaning what is holy through indiscriminate disseminating of it (v. 6), asking God for what we need (vv. 7–11), and doing to others as we wish them to do to us (v. 12).

7 ᵇ"Judge not, that you be not judged. ²For with the judgment you pronounce you will be judged, and with the measure you use it will be measured to you. ³Why do you see the speck that is in your brother's eye, but do not notice the log that is in your own eye? ⁴Or how can you say to your brother, 'Let me take the speck out of your eye,' when there is the log in your own eye? ⁵You hypocrite, first take the log out of your own eye, and then you will see clearly to take the speck out of your brother's eye.

⁶"Do not give dogs what is holy, and do not throw your pearls before pigs, lest they trample them underfoot and turn to attack you.

⁷ ᶜ"Ask, and it will be given to you; seek, and you will find; knock, and it will be opened to you. ⁸For everyone who asks receives, and the one who seeks finds, and to the one who knocks it will be opened. ⁹Or which one of you, if his son asks him for bread, will give him a stone? ¹⁰Or if he asks for a fish, will give him a serpent? ¹¹If you then, who are evil, know how to give good gifts to your children, how much more will your Father who is in heaven give good things to those who ask him!

¹²"So whatever you wish that others would do to you, do also to them, for this is the Law and the Prophets.

Three great contrasts and an epilogue [7:13–29]. As Jesus nears the end of his persuasive sermon, he nudges his listeners to make a choice by posing three great con-

---

¹ Or *a single cubit to his stature; a cubit* was about 18 inches or 45 centimeters ᵃ For 6:25-33 see parallel Luke 12:22-31 ᵇ For 7:1-5 see parallel Luke 6:37, 38, 41, 42 ᶜ For 7:7-11 see parallel Luke 11:9-13

trasts, a rhetorical strategy that shows that we need to make a decision. The heightened contrasts are between the narrow and broad ways (vv. 13–14), true and false prophets (vv. 15–23), and a house built on a rock versus one built on the sand (vv. 24–27). This great choice in life has been implicit throughout the sermon, as we have continuously had to choose whether we are ready to live the life that is pleasing to God as described by Jesus. To embody meaning in great *images and *similes like this is to use the resources of *poetry. The concluding verses (28–29) show the impact of Jesus' sermon on his listeners.

[13]"Enter by the narrow gate. For the gate is wide and the way is easy[1] that leads to destruction, and those who enter by it are many. [14]For the gate is narrow and the way is hard that leads to life, and those who find it are few.

[15]"Beware of false prophets, who come to you in sheep's clothing but inwardly are ravenous wolves. [16]You will recognize them by their fruits. Are grapes gathered from thornbushes, or figs from thistles? [17]So, every healthy tree bears good fruit, but the diseased tree bears bad fruit. [18]A healthy tree cannot bear bad fruit, nor can a diseased tree bear good fruit. [19]Every tree that does not bear good fruit is cut down and thrown into the fire. [20]Thus you will recognize them by their fruits.

[21]"Not everyone who says to me, 'Lord, Lord,' will enter the kingdom of heaven, but the one who does the will of my Father who is in heaven. [22]On that day many will say to me, 'Lord, Lord, did we not prophesy in your name, and cast out demons in your name, and do many mighty works in your name?' [23]And then will I declare to them, 'I never knew you; depart from me, you workers of lawlessness.'

[24a]"Everyone then who hears these words of mine and does them will be like a wise man who built his house on the rock. [25]And the rain fell, and the floods came, and the winds blew and beat on that house, but it did not fall, because it had been founded on the rock. [26]And everyone who hears these words of mine and does not do them will be like a foolish man who built his house on the sand. [27]And the rain fell, and the floods came, and the winds blew and beat against that house, and it fell, and great was the fall of it."

[28]And when Jesus finished these sayings, the crowds were astonished at his teaching, [29]for he was teaching them as one who had authority, and not as their scribes.

A collection of miracle stories [chapter 8]. In keeping with the back-and-forth rhythm of the book, Matthew returns to narrative after a three-chapter block of discourse material. And in keeping with his tendency to cluster various categories, he tells stories of miracles that Jesus performed. In each case the conventions at work are those of the *miracle story. We can profitably note the range of miracles that Jesus performed, the range of people with whom he came into contact as he performed his miracles, and the picture of Jesus that emerges from his miracles. We can ponder what we learn about Jesus here that we had not yet seen in Matthew's Gospel. We should never lose sight of Matthew's implicit persuasive aim to bring his readers to faith in Jesus as the promised Messiah.

[1] Some manuscripts *For the way is wide and easy* [a] For 7:24-27 see parallel Luke 6:47-49

8 When he came down from the mountain, great crowds followed him. [2a]And behold, a leper[1] came to him and knelt before him, saying, "Lord, if you will, you can make me clean." [3]And Jesus[2] stretched out his hand and touched him, saying, "I will; be clean." And immediately his leprosy was cleansed. [4]And Jesus said to him, "See that you say nothing to anyone, but go, show yourself to the priest and offer the gift that Moses commanded, for a proof to them."

[5b]When he entered Capernaum, a centurion came forward to him, appealing to him, [6]"Lord, my servant is lying paralyzed at home, suffering terribly." [7]And he said to him, "I will come and heal him." [8]But the centurion replied, "Lord, I am not worthy to have you come under my roof, but only say the word, and my servant will be healed. [9]For I too am a man under authority, with soldiers under me. And I say to one, 'Go,' and he goes, and to another, 'Come,' and he comes, and to my servant,[3] 'Do this,' and he does it." [10]When Jesus heard this, he marveled and said to those who followed him, "Truly, I tell you, with no one in Israel[4] have I found such faith. [11]I tell you, many will come from east and west and recline at table with Abraham, Isaac, and Jacob in the kingdom of heaven, [12]while the sons of the kingdom will be thrown into the outer darkness. In that place there will be weeping and gnashing of teeth." [13]And to the centurion Jesus said, "Go; let it be done for you as you have believed." And the servant was healed at that very moment.

[14c]And when Jesus entered Peter's house, he saw his mother-in-law lying sick with a fever. [15]He touched her hand, and the fever left her, and she rose and began to serve him. [16]That evening they brought to him many who were oppressed by demons, and he cast out the spirits with a word and healed all who were sick. [17]This was to fulfill what was spoken by the prophet Isaiah: [d]"He took our illnesses and bore our diseases."

[18]Now when Jesus saw a crowd around him, he gave orders to go over to the other side. [19e]And a scribe came up and said to him, "Teacher, I will follow you wherever you go." [20]And Jesus said to him, "Foxes have holes, and birds of the air have nests, but the Son of Man has nowhere to lay his head." [21]Another of the disciples said to him, "Lord, let me first go and bury my father." [22]And Jesus said to him, "Follow me, and leave the dead to bury their own dead."

[23f]And when he got into the boat, his disciples followed him. [24]And behold, there arose a great storm on the sea, so that the boat was being swamped by the waves; but he was asleep. [25]And they went and woke him, saying, "Save us, Lord; we are perishing." [26]And he said to them, "Why are you afraid, O you of little faith?" Then he rose and rebuked the winds and the sea, and there was a great calm. [27]And the men marveled, saying, "What sort of man is this, that even winds and sea obey him?"

[28g]And when he came to the other side, to the country of the Gadarenes,[5] two demon-possessed[6] men met him, coming out of the tombs, so fierce that no one could pass that way. [29]And behold, they cried out, "What have you to do with us, O Son of God? Have you come here to torment us before the time?" [30]Now a herd of many pigs was feeding at some distance from them. [31]And the demons begged him, saying, "If you cast us out, send us away into the herd of pigs." [32]And he said to them, "Go." So they came out and went into the pigs, and behold, the whole herd rushed down the steep bank into the sea and drowned in the waters. [33]The herdsmen fled, and going

[1] Leprosy was a term for several skin diseases; see Leviticus 13 [2] Greek he [3] Greek bondservant [4] Some manuscripts not even in Israel [5] Some manuscripts Gergesenes; some Gerasenes [6] Greek daimonizomai; also verse 33; elsewhere rendered oppressed by demons [a] For 8:2-4 see parallels Mark 1:40-44; Luke 5:12-14 [b] For 8:5-13 see parallel Luke 7:1-10 [c] For 8:14-17 see parallels Mark 1:29-34; Luke 4:38-41 [d] Isa. 53:4 [e] For 8:19-22 see parallels Luke 9:57-62 [f] For 8:23-27 see parallels Mark 4:35-41; Luke 8:22-25 [g] For 8:28-34 see parallels Mark 5:1-21; Luke 8:26-39

into the city they told everything, especially what had happened to the demon-possessed men. [34]And behold, all the city came out to meet Jesus, and when they saw him, they begged him to leave their region.

A miscellany of material [chapter 9]. Matthew tells three more miracle stories in this chapter (vv. 1–8, 18–26, 27–34), but there are four additional blocks of interspersed material: a calling story (v. 9); a pronouncement story (vv. 10–13); Jesus' explanation of why his disciples did not fast (vv. 14–17); Jesus' comment on the need for laborers to harvest the field (vv. 35–38). In addition to continuing to pay attention to what these units tell us about the person and work of Jesus, we can profitably ponder what they tell us about people in their fallen state.

---

9 And getting into a boat he crossed over and came to his own city. [2a]And behold, some people brought to him a paralytic, lying on a bed. And when Jesus saw their faith, he said to the paralytic, "Take heart, my son; your sins are forgiven." [3]And behold, some of the scribes said to themselves, "This man is blaspheming." [4]But Jesus, knowing[1] their thoughts, said, "Why do you think evil in your hearts? [5]For which is easier, to say, 'Your sins are forgiven,' or to say, 'Rise and walk'? [6]But that you may know that the Son of Man has authority on earth to forgive sins"—he then said to the paralytic—"Rise, pick up your bed and go home." [7]And he rose and went home. [8]When the crowds saw it, they were afraid, and they glorified God, who had given such authority to men.

[9b]As Jesus passed on from there, he saw a man called Matthew sitting at the tax booth, and he said to him, "Follow me." And he rose and followed him.

[10]And as Jesus[2] reclined at table in the house, behold, many tax collectors and sinners came and were reclining with Jesus and his disciples. [11]And when the Pharisees saw this, they said to his disciples, "Why does your teacher eat with tax collectors and sinners?" [12]But when he heard it, he said, "Those who are well have no need of a physician, but those who are sick. [13]Go and learn what this means, [c]'I desire mercy, and not sacrifice.' For I came not to call the righteous, but sinners."

[14]Then the disciples of John came to him, saying, "Why do we and the Pharisees fast,[3] but your disciples do not fast?" [15]And Jesus said to them, "Can the wedding guests mourn as long as the bridegroom is with them? The days will come when the bridegroom is taken away from them, and then they will fast. [16]No one puts a piece of unshrunk cloth on an old garment, for the patch tears away from the garment, and a worse tear is made. [17]Neither is new wine put into old wineskins. If it is, the skins burst and the wine is spilled and the skins are destroyed. But new wine is put into fresh wineskins, and so both are preserved."

[18d]While he was saying these things to them, behold, a ruler came in and knelt before him, saying, "My daughter has just died, but come and lay your hand on her, and she will live." [19]And Jesus rose and followed him, with his disciples. [20]And behold, a woman who had suffered from a discharge of blood for twelve years came up behind him and touched the fringe of his garment, [21]for she said to herself, "If I only touch his garment, I will be made well." [22]Jesus turned, and seeing her he said, "Take heart, daughter; your faith has made you well." And instantly[4] the woman was made well. [23]And when Jesus came to the ruler's house and saw the flute players and the

---

[1] Some manuscripts *perceiving* [2] Greek *he* [3] Some manuscripts add *much, or often* [4] Greek *from that hour* [a] For 9:2-8 see parallels Mark 2:1-12; Luke 5:17-26 [b] For 9:9-17 see parallels Mark 2:13-22; Luke 5:27-39 [c] Hos. 6:6 [d] For 9:18-26 see parallels Mark 5:21-43; Luke 8:40-56

crowd making a commotion, ²⁴he said, "Go away, for the girl is not dead but sleeping." And they laughed at him. ²⁵But when the crowd had been put outside, he went in and took her by the hand, and the girl arose. ²⁶And the report of this went through all that district.

²⁷And as Jesus passed on from there, two blind men followed him, crying aloud, "Have mercy on us, Son of David." ²⁸When he entered the house, the blind men came to him, and Jesus said to them, "Do you believe that I am able to do this?" They said to him, "Yes, Lord." ²⁹Then he touched their eyes, saying, "According to your faith be it done to you." ³⁰And their eyes were opened. And Jesus sternly warned them, "See that no one knows about it." ³¹But they went away and spread his fame through all that district.

³²As they were going away, behold, a demon-oppressed man who was mute was brought to him. ³³And when the demon had been cast out, the mute man spoke. And the crowds marveled, saying, "Never was anything like this seen in Israel." ³⁴But the Pharisees said, "He casts out demons by the prince of demons."

³⁵And Jesus went throughout all the cities and villages, teaching in their synagogues and proclaiming the gospel of the kingdom and healing every disease and every affliction. ³⁶When he saw the crowds, he had compassion for them, because they were harassed and helpless, like sheep without a shepherd. ³⁷Then he said to his disciples, "The harvest is plentiful, but the laborers are few; ³⁸therefore pray earnestly to the Lord of the harvest to send out laborers into his harvest."

Commissioning of the disciples [chapter 10]. After the flurry of activity represented by the brief stories of the preceding two chapters, chapter 10 returns to a discourse by Jesus. The instructions to the disciples unfold as follows: a roll call of the disciples whom Jesus called (vv. 1–4); specific instructions regarding how the disciples should conduct their itinerant ministry (vv. 5–15); a prediction that the disciples would be persecuted as they went forth in Christ's name (vv. 16–25); an exhortation not to be fearful (vv. 26–33); an explanation that Jesus had come into the world in order to force people to take sides for or against him (vv. 34–39); an outline of spiritual rewards that will come to a faithful disciple (vv. 40–42). Although some of the instructions were uniquely intended for the original disciples, this discourse also shows us principles for Christian ministry in any age, leading us to ponder what we are called to do for Jesus and what we can expect in return, both from the world and from God.

10 And he called to him his twelve disciples and gave them authority over unclean spirits, to cast them out, and to heal every disease and every affliction. ²ᵃThe names of the twelve apostles are these: first, Simon, who is called Peter, and Andrew his brother; James the son of Zebedee, and John his brother; ³Philip and Bartholomew; Thomas and Matthew the tax collector; James the son of Alphaeus, and Thaddaeus;¹ ⁴Simon the Cananaean, and Judas Iscariot, who betrayed him.

⁵These twelve Jesus sent out, instructing them, "Go nowhere among the Gentiles and enter no town of the Samaritans, ⁶but go rather to the lost sheep of the house of Israel. ⁷And proclaim as you go, saying, 'The kingdom of heaven is at hand.' ⁸Heal the sick, raise the dead, cleanse lepers,² cast out demons. You received without paying; give without pay. ⁹ᵇAcquire no gold nor silver nor copper for your belts, ¹⁰no bag for

---

¹ Some manuscripts *Lebbaeus*, or *Lebbaeus called Thaddaeus* ² Leprosy was a term for several skin diseases; see Leviticus 13 ᵃ For 10:2-4 see parallels Mark 3:16-19; Luke 6:13-16 ᵇ For 10:9-15 see parallels Mark 6:8-11; Luke 9:3-5

your journey, nor two tunics[1] nor sandals nor a staff, for the laborer deserves his food. [11]And whatever town or village you enter, find out who is worthy in it and stay there until you depart. [12]As you enter the house, greet it. [13]And if the house is worthy, let your peace come upon it, but if it is not worthy, let your peace return to you. [14]And if anyone will not receive you or listen to your words, shake off the dust from your feet when you leave that house or town. [15]Truly, I say to you, it will be more bearable on the day of judgment for the land of Sodom and Gomorrah than for that town.

[16]"Behold, I am sending you out as sheep in the midst of wolves, so be wise as serpents and innocent as doves. [17]Beware of men, for they will deliver you over to courts and flog you in their synagogues, [18]and you will be dragged before governors and kings for my sake, to bear witness before them and the Gentiles. [19]When they deliver you over, do not be anxious how you are to speak or what you are to say, for what you are to say will be given to you in that hour. [20]For it is not you who speak, but the Spirit of your Father speaking through you. [21]Brother will deliver brother over to death, and the father his child, and children will rise against parents and have them put to death, [22]and you will be hated by all for my name's sake. But the one who endures to the end will be saved. [23]When they persecute you in one town, flee to the next, for truly, I say to you, you will not have gone through all the towns of Israel before the Son of Man comes.

[24]"A disciple is not above his teacher, nor a servant[2] above his master. [25]It is enough for the disciple to be like his teacher, and the servant like his master. If they have called the master of the house Beelzebul, how much more will they malign[3] those of his household.

[26]"So have no fear of them, [a]for nothing is covered that will not be revealed, or hidden that will not be known. [27]What I tell you in the dark, say in the light, and what you hear whispered, proclaim on the housetops. [28]And do not fear those who kill the body but cannot kill the soul. Rather fear him who can destroy both soul and body in hell.[4] [29]Are not two sparrows sold for a penny?[5] And not one of them will fall to the ground apart from your Father. [30]But even the hairs of your head are all numbered. [31]Fear not, therefore; you are of more value than many sparrows. [32]So everyone who acknowledges me before men, I also will acknowledge before my Father who is in heaven, [33]but whoever denies me before men, I also will deny before my Father who is in heaven.

[34][b]"Do not think that I have come to bring peace to the earth. I have not come to bring peace, but a sword. [35]For I have come to set a man against his father, and a daughter against her mother, and a daughter-in-law against her mother-in-law. [36]And a person's enemies will be those of his own household. [37]Whoever loves father or mother more than me is not worthy of me, and whoever loves son or daughter more than me is not worthy of me. [38]And whoever does not take his cross and follow me is not worthy of me. [39]Whoever finds his life will lose it, and whoever loses his life for my sake will find it.

[40]"Whoever receives you receives me, and whoever receives me receives him who sent me. [41]The one who receives a prophet because he is a prophet will receive a prophet's reward, and the one who receives a righteous person because he is a righteous person will receive a righteous person's reward. [42]And whoever gives one of

---

[1] Greek *chiton*, a long garment worn under the cloak next to the skin [2] Greek *bondservant*; also verse 25 [3] Greek lacks *will they malign* [4] Greek *Gehenna* [5] Greek *assarion*, Roman copper coin (Latin *quadrans*) worth about 1/16 of a *denarius* (which was a day's wage for a laborer) [a] For 10:26-33 see parallel Luke 12:2-9 [b] For 10:34, 35 see parallel Luke 12:51-53

these little ones even a cup of cold water because he is a disciple, truly, I say to you, he will by no means lose his reward."

> **Conflict stories involving the crowds** [chapter 11]. The next extended block of stories (chapters 11–12) at first might seem miscellaneous in nature, but if looked at carefully, events that in themselves need not have produced conflict will be seen to have led to criticism directed toward Jesus and then Jesus' rebuke of others. There is an edge to Jesus' interactions with various onlookers. For example, an innocuous question by John the Baptist's followers about whether Jesus was the promised Messiah (vv. 1–6) telescopes into Jesus' haranguing the crowds regarding their critical spirit and lack of belief (vv. 7–24). In that context, Jesus' discourse about taking his yoke upon oneself (vv. 28–30) has the force of being an antidote to the unbelief that has just been denounced.

11 When Jesus had finished instructing his twelve disciples, he went on from there to teach and preach in their cities.

²ᵃNow when John heard in prison about the deeds of the Christ, he sent word by his disciples ³and said to him, "Are you the one who is to come, or shall we look for another?" ⁴And Jesus answered them, "Go and tell John what you hear and see: ⁵the blind receive their sight and the lame walk, lepers¹ are cleansed and the deaf hear, and the dead are raised up, and the poor have good news preached to them. ⁶And blessed is the one who is not offended by me."

⁷As they went away, Jesus began to speak to the crowds concerning John: "What did you go out into the wilderness to see? A reed shaken by the wind? ⁸What then did you go out to see? A man² dressed in soft clothing? Behold, those who wear soft clothing are in kings' houses. ⁹What then did you go out to see? A prophet?³ Yes, I tell you, and more than a prophet. ¹⁰This is he of whom it is written,

> ᵇ"'Behold, I send my messenger before your face,
>   who will prepare your way before you.'

¹¹Truly, I say to you, among those born of women there has arisen no one greater than John the Baptist. Yet the one who is least in the kingdom of heaven is greater than he. ¹²From the days of John the Baptist until now the kingdom of heaven has suffered violence,⁴ and the violent take it by force. ¹³For all the Prophets and the Law prophesied until John, ¹⁴and if you are willing to accept it, he is Elijah who is to come. ¹⁵He who has ears to hear,⁵ let him hear.

¹⁶"But to what shall I compare this generation? It is like children sitting in the marketplaces and calling to their playmates,

¹⁷   "'We played the flute for you, and you did not dance;
>   we sang a dirge, and you did not mourn.'

¹⁸For John came neither eating nor drinking, and they say, 'He has a demon.' ¹⁹The Son of Man came eating and drinking, and they say, 'Look at him! A glutton and a drunkard, a friend of tax collectors and sinners!' Yet wisdom is justified by her deeds."⁶

²⁰Then he began to denounce the cities where most of his mighty works had been done, because they did not repent. ²¹ᶜ"Woe to you, Chorazin! Woe to you, Bethsaida!

---

¹ *Leprosy* was a term for several skin diseases; see Leviticus 13 ² Or *Why then did you go out? To see a man . . .* ³ Some manuscripts *Why then did you go out? To see a prophet?* ⁴ Or *has been coming violently* ⁵ Some manuscripts omit *to hear* ⁶ Some manuscripts *children* (compare Luke 7:35) ᵃ For 11:2-19 see parallel Luke 7:18-35 ᵇ Mal. 3:1 ᶜ For 11:21-24 see parallel Luke 10:13-15

For if the mighty works done in you had been done in Tyre and Sidon, they would have repented long ago in sackcloth and ashes. ²²But I tell you, it will be more bearable on the day of judgment for Tyre and Sidon than for you. ²³And you, Capernaum, will you be exalted to heaven? You will be brought down to Hades. For if the mighty works done in you had been done in Sodom, it would have remained until this day. ²⁴But I tell you that it will be more tolerable on the day of judgment for the land of Sodom than for you."

²⁵ᵃAt that time Jesus declared, "I thank you, Father, Lord of heaven and earth, that you have hidden these things from the wise and understanding and revealed them to little children; ²⁶yes, Father, for such was your gracious will.¹ ²⁷All things have been handed over to me by my Father, and no one knows the Son except the Father, and no one knows the Father except the Son and anyone to whom the Son chooses to reveal him. ²⁸Come to me, all who labor and are heavy laden, and I will give you rest. ²⁹Take my yoke upon you, and learn from me, for I am gentle and lowly in heart, and you will find rest for your souls. ³⁰For my yoke is easy, and my burden is light."

> **Conflict stories involving the religious leaders** [chapter 12]. The next block of conflict stories pits Jesus against the religious establishment, designated as "the Pharisees." The conflicts grow out of Sabbath observance (vv. 1–21), casting out a demon (vv. 22–37), and seeking a sign from Jesus (vv. 38–45). Even the brief epilogue in which Jesus' family asks to see him has an edge to it, as Jesus remains aloof from his earthly family and states that "whoever does the will of my Father in heaven" is his brother and sister and mother (vv. 46–50).

12 At that time ᵇJesus went through the grainfields on the Sabbath. His disciples were hungry, and they began to pluck heads of grain and to eat. ²But when the Pharisees saw it, they said to him, "Look, your disciples are doing what is not lawful to do on the Sabbath." ³He said to them, "Have you not read what David did when he was hungry, and those who were with him: ⁴how he entered the house of God and ate the bread of the Presence, which it was not lawful for him to eat nor for those who were with him, but only for the priests? ⁵Or have you not read in the Law how on the Sabbath the priests in the temple profane the Sabbath and are guiltless? ⁶I tell you, something greater than the temple is here. ⁷And if you had known what this means, ᶜ'I desire mercy, and not sacrifice,' you would not have condemned the guiltless. ⁸For the Son of Man is lord of the Sabbath."

⁹He went on from there and ᵈentered their synagogue. ¹⁰And a man was there with a withered hand. And they asked him, "Is it lawful to heal on the Sabbath?"—so that they might accuse him. ¹¹He said to them, "Which one of you who has a sheep, if it falls into a pit on the Sabbath, will not take hold of it and lift it out? ¹²Of how much more value is a man than a sheep! So it is lawful to do good on the Sabbath." ¹³Then he said to the man, "Stretch out your hand." And the man stretched it out, and it was restored, healthy like the other. ¹⁴But the Pharisees went out and conspired against him, how to destroy him.

¹⁵Jesus, aware of this, withdrew from there. And many followed him, and he healed them all ¹⁶and ordered them not to make him known. ¹⁷This was to fulfill what was spoken by the prophet Isaiah:

---

¹ Or *for so it pleased you well* ᵃ For 11:25-27 see parallel Luke 10:21, 22 ᵇ For 12:1-8 see parallels Mark 2:23-28; Luke 6:1-5 ᶜ Hos. 6:6 ᵈ For 12:9-14 see parallels Mark 3:1-6; Luke 6:6-11

18 a "Behold, my servant whom I have chosen,
      my beloved with whom my soul is well pleased.
   I will put my Spirit upon him,
      and he will proclaim justice to the Gentiles.
19 He will not quarrel or cry aloud,
      nor will anyone hear his voice in the streets;
20 a bruised reed he will not break,
      and a smoldering wick he will not quench,
   until he brings justice to victory;
21   and in his name the Gentiles will hope."

22 b Then a demon-oppressed man who was blind and mute was brought to him, and he healed him, so that the man spoke and saw. 23 And all the people were amazed, and said, "Can this be the Son of David?" 24 But when the Pharisees heard it, they said, "It is only by Beelzebul, the prince of demons, that this man casts out demons." 25 Knowing their thoughts, c he said to them, "Every kingdom divided against itself is laid waste, and no city or house divided against itself will stand. 26 And if Satan casts out Satan, he is divided against himself. How then will his kingdom stand? 27 And if I cast out demons by Beelzebul, by whom do your sons cast them out? Therefore they will be your judges. 28 But if it is by the Spirit of God that I cast out demons, then the kingdom of God has come upon you. 29 Or how can someone enter a strong man's house and plunder his goods, unless he first binds the strong man? Then indeed he may plunder his house. 30 Whoever is not with me is against me, and whoever does not gather with me scatters. 31 d Therefore I tell you, every sin and blasphemy will be forgiven people, but the blasphemy against the Spirit will not be forgiven. 32 And whoever speaks a word against the Son of Man will be forgiven, but whoever speaks against the Holy Spirit will not be forgiven, either in this age or in the age to come.

33 "Either make the tree good and its fruit good, or make the tree bad and its fruit bad, for the tree is known by its fruit. 34 You brood of vipers! How can you speak good, when you are evil? For out of the abundance of the heart the mouth speaks. 35 The good person out of his good treasure brings forth good, and the evil person out of his evil treasure brings forth evil. 36 I tell you, on the day of judgment people will give account for every careless word they speak, 37 for by your words you will be justified, and by your words you will be condemned."

38 Then some of the scribes and Pharisees answered him, saying, "Teacher, we wish to see a sign from you." 39 But he answered them, e "An evil and adulterous generation seeks for a sign, but no sign will be given to it except the sign of the prophet Jonah. 40 For just as Jonah was three days and three nights in the belly of the great fish, so will the Son of Man be three days and three nights in the heart of the earth. 41 The men of Nineveh will rise up at the judgment with this generation and condemn it, for they repented at the preaching of Jonah, and behold, something greater than Jonah is here. 42 The queen of the South will rise up at the judgment with this generation and condemn it, for she came from the ends of the earth to hear the wisdom of Solomon, and behold, something greater than Solomon is here.

43 "When f the unclean spirit has gone out of a person, it passes through waterless places seeking rest, but finds none. 44 Then it says, 'I will return to my house from

---

a Isa. 42:1-3 b For 12:22-24 see parallel Luke 11:14, 15 c For 12:25-29 see parallels Mark 3:23-27; Luke 11:17-22 d For 12:31, 32 see parallel Mark 3:28-30
e For 12:39-42 see parallel Luke 11:29-32 f For 12:43-45 see parallel Luke 11:24-26

which I came.' And when it comes, it finds the house empty, swept, and put in order. [45]Then it goes and brings with it seven other spirits more evil than itself, and they enter and dwell there, and the last state of that person is worse than the first. So also will it be with this evil generation."

[46]While he was still speaking to the people, behold, [a]his mother and his brothers stood outside, asking to speak to him.[1] [48]But he replied to the man who told him, "Who is my mother, and who are my brothers?" [49]And stretching out his hand toward his disciples, he said, "Here are my mother and my brothers! [50]For whoever does the will of my Father in heaven is my brother and sister and mother."

Collected parables [chapter 13]. While Matthew's general plan is to narrate the life of Jesus in chronological sequence, within that loose framework his approach is topical. As Jesus traveled through Galilee, the various ingredients that Matthew clusters together were doubtless mingled—miracles, discourses, parables, altercations, encounters, and the like. Matthew places most of the *parables that he chose to record in chapter 13. Taken as a group, these parables are known as the parables of the kingdom because they use the introductory formula "The kingdom of heaven is like . . ." Individually, the parables go by the following titles: the parable of the sower (vv. 1–8), the weeds (vv. 24–30), the mustard seed (vv. 31–32), the leaven (v. 33), the hidden treasure (v. 44), the pearl of great value (vv. 45–46), the net of fish (vv. 47–50), and new and old treasures (vv. 51–52). To know what these parables teach us, we need to apply the usual rules of interpreting parables. Besides the parables, there are two very important additional components in this chapter. First, Jesus shows us how to interpret all of the parables by providing an interpretive key when he explicates the parables of the sower (vv. 10–23) and the weeds (vv. 36–43). Second, at the end of the chapter we learn, to our surprise, that the parables of Jesus elicited antagonism from the people of Jesus' hometown (vv. 53–58). Overall, the parables of the kingdom assert the supreme value of entering God's kingdom (which is a metaphor for believing in God and submitting to his royal authority), but many subordinate themes also emerge. The response that the parables encourage is to believe the gospel as the means of entering the kingdom.

---

13 That same day Jesus went out of the house [b]and sat beside the sea. [2]And great crowds gathered about him, so that he got into a boat and sat down. And the whole crowd stood on the beach. [3]And he told them many things in parables, saying: "A sower went out to sow. [4]And as he sowed, some seeds fell along the path, and the birds came and devoured them. [5]Other seeds fell on rocky ground, where they did not have much soil, and immediately they sprang up, since they had no depth of soil, [6]but when the sun rose they were scorched. And since they had no root, they withered away. [7]Other seeds fell among thorns, and the thorns grew up and choked them. [8]Other seeds fell on good soil and produced grain, some a hundredfold, some sixty, some thirty. [9]He who has ears,[2] let him hear."

[10]Then the disciples came and said to him, "Why do you speak to them in parables?" [11]And he answered them, "To you it has been given to know the secrets of the kingdom of heaven, but to them it has not been given. [12]For to the one who has, more will be given, and he will have an abundance, but from the one who has not, even what he has will be taken away. [13]This is why I speak to them in parables, because

---

[1] Some manuscripts insert verse 47: Someone told him, "Your mother and your brothers are standing outside, asking to speak to you" [2] Some manuscripts add here and in verse 43 to hear [a] For 12:46-50 see parallels Mark 3:31-35; Luke 8:19-21 [b] For 13:1-15 see parallels Mark 4:1-12; Luke 8:4-10

seeing they do not see, and hearing they do not hear, nor do they understand. [14]Indeed, in their case the prophecy of Isaiah is fulfilled that says:

[a]"'You will indeed hear but never understand,
    and you will indeed see but never perceive.
[15] For this people's heart has grown dull,
    and with their ears they can barely hear,
    and their eyes they have closed,
  lest they should see with their eyes
    and hear with their ears
  and understand with their heart
    and turn, and I would heal them.'

[16]But blessed are your eyes, for they see, and your ears, for they hear. [17]For truly, I say to you, many prophets and righteous people longed to see what you see, and did not see it, and to hear what you hear, and did not hear it.

[18][b]"Hear then the parable of the sower: [19]When anyone hears the word of the kingdom and does not understand it, the evil one comes and snatches away what has been sown in his heart. This is what was sown along the path. [20]As for what was sown on rocky ground, this is the one who hears the word and immediately receives it with joy, [21]yet he has no root in himself, but endures for a while, and when tribulation or persecution arises on account of the word, immediately he falls away.[1] [22]As for what was sown among thorns, this is the one who hears the word, but the cares of the world and the deceitfulness of riches choke the word, and it proves unfruitful. [23]As for what was sown on good soil, this is the one who hears the word and understands it. He indeed bears fruit and yields, in one case a hundredfold, in another sixty, and in another thirty."

[24]He put another parable before them, saying, "The kingdom of heaven may be compared to a man who sowed good seed in his field, [25]but while his men were sleeping, his enemy came and sowed weeds[2] among the wheat and went away. [26]So when the plants came up and bore grain, then the weeds appeared also. [27]And the servants[3] of the master of the house came and said to him, 'Master, did you not sow good seed in your field? How then does it have weeds?' [28]He said to them, 'An enemy has done this.' So the servants said to him, 'Then do you want us to go and gather them?' [29]But he said, 'No, lest in gathering the weeds you root up the wheat along with them. [30]Let both grow together until the harvest, and at harvest time I will tell the reapers, Gather the weeds first and bind them in bundles to be burned, but gather the wheat into my barn.'"

[31]He put another parable before them, saying, [c]"The kingdom of heaven is like a grain of mustard seed that a man took and sowed in his field. [32]It is the smallest of all seeds, but when it has grown it is larger than all the garden plants and becomes a tree, so that the birds of the air come and make nests in its branches."

[33]He told them another parable. "The kingdom of heaven is like leaven that a woman took and hid in three measures of flour, till it was all leavened."

[34]All these things Jesus said to the crowds in parables; indeed, he said nothing to them without a parable. [35]This was to fulfill what was spoken by the prophet:[4]

---

[1] Or *stumbles* [2] Probably *darnel*, a wheat-like weed [3] Greek *bondservants*; also verse 28 [4] Some manuscripts *Isaiah the prophet* [a] Isa. 6:9, 10
[b] For 13:18-23 see parallels Mark 4:13-20; Luke 8:11-15 [c] For 13:31, 32 see parallels Mark 4:30-32; Luke 13:18, 19

[a]"I will open my mouth in parables;
    I will utter what has been hidden since the foundation of the world."

[36]Then he left the crowds and went into the house. And his disciples came to him, saying, "Explain to us the parable of the weeds of the field." [37]He answered, "The one who sows the good seed is the Son of Man. [38]The field is the world, and the good seed is the sons of the kingdom. The weeds are the sons of the evil one, [39]and the enemy who sowed them is the devil. The harvest is the close of the age, and the reapers are angels. [40]Just as the weeds are gathered and burned with fire, so will it be at the close of the age. [41]The Son of Man will send his angels, and they will gather out of his kingdom all causes of sin and all law-breakers, [42]and throw them into the fiery furnace. In that place there will be weeping and gnashing of teeth. [43]Then the righteous will shine like the sun in the kingdom of their Father. He who has ears, let him hear.

[44]"The kingdom of heaven is like treasure hidden in a field, which a man found and covered up. Then in his joy he goes and sells all that he has and buys that field.

[45]"Again, the kingdom of heaven is like a merchant in search of fine pearls, [46]who, on finding one pearl of great value, went and sold all that he had and bought it.

[47]"Again, the kingdom of heaven is like a net that was thrown into the sea and gathered fish of every kind. [48]When it was full, men drew it ashore and sat down and sorted the good into containers but threw away the bad. [49]So it will be at the close of the age. The angels will come out and separate the evil from the righteous [50]and throw them into the fiery furnace. In that place there will be weeping and gnashing of teeth.

[51]"Have you understood all these things?" They said to him, "Yes." [52]And he said to them, "Therefore every scribe who has been trained for the kingdom of heaven is like a master of a house, who brings out of his treasure what is new and what is old."

[53]And when Jesus had finished these parables, he went away from there, [54][b]and coming to his hometown he taught them in their synagogue, so that they were astonished, and said, "Where did this man get this wisdom and these mighty works? [55]Is not this the carpenter's son? Is not his mother called Mary? And are not his brothers James and Joseph and Simon and Judas? [56]And are not all his sisters with us? Where then did this man get all these things?" [57]And they took offense at him. But Jesus said to them, "A prophet is not without honor except in his hometown and in his own household." [58]And he did not do many mighty works there, because of their unbelief.

Tragedy and miracle [chapter 14]. After the chapter devoted to the parables, Matthew places a four-chapter block of narratives. The apparent randomness of the material captures the quality of Jesus' life on the road during his public years. Additionally, we need to remember that all of the far-flung material serves the purpose of explaining the person and work of Jesus. At the beginning of chapter 14, the impulse toward historical documentation overshadows the genre of the hero story, as Matthew includes the narrative of the death of John the Baptist (vv. 1–12), which does not involve Jesus at all. This is followed by two miracle stories—the feeding of the five thousand (vv. 13–21) and Jesus' walking on the water (vv. 22–36). Both stories incorporate lessons of faith and provide strong evidence for the divine identity of Jesus Christ as the God of providence and creation.

---

[a] Ps. 78:2 [b] For 13:54-58 see parallel Mark 6:1-6

14 [a]At that time Herod the tetrarch heard about the fame of Jesus, [2]and he said to his servants, "This is John the Baptist. He has been raised from the dead; that is why these miraculous powers are at work in him." [3]For Herod had seized John and bound him and put him in prison for the sake of Herodias, his brother Philip's wife,[1] [4]because John had been saying to him, "It is not lawful for you to have her." [5]And though he wanted to put him to death, he feared the people, because they held him to be a prophet. [6]But when Herod's birthday came, the daughter of Herodias danced before the company and pleased Herod, [7]so that he promised with an oath to give her whatever she might ask. [8]Prompted by her mother, she said, "Give me the head of John the Baptist here on a platter." [9]And the king was sorry, but because of his oaths and his guests he commanded it to be given. [10]He sent and had John beheaded in the prison, [11]and his head was brought on a platter and given to the girl, and she brought it to her mother. [12]And his disciples came and took the body and buried it, and they went and told Jesus.

[13]Now when Jesus heard this, [b]he withdrew from there in a boat to a desolate place by himself. But when the crowds heard it, they followed him on foot from the towns. [14]When he went ashore he saw a great crowd, and he had compassion on them and healed their sick. [15]Now when it was evening, the disciples came to him and said, "This is a desolate place, and the day is now over; send the crowds away to go into the villages and buy food for themselves." [16]But Jesus said, "They need not go away; you give them something to eat." [17]They said to him, "We have only five loaves here and two fish." [18]And he said, "Bring them here to me." [19]Then he ordered the crowds to sit down on the grass, and taking the five loaves and the two fish, he looked up to heaven and said a blessing. Then he broke the loaves and gave them to the disciples, and the disciples gave them to the crowds. [20]And they all ate and were satisfied. And they took up twelve baskets full of the broken pieces left over. [21]And those who ate were about five thousand men, besides women and children.

[22][c]Immediately he made the disciples get into the boat and go before him to the other side, while he dismissed the crowds. [23]And after he had dismissed the crowds, he went up on the mountain by himself to pray. When evening came, he was there alone, [24]but the boat by this time was a long way[2] from the land,[3] beaten by the waves, for the wind was against them. [25]And in the fourth watch of the night he came to them, walking on the sea. [26]But when the disciples saw him walking on the sea, they were terrified, and said, "It is a ghost!" and they cried out in fear. [27]But immediately Jesus spoke to them, saying, "Take heart; it is I. Do not be afraid."

[28]And Peter answered him, "Lord, if it is you, command me to come to you on the water." [29]He said, "Come." So Peter got out of the boat and walked on the water and came to Jesus. [30]But when he saw the wind,[4] he was afraid, and beginning to sink he cried out, "Lord, save me." [31]Jesus immediately reached out his hand and took hold of him, saying to him, "O you of little faith, why did you doubt?" [32]And when they got into the boat, the wind ceased. [33]And those in the boat worshiped him, saying, "Truly you are the Son of God."

[34][d]And when they had crossed over, they came to land at Gennesaret. [35]And when the men of that place recognized him, they sent around to all that region and brought

---

[1] Some manuscripts *his brother's wife* [2] Greek *many stadia, a stadion* was about 607 feet or 185 meters [3] Some manuscripts *was out on the sea* [4] Some manuscripts *strong wind* [a] For 14:1-12 see parallels Mark 6:14-29; Luke 9:7-9 [b] For 14:13-21 see parallels Mark 6:32-44; Luke 9:10-17; John 6:1-13 [c] For 14:22-33 see parallels Mark 6:45-52; John 6:16-21 [d] For 14:34-36 see parallel Mark 6:53-56

to him all who were sick ³⁶and implored him that they might only touch the fringe of his garment. And as many as touched it were made well.

> **Conflict and miracle** [chapter 15]. A second chapter of narrative material follows a threefold pattern similar to that in chapter 14: the conflict story involving the complaint of the religious leaders about Jesus' casualness regarding ceremonial cleansing (vv. 1–20) is followed by two miracle stories—the healing of the demon-possessed daughter of the Canaanite woman (vv. 21–28) and the feeding of the four thousand (vv. 29–39). These stories give us a wealth of insight into the spiritual life and into Jesus' power and compassion.

15 ᵃThen Pharisees and scribes came to Jesus from Jerusalem and said, ²"Why do your disciples break the tradition of the elders? For they do not wash their hands when they eat." ³He answered them, "And why do you break the commandment of God for the sake of your tradition? ⁴For God commanded, ᵇ'Honor your father and your mother,' and, ᶜ'Whoever reviles father or mother must surely die.' ⁵But you say, 'If anyone tells his father or his mother, "What you would have gained from me is given to God,"¹ ⁶he need not honor his father.' So for the sake of your tradition you have made void the word² of God. ⁷You hypocrites! Well did Isaiah prophesy of you, when he said:

⁸ᵈ"'This people honors me with their lips,
    but their heart is far from me;
⁹ in vain do they worship me,
    teaching as doctrines the commandments of men.'"

¹⁰And he called the people to him and said to them, "Hear and understand: ¹¹it is not what goes into the mouth that defiles a person, but what comes out of the mouth; this defiles a person." ¹²Then the disciples came and said to him, "Do you know that the Pharisees were offended when they heard this saying?" ¹³He answered, "Every plant that my heavenly Father has not planted will be rooted up. ¹⁴Let them alone; they are blind guides.³ And if the blind lead the blind, both will fall into a pit." ¹⁵But Peter said to him, "Explain the parable to us." ¹⁶And he said, "Are you also still without understanding? ¹⁷Do you not see that whatever goes into the mouth passes into the stomach and is expelled?⁴ ¹⁸But what comes out of the mouth proceeds from the heart, and this defiles a person. ¹⁹For out of the heart come evil thoughts, murder, adultery, sexual immorality, theft, false witness, slander. ²⁰These are what defile a person. But to eat with unwashed hands does not defile anyone."

²¹ᵉAnd Jesus went away from there and withdrew to the district of Tyre and Sidon. ²²And behold, a Canaanite woman from that region came out and was crying, "Have mercy on me, O Lord, Son of David; my daughter is severely oppressed by a demon." ²³But he did not answer her a word. And his disciples came and begged him, saying, "Send her away, for she is crying out after us." ²⁴He answered, "I was sent only to the lost sheep of the house of Israel." ²⁵But she came and knelt before him, saying, "Lord, help me." ²⁶And he answered, "It is not right to take the children's bread and throw it to the dogs." ²⁷She said, "Yes, Lord, yet even the dogs eat the crumbs that fall from

¹ Or is an offering ² Some manuscripts law ³ Some manuscripts add of the blind ⁴ Greek is expelled into the latrine ᵃ For 15:1-20 see parallel Mark 7:1-23 ᵇ Ex. 20:12 ᶜ Ex. 21:17 ᵈ Isa. 29:13 ᵉ For 15:21-28 see parallel Mark 7:24-30

their masters' table." ²⁸Then Jesus answered her, "O woman, great is your faith! Be it done for you as you desire." And her daughter was healed instantly.¹

²⁹Jesus went on from there and walked beside the Sea of Galilee. And he went up on the mountain and sat down there. ³⁰And great crowds came to him, bringing with them the lame, the blind, the crippled, the mute, and many others, and they put them at his feet, and he healed them, ³¹so that the crowd wondered, when they saw the mute speaking, the crippled healthy, the lame walking, and the blind seeing. And they glorified the God of Israel.

³²ᵃThen Jesus called his disciples to him and said, "I have compassion on the crowd because they have been with me now three days and have nothing to eat. And I am unwilling to send them away hungry, lest they faint on the way." ³³And the disciples said to him, "Where are we to get enough bread in such a desolate place to feed so great a crowd?" ³⁴And Jesus said to them, "How many loaves do you have?" They said, "Seven, and a few small fish." ³⁵And directing the crowd to sit down on the ground, ³⁶he took the seven loaves and the fish, and having given thanks he broke them and gave them to the disciples, and the disciples gave them to the crowds. ³⁷And they all ate and were satisfied. And they took up seven baskets full of the broken pieces left over. ³⁸Those who ate were four thousand men, besides women and children. ³⁹And after sending away the crowds, he got into the boat and went to the region of Magadan.

Stories of Jesus with his disciples [chapter 16]. The block of brief narratives continues in this unit. After a conflict story involving the religious leaders (vv. 1–4), the stories that Matthew chose to include involve Jesus' interactions with his disciples, as follows: Jesus' warning to avoid the false teaching of the Pharisees and Sadducees (vv. 5–12); Peter's great confession of Jesus as the Christ (vv. 13–20); Jesus' preparing of his disciples for his suffering, death, and resurrection (vv. 21–23); Jesus' discourse about the need to deny oneself as a prerequisite for following him, combined with further statements about his coming death (vv. 24–28). Peter's confession and Jesus' follow-up words are a climactic point in Matthew's Gospel. Peter's confession concludes the case Matthew has made that Jesus is the Christ. With his identity thus clarified, Jesus turns at once to his work, and the story now moves inexorably to the cross.

16 ᵇAnd the Pharisees and Sadducees came, and to test him they asked him to show them a sign from heaven. ²He answered them,² "When it is evening, you say, 'It will be fair weather, for the sky is red.' ³And in the morning, 'It will be stormy today, for the sky is red and threatening.' You know how to interpret the appearance of the sky, but you cannot interpret the signs of the times. ⁴An evil and adulterous generation seeks for a sign, but no sign will be given to it except the sign of Jonah." So he left them and departed.

⁵When the disciples reached the other side, they had forgotten to bring any bread. ⁶Jesus said to them, "Watch and beware of the leaven of the Pharisees and Sadducees." ⁷And they began discussing it among themselves, saying, "We brought no bread." ⁸But Jesus, aware of this, said, "O you of little faith, why are you discussing among yourselves the fact that you have no bread? ⁹Do you not yet perceive? Do you not remember the five loaves for the five thousand, and how many baskets you gath-

¹ Greek *from that hour* ² Some manuscripts omit the following words to the end of verse 3 ᵃ For 15:32-39 see parallel Mark 8:1-10 ᵇ For 16:1-12 see parallel Mark 8:11-21

ered? ¹⁰Or the seven loaves for the four thousand, and how many baskets you gathered? ¹¹How is it that you fail to understand that I did not speak about bread? Beware of the leaven of the Pharisees and Sadducees." ¹²Then they understood that he did not tell them to beware of the leaven of bread, but of the teaching of the Pharisees and Sadducees.

¹³ᵃNow when Jesus came into the district of Caesarea Philippi, he asked his disciples, "Who do people say that the Son of Man is?" ¹⁴And they said, "Some say John the Baptist, others say Elijah, and others Jeremiah or one of the prophets." ¹⁵He said to them, "But who do you say that I am?" ¹⁶Simon Peter replied, "You are the Christ, the Son of the living God." ¹⁷And Jesus answered him, "Blessed are you, Simon Bar-Jonah! For flesh and blood has not revealed this to you, but my Father who is in heaven. ¹⁸And I tell you, you are Peter, and on this rock¹ I will build my church, and the gates of hell² shall not prevail against it. ¹⁹I will give you the keys of the kingdom of heaven, and whatever you bind on earth shall be bound in heaven, and whatever you loose on earth shall be loosed³ in heaven." ²⁰Then he strictly charged the disciples to tell no one that he was the Christ.

²¹ᵇFrom that time Jesus began to show his disciples that he must go to Jerusalem and suffer many things from the elders and chief priests and scribes, and be killed, and on the third day be raised. ²²And Peter took him aside and began to rebuke him, saying, "Far be it from you, Lord!⁴ This shall never happen to you." ²³But he turned and said to Peter, "Get behind me, Satan! You are a hindrance⁵ to me. For you are not setting your mind on the things of God, but on the things of man."

²⁴Then Jesus told his disciples, "If anyone would come after me, let him deny himself and take up his cross and follow me. ²⁵For whoever would save his life⁶ will lose it, but whoever loses his life for my sake will find it. ²⁶For what will it profit a man if he gains the whole world and forfeits his soul? Or what shall a man give in return for his soul? ²⁷For the Son of Man is going to come with his angels in the glory of his Father, and then he will repay each person according to what he has done. ²⁸Truly, I say to you, there are some standing here who will not taste death until they see the Son of Man coming in his kingdom."

Varied events in the life of Jesus [chapter 17]. Matthew rounds out his four-chapter block of narrative with four divergent events, capturing the varied nature of Jesus' life: the transfiguration (vv. 1–13); healing of the epileptic boy (vv. 14–20); prediction of Jesus' death and resurrection (vv. 22–23); a miracle related to the question of paying taxes (vv. 24–27). Each of these events contributes to the characterization of Jesus.

17 ᶜAnd after six days Jesus took with him Peter and James, and John his brother, and led them up a high mountain by themselves. ²And he was transfigured before them, and his face shone like the sun, and his clothes became white as light. ³And behold, there appeared to them Moses and Elijah, talking with him. ⁴And Peter said to Jesus, "Lord, it is good that we are here. If you wish, I will make three tents here, one for you and one for Moses and one for Elijah." ⁵He was still speaking when, behold, a bright cloud overshadowed them, and a voice from the cloud said, "This is

¹ The Greek words for *Peter* and *rock* sound similar ² Greek *the gates of Hades* ³ Or *shall have been bound . . . shall have been loosed* ⁴ Or "[May God be] merciful to you, Lord!" ⁵ Greek *stumbling block* ⁶ The same Greek word can mean either *soul* or *life*, depending on the context; twice in this verse and twice in verse 26 ᵃ For 16:13-16 see parallels Mark 8:27-29; Luke 9:18-20 ᵇ For 16:21-28 see parallels Mark 8:31–9:1; Luke 9:22-27 ᶜ For 17:1-8 see parallels Mark 9:2-8; Luke 9:28-36

my beloved Son,[1] with whom I am well pleased; listen to him." [6]When the disciples heard this, they fell on their faces and were terrified. [7]But Jesus came and touched them, saying, "Rise, and have no fear." [8]And when they lifted up their eyes, they saw no one but Jesus only.

[9a]And as they were coming down the mountain, Jesus commanded them, "Tell no one the vision, until the Son of Man is raised from the dead." [10]And the disciples asked him, "Then why do the scribes say that first Elijah must come?" [11]He answered, "Elijah does come, and he will restore all things. [12]But I tell you that Elijah has already come, and they did not recognize him, but did to him whatever they pleased. So also the Son of Man will certainly suffer at their hands." [13]Then the disciples understood that he was speaking to them of John the Baptist.

[14b]And when they came to the crowd, a man came up to him and, kneeling before him, [15]said, "Lord, have mercy on my son, for he is an epileptic and he suffers terribly. For often he falls into the fire, and often into the water. [16]And I brought him to your disciples, and they could not heal him." [17]And Jesus answered, "O faithless and twisted generation, how long am I to be with you? How long am I to bear with you? Bring him here to me." [18]And Jesus rebuked the demon,[2] and it[3] came out of him, and the boy was healed instantly.[4] [19]Then the disciples came to Jesus privately and said, "Why could we not cast it out?" [20]He said to them, "Because of your little faith. For truly, I say to you, if you have faith like a grain of mustard seed, you will say to this mountain, 'Move from here to there,' and it will move, and nothing will be impossible for you."[5]

[22c]As they were gathering[6] in Galilee, Jesus said to them, "The Son of Man is about to be delivered into the hands of men, [23]and they will kill him, and he will be raised on the third day." And they were greatly distressed.

[24]When they came to Capernaum, the collectors of the two-drachma tax went up to Peter and said, "Does your teacher not pay the tax?" [25]He said, "Yes." And when he came into the house, Jesus spoke to him first, saying, "What do you think, Simon? From whom do kings of the earth take toll or tax? From their sons or from others?" [26]And when he said, "From others," Jesus said to him, "Then the sons are free. [27]However, not to give offense to them, go to the sea and cast a hook and take the first fish that comes up, and when you open its mouth you will find a shekel.[7] Take that and give it to them for me and for yourself."

Discourse on not hindering entrance into the kingdom, and on forgiveness [chapter 18]. The event that gave rise to this discourse was the disciples' crass and self-seeking question "Who is greatest in the kingdom of heaven?" (v. 1). The entire remainder of the chapter is a discourse by Jesus, and it covers the following topics: the need to become like a child, accompanied by a warning not to cause a child to sin (vv. 2–6); a further warning to avoid temptations to sins that would prevent one from entering the kingdom, even to the hyperbolic point of cutting off a limb (vv. 7–9); the parable of the lost sheep as further evidence that God does not want any "of these little ones" to perish (vv. 10–14); instructions on what to do "if your brother sins against you," accompanied by the possibility of being excluded from the kingdom (vv. 15–20); instructions about forgiveness, accompanied by the parable of the unforgiving servant (vv. 21–35). The first half of the chapter focuses on the urgency of not hindering someone (including

---

[1] Or my Son, my (or the) Beloved [2] Greek it [3] Greek the demon [4] Greek from that hour [5] Some manuscripts insert verse 21: But this kind never comes out except by prayer and fasting [6] Some manuscripts remained [7] Greek stater, a silver coin worth four drachmas or approximately one shekel [a] For 17:9-13 see parallel Mark 9:9-13 [b] For 17:14-19 see parallels Mark 9:14-28; Luke 9:37-42 [c] For 17:22, 23 see parallels Mark 9:30-32; Luke 9:43-45

oneself) from entering the kingdom of heaven (even the section dealing with an unre- pentant brother is an implied warning not to indulge in such behavior, since it would exclude one from the kingdom [vv. 17–20]). Similarly, the last verse of the parable of the unforgiving servant (v. 35) raises the possibility of not entering the kingdom if one refuses to extend forgiveness. This section is oriented to the disciples' spiritual care for others—not hindering them but seeking the lost and pursuing reconciliation.

18 [a]At that time the disciples came to Jesus, saying, "Who is the greatest in the kingdom of heaven?" [2]And calling to him a child, he put him in the midst of them [3]and said, "Truly, I say to you, unless you turn and become like children, you will never enter the kingdom of heaven. [4]Whoever humbles himself like this child is the greatest in the kingdom of heaven.

[5]"Whoever receives one such child in my name receives me, [6]but whoever causes one of these little ones who believe in me to sin,[1] it would be better for him to have a great millstone fastened around his neck and to be drowned in the depth of the sea.

[7]"Woe to the world for temptations to sin![2] For it is necessary that temptations come, but woe to the one by whom the temptation comes! [8]And if your hand or your foot causes you to sin, cut it off and throw it away. It is better for you to enter life crippled or lame than with two hands or two feet to be thrown into the eternal fire. [9]And if your eye causes you to sin, tear it out and throw it away. It is better for you to enter life with one eye than with two eyes to be thrown into the hell[3] of fire.

[10]"See that you do not despise one of these little ones. For I tell you that in heaven their angels always see the face of my Father who is in heaven.[4] [12]What do you think? If a man has a hundred sheep, and one of them has gone astray, does he not leave the ninety-nine on the mountains and go in search of the one that went astray? [13]And if he finds it, truly, I say to you, he rejoices over it more than over the ninety-nine that never went astray. [14]So it is not the will of my[5] Father who is in heaven that one of these little ones should perish.

[15]"If your brother sins against you, go and tell him his fault, between you and him alone. If he listens to you, you have gained your brother. [16]But if he does not listen, take one or two others along with you, that every charge may be established by the evidence of two or three witnesses. [17]If he refuses to listen to them, tell it to the church. And if he refuses to listen even to the church, let him be to you as a Gentile and a tax collector. [18]Truly, I say to you, whatever you bind on earth shall be bound in heaven, and whatever you loose on earth shall be loosed[6] in heaven. [19]Again I say to you, if two of you agree on earth about anything they ask, it will be done for them by my Father in heaven. [20]For where two or three are gathered in my name, there am I among them."

[21]Then Peter came up and said to him, "Lord, how often will my brother sin against me, and I forgive him? As many as seven times?" [22]Jesus said to him, "I do not say to you seven times, but seventy times seven.[7]

[23]"Therefore the kingdom of heaven may be compared to a king who wished to set- tle accounts with his servants.[8] [24]When he began to settle, one was brought to him who owed him ten thousand talents.[9] [25]And since he could not pay, his master ordered him to be sold, with his wife and children and all that he had, and payment

---

[1] Greek causes . . . to stumble; also verses 8, 9 [2] Greek stumbling blocks [3] Greek Gehenna [4] Some manuscripts add verse 11: For the Son of Man came to save the lost [5] Some manuscripts your [6] Or shall have been bound . . . shall have been loosed [7] Or seventy-seven times [8] Greek bondservants; also verses 28, 31 [9] A talent was a monetary unit worth about twenty years' wages for a laborer [a] For 18:1-5 see parallels Mark 9:33-37; Luke 9:46-48

to be made. ²⁶So the servant¹ fell on his knees, imploring him, 'Have patience with me, and I will pay you everything.' ²⁷And out of pity for him, the master of that servant released him and forgave him the debt. ²⁸But when that same servant went out, he found one of his fellow servants who owed him a hundred denarii,² and seizing him, he began to choke him, saying, 'Pay what you owe.' ²⁹So his fellow servant fell down and pleaded with him, 'Have patience with me, and I will pay you.' ³⁰He refused and went and put him in prison until he should pay the debt. ³¹When his fellow servants saw what had taken place, they were greatly distressed, and they went and reported to their master all that had taken place. ³²Then his master summoned him and said to him, 'You wicked servant! I forgave you all that debt because you pleaded with me. ³³And should not you have had mercy on your fellow servant, as I had mercy on you?' ³⁴And in anger his master delivered him to the jailers,³ until he should pay all his debt. ³⁵So also my heavenly Father will do to every one of you, if you do not forgive your brother from your heart."

Lessons for the disciples [19:1–20:16]. Even though chapters 19–23 are sufficiently diverse to require dividing the material into separate units, we should notice that this entire block recounts events leading up to the crucifixion, as signaled by the transition verse at the beginning: "Now when Jesus had finished these sayings, he went away from Galilee and entered the region of Judea" (19:1). Chapter 19 starts out as a conflict story in which the Pharisees try to trip Jesus with a trick question regarding divorce (19:1–9), but Jesus' reply to the Pharisees prompts a question about marriage from the disciples (19:10–12). The disciples learn a second lesson when they try to prevent children from coming to Jesus (19:13–15). Following that, Jesus' standing up to the rich young man who values possessions over entrance into the kingdom of God (19:16–22) leads Jesus to instruct the disciples further about the requirements for entering the kingdom (19:23–30). The discourse to the disciples ends with the parable of the laborers in the vineyard (20:1–16), which teaches the additional point that heavenly reward depends on divine grace rather than human merit. As always, what the disciples learned we as readers today are expected to learn.

19 Now when Jesus had finished these sayings, he went away from Galilee and ªentered the region of Judea beyond the Jordan. ²And large crowds followed him, and he healed them there.

³And Pharisees came up to him and tested him by asking, "Is it lawful to divorce one's wife for any cause?" ⁴He answered, "Have you not read that he who created them from the beginning made them male and female, ⁵and said, ᵇ'Therefore a man shall leave his father and his mother and hold fast to his wife, and the two shall become one flesh'? ⁶So they are no longer two but one flesh. What therefore God has joined together, let not man separate." ⁷They said to him, "Why then did Moses command one to give a certificate of divorce and to send her away?" ⁸He said to them, "Because of your hardness of heart Moses allowed you to divorce your wives, but from the beginning it was not so. ⁹And I say to you: whoever divorces his wife, except for sexual immorality, and marries another, commits adultery."⁴

¹⁰The disciples said to him, "If such is the case of a man with his wife, it is better

¹ Greek *bondservant*; also verses 27, 28, 29, 32, 33 ² A *denarius* was a day's wage for a laborer ³ Greek *torturers* ⁴ Some manuscripts add *and whoever marries a divorced woman commits adultery*; other manuscripts *except for sexual immorality, makes her commit adultery, and whoever marries a divorced woman commits adultery* ª For 19:1-9 see parallel Mark 10:1-12 ᵇ Gen. 2:24

not to marry." [11]But he said to them, "Not everyone can receive this saying, but only those to whom it is given. [12]For there are eunuchs who have been so from birth, and there are eunuchs who have been made eunuchs by men, and there are eunuchs who have made themselves eunuchs for the sake of the kingdom of heaven. Let the one who is able to receive this receive it."

[13a]Then children were brought to him that he might lay his hands on them and pray. The disciples rebuked the people, [14]but Jesus said, "Let the little children come to me and do not hinder them, for to such belongs the kingdom of heaven." [15]And he laid his hands on them and went away.

[16b]And behold, a man came up to him, saying, "Teacher, what good deed must I do to have eternal life?" [17]And he said to him, "Why do you ask me about what is good? There is only one who is good. If you would enter life, keep the commandments." [18]He said to him, "Which ones?" And Jesus said, [c]"You shall not murder, You shall not commit adultery, You shall not steal, You shall not bear false witness, [19]Honor your father and mother, and, [d]You shall love your neighbor as yourself." [20]The young man said to him, "All these I have kept. What do I still lack?" [21]Jesus said to him, "If you would be perfect, go, sell what you possess and give to the poor, and you will have treasure in heaven; and come, follow me." [22]When the young man heard this he went away sorrowful, for he had great possessions.

[23]And Jesus said to his disciples, "Truly, I say to you, only with difficulty will a rich person enter the kingdom of heaven. [24]Again I tell you, it is easier for a camel to go through the eye of a needle than for a rich person to enter the kingdom of God." [25]When the disciples heard this, they were greatly astonished, saying, "Who then can be saved?" [26]But Jesus looked at them and said, "With man this is impossible, but with God all things are possible." [27]Then Peter said in reply, "See, we have left everything and followed you. What then will we have?" [28]Jesus said to them, "Truly, I say to you, in the new world,[1] when the Son of Man will sit on his glorious throne, you who have followed me will also sit on twelve thrones, judging the twelve tribes of Israel. [29]And everyone who has left houses or brothers or sisters or father or mother or children or lands, for my name's sake, will receive a hundredfold[2] and will inherit eternal life. [30]But many who are first will be last, and the last first.

20 "For the kingdom of heaven is like a master of a house who went out early in the morning to hire laborers for his vineyard. [2]After agreeing with the laborers for a denarius[3] a day, he sent them into his vineyard. [3]And going out about the third hour he saw others standing idle in the marketplace, [4]and to them he said, 'You go into the vineyard too, and whatever is right I will give you.' [5]So they went. Going out again about the sixth hour and the ninth hour, he did the same. [6]And about the eleventh hour he went out and found others standing. And he said to them, 'Why do you stand here idle all day?' [7]They said to him, 'Because no one has hired us.' He said to them, 'You go into the vineyard too.' [8]And when evening came, the owner of the vineyard said to his foreman, 'Call the laborers and pay them their wages, beginning with the last, up to the first.' [9]And when those hired about the eleventh hour came, each of them received a denarius. [10]Now when those hired first came, they thought they would receive more, but each of them also received a denarius. [11]And on receiv-

---

[1] Greek *in the regeneration* [2] Some manuscripts *manifold* [3] A *denarius* was a day's wage for a laborer [a] For 19:13-15 see parallels Mark 10:13-16; Luke 18:15-17 [b] For 19:16-30 see parallels Mark 10:17-31; Luke 18:18-30 [c] Ex. 20:12-16; Deut. 5:16-20 [d] Lev. 19:18

ing it they grumbled at the master of the house, ¹²saying, 'These last worked only one hour, and you have made them equal to us who have borne the burden of the day and the scorching heat.' ¹³But he replied to one of them, 'Friend, I am doing you no wrong. Did you not agree with me for a denarius? ¹⁴Take what belongs to you and go. I choose to give to this last worker as I give to you. ¹⁵Am I not allowed to do what I choose with what belongs to me? Or do you begrudge my generosity?'¹ ¹⁶So the last will be first, and the first last."

Jesus' journey to Jerusalem [20:17–21:11]. The ongoing narrative now reaches the events leading to the crucifixion. The first collection of these stories constitutes a travel story in which Jesus and his companions go "up to Jerusalem" (20:17). The sequence is as follows: Jesus tells his disciples about his impending passion and death (20:17–19); Jesus has to contend with the ambition of the mother of James and John and the follow-up anger of the other disciples (20:20–28); Jesus heals two blind men on the outskirts of Jericho (20:29–34); Jesus makes the triumphal entry (21:1–11). As we ponder the individual units, we learn about Jesus and about his sacrifice. Further, the triumphal entry fits in with Matthew's overall purpose to show that Jesus is the prophesied Messiah and also the true King.

¹⁷ᵃAnd as Jesus was going up to Jerusalem, he took the twelve disciples aside, and on the way he said to them, ¹⁸"See, we are going up to Jerusalem. And the Son of Man will be delivered over to the chief priests and scribes, and they will condemn him to death ¹⁹and deliver him over to the Gentiles to be mocked and flogged and crucified, and he will be raised on the third day."

²⁰ᵇThen the mother of the sons of Zebedee came up to him with her sons, and kneeling before him she asked him for something. ²¹And he said to her, "What do you want?" She said to him, "Say that these two sons of mine are to sit, one at your right hand and one at your left, in your kingdom." ²²Jesus answered, "You do not know what you are asking. Are you able to drink the cup that I am to drink?" They said to him, "We are able." ²³He said to them, "You will drink my cup, but to sit at my right hand and at my left is not mine to grant, but it is for those for whom it has been prepared by my Father." ²⁴And when the ten heard it, they were indignant at the two brothers. ²⁵But Jesus called them to him and said, "You know that the rulers of the Gentiles lord it over them, and their great ones exercise authority over them. ²⁶It shall not be so among you. But whoever would be great among you must be your servant,² ²⁷and whoever would be first among you must be your slave,³ ²⁸even as the Son of Man came not to be served but to serve, and to give his life as a ransom for many."

²⁹ᶜAnd as they went out of Jericho, a great crowd followed him. ³⁰And behold, there were two blind men sitting by the roadside, and when they heard that Jesus was passing by, they cried out, "Lord,⁴ have mercy on us, Son of David!" ³¹The crowd rebuked them, telling them to be silent, but they cried out all the more, "Lord, have mercy on us, Son of David!" ³²And stopping, Jesus called them and said, "What do you want me to do for you?" ³³They said to him, "Lord, let our eyes be opened." ³⁴And Jesus in pity touched their eyes, and immediately they recovered their sight and followed him.

¹ Or is your eye bad because I am good? ² Greek diakonos ³ Greek bondservant (doulos) ⁴ Some manuscripts omit Lord ᵃ For 20:17-19 see parallels Mark 10:32-34; Luke 18:31-33 ᵇ For 20:20-28 see parallel Mark 10:35-45 ᶜ For 20:29-34 see parallels Mark 10:46-52; Luke 18:35-43

21 [a]Now when they drew near to Jerusalem and came to Bethphage, to the Mount of Olives, then Jesus sent two disciples, [2]saying to them, "Go into the village in front of you, and immediately you will find a donkey tied, and a colt with her. Untie them and bring them to me. [3]If anyone says anything to you, you shall say, 'The Lord needs them,' and he will send them at once." [4]This took place to fulfill what was spoken by the prophet, saying,

[5] [b]"Say to the daughter of Zion,
'Behold, your king is coming to you,
    humble, and mounted on a donkey,
    and[1] on a colt, the foal of a beast of burden.'"

[6]The disciples went and did as Jesus had directed them. [7]They brought the donkey and the colt and put on them their cloaks, and he sat on them. [8]Most of the crowd spread their cloaks on the road, and others cut branches from the trees and spread them on the road. [9]And the crowds that went before him and that followed him were shouting, "Hosanna to the Son of David! Blessed is he who comes in the name of the Lord! Hosanna in the highest!" [10]And when he entered Jerusalem, the whole city was stirred up, saying, "Who is this?" [11]And the crowds said, "This is the prophet Jesus, from Nazareth of Galilee."

> **Jesus at the temple** [21:12–27]. Everything is laden with special meaning in the events and discourses that occurred just before Jesus' arrest and crucifixion. The sequence in Matthew's account is as follows: the cleansing of the temple (vv. 12–17); the barren fig tree, accompanied by Jesus' teaching about the power of faith (vv. 18–22); a conflict story in which the religious leaders try unsuccessfully to challenge Jesus' authority (vv. 23–27). The effect of these events at the temple is to intensify the plot conflict between Jesus and his opponents.

[12][c]And Jesus entered the temple[2] and drove out all who sold and bought in the temple, and he overturned the tables of the money-changers and the seats of those who sold pigeons. [13]He said to them, "It is written, [d]'My house shall be called a house of prayer,' but you make it a den of robbers."

[14]And the blind and the lame came to him in the temple, and he healed them. [15]But when the chief priests and the scribes saw the wonderful things that he did, and the children crying out in the temple, "Hosanna to the Son of David!" they were indignant, [16]and they said to him, "Do you hear what these are saying?" And Jesus said to them, "Yes; have you never read,

[e]"'Out of the mouth of infants and nursing babies
    you have prepared praise'?"

[17]And leaving them, he went out of the city to Bethany and lodged there.

[18][f]In the morning, as he was returning to the city, he became hungry. [19]And seeing a fig tree by the wayside, he went to it and found nothing on it but only leaves. And he said to it, "May no fruit ever come from you again!" And the fig tree withered at once.

[1] Or even [2] Some manuscripts add of God [a] For 21:1-9 see parallels Mark 11:1-10; Luke 19:28-38; John 12:12-15 [b] Zech. 9:9 [c] For 21:12-16 see parallels Mark 11:15-18; Luke 19:45-47 [d] Isa. 56:7 [e] Ps. 8:2 (Gk.) [f] For 21:18-22 see parallel Mark 11:12-14, 20-24

²⁰When the disciples saw it, they marveled, saying, "How did the fig tree wither at once?" ²¹And Jesus answered them, "Truly, I say to you, if you have faith and do not doubt, you will not only do what has been done to the fig tree, but even if you say to this mountain, 'Be taken up and thrown into the sea,' it will happen. ²²And whatever you ask in prayer, you will receive, if you have faith."

²³ᵃAnd when he entered the temple, the chief priests and the elders of the people came up to him as he was teaching, and said, "By what authority are you doing these things, and who gave you this authority?" ²⁴Jesus answered them, "I also will ask you one question, and if you tell me the answer, then I also will tell you by what authority I do these things. ²⁵The baptism of John, from where did it come? From heaven or from man?" And they discussed it among themselves, saying, "If we say, 'From heaven,' he will say to us, 'Why then did you not believe him?' ²⁶But if we say, 'From man,' we are afraid of the crowd, for they all hold that John was a prophet." ²⁷So they answered Jesus, "We do not know." And he said to them, "Neither will I tell you by what authority I do these things.

More parables of the kingdom [21:28–22:14]. The context of another block of parables remains that of Jesus' final days spent at the temple. This context charges the parables with added intensity, and because the parables are critical of the religious establishment, they are in effect yet another conflict story as Jesus moves toward the point of no return with the Jewish authorities. The parables are as follows: the two sons and their father's vineyard (21:28–32); the wicked tenants who killed the owner's son (21:33–46); the marriage feast (22:1–14). Good interpretive frameworks for interacting with these parables are these: what they teach about entering God's kingdom; what they say about Jesus' identity; how they constitute a conflict story leading toward Jesus' death at the hands of the Jewish authorities.

²⁸"What do you think? A man had two sons. And he went to the first and said, 'Son, go and work in the vineyard today.' ²⁹And he answered, 'I will not,' but afterward he changed his mind and went. ³⁰And he went to the other son and said the same. And he answered, 'I go, sir,' but did not go. ³¹Which of the two did the will of his father?" They said, "The first." Jesus said to them, "Truly, I say to you, the tax collectors and the prostitutes go into the kingdom of God before you. ³²For John came to you in the way of righteousness, and you did not believe him, but the tax collectors and the prostitutes believed him. And even when you saw it, you did not afterward change your minds and believe him.

³³ᵇ"Hear another parable. There was a master of a house who planted a vineyard and put a fence around it and dug a winepress in it and built a tower and leased it to tenants, and went into another country. ³⁴When the season for fruit drew near, he sent his servants¹ to the tenants to get his fruit. ³⁵And the tenants took his servants and beat one, killed another, and stoned another. ³⁶Again he sent other servants, more than the first. And they did the same to them. ³⁷Finally he sent his son to them, saying, 'They will respect my son.' ³⁸But when the tenants saw the son, they said to themselves, 'This is the heir. Come, let us kill him and have his inheritance.' ³⁹And they took him and threw him out of the vineyard and killed him. ⁴⁰When therefore the owner of the vineyard comes, what will he do to those tenants?" ⁴¹They said to

¹ Greek *bondservants*; also verses 35, 36 ª For 21:23-27 see parallels Mark 11:27-33; Luke 20:1-8 ᵇ For 21:33-46 see parallels Mark 12:1-12; Luke 20:9-18

him, "He will put those wretches to a miserable death and let out the vineyard to other tenants who will give him the fruits in their seasons."

[42]Jesus said to them, "Have you never read in the Scriptures:

> [a]"'The stone that the builders rejected
>   has become the cornerstone;[1]
>   this was the Lord's doing,
>   and it is marvelous in our eyes'?

[43]Therefore I tell you, the kingdom of God will be taken away from you and given to a people producing its fruits. [44]And the one who falls on this stone will be broken to pieces; and when it falls on anyone, it will crush him."[2]

[45]When the chief priests and the Pharisees heard his parables, they perceived that he was speaking about them. [46]And although they were seeking to arrest him, they feared the crowds, because they held him to be a prophet.

22 And again Jesus spoke to them in parables, saying, [2]"The kingdom of heaven may be compared to a king who gave a wedding feast for his son, [3]and sent his servants[3] to call those who were invited to the wedding feast, but they would not come. [4]Again he sent other servants, saying, 'Tell those who are invited, See, I have prepared my dinner, my oxen and my fat calves have been slaughtered, and everything is ready. Come to the wedding feast.' [5]But they paid no attention and went off, one to his farm, another to his business, [6]while the rest seized his servants, treated them shamefully, and killed them. [7]The king was angry, and he sent his troops and destroyed those murderers and burned their city. [8]Then he said to his servants, 'The wedding feast is ready, but those invited were not worthy. [9]Go therefore to the main roads and invite to the wedding feast as many as you find.' [10]And those servants went out into the roads and gathered all whom they found, both bad and good. So the wedding hall was filled with guests.

[11]"But when the king came in to look at the guests, he saw there a man who had no wedding garment. [12]And he said to him, 'Friend, how did you get in here without a wedding garment?' And he was speechless. [13]Then the king said to the attendants, 'Bind him hand and foot and cast him into the outer darkness. In that place there will be weeping and gnashing of teeth.' [14]For many are called, but few are chosen."

Conflict stories [22:15–46]. The hostility of the religious establishment against Jesus becomes even more intense in this threefold series of questions and answers. The Jewish leaders wrangle with Jesus over three questions—the paying of taxes (vv. 15–22), the nature of married relationships in resurrection (vv. 23–33), and what the greatest commandment is (vv. 34–40). In turn, Jesus accosts the religious establishment with the question "What do you think about the Christ?" (vv. 41–46). The unit has been an extended battle of wits between Jesus and his opponents, ending with Jesus' triumph each time. Humanly speaking, the crucifixion would never have occurred if the Jewish leaders had not become incorrigible to the point of executing Jesus. Events such as those narrated in this unit clue us in to how the religious leaders became provoked to that point.

---

[1] Greek *the head of the corner* [2] Some manuscripts omit verse 44 [3] Greek *bondservants*; also verses 4, 6, 8, 10 [a] Ps. 118:22, 23

¹⁵ᵃThen the Pharisees went and plotted how to entangle him in his words. ¹⁶And they sent their disciples to him, along with the Herodians, saying, "Teacher, we know that you are true and teach the way of God truthfully, and you do not care about anyone's opinion, for you are not swayed by appearances.¹ ¹⁷Tell us, then, what you think. Is it lawful to pay taxes to Caesar, or not?" ¹⁸But Jesus, aware of their malice, said, "Why put me to the test, you hypocrites? ¹⁹Show me the coin for the tax." And they brought him a denarius.² ²⁰And Jesus said to them, "Whose likeness and inscription is this?" ²¹They said, "Caesar's." Then he said to them, "Therefore render to Caesar the things that are Caesar's, and to God the things that are God's." ²²When they heard it, they marveled. And they left him and went away.

²³The same day Sadducees came to him, who say that there is no resurrection, and they asked him a question, ²⁴saying, "Teacher, Moses said, 'If a man dies having no children, his brother must marry the widow and raise up children for his brother.' ²⁵Now there were seven brothers among us. The first married and died, and having no children left his wife to his brother. ²⁶So too the second and third, down to the seventh. ²⁷After them all, the woman died. ²⁸In the resurrection, therefore, of the seven, whose wife will she be? For they all had her."

²⁹But Jesus answered them, "You are wrong, because you know neither the Scriptures nor the power of God. ³⁰For in the resurrection they neither marry nor are given in marriage, but are like angels in heaven. ³¹And as for the resurrection of the dead, have you not read what was said to you by God: ³²ᵇ'I am the God of Abraham, and the God of Isaac, and the God of Jacob'? He is not God of the dead, but of the living." ³³And when the crowd heard it, they were astonished at his teaching.

³⁴ᶜBut when the Pharisees heard that he had silenced the Sadducees, they gathered together. ³⁵And one of them, a lawyer, asked him a question to test him. ³⁶"Teacher, which is the great commandment in the Law?" ³⁷And he said to him, "You shall love the Lord your God with all your heart and with all your soul and with all your mind. ³⁸This is the great and first commandment. ³⁹And a second is like it: You shall love your neighbor as yourself. ⁴⁰On these two commandments depend all the Law and the Prophets."

⁴¹ᵈNow while the Pharisees were gathered together, Jesus asked them a question, ⁴²saying, "What do you think about the Christ? Whose son is he?" They said to him, "The son of David." ⁴³He said to them, "How is it then that David, in the Spirit, calls him Lord, saying,

⁴⁴ᵉ"'The Lord said to my Lord,
   Sit at my right hand,
      until I put your enemies under your feet'?

⁴⁵If then David calls him Lord, how is he his son?" ⁴⁶And no one was able to answer him a word, nor from that day did anyone dare to ask him any more questions.

Jesus' satiric attack on the Pharisees [chapter 23]. Chapter 23 is a "swing" chapter that has affinities with both the preceding and following material. As a discourse, it has something in common with the Olivet Discourse that follows, but its content places it with the preceding material, where it functions as the climax of Jesus' conflict with the Pharisees—the most unrestrained attack that Jesus made on them. The chapter is

---

¹ Greek *for you do not look at people's faces* ² A *denarius* was a day's wage for a laborer ᵃ For 22:15-32 see parallels Mark 12:13-27; Luke 20:20-38 ᵇ Ex. 3:6
ᶜ For 22:34-40 see parallel Mark 12:28-33 ᵈ For 22:41-45 see parallels Mark 12:35-37; Luke 20:41-44 ᵉ Ps. 110:1

a plain-spoken *satire. Jesus' satiric weapons include the "woe formula" (as he pronounces a sevenfold "woe" against the Pharisees), vituperation (direct rebuke), name-
calling ("you blind guides"), the catalog of abuses, *hyperbole, *metaphor ("you serpents"), and *simile ("you are like whitewashed tombs"). A good approach to the chapter
is to compile a running list of the abuses for which Jesus attacks the Pharisees, in an
awareness that if these abuses were wrong for the Pharisees to practice, they are wrong
for us to practice.

23 Then Jesus ªsaid to the crowds and to his disciples, ²"The scribes and the
Pharisees sit on Moses' seat, ³so practice and observe whatever they tell
you—but not what they do. For they preach, but do not practice. ⁴They tie up heavy
burdens, hard to bear,¹ and lay them on people's shoulders, but they themselves are
not willing to move them with their finger. ⁵They do all their deeds to be seen by others. For they make their phylacteries broad and their fringes long, ⁶and they love the
place of honor at feasts and the best seats in the synagogues ⁷and greetings in the
marketplaces and being called rabbi² by others. ⁸But you are not to be called rabbi,
for you have one teacher, and you are all brothers.³ ⁹And call no man your father on
earth, for you have one Father, who is in heaven. ¹⁰Neither be called instructors, for
you have one instructor, the Christ. ¹¹The greatest among you shall be your servant.
¹²Whoever exalts himself will be humbled, and whoever humbles himself will be
exalted.

¹³"But woe to you, scribes and Pharisees, hypocrites! For you shut the kingdom of
heaven in people's faces. For you neither enter yourselves nor allow those who would
enter to go in.⁴ ¹⁵Woe to you, scribes and Pharisees, hypocrites! For you travel across
sea and land to make a single proselyte, and when he becomes a proselyte, you make
him twice as much a child of hell⁵ as yourselves.

¹⁶"Woe to you, blind guides, who say, 'If anyone swears by the temple, it is nothing,
but if anyone swears by the gold of the temple, he is bound by his oath.' ¹⁷You blind
fools! For which is greater, the gold or the temple that has made the gold sacred?
¹⁸And you say, 'If anyone swears by the altar, it is nothing, but if anyone swears by
the gift that is on the altar, he is bound by his oath.' ¹⁹You blind men! For which is
greater, the gift or the altar that makes the gift sacred? ²⁰So whoever swears by the
altar swears by it and by everything on it. ²¹And whoever swears by the temple swears
by it and by him who dwells in it. ²²And whoever swears by heaven swears by the
throne of God and by him who sits upon it.

²³"Woe to you, scribes and Pharisees, hypocrites! For you tithe mint and dill and
cumin, and have neglected the weightier matters of the law: justice and mercy and
faithfulness. These you ought to have done, without neglecting the others. ²⁴You blind
guides, straining out a gnat and swallowing a camel!

²⁵"Woe to you, scribes and Pharisees, hypocrites! For you clean the outside of the
cup and the plate, but inside they are full of greed and self-indulgence. ²⁶You blind
Pharisee! First clean the inside of the cup and the plate, that the outside also may be
clean.

²⁷"Woe to you, scribes and Pharisees, hypocrites! For you are like whitewashed
tombs, which outwardly appear beautiful, but within are full of dead people's bones

---

¹ Some manuscripts omit *hard to bear* ² *Rabbi* means *my teacher*, or *my master*; also verse 8 ³ Or *brothers and sisters* ⁴ Some manuscripts add here (or
after verse 12) verse 14: *Woe to you, scribes and Pharisees, hypocrites! For you devour widows' houses and for a pretense you make long prayers; therefore
you will receive the greater condemnation* ⁵ Greek *Gehenna*; also verse 33 ª For 23:1, 2, 5-7 see parallels Mark 12:38-40; Luke 20:45, 46

and all uncleanness. [28]So you also outwardly appear righteous to others, but within you are full of hypocrisy and lawlessness.

[29]"Woe to you, scribes and Pharisees, hypocrites! For you build the tombs of the prophets and decorate the monuments of the righteous, [30]saying, 'If we had lived in the days of our fathers, we would not have taken part with them in shedding the blood of the prophets.' [31]Thus you witness against yourselves that you are sons of those who murdered the prophets. [32]Fill up, then, the measure of your fathers. [33]You serpents, you brood of vipers, how are you to escape being sentenced to hell? [34]Therefore I send you prophets and wise men and scribes, some of whom you will kill and crucify, and some you will flog in your synagogues and persecute from town to town, [35]so that on you may come all the righteous blood shed on earth, from the blood of innocent Abel to the blood of Zechariah the son of Barachiah,[1] whom you murdered between the sanctuary and the altar. [36]Truly, I say to you, all these things will come upon this generation.

[37][a]"O Jerusalem, Jerusalem, the city that kills the prophets and stones those who are sent to it! How often would I have gathered your children together as a hen gathers her brood under her wings, and you would not! [38]See, your house is left to you desolate. [39]For I tell you, you will not see me again, until you say, [b]'Blessed is he who comes in the name of the Lord.'"

The Olivet Discourse, part 1 [chapter 24]. Next to the book of Revelation, the Olivet Discourse is the most extended New Testament passage dealing with the last things. The discourse is occasioned by the disciples' twofold question about when Jerusalem will be destroyed and what the sign of the close of the age will be (vv. 1–3). This question sets up a double focus for the visions of destruction that make up this chapter, which predicts what would happen with the destruction of Jerusalem in A.D. 70 as a lens for seeing what will happen at the end of time. Jesus' answer to the disciples' questions unfolds a chronological sequence, as signaled by the transition formulas "then" (v. 9), "so when" (v. 15), "immediately after" (v. 29), "then" (v. 30). Jesus outlines a fivefold sequence, and the first four events are presented in chapter 24, as follows: (1) international warfare and natural catastrophes (vv. 4–8); (2) great persecution for believers, including the appearance of false prophets (vv. 9–14); (3) earthly disaster (including the fall of Jerusalem), great tribulation, and the appearance of false christs and false prophets (vv. 15–28); (4) the coming of Christ to gather the elect (vv. 29–31). The remainder of chapter 24 is an interlude in the chronological sequence, as Jesus comments on the imminence of the coming destruction (vv. 32–35) and the unexpectedness with which the end will come (vv. 36–51).

---

24 [c]Jesus left the temple and was going away, when his disciples came to point out to him the buildings of the temple. [2]But he answered them, "You see all these, do you not? Truly, I say to you, there will not be left here one stone upon another that will not be thrown down."

[3]As he sat on the Mount of Olives, the disciples came to him privately, saying, "Tell us, when will these things be, and what will be the sign of your coming and of the close of the age?" [4]And Jesus answered them, "See that no one leads you astray. [5]For many will come in my name, saying, 'I am the Christ,' and they will lead many astray.

---

[1] Some manuscripts omit *the son of Barachiah* [a]For 23:37-39 see parallel Luke 13:34, 35 [b] Ps. 118:26 [c]For 24:1-51 see parallels Mark 13:1-37; Luke 21:5-36

⁶And you will hear of wars and rumors of wars. See that you are not alarmed, for this must take place, but the end is not yet. ⁷For nation will rise against nation, and kingdom against kingdom, and there will be famines and earthquakes in various places. ⁸All these are but the beginning of the birth pains.

⁹"Then they will deliver you up to tribulation and put you to death, and you will be hated by all nations for my name's sake. ¹⁰And then many will fall away¹ and betray one another and hate one another. ¹¹And many false prophets will arise and lead many astray. ¹²And because lawlessness will be increased, the love of many will grow cold. ¹³But the one who endures to the end will be saved. ¹⁴And this gospel of the kingdom will be proclaimed throughout the whole world as a testimony to all nations, and then the end will come.

¹⁵"So when you see the abomination of desolation spoken of by the prophet Daniel, standing in the holy place (let the reader understand), ¹⁶then let those who are in Judea flee to the mountains. ¹⁷Let the one who is on the housetop not go down to take what is in his house, ¹⁸and let the one who is in the field not turn back to take his cloak. ¹⁹And alas for women who are pregnant and for those who are nursing infants in those days! ²⁰Pray that your flight may not be in winter or on a Sabbath. ²¹For then there will be great tribulation, such as has not been from the beginning of the world until now, no, and never will be. ²²And if those days had not been cut short, no human being would be saved. But for the sake of the elect those days will be cut short. ²³Then if anyone says to you, 'Look, here is the Christ!' or 'There he is!' do not believe it. ²⁴For false christs and false prophets will arise and perform great signs and wonders, so as to lead astray, if possible, even the elect. ²⁵See, I have told you beforehand. ²⁶So, if they say to you, 'Look, he is in the wilderness,' do not go out. If they say, 'Look, he is in the inner rooms,' do not believe it. ²⁷For as the lightning comes from the east and shines as far as the west, so will be the coming of the Son of Man. ²⁸Wherever the corpse is, there the vultures will gather.

²⁹"Immediately after the tribulation of those days the sun will be darkened, and the moon will not give its light, and the stars will fall from heaven, and the powers of the heavens will be shaken. ³⁰Then will appear in heaven the sign of the Son of Man, and then all the tribes of the earth will mourn, and they will see the Son of Man coming on the clouds of heaven with power and great glory. ³¹And he will send out his angels with a loud trumpet call, and they will gather his elect from the four winds, from one end of heaven to the other.

³²"From the fig tree learn its lesson: as soon as its branch becomes tender and puts out its leaves, you know that summer is near. ³³So also, when you see all these things, you know that he is near, at the very gates. ³⁴Truly, I say to you, this generation will not pass away until all these things take place. ³⁵Heaven and earth will pass away, but my words will not pass away.

³⁶"But concerning that day and hour no one knows, not even the angels of heaven, nor the Son,² but the Father only. ³⁷For as were the days of Noah, so will be the coming of the Son of Man. ³⁸For as in those days before the flood they were eating and drinking, marrying and giving in marriage, until the day when Noah entered the ark, ³⁹and they were unaware until the flood came and swept them all away, so will be the coming of the Son of Man. ⁴⁰Then two men will be in the field; one will be taken and one left. ⁴¹Two women will be grinding at the mill; one will be taken and one left. ⁴²Therefore, stay awake, for you do not know on what day your Lord is coming. ⁴³But

¹ Or *stumble* ² Some manuscripts omit *nor the Son*

know this, that if the master of the house had known in what part of the night the thief was coming, he would have stayed awake and would not have let his house be broken into. [44]Therefore you also must be ready, for the Son of Man is coming at an hour you do not expect.

[45]"Who then is the faithful and wise servant,[1] whom his master has set over his household, to give them their food at the proper time? [46]Blessed is that servant whom his master will find so doing when he comes. [47]Truly, I say to you, he will set him over all his possessions. [48]But if that wicked servant says to himself, 'My master is delayed,' [49]and begins to beat his fellow servants[2] and eats and drinks with drunkards, [50]the master of that servant will come on a day when he does not expect him and at an hour he does not know [51]and will cut him in pieces and put him with the hypocrites. In that place there will be weeping and gnashing of teeth.

> **The Olivet Discourse, part 2** [chapter 25]. The fifth phase of future events that Jesus predicts is final judgment. In chapter 25 this is pictured in the form of two eschatological-cal parables—the wise and foolish virgins (vv. 1–13) and the stewards entrusted with talents (vv. 14–30)—and the awe-inspiring narrative of the separation of the sheep and the goats "when the Son of Man comes in his glory" (vv. 31–46). Each of these units is laden with themes in addition to their primary assertion that there will be a final judgment. For example, we can see the need to be ready for Jesus' return at any time; the need to be busy working for God until the end comes; and the need to feel the urgency that stems from knowing that there will be a final and eternal separation between the redeemed and the damned.

25 "Then the kingdom of heaven will be like ten virgins who took their lamps[3] and went to meet the bridegroom.[4] [2]Five of them were foolish, and five were wise. [3]For when the foolish took their lamps, they took no oil with them, [4]but the wise took flasks of oil with their lamps. [5]As the bridegroom was delayed, they all became drowsy and slept. [6]But at midnight there was a cry, 'Here is the bridegroom! Come out to meet him.' [7]Then all those virgins rose and trimmed their lamps. [8]And the foolish said to the wise, 'Give us some of your oil, for our lamps are going out.' [9]But the wise answered, saying, 'Since there will not be enough for us and for you, go rather to the dealers and buy for yourselves.' [10]And while they were going to buy, the bridegroom came, and those who were ready went in with him to the marriage feast, and the door was shut. [11]Afterward the other virgins came also, saying, 'Lord, lord, open to us.' [12]But he answered, 'Truly, I say to you, I do not know you.' [13]Watch therefore, for you know neither the day nor the hour.

[14]"For it will be like a man going on a journey, who called his servants[5] and entrusted to them his property. [15]To one he gave five talents,[6] to another two, to another one, to each according to his ability. Then he went away. [16]He who had received the five talents went at once and traded with them, and he made five talents more. [17]So also he who had the two talents made two talents more. [18]But he who had received the one talent went and dug in the ground and hid his master's money. [19]Now after a long time the master of those servants came and settled accounts with them. [20]And he who had received the five talents came forward, bringing five talents more, saying, 'Master, you delivered to me five talents; here I have made five talents more.'

---

[1] Greek *bondservant*; also verses 46, 48, 50 [2] Greek *bondservants* [3] Or *torches* [4] Some manuscripts add *and the bride* [5] Greek *bondservants*; also verse 19 [6] A *talent* was a monetary unit worth about twenty years' wages for a laborer

[21]His master said to him, 'Well done, good and faithful servant.[1] You have been faithful over a little; I will set you over much. Enter into the joy of your master.' [22]And he also who had the two talents came forward, saying, 'Master, you delivered to me two talents; here I have made two talents more.' [23]His master said to him, 'Well done, good and faithful servant. You have been faithful over a little; I will set you over much. Enter into the joy of your master.' [24]He also who had received the one talent came forward, saying, 'Master, I knew you to be a hard man, reaping where you did not sow, and gathering where you scattered no seed, [25]so I was afraid, and I went and hid your talent in the ground. Here you have what is yours.' [26]But his master answered him, 'You wicked and slothful servant! You knew that I reap where I have not sown and gather where I scattered no seed? [27]Then you ought to have invested my money with the bankers, and at my coming I should have received what was my own with interest. [28]So take the talent from him and give it to him who has the ten talents. [29]For to everyone who has will more be given, and he will have an abundance. But from the one who has not, even what he has will be taken away. [30]And cast the worthless servant into the outer darkness. In that place there will be weeping and gnashing of teeth.'

[31]"When the Son of Man comes in his glory, and all the angels with him, then he will sit on his glorious throne. [32]Before him will be gathered all the nations, and he will separate people one from another as a shepherd separates the sheep from the goats. [33]And he will place the sheep on his right, but the goats on the left. [34]Then the King will say to those on his right, 'Come, you who are blessed by my Father, inherit the kingdom prepared for you from the foundation of the world. [35]For I was hungry and you gave me food, I was thirsty and you gave me drink, I was a stranger and you welcomed me, [36]I was naked and you clothed me, I was sick and you visited me, I was in prison and you came to me.' [37]Then the righteous will answer him, saying, 'Lord, when did we see you hungry and feed you, or thirsty and give you drink? [38]And when did we see you a stranger and welcome you, or naked and clothe you? [39]And when did we see you sick or in prison and visit you?' [40]And the King will answer them, 'Truly, I say to you, as you did it to one of the least of these my brothers,[2] you did it to me.'

[41]"Then he will say to those on his left, 'Depart from me, you cursed, into the eternal fire prepared for the devil and his angels. [42]For I was hungry and you gave me no food, I was thirsty and you gave me no drink, [43]I was a stranger and you did not welcome me, naked and you did not clothe me, sick and in prison and you did not visit me.' [44]Then they also will answer, saying, 'Lord, when did we see you hungry or thirsty or a stranger or naked or sick or in prison, and did not minister to you?' [45]Then he will answer them, saying, 'Truly, I say to you, as you did not do it to one of the least of these, you did not do it to me.' [46]And these will go away into eternal punishment, but the righteous into eternal life."

Two precrucifixion meals [26:1–29]. With this unit we ease into the passion story (the account of Jesus' suffering, death, and burial). A note of foreshadowing is sounded by the narrative lead-in that Jesus' adversaries are plotting to kill him after the Passover is finished (vv. 1–5). The anointing of Jesus by a woman (vv. 6–11) is an act that testifies to his worthiness, and additionally Jesus interprets it as an anticipation of his imminent death (vv. 12–13). A brief narrative interpolation about Judas Iscariot's intrigue to betray Jesus (vv. 14–16) builds the suspense. Then we get an account of the Passover meal that Jesus eats with his disciples (vv. 17–25), during which he institutes the Lord's

---

[1] Greek bondservant; also verses 23, 26, 30 [2] Or brothers and sisters

Supper (vv. 26–29). Virtually every verse at this stage of the story is anticipatory of Christ's passion.

26 When Jesus had finished all these sayings, he said to his disciples, [2a]"You know that after two days the Passover is coming, and the Son of Man will be delivered up to be crucified."

[3]Then the chief priests and the elders of the people gathered in the palace of the high priest, whose name was Caiaphas, [4]and plotted together in order to arrest Jesus by stealth and kill him. [5]But they said, "Not during the feast, lest there be an uproar among the people."

[6b]Now when Jesus was at Bethany in the house of Simon the leper,[1] [7a]a woman came up to him with an alabaster flask of very expensive ointment, and she poured it on his head as he reclined at table. [8]And when the disciples saw it, they were indignant, saying, "Why this waste? [9]For this could have been sold for a large sum and given to the poor." [10]But Jesus, aware of this, said to them, "Why do you trouble the woman? For she has done a beautiful thing to me. [11]For you always have the poor with you, but you will not always have me. [12]In pouring this ointment on my body, she has done it to prepare me for burial. [13]Truly, I say to you, wherever this gospel is proclaimed in the whole world, what she has done will also be told in memory of her."

[14c]Then one of the twelve, whose name was Judas Iscariot, went to the chief priests [15]and said, "What will you give me if I deliver him over to you?" And they paid him thirty pieces of silver. [16]And from that moment he sought an opportunity to betray him.

[17d]Now on the first day of Unleavened Bread the disciples came to Jesus, saying, "Where will you have us prepare for you to eat the Passover?" [18]He said, "Go into the city to a certain man and say to him, 'The Teacher says, My time is at hand. I will keep the Passover at your house with my disciples.'" [19]And the disciples did as Jesus had directed them, and they prepared the Passover.

[20e]When it was evening, he reclined at table with the twelve.[2] [21]And as they were eating, he said, "Truly, I say to you, one of you will betray me." [22]And they were very sorrowful and began to say to him one after another, "Is it I, Lord?" [23]He answered, "He who has dipped his hand in the dish with me will betray me. [24]The Son of Man goes as it is written of him, but woe to that man by whom the Son of Man is betrayed! It would have been better for that man if he had not been born." [25]Judas, who would betray him, answered, "Is it I, Rabbi?" He said to him, "You have said so."

[26f]Now as they were eating, Jesus took bread, and after blessing it broke it and gave it to the disciples, and said, "Take, eat; this is my body." [27]And he took a cup, and when he had given thanks he gave it to them, saying, "Drink of it, all of you, [28]for this is my blood of the[3] covenant, which is poured out for many for the forgiveness of sins. [29]I tell you I will not drink again of this fruit of the vine until that day when I drink it new with you in my Father's kingdom."

A night of terror [26:30–75]. The remainder of the chapter takes us from the evening Passover meal to events at daybreak. The action consists of moving scenes of suffering in the following sequence: Jesus predicts Peter's denial of him (vv. 30–35); Jesus' agony in Gethsemane (vv. 36–46); Jesus' betrayal and arrest (vv. 47–56); Jesus' furtive

---

[1] *Leprosy* was a term for several skin diseases; see Leviticus 13 [2] Some manuscripts add *disciples* [3] Some manuscripts insert *new* [a] For 26:2-5 see parallels Mark 14:1, 2; Luke 22:1, 2 [b] For 26:6-13 see parallels Mark 14:3-9; John 12:1-8 [c] For 26:14-16 see parallels Mark 14:10, 11; Luke 22:3-6 [d] For 26:17-19 see parallels Mark 14:12-16; Luke 22:7-13 [e] For 26:20-24 see parallel Mark 14:17-21 [f] For 26:26-29 see parallels Mark 14:22-25; Luke 22:18-20

trial before the high priest Caiaphas (vv. 57–68); Peter's denial of Jesus (vv. 69–75). Every detail counts in this story, so we need to read slowly and allow the details to sink in. Note how many directly quoted speeches there are in the account. Thematically, the separate scenes demonstrate the extreme cost of redemption seen in the suffering of Jesus. It is a truism that all the sins of those for whom Christ died were poured out on him; in these brief scenes we see some of the range of the sins for which Christ died.

[30][a] And when they had sung a hymn, they went out to the Mount of Olives. [31] Then Jesus said to them, "You will all fall away because of me this night. For it is written, 'I will [b] strike the shepherd, and the sheep of the flock will be scattered.' [32] But after I am raised up, I will go before you to Galilee." [33] Peter answered him, "Though they all fall away because of you, I will never fall away." [34] Jesus said to him, "Truly, I tell you, this very night, before the rooster crows, you will deny me three times." [35] Peter said to him, "Even if I must die with you, I will not deny you!" And all the disciples said the same.

[36][c] Then Jesus went with them to a place called Gethsemane, and he said to his disciples, "Sit here, while I go over there and pray." [37] And taking with him Peter and the two sons of Zebedee, he began to be sorrowful and troubled. [38] Then he said to them, "My soul is very sorrowful, even to death; remain here, and watch[1] with me." [39] And going a little farther he fell on his face and prayed, saying, "My Father, if it be possible, let this cup pass from me; nevertheless, not as I will, but as you will." [40] And he came to the disciples and found them sleeping. And he said to Peter, "So, could you not watch with me one hour? [41] Watch and pray that you may not enter into temptation. The spirit indeed is willing, but the flesh is weak." [42] Again, for the second time, he went away and prayed, "My Father, if this cannot pass unless I drink it, your will be done." [43] And again he came and found them sleeping, for their eyes were heavy. [44] So, leaving them again, he went away and prayed for the third time, saying the same words again. [45] Then he came to the disciples and said to them, "Sleep and take your rest later on.[2] See, the hour is at hand, and the Son of Man is betrayed into the hands of sinners. [46] Rise, let us be going; see, my betrayer is at hand."

[47][d] While he was still speaking, Judas came, one of the twelve, and with him a great crowd with swords and clubs, from the chief priests and the elders of the people. [48] Now the betrayer had given them a sign, saying, "The one I will kiss is the man; seize him." [49] And he came up to Jesus at once and said, "Greetings, Rabbi!" And he kissed him. [50] Jesus said to him, "Friend, do what you came to do."[3] Then they came up and laid hands on Jesus and seized him. [51] And behold, one of those who were with Jesus stretched out his hand and drew his sword and struck the servant[4] of the high priest and cut off his ear. [52] Then Jesus said to him, "Put your sword back into its place. For all who take the sword will perish by the sword. [53] Do you think that I cannot appeal to my Father, and he will at once send me more than twelve legions of angels? [54] But how then should the Scriptures be fulfilled, that it must be so?" [55] At that hour Jesus said to the crowds, "Have you come out as against a robber, with swords and clubs to capture me? Day after day I sat in the temple teaching, and you did not seize me. [56] But all this has taken place that the Scriptures of the prophets might be fulfilled." Then all the disciples left him and fled.

---

[1] Or keep awake; also verses 40, 41 [2] Or Are you still sleeping and taking your rest? [3] Or Friend, why are you here? [4] Greek bondservant [a] For 26:30-35 see parallel Mark 14:26-31 [b] Zech. 13:7 [c] For 26:36-46 see parallels Mark 14:32-42; Luke 22:39-46 [d] For 26:47-56 see parallels Mark 14:43-50; Luke 22:47-53; John 18:3-11

⁵⁷Then ªthose who had seized Jesus led him to Caiaphas the high priest, where the scribes and the elders had gathered. ⁵⁸And Peter was following him at a distance, as far as the courtyard of the high priest, and going inside he sat with the guards to see the end. ⁵⁹Now the chief priests and the whole Council¹ were seeking false testimony against Jesus that they might put him to death, ⁶⁰but they found none, though many false witnesses came forward. At last two came forward ⁶¹and said, "This man said, 'I am able to destroy the temple of God, and to rebuild it in three days.'" ⁶²And the high priest stood up and said, "Have you no answer to make? What is it that these men testify against you?"² ⁶³But Jesus remained silent. And the high priest said to him, "I adjure you by the living God, tell us if you are the Christ, the Son of God." ⁶⁴Jesus said to him, "You have said so. But I tell you, from now on you will see the Son of Man seated at the right hand of Power and coming on the clouds of heaven." ⁶⁵Then the high priest tore his robes and said, "He has uttered blasphemy. What further witnesses do we need? You have now heard his blasphemy. ⁶⁶What is your judgment?" They answered, "He deserves death." ⁶⁷Then they spit in his face and struck him. And some slapped him, ⁶⁸saying, "Prophesy to us, you Christ! Who is it that struck you?"

⁶⁹ᵇNow Peter was sitting outside in the courtyard. And a servant girl came up to him and said, "You also were with Jesus the Galilean." ⁷⁰But he denied it before them all, saying, "I do not know what you mean." ⁷¹And when he went out to the entrance, another servant girl saw him, and she said to the bystanders, "This man was with Jesus of Nazareth." ⁷²And again he denied it with an oath: "I do not know the man." ⁷³After a little while the bystanders came up and said to Peter, "Certainly you too are one of them, for your accent betrays you." ⁷⁴Then he began to invoke a curse on himself and to swear, "I do not know the man." And immediately the rooster crowed. ⁷⁵And Peter remembered the saying of Jesus, "Before the rooster crows, you will deny me three times." And he went out and wept bitterly.

Final maneuverings before the crucifixion [27:1–26]. It is well attested that the trials to which Jesus was subjected in the hours just before his execution were a mockery of justice. The action that unfolds in this unit falls into the following scenes: the binding of Jesus and delivery of him to the Roman governor Pilate (vv. 1–2); Judas Iscariot's regret and return of the thirty pieces of silver (vv. 3–10); Jesus' trial before Pilate (vv. 11–14); Pilate's release of Barabbas in exchange for Jesus (vv. 15–26). We read this segment in a double awareness that weighs heavily on us—the injustice of it all and the necessity of it for the accomplishment of salvation.

27 When morning came, all the chief priests and the elders of the people took counsel against Jesus to put him to death. ²And they bound him and led him away and delivered him over to Pilate the governor.

³Then when Judas, his betrayer, saw that Jesus³ was condemned, he changed his mind and brought back the thirty pieces of silver to the chief priests and the elders, ⁴saying, "I have sinned by betraying innocent blood." They said, "What is that to us? See to it yourself." ⁵And throwing down the pieces of silver into the temple, he departed, and he went and hanged himself. ⁶But the chief priests, taking the pieces of silver, said, "It is not lawful to put them into the treasury, since it is blood money." ⁷So they took counsel and bought with them the potter's field as a burial place for strang-

¹ Greek Sanhedrin ² Or Have you no answer to what these men testify against you? ³ Greek he ª For 26:57-68 see parallel Mark 14:53-65 ᵇ For 26:69-75 see parallels Mark 14:66-72; Luke 22:55-62; John 18:16-18, 25-27

ers. [8]Therefore that field has been called the Field of Blood to this day. [9]Then was fulfilled what had been spoken by the prophet Jeremiah, saying, [a]"And they took the thirty pieces of silver, the price of him on whom a price had been set by some of the sons of Israel, [10]and they gave them for the potter's field, as the Lord directed me."

[11][b]Now Jesus stood before the governor, and the governor asked him, "Are you the King of the Jews?" Jesus said, "You have said so." [12]But when he was accused by the chief priests and elders, he gave no answer. [13]Then Pilate said to him, "Do you not hear how many things they testify against you?" [14]But he gave him no answer, not even to a single charge, so that the governor was greatly amazed.

[15][c]Now at the feast the governor was accustomed to release for the crowd any one prisoner whom they wanted. [16]And they had then a notorious prisoner called Barabbas. [17]So when they had gathered, Pilate said to them, "Whom do you want me to release for you: Barabbas, or Jesus who is called Christ?" [18]For he knew that it was out of envy that they had delivered him up. [19]Besides, while he was sitting on the judgment seat, his wife sent word to him, "Have nothing to do with that righteous man, for I have suffered much because of him today in a dream." [20]Now the chief priests and the elders persuaded the crowd to ask for Barabbas and destroy Jesus. [21]The governor again said to them, "Which of the two do you want me to release for you?" And they said, "Barabbas." [22]Pilate said to them, "Then what shall I do with Jesus who is called Christ?" They all said, "Let him be crucified!" [23]And he said, "Why, what evil has he done?" But they shouted all the more, "Let him be crucified!"

[24]So when Pilate saw that he was gaining nothing, but rather that a riot was beginning, he took water and washed his hands before the crowd, saying, "I am innocent of this man's blood;[1] see to it yourselves." [25]And all the people answered, "His blood be on us and on our children!" [26]Then he released for them Barabbas, and having scourged[2] Jesus, delivered him to be crucified.

The crucifixion and burial of Jesus [27:27–66]. Because the death of Jesus is the climax of the story of redemptive atonement in the Bible, every detail that the four Gospel writers recorded is heavy with significance and pathos. The events that Matthew chose to record are as follows: the mockery and torture of Jesus (vv. 27–31); the procession to Golgotha (v. 32) and the events that transpired there during the crucifixion (vv. 33–49); the moment of death, accompanied by awe-inspiring and symbolism-laden miracles (vv. 50–53); responses of onlookers (vv. 54–56); the burial of Jesus at the end of the day (vv. 57–61); the sealing of the tomb (vv. 62–66). The details of the story carry a meaning greater than themselves: this is what it took to accomplish the salvation of sinners. The sadness of the individual events is nearly unbearable, and yet we would not want the story other than it is, because it is what accomplished our salvation. As we read, we simultaneously protest and desire what is happening.

[27][d]Then the soldiers of the governor took Jesus into the governor's headquarters,[3] and they gathered the whole battalion[4] before him. [28]And they stripped him and put a scarlet robe on him, [29]and twisting together a crown of thorns, they put it on his head and put a reed in his right hand. And kneeling before him, they mocked him, saying, "Hail, King of the Jews!" [30]And they spit on him and took the reed and struck him on

---

[1] Some manuscripts *this righteous blood*, or *this righteous man's blood* [2] A Roman judicial penalty, consisting of a severe beating with a multi-lashed whip containing imbedded pieces of bone and metal [3] Greek *the praetorium* [4] Greek *cohort*; a tenth of a Roman legion, usually about 600 men [a] Zech. 11:13 [b] For 27:11-14 see parallels Mark 15:1-5; Luke 23:1-3; John 18:28-38 [c] For 27:15-26 see parallels Mark 15:6-15; Luke 23:18-25; John 18:39, 40; 19:16 [d] For 27:27-31 see parallels Mark 15:16-20; John 19:2, 3

the head. [31]And when they had mocked him, they stripped him of the robe and put his own clothes on him and led him away to crucify him.

[32]As they went out, they found a man of Cyrene, Simon by name. They compelled this man to carry his cross. [33][a]And when they came to a place called Golgotha (which means Place of a Skull), [34]they offered him wine to drink, mixed with gall, but when he tasted it, he would not drink it. [35]And when they had crucified him, they divided his garments among them by casting lots. [36]Then they sat down and kept watch over him there. [37]And over his head they put the charge against him, which read, "This is Jesus, the King of the Jews." [38]Then two robbers were crucified with him, one on the right and one on the left. [39]And those who passed by derided him, wagging their heads [40]and saying, "You who would destroy the temple and rebuild it in three days, save yourself! If you are the Son of God, come down from the cross." [41]So also the chief priests, with the scribes and elders, mocked him, saying, [42]"He saved others; he cannot save himself. He is the King of Israel; let him come down now from the cross, and we will believe in him. [43]He trusts in God; let God deliver him now, if he desires him. For he said, 'I am the Son of God.'" [44]And the robbers who were crucified with him also reviled him in the same way.

[45]Now from the sixth hour[1] there was darkness over all the land[2] until the ninth hour.[3] [46]And about the ninth hour Jesus cried out with a loud voice, saying, [b]"Eli, Eli, lema sabachthani?" that is, "My God, my God, why have you forsaken me?" [47]And some of the bystanders, hearing it, said, "This man is calling Elijah." [48]And one of them at once ran and took a sponge, filled it with sour wine, and put it on a reed and gave it to him to drink. [49]But the others said, "Wait, let us see whether Elijah will come to save him." [50]And Jesus cried out again with a loud voice and yielded up his spirit.

[51]And behold, the curtain of the temple was torn in two, from top to bottom. And the earth shook, and the rocks were split. [52]The tombs also were opened. And many bodies of the saints who had fallen asleep were raised, [53]and coming out of the tombs after his resurrection they went into the holy city and appeared to many. [54][c]When the centurion and those who were with him, keeping watch over Jesus, saw the earthquake and what took place, they were filled with awe and said, "Truly this was the Son[4] of God!"

[55]There were also many women there, looking on from a distance, who had followed Jesus from Galilee, ministering to him, [56]among whom were Mary Magdalene and Mary the mother of James and Joseph and the mother of the sons of Zebedee.

[57][d]When it was evening, there came a rich man from Arimathea, named Joseph, who also was a disciple of Jesus. [58]He went to Pilate and asked for the body of Jesus. Then Pilate ordered it to be given to him. [59]And Joseph took the body and wrapped it in a clean linen shroud [60]and laid it in his own new tomb, which he had cut in the rock. And he rolled a great stone to the entrance of the tomb and went away. [61]Mary Magdalene and the other Mary were there, sitting opposite the tomb.

[62]The next day, that is, after the day of Preparation, the chief priests and the Pharisees gathered before Pilate [63]and said, "Sir, we remember how that impostor said, while he was still alive, 'After three days I will rise.' [64]Therefore order the tomb to be made secure until the third day, lest his disciples go and steal him away and tell the people, 'He has risen from the dead,' and the last fraud will be worse than the first."

---

[1] That is, noon [2] Or *earth* [3] That is, 3 P.M. [4] Or *a son* [a] For 27:33-51 see parallels Mark 15:22-38; Luke 23:32-38, 44-46; John 19:17-19, 23, 24, 28-30
[b] Ps. 22:1 [c] For 27:54-56 see parallels Mark 15:39-41; Luke 23:47, 49 [d] For 27:57-61 see parallels Mark 15:42-47; Luke 23:50-56; John 19:38-42

[65]Pilate said to them, "You have a guard[1] of soldiers. Go, make it as secure as you can." [66]So they went and made the tomb secure by sealing the stone and setting a guard.

> **The resurrection and its aftermath** [chapter 28]. Matthew's account of the resurrection is businesslike and brief, consisting of three narrative units: the discovery of Jesus' resurrection, accompanied by appearance to selected followers (vv. 1–10); the bribing of the soldiers to perpetuate the false story of the theft of Jesus' body (vv. 11–15); Jesus' meeting with his disciples on a mountain, where he delivers to them what became known as the Great Commission (vv. 16–20). The effect of this chapter is to propel us outward from the atoning life of Jesus on earth to the implications of that life for the rest of human history. As we read, we are aware that Jesus is forever alive and has entrusted his followers with the global mission of proclaiming the gospel.

28 [a]Now after the Sabbath, toward the dawn of the first day of the week, Mary Magdalene and the other Mary went to see the tomb. [2]And behold, there was a great earthquake, for an angel of the Lord descended from heaven and came and rolled back the stone and sat on it. [3]His appearance was like lightning, and his clothing white as snow. [4]And for fear of him the guards trembled and became like dead men. [5]But the angel said to the women, "Do not be afraid, for I know that you seek Jesus who was crucified. [6]He is not here, for he has risen, as he said. Come, see the place where he[2] lay. [7]Then go quickly and tell his disciples that he has risen from the dead, and behold, he is going before you to Galilee; there you will see him. See, I have told you." [8]So they departed quickly from the tomb with fear and great joy, and ran to tell his disciples. [9]And behold, Jesus met them and said, "Greetings!" And they came up and took hold of his feet and worshiped him. [10]Then Jesus said to them, "Do not be afraid; go and tell my brothers to go to Galilee, and there they will see me."

[11]While they were going, behold, some of the guard went into the city and told the chief priests all that had taken place. [12]And when they had assembled with the elders and taken counsel, they gave a sufficient sum of money to the soldiers [13]and said, "Tell people, 'His disciples came by night and stole him away while we were asleep.' [14]And if this comes to the governor's ears, we will satisfy him and keep you out of trouble." [15]So they took the money and did as they were directed. And this story has been spread among the Jews to this day.

[16]Now the eleven disciples went to Galilee, to the mountain to which Jesus had directed them. [17]And when they saw him they worshiped him, but some doubted. [18]And Jesus came and said to them, "All authority in heaven and on earth has been given to me. [19]Go therefore and make disciples of all nations, baptizing them in[3] the name of the Father and of the Son and of the Holy Spirit, [20]teaching them to observe all that I have commanded you. And behold, I am with you always, to the end of the age."

---

[1] Or *Take a guard* [2] Some manuscripts *the Lord* [3] Or *into* [a] For 28:1-8 see parallels Mark 16:1-8; Luke 24:1-10; John 20:1

THE GOSPEL ACCORDING TO

MARK

The book at a glance. 16 chapters, 678 verses. The Gospel of Mark is a
documentary life of Jesus. It is the fastest moving of the four Gospels, a feature
accentuated by Mark's fondness for the word *immediately*, which appears
approximately forty times. Mark's implied purpose in writing is to record a
selection of what Jesus did and said during his public years. Although Mark
reports the events objectively, his selection of material shows that he was a
believer in Christ who wanted his readers to follow Jesus as well. Even though
Mark was not one of the twelve disciples, his Gospel is the most circumstantial
of the four Gospels, excelling in vivid descriptions of characters and events.
From early Christian times, the theory has been widely accepted that Mark
learned these details directly from the apostle Peter. The key verse of the book
is Mark 10:45—"The Son of Man came not to be served but to serve, and to
give his life as a ransom for many." With any unit in Mark's Gospel, it is
appropriate to ask what the passage tells us about Jesus and his mission.

▌**Genres.** The Gospel of Mark is first of all a *Gospel, a *narrative that focuses on the
person and work of Jesus. Of all the Gospels, Mark is most overtly a *docudrama. The
approach to the biographical data is that of a careful recorder. Of course Mark's book
is at the same time an implied proclamation and apologetic work that hints at the
redemptive meaning of the events that are recorded. All of the Gospels are *hero
stories. Mark's Gospel is made up of the usual array of subgenres that we find in the
New Testament Gospels, including *calling stories, *recognition stories, *witness/
testimony stories, *encounter stories, *conflict or controversy stories, *pronouncement
stories, *miracle stories, *parables, *discourses and sermons, *proverbs or sayings,
*passion stories, and *resurrection stories. (For more information on items accompa-
nied by an asterisk, see the glossary at the back of this Bible.)

▌**Organization of the story.** The Gospel of Mark does not give us a continuous,
seamless story line. Even though the overall format is narrative, in fact it is a collection
of discrete units. Like the television docudrama, this account includes clips of famous
events and also of typical or representative ordinary events; snatches of speeches or
interviews; and commentary by the narrator and people familiar with the person who is
featured. There are crowd scenes, small-group scenes, public scenes, and private
scenes. The resulting book is a collage or mosaic on the life of Jesus. The best way to
negotiate this format is to regard yourself as Mark's traveling companion as he
assembles his documentary life of Christ. The only firm chronology is that we first
follow Christ's public ministry and then move inexorably to the crucifixion story. Things

Passage	Content	Main Story Line	Scene of Action	Role of Jesus
1:1-45	Initiation of Jesus' ministry			
2:1-3:35	Conflict stories			
4:1-5:43	Parables and miracle stories	Jesus reveals himself in his public ministry	Travel story that moves about Galilee	Jesus as itinerant teacher and miracle worker
6:1-8:26	Typical specimens from the life of Jesus			
8:27-9:50	Jesus with his disciples			
10:1-52	Final glimpse of Jesus' ministry			
11:1-12:44	Toward the crucifixion	Jesus presses his claims in such a way as to lead to his crucifixion	Concentrated action in Jerusalem	Jesus as sacrifice
13:1-37	Olivet Discourse			
14:1-15:47	Passion story			
16:1-20	Story of the resurrection			

that help to unify the mosaic of details include the following: a focus on the central character, Christ; the travel motif; the "world" of the story, whose recurrent features become familiar to us (for example, much of the action occurs in the countryside, and the world of the story continuously opens up into the miraculous and supernatural); the conflict motif; the disciples' slowness to understand Jesus' messianic meaning.

▌**Storytelling technique.** Mark's Gospel is a fast-paced narrative. It is the shortest Gospel, and through the years scholars have theorized that it is the "core Gospel," the first one compiled and the basis for the Gospels of Matthew and Luke (with these three together constituting the Synoptic Gospels). Mark is given to the inclusion of vivid descriptive details, and he prefers Greek verbs that portray an action in process. Mark often records the responses of people to what Jesus did and said. Like all storytellers, Mark selected his material by two criteria: he chose events that were typical of or representative in the life of Jesus (such as miracles of healing and the telling of parables), and unique, once-only events (especially those connected with the crucifixion and resurrection of Jesus).

▌**Key places.** Geography plays a key role in Mark's Gospel, and it is symbolic as well as literal. Jesus' life as a traveling preacher and miracle worker occurs largely in the towns and countryside of Galilee. This is where the beginning and middle of Jesus' public ministry occurred. It is the place where the gospel is revealed, though it would be wrong to equate Galilee with success as over against the rejection that occurred in Jerusalem; actually Jesus was often rejected in Galilee as well as in Jerusalem. The crucifixion occurs in Jerusalem, which symbolizes rejection and hostility. This is where Jesus' ministry ends.

▌Leading characters. The *protagonist of the story is Jesus. The central *plot conflict pits Jesus against those who reject or oppose him, chiefly the religious establishment. If the scribes and Pharisees are the villains of the story, the disciples are the loyal confidants of the hero (except during the events surrounding the crucifixion, when they abandon him). The nameless crowds are the final major character. In Mark's story there are numerous important minor characters, such as the pathetic demoniac who is healed, the woman with the issue of blood, and blind Bartimaeus.

▌Inferred literary intentions. The book is designed to achieve the following literary purposes:

- tell a concise documentary life of Jesus

- express admiration and faith regarding the hero of the story

- present the individual stories in a fast-moving way but also with maximum descriptive vividness

- show the broad range of what Jesus said and did

- capture the flavor of Jesus' life during his three years of public ministry

- cast the individual units in a format that today we call the docudrama

- interweave a geographical polarity or progression in which Jesus performs his miracles and reveals himself in Galilee and sacrifices himself in Jerusalem

- provide a full evidential account of Jesus' trial, death, and resurrection

▌Theological themes. (1) The Incarnation: the whole story fills out our understanding of the life of Jesus as someone who was simultaneously divine and human. (2) Salvation and faith: Mark's Gospel explains the way of salvation and the nature of saving faith. (3) Ethics: the life of Jesus is offered as an implied model of how to live a moral life. (4) Eschatology: chapter 13, as well as interspersed comments by Jesus, teaches about the end times.

▌The Gospel of Mark as a chapter in the master story of the Bible. The Bible's salvation history is a story in which the entire Old Testament points forward to the redemption that Jesus came to accomplish. With the Gospels, including Mark's, we finally come to the climax of the story. Distinctive features of Mark's account include an emphasis on the humanity of the Savior and at the same time a portrayal of Christ as active and powerful.

Initiation into the story of Jesus' public ministry [chapter 1]. The first thing into which the opening chapter initiates us is the storytelling technique and organizational strategy that Mark will use throughout his Gospel. The technique of the collage or mosaic is in full evidence. Most of the units are too brief to lend themselves to ordinary literary analysis, so instead we need to treat the individual units as building blocks of an initiation story. In addition to our initiation into the technique of the book of Mark, we are introduced to the protagonist of the account. The questions to ask of this initiation story include the following: What do we learn about Jesus in our first glimpses of him in this account? What characterizes his life during his public years? What things make up the world in which he lived, taught, and performed miracles? If I were a reporter covering these events, what headline would I give to my news article?

1

The beginning of the gospel of Jesus Christ, the Son of God.[1] [2a] As it is written in Isaiah the prophet,[2]

[b] "Behold, I send my messenger before your face,
      who will prepare your way,
[3] [c] the voice of one crying in the wilderness:
      'Prepare[3] the way of the Lord,
      make his paths straight,'"

[4] John appeared, baptizing in the wilderness and proclaiming a baptism of repentance for the forgiveness of sins. [5] And all the country of Judea and all Jerusalem were going out to him and were being baptized by him in the river Jordan, confessing their sins. [6] Now John was clothed with camel's hair and wore a leather belt around his waist and ate locusts and wild honey. [7] And he preached, saying, "After me comes he who is mightier than I, the strap of whose sandals I am not worthy to stoop down and untie. [8] I have baptized you with water, but he will baptize you with the Holy Spirit."

[9d] In those days Jesus came from Nazareth of Galilee and was baptized by John in the Jordan. [10] And when he came up out of the water, immediately he saw the heavens being torn open and the Spirit descending on him like a dove. [11] And a voice came from heaven, "You are my beloved Son;[d] with you I am well pleased."

[12] The Spirit immediately drove him out into the wilderness. [13] And he was in the wilderness forty days, being tempted by Satan. And he was with the wild animals, and the angels were ministering to him.

[14] Now after John was arrested, Jesus came into Galilee, proclaiming the gospel of God, [15] and saying, "The time is fulfilled, and the kingdom of God is at hand; repent and believe in the gospel."

[16e] Passing alongside the Sea of Galilee, he saw Simon and Andrew the brother of Simon casting a net into the sea, for they were fishermen. [17] And Jesus said to them, "Follow me, and I will make you become fishers of men." [18] And immediately they left their nets and followed him. [19] And going on a little farther, he saw James the son of Zebedee and John his brother, who were in their boat mending the nets. [20] And immediately he called them, and they left their father Zebedee in the boat with the hired servants and followed him.

[21f] And they went into Capernaum, and immediately on the Sabbath he entered the synagogue and was teaching. [22] And they were astonished at his teaching, for he taught them as one who had authority, and not as the scribes. [23] And immediately there was in their synagogue a man with an unclean spirit. And he cried out, [24] "What have you to do with us, Jesus of Nazareth? Have you come to destroy us? I know who you are—the Holy One of God." [25] But Jesus rebuked him, saying, "Be silent, and come out of him!" [26] And the unclean spirit, convulsing him and crying out with a loud

---

[1] Some manuscripts omit *the Son of God* [2] Some manuscripts *in the prophets* [3] Or *crying: Prepare in the wilderness* [4] Or *my Son, my (or the) Beloved* [a] For 1:2-8 see parallels Matt. 3:1-12; Luke 3:2-17 [b] Mal. 3:1 [c] Isa. 40:3 [d] For 1:9-11 see parallels Matt. 3:13-17; Luke 3:21, 22 [e] For 1:16-20 see parallel Matt. 4:18-22 [f] For 1:21-28 see parallel Luke 4:31-37

voice, came out of him. ²⁷And they were all amazed, so that they questioned among themselves, saying, "What is this? A new teaching with authority! He commands even the unclean spirits, and they obey him." ²⁸And at once his fame spread everywhere throughout all the surrounding region of Galilee.

²⁹ᵃAnd immediately heʲ left the synagogue and entered the house of Simon and Andrew, with James and John. ³⁰Now Simon's mother-in-law lay ill with a fever, and immediately they told him about her. ³¹And he came and took her by the hand and lifted her up, and the fever left her, and she began to serve them.

³²That evening at sundown they brought to him all who were sick or oppressed by demons. ³³And the whole city was gathered together at the door. ³⁴And he healed many who were sick with various diseases, and cast out many demons. And he would not permit the demons to speak, because they knew him.

³⁵ᵇAnd rising very early in the morning, while it was still dark, he departed and went out to a desolate place, and there he prayed. ³⁶And Simon and those who were with him searched for him, ³⁷and they found him and said to him, "Everyone is looking for you." ³⁸And he said to them, "Let us go on to the next towns, that I may preach there also, for that is why I came out." ³⁹And he went throughout all Galilee, preaching in their synagogues and casting out demons.

⁴⁰ᶜAnd a leper² came to him, imploring him, and kneeling said to him, "If you will, you can make me clean." ⁴¹Moved with pity, he stretched out his hand and touched him and said to him, "I will; be clean." ⁴²And immediately the leprosy left him, and he was made clean. ⁴³And Jesus³ sternly charged him and sent him away at once, ⁴⁴and said to him, "See that you say nothing to anyone, but go, show yourself to the priest and offer for your cleansing what Moses commanded, for a proof to them." ⁴⁵But he went out and began to talk freely about it, and to spread the news, so that Jesus could no longer openly enter a town, but was out in desolate places, and people were coming to him from every quarter.

Conflict stories [chapters 2–3]. With only one or two exceptions, all of the brief narratives that make up chapters 2–3 are conflict stories in which a saying or action of Jesus elicits controversy or opposition from others, usually the Jewish religious establishment. The right questions to ask of the text include the following: Exactly what did Jesus do or say? Why did others object to it? How did Jesus respond to the objections or criticism? The emerging portrait of Jesus continues to be important, inasmuch as the overall purpose of Mark is to document the life of Jesus and the spiritual meaning of that life. If Jesus is the great example to follow, what things typify his character and actions? And if Jesus is the great positive example in the story, his opponents are people from whose behavior we are expected to learn by way of negative example: according to the behavior of the villains of the story, what attitudes and responses to Jesus are ignominious?

2 And when he returned to Capernaum after some days, it was reported that he was at home. ²And many were gathered together, so that there was no more room, not even at the door. And he was preaching the word to them. ³ᵈAnd they came, bringing to him a paralytic carried by four men. ⁴And when they could not get near him because of the crowd, they removed the roof above him, and when they had

---

¹ Some manuscripts *they* ² *Leprosy* was a term for several skin diseases; see Leviticus 13 ³ Greek *he*; also verse 45 ᵃ For 1:29-34 see parallels Matt. 8:14-16; Luke 4:38-41 ᵇ For 1:35-38 see parallel Luke 4:42, 43 ᶜ For 1:40-44 see parallels Matt. 8:2-4; Luke 5:12-14 ᵈ For 2:3-12 see parallels Matt. 9:2-8; Luke 5:17-26

made an opening, they let down the bed on which the paralytic lay. ⁵And when Jesus saw their faith, he said to the paralytic, "Son, your sins are forgiven." ⁶Now some of the scribes were sitting there, questioning in their hearts, ⁷"Why does this man speak like that? He is blaspheming! Who can forgive sins but God alone?" ⁸And immediately Jesus, perceiving in his spirit that they thus questioned within themselves, said to them, "Why do you question these things in your hearts? ⁹Which is easier, to say to the paralytic, 'Your sins are forgiven,' or to say, 'Rise, take up your bed and walk'? ¹⁰But that you may know that the Son of Man has authority on earth to forgive sins"—he said to the paralytic— ¹¹"I say to you, rise, pick up your bed, and go home." ¹²And he rose and immediately picked up his bed and went out before them all, so that they were all amazed and glorified God, saying, "We never saw anything like this!"

¹³He went out again beside the sea, and all the crowd was coming to him, and he was teaching them. ¹⁴ᵃAnd as he passed by, he saw Levi the son of Alphaeus sitting at the tax booth, and he said to him, "Follow me." And he rose and followed him.

¹⁵And as he reclined at table in his house, many tax collectors and sinners were reclining with Jesus and his disciples, for there were many who followed him. ¹⁶And the scribes of¹ the Pharisees, when they saw that he was eating with sinners and tax collectors, said to his disciples, "Why does he eat² with tax collectors and sinners?" ¹⁷And when Jesus heard it, he said to them, "Those who are well have no need of a physician, but those who are sick. I came not to call the righteous, but sinners."

¹⁸Now John's disciples and the Pharisees were fasting. And people came and said to him, "Why do John's disciples and the disciples of the Pharisees fast, but your disciples do not fast?" ¹⁹And Jesus said to them, "Can the wedding guests fast while the bridegroom is with them? As long as they have the bridegroom with them, they cannot fast. ²⁰The days will come when the bridegroom is taken away from them, and then they will fast in that day. ²¹No one sews a piece of unshrunk cloth on an old garment. If he does, the patch tears away from it, the new from the old, and a worse tear is made. ²²And no one puts new wine into old wineskins. If he does, the wine will burst the skins—and the wine is destroyed, and so are the skins. But new wine is for fresh wineskins."³

²³ᵇOne Sabbath he was going through the grainfields, and as they made their way, his disciples began to pluck heads of grain. ²⁴And the Pharisees were saying to him, "Look, why are they doing what is not lawful on the Sabbath?" ²⁵And he said to them, "Have you never read what David did, when he was in need and was hungry, he and those who were with him: ²⁶how he entered the house of God, in the time of Abiathar the high priest, and ate the bread of the Presence, which it is not lawful for any but the priests to eat, and also gave it to those who were with him?" ²⁷And he said to them, "The Sabbath was made for man, not man for the Sabbath. ²⁸So the Son of Man is lord even of the Sabbath."

3 ᶜAgain he entered the synagogue, and a man was there with a withered hand. ²And they watched Jesus,⁴ to see whether he would heal him on the Sabbath, so that they might accuse him. ³And he said to the man with the withered hand, "Come here." ⁴And he said to them, "Is it lawful on the Sabbath to do good or to do harm, to save life or to kill?" But they were silent. ⁵And he looked around at them with anger,

---

¹ Some manuscripts and ² Some manuscripts add and drink ³ Some manuscripts omit But new wine is for fresh wineskins ⁴ Greek him ᵃFor 2:14-22 see parallels Matt. 9:9-17; Luke 5:27-39 ᵇFor 2:23-28 see parallels Matt. 12:1-8; Luke 6:1-5 ᶜFor 3:1-6 see parallels Matt. 12:9-14; Luke 6:6-11

grieved at their hardness of heart, and said to the man, "Stretch out your hand." He stretched it out, and his hand was restored. ⁶The Pharisees went out and immediately held counsel with the Herodians against him, how to destroy him.

⁷Jesus withdrew with his disciples to the sea, and a great crowd followed, from Galilee and Judea ⁸and Jerusalem and Idumea and from beyond the Jordan and from around Tyre and Sidon. When the great crowd heard all that he was doing, they came to him. ⁹And he told his disciples to have a boat ready for him because of the crowd, lest they crush him, ¹⁰for he had healed many, so that all who had diseases pressed around him to touch him. ¹¹And whenever the unclean spirits saw him, they fell down before him and cried out, "You are the Son of God." ¹²And he strictly ordered them not to make him known.

¹³And he went up on the mountain and called to him those whom he desired, and they came to him. ¹⁴And he appointed twelve (whom he also named apostles) so that they might be with him and he might send them out to preach ¹⁵and have authority to cast out demons. ¹⁶He appointed the twelve: ᵃSimon (to whom he gave the name Peter); ¹⁷James the son of Zebedee and John the brother of James (to whom he gave the name Boanerges, that is, Sons of Thunder); ¹⁸Andrew, and Philip, and Bartholomew, and Matthew, and Thomas, and James the son of Alphaeus, and Thaddaeus, and Simon the Cananaean, ¹⁹and Judas Iscariot, who betrayed him.

²⁰Then he went home, and the crowd gathered again, so that they could not even eat. ²¹And when his family heard it, they went out to seize him, for they were saying, "He is out of his mind."

²²And the scribes who came down from Jerusalem were saying, "He is possessed by Beelzebul," and "by the prince of demons he casts out the demons." ²³ᵇAnd he called them to him and said to them in parables, "How can Satan cast out Satan? ²⁴If a kingdom is divided against itself, that kingdom cannot stand. ²⁵And if a house is divided against itself, that house will not be able to stand. ²⁶And if Satan has risen up against himself and is divided, he cannot stand, but is coming to an end. ²⁷But no one can enter a strong man's house and plunder his goods, unless he first binds the strong man. Then indeed he may plunder his house.

²⁸ᶜ"Truly, I say to you, all sins will be forgiven the children of man, and whatever blasphemies they utter, ²⁹but whoever blasphemes against the Holy Spirit never has forgiveness, but is guilty of an eternal sin"— ³⁰for they were saying, "He has an unclean spirit."

³¹ᵈAnd his mother and his brothers came, and standing outside they sent to him and called him. ³²And a crowd was sitting around him, and they said to him, "Your mother and your brothers¹ are outside, seeking you." ³³And he answered them, "Who are my mother and my brothers?" ³⁴And looking about at those who sat around him, he said, "Here are my mother and my brothers! ³⁵For whoever does the will of God, he is my brother and sister and mother."

Parables [4:1–34]. Even though the Gospel writers organize their material by a loose chronology of Jesus' life, within that format their approach is to cluster material by topical categories. After two chapters of conflict stories, Mark now gives us two blocks of material arranged by genre. The first thirty-four verses of chapter 4 are a collection of four parables, along with Jesus' explanation of why he told parables (vv. 10–12). As nar-

---

¹ Other early manuscripts add *and your sisters* ᵃ For 3:16-19 see parallels Matt. 10:2-4; Luke 6:13-16 ᵇ For 3:23-27 see parallels Matt. 12:25-29; Luke 11:17-22 ᶜ For 3:28-30 see parallel Matt. 12:31, 32 ᵈ For 3:31-35 see parallels Matt. 12:46-50; Luke 8:19-21

ratives within themselves, these parables can be analyzed by the usual narrative grid of plot, characterization, and setting, with those yielding one or more ideas or themes.

4 Again [a]he began to teach beside the sea. And a very large crowd gathered about him, so that he got into a boat and sat in it on the sea, and the whole crowd was beside the sea on the land. [2]And he was teaching them many things in parables, and in his teaching he said to them: [3]"Listen! A sower went out to sow. [4]And as he sowed, some seed fell along the path, and the birds came and devoured it. [5]Other seed fell on rocky ground, where it did not have much soil, and immediately it sprang up, since it had no depth of soil. [6]And when the sun rose, it was scorched, and since it had no root, it withered away. [7]Other seed fell among thorns, and the thorns grew up and choked it, and it yielded no grain. [8]And other seeds fell into good soil and produced grain, growing up and increasing and yielding thirtyfold and sixtyfold and a hundredfold." [9]And he said, "He who has ears to hear, let him hear."

[10]And when he was alone, those around him with the twelve asked him about the parables. [11]And he said to them, "To you has been given the secret of the kingdom of God, but for those outside everything is in parables, [12]so that

"they may indeed see but not perceive,
    and may indeed hear but not understand,
  lest they should turn and be forgiven."

[13][b]And he said to them, "Do you not understand this parable? How then will you understand all the parables? [14]The sower sows the word. [15]And these are the ones along the path, where the word is sown: when they hear, Satan immediately comes and takes away the word that is sown in them. [16]And these are the ones sown on rocky ground: the ones who, when they hear the word, immediately receive it with joy. [17]And they have no root in themselves, but endure for a while; then, when tribulation or persecution arises on account of the word, immediately they fall away.[1] [18]And others are the ones sown among thorns. They are those who hear the word, [19]but the cares of the world and the deceitfulness of riches and the desires for other things enter in and choke the word, and it proves unfruitful. [20]But those that were sown on the good soil are the ones who hear the word and accept it and bear fruit, thirtyfold and sixtyfold and a hundredfold."

[21][c]And he said to them, "Is a lamp brought in to be put under a basket, or under a bed, and not on a stand? [22]For nothing is hidden except to be made manifest; nor is anything secret except to come to light. [23]If anyone has ears to hear, let him hear." [24]And he said to them, "Pay attention to what you hear: with the measure you use, it will be measured to you, and still more will be added to you. [25]For to the one who has, more will be given, and from the one who has not, even what he has will be taken away."

[26]And he said, "The kingdom of God is as if a man should scatter seed on the ground. [27]He sleeps and rises night and day, and the seed sprouts and grows; he knows not how. [28]The earth produces by itself, first the blade, then the ear, then the full grain in the ear. [29]But when the grain is ripe, at once he puts in the sickle, because the harvest has come."

[30][d]And he said, "With what can we compare the kingdom of God, or what parable

[1] Or stumble [a] For 4:1-12 see parallels Matt. 13:1-15; Luke 8:4-10 [b] For 4:13-20 see parallels Matt. 13:18-23; Luke 8:11-15 [c] For 4:21-25 see parallel Luke 8:16-18 [d] For 4:30-32 see parallels Matt. 13:31, 32; Luke 13:18, 19

shall we use for it? [31]It is like a grain of mustard seed, which, when sown on the ground, is the smallest of all the seeds on earth, [32]yet when it is sown it grows up and becomes larger than all the garden plants and puts out large branches, so that the birds of the air can make nests in its shade."

[33]With many such parables he spoke the word to them, as they were able to hear it. [34]He did not speak to them without a parable, but privately to his own disciples he explained everything.

Miracle stories [4:35–5:43]. The block of parables is followed by a block of miracle stories. The right grid by which to analyze a miracle story is to note as many of the following as apply: the need that is established; the seeking of Jesus' help; the faith displayed by the recipient of the miracle, or the recipient's acquaintances or family; the performance of the miracle; the response of characters to the miracle or to Jesus. There are many variations within this paradigm, and the range of types of miracles that Jesus performed is noteworthy.

[35][a]On that day, when evening had come, he said to them, "Let us go across to the other side." [36]And leaving the crowd, they took him with them in the boat, just as he was. And other boats were with him. [37]And a great windstorm arose, and the waves were breaking into the boat, so that the boat was already filling. [38]But he was in the stern, asleep on the cushion. And they woke him and said to him, "Teacher, do you not care that we are perishing?" [39]And he awoke and rebuked the wind and said to the sea, "Peace! Be still!" And the wind ceased, and there was a great calm. [40]He said to them, "Why are you so afraid? Have you still no faith?" [41]And they were filled with great fear and said to one another, "Who then is this, that even the wind and the sea obey him?"

5 [b]They came to the other side of the sea, to the country of the Gerasenes.[1] [2]And when Jesus[2] had stepped out of the boat, immediately there met him out of the tombs a man with an unclean spirit. [3]He lived among the tombs. And no one could bind him anymore, not even with a chain, [4]for he had often been bound with shackles and chains, but he wrenched the chains apart, and he broke the shackles in pieces. No one had the strength to subdue him. [5]Night and day among the tombs and on the mountains he was always crying out and cutting himself with stones. [6]And when he saw Jesus from afar, he ran and fell down before him. [7]And crying out with a loud voice, he said, "What have you to do with me, Jesus, Son of the Most High God? I adjure you by God, do not torment me." [8]For he was saying to him, "Come out of the man, you unclean spirit!" [9]And Jesus asked him, "What is your name?" He replied, "My name is Legion, for we are many." [10]And he begged him earnestly not to send them out of the country. [11]Now a great herd of pigs was feeding there on the hillside, [12]and they begged him, saying, "Send us to the pigs; let us enter them." [13]So he gave them permission. And the unclean spirits came out, and entered the pigs, and the herd, numbering about two thousand, rushed down the steep bank into the sea and were drowned in the sea.

[14]The herdsmen fled and told it in the city and in the country. And people came to see what it was that had happened. [15]And they came to Jesus and saw the demon-

---

[1] Some manuscripts *Gergesenes*; some *Gadarenes* [2] Greek *he*; also verse 9 [a] For 4:35-41 see parallels Matt. 8:18, 23-27; Luke 8:22-25 [b] For 5:1-20 see parallels Matt. 8:28-34; Luke 8:26-39

possessed[1] man, the one who had had the legion, sitting there, clothed and in his right mind, and they were afraid. [16]And those who had seen it described to them what had happened to the demon-possessed man and to the pigs. [17]And they began to beg Jesus[2] to depart from their region. [18]As he was getting into the boat, the man who had been possessed with demons begged him that he might be with him. [19]And he did not permit him but said to him, "Go home to your friends and tell them how much the Lord has done for you, and how he has had mercy on you." [20]And he went away and began to proclaim in the Decapolis how much Jesus had done for him, and everyone marveled.

[21]And when Jesus had crossed again in the boat to the other side, a great crowd gathered about him, and he was beside the sea. [22a]Then came one of the rulers of the synagogue, Jairus by name, and seeing him, he fell at his feet [23]and implored him earnestly, saying, "My little daughter is at the point of death. Come and lay your hands on her, so that she may be made well and live." [24]And he went with him.

And a great crowd followed him and thronged about him. [25]And there was a woman who had had a discharge of blood for twelve years, [26]and who had suffered much under many physicians, and had spent all that she had, and was no better but rather grew worse. [27]She had heard the reports about Jesus and came up behind him in the crowd and touched his garment. [28]For she said, "If I touch even his garments, I will be made well." [29]And immediately the flow of blood dried up, and she felt in her body that she was healed of her disease. [30]And Jesus, perceiving in himself that power had gone out from him, immediately turned about in the crowd and said, "Who touched my garments?" [31]And his disciples said to him, "You see the crowd pressing around you, and yet you say, 'Who touched me?'" [32]And he looked around to see who had done it. [33]But the woman, knowing what had happened to her, came in fear and trembling and fell down before him and told him the whole truth. [34]And he said to her, "Daughter, your faith has made you well; go in peace, and be healed of your disease."

[35]While he was still speaking, there came from the ruler's house some who said, "Your daughter is dead. Why trouble the Teacher any further?" [36]But overhearing[3] what they said, Jesus said to the ruler of the synagogue, "Do not fear, only believe." [37]And he allowed no one to follow him except Peter and James and John the brother of James. [38]They came to the house of the ruler of the synagogue, and Jesus[4] saw a commotion, people weeping and wailing loudly. [39]And when he had entered, he said to them, "Why are you making a commotion and weeping? The child is not dead but sleeping." [40]And they laughed at him. But he put them all outside and took the child's father and mother and those who were with him and went in where the child was. [41]Taking her by the hand he said to her, "Talitha cumi," which means, "Little girl, I say to you, arise." [42]And immediately the girl got up and began walking (for she was twelve years of age), and they were immediately overcome with amazement. [43]And he strictly charged them that no one should know this, and told them to give her something to eat.

A "week" in the life of Jesus [chapter 6]. The strategy of Mark the storyteller is to share either unique or representative events in Jesus' public ministry. The purpose is to enable us to know who Jesus was and what he did. The governing question as we read the material is, What do I know about Jesus on the basis of this unit?

---

[1] Greek *daimonizomai*; also verses 16, 18; elsewhere rendered *oppressed by demons* [2] Greek *him* [3] Or *ignoring*; some manuscripts *hearing* [4] Greek *he*
[a] For 5:22-43 see parallels Matt. 9:18-26; Luke 8:40-56

6 [a]He went away from there and came to his hometown, and his disciples followed him. [2]And on the Sabbath he began to teach in the synagogue, and many who heard him were astonished, saying, "Where did this man get these things? What is the wisdom given to him? How are such mighty works done by his hands? [3]Is not this the carpenter, the son of Mary and brother of James and Joses and Judas and Simon? And are not his sisters here with us?" And they took offense at him. [4]And Jesus said to them, "A prophet is not without honor, except in his hometown and among his relatives and in his own household." [5]And he could do no mighty work there, except that he laid his hands on a few sick people and healed them. [6]And he marveled because of their unbelief.

And he went about among the villages teaching.

[7b]And he called the twelve and began to send them out two by two, and gave them authority over the unclean spirits. [8]He charged them to take nothing for their journey except a staff—no bread, no bag, no money in their belts— [9]but to wear sandals and not put on two tunics.[1] [10]And he said to them, "Whenever you enter a house, stay there until you depart from there. [11]And if any place will not receive you and they will not listen to you, when you leave, shake off the dust that is on your feet as a testimony against them." [12]So they went out and proclaimed that people should repent. [13]And they cast out many demons and anointed with oil many who were sick and healed them.

[14c]King Herod heard of it, for Jesus'[2] name had become known. Some[3] said, "John the Baptist[4] has been raised from the dead. That is why these miraculous powers are at work in him." [15]But others said, "He is Elijah." And others said, "He is a prophet, like one of the prophets of old." [16]But when Herod heard of it, he said, "John, whom I beheaded, has been raised." [17]For it was Herod who had sent and seized John and bound him in prison for the sake of Herodias, his brother Philip's wife, because he had married her. [18]For John had been saying to Herod, "It is not lawful for you to have your brother's wife." [19]And Herodias had a grudge against him and wanted to put him to death. But she could not, [20]for Herod feared John, knowing that he was a righteous and holy man, and he kept him safe. When he heard him, he was greatly perplexed, and yet he heard him gladly.

[21]But an opportunity came when Herod on his birthday gave a banquet for his nobles and military commanders and the leading men of Galilee. [22]For when Herodias's daughter came in and danced, she pleased Herod and his guests. And the king said to the girl, "Ask me for whatever you wish, and I will give it to you." [23]And he vowed to her, "Whatever you ask me, I will give you, up to half of my kingdom." [24]And she went out and said to her mother, "For what should I ask?" And she said, "The head of John the Baptist." [25]And she came in immediately with haste to the king and asked, saying, "I want you to give me at once the head of John the Baptist on a platter." [26]And the king was exceedingly sorry, but because of his oaths and his guests he did not want to break his word to her. [27]And immediately the king sent an executioner with orders to bring John's[5] head. He went and beheaded him in the prison [28]and brought his head on a platter and gave it to the girl, and the girl gave it to her mother. [29]When his disciples heard of it, they came and took his body and laid it in a tomb.

[30]The apostles returned to Jesus and told him all that they had done and taught. [31]And he said to them, "Come away by yourselves to a desolate place and rest a

---

[1] Greek chiton, a long garment worn under the cloak next to the skin [2] Greek his [3] Some manuscripts He [4] Greek baptizer; also verse 24 [5] Greek his [a] For 6:1-6 see parallel Matt. 13:54-58 [b] For 6:7-11 see parallels Matt. 10:1, 5, 9-14; Luke 9:1, 3-5 [c] For 6:14-29 see parallels Matt. 14:1-12; Luke 9:7-9

while." For many were coming and going, and they had no leisure even to eat. ³²ᵃAnd they went away in the boat to a desolate place by themselves. ³³Now many saw them going and recognized them, and they ran there on foot from all the towns and got there ahead of them. ³⁴When he went ashore he saw a great crowd, and he had compassion on them, because they were like sheep without a shepherd. And he began to teach them many things. ³⁵And when it grew late, his disciples came to him and said, "This is a desolate place, and the hour is now late. ³⁶Send them away to go into the surrounding countryside and villages and buy themselves something to eat." ³⁷But he answered them, "You give them something to eat." And they said to him, "Shall we go and buy two hundred denarii¹ worth of bread and give it to them to eat?" ³⁸And he said to them, "How many loaves do you have? Go and see." And when they had found out, they said, "Five, and two fish." ³⁹Then he commanded them all to sit down in groups on the green grass. ⁴⁰So they sat down in groups, by hundreds and by fifties. ⁴¹And taking the five loaves and the two fish he looked up to heaven and said a blessing and broke the loaves and gave them to the disciples to set before the people. And he divided the two fish among them all. ⁴²And they all ate and were satisfied. ⁴³And they took up twelve baskets full of broken pieces and of the fish. ⁴⁴And those who ate the loaves were five thousand men.

⁴⁵ᵇImmediately he made his disciples get into the boat and go before him to the other side, to Bethsaida, while he dismissed the crowd. ⁴⁶And after he had taken leave of them, he went up on the mountain to pray. ⁴⁷And when evening came, the boat was out on the sea, and he was alone on the land. ⁴⁸And he saw that they were making headway painfully, for the wind was against them. And about the fourth watch of the night² he came to them, walking on the sea. He meant to pass by them, ⁴⁹but when they saw him walking on the sea they thought it was a ghost, and cried out, ⁵⁰for they all saw him and were terrified. But immediately he spoke to them and said, "Take heart; it is I. Do not be afraid." ⁵¹And he got into the boat with them, and the wind ceased. And they were utterly astounded, ⁵²for they did not understand about the loaves, but their hearts were hardened.

⁵³ᶜWhen they had crossed over, they came to land at Gennesaret and moored to the shore. ⁵⁴And when they got out of the boat, the people immediately recognized him ⁵⁵and ran about the whole region and began to bring the sick people on their beds to wherever they heard he was. ⁵⁶And wherever he came, in villages, cities, or countryside, they laid the sick in the marketplaces and implored him that they might touch even the fringe of his garment. And as many as touched it were made well.

On the road with Jesus: specimen stories [7:1–8:26]. This material, completely typical of Mark's techniques, sets up resistance to any attempt we might make to find a narrative unity in the collection of units. The organization is that of the docudrama—a collection of "clips" of typical or extraordinary events in the hero's life, snatches of speeches and conversations, overviews, close-ups, crowd scenes, and encounters with individuals. The goal is to get to know Jesus as completely as possible. The narrative units require the usual questions: who? where? what happens? how does it end? The dialogues of Jesus, which usually involve controversy with opponents, are speech acts that have much the same effect as a story; they are dramas in miniature, so that the questions who, where, and what are relevant.

¹ A *denarius* was a day's wage for a laborer ² That is, between 3 A.M. and 6 A.M. ᵃ For 6:32-44 see parallels Matt. 14:13-21; Luke 9:10-17; John 6:1-13 ᵇ For 6:45-52 see parallels Matt. 14:22-33; John 6:16-21 ᶜ For 6:53-56 see parallel Matt. 14:34-36

7 ᵃNow when the Pharisees gathered to him, with some of the scribes who had come from Jerusalem, ²they saw that some of his disciples ate with hands that were defiled, that is, unwashed. ³(For the Pharisees and all the Jews do not eat unless they wash¹ their hands, holding to the tradition of the elders, ⁴and when they come from the marketplace, they do not eat unless they wash.² And there are many other traditions that they observe, such as the washing of cups and pots and copper vessels and dining couches.³) ⁵And the Pharisees and the scribes asked him, "Why do your disciples not walk according to the tradition of the elders, but eat with defiled hands?" ⁶And he said to them, "Well did Isaiah prophesy of you hypocrites, as it is written,

ᵇ"'This people honors me with their lips,
    but their heart is far from me;
⁷ in vain do they worship me,
    teaching as doctrines the commandments of men.'

⁸You leave the commandment of God and hold to the tradition of men."

⁹And he said to them, "You have a fine way of rejecting the commandment of God in order to establish your tradition! ¹⁰For Moses said, ᶜ'Honor your father and your mother'; and, ᵈ'Whoever reviles father or mother must surely die.' ¹¹But you say, 'If a man tells his father or his mother, "Whatever you would have gained from me is Corban"' (that is, given to God)⁴— ¹²then you no longer permit him to do anything for his father or mother, ¹³thus making void the word of God by your tradition that you have handed down. And many such things you do."

¹⁴And he called the people to him again and said to them, "Hear me, all of you, and understand: ¹⁵There is nothing outside a person that by going into him can defile him, but the things that come out of a person are what defile him."⁵ ¹⁷And when he had entered the house and left the people, his disciples asked him about the parable. ¹⁸And he said to them, "Then are you also without understanding? Do you not see that whatever goes into a person from outside cannot defile him, ¹⁹since it enters not his heart but his stomach, and is expelled?"⁶ (Thus he declared all foods clean.) ²⁰And he said, "What comes out of a person is what defiles him. ²¹For from within, out of the heart of man, come evil thoughts, sexual immorality, theft, murder, adultery, ²²coveting, wickedness, deceit, sensuality, envy, slander, pride, foolishness. ²³All these evil things come from within, and they defile a person."

²⁴And from there he arose and went away to the region of Tyre and Sidon.⁷ And he entered a house and did not want anyone to know, yet he could not be hidden. ²⁵But immediately a woman whose little daughter had an unclean spirit heard of him and came and fell down at his feet. ²⁶Now the woman was a Gentile, a Syrophoenician by birth. And she begged him to cast the demon out of her daughter. ²⁷And he said to her, "Let the children be fed first, for it is not right to take the children's bread and throw it to the dogs." ²⁸But she answered him, "Yes, Lord; yet even the dogs under the table eat the children's crumbs." ²⁹And he said to her, "For this statement you may go your way; the demon has left your daughter." ³⁰And she went home and found the child lying in bed and the demon gone.

³¹Then he returned from the region of Tyre and went through Sidon to the Sea of

---

¹ Greek *unless they wash with a fist*, probably indicating a kind of ceremonial washing ² Greek *unless they baptize*; some manuscripts *unless they purify themselves* ³ Some manuscripts omit *and dining couches* ⁴ Or *an offering* ⁵ Some manuscripts add verse 16: *If anyone has ears to hear, let him hear* ⁶ Greek *goes out into the latrine* ⁷ Some manuscripts omit *and Sidon* ᵃ For 7:1-30 see parallel Matt. 15:1-28 ᵇ Isa. 29:13 ᶜ Ex. 20:12 ᵈ Ex. 21:17

Galilee, in the region of the Decapolis. ³²And they brought to him a man who was deaf and had a speech impediment, and they begged him to lay his hand on him. ³³And taking him aside from the crowd privately, he put his fingers into his ears, and after spitting touched his tongue. ³⁴And looking up to heaven, he sighed and said to him, "Ephphatha," that is, "Be opened." ³⁵And his ears were opened, his tongue was released, and he spoke plainly. ³⁶And Jesus[1] charged them to tell no one. But the more he charged them, the more zealously they proclaimed it. ³⁷And they were astonished beyond measure, saying, "He has done all things well. He even makes the deaf hear and the mute speak."

8 [a]In those days, when again a great crowd had gathered, and they had nothing to eat, he called his disciples to him and said to them, ²"I have compassion on the crowd, because they have been with me now three days and have nothing to eat. ³And if I send them away hungry to their homes, they will faint on the way. And some of them have come from far away." ⁴And his disciples answered him, "How can one feed these people with bread here in this desolate place?" ⁵And he asked them, "How many loaves do you have?" They said, "Seven." ⁶And he directed the crowd to sit down on the ground. And he took the seven loaves, and having given thanks, he broke them and gave them to his disciples to set before the people; and they set them before the crowd. ⁷And they had a few small fish. And having blessed them, he said that these also should be set before them. ⁸And they ate and were satisfied. And they took up the broken pieces left over, seven baskets full. ⁹And there were about four thousand people. And he sent them away. ¹⁰And immediately he got into the boat with his disciples and went to the district of Dalmanutha.[2]

¹¹[b]The Pharisees came and began to argue with him, seeking from him a sign from heaven to test him. ¹²And he sighed deeply in his spirit and said, "Why does this generation seek a sign? Truly, I say to you, no sign will be given to this generation." ¹³And he left them, got into the boat again, and went to the other side.

¹⁴Now they had forgotten to bring bread, and they had only one loaf with them in the boat. ¹⁵And he cautioned them, saying, "Watch out; beware of the leaven of the Pharisees and the leaven of Herod."[3] ¹⁶And they began discussing with one another the fact that they had no bread. ¹⁷And Jesus, aware of this, said to them, "Why are you discussing the fact that you have no bread? Do you not yet perceive or understand? Are your hearts hardened? ¹⁸Having eyes do you not see, and having ears do you not hear? And do you not remember? ¹⁹When I broke the five loaves for the five thousand, how many baskets full of broken pieces did you take up?" They said to him, "Twelve." ²⁰"And the seven for the four thousand, how many baskets full of broken pieces did you take up?" And they said to him, "Seven." ²¹And he said to them, "Do you not yet understand?"

²²And they came to Bethsaida. And some people brought to him a blind man and begged him to touch him. ²³And he took the blind man by the hand and led him out of the village, and when he had spit on his eyes and laid his hands on him, he asked him, "Do you see anything?" ²⁴And he looked up and said, "I see men, but they look like trees, walking." ²⁵Then Jesus[4] laid his hands on his eyes again; and he opened his eyes, his sight was restored, and he saw everything clearly. ²⁶And he sent him to his home, saying, "Do not even enter the village."

---

[1] Greek *he* [2] Some manuscripts *Magadan*, or *Magdala* [3] Some manuscripts *the Herodians* [4] Greek *he* [a] For 8:1-10 see parallel Matt. 15:32-39 [b] For 8:11-21 see parallel Matt. 16:1-12

Jesus with his disciples [8:27–9:50]. The circle of characters constricts in this mini-collection of stories, dialogues, and discourses, as Jesus interacts chiefly with his disciples. The events and revelations are not public but private (with the disciples), as the following index of units suggests: Peter's confession that Jesus is the Christ (8:27–29); Jesus' foretelling of his death and resurrection (8:31–9:1 and 9:30–32); the transfiguration (9:2–13); Jesus' casting out of a demon that the disciples had been powerless to exorcise (9:14–29); Jesus' discourse on humility (9:33–37), dialogue about how to deal with nondisciples who perform miracles (9:38–41), and discourse on avoiding obstacles to entering God's kingdom (9:42–50). The governing rhetorical pattern is a teaching-learning format. Our goal as readers should continue to be getting to know what Jesus did and taught, with a view toward being and thinking like him. Further, Mark composed this unit on what the disciples learned from their Master so that we could learn the same lessons the disciples learned.

²⁷ᵃ And Jesus went on with his disciples to the villages of Caesarea Philippi. And on the way he asked his disciples, "Who do people say that I am?" ²⁸And they told him, "John the Baptist; and others say, Elijah; and others, one of the prophets." ²⁹And he asked them, "But who do you say that I am?" Peter answered him, "You are the Christ." ³⁰And he strictly charged them to tell no one about him.

³¹ᵇ And he began to teach them that the Son of Man must suffer many things and be rejected by the elders and the chief priests and the scribes and be killed, and after three days rise again. ³²And he said this plainly. And Peter took him aside and began to rebuke him. ³³But turning and seeing his disciples, he rebuked Peter and said, "Get behind me, Satan! For you are not setting your mind on the things of God, but on the things of man."

³⁴And calling the crowd to him with his disciples, he said to them, "If anyone would come after me, let him deny himself and take up his cross and follow me. ³⁵For whoever would save his life¹ will lose it, but whoever loses his life for my sake and the gospel's will save it. ³⁶For what does it profit a man to gain the whole world and forfeit his soul? ³⁷For what can a man give in return for his soul? ³⁸For whoever is ashamed of me and of my words in this adulterous and sinful generation, of him will the Son of Man also be ashamed when he comes in the glory of his Father with the holy angels."

9 And he said to them, "Truly, I say to you, there are some standing here who will not taste death until they see the kingdom of God after it has come with power."

²ᶜ And after six days Jesus took with him Peter and James and John, and led them up a high mountain by themselves. And he was transfigured before them, ³and his clothes became radiant, intensely white, as no one² on earth could bleach them. ⁴And there appeared to them Elijah with Moses, and they were talking with Jesus. ⁵And Peter said to Jesus, "Rabbi,³ it is good that we are here. Let us make three tents, one for you and one for Moses and one for Elijah." ⁶For he did not know what to say, for they were terrified. ⁷And a cloud overshadowed them, and a voice came out of the cloud, "This is my beloved Son;⁴ listen to him." ⁸And suddenly, looking around, they no longer saw anyone with them but Jesus only.

⁹ᵈ And as they were coming down the mountain, he charged them to tell no one

---

¹ The same Greek word can mean either *soul* or *life*, depending on the context; twice in this verse and once in verse 36 and once in verse 37 ² Greek *no cloth refiner* ³ *Rabbi* means *my teacher*, or *my master* ⁴ Or *my Son, my* (or *the*) *Beloved* ᵃ For 8:27-29 see parallels Matt. 16:13-16; Luke 9:18-20 ᵇ For 8:31–9:1 see parallels Matt. 16:21-28; Luke 9:22-27 ᶜ For 9:2-8 see parallels Matt. 17:1-8; Luke 9:28-36 ᵈ For 9:9-13 see parallel Matt. 17:9-13

what they had seen, until the Son of Man had risen from the dead. ¹⁰So they kept the matter to themselves, questioning what this rising from the dead might mean. ¹¹And they asked him, "Why do the scribes say that first Elijah must come?" ¹²And he said to them, "Elijah does come first to restore all things. And how is it written of the Son of Man that he should suffer many things and be treated with contempt? ¹³But I tell you that Elijah has come, and they did to him whatever they pleased, as it is written of him."

¹⁴ᵃAnd when they came to the disciples, they saw a great crowd around them, and scribes arguing with them. ¹⁵And immediately all the crowd, when they saw him, were greatly amazed and ran up to him and greeted him. ¹⁶And he asked them, "What are you arguing about with them?" ¹⁷And someone from the crowd answered him, "Teacher, I brought my son to you, for he has a spirit that makes him mute. ¹⁸And whenever it seizes him, it throws him down, and he foams and grinds his teeth and becomes rigid. So I asked your disciples to cast it out, and they were not able." ¹⁹And he answered them, "O faithless generation, how long am I to be with you? How long am I to bear with you? Bring him to me." ²⁰And they brought the boy to him. And when the spirit saw him, immediately it convulsed the boy, and he fell on the ground and rolled about, foaming at the mouth. ²¹And Jesus asked his father, "How long has this been happening to him?" And he said, "From childhood. ²²And it has often cast him into fire and into water, to destroy him. But if you can do anything, have compassion on us and help us." ²³And Jesus said to him, "'If you can'! All things are possible for one who believes." ²⁴Immediately the father of the child cried out¹ and said, "I believe; help my unbelief!" ²⁵And when Jesus saw that a crowd came running together, he rebuked the unclean spirit, saying to it, "You mute and deaf spirit, I command you, come out of him and never enter him again." ²⁶And after crying out and convulsing him terribly, it came out, and the boy was like a corpse, so that most of them said, "He is dead." ²⁷But Jesus took him by the hand and lifted him up, and he arose. ²⁸And when he had entered the house, his disciples asked him privately, "Why could we not cast it out?" ²⁹And he said to them, "This kind cannot be driven out by anything but prayer."²

³⁰ᵇThey went on from there and passed through Galilee. And he did not want anyone to know, ³¹for he was teaching his disciples, saying to them, "The Son of Man is going to be delivered into the hands of men, and they will kill him. And when he is killed, after three days he will rise." ³²But they did not understand the saying, and were afraid to ask him.

³³And they came to Capernaum. And when he was in the house ᶜhe asked them, "What were you discussing on the way?" ³⁴But they kept silent, for on the way they had argued with one another about who was the greatest. ³⁵And he sat down and called the twelve. And he said to them, "If anyone would be first, he must be last of all and servant of all." ³⁶And he took a child and put him in the midst of them, and taking him in his arms, he said to them, ³⁷"Whoever receives one such child in my name receives me, and whoever receives me, receives not me but him who sent me."

³⁸ᵈJohn said to him, "Teacher, we saw someone casting out demons in your name,³ and we tried to stop him, because he was not following us." ³⁹But Jesus said, "Do not stop him, for no one who does a mighty work in my name will be able soon afterward

¹ Some manuscripts add *with tears* ² Some manuscripts add *and fasting* ³ Some manuscripts add *who does not follow us* ᵃ For 9:14-28 see parallels Matt. 17:14-19; Luke 9:37-42 ᵇ For 9:30-32 see parallels Matt. 17:22, 23; Luke 9:43-45 ᶜ For 9:33-37 see parallels Matt. 18:1-5; Luke 9:46-48 ᵈ For 9:38-40 see parallel Luke 9:49, 50

to speak evil of me. ⁴⁰For the one who is not against us is for us. ⁴¹For truly, I say to you, whoever gives you a cup of water to drink because you belong to Christ will by no means lose his reward.

⁴²"Whoever causes one of these little ones who believe in me to sin,¹ it would be better for him if a great millstone were hung around his neck and he were thrown into the sea. ⁴³And if your hand causes you to sin, cut it off. It is better for you to enter life crippled than with two hands to go to hell,² to the unquenchable fire.³ ⁴⁵And if your foot causes you to sin, cut it off. It is better for you to enter life lame than with two feet to be thrown into hell. ⁴⁷And if your eye causes you to sin, tear it out. It is better for you to enter the kingdom of God with one eye than with two eyes to be thrown into hell, ⁴⁸'where their worm does not die and the fire is not quenched.' ⁴⁹For everyone will be salted with fire.⁴ ⁵⁰Salt is good, but if the salt has lost its saltiness, how will you make it salty again? Have salt in yourselves, and be at peace with one another."

> **Final glimpses of Jesus' earthly ministry** [chapter 10]. The content of chapter 10 is exactly like what we have seen throughout Mark's Gospel up to this point. Jesus continues to travel (v. 1), teach (vv. 2–12), interact with groups (vv. 13–16) and individuals (vv. 17–31), foretell his crucifixion and resurrection (vv. 32–34), handle immature behavior from the disciples (vv. 35–45), and perform miracles (vv. 46–52). But since this is the last mosaic of such material before the story of the crucifixion, its narrative function is to serve as a recap of Jesus' career.

10 ᵃAnd he left there and went to the region of Judea and beyond the Jordan, and crowds gathered to him again. And again, as was his custom, he taught them.
²And Pharisees came up and in order to test him asked, "Is it lawful for a man to divorce his wife?" ³He answered them, "What did Moses command you?" ⁴They said, "Moses allowed a man to write a certificate of divorce and to send her away." ⁵And Jesus said to them, "Because of your hardness of heart he wrote you this commandment. ⁶But from the beginning of creation, 'God made them ᵇmale and female.' ⁷'Therefore a man shall leave his father and mother and hold fast to his wife,⁵ ⁸and the two shall become one flesh.' So they are no longer two but one flesh. ⁹What therefore God has joined together, let not man separate."

¹⁰And in the house the disciples asked him again about this matter. ¹¹And he said to them, "Whoever divorces his wife and marries another commits adultery against her, ¹²and if she divorces her husband and marries another, she commits adultery."

¹³ᵈAnd they were bringing children to him that he might touch them, and the disciples rebuked them. ¹⁴But when Jesus saw it, he was indignant and said to them, "Let the children come to me; do not hinder them, for to such belongs the kingdom of God. ¹⁵Truly, I say to you, whoever does not receive the kingdom of God like a child shall not enter it." ¹⁶And he took them in his arms and blessed them, laying his hands on them.

¹⁷ᵉAnd as he was setting out on his journey, a man ran up and knelt before him and asked him, "Good Teacher, what must I do to inherit eternal life?" ¹⁸And Jesus said to him, "Why do you call me good? No one is good except God alone. ¹⁹You know

---

¹ Greek *to stumble*; also verses 43, 45, 47 ² Greek *Gehenna*; also verse 47 ³ Some manuscripts add verses 44 and 46 (which are identical with verse 48)
⁴ Some manuscripts add *and every sacrifice will be salted with salt* ⁵ Some manuscripts omit *and hold fast to his wife* ᵃ For 10:1-12 see parallel Matt. 19:1-9
ᵇ Gen. 1:27; 5:2 ᶜ Gen. 2:24 ᵈ For 10:13-16 see parallels Matt. 19:13-15; Luke 18:15-17 ᵉ For 10:17-31 see parallels Matt. 19:16-30; Luke 18:18-30

the commandments: [a]'Do not murder, Do not commit adultery, Do not steal, Do not bear false witness, Do not defraud, Honor your father and mother.'" [20]And he said to him, "Teacher, all these I have kept from my youth." [21]And Jesus, looking at him, loved him, and said to him, "You lack one thing: go, sell all that you have and give to the poor, and you will have treasure in heaven; and come, follow me." [22]Disheartened by the saying, he went away sorrowful, for he had great possessions.

[23]And Jesus looked around and said to his disciples, "How difficult it will be for those who have wealth to enter the kingdom of God!" [24]And the disciples were amazed at his words. But Jesus said to them again, "Children, how difficult it is[1] to enter the kingdom of God! [25]It is easier for a camel to go through the eye of a needle than for a rich person to enter the kingdom of God." [26]And they were exceedingly astonished, and said to him,[2] "Then who can be saved?" [27]Jesus looked at them and said, "With man it is impossible, but not with God. For all things are possible with God." [28]Peter began to say to him, "See, we have left everything and followed you." [29]Jesus said, "Truly, I say to you, there is no one who has left house or brothers or sisters or mother or father or children or lands, for my sake and for the gospel, [30]who will not receive a hundredfold now in this time, houses and brothers and sisters and mothers and children and lands, with persecutions, and in the age to come eternal life. [31]But many who are first will be last, and the last first."

[32][b]And they were on the road, going up to Jerusalem, and Jesus was walking ahead of them. And they were amazed, and those who followed were afraid. And taking the twelve again, he began to tell them what was to happen to him, [33]saying, "See, we are going up to Jerusalem, and the Son of Man will be delivered over to the chief priests and the scribes, and they will condemn him to death and deliver him over to the Gentiles. [34]And they will mock him and spit on him, and flog him and kill him. And after three days he will rise."

[35][c]And James and John, the sons of Zebedee, came up to him and said to him, "Teacher, we want you to do for us whatever we ask of you." [36]And he said to them, "What do you want me to do for you?" [37]And they said to him, "Grant us to sit, one at your right hand and one at your left, in your glory." [38]Jesus said to them, "You do not know what you are asking. Are you able to drink the cup that I drink, or to be baptized with the baptism with which I am baptized?" [39]And they said to him, "We are able." And Jesus said to them, "The cup that I drink you will drink, and with the baptism with which I am baptized, you will be baptized, [40]but to sit at my right hand or at my left is not mine to grant, but it is for those for whom it has been prepared." [41]And when the ten heard it, they began to be indignant at James and John. [42]And Jesus called them to him and said to them, "You know that those who are considered rulers of the Gentiles lord it over them, and their great ones exercise authority over them. [43]But it shall not be so among you. But whoever would be great among you must be your servant,[3] [44]and whoever would be first among you must be slave[4] of all. [45]For even the Son of Man came not to be served but to serve, and to give his life as a ransom for many."

[46][d]And they came to Jericho. And as he was leaving Jericho with his disciples and a great crowd, Bartimaeus, a blind beggar, the son of Timaeus, was sitting by the roadside. [47]And when he heard that it was Jesus of Nazareth, he began to cry out and say,

[1] Some manuscripts add for those who trust in riches [2] Some manuscripts to one another [3] Greek diakonos [4] Greek bondservant (doulos) [a] Ex. 20:12-16; Deut. 5:16-20 [b] For 10:32-34 see parallels Matt. 20:17-19; Luke 18:31-33 [c] For 10:35-45 see parallel Matt. 20:20-28 [d] For 10:46-52 see parallels Matt. 20:29-34; Luke 18:35-43

"Jesus, Son of David, have mercy on me!" [48]And many rebuked him, telling him to be silent. But he cried out all the more, "Son of David, have mercy on me!" [49]And Jesus stopped and said, "Call him." And they called the blind man, saying to him, "Take heart. Get up; he is calling you." [50]And throwing off his cloak, he sprang up and came to Jesus. [51]And Jesus said to him, "What do you want me to do for you?" And the blind man said to him, "Rabbi, let me recover my sight." [52]And Jesus said to him, "Go your way; your faith has made you well." And immediately he recovered his sight and followed him on the way.

Events leading to the crucifixion [chapter 11]. With the story of the triumphal entry into Jerusalem at the beginning of this chapter (vv. 1–11), the current of the action leads us inexorably to the final confrontation with the Jewish authorities. Our first responsibility with this famous event is to relive it as vividly as possible in our imagination, and then to reflect on its importance for Jesus' life and the story of redemptive history. The story of the barren fig tree that Jesus cursed on the way into Jerusalem (vv. 12–14, 20–25) takes on the character of an enacted parable with direct instruction attached. Mark's accounts of events within Jerusalem—the cleansing of the temple (vv. 15–19) and Jesus' retort to the Jewish leaders' challenge of his authority (vv. 27–33)—portray a combative Savior; we can reflect on how this fits into the imminent passion story.

11 [a]Now when they drew near to Jerusalem, to Bethphage and Bethany, at the Mount of Olives, Jesus[1] sent two of his disciples [2]and said to them, "Go into the village in front of you, and immediately as you enter it you will find a colt tied, on which no one has ever sat. Untie it and bring it. [3]If anyone says to you, 'Why are you doing this?' say, 'The Lord has need of it and will send it back here immediately.'" [4]And they went away and found a colt tied at a door outside in the street, and they untied it. [5]And some of those standing there said to them, "What are you doing, untying the colt?" [6]And they told them what Jesus had said, and they let them go. [7]And they brought the colt to Jesus and threw their cloaks on it, and he sat on it. [8]And many spread their cloaks on the road, and others spread leafy branches that they had cut from the fields. [9]And those who went before and those who followed were shouting, "Hosanna! Blessed is he who comes in the name of the Lord! [10]Blessed is the coming kingdom of our father David! Hosanna in the highest!"

[11]And he entered Jerusalem and went into the temple. And when he had looked around at everything, as it was already late, he went out to Bethany with the twelve.

[12]On the following day, when they came from Bethany, he was hungry. [13]And seeing in the distance a fig tree in leaf, he went to see if he could find anything on it. When he came to it, he found nothing but leaves, for it was not the season for figs. [14]And he said to it, "May no one ever eat fruit from you again." And his disciples heard it.

[15b]And they came to Jerusalem. And he entered the temple and began to drive out those who sold and those who bought in the temple, and he overturned the tables of the money-changers and the seats of those who sold pigeons. [16]And he would not allow anyone to carry anything through the temple. [17]And he was teaching them and saying to them, "Is it not written, [c]'My house shall be called a house of prayer for all the nations'? But you have made it a den of robbers." [18]And the chief priests and the scribes heard it and were seeking a way to destroy him, for they feared him, because

---

[1] Greek *he* [a] For 11:1-10 see parallels Matt. 21:1-9; Luke 19:28-38; John 12:12-15 [b] For 11:15-18 see parallels Matt. 21:12-16; Luke 19:45-47 [c] Isa. 56:7

all the crowd was astonished at his teaching. [19]And when evening came they[1] went out of the city.

[20a]As they passed by in the morning, they saw the fig tree withered away to its roots. [21]And Peter remembered and said to him, "Rabbi, look! The fig tree that you cursed has withered." [22]And Jesus answered them, "Have faith in God. [23]Truly, I say to you, whoever says to this mountain, 'Be taken up and thrown into the sea,' and does not doubt in his heart, but believes that what he says will come to pass, it will be done for him. [24]Therefore I tell you, whatever you ask in prayer, believe that you have received[2] it, and it will be yours. [25]And whenever you stand praying, forgive, if you have anything against anyone, so that your Father also who is in heaven may forgive you your trespasses."[3]

[27b]And they came again to Jerusalem. And as he was walking in the temple, the chief priests and the scribes and the elders came to him, [28]and they said to him, "By what authority are you doing these things, or who gave you this authority to do them?" [29]Jesus said to them, "I will ask you one question; answer me, and I will tell you by what authority I do these things. [30]Was the baptism of John from heaven or from man? Answer me." [31]And they discussed it with one another, saying, "If we say, 'From heaven,' he will say, 'Why then did you not believe him?' [32]But shall we say, 'From man'?"—they were afraid of the people, for they all held that John really was a prophet. [33]So they answered Jesus, "We do not know." And Jesus said to them, "Neither will I tell you by what authority I do these things."

Teaching interlude [chapter 12]. The march toward the crucifixion receives a momentary halt in this chapter. Although the placement of the chapter seems to suggest that the events occurred after Jesus' final entry into Jerusalem, they resemble things that could have happened at any point in Jesus' earthly ministry. The sequence of literary forms is as follows: parable (vv. 1–12); conflated conflict story and pronouncement story (vv. 13–17); pronouncement story (vv. 18–27); encounter story (vv. 28–34); discourse material—snatches of addresses by Jesus (vv. 35–40); pronouncement story (vv. 41–44).

12 [c]And he began to speak to them in parables. "A man planted a vineyard and put a fence around it and dug a pit for the winepress and built a tower, and leased it to tenants and went into another country. [2]When the season came, he sent a servant[4] to the tenants to get from them some of the fruit of the vineyard. [3]And they took him and beat him and sent him away empty-handed. [4]Again he sent to them another servant, and they struck him on the head and treated him shamefully. [5]And he sent another, and him they killed. And so with many others: some they beat, and some they killed. [6]He had still one other, a beloved son. Finally he sent him to them, saying, 'They will respect my son.' [7]But those tenants said to one another, 'This is the heir. Come, let us kill him, and the inheritance will be ours.' [8]And they took him and killed him and threw him out of the vineyard. [9]What will the owner of the vineyard do? He will come and destroy the tenants and give the vineyard to others. [10]Have you not read this Scripture:

[d]"'The stone that the builders rejected
     has become the cornerstone;[5]

[1] Some manuscripts *he* [2] Some manuscripts *are receiving* [3] Some manuscripts add verse 26: *But if you do not forgive, neither will your Father who is in heaven forgive your trespasses* [4] Greek *bondservant*; also verse 4 [5] Greek *the head of the corner* [a] For 11:20-24 see parallel Matt. 21:19-22 [b] For 11:27-33 see parallels Matt. 21:23-27; Luke 20:1-8 [c] For 12:1-12 see parallels Matt. 21:33-46; Luke 20:9-18 [d] Ps. 118:22, 23

11   this was the Lord's doing,
        and it is marvelous in our eyes'?"

¹²And they were seeking to arrest him but feared the people, for they perceived that he had told the parable against them. So they left him and went away.

¹³ᵃAnd they sent to him some of the Pharisees and some of the Herodians, to trap him in his talk. ¹⁴And they came and said to him, "Teacher, we know that you are true and do not care about anyone's opinion. For you are not swayed by appearances,ⁱ but truly teach the way of God. Is it lawful to pay taxes to Caesar, or not? Should we pay them, or should we not?" ¹⁵But, knowing their hypocrisy, he said to them, "Why put me to the test? Bring me a denarius² and let me look at it." ¹⁶And they brought one. And he said to them, "Whose likeness and inscription is this?" They said to him, "Caesar's." ¹⁷Jesus said to them, "Render to Caesar the things that are Caesar's, and to God the things that are God's." And they marveled at him.

¹⁸And Sadducees came to him, who say that there is no resurrection. And they asked him a question, saying, ¹⁹"Teacher, Moses wrote for us that if a man's brother dies and leaves a wife, but leaves no child, the man³ must take the widow and raise up offspring for his brother. ²⁰There were seven brothers; the first took a wife, and when he died left no offspring. ²¹And the second took her, and died, leaving no offspring. And the third likewise. ²²And the seven left no offspring. Last of all the woman also died. ²³In the resurrection, when they rise again, whose wife will she be? For the seven had her as wife."

²⁴Jesus said to them, "Is this not the reason you are wrong, because you know neither the Scriptures nor the power of God? ²⁵For when they rise from the dead, they neither marry nor are given in marriage, but are like angels in heaven. ²⁶And as for the dead being raised, have you not read in the book of Moses, in the passage about the bush, how God spoke to him, saying, ᵇ'I am the God of Abraham, and the God of Isaac, and the God of Jacob'? ²⁷He is not God of the dead, but of the living. You are quite wrong."

²⁸ᶜAnd one of the scribes came up and heard them disputing with one another, and seeing that he answered them well, asked him, "Which commandment is the most important of all?" ²⁹Jesus answered, "The most important is, ᵈ'Hear, O Israel: The Lord our God, the Lord is one. ³⁰And you shall love the Lord your God with all your heart and with all your soul and with all your mind and with all your strength.' ³¹The second is this: ᵉ'You shall love your neighbor as yourself.' There is no other commandment greater than these." ³²And the scribe said to him, "You are right, Teacher. You have truly said that he is one, and there is no other besides him. ³³And to love him with all the heart and with all the understanding and with all the strength, and to love one's neighbor as oneself, is much more than all whole burnt offerings and sacrifices." ³⁴And when Jesus saw that he answered wisely, he said to him, "You are not far from the kingdom of God." And after that no one dared to ask him any more questions.

³⁵ᶠAnd as Jesus taught in the temple, he said, "How can the scribes say that the Christ is the son of David? ³⁶David himself, in the Holy Spirit, declared,

---

ⁱ Greek *you do not look at people's faces* ² A *denarius* was a day's wage for a laborer ³ Greek *his brother* ᵃ For 12:13-27 see parallels Matt. 22:15-32; Luke 20:20-38 ᵇ Ex. 3:6 ᶜ For 12:28-34 see parallel Matt. 22:34-40, 46 ᵈ Deut. 6:4, 5 ᵉ Lev. 19:18 ᶠ For 12:35-37 see parallels Matt. 22:41-45; Luke 20:41-44

[a]"'The Lord said to my Lord,
    Sit at my right hand,
        until I put your enemies under your feet.'

[37]David himself calls him Lord. So how is he his son?" And the great throng heard him gladly.

[38][b]And in his teaching he said, "Beware of the scribes, who like to walk around in long robes and like greetings in the marketplaces [39]and have the best seats in the synagogues and the places of honor at feasts, [40]who devour widows' houses and for a pretense make long prayers. They will receive the greater condemnation."

[41][c]And he sat down opposite the treasury and watched the people putting money into the offering box. Many rich people put in large sums. [42]And a poor widow came and put in two small copper coins, which make a penny.[1] [43]And he called his disciples to him and said to them, "Truly, I say to you, this poor widow has put in more than all those who are contributing to the offering box. [44]For they all contributed out of their abundance, but she out of her poverty has put in everything she had, all she had to live on."

> **The Olivet Discourse** [chapter 13]. The Olivet Discourse, also recorded in Matthew 24–25, is Jesus' most extended block of eschatological teaching. The discourse is Jesus' reply to his disciples' question about when the temple will be destroyed and "what will be the sign when all these things are about to be accomplished" (v. 4). An overall strategy is to read the chapter as Jesus' farewell discourse, in which he instructs his followers regarding what to expect after his death. Since the chapter is an ever-expanding outline of the last days, we also need to take the time to assemble a list of what will happen at the end of history. The discourse takes the form of a blueprint of events to come.

13 [d]And as he came out of the temple, one of his disciples said to him, "Look, Teacher, what wonderful stones and what wonderful buildings!" [2]And Jesus said to him, "Do you see these great buildings? There will not be left here one stone upon another that will not be thrown down."

[3]And as he sat on the Mount of Olives opposite the temple, Peter and James and John and Andrew asked him privately, [4]"Tell us, when will these things be, and what will be the sign when all these things are about to be accomplished?" [5]And Jesus began to say to them, "See that no one leads you astray. [6]Many will come in my name, saying, 'I am he!' and they will lead many astray. [7]And when you hear of wars and rumors of wars, do not be alarmed. This must take place, but the end is not yet. [8]For nation will rise against nation, and kingdom against kingdom. There will be earthquakes in various places; there will be famines. These are but the beginning of the birth pains.

[9]"But be on your guard. For they will deliver you over to councils, and you will be beaten in synagogues, and you will stand before governors and kings for my sake, to bear witness before them. [10]And the gospel must first be proclaimed to all nations. [11]And when they bring you to trial and deliver you over, do not be anxious beforehand what you are to say, but say whatever is given you in that hour, for it is not you who speak, but the Holy Spirit. [12]And brother will deliver brother over to death, and the father his child, and children will rise against parents and have them put to

---

[1] Greek *two lepta*, which make a *kodrantes*; a *kodrantes* (Latin *quadrans*) was a Roman copper coin worth about 1/64 of a *denarius* (which was a day's wage for a laborer) [a] Ps. 110:1 [b] For 12:38-40 see parallels Matt. 23:1, 2, 5-7; Luke 20:45, 46 [c] For 12:41-44 see parallel Luke 21:1-4 [d] For 13:1-37 see parallels Matt. 24:1-51; Luke 21:5-36

death. ¹³And you will be hated by all for my name's sake. But the one who endures to the end will be saved.

¹⁴"But when you see the abomination of desolation standing where he ought not to be (let the reader understand), then let those who are in Judea flee to the mountains. ¹⁵Let the one who is on the housetop not go down, nor enter his house, to take anything out, ¹⁶and let the one who is in the field not turn back to take his cloak. ¹⁷And alas for women who are pregnant and for those who are nursing infants in those days! ¹⁸Pray that it may not happen in winter. ¹⁹For in those days there will be such tribulation as has not been from the beginning of the creation that God created until now, and never will be. ²⁰And if the Lord had not cut short the days, no human being would be saved. But for the sake of the elect, whom he chose, he shortened the days. ²¹And then if anyone says to you, 'Look, here is the Christ!' or 'Look, there he is!' do not believe it. ²²For false christs and false prophets will arise and perform signs and wonders, to lead astray, if possible, the elect. ²³But be on guard; I have told you all things beforehand.

²⁴"But in those days, after that tribulation, the sun will be darkened, and the moon will not give its light, ²⁵and the stars will be falling from heaven, and the powers in the heavens will be shaken. ²⁶And then they will see the Son of Man coming in clouds with great power and glory. ²⁷And then he will send out the angels and gather his elect from the four winds, from the ends of the earth to the ends of heaven.

²⁸"From the fig tree learn its lesson: as soon as its branch becomes tender and puts out its leaves, you know that summer is near. ²⁹So also, when you see these things taking place, you know that he is near, at the very gates. ³⁰Truly, I say to you, this generation will not pass away until all these things take place. ³¹Heaven and earth will pass away, but my words will not pass away.

³²"But concerning that day or that hour, no one knows, not even the angels in heaven, nor the Son, but only the Father. ³³Be on guard, keep awake.¹ For you do not know when the time will come. ³⁴It is like a man going on a journey, when he leaves home and puts his servants² in charge, each with his work, and commands the doorkeeper to stay awake. ³⁵Therefore stay awake—for you do not know when the master of the house will come, in the evening, or at midnight, or when the rooster crows,³ or in the morning— ³⁶lest he come suddenly and find you asleep. ³⁷And what I say to you I say to all: Stay awake."

The night before Jesus' crucifixion [chapter 14]. The events in this chapter are part of Mark's passion story. They occurred on Thursday night extending into early Friday morning. Since the story of Jesus' trial and crucifixion is the climax of Mark's Gospel, he narrates the action in copious detail (this chapter has a whopping seventy-two verses). One way to organize the chapter is to note the shifts of setting, as Jesus is shown to be on the move during the night of his arrest and first trial. Every one of the settings is etched in the memory of Christians' experience. The cast of characters keeps expanding. There are fragments of foreshadowing (vv. 1–2; 10–11; 27–31); a scene commemorating the worthiness of Christ (vv. 3–9); a sacred meal eaten for the last time, which is at the same time a scene of sorrow (vv. 12–25); scenes of agony (vv. 32–42), betrayal (vv. 43–46, 66–72), arrest (vv. 47–52), trial (vv. 53–64), and torture (v. 65). The way to relive the story is to imagine ourselves present at the events.

¹ Some manuscripts add *and pray* ² Greek *bondservants* ³ That is, the third watch of the night, between midnight and 3 A.M.

14 [a] It was now two days before the Passover and the Feast of Unleavened Bread. And the chief priests and the scribes were seeking how to arrest him by stealth and kill him, [2] for they said, "Not during the feast, lest there be an uproar from the people."

[3b] And while he was at Bethany in the house of Simon the leper,[1] as he was reclining at table, a woman came with an alabaster flask of ointment of pure nard, very costly, and she broke the flask and poured it over his head. [4] There were some who said to themselves indignantly, "Why was the ointment wasted like that? [5] For this ointment could have been sold for more than three hundred denarii[2] and given to the poor." And they scolded her. [6] But Jesus said, "Leave her alone. Why do you trouble her? She has done a beautiful thing to me. [7] For you always have the poor with you, and whenever you want, you can do good for them. But you will not always have me. [8] She has done what she could; she has anointed my body beforehand for burial. [9] And truly, I say to you, wherever the gospel is proclaimed in the whole world, what she has done will be told in memory of her."

[10c] Then Judas Iscariot, who was one of the twelve, went to the chief priests in order to betray him to them. [11] And when they heard it, they were glad and promised to give him money. And he sought an opportunity to betray him.

[12d] And on the first day of Unleavened Bread, when they sacrificed the Passover lamb, his disciples said to him, "Where will you have us go and prepare for you to eat the Passover?" [13] And he sent two of his disciples and said to them, "Go into the city, and a man carrying a jar of water will meet you. Follow him, [14] and wherever he enters, say to the master of the house, 'The Teacher says, Where is my guest room, where I may eat the Passover with my disciples?' [15] And he will show you a large upper room furnished and ready; there prepare for us." [16] And the disciples set out and went to the city and found it just as he had told them, and they prepared the Passover.

[17e] And when it was evening, he came with the twelve. [18] And as they were reclining at table and eating, Jesus said, "Truly, I say to you, one of you will betray me, one who is eating with me." [19] They began to be sorrowful and to say to him one after another, "Is it I?" [20] He said to them, "It is one of the twelve, one who is dipping bread into the dish with me. [21] For the Son of Man goes as it is written of him, but woe to that man by whom the Son of Man is betrayed! It would have been better for that man if he had not been born."

[22f] And as they were eating, he took bread, and after blessing it broke it and gave it to them, and said, "Take; this is my body." [23] And he took a cup, and when he had given thanks he gave it to them, and they all drank of it. [24] And he said to them, "This is my blood of the[3] covenant, which is poured out for many. [25] Truly, I say to you, I will not drink again of the fruit of the vine until that day when I drink it new in the kingdom of God."

[26g] And when they had sung a hymn, they went out to the Mount of Olives. [27] And Jesus said to them, "You will all fall away, for it is written, 'I will [h] strike the shepherd, and the sheep will be scattered.' [28] But after I am raised up, I will go before you to Galilee." [29] Peter said to him, "Even though they all fall away, I will not." [30] And Jesus said to him, "Truly, I tell you, this very night, before the rooster crows twice, you will deny me three times." [31] But he said emphatically, "If I must die with you, I will not deny you." And they all said the same.

---

[1] *Leprosy* was a term for several skin diseases; see Leviticus 13 [2] A *denarius* was a day's wage for a laborer [3] Some manuscripts insert *new* [a] For 14:1, 2 see parallels Matt. 26:2-5; Luke 22:1, 2 [b] For 14:3-9 see parallels Matt. 26:6-13; John 12:1-8 [c] For 14:10, 11 see parallels Matt. 26:14-16; Luke 22:3-6 [d] For 14:12-16 see parallels Matt. 26:17-19; Luke 22:7-13 [e] For 14:17-21 see parallel Matt. 26:20-24 [f] For 14:22-25 see parallels Matt. 26:26-29; Luke 22:18-20 [g] For 14:26-31 see parallel Matt. 26:30-35 [h] Zech. 13:7

[32a]And they went to a place called Gethsemane. And he said to his disciples, "Sit here while I pray." [33]And he took with him Peter and James and John, and began to be greatly distressed and troubled. [34]And he said to them, "My soul is very sorrowful, even to death. Remain here and watch."[1] [35]And going a little farther, he fell on the ground and prayed that, if it were possible, the hour might pass from him. [36]And he said, "Abba, Father, all things are possible for you. Remove this cup from me. Yet not what I will, but what you will." [37]And he came and found them sleeping, and he said to Peter, "Simon, are you asleep? Could you not watch one hour? [38]Watch and pray that you may not enter into temptation. The spirit indeed is willing, but the flesh is weak." [39]And again he went away and prayed, saying the same words. [40]And again he came and found them sleeping, for their eyes were very heavy, and they did not know what to answer him. [41]And he came the third time and said to them, "Are you still sleeping and taking your rest? It is enough; the hour has come. The Son of Man is betrayed into the hands of sinners. [42]Rise, let us be going; see, my betrayer is at hand."

[43b]And immediately, while he was still speaking, Judas came, one of the twelve, and with him a crowd with swords and clubs, from the chief priests and the scribes and the elders. [44]Now the betrayer had given them a sign, saying, "The one I will kiss is the man. Seize him and lead him away under guard." [45]And when he came, he went up to him at once and said, "Rabbi!" And he kissed him. [46]And they laid hands on him and seized him. [47]But one of those who stood by drew his sword and struck the servant[2] of the high priest and cut off his ear. [48]And Jesus said to them, "Have you come out as against a robber, with swords and clubs to capture me? [49]Day after day I was with you in the temple teaching, and you did not seize me. But let the Scriptures be fulfilled." [50]And they all left him and fled.

[51]And a young man followed him, with nothing but a linen cloth about his body. And they seized him, [52]but he left the linen cloth and ran away naked.

[53c]And they led Jesus to the high priest. And all the chief priests and the elders and the scribes came together. [54]And Peter had followed him at a distance, right into the courtyard of the high priest. And he was sitting with the guards and warming himself at the fire. [55]Now the chief priests and the whole Council[3] were seeking testimony against Jesus to put him to death, but they found none. [56]For many bore false witness against him, but their testimony did not agree. [57]And some stood up and bore false witness against him, saying, [58]"We heard him say, 'I will destroy this temple that is made with hands, and in three days I will build another, not made with hands.'" [59]Yet even about this their testimony did not agree. [60]And the high priest stood up in the midst and asked Jesus, "Have you no answer to make? What is it that these men testify against you?"[4] [61]But he remained silent and made no answer. Again the high priest asked him, "Are you the Christ, the Son of the Blessed?" [62]And Jesus said, "I am, and you will see the Son of Man seated at the right hand of Power, and coming with the clouds of heaven." [63]And the high priest tore his garments and said, "What further witnesses do we need? [64]You have heard his blasphemy. What is your decision?" And they all condemned him as deserving death. [65]And some began to spit on him and to cover his face and to strike him, saying to him, "Prophesy!" And the guards received him with blows.

[66d]And as Peter was below in the courtyard, one of the servant girls of the high

---

[1] Or keep awake; also verses 37, 38 [2] Greek bondservant [3] Greek Sanhedrin [4] Or Have you no answer to what these men testify against you? [a] For 14:32-42 see parallels Matt. 26:36-46; Luke 22:39-46 [b] For 14:43-50 see parallels Matt. 26:47-56; Luke 22:47-53; John 18:3-11 [c] For 14:53-65 see parallel Matt. 26:57-68 [d] For 14:66-72 see parallels Matt. 26:69-75; Luke 22:55-62; John 18:16-18, 25-27

priest came, ⁶⁷and seeing Peter warming himself, she looked at him and said, "You also were with the Nazarene, Jesus." ⁶⁸But he denied it, saying, "I neither know nor understand what you mean." And he went out into the gateway¹ and the rooster crowed.² ⁶⁹And the servant girl saw him and began again to say to the bystanders, "This man is one of them." ⁷⁰But again he denied it. And after a little while the bystanders again said to Peter, "Certainly you are one of them, for you are a Galilean." ⁷¹But he began to invoke a curse on himself and to swear, "I do not know this man of whom you speak." ⁷²And immediately the rooster crowed a second time. And Peter remembered how Jesus had said to him, "Before the rooster crows twice, you will deny me three times." And he broke down and wept.³

> **The day of crucifixion** [chapter 15]. A temporal formula ("as soon as it was morning"—v. 1) provides the transition from the night before the crucifixion to the day of it. The tragic events happen at breakneck speed. The trial before the high priest Caiaphas is now succeeded by the more sinister trial before the Roman governor Pilate (vv. 1–5). A mob scene ensues in which a murderer and insurrectionist is exchanged for the innocent Jesus (vv. 6–15). After that the action marches grimly to its foreordained conclusion: torturing of Jesus (vv. 16–20); the procession to the place of crucifixion and then the crucifixion itself (vv. 21–32); the death of Jesus (vv. 33–41); the burial of Jesus (vv. 42–47). To read any story well, we need to be receptive to the feelings that the story evokes and awakens; this is the saddest of all stories. As we read it, we need to note that the Gospels tell us the facts of what happened, with very little theological explanation of the events. Most of the Bible's theological interpretation of the significance of what happens in the passion stories is found in the OT sacrificial system and messianic prophecies and the NT epistles' commentary on Jesus' atonement.

15 And as soon as it was morning, the chief priests held a consultation with the elders and scribes and the whole Council. And they bound Jesus and led him away and delivered him over to Pilate. ^{2a}And Pilate asked him, "Are you the King of the Jews?" And he answered him, "You have said so." ³And the chief priests accused him of many things. ⁴And Pilate again asked him, "Have you no answer to make? See how many charges they bring against you." ⁵But Jesus made no further answer, so that Pilate was amazed.

^{6b}Now at the feast he used to release for them one prisoner for whom they asked. ⁷And among the rebels in prison, who had committed murder in the insurrection, there was a man called Barabbas. ⁸And the crowd came up and began to ask Pilate to do as he usually did for them. ⁹And he answered them, saying, "Do you want me to release for you the King of the Jews?" ¹⁰For he perceived that it was out of envy that the chief priests had delivered him up. ¹¹But the chief priests stirred up the crowd to have him release for them Barabbas instead. ¹²And Pilate again said to them, "Then what shall I do with the man you call the King of the Jews?" ¹³And they cried out again, "Crucify him." ¹⁴And Pilate said to them, "Why, what evil has he done?" But they shouted all the more, "Crucify him." ¹⁵So Pilate, wishing to satisfy the crowd, released for them Barabbas, and having scourged⁴ Jesus, he delivered him to be crucified.

^{16c}And the soldiers led him away inside the palace (that is, the governor's

---

¹ Or forecourt ² Some manuscripts omit and the rooster crowed ³ Or And when he had thought about it, he wept ⁴ A Roman judicial penalty, consisting of a severe beating with a multi-lashed whip containing imbedded pieces of bone and metal ^a For 15:2-5 see parallels Matt. 27:11-14; Luke 23:1-3; John 18:28-38 ^b For 15:6-15 see parallels Matt. 27:15-26; Luke 23:18-25; John 18:39, 40; 19:16 ^c For 15:16-20 see parallels Matt. 27:27-31; John 19:2, 3

headquarters),[1] and they called together the whole battalion.[2] [17]And they clothed him in a purple cloak, and twisting together a crown of thorns, they put it on him. [18]And they began to salute him, "Hail, King of the Jews!" [19]And they were striking his head with a reed and spitting on him and kneeling down in homage to him. [20]And when they had mocked him, they stripped him of the purple cloak and put his own clothes on him. And they led him out to crucify him.

[21]And they compelled a passerby, Simon of Cyrene, who was coming in from the country, the father of Alexander and Rufus, to carry his cross. [22][a]And they brought him to the place called Golgotha (which means Place of a Skull). [23]And they offered him wine mixed with myrrh, but he did not take it. [24]And they crucified him and divided his garments among them, casting lots for them, to decide what each should take. [25]And it was the third hour[3] when they crucified him. [26]And the inscription of the charge against him read, "The King of the Jews." [27]And with him they crucified two robbers, one on his right and one on his left.[4] [29]And those who passed by derided him, wagging their heads and saying, "Aha! You who would destroy the temple and rebuild it in three days, [30]save yourself, and come down from the cross!" [31]So also the chief priests with the scribes mocked him to one another, saying, "He saved others; he cannot save himself. [32]Let the Christ, the King of Israel, come down now from the cross that we may see and believe." Those who were crucified with him also reviled him.

[33]And when the sixth hour[5] had come, there was darkness over the whole land until the ninth hour.[6] [34]And at the ninth hour Jesus cried with a loud voice, [b]"Eloi, Eloi, lema sabachthani?" which means, "My God, my God, why have you forsaken me?" [35]And some of the bystanders hearing it said, "Behold, he is calling Elijah." [36]And someone ran and filled a sponge with sour wine, put it on a reed and gave it to him to drink, saying, "Wait, let us see whether Elijah will come to take him down." [37]And Jesus uttered a loud cry and breathed his last. [38]And the curtain of the temple was torn in two, from top to bottom. [39][c]And when the centurion, who stood facing him, saw that in this way he[7] breathed his last, he said, "Truly this man was the Son[8] of God!"

[40]There were also women looking on from a distance, among whom were Mary Magdalene, and Mary the mother of James the younger and of Joses, and Salome. [41]When he was in Galilee, they followed him and ministered to him, and there were also many other women who came up with him to Jerusalem.

[42][d]And when evening had come, since it was the day of Preparation, that is, the day before the Sabbath, [43]Joseph of Arimathea, a respected member of the Council, who was also himself looking for the kingdom of God, took courage and went to Pilate and asked for the body of Jesus. [44]Pilate was surprised to hear that he should have already died.[9] And summoning the centurion, he asked him whether he was already dead. [45]And when he learned from the centurion that he was dead, he granted the corpse to Joseph. [46]And Joseph[10] bought a linen shroud, and taking him down, wrapped him in the linen shroud and laid him in a tomb that had been cut out of the rock. And he rolled a stone against the entrance of the tomb. [47]Mary Magdalene and Mary the mother of Joses saw where he was laid.

---

[1] Greek the praetorium [2] Greek cohort; a tenth of a Roman legion, usually about 600 men [3] That is, 9 A.M. [4] Some manuscripts insert verse 28: And the Scripture was fulfilled that says, "He was numbered with the transgressors" [5] That is, noon [6] That is, 3 P.M. [7] Some manuscripts insert cried out and [8] Or a son [9] Or Pilate wondered whether he had already died [10] Greek he [a] For 15:22-38 see parallels Matt. 27:33-51; Luke 23:32-51; John 19:17-19, 23, 24, 28-30 [b] Ps. 22:1 [c] For 15:39-41 see parallels Matt. 27:54-56; Luke 23:47, 49 [d] For 15:42-47 see parallels Matt. 27:57-61; Luke 23:50-56; John 19:38-42

The resurrection and postresurrection appearances of Jesus [chapter 16]. The power of the resurrection story is matchless, and it never loses its sway over the imagination and emotions. The visual details are carefully selected so as to make the whole scene come alive. The astonishment of those who were the first witnesses to the resurrection never palls in our rereading of the story. Although the Gospel writers do not belabor the point, the story is told in such a way as to embody a latent apologetic or evidential cast, offering proof that the resurrection really occurred. Jesus' final discourse to the disciples (vv. 14–18), followed by a narrative summary of Jesus' ascension (v. 19) and the disciples' preaching (v. 20), lends an artistic sense of closure to Mark's narrative. We should note that some of the early manuscripts of Mark do not include verses 9–20.

16 [a]When the Sabbath was past, Mary Magdalene and Mary the mother of James and Salome bought spices, so that they might go and anoint him. [2]And very early on the first day of the week, when the sun had risen, they went to the tomb. [3]And they were saying to one another, "Who will roll away the stone for us from the entrance of the tomb?" [4]And looking up, they saw that the stone had been rolled back—it was very large. [5]And entering the tomb, they saw a young man sitting on the right side, dressed in a white robe, and they were alarmed. [6]And he said to them, "Do not be alarmed. You seek Jesus of Nazareth, who was crucified. He has risen; he is not here. See the place where they laid him. [7]But go, tell his disciples and Peter that he is going before you to Galilee. There you will see him, just as he told you." [8]And they went out and fled from the tomb, for trembling and astonishment had seized them, and they said nothing to anyone, for they were afraid.

[SOME OF THE EARLIEST MANUSCRIPTS DO NOT INCLUDE 16:9-20.][1]

[9][[Now when he rose early on the first day of the week, he appeared first to Mary Magdalene, from whom he had cast out seven demons. [10]She went and told those who had been with him, as they mourned and wept. [11]But when they heard that he was alive and had been seen by her, they would not believe it.

[12]After these things he appeared in another form to two of them, as they were walking into the country. [13]And they went back and told the rest, but they did not believe them.

[14]Afterward he appeared to the eleven themselves as they were reclining at table, and he rebuked them for their unbelief and hardness of heart, because they had not believed those who saw him after he had risen. [15]And he said to them, "Go into all the world and proclaim the gospel to the whole creation. [16]Whoever believes and is baptized will be saved, but whoever does not believe will be condemned. [17]And these signs will accompany those who believe: in my name they will cast out demons; they will speak in new tongues; [18]they will pick up serpents with their hands; and if they drink any deadly poison, it will not hurt them; they will lay their hands on the sick, and they will recover."

[19]So then the Lord Jesus, after he had spoken to them, was taken up into heaven and sat down at the right hand of God. [20]And they went out and preached everywhere, while the Lord worked with them and confirmed the message by accompanying signs.]]

---

[1] Some manuscripts end the book with 16:8; others include verses 9-20 immediately after verse 8. A few manuscripts insert additional material after verse 14; one Latin manuscript adds after verse 8 the following: *But they reported briefly to Peter and those with him all that they had been told. And after this, Jesus himself sent out by means of them, from east to west, the sacred and imperishable proclamation of eternal salvation.* Other manuscripts include this same wording after verse 8, then continue with verses 9-20 [a] For 16:1-8 see parallels Matt. 28:1-8; Luke 24:1-10; John 20:1

LUKE

The book at a glance. 24 chapters, 1,151 verses. Like the other gospels, Luke tells the good-news story of the life, death, and resurrection of Jesus Christ. The book's many close parallels with Matthew and Mark also serve to highlight some important differences. If Mark was a storyteller and Matthew was something of a Bible scholar, then Luke was an investigative reporter. With a doctor's eye for detail and a journalist's passion for getting the facts straight, Luke carefully records the full gospel story of the God-man who was mighty in word and deed before dying for sinners and rising again with life for the world. He writes for the benefit of fellow Gentiles who want and need to know Jesus. Luke also shows a special concern for people who are marginalized by society, including women, children, and the poor. In keeping with this concern, many of the episodes that appear only in Luke's Gospel feature the welcome of an outcast (the Christmas shepherds, the Prodigal Son, the persistent widow, Zacchaeus, and so forth). There is also a strong sense of movement in the Gospel. In his teaching on discipleship, in his repeated predictions of his sufferings and death, and in his resolute journey toward Jerusalem, Jesus is always moving toward the cross—and beyond its agonies, to the triumph of the empty tomb.

▌ **Genres.** As its title indicates, the Gospel of Luke is a Gospel: a good-news proclamation of salvation through the incarnation, crucifixion, and resurrection of the Son of Man. Although there are many subgenres within Gospel, the narrative as a whole follows the chronology of Christ's own life and death. Despite the space that Luke devotes to the birth and boyhood of Jesus, he gives most attention to the three brief years of Christ's earthly ministry and especially to the world-changing events that took place in the last week of his life on earth. The many subgenres in the Gospel include *annunciation story, *birth narrative, *lyric *praise psalm, Christmas carol, *prophecy, *genealogy, preparation story, *temptation story, *calling story, *recognition story, *conflict story, *encounter story, *miracle story, *pronouncement story, *parable, *beatitude, *sermon, *proverb, passion story, trial narrative, and *resurrection account. (For more information on items accompanied by an asterisk, see the glossary at the back of this Bible.)

▌ **Unifying elements.** The Gospel of Luke finds its fundamental unity in the person of Jesus Christ and his mission to seek and to save the lost. From the first announcement of his coming to his ascension into heaven, Jesus is at the center of everything: the songs are for his praise, the miracles are by his power, the teaching is from his wisdom,

Passage	Content	The Son of Man	Geographical Location	Stage of Ministry
1:1–4	Prologue: Luke's purpose			
1:5–2:52	Birth and boyhood of Jesus	His advent	Israel	
3:1–4:13	Baptism and temptation			
4:14–6:16	Early ministry and calling of the first disciples			
6:17–8:56	Beatitudes, parables, and miracles	His ministry	Galilee	
9:1–50	Teaching on discipleship			Seeking the lost
9:51–10:37	In Samaria: the hard road of discipleship			
10:38–13:21	In Bethany and Judea: life's priorities			
13:22–17:10	Journey to Jerusalem: the destiny that awaits us	His rejection	On the way to Jerusalem	
17:11–19:27	Between Samaria and Galilee: faith and repentance			
19:28–21:38	Triumphal entry and teaching at the temple			
22:1–23:25	Last supper, arrest, trials	His death	Jerusalem	
23:26–56	Crucifixion and burial			Saving the lost
24:1–53	Resurrection and ascension	His triumph	From Jerusalem to the ends of the earth	

the conflict is over his claims, and the cross is the burden that only he could bear. Luke gives his account further literary unity by intertwining the stories of Jesus and John the Baptist; by beginning and ending his story at the temple; by presenting the life of Jesus as a journey toward Jerusalem; and by following the progress of the disciples as they learn to count the cost of discipleship. The unity of the gospel is also expressed in the climactic pronouncement that Jesus makes to Zacchaeus: "The Son of Man came to seek and to save the lost" (19:10). After coming to earth at the first Christmas (chapters 1–3), throughout most of the Gospel Jesus spends his time seeking people who are lost in all kinds of ways (chapters 4–21), before finally giving his life as the atonement for their sins (chapters 22–24). Other recurring motifs include the cost of discipleship; the importance of prayer; the call to faithful stewardship; the finding of what is lost; the growing opposition to Jesus and his kingdom work; and the special love that godly women had for Jesus.

▍**Inferred literary intentions.** Luke makes his purpose explicit in the opening verses, where he both acknowledges the existence of other gospels and states his own authorial intention of writing a Jesus narrative that is historically accurate, thoroughly researched, and carefully organized. His specific goal is to give his friend Theophilus (and by implication anyone else who loves God) a solid basis for having full certainty of salvation in Christ. The Gospel According to Luke is "the gospel of knowing for sure." The book is also designed to achieve the following literary purposes:

- show the anticipation and expectation that surrounded the coming of Christ

- demonstrate the power and mercy of Jesus in meeting the needs of both the body and the soul

- introduce the main themes in the parables, discourses, and other teaching ministry of Jesus

- show what is at stake in deciding either to reject Jesus or to become his disciple

- give a glimpse of the glorious welcome that awaits every child of God

- present the gospel facts of the cross and the empty tomb, together with their implications for the salvation of sinners and the evangelization of the world

- tell the life of Jesus in story form

- make the characters and settings come alive with unusual attention to concrete descriptive details

- give conspicuous attention to the marginalized members of society (including the poor and women)

▌**Theological themes.** (1) Incarnation: Luke's favorite title for Jesus, "the Son of Man," shows his deity, while many of the details surrounding his birth and death highlight his humanity. (2) Salvation: on the basis of his death on the cross and by the power of his resurrection life, Jesus brings total physical and spiritual restoration to the body and the soul. (3) The kingdom of God: in the coming of Christ, God is establishing his sovereign rule over the universe. (4) The Holy Spirit: more than any other Gospel, Luke highlights the role of the Holy Spirit in empowering the ministry of Jesus Christ. (5) Forgiveness: at both the human and the divine levels, forgiveness is exemplified in the healing of the paralytic (5:17–26), the story of the prodigal son (15:11–32), the parable of the Pharisee and the publican (18:9–14), the conversion of Zacchaeus (19:1–10), and other episodes from the Gospel. (5) Discipleship: for the sake of his gospel, Jesus calls every one of his followers to share in his sufferings. (6) Missions and evangelism: the gospel is not just for the Jews but also for the lost sinners of all nations. (7) Prayer: in addition to his specific teaching on prayer, Jesus exemplifies the life of prayer by his own intercession with the Father.

▌**The book of Luke as a chapter in the master story of the Bible.** Like the other evangelists, Luke tells the gospel story at the heart of the Bible's saving message. The coming of Christ is the fulfillment of all the ancient prophecies of the long-expected Messiah (see especially 24:27). Luke shows the compassion of Christ as the friend of poor, lost, brokenhearted, alienated, oppressed, and abandoned sinners.

The forerunner foretold [1:1–25]. Luke opens by dedicating his Gospel to Theophilus (vv. 1–4), with the hope of giving his friend complete certainty about the claims of Christ. He then begins to tell the story of Jesus by first telling the story of John the Baptist, starting with the prophecy of his birth to the old priest Zechariah and his barren wife Elizabeth. The effect of this opening (in which John the Baptist serves as a literary *foil to Jesus) is to heighten anticipation for the coming of Christ and to show his greatness by way of comparison: as great as John is, and as miraculous as the circumstances surrounding his birth are, his calling is to prepare the way for someone infinitely greater.

1 Inasmuch as many have undertaken to compile a narrative of the things that have been accomplished among us, ²just as those who from the beginning were eyewitnesses and ministers of the word have delivered them to us, ³it seemed good to me also, having followed all things closely for some time past, to write an orderly account for you, most excellent Theophilus, ⁴that you may have certainty concerning the things you have been taught.

⁵In the days of Herod, king of Judea, there was a priest named Zechariah,¹ of the division of Abijah. And he had a wife from the daughters of Aaron, and her name was Elizabeth. ⁶And they were both righteous before God, walking blamelessly in all the commandments and statutes of the Lord. ⁷But they had no child, because Elizabeth was barren, and both were advanced in years.

⁸Now while he was serving as priest before God when his division was on duty, ⁹according to the custom of the priesthood, he was chosen by lot to enter the temple of the Lord and burn incense. ¹⁰And the whole multitude of the people were praying outside at the hour of incense. ¹¹And there appeared to him an angel of the Lord standing on the right side of the altar of incense. ¹²And Zechariah was troubled when he saw him, and fear fell upon him. ¹³But the angel said to him, "Do not be afraid, Zechariah, for your prayer has been heard, and your wife Elizabeth will bear you a son, and you shall call his name John. ¹⁴And you will have joy and gladness, and many will rejoice at his birth, ¹⁵for he will be great before the Lord. And he must not drink wine or strong drink, and he will be filled with the Holy Spirit, even from his mother's womb. ¹⁶And he will turn many of the children of Israel to the Lord their God, ¹⁷and he will go before him in the spirit and power of Elijah, to turn the hearts of the fathers to the children, and the disobedient to the wisdom of the just, to make ready for the Lord a people prepared."

¹⁸And Zechariah said to the angel, "How shall I know this? For I am an old man, and my wife is advanced in years." ¹⁹And the angel answered him, "I am Gabriel. I stand in the presence of God, and I was sent to speak to you and to bring you this good news. ²⁰And behold, you will be silent and unable to speak until the day that these things take place, because you did not believe my words, which will be fulfilled in their time." ²¹And the people were waiting for Zechariah, and they were wondering at his delay in the temple. ²²And when he came out, he was unable to speak to them, and they realized that he had seen a vision in the temple. And he kept making signs to them and remained mute. ²³And when his time of service was ended, he went to his home.

²⁴After these days his wife Elizabeth conceived, and for five months she kept herself hidden, saying, ²⁵"Thus the Lord has done for me in the days when he looked on me, to take away my reproach among people."

¹ Greek *Zacharias*

> **Birth announcement [1:26–56].** The Gospel of Luke is one of two NT Gospels to tell the story of Jesus' birth and infancy. The announcement of Jesus' birth belongs to a biblical genre known as the *annunciation story. The annunciation of the birth of Jesus to Mary parallels the preceding annunciation story involving the birth of John the Baptist. But there are contrasts as well as parallels: Mary's willing submission shines all the more brightly when compared to Zechariah's initial unbelief. Gabriel's announcement serves as the reader's first introduction (an *initiation) to the person and work of Jesus as the Son of God and the Savior. Mary's visit with her cousin Elizabeth provides further confirmation that the child in Mary's womb is the Lord (vv. 39–45). In her hymn of praise (the Magnificat), Mary borrows liberally from the language of the Psalms and the Song of Hannah (1 Sam. 2:1–10) to sing a new song of praise to her God as the Savior of the poor and humble (vv. 46–55).

[26] In the sixth month the angel Gabriel was sent from God to a city of Galilee named Nazareth, [27] to a virgin betrothed[1] to a man whose name was Joseph, of the house of David. And the virgin's name was Mary. [28] And he came to her and said, "Greetings, O favored one, the Lord is with you!"[2] [29] But she was greatly troubled at the saying, and tried to discern what sort of greeting this might be. [30] And the angel said to her, "Do not be afraid, Mary, for you have found favor with God. [31] And behold, you will conceive in your womb and bear a son, and you shall call his name Jesus. [32] He will be great and will be called the Son of the Most High. And the Lord God will give to him the throne of his father David, [33] and he will reign over the house of Jacob forever, and of his kingdom there will be no end."

[34] And Mary said to the angel, "How will this be, since I am a virgin?"[3]

[35] And the angel answered her, "The Holy Spirit will come upon you, and the power of the Most High will overshadow you; therefore the child to be born[4] will be called holy—the Son of God. [36] And behold, your relative Elizabeth in her old age has also conceived a son, and this is the sixth month with her who was called barren. [37] For nothing will be impossible with God." [38] And Mary said, "Behold, I am the servant[5] of the Lord; let it be to me according to your word." And the angel departed from her.

[39] In those days Mary arose and went with haste into the hill country, to a town in Judah, [40] and she entered the house of Zechariah and greeted Elizabeth. [41] And when Elizabeth heard the greeting of Mary, the baby leaped in her womb. And Elizabeth was filled with the Holy Spirit, [42] and she exclaimed with a loud cry, "Blessed are you among women, and blessed is the fruit of your womb! [43] And why is this granted to me that the mother of my Lord should come to me? [44] For behold, when the sound of your greeting came to my ears, the baby in my womb leaped for joy. [45] And blessed is she who believed that there would be[6] a fulfillment of what was spoken to her from the Lord."

[46] And Mary said,

"My soul magnifies the Lord,
[47]   and my spirit rejoices in God my Savior,
[48]   for he has looked on the humble estate of his servant.
    For behold, from now on all generations will call me blessed;
[49]   for he who is mighty has done great things for me,
    and holy is his name.

---

[1] That is, legally pledged to be married [2] Some manuscripts add *Blessed are you among women!* [3] Greek *since I do not know a man* [4] Some manuscripts add *of you* [5] Greek *bondservant*; also verse 48 [6] Or *believed, for there will be*

⁵⁰ And his mercy is for those who fear him
from generation to generation.
⁵¹ He has shown strength with his arm;
he has scattered the proud in the thoughts of their hearts;
⁵² he has brought down the mighty from their thrones
and exalted those of humble estate;
⁵³ he has filled the hungry with good things,
and the rich he has sent away empty.
⁵⁴ He has helped his servant Israel,
in remembrance of his mercy,
⁵⁵ as he spoke to our fathers,
to Abraham and to his offspring forever."

⁵⁶And Mary remained with her about three months and returned to her home.

The birth of John the Baptist [1:57–80]. As the fulfillment of God's promise, the birth of the forerunner (as well as the restoration of Zechariah's speech) heightens everyone's expectations about what God will do for his people. Zechariah responds with a psalmlike hymn of praise that has come to be known as the Benedictus. Like everything else at the beginning of Luke's Gospel, the hymn moves from John the Baptist to the saving work of God in Christ. Among the Gospels, Luke is unique for including lyrics in the Christmas story.

⁵⁷Now the time came for Elizabeth to give birth, and she bore a son. ⁵⁸And her neighbors and relatives heard that the Lord had shown great mercy to her, and they rejoiced with her. ⁵⁹And on the eighth day they came to circumcise the child. And they would have called him Zechariah after his father, ⁶⁰but his mother answered, "No; he shall be called John." ⁶¹And they said to her, "None of your relatives is called by this name." ⁶²And they made signs to his father, inquiring what he wanted him to be called. ⁶³And he asked for a writing tablet and wrote, "His name is John." And they all wondered. ⁶⁴And immediately his mouth was opened and his tongue loosed, and he spoke, blessing God. ⁶⁵And fear came on all their neighbors. And all these things were talked about through all the hill country of Judea, ⁶⁶and all who heard them laid them up in their hearts, saying, "What then will this child be?" For the hand of the Lord was with him.

⁶⁷And his father Zechariah was filled with the Holy Spirit and prophesied, saying,

⁶⁸ "Blessed be the Lord God of Israel,
for he has visited and redeemed his people
⁶⁹ and has raised up a horn of salvation for us
in the house of his servant David,
⁷⁰ as he spoke by the mouth of his holy prophets from of old,
⁷¹ that we should be saved from our enemies
and from the hand of all who hate us;
⁷² to show the mercy promised to our fathers
and to remember his holy covenant,

⁷³ the oath that he swore to our father Abraham, to grant us
⁷⁴   that we, being delivered from the hand of our enemies,
          might serve him without fear,
⁷⁵   in holiness and righteousness before him all our days.
⁷⁶ And you, child, will be called the prophet of the Most High;
          for you will go before the Lord to prepare his ways,
⁷⁷ to give knowledge of salvation to his people
          in the forgiveness of their sins,
⁷⁸ because of the tender mercy of our God,
          whereby the sunrise shall visit us¹ from on high
⁷⁹ to give light to those who sit in darkness and in the shadow of death,
          to guide our feet into the way of peace."

⁸⁰And the child grew and became strong in spirit, and he was in the wilderness until the day of his public appearance to Israel.

> **The birth of Jesus Christ** [2:1–21]. This best known of all Bible passages—so carefully located in time and place (a style that literary critics call circumstantial)—draws a contrast between the humble circumstances of Christ's birth and the glorious praise that he deservedly receives from multitudes of the heavenly host. Reinforcing the motif of humility, the style is simple and the effect one of understatement as the world-changing events are narrated in a matter-of-fact way. In this birth narrative Luke introduces two of the main themes of his Gospel: as the Son of David, Jesus has come to bring salvation to Israel, especially poor and lowly outcasts like the shepherds; as the Savior of the world, he has come to bring salvation to all people.

2 In those days a decree went out from Caesar Augustus that all the world should be registered. ²This was the first registration when² Quirinius was governor of Syria. ³And all went to be registered, each to his own town. ⁴And Joseph also went up from Galilee, from the town of Nazareth, to Judea, to the city of David, which is called Bethlehem, because he was of the house and lineage of David, ⁵to be registered with Mary, his betrothed,³ who was with child. ⁶And while they were there, the time came for her to give birth. ⁷And she gave birth to her firstborn son and wrapped him in swaddling cloths and laid him in a manger, because there was no place for them in the inn.

⁸And in the same region there were shepherds out in the field, keeping watch over their flock by night. ⁹And an angel of the Lord appeared to them, and the glory of the Lord shone around them, and they were filled with fear. ¹⁰And the angel said to them, "Fear not, for behold, I bring you good news of great joy that will be for all the people. ¹¹For unto you is born this day in the city of David a Savior, who is Christ the Lord. ¹²And this will be a sign for you: you will find a baby wrapped in swaddling cloths and lying in a manger." ¹³And suddenly there was with the angel a multitude of the heavenly host praising God and saying,

¹⁴   "Glory to God in the highest,
          and on earth peace among those with whom he is pleased!"⁴

---

¹ Or *when the sunrise shall dawn upon us;* some manuscripts *since the sunrise has visited us* ² Or *This was the registration before* ³ That is, one legally pledged to be married ⁴ Some manuscripts *peace, good will among men*

¹⁵When the angels went away from them into heaven, the shepherds said to one another, "Let us go over to Bethlehem and see this thing that has happened, which the Lord has made known to us." ¹⁶And they went with haste and found Mary and Joseph, and the baby lying in a manger. ¹⁷And when they saw it, they made known the saying that had been told them concerning this child. ¹⁸And all who heard it wondered at what the shepherds told them. ¹⁹But Mary treasured up all these things, pondering them in her heart. ²⁰And the shepherds returned, glorifying and praising God for all they had heard and seen, as it had been told them.

²¹And at the end of eight days, when he was circumcised, he was called Jesus, the name given by the angel before he was conceived in the womb.

The Christ child at the temple [2:22–52]. As the baby Jesus is presented at the temple, two old and godly Israelites (once again, Luke is presenting things in pairs) show how everyone should receive him. In his song of praise (the Nunc Dimittis), Simeon borrows language from the Old Testament to praise Jesus as the universal Savior; he is both a light for the Gentiles and a glory for Israel. Similarly, Anna gives thanks to God for the redemption of Israel in Christ. Then, although Luke says little about the boyhood of Jesus, he does tell a coming-of-age story that is omitted from the other Gospels. The famous incident of Jesus' staying behind in Jerusalem after Passover (the only canonical story of Jesus' childhood that we possess) shows the Savior at home in his Father's house. Luke portrays a boy growing into a man, submitting to his parents while at the same time making the will of God his main purpose in life. In Luke's picture of the boy Jesus at the center of attention in the temple, we see the main structural principle of all four NT Gospels—a structure in which Jesus is the focus and a large cast of characters revolves around him.

²²And when the time came for their purification according to the Law of Moses, they brought him up to Jerusalem to present him to the Lord ²³(as it is written in the Law of the Lord, ᵃ"Every male who first opens the womb shall be called holy to the Lord") ²⁴and to offer a sacrifice according to what is said in the Law of the Lord, ᵇ"a pair of turtledoves, or two young pigeons." ²⁵Now there was a man in Jerusalem, whose name was Simeon, and this man was righteous and devout, waiting for the consolation of Israel, and the Holy Spirit was upon him. ²⁶And it had been revealed to him by the Holy Spirit that he would not see death before he had seen the Lord's Christ. ²⁷And he came in the Spirit into the temple, and when the parents brought in the child Jesus, to do for him according to the custom of the Law, ²⁸he took him up in his arms and blessed God and said,

²⁹ "Lord, now you are letting your servant¹ depart in peace,
       according to your word;
³⁰ for my eyes have seen your salvation
³¹   that you have prepared in the presence of all peoples,
³² a light for revelation to the Gentiles,
       and for glory to your people Israel."

³³And his father and his mother marveled at what was said about him. ³⁴And Simeon blessed them and said to Mary his mother, "Behold, this child is appointed for the fall and rising of many in Israel, and for a sign that is opposed ³⁵(and a sword

will pierce through your own soul also), so that thoughts from many hearts may be revealed."

[36] And there was a prophetess, Anna, the daughter of Phanuel, of the tribe of Asher. She was advanced in years, having lived with her husband seven years from when she was a virgin, [37] and then as a widow until she was eighty-four.[1] She did not depart from the temple, worshiping with fasting and prayer night and day. [38] And coming up at that very hour she began to give thanks to God and to speak of him to all who were waiting for the redemption of Jerusalem.

[39] And when they had performed everything according to the Law of the Lord, they returned into Galilee, to their own town of Nazareth. [40] And the child grew and became strong, filled with wisdom. And the favor of God was upon him.

[41] Now his parents went to Jerusalem every year at the Feast of the Passover. [42] And when he was twelve years old, they went up according to custom. [43] And when the feast was ended, as they were returning, the boy Jesus stayed behind in Jerusalem. His parents did not know it, [44] but supposing him to be in the group they went a day's journey, but then they began to search for him among their relatives and acquaintances, [45] and when they did not find him, they returned to Jerusalem, searching for him. [46] After three days they found him in the temple, sitting among the teachers, listening to them and asking them questions. [47] And all who heard him were amazed at his understanding and his answers. [48] And when his parents[2] saw him, they were astonished. And his mother said to him, "Son, why have you treated us so? Behold, your father and I have been searching for you in great distress." [49] And he said to them, "Why were you looking for me? Did you not know that I must be in my Father's house?"[3] [50] And they did not understand the saying that he spoke to them. [51] And he went down with them and came to Nazareth and was submissive to them. And his mother treasured up all these things in her heart.

[52] And Jesus increased in wisdom and in stature[4] and in favor with God and man.

The baptism of the Son [3:1–22]. Luke continues to weave the story of John into the story of Jesus. In preparation for the coming Savior, John the Baptist begins his public ministry of preaching the good news, calling sinners to repentance, and baptizing his followers with water for the forgiveness of their sins. Already in John's call to repentance and in his public rebuke of King Herod there are hints of a coming conflict with the authorities. Meanwhile, John's followers are wrestling with one of the central questions of the gospel: who is the Christ? John answers by pointing them to a greater Baptist—one who will baptize with the Holy Spirit and with fire. The baptism of Jesus comes with the blessing of the Father and the anointing of the Holy Spirit (vv. 21–22), preparing Jesus to do his great life's work.

---

3 In the fifteenth year of the reign of Tiberius Caesar, Pontius Pilate being governor of Judea, and Herod being tetrarch of Galilee, and his brother Philip tetrarch of the region of Ituraea and Trachonitis, and Lysanias tetrarch of Abilene, [2] during the high priesthood of Annas and Caiaphas, [a] the word of God came to John the son of Zechariah in the wilderness. [3] And he went into all the region around the Jordan, proclaiming a baptism of repentance for the forgiveness of sins. [4] As it is written in the book of the words of Isaiah the prophet,

---

[1] Or *as a widow for eighty-four years* [2] Greek *they* [3] Or *about my Father's business* [4] Or *years* [a] For 3:2-17 see parallels Matt. 3:1-12; Mark 1:2-8

ª"The voice of one crying in the wilderness:
  'Prepare the way of the Lord,[1]
    make his paths straight.
⁵ Every valley shall be filled,
    and every mountain and hill shall be made low,
  and the crooked shall become straight,
    and the rough places shall become level ways,
⁶ and all flesh shall see the salvation of God.'"

⁷He said therefore to the crowds that came out to be baptized by him, "You brood of vipers! Who warned you to flee from the wrath to come? ⁸Bear fruits in keeping with repentance. And do not begin to say to yourselves, 'We have Abraham as our father.' For I tell you, God is able from these stones to raise up children for Abraham. ⁹Even now the axe is laid to the root of the trees. Every tree therefore that does not bear good fruit is cut down and thrown into the fire."

¹⁰And the crowds asked him, "What then shall we do?" ¹¹And he answered them, "Whoever has two tunics[2] is to share with him who has none, and whoever has food is to do likewise." ¹²Tax collectors also came to be baptized and said to him, "Teacher, what shall we do?" ¹³And he said to them, "Collect no more than you are authorized to do." ¹⁴Soldiers also asked him, "And we, what shall we do?" And he said to them, "Do not extort money from anyone by threats or by false accusation, and be content with your wages."

¹⁵As the people were in expectation, and all were questioning in their hearts concerning John, whether he might be the Christ, ¹⁶John answered them all, saying, "I baptize you with water, but he who is mightier than I is coming, the strap of whose sandals I am not worthy to untie. He will baptize you with the Holy Spirit and with fire. ¹⁷His winnowing fork is in his hand, to clear his threshing floor and to gather the wheat into his barn, but the chaff he will burn with unquenchable fire."

¹⁸So with many other exhortations he preached good news to the people. ¹⁹But Herod the tetrarch, who had been reproved by him for Herodias, his brother's wife, and for all the evil things that Herod had done, ²⁰added this to them all, that he locked up John in prison.

²¹Now when all the people were baptized, and when ᵇJesus also had been baptized and was praying, the heavens were opened, ²²and the Holy Spirit descended on him in bodily form, like a dove; and a voice came from heaven, "You are my beloved Son;[3] with you I am well pleased."[4]

The temptation of the Son [3:23–4:13]. Jesus is reintroduced with a formal genealogy that serves to emphasize the dignity of his person (3:23–38). By going all the way back to Adam, Luke identifies Jesus as the universal Savior of humanity. Then Jesus is led into the wilderness, where in forty days he successfully resists three temptations from the devil (to meet his own needs by turning stones into bread, to avoid the cross by seizing Satan's crown, and to force God to prove his Sonship by leaping from the temple). Luke is alluding here to the exodus. In effect, Jesus is repeating the experience of Old Testament Israel, which was baptized in the Red Sea before facing forty years of temptation in the wilderness. The difference is that Jesus resists every temptation by trusting in the Word of God. The departure of the devil "until an opportune time" (4:13) ominously

---

[1] Or crying, Prepare in the wilderness the way of the Lord [2] Greek chiton, a long garment worn under the cloak next to the skin [3] Or my Son, my (or the) Beloved [4] Some manuscripts beloved Son; today I have begotten you ª Isa. 40:3-5 ᵇ For 3:21, 22 see parallels Matt. 3:13-17; Mark 1:9-11

foreshadows the deadly attack Satan will make near the end of Luke's Gospel. One of the underlying motifs in all four Gospels is known as Christus Victor—Christ victorious over Satan, sin, and death. The temptation story famously highlights this motif.

²³Jesus, when he began his ministry, was about thirty years of age, being the son (as was supposed) of Joseph, the son of Heli, ²⁴the son of Matthat, the son of Levi, the son of Melchi, the son of Jannai, the son of Joseph, ²⁵the son of Mattathias, the son of Amos, the son of Nahum, the son of Esli, the son of Naggai, ²⁶the son of Maath, the son of Mattathias, the son of Semein, the son of Josech, the son of Joda, ²⁷the son of Joanan, the son of Rhesa, the son of Zerubbabel, the son of Shealtiel,[1] the son of Neri, ²⁸the son of Melchi, the son of Addi, the son of Cosam, the son of Elmadam, the son of Er, ²⁹the son of Joshua, the son of Eliezer, the son of Jorim, the son of Matthat, the son of Levi, ³⁰the son of Simeon, the son of Judah, the son of Joseph, the son of Jonam, the son of Eliakim, ³¹the son of Melea, the son of Menna, the son of Mattatha, the son of Nathan, the son of David, ³²the son of Jesse, the son of Obed, the son of Boaz, the son of Sala, the son of Nahshon, ³³the son of Amminadab, the son of Admin, the son of Arni, the son of Hezron, the son of Perez, the son of Judah, ³⁴the son of Jacob, the son of Isaac, the son of Abraham, the son of Terah, the son of Nahor, ³⁵the son of Serug, the son of Reu, the son of Peleg, the son of Eber, the son of Shelah, ³⁶the son of Cainan, the son of Arphaxad, the son of Shem, the son of Noah, the son of Lamech, ³⁷the son of Methuselah, the son of Enoch, the son of Jared, the son of Mahalaleel, the son of Cainan, ³⁸the son of Enos, the son of Seth, the son of Adam, the son of God.

4 ᵃAnd Jesus, full of the Holy Spirit, returned from the Jordan and was led by the Spirit in the wilderness ²for forty days, being tempted by the devil. And he ate nothing during those days. And when they were ended, he was hungry. ³The devil said to him, "If you are the Son of God, command this stone to become bread." ⁴And Jesus answered him, "It is written, ᵇ'Man shall not live by bread alone.'" ⁵And the devil took him up and showed him all the kingdoms of the world in a moment of time, ⁶and said to him, "To you I will give all this authority and their glory, for it has been delivered to me, and I give it to whom I will. ⁷If you, then, will worship me, it will all be yours." ⁸And Jesus answered him, "It is written,

ᶜ"'You shall worship the Lord your God,
    and him only shall you serve.'"

⁹And he took him to Jerusalem and set him on the pinnacle of the temple and said to him, "If you are the Son of God, throw yourself down from here, ¹⁰for it is written,

ᵈ"'He will command his angels concerning you,
    to guard you,'

¹¹and

ᵉ"'On their hands they will bear you up,
    lest you strike your foot against a stone.'"

¹²And Jesus answered him, "It is said, ᶠ'You shall not put the Lord your God to the test.'" ¹³And when the devil had ended every temptation, he departed from him until an opportune time.

---

[1] Greek *Salathiel* ᵃFor 4:1-13 see parallels Matt. 4:1-11; Mark 1:12, 13 ᵇDeut. 8:3 ᶜDeut. 6:13 ᵈPs. 91:11 ᵉPs. 91:12 ᶠDeut. 6:16

The prophet rejected in his own hometown [4:14–44]. Jesus begins his public ministry by reading and teaching the Bible in the synagogues of Galilee. Jesus claims that the main purpose of his ministry is to "preach the good news of the kingdom" (v. 43). The sermon he gives in Nazareth typifies his method of biblical exposition: Jesus reads the Old Testament Scriptures and explains how they find their fulfillment in his own gospel ministry to the poor and oppressed (vv. 16–21). These claims are fully vindicated by his miracles of healing people from diseases and delivering them from demons. However, the preaching ministry of Jesus is hardly appreciated in his own hometown, where people are so offended by his message that they seek to stone him, as the story becomes an intense conflict story. Although the opposition will build throughout his ministry, it is present from the outset.

¹⁴And Jesus returned in the power of the Spirit to Galilee, and a report about him went out through all the surrounding country. ¹⁵And he taught in their synagogues, being glorified by all.

¹⁶And he came to Nazareth, where he had been brought up. And as was his custom, he went to the synagogue on the Sabbath day, and he stood up to read. ¹⁷And the scroll of the prophet Isaiah was given to him. He unrolled the scroll and found the place where it was written,

¹⁸ ᵃ"The Spirit of the Lord is upon me,
  because he has anointed me
  to proclaim good news to the poor.
He has sent me to proclaim liberty to the captives
  and recovering of sight to the blind,
  to set at liberty those who are oppressed,
¹⁹ to proclaim the year of the Lord's favor."

²⁰And he rolled up the scroll and gave it back to the attendant and sat down. And the eyes of all in the synagogue were fixed on him. ²¹And he began to say to them, "Today this Scripture has been fulfilled in your hearing." ²²And all spoke well of him and marveled at the gracious words that were coming from his mouth. And they said, "Is not this Joseph's son?" ²³And he said to them, "Doubtless you will quote to me this proverb, 'Physician, heal yourself.' What we have heard you did at Capernaum, do here in your hometown as well." ²⁴And he said, "Truly, I say to you, no prophet is acceptable in his hometown. ²⁵But in truth, I tell you, there were many widows in Israel in the days of Elijah, when the heavens were shut up three years and six months, and a great famine came over all the land, ²⁶and Elijah was sent to none of them but only to Zarephath, in the land of Sidon, to a woman who was a widow. ²⁷And there were many lepers¹ in Israel in the time of the prophet Elisha, and none of them was cleansed, but only Naaman the Syrian." ²⁸When they heard these things, all in the synagogue were filled with wrath. ²⁹And they rose up and drove him out of the town and brought him to the brow of the hill on which their town was built, so that they could throw him down the cliff. ³⁰But passing through their midst, he went away.

³¹ᵇAnd he went down to Capernaum, a city of Galilee. And he was teaching them on the Sabbath, ³²and they were astonished at his teaching, for his word possessed authority. ³³And in the synagogue there was a man who had the spirit of an unclean demon, and he cried out with a loud voice, ³⁴"Ha!² What have you to do with us, Jesus

---

¹ *Leprosy* was a term for several skin diseases; see Leviticus 13 ² Or *Leave us alone* ᵃ Isa. 61:1, 2 ᵇ For 4:31-37 see parallel Mark 1:21-28

of Nazareth? Have you come to destroy us? I know who you are—the Holy One of God." [35]But Jesus rebuked him, saying, "Be silent and come out of him!" And when the demon had thrown him down in their midst, he came out of him, having done him no harm. [36]And they were all amazed and said to one another, "What is this word? For with authority and power he commands the unclean spirits, and they come out!" [37]And reports about him went out into every place in the surrounding region.

[38a]And he arose and left the synagogue and entered Simon's house. Now Simon's mother-in-law was ill with a high fever, and they appealed to him on her behalf. [39]And he stood over her and rebuked the fever, and it left her, and immediately she rose and began to serve them.

[40]Now when the sun was setting, all those who had any who were sick with various diseases brought them to him, and he laid his hands on every one of them and healed them. [41]And demons also came out of many, crying, "You are the Son of God!" But he rebuked them and would not allow them to speak, because they knew that he was the Christ.

[42b]And when it was day, he departed and went into a desolate place. And the people sought him and came to him, and would have kept him from leaving them, [43]but he said to them, "I must preach the good news of the kingdom of God to the other towns as well; for I was sent for this purpose." [44]And he was preaching in the synagogues of Judea.[1]

The calling of the Twelve [5:1–6:16]. Some of the first people Jesus came seeking to save were his own disciples, whom he also named apostles (6:12–15). The calling of Simon (Peter) and the calling of Levi (Matthew) both show that to follow Jesus means leaving everything else behind (5:11, 28). The words of Jesus in these early call narratives and the nearby miracle stories (the leper, the paralytic, the man with the withered hand) are as profound as they are simple: "From now on you will be catching men" (5:10); "Be clean" (5:13); "Your sins are forgiven" (5:20); "Follow me" (5:27); "I have not come to call the righteous but sinners to repentance" (5:32); "The Son of Man is lord of the Sabbath" (6:5). Luke's purpose throughout is to show that Jesus Christ is Savior, Lord, and God. Who else has the power to forgive sins or demand discipleship?

5 On one occasion, while the crowd was pressing in on him to hear the word of God, he was standing by the lake of Gennesaret, [2]and he saw two boats by the lake, but the fishermen had gone out of them and were washing their nets. [3]Getting into one of the boats, which was Simon's, he asked him to put out a little from the land. And he sat down and taught the people from the boat. [4]And when he had finished speaking, he said to Simon, "Put out into the deep and let down your nets for a catch." [5]And Simon answered, "Master, we toiled all night and took nothing! But at your word I will let down the nets." [6]And when they had done this, they enclosed a large number of fish, and their nets were breaking. [7]They signaled to their partners in the other boat to come and help them. And they came and filled both the boats, so that they began to sink. [8]But when Simon Peter saw it, he fell down at Jesus' knees, saying, "Depart from me, for I am a sinful man, O Lord." [9]For he and all who were with him were astonished at the catch of fish that they had taken, [10]and so also were James and John, sons of Zebedee, who were partners with Simon. And Jesus said to

[1] Some manuscripts Galilee [a] For 4:38-41 see parallels Matt. 8:14-17; Mark 1:29-34 [b] For 4:42, 43 see parallel Mark 1:35-38

Simon, "Do not be afraid; from now on you will be catching men." ¹¹And when they had brought their boats to land, they left everything and followed him.

¹²While he was in one of the cities, ªthere came a man full of leprosy.¹ And when he saw Jesus, he fell on his face and begged him, "Lord, if you will, you can make me clean." ¹³And Jesus² stretched out his hand and touched him, saying, "I will; be clean." And immediately the leprosy left him. ¹⁴And he charged him to tell no one, but "go and show yourself to the priest, and make an offering for your cleansing, as Moses commanded, for a proof to them." ¹⁵But now even more the report about him went abroad, and great crowds gathered to hear him and to be healed of their infirmities. ¹⁶But he would withdraw to desolate places and pray.

¹⁷On one of those days, as he was teaching, Pharisees and teachers of the law were sitting there, who had come from every village of Galilee and Judea and from Jerusalem. And the power of the Lord was with him to heal.³ ¹⁸ᵇAnd behold, some men were bringing on a bed a man who was paralyzed, and they were seeking to bring him in and lay him before Jesus, ¹⁹but finding no way to bring him in, because of the crowd, they went up on the roof and let him down with his bed through the tiles into the midst before Jesus. ²⁰And when he saw their faith, he said, "Man, your sins are forgiven you." ²¹And the scribes and the Pharisees began to question, saying, "Who is this who speaks blasphemies? Who can forgive sins but God alone?" ²²When Jesus perceived their thoughts, he answered them, "Why do you question in your hearts? ²³Which is easier, to say, 'Your sins are forgiven you,' or to say, 'Rise and walk'? ²⁴But that you may know that the Son of Man has authority on earth to forgive sins"—he said to the man who was paralyzed—"I say to you, rise, pick up your bed and go home." ²⁵And immediately he rose up before them and picked up what he had been lying on and went home, glorifying God. ²⁶And amazement seized them all, and they glorified God and were filled with awe, saying, "We have seen extraordinary things today."

²⁷ᶜAfter this he went out and saw a tax collector named Levi, sitting at the tax booth. And he said to him, "Follow me." ²⁸And leaving everything, he rose and followed him.

²⁹And Levi made him a great feast in his house, and there was a large company of tax collectors and others reclining at table with them. ³⁰And the Pharisees and their scribes grumbled at his disciples, saying, "Why do you eat and drink with tax collectors and sinners?" ³¹And Jesus answered them, "Those who are well have no need of a physician, but those who are sick. ³²I have not come to call the righteous but sinners to repentance."

³³And they said to him, "The disciples of John fast often and offer prayers, and so do the disciples of the Pharisees, but yours eat and drink." ³⁴And Jesus said to them, "Can you make wedding guests fast while the bridegroom is with them? ³⁵The days will come when the bridegroom is taken away from them, and then they will fast in those days." ³⁶He also told them a parable: "No one tears a piece from a new garment and puts it on an old garment. If he does, he will tear the new, and the piece from the new will not match the old. ³⁷And no one puts new wine into old wineskins. If he does, the new wine will burst the skins and it will be spilled, and the skins will be destroyed. ³⁸But new wine must be put into fresh wineskins. ³⁹And no one after drinking old wine desires new, for he says, 'The old is good.'"⁴

---

¹ *Leprosy* was a term for several skin diseases; see Leviticus 13 ² Greek *he* ³ Some manuscripts *was present to heal them* ⁴ Some manuscripts *better* ª For 5:12-14 see parallels Matt. 8:2-4; Mark 1:40-44 ᵇ For 5:18-26 see parallels Matt. 9:2-8; Mark 2:1-12 ᶜ For 5:27-38 see parallels Matt. 9:9-17; Mark 2:13-22

6 [a]On a Sabbath,[1] while he was going through the grainfields, his disciples plucked and ate some heads of grain, rubbing them in their hands. [2]But some of the Pharisees said, "Why are you doing what is not lawful to do on the Sabbath?" [3]And Jesus answered them, "Have you not read what David did when he was hungry, he and those who were with him: [4]how he entered the house of God and took and ate the bread of the Presence, which is not lawful for any but the priests to eat, and also gave it to those with him?" [5]And he said to them, "The Son of Man is lord of the Sabbath."

[6]On another Sabbath, [b]he entered the synagogue and was teaching, and a man was there whose right hand was withered. [7]And the scribes and the Pharisees watched him, to see whether he would heal on the Sabbath, so that they might find a reason to accuse him. [8]But he knew their thoughts, and he said to the man with the withered hand, "Come and stand here." And he rose and stood there. [9]And Jesus said to them, "I ask you, is it lawful on the Sabbath to do good or to do harm, to save life or to destroy it?" [10]And after looking around at them all he said to him, "Stretch out your hand." And he did so, and his hand was restored. [11]But they were filled with fury and discussed with one another what they might do to Jesus.

[12]In these days he went out to the mountain to pray, and all night he continued in prayer to God. [13]And when day came, he called his disciples [c]and chose from them twelve, whom he named apostles: [14]Simon, whom he named Peter, and Andrew his brother, and James and John, and Philip, and Bartholomew, [15]and Matthew, and Thomas, and James the son of Alphaeus, and Simon who was called the Zealot, [16]and Judas the son of James, and Judas Iscariot, who became a traitor.

The sermon on the plain [6:17–49]. As a result of his teaching and miracles, the fame of Jesus quickly spread, and he gained a large following. Although it is not as lengthy as Matthew's more famous "Sermon on the Mount," the teaching that Luke records in this chapter forms the longest discourse in the first part of Luke's Gospel. In this subversive sermon Jesus repeatedly challenges the conventional religious wisdom. Who is blessed? The poor, the hungry, the mournful, and the persecuted. Who will come to woe and ruin? The rich, the fat, the happy, and the popular. Rather than hating their enemies, people should love them. Rather than holding on to possessions, people should give them away. Rather than always looking at what is wrong with others, people should first see what is wrong with themselves. The discourse is typical of the teaching ministry of Jesus Christ as a whole: it is full of sharp contrasts, vivid images, stern warnings, and seemingly impossible demands to hear and obey.

[17]And he came down with them and stood on a level place, with a great crowd of his disciples and a great multitude of people from all Judea and Jerusalem and the seacoast of Tyre and Sidon, [18]who came to hear him and to be healed of their diseases. And those who were troubled with unclean spirits were cured. [19]And all the crowd sought to touch him, for power came out from him and healed them all.

[20]And he lifted up his eyes on his disciples, and said:

"Blessed are you who are poor, for yours is the kingdom of God.
[21]"Blessed are you who are hungry now, for you shall be satisfied.
"Blessed are you who weep now, for you shall laugh.

---

[1] Some manuscripts *On the second first Sabbath* (that is, on the second Sabbath after the first) [a] For 6:1-5 see parallels Matt. 12:1-8; Mark 2:23-28 [b] For 6:6-11 see parallels Matt. 12:9-14; Mark 3:1-6 [c] For 6:13-16 see parallels Matt. 10:2-4; Mark 3:16-19

²²"Blessed are you when people hate you and when they exclude you and revile you and spurn your name as evil, on account of the Son of Man! ²³Rejoice in that day, and leap for joy, for behold, your reward is great in heaven; for so their fathers did to the prophets.

²⁴"But woe to you who are rich, for you have received your consolation.

²⁵"Woe to you who are full now, for you shall be hungry.

"Woe to you who laugh now, for you shall mourn and weep.

²⁶"Woe to you, when all people speak well of you, for so their fathers did to the false prophets.

²⁷"But I say to you who hear, Love your enemies, do good to those who hate you, ²⁸bless those who curse you, pray for those who abuse you. ²⁹ᵃTo one who strikes you on the cheek, offer the other also, and from one who takes away your cloak do not withhold your tunic¹ either. ³⁰Give to everyone who begs from you, and from one who takes away your goods do not demand them back. ³¹And as you wish that others would do to you, do so to them.

³²"If you love those who love you, what benefit is that to you? For even sinners love those who love them. ³³And if you do good to those who do good to you, what benefit is that to you? For even sinners do the same. ³⁴And if you lend to those from whom you expect to receive, what credit is that to you? Even sinners lend to sinners, to get back the same amount. ³⁵But love your enemies, and do good, and lend, expecting nothing in return, and your reward will be great, and you will be sons of the Most High, for he is kind to the ungrateful and the evil. ³⁶Be merciful, even as your Father is merciful.

³⁷ᵇ"Judge not, and you will not be judged; condemn not, and you will not be condemned; forgive, and you will be forgiven; ³⁸give, and it will be given to you. Good measure, pressed down, shaken together, running over, will be put into your lap. For with the measure you use it will be measured back to you."

³⁹He also told them a parable: "Can a blind man lead a blind man? Will they not both fall into a pit? ⁴⁰A disciple is not above his teacher, but everyone when he is fully trained will be like his teacher. ⁴¹Why do you see the speck that is in your brother's eye, but do not notice the log that is in your own eye? ⁴²How can you say to your brother, 'Brother, let me take out the speck that is in your eye,' when you yourself do not see the log that is in your own eye? You hypocrite, first take the log out of your own eye, and then you will see clearly to take out the speck that is in your brother's eye.

⁴³"For ᶜno good tree bears bad fruit, nor again does a bad tree bear good fruit, ⁴⁴for each tree is known by its own fruit. For figs are not gathered from thornbushes, nor are grapes picked from a bramble bush. ⁴⁵The good person out of the good treasure of his heart produces good, and the evil person out of his evil treasure produces evil, for out of the abundance of the heart his mouth speaks.

⁴⁶"Why do you call me 'Lord, Lord,' and not do what I tell you? ⁴⁷ᵈEveryone who comes to me and hears my words and does them, I will show you what he is like: ⁴⁸he is like a man building a house, who dug deep and laid the foundation on the rock. And when a flood arose, the stream broke against that house and could not shake it, because it had been well built.² ⁴⁹But the one who hears and does not do them is like a man who built a house on the ground without a foundation. When the stream broke against it, immediately it fell, and the ruin of that house was great."

---

¹ Greek *chiton*, a long garment worn under the cloak next to the skin ² Some manuscripts *founded upon the rock* ᵃ For 6:29, 30 see parallel Matt. 5:39-42 ᵇ For 6:37, 38, 41, 42 see parallel Matt. 7:1-5 ᶜ For 6:43, 44 see parallel Matt. 7:16, 20 ᵈ For 6:47-49 see parallel Matt. 7:24-27

Is Jesus the one, or not? [7:1–35]. The miracle stories in this section—healing from a deadly disease (vv. 1–10) and deliverance from death itself (vv. 11–17)—provide further confirmation that Jesus is the Savior whom God had always promised to send. For his part, the centurion has total faith in Jesus and his power to heal. But for some reason John the Baptist is entertaining some doubts: Is Jesus really the Christ or not? For proof, Jesus points to his miracles and to his ministry of preaching good news to the poor. As John well knows, and as Luke has already told us (see 4:18–21), these are exactly the things God always promised that the Messiah would do. The comments that Jesus makes about John (vv. 24–35) effectively bring the Baptist's role in Luke's Gospel to a close. Jesus strongly affirms John's ministry while at the same time claiming that something far greater has come.

7 After he had finished all his sayings in the hearing of the people, ᵃhe entered Capernaum. ²Now a centurion had a servant¹ who was sick and at the point of death, who was highly valued by him. ³When the centurion² heard about Jesus, he sent to him elders of the Jews, asking him to come and heal his servant. ⁴And when they came to Jesus, they pleaded with him earnestly, saying, "He is worthy to have you do this for him, ⁵for he loves our nation, and he is the one who built us our synagogue." ⁶And Jesus went with them. When he was not far from the house, the centurion sent friends, saying to him, "Lord, do not trouble yourself, for I am not worthy to have you come under my roof. ⁷Therefore I did not presume to come to you. But say the word, and let my servant be healed. ⁸For I too am a man set under authority, with soldiers under me: and I say to one, 'Go,' and he goes; and to another, 'Come,' and he comes; and to my servant, 'Do this,' and he does it." ⁹When Jesus heard these things, he marveled at him, and turning to the crowd that followed him, said, "I tell you, not even in Israel have I found such faith." ¹⁰And when those who had been sent returned to the house, they found the servant well.

¹¹Soon afterward³ he went to a town called Nain, and his disciples and a great crowd went with him. ¹²As he drew near to the gate of the town, behold, a man who had died was being carried out, the only son of his mother, and she was a widow, and a considerable crowd from the town was with her. ¹³And when the Lord saw her, he had compassion on her and said to her, "Do not weep." ¹⁴Then he came up and touched the bier, and the bearers stood still. And he said, "Young man, I say to you, arise." ¹⁵And the dead man sat up and began to speak, and Jesus⁴ gave him to his mother. ¹⁶Fear seized them all, and they glorified God, saying, "A great prophet has arisen among us!" and "God has visited his people!" ¹⁷And this report about him spread through the whole of Judea and all the surrounding country.

¹⁸ᵇThe disciples of John reported all these things to him. And John, ¹⁹calling two of his disciples to him, sent them to the Lord, saying, "Are you the one who is to come, or shall we look for another?" ²⁰And when the men had come to him, they said, "John the Baptist has sent us to you, saying, 'Are you the one who is to come, or shall we look for another?'" ²¹In that hour he healed many people of diseases and plagues and evil spirits, and on many who were blind he bestowed sight. ²²And he answered them, "Go and tell John what you have seen and heard: the blind receive their sight, the lame walk, lepers⁵ are cleansed, and the deaf hear, the dead are raised up, the

¹ Greek *bondservant*; also verses 3, 8, 10 ² Greek *he* ³ Some manuscripts *The next day* ⁴ Greek *he* ⁵ *Leprosy* was a term for several skin diseases; see Leviticus 13 ᵃ For 7:1-10 see parallel Matt. 8:5-13 ᵇ For 7:18-35 see parallel Matt. 11:2-19

poor have good news preached to them. ²³And blessed is the one who is not offended by me."

²⁴When John's messengers had gone, Jesus[1] began to speak to the crowds concerning John: "What did you go out into the wilderness to see? A reed shaken by the wind? ²⁵What then did you go out to see? A man dressed in soft clothing? Behold, those who are dressed in splendid clothing and live in luxury are in kings' courts. ²⁶What then did you go out to see? A prophet? Yes, I tell you, and more than a prophet. ²⁷This is he of whom it is written,

> ᵃ "'Behold, I send my messenger before your face,
> who will prepare your way before you.'

²⁸I tell you, among those born of women none is greater than John. Yet the one who is least in the kingdom of God is greater than he." ²⁹(When all the people heard this, and the tax collectors too, they declared God just,[2] having been baptized with the baptism of John, ³⁰but the Pharisees and the lawyers rejected the purpose of God for themselves, not having been baptized by him.)

³¹"To what then shall I compare the people of this generation, and what are they like? ³²They are like children sitting in the marketplace and calling to one another,

> "'We played the flute for you, and you did not dance;
> we sang a dirge, and you did not weep.'

³³For John the Baptist has come eating no bread and drinking no wine, and you say, 'He has a demon.' ³⁴The Son of Man has come eating and drinking, and you say, 'Look at him! A glutton and a drunkard, a friend of tax collectors and sinners!' ³⁵Yet wisdom is justified by all her children."

Women who were forgiven [7:36–8:3]. The story of the sinful woman who anointed Jesus' feet at the house of Simon the Pharisee is typical of the interest Luke takes in the caring relationships Jesus had with various women. It is also a study in contrasts: between a wealthy Pharisee and a notorious woman; between self-righteousness and self-confessed sin; between cold indifference to Jesus and the love for him that grace compels. It is by faith in Jesus that the woman is forgiven. Nor is she the only one: many women supported Jesus in his ministry of preaching the good news of the kingdom of God (8:1–3). The Gospel of Luke is sometimes called the humanitarian Gospel because of Luke's special attention to the marginalized members of society. Through sheer accumulation, the unfolding story gives a stronger and stronger impression of the universality of Christ's salvation as Lord.

---

³⁶One of the Pharisees asked him to eat with him, and he went into the Pharisee's house and took his place at the table. ³⁷And behold, a woman of the city, who was a sinner, when she learned that he was reclining at table in the Pharisee's house, brought an alabaster flask of ointment, ³⁸and standing behind him at his feet, weeping, she began to wet his feet with her tears and wiped them with the hair of her head and kissed his feet and anointed them with the ointment. ³⁹Now when the Pharisee who had invited him saw this, he said to himself, "If this man were a prophet, he would have known who and what sort of woman this is who is touching him, for she

---

[1] Greek *he* [2] Greek *they justified God* ᵃ Mal. 3:1

is a sinner." ⁴⁰And Jesus answering said to him, "Simon, I have something to say to you." And he answered, "Say it, Teacher."

⁴¹"A certain moneylender had two debtors. One owed five hundred denarii, and the other fifty. ⁴²When they could not pay, he cancelled the debt of both. Now which of them will love him more?" ⁴³Simon answered, "The one, I suppose, for whom he cancelled the larger debt." And he said to him, "You have judged rightly." ⁴⁴Then turning toward the woman he said to Simon, "Do you see this woman? I entered your house; you gave me no water for my feet, but she has wet my feet with her tears and wiped them with her hair. ⁴⁵You gave me no kiss, but from the time I came in she has not ceased to kiss my feet. ⁴⁶You did not anoint my head with oil, but she has anointed my feet with ointment. ⁴⁷Therefore I tell you, her sins, which are many, are forgiven—for she loved much. But he who is forgiven little, loves little." ⁴⁸And he said to her, "Your sins are forgiven." ⁴⁹Then those who were at table with him began to say among¹ themselves, "Who is this, who even forgives sins?" ⁵⁰And he said to the woman, "Your faith has saved you; go in peace."

8 Soon afterward he went on through cities and villages, proclaiming and bringing the good news of the kingdom of God. And the twelve were with him, ²and also some women who had been healed of evil spirits and infirmities: Mary, called Magdalene, from whom seven demons had gone out, ³and Joanna, the wife of Chuza, Herod's household manager, and Susanna, and many others, who provided for them² out of their means.

The parable of parables [8:4–21]. The parable of the sower is the first of twenty-nine parables that Luke records in his Gospel—more than we find in any other Gospel. As Jesus explains, the story of the sower is a paradigm for all the parables. The story itself is characterized by folktale simplicity and literary *realism. But in parables the simple, realistic details are often symbols that correspond to other less literal meanings (the word parable comes from the Greek work meaning "to throw alongside"). The spiritual meaning of this particular symbolic story is that many people hear what Jesus says, but not all of them listen to it for salvation. Some hearts are hard, and the devil snatches the Word away; others are shallow, and the words of Jesus never take root; still others allow the Word to be choked out by the joys and trials of life. But those who hear and obey—the true children of God—will bear abundant fruit.

⁴ᵃAnd when a great crowd was gathering and people from town after town came to him, he said in a parable: ⁵"A sower went out to sow his seed. And as he sowed, some fell along the path and was trampled underfoot, and the birds of the air devoured it. ⁶And some fell on the rock, and as it grew up, it withered away, because it had no moisture. ⁷And some fell among thorns, and the thorns grew up with it and choked it. ⁸And some fell into good soil and grew and yielded a hundredfold." As he said these things, he called out, "He who has ears to hear, let him hear."

⁹And when his disciples asked him what this parable meant, ¹⁰he said, "To you it has been given to know the secrets of the kingdom of God, but for others they are in parables, so ᵇthat 'seeing they may not see, and hearing they may not understand.' ¹¹ᶜNow the parable is this: The seed is the word of God. ¹²The ones along the path are those who have heard; then the devil comes and takes away the word from their

¹ Or to ² Some manuscripts him ᵃ For 8:4-10 see parallels Matt. 13:1-15; Mark 4:1-12 ᵇ Isa. 6:9, 10 ᶜ For 8:11-15 see parallels Matt. 13:18-23; Mark 4:13-20

hearts, so that they may not believe and be saved. [13]And the ones on the rock are those who, when they hear the word, receive it with joy. But these have no root; they believe for a while, and in time of testing fall away. [14]And as for what fell among the thorns, they are those who hear, but as they go on their way they are choked by the cares and riches and pleasures of life, and their fruit does not mature. [15]As for that in the good soil, they are those who, hearing the word, hold it fast in an honest and good heart, and bear fruit with patience.

[16a]"No one after lighting a lamp covers it with a jar or puts it under a bed, but puts it on a stand, so that those who enter may see the light. [17]For nothing is hidden that will not be made manifest, nor is anything secret that will not be known and come to light. [18]Take care then how you hear, for to the one who has, more will be given, and from the one who has not, even what he thinks that he has will be taken away."

[19b]Then his mother and his brothers came to him, but they could not reach him because of the crowd. [20]And he was told, "Your mother and your brothers are standing outside, desiring to see you." [21]But he answered them, "My mother and my brothers are those who hear the word of God and do it."

> **More miracles** [8:22–56]. Luke records a wide variety of miracles, especially in the first half of his Gospel. In general, these miracle stories have the dual purpose of demonstrating the divine power of Jesus Christ and showing how people respond to him in faith and repentance. The miracles in this section of the Gospel—the stilling of a storm (vv. 22–25), the deliverance of a demon (vv. 26–39), and two healing miracles that are told together in one story (vv. 40–56)—show the power of Jesus over creation, over the unseen spirit world, over disease, and even over death. These narratives also give notable examples of people coming to faith and telling others what Jesus has done for them. The question that Jesus once posed to his disciples becomes the question that Luke puts before his readers: "Where is your faith?" (v. 25). And the encouragement Luke gives is the encouragement Jesus gave to the man who feared that his daughter was dead: "Do not fear; only believe" (v. 50).

[22c]One day he got into a boat with his disciples, and he said to them, "Let us go across to the other side of the lake." So they set out, [23]and as they sailed he fell asleep. And a windstorm came down on the lake, and they were filling with water and were in danger. [24]And they went and woke him, saying, "Master, Master, we are perishing!" And he awoke and rebuked the wind and the raging waves, and they ceased, and there was a calm. [25]He said to them, "Where is your faith?" And they were afraid, and they marveled, saying to one another, "Who then is this, that he commands even winds and water, and they obey him?"

[26d]Then they sailed to the country of the Gerasenes,[1] which is opposite Galilee. [27]When Jesus[2] had stepped out on land, there met him a man from the city who had demons. For a long time he had worn no clothes, and he had not lived in a house but among the tombs. [28]When he saw Jesus, he cried out and fell down before him and said with a loud voice, "What have you to do with me, Jesus, Son of the Most High God? I beg you, do not torment me." [29]For he had commanded the unclean spirit to come out of the man. (For many a time it had seized him. He was kept under guard and bound with chains and shackles, but he would break the bonds and be driven by

---

[1] Some manuscripts *Gadarenes*; others *Gergesenes*; also verse 37 [2] Greek *he*; also verses 38, 42 [a] For 8:16-18 see parallel Mark 4:21-25 [b] For 8:19-21 see parallels Matt. 12:46-50; Mark 3:31-35 [c] For 8:22-25 see parallels Matt. 8:23-27; Mark 4:35-41 [d] For 8:26-39 see parallels Matt. 8:28-34; Mark 5:1-20

the demon into the desert.) [30]Jesus then asked him, "What is your name?" And he said, "Legion," for many demons had entered him. [31]And they begged him not to command them to depart into the abyss. [32]Now a large herd of pigs was feeding there on the hillside, and they begged him to let them enter these. So he gave them permission. [33]Then the demons came out of the man and entered the pigs, and the herd rushed down the steep bank into the lake and were drowned.

[34]When the herdsmen saw what had happened, they fled and told it in the city and in the country. [35]Then people went out to see what had happened, and they came to Jesus and found the man from whom the demons had gone, sitting at the feet of Jesus, clothed and in his right mind, and they were afraid. [36]And those who had seen it told them how the demon-possessed[1] man had been healed. [37]Then all the people of the surrounding country of the Gerasenes asked him to depart from them, for they were seized with great fear. So he got into the boat and returned. [38]The man from whom the demons had gone begged that he might be with him, but Jesus sent him away, saying, [39]"Return to your home, and declare how much God has done for you." And he went away, proclaiming throughout the whole city how much Jesus had done for him.

[40]Now when Jesus returned, the crowd welcomed him, for they were all waiting for him. [41][a]And there came a man named Jairus, who was a ruler of the synagogue. And falling at Jesus' feet, he implored him to come to his house, [42]for he had an only daughter, about twelve years of age, and she was dying.

As Jesus went, the people pressed around him. [43]And there was a woman who had had a discharge of blood for twelve years, and though she had spent all her living on physicians,[2] she could not be healed by anyone. [44]She came up behind him and touched the fringe of his garment, and immediately her discharge of blood ceased. [45]And Jesus said, "Who was it that touched me?" When all denied it, Peter[3] said, "Master, the crowds surround you and are pressing in on you!" [46]But Jesus said, "Someone touched me, for I perceive that power has gone out from me." [47]And when the woman saw that she was not hidden, she came trembling, and falling down before him declared in the presence of all the people why she had touched him, and how she had been immediately healed. [48]And he said to her, "Daughter, your faith has made you well; go in peace."

[49]While he was still speaking, someone from the ruler's house came and said, "Your daughter is dead; do not trouble the Teacher any more." [50]But Jesus on hearing this answered him, "Do not fear; only believe, and she will be well." [51]And when he came to the house, he allowed no one to enter with him, except Peter and John and James, and the father and mother of the child. [52]And all were weeping and mourning for her, but he said, "Do not weep, for she is not dead but sleeping." [53]And they laughed at him, knowing that she was dead. [54]But taking her by the hand he called, saying, "Child, arise." [55]And her spirit returned, and she got up at once. And he directed that something should be given her to eat. [56]And her parents were amazed, but he charged them to tell no one what had happened.

The cross of discipleship [9:1–50]. Although this section contains a variety of material—including a couple of notable miracles and the announcement that Herod has beheaded John the Baptist—the emphasis falls on what it means for Jesus to be the

---

[1] Greek *daimonizomai*; elsewhere rendered *oppressed by demons* [2] Some manuscripts omit *and though she had spent all her living on physicians*, [3] Some manuscripts add *and those who were with him* [a] For 8:41-56 see parallels Matt. 9:18-26; Mark 5:21-43

Christ and for his disciples to follow him. No sooner does Peter make his dramatic confession that Jesus is "the Christ of God" than Jesus proceeds to explain exactly what he has come to do: suffer, die, and rise again (vv. 20–22, 44). To put this in another way, it is only when the disciples correctly identify his person that Jesus begins to explain his work. His work will set the pattern for their own ministry, for all disciples are called to take up their daily cross to die with Jesus. But the Christ is not called only to suffer; he is also destined for glory, as revealed in his dazzling transfiguration on the mountain (vv. 28–36). Although there is a sense in which the whole Gospel is a divine-human encounter, this story—which awakens many echoes of the encounters people have with God in the Old Testament—is the example par excellence.

9 And he called the twelve together and gave them power and authority over all demons and to cure diseases, ²and he sent them out to proclaim the kingdom of God and to heal. ³ªAnd he said to them, "Take nothing for your journey, no staff, nor bag, nor bread, nor money; and do not have two tunics.¹ ⁴And whatever house you enter, stay there, and from there depart. ⁵And wherever they do not receive you, when you leave that town shake off the dust from your feet as a testimony against them." ⁶And they departed and went through the villages, preaching the gospel and healing everywhere.

⁷ᵇNow Herod the tetrarch heard about all that was happening, and he was perplexed, because it was said by some that John had been raised from the dead, ⁸by some that Elijah had appeared, and by others that one of the prophets of old had risen. ⁹Herod said, "John I beheaded, but who is this about whom I hear such things?" And he sought to see him.

¹⁰On their return the apostles told him all that they had done. ᶜAnd he took them and withdrew apart to a town called Bethsaida. ¹¹When the crowds learned it, they followed him, and he welcomed them and spoke to them of the kingdom of God and cured those who had need of healing. ¹²Now the day began to wear away, and the twelve came and said to him, "Send the crowd away to go into the surrounding villages and countryside to find lodging and get provisions, for we are here in a desolate place." ¹³But he said to them, "You give them something to eat." They said, "We have no more than five loaves and two fish—unless we are to go and buy food for all these people." ¹⁴For there were about five thousand men. And he said to his disciples, "Have them sit down in groups of about fifty each." ¹⁵And they did so, and had them all sit down. ¹⁶And taking the five loaves and the two fish, he looked up to heaven and said a blessing over them. Then he broke the loaves and gave them to the disciples to set before the crowd. ¹⁷And they all ate and were satisfied. And what was left over was picked up, twelve baskets of broken pieces.

¹⁸ᵈNow it happened that as he was praying alone, the disciples were with him. And he asked them, "Who do the crowds say that I am?" ¹⁹And they answered, "John the Baptist. But others say, Elijah, and others, that one of the prophets of old has risen." ²⁰Then he said to them, "But who do you say that I am?" And Peter answered, "The Christ of God."

²¹And he strictly charged and commanded them to tell this to no one, ²²ᵉsaying,

---

¹ Greek *chiton*, a long garment worn under the cloak next to the skin ª For 9:3-5 see parallels Matt. 10:9-15; Mark 6:8-11 ᵇ For 9:7-9 see parallels Matt. 14:1-12; Mark 6:14-29 ᶜ For 9:10-17 see parallels Matt. 14:13-21; Mark 6:32-44; John 6:1-13 ᵈ For 9:18-20 see parallels Matt. 16:13-16; Mark 8:27-29 ᵉ For 9:22-27 see parallels Matt. 16:21-28; Mark 8:31–9:1

"The Son of Man must suffer many things and be rejected by the elders and chief priests and scribes, and be killed, and on the third day be raised."

²³And he said to all, "If anyone would come after me, let him deny himself and take up his cross daily and follow me. ²⁴For whoever would save his life will lose it, but whoever loses his life for my sake will save it. ²⁵For what does it profit a man if he gains the whole world and loses or forfeits himself? ²⁶For whoever is ashamed of me and of my words, of him will the Son of Man be ashamed when he comes in his glory and the glory of the Father and of the holy angels. ²⁷But I tell you truly, there are some standing here who will not taste death until they see the kingdom of God."

²⁸Now about eight days after these sayings he took with him Peter and John and James and went up on the mountain to pray. ²⁹And as he was praying, the appearance of his face was altered, and his clothing became dazzling white. ³⁰And behold, two men were talking with him, Moses and Elijah, ³¹who appeared in glory and spoke of his departure,¹ which he was about to accomplish at Jerusalem. ³²Now Peter and those who were with him were heavy with sleep, but when they became fully awake they saw his glory and the two men who stood with him. ³³And as the men were parting from him, Peter said to Jesus, "Master, it is good that we are here. Let us make three tents, one for you and one for Moses and one for Elijah"—not knowing what he said. ³⁴As he was saying these things, a cloud came and overshadowed them, and they were afraid as they entered the cloud. ³⁵And a voice came out of the cloud, saying, "This is my Son, my Chosen One;² listen to him!" ³⁶And when the voice had spoken, Jesus was found alone. And they kept silent and told no one in those days anything of what they had seen.

³⁷On the next day, when they had come down from the mountain, a great crowd met him. ³⁸And behold, a man from the crowd cried out, "Teacher, I beg you to look at my son, for he is my only child. ³⁹And behold, a spirit seizes him, and he suddenly cries out. It convulses him so that he foams at the mouth, and shatters him, and will hardly leave him. ⁴⁰And I begged your disciples to cast it out, but they could not." ⁴¹Jesus answered, "O faithless and twisted generation, how long am I to be with you and bear with you? Bring your son here." ⁴²While he was coming, the demon threw him to the ground and convulsed him. But Jesus rebuked the unclean spirit and healed the boy, and gave him back to his father. ⁴³And all were astonished at the majesty of God.

But while they were all marveling at everything he was doing, Jesus³ said to his disciples, ⁴⁴"Let these words sink into your ears: The Son of Man is about to be delivered into the hands of men." ⁴⁵But they did not understand this saying, and it was concealed from them, so that they might not perceive it. And they were afraid to ask him about this saying.

⁴⁶An argument arose among them as to which of them was the greatest. ⁴⁷But Jesus, knowing the reasoning of their hearts, took a child and put him by his side ⁴⁸and said to them, "Whoever receives this child in my name receives me, and whoever receives me receives him who sent me. For he who is least among you all is the one who is great."

⁴⁹John answered, "Master, we saw someone casting out demons in your name, and we tried to stop him, because he does not follow with us." ⁵⁰But Jesus said to him, "Do not stop him, for the one who is not against you is for you."

---

¹ Greek exodus ² Some manuscripts my Beloved ³ Greek he

Jesus turns toward Jerusalem [9:51–10:24]. The journey or travel motif is the narrative skeleton on which Luke builds much of his story, and an apt subtitle for the Gospel of Luke would be "On the Road with Jesus." The chief role of Jesus as protagonist in the middle of the book is that of an itinerant teacher and miracle worker. The travels of Jesus take a significant new turn in Luke 9:51, as he steadfastly sets his face toward Jerusalem and the cross. Those who follow him—especially the seventy-two followers he sends out in pairs to preach the good news (10:1–24)—will share in his sufferings: homelessness, loneliness, and rejection. But they will also see the kingdom of God come in the person of the Christ and the power of the Holy Spirit, and for this Jesus rejoices.

⁵¹When the days drew near for him to be taken up, he set his face to go to Jerusalem. ⁵²And he sent messengers ahead of him, who went and entered a village of the Samaritans, to make preparations for him. ⁵³But the people did not receive him, because his face was set toward Jerusalem. ⁵⁴And when his disciples James and John saw it, they said, "Lord, do you want us to tell fire to come down from heaven and consume them?"[1] ⁵⁵But he turned and rebuked them.[2] ⁵⁶And they went on to another village.

⁵⁷ᵃAs they were going along the road, someone said to him, "I will follow you wherever you go." ⁵⁸And Jesus said to him, "Foxes have holes, and birds of the air have nests, but the Son of Man has nowhere to lay his head." ⁵⁹To another he said, "Follow me." But he said, "Lord, let me first go and bury my father." ⁶⁰And Jesus[3] said to him, "Leave the dead to bury their own dead. But as for you, go and proclaim the kingdom of God." ⁶¹Yet another said, "I will follow you, Lord, but let me first say farewell to those at my home." ⁶²Jesus said to him, "No one who puts his hand to the plow and looks back is fit for the kingdom of God."

10 After this the Lord appointed seventy-two[4] others and sent them on ahead of him, two by two, into every town and place where he himself was about to go. ²And he said to them, "The harvest is plentiful, but the laborers are few. Therefore pray earnestly to the Lord of the harvest to send out laborers into his harvest. ³Go your way; behold, I am sending you out as lambs in the midst of wolves. ⁴Carry no moneybag, no knapsack, no sandals, and greet no one on the road. ⁵Whatever house you enter, first say, 'Peace be to this house!' ⁶And if a son of peace is there, your peace will rest upon him. But if not, it will return to you. ⁷And remain in the same house, eating and drinking what they provide, for the laborer deserves his wages. Do not go from house to house. ⁸Whenever you enter a town and they receive you, eat what is set before you. ⁹Heal the sick in it and say to them, 'The kingdom of God has come near to you.' ¹⁰But whenever you enter a town and they do not receive you, go into its streets and say, ¹¹'Even the dust of your town that clings to our feet we wipe off against you. Nevertheless know this, that the kingdom of God has come near.' ¹²ᵇI tell you, it will be more bearable on that day for Sodom than for that town.

¹³"Woe to you, Chorazin! Woe to you, Bethsaida! For if the mighty works done in you had been done in Tyre and Sidon, they would have repented long ago, sitting in sackcloth and ashes. ¹⁴But it will be more bearable in the judgment for Tyre and Sidon than for you. ¹⁵And you, Capernaum, will you be exalted to heaven? You shall be brought down to Hades.

---

[1] Some manuscripts add *as Elijah did* [2] Some manuscripts add *and he said, "You do not know what manner of spirit you are of; for the Son of Man came not to destroy people's lives but to save them"* [3] Greek *he* [4] Some manuscripts *seventy*; also verse 17 ᵃ For 9:57-62 see parallel Matt. 8:19-22 ᵇ For 10:13-15 see parallel Matt. 11:21-24

[16]"The one who hears you hears me, and the one who rejects you rejects me, and the one who rejects me rejects him who sent me."

[17]The seventy-two returned with joy, saying, "Lord, even the demons are subject to us in your name!" [18]And he said to them, "I saw Satan fall like lightning from heaven. [19]Behold, I have given you authority to tread on serpents and scorpions, and over all the power of the enemy, and nothing shall hurt you. [20]Nevertheless, do not rejoice in this, that the spirits are subject to you, but rejoice that your names are written in heaven."

[21][a]In that same hour he rejoiced in the Holy Spirit and said, "I thank you, Father, Lord of heaven and earth, that you have hidden these things from the wise and understanding and revealed them to little children; yes, Father, for such was your gracious will.[1] [22]All things have been handed over to me by my Father, and no one knows who the Son is except the Father, or who the Father is except the Son and anyone to whom the Son chooses to reveal him."

[23]Then turning to the disciples he said privately, "Blessed are the eyes that see what you see! [24]For I tell you that many prophets and kings desired to see what you see, and did not see it, and to hear what you hear, and did not hear it."

Kingdom priorities [10:25–42]. The parable of the good Samaritan (vv. 25–37) and Martha's sisterly spat with her sister Mary (vv. 38–42) are unique to Luke's Gospel. These episodes are good examples of Luke's concern for the poor and his interest in the close relationships Jesus had with the women who were among his disciples. In both stories Luke makes masterful use of foils: characters whose true nature is revealed by the way their attitudes and actions contrast with those of others. Both episodes also serve to highlight priorities of Jesus: the call to love one's neighbor—even across ethnic lines and other social barriers—and the superior pleasure of giving full and undivided attention to the teaching of Jesus.

[25]And behold, a lawyer stood up to put him to the test, saying, "Teacher, what shall I do to inherit eternal life?" [26]He said to him, "What is written in the Law? How do you read it?" [27]And he answered, [b]"You shall love the Lord your God with all your heart and with all your soul and with all your strength and with all your mind, and [c]your neighbor as yourself." [28]And he said to him, "You have answered correctly; do this, and you will live."

[29]But he, desiring to justify himself, said to Jesus, "And who is my neighbor?" [30]Jesus replied, "A man was going down from Jerusalem to Jericho, and he fell among robbers, who stripped him and beat him and departed, leaving him half dead. [31]Now by chance a priest was going down that road, and when he saw him he passed by on the other side. [32]So likewise a Levite, when he came to the place and saw him, passed by on the other side. [33]But a Samaritan, as he journeyed, came to where he was, and when he saw him, he had compassion. [34]He went to him and bound up his wounds, pouring on oil and wine. Then he set him on his own animal and brought him to an inn and took care of him. [35]And the next day he took out two denarii[2] and gave them to the innkeeper, saying, 'Take care of him, and whatever more you spend, I will repay you when I come back.' [36]Which of these three, do you think, proved to be a neighbor to the man who fell among the robbers?"

[1] Or for so it pleased you well [2] A denarius was a day's wage for a laborer [a] For 10:21, 22 see parallel Matt. 11:25-27 [b] Deut. 6:5 [c] Lev. 19:18

[37] He said, "The one who showed him mercy." And Jesus said to him, "You go, and do likewise."

[38] Now as they went on their way, Jesus[1] entered a village. And a woman named Martha welcomed him into her house. [39] And she had a sister called Mary, who sat at the Lord's feet and listened to his teaching. [40] But Martha was distracted with much serving. And she went up to him and said, "Lord, do you not care that my sister has left me to serve alone? Tell her then to help me." [41] But the Lord answered her, "Martha, Martha, you are anxious and troubled about many things, [42] but one thing is necessary.[2] Mary has chosen the good portion, which will not be taken away from her."

Kingdoms in conflict [11:1–36]. The chapter opens with Luke's somewhat shorter version of the Lord's Prayer—a family prayer for the coming of the kingdom of God (vv. 1–4). This is followed by several miniparables that encourage the disciples to pray, especially for the Father's gift of the Holy Spirit (vv. 5–13). It is by the power of the Holy Spirit—not by the power of Satan, as some people tried to claim—that Jesus casts out demons. His miraculous exorcisms prove that he is on the side of God in the great supernatural conflict between good and evil. The teaching that Jesus gives in this section is punctuated by famous aphorisms about a house divided (v. 17), the sign of Jonah (v. 29), and a light hidden under a basket (v. 33).

11

Now Jesus[3] was praying in a certain place, and when he finished, one of his disciples said to him, "Lord, teach us to pray, as John taught his disciples." [2] And he said to them, "When you pray, say:

"Father, hallowed be your name.
Your kingdom come.
[3]   Give us each day our daily bread,[4]
[4]   and forgive us our sins,
       for we ourselves forgive everyone who is indebted to us.
And lead us not into temptation."

[5] And he said to them, "Which of you who has a friend will go to him at midnight and say to him, 'Friend, lend me three loaves, [6] for a friend of mine has arrived on a journey, and I have nothing to set before him'; [7] and he will answer from within, 'Do not bother me; the door is now shut, and my children are with me in bed. I cannot get up and give you anything'? [8] I tell you, though he will not get up and give him anything because he is his friend, yet because of his impudence[5] he will rise and give him whatever he needs. [9] And I tell you, [a] ask, and it will be given to you; seek, and you will find; knock, and it will be opened to you. [10] For everyone who asks receives, and the one who seeks finds, and to the one who knocks it will be opened. [11] What father among you, if his son asks for[6] a fish, will instead of a fish give him a serpent; [12] or if he asks for an egg, will give him a scorpion? [13] If you then, who are evil, know how to give good gifts to your children, how much more will the heavenly Father give the Holy Spirit to those who ask him!"

[14] [b] Now he was casting out a demon that was mute. When the demon had gone out, the mute man spoke, and the people marveled. [15] But some of them said, "He casts out demons by Beelzebul, the prince of demons," [16] while others, to test him, kept seeking

---

[1] Greek *he* [2] Some manuscripts *few things are necessary, or only one* [3] Greek *he* [4] Or *our bread for tomorrow* [5] Or *persistence* [6] Some manuscripts insert *bread, will give him a stone; or if he asks for* [a] For 11:9-13 see parallel Matt. 7:7-11 [b] For 11:14, 15 see parallel Matt. 12:22-24

from him a sign from heaven. [17a] But he, knowing their thoughts, said to them, "Every kingdom divided against itself is laid waste, and a divided household falls. [18] And if Satan also is divided against himself, how will his kingdom stand? For you say that I cast out demons by Beelzebul. [19] And if I cast out demons by Beelzebul, by whom do your sons cast them out? Therefore they will be your judges. [20] But if it is by the finger of God that I cast out demons, then the kingdom of God has come upon you. [21] When a strong man, fully armed, guards his own palace, his goods are safe; [22] but when one stronger than he attacks him and overcomes him, he takes away his armor in which he trusted and divides his spoil. [23] Whoever is not with me is against me, and whoever does not gather with me scatters.

[24b] "When the unclean spirit has gone out of a person, it passes through waterless places seeking rest, and finding none it says, 'I will return to my house from which I came.' [25] And when it comes, it finds the house swept and put in order. [26] Then it goes and brings seven other spirits more evil than itself, and they enter and dwell there. And the last state of that person is worse than the first."

[27] As he said these things, a woman in the crowd raised her voice and said to him, "Blessed is the womb that bore you, and the breasts at which you nursed!" [28] But he said, "Blessed rather are those who hear the word of God and keep it!"

[29] When the crowds were increasing, he began to say, [c] "This generation is an evil generation. It seeks for a sign, but no sign will be given to it except the sign of Jonah. [30] For as Jonah became a sign to the people of Nineveh, so will the Son of Man be to this generation. [31] The queen of the South will rise up at the judgment with the men of this generation and condemn them, for she came from the ends of the earth to hear the wisdom of Solomon, and behold, something greater than Solomon is here. [32] The men of Nineveh will rise up at the judgment with this generation and condemn it, for they repented at the preaching of Jonah, and behold, something greater than Jonah is here.

[33] "No one after lighting a lamp puts it in a cellar or under a basket, but on a stand, so that those who enter may see the light. [34] Your eye is the lamp of your body. When your eye is healthy, your whole body is full of light, but when it is bad, your body is full of darkness. [35] Therefore be careful lest the light in you be darkness. [36] If then your whole body is full of light, having no part dark, it will be wholly bright, as when a lamp with its rays gives you light."

Beware of hypocrisy [11:37–12:12]. Never one to shy away from controversy, Jesus enters into direct disputation with the ruling elite by pronouncing three woes against the Pharisees (11:39–44) and three woes against the lawyers or Bible scholars (11:46–52). The point of his carefully patterned critique is that Israel's spiritual leaders are not the same on the inside as they seem to be on the outside. In their hypocrisy they are weighing people down with legalism. Even worse, in their opposition to Jesus they are in danger of killing the Messiah. The disciples of Jesus are called to avoid the leaven of such Pharisees by being on the outside whatever they are on the inside (12:1–3). The real thing to fear is not what other people think but what God will declare in the courts of heaven on the Day of Judgment, when some people will be cast into hell while others will be openly acknowledged by the Son of Man himself (12:4–12). The genre at work in this passage is *satire, and we find the usual ingredients of objects of attack, literary forms

---

[a] For 11:17-22 see parallels Matt. 12:25-29; Mark 3:23-27 [b] For 11:24-26 see parallel Matt. 12:43-45 [c] For 11:29-32 see parallel Matt. 12:39-42

in which the attack is embodied (including the "woe" formula), and implied norms or standards by which the criticism is conducted.

[37]While Jesus[1] was speaking, a Pharisee asked him to dine with him, so he went in and reclined at table. [38]The Pharisee was astonished to see that he did not first wash before dinner. [39]And the Lord said to him, "Now you Pharisees cleanse the outside of the cup and of the dish, but inside you are full of greed and wickedness. [40]You fools! Did not he who made the outside make the inside also? [41]But give as alms those things that are within, and behold, everything is clean for you.

[42]"But woe to you Pharisees! For you tithe mint and rue and every herb, and neglect justice and the love of God. These you ought to have done, without neglecting the others. [43]Woe to you Pharisees! For you love the best seat in the synagogues and greetings in the marketplaces. [44]Woe to you! For you are like unmarked graves, and people walk over them without knowing it."

[45]One of the lawyers answered him, "Teacher, in saying these things you insult us also." [46]And he said, "Woe to you lawyers also! For you load people with burdens hard to bear, and you yourselves do not touch the burdens with one of your fingers. [47]Woe to you! For you build the tombs of the prophets whom your fathers killed. [48]So you are witnesses and you consent to the deeds of your fathers, for they killed them, and you build their tombs. [49]Therefore also the Wisdom of God said, 'I will send them prophets and apostles, some of whom they will kill and persecute,' [50]so that the blood of all the prophets, shed from the foundation of the world, may be charged against this generation, [51]from the blood of Abel to the blood of Zechariah, who perished between the altar and the sanctuary. Yes, I tell you, it will be required of this generation. [52]Woe to you lawyers! For you have taken away the key of knowledge. You did not enter yourselves, and you hindered those who were entering."

[53]As he went away from there, the scribes and the Pharisees began to press him hard and to provoke him to speak about many things, [54]lying in wait for him, to catch him in something he might say.

12 In the meantime, when so many thousands of the people had gathered together that they were trampling one another, he began to say to his disciples first, "Beware of the leaven of the Pharisees, which is hypocrisy. [2a]Nothing is covered up that will not be revealed, or hidden that will not be known. [3]Therefore whatever you have said in the dark shall be heard in the light, and what you have whispered in private rooms shall be proclaimed on the housetops.

[4]"I tell you, my friends, do not fear those who kill the body, and after that have nothing more that they can do. [5]But I will warn you whom to fear: fear him who, after he has killed, has authority to cast into hell.[2] Yes, I tell you, fear him! [6]Are not five sparrows sold for two pennies?[3] And not one of them is forgotten before God. [7]Why, even the hairs of your head are all numbered. Fear not; you are of more value than many sparrows.

[8]"And I tell you, everyone who acknowledges me before men, the Son of Man also will acknowledge before the angels of God, [9]but the one who denies me before men will be denied before the angels of God. [10]And everyone who speaks a word against the Son of Man will be forgiven, but the one who blasphemes against the Holy Spirit

---

[1] Greek he [2] Greek Gehenna [3] Greek two assaria; an assarion was a Roman copper coin worth about 1/16 of a *denarius* (which was a day's wage for a laborer) [a] For 12:2-9 see parallel Matt. 10:26-33

will not be forgiven. [11]And when they bring you before the synagogues and the rulers and the authorities, do not be anxious about how you should defend yourself or what you should say, [12]for the Holy Spirit will teach you in that very hour what you ought to say."

> **Be prepared** [12:13–48]. The parables and other forms of teaching about stewardship in this discourse are all given in the context of eternity. In view of death, judgment, and the second coming of the Son of Man, what is the best investment that people can make with their earthly treasure? The man in the first parable is a fool because in all the plans he made for his financial future he never prepared for his own inevitable demise, which separated him from all his earthly treasure forever (12:13–21). The wise thing to do is to trust God for every daily need, seek the kingdom of God, give generously to the poor, and store up treasure in heaven (12:22–34). No one knows when the Son of Man will come again, but in any case, every servant of God is called to be ready, constantly making good use of whatever God has given (vv. 35–48).

[13]Someone in the crowd said to him, "Teacher, tell my brother to divide the inheritance with me." [14]But he said to him, "Man, who made me a judge or arbitrator over you?" [15]And he said to them, "Take care, and be on your guard against all covetousness, for one's life does not consist in the abundance of his possessions." [16]And he told them a parable, saying, "The land of a rich man produced plentifully, [17]and he thought to himself, 'What shall I do, for I have nowhere to store my crops?' [18]And he said, 'I will do this: I will tear down my barns and build larger ones, and there I will store all my grain and my goods. [19]And I will say to my soul, Soul, you have ample goods laid up for many years; relax, eat, drink, be merry.' [20]But God said to him, 'Fool! This night your soul is required of you, and the things you have prepared, whose will they be?' [21]So is the one who lays up treasure for himself and is not rich toward God."

[22]And he said to his disciples, [a]"Therefore I tell you, do not be anxious about your life, what you will eat, nor about your body, what you will put on. [23]For life is more than food, and the body more than clothing. [24]Consider the ravens: they neither sow nor reap, they have neither storehouse nor barn, and yet God feeds them. Of how much more value are you than the birds! [25]And which of you by being anxious can add a single hour to his span of life?[1] [26]If then you are not able to do as small a thing as that, why are you anxious about the rest? [27]Consider the lilies, how they grow: they neither toil nor spin,[2] yet I tell you, even Solomon in all his glory was not arrayed like one of these. [28]But if God so clothes the grass, which is alive in the field today, and tomorrow is thrown into the oven, how much more will he clothe you, O you of little faith! [29]And do not seek what you are to eat and what you are to drink, nor be worried. [30]For all the nations of the world seek after these things, and your Father knows that you need them. [31]Instead, seek his[3] kingdom, and these things will be added to you.

[32]"Fear not, little flock, for it is your Father's good pleasure to give you the kingdom. [33]Sell your possessions, and give to the needy. Provide yourselves with moneybags that do not grow old, with a treasure in the heavens that does not fail, where no thief approaches and no moth destroys. [34]For where your treasure is, there will your heart be also.

[35]"Stay dressed for action[4] and keep your lamps burning, [36]and be like men who

---

[1] Or *a single cubit to his stature; a cubit* was about 18 inches or 45 centimeters [2] Some manuscripts *Consider the lilies; they neither spin nor weave* [3] Some manuscripts *God's* [4] Greek *Let your loins stay girded;* compare Exodus 12:11 [a] For 12:22-31 see parallel Matt. 6:25-33

are waiting for their master to come home from the wedding feast, so that they may open the door to him at once when he comes and knocks. [37]Blessed are those servants[1] whom the master finds awake when he comes. Truly, I say to you, he will dress himself for service and have them recline at table, and he will come and serve them. [38]If he comes in the second watch, or in the third, and finds them awake, blessed are those servants! [39]But know this, that if the master of the house had known at what hour the thief was coming, he[2] would not have left his house to be broken into. [40]You also must be ready, for the Son of Man is coming at an hour you do not expect."

[41]Peter said, "Lord, are you telling this parable for us or for all?" [42]And the Lord said, "Who then is the faithful and wise manager, whom his master will set over his household, to give them their portion of food at the proper time? [43]Blessed is that servant[3] whom his master will find so doing when he comes. [44]Truly, I say to you, he will set him over all his possessions. [45]But if that servant says to himself, 'My master is delayed in coming,' and begins to beat the male and female servants, and to eat and drink and get drunk, [46]the master of that servant will come on a day when he does not expect him and at an hour he does not know, and will cut him in pieces and put him with the unfaithful. [47]And that servant who knew his master's will but did not get ready or act according to his will, will receive a severe beating. [48]But the one who did not know, and did what deserved a beating, will receive a light beating. Everyone to whom much was given, of him much will be required, and from him to whom they entrusted much, they will demand the more.

Understanding the times [12:49–13:9]. Jesus continues his discourse on readiness with serious warnings about the intense conflict that his ministry will arouse (12:49–53) and the urgent need to reconcile with God while there is still time (12:54–59). Those who neither repent (13:1–5) nor bear good fruit (13:6–9) will perish. This section of the Gospel demonstrates the ease with which Jesus used the events of daily life, the wonders of the natural world, and the interest in current events as vehicles for teaching spiritual truth.

[49]"I came to cast fire on the earth, and would that it were already kindled! [50]I have a baptism to be baptized with, and how great is my distress until it is accomplished! [51][a]Do you think that I have come to give peace on earth? No, I tell you, but rather division. [52]For from now on in one house there will be five divided, three against two and two against three. [53]They will be divided, father against son and son against father, mother against daughter and daughter against mother, mother-in-law against her daughter-in-law and daughter-in-law against mother-in-law."

[54]He also said to the crowds, "When you see a cloud rising in the west, you say at once, 'A shower is coming.' And so it happens. [55]And when you see the south wind blowing, you say, 'There will be scorching heat,' and it happens. [56]You hypocrites! You know how to interpret the appearance of earth and sky, but why do you not know how to interpret the present time?

[57]"And why do you not judge for yourselves what is right? [58]As you go with your accuser before the magistrate, make an effort to settle with him on the way, lest he drag you to the judge, and the judge hand you over to the officer, and the officer put you in prison. [59]I tell you, you will never get out until you have paid the very last penny."[4]

---

[1] Greek bondservants [2] Some manuscripts add would have stayed awake and [3] Greek bondservant; also verses 45, 46, 47 [4] Greek lepton, a Jewish bronze or copper coin worth about 1/128 of a denarius (which was a day's wage for a laborer) [a] For 12:51-53 see parallel Matt. 10:34, 35

13 There were some present at that very time who told him about the Galileans whose blood Pilate had mingled with their sacrifices. ²And he answered them, "Do you think that these Galileans were worse sinners than all the other Galileans, because they suffered in this way? ³No, I tell you; but unless you repent, you will all likewise perish. ⁴Or those eighteen on whom the tower in Siloam fell and killed them: do you think that they were worse offenders than all the others who lived in Jerusalem? ⁵No, I tell you; but unless you repent, you will all likewise perish."

⁶And he told this parable: "A man had a fig tree planted in his vineyard, and he came seeking fruit on it and found none. ⁷And he said to the vinedresser, 'Look, for three years now I have come seeking fruit on this fig tree, and I find none. Cut it down. Why should it use up the ground?' ⁸And he answered him, 'Sir, let it alone this year also, until I dig around it and put on manure. ⁹Then if it should bear fruit next year, well and good; but if not, you can cut it down.'"

On the road to Jerusalem [13:10–35]. Yet another miracle on yet another Sabbath sets up yet another conflict between Jesus and a local spiritual leader (vv. 10–17). This is followed by two little parables that show the life and growth of the kingdom of God (vv. 18–21). Meanwhile, Jesus is still on his way to Jerusalem and the cross (v. 22). Many people (especially in Israel) claim to follow God, but only a few (including many Gentiles) will enter the narrow door and find the one true road that leads to eternal life (vv. 23–30). To their everlasting dismay—and to the lament of Jesus himself (vv. 31–35)—many religious people who think they are saved will reject the Savior and be cast out of God's presence forever. Literary genres in this unit include satire, the conflict story, and the hero story.

¹⁰Now he was teaching in one of the synagogues on the Sabbath. ¹¹And there was a woman who had had a disabling spirit for eighteen years. She was bent over and could not fully straighten herself. ¹²When Jesus saw her, he called her over and said to her, "Woman, you are freed from your disability." ¹³And he laid his hands on her, and immediately she was made straight, and she glorified God. ¹⁴But the ruler of the synagogue, indignant because Jesus had healed on the Sabbath, said to the people, "There are six days in which work ought to be done. Come on those days and be healed, and not on the Sabbath day." ¹⁵Then the Lord answered him, "You hypocrites! Does not each of you on the Sabbath untie his ox or his donkey from the manger and lead it away to water it? ¹⁶And ought not this woman, a daughter of Abraham whom Satan bound for eighteen years, be loosed from this bond on the Sabbath day?" ¹⁷As he said these things, all his adversaries were put to shame, and all the people rejoiced at all the glorious things that were done by him.

¹⁸ᵃHe said therefore, "What is the kingdom of God like? And to what shall I compare it? ¹⁹It is like a grain of mustard seed that a man took and sowed in his garden, and it grew and became a tree, and the birds of the air made nests in its branches."

²⁰And again he said, "To what shall I compare the kingdom of God? ²¹It is like leaven that a woman took and hid in three measures of flour, until it was all leavened."

²²He went on his way through towns and villages, teaching and journeying toward Jerusalem. ²³And someone said to him, "Lord, will those who are saved be few?" And he said to them, ²⁴"Strive to enter through the narrow door. For many, I

ᵃ For 13:18, 19 see parallels Matt. 13:31, 32; Mark 4:30-32

tell you, will seek to enter and will not be able. ²⁵When once the master of the house has risen and shut the door, and you begin to stand outside and to knock at the door, saying, 'Lord, open to us,' then he will answer you, 'I do not know where you come from.' ²⁶Then you will begin to say, 'We ate and drank in your presence, and you taught in our streets.' ²⁷But he will say, 'I tell you, I do not know where you come from. Depart from me, all you workers of evil!' ²⁸In that place there will be weeping and gnashing of teeth, when you see Abraham and Isaac and Jacob and all the prophets in the kingdom of God but you yourselves cast out. ²⁹And people will come from east and west, and from north and south, and recline at table in the kingdom of God. ³⁰And behold, some are last who will be first, and some are first who will be last."

³¹At that very hour some Pharisees came and said to him, "Get away from here, for Herod wants to kill you." ³²And he said to them, "Go and tell that fox, 'Behold, I cast out demons and perform cures today and tomorrow, and the third day I finish my course. ³³Nevertheless, I must go on my way today and tomorrow and the day following, for it cannot be that a prophet should perish away from Jerusalem.' ³⁴ᵃO Jerusalem, Jerusalem, the city that kills the prophets and stones those who are sent to it! How often would I have gathered your children together as a hen gathers her brood under her wings, and you would not! ³⁵Behold, your house is forsaken. And I tell you, you will not see me until you say, ᵇ'Blessed is he who comes in the name of the Lord!'"

The great banquet [chapter 14]. The ongoing conflict with the Pharisees continues with yet another Sabbath-day healing, in which Jesus cleverly silences his opposition (vv. 1–6). The miracle does not take place at the synagogue this time but in the home of one of the leading Pharisees. Observing the way most people try to claim a seat of honor at the dinner table, Jesus tells a parable about taking a lower place (vv. 7–10). The values of God's kingdom are subversive: the humble will be exalted, while those who exalt themselves will be humbled (v. 11). Rather than inviting dinner guests who are rich enough to return the favor, the servants of God should invite the poor, the lame, and the blind—all the lost people whom Jesus came to save (vv. 12–14). Indeed, according to Jesus this is what God himself will do at the last of all banquets (vv. 15–24). Many people will be so caught up in their own affairs that they will refuse to come to his heavenly table. But many poor and broken people who are outside the religious establishment will come in and feast with God forever—provided, that is, they give up everything they have, counting the cost to follow Jesus in cross-bearing discipleship (vv. 25–33). This chapter epitomizes the discourse methods of Jesus, with his typical reliance on storytelling (parable) and poetry (figurative language).

14 One Sabbath, when he went to dine at the house of a ruler of the Pharisees, they were watching him carefully. ²And behold, there was a man before him who had dropsy. ³And Jesus responded to the lawyers and Pharisees, saying, "Is it lawful to heal on the Sabbath, or not?" ⁴But they remained silent. Then he took him and healed him and sent him away. ⁵And he said to them, "Which of you, having a son¹ or an ox that has fallen into a well on a Sabbath day, will not immediately pull him out?" ⁶And they could not reply to these things.

¹ Some manuscripts *a donkey* ᵃ For 13:34, 35 see parallel Matt. 25:37-39 ᵇ Ps. 118:26

⁷Now he told a parable to those who were invited, when he noticed how they chose the places of honor, saying to them, ⁸"When you are invited by someone to a wedding feast, do not sit down in a place of honor, lest someone more distinguished than you be invited by him, ⁹and he who invited you both will come and say to you, 'Give your place to this person,' and then you will begin with shame to take the lowest place. ¹⁰But when you are invited, go and sit in the lowest place, so that when your host comes he may say to you, 'Friend, move up higher.' Then you will be honored in the presence of all who sit at table with you. ¹¹For everyone who exalts himself will be humbled, and he who humbles himself will be exalted."

¹²He said also to the man who had invited him, "When you give a dinner or a banquet, do not invite your friends or your brothers¹ or your relatives or rich neighbors, lest they also invite you in return and you be repaid. ¹³But when you give a feast, invite the poor, the crippled, the lame, the blind, ¹⁴and you will be blessed, because they cannot repay you. For you will be repaid at the resurrection of the just."

¹⁵When one of those who reclined at table with him heard these things, he said to him, "Blessed is everyone who will eat bread in the kingdom of God!" ¹⁶But he said to him, "A man once gave a great banquet and invited many. ¹⁷And at the time for the banquet he sent his servant² to say to those who had been invited, 'Come, for everything is now ready.' ¹⁸But they all alike began to make excuses. The first said to him, 'I have bought a field, and I must go out and see it. Please have me excused.' ¹⁹And another said, 'I have bought five yoke of oxen, and I go to examine them. Please have me excused.' ²⁰And another said, 'I have married a wife, and therefore I cannot come.' ²¹So the servant came and reported these things to his master. Then the master of the house became angry and said to his servant, 'Go out quickly to the streets and lanes of the city, and bring in the poor and crippled and blind and lame.' ²²And the servant said, 'Sir, what you commanded has been done, and still there is room.' ²³And the master said to the servant, 'Go out to the highways and hedges and compel people to come in, that my house may be filled. ²⁴For I tell you,³ none of those men who were invited shall taste my banquet.'"

²⁵Now great crowds accompanied him, and he turned and said to them, ²⁶"If anyone comes to me and does not hate his own father and mother and wife and children and brothers and sisters, yes, and even his own life, he cannot be my disciple. ²⁷Whoever does not bear his own cross and come after me cannot be my disciple. ²⁸For which of you, desiring to build a tower, does not first sit down and count the cost, whether he has enough to complete it? ²⁹Otherwise, when he has laid a foundation and is not able to finish, all who see it begin to mock him, ³⁰saying, 'This man began to build and was not able to finish.' ³¹Or what king, going out to encounter another king in war, will not sit down first and deliberate whether he is able with ten thousand to meet him who comes against him with twenty thousand? ³²And if not, while the other is yet a great way off, he sends a delegation and asks for terms of peace. ³³So therefore, any one of you who does not renounce all that he has cannot be my disciple.

³⁴"Salt is good, but if salt has lost its taste, how shall its saltiness be restored? ³⁵It is of no use either for the soil or for the manure pile. It is thrown away. He who has ears to hear, let him hear."

---

¹ Or *your brothers and sisters.* The plural Greek word *adelphoi* (translated "brothers") refers to siblings in a family. In New Testament usage, depending on the context, *adelphoi* may refer either to *brothers* or to *brothers and sisters* ² Greek *bondservant;* also verses 21, 22, 23 ³ The Greek word for *you* here is plural

Lost and found [chapter 15]. The mission of Jesus to seek and to save the lost is the very thing that alienates him from Israel's religious leaders. While Jesus happily enjoys table fellowship with all the needy people he loves to welcome into the kingdom of God, the Pharisees and scribes complain that he is receiving sinners and eating with them (vv. 1–2). In response, Jesus tells a triple parable about the joy that God has in finding lost sinners—a joy that everyone should share. In the stories of the lost sheep (vv. 3–7), the lost coin (vv. 8–10), and the lost son (vv. 11–32), there is a progression in rarity (one out of a hundred sheep, one out of ten coins, one out of two sons) and value (from an animal to a son). The parable comes to its climax in the masterpiece of the prodigal son. This story is about a lost son, of course, but even more about the welcoming father who goes out to his rebellious son in the embrace of forgiveness and grace. It is also about the other son, who is just as lost as his younger brother, having never truly grasped what it means to be his father's son. The keynote of all three parables is joy—the joy that God has with his children in finding what is lost. But this is exactly what the Pharisees are missing, which is the real point of this sharply polemical parable. In their joyless hypocrisy the Pharisees refuse to share the welcome that God loves to give lost sinners.

15 Now the tax collectors and sinners were all drawing near to hear him. ²And the Pharisees and the scribes grumbled, saying, "This man receives sinners and eats with them."

³So he told them this parable: ⁴"What man of you, having a hundred sheep, if he has lost one of them, does not leave the ninety-nine in the open country, and go after the one that is lost, until he finds it? ⁵And when he has found it, he lays it on his shoulders, rejoicing. ⁶And when he comes home, he calls together his friends and his neighbors, saying to them, 'Rejoice with me, for I have found my sheep that was lost.' ⁷Just so, I tell you, there will be more joy in heaven over one sinner who repents than over ninety-nine righteous persons who need no repentance.

⁸"Or what woman, having ten silver coins,[1] if she loses one coin, does not light a lamp and sweep the house and seek diligently until she finds it? ⁹And when she has found it, she calls together her friends and neighbors, saying, 'Rejoice with me, for I have found the coin that I had lost.' ¹⁰Just so, I tell you, there is joy before the angels of God over one sinner who repents."

¹¹And he said, "There was a man who had two sons. ¹²And the younger of them said to his father, 'Father, give me the share of property that is coming to me.' And he divided his property between them. ¹³Not many days later, the younger son gathered all he had and took a journey into a far country, and there he squandered his property in reckless living. ¹⁴And when he had spent everything, a severe famine arose in that country, and he began to be in need. ¹⁵So he went and hired himself out to[2] one of the citizens of that country, who sent him into his fields to feed pigs. ¹⁶And he was longing to be fed with the pods that the pigs ate, and no one gave him anything.

¹⁷"But when he came to himself, he said, 'How many of my father's hired servants have more than enough bread, but I perish here with hunger! ¹⁸I will arise and go to my father, and I will say to him, "Father, I have sinned against heaven and before you. ¹⁹I am no longer worthy to be called your son. Treat me as one of your hired servants."' ²⁰And he arose and came to his father. But while he was still a long way off, his father saw him and felt compassion, and ran and embraced him and kissed him. ²¹And the

[1] Greek ten drachmas; a drachma was a Greek coin approximately equal in value to a Roman denarius, worth about a day's wage for a laborer [2] Greek joined himself to

son said to him, 'Father, I have sinned against heaven and before you. I am no longer worthy to be called your son.'[1] [22]But the father said to his servants,[2] 'Bring quickly the best robe, and put it on him, and put a ring on his hand, and shoes on his feet. [23]And bring the fattened calf and kill it, and let us eat and celebrate. [24]For this my son was dead, and is alive again; he was lost, and is found.' And they began to celebrate.

[25]"Now his older son was in the field, and as he came and drew near to the house, he heard music and dancing. [26]And he called one of the servants and asked what these things meant. [27]And he said to him, 'Your brother has come, and your father has killed the fattened calf, because he has received him back safe and sound.' [28]But he was angry and refused to go in. His father came out and entreated him, [29]but he answered his father, 'Look, these many years I have served you, and I never disobeyed your command, yet you never gave me a young goat, that I might celebrate with my friends. [30]But when this son of yours came, who has devoured your property with prostitutes, you killed the fattened calf for him!' [31]And he said to him, 'Son, you are always with me, and all that is mine is yours. [32]It was fitting to celebrate and be glad, for this your brother was dead, and is alive; he was lost, and is found.' "

Stewardship and servanthood [16:1–17:10]. Most of the teaching in this section concerns faithfulness and unfaithfulness in the stewardship of spiritual and material possessions (Jesus also has important things to say about the law, divorce, and forgiveness) and how that relates to one's eternal destiny. The teaching Jesus gives in chapter 16 is mainly for the money-loving Pharisees (see 16:14). The main point of the parable of the dishonest manager is that rather than being mastered by money, a wise and faithful servant will use material wealth to gain eternal treasure (16:1–13). The rich man who ignored poor Lazarus is a cautionary counterexample: for all the finery and feasting he enjoyed on earth, he still ended up burning in hell (16:19–31). It is doubtful whether many of the things Jesus says here will ever be popular with fallen humanity: no one can serve both God and money; unlawful divorce is sinful adultery; there is an eternal chasm between heaven and hell; forgive people up to seven times a day; to serve God intensely is only to do one's duty. Pervasive literary forms here include conflict and satire; notice also how subversive Jesus' rhetoric is.

16 He also said to the disciples, "There was a rich man who had a manager, and charges were brought to him that this man was wasting his possessions. [2]And he called him and said to him, 'What is this that I hear about you? Turn in the account of your management, for you can no longer be manager.' [3]And the manager said to himself, 'What shall I do, since my master is taking the management away from me? I am not strong enough to dig, and I am ashamed to beg. [4]I have decided what to do, so that when I am removed from management, people may receive me into their houses.' [5]So, summoning his master's debtors one by one, he said to the first, 'How much do you owe my master?' [6]He said, 'A hundred measures[3] of oil.' He said to him, 'Take your bill, and sit down quickly and write fifty.' [7]Then he said to another, 'And how much do you owe?' He said, 'A hundred measures[4] of wheat.' He said to him, 'Take your bill, and write eighty.' [8]The master commended the dishonest manager for his shrewdness. For the sons of this world[5] are more shrewd in dealing with their own generation than the sons of light. [9]And I tell you, make friends for

---

[1] Some manuscripts add *treat me as one of your hired servants* [2] Greek *bondservants* [3] About 875 gallons [4] Between 1,000 and 1,200 bushels [5] Greek *age*

yourselves by means of unrighteous wealth,[1] so that when it fails they may receive you into the eternal dwellings.

[10]"One who is faithful in a very little is also faithful in much, and one who is dishonest in a very little is also dishonest in much. [11]If then you have not been faithful in the unrighteous wealth, who will entrust to you the true riches? [12]And if you have not been faithful in that which is another's, who will give you that which is your own? [13]No servant can serve two masters, for either he will hate the one and love the other, or he will be devoted to the one and despise the other. You cannot serve God and money."

[14]The Pharisees, who were lovers of money, heard all these things, and they ridiculed him. [15]And he said to them, "You are those who justify yourselves before men, but God knows your hearts. For what is exalted among men is an abomination in the sight of God.

[16]"The Law and the Prophets were until John; since then the good news of the kingdom of God is preached, and everyone forces his way into it.[2] [17]But it is easier for heaven and earth to pass away than for one dot of the Law to become void.

[18]"Everyone who divorces his wife and marries another commits adultery, and he who marries a woman divorced from her husband commits adultery.

[19]"There was a rich man who was clothed in purple and fine linen and who feasted sumptuously every day. [20]And at his gate was laid a poor man named Lazarus, covered with sores, [21]who desired to be fed with what fell from the rich man's table. Moreover, even the dogs came and licked his sores. [22]The poor man died and was carried by the angels to Abraham's side.[3] The rich man also died and was buried, [23]and in Hades, being in torment, he lifted up his eyes and saw Abraham far off and Lazarus at his side. [24]And he called out, 'Father Abraham, have mercy on me, and send Lazarus to dip the end of his finger in water and cool my tongue, for I am in anguish in this flame.' [25]But Abraham said, 'Child, remember that you in your lifetime received your good things, and Lazarus in like manner bad things; but now he is comforted here, and you are in anguish. [26]And besides all this, between us and you a great chasm has been fixed, in order that those who would pass from here to you may not be able, and none may cross from there to us.' [27]And he said, 'Then I beg you, father, to send him to my father's house— [28]for I have five brothers[4]—so that he may warn them, lest they also come into this place of torment.' [29]But Abraham said, 'They have Moses and the Prophets; let them hear them.' [30]And he said, 'No, father Abraham, but if someone goes to them from the dead, they will repent.' [31]He said to him, 'If they do not hear Moses and the Prophets, neither will they be convinced if someone should rise from the dead.'"

17 And he said to his disciples, "Temptations to sin[5] are sure to come, but woe to the one through whom they come! [2]It would be better for him if a millstone were hung around his neck and he were cast into the sea than that he should cause one of these little ones to sin.[6] [3]Pay attention to yourselves! If your brother sins, rebuke him, and if he repents, forgive him, [4]and if he sins against you seven times in the day, and turns to you seven times, saying, 'I repent,' you must forgive him."

[5]The apostles said to the Lord, "Increase our faith!" [6]And the Lord said, "If you had

---

[1] Greek *mammon*, a Semitic word for money or possessions; also verse 11; rendered *money* in verse 13 [2] Or *everyone is forcefully urged into it* [3] Greek *bosom*; also verse 23 [4] Or *brothers and sisters* [5] Greek *Stumbling blocks* [6] Greek *stumble*

faith like a grain of mustard seed, you could say to this mulberry tree, 'Be uprooted and planted in the sea,' and it would obey you.

⁷"Will any one of you who has a servant¹ plowing or keeping sheep say to him when he has come in from the field, 'Come at once and recline at table'? ⁸Will he not rather say to him, 'Prepare supper for me, and dress properly,² and serve me while I eat and drink, and afterward you will eat and drink'? ⁹Does he thank the servant because he did what was commanded? ¹⁰So you also, when you have done all that you were commanded, say, 'We are unworthy servants;³ we have only done what was our duty.'"

> **Kingdom come** [17:11–37]. Jesus is somewhere between Samaria and Galilee, still making his way to Jerusalem and the cross. The healing of the ten lepers (only one of whom ever came back to say "thank you") is recounted as a notable example of the difference between gratitude and ingratitude (17:11–19). The other prophecies and personal encounters in this section relate in one way or another to the coming of the kingdom. In one sense, since Jesus is the King, the kingdom has already come (17:20–21). However, the King is also coming again—unexpectedly, after his sufferings, and with the power of God's judgment (17:22–37).

¹¹On the way to Jerusalem he was passing along between Samaria and Galilee. ¹²And as he entered a village, he was met by ten lepers,⁴ who stood at a distance ¹³and lifted up their voices, saying, "Jesus, Master, have mercy on us." ¹⁴When he saw them he said to them, "Go and show yourselves to the priests." And as they went they were cleansed. ¹⁵Then one of them, when he saw that he was healed, turned back, praising God with a loud voice; ¹⁶and he fell on his face at Jesus' feet, giving him thanks. Now he was a Samaritan. ¹⁷Then Jesus answered, "Were not ten cleansed? Where are the nine? ¹⁸Was no one found to return and give praise to God except this foreigner?" ¹⁹And he said to him, "Rise and go your way; your faith has made you well."⁵

²⁰Being asked by the Pharisees when the kingdom of God would come, he answered them, "The kingdom of God is not coming with signs to be observed, ²¹nor will they say, 'Look, here it is!' or 'There!' for behold, the kingdom of God is in the midst of you."⁶

²²And he said to the disciples, "The days are coming when you will desire to see one of the days of the Son of Man, and you will not see it. ²³And they will say to you, 'Look, there!' or 'Look, here!' Do not go out or follow them. ²⁴For as the lightning flashes and lights up the sky from one side to the other, so will the Son of Man be in his day.⁷ ²⁵But first he must suffer many things and be rejected by this generation. ²⁶Just as it was in the days of Noah, so will it be in the days of the Son of Man. ²⁷They were eating and drinking and marrying and being given in marriage, until the day when Noah entered the ark, and the flood came and destroyed them all. ²⁸Likewise, just as it was in the days of Lot—they were eating and drinking, buying and selling, planting and building, ²⁹but on the day when Lot went out from Sodom, fire and sulfur rained from heaven and destroyed them all— ³⁰so will it be on the day when the Son of Man is revealed. ³¹On that day, let the one who is on the housetop, with his goods in the house, not come down to take them away, and likewise let the one who is in the field not turn back. ³²Remember Lot's wife. ³³Whoever seeks to preserve his life

---

¹ Greek bondservant; also verse 9 ² Greek gird yourself ³ Greek bondservants ⁴ Leprosy was a term for several skin diseases; see Leviticus 13 ⁵ Or has saved you ⁶ Or within you, or within your grasp ⁷ Some manuscripts omit in his day

will lose it, but whoever loses his life will keep it. ³⁴I tell you, in that night there will be two in one bed. One will be taken and the other left. ³⁵There will be two women grinding together. One will be taken and the other left."¹ ³⁷And they said to him, "Where, Lord?" He said to them, "Where the corpse² is, there the vultures³ will gather."

> **Parables and principles of the kingdom** [18:1–30]. How can people enter God's kingdom? Only with persistent prayer (vv. 1–8), humble repentance (vv. 9–14), child-like dependency (vv. 15–17), and the release of any and every possession that gets in the way of following Jesus (vv. 18–30). The parables in this section of Luke's Gospel are linked by the theme of prayer. Both parables feature strong and contrasting character types (the persistent widow who wears out the unjust judge; the proud Pharisee who serves as a *foil to the penitent tax collector). These and other parables show Jesus as a shrewd judge of human character, with a storyteller's knack for the telling detail. Luke's main purpose in telling about the little children and the rich young ruler who came to Jesus is to set up the dramatic statements Jesus makes about the terms of entrance into the kingdom of God. However, Luke is also showing the love of Jesus for little children (v. 16), his compassion for people outside the kingdom (v. 24), and his generosity toward his disciples (vv. 29–30).

18 And he told them a parable to the effect that they ought always to pray and not lose heart. ²He said, "In a certain city there was a judge who neither feared God nor respected man. ³And there was a widow in that city who kept coming to him and saying, 'Give me justice against my adversary.' ⁴For a while he refused, but afterward he said to himself, 'Though I neither fear God nor respect man, ⁵yet because this widow keeps bothering me, I will give her justice, so that she will not beat me down by her continual coming.'" ⁶And the Lord said, "Hear what the unrighteous judge says. ⁷And will not God give justice to his elect, who cry to him day and night? Will he delay long over them? ⁸I tell you, he will give justice to them speedily. Nevertheless, when the Son of Man comes, will he find faith on earth?"

⁹He also told this parable to some who trusted in themselves that they were righteous, and treated others with contempt: ¹⁰"Two men went up into the temple to pray, one a Pharisee and the other a tax collector. ¹¹The Pharisee, standing by himself, prayed⁴ thus: 'God, I thank you that I am not like other men, extortioners, unjust, adulterers, or even like this tax collector. ¹²I fast twice a week; I give tithes of all that I get.' ¹³But the tax collector, standing far off, would not even lift up his eyes to heaven, but beat his breast, saying, 'God, be merciful to me, a sinner!' ¹⁴I tell you, this man went down to his house justified, rather than the other. For everyone who exalts himself will be humbled, but the one who humbles himself will be exalted."

¹⁵ᵃNow they were bringing even infants to him that he might touch them. And when the disciples saw it, they rebuked them. ¹⁶But Jesus called them to him, saying, "Let the children come to me, and do not hinder them, for to such belongs the kingdom of God. ¹⁷Truly, I say to you, whoever does not receive the kingdom of God like a child shall not enter it."

¹⁸ᵇAnd a ruler asked him, "Good Teacher, what must I do to inherit eternal life?" ¹⁹And Jesus said to him, "Why do you call me good? No one is good except God alone. ²⁰You know the commandments: ᶜ'Do not commit adultery, Do not murder, Do not

---

¹ Some manuscripts add verse 36: *Two men will be in the field; one will be taken and the other left* ² Greek *body* ³ Or *eagles* ⁴ Or *standing, prayed to himself*
ᵃ For 18:15-17 see parallels Matt. 19:13-15; Mark 10:13-16 ᵇ For 18:18-30 see parallels Matt. 19:16-30; Mark 10:17-31 ᶜ Ex. 20:12-16; Deut. 5:16-20

steal, Do not bear false witness, Honor your father and mother.'" ²¹And he said, "All these I have kept from my youth." ²²When Jesus heard this, he said to him, "One thing you still lack. Sell all that you have and distribute to the poor, and you will have treasure in heaven; and come, follow me." ²³But when he heard these things, he became very sad, for he was extremely rich. ²⁴Jesus, seeing that he had become sad, said, "How difficult it is for those who have wealth to enter the kingdom of God! ²⁵For it is easier for a camel to go through the eye of a needle than for a rich person to enter the kingdom of God." ²⁶Those who heard it said, "Then who can be saved?" ²⁷But he said, "What is impossible with men is possible with God." ²⁸And Peter said, "See, we have left our homes and followed you." ²⁹And he said to them, "Truly, I say to you, there is no one who has left house or wife or brothers¹ or parents or children, for the sake of the kingdom of God, ³⁰who will not receive many times more in this time, and in the age to come eternal life."

The return of the King [18:31–19:27]. The long journey to Jerusalem is nearing its end. Jerusalem is more than a geographical goal for a physical journey; it is also a symbolic place where everything ever promised about the Son of Man will take place. He will suffer shameful treatment, die, and on the third day rise again (18:31–33). This is now the third time that Jesus has prophesied about his passion, and although the disciples still don't understand what he is talking about (see 18:34), Luke is obviously preparing his readers for the climactic events at the end of his Gospel. The two encounters that Jesus has in Jericho show what it means to come to God in faith (the blind man recovers his sight by faith, 18:35–43) and repentance (Zacchaeus makes restitution for all the money he stole, 19:1–9). These two men are exactly the kinds of people that Jesus came to save, for as the Savior announces—in what may well be regarded as the theme verse for Luke's Gospel—"the Son of Man came to seek and to save the lost" (19:10). Jesus tells the parable of the ten minas (19:11–27) in order to prepare his disciples for the interval between his first and second comings, though the parable is also a famous repository of teaching about stewardship (making maximum use of the gifts and opportunities that God gives). As disciples wait for the King to come again, their calling is to be faithful in service, making wise spiritual investments in the kingdom of God.

³¹ᵃ And taking the twelve, he said to them, "See, we are going up to Jerusalem, and everything that is written about the Son of Man by the prophets will be accomplished. ³²For he will be delivered over to the Gentiles and will be mocked and shamefully treated and spit upon. ³³And after flogging him, they will kill him, and on the third day he will rise." ³⁴But they understood none of these things. This saying was hidden from them, and they did not grasp what was said.

³⁵ᵇ As he drew near to Jericho, a blind man was sitting by the roadside begging. ³⁶And hearing a crowd going by, he inquired what this meant. ³⁷They told him, "Jesus of Nazareth is passing by." ³⁸And he cried out, "Jesus, Son of David, have mercy on me!" ³⁹And those who were in front rebuked him, telling him to be silent. But he cried out all the more, "Son of David, have mercy on me!" ⁴⁰And Jesus stopped and commanded him to be brought to him. And when he came near, he asked him, ⁴¹"What do you want me to do for you?" He said, "Lord, let me recover my sight." ⁴²And Jesus said to him, "Recover your sight; your faith has made you well." ⁴³And immediately he

---

¹ Or *wife or brothers and sisters* ᵃ For 18:31-33 see parallels Matt. 20:17-19; Mark 10:32-34 ᵇ For 18:35-43 see parallels Matt. 20:29-34; Mark 10:46-52

recovered his sight and followed him, glorifying God. And all the people, when they saw it, gave praise to God.

19 He entered Jericho and was passing through. [2]And there was a man named Zacchaeus. He was a chief tax collector and was rich. [3]And he was seeking to see who Jesus was, but on account of the crowd he could not, because he was small of stature. [4]So he ran on ahead and climbed up into a sycamore tree to see him, for he was about to pass that way. [5]And when Jesus came to the place, he looked up and said to him, "Zacchaeus, hurry and come down, for I must stay at your house today." [6]So he hurried and came down and received him joyfully. [7]And when they saw it, they all grumbled, "He has gone in to be the guest of a man who is a sinner." [8]And Zacchaeus stood and said to the Lord, "Behold, Lord, the half of my goods I give to the poor. And if I have defrauded anyone of anything, I restore it fourfold." [9]And Jesus said to him, "Today salvation has come to this house, since he also is a son of Abraham. [10]For the Son of Man came to seek and to save the lost."

[11]As they heard these things, he proceeded to tell a parable, because he was near to Jerusalem, and because they supposed that the kingdom of God was to appear immediately. [12]He said therefore, "A nobleman went into a far country to receive for himself a kingdom and then return. [13]Calling ten of his servants,[1] he gave them ten minas,[2] and said to them, 'Engage in business until I come.' [14]But his citizens hated him and sent a delegation after him, saying, 'We do not want this man to reign over us.' [15]When he returned, having received the kingdom, he ordered these servants to whom he had given the money to be called to him, that he might know what they had gained by doing business. [16]The first came before him, saying, 'Lord, your mina has made ten minas more.' [17]And he said to him, 'Well done, good servant![3] Because you have been faithful in a very little, you shall have authority over ten cities.' [18]And the second came, saying, 'Lord, your mina has made five minas.' [19]And he said to him, 'And you are to be over five cities.' [20]Then another came, saying, 'Lord, here is your mina, which I kept laid away in a handkerchief; [21]for I was afraid of you, because you are a severe man. You take what you did not deposit, and reap what you did not sow.' [22]He said to him, 'I will condemn you with your own words, you wicked servant! You knew that I was a severe man, taking what I did not deposit and reaping what I did not sow? [23]Why then did you not put my money in the bank, and at my coming I might have collected it with interest?' [24]And he said to those who stood by, 'Take the mina from him, and give it to the one who has the ten minas.' [25]And they said to him, 'Lord, he has ten minas!' [26]'I tell you that to everyone who has, more will be given, but from the one who has not, even what he has will be taken away. [27]But as for these enemies of mine, who did not want me to reign over them, bring them here and slaughter them before me.'"

Jesus enters Jerusalem [19:28–46]. This episode is usually known as the triumphal entry, but it is as much a tragedy as a triumph. Jesus rides into Jerusalem with gentle majesty, swept up by large crowds of cheering disciples who wish to crown him as their king. But Jesus himself is distraught. As he catches his first glimpse of the holy city, his eyes well up with tears. He knows that the people who praise him will soon seek to bury him and that for this rebellion the city will be destroyed. By the time Jesus reaches the

---

[1] Greek *bondservants*; also verse 15 [2] A *mina* was about three months' wages for a laborer [3] Greek *bondservant*; also verse 22

temple, his sorrow turns to anger. His Father's house is meant for prayer, but the religious leaders have turned its outer courts into a veritable supermarket.

²⁸And when he had said these things, he went on ahead, going up to Jerusalem. ²⁹ᵃWhen he drew near to Bethphage and Bethany, at the mount that is called Olivet, he sent two of the disciples, ³⁰saying, "Go into the village in front of you, where on entering you will find a colt tied, on which no one has ever yet sat. Untie it and bring it here. ³¹If anyone asks you, 'Why are you untying it?' you shall say this: 'The Lord has need of it.'" ³²So those who were sent away and found it just as he had told them. ³³And as they were untying the colt, its owners said to them, "Why are you untying the colt?" ³⁴And they said, "The Lord has need of it." ³⁵And they brought it to Jesus, and throwing their cloaks on the colt, they set Jesus on it. ³⁶And as he rode along, they spread their cloaks on the road. ³⁷As he was drawing near—already on the way down the Mount of Olives—the whole multitude of his disciples began to rejoice and praise God with a loud voice for all the mighty works that they had seen, ³⁸saying, "Blessed is the King who comes in the name of the Lord! Peace in heaven and glory in the highest!" ³⁹And some of the Pharisees in the crowd said to him, "Teacher, rebuke your disciples." ⁴⁰He answered, "I tell you, if these were silent, the very stones would cry out."

⁴¹And when he drew near and saw the city, he wept over it, ⁴²saying, "Would that you, even you, had known on this day the things that make for peace! But now they are hidden from your eyes. ⁴³For the days will come upon you, when your enemies will set up a barricade around you and surround you and hem you in on every side ⁴⁴and tear you down to the ground, you and your children within you. And they will not leave one stone upon another in you, because you did not know the time of your visitation."

⁴⁵ᵇAnd he entered the temple and began to drive out those who sold, ⁴⁶saying to them, "It is written, ᶜ'My house shall be a house of prayer,' but you have made it a den of robbers."

Jesus teaches at the temple [19:47–20:44]. Jesus spends most of the last week of his earthly ministry at the temple, where he teaches people and preaches the gospel (see 20:1). Luke presents this period as a time of rising conflict between Jesus and the religious establishment, which has decided to destroy him but is having trouble figuring out exactly how (see 19:47–48). When questioned as to whether he has authority to teach at the temple, Jesus responds with an unanswerable question that exposes the unbelief of his enemies (20:2–8). He also tells the most directly autobiographical and sharply polemical of all his parables, in which he prophesies his own death as the beloved Son of God and plainly indicates that the religious leaders will be thrown out of God's kingdom (20:9–18). Frustrated at every turn but still desperate to kill Jesus, the scribes and the chief priests try to trap him in either treason or tax evasion on the question of paying tribute to Caesar. The famous *aphorism Jesus gives by way of answer ("Render to Caesar the things that are Caesar's, and to God the things that are God's") silences them once again (20:19–26). Next up are the Sadducees, who try to confound Jesus with an outlandish objection to the resurrection. Once again, he gives a brilliant answer, defending the resurrection by his personal knowledge of heaven and his careful reading of the Old Testament (20:27–40). He completes his tour de force by asking a question that can be answered only in the person of the God-man who asks it: How can David's son also be David's Lord (20:41–44)? A leading role of Jesus in the Gospels is that of controversialist, and the literary form that typically embodies that role is the conflict story.

[47]And he was teaching daily in the temple. The chief priests and the scribes and the principal men of the people were seeking to destroy him, [48]but they did not find anything they could do, for all the people were hanging on his words.

20 [a][1]One day, as Jesus[1] was teaching the people in the temple and preaching the gospel, the chief priests and the scribes with the elders came up [2]and said to him, "Tell us by what authority you do these things, or who it is that gave you this authority." [3]He answered them, "I also will ask you a question. Now tell me, [4]was the baptism of John from heaven or from man?" [5]And they discussed it with one another, saying, "If we say, 'From heaven,' he will say, 'Why did you not believe him?' [6]But if we say, 'From man,' all the people will stone us to death, for they are convinced that John was a prophet." [7]So they answered that they did not know where it came from. [8]And Jesus said to them, "Neither will I tell you by what authority I do these things."

[9][b]And he began to tell the people this parable: "A man planted a vineyard and let it out to tenants and went into another country for a long while. [10]When the time came, he sent a servant[2] to the tenants, so that they would give him some of the fruit of the vineyard. But the tenants beat him and sent him away empty-handed. [11]And he sent another servant. But they also beat and treated him shamefully, and sent him away empty-handed. [12]And he sent yet a third. This one also they wounded and cast out. [13]Then the owner of the vineyard said, 'What shall I do? I will send my beloved son; perhaps they will respect him.' [14]But when the tenants saw him, they said to themselves, 'This is the heir. Let us kill him, so that the inheritance may be ours.' [15]And they threw him out of the vineyard and killed him. What then will the owner of the vineyard do to them? [16]He will come and destroy those tenants and give the vineyard to others." When they heard this, they said, "Surely not!" [17]But he looked directly at them and said, "What then is this that is written:

[c]"'The stone that the builders rejected
　　has become the cornerstone'?[3]

[18]Everyone who falls on that stone will be broken to pieces, and when it falls on anyone, it will crush him."

[19]The scribes and the chief priests sought to lay hands on him at that very hour, for they perceived that he had told this parable against them, but they feared the people. [20][d]So they watched him and sent spies, who pretended to be sincere, that they might catch him in something he said, so as to deliver him up to the authority and jurisdiction of the governor. [21]So they asked him, "Teacher, we know that you speak and teach rightly, and show no partiality,[4] but truly teach the way of God. [22]Is it lawful for us to give tribute to Caesar, or not?" [23]But he perceived their craftiness, and said to them, [24]"Show me a denarius.[5] Whose likeness and inscription does it have?" They said, "Caesar's." [25]He said to them, "Then render to Caesar the things that are Caesar's, and to God the things that are God's." [26]And they were not able in the pres-

---

[1] Greek he [2] Greek bondservant; also verse 11 [3] Greek the head of the corner [4] Greek and do not receive a face [5] A denarius was a day's wage for a laborer
[a] For 20:1-8 see parallels Matt. 21:23-27; Mark 11:27-33 [b] For 20:9-18 see parallels Matt. 21:33-46; Mark 12:1-12 [c] Ps. 118:22 [d] For 20:20-38 see parallels Matt. 22:15-32; Mark 12:13-27

ence of the people to catch him in what he said, but marveling at his answer they became silent.

²⁷There came to him some Sadducees, those who deny that there is a resurrection, ²⁸and they asked him a question, saying, "Teacher, Moses wrote for us that if a man's brother dies, having a wife but no children, the man¹ must take the widow and raise up offspring for his brother. ²⁹Now there were seven brothers. The first took a wife, and died without children. ³⁰And the second ³¹and the third took her, and likewise all seven left no children and died. ³²Afterward the woman also died. ³³In the resurrection, therefore, whose wife will the woman be? For the seven had her as wife."

³⁴And Jesus said to them, "The sons of this age marry and are given in marriage, ³⁵but those who are considered worthy to attain to that age and to the resurrection from the dead neither marry nor are given in marriage, ³⁶for they cannot die anymore, because they are equal to angels and are sons of God, being sons² of the resurrection. ³⁷But that the dead are raised, even Moses showed, in the passage about the bush, where he calls the Lord the God of Abraham and the God of Isaac and the God of Jacob. ³⁸Now he is not God of the dead, but of the living, for all live to him." ³⁹Then some of the scribes answered, "Teacher, you have spoken well." ⁴⁰For they no longer dared to ask him any question.

⁴¹ᵃBut he said to them, "How can they say that the Christ is David's son? ⁴²For David himself says in the Book of Psalms,

ᵇ"'The Lord said to my Lord,
   Sit at my right hand,
⁴³   until I make your enemies your footstool.'

⁴⁴David thus calls him Lord, so how is he his son?"

The fall of Jerusalem predicted [20:45–21:38]. The temple is also the setting for the teaching Jesus gives on the fall of Jerusalem and the end of the world (a speech that is often called the Olivet Discourse). His startling prediction that the temple will be torn down stone by stone prompts the disciples to ask for more details. Jesus warns his followers not to be led astray by false speculations about the Second Coming or to be terrified by all the suffering the future will bring, but to discern the many signs God will give of the coming judgment and to have confidence that he will enable them to endure. In addition to making specific predictions about the fall of Jerusalem (which took place in A.D. 70), Jesus widens the scope of his prophecy to include the glorious coming of the Son of Man at the catastrophic end of the universe (21:25–27). Many of the details surrounding the fall of Jerusalem and the end of the world remain mysterious, as is typical in *apocalyptic literature. However, the practical implications of these prophecies are fairly simple and straightforward: the kingdom of God is near, and when it suddenly comes, as it certainly will, people who are watching and waiting in faith will find their safety with the Son of Man (21:28–36).

⁴⁵ᶜAnd in the hearing of all the people he said to his disciples, ⁴⁶"Beware of the scribes, who like to walk around in long robes, and love greetings in the marketplaces and the best seats in the synagogues and the places of honor at feasts, ⁴⁷who devour

---

¹ Greek *his brother* ² Greek *huioi*; see preface ᵃ For 20:41-44 see parallels Matt. 22:41-45; Mark 12:35-37 ᵇ Ps. 110:1 ᶜ For 20:45, 46 see parallels Matt. 23:1, 2, 5-7; Mark 12:38-40

widows' houses and for a pretense make long prayers. They will receive the greater condemnation."

21 [a]Jesus[1] looked up and saw the rich putting their gifts into the offering box, [2]and he saw a poor widow put in two small copper coins.[2] [3]And he said, "Truly, I tell you, this poor widow has put in more than all of them. [4]For they all contributed out of their abundance, but she out of her poverty put in all she had to live on."

[5b]And while some were speaking of the temple, how it was adorned with noble stones and offerings, he said, [6]"As for these things that you see, the days will come when there will not be left here one stone upon another that will not be thrown down." [7]And they asked him, "Teacher, when will these things be, and what will be the sign when these things are about to take place?" [8]And he said, "See that you are not led astray. For many will come in my name, saying, 'I am he!' and, 'The time is at hand!' Do not go after them. [9]And when you hear of wars and tumults, do not be terrified, for these things must first take place, but the end will not be at once."

[10]Then he said to them, "Nation will rise against nation, and kingdom against kingdom. [11]There will be great earthquakes, and in various places famines and pestilences. And there will be terrors and great signs from heaven. [12]But before all this they will lay their hands on you and persecute you, delivering you up to the synagogues and prisons, and you will be brought before kings and governors for my name's sake. [13]This will be your opportunity to bear witness. [14]Settle it therefore in your minds not to meditate beforehand how to answer, [15]for I will give you a mouth and wisdom, which none of your adversaries will be able to withstand or contradict. [16]You will be delivered up even by parents and brothers[3] and relatives and friends, and some of you they will put to death. [17]You will be hated by all for my name's sake. [18]But not a hair of your head will perish. [19]By your endurance you will gain your lives.

[20]"But when you see Jerusalem surrounded by armies, then know that its desolation has come near. [21]Then let those who are in Judea flee to the mountains, and let those who are inside the city depart, and let not those who are out in the country enter it, [22]for these are days of vengeance, to fulfill all that is written. [23]Alas for women who are pregnant and for those who are nursing infants in those days! For there will be great distress upon the earth and wrath against this people. [24]They will fall by the edge of the sword and be led captive among all nations, and Jerusalem will be trampled underfoot by the Gentiles, until the times of the Gentiles are fulfilled.

[25]"And there will be signs in sun and moon and stars, and on the earth distress of nations in perplexity because of the roaring of the sea and the waves, [26]people fainting with fear and with foreboding of what is coming on the world. For the powers of the heavens will be shaken. [27]And then they will see the Son of Man coming in a cloud with power and great glory. [28]Now when these things begin to take place, straighten up and raise your heads, because your redemption is drawing near."

[29]And he told them a parable: "Look at the fig tree, and all the trees. [30]As soon as they come out in leaf, you see for yourselves and know that the summer is already near. [31]So also, when you see these things taking place, you know that the kingdom of God is near. [32]Truly, I say to you, this generation will not pass away until all has taken place. [33]Heaven and earth will pass away, but my words will not pass away.

[34]"But watch yourselves lest your hearts be weighed down with dissipation and

---

[1] Greek *He* [2] Greek *two lepta*; a *lepton* was a Jewish bronze or copper coin worth about 1/128 of a *denarius* (which was a day's wage for a laborer) [3] Or *parents and brothers and sisters* [a] For 21:1-4 see parallel Mark 12:41-44 [b] For 21:5-36 see parallels Matt. 24:1-51; Mark 13:1-37

drunkenness and cares of this life, and that day come upon you suddenly like a trap. [35]For it will come upon all who dwell on the face of the whole earth. [36]But stay awake at all times, praying that you may have strength to escape all these things that are going to take place, and to stand before the Son of Man."

[37]And every day he was teaching in the temple, but at night he went out and lodged on the mount called Olivet. [38]And early in the morning all the people came to him in the temple to hear him.

The Last Supper [22:1–46]. After years of arguing with Jesus and months of secretly plotting against him, the chief priests and the scribes finally get their opportunity to kill him. It will be an inside job, for their coconspirator is none other than Judas Iscariot, one of the twelve disciples. But darker powers are also at work as Satan seizes the "opportune time" (see 4:13) to make his last and deadliest attack on Jesus. Jesus begins his last night with his closest friends, sharing an intimate Passover with them in an upper room. In addition to giving his disciples the bread and the cup that institute the sacrament of the Lord's Supper (vv. 14–20), Jesus gives them some important warnings and instructions. A member of their own fellowship will be the betrayer. When this warning rekindles an old debate about which disciple is the greatest, Jesus reminds them that true greatness is measured by service, not status (vv. 22–30). The famous prophecy Jesus makes about Peter sets the stage both for Peter's denial and for his subsequent restoration (vv. 31–34; cf. 22:54–62). While the disciples sleep, against all warnings to watch and pray, their Lord struggles alone in the garden with the divine will for his sacrifice, finally choosing in favor of the Father's pleasure. The leading literary motifs are abandonment, treason, and the solitary sufferer.

22 Now the Feast of Unleavened Bread drew near, which is called the Passover. [2]And the chief priests and the scribes were seeking how to put him to death, for they feared the people.

[3a]Then Satan entered into Judas called Iscariot, who was of the number of the twelve. [4]He went away and conferred with the chief priests and officers how he might betray him to them. [5]And they were glad, and agreed to give him money. [6]So he consented and sought an opportunity to betray him to them in the absence of a crowd.

[7b]Then came the day of Unleavened Bread, on which the Passover lamb had to be sacrificed. [8]So Jesus[1] sent Peter and John, saying, "Go and prepare the Passover for us, that we may eat it." [9]They said to him, "Where will you have us prepare it?" [10]He said to them, "Behold, when you have entered the city, a man carrying a jar of water will meet you. Follow him into the house that he enters [11]and tell the master of the house, 'The Teacher says to you, Where is the guest room, where I may eat the Passover with my disciples?' [12]And he will show you a large upper room furnished; prepare it there." [13]And they went and found it just as he had told them, and they prepared the Passover.

[14]And when the hour came, he reclined at table, and the apostles with him. [15]And he said to them, "I have earnestly desired to eat this Passover with you before I suffer. [16]For I tell you I will not eat it[2] until it is fulfilled in the kingdom of God." [17]And he took a cup, and when he had given thanks he said, "Take this, and divide it among yourselves. [18]For I tell you that from now on I will not drink of the fruit of the vine until the

---

[1] Greek *he* [2] Some manuscripts *never eat it again* [a] For 22:3-6 see parallels Matt. 26:14-16; Mark 14:10, 11 [b] For 22:7-13 see parallels Matt. 26:17-19; Mark 14:12-16

kingdom of God comes." [19a] And he took bread, and when he had given thanks, he broke it and gave it to them, saying, "This is my body, which is given for you. Do this in remembrance of me." [20] And likewise the cup after they had eaten, saying, "This cup that is poured out for you is the new covenant in my blood.[1] [21b] But behold, the hand of him who betrays me is with me on the table. [22] For the Son of Man goes as it has been determined, but woe to that man by whom he is betrayed!" [23] And they began to question one another, which of them it could be who was going to do this.

[24] A dispute also arose among them, as to which of them was to be regarded as the greatest. [25] And he said to them, "The kings of the Gentiles exercise lordship over them, and those in authority over them are called benefactors. [26] But not so with you. Rather, let the greatest among you become as the youngest, and the leader as one who serves. [27] For who is the greater, one who reclines at table or one who serves? Is it not the one who reclines at table? But I am among you as the one who serves.

[28] "You are those who have stayed with me in my trials, [29] and I assign to you, as my Father assigned to me, a kingdom, [30] that you may eat and drink at my table in my kingdom and sit on thrones judging the twelve tribes of Israel.

[31] "Simon, Simon, behold, Satan demanded to have you,[2] that he might sift you like wheat, [32] but I have prayed for you that your faith may not fail. And when you have turned again, strengthen your brothers." [33] Peter[3] said to him, "Lord, I am ready to go with you both to prison and to death." [34] Jesus[4] said, "I tell you, Peter, the rooster will not crow this day, until you deny three times that you know me."

[35] And he said to them, "When I sent you out with no moneybag or knapsack or sandals, did you lack anything?" They said, "Nothing." [36] He said to them, "But now let the one who has a moneybag take it, and likewise a knapsack. And let the one who has no sword sell his cloak and buy one. [37] For I tell you that this Scripture must be fulfilled in me: [c]'And he was numbered with the transgressors.' For what is written about me has its fulfillment." [38] And they said, "Look, Lord, here are two swords." And he said to them, "It is enough."

[39] And he came out and went, as was his custom, to the Mount of Olives, and the disciples followed him. [40d] And when he came to the place, he said to them, "Pray that you may not enter into temptation." [41] And he withdrew from them about a stone's throw, and knelt down and prayed, [42] saying, "Father, if you are willing, remove this cup from me. Nevertheless, not my will, but yours, be done." [43] And there appeared to him an angel from heaven, strengthening him. [44] And being in an agony he prayed more earnestly; and his sweat became like great drops of blood falling down to the ground.[5] [45] And when he rose from prayer, he came to the disciples and found them sleeping for sorrow, [46] and he said to them, "Why are you sleeping? Rise and pray that you may not enter into temptation."

Jesus on trial [22:47–23:25]. It is the hour of "the power of darkness" (22:53), as Jesus calls it—the hour when evil persons will treacherously betray, mockingly abuse, falsely accuse, and wrongly condemn the Son of Man. Luke crafts the narrative to show that Jesus is both the Son of God (22:69–70) and the King of the Jews (23:3) and that his death is orchestrated by an unholy alliance of Jews and Gentiles. The trials before the Sanhedrin (22:66–71), before Pilate (23:1–5), before Herod (23:6–12), and before

[1] Some manuscripts omit, in whole or in part, verses 19b-20 (*which is given . . . in my blood*) [2] The Greek word for *you* (twice in this verse) is plural; in verse 32, all four instances are singular [3] Greek *He* [4] Greek *He* [5] Some manuscripts omit verses 43 and 44 [a] For 22:19, 20 see parallels Matt. 26:26-28; Mark 14:22-24 [b] For 22:21-23 see parallels Matt. 26:21-24; Mark 14:18-21 [c] Isa. 53:12 [d] For 22:40-46 see parallels Matt. 26:36-46; Mark 14:32-42

Pilate once again (23:13–25) prove the innocence of Jesus and the malevolence of his enemies. It becomes increasingly obvious that Jesus has done nothing wrong and that any attempt to establish his guilt by legitimate means is futile. In a dramatic irony, the legal proceedings end with a guilty man (Barabbas) going free, while the only completely innocent man who ever lived is condemned to die (23:18–25).

[47a]While he was still speaking, there came a crowd, and the man called Judas, one of the twelve, was leading them. He drew near to Jesus to kiss him, [48]but Jesus said to him, "Judas, would you betray the Son of Man with a kiss?" [49]And when those who were around him saw what would follow, they said, "Lord, shall we strike with the sword?" [50]And one of them struck the servant[1] of the high priest and cut off his right ear. [51]But Jesus said, "No more of this!" And he touched his ear and healed him. [52]Then Jesus said to the chief priests and officers of the temple and elders, who had come out against him, "Have you come out as against a robber, with swords and clubs? [53]When I was with you day after day in the temple, you did not lay hands on me. But this is your hour, and the power of darkness."

[54]Then they seized him and led him away, bringing him into the high priest's house, and Peter was following at a distance. [55b]And when they had kindled a fire in the middle of the courtyard and sat down together, Peter sat down among them. [56]Then a servant girl, seeing him as he sat in the light and looking closely at him, said, "This man also was with him." [57]But he denied it, saying, "Woman, I do not know him." [58]And a little later someone else saw him and said, "You also are one of them." But Peter said, "Man, I am not." [59]And after an interval of about an hour still another insisted, saying, "Certainly this man also was with him, for he too is a Galilean." [60]But Peter said, "Man, I do not know what you are talking about." And immediately, while he was still speaking, the rooster crowed. [61]And the Lord turned and looked at Peter. And Peter remembered the saying of the Lord, how he had said to him, "Before the rooster crows today, you will deny me three times." [62]And he went out and wept bitterly.

[63]Now the men who were holding Jesus in custody were mocking him as they beat him. [64]They also blindfolded him and kept asking him, "Prophesy! Who is it that struck you?" [65]And they said many other things against him, blaspheming him.

[66]When day came, the assembly of the elders of the people gathered together, both chief priests and scribes. And they led him away to their council, and they said, [67]"If you are the Christ, tell us." But he said to them, "If I tell you, you will not believe, [68]and if I ask you, you will not answer. [69]But from now on the Son of Man shall be seated at the right hand of the power of God." [70]So they all said, "Are you the Son of God, then?" And he said to them, "You say that I am." [71]Then they said, "What further testimony do we need? We have heard it ourselves from his own lips."

23 Then the whole company of them arose and brought him before Pilate. [2]And they began to accuse him, saying, "We found this man misleading our nation and forbidding us to give tribute to Caesar, and saying that he himself is Christ, a king." [3]And Pilate asked him, "Are you the King of the Jews?" And he answered him, "You have said so." [4]Then Pilate said to the chief priests and the crowds, "I find no guilt in this man." [5]But they were urgent, saying, "He stirs up the people, teaching throughout all Judea, from Galilee even to this place."

[1] Greek *bondservant* [a] For 22:47-53 see parallels Matt. 26:47-56; Mark 14:43-50; John 18:3-11 [b] For 22:55-62 see parallels Matt. 26:69-75; Mark 14:66-72; John 18:16-18, 25-27

⁶When Pilate heard this, he asked whether the man was a Galilean. ⁷And when he learned that he belonged to Herod's jurisdiction, he sent him over to Herod, who was himself in Jerusalem at that time. ⁸When Herod saw Jesus, he was very glad, for he had long desired to see him, because he had heard about him, and he was hoping to see some sign done by him. ⁹So he questioned him at some length, but he made no answer. ¹⁰The chief priests and the scribes stood by, vehemently accusing him. ¹¹And Herod with his soldiers treated him with contempt and mocked him. Then, arraying him in splendid clothing, he sent him back to Pilate. ¹²And Herod and Pilate became friends with each other that very day, for before this they had been at enmity with each other.

¹³Pilate then called together the chief priests and the rulers and the people, ¹⁴and said to them, "You brought me this man as one who was misleading the people. And after examining him before you, behold, I did not find this man guilty of any of your charges against him. ¹⁵Neither did Herod, for he sent him back to us. Look, nothing deserving death has been done by him. ¹⁶I will therefore punish and release him."¹

¹⁸ªBut they all cried out together, "Away with this man, and release to us Barabbas"— ¹⁹a man who had been thrown into prison for an insurrection started in the city and for murder. ²⁰Pilate addressed them once more, desiring to release Jesus, ²¹but they kept shouting, "Crucify, crucify him!" ²²A third time he said to them, "Why, what evil has he done? I have found in him no guilt deserving death. I will therefore punish and release him." ²³But they were urgent, demanding with loud cries that he should be crucified. And their voices prevailed. ²⁴So Pilate decided that their demand should be granted. ²⁵He released the man who had been thrown into prison for insurrection and murder, for whom they asked, but he delivered Jesus over to their will.

The cross and the tomb [23:26–56]. Each Gospel account of the crucifixion calls attention to different details. Luke chooses to include the following words of Jesus: another sad lament for Jerusalem (vv. 28–31); a free offer of forgiveness for his killers (v. 33); an open invitation to paradise for one of the criminals crucified next to him (v. 43); and a final prayer of faith that the Father will receive his spirit (v. 46). When Jesus breathes his last, the centurion declares the verdict that Herod and Pilate were too afraid to render: "Certainly this man was innocent!" (v. 47). This statement serves to make the crucifixion narrative a *recognition story in which the true identity of Jesus Christ is revealed. The ensuing description of Christ's burial calls attention to the pious devotion of Joseph of Arimathea and the godly women from Galilee, who watched Jesus to the end and lovingly prepared to lay his body to rest. The sheer quantity of characters and details that make an appearance in this passage give a dramatic sense of realism and capture the fast-moving nature of this horrific experience as it actually happened.

²⁶And as they led him away, they seized one Simon of Cyrene, who was coming in from the country, and laid on him the cross, to carry it behind Jesus. ²⁷And there followed him a great multitude of the people and of women who were mourning and lamenting for him. ²⁸But turning to them Jesus said, "Daughters of Jerusalem, do not weep for me, but weep for yourselves and for your children. ²⁹For behold, the days are coming when they will say, 'Blessed are the barren and the wombs that never bore and the breasts that never nursed!' ³⁰Then they will begin to say to the moun-

---

¹ Here, or after verse 19, some manuscripts add verse 17: *Now he was obliged to release one man to them at the festival* ª For 23:18-25 see parallels Matt. 27:15-26; Mark 15:6-15; John 18:39, 40; 19:16

tains, 'Fall on us,' and to the hills, 'Cover us.' [31]For if they do these things when the wood is green, what will happen when it is dry?"

[32]Two others, who were criminals, were led away to be put to death with him. [33]And when they came to the place that is called The Skull, there they crucified him, and the criminals, one on his right and one on his left. [34]And Jesus said, "Father, forgive them, for they know not what they do."[1] And they cast lots to divide his garments. [35]And the people stood by, watching, but the rulers scoffed at him, saying, "He saved others; let him save himself, if he is the Christ of God, his Chosen One!" [36]The soldiers also mocked him, coming up and offering him sour wine [37]and saying, "If you are the King of the Jews, save yourself!" [38]There was also an inscription over him,[2] "This is the King of the Jews."

[39]One of the criminals who were hanged railed at him,[3] saying, "Are you not the Christ? Save yourself and us!" [40]But the other rebuked him, saying, "Do you not fear God, since you are under the same sentence of condemnation? [41]And we indeed justly, for we are receiving the due reward of our deeds; but this man has done nothing wrong." [42]And he said, "Jesus, remember me when you come into your kingdom." [43]And he said to him, "Truly, I say to you, today you will be with me in Paradise."

[44]It was now about the sixth hour,[4] and there was darkness over the whole land until the ninth hour,[5] [45]while the sun's light failed. And the curtain of the temple was torn in two. [46]Then Jesus, calling out with a loud voice, said, "Father, into your hands I commit my spirit!" And having said this he breathed his last. [47]Now when the centurion saw what had taken place, he praised God, saying, "Certainly this man was innocent!" [48]And all the crowds that had assembled for this spectacle, when they saw what had taken place, returned home beating their breasts. [49]And all his acquaintances and the women who had followed him from Galilee stood at a distance watching these things.

[50][a]Now there was a man named Joseph, from the Jewish town of Arimathea. He was a member of the council, a good and righteous man, [51]who had not consented to their decision and action; and he was looking for the kingdom of God. [52]This man went to Pilate and asked for the body of Jesus. [53]Then he took it down and wrapped it in a linen shroud and laid him in a tomb cut in stone, where no one had ever yet been laid. [54]It was the day of Preparation, and the Sabbath was beginning.[6] [55]The women who had come with him from Galilee followed and saw the tomb and how his body was laid. [56]Then they returned and prepared spices and ointments.

On the Sabbath they rested according to the commandment.

The day of resurrection [chapter 24]. The resurrection narratives begin with the mystery of a missing body—a mystery resolved in the bright light of day with a risen Lord. Only Luke records the long conversation Jesus has with two disciples on the road to Emmaus, during which he proves the necessity of his sufferings, death, and resurrection from the total teaching of the Old Testament (see vv. 25–27, 44–46). The recognition of Jesus in the breaking of bread at an ordinary meal (vv. 30–32) is one of the great moments of *epiphany in the whole Bible. After recording various resurrection appearances that Jesus made to his disciples, Luke gives his version of the Great Commission, together with a promise of the Holy Spirit (vv. 47–49). After this *farewell discourse, the Gospel ends as it began: with joyful worship at the house of God in Jerusalem (vv.

---

[1] Some manuscripts omit the sentence And Jesus . . . what they do [2] Some manuscripts add in letters of Greek and Latin and Hebrew [3] Or blasphemed him [4] That is, noon [5] That is, 3 P.M. [6] Greek was dawning [a] For 23:50-56 see parallels Matt. 27:57-61; Mark 15:42-47; John 19:38-42

51–53). But even this is only the beginning, because in his next book (commonly known as the Acts of the Apostles) Luke will tell how the apostles received the Holy Spirit and bore witness to the crucified and risen Christ from Jerusalem to the ends of the earth.

24 [a]But on the first day of the week, at early dawn, they went to the tomb, taking the spices they had prepared. [2]And they found the stone rolled away from the tomb, [3]but when they went in they did not find the body of the Lord Jesus. [4]While they were perplexed about this, behold, two men stood by them in dazzling apparel. [5]And as they were frightened and bowed their faces to the ground, the men said to them, "Why do you seek the living among the dead? [6]He is not here, but has risen. Remember how he told you, while he was still in Galilee, [7]that the Son of Man must be delivered into the hands of sinful men and be crucified and on the third day rise." [8]And they remembered his words, [9]and returning from the tomb they told all these things to the eleven and to all the rest. [10]Now it was Mary Magdalene and Joanna and Mary the mother of James and the other women with them who told these things to the apostles, [11]but these words seemed to them an idle tale, and they did not believe them. [12]But Peter rose and ran to the tomb; stooping and looking in, he saw the linen cloths by themselves; and he went home marveling at what had happened.

[13]That very day two of them were going to a village named Emmaus, about seven miles[1] from Jerusalem, [14]and they were talking with each other about all these things that had happened. [15]While they were talking and discussing together, Jesus himself drew near and went with them. [16]But their eyes were kept from recognizing him. [17]And he said to them, "What is this conversation that you are holding with each other as you walk?" And they stood still, looking sad. [18]Then one of them, named Cleopas, answered him, "Are you the only visitor to Jerusalem who does not know the things that have happened there in these days?" [19]And he said to them, "What things?" And they said to him, "Concerning Jesus of Nazareth, a man who was a prophet mighty in deed and word before God and all the people, [20]and how our chief priests and rulers delivered him up to be condemned to death, and crucified him. [21]But we had hoped that he was the one to redeem Israel. Yes, and besides all this, it is now the third day since these things happened. [22]Moreover, some women of our company amazed us. They were at the tomb early in the morning, [23]and when they did not find his body, they came back saying that they had even seen a vision of angels, who said that he was alive. [24]Some of those who were with us went to the tomb and found it just as the women had said, but him they did not see." [25]And he said to them, "O foolish ones, and slow of heart to believe all that the prophets have spoken! [26]Was it not necessary that the Christ should suffer these things and enter into his glory?" [27]And beginning with Moses and all the Prophets, he interpreted to them in all the Scriptures the things concerning himself.

[28]So they drew near to the village to which they were going. He acted as if he were going farther, [29]but they urged him strongly, saying, "Stay with us, for it is toward evening and the day is now far spent." So he went in to stay with them. [30]When he was at table with them, he took the bread and blessed and broke it and gave it to them. [31]And their eyes were opened, and they recognized him. And he vanished from their sight. [32]They said to each other, "Did not our hearts burn within us while he talked to us on the road, while he opened to us the Scriptures?" [33]And they rose that same hour and

---

[1] Greek sixty *stadia; a stadion* was about 607 feet or 185 meters [a] For 24:1-10 see parallels Matt. 28:1-8; Mark 16:1-8; John 20:1

returned to Jerusalem. And they found the eleven and those who were with them gathered together, [34]saying, "The Lord has risen indeed, and has appeared to Simon!" [35]Then they told what had happened on the road, and how he was known to them in the breaking of the bread.

[36]As they were talking about these things, Jesus himself stood among them, and said to them, "Peace to you!" [37]But they were startled and frightened and thought they saw a spirit. [38]And he said to them, "Why are you troubled, and why do doubts arise in your hearts? [39]See my hands and my feet, that it is I myself. Touch me, and see. For a spirit does not have flesh and bones as you see that I have." [40]And when he had said this, he showed them his hands and his feet. [41]And while they still disbelieved for joy and were marveling, he said to them, "Have you anything here to eat?" [42]They gave him a piece of broiled fish,[1] [43]and he took it and ate before them.

[44]Then he said to them, "These are my words that I spoke to you while I was still with you, that everything written about me in the Law of Moses and the Prophets and the Psalms must be fulfilled." [45]Then he opened their minds to understand the Scriptures, [46]and said to them, "Thus it is written, that the Christ should suffer and on the third day rise from the dead, [47]and that repentance and forgiveness of sins should be proclaimed in his name to all nations, beginning from Jerusalem. [48]You are witnesses of these things. [49]And behold, I am sending the promise of my Father upon you. But stay in the city until you are clothed with power from on high."

[50]Then he led them out as far as Bethany, and lifting up his hands he blessed them. [51]While he blessed them, he parted from them and was carried up into heaven. [52]And they worshiped him and returned to Jerusalem with great joy, [53]and were continually in the temple blessing God.

---

[1] Some manuscripts add *and some honeycomb*

JOHN

The book at a glance. 21 chapters, 878 verses. Like the other Gospel writers, John recorded events and discourses from the life of Jesus that would lead his readers to believe in Jesus as the Savior of the world. In his own purpose statement, John states his reason for writing: "so that you may believe that Jesus is the Christ, the Son of God, and that by believing you may have life in his name" (20:31). The author of the book was one of the inner circle of disciples—in fact, he identifies himself as the "disciple whom Jesus loved" (21:7). John was an eyewitness to the events that he records. The Gospel of John is both the cosmic Gospel, portraying Jesus as the answer to universal human longings, and a Jewish Gospel that contains numerous references to Jewish feasts and rituals. Further, it is a poetic Gospel in its reliance on great images and symbols as means of expressing who Jesus is (light, bread, water). The Gospel of John is also known as the Gospel of belief because it says so much about faith and because it repeatedly shows people confronted with the need to choose to believe or disbelieve Jesus' claims about himself.

▌Genres. The main genre is *Gospel. Within that rubric, we find the usual array of gospel subgenres, including *calling or vocation stories, *recognition stories, *witness stories, *conflict stories, *encounter stories,*miracle stories, *discourses, *proverbs or sayings, *passion stories, *resurrection stories, and postresurrection appearances. The overriding framework of the Gospels is narrative or story, and the Gospel of John features a stronger unity of plot than the other Gospels, built around the conflict of belief versus unbelief. The major discourses are so awe-inspiring that they rank as orations, and a distinguishing feature of the Gospel of John is the attention that it gives to Jesus' discourses. (For more information on items accompanied by an asterisk, see the glossary at the end of this Bible.)

▌Format. A major organizing principle of John's Gospel is that the first half of the book is built around seven great "signs" (John's word for miracles) that Jesus performed. Another distinctive feature of the Gospel of John is the linking of a sign or other great symbol with a corresponding statement made by Jesus in the form of either a conver- sation or a full-fledged discourse. For example, Jesus asks the Samaritan woman for a drink from the well (4:7–8) and then pursues a conversation with the woman about water that climaxes in Jesus' claim to be the source of living water that wells up to eternal life (4:9–15). To cite another example, Jesus feeds five thousand (6:1–14), and a few verses later we read his discourse on Jesus' being the bread of life (6:25–40). The story as a whole enacts a pattern of increasing expansion (as Jesus begins his

Passage	Content	Type of Material	Place in Jesus' Life	Time Span
1:1–18	Prologue			
1:19–4:54	Jesus' initiation into public ministry	Signs, discourses, and conflicts with Jewish leaders	Ministry in the public sphere	Three years
5:1–12:50	Jesus' public career as teacher, miracle worker, and controversialist			
13:1–17:26	Jesus with his disciples	Teaching		
18:1–19:42	Crucifixion and burial	Suffering and atonement	Jesus with his disciples or as lone sufferer	A few weeks
20:1–21:25	Resurrection and appearances to the disciples	Victory		

ministry with a handful of followers and becomes a public figure at the center of his society's attention) and then increasing constriction (as Jesus lives his final days chiefly in the company of his disciples).

▌**Motifs.** (1) The motif of the misunderstood statement appears nine times: Jesus makes a pronouncement; a bystander expresses misunderstanding of the utterance; Jesus explains the meaning of his original statement. (2) There are numerous items that happen in threes and in sevens (including seven interspersed "I am" self-designations by Jesus). (3) The conflict between belief and unbelief in Jesus organizes the entire book. (4) The plot of the story forms a pattern of increasingly severe conflict between Jesus and his opponents, ending in the crucifixion of Jesus. (5) Great symbols become means of embodying the truth about Jesus—symbols like light, darkness, water, bread, and shepherd. (6) Heightened contrasts mark the book—light versus darkness; life versus death; the fleeting versus the eternal; disease versus health; love versus hate.

▌**Inferred literary intentions.** The book is designed to achieve the following literary purposes:

- paint a winsome portrait of Jesus as teacher and Savior
- tell the story of Jesus' life as a traveling teacher and miracle worker
- allow us to feel the conflict that Jesus faced during his public ministry
- confront readers with a need to choose to believe or disbelieve the claims that John makes about Jesus (and that Jesus makes about himself)
- embody the truth about Jesus in the form of "signs" and symbols
- balance what Jesus did with memorable conversations and speeches of Jesus

▌**Theological themes.** (1) Christology: the Gospel of John is a major source of NT truth about the person and work of Jesus. (2) Faith and salvation: Jesus makes numerous claims about how a person can be saved through faith in him, and many of the stories, in turn, show people expressing that faith. (3) Unbelief leading to damnation: the book also teaches the way of salvation by negative example, with stories of people who rejected Christ. (4) Resurrection: the story of the raising of Lazarus, in addition to the story of Jesus' resurrection, elevates the theme of resurrection to prominence. (5) The Holy Spirit: Jesus' Upper Room Discourse includes a key unit on the Holy Spirit (16:5–15). (6) Union with Christ: chapter 15 is a key NT text on this subject, which we correctly associate mainly with the Epistles.

▌**The Gospel of John as a chapter in the master story of the Bible.** The master story of the Bible tells us how people can be saved into eternal life. The Gospel of John is built around this very motif, portraying Jesus as the Savior of the whole world and showing by means of narrative examples and Jesus' discourses how a person can come to a saving faith in the person and work of Jesus.

Prologue to the book [1:1–18]. The Gospel of Matthew begins with a human genealogy for Jesus; John begins with a divine genealogy. The genre of this opening unit of the book is known as the *Christ hymn—a poem in praise of the person and work of Christ. Though printed in English Bibles as prose, this passage is so patterned and poetic that it could profitably be printed in poetic form. We can progress through the poem looking for two main topics regarding the incarnate Christ—his status as the revelation of God to people and as the bringer of spiritual life. Additionally, this poem initiates us into two leading stylistic traits of the book as a whole—the reliance on great images and symbols (like Jesus as a metaphoric "word" and light), and the reliance on antithesis (such as light vs. darkness and belief vs. unbelief).

1 In the beginning was the Word, and the Word was with God, and the Word was God. ²He was in the beginning with God. ³All things were made through him, and without him was not any thing made that was made. ⁴In him was life,¹ and the life was the light of men. ⁵The light shines in the darkness, and the darkness has not overcome it.

⁶There was a man sent from God, whose name was John. ⁷He came as a witness, to bear witness about the light, that all might believe through him. ⁸He was not the light, but came to bear witness about the light.

⁹The true light, which enlightens everyone, was coming into the world. ¹⁰He was in the world, and the world was made through him, yet the world did not know him. ¹¹He came to his own,² and his own people³ did not receive him. ¹²But to all who did receive him, who believed in his name, he gave the right to become children of God, ¹³who were born, not of blood nor of the will of the flesh nor of the will of man, but of God.

¹⁴And the Word became flesh and dwelt among us, and we have seen his glory, glory as of the only Son from the Father, full of grace and truth. ¹⁵(John bore witness about him, and cried out, "This was he of whom I said, 'He who comes after me ranks before me, because he was before me.'") ¹⁶And from his fullness we have all received, grace upon grace. ¹⁷For the law was given through Moses; grace and truth came

¹ Or *was not any thing made. That which has been made was life in him* ² Greek *to his own things;* that is, to his own domain, or to his own people
³ *People* is implied in Greek

through Jesus Christ. [18]No one has ever seen God; the only God,[1] who is at the Father's side,[2] he has made him known.

> **Initiation into ministry [1:19–51].** After the stately and formal prologue to the book, we might well be surprised by the abruptness with which John next plunges us into the middle of an action in verse 19. The remainder of the opening chapter is our initiation into the story that John the Evangelist will now tell. The units unfold according to the following sequence: John the Baptist's self-characterization as the forerunner of the Christ (vv. 19–28); John the Baptist's testimony regarding Jesus based on his reconstruction of what happened at the baptism of Jesus (vv. 29–34); two calling stories—the calling of Andrew and Peter (vv. 35–42) and of Philip and Nathanael (vv. 43–51). Everything about these episodes has the flavor of an initiation story that tells us how Jesus' public ministry began. Further, we need to probe everything that John wrote for its explicit and latent information about Jesus and his work. For example, what does the calling of the first disciples teach us about Jesus and the relationship that he wants believers to have with him? Finally, the Gospel of John specializes in conveying a sense of mystery surrounding Jesus; there are many unexplained details and mysterious sayings that prompt us to ponder what they mean. For example, why did the mere declaration "Behold, the Lamb of God!" (v. 36) lead two of Jesus' disciples to follow him? Why did two followers ask to see where Jesus was staying (v. 38)? Why does Jesus at once predict a name change for Peter (v. 42)? What is the import of Jesus' having seen Nathanael under a fig tree (v. 50)?

[19]And this is the testimony of John, when the Jews sent priests and Levites from Jerusalem to ask him, "Who are you?" [20]He confessed, and did not deny, but confessed, "I am not the Christ." [21]And they asked him, "What then? Are you Elijah?" He said, "I am not." "Are you the Prophet?" And he answered, "No." [22]So they said to him, "Who are you? We need to give an answer to those who sent us. What do you say about yourself?" [23]He said, "I am [a]the voice of one crying out in the wilderness, 'Make straight[3] the way of the Lord,' as the prophet Isaiah said."

[24](Now they had been sent from the Pharisees.) [25]They asked him, "Then why are you baptizing, if you are neither the Christ, nor Elijah, nor the Prophet?" [26]John answered them, "I baptize with water, but among you stands one you do not know, [27]even he who comes after me, the strap of whose sandal I am not worthy to untie." [28]These things took place in Bethany across the Jordan, where John was baptizing.

[29]The next day he saw Jesus coming toward him, and said, "Behold, the Lamb of God, who takes away the sin of the world! [30]This is he of whom I said, 'After me comes a man who ranks before me, because he was before me.' [31]I myself did not know him, but for this purpose I came baptizing with water, that he might be revealed to Israel." [32]And John bore witness: "I saw the Spirit descend from heaven like a dove, and it remained on him. [33]I myself did not know him, but he who sent me to baptize with water said to me, 'He on whom you see the Spirit descend and remain, this is he who baptizes with the Holy Spirit.' [34]And I have seen and have borne witness that this is the Son of God."

[35]The next day again John was standing with two of his disciples, [36]and he looked at Jesus as he walked by and said, "Behold, the Lamb of God!" [37]The two disciples heard him say this, and they followed Jesus. [38]Jesus turned and saw them following

[1] Or the only One, who is God; some manuscripts the only Son [2] Greek in the bosom of the Father [3] Or crying out, 'In the wilderness make straight [a] Isa. 40:3

and said to them, "What are you seeking?" And they said to him, "Rabbi" (which means Teacher), "where are you staying?" [39]He said to them, "Come and you will see." So they came and saw where he was staying, and they stayed with him that day, for it was about the tenth hour.[1] [40]One of the two who heard John speak and followed Jesus[2] was Andrew, Simon Peter's brother. [41]He first found his own brother Simon and said to him, "We have found the Messiah" (which means Christ). [42]He brought him to Jesus. Jesus looked at him and said, "So you are Simon the son of John? You shall be called Cephas" (which means Peter[3]).

[43]The next day Jesus decided to go to Galilee. He found Philip and said to him, "Follow me." [44]Now Philip was from Bethsaida, the city of Andrew and Peter. [45]Philip found Nathanael and said to him, "We have found him of whom Moses in the Law and also the prophets wrote, Jesus of Nazareth, the son of Joseph." [46]Nathanael said to him, "Can anything good come out of Nazareth?" Philip said to him, "Come and see." [47]Jesus saw Nathanael coming toward him and said of him, "Behold, an Israelite indeed, in whom there is no deceit!" [48]Nathanael said to him, "How do you know me?" Jesus answered him, "Before Philip called you, when you were under the fig tree, I saw you." [49]Nathanael answered him, "Rabbi, you are the Son of God! You are the King of Israel!" [50]Jesus answered him, "Because I said to you, 'I saw you under the fig tree,' do you believe? You will see greater things than these." [51]And he said to him, "Truly, truly, I say to you,[4] you will see heaven opened, and the angels of God ascending and descending on the Son of Man."

Water into wine and the cleansing of the temple [chapter 2]. The first miracle recorded in John is Jesus' turning water into wine at a wedding feast (vv. 1–12). John calls this "the first of his signs" (v. 11). In the Gospel of John, the word sign calls our attention to the fact that Jesus' miracles are not only physical events but also spiritual symbols that embody the truth about Jesus. We can therefore explore the miracle story of the water turned into wine for its spiritual meanings, including the divine power of Jesus and his bringing the OT ceremonial rituals of cleansing to an end. By means of a single verse (v. 13) we travel from Capernaum to Jerusalem. Thus far in the book we have seen Jesus as primarily a private figure, with his family and disciples. The episode of the cleansing of the temple (vv. 14–25) introduces Jesus into the public limelight. Although this conflict story is not one of Jesus' great "signs," it is like the signs in being a symbolic action. A picture of Jesus the revolutionary emerges in this event, but we must interpret Jesus' action not as a private crusade but a messianic entering of the temple as a divine presence.

2 On the third day there was a wedding at Cana in Galilee, and the mother of Jesus was there. [2]Jesus also was invited to the wedding with his disciples. [3]When the wine ran out, the mother of Jesus said to him, "They have no wine." [4]And Jesus said to her, "Woman, what does this have to do with me? My hour has not yet come." [5]His mother said to the servants, "Do whatever he tells you."

[6]Now there were six stone water jars there for the Jewish rites of purification, each holding twenty or thirty gallons.[5] [7]Jesus said to the servants, "Fill the jars with water." And they filled them up to the brim. [8]And he said to them, "Now draw some out and take it to the master of the feast." So they took it. [9]When the master of the feast tasted

---

[1] That is, about 4 P.M. [2] Greek him [3] Cephas and Peter are from the word for rock in Aramaic and Greek, respectively [4] The Greek for you is plural; twice in this verse [5] Greek two or three measures (metrētas); a metrētēs was about 10 gallons or 35 liters

the water now become wine, and did not know where it came from (though the servants who had drawn the water knew), the master of the feast called the bridegroom
[10]and said to him, "Everyone serves the good wine first, and when people have drunk
freely, then the poor wine. But you have kept the good wine until now." [11]This, the
first of his signs, Jesus did at Cana in Galilee, and manifested his glory. And his disciples believed in him.

[12]After this he went down to Capernaum, with his mother and his brothers[1] and
his disciples, and they stayed there for a few days.

[13]The Passover of the Jews was at hand, and Jesus went up to Jerusalem. [14]In the
temple he found those who were selling oxen and sheep and pigeons, and the money-
changers sitting there. [15]And making a whip of cords, he drove them all out of the
temple, with the sheep and oxen. And he poured out the coins of the money-changers
and overturned their tables. [16]And he told those who sold the pigeons, "Take these
things away; do not make my Father's house a house of trade." [17]His disciples remembered that it was written, [a]"Zeal for your house will consume me."

[18]So the Jews said to him, "What sign do you show us for doing these things?"
[19]Jesus answered them, "Destroy this temple, and in three days I will raise it up." [20]The
Jews then said, "It has taken forty-six years to build this temple, and will you raise it
up in three days?" [21]But he was speaking about the temple of his body. [22]When therefore he was raised from the dead, his disciples remembered that he had said this, and
they believed the Scripture and the word that Jesus had spoken.

[23]Now when he was in Jerusalem at the Passover Feast, many believed in his name
when they saw the signs that he was doing. [24]But Jesus on his part did not entrust
himself to them, because he knew all people [25]and needed no one to bear witness
about man, for he himself knew what was in man.

Jesus and Nicodemus [3:1–21]. This is the first in a string of famous encounter stories in John's Gospel. The vehicle of the encounter is conversation. Jesus steps forward
in a new role in the story, namely, teacher and revealer of truth. A mainspring of the
conversation is the motif of the misunderstood statement by Jesus, as when Nicodemus
mistakes Jesus' statement about being born again as referring to physical birth (v. 4).
Symbolism pervades the unit—birth imagery, wind, light. The episode also fits into the
ongoing story of belief versus unbelief. Those who believe in Christ will find everlasting
life, while those who refuse to believe in him will perish.

3 Now there was a man of the Pharisees named Nicodemus, a ruler of the Jews.
[2]This man came to Jesus[2] by night and said to him, "Rabbi, we know that you are
a teacher come from God, for no one can do these signs that you do unless God is
with him." [3]Jesus answered him, "Truly, truly, I say to you, unless one is born again[3]
he cannot see the kingdom of God." [4]Nicodemus said to him, "How can a man be
born when he is old? Can he enter a second time into his mother's womb and be
born?" [5]Jesus answered, "Truly, truly, I say to you, unless one is born of water and the
Spirit, he cannot enter the kingdom of God. [6]That which is born of the flesh is flesh,
and that which is born of the Spirit is spirit.[4] [7]Do not marvel that I said to you, 'You[5]
must be born again.' [8]The wind[6] blows where it wishes, and you hear its sound, but

---

[1] Or brothers and sisters. The plural Greek word adelphoi (translated "brothers") refers to siblings in a family. In New Testament usage, depending on the
context, adelphoi may refer either to brothers or to brothers and sisters [2] Greek him [3] Or from above; the Greek is purposely ambiguous and can mean
both again and from above; also verse 7 [4] The same Greek word means both wind and spirit [5] The Greek for you is plural here [6] The same Greek word
means both wind and spirit [a] Ps. 69:9

you do not know where it comes from or where it goes. So it is with everyone who is born of the Spirit."

⁹Nicodemus said to him, "How can these things be?" ¹⁰Jesus answered him, "Are you the teacher of Israel and yet you do not understand these things? ¹¹Truly, truly, I say to you, we speak of what we know, and bear witness to what we have seen, but you¹ do not receive our testimony. ¹²If I have told you earthly things and you do not believe, how can you believe if I tell you heavenly things? ¹³No one has ascended into heaven except he who descended from heaven, the Son of Man.² ¹⁴And as Moses lifted up the serpent in the wilderness, so must the Son of Man be lifted up, ¹⁵that whoever believes in him may have eternal life.³

¹⁶"For God so loved the world,⁴ that he gave his only Son, that whoever believes in him should not perish but have eternal life. ¹⁷For God did not send his Son into the world to condemn the world, but in order that the world might be saved through him. ¹⁸Whoever believes in him is not condemned, but whoever does not believe is condemned already, because he has not believed in the name of the only Son of God. ¹⁹And this is the judgment: the light has come into the world, and people loved the darkness rather than the light because their works were evil. ²⁰For everyone who does wicked things hates the light and does not come to the light, lest his works should be exposed. ²¹But whoever does what is true comes to the light, so that it may be clearly seen that his works have been carried out in God."

Jesus and John the Baptist [3:22–36]. A lead-in (v. 22) again reminds us that we are reading a travel story in which Jesus and his entourage live on the road from day to day. The key ingredient in the passage is the testimony of John the Baptist and perhaps also of John the author regarding Jesus (interpreters vary on whether to ascribe vv. 27–36 entirely to John the Baptist or whether vv. 31–36 belong to the author John). The keynote of the passage is christology—teaching about Christ.

²²After this Jesus and his disciples went into the Judean countryside, and he remained there with them and was baptizing. ²³John also was baptizing at Aenon near Salim, because water was plentiful there, and people were coming and being baptized ²⁴(for John had not yet been put in prison). ²⁵Now a discussion arose between some of John's disciples and a Jew over purification. ²⁶And they came to John and said to him, "Rabbi, he who was with you across the Jordan, to whom you bore witness—look, he is baptizing, and all are going to him." ²⁷John answered, "A person cannot receive even one thing unless it is given him from heaven. ²⁸You yourselves bear me witness, that I said, 'I am not the Christ, but I have been sent before him.' ²⁹The one who has the bride is the bridegroom. The friend of the bridegroom, who stands and hears him, rejoices greatly at the bridegroom's voice. Therefore this joy of mine is now complete. ³⁰He must increase, but I must decrease."⁵

³¹He who comes from above is above all. He who is of the earth belongs to the earth and speaks in an earthly way. He who comes from heaven is above all. ³²He bears witness to what he has seen and heard, yet no one receives his testimony. ³³Whoever receives his testimony sets his seal to this, that God is true. ³⁴For he whom God has sent utters the words of God, for he gives the Spirit without measure. ³⁵The

¹ The Greek for *you* is plural here; also four times in verse 12 ² Some manuscripts add *who is in heaven* ³ Some interpreters hold that the quotation ends at verse 15 ⁴ Or *For this is how God loved the world* ⁵ Some interpreters hold that the quotation continues through verse 36

Father loves the Son and has given all things into his hand. ³⁶Whoever believes in the Son has eternal life; whoever does not obey the Son shall not see life, but the wrath of God remains on him.

> **Jesus and the woman at the well** [4:1–42]. This is another famous encounter story, and a drama in miniature. The unit is structured as a two-act drama in which the two acts are surrounded with narrative material, as follows: a narrative prologue that gives the physical setting and participants in the dialogue (vv. 1–6); Jesus' conversation with the woman of Samaria (vv. 7–26); a narrative interlude in which the woman is dismissed from the scene and the disciples introduced into it (vv. 27–38); Jesus' discourse to the disciples (vv. 31–38); a narrative epilogue in which many Samaritans come to faith (vv. 39–42). The dialogue between Jesus and the woman at the well (vv. 7–26) is an encounter story in which dialogue is the vehicle for a quest in which, step by step, Jesus brings the woman to faith. The back-and-forth movement of the dialogue is a seamless sequence in which a statement by one of the two conversers leads to a response by the other. The discourse of Jesus to the disciples (vv. 31–38) is an interpretive lens through which to look at the story of the conversion of many Samaritans: the story is proof of Jesus' statement in the discourse that "the fields are white for harvest" (v. 35). A picture of Jesus emerges as someone who disregards human taboos; in fact, he breaks two taboos when as a Jew he speaks to a Samaritan and as a man he discourses about theology with a woman.

4 Now when Jesus learned that the Pharisees had heard that Jesus was making and baptizing more disciples than John ²(although Jesus himself did not baptize, but only his disciples), ³he left Judea and departed again for Galilee. ⁴And he had to pass through Samaria. ⁵So he came to a town of Samaria called Sychar, near the field that Jacob had given to his son Joseph. ⁶Jacob's well was there; so Jesus, wearied as he was from his journey, was sitting beside the well. It was about the sixth hour.¹

⁷A woman from Samaria came to draw water. Jesus said to her, "Give me a drink." ⁸(For his disciples had gone away into the city to buy food.) ⁹The Samaritan woman said to him, "How is it that you, a Jew, ask for a drink from me, a woman of Samaria?" (For Jews have no dealings with Samaritans.) ¹⁰Jesus answered her, "If you knew the gift of God, and who it is that is saying to you, 'Give me a drink,' you would have asked him, and he would have given you living water." ¹¹The woman said to him, "Sir, you have nothing to draw water with, and the well is deep. Where do you get that living water? ¹²Are you greater than our father Jacob? He gave us the well and drank from it himself, as did his sons and his livestock." ¹³Jesus said to her, "Everyone who drinks of this water will be thirsty again, ¹⁴but whoever drinks of the water that I will give him will never be thirsty again.² The water that I will give him will become in him a spring of water welling up to eternal life." ¹⁵The woman said to him, "Sir, give me this water, so that I will not be thirsty or have to come here to draw water."

¹⁶Jesus said to her, "Go, call your husband, and come here." ¹⁷The woman answered him, "I have no husband." Jesus said to her, "You are right in saying, 'I have no husband'; ¹⁸for you have had five husbands, and the one you now have is not your husband. What you have said is true." ¹⁹The woman said to him, "Sir, I perceive that you are a prophet. ²⁰Our fathers worshiped on this mountain, but you say that in Jerusalem is the place where people ought to worship." ²¹Jesus said to her, "Woman,

¹ That is, about noon ² Greek *forever*

believe me, the hour is coming when neither on this mountain nor in Jerusalem will you worship the Father. [22]You worship what you do not know; we worship what we know, for salvation is from the Jews. [23]But the hour is coming, and is now here, when the true worshipers will worship the Father in spirit and truth, for the Father is seeking such people to worship him. [24]God is spirit, and those who worship him must worship in spirit and truth." [25]The woman said to him, "I know that Messiah is coming (he who is called Christ). When he comes, he will tell us all things." [26]Jesus said to her, "I who speak to you am he."

[27]Just then his disciples came back. They marveled that he was talking with a woman, but no one said, "What do you seek?" or, "Why are you talking with her?" [28]So the woman left her water jar and went away into town and said to the people, [29]"Come, see a man who told me all that I ever did. Can this be the Christ?" [30]They went out of the town and were coming to him.

[31]Meanwhile the disciples were urging him, saying, "Rabbi, eat." [32]But he said to them, "I have food to eat that you do not know about." [33]So the disciples said to one another, "Has anyone brought him something to eat?" [34]Jesus said to them, "My food is to do the will of him who sent me and to accomplish his work. [35]Do you not say, 'There are yet four months, then comes the harvest'? Look, I tell you, lift up your eyes, and see that the fields are white for harvest. [36]Already the one who reaps is receiving wages and gathering fruit for eternal life, so that sower and reaper may rejoice together. [37]For here the saying holds true, 'One sows and another reaps.' [38]I sent you to reap that for which you did not labor. Others have labored, and you have entered into their labor."

[39]Many Samaritans from that town believed in him because of the woman's testimony, "He told me all that I ever did." [40]So when the Samaritans came to him, they asked him to stay with them, and he stayed there two days. [41]And many more believed because of his word. [42]They said to the woman, "It is no longer because of what you said that we believe, for we have heard for ourselves, and we know that this is indeed the Savior of the world."

Two miracle stories [4:43–5:18]. After the now-expected travel link (4:43–46a), John narrates two miracle stories (the second and third of the seven signs around which this Gospel is partly organized). The first is the healing of the official's son (vv. 46b–54), which John labels "the second sign that Jesus did" (4:54). Before extracting thematic meaning from such an event, we need to relive its details in our imagination. The healing of the lame man on the Sabbath (5:1–18) is likewise filled with particularized details. It ends as a conflict story between Jesus and the religious establishment, and this is a unifying plot motif in the Gospel of John. Again we see Jesus as someone who challenges traditional practices, in this case the religious observance of the Sabbath.

[43]After the two days he departed for Galilee. [44](For Jesus himself had testified that a prophet has no honor in his own hometown.) [45]So when he came to Galilee, the Galileans welcomed him, having seen all that he had done in Jerusalem at the feast. For they too had gone to the feast.

[46]So he came again to Cana in Galilee, where he had made the water wine. And at Capernaum there was an official whose son was ill. [47]When this man heard that Jesus

had come from Judea to Galilee, he went to him and asked him to come down and heal his son, for he was at the point of death. ⁴⁸So Jesus said to him, "Unless you see signs and wonders you will not believe." ⁴⁹The official said to him, "Sir, come down before my child dies." ⁵⁰Jesus said to him, "Go; your son will live." The man believed the word that Jesus spoke to him and went on his way. ⁵¹As he was going down, his servants¹ met him and told him that his son was recovering. ⁵²So he asked them the hour when he began to get better, and they said to him, "Yesterday at the seventh hour² the fever left him." ⁵³The father knew that was the hour when Jesus had said to him, "Your son will live." And he himself believed, and all his household. ⁵⁴This was now the second sign that Jesus did when he had come from Judea to Galilee.

5 After this there was a feast of the Jews, and Jesus went up to Jerusalem. ²Now there is in Jerusalem by the Sheep Gate a pool, in Aramaic³ called Bethesda,⁴ which has five roofed colonnades. ³In these lay a multitude of invalids— blind, lame, and paralyzed.⁵ ⁵One man was there who had been an invalid for thirty-eight years. ⁶When Jesus saw him lying there and knew that he had already been there a long time, he said to him, "Do you want to be healed?" ⁷The sick man answered him, "Sir, I have no one to put me into the pool when the water is stirred up, and while I am going another steps down before me." ⁸Jesus said to him, "Get up, take up your bed, and walk." ⁹And at once the man was healed, and he took up his bed and walked.

Now that day was the Sabbath. ¹⁰So the Jews said to the man who had been healed, "It is the Sabbath, and it is not lawful for you to take up your bed." ¹¹But he answered them, "The man who healed me, that man said to me, 'Take up your bed, and walk.'" ¹²They asked him, "Who is the man who said to you, 'Take up your bed and walk'?" ¹³Now the man who had been healed did not know who it was, for Jesus had withdrawn, as there was a crowd in the place. ¹⁴Afterward Jesus found him in the temple and said to him, "See, you are well! Sin no more, that nothing worse may happen to you." ¹⁵The man went away and told the Jews that it was Jesus who had healed him. ¹⁶And this was why the Jews were persecuting Jesus, because he was doing these things on the Sabbath. ¹⁷But Jesus answered them, "My Father is working until now, and I am working."

¹⁸This was why the Jews were seeking all the more to kill him, because not only was he breaking the Sabbath, but he was even calling God his own Father, making himself equal with God.

Jesus' discourse of self-characterization [5:19–47]. A notable feature of John's Gospel is the large amount of space that the storyteller devotes to the discourses of Jesus. The discourse in this unit is a speech in which Jesus characterizes himself, and a further point of unity is that throughout the entire discourse Jesus speaks in terms of his relation to the Father. No strict sequence of ideas is discernible, but the general progress in the discourse is as follows: Jesus' position of honor with the Father, especially in regard to resurrection and judgment (vv. 19–29); Jesus' exalted position in the eyes of various witnesses—John the Baptist, the Father, and the Scriptures (vv. 30–47).

---

¹ Greek bondservants ² That is, at 1 P.M. ³ Or Hebrew ⁴ Some manuscripts Bethsaida ⁵ Some manuscripts insert, wholly or in part, waiting for the moving of the water; ⁶for an angel of the Lord went down at certain seasons into the pool, and stirred the water: whoever stepped in first after the stirring of the water was healed of whatever disease he had

¹⁹So Jesus said to them, "Truly, truly, I say to you, the Son can do nothing of his own accord, but only what he sees the Father doing. For whatever the Father[1] does, that the Son does likewise. ²⁰For the Father loves the Son and shows him all that he himself is doing. And greater works than these will he show him, so that you may marvel. ²¹For as the Father raises the dead and gives them life, so also the Son gives life to whom he will. ²²The Father judges no one, but has given all judgment to the Son, ²³that all may honor the Son, just as they honor the Father. Whoever does not honor the Son does not honor the Father who sent him. ²⁴Truly, truly, I say to you, whoever hears my word and believes him who sent me has eternal life. He does not come into judgment, but has passed from death to life.

²⁵"Truly, truly, I say to you, an hour is coming, and is now here, when the dead will hear the voice of the Son of God, and those who hear will live. ²⁶For as the Father has life in himself, so he has granted the Son also to have life in himself. ²⁷And he has given him authority to execute judgment, because he is the Son of Man. ²⁸Do not marvel at this, for an hour is coming when all who are in the tombs will hear his voice ²⁹and come out, those who have done good to the resurrection of life, and those who have done evil to the resurrection of judgment.

³⁰"I can do nothing on my own. As I hear, I judge, and my judgment is just, because I seek not my own will but the will of him who sent me. ³¹If I alone bear witness about myself, my testimony is not deemed true. ³²There is another who bears witness about me, and I know that the testimony that he bears about me is true. ³³You sent to John, and he has borne witness to the truth. ³⁴Not that the testimony that I receive is from man, but I say these things so that you may be saved. ³⁵He was a burning and shining lamp, and you were willing to rejoice for a while in his light. ³⁶But the testimony that I have is greater than that of John. For the works that the Father has given me to accomplish, the very works that I am doing, bear witness about me that the Father has sent me. ³⁷And the Father who sent me has himself borne witness about me. His voice you have never heard, his form you have never seen, ³⁸and you do not have his word abiding in you, for you do not believe the one whom he has sent. ³⁹You search the Scriptures because you think that in them you have eternal life; and it is they that bear witness about me, ⁴⁰yet you refuse to come to me that you may have life. ⁴¹I do not receive glory from people. ⁴²But I know that you do not have the love of God within you. ⁴³I have come in my Father's name, and you do not receive me. If another comes in his own name, you will receive him. ⁴⁴How can you believe, when you receive glory from one another and do not seek the glory that comes from the only God? ⁴⁵Do not think that I will accuse you to the Father. There is one who accuses you: Moses, on whom you have set your hope. ⁴⁶For if you believed Moses, you would believe me; for he wrote of me. ⁴⁷But if you do not believe his writings, how will you believe my words?"

Two more signs [6:1–21]. The miracle of the feeding of the five thousand (vv. 1–14), Jesus' fourth great sign, is a highly public event, while Jesus' walking on the water (vv. 16–21), the fifth great sign of John's Gospel, is witnessed by only the disciples. Both miracles are signs that embody meanings about who Jesus is. The physical bread that Jesus provides the crowd is like the abundance of spiritual provision that he provides his people in all ages. Jesus' walking on the water testifies to his deity.

---

[1] Greek *he*

6 After this ªJesus went away to the other side of the Sea of Galilee, which is the Sea of Tiberias. ²And a large crowd was following him, because they saw the signs that he was doing on the sick. ³Jesus went up on the mountain, and there he sat down with his disciples. ⁴Now the Passover, the feast of the Jews, was at hand. ⁵Lifting up his eyes, then, and seeing that a large crowd was coming toward him, Jesus said to Philip, "Where are we to buy bread, so that these people may eat?" ⁶He said this to test him, for he himself knew what he would do. ⁷Philip answered him, "Two hundred denarii¹ would not buy enough bread for each of them to get a little." ⁸One of his disciples, Andrew, Simon Peter's brother, said to him, ⁹"There is a boy here who has five barley loaves and two fish, but what are they for so many?" ¹⁰Jesus said, "Have the people sit down." Now there was much grass in the place. So the men sat down, about five thousand in number. ¹¹Jesus then took the loaves, and when he had given thanks, he distributed them to those who were seated. So also the fish, as much as they wanted. ¹²And when they had eaten their fill, he told his disciples, "Gather up the leftover fragments, that nothing may be lost." ¹³So they gathered them up and filled twelve baskets with fragments from the five barley loaves left by those who had eaten. ¹⁴When the people saw the sign that he had done, they said, "This is indeed the Prophet who is to come into the world!"

¹⁵Perceiving then that they were about to come and take him by force to make him king, Jesus ᵇwithdrew again to the mountain by himself.

¹⁶When evening came, his disciples went down to the sea, ¹⁷got into a boat, and started across the sea to Capernaum. It was now dark, and Jesus had not yet come to them. ¹⁸The sea became rough because a strong wind was blowing. ¹⁹When they had rowed about three or four miles,² they saw Jesus walking on the sea and coming near the boat, and they were frightened. ²⁰But he said to them, "It is I; do not be afraid." ²¹Then they were glad to take him into the boat, and immediately the boat was at the land to which they were going.

> **Discourses and conversations** [6:22–71]. The most customary forms by which John narrates the life of Jesus are discourse and conversation or dialogue, and both of these are prominent in this unit. After a travelogue link (vv. 22–24), the miracle of the feeding of the five thousand is connected to Jesus' discourse on being the bread of life (vv. 25–51a). Additionally, Jesus' statement about giving his flesh to eat (v. 51b) becomes one of Jesus' misunderstood statements (v. 52) that he needs to explain (vv. 53–59). We have a variation on that pattern when the disciples complain that what Jesus has just said is "a hard saying" (v. 60), requiring Jesus to do more explaining (vv. 61–65). This high-intensity unit ends with a brief narrative about a defection of disciples (vv. 66–67), countered by Peter's great affirmation of loyalty to Jesus (vv. 68–69), to which Jesus replies with an observation about the fewness of true disciples (vv. 70–71).

²²On the next day the crowd that remained on the other side of the sea saw that there had been only one boat there, and that Jesus had not entered the boat with his disciples, but that his disciples had gone away alone. ²³Other boats from Tiberias came near the place where they had eaten the bread after the Lord had given thanks. ²⁴So when the crowd saw that Jesus was not there, nor his disciples, they themselves got into the boats and went to Capernaum, seeking Jesus.

---

¹ A *denarius* was a day's wage for a laborer ² Greek *twenty-five or thirty stadia*; a *stadion* was about 607 feet or 185 meters ª For 6:1-13 see parallels Matt. 14:13-21; Mark 6:32-44; Luke 9:10-17 ᵇ For 6:15-21 see parallels Matt. 14:22-33; Mark 6:45-52

²⁵When they found him on the other side of the sea, they said to him, "Rabbi, when did you come here?" ²⁶Jesus answered them, "Truly, truly, I say to you, you are seeking me, not because you saw signs, but because you ate your fill of the loaves. ²⁷Do not labor for the food that perishes, but for the food that endures to eternal life, which the Son of Man will give to you. For on him God the Father has set his seal." ²⁸Then they said to him, "What must we do, to be doing the works of God?" ²⁹Jesus answered them, "This is the work of God, that you believe in him whom he has sent." ³⁰So they said to him, "Then what sign do you do, that we may see and believe you? What work do you perform? ³¹Our fathers ate the manna in the wilderness; as it is written, ᵃ'He gave them bread from heaven to eat.'" ³²Jesus then said to them, "Truly, truly, I say to you, it was not Moses who gave you the bread from heaven, but my Father gives you the true bread from heaven. ³³For the bread of God is he who comes down from heaven and gives life to the world." ³⁴They said to him, "Sir, give us this bread always."

³⁵Jesus said to them, "I am the bread of life; whoever comes to me shall not hunger, and whoever believes in me shall never thirst. ³⁶But I said to you that you have seen me and yet do not believe. ³⁷All that the Father gives me will come to me, and whoever comes to me I will never cast out. ³⁸For I have come down from heaven, not to do my own will but the will of him who sent me. ³⁹And this is the will of him who sent me, that I should lose nothing of all that he has given me, but raise it up on the last day. ⁴⁰For this is the will of my Father, that everyone who looks on the Son and believes in him should have eternal life, and I will raise him up on the last day."

⁴¹So the Jews grumbled about him, because he said, "I am the bread that came down from heaven." ⁴²They said, "Is not this Jesus, the son of Joseph, whose father and mother we know? How does he now say, 'I have come down from heaven'?" ⁴³Jesus answered them, "Do not grumble among yourselves. ⁴⁴No one can come to me unless the Father who sent me draws him. And I will raise him up on the last day. ⁴⁵It is written in the Prophets, ᵇ'And they will all be taught by God.' Everyone who has heard and learned from the Father comes to me— ⁴⁶not that anyone has seen the Father except he who is from God; he has seen the Father. ⁴⁷Truly, truly, I say to you, whoever believes has eternal life. ⁴⁸I am the bread of life. ⁴⁹Your fathers ate the manna in the wilderness, and they died. ⁵⁰This is the bread that comes down from heaven, so that one may eat of it and not die. ⁵¹I am the living bread that came down from heaven. If anyone eats of this bread, he will live forever. And the bread that I will give for the life of the world is my flesh."

⁵²The Jews then disputed among themselves, saying, "How can this man give us his flesh to eat?" ⁵³So Jesus said to them, "Truly, truly, I say to you, unless you eat the flesh of the Son of Man and drink his blood, you have no life in you. ⁵⁴Whoever feeds on my flesh and drinks my blood has eternal life, and I will raise him up on the last day. ⁵⁵For my flesh is true food, and my blood is true drink. ⁵⁶Whoever feeds on my flesh and drinks my blood abides in me, and I in him. ⁵⁷As the living Father sent me, and I live because of the Father, so whoever feeds on me, he also will live because of me. ⁵⁸This is the bread that came down from heaven, not like the bread¹ the fathers ate and died. Whoever feeds on this bread will live forever." ⁵⁹Jesus² said these things in the synagogue, as he taught at Capernaum.

⁶⁰When many of his disciples heard it, they said, "This is a hard saying; who can listen to it?" ⁶¹But Jesus, knowing in himself that his disciples were grumbling about this, said to them, "Do you take offense at this? ⁶²Then what if you were to see the Son

---

¹ Greek lacks *the bread* ² Greek *He* ᵃ Neh. 9:15 ᵇ Isa. 54:13

of Man ascending to where he was before? ⁶³It is the Spirit who gives life; the flesh is no help at all. The words that I have spoken to you are spirit and life. ⁶⁴But there are some of you who do not believe." (For Jesus knew from the beginning who those were who did not believe, and who it was who would betray him.) ⁶⁵And he said, "This is why I told you that no one can come to me unless it is granted him by the Father."

⁶⁶After this many of his disciples turned back and no longer walked with him. ⁶⁷So Jesus said to the Twelve, "Do you want to go away as well?" ⁶⁸Simon Peter answered him, "Lord, to whom shall we go? You have the words of eternal life, ⁶⁹and we have believed, and have come to know, that you are the Holy One of God." ⁷⁰Jesus answered them, "Did I not choose you, the Twelve? And yet one of you is a devil." ⁷¹He spoke of Judas the son of Simon Iscariot, for he, one of the Twelve, was going to betray him.

Jesus attends the Feast of Booths [chapter 7]. Although John's Gospel is rightly called the cosmic Gospel, portraying Christ as the Savior of the whole world and employing universal symbols that speak to all people everywhere, paradoxically it is also a Jewish Gospel that gives prominence to the temple and Jewish rituals. This entire chapter takes place at the annual Feast of Booths and the temple in Jerusalem. The unifying motif in the chapter is the controversy that arose regarding who Jesus is. As the chapter unfolds, we overhear various theories among the populace regarding who Jesus is. The narrative unfolds as follows: after initially declining to accompany his family to Jerusalem (vv. 1–9), Jesus does go to Jerusalem without public fanfare (vv. 10–13); amid controversy, Jesus teaches and enters into debate in public in the temple area (vv. 14–36); a brief glimpse of Jesus' self-designation as the one from whom believers can drink to receive spiritual life (vv. 37–39) is followed by a recording of the divided opinion that such claims made in the populace (vv. 40–44); the religious leaders attempt to arrest Jesus (vv. 45–52). In the ongoing flow of the passage, Jesus' great declaration that all who are thirsty should drink of him (vv. 37–38) leaps out as the climax.

7 After this Jesus went about in Galilee. He would not go about in Judea, because the Jews¹ were seeking to kill him. ²Now the Jews' Feast of Booths was at hand. ³So his brothers² said to him, "Leave here and go to Judea, that your disciples also may see the works you are doing. ⁴For no one works in secret if he seeks to be known openly. If you do these things, show yourself to the world." ⁵For not even his brothers believed in him. ⁶Jesus said to them, "My time has not yet come, but your time is always here. ⁷The world cannot hate you, but it hates me because I testify about it that its works are evil. ⁸You go up to the feast. I am not³ going up to this feast, for my time has not yet fully come." ⁹After saying this, he remained in Galilee.

¹⁰But after his brothers had gone up to the feast, then he also went up, not publicly but in private. ¹¹The Jews were looking for him at the feast, and saying, "Where is he?" ¹²And there was much muttering about him among the people. While some said, "He is a good man," others said, "No, he is leading the people astray." ¹³Yet for fear of the Jews no one spoke openly of him.

¹⁴About the middle of the feast Jesus went up into the temple and began teaching. ¹⁵The Jews therefore marveled, saying, "How is it that this man has learning,⁴ when he has never studied?" ¹⁶So Jesus answered them, "My teaching is not mine, but his who sent me. ¹⁷If anyone's will is to do God's⁵ will, he will know whether the teaching

---

¹ Or *Judeans* ² Or *brothers and sisters*; also verses 5, 10 ³ Some manuscripts add *yet* ⁴ Or *this man knows his letters* ⁵ Greek *his*

is from God or whether I am speaking on my own authority. [18]The one who speaks on his own authority seeks his own glory; but the one who seeks the glory of him who sent him is true, and in him there is no falsehood. [19]Has not Moses given you the law? Yet none of you keeps the law. Why do you seek to kill me?" [20]The crowd answered, "You have a demon! Who is seeking to kill you?" [21]Jesus answered them, "I did one work, and you all marvel at it. [22]Moses gave you circumcision (not that it is from Moses, but from the fathers), and you circumcise a man on the Sabbath. [23]If on the Sabbath a man receives circumcision, so that the law of Moses may not be broken, are you angry with me because on the Sabbath I made a man's whole body well? [24]Do not judge by appearances, but judge with right judgment."

[25]Some of the people of Jerusalem therefore said, "Is not this the man whom they seek to kill? [26]And here he is, speaking openly, and they say nothing to him! Can it be that the authorities really know that this is the Christ? [27]But we know where this man comes from, and when the Christ appears, no one will know where he comes from." [28]So Jesus proclaimed, as he taught in the temple, "You know me, and you know where I come from? But I have not come of my own accord. He who sent me is true, and him you do not know. [29]I know him, for I come from him, and he sent me." [30]So they were seeking to arrest him, but no one laid a hand on him, because his hour had not yet come. [31]Yet many of the people believed in him. They said, "When the Christ appears, will he do more signs than this man has done?"

[32]The Pharisees heard the crowd muttering these things about him, and the chief priests and Pharisees sent officers to arrest him. [33]Jesus then said, "I will be with you a little longer, and then I am going to him who sent me. [34]You will seek me and you will not find me. Where I am you cannot come." [35]The Jews said to one another, "Where does this man intend to go that we will not find him? Does he intend to go to the Dispersion among the Greeks and teach the Greeks? [36]What does he mean by saying, 'You will seek me and you will not find me,' and, 'Where I am you cannot come'?"

[37]On the last day of the feast, the great day, Jesus stood up and cried out, "If anyone thirsts, let him come to me and drink. [38]Whoever believes in me, as[1] the Scripture has said, 'Out of his heart will flow rivers of living water.'" [39]Now this he said about the Spirit, whom those who believed in him were to receive, for as yet the Spirit had not been given, because Jesus was not yet glorified.

[40]When they heard these words, some of the people said, "This really is the Prophet." [41]Others said, "This is the Christ." But some said, "Is the Christ to come from Galilee? [42]Has not the Scripture said that the Christ comes from the offspring of David, and comes from Bethlehem, the village where David was?" [43]So there was a division among the people over him. [44]Some of them wanted to arrest him, but no one laid hands on him.

[45]The officers then came to the chief priests and Pharisees, who said to them, "Why did you not bring him?" [46]The officers answered, "No one ever spoke like this man!" [47]The Pharisees answered them, "Have you also been deceived? [48]Have any of the authorities or the Pharisees believed in him? [49]But this crowd that does not know the law is accursed." [50]Nicodemus, who had gone to him before, and who was one of them, said to them, [51]"Does our law judge a man without first giving him a hearing and learning what he does?" [52]They replied, "Are you from Galilee too? Search and see that no prophet arises from Galilee."

---

[1] Or let him come to me, and let him who believes in me drink. As

Conflict stories [chapter 8]. Narrative and conversation continue to intermingle, and together they tell a story of conflict between Jesus and Jewish leaders, adding up to a prolonged conflict story in this chapter. The sequence is as follows: Jesus cleverly defeats his enemies when he defends the woman caught in adultery (vv. 1–11); an altercation arises about the legitimacy of Jesus' claims about himself (vv. 12–20); Jesus warns against unbelief and speaks of himself as the Father's appointed teacher (vv. 21–30); an acrimonious controversy between Jesus and the religious leaders focuses in various ways on the OT figure of Abraham (vv. 31–59). The material in the chapter is varied, and there is no single line of thought or action. Overall, though, the subject is the person and work of Jesus. We can comb the passage looking for the following motifs: (1) Jesus as a controversialist who stands up to those who are hostile to him and the truth; (2) evidences that Jesus is divine; (3) the story line of hostility between the religious leaders and Jesus; (4) teaching from Jesus about sin and its forgiveness; (5) the authority of Jesus.

[THE EARLIEST MANUSCRIPTS DO NOT INCLUDE 7:53-8:11.][1]

8 [53][[They went each to his own house, [1]but Jesus went to the Mount of Olives. [2]Early in the morning he came again to the temple. All the people came to him, and he sat down and taught them. [3]The scribes and the Pharisees brought a woman who had been caught in adultery, and placing her in the midst [4]they said to him, "Teacher, this woman has been caught in the act of adultery. [5]Now in the Law Moses commanded us to stone such women. So what do you say?" [6]This they said to test him, that they might have some charge to bring against him. Jesus bent down and wrote with his finger on the ground. [7]And as they continued to ask him, he stood up and said to them, "Let him who is without sin among you be the first to throw a stone at her." [8]And once more he bent down and wrote on the ground. [9]But when they heard it, they went away one by one, beginning with the older ones, and Jesus was left alone with the woman standing before him. [10]Jesus stood up and said to her, "Woman, where are they? Has no one condemned you?" [11]She said, "No one, Lord." And Jesus said, "Neither do I condemn you; go, and from now on sin no more."]]

[12]Again Jesus spoke to them, saying, "I am the light of the world. Whoever follows me will not walk in darkness, but will have the light of life." [13]So the Pharisees said to him, "You are bearing witness about yourself; your testimony is not true." [14]Jesus answered, "Even if I do bear witness about myself, my testimony is true, for I know where I came from and where I am going, but you do not know where I come from or where I am going. [15]You judge according to the flesh; I judge no one. [16]Yet even if I do judge, my judgment is true, for it is not I alone who judge, but I and the Father[2] who sent me. [17]In your Law it is written that the testimony of two people is true. [18]I am the one who bears witness about myself, and the Father who sent me bears witness about me." [19]They said to him therefore, "Where is your Father?" Jesus answered, "You know neither me nor my Father. If you knew me, you would know my Father also." [20]These words he spoke in the treasury, as he taught in the temple; but no one arrested him, because his hour had not yet come.

[21]So he said to them again, "I am going away, and you will seek me, and you will die in your sin. Where I am going, you cannot come." [22]So the Jews said, "Will he kill him-

---

[1] Some manuscripts do not include 7:53–8:11; others add the passage here or after 7:36 or after 21:25 or after Luke 21:38, with variations in the text
[2] Some manuscripts *he*

self, since he says, 'Where I am going, you cannot come'?" ²³He said to them, "You are from below; I am from above. You are of this world; I am not of this world. ²⁴I told you that you would die in your sins, for unless you believe that I am he you will die in your sins." ²⁵So they said to him, "Who are you?" Jesus said to them, "Just what I have been telling you from the beginning. ²⁶I have much to say about you and much to judge, but he who sent me is true, and I declare to the world what I have heard from him." ²⁷They did not understand that he had been speaking to them about the Father. ²⁸So Jesus said to them, "When you have lifted up the Son of Man, then you will know that I am he, and that I do nothing on my own authority, but speak just as the Father taught me. ²⁹And he who sent me is with me. He has not left me alone, for I always do the things that are pleasing to him." ³⁰As he was saying these things, many believed in him.

³¹So Jesus said to the Jews who had believed in him, "If you abide in my word, you are truly my disciples, ³²and you will know the truth, and the truth will set you free." ³³They answered him, "We are offspring of Abraham and have never been enslaved to anyone. How is it that you say, 'You will become free'?"

³⁴Jesus answered them, "Truly, truly, I say to you, everyone who commits sin is a slave¹ to sin. ³⁵The slave does not remain in the house forever; the son remains forever. ³⁶So if the Son sets you free, you will be free indeed. ³⁷I know that you are offspring of Abraham; yet you seek to kill me because my word finds no place in you. ³⁸I speak of what I have seen with my Father, and you do what you have heard from your father."

³⁹They answered him, "Abraham is our father." Jesus said to them, "If you were Abraham's children, you would be doing the works Abraham did, ⁴⁰but now you seek to kill me, a man who has told you the truth that I heard from God. This is not what Abraham did. ⁴¹You are doing the works your father did." They said to him, "We were not born of sexual immorality. We have one Father—even God." ⁴²Jesus said to them, "If God were your Father, you would love me, for I came from God and I am here. I came not of my own accord, but he sent me. ⁴³Why do you not understand what I say? It is because you cannot bear to hear my word. ⁴⁴You are of your father the devil, and your will is to do your father's desires. He was a murderer from the beginning, and has nothing to do with the truth, because there is no truth in him. When he lies, he speaks out of his own character, for he is a liar and the father of lies. ⁴⁵But because I tell the truth, you do not believe me. ⁴⁶Which one of you convicts me of sin? If I tell the truth, why do you not believe me? ⁴⁷Whoever is of God hears the words of God. The reason why you do not hear them is that you are not of God."

⁴⁸The Jews answered him, "Are we not right in saying that you are a Samaritan and have a demon?" ⁴⁹Jesus answered, "I do not have a demon, but I honor my Father, and you dishonor me. ⁵⁰Yet I do not seek my own glory; there is One who seeks it, and he is the judge. ⁵¹Truly, truly, I say to you, if anyone keeps my word, he will never see death." ⁵²The Jews said to him, "Now we know that you have a demon! Abraham died, as did the prophets, yet you say, 'If anyone keeps my word, he will never taste death.' ⁵³Are you greater than our father Abraham, who died? And the prophets died! Who do you make yourself out to be?" ⁵⁴Jesus answered, "If I glorify myself, my glory is nothing. It is my Father who glorifies me, of whom you say, 'He is our God.'² ⁵⁵But you have not known him. I know him. If I were to say that I do not know him, I would be a liar like you, but I do know him and I keep his word. ⁵⁶Your father Abraham rejoiced that he would see my day. He saw it and was glad." ⁵⁷So the Jews said to him,

¹ Greek bondservant; also verse 35 ² Some manuscripts your God

"You are not yet fifty years old, and have you seen Abraham?"[1] [58]Jesus said to them, "Truly, truly, I say to you, before Abraham was, I am." [59]So they picked up stones to throw at him, but Jesus hid himself and went out of the temple.

Jesus heals the man born blind [chapter 9]. It may seem incongruous to call this miracle story a comic masterpiece, but the Jewish leaders make it such with their foolish attempts to evade the fact that Jesus has performed a miracle. The story is a combined miracle story (the sixth great sign in John's Gospel) and controversy story. From start to finish, the story is mainly conducted by means of snatches of dialogue that we overhear. The portrayal of the Jewish leaders is a satiric portrait in which the leaders exhibit the folly of disbelieving in Jesus' miraculous power and denying the fact that the blind man now sees. At the end of the story, pathos replaces comedy when the Pharisees expel the healed man from the community (v. 34), and Jesus steps forward as the consoler of the outcast (vv. 35–38).

9 As he passed by, he saw a man blind from birth. [2]And his disciples asked him, "Rabbi, who sinned, this man or his parents, that he was born blind?" [3]Jesus answered, "It was not that this man sinned, or his parents, but that the works of God might be displayed in him. [4]We must work the works of him who sent me while it is day; night is coming, when no one can work. [5]As long as I am in the world, I am the light of the world." [6]Having said these things, he spat on the ground and made mud with the saliva. Then he anointed the man's eyes with the mud [7]and said to him, "Go, wash in the pool of Siloam" (which means Sent). So he went and washed and came back seeing.

[8]The neighbors and those who had seen him before as a beggar were saying, "Is this not the man who used to sit and beg?" [9]Some said, "It is he." Others said, "No, but he is like him." He kept saying, "I am the man." [10]So they said to him, "Then how were your eyes opened?" [11]He answered, "The man called Jesus made mud and anointed my eyes and said to me, 'Go to Siloam and wash.' So I went and washed and received my sight." [12]They said to him, "Where is he?" He said, "I do not know."

[13]They brought to the Pharisees the man who had formerly been blind. [14]Now it was a Sabbath day when Jesus made the mud and opened his eyes. [15]So the Pharisees again asked him how he had received his sight. And he said to them, "He put mud on my eyes, and I washed, and I see." [16]Some of the Pharisees said, "This man is not from God, for he does not keep the Sabbath." But others said, "How can a man who is a sinner do such signs?" And there was a division among them. [17]So they said again to the blind man, "What do you say about him, since he has opened your eyes?" He said, "He is a prophet."

[18]The Jews did not believe that he had been blind and had received his sight, until they called the parents of the man who had received his sight [19]and asked them, "Is this your son, who you say was born blind? How then does he now see?" [20]His parents answered, "We know that this is our son and that he was born blind. [21]But how he now sees we do not know, nor do we know who opened his eyes. Ask him; he is of age. He will speak for himself." [22](His parents said these things because they feared the Jews, for the Jews had already agreed that if anyone should confess Jesus[2] to be Christ, he was to be put out of the synagogue.) [23]Therefore his parents said, "He is of age; ask him."

[1] Some manuscripts *has Abraham seen you?* [2] Greek *him*

²⁴So for the second time they called the man who had been blind and said to him, "Give glory to God. We know that this man is a sinner." ²⁵He answered, "Whether he is a sinner I do not know. One thing I do know, that though I was blind, now I see." ²⁶They said to him, "What did he do to you? How did he open your eyes?" ²⁷He answered them, "I have told you already, and you would not listen. Why do you want to hear it again? Do you also want to become his disciples?" ²⁸And they reviled him, saying, "You are his disciple, but we are disciples of Moses. ²⁹We know that God has spoken to Moses, but as for this man, we do not know where he comes from." ³⁰The man answered, "Why, this is an amazing thing! You do not know where he comes from, and yet he opened my eyes. ³¹We know that God does not listen to sinners, but if anyone is a worshiper of God and does his will, God listens to him. ³²Never since the world began has it been heard that anyone opened the eyes of a man born blind. ³³If this man were not from God, he could do nothing." ³⁴They answered him, "You were born in utter sin, and would you teach us?" And they cast him out.

³⁵Jesus heard that they had cast him out, and having found him he said, "Do you believe in the Son of Man?"¹ ³⁶He answered, "And who is he, sir, that I may believe in him?" ³⁷Jesus said to him, "You have seen him, and it is he who is speaking to you." ³⁸He said, "Lord, I believe," and he worshiped him. ³⁹Jesus said, "For judgment I came into this world, that those who do not see may see, and those who see may become blind." ⁴⁰Some of the Pharisees near him heard these things, and said to him, "Are we also blind?" ⁴¹Jesus said to them, "If you were blind, you would have no guilt;² but now that you say, 'We see,' your guilt remains.

The good shepherd discourse [10:1–18]. This famous discourse is another speech of self-characterization from the mouth of Jesus. After the Pharisees have shown themselves to be ignominious religious leaders in the episode of the blind man who was healed, Jesus now portrays himself as the good shepherd and satirizes bad shepherds. The entire discourse draws upon an ancient literary genre known as pastoral literature—literature in which the characters are shepherds and the action consists of things that shepherds do. Often the pastoral mode is a metaphoric disguise for real people, and that is what we find here. When Jesus describes the good shepherd, he is speaking autobiographically, even to the point of predicting his own death (v. 11). Equally obviously, the bad shepherds are a picture of the religious leaders. The theological teaching of the passage lies in the statements that Jesus makes about laying down his life for his sheep of his own accord and having power to take up his life again (v. 18).

10 "Truly, truly, I say to you, he who does not enter the sheepfold by the door but climbs in by another way, that man is a thief and a robber. ²But he who enters by the door is the shepherd of the sheep. ³To him the gatekeeper opens. The sheep hear his voice, and he calls his own sheep by name and leads them out. ⁴When he has brought out all his own, he goes before them, and the sheep follow him, for they know his voice. ⁵A stranger they will not follow, but they will flee from him, for they do not know the voice of strangers." ⁶This figure of speech Jesus used with them, but they did not understand what he was saying to them.

⁷So Jesus again said to them, "Truly, truly, I say to you, I am the door of the sheep. ⁸All who came before me are thieves and robbers, but the sheep did not listen to them. ⁹I am the door. If anyone enters by me, he will be saved and will go in and out

¹ Some manuscripts *the Son of God* ² Greek *you would not have sin*

and find pasture. [10]The thief comes only to steal and kill and destroy. I came that they may have life and have it abundantly. [11]I am the good shepherd. The good shepherd lays down his life for the sheep. [12]He who is a hired hand and not a shepherd, who does not own the sheep, sees the wolf coming and leaves the sheep and flees, and the wolf snatches them and scatters them. [13]He flees because he is a hired hand and cares nothing for the sheep. [14]I am the good shepherd. I know my own and my own know me, [15]just as the Father knows me and I know the Father; and I lay down my life for the sheep. [16]And I have other sheep that are not of this fold. I must bring them also, and they will listen to my voice. So there will be one flock, one shepherd. [17]For this reason the Father loves me, because I lay down my life that I may take it up again. [18]No one takes it from me, but I lay it down of my own accord. I have authority to lay it down, and I have authority to take it up again. This charge I have received from my Father."

> **Jesus generates controversy** [10:19–42]. The effect of this unit is to dramatize the degree of controversy that Jesus generated during his public ministry, especially as a result of his teaching. We can analyze this passage looking for three things: (1) the obtuseness of those who refused to believe in Jesus or even view him favorably; (2) data about the faith of some of those who heard Jesus' claims; (3) continued statements from Jesus about who he is.

[19]There was again a division among the Jews because of these words. [20]Many of them said, "He has a demon, and is insane; why listen to him?" [21]Others said, "These are not the words of one who is oppressed by a demon. Can a demon open the eyes of the blind?"

[22]At that time the Feast of Dedication took place at Jerusalem. It was winter, [23]and Jesus was walking in the temple, in the colonnade of Solomon. [24]So the Jews gathered around him and said to him, "How long will you keep us in suspense? If you are the Christ, tell us plainly." [25]Jesus answered them, "I told you, and you do not believe. The works that I do in my Father's name bear witness about me, [26]but you do not believe because you are not part of my flock. [27]My sheep hear my voice, and I know them, and they follow me. [28]I give them eternal life, and they will never perish, and no one will snatch them out of my hand. [29]My Father, who has given them to me,[1] is greater than all, and no one is able to snatch them out of the Father's hand. [30]I and the Father are one."

[31]The Jews picked up stones again to stone him. [32]Jesus answered them, "I have shown you many good works from the Father; for which of them are you going to stone me?" [33]The Jews answered him, "It is not for a good work that we are going to stone you but for blasphemy, because you, being a man, make yourself God." [34]Jesus answered them, "Is it not written in your Law, [a]'I said, you are gods'? [35]If he called them gods to whom the word of God came—and Scripture cannot be broken— [36]do you say of him whom the Father consecrated and sent into the world, 'You are blaspheming,' because I said, 'I am the Son of God'? [37]If I am not doing the works of my Father, then do not believe me; [38]but if I do them, even though you do not believe me, believe the works, that you may know and understand that the Father is in me and I am in the Father." [39]Again they sought to arrest him, but he escaped from their hands.

---

[1] Some manuscripts *What my Father has given to me* [a] Ps. 82:6

⁴⁰He went away again across the Jordan to the place where John had been baptizing at first, and there he remained. ⁴¹And many came to him. And they said, "John did no sign, but everything that John said about this man was true." ⁴²And many believed in him there.

> **The raising of Lazarus** [11:1–54]. Jesus' raising of Lazarus belongs to a biblical genre known as the death-rebirth story, and it is the last of the seven great signs that punctuate John's Gospel. The famous story unfolds by the following sequence: prologue in which Jesus is told about Lazarus' illness (vv. 1–14); Jesus delays (generating narrative suspense about why he "fails" to respond to a dire need) and then journeys to Bethany, accompanied by mysterious sayings about the situation (vv. 5–16); Jesus' discourse with Martha in which he leads her to recognize the truth about Jesus' being the resurrection and the life (vv. 17–27); Jesus shares Mary's grief about the death of Lazarus (vv. 28–37); Jesus raises Lazarus from death to life by the power of his word and restores Lazarus to his family (vv. 38–44); the religious leaders react with extreme hostility to the raising of Lazarus (vv. 45–54). Jesus is the center of the action throughout the narrative, and we do well to pay close attention to the portrait of Jesus that emerges from this story. We see Jesus' humanity in his loving compassion for the dying and grieving and his divinity highlighted in his miraculous power over death.

11 Now a certain man was ill, Lazarus of Bethany, the village of Mary and her sister Martha. ²It was Mary who anointed the Lord with ointment and wiped his feet with her hair, whose brother Lazarus was ill. ³So the sisters sent to him, saying, "Lord, he whom you love is ill." ⁴But when Jesus heard it he said, "This illness does not lead to death. It is for the glory of God, so that the Son of God may be glorified through it."

⁵Now Jesus loved Martha and her sister and Lazarus. ⁶So, when he heard that Lazarus¹ was ill, he stayed two days longer in the place where he was. ⁷Then after this he said to the disciples, "Let us go to Judea again." ⁸The disciples said to him, "Rabbi, the Jews were just now seeking to stone you, and are you going there again?" ⁹Jesus answered, "Are there not twelve hours in the day? If anyone walks in the day, he does not stumble, because he sees the light of this world. ¹⁰But if anyone walks in the night, he stumbles, because the light is not in him." ¹¹After saying these things, he said to them, "Our friend Lazarus has fallen asleep, but I go to awaken him." ¹²The disciples said to him, "Lord, if he has fallen asleep, he will recover." ¹³Now Jesus had spoken of his death, but they thought that he meant taking rest in sleep. ¹⁴Then Jesus told them plainly, "Lazarus has died, ¹⁵and for your sake I am glad that I was not there, so that you may believe. But let us go to him." ¹⁶So Thomas, called the Twin,² said to his fellow disciples, "Let us also go, that we may die with him."

¹⁷Now when Jesus came, he found that Lazarus had already been in the tomb four days. ¹⁸Bethany was near Jerusalem, about two miles³ off, ¹⁹and many of the Jews had come to Martha and Mary to console them concerning their brother. ²⁰So when Martha heard that Jesus was coming, she went and met him, but Mary remained seated in the house. ²¹Martha said to Jesus, "Lord, if you had been here, my brother would not have died. ²²But even now I know that whatever you ask from God, God will give you." ²³Jesus said to her, "Your brother will rise again." ²⁴Martha said to him, "I know that he will rise again in the resurrection on the last day." ²⁵Jesus said to her,

¹ Greek *he*; also verse 17 ² Greek *Didymus* ³ Greek *fifteen stadia*; a *stadion* was about 607 feet or 185 meters

"I am the resurrection and the life.[1] Whoever believes in me, though he die, yet shall he live, [26]and everyone who lives and believes in me shall never die. Do you believe this?" [27]She said to him, "Yes, Lord; I believe that you are the Christ, the Son of God, who is coming into the world."

[28]When she had said this, she went and called her sister Mary, saying in private, "The Teacher is here and is calling for you." [29]And when she heard it, she rose quickly and went to him. [30]Now Jesus had not yet come into the village, but was still in the place where Martha had met him. [31]When the Jews who were with her in the house, consoling her, saw Mary rise quickly and go out, they followed her, supposing that she was going to the tomb to weep there. [32]Now when Mary came to where Jesus was and saw him, she fell at his feet, saying to him, "Lord, if you had been here, my brother would not have died." [33]When Jesus saw her weeping, and the Jews who had come with her also weeping, he was deeply moved in his spirit and greatly troubled. [34]And he said, "Where have you laid him?" They said to him, "Lord, come and see." [35]Jesus wept. [36]So the Jews said, "See how he loved him!" [37]But some of them said, "Could not he who opened the eyes of the blind man also have kept this man from dying?"

[38]Then Jesus, deeply moved again, came to the tomb. It was a cave, and a stone lay against it. [39]Jesus said, "Take away the stone." Martha, the sister of the dead man, said to him, "Lord, by this time there will be an odor, for he has been dead four days." [40]Jesus said to her, "Did I not tell you that if you believed you would see the glory of God?" [41]So they took away the stone. And Jesus lifted up his eyes and said, "Father, I thank you that you have heard me. [42]I knew that you always hear me, but I said this on account of the people standing around, that they may believe that you sent me." [43]When he had said these things, he cried out with a loud voice, "Lazarus, come out." [44]The man who had died came out, his hands and feet bound with linen strips, and his face wrapped with a cloth. Jesus said to them, "Unbind him, and let him go."

[45]Many of the Jews therefore, who had come with Mary and had seen what he did, believed in him, [46]but some of them went to the Pharisees and told them what Jesus had done. [47]So the chief priests and the Pharisees gathered the Council and said, "What are we to do? For this man performs many signs. [48]If we let him go on like this, everyone will believe in him, and the Romans will come and take away both our place and our nation." [49]But one of them, Caiaphas, who was high priest that year, said to them, "You know nothing at all. [50]Nor do you understand that it is better for you that one man should die for the people, not that the whole nation should perish." [51]He did not say this of his own accord, but being high priest that year he prophesied that Jesus would die for the nation, [52]and not for the nation only, but also to gather into one the children of God who are scattered abroad. [53]So from that day on they made plans to put him to death.

[54]Jesus therefore no longer walked openly among the Jews, but went from there to the region near the wilderness, to a town called Ephraim, and there he stayed with the disciples.

Jesus as center of public attention [11:55–12:19]. This unit serves as the transition between the raising of Lazarus and events in Jerusalem during the final week of Jesus' life before his death and resurrection. Two main events are narrated—the anointing of Jesus by Mary and the Triumphal Entry. Intermingled with these two events is the larger story of the responses of the public and various individuals to Jesus. The groups

---

[1] Some manuscripts omit *and the life*

of responders are as follows: the religious leaders, especially the chief priests; the curious public at large; the disciples, with Judas Iscariot as the aberration among them; the family members Mary, Martha, and Lazarus. These, in turn, fit into the overall story line of the Gospel of John—the contrast between belief and unbelief. Because the action narrated in this unit occurs in the days preceding Passion Week, we can also scrutinize the passage for premonitions of Jesus' coming crucifixion and his ultimate royal triumph.

[55] Now the Passover of the Jews was at hand, and many went up from the country to Jerusalem before the Passover to purify themselves. [56] They were looking for[1] Jesus and saying to one another as they stood in the temple, "What do you think? That he will not come to the feast at all?" [57] Now the chief priests and the Pharisees had given orders that if anyone knew where he was, he should let them know, so that they might arrest him.

12 Six days before the Passover, Jesus therefore came to Bethany, where Lazarus was, whom Jesus had raised from the dead. [2] So they gave a dinner for him there. Martha served, and Lazarus was one of those reclining with him at table. [3] Mary therefore took a pound[2] of expensive ointment made from pure nard, and anointed the feet of Jesus and wiped his feet with her hair. The house was filled with the fragrance of the perfume. [4] But Judas Iscariot, one of his disciples (he who was about to betray him), said, [5] "Why was this ointment not sold for three hundred denarii[3] and given to the poor?" [6] He said this, not because he cared about the poor, but because he was a thief, and having charge of the moneybag he used to help himself to what was put into it. [7] Jesus said, "Leave her alone, so that she may keep it[4] for the day of my burial. [8] For the poor you always have with you, but you do not always have me."

[9] When the large crowd of the Jews learned that Jesus[5] was there, they came, not only on account of him but also to see Lazarus, whom he had raised from the dead. [10] So the chief priests made plans to put Lazarus to death as well, [11] because on account of him many of the Jews were going away and believing in Jesus.

[12] The next day [a] the large crowd that had come to the feast heard that Jesus was coming to Jerusalem. [13] So they took branches of palm trees and went out to meet him, crying out, "Hosanna! Blessed is he who comes in the name of the Lord, even the King of Israel!" [14] And Jesus found a young donkey and sat on it, just as it is written,

[15] [b] "Fear not, daughter of Zion;
    behold, your king is coming,
        sitting on a donkey's colt!"

[16] His disciples did not understand these things at first, but when Jesus was glorified, then they remembered that these things had been written about him and had been done to him. [17] The crowd that had been with him when he called Lazarus out of the tomb and raised him from the dead continued to bear witness. [18] The reason why the crowd went to meet him was that they heard he had done this sign. [19] So the Pharisees said to one another, "You see that you are gaining nothing. Look, the world has gone after him."

---

[1] Greek were seeking for [2] Greek litra; a litra (or Roman pound) was equal to about 11 1/2 ounces or 327 grams [3] A denarius was a day's wage for a laborer [4] Or Leave her alone; she intended to keep it [5] Greek he [a] For 12:12-15 see parallels Matt. 21:4-9; Mark 11:7-10; Luke 19:35-38 [b] Zech. 9:9

Jesus' final public statements [12:20–50]. This unit, like the preceding one, is a kaleidoscope of individual details—impressionistic snapshots of the busy events of Jesus' last days. Intermingled with narrative material (vv. 20–22 and 36–43) we have Jesus' last public claims about himself (vv. 23–36 and 44–50). These speeches constitute christological teaching, and we should analyze them for what they say about Christ and his atoning work. Specimen examples are Jesus' statements that by his death he would draw all people to himself (vv. 32–33) and that he came into the world to save it (v. 47). Intermingled with Jesus' claims about himself are statements that relate to the ever-present conflict between belief and unbelief in the Gospel of John.

[20] Now among those who went up to worship at the feast were some Greeks. [21] So these came to Philip, who was from Bethsaida in Galilee, and asked him, "Sir, we wish to see Jesus." [22] Philip went and told Andrew; Andrew and Philip went and told Jesus. [23] And Jesus answered them, "The hour has come for the Son of Man to be glorified. [24] Truly, truly, I say to you, unless a grain of wheat falls into the earth and dies, it remains alone; but if it dies, it bears much fruit. [25] Whoever loves his life loses it, and whoever hates his life in this world will keep it for eternal life. [26] If anyone serves me, he must follow me; and where I am, there will my servant be also. If anyone serves me, the Father will honor him.

[27] "Now is my soul troubled. And what shall I say? 'Father, save me from this hour'? But for this purpose I have come to this hour. [28] Father, glorify your name." Then a voice came from heaven: "I have glorified it, and I will glorify it again." [29] The crowd that stood there and heard it said that it had thundered. Others said, "An angel has spoken to him." [30] Jesus answered, "This voice has come for your sake, not mine. [31] Now is the judgment of this world; now will the ruler of this world be cast out. [32] And I, when I am lifted up from the earth, will draw all people to myself." [33] He said this to show by what kind of death he was going to die. [34] So the crowd answered him, "We have heard from the Law that the Christ remains forever. How can you say that the Son of Man must be lifted up? Who is this Son of Man?" [35] So Jesus said to them, "The light is among you for a little while longer. Walk while you have the light, lest darkness overtake you. The one who walks in the darkness does not know where he is going. [36] While you have the light, believe in the light, that you may become sons of light."

When Jesus had said these things, he departed and hid himself from them. [37] Though he had done so many signs before them, they still did not believe in him, [38] so that the word spoken by the prophet Isaiah might be fulfilled:

[a]"Lord, who has believed what he heard from us,
    and to whom has the arm of the Lord been revealed?"

[39] Therefore they could not believe. For again Isaiah said,

[40] [b]"He has blinded their eyes
        and hardened their heart,
    lest they see with their eyes,
        and understand with their heart, and turn,
        and I would heal them."

[a] Isa. 53:1 [b] Isa. 6:10

⁴¹Isaiah said these things because he saw his glory and spoke of him. ⁴²Nevertheless, many even of the authorities believed in him, but for fear of the Pharisees they did not confess it, so that they would not be put out of the synagogue; ⁴³for they loved the glory that comes from man more than the glory that comes from God.

⁴⁴And Jesus cried out and said, "Whoever believes in me, believes not in me but in him who sent me. ⁴⁵And whoever sees me sees him who sent me. ⁴⁶I have come into the world as light, so that whoever believes in me may not remain in darkness. ⁴⁷If anyone hears my words and does not keep them, I do not judge him; for I did not come to judge the world but to save the world. ⁴⁸The one who rejects me and does not receive my words has a judge; the word that I have spoken will judge him on the last day. ⁴⁹For I have not spoken on my own authority, but the Father who sent me has himself given me a commandment—what to say and what to speak. ⁵⁰And I know that his commandment is eternal life. What I say, therefore, I say as the Father has told me."

> **Jesus and the disciples convene in the upper room** [chapter 13]. John devotes five whole chapters to the narrative of what Jesus did and said in the upper room as he met there with his disciples for the Passover supper. Chapter 13 is largely narrative and dialogue, whereas the next four chapters record Jesus' speech and prayer in the upper room. The sequence of events is as follows: Jesus defies convention by condescending to wash the disciples' feet (vv. 1–11); Jesus then commands that what he has done is an example of servanthood that the disciples must imitate (vv. 12–17); Jesus predicts Judas' defection, and the disciples respond in various ways (vv. 18–30); Jesus predicts his imminent departure from life and accompanies it with a command that the disciples love each other (vv. 31–35); Jesus predicts Peter's denial of him (vv. 36–38). Every detail of what happened is important and memorable in the accounts of Jesus' final days, and we can accordingly extract historical facts and spiritual knowledge from the passage. The opening action of the foot washing foreshadows the even more ultimate display of Jesus' love in his sacrifice. Even though the sphere of action is here very different from that of earlier parts of the Gospel, we still find characters responding to Jesus in the contrary ways of acceptance and rejection, belief and unbelief.

13 Now before the Feast of the Passover, when Jesus knew that his hour had come to depart out of this world to the Father, having loved his own who were in the world, he loved them to the end. ²During supper, when the devil had already put it into the heart of Judas Iscariot, Simon's son, to betray him, ³Jesus, knowing that the Father had given all things into his hands, and that he had come from God and was going back to God, ⁴rose from supper. He laid aside his outer garments, and taking a towel, tied it around his waist. ⁵Then he poured water into a basin and began to wash the disciples' feet and to wipe them with the towel that was wrapped around him. ⁶He came to Simon Peter, who said to him, "Lord, do you wash my feet?" ⁷Jesus answered him, "What I am doing you do not understand now, but afterward you will understand." ⁸Peter said to him, "You shall never wash my feet." Jesus answered him, "If I do not wash you, you have no share with me." ⁹Simon Peter said to him, "Lord, not my feet only but also my hands and my head!" ¹⁰Jesus said to him, "The one who has bathed does not need to wash, except for his feet,¹ but is completely clean. And

¹ Some manuscripts omit *except for his feet*

you[1] are clean, but not every one of you." [11]For he knew who was to betray him; that was why he said, "Not all of you are clean."

[12]When he had washed their feet and put on his outer garments and resumed his place, he said to them, "Do you understand what I have done to you? [13]You call me Teacher and Lord, and you are right, for so I am. [14]If I then, your Lord and Teacher, have washed your feet, you also ought to wash one another's feet. [15]For I have given you an example, that you also should do just as I have done to you. [16]Truly, truly, I say to you, a servant[2] is not greater than his master, nor is a messenger greater than the one who sent him. [17]If you know these things, blessed are you if you do them. [18]I am not speaking of all of you; I know whom I have chosen. But the Scripture will be fulfilled,[3] [a]'He who ate my bread has lifted his heel against me.' [19]I am telling you this now, before it takes place, that when it does take place you may believe that I am he. [20]Truly, truly, I say to you, whoever receives the one I send receives me, and whoever receives me receives the one who sent me."

[21]After saying these things, Jesus was troubled in his spirit, and testified, "Truly, truly, I say to you, one of you will betray me." [22]The disciples looked at one another, uncertain of whom he spoke. [23]One of his disciples, whom Jesus loved, was reclining at table close to Jesus,[4] [24]so Simon Peter motioned to him to ask Jesus[5] of whom he was speaking. [25]So that disciple, leaning back against Jesus, said to him, "Lord, who is it?" [26]Jesus answered, "It is he to whom I will give this morsel of bread when I have dipped it." So when he had dipped the morsel, he gave it to Judas, the son of Simon Iscariot. [27]Then after he had taken the morsel, Satan entered into him. Jesus said to him, "What you are going to do, do quickly." [28]Now no one at the table knew why he said this to him. [29]Some thought that, because Judas had the moneybag, Jesus was telling him, "Buy what we need for the feast," or that he should give something to the poor. [30]So, after receiving the morsel of bread, he immediately went out. And it was night.

[31]When he had gone out, Jesus said, "Now is the Son of Man glorified, and God is glorified in him. [32]If God is glorified in him, God will also glorify him in himself, and glorify him at once. [33]Little children, yet a little while I am with you. You will seek me, and just as I said to the Jews, so now I also say to you, 'Where I am going you cannot come.' [34]A new commandment I give to you, that you love one another: just as I have loved you, you also are to love one another. [35]By this all people will know that you are my disciples, if you have love for one another."

[36]Simon Peter said to him, "Lord, where are you going?" Jesus answered him, "Where I am going you cannot follow me now, but you will follow afterward." [37]Peter said to him, "Lord, why can I not follow you now? I will lay down my life for you." [38]Jesus answered, "Will you lay down your life for me? Truly, truly, I say to you, the rooster will not crow till you have denied me three times.

Jesus teaches about the Holy Spirit [chapter 14]. This chapter is a main NT repository of information about the person and work of the Holy Spirit, and we should read it as a manual that teaches us what we need to know about the third person of the Trinity (vv. 12–31). Before the subject turns to the Holy Spirit, though, Jesus talks about heaven and his return to heaven after his resurrection (vv. 1–3) and about the Son's relation to the Father (vv. 5–11). The literary genre at work is the *farewell discourse in which a leader addresses his followers on the eve of his death. Conventional motifs include the follow-

---

[1] The Greek words for you in this verse are plural [2] Greek bondservant [3] Greek But in order that the Scripture may be fulfilled [4] Greek in the bosom of Jesus [5] Greek lacks Jesus [a] Ps. 41:9

ing; the speaker's announcement of his imminent departure; the listeners' sorrow and the speaker's words of comfort; the speaker's directive to keep God's commandments and love each other; a prediction of what will happen to the listeners in the future; the invocation of peace upon the listeners; the naming of a successor (in this case, the Holy Spirit); a concluding prayer for the followers.

14 "Let not your hearts be troubled. Believe in God;[1] believe also in me. [2]In my Father's house are many rooms. If it were not so, would I have told you that I go to prepare a place for you?[2] [3]And if I go and prepare a place for you, I will come again and will take you to myself, that where I am you may be also. [4]And you know the way to where I am going."[3] [5]Thomas said to him, "Lord, we do not know where you are going. How can we know the way?" [6]Jesus said to him, "I am the way, and the truth, and the life. No one comes to the Father except through me. [7]If you had known me, you would have known my Father also.[4] From now on you do know him and have seen him."

[8]Philip said to him, "Lord, show us the Father, and it is enough for us." [9]Jesus said to him, "Have I been with you so long, and you still do not know me, Philip? Whoever has seen me has seen the Father. How can you say, 'Show us the Father'? [10]Do you not believe that I am in the Father and the Father is in me? The words that I say to you I do not speak on my own authority, but the Father who dwells in me does his works. [11]Believe me that I am in the Father and the Father is in me, or else believe on account of the works themselves.

[12]"Truly, truly, I say to you, whoever believes in me will also do the works that I do; and greater works than these will he do, because I am going to the Father. [13]Whatever you ask in my name, this I will do, that the Father may be glorified in the Son. [14]If you ask me[5] anything in my name, I will do it.

[15]"If you love me, you will keep my commandments. [16]And I will ask the Father, and he will give you another Helper,[6] to be with you forever, [17]even the Spirit of truth, whom the world cannot receive, because it neither sees him nor knows him. You know him, for he dwells with you and will be in you.

[18]"I will not leave you as orphans; I will come to you. [19]Yet a little while and the world will see me no more, but you will see me. Because I live, you also will live. [20]In that day you will know that I am in my Father, and you in me, and I in you. [21]Whoever has my commandments and keeps them, he it is who loves me. And he who loves me will be loved by my Father, and I will love him and manifest myself to him." [22]Judas (not Iscariot) said to him, "Lord, how is it that you will manifest yourself to us, and not to the world?" [23]Jesus answered him, "If anyone loves me, he will keep my word, and my Father will love him, and we will come to him and make our home with him. [24]Whoever does not love me does not keep my words. And the word that you hear is not mine but the Father's who sent me.

[25]"These things I have spoken to you while I am still with you. [26]But the Helper, the Holy Spirit, whom the Father will send in my name, he will teach you all things and bring to your remembrance all that I have said to you. [27]Peace I leave with you; my peace I give to you. Not as the world gives do I give to you. Let not your hearts be troubled, neither let them be afraid. [28]You heard me say to you, 'I am going away, and

---

[1] Or You believe in God [2] Or In my Father's house are many rooms; if it were not so, I would have told you; for I go to prepare a place for you [3] Some manuscripts Where I am going you know, and the way you know [4] Or If you know me, you will know my Father also, or If you have known me, you will know my Father also [5] Some manuscripts omit me [6] Or Advocate, or Counselor; also 14:26; 15:26; 16:7

I will come to you.' If you loved me, you would have rejoiced, because I am going to the Father, for the Father is greater than I. ²⁹And now I have told you before it takes place, so that when it does take place you may believe. ³⁰I will no longer talk much with you, for the ruler of this world is coming. He has no claim on me, ³¹but I do as the Father has commanded me, so that the world may know that I love the Father. Rise, let us go from here.

> **Christ the true vine** [15:1–17]. Jesus talked to the disciples a long time in the upper room. This unit records his famous discourse on being the true vine. The literary technique at work is analogy—an extended comparison between a vine and its branches and Jesus and his believers. If we analyze the comparison carefully, we learn about how believers are spiritually united to Christ and the life-giving effect that this has on their lives. The concluding command that the disciples love one another (vv. 12–17) is a conventional motif in farewell discourses.

15 "I am the true vine, and my Father is the vinedresser. ²Every branch in me that does not bear fruit he takes away, and every branch that does bear fruit he prunes, that it may bear more fruit. ³Already you are clean because of the word that I have spoken to you. ⁴Abide in me, and I in you. As the branch cannot bear fruit by itself, unless it abides in the vine, neither can you, unless you abide in me. ⁵I am the vine; you are the branches. Whoever abides in me and I in him, he it is that bears much fruit, for apart from me you can do nothing. ⁶If anyone does not abide in me he is thrown away like a branch and withers; and the branches are gathered, thrown into the fire, and burned. ⁷If you abide in me, and my words abide in you, ask whatever you wish, and it will be done for you. ⁸By this my Father is glorified, that you bear much fruit and so prove to be my disciples. ⁹As the Father has loved me, so have I loved you. Abide in my love. ¹⁰If you keep my commandments, you will abide in my love, just as I have kept my Father's commandments and abide in his love. ¹¹These things I have spoken to you, that my joy may be in you, and that your joy may be full.

¹²"This is my commandment, that you love one another as I have loved you. ¹³Greater love has no one than this, that someone lay down his life for his friends. ¹⁴You are my friends if you do what I command you. ¹⁵No longer do I call you servants,¹ for the servant² does not know what his master is doing; but I have called you friends, for all that I have heard from my Father I have made known to you. ¹⁶You did not choose me, but I chose you and appointed you that you should go and bear fruit and that your fruit should abide, so that whatever you ask the Father in my name, he may give it to you. ¹⁷These things I command you, so that you will love one another.

> **Further farewell statements** [15:18–16:15]. As Jesus addresses his disciples, the topics keep expanding. First Jesus declares that after he departs the world will hate the disciples as it has hated him (15:18–16:3). Then he says more about the subject of his successor after his departure, namely, the Holy Spirit (16:4–15). Jesus also tells his disciples what opposition they will suffer in coming days and what their source of help will be in face of the opposition.

¹ Greek bondservants ² Greek bondservant; also verse 20

[18]"If the world hates you, know that it has hated me before it hated you. [19]If you were of the world, the world would love you as its own; but because you are not of the world, but I chose you out of the world, therefore the world hates you. [20]Remember the word that I said to you: 'A servant is not greater than his master.' If they persecuted me, they will also persecute you. If they kept my word, they will also keep yours. [21]But all these things they will do to you on account of my name, because they do not know him who sent me. [22]If I had not come and spoken to them, they would not have been guilty of sin,[1] but now they have no excuse for their sin. [23]Whoever hates me hates my Father also. [24]If I had not done among them the works that no one else did, they would not be guilty of sin, but now they have seen and hated both me and my Father. [25]But the word that is written in their Law must be fulfilled: [a]'They hated me without a cause.'

[26]"But when the Helper comes, whom I will send to you from the Father, the Spirit of truth, who proceeds from the Father, he will bear witness about me. [27]And you also will bear witness, because you have been with me from the beginning.

16 "I have said all these things to you to keep you from falling away. [2]They will put you out of the synagogues. Indeed, the hour is coming when whoever kills you will think he is offering service to God. [3]And they will do these things because they have not known the Father, nor me. [4]But I have said these things to you, that when their hour comes you may remember that I told them to you.

"I did not say these things to you from the beginning, because I was with you. [5]But now I am going to him who sent me, and none of you asks me, 'Where are you going?' [6]But because I have said these things to you, sorrow has filled your heart. [7]Nevertheless, I tell you the truth: it is to your advantage that I go away, for if I do not go away, the Helper will not come to you. But if I go, I will send him to you. [8]And when he comes, he will convict the world concerning sin and righteousness and judgment: [9]concerning sin, because they do not believe in me; [10]concerning righteousness, because I go to the Father, and you will see me no longer; [11]concerning judgment, because the ruler of this world is judged.

[12]"I still have many things to say to you, but you cannot bear them now. [13]When the Spirit of truth comes, he will guide you into all the truth, for he will not speak on his own authority, but whatever he hears he will speak, and he will declare to you the things that are to come. [14]He will glorify me, for he will take what is mine and declare it to you. [15]All that the Father has is mine; therefore I said that he will take what is mine and declare it to you.

Jesus' farewell to his disciples [16:16–33]. The last segment of Jesus' farewell discourse turns to his actual departure from the disciples. Jesus' remarks cover a range of subjects, but what they have in common is that they are expressed in the future tense and predict what the disciples can expect in the immediate future. The disciples in this instance are our representatives: what Jesus says about their life in him is true for all believers. The keynote is that believers in Christ will face tribulation in the world but will have the triune God as their great resource in the face of the world's hostility.

[16]"A little while, and you will see me no longer; and again a little while, and you will see me." [17]So some of his disciples said to one another, "What is this that he says

---

[1] Greek *they would not have sin;* also verse 24   [a] Ps. 35:19 or 69:4

to us, 'A little while, and you will not see me, and again a little while, and you will see me'; and, 'because I am going to the Father'?" ¹⁸So they were saying, "What does he mean by 'a little while'? We do not know what he is talking about." ¹⁹Jesus knew that they wanted to ask him, so he said to them, "Is this what you are asking yourselves, what I meant by saying, 'A little while and you will not see me, and again a little while and you will see me'? ²⁰Truly, truly, I say to you, you will weep and lament, but the world will rejoice. You will be sorrowful, but your sorrow will turn into joy. ²¹When a woman is giving birth, she has sorrow because her hour has come, but when she has delivered the baby, she no longer remembers the anguish, for joy that a human being has been born into the world. ²²So also you have sorrow now, but I will see you again, and your hearts will rejoice, and no one will take your joy from you. ²³In that day you will ask nothing of me. Truly, truly, I say to you, whatever you ask of the Father in my name, he will give it to you. ²⁴Until now you have asked nothing in my name. Ask, and you will receive, that your joy may be full.

²⁵"I have said these things to you in figures of speech. The hour is coming when I will no longer speak to you in figures of speech but will tell you plainly about the Father. ²⁶In that day you will ask in my name, and I do not say to you that I will ask the Father on your behalf; ²⁷for the Father himself loves you, because you have loved me and have believed that I came from God.¹ ²⁸I came from the Father and have come into the world, and now I am leaving the world and going to the Father."

²⁹His disciples said, "Ah, now you are speaking plainly and not using figurative speech! ³⁰Now we know that you know all things and do not need anyone to question you; this is why we believe that you came from God." ³¹Jesus answered them, "Do you now believe? ³²Behold, the hour is coming, indeed it has come, when you will be scattered, each to his own home, and will leave me alone. Yet I am not alone, for the Father is with me. ³³I have said these things to you, that in me you may have peace. In the world you will have tribulation. But take heart; I have overcome the world."

Jesus' high-priestly prayer [chapter 17]. The climax of Jesus' farewell discourse is his intercessory prayer for his followers, starting with the faithful disciples but extending beyond them to all believers throughout history. The literary genre is the *dramatic monologue, in which we overhear a speaker addressing a listener, and in this case it is specifically a prayer addressed by the Son to the Father. Specific topics unfold as follows: prayer that Jesus would be glorified (vv. 1–5); prayer for the disciples (vv. 6–19); prayer for followers of Christ throughout history (vv. 20–26). Two good questions around which to organize a study of the passage are these: What does Jesus desire for his followers? How should followers of Jesus live in light of his prayer for them? The prayer can also be explored for what it says about the following themes: the nature of the relationship between the Son and Father; truth; the relationship of believers to each other and the world.

17 When Jesus had spoken these words, he lifted up his eyes to heaven, and said, "Father, the hour has come; glorify your Son that the Son may glorify you, ²since you have given him authority over all flesh, to give eternal life to all whom you have given him. ³And this is eternal life, that they know you the only true God, and Jesus Christ whom you have sent. ⁴I glorified you on earth, having accomplished the

¹ Some manuscripts from the Father

work that you gave me to do. [5]And now, Father, glorify me in your own presence with the glory that I had with you before the world existed.

[6]"I have manifested your name to the people whom you gave me out of the world. Yours they were, and you gave them to me, and they have kept your word. [7]Now they know that everything that you have given me is from you. [8]For I have given them the words that you gave me, and they have received them and have come to know in truth that I came from you; and they have believed that you sent me. [9]I am praying for them. I am not praying for the world but for those whom you have given me, for they are yours. [10]All mine are yours, and yours are mine, and I am glorified in them. [11]And I am no longer in the world, but they are in the world, and I am coming to you. Holy Father, keep them in your name, which you have given me, that they may be one, even as we are one. [12]While I was with them, I kept them in your name, which you have given me. I have guarded them, and not one of them has been lost except the son of destruction, that the Scripture might be fulfilled. [13]But now I am coming to you, and these things I speak in the world, that they may have my joy fulfilled in themselves. [14]I have given them your word, and the world has hated them because they are not of the world, just as I am not of the world. [15]I do not ask that you take them out of the world, but that you keep them from the evil one.[1] [16]They are not of the world, just as I am not of the world. [17]Sanctify them[2] in the truth; your word is truth. [18]As you sent me into the world, so I have sent them into the world. [19]And for their sake I consecrate myself,[3] that they also may be sanctified[4] in truth.

[20]"I do not ask for these only, but also for those who will believe in me through their word, [21]that they may all be one, just as you, Father, are in me, and I in you, that they also may be in us, so that the world may believe that you have sent me. [22]The glory that you have given me I have given to them, that they may be one even as we are one, [23]I in them and you in me, that they may become perfectly one, so that the world may know that you sent me and loved them even as you loved me. [24]Father, I desire that they also, whom you have given me, may be with me where I am, to see my glory that you have given me because you loved me before the foundation of the world. [25]O righteous Father, even though the world does not know you, I know you, and these know that you have sent me. [26]I made known to them your name, and I will continue to make it known, that the love with which you have loved me may be in them, and I in them."

First events leading to the Passion [18:1–27]. The countdown to Jesus' execution unfolds as a series of dire events, and the first wave of these occurs in this unit. The sequence is as follows: Jesus' betrayal by Judas and arrest in the garden (vv. 1–11); narrative account of Jesus' removal to face Annas the high priest (vv. 12–14); Peter's denial of Jesus during his arraignment (vv. 15–18, 25–27); the questioning of Jesus by the Jewish authorities (vv. 19–24). On the narrative level, the story conveys the chaotic nature of what is happening as it would have been observed by an eyewitness. Thematically we can see the myriad ways in which Jesus the Messiah was rejected by people (Isaiah 53:3 is a good commentary on the action).

---

[1] Or from evil [2] Greek Set them apart (for holy service to God) [3] Or I sanctify myself; or I set myself apart (for holy service to God) [4] Greek may be set apart (for holy service to God)

18

When Jesus had spoken these words, he went out with his disciples across the Kidron Valley, where there was a garden, which he and his disciples entered. ²Now Judas, who betrayed him, also knew the place, for Jesus often met there with his disciples. ³ᵃSo Judas, having procured a band of soldiers and some officers from the chief priests and the Pharisees, went there with lanterns and torches and weapons. ⁴Then Jesus, knowing all that would happen to him, came forward and said to them, "Whom do you seek?" ⁵They answered him, "Jesus of Nazareth." Jesus said to them, "I am he."¹ Judas, who betrayed him, was standing with them. ⁶When Jesus² said to them, "I am he," they drew back and fell to the ground. ⁷So he asked them again, "Whom do you seek?" And they said, "Jesus of Nazareth." ⁸Jesus answered, "I told you that I am he. So, if you seek me, let these men go." ⁹This was to fulfill the word that he had spoken: "Of those whom you gave me I have lost not one." ¹⁰Then Simon Peter, having a sword, drew it and struck the high priest's servant³ and cut off his right ear. (The servant's name was Malchus.) ¹¹So Jesus said to Peter, "Put your sword into its sheath; shall I not drink the cup that the Father has given me?"

¹²So the band of soldiers and their captain and the officers of the Jews arrested Jesus and bound him. ¹³First they led him to Annas, for he was the father-in-law of Caiaphas, who was high priest that year. ¹⁴It was Caiaphas who had advised the Jews that it would be expedient that one man should die for the people.

¹⁵Simon Peter followed Jesus, and so did another disciple. Since that disciple was known to the high priest, he entered with Jesus into the court of the high priest, ¹⁶ᵇbut Peter stood outside at the door. So the other disciple, who was known to the high priest, went out and spoke to the servant girl who kept watch at the door, and brought Peter in. ¹⁷The servant girl at the door said to Peter, "You also are not one of this man's disciples, are you?" He said, "I am not." ¹⁸Now the servants⁴ and officers had made a charcoal fire, because it was cold, and they were standing and warming themselves. Peter also was with them, standing and warming himself.

¹⁹The high priest then questioned Jesus about his disciples and his teaching. ²⁰Jesus answered him, "I have spoken openly to the world. I have always taught in synagogues and in the temple, where all Jews come together. I have said nothing in secret. ²¹Why do you ask me? Ask those who have heard me what I said to them; they know what I said." ²²When he had said these things, one of the officers standing by struck Jesus with his hand, saying, "Is that how you answer the high priest?" ²³Jesus answered him, "If what I said is wrong, bear witness about the wrong; but if what I said is right, why do you strike me?" ²⁴Annas then sent him bound to Caiaphas the high priest.

²⁵ᶜNow Simon Peter was standing and warming himself. So they said to him, "You also are not one of his disciples, are you?" He denied it and said, "I am not." ²⁶One of the servants of the high priest, a relative of the man whose ear Peter had cut off, asked, "Did I not see you in the garden with him?" ²⁷Peter again denied it, and at once a rooster crowed.

Jesus' trial before Pilate [18:28–19:16]. The next step in the journey to execution is Jesus' removal from the high priest to the jurisdiction of the Roman governor Pontius Pilate. The exchange between Jesus and Pilate is recounted in full detail, leading us to

---

¹ Greek *I am*; also verses 6, 8 ² Greek *he* ³ Greek *bondservant*; twice in this verse ⁴ Greek *bondservants*; also verse 26 ᵃ For 18:3-11 see parallels Matt. 26:47-56; Mark 14:43-50; Luke 22:47-53 ᵇ For 18:16-18 see parallels Matt. 26:69, 70; Mark 14:66-68; Luke 22:55-57 ᶜ For 18:25-27 see parallels Matt. 26:71-75; Mark 14:69-72; Luke 22:58-62

relive the mistreatment of Jesus vicariously. Two motifs require our attention: the behavior of Jesus, whose conduct is governed by his role as the one who will die an atoning death, and the emerging portrait of the weak-willed Pilate. The hostile force that keeps the momentum of evil going is the Jewish crowd. The sequence of events is as follows: Pilate secures an indictment against Jesus from the Jews (18:18–32); Pilate questions Jesus (18:33–38a); Pilate returns to the Jews waiting outside his headquarters and announces that he has found no crime of which Jesus is guilty, while at the same time offering them an opportunity to have either Jesus or the robber Barabbas released from prison (18:38b–40); Pilate orchestrates the torture of Jesus, the Jews demand his crucifixion, and Pilate questions Jesus further (19:1–11); Pilate attempts to release Jesus but is overruled by the Jewish mob (19:12–16). In terms of literary form, John narrates the passion of Jesus with a combination of factual narrative and continuous snatches of dialogue. Certainly we experience and remember Jesus' passion by the voices that we hear—voices accusing, interrogating, denying, shouting. Finally, Pilate's questioning of Jesus (18:33–38) ties into unifying motifs of John's Gospel, including the question of who Jesus is, truth, and the nature of Jesus' kingdom.

[28]Then they led Jesus from the house of Caiaphas to the governor's headquarters.[1] It was early morning. They themselves did not enter the governor's headquarters, so that they would not be defiled, but could eat the Passover. [29][a]So Pilate went outside to them and said, "What accusation do you bring against this man?" [30]They answered him, "If this man were not doing evil, we would not have delivered him over to you." [31]Pilate said to them, "Take him yourselves and judge him by your own law." The Jews said to him, "It is not lawful for us to put anyone to death." [32]This was to fulfill the word that Jesus had spoken to show by what kind of death he was going to die.

[33]So Pilate entered his headquarters again and called Jesus and said to him, "Are you the King of the Jews?" [34]Jesus answered, "Do you say this of your own accord, or did others say it to you about me?" [35]Pilate answered, "Am I a Jew? Your own nation and the chief priests have delivered you over to me. What have you done?" [36]Jesus answered, "My kingdom is not of this world. If my kingdom were of this world, my servants would have been fighting, that I might not be delivered over to the Jews. But my kingdom is not from the world." [37]Then Pilate said to him, "So you are a king?" Jesus answered, "You say that I am a king. For this purpose I was born and for this purpose I have come into the world—to bear witness to the truth. Everyone who is of the truth listens to my voice." [38]Pilate said to him, "What is truth?"

After he had said this, he went back outside to the Jews and told them, "I find no guilt in him. [39][b]But you have a custom that I should release one man for you at the Passover. So do you want me to release to you the King of the Jews?" [40]They cried out again, "Not this man, but Barabbas!" Now Barabbas was a robber.[2]

19 Then Pilate took Jesus and flogged him. [2]And the soldiers twisted together a crown of thorns and put it on his head and arrayed him in a purple robe. [3]They came up to him, saying, "Hail, King of the Jews!" and struck him with their hands. [4]Pilate went out again and said to them, "See, I am bringing him out to you that you may know that I find no guilt in him." [5]So Jesus came out, wearing the crown of thorns and the purple robe. Pilate said to them, "Behold the man!" [6]When the chief

---

[1] Greek *the praetorium* [2] Or *an insurrectionist* [a] For 18:29-38 see parallels Matt. 27:11-14; Mark 15:1-5; Luke 23:1-3 [b] For 18:39, 40 see parallels Matt. 27:15-18, 20-23; Mark 15:6-14; Luke 23:18-23

priests and the officers saw him, they cried out, "Crucify him, crucify him!" Pilate said to them, "Take him yourselves and crucify him, for I find no guilt in him." [7]The Jews answered him, "We have a law, and according to that law he ought to die because he has made himself the Son of God." [8]When Pilate heard this statement, he was even more afraid. [9]He entered his headquarters again and said to Jesus, "Where are you from?" But Jesus gave him no answer. [10]So Pilate said to him, "You will not speak to me? Do you not know that I have authority to release you and authority to crucify you?" [11]Jesus answered him, "You would have no authority over me at all unless it had been given you from above. Therefore he who delivered me over to you has the greater sin."

[12]From then on Pilate sought to release him, but the Jews cried out, "If you release this man, you are not Caesar's friend. Everyone who makes himself a king opposes Caesar." [13]So when Pilate heard these words, he brought Jesus out and sat down on the judgment seat at a place called The Stone Pavement, and in Aramaic[1] Gabbatha. [14]Now it was the day of Preparation of the Passover. It was about the sixth hour.[2] He said to the Jews, "Behold your King!" [15]They cried out, "Away with him, away with him, crucify him!" Pilate said to them, "Shall I crucify your King?" The chief priests answered, "We have no king but Caesar." [16]So he delivered him over to them to be crucified.

The crucifixion and burial of Jesus [19:17–42]. John does not record the events of the crucifixion in strict chronology but as a series of snapshots. John chose to record these events: a summary account of the crucifixion (vv. 17–18); the inscription that Pilate had placed over Jesus on the cross (vv. 19–22); the parceling out of Jesus' clothes among the solders who crucified him (vv. 23–24); Jesus' words to his mother and John (vv. 25–27); Jesus' final words from the cross (vv. 28–30); the actions of the soldiers whose task was to ensure that the men on the crosses would die before sundown (vv. 31–37); the burying of Jesus (vv. 38–42). We can profitably look for the following things: the specific things that happened to Jesus; the words that Jesus uttered from the cross and their deeper meanings; the cast of characters in addition to Jesus who were present at the crucifixion, and their implied stories; the responses of onlookers to Jesus; evidences of John's concern that we interpret the events as the fulfillment of OT prophecy.

So they took Jesus, [17]and he went out, bearing his own cross, to the place called The Place of a Skull, which in Aramaic is called Golgotha. [18]There they crucified him, and with him two others, one on either side, and Jesus between them. [19]Pilate also wrote an inscription and put it on the cross. It read, "Jesus of Nazareth, the King of the Jews." [20]Many of the Jews read this inscription, for the place where Jesus was crucified was near the city, and it was written in Aramaic, in Latin, and in Greek. [21]So the chief priests of the Jews said to Pilate, "Do not write, 'The King of the Jews,' but rather, 'This man said, I am King of the Jews.'" [22]Pilate answered, "What I have written I have written."

[23]When the soldiers had crucified Jesus, they took his garments and divided them into four parts, one part for each soldier; also his tunic.[3] But the tunic was seamless, woven in one piece from top to bottom, [24]so they said to one another, "Let us not tear it, but cast lots for it to see whose it shall be." This was to fulfill the Scripture which says,

---

[1] Or *Hebrew*; also verses 17, 20 [2] That is, about noon [3] Greek *chiton*, a long garment worn under the cloak next to the skin

ᵃ"They divided my garments among them,
    and for my clothing they cast lots."

So the soldiers did these things, ²⁵but standing by the cross of Jesus were his mother and his mother's sister, Mary the wife of Clopas, and Mary Magdalene. ²⁶When Jesus saw his mother and the disciple whom he loved standing nearby, he said to his mother, "Woman, behold, your son!" ²⁷Then he said to the disciple, "Behold, your mother!" And from that hour the disciple took her to his own home.

²⁸After this, Jesus, knowing that all was now finished, said (to fulfill the Scripture), "I thirst." ²⁹A jar full of sour wine stood there, so they put a sponge full of the sour wine on a hyssop branch and held it to his mouth. ³⁰When Jesus had received the sour wine, he said, "It is finished," and he bowed his head and gave up his spirit.

³¹Since it was the day of Preparation, and so that the bodies would not remain on the cross on the Sabbath (for that Sabbath was a high day), the Jews asked Pilate that their legs might be broken and that they might be taken away. ³²So the soldiers came and broke the legs of the first, and of the other who had been crucified with him. ³³But when they came to Jesus and saw that he was already dead, they did not break his legs. ³⁴But one of the soldiers pierced his side with a spear, and at once there came out blood and water. ³⁵He who saw it has borne witness—his testimony is true, and he knows that he is telling the truth—that you also may believe. ³⁶For these things took place that the Scripture might be fulfilled: ᵇ"Not one of his bones will be broken." ³⁷And again another Scripture says, ᶜ"They will look on him whom they have pierced."

³⁸ᵈAfter these things Joseph of Arimathea, who was a disciple of Jesus, but secretly for fear of the Jews, asked Pilate that he might take away the body of Jesus, and Pilate gave him permission. So he came and took away his body. ³⁹Nicodemus also, who earlier had come to Jesus¹ by night, came bringing a mixture of myrrh and aloes, about seventy-five pounds² in weight. ⁴⁰So they took the body of Jesus and bound it in linen cloths with the spices, as is the burial custom of the Jews. ⁴¹Now in the place where he was crucified there was a garden, and in the garden a new tomb in which no one had yet been laid. ⁴²So because of the Jewish day of Preparation, since the tomb was close at hand, they laid Jesus there.

The resurrection of Jesus [chapter 20]. All the Gospel writers make the resurrection of Jesus the final and climactic "chapter" of their story of the life of Jesus. They all include circumstantial data that allow us to know that and how the resurrection of Jesus happened, but they vary as to the specific pieces of evidence that they choose to provide. John was an eyewitness of the events of resurrection morning, and he chose the following vignettes from the event: Mary Magdalene finds the tomb empty and runs to inform Peter and John, who run to the tomb and share Mary's discovery, returning home afterward (vv. 1–10); as Mary Magdalene weeps outside the tomb, the risen Jesus speaks to her (vv. 11–18); on the evening of that day, Jesus appears to the assembled disciples and briefly instructs them (vv. 19–23); eight days later Jesus appears to Thomas, who had been absent from the earlier appearance (vv. 24–29). The narrative is followed by John's summary explanation regarding the Gospel that he has composed (vv. 30–31). It is profitable to look for unifying motifs that permeate the sequence of events, including the following: evidential proof that Jesus really did rise from death; related to that, the motifs of belief and unbelief that have been central to John's Gospel; reunion scenes

---

¹ Greek *him* ² Greek *one hundred litras; a litra* (or Roman pound) was equal to about 11 1/2 ounces or 327 grams ᵃ Ps. 22:18 ᵇ Ex. 12:46; Num. 9:12 ᶜ Zech. 12:10 ᵈ For 19:38-42 see parallels Matt. 27:57-61; Mark 15:42-47; Luke 23:50-56

between the risen Jesus and those who love him; the way in which this chapter and the entire preceding Gospel fit into John's stated purpose in writing his book (vv. 30–31).

20 Now on the first day of the week Mary Magdalene came to the tomb early, while it was still dark, and saw that the stone had been taken away from the tomb. ²So she ran and went to Simon Peter and the other disciple, the one whom Jesus loved, and said to them, "They have taken the Lord out of the tomb, and we do not know where they have laid him." ³So Peter went out with the other disciple, and they were going toward the tomb. ⁴Both of them were running together, but the other disciple outran Peter and reached the tomb first. ⁵And stooping to look in, he saw the linen cloths lying there, but he did not go in. ⁶Then Simon Peter came, following him, and went into the tomb. He saw the linen cloths lying there, ⁷and the face cloth, which had been on Jesus'[1] head, not lying with the linen cloths but folded up in a place by itself. ⁸Then the other disciple, who had reached the tomb first, also went in, and he saw and believed; ⁹for as yet they did not understand the Scripture, that he must rise from the dead. ¹⁰Then the disciples went back to their homes.

¹¹But Mary stood weeping outside the tomb, and as she wept she stooped to look into the tomb. ¹²And she saw two angels in white, sitting where the body of Jesus had lain, one at the head and one at the feet. ¹³They said to her, "Woman, why are you weeping?" She said to them, "They have taken away my Lord, and I do not know where they have laid him." ¹⁴Having said this, she turned around and saw Jesus standing, but she did not know that it was Jesus. ¹⁵Jesus said to her, "Woman, why are you weeping? Whom are you seeking?" Supposing him to be the gardener, she said to him, "Sir, if you have carried him away, tell me where you have laid him, and I will take him away." ¹⁶Jesus said to her, "Mary." She turned and said to him in Aramaic,[2] "Rabboni!" (which means Teacher). ¹⁷Jesus said to her, "Do not cling to me, for I have not yet ascended to the Father; but go to my brothers and say to them, 'I am ascending to my Father and your Father, to my God and your God.'" ¹⁸Mary Magdalene went and announced to the disciples, "I have seen the Lord"—and that he had said these things to her.

¹⁹On the evening of that day, the first day of the week, the doors being locked where the disciples were for fear of the Jews, Jesus came and stood among them and said to them, "Peace be with you." ²⁰When he had said this, he showed them his hands and his side. Then the disciples were glad when they saw the Lord. ²¹Jesus said to them again, "Peace be with you. As the Father has sent me, even so I am sending you." ²²And when he had said this, he breathed on them and said to them, "Receive the Holy Spirit. ²³If you forgive the sins of any, they are forgiven them; if you withhold forgiveness from any, it is withheld."

²⁴Now Thomas, one of the Twelve, called the Twin,[3] was not with them when Jesus came. ²⁵So the other disciples told him, "We have seen the Lord." But he said to them, "Unless I see in his hands the mark of the nails, and place my finger into the mark of the nails, and place my hand into his side, I will never believe."

²⁶Eight days later, his disciples were inside again, and Thomas was with them. Although the doors were locked, Jesus came and stood among them and said, "Peace be with you." ²⁷Then he said to Thomas, "Put your finger here, and see my hands; and put out your hand, and place it in my side. Do not disbelieve, but believe." ²⁸Thomas

[1] Greek his [2] Or Hebrew [3] Greek Didymus

answered him, "My Lord and my God!" [29]Jesus said to him, "Have you believed because you have seen me? Blessed are those who have not seen and yet have believed."

[30]Now Jesus did many other signs in the presence of the disciples, which are not written in this book; [31]but these are written so that you may believe that Jesus is the Christ, the Son of God, and that by believing you may have life in his name.

Further postresurrection appearances by Jesus [chapter 21]. The Gospel writers are very concerned about the evidential and apologetic issue of proving the resurrection. John has already given abundant anecdotal evidence in the preceding chapter, but here at the end of his Gospel he includes even more. Chapter 21 is a fully embellished account of a single postresurrection appearance—the one that Jesus made to the disciples at daybreak on the shore of the Sea of Tiberias. The whole scene comes alive in our imagination, and one of the endearing portraits that we have of Jesus is his standing on the shore, having prepared breakfast for the disciples over a charcoal fire, along with the miraculous haul of fish (vv. 4–14). The restoration of Peter in three phases to match his threefold denial of Jesus is likewise laden with human and spiritual voltage (vv. 15–19). It is a climactic call to love the sheep for whom the Good Shepherd died and to carry on the teaching ministry of Jesus that has pervaded John's Gospel.

21

After this Jesus revealed himself again to the disciples by the Sea of Tiberias, and he revealed himself in this way. [2]Simon Peter, Thomas (called the Twin), Nathanael of Cana in Galilee, the sons of Zebedee, and two others of his disciples were together. [3]Simon Peter said to them, "I am going fishing." They said to him, "We will go with you." They went out and got into the boat, but that night they caught nothing.

[4]Just as day was breaking, Jesus stood on the shore; yet the disciples did not know that it was Jesus. [5]Jesus said to them, "Children, do you have any fish?" They answered him, "No." [6]He said to them, "Cast the net on the right side of the boat, and you will find some." So they cast it, and now they were not able to haul it in, because of the quantity of fish. [7]That disciple whom Jesus loved therefore said to Peter, "It is the Lord!" When Simon Peter heard that it was the Lord, he put on his outer garment, for he was stripped for work, and threw himself into the sea. [8]The other disciples came in the boat, dragging the net full of fish, for they were not far from the land, but about a hundred yards[1] off.

[9]When they got out on land, they saw a charcoal fire in place, with fish laid out on it, and bread. [10]Jesus said to them, "Bring some of the fish that you have just caught." [11]So Simon Peter went aboard and hauled the net ashore, full of large fish, 153 of them. And although there were so many, the net was not torn. [12]Jesus said to them, "Come and have breakfast." Now none of the disciples dared ask him, "Who are you?" They knew it was the Lord. [13]Jesus came and took the bread and gave it to them, and so with the fish. [14]This was now the third time that Jesus was revealed to the disciples after he was raised from the dead.

[15]When they had finished breakfast, Jesus said to Simon Peter, "Simon, son of John, do you love me more than these?" He said to him, "Yes, Lord; you know that I love you." He said to him, "Feed my lambs." [16]He said to him a second time, "Simon, son of John, do you love me?" He said to him, "Yes, Lord; you know that I love you." He said to him, "Tend my sheep." [17]He said to him the third time, "Simon, son of John, do you

---

[1] Greek *two hundred cubits*; a *cubit* was about 18 inches or 45 centimeters

love me?" Peter was grieved because he said to him the third time, "Do you love me?" and he said to him, "Lord, you know everything; you know that I love you." Jesus said to him, "Feed my sheep. [18]Truly, truly, I say to you, when you were young, you used to dress yourself and walk wherever you wanted, but when you are old, you will stretch out your hands, and another will dress you and carry you where you do not want to go." [19](This he said to show by what kind of death he was to glorify God.) And after saying this he said to him, "Follow me."

[20]Peter turned and saw the disciple whom Jesus loved following them, the one who had been reclining at table close to him and had said, "Lord, who is it that is going to betray you?" [21]When Peter saw him, he said to Jesus, "Lord, what about this man?" [22]Jesus said to him, "If it is my will that he remain until I come, what is that to you? You follow me!" [23]So the saying spread abroad among the brothers[1] that this disciple was not to die; yet Jesus did not say to him that he was not to die, but, "If it is my will that he remain until I come, what is that to you?"

[24]This is the disciple who is bearing witness about these things, and who has written these things, and we know that his testimony is true.

[25]Now there are also many other things that Jesus did. Were every one of them to be written, I suppose that the world itself could not contain the books that would be written.

---

[1] Or brothers and sisters

THE

ACTS

OF THE APOSTLES

The book at a glance. 28 chapters, 1,007 verses. The book of Acts tells the *epic story of the origin and growth of the Christian church from the time of Christ's ascension to Paul's final imprisonment. The focus is not on dates or institutional history but on the exploits of key leaders, especially Peter and Paul. The book follows an outward expansion of the early church from Jerusalem to Judea and Samaria to "the end of the earth" (1:8). The author of Acts was Luke, who had also written a Gospel on the life of Jesus. The book of Acts should be regarded as a continuation of the story of the gospel (good news) that Luke had proclaimed to Theophilus in his former book (1:1–2). The opening verse of Acts claims that the earlier Gospel had "dealt with all that Jesus began to do and teach," suggesting that the book of Acts tells what Jesus continued to do through the apostles, by the power of the Holy Spirit.

▌**The cyclic structure of the book.** Following the story line becomes easy when we realize that the book of Acts is structured on a cyclic principle in which a common pattern keeps getting repeated. Here are the ingredients of the pattern, in the order in which they appear in each sequence: (1) Christian leaders arise and preach the gospel; (2) listeners are converted and added to the church; (3) opponents (often Jewish but sometimes Gentile) begin to persecute the Christian leaders; (4) God intervenes to rescue the leaders or otherwise protect the church. While this pattern is most obvious in the first half of the book, it extends in modified form to the journeys of Paul, whose repeated buffetings are followed by the expansion of the church.

▌**Genres in the book of Acts.** The book of Acts is a small anthology of individual literary *genres. The list includes *hero story, *adventure story, *travel story, *conversion story, and *miracle story. *Drama also figures prominently; in fact, there are thirty-two speeches in Acts, and these, along with their contexts, make up one-fourth of the book. (For more information on items accompanied by an asterisk, see the glossary at the back of this Bible.)

▌**Ingredients of the story.** The book of Acts is noteworthy for its narrative qualities. We might say that this historically factual story has nearly all the ingredients that audiences love best in a story. The book narrates a series of journeys. It is an adventure story replete with arrests, imprisonments, beatings, riots, narrow escapes, a resurrection from death, a shipwreck, trial scenes, and rescues.

▌**Geography and places in Acts.** Places play a key role in the book of Acts. The places that matter most are the great cities of the Mediterranean region in the first

Passage	Contribution to the Story Line of Acts	Function in the Overall Design of the Book	History of the Early church	Leading Character	Key Event(s)
1:1–7:60	Coming of the Holy Spirit to give birth to the church	Witness in Jerusalem	The church discovers its identity and receives the resources to carry it out	Peter	Coming of the Holy Spirit at Pentecost; Stephen's martyrdom
8:1–12:25	The church expands beyond Jerusalem	Witness to Judea and Samaria	The church reaches into the world	Peter	Peter's vision of the Gentiles' inclusion in the Christian church
13:1–21:26	Paul's missionary journeys	Witness to the end of the earth	The church becomes an international presence	Paul	Paul's conversion and call to be the apostle to the Gentiles
21:27–28:31	Paul's career as a prisoner for the Gospel	Continued witness to the end of the earth	The church reaches to the world capital	Paul	Paul's sea voyage to Rome

century. Geography assumes a symbolic as well as literal importance, as Jerusalem, where the story begins, symbolizes the Jewish religion from which Christianity emerged, and Rome, where the story ends, symbolizes the Gentile world to which Christianity becomes transferred as the early history of the church unfolds.

▮ The representative nature of some of the events that Luke selected for inclusion.
Out of a large body of available data, storytellers select the details that fit their design and purpose. It is a plausible premise that sometimes Luke chose to give us *specimen or representative examples* of categories of experiences—examples of miraculous healings that were no doubt duplicated many times (e.g., 3:1–10 and 19:11–12), a specimen of preaching in the temple (3:11–26) and preaching to Greek intellectuals (17:16–34), an example of a martyrdom (chapter 7), instances of individuals' being converted (e.g., a Jew in 9:1–19 and an Ethiopian in 8:26–38) and groups' being converted (e.g., in Jerusalem in 2:37–41 and in Greek Ephesus in 19:17–20).

▮ The apostles as witnesses.
Witness is a major motif in the book of Acts. At the outset, the risen Christ calls the apostles to be his "witnesses" from Jerusalem to the end of the earth (1:8; Luke 24:48 records Jesus' statement to the disciples "You are witnesses of these things"). As eyewitnesses of the crucifixion and the resurrection, the apostles bear public witness to the saving gospel of Jesus Christ. "We are witnesses," they say (e.g. 2:32; 10:39), and then they proclaim the forgiveness of sins and the free gift of eternal life to the nations. Even Paul—the latest of the apostles—is a witness, for in his conversion he, too, becomes an eyewitness of the risen Christ (9:3–5). Beyond

these specific references, the image of witnessing is an unstated controlling *metaphor for the book of Acts.

▌The apostles as examples. The ministry of the apostles is exemplary. As witnesses for Christ in the face of persecution and death, they are models for us of courageous Christianity. Furthermore, their organization of the basic pattern of church life—its worship, witness, and authority structure—is the same essential pattern that the church follows all over the world today. However, the ministry of the apostles was also unique—a once-for-all gift to the church. The church is "built on the foundation of the apostles" (Eph. 2:20), and of course a building has only one foundation. We should not expect, therefore, that we will be able to replicate all the experiences of the early church or to exercise the same miraculous ministry as the apostles. What we can expect is to share in the same fundamental realities of the gospel and the Holy Spirit that were given once and for all to the church on Good Friday, Easter Sunday, and Pentecost.

▌Inferred literary intentions. The book is designed to achieve the following literary purposes:

- tell the story of the origin of the Christian church and its development during its first few decades

- embody that history in narrative form, with emphasis on personalities and events rather than dates and institutional developments

- lead us to thrill to the adventure and narrative qualities of the events recounted

- prompt us to marvel at God's protection of his church and empowerment of it by the Holy Spirit (leading someone to call the book "the Acts of the Holy Spirit")

- enable us to relive the speeches (including evangelistic sermons and courtroom defenses) that make up an important part of the story Luke tells

- impress upon us the courage of the early witnesses to the gospel, along with the continual hostility that these witnesses endured

- show the expanding witness of the church in the world, fulfilling the commission of Christ by moving from Judea and Samaria to the rest of the world

- prove that Jesus is not for the Jews only but also for Gentiles

▌Theological themes. (1) Ecclesiology: Acts is a repository of teaching about the nature and organization of the church. (2) The Holy Spirit: the book of Acts is a leading NT source on the person and work of the Holy Spirit. (3) The gospel: as the apostles preach to various audiences, their sermons and dialogues explain the theological meaning of the events in Christ's redemptive life, death, and resurrection.

▌The book of Acts as a chapter in the master story of the Bible. The history of the OT nation of Israel tells the story of God's earthly kingdom up to the redemptive life of Christ recorded in the four Gospels. The book of Acts is the first chapter of God's kingdom on earth following the incarnate life of Christ, and it inaugurates the final earthly phase of God's kingdom. Whereas the OT history of salvation pointed forward to the atoning life and death of Jesus, the history of the early church as we find it in Acts looks back to the atonement of Christ. Additionally, the evangelistic content of the message proclaimed by the early church represents a crucial theological interpretation of the events recorded in the four Gospels. An important aspect of this is that the book of Acts shows more strongly than anything else before it that God's way of salvation is for all the world, including Gentiles and not only Jews.

Prologue [chapter 1]. Every story begins with *exposition—background information that we need to know before the *plot can begin to unfold. Chapter 1 serves that function in the book of Acts. Each of the following phases contributes a piece of foreshadowing, whether large or small, to the ensuing book: vv. 1–5, the resurrected Jesus with his disciples; vv. 6–8, Jesus' missionary strategy for the church; vv. 9–11, Jesus' ascension into heaven; vv. 12–26, selection of Matthias as a replacement disciple for Judas Iscariot.

---

1 In the first book, O Theophilus, I have dealt with all that Jesus began to do and teach, [2]until the day when he was taken up, after he had given commands through the Holy Spirit to the apostles whom he had chosen. [3]He presented himself alive to them after his suffering by many proofs, appearing to them during forty days and speaking about the kingdom of God.

[4]And while staying[1] with them he ordered them not to depart from Jerusalem, but to wait for the promise of the Father, which, he said, "you heard from me; [5]for John baptized with water, but you will be baptized with[2] the Holy Spirit not many days from now."

[6]So when they had come together, they asked him, "Lord, will you at this time restore the kingdom to Israel?" [7]He said to them, "It is not for you to know times or seasons that the Father has fixed by his own authority. [8]But you will receive power when the Holy Spirit has come upon you, and you will be my witnesses in Jerusalem and in all Judea and Samaria, and to the end of the earth." [9]And when he had said these things, as they were looking on, he was lifted up, and a cloud took him out of their sight. [10]And while they were gazing into heaven as he went, behold, two men stood by them in white robes, [11]and said, "Men of Galilee, why do you stand looking into heaven? This Jesus, who was taken up from you into heaven, will come in the same way as you saw him go into heaven."

[12]Then they returned to Jerusalem from the mount called Olivet, which is near Jerusalem, a Sabbath day's journey away. [13]And when they had entered, they went up to the upper room, where they were staying, Peter and John and James and Andrew, Philip and Thomas, Bartholomew and Matthew, James the son of Alphaeus and Simon the Zealot and Judas the son of James. [14]All these with one accord were devoting themselves to prayer, together with the women and Mary the mother of Jesus, and his brothers.[3]

[15]In those days Peter stood up among the brothers (the company of persons was in

---

[1] Or *eating* [2] Or in [3] Or *brothers and sisters*. The plural Greek word *adelphoi* (translated "brothers") refers to siblings in a family. In New Testament usage, depending on the context, *adelphoi* may refer either to men or to both men and women who are siblings (brothers and sisters) in God's family, the church; also verse 15

all about 120) and said, ¹⁶"Brothers, the Scripture had to be fulfilled, which the Holy Spirit spoke beforehand by the mouth of David concerning Judas, who became a guide to those who arrested Jesus. ¹⁷For he was numbered among us and was allotted his share in this ministry." ¹⁸(Now this man acquired a field with the reward of his wickedness, and falling headlong¹ he burst open in the middle and all his bowels gushed out. ¹⁹And it became known to all the inhabitants of Jerusalem, so that the field was called in their own language Akeldama, that is, Field of Blood.) ²⁰"For it is written in the Book of Psalms,

> ᵃ"'May his camp become desolate,
>   and let there be no one to dwell in it';

and

> ᵇ"'Let another take his office.'

²¹So one of the men who have accompanied us during all the time that the Lord Jesus went in and out among us, ²²beginning from the baptism of John until the day when he was taken up from us—one of these men must become with us a witness to his resurrection." ²³And they put forward two, Joseph called Barsabbas, who was also called Justus, and Matthias. ²⁴And they prayed and said, "You, Lord, who know the hearts of all, show which one of these two you have chosen ²⁵to take the place in this ministry and apostleship from which Judas turned aside to go to his own place." ²⁶And they cast lots for them, and the lot fell on Matthias, and he was numbered with the eleven apostles.

> **Pentecost** [chapter 2]. Chapter 2 is the *inciting event for the plot that Luke com- posed. It is a self-contained action having the conventional plot pattern of begin- ning—middle—end. The beginning of the action is the appearance of the Holy Spirit in the form of tongues of fire (vv. 1–3). The middle consists of the speaking in tongues and its effects (vv. 4–12) and Peter's sermon and its effects (vv. 13–41). The end is the aftermath of Pentecost, consisting of the fellowship of the believing community that was formed on the day of Pentecost (vv. 42–47). The genius of a good story like this is that it places us in the middle of the place and events that are narrated, so that we can relive them in our imagination.

2 When the day of Pentecost arrived, they were all together in one place. ²And sud- denly there came from heaven a sound like a mighty rushing wind, and it filled the entire house where they were sitting. ³And divided tongues as of fire appeared to them and rested² on each one of them. ⁴And they were all filled with the Holy Spirit and began to speak in other tongues as the Spirit gave them utterance.

⁵Now there were dwelling in Jerusalem Jews, devout men from every nation under heaven. ⁶And at this sound the multitude came together, and they were bewildered, because each one was hearing them speak in his own language. ⁷And they were amazed and astonished, saying, "Are not all these who are speaking Galileans? ⁸And how is it that we hear, each of us in his own native language? ⁹Parthians and Medes and Elamites and residents of Mesopotamia, Judea and Cappadocia, Pontus and Asia, ¹⁰Phrygia and Pamphylia, Egypt and the parts of Libya belonging to Cyrene, and

---

¹ Or *swelling up* ² Or *And tongues as of fire appeared to them, distributed among them, and rested* ᵃ Ps. 69:25 ᵇ Ps. 109:8

visitors from Rome, [11]both Jews and proselytes, Cretans and Arabians—we hear them telling in our own tongues the mighty works of God." [12]And all were amazed and perplexed, saying to one another, "What does this mean?" [13]But others mocking said, "They are filled with new wine."

[14]But Peter, standing with the eleven, lifted up his voice and addressed them: "Men of Judea and all who dwell in Jerusalem, let this be known to you, and give ear to my words. [15]For these people are not drunk, as you suppose, since it is only the third hour of the day.[1] [16]But this is what was uttered through the prophet Joel:

[17][a]"'And in the last days it shall be, God declares,
> that I will pour out my Spirit on all flesh,
> and your sons and your daughters shall prophesy,
>> and your young men shall see visions,
>> and your old men shall dream dreams;
[18] even on my male servants[2] and female servants
>> in those days I will pour out my Spirit, and they shall prophesy.
[19] And I will show wonders in the heavens above
>> and signs on the earth below,
>> blood, and fire, and vapor of smoke;
[20] the sun shall be turned to darkness
>> and the moon to blood,
>> before the day of the Lord comes, the great and magnificent day.
[21] And it shall come to pass that everyone who calls upon the name of the Lord shall
>> be saved.'

[22]"Men of Israel, hear these words: Jesus of Nazareth, a man attested to you by God with mighty works and wonders and signs that God did through him in your midst, as you yourselves know— [23]this Jesus, delivered up according to the definite plan and foreknowledge of God, you crucified and killed by the hands of lawless men. [24]God raised him up, loosing the pangs of death, because it was not possible for him to be held by it. [25]For David says concerning him,

[b]"'I saw the Lord always before me,
> for he is at my right hand that I may not be shaken;
[26] therefore my heart was glad, and my tongue rejoiced;
> my flesh also will dwell in hope.
[27] For you will not abandon my soul to Hades,
> or let your Holy One see corruption.
[28] You have made known to me the paths of life;
> you will make me full of gladness with your presence.'

[29]"Brothers, I may say to you with confidence about the patriarch David that he both died and was buried, and his tomb is with us to this day. [30]Being therefore a prophet, and knowing that God had sworn with an oath to him that he would set one of his descendants on his throne, [31]he foresaw and spoke about the resurrection of the Christ, that he was not abandoned to Hades, nor did his flesh see corruption. [32]This Jesus God raised up, and of that we all are witnesses. [33]Being therefore exalted at the right hand of God, and having received from the Father the promise of the

---

[1] That is, 9 a.m. [2] Greek bondservants; twice in this verse [a] Joel 2:28-32 [b] Ps. 16:8-11

Holy Spirit, he has poured out this that you yourselves are seeing and hearing. [34] For David did not ascend into the heavens, but he himself says,

> [a] "'The Lord said to my Lord,
> Sit at my right hand,
> [35] until I make your enemies your footstool.'

[36] Let all the house of Israel therefore know for certain that God has made him both Lord and Christ, this Jesus whom you crucified."

[37] Now when they heard this they were cut to the heart, and said to Peter and the rest of the apostles, "Brothers, what shall we do?" [38] And Peter said to them, "Repent and be baptized every one of you in the name of Jesus Christ for the forgiveness of your sins, and you will receive the gift of the Holy Spirit. [39] For the promise is for you and for your children and for all who are far off, everyone whom the Lord our God calls to himself." [40] And with many other words he bore witness and continued to exhort them, saying, "Save yourselves from this crooked generation." [41] So those who received his word were baptized, and there were added that day about three thousand souls.

[42] And they devoted themselves to the apostles' teaching and the fellowship, to the breaking of bread and the prayers. [43] And awe[1] came upon every soul, and many wonders and signs were being done through the apostles. [44] And all who believed were together and had all things in common. [45] And they were selling their possessions and belongings and distributing the proceeds to all, as any had need. [46] And day by day, attending the temple together and breaking bread in their homes, they received their food with glad and generous hearts, [47] praising God and having favor with all the people. And the Lord added to their number day by day those who were being saved.

Peter and John's epic feats [3:1–4:31]. After the day of Pentecost has been re-created at moderate narrative length, Luke the storyteller chooses to give an extended account of events surrounding the bold actions of Peter and John. The first item on our agenda as we read this unit is to relive the sensational events in our imagination as vividly as possible. As we do so, we find successive spheres in which Peter and John exercise their Spirit-directed boldness: a private encounter with a lame beggar at the entrance to the temple (3:1–10); a sermon in the temple area to people who have been caught up in the drama of the healing of the lame man (3:11–26); retaliation against Peter and John by the Jewish religious leaders (4:1–22); and a prayer meeting of Christian believers who have been invigorated by the example of Peter and John and by the work of the Holy Spirit in Jerusalem (4:23–31). Unifying motifs include the following: (1) Peter, John, and the believing community as in some ways exemplary models of behavior that Christians in all generations need to emulate; (2) strategies by which Christians should interact with the outside world, including the opposition that they encounter in it; (3) the content of the gospel message that the early Christians proclaimed in the days immediately after the ascension of Jesus.

3 Now Peter and John were going up to the temple at the hour of prayer, the ninth hour.[2] [2] And a man lame from birth was being carried, whom they laid daily at the gate of the temple that is called the Beautiful Gate to ask alms of those entering the temple. [3] Seeing Peter and John about to go into the temple, he asked to receive

---

[1] Or fear [2] That is, 3 P.M. [a] Ps. 110:1

alms. ⁴And Peter directed his gaze at him, as did John, and said, "Look at us." ⁵And he fixed his attention on them, expecting to receive something from them. ⁶But Peter said, "I have no silver and gold, but what I do have I give to you. In the name of Jesus Christ of Nazareth, rise up and walk!" ⁷And he took him by the right hand and raised him up, and immediately his feet and ankles were made strong. ⁸And leaping up he stood and began to walk, and entered the temple with them, walking and leaping and praising God. ⁹And all the people saw him walking and praising God, ¹⁰and recognized him as the one who sat at the Beautiful Gate of the temple, asking for alms. And they were filled with wonder and amazement at what had happened to him.

¹¹While he clung to Peter and John, all the people, utterly astounded, ran together to them in the portico called Solomon's. ¹²And when Peter saw it he addressed the people: "Men of Israel, why do you wonder at this, or why do you stare at us, as though by our own power or piety we have made him walk? ¹³The God of Abraham, the God of Isaac, and the God of Jacob, the God of our fathers, glorified his servant[1] Jesus, whom you delivered over and denied in the presence of Pilate, when he had decided to release him. ¹⁴But you denied the Holy and Righteous One, and asked for a murderer to be granted to you, ¹⁵and you killed the Author of life, whom God raised from the dead. To this we are witnesses. ¹⁶And his name—by faith in his name—has made this man strong whom you see and know, and the faith that is through Jesus[2] has given the man this perfect health in the presence of you all.

¹⁷"And now, brothers, I know that you acted in ignorance, as did also your rulers. ¹⁸But what God foretold by the mouth of all the prophets, that his Christ would suffer, he thus fulfilled. ¹⁹Repent therefore, and turn again, that your sins may be blotted out, ²⁰that times of refreshing may come from the presence of the Lord, and that he may send the Christ appointed for you, Jesus, ²¹whom heaven must receive until the time for restoring all the things about which God spoke by the mouth of his holy prophets long ago. ²²Moses said, 'The Lord God will raise up for you [a]a prophet like me from your brothers. You shall listen to him in whatever he tells you. ²³And it shall be that every soul who does not listen to that prophet shall be destroyed from the people.' ²⁴And all the prophets who have spoken, from Samuel and those who came after him, also proclaimed these days. ²⁵You are the sons of the prophets and of the covenant that God made with your fathers, saying to Abraham, [b]'And in your offspring shall all the families of the earth be blessed.' ²⁶God, having raised up his servant, sent him to you first, to bless you by turning every one of you from your wickedness."

4 And as they were speaking to the people, the priests and the captain of the temple and the Sadducees came upon them, ²greatly annoyed because they were teaching the people and proclaiming in Jesus the resurrection from the dead. ³And they arrested them and put them in custody until the next day, for it was already evening. ⁴But many of those who had heard the word believed, and the number of the men came to about five thousand.

⁵On the next day their rulers and elders and scribes gathered together in Jerusalem, ⁶with Annas the high priest and Caiaphas and John and Alexander, and all who were of the high-priestly family. ⁷And when they had set them in the midst, they inquired, "By what power or by what name did you do this?" ⁸Then Peter, filled with the Holy Spirit, said to them, "Rulers of the people and elders, ⁹if we are being examined today concerning a good deed done to a crippled man, by what means this man has been

[1] Or child; also verse 26 [2] Greek him [a] Deut. 18:15, 18, 19 [b] Gen. 22:18

healed, ¹⁰let it be known to all of you and to all the people of Israel that by the name of Jesus Christ of Nazareth, whom you crucified, whom God raised from the dead— by him this man is standing before you well. ¹¹This Jesus¹ is the stone that was rejected by you, the builders, which has become the cornerstone.² ¹²And there is salvation in no one else, for there is no other name under heaven given among men by which we must be saved."

¹³Now when they saw the boldness of Peter and John, and perceived that they were uneducated, common men, they were astonished. And they recognized that they had been with Jesus. ¹⁴But seeing the man who was healed standing beside them, they had nothing to say in opposition. ¹⁵But when they had commanded them to leave the council, they conferred with one another, ¹⁶saying, "What shall we do with these men? For that a notable sign has been performed through them is evident to all the inhabitants of Jerusalem, and we cannot deny it. ¹⁷But in order that it may spread no further among the people, let us warn them to speak no more to anyone in this name." ¹⁸So they called them and charged them not to speak or teach at all in the name of Jesus. ¹⁹But Peter and John answered them, "Whether it is right in the sight of God to listen to you rather than to God, you must judge, ²⁰for we cannot but speak of what we have seen and heard." ²¹And when they had further threatened them, they let them go, finding no way to punish them, because of the people, for all were praising God for what had happened. ²²For the man on whom this sign of healing was performed was more than forty years old.

²³When they were released, they went to their friends and reported what the chief priests and the elders had said to them. ²⁴And when they heard it, they lifted their voices together to God and said, "Sovereign Lord, who made the heaven and the earth and the sea and everything in them, ²⁵who through the mouth of our father David, your servant,³ said by the Holy Spirit,

> ᵃ"'Why did the Gentiles rage,
>   and the peoples plot in vain?
> ²⁶   The kings of the earth set themselves,
>   and the rulers were gathered together,
>   against the Lord and against his Anointed'⁴—

²⁷for truly in this city there were gathered together against your holy servant Jesus, whom you anointed, both Herod and Pontius Pilate, along with the Gentiles and the peoples of Israel, ²⁸to do whatever your hand and your plan had predestined to take place. ²⁹And now, Lord, look upon their threats and grant to your servants⁵ to continue to speak your word with all boldness, ³⁰while you stretch out your hand to heal, and signs and wonders are performed through the name of your holy servant Jesus." ³¹And when they had prayed, the place in which they were gathered together was shaken, and they were all filled with the Holy Spirit and continued to speak the word of God with boldness.

The fledgling church discovers its identity [4:32–6:7]. After the close-ups of the heroics of faith by Peter and John, the next phase of Acts gives us a wide-angle picture of the community of faith that was in the process of forming. First we get a picture of the sharing of possessions of the new community (4:32–37) and, growing out of that,

¹ Greek *This one* ² Greek *the head of the corner* ³ Or *child; also verses* 27, 30 ⁴ Or *Christ* ⁵ Greek *bondservants* ᵃ Ps. 2:1, 2

the need for Peter to discipline members of the community who have misbehaved (5:1–11). Balancing the negative picture is an account of "signs and wonders" accompanied by conversions (5:12–16), followed by an expanded narrative of the arrest and release of church leaders by the Jewish religious establishment (5:17–42). In quite another vein but still in keeping with the theme of the church's discovering who it is, the small church is shown evolving institutional structures, namely, the appointment of men to oversee the ministry of mercy so the disciples can devote themselves to preaching and prayer (6:1–7). The book of Acts is a book of beginnings, and a leading aim of the narrative is to enable us to relive the excitement, suspense, and danger of life in the early days of the Christian church.

[32]Now the full number of those who believed were of one heart and soul, and no one said that any of the things that belonged to him was his own, but they had everything in common. [33]And with great power the apostles were giving their testimony to the resurrection of the Lord Jesus, and great grace was upon them all. [34]There was not a needy person among them, for as many as were owners of lands or houses sold them and brought the proceeds of what was sold [35]and laid it at the apostles' feet, and it was distributed to each as any had need. [36]Thus Joseph, who was also called by the apostles Barnabas (which means son of encouragement), a Levite, a native of Cyprus, [37]sold a field that belonged to him and brought the money and laid it at the apostles' feet.

5 But a man named Ananias, with his wife Sapphira, sold a piece of property, [2]and with his wife's knowledge he kept back for himself some of the proceeds and brought only a part of it and laid it at the apostles' feet. [3]But Peter said, "Ananias, why has Satan filled your heart to lie to the Holy Spirit and to keep back for yourself part of the proceeds of the land? [4]While it remained unsold, did it not remain your own? And after it was sold, was it not at your disposal? Why is it that you have contrived this deed in your heart? You have not lied to men but to God." [5]When Ananias heard these words, he fell down and breathed his last. And great fear came upon all who heard of it. [6]The young men rose and wrapped him up and carried him out and buried him.

[7]After an interval of about three hours his wife came in, not knowing what had happened. [8]And Peter said to her, "Tell me whether you[1] sold the land for so much." And she said, "Yes, for so much." [9]But Peter said to her, "How is it that you have agreed together to test the Spirit of the Lord? Behold, the feet of those who have buried your husband are at the door, and they will carry you out." [10]Immediately she fell down at his feet and breathed her last. When the young men came in they found her dead, and they carried her out and buried her beside her husband. [11]And great fear came upon the whole church and upon all who heard of these things.

[12]Now many signs and wonders were regularly done among the people by the hands of the apostles. And they were all together in Solomon's Portico. [13]None of the rest dared join them, but the people held them in high esteem. [14]And more than ever believers were added to the Lord, multitudes of both men and women, [15]so that they even carried out the sick into the streets and laid them on cots and mats, that as Peter came by at least his shadow might fall on some of them. [16]The people also gathered

---

[1] The Greek for you is plural here

from the towns around Jerusalem, bringing the sick and those afflicted with unclean spirits, and they were all healed. [17]But the high priest rose up, and all who were with him (that is, the party of the Sadducees), and filled with jealousy [18]they arrested the apostles and put them in the public prison. [19]But during the night an angel of the Lord opened the prison doors and brought them out, and said, [20]"Go and stand in the temple and speak to the people all the words of this Life." [21]And when they heard this, they entered the temple at daybreak and began to teach.

Now when the high priest came, and those who were with him, they called together the council and all the senate of the people of Israel and sent to the prison to have them brought. [22]But when the officers came, they did not find them in the prison, so they returned and reported, [23]"We found the prison securely locked and the guards standing at the doors, but when we opened them we found no one inside." [24]Now when the captain of the temple and the chief priests heard these words, they were greatly perplexed about them, wondering what this would come to. [25]And someone came and told them, "Look! The men whom you put in prison are standing in the temple and teaching the people." [26]Then the captain with the officers went and brought them, but not by force, for they were afraid of being stoned by the people.

[27]And when they had brought them, they set them before the council. And the high priest questioned them, [28]saying, "We strictly charged you not to teach in this name, yet here you have filled Jerusalem with your teaching, and you intend to bring this man's blood upon us." [29]But Peter and the apostles answered, "We must obey God rather than men. [30]The God of our fathers raised Jesus, whom you killed by hanging him on a tree. [31]God exalted him at his right hand as Leader and Savior, to give repentance to Israel and forgiveness of sins. [32]And we are witnesses to these things, and so is the Holy Spirit, whom God has given to those who obey him."

[33]When they heard this, they were enraged and wanted to kill them. [34]But a Pharisee in the council named Gamaliel, a teacher of the law held in honor by all the people, stood up and gave orders to put the men outside for a little while. [35]And he said to them, "Men of Israel, take care what you are about to do with these men. [36]For before these days Theudas rose up, claiming to be somebody, and a number of men, about four hundred, joined him. He was killed, and all who followed him were dispersed and came to nothing. [37]After him Judas the Galilean rose up in the days of the census and drew away some of the people after him. He too perished, and all who followed him were scattered. [38]So in the present case I tell you, keep away from these men and let them alone, for if this plan or this undertaking is of man, it will fail; [39]but if it is of God, you will not be able to overthrow them. You might even be found opposing God!" So they took his advice, [40]and when they had called in the apostles, they beat them and charged them not to speak in the name of Jesus, and let them go. [41]Then they left the presence of the council, rejoicing that they were counted worthy to suffer dishonor for the name. [42]And every day, in the temple and from house to house, they did not cease teaching and preaching Jesus as the Christ.

6 Now in these days when the disciples were increasing in number, a complaint by the Hellenists[1] arose against the Hebrews because their widows were being neglected in the daily distribution. [2]And the twelve summoned the full number of the disciples and said, "It is not right that we should give up preaching the word of God

[1] That is, Greek-speaking Jews

to serve tables. ³Therefore, brothers,¹ pick out from among you seven men of good repute, full of the Spirit and of wisdom, whom we will appoint to this duty. ⁴But we will devote ourselves to prayer and to the ministry of the word." ⁵And what they said pleased the whole gathering, and they chose Stephen, a man full of faith and of the Holy Spirit, and Philip, and Prochorus, and Nicanor, and Timon, and Parmenas, and Nicolaus, a proselyte of Antioch. ⁶These they set before the apostles, and they prayed and laid their hands on them.

⁷And the word of God continued to increase, and the number of the disciples multiplied greatly in Jerusalem, and a great many of the priests became obedient to the faith.

Stephen's martyrdom [6:8–7:60]. After the overview, we return to a close-up of a single heroic individual. In the background to the action lies a historical situation that baffles people who live in democratic societies, where imprisonments and executions are conducted by the state. As we see in the book of Acts, the Roman government turned a blind eye as Jewish authorities persecuted and executed people who practiced a religion that deviated from the Jewish faith. The story of Stephen's martyrdom is a hero story that unfolds as a self-contained action: Stephen's spiritual successes lead the Jewish authorities to arrest him and bring him to trial (6:8–15); Stephen replies to the charges with a long sermon that highlights OT history as a preparation for Christ and ends as a prophet's attack on the Jews for murdering Jesus (7:1–53); the resultant stoning of Stephen (7:54–60). The climax of the story is Stephen's vision of the risen Christ at the moment he is being executed. To experience this material as a story, we should pay attention to (1) the unfolding plot conflict between Stephen and his antagonists, (2) the specific things that constitute Stephen's heroism, and (3) the ways in which Stephen's sermon can be regarded as both a defense of himself and a proclamation of the gospel.

⁸And Stephen, full of grace and power, was doing great wonders and signs among the people. ⁹Then some of those who belonged to the synagogue of the Freedmen (as it was called), and of the Cyrenians, and of the Alexandrians, and of those from Cilicia and Asia, rose up and disputed with Stephen. ¹⁰But they could not withstand the wisdom and the Spirit with which he was speaking. ¹¹Then they secretly instigated men who said, "We have heard him speak blasphemous words against Moses and God." ¹²And they stirred up the people and the elders and the scribes, and they came upon him and seized him and brought him before the council, ¹³and they set up false witnesses who said, "This man never ceases to speak words against this holy place and the law, ¹⁴for we have heard him say that this Jesus of Nazareth will destroy this place and will change the customs that Moses delivered to us." ¹⁵And gazing at him, all who sat in the council saw that his face was like the face of an angel.

7 And the high priest said, "Are these things so?" ²And Stephen said:
"Brothers and fathers, hear me. The God of glory appeared to our father Abraham when he was in Mesopotamia, before he lived in Haran, ³and said to him, ª'Go out from your land and from your kindred and go into the land that I will show you.' ⁴Then he went out from the land of the Chaldeans and lived in Haran. And after his father died, God removed him from there into this land in which you are now liv-

¹ Or brothers and sisters ª Gen. 12:1

ing. ⁵Yet he gave him no inheritance in it, not even a foot's length, but promised to give it to him as a possession and to his offspring after him, though he had no child. ⁶And God spoke to this effect—that ᵃhis offspring would be sojourners in a land belonging to others, who would enslave them and afflict them four hundred years. ⁷'But I will judge the nation that they serve,' said God, 'and after that they shall come out and worship me in this place.' ⁸And he gave him the covenant of circumcision. And so Abraham became the father of Isaac, and circumcised him on the eighth day, and Isaac became the father of Jacob, and Jacob of the twelve patriarchs.

⁹"And the patriarchs, jealous of Joseph, sold him into Egypt; but God was with him ¹⁰and rescued him out of all his afflictions and gave him favor and wisdom before Pharaoh, king of Egypt, who made him ruler over Egypt and over all his household. ¹¹Now there came a famine throughout all Egypt and Canaan, and great affliction, and our fathers could find no food. ¹²But when Jacob heard that there was grain in Egypt, he sent out our fathers on their first visit. ¹³And on the second visit Joseph made himself known to his brothers, and Joseph's family became known to Pharaoh. ¹⁴And Joseph sent and summoned Jacob his father and all his kindred, seventy-five persons in all. ¹⁵And Jacob went down into Egypt, and he died, he and our fathers, ¹⁶and they were carried back to Shechem and laid in the tomb that Abraham had bought for a sum of silver from the sons of Hamor in Shechem.

¹⁷"But as the time of the promise drew near, which God had granted to Abraham, the people increased and multiplied in Egypt ¹⁸until there arose over Egypt another king who did not know Joseph. ¹⁹He dealt shrewdly with our race and forced our fathers to expose their infants, so that they would not be kept alive. ²⁰At this time Moses was born; and he was beautiful in God's sight. And he was brought up for three months in his father's house, ²¹and when he was exposed, Pharaoh's daughter adopted him and brought him up as her own son. ²²And Moses was instructed in all the wisdom of the Egyptians, and he was mighty in his words and deeds.

²³"When he was forty years old, it came into his heart to visit his brothers, the children of Israel. ²⁴And seeing one of them being wronged, he defended the oppressed man and avenged him by striking down the Egyptian. ²⁵He supposed that his brothers would understand that God was giving them salvation by his hand, but they did not understand. ²⁶And on the following day he appeared to them as they were quarreling and tried to reconcile them, saying, 'Men, you are brothers. Why do you wrong each other?' ²⁷But the man who was wronging his neighbor thrust him aside, saying, 'Who made you a ruler and a judge over us? ²⁸Do you want to kill me as you killed the Egyptian yesterday?' ²⁹At this retort Moses fled and became an exile in the land of Midian, where he became the father of two sons.

³⁰"Now when forty years had passed, an angel appeared to him in the wilderness of Mount Sinai, in a flame of fire in a bush. ³¹When Moses saw it, he was amazed at the sight, and as he drew near to look, there came the voice of the Lord: ³²ᵇ'I am the God of your fathers, the God of Abraham and of Isaac and of Jacob.' And Moses trembled and did not dare to look. ³³Then the Lord said to him, 'Take off the sandals from your feet, for the place where you are standing is holy ground. ³⁴I have surely seen the affliction of my people who are in Egypt, and have heard their groaning, and I have come down to deliver them. And now come, I will send you to Egypt.'

³⁵"This Moses, whom they rejected, saying, 'Who made you a ruler and a judge?'— this man God sent as both ruler and redeemer by the hand of the angel who appeared

---

ᵃ Gen. 15:13, 14   ᵇ Ex. 3:6

to him in the bush. ³⁶This man led them out, performing wonders and signs in Egypt and at the Red Sea and in the wilderness for forty years. ³⁷This is the Moses who said to the Israelites, 'God will raise up for you ªa prophet like me from your brothers.' ³⁸This is the one who was in the congregation in the wilderness with the angel who spoke to him at Mount Sinai, and with our fathers. He received living oracles to give to us. ³⁹Our fathers refused to obey him, but thrust him aside, and in their hearts they turned to Egypt, ⁴⁰saying to Aaron, ᵇ'Make for us gods who will go before us. As for this Moses who led us out from the land of Egypt, we do not know what has become of him.' ⁴¹And they made a calf in those days, and offered a sacrifice to the idol and were rejoicing in the works of their hands. ⁴²But God turned away and gave them over to worship the host of heaven, as it is written in the book of the prophets:

> ᶜ"'Did you bring to me slain beasts and sacrifices,
>   during the forty years in the wilderness, O house of Israel?
> ⁴³ You took up the tent of Moloch
>   and the star of your god Rephan,
>   the images that you made to worship;
>   and I will send you into exile beyond Babylon.'

⁴⁴"Our fathers had the tent of witness in the wilderness, just as he who spoke to Moses directed him to make it, according to the pattern that he had seen. ⁴⁵Our fathers in turn brought it in with Joshua when they dispossessed the nations that God drove out before our fathers. So it was until the days of David, ⁴⁶who found favor in the sight of God and asked to find a dwelling place for the God of Jacob.¹ ⁴⁷But it was Solomon who built a house for him. ⁴⁸Yet the Most High does not dwell in houses made by hands, as the prophet says,

> ⁴⁹ᵈ"'Heaven is my throne,
>   and the earth is my footstool.
> What kind of house will you build for me, says the Lord,
>   or what is the place of my rest?
> ⁵⁰ Did not my hand make all these things?'

⁵¹"You stiff-necked people, uncircumcised in heart and ears, you always resist the Holy Spirit. As your fathers did, so do you. ⁵²Which of the prophets did your fathers not persecute? And they killed those who announced beforehand the coming of the Righteous One, whom you have now betrayed and murdered, ⁵³you who received the law as delivered by angels and did not keep it."

⁵⁴Now when they heard these things they were enraged, and they ground their teeth at him. ⁵⁵But he, full of the Holy Spirit, gazed into heaven and saw the glory of God, and Jesus standing at the right hand of God. ⁵⁶And he said, "Behold, I see the heavens opened, and the Son of Man standing at the right hand of God." ⁵⁷But they cried out with a loud voice and stopped their ears and rushed together² at him. ⁵⁸Then they cast him out of the city and stoned him. And the witnesses laid down their garments at the feet of a young man named Saul. ⁵⁹And as they were stoning Stephen, he called out, "Lord Jesus, receive my spirit." ⁶⁰And falling to his knees he cried out with a loud voice, "Lord, do not hold this sin against them." And when he had said this, he fell asleep.

---

¹ Some manuscripts *for the house of Jacob* ² Or *rushed with one mind* ª Deut. 18:15 ᵇ Ex. 32:1, 23 ᶜ Amos 5:25-27 ᵈ Isa. 66:1, 2

The dispersion of the church outward from Jerusalem [chapter 8]. Chapter 8 marks a new stage of action in the ongoing story. The extreme persecution of Christians in Jerusalem leaves them with no option but to start leaving Jerusalem, the city that in the book of Acts is symbolic of the Jewish origins of the Christian faith. Chapter 8 fills in the picture of the first wave of the dispersion, according to the following sequence: explanation of the persecution that made the dispersion necessary (8:1–3); the preaching and healing ministry of Philip in Samaria (8:4–8); the conversion of Simon the sorcerer and others in Samaria (8:9–17); Simon's misguided attempt to purchase the power of the Holy Spirit (8:18–24); another conversion story as the Ethiopian eunuch is converted through the preaching of Philip (8:25–40). Things to notice include the following: (1) the geographic references that show the back-and-forth movement between Jerusalem and the surrounding region; (2) the extensive cast of characters in this chapter, suggesting how much action has been packed into the book of Acts; and (3) once again, the content of the gospel that is proclaimed in the evangelistic actions of the early Christians.

8 And Saul approved of his execution.
And there arose on that day a great persecution against the church in Jerusalem, and they were all scattered throughout the regions of Judea and Samaria, except the apostles. ²Devout men buried Stephen and made great lamentation over him. ³But Saul was ravaging the church, and entering house after house, he dragged off men and women and committed them to prison.

⁴Now those who were scattered went about preaching the word. ⁵Philip went down to the city[1] of Samaria and proclaimed to them the Christ. ⁶And the crowds with one accord paid attention to what was being said by Philip when they heard him and saw the signs that he did. ⁷For unclean spirits, crying out with a loud voice, came out of many who had them, and many who were paralyzed or lame were healed. ⁸So there was much joy in that city.

⁹But there was a man named Simon, who had previously practiced magic in the city and amazed the people of Samaria, saying that he himself was somebody great. ¹⁰They all paid attention to him, from the least to the greatest, saying, "This man is the power of God that is called Great." ¹¹And they paid attention to him because for a long time he had amazed them with his magic. ¹²But when they believed Philip as he preached good news about the kingdom of God and the name of Jesus Christ, they were baptized, both men and women. ¹³Even Simon himself believed, and after being baptized he continued with Philip. And seeing signs and great miracles[2] performed, he was amazed.

¹⁴Now when the apostles at Jerusalem heard that Samaria had received the word of God, they sent to them Peter and John, ¹⁵who came down and prayed for them that they might receive the Holy Spirit, ¹⁶for he had not yet fallen on any of them, but they had only been baptized in the name of the Lord Jesus. ¹⁷Then they laid their hands on them and they received the Holy Spirit. ¹⁸Now when Simon saw that the Spirit was given through the laying on of the apostles' hands, he offered them money, ¹⁹saying, "Give me this power also, so that anyone on whom I lay my hands may receive the Holy Spirit." ²⁰But Peter said to him, "May your silver perish with you, because you thought you could obtain the gift of God with money! ²¹You have neither part nor lot in this matter, for your heart is not right before God. ²²Repent, therefore, of this wickedness of yours, and pray to the Lord that, if possible, the intent of your heart may be

---

[1] Some manuscripts *a city* [2] Greek *works of power*

forgiven you. [23]For I see that you are in the gall[1] of bitterness and in the bond of iniquity." [24]And Simon answered, "Pray for me to the Lord, that nothing of what you have said may come upon me."

[25]Now when they had testified and spoken the word of the Lord, they returned to Jerusalem, preaching the gospel to many villages of the Samaritans.

[26]Now an angel of the Lord said to Philip, "Rise and go toward the south[2] to the road that goes down from Jerusalem to Gaza." This is a desert place. [27]And he rose and went. And there was an Ethiopian, a eunuch, a court official of Candace, queen of the Ethiopians, who was in charge of all her treasure. He had come to Jerusalem to worship [28]and was returning, seated in his chariot, and he was reading the prophet Isaiah. [29]And the Spirit said to Philip, "Go over and join this chariot." [30]So Philip ran to him and heard him reading Isaiah the prophet and asked, "Do you understand what you are reading?" [31]And he said, "How can I, unless someone guides me?" And he invited Philip to come up and sit with him. [32]Now the passage of the Scripture that he was reading was this:

[a]"Like a sheep he was led to the slaughter
   and like a lamb before its shearer is silent,
   so he opens not his mouth.
[33] In his humiliation justice was denied him.
   Who can describe his generation?
   For his life is taken away from the earth."

[34]And the eunuch said to Philip, "About whom, I ask you, does the prophet say this, about himself or about someone else?" [35]Then Philip opened his mouth, and beginning with this Scripture he told him the good news about Jesus. [36]And as they were going along the road they came to some water, and the eunuch said, "See, here is water! What prevents me from being baptized?"[3] [38]And he commanded the chariot to stop, and they both went down into the water, Philip and the eunuch, and he baptized him. [39]And when they came up out of the water, the Spirit of the Lord carried Philip away, and the eunuch saw him no more, and went on his way rejoicing. [40]But Philip found himself at Azotus, and as he passed through he preached the gospel to all the towns until he came to Caesarea.

The conversion of Paul [9:1–31]. The most famous single story in the book of Acts— the pivot on which the story turns—is actually an interlude within the first eleven chapters of the book, for following the conversion of Paul the story restores Peter to the status of protagonist until chapter 13 (thereby introducing an element of suspense as we wonder what has become of the converted Paul). Stories are unified entities in themselves, and they fall into a small cluster of possible paradigms. One of these is as follows: (1) exposition (background information); (2) inciting event; (3) a wavelike sequence of consequences from the inciting event; (4) closure to the action. In the story of Paul's conversion, we progress from the background account of Saul's causing havoc to the Christian church (vv. 1–2, with 7:58 and 8:1 serving as earlier foreshadowings of this motif), through the inciting event of his being struck down by the light from heaven (vv. 3–7), and thence to Saul's journey to Damascus for assimilation into the Christian community (vv. 8–19), his subsequent preaching of the gospel (vv. 20–22), and his forced

---

[1] That is, a bitter fluid secreted by the liver; bile [2] Or *go at about noon* [3] Some manuscripts add all or most of verse 37: *And Philip said, "If you believe with all your heart, you may." And he replied, "I believe that Jesus Christ is the Son of God."* [a] Isa. 53:7, 8

escape to Jerusalem in the wake of his preaching (vv. 23–25). Paul's acceptance into the Jerusalem circle of believers (vv. 26–31) provides closure to the story, which can be assimilated as a prototypical conversion story.

9 But Saul, still breathing threats and murder against the disciples of the Lord, went to the high priest ²and asked him for letters to the synagogues at Damascus, so that if he found any belonging to the Way, men or women, he might bring them bound to Jerusalem. ³Now as he went on his way, he approached Damascus, and suddenly a light from heaven flashed around him. ⁴And falling to the ground he heard a voice saying to him, "Saul, Saul, why are you persecuting me?" ⁵And he said, "Who are you, Lord?" And he said, "I am Jesus, whom you are persecuting. ⁶But rise and enter the city, and you will be told what you are to do." ⁷The men who were traveling with him stood speechless, hearing the voice but seeing no one. ⁸Saul rose from the ground, and although his eyes were opened, he saw nothing. So they led him by the hand and brought him into Damascus. ⁹And for three days he was without sight, and neither ate nor drank.

¹⁰Now there was a disciple at Damascus named Ananias. The Lord said to him in a vision, "Ananias." And he said, "Here I am, Lord." ¹¹And the Lord said to him, "Rise and go to the street called Straight, and at the house of Judas look for a man of Tarsus named Saul, for behold, he is praying, ¹²and he has seen in a vision a man named Ananias come in and lay his hands on him so that he might regain his sight." ¹³But Ananias answered, "Lord, I have heard from many about this man, how much evil he has done to your saints at Jerusalem. ¹⁴And here he has authority from the chief priests to bind all who call on your name." ¹⁵But the Lord said to him, "Go, for he is a chosen instrument of mine to carry my name before the Gentiles and kings and the children of Israel. ¹⁶For I will show him how much he must suffer for the sake of my name." ¹⁷So Ananias departed and entered the house. And laying his hands on him he said, "Brother Saul, the Lord Jesus who appeared to you on the road by which you came has sent me so that you may regain your sight and be filled with the Holy Spirit." ¹⁸And immediately something like scales fell from his eyes, and he regained his sight. Then he rose and was baptized; ¹⁹and taking food, he was strengthened.

For some days he was with the disciples at Damascus. ²⁰And immediately he proclaimed Jesus in the synagogues, saying, "He is the Son of God." ²¹And all who heard him were amazed and said, "Is not this the man who made havoc in Jerusalem of those who called upon this name? And has he not come here for this purpose, to bring them bound before the chief priests?" ²²But Saul increased all the more in strength, and confounded the Jews who lived in Damascus by proving that Jesus was the Christ.

²³When many days had passed, the Jews plotted to kill him, ²⁴but their plot became known to Saul. They were watching the gates day and night in order to kill him, ²⁵but his disciples took him by night and let him down through an opening in the wall,[1] lowering him in a basket.

²⁶And when he had come to Jerusalem, he attempted to join the disciples. And they were all afraid of him, for they did not believe that he was a disciple. ²⁷But Barnabas took him and brought him to the apostles and declared to them how on the road he had seen the Lord, who spoke to him, and how at Damascus he had preached boldly

---

[1] Greek *through the wall*

in the name of Jesus. ²⁸So he went in and out among them at Jerusalem, preaching boldly in the name of the Lord. ²⁹And he spoke and disputed against the Hellenists.¹ But they were seeking to kill him. ³⁰And when the brothers learned this, they brought him down to Caesarea and sent him off to Tarsus.

³¹So the church throughout all Judea and Galilee and Samaria had peace and was being built up. And walking in the fear of the Lord and in the comfort of the Holy Spirit, it multiplied.

Peter's miracles [9:32–43]. Tucked between the two major conversion stories of the book of Acts is an interlude narrating two miracles (one of healing, the other of raising the dead) performed by Peter. We are left to speculate about why Luke inserted these two events here. Their narrative effect is to reinstate Peter as the protagonist in the story of his mission to the Jews. They may have been signs and wonders that were particularly noteworthy in the life of the early church—not representative events but unique ones. They yield their narrative artistry if we simply approach them through the usual grid of the miracle story.

³²Now as Peter went here and there among them all, he came down also to the saints who lived at Lydda. ³³There he found a man named Aeneas, bedridden for eight years, who was paralyzed. ³⁴And Peter said to him, "Aeneas, Jesus Christ heals you; rise and make your bed." And immediately he rose. ³⁵And all the residents of Lydda and Sharon saw him, and they turned to the Lord.

³⁶Now there was in Joppa a disciple named Tabitha, which, translated, means Dorcas.² She was full of good works and acts of charity. ³⁷In those days she became ill and died, and when they had washed her, they laid her in an upper room. ³⁸Since Lydda was near Joppa, the disciples, hearing that Peter was there, sent two men to him, urging him, "Please come to us without delay." ³⁹So Peter rose and went with them. And when he arrived, they took him to the upper room. All the widows stood beside him weeping and showing tunics³ and other garments that Dorcas made while she was with them. ⁴⁰But Peter put them all outside, and knelt down and prayed; and turning to the body he said, "Tabitha, arise." And she opened her eyes, and when she saw Peter she sat up. ⁴¹And he gave her his hand and raised her up. Then calling the saints and widows, he presented her alive. ⁴²And it became known throughout all Joppa, and many believed in the Lord. ⁴³And he stayed in Joppa for many days with one Simon, a tanner.

Peter's "conversion" [10:1–11:18]. Virgil's *Aeneid* is built around the motif of the transfer of an empire from Troy to Rome. The book of Acts gives us a variation on that motif as it narrates how the focus of God's kingdom shifted from the Jewish religion to the Gentiles as the Jews continued to reject the Christian gospel. This is not to say that Jews were excluded from the kingdom if they accepted the gospel of Christ's atonement. In terms of the story that we read in Acts, though, the audience to which the gospel is chiefly preached and the geographic regions where it is proclaimed change halfway through the book. Paul's conversion was a key event in this shift because Paul became the prime apostle to the Gentiles. But the revolution of thinking in the mind of Peter was just as pivotal in the history of the early church. It is the subject of this narrative

¹ That is, Greek-speaking Jews ² The Aramaic name *Tabitha* and the Greek name *Dorcas* both mean *gazelle* ³ Greek *chiton*, a long garment worn under the cloak next to the skin

unit. The story follows the narrative paradigm of exposition–inciting event–aftermath. The story begins with a note of suspense, as we are led to wonder what will ensue when Cornelius of Caesarea is prompted by an angelic vision to send emissaries to Joppa to enlist a visit from Peter (10:1–8). Neither Cornelius nor we are told what Cornelius will accomplish by meeting Peter. While the journey is under way, the docudrama whisks us to Joppa, where Peter receives his famous vision of the sheet holding unclean animals, accompanied by the oracular voice telling Peter to eat the animals (10:9–16). The mystery surrounding the unexplained command to Cornelius to request a visit from Peter pales in comparison to Peter's perplexity as to the meaning of his vision (10:17a). The story has become a riddle. It is solved for Peter and us when Peter encounters Cornelius and then by stages pieces things together, in the following sequence: having been commanded by the Holy Spirit to accompany the men from Cornelius, Peter makes contact with the servants of Cornelius (10:17b–23); Peter travels to Caesarea and listens to Cornelius's account of his vision (10:24–33); the earlier riddles are answered as Peter interprets both his vision and the vision of Cornelius as evidence that the gospel is for all people and proceeds to preach an evangelistic sermon to the assembled party (10:34–43); the Holy Spirit falls on the assembled Gentiles, and they are baptized (10:44–48). When Peter later travels to Jerusalem, he adduces the narrative that has unfolded here as proof that God has included Gentiles in the Christian church (11:1–18).

10 At Caesarea there was a man named Cornelius, a centurion of what was known as the Italian Cohort, ²a devout man who feared God with all his household, gave alms generously to the people, and prayed continually to God. ³About the ninth hour of the day¹ he saw clearly in a vision an angel of God come in and say to him, "Cornelius." ⁴And he stared at him in terror and said, "What is it, Lord?" And he said to him, "Your prayers and your alms have ascended as a memorial before God. ⁵And now send men to Joppa and bring one Simon who is called Peter. ⁶He is lodging with one Simon, a tanner, whose house is by the sea." ⁷When the angel who spoke to him had departed, he called two of his servants and a devout soldier from among those who attended him, ⁸and having related everything to them, he sent them to Joppa.

⁹The next day, as they were on their journey and approaching the city, Peter went up on the housetop about the sixth hour² to pray. ¹⁰And he became hungry and wanted something to eat, but while they were preparing it, he fell into a trance ¹¹and saw the heavens opened and something like a great sheet descending, being let down by its four corners upon the earth. ¹²In it were all kinds of animals and reptiles and birds of the air. ¹³And there came a voice to him: "Rise, Peter; kill and eat." ¹⁴But Peter said, "By no means, Lord; for I have never eaten anything that is common or unclean." ¹⁵And the voice came to him again a second time, "What God has made clean, do not call common." ¹⁶This happened three times, and the thing was taken up at once to heaven.

¹⁷Now while Peter was inwardly perplexed as to what the vision that he had seen might mean, behold, the men who were sent by Cornelius, having made inquiry for Simon's house, stood at the gate ¹⁸and called out to ask whether Simon who was called Peter was lodging there. ¹⁹And while Peter was pondering the vision, the Spirit said to him, "Behold, three men are looking for you. ²⁰Rise and go down and accompany them without hesitation, for I have sent them." ²¹And Peter went down to the

¹ That is, 3 P.M. ² That is, noon

men and said, "I am the one you are looking for. What is the reason for your coming?" ²²And they said, "Cornelius, a centurion, an upright and God-fearing man, who is well spoken of by the whole Jewish nation, was directed by a holy angel to send for you to come to his house and to hear what you have to say." ²³So he invited them in to be his guests.

The next day he rose and went away with them, and some of the brothers from Joppa accompanied him. ²⁴And on the following day they entered Caesarea. Cornelius was expecting them and had called together his relatives and close friends. ²⁵When Peter entered, Cornelius met him and fell down at his feet and worshiped him. ²⁶But Peter lifted him up, saying, "Stand up; I too am a man." ²⁷And as he talked with him, he went in and found many persons gathered. ²⁸And he said to them, "You yourselves know how unlawful it is for a Jew to associate with or to visit anyone of another nation, but God has shown me that I should not call any person common or unclean. ²⁹So when I was sent for, I came without objection. I ask then why you sent for me."

³⁰And Cornelius said, "Four days ago, about this hour, I was praying in my house at the ninth hour,[1] and behold, a man stood before me in bright clothing ³¹and said, 'Cornelius, your prayer has been heard and your alms have been remembered before God. ³²Send therefore to Joppa and ask for Simon who is called Peter. He is lodging in the house of Simon, a tanner, by the sea.' ³³So I sent for you at once, and you have been kind enough to come. Now therefore we are all here in the presence of God to hear all that you have been commanded by the Lord."

³⁴So Peter opened his mouth and said: "Truly I understand that God shows no partiality, ³⁵but in every nation anyone who fears him and does what is right is acceptable to him. ³⁶As for the word that he sent to Israel, preaching good news of peace through Jesus Christ (he is Lord of all), ³⁷you yourselves know what happened throughout all Judea, beginning from Galilee after the baptism that John proclaimed: ³⁸how God anointed Jesus of Nazareth with the Holy Spirit and with power. He went about doing good and healing all who were oppressed by the devil, for God was with him. ³⁹And we are witnesses of all that he did both in the country of the Jews and in Jerusalem. They put him to death by hanging him on a tree, ⁴⁰but God raised him on the third day and made him to appear, ⁴¹not to all the people but to us who had been chosen by God as witnesses, who ate and drank with him after he rose from the dead. ⁴²And he commanded us to preach to the people and to testify that he is the one appointed by God to be judge of the living and the dead. ⁴³To him all the prophets bear witness that everyone who believes in him receives forgiveness of sins through his name."

⁴⁴While Peter was still saying these things, the Holy Spirit fell on all who heard the word. ⁴⁵And the believers from among the circumcised who had come with Peter were amazed, because the gift of the Holy Spirit was poured out even on the Gentiles. ⁴⁶For they were hearing them speaking in tongues and extolling God. Then Peter declared, ⁴⁷"Can anyone withhold water for baptizing these people, who have received the Holy Spirit just as we have?" ⁴⁸And he commanded them to be baptized in the name of Jesus Christ. Then they asked him to remain for some days.

11 Now the apostles and the brothers[2] who were throughout Judea heard that the Gentiles also had received the word of God. ²So when Peter went up to Jerusalem, the circumcision party criticized him, saying, ³"You went to uncircumcised

---

¹ That is, 3 P.M. ² Or *brothers and sisters*

men and ate with them." ⁴But Peter began and explained it to them in order: ⁵"I was in the city of Joppa praying, and in a trance I saw a vision, something like a great sheet descending, being let down from heaven by its four corners, and it came down to me. ⁶Looking at it closely, I observed animals and beasts of prey and reptiles and birds of the air. ⁷And I heard a voice saying to me, 'Rise, Peter; kill and eat.' ⁸But I said, 'By no means, Lord; for nothing common or unclean has ever entered my mouth.' ⁹But the voice answered a second time from heaven, 'What God has made clean, do not call common.' ¹⁰This happened three times, and all was drawn up again into heaven. ¹¹And behold, at that very moment three men arrived at the house in which we were, sent to me from Caesarea. ¹²And the Spirit told me to go with them, making no distinction. These six brothers also accompanied me, and we entered the man's house. ¹³And he told us how he had seen the angel stand in his house and say, 'Send to Joppa and bring Simon who is called Peter; ¹⁴he will declare to you a message by which you will be saved, you and all your household.' ¹⁵As I began to speak, the Holy Spirit fell on them just as on us at the beginning. ¹⁶And I remembered the word of the Lord, how he said, 'John baptized with water, but you will be baptized with the Holy Spirit.' ¹⁷If then God gave the same gift to them as he gave to us when we believed in the Lord Jesus Christ, who was I that I could stand in God's way?" ¹⁸When they heard these things they fell silent. And they glorified God, saying, "Then to the Gentiles also God has granted repentance that leads to life."

> **Focus on the church in Antioch** [11:19–30]. By now a rhythm has evolved in which fully narrated, epoch-making events are followed by brief entries in a historical chronicle. This unit gives us a glimpse into one corner of the emerging church, namely the church at Antioch. The key events are the arrival of Hellenists (Gentiles) who preach the gospel with great effectiveness (vv. 19–21); the arrival of Barnabas and Saul to observe and participate in this remarkable new development (vv. 22–26); the collection of relief money from Christians in Antioch to help victims of a famine in Judea (11:27–30). Here is proof that the kingdom has taken root in the non-Jewish world.

¹⁹Now those who were scattered because of the persecution that arose over Stephen traveled as far as Phoenicia and Cyprus and Antioch, speaking the word to no one except Jews. ²⁰But there were some of them, men of Cyprus and Cyrene, who on coming to Antioch spoke to the Hellenists[1] also, preaching the Lord Jesus. ²¹And the hand of the Lord was with them, and a great number who believed turned to the Lord. ²²The report of this came to the ears of the church in Jerusalem, and they sent Barnabas to Antioch. ²³When he came and saw the grace of God, he was glad, and he exhorted them all to remain faithful to the Lord with steadfast purpose, ²⁴for he was a good man, full of the Holy Spirit and of faith. And a great many people were added to the Lord. ²⁵So Barnabas went to Tarsus to look for Saul, ²⁶and when he had found him, he brought him to Antioch. For a whole year they met with the church and taught a great many people. And in Antioch the disciples were first called Christians. ²⁷Now in these days prophets came down from Jerusalem to Antioch. ²⁸And one of them named Agabus stood up and foretold by the Spirit that there would be a great famine over all the world (this took place in the days of Claudius). ²⁹So the disciples

---

[1] Or *Greeks* (that is, Greek-speaking non-Jews)

determined, everyone according to his ability, to send relief to the brothers[1] living in Judea. [30]And they did so, sending it to the elders by the hand of Barnabas and Saul.

> **The rescue of Peter** [chapter 12]. The story of Peter's rescue from prison is a *rescue story par excellence. It is told from beginning to end in vivid detail and a seamless step-by-step sequence from a seemingly insurmountable danger to a great escape. The story is based on a premise of *reversal, as the action begins with Herod's despotic persecution of the Christians and ends with his own sordid death as he is eaten by worms. Latent humor emerges when Peter is unable to make it into a prayer meeting being held on his behalf, and in the group's concluding that the person outside cannot be Peter but must be his angel (v. 15).

12 About that time Herod the king laid violent hands on some who belonged to the church. [2]He killed James the brother of John with the sword, [3]and when he saw that it pleased the Jews, he proceeded to arrest Peter also. This was during the days of Unleavened Bread. [4]And when he had seized him, he put him in prison, delivering him over to four squads of soldiers to guard him, intending after the Passover to bring him out to the people. [5]So Peter was kept in prison, but earnest prayer for him was made to God by the church.

[6]Now when Herod was about to bring him out, on that very night, Peter was sleeping between two soldiers, bound with two chains, and sentries before the door were guarding the prison. [7]And behold, an angel of the Lord stood next to him, and a light shone in the cell. He struck Peter on the side and woke him, saying, "Get up quickly." And the chains fell off his hands. [8]And the angel said to him, "Dress yourself and put on your sandals." And he did so. And he said to him, "Wrap your cloak around you and follow me." [9]And he went out and followed him. He did not know that what was being done by the angel was real, but thought he was seeing a vision. [10]When they had passed the first and the second guard, they came to the iron gate leading into the city. It opened for them of its own accord, and they went out and went along one street, and immediately the angel left him. [11]When Peter came to himself, he said, "Now I am sure that the Lord has sent his angel and rescued me from the hand of Herod and from all that the Jewish people were expecting."

[12]When he realized this, he went to the house of Mary, the mother of John whose other name was Mark, where many were gathered together and were praying. [13]And when he knocked at the door of the gateway, a servant girl named Rhoda came to answer. [14]Recognizing Peter's voice, in her joy she did not open the gate but ran in and reported that Peter was standing at the gate. [15]They said to her, "You are out of your mind." But she kept insisting that it was so, and they kept saying, "It is his angel!" [16]But Peter continued knocking, and when they opened, they saw him and were amazed. [17]But motioning to them with his hand to be silent, he described to them how the Lord had brought him out of the prison. And he said, "Tell these things to James and to the brothers."[2] Then he departed and went to another place.

[18]Now when day came, there was no little disturbance among the soldiers over what had become of Peter. [19]And after Herod searched for him and did not find him, he examined the sentries and ordered that they should be put to death. Then he went down from Judea to Caesarea and spent time there.

[1] Or brothers and sisters [2] Or brothers and sisters

²⁰Now Herod was angry with the people of Tyre and Sidon, and they came to him with one accord, and having persuaded Blastus, the king's chamberlain, they asked for peace, because their country depended on the king's country for food. ²¹On an appointed day Herod put on his royal robes, took his seat upon the throne, and delivered an oration to them. ²²And the people were shouting, "The voice of a god, and not of a man!" ²³Immediately an angel of the Lord struck him down, because he did not give God the glory, and he was eaten by worms and breathed his last.

²⁴But the word of God increased and multiplied.

²⁵And Barnabas and Saul returned from¹ Jerusalem when they had completed their service, bringing with them John, whose other name was Mark.

Paul's first missionary journey [chapters 13–14]. This narrative unit starts when the church at Antioch sets Barnabas and Paul apart for missionary work (13:1–3) and ends with the return of these two missionaries to give an account of their activity (14:24–28). Between these bookends we get the story of what is familiarly known as Paul's first missionary journey. The first thing to do when assimilating this section is to follow the geographic journey that Paul and Barnabas took, in an awareness that the genre at work is the travel story. The second thing to note is the exact outcome of the visit to each successive city—a story of mingled opposition, receptivity, success, and apparent failure (apparent only because churches are established even when the missionaries are expelled from a city). Today we would label the ministry of Paul and Barnabas church planting. Since the story can be viewed as the story of the Holy Spirit's action, it is important to trace the overall success of the gospel in the world in which it was proclaimed. Finally, it is important to note the content of the message that Paul and Barnabas proclaimed, the essence of which is salvation through the death and resurrection of Jesus Christ.

---

13 Now there were in the church at Antioch prophets and teachers, Barnabas, Simeon who was called Niger,² Lucius of Cyrene, Manaen a member of the court of Herod the tetrarch, and Saul. ²While they were worshiping the Lord and fasting, the Holy Spirit said, "Set apart for me Barnabas and Saul for the work to which I have called them." ³Then after fasting and praying they laid their hands on them and sent them off.

⁴So, being sent out by the Holy Spirit, they went down to Seleucia, and from there they sailed to Cyprus. ⁵When they arrived at Salamis, they proclaimed the word of God in the synagogues of the Jews. And they had John to assist them. ⁶When they had gone through the whole island as far as Paphos, they came upon a certain magician, a Jewish false prophet named Bar-Jesus. ⁷He was with the proconsul, Sergius Paulus, a man of intelligence, who summoned Barnabas and Saul and sought to hear the word of God. ⁸But Elymas the magician (for that is the meaning of his name) opposed them, seeking to turn the proconsul away from the faith. ⁹But Saul, who was also called Paul, filled with the Holy Spirit, looked intently at him ¹⁰and said, "You son of the devil, you enemy of all righteousness, full of all deceit and villainy, will you not stop making crooked the straight paths of the Lord? ¹¹And now, behold, the hand of the Lord is upon you, and you will be blind and unable to see the sun for a time." Immediately mist and darkness fell upon him, and he went about seeking people to

---

¹ Some manuscripts *to* ² *Niger* is a Latin word meaning *black*, or *dark*

lead him by the hand. [12]Then the proconsul believed, when he saw what had occurred, for he was astonished at the teaching of the Lord.

[13]Now Paul and his companions set sail from Paphos and came to Perga in Pamphylia. And John left them and returned to Jerusalem, [14]but they went on from Perga and came to Antioch in Pisidia. And on the Sabbath day they went into the synagogue and sat down. [15]After the reading from the Law and the Prophets, the rulers of the synagogue sent a message to them, saying, "Brothers, if you have any word of encouragement for the people, say it." [16]So Paul stood up, and motioning with his hand said:

"Men of Israel and you who fear God, listen. [17]The God of this people Israel chose our fathers and made the people great during their stay in the land of Egypt, and with uplifted arm he led them out of it. [18]And for about forty years he put up with[1] them in the wilderness. [19]And after destroying seven nations in the land of Canaan, he gave them their land as an inheritance. [20]All this took about 450 years. And after that he gave them judges until Samuel the prophet. [21]Then they asked for a king, and God gave them Saul the son of Kish, a man of the tribe of Benjamin, for forty years. [22]And when he had removed him, he raised up David to be their king, of whom he testified and said, [a]'I have found in David the son of Jesse [b]a man after my heart, who will do all my will.' [23]Of this man's offspring God has brought to Israel a Savior, Jesus, as he promised. [24]Before his coming, John had proclaimed a baptism of repentance to all the people of Israel. [25]And as John was finishing his course, he said, 'What do you suppose that I am? I am not he. No, but behold, after me one is coming, the sandals of whose feet I am not worthy to untie.'

[26]"Brothers, sons of the family of Abraham, and those among you who fear God, to us has been sent the message of this salvation. [27]For those who live in Jerusalem and their rulers, because they did not recognize him nor understand the utterances of the prophets, which are read every Sabbath, fulfilled them by condemning him. [28]And though they found in him no guilt worthy of death, they asked Pilate to have him executed. [29]And when they had carried out all that was written of him, they took him down from the tree and laid him in a tomb. [30]But God raised him from the dead, [31]and for many days he appeared to those who had come up with him from Galilee to Jerusalem, who are now his witnesses to the people. [32]And we bring you the good news that what God promised to the fathers, [33]this he has fulfilled to us their children by raising Jesus, as also it is written in the second Psalm,

[c]"'You are my Son,
       today I have begotten you.'

[34]And as for the fact that he raised him from the dead, no more to return to corruption, he has spoken in this way,

"'I will give you [d]the holy and sure blessings of David.'

[35]Therefore he says also in another psalm,

[e]"'You will not let your Holy One see corruption.'

[36]For David, after he had served the purpose of God in his own generation, fell asleep and was laid with his fathers and saw corruption, [37]but he whom God raised up did

---

[1] Some manuscripts *he carried* (compare Deuteronomy 1:31)   [a] Ps. 89:20   [b] 1 Sam. 13:14   [c] Ps. 2:7   [d] Isa. 55:3   [e] Ps. 16:10

not see corruption. [38]Let it be known to you therefore, brothers, that through this man forgiveness of sins is proclaimed to you, [39]and by him everyone who believes is freed[1] from everything from which you could not be freed by the law of Moses. [40]Beware, therefore, lest what is said in the Prophets should come about:

[41][a]"'Look, you scoffers,
  be astounded and perish;
for I am doing a work in your days,
  a work that you will not believe, even if one tells it to you.'"

[42]As they went out, the people begged that these things might be told them the next Sabbath. [43]And after the meeting of the synagogue broke up, many Jews and devout converts to Judaism followed Paul and Barnabas, who, as they spoke with them, urged them to continue in the grace of God.

[44]The next Sabbath almost the whole city gathered to hear the word of the Lord. [45]But when the Jews saw the crowds, they were filled with jealousy and began to contradict what was spoken by Paul, reviling him. [46]And Paul and Barnabas spoke out boldly, saying, "It was necessary that the word of God be spoken first to you. Since you thrust it aside and judge yourselves unworthy of eternal life, behold, we are turning to the Gentiles. [47]For so the Lord has commanded us, saying,

[b]"'I have made you a light for the Gentiles,
  that you may bring salvation to the ends of the earth.'"

[48]And when the Gentiles heard this, they began rejoicing and glorifying the word of the Lord, and as many as were appointed to eternal life believed. [49]And the word of the Lord was spreading throughout the whole region. [50]But the Jews incited the devout women of high standing and the leading men of the city, stirred up persecution against Paul and Barnabas, and drove them out of their district. [51]But they shook off the dust from their feet against them and went to Iconium. [52]And the disciples were filled with joy and with the Holy Spirit.

14 Now at Iconium they entered together into the Jewish synagogue and spoke in such a way that a great number of both Jews and Greeks believed. [2]But the unbelieving Jews stirred up the Gentiles and poisoned their minds against the brothers.[2] [3]So they remained for a long time, speaking boldly for the Lord, who bore witness to the word of his grace, granting signs and wonders to be done by their hands. [4]But the people of the city were divided; some sided with the Jews and some with the apostles. [5]When an attempt was made by both Gentiles and Jews, with their rulers, to mistreat them and to stone them, [6]they learned of it and fled to Lystra and Derbe, cities of Lycaonia, and to the surrounding country, [7]and there they continued to preach the gospel.

[8]Now at Lystra there was a man sitting who could not use his feet. He was crippled from birth and had never walked. [9]He listened to Paul speaking. And Paul, looking intently at him and seeing that he had faith to be made well,[3] [10]said in a loud voice, "Stand upright on your feet." And he sprang up and began walking. [11]And when the crowds saw what Paul had done, they lifted up their voices, saying in Lycaonian, "The gods have come down to us in the likeness of men!" [12]Barnabas they called Zeus, and Paul, Hermes, because he was the chief speaker. [13]And the priest of Zeus, whose tem-

---

[1] Greek *justified*; twice in this verse [2] Or *brothers and sisters* [3] Or *be saved* [a] Hab. 1:5 [b] Isa. 49:6

ple was at the entrance to the city, brought oxen and garlands to the gates and wanted to offer sacrifice with the crowds. ¹⁴But when the apostles Barnabas and Paul heard of it, they tore their garments and rushed out into the crowd, crying out, ¹⁵"Men, why are you doing these things? We also are men, of like nature with you, and we bring you good news, that you should turn from these vain things to a living God, who made the heaven and the earth and the sea and all that is in them. ¹⁶In past generations he allowed all the nations to walk in their own ways. ¹⁷Yet he did not leave himself without witness, for he did good by giving you rains from heaven and fruitful seasons, satisfying your hearts with food and gladness." ¹⁸Even with these words they scarcely restrained the people from offering sacrifice to them.

¹⁹But Jews came from Antioch and Iconium, and having persuaded the crowds, they stoned Paul and dragged him out of the city, supposing that he was dead. ²⁰But when the disciples gathered about him, he rose up and entered the city, and on the next day he went on with Barnabas to Derbe. ²¹When they had preached the gospel to that city and had made many disciples, they returned to Lystra and to Iconium and to Antioch, ²²strengthening the souls of the disciples, encouraging them to continue in the faith, and saying that through many tribulations we must enter the kingdom of God. ²³And when they had appointed elders for them in every church, with prayer and fasting they committed them to the Lord in whom they had believed.

²⁴Then they passed through Pisidia and came to Pamphylia. ²⁵And when they had spoken the word in Perga, they went down to Attalia, ²⁶and from there they sailed to Antioch, where they had been commended to the grace of God for the work that they had fulfilled. ²⁷And when they arrived and gathered the church together, they declared all that God had done with them, and how he had opened a door of faith to the Gentiles. ²⁸And they remained no little time with the disciples.

The Jerusalem Council [15:1–35]. This unit narrates what happened at the famous first church council (a deliberative meeting of church leaders to determine policy for a whole body of churches). Its subject was one of the pressing issues facing the Christian church in the first century—whether or not non-Jewish Gentiles needed to practice the rituals of the OT believing community as a necessary part of attaining salvation in Christ. The genre of the story is the *docudrama, and it is easy to read the account as though it were an article in a newspaper or church periodical. The unit unfolds as follows: the controversy that required a decision (vv. 1–5); Peter's address urging the council not to impose the Jewish ritual of circumcision on Gentile converts to Christianity (vv. 6–11); confirming statements by Barnabas, Paul, and James (vv. 12–21); the sending out of messengers to disseminate a letter bearing the official decision of the council (vv. 22–35). We can note in passing that both Peter and Paul play a prominent role in the Jerusalem Council, and that in this event the baton is passed from Peter as the leading character in the first half of Acts to Paul, who is the leading figure in the second half.

15

But some men came down from Judea and were teaching the brothers, "Unless you are circumcised according to the custom of Moses, you cannot be saved." ²And after Paul and Barnabas had no small dissension and debate with them, Paul and Barnabas and some of the others were appointed to go up to Jerusalem to the apostles and the elders about this question. ³So, being sent on their way by the church, they passed through both Phoenicia and Samaria, describing in detail the conversion of the Gentiles, and brought great joy to all the brothers.[1] ⁴When they came to Jerusalem, they were welcomed by the church and the apostles and the elders, and they declared all that God had done with them. ⁵But some believers who belonged to the party of the Pharisees rose up and said, "It is necessary to circumcise them and to order them to keep the law of Moses."

⁶The apostles and the elders were gathered together to consider this matter. ⁷And after there had been much debate, Peter stood up and said to them, "Brothers, you know that in the early days God made a choice among you, that by my mouth the Gentiles should hear the word of the gospel and believe. ⁸And God, who knows the heart, bore witness to them, by giving them the Holy Spirit just as he did to us, ⁹and he made no distinction between us and them, having cleansed their hearts by faith. ¹⁰Now, therefore, why are you putting God to the test by placing a yoke on the neck of the disciples that neither our fathers nor we have been able to bear? ¹¹But we believe that we will be saved through the grace of the Lord Jesus, just as they will."

¹²And all the assembly fell silent, and they listened to Barnabas and Paul as they related what signs and wonders God had done through them among the Gentiles. ¹³After they finished speaking, James replied, "Brothers, listen to me. ¹⁴Simeon has related how God first visited the Gentiles, to take from them a people for his name. ¹⁵And with this the words of the prophets agree, just as it is written,

¹⁶ᵃ"'After this I will return,
and I will rebuild the tent of David that has fallen;
I will rebuild its ruins,
and I will restore it,
¹⁷   that the remnant[2] of mankind may seek the Lord,
and all the Gentiles who are called by my name,
says the Lord, who makes these things ¹⁸known from of old.'

¹⁹Therefore my judgment is that we should not trouble those of the Gentiles who turn to God, ²⁰but should write to them to abstain from the things polluted by idols, and from sexual immorality, and from what has been strangled, and from blood. ²¹For from ancient generations Moses has had in every city those who proclaim him, for he is read every Sabbath in the synagogues."

²²Then it seemed good to the apostles and the elders, with the whole church, to choose men from among them and send them to Antioch with Paul and Barnabas. They sent Judas called Barsabbas, and Silas, leading men among the brothers, ²³with the following letter: "The brothers, both the apostles and the elders, to the brothers[3] who are of the Gentiles in Antioch and Syria and Cilicia, greetings. ²⁴Since we have heard that some persons have gone out from us and troubled you[4] with words, unsettling your minds, although we gave them no instructions, ²⁵it has seemed good to us, having come to one accord, to choose men and send them to you with our beloved Barnabas and Paul, ²⁶men who have risked their lives for the sake of our Lord Jesus Christ. ²⁷We have therefore sent Judas and Silas, who themselves will tell you the same things by word of mouth. ²⁸For it has seemed good to the Holy Spirit and to us to lay on you no greater burden than these requirements: ²⁹that you abstain from what has been sacrificed to idols, and from blood, and from what has been strangled, and from sexual immorality. If you keep yourselves from these, you will do well. Farewell."

[1] Or brothers and sisters; also verse 22 [2] Or rest [3] Or brothers and sisters; also verses 32, 33, 36 [4] Some manuscripts some persons from us have troubled you ᵃ Amos 9:11, 12

[30] So when they were sent off, they went down to Antioch, and having gathered the congregation together, they delivered the letter. [31] And when they had read it, they rejoiced because of its encouragement. [32] And Judas and Silas, who were themselves prophets, encouraged and strengthened the brothers with many words. [33] And after they had spent some time, they were sent off in peace by the brothers to those who had sent them.[1] [35] But Paul and Barnabas remained in Antioch, teaching and preaching the word of the Lord, with many others also.

The first leg of Paul's second missionary journey [15:36–17:15]. The conventions of the travel story now resume as the storyteller narrates the second missionary journey of Paul, the purpose of which is for Paul to revisit cities where he had earlier planted churches (15:36). Things to analyze in a travel story include the geographical movements of the leading characters, the places that these characters visit, the cast of characters with whom the travelers are brought into encounter, and the appearance of such stock devices of plot as conflict, danger, risk, suspense, and testing. This section of Acts is a triumph of storytelling, and it is important to relive the adventure and excitement of the action. You will be hard pressed to find a more exciting story than Paul's second missionary journey. Literary critics use the phrase point of view to identify the perspective of the storyteller. Most of the book of Acts is told in the third-person point of view, meaning that the narrator refers to the characters as "he" or "they" or by the characters' names. But there are "we" sections in Acts where the perspective is first-person plural, and the first of these sections is 16:10–17. We can infer that Luke was present with Paul in the events narrated in the first person.

[36] And after some days Paul said to Barnabas, "Let us return and visit the brothers in every city where we proclaimed the word of the Lord, and see how they are." [37] Now Barnabas wanted to take with them John called Mark. [38] But Paul thought best not to take with them one who had withdrawn from them in Pamphylia and had not gone with them to the work. [39] And there arose a sharp disagreement, so that they separated from each other. Barnabas took Mark with him and sailed away to Cyprus, [40] but Paul chose Silas and departed, having been commended by the brothers to the grace of the Lord. [41] And he went through Syria and Cilicia, strengthening the churches.

16 Paul[2] came also to Derbe and to Lystra. A disciple was there, named Timothy, the son of a Jewish woman who was a believer, but his father was a Greek. [2] He was well spoken of by the brothers[3] at Lystra and Iconium. [3] Paul wanted Timothy to accompany him, and he took him and circumcised him because of the Jews who were in those places, for they all knew that his father was a Greek. [4] As they went on their way through the cities, they delivered to them for observance the decisions that had been reached by the apostles and elders who were in Jerusalem. [5] So the churches were strengthened in the faith, and they increased in numbers daily.

[6] And they went through the region of Phrygia and Galatia, having been forbidden by the Holy Spirit to speak the word in Asia. [7] And when they had come up to Mysia, they attempted to go into Bithynia, but the Spirit of Jesus did not allow them. [8] So, passing by Mysia, they went down to Troas. [9] And a vision appeared to Paul in the night: a man of Macedonia was standing there, urging him and saying, "Come over to Macedonia and help us." [10] And when Paul[4] had seen the vision, immediately we

---

[1] Some manuscripts insert verse 34: *But it seemed good to Silas to remain there* [2] Greek *He* [3] Or *brothers and sisters;* also verse 40 [4] Greek *he*

sought to go on into Macedonia, concluding that God had called us to preach the gospel to them.

¹¹So, setting sail from Troas, we made a direct voyage to Samothrace, and the following day to Neapolis, ¹²and from there to Philippi, which is a leading city of the¹ district of Macedonia and a Roman colony. We remained in this city some days. ¹³And on the Sabbath day we went outside the gate to the riverside, where we supposed there was a place of prayer, and we sat down and spoke to the women who had come together. ¹⁴One who heard us was a woman named Lydia, from the city of Thyatira, a seller of purple goods, who was a worshiper of God. The Lord opened her heart to pay attention to what was said by Paul. ¹⁵And after she was baptized, and her household as well, she urged us, saying, "If you have judged me to be faithful to the Lord, come to my house and stay." And she prevailed upon us.

¹⁶As we were going to the place of prayer, we were met by a slave girl who had a spirit of divination and brought her owners much gain by fortune-telling. ¹⁷She followed Paul and us, crying out, "These men are servants² of the Most High God, who proclaim to you the way of salvation." ¹⁸And this she kept doing for many days. Paul, having become greatly annoyed, turned and said to the spirit, "I command you in the name of Jesus Christ to come out of her." And it came out that very hour.

¹⁹But when her owners saw that their hope of gain was gone, they seized Paul and Silas and dragged them into the marketplace before the rulers. ²⁰And when they had brought them to the magistrates, they said, "These men are Jews, and they are disturbing our city. ²¹They advocate customs that are not lawful for us as Romans to accept or practice." ²²The crowd joined in attacking them, and the magistrates tore the garments off them and gave orders to beat them with rods. ²³And when they had inflicted many blows upon them, they threw them into prison, ordering the jailer to keep them safely. ²⁴Having received this order, he put them into the inner prison and fastened their feet in the stocks.

²⁵About midnight Paul and Silas were praying and singing hymns to God, and the prisoners were listening to them, ²⁶and suddenly there was a great earthquake, so that the foundations of the prison were shaken. And immediately all the doors were opened, and everyone's bonds were unfastened. ²⁷When the jailer woke and saw that the prison doors were open, he drew his sword and was about to kill himself, supposing that the prisoners had escaped. ²⁸But Paul cried with a loud voice, "Do not harm yourself, for we are all here." ²⁹And the jailer³ called for lights and rushed in, and trembling with fear he fell down before Paul and Silas. ³⁰Then he brought them out and said, "Sirs, what must I do to be saved?" ³¹And they said, "Believe in the Lord Jesus, and you will be saved, you and your household." ³²And they spoke the word of the Lord to him and to all who were in his house. ³³And he took them the same hour of the night and washed their wounds; and he was baptized at once, he and all his family. ³⁴Then he brought them up into his house and set food before them. And he rejoiced along with his entire household that he had believed in God.

³⁵But when it was day, the magistrates sent the police, saying, "Let those men go." ³⁶And the jailer reported these words to Paul, saying, "The magistrates have sent to let you go. Therefore come out now and go in peace." ³⁷But Paul said to them, "They have beaten us publicly, uncondemned, men who are Roman citizens, and have thrown us into prison; and do they now throw us out secretly? No! Let them come themselves and take us out." ³⁸The police reported these words to the magistrates, and they were

¹ Or that ² Greek bondservants ³ Greek he

afraid when they heard that they were Roman citizens. ³⁹So they came and apologized to them. And they took them out and asked them to leave the city. ⁴⁰So they went out of the prison and visited Lydia. And when they had seen the brothers, they encouraged them and departed.

17 Now when they had passed through Amphipolis and Apollonia, they came to Thessalonica, where there was a synagogue of the Jews. ²And Paul went in, as was his custom, and on three Sabbath days he reasoned with them from the Scriptures, ³explaining and proving that it was necessary for the Christ to suffer and to rise from the dead, and saying, "This Jesus, whom I proclaim to you, is the Christ." ⁴And some of them were persuaded and joined Paul and Silas, as did a great many of the devout Greeks and not a few of the leading women. ⁵But the Jews were jealous, and taking some wicked men of the rabble, they formed a mob, set the city in an uproar, and attacked the house of Jason, seeking to bring them out to the crowd. ⁶And when they could not find them, they dragged Jason and some of the brothers before the city authorities, shouting, "These men who have turned the world upside down have come here also, ⁷and Jason has received them, and they are all acting against the decrees of Caesar, saying that there is another king, Jesus." ⁸And the people and the city authorities were disturbed when they heard these things. ⁹And when they had taken money as security from Jason and the rest, they let them go.

¹⁰The brothers¹ immediately sent Paul and Silas away by night to Berea, and when they arrived they went into the Jewish synagogue. ¹¹Now these Jews were more noble than those in Thessalonica; they received the word with all eagerness, examining the Scriptures daily to see if these things were so. ¹²Many of them therefore believed, with not a few Greek women of high standing as well as men. ¹³But when the Jews from Thessalonica learned that the word of God was proclaimed by Paul at Berea also, they came there too, agitating and stirring up the crowds. ¹⁴Then the brothers immediately sent Paul off on his way to the sea, but Silas and Timothy remained there. ¹⁵Those who conducted Paul brought him as far as Athens, and after receiving a command for Silas and Timothy to come to him as soon as possible, they departed.

Paul's address to the Areopagus [17:16–34]. This is one of the famous events in the book of Acts. Rome ruled the world, but Greece was the intellectual fountain of the classical world. The lead-in to the address establishes Paul's anguish of soul as he walked the streets of a godless but influential city (vv. 16–21). The Areopagus was both a place (a hill in Athens where intellectuals gathered and speeches were given) and a council of men who exercised control over the public speaking that occurred in Athens. Paul in effect was invited by an august group of intellectuals to establish his credentials as a speaker in the marketplace of ideas. The address that Luke gives us follows the conventions of classical oratory. According to classical rhetoric, a formal address was supposed to begin with an exordium—an introduction in which the speaker secured the goodwill of his audience and aroused their interest. Paul's speech, replete with the conventional opening "Men of Athens," long, flowing syntax, and allusions to classical literature, is virtually all exordium (vv. 22–28). As Paul nears the end of his exordium, he summarizes the general drift of his remarks up to that point (v. 29) and moves toward the second part of a classical oration, known as the propositio—the statement of thesis. Up to this point, Paul has engaged in natural theology (theology based on human reason rather than supernatural revelation) and has asserted universal theism. In his *propo-*

¹ Or *brothers and sisters*; also verse 14

sitio (vv. 30–31), Paul abandons this strategy in favor of the distinctives of Christian revelation. But the moment he mentions the resurrection, the crowd turns against him, and he is unable to continue his oration (vv. 32–33). Even this failure by external standards produced converts (v. 34), including the famous mystic of the early Christian church Dionysius the Areopagite.

¹⁶Now while Paul was waiting for them at Athens, his spirit was provoked within him as he saw that the city was full of idols. ¹⁷So he reasoned in the synagogue with the Jews and the devout persons, and in the marketplace every day with those who happened to be there. ¹⁸Some of the Epicurean and Stoic philosophers also conversed with him. And some said, "What does this babbler wish to say?" Others said, "He seems to be a preacher of foreign divinities"—because he was preaching Jesus and the resurrection. ¹⁹And they took him and brought him to the Areopagus, saying, "May we know what this new teaching is that you are presenting? ²⁰For you bring some strange things to our ears. We wish to know therefore what these things mean." ²¹Now all the Athenians and the foreigners who lived there would spend their time in nothing except telling or hearing something new.

²²So Paul, standing in the midst of the Areopagus, said: "Men of Athens, I perceive that in every way you are very religious. ²³For as I passed along and observed the objects of your worship, I found also an altar with this inscription, 'To the unknown god.' What therefore you worship as unknown, this I proclaim to you. ²⁴The God who made the world and everything in it, being Lord of heaven and earth, does not live in temples made by man,[1] ²⁵nor is he served by human hands, as though he needed anything, since he himself gives to all mankind life and breath and everything. ²⁶And he made from one man every nation of mankind to live on all the face of the earth, having determined allotted periods and the boundaries of their dwelling place, ²⁷that they should seek God, in the hope that they might feel their way toward him and find him. Yet he is actually not far from each one of us, ²⁸for

"'In him we live and move and have our being';[2]

as even some of your own poets have said,

"'For we are indeed his offspring.'[3]

²⁹Being then God's offspring, we ought not to think that the divine being is like gold or silver or stone, an image formed by the art and imagination of man. ³⁰The times of ignorance God overlooked, but now he commands all people everywhere to repent, ³¹because he has fixed a day on which he will judge the world in righteousness by a man whom he has appointed; and of this he has given assurance to all by raising him from the dead."

³²Now when they heard of the resurrection of the dead, some mocked. But others said, "We will hear you again about this." ³³So Paul went out from their midst. ³⁴But some men joined him and believed, among whom also were Dionysius the Areopagite and a woman named Damaris and others with them.

Conclusion of Paul's second missionary journey [18:1–22]. The narrative motifs remain constant: travel, arrival, conflict or opposition, being dragged before judges, and

---

[1] Greek *made by hands* [2] Probably from Epimenides of Crete [3] From Aratus's poem "Phainomena"

leave-taking. The appearance of Jesus to Paul in a dream (vv. 9–10) reminds us of the overall motif that the book of Acts narrates what Jesus continued to do after his ascension into heaven.

18 After this Paul[1] left Athens and went to Corinth. [2]And he found a Jew named Aquila, a native of Pontus, recently come from Italy with his wife Priscilla, because Claudius had commanded all the Jews to leave Rome. And he went to see them, [3]and because he was of the same trade he stayed with them and worked, for they were tentmakers by trade. [4]And he reasoned in the synagogue every Sabbath, and tried to persuade Jews and Greeks.

[5]When Silas and Timothy arrived from Macedonia, Paul was occupied with the word, testifying to the Jews that the Christ was Jesus. [6]And when they opposed and reviled him, he shook out his garments and said to them, "Your blood be on your own heads! I am innocent. From now on I will go to the Gentiles." [7]And he left there and went to the house of a man named Titius Justus, a worshiper of God. His house was next door to the synagogue. [8]Crispus, the ruler of the synagogue, believed in the Lord, together with his entire household. And many of the Corinthians hearing Paul believed and were baptized. [9]And the Lord said to Paul one night in a vision, "Do not be afraid, but go on speaking and do not be silent, [10]for I am with you, and no one will attack you to harm you, for I have many in this city who are my people." [11]And he stayed a year and six months, teaching the word of God among them.

[12]But when Gallio was proconsul of Achaia, the Jews made a united attack on Paul and brought him before the tribunal, [13]saying, "This man is persuading people to worship God contrary to the law." [14]But when Paul was about to open his mouth, Gallio said to the Jews, "If it were a matter of wrongdoing or vicious crime, O Jews, I would have reason to accept your complaint. [15]But since it is a matter of questions about words and names and your own law, see to it yourselves. I refuse to be a judge of these things." [16]And he drove them from the tribunal. [17]And they all seized Sosthenes, the ruler of the synagogue, and beat him in front of the tribunal. But Gallio paid no attention to any of this.

[18]After this, Paul stayed many days longer and then took leave of the brothers[2] and set sail for Syria, and with him Priscilla and Aquila. At Cenchreae he had cut his hair, for he was under a vow. [19]And they came to Ephesus, and he left them there, but he himself went into the synagogue and reasoned with the Jews. [20]When they asked him to stay for a longer period, he declined. [21]But on taking leave of them he said, "I will return to you if God wills," and he set sail from Ephesus.

[22]When he had landed at Caesarea, he went up and greeted the church, and then went down to Antioch.

The first leg of Paul's third missionary journey [18:23–19:22]. The places that Paul visits in this unit change, but the narrative strategy continues the same, with the travel story as the dominant organizing framework. A good reading strategy is to view oneself as the observant traveling companion of the *protagonist, reliving the events as vividly as possible. The opening segment of the journey suggests the range of things that occurred: traveling, preaching, baptizing, debating in a synagogue, encountering opposition, performing miracles, exorcising evil spirits.

---

[1] Greek he [2] Or brothers and sisters; also verse 27

[23] After spending some time there, he departed and went from one place to the next through the region of Galatia and Phrygia, strengthening all the disciples.

[24] Now a Jew named Apollos, a native of Alexandria, came to Ephesus. He was an eloquent man, competent in the Scriptures. [25] He had been instructed in the way of the Lord. And being fervent in spirit,[1] he spoke and taught accurately the things concerning Jesus, though he knew only the baptism of John. [26] He began to speak boldly in the synagogue, but when Priscilla and Aquila heard him, they took him and explained to him the way of God more accurately. [27] And when he wished to cross to Achaia, the brothers encouraged him and wrote to the disciples to welcome him. When he arrived, he greatly helped those who through grace had believed, [28] for he powerfully refuted the Jews in public, showing by the Scriptures that the Christ was Jesus.

19 And it happened that while Apollos was at Corinth, Paul passed through the inland[2] country and came to Ephesus. There he found some disciples. [2] And he said to them, "Did you receive the Holy Spirit when you believed?" And they said, "No, we have not even heard that there is a Holy Spirit." [3] And he said, "Into what then were you baptized?" They said, "Into John's baptism." [4] And Paul said, "John baptized with the baptism of repentance, telling the people to believe in the one who was to come after him, that is, Jesus." [5] On hearing this, they were baptized in[3] the name of the Lord Jesus. [6] And when Paul had laid his hands on them, the Holy Spirit came on them, and they began speaking in tongues and prophesying. [7] There were about twelve men in all.

[8] And he entered the synagogue and for three months spoke boldly, reasoning and persuading them about the kingdom of God. [9] But when some became stubborn and continued in unbelief, speaking evil of the Way before the congregation, he withdrew from them and took the disciples with him, reasoning daily in the hall of Tyrannus.[4] [10] This continued for two years, so that all the residents of Asia heard the word of the Lord, both Jews and Greeks.

[11] And God was doing extraordinary miracles by the hands of Paul, [12] so that even handkerchiefs or aprons that had touched his skin were carried away to the sick, and their diseases left them and the evil spirits came out of them. [13] Then some of the itinerant Jewish exorcists undertook to invoke the name of the Lord Jesus over those who had evil spirits, saying, "I adjure you by the Jesus whom Paul proclaims." [14] Seven sons of a Jewish high priest named Sceva were doing this. [15] But the evil spirit answered them, "Jesus I know, and Paul I recognize, but who are you?" [16] And the man in whom was the evil spirit leaped on them, mastered all[5] of them and overpowered them, so that they fled out of that house naked and wounded. [17] And this became known to all the residents of Ephesus, both Jews and Greeks. And fear fell upon them all, and the name of the Lord Jesus was extolled. [18] Also many of those who were now believers came, confessing and divulging their practices. [19] And a number of those who had practiced magic arts brought their books together and burned them in the sight of all. And they counted the value of them and found it came to fifty thousand pieces of silver. [20] So the word of the Lord continued to increase and prevail mightily.

[21] Now after these events Paul resolved in the Spirit to pass through Macedonia and Achaia and go to Jerusalem, saying, "After I have been there, I must also see

---

[1] Or in the Spirit [2] Greek upper (that is, highland) [3] Or into [4] Some manuscripts add from the fifth hour to the tenth (that is, from 11 A.M. to 4 P.M.) [5] Or both

Rome." ²²And having sent into Macedonia two of his helpers, Timothy and Erastus, he himself stayed in Asia for a while.

The riot at Ephesus and further travels [19:23–20:16]. The most sensational event of the third missionary journey was the riot at Ephesus. The event comes alive in our imaginations as we follow the sequence. Humor enters the story when, after frenzied shouting for two hours of the chant "Great is Artemis of the Ephesians," the town clerk tells the rioters that everyone already knows that Artemis is great (19:35). After the high voltage of the riot scene, the further travels return us to more normal events. Luke the author enters as a participant again with the resumption of the "we" point of view in 20:5, which extends to the end of the book. The story of Eutychus (20:7–12) is one of the great death-rebirth stories in the Bible.

²³About that time there arose no little disturbance concerning the Way. ²⁴For a man named Demetrius, a silversmith, who made silver shrines of Artemis, brought no little business to the craftsmen. ²⁵These he gathered together, with the workmen in similar trades, and said, "Men, you know that from this business we have our wealth. ²⁶And you see and hear that not only in Ephesus but in almost all of Asia this Paul has persuaded and turned away a great many people, saying that gods made with hands are not gods. ²⁷And there is danger not only that this trade of ours may come into disrepute but also that the temple of the great goddess Artemis may be counted as nothing, and that she may even be deposed from her magnificence, she whom all Asia and the world worship."

²⁸When they heard this they were enraged and were crying out, "Great is Artemis of the Ephesians!" ²⁹So the city was filled with the confusion, and they rushed together into the theater, dragging with them Gaius and Aristarchus, Macedonians who were Paul's companions in travel. ³⁰But when Paul wished to go in among the crowd, the disciples would not let him. ³¹And even some of the Asiarchs,¹ who were friends of his, sent to him and were urging him not to venture into the theater. ³²Now some cried out one thing, some another, for the assembly was in confusion, and most of them did not know why they had come together. ³³Some of the crowd prompted Alexander, whom the Jews had put forward. And Alexander, motioning with his hand, wanted to make a defense to the crowd. ³⁴But when they recognized that he was a Jew, for about two hours they all cried out with one voice, "Great is Artemis of the Ephesians!"

³⁵And when the town clerk had quieted the crowd, he said, "Men of Ephesus, who is there who does not know that the city of the Ephesians is temple keeper of the great Artemis, and of the sacred stone that fell from the sky?² ³⁶Seeing then that these things cannot be denied, you ought to be quiet and do nothing rash. ³⁷For you have brought these men here who are neither sacrilegious nor blasphemers of our goddess. ³⁸If therefore Demetrius and the craftsmen with him have a complaint against anyone, the courts are open, and there are proconsuls. Let them bring charges against one another. ³⁹But if you seek anything further,³ it shall be settled in the regular assembly. ⁴⁰For we really are in danger of being charged with rioting today, since there is no cause that we can give to justify this commotion." ⁴¹And when he had said these things, he dismissed the assembly.

---

¹ That is, high-ranking officers of the province of Asia ² The meaning of the Greek is uncertain ³ Some manuscripts *seek about other matters*

20 After the uproar ceased, Paul sent for the disciples, and after encouraging them, he said farewell and departed for Macedonia. ²When he had gone through those regions and had given them much encouragement, he came to Greece. ³There he spent three months, and when a plot was made against him by the Jews as he was about to set sail for Syria, he decided to return through Macedonia. ⁴Sopater the Berean, son of Pyrrhus, accompanied him; and of the Thessalonians, Aristarchus and Secundus; and Gaius of Derbe, and Timothy; and the Asians, Tychicus and Trophimus. ⁵These went on ahead and were waiting for us at Troas, ⁶but we sailed away from Philippi after the days of Unleavened Bread, and in five days we came to them at Troas, where we stayed for seven days.

⁷On the first day of the week, when we were gathered together to break bread, Paul talked with them, intending to depart on the next day, and he prolonged his speech until midnight. ⁸There were many lamps in the upper room where we were gathered. ⁹And a young man named Eutychus, sitting at the window, sank into a deep sleep as Paul talked still longer. And being overcome by sleep, he fell down from the third story and was taken up dead. ¹⁰But Paul went down and bent over him, and taking him in his arms, said, "Do not be alarmed, for his life is in him." ¹¹And when Paul had gone up and had broken bread and eaten, he conversed with them a long while, until daybreak, and so departed. ¹²And they took the youth away alive, and were not a little comforted.

¹³But going ahead to the ship, we set sail for Assos, intending to take Paul aboard there, for so he had arranged, intending himself to go by land. ¹⁴And when he met us at Assos, we took him on board and went to Mitylene. ¹⁵And sailing from there we came the following day opposite Chios; the next day we touched at Samos; and¹ the day after that we went to Miletus. ¹⁶For Paul had decided to sail past Ephesus, so that he might not have to spend time in Asia, for he was hastening to be at Jerusalem, if possible, on the day of Pentecost.

> **Meeting with the elders at Ephesus, and further travels** [20:17–21:16]. If the riot at Ephesus was the most sensational event on Paul's third missionary journey, his meeting with the elders of Ephesus at Miletus is the most emotionally charged. The speech has overtones of a *farewell discourse by a religious leader to his followers on the occasion of his final meeting with them (a situation hinted at in 19:36–38). Paul covers two main topics in his farewell discourse—a recap and defense of his life and ministry, implicitly offered as an example to follow (20:18–27, 33–35), and exhortations regarding how the elders are to rule after his departure (20:28–32). The travelogue that follows (21:1–16) serves the narrative function of getting Paul back to Jerusalem for the beginning of the final phase of his pilgrimage.

¹⁷Now from Miletus he sent to Ephesus and called the elders of the church to come to him. ¹⁸And when they came to him, he said to them:

"You yourselves know how I lived among you the whole time from the first day that I set foot in Asia, ¹⁹serving the Lord with all humility and with tears and with trials that happened to me through the plots of the Jews; ²⁰how I did not shrink from declaring to you anything that was profitable, and teaching you in public and from house to house, ²¹testifying both to Jews and to Greeks of repentance toward God and of faith in our Lord Jesus Christ. ²²And now, behold, I am going to Jerusalem, con-

---

¹ Some manuscripts add *after remaining at Trogyllium*

strained by[1] the Spirit, not knowing what will happen to me there, [23]except that the Holy Spirit testifies to me in every city that imprisonment and afflictions await me. [24]But I do not account my life of any value nor as precious to myself, if only I may finish my course and the ministry that I received from the Lord Jesus, to testify to the gospel of the grace of God. [25]And now, behold, I know that none of you among whom I have gone about proclaiming the kingdom will see my face again. [26]Therefore I testify to you this day that I am innocent of the blood of all of you, [27]for I did not shrink from declaring to you the whole counsel of God. [28]Pay careful attention to yourselves and to all the flock, in which the Holy Spirit has made you overseers, to care for the church of God,[2] which he obtained with his own blood.[3] [29]I know that after my departure fierce wolves will come in among you, not sparing the flock; [30]and from among your own selves will arise men speaking twisted things, to draw away the disciples after them. [31]Therefore be alert, remembering that for three years I did not cease night or day to admonish everyone with tears. [32]And now I commend you to God and to the word of his grace, which is able to build you up and to give you the inheritance among all those who are sanctified. [33]I coveted no one's silver or gold or apparel. [34]You yourselves know that these hands ministered to my necessities and to those who were with me. [35]In all things I have shown you that by working hard in this way we must help the weak and remember the words of the Lord Jesus, how he himself said, 'It is more blessed to give than to receive.'"

[36]And when he had said these things, he knelt down and prayed with them all. [37]And there was much weeping on the part of all; they embraced Paul and kissed him, [38]being sorrowful most of all because of the word he had spoken, that they would not see his face again. And they accompanied him to the ship.

21 And when we had parted from them and set sail, we came by a straight course to Cos, and the next day to Rhodes, and from there to Patara.[4] [2]And having found a ship crossing to Phoenicia, we went aboard and set sail. [3]When we had come in sight of Cyprus, leaving it on the left we sailed to Syria and landed at Tyre, for there the ship was to unload its cargo. [4]And having sought out the disciples, we stayed there for seven days. And through the Spirit they were telling Paul not to go on to Jerusalem. [5]When our days there were ended, we departed and went on our journey, and they all, with wives and children, accompanied us until we were outside the city. And kneeling down on the beach, we prayed [6]and said farewell to one another. Then we went on board the ship, and they returned home.

[7]When we had finished the voyage from Tyre, we arrived at Ptolemais, and we greeted the brothers[5] and stayed with them for one day. [8]On the next day we departed and came to Caesarea, and we entered the house of Philip the evangelist, who was one of the seven, and stayed with him. [9]He had four unmarried daughters, who prophesied. [10]While we were staying for many days, a prophet named Agabus came down from Judea. [11]And coming to us, he took Paul's belt and bound his own feet and hands and said, "Thus says the Holy Spirit, 'This is how the Jews at Jerusalem will bind the man who owns this belt and deliver him into the hands of the Gentiles.'" [12]When we heard this, we and the people there urged him not to go up to Jerusalem. [13]Then Paul answered, "What are you doing, weeping and breaking my heart? For I am ready not only to be imprisoned but even to die in Jerusalem for the name of the

---

[1] Or bound in [2] Some manuscripts of the Lord [3] Or with the blood of his Own [4] Some manuscripts add and Myra [5] Or brothers and sisters; also verse 17

Lord Jesus." ¹⁴And since he would not be persuaded, we ceased and said, "Let the will of the Lord be done."

¹⁵After these days we got ready and went up to Jerusalem. ¹⁶And some of the disciples from Caesarea went with us, bringing us to the house of Mnason of Cyprus, an early disciple, with whom we should lodge.

Paul and the Jewish mob in Jerusalem: arrest and defenses [21:17–23:11]. With this unit Luke enters new territory, consisting of Paul's career as a prisoner for the gospel. The two chief narrative ingredients are plot conflict and dramatized trial/defense scenes. The first arrest and defense occur in Jewish-controlled Jerusalem. The sequence is as follows: upon arrival in Jerusalem, Paul agrees to perform suggested Jewish rituals to prove his obedience to the Jewish law (21:17–26); Paul's arrest at the site of the temple by enraged Jews (21:27–36); Paul's defense speech to the mob (22:1–21); Paul's rescue from the enraged mob when the Roman tribune learns that Paul is a Roman citizen (22:22–29); Paul's defense the next day to the Sanhedrin (22:30–23:11). A good way to read the chapters is to relive the action, imagining yourself to be on the scene with a television crew. This narrative unit ends with the appearance of the Lord informing Paul that he "must testify also in Rome" (23:11); not only is this a foreshadowing, but it also establishes the journey to Rome as a quest that will govern the rest of the story of Acts.

¹⁷When we had come to Jerusalem, the brothers received us gladly. ¹⁸On the following day Paul went in with us to James, and all the elders were present. ¹⁹After greeting them, he related one by one the things that God had done among the Gentiles through his ministry. ²⁰And when they heard it, they glorified God. And they said to him, "You see, brother, how many thousands there are among the Jews of those who have believed. They are all zealous for the law, ²¹and they have been told about you that you teach all the Jews who are among the Gentiles to forsake Moses, telling them not to circumcise their children or walk according to our customs. ²²What then is to be done? They will certainly hear that you have come. ²³Do therefore what we tell you. We have four men who are under a vow; ²⁴take these men and purify yourself along with them and pay their expenses, so that they may shave their heads. Thus all will know that there is nothing in what they have been told about you, but that you yourself also live in observance of the law. ²⁵But as for the Gentiles who have believed, we have sent a letter with our judgment that they should abstain from what has been sacrificed to idols, and from blood, and from what has been strangled,¹ and from sexual immorality." ²⁶Then Paul took the men, and the next day he purified himself along with them and went into the temple, giving notice when the days of purification would be fulfilled and the offering presented for each one of them.

²⁷When the seven days were almost completed, the Jews from Asia, seeing him in the temple, stirred up the whole crowd and laid hands on him, ²⁸crying out, "Men of Israel, help! This is the man who is teaching everyone everywhere against the people and the law and this place. Moreover, he even brought Greeks into the temple and has defiled this holy place." ²⁹For they had previously seen Trophimus the Ephesian with him in the city, and they supposed that Paul had brought him into the temple. ³⁰Then all the city was stirred up, and the people ran together. They seized Paul and dragged him out of the temple, and at once the gates were shut. ³¹And as they were

---

¹ Some manuscripts omit *and from what has been strangled*

seeking to kill him, word came to the tribune of the cohort that all Jerusalem was in confusion. ³²He at once took soldiers and centurions and ran down to them. And when they saw the tribune and the soldiers, they stopped beating Paul. ³³Then the tribune came up and arrested him and ordered him to be bound with two chains. He inquired who he was and what he had done. ³⁴Some in the crowd were shouting one thing, some another. And as he could not learn the facts because of the uproar, he ordered him to be brought into the barracks. ³⁵And when he came to the steps, he was actually carried by the soldiers because of the violence of the crowd, ³⁶for the mob of the people followed, crying out, "Away with him!"

³⁷As Paul was about to be brought into the barracks, he said to the tribune, "May I say something to you?" And he said, "Do you know Greek? ³⁸Are you not the Egyptian, then, who recently stirred up a revolt and led the four thousand men of the Assassins out into the wilderness?" ³⁹Paul replied, "I am a Jew, from Tarsus in Cilicia, a citizen of no obscure city. I beg you, permit me to speak to the people." ⁴⁰And when he had given him permission, Paul, standing on the steps, motioned with his hand to the people. And when there was a great hush, he addressed them in the Hebrew language,¹ saying:

22 "Brothers and fathers, hear the defense that I now make before you." ²And when they heard that he was addressing them in the Hebrew language, they became even more quiet. And he said:

³"I am a Jew, born in Tarsus in Cilicia, but brought up in this city, educated at the feet of Gamaliel² according to the strict manner of the law of our fathers, being zealous for God as all of you are this day. ⁴I persecuted this Way to the death, binding and delivering to prison both men and women, ⁵as the high priest and the whole council of elders can bear me witness. From them I received letters to the brothers, and I journeyed toward Damascus to take those also who were there and bring them in bonds to Jerusalem to be punished.

⁶"As I was on my way and drew near to Damascus, about noon a great light from heaven suddenly shone around me. ⁷And I fell to the ground and heard a voice saying to me, 'Saul, Saul, why are you persecuting me?' ⁸And I answered, 'Who are you, Lord?' And he said to me, 'I am Jesus of Nazareth, whom you are persecuting.' ⁹Now those who were with me saw the light but did not understand³ the voice of the one who was speaking to me. ¹⁰And I said, 'What shall I do, Lord?' And the Lord said to me, 'Rise, and go into Damascus, and there you will be told all that is appointed for you to do.' ¹¹And since I could not see because of the brightness of that light, I was led by the hand by those who were with me, and came into Damascus.

¹²"And one Ananias, a devout man according to the law, well spoken of by all the Jews who lived there, ¹³came to me, and standing by me said to me, 'Brother Saul, receive your sight.' And at that very hour I received my sight and saw him. ¹⁴And he said, 'The God of our fathers appointed you to know his will, to see the Righteous One and to hear a voice from his mouth; ¹⁵for you will be a witness for him to everyone of what you have seen and heard. ¹⁶And now why do you wait? Rise and be baptized and wash away your sins, calling on his name.'

¹⁷"When I had returned to Jerusalem and was praying in the temple, I fell into a trance ¹⁸and saw him saying to me, 'Make haste and get out of Jerusalem quickly, because they will not accept your testimony about me.' ¹⁹And I said, 'Lord, they them-

---

¹ Or *the Hebrew dialect* (that is, Aramaic); also 22:2 ² Or *city at the feet of Gamaliel, educated* ³ Or *hear with understanding*

selves know that in one synagogue after another I imprisoned and beat those who believed in you. ²⁰And when the blood of Stephen your witness was being shed, I myself was standing by and approving and watching over the garments of those who killed him.' ²¹And he said to me, 'Go, for I will send you far away to the Gentiles.'"

²²Up to this word they listened to him. Then they raised their voices and said, "Away with such a fellow from the earth! For he should not be allowed to live." ²³And as they were shouting and throwing off their cloaks and flinging dust into the air, ²⁴the tribune ordered him to be brought into the barracks, saying that he should be examined by flogging, to find out why they were shouting against him like this. ²⁵But when they had stretched him out for the whips,¹ Paul said to the centurion who was standing by, "Is it lawful for you to flog a man who is a Roman citizen and uncondemned?" ²⁶When the centurion heard this, he went to the tribune and said to him, "What are you about to do? For this man is a Roman citizen." ²⁷So the tribune came and said to him, "Tell me, are you a Roman citizen?" And he said, "Yes." ²⁸The tribune answered, "I bought this citizenship for a large sum." Paul said, "But I am a citizen by birth." ²⁹So those who were about to examine him withdrew from him immediately, and the tribune also was afraid, for he realized that Paul was a Roman citizen and that he had bound him.

³⁰But on the next day, desiring to know the real reason why he was being accused by the Jews, he unbound him and commanded the chief priests and all the council to meet, and he brought Paul down and set him before them.

23 And looking intently at the council, Paul said, "Brothers, I have lived my life before God in all good conscience up to this day." ²And the high priest Ananias commanded those who stood by him to strike him on the mouth. ³Then Paul said to him, "God is going to strike you, you whitewashed wall! Are you sitting to judge me according to the law, and yet contrary to the law you order me to be struck?" ⁴Those who stood by said, "Would you revile God's high priest?" ⁵And Paul said, "I did not know, brothers, that he was the high priest, for it is written, ᵃ'You shall not speak evil of a ruler of your people.'"

⁶Now when Paul perceived that one part were Sadducees and the other Pharisees, he cried out in the council, "Brothers, I am a Pharisee, a son of Pharisees. It is with respect to the hope and the resurrection of the dead that I am on trial." ⁷And when he had said this, a dissension arose between the Pharisees and the Sadducees, and the assembly was divided. ⁸For the Sadducees say that there is no resurrection, nor angel, nor spirit, but the Pharisees acknowledge them all. ⁹Then a great clamor arose, and some of the scribes of the Pharisees' party stood up and contended sharply, "We find nothing wrong in this man. What if a spirit or an angel spoke to him?" ¹⁰And when the dissension became violent, the tribune, afraid that Paul would be torn to pieces by them, commanded the soldiers to go down and take him away from among them by force and bring him into the barracks.

¹¹The following night the Lord stood by him and said, "Take courage, for as you have testified to the facts about me in Jerusalem, so you must testify also in Rome."

Paul's hearing and defense before the Roman governor Felix [23:12–24:27]. The action continues at a fever pitch of danger and suspense, and once again as we read we find ourselves in the world of courtroom protocol and drama. To capture the spirit of

¹ Or when they had tied him up with leather strips ᵃ Ex. 22:28

the events, we need to draw upon our experiences (firsthand or through television and the media) of courtroom proceedings or fictional courtroom scenes. The action unfolds as follows: the Jews' oath to kill Paul (23:12–15); the discovery of the plot (23:16–22); Paul's removal from Jerusalem under cloak of night to the house of the regional governor Felix, accompanied by a letter from the tribune explaining Paul's situation (23:23–35); the Jews' charges against Paul before Felix the governor, Paul's reply to the charges (24:1–21), and Paul's two-year house arrest (24:22–27). The story by this point has become an adventure story that is not only exciting narrative material but also a spiritual epic of the spread of the gospel through the heroism of Paul under the direction of the Holy Spirit.

¹²When it was day, the Jews made a plot and bound themselves by an oath neither to eat nor drink till they had killed Paul. ¹³There were more than forty who made this conspiracy. ¹⁴They went to the chief priests and elders and said, "We have strictly bound ourselves by an oath to taste no food till we have killed Paul. ¹⁵Now therefore you, along with the council, give notice to the tribune to bring him down to you, as though you were going to determine his case more exactly. And we are ready to kill him before he comes near."

¹⁶Now the son of Paul's sister heard of their ambush, so he went and entered the barracks and told Paul. ¹⁷Paul called one of the centurions and said, "Take this young man to the tribune, for he has something to tell him." ¹⁸So he took him and brought him to the tribune and said, "Paul the prisoner called me and asked me to bring this young man to you, as he has something to say to you." ¹⁹The tribune took him by the hand, and going aside asked him privately, "What is it that you have to tell me?" ²⁰And he said, "The Jews have agreed to ask you to bring Paul down to the council tomorrow, as though they were going to inquire somewhat more closely about him. ²¹But do not be persuaded by them, for more than forty of their men are lying in ambush for him, who have bound themselves by an oath neither to eat nor drink till they have killed him. And now they are ready, waiting for your consent." ²²So the tribune dismissed the young man, charging him, "Tell no one that you have informed me of these things."

²³Then he called two of the centurions and said, "Get ready two hundred soldiers, with seventy horsemen and two hundred spearmen to go as far as Caesarea at the third hour of the night.¹ ²⁴Also provide mounts for Paul to ride and bring him safely to Felix the governor." ²⁵And he wrote a letter to this effect:

²⁶"Claudius Lysias, to his Excellency the governor Felix, greetings. ²⁷This man was seized by the Jews and was about to be killed by them when I came upon them with the soldiers and rescued him, having learned that he was a Roman citizen. ²⁸And desiring to know the charge for which they were accusing him, I brought him down to their council. ²⁹I found that he was being accused about questions of their law, but charged with nothing deserving death or imprisonment. ³⁰And when it was disclosed to me that there would be a plot against the man, I sent him to you at once, ordering his accusers also to state before you what they have against him."

³¹So the soldiers, according to their instructions, took Paul and brought him by night to Antipatris. ³²And on the next day they returned to the barracks, letting the horsemen go on with him. ³³When they had come to Caesarea and delivered the letter to the governor, they presented Paul also before him. ³⁴On reading the letter, he

¹ That is, 9 P.M.

asked what province he was from. And when he learned that he was from Cilicia, [35]he said, "I will give you a hearing when your accusers arrive." And he commanded him to be guarded in Herod's praetorium.

24 And after five days the high priest Ananias came down with some elders and a spokesman, one Tertullus. They laid before the governor their case against Paul. [2]And when he had been summoned, Tertullus began to accuse him, saying:

"Since through you we enjoy much peace, and since by your foresight, most excellent Felix, reforms are being made for this nation, [3]in every way and everywhere we accept this with all gratitude. [4]But, to detain[1] you no further, I beg you in your kindness to hear us briefly. [5]For we have found this man a plague, one who stirs up riots among all the Jews throughout the world and is a ringleader of the sect of the Nazarenes. [6]He even tried to profane the temple, but we seized him.[2] [8]By examining him yourself you will be able to find out from him about everything of which we accuse him."

[9]The Jews also joined in the charge, affirming that all these things were so.

[10]And when the governor had nodded to him to speak, Paul replied:

"Knowing that for many years you have been a judge over this nation, I cheerfully make my defense. [11]You can verify that it is not more than twelve days since I went up to worship in Jerusalem, [12]and they did not find me disputing with anyone or stirring up a crowd, either in the temple or in the synagogues or in the city. [13]Neither can they prove to you what they now bring up against me. [14]But this I confess to you, that according to the Way, which they call a sect, I worship the God of our fathers, believing everything laid down by the Law and written in the Prophets, [15]having a hope in God, which these men themselves accept, that there will be a resurrection of both the just and the unjust. [16]So I always take pains to have a clear conscience toward both God and man. [17]Now after several years I came to bring alms to my nation and to present offerings. [18]While I was doing this, they found me purified in the temple, without any crowd or tumult. But some Jews from Asia— [19]they ought to be here before you and to make an accusation, should they have anything against me. [20]Or else let these men themselves say what wrongdoing they found when I stood before the council, [21]other than this one thing that I cried out while standing among them: 'It is with respect to the resurrection of the dead that I am on trial before you this day.'"

[22]But Felix, having a rather accurate knowledge of the Way, put them off, saying, "When Lysias the tribune comes down, I will decide your case." [23]Then he gave orders to the centurion that he should be kept in custody but have some liberty, and that none of his friends should be prevented from attending to his needs.

[24]After some days Felix came with his wife Drusilla, who was Jewish, and he sent for Paul and heard him speak about faith in Christ Jesus. [25]And as he reasoned about righteousness and self-control and the coming judgment, Felix was alarmed and said, "Go away for the present. When I get an opportunity I will summon you." [26]At the same time he hoped that money would be given him by Paul. So he sent for him often and conversed with him. [27]When two years had elapsed, Felix was succeeded by Porcius Festus. And desiring to do the Jews a favor, Felix left Paul in prison.

---

[1] Or weary [2] Some manuscripts add *and we would have judged him according to our law.* [7]*But the chief captain Lysias came and with great violence took him out of our hands,* [8]*commanding his accusers to come before you.*

Two additional landmark defenses by Paul [chapters 25–26]. These chapters are a story of behind-the-scenes intrigue between Roman rulers and Paul's Jewish accusers and of Paul's formal defenses of himself. The action unfolds as follows: Paul's appearance before the Roman governor Festus, ending with Paul's request to be tried in Rome rather than Jerusalem (25:1–12); the discussion between Governor Festus and King Agrippa regarding Paul, ending with the staging of a public hearing (25:13–27), and Paul's defense speech (chapter 26). Chapter 25 has all the eyewitness precision of a docudrama, while chapter 26 is a dramatized speech, ending with memorable dialogue between Paul and Agrippa. While the official proceedings are judicial in nature, we should analyze the ways in which Paul's speech is actually evangelistic in nature, adding further to witness as a governing image pattern of the book of Acts. The pivotal moment in the last movement of Paul's life is his famous appeal to Caesar (25:11), which propels him to Rome when (according to a marveling King Agrippa in 26:32) he could have gone free.

25 Now three days after Festus had arrived in the province, he went up to Jerusalem from Caesarea. ²And the chief priests and the principal men of the Jews laid out their case against Paul, and they urged him, ³asking as a favor against Paul[1] that he summon him to Jerusalem—because they were planning an ambush to kill him on the way. ⁴Festus replied that Paul was being kept at Caesarea and that he himself intended to go there shortly. ⁵"So," said he, "let the men of authority among you go down with me, and if there is anything wrong about the man, let them bring charges against him."

⁶After he stayed among them not more than eight or ten days, he went down to Caesarea. And the next day he took his seat on the tribunal and ordered Paul to be brought. ⁷When he had arrived, the Jews who had come down from Jerusalem stood around him, bringing many and serious charges against him that they could not prove. ⁸Paul argued in his defense, "Neither against the law of the Jews, nor against the temple, nor against Caesar have I committed any offense." ⁹But Festus, wishing to do the Jews a favor, said to Paul, "Do you wish to go up to Jerusalem and there be tried on these charges before me?" ¹⁰But Paul said, "I am standing before Caesar's tribunal, where I ought to be tried. To the Jews I have done no wrong, as you yourself know very well. ¹¹If then I am a wrongdoer and have committed anything for which I deserve to die, I do not seek to escape death. But if there is nothing to their charges against me, no one can give me up to them. I appeal to Caesar." ¹²Then Festus, when he had conferred with his council, answered, "To Caesar you have appealed; to Caesar you shall go."

¹³Now when some days had passed, Agrippa the king and Bernice arrived at Caesarea and greeted Festus. ¹⁴And as they stayed there many days, Festus laid Paul's case before the king, saying, "There is a man left prisoner by Felix, ¹⁵and when I was at Jerusalem, the chief priests and the elders of the Jews laid out their case against him, asking for a sentence of condemnation against him. ¹⁶I answered them that it was not the custom of the Romans to give up anyone before the accused met the accusers face to face and had opportunity to make his defense concerning the charge laid against him. ¹⁷So when they came together here, I made no delay, but on the next day took my seat on the tribunal and ordered the man to be brought. ¹⁸When the accusers stood up, they brought no charge in his case of such evils as I supposed.

[1] Greek *him*

¹⁹Rather they had certain points of dispute with him about their own religion and about a certain Jesus, who was dead, but whom Paul asserted to be alive. ²⁰Being at a loss how to investigate these questions, I asked whether he wanted to go to Jerusalem and be tried there regarding them. ²¹But when Paul had appealed to be kept in custody for the decision of the emperor, I ordered him to be held until I could send him to Caesar." ²²Then Agrippa said to Festus, "I would like to hear the man myself." "Tomorrow," said he, "you will hear him."

²³So on the next day Agrippa and Bernice came with great pomp, and they entered the audience hall with the military tribunes and the prominent men of the city. Then, at the command of Festus, Paul was brought in. ²⁴And Festus said, "King Agrippa and all who are present with us, you see this man about whom the whole Jewish people petitioned me, both in Jerusalem and here, shouting that he ought not to live any longer. ²⁵But I found that he had done nothing deserving death. And as he himself appealed to the emperor, I decided to go ahead and send him. ²⁶But I have nothing definite to write to my lord about him. Therefore I have brought him before you all, and especially before you, King Agrippa, so that, after we have examined him, I may have something to write. ²⁷For it seems to me unreasonable, in sending a prisoner, not to indicate the charges against him."

26 So Agrippa said to Paul, "You have permission to speak for yourself." Then Paul stretched out his hand and made his defense:

²"I consider myself fortunate that it is before you, King Agrippa, I am going to make my defense today against all the accusations of the Jews, ³especially because you are familiar with all the customs and controversies of the Jews. Therefore I beg you to listen to me patiently.

⁴"My manner of life from my youth, spent from the beginning among my own nation and in Jerusalem, is known by all the Jews. ⁵They have known for a long time, if they are willing to testify, that according to the strictest party of our religion I have lived as a Pharisee. ⁶And now I stand here on trial because of my hope in the promise made by God to our fathers, ⁷to which our twelve tribes hope to attain, as they earnestly worship night and day. And for this hope I am accused by Jews, O king! ⁸Why is it thought incredible by any of you that God raises the dead?

⁹"I myself was convinced that I ought to do many things in opposing the name of Jesus of Nazareth. ¹⁰And I did so in Jerusalem. I not only locked up many of the saints in prison after receiving authority from the chief priests, but when they were put to death I cast my vote against them. ¹¹And I punished them often in all the synagogues and tried to make them blaspheme, and in raging fury against them I persecuted them even to foreign cities.

¹²"In this connection I journeyed to Damascus with the authority and commission of the chief priests. ¹³At midday, O king, I saw on the way a light from heaven, brighter than the sun, that shone around me and those who journeyed with me. ¹⁴And when we had all fallen to the ground, I heard a voice saying to me in the Hebrew language,¹ 'Saul, Saul, why are you persecuting me? It is hard for you to kick against the goads.' ¹⁵And I said, 'Who are you, Lord?' And the Lord said, 'I am Jesus whom you are persecuting. ¹⁶But rise and stand upon your feet, for I have appeared to you for this purpose, to appoint you as a servant and witness to the things in which you have seen me and to those in which I will appear to you, ¹⁷delivering you from your people and

---

¹ Or *the Hebrew dialect* (that is, Aramaic)

from the Gentiles—to whom I am sending you ¹⁸to open their eyes, so that they may turn from darkness to light and from the power of Satan to God, that they may receive forgiveness of sins and a place among those who are sanctified by faith in me.'

¹⁹"Therefore, O King Agrippa, I was not disobedient to the heavenly vision, ²⁰but declared first to those in Damascus, then in Jerusalem and throughout all the region of Judea, and also to the Gentiles, that they should repent and turn to God, performing deeds in keeping with their repentance. ²¹For this reason the Jews seized me in the temple and tried to kill me. ²²To this day I have had the help that comes from God, and so I stand here testifying both to small and great, saying nothing but what the prophets and Moses said would come to pass: ²³that the Christ must suffer and that, by being the first to rise from the dead, he would proclaim light both to our people and to the Gentiles."

²⁴And as he was saying these things in his defense, Festus said with a loud voice, "Paul, you are out of your mind; your great learning is driving you out of your mind." ²⁵But Paul said, "I am not out of my mind, most excellent Festus, but I am speaking true and rational words. ²⁶For the king knows about these things, and to him I speak boldly. For I am persuaded that none of these things has escaped his notice, for this has not been done in a corner. ²⁷King Agrippa, do you believe the prophets? I know that you believe." ²⁸And Agrippa said to Paul, "In a short time would you persuade me to be a Christian?"¹ ²⁹And Paul said, "Whether short or long, I would to God that not only you but also all who hear me this day might become such as I am—except for these chains."

³⁰Then the king rose, and the governor and Bernice and those who were sitting with them. ³¹And when they had withdrawn, they said to one another, "This man is doing nothing to deserve death or imprisonment." ³²And Agrippa said to Festus, "This man could have been set free if he had not appealed to Caesar."

Paul's journey to Rome [27:1–28:15]. This material is even more thoroughly a *travel story than the missionary journeys are. Although the narrative is factual rather than fictional, the story that we read reminds us of the journey of Homer's Odysseus on the Mediterranean Sea. Docudrama is replaced by a journalistic or diarylike recording of the details of the sea voyage to Italy. The units are as follows: the early days of the dangerous voyage (27:1–12); the storm at sea (27:13–38); the shipwreck (27:39–44); rescue on the island of Malta (28:1–10); the last leg of the journey and arrival in Rome (28:11–15). This story belongs to the genre of adventure on the high sea.

27 And when it was decided that we should sail for Italy, they delivered Paul and some other prisoners to a centurion of the Augustan Cohort named Julius. ²And embarking in a ship of Adramyttium, which was about to sail to the ports along the coast of Asia, we put to sea, accompanied by Aristarchus, a Macedonian from Thessalonica. ³The next day we put in at Sidon. And Julius treated Paul kindly and gave him leave to go to his friends and be cared for. ⁴And putting out to sea from there we sailed under the lee of Cyprus, because the winds were against us. ⁵And when we had sailed across the open sea along the coast of Cilicia and Pamphylia, we came to Myra in Lycia. ⁶There the centurion found a ship of Alexandria sailing for Italy and put us on board. ⁷We sailed slowly for a number of days and arrived with

¹ Or In a short time you would persuade me to act like a Christian!

difficulty off Cnidus, and as the wind did not allow us to go farther, we sailed under the lee of Crete off Salmone. [9]Coasting along it with difficulty, we came to a place called Fair Havens, near which was the city of Lasea.

[9]Since much time had passed, and the voyage was now dangerous because even the Fast[1] was already over, Paul advised them, [10]saying, "Sirs, I perceive that the voyage will be with injury and much loss, not only of the cargo and the ship, but also of our lives." [11]But the centurion paid more attention to the pilot and to the owner of the ship than to what Paul said. [12]And because the harbor was not suitable to spend the winter in, the majority decided to put out to sea from there, on the chance that somehow they could reach Phoenix, a harbor of Crete, facing both southwest and northwest, and spend the winter there.

[13]Now when the south wind blew gently, supposing that they had obtained their purpose, they weighed anchor and sailed along Crete, close to the shore. [14]But soon a tempestuous wind, called the northeaster, struck down from the land. [15]And when the ship was caught and could not face the wind, we gave way to it and were driven along. [16]Running under the lee of a small island called Cauda,[2] we managed with difficulty to secure the ship's boat. [17]After hoisting it up, they used supports to undergird the ship. Then, fearing that they would run aground on the Syrtis, they lowered the gear,[3] and thus they were driven along. [18]Since we were violently storm-tossed, they began the next day to jettison the cargo. [19]And on the third day they threw the ship's tackle overboard with their own hands. [20]When neither sun nor stars appeared for many days, and no small tempest lay on us, all hope of our being saved was at last abandoned.

[21]Since they had been without food for a long time, Paul stood up among them and said, "Men, you should have listened to me and not have set sail from Crete and incurred this injury and loss. [22]Yet now I urge you to take heart, for there will be no loss of life among you, but only of the ship. [23]For this very night there stood before me an angel of the God to whom I belong and whom I worship, [24]and he said, 'Do not be afraid, Paul; you must stand before Caesar. And behold, God has granted you all those who sail with you.' [25]So take heart, men, for I have faith in God that it will be exactly as I have been told. [26]But we must run aground on some island."

[27]When the fourteenth night had come, as we were being driven across the Adriatic Sea, about midnight the sailors suspected that they were nearing land. [28]So they took a sounding and found twenty fathoms.[4] A little farther on they took a sounding again and found fifteen fathoms.[5] [29]And fearing that we might run on the rocks, they let down four anchors from the stern and prayed for day to come. [30]And as the sailors were seeking to escape from the ship, and had lowered the ship's boat into the sea under pretense of laying out anchors from the bow, [31]Paul said to the centurion and the soldiers, "Unless these men stay in the ship, you cannot be saved." [32]Then the soldiers cut away the ropes of the ship's boat and let it go.

[33]As day was about to dawn, Paul urged them all to take some food, saying, "Today is the fourteenth day that you have continued in suspense and without food, having taken nothing. [34]Therefore I urge you to take some food. For it will give you strength, for not a hair is to perish from the head of any of you." [35]And when he had said these things, he took bread, and giving thanks to God in the presence of all he broke it and began to eat. [36]Then they all were encouraged and ate some food themselves. [37](We

---

[1] That is, the Day of Atonement [2] Some manuscripts *Clauda* [3] That is, the sea-anchor (or possibly the mainsail) [4] About 120 feet; a fathom (Greek *orguia*) was about 6 feet or 2 meters [5] About 90 feet (see previous note)

were in all 276[1] persons in the ship.) [38]And when they had eaten enough, they lightened the ship, throwing out the wheat into the sea.

[39]Now when it was day, they did not recognize the land, but they noticed a bay with a beach, on which they planned if possible to run the ship ashore. [40]So they cast off the anchors and left them in the sea, at the same time loosening the ropes that tied the rudders. Then hoisting the foresail to the wind they made for the beach. [41]But striking a reef,[2] they ran the vessel aground. The bow stuck and remained immovable, and the stern was being broken up by the surf. [42]The soldiers' plan was to kill the prisoners, lest any should swim away and escape. [43]But the centurion, wishing to save Paul, kept them from carrying out their plan. He ordered those who could swim to jump overboard first and make for the land, [44]and the rest on planks or on pieces of the ship. And so it was that all were brought safely to land.

28 After we were brought safely through, we then learned that the island was called Malta. [2]The native people[3] showed us unusual kindness, for they kindled a fire and welcomed us all, because it had begun to rain and was cold. [3]When Paul had gathered a bundle of sticks and put them on the fire, a viper came out because of the heat and fastened on his hand. [4]When the native people saw the creature hanging from his hand, they said to one another, "No doubt this man is a murderer. Though he has escaped from the sea, Justice[4] has not allowed him to live." [5]He, however, shook off the creature into the fire and suffered no harm. [6]They were waiting for him to swell up or suddenly fall down dead. But when they had waited a long time and saw no misfortune come to him, they changed their minds and said that he was a god.

[7]Now in the neighborhood of that place were lands belonging to the chief man of the island, named Publius, who received us and entertained us hospitably for three days. [8]It happened that the father of Publius lay sick with fever and dysentery. And Paul visited him and prayed, and putting his hands on him healed him. [9]And when this had taken place, the rest of the people on the island who had diseases also came and were cured. [10]They also honored us greatly,[5] and when we were about to sail, they put on board whatever we needed.

[11]After three months we set sail in a ship that had wintered in the island, a ship of Alexandria, with the twin gods[6] as a figurehead. [12]Putting in at Syracuse, we stayed there for three days. [13]And from there we made a circuit and arrived at Rhegium. And after one day a south wind sprang up, and on the second day we came to Puteoli. [14]There we found brothers[7] and were invited to stay with them for seven days. And so we came to Rome. [15]And the brothers there, when they heard about us, came as far as the Forum of Appius and Three Taverns to meet us. On seeing them, Paul thanked God and took courage.

Paul under house arrest in Rome [28:16–31]. After so much suspense and adventure in the book of Acts as a whole, the narrative ends on a note of quietude, as though the great things are now over and the storyteller is bringing the soaring intensity of the narrative back down to earth. We do not get a picture of Paul in a prison dungeon; rather, he lives a confined life that today we would call house arrest. He is bound by a chain (v. 20) and must receive visitors in his lodging instead of being free to meet them elsewhere

[1] Some manuscripts seventy-six, or about seventy-six [2] Or sandbank, or crosscurrent; Greek place between two seas [3] Greek barbaroi (that is, non–Greek speakers); also verse 4 [4] Or justice [5] Greek honored us with many honors [6] That is, the Greek gods Castor and Pollux [7] Or brothers and sisters; also verses 15, 21

(vv. 23, 30). The ending of the book of Acts is famous for its open-ended quality. All that Luke records is Paul's evangelistic dialogue with the Jews, followed by the statement that Paul lived at his own expense for two years. We hear nothing about Paul's last days and death. The notes of evangelism and witness make their final appearance in Luke's summary of Paul's day-long conversation with the Jews who visited him (vv. 23–29). One of the things that the conclusion of a long narrative needs to do is bring the issues that have been raised to satisfying closure. After the tumultuous lives of Peter and Paul in which their witness to the gospel met with repeated hostility and persecution, there is a sense of relief in the last cadences of the book, which tell us that Paul taught "about the Lord Jesus Christ with all boldness and without hindrance" (v. 31). Ordinarily the conclusion of a long story also echoes the opening, as we are reminded of how much territory has been covered; here at the end of Acts, Paul is fulfilling the calling that had been laid by Jesus on his disciples at the beginning of the book: he is witnessing about Christ at the end of the earth. The story has come full circle. Some literary critics also see the ending as adhering to the formula "to be continued," inasmuch as the Christian church picked up where the book of Acts ends.

[16]And when we came into Rome, Paul was allowed to stay by himself, with the soldier that guarded him.

[17]After three days he called together the local leaders of the Jews, and when they had gathered, he said to them, "Brothers, though I had done nothing against our people or the customs of our fathers, yet I was delivered as a prisoner from Jerusalem into the hands of the Romans. [18]When they had examined me, they wished to set me at liberty, because there was no reason for the death penalty in my case. [19]But because the Jews objected, I was compelled to appeal to Caesar—though I had no charge to bring against my nation. [20]For this reason, therefore, I have asked to see you and speak with you, since it is because of the hope of Israel that I am wearing this chain." [21]And they said to him, "We have received no letters from Judea about you, and none of the brothers coming here has reported or spoken any evil about you. [22]But we desire to hear from you what your views are, for with regard to this sect we know that everywhere it is spoken against."

[23]When they had appointed a day for him, they came to him at his lodging in greater numbers. From morning till evening he expounded to them, testifying to the kingdom of God and trying to convince them about Jesus both from the Law of Moses and from the Prophets. [24]And some were convinced by what he said, but others disbelieved. [25]And disagreeing among themselves, they departed after Paul had made one statement: "The Holy Spirit was right in saying to your fathers through Isaiah the prophet:

[26][a]"'Go to this people, and say,
        You will indeed hear but never understand,
            and you will indeed see but never perceive.
[27]   For this people's heart has grown dull,
            and with their ears they can barely hear,
            and their eyes they have closed;
        lest they should see with their eyes
            and hear with their ears

---

[a] Isa. 6:9, 10

and understand with their heart
    and turn, and I would heal them.'

[28]Therefore let it be known to you that this salvation of God has been sent to the Gentiles; they will listen."[1]

[30]He lived there two whole years at his own expense,[2] and welcomed all who came to him, [31]proclaiming the kingdom of God and teaching about the Lord Jesus Christ with all boldness and without hindrance.

---

[1] Some manuscripts add verse 29: *And when he had said these words, the Jews departed, having much dispute among themselves* [2] Or *in his own hired dwelling*

ROMANS

The book at a glance. 16 chapters, 433 verses. Romans is rightly regarded as the most comprehensive and systematic summary of Christian doctrine anywhere in Scripture. It is the Bible's own systematic theology—a summary of saving doctrines that serves as a Bible within the Bible. Like the other NT epistles, Romans was written by one of the apostles (Paul) to the church in a particular city (Rome). In this case, though, it was a church the apostle had not yet visited in person. So rather than addressing his own pastoral concerns about the church or answering specific questions that had arisen in the course of a partnership in ministry, Paul instead introduces himself to the Romans by offering a full statement of his understanding of sin and salvation in Christ. Although the interpersonal context is evident from the opening greeting and closing remarks, the main body of the letter is a sustained doctrinal argument that is directly relevant to any person, at any time, in any place. The universality of the book is highlighted by its theological scope. Romans addresses the plight of every guilty sinner in the whole human race, whether Jew or Gentile, laying out the whole plan of salvation from eternity past to eternity future.

▌**Genres.** Romans contains all of the standard features of a biblical *epistle, including the *salutation, *thanksgiving, body, list of moral exhortations (the *paraenesis), personal greetings, and *benediction. What distinguishes the letter is its long and carefully constructed body, which presents a sustained theological argument. Romans is perhaps the least occasional and most tightly organized of all the NT letters, which helps explain why it reads as much like a theological treatise as it does like an epistle. Understanding Romans thus demands careful attention to the details of its doctrine. (For more information on items accompanied by an asterisk, see the glossary at the back of this Bible.)

▌**The diatribe.** As a theological treatise, the book of Romans is a grand edifice. It is filled with lofty theological ideas and vocabulary. The rhetoric is grand, often taking the form of elaborate sentence patterns (syntax) and patterns of repetition. What is sometimes overlooked is the continuous presence of a genre that tends toward the informal and even lends a colloquial vigor that balances the evident grandeur of the book of Romans. This genre, known as the *diatribe, was the mainstay of ancient teachers and orators (also known as preachers). Characteristics of the form include the following: dialogue with imaginary questioners or opponents; question-and-answer constructions, sometimes catechism-like in effect; use of questions or hypothetical objections as a transition to the next topic; rhetorical questions; adducing famous and

Passage	Content	Central doctrine	The righteousness of God	Logical flow of the argument
1:1–17	Opening thesis statement	Total depravity	Revealed in wrath	The problem of sin
1:18–3:20	The whole world guilty before God			
3:21–4:25	Justification by grace, through faith	Justification by faith	Imputed by grace	
5:1–21	The benefits of justification			
6:1–23	Dead to sin, alive in Christ	Sanctification in Christ	Imparted by the Spirit	The solution of salvation
7:1–25	Freedom from bondage to the law			
8:1–39	Life in the Spirit, the hope of glory			
9:1–29	Past: Israel's election	Election by grace	Demonstrated in sovereignty	
9:30–10:21	Present: Israel's unbelief			
11:1–36	Future: Israel's restoration			
12:1–8	Gifts and sacrifices for God	Transformation by the Spirit	Lived out in the church	The response of service
12:9–13:14	Love for everyone and submission to the state			
14:1–15:13	The strong and the weak			
15:14–33	Paul's plans for ministry			
16:1–27	Closing greetings and doxology			

representative figures from the past as examples; use of analogy as a rhetorical device; *aphoristic style. A literary reading of Romans must be sensitive to these stylistic traits.

■ **Unifying elements.** The book is unified primarily by the coherence of its central argument, which outlines and explains the eternal plan of God for the salvation of sinners. The book's thesis statement (1:16–17) alerts us to the central place that the righteousness of God occupies in this plan—the righteousness that God both demands in our obedience and offers to us as a free gift in Christ, received by faith. The book is also unified by its dual concern with the place of Jews and Gentiles in the church and by the strongly Trinitarian thrust of its teaching: the Father, the Son, and the Holy Spirit are each given full and equal attention for their sovereign and gracious work in salvation.

■ **Inferred literary intentions.** The book is designed to achieve the following literary purposes:

■ give a systematic summary of the main doctrines of salvation

- appeal to the mind through rational argumentation

- convince us of our guilty sin before a holy God

- assure us that we are loved and accepted forever in Jesus Christ

- explain the inward dynamics of spiritual change by the work of the Holy Spirit

- show how God's ongoing plan for the Jews fits in with his plan for the Gentiles

- exhort us to live the transformed life that comes from knowing and believing the truth about salvation

- lay the personal and theological groundwork for Paul's future partnership with the Romans for evangelizing the world

- embody the theological content of the letter in a style that is rhetorically embellished and replete with literary techniques

■ **Theological themes.** (1) Total depravity: the whole human race is dead in Adam's sin. (2) Judgment: fallen sinners are under the wrath of God. (3) Justification: God declares sinners righteous by faith, imputing to us the righteousness of Jesus Christ. (4) Sanctification: the Spirit makes us holy by grace. (5) Adoption: the Holy Spirit assures us that we are the children of God. (6) Glorification: the same Spirit who sanctifies us will also glorify us at the resurrection. (7) Perseverance: since nothing can separate us from the love of God, those who truly believe in Christ will never fall away. (8) Election: the sovereign God chose his people in Christ before the beginning of time.

■ **The book of Romans as a chapter in the master story of the Bible.** Romans presents the whole doctrine of salvation from beginning to end, providing the systematic categories to understand the gospel in theological terms. Since it makes frequent reference to events and characters from the OT as well as to the life and ministry of Jesus Christ, Romans serves as a lens through which to see all of Scripture. Its main emphasis is on the basic biblical truths of our need for salvation because of our sin and God's provision of grace through the atoning work of Jesus Christ.

Greeting, occasion, and statement of thesis [1:1–17]. In keeping with epistolary convention, Paul opens with an apostolic salutation (vv. 1–7), although even this gives ample indication that the letter to follow will be profound in its Trinitarian theology. The apostle's thanksgiving (vv. 8–15) mentions the occasion for the letter: Paul prays regularly for the Christians in Rome and longs to visit them, but he has not yet had the opportunity to preach the gospel to them in person. His thesis statement (vv. 16–17) introduces the main themes of his letter, and indeed of his theology as a whole: the gospel of grace, salvation for Jews and Gentiles, the righteousness of God, and justification by faith.

1 Paul, a servant[1] of Christ Jesus, called to be an apostle, set apart for the gospel of God, [2]which he promised beforehand through his prophets in the holy Scriptures, [3]concerning his Son, who was descended from David[2] according to the flesh [4]and

---

[1] Or slave; Greek bondservant [2] Or who came from the offspring of David

was declared to be the Son of God in power according to the Spirit of holiness by his resurrection from the dead, Jesus Christ our Lord, ⁵through whom we have received grace and apostleship to bring about the obedience of faith for the sake of his name among all the nations, ⁶including you who are called to belong to Jesus Christ,

⁷To all those in Rome who are loved by God and called to be saints:

Grace to you and peace from God our Father and the Lord Jesus Christ.

⁸First, I thank my God through Jesus Christ for all of you, because your faith is proclaimed in all the world. ⁹For God is my witness, whom I serve with my spirit in the gospel of his Son, that without ceasing I mention you ¹⁰always in my prayers, asking that somehow by God's will I may now at last succeed in coming to you. ¹¹For I long to see you, that I may impart to you some spiritual gift to strengthen you— ¹²that is, that we may be mutually encouraged by each other's faith, both yours and mine. ¹³I want you to know, brothers,¹ that I have often intended to come to you (but thus far have been prevented), in order that I may reap some harvest among you as well as among the rest of the Gentiles. ¹⁴I am under obligation both to Greeks and to barbarians,² both to the wise and to the foolish. ¹⁵So I am eager to preach the gospel to you also who are in Rome.

¹⁶For I am not ashamed of the gospel, for it is the power of God for salvation to everyone who believes, to the Jew first and also to the Greek. ¹⁷For in it the righteousness of God is revealed from faith for faith,³ ᵃas it is written, "The righteous shall live by faith."⁴

Immoral people are guilty before God [1:18–32]. The apostle begins with a statement of the problem of all problems: sinful humanity is under the wrath of God. The guilt of fallen humanity is proven first from the condition of godless pagans who revel in immorality. Although they do not have the law of God in written form, they do have it plainly written on their hearts, and in any case they are obligated to keep it. Nevertheless, they are guilty of all kinds of terrible sins against God, including idolatry, homosexuality, and unbelief. Because they deny the God they ought to know (and in fact do know, even if they refuse to admit it), they are already under the judgment of God. Several literary techniques stand out: a narrative sequence underlies the story Paul tells of the downward spiral of the human race into more and more sordid depths of depravity; antithesis permeates the passage in individual verses; and sheer exuberance of style is evident in the catalog of vices that tumbles out in verses 29–31.

¹⁸For the wrath of God is revealed from heaven against all ungodliness and unrighteousness of men, who by their unrighteousness suppress the truth. ¹⁹For what can be known about God is plain to them, because God has shown it to them. ²⁰For his invisible attributes, namely, his eternal power and divine nature, have been clearly perceived, ever since the creation of the world, in the things that have been made. So they are without excuse. ²¹For although they knew God, they did not honor him as God or give thanks to him, but they became futile in their thinking, and their foolish hearts were darkened. ²²Claiming to be wise, they became fools, ²³and exchanged the glory of the immortal God for images resembling mortal man and birds and animals and creeping things.

---

¹ Or *brothers and sisters*. The plural Greek word *adelphoi* (translated "brothers") refers to siblings in a family. In New Testament usage, depending on the context, *adelphoi* may refer either to men or to both men and women who are siblings (brothers and sisters) in God's family, the church ² That is, non-Greeks ³ Or *beginning and ending in faith* ⁴ Or *The one who by faith is righteous shall live* ᵃ Hab. 2:4

²⁴Therefore God gave them up in the lusts of their hearts to impurity, to the dishonoring of their bodies among themselves, ²⁵because they exchanged the truth about God for a lie and worshiped and served the creature rather than the Creator, who is blessed forever! Amen.

²⁶For this reason God gave them up to dishonorable passions. For their women exchanged natural relations for those that are contrary to nature; ²⁷and the men likewise gave up natural relations with women and were consumed with passion for one another, men committing shameless acts with men and receiving in themselves the due penalty for their error.

²⁸And since they did not see fit to acknowledge God, God gave them up to a debased mind to do what ought not to be done. ²⁹They were filled with all manner of unrighteousness, evil, covetousness, malice. They are full of envy, murder, strife, deceit, maliciousness. They are gossips, ³⁰slanderers, haters of God, insolent, haughty, boastful, inventors of evil, disobedient to parents, ³¹foolish, faithless, heartless, ruthless. ³²Though they know God's decree that those who practice such things deserve to die, they not only do them but give approval to those who practice them.

> **Moral people are guilty too** [2:1–16]. Rather than confessing their sins, most people would prefer to think that they are able to meet God's basic demands for their behavior. This is the second case that Paul considers: the moral person who tries to keep the law of God and usually looks down on people who don't (vv. 1–3). Is such a person good enough for God? No, the apostle says, because people who have the law and try to keep its high moral standards still commit the same kinds of sins as people who don't have the law at all (vv. 1, 5–8). People without the law (the immoral pagans described in chapter 1) will perish without the law, but people who know God's law and sin anyway (whether Jews or Gentiles) will also be condemned—condemned by the very law that they fail to keep (vv. 5, 12). The first eleven verses employ the rhetoric of a popular Greek form of *satire known as the diatribe; the features that Paul uses here include harsh addresses to the reader; imaginary dialogues; *apostrophe (direct address to absent people as though they were present); question-and-answer constructions. In verses 12–16 Paul employs the rhetoric of doctrinal analysis.

2 Therefore you have no excuse, O man, every one of you who judges. For in passing judgment on another you condemn yourself, because you, the judge, practice the very same things. ²We know that the judgment of God rightly falls on those who practice such things. ³Do you suppose, O man—you who judge those who practice such things and yet do them yourself—that you will escape the judgment of God? ⁴Or do you presume on the riches of his kindness and forbearance and patience, not knowing that God's kindness is meant to lead you to repentance? ⁵But because of your hard and impenitent heart you are storing up wrath for yourself on the day of wrath when God's righteous judgment will be revealed.

⁶He will render to each one according to his works: ⁷to those who by patience in well-doing seek for glory and honor and immortality, he will give eternal life; ⁸but for those who are self-seeking¹ and do not obey the truth, but obey unrighteousness, there will be wrath and fury. ⁹There will be tribulation and distress for every human being who does evil, the Jew first and also the Greek, ¹⁰but glory and honor and peace

¹ Or contentious

for everyone who does good, the Jew first and also the Greek. [11]For God shows no partiality.

[12]For all who have sinned without the law will also perish without the law, and all who have sinned under the law will be judged by the law. [13]For it is not the hearers of the law who are righteous before God, but the doers of the law who will be justified. [14]For when Gentiles, who do not have the law, by nature do what the law requires, they are a law to themselves, even though they do not have the law. [15]They show that the work of the law is written on their hearts, while their conscience also bears witness, and their conflicting thoughts accuse or even excuse them [16]on that day when, according to my gospel, God judges the secrets of men by Christ Jesus.

Even religious people are guilty [2:17–3:8]. The third case that Paul considers is the religious person—specifically the Jewish person who knows and teaches God's law and has been circumcised as a sign of belonging to God's family (2:17–20; 25–29). Surely a practicing Jew will be justified by God? Not on the basis of keeping the law, because even the devout Jew who tries to keep the law is guilty of breaking its commandments nonetheless (2:21–24). That is not to say that it is disadvantageous to be Jewish. On the contrary, Jews like Paul have certain spiritual advantages (3:1–4). However, outward obedience to the law or participation in the sacraments is not the same as inward obedience by the Spirit or having a heart that belongs to God (2:25–29). And since even the most religious person is sometimes unrighteous, that person too is therefore under the wrath of God (3:5–8). The rhetoric of the diatribe keeps surfacing in the epistle to the Romans. In this passage we find examples of direct and harsh addresses to the reader, imaginary dialogues with theological opponents, rhetorical questions, and colloquial exclamations.

[17]But if you call yourself a Jew and rely on the law and boast in God [18]and know his will and approve what is excellent, because you are instructed from the law; [19]and if you are sure that you yourself are a guide to the blind, a light to those who are in darkness, [20]an instructor of the foolish, a teacher of children, having in the law the embodiment of knowledge and truth— [21]you then who teach others, do you not teach yourself? While you preach against stealing, do you steal? [22]You who say that one must not commit adultery, do you commit adultery? You who abhor idols, do you rob temples? [23]You who boast in the law dishonor God by breaking the law. [24]For, [a]as it is written, "The name of God is blasphemed among the Gentiles because of you."

[25]For circumcision indeed is of value if you obey the law, but if you break the law, your circumcision becomes uncircumcision. [26]So, if a man who is uncircumcised keeps the precepts of the law, will not his uncircumcision be regarded[1] as circumcision? [27]Then he who is physically uncircumcised but keeps the law will condemn you who have the written code[2] and circumcision but break the law. [28]For no one is a Jew who is merely one outwardly, nor is circumcision outward and physical. [29]But a Jew is one inwardly, and circumcision is a matter of the heart, by the Spirit, not by the letter. His praise is not from man but from God.

---

[1] Or *counted* [2] Or *the letter* [a] Isa. 52:5

3 Then what advantage has the Jew? Or what is the value of circumcision? ²Much in every way. To begin with, the Jews were entrusted with the oracles of God. ³What if some were unfaithful? Does their faithlessness nullify the faithfulness of God? ⁴By no means! Let God be true though every one were a liar, as it is written,

> ᵃ"That you may be justified in your words,
>   and prevail when you are judged."

⁵But if our unrighteousness serves to show the righteousness of God, what shall we say? That God is unrighteous to inflict wrath on us? (I speak in a human way.) ⁶By no means! For then how could God judge the world? ⁷But if through my lie God's truth abounds to his glory, why am I still being condemned as a sinner? ⁸And why not do evil that good may come?—as some people slanderously charge us with saying. Their condemnation is just.

The whole world is guilty before God [3:9–20]. Paul concludes his statement of the problem by charging that all people, "both Jews and Greeks, are under sin" (v. 9). Until now the apostle's condemnation of the human race has been based on his observation of the way people actually behave. However, here he proves his case biblically as well as empirically by citing Scriptures drawn from many different places in the Old Testament (vv. 10–18). Everyone is guilty before God. If that is true, then no one can be saved by keeping the law; the only thing the law can do for us is to prove that we are sinners (vv. 19–20).

⁹What then? Are we Jews¹ any better off?² No, not at all. For we have already charged that all, both Jews and Greeks, are under sin, ¹⁰as it is written:

> ᵇ"None is righteous, no, not one;
> ¹¹   no one understands;
>   no one seeks for God.
> ¹²   All have turned aside; together they have become worthless;
>   no one does good,
>   not even one."
> ¹³ ᶜ"Their throat is an open grave;
>   they use their tongues to deceive."
>   ᵈ"The venom of asps is under their lips."
> ¹⁴   ᵉ"Their mouth is full of curses and bitterness."
> ¹⁵ ᶠ"Their feet are swift to shed blood;
> ¹⁶   in their paths are ruin and misery,
> ¹⁷   and the way of peace they have not known."
> ¹⁸   ᵍ"There is no fear of God before their eyes."

¹⁹Now we know that whatever the law says it speaks to those who are under the law, so that every mouth may be stopped, and the whole world may be held accountable to God. ²⁰For by works of the law no human being³ will be justified in his sight, since through the law comes knowledge of sin.

The righteousness of God through faith [3:21–31]. The theological argument of the epistle turns on a logical distinction. "But now," the apostle says, contrasting the righ-

---

¹ Greek *Are we* ² Or *at any disadvantage?* ³ Greek *flesh* ᵃ Ps. 51:4 (Gk.) ᵇ Ps. 14:1-3; 53:1-3 ᶜ Ps. 5:9 ᵈ Ps. 140:3 ᵉ Ps. 10:7 (Gk.) ᶠ Prov. 1:16; 3:15-17; Isa. 59:7, 8 ᵍ Ps. 36:1

teousness that comes from trying to keep God's law with the righteousness that comes as a gift of grace through faith in Christ. This is the answer to the universal problem of human sin: faith in Jesus. Paul's pithy summary of salvation in Christ is saturated with weighty theological terms that describe Christ's atoning work on the cross: justification (a legal declaration of righteousness), redemption (the procuring of a release through the payment of a price), and propitiation (the turning aside of wrath by means of a blood sacrifice). Although no one can be saved by observing the law, both Jews and Gentiles can be justified by faith in what Jesus has done (vv. 28–29). Passages like this in Romans require our best exercise of logical thinking to follow the argument. Imaginary dialogues and question-and-answer constructions help to carry the theological rhetoric forward.

²¹But now the righteousness of God has been manifested apart from the law, although the Law and the Prophets bear witness to it— ²²the righteousness of God through faith in Jesus Christ for all who believe. For there is no distinction: ²³for all have sinned and fall short of the glory of God, ²⁴and are justified by his grace as a gift, through the redemption that is in Christ Jesus, ²⁵whom God put forward as a propitiation by his blood, to be received by faith. This was to show God's righteousness, because in his divine forbearance he had passed over former sins. ²⁶It was to show his righteousness at the present time, so that he might be just and the justifier of the one who has faith in Jesus.

²⁷Then what becomes of our boasting? It is excluded. By what kind of law? By a law of works? No, but by the law of faith. ²⁸For we hold that one is justified by faith apart from works of the law. ²⁹Or is God the God of Jews only? Is he not the God of Gentiles also? Yes, of Gentiles also, ³⁰since God is one—who will justify the circumcised by faith and the uncircumcised through faith. ³¹Do we then overthrow the law by this faith? By no means! On the contrary, we uphold the law.

The example of Abraham's faith [chapter 4]. The apostle now proves that justification comes by faith—not works—by appealing to the famous OT example of Abraham. If ever a man was righteous, it was Abraham. But how did he become righteous? Was it by doing good works (like receiving the sacrament of circumcision, for example), or was it by unwavering faith in the promises of God? The Bible says the patriarch believed God, and righteousness was credited or imputed to him on this basis (vv. 3, 5, 9, 22). Abraham was declared righteous simply by faith, even before he was circumcised (vv. 10–12). The same is true for us today: whether we are circumcised or uncircumcised, if we believe in the crucified and risen Christ, God has promised that he will credit to us his righteousness by faith (vv. 23–25). Practitioners of the Greek genre of the diatribe alluded to representative examples from the past as illustrations of the topic under discussion, which is how Paul uses his extended references to Abraham in this chapter. Abraham is a representative figure—the representative father of faith for all subsequent believers.

4 What then shall we say was gained by¹ Abraham, our forefather according to the flesh? ²For if Abraham was justified by works, he has something to boast about, but not before God. ³For what does the Scripture say? ᵃ"Abraham believed God, and it was counted to him as righteousness." ⁴Now to the one who works, his

¹ Some manuscripts *say about* ᵃ Gen. 15:6 (Gk.)

wages are not counted as a gift but as his due. [5]And to the one who does not work but believes in[1] him who justifies the ungodly, his faith is counted as righteousness, [6]just as David also speaks of the blessing of the one to whom God counts righteousness apart from works:

[7] [a]"Blessed are those whose lawless deeds are forgiven,
     and whose sins are covered;
[8]   blessed is the man against whom the Lord will not count his sin."

[9]Is this blessing then only for the circumcised, or also for the uncircumcised? We say that faith was counted to Abraham as righteousness. [10]How then was it counted to him? Was it before or after he had been circumcised? It was not after, but before he was circumcised. [11]He received the sign of circumcision as a seal of the righteousness that he had by faith while he was still uncircumcised. The purpose was to make him the father of all who believe without being circumcised, so that righteousness would be counted to them as well, [12]and to make him the father of the circumcised who are not merely circumcised but who also walk in the footsteps of the faith that our father Abraham had before he was circumcised.

[13]For the promise to Abraham and his offspring that he would be heir of the world did not come through the law but through the righteousness of faith. [14]For if it is the adherents of the law who are to be the heirs, faith is null and the promise is void. [15]For the law brings wrath, but where there is no law there is no transgression.

[16]That is why it depends on faith, in order that the promise may rest on grace and be guaranteed to all his offspring—not only to the adherent of the law but also to the one who shares the faith of Abraham, who is the father of us all, [17]as it is written, [b]"I have made you the father of many nations"—in the presence of the God in whom he believed, who gives life to the dead and calls into existence the things that do not exist. [18]In hope he believed against hope, that he should become the father of many nations, as he had been told, [c]"So shall your offspring be." [19]He did not weaken in faith when he considered his own body, which was as good as dead (since he was about a hundred years old), or when he considered the barrenness of Sarah's womb. [20]No distrust made him waver concerning the promise of God, but he grew strong in his faith as he gave glory to God, [21]fully convinced that God was able to do what he had promised. [22]That is why his faith was "counted to him as righteousness." [23]But the words "it was counted to him" were not written for his sake alone, [24]but for ours also. It will be counted to us who believe in him who raised from the dead Jesus our Lord, [25]who was delivered up for our trespasses and raised for our justification.

The blessings of justification [5:1–11]. The word therefore at the beginning of this section signals that what comes next follows logically from the doctrine that Paul has just been defending. In being justified by faith in the blood of Christ, the believer gains many further benefits: peace with God, access to grace, the hope of glory, joy in suffering, reconciliation with God, salvation from wrath, and the love of the Father, the Son, and the Holy Spirit.

---

[1] Or but trusts; compare verse 24 [a] Ps. 32:1, 2 [b] Gen. 17:5 [c] Gen. 15:5

5 Therefore, since we have been justified by faith, we[1] have peace with God through our Lord Jesus Christ. [2]Through him we have also obtained access by faith[2] into this grace in which we stand, and we[3] rejoice[4] in hope of the glory of God. [3]More than that, we rejoice in our sufferings, knowing that suffering produces endurance, [4]and endurance produces character, and character produces hope, [5]and hope does not put us to shame, because God's love has been poured into our hearts through the Holy Spirit who has been given to us.

[6]For while we were still weak, at the right time Christ died for the ungodly. [7]For one will scarcely die for a righteous person—though perhaps for a good person one would dare even to die— [8]but God shows his love for us in that while we were still sinners, Christ died for us. [9]Since, therefore, we have now been justified by his blood, much more shall we be saved by him from the wrath of God. [10]For if while we were enemies we were reconciled to God by the death of his Son, much more, now that we are reconciled, shall we be saved by his life. [11]More than that, we also rejoice in God through our Lord Jesus Christ, through whom we have now received reconciliation.

Adam's sin, Christ's righteousness [5:12–21]. The blessings of justification are all based on the obedient righteousness of Jesus Christ. The apostle shows this by going all the way back to Adam to make another representative argument from the Old Testament. In the same way that God once justly imputed Adam's sin to the entire human race (resulting in condemnation and death), so now God freely and graciously imputes the righteousness of Christ to everyone who has faith in him (bringing justification and life). The apostle uses this comparison and contrast to emphasize that God's abundant grace is greater than all our sin (vv. 20–21). The analogy draws a comparison between Adam and Christ as the second Adam, but as the passage unfolds we see that the contrasts take priority over the similarities.

[12]Therefore, just as sin came into the world through one man, and death through sin, and so death spread to all men because all sinned— [13]for sin indeed was in the world before the law was given, but sin is not counted where there is no law. [14]Yet death reigned from Adam to Moses, even over those whose sinning was not like the transgression of Adam, who was a type of the one who was to come.

[15]But the free gift is not like the trespass. For if many died through one man's trespass, much more have the grace of God and the free gift by the grace of that one man Jesus Christ abounded for many. [16]And the free gift is not like the result of that one man's sin. For the judgment following one trespass brought condemnation, but the free gift following many trespasses brought justification. [17]For if, because of one man's trespass, death reigned through that one man, much more will those who receive the abundance of grace and the free gift of righteousness reign in life through the one man Jesus Christ.

[18]Therefore, as one trespass[5] led to condemnation for all men, so one act of righteousness[6] leads to justification and life for all men. [19]For as by the one man's disobedience the many were made sinners, so by the one man's obedience the many will be made righteous. [20]Now the law came in to increase the trespass, but where sin increased, grace abounded all the more, [21]so that, as sin reigned in death, grace

---

[1] Some manuscripts *let us* [2] Some manuscripts omit *by faith* [3] Or *let us*; also verse 3 [4] Or *boast*; also verses 3, 11 [5] Or *the trespass of one* [6] Or *the act of righteousness of one*

also might reign through righteousness leading to eternal life through Jesus Christ our Lord.

> **The believer's freedom from the dominion of sin** [chapter 6]. At this point the apostle turns from the doctrine of justification to its logical consequence: the doctrine of sanctification. He also begins to consider possible objections to his argument—a common rhetorical strategy in speeches and writings of the day. If God responds to our sin with grace, then should we keep on sinning in order to show how gracious God is (vv. 1, 15)? On the contrary, the very reason that God has saved us is to set us free from sin by putting our sin to death. Because we are united to Christ in his crucifixion and resurrection, his death is our death and his life is our life (vv. 2–7), and now we must consider ourselves dead to sin and alive to God forever (vv. 8–11). Practically speaking, this means that we must not continue to be enslaved to sin (vv. 12–14, 20–21) but must offer ourselves to God as slaves for righteousness (vv. 15–19, 22–23).

6 What shall we say then? Are we to continue in sin that grace may abound? ²By no means! How can we who died to sin still live in it? ³Do you not know that all of us who have been baptized into Christ Jesus were baptized into his death? ⁴We were buried therefore with him by baptism into death, in order that, just as Christ was raised from the dead by the glory of the Father, we too might walk in newness of life.

⁵For if we have been united with him in a death like his, we shall certainly be united with him in a resurrection like his. ⁶We know that our old self[1] was crucified with him in order that the body of sin might be brought to nothing, so that we would no longer be enslaved to sin. ⁷For one who has died has been set free[2] from sin. ⁸Now if we have died with Christ, we believe that we will also live with him. ⁹We know that Christ, being raised from the dead, will never die again; death no longer has dominion over him. ¹⁰For the death he died he died to sin, once for all, but the life he lives he lives to God. ¹¹So you also must consider yourselves dead to sin and alive to God in Christ Jesus.

¹²Let not sin therefore reign in your mortal body, to make you obey its passions. ¹³Do not present your members to sin as instruments for unrighteousness, but present yourselves to God as those who have been brought from death to life, and your members to God as instruments for righteousness. ¹⁴For sin will have no dominion over you, since you are not under law but under grace.

¹⁵What then? Are we to sin because we are not under law but under grace? By no means! ¹⁶Do you not know that if you present yourselves to anyone as obedient slaves,[3] you are slaves of the one whom you obey, either of sin, which leads to death, or of obedience, which leads to righteousness? ¹⁷But thanks be to God, that you who were once slaves of sin have become obedient from the heart to the standard of teaching to which you were committed, ¹⁸and, having been set free from sin, have become slaves of righteousness. ¹⁹I am speaking in human terms, because of your natural limitations. For just as you once presented your members as slaves to impurity and to lawlessness leading to more lawlessness, so now present your members as slaves to righteousness leading to sanctification.

²⁰For when you were slaves of sin, you were free in regard to righteousness. ²¹But what fruit were you getting at that time from the things of which you are now

---

[1] Greek man [2] Greek has been justified [3] Greek bondservants. Twice in this verse and verse 19; also once in verses 17, 20

ashamed? For the end of those things is death. ²²But now that you have been set free from sin and have become slaves of God, the fruit you get leads to sanctification and its end, eternal life. ²³For the wages of sin is death, but the free gift of God is eternal life in Christ Jesus our Lord.

> **The believer's struggle with the remnants of sin** [chapter 7]. The believer's freedom from sin finds further confirmation in an analogy with marriage. Just as death brings an end to the marriage covenant, so also death to sin releases the believer from the condemning bondage of the law of God (vv. 1–6). This is not to say that there is anything wrong with the law itself, which actually helps to save us by showing us our sin (vv. 7–11). Indeed, the law is holy, righteous, and good (v. 12). The problem is that we are unholy, unrighteous, and evil, as the law shows us (v. 13). This is even true of our sinful nature after we have come to faith in Christ. The apostle proves this by poignantly describing his own ongoing conflict with remaining sin, in which he sometimes finds himself doing the very things that he hates to do (vv. 14–24). But there is hope for Paul and for every believer in Jesus Christ (v. 25). As always in the book of Romans, the logical structure that requires careful attention to unpack is balanced by a certain informality of style—a style replete with direct addresses to the reader, question-and-answer constructions, personification of abstractions (chiefly sin), and autobiography (as Paul shares his own spiritual struggles).

7 Or do you not know, brothers¹—for I am speaking to those who know the law— that the law is binding on a person only as long as he lives? ²For a married woman is bound by law to her husband while he lives, but if her husband dies she is released from the law of marriage.² ³Accordingly, she will be called an adulteress if she lives with another man while her husband is alive. But if her husband dies, she is free from that law, and if she marries another man she is not an adulteress.

⁴Likewise, my brothers, you also have died to the law through the body of Christ, so that you may belong to another, to him who has been raised from the dead, in order that we may bear fruit for God. ⁵For while we were living in the flesh, our sinful passions, aroused by the law, were at work in our members to bear fruit for death. ⁶But now we are released from the law, having died to that which held us captive, so that we serve in the new way of the Spirit and not in the old way of the written code.³

⁷What then shall we say? That the law is sin? By no means! Yet if it had not been for the law, I would not have known sin. For I would not have known what it is to covet if ªthe law had not said, "You shall not covet." ⁸But sin, seizing an opportunity through the commandment, produced in me all kinds of covetousness. For apart from the law, sin lies dead. ⁹I was once alive apart from the law, but when the commandment came, sin came alive and I died. ¹⁰The very commandment that promised life proved to be death to me. ¹¹For sin, seizing an opportunity through the commandment, deceived me and through it killed me. ¹²So the law is holy, and the commandment is holy and righteous and good.

¹³Did that which is good, then, bring death to me? By no means! It was sin, producing death in me through what is good, in order that sin might be shown to be sin, and through the commandment might become sinful beyond measure. ¹⁴For we know that the law is spiritual, but I am of the flesh, sold under sin. ¹⁵For I do not understand my own actions. For I do not do what I want, but I do the very thing I hate.

---

¹ Or brothers and sisters; also verse 4 ² Greek law concerning the husband ³ Greek of the letter ª Ex. 20:17; Deut. 5:21

¹⁶Now if I do what I do not want, I agree with the law, that it is good. ¹⁷So now it is no longer I who do it, but sin that dwells within me. ¹⁸For I know that nothing good dwells in me, that is, in my flesh. For I have the desire to do what is right, but not the ability to carry it out. ¹⁹For I do not do the good I want, but the evil I do not want is what I keep on doing. ²⁰Now if I do what I do not want, it is no longer I who do it, but sin that dwells within me.

²¹So I find it to be a law that when I want to do right, evil lies close at hand. ²²For I delight in the law of God, in my inner being, ²³but I see in my members another law waging war against the law of my mind and making me captive to the law of sin that dwells in my members. ²⁴Wretched man that I am! Who will deliver me from this body of death? ²⁵Thanks be to God through Jesus Christ our Lord! So then, I myself serve the law of God with my mind, but with my flesh I serve the law of sin.

> **Life in the Spirit** [8:1–17]. Once again the apostle's argument comes to a logical con-
> clusion. If it is true that faith in Christ means death to sin and freedom from its bond-
> age, then we who believe have every assurance that we are not condemned but saved
> forever (v. 1). Objectively speaking, this assurance is based on the saving work of the
> Son of God (vv. 2–3). Subjectively speaking, this assurance comes through the indwell-
> ing of the Holy Spirit, who brings us life, freedom, obedience, and adoption as sons who
> know God as Father (vv. 4–17). The constant interplay between life and death, flesh
> and Spirit, provides a strong thematic unity, with the passage unfolding as a classic
> example of the rhetorical mode of antithesis. This passage is also one of the central NT
> repositories of teaching on the Holy Spirit.

8 There is therefore now no condemnation for those who are in Christ Jesus.¹ ²For the law of the Spirit of life has set you² free in Christ Jesus from the law of sin and death. ³For God has done what the law, weakened by the flesh, could not do. By sending his own Son in the likeness of sinful flesh and for sin,³ he condemned sin in the flesh, ⁴in order that the righteous requirement of the law might be fulfilled in us, who walk not according to the flesh but according to the Spirit. ⁵For those who live according to the flesh set their minds on the things of the flesh, but those who live according to the Spirit set their minds on the things of the Spirit. ⁶For to set the mind on the flesh is death, but to set the mind on the Spirit is life and peace. ⁷For the mind that is set on the flesh is hostile to God, for it does not submit to God's law; indeed, it cannot. ⁸Those who are in the flesh cannot please God.

⁹You, however, are not in the flesh but in the Spirit, if in fact the Spirit of God dwells in you. Anyone who does not have the Spirit of Christ does not belong to him. ¹⁰But if Christ is in you, although the body is dead because of sin, the Spirit is life because of righteousness. ¹¹If the Spirit of him who raised Jesus from the dead dwells in you, he who raised Christ Jesus from the dead will also give life to your mortal bodies through his Spirit who dwells in you.

¹²So then, brothers,⁴ we are debtors, not to the flesh, to live according to the flesh. ¹³For if you live according to the flesh you will die, but if by the Spirit you put to death the deeds of the body, you will live. ¹⁴For all who are led by the Spirit of God are sons⁵ of God. ¹⁵For you did not receive the spirit of slavery to fall back into fear, but you have received the Spirit of adoption as sons, by whom we cry, "Abba! Father!" ¹⁶The

---

¹ Some manuscripts add *who walk not according to the flesh (but according to the Spirit)* ² Some manuscripts *me* ³ Or *and as a sin offering* ⁴ Or *brothers and sisters; also verse 29* ⁵ See discussion on "sons" in the preface

Spirit himself bears witness with our spirit that we are children of God, [17]and if children, then heirs—heirs of God and fellow heirs with Christ, provided we suffer with him in order that we may also be glorified with him.

> **Future glory and everlasting love** [8:18–39]. The end of chapter 8 is one of the high points of Romans. The mention of the believer's future glory in verse 17 leads the apostle to develop another strong contrast, in which he compares our present sufferings with the incomparably magnificent glory that will be ours in Christ. With the whole creation, now fallen in sin (vv. 19–22), we are longing desperately for the freedom that will come in the resurrection of our bodies by the power of the Spirit (vv. 23–25). In the meantime, as we suffer in weakness and sin, the Spirit helps turn our groaning into prayer (vv. 26–27). Nor should we have any doubts about our final salvation, for God is working everything for our good, from our predestination before the beginning of time to our glorification at the end of the world (vv. 28–30). In case any further assurance is needed, Paul asks a series of rhetorical questions to prove that if God is for us—the God who justified us by giving his Son to die for us and rise again—no one can condemn us (vv. 31–34). Indeed, absolutely nothing can ever separate us from the love of God, which Paul demonstrates by providing a lengthy catalog of things that cannot keep us from Christ (vv. 35–39). The exuberance of verses 31–39 rests on two techniques: highly charged question-and-answer constructions, followed by a catalog of things that cannot separate us from Christ, with some of the items receiving further voltage from antithesis (e.g., death and life, things present and things to come).

[18]For I consider that the sufferings of this present time are not worth comparing with the glory that is to be revealed to us. [19]For the creation waits with eager longing for the revealing of the sons of God. [20]For the creation was subjected to futility, not willingly, but because of him who subjected it, in hope [21]that the creation itself will be set free from its bondage to corruption and obtain the freedom of the glory of the children of God. [22]For we know that the whole creation has been groaning together in the pains of childbirth until now. [23]And not only the creation, but we ourselves, who have the firstfruits of the Spirit, groan inwardly as we wait eagerly for adoption as sons, the redemption of our bodies. [24]For in this hope we were saved. Now hope that is seen is not hope. For who hopes for what he sees? [25]But if we hope for what we do not see, we wait for it with patience.

[26]Likewise the Spirit helps us in our weakness. For we do not know what to pray for as we ought, but the Spirit himself intercedes for us with groanings too deep for words. [27]And he who searches hearts knows what is the mind of the Spirit, because[1] the Spirit intercedes for the saints according to the will of God. [28]And we know that for those who love God all things work together for good,[2] for those who are called according to his purpose. [29]For those whom he foreknew he also predestined to be conformed to the image of his Son, in order that he might be the firstborn among many brothers. [30]And those whom he predestined he also called, and those whom he called he also justified, and those whom he justified he also glorified.

[31]What then shall we say to these things? If God is for us, who can be[3] against us? [32]He who did not spare his own Son but gave him up for us all, how will he not also with him graciously give us all things? [33]Who shall bring any charge against God's elect? It is God who justifies. [34]Who is to condemn? Christ Jesus is the one who

---

[1] Or *that* [2] Some manuscripts *God works all things together for good,* or *God works in all things for the good* [3] Or *who is*

died—more than that, who was raised—who is at the right hand of God, who indeed is interceding for us.[1] ³⁵Who shall separate us from the love of Christ? Shall tribulation, or distress, or persecution, or famine, or nakedness, or danger, or sword? ³⁶As it is written,

> ᵃ"For your sake we are being killed all the day long;
>   we are regarded as sheep to be slaughtered."

³⁷No, in all these things we are more than conquerors through him who loved us. ³⁸For I am sure that neither death nor life, nor angels nor rulers, nor things present nor things to come, nor powers, ³⁹nor height nor depth, nor anything else in all creation, will be able to separate us from the love of God in Christ Jesus our Lord.

Israel's election [9:1–29]. Chapter 9 marks the beginning of a major new section in the body of the epistle. The apostle has just stated that nothing can separate us from the love of God in Christ. But what about the Jews? Hasn't God rejected them for rejecting the Christ? The next three chapters will explain God's purpose for Paul's fellow Israelites and in doing so will also probe the mysteries of divine sovereignty and the doctrine of election. The main point of the first section is that God is absolutely sovereign in saving some people and rejecting others. The apostle advances this biblical, logical, and theological argument by making the following points, many of them with reference to specific examples and prophecies in the Old Testament: to Paul's distress, and despite having every spiritual advantage, many of his beloved fellow Jews have rejected the Christ (vv. 1–5); this does not mean that God's promise has failed, however, because the doctrine of election teaches that God never intended to save each and every person (vv. 6–13); to answer the objection that election is unfair, Paul proves God's justice by appealing to the example of his sovereign dealings with Moses and Pharaoh (vv. 14–18); to answer the objection that divine sovereignty eliminates human responsibility, Paul shows that it is God's unquestionable prerogative to glorify himself by showing mercy to the people he chooses to save and wrath to the people he chooses to destroy, whether Jews or Gentiles (vv. 20–29). The rhetorical strategy of raising questions and then immediately answering them continues to dominate the letter.

9 I am speaking the truth in Christ—I am not lying; my conscience bears me witness in the Holy Spirit— ²that I have great sorrow and unceasing anguish in my heart. ³For I could wish that I myself were accursed and cut off from Christ for the sake of my brothers,[2] my kinsmen according to the flesh. ⁴They are Israelites, and to them belong the adoption, the glory, the covenants, the giving of the law, the worship, and the promises. ⁵To them belong the patriarchs, and from their race, according to the flesh, is the Christ who is God over all, blessed forever. Amen.

⁶But it is not as though the word of God has failed. For not all who are descended from Israel belong to Israel, ⁷and not all are children of Abraham because they are his offspring, but ᵇ"Through Isaac shall your offspring be named." ⁸This means that it is not the children of the flesh who are the children of God, but the children of the promise are counted as offspring. ⁹For this is what the promise said: ᶜ"About this time next year I will return, and Sarah shall have a son." ¹⁰And not only so, but also when Rebekah had conceived children by one man, our forefather Isaac, ¹¹though they were not yet born and had done nothing either good or bad—in order that God's

---

¹ Or Is it Christ Jesus who died . . . for us? ² Or brothers and sisters ᵃ Ps. 44:22 ᵇ Gen. 21:12 ᶜ Gen. 18:10, 14

purpose of election might continue, not because of works but because of him who calls— [12]she was told, [a]"The older will serve the younger." [13]As it is written, [b]"Jacob I loved, but Esau I hated."

[14]What shall we say then? Is there injustice on God's part? By no means! [15]For he says to Moses, [c]"I will have mercy on whom I have mercy, and I will have compassion on whom I have compassion." [16]So then it depends not on human will or exertion,[1] but on God, who has mercy. [17]For the Scripture says to Pharaoh, [d]"For this very purpose I have raised you up, that I might show my power in you, and that my name might be proclaimed in all the earth." [18]So then he has mercy on whomever he wills, and he hardens whomever he wills.

[19]You will say to me then, "Why does he still find fault? For who can resist his will?" [20]But who are you, O man, to answer back to God? Will what is molded say to its molder, "Why have you made me like this?" [21]Has the potter no right over the clay, to make out of the same lump one vessel for honorable use and another for dishonorable use? [22]What if God, desiring to show his wrath and to make known his power, has endured with much patience vessels of wrath prepared for destruction, [23]in order to make known the riches of his glory for vessels of mercy, which he has prepared beforehand for glory— [24]even us whom he has called, not from the Jews only but also from the Gentiles? [25]As indeed he says in Hosea,

> [e]"Those who were not my people I will call 'my people,'
> and her who was not beloved I will call 'beloved.'"
> [26] [f]"And in the very place where it was said to them, 'You are not my people,'
> there they will be called 'sons of the living God.'"

[27]And Isaiah cries out concerning Israel: [g]"Though the number of the sons of Israel[2] be as the sand of the sea, only a remnant of them will be saved, [28]for the Lord will carry out his sentence upon the earth fully and without delay." [29]And as Isaiah predicted,

> [h]"If the Lord of hosts had not left us offspring,
> we would have been like Sodom
> and become like Gomorrah."

Israel's unbelief [9:30–10:21]. Within the wider context of God's sovereignty in salvation, Paul considers the present situation of the Jews. A catechism-like sequence of questions and answers remains the apostle's preferred mode of discourse. In contrast to Gentiles who are coming to God in faith, many Israelites are not righteous before God (9:30–31). Why not? Because they have been seeking salvation by works of the law rather than faith in Jesus Christ (9:32–33). This leads the apostle to offer heartfelt intercession for the salvation of the Jews (10:1–2). Whether one is Jew or Greek, the only way to be saved is by believing the saving message that is offered to everyone and thus receiving the righteousness of God in Christ (10:3–13). This is the gospel of justification by faith. But the fact remains that many Jews have rejected that gospel in unbelief, as the prophets warned (10:14–21). For all the complexity of Paul's theological argument, what he says in 10:9–10 is one of the Bible's clearest and simplest statements of how to be saved.

---

[1] Greek *not of him who wills or runs* [2] Or *children of Israel* [a] Gen. 25:23 [b] Mal. 1:2, 3 [c] Ex. 33:19 [d] Ex. 9:16 [e] Hos. 2:23 [f] Hos. 1:10 [g] Isa. 10:22, 23 [h] Isa. 1:9

³⁰What shall we say, then? That Gentiles who did not pursue righteousness have attained it, that is, a righteousness that is by faith; ³¹but that Israel who pursued a law that would lead to righteousness¹ did not succeed in reaching that law. ³²Why? Because they did not pursue it by faith, but as if it were based on works. They have stumbled over the stumbling stone, ³³as it is written,

ᵃ"Behold, I am laying in Zion a stone of stumbling, and a rock of offense;
   and whoever believes in him will not be put to shame."

10 Brothers,² my heart's desire and prayer to God for them is that they may be saved. ²For I bear them witness that they have a zeal for God, but not according to knowledge. ³For, being ignorant of the righteousness of God, and seeking to establish their own, they did not submit to God's righteousness. ⁴For Christ is the end of the law for righteousness to everyone who believes.³

⁵For Moses writes about the righteousness that is based on the law, that the person who does the commandments shall live by them. ⁶But the righteousness based on faith says, "Do not say in your heart, 'Who will ascend into heaven?'" (that is, to bring Christ down) ⁷or "'Who will descend into the abyss?'" (that is, to bring Christ up from the dead). ⁸But what does it say? ᵇ"The word is near you, in your mouth and in your heart" (that is, the word of faith that we proclaim); ⁹because, if you confess with your mouth that Jesus is Lord and believe in your heart that God raised him from the dead, you will be saved. ¹⁰For with the heart one believes and is justified, and with the mouth one confesses and is saved. ¹¹For the Scripture says, "Everyone who believes in him will not be put to shame." ¹²For there is no distinction between Jew and Greek; for the same Lord is Lord of all, bestowing his riches on all who call on him. ¹³For ᶜ"everyone who calls on the name of the Lord will be saved."

¹⁴How then will they call on him in whom they have not believed? And how are they to believe in him of whom they have never heard?⁴ And how are they to hear without someone preaching? ¹⁵And how are they to preach unless they are sent? As it is written, ᵈ"How beautiful are the feet of those who preach the good news!" ¹⁶But they have not all obeyed the gospel. For Isaiah says, ᵉ"Lord, who has believed what he has heard from us?" ¹⁷So faith comes from hearing, and hearing through the word of Christ.

¹⁸But I ask, have they not heard? Indeed they have, for

ᶠ"Their voice has gone out to all the earth,
   and their words to the ends of the world."

¹⁹But I ask, did Israel not understand? First Moses says,

ᵍ"I will make you jealous of those who are not a nation;
   with a foolish nation I will make you angry."

²⁰Then Isaiah is so bold as to say,

ʰ"I have been found by those who did not seek me;
   I have shown myself to those who did not ask for me."

²¹But of Israel he says, ⁱ"All day long I have held out my hands to a disobedient and contrary people."

---

¹ Greek a law of righteousness ² Or Brothers and sisters ³ Or end of the law, that everyone who believes may be justified ⁴ Or him whom they have never heard ᵃ Isa. 28:16 ᵇ Deut. 30:14 ᶜ Joel 2:32 ᵈ Isa. 52:7 ᵉ Isa. 53:1 ᶠ Ps. 19:4 ᵍ Deut. 32:21 ʰ Isa. 65:1 ⁱ Isa. 65:2

Israel's restoration [chapter 11]. Despite their rejection of the gospel, God still has a plan for his people Israel, which Paul explains by making frequent reference to the promises of the Old Testament. To begin with, Israel's rejection is not total; although many have hardened their hearts, there is still a righteous remnant, elected by grace, not by works (vv. 1–10). Furthermore, the entrance of Gentiles into the kingdom of God has the gracious purpose of arousing some Jews to the kind of jealousy that will lead them to Christ (vv. 11–24). Here Paul uses an extended metaphor to show that if the Gentiles have been graciously included in the tree of salvation (like wild branches grafted into a domesticated olive tree), it will be even easier to include the Jews (like natural branches grafted back into the root of their native tree). By way of summary, the apostle appeals to the Gentiles in Rome not to be arrogant toward the Jews but to recognize that even though many of them are presently rejecting the gospel, God still has a merciful plan for saving all his people, both Jews and Gentiles (vv. 25–32). Paul closes his exploration of these mysteries with a famous doxology that glorifies God for the wisdom of his sovereignty (vv. 33–36).

11 I ask, then, has God rejected his people? By no means! For I myself am an Israelite, a descendant of Abraham,[1] a member of the tribe of Benjamin. [2]God has not rejected his people whom he foreknew. Do you not know what the Scripture says of Elijah, how he appeals to God against Israel? [3a]"Lord, they have killed your prophets, they have demolished your altars, and I alone am left, and they seek my life." [4]But what is God's reply to him? [b]"I have kept for myself seven thousand men who have not bowed the knee to Baal." [5]So too at the present time there is a remnant, chosen by grace. [6]But if it is by grace, it is no longer on the basis of works; otherwise grace would no longer be grace.

[7]What then? Israel failed to obtain what it was seeking. The elect obtained it, but the rest were hardened, [8]as it is written,

"God gave them a spirit of stupor,
　eyes that would not see
　and ears that would not hear,
down to this very day."

[9]And David says,

[c]"Let their table become a snare and a trap,
　a stumbling block and a retribution for them;
[10]　let their eyes be darkened so that they cannot see,
　and bend their backs forever."

[11]So I ask, did they stumble in order that they might fall? By no means! Rather through their trespass salvation has come to the Gentiles, so as to make Israel jealous. [12]Now if their trespass means riches for the world, and if their failure means riches for the Gentiles, how much more will their full inclusion[2] mean!

[13]Now I am speaking to you Gentiles. Inasmuch then as I am an apostle to the Gentiles, I magnify my ministry [14]in order somehow to make my fellow Jews jealous, and thus save some of them. [15]For if their rejection means the reconciliation of the world, what will their acceptance mean but life from the dead? [16]If the dough offered as firstfruits is holy, so is the whole lump, and if the root is holy, so are the branches.

---

[1] Or one of the offspring of Abraham [2] Greek their fullness [a] 1 Kgs. 19:10, 14 [b] 1 Kgs. 19:18 [c] Ps. 69:22, 23

[17] But if some of the branches were broken off, and you, although a wild olive shoot, were grafted in among the others and now share in the nourishing root[1] of the olive tree, [18] do not be arrogant toward the branches. If you are, remember it is not you who support the root, but the root that supports you. [19] Then you will say, "Branches were broken off so that I might be grafted in." [20] That is true. They were broken off because of their unbelief, but you stand fast through faith. So do not become proud, but fear. [21] For if God did not spare the natural branches, neither will he spare you. [22] Note then the kindness and the severity of God: severity toward those who have fallen, but God's kindness to you, provided you continue in his kindness. Otherwise you too will be cut off. [23] And even they, if they do not continue in their unbelief, will be grafted in, for God has the power to graft them in again. [24] For if you were cut from what is by nature a wild olive tree, and grafted, contrary to nature, into a cultivated olive tree, how much more will these, the natural branches, be grafted back into their own olive tree.

[25] Lest you be wise in your own sight, I want you to understand this mystery, brothers:[2] a partial hardening has come upon Israel, until the fullness of the Gentiles has come in. [26] And in this way all Israel will be saved, as it is written,

[a] "The Deliverer will come from Zion,
     he will banish ungodliness from Jacob";
[27] "and this will be my covenant with them
     when I take away their sins."

[28] As regards the gospel, they are enemies of God for your sake. But as regards election, they are beloved for the sake of their forefathers. [29] For the gifts and the calling of God are irrevocable. [30] For just as you were at one time disobedient to God but now have received mercy because of their disobedience, [31] so they too have now been disobedient in order that by the mercy shown to you they also may now[3] receive mercy. [32] For God has consigned all to disobedience, that he may have mercy on all.

[33] Oh, the depth of the riches and wisdom and knowledge of God! How unsearchable are his judgments and how inscrutable his ways!

[34] "For who has known the mind of the Lord,
     or who has been his counselor?"
[35] "Or who has given a gift to him
     that he might be repaid?"

[36] For from him and through him and to him are all things. To him be glory forever. Amen.

The transformed life [chapter 12]. Like most of Paul's letters, Romans moves from doctrine to application. In the *paraenesis* of this epistle, the apostle considers the right and proper way to respond to the mercy that God has shown in granting the free gift of righteousness in Christ. We are to offer ourselves as living sacrifices for the service of God (v. 1). Such service includes life-transforming, mind-renewing discipleship (v. 2); the proper recognition and use of our spiritual gifts in the body of Christ (vv. 3–8); showing brotherly love and hospitality to the family of God (vv. 9–13); and humbly blessing our enemies with peace and mercy (vv. 14–21).

---

[1] Greek *root of richness*; some manuscripts *richness* [2] Or *brothers and sisters* [3] Some manuscripts omit *now* [a] Isa. 59:20, 21

12 I appeal to you therefore, brothers,[1] by the mercies of God, to present your bodies as a living sacrifice, holy and acceptable to God, which is your spiritual worship.[2] [2]Do not be conformed to this world,[3] but be transformed by the renewal of your mind, that by testing you may discern what is the will of God, what is good and acceptable and perfect.[4]

[3]For by the grace given to me I say to everyone among you not to think of himself more highly than he ought to think, but to think with sober judgment, each according to the measure of faith that God has assigned. [4]For as in one body we have many members,[5] and the members do not all have the same function, [5]so we, though many, are one body in Christ, and individually members one of another. [6]Having gifts that differ according to the grace given to us, let us use them: if prophecy, in proportion to our faith; [7]if service, in our serving; the one who teaches, in his teaching; [8]the one who exhorts, in his exhortation; the one who contributes, in generosity; the one who leads,[6] with zeal; the one who does acts of mercy, with cheerfulness.

[9]Let love be genuine. Abhor what is evil; hold fast to what is good. [10]Love one another with brotherly affection. Outdo one another in showing honor. [11]Do not be slothful in zeal, be fervent in spirit,[7] serve the Lord. [12]Rejoice in hope, be patient in tribulation, be constant in prayer. [13]Contribute to the needs of the saints and seek to show hospitality.

[14]Bless those who persecute you; bless and do not curse them. [15]Rejoice with those who rejoice, weep with those who weep. [16]Live in harmony with one another. Do not be haughty, but associate with the lowly.[8] Never be wise in your own sight. [17]Repay no one evil for evil, but give thought to do what is honorable in the sight of all. [18]If possible, so far as it depends on you, live peaceably with all. [19]Beloved, never avenge yourselves, but leave it[9] to the wrath of God, for it is written, [a]"Vengeance is mine, I will repay, says the Lord." [20]To the contrary, [b]"if your enemy is hungry, feed him; if he is thirsty, give him something to drink; for by so doing you will heap burning coals on his head." [21]Do not be overcome by evil, but overcome evil with good.

The transformed community [chapter 13]. In commanding Christians to obey God's rules for holy living, Paul shows that these commands extend to three spheres: civil authorities (vv. 1–7), society at large (vv. 8–10), and one's personal spiritual life in relation to Christ (vv. 11–14). To submit to the governing authorities is to submit to God; to fulfill the law of love is to effectively keep all the commandments of God.

13 Let every person be subject to the governing authorities. For there is no authority except from God, and those that exist have been instituted by God. [2]Therefore whoever resists the authorities resists what God has appointed, and those who resist will incur judgment. [3]For rulers are not a terror to good conduct, but to bad. Would you have no fear of the one who is in authority? Then do what is good, and you will receive his approval, [4]for he is God's servant for your good. But if you do wrong, be afraid, for he does not bear the sword in vain. For he is the servant of God, an avenger who carries out God's wrath on the wrongdoer. [5]Therefore one must be in subjection, not only to avoid God's wrath but also for the sake of conscience. [6]For because of this you also pay taxes, for the authorities are ministers of God, attending to this very thing. [7]Pay to all what is owed to them: taxes to whom taxes are owed, rev-

[1] Or brothers and sisters [2] Or your rational service [3] Greek age [4] Or what is the good and acceptable and perfect will of God [5] Greek parts; also verse 5 [6] Or gives aid [7] Or fervent in the Spirit [8] Or give yourselves to humble tasks [9] Greek give place [a] Deut. 32:35 [b] Prov. 25:21, 22

enue to whom revenue is owed, respect to whom respect is owed, honor to whom honor is owed.

⁸Owe no one anything, except to love each other, for the one who loves another has fulfilled the law. ⁹For the commandments, ᵃ"You shall not commit adultery, You shall not murder, You shall not steal, You shall not covet," and any other commandment, are summed up in this word: ᵇ"You shall love your neighbor as yourself." ¹⁰Love does no wrong to a neighbor; therefore love is the fulfilling of the law.

¹¹Besides this you know the time, that the hour has come for you to wake from sleep. For salvation is nearer to us now than when we first believed. ¹²The night is far gone; the day is at hand. So then let us cast off the works of darkness and put on the armor of light. ¹³Let us walk properly as in the daytime, not in orgies and drunkenness, not in sexual immorality and sensuality, not in quarreling and jealousy. ¹⁴But put on the Lord Jesus Christ, and make no provision for the flesh, to gratify its desires.

Christian liberty [chapter 14]. Paul gives special attention to an issue that was often a problem in the early church (and has been ever since), namely, disagreements within the church about what constituted proper Christian behavior. The "weak" in this case were believers who had personal scruples about their diet (vv. 2, 6) and the observance of special holy days (vv. 5–6)—things that are not required of Christ's followers but that "the weak" did to honor the Lord nonetheless (see v. 6). The "strong" were believers who recognized (quite rightly, in Paul's view; see vv. 14, 20) that these personal scruples should not be allowed to become tests of orthodoxy. Eating and drinking aside, the really important thing is for both the strong and the weak to maintain peaceful bonds of fellowship without passing judgment on one another (vv. 3–4, 10–12) and without letting their freedom in Christ cause others to sin against their own conscience (vv. 13–23).

14 As for the one who is weak in faith, welcome him, but not to quarrel over opinions. ²One person believes he may eat anything, while the weak person eats only vegetables. ³Let not the one who eats despise the one who abstains, and let not the one who abstains pass judgment on the one who eats, for God has welcomed him. ⁴Who are you to pass judgment on the servant of another? It is before his own master¹ that he stands or falls. And he will be upheld, for the Lord is able to make him stand.

⁵One person esteems one day as better than another, while another esteems all days alike. Each one should be fully convinced in his own mind. ⁶The one who observes the day, observes it in honor of the Lord. The one who eats, eats in honor of the Lord, since he gives thanks to God, while the one who abstains, abstains in honor of the Lord and gives thanks to God. ⁷For none of us lives to himself, and none of us dies to himself. ⁸For if we live, we live to the Lord, and if we die, we die to the Lord. So then, whether we live or whether we die, we are the Lord's. ⁹For to this end Christ died and lived again, that he might be Lord both of the dead and of the living.

¹⁰Why do you pass judgment on your brother? Or you, why do you despise your brother? For we will all stand before the judgment seat of God; ¹¹for it is written,

ᶜ"As I live, says the Lord, every knee shall bow to me,
    and every tongue shall confess² to God."

¹²So then each of us will give an account of himself to God.

¹ Or lord ² Or shall give praise ᵃ Ex. 20:13-17; Deut. 5:17-21 ᵇ Lev. 19:18 ᶜ Isa. 45:23

¹³Therefore let us not pass judgment on one another any longer, but rather decide never to put a stumbling block or hindrance in the way of a brother. ¹⁴I know and am persuaded in the Lord Jesus that nothing is unclean in itself, but it is unclean for anyone who thinks it unclean. ¹⁵For if your brother is grieved by what you eat, you are no longer walking in love. By what you eat, do not destroy the one for whom Christ died. ¹⁶So do not let what you regard as good be spoken of as evil. ¹⁷For the kingdom of God is not a matter of eating and drinking but of righteousness and peace and joy in the Holy Spirit. ¹⁸Whoever thus serves Christ is acceptable to God and approved by men. ¹⁹So then let us pursue what makes for peace and for mutual upbuilding.

²⁰Do not, for the sake of food, destroy the work of God. Everything is indeed clean, but it is wrong for anyone to make another stumble by what he eats. ²¹It is good not to eat meat or drink wine or do anything that causes your brother to stumble.¹ ²²The faith that you have, keep between yourself and God. Blessed is the one who has no reason to pass judgment on himself for what he approves. ²³But whoever has doubts is condemned if he eats, because the eating is not from faith. For whatever does not proceed from faith is sin.²

The example of Christ [15:1–13]. Our model for love and service in the church—for the strong supporting the weak, for each encouraging others, and for everyone worshiping God with one voice—is Jesus Christ (vv. 1–6). Just as he welcomed us, so we are to welcome one another (v. 7). This welcome is to be extended to everyone, just as Jesus came to serve both Jews and Gentiles, giving joy to every believer (vv. 8–13). The prominence of biblical allusions in this chapter serves as a reminder of how important OT references are in the epistle to the Romans. In an argumentative discourse, the Hebrew mind of Bible times preferred to prove a point on the basis of Scripture.

15 We who are strong have an obligation to bear with the failings of the weak, and not to please ourselves. ²Let each of us please his neighbor for his good, to build him up. ³For Christ did not please himself, but as it is written, ᵃ"The reproaches of those who reproached you fell on me." ⁴For whatever was written in former days was written for our instruction, that through endurance and through the encouragement of the Scriptures we might have hope. ⁵May the God of endurance and encouragement grant you to live in such harmony with one another, in accord with Christ Jesus, ⁶that together you may with one voice glorify the God and Father of our Lord Jesus Christ. ⁷Therefore welcome one another as Christ has welcomed you, for the glory of God.

⁸For I tell you that Christ became a servant to the circumcised to show God's truthfulness, in order to confirm the promises given to the patriarchs, ⁹and in order that the Gentiles might glorify God for his mercy. As it is written,

ᵇ"Therefore I will praise you among the Gentiles,
and sing to your name."

¹⁰And again it is said,

ᶜ"Rejoice, O Gentiles, with his people."

¹ Some manuscripts add *or be hindered or be weakened* ² Some manuscripts insert here 16:25-27 ᵃ Ps. 69:9 ᵇ 2 Sam. 22:50; Ps. 18:49 ᶜ Deut. 32:43

[11]And again,

> [a]"Praise the Lord, all you Gentiles,
>   and let all the peoples extol him."

[12]And again Isaiah says,

> [b]"The root of Jesse will come,
>   even he who arises to rule the Gentiles;
>   in him will the Gentiles hope."

[13]May the God of hope fill you with all joy and peace in believing, so that by the power of the Holy Spirit you may abound in hope.

Paul's ministry to Jews and Gentiles [15:14–33]. As he presses toward the conclusion of his letter, Paul gives the Romans a testimony of his calling in ministry: as an apostle to the Gentiles, he has served God around the world by preaching the gospel to people who had never heard about Jesus (vv. 14–21). This divine calling explains both his keen desire to visit the Romans before going on to Spain (vv. 22–24, 28–29, 32–33) and his present endeavor of taking a monetary gift from Christians in Asia to their suffering brothers and sisters in Jerusalem (vv. 25–27, 30–32). The delivery of this gift is not simply an errand of mercy but a living demonstration of the message of Romans: the free gift of God's righteousness has brought Jews and Gentiles together in Christ. The genre underlying the passage is the missionary autobiography.

[14]I myself am satisfied about you, my brothers,[1] that you yourselves are full of goodness, filled with all knowledge and able to instruct one another. [15]But on some points I have written to you very boldly by way of reminder, because of the grace given me by God [16]to be a minister of Christ Jesus to the Gentiles in the priestly service of the gospel of God, so that the offering of the Gentiles may be acceptable, sanctified by the Holy Spirit. [17]In Christ Jesus, then, I have reason to be proud of my work for God. [18]For I will not venture to speak of anything except what Christ has accomplished through me to bring the Gentiles to obedience—by word and deed, [19]by the power of signs and wonders, by the power of the Spirit of God—so that from Jerusalem and all the way around to Illyricum I have fulfilled the ministry of the gospel of Christ; [20]and thus I make it my ambition to preach the gospel, not where Christ has already been named, lest I build on someone else's foundation, [21]but as it is written,

> [c]"Those who have never been told of him will see,
>   and those who have never heard will understand."

[22]This is the reason why I have so often been hindered from coming to you. [23]But now, since I no longer have any room for work in these regions, and since I have longed for many years to come to you, [24]I hope to see you in passing as I go to Spain, and to be helped on my journey there by you, once I have enjoyed your company for a while. [25]At present, however, I am going to Jerusalem bringing aid to the saints. [26]For Macedonia and Achaia have been pleased to make some contribution for the poor among the saints at Jerusalem. [27]For they were pleased to do it, and indeed they owe

---

[1] Or *brothers and sisters*; also verse 30 [a] Ps. 117:1 [b] Isa. 11:10 [c] Isa. 52:15

it to them. For if the Gentiles have come to share in their spiritual blessings, they ought also to be of service to them in material blessings. [28]When therefore I have completed this and have delivered to them what has been collected,[1] I will leave for Spain by way of you. [29]I know that when I come to you I will come in the fullness of the blessing[2] of Christ.

[30]I appeal to you, brothers, by our Lord Jesus Christ and by the love of the Spirit, to strive together with me in your prayers to God on my behalf, [31]that I may be delivered from the unbelievers in Judea, and that my service for Jerusalem may be acceptable to the saints, [32]so that by God's will I may come to you with joy and be refreshed in your company. [33]May the God of peace be with you all. Amen.

> **Personal greetings and final doxology** [chapter 16]. Romans ends with a long list of greetings to a wide variety of men and women in Rome, many of them Paul's partners in ministry. The list serves as a reminder that the service of ordinary people matters to God and also as a testimony of the apostle's own commitment to loving his brothers and sisters in Christ. The closing doxology is one of the longest in the New Testament (vv. 25–27). Its rich theology nicely balances the opening of Romans and recapitulates some of the main doctrinal and practical themes of the letter.

16 I commend to you our sister Phoebe, a servant[3] of the church at Cenchreae, [2]that you may welcome her in the Lord in a way worthy of the saints, and help her in whatever she may need from you, for she has been a patron of many and of myself as well.

[3]Greet Prisca and Aquila, my fellow workers in Christ Jesus, [4]who risked their necks for my life, to whom not only I give thanks but all the churches of the Gentiles give thanks as well. [5]Greet also the church in their house. Greet my beloved Epaenetus, who was the first convert[4] to Christ in Asia. [6]Greet Mary, who has worked hard for you. [7]Greet Andronicus and Junia,[5] my kinsmen and my fellow prisoners. They are well known to the apostles,[6] and they were in Christ before me. [8]Greet Ampliatus, my beloved in the Lord. [9]Greet Urbanus, our fellow worker in Christ, and my beloved Stachys. [10]Greet Apelles, who is approved in Christ. Greet those who belong to the family of Aristobulus. [11]Greet my kinsman Herodion. Greet those in the Lord who belong to the family of Narcissus. [12]Greet those workers in the Lord, Tryphaena and Tryphosa. Greet the beloved Persis, who has worked hard in the Lord. [13]Greet Rufus, chosen in the Lord; also his mother, who has been a mother to me as well. [14]Greet Asyncritus, Phlegon, Hermes, Patrobas, Hermas, and the brothers[7] who are with them. [15]Greet Philologus, Julia, Nereus and his sister, and Olympas, and all the saints who are with them. [16]Greet one another with a holy kiss. All the churches of Christ greet you.

[17]I appeal to you, brothers, to watch out for those who cause divisions and create obstacles contrary to the doctrine that you have been taught; avoid them. [18]For such persons do not serve our Lord Christ, but their own appetites,[8] and by smooth talk and flattery they deceive the hearts of the naive. [19]For your obedience is known to all, so that I rejoice over you, but I want you to be wise as to what is good and innocent as to what is evil. [20]The God of peace will soon crush Satan under your feet. The grace of our Lord Jesus Christ be with you.

---

[1] Greek *sealed to them this fruit* [2] Some manuscripts insert *of the gospel* [3] Or *deaconess* [4] Greek *firstfruit* [5] Or *Junias* [6] Or *messengers* [7] Or *brothers and sisters*; also verse 17 [8] Greek *their own belly*

²¹Timothy, my fellow worker, greets you; so do Lucius and Jason and Sosipater, my kinsmen.

²²I Tertius, who wrote this letter, greet you in the Lord.

²³Gaius, who is host to me and to the whole church, greets you. Erastus, the city treasurer, and our brother Quartus, greet you.[1]

²⁵Now to him who is able to strengthen you according to my gospel and the preaching of Jesus Christ, according to the revelation of the mystery that was kept secret for long ages ²⁶but has now been disclosed and through the prophetic writings has been made known to all nations, according to the command of the eternal God, to bring about the obedience of faith— ²⁷to the only wise God be glory forevermore through Jesus Christ! Amen.

---

[1] Some manuscripts insert verse 24: *The grace of our Lord Jesus Christ be with you all. Amen.*

1 CORINTHIANS

The book at a glance. 16 chapters, 433 verses. First Corinthians is a pastoral letter to a spiritually troubled church. Paul had founded the Corinthian church on his second missionary journey (Acts 18). He wrote this letter in response to a report of problems that were threatening to divide the church. He also answers questions that had been posed by church members. The NT epistles are *occasional letters, and by noting the signals that Paul gives us right in the text, we can quite readily piece together the things that occasioned 1 Corinthians. The relevance of this letter to our own day is high. Some of the issues involve the relationship between Christians and their surrounding pagan culture. Others are issues within the church, such as divisiveness expressed in church practices such as the Lord's Supper and spiritual gifts. Still other issues concern personal morality, such as sex, marriage, celibacy, and the virtues (especially love).

▌**Genres.** 1 Corinthians is in every way a typical NT *epistle. However, it is so thoroughly an *occasional letter in which the content is governed by the specific situation in the Corinthian church that the usual epistolary elements of *salutation, *thanksgiving, and *paraenesis* receive scant treatment. The body of the letter addresses situations and questions from the Corinthian church, and the epistolary close (chapter 16) is extensive. The rhetorical modes of exhortation and instruction dominate the letter. Chapter 13 is an *encomium in praise of love. (For more information on items accompanied by an asterisk, see the glossary at the back of this Bible.)

▌**Special features.** 1 Corinthians has a flavor all its own, and its distinguishing features include the following: (1) The author has received extensive information from a church with which he is on intimate terms, with the result that he writes with impassioned fervor on a wide range of topics. (2) Because Paul regards the Corinthian Christians as being out of line in a number of areas, the letter possesses a strong corrective tone. (3) First Corinthians is perhaps the most famous NT repository of information on a number of key subjects: sex, marriage, and celibacy (chapter 7); the institution of the Lord's Supper (11:23–29); church unity amid diversity of gifts, illuminated by the analogy between the church and the human body (chapter 12); the supremacy of love (chapter 13); spiritual gifts (chapter 14); the bodily resurrection of both Christ and the Christian (chapter 15). (4) The pagan context that keeps surfacing in the book is very similar to the modern world, so that the contemporary relevance of the book is high.

Passage	Content	Topic	What Paul Does in the Passage	Rhetorical Stance
1:1–9	Salutation and thanksgiving	Epistolary opening	Paul begins his letter	Exuberance
1:10–17	Reports of divisions	Divisions in the church	Paul responds to Chloe's report of divisions in the church	Concern
1:18–3:23	Spiritual wisdom offered as the solution to the problems that afflict the Corinthian church			
4:1–21	Paul offers himself as an example of servanthood			
5:1–6:20	Three problem areas in the Corinthian church: incest, lawsuits, sexual misconduct	Immorality in the church	Paul responds to reports of immorality in the church	Correction
7:1–40	Sex and marriage	Difficult issues in the church	Paul answers questions that have been raised	Counsel
8:1–11:1	Food offered to idols			
11:2–34	Worship and the Lord's Supper			
12:1–31	Unity within diversity in the church			
13:1–13	The superiority of love			
14:1–40	Spiritual gifts			
15:1–58	The resurrection			
16:1–24	Personal matters	Epistolary conclusion	Paul ends his letter	Practical discharge of "housekeeping" matters

▌**Inferred literary intentions.** The book is designed to achieve the following literary purposes:

- express moral and spiritual truth on a range of subjects by means of the conventions of an occasional epistle

- make the truth forceful by rhetorical techniques such as contrast, repetition, and analogy

- draw sharp contrasts between truth and error and between moral good and evil

- show how broad ranging the issues in the Christian life are, from sexual behavior to protocol in public worship to the doctrine of the resurrection

▌**Theological themes.** (1) Ethics: much of the content of the book relates to the conduct of the moral life, especially as regards the physical body. (2) The church: by means of Paul's response to specific issues in a single ancient church, this letter becomes a main NT repository of teaching about how church life should be conducted. (3) The resurrection: the long fifteenth chapter is a classic NT passage on the doctrine of the resurrection. (4) Spirituality: not only the chapter on spiritual gifts but also many other chapters (such as those on control of the body and the need for love) paint a portrait of what it means to live the spiritual life.

▌1 Corinthians as a chapter in the master story of the Bible. In the OT, the story of God's demands for how his followers were to live focused on the covenant nation of Israel. In the NT, the corresponding focus is the body of believers known as the church. First Corinthians is an expanded manual for how Christians who make up the church must conduct their individual and corporate lives.

Making contact with the audience [1:1–17]. In this opening unit, Paul transacts the necessary first business of any letter: making connection with the recipients. At first this occurs in the customary way, with a salutation consisting of the familiar identification of the sender (v. 1) and recipients (v. 2), followed by the familiar "grace and peace" prayer (v. 3). Equally expected is the section of thanksgiving (vv. 4–9). But then a surprise greets us, as the thanksgiving is shortened and immediately followed by an acknowledgment of reports of divisions in the Corinthian church (vv. 10–17). We always need to operate on the literary and spiritual premise that what was true for one church is true for Christians and churches throughout history.

1 Paul, called by the will of God to be an apostle of Christ Jesus, and our brother Sosthenes,

²To the church of God that is in Corinth, to those sanctified in Christ Jesus, called to be saints together with all those who in every place call upon the name of our Lord Jesus Christ, both their Lord and ours:

³Grace to you and peace from God our Father and the Lord Jesus Christ.

⁴I give thanks to my God always for you because of the grace of God that was given you in Christ Jesus, ⁵that in every way you were enriched in him in all speech and all knowledge— ⁶even as the testimony about Christ was confirmed among you— ⁷so that you are not lacking in any spiritual gift, as you wait for the revealing of our Lord Jesus Christ, ⁸who will sustain you to the end, guiltless in the day of our Lord Jesus Christ. ⁹God is faithful, by whom you were called into the fellowship of his Son, Jesus Christ our Lord.

¹⁰I appeal to you, brothers,ⁱ by the name of our Lord Jesus Christ, that all of you agree, and that there be no divisions among you, but that you be united in the same mind and the same judgment. ¹¹For it has been reported to me by Chloe's people that there is quarreling among you, my brothers. ¹²What I mean is that each one of you says, "I follow Paul," or "I follow Apollos," or "I follow Cephas," or "I follow Christ." ¹³Is Christ divided? Was Paul crucified for you? Or were you baptized in the name of Paul? ¹⁴I thank God that I baptized none of you except Crispus and Gaius, ¹⁵so that no one may say that you were baptized in my name. ¹⁶(I did baptize also the household of Stephanas. Beyond that, I do not know whether I baptized anyone else.) ¹⁷For Christ did not send me to baptize but to preach the gospel, and not with words of eloquent wisdom, lest the cross of Christ be emptied of its power.

ⁱ Or *brothers and sisters*. The plural Greek word *adelphoi* (translated "brothers") refers to siblings in a family. In New Testament usage, depending on the context, *adelphoi* may refer either to men or to both men and women who are siblings (brothers and sisters) in God's family, the church; also verses 11, 26

God's choice of the lowly [1:18–31]. This unit is one of the *rhetorical high points of the NT. The opening verse sets the keynote by calling the gospel "folly." The rest of the passage then unleashes a barrage on contrasts between wise and foolish, God and the world, strong and weak. But the rhetoric is stronger than that of simple antithesis; it keeps moving into the high-voltage rhetoric of *paradox, in which worldly wisdom is said to be folly and worldly folly is said to be divine wisdom, or in which the weakness of humankind is really strength to God. By means of this rhetoric, Paul asserts that God's values are exactly the opposite of the values of fallen humanity. *Satire figures strongly in the passage, as human standards of value and impressiveness are continually ridiculed. Then at the end of the passage (vv. 30–31), the elevation of God's wisdom takes an explicitly christological turn (foreshadowed in vv. 22–24), as Christ is said to be the wisdom, righteousness, sanctification, and redemption of the believer.

[18] For the word of the cross is folly to those who are perishing, but to us who are being saved it is the power of God. [19] For it is written,

[a] "I will destroy the wisdom of the wise,
     and the discernment of the discerning I will thwart."

[20] Where is the one who is wise? Where is the scribe? Where is the debater of this age? Has not God made foolish the wisdom of the world? [21] For since, in the wisdom of God, the world did not know God through wisdom, it pleased God through the folly of what we preach to save those who believe. [22] For Jews demand signs and Greeks seek wisdom, [23] but we preach Christ crucified, a stumbling block to Jews and folly to Gentiles, [24] but to those who are called, both Jews and Greeks, Christ the power of God and the wisdom of God. [25] For the foolishness of God is wiser than men, and the weakness of God is stronger than men.

[26] For consider your calling, brothers: not many of you were wise according to worldly standards,[1] not many were powerful, not many were of noble birth. [27] But God chose what is foolish in the world to shame the wise; God chose what is weak in the world to shame the strong; [28] God chose what is low and despised in the world, even things that are not, to bring to nothing things that are, [29] so that no human being[2] might boast in the presence of God. [30] And because of him[3] you are in Christ Jesus, who became to us wisdom from God, righteousness and sanctification and redemption, [31] so that, as it is written, "Let the one who boasts, boast in the Lord."

The wisdom of the Spirit [chapter 2]. This unit extends the general tenor of the preceding unit by again deflating human standards of wisdom and power and exalting God's standards. The christological emphasis of the preceding unit is now succeeded by an emphasis on the Holy Spirit. The motif of wisdom remains prominent. A good grid for assimilating the chapter is to look for what it says about (1) the Holy Spirit and (2) the nature of true spiritual wisdom. In view of those things, what characterizes the spiritual person?

2 And I, when I came to you, brothers,[4] did not come proclaiming to you the testimony[5] of God with lofty speech or wisdom. [2] For I decided to know nothing among you except Jesus Christ and him crucified. [3] And I was with you in weakness and in fear and much trembling, [4] and my speech and my message were not in plau-

---

[1] Greek *according to the flesh* [2] Greek *no flesh* [3] Greek *And from him* [4] Or *brothers and sisters* [5] Some manuscripts *mystery* (or *secret*) [a] Isa. 29:14

sible words of wisdom, but in demonstration of the Spirit and of power, [5]that your faith might not rest in the wisdom of men but in the power of God.

[6]Yet among the mature we do impart wisdom, although it is not a wisdom of this age or of the rulers of this age, who are doomed to pass away. [7]But we impart a secret and hidden wisdom of God, which God decreed before the ages for our glory. [8]None of the rulers of this age understood this, for if they had, they would not have crucified the Lord of glory. [9]But, as it is written,

"What no eye has seen, nor ear heard,
    nor the heart of man imagined,
  what God has prepared for those who love him"—

[10]these things God has revealed to us through the Spirit. For the Spirit searches everything, even the depths of God. [11]For who knows a person's thoughts except the spirit of that person, which is in him? So also no one comprehends the thoughts of God except the Spirit of God. [12]Now we have received not the spirit of the world, but the Spirit who is from God, that we might understand the things freely given us by God. [13]And we impart this in words not taught by human wisdom but taught by the Spirit, interpreting spiritual truths to those who are spiritual.[1]

[14]The natural person does not accept the things of the Spirit of God, for they are folly to him, and he is not able to understand them because they are spiritually discerned. [15]The spiritual person judges all things, but is himself to be judged by no one. [16a]"For who has understood the mind of the Lord so as to instruct him?" But we have the mind of Christ.

The folly of humanity [chapter 3]. After two rapturous passages dealing with the spiritual wisdom of God, Christ, and the Spirit, chapter 3 brings us down with a thud to the spectacle of human folly in the church at Corinth. The preceding two units make disparaging references to human folly, but those references are foils to the foreground subject of God's wisdom. With chapter 3, human folly is foregrounded. Two intertwined motifs can be explored: (1) bad conduct in the Corinthian church and (2) the doctrines that, if applied and lived out, would serve as corrective to the abuses that are pictured. For example, partisan devotion to particular leaders like Apollos and Paul would dissipate if people realized that Jesus Christ is the one on whom the church is founded.

3 But I, brothers,[2] could not address you as spiritual people, but as people of the flesh, as infants in Christ. [2]I fed you with milk, not solid food, for you were not ready for it. And even now you are not yet ready, [3]for you are still of the flesh. For while there is jealousy and strife among you, are you not of the flesh and behaving only in a human way? [4]For when one says, "I follow Paul," and another, "I follow Apollos," are you not being merely human?

[5]What then is Apollos? What is Paul? Servants through whom you believed, as the Lord assigned to each. [6]I planted, Apollos watered, but God gave the growth. [7]So neither he who plants nor he who waters is anything, but only God who gives the growth. [8]He who plants and he who waters are one, and each will receive his wages according to his labor. [9]For we are God's fellow workers. You are God's field, God's building.

[10]According to the grace of God given to me, like a skilled master builder I laid a

[1] Or interpreting spiritual truths in spiritual language, or comparing spiritual things with spiritual [2] Or brothers and sisters [a] Isa. 40:13

foundation, and someone else is building upon it. Let each one take care how he builds upon it. [11] For no one can lay a foundation other than that which is laid, which is Jesus Christ. [12] Now if anyone builds on the foundation with gold, silver, precious stones, wood, hay, straw— [13] each one's work will become manifest, for the Day will disclose it, because it will be revealed by fire, and the fire will test what sort of work each one has done. [14] If the work that anyone has built on the foundation survives, he will receive a reward. [15] If anyone's work is burned up, he will suffer loss, though he himself will be saved, but only as through fire.

[16] Do you not know that you[1] are God's temple and that God's Spirit dwells in you? [17] If anyone destroys God's temple, God will destroy him. For God's temple is holy, and you are that temple.

[18] Let no one deceive himself. If anyone among you thinks that he is wise in this age, let him become a fool that he may become wise. [19] For the wisdom of this world is folly with God. For it is written, [a]"He catches the wise in their craftiness," [20] and again, [b]"The Lord knows the thoughts of the wise, that they are futile." [21] So let no one boast in men. For all things are yours, [22] whether Paul or Apollos or Cephas or the world or life or death or the present or the future—all are yours, [23] and you are Christ's, and Christ is God's.

Paul offers himself as an example [chapter 4]. This chapter is closely related to the preceding unit. Having sketched out how true spiritual wisdom differs from the unspiritual behavior of some of the Corinthian Christians, Paul now describes his own ministry among the Corinthians, implicitly offering it as an example for the Corinthians to imitate. The self-portrait that Paul offers is an implied defense of his ministry, and we can analyze the passage in terms of how the description that Paul gives of his ministry is also a defense of that ministry. How does Paul's ministry demonstrate the spiritual paradoxes of wisdom and folly that should characterize the life of every servant of God?

4 This is how one should regard us, as servants of Christ and stewards of the mysteries of God. [2] Moreover, it is required of stewards that they be found trustworthy. [3] But with me it is a very small thing that I should be judged by you or by any human court. In fact, I do not even judge myself. [4] For I am not aware of anything against myself, but I am not thereby acquitted. It is the Lord who judges me. [5] Therefore do not pronounce judgment before the time, before the Lord comes, who will bring to light the things now hidden in darkness and will disclose the purposes of the heart. Then each one will receive his commendation from God.

[6] I have applied all these things to myself and Apollos for your benefit, brothers,[2] that you may learn by us not to go beyond what is written, that none of you may be puffed up in favor of one against another. [7] For who sees anything different in you? What do you have that you did not receive? If then you received it, why do you boast as if you did not receive it?

[8] Already you have all you want! Already you have become rich! Without us you have become kings! And would that you did reign, so that we might share the rule with you! [9] For I think that God has exhibited us apostles as last of all, like men sentenced to death, because we have become a spectacle to the world, to angels, and to men. [10] We are fools for Christ's sake, but you are wise in Christ. We are weak, but

[1] The Greek for *you* is plural in verses 16 and 17 [2] Or *brothers and sisters* [a] Job 5:13 [b] Ps. 94:11

you are strong. You are held in honor, but we in disrepute. ¹¹To the present hour we hunger and thirst, we are poorly dressed and buffeted and homeless, ¹²and we labor, working with our own hands. When reviled, we bless; when persecuted, we endure; ¹³when slandered, we entreat. We have become, and are still, like the scum of the world, the refuse of all things.

¹⁴I do not write these things to make you ashamed, but to admonish you as my beloved children. ¹⁵For though you have countless guides in Christ, you do not have many fathers. For I became your father in Christ Jesus through the gospel. ¹⁶I urge you, then, be imitators of me. ¹⁷That is why I sent¹ you Timothy, my beloved and faithful child in the Lord, to remind you of my ways in Christ,² as I teach them everywhere in every church. ¹⁸Some are arrogant, as though I were not coming to you. ¹⁹But I will come to you soon, if the Lord wills, and I will find out not the talk of these arrogant people but their power. ²⁰For the kingdom of God does not consist in talk but in power. ²¹What do you wish? Shall I come to you with a rod, or with love in a spirit of gentleness?

How to deal with incest in the church [chapter 5]. With this chapter Paul zeroes in on the reports that he has received regarding bad behavior in the Corinthian church. The first of these problems is a church member who is cohabiting with his father's wife. Paul's slant on this topic is primarily to instruct the corporate church how to deal with the sinful behavior of one of its members. We can start by making sure that we have a grip on the specific steps of discipline that Paul outlines. From that we look for the broader principles that Paul gives for relating to people who are living a sinful lifestyle.

5 It is actually reported that there is sexual immorality among you, and of a kind that is not tolerated even among pagans, for a man has his father's wife. ²And you are arrogant! Ought you not rather to mourn? Let him who has done this be removed from among you.

³For though absent in body, I am present in spirit; and as if present, I have already pronounced judgment on the one who did such a thing. ⁴When you are assembled in the name of the Lord Jesus and my spirit is present, with the power of our Lord Jesus, ⁵you are to deliver this man to Satan for the destruction of the flesh, so that his spirit may be saved in the day of the Lord.³

⁶Your boasting is not good. Do you not know that a little leaven leavens the whole lump? ⁷Cleanse out the old leaven that you may be a new lump, as you really are unleavened. For Christ, our Passover lamb, has been sacrificed. ⁸Let us therefore celebrate the festival, not with the old leaven, the leaven of malice and evil, but with the unleavened bread of sincerity and truth.

⁹I wrote to you in my letter not to associate with sexually immoral people— ¹⁰not at all meaning the sexually immoral of this world, or the greedy and swindlers, or idolaters, since then you would need to go out of the world. ¹¹But now I am writing to you not to associate with anyone who bears the name of brother if he is guilty of sexual immorality or greed, or is an idolater, reviler, drunkard, or swindler—not even to eat with such a one. ¹²For what have I to do with judging outsiders? Is it not those inside the church whom you are to judge? ¹³God judges⁴ those outside. "Purge the evil person from among you."

¹ Or am sending ² Some manuscripts add Jesus ³ Some manuscripts add Jesus ⁴ Or will judge

6 When one of you has a grievance against another, does he dare go to law before the unrighteous instead of the saints? [2]Or do you not know that the saints will judge the world? And if the world is to be judged by you, are you incompetent to try trivial cases? [3]Do you not know that we are to judge angels? How much more, then, matters pertaining to this life! [4]So if you have such cases, why do you lay them before those who have no standing in the church? [5]I say this to your shame. Can it be that there is no one among you wise enough to settle a dispute between the brothers, [6]but brother goes to law against brother, and that before unbelievers? [7]To have lawsuits at all with one another is already a defeat for you. Why not rather suffer wrong? Why not rather be defrauded? [8]But you yourselves wrong and defraud—even your own brothers![1]

[9]Or do you not know that the unrighteous[2] will not inherit the kingdom of God? Do not be deceived: neither the sexually immoral, nor idolaters, nor adulterers, nor men who practice homosexuality,[3] [10]nor thieves, nor the greedy, nor drunkards, nor revilers, nor swindlers will inherit the kingdom of God. [11]And such were some of you. But you were washed, you were sanctified, you were justified in the name of the Lord Jesus Christ and by the Spirit of our God.

[12]"All things are lawful for me," but not all things are helpful. "All things are lawful for me," but I will not be enslaved by anything. [13]"Food is meant for the stomach and the stomach for food"—and God will destroy both one and the other. The body is not meant for sexual immorality, but for the Lord, and the Lord for the body. [14]And God raised the Lord and will also raise us up by his power. [15]Do you not know that your bodies are members of Christ? Shall I then take the members of Christ and make them members of a prostitute? Never! [16]Or do you not know that he who is joined[4] to a prostitute becomes one body with her? For, as it is written, [a]"The two will become one flesh." [17]But he who is joined to the Lord becomes one spirit with him. [18]Flee from sexual immorality. Every other sin[5] a person commits is outside the body, but the sexually immoral person sins against his own body. [19]Or do you not know that your body is a temple of the Holy Spirit within you, whom you have from God? You are not your own, [20]for you were bought with a price. So glorify God in your body.

[1] Or brothers and sisters [2] Or wrongdoers [3] The two Greek terms translated by this phrase refer to the passive and active partners in consensual homosexual acts [4] Or who holds fast (compare Genesis 2:24 and Deuteronomy 10:20); also verse 17 [5] Or Every sin [a] Gen. 2:24

which Paul expresses his viewpoints on these subjects is a strong awareness that the end of history may be approaching (vv. 29–31). Within that context, Paul covers these topics: the need for married couples to share sexual relations (vv. 1–7); instructions to the unmarried (vv. 8–9); rules governing Christians who are married to unbelievers (vv. 10–16); by extension, rules about how conversion affects other areas of life as well as marriage (vv. 17–24); instructions to single people regarding the advisability of marriage and the spiritual advantages of celibacy (vv. 25–35); the same principles applied to couples who are betrothed (vv. 36–38); instruction to widows regarding remarriage (vv. 39–40).

7 Now concerning the matters about which you wrote: "It is good for a man not to have sexual relations with a woman." [2] But because of the temptation to sexual immorality, each man should have his own wife and each woman her own husband. [3] The husband should give to his wife her conjugal rights, and likewise the wife to her husband. [4] For the wife does not have authority over her own body, but the husband does. Likewise the husband does not have authority over his own body, but the wife does. [5] Do not deprive one another, except perhaps by agreement for a limited time, that you may devote yourselves to prayer; but then come together again, so that Satan may not tempt you because of your lack of self-control.

[6] Now as a concession, not a command, I say this.[1] [7] I wish that all were as I myself am. But each has his own gift from God, one of one kind and one of another.

[8] To the unmarried and the widows I say that it is good for them to remain single as I am. [9] But if they cannot exercise self-control, they should marry. For it is better to marry than to burn with passion.

[10] To the married I give this charge (not I, but the Lord): the wife should not separate from her husband [11] (but if she does, she should remain unmarried or else be reconciled to her husband), and the husband should not divorce his wife.

[12] To the rest I say (I, not the Lord) that if any brother has a wife who is an unbeliever, and she consents to live with him, he should not divorce her. [13] If any woman has a husband who is an unbeliever, and he consents to live with her, she should not divorce him. [14] For the unbelieving husband is made holy because of his wife, and the unbelieving wife is made holy because of her husband. Otherwise your children would be unclean, but as it is, they are holy. [15] But if the unbelieving partner separates, let it be so. In such cases the brother or sister is not enslaved. God has called you[2] to peace. [16] For how do you know, wife, whether you will save your husband? Or how do you know, husband, whether you will save your wife?

[17] Only let each person lead the life that the Lord has assigned to him, and to which God has called him. This is my rule in all the churches. [18] Was anyone at the time of his call already circumcised? Let him not seek to remove the marks of circumcision. Was anyone at the time of his call uncircumcised? Let him not seek circumcision. [19] For neither circumcision counts for anything nor uncircumcision, but keeping the commandments of God. [20] Each one should remain in the condition in which he was called. [21] Were you a slave[3] when called? Do not be concerned about it. (But if you can gain your freedom, avail yourself of the opportunity.) [22] For he who was called in the Lord as a slave is a freedman of the Lord. Likewise he who was free when called is a slave of Christ. [23] You were bought with a price; do not become slaves of men. [24] So, brothers,[4] in whatever condition each was called, there let him remain with God.

---

[1] Or I say this: [2] Some manuscripts us [3] Greek bondservant; also twice in verse 22 and once in verse 23 (plural) [4] Or brothers and sisters; also verse 29

²⁵Now concerning¹ the betrothed,² I have no command from the Lord, but I give my judgment as one who by the Lord's mercy is trustworthy. ²⁶I think that in view of the present³ distress it is good for a person to remain as he is. ²⁷Are you bound to a wife? Do not seek to be free. Are you free from a wife? Do not seek a wife. ²⁸But if you do marry, you have not sinned, and if a betrothed woman⁴ marries, she has not sinned. Yet those who marry will have worldly troubles, and I would spare you that. ²⁹This is what I mean, brothers: the appointed time has grown very short. From now on, let those who have wives live as though they had none, ³⁰and those who mourn as though they were not mourning, and those who rejoice as though they were not rejoicing, and those who buy as though they had no goods, ³¹and those who deal with the world as though they had no dealings with it. For the present form of this world is passing away.

³²I want you to be free from anxieties. The unmarried man is anxious about the things of the Lord, how to please the Lord. ³³But the married man is anxious about worldly things, how to please his wife, ³⁴and his interests are divided. And the unmarried or betrothed woman is anxious about the things of the Lord, how to be holy in body and spirit. But the married woman is anxious about worldly things, how to please her husband. ³⁵I say this for your own benefit, not to lay any restraint upon you, but to promote good order and to secure your undivided devotion to the Lord.

³⁶If anyone thinks that he is not behaving properly toward his betrothed,⁵ if his⁶ passions are strong, and it has to be, let him do as he wishes: let them marry—it is no sin. ³⁷But whoever is firmly established in his heart, being under no necessity but having his desire under control, and has determined this in his heart, to keep her as his betrothed, he will do well. ³⁸So then he who marries his betrothed does well, and he who refrains from marriage will do even better.

³⁹A wife is bound to her husband as long as he lives. But if her husband dies, she is free to be married to whom she wishes, only in the Lord. ⁴⁰Yet in my judgment she is happier if she remains as she is. And I think that I too have the Spirit of God.

Food offered to idols [chapter 8]. Again the opening verse of this unit tells us that Paul is responding to a question that has been raised regarding whether Christians are free to eat food that had been offered to idols before being served as a meal. This precise situation is not a relevant issue for most Christians today, so we need to analyze the passage for the principles underlying the behavior and attitudes that Paul commands in regard to the first-century issue of food offered to idols. The message that Paul articulates here is known as the doctrine of Christian liberty, and at its core lies a balancing act between personal rights and privileges on the one hand (the freedom of an individual's conscience before God) and loving obligation to the feelings and attitudes of stricter believers on the other hand (and we should note that it is the stricter believers whom Paul calls "the weak"). A good way to process the passage is to see how this balancing act works itself out.

8 Now concerning⁷ food offered to idols: we know that "all of us possess knowledge." This "knowledge" puffs up, but love builds up. ²If anyone imagines that he knows something, he does not yet know as he ought to know. ³But if anyone loves God, he is known by God.⁸

---

¹ The expression *Now concerning* introduces a reply to a question in the Corinthians' letter; see 7:1 ² Greek *virgins* ³ Or *impending* ⁴ Greek *virgin*; also verse 34 ⁵ Greek *virgin*; also verses 37, 38 ⁶ Or *her* ⁷ The expression *Now concerning* introduces a reply to a question in the Corinthians' letter; see 7:1 ⁸ Greek *him*

[4]Therefore, as to the eating of food offered to idols, we know that "an idol has no real existence," and that "there is no God but one." [5]For although there may be so-called gods in heaven or on earth—as indeed there are many "gods" and many "lords"— [6]yet for us there is one God, the Father, from whom are all things and for whom we exist, and one Lord, Jesus Christ, through whom are all things and through whom we exist.

[7]However, not all possess this knowledge. But some, through former association with idols, eat food as really offered to an idol, and their conscience, being weak, is defiled. [8]Food will not commend us to God. We are no worse off if we do not eat, and no better off if we do. [9]But take care that this right of yours does not somehow become a stumbling block to the weak. [10]For if anyone sees you who have knowledge eating[1] in an idol's temple, will he not be encouraged,[2] if his conscience is weak, to eat food offered to idols? [11]And so by your knowledge this weak person is destroyed, the brother for whom Christ died. [12]Thus, sinning against your brothers[3] and wounding their conscience when it is weak, you sin against Christ. [13]Therefore, if food makes my brother stumble, I will never eat meat, lest I make my brother stumble.

Paul's personal application of the principle of Christian liberty [chapter 9]. Chapter 9 extends the argument of chapter 8. The new development is that Paul displays how he himself applies the principles stated earlier. It takes patience to piece together all that Paul says on the subject, and there are numerous side paths to the main argument, including the subject of ministers' deserving to be paid for their ministry. At the heart of this chapter is Paul's claim that the truest freedom comes when we become a servant of others.

9 Am I not free? Am I not an apostle? Have I not seen Jesus our Lord? Are not you my workmanship in the Lord? [2]If to others I am not an apostle, at least I am to you, for you are the seal of my apostleship in the Lord.

[3]This is my defense to those who would examine me. [4]Do we not have the right to eat and drink? [5]Do we not have the right to take along a believing wife,[4] as do the other apostles and the brothers of the Lord and Cephas? [6]Or is it only Barnabas and I who have no right to refrain from working for a living? [7]Who serves as a soldier at his own expense? Who plants a vineyard without eating any of its fruit? Or who tends a flock without getting some of the milk?

[8]Do I say these things on human authority? Does not the Law say the same? [9]For it is written in the Law of Moses, [a]"You shall not muzzle an ox when it treads out the grain." Is it for oxen that God is concerned? [10]Does he not speak entirely for our sake? It was written for our sake, because the plowman should plow in hope and the thresher thresh in hope of sharing in the crop. [11]If we have sown spiritual things among you, is it too much if we reap material things from you? [12]If others share this rightful claim on you, do not we even more?

Nevertheless, we have not made use of this right, but we endure anything rather than put an obstacle in the way of the gospel of Christ. [13]Do you not know that those who are employed in the temple service get their food from the temple, and those who serve at the altar share in the sacrificial offerings? [14]In the same way, the Lord commanded that those who proclaim the gospel should get their living by the gospel.

---

[1] Greek *reclining at table* [2] Or *fortified*; Greek *built up* [3] Or *brothers and sisters* [4] Greek *a sister as wife* [a] Deut. 25:4

¹⁵But I have made no use of any of these rights, nor am I writing these things to secure any such provision. For I would rather die than have anyone deprive me of my ground for boasting. ¹⁶For if I preach the gospel, that gives me no ground for boasting. For necessity is laid upon me. Woe to me if I do not preach the gospel! ¹⁷For if I do this of my own will, I have a reward, but if not of my own will, I am still entrusted with a stewardship. ¹⁸What then is my reward? That in my preaching I may present the gospel free of charge, so as not to make full use of my right in the gospel.

¹⁹For though I am free from all, I have made myself a servant to all, that I might win more of them. ²⁰To the Jews I became as a Jew, in order to win Jews. To those under the law I became as one under the law (though not being myself under the law) that I might win those under the law. ²¹To those outside the law I became as one outside the law (not being outside the law of God but under the law of Christ) that I might win those outside the law. ²²To the weak I became weak, that I might win the weak. I have become all things to all people, that by all means I might save some. ²³I do it all for the sake of the gospel, that I may share with them in its blessings.

²⁴Do you not know that in a race all the runners run, but only one receives the prize? So run that you may obtain it. ²⁵Every athlete exercises self-control in all things. They do it to receive a perishable wreath, but we an imperishable. ²⁶So I do not run aimlessly; I do not box as one beating the air. ²⁷But I discipline my body and keep it under control,¹ lest after preaching to others I myself should be disqualified.

Final thoughts on food offered to idols [10:1–11:1]. When scrutinized carefully, this chapter can be seen as a third chapter on the general issue of how much freedom individual Christians should claim as their privilege. The chapter begins in a way that seems to be remote from that subject, as it offers important interpretive insights into the OT exodus. The preceding discussion has claimed that eating food offered to idols is not an inherently contaminating practice. To show that it is not what one *eats* that contaminates but what one is, Paul offers a shocking example: the OT covenant people had the best possible food and drink (10:1–4), and yet they were idolatrous (10:5–7). This is the sin that Christians need to avoid—not some external association with idols but an inward affection for them (10:8–13). From there Paul proceeds to the following subjects: the need for believers who participate in communion with Christ to avoid participating with pagan idolatry (10:14–22); final instructions regarding food offered to idols (10:23–30); concluding summary (10:31–11:1).

10 For I want you to know, brothers,² that our fathers were all under the cloud, and all passed through the sea, ²and all were baptized into Moses in the cloud and in the sea, ³and all ate the same spiritual food, ⁴and all drank the same spiritual drink. For they drank from the spiritual Rock that followed them, and the Rock was Christ. ⁵Nevertheless, with most of them God was not pleased, for they were overthrown in the wilderness.

⁶Now these things took place as examples for us, that we might not desire evil as they did. ⁷Do not be idolaters as some of them were; as it is written, ª"The people sat down to eat and drink and rose up to play." ⁸We must not indulge in sexual immorality as some of them did, and twenty-three thousand fell in a single day. ⁹We must not put Christ³ to the test, as some of them did and were destroyed by serpents, ¹⁰nor grumble, as some of them did and were destroyed by the Destroyer. ¹¹Now these

¹ Greek *I pummel my body and make it a slave* ² Or *brothers and sisters* ³ Some manuscripts *the Lord* ª Ex. 32:6

things happened to them as an example, but they were written down for our instruction, on whom the end of the ages has come. ¹²Therefore let anyone who thinks that he stands take heed lest he fall. ¹³No temptation has overtaken you that is not common to man. God is faithful, and he will not let you be tempted beyond your ability, but with the temptation he will also provide the way of escape, that you may be able to endure it.

¹⁴Therefore, my beloved, flee from idolatry. ¹⁵I speak as to sensible people; judge for yourselves what I say. ¹⁶The cup of blessing that we bless, is it not a participation in the blood of Christ? The bread that we break, is it not a participation in the body of Christ? ¹⁷Because there is one bread, we who are many are one body, for we all partake of the one bread. ¹⁸Consider the people of Israel:¹ are not those who eat the sacrifices participants in the altar? ¹⁹What do I imply then? That food offered to idols is anything, or that an idol is anything? ²⁰No, I imply that what pagans sacrifice they offer to demons and not to God. I do not want you to be participants with demons. ²¹You cannot drink the cup of the Lord and the cup of demons. You cannot partake of the table of the Lord and the table of demons. ²²Shall we provoke the Lord to jealousy? Are we stronger than he?

²³"All things are lawful," but not all things are helpful. "All things are lawful," but not all things build up. ²⁴Let no one seek his own good, but the good of his neighbor. ²⁵Eat whatever is sold in the meat market without raising any question on the ground of conscience. ²⁶For ᵃ"the earth is the Lord's, and the fullness thereof." ²⁷If one of the unbelievers invites you to dinner and you are disposed to go, eat whatever is set before you without raising any question on the ground of conscience. ²⁸But if someone says to you, "This has been offered in sacrifice," then do not eat it, for the sake of the one who informed you, and for the sake of conscience— ²⁹I do not mean your conscience, but his. For why should my liberty be determined by someone else's conscience? ³⁰If I partake with thankfulness, why am I denounced because of that for which I give thanks?

³¹So, whether you eat or drink, or whatever you do, do all to the glory of God. ³²Give no offense to Jews or to Greeks or to the church of God, ³³just as I try to please everyone in everything I do, not seeking my own advantage, but that of many, that they may be saved.

11

Be imitators of me, as I am of Christ.

Rules for public worship [11:2–34]. As we read the opening section dealing with differing protocol for women and men in public worship (vv. 2–16), we need to operate in an awareness of a basic literary principle: particularized details are intended to express universal principles. The chief interpretive issue with this passage is to ascertain what the general principles are. In Paul's day, long hair was a cultural symbol of respect for male leadership; we therefore need to ask how a woman today might show a similar respect. The rest of the chapter (vv. 17–34) expresses rules for how to administer and receive the Lord's Supper that still apply today, with a concluding appeal for unity in the church.

¹ Greek *Consider Israel according to the flesh* ᵃ Ps. 24:1

[2]Now I commend you because you remember me in everything and maintain the traditions even as I delivered them to you. [3]But I want you to understand that the head of every man is Christ, the head of a wife[1] is her husband, and the head of Christ is God. [4]Every man who prays or prophesies with his head covered dishonors his head, [5]but every wife[2] who prays or prophesies with her head uncovered dishonors her head, since it is the same as if her head were shaven. [6]For if a wife will not cover her head, then she should cut her hair short. But since it is disgraceful for a wife to cut off her hair or shave her head, let her cover her head. [7]For a man ought not to cover his head, since he is the image and glory of God, but woman is the glory of man. [8]For man was not made from woman, but woman from man. [9]Neither was man created for woman, but woman for man. [10]That is why a wife ought to have a symbol of authority on her head, because of the angels.[3] [11]Nevertheless, in the Lord woman is not independent of man nor man of woman; [12]for as woman was made from man, so man is now born of woman. And all things are from God. [13]Judge for yourselves: is it proper for a wife to pray to God with her head uncovered? [14]Does not nature itself teach you that if a man wears long hair it is a disgrace for him, [15]but if a woman has long hair, it is her glory? For her hair is given to her for a covering. [16]If anyone is inclined to be contentious, we have no such practice, nor do the churches of God.

[17]But in the following instructions I do not commend you, because when you come together it is not for the better but for the worse. [18]For, in the first place, when you come together as a church, I hear that there are divisions among you. And I believe it in part,[4] [19]for there must be factions among you in order that those who are genuine among you may be recognized. [20]When you come together, it is not the Lord's supper that you eat. [21]For in eating, each one goes ahead with his own meal. One goes hungry, another gets drunk. [22]What! Do you not have houses to eat and drink in? Or do you despise the church of God and humiliate those who have nothing? What shall I say to you? Shall I commend you in this? No, I will not.

[23]For I received from the Lord what I also delivered to you, that the Lord Jesus on the night when he was betrayed took bread, [24]and when he had given thanks, he broke it, and said, "This is my body which is for[5] you. Do this in remembrance of me."[6] [25]In the same way also he took the cup, after supper, saying, "This cup is the new covenant in my blood. Do this, as often as you drink it, in remembrance of me." [26]For as often as you eat this bread and drink the cup, you proclaim the Lord's death until he comes.

[27]Whoever, therefore, eats the bread or drinks the cup of the Lord in an unworthy manner will be guilty concerning the body and blood of the Lord. [28]Let a person examine himself, then, and so eat of the bread and drink of the cup. [29]For anyone who eats and drinks without discerning the body eats and drinks judgment on himself. [30]That is why many of you are weak and ill, and some have died.[7] [31]But if we judged[8] ourselves truly, we would not be judged. [32]But when we are judged by the Lord, we are disciplined[9] so that we may not be condemned along with the world.

[33]So then, my brothers,[10] when you come together to eat, wait for[11] one another— [34]if anyone is hungry, let him eat at home—so that when you come together it will not be for judgment. About the other things I will give directions when I come.

---

[1] Greek gunē. This term may refer to a *woman* or a *wife*, depending on the context [2] In verses 5-13, the Greek word gunē is translated *wife* in verses that deal with wearing a veil, a sign of being married in first-century culture [3] Or *messengers*, that is, people sent to observe and report [4] Or *I believe a certain report* [5] Some manuscripts broken for [6] Or *as my memorial*; also verse 25 [7] Greek *have fallen asleep* (as in 15:6, 20) [8] Or *discerned* [9] Or *when we are judged we are being disciplined by the Lord* [10] Or *brothers and sisters* [11] Or *share with*

Unity in diversity within the church [chapter 12]. This chapter is the classic NT passage on unity and diversity in the functioning of the church. Paul's point of departure
is to answer a question that has been raised about spiritual gifts (vv. 1–3). But the
flow of thought quickly turns toward the main subject of the chapter, which is elaborated as follows: the variety of gifts bestowed on the church by "the same Spirit" (vv.
4–11); assertion that the church is unified just as a physical body is a unity (vv. 12–13);
detailed elaboration of the analogy between the parts of the human body and the variety of gifts within the church to show that all gifts play an essential role in the unified
functioning of the body (vv. 14–26); a list of some of the gifts that God has given to the
church, accompanied by an implied declaration (by means of rhetorical questions) that
no one practices all the gifts, with a concluding command to desire the higher gifts (vv.
27–31). The passage is a rhetorical showcase of such techniques as repetition, parallel
constructions, analogy, imaginary dialogue, rhetorical question, and personification.

12 Now concerning[1] spiritual gifts,[2] brothers,[3] I do not want you to be uninformed. [2]You know that when you were pagans you were led astray to mute
idols, however you were led. [3]Therefore I want you to understand that no one speaking in the Spirit of God ever says "Jesus is accursed!" and no one can say "Jesus is
Lord" except in the Holy Spirit.

[4]Now there are varieties of gifts, but the same Spirit; [5]and there are varieties of service, but the same Lord; [6]and there are varieties of activities, but it is the same God
who empowers them all in everyone. [7]To each is given the manifestation of the Spirit
for the common good. [8]For to one is given through the Spirit the utterance of wisdom,
and to another the utterance of knowledge according to the same Spirit, [9]to another
faith by the same Spirit, to another gifts of healing by the one Spirit, [10]to another the
working of miracles, to another prophecy, to another the ability to distinguish
between spirits, to another various kinds of tongues, to another the interpretation of
tongues. [11]All these are empowered by one and the same Spirit, who apportions to
each one individually as he wills.

[12]For just as the body is one and has many members, and all the members of the
body, though many, are one body, so it is with Christ. [13]For in one Spirit we were all
baptized into one body—Jews or Greeks, slaves[4] or free—and all were made to drink
of one Spirit.

[14]For the body does not consist of one member but of many. [15]If the foot should
say, "Because I am not a hand, I do not belong to the body," that would not make it
any less a part of the body. [16]And if the ear should say, "Because I am not an eye, I do
not belong to the body," that would not make it any less a part of the body. [17]If the
whole body were an eye, where would be the sense of hearing? If the whole body
were an ear, where would be the sense of smell? [18]But as it is, God arranged the members in the body, each one of them, as he chose. [19]If all were a single member, where
would the body be? [20]As it is, there are many parts,[5] yet one body.

[21]The eye cannot say to the hand, "I have no need of you," nor again the head to the
feet, "I have no need of you." [22]On the contrary, the parts of the body that seem to be
weaker are indispensable, [23]and on those parts of the body that we think less honorable we bestow the greater honor, and our unpresentable parts are treated with
greater modesty, [24]which our more presentable parts do not require. But God has so

composed the body, giving greater honor to the part that lacked it, [25]that there may be no division in the body, but that the members may have the same care for one another. [26]If one member suffers, all suffer together; if one member is honored, all rejoice together.

[27]Now you are the body of Christ and individually members of it. [28]And God has appointed in the church first apostles, second prophets, third teachers, then miracles, then gifts of healing, helping, administrating, and various kinds of tongues. [29]Are all apostles? Are all prophets? Are all teachers? Do all work miracles? [30]Do all possess gifts of healing? Do all speak with tongues? Do all interpret? [31]But earnestly desire the higher gifts.

And I will show you a still more excellent way.

The supremacy of love [chapter 13]. The famous "love chapter" is an *encomium—a composition in praise of an abstract quality. The usual motifs are present: the indispensability of love (vv. 1–3); the acts and attributes of love (vv. 4–7); the superiority of love, expressed by means of comparison to lesser things (vv. 8–13). The usual command to emulate appears at the very beginning of the next chapter. This chapter, like the preceding one, is a showcase of such rhetorical techniques as parallel constructions, patterns of threefold repetition, wavelike prose rhythm (including rising and falling cadences), and elaborate patterns of syntactical units (such as long, flowing sentences).

13 If I speak in the tongues of men and of angels, but have not love, I am a noisy gong or a clanging cymbal. [2]And if I have prophetic powers, and understand all mysteries and all knowledge, and if I have all faith, so as to remove mountains, but have not love, I am nothing. [3]If I give away all I have, and if I deliver up my body to be burned,[1] but have not love, I gain nothing.

[4]Love is patient and kind; love does not envy or boast; it is not arrogant [5]or rude. It does not insist on its own way; it is not irritable or resentful;[2] [6]it does not rejoice at wrongdoing, but rejoices with the truth. [7]Love bears all things, believes all things, hopes all things, endures all things.

[8]Love never ends. As for prophecies, they will pass away; as for tongues, they will cease; as for knowledge, it will pass away. [9]For we know in part and we prophesy in part, [10]but when the perfect comes, the partial will pass away. [11]When I was a child, I spoke like a child, I thought like a child, I reasoned like a child. When I became a man, I gave up childish ways. [12]For now we see in a mirror dimly, but then face to face. Now I know in part; then I shall know fully, even as I have been fully known.

[13]So now faith, hope, and love abide, these three; but the greatest of these is love.

Spiritual gifts [chapter 14]. The focus of this chapter is on the gifts of prophecy and speaking in tongues. The flow of thought is as follows: a weighing of the relative merits of prophecy and tongues (vv. 1–5); cautions about speaking in tongues in public worship (vv. 6–12); instructions governing speaking in tongues in public worship (vv. 13–19); back to the comparison between prophecy and speaking in tongues (vv. 20–25); general rules for exercising the spiritual gifts in public worship, especially the gifts of prophecy and tongues (vv. 26–39).

---

[1] Some manuscripts *deliver up my body* [to death] *that I may boast* [2] Greek *irritable and does not count up wrongdoing*

14 Pursue love, and earnestly desire the spiritual gifts, especially that you may prophesy. [2]For one who speaks in a tongue speaks not to men but to God; for no one understands him, but he utters mysteries in the Spirit. [3]On the other hand, the one who prophesies speaks to people for their upbuilding and encouragement and consolation. [4]The one who speaks in a tongue builds up himself, but the one who prophesies builds up the church. [5]Now I want you all to speak in tongues, but even more to prophesy. The one who prophesies is greater than the one who speaks in tongues, unless someone interprets, so that the church may be built up.

[6]Now, brothers,[1] if I come to you speaking in tongues, how will I benefit you unless I bring you some revelation or knowledge or prophecy or teaching? [7]If even lifeless instruments, such as the flute or the harp, do not give distinct notes, how will anyone know what is played? [8]And if the bugle gives an indistinct sound, who will get ready for battle? [9]So with yourselves, if with your tongue you utter speech that is not intelligible, how will anyone know what is said? For you will be speaking into the air. [10]There are doubtless many different languages in the world, and none is without meaning, [11]but if I do not know the meaning of the language, I will be a foreigner to the speaker and the speaker a foreigner to me. [12]So with yourselves, since you are eager for manifestations of the Spirit, strive to excel in building up the church.

[13]Therefore, one who speaks in a tongue should pray for the power to interpret. [14]For if I pray in a tongue, my spirit prays but my mind is unfruitful. [15]What am I to do? I will pray with my spirit, but I will pray with my mind also; I will sing praise with my spirit, but I will sing with my mind also. [16]Otherwise, if you give thanks with your spirit, how can anyone in the position of an outsider[2] say "Amen" to your thanksgiving when he does not know what you are saying? [17]For you may be giving thanks well enough, but the other person is not being built up. [18]I thank God that I speak in tongues more than all of you. [19]Nevertheless, in church I would rather speak five words with my mind in order to instruct others, than ten thousand words in a tongue.

[20]Brothers, do not be children in your thinking. Be infants in evil, but in your thinking be mature. [21]In the Law it is written, [a]"By people of strange tongues and by the lips of foreigners will I speak to this people, and even then they will not listen to me, says the Lord." [22]Thus tongues are a sign not for believers but for unbelievers, while prophecy is a sign[3] not for unbelievers but for believers. [23]If, therefore, the whole church comes together and all speak in tongues, and outsiders or unbelievers enter, will they not say that you are out of your minds? [24]But if all prophesy, and an unbeliever or outsider enters, he is convicted by all, he is called to account by all, [25]the secrets of his heart are disclosed, and so, falling on his face, he will worship God and declare that God is really among you.

[26]What then, brothers? When you come together, each one has a hymn, a lesson, a revelation, a tongue, or an interpretation. Let all things be done for building up. [27]If any speak in a tongue, let there be only two or at most three, and each in turn, and let someone interpret. [28]But if there is no one to interpret, let each of them keep silent in church and speak to himself and to God. [29]Let two or three prophets speak, and let the others weigh what is said. [30]If a revelation is made to another sitting there, let the first be silent. [31]For you can all prophesy one by one, so that all may learn and all be encouraged, [32]and the spirits of prophets are subject to prophets. [33]For God is not a God of confusion but of peace.

As in all the churches of the saints, [34]the women should keep silent in the

---

[1] Or brothers and sisters; also verses 20, 26, 39 [2] Or of him that is without gifts [3] Greek lacks a sign [a] Isa. 28:11, 12

churches. For they are not permitted to speak, but should be in submission, as the Law also says. ³⁵If there is anything they desire to learn, let them ask their husbands at home. For it is shameful for a woman to speak in church.

³⁶Or was it from you that the word of God came? Or are you the only ones it has reached? ³⁷If anyone thinks that he is a prophet, or spiritual, he should acknowledge that the things I am writing to you are a command of the Lord. ³⁸If anyone does not recognize this, he is not recognized. ³⁹So, my brothers, earnestly desire to prophesy, and do not forbid speaking in tongues. ⁴⁰But all things should be done decently and in order.

The doctrine of the resurrection [chapter 15]. This long chapter is the classic NT passage on the resurrection of the physical body at the last day. The following is one way to divide the material: an assertion and proof of the fact of Christ's physical resurrection from the dead (vv. 1–11); how the whole gospel depends on Christ's resurrection from death (vv. 12–19); information about the eschatological future, including Christ's return and the resurrection of believers (vv. 20–28); the futility of the Christian life if there were no resurrection (vv. 29–34); information about the nature of the resurrection body (vv. 35–50); information about, and celebration of, the moment of the resurrection (vv. 51–57), with a concluding comment about the inspiration that this should provide Christians right now (v. 58). The rhetorical genre is the persuasive discourse based on argument. Subordinate rhetorical forms are the hypothetical question to which the author replies and the use of dialogue for the sake of argument.

15 Now I would remind you, brothers,¹ of the gospel I preached to you, which you received, in which you stand, ²and by which you are being saved, if you hold fast to the word I preached to you—unless you believed in vain.

³For I delivered to you as of first importance what I also received: that Christ died for our sins in accordance with the Scriptures, ⁴that he was buried, that he was raised on the third day in accordance with the Scriptures, ⁵and that he appeared to Cephas, then to the twelve. ⁶Then he appeared to more than five hundred brothers at one time, most of whom are still alive, though some have fallen asleep. ⁷Then he appeared to James, then to all the apostles. ⁸Last of all, as to one untimely born, he appeared also to me. ⁹For I am the least of the apostles, unworthy to be called an apostle, because I persecuted the church of God. ¹⁰But by the grace of God I am what I am, and his grace toward me was not in vain. On the contrary, I worked harder than any of them, though it was not I, but the grace of God that is with me. ¹¹Whether then it was I or they, so we preach and so you believed.

¹²Now if Christ is proclaimed as raised from the dead, how can some of you say that there is no resurrection of the dead? ¹³But if there is no resurrection of the dead, then not even Christ has been raised. ¹⁴And if Christ has not been raised, then our preaching is in vain and your faith is in vain. ¹⁵We are even found to be misrepresenting God, because we testified about God that he raised Christ, whom he did not raise if it is true that the dead are not raised. ¹⁶For if the dead are not raised, not even Christ has been raised. ¹⁷And if Christ has not been raised, your faith is futile and you are still in your sins. ¹⁸Then those also who have fallen asleep in Christ have perished. ¹⁹If in Christ we have hope² in this life only, we are of all people most to be pitied.

²⁰But in fact Christ has been raised from the dead, the firstfruits of those who have fallen asleep. ²¹For as by a man came death, by a man has come also the resurrection

¹ Or brothers and sisters; also verses 6, 31, 50, 58 ² Or we have hoped

of the dead. [22]For as in Adam all die, so also in Christ shall all be made alive. [23]But each in his own order: Christ the firstfruits, then at his coming those who belong to Christ. [24]Then comes the end, when he delivers the kingdom to God the Father after destroying every rule and every authority and power. [25]For he must reign until he has put all his enemies under his feet. [26]The last enemy to be destroyed is death. [27]For [a]"God[1] has put all things in subjection under his feet." But when it says, "all things are put in subjection," it is plain that he is excepted who put all things in subjection under him. [28]When all things are subjected to him, then the Son himself will also be subjected to him who put all things in subjection under him, that God may be all in all.

[29]Otherwise, what do people mean by being baptized on behalf of the dead? If the dead are not raised at all, why are people baptized on their behalf? [30]Why are we in danger every hour? [31]I protest, brothers, by my pride in you, which I have in Christ Jesus our Lord, I die every day! [32]What do I gain if, humanly speaking, I fought with beasts at Ephesus? If the dead are not raised, [b]"Let us eat and drink, for tomorrow we die." [33]Do not be deceived: "Bad company ruins good morals."[2] [34]Wake up from your drunken stupor, as is right, and do not go on sinning. For some have no knowledge of God. I say this to your shame.

[35]But someone will ask, "How are the dead raised? With what kind of body do they come?" [36]You foolish person! What you sow does not come to life unless it dies. [37]And what you sow is not the body that is to be, but a bare kernel, perhaps of wheat or of some other grain. [38]But God gives it a body as he has chosen, and to each kind of seed its own body. [39]For not all flesh is the same, but there is one kind for humans, another for animals, another for birds, and another for fish. [40]There are heavenly bodies and earthly bodies, but the glory of the heavenly is of one kind, and the glory of the earthly is of another. [41]There is one glory of the sun, and another glory of the moon, and another glory of the stars; for star differs from star in glory.

[42]So is it with the resurrection of the dead. What is sown is perishable; what is raised is imperishable. [43]It is sown in dishonor; it is raised in glory. It is sown in weakness; it is raised in power. [44]It is sown a natural body; it is raised a spiritual body. If there is a natural body, there is also a spiritual body. [45]Thus it is written, [c]"The first man Adam became a living being";[3] the last Adam became a life-giving spirit. [46]But it is not the spiritual that is first but the natural, and then the spiritual. [47]The first man was from the earth, a man of dust; the second man is from heaven. [48]As was the man of dust, so also are those who are of the dust, and as is the man of heaven, so also are those who are of heaven. [49]Just as we have borne the image of the man of dust, we shall[4] also bear the image of the man of heaven.

[50]I tell you this, brothers: flesh and blood cannot inherit the kingdom of God, nor does the perishable inherit the imperishable. [51]Behold! I tell you a mystery. We shall not all sleep, but we shall all be changed, [52]in a moment, in the twinkling of an eye, at the last trumpet. For the trumpet will sound, and the dead will be raised imperishable, and we shall be changed. [53]For this perishable body must put on the imperishable, and this mortal body must put on immortality. [54]When the perishable puts on the imperishable, and the mortal puts on immortality, then shall come to pass the saying that is written:

[d]"Death is swallowed up in victory."
[55]   "O death, where is your victory?
        O death, where is your sting?"

---

[1] Greek he [2] Probably from Menander's comedy Thais [3] Greek a living soul [4] Some manuscripts let us [a] Ps. 8:6 [b] Isa. 22:13 [c] Gen. 2:7 [d] Isa. 25:8

⁵⁶The sting of death is sin, and the power of sin is the law. ⁵⁷But thanks be to God, who gives us the victory through our Lord Jesus Christ.

⁵⁸Therefore, my beloved brothers, be steadfast, immovable, always abounding in the work of the Lord, knowing that in the Lord your labor is not in vain.

> **Epistolary conclusion** [chapter 16]. In the extended conclusion to this particular letter, Paul covers the usual personal concerns and much in addition, as follows: giving the details of a collection for the poor in Jerusalem (vv. 1–4); Paul's anticipated itinerary (vv. 5–12); exhortations (an abbreviated *paraenesis*, vv. 13–14); references to specific people (vv. 15–18); epistolary greetings (vv. 19–20); the author's signature (v. 21); a concluding curse (v. 22) and benedictions (vv. 23–24).

16 Now concerning[1] the collection for the saints: as I directed the churches of Galatia, so you also are to do. ²On the first day of every week, each of you is to put something aside and store it up, as he may prosper, so that there will be no collecting when I come. ³And when I arrive, I will send those whom you accredit by letter to carry your gift to Jerusalem. ⁴If it seems advisable that I should go also, they will accompany me.

⁵I will visit you after passing through Macedonia, for I intend to pass through Macedonia, ⁶and perhaps I will stay with you or even spend the winter, so that you may help me on my journey, wherever I go. ⁷For I do not want to see you now just in passing. I hope to spend some time with you, if the Lord permits. ⁸But I will stay in Ephesus until Pentecost, ⁹for a wide door for effective work has opened to me, and there are many adversaries.

¹⁰When Timothy comes, see that you put him at ease among you, for he is doing the work of the Lord, as I am. ¹¹So let no one despise him. Help him on his way in peace, that he may return to me, for I am expecting him with the brothers.

¹²Now concerning our brother Apollos, I strongly urged him to visit you with the other brothers, but it was not at all his will[2] to come now. He will come when he has opportunity.

¹³Be watchful, stand firm in the faith, act like men, be strong. ¹⁴Let all that you do be done in love.

¹⁵Now I urge you, brothers[3]—you know that the household[4] of Stephanas were the first converts in Achaia, and that they have devoted themselves to the service of the saints— ¹⁶be subject to such as these, and to every fellow worker and laborer. ¹⁷I rejoice at the coming of Stephanas and Fortunatus and Achaicus, because they have made up for your absence, ¹⁸for they refreshed my spirit as well as yours. Give recognition to such men.

¹⁹The churches of Asia send you greetings. Aquila and Prisca, together with the church in their house, send you hearty greetings in the Lord. ²⁰All the brothers send you greetings. Greet one another with a holy kiss.

²¹I, Paul, write this greeting with my own hand. ²²If anyone has no love for the Lord, let him be accursed. Our Lord, come![5] ²³The grace of the Lord Jesus be with you. ²⁴My love be with you all in Christ Jesus. Amen.

---

[1] The expression *Now concerning* introduces a reply to a question in the Corinthians' letter; see 7:1; also verse 12 [2] Or *God's will for him* [3] Or *brothers and sisters*; also verse 20 [4] Greek *house* [5] Greek *Maranatha* (a transliteration of Aramaic)

2 CORINTHIANS

The book at a glance. 13 chapters, 257 verses. A common designation for this letter through the centuries has been encapsulated in the Latin phrase *apologia pro vita sua*, which means "defense of his life." This title stems from the conspicuous place given to Paul's defense of his past apostolic ministry against detractors in the Corinthian church. By means of this defense, Paul steps forward as an example of how to live the Christian life and engage in Christian ministry that all Christians are expected to imitate. A keynote of the portrait is the inevitable occurrence of suffering in the life of a true servant of God. Like the preceding letter to the Corinthians, 2 Corinthians is an informal *occasional epistle, with a disjointed organization and numerous asides that are introduced without smooth tie-in to the preceding material. The letter is also a missionary manual, based on the author's real-life missionary experiences.

▌**Genres.** The usual conventions of the *epistle appear early and late with the epistolary salutation, *thanksgiving, and closing. The conventional *paraenesis* is absent. Occupying prominent places in the body of the letter are an extended defense of the author's life and ministry and a formal *boast in a spiritualized version. The letter is heavily *occasional, meaning that it is filled with references to specific events in Paul's life and ministry. In the background we can see the familiar genre of autobiography. Second Corinthians is also a missionary support letter that requests spiritual and financial support. (For more information on items accompanied by an asterisk, see the glossary at the back of this Bible.)

▌**Format and style.** Second Corinthians mingles a number of stylistic features or ingredients, including self-portraiture, *lyric outbursts of emotion, denunciation of opponents, sarcasm, threats, and expressions of personal affection. Further, the style is very personal and autobiographical, filled with references to Paul's own life. Exalted style frequently surfaces, with impressive vocabulary, catalogs or lists, parallel constructions, and rhetorical embellishments such as contrast and paradox ("as unknown, and yet well known; as dying, and behold, we live," 6:9). With all these stylistic fireworks, the flow is of course often disjointed, with sudden changes of direction, introduction of new topics, and changes of tone.

▌**The interpretive key.** Second Corinthians is filled with biographical references to Paul's life and ministry. In regard to this content, we face a basic interpretive decision: either this material is of antiquarian interest only, giving us information about a single individual from the distant past, or we are expected to see in Paul's example universal

Passage	Content	Relationship to Paul's Life	Paul's Role
1:1–11	Epistolary opening	Paul's current situation	Paul as missionary
1:12–2:11	Paul's past history with the Corinthians		
2:12–6:10	Paul explains and defends his ministry	Paul's life of ministry up to this point	Paul as exemplary minister of the new covenant
6:11–7:16	Mingled commands and personal reminiscences of past dealings with the Corinthians	Paul exhorts his spiritual children	Paul as moral counselor
8:1–9:15	Appeal for generous giving	Paul seeks to instill a spirit of generosity	Paul as fundraiser
10:1–12	Paul's defense against the charge of weakness	Paul defends his apostolic credentials	Paul as boaster
10:13–12:13	Paul's apostolic boast		
12:14–13:10	Preparations for a visit by Paul to Corinth	Paul lays the foundation for future dealings with the Corinthians	Paul as future visitor
13:11–14	Epistolary closing		

principles of the Christian life. The latter is surely the correct approach to take to this epistle, and it accords with an established literary principle of first reliving the particulars of the text but then looking through those particulars to human experience in its universal aspects. This letter is about principles of doing ministry.

▊ Inferred literary intentions. The book is designed to achieve the following literary purposes:

- provide an apology of the author's life in the standard literary genre known as *apologia pro vita sua*

- paint a portrait of the author and his life in such a way that in our imagination we become his traveling companion

- inspire us with literary and rhetorical flourishes that appear in abundance

- lead us to ponder the nature of the Christian life and ministry, including the suffering that inevitably accompanies them

- win us with *aphoristic flair ("we walk by faith, not by sight" [5:7]; "if anyone is in Christ, he is a new creation" [5:17]; "my grace is sufficient for you" [12:9])

- persuade readers to support faithful and genuine ministry of the gospel

▊ Theological themes. (1) Reconciliation: the letter expounds on how the sacrifice of Jesus restores the relationship between fallen people and the holy God. (2) Atonement: we are also led to see how closely the death of Christ on the cross fully pays the penalty for sin. (3) Suffering: the book repeatedly shows us that the Christian life is a life of suffering, which God can use for his glory. (4) Authority for belief: Paul's defense of his apostolic credentials is a reminder that God entrusted much of the content of the NT to the apostles as his official representatives.

▌2 Corinthians as a chapter in the master story of the Bible. The master story of the Bible is partly the story of how God intends his followers to live. In 2 Corinthians, Paul the author steps forward as our example of the follower of Christ—the archetypal Christian Everyman in whose steps we can walk. Additionally, the shape of Paul's ministry as a suffering servant is patterned after the gospel truth of dying with Christ and having life in his resurrection.

Epistolary opening [1:1–11]. The letter begins as we expect, given the conventions of the NT epistles. We find a salutation consisting of the name of the sender, the recipients, and the "grace and peace" prayer (vv. 1–2). The conventional thanksgiving then celebrates the comfort that believers have through Christ in all their afflictions (vv. 3–7). Verses 8–11 are a transition passage: the thanksgiving had ended with a reference to Paul's sufferings in ministry, and this following paragraph is an autobiographical passage in which Paul informs the Corinthians of his sufferings in his missionary travels; this autobiographical thread will continue in the next unit. The apostle is not ashamed to speak of his struggles in ministry, which have actually demonstrated that God alone can save.

1 Paul, an apostle of Christ Jesus by the will of God, and Timothy our brother,
    To the church of God that is at Corinth, with all the saints who are in the whole of Achaia:
    ²Grace to you and peace from God our Father and the Lord Jesus Christ.
    ³Blessed be the God and Father of our Lord Jesus Christ, the Father of mercies and God of all comfort, ⁴who comforts us in all our affliction, so that we may be able to comfort those who are in any affliction, with the comfort with which we ourselves are comforted by God. ⁵For as we share abundantly in Christ's sufferings, so through Christ we share abundantly in comfort too.[1] ⁶If we are afflicted, it is for your comfort and salvation; and if we are comforted, it is for your comfort, which you experience when you patiently endure the same sufferings that we suffer. ⁷Our hope for you is unshaken, for we know that as you share in our sufferings, you will also share in our comfort.
    ⁸For we do not want you to be ignorant, brothers,[2] of the affliction we experienced in Asia. For we were so utterly burdened beyond our strength that we despaired of life itself. ⁹Indeed, we felt that we had received the sentence of death. But that was to make us rely not on ourselves but on God who raises the dead. ¹⁰He delivered us from such a deadly peril, and he will deliver us. On him we have set our hope that he will deliver us again. ¹¹You also must help us by prayer, so that many will give thanks on our behalf for the blessing granted us through the prayers of many.

Paul's previous history with the Corinthian church [1:12–2:11]. The ostensible purpose of this unit is autobiographical, as Paul recalls his past experiences with the

---

[1] Or For as the sufferings of Christ abound for us, so also our comfort abounds through Christ [2] Or brothers and sisters. The plural Greek word adelphoi (translated "brothers") refers to siblings in a family. In New Testament usage, depending on the context, adelphoi may refer either to men or to both men and women who are siblings (brothers and sisters) in God's family, the church

Corinthian church. The passage also shows Paul's heart for his recipients and his true motives for sending them a message that on occasion has given them pain. A good way to progress through the passage is to compile a brief profile of Paul's relations with the Corinthian church. The underlying message of all the epistles is Christ, so we also need to keep alert to what a passage such as this tells us about Christ.

[12]For our boast is this, the testimony of our conscience, that we behaved in the world with simplicity[1] and godly sincerity, not by earthly wisdom but by the grace of God, and supremely so toward you. [13]For we are not writing to you anything other than what you read and acknowledge[2] and I hope you will fully acknowledge— [14]just as you did partially acknowledge us—that on the day of our Lord Jesus you will boast of us as we will boast of you.

[15]Because I was sure of this, I wanted to come to you first, so that you might have a second experience of grace. [16]I wanted to visit you on my way to Macedonia, and to come back to you from Macedonia and have you send me on my way to Judea. [17]Was I vacillating when I wanted to do this? Do I make my plans according to the flesh, ready to say "Yes, yes" and "No, no" at the same time? [18]As surely as God is faithful, our word to you has not been Yes and No. [19]For the Son of God, Jesus Christ, whom we proclaimed among you, Silvanus and Timothy and I, was not Yes and No, but in him it is always Yes. [20]For all the promises of God find their Yes in him. That is why it is through him that we utter our Amen to God for his glory. [21]And it is God who establishes us with you in Christ, and has anointed us, [22]and who has also put his seal on us and given us his Spirit in our hearts as a guarantee.[3]

[23]But I call God to witness against me—it was to spare you that I refrained from coming again to Corinth. [24]Not that we lord it over your faith, but we work with you for your joy, for you stand firm in your faith.

2 For I made up my mind not to make another painful visit to you. [2]For if I cause you pain, who is there to make me glad but the one whom I have pained? [3]And I wrote as I did, so that when I came I might not suffer pain from those who should have made me rejoice, for I felt sure of all of you, that my joy would be the joy of you all. [4]For I wrote to you out of much affliction and anguish of heart and with many tears, not to cause you pain but to let you know the abundant love that I have for you.

[5]Now if anyone has caused pain, he has caused it not to me, but in some measure—not to put it too severely—to all of you. [6]For such a one, this punishment by the majority is enough, [7]so you should rather turn to forgive and comfort him, or he may be overwhelmed by excessive sorrow. [8]So I beg you to reaffirm your love for him. [9]For this is why I wrote, that I might test you and know whether you are obedient in everything. [10]Anyone whom you forgive, I also forgive. Indeed, what I have forgiven, if I have forgiven anything, has been for your sake in the presence of Christ, [11]so that we would not be outwitted by Satan; for we are not ignorant of his designs.

The beginning of Paul's self-defense [2:12–3:18]. This unit begins an extended block in which Paul conducts an earnest defense of his own apostolic ministry. The best way to explain this unusual material in a NT epistle is to relate it to an inferred context in which a leading element in the disruption of the Corinthian church was a campaign to delegitimize Paul as an authority in the church (we will get a fuller picture of the detractors in

---

[1] Some manuscripts *holiness* [2] Or *understand*; twice in this verse; also verse 14 [3] Or *down payment*

chapter 11). Paul is not defending his own person as much as he is defending his God-given call as an apostle, and he does this in order to defend the gospel itself. We need first to note the literal details of Paul's self-defense, in effect compiling a portrait of Paul from the information that he gives us. But we also need to look for what is universal in this material, which paints a picture of all true Christian ministry and dispenses a lot of theological doctrine in addition. We can also relish the memorable *aphorisms that are always in abundance in the NT epistles. The general progression is as follows: brief missionary itinerary (2:12–13); statement of the believer's triumph in Christ, which simultaneously smells like death to unbelievers and life to believers (2:14–17); the Corinthian Christians as Paul's commendation in ministry (3:1–3); the confidence in Christ that Paul has for ministry (3:4–6); celebration of the superior splendor of the glorious new spiritual covenant in Christ and his Spirit (3:7–18).

[12]When I came to Troas to preach the gospel of Christ, even though a door was opened for me in the Lord, [13]my spirit was not at rest because I did not find my brother Titus there. So I took leave of them and went on to Macedonia.

[14]But thanks be to God, who in Christ always leads us in triumphal procession, and through us spreads the fragrance of the knowledge of him everywhere. [15]For we are the aroma of Christ to God among those who are being saved and among those who are perishing, [16]to one a fragrance from death to death, to the other a fragrance from life to life. Who is sufficient[1] for these things? [17]For we are not, like so many, peddlers of God's word, but as men of sincerity, as commissioned by God, in the sight of God we speak in Christ.

3 Are we beginning to commend ourselves again? Or do we need, as some do, letters of recommendation to you, or from you? [2]You yourselves are our letter of recommendation, written on our[2] hearts, to be known and read by all. [3]And you show that you are a letter from Christ delivered by us, written not with ink but with the Spirit of the living God, not on tablets of stone but on tablets of human hearts.[3]

[4]Such is the confidence that we have through Christ toward God. [5]Not that we are sufficient in ourselves to claim anything as coming from us, but our sufficiency is from God, [6]who has made us competent[4] to be ministers of a new covenant, not of the letter but of the Spirit. For the letter kills, but the Spirit gives life.

[7]Now if the ministry of death, carved in letters on stone, came with such glory that the Israelites could not gaze at Moses' face because of its glory, which was being brought to an end, [8]will not the ministry of the Spirit have even more glory? [9]For if there was glory in the ministry of condemnation, the ministry of righteousness must far exceed it in glory. [10]Indeed, in this case, what once had glory has come to have no glory at all, because of the glory that surpasses it. [11]For if what was being brought to an end came with glory, much more will what is permanent have glory.

[12]Since we have such a hope, we are very bold, [13]not like Moses, who would put a veil over his face so that the Israelites might not gaze at the outcome of what was being brought to an end. [14]But their minds were hardened. For to this day, when they read the old covenant, that same veil remains unlifted, because only through Christ is it taken away. [15]Yes, to this day whenever Moses is read a veil lies over their hearts. [16]But when one[5] turns to the Lord, the veil is removed. [17]Now the Lord[6] is the Spirit, and where the Spirit of the Lord is, there is freedom. [18]And we all, with unveiled face,

---

[1] Or competent [2] Some manuscripts your [3] Greek fleshly hearts [4] Or sufficient [5] Greek he [6] Or this Lord

beholding the glory of the Lord,[1] are being transformed into the same image from one degree of glory to another. For this comes from the Lord who is the Spirit.

> **Divine strength in human weakness** [4:1–5:10]. The subject continues to be Paul's description of his ministry, but within that subject, the movement of thought is fluid. The passage is not organized primarily as a progression from one thought to another but rather as an extended and paradoxical contrast between the strength that comes from Christ and the human weakness that depends on Christ's infilling to accomplish its purposes, and also between present sufferings and future glory. A good approach to the passage is to work out the details of these contrasts, noting variations on the theme of human weakness and the counterbalancing reasons that Paul does not falter under the weight of his inadequacy. His very weakness displays the life-giving power of Christ. But topical outlines like this should not be pressed too rigorously, because there are numerous asides in the form of freestanding verses. The passage is filled with famous aphorisms. Verses 7–9 of chapter 4 are a rhetorical flourish of paradoxes, and verses 1–4 of chapter 5 set up a famous analogy between the human body and a tent/home.

4 Therefore, having this ministry by the mercy of God,[2] we do not lose heart. [2]But we have renounced disgraceful, underhanded ways. We refuse to practice cunning or to tamper with God's word, but by the open statement of the truth we would commend ourselves to everyone's conscience in the sight of God. [3]And even if our gospel is veiled, it is veiled only to those who are perishing. [4]In their case the god of this world has blinded the minds of the unbelievers, to keep them from seeing the light of the gospel of the glory of Christ, who is the image of God. [5]For what we proclaim is not ourselves, but Jesus Christ as Lord, with ourselves as your servants[3] for Jesus' sake. [6]For God, who said, "Let light shine out of darkness," has shone in our hearts to give the light of the knowledge of the glory of God in the face of Jesus Christ.

[7]But we have this treasure in jars of clay, to show that the surpassing power belongs to God and not to us. [8]We are afflicted in every way, but not crushed; perplexed, but not driven to despair; [9]persecuted, but not forsaken; struck down, but not destroyed; [10]always carrying in the body the death of Jesus, so that the life of Jesus may also be manifested in our bodies. [11]For we who live are always being given over to death for Jesus' sake, so that the life of Jesus also may be manifested in our mortal flesh. [12]So death is at work in us, but life in you.

[13]Since we have the same spirit of faith according to what has been written, [a]"I believed, and so I spoke," we also believe, and so we also speak, [14]knowing that he who raised the Lord Jesus will raise us also with Jesus and bring us with you into his presence. [15]For it is all for your sake, so that as grace extends to more and more people it may increase thanksgiving, to the glory of God.

[16]So we do not lose heart. Though our outer self[4] is wasting away, our inner self is being renewed day by day. [17]For this light momentary affliction is preparing for us an eternal weight of glory beyond all comparison, [18]as we look not to the things that are seen but to the things that are unseen. For the things that are seen are transient, but the things that are unseen are eternal.

---

[1] Or reflecting the glory of the Lord [2] Greek as we have received mercy [3] Greek bondservants [4] Greek man [a] Ps. 116:10

5 For we know that if the tent that is our earthly home is destroyed, we have a building from God, a house not made with hands, eternal in the heavens. ²For in this tent we groan, longing to put on our heavenly dwelling, ³if indeed by putting it on¹ we may not be found naked. ⁴For while we are still in this tent, we groan, being burdened—not that we would be unclothed, but that we would be further clothed, so that what is mortal may be swallowed up by life. ⁵He who has prepared us for this very thing is God, who has given us the Spirit as a guarantee.

⁶So we are always of good courage. We know that while we are at home in the body we are away from the Lord, ⁷for we walk by faith, not by sight. ⁸Yes, we are of good courage, and we would rather be away from the body and at home with the Lord. ⁹So whether we are at home or away, we make it our aim to please him. ¹⁰For we must all appear before the judgment seat of Christ, so that each one may receive what is due for what he has done in the body, whether good or evil.

Paul's ministry of reconciliation [5:11–6:10]. By now it is evident that Paul's defense of his ministry in this part of the letter is actually a celebration of what Christ has done in Paul, for Paul, and through Paul. That is why it is easy to generalize from the specific example of Paul to the experience of all believers in Christ, who also suffer for Christ and live by his resurrection power. Famous NT proverbs continue to abound in this unit, which moves through the following topics in a fluid manner: Paul's total abandonment to declaring the message of Christ's atoning death and victorious resurrection (5:11–15); lyric celebration of the reconciliation that being in Christ brings and an assertion that believers are ambassadors for Christ (5:16–21); the urgency of accepting God's grace (6:1–2); Paul's eagerness to endure all possible hardship as an ambassador for Christ (6:3–10). This last unit is another example of Paul's rhetorical eloquence, consisting of an imposing catalog of disasters (6:4–7) and paradoxes (6:8–10).

¹¹Therefore, knowing the fear of the Lord, we persuade others. But what we are is known to God, and I hope it is known also to your conscience. ¹²We are not commending ourselves to you again but giving you cause to boast about us, so that you may be able to answer those who boast about outward appearance and not about what is in the heart. ¹³For if we are beside ourselves, it is for God; if we are in our right mind, it is for you. ¹⁴For the love of Christ controls us, because we have concluded this: that one has died for all, therefore all have died; ¹⁵and he died for all, that those who live might no longer live for themselves but for him who for their sake died and was raised.

¹⁶From now on, therefore, we regard no one according to the flesh. Even though we once regarded Christ according to the flesh, we regard him thus no longer. ¹⁷Therefore, if anyone is in Christ, he is a new creation.² The old has passed away; behold, the new has come. ¹⁸All this is from God, who through Christ reconciled us to himself and gave us the ministry of reconciliation; ¹⁹that is, in Christ God was reconciling³ the world to himself, not counting their trespasses against them, and entrusting to us the message of reconciliation. ²⁰Therefore, we are ambassadors for Christ, God making his appeal through us. We implore you on behalf of Christ, be reconciled to God. ²¹For our sake he made him to be sin who knew no sin, so that in him we might become the righteousness of God.

¹ Some manuscripts *putting it off* ² Or *creature* ³ Or *God was in Christ, reconciling*

6 Working together with him, then, we appeal to you not to receive the grace of God in vain. [2]For he says,

[a]"In a favorable time I listened to you,
and in a day of salvation I have helped you."

Behold, now is the favorable time; behold, now is the day of salvation. [3]We put no obstacle in anyone's way, so that no fault may be found with our ministry, [4]but as servants of God we commend ourselves in every way: by great endurance, in afflictions, hardships, calamities, [5]beatings, imprisonments, riots, labors, sleepless nights, hunger; [6]by purity, knowledge, patience, kindness, the Holy Spirit, genuine love; [7]by truthful speech, and the power of God; with the weapons of righteousness for the right hand and for the left; [8]through honor and dishonor, through slander and praise. We are treated as impostors, and yet are true; [9]as unknown, and yet well known; as dying, and behold, we live; as punished, and yet not killed; [10]as sorrowful, yet always rejoicing; as poor, yet making many rich; as having nothing, yet possessing everything.

Paul and his spiritual children [6:11–7:16]. This is a mingled unit in which Paul issues commands to his spiritual children at Corinth (6:11–7:4), recalls a past interval in his missionary endeavors (7:5–7), reflects on the Corinthians' response to a letter of criticism that Paul had sent (7:8–13a), and commends the Corinthians for their Christian lives (7:13b–16). What Paul commands of the Corinthians, God still commands of those who follow him, and the commendable behavior of the Corinthians represents behavior that all Christians should aspire to emulate.

[11]We have spoken freely to you,[1] Corinthians; our heart is wide open. [12]You are not restricted by us, but you are restricted in your own affections. [13]In return (I speak as to children) widen your hearts also.

[14]Do not be unequally yoked with unbelievers. For what partnership has righteousness with lawlessness? Or what fellowship has light with darkness? [15]What accord has Christ with Belial?[2] Or what portion does a believer share with an unbeliever? [16]What agreement has the temple of God with idols? For we are the temple of the living God; as God said,

[b]"I will make my dwelling among them and walk among them,
and I will be their God,
and they shall be my people.
[17] Therefore [c]go out from their midst,
and be separate from them, says the Lord,
and touch no unclean thing;
then I will welcome you,
[18] and I will be a father to you,
and you shall be sons and daughters to me,
says the Lord Almighty."

7 Since we have these promises, beloved, let us cleanse ourselves from every defilement of body[3] and spirit, bringing holiness to completion in the fear of God. [2]Make room in your hearts[4] for us. We have wronged no one, we have corrupted

---

[1] Greek Our mouth is open to you [2] Greek Beliar [3] Greek flesh [4] Greek lacks in your hearts [a] Isa. 49:8 [b] Lev. 26:12 [c] Isa. 52:11

no one, we have taken advantage of no one. ³I do not say this to condemn you, for I said before that you are in our hearts, to die together and to live together. ⁴I am acting with great boldness toward you; I have great pride in you; I am filled with comfort. In all our affliction, I am overflowing with joy.

⁵For even when we came into Macedonia, our bodies had no rest, but we were afflicted at every turn—fighting without and fear within. ⁶But God, who comforts the downcast, comforted us by the coming of Titus, ⁷and not only by his coming but also by the comfort with which he was comforted by you, as he told us of your longing, your mourning, your zeal for me, so that I rejoiced still more. ⁸For even if I made you grieve with my letter, I do not regret it—though I did regret it, for I see that that letter grieved you, though only for a while. ⁹As it is, I rejoice, not because you were grieved, but because you were grieved into repenting. For you felt a godly grief, so that you suffered no loss through us.

¹⁰For godly grief produces a repentance that leads to salvation without regret, whereas worldly grief produces death. ¹¹For see what earnestness this godly grief has produced in you, but also what eagerness to clear yourselves, what indignation, what fear, what longing, what zeal, what punishment! At every point you have proved yourselves innocent in the matter. ¹²So although I wrote to you, it was not for the sake of the one who did the wrong, nor for the sake of the one who suffered the wrong, but in order that your earnestness for us might be revealed to you in the sight of God. ¹³Therefore we are comforted.

And besides our own comfort, we rejoiced still more at the joy of Titus, because his spirit has been refreshed by you all. ¹⁴For whatever boasts I made to him about you, I was not put to shame. But just as everything we said to you was true, so also our boasting before Titus has proved true. ¹⁵And his affection for you is even greater, as he remembers the obedience of you all, how you received him with fear and trembling. ¹⁶I rejoice, because I have perfect confidence in you.

Generous giving [chapters 8–9]. The letter now takes an entirely different direction, as two chapters are devoted to the subject of a collection that Paul hopes to take to poor Christians in Jerusalem. This material is a small treatise on generous giving. Paul's discussion winds through the following topics: the example of the generosity of the Macedonian Christians in contributing to "the relief of the saints" (8:1–4); exhortation to the Corinthian Christians likewise to be generous (8:5–15); details about an upcoming visit by Titus and a delegation to collect money (8:16–24); appeal to the Corinthians to be generous, with principles for godly stewardship (chapter 9). This whole passage is a masterpiece of persuasion, and a good approach is to note the various rhetorical techniques by which Paul seeks to move his audience to be generous in their giving.

8 We want you to know, brothers,¹ about the grace of God that has been given among the churches of Macedonia, ²for in a severe test of affliction, their abundance of joy and their extreme poverty have overflowed in a wealth of generosity on their part. ³For they gave according to their means, as I can testify, and beyond their means, of their own accord, ⁴begging us earnestly for the favor² of taking part in the relief of the saints— ⁵and this, not as we expected, but they gave themselves first to the Lord and then by the will of God to us. ⁶Accordingly, we urged Titus that as he had started, so he should complete among you this act of grace. ⁷But as you excel in

---

¹ Or brothers and sisters ² The Greek word *charis* can mean *favor* or *grace* or *thanks*, depending on the context

everything—in faith, in speech, in knowledge, in all earnestness, and in our love for you[1]—see that you excel in this act of grace also.

[8]I say this not as a command, but to prove by the earnestness of others that your love also is genuine. [9]For you know the grace of our Lord Jesus Christ, that though he was rich, yet for your sake he became poor, so that you by his poverty might become rich. [10]And in this matter I give my judgment: this benefits you, who a year ago started not only to do this work but also to desire to do it. [11]So now finish doing it as well, so that your readiness in desiring it may be matched by your completing it out of what you have. [12]For if the readiness is there, it is acceptable according to what a person has, not according to what he does not have. [13]For I do not mean that others should be eased and you burdened, but that as a matter of fairness [14]your abundance at the present time should supply their need, so that their abundance may supply your need, that there may be fairness. [15]As it is written, [a]"Whoever gathered much had nothing left over, and whoever gathered little had no lack."

[16]But thanks be to God, who put into the heart of Titus the same earnest care I have for you. [17]For he not only accepted our appeal, but being himself very earnest he is going[2] to you of his own accord. [18]With him we are sending[3] the brother who is famous among all the churches for his preaching of the gospel. [19]And not only that, but he has been appointed by the churches to travel with us as we carry out this act of grace that is being ministered by us, for the glory of the Lord himself and to show our good will. [20]We take this course so that no one should blame us about this generous gift that is being administered by us, [21]for we aim at what is honorable not only in the Lord's sight but also in the sight of man. [22]And with them we are sending our brother whom we have often tested and found earnest in many matters, but who is now more earnest than ever because of his great confidence in you. [23]As for Titus, he is my partner and fellow worker for your benefit. And as for our brothers, they are messengers[4] of the churches, the glory of Christ. [24]So give proof before the churches of your love and of our boasting about you to these men.

9 Now it is superfluous for me to write to you about the ministry for the saints, [2]for I know your readiness, of which I boast about you to the people of Macedonia, saying that Achaia has been ready since last year. And your zeal has stirred up most of them. [3]But I am sending[5] the brothers so that our boasting about you may not prove empty in this matter, so that you may be ready, as I said you would be. [4]Otherwise, if some Macedonians come with me and find that you are not ready, we would be humiliated—to say nothing of you—for being so confident. [5]So I thought it necessary to urge the brothers to go on ahead to you and arrange in advance for the gift[6] you have promised, so that it may be ready as a willing gift, not as an exaction.[7]

[6]The point is this: whoever sows sparingly will also reap sparingly, and whoever sows bountifully[8] will also reap bountifully. [7]Each one must give as he has decided in his heart, not reluctantly or under compulsion, for God loves a cheerful giver. [8]And God is able to make all grace abound to you, so that having all sufficiency[9] in all things at all times, you may abound in every good work. [9]As it is written,

> [b]"He has distributed freely, he has given to the poor;
>   his righteousness endures forever."

---

[1] Some manuscripts *in your love for us* [2] Or *he went* [3] Or *we sent*; also verse 22 [4] Greek *apostles* [5] Or *I have sent* [6] Greek *blessing*; twice in this verse [7] Or *a gift expecting something in return*; Greek *greed* [8] Greek *with blessings*; twice in this verse [9] Or *all contentment* [a] Ex. 16:18 [b] Ps. 112:9

¹⁰He who supplies seed to the sower and bread for food will supply and multiply your seed for sowing and increase the harvest of your righteousness. ¹¹You will be enriched in every way to be generous in every way, which through us will produce thanksgiving to God. ¹²For the ministry of this service is not only supplying the needs of the saints but is also overflowing in many thanksgivings to God. ¹³By their approval of this service, they¹ will glorify God because of your submission flowing from your confession of the gospel of Christ, and the generosity of your contribution for them and for all others, ¹⁴while they long for you and pray for you, because of the surpassing grace of God upon you. ¹⁵Thanks be to God for his inexpressible gift!

Paul replies to accusations of weakness [10:1–12]. With the subject of the collection of money now complete, Paul returns to the thing that partly occasioned this letter: detractors who had disparaged Paul's authority and therefore his message. In this brief unit, we should note how Paul handles the claim that he is unimpressive in personal presence, and what this teaches us about authentic Christian ministry.

10 I, Paul, myself entreat you, by the meekness and gentleness of Christ—I who am humble when face to face with you, but bold toward you when I am away!— ²I beg of you that when I am present I may not have to show boldness with such confidence as I count on showing against some who suspect us of walking according to the flesh. ³For though we walk in the flesh, we are not waging war according to the flesh. ⁴For the weapons of our warfare are not of the flesh but have divine power to destroy strongholds. ⁵We destroy arguments and every lofty opinion raised against the knowledge of God, and take every thought captive to obey Christ, ⁶being ready to punish every disobedience, when your obedience is complete.

⁷Look at what is before your eyes. If anyone is confident that he is Christ's, let him remind himself that just as he is Christ's, so also are we. ⁸For even if I boast a little too much of our authority, which the Lord gave for building you up and not for destroying you, I will not be ashamed. ⁹I do not want to appear to be frightening you with my letters. ¹⁰For they say, "His letters are weighty and strong, but his bodily presence is weak, and his speech of no account." ¹¹Let such a person understand that what we say by letter when absent, we do when present. ¹²Not that we dare to classify or compare ourselves with some of those who are commending themselves. But when they measure themselves by one another and compare themselves with one another, they are without understanding.

Paul's apostolic boast [10:13–12:13]. Again we need to remind ourselves of the threat that has been posed not simply to Paul as a person but to the Corinthian church if it succumbs to the false teachers who have attacked the apostle as a way of disparaging his message. The issue at stake is the truth of the gospel. Chapter 11 contains the most extended glimpses of the detractors and their viewpoint that we find in 2 Corinthians. The dominant literary genre at work in this unit is the *boast. Ordinarily a boast is uttered by warriors in battle stories. Paul gives us a spiritualized version of the boast, and more particularly he defends his apostolic authority in addition to his personal integrity. As we progress through the passage, we can compile a list of the specific things of which Paul boasts (chiefly Christ). We can also work out the contrasts that

¹ Or you

underlie the passage, including the following: human boasting versus boasting in Christ; false teachers versus Paul as teacher of truth; human weakness versus divine strength.

[13]But we will not boast beyond limits, but will boast only with regard to the area of influence God assigned to us, to reach even to you. [14]For we are not overextending ourselves, as though we did not reach you. For we were the first to come all the way to you with the gospel of Christ. [15]We do not boast beyond limit in the labors of others. But our hope is that as your faith increases, our area of influence among you may be greatly enlarged, [16]so that we may preach the gospel in lands beyond you, without boasting of work already done in another's area of influence. [17]"Let the one who boasts, boast in the Lord." [18]For it is not the one who commends himself who is approved, but the one whom the Lord commends.

11 I wish you would bear with me in a little foolishness. Do bear with me! [2]For I feel a divine jealousy for you, since I betrothed you to one husband, to present you as a pure virgin to Christ. [3]But I am afraid that as the serpent deceived Eve by his cunning, your thoughts will be led astray from a sincere and pure devotion to Christ. [4]For if someone comes and proclaims another Jesus than the one we proclaimed, or if you receive a different spirit from the one you received, or if you accept a different gospel from the one you accepted, you put up with it readily enough. [5]Indeed, I consider that I am not in the least inferior to these super-apostles. [6]Even if I am unskilled in speaking, I am not so in knowledge; indeed, in every way we have made this plain to you in all things.

[7]Or did I commit a sin in humbling myself so that you might be exalted, because I preached God's gospel to you free of charge? [8]I robbed other churches by accepting support from them in order to serve you. [9]And when I was with you and was in need, I did not burden anyone, for the brothers who came from Macedonia supplied my need. So I refrained and will refrain from burdening you in any way. [10]As the truth of Christ is in me, this boasting of mine will not be silenced in the regions of Achaia. [11]And why? Because I do not love you? God knows I do!

[12]And what I do I will continue to do, in order to undermine the claim of those who would like to claim that in their boasted mission they work on the same terms as we do. [13]For such men are false apostles, deceitful workmen, disguising themselves as apostles of Christ. [14]And no wonder, for even Satan disguises himself as an angel of light. [15]So it is no surprise if his servants, also, disguise themselves as servants of righteousness. Their end will correspond to their deeds.

[16]I repeat, let no one think me foolish. But even if you do, accept me as a fool, so that I too may boast a little. [17]What I am saying with this boastful confidence, I say not with the Lord's authority but as a fool. [18]Since many boast according to the flesh, I too will boast. [19]For you gladly bear with fools, being wise yourselves! [20]For you bear it if someone makes slaves of you, or devours you, or takes advantage of you, or puts on airs, or strikes you in the face. [21]To my shame, I must say, we were too weak for that!

But whatever anyone else dares to boast of—I am speaking as a fool—I also dare to boast of that. [22]Are they Hebrews? So am I. Are they Israelites? So am I. Are they offspring of Abraham? So am I. [23]Are they servants of Christ? I am a better one—I am talking like a madman—with far greater labors, far more imprisonments, with countless beatings, and often near death. [24]Five times I received at the hands of the Jews the forty lashes less one. ²⁵Three times I was beaten with rods. Once I was stoned. Three times I was shipwrecked; a night and a day I was adrift at sea; ²⁶on frequent journeys, in danger from rivers, danger from robbers, danger from my own people, danger from Gentiles, danger in the city, danger in the wilderness, danger at sea, danger from false brothers; ²⁷in toil and hardship, through many a sleepless night, in hunger and thirst, often without food,¹ in cold and exposure. ²⁸And, apart from other things, there is the daily pressure on me of my anxiety for all the churches. ²⁹Who is weak, and I am not weak? Who is made to fall, and I am not indignant?

³⁰If I must boast, I will boast of the things that show my weakness. ³¹The God and Father of the Lord Jesus, he who is blessed forever, knows that I am not lying. ³²At Damascus, the governor under King Aretas was guarding the city of Damascus in order to seize me, ³³but I was let down in a basket through a window in the wall and escaped his hands.

12 I must go on boasting. Though there is nothing to be gained by it, I will go on to visions and revelations of the Lord. ²I know a man in Christ who fourteen years ago was caught up to the third heaven—whether in the body or out of the body I do not know, God knows. ³And I know that this man was caught up into paradise— whether in the body or out of the body I do not know, God knows— ⁴and he heard things that cannot be told, which man may not utter. ⁵On behalf of this man I will boast, but on my own behalf I will not boast, except of my weaknesses. ⁶Though if I should wish to boast, I would not be a fool, for I would be speaking the truth. But I refrain from it, so that no one may think more of me than he sees in me or hears from me. ⁷So to keep me from becoming conceited because of the surpassing greatness of the revelations,² a thorn was given me in the flesh, a messenger of Satan to harass me, to keep me from becoming conceited. ⁸Three times I pleaded with the Lord about this, that it should leave me. ⁹But he said to me, "My grace is sufficient for you, for my power is made perfect in weakness." Therefore I will boast all the more gladly of my weaknesses, so that the power of Christ may rest upon me. ¹⁰For the sake of Christ, then, I am content with weaknesses, insults, hardships, persecutions, and calamities. For when I am weak, then I am strong.

¹¹I have been a fool! You forced me to it, for I ought to have been commended by you. For I was not at all inferior to these super-apostles, even though I am nothing. ¹²The signs of a true apostle were performed among you with utmost patience, with signs and wonders and mighty works. ¹³For in what were you less favored than the rest of the churches, except that I myself did not burden you? Forgive me this wrong!

Epistolary closing [12:14–13:14]. We gradually modulate from Paul's fiery apostolic boast to his preparations for an envisioned visit to Corinth. There is still an admixture of sternness in what Paul writes, along with an ongoing defensive thread. The specific topics that Paul takes up are as follows: announcement that when he comes for a visit he will not be a burden to the Corinthians (12:14–18); appeal that the Corinthians reform what is evil in their corporate behavior (12:19–21); warnings that Paul will not tolerate false accusations against him (13:1–4); further commands and preparations regarding the imminent visit by Paul (13:5–10); concluding greetings (13:11–13) and benediction (13:14).

---

¹ Or often in fasting ² Or hears from me, even because of the surpassing greatness of the revelations. So to keep me from becoming conceited

[14]Here for the third time I am ready to come to you. And I will not be a burden, for I seek not what is yours but you. For children are not obligated to save up for their parents, but parents for their children. [15]I will most gladly spend and be spent for your souls. If I love you more, am I to be loved less? [16]But granting that I myself did not burden you, I was crafty, you say, and got the better of you by deceit. [17]Did I take advantage of you through any of those whom I sent to you? [18]I urged Titus to go, and sent the brother with him. Did Titus take advantage of you? Did we not act in the same spirit? Did we not take the same steps?

[19]Have you been thinking all along that we have been defending ourselves to you? It is in the sight of God that we have been speaking in Christ, and all for your upbuilding, beloved. [20]For I fear that perhaps when I come I may find you not as I wish, and that you may find me not as you wish—that perhaps there may be quarreling, jealousy, anger, hostility, slander, gossip, conceit, and disorder. [21]I fear that when I come again my God may humble me before you, and I may have to mourn over many of those who sinned earlier and have not repented of the impurity, sexual immorality, and sensuality that they have practiced.

13 This is the third time I am coming to you. Every charge must be established by the evidence of two or three witnesses. [2]I warned those who sinned before and all the others, and I warn them now while absent, as I did when present on my second visit, that if I come again I will not spare them— [3]since you seek proof that Christ is speaking in me. He is not weak in dealing with you, but is powerful among you. [4]For he was crucified in weakness, but lives by the power of God. For we also are weak in him, but in dealing with you we will live with him by the power of God.

[5]Examine yourselves, to see whether you are in the faith. Test yourselves. Or do you not realize this about yourselves, that Jesus Christ is in you?—unless indeed you fail to meet the test! [6]I hope you will find out that we have not failed the test. [7]But we pray to God that you may not do wrong—not that we may appear to have met the test, but that you may do what is right, though we may seem to have failed. [8]For we cannot do anything against the truth, but only for the truth. [9]For we are glad when we are weak and you are strong. Your restoration is what we pray for. [10]For this reason I write these things while I am away from you, that when I come I may not have to be severe in my use of the authority that the Lord has given me for building up and not for tearing down.

[11]Finally, brothers,[1] rejoice. Aim for restoration, comfort one another,[2] agree with one another, live in peace; and the God of love and peace will be with you. [12]Greet one another with a holy kiss. [13]All the saints greet you.

[14]The grace of the Lord Jesus Christ and the love of God and the fellowship of the Holy Spirit be with you all.

---

[1] Or brothers and sisters [2] Or listen to my appeal

THE LETTER OF PAUL TO THE

GALATIANS

The book at a glance. 6 chapters, 149 verses. Galatians is perhaps the most polemical of all Paul's letters. It was written to address a sudden crisis in Galatia (a region in modern-day Turkey), where Jewish-Christian missionaries (often called the "Judaizers") were telling Gentiles that in order to be Christians they had to obey Jewish tradition, especially by receiving the sign of circumcision. The apostle rightly saw this teaching as a threat to God's free grace in the gospel. We cannot receive the blessings of salvation by doing any works of the law but only by trusting in Jesus Christ. This doctrine of justification by faith alone liberates the church from the legalism of performance-based Christianity and preserves the grace of God in the gospel. In his letter to the Galatians, Paul passionately defends his apostolic authority to preach the gospel of free grace, vigorously defies his opponents by proving his theology from the very OT Scriptures they used to support their doctrinal position, and earnestly exhorts the people of God to live in the spiritual freedom that belongs to them by grace.

▮ **Genres.** Like the rest of Paul's letters, the book of Galatians generally follows the conventions of the NT *epistles. There is a *salutation, body, *paraenesis*, greeting, and *benediction. There is no *thanksgiving, however, and this lack indicates the apostle's agitation and alarm over the theological situation in Galatia. Paul gets right to the point, which is that the Galatians are in danger of turning to a different gospel, thereby risking everlasting peril. The main argument of the epistle is advanced by the use of autobiography, example, *allegory, *satiric rebuke, and exhortation. (For more information on items accompanied by an asterisk, see the glossary at the end of this Bible.)

▮ **Unifying elements.** The doctrinal thrust of Galatians gives it a strong internal unity. In one way or another, everything in the epistle is related to Paul's defense of justification by faith alone. The letter is also unified by the personality of the apostle himself, which comes through as strongly here as it does in any of his writings—especially his intolerance of false doctrine and indignation with people who promote it. Intensity of tone thus also unifies the letter. Stylistically, Galatians finds literary coherence in its thematic contrasts: the true gospel versus a false gospel, faith versus works, law versus grace, liberty versus legalism, sonship versus slavery, the fruit of the Spirit versus the desires of the flesh.

▮ **Inferred literary intentions.** The book is designed to achieve the following literary purposes:

Passage	Content	Mode of discourse	Thrust of argument
1:1–5	Salutation: grace from a true apostle		
1:6–10	Paul's astonishment at the Galatians		Paul defends his apostolic authority in order to defend the one true gospel
1:11–24	Paul's calling by the gospel	Autobiography	
2:1–14	Paul's acceptance among the apostles		
2:15–21	Paul's doctrine of justification by faith		
3:1–5	Works of the law vs. hearing with faith		
3:6–14	The example of Abraham: the righteous shall live by faith		
3:15–29	The example of Abraham: the promise precedes the law	Theology	Paul explains his doctrine of justification by faith from the Old Testament
4:1–11	No longer slaves, but sons		
4:12–20	Paul's perplexity regarding the Galatians		
4:21–31	The allegory of Hagar and Sarah		
5:1–15	Call to freedom in Christ		
5:16–26	Exhortation to walk by the Spirit		Paul applies the gospel of free grace to a life of spiritual liberty and love
6:1–10	Further practical exhortations	Ethics	
6:11–18	Signature: warning and blessing		

- defend God's free grace in the gospel

- employ sharp language to warn readers against the dangers of false doctrine

- explain why the author has the authority to write what he writes and why he writes as he does

- prove the doctrine of justification by faith by means of historical examples

- defeat the author's theological opponents by rational argumentation, while holding these opponents up to satiric scorn for their denial of the gospel

▌Theological themes. (1) Justification by faith: the central focus of Galatians is that sinners cannot be declared righteous by God on the basis of their works but only on the basis of the crucifixion and resurrection of Jesus Christ, received by faith. (2) Works of the law: since fallen human beings are unable to keep the law of God in all its perfection, the law cannot save but only bring us under its curse. (3) Adoption: believers in Jesus Christ are the free sons of God and the true children of Abraham. (4) The Holy Spirit: as the gift of God to believers in Christ, the third person of the Trinity is both the assurance of salvation and the source of freedom and fruitfulness in the Christian life. (5) Christian liberty: since believers are under grace, not under the law, we are free to live in love.

▌ **The book of Galatians as a chapter in the master story of the Bible.** Like most of the NT epistles, the letter to the Galatians works out some of the implications of the gospel. In particular, it preserves the free grace that God has provided in the cross of Christ by resisting any temptation to think that sinners can be saved by something they do, when in fact sinners can be saved only by believing in what Jesus has done.

Only one gospel [1:1–10]. Already in his opening greeting (vv. 1–5), Paul is busy proclaiming the gospel of the crucified and risen Christ and defending his apostleship as something he received from the triune God and not from any human being. As always with the Epistles, it pays dividends to note the specific form that the conventions of the salutation take (sender, addressee, grace-and-peace formula). Paul's reason for defending his apostolic credentials becomes apparent in his urgent appeal to the Galatians not to believe any other gospel except the one that he preached to them—the gospel of God. The apostle makes no effort to conceal his amazement that anyone would even think of believing another gospel. His tone is unashamedly polemical, especially when he anathematizes anyone who preaches any other gospel than the one true gospel of Christ (v. 9). The techniques of elaborate syntax, repetition, and rhetorical questions make the passage explode with rhetorical force.

1 Paul, an apostle—not from men nor through man, but through Jesus Christ and God the Father, who raised him from the dead— ²and all the brothers¹ who are with me,

To the churches of Galatia:

³Grace to you and peace from God our Father and the Lord Jesus Christ, ⁴who gave himself for our sins to deliver us from the present evil age, according to the will of our God and Father, ⁵to whom be the glory forever and ever. Amen.

⁶I am astonished that you are so quickly deserting him who called you in the grace of Christ and are turning to a different gospel— ⁷not that there is another one, but there are some who trouble you and want to distort the gospel of Christ. ⁸But even if we or an angel from heaven should preach to you a gospel contrary to the one we preached to you, let him be accursed. ⁹As we have said before, so now I say again: If anyone is preaching to you a gospel contrary to the one you received, let him be accursed.

¹⁰For am I now seeking the approval of man, or of God? Or am I trying to please man? If I were still trying to please man, I would not be a servant² of Christ.

The origin of Paul's religion [1:11–24]. To say that Paul is an apostle is to say that he has been sent with a message from God. His gospel is not his own gospel; it is God's gospel. But in order for people to accept his apostolic authority, Paul must demonstrate that he received his gospel firsthand (by revelation from God) rather than secondhand (by the testimony of another human being). Here Paul recounts the circumstances of his conversion and his early experiences as a Christian to show that his gospel came

---

¹ Or brothers and sisters. The plural Greek word adelphoi (translated "brothers") refers to siblings in a family. In New Testament usage, depending on the context, adelphoi may refer either to men or to both men and women who are siblings (brothers and sisters) in God's family, the church; also verse 11
² Or slave; Greek bondservant

directly from God and not from any other source. The rhetorical form of the passage is the brief missionary *biography, here used for purposes of defending the missionary's credentials.

[11] For I would have you know, brothers, that the gospel that was preached by me is not man's gospel.[1] [12] For I did not receive it from any man, nor was I taught it, but I received it through a revelation of Jesus Christ. [13] For you have heard of my former life in Judaism, how I persecuted the church of God violently and tried to destroy it. [14] And I was advancing in Judaism beyond many of my own age among my people, so extremely zealous was I for the traditions of my fathers. [15] But when he who had set me apart before I was born,[2] and who called me by his grace, [16] was pleased to reveal his Son to[3] me, in order that I might preach him among the Gentiles, I did not immediately consult with anyone;[4] [17] nor did I go up to Jerusalem to those who were apostles before me, but I went away into Arabia, and returned again to Damascus.

[18] Then after three years I went up to Jerusalem to visit Cephas and remained with him fifteen days. [19] But I saw none of the other apostles except James the Lord's brother. [20] (In what I am writing to you, before God, I do not lie!) [21] Then I went into the regions of Syria and Cilicia. [22] And I was still unknown in person to the churches of Judea that are in Christ. [23] They only were hearing it said, "He who used to persecute us is now preaching the faith he once tried to destroy." [24] And they glorified God because of me.

The independence of Paul's apostleship [chapter 2]. Reading between the lines, we surmise that Paul's theological opponents were trying to discredit him by saying that he was a second-rate apostle who preached a secondhand gospel. To respond to this charge, Paul takes time to explain the details of his relationship with the other apostles, especially in Jerusalem. Although his gospel is in full agreement with their gospel, it is independent of their endorsement (vv. 1–10). In fact, on one notable occasion Paul even had to rebuke Peter for failing to live fully in line with the implications of the gospel they both preached (vv. 11–14). The repeated mention of circumcision in this chapter (vv. 3–5, 7–9, 12) is a clue that this was an important issue for the Galatians: Paul's opponents were trying to add the Law of Moses to the gospel of Christ, and getting circumcised was the most obvious outward sign that a Gentile was committed to living like a Jew. But no one can be justified before God by getting circumcised, or by keeping any other works of the law for that matter; the only way to be justified is through faith in Jesus Christ (see especially v. 16, which could well serve as the theme verse for the entire epistle). The literary form underlying this chapter is autobiography turned to the argumentative purpose of establishing the apostle's authority.

2 Then after fourteen years I went up again to Jerusalem with Barnabas, taking Titus along with me. [2] I went up because of a revelation and set before them (though privately before those who seemed influential) the gospel that I proclaim among the Gentiles, in order to make sure I was not running or had not run in vain. [3] But even Titus, who was with me, was not forced to be circumcised, though he was a Greek. [4] Yet because of false brothers secretly brought in—who slipped in to spy out our freedom that we have in Christ Jesus, so that they might bring us into slavery— [5] to them we did not yield in submission even for a moment, so that the truth of the

---

[1] Greek *not according to man* [2] Greek *set me apart from my mother's womb* [3] Greek *in* [4] Greek *with flesh and blood*

gospel might be preserved for you. ⁶And from those who seemed to be influential (what they were makes no difference to me; God shows no partiality)—those, I say, who seemed influential added nothing to me. ⁷On the contrary, when they saw that I had been entrusted with the gospel to the uncircumcised, just as Peter had been entrusted with the gospel to the circumcised ⁸(for he who worked through Peter for his apostolic ministry to the circumcised worked also through me for mine to the Gentiles), ⁹and when James and Cephas and John, who seemed to be pillars, perceived the grace that was given to me, they gave the right hand of fellowship to Barnabas and me, that we should go to the Gentiles and they to the circumcised. ¹⁰Only, they asked us to remember the poor, the very thing I was eager to do.

¹¹But when Cephas came to Antioch, I opposed him to his face, because he stood condemned. ¹²For before certain men came from James, he was eating with the Gentiles; but when they came he drew back and separated himself, fearing the circumcision party. ¹³And the rest of the Jews acted hypocritically along with him, so that even Barnabas was led astray by their hypocrisy. ¹⁴But when I saw that their conduct was not in step with the truth of the gospel, I said to Cephas before them all, "If you, though a Jew, live like a Gentile and not like a Jew, how can you force the Gentiles to live like Jews?" ¹⁵We ourselves are Jews by birth and not Gentile sinners; ¹⁶yet we know that a person is not justified¹ by works of the law but through faith in Jesus Christ, so we also have believed in Christ Jesus, in order to be justified by faith in Christ and not by works of the law, because by works of the law no one will be justified.

¹⁷But if, in our endeavor to be justified in Christ, we too were found to be sinners, is Christ then a servant of sin? Certainly not! ¹⁸For if I rebuild what I tore down, I prove myself to be a transgressor. ¹⁹For through the law I died to the law, so that I might live to God. ²⁰I have been crucified with Christ. It is no longer I who live, but Christ who lives in me. And the life I now live in the flesh I live by faith in the Son of God, who loved me and gave himself for me. ²¹I do not nullify the grace of God, for if righteousness² were through the law, then Christ died for no purpose.

By faith alone [chapter 3]. Having asserted his apostolic authority, Paul at once launches into an impassioned satiric attack. In order to bring the Galatians back to their senses, he presents a series of arguments to prove that justification is by faith alone and not by works, or even faith plus works. First he appeals to their spiritual experience: they themselves received the Spirit by faith in Christ, not by works of the law (vv. 2–5). Next he appeals to Abraham, who was counted righteous by believing in God, not by doing works of the law (vv. 6–10). Finally, he refers to the structure of the covenant, in which the promises of grace came before the requirements of the law (vv. 15–22). The apostle's point is that justification has always come by faith, never by keeping the law (see v. 11). Although his mode of argumentation is rational, the examples he chooses have a good deal of emotional impact. In all likelihood, the apostle's opponents used Abraham as a prime example of someone who had to be circumcised in order to be saved. But Paul turned that argument on its head: since Abraham is the supreme example of faith, the true sons of Abraham are people who believe, not people who get circumcised (vv. 7, 14, 29). The rhetorical form of the chapter is theological argument, enlivened by *rhetorical questions, question-and-answer constructions, allusions to OT history, and analogies from familiar experience.

¹ Or *counted righteous* (three times in verse 16); also verse 17 ² Or *justification*

3 O foolish Galatians! Who has bewitched you? It was before your eyes that Jesus Christ was publicly portrayed as crucified. [2]Let me ask you only this: Did you receive the Spirit by works of the law or by hearing with faith? [3]Are you so foolish? Having begun by the Spirit, are you now being perfected by[1] the flesh? [4]Did you suffer[2] so many things in vain—if indeed it was in vain? [5]Does he who supplies the Spirit to you and works miracles among you do so by works of the law, or by hearing with faith— [6]just as [a]Abraham "believed God, and it was counted to him as righteousness"?

[7]Know then that it is those of faith who are the sons of Abraham. [8]And the Scripture, foreseeing that God would justify[3] the Gentiles by faith, preached the gospel beforehand to Abraham, saying, [b]"In you shall all the nations be blessed." [9]So then, those who are of faith are blessed along with Abraham, the man of faith.

[10]For all who rely on works of the law are under a curse; for it is written, [c]"Cursed be everyone who does not abide by all things written in the Book of the Law, and do them." [11]Now it is evident that no one is justified before God by the law, for [d]"The righteous shall live by faith."[4] [12]But the law is not of faith, rather [e]"The one who does them shall live by them." [13]Christ redeemed us from the curse of the law by becoming a curse for us—for it is written, [f]"Cursed is everyone who is hanged on a tree"— [14]so that in Christ Jesus the blessing of Abraham might come to the Gentiles, so that we might receive the promised Spirit[5] through faith.

[15]To give a human example, brothers:[6] even with a man-made covenant, no one annuls it or adds to it once it has been ratified. [16]Now the promises were made to Abraham and to his offspring. It does not say, "And to offsprings," referring to many, but referring to one, "And to your offspring," who is Christ. [17]This is what I mean: the law, which came 430 years afterward, does not annul a covenant previously ratified by God, so as to make the promise void. [18]For if the inheritance comes by the law, it no longer comes by promise; but God gave it to Abraham by a promise.

[19]Why then the law? It was added because of transgressions, until the offspring should come to whom the promise had been made, and it was put in place through angels by an intermediary. [20]Now an intermediary implies more than one, but God is one.

[21]Is the law then contrary to the promises of God? Certainly not! For if a law had been given that could give life, then righteousness would indeed be by the law. [22]But the Scripture imprisoned everything under sin, so that the promise by faith in Jesus Christ might be given to those who believe.

[23]Now before faith came, we were held captive under the law, imprisoned until the coming faith would be revealed. [24]So then, the law was our guardian until Christ came, in order that we might be justified by faith. [25]But now that faith has come, we are no longer under a guardian, [26]for in Christ Jesus you are all sons of God, through faith. [27]For as many of you as were baptized into Christ have put on Christ. [28]There is neither Jew nor Greek, there is neither slave[7] nor free, there is no male and female, for you are all one in Christ Jesus. [29]And if you are Christ's, then you are Abraham's offspring, heirs according to promise.

From slavery to sonship [chapter 4]. If the main contrast in chapter 3 was between faith and works, the main contrast in this section is between slavery and sonship. As

---

[1] Or now ending with [2] Or experience [3] Or count righteous; also verses 11, 24 [4] Or The one who by faith is righteous will live [5] Greek receive the promise of the Spirit [6] Or brothers and sisters [7] Greek bondservant [a] Gen. 15:6 [b] Gen. 12:3 [c] Deut. 27:26 [d] Hab. 2:4 [e] Lev. 18:5 [f] Deut. 21:23

long as the Galatians insist on being saved by keeping the law, they will be enslaved to its demands. But faith in Christ brings spiritual freedom to the sons of God (both men and women, who are identified here as sons to show that they too have full rights of inheritance, which in the ancient world were given only to sons). Paul first develops this contrast between slavery and sonship by making an analogy with the situation of an heir who is still a minor and thus remains under certain restrictions until he gains the full freedom of his inheritance as a son (vv. 1–7). Paul's passion for the Galatians to experience the freedom of their sonship and his perplexity over their present theological confusion come through strongly in his personal appeal (vv. 12–20). Although it is somewhat complex, the allegory of Abraham's sons is also built around the contrast between slavery and sonship (4:21–31). It is only those who believe the gospel promise who are the free sons of God (like Isaac, the son God gave to Abraham by promise). People like Paul's opponents, who insist on staying under the law, are spiritual slaves who do not belong to the family of God. The discourse throughout Galatians is highly charged with literary technique; in this chapter we find analogies, *apostrophes (direct addresses to the recipients of the letter), rhetorical questions, satiric put-downs, allegory combined with allusion, and *aphorisms.

4 I mean that the heir, as long as he is a child, is no different from a slave,[1] though he is the owner of everything, [2]but he is under guardians and managers until the date set by his father. [3]In the same way we also, when we were children, were enslaved to the elementary principles[2] of the world. [4]But when the fullness of time had come, God sent forth his Son, born of woman, born under the law, [5]to redeem those who were under the law, so that we might receive adoption as sons. [6]And because you are sons, God has sent the Spirit of his Son into our hearts, crying, "Abba! Father!" [7]So you are no longer a slave, but a son, and if a son, then an heir through God.

[8]Formerly, when you did not know God, you were enslaved to those that by nature are not gods. [9]But now that you have come to know God, or rather to be known by God, how can you turn back again to the weak and worthless elementary principles of the world, whose slaves you want to be once more? [10]You observe days and months and seasons and years! [11]I am afraid I may have labored over you in vain.

[12]Brothers,[3] I entreat you, become as I am, for I also have become as you are. You did me no wrong. [13]You know it was because of a bodily ailment that I preached the gospel to you at first, [14]and though my condition was a trial to you, you did not scorn or despise me, but received me as an angel of God, as Christ Jesus. [15]What then has become of the blessing you felt? For I testify to you that, if possible, you would have gouged out your eyes and given them to me. [16]Have I then become your enemy by telling you the truth?[4] [17]They make much of you, but for no good purpose. They want to shut you out, that you may make much of them. [18]It is always good to be made much of for a good purpose, and not only when I am present with you, [19]my little children, for whom I am again in the anguish of childbirth until Christ is formed in you! [20]I wish I could be present with you now and change my tone, for I am perplexed about you.

[21]Tell me, you who desire to be under the law, do you not listen to the law? [22]For it is written that Abraham had two sons, one by a slave woman and one by a free woman. [23]But the son of the slave was born according to the flesh, while the son of

---

[1] Greek bondservant; also verse 7　[2] Or elemental spirits; also verse 9　[3] Or Brothers and sisters; also verses 28, 31　[4] Or by dealing truthfully with you

the free woman was born through promise. ²⁴Now this may be interpreted allegorically: these women are two covenants. One is from Mount Sinai, bearing children for slavery; she is Hagar. ²⁵Now Hagar is Mount Sinai in Arabia;¹ she corresponds to the present Jerusalem, for she is in slavery with her children. ²⁶But the Jerusalem above is free, and she is our mother. ²⁷For it is written,

> ª"Rejoice, O barren one who does not bear;
>   break forth and cry aloud, you who are not in labor!
> For the children of the desolate one will be more
>   than those of the one who has a husband."

²⁸Now you,² brothers, like Isaac, are children of promise. ²⁹But just as at that time he who was born according to the flesh persecuted him who was born according to the Spirit, so also it is now. ³⁰But what does the Scripture say? ᵇ"Cast out the slave woman and her son, for the son of the slave woman shall not inherit with the son of the free woman." ³¹So, brothers, we are not children of the slave but of the free woman.

> **Faith working through love** [chapter 5]. Like a good pastor, Paul invariably turns to practical application at the end of his doctrinal letters. If we have been freely justified by God's grace in the gospel, then we are called to live in Christian freedom rather than spiritual slavery (vv. 1–15). People who insist on circumcision for salvation are not under grace; on the contrary, they remain in bondage because they still have to meet the full demands of the law by their own obedience. Only believers in Christ are free: free to serve one another in love. Such freedom comes when we "walk by the Spirit" (vv. 16–26). Here Paul guards against license, which is the opposite danger from legalism. We do not exercise our freedom in Christ by following the desires of our old sinful nature (many of which are listed in vv. 19–21) but by keeping in step with the Spirit, who produces supernatural fruit in our lives (which is described in vv. 22–23). There are so many metaphors in this chapter that it verges on a genre known as prose poetry. Antithesis is another prominent rhetorical technique in the chapter. The two contrasting lists of the works of the flesh and the fruits of the Spirit belong to a time-honored literary technique of the catalog—a list that serves as a mnemonic ("remembering") device and relies on the principle of accumulation to achieve a crescendo. As always, Paul's style tends toward an aphoristic effect.

5 For freedom Christ has set us free; stand firm therefore, and do not submit again to a yoke of slavery.

²Look: I, Paul, say to you that if you accept circumcision, Christ will be of no advantage to you. ³I testify again to every man who accepts circumcision that he is obligated to keep the whole law. ⁴You are severed from Christ, you who would be justified³ by the law; you have fallen away from grace. ⁵For through the Spirit, by faith, we ourselves eagerly wait for the hope of righteousness. ⁶For in Christ Jesus neither circumcision nor uncircumcision counts for anything, but only faith working through love.

⁷You were running well. Who hindered you from obeying the truth? ⁸This persuasion is not from him who calls you. ⁹A little leaven leavens the whole lump. ¹⁰I have confidence in the Lord that you will take no other view than mine, and the one who is

¹ Some manuscripts *For Sinai is a mountain in Arabia* ² Some manuscripts *we* ³ Or *counted righteous* ª Isa. 54:1 ᵇ Gen. 21:10

troubling you will bear the penalty, whoever he is. [11]But if I, brothers,[1] still preach[2] circumcision, why am I still being persecuted? In that case the offense of the cross has been removed. [12]I wish those who unsettle you would emasculate themselves!

[13]For you were called to freedom, brothers. Only do not use your freedom as an opportunity for the flesh, but through love serve one another. [14]For the whole law is fulfilled in one word: [a]"You shall love your neighbor as yourself." [15]But if you bite and devour one another, watch out that you are not consumed by one another.

[16]But I say, walk by the Spirit, and you will not gratify the desires of the flesh. [17]For the desires of the flesh are against the Spirit, and the desires of the Spirit are against the flesh, for these are opposed to each other, to keep you from doing the things you want to do. [18]But if you are led by the Spirit, you are not under the law. [19]Now the works of the flesh are evident: sexual immorality, impurity, sensuality, [20]idolatry, sorcery, enmity, strife, jealousy, fits of anger, rivalries, dissensions, divisions, [21]envy,[3] drunkenness, orgies, and things like these. I warn you, as I warned you before, that those who do such things will not inherit the kingdom of God. [22]But the fruit of the Spirit is love, joy, peace, patience, kindness, goodness, faithfulness, [23]gentleness, self-control; against such things there is no law. [24]And those who belong to Christ Jesus have crucified the flesh with its passions and desires.

[25]If we live by the Spirit, let us also walk by the Spirit. [26]Let us not become conceited, provoking one another, envying one another.

Final warnings and exhortations [chapter 6]. The apostle's concluding list of instructions for life in the church (vv. 1–10) appears to be somewhat less thematically focused than the rest of his epistle, but collections of proverbs like this are a familiar feature of the NT epistles; this section is a modification of the *paraenesis* (list of moral commands) that appears in most of the epistles. Given the spiritual danger that the Galatians may abandon the freedom of faith in Christ for the slavery of obedience to the law, it is not surprising that Paul returns at the end to the contrast between his true gospel of the cross and the false gospel of circumcision (vv. 11–18).

6 Brothers,[4] if anyone is caught in any transgression, you who are spiritual should restore him in a spirit of gentleness. Keep watch on yourself, lest you too be tempted. [2]Bear one another's burdens, and so fulfill the law of Christ. [3]For if anyone thinks he is something, when he is nothing, he deceives himself. [4]But let each one test his own work, and then his reason to boast will be in himself alone and not in his neighbor. [5]For each will have to bear his own load.

[6]One who is taught the word must share all good things with the one who teaches. [7]Do not be deceived: God is not mocked, for whatever one sows, that will he also reap. [8]For the one who sows to his own flesh will from the flesh reap corruption, but the one who sows to the Spirit will from the Spirit reap eternal life. [9]And let us not grow weary of doing good, for in due season we will reap, if we do not give up. [10]So then, as we have opportunity, let us do good to everyone, and especially to those who are of the household of faith.

[11]See with what large letters I am writing to you with my own hand. [12]It is those who want to make a good showing in the flesh who would force you to be circumcised, and only in order that they may not be persecuted for the cross of Christ. [13]For

---

[1] Or *brothers and sisters*; also verse 13 [2] Greek *proclaim* [3] Some manuscripts add *murder* [4] Or *Brothers and sisters*; also verse 18 [a] Lev. 19:18

even those who are circumcised do not themselves keep the law, but they desire to have you circumcised that they may boast in your flesh. [14]But far be it from me to boast except in the cross of our Lord Jesus Christ, by which[1] the world has been crucified to me, and I to the world. [15]For neither circumcision counts for anything, nor uncircumcision, but a new creation. [16]And as for all who walk by this rule, peace and mercy be upon them, and upon the Israel of God.

[17]From now on let no one cause me trouble, for I bear on my body the marks of Jesus.

[18]The grace of our Lord Jesus Christ be with your spirit, brothers. Amen.

---

[1] Or through whom

THE LETTER OF PAUL TO THE
EPHESIANS

The book at a glance. 6 chapters, 155 verses. The letter to the Ephesians is a practical handbook of Christian doctrine—a theological manifesto like Romans, only written on a smaller scale (there are also important parallels to Colossians, especially in the second half of the letter). Ephesians is cosmic in its scope. Lacking the personal references and local concerns that are found in most of Paul's other writings, the letter deals broadly with the unity and community of Jews and Gentiles in Christ, in the context of God's eternal plans for his church and the supernatural struggle between good and evil. Ephesians is one of the most Christ-centered of all the books in a Christ-centered New Testament, revealing the glory of God in Christ. It is also one of the most church-centered books in the New Testament, revealing the glory of God in the church. From beginning to end, there is an exuberant celebration of the blessings God has for his new community in Christ, from their election in eternity past to their final triumph. Whereas the first half of the epistle establishes the identity of believers in Christ, the second half exhorts believers to be who they are in Christ in every situation and every relationship.

▌**Genres.** Ephesians exemplifies the *genre of the NT epistle, with its *salutation (including sender, recipients, and greeting), *thanksgiving, exposition, exhortation, and close (including final greetings and *benediction). The main argument of the letter is punctuated by several prayers and an interior benediction (3:20–21) that marks the transition from doctrinal affirmations to practical exhortations. Chapter 2 takes the form of a spiritual *biography in which Paul recounts the saving work of Christ in the life of every believer, and especially in the lives of Gentiles who are now included in the one new people of God. In chapter 3 the apostle takes an autobiographical turn as he testifies about his calling to the Gentiles and his prayers for the Ephesian church. The *paraenesis consists mainly of instructions for household conduct, both for the church as the household of faith and for individual believers in their domestic relationships. The famous description of the complete armor in the last chapter is an extended *metaphor—what in the poetry of John Donne is called a conceit: a "little idea" in which the metaphor takes on an independent existence. (For more information on items accompanied by an asterisk, see the glossary at the end of this Bible.)

▌**Unifying elements.** Ephesians finds its central unity in the work of Jesus Christ and in the community of people (both Jews and Gentiles) who are corporately united in him. The strong opening statement of praise and the absence of any theological polemics make Ephesians pervasively positive in tone. The clear division of the epistle

Passage	Content	Theme	Structure	Mood
1:1–14	Salutation and benediction for all God's blessings in Christ			
1:15–23	Prayer of thanksgiving for knowing God's glorious work in Christ	Salvation	New life	
2:1–10	Saved by grace through faith in Christ			Indicative: What God has done for believers in Christ
2:11–22	Gentiles and Jews are united in Christ			
3:1–13	Paul's calling to preach the gospel of Christ to the Gentiles	Reconciliation	New society	
3:14–21	Prayer of intercession for Christ's love, power, and glory in the church			
4:1–16	Exhortation to use a diversity of gifts to promote unity in the body of Christ			
4:17–32	Exhortation to put off the old self and put on the new self in Christ	Sanctification	New standards	
5:1–21	Exhortation to walk in the love and the light of Christ			Imperative: What God tells believers to do in Christ
5:22–33	Husbands and wives	Domestic duties		
6:1–9	Parents and children, masters and servants		New relationships	
6:10–20	The full armor of God	Spiritual warfare		
6:21–24	Closing greetings and benediction			

into two halves of nearly equal length (namely, the doctrinal section in chapters 1–3 and the practical section in chapters 4–6) also provides a strong sense of structural unity.

▌Inferred literary intentions. The book is designed to achieve the following literary purposes:

- celebrate the sovereign grace that God has shown to his people in Christ

- catalog the blessings of salvation in a lofty and exhilarating lyrical style that inspires people to glorify the Father, the Son, and the Holy Spirit

- exult in the heavenly exaltation of Jesus Christ and expand people's knowledge of his awesome power and surpassing love

- model the spiritual vocabulary and passionate sentiment that should characterize fervent prayer for the church

- locate believers in their relationships to Christ and to one another in the church

- exhort Gentile and Jewish Christians to live out the reconciliation they have in Christ and the unity they have in the Holy Spirit

- contrast the old life of sin and death with the new life of love and unity in Christ

- show believers how to walk in a way that is pleasing to God, both at home and in the world

- use the extended metaphors of a building, the body, and marriage to describe life in the Christian community

- equip the believer with a full arsenal for spiritual warfare

▌**Theological themes.** (1) Predestination: the letter opens with one of the Bible's major statements on God's sovereign grace in choosing his people before the beginning of time. (2) Christology: Christ is praised for his crucifixion for sin, resurrection from the dead, headship over the church, and exaltation to God's throne over the universe. (3) Soteriology: the triune God is glorified for his saving work in election, adoption, redemption, and glorification. (4) Union with Christ: all the blessings of salvation are located in Christ. (5) Ecclesiology: the union of Jewish and Gentile believers with Christ establishes their communion with one another and their unity in the church. (6) Sanctification: the Christian life is described in terms of putting on the new self, walking in love, submitting to others according to our station in life, and waging spiritual warfare. (7) Holy Spirit: the Holy Spirit is present throughout the book as the Person who effectively applies the blessings of Christ, maintains unity in the church, enables Christians to live what they believe, and protects them from spiritual danger.

▌**The book of Ephesians as a chapter in the master story of the Bible.** Ephesians puts personal salvation in the context of a saved community by showing how the people of God throughout history—including both Jews and Gentiles—are now united in Christ and in his church. The letter starts before the first chapter in the Bible, all the way back in eternity past, when God predestined the people he would save in Christ. It sweeps forward to encompass the whole span of salvation, up to and including the glorious inheritance that the Holy Spirit guarantees for every believer in Christ. It ends with God's ultimate victory in the believer's mortal combat with Satan.

Every spiritual blessing in Christ [chapter 1]. After the customary apostolic greeting, Ephesians begins with an exuberant celebration of all the blessings that believers have in Jesus Christ. Verses 3–14 constitute a single run-on sentence in the original Greek, giving the passage a strong sense of forward momentum. In *rhetoric soaring with superlatives, Paul catalogs the multiple benefits of salvation, from our predestination in eternity past to our glorious destiny in eternity future. The logical structure of these verses is strongly Trinitarian: the salvation administered according to the Father's plan is accomplished by the Son's redemption and applied by the Spirit's guarantee. In verse 15 the apostle shifts from praise to prayer as he thanks God for the Ephesians and intercedes for the church to know the glorious riches that are their inheritance in the risen Christ. The mood of the chapter is sustained exaltation, to the glory of God.

1

Paul, an apostle of Christ Jesus by the will of God,

To the saints who are in Ephesus, and are faithful[1] in Christ Jesus:

[2]Grace to you and peace from God our Father and the Lord Jesus Christ.

[3]Blessed be the God and Father of our Lord Jesus Christ, who has blessed us in Christ with every spiritual blessing in the heavenly places, [4]even as he chose us in him before the foundation of the world, that we should be holy and blameless before him. In love [5]he predestined us[2] for adoption as sons through Jesus Christ, according to the purpose of his will, [6]to the praise of his glorious grace, with which he has blessed us in the Beloved. [7]In him we have redemption through his blood, the forgiveness of our trespasses, according to the riches of his grace, [8]which he lavished upon us, in all wisdom and insight [9]making known[3] to us the mystery of his will, according to his purpose, which he set forth in Christ [10]as a plan for the fullness of time, to unite all things in him, things in heaven and things on earth.

[11]In him we have obtained an inheritance, having been predestined according to the purpose of him who works all things according to the counsel of his will, [12]so that we who were the first to hope in Christ might be to the praise of his glory. [13]In him you also, when you heard the word of truth, the gospel of your salvation, and believed in him, were sealed with the promised Holy Spirit, [14]who is the guarantee[4] of our inheritance until we acquire possession of it,[5] to the praise of his glory.

[15]For this reason, because I have heard of your faith in the Lord Jesus and your love[6] toward all the saints, [16]I do not cease to give thanks for you, remembering you in my prayers, [17]that the God of our Lord Jesus Christ, the Father of glory, may give you a spirit of wisdom and of revelation in the knowledge of him, [18]having the eyes of your hearts enlightened, that you may know what is the hope to which he has called you, what are the riches of his glorious inheritance in the saints, [19]and what is the immeasurable greatness of his power toward us who believe, according to the working of his great might [20]that he worked in Christ when he raised him from the dead and seated him at his right hand in the heavenly places, [21]far above all rule and authority and power and dominion, and above every name that is named, not only in this age but also in the one to come. [22]And he put all things under his feet and gave him as head over all things to the church, [23]which is his body, the fullness of him who fills all in all.

One people saved by grace through faith [chapter 2]. The first half of the chapter (vv. 1–10) is a corporate spiritual biography that tells the story of Gentile salvation. Verses 1–3 are the "before": the Gentiles were dead in their sins; but verses 4–10 are the "after": they were made alive in Christ. This life-giving transformation is a gift of God's grace, received through faith rather than on the basis of works—a doctrinal construction at the heart of Paul's theology of salvation by grace. This grace is not simply for individuals as individuals; it is for all the people of God. So in the second half of the chapter (vv. 11–22) Paul widens the story to show how Gentiles who were once spiritual outsiders have now been included with Jews to make the one true body of Christ. The blood of Christ that reconciles us to God also reconciles us to one another. The rhetoric

---

[1] Some manuscripts *saints who are also faithful* (omitting *in Ephesus*) [2] Or *before him in love, having predestined us* [3] Or *he lavished upon us in all wisdom and insight, making known . . .* [4] Or *down payment* [5] Or *until God redeems his possession* [6] Some manuscripts omit *your love*

of the chapter is characterized by pairs of opposites (life and death, sin and grace, faith and works, aliens and citizens) and by various metaphors for the people of God, who are variously described as citizens of a commonwealth, parts of a body, members of a household, and building blocks in a holy temple.

2 And you were dead in the trespasses and sins ²in which you once walked, following the course of this world, following the prince of the power of the air, the spirit that is now at work in the sons of disobedience— ³among whom we all once lived in the passions of our flesh, carrying out the desires of the body¹ and the mind, and were by nature children of wrath, like the rest of mankind. ⁴But² God, being rich in mercy, because of the great love with which he loved us, ⁵even when we were dead in our trespasses, made us alive together with Christ—by grace you have been saved— ⁶and raised us up with him and seated us with him in the heavenly places in Christ Jesus, ⁷so that in the coming ages he might show the immeasurable riches of his grace in kindness toward us in Christ Jesus. ⁸For by grace you have been saved through faith. And this is not your own doing; it is the gift of God, ⁹not a result of works, so that no one may boast. ¹⁰For we are his workmanship, created in Christ Jesus for good works, which God prepared beforehand, that we should walk in them.

¹¹Therefore remember that at one time you Gentiles in the flesh, called "the uncircumcision" by what is called the circumcision, which is made in the flesh by hands— ¹²remember that you were at that time separated from Christ, alienated from the commonwealth of Israel and strangers to the covenants of promise, having no hope and without God in the world. ¹³But now in Christ Jesus you who once were far off have been brought near by the blood of Christ. ¹⁴For he himself is our peace, who has made us both one and has broken down in his flesh the dividing wall of hostility ¹⁵by abolishing the law of commandments expressed in ordinances, that he might create in himself one new man in place of the two, so making peace, ¹⁶and might reconcile us both to God in one body through the cross, thereby killing the hostility. ¹⁷And he came and preached peace to you who were far off and peace to those who were near. ¹⁸For through him we both have access in one Spirit to the Father. ¹⁹So then you are no longer strangers and aliens,³ but you are fellow citizens with the saints and members of the household of God, ²⁰built on the foundation of the apostles and prophets, Christ Jesus himself being the cornerstone, ²¹in whom the whole structure, being joined together, grows into a holy temple in the Lord. ²²In him you also are being built together into a dwelling place for God by⁴ the Spirit.

Paul preaches to and prays for the Gentiles [chapter 3]. The apostle shifts from biography to autobiography as he tells the story of his own calling as a Jew to preach the gospel to Gentiles. A key word in this chapter is mystery (vv. 3, 4, 6, 9)—in the sense not of something that is still unknown or uncertain, but of something long concealed that has finally been revealed. The gracious mystery of God is simply his eternal plan for the Gentiles to belong together with the Jews in hearing the gospel and having the riches of Jesus Christ. The apostle's prayer (vv. 14–19) is for the whole church to know the full dimensions of the surpassing love of Christ. This prayer ends with an exalted benediction or *doxology (vv. 20–21) that closes the main doctrinal section of the letter and recapitulates two of its main themes: the glory of God in Christ and in the church.

¹ Greek flesh ² Or And ³ Or sojourners ⁴ Or in

3 For this reason I, Paul, a prisoner for Christ Jesus on behalf of you Gentiles— ²assuming that you have heard of the stewardship of God's grace that was given to me for you, ³how the mystery was made known to me by revelation, as I have written briefly. ⁴When you read this, you can perceive my insight into the mystery of Christ, ⁵which was not made known to the sons of men in other generations as it has now been revealed to his holy apostles and prophets by the Spirit. ⁶This mystery is[1] that the Gentiles are fellow heirs, members of the same body, and partakers of the promise in Christ Jesus through the gospel.

⁷Of this gospel I was made a minister according to the gift of God's grace, which was given me by the working of his power. ⁸To me, though I am the very least of all the saints, this grace was given, to preach to the Gentiles the unsearchable riches of Christ, ⁹and to bring to light for everyone what is the plan of the mystery hidden for ages in[2] God who created all things, ¹⁰so that through the church the manifold wisdom of God might now be made known to the rulers and authorities in the heavenly places. ¹¹This was according to the eternal purpose that he has realized in Christ Jesus our Lord, ¹²in whom we have boldness and access with confidence through our faith in him. ¹³So I ask you not to lose heart over what I am suffering for you, which is your glory.

¹⁴For this reason I bow my knees before the Father, ¹⁵from whom every family[3] in heaven and on earth is named, ¹⁶that according to the riches of his glory he may grant you to be strengthened with power through his Spirit in your inner being, ¹⁷so that Christ may dwell in your hearts through faith—that you, being rooted and grounded in love, ¹⁸may have strength to comprehend with all the saints what is the breadth and length and height and depth, ¹⁹and to know the love of Christ that surpasses knowledge, that you may be filled with all the fullness of God.

²⁰Now to him who is able to do far more abundantly than all that we ask or think, according to the power at work within us, ²¹to him be glory in the church and in Christ Jesus throughout all generations, forever and ever. Amen.

Unity in diversity [4:1–16]. The word "therefore" marks the transition from doctrinal affirmation to practical exhortation. Having established the theological basis for Christian unity in the church, the apostle now encourages the Ephesians to maintain the oneness they have in Christ. Members of the church hold many things in common: one body, one Spirit, one hope, one Lord, one faith, one baptism, one God. Nevertheless, God has given his people a variety of spiritual gifts. Yet even the diversity of these gifts is intended to promote their maturity and unity in the faith as they build one another up and grow together in Christ. The controlling image at the end of the passage is once again the body—an apt metaphor for expressing unity in diversity.

---

4 I therefore, a prisoner for the Lord, urge you to walk in a manner worthy of the calling to which you have been called, ²with all humility and gentleness, with patience, bearing with one another in love, ³eager to maintain the unity of the Spirit in the bond of peace. ⁴There is one body and one Spirit—just as you were called to the one hope that belongs to your call— ⁵one Lord, one faith, one baptism, ⁶one God and Father of all, who is over all and through all and in all. ⁷But grace was given to each one of us according to the measure of Christ's gift. ⁸Therefore it says,

---

[1] The words *This mystery is* are inferred from verse 4 [2] Or *by* [3] Or *fatherhood;* the Greek word *patria* is closely related to the word for *Father* in verse 14

[a]"When he ascended on high he led a host of captives,
    and he gave gifts to men."

[9](In saying, "He ascended," what does it mean but that he had also descended into the lower regions, the earth?[1] [10]He who descended is the one who also ascended far above all the heavens, that he might fill all things.) [11]And he gave the apostles, the prophets, the evangelists, the shepherds[2] and teachers,[3] [12]to equip the saints for the work of ministry, for building up the body of Christ, [13]until we all attain to the unity of the faith and of the knowledge of the Son of God, to mature manhood,[4] to the measure of the stature of the fullness of Christ, [14]so that we may no longer be children, tossed to and fro by the waves and carried about by every wind of doctrine, by human cunning, by craftiness in deceitful schemes. [15]Rather, speaking the truth in love, we are to grow up in every way into him who is the head, into Christ, [16]from whom the whole body, joined and held together by every joint with which it is equipped, when each part is working properly, makes the body grow so that it builds itself up in love.

> **Old self, new self** [4:17–32]. Back in chapter 2 Paul contrasted the deadly old life of sin with the new and saving life that Gentiles have received in Christ. Here he exhorts them not to keep living the selfish and sensual way that they used to live but to live out what they have learned from Christ. To use a metaphor drawn from the everyday activity of changing clothes, they are to put off the old self and put on the new self, which is created to be like God (vv. 22–24). The list of things to put off and put on covers a wide range of ethical issues, especially ones that deal with interpersonal relationships: truth, falsehood, anger, theft, work, charity, speech, conflict, and reconciliation.

[17]Now this I say and testify in the Lord, that you must no longer walk as the Gentiles do, in the futility of their minds. [18]They are darkened in their understanding, alienated from the life of God because of the ignorance that is in them, due to their hardness of heart. [19]They have become callous and have given themselves up to sensuality, greedy to practice every kind of impurity. [20]But that is not the way you learned Christ!— [21]assuming that you have heard about him and were taught in him, as the truth is in Jesus, [22]to put off your old self,[5] which belongs to your former manner of life and is corrupt through deceitful desires, [23]and to be renewed in the spirit of your minds, [24]and to put on the new self, created after the likeness of God in true righteousness and holiness.

[25]Therefore, having put away falsehood, let each one of you speak the truth with his neighbor, for we are members one of another. [26]Be angry and do not sin; do not let the sun go down on your anger, [27]and give no opportunity to the devil. [28]Let the thief no longer steal, but rather let him labor, doing honest work with his own hands, so that he may have something to share with anyone in need. [29]Let no corrupting talk come out of your mouths, but only such as is good for building up, as fits the occasion, that it may give grace to those who hear. [30]And do not grieve the Holy Spirit of God, by whom you were sealed for the day of redemption. [31]Let all bitterness and wrath and anger and clamor and slander be put away from you, along with all malice. [32]Be kind to one another, tenderhearted, forgiving one another, as God in Christ forgave you.

---

[1] Or the lower parts of the earth? [2] Or pastors [3] Or the shepherd-teachers [4] Greek to a full-grown man [5] Greek man; also verse 24 [a] Ps. 68:18

Walk the walk [5:1–21]. The image of walking has already appeared a couple of times in Ephesians (4:1, 17) but comes to greater prominence in chapter 5. The Ephesians are to walk in love (v. 1), walk as children of the light (v. 8), and walk in wisdom (v. 15). This metaphor for the godly life has a rich background in the OT and is used here to emphasize that Christians are not just people who talk a certain kind of talk but people who walk a certain kind of walk. Once again, the apostle's *paraenesis* contrasts the right way with the wrong way to live, a contrast reinforced with images of light and darkness. His main technique is to catalog the behaviors that the children of God should either avoid or emulate—a rhetorical strategy that enables him to give a wide range of loosely structured exhortations on everything from sexual conduct and the abuse of alcohol to music and worship in the church.

5 Therefore be imitators of God, as beloved children. [2]And walk in love, as Christ loved us and gave himself up for us, a fragrant offering and sacrifice to God.

[3]But sexual immorality and all impurity or covetousness must not even be named among you, as is proper among saints. [4]Let there be no filthiness nor foolish talk nor crude joking, which are out of place, but instead let there be thanksgiving. [5]For you may be sure of this, that everyone who is sexually immoral or impure, or who is covetous (that is, an idolater), has no inheritance in the kingdom of Christ and God. [6]Let no one deceive you with empty words, for because of these things the wrath of God comes upon the sons of disobedience. [7]Therefore do not become partners with them; [8]for at one time you were darkness, but now you are light in the Lord. Walk as children of light [9](for the fruit of light is found in all that is good and right and true), [10]and try to discern what is pleasing to the Lord. [11]Take no part in the unfruitful works of darkness, but instead expose them. [12]For it is shameful even to speak of the things that they do in secret. [13]But when anything is exposed by the light, it becomes visible, [14]for anything that becomes visible is light. Therefore it says,

"Awake, O sleeper,
   and arise from the dead,
   and Christ will shine on you."

[15]Look carefully then how you walk, not as unwise but as wise, [16]making the best use of the time, because the days are evil. [17]Therefore do not be foolish, but understand what the will of the Lord is. [18]And do not get drunk with wine, for that is debauchery, but be filled with the Spirit, [19]addressing one another in psalms and hymns and spiritual songs, singing and making melody to the Lord with your heart, [20]giving thanks always and for everything to God the Father in the name of our Lord Jesus Christ, [21]submitting to one another out of reverence for Christ.

Household rules [5:22–6:9]. The ethical instructions in this section of the epistle are more tightly structured. They govern three sets of domestic relationships: husbands and wives (5:22–33), parents and children (6:1–4), and masters and slaves (or bondservants; 6:5–9). Each of these day-to-day relationships is explicitly set in the context of the believer's relationship to Christ as Savior and Lord; these are family rules for life in the household of God. The roles we have in these relationships are reciprocal but not symmetrical. The apostle addresses each person directly, depending on his or her situation in life. In each case, he pinpoints the area of individual responsibility that is most necessary (and perhaps also most spiritually demanding!) for the total relationship to fulfill its God-given purpose. The instructions to husbands and wives are justifiably famous for their stress on submissive (for wives) and sacrificial (for husbands) love. But marriage itself turns out to reveal a deeper mystery: it is a real-life metaphor for the love relationship between Christ and his church (5:32).

²²Wives, submit to your own husbands, as to the Lord. ²³For the husband is the head of the wife even as Christ is the head of the church, his body, and is himself its Savior. ²⁴Now as the church submits to Christ, so also wives should submit in everything to their husbands.

²⁵Husbands, love your wives, as Christ loved the church and gave himself up for her, ²⁶that he might sanctify her, having cleansed her by the washing of water with the word, ²⁷so that he might present the church to himself in splendor, without spot or wrinkle or any such thing, that she might be holy and without blemish.¹ ²⁸In the same way husbands should love their wives as their own bodies. He who loves his wife loves himself. ²⁹For no one ever hated his own flesh, but nourishes and cherishes it, just as Christ does the church, ³⁰because we are members of his body. ³¹ᵃ"Therefore a man shall leave his father and mother and hold fast to his wife, and the two shall become one flesh." ³²This mystery is profound, and I am saying that it refers to Christ and the church. ³³However, let each one of you love his wife as himself, and let the wife see that she respects her husband.

6 Children, obey your parents in the Lord, for this is right. ²ᵇ"Honor your father and mother" (this is the first commandment with a promise), ³"that it may go well with you and that you may live long in the land." ⁴Fathers, do not provoke your children to anger, but bring them up in the discipline and instruction of the Lord.

⁵Slaves,² obey your earthly masters³ with fear and trembling, with a sincere heart, as you would Christ, ⁶not by the way of eye-service, as people-pleasers, but as servants⁴ of Christ, doing the will of God from the heart, ⁷rendering service with a good will as to the Lord and not to man, ⁸knowing that whatever good anyone does, this he will receive back from the Lord, whether he is a slave or free. ⁹Masters, do the same to them, and stop your threatening, knowing that he who is both their Master⁵ and yours is in heaven, and that there is no partiality with him.

The Christian in complete armor [6:10–24]. This dramatic passage is a call to arms for spiritual warfare. The controlling metaphor is a warrior preparing for battle—in this case a supernatural struggle with the devil and all the principalities of evil. The cosmic scope of Ephesians thus encompasses the unseen dimensions of the spiritual world as well as the wide sweep of redemptive history from eternity to eternity. Each piece of conventional armor or weaponry is compared to a blessing or virtue that God provides for his people through the ministry of the Holy Spirit, protecting us from head to toe. We will win this supernatural conflict by standing strong in the power of God. The personal greetings at the end of the letter are uncharacteristically brief. Paul sends his letter off with peace, love, faith, and grace from God the Father and Jesus Christ.

¹ Or holy and blameless ² Or servants; Greek bondservants; similarly verse 8 ³ Or your masters according to the flesh ⁴ Or slaves; Greek bondservants ⁵ Greek Lord ᵃ Gen. 2:24 ᵇ Ex. 20:12

[10]Finally, be strong in the Lord and in the strength of his might. [11]Put on the whole armor of God, that you may be able to stand against the schemes of the devil. [12]For we do not wrestle against flesh and blood, but against the rulers, against the authorities, against the cosmic powers over this present darkness, against the spiritual forces of evil in the heavenly places. [13]Therefore take up the whole armor of God, that you may be able to withstand in the evil day, and having done all, to stand firm. [14]Stand therefore, having fastened on the belt of truth, and having put on the breastplate of righteousness, [15]and, as shoes for your feet, having put on the readiness given by the gospel of peace. [16]In all circumstances take up the shield of faith, with which you can extinguish all the flaming darts of the evil one; [17]and take the helmet of salvation, and the sword of the Spirit, which is the word of God, [18]praying at all times in the Spirit, with all prayer and supplication. To that end keep alert with all perseverance, making supplication for all the saints, [19]and also for me, that words may be given to me in opening my mouth boldly to proclaim the mystery of the gospel, [20]for which I am an ambassador in chains, that I may declare it boldly, as I ought to speak.

[21]So that you also may know how I am and what I am doing, Tychicus the beloved brother and faithful minister in the Lord will tell you everything. [22]I have sent him to you for this very purpose, that you may know how we are, and that he may encourage your hearts.

[23]Peace be to the brothers,[1] and love with faith, from God the Father and the Lord Jesus Christ. [24]Grace be with all who love our Lord Jesus Christ with love incorruptible.

---

[1] Or brothers and sisters

THE LETTER OF PAUL TO THE
PHILIPPIANS

The book at a glance. 4 chapters, 104 verses. The Philippians were among
Paul's closest friends and most valuable partners in ministry. This church was
planted by the apostle himself; the remarkable story of its founding (complete
with nighttime visions, riverside conversions, and prison cell earthquakes) is
told in Acts 16. The Philippians had been strong supporters of Paul's missionary work ever since they came to Christ, and their former pastor writes this
letter of friendship to thank them for their ongoing assistance. The specific
occasion for the letter becomes clear at the end of chapter 2: the Philippians
had sent Paul financial support while he was in prison (probably in Rome).
Unfortunately, their emissary (a man named Epaphroditus) had come down
with a life-threatening illness and was only just now healthy enough to make the
return journey to Philippi. Happily, Epaphroditus would return with Paul's letter
in hand—a letter in which the apostle joyfully celebrates his partnership with
the Philippians in the gospel and passionately exhorts them to join him in
following the example of Jesus Christ in life, in death, and in the life to come.

▌**Genres.** Philippians follows many of the same conventions as the other Pauline
epistles. The *salutation, *thanksgiving, prayer, body, *paraenesis*, greeting, and
*benediction are all readily identifiable. Today churchgoers would call Philippians a
missionary letter. Paul is writing to people who help provide the prayer support and
financial assistance that is necessary for his ministry as an apostle to the Gentiles. To
fulfill his end of the partnership, Paul assures the Philippians of his prayers, updates
them on his personal circumstances, reports on the effectiveness of gospel ministry in
his area, offers spiritual encouragement, and expresses heartfelt gratitude for the many
ways they support his ministry. With its highly patterned lines of praise to Christ,
Philippians 2:5–11 is usually identified as one of the earliest *Christ hymns or
confessions of the Christian church. (For more information on items accompanied by
an asterisk, see the glossary at the end of this Bible.)

▌**Unifying elements.** Philippians is unified by its joyful, almost exuberant mood (words
for "joy" or "rejoice" occur more than a dozen times); by the strong personal relationship between its author and its recipients—a relationship that is almost constantly in
view from beginning to end; and by the many connections Paul draws between the
saving work of Jesus Christ and the servant ministry of his followers, who are called to
live and die according to the pattern of the sufferings, death, resurrection, and
exaltation of Jesus himself.

Passage	Content	Person(s) in focus	Jesus as . . .
1:1–11	Greeting and prayer of thanksgiving	The saints in Philippi	The source of our life
1:12–26	Living and dying in Christ	Paul in prison	
1:27–2:11	Having the mind of Christ	Christ humiliated and exalted	The pattern for our service
2:12–30	Exhortations and examples	Timothy and Epaphroditus	
3:1–11	Being found in Christ's righteousness	Christ dying and rising again	The goal of our existence
3:12–4:1	Pressing on to the heavenly prize	Christ glorified and enthroned	
4:2–9	Further exhortations	Euodia and Syntyche	The joy of our fellowship
4:10–23	Final greeting and thanksgiving	Paul's partners, the Philippians	

▌**Inferred literary intentions.** The book is designed to achieve the following literary purposes:

- package its content in the familiar letter-writing conventions of NT epistles

- give an inside look at Paul's ministry in a Roman prison

- motivate the Philippians to continue to be faithful in their ongoing support of the apostle Paul

- show what joy Christians can have in working together to advance the gospel

- give high praise to Jesus Christ as the crucified, risen, and exalted Lord

- use both positive (Jesus, Timothy, and Epaphroditus) and negative (Euodia and Syntyche) examples to show what kind of service and love ought to characterize Christians who are working in the church

- provide a model for missionaries in expressing grateful thanksgiving for their faithful supporters in gospel work

- use such stylistic techniques as *aphorism, *metaphor, and *lyric to heighten the impact of the writing

▌**Theological themes.** (1) The humiliation of Christ: God the Son humbled himself in his incarnation and crucifixion. (2) The exaltation of Christ: the Father has raised the Son to the place of supreme lordship, where he is destined to receive universal praise. (3) Justification: our standing before God does not depend on any qualifications of our own but on the righteousness of Jesus Christ, which we can only receive by faith. (4) Union with Christ: knowing the crucified and risen Lord is the source of all spiritual life and the pattern for all Christian service. (5) The communion of saints: believers are united to one another as well as to Christ, and our fellowship in Christ makes us partners in the global work of his gospel.

▌ The book of Philippians as a chapter in the master story of the Bible. The story of
the Bible is the story of the gospel—God's saving sinners through the crucifixion and
resurrection of his Son Jesus Christ. Philippians shows how the saving mission of Jesus
is carried forward by people who share in his resurrection life and follow the servant
pattern of his sufferings and death.

Letter from prison [1:1–26]. The opening greeting (vv. 1–2) plainly identifies who is
sending this letter (the apostle Paul and his associate Timothy) and who is receiving it
(the Philippian church, under the leadership of its elders and deacons). The personal
thanksgiving (vv. 3–8) and prayer for God's blessing (vv. 9–11) indicate the situation:
Paul is in prison for defending the gospel, but even in his prison cell he can thank God
and rejoice in his long-standing, heartwarming partnership with the Philippians, who
have supported his missionary work from day one. As he begins to tell his friends about
his progress in ministry, Paul reports that far from hindering his effectiveness as an
evangelist, his imprisonment has actually served to advance the gospel among the
prison guards and others (vv. 12–18). This apparent setback has also served to focus
the apostle's attention on the great dilemma of life and death: whether he lives (as he
eagerly expects) or dies (as in some ways he might prefer), he is determined to live and
to die with Christ and for his glory (vv. 19–26).

1 Paul and Timothy, servants[1] of Christ Jesus,
To all the saints in Christ Jesus who are at Philippi, with the overseers[2] and
deacons:[3]
²Grace to you and peace from God our Father and the Lord Jesus Christ.
³I thank my God in all my remembrance of you, ⁴always in every prayer of mine
for you all making my prayer with joy, ⁵because of your partnership in the gospel
from the first day until now. ⁶And I am sure of this, that he who began a good work
in you will bring it to completion at the day of Jesus Christ. ⁷It is right for me to feel
this way about you all, because I hold you in my heart, for you are all partakers with
me of grace,[4] both in my imprisonment and in the defense and confirmation of the
gospel. ⁸For God is my witness, how I yearn for you all with the affection of Christ
Jesus. ⁹And it is my prayer that your love may abound more and more, with knowledge and all discernment, ¹⁰so that you may approve what is excellent, and so be pure
and blameless for the day of Christ, ¹¹filled with the fruit of righteousness that comes
through Jesus Christ, to the glory and praise of God.
¹²I want you to know, brothers,[5] that what has happened to me has really served to
advance the gospel, ¹³so that it has become known throughout the whole imperial
guard[6] and to all the rest that my imprisonment is for Christ. ¹⁴And most of the brothers, having become confident in the Lord by my imprisonment, are much more bold
to speak the word[7] without fear.
¹⁵Some indeed preach Christ from envy and rivalry, but others from good will.
¹⁶The latter do it out of love, knowing that I am put here for the defense of the gospel.
¹⁷The former proclaim Christ out of rivalry, not sincerely but thinking to afflict me in

---

[1] Or slaves; Greek bondservants [2] Or bishops; Greek episkopoi [3] Or servants, or ministers; Greek diakonoi [4] Or you all have fellowship with me in grace [5] Or brothers and sisters. The plural Greek word adelphoi (translated "brothers") refers to siblings in a family. In New Testament usage, depending on the context, adelphoi may refer either to men or to both men and women who are siblings (brothers and sisters) in God's family, the church; also verse 14 [6] Greek in the whole praetorium [7] Some manuscripts add of God

my imprisonment. ¹⁸What then? Only that in every way, whether in pretense or in truth, Christ is proclaimed, and in that I rejoice.

Yes, and I will rejoice, ¹⁹for I know that through your prayers and the help of the Spirit of Jesus Christ this will turn out for my deliverance, ²⁰as it is my eager expectation and hope that I will not be at all ashamed, but that with full courage now as always Christ will be honored in my body, whether by life or by death. ²¹For to me to live is Christ, and to die is gain. ²²If I am to live in the flesh, that means fruitful labor for me. Yet which I shall choose I cannot tell. ²³I am hard pressed between the two. My desire is to depart and be with Christ, for that is far better. ²⁴But to remain in the flesh is more necessary on your account. ²⁵Convinced of this, I know that I will remain and continue with you all, for your progress and joy in the faith, ²⁶so that in me you may have ample cause to glory in Christ Jesus, because of my coming to you again.

The perfect example [1:27–2:11]. Paul exhorts his missionary partners to live worthy of the gospel of Christ, which means standing as one, fighting with courage, suffering with patience, and loving one another with complete humility and total unity. In short, the Philippians are to share the mind of Christ. The apostle illustrates this servant mentality by tracing the contours of Christ's saving work—the great parabola of redemption that sweeps down from heaven all the way to the cross before rising back again to glory (2:5–11). The first half of this beautifully balanced Christ hymn recounts the humiliation of the Christ. Paul begins in eternity past, where God the Son enjoyed all the glorious prerogatives of his deity. He then goes down step by step to the incarnation and then to the cross, where Christ humbled himself to the very death. The second half of the hymn celebrates the exaltation of the Christ. It is just because he has served us to the very death that God has exalted Jesus to the highest place and given him the highest name in the universe: "Jesus Christ is Lord, to the glory of God the Father" (2:11). This is all by way of illustration, for the apostle uses the perfect example of Christ as a paradigm to make the very practical point that rather than serving ourselves we are to serve others, as Jesus did.

²⁷Only let your manner of life be worthy¹ of the gospel of Christ, so that whether I come and see you or am absent, I may hear of you that you are standing firm in one spirit, with one mind striving side by side for the faith of the gospel, ²⁸and not frightened in anything by your opponents. This is a clear sign to them of their destruction, but of your salvation, and that from God. ²⁹For it has been granted to you that for the sake of Christ you should not only believe in him but also suffer for his sake, ³⁰engaged in the same conflict that you saw I had and now hear that I still have.

2 So if there is any encouragement in Christ, any comfort from love, any participation in the Spirit, any affection and sympathy, ²complete my joy by being of the same mind, having the same love, being in full accord and of one mind. ³Do nothing from rivalry or conceit, but in humility count others more significant than yourselves. ⁴Let each of you look not only to his own interests, but also to the interests of others. ⁵Have this mind among yourselves, which is yours in Christ Jesus,² ⁶who, though he was in the form of God, did not count equality with God a thing to be grasped, ⁷but made himself nothing, taking the form of a servant,³ being born in the likeness of men. ⁸And being found in human form, he humbled himself by becoming obedient

¹ Greek Only behave as citizens worthy ² Or which was also in Christ Jesus ³ Greek bondservant

to the point of death, even death on a cross. ⁹Therefore God has highly exalted him and bestowed on him the name that is above every name, ¹⁰so that at the name of Jesus every knee should bow, in heaven and on earth and under the earth, ¹¹and every tongue confess that Jesus Christ is Lord, to the glory of God the Father.

> **Two good examples** [2:12–30]. The body of Paul's letter continues with further exhortations to practical godliness as the outworking of God's grace in salvation, especially in the areas of obedience, purity, and contentment. The apostle's personal remarks about two of his colleagues fill in some of the details about Paul's past, present, and future relationship with the Philippians. But they also do something more: they provide practical examples of putting other people first (Timothy, vv. 19–24) and serving Christ to the point of death (Epaphroditus, vv. 25–30)—the very attitudes of Christlike servanthood that Paul has been commending. Paul's metaphoric imagination is fully evident is this passage, as is his use of minibiographies to commend a life of service and godliness.

¹²Therefore, my beloved, as you have always obeyed, so now, not only as in my presence but much more in my absence, work out your own salvation with fear and trembling, ¹³for it is God who works in you, both to will and to work for his good pleasure.

¹⁴Do all things without grumbling or questioning, ¹⁵that you may be blameless and innocent, children of God without blemish in the midst of a crooked and twisted generation, among whom you shine as lights in the world, ¹⁶holding fast to the word of life, so that in the day of Christ I may be proud that I did not run in vain or labor in vain. ¹⁷Even if I am to be poured out as a drink offering upon the sacrificial offering of your faith, I am glad and rejoice with you all. ¹⁸Likewise you also should be glad and rejoice with me.

¹⁹I hope in the Lord Jesus to send Timothy to you soon, so that I too may be cheered by news of you. ²⁰For I have no one like him, who will be genuinely concerned for your welfare. ²¹For they all seek their own interests, not those of Jesus Christ. ²²But you know Timothy's[1] proven worth, how as a son[2] with a father he has served with me in the gospel. ²³I hope therefore to send him just as soon as I see how it will go with me, ²⁴and I trust in the Lord that shortly I myself will come also.

²⁵I have thought it necessary to send to you Epaphroditus my brother and fellow worker and fellow soldier, and your messenger and minister to my need, ²⁶for he has been longing for you all and has been distressed because you heard that he was ill. ²⁷Indeed he was ill, near to death. But God had mercy on him, and not only on him but on me also, lest I should have sorrow upon sorrow. ²⁸I am the more eager to send him, therefore, that you may rejoice at seeing him again, and that I may be less anxious. ²⁹So receive him in the Lord with all joy, and honor such men, ³⁰for he nearly died for the work of Christ, risking his life to complete what was lacking in your service to me.

> **Warnings against legalism and license** [3:1–4:1]. In this section of the letter—which is both theological and autobiographical—Paul uses his own testimony to warn against two opposite and perennial dangers in the Christian community: legalism (or trying to be justified before God by one's own accomplishments, 3:1–11) and license (or living

---

¹ Greek *his* ² Greek *child*

for earthly as opposed to heavenly pleasures, 3:12–4:1). In order to combat legalism, the apostle shows how he balances his own spiritual accounts with God. He does this by writing off all his own spiritual achievements as liabilities and simultaneously claiming the righteousness of Christ as his only asset. But knowing the crucified and risen Christ by faith should never become an excuse for spiritual complacency. On the contrary, Christians should follow the example of Paul by continuing to live for God while waiting for Jesus to come again and raise his people up to glory. Verses 4–11 belong to the literary form known as *parody: they use the *rhetoric of the conventional *boast for the paradoxical purpose of rejecting any conventional boasting in human greatness.

3 Finally, my brothers,[1] rejoice in the Lord. To write the same things to you is no trouble to me and is safe for you.

[2] Look out for the dogs, look out for the evildoers, look out for those who mutilate the flesh. [3] For we are the circumcision, who worship by the Spirit of God[2] and glory in Christ Jesus and put no confidence in the flesh— [4] though I myself have reason for confidence in the flesh also. If anyone else thinks he has reason for confidence in the flesh, I have more: [5] circumcised on the eighth day, of the people of Israel, of the tribe of Benjamin, a Hebrew of Hebrews; as to the law, a Pharisee; [6] as to zeal, a persecutor of the church; as to righteousness under the law,[3] blameless. [7] But whatever gain I had, I counted as loss for the sake of Christ. [8] Indeed, I count everything as loss because of the surpassing worth of knowing Christ Jesus my Lord. For his sake I have suffered the loss of all things and count them as rubbish, in order that I may gain Christ [9] and be found in him, not having a righteousness of my own that comes from the law, but that which comes through faith in Christ, the righteousness from God that depends on faith— [10] that I may know him and the power of his resurrection, and may share his sufferings, becoming like him in his death, [11] that by any means possible I may attain the resurrection from the dead.

[12] Not that I have already obtained this or am already perfect, but I press on to make it my own, because Christ Jesus has made me his own. [13] Brothers, I do not consider that I have made it my own. But one thing I do: forgetting what lies behind and straining forward to what lies ahead, [14] I press on toward the goal for the prize of the upward call of God in Christ Jesus. [15] Let those of us who are mature think this way, and if in anything you think otherwise, God will reveal that also to you. [16] Only let us hold true to what we have attained.

[17] Brothers, join in imitating me, and keep your eyes on those who walk according to the example you have in us. [18] For many, of whom I have often told you and now tell you even with tears, walk as enemies of the cross of Christ. [19] Their end is destruction, their god is their belly, and they glory in their shame, with minds set on earthly things. [20] But our citizenship is in heaven, and from it we await a Savior, the Lord Jesus Christ, [21] who will transform our lowly body to be like his glorious body, by the power that enables him even to subject all things to himself.

4 Therefore, my brothers,[4] whom I love and long for, my joy and crown, stand firm thus in the Lord, my beloved.

Final remarks [4:2–23]. Following his concluding exhortations regarding peace in the church, joy in the Lord, prayerful trust in God's provision, and love for what is true and

---

[1] Or brothers and sisters; also verses 13, 17 [2] Some manuscripts God in spirit [3] Greek in the law [4] Or brothers and sisters; also verses 8, 21

good (vv. 2–9), Paul finally comes to his main reason for writing: he wants to thank the Philippians for their loyalty and generosity in meeting his ongoing needs while he is in prison (vv. 10–19). He also wants to reassure them that in the context of their sharing, loving, praying partnership in the gospel, his needs have been fully met. Although Paul has nothing material to give back to the Philippians within the give-and-take of this reciprocal relationship, he knows that God will meet their every need in Christ. Indeed, this is the deep secret of contentment that he has learned in his ministry as a servant of the gospel: he can do everything in God's strength.

²I entreat Euodia and I entreat Syntyche to agree in the Lord. ³Yes, I ask you also, true companion,¹ help these women, who have labored side by side with me in the gospel together with Clement and the rest of my fellow workers, whose names are in the book of life.

⁴Rejoice in the Lord always; again I will say, Rejoice. ⁵Let your reasonableness be known to everyone. The Lord is at hand; ⁶do not be anxious about anything, but in everything by prayer and supplication with thanksgiving let your requests be made known to God. ⁷And the peace of God, which surpasses all understanding, will guard your hearts and your minds in Christ Jesus.

⁸Finally, brothers, whatever is true, whatever is honorable, whatever is just, whatever is pure, whatever is lovely, whatever is commendable, if there is any excellence, if there is anything worthy of praise, think about these things. ⁹What you have learned and received and heard and seen in me—practice these things, and the God of peace will be with you.

¹⁰I rejoiced in the Lord greatly that now at length you have revived your concern for me. You were indeed concerned for me, but you had no opportunity. ¹¹Not that I am speaking of being in need, for I have learned in whatever situation I am to be content. ¹²I know how to be brought low, and I know how to abound. In any and every circumstance, I have learned the secret of facing plenty and hunger, abundance and need. ¹³I can do all things through him who strengthens me.

¹⁴Yet it was kind of you to share² my trouble. ¹⁵And you Philippians yourselves know that in the beginning of the gospel, when I left Macedonia, no church entered into partnership with me in giving and receiving, except you only. ¹⁶Even in Thessalonica you sent me help for my needs once and again. ¹⁷Not that I seek the gift, but I seek the fruit that increases to your credit.³ ¹⁸I have received full payment, and more. I am well supplied, having received from Epaphroditus the gifts you sent, a fragrant offering, a sacrifice acceptable and pleasing to God. ¹⁹And my God will supply every need of yours according to his riches in glory in Christ Jesus. ²⁰To our God and Father be glory forever and ever. Amen.

²¹Greet every saint in Christ Jesus. The brothers who are with me greet you. ²²All the saints greet you, especially those of Caesar's household.

²³The grace of the Lord Jesus Christ be with your spirit.

¹ Or loyal Syzygus; Greek true yokefellow ² Or have fellowship in ³ Or I seek the profit that accrues to your account

THE LETTER OF PAUL TO THE

COLOSSIANS

The book at a glance. 4 chapters, 95 verses. The early church was often confronted by theological errors that contradicted fundamentals of the Christian faith. This was true in Colossae, where religious ideas drawn from Greek philosophy and Jewish tradition tempted some Christians to doubt the supremacy and sufficiency of Christ. Alarmed by this development, the pastor of the Colossian church—a convert named Epaphras—sought counsel from the apostle Paul, who was then in prison. Since Paul had never been to Colossae, this letter is somewhat less personal than his other epistles. It is no less passionate, however, for the apostle is eager to combat the asceticism and Old Testament ritualism, the adoration of angelic mediators, the fascination with the occult, the false claims to secret spiritual knowledge, the belief that Jesus was only one of a series of divine beings connecting the world to God, and the other heterodox notions that were threatening the Colossian church. Paul rightly understood that these heresies (commonly regarded as an early form of Gnosticism) denied Jesus his unique status as the only Son of God, the crucified and risen Savior. His strategy is partly polemical (refuting theological error) and partly doxological (praising God for the supreme Christ and his all-sufficient salvation).

▌**Genres.** Colossians closely follows the epistolary conventions of Paul's other letters to congregations in the early church. The correspondence opens with the customary greetings, including *thanksgiving and prayer. The main body of the letter is divided fairly equally between theological exposition and practical application (including household instructions), followed by personal greetings that reinforce the relationship between the writer and his correspondents. Because of its polemical (persuasive and argumentative) thrust, Colossians also takes the form of a disputation in which the apostle argues the gospel side of a debate between the all-sufficiency of Christ and the spurious claims of man-made religion. The lines of praise given to Christ in 1:15–20 are sometimes regarded as having the form of a *Christ hymn or *creed. (For more information on items accompanied by an asterisk, see the glossary at the end of this Bible.)

▌**Unifying elements.** As one of the most thoroughly Christ-centered books in the Bible, Colossians finds its essential unity in the divine and exalted person of the preeminent Christ. The letter presents variations on this central theme: Christ is variously celebrated as the object of the believer's faith, the image of the invisible God, the Creator of all dominions, the head of the church, the firstborn from the dead, the

Passage	Content	Context	Christ	Theme
1:1–14	Greeting, thanksgiving, prayers	The Colossian Christians	His salvation for the church	
1:15–23	Praise to the preeminent Christ	Creation and the church		Doctrinal explanation
1:24–2:5	The mystery of Christ and the manifestation of his Word	Paul's ministry as an apostle	His supremacy in creation, redemption, and revelation	Doctrinal explanation
2:6–23	The fullness and freedom of life in Christ	False religious philosophies		
3:1–17	The old and the new self	A life that is hidden in heaven with Christ	His lordship over the church	
3:18–4:6	Rules for social and spiritual conduct	The home, the workplace, and the wider culture		Practical exhortation
4:7–18	Final greetings	Paul's friends and colleagues	His ministry in the church	

unifier and reconciler of all things, the Savior through his sufferings on the cross, the treasury of all wisdom and knowledge, the triumphant victor over sin and Satan, the exalted Lord of life and glory, and the true pattern for the life of Christian faith. The letter is also unified by Paul's pastoral concern to dissuade the Colossians from getting caught up in useless religious regulations.

∎ **Inferred literary intentions.** The book is designed to achieve the following literary purposes:

- make a personal connection between the author and his readers, based especially on Paul's work, prayer, and suffering on their behalf

- praise the glory of Christ by using heightened language to describe his person and work in creation and redemption

- portray Christ in such exalted terms that readers will give him the full honor that he alone deserves

- awaken this exaltation with stylistic flair and aphoristic brilliance

- warn against the dangers of ritualism and religious speculation, as opposed to the life of true faith in Christ

- draw a sharp contrast between the old self in sin and the new self in Christ, which is so much more attractive

- offer clear instructions for Christian relationships in the home, the church, and the world

∎ **Theological themes.** (1) Christology: as God the Son, Jesus is in full personal and eternal possession of all the divine attributes; the whole fullness of deity dwells bodily in him. (2) Creation: Jesus Christ is both the origin and the goal of everything in creation. (3) Resurrection: as the firstborn from the dead, Jesus Christ is the living Savior and preeminent Lord. (4) Union with Christ: the believer has been crucified, buried, raised, and exalted with Christ, so that everything Christ has done for our salvation belongs to us by faith in him. (5) Sanctification: Paul encourages the Colossians not to get distracted by man-made rules for religious behavior but to live in a way that is truly pleasing to God: putting on the "new self" in Christ, setting their minds on things above, and bearing fruit in every good work. (6) Prayer: in addition to offering a model prayer for the Christian church, the letter to the Colossians exhorts Christians to pray for the ongoing work of the gospel.

■ **The book of Colossians as a chapter in the master story of the Bible.** At its widest angle, Colossians takes in the whole story of Jesus Christ from his being before the beginning of creation to his destiny as the glorious goal of all things that exist. Here the Bible makes its most explicit statements about the work of Christ as Creator. If it is true that in Jesus "all things hold together" (1:17), then this must include the Bible itself, which is his story. But Colossians also shows how the story of Jesus becomes our own story by faith: we have been crucified, buried, raised, and exalted with Christ, and now his life in us is the hope of our own eventual glory.

All praise to Christ [1:1–20]. The customary greeting (vv. 1–2), thanksgiving (vv. 3–8), and prayer (vv. 9–14) have a celebratory mood as Paul rejoices in the faith the Colossians have in Christ—the result of the gospel ministry of his friend Epaphras. But the heights of the apostle's exultation are reserved for Jesus himself, to whom he offers lyrical praise as the preeminent Christ. This Christ hymn falls into two stanzas, one praising Christ's supremacy in creation (vv. 15–17) and the other praising his supremacy in the church (vv. 18–20). Particular emphasis is given to Christ's full deity, his comprehensive involvement in the creation of the seen and the unseen world, his resurrection from the dead for the church, and his reconciling work through the cross.

---

1 Paul, an apostle of Christ Jesus by the will of God, and Timothy our brother,
²To the saints and faithful brothers¹ in Christ at Colossae:
Grace to you and peace from God our Father.
³We always thank God, the Father of our Lord Jesus Christ, when we pray for you, ⁴since we heard of your faith in Christ Jesus and of the love that you have for all the saints, ⁵because of the hope laid up for you in heaven. Of this you have heard before in the word of the truth, the gospel, ⁶which has come to you, as indeed in the whole world it is bearing fruit and growing—as it also does among you, since the day you heard it and understood the grace of God in truth, ⁷just as you learned it from Epaphras our beloved fellow servant.² He is a faithful minister of Christ on your³ behalf ⁸and has made known to us your love in the Spirit.
⁹And so, from the day we heard, we have not ceased to pray for you, asking that you may be filled with the knowledge of his will in all spiritual wisdom and understanding, ¹⁰so as to walk in a manner worthy of the Lord, fully pleasing to him, bear-

---

¹ Or *brothers and sisters*. The plural Greek word *adelphoi* (translated "brothers") refers to siblings in a family. In New Testament usage, depending on the context, *adelphoi* may refer either to men or to both men and women who are siblings (brothers and sisters) in God's family, the church ² Greek *fellow bondservant* ³ Some manuscripts *our*

ing fruit in every good work and increasing in the knowledge of God. [11]May you be strengthened with all power, according to his glorious might, for all endurance and patience with joy, [12]giving thanks[1] to the Father, who has qualified you[2] to share in the inheritance of the saints in light. [13]He has delivered us from the domain of darkness and transferred us to the kingdom of his beloved Son, [14]in whom we have redemption, the forgiveness of sins.

[15]He is the image of the invisible God, the firstborn of all creation. [16]For by[3] him all things were created, in heaven and on earth, visible and invisible, whether thrones or dominions or rulers or authorities—all things were created through him and for him. [17]And he is before all things, and in him all things hold together. [18]And he is the head of the body, the church. He is the beginning, the firstborn from the dead, that in everything he might be preeminent. [19]For in him all the fullness of God was pleased to dwell, [20]and through him to reconcile to himself all things, whether on earth or in heaven, making peace by the blood of his cross.

The goal of gospel ministry [1:21–2:5]. What are the implications of Christ's saving work, both for the Colossians and for Paul? Having been rescued from their evil ways and reconciled to God, the Colossians must continue to hold on to Jesus by faith. This is the goal of Paul's own gospel ministry, with all its hardship and suffering: to give people the treasure of knowing Christ so that they will have the hope of glory. Although Paul has never visited the Colossians, the personal appeal he makes in these verses reveals the heart that he has for their ministry. In passages like this one, Colossians possesses a lyric tone of exaltation.

[21]And you, who once were alienated and hostile in mind, doing evil deeds, [22]he has now reconciled in his body of flesh by his death, in order to present you holy and blameless and above reproach before him, [23]if indeed you continue in the faith, stable and steadfast, not shifting from the hope of the gospel that you heard, which has been proclaimed in all creation[4] under heaven, and of which I, Paul, became a minister.

[24]Now I rejoice in my sufferings for your sake, and in my flesh I am filling up what is lacking in Christ's afflictions for the sake of his body, that is, the church, [25]of which I became a minister according to the stewardship from God that was given to me for you, to make the word of God fully known, [26]the mystery hidden for ages and generations but now revealed to his saints. [27]To them God chose to make known how great among the Gentiles are the riches of the glory of this mystery, which is Christ in you, the hope of glory. [28]Him we proclaim, warning everyone and teaching everyone with all wisdom, that we may present everyone mature in Christ. [29]For this I toil, struggling with all his energy that he powerfully works within me.

2 For I want you to know how great a struggle I have for you and for those at Laodicea and for all who have not seen me face to face, [2]that their hearts may be encouraged, being knit together in love, to reach all the riches of full assurance of understanding and the knowledge of God's mystery, which is Christ, [3]in whom are hidden all the treasures of wisdom and knowledge. [4]I say this in order that no one may delude you with plausible arguments. [5]For though I am absent in body, yet I am

---

[1] Or patience, with joy giving thanks [2] Some manuscripts us [3] That is, by means of; or in [4] Or to every creature

with you in spirit, rejoicing to see your good order and the firmness of your faith in Christ.

> **Dead and alive in Christ** [2:6–23]. The Colossians must continue in Christ. However, they are in real danger of going in the wrong spiritual, theological, and practical direction. From the warnings the apostle gives, it is apparent that the Colossians are being tempted by a wide variety of false religious ideas: pagan worship, Old Testament rituals that are no longer necessary because they have been fulfilled in Christ, legalistic practices for human conduct, ascetic attitudes toward food and drink, the worship of angels, spurious appeals to religious knowledge, and the like. These man-made rules may have the external appearance of wisdom, but they do not produce any real, inward spiritual change. True spiritual life comes only through being connected to the incarnate Christ by faith in his death and resurrection, as signified and symbolized in Christian baptism. Once we were dead in our sin, but now God has made us alive together with Christ, who is the all-sufficient Savior. His death is death to our sin; his life enables us to live free from merely human religious regulations and in obedience to God alone. The passage embodies much of its meaning in *metaphors like clothing, burial, a canceled legal bond or contract, and the church as a body. Metaphors like these require that we identify the literal level of the comparison and then carry the meaning over to the spiritual topic Paul is addressing.

⁶Therefore, as you received Christ Jesus the Lord, so walk in him, ⁷rooted and built up in him and established in the faith, just as you were taught, abounding in thanksgiving.

⁸See to it that no one takes you captive by philosophy and empty deceit, according to human tradition, according to the elemental spirits¹ of the world, and not according to Christ. ⁹For in him the whole fullness of deity dwells bodily, ¹⁰and you have been filled in him, who is the head of all rule and authority. ¹¹In him also you were circumcised with a circumcision made without hands, by putting off the body of the flesh, by the circumcision of Christ, ¹²having been buried with him in baptism, in which you were also raised with him through faith in the powerful working of God, who raised him from the dead. ¹³And you, who were dead in your trespasses and the uncircumcision of your flesh, God made alive together with him, having forgiven us all our trespasses, ¹⁴by canceling the record of debt that stood against us with its legal demands. This he set aside, nailing it to the cross. ¹⁵He disarmed the rulers and authorities² and put them to open shame, by triumphing over them in him.³

¹⁶Therefore let no one pass judgment on you in questions of food and drink, or with regard to a festival or a new moon or a Sabbath. ¹⁷These are a shadow of the things to come, but the substance belongs to Christ. ¹⁸Let no one disqualify you, insisting on asceticism and worship of angels, going on in detail about visions,⁴ puffed up without reason by his sensuous mind, ¹⁹and not holding fast to the Head, from whom the whole body, nourished and knit together through its joints and ligaments, grows with a growth that is from God.

²⁰If with Christ you died to the elemental spirits of the world, why, as if you were still alive in the world, do you submit to regulations— ²¹"Do not handle, Do not taste, Do not touch" ²²(referring to things that all perish as they are used)—according to human precepts and teachings? ²³These have indeed an appearance of wisdom in

---

¹ Or *elementary principles*; also verse 20 ² Probably demonic rulers and authorities ³ Or *in it* (that is, the cross) ⁴ Or *about the things he has seen*

promoting self-made religion and asceticism and severity to the body, but they are of no value in stopping the indulgence of the flesh.

Off with the old, on with the new [3:1–17]. Paul draws out the implications of dying and rising with Christ by drawing a sharp contrast between the old and the new self. The old self and all its sinful ways must be put to death (vv. 5–9). In its place we must put on the new self, which is patterned after the character of Christ. The apostle's extended metaphor of putting off and putting on (like a change of clothes) is a variation on the traditional lists of vices and virtues, a convention of the Epistles known as *paraenesis*. The concluding verse of this section is one of the Bible's great epigrams on the Christian life.

3 If then you have been raised with Christ, seek the things that are above, where Christ is, seated at the right hand of God. ²Set your minds on things that are above, not on things that are on earth. ³For you have died, and your life is hidden with Christ in God. ⁴When Christ who is your[1] life appears, then you also will appear with him in glory.

⁵Put to death therefore what is earthly in you:[2] sexual immorality, impurity, passion, evil desire, and covetousness, which is idolatry. ⁶On account of these the wrath of God is coming.[3] ⁷In these you too once walked, when you were living in them. ⁸But now you must put them all away: anger, wrath, malice, slander, and obscene talk from your mouth. ⁹Do not lie to one another, seeing that you have put off the old self[4] with its practices ¹⁰and have put on the new self, which is being renewed in knowledge after the image of its creator. ¹¹Here there is not Greek and Jew, circumcised and uncircumcised, barbarian, Scythian, slave,[5] free; but Christ is all, and in all.

¹²Put on then, as God's chosen ones, holy and beloved, compassionate hearts, kindness, humility, meekness, and patience, ¹³bearing with one another and, if one has a complaint against another, forgiving each other; as the Lord has forgiven you, so you also must forgive. ¹⁴And above all these put on love, which binds everything together in perfect harmony. ¹⁵And let the peace of Christ rule in your hearts, to which indeed you were called in one body. And be thankful. ¹⁶Let the word of Christ dwell in you richly, teaching and admonishing one another in all wisdom, singing psalms and hymns and spiritual songs, with thankfulness in your hearts to God. ¹⁷And whatever you do, in word or deed, do everything in the name of the Lord Jesus, giving thanks to God the Father through him.

Living the Christian life at home, in the church, and in the world [3:18–4:18]. Here the general principle of doing everything in the name of Jesus, with thanksgiving to the Father, is specifically applied to practical matters such as life in the home (3:18–21), work (3:22–4:1), prayer for missionaries (4:2–4), and conversations with people outside the church (4:5–6). This intensely theological and spiritually practical letter ends on a more intimate note as Paul uses his final greetings to encourage the Colossians and make a personal connection with them through mutual friends in ministry.

¹⁸Wives, submit to your husbands, as is fitting in the Lord. ¹⁹Husbands, love your wives, and do not be harsh with them. ²⁰Children, obey your parents in everything,

---

[1] Some manuscripts *our* [2] Greek *therefore your members that are on the earth* [3] Some manuscripts add *upon the sons of disobedience* [4] Greek *man;* also as supplied in verse 10 [5] Greek *bondservant*

for this pleases the Lord. [21]Fathers, do not provoke your children, lest they become discouraged. [22]Slaves,[1] obey in everything those who are your earthly masters,[2] not by way of eye-service, as people-pleasers, but with sincerity of heart, fearing the Lord. [23]Whatever you do, work heartily, as for the Lord and not for men, [24]knowing that from the Lord you will receive the inheritance as your reward. You are serving the Lord Christ. [25]For the wrongdoer will be paid back for the wrong he has done, and there is no partiality.

4 Masters, treat your slaves[3] justly and fairly, knowing that you also have a Master in heaven.

[2]Continue steadfastly in prayer, being watchful in it with thanksgiving. [3]At the same time, pray also for us, that God may open to us a door for the word, to declare the mystery of Christ, on account of which I am in prison— [4]that I may make it clear, which is how I ought to speak.

[5]Walk in wisdom toward outsiders, making the best use of the time. [6]Let your speech always be gracious, seasoned with salt, so that you may know how you ought to answer each person.

[7]Tychicus will tell you all about my activities. He is a beloved brother and faithful minister and fellow servant[4] in the Lord. [8]I have sent him to you for this very purpose, that you may know how we are and that he may encourage your hearts, [9]and with him Onesimus, our faithful and beloved brother, who is one of you. They will tell you of everything that has taken place here.

[10]Aristarchus my fellow prisoner greets you, and Mark the cousin of Barnabas (concerning whom you have received instructions—if he comes to you, welcome him), [11]and Jesus who is called Justus. These are the only men of the circumcision among my fellow workers for the kingdom of God, and they have been a comfort to me. [12]Epaphras, who is one of you, a servant of Christ Jesus, greets you, always struggling on your behalf in his prayers, that you may stand mature and fully assured in all the will of God. [13]For I bear him witness that he has worked hard for you and for those in Laodicea and in Hierapolis. [14]Luke the beloved physician greets you, as does Demas. [15]Give my greetings to the brothers[5] at Laodicea, and to Nympha and the church in her house. [16]And when this letter has been read among you, have it also read in the church of the Laodiceans; and see that you also read the letter from Laodicea. [17]And say to Archippus, "See that you fulfill the ministry that you have received in the Lord."

[18]I, Paul, write this greeting with my own hand. Remember my chains. Grace be with you.

[1] Or Servants; Greek Bondservants [2] Or your masters according to the flesh [3] Or servants; Greek bondservants [4] Greek fellow bondservant; also verse 12 [5] Or brothers and sisters

I THESSALONIANS

The book at a glance. 5 chapters, 89 verses. First Thessalonians is an "open letter" to a Christian congregation. The author is an exiled missionary who had founded the fledgling church to which he writes (Acts 17:1–9). Prevented from paying a return visit (1 Thess. 2:17–20), Paul writes in letter form what he would have preferred to say in person. The letter is warm and even intimate in tone and contains repeated addresses to the recipients. The main topics covered are personal greetings to the recipients, Paul's reflections on his experiences with the Thessalonian Christians, instruction in Christian living, and eschatological (end times) instruction—both doctrinal and practical. Because the letter covers multiple topics, we can read it as giving us "program notes" on living the Christian life. Even though the book is a letter rather than an essay with a unifying thesis, it keeps the doctrine of the glorious return of Christ before us (1:10; 2:19–20; 3:13; 4:13–18; 5:1–11; 5:23).

▌**Genre.** First Thessalonians is an informal *epistle that contains all of the usual ingredients of New Testament letters. It is a public letter in the sense of being addressed to a whole group, but at many points it reads more like a personal letter to an individual. The relationship between author and recipients is highlighted, and there is a strong autobiographical element. The purpose of letters is to inform, and this letter informs the Thessalonian church about Paul's feelings toward them, events in his own life, and Christian doctrine and practice. The right way to interpret this epistle is to assume that what Paul wrote to a largely Greek group of Christians in the middle of the first century A.D. is addressed to us as well. We are called to lead the same holy life, and like the Thessalonians, we also live in the hope of the second coming of Christ.

▌**Special features.** Elements that characterize this epistle specifically include the following: (1) strong autobiographical element; (2) exuberant expressions of thanksgiving for people who are living the Christian life correctly; (3) repeated direct addresses to the recipients of the letter; (4) extended teaching on the second coming of Christ, so that even some of the moral exhortations are related to that doctrine; (5) a reference to Christ's second coming at the end of each of the five chapters.

▌**Inferred literary intentions.** The book is designed to achieve the following literary purposes:

- increase our fund of knowledge about key Christian doctrines, especially the second coming of Christ

Passage	Content	Conventional Epistolary Motif
1:1	Sender; recipient; "grace and peace" prayer	Salutation
1:2–10	Reasons that Paul is thankful for the Thessalonians	Thanksgiving
2:1–16	Recollection of past friendship	Autobiographical reflection
2:17–3:13	Joy at good news of the present situation; Paul's prayer for the Thessalonians	Autobiographical information
4:1–12	Exhortations to holy living	*Paraenesis*
4:13–5:11	Doctrine of the second coming of Christ	Instruction
5:12–22	Further exhortations regarding Christian living	*Paraenesis*
5:23–28	Concluding prayers, requests, benediction	Closing

- encourage Christians to endure and inspire them to hope in the return of Christ

- give us a firsthand glimpse into life in a first-century church

- enable us to see in Paul the letter writer a picture of a Christian who inspires our emulation

- raise our awareness about the Christian virtues that should characterize our lives, along with reminders of the vices that we need to avoid

- present all of the foregoing in the conventional epistolary format of NT letters

▌Theological themes. (1) Sanctification: this letter is a handbook on how to live the sanctified life until Jesus returns, and the author's concluding prayer for his readers is that "the God of peace himself sanctify you completely" (5:23). (2) Eschatology: 1 Thessalonians is one of the leading New Testament repositories of teaching about the end times and Christ's return. (3) Communion of the saints: much of the letter outlines how Christians should relate to each other, and Paul's affectionate and encouraging stance toward his recipients is a model. (4) Scripture: scattered throughout the letter are strong statements about the Bible as God's Word, with 2:13 being a classic statement on the subject.

▌1 Thessalonians as a chapter in the master story of the Bible. All of the NT epistles are chapters in the life of the Christian church during its first few decades. Additionally, 1 Thessalonians is a guide to the culminating chapter in salvation history, the eschaton. Many of the references to Christ in this letter link him to the parousia ("presence" or "arrival"), and all five chapters end with a reference to the return of Christ.

Epistolary opening: salutation and thanksgiving [chapter 1]. The opening of 1 Thessalonians is a case study in the conventional opening of NT epistles. Letters in the Greek and Roman world of the first century A.D. began with the names of the sender and recipient, followed by a salutation along the lines of "Greetings!" NT writers also begin with these three components (v. 1), but the greetings are evocative, spiritually charged statements. In Paul's letters, this moving greeting is the "grace and peace" prayer (which can also be regarded as a blessing or benediction), as we find it here. Even more innovative than the modification in the greeting is the addition of a "thanksgiving" that is wholly lacking in contemporaneous Greco-Roman letters. In this case (vv. 2–10), Paul lists the things for which he is thankful regarding the recipients of his letter; a good way to organize the passage is to compile a running list of things for which Paul is grateful. To take a further step, we can summarize the composite portrait of the ideal Christian that emerges both from the Thessalonians as Paul describes them and from the example of Paul himself as we observe him in this passage. Finally, because letters are not theological essays, whatever theology we derive from them generally must be inferred from the ostensible or main business of a passage. If we read between the proverbial lines, for example, we can find an incipient Trinitarian theology in the opening chapter of 1 Thessalonians, which contains references to God the Father (v. 3), Christ (vv. 3, 10), and the Holy Spirit (vv. 5–6).

1

Paul, Silvanus, and Timothy,

To the church of the Thessalonians in God the Father and the Lord Jesus Christ: Grace to you and peace.

[2]We give thanks to God always for all of you, constantly[1] mentioning you in our prayers, [3]remembering before our God and Father your work of faith and labor of love and steadfastness of hope in our Lord Jesus Christ. [4]For we know, brothers[2] loved by God, that he has chosen you, [5]because our gospel came to you not only in word, but also in power and in the Holy Spirit and with full conviction. You know what kind of men we proved to be among you for your sake. [6]And you became imitators of us and of the Lord, for you received the word in much affliction, with the joy of the Holy Spirit, [7]so that you became an example to all the believers in Macedonia and in Achaia. [8]For not only has the word of the Lord sounded forth from you in Macedonia and Achaia, but your faith in God has gone forth everywhere, so that we need not say anything. [9]For they themselves report concerning us the kind of reception we had among you, and how you turned to God from idols to serve the living and true God, [10]and to wait for his Son from heaven, whom he raised from the dead, Jesus who delivers us from the wrath to come.

Recollection of past relationship [2:1–16]. This unit begins a section of autobiographical recollection and reflection that carries over into the next chapter. The opening unit is retrospective in nature, focusing on Paul's past, on-site acquaintance with the Thessalonians when he was a missionary helping to found the church. The rhetorical mode of this autobiographical material is that of a defense or *apologia* ("apology for one's life"); such a defense may have been occasioned by detractors who had cast doubt on his legitimacy as a church leader. Regarding the quantity of autobiography in the epistles, we need to remember that literature is first of all a representation of lived human experience. While we are intended eventually to see what is universal and relevant to us in literature that comes from the past, the way to the universal is through the particular. So the first item on our agenda for this passage is to do what Paul does— relive his past experiences with the Thessalonians. Second, we can assume that Paul

---

[1] Or *without ceasing* [2] Or *brothers and sisters.* The plural Greek word *adelphoi* (translated "brothers") refers to siblings in a family. In New Testament usage, depending on the context, *adelphoi* may refer either to men or to both men and women who are siblings (brothers and sisters) in God's family, the church

and the Thessalonians whom he praises are models for us, showing us what we, too, should believe and practice. Remembering that the Thessalonians whom Paul describes constituted a church, we can also analyze the passage as giving us "program notes" regarding what a Christian church should be like.

2 For you yourselves know, brothers,[1] that our coming to you was not in vain. [2]But though we had already suffered and been shamefully treated at Philippi, as you know, we had boldness in our God to declare to you the gospel of God in the midst of much conflict. [3]For our appeal does not spring from error or impurity or any attempt to deceive, [4]but just as we have been approved by God to be entrusted with the gospel, so we speak, not to please man, but to please God who tests our hearts. [5]For we never came with words of flattery,[2] as you know, nor with a pretext for greed—God is witness. [6]Nor did we seek glory from people, whether from you or from others, though we could have made demands as apostles of Christ. [7]But we were gentle[3] among you, like a nursing mother taking care of her own children. [8]So, being affectionately desirous of you, we were ready to share with you not only the gospel of God but also our own selves, because you had become very dear to us.

[9]For you remember, brothers, our labor and toil: we worked night and day, that we might not be a burden to any of you, while we proclaimed to you the gospel of God. [10]You are witnesses, and God also, how holy and righteous and blameless was our conduct toward you believers. [11]For you know how, like a father with his children, [12]we exhorted each one of you and encouraged you and charged you to walk in a manner worthy of God, who calls you into his own kingdom and glory.

[13]And we also thank God constantly[4] for this, that when you received the word of God, which you heard from us, you accepted it not as the word of men but as what it really is, the word of God, which is at work in you believers. [14]For you, brothers, became imitators of the churches of God in Christ Jesus that are in Judea. For you suffered the same things from your own countrymen as they did from the Jews, [15]who killed both the Lord Jesus and the prophets, and drove us out, and displease God and oppose all mankind [16]by hindering us from speaking to the Gentiles that they might be saved—so as always to fill up the measure of their sins. But God's wrath has come upon them at last![5]

Joy at good news in the present [2:17–3:13]. The material continues to be heavily autobiographical, but the focus shifts from recollection of the past to Paul's joy at the Thessalonians' present situation, as reported by his emissary Timothy. We should continue to (a) pay attention to the literal details and (b) ask what universal human experiences we can glimpse through the historical facts. As we do so, here are some good paths to pursue: the things Paul became anxious about during his absence from the Thessalonians; specific items that constitute the good news from the Thessalonian church; Paul's prayer list regarding the Thessalonians; Paul himself as a model Christian whom we can emulate.

[17]But since we were torn away from you, brothers, for a short time, in person not in heart, we endeavored the more eagerly and with great desire to see you face to face, [18]because we wanted to come to you—I, Paul, again and again—but Satan hindered

---

[1] Or brothers and sisters; also verses 9, 14, 17 [2] Or with a flattering speech [3] Some manuscripts infants [4] Or without ceasing [5] Or completely, or forever

us. [19]For what is our hope or joy or crown of boasting before our Lord Jesus at his coming? Is it not you? [20]For you are our glory and joy.

3 Therefore when we could bear it no longer, we were willing to be left behind at Athens alone, [2]and we sent Timothy, our brother and God's coworker[1] in the gospel of Christ, to establish and exhort you in your faith, [3]that no one be moved by these afflictions. For you yourselves know that we are destined for this. [4]For when we were with you, we kept telling you beforehand that we were to suffer affliction, just as it has come to pass, and just as you know. [5]For this reason, when I could bear it no longer, I sent to learn about your faith, for fear that somehow the tempter had tempted you and our labor would be in vain.

[6]But now that Timothy has come to us from you, and has brought us the good news of your faith and love and reported that you always remember us kindly and long to see us, as we long to see you— [7]for this reason, brothers,[2] in all our distress and affliction we have been comforted about you through your faith. [8]For now we live, if you are standing fast in the Lord. [9]For what thanksgiving can we return to God for you, for all the joy that we feel for your sake before our God, [10]as we pray most earnestly night and day that we may see you face to face and supply what is lacking in your faith?

[11]Now may our God and Father himself, and our Lord Jesus, direct our way to you, [12]and may the Lord make you increase and abound in love for one another and for all, as we do for you, [13]so that he may establish your hearts blameless in holiness before our God and Father, at the coming of our Lord Jesus with all his saints.

Exhortations to holy living [4:1–12]. Up to this point Paul has described the Thessalonian church, in effect painting a picture of an ideal Christian community of believers. With chapter 4 Paul shifts from the descriptive mode to an instructional mode. Taking a cue from 3:10, with its passing reference to Paul's desire to "supply what is lacking in your faith," we can profitably read 4:1–12 as an implied addressing of that subject. These verses are the *paraenesis* section of this letter—the list of virtues and vices that is included in most NT epistles. We can profitably organize the passage around the two themes of (a) what Christians are supposed to do and (b) what they are supposed to avoid as followers of Christ.

4 Finally, then, brothers,[3] we ask and urge you in the Lord Jesus, that as you received from us how you ought to walk and to please God, just as you are doing, that you do so more and more. [2]For you know what instructions we gave you through the Lord Jesus. [3]For this is the will of God, your sanctification:[4] that you abstain from sexual immorality; [4]that each one of you know how to control his own body[5] in holiness and honor, [5]not in the passion of lust like the Gentiles who do not know God; [6]that no one transgress and wrong his brother in this matter, because the Lord is an avenger in all these things, as we told you beforehand and solemnly warned you. [7]For God has not called us for impurity, but in holiness. [8]Therefore whoever disregards this, disregards not man but God, who gives his Holy Spirit to you.

[9]Now concerning brotherly love you have no need for anyone to write to you, for you yourselves have been taught by God to love one another, [10]for that indeed is what

---

[1] Some manuscripts *servant* [2] Or *brothers and sisters* [3] Or *brothers and sisters; also verses 10, 13* [4] Or *your holiness* [5] Or *how to take a wife for himself;* Greek *how to possess his own vessel*

you are doing to all the brothers throughout Macedonia. But we urge you, brothers, to do this more and more, [11]and to aspire to live quietly, and to mind your own affairs, and to work with your hands, as we instructed you, [12]so that you may walk properly before outsiders and be dependent on no one.

The doctrine of the second coming of Christ [4:13–5:11]. Whereas most epistles begin with a doctrinal section and then move to practical application and moral implications of what has been taught, this letter partly reverses that conventional pattern. The chief instructional section of 1 Thessalonians comes after the *paraenesis*. It is one of the leading NT eschatological passages, and the lead-in (4:13) may hint that Paul is responding to a known deficiency in the Thessalonians' fund of knowledge. Paul takes up two related topics—what happens to those who have died (4:13–18) and general teaching about the return (parousia, "presence" or "arrival") of Christ (5:1–11). Piecing everything together requires our best concentration and analytic skills, but with patience we can discern these things: (1) pictures of the specific events that will happen at the end of human history; (2) a general sequence in which these events will happen; (3) a hidden warning regarding the second coming of Christ; (4) reasons for hope if one is a believer in Christ; (5) implications of the doctrine of the second coming for how Christians should live in the present.

[13]But we do not want you to be uninformed, brothers, about those who are asleep, that you may not grieve as others do who have no hope. [14]For since we believe that Jesus died and rose again, even so, through Jesus, God will bring with him those who have fallen asleep. [15]For this we declare to you by a word from the Lord,[1] that we who are alive, who are left until the coming of the Lord, will not precede those who have fallen asleep. [16]For the Lord himself will descend from heaven with a cry of command, with the voice of an archangel, and with the sound of the trumpet of God. And the dead in Christ will rise first. [17]Then we who are alive, who are left, will be caught up together with them in the clouds to meet the Lord in the air, and so we will always be with the Lord. [18]Therefore encourage one another with these words.

5 Now concerning the times and the seasons, brothers,[2] you have no need to have anything written to you. [2]For you yourselves are fully aware that the day of the Lord will come like a thief in the night. [3]While people are saying, "There is peace and security," then sudden destruction will come upon them as labor pains come upon a pregnant woman, and they will not escape. [4]But you are not in darkness, brothers, for that day to surprise you like a thief. [5]For you are all children[3] of light, children of the day. We are not of the night or of the darkness. [6]So then let us not sleep, as others do, but let us keep awake and be sober. [7]For those who sleep, sleep at night, and those who get drunk, are drunk at night. [8]But since we belong to the day, let us be sober, having put on the breastplate of faith and love, and for a helmet the hope of salvation. [9]For God has not destined us for wrath, but to obtain salvation through our Lord Jesus Christ, [10]who died for us so that whether we are awake or asleep we might live with him. [11]Therefore encourage one another and build one another up, just as you are doing.

---

[1] Or by the word of the Lord [2] Or brothers and sisters; also verses 4, 12, 14, 25, 26, 27 [3] Or sons; twice in this verse

Further exhortations regarding Christian living [5:12–22]. After the doctrinal section, Paul returns to a list of dos and don'ts. We can compose them into a brief portrait of the ideal Christian.

¹²We ask you, brothers, to respect those who labor among you and are over you in the Lord and admonish you, ¹³and to esteem them very highly in love because of their work. Be at peace among yourselves. ¹⁴And we urge you, brothers, admonish the idle,[1] encourage the fainthearted, help the weak, be patient with them all. ¹⁵See that no one repays anyone evil for evil, but always seek to do good to one another and to everyone. ¹⁶Rejoice always, ¹⁷pray without ceasing, ¹⁸give thanks in all circumstances; for this is the will of God in Christ Jesus for you. ¹⁹Do not quench the Spirit. ²⁰Do not despise prophecies, ²¹but test everything; hold fast what is good. ²²Abstain from every form of evil.

Epistolary conclusion [5:23–28]. Paul avoids personal references at the end of this letter and instead expresses general prayers and requests, plus the customary benediction. We can ponder how these concluding sentiments serve as a summary of the letter that has preceded.

²³Now may the God of peace himself sanctify you completely, and may your whole spirit and soul and body be kept blameless at the coming of our Lord Jesus Christ. ²⁴He who calls you is faithful; he will surely do it.
²⁵Brothers, pray for us.
²⁶Greet all the brothers with a holy kiss.
²⁷I put you under oath before the Lord to have this letter read to all the brothers.
²⁸The grace of our Lord Jesus Christ be with you.

[1] Or *disorderly, or undisciplined*

2 THESSALONIANS

The book at a glance. 3 chapters, 47 verses. The NT *epistles are examples of
*occasional literature, and 2 Thessalonians will fall into place if we read
between the lines to piece together its occasion. We can infer that 2 Thessalonians was a follow-up letter to 1 Thessalonians, occasioned by the fact the first
letter either had been misunderstood or had given rise to further questions.
Second Thessalonians offers further instruction and clarification on the
subjects that Paul had addressed in his earlier letter to the church at Thessalonica, including the following: the second coming of Christ; how to live a life
that is pleasing to God; behavior that needs to be avoided in the Christian's life.

▌ **Genre and format.** Second Thessalonians follows the customary order of a
NT letter. It begins with a salutation and ends with a prayer and benediction.
Between these bookends we find an informal letter that meanders through a series
of topics as our own informal letters often do. There is the usual mixture of personalia (references to the letter writer's relationship with his recipients) and public
information, Christian doctrine and practical application. The general lay of the land
is as follows: personal messages to the Thessalonians (chapter 1), an eschatological
passage (2:1–12), exuberant and inspiring sentiments (2:13–3:5), and a command
to work (3:6–15).

Passage	Content	Conventional Epistolary Motif
1:1–2	Sender; recipients; "grace and peace" prayer	Salutation
1:3–12	Thanksgiving for the Thessalonians; encouragement and warning about the return of Christ; prayer for the Thessalonians	Thanksgiving
2:1–12	Correcting wrong thinking about the second coming of Christ	Instruction
2:13–3:5	Encouragement and celebration	Lyric interlude
3:6–15	Denunciation of those who are idle	Satiric diatribe
3:16–18	Prayer, greetings, benediction	Closing

▌ **Tone.** In contrast to the warm and effusive tone of 1 Thessalonians, the tone of
2 Thessalonians is almost shocking. There is a strong element of *satire in 2 Thessalonians, as Paul puts down bad behavior and bad thinking. Further, this letter is
noteworthy for the author's tough-mindedness in predicting judgment on the ungodly

and rebuking church members who behave and think incorrectly. Still, there is a regular swing back and forth between reproof and encouragement.

▌**Inferred literary intentions.** The book is designed to achieve the following literary purposes:

- clarify and expand topics about which Paul had written in 1 Thessalonians

- give us detailed information about the second coming of Christ and a Christian work ethic

- facilitate our reading by the author's adherence to the customary rules of letter writing

- lift our spirit and imagination with vivid imagery and exalted vocabulary

▌**Theological themes.** (1) Eschatology: this epistle picks up and extends the teaching about the last days that had begun in the previous epistle. (2) Salvation: we find repeated side comments in which Paul asserts and expresses gratitude for the Thessalonians' salvation in Christ, and from these references we get a picture of what salvation entails. (3) The doctrine of work: the last chapter contains the most extended biblical passage on the subject of work.

▌**2 Thessalonians as a chapter in the master story of the Bible.** One of the story lines of the Bible is how God wants people to live and not live. Second Thessalonians contributes important information on both of these subjects. It particularly focuses on the second coming, the last "chapter" of human history, and its implications for how Christians should live.

Epistolary opening [chapter 1]. The opening chapter is organized along the familiar contours of New Testament epistles as a whole: salutation (vv. 1–2); thanksgiving for the recipients' endurance in the midst of affliction (vv. 3–4), which telescopes into a combined encouragement and warning regarding the return of Christ (vv. 5–10); prayer for the recipients (vv. 11–12). Reading between the lines, we can compile notes regarding what Christians should believe and how they should live, and additionally there are hints of the eschatological (end times) teaching that will dominate the body of the letter.

1 Paul, Silvanus, and Timothy,
To the church of the Thessalonians in God our Father and the Lord Jesus Christ:
²Grace to you and peace from God our Father and the Lord Jesus Christ.
³We ought always to give thanks to God for you, brothers,[1] as is right, because your faith is growing abundantly, and the love of every one of you for one another is increasing. ⁴Therefore we ourselves boast about you in the churches of God for your steadfastness and faith in all your persecutions and in the afflictions that you are enduring.
⁵This is evidence of the righteous judgment of God, that you may be considered worthy of the kingdom of God, for which you are also suffering— ⁶since indeed God considers it just to repay with affliction those who afflict you, ⁷and to grant relief to

---

[1] Or *brothers and sisters*. The plural Greek word *adelphoi* (translated "brothers") refers to siblings in a family. In New Testament usage, depending on the context, *adelphoi* may refer either to men or to both men and women who are siblings (brothers and sisters) in God's family, the church

you who are afflicted as well as to us, when the Lord Jesus is revealed from heaven with his mighty angels [8]in flaming fire, inflicting vengeance on those who do not know God and on those who do not obey the gospel of our Lord Jesus. [9]They will suffer the punishment of eternal destruction, away from[1] the presence of the Lord and from the glory of his might, [10]when he comes on that day to be glorified in his saints, and to be marveled at among all who have believed, because our testimony to you was believed. [11]To this end we always pray for you, that our God may make you worthy of his calling and may fulfill every resolve for good and every work of faith by his power, [12]so that the name of our Lord Jesus may be glorified in you, and you in him, according to the grace of our God and the Lord Jesus Christ.

Correcting erroneous thinking about the second coming of Christ [2:1–12]. With this section the occasion of the letter becomes foregrounded: the teaching of 1 Thessalonians had apparently not achieved its desired clarity and application. So Paul addresses the topic directly: "Now concerning the coming of our Lord Jesus Christ and our being gathered together to him. . ." (v. 1). We can analyze the text for these things: (1) evidences of Paul's anxiety about how the Thessalonians are handling the subject of eschatology; (2) the specific abuses that are agitating Paul; (3) the ideas that make up Paul's doctrinal teaching about the second coming in this passage; (4) the practical implications of what Paul teaches; (5) warnings to the human race regarding the eschaton.

2 Now concerning the coming of our Lord Jesus Christ and our being gathered together to him, we ask you, brothers,[2] [2]not to be quickly shaken in mind or alarmed, either by a spirit or a spoken word, or a letter seeming to be from us, to the effect that the day of the Lord has come. [3]Let no one deceive you in any way. For that day will not come, unless the rebellion comes first, and the man of lawlessness[3] is revealed, the son of destruction,[4] [4]who opposes and exalts himself against every so-called god or object of worship, so that he takes his seat in the temple of God, proclaiming himself to be God. [5]Do you not remember that when I was still with you I told you these things? [6]And you know what is restraining him now so that he may be revealed in his time. [7]For the mystery of lawlessness is already at work. Only he who now restrains it will do so until he is out of the way. [8]And then the lawless one will be revealed, whom the Lord Jesus will kill with the breath of his mouth and bring to nothing by the appearance of his coming. [9]The coming of the lawless one is by the activity of Satan with all power and false signs and wonders, [10]and with all wicked deception for those who are perishing, because they refused to love the truth and so be saved. [11]Therefore God sends them a strong delusion, so that they may believe what is false, [12]in order that all may be condemned who did not believe the truth but had pleasure in unrighteousness.

Expressions of encouragement [2:13–3:5]. The sternness of the eschatological passage is followed by a vintage Pauline outpouring that sweeps us upward with its lyric tone and eloquence of expression. We can discern elements of thanksgiving (noting for what Christians should be most thankful), exhortation, prayer, and benediction. It is an archetypal "feel good" passage to read. There is a pervasive note, however, of the need to persevere and remain steadfast, implying that the exuberance Paul expresses exists

---

[1] Or *destruction that comes from* [2] Or *brothers and sisters*; also verses 13, 15 [3] Some manuscripts *sin* [4] Greek *the son of perdition* (a Hebrew idiom)

in an awareness that there are forces in the world that might dampen a Christian's commitment.

[13]But we ought always to give thanks to God for you, brothers beloved by the Lord, because God chose you as the firstfruits[1] to be saved, through sanctification by the Spirit and belief in the truth. [14]To this he called you through our gospel, so that you may obtain the glory of our Lord Jesus Christ. [15]So then, brothers, stand firm and hold to the traditions that you were taught by us, either by our spoken word or by our letter.

[16]Now may our Lord Jesus Christ himself, and God our Father, who loved us and gave us eternal comfort and good hope through grace, [17]comfort your hearts and establish them in every good work and word.

3 Finally, brothers,[2] pray for us, that the word of the Lord may speed ahead and be honored,[3] as happened among you, [2]and that we may be delivered from wicked and evil men. For not all have faith. [3]But the Lord is faithful. He will establish you and guard you against the evil one.[4] [4]And we have confidence in the Lord about you, that you are doing and will do the things that we command. [5]May the Lord direct your hearts to the love of God and to the steadfastness of Christ.

Denunciation of those who are idle [3:6–15]. The lyric passage gives way to satire and rebuke. The object of satiric attack is idle people who refuse to work. While it is possible that these idle busybodies (v. 11) may be neglecting to work because of wrong thinking about the second coming, the letter itself does not explicitly draw that connection. We can scrutinize the passage for what it teaches about work in the following areas: (1) the fact that idleness is wrong; (2) the specific ways people can violate God's prescription for work; (3) appropriate penalties for those who refuse to work; (4) the positive antidote to idleness.

[6]Now we command you, brothers, in the name of our Lord Jesus Christ, that you keep away from any brother who is walking in idleness and not in accord with the tradition that you received from us. [7]For you yourselves know how you ought to imitate us, because we were not idle when we were with you, [8]nor did we eat anyone's bread without paying for it, but with toil and labor we worked night and day, that we might not be a burden to any of you. [9]It was not because we do not have that right, but to give you in ourselves an example to imitate. [10]For even when we were with you, we would give you this command: If anyone is not willing to work, let him not eat. [11]For we hear that some among you walk in idleness, not busy at work, but busybodies. [12]Now such persons we command and encourage in the Lord Jesus Christ to do their work quietly and to earn their own living.[5]

[13]As for you, brothers, do not grow weary in doing good. [14]If anyone does not obey what we say in this letter, take note of that person, and have nothing to do with him, that he may be ashamed. [15]Do not regard him as an enemy, but warn him as a brother.

Epistolary conclusion [3:16–18]. Prayer, greetings, and benediction. It is always important to note the exact content of these formulas in a given NT letter, since they

---

[1] Some manuscripts *chose you from the beginning* [2] Or *brothers and sisters*; also verses 6, 13 [3] Or *glorified* [4] Or *evil* [5] Greek *eat their own bread*

often tell a unique story despite the set form. Here, for example, Paul refers to writing the greeting in his own hand.

[16]Now may the Lord of peace himself give you peace at all times in every way. The Lord be with you all.

[17]I, Paul, write this greeting with my own hand. This is the sign of genuineness in every letter of mine; it is the way I write. [18]The grace of our Lord Jesus Christ be with you all.

I TIMOTHY

The book at a glance. 6 chapters, 113 verses. The "pastoral epistles" start here and include both letters to Timothy and the letter to Titus. They are called "pastorals" because they are addressed to individuals rather than churches, and to individuals, moreover, who are pastors of local churches. Timothy was a young pastor, Paul's protégé in pastoral ministry. Paul writes as an older, experienced missionary, church planter, and apostle; he is Timothy's mentor, instructing him in what to say and do as he confronts doctrinal deviation and other difficulties in a relatively new church at Ephesus. Although the letter is addressed to Timothy, Paul assumes that the church in Ephesus will also hear the letter and benefit from its instruction, and beyond that, what this letter says about church life is normative for the Christian church in all ages. Paul's own purpose statement is that he has written in order that Christians "may know how . . . to behave in the household of God, which is the church of the living God" (3:15).

■ **Genre and format.** The general form is the *epistle, and the subtype is the pastoral epistle—a letter written to a pastor, giving advice on the issues of church life on which the pastor-recipient needs guidance and encouragement. The resulting letter is heavily *occasional, meaning that the author of the letter addresses specific situations in the recipient's church that need attention. The pastoral letters are not theological treatises in which Paul systematically explores a topic of his choice. Rather, he takes up the topics that we find in this letter because they are the topics that have been raised. Finally, near the end of the opening chapter, Paul labels his remarks up to that point as "this charge" that he has committed to Timothy. It is helpful for the entire letter to be regarded as a formal, authoritative charge—a list of duties that Paul is challenging and directing Timothy to perform. (For more information on items accompanied by an asterisk, see the glossary at the end of this Bible.)

■ **Distinguishing features.** The stance of the author is that of a friend and father in the faith expressing personal concern for the well-being of a young pastor and his church. The overarching concern of the letter is to combat false teaching and false teachers. We accordingly find detailed contrasts between good and bad spiritual leadership in the church. Additionally, this letter provides the most complete summary in the Bible of a pastor's theology, ministry, and spirituality. We also find lists of spiritual qualifications for officers in the church, as well as advice about caring for people with special needs, such as widows and slaves. Three times Paul uses the formula that a statement he makes is "trustworthy" (1:15; 3:1; 4:9).

Passage	Content	Conventional Epistolary Motif
1:1–2	Sender; recipient; "grace, mercy, and peace" prayer	Salutation
1:3–20	Command to Timothy to resist false teachers; autobiographical assertion; charge to Timothy to hold the faith in good conscience	Exhortation
2:1–15	Prayer and the conduct of men and women in public worship	Instruction
3:1–13	Qualifications of elders and deacons	
3:14–16	Purpose statement; Christ hymn	Interlude
4:1–16	Charge to Timothy regarding how to conduct his life as a pastor	Combined exhortation and instruction
5:1–6:2	"Household rules" outlining how Timothy should relate to various groups in the church; intermingled advice about personal matters important in the life of a minister	Instruction
6:3–19	Godly motivation for ministry, combined with warnings about the love of money	Instruction and exhortation
6:20–21	Renewal of charge to Timothy; benediction	Closing

Inferred literary intentions. The book is designed to achieve the following literary purposes:

- give us instructions regarding how to live "in the household of God" (3:15)

- allow us to overhear spiritually oriented "shop talk" between an apostle and a young pastor from early church history

- inform us about how the institutional church should be structured and how it should conduct its ongoing life and ministry

- enable us to enjoy seeing how the letter-writing conventions of the Greco-Roman world were modified by Paul to fit a distinctively Christian purpose

Theological themes. (1) Ecclesiology: this letter is a manual for church organization and practice. (2) Salvation: we find references to the Fall (2:13–14), the Incarnation (3:16), and the way of salvation in Christ (1:15–16; 2:3–6). (3) Eschatology: Jesus Christ will return to earth in all the glory of heaven (6:13–16).

1 Timothy as a chapter in the master story of the Bible. In the NT era, God's kingdom on earth partly takes the form of the local church, composed of its members and ministry, replacing the OT nation of Israel as the locus of God's kingdom on earth. First Timothy gives a wealth of information about the community known as the church and about its calling to promote the truth of Jesus Christ in the world.

A charge relating to theology [chapter 1]. The most immediate impression that we get is the businesslike urgency with which Paul arranges his letter (in fact, this letter lacks such conventional features as the thanksgiving, prayer requests, and greetings to specific people). Following the conventional salutation (vv. 1–2), without transition or lead-in, Paul proceeds to exhort and command Timothy what to do, and near the end of the chapter he labels the passage a "charge" to Timothy (v. 18). Within this rhetorical form of the charge, Paul roams rather widely as he pursues the following sequence of material: a command to Timothy to stay in Ephesus and "charge" false teachers to cease from their errors (vv. 3–7); a discussion of the goodness and purpose of the law (vv. 8–11); an autobiographical statement of thanks by Paul that he was chosen by God to be a model of how Christ saves sinners (vv. 12–17); and a return to the charge to Timothy to stand up to false teaching, along with a reminder of the bad effects of such teaching (vv. 18–20). We should begin with the assumption that in Paul's mind this rather diverse material holds together as a charge to Timothy. We are helped in that analysis if we assume that the general subject of this chapter is the importance of sound theology in the life of a pastor and the local church. It is evident that Paul aims to fortify Timothy for the rigors of pastoral ministry, and specifically to defend against the threat of false doctrine.

1 Paul, an apostle of Christ Jesus by command of God our Savior and of Christ Jesus our hope,

[2]To Timothy, my true child in the faith:

Grace, mercy, and peace from God the Father and Christ Jesus our Lord.

[3]As I urged you when I was going to Macedonia, remain at Ephesus so that you may charge certain persons not to teach any different doctrine, [4]nor to devote themselves to myths and endless genealogies, which promote speculations rather than the stewardship[1] from God that is by faith. [5]The aim of our charge is love that issues from a pure heart and a good conscience and a sincere faith. [6]Certain persons, by swerving from these, have wandered away into vain discussion, [7]desiring to be teachers of the law, without understanding either what they are saying or the things about which they make confident assertions.

[8]Now we know that the law is good, if one uses it lawfully, [9]understanding this, that the law is not laid down for the just but for the lawless and disobedient, for the ungodly and sinners, for the unholy and profane, for those who strike their fathers and mothers, for murderers, [10]the sexually immoral, men who practice homosexuality, enslavers,[2] liars, perjurers, and whatever else is contrary to sound[3] doctrine, [11]in accordance with the gospel of the glory of the blessed God with which I have been entrusted.

[12]I thank him who has given me strength, Christ Jesus our Lord, because he judged me faithful, appointing me to his service, [13]though formerly I was a blasphemer, persecutor, and insolent opponent. But I received mercy because I had acted ignorantly in unbelief, [14]and the grace of our Lord overflowed for me with the faith and love that are in Christ Jesus. [15]The saying is trustworthy and deserving of full acceptance, that Christ Jesus came into the world to save sinners, of whom I am the foremost. [16]But I received mercy for this reason, that in me, as the foremost, Jesus Christ might display his perfect patience as an example to those who were to believe in him for eternal life. [17]To the King of ages, immortal, invisible, the only God, be honor and glory forever and ever.[4] Amen.

[18]This charge I entrust to you, Timothy, my child, in accordance with the prophe-

---

[1] Or *good order* [2] That is, those who take someone captive in order to sell him into slavery [3] Or *healthy* [4] Greek *to the ages of ages*

cies previously made about you, that by them you may wage the good warfare, ¹⁹holding faith and a good conscience. By rejecting this, some have made shipwreck of their faith, ²⁰among whom are Hymenaeus and Alexander, whom I have handed over to Satan that they may learn not to blaspheme.

A liturgical charge relating to public worship [chapter 2]. From theology, Paul turns to public worship. The two general topics covered are the conduct of prayer in church services (vv. 1–7) and the conduct of men and especially women in church services (vv. 8–15). In regard to the first, we should scrutinize the general orientation that Paul recommends (for example, prayer for state and missions/evangelism). In regard to women's participation in church services, it is likewise useful to identify the underlying principles and attitudes that Paul commends (especially studiousness and submission).

2 First of all, then, I urge that supplications, prayers, intercessions, and thanksgivings be made for all people, ²for kings and all who are in high positions, that we may lead a peaceful and quiet life, godly and dignified in every way. ³This is good, and it is pleasing in the sight of God our Savior, ⁴who desires all people to be saved and to come to the knowledge of the truth. ⁵For there is one God, and there is one mediator between God and men, the man¹ Christ Jesus, ⁶who gave himself as a ransom for all, which is the testimony given at the proper time. ⁷For this I was appointed a preacher and an apostle (I am telling the truth, I am not lying), a teacher of the Gentiles in faith and truth.

⁸I desire then that in every place the men should pray, lifting holy hands without anger or quarreling; ⁹likewise also that women should adorn themselves in respectable apparel, with modesty and self-control, not with braided hair and gold or pearls or costly attire, ¹⁰but with what is proper for women who profess godliness—with good works. ¹¹Let a woman learn quietly with all submissiveness. ¹²I do not permit a woman to teach or to exercise authority over a man; rather, she is to remain quiet. ¹³For Adam was formed first, then Eve; ¹⁴and Adam was not deceived, but the woman was deceived and became a transgressor. ¹⁵Yet she will be saved through childbearing—if they continue in faith and love and holiness, with self-control.

A charge relating to church polity [3:1–13]. The focus continues to be on life in the institutional church, as Paul lists the qualifications of "overseers" or elders (vv. 1–7) and deacons and "the women," who may be the wives of the elders or, alternately, other godly women who serve in the church (vv. 8–13). The rhetorical form is the list or catalog of qualifications.

3 The saying is trustworthy: If anyone aspires to the office of overseer, he desires a noble task. ²Therefore an overseer² must be above reproach, the husband of one wife,³ sober-minded, self-controlled, respectable, hospitable, able to teach, ³not a drunkard, not violent but gentle, not quarrelsome, not a lover of money. ⁴He must manage his own household well, with all dignity keeping his children submissive, ⁵for if someone does not know how to manage his own household, how will he care for God's church? ⁶He must not be a recent convert, or he may become puffed up

---

¹ men and man render the same Greek word that is translated people in verses 1 and 4 ² Or bishop; Greek episkopos; a similar term occurs in verse 1
³ Or a man of one woman; also verse 12

with conceit and fall into the condemnation of the devil. [7]Moreover, he must be well thought of by outsiders, so that he may not fall into disgrace, into a snare of the devil.

[8]Deacons likewise must be dignified, not double-tongued,[1] not addicted to much wine, not greedy for dishonest gain. [9]They must hold the mystery of the faith with a clear conscience. [10]And let them also be tested first; then let them serve as deacons if they prove themselves blameless. [11]Their wives likewise must[2] be dignified, not slanderers, but sober-minded, faithful in all things. [12]Let deacons each be the husband of one wife, managing their children and their own households well. [13]For those who serve well as deacons gain a good standing for themselves and also great confidence in the faith that is in Christ Jesus.

Interlude: purpose statement plus Christ hymn [3:14–16]. In keeping with the informal nature of Paul's letters, here his statement of purpose in writing the letter is inserted into the middle (3:14–15) rather than included in his salutation. Then, even more unexpectedly, Paul inserts a *Christ hymn (3:16), which is written in the verse form of parallelism and noteworthy for its hammerlike succession of short, succinct creedal affirmations.

[14]I hope to come to you soon, but I am writing these things to you so that, [15]if I delay, you may know how one ought to behave in the household of God, which is the church of the living God, a pillar and buttress of the truth. [16]Great indeed, we confess, is the mystery of godliness:

> He[3] was manifested in the flesh,
>   vindicated[4] by the Spirit,[5]
>   seen by angels,
>   proclaimed among the nations,
>   believed on in the world,
>   taken up in glory.

Personal pastoral charge [chapter 4]. The opening paragraph (vv. 1–5) takes the form of straightforward doctrinal assertion, so this may look like a free-standing passage of doctrine, but verse 6 turns it in the direction of a charge to Timothy in his discharge of his pastoral duties: "if you put these things before the brothers, you will be a good servant of Christ Jesus" (see also v. 11: "command and teach these things."). The rest of the chapter is more obviously a personal charge to Timothy, but of course what Paul commands to Timothy is commanded to all pastors in all churches and ultimately to all Christians. The exhortations in verses 6–10 cover a range of subjects but chiefly cover truth and godliness, while the rest of the chapter (vv. 11–16) specifically concerns the pastor's life. One way to understand the chapter is to regard it as giving a composite portrait of the ideal pastor, telling congregations what they should look for, value, and pray for in a pastor.

4 Now the Spirit expressly says that in later times some will depart from the faith by devoting themselves to deceitful spirits and teachings of demons, [2]through the insincerity of liars whose consciences are seared, [3]who forbid marriage and

---

[1] Or devious in speech [2] Or Wives, likewise, must, or Women, likewise, must [3] Greek Who; some manuscripts God; others Which [4] Or justified [5] Or vindicated in spirit

require abstinence from foods that God created to be received with thanksgiving by those who believe and know the truth. ⁴For everything created by God is good, and nothing is to be rejected if it is received with thanksgiving, ⁵for it is made holy by the word of God and prayer.

⁶If you put these things before the brothers,¹ you will be a good servant of Christ Jesus, being trained in the words of the faith and of the good doctrine that you have followed. ⁷Have nothing to do with irreverent, silly myths. Rather train yourself for godliness; ⁸for while bodily training is of some value, godliness is of value in every way, as it holds promise for the present life and also for the life to come. ⁹The saying is trustworthy and deserving of full acceptance. ¹⁰For to this end we toil and strive,² because we have our hope set on the living God, who is the Savior of all people, especially of those who believe.

¹¹Command and teach these things. ¹²Let no one despise you for your youth, but set the believers an example in speech, in conduct, in love, in faith, in purity. ¹³Until I come, devote yourself to the public reading of Scripture, to exhortation, to teaching. ¹⁴Do not neglect the gift you have, which was given you by prophecy when the council of elders laid their hands on you. ¹⁵Practice these things, immerse yourself in them,³ so that all may see your progress. ¹⁶Keep a close watch on yourself and on the teaching. Persist in this, for by so doing you will save both yourself and your hearers.

"Household" rules [5:1–6:2]. The rhetoric continues to be that of a formal charge or set of commands to the recipient of the charge. The subject is the pastor's duties in regard to groups and relationships in the church, along with what Timothy should teach church members regarding their relationships. The sequence of specific subjects is this: how to relate to people older and younger than oneself (5:1–2); rules governing widows (5:3–16); rules governing elders (5:17–22); advice regarding the medicinal use of wine (5:23); a nugget of wisdom about the visibility and hiddenness of sins and virtues (5:24–25); rules regarding slaves (6:1–2). One way to master the passage is transpose the rules that Paul states in prose form into an itemized list.

5 Do not rebuke an older man but encourage him as you would a father, younger men as brothers, ²older women as mothers, younger women as sisters, in all purity.

³Honor widows who are truly widows. ⁴But if a widow has children or grandchildren, let them first learn to show godliness to their own household and to make some return to their parents, for this is pleasing in the sight of God. ⁵She who is truly a widow, left all alone, has set her hope on God and continues in supplications and prayers night and day, ⁶but she who is self-indulgent is dead even while she lives. ⁷Command these things as well, so that they may be without reproach. ⁸But if anyone does not provide for his relatives, and especially for members of his household, he has denied the faith and is worse than an unbeliever.

⁹Let a widow be enrolled if she is not less than sixty years of age, having been the wife of one husband,⁴ ¹⁰and having a reputation for good works: if she has brought up children, has shown hospitality, has washed the feet of the saints, has cared for the afflicted, and has devoted herself to every good work. ¹¹But refuse to enroll

---

¹ Or *brothers and sisters.* The plural Greek word *adelphoi* (translated "brothers") refers to siblings in a family. In New Testament usage, depending on the context, *adelphoi* may refer either to men or to both men and women who are siblings (brothers and sisters) in God's family, the church ² Some manuscripts *and suffer reproach* ³ Greek *be in them* ⁴ Or *a woman of one man*

younger widows, for when their passions draw them away from Christ, they desire to marry [12]and so incur condemnation for having abandoned their former faith. [13]Besides that, they learn to be idlers, going about from house to house, and not only idlers, but also gossips and busybodies, saying what they should not. [14]So I would have younger widows marry, bear children, manage their households, and give the adversary no occasion for slander. [15]For some have already strayed after Satan. [16]If any believing woman has relatives who are widows, let her care for them. Let the church not be burdened, so that it may care for those who are truly widows.

[17]Let the elders who rule well be considered worthy of double honor, especially those who labor in preaching and teaching. [18]For the Scripture says, [a]"You shall not muzzle an ox when it treads out the grain," and, "The laborer deserves his wages." [19]Do not admit a charge against an elder except on the evidence of two or three witnesses. [20]As for those who persist in sin, rebuke them in the presence of all, so that the rest may stand in fear. [21]In the presence of God and of Christ Jesus and of the elect angels I charge you to keep these rules without prejudging, doing nothing from partiality. [22]Do not be hasty in the laying on of hands, nor take part in the sins of others; keep yourself pure. [23](No longer drink only water, but use a little wine for the sake of your stomach and your frequent ailments.) [24]The sins of some men are conspicuous, going before them to judgment, but the sins of others appear later. [25]So also good works are conspicuous, and even those that are not cannot remain hidden.

6 Let all who are under a yoke as slaves[1] regard their own masters as worthy of all honor, so that the name of God and the teaching may not be reviled. [2]Those who have believing masters must not be disrespectful on the ground that they are brothers; rather they must serve all the better since those who benefit by their good service are believers and beloved.

A charge regarding the motives for ministry [6:3–21]. Although there is additional material tucked into the flow of this passage, it chiefly concerns the motivation for ministry and, by extension, Christian service more generally. Permeating Paul's injunctions is an underlying contrast between monetary gain as a motivation for ministry and spiritual virtues as the motivation (summarized in v. 11). There is also an implied contrast between temporal and eternal rewards. Money is such a focus of the passage, though, that it becomes more than a charge to a pastor; it is also a major NT repository of teaching about the uses and abuses of money. Paul ends with a renewal of his charge to Timothy ("guard the deposit entrusted to you") and with the conventional benediction.

Teach and urge these things. [3]If anyone teaches a different doctrine and does not agree with the sound[2] words of our Lord Jesus Christ and the teaching that accords with godliness, [4]he is puffed up with conceit and understands nothing. He has an unhealthy craving for controversy and for quarrels about words, which produce envy, dissension, slander, evil suspicions, [5]and constant friction among people who are depraved in mind and deprived of the truth, imagining that godliness is a means of gain. [6]Now there is great gain in godliness with contentment, [7]for we brought nothing into the world, and[3] we cannot take anything out of the world. [8]But if we have food and clothing, with these we will be content. [9]But those who desire to be rich fall into temptation, into a snare, into many senseless and harmful desires that

---

[1] Greek *bondservants* [2] Or *healthy* [3] Greek *for*; some manuscripts insert [it is] *certain* [that] [a] Deut. 25:4

plunge people into ruin and destruction. ¹⁰For the love of money is a root of all kinds of evils. It is through this craving that some have wandered away from the faith and pierced themselves with many pangs.

¹¹But as for you, O man of God, flee these things. Pursue righteousness, godliness, faith, love, steadfastness, gentleness. ¹²Fight the good fight of the faith. Take hold of the eternal life to which you were called and about which you made the good confession in the presence of many witnesses. ¹³I charge you in the presence of God, who gives life to all things, and of Christ Jesus, who in his testimony before¹ Pontius Pilate made the good confession, ¹⁴to keep the commandment unstained and free from reproach until the appearing of our Lord Jesus Christ, ¹⁵which he will display at the proper time—he who is the blessed and only Sovereign, the King of kings and Lord of lords, ¹⁶who alone has immortality, who dwells in unapproachable light, whom no one has ever seen or can see. To him be honor and eternal dominion. Amen.

¹⁷As for the rich in this present age, charge them not to be haughty, nor to set their hopes on the uncertainty of riches, but on God, who richly provides us with everything to enjoy. ¹⁸They are to do good, to be rich in good works, to be generous and ready to share, ¹⁹thus storing up treasure for themselves as a good foundation for the future, so that they may take hold of that which is truly life.

²⁰O Timothy, guard the deposit entrusted to you. Avoid the irreverent babble and contradictions of what is falsely called "knowledge," ²¹for by professing it some have swerved from the faith.

Grace be with you.²

---

¹ Or in the time of ² The Greek for you is plural

2 TIMOTHY

The book at a glance. 4 chapters, 83 verses. Although this letter is technically a pastoral epistle like 1 Timothy, it is actually very different. It is true that Paul again addresses Timothy as a Christian friend and confidant, but the focus is not primarily on the practical execution of Timothy's role as a pastor. Second Timothy was written while Paul was waiting on death row in a Roman prison, and therefore this epistle is what might loosely be called a last will and testament. Its author writes as someone who is aware of being in the final days of his life and thus sums up his life for Timothy and posterity. The implied purpose of the letter is to inspire Christ's followers to follow Paul's example by persevering in the midst of the sufferings of Christian life and ministry. Additionally, Paul's farewell words implicitly pass the torch of ministry to Timothy and ultimately to the church throughout all time.

■ **Genre.** The *genre of 2 Timothy is a literary form known as the *farewell discourse. There are famous farewell discourses in the Bible—for example, by Moses (the book of Deuteronomy), Joshua (Joshua 23–24), David (1 Chronicles 28–29), and Jesus (the Upper Room Discourse in John 14–16). Conventional motifs include the speaker's announcement of his imminent departure, directives to keep God's commandments, predictions of what will happen after the speaker's departure, words of comfort and instruction for the benefit of those who will survive the speaker, and appeals to the addressees to remember what the speaker has taught. If we read 2 Timothy, Paul's last letter, with these features in mind, the book will fall neatly into place. The charges that Paul gives to Timothy in this letter are not occasioned by a specific situation (as 1 Timothy was) but are what Paul most wants Timothy to heed for the rest of his life and ministry—the last word from a spiritual father. (For more information on items accompanied by an asterisk, see the glossary at the end of this Bible.)

■ **Inferred literary intentions.** The book is designed to achieve the following literary purposes:

- lead us to see how Paul the apostle passed the torch of ministry not just to Timothy but to the continuing church

- share Paul's reflective mood as he looks back over past experiences

- lead us to a sober and thoughtful awareness of the bad spiritual times that Christians living in the last times continue to experience and assessment of how well or poorly we have followed Paul's commands regarding how to live in such a culture

Passage	Content	Conventional Epistolary Motif
1:1–7	Sender, recipient, "grace, mercy, and peace" prayer, thanksgiving	Salutation
1:8–18	Charge to not be ashamed of the gospel and to guard the truth	
2:1–26	Charge to be an approved workman	Exhortation
3:1–9	Charge to understand the last days	
3:10–4:8	Charge to Timothy to continue in what he has firmly believed	
4:9–22	Personalia: requests, account of current situation, recollections of past experiences, greetings to friends, benediction	Closing

▌**Theological themes.** (1) Perseverance in the faith: by both his personal example and his exhortations, Paul emphasizes the need to endure to the end. (2) Scripture: this letter includes Paul's famous manifesto about the inspiration of Scripture and its usefulness for all of life (3:16–17), and Timothy is repeatedly enjoined to believe and preach God's reliable Word. (3) Eschatology: looking beyond the end of his own life, Paul discusses such topics as the difficulty that will characterize the last days and the glories that God is waiting to reveal.

▌**2 Timothy as a chapter in the master story of the Bible.** The Bible's story of salvation history is not only universal (extending to the whole human race throughout all of history) but also personal and individual. Every individual needs to be saved, and every individual ends his or her life either in the kingdom or outside of it. Second Timothy tells the story of one Christian's final days as they are lived out in recollection of the life of faith that has preceded; Paul's experience is intended as a model for every Christian's experience, inasmuch as every Christian faces the same glorious future that Paul did and faces the same struggle to persevere until death. A Puritan writer, Edmund Barker, once wrote that "every Christian hath two great works to do in the world, to live well, and to die well." Second Timothy gives us a glimpse of someone who did both of those things.

Epistolary opening [1:1–7]. Author, recipient, religiously and emotionally charged salutation, and thanksgiving. As Paul appeals the legacy in faith that was traceable in Timothy's family line (v. 5), we already catch a hint of the situation that underlies the whole letter—a passing of the torch from one generation to the next.

1 Paul, an apostle of Christ Jesus by the will of God according to the promise of the life that is in Christ Jesus,

²To Timothy, my beloved child:

Grace, mercy, and peace from God the Father and Christ Jesus our Lord.

³I thank God whom I serve, as did my ancestors, with a clear conscience, as I remember you constantly in my prayers night and day. ⁴As I remember your tears, I long to see you, that I may be filled with joy. ⁵I am reminded of your sincere faith, a

faith that dwelt first in your grandmother Lois and your mother Eunice and now, I am sure, dwells in you as well. [6] For this reason I remind you to fan into flame the gift of God, which is in you through the laying on of my hands, [7] for God gave us a spirit not of fear but of power and love and self-control.

A charge to not be ashamed of the gospel and to guard the truth [1:8–18]. There are multiple good ways to divide and label the parts of 2 Timothy; the following division is one among several good options. Second Timothy contains helpful summarizing formulas, and chapter 1 contains two that bring the material into focus: "do not be ashamed of the testimony about our Lord" (v. 8), and "guard the good deposit entrusted to you" (v. 14). The rhetoric of the passage is (like 1 Timothy) the formal charge (list of commands and duties) to Timothy. The charge can profitably be scrutinized looking for the following motifs: (1) outworking of the twofold theme of not being ashamed of the gospel and guarding the truth; (2) the growing list of duties that Paul places on Timothy; (3) interspersed claims by Paul that he himself has followed what he commands Timothy to do; (4) statements that imply that living the Christian life as Paul outlines takes place in a context of hostility to the gospel and personal hardship; (5) God's grace in the gospel that makes it possible to follow what Paul commands and has himself modeled.

[8] Therefore do not be ashamed of the testimony about our Lord, nor of me his prisoner, but share in suffering for the gospel by the power of God, [9] who saved us and called us to[1] a holy calling, not because of our works but because of his own purpose and grace, which he gave us in Christ Jesus before the ages began,[2] [10] and which now has been manifested through the appearing of our Savior Christ Jesus, who abolished death and brought life and immortality to light through the gospel, [11] for which I was appointed a preacher and apostle and teacher, [12] which is why I suffer as I do. But I am not ashamed, for I know whom I have believed, and I am convinced that he is able to guard until that Day what has been entrusted to me.[3] [13] Follow the pattern of the sound[4] words that you have heard from me, in the faith and love that are in Christ Jesus. [14] By the Holy Spirit who dwells within us, guard the good deposit entrusted to you.

[15] You are aware that all who are in Asia turned away from me, among whom are Phygelus and Hermogenes. [16] May the Lord grant mercy to the household of Onesiphorus, for he often refreshed me and was not ashamed of my chains, [17] but when he arrived in Rome he searched for me earnestly and found me— [18] may the Lord grant him to find mercy from the Lord on that Day!—and you well know all the service he rendered at Ephesus.

A charge to be an approved workman [chapter 2]. We can take our clue from verse 15: "present yourself to God as one approved, a worker who has no need to be ashamed, rightly handling the word of truth." The chapter as a whole shows what it looks like to be an approved workman, especially for a minister but by extension for all Christians. As the portrait gets painted, here are the chief ingredients: an approved workman conducts a ministry that reproduces itself (vv. 1–2), endures hardship for the sake of the ministry (vv. 3–13), sticks to the word of truth and avoids false teaching (vv. 14–19), and pursues holiness while avoiding contentiousness (vv. 20–26). A good analytic grid to use is how the text supports and fills out these generalizations.

---

[1] Or with [2] Greek before times eternal [3] Or what I have entrusted to him; Greek my deposit [4] Or healthy

2 You then, my child, be strengthened by the grace that is in Christ Jesus, ²and what you have heard from me in the presence of many witnesses entrust to faithful men who will be able to teach others also. ³Share in suffering as a good soldier of Christ Jesus. ⁴No soldier gets entangled in civilian pursuits, since his aim is to please the one who enlisted him. ⁵An athlete is not crowned unless he competes according to the rules. ⁶It is the hard-working farmer who ought to have the first share of the crops. ⁷Think over what I say, for the Lord will give you understanding in everything.

⁸Remember Jesus Christ, risen from the dead, the offspring of David, as preached in my gospel, ⁹for which I am suffering, bound with chains as a criminal. But the word of God is not bound! ¹⁰Therefore I endure everything for the sake of the elect, that they also may obtain the salvation that is in Christ Jesus with eternal glory. ¹¹The saying is trustworthy, for:

> If we have died with him, we will also live with him;
> ¹² if we endure, we will also reign with him;
> if we deny him, he also will deny us;
> ¹³ if we are faithless, he remains faithful—

for he cannot deny himself.

¹⁴Remind them of these things, and charge them before God[1] not to quarrel about words, which does no good, but only ruins the hearers. ¹⁵Do your best to present yourself to God as one approved,[2] a worker who has no need to be ashamed, rightly handling the word of truth. ¹⁶But avoid irreverent babble, for it will lead people into more and more ungodliness, ¹⁷and their talk will spread like gangrene. Among them are Hymenaeus and Philetus, ¹⁸who have swerved from the truth, saying that the resurrection has already happened. They are upsetting the faith of some. ¹⁹But God's firm foundation stands, bearing this seal: "The Lord knows those who are his," and, "Let everyone who names the name of the Lord depart from iniquity."

²⁰Now in a great house there are not only vessels of gold and silver but also of wood and clay, some for honorable use, some for dishonorable. ²¹Therefore, if anyone cleanses himself from what is dishonorable,[3] he will be a vessel for honorable use, set apart as holy, useful to the master of the house, ready for every good work.

²²So flee youthful passions and pursue righteousness, faith, love, and peace, along with those who call on the Lord from a pure heart. ²³Have nothing to do with foolish, ignorant controversies; you know that they breed quarrels. ²⁴And the Lord's servant[4] must not be quarrelsome but kind to everyone, able to teach, patiently enduring evil, ²⁵correcting his opponents with gentleness. God may perhaps grant them repentance leading to a knowledge of the truth, ²⁶and they may come to their senses and escape from the snare of the devil, after being captured by him to do his will.

A charge to understand the last days [3:1–9]. When Paul speaks of the "last days" (v. 1), he is not referring to the very end of history (the eschaton) but to the decline of the world over a long span as history winds its way toward the *apocalypse. The rhetorical pattern is the catalog of vices, and it is one of Paul's nightmare passages. How bad can a society become? This brief apocalyptic vision tells us. As often in the NT epistles, the list includes both obviously heinous sins and vices that we are often tempted to excuse as mere character flaws.

---

[1] Some manuscripts *the Lord* [2] That is, one approved after being tested [3] Greek *from these things* [4] Greek *bondservant*

3 But understand this, that in the last days there will come times of difficulty. ²For people will be lovers of self, lovers of money, proud, arrogant, abusive, disobedient to their parents, ungrateful, unholy, ³heartless, unappeasable, slanderous, without self-control, brutal, not loving good, ⁴treacherous, reckless, swollen with conceit, lovers of pleasure rather than lovers of God, ⁵having the appearance of godliness, but denying its power. Avoid such people. ⁶For among them are those who creep into households and capture weak women, burdened with sins and led astray by various passions, ⁷always learning and never able to arrive at a knowledge of the truth. ⁸Just as Jannes and Jambres opposed Moses, so these men also oppose the truth, men corrupted in mind and disqualified regarding the faith. ⁹But they will not get very far, for their folly will be plain to all, as was that of those two men.

A charge to Timothy to continue in what he has firmly believed [3:10–4:8]. The "theme verse" of this section is 3:14: "continue in what you have learned and have firmly believed." Of course Timothy has learned a lot, so the passage covers a wide range of material. A good starting point for mastering the passage is to compile a list of categories and specific things that are encompassed in the formula "have learned and firmly believed." Second, one can discern in this section numerous echoes from previous parts of the letter. Third, the conventions of the farewell discourse are evident in this unit, as Paul appeals to his own life and seeks to recall Timothy to what Paul has taught him. Finally, we should look for ways in which the *motif of the Word permeates the passage (3:15–17; 4:2–4).

¹⁰You, however, have followed my teaching, my conduct, my aim in life, my faith, my patience, my love, my steadfastness, ¹¹my persecutions and sufferings that happened to me at Antioch, at Iconium, and at Lystra—which persecutions I endured; yet from them all the Lord rescued me. ¹²Indeed, all who desire to live a godly life in Christ Jesus will be persecuted, ¹³while evil people and impostors will go on from bad to worse, deceiving and being deceived. ¹⁴But as for you, continue in what you have learned and have firmly believed, knowing from whom¹ you learned it ¹⁵and how from childhood you have been acquainted with the sacred writings, which are able to make you wise for salvation through faith in Christ Jesus. ¹⁶All Scripture is breathed out by God and profitable for teaching, for reproof, for correction, and for training in righteousness, ¹⁷that the man of God² may be competent, equipped for every good work.

4 I charge you in the presence of God and of Christ Jesus, who is to judge the living and the dead, and by his appearing and his kingdom: ²preach the word; be ready in season and out of season; reprove, rebuke, and exhort, with complete patience and teaching. ³For the time is coming when people will not endure sound³ teaching, but having itching ears they will accumulate for themselves teachers to suit their own passions, ⁴and will turn away from listening to the truth and wander off into myths. ⁵As for you, always be sober-minded, endure suffering, do the work of an evangelist, fulfill your ministry.

⁶For I am already being poured out as a drink offering, and the time of my departure has come. ⁷I have fought the good fight, I have finished the race, I have kept the faith. ⁸Henceforth there is laid up for me the crown of righteousness, which the Lord,

---

¹ The Greek for *whom* is plural ² That is, a messenger of God (the phrase echoes a common Old Testament expression) ³ Or *healthy*

the righteous judge, will award to me on that Day, and not only to me but also to all who have loved his appearing.

Epistolary conclusion [4:9–22]. The conclusion of this epistle is longer than customary for Paul's letters. There is an extended section of personalia (personal information). It includes requests from Paul to others; an account of Paul's current situation; recollections of past experiences with various people (chiefly bad, as Paul takes stock of disappointments that still rankle him); recollection of past triumphs with Christ; friends to whom Paul wants greetings forwarded; and concluding benediction.

[9] Do your best to come to me soon. [10] For Demas, in love with this present world, has deserted me and gone to Thessalonica. Crescens has gone to Galatia,[1] Titus to Dalmatia. [11] Luke alone is with me. Get Mark and bring him with you, for he is very useful to me for ministry. [12] Tychicus I have sent to Ephesus. [13] When you come, bring the cloak that I left with Carpus at Troas, also the books, and above all the parchments. [14] Alexander the coppersmith did me great harm; the Lord will repay him according to his deeds. [15] Beware of him yourself, for he strongly opposed our message. [16] At my first defense no one came to stand by me, but all deserted me. May it not be charged against them! [17] But the Lord stood by me and strengthened me, so that through me the message might be fully proclaimed and all the Gentiles might hear it. So I was rescued from the lion's mouth. [18] The Lord will rescue me from every evil deed and bring me safely into his heavenly kingdom. To him be the glory forever and ever. Amen.

[19] Greet Prisca and Aquila, and the household of Onesiphorus. [20] Erastus remained at Corinth, and I left Trophimus, who was ill, at Miletus. [21] Do your best to come before winter. Eubulus sends greetings to you, as do Pudens and Linus and Claudia and all the brothers.[2]

[22] The Lord be with your spirit. Grace be with you.[3]

---

[1] Some manuscripts Gaul [2] Or brothers and sisters. The plural Greek word adelphoi (translated "brothers") refers to siblings in a family. In New Testament usage, depending on the context, adelphoi may refer either to men or to both men and women who are siblings (brothers and sisters) in God's family, the church [3] The Greek for you is plural

TITUS

The book at a glance. 3 chapters, 46 verses. Titus was a young pastor serving a church on the island of Crete, whose citizens were notorious for bad behavior (see 1:12–13). Paul's letter to this young man in a tight spot is a pastor's manual for leading a local church. Beyond its stated recipient, though, this is a letter of instruction for all pastors and laypeople. Again Paul writes as a religious "elder statesman" giving advice to a young pastor. The name of Titus appears numerous times in other epistles, and the picture we get is that of a coworker with Paul. The local church is the implied context within which Paul composes his directives.

▌**Genre.** This is a pastoral epistle, written by Paul to a pastor and giving directions that deal directly with a pastor's work in a local congregation. In keeping with the conventions of this genre, Paul writes with apostolic authority. To pack in all of the instruction that he can in a letter that is short even by NT epistolary standards, Paul writes in a curt and businesslike manner.

Passage	Content	Conventional Epistolary Motif
1:1–4	Sender; recipient; "grace and peace" prayer	Salutation
1:5–16	Contrast between good religious leaders (vv. 5–9) and bad religious leaders (vv. 10–16)	Instruction
2:1–15	Moral commands and their theological foundation	*Paraenesis*
3:1–8a	Moral commands and their theological foundation	*Paraenesis*
3:8b–11	Advice to a pastor	Instruction
3:12–15	Personalia; parting advice; greetings; benediction	Closing

▌**Rhetoric and style.** The authoritative and directive stance of the writer to his recipient is evident throughout. Most of Paul's advice is phrased in the imperative mood, producing an urgency of tone. The content, moreover, is condensed, with the effect being similar to that of a telephone conversation in which a speaker knows that he has only a few minutes available to talk.

▌**Inferred literary intentions.** The book is designed to achieve the following literary purposes:

- make a sharp impact on us with its recurring lists of commands

- win us with its succinct style

■ prompt us to think about church life, inasmuch as this book is a manual for life in the local church

▌Theological themes. (1) Christology: the letter has some of the most moving NT statements about the glory of salvation in Christ (additionally, 2:13 is one of the few direct statements in the NT about the deity of Christ). (2) Ethics: half of the letter deals with how elders and laity are supposed to live as followers of Christ, and the book is noteworthy for rooting ethics in theology in a cause-effect way. (3) Ecclesiology: the entire letter focuses on life in the church. (4) Conversion: Paul paints a vivid before-and-after picture of the prototypical Christian life (3:3–7).

▌Titus as a chapter in the master story of the Bible. The master story of the Bible is partly the history of God's kingdom on earth and in heaven. The church is the NT manifestation of God's kingdom on earth. The book of Titus tells the story of how pastors and congregations should live as embodiments of God's kingdom.

Epistolary opening [1:1–4]. Sender, recipient, and salutation in the form of a prayer or benediction.

1 Paul, a servant[1] of God and an apostle of Jesus Christ, for the sake of the faith of God's elect and their knowledge of the truth, which accords with godliness, ²in hope of eternal life, which God, who never lies, promised before the ages began[2] ³and at the proper time manifested in his word through the preaching with which I have been entrusted by the command of God our Savior;
⁴To Titus, my true child in a common faith:
Grace and peace from God the Father and Christ Jesus our Savior.

A contrast between good and bad religious leaders [1:5–16]. We should note first that Paul is so intent on getting to his business of instructing Titus that he dispenses with the conventional section of thanksgiving (the same happened in 1 Timothy). In an opening declaration that must have startled Titus, Paul declares that he left Titus in Crete so that he might put a difficult church situation "into order" (v. 5). At first sight, the two halves of this opening chapter might seem to be unrelated. First Paul outlines the qualifications for the elders whom he wants Titus to appoint in every town (vv. 5–9), and then he paints a lurid picture of bad teachers who are upsetting people in the church (vv. 10–16). But what both groups have in common is that they are leaders who have an impact on the church. Paul makes the connection clear with the coordinate "for" at the beginning of verse 10: Titus needs to appoint strong and godly men as elders because there are religious talkers who are having a bad influence on the church scene. The rhetorical structure, then, is first (a) a solution and then (b) the problem that requires this solution. The logic of the passage is that the elders described by Paul are exactly what is needed to bring the situation into line.

⁵This is why I left you in Crete, so that you might put what remained into order, and appoint elders in every town as I directed you— ⁶if anyone is above reproach, the husband of one wife,[3] and his children are believers and not open to the charge of

---

[1] Or *slave;* Greek *bondservant* [2] Greek *before times eternal* [3] Or *a man of one woman*

debauchery or insubordination. [7]For an overseer,[1] as God's steward, must be above reproach. He must not be arrogant or quick-tempered or a drunkard or violent or greedy for gain, [8]but hospitable, a lover of good, self-controlled, upright, holy, and disciplined. [9]He must hold firm to the trustworthy word as taught, so that he may be able to give instruction in sound[2] doctrine and also to rebuke those who contradict it.

[10]For there are many who are insubordinate, empty talkers and deceivers, especially those of the circumcision party. [11]They must be silenced, since they are upsetting whole families by teaching for shameful gain what they ought not to teach. [12]One of the Cretans,[3] a prophet of their own, said, "Cretans are always liars, evil beasts, lazy gluttons."[4] [13]This testimony is true. Therefore rebuke them sharply, that they may be sound in the faith, [14]not devoting themselves to Jewish myths and the commands of people who turn away from the truth. [15]To the pure, all things are pure, but to the defiled and unbelieving, nothing is pure; but both their minds and their consciences are defiled. [16]They profess to know God, but they deny him by their works. They are detestable, disobedient, unfit for any good work.

Ethics rooted in sound theology [chapter 2]. This chapter, too, pairs two seemingly different topics into a pair of balanced aspects of the Christian life. Verses 1–10 are a familiar section of *paraenesis*—lists of virtues and vices, dos and don'ts of Christian morality. Then we get the coordinating word "for", followed by a section devoted to a theological survey of how Christ has redeemed his followers (vv. 11–14). Salvation is thus offered as the reason and foundation and enabling grace to live the Christian life as Paul outlines it in the first ten verses. The concluding verse of the chapter returns us to the rhetorical situation of the letter: Paul's telling a young pastor to exert his pastoral authority (v. 15).

2 But as for you, teach what accords with sound[5] doctrine. [2]Older men are to be sober-minded, dignified, self-controlled, sound in faith, in love, and in steadfastness. [3]Older women likewise are to be reverent in behavior, not slanderers or slaves to much wine. They are to teach what is good, [4]and so train the young women to love their husbands and children, [5]to be self-controlled, pure, working at home, kind, and submissive to their own husbands, that the word of God may not be reviled. [6]Likewise, urge the younger men to be self-controlled. [7]Show yourself in all respects to be a model of good works, and in your teaching show integrity, dignity, [8]and sound speech that cannot be condemned, so that an opponent may be put to shame, having nothing evil to say about us. [9]Slaves[6] are to be submissive to their own masters in everything; they are to be well-pleasing, not argumentative, [10]not pilfering, but showing all good faith, so that in everything they may adorn the doctrine of God our Savior.

[11]For the grace of God has appeared, bringing salvation for all people, [12]training us to renounce ungodliness and worldly passions, and to live self-controlled, upright, and godly lives in the present age, [13]waiting for our blessed hope, the appearing of the glory of our great God and Savior Jesus Christ, [14]who gave himself for us to redeem us from all lawlessness and to purify for himself a people for his own possession who are zealous for good works.

[1] Or bishop; Greek episkopos [2] Or healthy; also verse 13 [3] Greek One of them [4] Probably from Epimenides of Crete [5] Or healthy; also verses 2, 8 [6] Or servants; Greek bondservants

¹⁵Declare these things; exhort and rebuke with all authority. Let no one disregard you.

The cycle repeated: moral living rooted in theological reality [3:1–8a]. Paul repeats the cause-effect relationship between ethics and theology. First he states a list of moral commands of virtues and vices (vv. 1–3) and then he outlines how salvation in Christ makes moral living possible (vv. 4–8a).

3 Remind them to be submissive to rulers and authorities, to be obedient, to be ready for every good work, ²to speak evil of no one, to avoid quarreling, to be gentle, and to show perfect courtesy toward all people. ³For we ourselves were once foolish, disobedient, led astray, slaves to various passions and pleasures, passing our days in malice and envy, hated by others and hating one another. ⁴But when the goodness and loving kindness of God our Savior appeared, ⁵he saved us, not because of works done by us in righteousness, but according to his own mercy, by the washing of regeneration and renewal of the Holy Spirit, ⁶whom he poured out on us richly through Jesus Christ our Savior, ⁷so that being justified by his grace we might become heirs according to the hope of eternal life. ⁸The saying is trustworthy, and I want you to insist on these things, so that those who have believed in God may be careful to devote themselves to good works.

Advice to a pastor [3:8b–11]. Paul here directs Titus in his work as a pastor, specifically in the areas of controversy and discipline.

These things are excellent and profitable for people. ⁹But avoid foolish controversies, genealogies, dissensions, and quarrels about the law, for they are unprofitable and worthless. ¹⁰As for a person who stirs up division, after warning him once and then twice, have nothing more to do with him, ¹¹knowing that such a person is warped and sinful; he is self-condemned.

Epistolary conclusion [3:12–15]. Personalia, parting advice, greetings, benediction.

¹²When I send Artemas or Tychicus to you, do your best to come to me at Nicopolis, for I have decided to spend the winter there. ¹³Do your best to speed Zenas the lawyer and Apollos on their way; see that they lack nothing. ¹⁴And let our people learn to devote themselves to good works, so as to help cases of urgent need, and not be unfruitful.

¹⁵All who are with me send greetings to you. Greet those who love us in the faith. Grace be with you all.

THE LETTER OF PAUL TO

PHILEMON

The book at a glance. One chapter, 25 verses. This is one of five single-chapter books in the Bible. From one point of view, it exhibits the literary impulse in its pure form: instead of discoursing about a subject, the letter sets the issues in a concrete narrative situation. This narrative situation, moreover, is so striking and heightened as to be a fit subject for a television drama. A runaway slave has met up with Paul and been converted, and Paul sends him back to his former master, Philemon, with a letter explaining how Paul wants Philemon to handle the situation of a returned slave who is now a brother in Christ. For narrative tension, it is hard to beat this.

▌**Structure of the letter.** This simplified letter approximates the letters that we ordinarily write, in contrast to the more stylized and literary five-part format that characterizes most NT epistles. The outline of the letter is as follows: salutation (vv. 1–3); Paul's praise of Philemon's love and faith (vv. 4–7); Paul's appeal on behalf of the returning slave (vv. 8–22); final greetings and benediction (vv. 23–25).

Passage	Content	Conventional Epistolary Motif
1–3	Author, recipient, "grace and peace" prayer	Salutation
4–7	Things in Philemon's life for which Paul is thankful	Thanksgiving
8–22	Paul's appeal to Philemon to accept Onesimus into fellowship	Persuasive appeal
23–25	Greetings and benediction	Closing

▌**The underlying story.** Although the book has the external format of a letter, this format is an indirect way of telling a gripping story. The cast of leading characters consists of Philemon the slave owner; the runaway slave Onesimus, newly converted; and Paul the mediator. The story is familiar among slave narratives the world over: a slave runs away and the master wants him back, usually with punishment in mind. When the slave is caught or turns himself in, the story becomes an archetypal *return story.

▌**The rhetorical situation.** With the conventional situation as a context, Paul's letter emerges as a masterpiece of persuasion (opinion divides on how gentle or forceful the persuasion is). The entire letter can be analyzed in terms of how Paul conducts his persuasion. His goal is to induce a favorable reception for the returning slave, whereas the normal attitude of the slave owner is to be vindictive. Paul needs to reverse the normal course of events. How does he do it? And how does the shared Christian faith of the owner and the returning slave factor into the persuasive appeal? In the background may lie a rhetorical practice prescribed by Greek and Roman rhetoricians: begin by building rapport and goodwill with an audience (vv. 4–10), then lay out the facts in such a way as to convince the mind or intellect (vv. 11–19), and finally appeal to the emotions of the audience (vv. 20–21).

▌**Inferred literary intentions.** The book is designed to achieve the following literary purposes:

- enable us to see what the Christian gospel and Christian morality look like in a difficult real-life situation

- display the rhetorical or persuasive skill of Paul

- grip us with the dramatic force of the situation

▌**Theological themes.** (1) Forgiveness: the main thrust of the letter is that Christians are obliged to forgive those who wrong them. (2) Equality of believers in Christ: this letter asserts a spiritual equality of believers in Christ, even though hierarchies of authority and social roles legitimately exist. (3) Christian community: this letter shows Christians living out their faith in a context of relationship to other Christians.

▌**Philemon as a chapter in the master story of the Bible.** The master story of the Bible is the story of how God calls out a people for himself. The letter to Philemon is a case study in how Christians can live the redeemed life in actual history. Much of the Bible is devoted to "big players" on the stage of world history and believers' history. The letter to Philemon shows the Christian drama of forgiveness being played out by ordinary people who would be unknown to us except for their inclusion in the biblical canon, and whose experiences echo the gospel story of alienation and reconciliation.

Epistolary opening [verses 1–3]. In another context, this would appear to be a merely conventional salutation, but we need to read Philemon with a heightened awareness of subtle (but not devious) attempts at persuasion and with our antennae ready to pick up something approximating a code language. For example, even though Philemon is the one who has the legal authority to determine the fate of Onesimus, observe how Paul enlarges the list of recipients of his missive, thereby holding Philemon accountable to the Christian community and making it harder for him to respond negatively as someone reaching a decision on his own.

¹Paul, a prisoner for Christ Jesus, and Timothy our brother,
To Philemon our beloved fellow worker ²and Apphia our sister and Archippus our fellow soldier, and the church in your house:
³Grace to you and peace from God our Father and the Lord Jesus Christ.

Thanksgiving [verses 4–7]. Once again, while this is an entirely expected statement of thanksgiving after the salutation of a letter, if we picture the charged situation in which this thanksgiving will be read, additional nuances spring up all over the place. For example, by painting such an idealized picture of Philemon's Christian faith and life, Paul is making it difficult for Philemon to take anything less than the high road of Christian behavior in his response to Onesimus.

⁴I thank my God always when I remember you in my prayers, ⁵because I hear of your love and of the faith that you have toward the Lord Jesus and for all the saints, ⁶and I pray that the sharing of your faith may become effective for the full knowledge of every good thing that is in us for the sake of Christ.¹ ⁷For I have derived much joy and comfort from your love, my brother, because the hearts of the saints have been refreshed through you.

The appeal to Philemon on behalf of Onesimus [verses 8–22]. The way to assimilate the passage is to analyze its persuasive strategies. It is as masterful as Mark Antony's funeral oration in Shakespeare's *Julius Caesar*. We should note that in verses 8–10 Paul refuses to pull apostolic rank and instead decides to use ordinary means of persuasion and appeal. Intermingled with the persuasive element in the passage we find implied teaching about Christian ethics and theology.

⁸Accordingly, though I am bold enough in Christ to command you to do what is required, ⁹yet for love's sake I prefer to appeal to you—I, Paul, an old man and now a prisoner also for Christ Jesus— ¹⁰I appeal to you for my child, Onesimus,² whose father I became in my imprisonment. ¹¹(Formerly he was useless to you, but now he is indeed useful to you and to me.) ¹²I am sending him back to you, sending my very heart. ¹³I would have been glad to keep him with me, in order that he might serve me on your behalf during my imprisonment for the gospel, ¹⁴but I preferred to do nothing without your consent in order that your goodness might not be by compulsion but of your own accord. ¹⁵For this perhaps is why he was parted from you for a while, that you might have him back forever, ¹⁶no longer as a slave³ but more than a slave, as a beloved brother—especially to me, but how much more to you, both in the flesh and in the Lord.

¹⁷So if you consider me your partner, receive him as you would receive me. ¹⁸If he has wronged you at all, or owes you anything, charge that to my account. ¹⁹I, Paul, write this with my own hand: I will repay it—to say nothing of your owing me even your own self. ²⁰Yes, brother, I want some benefit from you in the Lord. Refresh my heart in Christ.

²¹Confident of your obedience, I write to you, knowing that you will do even more than I say. ²²At the same time, prepare a guest room for me, for I am hoping that through your prayers I will be graciously given to you.

Epistolary conclusion [verses 23–25]. Greetings and benediction.

²³Epaphras, my fellow prisoner in Christ Jesus, sends greetings to you, ²⁴and so do Mark, Aristarchus, Demas, and Luke, my fellow workers. ²⁵The grace of the Lord Jesus Christ be with your spirit.

¹ Or for Christ's service ² Onesimus means useful (see verse 11) or beneficial (see verse 20) ³ Greek bondservant; twice in this verse

THE LETTER TO THE

HEBREWS

The book at a glance. 13 chapters, 303 verses. The implied purpose of the book is to warn readers not to relinquish their faith in Christ but instead to endure and grow in it. Although the letter names no recipient, there are clues that the author is writing to a group of persecuted Christians with whom he is acquainted. We can infer that they were Jewish converts to the Christian faith and were in danger of drifting from their Christian faith and practice. Next to the book of Romans, Hebrews is the most sustained work of theology in the Bible. Its subject is Christology, with emphasis on Christ's person, priesthood, and sacrifice, but the book is equally about Christians—about what they need to believe and practice. There is a connection between those two themes: it is because of who Christ is and what he has done that we must persevere and not pin our hopes on religious practices that cannot save us.

▌**Genres.** The book of Hebrews is a hybrid. It is commonly classified as an *epistle, and it is true that the book has the feel of other NT epistles. However, epistolary conventions appear overtly only in the last eight verses of the book. The book is also often said to be cast into the form of a sermon, but it does not resemble a sermon such as we commonly hear. Sermonic elements consist mainly of the fervent appeals of the writer, which resemble what a preacher might say to a congregation by way of application. These become dominant only halfway through chapter 10, though they are scattered throughout the earlier parts of the book as well. The main *genre is simply the theological treatise, such as we might read in a theological journal or hear in a seminary classroom. The first nine and a half chapters conduct a sustained theological argument about the superiority of Christ over a number of rivals. These chapters are in effect an essay with a thesis, a series of subordinate generalizations, and supporting proof consisting of data and commentary on it. (For more information on items accompanied by an asterisk, see the glossary at the back of this Bible.)

▌**The style of the book.** Scholars who know Greek literature well say that the book of Hebrews is one of the most stylistically polished books in the NT. The writer is a master of *imagery and *metaphor, allusions to the OT, comparison and analogy, contrast, and long flowing sentences that build to a climax and often use parallel construction of clauses (vv. 18–24 of chapter 12 are a good example of all these techniques).

▌**The rhetorical situation.** Even though the letter does not name its intended audience, we can infer the rhetorical situation from the text itself. The author believes that his readers are caught in a crisis of faith, with reversion to the Jewish religion the

Passage	Subjects Covered	Persons in Addition to Christ Who Are Referenced	Contribution to the Christology	Superiority Motif
1:1–14	Christ's superiority to angels	Prophets and angels	Christ's person	The superior Savior
2:1–18	Christ as the perfect Savior			
3:1–6	Christ's superiority to Moses	Moses and the Jews of the exodus		
3:7–4:13	Warning against unbelief; exhortation to enter Christ's rest			
4:14–5:10	Christ as sympathetic high priest	Priests	Christ's priesthood	
5:11–6:20	Mingled warning and encouragement	Christians at risk		
7:1–28	Christ as superior priest	Priests		
8:1–10:18	The new and better covenant	Recipients of the new covenant	Christ's sacrifice	The superior covenant
10:19–39	Exhortation to endure in the faith	Christians at risk	Christ's followers	The superior life of faith
11:1–12:2	Honor roll of faith	Heroes of the faith		
12:3–29	Variations on the theme of endurance	Christians in need of instruction and the will to endure		
13:1–25	Rules for living the Christian life			

specific danger. We can even catch hints of what prompted the crisis: fear of persecution and the continuing appeal of Judaism. This situation determines the rhetorical stance of the writer—urgency about the crisis. The author displays a pastoral concern to dissuade his readers from drifting from their faith. It is customary to refer to the NT epistles as *occasional letters, and the book of Hebrews is thoroughly rooted in the situation just described.

▎**The rhetorical content.** The *rhetoric of the book is partly argumentative, as the author conducts a sustained theological argument such as we might expect in a debate or a theology book. In terms of how the author conducts his theological argument, the book shows a Jewish orientation. The Jewish way of arguing a thesis was to repeat the main idea so often and from so many angles that an audience would finally agree with the proposition that had been advanced (the book of Ecclesiastes is a classic case). In addition to the rhetoric of argument and debate, we find in the book of Hebrews a persuasive rhetoric of exhortation, as the writer appeals to his readers not to abandon their faith. Outlines of the book usually give the impression that the book is a continuous theological argument, but in fact the book swings back and forth between theological argument and persuasive appeal (if we read most of chapters 2–4, 6, 10:19–39, and most of 12, it is obvious that this material is only slightly tied to the theological argument about the superiority of Christ, being instead an appeal not to abandon the faith but to pursue Christ earnestly).

▌**Rhetorical motifs.** The central *motif of the book is the formula "better," with the cluster of words *better, more,* and *greater* appearing a combined total of twenty-five times. This confirms that the comparative motif, with one thing declared superior to another thing, is the main rhetorical strategy of the book. A common rhetorical form by which the comparison is conducted is analogy, with something in the OT being declared similar to the person and work of Christ. But the analogies are not between two equal things; rather, the author argues from the lesser to the greater. Related to the superiority motif is the motif of progression in God's revelation and his unfolding plan of redemption: what preceded the death, resurrection, and atonement of Christ was anticipatory, while Christ's work has the quality of being final in God's revelation and plan of redemption. Foreshadowing and fulfillment are thus recurrent motifs, and these, in turn, are related to the interpretive practice known as typology—seeing OT events and characters as foreshadowings of Christ's person and work.

▌**Further unifying elements.** (1) A continuous OT or Hebraic frame of reference, resulting in a multitude of allusions to the OT. (2) Repetition of key ideas and citing of examples and authorities from the past as the preferred means of persuading an audience that an idea is true or of moving them to a desired action. (3) Preoccupation with the OT temple and its practices, especially sacrifices. (4) Within exhortations to readers to keep practicing the Christian faith, the formula "let us . . ." (used fourteen times). (5) Alongside Jewish ways of thinking, the Greek mindset and incipient Platonism, seen in contrasts between the earthly and the transcendent or heavenly, the temporal and the eternal, the imperfect earthly copies of realities and the perfect model of those copies.

▌**Inferred literary intentions.** The book is designed to achieve the following literary purposes:

- move readers to keep on practicing the Christian faith

- exalt Christ as being superior to all other beings

- convince us of the truthfulness of the Christian doctrine of Christ's atonement

- put us through a back-and-forth rhythm between theological argument regarding the superiority of Christ's atonement and practical exhortation regarding the need to remain loyal to Christ

- show us how the OT relates to the NT in the plan of redemption

- celebrate the life of faith, especially in the famous *encomium in praise of faith in chapter 11

▌**Theological themes.** (1) Christology: the book of Hebrews is a major NT repository of truth about the atonement of Christ. (2) Progressive revelation: we can infer a thoroughgoing theory of how God's revelation progressed from the OT to the NT.

(3) Salvation: next to the book of Romans, Hebrews is the NT's most extended discussion of the nature of redemption in Christ. (4) Covenant: the book delineates in detail how the old covenant was fulfilled and in some ways superseded by the new covenant.

■ **The book of Hebrews as a chapter in the master story of the Bible.** The most important story that the Bible tells is the story of God's plan of redemption as it unfolded progressively through history. The book of Hebrews reveals how the story of atonement reached its final fulfillment in the sacrifice of Christ. The OT is a series of foreshadowings; the book of Hebrews explains in detail how the atonement of Christ constitutes the actual story, the reality behind the shadows.

Christ's superiority to angels [chapter 1]. The famous first three verses are a prologue to the entire book. They establish Christ as the culmination of God's progressive revelation of his plan of salvation. The rest of the chapter is built on the rhetorical pattern of a comparison between Christ and angels, with a view toward showing the superiority of Christ. The Hebrew mindset is immediately displayed in the technique of extensive quotation from the OT, as well as the honor accorded to angels. The logic of the passage is editorialized for us at the beginning of verse 5: none of the quoted passages from the OT could be applied to angels; they are reserved for Christ alone.

1 Long ago, at many times and in many ways, God spoke to our fathers by the prophets, ²but in these last days he has spoken to us by his Son, whom he appointed the heir of all things, through whom also he created the world. ³He is the radiance of the glory of God and the exact imprint of his nature, and he upholds the universe by the word of his power. After making purification for sins, he sat down at the right hand of the Majesty on high, ⁴having become as much superior to angels as the name he has inherited is more excellent than theirs.

⁵For to which of the angels did God ever say,

ᵃ"You are my Son,
    today I have begotten you"?

Or again,

ᵇ"I will be to him a father,
    and he shall be to me a son"?

⁶And again, when he brings the firstborn into the world, he says,

ᶜ"Let all God's angels worship him."

⁷Of the angels he says,

ᵈ"He makes his angels winds,
    and his ministers a flame of fire."

⁸But of the Son he says,

ᵉ"Your throne, O God, is forever and ever,
    the scepter of uprightness is the scepter of your kingdom.

ᵃ Ps. 2:7 ᵇ 2 Sam. 7:14 ᶜ Deut. 32:43 (Gk.) ᵈ Ps. 104:4 ᵉ Ps. 45:6, 7

9   You have loved righteousness and hated wickedness;
        therefore God, your God, has anointed you
            with the oil of gladness beyond your companions."

¹⁰And,

    ᵃ"You, Lord, laid the foundation of the earth in the beginning,
            and the heavens are the work of your hands;
¹¹   they will perish, but you remain;
            they will all wear out like a garment,
¹²   like a robe you will roll them up,
            like a garment they will be changed.¹
        But you are the same,
            and your years will have no end."

¹³And to which of the angels has he ever said,

    ᵇ"Sit at my right hand
            until I make your enemies a footstool for your feet"?

¹⁴Are they not all ministering spirits sent out to serve for the sake of those who are to inherit salvation?

Christ as the perfect Savior [chapter 2]. Although the general drift of the chapter is to exalt Christ, the author here drops the superiority motif (except for a brief reappearance in v. 5, with its comparison to angels). The author's pastoral impulse to exhort his audience is prominent, in particular the exhortation not to drift from belief in such a wonderful Savior. The sequence of topics is as follows: the ignominy and tragedy of drifting away from the faith (vv. 1–4); God's intention to subject all things to Christ, accompanied by a reminder that although we do not yet see this complete subjection, we nonetheless see Jesus crowned with glory because of his atoning death (vv. 5–9); assertion that Christ's salvation was achieved through suffering (v. 10); the common human identity between the incarnate Christ and those who believe in him (vv. 11–13); as an extension of that human bond, Christ's sympathetic identification with our human weakness (vv. 14–18).

2 Therefore we must pay much closer attention to what we have heard, lest we drift away from it. ²For since the message declared by angels proved to be reliable, and every transgression or disobedience received a just retribution, ³how shall we escape if we neglect such a great salvation? It was declared at first by the Lord, and it was attested to us by those who heard, ⁴while God also bore witness by signs and wonders and various miracles and by gifts of the Holy Spirit distributed according to his will.

⁵Now it was not to angels that God subjected the world to come, of which we are speaking. ⁶It has been testified somewhere,

    ᶜ"What is man, that you are mindful of him,
            or the son of man, that you care for him?
⁷   You made him for a little while lower than the angels;

---

¹ Some manuscripts omit *like a garment* ᵃ Ps. 102:25-27 ᵇ Ps. 110:1 ᶜ Ps. 8:4-6

you have crowned him with glory and honor,[1]

8   putting everything in subjection under his feet."

Now in putting everything in subjection to him, he left nothing outside his control. At present, we do not yet see everything in subjection to him. [9]But we see him who for a little while was made lower than the angels, namely Jesus, crowned with glory and honor because of the suffering of death, so that by the grace of God he might taste death for everyone.

[10]For it was fitting that he, for whom and by whom all things exist, in bringing many sons to glory, should make the founder of their salvation perfect through suffering. [11]For he who sanctifies and those who are sanctified all have one source.[2] That is why he is not ashamed to call them brothers,[3] [12]saying,

[a]"I will tell of your name to my brothers;
    in the midst of the congregation I will sing your praise."

[13]And again,

"I will put my trust in him."

And again,

[b]"Behold, I and the children God has given me."

[14]Since therefore the children share in flesh and blood, he himself likewise partook of the same things, that through death he might destroy the one who has the power of death, that is, the devil, [15]and deliver all those who through fear of death were subject to lifelong slavery. [16]For surely it is not angels that he helps, but he helps the offspring of Abraham. [17]Therefore he had to be made like his brothers in every respect, so that he might become a merciful and faithful high priest in the service of God, to make propitiation for the sins of the people. [18]For because he himself has suffered when tempted, he is able to help those who are being tempted.

Christ's superiority to Moses [3:1–6]. The Jews venerated not only angels but also the towering OT figure of Moses. In this brief segment, the author offers reasons for regarding Jesus as superior to Moses. Two major motifs of the book as a whole make an appearance: the command to "consider Jesus" (v. 1) occurs at several key moments in the book, and the writer never loses sight of his persuasive purpose to enjoin his readers to "hold fast" their confidence and hope (v. 6).

3 Therefore, holy brothers,[4] you who share in a heavenly calling, consider Jesus, the apostle and high priest of our confession, [2]who was faithful to him who appointed him, just as Moses also was faithful in all God's[5] house. [3]For Jesus has been counted worthy of more glory than Moses—as much more glory as the builder of a house has more honor than the house itself. [4](For every house is built by someone, but the builder of all things is God.) [5]Now Moses was faithful in all God's house as a servant, to testify to the things that were to be spoken later, [6]but Christ is faithful

---

[1] Some manuscripts insert *and set him over the works of your hands* [2] Greek *all are of one* [3] Or *brothers and sisters.* The plural Greek word *adelphoi* (translated "brothers") refers to siblings in a family. In New Testament usage, depending on the context, *adelphoi* may refer either to men or to both men and women who are siblings (brothers and sisters) in God's family, the church; also verse 12 [4] Or *brothers and sisters;* also verse 12 [5] Greek *his;* also verses 5, 6 [a] Ps. 22:22 [b] Isa. 8:18

over God's house as a son. And we are his house if indeed we hold fast our confidence and our boasting in our hope.[1]

Exhortation to enter into Christ's rest [3:7–4:13]. The rhetoric now swings back from the theological argument about Christ's superiority to an exhortation to remain faithful. The point of departure (vv. 7–11) is a quotation from Psalm 95:7–11, with its stern warning not to harden one's heart and incur God's penalty of not entering his rest. Taking his cue from the concluding image of not entering God's rest (3:11), the author then unifies the entire remaining part of this unit around the motif of entering God's rest. The variations on the theme are as follows: a warning not be numbered among those who fail to enter God's rest because of unbelief (3:12–19); an intricate argument that God has promised a rest yet to occur in the eschaton (4:1–10); a solemn exhortation to "strive to enter that rest" (4:11), accompanied by a reminder that God's word of judgment can be trusted to occur (4:12–13).

[7] Therefore, as the Holy Spirit says,

[a]"Today, if you hear his voice,
[8] do not harden your hearts as in the rebellion,
on the day of testing in the wilderness,
[9] where your fathers put me to the test
and saw my works for forty years.
[10] Therefore I was provoked with that generation,
and said, 'They always go astray in their heart;
they have not known my ways.'
[11] As I swore in my wrath,
'They shall not enter my rest.'"

[12] Take care, brothers, lest there be in any of you an evil, unbelieving heart, leading you to fall away from the living God. [13] But exhort one another every day, as long as it is called "today," that none of you may be hardened by the deceitfulness of sin. [14] For we have come to share in Christ, if indeed we hold our original confidence firm to the end. [15] As it is said,

[b]"Today, if you hear his voice,
do not harden your hearts as in the rebellion."

[16] For who were those who heard and yet rebelled? Was it not all those who left Egypt led by Moses? [17] And with whom was he provoked for forty years? Was it not with those who sinned, whose bodies fell in the wilderness? [18] And to whom did he swear that they would not enter his rest, but to those who were disobedient? [19] So we see that they were unable to enter because of unbelief.

4 Therefore, while the promise of entering his rest still stands, let us fear lest any of you should seem to have failed to reach it. [2] For good news came to us just as to them, but the message they heard did not benefit them, because they were not united by faith with those who listened.[2] [3] For we who have believed enter that rest, as he has said,

---

[1] Some manuscripts insert *firm to the end* [2] Some manuscripts *it did not meet with faith in the hearers* [a] Ps. 95:7-11 [b] Ps. 95:7, 8

[a]"As I swore in my wrath,
  'They shall not enter my rest,'"

although his works were finished from the foundation of the world. [4]For he has somewhere spoken of the seventh day in this way: [b]"And God rested on the seventh day from all his works." [5]And again in this passage he said,

[c]"They shall not enter my rest."

[6]Since therefore it remains for some to enter it, and those who formerly received the good news failed to enter because of disobedience, [7]again he appoints a certain day, "Today," saying through David so long afterward, in the words already quoted,

[d]"Today, if you hear his voice,
  do not harden your hearts."

[8]For if Joshua had given them rest, God[1] would not have spoken of another day later on. [9]So then, there remains a Sabbath rest for the people of God, [10]for whoever has entered God's rest has also rested from his works as God did from his.

[11]Let us therefore strive to enter that rest, so that no one may fall by the same sort of disobedience. [12]For the word of God is living and active, sharper than any two-edged sword, piercing to the division of soul and of spirit, of joints and of marrow, and discerning the thoughts and intentions of the heart. [13]And no creature is hidden from his sight, but all are naked and exposed to the eyes of him to whom we must give account.

Christ as sympathetic high priest [4:14–5:10]. Although a later unit will stress Christ's superiority to OT priests, this passage uses analogy rather than comparison as its rhetorical mode. The unit unfolds as follows: exhortation to draw near to Christ in confidence because he is a high priest who can sympathize with our neediness (4:14–16); an extended analogy in which the fact that OT priests were called by God to represent the people to God (5:1–4) is offered as a parallel to Christ's humility in becoming a priest who suffered for those who believe in him (5:5–10). Although the rhetorical mode in most of Hebrews is from the lesser to the greater, this passage uses a straight analogy to set forth the case that Christ is a sympathetic high priest. In fact, the analogy is the essential point: because Christ is a man, he is able to sympathize with us as men and women.

[14]Since then we have a great high priest who has passed through the heavens, Jesus, the Son of God, let us hold fast our confession. [15]For we do not have a high priest who is unable to sympathize with our weaknesses, but one who in every respect has been tempted as we are, yet without sin. [16]Let us then with confidence draw near to the throne of grace, that we may receive mercy and find grace to help in time of need.

5 For every high priest chosen from among men is appointed to act on behalf of men in relation to God, to offer gifts and sacrifices for sins. [2]He can deal gently with the ignorant and wayward, since he himself is beset with weakness. [3]Because of this he is obligated to offer sacrifice for his own sins just as he does for those of the

---

[1] Greek *he* [a] Ps. 95:11 [b] Gen. 2:2 [c] Ps. 95:11 [d] Ps. 95:7, 8

people. ⁴And no one takes this honor for himself, but only when called by God, just as Aaron was.

⁵So also Christ did not exalt himself to be made a high priest, but was appointed by him who said to him,

> ᵃ"You are my Son,
>   today I have begotten you";

⁶as he says also in another place,

> ᵇ"You are a priest forever,
>   after the order of Melchizedek."

⁷In the days of his flesh, Jesus¹ offered up prayers and supplications, with loud cries and tears, to him who was able to save him from death, and he was heard because of his reverence. ⁸Although he was a son, he learned obedience through what he suffered. ⁹And being made perfect, he became the source of eternal salvation to all who obey him, ¹⁰being designated by God a high priest after the order of Melchizedek.

Mingled warning and encouragement [5:11–6:20]. The organization of the book has by now become miscellaneous. This passage unfolds as follows: criticism of the readers for being immature in their grasp of doctrine (5:11–6:3); the impossibility of restoring genuine apostates to repentance (vv. 4–8); encouragement to the readers to remain strong in faith (vv. 9–12); the certainty of God's promise to save (vv. 13–20). The way to assimilate the passage is to look carefully at what the author says about these topics, and in particular what he says Christians need to rectify in their lives and what he offers as the basis for their spiritual hope.

¹¹About this we have much to say, and it is hard to explain, since you have become dull of hearing. ¹²For though by this time you ought to be teachers, you need someone to teach you again the basic principles of the oracles of God. You need milk, not solid food, ¹³for everyone who lives on milk is unskilled in the word of righteousness, since he is a child. ¹⁴But solid food is for the mature, for those who have their powers of discernment trained by constant practice to distinguish good from evil.

6 Therefore let us leave the elementary doctrine of Christ and go on to maturity, not laying again a foundation of repentance from dead works and of faith toward God, ²and of instruction about washings,² the laying on of hands, the resurrection of the dead, and eternal judgment. ³And this we will do if God permits. ⁴For it is impossible, in the case of those who have once been enlightened, who have tasted the heavenly gift, and have shared in the Holy Spirit, ⁵and have tasted the goodness of the word of God and the powers of the age to come, ⁶and then have fallen away, to restore them again to repentance, since they are crucifying once again the Son of God to their own harm and holding him up to contempt. ⁷For land that has drunk the rain that often falls on it, and produces a crop useful to those for whose sake it is cultivated, receives a blessing from God. ⁸But if it bears thorns and thistles, it is worthless and near to being cursed, and its end is to be burned.

⁹Though we speak in this way, yet in your case, beloved, we feel sure of better things—things that belong to salvation. ¹⁰For God is not unjust so as to overlook your

---

¹ Greek he ² Or baptisms (that is, cleansing rites) ᵃ Ps. 2:7 ᵇ Ps. 110:4

work and the love that you have shown for his name in serving the saints, as you still do. [11]And we desire each one of you to show the same earnestness to have the full assurance of hope until the end, [12]so that you may not be sluggish, but imitators of those who through faith and patience inherit the promises.

[13]For when God made a promise to Abraham, since he had no one greater by whom to swear, he swore by himself, [14]saying, [a]"Surely I will bless you and multiply you." [15]And thus Abraham,[1] having patiently waited, obtained the promise. [16]For people swear by something greater than themselves, and in all their disputes an oath is final for confirmation. [17]So when God desired to show more convincingly to the heirs of the promise the unchangeable character of his purpose, he guaranteed it with an oath, [18]so that by two unchangeable things, in which it is impossible for God to lie, we who have fled for refuge might have strong encouragement to hold fast to the hope set before us. [19]We have this as a sure and steadfast anchor of the soul, a hope that enters into the inner place behind the curtain, [20]where Jesus has gone as a forerunner on our behalf, having become a high priest forever after the order of Melchizedek.

Christ as superior priest [chapter 7]. The last verse of the preceding chapter makes the famous assertion that Christ was "a high priest forever after the order of Melchizedek" (6:20). The author now elaborates the link between Christ and Melchizedek. In the first three verses the author reconstructs the story of Melchizedek as narrated in Genesis 14:18–20. Additionally, he comments on the OT story in such a way as to exalt the mysterious figure of Melchizedek over the Levitical priests (vv. 4–10). Then in the second of three units in this chapter (vv. 11–19), the author declares Christ to be like Melchizedek and superior to the Levitical priests. To assimilate the passage, we need to ponder why the author considers Christ to be a priest like Melchizedek rather than like Aaron and his descendants. In the last third of the chapter (vv. 20–28), the author allows Melchizedek to drop out of the discussion and continues his theme that Christ is a better priest than the OT Jewish priesthood. We need to follow the author's line of thinking to see how he arrives at his conclusion.

7 For this Melchizedek, king of Salem, priest of the Most High God, met Abraham returning from the slaughter of the kings and blessed him, [2]and to him Abraham apportioned a tenth part of everything. He is first, by translation of his name, king of righteousness, and then he is also king of Salem, that is, king of peace. [3]He is without father or mother or genealogy, having neither beginning of days nor end of life, but resembling the Son of God he continues a priest forever.

[4]See how great this man was to whom Abraham the patriarch gave a tenth of the spoils! [5]And those descendants of Levi who receive the priestly office have a commandment in the law to take tithes from the people, that is, from their brothers,[2] though these also are descended from Abraham. [6]But this man who does not have his descent from them received tithes from Abraham and blessed him who had the promises. [7]It is beyond dispute that the inferior is blessed by the superior. [8]In the one case tithes are received by mortal men, but in the other case, by one of whom it is testified that he lives. [9]One might even say that Levi himself, who receives tithes, paid tithes through Abraham, [10]for he was still in the loins of his ancestor when Melchizedek met him.

[11]Now if perfection had been attainable through the Levitical priesthood (for under

---

[1] Greek *he* [2] Or *brothers and sisters* [a] Gen. 22:17

it the people received the law), what further need would there have been for another priest to arise after the order of Melchizedek, rather than one named after the order of Aaron? [12]For when there is a change in the priesthood, there is necessarily a change in the law as well. [13]For the one of whom these things are spoken belonged to another tribe, from which no one has ever served at the altar. [14]For it is evident that our Lord was descended from Judah, and in connection with that tribe Moses said nothing about priests.

[15]This becomes even more evident when another priest arises in the likeness of Melchizedek, [16]who has become a priest, not on the basis of a legal requirement concerning bodily descent, but by the power of an indestructible life. [17]For it is witnessed of him,

[a]"You are a priest forever,
      after the order of Melchizedek."

[18]For on the one hand, a former commandment is set aside because of its weakness and uselessness [19](for the law made nothing perfect); but on the other hand, a better hope is introduced, through which we draw near to God.

[20]And it was not without an oath. For those who formerly became priests were made such without an oath, [21]but this one was made a priest with an oath by the one who said to him:

[b]"The Lord has sworn
      and will not change his mind,
  'You are a priest forever.'"

[22]This makes Jesus the guarantor of a better covenant.

[23]The former priests were many in number, because they were prevented by death from continuing in office, [24]but he holds his priesthood permanently, because he continues forever. [25]Consequently, he is able to save to the uttermost[1] those who draw near to God through him, since he always lives to make intercession for them.

[26]For it was indeed fitting that we should have such a high priest, holy, innocent, unstained, separated from sinners, and exalted above the heavens. [27]He has no need, like those high priests, to offer sacrifices daily, first for his own sins and then for those of the people, since he did this once for all when he offered up himself. [28]For the law appoints men in their weakness as high priests, but the word of the oath, which came later than the law, appoints a Son who has been made perfect forever.

The inferiority of the old covenant [8:1–9:10]. The book now moves from the earlier comparison of two priestly orders to a comparison of the old and new covenants. In this first unit devoted to this topic, the subject is the inferior nature of the OT covenant. The specific arguments are these: the earthly nature of the OT priests and tabernacle makes it inferior to the heavenly position of Christ (8:1–7); a series of OT quotations that show that the old covenant was intended by God to become obsolete (8:8–13); the OT sacrificial system's temporary and external/physical nature shows it to be inferior to the spiritual and once-for-all sacrifice of Christ. Those are the main arguments; the reader's task is to see how the details support the arguments.

[1] That is, completely; or at all times [a] Ps. 110:4 [b] Ps. 110:4

8 Now the point in what we are saying is this: we have such a high priest, one who is seated at the right hand of the throne of the Majesty in heaven, ²a minister in the holy places, in the true tent[1] that the Lord set up, not man. ³For every high priest is appointed to offer gifts and sacrifices; thus it is necessary for this priest also to have something to offer. ⁴Now if he were on earth, he would not be a priest at all, since there are priests who offer gifts according to the law. ⁵They serve a copy and shadow of the heavenly things. For when Moses was about to erect the tent, he was instructed by God, saying, [a]"See that you make everything according to the pattern that was shown you on the mountain." ⁶But as it is, Christ[2] has obtained a ministry that is as much more excellent than the old as the covenant he mediates is better, since it is enacted on better promises. ⁷For if that first covenant had been faultless, there would have been no occasion to look for a second.

⁸For he finds fault with them when he says:[3]

[b]"Behold, the days are coming, declares the Lord,
    when I will establish a new covenant with the house of Israel
    and with the house of Judah,
⁹   not like the covenant that I made with their fathers
        on the day when I took them by the hand to bring them out of the land of Egypt.
    For they did not continue in my covenant,
        and so I showed no concern for them, declares the Lord.
¹⁰ For this is the covenant that I will make with the house of Israel
        after those days, declares the Lord:
    I will put my laws into their minds,
        and write them on their hearts,
    and I will be their God,
        and they shall be my people.
¹¹ And they shall not teach, each one his neighbor
        and each one his brother, saying, 'Know the Lord,'
    for they shall all know me,
        from the least of them to the greatest.
¹² For I will be merciful toward their iniquities,
        and I will remember their sins no more."

¹³In speaking of a new covenant, he makes the first one obsolete. And what is becoming obsolete and growing old is ready to vanish away.

9 Now even the first covenant had regulations for worship and an earthly place of holiness. ²For a tent[4] was prepared, the first section, in which were the lampstand and the table and the bread of the Presence.[5] It is called the Holy Place. ³Behind the second curtain was a second section[6] called the Most Holy Place, ⁴having the golden altar of incense and the ark of the covenant covered on all sides with gold, in which was a golden urn holding the manna, and Aaron's staff that budded, and the tablets of the covenant. ⁵Above it were the cherubim of glory overshadowing the mercy seat. Of these things we cannot now speak in detail.

⁶These preparations having thus been made, the priests go regularly into the first section, performing their ritual duties, ⁷but into the second only the high priest goes,

---

[1] Or tabernacle; also verse 5 [2] Greek he [3] Some manuscripts For finding fault with it he says to them [4] Or tabernacle; also verses 11, 21 [5] Greek the presentation of the loaves [6] Greek tent; also verses 6, 8 [a] Ex. 25:40 [b] Jer. 31:31-34

and he but once a year, and not without taking blood, which he offers for himself and for the unintentional sins of the people. ⁸By this the Holy Spirit indicates that the way into the holy places is not yet opened as long as the first section is still standing ⁹(which is symbolic for the present age).ᴵ According to this arrangement, gifts and sacrifices are offered that cannot perfect the conscience of the worshiper, ¹⁰but deal only with food and drink and various washings, regulations for the body imposed until the time of reformation.

> **The superiority of the new covenant** [9:11–10:18]. As we ponder the preceding section on the inferiority of the old covenant, we keep anticipating the counterpart of that argument, and the pivot occurs at the outset of this unit with the formula "But when Christ appeared . . ." (9:11). The specific variations on the theme of the superiority of the new covenant are as follows: Christ's sacrifice is eternal, not something that needs to be done repeatedly (9:11–14); in the new covenant, Christ's death ratifies a believer's salvation, as contrasted to the blood of bulls and goats in the old covenant, which did not have the power of atonement in themselves but only in connection to the subsequent sacrifice of the true Messiah (9:15–22); Christ entered heaven once for all after he obtained salvation, and that is superior to the OT priest's entering the earthly Holy Place year after year (9:23–28); the once-only sacrifice of Christ is better than the perpetual sacrifices of the old covenant (10:1–10); summary statement exalting the once-for-all over the repeated (10:11–18). To catch the drift of the argument, we need to pay attention to the rhetorical mode, which involves contrast and comparison.

¹¹But when Christ appeared as a high priest of the good things that have come,² then through the greater and more perfect tent (not made with hands, that is, not of this creation) ¹²he entered once for all into the holy places, not by means of the blood of goats and calves but by means of his own blood, thus securing an eternal redemption. ¹³For if the blood of goats and bulls, and the sprinkling of defiled persons with the ashes of a heifer, sanctify³ for the purification of the flesh, ¹⁴how much more will the blood of Christ, who through the eternal Spirit offered himself without blemish to God, purify our⁴ conscience from dead works to serve the living God.

¹⁵Therefore he is the mediator of a new covenant, so that those who are called may receive the promised eternal inheritance, since a death has occurred that redeems them from the transgressions committed under the first covenant.⁵ ¹⁶For where a will is involved, the death of the one who made it must be established. ¹⁷For a will takes effect only at death, since it is not in force as long as the one who made it is alive. ¹⁸Therefore not even the first covenant was inaugurated without blood. ¹⁹For when every commandment of the law had been declared by Moses to all the people, he took the blood of calves and goats, with water and scarlet wool and hyssop, and sprinkled both the book itself and all the people, ²⁰saying, ᵃ"This is the blood of the covenant that God commanded for you." ²¹And in the same way he sprinkled with the blood both the tent and all the vessels used in worship. ²²Indeed, under the law almost everything is purified with blood, and without the shedding of blood there is no forgiveness of sins.

²³Thus it was necessary for the copies of the heavenly things to be purified with

---

¹ Or which is symbolic for the age then present ² Some manuscripts good things to come ³ Or For if the blood of goats and bulls, and the sprinkling of defiled persons with the ashes of a heifer, sanctifies ⁴ Some manuscripts your ⁵ The Greek word means both covenant and will; also verses 16, 17 ᵃ Ex. 24:8

these rites, but the heavenly things themselves with better sacrifices than these. ²⁴For Christ has entered, not into holy places made with hands, which are copies of the true things, but into heaven itself, now to appear in the presence of God on our behalf. ²⁵Nor was it to offer himself repeatedly, as the high priest enters the holy places every year with blood not his own, ²⁶for then he would have had to suffer repeatedly since the foundation of the world. But as it is, he has appeared once for all at the end of the ages to put away sin by the sacrifice of himself. ²⁷And just as it is appointed for man to die once, and after that comes judgment, ²⁸so Christ, having been offered once to bear the sins of many, will appear a second time, not to deal with sin but to save those who are eagerly waiting for him.

10 For since the law has but a shadow of the good things to come instead of the true form of these realities, it can never, by the same sacrifices that are continually offered every year, make perfect those who draw near. ²Otherwise, would they not have ceased to be offered, since the worshipers, having once been cleansed, would no longer have any consciousness of sins? ³But in these sacrifices there is a reminder of sins every year. ⁴For it is impossible for the blood of bulls and goats to take away sins.

⁵Consequently, when Christ¹ came into the world, he said,

ᵃ"Sacrifices and offerings you have not desired,
>   but a body have you prepared for me;
⁶   in burnt offerings and sin offerings
>   you have taken no pleasure.
⁷   Then I said, 'Behold, I have come to do your will, O God,
>   as it is written of me in the scroll of the book.'"

⁸When he said above, "You have neither desired nor taken pleasure in sacrifices and offerings and burnt offerings and sin offerings" (these are offered according to the law), ⁹then he added, "Behold, I have come to do your will." He does away with the first in order to establish the second. ¹⁰And by that will we have been sanctified through the offering of the body of Jesus Christ once for all.

¹¹And every priest stands daily at his service, offering repeatedly the same sacrifices, which can never take away sins. ¹²But when Christ² had offered for all time a single sacrifice for sins, he sat down at the right hand of God, ¹³waiting from that time until his enemies should be made a footstool for his feet. ¹⁴For by a single offering he has perfected for all time those who are being sanctified.

¹⁵And the Holy Spirit also bears witness to us; for after saying,

¹⁶ ᵇ"This is the covenant that I will make with them
>   after those days, declares the Lord:
> I will put my laws on their hearts,
>   and write them on their minds,"

¹⁷then he adds,

ᶜ"I will remember their sins and their lawless deeds no more."

¹⁸Where there is forgiveness of these, there is no longer any offering for sin.

---

¹ Greek *he* ² Greek *this one* ᵃ Ps. 40:6-8 ᵇ Jer. 31:33 ᶜ Jer. 31:34

Exhortation to endure in the faith [10:19–39]. This unit leads scholars to say that Hebrews has affinities to a sermon, though the pastoral intensity of the passage would feel right at home in the NT epistles as well. The opening connective word "therefore" (v. 19) signals the relation between this passage of practical exhortation and the preceding Christological arguments. Reinforcing this are the "since" clauses that lead up to the main appeal (vv. 19, 21). With the weight of preceding arguments about the superiority of Christ and the new covenant as a backdrop, the author now makes a persuasive appeal to his readers to endure in their loyalty to such a Savior and such a covenant. The first movement of the appeal consists of three "let us" commands (vv. 22, 23, 24). This is followed by a paragraph warning the reader not to abandon belief in Christ's sacrifice (vv. 26–31). This negative approach—a dissuasion—leads to a positive persuasion or exhortation to persist even in the face of persecution, with God's eternal reward offered as an incentive to persevere in faith (vv. 32–39).

[19]Therefore, brothers,[1] since we have confidence to enter the holy places by the blood of Jesus, [20]by the new and living way that he opened for us through the curtain, that is, through his flesh, [21]and since we have a great priest over the house of God, [22]let us draw near with a true heart in full assurance of faith, with our hearts sprinkled clean from an evil conscience and our bodies washed with pure water. [23]Let us hold fast the confession of our hope without wavering, for he who promised is faithful. [24]And let us consider how to stir up one another to love and good works, [25]not neglecting to meet together, as is the habit of some, but encouraging one another, and all the more as you see the Day drawing near.

[26]For if we go on sinning deliberately after receiving the knowledge of the truth, there no longer remains a sacrifice for sins, [27]but a fearful expectation of judgment, and a fury of fire that will consume the adversaries. [28]Anyone who has set aside the law of Moses dies without mercy on the evidence of two or three witnesses. [29]How much worse punishment, do you think, will be deserved by the one who has spurned the Son of God, and has profaned the blood of the covenant by which he was sanctified, and has outraged the Spirit of grace? [30]For we know him who said, [a]"Vengeance is mine; I will repay." And again, [b]"The Lord will judge his people." [31]It is a fearful thing to fall into the hands of the living God.

[32]But recall the former days when, after you were enlightened, you endured a hard struggle with sufferings, [33]sometimes being publicly exposed to reproach and affliction, and sometimes being partners with those so treated. [34]For you had compassion on those in prison, and you joyfully accepted the plundering of your property, since you knew that you yourselves had a better possession and an abiding one. [35]Therefore do not throw away your confidence, which has a great reward. [36]For you have need of endurance, so that when you have done the will of God you may receive what is promised. [37]For,

> "Yet a little while,
>   and [c]the coming one will come and will not delay;
> [38]   but my righteous one shall live by faith,
>   and if he shrinks back,
>   my soul has no pleasure in him."

---

[1] Or *brothers and sisters* [a] Deut. 32:35 [b] Deut. 32:36 [c] Hab. 2:3, 4

[39] But we are not of those who shrink back and are destroyed, but of those who have faith and preserve their souls.

An encomium in praise of faith [11:1–12:2]. The famous encomium in praise of faith is the climax of the book of Hebrews and one of the literary high points of the NT. An encomium is a poem or prose piece written in praise of either a character type (for example, the virtuous wife of Prov. 31:10–31) or an abstract quality (such as love in 1 Corinthians 13). This encomium in praise of faith includes the usual motifs: a formal introduction or definition of the quality being praised (11:1); the distinguished ancestry of the subject (11:2); the catalog of praiseworthy acts and attributes of the subject (11:3–40); the command to emulate the subject of praise (12:1–2). Additionally, it is common for the writer of an encomium to praise the superiority of the subject of praise to other things, and we find this motif in the intermittent comparative vocabulary of better (v. 16), more (v. 4), and greater (v. 26). The main rhetorical pattern is a series of eighteen statements beginning with the phrase "By faith." The author marches straight through OT history from the creation forward, ending with the supreme example, Christ (12:2). The author's approach to OT history is to give us a gallery of famous characters, and the list emerges in our imagination as a mini-anthology of hero stories from the OT.

11 Now faith is the assurance of things hoped for, the conviction of things not seen. [2] For by it the people of old received their commendation. [3] By faith we understand that the universe was created by the word of God, so that what is seen was not made out of things that are visible.

[4] By faith Abel offered to God a more acceptable sacrifice than Cain, through which he was commended as righteous, God commending him by accepting his gifts. And through his faith, though he died, he still speaks. [5] By faith Enoch was taken up so that he should not see death, and he was not found, because God had taken him. Now before he was taken he was commended as having pleased God. [6] And without faith it is impossible to please him, for whoever would draw near to God must believe that he exists and that he rewards those who seek him. [7] By faith Noah, being warned by God concerning events as yet unseen, in reverent fear constructed an ark for the saving of his household. By this he condemned the world and became an heir of the righteousness that comes by faith.

[8] By faith Abraham obeyed when he was called to go out to a place that he was to receive as an inheritance. And he went out, not knowing where he was going. [9] By faith he went to live in the land of promise, as in a foreign land, living in tents with Isaac and Jacob, heirs with him of the same promise. [10] For he was looking forward to the city that has foundations, whose designer and builder is God. [11] By faith Sarah herself received power to conceive, even when she was past the age, since she considered him faithful who had promised. [12] Therefore from one man, and him as good as dead, were born descendants as many as the stars of heaven and as many as the innumerable grains of sand by the seashore.

[13] These all died in faith, not having received the things promised, but having seen them and greeted them from afar, and having acknowledged that they were strangers and exiles on the earth. [14] For people who speak thus make it clear that they are seeking a homeland. [15] If they had been thinking of that land from which they had gone out, they would have had opportunity to return. [16] But as it is, they desire a better

country, that is, a heavenly one. Therefore God is not ashamed to be called their God, for he has prepared for them a city.

[17] By faith Abraham, when he was tested, offered up Isaac, and he who had received the promises was in the act of offering up his only son, [18] of whom it was said, [a]"Through Isaac shall your offspring be named." [19] He considered that God was able even to raise him from the dead, from which, figuratively speaking, he did receive him back. [20] By faith Isaac invoked future blessings on Jacob and Esau. [21] By faith Jacob, when dying, blessed each of the sons of Joseph, bowing in worship over the head of his staff. [22] By faith Joseph, at the end of his life, made mention of the exodus of the Israelites and gave directions concerning his bones.

[23] By faith Moses, when he was born, was hidden for three months by his parents, because they saw that the child was beautiful, and they were not afraid of the king's edict. [24] By faith Moses, when he was grown up, refused to be called the son of Pharaoh's daughter, [25] choosing rather to be mistreated with the people of God than to enjoy the fleeting pleasures of sin. [26] He considered the reproach of Christ greater wealth than the treasures of Egypt, for he was looking to the reward. [27] By faith he left Egypt, not being afraid of the anger of the king, for he endured as seeing him who is invisible. [28] By faith he kept the Passover and sprinkled the blood, so that the Destroyer of the firstborn might not touch them.

[29] By faith the people crossed the Red Sea as on dry land, but the Egyptians, when they attempted to do the same, were drowned. [30] By faith the walls of Jericho fell down after they had been encircled for seven days. [31] By faith Rahab the prostitute did not perish with those who were disobedient, because she had given a friendly welcome to the spies.

[32] And what more shall I say? For time would fail me to tell of Gideon, Barak, Samson, Jephthah, of David and Samuel and the prophets— [33] who through faith conquered kingdoms, enforced justice, obtained promises, stopped the mouths of lions, [34] quenched the power of fire, escaped the edge of the sword, were made strong out of weakness, became mighty in war, put foreign armies to flight. [35] Women received back their dead by resurrection. Some were tortured, refusing to accept release, so that they might rise again to a better life. [36] Others suffered mocking and flogging, and even chains and imprisonment. [37] They were stoned, they were sawn in two,[1] they were killed with the sword. They went about in skins of sheep and goats, destitute, afflicted, mistreated— [38] of whom the world was not worthy—wandering about in deserts and mountains, and in dens and caves of the earth.

[39] And all these, though commended through their faith, did not receive what was promised, [40] since God had provided something better for us, that apart from us they should not be made perfect.

12 Therefore, since we are surrounded by so great a cloud of witnesses, let us also lay aside every weight, and sin which clings so closely, and let us run with endurance the race that is set before us, [2] looking to Jesus, the founder and perfecter of our faith, who for the joy that was set before him endured the cross, despising the shame, and is seated at the right hand of the throne of God.

Variations on the theme of endurance [12:3–29]. The writing remains at a high level of intensity and eloquence as the author continues to exhort his readers to persist in

[1] Some manuscripts add *they were tempted* [a] Gen. 21:12

their faith. The specific topics include the following: the benefits of God's discipline in a believer's life (vv. 3–11); commands to encourage fellow Christians (vv. 12–13) and seek peace and holiness (v. 14); exhortation to resist temptations to bitterness (v. 15) and misprizing of spiritual things (vv. 16–17); a lyric passage that describes the glorious kingdom into which believers have been inducted (vv. 18–24); a solemn warning not to reject membership in such a glorious kingdom (vv. 25–29). What breathes through all of these units is the momentousness of the issues about which the author writes. As we read, we are aware that we are dealing with life-and-death issues.

³Consider him who endured from sinners such hostility against himself, so that you may not grow weary or fainthearted. ⁴In your struggle against sin you have not yet resisted to the point of shedding your blood. ⁵And have you forgotten the exhortation that addresses you as sons?

ª"My son, do not regard lightly the discipline of the Lord,
　　nor be weary when reproved by him.
⁶　For the Lord disciplines the one he loves,
　　and chastises every son whom he receives."

⁷It is for discipline that you have to endure. God is treating you as sons. For what son is there whom his father does not discipline? ⁸If you are left without discipline, in which all have participated, then you are illegitimate children and not sons. ⁹Besides this, we have had earthly fathers who disciplined us and we respected them. Shall we not much more be subject to the Father of spirits and live? ¹⁰For they disciplined us for a short time as it seemed best to them, but he disciplines us for our good, that we may share his holiness. ¹¹For the moment all discipline seems painful rather than pleasant, but later it yields the peaceful fruit of righteousness to those who have been trained by it.

¹²Therefore lift your drooping hands and strengthen your weak knees, ¹³and make straight paths for your feet, so that what is lame may not be put out of joint but rather be healed. ¹⁴Strive for peace with everyone, and for the holiness without which no one will see the Lord. ¹⁵See to it that no one fails to obtain the grace of God; that no one "root of bitterness" springs up and causes trouble, and by it many become defiled; ¹⁶that no one is sexually immoral or unholy like Esau, who sold his birthright for a single meal. ¹⁷For you know that afterward, when he desired to inherit the blessing, he was rejected, for he found no chance to repent, though he sought it with tears.

¹⁸For you have not come to what may be touched, a blazing fire and darkness and gloom and a tempest ¹⁹and the sound of a trumpet and a voice whose words made the hearers beg that no further messages be spoken to them. ²⁰For they could not endure the order that was given, ᵇ"If even a beast touches the mountain, it shall be stoned." ²¹Indeed, so terrifying was the sight that Moses said, "I tremble with fear." ²²But you have come to Mount Zion and to the city of the living God, the heavenly Jerusalem, and to innumerable angels in festal gathering, ²³and to the assembly¹ of the firstborn who are enrolled in heaven, and to God, the judge of all, and to the spirits of the righteous made perfect, ²⁴and to Jesus, the mediator of a new covenant, and to the sprinkled blood that speaks a better word than the blood of Abel.

²⁵See that you do not refuse him who is speaking. For if they did not escape when

¹ Or church ª Prov. 3:11, 12 ᵇ Ex. 19:12, 13

they refused him who warned them on earth, much less will we escape if we reject him who warns from heaven. [26]At that time his voice shook the earth, but now he has promised, [a]"Yet once more I will shake not only the earth but also the heavens." [27]This phrase, "Yet once more," indicates the removal of things that are shaken—that is, things that have been made—in order that the things that cannot be shaken may remain. [28]Therefore let us be grateful for receiving a kingdom that cannot be shaken, and thus let us offer to God acceptable worship, with reverence and awe, [29]for our God is a consuming fire.

> **Rules for Christian living** [13:1–19]. Chapters 10 (vv. 19–39) and 12 have contained lists of commands such as are part of every NT epistle, but as we begin chapter 13 it is obvious that we have entered upon a full-fledged *paraenesis*—a list of commands covering many aspects of the Christian life. There is little topical unity other than the general idea of God's prescriptions for living the life of faith.

13 Let brotherly love continue. [2]Do not neglect to show hospitality to strangers, for thereby some have entertained angels unawares. [3]Remember those who are in prison, as though in prison with them, and those who are mistreated, since you also are in the body. [4]Let marriage be held in honor among all, and let the marriage bed be undefiled, for God will judge the sexually immoral and adulterous. [5]Keep your life free from love of money, and be content with what you have, for he has said, [b]"I will never leave you nor forsake you." [6]So we can confidently say,

[c]"The Lord is my helper;
  I will not fear;
  what can man do to me?"

[7]Remember your leaders, those who spoke to you the word of God. Consider the outcome of their way of life, and imitate their faith. [8]Jesus Christ is the same yesterday and today and forever. [9]Do not be led away by diverse and strange teachings, for it is good for the heart to be strengthened by grace, not by foods, which have not benefited those devoted to them. [10]We have an altar from which those who serve the tent have no right to eat. [11]For the bodies of those animals whose blood is brought into the holy places by the high priest as a sacrifice for sin are burned outside the camp. [12]So Jesus also suffered outside the gate in order to sanctify the people through his own blood. [13]Therefore let us go to him outside the camp and bear the reproach he endured. [14]For here we have no lasting city, but we seek the city that is to come. [15]Through him then let us continually offer up a sacrifice of praise to God, that is, the fruit of lips that acknowledge his name. [16]Do not neglect to do good and to share what you have, for such sacrifices are pleasing to God.

[17]Obey your leaders and submit to them, for they are keeping watch over your souls, as those who will have to give an account. Let them do this with joy and not with groaning, for that would be of no advantage to you.

[18]Pray for us, for we are sure that we have a clear conscience, desiring to act honorably in all things. [19]I urge you the more earnestly to do this in order that I may be restored to you the sooner.

[a] Hag. 2:6 [b] Josh. 1:5 [c] Ps. 118:6

Epistolary closing [13:20–25]. The author ends with an exalted benediction (vv. 20–21); an appeal to the reader to heed the message of the letter (v. 22); a personal reference to Timothy (v. 23); greetings (v. 24); and a brief *benediction (v. 25).

²⁰Now may the God of peace who brought again from the dead our Lord Jesus, the great shepherd of the sheep, by the blood of the eternal covenant, ²¹equip you with everything good that you may do his will, working in us¹ that which is pleasing in his sight, through Jesus Christ, to whom be glory forever and ever. Amen.

²²I appeal to you, brothers,² bear with my word of exhortation, for I have written to you briefly. ²³You should know that our brother Timothy has been released, with whom I shall see you if he comes soon. ²⁴Greet all your leaders and all the saints. Those who come from Italy send you greetings. ²⁵Grace be with all of you.

¹ Some manuscripts *you* ² Or *brothers and sisters*

THE LETTER OF

JAMES

The book at a glance. 5 chapters, 108 verses. The book of James is the NT "book of Proverbs." It is the only NT book that falls into the form known as *wisdom literature. It is arranged mainly into small units but contains some larger proverb clusters on a common theme. The books of Ecclesiastes and Proverbs provide the most helpful model for what we should expect in the book of James. The author's goal is to instill right thinking and correct behavior. His stance is practical, and a suitable subtitle for the book would be "Faith That Works." The author's directives are so convicting that his letter has something in it somewhere that will offend pretty much everyone. Even though the book begins with an epistolary salutation, the rest of the book does not have the format of an *epistle but rather that of a collection of wisdom sayings. The book of James is not a theological treatise in which the author pursues a single thesis or continuous line of thought.

■ **Genres.** The general genre is *wisdom literature as we know it from the OT. The specific format of that wisdom literature is the collection of *proverbs. This means that we continuously need to apply the usual rules for interpreting individual proverbs (see glossary). Additionally, the book of James belongs to an ancient Greek form of *satire known as the *diatribe, whose traits include the following: imaginary dialogues, including question-and-answer constructions; *apostrophe (direct address to absent people or things as though they are present and can hear); *metaphors taken from nature and everyday life; allusions to famous people from the past (stock instances, or well-known representations of the qualities that are under discussion); harsh addresses to readers; heightened contrasts. As for the customary label epistle, the only obvious epistolary feature is the opening salutation, though repeated direct address to the audience (whom the author calls "brothers") is a feature of letter writing as well as addresses and sermons. (For more information on items accompanied by an asterisk, see the glossary at the back of this Bible.)

■ **Distinguishing features.** The most pervasive technique in the book of James is the proverb or *aphorism, in the mode of ancient wisdom teachers. Next in frequency is the rhetorical device of direct command, expressed in the imperative mood of the verb (for example, "be doers of the word, and not hearers only" [1:22]). In fact, there are more than 50 imperatives in 108 verses. This abundance of commands is a signal that the writer has a practical bent and is interested in action rather than mere belief as the distinguishing characteristic of Christians. We also find a strongly persuasive stance as the author seeks to move his readers to action. The focus tends to be moral and ethical

Passage	Content	Format
1:1	Salutation	Single-verse unit
1:2–27	Proverbial wisdom on testing, asking for wisdom, riches, words, active faith, true religion	Short paragraphs of proverbs on a range of diverse subjects
2:1–13	Stern denunciation of showing favoritism	
2:14–26	The need to validate one's Christian faith by action	Four mini-essays in proverb form (longer units)
3:1–12	The need to control one's speech	
3:13–18	A definition of true wisdom	
4:1–10	Aphoristic commands on diverse subjects	A list of proverbs
4:11–12	Prohibition of slander	
4:13–17	Warning against presumption on God's providence	Paragraph-length proverb clusters (longer units)
5:1–6	Warning against trusting in riches	
5:7–12	The need for patience when suffering	
5:13–20	Two practices in the church—praying in faith for the ill and restoring a sinner	Items for a church manual

rather than abstractly theological. The tone is continuously energetic, and satire is never far from the surface, sometimes couched in a somewhat scolding manner.

▌**Unity.** There is no structural unity in the sense of a single line of argument. To attempt to relate one brief unit of proverbs to the next one as though James had a continuous line of thought would produce only fanciful connections. We therefore need to look for other types of unity. The book as a whole is unified by the format of the anthology of proverbs. The rhetorical features noted above—proverbial discourse, the rhetoric of command, the energy of the discourse, the satiric impulse to expose Christians' failings—are so continuously present as to constitute a unifying element. Finally, if we take 2:26 as the theme verse ("faith apart from works is dead"), the book itself, with its abundance of observations and commands, is a catalog of the works that faith should produce.

▌**Inferred literary intentions.** The book is designed to achieve the following literary purposes:

- rouse readers from their moral and spiritual lethargy

- move readers to demonstrate their faith by their actions

- raise our consciousness about the need to behave correctly in many areas of life

- win our assent through aphoristic flair

- make us discontent with our level of spiritual attainment and prompt us to undertake a holy reformation of our life

- fire our literary response with a host of literary techniques

▌Theological themes. (1) Ethics: the book of James is a primer on how to conduct our lives in a moral way and reverse our immoral practices. (2) Sanctification: the book is equally a handbook on becoming holy as God conceives of holiness. (3) Faith and works: along with the book of Romans (to which James stands as a complement and balance), the book of James discusses the roles of faith and works in a Christian's life.

▌The book of James as a chapter in the master story of the Bible. The Bible tells us how to live as God wants us to live. The book of James, with its myriad commands and vignettes of Christian living, is a highly condensed and major "chapter" in the story of how God demands that people live. Further, the Bible is addressed primarily to people who follow God, and the book of James covers areas of behavior where religious people often fail, such as not controlling the tongue, not caring for the lowly, and embracing a religion of the mind rather than moral obligation.

A mini-anthology of proverbs [chapter 1]. Following the epistolary salutation (v. 1), the opening chapter consists of a collection of proverbs on a wide range of subjects. The format does not have the logical flow of an essay, with a continuous line of argument. Here is an accurate (but not the only possible) way of dividing the material: the benefits of testing in a believer's life (vv. 2–4); how to ask God for wisdom and how not to do so (vv. 5–8); the fleetingness of earthly life and riches (vv. 9–11); the blessing of enduring trial, along with the inappropriateness of blaming God for temptations that are actually self-generated (vv. 12–15); God as the source of all good gifts (vv. 16–18); the evil of anger (vv. 19–20); the need to put away evil and to embrace God's word (v. 21); commands to be a doer of the word and not just a hearer of it (vv. 22–25); tests of true religion (vv. 26–27). To appropriate the wisdom of the chapter, we need to apply the usual rules for reading and interpreting proverbs, such as identifying the general principle involved, applying that principle to our own experiences and observations, and paying attention to a stated or implied virtue that is commanded and vice that is prohibited by a given proverb.

1 James, a servant[1] of God and of the Lord Jesus Christ,
To the twelve tribes in the Dispersion:
Greetings.
[2] Count it all joy, my brothers,[2] when you meet trials of various kinds, [3] for you know that the testing of your faith produces steadfastness. [4] And let steadfastness have its full effect, that you may be perfect and complete, lacking in nothing.
[5] If any of you lacks wisdom, let him ask God, who gives generously to all without reproach, and it will be given him. [6] But let him ask in faith, with no doubting, for the one who doubts is like a wave of the sea that is driven and tossed by the wind. [7] For that person must not suppose that he will receive anything from the Lord; [8] he is a double-minded man, unstable in all his ways.
[9] Let the lowly brother boast in his exaltation, [10] and the rich in his humiliation, because like a flower of the grass[3] he will pass away. [11] For the sun rises with its scorching heat and withers the grass; its flower falls, and its beauty perishes. So also will the rich man fade away in the midst of his pursuits.

[1] Or slave; Greek bondservant [2] Or brothers and sisters. The plural Greek word adelphoi (translated "brothers") refers to siblings in a family. In New Testament usage, depending on the context, adelphoi may refer either to men or to both men and women who are siblings (brothers and sisters) in God's family, the church; also verses 16, 19 [3] Or a wild flower

¹²Blessed is the man who remains steadfast under trial, for when he has stood the test he will receive the crown of life, which God has promised to those who love him. ¹³Let no one say when he is tempted, "I am being tempted by God," for God cannot be tempted with evil, and he himself tempts no one. ¹⁴But each person is tempted when he is lured and enticed by his own desire. ¹⁵Then desire when it has conceived gives birth to sin, and sin when it is fully grown brings forth death.

¹⁶Do not be deceived, my beloved brothers. ¹⁷Every good gift and every perfect gift is from above, coming down from the Father of lights with whom there is no variation or shadow due to change.¹ ¹⁸Of his own will he brought us forth by the word of truth, that we should be a kind of firstfruits of his creatures.

¹⁹Know this, my beloved brothers: let every person be quick to hear, slow to speak, slow to anger; ²⁰for the anger of man does not produce the righteousness of God. ²¹Therefore put away all filthiness and rampant wickedness and receive with meekness the implanted word, which is able to save your souls.

²²But be doers of the word, and not hearers only, deceiving yourselves. ²³For if anyone is a hearer of the word and not a doer, he is like a man who looks intently at his natural face in a mirror. ²⁴For he looks at himself and goes away and at once forgets what he was like. ²⁵But the one who looks into the perfect law, the law of liberty, and perseveres, being no hearer who forgets but a doer who acts, he will be blessed in his doing.

²⁶If anyone thinks he is religious and does not bridle his tongue but deceives his heart, this person's religion is worthless. ²⁷Religion that is pure and undefiled before God, the Father, is this: to visit orphans and widows in their affliction, and to keep oneself unstained from the world.

On not showing favoritism [2:1–13]. This unit is the first of four comparatively longer units in the book of James. The subject is the importance of not showing favoritism to categories of people that a given culture regards as impressive (vv. 1–9). For James, clothing as a sign of wealth was a trigger for such favoritism, so this is the example that he adduces. However, the passage is not only about wealth or clothing but about showing favoritism to any group of people while discriminating against other groups. To follow up, James asserts that failing to keep even one command of God's law, such as by the seemingly minor offense of showing favoritism, condemns a person in God's sight (vv. 10–13).

2 My brothers,² show no partiality as you hold the faith in our Lord Jesus Christ, the Lord of glory. ²For if a man wearing a gold ring and fine clothing comes into your assembly, and a poor man in shabby clothing also comes in, ³and if you pay attention to the one who wears the fine clothing and say, "You sit here in a good place," while you say to the poor man, "You stand over there," or, "Sit down at my feet," ⁴have you not then made distinctions among yourselves and become judges with evil thoughts? ⁵Listen, my beloved brothers, has not God chosen those who are poor in the world to be rich in faith and heirs of the kingdom, which he has promised to those who love him? ⁶But you have dishonored the poor man. Are not the rich the ones who oppress you, and the ones who drag you into court? ⁷Are they not the ones who blaspheme the honorable name by which you were called?

¹ Some manuscripts *variation due to a shadow of turning* ² Or *brothers and sisters*; also verses 5, 14

⁸If you really fulfill the royal law according to the Scripture, ᵃ"You shall love your neighbor as yourself," you are doing well. ⁹But if you show partiality, you are committing sin and are convicted by the law as transgressors. ¹⁰For whoever keeps the whole law but fails in one point has become accountable for all of it. ¹¹For he who said, ᵇ"Do not commit adultery," also said, ᶜ"Do not murder." If you do not commit adultery but do murder, you have become a transgressor of the law. ¹²So speak and so act as those who are to be judged under the law of liberty. ¹³For judgment is without mercy to one who has shown no mercy. Mercy triumphs over judgment.

The need to demonstrate faith by action [2:14–26]. The second mini-essay is a classic NT passage on the perennial subject of faith versus works. The passage is arranged as James's half of a debate on that subject. The author's proposition is stated five times (vv. 14, 17, 22, 24, 26). Interspersed between these statements we find proof in the form of supporting examples (vv. 15–16, 21, 23, 25) and also refutation of an imaginary opponent (vv. 18–20). James's handling of the relationship between faith and works does not contradict Paul's statements on the same subject. Paul's statements answer the question of what it takes to justify a sinner before God, and the answer is "faith alone." James asks the very different question of what proves or justifies the genuineness of a Christian's faith, and the answer to that question is "works."

¹⁴What good is it, my brothers, if someone says he has faith but does not have works? Can that faith save him? ¹⁵If a brother or sister is poorly clothed and lacking in daily food, ¹⁶and one of you says to them, "Go in peace, be warmed and filled," without giving them the things needed for the body, what good¹ is that? ¹⁷So also faith by itself, if it does not have works, is dead.

¹⁸But someone will say, "You have faith and I have works." Show me your faith apart from your works, and I will show you my faith by my works. ¹⁹You believe that God is one; you do well. Even the demons believe—and shudder! ²⁰Do you want to be shown, you foolish person, that faith apart from works is useless? ²¹Was not Abraham our father justified by works when he offered up his son Isaac on the altar? ²²You see that faith was active along with his works, and faith was completed by his works; ²³and the Scripture was fulfilled that says, ᵈ"Abraham believed God, and it was counted to him as righteousness"—and he was called a friend of God. ²⁴You see that a person is justified by works and not by faith alone. ²⁵And in the same way was not also Rahab the prostitute justified by works when she received the messengers and sent them out by another way? ²⁶For as the body apart from the spirit is dead, so also faith apart from works is dead.

The need to control one's speech [3:1–12]. The third mini-essay in proverb form takes up the subject of how we use language. The main thesis is that the tongue (meaning human speech) is difficult to control and therefore a source of great destructiveness among people—one of the most dangerous parts of the body. The passage uses the familiar wisdom-literature technique of drawing analogies from nature to portray human experience (vv. 3–8) and also the device of listing *rhetorical questions that state analogies to the actual subject of the discourse, which is named last in the series (vv. 11–12). The mini-essay covers three topics: the power of the tongue (vv. 1–5a), the

¹ Or benefit ᵃLev. 19:18 ᵇEx. 20:14 ᶜEx. 20:13 ᵈGen. 15:6

destructive and untamable nature of the tongue (vv. 5b–8), and the perverseness of the
tongue in uttering both good and evil (vv. 9–12).

3 Not many of you should become teachers, my brothers, for you know that we
who teach will be judged with greater strictness. ²For we all stumble in many
ways. And if anyone does not stumble in what he says, he is a perfect man, able also
to bridle his whole body. ³If we put bits into the mouths of horses so that they obey
us, we guide their whole bodies as well. ⁴Look at the ships also: though they are so
large and are driven by strong winds, they are guided by a very small rudder wherever the will of the pilot directs. ⁵So also the tongue is a small member, yet it boasts of
great things.

How great a forest is set ablaze by such a small fire! ⁶And the tongue is a fire, a
world of unrighteousness. The tongue is set among our members, staining the whole
body, setting on fire the entire course of life,¹ and set on fire by hell.² ⁷For every kind
of beast and bird, of reptile and sea creature, can be tamed and has been tamed by
mankind, ⁸but no human being can tame the tongue. It is a restless evil, full of deadly
poison. ⁹With it we bless our Lord and Father, and with it we curse people who are
made in the likeness of God. ¹⁰From the same mouth come blessing and cursing. My
brothers,³ these things ought not to be so. ¹¹Does a spring pour forth from the same
opening both fresh and salt water? ¹²Can a fig tree, my brothers, bear olives, or a
grapevine produce figs? Neither can a salt pond yield fresh water.

A definition of true wisdom [3:13–18]. This unit lists the qualities of true wisdom and
sets it over against its opposite. The main rhetorical form is thus definition by description and by *foil or contrast, and a good way to assimilate the passage is to work out the
system of contrasts that James puts before us.

¹³Who is wise and understanding among you? By his good conduct let him show
his works in the meekness of wisdom. ¹⁴But if you have bitter jealousy and selfish
ambition in your hearts, do not boast and be false to the truth. ¹⁵This is not the wisdom that comes down from above, but is earthly, unspiritual, demonic. ¹⁶For where
jealousy and selfish ambition exist, there will be disorder and every vile practice.
¹⁷But the wisdom from above is first pure, then peaceable, gentle, open to reason, full
of mercy and good fruits, impartial and sincere. ¹⁸And a harvest of righteousness is
sown in peace by those who make peace.

Collection of individual proverbs [4:1–10]. Although this unit is printed as two prose
paragraphs, it is really a list of individual proverbs. In fact, if each verse were printed
separately, the material would be right at home in the OT book of Proverbs, with its format of one-verse or two-verse proverbs. We can explore the passage looking for underlying principles such as the following: the attitudes that God loves and abhors in people;
how to please God; the dangers of self-assertion and selfish behavior; ways of behaving
that we should avoid because they are sinful; the need for Christians to serve God rather
than the world.

¹ Or *wheel of birth* ² Greek *Gehenna* ³ Or *brothers and sisters*; also verse 12

4 What causes quarrels and what causes fights among you? Is it not this, that your passions[1] are at war within you?[2] [2]You desire and do not have, so you murder. You covet and cannot obtain, so you fight and quarrel. You do not have, because you do not ask. [3]You ask and do not receive, because you ask wrongly, to spend it on your passions. [4]You adulterous people![3] Do you not know that friendship with the world is enmity with God? Therefore whoever wishes to be a friend of the world makes himself an enemy of God. [5]Or do you suppose it is to no purpose that the Scripture says, "He yearns jealously over the spirit that he has made to dwell in us"? [6]But he gives more grace. Therefore it says, [a]"God opposes the proud, but gives grace to the humble." [7]Submit yourselves therefore to God. Resist the devil, and he will flee from you. [8]Draw near to God, and he will draw near to you. Cleanse your hands, you sinners, and purify your hearts, you double-minded. [9]Be wretched and mourn and weep. Let your laughter be turned to mourning and your joy to gloom. [10]Humble yourselves before the Lord, and he will exalt you.

Four proverb clusters [4:11–5:12]. Following the individual proverbs of the preceding unit, we now get proverb clusters on four subjects, as follows: slander (4:11–12); presumption on God's providence (4:13–17); warnings against the negatives of a wealthy lifestyle and affluent mindset (5:1–6); patience in suffering, with a one-verse addendum on avoiding oaths (5:7–12).

[11]Do not speak evil against one another, brothers.[4] The one who speaks against a brother or judges his brother, speaks evil against the law and judges the law. But if you judge the law, you are not a doer of the law but a judge. [12]There is only one lawgiver and judge, he who is able to save and to destroy. But who are you to judge your neighbor?

[13]Come now, you who say, "Today or tomorrow we will go into such and such a town and spend a year there and trade and make a profit"— [14]yet you do not know what tomorrow will bring. What is your life? For you are a mist that appears for a little time and then vanishes. [15]Instead you ought to say, "If the Lord wills, we will live and do this or that." [16]As it is, you boast in your arrogance. All such boasting is evil. [17]So whoever knows the right thing to do and fails to do it, for him it is sin.

5 Come now, you rich, weep and howl for the miseries that are coming upon you. [2]Your riches have rotted and your garments are moth-eaten. [3]Your gold and silver have corroded, and their corrosion will be evidence against you and will eat your flesh like fire. You have laid up treasure in the last days. [4]Behold, the wages of the laborers who mowed your fields, which you kept back by fraud, are crying out against you, and the cries of the harvesters have reached the ears of the Lord of hosts. [5]You have lived on the earth in luxury and in self-indulgence. You have fattened your hearts in a day of slaughter. [6]You have condemned and murdered the righteous person. He does not resist you.

[7]Be patient, therefore, brothers,[5] until the coming of the Lord. See how the farmer waits for the precious fruit of the earth, being patient about it, until it receives the early and the late rains. [8]You also, be patient. Establish your hearts, for the coming of the Lord is at hand. [9]Do not grumble against one another, brothers, so that you may

[1] Greek *pleasures*; also verse 3 [2] Greek *in your members* [3] Greek *You adulteresses!* [4] Or *brothers and sisters* [5] Or *brothers and sisters*; also verses 9, 10, 12, 19
[a] Prov. 3:34

not be judged; behold, the Judge is standing at the door. ¹⁰As an example of suffering and patience, brothers, take the prophets who spoke in the name of the Lord. ¹¹Behold, we consider those blessed who remained steadfast. You have heard of the steadfastness of Job, and you have seen the purpose of the Lord, how the Lord is compassionate and merciful.

¹²But above all, my brothers, do not swear, either by heaven or by earth or by any other oath, but let your "yes" be yes and your "no" be no, so that you may not fall under condemnation.

Two practices in the church [5:13–20]. While not abandoning the use of aphorisms, James concludes with two passages of instruction that resemble instructional sections in other NT epistles. The first passage outlines the church practice of the prayer of faith for those undergoing illness (vv. 13–18). The other unit concerns restoring a fellow believer who has sinned (vv. 19–20).

¹³Is anyone among you suffering? Let him pray. Is anyone cheerful? Let him sing praise. ¹⁴Is anyone among you sick? Let him call for the elders of the church, and let them pray over him, anointing him with oil in the name of the Lord. ¹⁵And the prayer of faith will save the one who is sick, and the Lord will raise him up. And if he has committed sins, he will be forgiven. ¹⁶Therefore, confess your sins to one another and pray for one another, that you may be healed. The prayer of a righteous person has great power as it is working.[1] ¹⁷Elijah was a man with a nature like ours, and he prayed fervently that it might not rain, and for three years and six months it did not rain on the earth. ¹⁸Then he prayed again, and heaven gave rain, and the earth bore its fruit.

¹⁹My brothers, if anyone among you wanders from the truth and someone brings him back, ²⁰let him know that whoever brings back a sinner from his wandering will save his soul from death and will cover a multitude of sins.

---

[1] Or *The effective prayer of a righteous person has great power*

1 PETER

The book at a glance. 5 chapters, 105 verses. First Peter is written to Christians living in alien territory, as a beleaguered minority in the culture. The controlling *metaphor by which we can best assimilate the book is the exile *motif. Given the difficulties of an exilic existence, it is small wonder that in its later stages the letter becomes a small classic on the subject of suffering for Christ's sake. Yet the letter begins with one of the most exuberant *lyric passages of celebration of the riches that believers have in Christ that we find anywhere in the NT. Between these bookends of exhilaration and suffering, the letter has the same abundance of instructions for living the Christian life that we find in other NT *epistles. The structure of the letter is informal and miscellaneous, but four good questions to ask as we work our way through the book are these: (1) What spiritual possessions do Christians living in exile have in Christ? (2) What duties accompany such great privileges? (3) What is it about our new nature that enables Christians in exile to perform these duties? (4) What advice does the book give to exiles as they endure suffering for the sake of Christ?

▌Genre and format. First Peter follows the usual contours of the NT epistles. Along with the usual ingredients of salutation-thanksgiving-body-*paraenesis*-closing, we find a pattern of back-and-forth movement between theological assertions and either practical application or lyric celebration. The book moves in a fluid manner between the poles of the riches that believers have in Christ and the duties they need to shoulder, within the implied situation of their living in a hostile surrounding culture.

▌Style and rhetoric. First Peter is exuberant in tone and exalted in language. In virtually every paragraph we find vivid *imagery and a skillful use of figurative language. The tone of the book is urgent and intense, as signaled by the presence of more than thirty imperative verbs (or an average of one command in every three verses). The content and style are thus elevated and elevating.

▌Inferred literary intentions. The book is designed to achieve the following literary purposes:

- embody the content that the author aims to communicate in the conventional categories of the NT epistle

- infuse a spirit of exaltation in readers as they contemplate their riches in Christ

- leave believers with a sense of obligation to obey the commands of God

Passage	Content	Conventional Epistolary Motif
1:1–2	Sender, recipients, "grace and peace" prayer	Salutation
1:3–12	Lyric celebration of the Christian's living hope	Lyric celebration (a version of the conventional thanksgiving)
1:13–2:3	Exhortation to live a holy life	*Paraenesis*
2:4–10	The believer's identity in Christ	Description
2:11–3:12	Duties of Christians, especially to others	*Paraenesis*
3:13–4:19	Treatise on suffering	Instruction, with an interpolated *paraenesis*
5:1–5	Instructions regarding elders	Instruction
5:6–11	Commands for living the Christian life	*Paraenesis*
5:12–14	Naming of amanuensis and/or bearer of the letter; greetings; benediction	Closing

- make readers receptive through stylistic excellence

- present a balanced picture between the blessings of the Christian life and the difficulties that Christians face in the world

- appeal to our imagination (our image-making and image-perceiving capacity) with a continuous thread of vivid images and metaphors

▌**Theological themes.** (1) Christology: the name of Christ appears twenty-one times in the book, which elaborates the complementary themes of what believers possess in Christ and how they are to live on the basis of that possession. (2) New life in Christ: Peter is rapturous about the ways in which believers in Christ possess the privileges of being in Christ. (3) The ethics of kingdom living: the book is filled with commands that outline the duties that attend the Christian life. (4) Suffering: the book predicts suffering as the lot of Christians and accompanies that premise with directives regarding how to live with suffering, along with a reminder that Christ himself is the supreme example of suffering.

▌**1 Peter as a chapter in the master story of the Bible.** The story of redemption in the Bible finds its culmination in the atoning death and resurrection of Jesus. First Peter takes up the subject of how Christians should live in the world on the basis of their new life in Christ. Christ is offered as the example of the pattern of suffering leading to glory—the cross before the crown.

> **Epistolary opening [1:1–12].** Following the conventional salutation of sender, recipients, and "grace and peace" prayer, the writer launches into a lyric equivalent of what is usually a section of thanksgiving in NT epistles. Writing in a flowing syntax and elevated vocabulary, Peter uses the rhetorical form of a blessing to rehearse with ecstatic feeling the riches that believers possess in Christ on the basis of his sufferings and death (vv. 3–9). Having thus rehearsed the riches of grace, Peter branches out into the related thought that the OT prophets who prophesied of this grace in Christ were serving not

themselves but NT believers, who have the fuller revelation of what Christ has accomplished (vv. 10–12).

1

Peter, an apostle of Jesus Christ,

To those who are elect exiles of the dispersion in Pontus, Galatia, Cappadocia, Asia, and Bithynia, ²according to the foreknowledge of God the Father, in the sanctification of the Spirit, for obedience to Jesus Christ and for sprinkling with his blood:

May grace and peace be multiplied to you.

³Blessed be the God and Father of our Lord Jesus Christ! According to his great mercy, he has caused us to be born again to a living hope through the resurrection of Jesus Christ from the dead, ⁴to an inheritance that is imperishable, undefiled, and unfading, kept in heaven for you, ⁵who by God's power are being guarded through faith for a salvation ready to be revealed in the last time. ⁶In this you rejoice, though now for a little while, if necessary, you have been grieved by various trials, ⁷so that the tested genuineness of your faith—more precious than gold that perishes though it is tested by fire—may be found to result in praise and glory and honor at the revelation of Jesus Christ. ⁸Though you have not seen him, you love him. Though you do not now see him, you believe in him and rejoice with joy that is inexpressible and filled with glory, ⁹obtaining the outcome of your faith, the salvation of your souls.

¹⁰Concerning this salvation, the prophets who prophesied about the grace that was to be yours searched and inquired carefully, ¹¹inquiring what person or time the Spirit of Christ in them was indicating when he predicted the sufferings of Christ and the subsequent glories. ¹²It was revealed to them that they were serving not themselves but you, in the things that have now been announced to you through those who preached the good news to you by the Holy Spirit sent from heaven, things into which angels long to look.

Exhortation to live a holy life [1:13–2:3]. The word "therefore" at the beginning of the next unit signals the author's intention to base his ensuing remarks on the foundation of his assertions about the believer's privileged blessings in Christ. Adhering to a common epistolary pattern of following doctrinal instruction with a section of practical application, Peter in this unit exhorts his readers to godly living. We can assimilate the passage by noting the specific moral and spiritual actions that Peter regards as constituting a life of loyalty to Christ.

¹³Therefore, preparing your minds for action,¹ and being sober-minded, set your hope fully on the grace that will be brought to you at the revelation of Jesus Christ. ¹⁴As obedient children, do not be conformed to the passions of your former ignorance, ¹⁵but as he who called you is holy, you also be holy in all your conduct, ¹⁶since it is written, ᵃ"You shall be holy, for I am holy." ¹⁷And if you call on him as Father who judges impartially according to each one's deeds, conduct yourselves with fear throughout the time of your exile, ¹⁸knowing that you were ransomed from the futile ways inherited from your forefathers, not with perishable things such as silver or gold, ¹⁹but with the precious blood of Christ, like that of a lamb without blemish or spot. ²⁰He was foreknown before the foundation of the world but was made manifest

---

¹ Greek *girding up the loins of your mind* ᵃ Lev. 11:44

in the last times for the sake of you [21]who through him are believers in God, who raised him from the dead and gave him glory, so that your faith and hope are in God.

[22]Having purified your souls by your obedience to the truth for a sincere brotherly love, love one another earnestly from a pure heart, [23]since you have been born again, not of perishable seed but of imperishable, through the living and abiding word of God; [24]for

[a]"All flesh is like grass
    and all its glory like the flower of grass.
The grass withers,
    and the flower falls,
[25] but the word of the Lord remains forever."

And this word is the good news that was preached to you.

2 So put away all malice and all deceit and hypocrisy and envy and all slander. [2]Like newborn infants, long for the pure spiritual milk, that by it you may grow up into salvation— [3]if indeed you have tasted that the Lord is good.

The believer's identity in Christ [2:4–10]. Peter next returns to the mode of the opening of the letter, as he reminds his readers of who they are as believers in Christ. Again the sentiment and vocabulary are elevating, as in the lists that begin (vv. 4–5) and end (vv. 9–10) the passage. The passage is famous for its list of metaphors used to identify the church.

[4]As you come to him, a living stone rejected by men but in the sight of God chosen and precious, [5]you yourselves like living stones are being built up as a spiritual house, to be a holy priesthood, to offer spiritual sacrifices acceptable to God through Jesus Christ. [6]For it stands in Scripture:

[b]"Behold, I am laying in Zion a stone,
    a cornerstone chosen and precious,
and whoever believes in him will not be put to shame."

[7]So the honor is for you who believe, but for those who do not believe,

[c]"The stone that the builders rejected
    has become the cornerstone,"[1]

[8]and

[d]"A stone of stumbling,
    and a rock of offense."

They stumble because they disobey the word, as they were destined to do.

[9]But you are a chosen race, a royal priesthood, a holy nation, a people for his own possession, that you may proclaim the excellencies of him who called you out of darkness into his marvelous light. [10]Once you were not a people, but now you are God's people; once you had not received mercy, but now you have received mercy.

[1] Greek *the head of the corner* [a] Isa. 40:6, 8 [b] Isa. 28:16 [c] Ps. 118:22 [d] Isa. 8:14

Duties of Christians, especially to others [2:11–3:12]. In the back-and-forth rhythm of this letter, Peter next returns to a list of commands (the familiar *paraenesis* of NT epistles). These commands chiefly state how we must relate to others, as follows: how to behave toward the surrounding unbelieving culture (2:11–12); how to behave toward the state, in light of one's simultaneous loyalty to God (2:13–17); servants' submission to masters (2:18–20), with an addendum on suffering as a Christian calling (2:21–25); relations of wives toward husbands (3:1–6) and husbands toward wives (3:7); relations toward fellow believers (3:8–12).

[11] Beloved, I urge you as sojourners and exiles to abstain from the passions of the flesh, which wage war against your soul. [12] Keep your conduct among the Gentiles honorable, so that when they speak against you as evildoers, they may see your good deeds and glorify God on the day of visitation.

[13] Be subject for the Lord's sake to every human institution,[1] whether it be to the emperor[2] as supreme, [14] or to governors as sent by him to punish those who do evil and to praise those who do good. [15] For this is the will of God, that by doing good you should put to silence the ignorance of foolish people. [16] Live as people who are free, not using your freedom as a cover-up for evil, but living as servants[3] of God. [17] Honor everyone. Love the brotherhood. Fear God. Honor the emperor.

[18] Servants, be subject to your masters with all respect, not only to the good and gentle but also to the unjust. [19] For this is a gracious thing, when, mindful of God, one endures sorrows while suffering unjustly. [20] For what credit is it if, when you sin and are beaten for it, you endure? But if when you do good and suffer for it you endure, this is a gracious thing in the sight of God. [21] For to this you have been called, because Christ also suffered for you, leaving you an example, so that you might follow in his steps. [22] He committed no sin, neither was deceit found in his mouth. [23] When he was reviled, he did not revile in return; when he suffered, he did not threaten, but continued entrusting himself to him who judges justly. [24] He himself bore our sins in his body on the tree, that we might die to sin and live to righteousness. By his wounds you have been healed. [25] For you were straying like sheep, but have now returned to the Shepherd and Overseer of your souls.

3 Likewise, wives, be subject to your own husbands, so that even if some do not obey the word, they may be won without a word by the conduct of their wives, [2] when they see your respectful and pure conduct. [3] Do not let your adorning be external—the braiding of hair and the putting on of gold jewelry, or the clothing you wear— [4] but let your adorning be the hidden person of the heart with the imperishable beauty of a gentle and quiet spirit, which in God's sight is very precious. [5] For this is how the holy women who hoped in God used to adorn themselves, by submitting to their own husbands, [6] as Sarah obeyed Abraham, calling him lord. And you are her children, if you do good and do not fear anything that is frightening.

[7] Likewise, husbands, live with your wives in an understanding way, showing honor to the woman as the weaker vessel, since they are heirs with you[4] of the grace of life, so that your prayers may not be hindered.

[8] Finally, all of you, have unity of mind, sympathy, brotherly love, a tender heart, and a humble mind. [9] Do not repay evil for evil or reviling for reviling, but on the contrary, bless, for to this you were called, that you may obtain a blessing. [10] For

---

[1] Or *every institution ordained for people*   [2] Or *king;* also verse 17   [3] Greek *bondservants*   [4] Some manuscripts *since you are joint heirs*

> ^a"Whoever desires to love life
>   and see good days,
>   let him keep his tongue from evil
>   and his lips from speaking deceit;
> ¹¹ let him turn away from evil and do good;
>   let him seek peace and pursue it.
> ¹² For the eyes of the Lord are on the righteous,
>   and his ears are open to their prayer.
>   But the face of the Lord is against those who do evil."

Treatise on suffering [3:13–4:19]. This is the part of 1 Peter that leads people to remember it as a small classic on the subject of suffering. The passage can be analyzed by looking for directives on the actions and attitudes that should characterize Christians who are undergoing suffering, especially suffering because of their loyalty to Christ. The example of Christ pervades the passage, and we should analyze how the suffering of Christ relates to our suffering for the sake of Christ. An interlude in the argument on suffering comes in 4:7–11, which is in effect a mini-*paraenesis*.

¹³Now who is there to harm you if you are zealous for what is good? ¹⁴But even if you should suffer for righteousness' sake, you will be blessed. Have no fear of them, nor be troubled, ¹⁵but in your hearts honor Christ the Lord as holy, always being prepared to make a defense to anyone who asks you for a reason for the hope that is in you; yet do it with gentleness and respect, ¹⁶having a good conscience, so that, when you are slandered, those who revile your good behavior in Christ may be put to shame. ¹⁷For it is better to suffer for doing good, if that should be God's will, than for doing evil.

¹⁸For Christ also suffered[1] once for sins, the righteous for the unrighteous, that he might bring us to God, being put to death in the flesh but made alive in the spirit, ¹⁹in which[2] he went and proclaimed[3] to the spirits in prison, ²⁰because[4] they formerly did not obey, when God's patience waited in the days of Noah, while the ark was being prepared, in which a few, that is, eight persons, were brought safely through water. ²¹Baptism, which corresponds to this, now saves you, not as a removal of dirt from the body but as an appeal to God for a good conscience, through the resurrection of Jesus Christ, ²²who has gone into heaven and is at the right hand of God, with angels, authorities, and powers having been subjected to him.

4 Since therefore Christ suffered in the flesh,[5] arm yourselves with the same way of thinking, for whoever has suffered in the flesh has ceased from sin, ²so as to live for the rest of the time in the flesh no longer for human passions but for the will of God. ³For the time that is past suffices for doing what the Gentiles want to do, living in sensuality, passions, drunkenness, orgies, drinking parties, and lawless idolatry. ⁴With respect to this they are surprised when you do not join them in the same flood of debauchery, and they malign you; ⁵but they will give account to him who is ready to judge the living and the dead. ⁶For this is why the gospel was preached even to those who are dead, that though judged in the flesh the way people are, they might live in the spirit the way God does.

⁷The end of all things is at hand; therefore be self-controlled and sober-minded for the sake of your prayers. ⁸Above all, keep loving one another earnestly, since love cov-

---

[1] Some manuscripts *died* [2] Or *the Spirit, in whom* [3] Or *preached* [4] Or *when* [5] Some manuscripts add *for us; some for you* [a] Ps. 34:12-16

ers a multitude of sins. [9]Show hospitality to one another without grumbling. [10]As each has received a gift, use it to serve one another, as good stewards of God's varied grace: [11]whoever speaks, as one who speaks oracles of God; whoever serves, as one who serves by the strength that God supplies—in order that in everything God may be glorified through Jesus Christ. To him belong glory and dominion forever and ever. Amen.

[12]Beloved, do not be surprised at the fiery trial when it comes upon you to test you, as though something strange were happening to you. [13]But rejoice insofar as you share Christ's sufferings, that you may also rejoice and be glad when his glory is revealed. [14]If you are insulted for the name of Christ, you are blessed, because the Spirit of glory[1] and of God rests upon you. [15]But let none of you suffer as a murderer or a thief or an evildoer or as a meddler. [16]Yet if anyone suffers as a Christian, let him not be ashamed, but let him glorify God in that name. [17]For it is time for judgment to begin at the household of God; and if it begins with us, what will be the outcome for those who do not obey the gospel of God? [18]And

> "If the righteous is scarcely saved,
>   what will become of the ungodly and the sinner?"[2]

[19]Therefore let those who suffer according to God's will entrust their souls to a faithful Creator while doing good.

Conclusion of the letter [chapter 5]. The concluding chapter falls into three sections—instructions to elders in the church (vv. 1–5); another section of *paraenesis*, filled with aphoristic splendor (vv. 6–11); conventional epistolary closing (vv. 12–14).

5 So I exhort the elders among you, as a fellow elder and a witness of the sufferings of Christ, as well as a partaker in the glory that is going to be revealed: [2]shepherd the flock of God that is among you, exercising oversight,[3] not under compulsion, but willingly, as God would have you;[4] not for shameful gain, but eagerly; [3]not domineering over those in your charge, but being examples to the flock. [4]And when the chief Shepherd appears, you will receive the unfading crown of glory. [5]Likewise, you who are younger, be subject to the elders. Clothe yourselves, all of you, with humility toward one another, for "God opposes the proud but gives grace to the humble."

[6]Humble yourselves, therefore, under the mighty hand of God so that at the proper time he may exalt you, [7]casting all your anxieties on him, because he cares for you. [8]Be sober-minded; be watchful. Your adversary the devil prowls around like a roaring lion, seeking someone to devour. [9]Resist him, firm in your faith, knowing that the same kinds of suffering are being experienced by your brotherhood throughout the world. [10]And after you have suffered a little while, the God of all grace, who has called you to his eternal glory in Christ, will himself restore, confirm, strengthen, and establish you. [11]To him be the dominion forever and ever. Amen.

[12]By Silvanus, a faithful brother as I regard him, I have written briefly to you, exhorting and declaring that this is the true grace of God. Stand firm in it. [13]She who is at Babylon, who is likewise chosen, sends you greetings, and so does Mark, my son. [14]Greet one another with the kiss of love.

Peace to all of you who are in Christ.

---

[1] Some manuscripts insert *and of power* [2] Greek *where will the ungodly and sinner appear?* [3] Some manuscripts omit *exercising oversight* [4] Some manuscripts omit *as God would have you*

2 PETER

The book at a glance. 3 chapters, 61 verses. Peter's first *epistle had addressed Christians who were suffering for the sake of their faith while living in an alien, unbelieving culture. After thus strengthening his readers against outside threats, Peter apparently learned of a more serious threat from within: false doctrine. While false doctrine is a *motif in virtually all NT epistles, it is particularly pronounced in 2 Peter. With false teaching as the occasion, Peter follows three primary aims—to encourage growth in Christ, to warn against false teachers, and to strengthen conviction regarding Christian doctrine about the last days. Because no specific audience is addressed, this epistle has the nature of an "open letter" to all Christians, identified in the salutation (1:1) as "those who have obtained a faith of equal standing with ours."

▌ **Genres.** The primary form is the epistle, with its usual elements. Second, partly on the basis of 1:13–14, where Peter asserts that he will soon depart this life, it is customary to view 2 Peter as adhering to some of the conventions of the *farewell discourse. Motifs that belong to that genre include the author's (a) announcing that he is near the end of his earthly life, (b) reminding his followers of what he has taught them, (c) commanding his followers how to live, and (d) predicting what will happen in the future. In a farewell discourse, a leader has his last chance to influence his followers in the right direction for the sake of the movement in which he has been a guiding light. Second Peter is also filled with famous *proverbs and *aphoristic statements, vivid *poetry and *imagery, and an *eschatological discourse (chapter 3). (For more information on items accompanied by an asterisk, see the glossary at the back of this Bible.)

Passage	Content	Conventional Epistolary Motif
1:1–2	Sender, recipient, "grace and peace" prayer	Salutation
1:3–11	Exhortation to build upon what Christ has given the believer	Exhortation
1:12–21	Peter's assertion of his reliable authority to teach	Information
2:1–22	Description and denunciation of false teachers	Satiric diatribe
3:1–18a	The certainty of Christ's second coming	Eschatological discourse (instruction)
3:18b	Benediction	Closing

❚ Format and structure. The chart above gives the topical outline of the book, arranged according to epistolary motifs. If we stand back at a greater distance from the text, it is possible to arrange the material more generally according to the three-chapter arrangement of English Bibles. One such outline is as follows: be zealous to live and believe the Christian gospel (chapter 1); beware of false teachers (chapter 2); be prepared for the return of Christ (chapter 3). Or, to give another outline: true knowledge (chapter 1), false teachers (chapter 2), and a sure promise (chapter 3).

❚ Unifying motifs. By using such words as remind, remember, reminder, and recall, Peter emphasizes that he is reminding his readers of truth they already know (showing his agreement with a principle that eighteenth-century author Samuel Johnson expressed when he said famously that we need to be reminded more often than we need to be informed). Second, the theme of knowledge is very important to Peter in this letter, with the words know and knowledge appearing sixteen times. Third, much of the letter falls into place if we grasp that Peter's horror at false teaching (which is concentrated in chapter 2) is set over against the reliability of God's prophetic word (1:19–21; 3:1–2). These two motifs converge in the eschatological vision of the last chapter, where biblical *prophecy about the return of Christ is aggressively offered as a rebuttal of scoffers (false teachers) who denigrate such prophecy. In 2 Peter, true and false teaching engage in a single combat of huge proportions.

❚ Inferred literary intentions. The book is designed to achieve the following literary purposes:

- convey doctrinal truth with an urgency that arises from the situation of the farewell discourse

- impart Christian truth to our imagination as well as our mind and will

- use the resources of poetry to move us

- inspire us with a passion for truth as opposed to error

- catch us up in the exaltation of the book's style and content

- remind us that the faith we embrace is founded on the reliable word and prophecy of God

- encourage us not to entertain doubt about Christ's return simply because it is delayed

❚ Theological themes. (1) God's revelation and Scripture: 2 Peter contains key statements about the authority and inspiration of the Bible. (2) Eschatology: the last chapter is a major NT passage on the end times and the second coming of Jesus Christ. (3) Truth: a major emphasis of the book is the need to embrace doctrinal truth (and put it into practice) and reject false doctrine.

❚ 2 Peter as a chapter in the master story of the Bible. In the OT, the story of God's covenant dealings with his people was largely a history of national Israel; in the NT, that story takes the form of God's dealings with the believers across the world called the church. Second Peter is part of the NT story of how God expects his followers to live, with emphasis on godly living, acceptance of God's revealed truth as reliable, and belief in biblical prophecy about the end of history. Second Peter thus gives us glimpses of the concluding chapter in the master story of the Bible.

Epistolary opening [1:1–11]. Following the usual salutation (vv. 1–2), Peter dispenses with the conventional thanksgiving and instead exhorts his readers to godly living. He first reminds his readers that Christ has given them everything they need to live godly lives (vv. 3–4). Using the formula "For this very reason" (v. 5) as his transition, Peter then commands and lists the actions (vv. 5–11) that should characterize those who have received "all things that pertain to life and godliness," as he had said in verse 3. Exalted words tumble out of Peter's imagination and spill onto the page with splendor and exuberance.

1 Simeon[1] Peter, a servant[2] and apostle of Jesus Christ,
To those who have obtained a faith of equal standing with ours by the righteousness of our God and Savior Jesus Christ:

[2] May grace and peace be multiplied to you in the knowledge of God and of Jesus our Lord.

[3] His divine power has granted to us all things that pertain to life and godliness, through the knowledge of him who called us to[3] his own glory and excellence,[4] [4] by which he has granted to us his precious and very great promises, so that through them you may become partakers of the divine nature, having escaped from the corruption that is in the world because of sinful desire. [5] For this very reason, make every effort to supplement your faith with virtue,[5] and virtue with knowledge, [6] and knowledge with self-control, and self-control with steadfastness, and steadfastness with godliness, [7] and godliness with brotherly affection, and brotherly affection with love. [8] For if these qualities[6] are yours and are increasing, they keep you from being ineffective or unfruitful in the knowledge of our Lord Jesus Christ. [9] For whoever lacks these qualities is so nearsighted that he is blind, having forgotten that he was cleansed from his former sins. [10] Therefore, brothers,[7] be all the more diligent to make your calling and election sure, for if you practice these qualities you will never fall. [11] For in this way there will be richly provided for you an entrance into the eternal kingdom of our Lord and Savior Jesus Christ.

Peter's apostolic authority [1:12–21]. With this unit the characteristics of the farewell discourse enter the letter. The first motif to fit that *genre is Peter's claim that he intends to remind his readers of certain foundational truths, accompanied by a direct statement that his death is imminent (vv. 12–15). Then he recalls the integrity of his ministry as based on the gospel of Christ, which he declares to be the fulfillment of prophetic predictions (vv. 16–21). Verses 20–21 are a key biblical assertion about the inspiration of the Bible, with emphasis on God himself as the source of the Bible's authority.

---

[1] Some manuscripts *Simon* [2] Or *slave*; Greek *bondservant* [3] Or *by* [4] Or *virtue* [5] Or *excellence*; twice in this verse [6] Greek *these things*; also verses 9, 10, 12 [7] Or *brothers and sisters*. The plural Greek word *adelphoi* (translated "brothers") refers to siblings in a family. In New Testament usage, depending on the context, *adelphoi* may refer either to men or to both men and women who are siblings (brothers and sisters) in God's family, the church

¹²Therefore I intend always to remind you of these qualities, though you know them and are established in the truth that you have. ¹³I think it right, as long as I am in this body,¹ to stir you up by way of reminder, ¹⁴since I know that the putting off of my body will be soon, as our Lord Jesus Christ made clear to me. ¹⁵And I will make every effort so that after my departure you may be able at any time to recall these things.

¹⁶For we did not follow cleverly devised myths when we made known to you the power and coming of our Lord Jesus Christ, but we were eyewitnesses of his majesty. ¹⁷For when he received honor and glory from God the Father, and the voice was borne to him by the Majestic Glory, "This is my beloved Son,² with whom I am well pleased," ¹⁸we ourselves heard this very voice borne from heaven, for we were with him on the holy mountain. ¹⁹And we have something more sure, the prophetic word, to which you will do well to pay attention as to a lamp shining in a dark place, until the day dawns and the morning star rises in your hearts, ²⁰knowing this first of all, that no prophecy of Scripture comes from someone's own interpretation. ²¹For no prophecy was ever produced by the will of man, but men spoke from God as they were carried along by the Holy Spirit.

False teachers [chapter 2]. On the heels of a passage that has asserted the reliability of prophecies regarding Christ, Peter now describes and denounces false teachers. The specific topics covered are as follows: a prediction that false teachers will arise after Peter's death (vv. 1–3); God will punish false teachers but save the godly from them (vv. 4–10a); a detailed description of the false teachers (vv. 10b–16); prediction of coming judgment against the false teachers, who have repudiated the truth they once embraced (vv. 17–22). Rhetorically, this is one of the fireworks passages of the NT epistles. The imagery and *metaphors explode off the page. Placed in the context of a farewell discourse, this is the leader's prediction to his followers of what will happen after his death.

2 But false prophets also arose among the people, just as there will be false teachers among you, who will secretly bring in destructive heresies, even denying the Master who bought them, bringing upon themselves swift destruction. ²And many will follow their sensuality, and because of them the way of truth will be blasphemed. ³And in their greed they will exploit you with false words. Their condemnation from long ago is not idle, and their destruction is not asleep.

⁴For if God did not spare angels when they sinned, but cast them into hell³ and committed them to chains⁴ of gloomy darkness to be kept until the judgment; ⁵if he did not spare the ancient world, but preserved Noah, a herald of righteousness, with seven others, when he brought a flood upon the world of the ungodly; ⁶if by turning the cities of Sodom and Gomorrah to ashes he condemned them to extinction, making them an example of what is going to happen to the ungodly;⁵ ⁷and if he rescued righteous Lot, greatly distressed by the sensual conduct of the wicked ⁸(for as that righteous man lived among them day after day, he was tormenting his righteous soul over their lawless deeds that he saw and heard); ⁹then the Lord knows how to rescue the godly from trials,⁶ and to keep the unrighteous under punishment until the day of judgment, ¹⁰and especially those who indulge in the lust of defiling passion and despise authority.

---

¹ Greek tent; also verse 14 ² Or my Son, my (or the) Beloved ³ Greek Tartarus ⁴ Some manuscripts pits ⁵ Some manuscripts an example to those who were to be ungodly ⁶ Or temptations

Bold and willful, they do not tremble as they blaspheme the glorious ones, [11]whereas angels, though greater in might and power, do not pronounce a blasphemous judgment against them before the Lord. [12]But these, like irrational animals, creatures of instinct, born to be caught and destroyed, blaspheming about matters of which they are ignorant, will also be destroyed in their destruction, [13]suffering wrong as the wage for their wrongdoing. They count it pleasure to revel in the daytime. They are blots and blemishes, reveling in their deceptions,[1] while they feast with you. [14]They have eyes full of adultery, insatiable for sin. They entice unsteady souls. They have hearts trained in greed. Accursed children! [15]Forsaking the right way, they have gone astray. They have followed the way of Balaam, the son of Beor, who loved gain from wrongdoing, [16]but was rebuked for his own transgression; a speechless donkey spoke with human voice and restrained the prophet's madness.

[17]These are waterless springs and mists driven by a storm. For them the gloom of utter darkness has been reserved. [18]For, speaking loud boasts of folly, they entice by sensual passions of the flesh those who are barely escaping from those who live in error. [19]They promise them freedom, but they themselves are slaves[2] of corruption. For whatever overcomes a person, to that he is enslaved. [20]For if, after they have escaped the defilements of the world through the knowledge of our Lord and Savior Jesus Christ, they are again entangled in them and overcome, the last state has become worse for them than the first. [21]For it would have been better for them never to have known the way of righteousness than after knowing it to turn back from the holy commandment delivered to them. [22]What the true proverb says has happened to them: "The dog returns to its own vomit, and the sow, after washing herself, returns to wallow in the mire."

The certainty of Christ's second coming [chapter 3]. This is one of the glorious eschatological passages of the NT. Its specific topic is the return of Christ. The key to assimilating the passage is to realize that it follows the form of a debate. Peter gives us his half of the debate, following the conventional format of that form: a statement of the proposition that believers should believe the predictions of the biblical prophets (vv. 1–2); a summary of the opponent's viewpoint, in this case scorn at the idea that Christ will return (vv. 3–4); rebuttal of the opponent's viewpoint, including an analysis of how the opponent's view is faulty (vv. 5–9); counterstatement in the form of Peter's proposition that Christ will return (v. 10); recapitulation of the main proposition—that the eschaton will happen as God has promised it—and remarks on the practical effects of believing this (vv. 11–15a); corroboration of the proposition from an additional authority (vv. 15b–16); final exhortation to put the author's insight into practice (vv. 17–18a); concluding *benediction (v. 18b).

3 This is now the second letter that I am writing to you, beloved. In both of them I am stirring up your sincere mind by way of reminder, [2]that you should remember the predictions of the holy prophets and the commandment of the Lord and Savior through your apostles, [3]knowing this first of all, that scoffers will come in the last days with scoffing, following their own sinful desires. [4]They will say, "Where is the promise of his coming? For ever since the fathers fell asleep, all things are continuing as they were from the beginning of creation." [5]For they deliberately overlook this fact, that the heavens existed long ago, and the earth was formed out of water

---

[1] Some manuscripts *love feasts* [2] Greek *bondservants*

and through water by the word of God, [6]and that by means of these the world that then existed was deluged with water and perished. [7]But by the same word the heavens and earth that now exist are stored up for fire, being kept until the day of judgment and destruction of the ungodly.

[8]But do not overlook this one fact, beloved, that with the Lord one day is as a thousand years, and a thousand years as one day. [9]The Lord is not slow to fulfill his promise as some count slowness, but is patient toward you,[1] not wishing that any should perish, but that all should reach repentance. [10]But the day of the Lord will come like a thief, and then the heavens will pass away with a roar, and the heavenly bodies[2] will be burned up and dissolved, and the earth and the works that are done on it will be exposed.[3]

[11]Since all these things are thus to be dissolved, what sort of people ought you to be in lives of holiness and godliness, [12]waiting for and hastening the coming of the day of God, because of which the heavens will be set on fire and dissolved, and the heavenly bodies will melt as they burn! [13]But according to his promise we are waiting for new heavens and a new earth in which righteousness dwells.

[14]Therefore, beloved, since you are waiting for these, be diligent to be found by him without spot or blemish, and at peace. [15]And count the patience of our Lord as salvation, just as our beloved brother Paul also wrote to you according to the wisdom given him, [16]as he does in all his letters when he speaks in them of these matters. There are some things in them that are hard to understand, which the ignorant and unstable twist to their own destruction, as they do the other Scriptures. [17]You therefore, beloved, knowing this beforehand, take care that you are not carried away with the error of lawless people and lose your own stability. [18]But grow in the grace and knowledge of our Lord and Savior Jesus Christ. To him be the glory both now and to the day of eternity. Amen.

---

[1] Some manuscripts *on your account* [2] Or *elements*; also verse 12 [3] Greek *found*; some manuscripts *will be burned up*

1 JOHN

The book at a glance. 5 chapters, 105 verses. The subject of 1 John is how people can know if they are Christians. The letter develops a series of tests to demonstrate whether or not a person is in Christ. The tests are objective (a test of intellectual assent to the truth of the gospel), subjective (inner awareness of having been born of God), and communal (love for the people of God). These tests are presented in an informal letter that has a fluid structure. The *epistle is easy to read: it is organized as a fireside conversation with John on the Christian life. First John is also a small classic on the subject of love.

▍**Genres.** First John is ostensibly an epistle, but its content is more fluid than what we find in most NT epistles. There is no epistolary salutation, nor is there a conventional epistolary conclusion. A more accurate designation for this book is a treatise or pamphlet. Alternately, we can read it as an address or loosely structured sermon.

Passage	Content	Conventional Epistolary Motifs
1:1–4	Purpose statement: to proclaim the reality of the Incarnation	Introduction
1:5–2:6	Tests of true faith that center on confession of sin and walking in obedience to God's law	Instruction
2:7–11	Tests of true faith that center on loving rather than hating	
2:12–14	John's reasons for writing the letter	Interlude
2:15–17	Commands not to love the world	Exhortation
2:18–3:3	Tests of true faith that center on believing the truth about Christ and living in light of his second coming	
3:4–24	Tests of true faith that center on doing what is right according to God's law, loving one's fellow Christians, and believing in Christ	Instruction
4:1–21	Tests of true faith that center on confessing Christ's incarnation and loving one's fellow Christians	
5:1–12	Tests of true faith that center on loving God and believing the truth about Christ	
5:13–21	Summary statement: seven assertions of what a Christian can know	Conclusion

▌Format. The topic changes with virtually every paragraph, so the best advice for reading the book is "think paragraph." Nonetheless, even though the structure is not strictly linear, the author keeps coming back to topics that have been introduced earlier, so that we can profitably think of the book as arranged like a musical symphony. The main theme is *tests by which we can know if we are in Christ*—beliefs and attitudes that authenticate one's claims to be a Christian. Under that umbrella, subordinate themes appear: Christology (doctrine about the person and work of Christ); walking in the light; love; the need to reject fallen culture. These topics weave in and out of the book.

▌Inferred context and occasion. We can infer that John is writing to Christians who want to know how to (1) tell when one's Christian faith is genuine and (2) exhibit love in their lives. It is possible that there has been a church split (see 2:19, 26) and that in the wake of it the Christians who remained in the church wondered whether they were on the right track and were behaving as Christians toward those who had left the church. There is a tone of urgency in what John writes, and further, John obviously wishes to discredit false teaching and strongly exhort believers to love, which is offered as the supreme virtue of the Christian life. John writes as an elderly apostle to his "little children" in the faith.

▌Tips for reading 1 John. Do not look for a single line of argument. Instead, think in terms of theme and variation, with the main theme being tests of authentic Christian faith. The movement from one paragraph to the next is fluid, though within the relatively brief paragraphs the material is unified. A good reading strategy is to keep a running list of tests of true faith. These tests, which offer grounds for certainty, are not simply doctrinal; they are consistently accompanied by moral commands for living the doctrines in everyday life. Further, the book is structured on an implied dialectical principle as John continually seeks to oppose viewpoints that are contrary to his assertions. For example, John's assertions that Christ has come in the flesh (1:1–3; 4:2) are an implied refutation of those who deny the Incarnation. Finally, there is an incipient poetry and mysticism in John's writing, so that (for example) many of his assertions about the Christian life are conveyed in great symbols like light and darkness or walking and abiding in Christ.

▌Inferred literary intentions. The book is designed to achieve the following literary purposes:

- state clear criteria for testing whether someone's Christian faith is genuine

- prompt readers toward moral conduct, especially love

- express the timeless truths of the Christian faith in memorable, *aphoristic form ("we love because he first loved us" [4:19]; "this is the victory that has overcome the world—our faith" [5:4])

- highlight the truth by implicitly setting it over against error

▌Theological themes. (1) Christology: the book contains famous statements about the person and work of Christ. (2) Sanctification: John outlines how Christians need to live in demonstration of their genuine faith, especially in regard to loving others. (3) Sin, confession, repentance, forgiveness: this book contains key NT statements about the nature of sin (especially love of the world), the need to confess sin, and the assurance of forgiveness.

▌ **1 John as a chapter in the master story of the Bible.** The master story of the Bible outlines how God's followers are to live and what they are to love. First John contributes to that story by offering tests of true belief and of conduct that pleases God.

Introduction and early tests of faith [1:1–2:6]. The first four verses are a key NT assertion of the incarnation of Jesus Christ. John makes a very strong assertion of empirical (based on sensory observation) validation of the Incarnation. By beginning in this way, John invites us to ponder as we read the ensuing letter how the incarnation of Christ permeates all that he says about the Christian life. At the outset John is also alerting us of his credentials to write about Christ: he was a personal disciple of Christ during his earthly ministry. With the preamble complete, John then turns to some pre-liminary tests of faith. The material is organized very fluidly, and this means that we cannot simply number the tests. We need to read slowly, noting themes that are intro-duced, succeeded by something different, and then picked up again. Here is a starting list: walking in the light rather than darkness; confessing sin and receiving God's for-giveness; the need to love rather than hate.

---

1 That which was from the beginning, which we have heard, which we have seen with our eyes, which we looked upon and have touched with our hands, concern-ing the word of life— ²the life was made manifest, and we have seen it, and testify to it and proclaim to you the eternal life, which was with the Father and was made man-ifest to us— ³that which we have seen and heard we proclaim also to you, so that you too may have fellowship with us; and indeed our fellowship is with the Father and with his Son Jesus Christ. ⁴And we are writing these things so that our¹ joy may be complete.

⁵This is the message we have heard from him and proclaim to you, that God is light, and in him is no darkness at all. ⁶If we say we have fellowship with him while we walk in darkness, we lie and do not practice the truth. ⁷But if we walk in the light, as he is in the light, we have fellowship with one another, and the blood of Jesus his Son cleanses us from all sin. ⁸If we say we have no sin, we deceive ourselves, and the truth is not in us. ⁹If we confess our sins, he is faithful and just to forgive us our sins and to cleanse us from all unrighteousness. ¹⁰If we say we have not sinned, we make him a liar, and his word is not in us.

2 My little children, I am writing these things to you so that you may not sin. But if anyone does sin, we have an advocate with the Father, Jesus Christ the righteous. ²He is the propitiation for our sins, and not for ours only but also for the sins of the whole world. ³And by this we know that we have come to know him, if we keep his commandments. ⁴Whoever says "I know him" but does not keep his commandments is a liar, and the truth is not in him, ⁵but whoever keeps his word, in him truly the

---

¹ Some manuscripts *your*

love of God is perfected. By this we may know that we are in him: [6]whoever says he abides in him ought to walk in the same way in which he walked.

> **Epistolary preliminaries** [2:7–17]. We need continually to remind ourselves of the very fluid structure of this letter. In some ways, verses 7–14 of this unit more closely resemble the beginning of a letter than anything up to this point in 1 John. John first clarifies the content of his letter by asserting that his message is both old and new (vv. 7–8) and then in effect states the gist of this message: the need to love and walk in the light (vv. 9–11). Then John identifies his intended audiences, matching each of the audiences with a reason that he has written to them (vv. 12–14). Finally, in an aphoristic passage that reads like a theme statement, John commands his readers not to love the world (his word for the fallen order of things), giving a reason for the command: loving the world is inferior to doing the will of God (vv. 15–17).

[7]Beloved, I am writing you no new commandment, but an old commandment that you had from the beginning. The old commandment is the word that you have heard. [8]At the same time, it is a new commandment that I am writing to you, which is true in him and in you, because[1] the darkness is passing away and the true light is already shining. [9]Whoever says he is in the light and hates his brother is still in darkness. [10]Whoever loves his brother abides in the light, and in him[2] there is no cause for stumbling. [11]But whoever hates his brother is in the darkness and walks in the darkness, and does not know where he is going, because the darkness has blinded his eyes.

[12]   I am writing to you, little children,
      because your sins are forgiven for his name's sake.
[13]   I am writing to you, fathers,
      because you know him who is from the beginning.
   I am writing to you, young men,
      because you have overcome the evil one.
   I write to you, children,
      because you know the Father.
[14]   I write to you, fathers,
      because you know him who is from the beginning.
   I write to you, young men,
      because you are strong,
      and the word of God abides in you,
      and you have overcome the evil one.

[15]Do not love the world or the things in the world. If anyone loves the world, the love of the Father is not in him. [16]For all that is in the world—the desires of the flesh and the desires of the eyes and pride in possessions—is not from the Father but is from the world. [17]And the world is passing away along with its desires, but whoever does the will of God abides forever.

> **Further tests of faith** [2:18–3:3]. The organization continues to be loose, consisting of a theme-and-variation format. Still, in this unit we get two primary tests of genuine-

---

[1] Or that [2] Or it

ness for faith: the test of believing the truth about Christ (2:18–25) and the test of living properly in light of Christ's anticipated appearance (2:28–3:3). But there are also interspersed exhortations and promises of a general nature, along with assurances to readers that they have the truth and should not be led into doubt by people who have left them and would seek to deceive them.

[18]Children, it is the last hour, and as you have heard that antichrist is coming, so now many antichrists have come. Therefore we know that it is the last hour. [19]They went out from us, but they were not of us; for if they had been of us, they would have continued with us. But they went out, that it might become plain that they all are not of us. [20]But you have been anointed by the Holy One, and you all have knowledge.[1] [21]I write to you, not because you do not know the truth, but because you know it, and because no lie is of the truth. [22]Who is the liar but he who denies that Jesus is the Christ? This is the antichrist, he who denies the Father and the Son. [23]No one who denies the Son has the Father. Whoever confesses the Son has the Father also. [24]Let what you heard from the beginning abide in you. If what you heard from the beginning abides in you, then you too will abide in the Son and in the Father. [25]And this is the promise that he made to us[2]—eternal life.

[26]I write these things to you about those who are trying to deceive you. [27]But the anointing that you received from him abides in you, and you have no need that anyone should teach you. But as his anointing teaches you about everything, and is true, and is no lie—just as it has taught you, abide in him.

[28]And now, little children, abide in him, so that when he appears we may have confidence and not shrink from him in shame at his coming. [29]If you know that he is righteous, you may be sure that everyone who practices righteousness has been born of him.

3 See what kind of love the Father has given to us, that we should be called children of God; and so we are. The reason why the world does not know us is that it did not know him. [2]Beloved, we are God's children now, and what we will be has not yet appeared; but we know that when he appears[3] we shall be like him, because we shall see him as he is. [3]And everyone who thus hopes in him purifies himself as he is pure.

Still more tests of faith [3:4–24]. We can pick up hints that John is seeking to infuse confidence in readers who are in danger of being intimidated by alternative claims regarding what constitutes true faith and right conduct. Here he presents a loosely organized kaleidoscope of further thoughts on how we can know that we are Christians. For starters, we are Christians if we abide in Christ, do what is right, shun sin, love others, have confidence before God, believe in Christ, obey God's commandments. At each point we can observe the rhetorical or persuasive stance John chooses in order to instill confidence. This unit is a spiritual pep talk.

[4]Everyone who makes a practice of sinning also practices lawlessness; sin is lawlessness. [5]You know that he appeared to take away sins, and in him there is no sin. [6]No one who abides in him keeps on sinning; no one who keeps on sinning has either seen him or known him. [7]Little children, let no one deceive you. Whoever practices

---

[1] Some manuscripts *you know everything* [2] Some manuscripts *you* [3] Or *when it appears*

righteousness is righteous, as he is righteous. ⁸Whoever makes a practice of sinning is of the devil, for the devil has been sinning from the beginning. The reason the Son of God appeared was to destroy the works of the devil. ⁹No one born of God makes a practice of sinning, for God's¹ seed abides in him, and he cannot keep on sinning because he has been born of God. ¹⁰By this it is evident who are the children of God, and who are the children of the devil: whoever does not practice righteousness is not of God, nor is the one who does not love his brother.

¹¹For this is the message that you have heard from the beginning, that we should love one another. ¹²We should not be like Cain, who was of the evil one and murdered his brother. And why did he murder him? Because his own deeds were evil and his brother's righteous. ¹³Do not be surprised, brothers,² that the world hates you. ¹⁴We know that we have passed out of death into life, because we love the brothers. Whoever does not love abides in death. ¹⁵Everyone who hates his brother is a murderer, and you know that no murderer has eternal life abiding in him.

¹⁶By this we know love, that he laid down his life for us, and we ought to lay down our lives for the brothers. ¹⁷But if anyone has the world's goods and sees his brother in need, yet closes his heart against him, how does God's love abide in him? ¹⁸Little children, let us not love in word or talk but in deed and in truth.

¹⁹By this we shall know that we are of the truth and reassure our heart before him; ²⁰for whenever our heart condemns us, God is greater than our heart, and he knows everything. ²¹Beloved, if our heart does not condemn us, we have confidence before God; ²²and whatever we ask we receive from him, because we keep his commandments and do what pleases him. ²³And this is his commandment, that we believe in the name of his Son Jesus Christ and love one another, just as he has commanded us. ²⁴Whoever keeps his commandments abides in God,³ and God⁴ in him. And by this we know that he abides in us, by the Spirit whom he has given us.

Testing the spirits [chapter 4]. Testing the spirits to see whether they are from God (v. 1) is this chapter's variation on the major theme of criteria for distinguishing true faith from its fraudulent counterfeits. The tests turn out to be intellectual (discerning truth from error) and moral (with primary emphasis on the virtue of love). Everything in this chapter has been stated in kernel form earlier, including the following emphases: the need to confess the incarnate Christ; the confidence that followers of Christ can have no matter what the world says; commands for Christians to love each other and God. We can read the chapter looking for evidences of John's triad of (1) confessing Christ, (2) loving, and (3) being confident.

4 Beloved, do not believe every spirit, but test the spirits to see whether they are from God, for many false prophets have gone out into the world. ²By this you know the Spirit of God: every spirit that confesses that Jesus Christ has come in the flesh is from God, ³and every spirit that does not confess Jesus is not from God. This is the spirit of the antichrist, which you heard was coming and now is in the world already. ⁴Little children, you are from God and have overcome them, for he who is in you is greater than he who is in the world. ⁵They are from the world; therefore they speak from the world, and the world listens to them. ⁶We are from God. Whoever

¹Greek *his* ²Or *brothers and sisters*. The plural Greek word *adelphoi* (translated "brothers") refers to siblings in a family. In New Testament usage, depending on the context, *adelphoi* may refer either to men or to both men and women who are siblings (brothers and sisters) in God's family, the church; also verses 14, 16 ³Greek *him* ⁴Greek *he*

knows God listens to us; whoever is not from God does not listen to us. By this we know the Spirit of truth and the spirit of error.

⁷Beloved, let us love one another, for love is from God, and whoever loves has been born of God and knows God. ⁸Anyone who does not love does not know God, because God is love. ⁹In this the love of God was made manifest among us, that God sent his only Son into the world, so that we might live through him. ¹⁰In this is love, not that we have loved God but that he loved us and sent his Son to be the propitiation for our sins. ¹¹Beloved, if God so loved us, we also ought to love one another. ¹²No one has ever seen God; if we love one another, God abides in us and his love is perfected in us.

¹³By this we know that we abide in him and he in us, because he has given us of his Spirit. ¹⁴And we have seen and testify that the Father has sent his Son to be the Savior of the world. ¹⁵Whoever confesses that Jesus is the Son of God, God abides in him, and he in God. ¹⁶So we have come to know and to believe the love that God has for us. God is love, and whoever abides in love abides in God, and God abides in him. ¹⁷By this is love perfected with us, so that we may have confidence for the day of judgment, because as he is so also are we in this world. ¹⁸There is no fear in love, but perfect love casts out fear. For fear has to do with punishment, and whoever fears has not been perfected in love. ¹⁹We love because he first loved us. ²⁰If anyone says, "I love God," and hates his brother, he is a liar; for he who does not love his brother whom he has seen cannot¹ love God whom he has not seen. ²¹And this commandment we have from him: whoever loves God must also love his brother.

Summary [chapter 5]. The concluding chapter is a twofold summary of the entire book. The first half (vv. 1–12), a strongly Christological passage, restates the theme that we know we are God's children if we believe in Christ and love and obey God. The second half (vv. 13–21) clinches the major theme of how we can confidently know that we are genuine believers with a list of seven things that a Christian can know (the word pattern that dominates the passage).

5 Everyone who believes that Jesus is the Christ has been born of God, and everyone who loves the Father loves whoever has been born of him. ²By this we know that we love the children of God, when we love God and obey his commandments. ³For this is the love of God, that we keep his commandments. And his commandments are not burdensome. ⁴For everyone who has been born of God overcomes the world. And this is the victory that has overcome the world—our faith. ⁵Who is it that overcomes the world except the one who believes that Jesus is the Son of God?

⁶This is he who came by water and blood—Jesus Christ; not by the water only but by the water and the blood. And the Spirit is the one who testifies, because the Spirit is the truth. ⁷For there are three that testify: ⁸the Spirit and the water and the blood; and these three agree. ⁹If we receive the testimony of men, the testimony of God is greater, for this is the testimony of God that he has borne concerning his Son. ¹⁰Whoever believes in the Son of God has the testimony in himself. Whoever does not believe God has made him a liar, because he has not believed in the testimony that God has borne concerning his Son. ¹¹And this is the testimony, that God gave us eternal life, and this life is in his Son. ¹²Whoever has the Son has life; whoever does not have the Son of God does not have life.

¹ Some manuscripts *how can he*

¹³I write these things to you who believe in the name of the Son of God that you may know that you have eternal life. ¹⁴And this is the confidence that we have toward him, that if we ask anything according to his will he hears us. ¹⁵And if we know that he hears us in whatever we ask, we know that we have the requests that we have asked of him.

¹⁶If anyone sees his brother committing a sin not leading to death, he shall ask, and God[1] will give him life—to those who commit sins that do not lead to death. There is sin that leads to death; I do not say that one should pray for that. ¹⁷All wrongdoing is sin, but there is sin that does not lead to death.

¹⁸We know that everyone who has been born of God does not keep on sinning, but he who was born of God protects him, and the evil one does not touch him.

¹⁹We know that we are from God, and the whole world lies in the power of the evil one.

²⁰And we know that the Son of God has come and has given us understanding, so that we may know him who is true; and we are in him who is true, in his Son Jesus Christ. He is the true God and eternal life. ²¹Little children, keep yourselves from idols.

---

[1] Greek he

2 JOHN

The book at a glance. One chapter, 13 verses. This is one of five one-chapter books in the Bible. The author calls himself "the elder" (v. 1) and calls the church "the elect lady and her children" (v. 1). This church that is addressed might be either a local church known to John or the church universal (to which the letter applies, in any case). In a manner akin to what we find in 1 John, the author warns his readers about false teachers who might arrive in their city and provides a standard by which to judge what is false in the message of such teachers. The purpose of the letter is thus to protect the church from error.

▌**Genre.** This brief book is a standard NT *epistle, consisting of a salutation, a body, and a conclusion. As in the conventional epistle, the body of the letter consists of mingled instruction and commands, and although we do not find the concentrated list of commands that constitutes the familiar paraenesis of NT letters, verses 8–11 have affinities with that conventional motif. (For more information on items accompanied by an asterisk, see the glossary at the end of this Bible.)

Passage	Content	Epistolary Convention
1–3	Epistolary opening: author, recipient, "grace, mercy, and peace" benediction	Salutation
4–11	Commands and instructions	Body
12–13	Personal matters and greetings	Closing

▌**Inferred literary intentions.** The book is designed to achieve the following literary purposes:

- instruct the church using the literary form of the epistle

- echo language and ideas from 1 John

- warn readers about error and false teachers

- exhort readers to embrace truth, Christ, and God's commands

- present the content in elevated and *aphoristic style

▌**Theological themes.** (1) The importance of truth: the word truth appears five times in the first four verses, signaling the book's concern with truth as opposed to false-hood. (2) The need to embrace true doctrine: despite its brevity, this letter is a concentrated expression of several doctrines (such as the need to obey God's commandment, the existence of the antichrist, and heavenly reward for the faithful), accompanied by commands to believe them and reject their opposites.

▌**2 John as a chapter in the master story of the Bible.** The master story of the Bible tells followers of God how to live the truth in a false world. This letter takes that as its subject.

The need to be vigilant in the Christian life [2 John]. The salutation (vv. 1–3) and conclusion (vv. 12–13) are predictable as epistolary conventions. The complexity comes in the packed middle paragraph that makes up the body. We can note a general division into the following units: a reminder (vv. 4–6), a warning (vv. 7–9), and an instruction (vv. 10–11). First, John reminds his readers of God's great command to love (vv. 4–6). Then he warns his readers about the need to protect their eternal hope by resisting any teaching that denies the doctrine of the Incarnation (vv. 7–9). By way of application, John instructs his readers not to extend hospitality or support to traveling teachers who deny the Incarnation (vv. 10–11). Having absorbed these ideas, we can reflect on how similar perils might manifest themselves in our own situation.

¹The elder to the elect lady and her children, whom I love in truth, and not only I, but also all who know the truth, ²because of the truth that abides in us and will be with us forever:

³Grace, mercy, and peace will be with us, from God the Father and from Jesus Christ the Father's Son, in truth and love.

⁴I rejoiced greatly to find some of your children walking in the truth, just as we were commanded by the Father. ⁵And now I ask you, dear lady—not as though I were writing you a new commandment, but the one we have had from the beginning—that we love one another. ⁶And this is love, that we walk according to his commandments; this is the commandment, just as you have heard from the beginning, so that you should walk in it. ⁷For many deceivers have gone out into the world, those who do not confess the coming of Jesus Christ in the flesh. Such a one is the deceiver and the antichrist. ⁸Watch yourselves, so that you may not lose what we¹ have worked for, but may win a full reward. ⁹Everyone who goes on ahead and does not abide in the teaching of Christ, does not have God. Whoever abides in the teaching has both the Father and the Son. ¹⁰If anyone comes to you and does not bring this teaching, do not receive him into your house or give him any greeting, ¹¹for whoever greets him takes part in his wicked works.

¹²Though I have much to write to you, I would rather not use paper and ink. Instead I hope to come to you and talk face to face, so that our joy may be complete.

¹³The children of your elect sister greet you.

---

¹ Some manuscripts you

3 JOHN

> **The book at a glance.** One chapter, 15 verses. Whereas 2 John was written to an unlocalized church, this letter is filled with references to specific people and situations. Its theme is hospitality to traveling Christians. The main motif is "a home away from home" and, accompanying that, a pattern of arrival and welcoming of guests. Although addressed to a specific person named Gaius, the letter applies to any Christian who is in a position to extend hospitality. People who refuse to extend hospitality, however, are denounced by John.

▌**Genre.** Third John is a personal *epistle, addressed to a friend of the author. The customary epistolary conventions are evident: an opening salutation, a body of instruction, and concluding greetings. Reinforcing the nature of this book as a personal letter is the way in which it is built around references to specific acquaintances from start to finish.

Passage	Content	Epistolary Convention
1–4	Epistolary opening: author, recipient, greetings and commendations	Salutation
5–12	Good conduct commended; bad conduct rebuked	Body
13–15	Personal matters and final greetings	Closing

▌**Inferred literary intentions.** The book is designed to achieve the following literary purposes:

- present teaching about the virtue of hospitality in the form of a personal letter

- hold up models of virtue for emulation and a model of vice for disapproval

▌**Theological theme.** (1) Christian ethics: 3 John is a repository of biblical teaching on hospitality. (2) Truth: a subtheme is the need for Christians to embrace truth, as the words truth and true appear seven times.

▌**3 John as a chapter in the master story of the Bible.** An important theme in the master story of the Bible is the great conflict between good and evil, right and wrong. This letter focuses on the contrast between good and bad behavior and the need to "not imitate evil but imitate good" (v. 11).

On showing hospitality [3 John]. The structure of 3 John is neatness itself: warm greetings to Gaius, who is commended for the report that has reached John of his hospitality and devotion to truth (vv. 1–4); commendation of the virtue of hospitality to Christian workers (vv. 5–8); rebuke of someone named Diotrephes for his self-centeredness and refusal to extend hospitality (vv. 9–10); commands to do good rather than evil, with Demetrius offered as an example of good conduct (vv. 11–12); concluding greetings to friends (vv. 13–15). A good literary approach to this material is what is known as "example theory," based on the premise that literature puts positive examples before us to imitate and negative examples to avoid.

¹The elder to the beloved Gaius, whom I love in truth.

²Beloved, I pray that all may go well with you and that you may be in good health, as it goes well with your soul. ³For I rejoiced greatly when the brothers¹ came and testified to your truth, as indeed you are walking in the truth. ⁴I have no greater joy than to hear that my children are walking in the truth.

⁵Beloved, it is a faithful thing you do in all your efforts for these brothers, strangers as they are, ⁶who testified to your love before the church. You will do well to send them on their journey in a manner worthy of God. ⁷For they have gone out for the sake of the name, accepting nothing from the Gentiles. ⁸Therefore we ought to support people like these, that we may be fellow workers for the truth.

⁹I have written something to the church, but Diotrephes, who likes to put himself first, does not acknowledge our authority. ¹⁰So if I come, I will bring up what he is doing, talking wicked nonsense against us. And not content with that, he refuses to welcome the brothers, and also stops those who want to and puts them out of the church.

¹¹Beloved, do not imitate evil but imitate good. Whoever does good is from God; whoever does evil has not seen God. ¹²Demetrius has received a good testimony from everyone, and from the truth itself. We also add our testimony, and you know that our testimony is true.

¹³I had much to write to you, but I would rather not write with pen and ink. ¹⁴I hope to see you soon, and we will talk face to face.

¹⁵Peace be to you. The friends greet you. Greet the friends, every one of them.

---

¹ Or brothers and sisters. The plural Greek word adelphoi (translated "brothers") refers to siblings in a family. In New Testament usage, depending on the context, adelphoi may refer either to men or to both men and women who are siblings (brothers and sisters) in God's family, the church; also verses 5, 10

THE LETTER OF

JUDE

The book at a glance. One chapter, 25 verses. The *epistle of Jude is one of
the fireworks books of the Bible. It is filled with vivid *imagery, and much of it
is written at the white heat of anger. Yet despite our sense that the writer has
been aroused by a specific situation, the recipients of the letter are not named;
the letter is apparently addressed to Christians in general. The writer displays
horror over the spectacle of apostasy and false teachers who induce it. The
only NT passage that surpasses Jude in angry intensity is Jesus' denunciation
of religious leaders in Matthew 23. But the letter begins with the usual soothing
notes of NT epistles, and in the last two verses it modulates into one of the
most moving benedictions in the NT.

▌**Genres.** The external format is that of the NT epistle, with its loose divisions of
salutation, body, and closing. But the central unit of the letter (vv. 5–16) falls
decisively into the genre of *satire: it has an object of attack, a many-sided vehicle in
which the attack is conveyed, a discernible satiric tone (harsh), and an implied
standard by which the attack is being conducted ("the faith that was once for all
delivered to the saints," v. 3). The description of the apostates (vv. 10–16) uses the
portrait technique: we learn more and more about the apostates until we have a
picture of their character and actions. Finally, the concentrated use of images and
*allusions (e.g., to Sodom and Gomorrah and the archangel Michael) lends a poetic
quality to the letter.

▌**Inferred literary intentions.** The book is designed to achieve the following literary
purposes:

- present its content in the form of an epistle

- denigrate the apostates against which Jude writes by means of satire

- make the utterance vivid by means of poetic imagery and allusions

- move the reader to reject the evil against which Jude writes

▌**Theological themes.** (1) Truth: the letter shows that Christians must defend the
truth and reject falsehood. (2) Faith: we are led to see that the Christian faith as
taught by Christ and the apostles is reliable. (3) Judgment and hell: we are equally led
to feel the certainty of God's eventual judgment against evil and accept the existence
of hell.

Passage	Content	Contribution to the Main Argument about Apostates	Epistolary Conventions
1–2	Epistolary opening: author, recipients, "mercy, peace, and love" benediction	Preamble	Salutation
3–4	Reason for writing	Summarizes the crisis that has occasioned the letter	Purpose statement
5–7	God's judgment against evildoers in the past	Adduces three examples from the past to show that God judges evildoers	Instruction
8–16	Description and denunciation of the apostates	Arouses a feeling of disgust toward apostasy	
17–23	Instruction in how to resist the efforts of the false teachers	Instills hope that the apostates can be defeated	Exhortation
24–25	Benediction	Invokes the divine antidote to the apostates	Closing

❙ **Jude as a chapter in the master story of the Bible.** The letter of Jude contributes to the overall story of conflict between good and evil, truth and error, that is a unifying thread throughout the Bible, and it is a building block in the story of how God wants his followers to live.

Dealing decisively with false teachers [Jude]. The chart above shows the topical arrangement of the book. Tips for reading the book include the following: We can compile a portrait or character sketch of the people against whom Jude writes. As we do so, we can also compile a list of their offenses (such as blasphemy against celestial beings, greed, and instability). By way of contrast, from other parts of the letter we can compile a list of virtues that we are commanded to practice. Finally, we need to unpack the meanings of the *metaphors and allusions that Jude uses to portray the ungodly against whom he writes.

¹Jude, a servant¹ of Jesus Christ and brother of James,

To those who are called, beloved in God the Father and kept for² Jesus Christ:

²May mercy, peace, and love be multiplied to you.

³Beloved, although I was very eager to write to you about our common salvation, I found it necessary to write appealing to you to contend for the faith that was once for all delivered to the saints. ⁴For certain people have crept in unnoticed who long ago were designated for this condemnation, ungodly people, who pervert the grace of our God into sensuality and deny our only Master and Lord, Jesus Christ.

⁵Now I want to remind you, although you once fully knew it, that Jesus, who saved³ a people out of the land of Egypt, afterward destroyed those who did not believe. ⁶And the angels who did not stay within their own position of authority, but left their proper dwelling, he has kept in eternal chains under gloomy darkness until the judgment of the great day— ⁷just as Sodom and Gomorrah and the surrounding cities,

---

¹ Or *slave*; Greek *bondservant* ² Or *by* ³ Some manuscripts *although you fully knew it, that the Lord who once saved*

which likewise indulged in sexual immorality and pursued unnatural desire,[1] serve as an example by undergoing a punishment of eternal fire.

[8]Yet in like manner these people also, relying on their dreams, defile the flesh, reject authority, and blaspheme the glorious ones. [9]But when the archangel Michael, contending with the devil, was disputing about the body of Moses, he did not presume to pronounce a blasphemous judgment, but said, "The Lord rebuke you." [10]But these people blaspheme all that they do not understand, and they are destroyed by all that they, like unreasoning animals, understand instinctively. [11]Woe to them! For they walked in the way of Cain and abandoned themselves for the sake of gain to Balaam's error and perished in Korah's rebellion. [12]These are hidden reefs[2] at your love feasts, as they feast with you without fear, shepherds feeding themselves; waterless clouds, swept along by winds; fruitless trees in late autumn, twice dead, uprooted; [13]wild waves of the sea, casting up the foam of their own shame; wandering stars, for whom the gloom of utter darkness has been reserved forever.

[14]It was also about these that Enoch, the seventh from Adam, prophesied, saying, "Behold, the Lord comes with ten thousands of his holy ones, [15]to execute judgment on all and to convict all the ungodly of all their deeds of ungodliness that they have committed in such an ungodly way, and of all the harsh things that ungodly sinners have spoken against him." [16]These are grumblers, malcontents, following their own sinful desires; they are loud-mouthed boasters, showing favoritism to gain advantage.

[17]But you must remember, beloved, the predictions of the apostles of our Lord Jesus Christ. [18]They[3] said to you, "In the last time there will be scoffers, following their own ungodly passions." [19]It is these who cause divisions, worldly people, devoid of the Spirit. [20]But you, beloved, building yourselves up in your most holy faith and praying in the Holy Spirit, [21]keep yourselves in the love of God, waiting for the mercy of our Lord Jesus Christ that leads to eternal life. [22]And have mercy on those who doubt; [23]save others by snatching them out of the fire; to others show mercy with fear, hating even the garment[4] stained by the flesh.

[24]Now to him who is able to keep you from stumbling and to present you blameless before the presence of his glory with great joy, [25]to the only God, our Savior, through Jesus Christ our Lord, be glory, majesty, dominion, and authority, before all time and now and forever. Amen.

---

[1] Greek other flesh [2] Or are blemishes [3] Or Christ, because they [4] Greek chiton, a long garment worn under the cloak next to the skin

THE
REVELATION
TO JOHN

The book at a glance. 22 chapters, 404 verses. If we come to the book of
Revelation with the right literary expectations, we will find it a great deal more
accessible and more similar to familiar literary *genres than most people
believe the book to be. The book uses the resources of *fantasy or *visionary
writing to whisk us away to realms of the imagination that, for all their far-flung
difference from waking reality, nonetheless portray events of real life, including
some of our own daily experiences. The author is a divinely inspired visionary
who takes us on a guided tour of heaven and the future. Of course, much of
what was future history for John the author has already happened (such as the
fall of Rome) or has been happening since John's time (such as the cosmic
struggle between God and Satan), or is daily reality for us who live two
thousand years later (for example, some of the ecological terrors that John
envisions). Additionally, much of what John portrays is not time-bound at all but
instead belongs to the heavenly realities behind the things that happen on
earth. By portraying the end of earthly history, the book of Revelation serves as
a fitting conclusion to the Bible as a whole, as God gains a total and eternal
triumph in Jesus Christ.

▌**Genres.** Numerous genres converge in the book of Revelation, which is one of the
most packed and complex books in the Bible. The overall genre is *prophecy (22:19).
Like biblical prophecy generally, the actual medium is visionary writing: the book
unfolds as a pageant of visions, much like a modern music video. Furthermore, the way
in which real persons and events are actually portrayed is the way of fantasy, with
unlifelike details. The title of the book—the Apocalypse (based on the Greek word
meaning "to unveil")—indicates further that the book belongs to the genre of *apocalyptic writing. At every turn the author uses the resources of *poetry—*imagery,
*metaphor, *simile, and *allusion. The book begins and ends with the standard
features of NT *epistles. The overall shape of the book is *narrative or story, with the
usual ingredients of setting, characters, and plot (including plot conflict, progression,
and resolution). Greek drama was also an influence, seen in the attention that John
gives to the staging of events, positioning of characters in settings, crowd scenes, and
costuming of characters. Many of the visions of Revelation are like political cartoons,
only in the form of words instead of drawings.

▌**Symbolism.** The most important thing to know about the literary form of the book of
Revelation is that it uses the technique of *symbolism from start to finish. Instead of
portraying characters and events directly, much of the time the author portrays them

Passage	Content	Characters, Places, and Symbols	Time Frame
1:1–20	Prologue to the book: theme and source (vv. 1–3); epistolary opening (vv. 4–8); introduction to the book's narrator (vv. 9–11) and hero (vv. 12–20)	John the seer; the exalted hero of the book (Christ); the seven golden lampstands	"The things . . . that are" [now happening] (1:19)
2:1–3:22	Letters to the seven churches of Asia Minor (modern day Turkey)	The epistolary format; the evocative names of the cities where the churches are located; brief pictures of the exalted Christ; oracular tone	
4:1–11	Heavenly worship	God's heavenly throne with worshiping creatures around it	
5:1–8:1	The seven seals	Images of heaven and God; the scroll and the Lamb; songs of praise to God and the Lamb; the four horsemen; cataclysmic destruction of nature; the martyrs under the altar; the sealing of believers	
8:2–11:19	The seven trumpets	Scenes of heavenly worship; cataclysmic destruction of nature; the two witnesses; a terrifying cavalry on fantastic horses	
12:1–14:20	The seven great signs	The woman, the child, and the dragon, culminating in war in heaven; beast from the sea; beast from the earth; the Lamb on Mount Zion; angelic messages; Christ's reaping of the earth; judgment of the wicked	"The things . . . that are to take place after this" [from the time of John forward] (1:19)
15:1–16:21	The seven bowls of wrath	Plagues on earth; splitting of the city of Babylon into three parts	
17:1–22:5	The seven last events	Judgment of Babylon; marriage supper of the Lamb; defeat of the beast and false prophet; binding of Satan and millennial reign of Christ; loosing of Satan and his defeat; final judgment; the new heaven and new earth	
22:6–21	Epilogue	Final words about the narrator and prophecy; concluding benedictions	

indirectly by means of symbols. For example, Jesus is portrayed as a lamb, churches as lamps on lampstands, and Satan as a dragon with seven heads and ten horns. The symbols are sometimes familiar and sometimes original and strange. Whenever a work of literature presents a preponderance of symbols instead of realistic details, we can speak of the technique of symbolic reality, meaning that as we enter the work in our imagination, we primarily move in a world of symbols.

■ To what do the symbols refer? The strange visions of Revelation keep referring to familiar doctrines and *eschatological ideas taught elsewhere in the NT. Here is a list of the images and *motifs that according to the NT will mark the end of human history (not arranged so as to imply a sequential order): moral degeneration (including the appearance of the "lawless one"); a spirit of apostasy (including the appearance of the Antichrist and others who mislead people); cataclysmic natural and military disasters; great tribulation (including persecution) for believers; the parousia (arrival of Christ); the millennium; intermediate and final judgment (including hell); final dissolution of earthly reality; glorification of believers in heaven; new heavens and new earth. This is the list of referents to which we need to keep relating the visions of Revelation, asking, What familiar NT doctrine (such as God's judgment against evil) or event in salvation history (such as Christ's defeat of evil) or eschatological teaching (such as the degeneration of human history in its final phases) is pictured by the visionary details of the text? The book of Revelation fleshes out the blueprint that we can construct from elsewhere in the NT.

■ The structure of the book. The book is organized as a pageant of visions. There is no single sequence of action. Instead, the visions are cyclical and repetitive, as we keep retreading similar material. However, there is an element of progression and intensification as the cycles unfold, so that as we reach the last cycle we have a definite sense of the final end. Except for the prologue and epilogue, all of the sections fall into a pattern of seven units. Additionally, within these sevenfold units, the general movement is from fallen human history, associated with evil and misery, to the final consummation of history in its two aspects of punishment of evil and glorification of believers in heaven.

■ Inferred literary intentions. The book is designed to achieve the following literary purposes:

- depict events of earthly history or the eternal spiritual realms in the literary forms of apocalyptic writing, visionary writing, and fantasy

- express eschatological doctrines by means of symbols, thereby constructing a world of symbolic reality in the reader's imagination

- incarnate the truths of the Christian faith in great images and symbols

- exalt Christ as a conquering hero

- portray the defeat of all evil and the final victory of the people of God

■ Theological themes. (1) Christology: the book portrays Christ's work of redemption and triumph over evil in great detail. (2) Satan: Revelation is also the Bible's most extended delineation of Satan and his legions, and his eventual destruction. (3) Divine sovereignty: despite all the evil that is shown as occurring on earth, God remains in control of the events portrayed in Revelation. (4) Judgment: the book of Revelation is the Bible's most emphatic assertion that evil will be defeated and judged, and as part of that, it gives us some of the Bible's most vivid pictures of the wrath of God. (5) Redemption and salvation: the book is equally filled with visions of the ultimate salvation of believers. (6) Heaven: the book gives us the most extended visions of heaven in the Bible. (7) The church: we see the church's present spiritual struggles and ultimate spiritual glory.

Revelation as a chapter in the master story of the Bible. Just as the book of Genesis opens the master story of the Bible with the story of creation, the book of Revelation brings it to a close with the story of the end of earthly history. The whole story of redemption reaches its climax and conclusion in this book. The book of Genesis told us how the world and human history began; the book of Revelation is the last chapter in the story, showing how earthly history will end with the glorious triumph of Jesus Christ and God's returning to dwell with his people.

Prologue [chapter 1]. The opening chapter is a fourfold introduction. We are introduced to the theme and source of the revelation (vv. 1–3); given an epistolary salutation (vv. 4–8); introduced to the narrator (vv. 9–11); and given a portrait of the hero (Jesus Christ) of the visions to follow (vv. 12–20). Each of these units is densely packed and requires to be pondered in detail. For example: What do we learn about the theme and source of the visions? What religious meanings are embodied in the salutation? What specific details do we learn about the narrator and the victorious Christ? The vision of Christ (vv. 12–20) is our introduction to the symbolic mode of the book. Instead of assembling the individual details into a grotesque composite picture of Christ, we should view the individual symbols as embodying the qualities of Christ (e.g., his flaming eyes and bronzelike feet represent his transcendence; the sword coming from his mouth symbolizes his word and judgment).

1 The revelation of Jesus Christ, which God gave him to show to his servants[1] the things that must soon take place. He made it known by sending his angel to his servant[2] John, ²who bore witness to the word of God and to the testimony of Jesus Christ, even to all that he saw. ³Blessed is the one who reads aloud the words of this prophecy, and blessed are those who hear, and who keep what is written in it, for the time is near.

⁴John to the seven churches that are in Asia:

Grace to you and peace from him who is and who was and who is to come, and from the seven spirits who are before his throne, ⁵and from Jesus Christ the faithful witness, the firstborn of the dead, and the ruler of kings on earth.

To him who loves us and has freed us from our sins by his blood ⁶and made us a kingdom, priests to his God and Father, to him be glory and dominion forever and ever. Amen. ⁷Behold, he is coming with the clouds, and every eye will see him, even those who pierced him, and all tribes of the earth will wail[3] on account of him. Even so. Amen.

⁸"I am the Alpha and the Omega," says the Lord God, "who is and who was and who is to come, the Almighty."

---

¹ Greek *bondservants* ² Greek *bondservant* ³ Or *mourn*

⁹I, John, your brother and partner in the tribulation and the kingdom and the patient endurance that are in Jesus, was on the island called Patmos on account of the word of God and the testimony of Jesus. ¹⁰I was in the Spirit on the Lord's day, and I heard behind me a loud voice like a trumpet ¹¹saying, "Write what you see in a book and send it to the seven churches, to Ephesus and to Smyrna and to Pergamum and to Thyatira and to Sardis and to Philadelphia and to Laodicea."

¹²Then I turned to see the voice that was speaking to me, and on turning I saw seven golden lampstands, ¹³and in the midst of the lampstands one like a son of man, clothed with a long robe and with a golden sash around his chest. ¹⁴The hairs of his head were white, like white wool, like snow. His eyes were like a flame of fire, ¹⁵his feet were like burnished bronze, refined in a furnace, and his voice was like the roar of many waters. ¹⁶In his right hand he held seven stars, from his mouth came a sharp two-edged sword, and his face was like the sun shining in full strength.

¹⁷When I saw him, I fell at his feet as though dead. But he laid his right hand on me, saying, "Fear not, I am the first and the last, ¹⁸and the living one. I died, and behold I am alive forevermore, and I have the keys of Death and Hades. ¹⁹Write therefore the things that you have seen, those that are and those that are to take place after this. ²⁰As for the mystery of the seven stars that you saw in my right hand, and the seven golden lampstands, the seven stars are the angels of the seven churches, and the seven lampstands are the seven churches.

The letters to the churches, part 1 [chapter 2]. Chapters 2–3 contain the famous letters to the seven churches. The individual letters are constructed of seven elements, slightly varied among the individual letters: (1) a greeting ("to the angel of the church in _____ write"); (2) a title for Christ taken from the vision of him that concluded chapter 1; (3) a commendation of the church; (4) a criticism; (5) a warning; (6) an exhortation to be attentive ("He who has an ear, let him hear"); (7) a promise (beginning with the formula "to the one who conquers . . ."). The messages to the churches are timeless, as applicable today as they were in the first century.

2 "To the angel of the church in Ephesus write: 'The words of him who holds the seven stars in his right hand, who walks among the seven golden lampstands.

²"'I know your works, your toil and your patient endurance, and how you cannot bear with those who are evil, but have tested those who call themselves apostles and are not, and found them to be false. ³I know you are enduring patiently and bearing up for my name's sake, and you have not grown weary. ⁴But I have this against you, that you have abandoned the love you had at first. ⁵Remember therefore from where you have fallen; repent, and do the works you did at first. If not, I will come to you and remove your lampstand from its place, unless you repent. ⁶Yet this you have: you hate the works of the Nicolaitans, which I also hate. ⁷He who has an ear, let him hear what the Spirit says to the churches. To the one who conquers I will grant to eat of the tree of life, which is in the paradise of God.'

⁸"And to the angel of the church in Smyrna write: 'The words of the first and the last, who died and came to life.

⁹"'I know your tribulation and your poverty (but you are rich) and the slander[1] of those who say that they are Jews and are not, but are a synagogue of Satan. ¹⁰Do not

---

[1] Greek *blasphemy*

fear what you are about to suffer. Behold, the devil is about to throw some of you into prison, that you may be tested, and for ten days you will have tribulation. Be faithful unto death, and I will give you the crown of life. ¹¹He who has an ear, let him hear what the Spirit says to the churches. The one who conquers will not be hurt by the second death.'

¹²"And to the angel of the church in Pergamum write: 'The words of him who has the sharp two-edged sword.

¹³"'I know where you dwell, where Satan's throne is. Yet you hold fast my name, and you did not deny my faith¹ even in the days of Antipas my faithful witness, who was killed among you, where Satan dwells. ¹⁴But I have a few things against you: you have some there who hold the teaching of Balaam, who taught Balak to put a stumbling block before the sons of Israel, so that they might eat food sacrificed to idols and practice sexual immorality. ¹⁵So also you have some who hold the teaching of the Nicolaitans. ¹⁶Therefore repent. If not, I will come to you soon and war against them with the sword of my mouth. ¹⁷He who has an ear, let him hear what the Spirit says to the churches. To the one who conquers I will give some of the hidden manna, and I will give him a white stone, with a new name written on the stone that no one knows except the one who receives it.'

¹⁸"And to the angel of the church in Thyatira write: 'The words of the Son of God, who has eyes like a flame of fire, and whose feet are like burnished bronze.

¹⁹"'I know your works, your love and faith and service and patient endurance, and that your latter works exceed the first. ²⁰But I have this against you, that you tolerate that woman Jezebel, who calls herself a prophetess and is teaching and seducing my servants² to practice sexual immorality and to eat food sacrificed to idols. ²¹I gave her time to repent, but she refuses to repent of her sexual immorality. ²²Behold, I will throw her onto a sickbed, and those who commit adultery with her I will throw into great tribulation, unless they repent of her works, ²³and I will strike her children dead. And all the churches will know that I am he who searches mind and heart, and I will give to each of you according to your works. ²⁴But to the rest of you in Thyatira, who do not hold this teaching, who have not learned what some call the deep things of Satan, to you I say, I do not lay on you any other burden. ²⁵Only hold fast what you have until I come. ²⁶The one who conquers and who keeps my works until the end, to him I will give authority over the nations, ²⁷and he will rule them with a rod of iron, as when earthen pots are broken in pieces, even as I myself have received authority from my Father. ²⁸And I will give him the morning star. ²⁹He who has an ear, let him hear what the Spirit says to the churches.'

The letters to the churches, part 2 [chapter 3]. Three more letters appear in this chapter, and they follow the same sevenfold pattern noted above. We need to pick up on the prevalence of symbolism (the nonliteral) already in the most historically rooted part of Revelation. For example, the godly in Sardis do not literally keep from ever soiling their clothes (v. 4), and believers will not literally be pillars in heaven (v. 12). To extract the applicable truth from chapters 2–3, we need to discern what qualities and conduct God wants from his followers and what he detests. The particular details of a specific historical moment point us to universal principles that characterize the church in the world at every point in history.

¹ Or your faith in me ² Greek bondservants

3 "And to the angel of the church in Sardis write: 'The words of him who has the seven spirits of God and the seven stars.

"'I know your works. You have the reputation of being alive, but you are dead. [2] Wake up, and strengthen what remains and is about to die, for I have not found your works complete in the sight of my God. [3] Remember, then, what you received and heard. Keep it, and repent. If you will not wake up, I will come like a thief, and you will not know at what hour I will come against you. [4] Yet you have still a few names in Sardis, people who have not soiled their garments, and they will walk with me in white, for they are worthy. [5] The one who conquers will be clothed thus in white garments, and I will never blot his name out of the book of life. I will confess his name before my Father and before his angels. [6] He who has an ear, let him hear what the Spirit says to the churches.'

[7] "And to the angel of the church in Philadelphia write: 'The words of the holy one, the true one, who has the key of David, who opens and no one will shut, who shuts and no one opens.

[8] "'I know your works. Behold, I have set before you an open door, which no one is able to shut. I know that you have but little power, and yet you have kept my word and have not denied my name. [9] Behold, I will make those of the synagogue of Satan who say that they are Jews and are not, but lie—behold, I will make them come and bow down before your feet and they will learn that I have loved you. [10] Because you have kept my word about patient endurance, I will keep you from the hour of trial that is coming on the whole world, to try those who dwell on the earth. [11] I am coming soon. Hold fast what you have, so that no one may seize your crown. [12] The one who conquers, I will make him a pillar in the temple of my God. Never shall he go out of it, and I will write on him the name of my God, and the name of the city of my God, the new Jerusalem, which comes down from my God out of heaven, and my own new name. [13] He who has an ear, let him hear what the Spirit says to the churches.'

[14] "And to the angel of the church in Laodicea write: 'The words of the Amen, the faithful and true witness, the beginning of God's creation.

[15] "'I know your works: you are neither cold nor hot. Would that you were either cold or hot! [16] So, because you are lukewarm, and neither hot nor cold, I will spit you out of my mouth. [17] For you say, I am rich, I have prospered, and I need nothing, not realizing that you are wretched, pitiable, poor, blind, and naked. [18] I counsel you to buy from me gold refined by fire, so that you may be rich, and white garments so that you may clothe yourself and the shame of your nakedness may not be seen, and salve to anoint your eyes, so that you may see. [19] Those whom I love, I reprove and discipline, so be zealous and repent. [20] Behold, I stand at the door and knock. If anyone hears my voice and opens the door, I will come in to him and eat with him, and he with me. [21] The one who conquers, I will grant him to sit with me on my throne, as I also conquered and sat down with my Father on his throne. [22] He who has an ear, let him hear what the Spirit says to the churches.'"

Heavenly worship [chapter 4]. Chapter 4 is a "swing chapter" that can be viewed as a climax to the letters to the churches and a preview of the seven seals that will follow. The letters to the churches had ended with very brief anticipations of ultimate glory; chapter 4 gives us the full vision of heavenly glory. But the chapter is also our entrance into the heavenly scenes that will follow. Symbolism is the basic mode, with interspersed *lyric hymns of praise. We should not try to visualize the details in a composite way; it is the symbolic meaning of each detail that counts: for example, the white garments and crowns of the elders (v. 4) symbolize the transcendent glory of the creatures in heaven, and creatures "full of eyes all around and within" (v. 8) symbolize omniscience.

4 After this I looked, and behold, a door standing open in heaven! And the first voice, which I had heard speaking to me like a trumpet, said, "Come up here, and I will show you what must take place after this." ²At once I was in the Spirit, and behold, a throne stood in heaven, with one seated on the throne. ³And he who sat there had the appearance of jasper and carnelian, and around the throne was a rainbow that had the appearance of an emerald. ⁴Around the throne were twenty-four thrones, and seated on the thrones were twenty-four elders, clothed in white garments, with golden crowns on their heads. ⁵From the throne came flashes of lightning, and rumblings[1] and peals of thunder, and before the throne were burning seven torches of fire, which are the seven spirits of God, ⁶and before the throne there was as it were a sea of glass, like crystal.

And around the throne, on each side of the throne, are four living creatures, full of eyes in front and behind: ⁷the first living creature like a lion, the second living creature like an ox, the third living creature with the face of a man, and the fourth living creature like an eagle in flight. ⁸And the four living creatures, each of them with six wings, are full of eyes all around and within, and day and night they never cease to say,

"Holy, holy, holy, is the Lord God Almighty,
    who was and is and is to come!"

⁹And whenever the living creatures give glory and honor and thanks to him who is seated on the throne, who lives forever and ever, ¹⁰the twenty-four elders fall down before him who is seated on the throne and worship him who lives forever and ever. They cast their crowns before the throne, saying,

¹¹ "Worthy are you, our Lord and God,
        to receive glory and honor and power,
    for you created all things,
        and by your will they existed and were created."

The Lamb declared worthy to open the seven seals [chapter 5]. The next sevenfold unit of the book is devoted to the opening of the seven seals of God's revelation, his decrees of judgment. Chapter 5 is the prelude to that sequence. This scene set in the throne room of God functions like the epic council of the gods, where events are determined in a celestial world to be enacted on earth. The sequence of the chapter is as follows: the problem is posed as to who is worthy to open the seals on the scroll that reveals the future (vv. 1–4); the problem is solved when Christ—the Lamb—is declared worthy to open the seals (vv. 5–7); the elders around the throne respond with praise to the Lamb (vv. 8–10); the rest of the heavenly hosts likewise praise the worthiness of the Lamb (vv. 11–14). The emotional voltage of the chapter makes it lyric in effect.

[1] Or *voices, or sounds*

5 Then I saw in the right hand of him who was seated on the throne a scroll written within and on the back, sealed with seven seals. ²And I saw a strong angel proclaiming with a loud voice, "Who is worthy to open the scroll and break its seals?" ³And no one in heaven or on earth or under the earth was able to open the scroll or to look into it, ⁴and I began to weep loudly because no one was found worthy to open the scroll or to look into it. ⁵And one of the elders said to me, "Weep no more; behold, the Lion of the tribe of Judah, the Root of David, has conquered, so that he can open the scroll and its seven seals."

⁶And between the throne and the four living creatures and among the elders I saw a Lamb standing, as though it had been slain, with seven horns and with seven eyes, which are the seven spirits of God sent out into all the earth. ⁷And he went and took the scroll from the right hand of him who was seated on the throne. ⁸And when he had taken the scroll, the four living creatures and the twenty-four elders fell down before the Lamb, each holding a harp, and golden bowls full of incense, which are the prayers of the saints. ⁹And they sang a new song, saying,

"Worthy are you to take the scroll
    and to open its seals,
for you were slain, and by your blood you ransomed people for God
    from every tribe and language and people and nation,
¹⁰ and you have made them a kingdom and priests to our God,
    and they shall reign on the earth."

¹¹Then I looked, and I heard around the throne and the living creatures and the elders the voice of many angels, numbering myriads of myriads and thousands of thousands, ¹²saying with a loud voice, "Worthy is the Lamb who was slain, to receive power and wealth and wisdom and might and honor and glory and blessing!" ¹³And I heard every creature in heaven and on earth and under the earth and in the sea, and all that is in them, saying, "To him who sits on the throne and to the Lamb be blessing and honor and glory and might forever and ever!" ¹⁴And the four living creatures said, "Amen!" and the elders fell down and worshiped.

The first six seals unloosed [chapter 6]. Each of the seals is a vision of what has happened and will continue to happen beginning at the time that John wrote. The mode is symbolism and fantasy, as events that will really happen are portrayed not literally but figuratively. For example, an increasingly sinister pageant of four horsemen (vv. 1–8) uses the mode of symbolism and fantasy to embody Jesus' prediction in the Olivet Discourse that "you will hear of wars and rumors of wars. . . . For nation will rise against nation, and kingdom against kingdom, and there will be famines . . . in various places" (Matt. 24:6–7). The four visions are symbolic visions of warfare and famine. The vision of the martyrs under the altar (vv. 9–11) parallels Jesus' prediction of a great tribulation (Matt. 24:9–13), while the vision of cosmic collapse in the sixth seal (vv. 12–17) is cut from the same cloth as Jesus' eschatological predictions in such passages as Matthew 24:29–30 and Luke 23:30.

6 Now I watched when the Lamb opened one of the seven seals, and I heard one of the four living creatures say with a voice like thunder, "Come!" [2]And I looked, and behold, a white horse! And its rider had a bow, and a crown was given to him, and he came out conquering, and to conquer.

[3]When he opened the second seal, I heard the second living creature say, "Come!" [4]And out came another horse, bright red. Its rider was permitted to take peace from the earth, so that people should slay one another, and he was given a great sword.

[5]When he opened the third seal, I heard the third living creature say, "Come!" And I looked, and behold, a black horse! And its rider had a pair of scales in his hand. [6]And I heard what seemed to be a voice in the midst of the four living creatures, saying, "A quart[1] of wheat for a denarius,[2] and three quarts of barley for a denarius, and do not harm the oil and wine!"

[7]When he opened the fourth seal, I heard the voice of the fourth living creature say, "Come!" [8]And I looked, and behold, a pale horse! And its rider's name was Death, and Hades followed him. And they were given authority over a fourth of the earth, to kill with sword and with famine and with pestilence and by wild beasts of the earth.

[9]When he opened the fifth seal, I saw under the altar the souls of those who had been slain for the word of God and for the witness they had borne. [10]They cried out with a loud voice, "O Sovereign Lord, holy and true, how long before you will judge and avenge our blood on those who dwell on the earth?" [11]Then they were each given a white robe and told to rest a little longer, until the number of their fellow servants[3] and their brothers[4] should be complete, who were to be killed as they themselves had been.

[12]When he opened the sixth seal, I looked, and behold, there was a great earthquake, and the sun became black as sackcloth, the full moon became like blood, [13]and the stars of the sky fell to the earth as the fig tree sheds its winter fruit when shaken by a gale. [14]The sky vanished like a scroll that is being rolled up, and every mountain and island was removed from its place. [15]Then the kings of the earth and the great ones and the generals and the rich and the powerful, and everyone, slave[5] and free, hid themselves in the caves and among the rocks of the mountains, [16]calling to the mountains and rocks, "Fall on us and hide us from the face of him who is seated on the throne, and from the wrath of the Lamb, [17]for the great day of their wrath has come, and who can stand?"

The sealing of believers [7:1–8:5]. John gives us a chapter-length interlude between the opening of the sixth and seventh seals. In this context, to seal something (vv. 1–8) is to put a mark of ownership on it. Here the redeemed are sealed, that is, saved by God. The number (144,000) is large (multiples of thousand, the ancient equivalent of "the largest number imaginable") and complete (12 times 12, or a symbolic four-square). The redemption scene is followed by a scene of heavenly worship (vv. 9–17); we should note that a leading theme or purpose of Revelation is to give us pictures and assurances of a heavenly reality that transcends the earthly sphere. The opening of the seventh seal and its awesome aftermath (8:1–5) are an extension of the scene of heavenly worship that comes at the end of chapter 7.

---

[1] Greek *choinix*, a dry measure equal to about a quart [2] A *denarius* was a day's wage for a laborer [3] Greek *fellow bondservants* [4] Or *brothers and sisters*. The plural Greek word *adelphoi* (translated "brothers") refers to siblings in a family. In New Testament usage, depending on the context, *adelphoi* may refer either to men or to both men and women who are siblings (brothers and sisters) in God's family, the church [5] Or *servant*; Greek *bondservant*

7 After this I saw four angels standing at the four corners of the earth, holding back the four winds of the earth, that no wind might blow on earth or sea or against any tree. ²Then I saw another angel ascending from the rising of the sun, with the seal of the living God, and he called with a loud voice to the four angels who had been given power to harm earth and sea, ³saying, "Do not harm the earth or the sea or the trees, until we have sealed the servants¹ of our God on their foreheads." ⁴And I heard the number of the sealed, 144,000, sealed from every tribe of the sons of Israel:

⁵   12,000 from the tribe of Judah were sealed,
   12,000 from the tribe of Reuben,
   12,000 from the tribe of Gad,
⁶   12,000 from the tribe of Asher,
   12,000 from the tribe of Naphtali,
   12,000 from the tribe of Manasseh,
⁷   12,000 from the tribe of Simeon,
   12,000 from the tribe of Levi,
   12,000 from the tribe of Issachar,
⁸   12,000 from the tribe of Zebulun,
   12,000 from the tribe of Joseph,
   12,000 from the tribe of Benjamin were sealed.

⁹After this I looked, and behold, a great multitude that no one could number, from every nation, from all tribes and peoples and languages, standing before the throne and before the Lamb, clothed in white robes, with palm branches in their hands, ¹⁰and crying out with a loud voice, "Salvation belongs to our God who sits on the throne, and to the Lamb!" ¹¹And all the angels were standing around the throne and around the elders and the four living creatures, and they fell on their faces before the throne and worshiped God, ¹²saying, "Amen! Blessing and glory and wisdom and thanksgiving and honor and power and might be to our God forever and ever! Amen."

¹³Then one of the elders addressed me, saying, "Who are these, clothed in white robes, and from where have they come?" ¹⁴I said to him, "Sir, you know." And he said to me, "These are the ones coming out of the great tribulation. They have washed their robes and made them white in the blood of the Lamb.

¹⁵   "Therefore they are before the throne of God,
   and serve him day and night in his temple;
   and he who sits on the throne will shelter them with his presence.
¹⁶   They shall hunger no more, neither thirst anymore;
   the sun shall not strike them,
   nor any scorching heat.
¹⁷   For the Lamb in the midst of the throne will be their shepherd,
   and he will guide them to springs of living water,
   and God will wipe away every tear from their eyes."

8 When the Lamb opened the seventh seal, there was silence in heaven for about half an hour. ²Then I saw the seven angels who stand before God, and seven trumpets were given to them. ³And another angel came and stood at the altar with a golden censer, and he was given much incense to offer with the prayers of

¹ Greek bondservants

all the saints on the golden altar before the throne, ⁴and the smoke of the incense, with the prayers of the saints, rose before God from the hand of the angel. ⁵Then the angel took the censer and filled it with fire from the altar and threw it on the earth, and there were peals of thunder, rumblings,¹ flashes of lightning, and an earthquake.

The first six trumpets [8:6–9:21]. We now begin a new cycle of sevenfold visions. Once again (as with the four horse visions) the first four visions (8:6–13) form a unified sequence, this time portraying the destruction of a third of the elemental forces of nature. At a moment such as this we can see Revelation's affinities to the genre of the *horror story. This continues with the terrifying vision of destructive locusts (9:1–11), which pictures the degeneration of life on earth as an expression of God's judgment against evil. The symbolic locusts are as up to date as our ecological crisis and the daily news about terrorism. This is equally true of the second half of chapter 9 (vv. 13–19), a vision of more-than-human military destructiveness. Verses 20–21, a picture of the human race's refusal to repent in the face of the devastating events, is a famous non sequitur—an action contrary to what we might logically expect.

⁶Now the seven angels who had the seven trumpets prepared to blow them.

⁷The first angel blew his trumpet, and there followed hail and fire, mixed with blood, and these were thrown upon the earth. And a third of the earth was burned up, and a third of the trees were burned up, and all green grass was burned up.

⁸The second angel blew his trumpet, and something like a great mountain, burning with fire, was thrown into the sea, and a third of the sea became blood. ⁹A third of the living creatures in the sea died, and a third of the ships were destroyed.

¹⁰The third angel blew his trumpet, and a great star fell from heaven, blazing like a torch, and it fell on a third of the rivers and on the springs of water. ¹¹The name of the star is Wormwood.² A third of the waters became wormwood, and many people died from the water, because it had been made bitter.

¹²The fourth angel blew his trumpet, and a third of the sun was struck, and a third of the moon, and a third of the stars, so that a third of their light might be darkened, and a third of the day might be kept from shining, and likewise a third of the night.

¹³Then I looked, and I heard an eagle crying with a loud voice as it flew directly overhead, "Woe, woe, woe to those who dwell on the earth, at the blasts of the other trumpets that the three angels are about to blow!"

9 And the fifth angel blew his trumpet, and I saw a star fallen from heaven to earth, and he was given the key to the shaft of the bottomless pit.³ ²He opened the shaft of the bottomless pit, and from the shaft rose smoke like the smoke of a great furnace, and the sun and the air were darkened with the smoke from the shaft. ³Then from the smoke came locusts on the earth, and they were given power like the power of scorpions of the earth. ⁴They were told not to harm the grass of the earth or any green plant or any tree, but only those people who do not have the seal of God on their foreheads. ⁵They were allowed to torment them for five months, but not to kill them, and their torment was like the torment of a scorpion when it stings someone. ⁶And in those days people will seek death and will not find it. They will long to die, but death will flee from them.

---

¹ Or *voices*, or *sounds* ² *Wormwood* is the name of a plant and of the bitter-tasting extract derived from it ³ Greek *the abyss*; also verses 2, 11

⁷In appearance the locusts were like horses prepared for battle: on their heads were what looked like crowns of gold; their faces were like human faces, ⁸their hair like women's hair, and their teeth like lions' teeth; ⁹they had breastplates like breastplates of iron, and the noise of their wings was like the noise of many chariots with horses rushing into battle. ¹⁰They have tails and stings like scorpions, and their power to hurt people for five months is in their tails. ¹¹They have as king over them the angel of the bottomless pit. His name in Hebrew is Abaddon, and in Greek he is called Apollyon.¹

¹²The first woe has passed; behold, two woes are still to come.

¹³Then the sixth angel blew his trumpet, and I heard a voice from the four horns of the golden altar before God, ¹⁴saying to the sixth angel who had the trumpet, "Release the four angels who are bound at the great river Euphrates." ¹⁵So the four angels, who had been prepared for the hour, the day, the month, and the year, were released to kill a third of mankind. ¹⁶The number of mounted troops was twice ten thousand times ten thousand; I heard their number. ¹⁷And this is how I saw the horses in my vision and those who rode them: they wore breastplates the color of fire and of sapphire² and of sulfur, and the heads of the horses were like lions' heads, and fire and smoke and sulfur came out of their mouths. ¹⁸By these three plagues a third of mankind was killed, by the fire and smoke and sulfur coming out of their mouths. ¹⁹For the power of the horses is in their mouths and in their tails, for their tails are like serpents with heads, and by means of them they wound.

²⁰The rest of mankind, who were not killed by these plagues, did not repent of the works of their hands nor give up worshiping demons and idols of gold and silver and bronze and stone and wood, which cannot see or hear or walk, ²¹nor did they repent of their murders or their sorceries or their sexual immorality or their thefts.

Prelude to the interlude [chapter 10]. Just as the sequence of the seven seals was interrupted after the sixth seal by an interlude (creating the effect of setting the seventh vision apart), John now gives us an elaborate interlude between the sixth and seventh trumpets. The chapter is dominated by a larger-than-life angelic figure who bestrides the earth like a colossus (vv. 1–7) and tells John to eat the scroll of revelation, symbolic of his prophetic task and message.

10 Then I saw another mighty angel coming down from heaven, wrapped in a cloud, with a rainbow over his head, and his face was like the sun, and his legs like pillars of fire. ²He had a little scroll open in his hand. And he set his right foot on the sea, and his left foot on the land, ³and called out with a loud voice, like a lion roaring. When he called out, the seven thunders sounded. ⁴And when the seven thunders had sounded, I was about to write, but I heard a voice from heaven saying, "Seal up what the seven thunders have said, and do not write it down." ⁵And the angel whom I saw standing on the sea and on the land raised his right hand to heaven ⁶and swore by him who lives forever and ever, who created heaven and what is in it, the earth and what is in it, and the sea and what is in it, that there would be no more delay, ⁷but that in the days of the trumpet call to be sounded by the seventh angel, the mystery of God would be fulfilled, just as he announced to his servants³ the prophets.

¹ *Abaddon means destruction; Apollyon means destroyer* ² Greek *hyacinth* ³ Greek *bondservants*

⁸Then the voice that I had heard from heaven spoke to me again, saying, "Go, take the scroll that is open in the hand of the angel who is standing on the sea and on the land." ⁹So I went to the angel and told him to give me the little scroll. And he said to me, "Take and eat it; it will make your stomach bitter, but in your mouth it will be sweet as honey." ¹⁰And I took the little scroll from the hand of the angel and ate it. It was sweet as honey in my mouth, but when I had eaten it my stomach was made bitter. ¹¹And I was told, "You must again prophesy about many peoples and nations and languages and kings."

Interlude and seventh trumpet [chapter 11]. The actions that the two witnesses of the interlude perform (vv. 1–14), such as measuring the temple and spewing forth fire from their mouths, are doubtless mysterious, and we do well to consider that one of the purposes of the visionary book of Revelation is to convey a due sense of mystery about the future and the heavenly sphere. The career of the two witnesses in this interlude parallels the other movements within the book of Revelation—the temporary defeat of the church followed by its ultimate triumph. This pattern is climaxed by the seventh trumpet, an awesome scene of heavenly triumph and worship (vv. 15–19).

11 Then I was given a measuring rod like a staff, and I was told, "Rise and measure the temple of God and the altar and those who worship there, ²but do not measure the court outside the temple; leave that out, for it is given over to the nations, and they will trample the holy city for forty-two months. ³And I will grant authority to my two witnesses, and they will prophesy for 1,260 days, clothed in sackcloth."

⁴These are the two olive trees and the two lampstands that stand before the Lord of the earth. ⁵And if anyone would harm them, fire pours from their mouth and consumes their foes. If anyone would harm them, this is how he is doomed to be killed. ⁶They have the power to shut the sky, that no rain may fall during the days of their prophesying, and they have power over the waters to turn them into blood and to strike the earth with every kind of plague, as often as they desire. ⁷And when they have finished their testimony, the beast that rises from the bottomless pit¹ will make war on them and conquer them and kill them, ⁸and their dead bodies will lie in the street of the great city that symbolically² is called Sodom and Egypt, where their Lord was crucified. ⁹For three and a half days some from the peoples and tribes and languages and nations will gaze at their dead bodies and refuse to let them be placed in a tomb, ¹⁰and those who dwell on the earth will rejoice over them and make merry and exchange presents, because these two prophets had been a torment to those who dwell on the earth. ¹¹But after the three and a half days a breath of life from God entered them, and they stood up on their feet, and great fear fell on those who saw them. ¹²Then they heard a loud voice from heaven saying to them, "Come up here!" And they went up to heaven in a cloud, and their enemies watched them. ¹³And at that hour there was a great earthquake, and a tenth of the city fell. Seven thousand people were killed in the earthquake, and the rest were terrified and gave glory to the God of heaven.

¹⁴The second woe has passed; behold, the third woe is soon to come.

¹⁵Then the seventh angel blew his trumpet, and there were loud voices in heaven, saying, "The kingdom of the world has become the kingdom of our Lord and of his

¹ Or the abyss ² Greek spiritually

Christ, and he shall reign forever and ever." [16]And the twenty-four elders who sit on their thrones before God fell on their faces and worshiped God, [17]saying,

> "We give thanks to you, Lord God Almighty,
>   who is and who was,
> for you have taken your great power
>   and begun to reign.
> [18] The nations raged,
>   but your wrath came,
> and the time for the dead to be judged,
> and for rewarding your servants,[1] the prophets and saints,
>   and those who fear your name,
>   both small and great,
> and for destroying the destroyers of the earth."

[19]Then God's temple in heaven was opened, and the ark of his covenant was seen within his temple. There were flashes of lightning, rumblings,[2] peals of thunder, an earthquake, and heavy hail.

The first great sign [chapter 12]. We should note in advance that chapters 12–14 are a self-contained unit with a U-shaped trajectory that epitomizes the general movement of the book of Revelation as a whole, as the temporary triumph of evil on earth is eventually countered by God's establishment of his heavenly kingdom. The material consists of seven great signs (so called in vv. 1 and 3), the first of which occupies chapter 12. The chief actors are the woman (symbolic of Israel in the beginning of the chapter, inasmuch as the woman is the one who gives birth to the son), the woman's son (Christ), and a dragon (Satan). This chapter is a flashback in the book of Revelation, narrating in symbolism and fantasy Satan's inability to defeat Christ during his life on earth (vv. 1–5) and, in fact, Christ's defeat of Satan and his cohorts. The woman protected in the wilderness (v. 6) is the church, on whom Satan turns with violent anger (v. 17) when he is defeated by the followers of Christ (vv. 7–12), both angels (vv. 7–8) and people (v. 11).

12 And a great sign appeared in heaven: a woman clothed with the sun, with the moon under her feet, and on her head a crown of twelve stars. [2]She was pregnant and was crying out in birth pains and the agony of giving birth. [3]And another sign appeared in heaven: behold, a great red dragon, with seven heads and ten horns, and on his heads seven diadems. [4]His tail swept down a third of the stars of heaven and cast them to the earth. And the dragon stood before the woman who was about to give birth, so that when she bore her child he might devour it. [5]She gave birth to a male child, one who is to rule all the nations with a rod of iron, but her child was caught up to God and to his throne, [6]and the woman fled into the wilderness, where she has a place prepared by God, in which she is to be nourished for 1,260 days.

[7]Now war arose in heaven, Michael and his angels fighting against the dragon. And the dragon and his angels fought back, [8]but he was defeated, and there was no longer any place for them in heaven. [9]And the great dragon was thrown down, that ancient serpent, who is called the devil and Satan, the deceiver of the whole world— he was thrown down to the earth, and his angels were thrown down with him. [10]And I heard a loud voice in heaven, saying, "Now the salvation and the power and the

---

[1] Greek bondservants [2] Or voices, or sounds

kingdom of our God and the authority of his Christ have come, for the accuser of our brothers[1] has been thrown down, who accuses them day and night before our God. [11]And they have conquered him by the blood of the Lamb and by the word of their testimony, for they loved not their lives even unto death. [12]Therefore, rejoice, O heavens and you who dwell in them! But woe to you, O earth and sea, for the devil has come down to you in great wrath, because he knows that his time is short!"

[13]And when the dragon saw that he had been thrown down to the earth, he pursued the woman who had given birth to the male child. [14]But the woman was given the two wings of the great eagle so that she might fly from the serpent into the wilderness, to the place where she is to be nourished for a time, and times, and half a time. [15]The serpent poured water like a river out of his mouth after the woman, to sweep her away with a flood. [16]But the earth came to the help of the woman, and the earth opened its mouth and swallowed the river that the dragon had poured from his mouth. [17]Then the dragon became furious with the woman and went off to make war on the rest of her offspring, on those who keep the commandments of God and hold to the testimony of Jesus. And he stood[2] on the sand of the sea.

The two beasts [chapter 13]. The second and third great signs center on two beasts— figures of demonic evil—rising, respectively, from the sea (vv. 1–10) and the earth (vv. 11–18). They are symbols of the damage that Satan does through earthly governments and institutions corrupted by evil. These beasts perform signs and wonders and wield great power, deceiving and persecuting many. It is easy to see them as a fleshing out in the mode of fantasy Jesus' prediction in the Olivet Discourse that "false christs and false prophets will arise and perform great signs and wonders, so as to lead astray, if possible, even the elect" (Matt. 24:24).

13 And I saw a beast rising out of the sea, with ten horns and seven heads, with ten diadems on its horns and blasphemous names on its heads. [2]And the beast that I saw was like a leopard; its feet were like a bear's, and its mouth was like a lion's mouth. And to it the dragon gave his power and his throne and great authority. [3]One of its heads seemed to have a mortal wound, but its mortal wound was healed, and the whole earth marveled as they followed the beast. [4]And they worshiped the dragon, for he had given his authority to the beast, and they worshiped the beast, saying, "Who is like the beast, and who can fight against it?"

[5]And the beast was given a mouth uttering haughty and blasphemous words, and it was allowed to exercise authority for forty-two months. [6]It opened its mouth to utter blasphemies against God, blaspheming his name and his dwelling,[3] that is, those who dwell in heaven. [7]Also it was allowed to make war on the saints and to conquer them.[4] And authority was given it over every tribe and people and language and nation, [8]and all who dwell on earth will worship it, everyone whose name has not been written before the foundation of the world in the book of life of the Lamb who was slain. [9]If anyone has an ear, let him hear:

[10]   If anyone is to be taken captive,
            to captivity he goes;
        if anyone is to be slain with the sword,
            with the sword must he be slain.

---

[1] Or brothers and sisters [2] Some manuscripts And I stood, connecting the sentence with 13:1 [3] Or tabernacle [4] Some manuscripts omit this sentence

Here is a call for the endurance and faith of the saints.

¹¹Then I saw another beast rising out of the earth. It had two horns like a lamb and it spoke like a dragon. ¹²It exercises all the authority of the first beast in its presence,¹ and makes the earth and its inhabitants worship the first beast, whose mortal wound was healed. ¹³It performs great signs, even making fire come down from heaven to earth in front of people, ¹⁴and by the signs that it is allowed to work in the presence of² the beast it deceives those who dwell on earth, telling them to make an image for the beast that was wounded by the sword and yet lived. ¹⁵And it was allowed to give breath to the image of the beast, so that the image of the beast might even speak and might cause those who would not worship the image of the beast to be slain. ¹⁶Also it causes all, both small and great, both rich and poor, both free and slave,³ to be marked on the right hand or the forehead, ¹⁷so that no one can buy or sell unless he has the mark, that is, the name of the beast or the number of its name. ¹⁸This calls for wisdom: let the one who has understanding calculate the number of the beast, for it is the number of a man, and his number is 666.⁴

Four more great signs [chapter 14]. This chapter fills out the sequence of seven great signs in chapters 12–14. The sequence is as follows: the Lamb worshiped by his redeemed on Mount Zion, that is, in heaven (vv. 1–5); angelic messages of judgment against evil (vv. 6–13); Christ's harvesting of the earth, a picture of the end of human history (vv. 14–16); the angelic reaping and judgment of the wicked at the end of history (vv. 17–20). All of these four visions depict events at the end of history and the beginning of the entrance of all people into the eternal afterlife. The author uses visionary symbols to represent the realities that are to come.

14 Then I looked, and behold, on Mount Zion stood the Lamb, and with him 144,000 who had his name and his Father's name written on their foreheads. ²And I heard a voice from heaven like the roar of many waters and like the sound of loud thunder. The voice I heard was like the sound of harpists playing on their harps, ³and they were singing a new song before the throne and before the four living creatures and before the elders. No one could learn that song except the 144,000 who had been redeemed from the earth. ⁴It is these who have not defiled themselves with women, for they are virgins. It is these who follow the Lamb wherever he goes. These have been redeemed from mankind as firstfruits for God and the Lamb, ⁵and in their mouth no lie was found, for they are blameless.

⁶Then I saw another angel flying directly overhead, with an eternal gospel to proclaim to those who dwell on earth, to every nation and tribe and language and people. ⁷And he said with a loud voice, "Fear God and give him glory, because the hour of his judgment has come, and worship him who made heaven and earth, the sea and the springs of water."

⁸Another angel, a second, followed, saying, "Fallen, fallen is Babylon the great, she who made all nations drink the wine of the passion⁵ of her sexual immorality."

⁹And another angel, a third, followed them, saying with a loud voice, "If anyone worships the beast and its image and receives a mark on his forehead or on his hand, ¹⁰he also will drink the wine of God's wrath, poured full strength into the cup of his anger, and he will be tormented with fire and sulfur in the presence of the holy

---

¹ Or on its behalf ² Or on behalf of ³ Greek bondservant ⁴ Some manuscripts 616 ⁵ Or wrath

angels and in the presence of the Lamb. ¹¹And the smoke of their torment goes up forever and ever, and they have no rest, day or night, these worshipers of the beast and its image, and whoever receives the mark of its name."

¹²Here is a call for the endurance of the saints, those who keep the commandments of God and their faith in Jesus.¹

¹³And I heard a voice from heaven saying, "Write this: Blessed are the dead who die in the Lord from now on." "Blessed indeed," says the Spirit, "that they may rest from their labors, for their deeds follow them!"

¹⁴Then I looked, and behold, a white cloud, and seated on the cloud one like a son of man, with a golden crown on his head, and a sharp sickle in his hand. ¹⁵And another angel came out of the temple, calling with a loud voice to him who sat on the cloud, "Put in your sickle, and reap, for the hour to reap has come, for the harvest of the earth is fully ripe." ¹⁶So he who sat on the cloud swung his sickle across the earth, and the earth was reaped.

¹⁷Then another angel came out of the temple in heaven, and he too had a sharp sickle. ¹⁸And another angel came out from the altar, the angel who has authority over the fire, and he called with a loud voice to the one who had the sharp sickle, "Put in your sickle and gather the clusters from the vine of the earth, for its grapes are ripe." ¹⁹So the angel swung his sickle across the earth and gathered the grape harvest of the earth and threw it into the great winepress of the wrath of God. ²⁰And the winepress was trodden outside the city, and blood flowed from the winepress, as high as a horse's bridle, for 1,600 stadia.²

Prelude to the seven bowls of wrath [chapter 15]. Just as the seven seals and seven trumpets were preceded by a scene set in heaven, so too chapter 15 is a heavenly prelude to the seven bowls of God's judgment. The announcement that the coming plagues "are the last, for with them the wrath of God is finished" (v. 1), alerts us to a progressive element that underlies the cycles of Revelation. Chapter 15 allows us to look in on scenes of heavenly ritual, with the chief motifs being praise of God's transcendent greatness and heavenly worship.

15 Then I saw another sign in heaven, great and amazing, seven angels with seven plagues, which are the last, for with them the wrath of God is finished.
²And I saw what appeared to be a sea of glass mingled with fire—and also those who had conquered the beast and its image and the number of its name, standing beside the sea of glass with harps of God in their hands. ³And they sing the song of Moses, the servant³ of God, and the song of the Lamb, saying,

"Great and amazing are your deeds,
    O Lord God the Almighty!
Just and true are your ways,
    O King of the nations!⁴
⁴ Who will not fear, O Lord,
    and glorify your name?
For you alone are holy.
    All nations will come

---

¹ Greek *and the faith of Jesus* ² About 184 miles; a *stadion* was about 607 feet or 185 meters ³ Greek *bondservant* ⁴ Some manuscripts *the ages*

> and worship you,
>> for your righteous acts have been revealed."

⁵After this I looked, and the sanctuary of the tent[1] of witness in heaven was opened, ⁶and out of the sanctuary came the seven angels with the seven plagues, clothed in pure, bright linen, with golden sashes around their chests. ⁷And one of the four living creatures gave to the seven angels seven golden bowls full of the wrath of God who lives forever and ever, ⁸and the sanctuary was filled with smoke from the glory of God and from his power, and no one could enter the sanctuary until the seven plagues of the seven angels were finished.

The seven bowls of wrath [chapter 16]. The cyclic organization of Revelation is by now unmistakable, as we keep retreading similar material, starting with the spread of evil on earth and God's judgment of it in history, and moving toward the consummation of history in its twofold elements of punishment of the unbelieving and redemption of Christ's followers. The seven bowls repeat rather than succeed the seven seals and seven trumpets. The keynote of the seven visions in chapter 16 is a vision of total collapse on the earth, chiefly in the spheres of nature and military conflict. The chapter belongs to the genre of the horror story, here used to portray God's judgment against evil and also the self-destructive nature of human sinfulness.

16

Then I heard a loud voice from the temple telling the seven angels, "Go and pour out on the earth the seven bowls of the wrath of God."

²So the first angel went and poured out his bowl on the earth, and harmful and painful sores came upon the people who bore the mark of the beast and worshiped its image.

³The second angel poured out his bowl into the sea, and it became like the blood of a corpse, and every living thing died that was in the sea.

⁴The third angel poured out his bowl into the rivers and the springs of water, and they became blood. ⁵And I heard the angel in charge of the waters[2] say,

> "Just are you, O Holy One, who is and who was,
>> for you brought these judgments.
> ⁶ For they have shed the blood of saints and prophets,
>> and you have given them blood to drink.
> It is what they deserve!"

⁷And I heard the altar saying,

> "Yes, Lord God the Almighty,
>> true and just are your judgments!"

⁸The fourth angel poured out his bowl on the sun, and it was allowed to scorch people with fire. ⁹They were scorched by the fierce heat, and they cursed[3] the name of God who had power over these plagues. They did not repent and give him glory.

¹⁰The fifth angel poured out his bowl on the throne of the beast, and its kingdom was plunged into darkness. People gnawed their tongues in anguish ¹¹and cursed the God of heaven for their pain and sores. They did not repent of their deeds.

¹²The sixth angel poured out his bowl on the great river Euphrates, and its water

---

[1] Or tabernacle [2] Greek angel of the waters [3] Greek blasphemed; also verses 11, 21

was dried up, to prepare the way for the kings from the east. ¹³And I saw, coming out of the mouth of the dragon and out of the mouth of the beast and out of the mouth of the false prophet, three unclean spirits like frogs. ¹⁴For they are demonic spirits, performing signs, who go abroad to the kings of the whole world, to assemble them for battle on the great day of God the Almighty. ¹⁵("Behold, I am coming like a thief! Blessed is the one who stays awake, keeping his garments on, that he may not go about naked and be seen exposed!") ¹⁶And they assembled them at the place that in Hebrew is called Armageddon.

¹⁷The seventh angel poured out his bowl into the air, and a loud voice came out of the temple, from the throne, saying, "It is done!" ¹⁸And there were flashes of lightning, rumblings,¹ peals of thunder, and a great earthquake such as there had never been since man was on the earth, so great was that earthquake. ¹⁹The great city was split into three parts, and the cities of the nations fell, and God remembered Babylon the great, to make her drain the cup of the wine of the fury of his wrath. ²⁰And every island fled away, and no mountains were to be found. ²¹And great hailstones, about one hundred pounds² each, fell from heaven on people; and they cursed God for the plague of the hail, because the plague was so severe.

The judgment of Babylon [chapter 17]. The final sevenfold unit in Revelation can be called the seven last events. They fall into the two categories of God's judgment of evil and the consummation of human history. The first of the seven last events is the defeat of Babylon, an event that spans two chapters. Chapter 17 introduces the evocative symbol Babylon, a composite city that symbolizes unregenerate humanity in community against God. The city has many qualities of the historical Rome (persecutor of Christians in John's day), but it is more profoundly the timeless city of evil, symbol of humankind in rebellion against God. As the city of Satan, it stands over against the city of God. As the chapter unfolds, other symbols of evil cluster around the city of Babylon—prostitution, cannibalism, blasphemy, murder, and monstrous beasts. Verses 1–6 describe the harlot, while verses 7–18 explain her meaning and significance. The symbolism of the city of evil is open-ended and applies to all forms of evil at every point in Christian history.

17 Then one of the seven angels who had the seven bowls came and said to me, "Come, I will show you the judgment of the great prostitute who is seated on many waters, ²with whom the kings of the earth have committed sexual immorality, and with the wine of whose sexual immorality the dwellers on earth have become drunk." ³And he carried me away in the Spirit into a wilderness, and I saw a woman sitting on a scarlet beast that was full of blasphemous names, and it had seven heads and ten horns. ⁴The woman was arrayed in purple and scarlet, and adorned with gold and jewels and pearls, holding in her hand a golden cup full of abominations and the impurities of her sexual immorality. ⁵And on her forehead was written a name of mystery: "Babylon the great, mother of prostitutes and of earth's abominations." ⁶And I saw the woman, drunk with the blood of the saints, the blood of the martyrs of Jesus.³

When I saw her, I marveled greatly. ⁷But the angel said to me, "Why do you marvel? I will tell you the mystery of the woman, and of the beast with seven heads and ten horns that carries her. ⁸The beast that you saw was, and is not, and is about to rise from the bottomless pit⁴ and go to destruction. And the dwellers on earth whose

¹ Or voices, or sounds ² Greek a talent in weight ³ Greek the witnesses to Jesus ⁴ Greek the abyss

names have not been written in the book of life from the foundation of the world will marvel to see the beast, because it was and is not and is to come. [9]This calls for a mind with wisdom: the seven heads are seven mountains on which the woman is seated; [10]they are also seven kings, five of whom have fallen, one is, the other has not yet come, and when he does come he must remain only a little while. [11]As for the beast that was and is not, it is an eighth but it belongs to the seven, and it goes to destruction. [12]And the ten horns that you saw are ten kings who have not yet received royal power, but they are to receive authority as kings for one hour, together with the beast. [13]These are of one mind, and they hand over their power and authority to the beast. [14]They will make war on the Lamb, and the Lamb will conquer them, for he is Lord of lords and King of kings, and those with him are called and chosen and faithful."

[15]And the angel[1] said to me, "The waters that you saw, where the prostitute is seated, are peoples and multitudes and nations and languages. [16]And the ten horns that you saw, they and the beast will hate the prostitute. They will make her desolate and naked, and devour her flesh and burn her up with fire, [17]for God has put it into their hearts to carry out his purpose by being of one mind and handing over their royal power to the beast, until the words of God are fulfilled. [18]And the woman that you saw is the great city that has dominion over the kings of the earth."

The fall of Babylon [chapter 18]. With the city of evil having been established in our imagination in chapter 17, we now witness the aftermath of the fall of the city, symbolic of God's defeat of evil. We traverse the fall of Babylon in five distinct units: a *doom song that rehearses the details of Babylon's demise (vv. 1–3); a prophetic *oracle that warns Christians to stay away from the sinful city and asserts the justice of the city's fall (vv. 4–8); a *lament over the fall of Babylon (here pictured as a world empire like the Roman Empire of John's day) by the evil world order that participated in Babylon's wicked exploits (vv. 9–19); an *apostrophe commanding believers to rejoice over the defeat of Babylon (v. 20); another doom song that catalogs the routines of life that will "no more" be found in Babylon (vv. 21–24). This chapter is a symbolic vision of God's decisive defeat of evil at the end of history.

18

After this I saw another angel coming down from heaven, having great authority, and the earth was made bright with his glory. [2]And he called out with a mighty voice,

"Fallen, fallen is Babylon the great!
    She has become a dwelling place for demons,
a haunt for every unclean spirit,
    a haunt for every unclean bird,
    a haunt for every unclean and detestable beast.
[3]   For all nations have drunk[2]
        the wine of the passion of her sexual immorality,
    and the kings of the earth have committed immorality with her,
        and the merchants of the earth have grown rich from the power of her luxurious
            living."

---

[1] Greek he [2] Some manuscripts fallen by

⁴Then I heard another voice from heaven saying,

   "Come out of her, my people,
      lest you take part in her sins,
     lest you share in her plagues;
⁵ for her sins are heaped high as heaven,
      and God has remembered her iniquities.
⁶ Pay her back as she herself has paid back others,
      and repay her double for her deeds;
      mix a double portion for her in the cup she mixed.
⁷ As she glorified herself and lived in luxury,
      so give her a like measure of torment and mourning,
    since in her heart she says,
     'I sit as a queen,
    I am no widow,
     and mourning I shall never see.'
⁸ For this reason her plagues will come in a single day,
      death and mourning and famine,
    and she will be burned up with fire;
      for mighty is the Lord God who has judged her."

⁹And the kings of the earth, who committed sexual immorality and lived in luxury with her, will weep and wail over her when they see the smoke of her burning. ¹⁰They will stand far off, in fear of her torment, and say,

   "Alas! Alas! You great city,
     you mighty city, Babylon!
   For in a single hour your judgment has come."

¹¹And the merchants of the earth weep and mourn for her, since no one buys their cargo anymore, ¹²cargo of gold, silver, jewels, pearls, fine linen, purple cloth, silk, scarlet cloth, all kinds of scented wood, all kinds of articles of ivory, all kinds of articles of costly wood, bronze, iron and marble, ¹³cinnamon, spice, incense, myrrh, frankincense, wine, oil, fine flour, wheat, cattle and sheep, horses and chariots, and slaves, that is, human souls.[1]

¹⁴ "The fruit for which your soul longed
      has gone from you,
    and all your delicacies and your splendors
      are lost to you,
      never to be found again!"

¹⁵The merchants of these wares, who gained wealth from her, will stand far off, in fear of her torment, weeping and mourning aloud,

¹⁶ "Alas, alas, for the great city
      that was clothed in fine linen,
        in purple and scarlet,
      adorned with gold,

---

[1] Or *and slaves, and human lives*

with jewels, and with pearls!

¹⁷ For in a single hour all this wealth has been laid waste."

And all shipmasters and seafaring men, sailors and all whose trade is on the sea, stood far off ¹⁸and cried out as they saw the smoke of her burning,

"What city was like the great city?"

¹⁹And they threw dust on their heads as they wept and mourned, crying out,

"Alas, alas, for the great city
     where all who had ships at sea
     grew rich by her wealth!
For in a single hour she has been laid waste.
²⁰ Rejoice over her, O heaven,
     and you saints and apostles and prophets,
for God has given judgment for you against her!"

²¹Then a mighty angel took up a stone like a great millstone and threw it into the sea, saying,

"So will Babylon the great city be thrown down with violence,
     and will be found no more;
²² and the sound of harpists and musicians, of flute players and trumpeters,
     will be heard in you no more,
and a craftsman of any craft
     will be found in you no more,
and the sound of the mill
     will be heard in you no more,
²³ and the light of a lamp
     will shine in you no more,
and the voice of bridegroom and bride
     will be heard in you no more,
for your merchants were the great ones of the earth,
     and all nations were deceived by your sorcery.
²⁴ And in her was found the blood of prophets and of saints,
     and of all who have been slain on earth."

Marriage supper of the Lamb and defeat of the beast and false prophet [chapter 19]. Chapter 19 narrates the second and third of the seven last events. The marriage supper of the Lamb (vv. 1–10) is the counterpart to the fall of Babylon. In fact, it is a celebration scene, filled with lyric praise of Christ and his claiming of his bride, the church. The vision is the culmination of the biblical archetype of God's people as his bride. The wedding is suddenly interrupted by the ensuing vision, as Christ appears in combat as a warrior leading an army (vv. 11–21). In this unit we observe a brief epic battlefield scene, symbolic of Christ's triumph over evil. This vision makes clear that the God of the Bible is the Lord of joyful love but also of vengeful wrath against all forms of evil.

19 After this I heard what seemed to be the loud voice of a great multitude in heaven, crying out,

"Hallelujah!
Salvation and glory and power belong to our God,
² 　for his judgments are true and just;
for he has judged the great prostitute
　who corrupted the earth with her immorality,
and has avenged on her the blood of his servants."¹

³Once more they cried out,

"Hallelujah!
The smoke from her goes up forever and ever."

⁴And the twenty-four elders and the four living creatures fell down and worshiped God who was seated on the throne, saying, "Amen. Hallelujah!" ⁵And from the throne came a voice saying,

"Praise our God,
　all you his servants,
you who fear him,
small and great."

⁶Then I heard what seemed to be the voice of a great multitude, like the roar of many waters and like the sound of mighty peals of thunder, crying out,

"Hallelujah!
For the Lord our God
　the Almighty reigns.
⁷ 　Let us rejoice and exult
　and give him the glory,
for the marriage of the Lamb has come,
　and his Bride has made herself ready;
⁸ 　it was granted her to clothe herself
　with fine linen, bright and pure"—

for the fine linen is the righteous deeds of the saints. ⁹And the angel said² to me, "Write this: Blessed are those who are invited to the marriage supper of the Lamb." And he said to me, "These are the true words of God." ¹⁰Then I fell down at his feet to worship him, but he said to me, "You must not do that! I am a fellow servant³ with you and your brothers who hold to the testimony of Jesus. Worship God." For the testimony of Jesus is the spirit of prophecy. ¹¹Then I saw heaven opened, and behold, a white horse! The one sitting on it is called Faithful and True, and in righteousness he judges and makes war. ¹²His eyes are like a flame of fire, and on his head are many diadems, and he has a name written that no one knows but himself. ¹³He is clothed in a robe dipped in⁴ blood, and the name by which he is called is The Word of God. ¹⁴And the armies of heaven, arrayed in fine linen, white and pure, were following him on white horses. ¹⁵From his mouth comes a sharp sword with which to strike down the nations, and he will rule them

---

¹ Greek bondservants; also verse 5 ² Greek he said ³ Greek fellow bondservant ⁴ Some manuscripts sprinkled with

with a rod of iron. He will tread the winepress of the fury of the wrath of God the Almighty. ¹⁶On his robe and on his thigh he has a name written, King of kings and Lord of lords.

¹⁷Then I saw an angel standing in the sun, and with a loud voice he called to all the birds that fly directly overhead, "Come, gather for the great supper of God, ¹⁸to eat the flesh of kings, the flesh of captains, the flesh of mighty men, the flesh of horses and their riders, and the flesh of all men, both free and slave,¹ both small and great." ¹⁹And I saw the beast and the kings of the earth with their armies gathered to make war against him who was sitting on the horse and against his army. ²⁰And the beast was captured, and with it the false prophet who in its presence² had done the signs by which he deceived those who had received the mark of the beast and those who worshiped its image. These two were thrown alive into the lake of fire that burns with sulfur. ²¹And the rest were slain by the sword that came from the mouth of him who was sitting on the horse, and all the birds were gorged with their flesh.

Binding and loosing of Satan, and final judgment [chapter 20]. Three more visions keep the sequence of seven last events alive. In visions replete with mystery, Satan is first bound while believers reign (vv. 1–6), and then he is loosed to pursue war against Christ's followers (vv. 7–10). The third vision in the chapter pictures God's final judgment of all people who have lived (vv. 11–15). Our safest interpretive guides to these mysterious visions are the familiar images of the end that we find in the NT. The millennium of verse 2 is a famous crux that has yielded three main interpretations: (1) the millennium will be an earthly reign of believers with Christ after he returns to claim them and before the new heavens and the new earth; (2) it is a period of time before the second coming of Christ when the church will enjoy an earthly reign; (3) it is a symbolic account of what has been happening ever since Christ broke Satan's power at the cross and empty tomb—a picture of how believers are already reigning with Christ.

20 Then I saw an angel coming down from heaven, holding in his hand the key to the bottomless pit³ and a great chain. ²And he seized the dragon, that ancient serpent, who is the devil and Satan, and bound him for a thousand years, ³and threw him into the pit, and shut it and sealed it over him, so that he might not deceive the nations any longer, until the thousand years were ended. After that he must be released for a little while.

⁴Then I saw thrones, and seated on them were those to whom the authority to judge was committed. Also I saw the souls of those who had been beheaded for the testimony of Jesus and for the word of God, and those who had not worshiped the beast or its image and had not received its mark on their foreheads or their hands. They came to life and reigned with Christ for a thousand years. ⁵The rest of the dead did not come to life until the thousand years were ended. This is the first resurrection. ⁶Blessed and holy is the one who shares in the first resurrection! Over such the second death has no power, but they will be priests of God and of Christ, and they will reign with him for a thousand years.

⁷And when the thousand years are ended, Satan will be released from his prison ⁸and will come out to deceive the nations that are at the four corners of the earth, Gog and Magog, to gather them for battle; their number is like the sand of the sea. ⁹And they marched up over the broad plain of the earth and surrounded the camp of

---

¹ Greek *bondservant* ² Or *on its behalf* ³ Greek *the abyss*; also verse 3

the saints and the beloved city, but fire came down from heaven[1] and consumed them, [10]and the devil who had deceived them was thrown into the lake of fire and sulfur where the beast and the false prophet were, and they will be tormented day and night forever and ever.

[11]Then I saw a great white throne and him who was seated on it. From his presence earth and sky fled away, and no place was found for them. [12]And I saw the dead, great and small, standing before the throne, and books were opened. Then another book was opened, which is the book of life. And the dead were judged by what was written in the books, according to what they had done. [13]And the sea gave up the dead who were in it, Death and Hades gave up the dead who were in them, and they were judged, each one of them, according to what they had done. [14]Then Death and Hades were thrown into the lake of fire. This is the second death, the lake of fire. [15]And if anyone's name was not found written in the book of life, he was thrown into the lake of fire.

The new heaven and new earth [21:1–22:5]. The climactic vision of Revelation is this vision of heaven. It is pictured in symbolic terms—as a transformed or new place and as a city that combines features that no earthly city can possess. The emphasis is on motifs of permanence and transcendence (hence the nonvegetative imagery of streets of gold and jewels); splendor; the bliss and perfection of the citizens of the city; the beauty of the place; freedom from intrusions of sin; absence of fallen experience; the banishment of all evil; the satisfaction of all human needs and longings; the life-giving, light-shining presence of the Lamb. The profusion of details is not intended to yield a composite visual picture but instead represents a symbolic richness. The garden of perfection at the beginning of the Bible is here completed in a city of perfection, implying an expansive inclusiveness that differs from an enclosed garden inhabited by two people.

21 Then I saw a new heaven and a new earth, for the first heaven and the first earth had passed away, and the sea was no more. [2]And I saw the holy city, new Jerusalem, coming down out of heaven from God, prepared as a bride adorned for her husband. [3]And I heard a loud voice from the throne saying, "Behold, the dwelling place[2] of God is with man. He will dwell with them, and they will be his people,[3] and God himself will be with them as their God.[4] [4]He will wipe away every tear from their eyes, and death shall be no more, neither shall there be mourning, nor crying, nor pain anymore, for the former things have passed away."

[5]And he who was seated on the throne said, "Behold, I am making all things new." Also he said, "Write this down, for these words are trustworthy and true." [6]And he said to me, "It is done! I am the Alpha and the Omega, the beginning and the end. To the thirsty I will give from the spring of the water of life without payment. [7]The one who conquers will have this heritage, and I will be his God and he will be my son. [8]But as for the cowardly, the faithless, the detestable, as for murderers, the sexually immoral, sorcerers, idolaters, and all liars, their portion will be in the lake that burns with fire and sulfur, which is the second death."

[9]Then came one of the seven angels who had the seven bowls full of the seven last plagues and spoke to me, saying, "Come, I will show you the Bride, the wife of the

[1] Some manuscripts *from God, out of heaven, or out of heaven from God* [2] Or *tabernacle* [3] Some manuscripts *peoples* [4] Some manuscripts omit *as their God*

Lamb." ¹⁰And he carried me away in the Spirit to a great, high mountain, and showed me the holy city Jerusalem coming down out of heaven from God, ¹¹having the glory of God, its radiance like a most rare jewel, like a jasper, clear as crystal. ¹²It had a great, high wall, with twelve gates, and at the gates twelve angels, and on the gates the names of the twelve tribes of the sons of Israel were inscribed— ¹³on the east three gates, on the north three gates, on the south three gates, and on the west three gates. ¹⁴And the wall of the city had twelve foundations, and on them were the twelve names of the twelve apostles of the Lamb.

¹⁵And the one who spoke with me had a measuring rod of gold to measure the city and its gates and walls. ¹⁶The city lies foursquare, its length the same as its width. And he measured the city with his rod, 12,000 stadia.¹ Its length and width and height are equal. ¹⁷He also measured its wall, 144 cubits² by human measurement, which is also an angel's measurement. ¹⁸The wall was built of jasper, while the city was pure gold, clear as glass. ¹⁹The foundations of the wall of the city were adorned with every kind of jewel. The first was jasper, the second sapphire, the third agate, the fourth emerald, ²⁰the fifth onyx, the sixth carnelian, the seventh chrysolite, the eighth beryl, the ninth topaz, the tenth chrysoprase, the eleventh jacinth, the twelfth amethyst. ²¹And the twelve gates were twelve pearls, each of the gates made of a single pearl, and the street of the city was pure gold, transparent as glass.

²²And I saw no temple in the city, for its temple is the Lord God the Almighty and the Lamb. ²³And the city has no need of sun or moon to shine on it, for the glory of God gives it light, and its lamp is the Lamb. ²⁴By its light will the nations walk, and the kings of the earth will bring their glory into it, ²⁵and its gates will never be shut by day—and there will be no night there. ²⁶They will bring into it the glory and the honor of the nations. ²⁷But nothing unclean will ever enter it, nor anyone who does what is detestable or false, but only those who are written in the Lamb's book of life.

22 Then the angel³ showed me the river of the water of life, bright as crystal, flowing from the throne of God and of the Lamb ²through the middle of the street of the city; also, on either side of the river, the tree of life⁴ with its twelve kinds of fruit, yielding its fruit each month. The leaves of the tree were for the healing of the nations. ³No longer will there be anything accursed, but the throne of God and of the Lamb will be in it, and his servants⁵ will worship him. ⁴They will see his face, and his name will be on their foreheads. ⁵And night will be no more. They will need no light of lamp or sun, for the Lord God will be their light, and they will reign forever and ever.

Epistolary closing [22:6–21]. Chapter 1 of Revelation includes an epistolary salutation, and the book now ends with familiar conventions of conclusion in NT letters. The keynote is the sense of urgency that John hopes to instill in his readers. The specific motifs are as follows: the certainty of the imminent return of Christ (vv. 6–7, 10, 12, 20); a practical emphasis on obeying John's revelations, couched as two of the seven beatitudes found in the book of Revelation (vv. 7b, 14; see also 1:3; 14:13; 16:15; 19:9; 20:6); reminders of spiritual warfare (vv. 11, 15); comments about the awesomeness of the revelation (vv. 6, 10, 18–19); an urgent invitation to come to Christ for life and salvation (v. 17); a benediction that brings the entire Bible to a close (v. 21).

¹ About 1,380 miles; a *stadion* was about 607 feet or 185 meters ² A *cubit* was about 18 inches or 45 centimeters ³ Greek *he* ⁴ Or *the Lamb. In the midst of the street of the city, and on either side of the river, was the tree of life* ⁵ Greek *bondservants*; also verse 6

⁶And he said to me, "These words are trustworthy and true. And the Lord, the God of the spirits of the prophets, has sent his angel to show his servants what must soon take place."

⁷"And behold, I am coming soon. Blessed is the one who keeps the words of the prophecy of this book."

⁸I, John, am the one who heard and saw these things. And when I heard and saw them, I fell down to worship at the feet of the angel who showed them to me, ⁹but he said to me, "You must not do that! I am a fellow servant¹ with you and your brothers the prophets, and with those who keep the words of this book. Worship God."

¹⁰And he said to me, "Do not seal up the words of the prophecy of this book, for the time is near. ¹¹Let the evildoer still do evil, and the filthy still be filthy, and the righteous still do right, and the holy still be holy."

¹²"Behold, I am coming soon, bringing my recompense with me, to repay everyone for what he has done. ¹³I am the Alpha and the Omega, the first and the last, the beginning and the end."

¹⁴Blessed are those who wash their robes,² so that they may have the right to the tree of life and that they may enter the city by the gates. ¹⁵Outside are the dogs and sorcerers and the sexually immoral and murderers and idolaters, and everyone who loves and practices falsehood.

¹⁶"I, Jesus, have sent my angel to testify to you about these things for the churches. I am the root and the descendant of David, the bright morning star."

¹⁷The Spirit and the Bride say, "Come." And let the one who hears say, "Come." And let the one who is thirsty come; let the one who desires take the water of life without price.

¹⁸I warn everyone who hears the words of the prophecy of this book: if anyone adds to them, God will add to him the plagues described in this book, ¹⁹and if anyone takes away from the words of the book of this prophecy, God will take away his share in the tree of life and in the holy city, which are described in this book.

²⁰He who testifies to these things says, "Surely I am coming soon." Amen. Come, Lord Jesus!

²¹The grace of the Lord Jesus be with all.³ Amen.

---

¹ Greek *fellow bondservant* ² Some manuscripts *do his commandments* ³ Some manuscripts *all the saints*

TABLE OF
WEIGHTS AND MEASURES
AND MONETARY UNITS

The following table is based on the best generally accepted information available for biblical weights, measures, and monetary units. All equivalents are approximate. Weights and measures also varied somewhat in different times and places in the ancient world. Most weights, measures, and monetary units are also explained in footnotes on the pages where they occur in the ESV text.

Biblical Unit	Approximate American and Metric Equivalents	Biblical Equivalent
bath	A *bath* was about 6 gallons or 22 liters	1 ephah
beka	A *beka* was about 1/5 ounce or 5.5 grams	10 gerahs
cor	A *cor* was about 6 bushels or 220 liters	10 ephahs
cubit	A *cubit* was about 18 inches or 45 centimeters	6 handbreadths
denarius	A *denarius* was a day's wage for a laborer	
daric	A *daric* was a coin of about 1/4 ounce or 8.5 grams	
ephah	An *ephah* was about 3/5 bushel or 22 liters	10 omers
gerah	A *gerah* was about 1/50 ounce or 0.6 gram	1/10 beka
handbreadth	A *handbreadth* was about 3 inches or 7.5 centimeters	1/6 cubit
hin	A *hin* was about 4 quarts or 3.5 liters	1/6 bath
homer	A *homer* was about 6 bushels or 220 liters	10 ephahs
kab	A *kab* was about 1 quart or 1 liter	1/22 ephah
lethech	A *lethech* was about 3 bushels or 110 liters	5 ephahs
log	A *log* was about 1/3 quart or 0.3 liter	1/72 bath
mina	A *mina* was about 1 1/4 pounds or 0.6 kilogram	50 shekels
omer	An *omer* was about 2 quarts or 2 liters	1/10 ephah
pim	A *pim* was about 1/3 ounce or 7.5 grams	2/3 shekel
seah	A *seah* was about 7 quarts or 7.3 liters	1/3 ephah
shekel	A *shekel* was about 2/5 ounce or 11 grams	2 bekas
span	A *span* was about 9 inches or 22 centimeters	3 handbreadths
stadion	A *stadion* was about 607 feet or 185 meters	
talent	A *talent* was about 75 pounds or 34 kilograms	60 minas

GLOSSARY
OF LITERARY TERMS AND GENRES

This glossary provides succinct definitions, sometimes accompanied by an illustration from the Bible, of the leading literary forms of the Bible. More detailed information on most of these terms can be found in the following sources: Leland Ryken, James C. Wilhoit, and Tremper Longman III, eds., *Dictionary of Biblical Imagery* (Downers Grove, Ill.: InterVarsity Press, 1998); Leland Ryken, *Words of Delight: A Literary Introduction to the Bible* (Grand Rapids: Baker, 1992); Leland Ryken, *How to Read the Bible as Literature* (Grand Rapids: Zondervan, 1984); James L. Bailey and Lyle D. Vander Broek, *Literary Forms in the New Testament: A Handbook* (Louisville, Ky.: Westminster John Knox, 1992).

acrostic. A poem in which the successive units begin with the consecutive letters of the Hebrew alphabet. The units might be single lines, pairs of lines, or stanzas (as in Psalm 119).

adventure story. A narrative genre in which stock ingredients create an atmosphere of excitement and the extraordinary. Stock ingredients include the following: variety and remoteness of settings; inclusion of the marvelous or supernatural; heightened conflict; danger or risk; suspense; surprise; arrests and escapes; chases; hiding; secrets and their discovery; journeys through dangerous landscapes; storms; disguises; shipwrecks; battles.

allegory. A work of literature in which many of the details have a corresponding "other" meaning. The basic technique is symbolism in the sense that a detail in the text stands for something else. Interpreting an allegorical text must not be confused with allegorizing a text. To interpret an allegorical text is to follow the intentions of the author. Allegorizing a text implies attaching symbolic meanings to a text that was not intended by the author to be allegorical. An example of an allegorical text is Jesus' parable of the sower (Matthew 13:1–9), for which Jesus himself gave every detail in the story except the sower a corresponding other meaning (Matthew 13:18–23).

allusion (*verb form:* alludes to). A reference, sometimes by means of a quotation, to past history or literature.

annunciation story. A story in which an angel or human agent announces to a barren wife that she will become pregnant and bear a child.

antagonist. Any person or force in a narrative that stands in the way of the protagonist of the story, or with which the protagonist is in conflict. Features of a
character's own personality or character can function as antagonists, such as
when Cain is in conflict with his own evil impulses (Genesis 4:5–16).

anthropomorphism (*adjective form:* anthropomorphic). The portrayal of deity as
possessing human body parts or emotions. To speak of God's hand or foot or of
his changing his mind is an example of anthropomorphism.

antithetic parallelism. Two lines of Hebrew poetry in which the second line states the
truth of the first line in a contrasting way: "The LORD knows the way of the
righteous, / but the way of the wicked will perish" (Ps. 1:6).

aphorism (*adjective form:* aphoristic). A concise, memorable statement of truth;
synonymous with *proverb.*

apocalypse; apocalyptic writing; apocalyptic vision. Literally the word *apocalypse*
means "unveiling" or "revelation." Apocalyptic writing is a branch of visionary
writing that specifically portrays the end of history and the eternity that succeeds
that end. At the same time, the events portrayed in apocalyptic writing often
embody universal principles (such as a conflict between good and evil or the
sovereignty of God over history) that are true at any point in history. Specific
motifs in apocalyptic writing include the following: dualism (the universe
envisioned as divided into good and evil); spiritism (angels and demons as
characters); judgment against evil; messianic focus; animal symbolism; color
symbolism; number symbolism; cataclysmic imagery; cosmic stage of action;
forces of nature as "characters" in the story. Daniel 7–12 and the book of
Revelation are the main (but not the only) examples of this genre in the Bible.

apostrophe. A figure of speech in which the writer addresses someone absent as
though present and capable of responding. By slight extension, an apostrophe
might be an address to something nonhuman as though it were human and
capable of responding, even if the speaker is in the presence of the object (for
example, the poet in Psalm 148:3 might well be looking up at the sun, moon, or
stars as he commands them to praise God).

archetype. A plot motif (such as the ordeal), character type (such as the hero), or
setting/image/symbol (such as the wicked city) that recurs throughout literature
and life.

ascension story. A story in which a person or angel takes leave from earth and
journeys to heaven.

battle story. A story of conflict between armies and individual warriors. A full-fledged
battle story incorporates a large array of motifs, falling into the three categories
of prelude to battle, conduct of the battle, and postbattle rituals. The prelude to
battle can include these motifs: provocation to battle; mustering of armies;
gathering of weapons; planning of battle strategy; arming of the hero; march to
the battlefield; taunting of enemies; sometimes a challenge to single combat.
Motifs of the battle itself include these: invasion; attack; ambush; hand-to-hand

combat; flight and chase; siege. Postbattle rituals include the following: exaltation by the victorious; offering of kingship to the leader of the winning side; shouts by the victorious; poems or songs of thanksgiving that rehearse the details of the battle as a way of prolonging the ecstasy of victory; triumphal procession; feasting and celebration; taking of spoils and of trophies for public display; mutilating the bodies of the defeated; beheading of the defeated leaders and/or public display of their bodies.

beatitude. A pronouncement of blessing, phrased in the formula "blessed is" or "blessed are." When beatitudes appear in the Bible, they do more than express a wish for blessing; they confer a quality of blessedness on a person or group. Sometimes beatitudes pronounce blessing on God.

benediction. A statement of God's blessing conferred on a person or group by his designated human agent, such as an OT priest or NT apostle.

biography. The story of a person's life, either in whole or in part.

birth story. A story that recounts the birth of a baby, usually a future hero. A full-fledged biblical birth story contains the following elements: a barren wife or couple; divine or angelic prediction that a child will be born; a birth that is accompanied by miracles; protection of the baby from hostile forces. Usually the baby thus born becomes a hero, saint, or savior.

boast. A work of literature in which the leading ingredient is a formalized boasting or extolling by a speaker or writer. Originally a genre associated with battle or other types of victory, in the Bible the boast is often turned to spiritual effect when people boast in God or their salvation.

calling story. A story in which either a prophet or a disciple receives a call from God to perform a task, enter a vocation, or follow Jesus. Also called a *vocation story.*

character; characterization. Characters are one of three elements (along with plot and setting) that make up a story. In regard to characters in a story, a reader's leading goal should be to get to know the characters as fully as possible from the data that the storyteller provides. Our acquaintance with characters in a story is based on the following things: a character's actions, including thoughts and feelings; personal traits and abilities; relationships and roles; archetypes to which a character belongs; what the narrator tells us about a character; other characters' responses to a character.

Christ hymn. A NT psalm that praises Christ by extolling his nature, his acts, his attributes, and/or the redemptive effects of his life and sacrifice.

climactic parallelism. Two or more parallel lines of poetry in which the first line is left incomplete until the second line (and sometimes third line) repeats part of it and adds to it: "Ascribe to the LORD, O heavenly beings, / ascribe to the LORD glory and strength" (Ps. 29:1).

comedy; comic plot. A U-shaped plot in which the action begins in prosperity, descends into potentially tragic events, and rises to a happy ending. Even if the first of these phases is missing, the plot can be called a comic plot.

complaint. A genre of psalm in which the speaker defines a crisis and invokes God to help. Five ingredients are usually present in a biblical lament psalm: invocation or cry to God; definition of the crisis (which the psalmists call a complaint); petition to God to deliver; statement of confidence in God; vow to praise God. All lament poems are occasional poems that refer to specific events that gave rise to the poem. Synonymous with *lament psalm*.

conflict story/controversy story. A story that is built primarily around the element of conflict between characters or groups. While plot conflict exists in virtually every good story, a conflict story subordinates other narrative elements to conflict or controversy.

confrontation story/narrative. A story in which the central situation is one character confronting another character or a group; synonymous with *encounter story*. God's accosting of Moses at the burning bush (Exodus 3) and Jesus' conversation with the Samaritan woman at the well (John 4:1–26) are classic confrontation stories.

conquest story. A story that narrates the victory of a person or group over enemies.

conversion story. A story in which the central event is one or more characters' coming to faith in God or Christ and having their lives turned around as a result.

creed. A formal statement of beliefs, often expressed with aphoristic flair and in a patterned manner (often by means of tight syntax). First Timothy 3:16 illustrates these features.

crime and punishment story. A story built around the threefold pattern of the antecedents of a crime (what led up to the crime), the occurrence of the crime, and the consequences of the crime.

denouement. The last phase of a story, following the climax; literally "tying up of loose ends."

diatribe. A literary form of teaching, street preaching, oratory, and satire that arose in classical Greece and Rome. Motifs include the following: dialogue with imaginary questioners or opponents; as part of that, question-and-answer constructions, sometimes catechismlike in effect; use of questions or hypothetical objections as a transition to the next topic; rhetorical questions; adducing famous and representative figures from the past as examples; use of analogy as a rhetorical device; aphoristic style.

discourse. A written or spoken address to an audience. The term usually refers to a formal or dignified oration or piece of writing.

docudrama. A genre of film or video that presents information about a person, place, or movement. Stock ingredients include interviews; a narrator; photographs or film clips; and facts gleaned from historical archives, including news sources contemporaneous with the subject of the docudrama. Many historical narratives in the Bible give us the same ingredients that we find in a docudrama.

doom song. A form of prophetic writing and satire in which the author predicts the downfall of a nation in vivid and sometimes taunting form. Often the author

GLOSSARY

pictures the downfall in the present or past tense, even though the events may still be in the future. A common rhetorical strategy is to list the things that will be "no more," lending the quality of an elegy (funeral poem) to the text.

doxology. A command to praise God. Although the term is sometimes extended to mean an actual song of praise, this is an undesirable extension because it leaves us without a term to denote specifically a command to praise God. Psalm 148 is a catalog of doxologies, and the familiar "Doxology" of Christian hymnody is similarly a list of commands to praise God.

drama. A narrative form in which the action is embodied in the form of dialogue among characters. The book of Job is a major work of drama in the Bible.

dramatic irony. A situation in a story where readers know something of which some or all of the characters in the story are ignorant.

dramatic monologue. A literary work in which a single speaker addresses an implied but silent audience and in which various details keep the dramatic situation alive in a reader's awareness. For example, the format into which Psalm 45 (a wedding poem) is cast makes it easy to imagine the poet as speaking in sequence to the groom (vv. 2–9) and then the bride (vv. 10–17), while Proverbs 2 is couched as an address by a father to his son.

elegy (*adjective form:* elegiac). A funeral poem. In its strict form, such as David's elegy for Saul and Jonathan in 2 Samuel 1:19–27, the motifs include the following: references to the circumstances of death; praising or eulogizing of the deceased; recollection of past friendship; lament or grief over the loss. The adjective *elegiac* is often attached to works of literature that embody a sorrowful mood or that are permeated by a sense of irretrievable loss; the book of Lamentations is governed by an elegiac mood.

emblematic blazon. A blazon is a love poem that praises the beauty and virtue of the beloved. An emblematic blazon catalogs the attractive features of the beloved and compares them to objects in nature; the Song of Solomon contains numerous examples.

encomium. A work of literature that praises either a general character type (e.g., Psalm 1 on the godly person and Proverbs 31:10–31 on the virtuous wife) or abstract quality (e.g., 1 Corinthians 13 on love and Hebrews 11 on faith). Conventional motifs are these: a formal introduction to the subject being praised; the distinguished and/or ancient ancestry of the subject of praise; a listing of the acts and attributes/qualities of the subject; the indispensable or superior nature of the subject (usually using the technique of comparison to demonstrate this superiority and often listing the rewards that accompany the subject of praise); a concluding command urging the reader to emulate the subject that has been praised.

encounter story/narrative. A story in which the central situation is one character's confronting another character or a group; synonymous with *confrontation story.* God's accosting of Moses at the burning bush (Exodus 3) and Jesus' conversation with the Samaritan woman at the well (John 4:1–26) are classic encounter stories.

epic. A long narrative having the following characteristics or ingredients: expansiveness and grandness; the story of a nation or group (nationalistic emphasis), not simply an individual; a unifying hero; motifs of warfare, conquest, kingdom, rulership; presence of supernatural characters and events (what literary critics have traditionally called "the marvelous"); exalted style. Epics are very important to societies; in fact, they sum up what a whole culture wants to say about itself and about life. The story of Israel's exodus from Egypt is the most obvious epic in the Bible, but there are epiclike stories in abundance, and the life of David can be considered an epic.

epiphany. A moment of heightened insight or revelation in a story; it usually comes late in a story and casts a retrospective light on the meaning of the story as a whole.

epistle. A NT letter that possesses the usual ingredients and structure of letters generally. An epistle is not a sermon or treatise. Most NT epistles are occasional letters, meaning that specific questions or crises gave rise to them and shaped their content. NT epistles, except for Romans, are thus not freestanding treatises; they are embedded in a specific occasion and setting. NT epistles follow the customary conventions of Greek and Roman letters of the same era, with modifications. Three of the stock ingredients of NT epistles correspond to the letters of the day: salutation, body, and conclusion. But even here we find innovations, as the salutation, for example, becomes a theologically charged "grace and peace" formula, and the body deals specifically with moral and religious issues. Additionally, NT letters have two unique units: a thanksgiving that consists of a liturgically formulated statement of thanks and praise for spiritual blessings, and a *paraenesis* composed of lists of virtues and vices, or moral commands.

epithalamion. A wedding poem that celebrates a specific occasion (a wedding), not simply the institution of marriage. Psalm 45 and the Song of Solomon are biblical epithalamia.

epithet. An exalted title for a person or thing; a feature of the high style. Examples are "the LORD of hosts" as a title for God and "Darius the Mede" as a title of the Persian king (Dan. 5:31).

eschatological discourse. A vision of what will happen at the very end of human history and just prior to that end; synonymous with *end times discourse*.

etiology. The nonliterary dictionary definition is "assignment of a cause or origin" to something. As a literary term, *etiology* is sometimes used in the broad sense as synonymous with story of origins, but more precisely it is a story that tells how a person or place received its name. An example is Genesis 11:1–9, which explains how the unfinished city of Babel received its name. Etiologies link the origin of a name to a historical event and are not fictional stories composed to explain an already-existing name.

exile motif; story of exile. An exile is a person or group that has been forced to leave home or nation. A poem or story based on exile recounts the process of being expelled and/or the experience of living in exile.

exposition. The opening phase of a story, in which the writer presents the background information that readers need to know in order to understand the plot that follows.

expository writing. Writing (ordinarily in prose) in which the main purpose is to convey information.

fantasy. A work of literature or a passage that portrays events, characters, settings, or images that do not literally exist in the real world (though details in a work of fantasy may be metaphors of real-life people or experiences). Whereas realistic literature gives us a replica of the known world, fantasy whisks us away to an alternate world of the imagination. In fantasy, horses can be red (Rev. 6:4), a branch can build a temple (Zech. 6:12), and a goat's horn can reach to the heavens and throw stars to the ground (Dan. 8:8–10). Fantasy presents real events, places, or characters, but it does not present them in their literal form. For example, a great red dragon that sweeps down a third of the stars of heaven (Rev. 12:3–4) refers to a real being, Satan, but does not give a literal portrayal of him.

farewell discourse. An address by a prophetic or political leader to followers at or close to his or her death. The aim of the discourse is to prepare followers for the loss of their leader. Customary motifs include the following: the leader's summoning of followers; announcement of impending death; review of the leader's past relations with his or her followers; exhortations to remain faithful to the leader's teachings; revelations about the future, including the difficulties that the followers will face in the absence of their leader; warnings; predictions of woes and controversies; words of comfort and promise; prayers and blessings pronounced on the followers; appointment of a successor.

foil. Something within a work of literature that heightens or "sets off" (the literal meaning of the word *foil*) a main element in the work; usually a foil is a contrast, but sometimes it is a parallel. In the story of the separation of Abraham and Lot (Genesis 13), Lot's selfishness and worldly-mindedness are foils that highlight Abraham's generosity and willingness to live a life of faith in God's promises.

genealogy. A list of ancestors. The genealogies of the Bible serve as many as five purposes: they reflect the interest of biblical cultures in family and individual origins or roots; they express the continuity of generations (for either good or evil); they show the importance that God places on individuals (named individuality is important in the genealogies); they root biblical faith in space-time history; they embody theological meaning (as, for example, in the genealogies that trace the messianic line).

genre. Literary type or kind. The two biggest genres are story (narrative) and poetry. But as we move across the continuum from these general categories to very specific ones, we end up with genres like doxology, taunt, and travel story.

Genres have their own conventions (ways of conducting their literary business), and they need to be interpreted in keeping with these conventions. Considerations of genre also help program our experience of a text, alerting us beforehand what to be looking for as we read.

golden age vision/prophecy. A picture of a future era of total bliss and abundance. This is a common genre in the OT prophetic books. Lavishness of imagery characterizes the genre.

good life motif. The portrayal of an ideal place and way of life. A leading impulse in literature is to portray the good life. Abraham and Sarah's entertainment of the heavenly visitors (Gen. 18:1–8) pictures the good life conceived in pastoral (rural) terms. The city scene portrayed in Zechariah 8:3–8 is an urban picture of the good life.

Gospel. A narrative genre of the NT that tells the story of the life of Jesus. Primarily the Gospels inform us about the person and work of Christ. The material is divided approximately evenly between narrative (events) and discourses. The Gospels combine three primary ingredients: Jesus' teaching and preaching (what Jesus said and taught); Jesus' actions (what Jesus did); the responses of people to Jesus (what others said and did). Jesus' conversations and controversies are a hybrid that combine all three ingredients: they are a form of teaching, they are speech acts that have the effect of an action, and they involve people's responses to Jesus. Numerous subgenres converge in the Gospels—birth stories; stories of calling, recognition, witness/testimony, conflict/controversy, encounter, miracle, pronouncement; sayings, parables, and discourses/sermons by Jesus; passion and resurrection stories. The overall aim of the Gospels is persuasive, as the writers seek to give readers adequate reasons for believing that Jesus is the Savior of the world and to appeal to them to place their faith in Jesus. The Gospels thus have affinities with biography, but biography tends to be packaged as a straightforward factual account, not as an embodiment of dialogues, stories, and discourses.

hero. A protagonist whose experience is representative of people generally and who is either wholly or largely ideal in behavior and character.

hero story; heroic narrative. A story built around the character and exploits of a protagonist who is (a) representative of a whole community and (b) largely or wholly exemplary/idealized. The Bible is in many ways a collection of hero stories, and one of the distinctive features of these stories is that only a few of its heroes are completely idealized, in keeping with the essential realism of the Bible.

horror story. A story that portrays frightening or grotesque experiences in such a way as to make a reader feel terror. The story of the ten plagues (Exodus 7–12) and the narrative of the murderous rape of the concubine (Judges 19) are examples of horror stories in the Bible.

hyperbole. A figure of speech in which a writer consciously exaggerates for the sake of effect; usually that effect is emotional, so that we can loosely say that hyperbole usually expresses emotional truth rather than literal truth. The psalmist's statement that "my tears have been my food day and night" (Ps. 42:3) is a hyperbole.

idyll (*also spelled* idyl). A short work of literature that describes a simple, pleasant aspect of rural and/or domestic life. The book of Ruth is an idyl.

image. A word or phrase that names a concrete action or thing. By extension, a character, setting, or event in a story is an image—a concrete embodiment of human experience or an idea.

image pattern. Multiple occurrences of an image in a passage or work of literature. Images of emptiness and fullness are an image pattern in the book of Ruth. An image pattern in Psalm 121 is words referring to a journey.

imagery. The whole span of images in a piece of writing, and/or patterns of images in a piece of writing. For example, in Psalm 1 we find the imagery of the path or way, the assembly, and nature or harvest.

inciting event/moment/agent. The second phase of a well-made plot, following the opening exposition; the thing that sets the main action and plot conflict into motion when it is added to the situation already introduced.

initiation motif; story of initiation. A story or situation in which characters are introduced to something for the first time and/or undergo an experience for the first time.

invitation to love. A genre of love poetry in which the speaker invites the beloved to a life of mutual love, or to some specific action such as going for a walk in nature (which is usually metaphoric of a life of mutual love). Song of Solomon 2:8–15 is a pastoral invitation to love.

irony. An incongruity or discrepancy. Three main categories of literary irony exist: (1) dramatic irony, in which a reader knows more than characters in a story know; (2) verbal irony, in which writers or speakers say the opposite of what they mean; (3) irony of situation, in which a situation is strikingly incongruous with (or even the opposite of) what is expected or appropriate. An example of irony of situation is Lot's arguing with his angelic rescuers about the escape route as his home city is about to go up in smoke (Gen. 19:17–20).

journey motif; journey narrative. A story in which the focus of the plot is on the journeying of a person or group, usually toward a goal.

lament; lament psalm; psalm of lament. A genre of psalm in which the speaker in the poem defines a crisis and invokes God for help. Five ingredients are usually present in a biblical lament psalm: invocation or cry to God; definition of the crisis (which the psalmists often call a complaint); petition to God to deliver; statement of confidence in God; vow to praise God. All lament poems are occasional poems, meaning that they arise from a specific event in an individual's or nation's life.

love story. A story in which the central story line involves romantic love between a man and a woman. Such a story almost always deals with courtship rather than married life, even though its goal is marriage. Common motifs include the following: an idealized man and woman who are worthy of each other; background observers to the romance; a go-between or matchmaker; a confidant for the lovers; a rival lover; a memorable first meeting; meetings or rendezvous in secret places; good-bye scenes; bestowing of favors on the beloved; overcoming of obstacles to the romance; betrothal as a high point; expressions of compliment and affection toward the beloved; heightened sentiments expressed in heightened language. The Song of Solomon serves as the chief example in the Bible.

lyric. A short poem that expresses the thoughts and/or feelings of a speaker. Lyrics capture an experience, feeling, or idea at the height of its intensity. Lyrics unfold according to a three-part structure: (1) introduction to the thought, feeling, or situation to which the poet is responding; (2) development of the main theme; (3) rounding off the poem on a note of resolution and closure. Lyric poets use as many as four ways of developing their theme: repetition; contrast; catalog or listing; association (in which the poet branches out from the initial motif to a related one). Lyrics do not ordinarily tell a story, and they often have a disjointed structure in which the poet jumps from one thought or feeling to another one.

metaphor. An implied comparison that does not use the formula *like* or *as*: "The LORD is my shepherd" (Ps. 23:1).

miracle story. An account of a supernatural action on behalf of one or more people. Standard elements in such a story are as follows: a need is established; the help of Jesus or a prophet is sought; the person in need expresses faith or obedience; a miracle occurs; characters in the story respond to the miracle and/or the miracle worker.

moment of epiphany. A point of heightened insight that occurs to a character in a story, with the reader of course sharing the insight or revelation. A moment of epiphany ordinarily comes late in a story and is in effect a statement of the main idea of the story. It also casts a retrospective light on the story and expresses an interpretive framework within which to understand the preceding action. For example, late in Joseph's story Joseph twice makes key statements about his experience of redemptive suffering (Gen. 45:5–8 and 50:20–21).

motif. A discernible pattern composed of similar individual units, either in a single work or in literature generally. Psalm 23 is built around the motif of a shepherd's daily provision for his sheep. Jesus' special concern for outcasts and marginalized people is a motif in the Gospel of Luke.

narrative. A sequence of events composed of the three ingredients of plot, setting, and character. Synonymous with *story*.

narrator. The voice or presenter in a work of literature; the speaker in the work, whom we get to know as an explicit or implied character.

nature poem; nature psalm. A poem that takes nature as its subject. Such poems describe and praise nature, usually by painting word pictures of nature and expressing emotional responses to nature.

occasional poem; occasional literature. A literary work that takes its origin from a specific historical event or situation in a writer's life. Psalm 84 is an occasional poem that arose from the experience of worshiping God at the temple in Jerusalem. The NT epistles are occasional letters that refer to specific problems and happenings in a given local church.

ode. An exalted lyric poem that deals with a dignified subject in an elevated style. An ode is the most exalted type of lyric. Examples include Psalms 104 and 139.

oracle. A pronouncement from God, usually mediated through a human prophet.

oracle of blessing. A prophetic genre in which either the prophet himself or the prophet as conveyer of God's message pronounces or predicts blessing on a group, nation, or individual. The rhetorical forms that appear in such oracles include straightforward pronouncements of blessing; promises of blessing; catalogs of the specific forms of prosperity that the blessing will take.

oracle of judgment. A prophetic genre in which either the prophet himself or the prophet as conveyer of God's message predicts calamity for a group, nation, or individual. The predicted judgment is pictured as God's punishment for sin. The rhetorical form by which the calamity is portrayed is either a catalog of catastrophes or a portrait of misfortune. An oracle of judgment is an example of satire: there are discernible objects of attack, a literary form in which the abuses are concretely embodied, and a stated or implied standard of judgment by which evildoers are being criticized.

oracle of redemption or salvation. A prophetic genre in which either the prophet himself or the prophet as conveyer of God's message predicts that God will save or redeem a group, nation, or individual. The oracle predicts that at a future time God will restore the fortunes of the recipients of the oracle. The most common rhetorical pattern is the catalog of blessings that God will bestow. Alternatively, the prophet paints a picture of an ideal situation. The picture of restored favor with God can focus on either earthly prosperity or spiritual salvation from sin.

parable. A brief allegorical story that embodies one or more themes. The allegorical nature of a parable means that we need to identify a corresponding "other" meaning for at least some of the details in the story. The word *parable* is based on two Greek words meaning "to throw alongside," signaling that double meaning is at the heart of the genre. As a story, a parable requires ordinary narrative analysis of plot, setting, and character.

paradox (*adjective form:* paradoxical). An apparent contradiction that, upon analysis, can be seen to express a truth. The contradiction in a paradox must be resolved or explained before we have identified its truth. Proverbs 12:10 states a paradox: "The mercy of the wicked is cruel."

paraenesis. Sections in the NT epistles that list moral virtues and vices, or collections of moral commands to practice specific virtues and avoid specific vices. The Greek word *paraenesis* (pronounced para-NEES-us) means moral instruction or exhortation. No substitute English term has gained currency.

parallelism. Any successive series of phrases or lines that have the same grammatical format, such as "whatever is honorable, whatever is just, whatever is pure, whatever is lovely" (Phil. 4:8). More technically, parallelism is the verse form in which virtually all biblical poetry is written. While there are specific types of the verse form of parallelism (antithetic parallelism, synonymous parallelism, synthetic parallelism, climactic parallelism), the overriding idea that covers all of them is this: parallelism consists of two or more lines that form a pattern based on repetition or balance of thought and grammar and/or syntax.

parody. A work or passage of literature that imitates or echoes a specific work of literature or a literary genre, but with altered (and sometimes opposite) effect compared to the original. The result is to drastically alter the meaning of the original. For example, when the prophet Amos says, "Come to Bethel, and transgress" (Amos 4:4), he is parodying the priestly exhortation to worship with inverted (satiric) effect.

passion story. A story that recounts the circumstances surrounding the trial and crucifixion of Jesus.

pastoral literature. Literature in which the setting, characters, and actions are those that belong to the world of shepherding. Usually the pastoral world is presented as an idealized "good place" and becomes symbolic of the good life. Much love poetry is pastoral poetry, on the ground that the beautiful rural setting provides an appropriate place for idealized love to occur. Sometimes the characters and events in a pastoral work are allegorical in nature, referring to real-life people and events.

penitential psalm. A psalm in which the speaker confesses sin, expresses sorrow for sin, describes the effects of guilt, and petitions God for forgiveness and/or celebrates God's forgiveness.

personification. A figure of speech in which human attributes are given to something nonhuman, such as animals, objects, or abstract qualities. Wisdom and Folly are personified as women in Proverbs 1–9. Light and truth are personified as guides in Psalm 43:3.

plot. The sequence of events in a story. The essence of plot is one or more conflicts that reach resolution and closure by the end of the story. Plot conflicts can pit the protagonist against the environment, other characters, the supernatural, or himself or herself. The sequence of a plot usually unfolds according to the following phases: exposition (background information); inciting moment/force/incident; rising action; turning point (the point from which, in retrospect, we can see how the action will be eventually be resolved, even though we do not know the details); further complication; denouement (tying up of loose ends).

poetic justice. A situation in which virtue is rewarded and vice is punished.

poetic license. The tendency of poetry to rely on figures of speech rather than literal statement.

poetry. Writing that employs a preponderance of imagery and figures of speech and that is written in a verse form (in the Bible, nearly always some form of parallelism).

praise psalm; psalm of praise. A lyric genre in which the speaker praises God, specifically. Praise psalms fall into three phases: (1) a formal call to praise, potentially including the command to praise, the recipient of the command, and the mode of praise; (2) a catalog of the praiseworthy acts and attributes of God (on rare occasions replaced by a portrait of God); (3) a note of resolution or closure (such as a concluding benediction or prayer). The overall purpose of a praise psalm is to elevate and exalt the worthiness of God.

pronouncement story. A Gospel subtype that pairs an event with one or more memorable statements by Jesus, so that the story and saying(s) are remembered together. An example of a pronouncement story is Mark 2:15–17, where the story of Jesus' being criticized for eating with sinners is linked to Jesus' saying about the sick rather than the healthy needing a physician.

prophecy. The discourse of a prophet. A prophet mainly *tells forth* the word of God. Often (though not always) the prophet's message also *foretells* the future. The utterance of a prophet is called an oracle—a message from God, ordinarily through the mediation of a prophet. Depending on the content of the message, an oracle can be an oracle of judgment, an oracle of salvation or redemption, or an oracle of blessing. The oracle of judgment usually focuses on a present state of affairs in the prophet's own nation or an adjoining nation, and because this social and moral critique contains an element of attack, the genre of satire is operative as well. In addition to *depicting* the evils of a society, prophecy incorporates *denunciation of* those evils. Visions of the future in prophetic writing include golden-age visions of a coming restoration and perfection. The three main themes of prophetic writing are sin, judgment, and restoration/redemption. Often prophetic writing is visionary writing, and much of it falls into the genres of apocalyptic writing and eschatology.

protagonist. Based on the Greek words for "first struggler," the main character in a story, whether sympathetic or unsympathetic.

proverb. A concise, memorable statement of a general truth. Proverbs express an insight into the repeatable situations of life. They are often so striking that they do not merely express an insight but compel it. Proverbs are simultaneously simple and profound, specific and universal. Proverbs achieve their memorable quality through tighter-than-normal syntax, figurative language, and (frequently) the verse form of parallelism. Proverbs are the human race's testimony to its own experience, and they grow out of close observation, usually of the social and human scene.

psalm. Strictly speaking, a psalm is a lyric poem that appears in the Psalter (the collection of 150 psalms that constitute the OT book of Psalms). But a lyric that appears elsewhere in the Bible can legitimately be called a psalm as well.

quest motif; quest story. A sequence of events in which a character or group progresses toward a goal.

realism. Writing marked by two different literary characteristics: at the level of subject matter, the portrayal of unideal or sordid human experiences; at the level of technique, reliance on an abundance of concrete details taken from everyday life. In both cases, realism gives us a "slice of life," and practitioners of realism claim as their goal to portray life "as it is."

recognition story. A story that turns upon one or more characters' perceiving something noteworthy. The designation is most often used of a subgenre in the NT Gospels in which characters recognize that Jesus is the Christ and further recognize the deeper meanings or implications of this. But a looser application of the term extends it to any narrative situation in which characters recognize something significant, usually about God. For example, the Israelites on Mount Carmel are led to recognize that the Lord is God (1 Kings 18).

reform story; reformation story. A story in which an individual or nation reverses a negative situation by resolving to follow God and a course of right action. Ordinarily the story narrates the circumstances leading up to the change and also the specific changes in behavior that followed the resolve to reform.

rescue story. A story that portrays deliverance from a dire situation or a situation of immediate and impending disaster. Such stories follow a U-shaped pattern: first we are shown the situation that requires deliverance and then the steps by which the characters in the dire situation are rescued from it. A rescue requires one or more people in need of rescue and an agent of rescue. The Bible is an anthology of rescue stories.

resurrection story. A story about a character who returns to life after having been dead. Often the label is limited to the events surrounding the resurrection of Jesus as narrated in the Gospels, but any story in the Bible in which a dead person comes back to life is a resurrection story.

return story. A story in which individuals or groups return to a place from which they have been absent. The return is often accompanied by a sense of restoration of what had been lost.

revenge story. A story in which the mainspring of the plot is a character's exacting justice against a hostile person or group.

reversal. An element of plot in which the action takes a turn opposite to what had prevailed up to that point; often reversal entails the added element that an action produces the opposite effect of that intended by the character who performed it.

rhetoric. Rhetoric has always meant two things to literary people: (1) a writer's strategies of persuasion and (2) discourse that is ornamented or embellished with certain conventional techniques (such as figurative language or patterns of repetition).

rhetorical question. A question that is asked for the sake of effect rather than to elicit an answer. The answer to a rhetorical question is obvious and is therefore left unstated. A rhetorical question is a standard way to express emotion or strong conviction.

royal psalm. A psalm that takes the king or kingship as its subject. Some of the royal psalms are spoken *by* a king. Motifs include rulership, the nation, God's covenant with David and the nation of Israel, and the coming Messiah as the perfect king.

salutation. The opening elements of a letter, including as many as three ingredients: sender/author, recipient, greeting.

satire. The exposure, through ridicule or abuse, of human vice or folly. Four main elements make up satire: (1) one or more objects of attack; (2) a discernible literary vehicle (such as story or a list of vices) in which the attack is embodied; (3) a satiric norm or standard of correctness by which the criticism is conducted; (4) a satiric tone (either biting or laughing).

saying. In a biblical context, a proverb or aphorism.

setting. The place(s) in a story or narrative within which the action occurs. When one is analyzing a story, it is important to explore the contribution that setting makes to the action. Possible functions include these: providing a suitable "container" for the characters and events; symbolizing qualities that are important in the story; establishing atmosphere.

simile. A figure of speech in which a writer compares two things using the formula *like* or *as*. Psalm 1:3 is a simile: "He is like a tree planted by streams of water."

soliloquy. A statement uttered by a speaker while alone; as readers or listeners, we overhear the speech. Examples are Jeremiah's musings in Jeremiah 15:10–14 and Job's taking stock of his own innocence in Job 31.

song of victory. A lyric genre belonging to war literature. A song of victory celebrates a military victory and thanks God for it. Often references in the poem create the impression that the poem is spoken on the battlefield immediately after the battle is over. Biblical songs of victory can be found in Exodus 15, Judges 5, and Psalm 18.

story. A sequence of events made up of plot, setting, and characters. Synonymous with *narrative*.

story of origins. A story that recounts how something began. The preeminent example is the Genesis account of creation and fall from innocence. Genesis, the Bible's "book of beginnings," also contains numerous individual stories of origin, and there are scattered examples beyond that. Exodus 12–13 tells the story of the origin of the Passover.

stream of consciousness. A literary structure in which the content of the work unfolds in a random way that corresponds to how the human mind organizes thoughts, feelings, and consciousness. Such a structure aims to re-create the flow of the mind, and it has a psychological cast. In Song of Solomon 2:3–7, the thoughts of the woman follow a stream-of-consciousness structure.

succession story. A story involving the transfer of leadership from one leader or prophet to the next. Sometimes the early exploits of the successor are also called a succession story.

symbol; symbolism. Any detail in a work of literature that stands for something else. In biblical poetry, for example, God's right arm symbolizes his power.

symbolic reality. A technique in which the details that we encounter as we read a work consist so thoroughly of symbols that we enter an imagined world consisting primarily of symbols. The book of Revelation is the supreme example of symbolic reality in the Bible, but the technique also is evident elsewhere in the prophetic books.

synonymous parallelism. A type of parallelism in which two or more lines state the same general idea in different words or images but in similar grammatical form; the second (and sometimes third) line repeats the content of all or part of the first line. Psalm 46:7 is an example: "The LORD of hosts is with us; / the God of Jacob is our fortress."

synthetic ("growing") parallelism. A type of parallelism in which the second line completes the thought of the first line without repeating anything from the first line. An example is Psalm 104:5: "He set the earth on its foundations, / so that it should never be moved."

taunt; taunt song. Any work of literature in which the central ingredient is a mocking, jeering, or put-down of an enemy or guilty party, often in a formalized manner (such as a list of coming woes or a rehearsal of the details of a defeat that has been inflicted on an enemy). The largest repository of taunts in the Bible is the prophetic books, and the next largest repository is battle stories.

temptation story. A story in which the plot revolves around the temptation of one or more characters by an agent of temptation. A temptation story features, at the very least, a victim of the temptation and an agent of temptation. In a full-fledged temptation story, we witness a threefold pattern: the luring of a victim toward an evil action by the agent of temptation; a process in which the agent of temptation manipulates the victim and in which (usually) the victim initially resists the temptation but gradually weakens; the final succumbing to the temptation (though there is always a possibility that the intended victim will successfully resist).

thanksgiving. A standard section of the NT epistles, usually coming immediately after the salutation. The usual content is a prayer for the spiritual welfare of the recipients of the letter, remembrance of past relations between author and recipients, and commendation or enumeration of the spiritual riches that the recipients have in Christ.

theme. A generalization about life that can be deduced from a work of literature. Works of literature usually embody multiple themes. A theme in the story of Cain (Genesis 4:1–16) is the self-destructiveness of uncontrolled sin in a person's life. A theme of Psalm 23 is the contentment that comes from resting in the sufficiency of God's provision.

theophany. A work of literature that describes an appearance of God in visible form. Often the description pictures spectacular forces of nature like thunder and lightning.

tragedy. A narrative form that presents an exceptional calamity stemming from a protagonist's wrong choice. At the heart of tragedy is the tragic hero's choice, and from the time of Aristotle critics have agreed that we can see a notable *hamartia*—a missing of the mark—in the wrong choice that the tragic hero makes. Tragedy is a story of retribution or punishment for sinful action. A full-fledged tragedy unfolds according to the following sequence: exposition (background or prelude to tragedy); dilemma (as the hero is drawn in two directions); choice; catastrophe; suffering; tragic perception or recognition (sometimes absent); death. The two full-fledged literary tragedies in the Bible are the OT stories of Samson and King Saul, but there are numerous brief tragedies scattered throughout the historical books and the parables of Jesus.

transformation story. A story in which a character undergoes a drastic change or reversal. Gideon is transformed from a reluctant leader suffering from an inferiority complex into a heroic leader who conquers his nation's enemy. The apostle Paul is transformed from a zealous persecutor of Christians into a Christian missionary.

travel story. A story in which a leading action is the journeying of a person or group through a series of places. One reason this genre is so prevalent (including in the Bible) is the literary motifs that converge in a travel story: variety of adventure; danger; risk; suspense; testing; encounters with a range of characters; quest; flight; escape; exile; wandering.

utopia; utopian literature. Portrayal of a "good place" or ideal society, along with an explanation of the institutions and rules that undergird and produce that society. The word *utopia* is based on two Greek words meaning "no place," but they are a pun on the Greek words meaning "good place." The book of Deuteronomy outlines the contours of a godly society and includes the laws that help to produce it.

visionary writing. The essential feature of visionary writing is that it presents material that is *envisioned* as opposed to something that exists in the real world. Another literary term for this genre is *fantasy*—writing that presents characters, events, or scenes that exist only in the imagination and not in the real world. A dragon with seven heads and trees clapping their hands belong to the realm of visionary writing. Even though such details are unlifelike at a literal level, they nonetheless picture events, people, places, and human emotions that really exist. The places in the Bible where we are most likely to confront visionary writing are the prophetic books and eschatological predictions surrounding the end times. Two kinds of alternate reality appear in visionary writing, and they may be combined in the same passage: (1) the writer transports us to a world of the imagination that transcends earthly reality; (2) the writer keeps us rooted in the known world but envisions a future time when conditions that now exist are radically altered (for example, the empire that is in power at the time of writing has been toppled). The structure of visionary writing is typically a pageant of brief, constantly shifting pictures.

vocation story. A story in which either a prophet or a disciple receives a call from God to perform a task, enter a vocation, or follow Jesus. Also goes by the label *calling story.*

wisdom literature. A branch of biblical literature in which the writer depends mainly on the proverb as the basic unit. The OT books of Proverbs and Ecclesiastes and the NT book of James are the leading biblical examples of wisdom literature.

witness story. A subgenre in the Gospels in which a character testifies about the person and work of Jesus. Three questions converge in such stories: who (the witness); what (the testimony); why (the proof, which might include circum-stances). Synonymous with *testimony story.*

worship psalm. A psalm built around the experience of worshiping God, almost always specifically in the temple in Jerusalem. Also called *song of Zion.*

DAILY READING PLAN

This schedule of daily Bible readings has been organized into reading portions that match the passage divisions in *The Literary Study Bible*. The schedule is designed to go through the entire Bible in one year.

There are four readings for each day (in a handful of instances it has proven necessary to include a fifth reading portion). These readings are divided into four main sections: Psalms and Wisdom Literature; Pentateuch and the History of Israel; Chronicles and Prophets; and Gospels and Epistles.

In order to make the readings come out evenly, four major books of the Bible are included twice in the schedule: the Psalms (the Bible's hymnal, and also its main body of teaching on the doctrine of God), Isaiah (the grandest of the Old Testament prophets), Luke (one of the four biblical Gospels), and Romans (the heart of the Bible's theology of salvation).

The list of readings from the Psalms and the Wisdom Literature begins and ends with special readings that are especially appropriate for the opening and closing of the year. The list of readings from the Pentateuch and the History of Israel proceeds canonically through the five books of Moses and then chronologically through the history of the Old Testament, before closing the year with the sufferings of Job. The list of readings from the Chronicles and the Prophets begins with the Chronicler's history of the people of God from Adam through the exile, followed by the major and minor prophets, which are organized chronologically rather than canonically.

The Gospels and Epistles are largely grouped according to authorship: first the writings of Luke in the Gospel that bears his name and also in the book of Acts; then the letters of Paul, from Romans through Philemon; next Matthew, followed by Hebrews (both of which seem to have been written to largely Jewish audiences); then Mark, which probably was based on the experiences of Peter, followed by Peter's own letters; then a repeat of Luke and Romans; finally, James and the writings of John, including his Gospel, his epistles, and Revelation.

This is one plan for reading through the Bible in one year. There are other good plans, of course, and they each have their special strengths. But the most important thing is to take your Bible and read it, praying to the Father that the Spirit will take what all the Scriptures teach about Christ and apply it to your mind and heart.

	Psalms and Wisdom Literature	Pentateuch and History of Israel	Chronicles and Prophets	Gospels and Epistles
January				
1	Ecclesiastes 3:1–8	Genesis 1	1 Chronicles 1	Luke 1:1–25
2	Psalm 1	Genesis 2	1 Chronicles 2	Luke 1:26–56
3	Psalm 2	Genesis 3	1 Chronicles 3	Luke 1:57–80
4	Psalm 3	Genesis 4	1 Chronicles 4	Luke 2:1–21
5	Psalm 4	Genesis 5	1 Chronicles 5	Luke 2:22–52
6	Psalm 5	Genesis 6	1 Chronicles 6	Luke 3:1–22
7	Psalm 6	Genesis 7	1 Chronicles 7	Luke 3:23–4:13
8	Psalm 7	Genesis 8:1–19	1 Chronicles 8	Luke 4:14–44
9	Psalm 8	Genesis 8:20–9:19	1 Chronicles 9	Luke 5:1–6:16
10	Psalm 9	Genesis 9:20–10:32	1 Chronicles 10	Luke 6:17–49
11	Psalm 10	Genesis 11	1 Chronicles 11	Luke 7:1–35
12	Psalm 11	Genesis 12–13:1	1 Chronicles 12	Luke 7:36–8:3
13	Psalm 12	Genesis 13:2–18	1 Chronicles 13	Luke 8:4–21
14	Psalm 13	Genesis 14	1 Chronicles 14	Luke 8:22–56
15	Psalm 14	Genesis 15	1 Chronicles 15:1–16:3	Luke 9:1–50
16	Psalm 15	Genesis 16	1 Chronicles 16:4–43	Luke 9:51–10:24
17	Psalm 16	Genesis 17	1 Chronicles 17	Luke 10:25–42
18	Psalm 17	Genesis 18:1–15	1 Chronicles 18–20	Luke 11:1–36
19	Psalm 18	Genesis 18:16–33	1 Chronicles 21:1–17	Luke 11:37–12:12
20	Psalm 19	Genesis 19	1 Chronicles 21:18–22:19	Luke 12:13–48
21	Psalm 20	Genesis 20	1 Chronicles 23–24	Luke 12:49–13:9
22	Psalm 21	Genesis 21:1–21	1 Chronicles 25	Luke 13:10–35
23	Psalm 22	Genesis 21:22–34	1 Chronicles 26	Luke 14
24	Psalm 23	Genesis 22	1 Chronicles 27	Luke 15
25	Psalm 24	Genesis 23	1 Chronicles 28	Luke 16:1–17:10
26	Psalm 25	Genesis 24	1 Chronicles 29:1–22a	Luke 17:11–37
27	Psalm 26	Genesis 25:1–18	1 Chronicles 29:22b–30	Luke 18:1–30
28	Psalm 27	Genesis 25:19–34	2 Chronicles 1	Luke 18:31–19:27
29	Psalm 28	Genesis 26	2 Chronicles 2	Luke 19:28–46
30	Psalm 29	Genesis 27:1–40	2 Chronicles 3	Luke 19:47–20:44
31	Psalm 30	Genesis 27:41–28:9	2 Chronicles 4	Luke 20:45–21:38

	Psalms and Wisdom Literature	Pentateuch and History of Israel	Chronicles and Prophets	Gospels and Epistles
February				
1	Psalm 31	Genesis 28:10–22	2 Chronicles 5	Luke 22:1–46
2	Psalm 32	Genesis 29:1–30	2 Chronicles 6	Luke 22:47–23:25
3	Psalm 33	Genesis 29:31–30:43	2 Chronicles 7	Luke 23:26–56
4	Psalm 34	Genesis 31	2 Chronicles 8	Luke 24
5	Psalm 35	Genesis 32	2 Chronicles 9	Acts 1
6	Psalm 36	Genesis 33	2 Chronicles 10	Acts 2
7	Psalm 37	Genesis 34	2 Chronicles 11	Acts 3:1–4:31
8	Psalm 38	Genesis 35	2 Chronicles 12	Acts 4:32–6:7
9	Psalm 39	Genesis 36	2 Chronicles 13	Acts 6:8–7:60
10	Psalm 40	Genesis 37	2 Chronicles 14	Acts 8
11	Psalm 41	Genesis 38	2 Chronicles 15	Acts 9:1–31
12	Psalm 42–43	Genesis 39	2 Chronicles 16	Acts 9:32–43
13	Psalm 44	Genesis 40	2 Chronicles 17	Acts 10:1–11:18
14	Psalm 45	Genesis 41:1–36	2 Chronicles 18:1–19:3	Acts 11:19–30
15	Psalm 46	Genesis 41:37–57	2 Chronicles 19:4–11	Acts 12
16	Psalm 47	Genesis 42	2 Chronicles 20	Acts 13–14
17	Psalm 48	Genesis 43	2 Chronicles 21	Acts 15:1–35
18	Psalm 49	Genesis 44	2 Chronicles 22	Acts 15:36–17:15
19	Psalm 50	Genesis 45	2 Chronicles 23	Acts 17:16–34
20	Psalm 51	Genesis 46:1–47:12	2 Chronicles 24	Acts 18:1–22
21	Psalm 52	Genesis 47:13–26	2 Chronicles 25	Acts 18:23–19:22
22	Psalm 53	Genesis 47:27–48:22	2 Chronicles 26	Acts 19:23–20:16
23	Psalm 54	Genesis 49	2 Chronicles 27	Acts 20:17–21:16
24	Psalm 55	Genesis 50:1–14	2 Chronicles 28	Acts 21:17–23:11
25	Psalm 56	Genesis 50:15–26	2 Chronicles 29	Acts 23:12–24:27
26	Psalm 57	Exodus 1:1–21	2 Chronicles 30	Acts 25–26
27	Psalm 58	Exodus 1:22–2:22	2 Chronicles 31	Acts 27:1–28:15
28/29	Psalm 59	Exodus 2:23–3:22	2 Chronicles 32	Acts 28:16–31

	Psalms and Wisdom Literature	Pentateuch and History of Israel	Chronicles and Prophets	Gospels and Epistles
March				
1	Psalm 60	Exodus 4	2 Chronicles 33	Romans 1:1–17
2	Psalm 61	Exodus 5:1–6:9	2 Chronicles 34	Romans 1:18–32
3	Psalm 62	Exodus 6:10–7:13	2 Chronicles 35:1–19	Romans 2:1–16
4	Psalm 63	Exodus 7:14–8:19	2 Chronicles 35:20–27	Romans 2:17–3:8
5	Psalm 64	Exodus 8:20–9:12	2 Chronicles 36	Romans 3:9–20
6	Psalm 65	Exodus 9:13–10:29	Ezra 1	Romans 3:21–31
7	Psalm 66	Exodus 11:1–12:30	Ezra 2	Romans 4
8	Psalm 67	Exodus 12:31–13:22	Ezra 3	Romans 5:1–11
9	Psalm 68	Exodus 14	Ezra 4	Romans 5:12–21
10	Psalm 69	Exodus 15:1–21	Ezra 5	Romans 6
11	Psalm 70	Exodus 15:22–16:36	Ezra 6	Romans 7
12	Psalm 71	Exodus 17	Ezra 7	Romans 8:1–17
13	Psalm 72	Exodus 18	Ezra 8	Romans 8:18–39
14	Psalm 73	Exodus 19	Ezra 9	Romans 9:1–29
15	Psalm 74	Exodus 20:1–17	Ezra 10	Romans 9:30–10:21
16	Psalm 75	Exodus 20:18–21:11	Nehemiah 1	Romans 11
17	Psalm 76	Exodus 21:12–22:15	Nehemiah 2	Romans 12
18	Psalm 77	Exodus 22:16–23:9	Nehemiah 3	Romans 13
19	Psalm 78	Exodus 23:10–33	Nehemiah 4	Romans 14
20	Psalm 79	Exodus 24	Nehemiah 5	Romans 15:1–13
21	Psalm 80	Exodus 25	Nehemiah 6	Romans 15:14–33
22	Psalm 81	Exodus 26	Nehemiah 7	Romans 16
23	Psalm 82	Exodus 27:1–19	Nehemiah 8	1 Cor. 1:1–17
24	Psalm 83	Exodus 27:20–28:43	Nehemiah 9	1 Cor. 1:18–31
25	Psalm 84	Exodus 29	Nehemiah 10	1 Cor. 2
26	Psalm 85	Exodus 30–31	Nehemiah 11:1–12:26	1 Cor. 3
27	Psalm 86	Exodus 32	Nehemiah 12:27–47	1 Cor. 4
28	Psalm 87	Exodus 33	Nehemiah 13	1 Cor. 5
29	Psalm 88	Exodus 34	Esther 1	1 Cor. 6
30	Psalm 89	Exodus 35:1–29	Esther 2	1 Cor. 7
31	Psalm 90	Exodus 35:30–36:38	Esther 3	1 Cor. 8

	Psalms and Wisdom Literature	Pentateuch and History of Israel	Chronicles and Prophets	Gospels and Epistles
April				
1	Psalm 91	Exodus 37	Esther 4	1 Cor. 9
2	Psalm 92	Exodus 38	Esther 5	1 Cor. 10:1–11:1
3	Psalm 93	Exodus 39	Esther 6	1 Cor. 11:2–34
4	Psalm 94	Exodus 40	Esther 7	1 Cor. 12
5	Psalm 95	Leviticus 1	Esther 8	1 Cor. 13
6	Psalm 96	Leviticus 2	Esther 9–10	1 Cor. 14
7	Psalm 97	Leviticus 3	Isaiah 1	1 Cor. 15
8	Psalm 98	Leviticus 4:1–5:13	Isaiah 2	1 Cor. 16
9	Psalm 99	Leviticus 5:14–6:7	Isaiah 3–4	2 Cor. 1:1–11
10	Psalm 100	Leviticus 6:8–7:38	Isaiah 5	2 Cor. 1:12–2:11
11	Psalm 101	Leviticus 8	Isaiah 6	2 Cor. 2:12–3:18
12	Psalm 102	Leviticus 9	Isaiah 7–8	2 Cor. 4:1–5:10
13	Psalm 103	Leviticus 10	Isaiah 9:1–7	2 Cor. 5:11–6:10
14	Psalm 104	Leviticus 11	Isaiah 9:8–10:34	2 Cor. 6:11–7:16
15	Psalm 105	Leviticus 12	Isaiah 11–12	2 Cor. 8–9
16	Psalm 106	Leviticus 13	Isaiah 13–14	2 Cor. 10:1–12
17	Psalm 107	Leviticus 14:1–32	Isaiah 15–16	2 Cor. 10:13–12:13
18	Psalm 108	Leviticus 14:33–57	Isaiah 17–18	2 Cor. 12:14–13:14
19	Psalm 109	Leviticus 15	Isaiah 19–20	Galatians 1:1–10
20	Psalm 110	Leviticus 16	Isaiah 21	Galatians 1:11–24
21	Psalm 111	Leviticus 17	Isaiah 22	Galatians 2
22	Psalm 112	Leviticus 18	Isaiah 23	Galatians 3
23	Psalm 113	Leviticus 19	Isaiah 24	Galatians 4
24	Psalm 114	Leviticus 20	Isaiah 25	Galatians 5
25	Psalm 115	Leviticus 21:1–22:16	Isaiah 26–27	Galatians 6
26	Psalm 116	Leviticus 22:17–33	Isaiah 28	Ephesians 1
27	Psalm 117	Leviticus 23	Isaiah 29:1–30:17	Ephesians 2
28	Psalm 118	Leviticus 24	Isaiah 30:18–32:20	Ephesians 3
29	Psalm 119:1–88	Leviticus 25	Isaiah 33–34	Ephesians 4:1–16
30	Psalm 119:89–176	Leviticus 26	Isaiah 35	Ephesians 4:17–32

	Psalms and Wisdom Literature	Pentateuch and History of Israel	Chronicles and Prophets	Gospels and Epistles
May				
1	Psalm 120	Leviticus 27	Isaiah 36–37	Ephesians 5:1–21
2	Psalm 121	Numbers 1	Isaiah 38	Ephesians 5:22–6:9
3	Psalm 122	Numbers 2	Isaiah 39	Ephesians 6:10–24
4	Psalm 123	Numbers 3–4	Isaiah 40	Philippians 1:1–26
5	Psalm 124	Numbers 5	Isaiah 41	Philippians 1:27–2:11
6	Psalm 125	Numbers 6	Isaiah 42	Philippians 2:12–30
7	Psalm 126	Numbers 7	Isaiah 43:1–44:5	Philippians 3:1–4:1
8	Psalm 127	Numbers 8	Isaiah 44:6–28	Philippians 4:2–23
9	Psalm 128	Numbers 9:1–14	Isaiah 45	Colossians 1:1–20
10	Psalm 129	Numbers 9:15–10:10	Isaiah 46–47	Colossians 1:21–2:5
11	Psalm 130	Numbers 10:11–36	Isaiah 48–49	Colossians 2:6–23
12	Psalm 131	Numbers 11	Isaiah 50	Colossians 3:1–17
13	Psalm 132	Numbers 12	Isaiah 51:1–52:12	Colossians 3:18–4:18
14	Psalm 133	Numbers 13–14	Isaiah 52:13–53:12	1 Thess. 1
15	Psalm 134	Numbers 15	Isaiah 54	1 Thess. 2:1–16
16	Psalm 135	Numbers 16–17	Isaiah 55	1 Thess. 2:17–3:13
17	Psalm 136	Numbers 18–19	Isaiah 56–57	1 Thess. 4:1–12
18	Psalm 137	Numbers 20–21	Isaiah 58	1 Thess. 4:13–5:11
19	Psalm 138	Numbers 22	Isaiah 59	1 Thess. 5:12–22
20	Psalm 139	Numbers 23–24	Isaiah 60	1 Thess. 5:23–28
21	Psalm 140	Numbers 25	Isaiah 61–62	2 Thess. 1
22	Psalm 141	Numbers 26	Isaiah 63–64	2 Thess. 2:1–12
23	Psalm 142	Numbers 27	Isaiah 65	2 Thess. 2:13–3:5
24	Psalm 143	Numbers 28–29	Isaiah 66	2 Thess. 3:6–18
25	Psalm 144	Numbers 30	Obadiah 1–14	1 Timothy 1
26	Psalm 145	Numbers 31	Obadiah 15–21	1 Timothy 2
27	Psalm 146	Numbers 32	Joel 1	1 Timothy 3
28	Psalm 147	Numbers 33:1–49	Joel 2:1–17	1 Timothy 4
29	Psalm 148	Numbers 33:50–34:29	Joel 2:18–27	1 Timothy 5:1–6:2
30	Psalm 149	Numbers 35–36	Joel 2:28–3:21	1 Timothy 6:3–21
31	Psalm 150	Deut. 1	Jonah 1	2 Timothy 1:1–7

	Psalms and Wisdom Literature	Pentateuch and History of Israel	Chronicles and Prophets	Gospels and Epistles
June				
1	Proverbs 1:1–7	Deut. 2	Jonah 2	2 Timothy 1:8–18
2	Proverbs 1:8–19	Deut. 3	Jonah 3	2 Timothy 2
3	Proverbs 1:20–33	Deut. 4	Jonah 4	2 Timothy 3:1–9
4	Proverbs 2	Deut. 5	Hosea 1:1–2:1	2 Timothy 3:10–4:8
5	Proverbs 3:1–12	Deut. 6	Hosea 2:2–23	2 Timothy 4:9–22
6	Proverbs 3:13–20	Deut. 7	Hosea 3	Titus 1:1–4
7	Proverbs 3:21–35	Deut. 8:1–9:5	Hosea 4–5	Titus 1:5–16
8	Proverbs 4	Deut. 9:6–10:11	Hosea 6–7	Titus 2
9	Proverbs 5	Deut. 10:12–11:32	Hosea 8	Titus 3:1–8a
10	Proverbs 6:1–19	Deut. 12	Hosea 9	Titus 3:8b–11
11	Proverbs 6:20–35	Deut. 13	Hosea 10	Titus 3:12–15
12	Proverbs 7	Deut. 14	Hosea 11:1–11	Philemon 1–3
13	Proverbs 8	Deut. 15:1–18	Hosea 11:12–13:16	Philemon 4–7
14	Proverbs 9	Deut. 15:19–16:17	Hosea 14	Philemon 8–22
15	Proverbs 10	Deut. 16:18–17:20	Amos 1:1–2:5	Philemon 23–25
16	Proverbs 11–12	Deut. 18	Amos 2:6–16	Matthew 1:1–17
17	Proverbs 13–14	Deut. 19	Amos 3	Matthew 1:18–2:12
18	Proverbs 15–16	Deut. 20	Amos 4	Matthew 2:13–23
19	Proverbs 17–18	Deut. 21:1–22:12	Amos 5	Matthew 3
20	Proverbs 19–20	Deut. 22:13–30	Amos 6	Matthew 4:1–11
21	Proverbs 21–22	Deut. 23:1–14	Amos 7–8	Matthew 4:12–25
22	Proverbs 23–24	Deut. 23:15–25:19	Amos 9	Matthew 5:1–16
23	Proverbs 25–26	Deut. 26	Micah 1–2	Matthew 5:17–48
24	Proverbs 27–28	Deut. 27	Micah 3	Matthew 6:1–18
25	Proverbs 29	Deut. 28:1–14	Micah 4	Matthew 6:19–24
26	Proverbs 30:1–31:9	Deut. 28:15–68	Micah 5	Matthew 6:25–34
27	Proverbs 31:10–31	Deut. 29:1–30:10	Micah 6	Matthew 7:1–12
28	Ecclesiastes 1:1–3	Deut. 30:11–20	Micah 7:1–13	Matthew 7:13–29
29	Ecclesiastes 1:4–11	Deut. 31:1–29	Micah 7:14–20	Matthew 8
30	Ecclesiastes 1:12–18	Deut. 31:30–32:47	Nahum 1	Matthew 9

	Psalms and Wisdom Literature	Pentateuch and History of Israel	Chronicles and Prophets	Gospels and Epistles
July				
1	Ecclesiastes 2:1–11	Deut. 32:48–33:29	Nahum 2:1–3:4	Matthew 10
2	Ecclesiastes 2:12–17	Deut. 34	Nahum 3:5–19	Matthew 11
3	Ecclesiastes 2:18–23	Joshua 1	Zephaniah 1:1–2:3	Matthew 12
4	Ecclesiastes 2:24–26	Joshua 2	Zephaniah 2:4–15	Matthew 13
5	Ecclesiastes 3:1–8	Joshua 3	Zephaniah 3:1–8	Matthew 14
6	Ecclesiastes 3:9–22	Joshua 4	Zephaniah 3:9–20	Matthew 15
7	Ecclesiastes 4	Joshua 5	Jeremiah 1:1–10	Matthew 16
8	Ecclesiastes 5:1–7	Joshua 6	Jeremiah 1:11–19	Matthew 17
9	Ecclesiastes 5:8–17	Joshua 7	Jeremiah 2:1–3:5	Matthew 18
10	Ecclesiastes 5:18–20	Joshua 8	Jeremiah 3:6–4:4	Matthew 19:1–20:16
11	Ecclesiastes 6	Joshua 9	Jeremiah 4:5–31	Matthew 20:17–21:11
12	Ecclesiastes 7:1–14	Joshua 10	Jeremiah 5	Matthew 21:12–27
13	Ecclesiastes 7:15–29	Joshua 11–12	Jeremiah 6	Matthew 21:28–22:14
14	Ecclesiastes 8	Joshua 13–14	Jeremiah 7:1–8:3	Matthew 22:15–46
15	Ecclesiastes 9:1–10	Joshua 15	Jeremiah 8:4–9:22	Matthew 23
16	Ecclesiastes 9:11–18	Joshua 16–17	Jeremiah 9:23–10:25	Matthew 24
17	Ecclesiastes 10	Joshua 18–19	Jeremiah 11:1–17	Matthew 25
18	Ecclesiastes 11:1–8	Joshua 20	Jeremiah 11:18–12:17	Matthew 26:1–29
19	Ecclesiastes 11:9–12:8	Joshua 21	Jeremiah 13	Matthew 26:30–75
20	Ecclesiastes 12:9–14	Joshua 22	Jeremiah 14:1–15:9	Matthew 27:1–26
21	Song 1:1–8	Joshua 23–24	Jeremiah 15:10–16:21	Matthew 27:27–66
22	Song 1:9–2:7	Judges 1	Jeremiah 17	Matthew 28
23	Song 2:8–17	Judges 2:1–3:6	Jeremiah 18	Hebrews 1
24	Song 3	Judges 3:7–31	Jeremiah 19	Hebrews 2
25	Song 4:1–8	Judges 4	Jeremiah 20	Hebrews 3:1–6
26	Song 4:9–5:1	Judges 5	Jeremiah 21	Hebrews 3:7–4:13
27	Song 5:2–9	Judges 6	Jeremiah 22:1–23:8	Hebrews 4:14–5:10
28	Song 5:10–6:3	Judges 7	Jeremiah 23:9–40	Hebrews 5:11–6:20
29	Song 6:4–12	Judges 8	Jeremiah 24	Hebrews 7
30	Song 6:13–7:9	Judges 9	Jeremiah 25:1–14	Hebrews 8:1–9:10
31	Song 7:10–13	Judges 10:1–11:3	Jeremiah 25:15–38	Hebrews 9:11–10:18

	Psalms and Wisdom Literature	Pentateuch and History of Israel	Chronicles and Prophets	Gospels and Epistles
August				
1	Song 8:1–7	Judges 11:4–40	Jeremiah 26	Hebrews 10:19–39
2	Song 8:8–14	Judges 12	Jeremiah 27–28	Hebrews 11:1–12:2
3	Psalm 1	Judges 13	Jeremiah 29	Hebrews 12:3–29
4	Psalm 2	Judges 14	Jeremiah 30	Hebrews 13:1–19
5	Psalm 3	Judges 15	Jeremiah 31	Hebrews 13:20–25
6	Psalm 4	Judges 16	Jeremiah 32	Mark 1
7	Psalm 5	Judges 17	Jeremiah 33	Mark 2–3
8	Psalm 6	Judges 18	Jeremiah 34	Mark 4:1–34
9	Psalm 7	Judges 19	Jeremiah 35	Mark 4:35–5:43
10	Psalm 8	Judges 20	Jeremiah 36	Mark 6
11	Psalm 9	Judges 21	Jeremiah 37	Mark 7:1–8:26
12	Psalm 10	Ruth 1	Jeremiah 38	Mark 8:27–9:50
13	Psalm 11	Ruth 2	Jeremiah 39	Mark 10
14	Psalm 12	Ruth 3	Jeremiah 40–41	Mark 11
15	Psalm 13	Ruth 4	Jeremiah 42–43	Mark 12
16	Psalm 14	1 Samuel 1:1–2:11	Jeremiah 44–45	Mark 13
17	Psalm 15	1 Samuel 2:12–36	Jeremiah 46–47	Mark 14
18	Psalm 16	1 Samuel 3	Jeremiah 48	Mark 15
19	Psalm 17	1 Samuel 4	Jeremiah 49	Mark 16
20	Psalm 18	1 Samuel 5:1–7:2	Jeremiah 50	1 Peter 1:1–12
21	Psalm 19	1 Samuel 7:3–17	Jeremiah 51	1 Peter 1:13–2:3
22	Psalm 20	1 Samuel 8	Jeremiah 52	1 Peter 2:4–10
23	Psalm 21	1 Samuel 9:1–10:16	Lamentations 1	1 Peter 2:11–3:12
24	Psalm 22	1 Samuel 10:17–11:15	Lamentations 2	1 Peter 3:13–4:19
25	Psalm 23	1 Samuel 12	Lamentations 3	1 Peter 5
26	Psalm 24	1 Samuel 13	Lamentations 4	2 Peter 1:1–11
27	Psalm 25	1 Samuel 14	Lamentations 5	2 Peter 1:12–21
28	Psalm 26	1 Samuel 15	Habakkuk 1:1–11	2 Peter 2
29	Psalm 27	1 Samuel 16	Habakkuk 1:12–2:20	2 Peter 3
30	Psalm 28	1 Samuel 17	Habakkuk 3	Luke 1:1–25
31	Psalm 29	1 Samuel 18	Daniel 1	Luke 1:26–56

	Psalms and Wisdom Literature	Pentateuch and History of Israel	Chronicles and Prophets	Gospels and Epistles
September				
1	Psalm 30	1 Samuel 19	Daniel 2	Luke 1:57–80
2	Psalm 31	1 Samuel 20	Daniel 3	Luke 2:1–21
3	Psalm 32	1 Samuel 21–22	Daniel 4	Luke 2:22–52
4	Psalm 33	1 Samuel 23–24	Daniel 5	Luke 3:1–22
5	Psalm 34	1 Samuel 25	Daniel 6	Luke 3:23–4:13
6	Psalm 35	1 Samuel 26	Daniel 7	Luke 4:14–44
7	Psalm 36	1 Samuel 27	Daniel 8	Luke 5:1–6:16
8	Psalm 37	1 Samuel 28	Daniel 9	Luke 6:17–49
9	Psalm 38	1 Samuel 29–30	Daniel 10:1–11:1	Luke 7:1–35
10	Psalm 39	1 Samuel 31	Daniel 11:2–45	Luke 7:36–8:3
11	Psalm 40	2 Samuel 1	Daniel 12	Luke 8:4–21
12	Psalm 41	2 Samuel 2	Ezekiel 1	Luke 8:22–56
13	Psalm 42–43	2 Samuel 3	Ezekiel 2–3	Luke 9:1–50
14	Psalm 44	2 Samuel 4	Ezekiel 4:1–5:4	Luke 9:51–10:24
15	Psalm 45	2 Samuel 5	Ezekiel 5:5–17	Luke 10:25–42
16	Psalm 46	2 Samuel 6	Ezekiel 6	Luke 11:1–36
17	Psalm 47	2 Samuel 7	Ezekiel 7	Luke 11:37–12:12
18	Psalm 48	2 Samuel 8	Ezekiel 8	Luke 12:13–48
19	Psalm 49	2 Samuel 9	Ezekiel 9	Luke 12:49–13:9
20	Psalm 50	2 Samuel 10	Ezekiel 10:1–11:13	Luke 13:10–35
21	Psalm 51	2 Samuel 11	Ezekiel 11:14–25	Luke 14
22	Psalm 52	2 Samuel 12	Ezekiel 12	Luke 15
23	Psalm 53	2 Samuel 13	Ezekiel 13	Luke 16:1–17:10
24	Psalm 54	2 Samuel 14:1–24	Ezekiel 14–15	Luke 17:11–37
25	Psalm 55	2 Samuel 14:25–15:12	Ezekiel 16	Luke 18:1–30
26	Psalm 56	2 Samuel 15:13–16:14	Ezekiel 17	Luke 18:31–19:27
27	Psalm 57	2 Samuel 16:15–17:23	Ezekiel 18	Luke 19:28–46
28	Psalm 58	2 Samuel 17:24–18:33	Ezekiel 19	Luke 19:47–20:44
29	Psalm 59	2 Samuel 19	Ezekiel 20	Luke 20:45–21:38
30	Psalm 60	2 Samuel 20	Ezekiel 21	Luke 22:1–46

	Psalms and Wisdom Literature	Pentateuch and History of Israel	Chronicles and Prophets	Gospels and Epistles
October				
1	Psalm 61	2 Samuel 21	Ezekiel 22	Luke 22:47–23:25
2	Psalm 62	2 Samuel 22:1–23:7	Ezekiel 23	Luke 23:26–56
3	Psalm 63	2 Samuel 23:8–39	Ezekiel 24	Luke 24
4	Psalm 64	2 Samuel 24	Ezekiel 25	Romans 1:1–17
5	Psalm 65	1 Kings 1:1–27	Ezekiel 26	Romans 1:18–32
6	Psalm 66	1 Kings 1:28–53	Ezekiel 27	Romans 2:1–16
7	Psalm 67	1 Kings 2	Ezekiel 28	Romans 2:17–3:8
8	Psalm 68	1 Kings 3	Ezekiel 29–30	Romans 3:9–20
9	Psalm 69	1 Kings 4	Ezekiel 31	Romans 3:21–31
10	Psalm 70	1 Kings 5	Ezekiel 32	Romans 4
11	Psalm 71	1 Kings 6	Ezekiel 33	Romans 5:1–11
12	Psalm 72	1 Kings 7	Ezekiel 34	Romans 5:12–21
13	Psalm 73	1 Kings 8:1–21	Ezekiel 35	Romans 6
14	Psalm 74	1 Kings 8:22–66	Ezekiel 36	Romans 7
15	Psalm 75	1 Kings 9:1–9	Ezekiel 37	Romans 8:1–17
16	Psalm 76	1 Kings 9:10–10:29	Ezekiel 38	Romans 8:18–39
17	Psalm 77	1 Kings 11	Ezekiel 39	Romans 9:1–29
18	Psalm 78	1 Kings 12:1–15	Ezekiel 40	Romans 9:30–10:21
19	Psalm 79	1 Kings 12:16–33	Ezekiel 41–42	Romans 11
20	Psalm 80	1 Kings 13	Ezekiel 43	Romans 12
21	Psalm 81	1 Kings 14:1–20	Ezekiel 44	Romans 13
22	Psalm 82	1 Kings 14:21–15:24	Ezekiel 45	Romans 14
23	Psalm 83	1 Kings 15:25–16:34	Ezekiel 46	Romans 15:1–13
24	Psalm 84	1 Kings 17	Ezekiel 47:1–12	Romans 15:14–33
25	Psalm 85	1 Kings 18:1–19	Ezekiel 47:13–48:35	Romans 16
26	Psalm 86	1 Kings 18:20–46	Haggai 1	James 1
27	Psalm 87	1 Kings 19	Haggai 2	James 2:1–13
28	Psalm 88	1 Kings 20	Zechariah 1:1–17	James 2:14–26
29	Psalm 89	1 Kings 21	Zechariah 1:18–2:13	James 3:1–12
30	Psalm 90	1 Kings 22:1–40	Zechariah 3	James 3:13–18
31	Psalm 91	1 Kings 22:41–53	Zechariah 4	James 4:1–10

	Psalms and Wisdom Literature	Pentateuch and History of Israel	Chronicles and Prophets	Gospels and Epistles
November				
1	Psalm 92	2 Kings 1	Zechariah 5	James 4:11–5:12
2	Psalm 93	2 Kings 2	Zechariah 6	James 5:13–20
3	Psalm 94	2 Kings 3	Zechariah 7	John 1:1–18
4	Psalm 95	2 Kings 4	Zechariah 8	John 1:19–51
5	Psalm 96	2 Kings 5	Zechariah 9	John 2
6	Psalm 97	2 Kings 6:1–23	Zechariah 10	John 3:1–21
7	Psalm 98	2 Kings 6:24–7:20	Zechariah 11	John 3:22–36
8	Psalm 99	2 Kings 8	Zechariah 12–13	John 4:1–42
9	Psalm 100	2 Kings 9	Zechariah 14	John 4:43–5:18
10	Psalm 101	2 Kings 10	Malachi 1:1–2:9	John 5:19–47
11	Psalm 102	2 Kings 11	Malachi 2:10–17	John 6:1–21
12	Psalm 103	2 Kings 12	Malachi 3:1–12	John 6:22–71
13	Psalm 104	2 Kings 13	Malachi 3:13–4:6	John 7
14	Psalm 105	2 Kings 14:1–22	Isaiah 1	John 8
15	Psalm 106	2 Kings 14:23–15:38	Isaiah 2	John 9
16	Psalm 107	2 Kings 16	Isaiah 3–4	John 10:1–18
17	Psalm 108	2 Kings 17:1–23	Isaiah 5	John 10:19–42
18	Psalm 109	2 Kings 17:24–41	Isaiah 6	John 11:1–54
19	Psalm 110	2 Kings 18	Isaiah 7–8	John 11:55–12:19
20	Psalm 111	2 Kings 19	Isaiah 9:1–7	John 12:20–50
21	Psalm 112	2 Kings 20	Isaiah 9:8–10:34	John 13
22	Psalm 113	2 Kings 21	Isaiah 11–12	John 14
23	Psalm 114	2 Kings 22	Isaiah 13–14	John 15:1–17
24	Psalm 115	2 Kings 23:1–30	Isaiah 15–16	John 15:18–16:15
25	Psalm 116	2 Kings 23:31–24:17	Isaiah 17–18	John 16:16–33
26	Psalm 117	2 Kings 24:18–25:21	Isaiah 19–20	John 17
27	Psalm 118	2 Kings 25:22–30	Isaiah 21	John 18:1–27
28	Psalm 119:1–88	Job 1	Isaiah 22	John 18:28–19:16
29	Psalm 119:89–176	Job 2	Isaiah 23	John 19:17–42
30	Psalm 120	Job 3	Isaiah 24	John 20

	Psalms and Wisdom Literature	Pentateuch and History of Israel	Chronicles and Prophets	Gospels and Epistles
December				
1	Psalm 121	Job 4–5	Isaiah 25	John 21
2	Psalm 122	Job 6–7	Isaiah 26–27	1 John 1:1–2:6
3	Psalm 123	Job 8	Isaiah 28	1 John 2:7–17
4	Psalm 124	Job 9–10	Isaiah 29:1–30:17	1 John 2:18–3:3
5	Psalm 125	Job 11	Isaiah 30:18–32:20	1 John 3:4–24
6	Psalm 126	Job 12	Isaiah 33–34	1 John 4
7	Psalm 127	Job 13	Isaiah 35	1 John 5
8	Psalm 128	Job 14	Isaiah 36–37	2 John
9	Psalm 129	Job 15	Isaiah 38	3 John
10	Psalm 130	Job 16–17	Isaiah 39	Jude
11	Psalm 131	Job 18	Isaiah 40	Revelation 1
12	Psalm 132	Job 19	Isaiah 41	Revelation 2
13	Psalm 133	Job 20	Isaiah 42	Revelation 3
14	Psalm 134	Job 21	Isaiah 43:1–44:5	Revelation 4
15	Psalm 135	Job 22	Isaiah 44:6–28	Revelation 5
16	Psalm 136	Job 23–24	Isaiah 45	Revelation 6
17	Psalm 137	Job 25–26	Isaiah 46–47	Revelation 7:1–8:5
18	Psalm 138	Job 27	Isaiah 48–49	Revelation 8:6–9:21
19	Psalm 139	Job 28	Isaiah 50	Revelation 10
20	Psalm 140	Job 29	Isaiah 51:1–52:12	Revelation 11
21	Psalm 141	Job 30	Isaiah 52:13–53:12	Revelation 12
22	Psalm 142	Job 31	Isaiah 54	Revelation 13
23	Psalm 143	Job 32	Isaiah 55	Revelation 14
24	Psalm 144	Job 33	Isaiah 56–57	Revelation 15
25	Psalm 145	Job 34–35	Isaiah 58	Revelation 16
26	Psalm 146	Job 36:1–21	Isaiah 59	Revelation 17
27	Psalm 147	Job 36:22–37:24	Isaiah 60	Revelation 18
28	Psalm 148	Job 38	Isaiah 61–62	Revelation 19
29	Psalm 149	Job 39:1–40:5	Isaiah 63–64	Revelation 20
30	Psalm 150	Job 40:6–42:6	Isaiah 65	Revelation 21:1–22:5
31	Psalm 90	Job 42:7–17	Isaiah 66	Revelation 22:6–21